new *Women's*
DEVOTIONAL BIBLE

ZONDERVAN®

Table of Contents

THE OLD TESTAMENT

THE NEW TESTAMENT

Table of Contents

Welcome to the ... NIV ... Bible
A Journey to God
Preface to the New International Version

WELCOME TO THE *New Women's Devotional Bible!*

We've designed this special Bible with you in mind. We know you're a busy woman who needs private time with God to stay spiritually strong. You want to keep God first in your heart, but you don't always have the time you'd like. So we've included some great features to help you as you pursue your relationship with God.

Why a Devotional Bible?

So you can be enveloped in God's transforming love. So you can know him better and trust him more. So you can find out how to share what you've learned with others. Let God use this Bible to change your life.

What Is a Devotional Bible?

The devotions in this Bible are designed to help you develop a daily time with God—to help you praise him, cultivate an intimate relationship with him and become more like him. Your devotional time will affect all areas of your life: heart, mind and spirit.

But these devotionals don't just benefit you; they allow you to help those around you with the wisdom you've gleaned from God's Word. Through your time spent with God each day, you'll be better equipped to meet the needs of those you come in contact with. You'll be challenged to apply what you have been taught so that you can share with others your knowledge and understanding of the loving and powerful God you serve.

How Do I Schedule My Time With God?

You have a busy schedule, and sometimes it seems impossible for you to cultivate a regular devotional habit. But you can have a meaningful daily devotional life. Here are some tips that may help you:

• Set aside a block of time each day to spend with God. Think of this as a scheduled appointment—something that can't be postponed or rescheduled. Guard your time with God. Set your alarm clock fifteen minutes earlier in the morning or go to bed fifteen minutes later in the evening. You can have your devotional during your lunch break, while waiting to pick up your kids or before you go to bed. Decide that spending time with God is the most important thing you can do for yourself and others. And remember, God is available anytime!

• Joyfully look forward to your time with God, as you would anticipate a luncheon with a friend or a date with your husband. Come prepared with your Bible, a notebook and a pen. Pray before you begin, asking God to give you wisdom and insight into his Word. Ponder and pray about the passages you don't quite understand. Mull over concepts that are new to you or that don't fit your preconceived ideas. Throughout the day call to mind what you've read so that it takes root in your heart. Ask your pastor or a mature believer any questions you may have.

• Devotions involve a variety of spiritual disciplines. As you spend time with God, try to develop any or all of the following devotional habits:

  • Memorize relevant Scripture passages.
  • Praise God for who he is and for what he has done and is doing.
  • Listen in silence for God's voice.
  • Sing songs of praise and thanksgiving.
  • Journal your thoughts, insights and answered prayers.

How Do I Get Started?

Are you ready to get started? Within the *New Women's Devotional Bible* you'll find features designed specifically to help you develop a devotional life that's just right for you.

• The New International Version of the Bible

The Bible text itself is the most important part of any Bible. Readable and accurate, the NIV is the most read, most trusted version of the Bible.

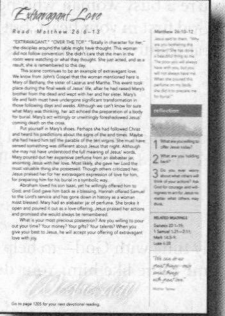

• 260 devotions, one for each weekday of the year

All of the daily devotions were written by godly women—women who have experienced the joys and struggles of living a Christian life in today's world. Some of them are names you'll recognize. Others will be new to you. But all of them have one thing in common: they love the Lord and want you to draw near to him in a fresh and exciting way. Each devotion also includes thought-provoking questions to help you personally apply what you've read. You'll also find links to related passages of Scripture for further study. Sometimes you'll find meaningful quotes to add depth to the day's devotion.

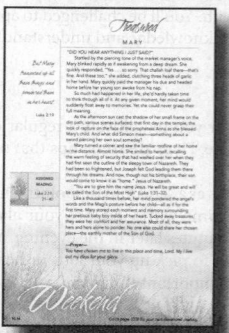

• 52 weekend devotions

Grounded in Scripture but incorporating some imaginative retelling, each weekend devotion profiles a woman in the Bible, offering insights into her character and helping you realize that she was a real woman who lived and breathed so many years ago. You may be surprised by the insights you'll find and the lessons you'll learn from her life. Each weekend devotion ends with a prayer of application to help you draw closer to God from your time spent in reading.

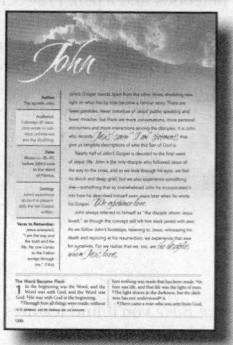

• Book introductions

Each book introduction gives information on the book of the Bible and its place in the canon of God's Word. A side-column section offers basic facts on each book.

• Reading plans

You'll be able to discover the devotional path that works best for you by exploring the reading plans included in the back of this book.

• Subject index

You can look up a wide variety of subjects in the index in the back of this Bible and can then turn to the listed page number for a devotion that fits your need.

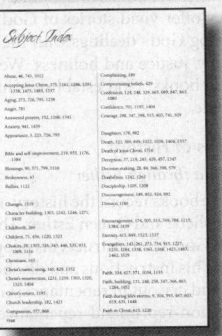

There's no better time than *now* to devote yourself to God and his Word. Start to build a strong and intimate relationship with the One who created you and loved you before the foundation of the earth by beginning a devotional relationship with God. May God reveal himself to you in profound ways as you open the door to his Word and his heart!

A Library in Itself

The Bible is comprised of 66 individual books ... written by different authors ... with different writing styles ... in different eras of history ... with different purposes. What separates the Bible from other anthologies is the fact that God himself guided the writing of Scripture. The result is one amazingly cohesive book made up of disparate parts. Here's a quick look at the different genres you'll find as you explore the books of Scripture.

OLD TESTAMENT

Books of the Law
Genesis through Deuteronomy

The first five books of the Bible (the Pentateuch) detail God's interaction with his human creation. They offer vivid stories of God making himself known to individuals. Specifically, these books catalog God's dealings with the Israelites, his chosen people. They give us snapshots of his love, mercy, justice and holiness. We see how he rewards faithfulness and punishes disobedience. In these books, God establishes his rules for living and how he expects to govern the lives of his people.

Books of History
Joshua through Esther

These books record the history of the Israelites, including stories of women such as Rahab, Delilah, Bathsheba and Queen Esther. This time period establishes a familiar pattern in Israel's relationship with God: God instructs his people and desires to reward them with blessings and fellowship; they reject his instructions and disobey him; God reprimands the disobedient; they recognize their error and cry out in repentance; God forgives them and restores them to fellowship. This pattern of rejection-reprimand-repentance-restoration is repeated throughout the books of history.

Books of Poetry
Job through Song of Songs

These books record the thoughts, personal struggles and hard-earned wisdom of God's people. They address timeless topics such as why people suffer, what kind of worship is pleasing to God and how God's wisdom can be applied to our lives today.

Books of the Prophets
Isaiah through Malachi

The books of prophecy are God's way of speaking to his people, making his intentions and plans known to them, as well as giving them directives for their attitudes and behaviors. Not only do the prophets offer warnings to the people of Israel, they also point to the long-awaited Messiah, the One who would ultimately restore the relationship between God and humans and will come again to establish his eternal kingdom.

NEW TESTAMENT

Books of History
Matthew through Acts

The first four books of the New Testament—the Gospels—present four different yet complementary accounts of the life of Christ.

Before Jesus returned to heaven, he instructed his followers to spread his Good News throughout the world. The book of Acts details the efforts of early believers—including many women—to do just that. Here you'll see the beginning of the church, the body of Christ on earth.

Letters
Romans through Revelation

The Epistles, which were written to the early churches and church leaders, encouraged believers and addressed problems they faced. Through them, the Lord outlined the basic doctrines of faith and the responsibilities of believers. Since women were a vital part of the early church, you can see the impact they had in the churches and how their lives can inspire and encourage you today.

Preface to the New International Version

THE NEW INTERNATIONAL VERSION is a completely new translation of the Holy Bible made by over a hundred scholars working directly from the best available Hebrew, Aramaic and Greek texts. It had its beginning in 1965 when, after several years of exploratory study by committees from the Christian Reformed Church and the National Association of Evangelicals, a group of scholars met at Palos Heights, Illinois, and concurred in the need for a new translation of the Bible in contemporary English. This group, though not made up of official church representatives, was transdenominational. Its conclusion was endorsed by a large number of leaders from many denominations who met in Chicago in 1966.

Responsibility for the new version was delegated by the Palos Heights group to a self-governing body of fifteen, the Committee on Bible Translation, composed for the most part of biblical scholars from colleges, universities and seminaries. In 1967 the New York Bible Society (now the International Bible Society) generously undertook the financial sponsorship of the project—a sponsorship that made it possible to enlist the help of many distinguished scholars. The fact that participants from the United States, Great Britain, Canada, Australia and New Zealand worked together gave the project its international scope. That they were from many denominations—including Anglican, Assemblies of God, Baptist, Brethren, Christian Reformed, Church of Christ, Evangelical Free, Lutheran, Mennonite, Methodist, Nazarene, Presbyterian, Wesleyan and other churches—helped to safeguard the translation from sectarian bias.

How it was made helps to give the New International Version its distinctiveness. The translation of each book was assigned to a team of scholars. Next, one of the Intermediate Editorial Committees revised the initial translation, with constant reference to the Hebrew, Aramaic or Greek. Their work then went to one of the General Editorial Committees, which checked it in detail and made another thorough revision. This revision in turn was carefully reviewed by the Committee on Bible Translation, which made further changes and then released the final version for publication. In this way the entire Bible underwent three revisions, during each of which the translation was examined for its faithfulness to the original languages and for its English style.

All this involved many thousands of hours of research and discussion regarding the meaning of the texts and the precise way of putting them into English. It may well be that no other translation has been made by a more thorough process of review and revision from committee to committee than this one.

From the beginning of the project, the Committee on Bible Translation held to certain goals for the New International Version: that it would be an accurate translation and one that would have clarity and literary quality and so prove suitable for public and private reading, teaching, preaching, memorizing and liturgical use. The Committee also sought to preserve some measure of continuity with the long tradition of translating the Scriptures into English.

In working toward these goals, the translators were united in their commitment to the authority and infallibility of the Bible as God's Word in written form. They believe that it contains the divine answer to the deepest needs of humanity, that it sheds unique light on our path in a dark world, and that it sets forth the way to our eternal well-being.

The first concern of the translators has been the accuracy of the translation and its fidelity to the thought of the biblical writers. They have weighed the significance of the lexical and grammatical details of the Hebrew, Aramaic and Greek texts. At the same time, they have striven for more than a word-for-word translation. Because thought patterns and syntax differ from language to language, faithful communication of the meaning of the writers of the Bible demands frequent modifications in sentence structure and constant regard for the contextual meanings of words.

A sensitive feeling for style does not always accompany scholarship. Accordingly the Committee on Bible Translation submitted the developing version to a number of stylistic consultants. Two of them read every book of both Old and New Testaments twice—once before and once after the last major revision—and made invaluable suggestions. Samples of the translation were tested for clarity and ease of reading by various kinds of people—young and old, highly educated and less well educated, ministers and laymen.

Concern for clear and natural English—that the New International Version should be idiomatic but not idiosyncratic, contemporary but not dated—motivated the translators and consultants. At the same time, they tried to reflect the differing styles of the biblical writers. In view of the international use of English, the translators sought to avoid obvious Americanisms on the one hand and obvious Anglicisms on the other. A British edition reflects the comparatively few differences of significant idiom and of spelling.

As for the traditional pronouns "thou," "thee" and "thine" in reference to the Deity, the translators judged that to use these archaisms (along with the old verb forms such as "doest," "wouldest" and "hadst") would violate accuracy in translation. Neither Hebrew, Aramaic nor Greek uses special pronouns for the persons of the Godhead. A present-day translation is not enhanced by forms that in the time of the King James Version were used in everyday speech, whether referring to God or man.

For the Old Testament the standard Hebrew text, the Masoretic Text as published in the latest editions of Biblia Hebraica, was used throughout. The Dead Sea Scrolls contain material bearing on an earlier stage of the Hebrew text. They were consulted, as were the Samaritan Pentateuch and the ancient scribal traditions relating to textual changes. Sometimes a variant Hebrew reading in the margin of the Masoretic Text was followed instead of the text itself. Such instances, being variants within the Masoretic tradition, are not specified by footnotes. In rare cases, words in the consonantal text were divided differently from the way they appear in the Masoretic Text. Footnotes indicate this. The translators also consulted the more important early versions—the Septuagint; Aquila, Symmachus and Theodotion; the Vulgate; the Syriac Peshitta; the Targums; and for the Psalms the Juxta Hebraica of Jerome. Readings from these versions were occasionally followed where the Masoretic Text seemed doubtful and where accepted principles of textual criticism showed that one or more of these textual witnesses appeared to provide the correct reading. Such instances are footnoted. Sometimes vowel letters and vowel signs did not, in the judgment of the translators, represent the correct vowels for the original consonantal text. Accordingly some words were read with a different set of vowels. These instances are usually not indicated by footnotes.

The Greek text used in translating the New Testament was an eclectic one. No other piece of ancient literature has such an abundance of manuscript witnesses as does the New Testament. Where existing manuscripts differ, the translators made their choice of readings according to accepted principles of New Testament textual criticism. Footnotes call attention to places where there was uncertainty about what the original text was. The best current printed texts of the Greek New Testament were used.

There is a sense in which the work of translation is never wholly finished. This applies to all great literature and uniquely so to the Bible. In 1973 the New Testament in the New International Version was published. Since then, suggestions for corrections and revisions have been received from various sources. The Committee on Bible Translation carefully considered the suggestions and adopted a number of them. These were incorporated in the first printing of the entire Bible in 1978. Additional revisions were made by the Committee on Bible Translation in 1983 and appear in printings after that date.

As in other ancient documents, the precise meaning of the biblical texts is sometimes uncertain. This is more often the case with the Hebrew and Aramaic texts than with the Greek text. Although archaeological and linguistic discoveries in this century aid in understanding difficult passages, some uncertainties remain. The more significant of these have been called to the reader's attention in the footnotes.

In regard to the divine name YHWH, commonly referred to as the Tetragrammaton, the translators adopted the device used in most English versions of rendering that name as "Lord" in capital letters to distinguish it from Adonai, another Hebrew word rendered "Lord," for which small letters are used. Wherever the two names stand together in the Old Testament as a compound name of God, they are rendered "Sovereign Lord."

Because for most readers today the phrases "the Lord of hosts" and "God of hosts" have little meaning, this version renders them "the Lord Almighty" and "God Almighty." These renderings convey the sense of the Hebrew, namely, "he who is sovereign over all the 'hosts' (powers) in heaven and on earth, especially over the 'hosts' (armies) of Israel." For readers unacquainted with Hebrew this does not make clear the distinction between Sabaoth ("hosts" or "Almighty") and Shaddai (which can also be translated "Almighty"), but the latter occurs infrequently and is always footnoted. When Adonai and YHWH Sabaoth occur together, they are rendered "the Lord, the LORD Almighty."

As for other proper nouns, the familiar spellings of the King James Version are generally retained. Names traditionally spelled with "ch," except where it is final, are usually spelled in this translation with "k" or "c," since the biblical languages do not have the sound that "ch" frequently indicates in English—for example, in chant. For well-known names such as Zechariah, however, the traditional spelling has been retained. Variation in the spelling of names in the original languages has usually not been indicated. Where a person or place has two or more different names in the Hebrew, Aramaic or Greek texts, the more familiar one has generally been used, with footnotes where needed.

To achieve clarity the translators sometimes supplied words not in the original texts but required by the context. If there was uncertainty about such material, it is enclosed in brackets. Also for the sake of clarity or style, nouns, including some proper nouns, are sometimes substituted for pronouns, and vice versa. And though the Hebrew writers often shifted back and forth between first, second and third personal pronouns without change of antecedent, this translation often makes them uniform, in accordance with English style and without the use of footnotes.

Poetical passages are printed as poetry, that is, with indentation of lines and with separate stanzas. These are generally designed to reflect the structure of Hebrew poetry. This poetry is normally characterized by parallelism in balanced lines. Most of the poetry in the Bible is in the Old Testament, and scholars differ regarding the scansion of Hebrew lines. The translators determined the stanza divisions for the most part by analysis of the subject matter. The stanzas therefore serve as poetic paragraphs.

As an aid to the reader, italicized sectional headings are inserted in most of the books. They are not to be regarded as part of the NIV text, are not for oral reading, and are not intended to dictate the interpretation of the sections they head.

The footnotes in this version are of several kinds, most of which need no explanation. Those giving alternative translations begin with "Or" and generally introduce the alternative with the last word preceding it in the text, except when it is a single-word alternative; in poetry quoted in a footnote a slant mark indicates a line division. Footnotes introduced by "Or" do not have uniform significance. In some cases two possible translations were considered to have about equal validity. In other cases, though the translators were convinced that the translation in the text was correct, they judged that another interpretation was possible and of sufficient importance to be represented in a footnote.

In the New Testament, footnotes that refer to uncertainty regarding the original text are introduced by "Some manuscripts" or similar expressions. In the Old Testament, evidence for the reading chosen is given first and evidence for the alternative is added after a semicolon (for example: Septuagint; Hebrew father). In such notes the term "Hebrew" refers to the Masoretic Text.

It should be noted that minerals, flora and fauna, architectural details, articles of clothing and jewelry, musical instruments and other articles cannot always be identified with precision. Also measures of capacity in the biblical period are particularly uncertain (see the table of weights and measures following the text).

Like all translations of the Bible, made as they are by imperfect man, this one undoubtedly falls short of its goals. Yet we are grateful to God for the extent to which he has enabled us to realize these goals and for the strength he has given us and our colleagues to complete our task. We offer this version of the Bible to him in whose name and for whose glory it has been made. We pray that it will lead many into a better understanding of the Holy Scriptures and a fuller knowledge of Jesus Christ the incarnate Word, of whom the Scriptures so faithfully testify.

The Committee on Bible Translation
June 1978
(Revised August 1983)

Names of the translators and editors may be secured
from the International Bible Society,
translation sponsors of the New International Version,
1820 Jet Stream Drive, Colorado Springs, CO 80921-3696 U.S.A

The Old Testament

Genesis

Every story has *a beginning,* a genesis. The beginning of God's story of his interactions with humanity is found in the very first words of the Bible. In the beginning God created. From the start God was present. He was at work.

However, in the freshness of *a new world* where the first man and woman walked and talked with God, sin slithered in, marring creation forever. But the God who hung every star in place and laid every grain of sand upon the shore had, from the beginning, a plan. The whole of Scripture, and indeed the whole of history, is unveiled within the seeds of Genesis. It will be many years before we see the fruit of those seeds, but they are not years of dormancy. Throughout the world and within individual lives, *God is actively working* to redeem his creation. In Genesis we see him form covenants, bestow blessings, test faithfulness and turn evil intentions into a greater good—all for the purpose of one day *redeeming the people* he created in his image. It's a work that will continue until the end of time, but the beginnings for all of it are found in Genesis.

Author:
Moses.

Audience:
The people of Israel.

Date:
Between 1446 and 1406 B.C.

Setting:
The area called the Middle East today.

Verse to Remember:
In the beginning God . . . (1:1)

The Beginning

1 In the beginning God created the heavens and the earth. ²Now the earth was[a] formless and empty, darkness was over the surface of the deep, and the Spirit of God was hovering over the waters.

³And God said, "Let there be light," and there was light. ⁴God saw that the light was good, and he separated the light from the darkness. ⁵God called the light "day," and the darkness he called "night." And there was evening, and there was morning—the first day.

⁶And God said, "Let there be an expanse between the waters to separate water from water." ⁷So God made the expanse and

[a] 2 Or possibly *became*

1

separated the water under the expanse from the water above it. And it was so. ⁸God called the expanse "sky." And there was evening, and there was morning—the second day.

⁹ And God said, "Let the water under the sky be gathered to one place, and let dry ground appear." And it was so. ¹⁰God called the dry ground "land," and the gathered waters he called "seas." And God saw that it was good.

¹¹Then God said, "Let the land produce vegetation: seed-bearing plants and trees on the land that bear fruit with seed in it, according to their various kinds." And it was so. ¹²The land produced vegetation: plants bearing seed according to their kinds and trees bearing fruit with seed in it according to their kinds. And God saw that it was good. ¹³And there was evening, and there was morning—the third day.

¹⁴And God said, "Let there be lights in the expanse of the sky to separate the day from the night, and let them serve as signs to mark seasons and days and years, ¹⁵and let them be lights in the expanse of the sky to give light on the earth." And it was so. ¹⁶God made two great lights—the greater light to govern the day and the lesser light to govern the night. He also made the stars. ¹⁷God set them in the expanse of the sky to give light on the earth, ¹⁸to govern the day and the night, and to separate light from darkness. And God saw that it was good. ¹⁹And there was evening, and there was morning—the fourth day.

²⁰And God said, "Let the water teem with living creatures, and let birds fly above the earth across the expanse of the sky." ²¹So God created the great creatures of the sea and every living and moving thing with which the water teems, according to their kinds, and every winged bird according to its kind. And God saw that it was good. ²²God blessed them and said, "Be fruitful and increase in number and fill the water in the seas, and let the birds increase on the earth." ²³And there was evening, and there was morning—the fifth day.

²⁴And God said, "Let the land produce living creatures according to their kinds: livestock, creatures that move along the ground, and wild animals, each according to its kind." And it was so. ²⁵God made the wild animals according to their kinds, the livestock according to their kinds, and all the creatures that move along the ground according to their kinds. And God saw that it was good.

²⁶Then God said, "Let us make man in our image, in our likeness, and let them rule over the fish of the sea and the birds of the air, over the livestock, over all the earth,ᵃ and over all the creatures that move along the ground."

²⁷So God created man in his own image,
in the image of God he created him;
male and female he created them.

²⁸God blessed them and said to them, "Be fruitful and increase in number; fill the earth and subdue it. Rule over the fish of the sea and the birds of the air and over every living creature that moves on the ground."

²⁹Then God said, "I give you every seed-bearing plant on the face of the whole earth and every tree that has fruit with seed in it. They will be yours for food. ³⁰And to all the beasts of the earth and all the birds of the air and all the creatures that move on the ground—everything that has the breath of life in it—I give every green plant for food." And it was so.

³¹God saw all that he had made, and it was very good. And there was evening, and there was morning—the sixth day.

Genesis 1:27

God Is Our Creator

So God created man
in his own image,
in the image of God
he created him;
male and female he
created them.

ᵃ26 Hebrew; Syriac *all the wild animals*

God's Image Bearers

Read: Genesis 1:27–31

IMAGINE THE SCENE. Holding her hair back with one hand, the woman kneels and leans forward to drink from the clear pool of water. As her cupped hand reaches for the clear liquid, she draws back, startled. Who is the long-haired stranger staring back at her?

Perhaps even since the time Eve first caught sight of her reflection in the Garden of Eden, women have dealt with the question of image. Polls consistently reveal that the majority of us are dissatisfied with our appearance. Confronted with a barrage of airbrushed photos of supermodels and celebrities adorning magazine covers, the average woman thinks she is too short, too fat, too unattractive, too imperfect. How can we ever measure up with the media's standards of perfection?

The first chapter of the Bible supplies the answer. We were created in the image of one paradigm of perfection: our Creator. Our height, weight and skin color may indicate our human origins, but our soul and spirit reflect our Sovereign God.

When a child is born, it's not unusual for someone to claim she's the very "image" of a relative. But what does it mean to be created in the image of our heavenly Father? An image is a likeness or resemblance—a reflection as seen in a mirror. Scripture teaches that Jesus Christ is the "image of the invisible God" (Colossians 1:15). As we grow in faith, we who believe are gradually "being transformed into [Christ's] likeness" (2 Corinthians 3:18). When we become like Jesus, we begin to look more and more like our heavenly Father.

God created us to convey the distinctive imprint of his divine nature to a world often blinded to his existence. Even our differences reflect the One who delighted in creating a world of dazzling diversity: peculiar penguins and majestic eagles; towering redwoods and dwarf pines; blondes, brunettes and redheads . . . every person created with the individual imprint of the Creator's hand to bear his image. So the next time you pass by a mirror, pause a moment to gaze in wonder at the designer original whom God loves so dearly—you!

Go to page 9 for your next devotional reading.

Genesis 1:27

So God created man in his own image, in the image of God he created him; male and female he created them.

reflection

1 How do you see God's image reflected in the lives of others you admire?

2 What factors from the past have damaged your sense of self-worth?

3 Think of three ways in which you can beautifully reflect the characteristics of your Creator by imitating Christ.

RELATED READINGS

Psalm 139:14;
2 Corinthians 3:18;
Colossians 1:15;
Revelation 7:9

"A handful of the earth to make God's image!"

Elizabeth Barrett Browning

3

2 Thus the heavens and the earth were completed in all their vast array.

²By the seventh day God had finished the work he had been doing; so on the seventh day he rested[a] from all his work. ³And God blessed the seventh day and made it holy, because on it he rested from all the work of creating that he had done.

Adam and Eve

⁴This is the account of the heavens and the earth when they were created.

When the LORD God made the earth and the heavens— ⁵and no shrub of the field had yet appeared on the earth[b] and no plant of the field had yet sprung up, for the LORD God had not sent rain on the earth[b] and there was no man to work the ground, ⁶but streams[c] came up from the earth and watered the whole surface of the ground— ⁷the LORD God formed the man[d] from the dust of the ground and breathed into his nostrils the breath of life, and the man became a living being.

⁸Now the LORD God had planted a garden in the east, in Eden; and there he put the man he had formed. ⁹And the LORD God made all kinds of trees grow out of the ground—trees that were pleasing to the eye and good for food. In the middle of the garden were the tree of life and the tree of the knowledge of good and evil.

¹⁰A river watering the garden flowed from Eden; from there it was separated into four headwaters. ¹¹The name of the first is the Pishon; it winds through the entire land of Havilah, where there is gold. ¹²(The gold of that land is good; aromatic resin[e] and onyx are also there.) ¹³The name of the second river is the Gihon; it winds through the entire land of Cush.[f] ¹⁴The name of the third river is the Tigris; it runs along the east side of Asshur. And the fourth river is the Euphrates.

¹⁵The LORD God took the man and put him in the Garden of Eden to work it and take care of it. ¹⁶And the LORD God commanded the man, "You are free to eat from any tree in the garden; ¹⁷but you must not eat from the tree of the knowledge of good and evil, for when you eat of it you will surely die."

¹⁸The LORD God said, "It is not good for the man to be alone. I will make a helper suitable for him." ¹⁹Now the LORD God had formed out of the ground all the beasts of the field and all the birds of the air. He brought them to the man to see what he would name them; and whatever the man called each living creature, that was its name. ²⁰So the man gave names to all the livestock, the birds of the air and all the beasts of the field.

But for Adam[g] no suitable helper was found. ²¹So the LORD God caused the man to fall into a deep sleep; and while he was sleeping, he took one of the man's ribs[h] and closed up the place with flesh. ²²Then the LORD God made a woman from the rib[i] he had taken out of the man, and he brought her to the man.

²³The man said,

"This is now bone of my bones
    and flesh of my flesh;
she shall be called 'woman,'[j]
    for she was taken out of man."

²⁴For this reason a man will leave his father and mother and be united to his wife, and they will become one flesh.

²⁵The man and his wife were both naked, and they felt no shame.

The Fall of Man

3 Now the serpent was more crafty than any of the wild animals the LORD God had made. He said to the woman, "Did God really say, 'You must not eat from any tree in the garden'?"

Genesis 2:24

God Ordains Marriage

For this reason a man will leave his father and mother and be united to his wife, and they will become one flesh.

---

a2 Or *ceased*; also in verse 3   b5 Or *land*; also in verse 6   c6 Or *mist*   d7 The Hebrew for *man (adam)* sounds like and may be related to the Hebrew for *ground (adamah)*; it is also the name *Adam* (see Gen. 2:20).   e12 Or *good; pearls*   f13 Possibly southeast Mesopotamia   g20 Or *the man*   h21 Or *took part of the man's side*   i22 Or *part*   j23 The Hebrew for *woman* sounds like the Hebrew for *man*.

²The woman said to the serpent, "We may eat fruit from the trees in the garden, ³but God did say, 'You must not eat fruit from the tree that is in the middle of the garden, and you must not touch it, or you will die.'"

⁴"You will not surely die," the serpent said to the woman. ⁵"For God knows that when you eat of it your eyes will be opened, and you will be like God, knowing good and evil."

⁶When the woman saw that the fruit of the tree was good for food and pleasing to the eye, and also desirable for gaining wisdom, she took some and ate it. She also gave some to her husband, who was with her, and he ate it. ⁷Then the eyes of both of them were opened, and they realized they were naked; so they sewed fig leaves together and made coverings for themselves.

⁸Then the man and his wife heard the sound of the LORD God as he was walking in the garden in the cool of the day, and they hid from the LORD God among the trees of the garden. ⁹But the LORD God called to the man, "Where are you?"

¹⁰He answered, "I heard you in the garden, and I was afraid because I was naked; so I hid."

¹¹And he said, "Who told you that you were naked? Have you eaten from the tree that I commanded you not to eat from?"

¹²The man said, "The woman you put here with me—she gave me some fruit from the tree, and I ate it."

¹³Then the LORD God said to the woman, "What is this you have done?"

The woman said, "The serpent deceived me, and I ate."

¹⁴So the LORD God said to the serpent, "Because you have done this,

"Cursed are you above all
    the livestock
and all the wild animals!
You will crawl on your belly
    and you will eat dust

all the days of your life.
¹⁵And I will put enmity
    between you and the woman,
    and between your offspring[a] and hers;
he will crush[b] your head,
    and you will strike his heel."

¹⁶To the woman he said,

"I will greatly increase your pains in
        childbearing;
    with pain you will give birth to children.
Your desire will be for your husband,
    and he will rule over you."

¹⁷To Adam he said, "Because you listened to your wife and ate from the tree about which I commanded you, 'You must not eat of it,'

"Cursed is the ground because of you;
    through painful toil you will eat of it
    all the days of your life.
¹⁸It will produce thorns and thistles for you,
    and you will eat the plants of the field.
¹⁹By the sweat of your brow
    you will eat your food
until you return to the ground,
    since from it you were taken;
for dust you are
    and to dust you will return."

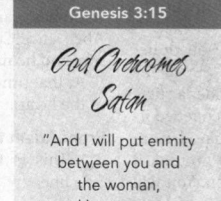

Genesis 3:15

God Overcomes Satan

"And I will put enmity between you and the woman, and between your offspring and hers; he will crush your head, and you will strike his heel."

²⁰Adam[c] named his wife Eve,[d] because she would become the mother of all the living.

²¹The LORD God made garments of skin for Adam and his wife and clothed them. ²²And the LORD God said, "The man has now become like one of us, knowing good and evil. He must not be allowed to reach out his hand and take also from the tree of life and eat, and live forever." ²³So the LORD God banished him from the Garden of Eden to work the ground from which he had been taken. ²⁴After he drove the man out, he placed on the east side[e] of the Garden of Eden cherubim and a flaming sword

---

a15 Or seed b15 Or strike c20 Or The man d20 Eve probably means living. e24 Or placed in front flashing back and forth to guard the way to the tree of life.

Cain and Abel

4 Adam[a] lay with his wife Eve, and she became pregnant and gave birth to Cain.[b] She said, "With the help of the Lord I have brought forth[c] a man." [2]Later she gave birth to his brother Abel.

Now Abel kept flocks, and Cain worked the soil. [3]In the course of time Cain brought some of the fruits of the soil as an offering to the Lord. [4]But Abel brought fat portions from some of the firstborn of his flock. The Lord looked with favor on Abel and his offering, [5]but on Cain and his offering he did not look with favor. So Cain was very angry, and his face was downcast.

[6]Then the Lord said to Cain, "Why are you angry? Why is your face downcast? [7]If you do what is right, will you not be accepted? But if you do not do what is right, sin is crouching at your door; it desires to have you, but you must master it."

[8]Now Cain said to his brother Abel, "Let's go out to the field."[d] And while they were in the field, Cain attacked his brother Abel and killed him.

[9]Then the Lord said to Cain, "Where is your brother Abel?"

"I don't know," he replied. "Am I my brother's keeper?"

[10]The Lord said, "What have you done? Listen! Your brother's blood cries out to me from the ground. [11]Now you are under a curse and driven from the ground, which opened its mouth to receive your brother's blood from your hand. [12]When you work the ground, it will no longer yield its crops for you. You will be a restless wanderer on the earth."

[13]Cain said to the Lord, "My punishment is more than I can bear. [14]Today you are driving me from the land, and I will be hidden from your presence; I will be a restless wanderer on the earth, and whoever finds me will kill me."

[15]But the Lord said to him, "Not so[e]; if anyone kills Cain, he will suffer vengeance seven times over." Then the Lord put a mark on Cain so that no one who found him would kill him. [16]So Cain went out from the Lord's presence and lived in the land of Nod,[f] east of Eden.

[17]Cain lay with his wife, and she became pregnant and gave birth to Enoch. Cain was then building a city, and he named it after his son Enoch. [18]To Enoch was born Irad, and Irad was the father of Mehujael, and Mehujael was the father of Methushael, and Methushael was the father of Lamech.

[19]Lamech married two women, one named Adah and the other Zillah. [20]Adah gave birth to Jabal; he was the father of those who live in tents and raise livestock. [21]His brother's name was Jubal; he was the father of all who play the harp and flute. [22]Zillah also had a son, Tubal-Cain, who forged all kinds of tools out of[g] bronze and iron. Tubal-Cain's sister was Naamah.

[23]Lamech said to his wives,

"Adah and Zillah, listen to me;
    wives of Lamech, hear my words.
I have killed[h] a man for wounding me,
    a young man for injuring me.
[24]If Cain is avenged seven times,
    then Lamech seventy-seven times."

[25]Adam lay with his wife again, and she gave birth to a son and named him Seth,[i] saying, "God has granted me another child in place of Abel, since Cain killed him." [26]Seth also had a son, and he named him Enosh.

At that time men began to call on[j] the name of the Lord.

From Adam to Noah

5 This is the written account of Adam's line.

When God created man, he made him in the likeness of God. [2]He created them male and female and blessed them. And when they were created, he called them "man."[k]

[3]When Adam had lived 130 years, he had a son in his own likeness, in his own image; and he named him Seth. [4]After Seth was born,

[a]1 Or The man   [b]1 Cain sounds like the Hebrew for brought forth or acquired.   [c]1 Or have acquired   [d]8 Samaritan Pentateuch, Septuagint, Vulgate and Syriac; Masoretic Text does not have "Let's go out to the field."   [e]15 Septuagint, Vulgate and Syriac; Hebrew Very well   [f]16 Nod means wandering (see verses 12 and 14).   [g]22 Or who instructed all who work in   [h]23 Or I will kill   [i]25 Seth probably means granted.   [j]26 Or to proclaim   [k]2 Hebrew adam

Adam lived 800 years and had other sons and daughters. ⁵Altogether, Adam lived 930 years, and then he died.

⁶When Seth had lived 105 years, he became the father*a* of Enosh. ⁷And after he became the father of Enosh, Seth lived 807 years and had other sons and daughters. ⁸Altogether, Seth lived 912 years, and then he died.

⁹When Enosh had lived 90 years, he became the father of Kenan. ¹⁰And after he became the father of Kenan, Enosh lived 815 years and had other sons and daughters. ¹¹Altogether, Enosh lived 905 years, and then he died.

¹²When Kenan had lived 70 years, he became the father of Mahalalel. ¹³And after he became the father of Mahalalel, Kenan lived 840 years and had other sons and daughters. ¹⁴Altogether, Kenan lived 910 years, and then he died.

¹⁵When Mahalalel had lived 65 years, he became the father of Jared. ¹⁶And after he became the father of Jared, Mahalalel lived 830 years and had other sons and daughters. ¹⁷Altogether, Mahalalel lived 895 years, and then he died.

¹⁸When Jared had lived 162 years, he became the father of Enoch. ¹⁹And after he became the father of Enoch, Jared lived 800 years and had other sons and daughters. ²⁰Altogether, Jared lived 962 years, and then he died.

²¹When Enoch had lived 65 years, he became the father of Methuselah. ²²And after he became the father of Methuselah, Enoch walked with God 300 years and had other sons and daughters. ²³Altogether, Enoch lived 365 years. ²⁴Enoch walked with God; then he was no more, because God took him away.

²⁵When Methuselah had lived 187 years, he became the father of Lamech. ²⁶And after he became the father of Lamech, Methuselah lived 782 years and had other sons and daughters. ²⁷Altogether, Methuselah lived 969 years, and then he died.

Genesis 5:24

God Walks With His People

Enoch walked with God; then he was no more, because God took him away.

---

²⁸When Lamech had lived 182 years, he had a son. ²⁹He named him Noah*b* and said, "He will comfort us in the labor and painful toil of our hands caused by the ground the LORD has cursed." ³⁰After Noah was born, Lamech lived 595 years and had other sons and daughters. ³¹Altogether, Lamech lived 777 years, and then he died.

³²After Noah was 500 years old, he became the father of Shem, Ham and Japheth.

The Flood

6 When men began to increase in number on the earth and daughters were born to them, ²the sons of God saw that the daughters of men were beautiful, and they married any of them they chose. ³Then the LORD said, "My Spirit will not contend with*c* man forever, for he is mortal*d*; his days will be a hundred and twenty years."

⁴The Nephilim were on the earth in those days—and also afterward—when the sons of God went to the daughters of men and had children by them. They were the heroes of old, men of renown.

⁵The LORD saw how great man's wickedness on the earth had become, and that every inclination of the thoughts of his heart was only evil all the time. ⁶The LORD was grieved that he had made man on the earth, and his heart was filled with pain. ⁷So the LORD said, "I will wipe mankind, whom I have created, from the face of the earth—men and animals, and creatures that move along the ground, and birds of the air—for I am grieved that I have made them." ⁸But Noah found favor in the eyes of the LORD.

⁹This is the account of Noah.

Noah was a righteous man, blameless among the people of his time, and he walked with God. ¹⁰Noah had three sons: Shem, Ham and Japheth.

¹¹Now the earth was corrupt in God's sight

---

*a*6 *Father* may mean *ancestor*; also in verses 7–26.   *b*29 *Noah* sounds like the Hebrew for *comfort*.   *c*3 Or *My spirit will not remain in*   *d*3 Or *corrupt* and was full of violence. ¹²God saw how corrupt the earth had become, for all the people on earth had corrupted their ways. ¹³So God said to Noah, "I am going to put an end to all people, for the earth is filled with violence because of them. I am surely going to destroy both them and the earth. ¹⁴So make yourself an ark of cypress*a* wood; make rooms in it and coat it with pitch inside and out. ¹⁵This is how you are to build it: The ark is to be 450 feet long, 75 feet wide and 45 feet high.*b* ¹⁶Make a roof for it and finish*c* the ark to within 18 inches*d* of the top. Put a door in the side of the ark and make lower, middle and upper decks. ¹⁷I am going to bring floodwaters on the earth to destroy all life under the heavens, every creature that has the breath of life in it. Everything on earth will perish. ¹⁸But I will establish my covenant with you, and you will enter the ark—you and your sons and your wife and your sons' wives with you. ¹⁹You are to bring into the ark two of all living creatures, male and female, to keep them alive with you. ²⁰Two of every kind of bird, of every kind of animal and of every kind of creature that moves along the ground will come to you to be kept alive. ²¹You are to take every kind of food that is to be eaten and store it away as food for you and for them."

²²Noah did everything just as God commanded him.

7 The LORD then said to Noah, "Go into the ark, you and your whole family, because I have found you righteous in this generation. ²Take with you seven*e* of every kind of clean animal, a male and its mate, and two of every kind of unclean animal, a male and its mate, ³and also seven of every kind of bird, male and female, to keep their various kinds alive throughout the earth. ⁴Seven days from now I will send rain on the earth for forty days and forty nights, and I will wipe from the face

Genesis 6:17–18

God Protects Us

"I am going to bring floodwaters on the earth…Everything on earth will perish. But I will establish my covenant with you, and you will enter the ark—you and your sons and your wife and your sons' wives with you."

of the earth every living creature I have made."

⁵And Noah did all that the LORD commanded him.

⁶Noah was six hundred years old when the floodwaters came on the earth. ⁷And Noah and his sons and his wife and his sons' wives entered the ark to escape the waters of the flood. ⁸Pairs of clean and unclean animals, of birds and of all creatures that move along the ground, ⁹male and female, came to Noah and entered the ark, as God had commanded Noah. ¹⁰And after the seven days the floodwaters came on the earth.

¹¹In the six hundredth year of Noah's life, on the seventeenth day of the second month—on that day all the springs of the great deep burst forth, and the floodgates of the heavens were opened. ¹²And rain fell on the earth forty days and forty nights.

¹³On that very day Noah and his sons, Shem, Ham and Japheth, together with his wife and the wives of his three sons, entered the ark. ¹⁴They had with them every wild animal according to its kind, all livestock according to their kinds, every creature that moves along the ground according to its kind and every bird according to its kind, everything with wings. ¹⁵Pairs of all creatures that have the breath of life in them came to Noah and entered the ark. ¹⁶The animals going in were male and female of every living thing, as God had commanded Noah. Then the LORD shut him in.

¹⁷For forty days the flood kept coming on the earth, and as the waters increased they lifted the ark high above the earth. ¹⁸The waters rose and increased greatly on the earth, and the ark floated on the surface of the water. ¹⁹They rose greatly on the earth, and all the high mountains under the entire heavens were covered. ²⁰The waters rose and covered the mountains to a depth of more than twenty feet.*f,g* ²¹Every living thing that moved

a14 The meaning of the Hebrew for this word is uncertain. *b15 Hebrew 300 cubits long, 50 cubits wide and 30 cubits high (about 140 meters long, 23 meters wide and 13.5 meters high)* *c16 Or Make an opening for light by finishing* *d16 Hebrew a cubit (about 0.5 meter)* *e2 Or seven pairs; also in verse 3* *f20 Hebrew fifteen cubits (about 6.9 meters)* *g20 Or rose more than twenty feet, and the mountains were covered*

When Floods Come

Read: Genesis 7:1–24

A NATURAL DISASTER hits a community, city or country, and the loss is mind-boggling. The media reports facts and figures to describe the devastation, but the tragedy doesn't hit home until we see the pictures and hear the stories. Tears. Faces etched in agony. Eyes roaming for lost loved ones. Families torn apart: A man who lost his son; a woman whose husband is missing; a child looking for a familiar face. The unbearable pain and sorrow become more personal.

Long ago there was a great flood. Noah and his family knew catastrophe was coming, so they built an ark at God's command. They followed instructions. They braced for impending crisis. They endured umpteen years of looking foolish. They faced criticism, ridicule, rejection. They plodded in the slow work of faith and love. Then the downpour came and the final command: "Go into the ark." So Noah and his family left everything and evacuated to the big boat. Noah led the eight members of his family into a floating zoo—out of harm's way. The devastation of the world they knew had to be heartbreaking. But they followed God, and his grace saved them from the disaster.

When storms come in your own life, they may not be a calamity on the scale of a flood. But they may bring just as much sorrow and pain—an illness, an accident, a betrayal. In the midst of the event, your decisions can help save you and your family. Let's face it; disaster can strike whether you're a saint or sinner. To survive requires spiritual preparation. When you build your home on the foundation of God's Word, you can find safety despite the downpour outside. You can help those you love to weather the storm. Begin now to prepare your house for the storms that are sure to come: Spend time in the Bible. Strengthen your relationship with God and with a godly community. Bring those you love before God in prayer. When (not if) the tempest strikes, you will have shelter.

Genesis 7:1

The LORD then said to Noah, "Go into the ark, you and your family, because I have found you righteous in this generation."

reflection

1 In the face of a flood, who would you take with you into the ark?

2 How are you preparing for the inevitable storms of life? How will your family benefit from your actions?

3 Has God commanded you to do things that may seem foolish to others? In what ways are you obeying him?

RELATED READINGS

Hebrews 11:1–16;
1 Peter 3:13–22;
2 Peter 3:11–18

"There are some things you learn best in calm, and some in storm."

Willa Cather

Go to page 13 for your next devotional reading.

on the earth perished—birds, livestock, wild animals, all the creatures that swarm over the earth, and all mankind. [22]Everything on dry land that had the breath of life in its nostrils died. [23]Every living thing on the face of the earth was wiped out; men and animals and the creatures that move along the ground and the birds of the air were wiped from the earth. Only Noah was left, and those with him in the ark.

[24]The waters flooded the earth for a hundred and fifty days.

8 But God remembered Noah and all the wild animals and the livestock that were with him in the ark, and he sent a wind over the earth, and the waters receded. [2]Now the springs of the deep and the floodgates of the heavens had been closed, and the rain had stopped falling from the sky. [3]The water receded steadily from the earth. At the end of the hundred and fifty days the water had gone down, [4]and on the seventeenth day of the seventh month the ark came to rest on the mountains of Ararat. [5]The waters continued to recede until the tenth month, and on the first day of the tenth month the tops of the mountains became visible.

[6]After forty days Noah opened the window he had made in the ark [7]and sent out a raven, and it kept flying back and forth until the water had dried up from the earth. [8]Then he sent out a dove to see if the water had receded from the surface of the ground. [9]But the dove could find no place to set its feet because there was water over all the surface of the earth; so it returned to Noah in the ark. He reached out his hand and took the dove and brought it back to himself in the ark. [10]He waited seven more days and again sent out the dove from the ark. [11]When the dove returned to him in the evening, there in its beak was a freshly plucked olive leaf! Then Noah knew that the water had receded from the earth. [12]He waited seven more days and sent the dove out again, but this time it did not return to him.

[13]By the first day of the first month of Noah's six hundred and first year, the water had dried up from the earth. Noah then removed the covering from the ark and saw that the surface of the ground was dry. [14]By the twenty-seventh day of the second month the earth was completely dry.

[15]Then God said to Noah, [16]"Come out of the ark, you and your wife and your sons and their wives. [17]Bring out every kind of living creature that is with you—the birds, the animals, and all the creatures that move along the ground—so they can multiply on the earth and be fruitful and increase in number upon it."

[18]So Noah came out, together with his sons and his wife and his sons' wives. [19]All the animals and all the creatures that move along the ground and all the birds—everything that moves on the earth—came out of the ark, one kind after another.

[20]Then Noah built an altar to the LORD and, taking some of all the clean animals and clean birds, he sacrificed burnt offerings on it. [21]The LORD smelled the pleasing aroma and said in his heart: "Never again will I curse the ground because of man, even though[a] every inclination of his heart is evil from childhood. And never again will I destroy all living creatures, as I have done.

[22]"As long as the earth endures,
    seedtime and harvest,
    cold and heat,
    summer and winter,
    day and night
    will never cease."

God's Covenant With Noah

9 Then God blessed Noah and his sons, saying to them, "Be fruitful and increase in number and fill the earth. [2]The fear and dread of you will fall upon all the beasts of the earth

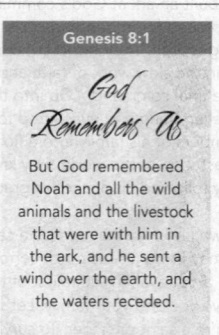

Genesis 8:1

God Remembers Us

But God remembered Noah and all the wild animals and the livestock that were with him in the ark, and he sent a wind over the earth, and the waters receded.

---

[a]21 Or *man, for*

and all the birds of the air, upon every creature that moves along the ground, and upon all the fish of the sea; they are given into your hands. ³Everything that lives and moves will be food for you. Just as I gave you the green plants, I now give you everything.

⁴"But you must not eat meat that has its lifeblood still in it. ⁵And for your lifeblood I will surely demand an accounting. I will demand an accounting from every animal. And from each man, too, I will demand an accounting for the life of his fellow man.

⁶"Whoever sheds the blood of man,
　by man shall his blood be shed;
for in the image of God
　has God made man.

⁷As for you, be fruitful and increase in number; multiply on the earth and increase upon it."

⁸Then God said to Noah and to his sons with him: ⁹"I now establish my covenant with you and with your descendants after you ¹⁰and with every living creature that was with you—the birds, the livestock and all the wild animals, all those that came out of the ark with you—every living creature on earth. ¹¹I establish my covenant with you: Never again will all life be cut off by the waters of a flood; never again will there be a flood to destroy the earth."

¹²And God said, "This is the sign of the covenant I am making between me and you and every living creature with you, a covenant for all generations to come: ¹³I have set my rainbow in the clouds, and it will be the sign of the covenant between me and the earth. ¹⁴Whenever I bring clouds over the earth and the rainbow appears in the clouds, ¹⁵I will remember my covenant between me and you and all living creatures of every kind. Never again will the waters become a flood to destroy all life. ¹⁶Whenever the rainbow appears in the clouds, I will see it and remember the everlast-

ing covenant between God and all living creatures of every kind on the earth." ¹⁷So God said to Noah, "This is the sign of the covenant I have established between me and all life on the earth."

The Sons of Noah

¹⁸The sons of Noah who came out of the ark were Shem, Ham and Japheth. (Ham was the father of Canaan.) ¹⁹These were the three sons of Noah, and from them came the people who were scattered over the earth.

²⁰Noah, a man of the soil, proceeded*a* to plant a vineyard. ²¹When he drank some of its wine, he became drunk and lay uncovered inside his tent. ²²Ham, the father of Canaan, saw his father's nakedness and told his two brothers outside. ²³But Shem and Japheth took a garment and laid it across their shoulders; then they walked in backward and covered their father's nakedness. Their faces were turned the other way so that they would not see their father's nakedness.

²⁴When Noah awoke from his wine and found out what his youngest son had done to him, ²⁵he said,

"Cursed be Canaan!
　The lowest of slaves
　will he be to his brothers."

²⁶He also said,

"Blessed be the LORD, the God of Shem!
　May Canaan be the slave of Shem.*b*
²⁷May God extend the territory of Japheth*c*;
　may Japheth live in the tents of Shem,
　and may Canaan be his*d* slave."

²⁸After the flood Noah lived 350 years. ²⁹Altogether, Noah lived 950 years, and then he died.

The Table of Nations

10 This is the account of Shem, Ham and Japheth, Noah's sons, who themselves had sons after the flood.

Genesis 9:15

God Keeps His Promises

"I will remember my covenant between me and you and all living creatures of every kind. Never again will the waters become a flood to destroy all life."

---

*a*20 Or *soil, was the first*　*b*26 Or *be his slave*　*c*27 *Japheth* sounds like the Hebrew for *extend.*　*d*27 Or *their*

The Japhethites

2 The sons[a] of Japheth:

Gomer, Magog, Madai, Javan, Tubal, Meshech and Tiras.

3 The sons of Gomer:

Ashkenaz, Riphath and Togarmah.

4 The sons of Javan:

Elishah, Tarshish, the Kittim and the Rodanim.[b] 5 (From these the maritime peoples spread out into their territories by their clans within their nations, each with its own language.)

The Hamites

6 The sons of Ham:

Cush, Mizraim,[c] Put and Canaan.

7 The sons of Cush:

Seba, Havilah, Sabtah, Raamah and Sabteca.

The sons of Raamah:

Sheba and Dedan.

8 Cush was the father[d] of Nimrod, who grew to be a mighty warrior on the earth. 9 He was a mighty hunter before the LORD; that is why it is said, "Like Nimrod, a mighty hunter before the LORD." 10 The first centers of his kingdom were Babylon, Erech, Akkad and Calneh, in[e] Shinar.[f] 11 From that land he went to Assyria, where he built Nineveh, Rehoboth Ir,[g] Calah 12 and Resen, which is between Nineveh and Calah; that is the great city.

13 Mizraim was the father of

the Ludites, Anamites, Lehabites, Naphtuhites, 14 Pathrusites, Casluhites (from whom the Philistines came) and Caphtorites.

15 Canaan was the father of

Sidon his firstborn,[h] and of the Hittites, 16 Jebusites, Amorites, Girgashites, 17 Hivites, Arkites, Sinites, 18 Arvadites, Zemarites and Hamathites.

Later the Canaanite clans scattered 19 and the borders of Canaan reached from Sidon toward Gerar as far as Gaza, and then toward Sodom, Gomorrah, Admah and Zeboiim, as far as Lasha.

20 These are the sons of Ham by their clans and languages, in their territories and nations.

The Semites

21 Sons were also born to Shem, whose older brother was[i] Japheth; Shem was the ancestor of all the sons of Eber.

22 The sons of Shem:

Elam, Asshur, Arphaxad, Lud and Aram.

23 The sons of Aram:

Uz, Hul, Gether and Meshech.[j]

24 Arphaxad was the father of[k] Shelah, and Shelah the father of Eber.

25 Two sons were born to Eber:

One was named Peleg,[l] because in his time the earth was divided; his brother was named Joktan.

26 Joktan was the father of

Almodad, Sheleph, Hazarmaveth, Jerah, 27 Hadoram, Uzal, Diklah, 28 Obal, Abimael, Sheba, 29 Ophir, Havilah and Jobab. All these were sons of Joktan.

30 The region where they lived stretched from Mesha toward Sephar, in the eastern hill country.

31 These are the sons of Shem by their clans and languages, in their territories and nations.

32 These are the clans of Noah's sons, according to their lines of descent, within their nations. From these the nations spread out over the earth after the flood.

The Tower of Babel

11 Now the whole world had one language and a common speech. 2 As men moved eastward,[m] they found a plain in Shinar[f] and settled there.

3 They said to each other, "Come, let's make bricks and bake them thoroughly." They used brick instead of stone, and tar for mortar. 4 Then they said, "Come, let us build ourselves a city, with a tower that reaches to the heavens, so that

---

*a2 *Sons* may mean *descendants* or *successors* or *nations*; also in verses 3, 4, 6, 7, 20–23, 29 and 31. *b4 *Some manuscripts of the Masoretic Text and Samaritan Pentateuch (see also Septuagint and 1 Chron. 1:7); most manuscripts of the Masoretic Text *Dodanim* *c6 *That is, Egypt; also in verse 13 *d8 *Father* may mean *ancestor* or *predecessor* or *founder*; also in verses 13, 15, 24 and 26. *e10 *Or *Erech and Akkad—all of them in *f10,2 *That is, Babylonia *g11 *Or *Nineveh with its city squares *h15 *Or *of the Sidonians, the foremost *i21 *Or *Shem, the older brother of *j23 *See Septuagint and 1 Chron. 1:17; Hebrew *Mash *k24 *Hebrew; Septuagint *father of Cainan, and Cainan was the father of *l25 *Peleg* means *division. *m2 *Or *from the east; or *in the east

12

Reaching for the Heavens

Read: Genesis 11:1–9

LOUIS SULLIVAN, the inventor of the modern skyscraper, said, "The tall building . . . should be a proud and soaring thing that makes a powerful appeal to the architectural imagination." Today, many women embody the same spirit of pride and self-sufficiency that is represented in the lofty towers that make up our cities. We focus on personal perfection. Many women seek the pinnacle of age-defying beauty through creams, procedures or surgeries. Some become obsessed with fashion or feel that they must conform to some media-driven image. Over time, it becomes easier and easier to build monuments to ourselves. After all, as the famous ad says, "I'm worth it."

The builders of the tower of Babel shared a key aspect of Sullivan's vision of the tall building: pride. And they had one purpose: to build a name for themselves. They wanted to claim glory that rightly belonged to God—after all, they were worth it.

The longing to climb higher than God didn't begin in Babel. Before time began Lucifer said, "I will raise my throne above the stars of God" (Isaiah 14:13). It didn't end with Babel, either. The pyramids of Egypt proclaim the power of the rulers buried beneath them. Many lives were lost in the building of the pyramids, "collateral damage" to the princes who built them. Often Egyptian slaves were killed when their masters died and were buried alongside them. But just as the Egyptian kings sacrificed everything to their own legacy, women often sacrifice the good of those around them for fleeting recognition, not to mention the humble spirit God desires. The rulers of ancient Egypt were not all-powerful—they died the deaths of mere men. Don't be deceived, your soul will not be saved by flawless skin or the perfect career any more than the towering mountains of stone raised over the mummies of kings saved them.

What do you take pride in? What keeps you from glorifying God? Has your focus become self-absorbed? Have you become self-glorifying? The solution is simple: Whatever is keeping you from God, give it to him for his glory. Let your relationship with Jesus be the source of your significance. When you humble yourself before God, you'll be lifted up.

Go to page 18 for your next devotional reading.

Genesis 11:4

"Come, let us build ourselves a city, with a tower that reaches to the heavens, so that we may make a name for ourselves and not be scattered over the face of the whole earth."

reflection

1 Name some of the towers you see others building around you that take glory away from God. What kinds of towers have you built?

2 Have you ever taken credit for work when another person really deserved it, or has someone taken credit for work you have done? How did that feel?

3 How do you think God feels when we take the credit for his work in our lives?

RELATED READINGS

Psalm 86:8–10; Proverbs 18:10–12; Matthew 23:12

"The one sole thing in myself in which I glory is that I see in myself nothing in which I can glory."

Catherine of Genoa

we may make a name for ourselves and not be scattered over the face of the whole earth."

⁵But the LORD came down to see the city and the tower that the men were building. ⁶The LORD said, "If as one people speaking the same language they have begun to do this, then nothing they plan to do will be impossible for them. ⁷Come, let us go down and confuse their language so they will not understand each other."

⁸So the LORD scattered them from there over all the earth, and they stopped building the city. ⁹That is why it was called Babel[a]—because there the LORD confused the language of the whole world. From there the LORD scattered them over the face of the whole earth.

From Shem to Abram

¹⁰This is the account of Shem.

Two years after the flood, when Shem was 100 years old, he became the father[b] of Arphaxad. ¹¹And after he became the father of Arphaxad, Shem lived 500 years and had other sons and daughters.

¹²When Arphaxad had lived 35 years, he became the father of Shelah. ¹³And after he became the father of Shelah, Arphaxad lived 403 years and had other sons and daughters.[c]

¹⁴When Shelah had lived 30 years, he became the father of Eber. ¹⁵And after he became the father of Eber, Shelah lived 403 years and had other sons and daughters.

¹⁶When Eber had lived 34 years, he became the father of Peleg. ¹⁷And after he became the father of Peleg, Eber lived 430 years and had other sons and daughters.

¹⁸When Peleg had lived 30 years, he became the father of Reu. ¹⁹And after he became the father of Reu, Peleg lived 209 years and had other sons and daughters.

²⁰When Reu had lived 32 years, he became the father of Serug. ²¹And after he became the

father of Serug, Reu lived 207 years and had other sons and daughters.

²²When Serug had lived 30 years, he became the father of Nahor. ²³And after he became the father of Nahor, Serug lived 200 years and had other sons and daughters.

²⁴When Nahor had lived 29 years, he became the father of Terah. ²⁵And after he became the father of Terah, Nahor lived 119 years and had other sons and daughters.

²⁶After Terah had lived 70 years, he became the father of Abram, Nahor and Haran.

²⁷This is the account of Terah.

Terah became the father of Abram, Nahor and Haran. And Haran became the father of Lot. ²⁸While his father Terah was still alive, Haran died in Ur of the Chaldeans, in the land of his birth. ²⁹Abram and Nahor both married. The name of Abram's wife was Sarai, and the name of Nahor's wife was Milcah; she was the daughter of Haran, the father of both Milcah and Iscah. ³⁰Now Sarai was barren; she had no children.

³¹Terah took his son Abram, his grandson Lot son of Haran, and his daughter-in-law Sarai, the wife of his son Abram, and together they set out from Ur of the Chaldeans to go to Canaan. But when they came to Haran, they settled there.

³²Terah lived 205 years, and he died in Haran.

The Call of Abram

12 The LORD had said to Abram, "Leave your country, your people and your father's household and go to the land I will show you.

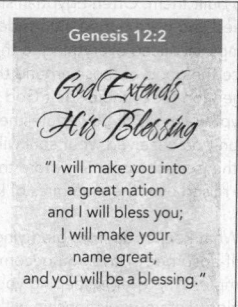

Genesis 12:2

God Extends His Blessing

"I will make you into a great nation and I will bless you; I will make your name great, and you will be a blessing."

²"I will make you into a great nation
    and I will bless you;
I will make your name great,
    and you will be a blessing;
³I will bless those who bless you,
    and whoever curses you I will curse;

---

[a]9 That is, Babylon; *Babel* sounds like the Hebrew for *confused.*   [b]10 *Father* may mean *ancestor*; also in verses 11–25.   [c]12,13 Hebrew; Septuagint (see also Luke 3:35, 36 and note at Gen. 10:24) *35 years, he became the father of Cainan. ¹³And after he became the father of Cainan, Arphaxad lived 430 years and had other sons and daughters, and then he died. When Cainan had lived 130 years, he became the father of Shelah. And after he became the father of Shelah, Cainan lived 330 years and had other sons and daughters*

and all peoples on earth
will be blessed through you."

⁴So Abram left, as the Lord had told him; and Lot went with him. Abram was seventy-five years old when he set out from Haran. ⁵He took his wife Sarai, his nephew Lot, all the possessions they had accumulated and the people they had acquired in Haran, and they set out for the land of Canaan, and they arrived there.

⁶Abram traveled through the land as far as the site of the great tree of Moreh at Shechem. At that time the Canaanites were in the land. ⁷The Lord appeared to Abram and said, "To your offspring*a* I will give this land." So he built an altar there to the Lord, who had appeared to him.

⁸From there he went on toward the hills east of Bethel and pitched his tent, with Bethel on the west and Ai on the east. There he built an altar to the Lord and called on the name of the Lord. ⁹Then Abram set out and continued toward the Negev.

Abram in Egypt

¹⁰Now there was a famine in the land, and Abram went down to Egypt to live there for a while because the famine was severe. ¹¹As he was about to enter Egypt, he said to his wife Sarai, "I know what a beautiful woman you are. ¹²When the Egyptians see you, they will say, 'This is his wife.' Then they will kill me but will let you live. ¹³Say you are my sister, so that I will be treated well for your sake and my life will be spared because of you."

¹⁴When Abram came to Egypt, the Egyptians saw that she was a very beautiful woman. ¹⁵And when Pharaoh's officials saw her, they praised her to Pharaoh, and she was taken into his palace. ¹⁶He treated Abram well for her sake, and Abram acquired sheep and cattle, male and female donkeys, menservants and maidservants, and camels.

¹⁷But the Lord inflicted serious diseases on Pharaoh and his household because of Abram's wife Sarai. ¹⁸So Pharaoh summoned Abram. "What have you done to me?" he said. "Why didn't you tell me she was your wife? ¹⁹Why did you say, 'She is my sister,' so that I took her

to be my wife? Now then, here is your wife. Take her and go!" ²⁰Then Pharaoh gave orders about Abram to his men, and they sent him on his way, with his wife and everything he had.

Abram and Lot Separate

13 So Abram went up from Egypt to the Negev, with his wife and everything he had, and Lot went with him. ²Abram had become very wealthy in livestock and in silver and gold.

³From the Negev he went from place to place until he came to Bethel, to the place between Bethel and Ai where his tent had been earlier ⁴and where he had first built an altar. There Abram called on the name of the Lord.

⁵Now Lot, who was moving about with Abram, also had flocks and herds and tents. ⁶But the land could not support them while they stayed together, for their possessions were so great that they were not able to stay together. ⁷And quarreling arose between Abram's herdsmen and the herdsmen of Lot. The Canaanites and Perizzites were also living in the land at that time.

⁸So Abram said to Lot, "Let's not have any quarreling between you and me, or between your herdsmen and mine, for we are brothers. ⁹Is not the whole land before you? Let's part company. If you go to the left, I'll go to the right; if you go to the right, I'll go to the left."

¹⁰Lot looked up and saw that the whole plain of the Jordan was well watered, like the garden of the Lord, like the land of Egypt, toward Zoar. (This was before the Lord destroyed Sodom and Gomorrah.) ¹¹So Lot chose for himself the whole plain of the Jordan and set out toward the east. The two men parted company: ¹²Abram lived in the land of Canaan, while Lot lived among the cities of the plain and pitched his tents near Sodom. ¹³Now the men of Sodom were wicked and were sinning greatly against the Lord.

¹⁴The Lord said to Abram after Lot had parted from him, "Lift up your eyes from where you are and look north and south, east and west. ¹⁵All the land that you see I will give to you and your offspring*b* forever. ¹⁶I will make your offspring like the dust of the earth,

a7 Or seed b15 Or seed; also in verse 16

so that if anyone could count the dust, then your offspring could be counted. **17**Go, walk through the length and breadth of the land, for I am giving it to you."

18So Abram moved his tents and went to live near the great trees of Mamre at Hebron, where he built an altar to the LORD.

Abram Rescues Lot

14 At this time Amraphel king of Shinar,[a] Arioch king of Ellasar, Kedorlaomer king of Elam and Tidal king of Goiim **2**went to war against Bera king of Sodom, Birsha king of Gomorrah, Shinab king of Admah, Shemeber king of Zeboiim, and the king of Bela (that is, Zoar). **3**All these latter kings joined forces in the Valley of Siddim (the Salt Sea[b]). **4**For twelve years they had been subject to Kedorlaomer, but in the thirteenth year they rebelled.

5In the fourteenth year, Kedorlaomer and the kings allied with him went out and defeated the Rephaites in Ashteroth Karnaim, the Zuzites in Ham, the Emites in Shaveh Kiriathaim **6**and the Horites in the hill country of Seir, as far as El Paran near the desert. **7**Then they turned back and went to En Mishpat (that is, Kadesh), and they conquered the whole territory of the Amalekites, as well as the Amorites who were living in Hazazon Tamar.

8Then the king of Sodom, the king of Gomorrah, the king of Admah, the king of Zeboiim and the king of Bela (that is, Zoar) marched out and drew up their battle lines in the Valley of Siddim **9**against Kedorlaomer king of Elam, Tidal king of Goiim, Amraphel king of Shinar and Arioch king of Ellasar—four kings against five. **10**Now the Valley of Siddim was full of tar pits, and when the kings of Sodom and Gomorrah fled, some of the men fell into them and the rest fled to the hills. **11**The four kings seized all the goods of Sodom and Gomorrah and all their food; then they went away. **12**They also carried off Abram's nephew Lot and his possessions, since he was living in Sodom.

13One who had escaped came and reported this to Abram the Hebrew. Now Abram was living near the great trees of Mamre the Amorite, a brother[c] of Eshcol and Aner, all of whom were allied with Abram. **14**When Abram heard that his relative had been taken captive, he called out the 318 trained men born in his household and went in pursuit as far as Dan. **15**During the night Abram divided his men to attack them and he routed them, pursuing them as far as Hobah, north of Damascus. **16**He recovered all the goods and brought back his relative Lot and his possessions, together with the women and the other people.

17After Abram returned from defeating Kedorlaomer and the kings allied with him, the king of Sodom came out to meet him in the Valley of Shaveh (that is, the King's Valley).

18Then Melchizedek king of Salem[d] brought out bread and wine. He was priest of God Most High, **19**and he blessed Abram, saying,

"Blessed be Abram by God Most High,
    Creator[e] of heaven and earth.
20And blessed be[f] God Most High,
    who delivered your enemies into your
    hand."

Then Abram gave him a tenth of everything.

21The king of Sodom said to Abram, "Give me the people and keep the goods for yourself."

22But Abram said to the king of Sodom, "I have raised my hand to the LORD, God Most High, Creator of heaven and earth, and have taken an oath **23**that I will accept nothing belonging to you, not even a thread or the thong of a sandal, so that you will never be able to say, 'I made Abram rich.' **24**I will accept nothing but what my men have eaten and the share that belongs to the men who went with me—to Aner, Eshcol and Mamre. Let them have their share."

God's Covenant With Abram

15 After this, the word of the LORD came to Abram in a vision:

"Do not be afraid, Abram.
    I am your shield,[g]
    your very great reward.[h]"

2But Abram said, "O Sovereign LORD, what can you give me since I remain childless and the one who will inherit[i] my estate is Eliezer

---

[a]1 That is, Babylonia; also in verse 9   [b]3 That is, the Dead Sea   [c]13 Or *a relative;* or *an ally*   [d]18 That is, Jerusalem   [e]19 Or *Possessor;* also in verse 22   [f]20 Or *And praise be to*   [g]1 Or *sovereign*   [h]1 Or *shield; I your reward will be very great*   [i]2 The meaning of the Hebrew for this phrase is uncertain.

of Damascus?" ³And Abram said, "You have given me no children; so a servant in my household will be my heir."

⁴Then the word of the LORD came to him: "This man will not be your heir, but a son coming from your own body will be your heir." ⁵He took him outside and said, "Look up at the heavens and count the stars—if indeed you can count them." Then he said to him, "So shall your offspring be."

⁶Abram believed the LORD, and he credited it to him as righteousness.

⁷He also said to him, "I am the LORD, who brought you out of Ur of the Chaldeans to give you this land to take possession of it."

⁸But Abram said, "O Sovereign LORD, how can I know that I will gain possession of it?"

⁹So the LORD said to him, "Bring me a heifer, a goat and a ram, each three years old, along with a dove and a young pigeon."

¹⁰Abram brought all these to him, cut them in two and arranged the halves opposite each other; the birds, however, he did not cut in half. ¹¹Then birds of prey came down on the carcasses, but Abram drove them away.

¹²As the sun was setting, Abram fell into a deep sleep, and a thick and dreadful darkness came over him. ¹³Then the LORD said to him, "Know for certain that your descendants will be strangers in a country not their own, and they will be enslaved and mistreated four hundred years. ¹⁴But I will punish the nation they serve as slaves, and afterward they will come out with great possessions. ¹⁵You, however, will go to your fathers in peace and be buried at a good old age. ¹⁶In the fourth generation your descendants will come back here, for the sin of the Amorites has not yet reached its full measure."

¹⁷When the sun had set and darkness had fallen, a smoking firepot with a blazing torch appeared and passed between the pieces. ¹⁸On that day the LORD made a covenant with Abram and said, "To your descendants I give this land, from the river[a] of Egypt to the great river, the

Euphrates— ¹⁹the land of the Kenites, Kenizzites, Kadmonites, ²⁰Hittites, Perizzites, Rephaites, ²¹Amorites, Canaanites, Girgashites and Jebusites."

Hagar and Ishmael

16 Now Sarai, Abram's wife, had borne him no children. But she had an Egyptian maidservant named Hagar; ²so she said to Abram, "The LORD has kept me from having children. Go, sleep with my maidservant; perhaps I can build a family through her."

Abram agreed to what Sarai said. ³So after Abram had been living in Canaan ten years, Sarai his wife took her Egyptian maidservant Hagar and gave her to her husband to be his wife. ⁴He slept with Hagar, and she conceived.

When she knew she was pregnant, she began to despise her mistress. ⁵Then Sarai said to Abram, "You are responsible for the wrong I am suffering. I put my servant in your arms, and now that she knows she is pregnant, she despises me. May the LORD judge between you and me."

⁶"Your servant is in your hands," Abram said. "Do with her whatever you think best." Then Sarai mistreated Hagar; so she fled from her.

⁷The angel of the LORD found Hagar near a spring in the desert; it was the spring that is beside the road to Shur. ⁸And he said, "Hagar, servant of Sarai, where have you come from, and where are you going?"

"I'm running away from my mistress Sarai," she answered.

⁹Then the angel of the LORD told her, "Go back to your mistress and submit to her." ¹⁰The angel added, "I will so increase your descendants that they will be too numerous to count."

¹¹The angel of the LORD also said to her:

"You are now with child
    and you will have a son.
You shall name him Ishmael,[b]
    for the LORD has heard of your misery.
¹²He will be a wild donkey of a man;
    his hand will be against everyone

---

[a]18 Or *Wadi*   [b]11 *Ishmael* means *God hears.*

Genesis 15:1

God Protects

"Do not be afraid, Abram.
I am your shield,
your very great reward."

Promises Worth Waiting For

Read: Genesis 16:1–16

Genesis 16:1–2

Now Sarai, Abram's wife, had borne him no children. But she had an Egyptian maidservant named Hagar; so she said to Abram, "The Lord has kept me from having children. Go, sleep with my maidservant; perhaps I can build a family through her."

reflection

1 Is there something you're waiting for right now? What has God promised through his Word?

2 Describe a time when you took matters into your own hands. What were the results? Was it worth it?

3 How do you respond when your actions have unexpected consequences? Do you blame someone else, as Sarai blamed Abram, or do you go to God and ask for his help and forgiveness?

RELATED READINGS

1 Samuel 1:3–17;
Romans 4:13–18;
Galatians 4:21–23

WHAT ARE YOU WAITING FOR? Who or what do you believe will satisfy and complete you? You may be waiting for Mr. Right, your dream job, a precious baby or any number of things to fulfill your hopes and dreams.

Waiting is hard when you just *know* your life will be so much better if your hopes become reality. Waiting is hard . . . especially when years pass and there is no sign of your expectations being met. Often, the longer you wait, the more desperate you become.

Sarai was fed up with waiting for the baby God had promised. She grew older every day, and her body showed no sign of pregnancy. Perhaps she questioned that God's promise of children for Abram included her: *Why is God taking so long? What if I'm not the one to bear the promised child?* So Sarai took matters into her own hands. She gave her maidservant Hagar to Abram to bear a child to fulfill God's promise.

However, things didn't quite turn out the way Sarai expected. Hagar became pregnant as planned, but Hagar's pride and Sarai's jealousy caused a jagged rift between the two women. And Abram was caught in the middle. The consequences of Sarai's actions not only affected Sarai's family and household, but also generations of people who came after them. To this day, the children of Hagar and Sarai war against one another as the Arabs and Jews fight for control over the land of Israel.

But God had a plan. A plan to bless Abram and Sarai with their very own baby. A plan to bless the world through their offspring. Isaac would be the fulfillment of God's promise. That plan was worth waiting for.

God has plans for your life, too. Plans that will make you thrive and not be knocked down by life's setbacks (see Jeremiah 29:11–13). God's plans are well worth waiting for. You may be tempted to take matters into your own hands, thinking God is just a little bit late. But don't risk God's perfect intentions for you by relying on your own schemes. Waiting for God's perfect timing can save you years of heartbreak. Remember, God is faithful and always keeps his promises . . . even if you have to wait.

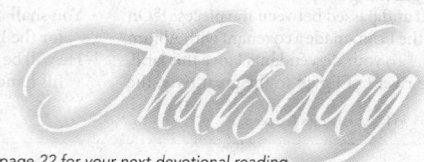

Thursday

Go to page 22 for your next devotional reading.

and everyone's hand against him,
and he will live in hostility
toward[a] all his brothers."

¹³She gave this name to the LORD who spoke to her: "You are the God who sees me," for she said, "I have now seen[b] the One who sees me." ¹⁴That is why the well was called Beer Lahai Roi[c]; it is still there, between Kadesh and Bered.

¹⁵So Hagar bore Abram a son, and Abram gave the name Ishmael to the son she had borne. ¹⁶Abram was eighty-six years old when Hagar bore him Ishmael.

The Covenant of Circumcision

17 When Abram was ninety-nine years old, the LORD appeared to him and said, "I am God Almighty[d]; walk before me and be blameless. ²I will confirm my covenant between me and you and will greatly increase your numbers."

³Abram fell facedown, and God said to him, ⁴"As for me, this is my covenant with you: You will be the father of many nations. ⁵No longer will you be called Abram[e]; your name will be Abraham,[f] for I have made you a father of many nations. ⁶I will make you very fruitful; I will make nations of you, and kings will come from you. ⁷I will establish my covenant as an everlasting covenant between me and you and your descendants after you for the generations to come, to be your God and the God of your descendants after you. ⁸The whole land of Canaan, where you are now an alien, I will give as an everlasting possession to you and your descendants after you; and I will be their God."

⁹Then God said to Abraham, "As for you, you must keep my covenant, you and your descendants after you for the generations to come. ¹⁰This is my covenant with you and your descendants after you, the covenant you are to keep: Every male among you shall be circumcised. ¹¹You are to undergo circumcision, and it will be the sign of the covenant between me and you. ¹²For the generations to come every male among you who is eight days old must be circumcised, including those born in your household or bought with money from a foreigner—those who are not your offspring. ¹³Whether born in your household or bought with your money, they must be circumcised. My covenant in your flesh is to be an everlasting covenant. ¹⁴Any uncircumcised male, who has not been circumcised in the flesh, will be cut off from his people; he has broken my covenant."

¹⁵God also said to Abraham, "As for Sarai your wife, you are no longer to call her Sarai; her name will be Sarah. ¹⁶I will bless her and will surely give you a son by her. I will bless her so that she will be the mother of nations; kings of peoples will come from her."

¹⁷Abraham fell facedown; he laughed and said to himself, "Will a son be born to a man a hundred years old? Will Sarah bear a child at the age of ninety?" ¹⁸And Abraham said to God, "If only Ishmael might live under your blessing!"

¹⁹Then God said, "Yes, but your wife Sarah will bear you a son, and you will call him Isaac.[g] I will establish my covenant with him as an everlasting covenant for his descendants after him. ²⁰And as for Ishmael, I have heard you: I will surely bless him; I will make him fruitful and will greatly increase his numbers. He will be the father of twelve rulers, and I will make him into a great nation. ²¹But my covenant I will establish with Isaac, whom Sarah will bear to you by this time next year." ²²When he had finished speaking with Abraham, God went up from him.

²³On that very day Abraham took his son Ishmael and all those born in his household or bought with his money, every male in his household, and circumcised them, as God told him. ²⁴Abraham was ninety-nine years old when he was circumcised, ²⁵and his son Ishmael was thirteen; ²⁶Abraham and his son Ishmael were both circumcised on that same day. ²⁷And every male in Abraham's household, including those born in his household or bought from a foreigner, was circumcised with him.

The Three Visitors

18 The LORD appeared to Abraham near the great trees of Mamre while he was sitting at the entrance to his tent in the heat of

---

[a]12 Or *live to the east / of* [b]13 Or *seen the back of* [c]14 *Beer Lahai Roi* means *well of the Living One who sees me.* [d]1 Hebrew *El-Shaddai* [e]5 *Abram* means *exalted father.* [f]5 *Abraham* means *father of many.* [g]19 *Isaac* means *he laughs.*

the day. ²Abraham looked up and saw three men standing nearby. When he saw them, he hurried from the entrance of his tent to meet them and bowed low to the ground.

³He said, "If I have found favor in your eyes, my lord,ᵃ do not pass your servant by. ⁴Let a little water be brought, and then you may all wash your feet and rest under this tree. ⁵Let me get you something to eat, so you can be refreshed and then go on your way—now that you have come to your servant."

"Very well," they answered, "do as you say."

⁶So Abraham hurried into the tent to Sarah. "Quick," he said, "get three seahsᵇ of fine flour and knead it and bake some bread."

⁷Then he ran to the herd and selected a choice, tender calf and gave it to a servant, who hurried to prepare it. ⁸He then brought some curds and milk and the calf that had been prepared, and set these before them. While they ate, he stood near them under a tree.

⁹"Where is your wife Sarah?" they asked him.

"There, in the tent," he said.

¹⁰Then the Lordᶜ said, "I will surely return to you about this time next year, and Sarah your wife will have a son."

Now Sarah was listening at the entrance to the tent, which was behind him. ¹¹Abraham and Sarah were already old and well advanced in years, and Sarah was past the age of childbearing. ¹²So Sarah laughed to herself as she thought, "After I am worn out and my masterᵈ is old, will I now have this pleasure?"

¹³Then the Lord said to Abraham, "Why did Sarah laugh and say, 'Will I really have a child, now that I am old?' ¹⁴Is anything too hard for the Lord? I will return to you at the appointed time next year and Sarah will have a son."

¹⁵Sarah was afraid, so she lied and said, "I did not laugh."

But he said, "Yes, you did laugh."

Abraham Pleads for Sodom

¹⁶When the men got up to leave, they looked down toward Sodom, and Abraham walked along with them to see them on their way. ¹⁷Then the Lord said, "Shall I hide from Abraham what I am about to do? ¹⁸Abraham will surely become a great and powerful nation, and all nations on earth will be blessed through him. ¹⁹For I have chosen him, so that he will direct his children and his household after him to keep the way of the Lord by doing what is right and just, so that the Lord will bring about for Abraham what he has promised him."

²⁰Then the Lord said, "The outcry against Sodom and Gomorrah is so great and their sin so grievous ²¹that I will go down and see if what they have done is as bad as the outcry that has reached me. If not, I will know."

²²The men turned away and went toward Sodom, but Abraham remained standing before the Lord.ᵉ ²³Then Abraham approached him and said: "Will you sweep away the righteous with the wicked? ²⁴What if there are fifty righteous people in the city? Will you really sweep it away and not spareᶠ the place for the sake of the fifty righteous people in it? ²⁵Far be it from you to do such a thing—to kill the righteous with the wicked, treating the righteous and the wicked alike. Far be it from you! Will not the Judgeᵍ of all the earth do right?"

²⁶The Lord said, "If I find fifty righteous people in the city of Sodom, I will spare the whole place for their sake."

²⁷Then Abraham spoke up again: "Now that I have been so bold as to speak to the Lord, though I am nothing but dust and ashes, ²⁸what if the number of the righteous is five less than fifty? Will you destroy the whole city because of five people?"

"If I find forty-five there," he said, "I will not destroy it."

²⁹Once again he spoke to him, "What if only forty are found there?"

Genesis 18:14

God Does the Impossible

"Is anything too hard for the Lord? I will return to you at the appointed time next year and Sarah will have a son."

ᵃ3 Or *O Lord*   ᵇ6 That is, probably about 20 quarts (about 22 liters)   ᶜ10 Hebrew *Then he*   ᵈ12 Or *husband*   ᵉ22 Masoretic Text; an ancient Hebrew scribal tradition *but the Lord remained standing before Abraham*   ᶠ24 Or *forgive*; also in verse 26   ᵍ25 Or *Ruler*

He said, "For the sake of forty, I will not do it."

³⁰Then he said, "May the Lord not be angry, but let me speak. What if only thirty can be found there?"

He answered, "I will not do it if I find thirty there."

³¹Abraham said, "Now that I have been so bold as to speak to the Lord, what if only twenty can be found there?"

He said, "For the sake of twenty, I will not destroy it."

³²Then he said, "May the Lord not be angry, but let me speak just once more. What if only ten can be found there?"

He answered, "For the sake of ten, I will not destroy it."

³³When the Lord had finished speaking with Abraham, he left, and Abraham returned home.

Sodom and Gomorrah Destroyed

19 The two angels arrived at Sodom in the evening, and Lot was sitting in the gateway of the city. When he saw them, he got up to meet them and bowed down with his face to the ground. ²"My lords," he said, "please turn aside to your servant's house. You can wash your feet and spend the night and then go on your way early in the morning."

"No," they answered, "we will spend the night in the square."

³But he insisted so strongly that they did go with him and entered his house. He prepared a meal for them, baking bread without yeast, and they ate. ⁴Before they had gone to bed, all the men from every part of the city of Sodom—both young and old—surrounded the house. ⁵They called to Lot, "Where are the men who came to you tonight? Bring them out to us so that we can have sex with them."

⁶Lot went outside to meet them and shut the door behind him ⁷and said, "No, my friends. Don't do this wicked thing. ⁸Look, I have two daughters who have never slept with a man. Let me bring them out to you, and you can do what you like with them. But don't do anything to these men, for they have come under the protection of my roof."

⁹"Get out of our way," they replied. And they said, "This fellow came here as an alien, and now he wants to play the judge! We'll treat you worse than them." They kept bringing pressure on Lot and moved forward to break down the door.

¹⁰But the men inside reached out and pulled Lot back into the house and shut the door. ¹¹Then they struck the men who were at the door of the house, young and old, with blindness so that they could not find the door.

¹²The two men said to Lot, "Do you have anyone else here—sons-in-law, sons or daughters, or anyone else in the city who belongs to you? Get them out of here, ¹³because we are going to destroy this place. The outcry to the Lord against its people is so great that he has sent us to destroy it."

¹⁴So Lot went out and spoke to his sons-in-law, who were pledged to marry*a* his daughters. He said, "Hurry and get out of this place, because the Lord is about to destroy the city!" But his sons-in-law thought he was joking.

¹⁵With the coming of dawn, the angels urged Lot, saying, "Hurry! Take your wife and your two daughters who are here, or you will be swept away when the city is punished."

¹⁶When he hesitated, the men grasped his hand and the hands of his wife and of his two daughters and led them safely out of the city, for the Lord was merciful to them. ¹⁷As soon as they had brought them out, one of them said, "Flee for your lives! Don't look back, and don't stop anywhere on the plain! Flee to the mountains or you will be swept away!"

¹⁸But Lot said to them, "No, my lords,*b* please! ¹⁹Your*c* servant has found favor in your*c* eyes, and you*c* have shown great kindness to me in sparing my life. But I can't flee to the mountains; this disaster will overtake me, and I'll die. ²⁰Look, here is a town near enough to run to, and it is small. Let me flee to it—it is very small, isn't it? Then my life will be spared."

²¹He said to him, "Very well, I will grant this request too; I will not overthrow the town you speak of. ²²But flee there quickly, because I cannot do anything until you reach it." (That is why the town was called Zoar.*d*)

²³By the time Lot reached Zoar, the sun

---

*a*14 Or *were married to*   *b*18 Or *No, Lord*; or *No, my lord*   *c*19 The Hebrew is singular.   *d*22 *Zoar* means *small.*

Letting Go of the Familiar

Genesis 19:26

But Lot's wife looked back, and she became a pillar of salt.

reflection

1 What does the passage in today's reading teach you about letting go in order to move forward?

2 Why is it so difficult sometimes to let go of the past?

3 What is one thing you think God may be asking you to let go of right now? Spend some time praying that God will help you let go of whatever is hindering you from moving forward in your spiritual journey.

RELATED READINGS

Genesis 12:1–7;
Numbers 14:1–38;
Philippians 3:13

Read: Genesis 19:1–26

LETTING GO OF THE FAMILIAR is tough. Changing careers or colleges or moving to a new city can take an emotional toll on us. It's even more difficult to leave behind old habits, attitudes and behaviors.

Lot's wife wasn't able to let go of her home in Sodom, even though God sent angels to warn her family to run for their lives because judgment was coming. In fact, the angels' warnings included such grave commands as "Don't look back" and "Don't stop." Why in the world did this woman choose to stop and look back? Could it be that she loved the life she was leaving too much? Though Sodom was full to overflowing with sin and vice, apparently the dark and oppressive city was comfortably familiar to Lot's wife.

It *is* difficult to leave the familiar behind. That fact is as true today as it was in the days of Sodom and Gomorrah's destruction—even when God himself is saying, "It's time to move on." If you've ever struggled with a destructive habit, you've felt the pull of the familiar—even as you've sensed God's nudge, "Move on now." You've experienced the temptation to turn back just one more time, for one last look, one last taste, one last "fix"—even as God has whispered, "Don't look back." Maybe you've agonized over a loved one's downward spiral, desperately attempting to rescue them time and time again—until finally God impressed upon you, "Stop. Let go."

Unlike Lot's wife, none of us has ever become a pillar of salt by turning back for one last peek. Yet we all struggle with the difficulties of letting go of the old in order to grasp the new. Take heart. God understands that letting go of the familiar is hard. Yet he has called us to move on to new life in Jesus Christ by letting go of our old worldly lives, our old habits, our old dreams—to boldly move forward without looking back. When you feel God's call to move, allow him to guide you. He will give you the grace to do whatever he has asked.

Go to page 26 for your next devotional reading.

had risen over the land. ²⁴Then the LORD rained down burning sulfur on Sodom and Gomorrah—from the LORD out of the heavens. ²⁵Thus he overthrew those cities and the entire plain, including all those living in the cities—and also the vegetation in the land. ²⁶But Lot's wife looked back, and she became a pillar of salt.

²⁷Early the next morning Abraham got up and returned to the place where he had stood before the LORD. ²⁸He looked down toward Sodom and Gomorrah, toward all the land of the plain, and he saw dense smoke rising from the land, like smoke from a furnace.

²⁹So when God destroyed the cities of the plain, he remembered Abraham, and he brought Lot out of the catastrophe that overthrew the cities where Lot had lived.

Lot and His Daughters

³⁰Lot and his two daughters left Zoar and settled in the mountains, for he was afraid to stay in Zoar. He and his two daughters lived in a cave. ³¹One day the older daughter said to the younger, "Our father is old, and there is no man around here to lie with us, as is the custom all over the earth. ³²Let's get our father to drink wine and then lie with him and preserve our family line through our father."

³³That night they got their father to drink wine, and the older daughter went in and lay with him. He was not aware of it when she lay down or when she got up.

³⁴The next day the older daughter said to the younger, "Last night I lay with my father. Let's get him to drink wine again tonight, and you go in and lie with him so we can preserve our family line through our father." ³⁵So they got their father to drink wine that night also, and the younger daughter went and lay with him. Again he was not aware of it when she lay down or when she got up.

³⁶So both of Lot's daughters became pregnant by their father. ³⁷The older daughter had a son, and she named him Moab*ᵃ*; he is the father of the Moabites of today. ³⁸The younger daughter also had a son, and she named him Ben-Ammi*ᵇ*; he is the father of the Ammonites of today.

Abraham and Abimelech

20 Now Abraham moved on from there into the region of the Negev and lived between Kadesh and Shur. For a while he stayed in Gerar, ²and there Abraham said of his wife Sarah, "She is my sister." Then Abimelech king of Gerar sent for Sarah and took her.

³But God came to Abimelech in a dream one night and said to him, "You are as good as dead because of the woman you have taken; she is a married woman."

⁴Now Abimelech had not gone near her, so he said, "Lord, will you destroy an innocent nation? ⁵Did he not say to me, 'She is my sister,' and didn't she also say, 'He is my brother'? I have done this with a clear conscience and clean hands."

⁶Then God said to him in the dream, "Yes, I know you did this with a clear conscience, and so I have kept you from sinning against me. That is why I did not let you touch her. ⁷Now return the man's wife, for he is a prophet, and he will pray for you and you will live. But if you do not return her, you may be sure that you and all yours will die."

⁸Early the next morning Abimelech summoned all his officials, and when he told them all that had happened, they were very much afraid. ⁹Then Abimelech called Abraham in and said, "What have you done to us? How have I wronged you that you have brought such great guilt upon me and my kingdom? You have done things to me that should not be done." ¹⁰And Abimelech asked Abraham, "What was your reason for doing this?"

¹¹Abraham replied, "I said to myself, 'There is surely no fear of God in this place, and they will kill me because of my wife.' ¹²Besides, she really is my sister, the daughter of my father though not of my mother; and she became my wife. ¹³And when God had me wander from my father's household, I said to her, 'This is how you can show your love to me: Everywhere we go, say of me, "He is my brother."'"

¹⁴Then Abimelech brought sheep and cattle and male and female slaves and gave them to Abraham, and he returned Sarah his wife to him. ¹⁵And Abimelech said, "My land is before you; live wherever you like."

ᵃ37 Moab sounds like the Hebrew for *from father.*   *ᵇ38 Ben-Ammi* means *son of my people.*

¹⁶To Sarah he said, "I am giving your brother a thousand shekels*a* of silver. This is to cover the offense against you before all who are with you; you are completely vindicated."

¹⁷Then Abraham prayed to God, and God healed Abimelech, his wife and his slave girls so they could have children again, ¹⁸for the LORD had closed up every womb in Abimelech's household because of Abraham's wife Sarah.

The Birth of Isaac

21 Now the LORD was gracious to Sarah as he had said, and the LORD did for Sarah what he had promised. ²Sarah became pregnant and bore a son to Abraham in his old age, at the very time God had promised him. ³Abraham gave the name Isaac*b* to the son Sarah bore him. ⁴When his son Isaac was eight days old, Abraham circumcised him, as God commanded him. ⁵Abraham was a hundred years old when his son Isaac was born to him.

⁶Sarah said, "God has brought me laughter, and everyone who hears about this will laugh with me." ⁷And she added, "Who would have said to Abraham that Sarah would nurse children? Yet I have borne him a son in his old age."

Hagar and Ishmael Sent Away

⁸The child grew and was weaned, and on the day Isaac was weaned Abraham held a great feast. ⁹But Sarah saw that the son whom Hagar the Egyptian had borne to Abraham was mocking, ¹⁰and she said to Abraham, "Get rid of that slave woman and her son, for that slave woman's son will never share in the inheritance with my son Isaac."

¹¹The matter distressed Abraham greatly because it concerned his son. ¹²But God said to him, "Do not be so distressed about the boy and your maidservant. Listen to whatever Sarah tells you, because it is through Isaac that your offspring*c* will be reckoned. ¹³I will make the son of the maidservant into a nation also, because he is your offspring."

¹⁴Early the next morning Abraham took some food and a skin of water and gave them to Hagar. He set them on her shoulders and then sent her off with the boy. She went on her way and wandered in the desert of Beersheba.

¹⁵When the water in the skin was gone, she put the boy under one of the bushes. ¹⁶Then she went off and sat down nearby, about a bowshot away, for she thought, "I cannot watch the boy die." And as she sat there nearby, she*d* began to sob.

¹⁷God heard the boy crying, and the angel of God called to Hagar from heaven and said to her, "What is the matter, Hagar? Do not be afraid; God has heard the boy crying as he lies there. ¹⁸Lift the boy up and take him by the hand, for I will make him into a great nation."

¹⁹Then God opened her eyes and she saw a well of water. So she went and filled the skin with water and gave the boy a drink.

²⁰God was with the boy as he grew up. He lived in the desert and became an archer. ²¹While he was living in the Desert of Paran, his mother got a wife for him from Egypt.

The Treaty at Beersheba

²²At that time Abimelech and Phicol the commander of his forces said to Abraham, "God is with you in everything you do. ²³Now swear to me here before God that you will not deal falsely with me or my children or my descendants. Show to me and the country where you are living as an alien the same kindness I have shown to you."

²⁴Abraham said, "I swear it."

²⁵Then Abraham complained to Abimelech about a well of water that Abimelech's servants had seized. ²⁶But Abimelech said, "I don't know who has done this. You did not tell me, and I heard about it only today."

²⁷So Abraham brought sheep and cattle and gave them to Abimelech, and the two men made a treaty. ²⁸Abraham set apart seven ewe lambs from the flock, ²⁹and Abimelech asked Abraham, "What is the meaning of these

---

Genesis 20:17

God Heals

Then Abraham prayed to God, and God healed Abimelech, his wife and his slave girls so they could have children again.

---

a16 That is, about 25 pounds (about 11.5 kilograms)   *b3 Isaac* means *he laughs.*   *c12* Or *seed*   *d16* Hebrew; Septuagint *the child* seven ewe lambs you have set apart by themselves?"

³⁰He replied, "Accept these seven lambs from my hand as a witness that I dug this well."

³¹So that place was called Beersheba,ᵃ because the two men swore an oath there.

³²After the treaty had been made at Beersheba, Abimelech and Phicol the commander of his forces returned to the land of the Philistines. ³³Abraham planted a tamarisk tree in Beersheba, and there he called upon the name of the LORD, the Eternal God. ³⁴And Abraham stayed in the land of the Philistines for a long time.

Abraham Tested

22 Some time later God tested Abraham. He said to him, "Abraham!"

"Here I am," he replied.

²Then God said, "Take your son, your only son, Isaac, whom you love, and go to the region of Moriah. Sacrifice him there as a burnt offering on one of the mountains I will tell you about."

³Early the next morning Abraham got up and saddled his donkey. He took with him two of his servants and his son Isaac. When he had cut enough wood for the burnt offering, he set out for the place God had told him about. ⁴On the third day Abraham looked up and saw the place in the distance. ⁵He said to his servants, "Stay here with the donkey while I and the boy go over there. We will worship and then we will come back to you."

⁶Abraham took the wood for the burnt offering and placed it on his son Isaac, and he himself carried the fire and the knife. As the two of them went on together, ⁷Isaac spoke up and said to his father Abraham, "Father?"

"Yes, my son?" Abraham replied.

"The fire and wood are here," Isaac said, "but where is the lamb for the burnt offering?"

⁸Abraham answered, "God himself will provide the lamb for the burnt offering, my son." And the two of them went on together.

⁹When they reached the place God had told

him about, Abraham built an altar there and arranged the wood on it. He bound his son Isaac and laid him on the altar, on top of the wood. ¹⁰Then he reached out his hand and took the knife to slay his son. ¹¹But the angel of the LORD called out to him from heaven, "Abraham! Abraham!"

"Here I am," he replied.

¹²"Do not lay a hand on the boy," he said.

Genesis 21:33

God Is Eternal

Abraham . . . called upon the name of the LORD, the Eternal God.

"Do not do anything to him. Now I know that you fear God, because you have not withheld from me your son, your only son."

¹³Abraham looked up and there in a thicket he saw a ramᵇ caught by its horns. He went over and took the ram and sacrificed it as a burnt offering instead of his son. ¹⁴So Abraham called that place The LORD Will Provide. And to this day it is said, "On the mountain of the LORD it will be provided."

¹⁵The angel of the LORD called to Abraham from heaven a second time ¹⁶and said, "I swear by myself, declares the LORD, that because you have done this and have not withheld your son, your only son, ¹⁷I will surely bless you and make your descendants as numerous as the stars in the sky and as the sand on the seashore. Your descendants will take possession of the cities of their enemies, ¹⁸and through your offspringᶜ all nations on earth will be blessed, because you have obeyed me."

¹⁹Then Abraham returned to his servants, and they set off together for Beersheba. And Abraham stayed in Beersheba.

Nahor's Sons

²⁰Some time later Abraham was told, "Milcah is also a mother; she has borne sons to your brother Nahor: ²¹Uz the firstborn, Buz his brother, Kemuel (the father of Aram), ²²Kesed, Hazo, Pildash, Jidlaph and Bethuel." ²³Bethuel became the father of Rebekah. Milcah bore these eight sons to Abraham's brother Nahor. ²⁴His concubine, whose name was Reumah, also had sons: Tebah, Gaham, Tahash and Maacah.

ᵃ31 *Beersheba* can mean *well of seven* or *well of the oath.* ᵇ13 Many manuscripts of the Masoretic Text, Samaritan Pentateuch, Septuagint and Syriac; most manuscripts of the Masoretic Text *a ram behind him.* ᶜ18 Or *seed*

The Heart of a Mother

EVE

[Eve] said,
"With the help
of the LORD
I have brought
forth a man."

Genesis 4:1

STRANGE CRAVINGS. That first flutter. Her body was changing, growing and stretching in unpredictable and unsettling ways. The first mother in history conceived a child, carried him to term and gave birth without ever knowing what to expect next.

She didn't have a girlfriend to confide in when Adam just didn't understand her moods. She had no one to assure the young mother that sudden clumsiness was normal or that the awful bloated feelings would pass. Her experience was the ultimate as natural childbirth goes—she made it without the benefit of an obstetrician, a midwife or a drop of morphine. She couldn't even run to her mother!

And that was just the pregnancy.

She recalled cradling Cain in her arms as a newborn and gently leading him to nurse for the first time. She remembered fingering his tiny hands and counting all his toes, one by one. She didn't know she could love someone so much.

How, oh how, would she ever be able to be what he needed her to be—his mother? Eve answered her own question when she spoke in the afterglow of giving birth. "With the help of the LORD I have brought forth a man."

No one was there to inform Eve about the significance of what had just transpired. They didn't have to. She got it. She instinctively knew what every mother knows in an instant: She had *not* brought forth this miracle by her own power. And almost simultaneously, she knew she would not be able to raise him in her own strength either. The very first mother in history would have to raise her child the very same way mothers throughout history have conceived and nurtured children—fully relying on God's help.

If that fact wasn't obvious then, it soon would be. Like when she had to steal away for a moment alone to cry because it was the first time she had to punish him. When he bickered with his brother. When his career choice went south. And whenever her own poor choices threatened to scar her children's future.

Eve was the first to experience joy and heartache as a mother. But no one could tell her then that she certainly wouldn't be the last.

ASSIGNED
READING:

Genesis
4:1–26

—Prayer—

Thank you, Lord, for never leaving me alone. I take comfort in your guidance and care.

Weekend

The Death of Sarah

23 Sarah lived to be a hundred and twenty-seven years old. [2]She died at Kiriath Arba (that is, Hebron) in the land of Canaan, and Abraham went to mourn for Sarah and to weep over her.

[3]Then Abraham rose from beside his dead wife and spoke to the Hittites.[a] He said, [4]"I am an alien and a stranger among you. Sell me some property for a burial site here so I can bury my dead."

[5]The Hittites replied to Abraham, [6]"Sir, listen to us. You are a mighty prince among us. Bury your dead in the choicest of our tombs. None of us will refuse you his tomb for burying your dead."

[7]Then Abraham rose and bowed down before the people of the land, the Hittites. [8]He said to them, "If you are willing to let me bury my dead, then listen to me and intercede with Ephron son of Zohar on my behalf [9]so he will sell me the cave of Machpelah, which belongs to him and is at the end of his field. Ask him to sell it to me for the full price as a burial site among you."

[10]Ephron the Hittite was sitting among his people and he replied to Abraham in the hearing of all the Hittites who had come to the gate of his city. [11]"No, my lord," he said. "Listen to me; I give[b] you the field, and I give[b] you the cave that is in it. I give[b] it to you in the presence of my people. Bury your dead."

[12]Again Abraham bowed down before the people of the land [13]and he said to Ephron in their hearing, "Listen to me, if you will. I will pay the price of the field. Accept it from me so I can bury my dead there."

[14]Ephron answered Abraham, [15]"Listen to me, my lord; the land is worth four hundred shekels[c] of silver, but what is that between me and you? Bury your dead."

[16]Abraham agreed to Ephron's terms and weighed out for him the price he had named in the hearing of the Hittites: four hundred shekels of silver, according to the weight current among the merchants.

[17]So Ephron's field in Machpelah near Mamre—both the field and the cave in it, and all the trees within the borders of the field—was deeded [18]to Abraham as his property in the presence of all the Hittites who had come to the gate of the city. [19]Afterward Abraham buried his wife Sarah in the cave in the field of Machpelah near Mamre (which is at Hebron) in the land of Canaan. [20]So the field and the cave in it were deeded to Abraham by the Hittites as a burial site.

Isaac and Rebekah

24 Abraham was now old and well advanced in years, and the LORD had blessed him in every way. [2]He said to the chief[d] servant in his household, the one in charge of all that he had, "Put your hand under my thigh. [3]I want you to swear by the LORD, the God of heaven and the God of earth, that you will not get a wife for my son from the daughters of the Canaanites, among whom I am living, [4]but will go to my country and my own relatives and get a wife for my son Isaac."

[5]The servant asked him, "What if the woman is unwilling to come back with me to this land? Shall I then take your son back to the country you came from?"

[6]"Make sure that you do not take my son back there," Abraham said. [7]"The LORD, the God of heaven, who brought me out of my father's household and my native land and who spoke to me and promised me on oath, saying, 'To your offspring[e] I will give this land'—he will send his angel before you so that you can get a wife for my son from there. [8]If the woman is unwilling to come back with you, then you will be released from this oath of mine. Only do not take my son back there." [9]So the servant put his hand under the thigh of his master Abraham and swore an oath to him concerning this matter.

[10]Then the servant took ten of his master's camels and left, taking with him all kinds of good things from his master. He set out for Aram Naharaim[f] and made his way to the town of Nahor. [11]He had the camels kneel down near the well outside the town; it was toward evening, the time the women go out to draw water.

---

[a]3 Or *the sons of Heth; also in verses* 5, 7, 10, 16, 18 and 20   [b]11 Or *sell*   [c]15 That is, about 10 pounds (about 4.5 kilograms)
[d]2 Or *oldest*   [e]7 Or *seed*   [f]10 That is, Northwest Mesopotamia

Making Hard Choices

[Abraham] said to the chief servant in his household, the one in charge of all that he had, . . . "I want you to swear by the LORD, the God of heaven and the God of earth, that you will not get a wife for my son from the daughters of the Canaanites, among whom I am living, but will go to my country and my own relatives and get a wife for my son Isaac."

reflection

1 What hard choice is confronting you today?

2 What factors make your decision difficult?

3 How is God asking you to trust him in this situation? Will you obey him?

RELATED READINGS

Joshua 24:15;
1 Kings 8:57–58;
Psalm 32:8–9

Read: Genesis 24:1–67

"HAVE IT YOUR WAY." Remember that popular advertising slogan? Our culture demands choice—the freedom to choose precisely what we want, exactly how we want it. One national coffee chain reportedly can serve your morning cup in as many as nineteen thousand different ways.[1] Some choices, such as *tall, grande* or *venti mocha*, are insignificant. Other choices can determine the course of a lifetime.

The story of Isaac and Rebekah is all about people making choices. Think about it. Wouldn't it have been infinitely easier for Abraham to choose a wife for his son from among local families he already knew? Next, consider the servant. He'd been assigned to find a matrimonial needle in a haystack. His job was to choose the perfect wife for his master's son. And then there was Rebekah. She was asked to choose to leave her home, family and everything familiar to travel to a distant country to marry a man she'd never met.

Choices. We all make them. Abraham chose to obey God's directive that his family not intermarry with the Canaanites. The servant chose to accept a complicated challenge from his employer, trusting God to lead him to the right woman. And Rebekah—Rebekah had to make a decision that would affect the rest of her life. She ultimately chose to trust her life and future to the servant of a distant relative whose God was her God. The story of the divinely arranged marriage between Isaac and Rebekah reminds us that nothing is too difficult for God.

Trust and obey—these two words go together like coffee and cream. Yet every day we face difficult situations that seem to defy simple solutions. As women, myriad difficult choices face us—the right course of care for a sick child, moving from everything familiar for a new opportunity, following God's leading even when the outcome is hazy, even when the right choice frightens us. You may toss and turn for nights without finding peace in your choice. The right choice is often the hard choice, but not always. How do we determine the right choice? *Obey* the guidance you find in God's Word, earnestly pray and seek trusted counsel, then *trust* God with the outcome. Will you have it your way or God's way? First trust God to have your best interest at heart, and then trust him to lead you to the right choice.

[1] Horovitz, Bruce. "You Want It Your Way." Posted March 5, 2004. USAToday.com. www.usatoday.com. (Accessed November 9, 2005.)

¹²Then he prayed, "O LORD, God of my master Abraham, give me success today, and show kindness to my master Abraham. ¹³See, I am standing beside this spring, and the daughters of the townspeople are coming out to draw water. ¹⁴May it be that when I say to a girl, 'Please let down your jar that I may have a drink,' and she says, 'Drink, and I'll water your camels too'—let her be the one you have chosen for your servant Isaac. By this I will know that you have shown kindness to my master."

¹⁵Before he had finished praying, Rebekah came out with her jar on her shoulder. She was the daughter of Bethuel son of Milcah, who was the wife of Abraham's brother Nahor. ¹⁶The girl was very beautiful, a virgin; no man had ever lain with her. She went down to the spring, filled her jar and came up again.

¹⁷The servant hurried to meet her and said, "Please give me a little water from your jar."

¹⁸"Drink, my lord," she said, and quickly lowered the jar to her hands and gave him a drink.

¹⁹After she had given him a drink, she said, "I'll draw water for your camels too, until they have finished drinking." ²⁰So she quickly emptied her jar into the trough, ran back to the well to draw more water, and drew enough for all his camels. ²¹Without saying a word, the man watched her closely to learn whether or not the LORD had made his journey successful.

²²When the camels had finished drinking, the man took out a gold nose ring weighing a beka*a* and two gold bracelets weighing ten shekels.*b* ²³Then he asked, "Whose daughter are you? Please tell me, is there room in your father's house for us to spend the night?"

²⁴She answered him, "I am the daughter of Bethuel, the son that Milcah bore to Nahor." ²⁵And she added, "We have plenty of straw and fodder, as well as room for you to spend the night."

²⁶Then the man bowed down and worshiped the LORD, ²⁷saying, "Praise be to the LORD, the God of my master Abraham, who has not abandoned his kindness and faithfulness to my master. As for me, the LORD has led me on the journey to the house of my master's relatives."

²⁸The girl ran and told her mother's household about these things. ²⁹Now Rebekah had a brother named Laban, and he hurried out to the man at the spring. ³⁰As soon as he had seen the nose ring, and the bracelets on his sister's arms, and had heard Rebekah tell what the man said to her, he went out to the man and found him standing by the camels near the spring. ³¹"Come, you who are blessed by the LORD," he said. "Why are you standing out here? I have prepared the house and a place for the camels."

³²So the man went to the house, and the camels were unloaded. Straw and fodder were brought for the camels, and water for him and his men to wash their feet. ³³Then food was set before him, but he said, "I will not eat until I have told you what I have to say."

"Then tell us," ⌊Laban⌋ said.

³⁴So he said, "I am Abraham's servant. ³⁵The LORD has blessed my master abundantly, and he has become wealthy. He has given him sheep and cattle, silver and gold, menservants and maidservants, and camels and donkeys. ³⁶My master's wife Sarah has borne him a son in her*c* old age, and he has given him everything he owns. ³⁷And my master made me swear an oath, and said, 'You must not get a wife for my son from the daughters of the Canaanites, in whose land I live, ³⁸but go to my father's family and to my own clan, and get a wife for my son.'

³⁹"Then I asked my master, 'What if the woman will not come back with me?'

⁴⁰"He replied, 'The LORD, before whom I have walked, will send his angel with you and

> ### Genesis 24:27
> ## *God Guides Our Paths*
>
> "Praise be to the LORD, the God of my master Abraham, who has not abandoned his kindness and faithfulness to my master. As for me, the LORD has led me on the journey."

---

*a*22 That is, about 1/5 ounce (about 5.5 grams) *b*22 That is, about 4 ounces (about 110 grams) *c*36 Or *his* make your journey a success, so that you can get a wife for my son from my own clan and from my father's family. **41**Then, when you go to my clan, you will be released from my oath even if they refuse to give her to you—you will be released from my oath.'

42"When I came to the spring today, I said, 'O LORD, God of my master Abraham, if you will, please grant success to the journey on which I have come. **43**See, I am standing beside this spring; if a maiden comes out to draw water and I say to her, "Please let me drink a little water from your jar," **44**and if she says to me, "Drink, and I'll draw water for your camels too," let her be the one the LORD has chosen for my master's son.'

45"Before I finished praying in my heart, Rebekah came out, with her jar on her shoulder. She went down to the spring and drew water, and I said to her, 'Please give me a drink.'

46"She quickly lowered her jar from her shoulder and said, 'Drink, and I'll water your camels too.' So I drank, and she watered the camels also.

47"I asked her, 'Whose daughter are you?'

"She said, 'The daughter of Bethuel son of Nahor, whom Milcah bore to him.'

"Then I put the ring in her nose and the bracelets on her arms, **48**and I bowed down and worshiped the LORD. I praised the LORD, the God of my master Abraham, who had led me on the right road to get the granddaughter of my master's brother for his son. **49**Now if you will show kindness and faithfulness to my master, tell me; and if not, tell me, so I may know which way to turn."

50Laban and Bethuel answered, "This is from the LORD; we can say nothing to you one way or the other. **51**Here is Rebekah; take her and go, and let her become the wife of your master's son, as the LORD has directed."

52When Abraham's servant heard what they said, he bowed down to the ground before the LORD. **53**Then the servant brought out gold and silver jewelry and articles of clothing and gave them to Rebekah; he also gave costly gifts to her brother and to her mother. **54**Then he and the men who were with him ate and drank and spent the night there.

When they got up the next morning, he said, "Send me on my way to my master."

55But her brother and her mother replied, "Let the girl remain with us ten days or so; then you*a* may go."

56But he said to them, "Do not detain me, now that the LORD has granted success to my journey. Send me on my way so I may go to my master."

57Then they said, "Let's call the girl and ask her about it." **58**So they called Rebekah and asked her, "Will you go with this man?"

"I will go," she said.

59So they sent their sister Rebekah on her way, along with her nurse and Abraham's servant and his men. **60**And they blessed Rebekah and said to her,

"Our sister, may you increase
   to thousands upon thousands;
may your offspring possess
   the gates of their enemies."

61Then Rebekah and her maids got ready and mounted their camels and went back with the man. So the servant took Rebekah and left.

62Now Isaac had come from Beer Lahai Roi, for he was living in the Negev. **63**He went out to the field one evening to meditate,*b* and as he looked up, he saw camels approaching. **64**Rebekah also looked up and saw Isaac. She got down from her camel **65**and asked the servant, "Who is that man in the field coming to meet us?"

"He is my master," the servant answered. So she took her veil and covered herself.

66Then the servant told Isaac all he had done. **67**Isaac brought her into the tent of his mother Sarah, and he married Rebekah. So she became his wife, and he loved her; and Isaac was comforted after his mother's death.

The Death of Abraham

25 Abraham took*c* another wife, whose name was Keturah. **2**She bore him Zimran, Jokshan, Medan, Midian, Ishbak and Shuah. **3**Jokshan was the father of Sheba and Dedan; the descendants of Dedan were the Asshurites, the Letushites and the Leummites.

---

*a*55 Or *she*   *b*63 The meaning of the Hebrew for this word is uncertain.   *c*1 Or *had taken*

[4]The sons of Midian were Ephah, Epher, Hanoch, Abida and Eldaah. All these were descendants of Keturah.

[5]Abraham left everything he owned to Isaac. [6]But while he was still living, he gave gifts to the sons of his concubines and sent them away from his son Isaac to the land of the east.

[7]Altogether, Abraham lived a hundred and seventy-five years. [8]Then Abraham breathed his last and died at a good old age, an old man and full of years; and he was gathered to his people. [9]His sons Isaac and Ishmael buried him in the cave of Machpelah near Mamre, in the field of Ephron son of Zohar the Hittite, [10]the field Abraham had bought from the Hittites.[a] There Abraham was buried with his wife Sarah. [11]After Abraham's death, God blessed his son Isaac, who then lived near Beer Lahai Roi.

Ishmael's Sons

[12]This is the account of Abraham's son Ishmael, whom Sarah's maidservant, Hagar the Egyptian, bore to Abraham.

[13]These are the names of the sons of Ishmael, listed in the order of their birth: Nebaioth the firstborn of Ishmael, Kedar, Adbeel, Mibsam, [14]Mishma, Dumah, Massa, [15]Hadad, Tema, Jetur, Naphish and Kedemah. [16]These were the sons of Ishmael, and these are the names of the twelve tribal rulers according to their settlements and camps. [17]Altogether, Ishmael lived a hundred and thirty-seven years. He breathed his last and died, and he was gathered to his people. [18]His descendants settled in the area from Havilah to Shur, near the border of Egypt, as you go toward Asshur. And they lived in hostility toward[b] all their brothers.

Jacob and Esau

[19]This is the account of Abraham's son Isaac.

Abraham became the father of Isaac, [20]and Isaac was forty years old when he married Rebekah daughter of Bethuel the Aramean from Paddan Aram[c] and sister of Laban the Aramean.

[21]Isaac prayed to the LORD on behalf of his wife, because she was barren. The LORD answered his prayer, and his wife Rebekah became pregnant. [22]The babies jostled each other within her, and she said, "Why is this happening to me?" So she went to inquire of the LORD.

[23]The LORD said to her,

"Two nations are in your womb,
    and two peoples from within you will be separated;
one people will be stronger than the other,
    and the older will serve the younger."

[24]When the time came for her to give birth, there were twin boys in her womb. [25]The first to come out was red, and his whole body was like a hairy garment; so they named him Esau.[d] [26]After this, his brother came out, with his hand grasping Esau's heel; so he was named Jacob.[e] Isaac was sixty years old when Rebekah gave birth to them.

[27]The boys grew up, and Esau became a skillful hunter, a man of the open country, while Jacob was a quiet man, staying among the tents. [28]Isaac, who had a taste for wild game, loved Esau, but Rebekah loved Jacob.

[29]Once when Jacob was cooking some stew, Esau came in from the open country, famished. [30]He said to Jacob, "Quick, let me have some of that red stew! I'm famished!" (That is why he was also called Edom.[f])

[31]Jacob replied, "First sell me your birthright."

[32]"Look, I am about to die," Esau said. "What good is the birthright to me?"

[33]But Jacob said, "Swear to me first." So he

Genesis 25:21

God Hears Prayers

Isaac prayed to the LORD on behalf of his wife, because she was barren. The LORD answered his prayer, and his wife Rebekah became pregnant.

---

[a]10 Or *the sons of Heth*   [b]18 Or *lived to the east of*   [c]20 That is, Northwest Mesopotamia   [d]25 *Esau* may mean *hairy*; he was also called Edom, which means *red*.   [e]26 *Jacob* means *he grasps the heel* (figuratively, *he deceives*).   [f]30 *Edom* means *red*.

swore an oath to him, selling his birthright to Jacob.

³⁴Then Jacob gave Esau some bread and some lentil stew. He ate and drank, and then got up and left.

So Esau despised his birthright.

Isaac and Abimelech

26 Now there was a famine in the land— besides the earlier famine of Abraham's time—and Isaac went to Abimelech king of the Philistines in Gerar. ²The LORD appeared to Isaac and said, "Do not go down to Egypt; live in the land where I tell you to live. ³Stay in this land for a while, and I will be with you and will bless you. For to you and your descendants I will give all these lands and will confirm the oath I swore to your father Abraham. ⁴I will make your descendants as numerous as the stars in the sky and will give them all these lands, and through your offspring[a] all nations on earth will be blessed, ⁵because Abraham obeyed me and kept my requirements, my commands, my decrees and my laws." ⁶So Isaac stayed in Gerar.

⁷When the men of that place asked him about his wife, he said, "She is my sister," because he was afraid to say, "She is my wife." He thought, "The men of this place might kill me on account of Rebekah, because she is beautiful."

⁸When Isaac had been there a long time, Abimelech king of the Philistines looked down from a window and saw Isaac caressing his wife Rebekah. ⁹So Abimelech summoned Isaac and said, "She is really your wife! Why did you say, 'She is my sister'?"

Isaac answered him, "Because I thought I might lose my life on account of her."

¹⁰Then Abimelech said, "What is this you have done to us? One of the men might well have slept with your wife, and you would have brought guilt upon us."

¹¹So Abimelech gave orders to all the people: "Anyone who molests this man or his wife shall surely be put to death."

¹²Isaac planted crops in that land and the same year reaped a hundredfold, because the LORD blessed him. ¹³The man became rich, and his wealth continued to grow until he became very wealthy. ¹⁴He had so many flocks and herds and servants that the Philistines envied him. ¹⁵So all the wells that his father's servants had dug in the time of his father Abraham, the Philistines stopped up, filling them with earth.

¹⁶Then Abimelech said to Isaac, "Move away from us; you have become too powerful for us."

¹⁷So Isaac moved away from there and encamped in the Valley of Gerar and settled there. ¹⁸Isaac reopened the wells that had been dug in the time of his father Abraham, which the Philistines had stopped up after Abraham died, and he gave them the same names his father had given them.

¹⁹Isaac's servants dug in the valley and discovered a well of fresh water there. ²⁰But the herdsmen of Gerar quarreled with Isaac's herdsmen and said, "The water is ours!" So he named the well Esek,[b] because they disputed with him. ²¹Then they dug another well, but they quarreled over that one also; so he named it Sitnah.[c] ²²He moved on from there and dug another well, and no one quarreled over it. He named it Rehoboth,[d] saying, "Now the LORD has given us room and we will flourish in the land."

²³From there he went up to Beersheba. ²⁴That night the LORD appeared to him and said, "I am the God of your father Abraham. Do not be afraid, for I am with you; I will bless you and will increase the number of your descendants for the sake of my servant Abraham."

²⁵Isaac built an altar there and called on the

Genesis 26:24

God Keeps Promises

The LORD appeared to him and said, "I am the God of your father Abraham. Do not be afraid, for I am with you; I will bless you and will increase the number of your descendants for the sake of my servant Abraham."

---

[a]4 Or *seed*   [b]20 *Esek* means *dispute*.   [c]21 *Sitnah* means *opposition*.   [d]22 *Rehoboth* means *room*.

name of the LORD. There he pitched his tent, and there his servants dug a well.

²⁶Meanwhile, Abimelech had come to him from Gerar, with Ahuzzath his personal adviser and Phicol the commander of his forces. ²⁷Isaac asked them, "Why have you come to me, since you were hostile to me and sent me away?"

²⁸They answered, "We saw clearly that the LORD was with you; so we said, 'There ought to be a sworn agreement between us'—between us and you. Let us make a treaty with you ²⁹that you will do us no harm, just as we did not molest you but always treated you well and sent you away in peace. And now you are blessed by the LORD."

³⁰Isaac then made a feast for them, and they ate and drank. ³¹Early the next morning the men swore an oath to each other. Then Isaac sent them on their way, and they left him in peace.

³²That day Isaac's servants came and told him about the well they had dug. They said, "We've found water!" ³³He called it Shibah,ᵃ and to this day the name of the town has been Beersheba.ᵇ

³⁴When Esau was forty years old, he married Judith daughter of Beeri the Hittite, and also Basemath daughter of Elon the Hittite. ³⁵They were a source of grief to Isaac and Rebekah.

Jacob Gets Isaac's Blessing

27 When Isaac was old and his eyes were so weak that he could no longer see, he called for Esau his older son and said to him, "My son."

"Here I am," he answered.

²Isaac said, "I am now an old man and don't know the day of my death. ³Now then, get your weapons—your quiver and bow—and go out to the open country to hunt some wild game for me. ⁴Prepare me the kind of tasty food I like and bring it to me to eat, so that I may give you my blessing before I die."

⁵Now Rebekah was listening as Isaac spoke to his son Esau. When Esau left for the open country to hunt game and bring it back, ⁶Rebekah said to her son Jacob, "Look, I overheard your father say to your brother Esau, ⁷'Bring me

some game and prepare me some tasty food to eat, so that I may give you my blessing in the presence of the LORD before I die.' ⁸Now, my son, listen carefully and do what I tell you: ⁹Go out to the flock and bring me two choice young goats, so I can prepare some tasty food for your father, just the way he likes it. ¹⁰Then take it to your father to eat, so that he may give you his blessing before he dies."

¹¹Jacob said to Rebekah his mother, "But my brother Esau is a hairy man, and I'm a man with smooth skin. ¹²What if my father touches me? I would appear to be tricking him and would bring down a curse on myself rather than a blessing."

¹³His mother said to him, "My son, let the curse fall on me. Just do what I say; go and get them for me."

¹⁴So he went and got them and brought them to his mother, and she prepared some tasty food, just the way his father liked it. ¹⁵Then Rebekah took the best clothes of Esau her older son, which she had in the house, and put them on her younger son Jacob. ¹⁶She also covered his hands and the smooth part of his neck with the goatskins. ¹⁷Then she handed to her son Jacob the tasty food and the bread she had made.

¹⁸He went to his father and said, "My father."

"Yes, my son," he answered. "Who is it?"

¹⁹Jacob said to his father, "I am Esau your firstborn. I have done as you told me. Please sit up and eat some of my game so that you may give me your blessing."

²⁰Isaac asked his son, "How did you find it so quickly, my son?"

"The LORD your God gave me success," he replied.

²¹Then Isaac said to Jacob, "Come near so I can touch you, my son, to know whether you really are my son Esau or not."

²²Jacob went close to his father Isaac, who touched him and said, "The voice is the voice of Jacob, but the hands are the hands of Esau." ²³He did not recognize him, for his hands were hairy like those of his brother Esau; so he blessed him. ²⁴"Are you really my son Esau?" he asked.

"I am," he replied.

ᵃ33 Shibah can mean *oath* or *seven*.   *ᵇ33* Beersheba can mean *well of the oath* or *well of seven*.

Meddling

Read: Genesis 27:1–40

Genesis 27:13–15

His mother said to him, "My son, let the curse fall on me. Just do what I say; go and get them for me." So he went and got them and brought them to his mother, and she prepared some tasty food, just the way his father liked it. Then Rebekah took the best clothes of Esau her older son, which she had in the house, and put them on her younger son Jacob.

reflection

1 When have you meddled your way through a problem instead of waiting on God to solve it? What were the results?

2 When have you seen God solve a problem in a way that surprised you?

3 What are you waiting on God for now? What will you meditate on rather than meddle in?

RELATED READINGS

Genesis 25:19–28;
Psalms 27:14; 77:10–14;
Proverbs 19:2

OH, HOW WE LOVE TO MEDDLE. We may call it by other names, of course. Motherly concern. Friendly advice. A word to the wise. But when we boil it down and take a good look at what's left in the bottom of the pot, it's really just plain, old-fashioned meddling.

Rebekah thought she had good reason to meddle. (But then, don't we always *think* we have a good reason?) During her pregnancy, her twin baby boys had wrestled in her womb for position. That's when God told her that Esau, her older son, would serve Jacob, the younger. Now her husband was preparing to give the blessing and all of its benefits to Esau. She had to do something—fast! So she meddled.

You know, a funny thing happens when we meddle. We usually succeed: something changes. But succeeding can come with a high price tag—much higher than we ever expected to pay. The price Rebekah paid for meddling was painfully high. She turned her sons against one another. She sent Jacob away to escape Esau's wrath, never to see him again. She alienated herself from her husband and her firstborn son. But worst of all, she deprived herself of seeing how God would have fulfilled his promise to her.

If you search your Bible, you won't find any verses telling you to trust in your own ways or to interfere in other people's business because God can't handle it. You won't find God telling you to meddle so that his perfect will can be done. God doesn't encourage his people to scheme or to plan or to quick, come up with something—anything! If you are frantically trying to figure out what to do, it's a good clue that you need to slow down, take a deep breath and take a giant step back.

Instead of wasting your energy meddling, try pouring your energy into meditating. Meditate on God's goodness, his faithfulness, his character traits and his promises. When you begin turning your eyes to the Lord rather than sticking your nose into other people's business, you'll soon discover that he is always busy intervening on behalf of his people—including you and the people you love.

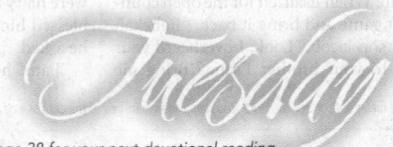

Tuesday

²⁵Then he said, "My son, bring me some of your game to eat, so that I may give you my blessing."

Jacob brought it to him and he ate; and he brought some wine and he drank. ²⁶Then his father Isaac said to him, "Come here, my son, and kiss me."

²⁷So he went to him and kissed him. When Isaac caught the smell of his clothes, he blessed him and said,

"Ah, the smell of my son
    is like the smell of a field
    that the LORD has blessed.
²⁸May God give you of heaven's dew
    and of earth's richness—
    an abundance of grain and new
        wine.
²⁹May nations serve you
    and peoples bow down to you.
Be lord over your brothers,
    and may the sons of your mother bow
        down to you.
May those who curse you be cursed
    and those who bless you be blessed."

³⁰After Isaac finished blessing him and Jacob had scarcely left his father's presence, his brother Esau came in from hunting. ³¹He too prepared some tasty food and brought it to his father. Then he said to him, "My father, sit up and eat some of my game, so that you may give me your blessing."

³²His father Isaac asked him, "Who are you?"

"I am your son," he answered, "your firstborn, Esau."

³³Isaac trembled violently and said, "Who was it, then, that hunted game and brought it to me? I ate it just before you came and I blessed him—and indeed he will be blessed!"

³⁴When Esau heard his father's words, he burst out with a loud and bitter cry and said to his father, "Bless me—me too, my father!"

³⁵But he said, "Your brother came deceitfully and took your blessing."

³⁶Esau said, "Isn't he rightly named Jacob[a]? He has deceived me these two times: He took my birthright, and now he's taken my bless-

ing!" Then he asked, "Haven't you reserved any blessing for me?"

³⁷Isaac answered Esau, "I have made him lord over you and have made all his relatives his servants, and I have sustained him with grain and new wine. So what can I possibly do for you, my son?"

³⁸Esau said to his father, "Do you have only one blessing, my father? Bless me too, my father!" Then Esau wept aloud.

³⁹His father Isaac answered him,

"Your dwelling will be
    away from the earth's richness,
    away from the dew of heaven above.
⁴⁰You will live by the sword
    and you will serve your brother.
But when you grow restless,
    you will throw his yoke
    from off your neck."

Jacob Flees to Laban

⁴¹Esau held a grudge against Jacob because of the blessing his father had given him. He said to himself, "The days of mourning for my father are near; then I will kill my brother Jacob."

⁴²When Rebekah was told what her older son Esau had said, she sent for her younger son Jacob and said to him, "Your brother Esau is consoling himself with the thought of killing you. ⁴³Now then, my son, do what I say: Flee at once to my brother Laban in Haran. ⁴⁴Stay with him for a while until your brother's fury subsides. ⁴⁵When your brother is no longer angry with you and forgets what you did to him, I'll send word for you to come back from there. Why should I lose both of you in one day?"

⁴⁶Then Rebekah said to Isaac, "I'm disgusted with living because of these Hittite women. If Jacob takes a wife from among the women of this land, from Hittite women like these, my life will not be worth living."

28 So Isaac called for Jacob and blessed[b] him and commanded him: "Do not marry a Canaanite woman. ²Go at once to Paddan Aram,[c] to the house of your mother's father Bethuel. Take a wife for yourself there, from among the daughters of Laban, your mother's brother. ³May God Almighty[d] bless

---

*a*36 *Jacob* means *he grasps the heel* (figuratively, *he deceives*).   *b*1 Or *greeted*   *c*2 That is, Northwest Mesopotamia; also in verses 5, 6 and 7   *d*3 Hebrew *El-Shaddai* you and make you fruitful and increase your numbers until you become a community of peoples. ⁴May he give you and your descendants the blessing given to Abraham, so that you may take possession of the land where you now live as an alien, the land God gave to Abraham." ⁵Then Isaac sent Jacob on his way, and he went to Paddan Aram, to Laban son of Bethuel the Aramean, the brother of Rebekah, who was the mother of Jacob and Esau.

⁶Now Esau learned that Isaac had blessed Jacob and had sent him to Paddan Aram to take a wife from there, and that when he blessed him he commanded him, "Do not marry a Canaanite woman," ⁷and that Jacob had obeyed his father and mother and had gone to Paddan Aram. ⁸Esau then realized how displeasing the Canaanite women were to his father Isaac; ⁹so he went to Ishmael and married Mahalath, the sister of Nebaioth and daughter of Ishmael son of Abraham, in addition to the wives he already had.

Jacob's Dream at Bethel

¹⁰Jacob left Beersheba and set out for Haran. ¹¹When he reached a certain place, he stopped for the night because the sun had set. Taking one of the stones there, he put it under his head and lay down to sleep. ¹²He had a dream in which he saw a stairway*a* resting on the earth, with its top reaching to heaven, and the angels of God were ascending and descending on it. ¹³There above it*b* stood the Lᴏʀᴅ, and he said: "I am the Lᴏʀᴅ, the God of your father Abraham and the God of Isaac. I will give you and your descendants the land on which you are lying. ¹⁴Your descendants will be like the dust of the earth, and you will spread out to the west and to the east, to the north and to the south. All peoples on earth will be blessed through you and your offspring. ¹⁵I am with you and will watch over you wherever you go,

and I will bring you back to this land. I will not leave you until I have done what I have promised you."

¹⁶When Jacob awoke from his sleep, he thought, "Surely the Lᴏʀᴅ is in this place, and I was not aware of it." ¹⁷He was afraid and said, "How awesome is this place! This is none other than the house of God; this is the gate of heaven."

¹⁸Early the next morning Jacob took the stone he had placed under his head and set it up as a pillar and poured oil on top of it. ¹⁹He called that place Bethel,*c* though the city used to be called Luz.

²⁰Then Jacob made a vow, saying, "If God will be with me and will watch over me on this journey I am taking and will give me food to eat and clothes to wear ²¹so that I return safely to my father's house, then the Lᴏʀᴅ*d* will be my God ²²and*e* this stone that I have set up as a pillar will be God's house, and of all that you give me I will give you a tenth."

Jacob Arrives in Paddan Aram

29 Then Jacob continued on his journey and came to the land of the eastern peoples. ²There he saw a well in the field, with three flocks of sheep lying near it because the flocks were watered from that well. The stone over the mouth of the well was large. ³When all the flocks were gathered there, the shepherds would roll the stone away from the well's mouth and water the sheep. Then they would return the stone to its place over the mouth of the well.

⁴Jacob asked the shepherds, "My brothers, where are you from?"

"We're from Haran," they replied.

⁵He said to them, "Do you know Laban, Nahor's grandson?"

"Yes, we know him," they answered.

⁶Then Jacob asked them, "Is he well?"

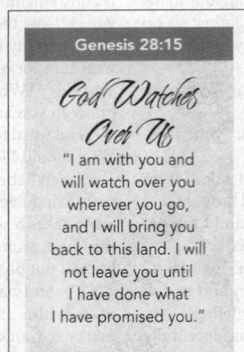

Genesis 28:15

God Watches Over Us

"I am with you and will watch over you wherever you go, and I will bring you back to this land. I will not leave you until I have done what I have promised you."

---

*a*12 Or *ladder*   *b*13 Or *There beside him*   *c*19 *Bethel* means *house of God.*   *d*20,21 Or *Since God... father's house, the* Lᴏʀᴅ
*e*21,22 Or *house, and the* Lᴏʀᴅ *will be my God,* *²²*then

"Yes, he is," they said, "and here comes his daughter Rachel with the sheep."

⁷"Look," he said, "the sun is still high; it is not time for the flocks to be gathered. Water the sheep and take them back to pasture."

⁸"We can't," they replied, "until all the flocks are gathered and the stone has been rolled away from the mouth of the well. Then we will water the sheep."

⁹While he was still talking with them, Rachel came with her father's sheep, for she was a shepherdess. ¹⁰When Jacob saw Rachel daughter of Laban, his mother's brother, and Laban's sheep, he went over and rolled the stone away from the mouth of the well and watered his uncle's sheep. ¹¹Then Jacob kissed Rachel and began to weep aloud. ¹²He had told Rachel that he was a relative of her father and a son of Rebekah. So she ran and told her father.

¹³As soon as Laban heard the news about Jacob, his sister's son, he hurried to meet him. He embraced him and kissed him and brought him to his home, and there Jacob told him all these things. ¹⁴Then Laban said to him, "You are my own flesh and blood."

Jacob Marries Leah and Rachel

After Jacob had stayed with him for a whole month, ¹⁵Laban said to him, "Just because you are a relative of mine, should you work for me for nothing? Tell me what your wages should be."

¹⁶Now Laban had two daughters; the name of the older was Leah, and the name of the younger was Rachel. ¹⁷Leah had weak*a* eyes, but Rachel was lovely in form, and beautiful. ¹⁸Jacob was in love with Rachel and said, "I'll work for you seven years in return for your younger daughter Rachel."

¹⁹Laban said, "It's better that I give her to you than to some other man. Stay here with me." ²⁰So Jacob served seven years to get Rachel, but they seemed like only a few days to him because of his love for her.

²¹Then Jacob said to Laban, "Give me my wife. My time is completed, and I want to lie with her."

²²So Laban brought together all the people of the place and gave a feast. ²³But when evening came, he took his daughter Leah and gave her to Jacob, and Jacob lay with her. ²⁴And Laban gave his servant girl Zilpah to his daughter as her maidservant.

²⁵When morning came, there was Leah! So Jacob said to Laban, "What is this you have done to me? I served you for Rachel, didn't I? Why have you deceived me?"

²⁶Laban replied, "It is not our custom here to give the younger daughter in marriage before the older one. ²⁷Finish this daughter's bridal week; then we will give you the younger one also, in return for another seven years of work."

²⁸And Jacob did so. He finished the week with Leah, and then Laban gave him his daughter Rachel to be his wife. ²⁹Laban gave his servant girl Bilhah to his daughter Rachel as her maidservant. ³⁰Jacob lay with Rachel also, and he loved Rachel more than Leah. And he worked for Laban another seven years.

Jacob's Children

³¹When the Lord saw that Leah was not loved, he opened her womb, but Rachel was barren. ³²Leah became pregnant and gave birth to a son. She named him Reuben,*b* for she said, "It is because the Lord has seen my misery. Surely my husband will love me now."

³³She conceived again, and when she gave birth to a son she said, "Because the Lord heard that I am not loved, he gave me this one too." So she named him Simeon.*c*

³⁴Again she conceived, and when she gave birth to a son she said, "Now at last my husband will become attached to me, because I have borne him three sons." So he was named Levi.*d*

³⁵She conceived again, and when she gave birth to a son she said, "This time I will praise the Lord." So she named him Judah.*e* Then she stopped having children.

30 When Rachel saw that she was not bearing Jacob any children, she became jealous of her sister. So she said to Jacob, "Give me children, or I'll die!"

²Jacob became angry with her and said,

---

*a*17 Or *delicate*   *b*32 *Reuben* sounds like the Hebrew for *he has seen my misery*; the name means *see, a son.*   *c*33 *Simeon* probably means *one who hears.*   *d*34 *Levi* sounds like and may be derived from the Hebrew for *attached.*   *e*35 *Judah* sounds like and may be derived from the Hebrew for *praise.*

When Morning Comes

Read: Genesis 29:16–30

Genesis 29:23,25

But when evening came, he took his daughter Leah and gave her to Jacob . . . When morning came, there was Leah!

reflection

1 Take a look in the mirror and describe the things you like about yourself.

2 What don't you like about yourself? Describe some of the things you'd change if you could.

3 What parts of yourself have you been afraid to show your loved ones (spiritually, emotionally or physically), and why? Take a chance and expose one part you've hidden behind the mask. Ask God to give you the strength to take this step. And ask God to surprise you with how much your loved ones accept the real you.

RELATED READINGS

Psalm 139:23–24;
1 John 1:5–7

IMAGINE THE SINKING FEELING you might feel when a beautiful, intelligent, accomplished woman arrives on the scene. She may be the new hire who took a promotion you've worked years to attain. She may be the charming wife of a friend. She may be the mother whose children have impeccable manners and dress. Whoever she is, she shakes your confidence, and ugly feelings of envy and self-loathing rear their heads, if only for a moment.

Leah came to her wedding night cloaked under layers of bridal veils. But her cover didn't last long: Morning came and her true identity came to light. Jacob was shocked to find that he had been deceived into marrying his beloved Rachel's sister.

The Bible places the blame squarely on Laban's shoulders: "He took his daughter Leah and gave her to Jacob." But did Leah play any part in the deceit? Was she simply obeying a conniving father, was she making a last-ditch effort to win a lover, or—on some hidden level—was she seeking to spite a sister more beautiful than herself? We will never know what kept Leah quiet as she went to marry Jacob, disguised beneath veils and robes, bangles and jewels. But we do know that in the clear light of morning, the game was up for the whole family.

If Leah hid beneath her veil, Laban hid behind the status quo. He failed to take responsibility for the pain Jacob, Leah and Rachel were to endure for years. He shifted the blame to his country's customs. And he shamelessly drove a hard bargain to keep Jacob in bondage. Laban's greed overcame common decency. He inflicted permanent and painful scars on his family.

Do you feel you have to hide your true self to gain a relationship? Perhaps you are elaborately and even beautifully veiling yourself with another person's interests, hobbies or pursuits to win their affections. Does the equivalent of a beautiful sister and deceitful father make you feel pushed to the sidelines, forced to veil yourself because you are afraid you won't be accepted as you are?

It could be that, like Leah, you fear that you are unlovely compared to others. But God created you—you are both lovely and lovable just as you are. Today, ask God for the courage to remove the veils covering your heart and recognize the beauty of his image in you.

38

Go to page 43 for your next devotional reading.

"Am I in the place of God, who has kept you from having children?"

³Then she said, "Here is Bilhah, my maidservant. Sleep with her so that she can bear children for me and that through her I too can build a family."

⁴So she gave him her servant Bilhah as a wife. Jacob slept with her, ⁵and she became pregnant and bore him a son. ⁶Then Rachel said, "God has vindicated me; he has listened to my plea and given me a son." Because of this she named him Dan.ᵃ

⁷Rachel's servant Bilhah conceived again and bore Jacob a second son. ⁸Then Rachel said, "I have had a great struggle with my sister, and I have won." So she named him Naphtali.ᵇ

⁹When Leah saw that she had stopped having children, she took her maidservant Zilpah and gave her to Jacob as a wife. ¹⁰Leah's servant Zilpah bore Jacob a son. ¹¹Then Leah said, "What good fortune!"ᶜ So she named him Gad.ᵈ

¹²Leah's servant Zilpah bore Jacob a second son. ¹³Then Leah said, "How happy I am! The women will call me happy." So she named him Asher.ᵉ

¹⁴During wheat harvest, Reuben went out into the fields and found some mandrake plants, which he brought to his mother Leah. Rachel said to Leah, "Please give me some of your son's mandrakes."

¹⁵But she said to her, "Wasn't it enough that you took away my husband? Will you take my son's mandrakes too?"

"Very well," Rachel said, "he can sleep with you tonight in return for your son's mandrakes."

¹⁶So when Jacob came in from the fields that evening, Leah went out to meet him. "You must sleep with me," she said. "I have hired you with my son's mandrakes." So he slept with her that night.

¹⁷God listened to Leah, and she became pregnant and bore Jacob a fifth son. ¹⁸Then Leah said, "God has rewarded me for giving my maidservant to my husband." So she named him Issachar.ᶠ

¹⁹Leah conceived again and bore Jacob a sixth son. ²⁰Then Leah said, "God has presented me with a precious gift. This time my husband will treat me with honor, because I have borne him six sons." So she named him Zebulun.ᵍ

²¹Some time later she gave birth to a daughter and named her Dinah.

²²Then God remembered Rachel; he listened to her and opened her womb. ²³She became pregnant and gave birth to a son and said, "God has taken away my disgrace." ²⁴She named him Joseph,ʰ and said, "May the Lord add to me another son."

Jacob's Flocks Increase

²⁵After Rachel gave birth to Joseph, Jacob said to Laban, "Send me on my way so I can go back to my own homeland. ²⁶Give me my wives and children, for whom I have served you, and I will be on my way. You know how much work I've done for you."

²⁷But Laban said to him, "If I have found favor in your eyes, please stay. I have learned by divination thatⁱ the Lord has blessed me because of you." ²⁸He added, "Name your wages, and I will pay them."

²⁹Jacob said to him, "You know how I have worked for you and how your livestock has fared under my care. ³⁰The little you had before I came has increased greatly, and the Lord has blessed you wherever I have been. But now, when may I do something for my own household?"

³¹"What shall I give you?" he asked.

"Don't give me anything," Jacob replied. "But if you will do this one thing for me, I will go on tending your flocks and watching over them: ³²Let me go through all your flocks today and remove from them every speckled or spotted sheep, every dark-colored lamb and every spotted or speckled goat. They will be my wages. ³³And my honesty will testify for me in the future, whenever you check on the wages you have paid me. Any goat in my possession that is not speckled or spotted, or any lamb that is not dark-colored, will be considered stolen."

³⁴"Agreed," said Laban. "Let it be as you have said." ³⁵That same day he removed all the male goats that were streaked or spotted, and all the speckled or spotted female goats (all that had

---

ᵃ6 *Dan* here means *he has vindicated.* ᵇ8 *Naphtali* means *my struggle.* ᶜ11 Or *"A troop is coming!"* ᵈ11 *Gad* can mean *good fortune* or *a troop.* ᵉ13 *Asher* means *happy.* ᶠ18 *Issachar* sounds like the Hebrew for *reward.* ᵍ20 *Zebulun* probably means *honor.* ʰ24 *Joseph* means *may he add.* ⁱ27 Or possibly *have become rich and* white on them) and all the dark-colored lambs, and he placed them in the care of his sons. [36] Then he put a three-day journey between himself and Jacob, while Jacob continued to tend the rest of Laban's flocks.

[37] Jacob, however, took fresh-cut branches from poplar, almond and plane trees and made white stripes on them by peeling the bark and exposing the white inner wood of the branches. [38] Then he placed the peeled branches in all the watering troughs, so that they would be directly in front of the flocks when they came to drink. When the flocks were in heat and came to drink, [39] they mated in front of the branches. And they bore young that were streaked or speckled or spotted. [40] Jacob set apart the young of the flock by themselves, but made the rest face the streaked and dark-colored animals that belonged to Laban. Thus he made separate flocks for himself and did not put them with Laban's animals. [41] Whenever the stronger females were in heat, Jacob would place the branches in the troughs in front of the animals so they would mate near the branches, [42] but if the animals were weak, he would not place them there. So the weak animals went to Laban and the strong ones to Jacob. [43] In this way the man grew exceedingly prosperous and came to own large flocks, and maidservants and menservants, and camels and donkeys.

Jacob Flees From Laban

31 Jacob heard that Laban's sons were saying, "Jacob has taken everything our father owned and has gained all this wealth from what belonged to our father." [2] And Jacob noticed that Laban's attitude toward him was not what it had been.

[3] Then the LORD said to Jacob, "Go back to the land of your fathers and to your relatives, and I will be with you."

[4] So Jacob sent word to Rachel and Leah to come out to the fields where his flocks were. [5] He said to them, "I see that your father's attitude toward me is not what it was before, but the God of my father has been with me. [6] You know that I've worked for your father with all my strength, [7] yet your father has cheated me by changing my wages ten times. However, God has not allowed him to harm me. [8] If he said, 'The speckled ones will be your wages,' then all the flocks gave birth to speckled young; and if he said, 'The streaked ones will be your wages,' then all the flocks bore streaked young. [9] So God has taken away your father's livestock and has given them to me.

[10] "In breeding season I once had a dream in which I looked up and saw that the male goats mating with the flock were streaked, speckled or spotted. [11] The angel of God said to me in the dream, 'Jacob.' I answered, 'Here I am.' [12] And he said, 'Look up and see that all the male goats mating with the flock are streaked, speckled or spotted, for I have seen all that Laban has been doing to you. [13] I am the God of Bethel, where you anointed a pillar and where you made a vow to me. Now leave this land at once and go back to your native land.'"

[14] Then Rachel and Leah replied, "Do we still have any share in the inheritance of our father's estate? [15] Does he not regard us as foreigners? Not only has he sold us, but he has used up what was paid for us. [16] Surely all the wealth that God took away from our father belongs to us and our children. So do whatever God has told you."

[17] Then Jacob put his children and his wives on camels, [18] and he drove all his livestock ahead of him, along with all the goods he had accumulated in Paddan Aram,[a] to go to his father Isaac in the land of Canaan.

[19] When Laban had gone to shear his sheep, Rachel stole her father's household gods. [20] Moreover, Jacob deceived Laban the Aramean by not telling him he was running

Genesis 31:6–7

God Defends the Disadvantaged

"You know that I've worked for your father with all my strength, yet your father has cheated me by changing my wages ten times. However, God has not allowed him to harm me."

---

[a] 18 That is, Northwest Mesopotamia

away. ²¹So he fled with all he had, and crossing the River,*ᵃ* he headed for the hill country of Gilead.

Laban Pursues Jacob

²²On the third day Laban was told that Jacob had fled. ²³Taking his relatives with him, he pursued Jacob for seven days and caught up with him in the hill country of Gilead. ²⁴Then God came to Laban the Aramean in a dream at night and said to him, "Be careful not to say anything to Jacob, either good or bad."

²⁵Jacob had pitched his tent in the hill country of Gilead when Laban overtook him, and Laban and his relatives camped there too. ²⁶Then Laban said to Jacob, "What have you done? You've deceived me, and you've carried off my daughters like captives in war. ²⁷Why did you run off secretly and deceive me? Why didn't you tell me, so I could send you away with joy and singing to the music of tambourines and harps? ²⁸You didn't even let me kiss my grandchildren and my daughters goodby. You have done a foolish thing. ²⁹I have the power to harm you; but last night the God of your father said to me, 'Be careful not to say anything to Jacob, either good or bad.' ³⁰Now you have gone off because you longed to return to your father's house. But why did you steal my gods?"

³¹Jacob answered Laban, "I was afraid, because I thought you would take your daughters away from me by force. ³²But if you find anyone who has your gods, he shall not live. In the presence of our relatives, see for yourself whether there is anything of yours here with me; and if so, take it." Now Jacob did not know that Rachel had stolen the gods.

³³So Laban went into Jacob's tent and into Leah's tent and into the tent of the two maidservants, but he found nothing. After he came out of Leah's tent, he entered Rachel's tent. ³⁴Now Rachel had taken the household gods and put them inside her camel's saddle and was sitting on them. Laban searched through everything in the tent but found nothing.

³⁵Rachel said to her father, "Don't be angry, my lord, that I cannot stand up in your presence; I'm having my period." So he searched but could not find the household gods.

³⁶Jacob was angry and took Laban to task. "What is my crime?" he asked Laban. "What sin have I committed that you hunt me down? ³⁷Now that you have searched through all my goods, what have you found that belongs to your household? Put it here in front of your relatives and mine, and let them judge between the two of us.

³⁸"I have been with you for twenty years now. Your sheep and goats have not miscarried, nor have I eaten rams from your flocks. ³⁹I did not bring you animals torn by wild beasts; I bore the loss myself. And you demanded payment from me for whatever was stolen by day or night. ⁴⁰This was my situation: The heat consumed me in the daytime and the cold at night, and sleep fled from my eyes. ⁴¹It was like this for the twenty years I was in your household. I worked for you fourteen years for your two daughters and six years for your flocks, and you changed my wages ten times. ⁴²If the God of my father, the God of Abraham and the Fear of Isaac, had not been with me, you would surely have sent me away empty-handed. But God has seen my hardship and the toil of my hands, and last night he rebuked you."

⁴³Laban answered Jacob, "The women are my daughters, the children are my children, and the flocks are my flocks. All you see is mine. Yet what can I do today about these daughters of mine, or about the children they have borne? ⁴⁴Come now, let's make a covenant, you and I, and let it serve as a witness between us."

⁴⁵So Jacob took a stone and set it up as a pillar. ⁴⁶He said to his relatives, "Gather some stones." So they took stones and piled them in a heap, and they ate there by the heap. ⁴⁷Laban called it Jegar Sahadutha,*ᵇ* and Jacob called it Galeed.*ᶜ*

⁴⁸Laban said, "This heap is a witness between you and me today." That is why it was called Galeed. ⁴⁹It was also called Mizpah,*ᵈ* because he said, "May the LORD keep watch between you and me when we are away from each other. ⁵⁰If you mistreat my daughters or if you take any wives besides my daughters, even

---

*ᵃ*21 That is, the Euphrates   *ᵇ*47 The Aramaic *Jegar Sahadutha* means *witness heap.*   *ᶜ*47 The Hebrew *Galeed* means *witness heap.*
*ᵈ*49 *Mizpah* means *watchtower.*

though no one is with us, remember that God is a witness between you and me."

51Laban also said to Jacob, "Here is this heap, and here is this pillar I have set up between you and me. 52This heap is a witness, and this pillar is a witness, that I will not go past this heap to your side to harm you and that you will not go past this heap and pillar to my side to harm me. 53May the God of Abraham and the God of Nahor, the God of their father, judge between us."

So Jacob took an oath in the name of the Fear of his father Isaac. 54He offered a sacrifice there in the hill country and invited his relatives to a meal. After they had eaten, they spent the night there.

55Early the next morning Laban kissed his grandchildren and his daughters and blessed them. Then he left and returned home.

Jacob Prepares to Meet Esau

32 Jacob also went on his way, and the angels of God met him. 2When Jacob saw them, he said, "This is the camp of God!" So he named that place Mahanaim.*a*

3Jacob sent messengers ahead of him to his brother Esau in the land of Seir, the country of Edom. 4He instructed them: "This is what you are to say to my master Esau: 'Your servant Jacob says, I have been staying with Laban and have remained there till now. 5I have cattle and donkeys, sheep and goats, menservants and maidservants. Now I am sending this message to my lord, that I may find favor in your eyes.'"

6When the messengers returned to Jacob, they said, "We went to your brother Esau, and now he is coming to meet you, and four hundred men are with him."

7In great fear and distress Jacob divided the people who were with him into two groups,*b* and the flocks and herds and camels as well. 8He thought, "If Esau comes and attacks one group,*c* the group*c* that is left may escape."

9Then Jacob prayed, "O God of my father Abraham, God of my father Isaac, O Lord, who said to me, 'Go back to your country and your relatives, and I will make you prosper,' 10I am unworthy of all the kindness and faithful-

ness you have shown your servant. I had only my staff when I crossed this Jordan, but now I have become two groups. 11Save me, I pray, from the hand of my brother Esau, for I am afraid he will come and attack me, and also the mothers with their children. 12But you have said, 'I will surely make you prosper and will make your descendants like the sand of the sea, which cannot be counted.'"

13He spent the night there, and from what he had with him he selected a gift for his brother Esau: 14two hundred female goats and twenty male goats, two hundred ewes and twenty rams, 15thirty female camels with their young, forty cows and ten bulls, and twenty female donkeys and ten male donkeys. 16He put them in the care of his servants, each herd by itself, and said to his servants, "Go ahead of me, and keep some space between the herds."

17He instructed the one in the lead: "When my brother Esau meets you and asks, 'To whom do you belong, and where are you going, and who owns all these animals in front of you?' 18then you are to say, 'They belong to your servant Jacob. They are a gift sent to my lord Esau, and he is coming behind us.'"

19He also instructed the second, the third and all the others who followed the herds: "You are to say the same thing to Esau when you meet him. 20And be sure to say, 'Your servant Jacob is coming behind us.'" For he thought, "I will pacify him with these gifts I am sending on ahead; later, when I see him, perhaps he will receive me." 21So Jacob's gifts went on ahead of him, but he himself spent the night in the camp.

Jacob Wrestles With God

22That night Jacob got up and took his two wives, his two maidservants and his eleven sons and crossed the ford of the Jabbok. 23After he had sent them across the stream, he sent over all his possessions. 24So Jacob was left alone, and a man wrestled with him till daybreak. 25When the man saw that he could not overpower him, he touched the socket of Jacob's hip so that his hip was wrenched as he wrestled with the man. 26Then the man said, "Let me go, for it is daybreak."

---

*a*2 *Mahanaim means* two camps.   *b*7 Or *camps; also in verse 10*   *c*8 Or *camp*

He Breaks Us to Make Us

Read: Genesis 32:22–32

THERE'S A GOOD REASON God calls his people sheep. Sometimes they act ba-a-a-ad and wander away from the paths he has mapped out for them.

A good shepherd will relentlessly search for a wayward sheep. Sometimes, if the sheep refuses to follow his master, the shepherd takes drastic action. He breaks the sheep's leg, places it upon his shoulders and carries the sheep until it learns total dependence. This is tough love—the shepherd breaks the sheep to make sure the sheep always follows the shepherd.

Jacob had always been a wanderer. He fled his home in Beer-sheba to escape his brother's wrath and find a wife in Haran. On his journey, he encountered God at a place called Bethel and saw a stairway leading to heaven. Years later, Jacob left Haran along with his wives, children and property. One night he found himself at Jabbok, utterly alone. At this solitary place God, in the form of "a man," sought out Jacob. God wanted to make Jacob into a different person, so he took drastic action. He initiated a wrestling match that lasted from dusk till dawn. Jacob's willfulness would not allow him to give up. So the man "broke" Jacob, touching his hip so that he walked with a limp for the rest of his life. Many people might become bitter and turn away from God for breaking them. But Jacob had just the opposite response. He clung to God saying, "I will not let you go unless you bless me."

We may think that a God of love would never allow his children to feel any pain. But sometimes God breaks us to make us better. He may break our hearts so we will make room for him there. He may break our will so we can discover his will for us. He may break our physical strength so we discover that God's strength is made perfect in our weakness (see 2 Corinthians 12:9). Like Jacob, the best response to God's tough love is to cling to him and earnestly pray, "I will not let you go unless you bless me."

If you've been acting like ba-a-a-ad sheep and have wandered off the path, climb up on the shepherd's shoulders and let him carry you home to healing.

Genesis 32:24–26

So Jacob was left alone, and a man wrestled with him till daybreak. When the man saw that he could not overpower him, he touched the socket of Jacob's hip so that his hip was wrenched as he wrestled with the man. Then the man said, "Let me go, for it is daybreak." But Jacob replied, "I will not let you go unless you bless me."

reflection

1 Describe the times you have wandered from God and how you sensed him relentlessly seeking you.

2 How has God broken you physically, emotionally or spiritually? What was the result?

3 God is a good shepherd; thank him for his care for you even when you don't always understand his methods.

RELATED READINGS

Psalms 23; 51:15–17;
James 1:2–5;
1 Peter 4:12–14

Thursday

Go to page 46 for your next devotional reading.

But Jacob replied, "I will not let you go unless you bless me."

27The man asked him, "What is your name?"

"Jacob," he answered.

28Then the man said, "Your name will no longer be Jacob, but Israel,*a* because you have struggled with God and with men and have overcome."

29Jacob said, "Please tell me your name."

But he replied, "Why do you ask my name?" Then he blessed him there.

30So Jacob called the place Peniel,*b* saying, "It is because I saw God face to face, and yet my life was spared."

31The sun rose above him as he passed Peniel,*c* and he was limping because of his hip. 32Therefore to this day the Israelites do not eat the tendon attached to the socket of the hip, because the socket of Jacob's hip was touched near the tendon.

Genesis 32:28

God Wrestles With His People

Then the man said, "Your name will no longer be Jacob, but Israel, because you have struggled with God and with men and have overcome."

Jacob Meets Esau

33 Jacob looked up and there was Esau, coming with his four hundred men; so he divided the children among Leah, Rachel and the two maidservants. 2He put the maidservants and their children in front, Leah and her children next, and Rachel and Joseph in the rear. 3He himself went on ahead and bowed down to the ground seven times as he approached his brother.

4But Esau ran to meet Jacob and embraced him; he threw his arms around his neck and kissed him. And they wept. 5Then Esau looked up and saw the women and children. "Who are these with you?" he asked.

Jacob answered, "They are the children God has graciously given your servant."

6Then the maidservants and their children approached and bowed down. 7Next, Leah and her children came and bowed down. Last of all came Joseph and Rachel, and they too bowed down.

8Esau asked, "What do you mean by all these droves I met?"

"To find favor in your eyes, my lord," he said.

9But Esau said, "I already have plenty, my brother. Keep what you have for yourself."

10"No, please!" said Jacob. "If I have found favor in your eyes, accept this gift from me. For to see your face is like seeing the face of God, now that you have received me favorably. 11Please accept the present that was brought to you, for God has been gracious to me and I have all I need." And because Jacob insisted, Esau accepted it.

12Then Esau said, "Let us be on our way; I'll accompany you."

13But Jacob said to him, "My lord knows that the children are tender and that I must care for the ewes and cows that are nursing their young. If they are driven hard just one day, all the animals will die. 14So let my lord go on ahead of his servant, while I move along slowly at the pace of the droves before me and that of the children, until I come to my lord in Seir."

15Esau said, "Then let me leave some of my men with you."

"But why do that?" Jacob asked. "Just let me find favor in the eyes of my lord."

16So that day Esau started on his way back to Seir. 17Jacob, however, went to Succoth, where he built a place for himself and made shelters for his livestock. That is why the place is called Succoth.*d*

18After Jacob came from Paddan Aram,*e* he arrived safely at the*f* city of Shechem in Canaan and camped within sight of the city. 19For a hundred pieces of silver,*g* he bought from the sons of Hamor, the father of Shechem, the plot of ground where he pitched his tent. 20There he set up an altar and called it El Elohe Israel.*h*

---

*a*28 *Israel* means *he struggles with God.*   *b*30 *Peniel* means *face of God.*   *c*31 Hebrew *Penuel,* a variant of *Peniel*   *d*17 *Succoth* means *shelters.*   *e*18 That is, Northwest Mesopotamia   *f*18 Or *arrived at Shalem, a*   *g*19 Hebrew *hundred kesitahs;* a kesitah was a unit of money of unknown weight and value.   *h*20 *El Elohe Israel* can mean *God, the God of Israel* or *mighty is the God of Israel.*

Dinah and the Shechemites

34 Now Dinah, the daughter Leah had borne to Jacob, went out to visit the women of the land. ²When Shechem son of Hamor the Hivite, the ruler of that area, saw her, he took her and violated her. ³His heart was drawn to Dinah daughter of Jacob, and he loved the girl and spoke tenderly to her. ⁴And Shechem said to his father Hamor, "Get me this girl as my wife."

⁵When Jacob heard that his daughter Dinah had been defiled, his sons were in the fields with his livestock; so he kept quiet about it until they came home.

⁶Then Shechem's father Hamor went out to talk with Jacob. ⁷Now Jacob's sons had come in from the fields as soon as they heard what had happened. They were filled with grief and fury, because Shechem had done a disgraceful thing in*a* Israel by lying with Jacob's daughter—a thing that should not be done.

⁸But Hamor said to them, "My son Shechem has his heart set on your daughter. Please give her to him as his wife. ⁹Intermarry with us; give us your daughters and take our daughters for yourselves. ¹⁰You can settle among us; the land is open to you. Live in it, trade*b* in it, and acquire property in it."

¹¹Then Shechem said to Dinah's father and brothers, "Let me find favor in your eyes, and I will give you whatever you ask. ¹²Make the price for the bride and the gift I am to bring as great as you like, and I'll pay whatever you ask me. Only give me the girl as my wife."

¹³Because their sister Dinah had been defiled, Jacob's sons replied deceitfully as they spoke to Shechem and his father Hamor. ¹⁴They said to them, "We can't do such a thing; we can't give our sister to a man who is not circumcised. That would be a disgrace to us. ¹⁵We will give our consent to you on one condition only: that you become like us by circumcising all your males. ¹⁶Then we will give you our daughters and take your daughters for ourselves. We'll settle among you and become one people with you. ¹⁷But if you will not agree to be circumcised, we'll take our sister*c* and go."

¹⁸Their proposal seemed good to Hamor and his son Shechem. ¹⁹The young man, who was the most honored of all his father's household, lost no time in doing what they said, because he was delighted with Jacob's daughter. ²⁰So Hamor and his son Shechem went to the gate of their city to speak to their fellow townsmen. ²¹"These men are friendly toward us," they said. "Let them live in our land and trade in it; the land has plenty of room for them. We can marry their daughters and they can marry ours. ²²But the men will consent to live with us as one people only on the condition that our males be circumcised, as they themselves are. ²³Won't their livestock, their property and all their other animals become ours? So let us give our consent to them, and they will settle among us."

²⁴All the men who went out of the city gate agreed with Hamor and his son Shechem, and every male in the city was circumcised.

²⁵Three days later, while all of them were still in pain, two of Jacob's sons, Simeon and Levi, Dinah's brothers, took their swords and attacked the unsuspecting city, killing every male. ²⁶They put Hamor and his son Shechem to the sword and took Dinah from Shechem's house and left. ²⁷The sons of Jacob came upon the dead bodies and looted the city where*d* their sister had been defiled. ²⁸They seized their flocks and herds and donkeys and everything else of theirs in the city and out in the fields. ²⁹They carried off all their wealth and all their women and children, taking as plunder everything in the houses.

³⁰Then Jacob said to Simeon and Levi, "You have brought trouble on me by making me a stench to the Canaanites and Perizzites, the people living in this land. We are few in number, and if they join forces against me and attack me, I and my household will be destroyed."

³¹But they replied, "Should he have treated our sister like a prostitute?"

Jacob Returns to Bethel

35 Then God said to Jacob, "Go up to Bethel and settle there, and build an altar there to God, who appeared to you when you were fleeing from your brother Esau."

²So Jacob said to his household and to all who were with him, "Get rid of the foreign

---

*a*7 Or *against*   *b*10 Or *move about freely*; also in verse 21   *c*17 Hebrew *daughter*   *d*27 Or *because*

Innocence Lost

Genesis 34:7

Now Jacob's sons had come in from the fields as soon as they heard what had happened. They were filled with grief and fury, because Shechem had done a disgraceful thing in Israel by lying with Jacob's daughter—a thing that should not be done.

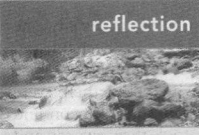

reflection

1 Describe a time when someone abused you either physically, mentally or emotionally.

2 How did it impact not just you but also those around you?

3 What are God's promises to you that he will forgive you and restore you? Write an exchange prayer, trading in your feelings of pain, sorrow or loss for the victory of being a believer (e.g., "I trade in my loss of innocence for the truth that I can regain purity through Christ's blood").

RELATED READINGS

Genesis 49:1,5–7;
Psalm 147:3–6;
Isaiah 43:18–19;
Romans 12:19–21

Read: Genesis 34:1–31

DINAH WAS JACOB'S ONLY DAUGHTER. When she ventured from her family's home to visit with the local people, she was taken and raped by Shechem, the son of a local ruler. Because of his position of power, he may have been able to take her without anyone intervening. Or perhaps he was adept at verbal manipulation, and he smoothly talked Dinah into a compromising position. Imagine Dinah's terror, vulnerability and defenselessness as she realized what Shechem intended. Add to Dinah's anguish the fact that only pure women could marry in Hebraic culture. Not being married meant having no social standing, no identity and no hope for the future.

No one is the same after sin—not the victim, not the perpetrator and not those who love the victim or victimizer. In this story, Shechem was a powerful man who thought he could have whatever he wanted. So he took it. Ultimately, he paid the price with his life, and his men paid the price with theirs.

Then there was Dinah's family. They, too, suffered because of Shechem's sin. Dinah's brothers became vigilantes, seeking vengeance not just on Shechem but on his helpless men. Two of the brothers acted with such brutality that Jacob cursed them from his deathbed.

And what about Dinah? She was violated, attacked, abused. Her pain is barely mentioned in this account. What must she have felt when her father did nothing? Or when her brothers overreacted? And what of her future? What would she do now?

No one suffers or sins in a vacuum. We can see that in the results of sin all around us. But we can see it in our own lives too. Maybe you have been abused or taken advantage of. You may feel that you have no future or no hope. Maybe others you know are suffering because of the actions of one person. God can work through any situation. He cannot change the past, but he can work through your present to help you cope, change, grow and ultimately thrive. God was victorious over sin at the cross. No matter what happened to you, God knows. Turn to him for comfort. Turn to him with your pain. Ask him to heal your hurting heart and restore you. He is the only one who can restore your soul.

Friday

Go to page 52 for your next devotional reading.

gods you have with you, and purify yourselves and change your clothes. ³Then come, let us go up to Bethel, where I will build an altar to God, who answered me in the day of my distress and who has been with me wherever I have gone." ⁴So they gave Jacob all the foreign gods they had and the rings in their ears, and Jacob buried them under the oak at Shechem. ⁵Then they set out, and the terror of God fell upon the towns all around them so that no one pursued them.

⁶Jacob and all the people with him came to Luz (that is, Bethel) in the land of Canaan. ⁷There he built an altar, and he called the place El Bethel,ᵃ because it was there that God revealed himself to him when he was fleeing from his brother.

⁸Now Deborah, Rebekah's nurse, died and was buried under the oak below Bethel. So it was named Allon Bacuth.ᵇ

⁹After Jacob returned from Paddan Aram,ᶜ God appeared to him again and blessed him. ¹⁰God said to him, "Your name is Jacob,ᵈ but you will no longer be called Jacob; your name will be Israel.ᵉ" So he named him Israel.

¹¹And God said to him, "I am God Almighty;ᶠ be fruitful and increase in number. A nation and a community of nations will come from you, and kings will come from your body. ¹²The land I gave to Abraham and Isaac I also give to you, and I will give this land to your descendants after you." ¹³Then God went up from him at the place where he had talked with him.

¹⁴Jacob set up a stone pillar at the place where God had talked with him, and he poured out a drink offering on it; he also poured oil on it. ¹⁵Jacob called the place where God had talked with him Bethel.ᵍ

The Deaths of Rachel and Isaac

¹⁶Then they moved on from Bethel. While they were still some distance from Ephrath, Rachel began to give birth and had great difficulty. ¹⁷And as she was having great difficulty in childbirth, the midwife said to her, "Don't be afraid, for you have another son." ¹⁸As she breathed her last—for she was dying—she named her son Ben-Oni.ʰ But his father named him Benjamin.ⁱ

¹⁹So Rachel died and was buried on the way to Ephrath (that is, Bethlehem). ²⁰Over her tomb Jacob set up a pillar, and to this day that pillar marks Rachel's tomb.

²¹Israel moved on again and pitched his tent beyond Migdal Eder. ²²While Israel was living in that region, Reuben went in and slept with his father's concubine Bilhah, and Israel heard of it.

Jacob had twelve sons:

²³The sons of Leah:
    Reuben the firstborn of Jacob,
    Simeon, Levi, Judah, Issachar and Zebulun.
²⁴The sons of Rachel:
    Joseph and Benjamin.
²⁵The sons of Rachel's maidservant Bilhah:
    Dan and Naphtali.
²⁶The sons of Leah's maidservant Zilpah:
    Gad and Asher.

These were the sons of Jacob, who were born to him in Paddan Aram.

²⁷Jacob came home to his father Isaac in Mamre, near Kiriath Arba (that is, Hebron), where Abraham and Isaac had stayed. ²⁸Isaac lived a hundred and eighty years. ²⁹Then he breathed his last and died and was gathered to his people, old and full of years. And his sons Esau and Jacob buried him.

Esau's Descendants

36
This is the account of Esau (that is, Edom).

²Esau took his wives from the women of Canaan: Adah daughter of Elon the

---

> ### Genesis 35:3
>
> *God Meets Our Distress*
>
> "Then come, let us go up to Bethel, where I will build an altar to God, who answered me in the day of my distress and who has been with me wherever I have gone."

ᵃ7 *El Bethel* means *God of Bethel.*   ᵇ8 *Allon Bacuth* means *oak of weeping.*   ᶜ9 That is, Northwest Mesopotamia; also in verse 26
ᵈ10 *Jacob* means *he grasps the heel* (figuratively, *he deceives*).   ᵉ10 *Israel* means *he struggles with God.*   ᶠ11 Hebrew *El-Shaddai*
ᵍ15 *Bethel* means *house of God.*   ʰ18 *Ben-Oni* means *son of my trouble.*   ⁱ18 *Benjamin* means *son of my right hand.*

Hittite, and Oholibamah daughter of Anah and granddaughter of Zibeon the Hivite— ³also Basemath daughter of Ishmael and sister of Nebaioth.

⁴Adah bore Eliphaz to Esau, Basemath bore Reuel, ⁵and Oholibamah bore Jeush, Jalam and Korah. These were the sons of Esau, who were born to him in Canaan.

⁶Esau took his wives and sons and daughters and all the members of his household, as well as his livestock and all his other animals and all the goods he had acquired in Canaan, and moved to a land some distance from his brother Jacob. ⁷Their possessions were too great for them to remain together; the land where they were staying could not support them both because of their livestock. ⁸So Esau (that is, Edom) settled in the hill country of Seir.

⁹This is the account of Esau the father of the Edomites in the hill country of Seir.

¹⁰These are the names of Esau's sons:

Eliphaz, the son of Esau's wife Adah, and Reuel, the son of Esau's wife Basemath.

¹¹The sons of Eliphaz:

Teman, Omar, Zepho, Gatam and Kenaz.

¹²Esau's son Eliphaz also had a concubine named Timna, who bore him Amalek. These were grandsons of Esau's wife Adah.

¹³The sons of Reuel:

Nahath, Zerah, Shammah and Mizzah. These were grandsons of Esau's wife Basemath.

¹⁴The sons of Esau's wife Oholibamah daughter of Anah and granddaughter of Zibeon, whom she bore to Esau:

Jeush, Jalam and Korah.

¹⁵These were the chiefs among Esau's descendants:

The sons of Eliphaz the firstborn of Esau:

Chiefs Teman, Omar, Zepho, Kenaz, ¹⁶Korah,ᵃ Gatam and Amalek. These were the chiefs descended from Eli-

phaz in Edom; they were grandsons of Adah.

¹⁷The sons of Esau's son Reuel:

Chiefs Nahath, Zerah, Shammah and Mizzah. These were the chiefs descended from Reuel in Edom; they were grandsons of Esau's wife Basemath.

¹⁸The sons of Esau's wife Oholibamah:

Chiefs Jeush, Jalam and Korah. These were the chiefs descended from Esau's wife Oholibamah daughter of Anah.

¹⁹These were the sons of Esau (that is, Edom), and these were their chiefs.

²⁰These were the sons of Seir the Horite, who were living in the region:

Lotan, Shobal, Zibeon, Anah, ²¹Dishon, Ezer and Dishan. These sons of Seir in Edom were Horite chiefs.

²²The sons of Lotan:

Hori and Homam.ᵇ Timna was Lotan's sister.

²³The sons of Shobal:

Alvan, Manahath, Ebal, Shepho and Onam.

²⁴The sons of Zibeon:

Aiah and Anah. This is the Anah who discovered the hot springsᶜ in the desert while he was grazing the donkeys of his father Zibeon.

²⁵The children of Anah:

Dishon and Oholibamah daughter of Anah.

²⁶The sons of Dishonᵈ:

Hemdan, Eshban, Ithran and Keran.

²⁷The sons of Ezer:

Bilhan, Zaavan and Akan.

²⁸The sons of Dishan:

Uz and Aran.

²⁹These were the Horite chiefs:

Lotan, Shobal, Zibeon, Anah, ³⁰Dishon, Ezer and Dishan. These were the Horite chiefs, according to their divisions, in the land of Seir.

The Rulers of Edom

³¹These were the kings who reigned in Edom before any Israelite king reignedᵉ:

ᵃ16 Masoretic Text; Samaritan Pentateuch (see also Gen. 36:11 and 1 Chron. 1:36) does not have *Korah*.   ᵇ22 Hebrew *Hemam*, a variant of *Homam* (see 1 Chron. 1:39)   ᶜ24 Vulgate; Syriac *discovered water*; the meaning of the Hebrew for this word is uncertain.   ᵈ26 Hebrew *Dishan*, a variant of *Dishon*   ᵉ31 Or *before an Israelite king reigned over them*

³²Bela son of Beor became king of Edom. His city was named Dinhabah.

³³When Bela died, Jobab son of Zerah from Bozrah succeeded him as king.

³⁴When Jobab died, Husham from the land of the Temanites succeeded him as king.

³⁵When Husham died, Hadad son of Bedad, who defeated Midian in the country of Moab, succeeded him as king. His city was named Avith.

³⁶When Hadad died, Samlah from Masrekah succeeded him as king.

³⁷When Samlah died, Shaul from Rehoboth on the river*ª* succeeded him as king.

³⁸When Shaul died, Baal-Hanan son of Acbor succeeded him as king.

³⁹When Baal-Hanan son of Acbor died, Hadad*ᵇ* succeeded him as king. His city was named Pau, and his wife's name was Mehetabel daughter of Matred, the daughter of Me-Zahab.

⁴⁰These were the chiefs descended from Esau, by name, according to their clans and regions: Timna, Alvah, Jetheth, ⁴¹Oholibamah, Elah, Pinon, ⁴²Kenaz, Teman, Mibzar, ⁴³Magdiel and Iram. These were the chiefs of Edom, according to their settlements in the land they occupied.

This was Esau the father of the Edomites.

Joseph's Dreams

37 Jacob lived in the land where his father had stayed, the land of Canaan.

²This is the account of Jacob.

Joseph, a young man of seventeen, was tending the flocks with his brothers, the sons of Bilhah and the sons of Zilpah, his father's wives, and he brought their father a bad report about them.

³Now Israel loved Joseph more than any of his other sons, because he had been born to him in his old age; and he made a richly ornamented*ᶜ* robe for him. ⁴When his brothers saw that their father loved him more than any of them, they hated him and could not speak a kind word to him.

⁵Joseph had a dream, and when he told it to his brothers, they hated him all the more. ⁶He said to them, "Listen to this dream I had: ⁷We were binding sheaves of grain out in the field when suddenly my sheaf rose and stood upright, while your sheaves gathered around mine and bowed down to it."

⁸His brothers said to him, "Do you intend to reign over us? Will you actually rule us?" And they hated him all the more because of his dream and what he had said.

⁹Then he had another dream, and he told it to his brothers. "Listen," he said, "I had another dream, and this time the sun and moon and eleven stars were bowing down to me."

¹⁰When he told his father as well as his brothers, his father rebuked him and said, "What is this dream you had? Will your mother and I and your brothers actually come and bow down to the ground before you?" ¹¹His brothers were jealous of him, but his father kept the matter in mind.

Joseph Sold by His Brothers

¹²Now his brothers had gone to graze their father's flocks near Shechem, ¹³and Israel said to Joseph, "As you know, your brothers are grazing the flocks near Shechem. Come, I am going to send you to them."

"Very well," he replied.

¹⁴So he said to him, "Go and see if all is well with your brothers and with the flocks, and bring word back to me." Then he sent him off from the Valley of Hebron.

When Joseph arrived at Shechem, ¹⁵a man found him wandering around in the fields and asked him, "What are you looking for?"

¹⁶He replied, "I'm looking for my brothers. Can you tell me where they are grazing their flocks?"

¹⁷"They have moved on from here," the man answered. "I heard them say, 'Let's go to Dothan.'"

So Joseph went after his brothers and found them near Dothan. ¹⁸But they saw him in the distance, and before he reached them, they plotted to kill him.

¹⁹"Here comes that dreamer!" they said to each other. ²⁰"Come now, let's kill him and

---

ª37 Possibly the Euphrates   *ᵇ39* Many manuscripts of the Masoretic Text, Samaritan Pentateuch and Syriac (see also 1 Chron. 1:50); most manuscripts of the Masoretic Text *Hadar*   *ᶜ3* The meaning of the Hebrew for *richly ornamented* is uncertain; also in verses 23 and 32.

throw him into one of these cisterns and say that a ferocious animal devoured him. Then we'll see what comes of his dreams."

²¹When Reuben heard this, he tried to rescue him from their hands. "Let's not take his life," he said. ²²"Don't shed any blood. Throw him into this cistern here in the desert, but don't lay a hand on him." Reuben said this to rescue him from them and take him back to his father.

²³So when Joseph came to his brothers, they stripped him of his robe—the richly ornamented robe he was wearing— ²⁴and they took him and threw him into the cistern. Now the cistern was empty; there was no water in it.

²⁵As they sat down to eat their meal, they looked up and saw a caravan of Ishmaelites coming from Gilead. Their camels were loaded with spices, balm and myrrh, and they were on their way to take them down to Egypt.

²⁶Judah said to his brothers, "What will we gain if we kill our brother and cover up his blood? ²⁷Come, let's sell him to the Ishmaelites and not lay our hands on him; after all, he is our brother, our own flesh and blood." His brothers agreed.

²⁸So when the Midianite merchants came by, his brothers pulled Joseph up out of the cistern and sold him for twenty shekels[a] of silver to the Ishmaelites, who took him to Egypt.

²⁹When Reuben returned to the cistern and saw that Joseph was not there, he tore his clothes. ³⁰He went back to his brothers and said, "The boy isn't there! Where can I turn now?"

³¹Then they got Joseph's robe, slaughtered a goat and dipped the robe in the blood. ³²They took the ornamented robe back to their father and said, "We found this. Examine it to see whether it is your son's robe."

³³He recognized it and said, "It is my son's robe! Some ferocious animal has devoured him. Joseph has surely been torn to pieces."

³⁴Then Jacob tore his clothes, put on sackcloth and mourned for his son many days. ³⁵All his sons and daughters came to comfort him, but he refused to be comforted. "No," he said, "in mourning will I go down to the grave[b] to my son." So his father wept for him.

³⁶Meanwhile, the Midianites[c] sold Joseph in Egypt to Potiphar, one of Pharaoh's officials, the captain of the guard.

Judah and Tamar

38 At that time, Judah left his brothers and went down to stay with a man of Adullam named Hirah. ²There Judah met the daughter of a Canaanite man named Shua. He married her and lay with her; ³she became pregnant and gave birth to a son, who was named Er. ⁴She conceived again and gave birth to a son and named him Onan. ⁵She gave birth to still another son and named him Shelah. It was at Kezib that she gave birth to him.

⁶Judah got a wife for Er, his firstborn, and her name was Tamar. ⁷But Er, Judah's firstborn, was wicked in the LORD's sight; so the LORD put him to death.

⁸Then Judah said to Onan, "Lie with your brother's wife and fulfill your duty to her as a brother-in-law to produce offspring for your brother." ⁹But Onan knew that the offspring would not be his; so whenever he lay with his brother's wife, he spilled his semen on the ground to keep from producing offspring for his brother. ¹⁰What he did was wicked in the LORD's sight; so he put him to death also.

Genesis 38:7

God Hates Sin

But Er, Judah's firstborn, was wicked in the LORD's sight; so the LORD put him to death.

¹¹Judah then said to his daughter-in-law Tamar, "Live as a widow in your father's house until my son Shelah grows up." For he thought, "He may die too, just like his brothers." So Tamar went to live in her father's house.

¹²After a long time Judah's wife, the daughter of Shua, died. When Judah had recovered from his grief, he went up to Timnah, to the men who were shearing his sheep, and his friend Hirah the Adullamite went with him.

---

*a*28 That is, about 8 ounces (about 0.2 kilogram)   *b*35 Hebrew *Sheol* also verse 28);   Masoretic Text *Medanites*   *c*36 Samaritan Pentateuch, Septuagint, Vulgate and Syriac (see

13When Tamar was told, "Your father-in-law is on his way to Timnah to shear his sheep," 14she took off her widow's clothes, covered herself with a veil to disguise herself, and then sat down at the entrance to Enaim, which is on the road to Timnah. For she saw that, though Shelah had now grown up, she had not been given to him as his wife.

15When Judah saw her, he thought she was a prostitute, for she had covered her face. 16Not realizing that she was his daughter-in-law, he went over to her by the roadside and said, "Come now, let me sleep with you."

"And what will you give me to sleep with you?" she asked.

17"I'll send you a young goat from my flock," he said.

"Will you give me something as a pledge until you send it?" she asked.

18He said, "What pledge should I give you?"

"Your seal and its cord, and the staff in your hand," she answered. So he gave them to her and slept with her, and she became pregnant by him. 19After she left, she took off her veil and put on her widow's clothes again.

20Meanwhile Judah sent the young goat by his friend the Adullamite in order to get his pledge back from the woman, but he did not find her. 21He asked the men who lived there, "Where is the shrine prostitute who was beside the road at Enaim?"

"There hasn't been any shrine prostitute here," they said.

22So he went back to Judah and said, "I didn't find her. Besides, the men who lived there said, 'There hasn't been any shrine prostitute here.'"

23Then Judah said, "Let her keep what she has, or we will become a laughingstock. After all, I did send her this young goat, but you didn't find her."

24About three months later Judah was told, "Your daughter-in-law Tamar is guilty of prostitution, and as a result she is now pregnant."

Judah said, "Bring her out and have her burned to death!"

25As she was being brought out, she sent a message to her father-in-law. "I am pregnant by the man who owns these," she said. And she added, "See if you recognize whose seal and cord and staff these are."

26Judah recognized them and said, "She is more righteous than I, since I wouldn't give her to my son Shelah." And he did not sleep with her again.

27When the time came for her to give birth, there were twin boys in her womb. 28As she was giving birth, one of them put out his hand; so the midwife took a scarlet thread and tied it on his wrist and said, "This one came out first." 29But when he drew back his hand, his brother came out, and she said, "So this is how you have broken out!" And he was named Perez.a 30Then his brother, who had the scarlet thread on his wrist, came out and he was given the name Zerah.b

Joseph and Potiphar's Wife

39 Now Joseph had been taken down to Egypt. Potiphar, an Egyptian who was one of Pharaoh's officials, the captain of the guard, bought him from the Ishmaelites who had taken him there.

2The LORD was with Joseph and he prospered, and he lived in the house of his Egyptian master. 3When his master saw that the LORD was with him and that the LORD gave him success in everything he did, 4Joseph found favor in his eyes and became his attendant. Potiphar put him in charge of his household, and he entrusted to his care everything he owned. 5From the time he put him in charge of his household and of all that he owned, the LORD blessed the household of the Egyptian because of Joseph. The blessing of the LORD was on everything Potiphar had, both in the house and in the field. 6So he left in Joseph's care everything he had; with Joseph in charge, he did not concern himself with anything except the food he ate.

Now Joseph was well-built and handsome, 7and after a while his master's wife took notice of Joseph and said, "Come to bed with me!"

8But he refused. "With me in charge," he told her, "my master does not concern himself with anything in the house; everything he owns he has entrusted to my care. 9No one is greater in this house than I am. My master has withheld

a29 Perez means breaking out.   b30 Zerah can mean scarlet or brightness.

More Than a Promise

SARAH

"*I will bless her
and will surely
give you a son
by her. I will bless
her so that she
will be the mother
of nations.*"

Genesis 17:16

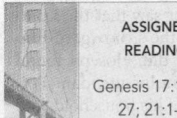

**ASSIGNED
READING:**

Genesis 17:1–
27; 21:1–6

"IT'S A BOY." Oh, the joy!

For her husband, this baby brought the prospect of being the father of a nation, of seeing his name carried throughout genera-tions. For Abraham, the baby meant his lineage was now secure. He smiled in satisfaction as he contemplated the future.

But not Sarah. The idea of mothering an entire race of people was beyond her for the moment. She was content to just let herself be entirely dazzled by the innocence in her baby's eyes, the scent of his flawless skin, the softness of his tiny hands.

Sarah was caught up in the "now." All she had ever wanted in life she could now cradle in the crook of her arm. She was a new mother; she likely wasn't thinking of the next generation. Nor of next year. Nor of tomorrow or even the next minute. She'd experienced a lifetime of being the daughter, the friend, the wife, the mistress of her household. Now, today, she reveled in her new primary identity—mother.

If given a choice, maybe she would have held the promise to her and kept him small forever. However, the much-anticipated promise also came with much-needed perspective. You see, the promise would one day grow up and grow old. More than likely, this baby boy would outlive his mom and dad altogether and, if he lived near them at all, bury them both. Maybe Sarah had a motherly tendency to focus on the now, and Abraham envisioned several generations into the future, but God had eternity clearly in view. It wasn't about the promise as much as it was about the Promise Maker.

Behind the promise Sarah could see the unseen Promise Maker. Far beyond the tiniest branch of the family tree that Abraham could envision, eternity stretched outward. The indescribable delight and pleasure of holding her son was meant to teach Sarah about the rapture of God cradling her in the palm of his hand. Beyond the joy of becoming a mother for the first time after 90 years and being in a unique relationship with another human being, there was a greater kind of happiness beyond measure: the joy of being in relationship with God.

—*Prayer*—
God, you know what my future holds. I can trust you no matter what I'm facing right now.

Weekend

Go to page 56 for your next devotional reading.

nothing from me except you, because you are his wife. How then could I do such a wicked thing and sin against God?" 10And though she spoke to Joseph day after day, he refused to go to bed with her or even be with her.

11One day he went into the house to attend to his duties, and none of the household servants was inside. 12She caught him by his cloak and said, "Come to bed with me!" But he left his cloak in her hand and ran out of the house.

13When she saw that he had left his cloak in her hand and had run out of the house, 14she called her household servants. "Look," she said to them, "this Hebrew has been brought to us to make sport of us! He came in here to sleep with me, but I screamed. 15When he heard me scream for help, he left his cloak beside me and ran out of the house."

16She kept his cloak beside her until his master came home. 17Then she told him this story: "That Hebrew slave you brought us came to me to make sport of me. 18But as soon as I screamed for help, he left his cloak beside me and ran out of the house."

19When his master heard the story his wife told him, saying, "This is how your slave treated me," he burned with anger. 20Joseph's master took him and put him in prison, the place where the king's prisoners were confined.

But while Joseph was there in the prison, 21the LORD was with him; he showed him kindness and granted him favor in the eyes of the prison warden. 22So the warden put Joseph in charge of all those held in the prison, and he was made responsible for all that was done there. 23The warden paid no attention to anything under Joseph's care, because the LORD was with Joseph and gave him success in whatever he did.

The Cupbearer and the Baker

40 Some time later, the cupbearer and the baker of the king of Egypt offended their master, the king of Egypt. 2Pharaoh was angry with his two officials, the chief cupbearer and the chief baker, 3and put them in custody in the house of the captain of the guard, in the same prison where Joseph was confined. 4The captain of the guard assigned them to Joseph, and he attended them.

After they had been in custody for some time, 5each of the two men—the cupbearer and the baker of the king of Egypt, who were being held in prison—had a dream the same night, and each dream had a meaning of its own.

6When Joseph came to them the next morning, he saw that they were dejected. 7So he asked Pharaoh's officials who were in custody with him in his master's house, "Why are your faces so sad today?"

8"We both had dreams," they answered, "but there is no one to interpret them."

Then Joseph said to them, "Do not interpretations belong to God? Tell me your dreams."

9So the chief cupbearer told Joseph his dream. He said to him, "In my dream I saw a vine in front of me, 10and on the vine were three branches. As soon as it budded, it blossomed, and its clusters ripened into grapes. 11Pharaoh's cup was in my hand, and I took the grapes, squeezed them into Pharaoh's cup and put the cup in his hand."

12"This is what it means," Joseph said to him. "The three branches are three days. 13Within three days Pharaoh will lift up your head and restore you to your position, and you will put Pharaoh's cup in his hand, just as you used to do when you were his cupbearer. 14But when all goes well with you, remember me and show me kindness; mention me to Pharaoh and get me out of this prison. 15For I was forcibly carried off from the land of the Hebrews, and even here I have done nothing to deserve being put in a dungeon."

16When the chief baker saw that Joseph had given a favorable interpretation, he said to Joseph, "I too had a dream: On my head were three baskets of bread.a 17In the top basket

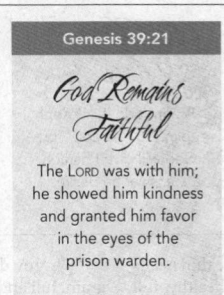

Genesis 39:21

God Remains Faithful

The LORD was with him; he showed him kindness and granted him favor in the eyes of the prison warden.

---

a16 Or *three wicker baskets*

were all kinds of baked goods for Pharaoh, but the birds were eating them out of the basket on my head."

[18] "This is what it means," Joseph said. "The three baskets are three days. [19] Within three days Pharaoh will lift off your head and hang you on a tree.[a] And the birds will eat away your flesh."

[20] Now the third day was Pharaoh's birthday, and he gave a feast for all his officials. He lifted up the heads of the chief cupbearer and the chief baker in the presence of his officials: [21] He restored the chief cupbearer to his position, so that he once again put the cup into Pharaoh's hand, [22] but he hanged[b] the chief baker, just as Joseph had said to them in his interpretation.

[23] The chief cupbearer, however, did not remember Joseph; he forgot him.

Pharaoh's Dreams

41 When two full years had passed, Pharaoh had a dream: He was standing by the Nile, [2] when out of the river there came up seven cows, sleek and fat, and they grazed among the reeds. [3] After them, seven other cows, ugly and gaunt, came up out of the Nile and stood beside those on the riverbank. [4] And the cows that were ugly and gaunt ate up the seven sleek, fat cows. Then Pharaoh woke up.

[5] He fell asleep again and had a second dream: Seven heads of grain, healthy and good, were growing on a single stalk. [6] After them, seven other heads of grain sprouted—thin and scorched by the east wind. [7] The thin heads of grain swallowed up the seven healthy, full heads. Then Pharaoh woke up; it had been a dream.

[8] In the morning his mind was troubled, so he sent for all the magicians and wise men of Egypt. Pharaoh told them his dreams, but no one could interpret them for him.

[9] Then the chief cupbearer said to Pharaoh, "Today I am reminded of my shortcomings. [10] Pharaoh was once angry with his servants,

and he imprisoned me and the chief baker in the house of the captain of the guard. [11] Each of us had a dream the same night, and each dream had a meaning of its own. [12] Now a young Hebrew was there with us, a servant of the captain of the guard. We told him our dreams, and he interpreted them for us, giving each man the interpretation of his dream. [13] And things turned out exactly as he interpreted them to us: I was restored to my position, and the other man was hanged.[b]"

[14] So Pharaoh sent for Joseph, and he was quickly brought from the dungeon. When he had shaved and changed his clothes, he came before Pharaoh.

[15] Pharaoh said to Joseph, "I had a dream, and no one can interpret it. But I have heard it said of you that when you hear a dream you can interpret it."

[16] "I cannot do it," Joseph replied to Pharaoh, "but God will give Pharaoh the answer he desires."

[17] Then Pharaoh said to Joseph, "In my dream I was standing on the bank of the Nile, [18] when out of the river there came up seven cows, fat and sleek, and they grazed among the reeds. [19] After them, seven other cows came up—scrawny and very ugly and lean. I had never seen such ugly cows in all the land of Egypt. [20] The lean, ugly cows ate up the seven fat cows that came up first. [21] But even after they ate them, no one could tell that they had done so; they looked just as ugly as before. Then I woke up.

[22] "In my dreams I also saw seven heads of grain, full and good, growing on a single stalk. [23] After them, seven other heads sprouted—withered and thin and scorched by the east wind. [24] The thin heads of grain swallowed up the seven good heads. I told this to the magicians, but none could explain it to me."

[25] Then Joseph said to Pharaoh, "The dreams of Pharaoh are one and the same. God has revealed to Pharaoh what he is about to do. [26] The seven good cows are seven years, and the seven

Genesis 41:16

God Provides Answers

"I cannot do it," Joseph replied to Pharaoh, "but God will give Pharaoh the answer he desires."

---

[a]19 Or *and impale you on a pole*   [b]22,13 Or *impaled*

good heads of grain are seven years; it is one and the same dream. 27The seven lean, ugly cows that came up afterward are seven years, and so are the seven worthless heads of grain scorched by the east wind: They are seven years of famine.

28"It is just as I said to Pharaoh: God has shown Pharaoh what he is about to do. 29Seven years of great abundance are coming throughout the land of Egypt, 30but seven years of famine will follow them. Then all the abundance in Egypt will be forgotten, and the famine will ravage the land. 31The abundance in the land will not be remembered, because the famine that follows it will be so severe. 32The reason the dream was given to Pharaoh in two forms is that the matter has been firmly decided by God, and God will do it soon.

33"And now let Pharaoh look for a discerning and wise man and put him in charge of the land of Egypt. 34Let Pharaoh appoint commissioners over the land to take a fifth of the harvest of Egypt during the seven years of abundance. 35They should collect all the food of these good years that are coming and store up the grain under the authority of Pharaoh, to be kept in the cities for food. 36This food should be held in reserve for the country, to be used during the seven years of famine that will come upon Egypt, so that the country may not be ruined by the famine."

37The plan seemed good to Pharaoh and to all his officials. 38So Pharaoh asked them, "Can we find anyone like this man, one in whom is the spirit of God[a]?"

39Then Pharaoh said to Joseph, "Since God has made all this known to you, there is no one so discerning and wise as you. 40You shall be in charge of my palace, and all my people are to submit to your orders. Only with respect to the throne will I be greater than you."

Joseph in Charge of Egypt

41So Pharaoh said to Joseph, "I hereby put you in charge of the whole land of Egypt." 42Then Pharaoh took his signet ring from his finger and put it on Joseph's finger. He dressed him in robes of fine linen and put a gold chain around his neck. 43He had him ride in a chariot as his second-in-command,[b] and men shouted before him, "Make way[c]!" Thus he put him in charge of the whole land of Egypt.

44Then Pharaoh said to Joseph, "I am Pharaoh, but without your word no one will lift hand or foot in all Egypt." 45Pharaoh gave Joseph the name Zaphenath-Paneah and gave him Asenath daughter of Potiphera, priest of On,[d] to be his wife. And Joseph went throughout the land of Egypt.

46Joseph was thirty years old when he entered the service of Pharaoh king of Egypt. And Joseph went out from Pharaoh's presence and traveled throughout Egypt. 47During the seven years of abundance the land produced plentifully. 48Joseph collected all the food produced in those seven years of abundance in Egypt and stored it in the cities. In each city he put the food grown in the fields surrounding it. 49Joseph stored up huge quantities of grain, like the sand of the sea; it was so much that he stopped keeping records because it was beyond measure.

50Before the years of famine came, two sons were born to Joseph by Asenath daughter of Potiphera, priest of On. 51Joseph named his firstborn Manasseh[e] and said, "It is because God has made me forget all my trouble and all my father's household." 52The second son he named Ephraim[f] and said, "It is because God has made me fruitful in the land of my suffering."

53The seven years of abundance in Egypt came to an end, 54and the seven years of famine began, just as Joseph had said. There was famine in all the other lands, but in the whole land of Egypt there was food. 55When all Egypt began to feel the famine, the people cried to Pharaoh for food. Then Pharaoh told all the Egyptians, "Go to Joseph and do what he tells you."

56When the famine had spread over the whole country, Joseph opened the storehouses and sold grain to the Egyptians, for the famine was severe throughout Egypt. 57And all the countries came to Egypt to buy grain from Joseph, because the famine was severe in all the world.

---

[a]38 Or of the gods   [b]43 Or in the chariot of his second-in-command; or in his second chariot   [c]43 Or Bow down   [d]45 That is, Heliopolis; also in verse 50   [e]51 Manasseh sounds like and may be derived from the Hebrew for forget.   [f]52 Ephraim sounds like the Hebrew for twice fruitful.

Joseph named his firstborn Manasseh and said, "It is because God has made me forget all my trouble and all my father's household." The second son he named Ephraim and said, "It is because God has made me fruitful in the land of my suffering."

reflection

1 What difficulties have you faced in the past? How did God use those times to shape you?

2 What situations are you currently facing that seem hopeless? How do you see God silently working to get you through them?

3 Sing Fanny Crosby's hymn "To God Be the Glory" as a way of thanking him for working behind the scenes in your life.

RELATED READINGS

Genesis 39:2–6,21–23; Romans 8:28–30

"Everything has its wonders, even darkness and silence, and I learn, whatever state I may be in, therein to be content."

Helen Adams Keller

God's Silent Work

Read: Genesis 41:41–57

IN MAY 1820 a six-week-old baby caught a cold. When her eyes became inflamed, a man posing as a doctor treated her with the wrong medication. Within days her eyesight was destroyed. But Fanny Crosby was not content to be a victim. She voraciously memorized five books of the Old Testament and most of the New Testament by the time she was ten years old. She attended the New York Institute for the Blind, where she became a teacher and gifted poet. After surviving the cholera epidemic in 1849, Fanny realized something was missing in her life and turned to Christ at the age of 30. God had been silently working in her heart. The poetry that formerly flowed from her heart turned into hymns of praise, many of which we still sing today. "To God Be the Glory," "Praise Him, Praise Him," "Tell Me the Story of Jesus" and many more songs speak of how Fanny loved God and the ways he worked in her life—even when she couldn't see it.

In Genesis 41 we see God silently working in Joseph's life. Joseph could have grown bitter and inflamed by the dreadful circumstances of his life. After all, he had been sold into slavery by his own brothers at the age of 17 and then sent to prison after refusing to sleep with his master's wife. Finally, after Joseph waited 13 long years, God transformed his wretched circumstances into something good. At the age of 30, Joseph experienced a new beginning. He rose to prominence within Pharaoh's court, saved the nation from famine and was blessed with a family of his own.

Joseph's sons' names poetically described his life story: *Manasseh*, "God has made me forget all my trouble"; and *Ephraim*, "God has made me fruitful in the land of my suffering." Amazingly, Joseph experienced God's silent work as much in slavery and in prison as he did when he rose to prominence.

Whatever your circumstances, you can trust that God is working behind the scenes. When you experience trouble—and you will—God can make you fruitful and full of praise, just as he did with Joseph and with Fanny Crosby.

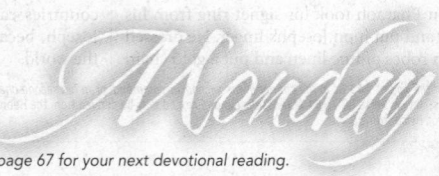

Monday

Go to page 67 for your next devotional reading.

Joseph's Brothers Go to Egypt

42 When Jacob learned that there was grain in Egypt, he said to his sons, "Why do you just keep looking at each other?" ²He continued, "I have heard that there is grain in Egypt. Go down there and buy some for us, so that we may live and not die."

³Then ten of Joseph's brothers went down to buy grain from Egypt. ⁴But Jacob did not send Benjamin, Joseph's brother, with the others, because he was afraid that harm might come to him. ⁵So Israel's sons were among those who went to buy grain, for the famine was in the land of Canaan also.

⁶Now Joseph was the governor of the land, the one who sold grain to all its people. So when Joseph's brothers arrived, they bowed down to him with their faces to the ground. ⁷As soon as Joseph saw his brothers, he recognized them, but he pretended to be a stranger and spoke harshly to them. "Where do you come from?" he asked.

"From the land of Canaan," they replied, "to buy food."

⁸Although Joseph recognized his brothers, they did not recognize him. ⁹Then he remembered his dreams about them and said to them, "You are spies! You have come to see where our land is unprotected."

¹⁰"No, my lord," they answered. "Your servants have come to buy food. ¹¹We are all the sons of one man. Your servants are honest men, not spies."

¹²"No!" he said to them. "You have come to see where our land is unprotected."

¹³But they replied, "Your servants were twelve brothers, the sons of one man, who lives in the land of Canaan. The youngest is now with our father, and one is no more."

¹⁴Joseph said to them, "It is just as I told you: You are spies! ¹⁵And this is how you will be tested: As surely as Pharaoh lives, you will not leave this place unless your youngest brother comes here. ¹⁶Send one of your number to get your brother; the rest of you will be kept in prison, so that your words may be tested to see if you are telling the truth. If you are not, then as surely as Pharaoh lives, you are spies!" ¹⁷And he put them all in custody for three days.

¹⁸On the third day, Joseph said to them, "Do this and you will live, for I fear God: ¹⁹If you are honest men, let one of your brothers stay here in prison, while the rest of you go and take grain back for your starving households. ²⁰But you must bring your youngest brother to me, so that your words may be verified and that you may not die." This they proceeded to do.

²¹They said to one another, "Surely we are being punished because of our brother. We saw how distressed he was when he pleaded with us for his life, but we would not listen; that's why this distress has come upon us."

²²Reuben replied, "Didn't I tell you not to sin against the boy? But you wouldn't listen! Now we must give an accounting for his blood." ²³They did not realize that Joseph could understand them, since he was using an interpreter.

²⁴He turned away from them and began to weep, but then turned back and spoke to them again. He had Simeon taken from them and bound before their eyes.

²⁵Joseph gave orders to fill their bags with grain, to put each man's silver back in his sack, and to give them provisions for their journey. After this was done for them, ²⁶they loaded their grain on their donkeys and left.

²⁷At the place where they stopped for the night one of them opened his sack to get feed for his donkey, and he saw his silver in the mouth of his sack. ²⁸"My silver has been returned," he said to his brothers. "Here it is in my sack."

Their hearts sank and they turned to each other trembling and said, "What is this that God has done to us?"

²⁹When they came to their father Jacob in the land of Canaan, they told him all that had happened to them. They said, ³⁰"The man who is lord over the land spoke harshly to us and treated us as though we were spying on the land. ³¹But we said to him, 'We are honest men; we are not spies. ³²We were twelve brothers, sons of one father. One is no more, and the youngest is now with our father in Canaan.'

³³"Then the man who is lord over the land said to us, 'This is how I will know whether you are honest men: Leave one of your brothers here with me, and take food for your starving households and go. ³⁴But bring your youngest brother to me so I will know that you are not spies but honest men. Then I will give your

brother back to you, and you can trade[a] in the land.'"

35 As they were emptying their sacks, there in each man's sack was his pouch of silver! When they and their father saw the money pouches, they were frightened. 36 Their father Jacob said to them, "You have deprived me of my children. Joseph is no more and Simeon is no more, and now you want to take Benjamin. Everything is against me!"

37 Then Reuben said to his father, "You may put both of my sons to death if I do not bring him back to you. Entrust him to my care, and I will bring him back."

38 But Jacob said, "My son will not go down there with you; his brother is dead and he is the only one left. If harm comes to him on the journey you are taking, you will bring my gray head down to the grave[b] in sorrow."

The Second Journey to Egypt

43 Now the famine was still severe in the land. 2 So when they had eaten all the grain they had brought from Egypt, their father said to them, "Go back and buy us a little more food."

3 But Judah said to him, "The man warned us solemnly, 'You will not see my face again unless your brother is with you.' 4 If you will send our brother along with us, we will go down and buy food for you. 5 But if you will not send him, we will not go down, because the man said to us, 'You will not see my face again unless your brother is with you.'"

6 Israel asked, "Why did you bring this trouble on me by telling the man you had another brother?"

7 They replied, "The man questioned us closely about ourselves and our family. 'Is your father still living?' he asked us. 'Do you have another brother?' We simply answered his questions. How were we to know he would say, 'Bring your brother down here'?"

8 Then Judah said to Israel his father, "Send the boy along with me and we will go at once, so that we and you and our children may live and not die. 9 I myself will guarantee his safety; you can hold me personally responsible for him. If I do not bring him back to you and set him here before you, I will bear the blame before you

all my life. 10 As it is, if we had not delayed, we could have gone and returned twice."

11 Then their father Israel said to them, "If it must be, then do this: Put some of the best products of the land in your bags and take them down to the man as a gift—a little balm and a little honey, some spices and myrrh, some pistachio nuts and almonds. 12 Take double the amount of silver with you, for you must return the silver that was put back into the mouths of your sacks. Perhaps it was a mistake. 13 Take your brother also and go back to the man at once. 14 And may God Almighty[c] grant you mercy before the man so that he will let your other brother and Benjamin come back with you. As for me, if I am bereaved, I am bereaved."

15 So the men took the gifts and double the amount of silver, and Benjamin also. They hurried down to Egypt and presented themselves to Joseph. 16 When Joseph saw Benjamin with them, he said to the steward of his house, "Take these men to my house, slaughter an animal and prepare dinner; they are to eat with me at noon."

17 The man did as Joseph told him and took the men to Joseph's house. 18 Now the men were frightened when they were taken to his house. They thought, "We were brought here because of the silver that was put back into our sacks the first time. He wants to attack us and overpower us and seize us as slaves and take our donkeys."

19 So they went up to Joseph's steward and spoke to him at the entrance to the house. 20 "Please, sir," they said, "we came down here the first time to buy food. 21 But at the place where we stopped for the night we opened our sacks and each of us found his silver—the exact weight—in the mouth of his sack. So we have brought it back with us. 22 We have also brought additional silver with us to buy food. We don't know who put our silver in our sacks."

23 "It's all right," he said. "Don't be afraid. Your God, the God of your father, has given you treasure in your sacks; I received your silver." Then he brought Simeon out to them.

24 The steward took the men into Joseph's house, gave them water to wash their feet and

[a]34 Or move about freely   [b]38 Hebrew Sheol   [c]14 Hebrew El-Shaddai

provided fodder for their donkeys. ²⁵They prepared their gifts for Joseph's arrival at noon, because they had heard that they were to eat there.

²⁶When Joseph came home, they presented to him the gifts they had brought into the house, and they bowed down before him to the ground. ²⁷He asked them how they were, and then he said, "How is your aged father you told me about? Is he still living?"

²⁸They replied, "Your servant our father is still alive and well." And they bowed low to pay him honor.

²⁹As he looked about and saw his brother Benjamin, his own mother's son, he asked, "Is this your youngest brother, the one you told me about?" And he said, "God be gracious to you, my son." ³⁰Deeply moved at the sight of his brother, Joseph hurried out and looked for a place to weep. He went into his private room and wept there.

³¹After he had washed his face, he came out and, controlling himself, said, "Serve the food."

³²They served him by himself, the brothers by themselves, and the Egyptians who ate with him by themselves, because Egyptians could not eat with Hebrews, for that is detestable to Egyptians. ³³The men had been seated before him in the order of their ages, from the firstborn to the youngest; and they looked at each other in astonishment. ³⁴When portions were served to them from Joseph's table, Benjamin's portion was five times as much as anyone else's. So they feasted and drank freely with him.

A Silver Cup in a Sack

44 Now Joseph gave these instructions to the steward of his house: "Fill the men's sacks with as much food as they can carry, and put each man's silver in the mouth of his sack. ²Then put my cup, the silver one, in the mouth of the youngest one's sack, along with the silver for his grain." And he did as Joseph said.

³As morning dawned, the men were sent on their way with their donkeys. ⁴They had not gone far from the city when Joseph said to his steward, "Go after those men at once, and when you catch up with them, say to them, 'Why have you repaid good with evil? ⁵Isn't this the cup my master drinks from and also

uses for divination? This is a wicked thing you have done.'"

⁶When he caught up with them, he repeated these words to them. ⁷But they said to him, "Why does my lord say such things? Far be it from your servants to do anything like that! ⁸We even brought back to you from the land of Canaan the silver we found inside the mouths of our sacks. So why would we steal silver or gold from your master's house? ⁹If any of your servants is found to have it, he will die; and the rest of us will become my lord's slaves."

¹⁰"Very well, then," he said, "let it be as you say. Whoever is found to have it will become my slave; the rest of you will be free from blame."

¹¹Each of them quickly lowered his sack to the ground and opened it. ¹²Then the steward proceeded to search, beginning with the oldest and ending with the youngest. And the cup was found in Benjamin's sack. ¹³At this, they tore their clothes. Then they all loaded their donkeys and returned to the city.

¹⁴Joseph was still in the house when Judah and his brothers came in, and they threw themselves to the ground before him. ¹⁵Joseph said to them, "What is this you have done? Don't you know that a man like me can find things out by divination?"

¹⁶"What can we say to my lord?" Judah replied. "What can we say? How can we prove our innocence? God has uncovered your servants' guilt. We are now my lord's slaves—we ourselves and the one who was found to have the cup."

¹⁷But Joseph said, "Far be it from me to do such a thing! Only the man who was found to have the cup will become my slave. The rest of you, go back to your father in peace."

¹⁸Then Judah went up to him and said: "Please, my lord, let your servant speak a word to my lord. Do not be angry with your servant, though you are equal to Pharaoh himself. ¹⁹My lord asked his servants, 'Do you have a father or a brother?' ²⁰And we answered, 'We have an aged father, and there is a young son born to him in his old age. His brother is dead, and he is the only one of his mother's sons left, and his father loves him.'

²¹"Then you said to your servants, 'Bring him down to me so I can see him for myself.'

22And we said to my lord, 'The boy cannot leave his father; if he leaves him, his father will die.' 23But you told your servants, 'Unless your youngest brother comes down with you, you will not see my face again.' 24When we went back to your servant my father, we told him what my lord had said.

25"Then our father said, 'Go back and buy a little more food.' 26But we said, 'We cannot go down. Only if our youngest brother is with us will we go. We cannot see the man's face unless our youngest brother is with us.'

27"Your servant my father said to us, 'You know that my wife bore me two sons. 28One of them went away from me, and I said, "He has surely been torn to pieces." And I have not seen him since. 29If you take this one from me too and harm comes to him, you will bring my gray head down to the grave*a* in misery.'

30"So now, if the boy is not with us when I go back to your servant my father and if my father, whose life is closely bound up with the boy's life, 31sees that the boy isn't there, he will die. Your servants will bring the gray head of our father down to the grave in sorrow. 32Your servant guaranteed the boy's safety to my father. I said, 'If I do not bring him back to you, I will bear the blame before you, my father, all my life!'

33"Now then, please let your servant remain here as my lord's slave in place of the boy, and let the boy return with his brothers. 34How can I go back to my father if the boy is not with me? No! Do not let me see the misery that would come upon my father."

Joseph Makes Himself Known

45 Then Joseph could no longer control himself before all his attendants, and he cried out, "Have everyone leave my presence!" So there was no one with Joseph when he made himself known to his brothers. 2And he wept so loudly that the Egyptians heard him, and Pharaoh's household heard about it.

3Joseph said to his brothers, "I am Joseph! Is my father still living?" But his brothers were not able to answer him, because they were terrified at his presence.

4Then Joseph said to his brothers, "Come close to me." When they had done so, he said, "I am your brother Joseph, the one you sold into Egypt! 5And now, do not be distressed and do not be angry with yourselves for selling me here, because it was to save lives that God sent me ahead of you. 6For two years now there has been famine in the land, and for the next five years there will not be plowing and reaping. 7But God sent me ahead of you to preserve for you a remnant on earth and to save your lives by a great deliverance.*b*

8"So then, it was not you who sent me here, but God. He made me father to Pharaoh, lord of his entire household and ruler of all Egypt. 9Now hurry back to my father and say to him, 'This is what your son Joseph says: God has made me lord of all Egypt. Come down to me; don't delay. 10You shall live in the region of Goshen and be near me—you, your children and grandchildren, your flocks and herds, and all you have. 11I will provide for you there, because five years of famine are still to come. Otherwise you and your household and all who belong to you will become destitute.'

12"You can see for yourselves, and so can my brother Benjamin, that it is really I who am speaking to you. 13Tell my father about all the honor accorded me in Egypt and about everything you have seen. And bring my father down here quickly."

14Then he threw his arms around his brother Benjamin and wept, and Benjamin embraced him, weeping. 15And he kissed all his brothers and wept over them. Afterward his brothers talked with him.

16When the news reached Pharaoh's palace that Joseph's brothers had come, Pharaoh and all his officials were pleased. 17Pharaoh said

---

> **Genesis 45:7**
>
> *God Plans Ahead*
>
> "But God sent me ahead of you to preserve for you a remnant on earth and to save your lives by a great deliverance."

---

*a*29 Hebrew *Sheol*; also in verse 31 *b*7 Or *save you as a great band of survivors* to Joseph, "Tell your brothers, 'Do this: Load your animals and return to the land of Canaan, [18]and bring your father and your families back to me. I will give you the best of the land of Egypt and you can enjoy the fat of the land.'

[19]"You are also directed to tell them, 'Do this: Take some carts from Egypt for your children and your wives, and get your father and come. [20]Never mind about your belongings, because the best of all Egypt will be yours.'"

[21]So the sons of Israel did this. Joseph gave them carts, as Pharaoh had commanded, and he also gave them provisions for their journey. [22]To each of them he gave new clothing, but to Benjamin he gave three hundred shekels[a] of silver and five sets of clothes. [23]And this is what he sent to his father: ten donkeys loaded with the best things of Egypt, and ten female donkeys loaded with grain and bread and other provisions for his journey. [24]Then he sent his brothers away, and as they were leaving he said to them, "Don't quarrel on the way!"

[25]So they went up out of Egypt and came to their father Jacob in the land of Canaan. [26]They told him, "Joseph is still alive! In fact, he is ruler of all Egypt." Jacob was stunned; he did not believe them. [27]But when they told him everything Joseph had said to them, and when he saw the carts Joseph had sent to carry him back, the spirit of their father Jacob revived. [28]And Israel said, "I'm convinced! My son Joseph is still alive. I will go and see him before I die."

Jacob Goes to Egypt

46 So Israel set out with all that was his, and when he reached Beersheba, he offered sacrifices to the God of his father Isaac.

[2]And God spoke to Israel in a vision at night and said, "Jacob! Jacob!"

"Here I am," he replied.

[3]"I am God, the God of your father," he said. "Do not be afraid to go down to Egypt, for I will make you into a great nation there. [4]I will go down to Egypt with you, and I will surely bring you back again. And Joseph's own hand will close your eyes."

[5]Then Jacob left Beersheba, and Israel's sons took their father Jacob and their children and their wives in the carts that Pharaoh had sent to transport him. [6]They also took with them their livestock and the possessions they had acquired in Canaan, and Jacob and all his offspring went to Egypt. [7]He took with him to Egypt his sons and grandsons and his daughters and grand-daughters—all his offspring.

[8]These are the names of the sons of Israel (Jacob and his descendants) who went to Egypt:

Reuben the firstborn of Jacob.
[9]The sons of Reuben:
    Hanoch, Pallu, Hezron and Carmi.
[10]The sons of Simeon:
    Jemuel, Jamin, Ohad, Jakin, Zohar and
    Shaul the son of a Canaanite woman.
[11]The sons of Levi:
    Gershon, Kohath and Merari.
[12]The sons of Judah:
    Er, Onan, Shelah, Perez and Zerah (but
    Er and Onan had died in the land of
    Canaan).
    The sons of Perez:
        Hezron and Hamul.
[13]The sons of Issachar:
    Tola, Puah,[b] Jashub[c] and Shimron.
[14]The sons of Zebulun:
    Sered, Elon and Jahleel.
[15]These were the sons Leah bore to Jacob in Paddan Aram,[d] besides his daughter Dinah. These sons and daughters of his were thirty-three in all.

[16]The sons of Gad:
    Zephon,[e] Haggi, Shuni, Ezbon, Eri,
    Arodi and Areli.
[17]The sons of Asher:
    Imnah, Ishvah, Ishvi and Beriah.
    Their sister was Serah.
    The sons of Beriah:
        Heber and Malkiel.
[18]These were the children born to Jacob by Zilpah, whom Laban had given to his daughter Leah—sixteen in all.

[a]22 That is, about 7 1/2 pounds (about 3.5 kilograms)   [b]13 Samaritan Pentateuch and Syriac (see also 1 Chron. 7:1); Masoretic Text *Puvah*   [c]13 Samaritan Pentateuch and some Septuagint manuscripts (see also Num. 26:24 and 1 Chron. 7:1); Masoretic Text *Iob*   [d]15 That is, Northwest Mesopotamia   [e]16 Samaritan Pentateuch and Septuagint (see also Num. 26:15); Masoretic Text *Ziphion*

19 The sons of Jacob's wife Rachel:

Joseph and Benjamin. **20** In Egypt, Manasseh and Ephraim were born to Joseph by Asenath daughter of Potiphera, priest of On.[a]

21 The sons of Benjamin:

Bela, Beker, Ashbel, Gera, Naaman, Ehi, Rosh, Muppim, Huppim and Ard.

22 These were the sons of Rachel who were born to Jacob—fourteen in all.

23 The son of Dan:

Hushim.

24 The sons of Naphtali:

Jahziel, Guni, Jezer and Shillem.

25 These were the sons born to Jacob by Bilhah, whom Laban had given to his daughter Rachel—seven in all.

26 All those who went to Egypt with Jacob—those who were his direct descendants, not counting his sons' wives—numbered sixty-six persons. **27** With the two sons[b] who had been born to Joseph in Egypt, the members of Jacob's family, which went to Egypt, were seventy[c] in all.

28 Now Jacob sent Judah ahead of him to Joseph to get directions to Goshen. When they arrived in the region of Goshen, **29** Joseph had his chariot made ready and went to Goshen to meet his father Israel. As soon as Joseph appeared before him, he threw his arms around his father[d] and wept for a long time.

30 Israel said to Joseph, "Now I am ready to die, since I have seen for myself that you are still alive."

31 Then Joseph said to his brothers and to his father's household, "I will go up and speak to Pharaoh and will say to him, 'My brothers and my father's household, who were living in the land of Canaan, have come to me. **32** The men are shepherds; they tend livestock, and they have brought along their flocks and herds and everything they own.' **33** When Pharaoh calls you in and asks, 'What is your occupation?' **34** you should answer, 'Your servants have tended livestock from our boyhood on, just as our fathers did.' Then you will be allowed to settle in the region of Goshen, for all shepherds are detestable to the Egyptians."

47 Joseph went and told Pharaoh, "My father and brothers, with their flocks and herds and everything they own, have come from the land of Canaan and are now in Goshen." **2** He chose five of his brothers and presented them before Pharaoh.

3 Pharaoh asked the brothers, "What is your occupation?"

"Your servants are shepherds," they replied to Pharaoh, "just as our fathers were." **4** They also said to him, "We have come to live here awhile, because the famine is severe in Canaan and your servants' flocks have no pasture. So now, please let your servants settle in Goshen."

5 Pharaoh said to Joseph, "Your father and your brothers have come to you, **6** and the land of Egypt is before you; settle your father and your brothers in the best part of the land. Let them live in Goshen. And if you know of any among them with special ability, put them in charge of my own livestock."

7 Then Joseph brought his father Jacob in and presented him before Pharaoh. After Jacob blessed[e] Pharaoh, **8** Pharaoh asked him, "How old are you?"

9 And Jacob said to Pharaoh, "The years of my pilgrimage are a hundred and thirty. My years have been few and difficult, and they do not equal the years of the pilgrimage of my fathers." **10** Then Jacob blessed[f] Pharaoh and went out from his presence.

11 So Joseph settled his father and his brothers in Egypt and gave them property in the best part of the land, the district of Rameses, as Pharaoh directed. **12** Joseph also provided his father and his brothers and all his father's household with food, according to the number of their children.

Joseph and the Famine

13 There was no food, however, in the whole region because the famine was severe; both Egypt and Canaan wasted away because of the famine. **14** Joseph collected all the money that was to be found in Egypt and Canaan in payment for the grain they were buying, and

---

[a] **20** That is, Heliopolis   [b] **27** Hebrew; Septuagint *the nine children* (Acts 7:14) *seventy-five*   [c] **27** Hebrew (see also Exodus 1:5 and footnote); Septuagint (see also Acts 7:14) *seventy-five*   [d] **29** Hebrew *around him*   [e] **7** Or *greeted*   [f] **10** Or *said farewell to*

he brought it to Pharaoh's palace. ¹⁵When the money of the people of Egypt and Canaan was gone, all Egypt came to Joseph and said, "Give us food. Why should we die before your eyes? Our money is used up."

¹⁶"Then bring your livestock," said Joseph. "I will sell you food in exchange for your livestock, since your money is gone." ¹⁷So they brought their livestock to Joseph, and he gave them food in exchange for their horses, their sheep and goats, their cattle and donkeys. And he brought them through that year with food in exchange for all their livestock.

¹⁸When that year was over, they came to him the following year and said, "We cannot hide from our lord the fact that since our money is gone and our livestock belongs to you, there is nothing left for our lord except our bodies and our land. ¹⁹Why should we perish before your eyes—we and our land as well? Buy us and our land in exchange for food, and we with our land will be in bondage to Pharaoh. Give us seed so that we may live and not die, and that the land may not become desolate."

²⁰So Joseph bought all the land in Egypt for Pharaoh. The Egyptians, one and all, sold their fields, because the famine was too severe for them. The land became Pharaoh's, ²¹and Joseph reduced the people to servitude,[a] from one end of Egypt to the other. ²²However, he did not buy the land of the priests, because they received a regular allotment from Pharaoh and had food enough from the allotment Pharaoh gave them. That is why they did not sell their land.

²³Joseph said to the people, "Now that I have bought you and your land today for Pharaoh, here is seed for you so you can plant the ground. ²⁴But when the crop comes in, give a fifth of it to Pharaoh. The other four-fifths you may keep as seed for the fields and as food for yourselves and your households and your children."

²⁵"You have saved our lives," they said. "May we find favor in the eyes of our lord; we will be in bondage to Pharaoh."

²⁶So Joseph established it as a law concerning land in Egypt—still in force today—that

a fifth of the produce belongs to Pharaoh. It was only the land of the priests that did not become Pharaoh's.

²⁷Now the Israelites settled in Egypt in the region of Goshen. They acquired property there and were fruitful and increased greatly in number.

²⁸Jacob lived in Egypt seventeen years, and the years of his life were a hundred and forty-seven. ²⁹When the time drew near for Israel to die, he called for his son Joseph and said to him, "If I have found favor in your eyes, put your hand under my thigh and promise that you will show me kindness and faithfulness. Do not bury me in Egypt, ³⁰but when I rest with my fathers, carry me out of Egypt and bury me where they are buried."

"I will do as you say," he said.

³¹"Swear to me," he said. Then Joseph swore to him, and Israel worshiped as he leaned on the top of his staff.[b]

Manasseh and Ephraim

48
Some time later Joseph was told, "Your father is ill." So he took his two sons Manasseh and Ephraim along with him. ²When Jacob was told, "Your son Joseph has come to you," Israel rallied his strength and sat up on the bed.

³Jacob said to Joseph, "God Almighty[c] appeared to me at Luz in the land of Canaan, and there he blessed me ⁴and said to me, 'I am going to make you fruitful and will increase your numbers. I will make you a community of peoples, and I will give this land as an everlasting possession to your descendants after you.'

⁵"Now then, your two sons born to you in Egypt before I came to you here will be reckoned as mine; Ephraim and Manasseh will be mine, just as Reuben and Simeon are mine. ⁶Any children born to you after them will be yours; in the territory they inherit they will be reckoned under the names of their brothers. ⁷As I was returning from Paddan,[d] to my sorrow Rachel died in the land of Canaan while we were still on the way, a little distance from Ephrath. So I buried her there beside the road to Ephrath" (that is, Bethlehem).

---

a21 Samaritan Pentateuch and Septuagint (see also Vulgate); Masoretic Text *and he moved the people into the cities*   b31 Or *Israel bowed down at the head of his bed*   c3 Hebrew *El-Shaddai*   d7 That is, Northwest Mesopotamia

⁸When Israel saw the sons of Joseph, he asked, "Who are these?"

⁹"They are the sons God has given me here," Joseph said to his father.

Then Israel said, "Bring them to me so I may bless them."

¹⁰Now Israel's eyes were failing because of old age, and he could hardly see. So Joseph brought his sons close to him, and his father kissed them and embraced them.

¹¹Israel said to Joseph, "I never expected to see your face again, and now God has allowed me to see your children too."

¹²Then Joseph removed them from Israel's knees and bowed down with his face to the ground. ¹³And Joseph took both of them, Ephraim on his right toward Israel's left hand and Manasseh on his left toward Israel's right hand, and brought them close to him. ¹⁴But Israel reached out his right hand and put it on Ephraim's head, though he was the younger, and crossing his arms, he put his left hand on Manasseh's head, even though Manasseh was the firstborn.

¹⁵Then he blessed Joseph and said,

> "May the God before whom
>   my fathers
>   Abraham and Isaac walked,
> the God who has been my shepherd
>   all my life to this day,
> ¹⁶the Angel who has delivered me from all
>   harm
>   —may he bless these boys.
> May they be called by my name
>   and the names of my fathers Abraham
>   and Isaac,
> and may they increase greatly
>   upon the earth."

¹⁷When Joseph saw his father placing his right hand on Ephraim's head he was displeased; so he took hold of his father's hand to move it from Ephraim's head to Manasseh's head. ¹⁸Joseph said to him, "No, my father, this one is the firstborn; put your right hand on his head."

¹⁹But his father refused and said, "I know, my son, I know. He too will become a people, and he too will become great. Nevertheless, his younger brother will be greater than he, and his descendants will become a group of nations." ²⁰He blessed them that day and said,

> "In your*ᵃ* name will Israel pronounce this
>   blessing:
>   'May God make you like Ephraim and
>   Manasseh.'"

So he put Ephraim ahead of Manasseh.

²¹Then Israel said to Joseph, "I am about to die, but God will be with you*ᵇ* and take you*ᵇ* back to the land of your*ᵇ* fathers. ²²And to you, as one who is over your brothers, I give the ridge of land*ᶜ* I took from the Amorites with my sword and my bow."

Jacob Blesses His Sons

49 Then Jacob called for his sons and said: "Gather around so I can tell you what will happen to you in days to come.

> ²"Assemble and listen, sons of Jacob;
>   listen to your father Israel.

> ³"Reuben, you are my firstborn,
>   my might, the first sign of my strength,
>   excelling in honor, excelling in power.
> ⁴Turbulent as the waters, you will no longer
>   excel,
>   for you went up onto your father's bed,
>   onto my couch and defiled it.

> ⁵"Simeon and Levi are brothers—
>   their swords*ᵈ* are weapons of
>   violence.
> ⁶Let me not enter their council,
>   let me not join their assembly,
>   for they have killed men in their anger

Genesis 48:15

God Is Our Shepherd

"May the God before whom my fathers Abraham and Isaac walked, the God who has been my shepherd all my life to this day…"

ᵃ20 The Hebrew is singular.   ᵇ21 The Hebrew is plural.   ᶜ22 Or *And to you I give one portion more than to your brothers—the portion*
ᵈ5 The meaning of the Hebrew for this word is uncertain.

and hamstrung oxen as they pleased.
⁷ Cursed be their anger, so fierce,
     and their fury, so cruel!
  I will scatter them in Jacob
     and disperse them in Israel.

⁸ "Judah,[a] your brothers will praise you;
     your hand will be on the neck of your
        enemies;
  your father's sons will bow down to
     you.
⁹ You are a lion's cub, O Judah;
     you return from the prey, my son.
  Like a lion he crouches and lies down,
     like a lioness—who dares to rouse
        him?
¹⁰ The scepter will not depart from Judah,
     nor the ruler's staff from between his
        feet,
  until he comes to whom it belongs[b]
     and the obedience of the nations is
        his.
¹¹ He will tether his donkey to a vine,
     his colt to the choicest branch;
  he will wash his garments in wine,
     his robes in the blood of grapes.
¹² His eyes will be darker than wine,
     his teeth whiter than milk.[c]

¹³ "Zebulun will live by the seashore
     and become a haven for ships;
  his border will extend toward Sidon.

¹⁴ "Issachar is a rawboned[d] donkey
     lying down between two saddlebags.[e]
¹⁵ When he sees how good is his resting
        place
     and how pleasant is his land,
  he will bend his shoulder to the burden
     and submit to forced labor.

¹⁶ "Dan[f] will provide justice for his people
     as one of the tribes of Israel.
¹⁷ Dan will be a serpent by the roadside,
     a viper along the path,
  that bites the horse's heels
     so that its rider tumbles backward.

¹⁸ "I look for your deliverance, O LORD.

¹⁹ "Gad[g] will be attacked by a band of
        raiders,
     but he will attack them at their heels.

²⁰ "Asher's food will be rich;
     he will provide delicacies fit for a king.

²¹ "Naphtali is a doe set free
     that bears beautiful fawns.[h]

²² "Joseph is a fruitful vine,
     a fruitful vine near a spring,
  whose branches climb over a wall.[i]
²³ With bitterness archers attacked him;
     they shot at him with hostility.
²⁴ But his bow remained steady,
     his strong arms stayed[j] limber,
  because of the hand of the Mighty One of
        Jacob,
     because of the Shepherd, the Rock of
        Israel,
²⁵ because of your father's God, who helps
        you,
     because of the Almighty,[k] who blesses
        you
  with blessings of the heavens above,
     blessings of the deep that lies below,
     blessings of the breast and womb.
²⁶ Your father's blessings are greater
     than the blessings of the ancient
        mountains,
  than[l] the bounty of the age-old hills.
  Let all these rest on the head of Joseph,
     on the brow of the prince among[m] his
        brothers.

²⁷ "Benjamin is a ravenous wolf;
     in the morning he devours the prey,
     in the evening he divides the plunder."

²⁸ All these are the twelve tribes of Israel, and
this is what their father said to them when he
blessed them, giving each the blessing appropriate to him.

The Death of Jacob

²⁹ Then he gave them these instructions: "I
am about to be gathered to my people. Bury me
with my fathers in the cave in the field of Ephron

---

[a]8 *Judah sounds like and may be derived from the Hebrew for praise.*   [b]10 Or *until Shiloh comes; or until he comes to whom tribute belongs*   [c]12 Or *will be dull from wine, / his teeth white from milk*   [d]14 Or *strong*   [e]14 Or *campfires*   [f]16 *Dan here means he provides justice.*   [g]19 *Gad can mean attack and band of raiders.*   [h]21 Or *free; he utters beautiful words*   [i]22 Or *Joseph is a wild colt, / a wild colt near a spring, / a wild donkey on a terraced hill*   [j]23,24 Or *archers will attack... will shoot... will remain... will stay*   [k]25 Hebrew *Shaddai*   [l]26 Or *of my progenitors, / as great as*   [m]26 Or *the one separated from*

the Hittite, 30the cave in the field of Machpelah, near Mamre in Canaan, which Abraham bought as a burial place from Ephron the Hittite, along with the field. 31There Abraham and his wife Sarah were buried, there Isaac and his wife Rebekah were buried, and there I buried Leah. 32The field and the cave in it were bought from the Hittites.*a*"

33When Jacob had finished giving instructions to his sons, he drew his feet up into the bed, breathed his last and was gathered to his people.

50 Joseph threw himself upon his father and wept over him and kissed him. 2Then Joseph directed the physicians in his service to embalm his father Israel. So the physicians embalmed him, 3taking a full forty days, for that was the time required for embalming. And the Egyptians mourned for him seventy days.

4When the days of mourning had passed, Joseph said to Pharaoh's court, "If I have found favor in your eyes, speak to Pharaoh for me. Tell him, 5'My father made me swear an oath and said, "I am about to die; bury me in the tomb I dug for myself in the land of Canaan." Now let me go up and bury my father; then I will return.'"

6Pharaoh said, "Go up and bury your father, as he made you swear to do."

7So Joseph went up to bury his father. All Pharaoh's officials accompanied him—the dignitaries of his court and all the dignitaries of Egypt— 8besides all the members of Joseph's household and his brothers and those belonging to his father's household. Only their children and their flocks and herds were left in Goshen.

9Chariots and horsemen*b* also went up with him. It was a very large company.

10When they reached the threshing floor of Atad, near the Jordan, they lamented loudly and bitterly; and there Joseph observed a seven-day period of mourning for his father. 11When the Canaanites who lived there saw the mourning at the threshing floor of Atad, they said, "The Egyptians are holding a solemn ceremony of mourning." That is why that place near the Jordan is called Abel Mizraim.*c*

12So Jacob's sons did as he had commanded them: 13They carried him to the land of Canaan and buried him in the cave in the field of Machpelah, near Mamre, which Abraham had bought as a burial place from Ephron the Hittite, along with the field. 14After burying his father, Joseph returned to Egypt, together with his brothers and all the others who had gone with him to bury his father.

Joseph Reassures His Brothers

15When Joseph's brothers saw that their father was dead, they said, "What if Joseph holds a grudge against us and pays us back for all the wrongs we did to him?" 16So they sent word to Joseph, saying, "Your father left these instructions before he died: 17'This is what you are to say to Joseph: I ask you to forgive your brothers the sins and the wrongs they committed in treating you so badly.' Now please forgive the sins of the servants of the God of your father." When their message came to him, Joseph wept.

18His brothers then came and threw themselves down before him. "We are your slaves," they said.

19But Joseph said to them, "Don't be afraid. Am I in the place of God? 20You intended to harm me, but God intended it for good to accomplish what is now being done, the saving of many lives. 21So then, don't be afraid. I will provide for you and your children." And he reassured them and spoke kindly to them.

The Death of Joseph

22Joseph stayed in Egypt, along with all his father's family. He lived a hundred and ten years 23and saw the third generation of Ephraim's children. Also the children of Makir son of Manasseh were placed at birth on Joseph's knees.*d*

24Then Joseph said to his brothers, "I am

Genesis 50:20

God Overcomes Evil

"You intended to harm me, but God intended it for good to accomplish what is now being done, the saving of many lives."

---

*a*32 Or the sons of Heth   *b*9 Or charioteers   *c*11 Abel Mizraim means mourning of the Egyptians.   *d*23 That is, were counted as his

A Good Gift from a Good God

Read: Genesis 50:15–21

Sometimes our worry is the thread by which we hang onto the belief that we can do something to change our situation and end our fear. As ridiculous as it is, we believe that our anxiety gives us some measure of control. Or we believe it keeps God mindful of our problem. We are afraid that without the pressure of our fear, He might forget what we want from Him. But our anxiety and demanding prayers accomplish nothing. We fear giving up our fear because if we don't worry, who will remember to care? If we don't worry, would God decide we really aren't concerned about the issue? If we don't worry, are we giving up hope of God involving Himself in our world?

Cutting across all our stubborn reasons for remaining in our fear, Paul wrote, "May the God of hope fill you with all joy and peace as you trust in him, so that you may overflow with hope by the power of the Holy Spirit" (Romans 15:13). God's joy and peace are available to us as we trust Him; they are not the result of absolute guarantees about the outcomes of our worries. We have a choice: will we trust Him and receive His joy and peace, or will we insist on seeking our joy and peace from resolved fears and changed circumstances?

The choice really is ours. We can hang onto our fears, insisting that until they are resolved, there is no way for us to enter into rest, or we can see those same fears as the door by which we can enter a rest far richer and sweeter than the rest that might arise from a tenuous arrangement of perfect circumstances. It is a rest that believes that a life without all the pieces in place, a life in which we do indeed suffer lack, is still a life to celebrate, a good gift from a good God.

—*Sally Breedlove*

Genesis 50:20–21

"You intended to harm me, but God intended it for good to accomplish what is now being done, the saving of many lives. So then, don't be afraid. I will provide for you and your children." And [Joseph] reassured them and spoke kindly to them.

reflection

1 Based on your knowledge of Joseph's life, how often might he have given into fear and worry over the course of his life?

2 What circumstances are causing you to feel fearful or worried?

3 Spend time with God asking him to use your fears as "the door" through which you can enter your rest, trusting that God will use your present circumstances for your good and his glory.

RELATED READINGS

Psalm 34;
Acts 7:9–17;
James 1:9–18

Go to page 71 for your next devotional reading.

about to die. But God will surely come to your aid and take you up out of this land to the land he promised on oath to Abraham, Isaac and Jacob." 25 And Joseph made the sons of Israel swear an oath and said, "God will surely come to your aid, and then you must carry my bones up from this place."

26 So Joseph died at the age of a hundred and ten. And after they embalmed him, he was placed in a coffin in Egypt.

Exodus

Four centuries pass from the time Jacob went to Egypt at the end of Genesis to the time the story picks up again in Exodus. The age of the patriarchs has ended, and we find the Israelites laboring as slaves under the Egyptian sun, *longing for a redeemer* to free them. God's promises to Abraham have become timeworn and faded. The Israelites are indeed numerous, as God promised, but their numbers seem to be not a blessing but a curse, the cause of their slavery. As for the land of promise—not one Israelite living has laid eyes on it. *And yet they hope.* Thin threads of promise can at least hold hope.

Exodus literally means *"exit,"* and that is precisely what the Israelites do, in a way that only God could orchestrate. God then sets about teaching them how to live in their newfound freedom. But knowing how to live it and actually living it are two very different things. With the Law comes the realization of *their need for another Redeemer,* one who could free the people from their bondage to sin.

Author:
Moses.

Audience:
The people of Israel.

Date:
Between 1450 and 1410 B.C.

Setting:
Opening scenes are in Egypt. The plot then moves to the region of the Sinai Peninsula.

Verse to Remember:
The LORD replied, "My Presence will go with you, and I will give you rest." (33:14)

The Israelites Oppressed

1 These are the names of the sons of Israel who went to Egypt with Jacob, each with his family: ²Reuben, Simeon, Levi and Judah; ³Issachar, Zebulun and Benjamin; ⁴Dan and Naphtali; Gad and Asher. ⁵The descendants of Jacob numbered seventy[a] in all; Joseph was already in Egypt.

⁶Now Joseph and all his brothers and all that generation died, ⁷but the Israelites were fruitful and multiplied greatly and became exceedingly numerous, so that the land was filled with them.

⁸Then a new king, who did not know about Joseph, came to power in Egypt. ⁹"Look," he said to his people, "the Israelites have become

---

[a]5 Masoretic Text (see also Gen. 46:27); Dead Sea Scrolls and Septuagint (see also Acts 7:14 and note at Gen. 46:27) *seventy-five*

much too numerous for us. ¹⁰Come, we must deal shrewdly with them or they will become even more numerous and, if war breaks out, will join our enemies, fight against us and leave the country."

¹¹So they put slave masters over them to oppress them with forced labor, and they built Pithom and Rameses as store cities for Pharaoh. ¹²But the more they were oppressed, the more they multiplied and spread; so the Egyptians came to dread the Israelites ¹³and worked them ruthlessly. ¹⁴They made their lives bitter with hard labor in brick and mortar and with all kinds of work in the fields; in all their hard labor the Egyptians used them ruthlessly.

¹⁵The king of Egypt said to the Hebrew midwives, whose names were Shiphrah and Puah, ¹⁶"When you help the Hebrew women in childbirth and observe them on the delivery stool, if it is a boy, kill him; but if it is a girl, let her live." ¹⁷The midwives, however, feared God and did not do what the king of Egypt had told them to do; they let the boys live. ¹⁸Then the king of Egypt summoned the midwives and asked them, "Why have you done this? Why have you let the boys live?"

¹⁹The midwives answered Pharaoh, "Hebrew women are not like Egyptian women; they are vigorous and give birth before the midwives arrive."

²⁰So God was kind to the midwives and the people increased and became even more numerous. ²¹And because the midwives feared God, he gave them families of their own.

²²Then Pharaoh gave this order to all his people: "Every boy that is born*ᵃ* you must throw into the Nile, but let every girl live."

The Birth of Moses

2 Now a man of the house of Levi married a Levite woman, ²and she became pregnant and gave birth to a son. When she saw that he was a fine child, she hid him for three months. ³But when she could hide him no longer, she got a papyrus basket for him and coated it with tar and pitch. Then she placed the child in it and put him among the reeds along the bank of the Nile. ⁴His sister stood at a distance to see what would happen to him.

⁵Then Pharaoh's daughter went down to the Nile to bathe, and her attendants were walking along the river bank. She saw the basket among the reeds and sent her slave girl to get it. ⁶She opened it and saw the baby. He was crying, and she felt sorry for him. "This is one of the Hebrew babies," she said.

⁷Then his sister asked Pharaoh's daughter, "Shall I go and get one of the Hebrew women to nurse the baby for you?"

⁸"Yes, go," she answered. And the girl went and got the baby's mother. ⁹Pharaoh's daughter said to her, "Take this baby and nurse him for me, and I will pay you." So the woman took the baby and nursed him. ¹⁰When the child grew older, she took him to Pharaoh's daughter and he became her son. She named him Moses,*ᵇ* saying, "I drew him out of the water."

Moses Flees to Midian

¹¹One day, after Moses had grown up, he went out to where his own people were and watched them at their hard labor. He saw an Egyptian beating a Hebrew, one of his own people. ¹²Glancing this way and that and seeing no one, he killed the Egyptian and hid him in the sand. ¹³The next day he went out and saw two Hebrews fighting. He asked the one in the wrong, "Why are you hitting your fellow Hebrew?"

¹⁴The man said, "Who made you ruler and judge over us? Are you thinking of killing me as you killed the Egyptian?" Then Moses was afraid and thought, "What I did must have become known."

¹⁵When Pharaoh heard of this, he tried to kill Moses, but Moses fled from Pharaoh and went to live in Midian, where he sat down by a well. ¹⁶Now a priest of Midian had seven daughters, and they came to draw water and fill the troughs to water their father's flock. ¹⁷Some shepherds came along and drove them away, but Moses got up and came to their rescue and watered their flock.

¹⁸When the girls returned to Reuel their father, he asked them, "Why have you returned so early today?"

¹⁹They answered, "An Egyptian rescued us

ᵃ22 Masoretic Text; Samaritan Pentateuch, Septuagint and Targums born to the Hebrews   *ᵇ10* Moses *sounds like the Hebrew for* draw out.

Wait and Watch

Read: Exodus 2:1–10

NOW THAT SHE WAS ALONE, the widow faced a decision: "Should I sell my house and move to a secure retirement community?" For years she had watched the changes in her neighborhood. Many things concerned her: unattended children, unkempt yards, unleashed pets and unwatched houses. But one personal tug kept her from moving. She observed one family and saw the unscrupulous behavior of the adults in the house: Strange cars would pull up, shady characters would come and go at all hours. She'd look out her window and see the young brother and sister who lived there climb into their tree house at odd times. Were they going there for shelter?

The widow wondered how she could leave these children. She had a mission . . . to keep a close eye on these two. The widow waited, watched and prayed for a chance to help. Though the children didn't know it, a neighbor became a part of their life story by keeping surveillance and interceding from the sidelines.

Before Moses was born, the pharaoh of Egypt issued a cruel edict: To keep the Hebrew people from becoming too powerful, every Hebrew baby boy must be killed. But the Hebrew women waited for the right opportunities to frustrate Pharaoh's genocidal plan. The midwives, mothers and sisters subverted the edict and saved some of the babies. Moses' mother put the baby Moses in a basket and placed it in the Nile. Moses' sister watched from the shore. Pharaoh's daughter joined in the cause by taking the baby Moses out of the reeds and into her heart. Even as Moses was saved from the fate of so many other children, Miriam "stood at a distance to see what would happen to him."

Every newborn baby enters the context of a human story, even though some of those stories are less than hopeful. You may see this and realize how unfair the world is. You want to do something to help but feel sidelined. You wait. You watch. You pray. You want to perform some act of practical compassion. The truth is, sometimes the best action is the sideline action: Wait, watch and pray. God will guide you to action when the time is right.

You're a part of others' stories. And they're a part of yours. Who needs your vigilant prayer protection? God may ask you to wait behind the scenes until he shows you how to step in.

Go to page 73 for your next devotional reading.

Exodus 2:4

[Moses'] sister stood at a distance to see what would happen to him.

reflection

1 Whom are you watching over right now?

2 How does prayer empower you as you wait?

3 How does this perspective of waiting and watching help you in your own life's story?

RELATED READINGS

Exodus 15:19–21;
1 Samuel 12:23

from the shepherds. He even drew water for us and watered the flock."

20"And where is he?" he asked his daughters. "Why did you leave him? Invite him to have something to eat."

21Moses agreed to stay with the man, who gave his daughter Zipporah to Moses in marriage. 22Zipporah gave birth to a son, and Moses named him Gershom,*a* saying, "I have become an alien in a foreign land."

23During that long period, the king of Egypt died. The Israelites groaned in their slavery and cried out, and their cry for help because of their slavery went up to God. 24God heard their groaning and he remembered his covenant with Abraham, with Isaac and with Jacob. 25So God looked on the Israelites and was concerned about them.

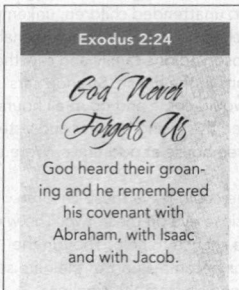

Exodus 2:24

God Never Forgets Us

God heard their groaning and he remembered his covenant with Abraham, with Isaac and with Jacob.

Moses and the Burning Bush

3 Now Moses was tending the flock of Jethro his father-in-law, the priest of Midian, and he led the flock to the far side of the desert and came to Horeb, the mountain of God. 2There the angel of the LORD appeared to him in flames of fire from within a bush. Moses saw that though the bush was on fire it did not burn up. 3So Moses thought, "I will go over and see this strange sight—why the bush does not burn up."

4When the LORD saw that he had gone over to look, God called to him from within the bush, "Moses! Moses!"

And Moses said, "Here I am."

5"Do not come any closer," God said. "Take off your sandals, for the place where you are standing is holy ground." 6Then he said, "I am the God of your father, the God of Abraham, the God of Isaac and the God of Jacob." At this, Moses hid his face, because he was afraid to look at God.

7The LORD said, "I have indeed seen the misery of my people in Egypt. I have heard them crying out because of their slave drivers, and I am concerned about their suffering. 8So I have come down to rescue them from the hand of the Egyptians and to bring them up out of that land into a good and spacious land, a land flowing with milk and honey—the home of the Canaanites, Hittites, Amorites, Perizzites, Hivites and Jebusites. 9And now the cry of the Israelites has reached me, and I have seen the way the Egyptians are oppressing them. 10So now, go. I am sending you to Pharaoh to bring my people the Israelites out of Egypt."

11But Moses said to God, "Who am I, that I should go to Pharaoh and bring the Israelites out of Egypt?"

12And God said, "I will be with you. And this will be the sign to you that it is I who have sent you: When you have brought the people out of Egypt, you*b* will worship God on this mountain."

13Moses said to God, "Suppose I go to the Israelites and say to them, 'The God of your fathers has sent me to you,' and they ask me, 'What is his name?' Then what shall I tell them?"

14God said to Moses, "I AM WHO I AM.*c* This is what you are to say to the Israelites: 'I AM has sent me to you.' "

15God also said to Moses, "Say to the Israelites, 'The LORD,*d* the God of your fathers—the God of Abraham, the God of Isaac and the God of Jacob—has sent me to you.' This is my name forever, the name by which I am to be remembered from generation to generation.

16"Go, assemble the elders of Israel and say to them, 'The LORD, the God of your fathers—the God of Abraham, Isaac and Jacob—appeared to me and said: I have watched over you and have seen what has been done to you in Egypt. 17And I have promised to bring you up out of your misery in Egypt into the land of the Canaanites, Hittites, Amorites, Perizzites, Hivites and Jebusites—a land flowing with milk and honey.'

---

*a*22 *Gershom* sounds like the Hebrew for *an alien there.*   *b*12 The Hebrew is plural.   *c*14 Or *I WILL BE WHAT I WILL BE*   *d*15 The Hebrew for LORD sounds like and may be derived from the Hebrew for *I AM* in verse 14.

Availability Check

Read: Exodus 3:1–22

THE GOOD OFTEN cannibalizes the best. Think about it: How often do schedules, long to-do lists and our immediate line of sight trump the things we claim to love the most? A pile of laundry certainly seems insignificant the day a close friend wrecks her car or a parent falls ill. Certainly, life involves responsibility, but it also involves a need for *responsiveness* to urgent situations—a child struggling in school or a severely depressed coworker.

Moses was tending sheep—fulfilling a needed task—when God intervened with an urgent call. A bush burned without being consumed. God called Moses' name from within the fiery bush. Moses immediately answered. Moses was available and obedient. But then God told him what he wanted: Moses was to go back to Egypt to lead a rescue mission for the Hebrew people.

In the midst of our ordinary days—tending to our families, our jobs, our friends—how do we respond to the persistent pull of God's call? Regardless of how God makes his wishes known—a burning bush, a burning desire or a burning need—are we willing to have our tidy plans and schedules interrupted to listen to his voice? Or are we too busy or too distracted to answer? Bottom line: Are we willing to be recruited at God's bidding?

Like Moses, we may feel inadequate for the job: "I'm just a student, just a mother, just an hourly employee. I'm not equipped for this mission!" However, when God calls us to do something bigger than we think we can accomplish, he will equip us by working through us. We learn to rely on his strength, not on our own abilities. Simply put, God doesn't look for abilities; he looks for availabilities. That's how we can be confident of success: His great power trumps our lack of talent. We act in the power of the great "I AM" (3:14).

So when you hear the voice of God calling your name, answer without hesitation, "Here I am."

God's call. God's strength. Your availability.

Go to page 78 for your next devotional reading.

Exodus 3:4

When the LORD saw that he had gone over to look, God called to him from within the bush, "Moses! Moses!" And Moses said, "Here I am."

reflection

1 In what ways has God indicated he has something for you to do, and how have you responded?

2 Recount a time when you felt inadequate to do something you knew God wanted you to do. How did God equip you to accomplish it?

3 What interferes with your availability to answer God's call?

RELATED READINGS

1 Samuel 3:1–10; Isaiah 6:8; 50:2; 2 Corinthians 12:9–10

"In a very real sense, not one of us is qualified, but it seems that God continually chooses the most unqualified to do his work, to bear his glory."

Madeleine L'Engle

18"The elders of Israel will listen to you. Then you and the elders are to go to the king of Egypt and say to him, 'The LORD, the God of the Hebrews, has met with us. Let us take a three-day journey into the desert to offer sacrifices to the LORD our God.' 19But I know that the king of Egypt will not let you go unless a mighty hand compels him. 20So I will stretch out my hand and strike the Egyptians with all the wonders that I will perform among them. After that, he will let you go.

21"And I will make the Egyptians favorably disposed toward this people, so that when you leave you will not go empty-handed. 22Every woman is to ask her neighbor and any woman living in her house for articles of silver and gold and for clothing, which you will put on your sons and daughters. And so you will plunder the Egyptians."

Signs for Moses

4 Moses answered, "What if they do not believe me or listen to me and say, 'The LORD did not appear to you'?"

2Then the LORD said to him, "What is that in your hand?"

"A staff," he replied.

3The LORD said, "Throw it on the ground."

Moses threw it on the ground and it became a snake, and he ran from it. 4Then the LORD said to him, "Reach out your hand and take it by the tail." So Moses reached out and took hold of the snake and it turned back into a staff in his hand. 5"This," said the LORD, "is so that they may believe that the LORD, the God of their fathers—the God of Abraham, the God of Isaac and the God of Jacob—has appeared to you."

6Then the LORD said, "Put your hand inside your cloak." So Moses put his hand into his cloak, and when he took it out, it was leprous,[a] like snow.

7"Now put it back into your cloak," he said. So Moses put his hand back into his cloak, and when he took it out, it was restored, like the rest of his flesh.

8Then the LORD said, "If they do not believe you or pay attention to the first miraculous sign, they may believe the second. 9But if they do not believe these two signs or listen to you, take some water from the Nile and pour it on the dry ground. The water you take from the river will become blood on the ground."

10Moses said to the LORD, "O Lord, I have never been eloquent, neither in the past nor since you have spoken to your servant. I am slow of speech and tongue."

11The LORD said to him, "Who gave man his mouth? Who makes him deaf or mute? Who gives him sight or makes him blind? Is it not I, the LORD? 12Now go; I will help you speak and will teach you what to say."

13But Moses said, "O Lord, please send someone else to do it."

14Then the LORD's anger burned against Moses and he said, "What about your brother, Aaron the Levite? I know he can speak well. He is already on his way to meet you, and his heart will be glad when he sees you. 15You shall speak to him and put words in his mouth; I will help both of you speak and will teach you what to do. 16He will speak to the people for you, and it will be as if he were your mouth and as if you were God to him. 17But take this staff in your hand so you can perform miraculous signs with it."

Moses Returns to Egypt

18Then Moses went back to Jethro his father-in-law and said to him, "Let me go back to my own people in Egypt to see if any of them are still alive."

Jethro said, "Go, and I wish you well."

19Now the LORD had said to Moses in Midian, "Go back to Egypt, for all the men who wanted to kill you are dead." 20So Moses took his wife and sons, put them on a donkey and started back to Egypt. And he took the staff of God in his hand.

21The LORD said to Moses, "When you re-

Exodus 4:11

God Prepares Us

The LORD said to him, "Who gave man his mouth? Who makes him deaf or mute? Who gives him sight or makes him blind? Is it not I, the LORD?"

---

a6 The Hebrew word was used for various diseases affecting the skin—not necessarily leprosy.

turn to Egypt, see that you perform before Pharaoh all the wonders I have given you the power to do. But I will harden his heart so that he will not let the people go. ²²Then say to Pharaoh, 'This is what the LORD says: Israel is my firstborn son, ²³and I told you, "Let my son go, so he may worship me." But you refused to let him go; so I will kill your firstborn son.'"

²⁴At a lodging place on the way, the LORD met ⌊Moses,⌋*a* and was about to kill him. ²⁵But Zipporah took a flint knife, cut off her son's foreskin and touched ⌊Moses'⌋ feet with it.*b* "Surely you are a bridegroom of blood to me," she said. ²⁶So the LORD let him alone. (At that time she said "bridegroom of blood," referring to circumcision.)

²⁷The LORD said to Aaron, "Go into the desert to meet Moses." So he met Moses at the mountain of God and kissed him. ²⁸Then Moses told Aaron everything the LORD had sent him to say, and also about all the miraculous signs he had commanded him to perform.

²⁹Moses and Aaron brought together all the elders of the Israelites, ³⁰and Aaron told them everything the LORD had said to Moses. He also performed the signs before the people, ³¹and they believed. And when they heard that the LORD was concerned about them and had seen their misery, they bowed down and worshiped.

Bricks Without Straw

5 Afterward Moses and Aaron went to Pharaoh and said, "This is what the LORD, the God of Israel, says: 'Let my people go, so that they may hold a festival to me in the desert.'"

²Pharaoh said, "Who is the LORD, that I should obey him and let Israel go? I do not know the LORD and I will not let Israel go."

³Then they said, "The God of the Hebrews has met with us. Now let us take a three-day journey into the desert to offer sacrifices to the LORD our God, or he may strike us with plagues or with the sword."

⁴But the king of Egypt said, "Moses and Aaron, why are you taking the people away from their labor? Get back to your work!" ⁵Then Pharaoh said, "Look, the people of the land are now numerous, and you are stopping them from working."

⁶That same day Pharaoh gave this order to the slave drivers and foremen in charge of the people: ⁷"You are no longer to supply the people with straw for making bricks; let them go and gather their own straw. ⁸But require them to make the same number of bricks as before; don't reduce the quota. They are lazy; that is why they are crying out, 'Let us go and sacrifice to our God.' ⁹Make the work harder for the men so that they keep working and pay no attention to lies."

¹⁰Then the slave drivers and the foremen went out and said to the people, "This is what Pharaoh says: 'I will not give you any more straw. ¹¹Go and get your own straw wherever you can find it, but your work will not be reduced at all.'" ¹²So the people scattered all over Egypt to gather stubble to use for straw. ¹³The slave drivers kept pressing them, saying, "Complete the work required of you for each day, just as when you had straw." ¹⁴The Israelite foremen appointed by Pharaoh's slave drivers were beaten and were asked, "Why didn't you meet your quota of bricks yesterday or today, as before?"

¹⁵Then the Israelite foremen went and appealed to Pharaoh: "Why have you treated your servants this way? ¹⁶Your servants are given no straw, yet we are told, 'Make bricks!' Your servants are being beaten, but the fault is with your own people."

¹⁷Pharaoh said, "Lazy, that's what you are—lazy! That is why you keep saying, 'Let us go and sacrifice to the LORD.' ¹⁸Now get to work. You will not be given any straw, yet you must produce your full quota of bricks."

¹⁹The Israelite foremen realized they were in trouble when they were told, "You are not to reduce the number of bricks required of you for each day." ²⁰When they left Pharaoh, they found Moses and Aaron waiting to meet them, ²¹and they said, "May the LORD look upon you and judge you! You have made us a stench to Pharaoh and his officials and have put a sword in their hand to kill us."

God Promises Deliverance

²²Moses returned to the LORD and said, "O Lord, why have you brought trouble upon this people? Is this why you sent me? ²³Ever

a24 Or ⌊Moses' son⌋; Hebrew him   b25 Or and drew near ⌊Moses'⌋ feet since I went to Pharaoh to speak in your name, he has brought trouble upon this people, and you have not rescued your people at all."

6 Then the LORD said to Moses, "Now you will see what I will do to Pharaoh: Because of my mighty hand he will let them go; because of my mighty hand he will drive them out of his country."

²God also said to Moses, "I am the LORD. ³I appeared to Abraham, to Isaac and to Jacob as God Almighty,ᵃ but by my name the LORDᵇ I did not make myself known to them.ᶜ ⁴I also established my covenant with them to give them the land of Canaan, where they lived as aliens. ⁵Moreover, I have heard the groaning of the Israelites, whom the Egyptians are enslaving, and I have remembered my covenant.

⁶"Therefore, say to the Israelites: 'I am the LORD, and I will bring you out from under the yoke of the Egyptians. I will free you from being slaves to them, and I will redeem you with an outstretched arm and with mighty acts of judgment. ⁷I will take you as my own people, and I will be your God. Then you will know that I am the LORD your God, who brought you out from under the yoke of the Egyptians. ⁸And I will bring you to the land I swore with uplifted hand to give to Abraham, to Isaac and to Jacob. I will give it to you as a possession. I am the LORD.'"

⁹Moses reported this to the Israelites, but they did not listen to him because of their discouragement and cruel bondage.

¹⁰Then the LORD said to Moses, ¹¹"Go, tell Pharaoh king of Egypt to let the Israelites go out of his country."

¹²But Moses said to the LORD, "If the Israelites will not listen to me, why would Pharaoh listen to me, since I speak with faltering lipsᵈ?"

Family Record of Moses and Aaron

¹³Now the LORD spoke to Moses and Aaron about the Israelites and Pharaoh king of Egypt, and he commanded them to bring the Israelites out of Egypt.

¹⁴These were the heads of their familiesᵉ:

The sons of Reuben the firstborn son of Israel were Hanoch and Pallu, Hezron and Carmi. These were the clans of Reuben.

¹⁵The sons of Simeon were Jemuel, Jamin, Ohad, Jakin, Zohar and Shaul the son of a Canaanite woman. These were the clans of Simeon.

¹⁶These were the names of the sons of Levi according to their records: Gershon, Kohath and Merari. Levi lived 137 years.

¹⁷The sons of Gershon, by clans, were Libni and Shimei.

¹⁸The sons of Kohath were Amram, Izhar, Hebron and Uzziel. Kohath lived 133 years.

¹⁹The sons of Merari were Mahli and Mushi.

These were the clans of Levi according to their records.

²⁰Amram married his father's sister Jochebed, who bore him Aaron and Moses. Amram lived 137 years.

²¹The sons of Izhar were Korah, Nepheg and Zicri.

²²The sons of Uzziel were Mishael, Elzaphan and Sithri.

²³Aaron married Elisheba, daughter of Amminadab and sister of Nahshon, and she bore him Nadab and Abihu, Eleazar and Ithamar.

²⁴The sons of Korah were Assir, Elkanah and Abiasaph. These were the Korahite clans.

²⁵Eleazar son of Aaron married one of the daughters of Putiel, and she bore him Phinehas.

These were the heads of the Levite families, clan by clan.

²⁶It was this same Aaron and Moses to whom the LORD said, "Bring the Israelites

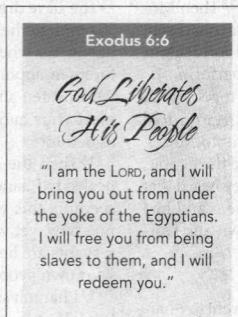

Exodus 6:6

God Liberates His People

"I am the LORD, and I will bring you out from under the yoke of the Egyptians. I will free you from being slaves to them, and I will redeem you."

ᵃ3 Hebrew *El-Shaddai* ᵇ3 See note at Exodus 3:15. ᶜ3 Or *Almighty, and by my name the LORD did I not let myself be known to them?* ᵈ12 Hebrew *I am uncircumcised of lips;* also in verse 30 ᵉ14 The Hebrew for *families* here and in verse 25 refers to units larger than clans.

out of Egypt by their divisions." 27They were the ones who spoke to Pharaoh king of Egypt about bringing the Israelites out of Egypt. It was the same Moses and Aaron.

Aaron to Speak for Moses

28Now when the LORD spoke to Moses in Egypt, 29he said to him, "I am the LORD. Tell Pharaoh king of Egypt everything I tell you."

30But Moses said to the LORD, "Since I speak with faltering lips, why would Pharaoh listen to me?"

7 Then the LORD said to Moses, "See, I have made you like God to Pharaoh, and your brother Aaron will be your prophet. 2You are to say everything I command you, and your brother Aaron is to tell Pharaoh to let the Israelites go out of his country. 3But I will harden Pharaoh's heart, and though I multiply my miraculous signs and wonders in Egypt, 4he will not listen to you. Then I will lay my hand on Egypt and with mighty acts of judgment I will bring out my divisions, my people the Israelites. 5And the Egyptians will know that I am the LORD when I stretch out my hand against Egypt and bring the Israelites out of it."

6Moses and Aaron did just as the LORD commanded them. 7Moses was eighty years old and Aaron eighty-three when they spoke to Pharaoh.

Aaron's Staff Becomes a Snake

8The LORD said to Moses and Aaron, 9"When Pharaoh says to you, 'Perform a miracle,' then say to Aaron, 'Take your staff and throw it down before Pharaoh,' and it will become a snake."

10So Moses and Aaron went to Pharaoh and did just as the LORD commanded. Aaron threw his staff down in front of Pharaoh and his officials, and it became a snake. 11Pharaoh then summoned wise men and sorcerers, and the Egyptian magicians also did the same things by their secret arts: 12Each one threw down his staff and it became a snake. But Aaron's staff swallowed up their staffs. 13Yet Pharaoh's heart became hard and he would not listen to them, just as the LORD had said.

The Plague of Blood

14Then the LORD said to Moses, "Pharaoh's heart is unyielding; he refuses to let the people go. 15Go to Pharaoh in the morning as he goes out to the water. Wait on the bank of the Nile to meet him, and take in your hand the staff that was changed into a snake. 16Then say to him, 'The LORD, the God of the Hebrews, has sent me to say to you: Let my people go, so that they may worship me in the desert. But until now you have not listened. 17This is what the LORD says: By this you will know that I am the LORD: With the staff that is in my hand I will strike the water of the Nile, and it will be changed into blood. 18The fish in the Nile will die, and the river will stink; the Egyptians will not be able to drink its water.' "

19The LORD said to Moses, "Tell Aaron, 'Take your staff and stretch out your hand over the waters of Egypt—over the streams and canals, over the ponds and all the reservoirs'—and they will turn to blood. Blood will be everywhere in Egypt, even in the wooden buckets and stone jars."

20Moses and Aaron did just as the LORD had commanded. He raised his staff in the presence of Pharaoh and his officials and struck the water of the Nile, and all the water was changed into blood. 21The fish in the Nile died, and the river smelled so bad that the Egyptians could not drink its water. Blood was everywhere in Egypt.

22But the Egyptian magicians did the same things by their secret arts, and Pharaoh's heart became hard; he would not listen to Moses and Aaron, just as the LORD had said. 23Instead, he turned and went into his palace, and did not take even this to heart. 24And all the Egyptians dug along the Nile to get drinking water, because they could not drink the water of the river.

The Plague of Frogs

25Seven days passed after the LORD struck the Nile. 8 1Then the LORD said to Moses, "Go to Pharaoh and say to him, 'This is what the LORD says: Let my people go, so that they may worship me. 2If you refuse to let them go, I will plague your whole country with frogs. 3The Nile will teem with frogs. They will come up into your palace and your bedroom and onto your bed, into the houses of your officials and on your people, and into your ovens and kneading troughs. 4The frogs will go up on you and your people and all your officials.' "

Let His People Go!

Exodus 7:5

"And the Egyptians will know that I am the LORD when I stretch out my hand against Egypt and bring the Israelites out of it."

Read: Exodus 7:1–24

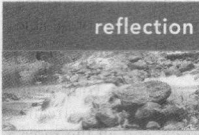

reflection

1 How do you see God revealing himself to you as the one true God?

2 Whom do you look on as God's enemies?

3 How can you share God's power in your life with others?

RELATED READINGS

Psalm 46:8–10;
Isaiah 10:33—11:10;
12:1–6;
2 Peter 3:9

IT WAS FAMILY MOVIE NIGHT, and Cecile B. DeMille's epic *The Ten Commandments* was playing on TV. Five-year-old Emily watched in fascination as Aaron's staff became a snake and swallowed the magically conjured snakes. She saw the river flowing blood and the plagues terrorize the Egyptians. But Yul Brenner as Pharaoh was unflinching when Charlton Heston as Moses demanded, "Let my people go!" The girl grew more and more agitated. Finally she cried out, "Why doesn't Moses just hit that bad guy?"

Reading about the plagues and Pharaoh's hard-hearted responses can leave us frustrated. Why did Moses and Aaron have to go through all of that hoopla? Why did the Egyptians have to suffer plague after plague? Why didn't God just "hit that bad guy" so the Hebrews could immediately leave Egypt? The answer is clear: "The Egyptians will know that I am the LORD when I stretch out my hand against Egypt and bring the Israelites out of it." God was just as concerned with the Egyptians as he was with the Israelites.

Yes, God wanted to free the Israelites from years of cruel bondage. But he wanted everyone—Egyptians and Israelites alike—to experience his power as the one true God. God used individual plagues to challenge the Egyptians' belief in their pagan gods. When God turned the Nile into blood, he proved that Re, their creator god, was powerless against his might. The sorcerers might turn water to blood, but Re couldn't turn blood back to water. Though the Egyptians believed the god Thoth brought frogs to life, God proved that Egyptian gods were defenseless against a plague of frogs.

Today, God still wants everyone to know that he is the only true God. And he shows his power through the events and circumstances of our lives. When we see the miracles of God, do we share those happenings with others? God still wants all people to know him. We usually think of the Egyptians as the "bad guys," and we wonder why God wasted his time on them. But unlike the black-and-white world portrayed in TV shows and movies, God goes beyond our expectations and spends some time showing the Egyptians and the Israelites about himself. The next time you see God reveal himself to you, don't hesitate to share your experiences with others—even those you might think don't have time for God.

⁵Then the LORD said to Moses, "Tell Aaron, 'Stretch out your hand with your staff over the streams and canals and ponds, and make frogs come up on the land of Egypt.'"

⁶So Aaron stretched out his hand over the waters of Egypt, and the frogs came up and covered the land. ⁷But the magicians did the same things by their secret arts; they also made frogs come up on the land of Egypt.

⁸Pharaoh summoned Moses and Aaron and said, "Pray to the LORD to take the frogs away from me and my people, and I will let your people go to offer sacrifices to the LORD."

⁹Moses said to Pharaoh, "I leave to you the honor of setting the time for me to pray for you and your officials and your people that you and your houses may be rid of the frogs, except for those that remain in the Nile."

¹⁰"Tomorrow," Pharaoh said.

Moses replied, "It will be as you say, so that you may know there is no one like the LORD our God. ¹¹The frogs will leave you and your houses, your officials and your people; they will remain only in the Nile."

¹²After Moses and Aaron left Pharaoh, Moses cried out to the LORD about the frogs he had brought on Pharaoh. ¹³And the LORD did what Moses asked. The frogs died in the houses, in the courtyards and in the fields. ¹⁴They were piled into heaps, and the land reeked of them. ¹⁵But when Pharaoh saw that there was relief, he hardened his heart and would not listen to Moses and Aaron, just as the LORD had said.

The Plague of Gnats

¹⁶Then the LORD said to Moses, "Tell Aaron, 'Stretch out your staff and strike the dust of the ground,' and throughout the land of Egypt the dust will become gnats." ¹⁷They did this, and when Aaron stretched out his hand with the staff and struck the dust of the ground, gnats came upon men and animals. All the dust throughout the land of Egypt became gnats. ¹⁸But when the magicians tried to produce gnats by their secret arts, they could not. And the gnats were on men and animals.

¹⁹The magicians said to Pharaoh, "This is the finger of God." But Pharaoh's heart was hard and he would not listen, just as the LORD had said.

The Plague of Flies

²⁰Then the LORD said to Moses, "Get up early in the morning and confront Pharaoh as he goes to the water and say to him, 'This is what the LORD says: Let my people go, so that they may worship me. ²¹If you do not let my people go, I will send swarms of flies on you and your officials, on your people and into your houses. The houses of the Egyptians will be full of flies, and even the ground where they are.

²²"'But on that day I will deal differently with the land of Goshen, where my people live; no swarms of flies will be there, so that you will know that I, the LORD, am in this land. ²³I will make a distinction[a] between my people and your people. This miraculous sign will occur tomorrow.'"

²⁴And the LORD did this. Dense swarms of flies poured into Pharaoh's palace and into the houses of his officials, and throughout Egypt the land was ruined by the flies.

²⁵Then Pharaoh summoned Moses and Aaron and said, "Go, sacrifice to your God here in the land."

²⁶But Moses said, "That would not be right. The sacrifices we offer the LORD our God would be detestable to the Egyptians. And if we offer sacrifices that are detestable in their eyes, will they not stone us? ²⁷We must take a three-day journey into the desert to offer sacrifices to the LORD our God, as he commands us."

²⁸Pharaoh said, "I will let you go to offer sacrifices to the LORD your God in the desert, but you must not go very far. Now pray for me."

²⁹Moses answered, "As soon as I leave you, I will pray to the LORD, and tomorrow the flies will leave Pharaoh and his officials and his people. Only be sure that Pharaoh does not act deceitfully again by not letting the people go to offer sacrifices to the LORD."

³⁰Then Moses left Pharaoh and prayed to the LORD, ³¹and the LORD did what Moses asked: The flies left Pharaoh and his officials and his people; not a fly remained. ³²But this time also Pharaoh hardened his heart and would not let the people go.

---

a23 Septuagint and Vulgate; Hebrew *will put a deliverance*

The Plague on Livestock

9 Then the LORD said to Moses, "Go to Pharaoh and say to him, 'This is what the LORD, the God of the Hebrews, says: "Let my people go, so that they may worship me." ²If you refuse to let them go and continue to hold them back, ³the hand of the LORD will bring a terrible plague on your livestock in the field—on your horses and donkeys and camels and on your cattle and sheep and goats. ⁴But the LORD will make a distinction between the livestock of Israel and that of Egypt, so that no animal belonging to the Israelites will die.'"

⁵The LORD set a time and said, "Tomorrow the LORD will do this in the land." ⁶And the next day the LORD did it: All the livestock of the Egyptians died, but not one animal belonging to the Israelites died. ⁷Pharaoh sent men to investigate and found that not even one of the animals of the Israelites had died. Yet his heart was unyielding and he would not let the people go.

The Plague of Boils

⁸Then the LORD said to Moses and Aaron, "Take handfuls of soot from a furnace and have Moses toss it into the air in the presence of Pharaoh. ⁹It will become fine dust over the whole land of Egypt, and festering boils will break out on men and animals throughout the land."

¹⁰So they took soot from a furnace and stood before Pharaoh. Moses tossed it into the air, and festering boils broke out on men and animals. ¹¹The magicians could not stand before Moses because of the boils that were on them and on all the Egyptians. ¹²But the LORD hardened Pharaoh's heart and he would not listen to Moses and Aaron, just as the LORD had said to Moses.

The Plague of Hail

¹³Then the LORD said to Moses, "Get up early in the morning, confront Pharaoh and say to him, 'This is what the LORD, the God of the Hebrews, says: Let my people go, so that they may worship me, ¹⁴or this time I will send the full force of my plagues against you and against your officials and your people, so you may know that there is no one like me in all the earth. ¹⁵For by now I could have stretched out my hand and struck you and your people with a plague that would have wiped you off the earth. ¹⁶But I have raised you up[a] for this very purpose, that I might show you my power and that my name might be proclaimed in all the earth. ¹⁷You still set yourself against my people and will not let them go. ¹⁸Therefore, at this time tomorrow I will send the worst hailstorm that has ever fallen on Egypt, from the day it was founded till now. ¹⁹Give an order now to bring your livestock and everything you have in the field to a place of shelter, because the hail will fall on every man and animal that has not been brought in and is still out in the field, and they will die.'"

²⁰Those officials of Pharaoh who feared the word of the LORD hurried to bring their slaves and their livestock inside. ²¹But those who ignored the word of the LORD left their slaves and livestock in the field.

²²Then the LORD said to Moses, "Stretch out your hand toward the sky so that hail will fall all over Egypt—on men and animals and on everything growing in the fields of Egypt." ²³When Moses stretched out his staff toward the sky, the LORD sent thunder and hail, and lightning flashed down to the ground. So the LORD rained hail on the land of Egypt; ²⁴hail fell and lightning flashed back and forth. It was the worst storm in all the land of Egypt since it had become a nation. ²⁵Throughout Egypt hail struck everything in the fields—both men and animals; it beat down everything growing in the fields and stripped every tree. ²⁶The only place it did not hail was the land of Goshen, where the Israelites were.

²⁷Then Pharaoh summoned Moses and Aaron. "This time I have sinned," he said to them. "The LORD is in the right, and I and my

---

Exodus 9:1

God Seeks Worshipers

This is what the LORD, the God of the Hebrews, says: "Let my people go, so that they may worship me."

---

[a] 16 Or *have spared you*

people are in the wrong. 28Pray to the Lord, for we have had enough thunder and hail. I will let you go; you don't have to stay any longer."

29Moses replied, "When I have gone out of the city, I will spread out my hands in prayer to the Lord. The thunder will stop and there will be no more hail, so you may know that the earth is the Lord's. 30But I know that you and your officials still do not fear the Lord God."

31(The flax and barley were destroyed, since the barley had headed and the flax was in bloom. 32The wheat and spelt, however, were not destroyed, because they ripen later.)

33Then Moses left Pharaoh and went out of the city. He spread out his hands toward the Lord; the thunder and hail stopped, and the rain no longer poured down on the land. 34When Pharaoh saw that the rain and hail and thunder had stopped, he sinned again: He and his officials hardened their hearts. 35So Pharaoh's heart was hard and he would not let the Israelites go, just as the Lord had said through Moses.

The Plague of Locusts

10 Then the Lord said to Moses, "Go to Pharaoh, for I have hardened his heart and the hearts of his officials so that I may perform these miraculous signs of mine among them 2that you may tell your children and grandchildren how I dealt harshly with the Egyptians and how I performed my signs among them, and that you may know that I am the Lord."

3So Moses and Aaron went to Pharaoh and said to him, "This is what the Lord, the God of the Hebrews, says: 'How long will you refuse to humble yourself before me? Let my people go, so that they may worship me. 4If you refuse to let them go, I will bring locusts into your country tomorrow. 5They will cover the face of the ground so that it cannot be seen. They will devour what little you have left after the hail, including every tree that is growing in your fields. 6They will fill your houses and those of all your officials and all the Egyptians—something neither your fathers nor your forefathers have ever seen from the day they settled in this land till now.'" Then Moses turned and left Pharaoh.

7Pharaoh's officials said to him, "How long

will this man be a snare to us? Let the people go, so that they may worship the Lord their God. Do you not yet realize that Egypt is ruined?"

8Then Moses and Aaron were brought back to Pharaoh. "Go, worship the Lord your God," he said. "But just who will be going?"

9Moses answered, "We will go with our young and old, with our sons and daughters, and with our flocks and herds, because we are to celebrate a festival to the Lord."

10Pharaoh said, "The Lord be with you—if I let you go, along with your women and children! Clearly you are bent on evil.a 11No! Have only the men go; and worship the Lord, since that's what you have been asking for." Then Moses and Aaron were driven out of Pharaoh's presence.

12And the Lord said to Moses, "Stretch out your hand over Egypt so that locusts will swarm over the land and devour everything growing in the fields, everything left by the hail."

13So Moses stretched out his staff over Egypt, and the Lord made an east wind blow across the land all that day and all that night. By morning the wind had brought the locusts; 14they invaded all Egypt and settled down in every area of the country in great numbers. Never before had there been such a plague of locusts, nor will there ever be again. 15They covered all the ground until it was black. They devoured all that was left after the hail—everything growing in the fields and the fruit on the trees. Nothing green remained on tree or plant in all the land of Egypt.

16Pharaoh quickly summoned Moses and Aaron and said, "I have sinned against the Lord your God and against you. 17Now forgive my sin once more and pray to the Lord your God to take this deadly plague away from me."

18Moses then left Pharaoh and prayed to the Lord. 19And the Lord changed the wind to a very strong west wind, which caught up the locusts and carried them into the Red Sea.b Not a locust was left anywhere in Egypt. 20But the Lord hardened Pharaoh's heart, and he would not let the Israelites go.

The Plague of Darkness

21Then the Lord said to Moses, "Stretch out your hand toward the sky so that darkness will

a10 Or Be careful, trouble is in store for you!   b19 Hebrew Yam Suph; that is, Sea of Reeds spread over Egypt—darkness that can be felt." ²²So Moses stretched out his hand toward the sky, and total darkness covered all Egypt for three days. ²³No one could see anyone else or leave his place for three days. Yet all the Israelites had light in the places where they lived.

²⁴Then Pharaoh summoned Moses and said, "Go, worship the LORD. Even your women and children may go with you; only leave your flocks and herds behind."

²⁵But Moses said, "You must allow us to have sacrifices and burnt offerings to present to the LORD our God. ²⁶Our livestock too must go with us; not a hoof is to be left behind. We have to use some of them in worshiping the LORD our God, and until we get there we will not know what we are to use to worship the LORD."

²⁷But the LORD hardened Pharaoh's heart, and he was not willing to let them go. ²⁸Pharaoh said to Moses, "Get out of my sight! Make sure you do not appear before me again! The day you see my face you will die."

²⁹"Just as you say," Moses replied, "I will never appear before you again."

The Plague on the Firstborn

11 Now the LORD had said to Moses, "I will bring one more plague on Pharaoh and on Egypt. After that, he will let you go from here, and when he does, he will drive you out completely. ²Tell the people that men and women alike are to ask their neighbors for articles of silver and gold." ³(The LORD made the Egyptians favorably disposed toward the people, and Moses himself was highly regarded in Egypt by Pharaoh's officials and by the people.)

⁴So Moses said, "This is what the LORD says: 'About midnight I will go throughout Egypt. ⁵Every firstborn son in Egypt will die, from the firstborn son of Pharaoh, who sits on the throne, to the firstborn son of the slave girl, who is at her hand mill, and all the firstborn of the cattle as well. ⁶There will be loud wailing throughout Egypt—worse than there has ever been or ever will be again. ⁷But among the Israelites not a dog will bark at any man or animal.' Then you will know that the LORD makes a distinction between Egypt and Israel. ⁸All these of-

ficials of yours will come to me, bowing down before me and saying, 'Go, you and all the people who follow you!' After that I will leave." Then Moses, hot with anger, left Pharaoh.

⁹The LORD had said to Moses, "Pharaoh will refuse to listen to you—so that my wonders may be multiplied in Egypt." ¹⁰Moses and Aaron performed all these wonders before Pharaoh, but the LORD hardened Pharaoh's heart, and he would not let the Israelites go out of his country.

The Passover

12 The LORD said to Moses and Aaron in Egypt, ²"This month is to be for you the first month, the first month of your year. ³Tell the whole community of Israel that on the tenth day of this month each man is to take a lamb*a* for his family, one for each household. ⁴If any household is too small for a whole lamb, they must share one with their nearest neighbor, having taken into account the number of people there are. You are to determine the amount of lamb needed in accordance with what each person will eat. ⁵The animals you choose must be year-old males without defect, and you may take them from the sheep or the goats. ⁶Take care of them until the fourteenth day of the month, when all the people of the community of Israel must slaughter them at twilight. ⁷Then they are to take some of the blood and put it on the sides and tops of the doorframes of the houses where they eat the lambs. ⁸That same night they are to eat the meat roasted over the fire, along with bitter herbs, and bread made without yeast. ⁹Do not eat the meat raw or cooked in water, but roast it over the fire—head, legs and inner parts. ¹⁰Do not leave any of it till morning; if some is left till morning, you must burn it. ¹¹This is how you are to eat it: with your cloak tucked into your belt, your sandals on your feet and your staff in your hand. Eat it in haste; it is the LORD's Passover.

¹²"On that same night I will pass through Egypt and strike down every firstborn—both men and animals—and I will bring judgment on all the gods of Egypt. I am the LORD. ¹³The blood will be a sign for you on the houses where you are; and when I see the blood, I will

a3 The Hebrew word can mean lamb *or* kid; *also in verse 4.*

Life at the Crossroads

HAGAR

WHERE HAVE YOU COME FROM and where are you going?

The question came to Hagar at the pinnacle of a crucial decision. She was torn between allegiance to her mistress, Sarai (known as Sarah later in the story), and the innate desire to be free to raise the baby now growing inside of her. As with most questions one faces when standing at one of life's many crossroads, it haunted her.

Where had she come from? Where was she going? It was painful for Hagar to reflect on her past, much less attempt to see through the gauze of an uncertain future, but the angel's question pierced her soul with its persistence.

Where have I come from . . .? Hagar thought to herself as she contemplated the events over the past few months. She concluded that she'd come from a place no woman should have to be.

I've come from the grasp of a woman who hates me. I've come from the burden of carrying a baby whose father loves someone else. I've come from a terrifying place of confusion, isolation and abandonment. *That's* where I have come from.

But that was only half of the equation. "*. . . And where are you going?*"

This question was even more painful than the previous one. She knew from where she'd come, but she had no idea where she was going. In fact, she was wandering the desert, considering her options at that very moment.

Could she make it? Would she die? As if the Lord's angel had traced her thoughts, he cut through her myriad of optional scenarios with a command. "Go back to your mistress and submit to her."

In truth, it was the last thing she felt like doing at the moment. *Go back? Had she heard the angel's message clearly?* Surely there was a misunderstanding.

However, there was no misunderstanding. The crossroads pointed to a path she did not want to take—had not planned to take. God had spoken, and Hagar must obey. She peered down the road that represented her future, but it looked suspiciously like the road that led to a painful past.

—Prayer—
Dear God, please help me accept your will for me even if it's not what I had planned for myself.

[The angel of the LORD] said, "Hagar, servant of Sarai, where have you come from, and where are you going?"

Genesis 16:8

ASSIGNED READING:

Genesis 16:1–16; 21:8–21

Weekend

Go to page 87 for your next devotional reading.

pass over you. No destructive plague will touch you when I strike Egypt.

14 "This is a day you are to commemorate; for the generations to come you shall celebrate it as a festival to the LORD—a lasting ordinance. 15 For seven days you are to eat bread made without yeast. On the first day remove the yeast from your houses, for whoever eats anything with yeast in it from the first day through the seventh must be cut off from Israel. 16 On the first day hold a sacred assembly, and another one on the seventh day. Do no work at all on these days, except to prepare food for everyone to eat—that is all you may do.

17 "Celebrate the Feast of Unleavened Bread, because it was on this very day that I brought your divisions out of Egypt. Celebrate this day as a lasting ordinance for the generations to come. 18 In the first month you are to eat bread made without yeast, from the evening of the fourteenth day until the evening of the twenty-first day. 19 For seven days no yeast is to be found in your houses. And whoever eats anything with yeast in it must be cut off from the community of Israel, whether he is an alien or native-born. 20 Eat nothing made with yeast. Wherever you live, you must eat unleavened bread."

21 Then Moses summoned all the elders of Israel and said to them, "Go at once and select the animals for your families and slaughter the Passover lamb. 22 Take a bunch of hyssop, dip it into the blood in the basin and put some of the blood on the top and on both sides of the doorframe. Not one of you shall go out the door of his house until morning. 23 When the LORD goes through the land to strike down the Egyptians, he will see the blood on the top and sides of the doorframe and will pass over that doorway, and he will not permit the destroyer to enter your houses and strike you down.

24 "Obey these instructions as a lasting ordinance for you and your descendants. 25 When you enter the land that the LORD will give you as he promised, observe this ceremony. 26 And when your children ask you, 'What does this ceremony mean to you?' 27 then tell them, 'It is the Passover sacrifice to the LORD, who passed over the houses of the Israelites in Egypt and spared our homes when he struck down the

Egyptians.' " Then the people bowed down and worshiped. 28 The Israelites did just what the LORD commanded Moses and Aaron.

29 At midnight the LORD struck down all the firstborn in Egypt, from the firstborn of Pharaoh, who sat on the throne, to the firstborn of the prisoner, who was in the dungeon, and the firstborn of all the livestock as well. 30 Pharaoh and all his officials and all the Egyptians got up during the night, and there was loud wailing in Egypt, for there was not a house without someone dead.

The Exodus

31 During the night Pharaoh summoned Moses and Aaron and said, "Up! Leave my people, you and the Israelites! Go, worship the LORD as you have requested. 32 Take your flocks and herds, as you have said, and go. And also bless me."

33 The Egyptians urged the people to hurry and leave the country. "For otherwise," they said, "we will all die!" 34 So the people took their dough before the yeast was added, and carried it on their shoulders in kneading troughs wrapped in clothing. 35 The Israelites did as Moses instructed and asked the Egyptians for articles of silver and gold and for clothing. 36 The LORD had made the Egyptians favorably disposed toward the people, and they gave them what they asked for; so they plundered the Egyptians.

37 The Israelites journeyed from Rameses to Succoth. There were about six hundred thousand men on foot, besides women and children. 38 Many other people went up with them, as well as large droves of livestock, both flocks and herds. 39 With the dough they had brought from Egypt, they baked cakes of unleavened bread. The dough was without yeast because they had been driven out of Egypt and did not have time to prepare food for themselves.

40 Now the length of time the Israelite people lived in Egypt[a] was 430 years. 41 At the end of the 430 years, to the very day, all the LORD's divisions left Egypt. 42 Because the LORD kept vigil that night to bring them out of Egypt, on this night all the Israelites are to keep vigil to honor the LORD for the generations to come.

---

a 40 Masoretic Text; Samaritan Pentateuch and Septuagint *Egypt and Canaan*

Passover Restrictions

43 The LORD said to Moses and Aaron, "These are the regulations for the Passover:

"No foreigner is to eat of it. **44** Any slave you have bought may eat of it after you have circumcised him, **45** but a temporary resident and a hired worker may not eat of it.

46 "It must be eaten inside one house; take none of the meat outside the house. Do not break any of the bones. **47** The whole community of Israel must celebrate it.

48 "An alien living among you who wants to celebrate the LORD's Passover must have all the males in his household circumcised; then he may take part like one born in the land. No uncircumcised male may eat of it. **49** The same law applies to the native-born and to the alien living among you."

50 All the Israelites did just what the LORD had commanded Moses and Aaron. **51** And on that very day the LORD brought the Israelites out of Egypt by their divisions.

Consecration of the Firstborn

13 The LORD said to Moses, **2** "Consecrate to me every firstborn male. The first offspring of every womb among the Israelites belongs to me, whether man or animal."

3 Then Moses said to the people, "Commemorate this day, the day you came out of Egypt, out of the land of slavery, because the LORD brought you out of it with a mighty hand. Eat nothing containing yeast. **4** Today, in the month of Abib, you are leaving. **5** When the LORD brings you into the land of the Canaanites, Hittites, Amorites, Hivites and Jebusites—the land he swore to your forefathers to give you, a land flowing with milk and honey—you are to observe this ceremony in this month: **6** For seven days eat bread made without yeast and on the seventh day hold a festival to the LORD. **7** Eat unleavened bread during those seven days; nothing with yeast in it is to be seen among you, nor shall any yeast be seen anywhere within your borders. **8** On that day tell your son, 'I do this because of what the LORD did for me when I came out of Egypt.' **9** This observance will be for you like a sign on your hand and a reminder on your forehead that the law of the LORD is to be on your lips. For the LORD brought you out of Egypt with his mighty hand. **10** You must keep this ordinance at the appointed time year after year.

11 "After the LORD brings you into the land of the Canaanites and gives it to you, as he promised on oath to you and your forefathers, **12** you are to give over to the LORD the first offspring of every womb. All the firstborn males of your livestock belong to the LORD. **13** Redeem with a lamb every firstborn donkey, but if you do not redeem it, break its neck. Redeem every firstborn among your sons.

14 "In days to come, when your son asks you, 'What does this mean?' say to him, 'With a mighty hand the LORD brought us out of Egypt, out of the land of slavery. **15** When Pharaoh stubbornly refused to let us go, the LORD killed every firstborn in Egypt, both man and animal. This is why I sacrifice to the LORD the first male offspring of every womb and redeem each of my firstborn sons.' **16** And it will be like a sign on your hand and a symbol on your forehead that the LORD brought us out of Egypt with his mighty hand."

Crossing the Sea

17 When Pharaoh let the people go, God did not lead them on the road through the Philistine country, though that was shorter. For God said, "If they face war, they might change their minds and return to Egypt." **18** So God led the people around by the desert road toward the Red Sea.[a] The Israelites went up out of Egypt armed for battle.

19 Moses took the bones of Joseph with him because Joseph had made the sons of Israel swear an oath. He had said, "God will surely come to your aid, and then you must carry my bones up with you from this place."[b]

> Exodus 12:41
>
> *God Has Perfect Timing*
>
> At the end of the 430 years, to the very day, all the LORD's divisions left Egypt.

---

[a]18 Hebrew *Yam Suph*; that is, Sea of Reeds   [b]19 See Gen. 50:25.

²⁰After leaving Succoth they camped at Etham on the edge of the desert. ²¹By day the LORD went ahead of them in a pillar of cloud to guide them on their way and by night in a pillar of fire to give them light, so that they could travel by day or night. ²²Neither the pillar of cloud by day nor the pillar of fire by night left its place in front of the people.

14 Then the LORD said to Moses, ²"Tell the Israelites to turn back and encamp near Pi Hahiroth, between Migdol and the sea. They are to encamp by the sea, directly opposite Baal Zephon. ³Pharaoh will think, 'The Israelites are wandering around the land in confusion, hemmed in by the desert.' ⁴And I will harden Pharaoh's heart, and he will pursue them. But I will gain glory for myself through Pharaoh and all his army, and the Egyptians will know that I am the LORD." So the Israelites did this.

⁵When the king of Egypt was told that the people had fled, Pharaoh and his officials changed their minds about them and said, "What have we done? We have let the Israelites go and have lost their services!" ⁶So he had his chariot made ready and took his army with him. ⁷He took six hundred of the best chariots, along with all the other chariots of Egypt, with officers over all of them. ⁸The LORD hardened the heart of Pharaoh king of Egypt, so that he pursued the Israelites, who were marching out boldly. ⁹The Egyptians—all Pharaoh's horses and chariots, horsemen*a* and troops—pursued the Israelites and overtook them as they camped by the sea near Pi Hahiroth, opposite Baal Zephon.

¹⁰As Pharaoh approached, the Israelites looked up, and there were the Egyptians, marching after them. They were terrified and cried out to the LORD. ¹¹They said to Moses, "Was it because there were no graves in Egypt that you brought us to the desert to die? What have you done to us by bringing us out of Egypt? ¹²Didn't we say to you in Egypt, 'Leave us alone; let us serve the Egyptians'? It would have been better for us to serve the Egyptians than to die in the desert!"

¹³Moses answered the people, "Do not be afraid. Stand firm and you will see the deliverance the LORD will bring you today. The Egyptians you see today you will never see again. ¹⁴The LORD will fight for you; you need only to be still."

¹⁵Then the LORD said to Moses, "Why are you crying out to me? Tell the Israelites to move on. ¹⁶Raise your staff and stretch out your hand over the sea to divide the water so that the Israelites can go through the sea on dry ground. ¹⁷I will harden the hearts of the Egyptians so that they will go in after them. And I will gain glory through Pharaoh and all his army, through his chariots and his horsemen. ¹⁸The Egyptians will know that I am the LORD when I gain glory through Pharaoh, his chariots and his horsemen."

¹⁹Then the angel of God, who had been traveling in front of Israel's army, withdrew and went behind them. The pillar of cloud also moved from in front and stood behind them, ²⁰coming between the armies of Egypt and Israel. Throughout the night the cloud brought darkness to the one side and light to the other side; so neither went near the other all night long.

²¹Then Moses stretched out his hand over the sea, and all that night the LORD drove the sea back with a strong east wind and turned it into dry land. The waters were divided, ²²and the Israelites went through the sea on dry ground, with a wall of water on their right and on their left.

²³The Egyptians pursued them, and all Pharaoh's horses and chariots and horsemen followed them into the sea. ²⁴During the last watch of the night the LORD looked down from the pillar of fire and cloud at the Egyptian army

Exodus 13:21

God Lights Our Path

By day the LORD went ahead of them in a pillar of cloud to guide them on their way and by night in a pillar of fire to give them light, so that they could travel by day or night.

---

*a*9 Or *charioteers*; also in verses 17, 18, 23, 26 and 28

Be Still

Read: Exodus 14:1–31

IMAGINE THE FEAR. You've just escaped from the most powerful kingdom on earth to follow an 80-year-old shepherd. Now Pharaoh is coming after you with 600 of his best chariots and "all Pharaoh's horses and chariots, horsemen and troops" (Exodus 14:9). The best trained army in the world is pursuing a ragtag group of Hebrew slaves and camp followers. Now might be a good time to panic.

We find the Israelites at Pi Hahiroth in an open space with their backs to the sea . . . and escape seemed impossible. But this fear was not just in their minds. Pharaoh was coming, and they had every right to panic. Rather than telling them to take up arms or run for their lives, Moses gave a surprising command, "Do not be afraid . . . The LORD will fight for you; you need only to be still." We all know the end of the story. The waters parted, and the Israelites crossed the sea on dry land while the sea closed over the pursuing army.

So what can we learn from this well-known story as women living in the twenty-first century? Perhaps God wants us to recognize that we all harbor some kind of fear—real or imagined. For some it may be a fear of the future or a fear of failure. For others it may be the fear of rejection. Many fear the threat of terrorism. Some of us may even have a phobia, a fear that seems irrational to others, but is overwhelming and life-altering to us. No matter what our fear may be, God's Word still resounds, "Do not be afraid." Did you notice that God didn't make fearlessness a suggestion but a command?

So how do we overcome our fears? We can begin by taking the time to be still—not always an easy thing to do in our culture. But with practice and deliberation, we can make the time and cultivate a lifestyle in which we learn to draw our courage from our times of stillness, quietness and prayer.

Go to page 90 for your next devotional reading.

Exodus 14:13–14

Moses answered the people, "Do not be afraid. Stand firm and you will see the deliverance the LORD will bring you today. The Egyptians you see today you will never see again. The LORD will fight for you; you need only to be still."

reflection

1 What do you most fear?

2 How has your fear caused you to fight or take flight rather than be still and trust God?

3 Take some time to "be still" before the Lord and ask him to deliver you from your fears.

RELATED READINGS

Psalms 37:1–7; 46:8–11; Mark 4:35–41

and threw it into confusion. 25 He made the wheels of their chariots come off[a] so that they had difficulty driving. And the Egyptians said, "Let's get away from the Israelites! The LORD is fighting for them against Egypt."

26 Then the LORD said to Moses, "Stretch out your hand over the sea so that the waters may flow back over the Egyptians and their chariots and horsemen." 27 Moses stretched out his hand over the sea, and at daybreak the sea went back to its place. The Egyptians were fleeing toward[b] it, and the LORD swept them into the sea. 28 The water flowed back and covered the chariots and horsemen—the entire army of Pharaoh that had followed the Israelites into the sea. Not one of them survived.

29 But the Israelites went through the sea on dry ground, with a wall of water on their right and on their left. 30 That day the LORD saved Israel from the hands of the Egyptians, and Israel saw the Egyptians lying dead on the shore. 31 And when the Israelites saw the great power the LORD displayed against the Egyptians, the people feared the LORD and put their trust in him and in Moses his servant.

The Song of Moses and Miriam

15 Then Moses and the Israelites sang this song to the LORD:

"I will sing to the LORD,
　for he is highly exalted.
The horse and its rider
　he has hurled into the sea.
2 The LORD is my strength and my song;
　he has become my salvation.
He is my God, and I will praise him,
　my father's God, and I will exalt him.
3 The LORD is a warrior;
　the LORD is his name.
4 Pharaoh's chariots and his army
　he has hurled into the sea.
The best of Pharaoh's officers
　are drowned in the Red Sea.[c]
5 The deep waters have covered them;
　they sank to the depths like a stone.

6 "Your right hand, O LORD,
　was majestic in power.
Your right hand, O LORD,

　shattered the enemy.
7 In the greatness of your majesty
　you threw down those who opposed
　　you.
You unleashed your burning anger;
　it consumed them like stubble.
8 By the blast of your nostrils
　the waters piled up.
The surging waters stood firm like a wall;
　the deep waters congealed in the heart
　　of the sea.

9 "The enemy boasted,
　'I will pursue, I will overtake them.
I will divide the spoils;
　I will gorge myself on them.
I will draw my sword
　and my hand will destroy them.'
10 But you blew with your breath,
　and the sea covered them.
They sank like lead
　in the mighty waters.

11 "Who among the gods is like you, O LORD?
　Who is like you—
　　majestic in holiness,
　　awesome in glory,
　　working wonders?
12 You stretched out your right hand
　and the earth swallowed them.

13 "In your unfailing love you will lead
　the people you have redeemed.
In your strength you will guide them
　to your holy dwelling.
14 The nations will hear and tremble;
　anguish will grip the people of Philistia.
15 The chiefs of Edom will be terrified,
　the leaders of Moab will be seized with
　　trembling,
the people[d] of Canaan will melt away;
16 　terror and dread will fall upon them.
By the power of your arm
　they will be as still as a stone—
until your people pass by, O LORD,
　until the people you bought[e] pass by.
17 You will bring them in and plant them
　on the mountain of your inheritance—
the place, O LORD, you made for your
　　dwelling,

---

a25 Or *He jammed the wheels of their chariots* (see Samaritan Pentateuch, Septuagint and Syriac)　　b27 Or *from*　　c4 Hebrew *Yam Suph*; that is, Sea of Reeds; also in verse 22　　d15 Or *rulers*　　e16 Or *created*

the sanctuary, O Lord, your hands
established.
[18] The LORD will reign
for ever and ever."

[19] When Pharaoh's horses, chariots and
horsemen[a] went into the sea, the LORD brought
the waters of the sea back over them, but the Israelites walked through the sea on dry ground.
[20] Then Miriam the prophetess, Aaron's sister,
took a tambourine in her hand, and all the
women followed her, with tambourines and
dancing. [21] Miriam sang to them:

"Sing to the LORD,
    for he is highly exalted.
The horse and its rider
    he has hurled into the sea."

The Waters of Marah and Elim

[22] Then Moses led Israel from the Red Sea
and they went into the Desert of Shur. For three
days they traveled in the desert without finding
water. [23] When they came to Marah, they could
not drink its water because it was bitter. (That is
why the place is called Marah.[b]) [24] So the people grumbled against Moses, saying, "What are
we to drink?"

[25] Then Moses cried out to the LORD, and the
LORD showed him a piece of wood. He threw it
into the water, and the water became sweet.

There the LORD made a de-
cree and a law for them, and
there he tested them. [26] He
said, "If you listen carefully
to the voice of the LORD your
God and do what is right in his
eyes, if you pay attention to his
commands and keep all his decrees, I will not bring on you
any of the diseases I brought
on the Egyptians, for I am the
LORD, who heals you."

[27] Then they came to Elim, where there were
twelve springs and seventy palm trees, and they
camped there near the water.

Manna and Quail

16
The whole Israelite community set out
from Elim and came to the Desert of
Sin, which is between Elim and Sinai, on the
fifteenth day of the second month after they
had come out of Egypt. [2] In the desert the
whole community grumbled against Moses
and Aaron. [3] The Israelites said to them, "If
only we had died by the LORD's hand in Egypt!
There we sat around pots of meat and ate all the
food we wanted, but you have brought us out
into this desert to starve this entire assembly
to death."

[4] Then the LORD said to Moses, "I will rain
down bread from heaven for you. The people
are to go out each day and gather enough for
that day. In this way I will test them and see
whether they will follow my instructions. [5] On
the sixth day they are to prepare what they
bring in, and that is to be twice as much as they
gather on the other days."

[6] So Moses and Aaron said to all the Israelites, "In the evening you will know that it was
the LORD who brought you out of Egypt, [7] and
in the morning you will see the glory of the
LORD, because he has heard your grumbling
against him. Who are we, that you should
grumble against us?" [8] Moses also said, "You
will know that it was the LORD when he gives
you meat to eat in the evening and all the bread
you want in the morning, because he has heard
your grumbling against him. Who are we?
You are not grumbling against us, but against
the LORD."

[9] Then Moses told Aaron,
"Say to the entire Israelite
community, 'Come before the
LORD, for he has heard your
grumbling.'"

[10] While Aaron was speaking to the whole Israelite community, they looked toward
the desert, and there was the
glory of the LORD appearing in
the cloud.

[11] The LORD said to Moses,
[12] "I have heard the grumbling of the Israelites.
Tell them, 'At twilight you will eat meat, and
in the morning you will be filled with bread.
Then you will know that I am the LORD your
God.'"

[13] That evening quail came and covered the
camp, and in the morning there was a layer of

Exodus 15:26

*God Heals
Our Wounds*

"I am the LORD,
who heals you."

---

a19 Or charioteers   b23 Marah means bitter.

How Quickly We Forget

Then the LORD said to Moses, "I will rain down bread from heaven for you. The people are to go out each day and gather enough for that day. In this way I will test them and see whether they will follow my instructions."

reflection

1 In what ways have you been brought "out of bondage"? What circumstances cause you to look back? What do you look back to?

2 How often do you blame others for circumstances God has allowed in your life?

3 How has God graciously provided for your needs despite your grumbling and complaining? Spend some time praising the bread of life, Jesus Christ, for feeding your soul.

RELATED READINGS

Deuteronomy 8:2–3;
John 6:32–35;
Philippians 4:6–7

FRIGID WEATHER ON THE CROSSING, a food shortage, a desperate need for shelter in a dark wilderness winter. Contrasted with the dire straits the Puritan pilgrims faced their first winter in America, religious persecution might have seemed downright appealing. At least in England they could have a hot meal while being ostracized. Their plight in the new world included death from sickness and starvation.

Suffering sears the human spirit so fully that we begin to believe lies about the past, and, even more dangerous, the future becomes a dead wasteland in our clouded vision. We tend to doubt God's goodness when we follow him through difficult experiences. Trapped by physical, emotional or spiritual pain, we long for happier times; we may even wish for death over pain before we acknowledge God's presence. God cares for us beyond imagination. Although we know that, how do we *feel* it when our guts tighten with fear and a sense of abandonment?

The moment the Israelites didn't get the food they craved, they began to blame Moses and Aaron. How quickly they forgot the God who had brought them out of Egypt. You might think God would react with anger: *Those ungrateful people. Grumbling after all I've done for them. I'll just let them starve.* But instead God chose to "rain down bread from heaven." Though the Israelites remembered Egypt fondly and blamed their deliverer, the Almighty still chose to provide what they needed.

Provision doesn't always arrive as tangibly as manna from heaven. Gut-wrenching starvation afflicted the Pilgrims in a very real way: many of them died that first winter. Sometimes we forget that the world groans under the weight of a curse, that God's love doesn't instantly remove all discomfort, the far-reaching effects of the fall, from our lives. But hidden in God's nature we find answers. When the world threatens to crush our hope, we must cling to the knowledge of God's goodness. Even when our *feelings* tell us otherwise, that we miss England or Egypt or another decade of our lives, *knowing* God's goodness will gradually restore our sight. Then we can see our situation clearly, as daughters of a heavenly Father who desires our good more than we possibly can imagine.

Go to page 93 for your next devotional reading.

dew around the camp. [14]When the dew was gone, thin flakes like frost on the ground appeared on the desert floor. [15]When the Israelites saw it, they said to each other, "What is it?" For they did not know what it was.

Moses said to them, "It is the bread the LORD has given you to eat. [16]This is what the LORD has commanded: 'Each one is to gather as much as he needs. Take an omer[a] for each person you have in your tent.'"

[17]The Israelites did as they were told; some gathered much, some little. [18]And when they measured it by the omer, he who gathered much did not have too much, and he who gathered little did not have too little. Each one gathered as much as he needed.

[19]Then Moses said to them, "No one is to keep any of it until morning."

[20]However, some of them paid no attention to Moses; they kept part of it until morning, but it was full of maggots and began to smell. So Moses was angry with them.

[21]Each morning everyone gathered as much as he needed, and when the sun grew hot, it melted away. [22]On the sixth day, they gathered twice as much—two omers[b] for each person—and the leaders of the community came and reported this to Moses. [23]He said to them, "This is what the LORD commanded: 'Tomorrow is to be a day of rest, a holy Sabbath to the LORD. So bake what you want to bake and boil what you want to boil. Save whatever is left and keep it until morning.'"

[24]So they saved it until morning, as Moses commanded, and it did not stink or get maggots in it. [25]"Eat it today," Moses said, "because today is a Sabbath to the LORD. You will not find any of it on the ground today. [26]Six days you are to gather it, but on the seventh day, the Sabbath, there will not be any."

[27]Nevertheless, some of the people went out on the seventh day to gather it, but they found none. [28]Then the LORD said to Moses, "How long will you[c] refuse to keep my commands and my instructions? [29]Bear in mind that the LORD has given you the Sabbath; that is why on the sixth day he gives you bread for two days. Everyone is to stay where he is on the seventh day; no one is to go out." [30]So the people rested on the seventh day.

[31]The people of Israel called the bread manna.[d] It was white like coriander seed and tasted like wafers made with honey. [32]Moses said, "This is what the LORD has commanded: 'Take an omer of manna and keep it for the generations to come, so they can see the bread I gave you to eat in the desert when I brought you out of Egypt.'"

[33]So Moses said to Aaron, "Take a jar and put an omer of manna in it. Then place it before the LORD to be kept for the generations to come."

[34]As the LORD commanded Moses, Aaron put the manna in front of the Testimony, that it might be kept. [35]The Israelites ate manna forty years, until they came to a land that was settled; they ate manna until they reached the border of Canaan.

[36](An omer is one tenth of an ephah.)

Water From the Rock

17 The whole Israelite community set out from the Desert of Sin, traveling from place to place as the LORD commanded. They camped at Rephidim, but there was no water for the people to drink. [2]So they quarreled with Moses and said, "Give us water to drink."

Moses replied, "Why do you quarrel with me? Why do you put the LORD to the test?"

[3]But the people were thirsty for water there, and they grumbled against Moses. They said, "Why did you bring us up out of Egypt to make us and our children and livestock die of thirst?"

[4]Then Moses cried out to the LORD, "What am I to do with these people? They are almost ready to stone me."

[5]The LORD answered Moses, "Walk on ahead of the people. Take with you some of the elders of Israel and take in your hand the staff with which you struck the Nile, and go. [6]I will stand there before you by the rock at Horeb. Strike the rock, and water will come out of it for the people to drink." So Moses did this in the sight of the elders of Israel. [7]And he called the place Massah[e] and Meribah[f] because the Israelites

[a]16 That is, probably about 2 quarts (about 2 liters); also in verses 18, 32, 33 and 36   [b]22 That is, probably about 4 quarts (about 4.5 liters)   [c]28 The Hebrew is plural.   [d]31 Manna means What is it? (see verse 15).   [e]7 Massah means testing.   [f]7 Meribah means quarreling.

quarreled and because they tested the Lord saying, "Is the Lord among us or not?"

The Amalekites Defeated

8 The Amalekites came and attacked the Israelites at Rephidim. 9 Moses said to Joshua, "Choose some of our men and go out to fight the Amalekites. Tomorrow I will stand on top of the hill with the staff of God in my hands."

10 So Joshua fought the Amalekites as Moses had ordered, and Moses, Aaron and Hur went to the top of the hill. 11 As long as Moses held up his hands, the Israelites were winning, but whenever he lowered his hands, the Amalekites were winning. 12 When Moses' hands grew tired, they took a stone and put it under him and he sat on it. Aaron and Hur held his hands up—one on one side, one on the other—so that his hands remained steady till sunset. 13 So Joshua overcame the Amalekite army with the sword.

14 Then the Lord said to Moses, "Write this on a scroll as something to be remembered and make sure that Joshua hears it, because I will completely blot out the memory of Amalek from under heaven."

15 Moses built an altar and called it The Lord is my Banner. 16 He said, "For hands were lifted up to the throne of the Lord. The[a] Lord will be at war against the Amalekites from generation to generation."

Jethro Visits Moses

18 Now Jethro, the priest of Midian and father-in-law of Moses, heard of everything God had done for Moses and for his people Israel, and how the Lord had brought Israel out of Egypt.

2 After Moses had sent away his wife Zipporah, his father-in-law Jethro received her 3 and her two sons. One son was named Gershom,[b] for Moses said, "I have become an alien in a foreign land"; 4 and the other was named Eliezer,[c] for he said, "My father's God was my helper; he saved me from the sword of Pharaoh."

5 Jethro, Moses' father-in-law, together with Moses' sons and wife, came to him in the desert, where he was camped near the mountain of God. 6 Jethro had sent word to him, "I, your father-in-law Jethro, am coming to you with your wife and her two sons."

7 So Moses went out to meet his father-in-law and bowed down and kissed him. They greeted each other and then went into the tent. 8 Moses told his father-in-law about everything the Lord had done to Pharaoh and the Egyptians for Israel's sake and about all the hardships they had met along the way and how the Lord had saved them.

9 Jethro was delighted to hear about all the good things the Lord had done for Israel in rescuing them from the hand of the Egyptians. 10 He said, "Praise be to the Lord, who rescued you from the hand of the Egyptians and of Pharaoh, and who rescued the people from the hand of the Egyptians. 11 Now I know that the Lord is greater than all other gods, for he did this to those who had treated Israel arrogantly." 12 Then Jethro, Moses' father-in-law, brought a burnt offering and other sacrifices to God, and Aaron came with all the elders of Israel to eat bread with Moses' father-in-law in the presence of God.

13 The next day Moses took his seat to serve as judge for the people, and they stood around him from morning till evening. 14 When his father-in-law saw all that Moses was doing for the people, he said, "What is this you are doing for the people? Why do you alone sit as judge, while all these people stand around you from morning till evening?"

15 Moses answered him, "Because the people come to me to seek God's will. 16 Whenever they have a dispute, it is brought to me, and I decide between the parties and inform them of God's decrees and laws."

17 Moses' father-in-law replied, "What you are doing is not good. 18 You and these people who come to you will only wear yourselves out. The work is too heavy for you; you cannot handle it alone. 19 Listen now to me and I will give you some advice, and may God be with you. You must be the people's representative before God and bring their disputes to him. 20 Teach them the decrees and laws, and show them the way to live and the duties they are to perform. 21 But select capable men from all the people—

---

[a]16 Or *"Because a hand was against the throne of the Lord, the"* [b]3 Gershom sounds like the Hebrew for *an alien there.* [c]4 Eliezer means *my God is helper.*

All Things to All People

Read: Exodus 18:1–27

AN ADVERTISEMENT in a colonial newspaper listed these qualifications for a housekeeper: "An affable, cheerful, and amiable Disposition; cleanly, industrious, perfectly qualified to direct and manage the female Concerns of country business, as raising small stock, dairying, marketing, combing, carding, spinning, knitting, sewing, pickling, preserving, etc., and occasionally to instruct two Young Ladies in those Branches of Economy." Whew! And we think we're busy!

Juggling a hectic life is not new or unique to women in our culture. However, our culture glorifies the multi-tasking woman. Many times we over-schedule our lives because we can't say no. Sometimes we don't want to miss out, so we try to do everything.

Moses could relate. He led Israel as a prophet, guide, intercessor, teacher, lawyer and judge. (Sound like good practice for motherhood?) In short, he was trying to be all things to the Israelites. But it was too much for him to handle by himself. Fortunately, his wise father-in-law saw that he was wearing himself out. Jethro made a great suggestion: You can't do it alone; share the burden with trusted friends. Moses recognized good advice when he heard it, and so he acted upon it, placing capable leaders over various groups of Israelites.

Many women struggle with the "need" to please everyone. But we simply can't be everywhere at once. We can't do everything everyone would like us to do. We can't even do everything we would like to do. Trying to be all things to all people puts us on the fast track to burnout. But when we delegate, we are freed up to focus on the things God has given us to do.

Delegating also creates the opportunity for another capable person to grow into a new role. The people around Moses might never have become leaders if he hadn't given them the opportunity. It's the same for us today. Sometimes we stay in a position because we think that we are irreplaceable. Sometimes we're afraid no one else will do it. Maybe there's some pride involved—we think no one else can do the work as well as we do. But failing to share the load may impede another person's God-given potential. Sometimes the best thing we can do, for others and ourselves, is to step aside so someone else can step up.

Exodus 18:17–18

Moses' father-in-law replied, "What you are doing is not good. You and these people who come to you will only wear yourselves out. The work is too heavy for you; you cannot handle it alone."

reflection

1 What things do you feel God is showing you as your highest priorities? What things are distracting you from that calling?

2 Look at the capable women in your life. Can you release a responsibility to someone else and encourage her to grow in serving God?

3 What chores and responsibilities can you delegate to your children, so that they, too, may grow in learning skills and serving others?

RELATED READINGS

Galatians 6:2;
2 Timothy 2:1–3

Wednesday

Go to page 96 for your next devotional reading.

men who fear God, trustworthy men who hate dishonest gain—and appoint them as officials over thousands, hundreds, fifties and tens. [22]Have them serve as judges for the people at all times, but have them bring every difficult case to you; the simple cases they can decide themselves. That will make your load lighter, because they will share it with you. [23]If you do this and God so commands, you will be able to stand the strain, and all these people will go home satisfied."

[24]Moses listened to his father-in-law and did everything he said. [25]He chose capable men from all Israel and made them leaders of the people, officials over thousands, hundreds, fifties and tens. [26]They served as judges for the people at all times. The difficult cases they brought to Moses, but the simple ones they decided themselves.

[27]Then Moses sent his father-in-law on his way, and Jethro returned to his own country.

At Mount Sinai

19 In the third month after the Israelites left Egypt—on the very day—they came to the Desert of Sinai. [2]After they set out from Rephidim, they entered the Desert of Sinai, and Israel camped there in the desert in front of the mountain.

[3]Then Moses went up to God, and the LORD called to him from the mountain and said, "This is what you are to say to the house of Jacob and what you are to tell the people of Israel: [4]'You yourselves have seen what I did to Egypt, and how I carried you on eagles' wings and brought you to myself. [5]Now if you obey me fully and keep my covenant, then out of all nations you will be my treasured possession. Although the whole earth is mine, [6]you[a] will be for me a kingdom of priests and a holy nation.' These are the words you are to speak to the Israelites."

[7]So Moses went back and summoned the elders of the people and set before them all the words the LORD had commanded him to speak. [8]The people all responded together, "We will do everything the LORD has said." So Moses brought their answer back to the LORD.

[9]The LORD said to Moses, "I am going to come to you in a dense cloud, so that the people will hear me speaking with you and will always put their trust in you." Then Moses told the LORD what the people had said.

[10]And the LORD said to Moses, "Go to the people and consecrate them today and tomorrow. Have them wash their clothes [11]and be ready by the third day, because on that day the LORD will come down on Mount Sinai in the sight of all the people. [12]Put limits for the people around the mountain and tell them, 'Be careful that you do not go up the mountain or touch the foot of it. Whoever touches the mountain shall surely be put to death. [13]He shall surely be stoned or shot with arrows; not a hand is to be laid on him. Whether man or animal, he shall not be permitted to live.' Only when the ram's horn sounds a long blast may they go up to the mountain."

[14]After Moses had gone down the mountain to the people, he consecrated them, and they washed their clothes. [15]Then he said to the people, "Prepare yourselves for the third day. Abstain from sexual relations."

[16]On the morning of the third day there was thunder and lightning, with a thick cloud over the mountain, and a very loud trumpet blast. Everyone in the camp trembled. [17]Then Moses led the people out of the camp to meet with God, and they stood at the foot of the mountain. [18]Mount Sinai was covered with smoke, because the LORD descended on it in fire. The smoke billowed up from it like smoke from a furnace, the whole mountain[b] trembled violently, [19]and the sound of the trumpet grew louder and louder. Then Moses spoke and the voice of God answered him.[c]

[20]The LORD descended to the top of Mount

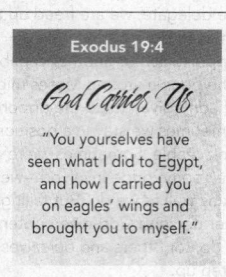

Exodus 19:4

God Carries Us

"You yourselves have seen what I did to Egypt, and how I carried you on eagles' wings and brought you to myself."

---

[a]5,6 Or *possession, for the whole earth is mine.* [6] *You* [b]18 Most Hebrew manuscripts; a few Hebrew manuscripts and Septuagint *all the people* [c]19 Or *and God answered him with thunder*

Sinai and called Moses to the top of the mountain. So Moses went up ²¹and the LORD said to him, "Go down and warn the people so they do not force their way through to see the LORD and many of them perish. ²²Even the priests, who approach the LORD, must consecrate themselves, or the LORD will break out against them."

²³Moses said to the LORD, "The people cannot come up Mount Sinai, because you yourself warned us, 'Put limits around the mountain and set it apart as holy.'"

²⁴The LORD replied, "Go down and bring Aaron up with you. But the priests and the people must not force their way through to come up to the LORD, or he will break out against them."

²⁵So Moses went down to the people and told them.

The Ten Commandments

20 And God spoke all these words:

²"I am the LORD your God, who brought you out of Egypt, out of the land of slavery.

³ "You shall have no other gods before*a* me.

⁴ "You shall not make for yourself an idol in the form of anything in heaven above or on the earth beneath or in the waters below. ⁵You shall not bow down to them or worship them; for I, the LORD your God, am a jealous God, punishing the children for the sin of the fathers to the third and fourth generation of those who hate me, ⁶but showing love to a thousand generations of those who love me and keep my commandments.

⁷ "You shall not misuse the name of the LORD your God, for the LORD will not hold anyone guiltless who misuses his name.

⁸ "Remember the Sabbath day by keeping it holy. ⁹Six days you shall labor and do all your work, ¹⁰but the seventh day is a Sabbath to the LORD your God. On it you shall not do any work, neither you, nor your son or daughter, nor your manservant or maidservant, nor your animals, nor the alien within your gates. ¹¹For in six days the LORD made the heavens and the earth, the sea, and all that is in them, but he rested on the seventh day. Therefore the LORD blessed the Sabbath day and made it holy.

¹² "Honor your father and your mother, so that you may live long in the land the LORD your God is giving you.

¹³ "You shall not murder.

¹⁴ "You shall not commit adultery.

¹⁵ "You shall not steal.

¹⁶ "You shall not give false testimony against your neighbor.

¹⁷ "You shall not covet your neighbor's house. You shall not covet your neighbor's wife, or his manservant or maidservant, his ox or donkey, or anything that belongs to your neighbor."

¹⁸When the people saw the thunder and lightning and heard the trumpet and saw the mountain in smoke, they trembled with fear. They stayed at a distance ¹⁹and said to Moses, "Speak to us yourself and we will listen. But do not have God speak to us or we will die."

²⁰Moses said to the people, "Do not be afraid. God has come to test you, so that the fear of God will be with you to keep you from sinning."

²¹The people remained at a distance, while Moses approached the thick darkness where God was.

Idols and Altars

²²Then the LORD said to Moses, "Tell the Israelites this: 'You have seen for yourselves that I have spoken to you from heaven: ²³Do not make any gods to be alongside me; do not make for yourselves gods of silver or gods of gold.

²⁴ "'Make an altar of earth for me and sacrifice on it your burnt offerings and fellowship offerings,*b* your sheep and goats and your cattle. Wherever I cause my name to be honored, I will come to you and bless you. ²⁵If you make an altar of stones for me, do not build it with dressed stones, for you will defile it if you use

*a*3 Or *besides*   *b*24 Traditionally *peace offerings*

Heart Troublers

Read: Exodus 20:1–26

Exodus 20:18–20

When the people saw the thunder and lightning and heard the trumpet and saw the mountain in smoke, they trembled with fear. They stayed at a distance and said to Moses, "Speak to us yourself and we will listen. But do not have God speak to us or we will die." Moses said to the people, "Do not be afraid. God has come to test you, so that the fear of God will be with you to keep you from sinning."

reflection

1 Have you ever found yourself fearing God in the way the Israelites feared him at Mt. Sinai?

2 How does the fear of the Lord keep you from sinning, as God said to Moses?

3 What "heart troubler" are you experiencing right now? As Jan suggested, turn to God in trust and ask him to perform his good work on your behalf.

RELATED READINGS

Proverbs 1:1–7;
Proverbs 3:5–6;
Luke 18:18–27

SO MANY THINGS can trouble our hearts. Unpaid bills. A frightening medical prognosis. Loss of a job. The death of a loved one. Upcoming surgery. An unexpected move. An argument with a close friend. A savage rumor. A church dispute.

The world is full of "heart troublers," and it always will be. Yet Jesus does not want our hearts to remain troubled. And he does not expect us to deal with those troubles so much by ignoring them as by turning toward him. As he said to his anxious disciples in John 14:1, "Trust in God, trust also in me."

When suffering and persecution and pain and difficulties do is not so much *make* us weak, as show us we *are* weak. Without them, we can deceive ourselves into believing we're prizefighters. With them, we're reminded that we're not constructed to function on our own power. The trick is to allow suffering to be used as a tool to help us depend on God and not on ourselves.

God didn't go halfway when he went to work on my behalf. He did it all. Even when I couldn't feel him, even when I couldn't sense him, even when I wasn't holding on to him anymore, God worked on my behalf. He didn't need me to do a thing!

When I faced far worse than my worst imaginings, something unexpected and wonderful happened. I realized that God is in control and God is good—even when bad things happen in our lives.

Even though I didn't know what I might have to go through next, I could rest and accept it. Because now I knew that when I let go, I would fall into the strong hands of God.

—Jan Dravecky

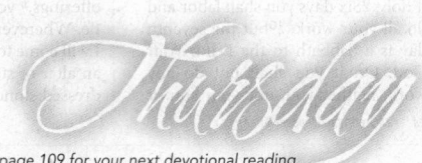

Go to page 109 for your next devotional reading.

a tool on it. ²⁶And do not go up to my altar on steps, lest your nakedness be exposed on it.'

21

¹"These are the laws you are to set before them:

Hebrew Servants

²"If you buy a Hebrew servant, he is to serve you for six years. But in the seventh year, he shall go free, without paying anything. ³If he comes alone, he is to go free alone; but if he has a wife when he comes, she is to go with him. ⁴If his master gives him a wife and she bears him sons or daughters, the woman and her children shall belong to her master, and only the man shall go free.

⁵"But if the servant declares, 'I love my master and my wife and children and do not want to go free,' ⁶then his master must take him before the judges.[a] He shall take him to the door or the doorpost and pierce his ear with an awl. Then he will be his servant for life.

⁷"If a man sells his daughter as a servant, she is not to go free as menservants do. ⁸If she does not please the master who has selected her for himself,[b] he must let her be redeemed. He has no right to sell her to foreigners, because he has broken faith with her. ⁹If he selects her for his son, he must grant her the rights of a daughter. ¹⁰If he marries another woman, he must not deprive the first one of her food, clothing and marital rights. ¹¹If he does not provide her with these three things, she is to go free, without any payment of money.

Personal Injuries

¹²"Anyone who strikes a man and kills him shall surely be put to death. ¹³However, if he does not do it intentionally, but God lets it happen, he is to flee to a place I will designate. ¹⁴But if a man schemes and kills another man deliberately, take him away from my altar and put him to death.

¹⁵"Anyone who attacks[c] his father or his mother must be put to death.

¹⁶"Anyone who kidnaps another and either sells him or still has him when he is caught must be put to death.

¹⁷"Anyone who curses his father or mother must be put to death.

¹⁸"If men quarrel and one hits the other with a stone or with his fist[d] and he does not die but is confined to bed, ¹⁹the one who struck the blow will not be held responsible if the other gets up and walks around outside with his staff; however, he must pay the injured man for the loss of his time and see that he is completely healed.

²⁰"If a man beats his male or female slave with a rod and the slave dies as a direct result, he must be punished, ²¹but he is not to be punished if the slave gets up after a day or two, since the slave is his property.

²²"If men who are fighting hit a pregnant woman and she gives birth prematurely[e] but there is no serious injury, the offender must be fined whatever the woman's husband demands and the court allows. ²³But if there is serious injury, you are to take life for life, ²⁴eye for eye, tooth for tooth, hand for hand, foot for foot, ²⁵burn for burn, wound for wound, bruise for bruise.

²⁶"If a man hits a manservant or maidservant in the eye and destroys it, he must let the servant go free to compensate for the eye. ²⁷And if he knocks out the tooth of a manservant or maidservant, he must let the servant go free to compensate for the tooth.

²⁸"If a bull gores a man or a woman to death, the bull must be stoned to death, and its meat must not be eaten. But the owner of the bull will not be held responsible. ²⁹If, however, the bull has had the habit of goring and the owner has been warned but has not kept it penned up and it kills a man or woman, the bull must be stoned and the owner also must be put to death. ³⁰However, if payment is demanded of him, he may redeem his life by paying whatever is demanded. ³¹This law also applies if the bull gores a son or daughter. ³²If the bull gores a male or female slave, the owner must pay thirty shekels[f] of silver to the master of the slave, and the bull must be stoned.

³³"If a man uncovers a pit or digs one and fails to cover it and an ox or a donkey falls into it, ³⁴the owner of the pit must pay for the loss;

---

^a6 Or *before God*   ^b8 Or *master so that he does not choose her*   ^c15 Or *kills*   ^d18 Or *with a tool*   ^e22 Or *she has a miscarriage*
^f32 That is, about 12 ounces (about 0.3 kilogram)

he must pay its owner, and the dead animal will be his.

³⁵"If a man's bull injures the bull of another and it dies, they are to sell the live one and divide both the money and the dead animal equally. ³⁶However, if it was known that the bull had the habit of goring, yet the owner did not keep it penned up, the owner must pay, animal for animal, and the dead animal will be his.

Protection of Property

22 "If a man steals an ox or a sheep and slaughters it or sells it, he must pay back five head of cattle for the ox and four sheep for the sheep.

²"If a thief is caught breaking in and is struck so that he dies, the defender is not guilty of bloodshed; ³but if it happens*a* after sunrise, he is guilty of bloodshed.

"A thief must certainly make restitution, but if he has nothing, he must be sold to pay for his theft.

⁴"If the stolen animal is found alive in his possession—whether ox or donkey or sheep— he must pay back double.

⁵"If a man grazes his livestock in a field or vineyard and lets them stray and they graze in another man's field, he must make restitution from the best of his own field or vineyard.

⁶"If a fire breaks out and spreads into thornbushes so that it burns shocks of grain or standing grain or the whole field, the one who started the fire must make restitution.

⁷"If a man gives his neighbor silver or goods for safekeeping and they are stolen from the neighbor's house, the thief, if he is caught, must pay back double. ⁸But if the thief is not found, the owner of the house must appear before the judges*b* to determine whether he has laid his hands on the other man's property. ⁹In all cases of illegal possession of an ox, a donkey, a sheep, a garment, or any other lost property about which somebody says, 'This is mine,'

both parties are to bring their cases before the judges. The one whom the judges declare*c* guilty must pay back double to his neighbor.

¹⁰"If a man gives a donkey, an ox, a sheep or any other animal to his neighbor for safekeeping and it dies or is injured or is taken away while no one is looking, ¹¹the issue between them will be settled by the taking of an oath before the LORD that the neighbor did not lay hands on the other person's property. The owner is to accept this, and no restitution is required. ¹²But if the animal was stolen from the neighbor, he must make restitution to the owner. ¹³If it was torn to pieces by a wild animal, he shall bring in the remains as evidence and he will not be required to pay for the torn animal.

¹⁴"If a man borrows an animal from his neighbor and it is injured or dies while the owner is not present, he must make restitution. ¹⁵But if the owner is with the animal, the borrower will not have to pay. If the animal was hired, the money paid for the hire covers the loss.

Social Responsibility

¹⁶"If a man seduces a virgin who is not pledged to be married and sleeps with her, he must pay the bride-price, and she shall be his wife. ¹⁷If her father absolutely refuses to give her to him, he must still pay the bride-price for virgins.

¹⁸"Do not allow a sorceress to live.

¹⁹"Anyone who has sexual relations with an animal must be put to death.

²⁰"Whoever sacrifices to any god other than the LORD must be destroyed.*d*

²¹"Do not mistreat an alien or oppress him, for you were aliens in Egypt.

²²"Do not take advantage of a widow or an orphan. ²³If you do and they cry out to me, I will certainly hear their cry. ²⁴My anger will be aroused, and I will kill you with the sword; your wives will become widows and your children fatherless.

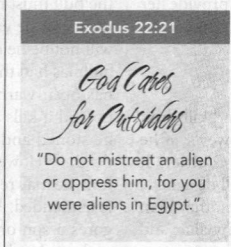

Exodus 22:21

God Cares for Outsiders

"Do not mistreat an alien or oppress him, for you were aliens in Egypt."

---

*a*3 Or *if he strikes him* *b*8 Or *before God*; also in verse 9 *c*9 Or *whom God declares* *d*20 The Hebrew term refers to the irrevocable giving over of things or persons to the LORD, often by totally destroying them.

²⁵"If you lend money to one of my people among you who is needy, do not be like a moneylender; charge him no interest.ᵃ ²⁶If you take your neighbor's cloak as a pledge, return it to him by sunset, ²⁷because his cloak is the only covering he has for his body. What else will he sleep in? When he cries out to me, I will hear, for I am compassionate.

²⁸"Do not blaspheme Godᵇ or curse the ruler of your people.

²⁹"Do not hold back offerings from your granaries or your vats.ᶜ

"You must give me the firstborn of your sons. ³⁰Do the same with your cattle and your sheep. Let them stay with their mothers for seven days, but give them to me on the eighth day.

³¹"You are to be my holy people. So do not eat the meat of an animal torn by wild beasts; throw it to the dogs.

Laws of Justice and Mercy

23 "Do not spread false reports. Do not help a wicked man by being a malicious witness.

²"Do not follow the crowd in doing wrong. When you give testimony in a lawsuit, do not pervert justice by siding with the crowd, ³and do not show favoritism to a poor man in his lawsuit.

⁴"If you come across your enemy's ox or donkey wandering off, be sure to take it back to him. ⁵If you see the donkey of someone who hates you fallen down under its load, do not leave it there; be sure you help him with it.

⁶"Do not deny justice to your poor people in their lawsuits. ⁷Have nothing to do with a false charge and do not put an innocent or honest person to death, for I will not acquit the guilty.

⁸"Do not accept a bribe, for a bribe blinds those who see and twists the words of the righteous.

⁹"Do not oppress an alien; you yourselves know how it feels to be aliens, because you were aliens in Egypt.

Sabbath Laws

¹⁰"For six years you are to sow your fields and harvest the crops, ¹¹but during the seventh year let the land lie unplowed and unused. Then the poor among your people may get food from it, and the wild animals may eat what they leave. Do the same with your vineyard and your olive grove.

¹²"Six days do your work, but on the seventh day do not work, so that your ox and your donkey may rest and the slave born in your household, and the alien as well, may be refreshed.

¹³"Be careful to do everything I have said to you. Do not invoke the names of other gods; do not let them be heard on your lips.

The Three Annual Festivals

¹⁴"Three times a year you are to celebrate a festival to me.

¹⁵"Celebrate the Feast of Unleavened Bread; for seven days eat bread made without yeast, as I commanded you. Do this at the appointed time in the month of Abib, for in that month you came out of Egypt.

"No one is to appear before me empty-handed.

¹⁶"Celebrate the Feast of Harvest with the firstfruits of the crops you sow in your field.

"Celebrate the Feast of Ingathering at the end of the year, when you gather in your crops from the field.

¹⁷"Three times a year all the men are to appear before the Sovereign Lᴏʀᴅ.

¹⁸"Do not offer the blood of a sacrifice to me along with anything containing yeast.

"The fat of my festival offerings must not be kept until morning.

¹⁹"Bring the best of the firstfruits of your soil to the house of the Lᴏʀᴅ your God.

"Do not cook a young goat in its mother's milk.

God's Angel to Prepare the Way

²⁰"See, I am sending an angel ahead of you to guard you along the way and to bring you

> **Exodus 23:20**
>
> *God Prepares Our Way*
>
> "See, I am sending an angel ahead of you to guard you along the way and to bring you to the place I have prepared."

ᵃ25 Or *excessive interest*   ᵇ28 Or *Do not revile the judges*   ᶜ29 The meaning of the Hebrew for this phrase is uncertain.

to the place I have prepared. ²¹Pay attention to him and listen to what he says. Do not rebel against him; he will not forgive your rebellion, since my Name is in him. ²²If you listen carefully to what he says and do all that I say, I will be an enemy to your enemies and will oppose those who oppose you. ²³My angel will go ahead of you and bring you into the land of the Amorites, Hittites, Perizzites, Canaanites, Hivites and Jebusites, and I will wipe them out. ²⁴Do not bow down before their gods or worship them or follow their practices. You must demolish them and break their sacred stones to pieces. ²⁵Worship the LORD your God, and his blessing will be on your food and water. I will take away sickness from among you, ²⁶and none will miscarry or be barren in your land. I will give you a full life span.

²⁷"I will send my terror ahead of you and throw into confusion every nation you encounter. I will make all your enemies turn their backs and run. ²⁸I will send the hornet ahead of you to drive the Hivites, Canaanites and Hittites out of your way. ²⁹But I will not drive them out in a single year, because the land would become desolate and the wild animals too numerous for you. ³⁰Little by little I will drive them out before you, until you have increased enough to take possession of the land.

³¹"I will establish your borders from the Red Sea*a* to the Sea of the Philistines,*b* and from the desert to the River.*c* I will hand over to you the people who live in the land and you will drive them out before you. ³²Do not make a covenant with them or with their gods. ³³Do not let them live in your land, or they will cause you to sin against me, because the worship of their gods will certainly be a snare to you."

The Covenant Confirmed

24 Then he said to Moses, "Come up to the LORD, you and Aaron, Nadab and Abihu, and seventy of the elders of Israel. You are to worship at a distance, ²but Moses alone is to approach the LORD; the others must not come near. And the people may not come up with him."

³When Moses went and told the people all the LORD's words and laws, they responded with one voice, "Everything the LORD has said we will do." ⁴Moses then wrote down everything the LORD had said.

He got up early the next morning and built an altar at the foot of the mountain and set up twelve stone pillars representing the twelve tribes of Israel. ⁵Then he sent young Israelite men, and they offered burnt offerings and sacrificed young bulls as fellowship offerings*d* to the LORD. ⁶Moses took half of the blood and put it in bowls, and the other half he sprinkled on the altar. ⁷Then he took the Book of the Covenant and read it to the people. They responded, "We will do everything the LORD has said; we will obey."

⁸Moses then took the blood, sprinkled it on the people and said, "This is the blood of the covenant that the LORD has made with you in accordance with all these words."

⁹Moses and Aaron, Nadab and Abihu, and the seventy elders of Israel went up ¹⁰and saw the God of Israel. Under his feet was something like a pavement made of sapphire,*e* clear as the sky itself. ¹¹But God did not raise his hand against these leaders of the Israelites; they saw God, and they ate and drank.

¹²The LORD said to Moses, "Come up to me on the mountain and stay here, and I will give you the tablets of stone, with the law and commands I have written for their instruction."

¹³Then Moses set out with Joshua his aide, and Moses went up on the mountain of God. ¹⁴He said to the elders, "Wait here for us until we come back to you. Aaron and Hur are with you, and anyone involved in a dispute can go to them."

Exodus 24:12

God Instructs Us

The LORD said to Moses, "Come up to me on the mountain and stay here, and I will give you the tablets of stone, with the law and commands I have written for their instruction."

---

*a*31 Hebrew *Yam Suph*; that is, Sea of Reeds   *b*31 That is, the Mediterranean   *c*31 That is, the Euphrates   *d*5 Traditionally *peace offerings*   *e*10 Or *lapis lazuli*

15When Moses went up on the mountain, the cloud covered it, 16and the glory of the LORD settled on Mount Sinai. For six days the cloud covered the mountain, and on the seventh day the LORD called to Moses from within the cloud. 17To the Israelites the glory of the LORD looked like a consuming fire on top of the mountain. 18Then Moses entered the cloud as he went on up the mountain. And he stayed on the mountain forty days and forty nights.

Offerings for the Tabernacle

25 The LORD said to Moses, 2"Tell the Israelites to bring me an offering. You are to receive the offering for me from each man whose heart prompts him to give. 3These are the offerings you are to receive from them: gold, silver and bronze; 4blue, purple and scarlet yarn and fine linen; goat hair; 5ram skins dyed red and hides of sea cows*a*; acacia wood; 6olive oil for the light; spices for the anointing oil and for the fragrant incense; 7and onyx stones and other gems to be mounted on the ephod and breastpiece.

8"Then have them make a sanctuary for me, and I will dwell among them. 9Make this tabernacle and all its furnishings exactly like the pattern I will show you.

The Ark

10"Have them make a chest of acacia wood—two and a half cubits long, a cubit and a half wide, and a cubit and a half high.*b* 11Overlay it with pure gold, both inside and out, and make a gold molding around it. 12Cast four gold rings for it and fasten them to its four feet, with two rings on one side and two rings on the other. 13Then make poles of acacia wood and overlay them with gold. 14Insert the poles into the rings on the sides of the chest to carry it. 15The poles are to remain in the rings of this ark; they are not to be removed. 16Then put in the ark the Testimony, which I will give you.

17"Make an atonement cover*c* of pure gold—two and a half cubits long and a cubit and a half wide.*d* 18And make two cherubim out of hammered gold at the ends of the cover.

19Make one cherub on one end and the second cherub on the other; make the cherubim of one piece with the cover, at the two ends. 20The cherubim are to have their wings spread upward, overshadowing the cover with them. The cherubim are to face each other, looking toward the cover. 21Place the cover on top of the ark and put in the ark the Testimony, which I will give you. 22There, above the cover between the two cherubim that are over the ark of the Testimony, I will meet with you and give you all my commands for the Israelites.

The Table

23"Make a table of acacia wood—two cubits long, a cubit wide and a cubit and a half high.*e* 24Overlay it with pure gold and make a gold molding around it. 25Also make around it a rim a handbreadth*f* wide and put a gold molding on the rim. 26Make four gold rings for the table and fasten them to the four corners, where the four legs are. 27The rings are to be close to the rim to hold the poles used in carrying the table. 28Make the poles of acacia wood, overlay them with gold and carry the table with them. 29And make its plates and dishes of pure gold, as well as its pitchers and bowls for the pouring out of offerings. 30Put the bread of the Presence on this table to be before me at all times.

The Lampstand

31"Make a lampstand of pure gold and hammer it out, base and shaft; its flowerlike cups, buds and blossoms shall be of one piece with it. 32Six branches are to extend from the sides of the lampstand—three on one side and three on the other. 33Three cups shaped like almond flowers with buds and blossoms are to be on one branch, three on the next branch, and the same for all six branches extending from the lampstand. 34And on the lampstand there are to be four cups shaped like almond flowers with buds and blossoms. 35One bud shall be under the first pair of branches extending from the lampstand, a second bud under the second pair, and a third bud under the third pair—six branches in all. 36The buds and branches shall

---

*a*5 That is, dugongs *b*10 That is, about 3 3/4 feet (about 1.1 meters) long and 2 1/4 feet (about 0.7 meter) wide and high
*c*17 Traditionally *a mercy seat* *d*17 That is, about 3 3/4 feet (about 1.1 meters) long and 2 1/4 feet (about 0.7 meter) wide *e*23 That is, about 3 feet (about 0.9 meter) long and 1 1/2 feet (about 0.5 meter) wide and 2 1/4 feet (about 0.7 meter) high *f*25 That is, about 3 inches (about 8 centimeters)

all be of one piece with the lampstand, hammered out of pure gold.

37"Then make its seven lamps and set them up on it so that they light the space in front of it. 38Its wick trimmers and trays are to be of pure gold. 39A talent*a* of pure gold is to be used for the lampstand and all these accessories. 40See that you make them according to the pattern shown you on the mountain.

The Tabernacle

26 "Make the tabernacle with ten curtains of finely twisted linen and blue, purple and scarlet yarn, with cherubim worked into them by a skilled craftsman. 2All the curtains are to be the same size—twenty-eight cubits long and four cubits wide.*b* 3Join five of the curtains together, and do the same with the other five. 4Make loops of blue material along the edge of the end curtain in one set, and do the same with the end curtain in the other set. 5Make fifty loops on one curtain and fifty loops on the end curtain of the other set, with the loops opposite each other. 6Then make fifty gold clasps and use them to fasten the curtains together so that the tabernacle is a unit.

7"Make curtains of goat hair for the tent over the tabernacle—eleven altogether. 8All eleven curtains are to be the same size—thirty cubits long and four cubits wide.*c* 9Join five of the curtains together into one set and the other six into another set. Fold the sixth curtain double at the front of the tent. 10Make fifty loops along the edge of the end curtain in one set and also along the edge of the end curtain in the other set. 11Then make fifty bronze clasps and put them in the loops to fasten the tent together as a unit. 12As for the additional length of the tent curtains, the half curtain that is left over is to hang down at the rear of the tabernacle. 13The tent curtains will be a cubit*d* longer on both sides; what is left will hang over the sides of the tabernacle so as to cover it. 14Make for the tent a covering of ram skins dyed red, and over that a covering of hides of sea cows.*e*

15"Make upright frames of acacia wood for the tabernacle. 16Each frame is to be ten cubits long and a cubit and a half wide,*f* 17with two projections set parallel to each other. Make all the frames of the tabernacle in this way. 18Make twenty frames for the south side of the tabernacle 19and make forty silver bases to go under them—two bases for each frame, one under each projection. 20For the other side, the north side of the tabernacle, make twenty frames 21and forty silver bases—two under each frame. 22Make six frames for the far end, that is, the west end of the tabernacle, 23and make two frames for the corners at the far end. 24At these two corners they must be double from the bottom all the way to the top, and fitted into a single ring; both shall be like that. 25So there will be eight frames and sixteen silver bases—two under each frame.

26"Also make crossbars of acacia wood: five for the frames on one side of the tabernacle, 27five for those on the other side, and five for the frames on the west, at the far end of the tabernacle. 28The center crossbar is to extend from end to end at the middle of the frames. 29Overlay the frames with gold and make gold rings to hold the crossbars. Also overlay the crossbars with gold.

30"Set up the tabernacle according to the plan shown you on the mountain.

31"Make a curtain of blue, purple and scarlet yarn and finely twisted linen, with cherubim worked into it by a skilled craftsman. 32Hang it with gold hooks on four posts of acacia wood overlaid with gold and standing on four silver bases. 33Hang the curtain from the clasps and place the ark of the Testimony behind the curtain. The curtain will separate the Holy Place from the Most Holy Place. 34Put the atonement cover on the ark of the Testimony in the Most Holy Place. 35Place the table outside the curtain on the north side of the tabernacle and put the lampstand opposite it on the south side.

36"For the entrance to the tent make a curtain of blue, purple and scarlet yarn and finely twisted linen—the work of an embroiderer. 37Make gold hooks for this curtain and five posts of acacia wood overlaid with gold. And cast five bronze bases for them.

---

*a*39 That is, about 75 pounds (about 34 kilograms)　*b*2 That is, about 42 feet (about 12.5 meters) long and 6 feet (about 1.8 meters) wide　*c*8 That is, about 45 feet (about 13.5 meters) long and 6 feet (about 1.8 meters) wide　*d*13 That is, about 1 1/2 feet (about 0.5 meter)　*e*14 That is, dugongs　*f*16 That is, about 15 feet (about 4.5 meters) long and 2 1/4 feet (about 0.7 meter) wide

The Altar of Burnt Offering

27 "Build an altar of acacia wood, three cubits[a] high; it is to be square, five cubits long and five cubits wide.[b] ²Make a horn at each of the four corners, so that the horns and the altar are of one piece, and overlay the altar with bronze. ³Make all its utensils of bronze—its pots to remove the ashes, and its shovels, sprinkling bowls, meat forks and firepans. ⁴Make a grating for it, a bronze network, and make a bronze ring at each of the four corners of the network. ⁵Put it under the ledge of the altar so that it is halfway up the altar. ⁶Make poles of acacia wood for the altar and overlay them with bronze. ⁷The poles are to be inserted into the rings so they will be on two sides of the altar when it is carried. ⁸Make the altar hollow, out of boards. It is to be made just as you were shown on the mountain.

The Courtyard

⁹"Make a courtyard for the tabernacle. The south side shall be a hundred cubits[c] long and is to have curtains of finely twisted linen, ¹⁰with twenty posts and twenty bronze bases and with silver hooks and bands on the posts. ¹¹The north side shall also be a hundred cubits long and is to have curtains, with twenty posts and twenty bronze bases and with silver hooks and bands on the posts.

¹²"The west end of the courtyard shall be fifty cubits[d] wide and have curtains, with ten posts and ten bases. ¹³On the east end, toward the sunrise, the courtyard shall also be fifty cubits wide. ¹⁴Curtains fifteen cubits[e] long are to be on one side of the entrance, with three posts and three bases, ¹⁵and curtains fifteen cubits long are to be on the other side, with three posts and three bases.

¹⁶"For the entrance to the courtyard, provide a curtain twenty cubits[f] long, of blue, purple and scarlet yarn and finely twisted linen—the work of an embroiderer—with four posts and four bases. ¹⁷All the posts around the courtyard are to have silver bands and hooks, and bronze bases. ¹⁸The courtyard shall be a hundred cubits long and fifty cubits

wide,[g] with curtains of finely twisted linen five cubits[h] high, and with bronze bases. ¹⁹All the other articles used in the service of the tabernacle, whatever their function, including all the tent pegs for it and those for the courtyard, are to be of bronze.

Oil for the Lampstand

²⁰"Command the Israelites to bring you clear oil of pressed olives for the light so that the lamps may be kept burning. ²¹In the Tent of Meeting, outside the curtain that is in front of the Testimony, Aaron and his sons are to keep the lamps burning before the LORD from evening till morning. This is to be a lasting ordinance among the Israelites for the generations to come.

The Priestly Garments

28 "Have Aaron your brother brought to you from among the Israelites, along with his sons Nadab and Abihu, Eleazar and Ithamar, so they may serve me as priests. ²Make sacred garments for your brother Aaron, to give him dignity and honor. ³Tell all the skilled men to whom I have given wisdom in such matters that they are to make garments for Aaron, for his consecration, so he may serve me as priest. ⁴These are the garments they are to make: a breastpiece, an ephod, a robe, a woven tunic, a turban and a sash. They are to make these sacred garments for your brother Aaron and his sons, so they may serve me as priests. ⁵Have them use gold, and blue, purple and scarlet yarn, and fine linen.

The Ephod

⁶"Make the ephod of gold, and of blue, purple and scarlet yarn, and of finely twisted linen—the work of a skilled craftsman. ⁷It is to have two shoulder pieces attached to two of its corners, so it can be fastened. ⁸Its skillfully woven waistband is to be like it—of one piece with the ephod and made with gold, and with blue, purple and scarlet yarn, and with finely twisted linen.

⁹"Take two onyx stones and engrave on them the names of the sons of Israel ¹⁰in the

---

[a]1 That is, about 4 1/2 feet (about 1.3 meters) [b]1 That is, about 7 1/2 feet (about 2.3 meters) long and wide [c]9 That is, about 150 feet (about 46 meters); also in verse 11 [d]12 That is, about 75 feet (about 23 meters); also in verse 13 [e]14 That is, about 22 1/2 feet (about 6.9 meters); also in verse 15 [f]16 That is, about 30 feet (about 9 meters) [g]18 That is, about 150 feet (about 46 meters) long and 75 feet (about 23 meters) wide [h]18 That is, about 7 1/2 feet (about 2.3 meters)

order of their birth—six names on one stone and the remaining six on the other. ¹¹Engrave the names of the sons of Israel on the two stones the way a gem cutter engraves a seal. Then mount the stones in gold filigree settings ¹²and fasten them on the shoulder pieces of the ephod as memorial stones for the sons of Israel. Aaron is to bear the names on his shoulders as a memorial before the LORD. ¹³Make gold filigree settings ¹⁴and two braided chains of pure gold, like a rope, and attach the chains to the settings.

The Breastpiece

¹⁵"Fashion a breastpiece for making decisions—the work of a skilled craftsman. Make it like the ephod: of gold, and of blue, purple and scarlet yarn, and of finely twisted linen. ¹⁶It is to be square—a span*a* long and a span wide—and folded double. ¹⁷Then mount four rows of precious stones on it. In the first row there shall be a ruby, a topaz and a beryl; ¹⁸in the second row a turquoise, a sapphire*b* and an emerald; ¹⁹in the third row a jacinth, an agate and an amethyst; ²⁰in the fourth row a chrysolite, an onyx and a jasper.*c* Mount them in gold filigree settings. ²¹There are to be twelve stones, one for each of the names of the sons of Israel, each engraved like a seal with the name of one of the twelve tribes.

²²"For the breastpiece make braided chains of pure gold, like a rope. ²³Make two gold rings for it and fasten them to two corners of the breastpiece. ²⁴Fasten the two gold chains to the rings at the corners of the breastpiece, ²⁵and the other ends of the chains to the two settings, attaching them to the shoulder pieces of the ephod at the front. ²⁶Make two gold rings and attach them to the other two corners of the breastpiece on the inside edge next to the ephod. ²⁷Make two more gold rings and attach them to the bottom of the shoulder pieces on the front of the ephod, close to the seam just above the waistband of the ephod. ²⁸The rings of the breastpiece are to be tied to the rings of the ephod with blue cord, connecting it to the waistband, so that the breastpiece will not swing out from the ephod.

²⁹"Whenever Aaron enters the Holy Place, he will bear the names of the sons of Israel over his heart on the breastpiece of decision as a continuing memorial before the LORD. ³⁰Also put the Urim and the Thummim in the breastpiece, so they may be over Aaron's heart whenever he enters the presence of the LORD. Thus Aaron will always bear the means of making decisions for the Israelites over his heart before the LORD.

Other Priestly Garments

³¹"Make the robe of the ephod entirely of blue cloth, ³²with an opening for the head in its center. There shall be a woven edge like a collar*d* around this opening, so that it will not tear. ³³Make pomegranates of blue, purple and scarlet yarn around the hem of the robe, with gold bells between them. ³⁴The gold bells and the pomegranates are to alternate around the hem of the robe. ³⁵Aaron must wear it when he ministers. The sound of the bells will be heard when he enters the Holy Place before the LORD and when he comes out, so that he will not die.

³⁶"Make a plate of pure gold and engrave on it as on a seal: HOLY TO THE LORD. ³⁷Fasten a blue cord to it to attach it to the turban; it is to be on the front of the turban. ³⁸It will be on Aaron's forehead, and he will bear the guilt involved in the sacred gifts the Israelites consecrate, whatever their gifts may be. It will be on Aaron's forehead continually so that they will be acceptable to the LORD.

³⁹"Weave the tunic of fine linen and make the turban of fine linen. The sash is to be the work of an embroiderer. ⁴⁰Make tunics, sashes and headbands for Aaron's sons, to give them dignity and honor. ⁴¹After you put these clothes on your brother Aaron and his sons, anoint and ordain them. Consecrate them so they may serve me as priests.

⁴²"Make linen undergarments as a covering for the body, reaching from the waist to the thigh. ⁴³Aaron and his sons must wear them whenever they enter the Tent of Meeting or approach the altar to minister in the Holy Place, so that they will not incur guilt and die.

"This is to be a lasting ordinance for Aaron and his descendants.

---

*a*16 That is, about 9 inches (about 22 centimeters)   *b*18 Or *lapis lazuli*   *c*20 The precise identification of some of these precious stones is uncertain.   *d*32 The meaning of the Hebrew for this word is uncertain.

Consecration of the Priests

29 "This is what you are to do to consecrate them, so they may serve me as priests: Take a young bull and two rams without defect. ²And from fine wheat flour, without yeast, make bread, and cakes mixed with oil, and wafers spread with oil. ³Put them in a basket and present them in it—along with the bull and the two rams. ⁴Then bring Aaron and his sons to the entrance to the Tent of Meeting and wash them with water. ⁵Take the garments and dress Aaron with the tunic, the robe of the ephod, the ephod itself and the breastpiece. Fasten the ephod on him by its skillfully woven waistband. ⁶Put the turban on his head and attach the sacred diadem to the turban. ⁷Take the anointing oil and anoint him by pouring it on his head. ⁸Bring his sons and dress them in tunics ⁹and put headbands on them. Then tie sashes on Aaron and his sons.*a* The priesthood is theirs by a lasting ordinance. In this way you shall ordain Aaron and his sons.

¹⁰"Bring the bull to the front of the Tent of Meeting, and Aaron and his sons shall lay their hands on its head. ¹¹Slaughter it in the LORD's presence at the entrance to the Tent of Meeting. ¹²Take some of the bull's blood and put it on the horns of the altar with your finger, and pour out the rest of it at the base of the altar. ¹³Then take all the fat around the inner parts, the covering of the liver, and both kidneys with the fat on them, and burn them on the altar. ¹⁴But burn the bull's flesh and its hide and its offal outside the camp. It is a sin offering.

¹⁵"Take one of the rams, and Aaron and his sons shall lay their hands on its head. ¹⁶Slaughter it and take the blood and sprinkle it against the altar on all sides. ¹⁷Cut the ram into pieces and wash the inner parts and the legs, putting them with the head and the other pieces. ¹⁸Then burn the entire ram on the altar. It is a burnt offering to the LORD, a pleasing aroma, an offering made to the LORD by fire.

¹⁹"Take the other ram, and Aaron and his sons shall lay their hands on its head. ²⁰Slaughter it, take some of its blood and put it on the lobes of the right ears of Aaron and his sons, on the thumbs of their right hands, and on the big toes of their right feet. Then sprinkle blood against the altar on all sides. ²¹And take some of the blood on the altar and some of the anointing oil and sprinkle it on Aaron and his garments and on his sons and their garments. Then he and his sons and their garments will be consecrated.

²²"Take from this ram the fat, the fat tail, the fat around the inner parts, the covering of the liver, both kidneys with the fat on them, and the right thigh. (This is the ram for the ordination.) ²³From the basket of bread made without yeast, which is before the LORD, take a loaf, and a cake made with oil, and a wafer. ²⁴Put all these in the hands of Aaron and his sons and wave them before the LORD as a wave offering. ²⁵Then take them from their hands and burn them on the altar along with the burnt offering for a pleasing aroma to the LORD, an offering made to the LORD by fire. ²⁶After you take the breast of the ram for Aaron's ordination, wave it before the LORD as a wave offering, and it will be your share.

²⁷"Consecrate those parts of the ordination ram that belong to Aaron and his sons: the breast that was waved and the thigh that was presented. ²⁸This is always to be the regular share from the Israelites for Aaron and his sons. It is the contribution the Israelites are to make to the LORD from their fellowship offerings.*b*

²⁹"Aaron's sacred garments will belong to his descendants so that they can be anointed and ordained in them. ³⁰The son who succeeds him as priest and comes to the Tent of Meeting to minister in the Holy Place is to wear them seven days.

³¹"Take the ram for the ordination and cook the meat in a sacred place. ³²At the entrance to the Tent of Meeting, Aaron and his sons are to eat the meat of the ram and the bread that is in the basket. ³³They are to eat these offerings by which atonement was made for their ordination and consecration. But no one else may eat them, because they are sacred. ³⁴And if any of the meat of the ordination ram or any bread is left over till morning, burn it up. It must not be eaten, because it is sacred.

³⁵"Do for Aaron and his sons everything I have commanded you, taking seven days to

---

a9 Hebrew; Septuagint *on them*   *b28* Traditionally *peace offerings* ordain them. ³⁶Sacrifice a bull each day as a sin offering to make atonement. Purify the altar by making atonement for it, and anoint it to consecrate it. ³⁷For seven days make atonement for the altar and consecrate it. Then the altar will be most holy, and whatever touches it will be holy.

³⁸"This is what you are to offer on the altar regularly each day: two lambs a year old. ³⁹Offer one in the morning and the other at twilight. ⁴⁰With the first lamb offer a tenth of an ephah*ᵃ* of fine flour mixed with a quarter of a hin*ᵇ* of oil from pressed olives, and a quarter of a hin of wine as a drink offering. ⁴¹Sacrifice the other lamb at twilight with the same grain offering and its drink offering as in the morning—a pleasing aroma, an offering made to the Lord by fire.

⁴²"For the generations to come this burnt offering is to be made regularly at the entrance to the Tent of Meeting before the Lord. There I will meet you and speak to you; ⁴³there also I will meet with the Israelites, and the place will be consecrated by my glory.

⁴⁴"So I will consecrate the Tent of Meeting and the altar and will consecrate Aaron and his sons to serve me as priests. ⁴⁵Then I will dwell among the Israelites and be their God. ⁴⁶They will know that I am the Lord their God, who brought them out of Egypt so that I might dwell among them. I am the Lord their God.

The Altar of Incense

30 "Make an altar of acacia wood for burning incense. ²It is to be square, a cubit long and a cubit wide, and two cubits high*ᶜ*—its horns of one piece with it. ³Overlay the top and all the sides and the horns with pure gold, and make a gold molding around it. ⁴Make two gold rings for the altar below the molding—two on opposite sides—to hold the *poles* used to carry it. ⁵Make the poles of acacia wood and overlay them with gold. ⁶Put the altar in front of the curtain that is before the ark

of the Testimony—before the atonement cover that is over the Testimony—where I will meet with you.

⁷"Aaron must burn fragrant incense on the altar every morning when he tends the lamps. ⁸He must burn incense again when he lights the lamps at twilight so incense will burn regularly before the Lord for the generations to come. ⁹Do not offer on this altar any other incense or any burnt offering or grain offering, and do not pour a drink offering on it. ¹⁰Once a year Aaron shall make atonement on its horns. This annual atonement must be made with the blood of the atoning sin offering for the generations to come. It is most holy to the Lord."

Atonement Money

¹¹Then the Lord said to Moses, ¹²"When you take a census of the Israelites to count them, each one must pay the Lord a ransom for his life at the time he is counted. Then no plague will come on them when you number them. ¹³Each one who crosses over to those already counted is to give a half shekel,*ᵈ* according to the sanctuary shekel, which weighs twenty gerahs. This half shekel is an offering to the Lord. ¹⁴All who cross over, those twenty years old or more, are to give an offering to the Lord. ¹⁵The rich are not to give more than a half shekel and the poor are not to give less when you make the offering to the Lord to atone for your lives. ¹⁶Receive the atonement money from the Israelites and use it for the service of the Tent of Meeting. It will be a memorial for the Israelites before the Lord, making atonement for your lives."

Basin for Washing

¹⁷Then the Lord said to Moses, ¹⁸"Make a bronze basin, with its bronze stand, for washing. Place it between the Tent of Meeting and the altar, and put water in it. ¹⁹Aaron and his sons are to wash their hands and feet with water from it. ²⁰Whenever they enter the Tent of

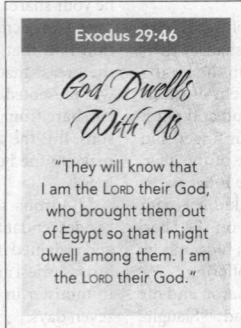

Exodus 29:46

God Dwells With Us

"They will know that I am the Lord their God, who brought them out of Egypt so that I might dwell among them. I am the Lord their God."

ᵃ40 That is, probably about 2 quarts (about 2 liters)   ᵇ40 That is, probably about 1 quart (about 1 liter)   ᶜ2 That is, about 1 1/2 feet (about 0.5 meter) long and wide and about 3 feet (about 0.9 meter) high   ᵈ13 That is, about 1/5 ounce (about 6 grams); also in verse 15

Meeting, they shall wash with water so that they will not die. Also, when they approach the altar to minister by presenting an offering made to the LORD by fire, ²¹they shall wash their hands and feet so that they will not die. This is to be a lasting ordinance for Aaron and his descendants for the generations to come."

Anointing Oil

²²Then the LORD said to Moses, ²³"Take the following fine spices: 500 shekels*ᵃ* of liquid myrrh, half as much (that is, 250 shekels) of fragrant cinnamon, 250 shekels of fragrant cane, ²⁴500 shekels of cassia—all according to the sanctuary shekel—and a hin*ᵇ* of olive oil. ²⁵Make these into a sacred anointing oil, a fragrant blend, the work of a perfumer. It will be the sacred anointing oil. ²⁶Then use it to anoint the Tent of Meeting, the ark of the Testimony, ²⁷the table and all its articles, the lampstand and its accessories, the altar of incense, ²⁸the altar of burnt offering and all its utensils, and the basin with its stand. ²⁹You shall consecrate them so they will be most holy, and whatever touches them will be holy.

³⁰"Anoint Aaron and his sons and consecrate them so they may serve me as priests. ³¹Say to the Israelites, 'This is to be my sacred anointing oil for the generations to come. ³²Do not pour it on men's bodies and do not make any oil with the same formula. It is sacred, and you are to consider it sacred. ³³Whoever makes perfume like it and whoever puts it on anyone other than a priest must be cut off from his people.'"

Incense

³⁴Then the LORD said to Moses, "Take fragrant spices—gum resin, onycha and galbanum—and pure frankincense, all in equal amounts, ³⁵and make a fragrant blend of incense, the work of a perfumer. It is to be salted and pure and sacred. ³⁶Grind some of it to powder and place it in front of the Testimony in the Tent of Meeting, where I will meet with you. It shall be most holy to you. ³⁷Do not make any incense with this formula for yourselves; consider it holy to the LORD. ³⁸Whoever makes any like it to enjoy its fragrance must be cut off from his people."

Bezalel and Oholiab

31 Then the LORD said to Moses, ²"See, I have chosen Bezalel son of Uri, the son of Hur, of the tribe of Judah, ³and I have filled him with the Spirit of God, with skill, ability and knowledge in all kinds of crafts— ⁴to make artistic designs for work in gold, silver and bronze, ⁵to cut and set stones, to work in wood, and to engage in all kinds of craftsmanship. ⁶Moreover, I have appointed Oholiab son of Ahisamach, of the tribe of Dan, to help him. Also I have given skill to all the craftsmen to make everything I have commanded you: ⁷the Tent of Meeting, the ark of the Testimony with the atonement cover on it, and all the other furnishings of the tent— ⁸the table and its articles, the pure gold lampstand and all its accessories, the altar of incense, ⁹the altar of burnt offering and all its utensils, the basin with its stand— ¹⁰and also the woven garments, both the sacred garments for Aaron the priest and the garments for his sons when they serve as priests, ¹¹and the anointing oil and fragrant incense for the Holy Place. They are to make them just as I commanded you."

The Sabbath

¹²Then the LORD said to Moses, ¹³"Say to the Israelites, 'You must observe my Sabbaths. This will be a sign between me and you for the generations to come, so you may know that I am the LORD, who makes you holy.*ᶜ*

¹⁴"'Observe the Sabbath, because it is holy to you. Anyone who desecrates it must be put to death; whoever does any work on that day must be cut off from his people. ¹⁵For six days,

> ### Exodus 31:2–3
>
> *God Assigns Our Talents*
>
> "See, I have chosen Bezalel son of Uri, the son of Hur, of the tribe of Judah, and I have filled him with the Spirit of God, with skill, ability and knowledge in all kinds of crafts."

ᵃ23 That is, about 12 1/2 pounds (about 6 kilograms) *ᵇ24* That is, probably about 4 quarts (about 4 liters) *ᶜ13* Or *who sanctifies you;* or *who sets you apart as holy* work is to be done, but the seventh day is a Sabbath of rest, holy to the LORD. Whoever does any work on the Sabbath day must be put to death. 16The Israelites are to observe the Sabbath, celebrating it for the generations to come as a lasting covenant. 17It will be a sign between me and the Israelites forever, for in six days the LORD made the heavens and the earth, and on the seventh day he abstained from work and rested.'"

18When the LORD finished speaking to Moses on Mount Sinai, he gave him the two tablets of the Testimony, the tablets of stone inscribed by the finger of God.

The Golden Calf

32 When the people saw that Moses was so long in coming down from the mountain, they gathered around Aaron and said, "Come, make us gods*a* who will go before us. As for this fellow Moses who brought us up out of Egypt, we don't know what has happened to him."

2Aaron answered them, "Take off the gold earrings that your wives, your sons and your daughters are wearing, and bring them to me." 3So all the people took off their earrings and brought them to Aaron. 4He took what they handed him and made it into an idol cast in the shape of a calf, fashioning it with a tool. Then they said, "These are your gods,*b* O Israel, who brought you up out of Egypt."

5When Aaron saw this, he built an altar in front of the calf and announced, "Tomorrow there will be a festival to the LORD." 6So the next day the people rose early and sacrificed burnt offerings and presented fellowship offerings.*c* Afterward they sat down to eat and drink and got up to indulge in revelry.

7Then the LORD said to Moses, "Go down, because your people, whom you brought up out of Egypt, have become corrupt. 8They have been quick to turn away from what I commanded them and have made themselves an idol cast in the shape of a calf. They have bowed down to it and sacrificed to it and have said, 'These are your gods, O Israel, who brought you up out of Egypt.'

9"I have seen these people," the LORD said

to Moses, "and they are a stiff-necked people. 10Now leave me alone so that my anger may burn against them and that I may destroy them. Then I will make you into a great nation."

11But Moses sought the favor of the LORD his God. "O LORD," he said, "why should your anger burn against your people, whom you brought out of Egypt with great power and a mighty hand? 12Why should the Egyptians say, 'It was with evil intent that he brought them out, to kill them in the mountains and to wipe them off the face of the earth'? Turn from your fierce anger; relent and do not bring disaster on your people. 13Remember your servants Abraham, Isaac and Israel, to whom you swore by your own self: 'I will make your descendants as numerous as the stars in the sky and I will give your descendants all this land I promised them, and it will be their inheritance forever.'" 14Then the LORD relented and did not bring on his people the disaster he had threatened.

15Moses turned and went down the mountain with the two tablets of the Testimony in his hands. They were inscribed on both sides, front and back. 16The tablets were the work of God; the writing was the writing of God, engraved on the tablets.

17When Joshua heard the noise of the people shouting, he said to Moses, "There is the sound of war in the camp."

18Moses replied:

"It is not the sound of victory,
    it is not the sound of defeat;
    it is the sound of singing that I hear."

19When Moses approached the camp and saw the calf and the dancing, his anger burned and he threw the tablets out of his hands, breaking them to pieces at the foot of the mountain. 20And he took the calf they had made and burned it in the fire; then he ground it to powder, scattered it on the water and made the Israelites drink it.

21He said to Aaron, "What did these people do to you, that you led them into such great sin?"

22"Do not be angry, my lord," Aaron answered. "You know how prone these people are to evil. 23They said to me, 'Make us gods

*a*1 Or *a god*; also in verses 23 and 31   *b*4 Or *This is your god*; also in verse 8   *c*6 Traditionally *peace offerings*

Gold or God?

Read: Exodus 32:1–35

IDOLATRY IS ALIVE and well in the modern world. People worship at the temple of self. They bow down to the god of money. They make sacrifices to elusive dreams of perfection—the perfect husband, the perfect family, the perfect body, the perfect life. Perfection becomes a substitute for the gold and jewels the Israelites used to create idols. As women, we often find it easier to worship temporal dreams of earthly perfection than the eternal God. The resplendent life we have planned shimmers before us, but the mirage will fail to satisfy our thirst.

When the Israelites fled Egypt, they left a land steeped in idolatry. The Egyptians worshiped thousands of deities, ascribing god-like qualities to animals, birds and trees. They created temples and statues swathed in gold and jewels to elevate these false gods. When Moses, the Israelites' spiritual leader, left to meet with God on Mount Sinai, the people quickly returned to idol worship. The fickle Israelites, delivered from slavery by the unseen God, quickly exchanged worshiping God for worshiping a golden dream they could control, a deity they could manipulate.

You may not think you're guilty of idol worship. You wouldn't bow down to an animal figurine. You go to church every Sunday. You have a Bible sitting on your bedside table. But do you long for a golden dream you can fashion to your own whims? God's goodness, his justice and his holiness do not necessarily make him safe. Our golden dreams of earthly perfection encapsulate only what we allow; they stay as safe as we like them, as shimmering and domestic as we dare. God is wild, unsafe, unpredictable even. He does not fit into the neat fairy tale we sometimes prefer to him.

What do you return to when God feels untamed? What do you adore? Perhaps a relationship fills your every waking thought; perhaps you spend your time dreaming of ascending to greatness as an artist or breaking new ground in your field; perhaps you idolize your children. When something catches your thoughts, eventually it captures your heart. Idol worship is alive and well, but the golden dream will not soothe your soul. The illusion of perfection does not comfort you when you mourn. Gold will not go with you into eternity. But God can, and will, do all these things when you worship him "in spirit and in truth" (John 4:24).

Go to page 111 for your next devotional reading.

Exodus 32:2–4

Aaron answered them, "Take off the gold earrings that your wives, your sons and your daughters are wearing, and bring them to me." So all the people took off their earrings and brought them to Aaron. He took what they handed him and made it into an idol cast in the shape of a calf, fashioning it with a tool. Then they said, "These are your gods, O Israel, who brought you up out of Egypt."

reflection

1 What types of idols have you noticed in the world around you?

2 In what subtle ways have you been guilty of putting things, people or ideas before God?

3 How will you show God that you love him more than any person, place or thing?

RELATED READINGS

Exodus 20:1–17; Micah 6:6–8; Matthew 6:19–21

who will go before us. As for this fellow Moses who brought us up out of Egypt, we don't know what has happened to him.' ²⁴So I told them, 'Whoever has any gold jewelry, take it off.' Then they gave me the gold, and I threw it into the fire, and out came this calf!"

²⁵Moses saw that the people were running wild and that Aaron had let them get out of control and so become a laughingstock to their enemies. ²⁶So he stood at the entrance to the camp and said, "Whoever is for the Lord, come to me." And all the Levites rallied to him.

²⁷Then he said to them, "This is what the Lord, the God of Israel, says: 'Each man strap a sword to his side. Go back and forth through the camp from one end to the other, each killing his brother and friend and neighbor.' " ²⁸The Levites did as Moses commanded, and that day about three thousand of the people died. ²⁹Then Moses said, "You have been set apart to the Lord today, for you were against your own sons and brothers, and he has blessed you this day."

³⁰The next day Moses said to the people, "You have committed a great sin. But now I will go up to the Lord; perhaps I can make atonement for your sin."

³¹So Moses went back to the Lord and said, "Oh, what a great sin these people have committed! They have made themselves gods of gold. ³²But now, please forgive their sin—but if not, then blot me out of the book you have written."

³³The Lord replied to Moses, "Whoever has sinned against me I will blot out of my book. ³⁴Now go, lead the people to the place I spoke of, and my angel will go before you. However, when the time comes for me to punish, I will punish them for their sin."

³⁵And the Lord struck the people with a plague because of what they did with the calf Aaron had made.

33 Then the Lord said to Moses, "Leave this place, you and the people you brought up out of Egypt, and go up to the land I promised on oath to Abraham, Isaac and Jacob, saying, 'I will give it to your descendants.' ²I will send an angel before you and drive out the Canaanites, Amorites, Hittites, Perizzites, Hivites and Jebusites. ³Go up to the land flow-

ing with milk and honey. But I will not go with you, because you are a stiff-necked people and I might destroy you on the way."

⁴When the people heard these distressing words, they began to mourn and no one put on any ornaments. ⁵For the Lord had said to Moses, "Tell the Israelites, 'You are a stiff-necked people. If I were to go with you even for a moment, I might destroy you. Now take off your ornaments and I will decide what to do with you.' " ⁶So the Israelites stripped off their ornaments at Mount Horeb.

The Tent of Meeting

⁷Now Moses used to take a tent and pitch it outside the camp some distance away, calling it the "tent of meeting." Anyone inquiring of the Lord would go to the tent of meeting outside the camp. ⁸And whenever Moses went out to the tent, all the people rose and stood at the entrances to their tents, watching Moses until he entered the tent. ⁹As Moses went into the tent, the pillar of cloud would come down and stay at the entrance, while the Lord spoke with Moses. ¹⁰Whenever the people saw the pillar of cloud standing at the entrance to the tent, they all stood and worshiped, each at the entrance to his tent. ¹¹The Lord would speak to Moses face to face, as a man speaks with his friend. Then Moses would return to the camp, but his young aide Joshua son of Nun did not leave the tent.

Moses and the Glory of the Lord

¹²Moses said to the Lord, "You have been telling me, 'Lead these people,' but you have not let me know whom you will send with me. You have said, 'I know you by name and you have found favor with me.' ¹³If you are pleased with me, teach me your ways so I may know you and continue to find favor with you. Remember that this nation is your people."

¹⁴The Lord replied, "My Presence will go with you, and I will give you rest."

¹⁵Then Moses said to him, "If your Presence does not go with us, do not send us up from here. ¹⁶How will anyone know that you are pleased with me and with your people unless you go with us? What else will distinguish me and your people from all the other people on the face of the earth?"

Sleepless in Sodom

LOT'S WIFE

SHE HEARD THE CROWD coming down the street, a discord of voices, echoes, shouts and drunken laughter. They stopped at the house she shared with her husband, Lot, and pressed their bodies up against the doorframe, jeering loudly.

"Another sleepless night in Sodom," she thought.

Earlier that evening, two strangers had entered her home, and she'd been on edge ever since. They looked like ordinary men. However, something told her there was nothing ordinary about them. The men certainly did not remind her of the flesh-and-blood world she was accustomed to. She had grown somewhat used to the sounds of Sodom—late night brawls and the like. But being in the same house as these unearthly, quiet men made her feel down-right anxious. Uncomfortable. Almost as if they could somehow see right through her.

It reminded her of when her family first moved to Sodom long ago. Whatever lifestyle she'd known before seemed quaint amid the unnatural ways of the diverse crowd. Nevertheless, it took less time than one could have ever imagined to grow accustomed to life in Sodom. The frightening soon became familiar. And, looking back now, it felt strange to think of living anywhere else.

"Who in your family is still here?" The voice of the strangers interrupted her thoughts. "Get them out of here now!" At once, she battled an indescribable urge to obey them against the desire to stay where she was. If it was easy to ignore her intuition to flee those first nights in Sodom, how much easier would it be now to downplay the men's warnings?

She didn't have time to decide. Still in her bedclothes, the two men rushed her and her family out of the house. Her feet barely seemed to touch the streets or the sandy path as the men fled with them out of the city and toward the mountains. Ahead, she could see a thin slice of pomegranate red spreading east against the night sky. Behind, the noise from the jeering crowd grew fainter. But she could still feel the city pulling her back.

—Prayer—
Father, I pray that I will hold true to Jesus' words and always remember Lot's wife as an example for my own life.

With the coming of dawn, the angels urged Lot, saying, "Hurry! Take your wife and your two daughters who are here, or you will be swept away when the city is punished."

Genesis 19:15

ASSIGNED READING:

Genesis 19:1–29

Weekend

Go to page 125 for your next devotional reading.

¹⁷And the LORD said to Moses, "I will do the very thing you have asked, because I am pleased with you and I know you by name."

¹⁸Then Moses said, "Now show me your glory."

¹⁹And the LORD said, "I will cause all my goodness to pass in front of you, and I will proclaim my name, the LORD, in your presence. I will have mercy on whom I will have mercy, and I will have compassion on whom I will have compassion. ²⁰But," he said, "you cannot see my face, for no one may see me and live."

²¹Then the LORD said, "There is a place near me where you may stand on a rock. ²²When my glory passes by, I will put you in a cleft in the rock and cover you with my hand until I have passed by. ²³Then I will remove my hand and you will see my back; but my face must not be seen."

Exodus 33:19

God Is Compassionate

"I will cause all my goodness to pass in front of you, and I will proclaim my name, the LORD, in your presence. I will have mercy on whom I will have mercy, and I will have compassion on whom I will have compassion."

leave the guilty unpunished; he punishes the children and their children for the sin of the fathers to the third and fourth generation."

⁸Moses bowed to the ground at once and worshiped. ⁹"O Lord, if I have found favor in your eyes," he said, "then let the Lord go with us. Although this is a stiff-necked people, forgive our wickedness and our sin, and take us as your inheritance."

¹⁰Then the LORD said: "I am making a covenant with you. Before all your people I will do wonders never before done in any nation in all the world. The people you live among will see how awesome is the work that I, the LORD, will do for you. ¹¹Obey what I command you today. I will drive out before you the Amorites, Canaanites, Hittites, Perizzites, Hivites and Jebusites. ¹²Be careful not to make a treaty with those who live in the land where you are going, or they will be a snare among you. ¹³Break down their altars, smash their sacred stones and cut down their Asherah poles.ᵃ ¹⁴Do not worship any other god, for the LORD, whose name is Jealous, is a jealous God.

¹⁵"Be careful not to make a treaty with those who live in the land; for when they prostitute themselves to their gods and sacrifice to them, they will invite you and you will eat their sacrifices. ¹⁶And when you choose some of their daughters as wives for your sons and those daughters prostitute themselves to their gods, they will lead your sons to do the same.

¹⁷"Do not make cast idols.

¹⁸"Celebrate the Feast of Unleavened Bread. For seven days eat bread made without yeast, as I commanded you. Do this at the appointed time in the month of Abib, for in that month you came out of Egypt.

¹⁹"The first offspring of every womb belongs to me, including all the firstborn males of your livestock, whether from herd or flock. ²⁰Redeem the firstborn donkey with a lamb, but if

The New Stone Tablets

34

The LORD said to Moses, "Chisel out two stone tablets like the first ones, and I will write on them the words that were on the first tablets, which you broke. ²Be ready in the morning, and then come up on Mount Sinai. Present yourself to me there on top of the mountain. ³No one is to come with you or be seen anywhere on the mountain; not even the flocks and herds may graze in front of the mountain."

⁴So Moses chiseled out two stone tablets like the first ones and went up Mount Sinai early in the morning, as the LORD had commanded him; and he carried the two stone tablets in his hands. ⁵Then the LORD came down in the cloud and stood there with him and proclaimed his name, the LORD. ⁶And he passed in front of Moses, proclaiming, "The LORD, the LORD, *the compassionate and gracious God*, slow to anger, abounding in love and faithfulness, ⁷maintaining love to thousands, and forgiving wickedness, rebellion and sin. Yet he does not

---

ᵃ13 That is, symbols of the goddess Asherah

you do not redeem it, break its neck. Redeem all your firstborn sons.

"No one is to appear before me empty-handed.

21"Six days you shall labor, but on the seventh day you shall rest; even during the plowing season and harvest you must rest.

22"Celebrate the Feast of Weeks with the firstfruits of the wheat harvest, and the Feast of Ingathering at the turn of the year.*a* 23Three times a year all your men are to appear before the Sovereign LORD, the God of Israel. 24I will drive out nations before you and enlarge your territory, and no one will covet your land when you go up three times each year to appear before the LORD your God.

25"Do not offer the blood of a sacrifice to me along with anything containing yeast, and do not let any of the sacrifice from the Passover Feast remain until morning.

26"Bring the best of the firstfruits of your soil to the house of the LORD your God.

"Do not cook a young goat in its mother's milk."

27Then the LORD said to Moses, "Write down these words, for in accordance with these words I have made a covenant with you and with Israel." 28Moses was there with the LORD forty days and forty nights without eating bread or drinking water. And he wrote on the tablets the words of the covenant—the Ten Commandments.

The Radiant Face of Moses

29When Moses came down from Mount Sinai with the two tablets of the Testimony in his hands, he was not aware that his face was radiant because he had spoken with the LORD. 30When Aaron and all the Israelites saw Moses, his face was radiant, and they were afraid to come near him. 31But Moses called to them; so Aaron and all the leaders of the community came back to him, and he spoke to them. 32Afterward all the Israelites came near him, and he gave them all the commands the LORD had given him on Mount Sinai.

33When Moses finished speaking to them, he put a veil over his face. 34But whenever he entered the LORD's presence to speak with him, he removed the veil until he came out. And when he came out and told the Israelites what he had been commanded, 35they saw that his face was radiant. Then Moses would put the veil back over his face until he went in to speak with the LORD.

Sabbath Regulations

35 Moses assembled the whole Israelite community and said to them, "These are the things the LORD has commanded you to do: 2For six days, work is to be done, but the seventh day shall be your holy day, a Sabbath of rest to the LORD. Whoever does any work on it must be put to death. 3Do not light a fire in any of your dwellings on the Sabbath day."

Materials for the Tabernacle

4Moses said to the whole Israelite community, "This is what the LORD has commanded: 5From what you have, take an offering for the LORD. Everyone who is willing is to bring to the LORD an offering of gold, silver and bronze; 6blue, purple and scarlet yarn and fine linen; goat hair; 7ram skins dyed red and hides of sea cows*b*; acacia wood; 8olive oil for the light; spices for the anointing oil and for the fragrant incense; 9and onyx stones and other gems to be mounted on the ephod and breastpiece.

10"All who are skilled among you are to come and make everything the LORD has commanded: 11the tabernacle with its tent and its covering, clasps, frames, crossbars, posts and bases; 12the ark with its poles and the atonement cover and the curtain that shields it; 13the table with its poles and all its articles and the bread of the Presence; 14the lampstand that is for light with its accessories, lamps and oil for the light; 15the altar of incense with its poles, the anointing oil and the fragrant incense; the curtain for the doorway at the entrance to the tabernacle; 16the altar of burnt offering with its bronze grating, its poles and all its utensils; the bronze basin with its stand; 17the curtains of the courtyard with its posts and bases, and the curtain for the entrance to the courtyard; 18the tent pegs for the tabernacle and for the courtyard, and their ropes; 19the woven garments worn for ministering in the sanctuary—both

*a*22 That is, in the fall   *b*7 That is, dugongs; also in verse 23

113

the sacred garments for Aaron the priest and the garments for his sons when they serve as priests."

20 Then the whole Israelite community withdrew from Moses' presence, 21 and everyone who was willing and whose heart moved him came and brought an offering to the LORD for the work on the Tent of Meeting, for all its service, and for the sacred garments. 22 All who were willing, men and women alike, came and brought gold jewelry of all kinds: brooches, earrings, rings and ornaments. They all presented their gold as a wave offering to the LORD. 23 Everyone who had blue, purple or scarlet yarn or fine linen, or goat hair, ram skins dyed red or hides of sea cows brought them. 24 Those presenting an offering of silver or bronze brought it as an offering to the LORD, and everyone who had acacia wood for any part of the work brought it. 25 Every skilled woman spun with her hands and brought what she had spun—blue, purple or scarlet yarn or fine linen. 26 And all the women who were willing and had the skill spun the goat hair. 27 The leaders brought onyx stones and other gems to be mounted on the ephod and breastpiece. 28 They also brought spices and olive oil for the light and for the anointing oil and for the fragrant incense. 29 All the Israelite men and women who were willing brought to the LORD freewill offerings for all the work the LORD had commanded them to do.

Bezalel and Oholiab

30 Then Moses said to the Israelites, "See, the LORD has chosen Bezalel son of Uri, the son of Hur, of the tribe of Judah, 31 and he has filled him with the Spirit of God, with skill, ability and knowledge in all kinds of crafts— 32 to make artistic designs for work in gold, silver and bronze, 33 to cut and set stones, to work in wood and to engage in all kinds of artistic craftsmanship. 34 And he has given both him and Oholiab son of Ahisamach, of the tribe of Dan, the ability to teach others. 35 He has filled them with skill to do all kinds of work as craftsmen, designers, embroiderers in blue, purple and scarlet yarn and fine linen, and weavers—all of them master craftsmen and designers.

36 So Bezalel, Oholiab and every skilled person to whom the LORD has given skill and ability to know how to carry out all the work of constructing the sanctuary are to do the work just as the LORD has commanded."

2 Then Moses summoned Bezalel and Oholiab and every skilled person to whom the LORD had given ability and who was willing to come and do the work. 3 They received from Moses all the offerings the Israelites had brought to carry out the work of constructing the sanctuary. And the people continued to bring freewill offerings morning after morning. 4 So all the skilled craftsmen who were doing all the work on the sanctuary left their work 5 and said to Moses, "The people are bringing more than enough for doing the work the LORD commanded to be done."

6 Then Moses gave an order and they sent this word throughout the camp: "No man or woman is to make anything else as an offering for the sanctuary." And so the people were restrained from bringing more, 7 because what they already had was more than enough to do all the work.

The Tabernacle

8 All the skilled men among the workmen made the tabernacle with ten curtains of finely twisted linen and blue, purple and scarlet yarn, with cherubim worked into them by a skilled craftsman. 9 All the curtains were the same size—twenty-eight cubits long and four cubits wide.a 10 They joined five of the curtains together and did the same with the other five. 11 Then they made loops of blue material along the edge of the end curtain in one set, and the same was done with the end curtain in the other set. 12 They also made fifty loops on one curtain and fifty loops on the end curtain of the other set, with the loops opposite each other. 13 Then they made fifty gold clasps and used them to fasten the two sets of curtains together so that the tabernacle was a unit.

14 They made curtains of goat hair for the tent over the tabernacle—eleven altogether. 15 All eleven curtains were the same size—thirty cubits long and four cubits wide.b 16 They joined five of the curtains into one set and the other six into

a9 That is, about 42 feet (about 12.5 meters) long and 6 feet (about 1.8 meters) wide   b15 That is, about 45 feet (about 13.5 meters) long and 6 feet (about 1.8 meters) wide another set. **17**Then they made fifty loops along the edge of the end curtain in one set and also along the edge of the end curtain in the other set. **18**They made fifty bronze clasps to fasten the tent together as a unit. **19**Then they made for the tent a covering of ram skins dyed red, and over that a covering of hides of sea cows.ᵃ

20They made upright frames of acacia wood for the tabernacle. **21**Each frame was ten cubits long and a cubit and a half wide,ᵇ **22**with two projections set parallel to each other. They made all the frames of the tabernacle in this way. **23**They made twenty frames for the south side of the tabernacle **24**and forty silver bases to go under them—two bases for each frame, one under each projection. **25**For the other side, the north side of the tabernacle, they made twenty frames **26**and forty silver bases—two under each frame. **27**They made six frames for the far end, that is, the west end of the tabernacle, **28**and two frames were made for the corners of the tabernacle at the far end. **29**At these two corners the frames were double from the bottom all the way to the top and fitted into a single ring; both were made alike. **30**So there were eight frames and sixteen silver bases—two under each frame.

31They also made crossbars of acacia wood: five for the frames on one side of the tabernacle, **32**five for those on the other side, and five for the frames on the west, at the far end of the tabernacle. **33**They made the center crossbar so that it extended from end to end at the middle of the frames. **34**They overlaid the frames with gold and made gold rings to hold the crossbars. They also overlaid the crossbars with gold.

35They made the curtain of blue, purple and scarlet yarn and finely twisted linen, with cherubim worked into it by a skilled craftsman. **36**They made four posts of acacia wood for it and overlaid them with gold. They made gold hooks for them and cast their four silver bases. **37**For the entrance to the tent they made a curtain of blue, purple and scarlet yarn and finely twisted linen—the work of an embroiderer; **38**and they made five posts with hooks for them. They overlaid the tops of the posts and

their bands with gold and made their five bases of bronze.

The Ark

37 Bezalel made the ark of acacia wood— two and a half cubits long, a cubit and a half wide, and a cubit and a half high.ᶜ **2**He overlaid it with pure gold, both inside and out, and made a gold molding around it. **3**He cast four gold rings for it and fastened them to its four feet, with two rings on one side and two rings on the other. **4**Then he made poles of acacia wood and overlaid them with gold. **5**And he inserted the poles into the rings on the sides of the ark to carry it.

6He made the atonement cover of pure gold—two and a half cubits long and a cubit and a half wide.ᵈ **7**Then he made two cherubim out of hammered gold at the ends of the cover. **8**He made one cherub on one end and the second cherub on the other; at the two ends he made them of one piece with the cover. **9**The cherubim had their wings spread upward, overshadowing the cover with them. The cherubim faced each other, looking toward the cover.

The Table

10Theyᵉ made the table of acacia wood—two cubits long, a cubit wide, and a cubit and a half high.ᶠ **11**Then they overlaid it with pure gold and made a gold molding around it. **12**They also made around it a rim a handbreadthᵍ wide and put a gold molding on the rim. **13**They cast four gold rings for the table and fastened them to the four corners, where the four legs were. **14**The rings were put close to the rim to hold the poles used in carrying the table. **15**The poles for carrying the table were made of acacia wood and were overlaid with gold. **16**And they made from pure gold the articles for the table—its plates and dishes and bowls and its pitchers for the pouring out of drink offerings.

The Lampstand

17They made the lampstand of pure gold and hammered it out, base and shaft; its flower-like cups, buds and blossoms were of one piece with it. **18**Six branches extended from the sides

ᵃ**19** That is, dugongs ᵇ**21** That is, about 15 feet (about 4.5 meters) long and 2 1/4 feet (about 0.7 meter) wide ᶜ**1** That is, about 3 3/4 feet (about 1.1 meters) long and 2 1/4 feet (about 0.7 meter) wide and high ᵈ**6** That is, about 3 3/4 feet (about 1.1 meters) long and 2 1/4 feet (about 0.7 meter) wide ᵉ**10** Or *He*; also in verses 11–29 ᶠ**10** That is, about 3 feet (about 0.9 meter) long, 1 1/2 feet (about 0.5 meter) wide, and 2 1/4 feet (about 0.7 meter) high ᵍ**12** That is, about 3 inches (about 8 centimeters) of the lampstand—three on one side and three on the other. ¹⁹Three cups shaped like almond flowers with buds and blossoms were on one branch, three on the next branch and the same for all six branches extending from the lampstand. ²⁰And on the lampstand were four cups shaped like almond flowers with buds and blossoms. ²¹One bud was under the first pair of branches extending from the lampstand, a second bud under the second pair, and a third bud under the third pair—six branches in all. ²²The buds and the branches were all of one piece with the lampstand, hammered out of pure gold.

²³They made its seven lamps, as well as its wick trimmers and trays, of pure gold. ²⁴They made the lampstand and all its accessories from one talent[a] of pure gold.

The Altar of Incense

²⁵They made the altar of incense out of acacia wood. It was square, a cubit long and a cubit wide, and two cubits high[b]—its horns of one piece with it. ²⁶They overlaid the top and all the sides and the horns with pure gold, and made a gold molding around it. ²⁷They made two gold rings below the molding—two on opposite sides—to hold the poles used to carry it. ²⁸They made the poles of acacia wood and overlaid them with gold.

²⁹They also made the sacred anointing oil and the pure, fragrant incense—the work of a perfumer.

The Altar of Burnt Offering

38 They[c] built the altar of burnt offering of acacia wood, three cubits[d] high; it was square, five cubits long and five cubits wide.[e] ²They made a horn at each of the four corners, so that the horns and the altar were of one piece, and they overlaid the altar with bronze. ³They made all its utensils of bronze—its pots, shovels, sprinkling bowls, meat forks and firepans. ⁴They made a grating for the altar, a bronze network, to be under its ledge, halfway up the altar. ⁵They cast bronze rings to hold the poles for the four corners of the bronze grating. ⁶They made the poles of acacia

wood and overlaid them with bronze. ⁷They inserted the poles into the rings so they would be on the sides of the altar for carrying it. They made it hollow, out of boards.

Basin for Washing

⁸They made the bronze basin and its bronze stand from the mirrors of the women who served at the entrance to the Tent of Meeting.

The Courtyard

⁹Next they made the courtyard. The south side was a hundred cubits[f] long and had curtains of finely twisted linen, ¹⁰with twenty posts and twenty bronze bases, and with silver hooks and bands on the posts. ¹¹The north side was also a hundred cubits long and had twenty posts and twenty bronze bases, with silver hooks and bands on the posts.

¹²The west end was fifty cubits[g] wide and had curtains, with ten posts and ten bases, with silver hooks and bands on the posts. ¹³The east end, toward the sunrise, was also fifty cubits wide. ¹⁴Curtains fifteen cubits[h] long were on one side of the entrance, with three posts and three bases, ¹⁵and curtains fifteen cubits long were on the other side of the entrance to the courtyard, with three posts and three bases. ¹⁶All the curtains around the courtyard were of finely twisted linen. ¹⁷The bases for the posts were bronze. The hooks and bands on the posts were silver, and their tops were overlaid with silver; so all the posts of the courtyard had silver bands.

¹⁸The curtain for the entrance to the courtyard was of blue, purple and scarlet yarn and finely twisted linen—the work of an embroiderer. It was twenty cubits[i] long and, like the curtains of the courtyard, five cubits[j] high, ¹⁹with four posts and four bronze bases. Their hooks and bands were silver, and their tops were overlaid with silver. ²⁰All the tent pegs of the tabernacle and of the surrounding courtyard were bronze.

The Materials Used

²¹These are the amounts of the materials used for the tabernacle, the tabernacle of the

---

[a]24 That is, about 75 pounds (about 34 kilograms)   [b]25 That is, about 1 1/2 feet (about 0.5 meter) long and wide, and about 3 feet (about 0.9 meter) high   [c]1 Or He; also in verses 2–9   [d]1 That is, about 4 1/2 feet (about 1.3 meters)   [e]1 That is, about 7 1/2 feet (about 2.3 meters) long and wide   [f]9 That is, about 150 feet (about 46 meters)   [g]12 That is, about 75 feet (about 23 meters)   [h]14 That is, about 22 1/2 feet (about 6.9 meters)   [i]18 That is, about 30 feet (about 9 meters)   [j]18 That is, about 7 1/2 feet (about 2.3 meters)

Testimony, which were recorded at Moses' command by the Levites under the direction of Ithamar son of Aaron, the priest. 22(Bezalel son of Uri, the son of Hur, of the tribe of Judah, made everything the LORD commanded Moses; 23with him was Oholiab son of Ahisamach, of the tribe of Dan—a craftsman and designer, and an embroiderer in blue, purple and scarlet yarn and fine linen.) 24The total amount of the gold from the wave offering used for all the work on the sanctuary was 29 talents and 730 shekels,*a* according to the sanctuary shekel.

25The silver obtained from those of the community who were counted in the census was 100 talents and 1,775 shekels,*b* according to the sanctuary shekel— 26one beka per person, that is, half a shekel,*c* according to the sanctuary shekel, from everyone who had crossed over to those counted, twenty years old or more, a total of 603,550 men. 27The 100 talents*d* of silver were used to cast the bases for the sanctuary and for the curtain—100 bases from the 100 talents, one talent for each base. 28They used the 1,775 shekels*e* to make the hooks for the posts, to overlay the tops of the posts, and to make their bands.

29The bronze from the wave offering was 70 talents and 2,400 shekels.*f* 30They used it to make the bases for the entrance to the Tent of Meeting, the bronze altar with its bronze grating and all its utensils, 31the bases for the surrounding courtyard and those for its entrance and all the tent pegs for the tabernacle and those for the surrounding courtyard.

The Priestly Garments

39 From the blue, purple and scarlet yarn they made woven garments for ministering in the sanctuary. They also made sacred garments for Aaron, as the LORD commanded Moses.

The Ephod

2They*g* made the ephod of gold, and of blue, purple and scarlet yarn, and of finely twisted linen. 3They hammered out thin sheets of gold and cut strands to be worked into the blue, purple and scarlet yarn and fine linen—the work of a skilled craftsman. 4They made shoulder pieces for the ephod, which were attached to two of its corners, so it could be fastened. 5Its skillfully woven waistband was like it—of one piece with the ephod and made with gold, and with blue, purple and scarlet yarn, and with finely twisted linen, as the LORD commanded Moses.

6They mounted the onyx stones in gold filigree settings and engraved them like a seal with the names of the sons of Israel. 7Then they fastened them on the shoulder pieces of the ephod as memorial stones for the sons of Israel, as the LORD commanded Moses.

The Breastpiece

8They fashioned the breastpiece—the work of a skilled craftsman. They made it like the ephod: of gold, and of blue, purple and scarlet yarn, and of finely twisted linen. 9It was square—a span*h* long and a span wide—and folded double. 10Then they mounted four rows of precious stones on it. In the first row there was a ruby, a topaz and a beryl; 11in the second row a turquoise, a sapphire*i* and an emerald; 12in the third row a jacinth, an agate and an amethyst; 13in the fourth row a chrysolite, an onyx and a jasper.*j* They were mounted in gold filigree settings. 14There were twelve stones, one for each of the names of the sons of Israel, each engraved like a seal with the name of one of the twelve tribes.

15For the breastpiece they made braided chains of pure gold, like a rope. 16They made two gold filigree settings and two gold rings, and fastened the rings to two of the corners of the breastpiece. 17They fastened the two gold chains to the rings at the corners of the breastpiece, 18and the other ends of the chains to the two settings, attaching them to the shoulder pieces of the ephod at the front. 19They made two gold rings and attached them to the other two corners of the breastpiece on the inside edge next to the ephod. 20Then they made two more gold rings and attached them to the bottom of the shoulder pieces on the front of the ephod, close to the seam just above the waist-

---

*a*24 The weight of the gold was a little over one ton (about 1 metric ton).   *b*25 The weight of the silver was a little over 3 3/4 tons (about 3.4 metric tons).   *c*26 That is, about 1/5 ounce (about 5.5 grams)   *d*27 That is, about 3 3/4 tons (about 3.4 metric tons)   *e*28 That is, about 45 pounds (about 20 kilograms)   *f*29 The weight of the bronze was about 2 1/2 tons (about 2.4 metric tons).   *g*2 Or *He*; also in verses 7, 8 and 22   *h*9 That is, about 9 inches (about 22 centimeters)   *i*11 Or *lapis lazuli*   *j*13 The precise identification of some of these precious stones is uncertain.

band of the ephod. [21]They tied the rings of the breastpiece to the rings of the ephod with blue cord, connecting it to the waistband so that the breastpiece would not swing out from the ephod—as the LORD commanded Moses.

Other Priestly Garments

[22]They made the robe of the ephod entirely of blue cloth—the work of a weaver— [23]with an opening in the center of the robe like the opening of a collar,[a] and a band around this opening, so that it would not tear. [24]They made pomegranates of blue, purple and scarlet yarn and finely twisted linen around the hem of the robe. [25]And they made bells of pure gold and attached them around the hem between the pomegranates. [26]The bells and pomegranates alternated around the hem of the robe to be worn for ministering, as the LORD commanded Moses.

[27]For Aaron and his sons, they made tunics of fine linen—the work of a weaver— [28]and the turban of fine linen, the linen headbands and the undergarments of finely twisted linen. [29]The sash was of finely twisted linen and blue, purple and scarlet yarn—the work of an embroiderer— as the LORD commanded Moses.

[30]They made the plate, the sacred diadem, out of pure gold and engraved on it, like an inscription on a seal: HOLY TO THE LORD. [31]Then they fastened a blue cord to it to attach it to the turban, as the LORD commanded Moses.

Moses Inspects the Tabernacle

[32]So all the work on the tabernacle, the Tent of Meeting, was completed. The Israelites did everything just as the LORD commanded Moses. [33]Then they brought the tabernacle to Moses: the tent and all its furnishings, its clasps, frames, crossbars, posts and bases; [34]the covering of ram skins dyed red, the covering of hides of sea cows[b] and the shielding curtain; [35]the ark of the Testimony with its poles and the atonement cover; [36]the table with all its articles and the bread of the Presence; [37]the pure gold lampstand with its row of lamps and all its accessories, and the oil for the light; [38]the gold altar, the anointing oil, the fragrant incense, and the curtain for the entrance to the tent; [39]the bronze altar with its bronze grating,

its poles and all its utensils; the basin with its stand; [40]the curtains of the courtyard with its posts and bases, and the curtain for the entrance to the courtyard; the ropes and tent pegs for the courtyard; all the furnishings for the tabernacle, the Tent of Meeting; [41]and the woven garments worn for ministering in the sanctuary, both the sacred garments for Aaron the priest and the garments for his sons when serving as priests.

[42]The Israelites had done all the work just as the LORD had commanded Moses. [43]Moses inspected the work and saw that they had done it just as the LORD had commanded. So Moses blessed them.

Setting Up the Tabernacle

40 Then the LORD said to Moses: [2]"Set up the tabernacle, the Tent of Meeting, on the first day of the first month. [3]Place the ark of the Testimony in it and shield the ark with the curtain. [4]Bring in the table and set out what belongs on it. Then bring in the lampstand and set up its lamps. [5]Place the gold altar of incense in front of the ark of the Testimony and put the curtain at the entrance to the tabernacle.

[6]"Place the altar of burnt offering in front of the entrance to the tabernacle, the Tent of Meeting; [7]place the basin between the Tent of Meeting and the altar and put water in it. [8]Set up the courtyard around it and put the curtain at the entrance to the courtyard.

[9]"Take the anointing oil and anoint the tabernacle and everything in it; consecrate it and all its furnishings, and it will be holy. [10]Then anoint the altar of burnt offering and all its utensils; consecrate the altar, and it will be most holy. [11]Anoint the basin and its stand and consecrate them.

[12]"Bring Aaron and his sons to the entrance to the Tent of Meeting and wash them with water. [13]Then dress Aaron in the sacred garments, anoint him and consecrate him so he may serve me as priest. [14]Bring his sons and dress them in tunics. [15]Anoint them just as you anointed their father, so they may serve me as priests. Their anointing will be to a priesthood that will continue for all generations to come." [16]Moses did everything just as the LORD commanded him.

---

[a]23 The meaning of the Hebrew for this word is uncertain.   [b]34 That is, dugongs

¹⁷So the tabernacle was set up on the first day of the first month in the second year. ¹⁸When Moses set up the tabernacle, he put the bases in place, erected the frames, inserted the crossbars and set up the posts. ¹⁹Then he spread the tent over the tabernacle and put the covering over the tent, as the LORD commanded him.

²⁰He took the Testimony and placed it in the ark, attached the poles to the ark and put the atonement cover over it. ²¹Then he brought the ark into the tabernacle and hung the shielding curtain and shielded the ark of the Testimony, as the LORD commanded him.

²²Moses placed the table in the Tent of Meeting on the north side of the tabernacle outside the curtain ²³and set out the bread on it before the LORD, as the LORD commanded him.

²⁴He placed the lampstand in the Tent of Meeting opposite the table on the south side of the tabernacle ²⁵and set up the lamps before the LORD, as the LORD commanded him.

²⁶Moses placed the gold altar in the Tent of Meeting in front of the curtain ²⁷and burned fragrant incense on it, as the LORD commanded him. ²⁸Then he put up the curtain at the entrance to the tabernacle.

²⁹He set the altar of burnt offering near the entrance to the tabernacle, the Tent of Meeting, and offered on it burnt offerings and grain offerings, as the LORD commanded him.

³⁰He placed the basin between the Tent of Meeting and the altar and put water in it for washing, ³¹and Moses and Aaron and his sons used it to wash their hands and feet. ³²They washed whenever they entered the Tent of Meeting or approached the altar, as the LORD commanded Moses.

³³Then Moses set up the courtyard around the tabernacle and altar and put up the curtain at the entrance to the courtyard. And so Moses finished the work.

The Glory of the LORD

³⁴Then the cloud covered the Tent of Meeting, and the glory of the LORD filled the tabernacle. ³⁵Moses could not enter the Tent of Meeting because the cloud had settled upon it, and the glory of the LORD filled the tabernacle.

³⁶In all the travels of the Israelites, whenever the cloud lifted from above the tabernacle, they would set out; ³⁷but if the cloud did not lift, they did not set out—until the day it lifted. ³⁸So the cloud of the LORD was over the tabernacle by day, and fire was in the cloud by night, in the sight of all the house of Israel during all their travels.

Exodus 40:38

God Remains With Us

So the cloud of the LORD was over the tabernacle by day, and fire was in the cloud by night, in the sight of all the house of Israel during all their travels.

Leviticus

Author:
Moses.

Audience:
The people of Israel.

Date:
During the 1400s B.C., while the Israelites were traveling in the desert.

Setting:
At the foot of Mount Sinai, God introduces laws for living.

Verse to Remember:
"I am the LORD who brought you up out of Egypt to be your God; therefore be holy, because I am holy." (11:45)

God's holiness demands purity, yet human perfection is impossible to attain. God provided a perfect sacrifice for sin in *Jesus Christ*, but until he arrived, the Law demanded continual sacrifices as the means by which God's people recognized their sinfulness and their need for repentance. The Law demanded that animals with no known blemishes be sacrificed, but animal sacrifices could never take away sin.

Leviticus is a book focused on holiness.

From the laws of personal hygiene to the scapegoat that was allowed to live while a second goat was killed, the book highlights the need for personal and moral purity of God's people— and it describes the provisions to deal with the inevitable lack of purity. Notice how costly sin was and how seriously it was treated. But notice, too, that *God provides a way* for his people to come to him.

The Burnt Offering

1 The LORD called to Moses and spoke to him from the Tent of Meeting. He said, ²"Speak to the Israelites and say to them: 'When any of you brings an offering to the LORD, bring as your offering an animal from either the herd or the flock.

³"'If the offering is a burnt offering from the herd, he is to offer a male without defect. He must present it at the entrance to the Tent of Meeting so that it*ᵃ* will be acceptable to the LORD. ⁴He is to lay his hand on the head of the burnt offering, and it will be accepted on his behalf to make atonement for him. ⁵He is to slaughter the young bull before the LORD, and then Aaron's sons the priests shall bring the

ᵃ3 Or he

blood and sprinkle it against the altar on all sides at the entrance to the Tent of Meeting. ⁶He is to skin the burnt offering and cut it into pieces. ⁷The sons of Aaron the priest are to put fire on the altar and arrange wood on the fire. ⁸Then Aaron's sons the priests shall arrange the pieces, including the head and the fat, on the burning wood that is on the altar. ⁹He is to wash the inner parts and the legs with water, and the priest is to burn all of it on the altar. It is a burnt offering, an offering made by fire, an aroma pleasing to the LORD.

¹⁰"If the offering is a burnt offering from the flock, from either the sheep or the goats, he is to offer a male without defect. ¹¹He is to slaughter it at the north side of the altar before the LORD, and Aaron's sons the priests shall sprinkle its blood against the altar on all sides. ¹²He is to cut it into pieces, and the priest shall arrange them, including the head and the fat, on the burning wood that is on the altar. ¹³He is to wash the inner parts and the legs with water, and the priest is to bring all of it and burn it on the altar. It is a burnt offering, an offering made by fire, an aroma pleasing to the LORD.

¹⁴"If the offering to the LORD is a burnt offering of birds, he is to offer a dove or a young pigeon. ¹⁵The priest shall bring it to the altar, wring off the head and burn it on the altar; its blood shall be drained out on the side of the altar. ¹⁶He is to remove the crop with its contents[a] and throw it to the east side of the altar, where the ashes are. ¹⁷He shall tear it open by the wings, not severing it completely, and then the priest shall burn it on the wood that is on the fire on the altar. It is a burnt offering, an offering made by fire, an aroma pleasing to the LORD.

The Grain Offering

2 "'When someone brings a grain offering to the LORD, his offering is to be of fine flour. He is to pour oil on it, put incense on it ²and take it to Aaron's sons the priests. The priest shall take a handful of the fine flour and oil, together with all the incense, and burn this as a memorial portion on the altar, an offering made by fire, an aroma pleasing to the LORD. ³The rest of the grain offering belongs to Aaron and his sons; it is a most holy part of the offerings made to the LORD by fire.

⁴"'If you bring a grain offering baked in an oven, it is to consist of fine flour: cakes made without yeast and mixed with oil, or[b] wafers made without yeast and spread with oil. ⁵If your grain offering is prepared on a griddle, it is to be made of fine flour mixed with oil, and without yeast. ⁶Crumble it and pour oil on it; it is a grain offering. ⁷If your grain offering is cooked in a pan, it is to be made of fine flour and oil. ⁸Bring the grain offering made of these things to the LORD; present it to the priest, who shall take it to the altar. ⁹He shall take out the memorial portion from the grain offering and burn it on the altar as an offering made by fire, an aroma pleasing to the LORD. ¹⁰The rest of the grain offering belongs to Aaron and his sons; it is a most holy part of the offerings made to the LORD by fire.

¹¹"'Every grain offering you bring to the LORD must be made without yeast, for you are not to burn any yeast or honey in an offering made to the LORD by fire. ¹²You may bring them to the LORD as an offering of the first-fruits, but they are not to be offered on the altar as a pleasing aroma. ¹³Season all your grain offerings with salt. Do not leave the salt of the covenant of your God out of your grain offerings; add salt to all your offerings.

¹⁴"'If you bring a grain offering of firstfruits to the LORD, offer crushed heads of new grain roasted in the fire. ¹⁵Put oil and incense on it; it is a grain offering. ¹⁶The priest shall burn the memorial portion of the crushed grain and the oil, together with all the incense, as an offering made to the LORD by fire.

The Fellowship Offering

3 "'If someone's offering is a fellowship offering,[c] and he offers an animal from the herd, whether male or female, he is to present

Leviticus 1:1

God Speaks

The LORD called to Moses and spoke to him from the Tent of Meeting.

---

a16 Or *crop and the feathers*; the meaning of the Hebrew for this word is uncertain.   b4 Or *and*   c1 Traditionally *peace offering*; also in verses 3, 6 and 9 before the LORD an animal without defect. ²He is to lay his hand on the head of his offering and slaughter it at the entrance to the Tent of Meeting. Then Aaron's sons the priests shall sprinkle the blood against the altar on all sides. ³From the fellowship offering he is to bring a sacrifice made to the LORD by fire: all the fat that covers the inner parts or is connected to them, ⁴both kidneys with the fat on them near the loins, and the covering of the liver, which he will remove with the kidneys. ⁵Then Aaron's sons are to burn it on the altar on top of the burnt offering that is on the burning wood, as an offering made by fire, an aroma pleasing to the LORD.

⁶"If he offers an animal from the flock as a fellowship offering to the LORD, he is to offer a male or female without defect. ⁷If he offers a lamb, he is to present it before the LORD. ⁸He is to lay his hand on the head of his offering and slaughter it in front of the Tent of Meeting. Then Aaron's sons shall sprinkle its blood against the altar on all sides. ⁹From the fellowship offering he is to bring a sacrifice made to the LORD by fire: its fat, the entire fat tail cut off close to the backbone, all the fat that covers the inner parts or is connected to them, ¹⁰both kidneys with the fat on them near the loins, and the covering of the liver, which he will remove with the kidneys. ¹¹The priest shall burn them on the altar as food, an offering made to the LORD by fire.

¹²"If his offering is a goat, he is to present it before the LORD. ¹³He is to lay his hand on its head and slaughter it in front of the Tent of Meeting. Then Aaron's sons shall sprinkle its blood against the altar on all sides. ¹⁴From what he offers he is to make this offering to the LORD by fire: all the fat that covers the inner parts or is connected to them, ¹⁵both kidneys with the fat on them near the loins, and the covering of the liver, which he will remove with the kidneys. ¹⁶The priest shall burn them on the al-

tar as food, an offering made by fire, a pleasing aroma. All the fat is the LORD's.

¹⁷"'This is a lasting ordinance for the generations to come, wherever you live: You must not eat any fat or any blood.'"

The Sin Offering

4 The LORD said to Moses, ²"Say to the Israelites: 'When anyone sins unintentionally and does what is forbidden in any of the LORD's commands—

³"'If the anointed priest sins, bringing guilt on the people, he must bring to the LORD a young bull without defect as a sin offering for the sin he has committed. ⁴He is to present the bull at the entrance to the Tent of Meeting before the LORD. He is to lay his hand on its head and slaughter it before the LORD. ⁵Then the anointed priest shall take some of the bull's blood and carry it into the Tent of Meeting. ⁶He is to dip his finger into the blood and sprinkle some of it seven times before the LORD, in front of the curtain of the sanctuary. ⁷The priest shall then put some of the blood on the horns of the altar of fragrant incense that is before the LORD in the Tent of Meeting. The rest of the bull's blood he shall pour out at the base of the altar of burnt offering at the entrance to the Tent of Meeting. ⁸He shall remove all the fat from the bull of the sin offering—the fat that covers the inner parts or is connected to them, ⁹both kidneys with the fat on them near the loins, and the covering of the liver, which he will remove with the kidneys— ¹⁰just as the fat is removed from the ox*a* sacrificed as a fellowship offering.*b* Then the priest shall burn them on the altar of burnt offering. ¹¹But the hide of the bull and all its flesh, as well as the head and legs, the inner parts and offal— ¹²that is, all the rest of the bull—he must take outside the camp to a place ceremonially clean, where the ashes are thrown, and burn it in a wood fire on the ash heap.

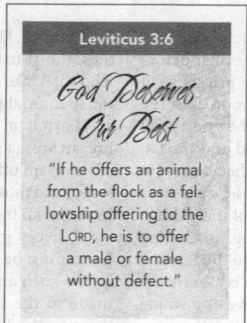

Leviticus 3:6

God Deserves Our Best

"If he offers an animal from the flock as a fellowship offering to the LORD, he is to offer a male or female without defect."

---

*a*10 The Hebrew word can include both male and female.   *b*10 Traditionally *peace offering*; also in verses 26, 31 and 35

13 "'If the whole Israelite community sins unintentionally and does what is forbidden in any of the LORD's commands, even though the community is unaware of the matter, they are guilty. 14When they become aware of the sin they committed, the assembly must bring a young bull as a sin offering and present it before the Tent of Meeting. 15The elders of the community are to lay their hands on the bull's head before the LORD, and the bull shall be slaughtered before the LORD. 16Then the anointed priest is to take some of the bull's blood into the Tent of Meeting. 17He shall dip his finger into the blood and sprinkle it before the LORD seven times in front of the curtain. 18He is to put some of the blood on the horns of the altar that is before the LORD in the Tent of Meeting. The rest of the blood he shall pour out at the base of the altar of burnt offering at the entrance to the Tent of Meeting. 19He shall remove all the fat from it and burn it on the altar, 20and do with this bull just as he did with the bull for the sin offering. In this way the priest will make atonement for them, and they will be forgiven. 21Then he shall take the bull outside the camp and burn it as he burned the first bull. This is the sin offering for the community.

22 "'When a leader sins unintentionally and does what is forbidden in any of the commands of the LORD his God, he is guilty. 23When he is made aware of the sin he committed, he must bring as his offering a male goat without defect. 24He is to lay his hand on the goat's head and slaughter it at the place where the burnt offering is slaughtered before the LORD. It is a sin offering. 25Then the priest shall take some of the blood of the sin offering with his finger and put it on the horns of the altar of burnt offering and pour out the rest of the blood at the base of the altar. 26He shall burn all the fat on the altar as he burned the fat of the fellowship offering. In this way the priest will make atonement for the man's sin, and he will be forgiven.

27 "'If a member of the community sins unintentionally and does what is forbidden in any of the LORD's commands, he is guilty. 28When he is made aware of the sin he committed, he must bring as his offering for the sin he committed a female goat without defect. 29He is to lay his hand on the head of the sin offering and slaughter it at the place of the burnt offering. 30Then the priest is to take some of the blood with his finger and put it on the horns of the altar of burnt offering and pour out the rest of the blood at the base of the altar. 31He shall remove all the fat, just as the fat is removed from the fellowship offering, and the priest shall burn it on the altar as an aroma pleasing to the LORD. In this way the priest will make atonement for him, and he will be forgiven.

32 "'If he brings a lamb as his sin offering, he is to bring a female without defect. 33He is to lay his hand on its head and slaughter it for a sin offering at the place where the burnt offering is slaughtered. 34Then the priest shall take some of the blood of the sin offering with his finger and put it on the horns of the altar of burnt offering and pour out the rest of the blood at the base of the altar. 35He shall remove all the fat, just as the fat is removed from the lamb of the fellowship offering, and the priest shall burn it on the altar on top of the offerings made to the LORD by fire. In this way the priest will make atonement for him for the sin he has committed, and he will be forgiven.

5 "'If a person sins because he does not speak up when he hears a public charge to testify regarding something he has seen or learned about, he will be held responsible.

2 "'Or if a person touches anything ceremonially unclean—whether the carcasses of unclean wild animals or of unclean livestock or of unclean creatures that move along the ground—even though he is unaware of it, he has become unclean and is guilty.

3 "'Or if he touches human uncleanness—anything that would make him unclean—even

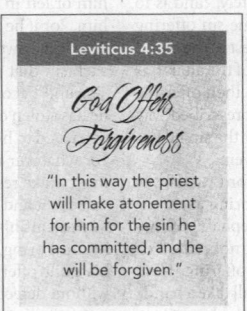

Leviticus 4:35

God Offers Forgiveness

"In this way the priest will make atonement for him for the sin he has committed, and he will be forgiven."

though he is unaware of it, when he learns of it he will be guilty.

⁴ "'Or if a person thoughtlessly takes an oath to do anything, whether good or evil—in any matter one might carelessly swear about—even though he is unaware of it, in any case when he learns of it he will be guilty.

⁵ "'When anyone is guilty in any of these ways, he must confess in what way he has sinned ⁶ and, as a penalty for the sin he has committed, he must bring to the LORD a female lamb or goat from the flock as a sin offering; and the priest shall make atonement for him for his sin.

⁷ "'If he cannot afford a lamb, he is to bring two doves or two young pigeons to the LORD as a penalty for his sin—one for a sin offering and the other for a burnt offering. ⁸ He is to bring them to the priest, who shall first offer the one for the sin offering. He is to wring its head from its neck, not severing it completely, ⁹ and is to sprinkle some of the blood of the sin offering against the side of the altar; the rest of the blood must be drained out at the base of the altar. It is a sin offering. ¹⁰ The priest shall then offer the other as a burnt offering in the prescribed way and make atonement for him for the sin he has committed, and he will be forgiven.

¹¹ "'If, however, he cannot afford two doves or two young pigeons, he is to bring as an offering for his sin a tenth of an ephah[a] of fine flour for a sin offering. He must not put oil or incense on it, because it is a sin offering. ¹² He is to bring it to the priest, who shall take a handful of it as a memorial portion and burn it on the altar on top of the offerings made to the LORD by fire. It is a sin offering. ¹³ In this way the priest will make atonement for him for any of these sins he has committed, and he will be forgiven. The rest of the offering will belong to the priest, as in the case of the grain offering.'"

The Guilt Offering

¹⁴ The LORD said to Moses: ¹⁵ "When a person commits a violation and sins unintentionally in regard to any of the LORD's holy things, he is to bring to the LORD as a penalty a ram from the flock, one without defect and of the proper value in silver, according to the sanctuary

shekel.[b] It is a guilt offering. ¹⁶ He must make restitution for what he has failed to do in regard to the holy things, add a fifth of the value to that and give it all to the priest, who will make atonement for him with the ram as a guilt offering, and he will be forgiven.

¹⁷ "If a person sins and does what is forbidden in any of the LORD's commands, even though he does not know it, he is guilty and will be held responsible. ¹⁸ He is to bring to the priest as a guilt offering a ram from the flock, one without defect and of the proper value. In this way the priest will make atonement for him for the wrong he has committed unintentionally, and he will be forgiven. ¹⁹ It is a guilt offering; he has been guilty of[c] wrongdoing against the LORD."

6 The LORD said to Moses: ² "If anyone sins and is unfaithful to the LORD by deceiving his neighbor about something entrusted to him or left in his care or stolen, or if he cheats him, ³ or if he finds lost property and lies about it, or if he swears falsely, or if he commits any such sin that people may do— ⁴ when he thus sins and becomes guilty, he must return what he has stolen or taken by extortion, or what was entrusted to him, or the lost property he found, ⁵ or whatever it was he swore falsely about. He must make restitution in full, add a fifth of the value to it and give it all to the owner on the day he presents his guilt offering. ⁶ And as a penalty he must bring to the priest, that is, to the LORD, his guilt offering, a ram from the flock, one without defect and of the proper value. ⁷ In this way the priest will make atonement for him before the LORD, and he will be forgiven for any of these things he did that made him guilty."

The Burnt Offering

⁸ The LORD said to Moses: ⁹ "Give Aaron and his sons this command: 'These are the regulations for the burnt offering: The burnt offering is to remain on the altar hearth throughout the night, till morning, and the fire must be kept burning on the altar. ¹⁰ The priest shall then put on his linen clothes, with linen undergarments next to his body, and shall remove the ashes of the burnt offering that the fire has consumed on the altar and place them beside the altar.

---

[a]11 That is, probably about 2 quarts (about 2 liters)   [b]15 That is, about 2/5 ounce (about 11.5 grams)   [c]19 Or *has made full expiation for his*

Not Guilty

Read: Leviticus 5:14–19

ISN'T IT PAINFUL to harm others intentionally? Premeditated evils can be set right by our finite sense of justice, even if guilt then rests on our own head. But imagine the fear and frustration of being held accountable for hundreds of violations that you committed without knowing it. Nothing you ever did would be good enough; you would carry around the guilt of wrongs you never intended to commit. Talk about paranoia.

Yet in Old Testament times, you would certainly have been guilty of such unwitting sins, and they would have required blood sacrifice. The Law of God was clear: no one could be good enough, not even those who sinned without awareness, unintentionally. Few of us think of sin in these terms today, but God remains the same. His standard of perfection cannot be attained, even by the best of us on our best day.

The sacrifices of the Old Testament foreshadowed the ultimate sacrifice: Jesus Christ. When Jesus offered himself on the cross, he paid the debt of sin in full. He declared his followers "not guilty." The law was fulfilled. We no longer need the sacrifice of a ram to cleanse us from the sins we knowingly commit or the sins we unintentionally commit. No other blood sacrifice will ever be required.

Women today are often burdened by guilt. We are inundated with "shoulds" and "oughts." We feel guilty if we work; guilty if we don't; guilty for not spending enough time with our husband, kids and friends; and guilty for not taking time for God and ourselves. We have a hard time knowing when we're really guilty and when we suffer from false guilt. But Jesus' declaration from the cross that we are not guilty covers all of our sins—even the unintentional ones. Instead of blood sacrifice, we can make offerings of gratitude: repentance, praise and service.

We all both unintentionally and intentionally wrong God and others. But Jesus Christ bought our forgiveness on the cross. Offer him the sacrifice of confession, and you'll be covered for overlooking the things you should have done and the things you ought not have. Then pour out the sacrifice of praise. Present the sacrifice of service, helping others in God's name, for "love covers over a multitude of sins" (1 Peter 4:8). Despair has no place here; our advocate perfectly kept even the hidden laws.

Monday

Go to page 130 for your next devotional reading.

Leviticus 5:18

"He is to bring to the priest as a guilt offering a ram from the flock, one without defect and of the proper value. In this way the priest will make atonement for him for the wrong he has committed unintentionally, and he will be forgiven."

reflection

1 What unintentional sins have you committed in the past few days? Spend some time asking God to reveal your sins to you.

2 Now offer God a sacrifice of repentance and of praise for declaring you not guilty.

3 Whom can you serve sacrificially? How will you go about this?

RELATED READINGS

Psalm 139:23–24;
Proverbs 28:13;
Isaiah 55:6–7;
Hebrews 8:8–12

125

11Then he is to take off these clothes and put on others, and carry the ashes outside the camp to a place that is ceremonially clean. 12The fire on the altar must be kept burning; it must not go out. Every morning the priest is to add firewood and arrange the burnt offering on the fire and burn the fat of the fellowship offerings*a* on it. 13The fire must be kept burning on the altar continuously; it must not go out.

The Grain Offering

14"'These are the regulations for the grain offering: Aaron's sons are to bring it before the LORD, in front of the altar. 15The priest is to take a handful of fine flour and oil, together with all the incense on the grain offering, and burn the memorial portion on the altar as an aroma pleasing to the LORD. 16Aaron and his sons shall eat the rest of it, but it is to be eaten without yeast in a holy place; they are to eat it in the courtyard of the Tent of Meeting. 17It must not be baked with yeast; I have given it as their share of the offerings made to me by fire. Like the sin offering and the guilt offering, it is most holy. 18Any male descendant of Aaron may eat it. It is his regular share of the offerings made to the LORD by fire for the generations to come. Whatever touches them will become holy.*b*' "

19The LORD also said to Moses, 20"This is the offering Aaron and his sons are to bring to the LORD on the day he*c* is anointed: a tenth of an ephah*d* of fine flour as a regular grain offering, half of it in the morning and half in the evening. 21Prepare it with oil on a griddle; bring it well-mixed and present the grain offering broken*e* in pieces as an aroma pleasing to the LORD. 22The son who is to succeed him as anointed priest shall prepare it. It is the LORD's regular share and is to be burned completely. 23Every grain offering of a priest shall be burned completely; it must not be eaten."

The Sin Offering

24The LORD said to Moses, 25"Say to Aaron and his sons: 'These are the regulations for the sin offering: The sin offering is to be slaughtered before the LORD in the place the burnt offering is slaughtered; it is most holy. 26The priest who offers it shall eat it; it is to be eaten in a holy place, in the courtyard of the Tent of Meeting. 27Whatever touches any of the flesh will become holy, and if any of the blood is spattered on a garment, you must wash it in a holy place. 28The clay pot the meat is cooked in must be broken; but if it is cooked in a bronze pot, the pot is to be scoured and rinsed with water. 29Any male in a priest's family may eat it; it is most holy. 30But any sin offering whose blood is brought into the Tent of Meeting to make atonement in the Holy Place must not be eaten; it must be burned.

The Guilt Offering

7 "'These are the regulations for the guilt offering, which is most holy: 2The guilt offering is to be slaughtered in the place where the burnt offering is slaughtered, and its blood is to be sprinkled against the altar on all sides. 3All its fat shall be offered: the fat tail and the fat that covers the inner parts, 4both kidneys with the fat on them near the loins, and the covering of the liver, which is to be removed with the kidneys. 5The priest shall burn them on the altar as an offering made to the LORD by fire. It is a guilt offering. 6Any male in a priest's family may eat it, but it must be eaten in a holy place; it is most holy.

7"'The same law applies to both the sin offering and the guilt offering: They belong to the priest who makes atonement with them. 8The priest who offers a burnt offering for anyone may keep its hide for himself. 9Every grain offering baked in an oven or cooked in a pan or on a griddle belongs to the priest who offers it, 10and every grain offering, whether mixed with oil or dry, belongs equally to all the sons of Aaron.

The Fellowship Offering

11"'These are the regulations for the fellowship offering*f* a person may present to the LORD:

12"'If he offers it as an expression of thankfulness, then along with this thank offering he is to offer cakes of bread made without yeast and mixed with oil, wafers made without yeast and

---

*a*12 Traditionally *peace offerings*   *b*18 Or *Whoever touches them must be holy*; similarly in verse 27   *c*20 Or *each*   *d*20 That is, probably about 2 quarts (about 2 liters)   *e*21 The meaning of the Hebrew for this word is uncertain.   *f*11 Traditionally *peace offering*; also in verses 13–37 spread with oil, and cakes of fine flour well-kneaded and mixed with oil. ¹³Along with his fellowship offering of thanksgiving he is to present an offering with cakes of bread made with yeast. ¹⁴He is to bring one of each kind as an offering, a contribution to the LORD; it belongs to the priest who sprinkles the blood of the fellowship offerings. ¹⁵The meat of his fellowship offering of thanksgiving must be eaten on the day it is offered; he must leave none of it till morning.

¹⁶"If, however, his offering is the result of a vow or is a freewill offering, the sacrifice shall be eaten on the day he offers it, but anything left over may be eaten on the next day. ¹⁷Any meat of the sacrifice left over till the third day must be burned up. ¹⁸If any meat of the fellowship offering is eaten on the third day, it will not be accepted. It will not be credited to the one who offered it, for it is impure; the person who eats any of it will be held responsible.

¹⁹"Meat that touches anything ceremonially unclean must not be eaten; it must be burned up. As for other meat, anyone ceremonially clean may eat it. ²⁰But if anyone who is unclean eats any meat of the fellowship offering belonging to the LORD, that person must be cut off from his people. ²¹If anyone touches something unclean—whether human uncleanness or an unclean animal or any unclean, detestable thing—and then eats any of the meat of the fellowship offering belonging to the LORD, that person must be cut off from his people.'"

Eating Fat and Blood Forbidden

²²The LORD said to Moses, ²³"Say to the Israelites: 'Do not eat any of the fat of cattle, sheep or goats. ²⁴The fat of an animal found dead or torn by wild animals may be used for any other purpose, but you must not eat it. ²⁵Anyone who eats the fat of an animal from which an offering by fire may be[a] made to the LORD must be cut off from his people. ²⁶And wherever you live, you must not eat the blood of any bird or animal. ²⁷If anyone eats blood, that person must be cut off from his people.'"

The Priests' Share

²⁸The LORD said to Moses, ²⁹"Say to the Israelites: 'Anyone who brings a fellowship offering to the LORD is to bring part of it as his sacrifice to the LORD. ³⁰With his own hands he is to bring the offering made to the LORD by fire; he is to bring the fat, together with the breast, and wave the breast before the LORD as a wave offering. ³¹The priest shall burn the fat on the altar, but the breast belongs to Aaron and his sons. ³²You are to give the right thigh of your fellowship offerings to the priest as a contribution. ³³The son of Aaron who offers the blood and the fat of the fellowship offering shall have the right thigh as his share. ³⁴From the fellowship offerings of the Israelites, I have taken the breast that is waved and the thigh that is presented and have given them to Aaron the priest and his sons as their regular share from the Israelites.'"

³⁵This is the portion of the offerings made to the LORD by fire that were allotted to Aaron and his sons on the day they were presented to serve the LORD as priests. ³⁶On the day they were anointed, the LORD commanded that the Israelites give this to them as their regular share for the generations to come.

³⁷These, then, are the regulations for the burnt offering, the grain offering, the sin offering, the guilt offering, the ordination offering and the fellowship offering, ³⁸which the LORD gave Moses on Mount Sinai on the day he commanded the Israelites to bring their offerings to the LORD, in the Desert of Sinai.

The Ordination of Aaron and His Sons

8 The LORD said to Moses, ²"Bring Aaron and his sons, their garments, the anointing oil, the bull for the sin offering, the two rams and the basket containing bread made without yeast, ³and gather the entire assembly at the entrance to the Tent of Meeting." ⁴Moses did as the LORD commanded him, and the assembly gathered at the entrance to the Tent of Meeting.

⁵Moses said to the assembly, "This is what the LORD has commanded to be done." ⁶Then Moses brought Aaron and his sons forward and washed them with water. ⁷He put the tunic on Aaron, tied the sash around him, clothed him with the robe and put the ephod on him. He also tied the ephod to him by its skillfully

a25 Or *fire is*

woven waistband; so it was fastened on him. [8]He placed the breastpiece on him and put the Urim and Thummim in the breastpiece. [9]Then he placed the turban on Aaron's head and set the gold plate, the sacred diadem, on the front of it, as the Lord commanded Moses.

[10]Then Moses took the anointing oil and anointed the tabernacle and everything in it, and so consecrated them. [11]He sprinkled some of the oil on the altar seven times, anointing the altar and all its utensils and the basin with its stand, to consecrate them. [12]He poured some of the anointing oil on Aaron's head and anointed him to consecrate him. [13]Then he brought Aaron's sons forward, put tunics on them, tied sashes around them and put headbands on them, as the Lord commanded Moses.

[14]He then presented the bull for the sin offering, and Aaron and his sons laid their hands on its head. [15]Moses slaughtered the bull and took some of the blood, and with his finger he put it on all the horns of the altar to purify the altar. He poured out the rest of the blood at the base of the altar. So he consecrated it to make atonement for it. [16]Moses also took all the fat around the inner parts, the covering of the liver, and both kidneys and their fat, and burned it on the altar. [17]But the bull with its hide and its flesh and its offal he burned up outside the camp, as the Lord commanded Moses.

[18]He then presented the ram for the burnt offering, and Aaron and his sons laid their hands on its head. [19]Then Moses slaughtered the ram and sprinkled the blood against the altar on all sides. [20]He cut the ram into pieces and burned the head, the pieces and the fat. [21]He washed the inner parts and the legs with water and burned the whole ram on the altar as a burnt offering, a pleasing aroma, an offering made to the Lord by fire, as the Lord commanded Moses.

[22]He then presented the other ram, the ram for the ordination, and Aaron and his sons laid their hands on its head. [23]Moses slaughtered the ram and took some of its blood and put it on the lobe of Aaron's right ear, on the thumb of his right hand and on the big toe of his right foot. [24]Moses also brought Aaron's sons forward and put some of the blood on the lobes

of their right ears, on the thumbs of their right hands and on the big toes of their right feet. Then he sprinkled blood against the altar on all sides. [25]He took the fat, the fat tail, all the fat around the inner parts, the covering of the liver, both kidneys and their fat and the right thigh. [26]Then from the basket of bread made without yeast, which was before the Lord, he took a cake of bread, and one made with oil, and a wafer; he put these on the fat portions and on the right thigh. [27]He put all these in the hands of Aaron and his sons and waved them before the Lord as a wave offering. [28]Then Moses took them from their hands and burned them on the altar on top of the burnt offering as an ordination offering, a pleasing aroma, an offering made to the Lord by fire. [29]He also took the breast—Moses' share of the ordination ram—and waved it before the Lord as a wave offering, as the Lord commanded Moses.

[30]Then Moses took some of the anointing oil and some of the blood from the altar and sprinkled them on Aaron and his garments and on his sons and their garments. So he consecrated Aaron and his garments and his sons and their garments.

[31]Moses then said to Aaron and his sons, "Cook the meat at the entrance to the Tent of Meeting and eat it there with the bread from the basket of ordination offerings, as I commanded, saying,[a] 'Aaron and his sons are to eat it.' [32]Then burn up the rest of the meat and the bread. [33]Do not leave the entrance to the Tent of Meeting for seven days, until the days of your ordination are completed, for your ordination will last seven days. [34]What has been done today was commanded by the Lord to make atonement for you. [35]You must stay at the entrance to the Tent of Meeting day and night for seven days and do what the Lord requires, so you will not die; for that is what I have been commanded." [36]So Aaron and his sons did everything the Lord commanded through Moses.

The Priests Begin Their Ministry

9 On the eighth day Moses summoned Aaron and his sons and the elders of Israel. [2]He said to Aaron, "Take a bull calf for

---

[a]31 Or I was commanded:

your sin offering and a ram for your burnt offering, both without defect, and present them before the Lord. ³Then say to the Israelites: 'Take a male goat for a sin offering, a calf and a lamb—both a year old and without defect—for a burnt offering, ⁴and an ox^a and a ram for a fellowship offering^b to sacrifice before the Lord, together with a grain offering mixed with oil. For today the Lord will appear to you.'"

⁵They took the things Moses commanded to the front of the Tent of Meeting, and the entire assembly came near and stood before the Lord. ⁶Then Moses said, "This is what the Lord has commanded you to do, so that the glory of the Lord may appear to you."

⁷Moses said to Aaron, "Come to the altar and sacrifice your sin offering and your burnt offering and make atonement for yourself and the people; sacrifice the offering that is for the people and make atonement for them, as the Lord has commanded."

⁸So Aaron came to the altar and slaughtered the calf as a sin offering for himself. ⁹His sons brought the blood to him, and he dipped his finger into the blood and put it on the horns of the altar; the rest of the blood he poured out at the base of the altar. ¹⁰On the altar he burned the fat, the kidneys and the covering of the liver from the sin offering, as the Lord commanded Moses; ¹¹the flesh and the hide he burned up outside the camp.

¹²Then he slaughtered the burnt offering. His sons handed him the blood, and he sprinkled it against the altar on all sides. ¹³They handed him the burnt offering piece by piece, including the head, and he burned them on the altar. ¹⁴He washed the inner parts and the legs and burned them on top of the burnt offering on the altar.

¹⁵Aaron then brought the offering that was for the people. He took the goat for the people's sin offering and slaughtered it and offered it for a sin offering as he did with the first one.

¹⁶He brought the burnt offering and offered it in the prescribed way. ¹⁷He also brought the grain offering, took a handful of it and burned it on the altar in addition to the morning's burnt offering.

¹⁸He slaughtered the ox and the ram as the fellowship offering for the people. His sons handed him the blood, and he sprinkled it against the altar on all sides. ¹⁹But the fat portions of the ox and the ram—the fat tail, the layer of fat, the kidneys and the covering of the liver— ²⁰these they laid on the breasts, and then Aaron burned the fat on the altar. ²¹Aaron waved the breasts and the right thigh before the Lord as a wave offering, as Moses commanded.

²²Then Aaron lifted his hands toward the people and blessed them. And having sacrificed the sin offering, the burnt offering and the fellowship offering, he stepped down.

²³Moses and Aaron then went into the Tent of Meeting. When they came out, they blessed the people; and the glory of the Lord appeared to all the people. ²⁴Fire came out from the presence of the Lord and consumed the burnt offering and the fat portions on the altar. And when all the people saw it, they shouted for joy and fell facedown.

Leviticus 9:24

God Inspires Awe

Fire came out from the presence of the Lord and consumed the burnt offering and the fat portions on the altar. And when all the people saw it, they shouted for joy and fell facedown.

The Death of Nadab and Abihu

10 Aaron's sons Nadab and Abihu took their censers, put fire in them and added incense; and they offered unauthorized fire before the Lord, contrary to his command. ²So fire came out from the presence of the Lord and consumed them, and they died before the Lord. ³Moses then said to Aaron, "This is what the Lord spoke of when he said:

"'Among those who approach me
  I will show myself holy;
in the sight of all the people
  I will be honored.'"

Aaron remained silent.

---

^a4 The Hebrew word can include both male and female; also in verses 18 and 19.   ^b4 Traditionally *peace offering*; also in verses 18 and 22

So fire came out from the presence of the LORD and consumed them, and they died before the LORD. Moses then said to Aaron, "This is what the LORD spoke of when he said: 'Among those who approach me I will show myself holy; in the sight of all the people I will be honored.'" Aaron remained silent.

reflection

1 What was the last command God gave you through his Word?

2 Did you obey or disobey?

3 How did your actions honor or dishonor God? If you disobeyed, what can you do to set things right, right now?

RELATED READINGS

Isaiah 55:8–9;
Hebrews 12:14;
1 Peter 2:4–9

"Holiness does not consist in doing extraordinary things. It consists in accepting, with a smile, what Jesus sends us. It consists in accepting and following the will of God."

Mother Teresa

Holy Fire

Read: Leviticus 10:1–3

YOU ARRIVE AT A DINNER PARTY, bottle of wine in hand, and your hostess meets you at the door with a scowl. You knew they didn't drink, but chalked it up to conservatism and thought a little loosening up was in order. You didn't know your friend's husband had struggled with a drinking problem for years. You had good intentions, but sometimes good intentions aren't good enough.

We can't always see the reasons for God's requirements, any more than we can divine the motivations of our friends. Nadab and Abihu might have assumed a good intention would find favor equal to obedience; perhaps God would even reward them for their ingenuity. As high priest, Aaron made the burnt offering decreed by God. Then, perhaps caught up in the enthusiasm of the moment, Nadab and Abihu offered their own "unauthorized fire." The sacrifice had already been offered. God's glory had appeared. Nadab and Abihu presumptuously tried to add to God's decree for sacrifice. The result? Instant death. Verse 3 takes us to the heart of the matter: The closer we come to God, the more we must honor his holiness by obeying his commands.

As women, we face numerous opportunities to second-guess God. We justify detours from God's will by believing we're following the spirit of the law in our own creative way. The double-edged sword of ingenuity gets us into trouble. In this age of grace, such an exacting standard may seem harsh. But God's ways are not our ways. His holiness surpasses our comprehension. He is just, while we only seek justice. He has intentions for us that we cannot, with our finite minds, grasp. That's why obedience to God and what his Word tells us is crucial. Obedience shows God we consider him holy and worthy of honor.

How can you honor God daily? When God says something to you in his Word, take it personally. Reading the passage on honoring your husband or taming the tongue doesn't fulfill your obligation; your actions reflect your heart toward God. Obedience honors God. Disobedience dishonors him. The practice of obedience will align your heart with God's own desire. For "just as he who called you is holy, so be holy in all you do; for it is written: 'Be holy, because I am holy'" (1 Peter 1:15–16).

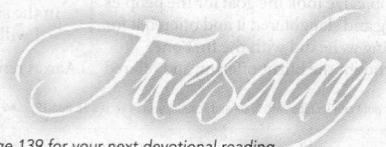

Tuesday

Go to page 139 for your next devotional reading.

⁴Moses summoned Mishael and Elzaphan, sons of Aaron's uncle Uzziel, and said to them, "Come here; carry your cousins outside the camp, away from the front of the sanctuary." ⁵So they came and carried them, still in their tunics, outside the camp, as Moses ordered.

⁶Then Moses said to Aaron and his sons Eleazar and Ithamar, "Do not let your hair become unkempt,ᵃ and do not tear your clothes, or you will die and the LORD will be angry with the whole community. But your relatives, all the house of Israel, may mourn for those the LORD has destroyed by fire. ⁷Do not leave the entrance to the Tent of Meeting or you will die, because the LORD's anointing oil is on you." So they did as Moses said.

⁸Then the LORD said to Aaron, ⁹"You and your sons are not to drink wine or other fermented drink whenever you go into the Tent of Meeting, or you will die. This is a lasting ordinance for the generations to come. ¹⁰You must distinguish between the holy and the common, between the unclean and the clean, ¹¹and you must teach the Israelites all the decrees the LORD has given them through Moses."

¹²Moses said to Aaron and his remaining sons, Eleazar and Ithamar, "Take the grain offering left over from the offerings made to the LORD by fire and eat it prepared without yeast, beside the altar, for it is most holy. ¹³Eat it in a holy place, because it is your share and your sons' share of the offerings made to the LORD by fire; for so I have been commanded. ¹⁴But you and your sons and your daughters may eat the breast that was waved and the thigh that was presented. Eat them in a ceremonially clean place; they have been given to you and your children as your share of the Israelites' fellowship offerings.ᵇ ¹⁵The thigh that was presented and the breast that was waved must be brought with the fat portions of the offerings made by fire, to be waved before the LORD as a wave offering. This will be the regular share for you and your children, as the LORD has commanded."

¹⁶When Moses inquired about the goat of the sin offering and found that it had been burned up, he was angry with Eleazar and Ithamar, Aaron's remaining sons, and asked,

¹⁷"Why didn't you eat the sin offering in the sanctuary area? It is most holy; it was given to you to take away the guilt of the community by making atonement for them before the LORD. ¹⁸Since its blood was not taken into the Holy Place, you should have eaten the goat in the sanctuary area, as I commanded."

¹⁹Aaron replied to Moses, "Today they sacrificed their sin offering and their burnt offering before the LORD, but such things as this have happened to me. Would the LORD have been pleased if I had eaten the sin offering today?" ²⁰When Moses heard this, he was satisfied.

Clean and Unclean Food

11 The LORD said to Moses and Aaron, ²"Say to the Israelites: 'Of all the animals that live on land, these are the ones you may eat: ³You may eat any animal that has a split hoof completely divided and that chews the cud.

⁴"'There are some that only chew the cud or only have a split hoof, but you must not eat them. The camel, though it chews the cud, does not have a split hoof; it is ceremonially unclean for you. ⁵The coney,ᶜ though it chews the cud, does not have a split hoof; it is unclean for you. ⁶The rabbit, though it chews the cud, does not have a split hoof; it is unclean for you. ⁷And the pig, though it has a split hoof completely divided, does not chew the cud; it is unclean for you. ⁸You must not eat their meat or touch their carcasses; they are unclean for you.

⁹"'Of all the creatures living in the water of the seas and the streams, you may eat any that have fins and scales. ¹⁰But all creatures in the seas or streams that do not have fins and scales—whether among all the swarming things or among all the other living creatures in the water—you are to detest. ¹¹And since you are to detest them, you must not eat their meat and you must detest their carcasses. ¹²Anything living in the water that does not have fins and scales is to be detestable to you.

¹³"'These are the birds you are to detest and not eat because they are detestable: the eagle, the vulture, the black vulture, ¹⁴the red kite, any kind of black kite, ¹⁵any kind of raven, ¹⁶the horned owl, the screech owl, the gull, any

---

ᵃ6 Or *Do not uncover your heads*   ᵇ14 Traditionally *peace offerings*   ᶜ5 That is, the hyrax or rock badger

131

kind of hawk, ¹⁷the little owl, the cormorant, the great owl, ¹⁸the white owl, the desert owl, the osprey, ¹⁹the stork, any kind of heron, the hoopoe and the bat.ᵃ

²⁰"'All flying insects that walk on all fours are to be detestable to you. ²¹There are, however, some winged creatures that walk on all fours that you may eat: those that have jointed legs for hopping on the ground. ²²Of these you may eat any kind of locust, katydid, cricket or grasshopper. ²³But all other winged creatures that have four legs you are to detest.

²⁴"'You will make yourselves unclean by these; whoever touches their carcasses will be unclean till evening. ²⁵Whoever picks up one of their carcasses must wash his clothes, and he will be unclean till evening.

²⁶"'Every animal that has a split hoof not completely divided or that does not chew the cud is unclean for you; whoever touches the carcass of any of them will be unclean. ²⁷Of all the animals that walk on all fours, those that walk on their paws are unclean for you; whoever touches their carcasses will be unclean till evening. ²⁸Anyone who picks up their carcasses must wash his clothes, and he will be unclean till evening. They are unclean for you.

²⁹"'Of the animals that move about on the ground, these are unclean for you: the weasel, the rat, any kind of great lizard, ³⁰the gecko, the monitor lizard, the wall lizard, the skink and the chameleon. ³¹Of all those that move along the ground, these are unclean for you. Whoever touches them when they are dead will be unclean till evening. ³²When one of them dies and falls on something, that article, whatever its use, will be unclean, whether it is made of wood, cloth, hide or sackcloth. Put it in water; it will be unclean till evening, and then it will be clean. ³³If one of them falls into a clay pot, everything in it will be unclean, and you must break the pot. ³⁴Any food that could be eaten but has water on it from such a pot is unclean, and any liquid that could be drunk from it is unclean. ³⁵Anything that one of their carcasses falls on becomes unclean; an oven or cooking pot must be broken up. They are unclean, and you are to regard them as unclean. ³⁶A spring, however, or a cistern for collecting water remains clean, but anyone who touches one of these carcasses is unclean. ³⁷If a carcass falls on any seeds that are to be planted, they remain clean. ³⁸But if water has been put on the seed and a carcass falls on it, it is unclean for you.

³⁹"'If an animal that you are allowed to eat dies, anyone who touches the carcass will be unclean till evening. ⁴⁰Anyone who eats some of the carcass must wash his clothes, and he will be unclean till evening. Anyone who picks up the carcass must wash his clothes, and he will be unclean till evening.

⁴¹"'Every creature that moves about on the ground is detestable; it is not to be eaten. ⁴²You are not to eat any creature that moves about on the ground, whether it moves on its belly or walks on all fours or on many feet; it is detestable. ⁴³Do not defile yourselves by any of these creatures. Do not make yourselves unclean by means of them or be made unclean by them. ⁴⁴I am the LORD your God; consecrate yourselves and be holy, because I am holy. Do not make yourselves unclean by any creature that moves about on the ground. ⁴⁵I am the LORD who brought you up out of Egypt to be your God; therefore be holy, because I am holy.

⁴⁶"'These are the regulations concerning animals, birds, every living thing that moves in the water and every creature that moves about on the ground. ⁴⁷You must distinguish between the unclean and the clean, between living creatures that may be eaten and those that may not be eaten.'"

Leviticus 11:45

God Is Holy

"I am the LORD who brought you up out of Egypt to be your God; therefore be holy, because I am holy."

Purification After Childbirth

12 The LORD said to Moses, ²"Say to the Israelites: 'A woman who becomes pregnant and gives birth to a son will be ceremonially unclean for seven days, just as she

---

ᵃ19 The precise identification of some of the birds, insects and animals in this chapter is uncertain.

is unclean during her monthly period. ³On the eighth day the boy is to be circumcised. ⁴Then the woman must wait thirty-three days to be purified from her bleeding. She must not touch anything sacred or go to the sanctuary until the days of her purification are over. ⁵If she gives birth to a daughter, for two weeks the woman will be unclean, as during her period. Then she must wait sixty-six days to be purified from her bleeding.

⁶"'When the days of her purification for a son or daughter are over, she is to bring to the priest at the entrance to the Tent of Meeting a year-old lamb for a burnt offering and a young pigeon or a dove for a sin offering. ⁷He shall offer them before the LORD to make atonement for her, and then she will be ceremonially clean from her flow of blood.

"'These are the regulations for the woman who gives birth to a boy or a girl. ⁸If she cannot afford a lamb, she is to bring two doves or two young pigeons, one for a burnt offering and the other for a sin offering. In this way the priest will make atonement for her, and she will be clean.'"

Regulations About Infectious Skin Diseases

13 The LORD said to Moses and Aaron, ²"When anyone has a swelling or a rash or a bright spot on his skin that may become an infectious skin disease,ᵃ he must be brought to Aaron the priest or to one of his sonsᵇ who is a priest. ³The priest is to examine the sore on his skin, and if the hair in the sore has turned white and the sore appears to be more than skin deep,ᶜ it is an infectious skin disease. When the priest examines him, he shall pronounce him ceremonially unclean. ⁴If the spot on his skin is white but does not appear to be more than skin deep and the hair in it has not turned white, the priest is to put the infected person in isolation for seven days. ⁵On the seventh day the priest is to examine him, and if he sees that the sore is unchanged and has not spread in the skin, he is to keep him in isolation another seven days. ⁶On the seventh day the priest is to examine him again, and if the sore has faded and has not spread in the skin, the priest shall pronounce him clean; it is only a rash. The man must wash his clothes, and he will be clean. ⁷But if the rash does spread in his skin after he has shown himself to the priest to be pronounced clean, he must appear before the priest again. ⁸The priest is to examine him, and if the rash has spread in the skin, he shall pronounce him unclean; it is an infectious disease.

⁹"When anyone has an infectious skin disease, he must be brought to the priest. ¹⁰The priest is to examine him, and if there is a white swelling in the skin that has turned the hair white and if there is raw flesh in the swelling, ¹¹it is a chronic skin disease and the priest shall pronounce him unclean. He is not to put him in isolation, because he is already unclean.

¹²"If the disease breaks out all over his skin and, so far as the priest can see, it covers all the skin of the infected person from head to foot, ¹³the priest is to examine him, and if the disease has covered his whole body, he shall pronounce that person clean. Since it has all turned white, he is clean. ¹⁴But whenever raw flesh appears on him, he will be unclean. ¹⁵When the priest sees the raw flesh, he shall pronounce him unclean. The raw flesh is unclean; he has an infectious disease. ¹⁶Should the raw flesh change and turn white, he must go to the priest. ¹⁷The priest is to examine him, and if the sores have turned white, the priest shall pronounce the infected person clean; then he will be clean.

¹⁸"When someone has a boil on his skin and it heals, ¹⁹and in the place where the boil was, a white swelling or reddish-white spot appears, he must present himself to the priest. ²⁰The priest is to examine it, and if it appears to be more than skin deep and the hair in it has turned white, the priest shall pronounce him unclean. It is an infectious skin disease that has broken out where the boil was. ²¹But if, when the priest examines it, there is no white hair in it and it is not more than skin deep and has faded, then the priest is to put him in isolation for seven days. ²²If it is spreading in the skin, the priest shall pronounce him unclean; it is infectious. ²³But if the spot is unchanged and has not spread, it is only a scar from the boil, and the priest shall pronounce him clean.

²⁴"When someone has a burn on his skin

ᵃ2 Traditionally *leprosy*; the Hebrew word was used for various diseases affecting the skin—not necessarily leprosy; also elsewhere in this chapter.   ᵇ2 Or *descendants*   ᶜ3 Or *be lower than the rest of the skin*; also elsewhere in this chapter and a reddish-white or white spot appears in the raw flesh of the burn, 25the priest is to examine the spot, and if the hair in it has turned white, and it appears to be more than skin deep, it is an infectious disease that has broken out in the burn. The priest shall pronounce him unclean; it is an infectious skin disease. 26But if the priest examines it and there is no white hair in the spot and if it is not more than skin deep and has faded, then the priest is to put him in isolation for seven days. 27On the seventh day the priest is to examine him, and if it is spreading in the skin, the priest shall pronounce him unclean; it is an infectious skin disease. 28If, however, the spot is unchanged and has not spread in the skin but has faded, it is a swelling from the burn, and the priest shall pronounce him clean; it is only a scar from the burn.

29"If a man or woman has a sore on the head or on the chin, 30the priest is to examine the sore, and if it appears to be more than skin deep and the hair in it is yellow and thin, the priest shall pronounce that person unclean; it is an itch, an infectious disease of the head or chin. 31But if, when the priest examines this kind of sore, it does not seem to be more than skin deep and there is no black hair in it, then the priest is to put the infected person in isolation for seven days. 32On the seventh day the priest is to examine the sore, and if the itch has not spread and there is no yellow hair in it and it does not appear to be more than skin deep, 33he must be shaved except for the diseased area, and the priest is to keep him in isolation another seven days. 34On the seventh day the priest is to examine the itch, and if it has not spread in the skin and appears to be no more than skin deep, the priest shall pronounce him clean. He must wash his clothes, and he will be clean. 35But if the itch does spread in the skin after he is pronounced clean, 36the priest is to examine him, and if the itch has spread in the skin, the priest does not need to look for yellow hair; the person is unclean. 37If, however, in his judgment it is unchanged and black hair has grown in it, the itch is healed. He is clean, and the priest shall pronounce him clean.

38"When a man or woman has white spots on the skin, 39the priest is to examine them,

and if the spots are dull white, it is a harmless rash that has broken out on the skin; that person is clean.

40"When a man has lost his hair and is bald, he is clean. 41If he has lost his hair from the front of his scalp and has a bald forehead, he is clean. 42But if he has a reddish-white sore on his bald head or forehead, it is an infectious disease breaking out on his head or forehead. 43The priest is to examine him, and if the swollen sore on his head or forehead is reddish-white like an infectious skin disease, 44the man is diseased and is unclean. The priest shall pronounce him unclean because of the sore on his head.

45"The person with such an infectious disease must wear torn clothes, let his hair be unkempt,a cover the lower part of his face and cry out, 'Unclean! Unclean!' 46As long as he has the infection he remains unclean. He must live alone; he must live outside the camp.

Regulations About Mildew

47"If any clothing is contaminated with mildew—any woolen or linen clothing, 48any woven or knitted material of linen or wool, any leather or anything made of leather— 49and if the contamination in the clothing, or leather, or woven or knitted material, or any leather article, is greenish or reddish, it is a spreading mildew and must be shown to the priest. 50The priest is to examine the mildew and isolate the affected article for seven days. 51On the seventh day he is to examine it, and if the mildew has spread in the clothing, or the woven or knitted material, or the leather, whatever its use, it is a destructive mildew; the article is unclean. 52He must burn up the clothing, or the woven or knitted material of wool or linen, or any leather article that has the contamination in it, because the mildew is destructive; the article must be burned up.

53"But if, when the priest examines it, the mildew has not spread in the clothing, or the woven or knitted material, or the leather article, 54he shall order that the contaminated article be washed. Then he is to isolate it for another seven days. 55After the affected article has been washed, the priest is to examine

a45 Or clothes, uncover his head

it, and if the mildew has not changed its appearance, even though it has not spread, it is unclean. Burn it with fire, whether the mildew has affected one side or the other. ⁵⁶If, when the priest examines it, the mildew has faded after the article has been washed, he is to tear the contaminated part out of the clothing, or the leather, or the woven or knitted material. ⁵⁷But if it reappears in the clothing, or in the woven or knitted material, or in the leather article, it is spreading, and whatever has the mildew must be burned with fire. ⁵⁸The clothing, or the woven or knitted material, or any leather article that has been washed and is rid of the mildew, must be washed again, and it will be clean."

⁵⁹These are the regulations concerning contamination by mildew in woolen or linen clothing, woven or knitted material, or any leather article, for pronouncing them clean or unclean.

Cleansing From Infectious Skin Diseases

14 The Lord said to Moses, ²"These are the regulations for the diseased person at the time of his ceremonial cleansing, when he is brought to the priest: ³The priest is to go outside the camp and examine him. If the person has been healed of his infectious skin disease,ᵃ ⁴the priest shall order that two live clean birds and some cedar wood, scarlet yarn and hyssop be brought for the one to be cleansed. ⁵Then the priest shall order that one of the birds be killed over fresh water in a clay pot. ⁶He is then to take the live bird and dip it, together with the cedar wood, the scarlet yarn and the hyssop, into the blood of the bird that was killed over the fresh water. ⁷Seven times he shall sprinkle the one to be cleansed of the infectious disease and pronounce him clean. Then he is to release the live bird in the open fields.

⁸"The person to be cleansed must wash his clothes, shave off all his hair and bathe with water; then he will be ceremonially clean. After this he may come into the camp, but he must stay outside his tent for seven days. ⁹On the seventh day he must shave off all his hair; he must shave his head, his beard, his eyebrows and the rest of his hair. He must wash his clothes and bathe himself with water, and he will be clean.

¹⁰"On the eighth day he must bring two male lambs and one ewe lamb a year old, each without defect, along with three-tenths of an ephahᵇ of fine flour mixed with oil for a grain offering, and one logᶜ of oil. ¹¹The priest who pronounces him clean shall present both the one to be cleansed and his offerings before the Lord at the entrance to the Tent of Meeting.

¹²"Then the priest is to take one of the male lambs and offer it as a guilt offering, along with the log of oil; he shall wave them before the Lord as a wave offering. ¹³He is to slaughter the lamb in the holy place where the sin offering and the burnt offering are slaughtered. Like the sin offering, the guilt offering belongs to the priest; it is most holy. ¹⁴The priest is to take some of the blood of the guilt offering and put it on the lobe of the right ear of the one to be cleansed, on the thumb of his right hand and on the big toe of his right foot. ¹⁵The priest shall then take some of the log of oil, pour it in the palm of his own left hand, ¹⁶dip his right forefinger into the oil in his palm, and with his finger sprinkle some of it before the Lord seven times. ¹⁷The priest is to put some of the oil remaining in his palm on the lobe of the right ear of the one to be cleansed, on the thumb of his right hand and on the big toe of his right foot, on top of the blood of the guilt offering. ¹⁸The rest of the oil in his palm the priest shall put on the head of the one to be cleansed and make atonement for him before the Lord.

¹⁹"Then the priest is to sacrifice the sin offering and make atonement for the one to be cleansed from his uncleanness. After that, the priest shall slaughter the burnt offering ²⁰and offer it on the altar, together with the grain offering, and make atonement for him, and he will be clean.

²¹"If, however, he is poor and cannot afford these, he must take one male lamb as a guilt offering to be waved to make atonement for him, together with a tenth of an ephahᵈ of fine flour mixed with oil for a grain offering, a log of oil, ²²and two doves or two young pigeons,

---

ᵃ3 Traditionally *leprosy*; the Hebrew word was used for various diseases affecting the skin—not necessarily leprosy; also elsewhere in this chapter.   ᵇ10 That is, probably about 6 quarts (about 6.5 liters)   ᶜ10 That is, probably about 2/3 pint (about 0.3 liter); also in verses 12, 15, 21 and 24   ᵈ21 That is, probably about 2 quarts (about 2 liters) which he can afford, one for a sin offering and the other for a burnt offering.

²³"On the eighth day he must bring them for his cleansing to the priest at the entrance to the Tent of Meeting, before the LORD. ²⁴The priest is to take the lamb for the guilt offering, together with the log of oil, and wave them before the LORD as a wave offering. ²⁵He shall slaughter the lamb for the guilt offering and take some of its blood and put it on the lobe of the right ear of the one to be cleansed, on the thumb of his right hand and on the big toe of his right foot. ²⁶The priest is to pour some of the oil into the palm of his own left hand, ²⁷and with his right forefinger sprinkle some of the oil from his palm seven times before the LORD. ²⁸Some of the oil in his palm he is to put on the same places he put the blood of the guilt offering—on the lobe of the right ear of the one to be cleansed, on the thumb of his right hand and on the big toe of his right foot. ²⁹The rest of the oil in his palm the priest shall put on the head of the one to be cleansed, to make atonement for him before the LORD. ³⁰Then he shall sacrifice the doves or the young pigeons, which the person can afford, ³¹one*a* as a sin offering and the other as a burnt offering, together with the grain offering. In this way the priest will make atonement before the LORD on behalf of the one to be cleansed."

³²These are the regulations for anyone who has an infectious skin disease and who cannot afford the regular offerings for his cleansing.

Cleansing From Mildew

³³The LORD said to Moses and Aaron, ³⁴"When you enter the land of Canaan, which I am giving you as your possession, and I put a spreading mildew in a house in that land, ³⁵the owner of the house must go and tell the priest, 'I have seen something that looks like mildew in my house.' ³⁶The priest is to order the house to be emptied before he goes in to examine the mildew, so that nothing in the house will be pronounced unclean. After this the priest is to go in and inspect the house. ³⁷He is to examine the mildew on the walls, and if it has greenish or reddish depressions that appear to be deeper than the surface of the wall, ³⁸the priest shall go out the doorway of the house and close it up for seven days. ³⁹On the seventh day the priest shall return to inspect the house. If the mildew has spread on the walls, ⁴⁰he is to order that the contaminated stones be torn out and thrown into an unclean place outside the town. ⁴¹He must have all the inside walls of the house scraped and the material that is scraped off dumped into an unclean place outside the town. ⁴²Then they are to take other stones to replace these and take new clay and plaster the house.

⁴³"If the mildew reappears in the house after the stones have been torn out and the house scraped and plastered, ⁴⁴the priest is to go and examine it and, if the mildew has spread in the house, it is a destructive mildew; the house is unclean. ⁴⁵It must be torn down—its stones, timbers and all the plaster—and taken out of the town to an unclean place.

⁴⁶"Anyone who goes into the house while it is closed up will be unclean till evening. ⁴⁷Anyone who sleeps or eats in the house must wash his clothes.

⁴⁸"But if the priest comes to examine it and the mildew has not spread after the house has been plastered, he shall pronounce the house clean, because the mildew is gone. ⁴⁹To purify the house he is to take two birds and some cedar wood, scarlet yarn and hyssop. ⁵⁰He shall kill one of the birds over fresh water in a clay pot. ⁵¹Then he is to take the cedar wood, the hyssop, the scarlet yarn and the live bird, dip them into the blood of the dead bird and the fresh water, and sprinkle the house seven times. ⁵²He shall purify the house with the bird's blood, the fresh water, the live bird, the cedar wood, the hyssop and the scarlet yarn. ⁵³Then he is to release the live bird in the open fields outside the town. In this way he will make atonement for the house, and it will be clean."

⁵⁴These are the regulations for any infectious skin disease, for an itch, ⁵⁵for mildew in clothing or in a house, ⁵⁶and for a swelling, a rash or a bright spot, ⁵⁷to determine when something is clean or unclean.

These are the regulations for infectious skin diseases and mildew.

---

*a*31 Septuagint and Syriac; Hebrew ³¹ *such as the person can afford, one*

Discharges Causing Uncleanness

15 The LORD said to Moses and Aaron, 2"Speak to the Israelites and say to them: 'When any man has a bodily discharge, the discharge is unclean. 3Whether it continues flowing from his body or is blocked, it will make him unclean. This is how his discharge will bring about uncleanness:

4"'Any bed the man with a discharge lies on will be unclean, and anything he sits on will be unclean. 5Anyone who touches his bed must wash his clothes and bathe with water, and he will be unclean till evening. 6Whoever sits on anything that the man with a discharge sat on must wash his clothes and bathe with water, and he will be unclean till evening.

7"'Whoever touches the man who has a discharge must wash his clothes and bathe with water, and he will be unclean till evening.

8"'If the man with the discharge spits on someone who is clean, that person must wash his clothes and bathe with water, and he will be unclean till evening.

9"'Everything the man sits on when riding will be unclean, 10and whoever touches any of the things that were under him will be unclean till evening; whoever picks up those things must wash his clothes and bathe with water, and he will be unclean till evening.

11"'Anyone the man with a discharge touches without rinsing his hands with water must wash his clothes and bathe with water, and he will be unclean till evening.

12"'A clay pot that the man touches must be broken, and any wooden article is to be rinsed with water.

13"'When a man is cleansed from his discharge, he is to count off seven days for his ceremonial cleansing; he must wash his clothes and bathe himself with fresh water, and he will be clean. 14On the eighth day he must take two doves or two young pigeons and come before the LORD to the entrance to the Tent of Meeting and give them to the priest. 15The priest is to sacrifice them, the one for a sin offering and the other for a burnt offering. In this way he will make atonement before the LORD for the man because of his discharge.

16"'When a man has an emission of semen, he must bathe his whole body with water, and he will be unclean till evening. 17Any clothing or leather that has semen on it must be washed with water, and it will be unclean till evening. 18When a man lies with a woman and there is an emission of semen, both must bathe with water, and they will be unclean till evening.

19"'When a woman has her regular flow of blood, the impurity of her monthly period will last seven days, and anyone who touches her will be unclean till evening.

20"'Anything she lies on during her period will be unclean, and anything she sits on will be unclean. 21Whoever touches her bed must wash his clothes and bathe with water, and he will be unclean till evening. 22Whoever touches anything she sits on must wash his clothes and bathe with water, and he will be unclean till evening. 23Whether it is the bed or anything she was sitting on, when anyone touches it, he will be unclean till evening.

24"'If a man lies with her and her monthly flow touches him, he will be unclean for seven days; any bed he lies on will be unclean.

25"'When a woman has a discharge of blood for many days at a time other than her monthly period or has a discharge that continues beyond her period, she will be unclean as long as she has the discharge, just as in the days of her period. 26Any bed she lies on while her discharge continues will be unclean, as is her bed during her monthly period, and anything she sits on will be unclean, as during her period. 27Whoever touches them will be unclean; he must wash his clothes and bathe with water, and he will be unclean till evening.

28"'When she is cleansed from her discharge, she must count off seven days, and after that she will be ceremonially clean. 29On the eighth day she must take two doves or two young pigeons and bring them to the priest at the entrance to the Tent of Meeting. 30The priest is to sacrifice one for a sin offering and the other for a burnt offering. In this way he will make atonement for her before the LORD for the uncleanness of her discharge.

31"'You must keep the Israelites separate from things that make them unclean, so they will not die in their uncleanness for defiling my dwelling place,*a* which is among them.'"

32 These are the regulations for a man with a discharge, for anyone made unclean by an emission of semen, **33** for a woman in her monthly period, for a man or a woman with a discharge, and for a man who lies with a woman who is ceremonially unclean.

The Day of Atonement

16 The LORD spoke to Moses after the death of the two sons of Aaron who died when they approached the LORD. **2** The LORD said to Moses: "Tell your brother Aaron not to come whenever he chooses into the Most Holy Place behind the curtain in front of the atonement cover on the ark, or else he will die, because I appear in the cloud over the atonement cover.

3 "This is how Aaron is to enter the sanctuary area: with a young bull for a sin offering and a ram for a burnt offering. **4** He is to put on the sacred linen tunic, with linen undergarments next to his body; he is to tie the linen sash around him and put on the linen turban. These are sacred garments; so he must bathe himself with water before he puts them on. **5** From the Israelite community he is to take two male goats for a sin offering and a ram for a burnt offering.

6 "Aaron is to offer the bull for his own sin offering to make atonement for himself and his household. **7** Then he is to take the two goats and present them before the LORD at the entrance to the Tent of Meeting. **8** He is to cast lots for the two goats—one lot for the LORD and the other for the scapegoat.*b* **9** Aaron shall bring the goat whose lot falls to the LORD and sacrifice it for a sin offering. **10** But the goat chosen by lot as the scapegoat shall be presented alive before the LORD to be used for making atonement by sending it into the desert as a scapegoat.

11 "Aaron shall bring the bull for his own sin offering to make atonement for himself and his household, and he is to slaughter the bull for his own sin offering. **12** He is to take a censer full of burning coals from the altar before the LORD and two handfuls of finely ground fragrant incense and take them behind the curtain. **13** He is to put the incense on the fire before the LORD, and the smoke of the incense will conceal the atonement cover above the Testimony, so that he will not die. **14** He is to take some of the bull's blood and with his finger sprinkle it on the front of the atonement cover; then he shall sprinkle some of it with his finger seven times before the atonement cover.

15 "He shall then slaughter the goat for the sin offering for the people and take its blood behind the curtain and do with it as he did with the bull's blood: He shall sprinkle it on the atonement cover and in front of it. **16** In this way he will make atonement for the Most Holy Place because of the uncleanness and rebellion of the Israelites, whatever their sins have been. He is to do the same for the Tent of Meeting, which is among them in the midst of their uncleanness. **17** No one is to be in the Tent of Meeting from the time Aaron goes in to make atonement in the Most Holy Place until he comes out, having made atonement for himself, his household and the whole community of Israel.

18 "Then he shall come out to the altar that is before the LORD and make atonement for it. He shall take some of the bull's blood and some of the goat's blood and put it on all the horns of the altar. **19** He shall sprinkle some of the blood on it with his finger seven times to cleanse it and to consecrate it from the uncleanness of the Israelites.

20 "When Aaron has finished making atonement for the Most Holy Place, the Tent of Meeting and the altar, he shall bring forward the live goat. **21** He is to lay both hands on the head of the live goat and confess over it all the wickedness and rebellion of the Israelites—all their sins—and put them on the goat's head. He shall send the goat away into the desert in the care of a man appointed for the task. **22** The goat will carry on itself all their sins to a solitary place; and the man shall release it in the desert.

23 "Then Aaron is to go into the Tent of Meeting and take off the linen garments he put on before he entered the Most Holy Place, and he is to leave them there. **24** He shall bathe himself with water in a holy place and put on his regular garments. Then he shall come out and sacrifice the burnt offering for himself and the burnt offering for the people, to make atonement for

a 31 Or *my tabernacle*   *b* 8 That is, the goat of removal; Hebrew *azazel*; also in verses 10 and 26

Once and for All

IN A DUSTY, DESERT WASTELAND, a man slowly unties a rope from the goat's neck. His fingers trace the dried blood on the goat's forehead, where a few hours before the priest had laid his hands. The transfer of sin is complete. All that remains is for it to be far removed from sight.

The man slaps the animal's rump and it jumps. It runs a few paces, then stops and looks back. "Go on," the man yells. "Run. Run away!" He claps his hands. He chases the goat. And it runs. But it keeps looking back, hesitating, waiting and wondering if the man will change his mind.

But the man doesn't change his mind—he can't. When he is sure the goat has gone far enough, he turns to leave. He makes the dusty journey back alone, without the sound of trotting hooves or bleating to keep him company. The sin of the Israelites has been temporarily atoned for, sent away on the head of the goat that was left in the desert.

The Day of Atonement was Israel's most solemn holy day. On that day, God made a way for his sinful people to set things right with him, the Holy One of Israel. But like the scapegoat that kept looking back, sin and guilt always returned. Year after year, goat after goat, the ritual was repeated: One goat slaughtered to atone for sin, the other sent far into the desert to remove the presence of guilt. But it wasn't enough. It merely symbolized what was to come.

When Jesus died on the cross and was banished to the tomb, he fulfilled the requirement for the two goats on the Day of Atonement. His sacrificial death on the cross atoned for our sin, finally making us one with God for all time. His journey to death removed our guilt for all time. He took our sins with him to the pit of hell, just as the scapegoat was banished into the solitary wasteland.

It was a high price to pay. The scapegoat didn't have a choice, but Jesus did. He chose to die because of his unfathomable love for us. "This is how we know what love is: Jesus Christ laid down his life for us" (1 John 3:16).

Leviticus 16:22

"The goat will carry on itself all their sins to a solitary place; and the man shall release it in the desert."

reflection

1 What do the images of the sacrificial goat and scapegoat tell you about the high price of sin?

2 What does the image of the scapegoat reveal about how far Christ was willing to go for you?

3 What guilt are you holding onto? Speak it out loud to Jesus today and ask his forgiveness so he can carry it far away, never to be seen again.

RELATED READINGS

Psalm 103:11–12; Isaiah 53:3–6; Hebrews 10:1–18

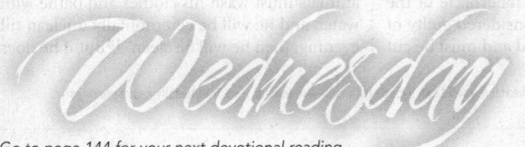

himself and for the people. ²⁵He shall also burn the fat of the sin offering on the altar.

²⁶"The man who releases the goat as a scapegoat must wash his clothes and bathe himself with water; afterward he may come into the camp. ²⁷The bull and the goat for the sin offerings, whose blood was brought into the Most Holy Place to make atonement, must be taken outside the camp; their hides, flesh and offal are to be burned up. ²⁸The man who burns them must wash his clothes and bathe himself with water; afterward he may come into the camp.

²⁹"This is to be a lasting ordinance for you: On the tenth day of the seventh month you must deny yourselves*a* and not do any work—whether native-born or an alien living among you— ³⁰because on this day atonement will be made for you, to cleanse you. Then, before the LORD, you will be clean from all your sins. ³¹It is a sabbath of rest, and you must deny yourselves; it is a lasting ordinance. ³²The priest who is anointed and ordained to succeed his father as high priest is to make atonement. He is to put on the sacred linen garments ³³and make atonement for the Most Holy Place, for the Tent of Meeting and the altar, and for the priests and all the people of the community.

³⁴"This is to be a lasting ordinance for you: Atonement is to be made once a year for all the sins of the Israelites."

And it was done, as the LORD commanded Moses.

Eating Blood Forbidden

17 The LORD said to Moses, ²"Speak to Aaron and his sons and to all the Israelites and say to them: 'This is what the LORD has commanded: ³Any Israelite who sacrifices an ox,*b* a lamb or a goat in the camp or outside of it ⁴instead of bringing it to the entrance to the Tent of Meeting to present it as an offering to the LORD in front of the tabernacle of the LORD—that man shall be considered guilty of bloodshed; he has shed blood and must be cut

off from his people. ⁵This is so the Israelites will bring to the LORD the sacrifices they are now making in the open fields. They must bring them to the priest, that is, to the LORD, at the entrance to the Tent of Meeting and sacrifice them as fellowship offerings.*c* ⁶The priest is to sprinkle the blood against the altar of the LORD at the entrance to the Tent of Meeting and burn the fat as an aroma pleasing to the LORD. ⁷They must no longer offer any of their sacrifices to the goat idols*d* to whom they prostitute themselves. This is to be a lasting ordinance for them and for the generations to come.'

⁸"Say to them: 'Any Israelite or any alien living among them who offers a burnt offering or sacrifice ⁹and does not bring it to the entrance to the Tent of Meeting to sacrifice it to the LORD—that man must be cut off from his people.

¹⁰"'Any Israelite or any alien living among them who eats any blood—I will set my face against that person who eats blood and will cut him off from his people. ¹¹For the life of a creature is in the blood, and I have given it to you to make atonement for yourselves on the altar; it is the blood that makes atonement for one's life. ¹²Therefore I say to the Israelites, "None of you may eat blood, nor may an alien living among you eat blood."

¹³"'Any Israelite or any alien living among you who hunts any animal or bird that may be eaten must drain out the blood and cover it with earth, ¹⁴because the life of every creature is its blood. That is why I have said to the Israelites, "You must not eat the blood of any creature, because the life of every creature is its blood; anyone who eats it must be cut off."

¹⁵"'Anyone, whether native-born or alien, who eats anything found dead or torn by wild animals must wash his clothes and bathe with water, and he will be ceremonially unclean till evening; then he will be clean. ¹⁶But if he does

Leviticus 17:11

God Requires Atonement

"For the life of a creature is in the blood, and I have given it to you to make atonement for yourselves on the altar; it is the blood that makes atonement for one's life."

---

*a*29 Or *must fast;* also in verse 31   *b*3 The Hebrew word can include both male and female.   *c*5 Traditionally *peace offerings*
*d*7 Or *demons*

not wash his clothes and bathe himself, he will be held responsible.'"

Unlawful Sexual Relations

18 The LORD said to Moses, ²"Speak to the Israelites and say to them: 'I am the LORD your God. ³You must not do as they do in Egypt, where you used to live, and you must not do as they do in the land of Canaan, where I am bringing you. Do not follow their practices. ⁴You must obey my laws and be careful to follow my decrees. I am the LORD your God. ⁵Keep my decrees and laws, for the man who obeys them will live by them. I am the LORD.

⁶'No one is to approach any close relative to have sexual relations. I am the LORD.

⁷'Do not dishonor your father by having sexual relations with your mother. She is your mother; do not have relations with her.

⁸'Do not have sexual relations with your father's wife; that would dishonor your father.

⁹'Do not have sexual relations with your sister, either your father's daughter or your mother's daughter, whether she was born in the same home or elsewhere.

¹⁰'Do not have sexual relations with your son's daughter or your daughter's daughter; that would dishonor you.

¹¹'Do not have sexual relations with the daughter of your father's wife, born to your father; she is your sister.

¹²'Do not have sexual relations with your father's sister; she is your father's close relative.

¹³'Do not have sexual relations with your mother's sister, because she is your mother's close relative.

¹⁴'Do not dishonor your father's brother by approaching his wife to have sexual relations; she is your aunt.

¹⁵'Do not have sexual relations with your daughter-in-law. She is your son's wife; do not have relations with her.

¹⁶'Do not have sexual relations with your brother's wife; that would dishonor your brother.

¹⁷'Do not have sexual relations with both a woman and her daughter. Do not have sexual relations with either her son's daughter or her daughter's daughter; they are her close relatives. That is wickedness.

¹⁸'Do not take your wife's sister as a rival wife and have sexual relations with her while your wife is living.

¹⁹'Do not approach a woman to have sexual relations during the uncleanness of her monthly period.

²⁰'Do not have sexual relations with your neighbor's wife and defile yourself with her.

²¹'Do not give any of your children to be sacrificed[a] to Molech, for you must not profane the name of your God. I am the LORD.

²²'Do not lie with a man as one lies with a woman; that is detestable.

²³'Do not have sexual relations with an animal and defile yourself with it. A woman must not present herself to an animal to have sexual relations with it; that is a perversion.

²⁴'Do not defile yourselves in any of these ways, because this is how the nations that I am going to drive out before you became defiled. ²⁵Even the land was defiled; so I punished it for its sin, and the land vomited out its inhabitants. ²⁶But you must keep my decrees and my laws. The native-born and the aliens living among you must not do any of these detestable things, ²⁷for all these things were done by the people who lived in the land before you, and the land became defiled. ²⁸And if you defile the land, it will vomit you out as it vomited out the nations that were before you.

²⁹'Everyone who does any of these detestable things—such persons must be cut off from their people. ³⁰Keep my requirements and do not follow any of the detestable customs that were practiced before you came and do not defile yourselves with them. I am the LORD your God.'"

> **Leviticus 18:4**
>
> *God Expects Obedience*
>
> "You must obey my laws and be careful to follow my decrees. I am the LORD your God."

---

[a]21 Or *to be passed through the fire*

Various Laws

19 The LORD said to Moses, ²"Speak to the entire assembly of Israel and say to them: 'Be holy because I, the LORD your God, am holy.

³"'Each of you must respect his mother and father, and you must observe my Sabbaths. I am the LORD your God.

⁴"'Do not turn to idols or make gods of cast metal for yourselves. I am the LORD your God.

⁵"'When you sacrifice a fellowship offering*a* to the LORD, sacrifice it in such a way that it will be accepted on your behalf. ⁶It shall be eaten on the day you sacrifice it or on the next day; anything left over until the third day must be burned up. ⁷If any of it is eaten on the third day, it is impure and will not be accepted. ⁸Whoever eats it will be held responsible because he has desecrated what is holy to the LORD; that person must be cut off from his people.

⁹"'When you reap the harvest of your land, do not reap to the very edges of your field or gather the gleanings of your harvest. ¹⁰Do not go over your vineyard a second time or pick up the grapes that have fallen. Leave them for the poor and the alien. I am the LORD your God.

¹¹"'Do not steal.

"'Do not lie.

"'Do not deceive one another.

¹²"'Do not swear falsely by my name and so profane the name of your God. I am the LORD.

¹³"'Do not defraud your neighbor or rob him.

"'Do not hold back the wages of a hired man overnight.

¹⁴"'Do not curse the deaf or put a stumbling block in front of the blind, but fear your God. I am the LORD.

¹⁵"'Do not pervert justice; do not show partiality to the poor or favoritism to the great, but judge your neighbor fairly.

¹⁶"'Do not go about spreading slander among your people.

"'Do not do anything that endangers your neighbor's life. I am the LORD.

¹⁷"'Do not hate your brother in your heart.

Rebuke your neighbor frankly so you will not share in his guilt.

¹⁸"'Do not seek revenge or bear a grudge against one of your people, but love your neighbor as yourself. I am the LORD.

¹⁹"'Keep my decrees.

"'Do not mate different kinds of animals.

"'Do not plant your field with two kinds of seed.

"'Do not wear clothing woven of two kinds of material.

²⁰"'If a man sleeps with a woman who is a slave girl promised to another man but who has not been ransomed or given her freedom, there must be due punishment. Yet they are not to be put to death, because she had not been freed. ²¹The man, however, must bring a ram to the entrance to the Tent of Meeting for a guilt offering to the LORD. ²²With the ram of the guilt offering the priest is to make atonement for him before the LORD for the sin he has committed, and his sin will be forgiven.

²³"'When you enter the land and plant any kind of fruit tree, regard its fruit as forbidden.*b* For three years you are to consider it forbidden*b*; it must not be eaten. ²⁴In the fourth year all its fruit will be holy, an offering of praise to the LORD. ²⁵But in the fifth year you may eat its fruit. In this way your harvest will be increased. I am the LORD your God.

²⁶"'Do not eat any meat with the blood still in it.

"'Do not practice divination or sorcery.

²⁷"'Do not cut the hair at the sides of your head or clip off the edges of your beard.

²⁸"'Do not cut your bodies for the dead or put tattoo marks on yourselves. I am the LORD.

²⁹"'Do not degrade your daughter by making her a prostitute, or the land will turn to prostitution and be filled with wickedness.

³⁰"'Observe my Sabbaths and have reverence for my sanctuary. I am the LORD.

³¹"'Do not turn to mediums or seek out

Leviticus 19:15

God Is Fair

"Do not pervert justice; do not show partiality to the poor or favoritism to the great, but judge your neighbor fairly."

---

*a*5 Traditionally *peace offering*   *b*23 Hebrew *uncircumcised* spiritists, for you will be defiled by them. I am the LORD your God.

³² "'Rise in the presence of the aged, show respect for the elderly and revere your God. I am the LORD.

³³ "'When an alien lives with you in your land, do not mistreat him. ³⁴ The alien living with you must be treated as one of your native-born. Love him as yourself, for you were aliens in Egypt. I am the LORD your God.

³⁵ "'Do not use dishonest standards when measuring length, weight or quantity. ³⁶ Use honest scales and honest weights, an honest ephah*a* and an honest hin.*b* I am the LORD your God, who brought you out of Egypt.

³⁷ "'Keep all my decrees and all my laws and follow them. I am the LORD.'"

Punishments for Sin

20 The LORD said to Moses, ² "Say to the Israelites: 'Any Israelite or any alien living in Israel who gives*c* any of his children to Molech must be put to death. The people of the community are to stone him. ³ I will set my face against that man and I will cut him off from his people; for by giving his children to Molech, he has defiled my sanctuary and profaned my holy name. ⁴ If the people of the community close their eyes when that man gives one of his children to Molech and they fail to put him to death, ⁵ I will set my face against that man and his family and will cut off from their people both him and all who follow him in prostituting themselves to Molech.

⁶ "'I will set my face against the person who turns to mediums and spiritists to prostitute himself by following them, and I will cut him off from his people.

⁷ "'Consecrate yourselves and be holy, because I am the LORD your God. ⁸ Keep my decrees and follow them. I am the LORD, who makes you holy.*d*

⁹ "'If anyone curses his father or mother, he must be put to death. He has cursed his father or his mother, and his blood will be on his own head.

¹⁰ "'If a man commits adultery with another man's wife—with the wife of his neighbor—both the adulterer and the adulteress must be put to death.

¹¹ "'If a man sleeps with his father's wife, he has dishonored his father. Both the man and the woman must be put to death; their blood will be on their own heads.

¹² "'If a man sleeps with his daughter-in-law, both of them must be put to death. What they have done is a perversion; their blood will be on their own heads.

¹³ "'If a man lies with a man as one lies with a woman, both of them have done what is detestable. They must be put to death; their blood will be on their own heads.

¹⁴ "'If a man marries both a woman and her mother, it is wicked. Both he and they must be burned in the fire, so that no wickedness will be among you.

¹⁵ "'If a man has sexual relations with an animal, he must be put to death, and you must kill the animal.

¹⁶ "'If a woman approaches an animal to have sexual relations with it, kill both the woman and the animal. They must be put to death; their blood will be on their own heads.

¹⁷ "'If a man marries his sister, the daughter of either his father or his mother, and they have sexual relations, it is a disgrace. They must be cut off before the eyes of their people. He has dishonored his sister and will be held responsible.

¹⁸ "'If a man lies with a woman during her monthly period and has sexual relations with her, he has exposed the source of her flow, and she has also uncovered it. Both of them must be cut off from their people.

¹⁹ "'Do not have sexual relations with the sister of either your mother or your father, for

Leviticus 20:8

God Makes Us Holy

"Keep my decrees and follow them. I am the LORD, who makes you holy."

---

*a*36 An ephah was a dry measure.   *b*36 A hin was a liquid measure.   *c*2 Or *sacrifices*; also in verses 3 and 4   *d*8 Or *who sanctifies you*; or *who sets you apart as holy*

Loving the Alien

Leviticus 19:33–34

"When an alien lives with you in your land, do not mistreat him. The alien living with you must be treated as one of your native-born. Love him as yourself, for you were aliens in Egypt. I am the LORD your God."

reflection

1 Have you ever felt like an alien because of your faith in Christ?

2 Have you ever treated someone like an alien because they didn't look, dress or believe as you do? How has this devotional changed your mind and heart?

3 Who in your sphere of influence is alienated from God? How can you apply the Golden Rule to help them see God in a new light?

RELATED READINGS

Ephesians 2:11–22;
Philippians 3:20–21;
Hebrews 11:13–16;
1 Peter 2:11–12

Read: Leviticus 19:33–34

MILDRED HOYT, "MID" TO HER FRIENDS, left this world and went to rest in the arms of Jesus at the age of 97. She was born December 24, 1899. Imagine what her eyes saw, the changes that transformed this world of ours—it's staggering if you think about it.

If we were beamed to an alien world—to a galaxy far, far away, would we experience any greater change than Mid did during her lifetime? Two world wars, not to mention several smaller ones, the advent of cars, planes, electricity, radio, television and, yes, computers and the Net. The list could go on for more pages than a New York City phone book.

Spending time with Mid left one with a longing . . . a longing to return to a different time. A time of simplicity, a time for family and community. A time when doors were left unlocked and neighbors would drop everything and help you rebuild a barn. A time when family and faith reigned supreme.

Perhaps a similar longing prompted a group of so-called aliens to accompany the Israelites out of Egypt. These weren't little green men; they were non-Hebrews who followed the Hebrews' God. So when the Hebrews left Egypt, they weren't alone, as "many other people went up with them." These aliens just didn't fit in Egypt anymore. They longed for a life that honored God. They had seen God's power and wanted what he offered. They left families, homes, businesses and country.

God honored their determination by protecting them with this commandment, reminding the Israelites that they, too, had once been aliens in a foreign land. God reminded them of the harsh treatment they'd endured so they would treat the aliens as they would want to be treated—the Golden Rule in the desert.

Who are the aliens today? Perhaps the alien is a neighbor who admires your faith and with a little encouragement would come to church with you. Perhaps the alien is a store clerk who notices the little cross around your neck as well as your kindness and patience. Perhaps the alien is someone at work whose lifestyle you would not choose, but who might be drawn to God through your gracious attitude. The challenge is to live the Golden Rule in the desert of life. Don't treat the aliens as strangers, but treat them as you would one of your friends or family. Treat the aliens in your life to a taste of God's love.

Thursday

144

Go to page 147 for your next devotional reading.

that would dishonor a close relative; both of you would be held responsible.

20 " 'If a man sleeps with his aunt, he has dishonored his uncle. They will be held responsible; they will die childless.

21 " 'If a man marries his brother's wife, it is an act of impurity; he has dishonored his brother. They will be childless.

22 " 'Keep all my decrees and laws and follow them, so that the land where I am bringing you to live may not vomit you out. 23 You must not live according to the customs of the nations I am going to drive out before you. Because they did all these things, I abhorred them. 24 But I said to you, "You will possess their land; I will give it to you as an inheritance, a land flowing with milk and honey." I am the LORD your God, who has set you apart from the nations.

25 " 'You must therefore make a distinction between clean and unclean animals and between unclean and clean birds. Do not defile yourselves by any animal or bird or anything that moves along the ground—those which I have set apart as unclean for you. 26 You are to be holy to me*a* because I, the LORD, am holy, and I have set you apart from the nations to be my own.

27 " 'A man or woman who is a medium or spiritist among you must be put to death. You are to stone them; their blood will be on their own heads.' "

Rules for Priests

21 The LORD said to Moses, "Speak to the priests, the sons of Aaron, and say to them: 'A priest must not make himself ceremonially unclean for any of his people who die, 2 except for a close relative, such as his mother or father, his son or daughter, his brother, 3 or an unmarried sister who is dependent on him since she has no husband—for her he may make himself unclean. 4 He must not make himself unclean for people related to him by marriage,*b* and so defile himself.

5 " 'Priests must not shave their heads or shave off the edges of their beards or cut their bodies. 6 They must be holy to their God and must not profane the name of their God. Because they present the offerings made to the

LORD by fire, the food of their God, they are to be holy.

7 " 'They must not marry women defiled by prostitution or divorced from their husbands, because priests are holy to their God. 8 Regard them as holy, because they offer up the food of your God. Consider them holy, because I the LORD am holy—I who make you holy.*c*

9 " 'If a priest's daughter defiles herself by becoming a prostitute, she disgraces her father; she must be burned in the fire.

10 " 'The high priest, the one among his brothers who has had the anointing oil poured on his head and who has been ordained to wear the priestly garments, must not let his hair become unkempt*d* or tear his clothes. 11 He must not enter a place where there is a dead body. He must not make himself unclean, even for his father or mother, 12 nor leave the sanctuary of his God or desecrate it, because he has been dedicated by the anointing oil of his God. I am the LORD.

13 " 'The woman he marries must be a virgin. 14 He must not marry a widow, a divorced woman, or a woman defiled by prostitution, but only a virgin from his own people, 15 so he will not defile his offspring among his people. I am the LORD, who makes him holy.*e* ' "

16 The LORD said to Moses, 17 "Say to Aaron: 'For the generations to come none of your descendants who has a defect may come near to offer the food of his God. 18 No man who has any defect may come near: no man who is blind or lame, disfigured or deformed; 19 no man with a crippled foot or hand, 20 or who is hunchbacked or dwarfed, or who has any eye defect, or who has festering or running sores or damaged testicles. 21 No descendant of Aaron the priest who has any defect is to come near to present the offerings made to the LORD by fire. He has a defect; he must not come near to offer the food of his God. 22 He may eat the most holy food of his God, as well as the holy food; 23 yet because of his defect, he must not go near the curtain or approach the altar, and so desecrate my sanctuary. I am the LORD, who makes them holy.*f* ' "

24 So Moses told this to Aaron and his sons and to all the Israelites.

---

*a*26 Or *be my holy ones*   *b*4 Or *unclean as a leader among his people*   *c*8 Or *who sanctify you; or who set you apart as holy*   *d*10 Or *not uncover his head*   *e*15 Or *who sanctifies him; or who sets him apart as holy*   *f*23 Or *who sanctifies them; or who sets them apart as holy*

22 The LORD said to Moses, ²"Tell Aaron and his sons to treat with respect the sacred offerings the Israelites consecrate to me, so they will not profane my holy name. I am the LORD.

³"Say to them: 'For the generations to come, if any of your descendants is ceremonially unclean and yet comes near the sacred offerings that the Israelites consecrate to the LORD, that person must be cut off from my presence. I am the LORD.

⁴"'If a descendant of Aaron has an infectious skin disease[a] or a bodily discharge, he may not eat the sacred offerings until he is cleansed. He will also be unclean if he touches something defiled by a corpse or by anyone who has an emission of semen, ⁵or if he touches any crawling thing that makes him unclean, or any person who makes him unclean, whatever the uncleanness may be. ⁶The one who touches any such thing will be unclean till evening. He must not eat any of the sacred offerings unless he has bathed himself with water. ⁷When the sun goes down, he will be clean, and after that he may eat the sacred offerings, for they are his food. ⁸He must not eat anything found dead or torn by wild animals, and so become unclean through it. I am the LORD.

⁹"'The priests are to keep my requirements so that they do not become guilty and die for treating them with contempt. I am the LORD, who makes them holy.[b]

¹⁰"'No one outside a priest's family may eat the sacred offering, nor may the guest of a priest or his hired worker eat it. ¹¹But if a priest buys a slave with money, or if a slave is born in his household, that slave may eat his food. ¹²If a priest's daughter marries anyone other than a priest, she may not eat any of the sacred contributions. ¹³But if a priest's daughter becomes a widow or is divorced, yet has no children, and she returns to live in her father's house as in her youth, she may eat of her father's food. No unauthorized person, however, may eat any of it.

¹⁴"'If anyone eats a sacred offering by mistake, he must make restitution to the priest for the offering and add a fifth of the value to it. ¹⁵The priests must not desecrate the sacred offerings the Israelites present to the LORD ¹⁶by allowing them to eat the sacred offerings and so bring upon them guilt requiring payment. I am the LORD, who makes them holy.'"

Unacceptable Sacrifices

¹⁷The LORD said to Moses, ¹⁸"Speak to Aaron and his sons and to all the Israelites and say to them: 'If any of you—either an Israelite or an alien living in Israel—presents a gift for a burnt offering to the LORD, either to fulfill a vow or as a freewill offering, ¹⁹you must present a male without defect from the cattle, sheep or goats in order that it may be accepted on your behalf. ²⁰Do not bring anything with a defect, because it will not be accepted on your behalf. ²¹When anyone brings from the herd or flock a fellowship offering[c] to the LORD to fulfill a special vow or as a freewill offering, it must be without defect or blemish to be acceptable. ²²Do not offer to the LORD the blind, the injured or the maimed, or anything with warts or festering or running sores. Do not place any of these on the altar as an offering made to the LORD by fire. ²³You may, however, present as a freewill offering an ox[d] or a sheep that is deformed or stunted, but it will not be accepted in fulfillment of a vow. ²⁴You must not offer to the LORD an animal whose testicles are bruised, crushed, torn or cut. You must not do this in your own land, ²⁵and you must not accept such animals from the hand of a foreigner and offer them as the food of your God. They will not be accepted on your behalf, because they are deformed and have defects.'"

²⁶The LORD said to Moses, ²⁷"When a calf, a lamb or a goat is born, it is to remain with its mother for seven days. From the eighth day on, it will be acceptable as an offering made to the LORD by fire. ²⁸Do not slaughter a cow or a sheep and its young on the same day.

²⁹"When you sacrifice a thank offering to the LORD, sacrifice it in such a way that it will be accepted on your behalf. ³⁰It must be eaten that same day; leave none of it till morning. I am the LORD.

³¹"Keep my commands and follow them. I am the LORD. ³²Do not profane my holy name.

---

a4 Traditionally *leprosy*; the Hebrew word was used for various diseases affecting the skin—not necessarily leprosy.   b9 Or *who sanctifies them*; or *who sets them apart as holy*; also in verse 16   c21 Traditionally *peace offering*   d23 The Hebrew word can include both male and female.

A Time Apart

Read Leviticus 23

TO ENTER INTO SOLITUDE and silence is to take the spiritual life seriously. It is to take seriously our need to quiet the noise of our lives, to cease the constant striving of human effort, to pull away from our absorption in human relationships for a time in order to give God our undivided attention. In solitude God begins to free us from our bondage to human expectations, for there we experience God as our ultimate reality—the One in whom we live and move and have our being. In solitude our thoughts and our mind, our will and our desires are reoriented Godward so we become less and less attracted by external forces and can be more deeply responsive to God's desire and prayer in us.

Silence deepens the experience of solitude. In silence we not only withdraw from the demands of life in the company of others but also allow the noise of our own thoughts, strivings and compulsions to settle down so we can hear a truer and more reliable Voice. Reliance on our own thoughts and words, even in our praying, can be one facet of a need to control things, to set the agenda, or at least to know what the agenda is even in our relationship with God. It is in silence that we habitually release our own agendas and our need to control and become more willing and able to give ourselves to God's loving initiative. In silence we create space for God's activity rather than filling every minute with our own . . .

Solitude and silence are not, in the end, about success and failure. They are about showing up and letting God do the rest. They are not an end in themselves; they are merely a *means* through which we regularly make ourselves available to God for the intimacy of relationship and for the work of transformation that only God can accomplish.

—*Ruth Haley Barton*

Leviticus 23:3
"There are six days when you may work, but the seventh day is a Sabbath of rest, a day of sacred assembly. You are not to do any work; wherever you live, it is a Sabbath to the LORD."

reflection

1 How often do you give God your undivided attention?

2 Picture in your mind a quiet place where you can "withdraw from the demands of life." When will you go there, so you can be alone with God?

3 No matter what day you chose to set apart to God, make sure that during that time you make yourself available to him for "the work of transformation" that he alone can accomplish in your life.

RELATED READINGS

Exodus 20:8–11;
Acts 17:24–28;
Romans 12:1–2

Go to page 152 for your next devotional reading.

I must be acknowledged as holy by the Israelites. I am the LORD, who makes[a] you holy[b] ³³and who brought you out of Egypt to be your God. I am the LORD."

23

The LORD said to Moses, ²"Speak to the Israelites and say to them: 'These are my appointed feasts, the appointed feasts of the LORD, which you are to proclaim as sacred assemblies.

The Sabbath

³" 'There are six days when you may work, but the seventh day is a Sabbath of rest, a day of sacred assembly. You are not to do any work; wherever you live, it is a Sabbath to the LORD.

The Passover and Unleavened Bread

⁴" 'These are the LORD's appointed feasts, the sacred assemblies you are to proclaim at their appointed times: ⁵The LORD's Passover begins at twilight on the fourteenth day of the first month. ⁶On the fifteenth day of that month the LORD's Feast of Unleavened Bread begins; for seven days you must eat bread made without yeast. ⁷On the first day hold a sacred assembly and do no regular work. ⁸For seven days present an offering made to the LORD by fire. And on the seventh day hold a sacred assembly and do no regular work.' "

Firstfruits

⁹The LORD said to Moses, ¹⁰"Speak to the Israelites and say to them: 'When you enter the land I am going to give you and you reap its harvest, bring to the priest a sheaf of the first grain you harvest. ¹¹He is to wave the sheaf before the LORD so it will be accepted on your behalf; the priest is to wave it on the day after the Sabbath. ¹²On the day you wave the sheaf, you must sacrifice as a burnt offering to the LORD a lamb a year old without defect, ¹³together with its grain offering of two-tenths of an ephah[c] of fine flour mixed with oil—an offering made to the LORD by fire, a pleasing aroma—and its drink offering of a quarter of a hin[d] of wine. ¹⁴You must not eat any bread, or roasted or new grain, until the very day you bring this offering to your God. This is to be a lasting ordinance for the generations to come, wherever you live.

Feast of Weeks

¹⁵" 'From the day after the Sabbath, the day you brought the sheaf of the wave offering, count off seven full weeks. ¹⁶Count off fifty days up to the day after the seventh Sabbath, and then present an offering of new grain to the LORD. ¹⁷From wherever you live, bring two loaves made of two-tenths of an ephah of fine flour, baked with yeast, as a wave offering of firstfruits to the LORD. ¹⁸Present with this bread seven male lambs, each a year old and without defect, one young bull and two rams. They will be a burnt offering to the LORD, together with their grain offerings and drink offerings—an offering made by fire, an aroma pleasing to the LORD. ¹⁹Then sacrifice one male goat for a sin offering and two lambs, each a year old, for a fellowship offering.[e] ²⁰The priest is to wave the two lambs before the LORD as a wave offering, together with the bread of the firstfruits. They are a sacred offering to the LORD for the priest. ²¹On that same day you are to proclaim a sacred assembly and do no regular work. This is to be a lasting ordinance for the generations to come, wherever you live.

²²" 'When you reap the harvest of your land, do not reap to the very edges of your field or gather the gleanings of your harvest. Leave them for the poor and the alien. I am the LORD your God.' "

Feast of Trumpets

²³The LORD said to Moses, ²⁴"Say to the Israelites: 'On the first day of the seventh month you are to have a day of rest, a sacred assembly commemorated with trumpet blasts. ²⁵Do no regular work, but present an offering made to the LORD by fire.' "

Day of Atonement

²⁶The LORD said to Moses, ²⁷"The tenth day of this seventh month is the Day of Atonement. Hold a sacred assembly and deny yourselves,[f] and present an offering made to the LORD by fire. ²⁸Do no work on that day, because it is the Day of Atonement, when atonement is made for you before the LORD your God. ²⁹Anyone

---

*a*32 Or *made*   *b*32 Or *who sanctifies you;* or *who sets you apart as holy*   *c*13 That is, probably about 4 quarts (about 4.5 liters); also in verse 17   *d*13 That is, probably about 1 quart (about 1 liter)   *e*19 Traditionally *peace offering*   *f*27 Or *and fast;* also in verses 29 and 32 who does not deny himself on that day must be cut off from his people. ³⁰I will destroy from among his people anyone who does any work on that day. ³¹You shall do no work at all. This is to be a lasting ordinance for the generations to come, wherever you live. ³²It is a sabbath of rest for you, and you must deny yourselves. From the evening of the ninth day of the month until the following evening you are to observe your sabbath."

Feast of Tabernacles

³³The LORD said to Moses, ³⁴"Say to the Israelites: 'On the fifteenth day of the seventh month the LORD's Feast of Tabernacles begins, and it lasts for seven days. ³⁵The first day is a sacred assembly; do no regular work. ³⁶For seven days present offerings made to the LORD by fire, and on the eighth day hold a sacred assembly and present an offering made to the LORD by fire. It is the closing assembly; do no regular work.

³⁷(" 'These are the LORD's appointed feasts, which you are to proclaim as sacred assemblies for bringing offerings made to the LORD by fire—the burnt offerings and grain offerings, sacrifices and drink offerings required for each day. ³⁸These offerings are in addition to those for the LORD's Sabbaths and[a] in addition to your gifts and whatever you have vowed and all the freewill offerings you give to the LORD.)

³⁹" 'So beginning with the fifteenth day of the seventh month, after you have gathered the crops of the land, celebrate the festival to the LORD for seven days; the first day is a day of rest, and the eighth day also is a day of rest. ⁴⁰On the first day you are to take choice fruit from the trees, and palm fronds, leafy branches and poplars, and rejoice before the LORD your God for seven days. ⁴¹Celebrate this as a festival to the LORD for seven days each year. This is to be a lasting ordinance for the generations to come; celebrate it in the seventh month. ⁴²Live in booths for seven days: All native-born Israelites are to live in booths ⁴³so your descendants will know that I had the Israelites live in booths when I brought them out of Egypt. I am the LORD your God.' "

⁴⁴So Moses announced to the Israelites the appointed feasts of the LORD.

Oil and Bread Set Before the LORD

24 The LORD said to Moses, ²"Command the Israelites to bring you clear oil of pressed olives for the light so that the lamps may be kept burning continually. ³Outside the curtain of the Testimony in the Tent of Meeting, Aaron is to tend the lamps before the LORD from evening till morning, continually. This is to be a lasting ordinance for the generations to come. ⁴The lamps on the pure gold lampstand before the LORD must be tended continually.

⁵"Take fine flour and bake twelve loaves of bread, using two-tenths of an ephah[b] for each loaf. ⁶Set them in two rows, six in each row, on the table of pure gold before the LORD. ⁷Along each row put some pure incense as a memorial portion to represent the bread and to be an offering made to the LORD by fire. ⁸This bread is to be set out before the LORD regularly, Sabbath after Sabbath, on behalf of the Israelites, as a lasting covenant. ⁹It belongs to Aaron and his sons, who are to eat it in a holy place, because it is a most holy part of their regular share of the offerings made to the LORD by fire."

A Blasphemer Stoned

¹⁰Now the son of an Israelite mother and an Egyptian father went out among the Israelites, and a fight broke out in the camp between him and an Israelite. ¹¹The son of the Israelite woman blasphemed the Name with a curse; so they brought him to Moses. (His mother's name was Shelomith, the daughter of Dibri the Danite.) ¹²They put him in custody until the will of the LORD should be made clear to them.

¹³Then the LORD said to Moses: ¹⁴"Take the blasphemer outside the camp. All those who heard him are to lay their hands on his head, and the entire assembly is to stone him. ¹⁵Say to the Israelites: 'If anyone curses his God, he will be held responsible; ¹⁶anyone who blasphemes the name of the LORD must be put to death. The entire assembly must stone him. Whether an alien or native-born, when he blasphemes the Name, he must be put to death.

¹⁷" 'If anyone takes the life of a human being, he must be put to death. ¹⁸Anyone who takes

*a*38 Or *These feasts are in addition to the LORD's Sabbaths, and these offerings are*   *b*5 That is, probably about 4 quarts (about 4.5 liters) the life of someone's animal must make restitution—life for life. [19]If anyone injures his neighbor, whatever he has done must be done to him: [20]fracture for fracture, eye for eye, tooth for tooth. As he has injured the other, so he is to be injured. [21]Whoever kills an animal must make restitution, but whoever kills a man must be put to death. [22]You are to have the same law for the alien and the native-born. I am the Lord your God.'"

[23]Then Moses spoke to the Israelites, and they took the blasphemer outside the camp and stoned him. The Israelites did as the Lord commanded Moses.

The Sabbath Year

25 The Lord said to Moses on Mount Sinai, [2]"Speak to the Israelites and say to them: 'When you enter the land I am going to give you, the land itself must observe a sabbath to the Lord. [3]For six years sow your fields, and for six years prune your vineyards and gather their crops. [4]But in the seventh year the land is to have a sabbath of rest, a sabbath to the Lord. Do not sow your fields or prune your vineyards. [5]Do not reap what grows of itself or harvest the grapes of your untended vines. The land is to have a year of rest. [6]Whatever the land yields during the sabbath year will be food for you—for yourself, your manservant and maidservant, and the hired worker and temporary resident who live among you, [7]as well as for your livestock and the wild animals in your land. Whatever the land produces may be eaten.

The Year of Jubilee

[8]'Count off seven sabbaths of years—seven times seven years—so that the seven sabbaths of years amount to a period of forty-nine years. [9]Then have the trumpet sounded everywhere on the tenth day of the seventh month; on the Day of Atonement sound the trumpet throughout your land. [10]Consecrate the fiftieth year and proclaim liberty throughout the land to all its inhabitants. It shall be a jubilee for you; each one of you is to return to his family property and each to his own clan. [11]The fiftieth year shall be a jubilee for you; do not sow and do not reap what grows of itself or harvest the untended vines. [12]For it is a jubilee and is to be holy for you; eat only what is taken directly from the fields.

[13]"'In this Year of Jubilee everyone is to return to his own property.

[14]"'If you sell land to one of your countrymen or buy any from him, do not take advantage of each other. [15]You are to buy from your countryman on the basis of the number of years since the Jubilee. And he is to sell to you on the basis of the number of years left for harvesting crops. [16]When the years are many, you are to increase the price, and when the years are few, you are to decrease the price, because what he is really selling you is the number of crops. [17]Do not take advantage of each other, but fear your God. I am the Lord your God.

[18]"'Follow my decrees and be careful to obey my laws, and you will live safely in the land. [19]Then the land will yield its fruit, and you will eat your fill and live there in safety. [20]You may ask, "What will we eat in the seventh year if we do not plant or harvest our crops?" [21]I will send you such a blessing in the sixth year that the land will yield enough for three years. [22]While you plant during the eighth year, you will eat from the old crop and will continue to eat from it until the harvest of the ninth year comes in.

[23]"'The land must not be sold permanently, because the land is mine and you are but aliens and my tenants. [24]Throughout the country that you hold as a possession, you must provide for the redemption of the land.

[25]"'If one of your countrymen becomes poor and sells some of his property, his nearest relative is to come and redeem what his countryman has sold. [26]If, however, a man has no one to redeem it for him but he himself prospers and acquires sufficient means to redeem it, [27]he is to determine the value for the years since he sold it and refund

Leviticus 25:23

God Owns Everything

"The land must not be sold permanently, because the land is mine and you are but aliens and my tenants."

the balance to the man to whom he sold it; he can then go back to his own property. ²⁸But if he does not acquire the means to repay him, what he sold will remain in the possession of the buyer until the Year of Jubilee. It will be returned in the Jubilee, and he can then go back to his property.

²⁹"'If a man sells a house in a walled city, he retains the right of redemption a full year after its sale. During that time he may redeem it. ³⁰If it is not redeemed before a full year has passed, the house in the walled city shall belong permanently to the buyer and his descendants. It is not to be returned in the Jubilee. ³¹But houses in villages without walls around them are to be considered as open country. They can be redeemed, and they are to be returned in the Jubilee.

³²"'The Levites always have the right to redeem their houses in the Levitical towns, which they possess. ³³So the property of the Levites is redeemable—that is, a house sold in any town they hold—and is to be returned in the Jubilee, because the houses in the towns of the Levites are their property among the Israelites. ³⁴But the pastureland belonging to their towns must not be sold; it is their permanent possession.

³⁵"'If one of your countrymen becomes poor and is unable to support himself among you, help him as you would an alien or a temporary resident, so he can continue to live among you. ³⁶Do not take interest of any kind*a* from him, but fear your God, so that your countryman may continue to live among you. ³⁷You must not lend him money at interest or sell him food at a profit. ³⁸I am the LORD your God, who brought you out of Egypt to give you the land of Canaan and to be your God.

³⁹"'If one of your countrymen becomes poor among you and sells himself to you, do not make him work as a slave. ⁴⁰He is to be treated as a hired worker or a temporary resident among you; he is to work for you until the Year of Jubilee. ⁴¹Then he and his children are to be released, and he will go back to his own clan and to the property of his forefathers. ⁴²Because the Israelites are my servants, whom I brought out of Egypt, they must not be sold as slaves. ⁴³Do not rule over them ruthlessly, but fear your God.

⁴⁴"'Your male and female slaves are to come from the nations around you; from them you may buy slaves. ⁴⁵You may also buy some of the temporary residents living among you and members of their clans born in your country, and they will become your property. ⁴⁶You can will them to your children as inherited property and can make them slaves for life, but you must not rule over your fellow Israelites ruthlessly.

⁴⁷"'If an alien or a temporary resident among you becomes rich and one of your countrymen becomes poor and sells himself to the alien living among you or to a member of the alien's clan, ⁴⁸he retains the right of redemption after he has sold himself. One of his relatives may redeem him: ⁴⁹An uncle or a cousin or any blood relative in his clan may redeem him. Or if he prospers, he may redeem himself. ⁵⁰He and his buyer are to count the time from the year he sold himself up to the Year of Jubilee. The price for his release is to be based on the rate paid to a hired man for that number of years. ⁵¹If many years remain, he must pay for his redemption a larger share of the price paid for him. ⁵²If only a few years remain until the Year of Jubilee, he is to compute that and pay for his redemption accordingly. ⁵³He is to be treated as a man hired from year to year; you must see to it that his owner does not rule over him ruthlessly.

⁵⁴"'Even if he is not redeemed in any of these ways, he and his children are to be released in the Year of Jubilee, ⁵⁵for the Israelites belong to me as servants. They are my servants, whom I brought out of Egypt. I am the LORD your God.

Reward for Obedience

26 "'Do not make idols or set up an image or a sacred stone for yourselves, and do not place a carved stone in your land to bow down before it. I am the LORD your God.

²"'Observe my Sabbaths and have reverence for my sanctuary. I am the LORD.

³"'If you follow my decrees and are careful to obey my commands, ⁴I will send you rain in its season, and the ground will yield its crops

---

a36 Or *take excessive interest*; similarly in verse 37

An Answer to Prayer

REBEKAH

Before he had finished praying, Rebekah came out with her jar on her shoulder.

Genesis 24:15

ONE MINUTE she was a single woman, going to fetch water—something she routinely did every day of her life—and the next minute she had a ring and a proposal of marriage to a man she had never met. One minute she was going about her normal routine, and then suddenly she was destined to be the answer to prayer.

Abraham was insistent that his son, his chosen son, Isaac, marry a woman from Abraham's own people. Abraham made his servant swear an oath that he would get the boy a bride. Both Abraham and the servant prayed that God would direct this marriage. The prayers had been specific. Certain. And entirely trusting. In response, and against all odds, the Lord intertwined the lives of a man and a woman many miles apart and drew a knot between their two hearts.

Upon meeting Abraham's servant, Rebekah didn't know she was an answer to prayer. She just saw a man who was thirsty and needing water. Because she was kind and hospitable, she quickly allowed the man water from her jar. And then she watered the man's camels too.

It wasn't until later that Rebekah realized that Isaac's family had *prayed* for someone like her. And here she was—voilà! Beautiful. Poised. Hospitable. A virgin. What an awesome feeling: to be someone's answer to prayer. Someone's "dream girl."

Armed with that knowledge, Rebekah was ready to take a radical step of faith. "Do you want to go right now with this servant or do you want to stay here for a few days to say goodbye to your friends, neighbors and family?" Rebekah's mom and brother asked, already feeling her loss. Rebekah looked at the man and took a deep breath. "I'm ready to go now."

—*Prayer*—
My Lord, thank you for the opportunities you give me every day to demonstrate my faith in you.

ASSIGNED READING:

Genesis 24–27

Weekend

and the trees of the field their fruit. ⁵Your threshing will continue until grape harvest and the grape harvest will continue until planting, and you will eat all the food you want and live in safety in your land.

⁶"'I will grant peace in the land, and you will lie down and no one will make you afraid. I will remove savage beasts from the land, and the sword will not pass through your country. ⁷You will pursue your enemies, and they will fall by the sword before you. ⁸Five of you will chase a hundred, and a hundred of you will chase ten thousand, and your enemies will fall by the sword before you.

⁹"'I will look on you with favor and make you fruitful and increase your numbers, and I will keep my covenant with you. ¹⁰You will still be eating last year's harvest when you will have to move it out to make room for the new. ¹¹I will put my dwelling place*a* among you, and I will not abhor you. ¹²I will walk among you and be your God, and you will be my people. ¹³I am the LORD your God, who brought you out of Egypt so that you would no longer be slaves to the Egyptians; I broke the bars of your yoke and enabled you to walk with heads held high.

Punishment for Disobedience

¹⁴"'But if you will not listen to me and carry out all these commands, ¹⁵and if you reject my decrees and abhor my laws and fail to carry out all my commands and so violate my covenant, ¹⁶then I will do this to you: I will bring upon you sudden terror, wasting diseases and fever that will destroy your sight and drain away your life. You will plant seed in vain, because your enemies will eat it. ¹⁷I will set my face against you so that you will be defeated by your enemies; those who hate you will rule over you, and you will flee even when no one is pursuing you.

¹⁸"'If after all this you will not listen to me, I will punish you for your sins seven times over. ¹⁹I will break down your stubborn pride and make the sky above you like iron and

Leviticus 26:12

God Identifies With Us

"I will walk among you and be your God, and you will be my people."

the ground beneath you like bronze. ²⁰Your strength will be spent in vain, because your soil will not yield its crops, nor will the trees of the land yield their fruit.

²¹"'If you remain hostile toward me and refuse to listen to me, I will multiply your afflictions seven times over, as your sins deserve. ²²I will send wild animals against you, and they will rob you of your children, destroy your cattle and make you so few in number that your roads will be deserted.

²³"'If in spite of these things you do not accept my correction but continue to be hostile toward me, ²⁴I myself will be hostile toward you and will afflict you for your sins seven times over. ²⁵And I will bring the sword upon you to avenge the breaking of the covenant. When you withdraw into your cities, I will send a plague among you, and you will be given into enemy hands. ²⁶When I cut off your supply of bread, ten women will be able to bake your bread in one oven, and they will dole out the bread by weight. You will eat, but you will not be satisfied.

²⁷"'If in spite of this you still do not listen to me but continue to be hostile toward me, ²⁸then in my anger I will be hostile toward you, and I myself will punish you for your sins seven times over. ²⁹You will eat the flesh of your sons and the flesh of your daughters. ³⁰I will destroy your high places, cut down your incense altars and pile your dead bodies on the lifeless forms of your idols, and I will abhor you. ³¹I will turn your cities into ruins and lay waste your sanctuaries, and I will take no delight in the pleasing aroma of your offerings. ³²I will lay waste the land, so that your enemies who live there will be appalled. ³³I will scatter you among the nations and will draw out my sword and pursue you. Your land will be laid waste, and your cities will lie in ruins. ³⁴Then the land will enjoy its sabbath years all the time that it lies desolate and you are in the country of your enemies; then the land will rest and enjoy its sabbaths. ³⁵All the time that it lies

a11 Or my tabernacle

desolate, the land will have the rest it did not have during the sabbaths you lived in it.

36 "'As for those of you who are left, I will make their hearts so fearful in the lands of their enemies that the sound of a windblown leaf will put them to flight. They will run as though fleeing from the sword, and they will fall, even though no one is pursuing them. 37 They will stumble over one another as though fleeing from the sword, even though no one is pursuing them. So you will not be able to stand before your enemies. 38 You will perish among the nations; the land of your enemies will devour you. 39 Those of you who are left will waste away in the lands of their enemies because of their sins; also because of their fathers' sins they will waste away.

40 "'But if they will confess their sins and the sins of their fathers—their treachery against me and their hostility toward me, 41 which made me hostile toward them so that I sent them into the land of their enemies—then when their uncircumcised hearts are humbled and they pay for their sin, 42 I will remember my covenant with Jacob and my covenant with Isaac and my covenant with Abraham, and I will remember the land. 43 For the land will be deserted by them and will enjoy its sabbaths while it lies desolate without them. They will pay for their sins because they rejected my laws and abhorred my decrees. 44 Yet in spite of this, when they are in the land of their enemies, I will not reject them or abhor them so as to destroy them completely, breaking my covenant with them. I am the LORD their God. 45 But for their sake I will remember the covenant with their ancestors whom I brought out of Egypt in the sight of the nations to be their God. I am the LORD.'"

46 These are the decrees, the laws and the regulations that the LORD established on Mount Sinai between himself and the Israelites through Moses.

Redeeming What Is the LORD's

27 The LORD said to Moses, 2 "Speak to the Israelites and say to them: 'If anyone makes a special vow to dedicate persons to the LORD by giving equivalent values, 3 set the value of a male between the ages of twenty and sixty at fifty shekels[a] of silver, according to the sanctuary shekel[b]; 4 and if it is a female, set her value at thirty shekels.[c] 5 If it is a person between the ages of five and twenty, set the value of a male at twenty shekels[d] and of a female at ten shekels.[e] 6 If it is a person between one month and five years, set the value of a male at five shekels[f] of silver and that of a female at three shekels[g] of silver. 7 If it is a person sixty years old or more, set the value of a male at fifteen shekels[h] and of a female at ten shekels. 8 If anyone making the vow is too poor to pay the specified amount, he is to present the person to the priest, who will set the value for him according to what the man making the vow can afford.

9 "'If what he vowed is an animal that is acceptable as an offering to the LORD, such an animal given to the LORD becomes holy. 10 He must not exchange it or substitute a good one for a bad one, or a bad one for a good one; if he should substitute one animal for another, both it and the substitute become holy. 11 If what he vowed is a ceremonially unclean animal—one that is not acceptable as an offering to the LORD—the animal must be presented to the priest, 12 who will judge its quality as good or bad. Whatever value the priest then sets, that is what it will be. 13 If the owner wishes to redeem the animal, he must add a fifth to its value.

14 "'If a man dedicates his house as something holy to the LORD, the priest will judge its quality as good or bad. Whatever value the priest then sets, so it will remain. 15 If the man who dedicates his house redeems it, he must add a fifth to its value, and the house will again become his.

16 "'If a man dedicates to the LORD part of his family land, its value is to be set according to the amount of seed required for it—fifty shekels of silver to a homer[i] of barley seed. 17 If he dedicates his field during the Year of Jubilee, the value that has been set remains. 18 But if he dedicates his field after the Jubilee, the priest will determine the value according to the num-

---

a 3 That is, about 1 1/4 pounds (about 0.6 kilogram); also in verse 16   b 3 That is, about 2/5 ounce (about 11.5 grams); also in verse 25   c 4 That is, about 12 ounces (about 0.3 kilogram)   d 5 That is, about 8 ounces (about 0.2 kilogram)   e 5 That is, about 4 ounces (about 110 grams); also in verse 7   f 6 That is, about 2 ounces (about 55 grams)   g 6 That is, about 1 1/4 ounces (about 35 grams)   h 7 That is, about 6 ounces (about 170 grams)   i 16 That is, probably about 6 bushels (about 220 liters) ber of years that remain until the next Year of Jubilee, and its set value will be reduced. [19]If the man who dedicates the field wishes to redeem it, he must add a fifth to its value, and the field will again become his. [20]If, however, he does not redeem the field, or if he has sold it to someone else, it can never be redeemed. [21]When the field is released in the Jubilee, it will become holy, like a field devoted to the LORD; it will become the property of the priests.[a]

[22]"'If a man dedicates to the LORD a field he has bought, which is not part of his family land, [23]the priest will determine its value up to the Year of Jubilee, and the man must pay its value on that day as something holy to the LORD. [24]In the Year of Jubilee the field will revert to the person from whom he bought it, the one whose land it was. [25]Every value is to be set according to the sanctuary shekel, twenty gerahs to the shekel.

[26]"'No one, however, may dedicate the firstborn of an animal, since the firstborn already belongs to the LORD; whether an ox[b] or a sheep, it is the LORD's. [27]If it is one of the unclean animals, he may buy it back at its set value, adding a fifth of the value to it. If he does not redeem it, it is to be sold at its set value.

[28]"'But nothing that a man owns and devotes[c] to the LORD—whether man or animal or family land—may be sold or redeemed; everything so devoted is most holy to the LORD.

[29]"'No person devoted to destruction[d] may be ransomed; he must be put to death.

[30]"'A tithe of everything from the land, whether grain from the soil or fruit from the trees, belongs to the LORD; it is holy to the LORD. [31]If a man redeems any of his tithe, he must add a fifth of the value to it. [32]The entire tithe of the herd and flock—every tenth animal that passes under the shepherd's rod—will be holy to the LORD. [33]He must not pick out the good from the bad or make any substitution. If he does make a substitution, both the animal and its substitute become holy and cannot be redeemed.'"

[34]These are the commands the LORD gave Moses on Mount Sinai for the Israelites.

---

[a]21 Or *priest*   [b]26 The Hebrew word can include both male and female.   [c]28 The Hebrew term refers to the irrevocable giving over of things or persons to the LORD.   [d]29 The Hebrew term refers to the irrevocable giving over of things or persons to the LORD, often by totally destroying them.

Numbers

Author:
Moses.

Audience:
The people of Israel.

Date:
Between 1446
and 1406 B.C.

Setting:
After a year in the Sinai
Desert, a census is taken.
Then the Israelites move
onward to Canaan and
spend 39 more years wan-
dering in the desert.

Verses to Remember:
"We went into the land to
which you sent us, and it
does flow with milk and
honey! Here is its fruit."
. . . But the men who had
gone up with him said,
"We can't attack those
people; they are stronger
than we are." (13:27,31)

The book of Numbers is named for the two "number-ings," or countings, of the Hebrew people that took place. The first census was taken to organize the camps by tribal clans (see Numbers 1–4). After this event, the people prepared to enter the land of promise. But when they *scouted out the promised land* preparing to enter, they balked in fear. Although they had seen God's provision over and over, they grumbled and disbelieved. So the *people journeyed* on a 40-year roller coaster of obedience and defiance.

The second census was taken of the next generation (see Numbers 26), a new faithful generation, as they stood poised by the Jordan River, *ready to cross over into Canaan.*

The Census

1 The LORD spoke to Moses in the Tent of Meeting in the Desert of Sinai on the first day of the second month of the second year after the Israelites came out of Egypt. He said: **2**"Take a census of the whole Israelite community by their clans and families, listing every man by name, one by one. **3**You and Aaron are to number by their divisions all the men in Israel twenty years old or more who are able to serve in the army. **4**One man from each tribe, each the head of his family, is to help you. **5**These are the names of the men who are to assist you:

from Reuben, Elizur son of Shedeur;

⁶from Simeon, Shelumiel son of Zurishaddai;

⁷from Judah, Nahshon son of Amminadab;

⁸from Issachar, Nethanel son of Zuar;

⁹from Zebulun, Eliab son of Helon;

¹⁰from the sons of Joseph:

from Ephraim, Elishama son of Ammihud;

from Manasseh, Gamaliel son of Pedahzur;

¹¹from Benjamin, Abidan son of Gideoni;

¹²from Dan, Ahiezer son of Ammishaddai;

¹³from Asher, Pagiel son of Ocran;

¹⁴from Gad, Eliasaph son of Deuel;

¹⁵from Naphtali, Ahira son of Enan."

¹⁶These were the men appointed from the community, the leaders of their ancestral tribes. They were the heads of the clans of Israel.

¹⁷Moses and Aaron took these men whose names had been given, ¹⁸and they called the whole community together on the first day of the second month. The people indicated their ancestry by their clans and families, and the men twenty years old or more were listed by name, one by one, ¹⁹as the LORD commanded Moses. And so he counted them in the Desert of Sinai:

²⁰From the descendants of Reuben the firstborn son of Israel:

All the men twenty years old or more who were able to serve in the army were listed by name, one by one, according to the records of their clans and families. ²¹The number from the tribe of Reuben was 46,500.

²²From the descendants of Simeon:

All the men twenty years old or more who were able to serve in the army were counted and listed by name, one by one, according to the records of their clans and families. ²³The number from the tribe of Simeon was 59,300.

²⁴From the descendants of Gad:

All the men twenty years old or more who were able to serve in the army were listed by name, according to the records of their clans and families. ²⁵The number from the tribe of Gad was 45,650.

²⁶From the descendants of Judah:

All the men twenty years old or more who were able to serve in the army were listed by name, according to the records of their clans and families. ²⁷The number from the tribe of Judah was 74,600.

²⁸From the descendants of Issachar:

All the men twenty years old or more who were able to serve in the army were listed by name, according to the records of their clans and families. ²⁹The number from the tribe of Issachar was 54,400.

³⁰From the descendants of Zebulun:

All the men twenty years old or more who were able to serve in the army were listed by name, according to the records of their clans and families. ³¹The number from the tribe of Zebulun was 57,400.

³²From the sons of Joseph:

From the descendants of Ephraim:

All the men twenty years old or more who were able to serve in the army were listed by name, according to the records of their clans and families. ³³The number from the tribe of Ephraim was 40,500.

³⁴From the descendants of Manasseh:

All the men twenty years old or more who were able to serve in the army were listed by name, according to the records of their clans and families. ³⁵The number from the tribe of Manasseh was 32,200.

Numbers 1:1

God Communicates

The LORD spoke to Moses in the Tent of Meeting in the Desert of Sinai on the first day of the second month of the second year after the Israelites came out of Egypt.

36From the descendants of Benjamin:
All the men twenty years old or more who were able to serve in the army were listed by name, according to the records of their clans and families. 37The number from the tribe of Benjamin was 35,400.

38From the descendants of Dan:
All the men twenty years old or more who were able to serve in the army were listed by name, according to the records of their clans and families. 39The number from the tribe of Dan was 62,700.

40From the descendants of Asher:
All the men twenty years old or more who were able to serve in the army were listed by name, according to the records of their clans and families. 41The number from the tribe of Asher was 41,500.

42From the descendants of Naphtali:
All the men twenty years old or more who were able to serve in the army were listed by name, according to the records of their clans and families. 43The number from the tribe of Naphtali was 53,400.

44These were the men counted by Moses and Aaron and the twelve leaders of Israel, each one representing his family. 45All the Israelites twenty years old or more who were able to serve in Israel's army were counted according to their families. 46The total number was 603,550.

47The families of the tribe of Levi, however, were not counted along with the others. 48The Lord had said to Moses: 49"You must not count the tribe of Levi or include them in the census of the other Israelites. 50Instead, appoint the Levites to be in charge of the tabernacle of the Testimony—over all its furnishings and everything belonging to it. They are to carry the tabernacle and all its furnishings; they are to take care of it and encamp around it. 51Whenever the tabernacle is to move, the Levites are to take

it down, and whenever the tabernacle is to be set up, the Levites shall do it. Anyone else who goes near it shall be put to death. 52The Israelites are to set up their tents by divisions, each man in his own camp under his own standard. 53The Levites, however, are to set up their tents around the tabernacle of the Testimony so that wrath will not fall on the Israelite community. The Levites are to be responsible for the care of the tabernacle of the Testimony."

54The Israelites did all this just as the Lord commanded Moses.

The Arrangement of the Tribal Camps

2 The Lord said to Moses and Aaron: 2"The Israelites are to camp around the Tent of Meeting some distance from it, each man under his standard with the banners of his family."

3On the east, toward the sunrise, the divisions of the camp of Judah are to encamp under their standard. The leader of the people of Judah is Nahshon son of Amminadab. 4His division numbers 74,600.

5The tribe of Issachar will camp next to them. The leader of the people of Issachar is Nethanel son of Zuar. 6His division numbers 54,400.

7The tribe of Zebulun will be next. The leader of the people of Zebulun is Eliab son of Helon. 8His division numbers 57,400.

9All the men assigned to the camp of Judah, according to their divisions, number 186,400. They will set out first.

10On the south will be the divisions of the camp of Reuben under their standard. The leader of the people of Reuben is Elizur son of Shedeur. 11His division numbers 46,500.

12The tribe of Simeon will camp next to them. The leader of the people of Simeon is Shelumiel son of Zurishaddai. 13His division numbers 59,300.

14The tribe of Gad will be next. The leader of the people of Gad is Eliasaph son of Deuel.*a* 15His division numbers 45,650.

16All the men assigned to the camp of

a14 Many manuscripts of the Masoretic Text, Samaritan Pentateuch and Vulgate (see also Num. 1:14); most manuscripts of the Masoretic Text Reuel

Reuben, according to their divisions, number 151,450. They will set out second.

¹⁷Then the Tent of Meeting and the camp of the Levites will set out in the middle of the camps. They will set out in the same order as they encamp, each in his own place under his standard.

¹⁸On the west will be the divisions of the camp of Ephraim under their standard. The leader of the people of Ephraim is Elishama son of Ammihud. ¹⁹His division numbers 40,500.

²⁰The tribe of Manasseh will be next to them. The leader of the people of Manasseh is Gamaliel son of Pedahzur. ²¹His division numbers 32,200.

²²The tribe of Benjamin will be next. The leader of the people of Benjamin is Abidan son of Gideoni. ²³His division numbers 35,400.

²⁴All the men assigned to the camp of Ephraim, according to their divisions, number 108,100. They will set out third.

²⁵On the north will be the divisions of the camp of Dan, under their standard. The leader of the people of Dan is Ahiezer son of Ammishaddai. ²⁶His division numbers 62,700.

²⁷The tribe of Asher will camp next to them. The leader of the people of Asher is Pagiel son of Ocran. ²⁸His division numbers 41,500.

²⁹The tribe of Naphtali will be next. The leader of the people of Naphtali is Ahira son of Enan. ³⁰His division numbers 53,400.

³¹All the men assigned to the camp of Dan number 157,600. They will set out last, under their standards.

³²These are the Israelites, counted according to their families. All those in the camps, by their divisions, number 603,550. ³³The Levites, however, were not counted along with the other Israelites, as the LORD commanded Moses.

³⁴So the Israelites did everything the LORD commanded Moses; that is the way they encamped under their standards, and that is the way they set out, each with his clan and family.

The Levites

3 This is the account of the family of Aaron and Moses at the time the LORD talked with Moses on Mount Sinai.

²The names of the sons of Aaron were Nadab the firstborn and Abihu, Eleazar and Ithamar. ³Those were the names of Aaron's sons, the anointed priests, who were ordained to serve as priests. ⁴Nadab and Abihu, however, fell dead before the LORD when they made an offering with unauthorized fire before him in the Desert of Sinai. They had no sons; so only Eleazar and Ithamar served as priests during the lifetime of their father Aaron.

⁵The LORD said to Moses, ⁶"Bring the tribe of Levi and present them to Aaron the priest to assist him. ⁷They are to perform duties for him and for the whole community at the Tent of Meeting by doing the work of the tabernacle. ⁸They are to take care of all the furnishings of the Tent of Meeting, fulfilling the obligations of the Israelites by doing the work of the tabernacle. ⁹Give the Levites to Aaron and his sons; they are the Israelites who are to be given wholly to him.^a ¹⁰Appoint Aaron and his sons to serve as priests; anyone else who approaches the sanctuary must be put to death."

¹¹The LORD also said to Moses, ¹²"I have taken the Levites from among the Israelites in place of the first male offspring of every Israelite woman. The Levites are mine, ¹³for all the firstborn are mine. When I struck down all the firstborn in Egypt, I set apart for myself every firstborn in Israel, whether man or animal. They are to be mine. I am the LORD."

¹⁴The LORD said to Moses in the Desert of Sinai, ¹⁵"Count the Levites by their families and clans. Count every male a month old or more." ¹⁶So Moses counted them, as he was commanded by the word of the LORD.

¹⁷These were the names of the sons of Levi:

Gershon, Kohath and Merari.

¹⁸These were the names of the Gershonite clans:

---

^a9 Most manuscripts of the Masoretic Text; some manuscripts of the Masoretic Text, Samaritan Pentateuch and Septuagint (see also Num. 8:16) *to me*

Libni and Shimei.

19 The Kohathite clans:

Amram, Izhar, Hebron and Uzziel.

20 The Merarite clans:

Mahli and Mushi.

These were the Levite clans, according to their families.

21 To Gershon belonged the clans of the Libnites and Shimeites; these were the Gershonite clans. 22 The number of all the males a month old or more who were counted was 7,500. 23 The Gershonite clans were to camp on the west, behind the tabernacle. 24 The leader of the families of the Gershonites was Eliasaph son of Lael. 25 At the Tent of Meeting the Gershonites were responsible for the care of the tabernacle and tent, its coverings, the curtain at the entrance to the Tent of Meeting, 26 the curtains of the courtyard, the curtain at the entrance to the courtyard surrounding the tabernacle and altar, and the ropes—and everything related to their use.

27 To Kohath belonged the clans of the Amramites, Izharites, Hebronites and Uzzielites; these were the Kohathite clans. 28 The number of all the males a month old or more was 8,600.[a] The Kohathites were responsible for the care of the sanctuary. 29 The Kohathite clans were to camp on the south side of the tabernacle. 30 The leader of the families of the Kohathite clans was Elizaphan son of Uzziel. 31 They were responsible for the care of the ark, the table, the lampstand, the altars, the articles of the sanctuary used in ministering, the curtain, and everything related to their use. 32 The chief leader of the Levites was Eleazar son of Aaron, the priest. He was appointed over those who were responsible for the care of the sanctuary.

33 To Merari belonged the clans of the Mahlites and the Mushites; these were the Merarite clans. 34 The number of all the males a month old or more who were counted was 6,200. 35 The leader of the families of the Merarite clans was Zuriel son of Abihail; they were to camp on the north side of the tabernacle. 36 The Merarites were appointed to take care of the frames of the tabernacle, its crossbars, posts, bases, all its equipment, and everything related to their use, 37 as well as the posts of the surrounding courtyard with their bases, tent pegs and ropes.

38 Moses and Aaron and his sons were to camp to the east of the tabernacle, toward the sunrise, in front of the Tent of Meeting. They were responsible for the care of the sanctuary on behalf of the Israelites. Anyone else who approached the sanctuary was to be put to death.

39 The total number of Levites counted at the LORD's command by Moses and Aaron according to their clans, including every male a month old or more, was 22,000.

40 The LORD said to Moses, "Count all the firstborn Israelite males who are a month old or more and make a list of their names. 41 Take the Levites for me in place of all the firstborn of the Israelites, and the livestock of the Levites in place of all the firstborn of the livestock of the Israelites. I am the LORD."

42 So Moses counted all the firstborn of the Israelites, as the LORD commanded him. 43 The total number of firstborn males a month old or more, listed by name, was 22,273.

44 The LORD also said to Moses, 45 "Take the Levites in place of all the firstborn of Israel, and the livestock of the Levites in place of their livestock. The Levites are to be mine. I am the LORD. 46 To redeem the 273 firstborn Israelites who exceed the number of the Levites, 47 collect five shekels[b] for each one, according to the sanctuary shekel, which weighs twenty gerahs. 48 Give the money for the redemption of the additional Israelites to Aaron and his sons."

49 So Moses collected the redemption money from those who exceeded the number redeemed by the Levites. 50 From the firstborn of the Israelites he collected silver weighing 1,365 shekels,[c] according to the sanctuary shekel. 51 Moses gave the redemption money to Aaron and his sons, as he was commanded by the word of the LORD.

---

*a*28 Hebrew; some Septuagint manuscripts *8,300*   *b*47 That is, about 2 ounces (about 55 grams)   *c*50 That is, about 35 pounds (about 15.5 kilograms)

The Kohathites

4 The LORD said to Moses and Aaron: [2]"Take a census of the Kohathite branch of the Levites by their clans and families. [3]Count all the men from thirty to fifty years of age who come to serve in the work in the Tent of Meeting.

[4]"This is the work of the Kohathites in the Tent of Meeting: the care of the most holy things. [5]When the camp is to move, Aaron and his sons are to go in and take down the shielding curtain and cover the ark of the Testimony with it. [6]Then they are to cover this with hides of sea cows,[a] spread a cloth of solid blue over that and put the poles in place.

[7]"Over the table of the Presence they are to spread a blue cloth and put on it the plates, dishes and bowls, and the jars for drink offerings; the bread that is continually there is to remain on it. [8]Over these they are to spread a scarlet cloth, cover that with hides of sea cows and put its poles in place.

[9]"They are to take a blue cloth and cover the lampstand that is for light, together with its lamps, its wick trimmers and trays, and all its jars for the oil used to supply it. [10]Then they are to wrap it and all its accessories in a covering of hides of sea cows and put it on a carrying frame.

[11]"Over the gold altar they are to spread a blue cloth and cover that with hides of sea cows and put its poles in place.

[12]"They are to take all the articles used for ministering in the sanctuary, wrap them in a blue cloth, cover that with hides of sea cows and put them on a carrying frame.

[13]"They are to remove the ashes from the bronze altar and spread a purple cloth over it. [14]Then they are to place on it all the utensils used for ministering at the altar, including the firepans, meat forks, shovels and sprinkling bowls. Over it they are to spread a covering of hides of sea cows and put its poles in place.

[15]"After Aaron and his sons have finished covering the holy furnishings and all the holy articles, and when the camp is ready to move, the Kohathites are to come to do the carrying. But they must not touch the holy things or they will die. The Kohathites are to carry those things that are in the Tent of Meeting.

[16]"Eleazar son of Aaron, the priest, is to have charge of the oil for the light, the fragrant incense, the regular grain offering and the anointing oil. He is to be in charge of the entire tabernacle and everything in it, including its holy furnishings and articles."

[17]The LORD said to Moses and Aaron, [18]"See that the Kohathite tribal clans are not cut off from the Levites. [19]So that they may live and not die when they come near the most holy things, do this for them: Aaron and his sons are to go into the sanctuary and assign to each man his work and what he is to carry. [20]But the Kohathites must not go in to look at the holy things, even for a moment, or they will die."

The Gershonites

[21]The LORD said to Moses, [22]"Take a census also of the Gershonites by their families and clans. [23]Count all the men from thirty to fifty years of age who come to serve in the work at the Tent of Meeting.

[24]"This is the service of the Gershonite clans as they work and carry burdens: [25]They are to carry the curtains of the tabernacle, the Tent of Meeting, its covering and the outer covering of hides of sea cows, the curtains for the entrance to the Tent of Meeting, [26]the curtains of the courtyard surrounding the tabernacle and altar, the curtain for the entrance, the ropes and all the equipment used in its service. The Gershonites are to do all that needs to be done with these things. [27]All their service, whether carrying or doing other work, is to be done under the direction of Aaron and his sons. You shall assign to them as their responsibility all they are to carry. [28]This is the service of the Gershonite clans at the Tent of Meeting. Their duties are to be under the direction of Ithamar son of Aaron, the priest.

The Merarites

[29]"Count the Merarites by their clans and families. [30]Count all the men from thirty to fifty years of age who come to serve in the work at the Tent of Meeting. [31]This is their duty as they perform service at the Tent of Meeting: to carry the frames of the tabernacle, its crossbars, posts and bases, [32]as well as the posts of the surrounding courtyard with their bases,

[a]6 That is, dugongs; also in verses 8, 10, 11, 12, 14 and 25

tent pegs, ropes, all their equipment and everything related to their use. Assign to each man the specific things he is to carry. [33]This is the service of the Merarite clans as they work at the Tent of Meeting under the direction of Ithamar son of Aaron, the priest."

The Numbering of the Levite Clans

[34]Moses, Aaron and the leaders of the community counted the Kohathites by their clans and families. [35]All the men from thirty to fifty years of age who came to serve in the work in the Tent of Meeting, [36]counted by clans, were 2,750. [37]This was the total of all those in the Kohathite clans who served in the Tent of Meeting. Moses and Aaron counted them according to the LORD's command through Moses.

[38]The Gershonites were counted by their clans and families. [39]All the men from thirty to fifty years of age who came to serve in the work at the Tent of Meeting, [40]counted by their clans and families, were 2,630. [41]This was the total of those in the Gershonite clans who served at the Tent of Meeting. Moses and Aaron counted them according to the LORD's command.

[42]The Merarites were counted by their clans and families. [43]All the men from thirty to fifty years of age who came to serve in the work at the Tent of Meeting, [44]counted by their clans, were 3,200. [45]This was the total of those in the Merarite clans. Moses and Aaron counted them according to the LORD's command through Moses.

[46]So Moses, Aaron and the leaders of Israel counted all the Levites by their clans and families. [47]All the men from thirty to fifty years of age who came to do the work of serving and carrying the Tent of Meeting [48]numbered 8,580. [49]At the LORD's command through Moses, each was assigned his work and told what to carry.

Thus they were counted, as the LORD commanded Moses.

The Purity of the Camp

5 The LORD said to Moses, [2]"Command the Israelites to send away from the camp anyone who has an infectious skin disease[a] or a discharge of any kind, or who is ceremonially unclean because of a dead body. [3]Send away male and female alike; send them outside the camp so they will not defile their camp, where I dwell among them." [4]The Israelites did this; they sent them outside the camp. They did just as the LORD had instructed Moses.

Restitution for Wrongs

[5]The LORD said to Moses, [6]"Say to the Israelites: 'When a man or woman wrongs another in any way[b] and so is unfaithful to the LORD, that person is guilty [7]and must confess the sin he has committed. He must make full restitution for his wrong, add one fifth to it and give it all to the person he has wronged. [8]But if that person has no close relative to whom restitution can be made for the wrong, the restitution belongs to the LORD and must be given to the priest, along with the ram with which atonement is made for him. [9]All the sacred contributions the Israelites bring to a priest will belong to him. [10]Each man's sacred gifts are his own, but what he gives to the priest will belong to the priest.'"

The Test for an Unfaithful Wife

[11]Then the LORD said to Moses, [12]"Speak to the Israelites and say to them: 'If a man's wife goes astray and is unfaithful to him [13]by sleeping with another man, and this is hidden from her husband and her impurity is undetected (since there is no witness against her and she has not been caught in the act), [14]and if feelings of jealousy come over her husband and he suspects his wife and she is impure—or if he is jealous and suspects her even though she is not impure— [15]then he is to take his wife to the priest. He must also take an offering of a tenth of an ephah[c] of barley flour on her behalf. He must not pour oil on it or put incense on it, because it is a grain offering for jealousy, a reminder offering to draw attention to guilt.

[16]"'The priest shall bring her and have her stand before the LORD. [17]Then he shall take some holy water in a clay jar and put some dust from the tabernacle floor into the water. [18]After the priest has had the woman stand before the LORD, he shall loosen her hair and place in her hands the reminder offering, the grain

---

[a]2 Traditionally *leprosy*; the Hebrew word was used for various diseases affecting the skin—not necessarily leprosy.   [b]6 Or *woman commits any wrong common to mankind*   [c]15 That is, probably about 2 quarts (about 2 liters)

How to Restore Relationships

Read: Numbers 5:5-8

SUE *LOVED* HER NEW SWEATER. She couldn't wait to show it to her friend Leslie. The two decided to meet for dinner and a movie. Leslie loved the sweater too. She immediately said, "That sweater would be perfect for my office party. Can I borrow it?" Sue hesitated, but decided a friend was more valuable than an article of clothing, so she agreed. When she got the sweater back, there was a hole under the arm. Leslie apologized profusely, saying, "It must have unraveled. I'm so sorry." Sue nodded and said, "Oh, it's okay." But things were never the same between the two of them. Sue felt that Leslie had taken advantage of her. Leslie thought Sue had overreacted over a simple article of clothing. Over time, the friendship unraveled like the sweater. What would have happened if Leslie had offered to repair or replace the sweater . . . and maybe added a scarf to apologize?

When God gave Moses the Law, he instituted a system of restitution: Anyone who injured another paid the price for what was stolen or destroyed and added 20 percent to the value. We may think of restitution as justice for the wronged party and punishment for the offender. But restitution offers more: It builds a bridge between the two parties, paving the way for relationships to be restored. By confessing the sin and compensating for any loss, the offender no longer has to deal with guilt. Receiving restitution and more frees the injured party from feeling unfairly treated.

Forgiveness from God coupled with responsibility toward the other person are key to restoring relationships. In Jesus' eyes, those broken relationships are always our responsibility. If someone has something against us, he calls us to go and make it right (see Matthew 5:23–24). If we have something against another, we're responsible to take the initiative to settle our differences with them (see Matthew 18:15). It's not always comfortable. But it's always the right thing to do.

Do you feel taken advantage of? Maybe it's time to engage someone in conversation rather than detach from your relationship with them. Or maybe you've unintentionally mistreated a friend . . . you owe them money or lunch or a favor. Consider what needs to be done and take action: Repay the debt, replace the item and apologize for a wrong. Do whatever it takes to restore the relationship. Do it because it pleases God and because your relationships will be richer for it.

Numbers 5:5–7

The Lord said to Moses, "Say to the Israelites: 'When a man or woman wrongs another in any way and so is unfaithful to the Lord, that person is guilty and must confess the sin he has committed. He must make full restitution for his wrong, add one fifth to it and give it all to the person he has wronged.' "

reflection

1 Why is restitution necessary?

2 Think about a relationship that is unraveling. How can you make restitution?

3 What are some ways you can reconcile with God after you have sinned? What restitution can you offer?

RELATED READINGS

Leviticus 6:1–7;
Luke 19:8–10

Go to page 165 for your next devotional reading.

offering for jealousy, while he himself holds the bitter water that brings a curse. [19]Then the priest shall put the woman under oath and say to her, "If no other man has slept with you and you have not gone astray and become impure while married to your husband, may this bitter water that brings a curse not harm you. [20]But if you have gone astray while married to your husband and you have defiled yourself by sleeping with a man other than your husband"— [21]here the priest is to put the woman under this curse of the oath—"may the LORD cause your people to curse and denounce you when he causes your thigh to waste away and your abdomen to swell.[a] [22]May this water that brings a curse enter your body so that your abdomen swells and your thigh wastes away.[b]"

"'Then the woman is to say, "Amen. So be it."

[23]"'The priest is to write these curses on a scroll and then wash them off into the bitter water. [24]He shall have the woman drink the bitter water that brings a curse, and this water will enter her and cause bitter suffering. [25]The priest is to take from her hands the grain offering for jealousy, wave it before the LORD and bring it to the altar. [26]The priest is then to take a handful of the grain offering as a memorial offering and burn it on the altar; after that, he is to have the woman drink the water. [27]If she has defiled herself and been unfaithful to her husband, then when she is made to drink the water that brings a curse, it will go into her and cause bitter suffering; her abdomen will swell and her thigh waste away,[c] and she will become accursed among her people. [28]If, however, the woman has not defiled herself and is free from impurity, she will be cleared of guilt and will be able to have children.

[29]"'This, then, is the law of jealousy when a woman goes astray and defiles herself while married to her husband, [30]or when feelings of jealousy come over a man because he suspects his wife. The priest is to have her stand before the LORD and is to apply this entire law to her. [31]The husband will be innocent of any wrongdoing, but the woman will bear the consequences of her sin.'"

The Nazirite

6 The LORD said to Moses, [2]"Speak to the Israelites and say to them: 'If a man or woman wants to make a special vow, a vow of separation to the LORD as a Nazirite, [3]he must abstain from wine and other fermented drink and must not drink vinegar made from wine or from other fermented drink. He must not drink grape juice or eat grapes or raisins. [4]As long as he is a Nazirite, he must not eat anything that comes from the grapevine, not even the seeds or skins.

[5]"'During the entire period of his vow of separation no razor may be used on his head. He must be holy until the period of his separation to the LORD is over; he must let the hair of his head grow long. [6]Throughout the period of his separation to the LORD he must not go near a dead body. [7]Even if his own father or mother or brother or sister dies, he must not make himself ceremonially unclean on account of them, because the symbol of his separation to God is on his head. [8]Throughout the period of his separation he is consecrated to the LORD.

[9]"'If someone dies suddenly in his presence, thus defiling the hair he has dedicated, he must shave his head on the day of his cleansing—the seventh day. [10]Then on the eighth day he must bring two doves or two young pigeons to the priest at the entrance to the Tent of Meeting. [11]The priest is to offer one as a sin offering and the other as a burnt offering to make atonement for him because he sinned by being in the presence of the dead body. That same day he is to consecrate his head. [12]He must dedicate himself to the LORD for the period of his separation and must bring a year-old male lamb as a guilt offering. The previous days do not count, because he became defiled during his separation.

[13]"'Now this is the law for the Nazirite when the period of his separation is over. He is to be brought to the entrance to the Tent of Meeting. [14]There he is to present his offerings to the LORD: a year-old male lamb without defect for a burnt offering, a year-old ewe lamb without defect for a sin offering, a ram without defect

---

[a]21 Or causes you to have a miscarrying womb and barrenness [b]22 Or body and cause you to be barren and have a miscarrying womb [c]27 Or suffering; she will have barrenness and a miscarrying womb

What's in a Name?

Read: Numbers 6:1–27

ONE POPULAR WEBSITE offers 970 books to help you name your baby. Titles like *Cool Names for Babies* and *75,000+ Baby Names for the 21st Century* reveal a truth most parents already know: Names mean something. We spend months agonizing over just the right name for the new baby coming into the world. Should we name the baby after the father or the mother's father? If we name the baby this will they call her that? What if we get it wrong—will she be scarred for life?

In the Old Testament, names were not chosen because they were cute or cool. They represented the parents' hopes, dreams and prayers for their child. Take Daniel the prophet, for example, held captive in Babylon. His name meant "God is my judge." Names sometimes represented the circumstances of the child's birth: Isaac's name reflected his mother's laughter; Esau's, his hairy appearance.

God's name is so revered to the Jews that, starting in the later Old Testament days, they would not say it out loud. Even today in synagogues, they won't say the sacred name YHWH (Jehovah). Instead they call him *Adonai*—the LORD.

When God instructed Aaron to bless the Israelites with his sacred name, he bestowed a great honor on the newborn nation. He was promising to bless them. He was setting them apart for his own special purpose. As the priests pronounced this blessing on the Israelites, they were, in effect, calling upon God to live in their midst and meet their needs as their heavenly provider. To be called by God's holy name meant that they would be expected to act as holy people. They would have to live up to the name they'd been given.

When we were born again, we received a new name: Christian. We now carry the name of our Savior. Just as the Israelites were expected to bear God's name with dignity, we are to honor Christ's name by reflecting his character with our words and actions. That also means not using his name in vain or allowing others to defame it.

Jesus' name is the name above all names. Wear it proudly. Defend it loudly. Make it mean something holy and wonderful to everyone you meet.

Go to page 171 for your next devotional reading.

Numbers 6:27

"So they will put my name on the Israelites, and I will bless them."

reflection

1 Think about your own name. How does your name reflect who you are?

2 How do you feel when you hear someone use Christ's name in vain? How do you respond?

3 How did today's devotion affect your understanding of the importance of bearing God's name?

RELATED READINGS

Genesis 2:19–20;
4:1,25–26;
Exodus 34:1–7;
Revelation 2:17

for a fellowship offering,[a] **15**together with their grain offerings and drink offerings, and a basket of bread made without yeast—cakes made of fine flour mixed with oil, and wafers spread with oil.

16"The priest is to present them before the LORD and make the sin offering and the burnt offering. **17**He is to present the basket of unleavened bread and is to sacrifice the ram as a fellowship offering to the LORD, together with its grain offering and drink offering.

18"Then at the entrance to the Tent of Meeting, the Nazirite must shave off the hair that he dedicated. He is to take the hair and put it in the fire that is under the sacrifice of the fellowship offering.

19"After the Nazirite has shaved off the hair of his dedication, the priest is to place in his hands a boiled shoulder of the ram, and a cake and a wafer from the basket, both made without yeast. **20**The priest shall then wave them before the LORD as a wave offering; they are holy and belong to the priest, together with the breast that was waved and the thigh that was presented. After that, the Nazirite may drink wine.

21"This is the law of the Nazirite who vows his offering to the LORD in accordance with his separation, in addition to whatever else he can afford. He must fulfill the vow he has made, according to the law of the Nazirite.'"

The Priestly Blessing

22The LORD said to Moses, **23**"Tell Aaron and his sons, 'This is how you are to bless the Israelites. Say to them:

24"'"The LORD bless you
    and keep you;
25the LORD make his face
        shine upon you
    and be gracious to you;
26the LORD turn his face
        toward you
    and give you peace."'

27"So they will put my name on the Israelites, and I will bless them."

Numbers 6:25

God Bless His People

"The LORD make his face shine upon you and be gracious to you."

Offerings at the Dedication of the Tabernacle

7 When Moses finished setting up the tabernacle, he anointed it and consecrated it and all its furnishings. He also anointed and consecrated the altar and all its utensils. **2**Then the leaders of Israel, the heads of families who were the tribal leaders in charge of those who were counted, made offerings. **3**They brought as their gifts before the LORD six covered carts and twelve oxen—an ox from each leader and a cart from every two. These they presented before the tabernacle.

4The LORD said to Moses, **5**"Accept these from them, that they may be used in the work at the Tent of Meeting. Give them to the Levites as each man's work requires."

6So Moses took the carts and oxen and gave them to the Levites. **7**He gave two carts and four oxen to the Gershonites, as their work required, **8**and he gave four carts and eight oxen to the Merarites, as their work required. They were all under the direction of Ithamar son of Aaron, the priest. **9**But Moses did not give any to the Kohathites, because they were to carry on their shoulders the holy things, for which they were responsible.

10When the altar was anointed, the leaders brought their offerings for its dedication and presented them before the altar. **11**For the LORD had said to Moses, "Each day one leader is to bring his offering for the dedication of the altar."

12The one who brought his offering on the first day was Nahshon son of Amminadab of the tribe of Judah.

13His offering was one silver plate weighing a hundred and thirty shekels,[b] and one silver sprinkling bowl weighing seventy shekels,[c] both according to the sanctuary shekel, each filled with fine flour mixed with oil as a grain offering; **14**one gold dish weighing ten shekels,[d] filled with incense;

---

[a]14 Traditionally *peace offering*; also in verses 17 and 18   [b]13 That is, about 3 1/4 pounds (about 1.5 kilograms); also elsewhere in this chapter   [c]13 That is, about 1 3/4 pounds (about 0.8 kilogram); also elsewhere in this chapter   [d]14 That is, about 4 ounces (about 110 grams); also elsewhere in this chapter

¹⁵one young bull, one ram and one male lamb a year old, for a burnt offering; ¹⁶one male goat for a sin offering; ¹⁷and two oxen, five rams, five male goats and five male lambs a year old, to be sacrificed as a fellowship offering.ᵃ This was the offering of Nahshon son of Amminadab.

¹⁸On the second day Nethanel son of Zuar, the leader of Issachar, brought his offering.

¹⁹The offering he brought was one silver plate weighing a hundred and thirty shekels, and one silver sprinkling bowl weighing seventy shekels, both according to the sanctuary shekel, each filled with fine flour mixed with oil as a grain offering; ²⁰one gold dish weighing ten shekels, filled with incense; ²¹one young bull, one ram and one male lamb a year old, for a burnt offering; ²²one male goat for a sin offering; ²³and two oxen, five rams, five male goats and five male lambs a year old, to be sacrificed as a fellowship offering. This was the offering of Nethanel son of Zuar.

²⁴On the third day, Eliab son of Helon, the leader of the people of Zebulun, brought his offering.

²⁵His offering was one silver plate weighing a hundred and thirty shekels, and one silver sprinkling bowl weighing seventy shekels, both according to the sanctuary shekel, each filled with fine flour mixed with oil as a grain offering; ²⁶one gold dish weighing ten shekels, filled with incense; ²⁷one young bull, one ram and one male lamb a year old, for a burnt offering; ²⁸one male goat for a sin offering; ²⁹and two oxen, five rams, five male goats and five male lambs a year old, to be sacrificed as a fellowship offering. This was the offering of Eliab son of Helon.

³⁰On the fourth day Elizur son of Shedeur, the leader of the people of Reuben, brought his offering.

³¹His offering was one silver plate weighing a hundred and thirty shekels, and one silver sprinkling bowl weighing seventy shekels, both according to the sanctuary shekel, each filled with fine flour mixed with oil as a grain offering; ³²one gold dish weighing ten shekels, filled with incense; ³³one young bull, one ram and one male lamb a year old, for a burnt offering; ³⁴one male goat for a sin offering; ³⁵and two oxen, five rams, five male goats and five male lambs a year old, to be sacrificed as a fellowship offering. This was the offering of Elizur son of Shedeur.

³⁶On the fifth day Shelumiel son of Zurishaddai, the leader of the people of Simeon, brought his offering.

³⁷His offering was one silver plate weighing a hundred and thirty shekels, and one silver sprinkling bowl weighing seventy shekels, both according to the sanctuary shekel, each filled with fine flour mixed with oil as a grain offering; ³⁸one gold dish weighing ten shekels, filled with incense; ³⁹one young bull, one ram and one male lamb a year old, for a burnt offering; ⁴⁰one male goat for a sin offering; ⁴¹and two oxen, five rams, five male goats and five male lambs a year old, to be sacrificed as a fellowship offering. This was the offering of Shelumiel son of Zurishaddai.

⁴²On the sixth day Eliasaph son of Deuel, the leader of the people of Gad, brought his offering.

⁴³His offering was one silver plate weighing a hundred and thirty shekels, and one silver sprinkling bowl weighing seventy shekels, both according to the sanctuary shekel, each filled with fine flour mixed with oil as a grain offering; ⁴⁴one gold dish weighing ten shekels, filled with incense; ⁴⁵one young bull, one ram and one male lamb a year old, for a burnt offering; ⁴⁶one male goat for a sin offering; ⁴⁷and two oxen, five rams, five male goats and five male lambs a year old, to be sacrificed as a fellowship offering. This was the offering of Eliasaph son of Deuel.

⁴⁸On the seventh day Elishama son of Ammihud, the leader of the people of Ephraim, brought his offering.

ᵃ17 Traditionally *peace offering*; also elsewhere in this chapter

49His offering was one silver plate weighing a hundred and thirty shekels, and one silver sprinkling bowl weighing seventy shekels, both according to the sanctuary shekel, each filled with fine flour mixed with oil as a grain offering; 50one gold dish weighing ten shekels, filled with incense; 51one young bull, one ram and one male lamb a year old, for a burnt offering; 52one male goat for a sin offering; 53and two oxen, five rams, five male goats and five male lambs a year old, to be sacrificed as a fellowship offering. This was the offering of Elishama son of Ammihud.

54On the eighth day Gamaliel son of Pedahzur, the leader of the people of Manasseh, brought his offering.

55His offering was one silver plate weighing a hundred and thirty shekels, and one silver sprinkling bowl weighing seventy shekels, both according to the sanctuary shekel, each filled with fine flour mixed with oil as a grain offering; 56one gold dish weighing ten shekels, filled with incense; 57one young bull, one ram and one male lamb a year old, for a burnt offering; 58one male goat for a sin offering; 59and two oxen, five rams, five male goats and five male lambs a year old, to be sacrificed as a fellowship offering. This was the offering of Gamaliel son of Pedahzur.

60On the ninth day Abidan son of Gideoni, the leader of the people of Benjamin, brought his offering.

61His offering was one silver plate weighing a hundred and thirty shekels, and one silver sprinkling bowl weighing seventy shekels, both according to the sanctuary shekel, each filled with fine flour mixed with oil as a grain offering; 62one gold dish weighing ten shekels, filled with incense; 63one young bull, one ram and one male lamb a year old, for a burnt offering; 64one male goat for a sin offering; 65and two oxen, five rams, five male goats and five male lambs a year old, to be sacrificed as a fellowship offering. This was the offering of Abidan son of Gideoni.

66On the tenth day Ahiezer son of Ammishaddai, the leader of the people of Dan, brought his offering.

67His offering was one silver plate weighing a hundred and thirty shekels, and one silver sprinkling bowl weighing seventy shekels, both according to the sanctuary shekel, each filled with fine flour mixed with oil as a grain offering; 68one gold dish weighing ten shekels, filled with incense; 69one young bull, one ram and one male lamb a year old, for a burnt offering; 70one male goat for a sin offering; 71and two oxen, five rams, five male goats and five male lambs a year old, to be sacrificed as a fellowship offering. This was the offering of Ahiezer son of Ammishaddai.

72On the eleventh day Pagiel son of Ocran, the leader of the people of Asher, brought his offering.

73His offering was one silver plate weighing a hundred and thirty shekels, and one silver sprinkling bowl weighing seventy shekels, both according to the sanctuary shekel, each filled with fine flour mixed with oil as a grain offering; 74one gold dish weighing ten shekels, filled with incense; 75one young bull, one ram and one male lamb a year old, for a burnt offering; 76one male goat for a sin offering; 77and two oxen, five rams, five male goats and five male lambs a year old, to be sacrificed as a fellowship offering. This was the offering of Pagiel son of Ocran.

78On the twelfth day Ahira son of Enan, the leader of the people of Naphtali, brought his offering.

79His offering was one silver plate weighing a hundred and thirty shekels, and one silver sprinkling bowl weighing seventy shekels, both according to the sanctuary shekel, each filled with fine flour mixed with oil as a grain offering; 80one gold dish weighing ten shekels, filled with incense; 81one young bull, one ram and one male lamb a year old, for a burnt offering; 82one male goat for a sin offering; 83and two oxen, five rams, five male goats and five male lambs a year old, to be sacrificed as a fellowship offering. This was the offering of Ahira son of Enan.

84These were the offerings of the Israelite leaders for the dedication of the altar when it was anointed: twelve silver plates, twelve silver sprinkling bowls and twelve gold dishes. 85Each silver plate weighed a hundred and thirty shekels, and each sprinkling bowl seventy shekels. Altogether, the silver dishes weighed two thousand four hundred shekels,a according to the sanctuary shekel. 86The twelve gold dishes filled with incense weighed ten shekels each, according to the sanctuary shekel. Altogether, the gold dishes weighed a hundred and twenty shekels.b 87The total number of animals for the burnt offering came to twelve young bulls, twelve rams and twelve male lambs a year old, together with their grain offering. Twelve male goats were used for the sin offering. 88The total number of animals for the sacrifice of the fellowship offering came to twenty-four oxen, sixty rams, sixty male goats and sixty male lambs a year old. These were the offerings for the dedication of the altar after it was anointed.

89When Moses entered the Tent of Meeting to speak with the LORD, he heard the voice speaking to him from between the two cherubim above the atonement cover on the ark of the Testimony. And he spoke with him.

Setting Up the Lamps

8 The LORD said to Moses, 2"Speak to Aaron and say to him, 'When you set up the seven lamps, they are to light the area in front of the lampstand.'"

3Aaron did so; he set up the lamps so that they faced forward on the lampstand, just as the LORD commanded Moses. 4This is how the lampstand was made: It was made of hammered gold—from its base to its blossoms. The lampstand was made exactly like the pattern the LORD had shown Moses.

Numbers 7:89

God Can Be Known

When Moses entered the Tent of Meeting to speak with the LORD, he heard the voice speaking to him from between the two cherubim above the atonement cover on the ark of the Testimony. And he spoke with him.

The Setting Apart of the Levites

5The LORD said to Moses: 6"Take the Levites from among the other Israelites and make them ceremonially clean. 7To purify them, do this: Sprinkle the water of cleansing on them; then have them shave their whole bodies and wash their clothes, and so purify themselves. 8Have them take a young bull with its grain offering of fine flour mixed with oil; then you are to take a second young bull for a sin offering. 9Bring the Levites to the front of the Tent of Meeting and assemble the whole Israelite community. 10You are to bring the Levites before the LORD, and the Israelites are to lay their hands on them. 11Aaron is to present the Levites before the LORD as a wave offering from the Israelites, so that they may be ready to do the work of the LORD.

12"After the Levites lay their hands on the heads of the bulls, use the one for a sin offering to the LORD and the other for a burnt offering, to make atonement for the Levites. 13Have the Levites stand in front of Aaron and his sons and then present them as a wave offering to the LORD. 14In this way you are to set the Levites apart from the other Israelites, and the Levites will be mine.

15"After you have purified the Levites and presented them as a wave offering, they are to come to do their work at the Tent of Meeting. 16They are the Israelites who are to be given wholly to me. I have taken them as my own in place of the firstborn, the first male offspring from every Israelite woman. 17Every firstborn male in Israel, whether man or animal, is mine. When I struck down all the firstborn in Egypt, I set them apart for myself. 18And I have taken the Levites in place of all the firstborn sons in Israel. 19Of all the Israelites, I have given the Levites as gifts to Aaron and his sons to do the work at the Tent of Meeting on behalf of the Israelites and to make atonement for them so that no plague will strike the Israelites when they go near the sanctuary."

a85 That is, about 60 pounds (about 28 kilograms)   b86 That is, about 3 pounds (about 1.4 kilograms)

²⁰Moses, Aaron and the whole Israelite community did with the Levites just as the LORD commanded Moses. ²¹The Levites purified themselves and washed their clothes. Then Aaron presented them as a wave offering before the LORD and made atonement for them to purify them. ²²After that, the Levites came to do their work at the Tent of Meeting under the supervision of Aaron and his sons. They did with the Levites just as the LORD commanded Moses.

²³The LORD said to Moses, ²⁴"This applies to the Levites: Men twenty-five years old or more shall come to take part in the work at the Tent of Meeting, ²⁵but at the age of fifty, they must retire from their regular service and work no longer. ²⁶They may assist their brothers in performing their duties at the Tent of Meeting, but they themselves must not do the work. This, then, is how you are to assign the responsibilities of the Levites."

The Passover

9 The LORD spoke to Moses in the Desert of Sinai in the first month of the second year after they came out of Egypt. He said, ²"Have the Israelites celebrate the Passover at the appointed time. ³Celebrate it at the appointed time, at twilight on the fourteenth day of this month, in accordance with all its rules and regulations."

⁴So Moses told the Israelites to celebrate the Passover, ⁵and they did so in the Desert of Sinai at twilight on the fourteenth day of the first month. The Israelites did everything just as the LORD commanded Moses.

⁶But some of them could not celebrate the Passover on that day because they were ceremonially unclean on account of a dead body. So they came to Moses and Aaron that same day ⁷and said to Moses, "We have become unclean because of a dead body, but why should we be kept from presenting the LORD's offering with the other Israelites at the appointed time?"

⁸Moses answered them, "Wait until I find out what the LORD commands concerning you."

⁹Then the LORD said to Moses, ¹⁰"Tell the Israelites: 'When any of you or your descendants are unclean because of a dead body or are away on a journey, they may still celebrate the LORD's Passover. ¹¹They are to celebrate it on the fourteenth day of the second month at twilight. They are to eat the lamb, together with unleavened bread and bitter herbs. ¹²They must not leave any of it till morning or break any of its bones. When they celebrate the Passover, they must follow all the regulations. ¹³But if a man who is ceremonially clean and not on a journey fails to celebrate the Passover, that person must be cut off from his people because he did not present the LORD's offering at the appointed time. That man will bear the consequences of his sin.

¹⁴"'An alien living among you who wants to celebrate the LORD's Passover must do so in accordance with its rules and regulations. You must have the same regulations for the alien and the native-born.'"

The Cloud Above the Tabernacle

¹⁵On the day the tabernacle, the Tent of the Testimony, was set up, the cloud covered it. From evening till morning the cloud above the tabernacle looked like fire. ¹⁶That is how it continued to be; the cloud covered it, and at night it looked like fire. ¹⁷Whenever the cloud lifted from above the Tent, the Israelites set out; wherever the cloud settled, the Israelites encamped. ¹⁸At the LORD's command the Israelites set out, and at his command they encamped. As long as the cloud stayed over the tabernacle, they remained in camp. ¹⁹When the cloud remained over the tabernacle a long time, the Israelites obeyed the LORD's order and did not set out. ²⁰Sometimes the cloud was over the tabernacle only a few days; at the LORD's command they would encamp, and then at his command they would set out. ²¹Sometimes the cloud stayed only from evening till morning, and when it lifted in the morning, they set out. Whether by day or by night, whenever the cloud lifted, they

Numbers 9:17

God Leads

Whenever the cloud lifted from above the Tent, the Israelites set out; wherever the cloud settled, the Israelites encamped.

Life in the Fast Lane

Read: Numbers 9:15-23

JOANIE COULD SCARCELY BELIEVE her eyes. The woman speeding along the Los Angeles freeway next to her balanced a cup of coffee and a cigarette in one hand and ignored her three children bouncing around in the back seat. At that moment, Joanie longed to quit her job and move to the mountains. She prayed, *Lord, I'm tired of this fast-paced life. Can I get off this merry-go-round?*

Maybe life in the fast lane doesn't appeal to you anymore either. You're tired. You need a break. Maybe you're thinking of buying a nice little cabin with a fireplace, a cat and a rocking chair. *Anywhere but here, Lord,* you think. But what does God think?

Following her release from Ravensbruck concentration camp, Corrie ten Boom purchased a house called Schapendunien and turned it into a home for disabled people and ex-prisoners. She thought that was where God wanted her to settle down. But in late 1945, she began to sense that God wanted her to travel to the United States to tell her story. So she crossed the Atlantic and became what she described as a "tramp for the Lord." It wasn't until 1977, when she suffered a stroke, that she finally retired to a home in Orange, California. Choosing to follow God's leading rather than her own comfort-level, Corrie ten Boom maintained an itinerant lifestyle of travel for Christ.

You may be facing unbearable pressures in your daily life, pressures you think will get better if you settle down in a peaceful location of your choice. But God showed the Israelites that he chooses our paths. He gave them a visible reminder of his presence to guide them: a cloud by day and a fire by night. When the cloud lifted, they set out; when it stopped, they camped. God's sign in the sky marked their course and set the pace. By looking up, the Israelites discovered that the Lord ordained the movements of his people; God saying "no" was just as important as God saying "go." God alone knew the reasons for the journey, the unseen dangers ahead and the ultimate purpose beyond each move.

God ordered the lives of the Israelites. And he'll order yours if you will let him. If you need to know which way to turn, look up.

Numbers 9:17-18

Whenever the cloud lifted from above the Tent, the Israelites set out; wherever the cloud settled, the Israelites encamped. At the LORD's command the Israelites set out, and at his command they encamped. As long as the cloud stayed over the tabernacle, they remained in camp.

reflection

1 What changes are you considering in your life? Have you asked God about them?

2 What are the obstacles (if any) that you face in making your life-changing decisions? Could God be telling you "no" instead of "go"?

3 Is it difficult for you to be patient, or are you willing to wait for God's guidance? Take the time to look up and ask the Lord to show you what he wants you to do.

RELATED READINGS

Deuteronomy 4:1; 28:1; Psalm 43:3-4

Wednesday

Go to page 174 for your next devotional reading.

171

set out. ²²Whether the cloud stayed over the tabernacle for two days or a month or a year, the Israelites would remain in camp and not set out; but when it lifted, they would set out. ²³At the Lord's command they encamped, and at the Lord's command they set out. They obeyed the Lord's order, in accordance with his command through Moses.

The Silver Trumpets

10 The Lord said to Moses: ²"Make two trumpets of hammered silver, and use them for calling the community together and for having the camps set out. ³When both are sounded, the whole community is to assemble before you at the entrance to the Tent of Meeting. ⁴If only one is sounded, the leaders—the heads of the clans of Israel—are to assemble before you. ⁵When a trumpet blast is sounded, the tribes camping on the east are to set out. ⁶At the sounding of a second blast, the camps on the south are to set out. The blast will be the signal for setting out. ⁷To gather the assembly, blow the trumpets, but not with the same signal.

⁸"The sons of Aaron, the priests, are to blow the trumpets. This is to be a lasting ordinance for you and the generations to come. ⁹When you go into battle in your own land against an enemy who is oppressing you, sound a blast on the trumpets. Then you will be remembered by the Lord your God and rescued from your enemies. ¹⁰Also at your times of rejoicing—your appointed feasts and New Moon festivals—you are to sound the trumpets over your burnt offerings and fellowship offerings,[a] and they will be a memorial for you before your God. I am the Lord your God."

The Israelites Leave Sinai

¹¹On the twentieth day of the second month of the second year, the cloud lifted from above the tabernacle of the Testimony. ¹²Then the Israelites set out from the Desert of Sinai and traveled from place to place until the cloud came to rest in the Desert of Paran. ¹³They set out, this first time, at the Lord's command through Moses.

¹⁴The divisions of the camp of Judah went first, under their standard. Nahshon son of Amminadab was in command. ¹⁵Nethanel son of Zuar was over the division of the tribe of Issachar, ¹⁶and Eliab son of Helon was over the division of the tribe of Zebulun. ¹⁷Then the tabernacle was taken down, and the Gershonites and Merarites, who carried it, set out.

¹⁸The divisions of the camp of Reuben went next, under their standard. Elizur son of Shedeur was in command. ¹⁹Shelumiel son of Zurishaddai was over the division of the tribe of Simeon, ²⁰and Eliasaph son of Deuel was over the division of the tribe of Gad. ²¹Then the Kohathites set out, carrying the holy things. The tabernacle was to be set up before they arrived.

²²The divisions of the camp of Ephraim went next, under their standard. Elishama son of Ammihud was in command. ²³Gamaliel son of Pedahzur was over the division of the tribe of Manasseh, ²⁴and Abidan son of Gideoni was over the division of the tribe of Benjamin.

²⁵Finally, as the rear guard for all the units, the divisions of the camp of Dan set out, under their standard. Ahiezer son of Ammishaddai was in command. ²⁶Pagiel son of Ocran was over the division of the tribe of Asher, ²⁷and Ahira son of Enan was over the division of the tribe of Naphtali. ²⁸This was the order of march for the Israelite divisions as they set out.

²⁹Now Moses said to Hobab son of Reuel the Midianite, Moses' father-in-law, "We are setting out for the place about which the Lord said, 'I will give it to you.' Come with us and we will treat you well, for the Lord has promised good things to Israel."

³⁰He answered, "No, I will not go; I am going back to my own land and my own people."

³¹But Moses said, "Please do not leave us. You know where we should camp in the desert, and you can be our eyes. ³²If you come with us, we will share with you whatever good things the Lord gives us."

³³So they set out from the mountain of the Lord and traveled for three days. The ark of the covenant of the Lord went before them during those three days to find them a place to rest. ³⁴The cloud of the Lord was over them by day when they set out from the camp. ³⁵Whenever the ark set out, Moses said,

---

^a10 Traditionally *peace offerings*

"Rise up, O LORD!
May your enemies be scattered;
may your foes flee before you."

³⁶Whenever it came to rest, he said,

"Return, O LORD,
to the countless thousands of Israel."

Fire From the LORD

11 Now the people complained about their hardships in the hearing of the LORD, and when he heard them his anger was aroused. Then fire from the LORD burned among them and consumed some of the outskirts of the camp. ²When the people cried out to Moses, he prayed to the LORD and the fire died down. ³So that place was called Taberah,ᵃ because fire from the LORD had burned among them.

Quail From the LORD

⁴The rabble with them began to crave other food, and again the Israelites started wailing and said, "If only we had meat to eat! ⁵We remember the fish we ate in Egypt at no cost—also the cucumbers, melons, leeks, onions and garlic. ⁶But now we have lost our appetite; we never see anything but this manna!"

⁷The manna was like coriander seed and looked like resin. ⁸The people went around gathering it, and then ground it in a handmill or crushed it in a mortar. They cooked it in a pot or made it into cakes. And it tasted like something made with olive oil. ⁹When the dew settled on the camp at night, the manna also came down.

¹⁰Moses heard the people of every family wailing, each at the entrance to his tent. The LORD became exceedingly angry, and Moses was troubled. ¹¹He asked the LORD, "Why have you brought this trouble on your servant? What have I done to displease you that you put the burden of all these people on me? ¹²Did I conceive all these people? Did I give them birth? Why do you tell me to carry them in my arms, as a nurse carries an infant, to the land you promised on oath to their forefathers? ¹³Where can I get meat for all these people? They keep wailing to me, 'Give us meat to eat!' ¹⁴I cannot carry all these people by myself; the burden is too heavy for me. ¹⁵If this is how you are going to treat me, put me to death right now—if I have found favor in your eyes—and do not let me face my own ruin."

¹⁶The LORD said to Moses: "Bring me seventy of Israel's elders who are known to you as leaders and officials among the people. Have them come to the Tent of Meeting, that they may stand there with you. ¹⁷I will come down and speak with you there, and I will take of the Spirit that is on you and put the Spirit on them. They will help you carry the burden of the people so that you will not have to carry it alone.

¹⁸"Tell the people: 'Consecrate yourselves in preparation for tomorrow, when you will eat meat. The LORD heard you when you wailed, "If only we had meat to eat! We were better off in Egypt!" Now the LORD will give you meat, and you will eat it. ¹⁹You will not eat it for just one day, or two days, or five, ten or twenty days, ²⁰but for a whole month—until it comes out of your nostrils and you loathe it—because you have rejected the LORD, who is among you, and have wailed before him, saying, "Why did we ever leave Egypt?"' "

²¹But Moses said, "Here I am among six hundred thousand men on foot, and you say, 'I will give them meat to eat for a whole month!' ²²Would they have enough if flocks and herds were slaughtered for them? Would they have enough if all the fish in the sea were caught for them?"

²³The LORD answered Moses, "Is the LORD's arm too short? You will now see whether or not what I say will come true for you."

Numbers 11:23

God Is Powerful

The LORD answered Moses, "Is the LORD's arm too short? You will now see whether or not what I say will come true for you."

²⁴So Moses went out and told the people what the LORD had said. He brought together seventy of their elders and had them stand around the Tent. ²⁵Then the LORD came down

---

ᵃ3 *Taberah* means *burning.*

The Light of His Love

Read: Numbers 11:1–35

Numbers 11:4–6

The rabble with them began to crave other food, and again the Israelites started wailing and said, "If only we had meat to eat! We remember the fish we ate in Egypt at no cost—also the cucumbers, melons, leeks, onions and garlic. But now we have lost our appetite; we never see anything but this manna!"

reflection

1 How might things have been different for the Israelites if they had encouraged one another rather than listening to the grumbles of the "rabble"?

2 What situation is causing you to grumble and lose perspective concerning God's provision?

3 Who do you know that needs a word of encouragement? Follow Christine's advice and remind her that God's ways are worth it.

RELATED READINGS

Psalm 25:1–22;
1 Thessalonians 5:8–11;
Hebrews 6:16–20

I WANT TO BE YOUR ENCOURAGER, a voice that cheers you on to believe that God is who he says he is and that walking in his ways will prosper your soul. There's a lot at stake. Without personal encouragement we begin to lose sight of the goal. We get lost in the isolation of making so many choices. The days blend into one another and we slowly lose perspective. To complicate matters, the voices that offer false promises are too alluring to refuse.

No wonder God told us to whisper the truth in each other's ears, because sin is deceitful. It lies. It makes promises it can ever deliver in the long run. Initially sin feels good. An affair is exhilarating. Controlling others is empowering. Taking revenge feels therapeutic. Building a bigger house is an anesthetic to the pain. Gossip makes us feel better about ourselves. Fighting for our rights massages the pain of unfairness. The list goes on.

The longer I choose to believe (and act on) the false promises of sin, the harder my heart becomes. If I sin today, I will be more hardened tomorrow. I'll be even less likely to be affected by the truth. God's voice will be more unwelcome. The purity of his ways will seem more perverted.

Let's put our arms around someone who is struggling with critical choices today. Let's remind them that God's ways are worth it. He delivers what he promises: peace, confidence, eternal rewards and the joy of living in the light of his love.

— Christine Wyrtzen

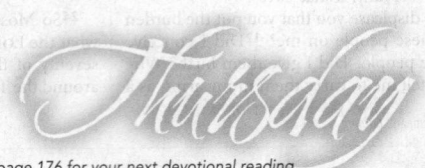

Thursday

in the cloud and spoke with him, and he took of the Spirit that was on him and put the Spirit on the seventy elders. When the Spirit rested on them, they prophesied, but they did not do so again.*a*

²⁶However, two men, whose names were Eldad and Medad, had remained in the camp. They were listed among the elders, but did not go out to the Tent. Yet the Spirit also rested on them, and they prophesied in the camp. ²⁷A young man ran and told Moses, "Eldad and Medad are prophesying in the camp."

²⁸Joshua son of Nun, who had been Moses' aide since youth, spoke up and said, "Moses, my lord, stop them!"

²⁹But Moses replied, "Are you jealous for my sake? I wish that all the LORD's people were prophets and that the LORD would put his Spirit on them!" ³⁰Then Moses and the elders of Israel returned to the camp.

³¹Now a wind went out from the LORD and drove quail in from the sea. It brought them*b* down all around the camp to about three feet*c* above the ground, as far as a day's walk in any direction. ³²All that day and night and all the next day the people went out and gathered quail. No one gathered less than ten homers.*d* Then they spread them out all around the camp. ³³But while the meat was still between their teeth and before it could be consumed, the anger of the LORD burned against the people, and he struck them with a severe plague. ³⁴Therefore the place was named Kibroth Hattaavah,*e* because there they buried the people who had craved other food.

³⁵From Kibroth Hattaavah the people traveled to Hazeroth and stayed there.

Miriam and Aaron Oppose Moses

12 Miriam and Aaron began to talk against Moses because of his Cushite wife, for he had married a Cushite. ²"Has the LORD spoken only through Moses?" they asked. "Hasn't he also spoken through us?" And the LORD heard this.

³(Now Moses was a very humble man, more humble than anyone else on the face of the earth.)

⁴At once the LORD said to Moses, Aaron and Miriam, "Come out to the Tent of Meeting, all three of you." So the three of them came out. ⁵Then the LORD came down in a pillar of cloud; he stood at the entrance to the Tent and summoned Aaron and Miriam. When both of them stepped forward, ⁶he said, "Listen to my words:

"When a prophet of the LORD is among you,
   I reveal myself to him in visions,
   I speak to him in dreams.
⁷But this is not true of my servant Moses;
   he is faithful in all my house.
⁸With him I speak face to face,
   clearly and not in riddles;
   he sees the form of the LORD.
Why then were you not afraid
   to speak against my servant Moses?"

⁹The anger of the LORD burned against them, and he left them.

¹⁰When the cloud lifted from above the Tent, there stood Miriam—leprous,*f* like snow. Aaron turned toward her and saw that she had leprosy; ¹¹and he said to Moses, "Please, my lord, do not hold against us the sin we have so foolishly committed. ¹²Do not let her be like a stillborn infant coming from its mother's womb with its flesh half eaten away."

¹³So Moses cried out to the LORD, "O God, please heal her!"

¹⁴The LORD replied to Moses, "If her father had spit in her face, would she not have been in disgrace for seven days? Confine her outside the camp for seven days; after that she can be brought back." ¹⁵So Miriam was confined outside the camp for seven days, and the people did not move on till she was brought back.

¹⁶After that, the people left Hazeroth and encamped in the Desert of Paran.

Exploring Canaan

13 The LORD said to Moses, ²"Send some men to explore the land of Canaan, which I am giving to the Israelites. From each ancestral tribe send one of its leaders."

³So at the LORD's command Moses sent

---

*a*25 Or *prophesied and continued to do so*   *b*31 Or *They flew*   *c*31 Hebrew *two cubits* (about 1 meter)   *d*32 That is, probably about 60 bushels (about 2.2 kiloliters)   *e*34 *Kibroth Hattaavah* means *graves of craving.*   *f*10 The Hebrew word was used for various diseases affecting the skin—not necessarily leprosy.

Boiling Over

Numbers 12:2

"Has the LORD spoken
only through Moses?"
they asked. "Hasn't he
also spoken through us?"
And the LORD heard this.

reflection

1 How do you respond
when you see others
receiving acclamation for
their spiritual or natural
gifts?

2 How do you act when
you receive acclama-
tion? How do you re-
spond when others are
jealous of you?

3 Jealousy is a sneaky
sin. What do you do
when you sense it start-
ing to simmer?

RELATED READINGS

Exodus 15:20–21;
28:1–5;
Proverbs 14:30;
James 3:14–18

Read: Numbers 12:1–15

APPLAUDING OTHERS can be surprisingly difficult. It's easy
enough to fake it, to smile approvingly and nod in agreement.
But sometimes when others are recognized for achievements, it's
hard to feel anything but that ugly burning twinge of jealousy.
Outwardly we're clapping and congratulating, but inwardly we're
slowly beginning to simmer. *Who does she think she is anyway?
What's so special about her? Why all the fuss over one person?*
And if we don't catch it in time, that simmer can turn into a hard
boil that erupts in anger, harsh words and broken relationships.

The root of jealousy, when we dig down deep enough, is often
insecurity. It's not so much a question of what's so special about
someone else as it is a question of what's so un-special about me?
What's wrong with me, we wonder, that God doesn't use me
like that?

When Miriam and Aaron saw the way God was using Moses,
they were jealous. They wanted to be what he was. And who
wouldn't? God actually talked to Moses face-to-face. He had a
unique role in history that no one else had ever played.

But Miriam and Aaron also had unique roles in history, roles
that Moses couldn't fill, roles that they alone could fill. God had
used them in wonderful ways. Miriam was a prophetess. Think
of how rare in that day—a female prophet! Aaron was the high
priest—the priest above all other priests. He was different from
Moses but amazingly gifted. Miriam and Aaron both had gifts used
by God, but their jealousy started to burn, and they allowed their
negative feelings to affect their positions.

God has made a place for you in his kingdom that only you can
fill. You may be a Moses, out front leading the way. Or you may
be serving in more behind-the-scenes ways like Miriam and Aaron.
Your job is not to compare your work to another's and attach value
based on what you can see. Your job is to turn down the heat of
jealousy and quietly go about the work God has given you to do:
"Each one should test his own actions. Then he can take pride in
himself, without comparing himself to somebody else, for each one
should carry his own load" (Galatians 6:4–5). When it's God's work,
it's valuable. When we allow jealousy to simmer up and boil over,
our own bitterness will only burn us.

Friday

them out from the Desert of Paran. All of them were leaders of the Israelites. ⁴These are their names:

from the tribe of Reuben, Shammua son of Zaccur;
⁵from the tribe of Simeon, Shaphat son of Hori;
⁶from the tribe of Judah, Caleb son of Jephunneh;
⁷from the tribe of Issachar, Igal son of Joseph;
⁸from the tribe of Ephraim, Hoshea son of Nun;
⁹from the tribe of Benjamin, Palti son of Raphu;
¹⁰from the tribe of Zebulun, Gaddiel son of Sodi;
¹¹from the tribe of Manasseh (a tribe of Joseph), Gaddi son of Susi;
¹²from the tribe of Dan, Ammiel son of Gemalli;
¹³from the tribe of Asher, Sethur son of Michael;
¹⁴from the tribe of Naphtali, Nahbi son of Vophsi;
¹⁵from the tribe of Gad, Geuel son of Maki.

¹⁶These are the names of the men Moses sent to explore the land. (Moses gave Hoshea son of Nun the name Joshua.)

¹⁷When Moses sent them to explore Canaan, he said, "Go up through the Negev and on into the hill country. ¹⁸See what the land is like and whether the people who live there are strong or weak, few or many. ¹⁹What kind of land do they live in? Is it good or bad? What kind of towns do they live in? Are they unwalled or fortified? ²⁰How is the soil? Is it fertile or poor? Are there trees on it or not? Do your best to bring back some of the fruit of the land." (It was the season for the first ripe grapes.)

²¹So they went up and explored the land from the Desert of Zin as far as Rehob, toward Lebo*ᵃ* Hamath. ²²They went up through the Negev and came to Hebron, where Ahiman, Sheshai and Talmai, the descendants of Anak, lived. (Hebron had been built seven years before Zoan in Egypt.) ²³When they reached the Valley of Eshcol,*ᵇ* they cut off a branch bearing a single cluster of grapes. Two of them carried it on a pole between them, along with some pomegranates and figs. ²⁴That place was called the Valley of Eshcol because of the cluster of grapes the Israelites cut off there. ²⁵At the end of forty days they returned from exploring the land.

Report on the Exploration

²⁶They came back to Moses and Aaron and the whole Israelite community at Kadesh in the Desert of Paran. There they reported to them and to the whole assembly and showed them the fruit of the land. ²⁷They gave Moses this account: "We went into the land to which you sent us, and it does flow with milk and honey! Here is its fruit. ²⁸But the people who live there are powerful, and the cities are fortified and very large. We even saw descendants of Anak there. ²⁹The Amalekites live in the Negev; the Hittites, Jebusites and Amorites live in the hill country; and the Canaanites live near the sea and along the Jordan."

³⁰Then Caleb silenced the people before Moses and said, "We should go up and take possession of the land, for we can certainly do it."

³¹But the men who had gone up with him said, "We can't attack those people; they are stronger than we are." ³²And they spread among the Israelites a bad report about the land they had explored. They said, "The land we explored devours those living in it. All the people we saw there are of great size. ³³We saw the Nephilim there (the descendants of Anak come from the Nephilim). We seemed like grasshoppers in our own eyes, and we looked the same to them."

The People Rebel

14 That night all the people of the community raised their voices and wept aloud. ²All the Israelites grumbled against Moses and Aaron, and the whole assembly said to them, "If only we had died in Egypt! Or in this desert! ³Why is the LORD bringing us to this land only to let us fall by the sword? Our wives and children will be taken as plunder. Wouldn't it be better for us to go back to Egypt?" ⁴And they said to each other, "We should choose a leader and go back to Egypt."

---

*ᵃ*21 Or *toward the entrance to*   *ᵇ*23 *Eshcol* means *cluster*; also in verse 24.

Just Out of Reach

RACHEL

"BUT, FATHER . . . MY DRESS," she tearfully argued. He had made his decision. "Everyone is ready . . ." she called after him as he turned to leave. He didn't hear.

What was meant to be the best day of her life—her wedding day—was suddenly just out of reach. And her father didn't seem to care.

Years ago, when Jacob and Rachel had fallen in love, she had clearly known that she'd won Jacob's heart. Where she stood with her own father, however, had never been as clear to her. It must have felt wonderful to know that Jacob loved her enough to work for her father for seven years. During that time, did Rachel hope that her father would look on her with love and favor since she was providing him with a desirable son-in-law? Was she worthwhile to her father after all?

A timeless principle between fathers and daughters plays out behind the scenes of this love story. Like every daughter, Rachel had surely sought her father's attention, affection and approval from the time she was a little girl. And like every daughter, her success (or failure) in doing so affected her in ways she couldn't explain.

On her wedding day, the day she had dreamed of for so long, Rachel realized that her usefulness to her father was over. The harsh reality: Laban viewed Rachel and her sister like currency, not like priceless daughters. She witnessed her father squeeze every sum of money out of them that he could, using them as a bartering tool with Jacob. And in the intervening years, he spent it all.

So when Jacob approached her with the idea of returning to his homeland, Rachel had no arguments. She had no ties.

"Our father treats us like we're not even his own." Rachel felt the sting in her eyes as she thought these words. It was as if someone else were saying those cruel words. If she distanced herself from the truth, maybe it wouldn't hurt so badly.

—Prayer—
Dear Jesus, I ask that you help me to forgive and to heal from the wounds caused by others.

Then Rachel and Leah replied, "Do we still have any share in the inheritance of our father's estate? Does he not regard us as foreigners? Not only has he sold us, but he has used up what was paid for us."

Genesis 31:14–15

ASSIGNED READING:

Genesis 29:1—35:20

Weekend

Go to page 182 for your next devotional reading.

⁵Then Moses and Aaron fell facedown in front of the whole Israelite assembly gathered there. ⁶Joshua son of Nun and Caleb son of Jephunneh, who were among those who had explored the land, tore their clothes ⁷and said to the entire Israelite assembly, "The land we passed through and explored is exceedingly good. ⁸If the LORD is pleased with us, he will lead us into that land, a land flowing with milk and honey, and will give it to us. ⁹Only do not rebel against the LORD. And do not be afraid of the people of the land, because we will swallow them up. Their protection is gone, but the LORD is with us. Do not be afraid of them."

¹⁰But the whole assembly talked about stoning them. Then the glory of the LORD appeared at the Tent of Meeting to all the Israelites. ¹¹The LORD said to Moses, "How long will these people treat me with contempt? How long will they refuse to believe in me, in spite of all the miraculous signs I have performed among them? ¹²I will strike them down with a plague and destroy them, but I will make you into a nation greater and stronger than they."

¹³Moses said to the LORD, "Then the Egyptians will hear about it! By your power you brought these people up from among them. ¹⁴And they will tell the inhabitants of this land about it. They have already heard that you, O LORD, are with these people and that you, O LORD, have been seen face to face, that your cloud stays over them, and that you go before them in a pillar of cloud by day and a pillar of fire by night. ¹⁵If you put these people to death all at one time, the nations who have heard this report about you will say, ¹⁶'The LORD was not able to bring these people into the land he promised them on oath; so he slaughtered them in the desert.'

¹⁷"Now may the Lord's strength be displayed, just as you have declared: ¹⁸'The LORD is slow to anger, abounding in love and forgiving sin and rebellion. Yet he does not leave the guilty unpunished; he punishes the children for the sin of the fathers to the third and fourth generation.' ¹⁹In accordance with your great love, forgive the sin of these people, just as you have pardoned them from the time they left Egypt until now."

²⁰The LORD replied, "I have forgiven them, as you asked. ²¹Nevertheless, as surely as I live and as surely as the glory of the LORD fills the whole earth, ²²not one of the men who saw my glory and the miraculous signs I performed in Egypt and in the desert but who disobeyed me and tested me ten times— ²³not one of them will ever see the land I promised on oath to their forefathers. No one who has treated me with contempt will ever see it. ²⁴But because my servant Caleb has a different spirit and follows me wholeheartedly, I will bring him into the land he went to, and his descendants will inherit it. ²⁵Since the Amalekites and Canaanites are living in the valleys, turn back tomorrow and set out toward the desert along the route to the Red Sea.ᵃ"

²⁶The LORD said to Moses and Aaron: ²⁷"How long will this wicked community grumble against me? I have heard the complaints of these grumbling Israelites. ²⁸So tell them, 'As surely as I live, declares the LORD, I will do to you the very things I heard you say: ²⁹In this desert your bodies will fall—every one of you twenty years old or more who was counted in the census and who has grumbled against me. ³⁰Not one of you will enter the land I swore with uplifted hand to make your home, except Caleb son of Jephunneh and Joshua son of Nun. ³¹As for your children that you said would be taken as plunder, I will bring them in to enjoy the land you have rejected. ³²But you—your bodies will fall in this desert. ³³Your children will be shepherds here for forty years, suffering for your unfaithfulness, until the last of your bodies lies in the desert. ³⁴For forty years—one year for each of the forty days you explored the land—you will suffer for your sins and know what it is like to have me against you.' ³⁵I, the LORD, have spoken, and I will surely do these things to this

Numbers 14:18

God Forgives Sin

"The LORD is slow to anger, abounding in love and forgiving sin and rebellion."

---

whole wicked community, which has banded together against me. They will meet their end in this desert; here they will die."

³⁶So the men Moses had sent to explore the land, who returned and made the whole community grumble against him by spreading a bad report about it— ³⁷these men responsible for spreading the bad report about the land were struck down and died of a plague before the Lord. ³⁸Of the men who went to explore the land, only Joshua son of Nun and Caleb son of Jephunneh survived.

³⁹When Moses reported this to all the Israelites, they mourned bitterly. ⁴⁰Early the next morning they went up toward the high hill country. "We have sinned," they said. "We will go up to the place the Lord promised."

⁴¹But Moses said, "Why are you disobeying the Lord's command? This will not succeed! ⁴²Do not go up, because the Lord is not with you. You will be defeated by your enemies, ⁴³for the Amalekites and Canaanites will face you there. Because you have turned away from the Lord, he will not be with you and you will fall by the sword."

⁴⁴Nevertheless, in their presumption they went up toward the high hill country, though neither Moses nor the ark of the Lord's covenant moved from the camp. ⁴⁵Then the Amalekites and Canaanites who lived in that hill country came down and attacked them and beat them down all the way to Hormah.

Supplementary Offerings

15 The Lord said to Moses, ²"Speak to the Israelites and say to them: 'After you enter the land I am giving you as a home ³and you present to the Lord offerings made by fire, from the herd or the flock, as an aroma pleasing to the Lord—whether burnt offerings or sacrifices, for special vows or freewill offerings or festival offerings— ⁴then the one who brings his offering shall present to the Lord a grain offering of a tenth of an ephah*ᵃ* of fine flour mixed with a quarter of a hin*ᵇ* of oil. ⁵With each lamb for the burnt offering or the sacrifice, prepare a quarter of a hin of wine as a drink offering.

⁶" 'With a ram prepare a grain offering of two-tenths of an ephah*ᶜ* of fine flour mixed with a third of a hin*ᵈ* of oil, ⁷and a third of a hin of wine as a drink offering. Offer it as an aroma pleasing to the Lord.

⁸" 'When you prepare a young bull as a burnt offering or sacrifice, for a special vow or a fellowship offering*ᵉ* to the Lord, ⁹bring with the bull a grain offering of three-tenths of an ephah*ᶠ* of fine flour mixed with half a hin*ᵍ* of oil. ¹⁰Also bring half a hin of wine as a drink offering. It will be an offering made by fire, an aroma pleasing to the Lord. ¹¹Each bull or ram, each lamb or young goat, is to be prepared in this manner. ¹²Do this for each one, for as many as you prepare.

¹³" 'Everyone who is native-born must do these things in this way when he brings an offering made by fire as an aroma pleasing to the Lord. ¹⁴For the generations to come, whenever an alien or anyone else living among you presents an offering made by fire as an aroma pleasing to the Lord, he must do exactly as you do. ¹⁵The community is to have the same rules for you and for the alien living among you; this is a lasting ordinance for the generations to come. You and the alien shall be the same before the Lord: ¹⁶The same laws and regulations will apply both to you and to the alien living among you.' "

¹⁷The Lord said to Moses, ¹⁸"Speak to the Israelites and say to them: 'When you enter the land to which I am taking you ¹⁹and you eat the food of the land, present a portion as an offering to the Lord. ²⁰Present a cake from the first of your ground meal and present it as an offering from the threshing floor. ²¹Throughout the generations to come you are to give this offering to the Lord from the first of your ground meal.

Offerings for Unintentional Sins

²²" 'Now if you unintentionally fail to keep any of these commands the Lord gave Moses— ²³any of the Lord's commands to you through him, from the day the Lord gave them and continuing through the generations to come— ²⁴and if this is done unintentionally

---

ᵃ 4 That is, probably about 2 quarts (about 2 liters)   *ᵇ* 4 That is, probably about 1 quart (about 1 liter); also in verse 5   *ᶜ* 6 That is, probably about 4 quarts (about 4.5 liters)   *ᵈ* 6 That is, probably about 1 1/4 quarts (about 1.2 liters); also in verse 7   *ᵉ* 8 Traditionally *peace offering*   *ᶠ* 9 That is, probably about 6 quarts (about 6.5 liters)   *ᵍ* 9 That is, probably about 2 quarts (about 2 liters); also in verse 10 without the community being aware of it, then the whole community is to offer a young bull for a burnt offering as an aroma pleasing to the LORD, along with its prescribed grain offering and drink offering, and a male goat for a sin offering. 25 The priest is to make atonement for the whole Israelite community, and they will be forgiven, for it was not intentional and they have brought to the LORD for their wrong an offering made by fire and a sin offering. 26 The whole Israelite community and the aliens living among them will be forgiven, because all the people were involved in the unintentional wrong.

27 "But if just one person sins unintentionally, he must bring a year-old female goat for a sin offering. 28 The priest is to make atonement before the LORD for the one who erred by sinning unintentionally, and when atonement has been made for him, he will be forgiven. 29 One and the same law applies to everyone who sins unintentionally, whether he is a native-born Israelite or an alien.

30 "But anyone who sins defiantly, whether native-born or alien, blasphemes the LORD, and that person must be cut off from his people. 31 Because he has despised the LORD's word and broken his commands, that person must surely be cut off; his guilt remains on him.' "

The Sabbath-Breaker Put to Death

32 While the Israelites were in the desert, a man was found gathering wood on the Sabbath day. 33 Those who found him gathering wood brought him to Moses and Aaron and the whole assembly, 34 and they kept him in custody, because it was not clear what should be done to him. 35 Then the LORD said to Moses, "The man must die. The whole assembly must stone him outside the camp." 36 So the assembly took him outside the camp and stoned him to death, as the LORD commanded Moses.

Tassels on Garments

37 The LORD said to Moses, 38 "Speak to the Israelites and say to them: 'Throughout the generations to come you are to make tassels on the corners of your garments, with a blue cord on each tassel. 39 You will have these tassels to look at and so you will remember all the commands

of the LORD, that you may obey them and not prostitute yourselves by going after the lusts of your own hearts and eyes. 40 Then you will remember to obey all my commands and will be consecrated to your God. 41 I am the LORD your God, who brought you out of Egypt to be your God. I am the LORD your God.' "

Korah, Dathan and Abiram

16 Korah son of Izhar, the son of Kohath, the son of Levi, and certain Reubenites—Dathan and Abiram, sons of Eliab, and On son of Peleth—became insolent*a* 2 and rose up against Moses. With them were 250 Israelite men, well-known community leaders who had been appointed members of the council. 3 They came as a group to oppose Moses and Aaron and said to them, "You have gone too far! The whole community is holy, every one of them, and the LORD is with them. Why then do you set yourselves above the LORD's assembly?"

4 When Moses heard this, he fell facedown. 5 Then he said to Korah and all his followers: "In the morning the LORD will show who belongs to him and who is holy, and he will have that person come near him. The man he chooses he will cause to come near him. 6 You, Korah, and all your followers are to do this: Take censers 7 and tomorrow put fire and incense in them before the LORD. The man the LORD chooses will be the one who is holy. You Levites have gone too far!"

8 Moses also said to Korah, "Now listen, you Levites! 9 Isn't it enough for you that the God of Israel has separated you from the rest of the Israelite community and brought you near himself to do the work at the LORD's tabernacle and to stand before the community and minister to them? 10 He has brought you and all your fellow Levites near himself, but now you are trying to get the priesthood too. 11 It is against the LORD that you and all your followers have banded together. Who is Aaron that you should grumble against him?"

12 Then Moses summoned Dathan and Abiram, the sons of Eliab. But they said, "We will not come! 13 Isn't it enough that you have brought us up out of a land flowing with milk and honey to kill us in the desert? And now

*a*1 Or Peleth—took men

A Grumbling Church

Read: Numbers 16:1–35

Numbers 16:1–2

Korah son of Izhar, the son of Kohath, the son of Levi, and certain Reubenites—Dathan and Abiram, sons of Eliab, and On son of Peleth— became insolent and rose up against Moses. With them were 250 Israelite men, well-known community leaders who had been appointed members of the council.

reflection

1 What are some ways you can show respect to the leaders in your church?

2 Recount a time of conflict within a church. Looking back, can you see ways that God was in control?

3 How have your actions or inactions negatively or positively affected your church?

RELATED READINGS

Philippians 4:2–3;
1 Timothy 5:17–20;
Titus 3:1–2

GAYLE WONDERED HOW she had gotten herself into this mess. She had agreed to oversee a women's Bible study this year, and while things started off great, somehow everything started going wrong. Her small group leaders were upset with curriculum; some of the women in the study were upset with the women's ministries leaders; and everyone seemed to be talking about everyone else. Gayle wondered if perhaps she should just resign and let someone else deal with the complaining, bickering and power struggles.

What would you do in this situation? Would you try to take control and fix the problems? Would you call five of your best friends to discuss it? Or would you pray and ask God to fix his ministry?

Clearly, Korah and the leaders didn't respect Aaron and Moses' positions, overlooking the fact that God had appointed the brothers to lead Israel. Today, we don't hear audible voices like Moses did, so it seems more difficult to perceive that God has appointed the leaders in our churches. But if we don't submit to and respect our leaders, in essence we are saying, "God, I don't believe you are in control." Often, we are part of the problems that we are complaining about. We point fingers at pastors and leaders instead of recognizing that our own actions or inactions might have been part of the problem. Dathan and Abiram blamed Aaron and Moses for their circumstances. They jeered, "Isn't it enough that you have brought us up out of a land flowing with milk and honey to kill us in the desert?" Their twisted thinking allowed them to remember Egypt as a paradise rather than a land of slavery. And they conveniently forgot their cowardly refusal to enter the promised land (see chapter 14), the true "land flowing with milk and honey."

Problems occur in every church and ministry. After all, God uses fallible human beings to accomplish his work. But it is God's church and he is in control. We may not always agree with all of our spiritual leaders' decisions, but we can pray that God will lead them and guard their hearts and minds. We can examine our own actions and attitudes to make sure we're not causing more problems. And we can trust God to finish the work he has started—especially the work he has called us to do.

Monday

Go to page 187 for your next devotional reading.

you also want to lord it over us? ¹⁴Moreover, you haven't brought us into a land flowing with milk and honey or given us an inheritance of fields and vineyards. Will you gouge out the eyes of*^a these men? No, we will not come!"

¹⁵Then Moses became very angry and said to the LORD, "Do not accept their offering. I have not taken so much as a donkey from them, nor have I wronged any of them."

¹⁶Moses said to Korah, "You and all your followers are to appear before the LORD tomorrow—you and they and Aaron. ¹⁷Each man is to take his censer and put incense in it—250 censers in all—and present it before the LORD. You and Aaron are to present your censers also." ¹⁸So each man took his censer, put fire and incense in it, and stood with Moses and Aaron at the entrance to the Tent of Meeting. ¹⁹When Korah had gathered all his followers in opposition to them at the entrance to the Tent of Meeting, the glory of the LORD appeared to the entire assembly. ²⁰The LORD said to Moses and Aaron, ²¹"Separate yourselves from this assembly so I can put an end to them at once."

²²But Moses and Aaron fell facedown and cried out, "O God, God of the spirits of all mankind, will you be angry with the entire assembly when only one man sins?"

²³Then the LORD said to Moses, ²⁴"Say to the assembly, 'Move away from the tents of Korah, Dathan and Abiram.'"

²⁵Moses got up and went to Dathan and Abiram, and the elders of Israel followed him. ²⁶He warned the assembly, "Move back from the tents of these wicked men! Do not touch anything belonging to them, or you will be swept away because of all their sins." ²⁷So they moved away from the tents of Korah, Dathan and Abiram. Dathan and Abiram had come out and were standing with their wives, children and little ones at the entrances to their tents.

²⁸Then Moses said, "This is how you will know that the LORD has sent me to do all these things and that it was not my idea: ²⁹If these men die a natural death and experience only what usually happens to men, then the LORD has not sent me. ³⁰But if the LORD brings about something totally new, and the earth opens its mouth and swallows them, with everything that belongs to them, and they go down alive into the grave,*^b then you will know that these men have treated the LORD with contempt."

³¹As soon as he finished saying all this, the ground under them split apart ³²and the earth opened its mouth and swallowed them, with their households and all Korah's men and all their possessions. ³³They went down alive into the grave, with everything they owned; the earth closed over them, and they perished and were gone from the community. ³⁴At their cries, all the Israelites around them fled, shouting, "The earth is going to swallow us too!"

³⁵And fire came out from the LORD and consumed the 250 men who were offering the incense.

³⁶The LORD said to Moses, ³⁷"Tell Eleazar son of Aaron, the priest, to take the censers out of the smoldering remains and scatter the coals some distance away, for the censers are holy— ³⁸the censers of the men who sinned at the cost of their lives. Hammer the censers into sheets to overlay the altar, for they were presented before the LORD and have become holy. Let them be a sign to the Israelites."

³⁹So Eleazar the priest collected the bronze censers brought by those who had been burned up, and he had them hammered out to overlay the altar, ⁴⁰as the LORD directed him through Moses. This was to remind the Israelites that no one except a descendant of Aaron should come to burn incense before the LORD, or he would become like Korah and his followers.

⁴¹The next day the whole Israelite community grumbled against Moses and Aaron. "You have killed the LORD's people," they said.

⁴²But when the assembly gathered in opposition to Moses and Aaron and turned toward the Tent of Meeting, suddenly the cloud covered it and the glory of the LORD appeared.

Numbers 16:21

God Addresses Sin

"Separate yourselves from this assembly so I can put an end to them at once."

---

*a*14 Or *you make slaves of*; or *you deceive*   *b*30 Hebrew *Sheol*; also in verse 33

⁴³Then Moses and Aaron went to the front of the Tent of Meeting, ⁴⁴and the LORD said to Moses, ⁴⁵"Get away from this assembly so I can put an end to them at once." And they fell facedown.

⁴⁶Then Moses said to Aaron, "Take your censer and put incense in it, along with fire from the altar, and hurry to the assembly to make atonement for them. Wrath has come out from the LORD; the plague has started." ⁴⁷So Aaron did as Moses said, and ran into the midst of the assembly. The plague had already started among the people, but Aaron offered the incense and made atonement for them. ⁴⁸He stood between the living and the dead, and the plague stopped. ⁴⁹But 14,700 people died from the plague, in addition to those who had died because of Korah. ⁵⁰Then Aaron returned to Moses at the entrance to the Tent of Meeting, for the plague had stopped.

The Budding of Aaron's Staff

17 The LORD said to Moses, ²"Speak to the Israelites and get twelve staffs from them, one from the leader of each of their ancestral tribes. Write the name of each man on his staff. ³On the staff of Levi write Aaron's name, for there must be one staff for the head of each ancestral tribe. ⁴Place them in the Tent of Meeting in front of the Testimony, where I meet with you. ⁵The staff belonging to the man I choose will sprout, and I will rid myself of this constant grumbling against you by the Israelites."

⁶So Moses spoke to the Israelites, and their leaders gave him twelve staffs, one for the leader of each of their ancestral tribes, and Aaron's staff was among them. ⁷Moses placed the staffs before the LORD in the Tent of the Testimony.

⁸The next day Moses entered the Tent of Testimony and saw that Aaron's staff, which represented the house of Levi, had not only sprouted but had budded, blossomed and produced almonds. ⁹Then Moses brought out all the staffs from the LORD's presence to all the Israelites. They looked at them, and each man took his own staff.

¹⁰The LORD said to Moses, "Put back Aaron's staff in front of the Testimony, to be kept as a sign to the rebellious. This will put an end to their grumbling against me, so that they will not die." ¹¹Moses did just as the LORD commanded him.

¹²The Israelites said to Moses, "We will die! We are lost, we are all lost! ¹³Anyone who even comes near the tabernacle of the LORD will die. Are we all going to die?"

Duties of Priests and Levites

18 The LORD said to Aaron, "You, your sons and your father's family are to bear the responsibility for offenses against the sanctuary, and you and your sons alone are to bear the responsibility for offenses against the priesthood. ²Bring your fellow Levites from your ancestral tribe to join you and assist you when you and your sons minister before the Tent of the Testimony. ³They are to be responsible to you and are to perform all the duties of the Tent, but they must not go near the furnishings of the sanctuary or the altar, or both they and you will die. ⁴They are to join you and be responsible for the care of the Tent of Meeting—all the work at the Tent—and no one else may come near where you are.

⁵"You are to be responsible for the care of the sanctuary and the altar, so that wrath will not fall on the Israelites again. ⁶I myself have selected your fellow Levites from among the Israelites as a gift to you, dedicated to the LORD to do the work at the Tent of Meeting. ⁷But only you and your sons may serve as priests in connection with everything at the altar and inside the curtain. I am giving you the service of the priesthood as a gift. Anyone else who comes near the sanctuary must be put to death."

Offerings for Priests and Levites

⁸Then the LORD said to Aaron, "I myself have put you in charge of the offerings presented to me; all the holy offerings the Israelites give me I give to you and your sons as your portion and regular share. ⁹You are to have the part of the most holy offerings that is kept from the fire. From all the gifts they bring me as most holy offerings, whether grain or sin or guilt offerings, that part belongs to you and your sons. ¹⁰Eat it as something most holy; every male shall eat it. You must regard it as holy.

¹¹"This also is yours: whatever is set aside from the gifts of all the wave offerings of the Israelites. I give this to you and your sons and

daughters as your regular share. Everyone in your household who is ceremonially clean may eat it.

¹²"I give you all the finest olive oil and all the finest new wine and grain they give the LORD as the firstfruits of their harvest. ¹³All the land's firstfruits that they bring to the LORD will be yours. Everyone in your household who is ceremonially clean may eat it.

¹⁴"Everything in Israel that is devoted*a* to the LORD is yours. ¹⁵The first offspring of every womb, both man and animal, that is offered to the LORD is yours. But you must redeem every firstborn son and every firstborn male of unclean animals. ¹⁶When they are a month old, you must redeem them at the redemption price set at five shekels*b* of silver, according to the sanctuary shekel, which weighs twenty gerahs.

¹⁷"But you must not redeem the firstborn of an ox, a sheep or a goat; they are holy. Sprinkle their blood on the altar and burn their fat as an offering made by fire, an aroma pleasing to the LORD. ¹⁸Their meat is to be yours, just as the breast of the wave offering and the right thigh are yours. ¹⁹Whatever is set aside from the holy offerings the Israelites present to the LORD I give to you and your sons and daughters as your regular share. It is an everlasting covenant of salt before the LORD for both you and your offspring."

²⁰The LORD said to Aaron, "You will have no inheritance in their land, nor will you have any share among them; I am your share and your inheritance among the Israelites.

²¹"I give to the Levites all the tithes in Israel as their inheritance in return for the work they do while serving at the Tent of Meeting. ²²From now on the Israelites must not go near the Tent of Meeting, or they will bear the consequences of their sin and will die. ²³It is the Levites who are to do the work at the Tent of Meeting and bear the responsibility for offenses against it. This is a lasting ordinance for the generations to come. They will receive no inheritance

among the Israelites. ²⁴Instead, I give to the Levites as their inheritance the tithes that the Israelites present as an offering to the LORD. That is why I said concerning them: 'They will have no inheritance among the Israelites.' "

²⁵The LORD said to Moses, ²⁶"Speak to the Levites and say to them: 'When you receive from the Israelites the tithe I give you as your inheritance, you must present a tenth of that tithe as the LORD's offering. ²⁷Your offering will be reckoned to you as grain from the threshing floor or juice from the winepress. ²⁸In this way you also will present an offering to the LORD from all the tithes you receive from the Israelites. From these tithes you must give the LORD's portion to Aaron the priest. ²⁹You must present as the LORD's portion the best and holiest part of everything given to you.'

³⁰"Say to the Levites: 'When you present the best part, it will be reckoned to you as the product of the threshing floor or the winepress. ³¹You and your households may eat the rest of it anywhere, for it is your wages for your work at the Tent of Meeting. ³²By presenting the best part of it you will not be guilty in this matter; then you will not defile the holy offerings of the Israelites, and you will not die.' "

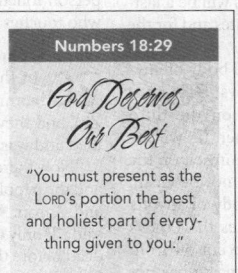

Numbers 18:29

God Deserves Our Best

"You must present as the LORD's portion the best and holiest part of everything given to you."

The Water of Cleansing

19 The LORD said to Moses and Aaron: ²"This is a requirement of the law that the LORD has commanded: Tell the Israelites to bring you a red heifer without defect or blemish and that has never been under a yoke. ³Give it to Eleazar the priest; it is to be taken outside the camp and slaughtered in his presence. ⁴Then Eleazar the priest is to take some of its blood on his finger and sprinkle it seven times toward the front of the Tent of Meeting. ⁵While he watches, the heifer is to be burned—its hide, flesh, blood and offal. ⁶The priest is to take some cedar wood, hyssop and scarlet wool and throw them onto the burning heifer. ⁷After that, the priest must wash his clothes and

---

*a*14 The Hebrew term refers to the irrevocable giving over of things or persons to the LORD.   *b*16 That is, about 2 ounces (about 55 grams) bathe himself with water. He may then come into the camp, but he will be ceremonially unclean till evening. **8**The man who burns it must also wash his clothes and bathe with water, and he too will be unclean till evening.

9"A man who is clean shall gather up the ashes of the heifer and put them in a ceremonially clean place outside the camp. They shall be kept by the Israelite community for use in the water of cleansing; it is for purification from sin. **10**The man who gathers up the ashes of the heifer must also wash his clothes, and he too will be unclean till evening. This will be a lasting ordinance both for the Israelites and for the aliens living among them.

11"Whoever touches the dead body of anyone will be unclean for seven days. **12**He must purify himself with the water on the third day and on the seventh day; then he will be clean. But if he does not purify himself on the third and seventh days, he will not be clean. **13**Whoever touches the dead body of anyone and fails to purify himself defiles the LORD's tabernacle. That person must be cut off from Israel. Because the water of cleansing has not been sprinkled on him, he is unclean; his uncleanness remains on him.

14"This is the law that applies when a person dies in a tent: Anyone who enters the tent and anyone who is in it will be unclean for seven days, **15**and every open container without a lid fastened on it will be unclean.

16"Anyone out in the open who touches someone who has been killed with a sword or someone who has died a natural death, or anyone who touches a human bone or a grave, will be unclean for seven days.

17"For the unclean person, put some ashes from the burned purification offering into a jar and pour fresh water over them. **18**Then a man who is ceremonially clean is to take some hyssop, dip it in the water and sprinkle the tent and all the furnishings and the people who were there. He must also sprinkle anyone who has touched a human bone or a grave or someone who has been killed or someone who has died a natural death. **19**The man who is clean is to sprinkle the unclean person on the third and seventh days, and on the seventh day he is to purify him. The person being cleansed must wash his clothes and bathe with water, and that evening he will be clean. **20**But if a person who is unclean does not purify himself, he must be cut off from the community, because he has defiled the sanctuary of the LORD. The water of cleansing has not been sprinkled on him, and he is unclean. **21**This is a lasting ordinance for them.

"The man who sprinkles the water of cleansing must also wash his clothes, and anyone who touches the water of cleansing will be unclean till evening. **22**Anything that an unclean person touches becomes unclean, and anyone who touches it becomes unclean till evening."

Water From the Rock

20 In the first month the whole Israelite community arrived at the Desert of Zin, and they stayed at Kadesh. There Miriam died and was buried.

2Now there was no water for the community, and the people gathered in opposition to Moses and Aaron. **3**They quarreled with Moses and said, "If only we had died when our brothers fell dead before the LORD! **4**Why did you bring the LORD's community into this desert, that we and our livestock should die here? **5**Why did you bring us up out of Egypt to this terrible place? It has no grain or figs, grapevines or pomegranates. And there is no water to drink!"

6Moses and Aaron went from the assembly to the entrance to the Tent of Meeting and fell facedown, and the glory of the LORD appeared to them. **7**The LORD said to Moses, **8**"Take the staff, and you and your brother Aaron gather the assembly together. Speak to that rock before their eyes and it will pour out its water. You will bring water out of the rock for the community so they and their livestock can drink."

9So Moses took the staff from the LORD's presence, just as he commanded him. **10**He and Aaron gathered the assembly together in front of the rock and Moses said to them, "Listen, you rebels, must we bring you water out of this rock?" **11**Then Moses raised his arm and struck the rock twice with his staff. Water gushed out, and the community and their livestock drank.

12But the LORD said to Moses and Aaron, "Because you did not trust in me enough to honor me as holy in the sight of the Israelites,

Credit Where Credit Is Due

Read: Numbers 20:2–13

SINCE SCHOOL DAYS, it's been drummed into our collective conscience to give credit where credit is due. If a person "borrows" a concept without properly giving recognition, they are guilty of plagiarizing—stealing ideas, words or creations. Oftentimes, the plagiarist pays the price by losing their reputation or career. The same is true spiritually. We must be willing to give God the credit for his work in our lives.

The Israelites had almost reached the end of their desert wanderings. The new generation was ready to enter the promised land. They had witnessed miracles and tasted manna. Yet they worried that God would not provide water. So they complained against Moses.

Moses went to the Lord and asked for guidance. God spelled out his instructions: Bring the staff and speak to the rock. God promised that water would pour forth to nourish the people and flocks. Then Moses made two big mistakes. First, he took credit for God's work by complaining about being forced to bring water out of the rock himself. Then he disobeyed God by overreacting. He struck the rock—WHAM! Then again—WHAM!

It's heartbreaking to realize that Moses, God's faithful servant, was left behind. He didn't get to go into the promised land. But God had his reasons: "You did not trust in me enough to honor me as holy in the sight of the Israelites" (Numbers 20:12). In other words, Moses did not give God credit where credit was due. He stole God's glory by striking the rock—twice. But in the end, God loved Moses so much he showed him the promised land from the top of Mount Nebo and then had him buried there.

But rather than being hard on Moses, perhaps we should look at our own attitudes and motives. When we accomplish God's work, do we take the credit and bask in our own sense of accomplishment? When we benefit from God's grace in our lives, do we take it for granted and think that we somehow deserve it? Take a moment each day to sort out who is doing what, and give God the credit—for the gifts and abilities he has given you and for everything he is able to do through you. In short, for everything.

Go to page 189 for your next devotional reading.

Numbers 20:10–11

[Moses] and Aaron gathered the assembly together in front of the rock and Moses said to them, "Listen, you rebels, must we bring you water out of this rock?" Then Moses raised his arm and struck the rock twice with his staff. Water gushed out, and the community and their livestock drank.

reflection

1 Have you ever taken credit for another person's accomplishments?

2 When was the last time you didn't give God credit for his work in your life?

3 How will you honor God in the presence of those you encounter today?

RELATED READINGS

1 Chronicles 16:7–36;
Psalm 106:1–2,32–48;
1 Corinthians 10:1–5

Tuesday

you will not bring this community into the land I give them."

13These were the waters of Meribah,*a* where the Israelites quarreled with the LORD and where he showed himself holy among them.

Edom Denies Israel Passage

14Moses sent messengers from Kadesh to the king of Edom, saying:

"This is what your brother Israel says: You know about all the hardships that have come upon us. 15Our forefathers went down into Egypt, and we lived there many years. The Egyptians mistreated us and our fathers, 16but when we cried out to the LORD, he heard our cry and sent an angel and brought us out of Egypt.

"Now we are here at Kadesh, a town on the edge of your territory. 17Please let us pass through your country. We will not go through any field or vineyard, or drink water from any well. We will travel along the king's highway and not turn to the right or to the left until we have passed through your territory."

18But Edom answered:

"You may not pass through here; if you try, we will march out and attack you with the sword."

19The Israelites replied:

"We will go along the main road, and if we or our livestock drink any of your water, we will pay for it. We only want to pass through on foot—nothing else."

20Again they answered:

"You may not pass through."

Then Edom came out against them with a large and powerful army. 21Since Edom refused to let them go through their territory, Israel turned away from them.

The Death of Aaron

22The whole Israelite community set out from Kadesh and came to Mount Hor. 23At Mount Hor, near the border of Edom, the LORD said to Moses and Aaron, 24"Aaron will be gathered to his people. He will not enter the land I give the Israelites, because both of you rebelled against my command at the waters of Meribah. 25Get Aaron and his son Eleazar and take them up Mount Hor. 26Remove Aaron's garments and put them on his son Eleazar, for Aaron will be gathered to his people; he will die there."

27Moses did as the LORD commanded: They went up Mount Hor in the sight of the whole community. 28Moses removed Aaron's garments and put them on his son Eleazar. And Aaron died there on top of the mountain. Then Moses and Eleazar came down from the mountain, 29and when the whole community learned that Aaron had died, the entire house of Israel mourned for him thirty days.

Arad Destroyed

21 When the Canaanite king of Arad, who lived in the Negev, heard that Israel was coming along the road to Atharim, he attacked the Israelites and captured some of them. 2Then Israel made this vow to the LORD: "If you will deliver these people into our hands, we will totally destroy*b* their cities." 3The LORD listened to Israel's plea and gave the Canaanites over to them. They completely destroyed them and their towns; so the place was named Hormah.*c*

The Bronze Snake

4They traveled from Mount Hor along the route to the Red Sea,*d* to go around Edom. But the people grew impatient on the way; 5they spoke against God and against Moses, and said, "Why have you brought us up out of Egypt to die in the desert? There is no bread! There is no water! And we detest this miserable food!"

6Then the LORD sent venomous snakes among them; they bit the people and many Israelites died. 7The people came to Moses and said, "We sinned when we spoke against the LORD and against you. Pray that the LORD will take the snakes away from us." So Moses prayed for the people.

8The LORD said to Moses, "Make a snake and put it up on a pole; anyone who is

---

*a*13 *Meribah* means *quarreling.*   *b*2 The Hebrew term refers to the irrevocable giving over of things or persons to the LORD, often by totally destroying them; also in verse 3.   *c*3 *Hormah* means *destruction.*   *d*4 Hebrew *Yam Suph*; that is, Sea of Reeds

Look Up and Live

Read: Numbers 21:4–9

WANDERING THROUGH OUR DAY, thirsting for evidence of God's presence, hungry for the blessings everyone else seems to enjoy . . . stumbling blindly in the same old drudgery. We, too, can begin to doubt whether God is really guiding us, whether he really has chosen us. And if he has, why is life so hard? And then we begin to doubt . . . just like the Israelites.

They tramped through a scorching desert, their feet dusty and sore. They faced yet another day of water rations and a menu of manna—the same as every other day. Sure, the Israelites had God's cloud to guide them by day and that fire to follow by night. Yes, he told them he had "chosen" them. The miracles to get them out of Egypt had been amazing. Yet the way was so rough, it was easy to forget all that. Looking out at the hot desert, it was easy to assume God had left them alone there.

Does this sound familiar as you tramp through your daily life?
If God really loved me, I'd get that promotion at work!
Mumble, mumble, mumble.
Why doesn't God heal me?
Grumble, grumble, grumble.
I pray and pray, but God never seems to answer.
Whine, whine, whine.

Eventually, the Israelites' grumbling exploded into venomous blasphemy against God. In retribution, God sent a plague of poisonous snakes to stop their poisonous treason. Sometimes God's rebuke might feel like one more reason to resent him. But God's compassion drives his punishments. When his people called out for help—wailing for the cure—he provided a remedy. The afflicted needed to look up at the picture of their sinful rebellion—the bronze serpent raised high on a pole. God raised their sin on a pole, and they were healed. And millennia later, he raised up a Savior on a cross so that humankind could look to him and be saved (see John 3:14–15).

Do frustration and discouragement sometimes drive you to mumble and complain? Have you begun to detest the things of God because they just aren't quite what you expected?

Stop. Look up to Jesus Christ. He took on your sin to heal your heart. He is the only way you can rid yourself of the venom of bitterness. Look up to him and live.

Numbers 21:8

The LORD said to Moses, "Make a snake and put it up on a pole; anyone who is bitten can look at it and live."

reflection

1 What "desert" experience has caused you to grumble?

2 What sin has poisoned your heart? Is it envy? Bitterness? Anger?

3 Today, lift your eyes up toward Jesus and ask him to take the poisonous thoughts from your heart.

RELATED READINGS

Psalm 121:1–2;
John 8:27–28

Wednesday

Go to page 198 for your next devotional reading.

bitten can look at it and live." ⁹So Moses made a bronze snake and put it up on a pole. Then when anyone was bitten by a snake and looked at the bronze snake, he lived.

The Journey to Moab

¹⁰The Israelites moved on and camped at Oboth. ¹¹Then they set out from Oboth and camped in Iye Abarim, in the desert that faces Moab toward the sunrise. ¹²From there they moved on and camped in the Zered Valley. ¹³They set out from there and camped alongside the Arnon, which is in the desert extending into Amorite territory. The Arnon is the border of Moab, between Moab and the Amorites. ¹⁴That is why the Book of the Wars of the LORD says:

> "… Waheb in Suphah*a* and the ravines,
>   the Arnon ¹⁵and*b* the slopes of the ravines
> that lead to the site of Ar
>   and lie along the border of Moab."

¹⁶From there they continued on to Beer, the well where the LORD said to Moses, "Gather the people together and I will give them water."

¹⁷Then Israel sang this song:

> "Spring up, O well!
>   Sing about it,
> ¹⁸about the well that the princes dug,
>   that the nobles of the people sank—
>   the nobles with scepters and staffs."

Then they went from the desert to Mattanah, ¹⁹from Mattanah to Nahaliel, from Nahaliel to Bamoth, ²⁰and from Bamoth to the valley in Moab where the top of Pisgah overlooks the wasteland.

Defeat of Sihon and Og

²¹Israel sent messengers to say to Sihon king of the Amorites:

> ²²"Let us pass through your country. We will not turn aside into any field or vineyard, or drink water from any well. We will travel along the king's highway until we have passed through your territory."

²³But Sihon would not let Israel pass through his territory. He mustered his entire army and marched out into the desert against Israel. When he reached Jahaz, he fought with Israel. ²⁴Israel, however, put him to the sword and took over his land from the Arnon to the Jabbok, but only as far as the Ammonites, because their border was fortified. ²⁵Israel captured all the cities of the Amorites and occupied them, including Heshbon and all its surrounding settlements. ²⁶Heshbon was the city of Sihon king of the Amorites, who had fought against the former king of Moab and had taken from him all his land as far as the Arnon.

²⁷That is why the poets say:

> "Come to Heshbon and let it be rebuilt;
>   let Sihon's city be restored.

> ²⁸"Fire went out from Heshbon,
>   a blaze from the city of Sihon.
> It consumed Ar of Moab,
>   the citizens of Arnon's heights.
> ²⁹Woe to you, O Moab!
>   You are destroyed, O people of Chemosh!
> He has given up his sons as fugitives
>   and his daughters as captives
> to Sihon king of the Amorites.

> ³⁰"But we have overthrown them;
>   Heshbon is destroyed all the way to Dibon.
> We have demolished them as far as Nophah,
>   which extends to Medeba."

³¹So Israel settled in the land of the Amorites.

³²After Moses had sent spies to Jazer, the Israelites captured its surrounding settlements and drove out the Amorites who were there. ³³Then they turned and went up along the road toward Bashan, and Og king of Bashan and his whole army marched out to meet them in battle at Edrei.

³⁴The LORD said to Moses, "Do not be afraid of him, for I have handed him over to you, with his whole army and his land. Do to him what you did to Sihon king of the Amorites, who reigned in Heshbon."

³⁵So they struck him down, together with his

---

a 14 The meaning of the Hebrew for this phrase is uncertain.   *b* 14,15 Or *"I have been given from Suphah and the ravines / of the Arnon ¹⁵to* sons and his whole army, leaving them no survivors. And they took possession of his land.

Balak Summons Balaam

22 Then the Israelites traveled to the plains of Moab and camped along the Jordan across from Jericho.[a]

2 Now Balak son of Zippor saw all that Israel had done to the Amorites, 3 and Moab was terrified because there were so many people. Indeed, Moab was filled with dread because of the Israelites.

4 The Moabites said to the elders of Midian, "This horde is going to lick up everything around us, as an ox licks up the grass of the field."

So Balak son of Zippor, who was king of Moab at that time, 5 sent messengers to summon Balaam son of Beor, who was at Pethor, near the River,[b] in his native land. Balak said:

"A people has come out of Egypt; they cover the face of the land and have settled next to me. 6 Now come and put a curse on these people, because they are too powerful for me. Perhaps then I will be able to defeat them and drive them out of the country. For I know that those you bless are blessed, and those you curse are cursed."

7 The elders of Moab and Midian left, taking with them the fee for divination. When they came to Balaam, they told him what Balak had said.

8 "Spend the night here," Balaam said to them, "and I will bring you back the answer the LORD gives me." So the Moabite princes stayed with him.

9 God came to Balaam and asked, "Who are these men with you?"

10 Balaam said to God, "Balak son of Zippor, king of Moab, sent me this message: 11 'A people that has come out of Egypt covers the face of the land. Now come and put a curse on them for me. Perhaps then I will be able to fight them and drive them away.'"

12 But God said to Balaam, "Do not go with them. You must not put a curse on those people, because they are blessed."

13 The next morning Balaam got up and said to Balak's princes, "Go back to your own country, for the LORD has refused to let me go with you."

14 So the Moabite princes returned to Balak and said, "Balaam refused to come with us."

15 Then Balak sent other princes, more numerous and more distinguished than the first. 16 They came to Balaam and said:

"This is what Balak son of Zippor says: Do not let anything keep you from coming to me, 17 because I will reward you handsomely and do whatever you say. Come and put a curse on these people for me."

18 But Balaam answered them, "Even if Balak gave me his palace filled with silver and gold, I could not do anything great or small to go beyond the command of the LORD my God. 19 Now stay here tonight as the others did, and I will find out what else the LORD will tell me."

20 That night God came to Balaam and said, "Since these men have come to summon you, go with them, but do only what I tell you."

Balaam's Donkey

21 Balaam got up in the morning, saddled his donkey and went with the princes of Moab. 22 But God was very angry when he went, and the angel of the LORD stood in the road to oppose him. Balaam was riding on his donkey, and his two servants were with him. 23 When the donkey saw the angel of the LORD standing in the road with a drawn sword in his hand, she turned off the road into a field. Balaam beat her to get her back on the road.

24 Then the angel of the LORD stood in a narrow path between two vineyards, with walls on both sides. 25 When the donkey saw the angel of the LORD, she pressed close to the wall, crushing Balaam's foot against it. So he beat her again.

26 Then the angel of the LORD moved on ahead and stood in a narrow place where there was no room to turn, either to the right or to the left. 27 When the donkey saw the angel of the LORD, she lay down under Balaam, and he was angry and beat her with his staff. 28 Then the LORD opened the donkey's mouth, and she

---

a 1 Hebrew *Jordan of Jericho*; possibly an ancient name for the Jordan River   b 5 That is, the Euphrates said to Balaam, "What have I done to you to make you beat me these three times?"

29Balaam answered the donkey, "You have made a fool of me! If I had a sword in my hand, I would kill you right now."

30The donkey said to Balaam, "Am I not your own donkey, which you have always ridden, to this day? Have I been in the habit of doing this to you?"

"No," he said.

31Then the LORD opened Balaam's eyes, and he saw the angel of the LORD standing in the road with his sword drawn. So he bowed low and fell facedown.

32The angel of the LORD asked him, "Why have you beaten your donkey these three times? I have come here to oppose you because your path is a reckless one before me.*a* 33The donkey saw me and turned away from me these three times. If she had not turned away, I would certainly have killed you by now, but I would have spared her."

34Balaam said to the angel of the LORD, "I have sinned. I did not realize you were standing in the road to oppose me. Now if you are displeased, I will go back."

35The angel of the LORD said to Balaam, "Go with the men, but speak only what I tell you." So Balaam went with the princes of Balak.

36When Balak heard that Balaam was coming, he went out to meet him at the Moabite town on the Arnon border, at the edge of his territory. 37Balak said to Balaam, "Did I not send you an urgent summons? Why didn't you come to me? Am I really not able to reward you?"

38"Well, I have come to you now," Balaam replied. "But can I say just anything? I must speak only what God puts in my mouth."

39Then Balaam went with Balak to Kiriath Huzoth. 40Balak sacrificed cattle and sheep, and gave some to Balaam and the princes who were with him. 41The next morning Balak took Balaam up to Bamoth Baal, and from there he saw part of the people.

Balaam's First Oracle

23 Balaam said, "Build me seven altars here, and prepare seven bulls and seven rams for me." 2Balak did as Balaam said, and the two of them offered a bull and a ram on each altar.

3Then Balaam said to Balak, "Stay here beside your offering while I go aside. Perhaps the LORD will come to meet with me. Whatever he reveals to me I will tell you." Then he went off to a barren height.

4God met with him, and Balaam said, "I have prepared seven altars, and on each altar I have offered a bull and a ram."

5The LORD put a message in Balaam's mouth and said, "Go back to Balak and give him this message."

6So he went back to him and found him standing beside his offering, with all the princes of Moab. 7Then Balaam uttered his oracle:

"Balak brought me from Aram,
 the king of Moab from the eastern
  mountains.
'Come,' he said, 'curse Jacob for me;
 come, denounce Israel.'
8 How can I curse
 those whom God has not cursed?
How can I denounce
 those whom the LORD has not
  denounced?
9 From the rocky peaks I see them,
 from the heights I view them.
I see a people who live apart
 and do not consider themselves one of
  the nations.
10 Who can count the dust of Jacob
 or number the fourth part of
  Israel?
Let me die the death of the righteous,
 and may my end be like theirs!"

11Balak said to Balaam, "What have you done to me? I brought you to curse my enemies, but you have done nothing but bless them!"

12He answered, "Must I not speak what the LORD puts in my mouth?"

Balaam's Second Oracle

13Then Balak said to him, "Come with me to another place where you can see them; you will see only a part but not all of them. And from there, curse them for me." 14So he took him to the field of Zophim on the top of Pisgah, and

---

a 32 The meaning of the Hebrew for this clause is uncertain.

there he built seven altars and offered a bull and a ram on each altar.

¹⁵ Balaam said to Balak, "Stay here beside your offering while I meet with him over there."

¹⁶ The LORD met with Balaam and put a message in his mouth and said, "Go back to Balak and give him this message."

¹⁷ So he went to him and found him standing beside his offering, with the princes of Moab. Balak asked him, "What did the LORD say?"

¹⁸ Then he uttered his oracle:

"Arise, Balak, and listen;
    hear me, son of Zippor.
¹⁹ God is not a man, that he should lie,
    nor a son of man, that he
        should change his
        mind.
Does he speak and then not
        act?
Does he promise and not
        fulfill?
²⁰ I have received a command
        to bless;
    he has blessed, and I
        cannot change it.

²¹ "No misfortune is seen in
        Jacob,
    no misery observed in
        Israel.[a]
The LORD their God is with
        them;
    the shout of the King is among them.
²² God brought them out of Egypt;
    they have the strength of a wild ox.
²³ There is no sorcery against Jacob,
    no divination against Israel.
It will now be said of Jacob
    and of Israel, 'See what God has done!'
²⁴ The people rise like a lioness;
    they rouse themselves like a lion
that does not rest till he devours his prey
    and drinks the blood of his victims."

²⁵ Then Balak said to Balaam, "Neither curse them at all nor bless them at all!"

²⁶ Balaam answered, "Did I not tell you I must do whatever the LORD says?"

Balaam's Third Oracle

²⁷ Then Balak said to Balaam, "Come, let me take you to another place. Perhaps it will please God to let you curse them for me from there."

²⁸ And Balak took Balaam to the top of Peor, overlooking the wasteland.

²⁹ Balaam said, "Build me seven altars here, and prepare seven bulls and seven rams for me." ³⁰ Balak did as Balaam had said, and offered a bull and a ram on each altar.

24 Now when Balaam saw that it pleased the LORD to bless Israel, he did not resort to sorcery as at other times, but turned his face toward the desert. ² When Balaam looked out and saw Israel encamped tribe by tribe, the Spirit of God came upon him ³ and he uttered his oracle:

"The oracle of Balaam son
        of Beor,
    the oracle of one whose
        eye sees clearly,
⁴ the oracle of one who hears
        the words of God,
    who sees a vision from
        the Almighty,[b]
who falls prostrate, and
        whose eyes are
        opened:
⁵ "How beautiful are your
        tents, O Jacob,
    your dwelling places,
        O Israel!

⁶ "Like valleys they spread out,
    like gardens beside a river,
like aloes planted by the LORD,
    like cedars beside the waters.
⁷ Water will flow from their buckets;
    their seed will have abundant water.

"Their king will be greater than Agag;
    their kingdom will be exalted.

⁸ "God brought them out of Egypt;
    they have the strength of a wild ox.
They devour hostile nations
    and break their bones in pieces;
    with their arrows they pierce them.
⁹ Like a lion they crouch and lie down,
    like a lioness—who dares to rouse them?

Numbers 23:19

God Is Truthful

"God is not a man,
that he should lie,
nor a son of man, that he
should change his mind.
Does he speak and
then not act?
Does he promise
and not fulfill?"

---

[a]21 Or *He has not looked on Jacob's offenses / or on the wrongs found in Israel.*   [b]4 Hebrew *Shaddai*; also in verse 16

"May those who bless you be blessed
and those who curse you be cursed!"

¹⁰Then Balak's anger burned against Balaam. He struck his hands together and said to him, "I summoned you to curse my enemies, but you have blessed them these three times. ¹¹Now leave at once and go home! I said I would reward you handsomely, but the LORD has kept you from being rewarded."

¹²Balaam answered Balak, "Did I not tell the messengers you sent me, ¹³'Even if Balak gave me his palace filled with silver and gold, I could not do anything of my own accord, good or bad, to go beyond the command of the LORD—and I must say only what the LORD says'? ¹⁴Now I am going back to my people, but come, let me warn you of what this people will do to your people in days to come."

Balaam's Fourth Oracle

¹⁵Then he uttered his oracle:

"The oracle of Balaam son of Beor,
    the oracle of one whose eye sees clearly,
¹⁶the oracle of one who hears the words of
        God,
    who has knowledge from the Most
        High,
who sees a vision from the Almighty,
    who falls prostrate, and whose eyes are
        opened:

¹⁷"I see him, but not now;
    I behold him, but not near.
A star will come out of Jacob;
    a scepter will rise out of Israel.
He will crush the foreheads of Moab,
    the skulls*a* of*b* all the sons of Sheth.*c*
¹⁸Edom will be conquered;
    Seir, his enemy, will be conquered,
    but Israel will grow strong.
¹⁹A ruler will come out of Jacob
    and destroy the survivors of the city."

Balaam's Final Oracles

²⁰Then Balaam saw Amalek and uttered his oracle:

"Amalek was first among the nations,
    but he will come to ruin at last."

²¹Then he saw the Kenites and uttered his oracle:

"Your dwelling place is secure,
    your nest is set in a rock;
²²yet you Kenites will be destroyed
    when Asshur takes you captive."

²³Then he uttered his oracle:

"Ah, who can live when God does this?*d*
²⁴   Ships will come from the shores of
        Kittim;
    they will subdue Asshur and Eber,
        but they too will come to ruin."

²⁵Then Balaam got up and returned home and Balak went his own way.

Moab Seduces Israel

25 While Israel was staying in Shittim, the men began to indulge in sexual immorality with Moabite women, ²who invited them to the sacrifices to their gods. The people ate and bowed down before these gods. ³So Israel joined in worshiping the Baal of Peor. And the LORD's anger burned against them.

⁴The LORD said to Moses, "Take all the leaders of these people, kill them and expose them in broad daylight before the LORD, so that the LORD's fierce anger may turn away from Israel."

⁵So Moses said to Israel's judges, "Each of you must put to death those of your men who have joined in worshiping the Baal of Peor."

⁶Then an Israelite man brought to his family a Midianite woman right before the eyes of Moses and the whole assembly of Israel while they were weeping at the entrance to the Tent of Meeting. ⁷When Phinehas son of Eleazar, the son of Aaron, the priest, saw this, he left the assembly, took a spear in his hand ⁸and followed the Israelite into the tent. He drove the spear through both of them—through the Israelite and into the woman's body. Then the plague against the Israelites was stopped; ⁹but those who died in the plague numbered 24,000.

¹⁰The LORD said to Moses, ¹¹"Phinehas son of Eleazar, the son of Aaron, the priest, has turned my anger away from the Israelites; for he was as zealous as I am for my honor among

---

*a*17 Samaritan Pentateuch (see also Jer. 48:45); the meaning of the word in the Masoretic Text is uncertain.   *b*17 Or possibly *Moab, /
batter*   *c*17 Or *all the noisy boasters*   *d*23 Masoretic Text; with a different word division of the Hebrew *A people will gather from the north.*

them, so that in my zeal I did not put an end to them. [12]Therefore tell him I am making my covenant of peace with him. [13]He and his descendants will have a covenant of a lasting priesthood, because he was zealous for the honor of his God and made atonement for the Israelites."

[14]The name of the Israelite who was killed with the Midianite woman was Zimri son of Salu, the leader of a Simeonite family. [15]And the name of the Midianite woman who was put to death was Cozbi daughter of Zur, a tribal chief of a Midianite family.

[16]The LORD said to Moses, [17]"Treat the Midianites as enemies and kill them, [18]because they treated you as enemies when they deceived you in the affair of Peor and their sister Cozbi, the daughter of a Midianite leader, the woman who was killed when the plague came as a result of Peor."

The Second Census

26 After the plague the LORD said to Moses and Eleazar son of Aaron, the priest, [2]"Take a census of the whole Israelite community by families—all those twenty years old or more who are able to serve in the army of Israel." [3]So on the plains of Moab by the Jordan across from Jericho,[a] Moses and Eleazar the priest spoke with them and said, [4]"Take a census of the men twenty years old or more, as the LORD commanded Moses."

These were the Israelites who came out of Egypt:

[5]The descendants of Reuben, the firstborn son of Israel, were:

through Hanoch, the Hanochite clan;
through Pallu, the Palluite clan;
[6]through Hezron, the Hezronite clan;
through Carmi, the Carmite clan.

[7]These were the clans of Reuben; those numbered were 43,730.

[8]The son of Pallu was Eliab, [9]and the sons of Eliab were Nemuel, Dathan and Abiram. The same Dathan and Abiram were the community officials who rebelled against Moses and Aaron and were among Korah's followers when they rebelled against the LORD. [10]The earth opened its mouth and swallowed them along with Korah, whose followers died when the fire devoured the 250 men. And they served as a warning sign. [11]The line of Korah, however, did not die out.

[12]The descendants of Simeon by their clans were:

through Nemuel, the Nemuelite clan;
through Jamin, the Jaminite clan;
through Jakin, the Jakinite clan;
[13]through Zerah, the Zerahite clan;
through Shaul, the Shaulite clan.

[14]These were the clans of Simeon; there were 22,200 men.

[15]The descendants of Gad by their clans were:

through Zephon, the Zephonite clan;
through Haggi, the Haggite clan;
through Shuni, the Shunite clan;
[16]through Ozni, the Oznite clan;
through Eri, the Erite clan;
[17]through Arodi,[b] the Arodite clan;
through Areli, the Arelite clan.

[18]These were the clans of Gad; those numbered were 40,500.

[19]Er and Onan were sons of Judah, but they died in Canaan. [20]The descendants of Judah by their clans were:

through Shelah, the Shelanite clan;
through Perez, the Perezite clan;
through Zerah, the Zerahite clan.
[21]The descendants of Perez were:

through Hezron, the Hezronite clan;
through Hamul, the Hamulite clan.

[22]These were the clans of Judah; those numbered were 76,500.

Numbers 25:11

God Is Zealous

"Phinehas son of Eleazar, the son of Aaron, the priest, has turned my anger away from the Israelites; for he was as zealous as I am for my honor among them, so that in my zeal I did not put an end to them."

---

[a]3 Hebrew *Jordan of Jericho*; possibly an ancient name for the Jordan River; also in verse 63   [b]17 Samaritan Pentateuch and Syriac (see also Gen. 46:16); Masoretic Text *Arod*

23 The descendants of Issachar by their clans were:

through Tola, the Tolaite clan;
through Puah, the Puite[a] clan;
24 through Jashub, the Jashubite clan;
through Shimron, the Shimronite clan.

25 These were the clans of Issachar; those numbered were 64,300.

26 The descendants of Zebulun by their clans were:

through Sered, the Seredite clan;
through Elon, the Elonite clan;
through Jahleel, the Jahleelite clan.

27 These were the clans of Zebulun; those numbered were 60,500.

28 The descendants of Joseph by their clans through Manasseh and Ephraim were:

29 The descendants of Manasseh:

through Makir, the Makirite clan (Makir was the father of Gilead);
through Gilead, the Gileadite clan.

30 These were the descendants of Gilead:

through Iezer, the Iezerite clan;
through Helek, the Helekite clan;
31 through Asriel, the Asrielite clan;
through Shechem, the Shechemite clan;
32 through Shemida, the Shemidaite clan;
through Hepher, the Hepherite clan.

33 (Zelophehad son of Hepher had no sons; he had only daughters, whose names were Mahlah, Noah, Hoglah, Milcah and Tirzah.)

34 These were the clans of Manasseh; those numbered were 52,700.

35 These were the descendants of Ephraim by their clans:

through Shuthelah, the Shuthelahite clan;
through Beker, the Bekerite clan;
through Tahan, the Tahanite clan.

36 These were the descendants of Shuthelah:

through Eran, the Eranite clan.

37 These were the clans of Ephraim; those numbered were 32,500.

These were the descendants of Joseph by their clans.

38 The descendants of Benjamin by their clans were:

through Bela, the Belaite clan;
through Ashbel, the Ashbelite clan;
through Ahiram, the Ahiramite clan;
39 through Shupham,[b] the Shuphamite clan;
through Hupham, the Huphamite clan.

40 The descendants of Bela through Ard and Naaman were:

through Ard,[c] the Ardite clan;
through Naaman, the Naamite clan.

41 These were the clans of Benjamin; those numbered were 45,600.

42 These were the descendants of Dan by their clans:

through Shuham, the Shuhamite clan.

These were the clans of Dan: 43 All of them were Shuhamite clans; and those numbered were 64,400.

44 The descendants of Asher by their clans were:

through Imnah, the Imnite clan;
through Ishvi, the Ishvite clan;
through Beriah, the Beriite clan;
45 and through the descendants of Beriah:

through Heber, the Heberite clan;
through Malkiel, the Malkielite clan.

46 (Asher had a daughter named Serah.)

47 These were the clans of Asher; those numbered were 53,400.

48 The descendants of Naphtali by their clans were:

through Jahzeel, the Jahzeelite clan;
through Guni, the Gunite clan;
49 through Jezer, the Jezerite clan;
through Shillem, the Shillemite clan.

50 These were the clans of Naphtali; those numbered were 45,400.

51 The total number of the men of Israel was 601,730.

52 The LORD said to Moses, 53 "The land is to be allotted to them as an inheritance based on

---

a23 Samaritan Pentateuch, Septuagint, Vulgate and Syriac (see also 1 Chron. 7:1); Masoretic Text *through Puvah, the Punite*   *b39* A few manuscripts of the Masoretic Text, Samaritan Pentateuch, Vulgate and Syriac (see also Septuagint); most manuscripts of the Masoretic Text *Shephupham*   *c40* Samaritan Pentateuch and Vulgate (see also Septuagint); Masoretic Text does not have *through Ard.*

the number of names. ⁵⁴To a larger group give a larger inheritance, and to a smaller group a smaller one; each is to receive its inheritance according to the number of those listed. ⁵⁵Be sure that the land is distributed by lot. What each group inherits will be according to the names for its ancestral tribe. ⁵⁶Each inheritance is to be distributed by lot among the larger and smaller groups."

⁵⁷These were the Levites who were counted by their clans:

through Gershon, the Gershonite clan;
through Kohath, the Kohathite clan;
through Merari, the Merarite clan.

⁵⁸These also were Levite clans:

the Libnite clan,
the Hebronite clan,
the Mahlite clan,
the Mushite clan,
the Korahite clan.

(Kohath was the forefather of Amram; ⁵⁹the name of Amram's wife was Jochebed, a descendant of Levi, who was born to the Levites*ᵃ* in Egypt. To Amram she bore Aaron, Moses and their sister Miriam. ⁶⁰Aaron was the father of Nadab and Abihu, Eleazar and Ithamar. ⁶¹But Nadab and Abihu died when they made an offering before the LORD with unauthorized fire.)

⁶²All the male Levites a month old or more numbered 23,000. They were not counted along with the other Israelites because they received no inheritance among them.

⁶³These are the ones counted by Moses and Eleazar the priest when they counted the Israelites on the plains of Moab by the Jordan across from Jericho. ⁶⁴Not one of them was among those counted by Moses and Aaron the priest when they counted the Israelites in the Desert of Sinai. ⁶⁵For the LORD had told those Israelites they would surely die in the desert, and not one of them was left except Caleb son of Jephunneh and Joshua son of Nun.

ᵃ59 Or *Jochebed, a daughter of Levi, who was born to Levi*

Zelophehad's Daughters

27 The daughters of Zelophehad son of Hepher, the son of Gilead, the son of Makir, the son of Manasseh, belonged to the clans of Manasseh son of Joseph. The names of the daughters were Mahlah, Noah, Hoglah, Milcah and Tirzah. They approached ²the entrance to the Tent of Meeting and stood before Moses, Eleazar the priest, the leaders and the whole assembly, and said, ³"Our father died in the desert. He was not among Korah's followers, who banded together against the LORD, but he died for his own sin and left no sons. ⁴Why should our father's name disappear from his clan because he had no son? Give us property among our father's relatives."

⁵So Moses brought their case before the LORD ⁶and the LORD said to him, ⁷"What Zelophehad's daughters are saying is right. You must certainly give them property as an inheritance among their father's relatives and turn their father's inheritance over to them.

⁸"Say to the Israelites, 'If a man dies and leaves no son, turn his inheritance over to his daughter. ⁹If he has no daughter, give his inheritance to his brothers. ¹⁰If he has no brothers, give his inheritance to his father's brothers. ¹¹If his father had no brothers, give his inheritance to the nearest relative in his clan, that he may possess it. This is to be a legal requirement for the Israelites, as the LORD commanded Moses.'"

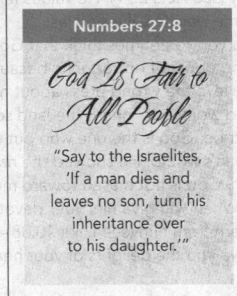

Numbers 27:8

God Is Fair to All People

"Say to the Israelites, 'If a man dies and leaves no son, turn his inheritance over to his daughter.'"

Joshua to Succeed Moses

¹²Then the LORD said to Moses, "Go up this mountain in the Abarim range and see the land I have given the Israelites. ¹³After you have seen it, you too will be gathered to your people, as your brother Aaron was, ¹⁴for when the community rebelled at the waters in the Desert of Zin, both of you disobeyed my command to honor me as holy before their eyes." (These were the waters of Meribah Kadesh, in the Desert of Zin.)

¹⁵Moses said to the LORD, ¹⁶"May the LORD, the God of the spirits of all mankind, appoint

Devotion and Dignity

Numbers 27:5-7

So Moses brought their case before the LORD and the LORD said to him, "What Zelophehad's daughters are saying is right. You must certainly give them property as an inheritance among their father's relatives and turn their father's inheritance over to them."

reflection

1 Has this passage helped you rethink your view of God and his treatment of women?

2 How can you treat God with devotion each and every day?

3 If you feel you've been treated unfairly, how can taking your feelings to God help you deal with the experience?

RELATED READINGS

Joshua 17:3–4;
Luke 24:1–10;
Romans 16:12;
Galatians 3:28

Read: Numbers 27:1–11

SINCE THE NINETEENTH CENTURY, *Pride and Prejudice* has been one of the most beloved of all love stories. Jane Austen's tale of five sisters bound by the rigid rules of Victorian society has captivated readers, television audiences and movie buffs for years. We all want the beautiful elder sister Jane to marry Mr. Bingley. We so want Lizzie to overcome her pride and Mr. Darcy to conquer his prejudice and finally admit they love each other so they can live happily ever after. We want Mr. Wickham to be discovered for the cad he truly is. And really, the old-fashioned inheritance law of entailment which required that the family estate be passed on to the nearest male relative puzzles us. Why couldn't Mr. Bennet bequeath the family fortune to his daughters so they could marry well? Why were society's laws so male-dominated that women were prevented from keeping the family estate?

Zelophehad's five daughters had a similar problem. Their father died in the desert with no male offspring left to inherit the land. God had given the land to the tribes of Israel in perpetuity. If there was no male to inherit, what should be done? The daughters came to Moses and asked for a hearing. They wanted their portion of the inheritance. They wanted to be treated with dignity. Moses listened to the sisters make their case, and then he brought it to the Lord. God's immediate response: "Of course they should have the land."

God is not sexist, as some believe him to be. He created all of his children as equals. He pours out his Spirit on both genders equally (see Acts 2:17). He values females who are devoted to him the same way he values males.

Do you sometimes think that God is limiting you rather than opening doors of opportunity because you are a woman? Then you believe the wrong press about him. God is the one who allowed women to inherit the land so long as they married into the same tribe. God is the one who put the Savior of the world into a woman's womb. He showed the risen Lord to women first, not to men. God is not biased toward men; he's an equal-opportunity deity. When you give him your devotion, when you sit at his feet and learn from him (see Luke 10:38–42), he'll treat you with dignity and give you the delights of your heart.

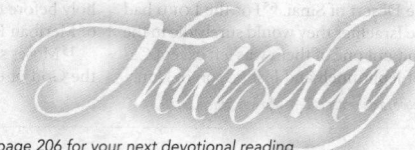

Thursday

Go to page 206 for your next devotional reading.

a man over this community [17]to go out and come in before them, one who will lead them out and bring them in, so the LORD's people will not be like sheep without a shepherd."

[18]So the LORD said to Moses, "Take Joshua son of Nun, a man in whom is the spirit,[a] and lay your hand on him. [19]Have him stand before Eleazar the priest and the entire assembly and commission him in their presence. [20]Give him some of your authority so the whole Israelite community will obey him. [21]He is to stand before Eleazar the priest, who will obtain decisions for him by inquiring of the Urim before the LORD. At his command he and the entire community of the Israelites will go out, and at his command they will come in."

[22]Moses did as the LORD commanded him. He took Joshua and had him stand before Eleazar the priest and the whole assembly. [23]Then he laid his hands on him and commissioned him, as the LORD instructed through Moses.

Daily Offerings

28 The LORD said to Moses, [2]"Give this command to the Israelites and say to them: 'See that you present to me at the appointed time the food for my offerings made by fire, as an aroma pleasing to me.' [3]Say to them: 'This is the offering made by fire that you are to present to the LORD: two lambs a year old without defect, as a regular burnt offering each day. [4]Prepare one lamb in the morning and the other at twilight, [5]together with a grain offering of a tenth of an ephah[b] of fine flour mixed with a quarter of a hin[c] of oil from pressed olives. [6]This is the regular burnt offering instituted at Mount Sinai as a pleasing aroma, an offering made to the LORD by fire. [7]The accompanying drink offering is to be a quarter of a hin of fermented drink with each lamb. Pour out the drink offering to the LORD at the sanctuary. [8]Prepare the second lamb at twilight, along with the same kind of grain offering and drink offering that you prepare in the morning. This is an offering made by fire, an aroma pleasing to the LORD.

Sabbath Offerings

[9]"'On the Sabbath day, make an offering of two lambs a year old without defect, together with its drink offering and a grain offering of two-tenths of an ephah[d] of fine flour mixed with oil. [10]This is the burnt offering for every Sabbath, in addition to the regular burnt offering and its drink offering.

Monthly Offerings

[11]"'On the first of every month, present to the LORD a burnt offering of two young bulls, one ram and seven male lambs a year old, all without defect. [12]With each bull there is to be a grain offering of three-tenths of an ephah[e] of fine flour mixed with oil; with the ram, a grain offering of two-tenths of an ephah of fine flour mixed with oil; [13]and with each lamb, a grain offering of a tenth of an ephah of fine flour mixed with oil. This is for a burnt offering, a pleasing aroma, an offering made to the LORD by fire. [14]With each bull there is to be a drink offering of half a hin[f] of wine; with the ram, a third of a hin[g]; and with each lamb, a quarter of a hin. This is the monthly burnt offering to be made at each new moon during the year. [15]Besides the regular burnt offering with its drink offering, one male goat is to be presented to the LORD as a sin offering.

The Passover

[16]"'On the fourteenth day of the first month the LORD's Passover is to be held. [17]On the fifteenth day of this month there is to be a festival; for seven days eat bread made without yeast. [18]On the first day hold a sacred assembly and do no regular work. [19]Present to the LORD an offering made by fire, a burnt offering of two young bulls, one ram and seven male lambs a year old, all without defect. [20]With each bull prepare a grain offering of three-tenths of an ephah of fine flour mixed with oil; with the ram, two-tenths; [21]and with each of the seven lambs, one-tenth. [22]Include one male goat as a sin offering to make atonement for you. [23]Prepare these in addition to the regular morning burnt offering. [24]In this way prepare the food for the offering made by fire every day for

a 18 Or *Spirit*   b 5 That is, probably about 2 quarts (about 2 liters); also in verses 13, 21 and 29   c 5 That is, probably about 1 quart (about 1 liter); also in verses 7 and 14   d 9 That is, probably about 4 quarts (about 4.5 liters); also in verses 12, 20 and 28   e 12 That is, probably about 6 quarts (about 6.5 liters); also in verses 20 and 28   f 14 That is, probably about 2 quarts (about 2 liters)   g 14 That is, probably about 1 1/4 quarts (about 1.2 liters) seven days as an aroma pleasing to the LORD; it is to be prepared in addition to the regular burnt offering and its drink offering. 25On the seventh day hold a sacred assembly and do no regular work.

Feast of Weeks

26"'On the day of firstfruits, when you present to the LORD an offering of new grain during the Feast of Weeks, hold a sacred assembly and do no regular work. 27Present a burnt offering of two young bulls, one ram and seven male lambs a year old as an aroma pleasing to the LORD. 28With each bull there is to be a grain offering of three-tenths of an ephah of fine flour mixed with oil; with the ram, two-tenths; 29and with each of the seven lambs, one-tenth. 30Include one male goat to make atonement for you. 31Prepare these together with their drink offerings, in addition to the regular burnt offering and its grain offering. Be sure the animals are without defect.

Feast of Trumpets

29 "'On the first day of the seventh month hold a sacred assembly and do no regular work. It is a day for you to sound the trumpets. 2As an aroma pleasing to the LORD, prepare a burnt offering of one young bull, one ram and seven male lambs a year old, all without defect. 3With the bull prepare a grain offering of three-tenths of an ephah*a* of fine flour mixed with oil; with the ram, two-tenths*b*; 4and with each of the seven lambs, one-tenth.*c* 5Include one male goat as a sin offering to make atonement for you. 6These are in addition to the monthly and daily burnt offerings with their grain offerings and drink offerings as specified. They are offerings made to the LORD by fire—a pleasing aroma.

Day of Atonement

7"'On the tenth day of this seventh month hold a sacred assembly. You must deny yourselves*d* and do no work. 8Present as an aroma pleasing to the LORD a burnt offering of one young bull, one ram and seven male lambs a year old, all without defect. 9With the bull prepare a grain offering of three-tenths of an ephah of fine flour mixed with oil; with the

ram, two-tenths; 10and with each of the seven lambs, one-tenth. 11Include one male goat as a sin offering, in addition to the sin offering for atonement and the regular burnt offering with its grain offering, and their drink offerings.

Feast of Tabernacles

12"'On the fifteenth day of the seventh month, hold a sacred assembly and do no regular work. Celebrate a festival to the LORD for seven days. 13Present an offering made by fire as an aroma pleasing to the LORD, a burnt offering of thirteen young bulls, two rams and fourteen male lambs a year old, all without defect. 14With each of the thirteen bulls prepare a grain offering of three-tenths of an ephah of fine flour mixed with oil; with each of the two rams, two-tenths; 15and with each of the fourteen lambs, one-tenth. 16Include one male goat as a sin offering, in addition to the regular burnt offering with its grain offering and drink offering.

17"'On the second day prepare twelve young bulls, two rams and fourteen male lambs a year old, all without defect. 18With the bulls, rams and lambs, prepare their grain offerings and drink offerings according to the number specified. 19Include one male goat as a sin offering, in addition to the regular burnt offering with its grain offering, and their drink offerings.

20"'On the third day prepare eleven bulls, two rams and fourteen male lambs a year old, all without defect. 21With the bulls, rams and lambs, prepare their grain offerings and drink offerings according to the number specified. 22Include one male goat as a sin offering, in addition to the regular burnt offering with its grain offering and drink offering.

23"'On the fourth day prepare ten bulls, two rams and fourteen male lambs a year old, all without defect. 24With the bulls, rams and lambs, prepare their grain offerings and drink offerings according to the number specified. 25Include one male goat as a sin offering, in addition to the regular burnt offering with its grain offering and drink offering.

26"'On the fifth day prepare nine bulls, two rams and fourteen male lambs a year old, all without defect. 27With the bulls, rams and

---

*a*3 That is, probably about 6 quarts (about 6.5 liters); also in verses 9 and 14   *b*3 That is, probably about 4 quarts (about 4.5 liters); also in verses 9 and 14   *c*4 That is, probably about 2 quarts (about 2 liters); also in verses 10 and 15   *d*7 Or *must fast* lambs, prepare their grain offerings and drink offerings according to the number specified. 28Include one male goat as a sin offering, in addition to the regular burnt offering with its grain offering and drink offering.

29"'On the sixth day prepare eight bulls, two rams and fourteen male lambs a year old, all without defect. 30With the bulls, rams and lambs, prepare their grain offerings and drink offerings according to the number specified. 31Include one male goat as a sin offering, in addition to the regular burnt offering with its grain offering and drink offering.

32"'On the seventh day prepare seven bulls, two rams and fourteen male lambs a year old, all without defect. 33With the bulls, rams and lambs, prepare their grain offerings and drink offerings according to the number specified. 34Include one male goat as a sin offering, in addition to the regular burnt offering with its grain offering and drink offering.

35"'On the eighth day hold an assembly and do no regular work. 36Present an offering made by fire as an aroma pleasing to the LORD, a burnt offering of one bull, one ram and seven male lambs a year old, all without defect. 37With the bull, the ram and the lambs, prepare their grain offerings and drink offerings according to the number specified. 38Include one male goat as a sin offering, in addition to the regular burnt offering with its grain offering and drink offering.

39"'In addition to what you vow and your freewill offerings, prepare these for the LORD at your appointed feasts: your burnt offerings, grain offerings, drink offerings and fellowship offerings.a'"

40Moses told the Israelites all that the LORD commanded him.

Vows

30 Moses said to the heads of the tribes of Israel: "This is what the LORD commands: 2When a man makes a vow to the LORD or takes an oath to obligate himself by a pledge, he must not break his word but must do everything he said.

3"When a young woman still living in her father's house makes a vow to the LORD or obli-gates herself by a pledge 4and her father hears about her vow or pledge but says nothing to her, then all her vows and every pledge by which she obligated herself will stand. 5But if her father forbids her when he hears about it, none of her vows or the pledges by which she obligated herself will stand; the LORD will release her because her father has forbidden her.

6"If she marries after she makes a vow or after her lips utter a rash promise by which she obligates herself 7and her husband hears about it but says nothing to her, then her vows or the pledges by which she obligated herself will stand. 8But if her husband forbids her when he hears about it, he nullifies the vow that obligates her or the rash promise by which she obligates herself, and the LORD will release her.

9"Any vow or obligation taken by a widow or divorced woman will be binding on her.

10"If a woman living with her husband makes a vow or obligates herself by a pledge under oath 11and her husband hears about it but says nothing to her and does not forbid her, then all her vows or the pledges by which she obligated herself will stand. 12But if her husband nullifies them when he hears about them, then none of the vows or pledges that came from her lips will stand. Her husband has nullified them, and the LORD will release her. 13Her husband may confirm or nullify any vow she makes or any sworn pledge to deny herself. 14But if her husband says nothing to her about it from day to day, then he confirms all her vows or the pledges binding on her. He confirms them by saying nothing to her when he hears about them. 15If, however, he nullifies them some time after he hears about them, then he is responsible for her guilt."

16These are the regulations the LORD gave Moses concerning relationships between a man and his wife, and between a father and his young daughter still living in his house.

Vengeance on the Midianites

31 The LORD said to Moses, 2"Take vengeance on the Midianites for the Israelites. After that, you will be gathered to your people."

3So Moses said to the people, "Arm so

---

a39 Traditionally *peace offerings*

your men to go to war against the Midianites and to carry out the LORD's vengeance on them. 4Send into battle a thousand men from each of the tribes of Israel." 5So twelve thousand men armed for battle, a thousand from each tribe, were supplied from the clans of Israel. 6Moses sent them into battle, a thousand from each tribe, along with Phinehas son of Eleazar, the priest, who took with him articles from the sanctuary and the trumpets for signaling.

7They fought against Midian, as the LORD commanded Moses, and killed every man. 8Among their victims were Evi, Rekem, Zur, Hur and Reba—the five kings of Midian. They also killed Balaam son of Beor with the sword. 9The Israelites captured the Midianite women and children and took all the Midianite herds, flocks and goods as plunder. 10They burned all the towns where the Midianites had settled, as well as all their camps. 11They took all the plunder and spoils, including the people and animals, 12and brought the captives, spoils and plunder to Moses and Eleazar the priest and the Israelite assembly at their camp on the plains of Moab, by the Jordan across from Jericho.a

13Moses, Eleazar the priest and all the leaders of the community went to meet them outside the camp. 14Moses was angry with the officers of the army—the commanders of thousands and commanders of hundreds—who returned from the battle.

15"Have you allowed all the women to live?" he asked them. 16"They were the ones who followed Balaam's advice and were the means of turning the Israelites away from the LORD in what happened at Peor, so that a plague struck the LORD's people. 17Now kill all the boys. And kill every woman who has slept with a man, 18but save for yourselves every girl who has never slept with a man.

19"All of you who have killed anyone or touched anyone who was killed must stay outside the camp seven days. On the third and seventh days you must purify yourselves and your captives. 20Purify every garment as well as everything made of leather, goat hair or wood."

21Then Eleazar the priest said to the soldiers who had gone into battle, "This is the requirement of the law that the LORD gave Moses:

22Gold, silver, bronze, iron, tin, lead 23and anything else that can withstand fire must be put through the fire, and then it will be clean. But it must also be purified with the water of cleansing. And whatever cannot withstand fire must be put through that water. 24On the seventh day wash your clothes and you will be clean. Then you may come into the camp."

Dividing the Spoils

25The LORD said to Moses, 26"You and Eleazar the priest and the family heads of the community are to count all the people and animals that were captured. 27Divide the spoils between the soldiers who took part in the battle and the rest of the community. 28From the soldiers who fought in the battle, set apart as tribute for the LORD one out of every five hundred, whether persons, cattle, donkeys, sheep or goats. 29Take this tribute from their half share and give it to Eleazar the priest as the LORD's part. 30From the Israelites' half, select one out of every fifty, whether persons, cattle, donkeys, sheep, goats or other animals. Give them to the Levites, who are responsible for the care of the LORD's tabernacle." 31So Moses and Eleazar the priest did as the LORD commanded Moses.

32The plunder remaining from the spoils that the soldiers took was 675,000 sheep, 3372,000 cattle, 3461,000 donkeys 35and 32,000 women who had never slept with a man.

36The half share of those who fought in the battle was:

> 337,500 sheep, 37of which the tribute for the LORD was 675;
> 38 36,000 cattle, of which the tribute for the LORD was 72;
> 39 30,500 donkeys, of which the tribute for the LORD was 61;
> 40 16,000 people, of which the tribute for the LORD was 32.

41Moses gave the tribute to Eleazar the priest as the LORD's part, as the LORD commanded Moses.

42The half belonging to the Israelites, which Moses set apart from that of the fighting men— 43the community's half—was 337,500 sheep, 4436,000 cattle, 4530,500 donkeys 46and

---

a ew Jordan of Jericho; possibly an ancient name for the Jordan River

16,000 people. ⁴⁷From the Israelites' half, Moses selected one out of every fifty persons and animals, as the LORD commanded him, and gave them to the Levites, who were responsible for the care of the LORD's tabernacle.

⁴⁸Then the officers who were over the units of the army—the commanders of thousands and commanders of hundreds—went to Moses ⁴⁹and said to him, "Your servants have counted the soldiers under our command, and not one is missing. ⁵⁰So we have brought as an offering to the LORD the gold articles each of us acquired—armlets, bracelets, signet rings, earrings and necklaces—to make atonement for ourselves before the LORD."

⁵¹Moses and Eleazar the priest accepted from them the gold—all the crafted articles. ⁵²All the gold from the commanders of thousands and commanders of hundreds that Moses and Eleazar presented as a gift to the LORD weighed 16,750 shekels.^a ⁵³Each soldier had taken plunder for himself. ⁵⁴Moses and Eleazar the priest accepted the gold from the commanders of thousands and commanders of hundreds and brought it into the Tent of Meeting as a memorial for the Israelites before the LORD.

The Transjordan Tribes

32 The Reubenites and Gadites, who had very large herds and flocks, saw that the lands of Jazer and Gilead were suitable for livestock. ²So they came to Moses and Eleazar the priest and to the leaders of the community, and said, ³"Ataroth, Dibon, Jazer, Nimrah, Heshbon, Elealeh, Sebam, Nebo and Beon— ⁴the land the LORD subdued before the people of Israel—are suitable for livestock, and your servants have livestock. ⁵If we have found favor in your eyes," they said, "let this land be given to your servants as our possession. Do not make us cross the Jordan."

⁶Moses said to the Gadites and Reubenites, "Shall your countrymen go to war while you sit here? ⁷Why do you discourage the Israelites from going over into the land the LORD has given them? ⁸This is what your fathers did when I sent them from Kadesh Barnea to look over the land. ⁹After they went up to

the Valley of Eshcol and viewed the land, they discouraged the Israelites from entering the land the LORD had given them. ¹⁰The LORD's anger was aroused that day and he swore this oath: ¹¹'Because they have not followed me wholeheartedly, not one of the men twenty years old or more who came up out of Egypt will see the land I promised on oath to Abraham, Isaac and Jacob— ¹²not one except Caleb son of Jephunneh the Kenizzite and Joshua son of Nun, for they followed the LORD wholeheartedly.' ¹³The LORD's anger burned against Israel and he made them wander in the desert forty years, until the whole generation of those who had done evil in his sight was gone.

¹⁴"And here you are, a brood of sinners, standing in the place of your fathers and making the LORD even more angry with Israel. ¹⁵If you turn away from following him, he will again leave all this people in the desert, and you will be the cause of their destruction."

¹⁶Then they came up to him and said, "We would like to build pens here for our livestock and cities for our women and children. ¹⁷But we are ready to arm ourselves and go ahead of the Israelites until we have brought them to their place. Meanwhile our women and children will live in fortified cities, for protection from the inhabitants of the land. ¹⁸We will not return to our homes until every Israelite has received his inheritance. ¹⁹We will not receive any inheritance with them on the other side of the Jordan, because our inheritance has come to us on the east side of the Jordan."

²⁰Then Moses said to them, "If you will do this—if you will arm yourselves before the LORD for battle, ²¹and if all of you will go armed over the Jordan before the LORD until he has driven his enemies out before him— ²²then when the land is subdued before the LORD, you may return and be free from your obligation to the LORD and to Israel. And this land will be your possession before the LORD.

²³"But if you fail to do this, you will be sinning against the LORD; and you may be sure that your sin will find you out. ²⁴Build cities for your women and children, and pens for your flocks, but do what you have promised."

²⁵The Gadites and Reubenites said to Moses,

^a52 That is, about 420 pounds (about 190 kilograms)

203

"We your servants will do as our lord commands. ²⁶Our children and wives, our flocks and herds will remain here in the cities of Gilead. ²⁷But your servants, every man armed for battle, will cross over to fight before the LORD, just as our lord says."

²⁸Then Moses gave orders about them to Eleazar the priest and Joshua son of Nun and to the family heads of the Israelite tribes. ²⁹He said to them, "If the Gadites and Reubenites, every man armed for battle, cross over the Jordan with you before the LORD, then when the land is subdued before you, give them the land of Gilead as their possession. ³⁰But if they do not cross over with you armed, they must accept their possession with you in Canaan."

³¹The Gadites and Reubenites answered, "Your servants will do what the LORD has said. ³²We will cross over before the LORD into Canaan armed, but the property we inherit will be on this side of the Jordan."

³³Then Moses gave to the Gadites, the Reubenites and the half-tribe of Manasseh son of Joseph the kingdom of Sihon king of the Amorites and the kingdom of Og king of Bashan—the whole land with its cities and the territory around them.

³⁴The Gadites built up Dibon, Ataroth, Aroer, ³⁵Atroth Shophan, Jazer, Jogbehah, ³⁶Beth Nimrah and Beth Haran as fortified cities, and built pens for their flocks. ³⁷And the Reubenites rebuilt Heshbon, Elealeh and Kiriathaim, ³⁸as well as Nebo and Baal Meon (these names were changed) and Sibmah. They gave names to the cities they rebuilt.

³⁹The descendants of Makir son of Manasseh went to Gilead, captured it and drove out the Amorites who were there. ⁴⁰So Moses gave Gilead to the Makirites, the descendants of Manasseh, and they settled there. ⁴¹Jair, a descendant of Manasseh, captured their settlements and called them Havvoth Jair.^a ⁴²And Nobah captured Kenath and its surrounding settlements and called it Nobah after himself.

Numbers 32:23

God Sees Everything

"But if you fail to do this, you will be sinning against the LORD; and you may be sure that your sin will find you out."

Stages in Israel's Journey

33 Here are the stages in the journey of the Israelites when they came out of Egypt by divisions under the leadership of Moses and Aaron. ²At the LORD's command Moses recorded the stages in their journey. This is their journey by stages:

³The Israelites set out from Rameses on the fifteenth day of the first month, the day after the Passover. They marched out boldly in full view of all the Egyptians, ⁴who were burying all their firstborn, whom the LORD had struck down among them; for the LORD had brought judgment on their gods.

⁵The Israelites left Rameses and camped at Succoth.

⁶They left Succoth and camped at Etham, on the edge of the desert.

⁷They left Etham, turned back to Pi Hahiroth, to the east of Baal Zephon, and camped near Migdol.

⁸They left Pi Hahiroth^b and passed through the sea into the desert, and when they had traveled for three days in the Desert of Etham, they camped at Marah.

⁹They left Marah and went to Elim, where there were twelve springs and seventy palm trees, and they camped there.

¹⁰They left Elim and camped by the Red Sea.^c

¹¹They left the Red Sea and camped in the Desert of Sin.

¹²They left the Desert of Sin and camped at Dophkah.

¹³They left Dophkah and camped at Alush.

¹⁴They left Alush and camped at Rephidim, where there was no water for the people to drink.

^a41 Or *them the settlements of Jair*   ^b8 Many manuscripts of the Masoretic Text, Samaritan Pentateuch and Vulgate; most manuscripts of the Masoretic Text *left from before Hahiroth*   ^c10 Hebrew *Yam Suph*; that is, Sea of Reeds; also in verse 11

¹⁵They left Rephidim and camped in the Desert of Sinai.

¹⁶They left the Desert of Sinai and camped at Kibroth Hattaavah.

¹⁷They left Kibroth Hattaavah and camped at Hazeroth.

¹⁸They left Hazeroth and camped at Rithmah.

¹⁹They left Rithmah and camped at Rimmon Perez.

²⁰They left Rimmon Perez and camped at Libnah.

²¹They left Libnah and camped at Rissah.

²²They left Rissah and camped at Kehelathah.

²³They left Kehelathah and camped at Mount Shepher.

²⁴They left Mount Shepher and camped at Haradah.

²⁵They left Haradah and camped at Makheloth.

²⁶They left Makheloth and camped at Tahath.

²⁷They left Tahath and camped at Terah.

²⁸They left Terah and camped at Mithcah.

²⁹They left Mithcah and camped at Hashmonah.

³⁰They left Hashmonah and camped at Moseroth.

³¹They left Moseroth and camped at Bene Jaakan.

³²They left Bene Jaakan and camped at Hor Haggidgad.

³³They left Hor Haggidgad and camped at Jotbathah.

³⁴They left Jotbathah and camped at Abronah.

³⁵They left Abronah and camped at Ezion Geber.

³⁶They left Ezion Geber and camped at Kadesh, in the Desert of Zin.

³⁷They left Kadesh and camped at Mount Hor, on the border of Edom. ³⁸At the Lord's command Aaron the priest went up Mount Hor, where he died on the first day of the fifth month of the fortieth year after the Israelites came out of Egypt. ³⁹Aaron was a hundred and twenty-three years old when he died on Mount Hor.

⁴⁰The Canaanite king of Arad, who lived in the Negev of Canaan, heard that the Israelites were coming.

⁴¹They left Mount Hor and camped at Zalmonah.

⁴²They left Zalmonah and camped at Punon.

⁴³They left Punon and camped at Oboth.

⁴⁴They left Oboth and camped at Iye Abarim, on the border of Moab.

⁴⁵They left Iyim*a* and camped at Dibon Gad.

⁴⁶They left Dibon Gad and camped at Almon Diblathaim.

⁴⁷They left Almon Diblathaim and camped in the mountains of Abarim, near Nebo.

⁴⁸They left the mountains of Abarim and camped on the plains of Moab by the Jordan across from Jericho.*b* ⁴⁹There on the plains of Moab they camped along the Jordan from Beth Jeshimoth to Abel Shittim.

⁵⁰On the plains of Moab by the Jordan across from Jericho the Lord said to Moses, ⁵¹"Speak to the Israelites and say to them: 'When you cross the Jordan into Canaan, ⁵²drive out all the inhabitants of the land before you. Destroy all their carved images and their cast idols, and demolish all their high places. ⁵³Take possession of the land and settle in it, for I have given you the land to possess. ⁵⁴Distribute the land by lot, according to your clans. To a larger group give a larger inheritance, and to a smaller group a smaller one. Whatever falls to them by lot will be theirs. Distribute it according to your ancestral tribes.

⁵⁵"'But if you do not drive out the inhabitants of the land, those you allow to remain will become barbs in your eyes and thorns in your sides. They will give you trouble in the land where you will live. ⁵⁶And then I will do to you what I plan to do to them.'"

---

*a*45 That is, Iye Abarim   *b*48 Hebrew *Jordan of Jericho*; possibly an ancient name for the Jordan River; also in verse 50

No Loopholes

Numbers 33:55–56

"But if you do not drive out the inhabitants of the land, those you allow to remain will become barbs in your eyes and thorns in your sides. They will give you trouble in the land where you will live. And then I will do to you what I plan to do to them."

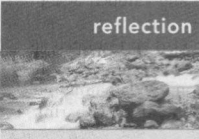

reflection

1 When do you find it especially difficult to obey God?

2 Have you experienced "barbs and thorns" because you insisted on doing things your own way?

3 How does it comfort you to know that God's ways are far above your ways?

RELATED READINGS

2 Chronicles 31:20–21;
Romans 8:28;
2 Timothy 3:16–17

Read: Numbers 33:50–56

SURE, DESTROY THE IDOLS. Can you hear the Israelites' thoughts as they finally entered the promised land? *Dividing up the land— that sounds good. After all, we want the land.* So far, they're liking what God tells them. Then comes the rub. God tells them to drive everyone from the land. Every single person living in the land has got to go. *Wait a minute! How could our good and loving God drive these folks from their homes? Even fragile women, helpless old people and innocent little children? That's just not fair!*

Sometimes we come to portions of the Bible we cannot reconcile with our notions of what is fair. But we can't avoid these difficult passages. God said, "Drive out everyone." And in our limited understanding we argue, question and challenge: "Surely 'everyone' doesn't mean *everyone*. You just mean a few—like the really bad guys. 'Cause you're loving and fair, right?"

But instead of responding to our demands, God points us back to his Word and reveals more of who he is: "'My thoughts are not your thoughts, neither are your ways my ways,' declares the LORD. 'As the heavens are higher than the earth, so are my ways higher than your ways and my thoughts than your thoughts' " (Isaiah 55:8–9). Yes, God is loving and fair. But God is also just. When he said "everyone," he meant every single person. He wasn't being cruel. He was being protective.

God recognized that the Canaanites were thoroughly infected with the highly contagious disease of idolatry. Allowing them to stay in the land would mean exposing the Israelites to their contamination. The moral illness would certainly destroy them.

Do you ever find yourself second-guessing God? Even when his instruction is clearly laid out in his Word? Do you bristle and say, "Wait! Surely 'all' doesn't mean *all*?" Yet when Paul wrote, "As we have opportunity, let us do good to *all* people" (Galatians 6:10, emphasis added), we don't find much wiggle room . . . "all people" means *all* people. We might try to say, "Surely 'every' doesn't mean *every*. I'm sure there are exceptions to your rules. Isn't there a loophole?" But God doesn't ask for our advice or our input—just our obedience, even when his ways don't seem to make sense. The truth is this: There is no better way than God's way. In every area, in all things, at all times, God is good and loving and just. And he always, in all ways, knows best.

Go to page 212 for your next devotional reading.

Boundaries of Canaan

34 The LORD said to Moses, 2"Command the Israelites and say to them: 'When you enter Canaan, the land that will be allotted to you as an inheritance will have these boundaries:

3"'Your southern side will include some of the Desert of Zin along the border of Edom. On the east, your southern boundary will start from the end of the Salt Sea,*a* 4cross south of Scorpion*b* Pass, continue on to Zin and go south of Kadesh Barnea. Then it will go to Hazar Addar and over to Azmon, 5where it will turn, join the Wadi of Egypt and end at the Sea.*c*

6"'Your western boundary will be the coast of the Great Sea. This will be your boundary on the west.

7"'For your northern boundary, run a line from the Great Sea to Mount Hor 8and from Mount Hor to Lebo*d* Hamath. Then the boundary will go to Zedad, 9continue to Ziphron and end at Hazar Enan. This will be your boundary on the north.

10"'For your eastern boundary, run a line from Hazar Enan to Shepham. 11The boundary will go down from Shepham to Riblah on the east side of Ain and continue along the slopes east of the Sea of Kinnereth.*e* 12Then the boundary will go down along the Jordan and end at the Salt Sea.

"'This will be your land, with its boundaries on every side.'"

13Moses commanded the Israelites: "Assign this land by lot as an inheritance. The LORD has ordered that it be given to the nine and a half tribes, 14because the families of the tribe of Reuben, the tribe of Gad and the half-tribe of Manasseh have received their inheritance. 15These two and a half tribes have received their inheritance on the east side of the Jordan of Jericho,*f* toward the sunrise."

16The LORD said to Moses, 17"These are the names of the men who are to assign the land for you as an inheritance: Eleazar the priest and Joshua son of Nun. 18And appoint one leader from each tribe to help assign the land. 19These are their names:

Caleb son of Jephunneh,
    from the tribe of Judah;
20Shemuel son of Ammihud,
    from the tribe of Simeon;
21Elidad son of Kislon,
    from the tribe of Benjamin;
22Bukki son of Jogli,
    the leader from the tribe of Dan;
23Hanniel son of Ephod,
    the leader from the tribe of Manasseh
    son of Joseph;
24Kemuel son of Shiphtan,
    the leader from the tribe of Ephraim
    son of Joseph;
25Elizaphan son of Parnach,
    the leader from the tribe of Zebulun;
26Paltiel son of Azzan,
    the leader from the tribe of Issachar;
27Ahihud son of Shelomi,
    the leader from the tribe of Asher;
28Pedahel son of Ammihud,
    the leader from the tribe of Naphtali."

29These are the men the LORD commanded to assign the inheritance to the Israelites in the land of Canaan.

Towns for the Levites

35 On the plains of Moab by the Jordan across from Jericho,*g* the LORD said to Moses, 2"Command the Israelites to give the Levites towns to live in from the inheritance the Israelites will possess. And give them pasturelands around the towns. 3Then they will have towns to live in and pasturelands for their cattle, flocks and all their other livestock.

4"The pasturelands around the towns that you give the Levites will extend out fifteen hundred feet*h* from the town wall. 5Outside the town, measure three thousand feet*i* on the east side, three thousand on the south side, three thousand on the west and three thousand on the north, with the town in the center. They will have this area as pastureland for the towns.

Cities of Refuge

6"Six of the towns you give the Levites will be cities of refuge, to which a person who has killed someone may flee. In addition, give them

*a*3 That is, the Dead Sea; also in verse 12   *b*4 Hebrew *Akrabbim*   *c*5 That is, the Mediterranean; also in verses 6 and 7   *d*8 Or *to the entrance to*   *e*11 That is, Galilee   *f*15 *Jordan of Jericho* was possibly an ancient name for the Jordan River.   *g*1 Hebrew *Jordan of Jericho*; possibly an ancient name for the Jordan River   *h*4 Hebrew *a thousand cubits* (about 450 meters)   *i*5 Hebrew *two thousand cubits* (about 900 meters) forty-two other towns. **7**In all you must give the Levites forty-eight towns, together with their pasturelands. **8**The towns you give the Levites from the land the Israelites possess are to be given in proportion to the inheritance of each tribe: Take many towns from a tribe that has many, but few from one that has few."

9Then the LORD said to Moses: **10**"Speak to the Israelites and say to them: 'When you cross the Jordan into Canaan, **11**select some towns to be your cities of refuge, to which a person who has killed someone accidentally may flee. **12**They will be places of refuge from the avenger, so that a person accused of murder may not die before he stands trial before the assembly. **13**These six towns you give will be your cities of refuge. **14**Give three on this side of the Jordan and three in Canaan as cities of refuge. **15**These six towns will be a place of refuge for Israelites, aliens and any other people living among them, so that anyone who has killed another accidentally can flee there.

16"'If a man strikes someone with an iron object so that he dies, he is a murderer; the murderer shall be put to death. **17**Or if anyone has a stone in his hand that could kill, and he strikes someone so that he dies, he is a murderer; the murderer shall be put to death. **18**Or if anyone has a wooden object in his hand that could kill, and he hits someone so that he dies, he is a murderer; the murderer shall be put to death. **19**The avenger of blood shall put the murderer to death; when he meets him, he shall put him to death. **20**If anyone with malice aforethought shoves another or throws something at him intentionally so that he dies **21**or if in hostility he hits him with his fist so that he dies, that person shall be put to death; he is a murderer. The avenger of blood shall put the murderer to *death when he meets him.*

22"'But if without hostility someone suddenly shoves another or throws something at him unintentionally **23**or, without seeing him, drops a stone on him that could kill him, and he dies, then since he was not his enemy and he did not intend to harm him, **24**the assembly must judge between him and the avenger of blood according to these regulations. **25**The assembly must protect the one accused of murder from the avenger of blood and send him back to the city of refuge to which he fled. He must stay there until the death of the high priest, who was anointed with the holy oil.

26"'But if the accused ever goes outside the limits of the city of refuge to which he has fled **27**and the avenger of blood finds him outside the city, the avenger of blood may kill the accused without being guilty of murder. **28**The accused must stay in his city of refuge until the death of the high priest; only after the death of the high priest may he return to his own property.

29"'These are to be legal requirements for you throughout the generations to come, wherever you live.

30"'Anyone who kills a person is to be put to death as a murderer only on the testimony of witnesses. But no one is to be put to death on the testimony of only one witness.

31"'Do not accept a ransom for the life of a murderer, who deserves to die. He must surely be put to death.

32"'Do not accept a ransom for anyone who has fled to a city of refuge and so allow him to go back and live on his own land before the death of the high priest.

33"'Do not pollute the land where you are. Bloodshed pollutes the land, and atonement cannot be made for the land on which blood has been shed, except by the blood of the one who shed it. **34**Do not defile the land where you live and where I dwell, for I, the LORD, dwell among the Israelites.'"

Numbers 35:34

God Lives With Us

"Do not defile the land where you live and where I dwell, for I, the LORD, dwell among the Israelites."

Inheritance of Zelophehad's Daughters

36 The family heads of the clan of Gilead son of Makir, the son of Manasseh, who were from the clans of the descendants of Joseph, came and spoke before Moses and the leaders, the heads of the Israelite families. **2**They said, "When the LORD commanded my lord to give the land as an inheritance to the Israelites by lot, he ordered you to give the inheritance of our brother Zelophehad to his daughters. ³Now suppose they marry men from other Israelite tribes; then their inheritance will be taken from our ancestral inheritance and added to that of the tribe they marry into. And so part of the inheritance allotted to us will be taken away. ⁴When the Year of Jubilee for the Israelites comes, their inheritance will be added to that of the tribe into which they marry, and their property will be taken from the tribal inheritance of our forefathers."

⁵Then at the LORD's command Moses gave this order to the Israelites: "What the tribe of the descendants of Joseph is saying is right. ⁶This is what the LORD commands for Zelophehad's daughters: They may marry anyone they please as long as they marry within the tribal clan of their father. ⁷No inheritance in

Israel is to pass from tribe to tribe, for every Israelite shall keep the tribal land inherited from his forefathers. ⁸Every daughter who inherits land in any Israelite tribe must marry someone in her father's tribal clan, so that every Israelite will possess the inheritance of his fathers. ⁹No inheritance may pass from tribe to tribe, for each Israelite tribe is to keep the land it inherits."

¹⁰So Zelophehad's daughters did as the LORD commanded Moses. ¹¹Zelophehad's daughters—Mahlah, Tirzah, Hoglah, Milcah and Noah—married their cousins on their father's side. ¹²They married within the clans of the descendants of Manasseh son of Joseph, and their inheritance remained in their father's clan and tribe.

¹³These are the commands and regulations the LORD gave through Moses to the Israelites on the plains of Moab by the Jordan across from Jericho.*

---

*13 Hebrew *Jordan of Jericho*; possibly an ancient name for the Jordan River

Deuteronomy

Author:
Moses.

Audience:
The people of Israel.

Date:
About 1406 B.C.

Setting:
In the desert east of the Jordan River, preparing to enter the promised land.

Verse to Remember:
Love the LORD your God with all your heart and with all your soul and with all your strength. (6:5)

Deuteronomy reads like a farewell address given by a leader to his beloved people. *Moses is 120 years old now,* still strong, still clear of vision and still very much a leader. But *it is time for a change.* He has watched a generation of the Israelites die in the wilderness. He knows that he too will soon die. He will not be the one to cross the Jordan River and lead the Israelites into *the promised land.* Before he departs he wants to impress upon the people who God is and what God requires. Moses won't be going with them, but he wants to be sure the people go with God. They must know what *God's Law says,* and they must live it out. The only way for them to reach and secure the promised land is to love God and obey him.

The Command to Leave Horeb

1 These are the words Moses spoke to all Israel in the desert east of the Jordan—that is, in the Arabah—opposite Suph, between Paran and Tophel, Laban, Hazeroth and Dizahab. ²(It takes eleven days to go from Horeb to Kadesh Barnea by the Mount Seir road.)

³In the fortieth year, on the first day of the eleventh month, Moses proclaimed to the Israelites all that the LORD had commanded him concerning them. ⁴This was after he had defeated Sihon king of the Amorites, who reigned in Heshbon, and at Edrei had defeated Og king of Bashan, who reigned in Ashtaroth.

⁵East of the Jordan in the territory of Moab, Moses began to expound this law, saying:

⁶The LORD our God said to us at Horeb, "You have stayed long enough at this mountain. ⁷Break camp and advance into the hill country of the Amorites; go to all the neighboring peoples in the Arabah, in the mountains, in the western foothills, in the Negev and along the coast, to the land of the Canaanites and to

Lebanon, as far as the great river, the Euphrates. **8**See, I have given you this land. Go in and take possession of the land that the Lord swore he would give to your fathers—to Abraham, Isaac and Jacob—and to their descendants after them."

The Appointment of Leaders

9At that time I said to you, "You are too heavy a burden for me to carry alone. **10**The Lord your God has increased your numbers so that today you are as many as the stars in the sky. **11**May the Lord, the God of your fathers, increase you a thousand times and bless you as he has promised! **12**But how can I bear your problems and your burdens and your disputes all by myself? **13**Choose some wise, understanding and respected men from each of your tribes, and I will set them over you."

14You answered me, "What you propose to do is good."

15So I took the leading men of your tribes, wise and respected men, and appointed them to have authority over you—as commanders of thousands, of hundreds, of fifties and of tens and as tribal officials. **16**And I charged your judges at that time: Hear the disputes between your brothers and judge fairly, whether the case is between brother Israelites or between one of them and an alien. **17**Do not show partiality in judging; hear both small and great alike. Do not be afraid of any man, for judgment belongs to God. Bring me any case too hard for you, and I will hear it. **18**And at that time I told you everything you were to do.

Spies Sent Out

19Then, as the Lord our God commanded us, we set out from Horeb and went toward the hill country of the Amorites through all that vast and dreadful desert that you have seen, and so we reached Kadesh Barnea. **20**Then I said to you, "You have reached the hill country of the Amorites, which the Lord our God is giving us. **21**See, the Lord your God has given you the land. Go up and take possession of it as the Lord, the God of your fathers, told you. Do not be afraid; do not be discouraged."

22Then all of you came to me and said, "Let us send men ahead to spy out the land for us and bring back a report about the route we are to take and the towns we will come to."

23The idea seemed good to me; so I selected twelve of you, one man from each tribe. **24**They left and went up into the hill country, and came to the Valley of Eshcol and explored it. **25**Taking with them some of the fruit of the land, they brought it down to us and reported, "It is a good land that the Lord our God is giving us."

Rebellion Against the Lord

26But you were unwilling to go up; you rebelled against the command of the Lord your God. **27**You grumbled in your tents and said, "The Lord hates us; so he brought us out of Egypt to deliver us into the hands of the Amorites to destroy us. **28**Where can we go? Our brothers have made us lose heart. They say, 'The people are stronger and taller than we are; the cities are large, with walls up to the sky. We even saw the Anakites there.'"

29Then I said to you, "Do not be terrified; do not be afraid of them. **30**The Lord your God, who is going before you, will fight for you, as he did for you in Egypt, before your very eyes, **31**and in the desert. There you saw how the Lord your God carried you, as a father carries his son, all the way you went until you reached this place."

Deuteronomy 1:31

God Carries Us

"There you saw how the Lord your God carried you, as a father carries his son, all the way you went until you reached this place."

32In spite of this, you did not trust in the Lord your God, **33**who went ahead of you on your journey, in fire by night and in a cloud by day, to search out places for you to camp and to show you the way you should go.

34When the Lord heard what you said, he was angry and solemnly swore: **35**"Not a man of this evil generation shall see the good land I swore to give your forefathers, **36**except Caleb son of Jephunneh. He will see it, and I will give him and his descendants the land he

LEAH

RACHEL, HER SISTER, had always had something she didn't. Rachel had beauty, Leah didn't. Rachel had Jacob's heart, Leah didn't. However, with the birth of her first child, she finally had something Rachel didn't: a son.

"Surely my husband will love me *now,*" she recalled thinking after Reuben was born. What she desperately wanted would finally belong to her and her alone. She had bargaining power, and she planned to use it.

This is the way that Leah considered each of her children. They served as a strange sort of currency, each one "buying" her a certain level of emotional security and social standing. However, whatever dividends she gained depreciated all too quickly. She had to have another baby, and another, to keep her emotional security afloat.

Unsettled in her own skin for most of her life, Leah longed to feel comfortable around other women. She would never be the prettiest. Never the smartest. Not even the wealthiest. She knew that. But a baby gave women reason to envy. "The women will call me happy!" she recalled, fantasizing at the time of yet another son's birth. She thought every eye would be on her. The odds would finally be in her favor.

After five strapping sons and with one on the way, she imagined herself becoming a queen among her princes. As she contemplated the next birth, she thought that surely her husband would finally look at her with eyes of love. This time, her peers would approve of her. This time, she would earn everyone's respect.

The last time hadn't worked out like she'd hoped. And the time before that, well . . . the rewards had been short-lived at best. Every "last time" was, after all, *last* time. She needed something new in order to feel good about herself today. As she looked up and saw her husband coming in from the fields, she absently stroked her pregnant belly. This time . . .

—Prayer—
Lord, the next time I look to some person, thing or idea to complete me, draw my eyes to you instead.

ASSIGNED READING:

Genesis 29–30

Weekend

Go to page 219 for your next devotional reading.

set his feet on, because he followed the LORD wholeheartedly."

37 Because of you the LORD became angry with me also and said, "You shall not enter it, either. 38 But your assistant, Joshua son of Nun, will enter it. Encourage him, because he will lead Israel to inherit it. 39 And the little ones that you said would be taken captive, your children who do not yet know good from bad—they will enter the land. I will give it to them and they will take possession of it. 40 But as for you, turn around and set out toward the desert along the route to the Red Sea.*a* 41 Then you replied, "We have sinned against the LORD. We will go up and fight, as the LORD our God commanded us." So every one of you put on his weapons, thinking it easy to go up into the hill country.

42 But the LORD said to me, "Tell them, 'Do not go up and fight, because I will not be with you. You will be defeated by your enemies.'"

43 So I told you, but you would not listen. You rebelled against the LORD's command and in your arrogance you marched up into the hill country. 44 The Amorites who lived in those hills came out against you; they chased you like a swarm of bees and beat you down from Seir all the way to Hormah. 45 You came back and wept before the LORD, but he paid no attention to your weeping and turned a deaf ear to you. 46 And so you stayed in Kadesh many days—all the time you spent there.

Wanderings in the Desert

2 Then we turned back and set out toward the desert along the route to the Red Sea,*a* as the LORD had directed me. For a long time we made our way around the hill country of Seir.

2 Then the LORD said to me, 3 "You have made your way around this hill country long enough; now turn north. 4 Give the people these orders: 'You are about to pass through

the territory of your brothers the descendants of Esau, who live in Seir. They will be afraid of you, but be very careful. 5 Do not provoke them to war, for I will not give you any of their land, not even enough to put your foot on. I have given Esau the hill country of Seir as his own. 6 You are to pay them in silver for the food you eat and the water you drink.'"

7 The LORD your God has blessed you in all the work of your hands. He has watched over your journey through this vast desert. These forty years the LORD your God has been with you, and you have not lacked anything.

8 So we went on past our brothers the descendants of Esau, who live in Seir. We turned from the Arabah road, which comes up from Elath and Ezion Geber, and traveled along the desert road of Moab.

9 Then the LORD said to me, "Do not harass the Moabites or provoke them to war, for I will not give you any part of their land. I have given Ar to the descendants of Lot as a possession."

10 (The Emites used to live there—a people strong and numerous, and as tall as the Anakites. 11 Like the Anakites, they too were considered Rephaites, but the Moabites called them Emites. 12 Horites used to live in Seir, but the descendants of Esau drove them out. They destroyed the Horites from before them and settled in their place, just as Israel did in the land the LORD gave them as their possession.)

13 And the LORD said, "Now get up and cross the Zered Valley." So we crossed the valley.

14 Thirty-eight years passed from the time we left Kadesh Barnea until we crossed the Zered Valley. By then, that entire generation of fighting men had perished from the camp, as the LORD had sworn to them. 15 The LORD's hand was against them until he had completely eliminated them from the camp.

16 Now when the last of these fighting men among the people had died, 17 the LORD said to me, 18 "Today you are to pass by the region

---

Deuteronomy 2:7

God Watches Over Us

He has watched over your journey through this vast desert. These forty years the LORD your God has been with you, and you have not lacked anything.

---

a 40,1 Hebrew Yam Suph; that is, Sea of Reeds

of Moab at Ar. ¹⁹When you come to the Ammonites, do not harass them or provoke them to war, for I will not give you possession of any land belonging to the Ammonites. I have given it as a possession to the descendants of Lot."

²⁰(That too was considered a land of the Rephaites, who used to live there; but the Ammonites called them Zamzummites. ²¹They were a people strong and numerous, and as tall as the Anakites. The LORD destroyed them from before the Ammonites, who drove them out and settled in their place. ²²The LORD had done the same for the descendants of Esau, who lived in Seir, when he destroyed the Horites from before them. They drove them out and have lived in their place to this day. ²³And as for the Avvites who lived in villages as far as Gaza, the Caphtorites coming out from Caphtor*a* destroyed them and settled in their place.)

Defeat of Sihon King of Heshbon

²⁴"Set out now and cross the Arnon Gorge. See, I have given into your hand Sihon the Amorite, king of Heshbon, and his country. Begin to take possession of it and engage him in battle. ²⁵This very day I will begin to put the terror and fear of you on all the nations under heaven. They will hear reports of you and will tremble and be in anguish because of you."

²⁶From the desert of Kedemoth I sent messengers to Sihon king of Heshbon offering peace and saying, ²⁷"Let us pass through your country. We will stay on the main road; we will not turn aside to the right or to the left. ²⁸Sell us food to eat and water to drink for their price in silver. Only let us pass through on foot— ²⁹as the descendants of Esau, who live in Seir, and the Moabites, who live in Ar, did for us—until we cross the Jordan into the land the LORD our God is giving us." ³⁰But Sihon king of Heshbon refused to let us pass through. For the LORD your God had made his spirit stubborn and his heart obstinate in order to give him into your hands, as he has now done.

³¹The LORD said to me, "See, I have begun to deliver Sihon and his country over to you. Now begin to conquer and possess his land."

³²When Sihon and all his army came out to meet us in battle at Jahaz, ³³the LORD our God delivered him over to us and we struck him down, together with his sons and his whole army. ³⁴At that time we took all his towns and completely destroyed*b* them—men, women and children. We left no survivors. ³⁵But the livestock and the plunder from the towns we had captured we carried off for ourselves. ³⁶From Aroer on the rim of the Arnon Gorge, and from the town in the gorge, even as far as Gilead, not one town was too strong for us. The LORD our God gave us all of them. ³⁷But in accordance with the command of the LORD our God, you did not encroach on any of the land of the Ammonites, neither the land along the course of the Jabbok nor that around the towns in the hills.

Defeat of Og King of Bashan

3 Next we turned and went up along the road toward Bashan, and Og king of Bashan with his whole army marched out to meet us in battle at Edrei. ²The LORD said to me, "Do not be afraid of him, for I have handed him over to you with his whole army and his land. Do to him what you did to Sihon king of the Amorites, who reigned in Heshbon."

³So the LORD our God also gave into our hands Og king of Bashan and all his army. We struck them down, leaving no survivors. ⁴At that time we took all his cities. There was not one of the sixty cities that we did not take from them—the whole region of Argob, Og's kingdom in Bashan. ⁵All these cities were fortified with high walls and with gates and bars, and there were also a great many unwalled villages. ⁶We completely destroyed*b* them, as we had done with Sihon king of Heshbon, destroying*b* every city—men, women and children. ⁷But all the livestock and the plunder from their cities we carried off for ourselves.

⁸So at that time we took from these two kings of the Amorites the territory east of the Jordan, from the Arnon Gorge as far as Mount Hermon. ⁹(Hermon is called Sirion by the Sidonians; the Amorites call it Senir.) ¹⁰We took all the towns on the plateau, and all Gilead, and all Bashan as far as Salecah and Edrei, towns of Og's kingdom in Bashan. ¹¹(Only Og king of Bashan was left of the remnant of the Repha-

---

*a*23 That is, Crete   *b*34,6 The Hebrew term refers to the irrevocable giving over of things or persons to the LORD, often by totally destroying them.

ites. His bed[a] was made of iron and was more than thirteen feet long and six feet wide.[b] It is still in Rabbah of the Ammonites.)

Division of the Land

12Of the land that we took over at that time, I gave the Reubenites and the Gadites the territory north of Aroer by the Arnon Gorge, including half the hill country of Gilead, together with its towns. 13The rest of Gilead and also all of Bashan, the kingdom of Og, I gave to the half-tribe of Manasseh. (The whole region of Argob in Bashan used to be known as a land of the Rephaites. 14Jair, a descendant of Manasseh, took the whole region of Argob as far as the border of the Geshurites and the Maacathites; it was named after him, so that to this day Bashan is called Havvoth Jair.[c]) 15And I gave Gilead to Makir. 16But to the Reubenites and the Gadites I gave the territory extending from Gilead down to the Arnon Gorge (the middle of the gorge being the border) and out to the Jabbok River, which is the border of the Ammonites. 17Its western border was the Jordan in the Arabah, from Kinnereth to the Sea of the Arabah (the Salt Sea[d]), below the slopes of Pisgah.

18I commanded you at that time: "The LORD your God has given you this land to take possession of it. But all your able-bodied men, armed for battle, must cross over ahead of your brother Israelites. 19However, your wives, your children and your livestock (I know you have much livestock) may stay in the towns I have given you, 20until the LORD gives rest to your brothers as he has to you, and they too have taken over the land that the LORD your God is giving them, across the Jordan. After that, each of you may go back to the possession I have given you."

Moses Forbidden to Cross the Jordan

21At that time I commanded Joshua: "You have seen with your own eyes all that the LORD your God has done to these two kings. The LORD will do the same to all the kingdoms over there where you are going. 22Do not be afraid of them; the LORD your God himself will fight for you."

23At that time I pleaded with the LORD: 24"O Sovereign LORD, you have begun to show to your servant your greatness and your strong hand. For what god is there in heaven or on earth who can do the deeds and mighty works you do? 25Let me go over and see the good land beyond the Jordan—that fine hill country and Lebanon."

26But because of you the LORD was angry with me and would not listen to me. "That is enough," the LORD said. "Do not speak to me anymore about this matter. 27Go up to the top of Pisgah and look west and north and south and east. Look at the land with your own eyes, since you are not going to cross this Jordan. 28But commission Joshua, and encourage and strengthen him, for he will lead this people across and will cause them to inherit the land that you will see." 29So we stayed in the valley near Beth Peor.

Obedience Commanded

4 Hear now, O Israel, the decrees and laws I am about to teach you. Follow them so that you may live and may go in and take possession of the land that the LORD, the God of your fathers, is giving you. 2Do not add to what I command you and do not subtract from it, but keep the commands of the LORD your God that I give you.

3You saw with your own eyes what the LORD did at Baal Peor. The LORD your God destroyed from among you everyone who followed the Baal of Peor, 4but all of you who held fast to the LORD your God are still alive today.

5See, I have taught you decrees and laws as the LORD my God commanded me, so that you

---

Deuteronomy 3:24

God Is Without Equal

"O Sovereign LORD, you have begun to show to your servant your greatness and your strong hand. For what god is there in heaven or on earth who can do the deeds and mighty works you do?"

---

a11 Or *sarcophagus* b11 Hebrew *nine cubits long and four cubits wide* (about 4 meters long and 1.8 meters wide) c14 Or *called the settlements of Jair* d17 That is, the Dead Sea may follow them in the land you are entering to take possession of it. **6**Observe them carefully, for this will show your wisdom and understanding to the nations, who will hear about all these decrees and say, "Surely this great nation is a wise and understanding people." **7**What other nation is so great as to have their gods near them the way the LORD our God is near us whenever we pray to him? **8**And what other nation is so great as to have such righteous decrees and laws as this body of laws I am setting before you today?

9Only be careful, and watch yourselves closely so that you do not forget the things your eyes have seen or let them slip from your heart as long as you live. Teach them to your children and to their children after them. **10**Remember the day you stood before the LORD your God at Horeb, when he said to me, "Assemble the people before me to hear my words so that they may learn to revere me as long as they live in the land and may teach them to their children." **11**You came near and stood at the foot of the mountain while it blazed with fire to the very heavens, with black clouds and deep darkness. **12**Then the LORD spoke to you out of the fire. You heard the sound of words but saw no form; there was only a voice. **13**He declared to you his covenant, the Ten Commandments, which he commanded you to follow and then wrote them on two stone tablets. **14**And the LORD directed me at that time to teach you the decrees and laws you are to follow in the land that you are crossing the Jordan to possess.

Idolatry Forbidden

15You saw no form of any kind the day the LORD spoke to you at Horeb on the fire. Therefore watch yourselves very carefully, **16**so that you do not become corrupt and make for yourselves an idol, an image of any shape, whether formed like a man or a woman, **17**or like any animal on earth or any bird that flies in the air, **18**or like any creature that moves along the ground or any fish in the waters below.

Deuteronomy 4:7

God Is Near

What other nation is so great as to have their gods near them the way the LORD our God is near us whenever we pray to him?

19And when you look up to the sky and see the sun, the moon and the stars—all the heavenly array—do not be enticed into bowing down to them and worshiping things the LORD your God has apportioned to all the nations under heaven. **20**But as for you, the LORD took you and brought you out of the iron-smelting furnace, out of Egypt, to be the people of his inheritance, as you now are.

21The LORD was angry with me because of you, and he solemnly swore that I would not cross the Jordan and enter the good land the LORD your God is giving you as your inheritance. **22**I will die in this land; I will not cross the Jordan; but you are about to cross over and take possession of that good land. **23**Be careful not to forget the covenant of the LORD your God that he made with you; do not make for yourselves an idol in the form of anything the LORD your God has forbidden. **24**For the LORD your God is a consuming fire, a jealous God.

25After you have had children and grandchildren and have lived in the land a long time—if you then become corrupt and make any kind of idol, doing evil in the eyes of the LORD your God and provoking him to anger, **26**I call heaven and earth as witnesses against you this day that you will quickly perish from the land that you are crossing the Jordan to possess. You will not live there long but will certainly be destroyed. **27**The LORD will scatter you among the peoples, and only a few of you will survive among the nations to which the LORD will drive you. **28**There you will worship man-made gods of wood and stone, which cannot see or hear or eat or smell. **29**But if from there you seek the LORD your God, you will find him if you look for him with all your heart and with all your soul. **30**When you are in distress and all these things have happened to you, then in later days you will return to the LORD your God and obey him. **31**For the LORD your God is a merciful God; he will not abandon or destroy you or forget the covenant with your forefathers, which he confirmed to them by oath.

The LORD Is God

32 Ask now about the former days, long before your time, from the day God created man on the earth; ask from one end of the heavens to the other. Has anything so great as this ever happened, or has anything like it ever been heard of? **33** Has any other people heard the voice of God[a] speaking out of fire, as you have, and lived? **34** Has any god ever tried to take for himself one nation out of another nation, by testings, by miraculous signs and wonders, by war, by a mighty hand and an outstretched arm, or by great and awesome deeds, like all the things the LORD your God did for you in Egypt before your very eyes?

35 You were shown these things so that you might know that the LORD is God; besides him there is no other. **36** From heaven he made you hear his voice to discipline you. On earth he showed you his great fire, and you heard his words from out of the fire. **37** Because he loved your forefathers and chose their descendants after them, he brought you out of Egypt by his Presence and his great strength, **38** to drive out before you nations greater and stronger than you and to bring you into their land to give it to you for your inheritance, as it is today.

39 Acknowledge and take to heart this day that the LORD is God in heaven above and on the earth below. There is no other. **40** Keep his decrees and commands, which I am giving you today, so that it may go well with you and your children after you and that you may live long in the land the LORD your God gives you for all time.

Cities of Refuge

41 Then Moses set aside three cities east of the Jordan, **42** to which anyone who had killed a person could flee if he had unintentionally killed his neighbor without malice aforethought. He could flee into one of these cities and save his life. **43** The cities were these: Bezer in the desert plateau, for the Reubenites; Ramoth in Gilead, for the Gadites; and Golan in Bashan, for the Manassites.

Introduction to the Law

44 This is the law Moses set before the Israelites. **45** These are the stipulations, decrees and laws Moses gave them when they came out of Egypt **46** and were in the valley near Beth Peor east of the Jordan, in the land of Sihon king of the Amorites, who reigned in Heshbon and was defeated by Moses and the Israelites as they came out of Egypt. **47** They took possession of his land and the land of Og king of Bashan, the two Amorite kings east of the Jordan. **48** This land extended from Aroer on the rim of the Arnon Gorge to Mount Siyon[b] (that is, Hermon), **49** and included all the Arabah east of the Jordan, as far as the Sea of the Arabah,[c] below the slopes of Pisgah.

The Ten Commandments

5 Moses summoned all Israel and said:

Hear, O Israel, the decrees and laws I declare in your hearing today. Learn them and be sure to follow them. **2** The LORD our God made a covenant with us at Horeb. **3** It was not with our fathers that the LORD made this covenant, but with us, with all of us who are alive here today. **4** The LORD spoke to you face to face out of the fire on the mountain. **5** (At that time I stood between the LORD and you to declare to you the word of the LORD, because you were afraid of the fire and did not go up the mountain.) And he said:

6 "I am the LORD your God, who brought you out of Egypt, out of the land of slavery.

7 "You shall have no other gods before[d] me.

8 "You shall not make for yourself an idol in the form of anything in heaven above or on the earth beneath or in the waters below. **9** You shall not bow down to them or worship them; for I, the LORD your God, am a jealous God, punishing the children for the sin of the fathers to the third and fourth generation of those who hate me, **10** but showing love to a thousand generations of those who love me and keep my commandments.

11 "You shall not misuse the name of the LORD your God, for the LORD will not hold anyone guiltless who misuses his name.

12 "Observe the Sabbath day by keeping it holy, as the LORD your God has commanded you. 13 Six days you shall labor and do all your work, 14 but the seventh day is a Sabbath to the LORD your God. On it you shall not do any work, neither you, nor your son or daughter, nor your manservant or maidservant, nor your ox, your donkey or any of your animals, nor the alien within your gates, so that your manservant and maidservant may rest, as you do. 15 Remember that you were slaves in Egypt and that the LORD your God brought you out of there with a mighty hand and an outstretched arm. Therefore the LORD your God has commanded you to observe the Sabbath day.

16 "Honor your father and your mother, as the LORD your God has commanded you, so that you may live long and that it may go well with you in the land the LORD your God is giving you.

17 "You shall not murder.

18 "You shall not commit adultery.

19 "You shall not steal.

20 "You shall not give false testimony against your neighbor.

21 "You shall not covet your neighbor's wife. You shall not set your desire on your neighbor's house or land, his manservant or maidservant, his ox or donkey, or anything that belongs to your neighbor."

22 These are the commandments the LORD proclaimed in a loud voice to your whole assembly there on the mountain from out of the fire, the cloud and the deep darkness; and he added nothing more. Then he wrote them on two stone tablets and gave them to me.

23 When you heard the voice out of the darkness, while the mountain was ablaze with fire, all the leading men of your tribes and your elders came to me. 24 And you said, "The LORD our God has shown us his glory and his majesty, and we have heard his voice from the fire. Today we have seen that a man can live even if God speaks with him. 25 But now, why should we die? This great fire will consume us, and we will die if we hear the voice of the LORD our God any longer. 26 For what mortal man has ever heard the voice of the living God speaking out of fire, as we have, and survived? 27 Go near and listen to all that the LORD our God says. Then tell us whatever the LORD our God tells you. We will listen and obey."

28 The LORD heard you when you spoke to me and the LORD said to me, "I have heard what this people said to you. Everything they said was good. 29 Oh, that their hearts would be inclined to fear me and keep all my commands always, so that it might go well with them and their children forever!

30 "Go, tell them to return to their tents. 31 But you stay here with me so that I may give you all the commands, decrees and laws you are to teach them to follow in the land I am giving them to possess."

32 So be careful to do what the LORD your God has commanded you; do not turn aside to the right or to the left. 33 Walk in all the way that the LORD your God has commanded you, so that you may live and prosper and prolong your days in the land that you will possess.

Love the LORD Your God

6 These are the commands, decrees and laws the LORD your God directed me to teach you to observe in the land that you are crossing the Jordan to possess, 2 so that you, your children and their children after them may fear the LORD your God as long as you live by keeping all his decrees and commands that I give you, and so that you may enjoy long life. 3 Hear, O Israel, and be careful to obey so that it may go well with you and that you may

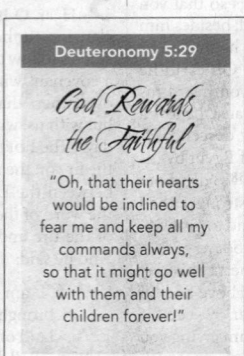

Deuteronomy 5:29

God Rewards the Faithful

"Oh, that their hearts would be inclined to fear me and keep all my commands always, so that it might go well with them and their children forever!"

Interior Designs

Read: Deuteronomy 6:1–9

"HE SEEMED LIKE SUCH A NICE BOY." How many times have we seen the neighbors of a convicted criminal interviewed on TV, shaking their heads in disbelief that an outwardly nice person could hide such evil intentions? Outer appearance can deceive, but the heart reveals itself eventually.

God provides a master guidebook to redesigning our spirits: the Bible. He directs us to tie his Word on our hands as we would tie a cord around a curtain, to bind his commandments to our foreheads as solidly as we would hang a valuable painting, to write his promises on our hearts as carefully as we would follow a blueprint. This is the ultimate form of home improvement.

Redesign must begin with our hearts. That is why God commanded the Israelites to pass on his holy commands, decrees and laws to their children and to allow them to permeate their lives and thought processes. Even today, Jewish families often fasten a small box called a mezuzah, containing Scriptures from Deuteronomy 6:4–9 and 11:13–21, to the doorposts of their homes to remind them that because "the LORD is one" they should "faithfully obey the commands . . . to love the LORD your God and to serve him with all your heart and with all your soul." Only God's Word can do the work of improving the lives of his people, generation to generation.

In Jesus' day, the Pharisees wore phylacteries, literally fastening Scripture to their foreheads. Some of the Pharisees wore their phylacteries pridefully to display how "religious" they were. Unfortunately, many failed to live out what the Scriptures inside their phylacteries said. Christ called them hypocrites. You may succeed in fooling the neighbors, but God is not deceived. He doesn't want his principles displayed outwardly if they don't impact us inwardly. When ingrained on our inmost being, his principles will change the way we think, act and live.

Would your neighbors be shocked to see inside your locked rooms? Would your own family? Perhaps you spend so much time on decorating your exterior that you've neglected what Teresa of Avila called your "interior castle," the cloistered rooms of your soul? Take the time to memorize Scripture, meditate on it and tell the children in your life about God. That kind of home improvement is eternal.

Deuteronomy 6:8–9

Tie them as symbols on your hands and bind them on your foreheads. Write them on the door-frames of your houses and on your gates.

reflection

1 What disconnects your spirit from your outer facade?

2 Who might God want you to "adopt" as a spiritual child so you can talk with them, teach them and train them to know and love him?

3 How much time do you spend redecorating the inner rooms of your soul through prayer and Bible reading? How can you deepen and nurture your faith?

RELATED READINGS

Exodus 13:1–16;
Deuteronomy 11:13–21;
Proverbs 7:1–4

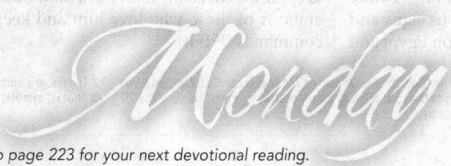

Monday

Go to page 223 for your next devotional reading.

increase greatly in a land flowing with milk and honey, just as the LORD, the God of your fathers, promised you.

[4]Hear, O Israel: The LORD our God, the LORD is one.[a] [5]Love the LORD your God with all your heart and with all your soul and with all your strength. [6]These commandments that I give you today are to be upon your hearts. [7]Impress them on your children. Talk about them when you sit at home and when you walk along the road, when you lie down and when you get up. [8]Tie them as symbols on your hands and bind them on your foreheads. [9]Write them on the doorframes of your houses and on your gates.

[10]When the LORD your God brings you into the land he swore to your fathers, to Abraham, Isaac and Jacob, to give you—a land with large, flourishing cities you did not build, [11]houses filled with all kinds of good things you did not provide, wells you did not dig, and vineyards and olive groves you did not plant—then when you eat and are satisfied, [12]be careful that you do not forget the LORD, who brought you out of Egypt, out of the land of slavery.

[13]Fear the LORD your God, serve him only and take your oaths in his name. [14]Do not follow other gods, the gods of the peoples around you; [15]for the LORD your God, who is among you, is a jealous God and his anger will burn against you, and he will destroy you from the face of the land. [16]Do not test the LORD your God as you did at Massah. [17]Be sure to keep the commands of the LORD your God and the stipulations and decrees he has given you. [18]Do what is right and good in the LORD's sight, so that it may go well with you and you may go in and take over the good land that the LORD promised on oath to your forefathers, [19]thrusting out all your enemies before you, as the LORD said.

[20]In the future, when your son asks you, "What is the meaning of the stipulations, decrees and laws the LORD our God has commanded you?" [21]tell him: "We were slaves of Pharaoh in Egypt, but the LORD brought us out of Egypt with a mighty hand. [22]Before our eyes the LORD sent miraculous signs and wonders—great and terrible—upon Egypt and Pharaoh and his whole household. [23]But he brought us out from there to bring us in and give us the land that he promised on oath to our forefathers. [24]The LORD commanded us to obey all these decrees and to fear the LORD our God, so that we might always prosper and be kept alive, as is the case today. [25]And if we are careful to obey all this law before the LORD our God, as he has commanded us, that will be our righteousness."

Driving Out the Nations

7 When the LORD your God brings you into the land you are entering to possess and drives out before you many nations—the Hittites, Girgashites, Amorites, Canaanites, Perizzites, Hivites and Jebusites, seven nations larger and stronger than you— [2]and when the LORD your God has delivered them over to you and you have defeated them, then you must destroy them totally.[b] Make no treaty with them, and show them no mercy. [3]Do not intermarry with them. Do not give your daughters to their sons or take their daughters for your sons, [4]for they will turn your sons away from following me to serve other gods, and the LORD's anger will burn against you and will quickly destroy you. [5]This is what you are to do to them: Break down their altars, smash their sacred stones, cut down their Asherah poles[c] and burn their idols in the fire. [6]For you are a people holy to the LORD your God. The LORD your God has chosen you out of all the peoples on the face of the earth to be his people, his treasured possession.

[7]The LORD did not set his affection on you and choose you because you were more numerous than other peoples, for you were the fewest of all peoples. [8]But it was because the LORD loved you and kept the oath he swore to your forefathers that he brought you out with a mighty hand and redeemed you from the land of slavery, from the power of Pharaoh king of Egypt. [9]Know therefore that the LORD your God is God; he is the faithful God, keeping his covenant of love to a thousand generations of those who love him and keep his commands. [10]But

---

[a]4 Or *The LORD our God is one LORD;* or *The LORD is our God, the LORD is one;* or *The LORD is our God, the LORD alone*   [b]2 The Hebrew term refers to the irrevocable giving over of things or persons to the LORD, often by totally destroying them; also in verse 26.   [c]5 That is, symbols of the goddess Asherah; here and elsewhere in Deuteronomy

those who hate him he will repay to their
    face by destruction;
  he will not be slow to repay to their face
    those who hate him.

11Therefore, take care to follow the commands, decrees and laws I give you today.

12If you pay attention to these laws and are careful to follow them, then the Lord your God will keep his covenant of love with you, as he swore to your forefathers. **13**He will love you and bless you and increase your numbers. He will bless the fruit of your womb, the crops of your land—your grain, new wine and oil—the calves of your herds and the lambs of your flocks in the land that he swore to your forefathers to give you. **14**You will be blessed more than any other people; none of your men or women will be childless, nor any of your livestock without young. **15**The Lord will keep you free from every disease. He will not inflict on you the horrible diseases you knew in Egypt, but he will inflict them on all who hate you. **16**You must destroy all the peoples the Lord your God gives over to you. Do not look on them with pity and do not serve their gods, for that will be a snare to you.

17You may say to yourselves, "These nations are stronger than we are. How can we drive them out?" **18**But do not be afraid of them; remember well what the Lord your God did to Pharaoh and to all Egypt. **19**You saw with your own eyes the great trials, the miraculous signs and wonders, the mighty hand and outstretched arm, with which the Lord your God brought you out. The Lord your God will do the same to all the peoples you now fear. **20**Moreover, the Lord your God will send the hornet among them until even the survivors who hide from you have perished. **21**Do not be terrified by them, for the Lord your God, who is among you, is a great and awesome God. **22**The Lord your God will drive out those nations before you, little by little. You will not be allowed to eliminate them all at once, or the wild

animals will multiply around you. **23**But the Lord your God will deliver them over to you, throwing them into great confusion until they are destroyed. **24**He will give their kings into your hand, and you will wipe out their names from under heaven. No one will be able to stand up against you; you will destroy them. **25**The images of their gods you are to burn in the fire. Do not covet the silver and gold on them, and do not take it for yourselves, or you will be ensnared by it, for it is detestable to the Lord your God. **26**Do not bring a detestable thing into your house or you, like it, will be set apart for destruction. Utterly abhor and detest it, for it is set apart for destruction.

Deuteronomy 7:9

God Is Faithful

Know therefore that the Lord your God is God; he is the faithful God, keeping his covenant of love to a thousand generations of those who love him and keep his commands.

Do Not Forget the Lord

8 Be careful to follow every command I am giving you today, so that you may live and increase and may enter and possess the land that the Lord promised on oath to your forefathers. **2**Remember how the Lord your God led you all the way in the desert these forty years, to humble you and to test you in order to know what was in your heart, whether or not you would keep his commands. **3**He humbled you, causing you to hunger and then feeding you with manna, which neither you nor your fathers had known, to teach you that man does not live on bread alone but on every word that comes from the mouth of the Lord. **4**Your clothes did not wear out and your feet did not swell during these forty years. **5**Know then in your heart that as a man disciplines his son, so the Lord your God disciplines you.

6Observe the commands of the Lord your God, walking in his ways and revering him. **7**For the Lord your God is bringing you into a good land—a land with streams and pools of water, with springs flowing in the valleys and hills; **8**a land with wheat and barley, vines and fig trees, pomegranates, olive oil and honey; **9**a land where bread will not be scarce and you will lack nothing; a land where the rocks are iron and you can dig copper out of the hills.

¹⁰When you have eaten and are satisfied, praise the LORD your God for the good land he has given you. ¹¹Be careful that you do not forget the LORD your God, failing to observe his commands, his laws and his decrees that I am giving you this day. ¹²Otherwise, when you eat and are satisfied, when you build fine houses and settle down, ¹³and when your herds and flocks grow large and your silver and gold increase and all you have is multiplied, ¹⁴then your heart will become proud and you will forget the LORD your God, who brought you out of Egypt, out of the land of slavery. ¹⁵He led you through the vast and dreadful desert, that thirsty and waterless land, with its venomous snakes and scorpions. He brought you water out of hard rock. ¹⁶He gave you manna to eat in the desert, something your fathers had never known, to humble and to test you so that in the end it might go well with you. ¹⁷You may say to yourself, "My power and the strength of my hands have produced this wealth for me." ¹⁸But remember the LORD your God, for it is he who gives you the ability to produce wealth, and so confirms his covenant, which he swore to your forefathers, as it is today.

¹⁹If you ever forget the LORD your God and follow other gods and worship and bow down to them, I testify against you today that you will surely be destroyed. ²⁰Like the nations the LORD destroyed before you, so you will be destroyed for not obeying the LORD your God.

Not Because of Israel's Righteousness

9 Hear, O Israel. You are now about to cross the Jordan to go in and dispossess nations greater and stronger than you, with large cities that have walls up to the sky. ²The people are strong and tall—Anakites! You know about them and have heard it said: "Who can stand up against the Anakites?" ³But be assured today that the LORD your God is the one who goes across ahead of you like a devouring fire. He will destroy them; he will subdue them before you. And you will drive them out and

annihilate them quickly, as the LORD has promised you.

⁴After the LORD your God has driven them out before you, do not say to yourself, "The LORD has brought me here to take possession of this land because of my righteousness." No, it is on account of the wickedness of these nations that the LORD is going to drive them out before you. ⁵It is not because of your righteousness or your integrity that you are going in to take possession of their land; but on account of the wickedness of these nations, the LORD your God will drive them out before you, to accomplish what he swore to your fathers, to Abraham, Isaac and Jacob. ⁶Understand, then, that it is not because of your righteousness that the LORD your God is giving you this good land to possess, for you are a stiff-necked people.

The Golden Calf

⁷Remember this and never forget how you provoked the LORD your God to anger in the desert. From the day you left Egypt until you arrived here, you have been rebellious against the LORD. ⁸At Horeb you aroused the LORD's wrath so that he was angry enough to destroy you. ⁹When I went up on the mountain to receive the tablets of stone, the tablets of the covenant that the LORD had made with you, I stayed on the mountain forty days and forty nights; I ate no bread and drank no water. ¹⁰The LORD gave me two stone tablets inscribed by the finger of God. On them were all the commandments the LORD proclaimed to you on the mountain out of the fire, on the day of the assembly.

¹¹At the end of the forty days and forty nights, the LORD gave me the two stone tablets, the tablets of the covenant. ¹²Then the LORD told me, "Go down from here at once, because your people whom you brought out of Egypt have become corrupt. They have turned away quickly from what I commanded them and have made a cast idol for themselves."

¹³And the LORD said to me, "I have seen this people, and they are a stiff-necked people

Deuteronomy 8:18

God Provides All

But remember the LORD your God, for it is he who gives you the ability to produce wealth, and so confirms his covenant, which he swore to your forefathers, as it is today.

Who Can Stand?

Read: Deuteronomy 9:1–6

SHE STARES DOWN at us from the wide screen or up from the magazine. She's the "perfect" woman. She's tall. She's willowy. She always knows just the right thing to say . . . and when to say it. She's the picture of who the world says we should be. We feel like the Israelites felt about the Anakites: "Who can stand up against that?"

No doubt the Hebrew nation trembled in their sandals at the thought of facing the mighty Anakites. However, God promised to be more than an ally to his people. He didn't just say, "I will go with you to conquer the enemy." Instead, he promised to go ahead of them. He promised to lead the charge into battle. God would conquer and take the land on their behalf. Of course, God kept his word. The Anakites were destroyed.

As believers, we're not really at war with "perfect" women. When you put yourself in their high-heeled sandals, you realize they have their own insecurities: Do people like me for me? Am I a slave to my looks? Opposition and uncertainties loom in every woman's heart. Do we really have to squeeze into the culture's mold to fit in? To get the man? To get the job? To have the friends? So many times our internal struggles are the real giants we must conquer. Conquering the heart and mind are the front line of the battle of faith.

When uncertainties about who you are make you feel small, remember that God is more than just a friendly ally. He is a trusted warrior who will go out ahead and battle your giants. As you grow in your faith and in grace, he will conquer your insecurities about your looks and abilities as you grow to realize that you are "fearfully and wonderfully made" (Psalm 139:14). He will conquer your lack of confidence in conversation by giving you the proper words to say through his Holy Spirit. He will fill you with security by giving you his righteousness. Then, when you've walked through the challenge, you'll know it was God who won the war, and you can give him all the glory.

What personal battles are causing your stomach to tie up in knots? What giant challenges are stopping you dead in your tracks? Rest assured; God will go before you to devour your doubts.

Go to page 225 for your next devotional reading.

Deuteronomy 9:2–3

The people are strong and tall—Anakites! You know about them and have heard it said: "Who can stand up against the Anakites?" But be assured today that the LORD your God is the one who goes across ahead of you like a devouring fire.

reflection

1 What personal battles seem huge and daunting?

2 What emotions are causing you to doubt your strength?

3 How has God shown you his love by fighting a battle for you? Recount a time in the past when God went ahead of you to conquer a situation.

RELATED READINGS

2 Chronicles 20:15–17;
Psalm 28:6–7;
Ephesians 6:10–18

"*Let nothing disturb you, let nothing frighten you: everything passes away except God; God alone is sufficient.*"

Teresa of Avila

indeed! **14**Let me alone, so that I may destroy them and blot out their name from under heaven. And I will make you into a nation stronger and more numerous than they."

15So I turned and went down from the mountain while it was ablaze with fire. And the two tablets of the covenant were in my hands.*a* **16**When I looked, I saw that you had sinned against the LORD your God; you had made for yourselves an idol cast in the shape of a calf. You had turned aside quickly from the way that the LORD had commanded you. **17**So I took the two tablets and threw them out of my hands, breaking them to pieces before your eyes.

18Then once again I fell prostrate before the LORD for forty days and forty nights; I ate no bread and drank no water, because of all the sin you had committed, doing what was evil in the LORD's sight and so provoking him to anger. **19**I feared the anger and wrath of the LORD, for he was angry enough with you to destroy you. But again the LORD listened to me. **20**And the LORD was angry enough with Aaron to destroy him, but at that time I prayed for Aaron too. **21**Also I took that sinful thing of yours, the calf you had made, and burned it in the fire. Then I crushed it and ground it to powder as fine as dust and threw the dust into a stream that flowed down the mountain.

22You also made the LORD angry at Taberah, at Massah and at Kibroth Hattaavah.

23And when the LORD sent you out from Kadesh Barnea, he said, "Go up and take possession of the land I have given you." But you rebelled against the command of the LORD your God. You did not trust him or obey him. **24**You have been rebellious against the LORD ever since I have known you.

25I lay prostrate before the LORD those forty days and forty nights because the LORD had said he would destroy you. **26**I prayed to the LORD and said, "O Sovereign LORD, do not destroy your people, your own inheritance that you redeemed by your great power and brought out of Egypt with a mighty hand. **27**Remember your servants Abraham, Isaac and Jacob. Overlook the stubbornness of this people, their wickedness and their sin. **28**Otherwise, the country from which you brought us will say, 'Because

the LORD was not able to take them into the land he had promised them, and because he hated them, he brought them out to put them to death in the desert.' **29**But they are your people, your inheritance that you brought out by your great power and your outstretched arm."

Tablets Like the First Ones

10 At that time the LORD said to me, "Chisel out two stone tablets like the first ones and come up to me on the mountain. Also make a wooden chest.*b* **2**I will write on the tablets the words that were on the first tablets, which you broke. Then you are to put them in the chest."

3So I made the ark out of acacia wood and chiseled out two stone tablets like the first ones, and I went up on the mountain with the two tablets in my hands. **4**The LORD wrote on these tablets what he had written before, the Ten Commandments he had proclaimed to you on the mountain, out of the fire, on the day of the assembly. And the LORD gave them to me. **5**Then I came back down the mountain and put the tablets in the ark I had made, as the LORD commanded me, and they are there now.

6(The Israelites traveled from the wells of the Jaakanites to Moserah. There Aaron died and was buried, and Eleazar his son succeeded him as priest. **7**From there they traveled to Gudgodah and on to Jotbathah, a land with streams of water. **8**At that time the LORD set apart the tribe of Levi to carry the ark of the covenant of the LORD, to stand before the LORD to minister and to pronounce blessings in his name, as they still do today. **9**That is why the Levites have no share or inheritance among their brothers; the LORD is their inheritance, as the LORD your God told them.)

10Now I had stayed on the mountain forty days and nights, as I did the first time, and the LORD listened to me at this time also. It was not his will to destroy you. **11**"Go," the LORD said to me, "and lead the people on their way, so that they may enter and possess the land that I swore to their fathers to give them."

Fear the LORD

12And now, O Israel, what does the LORD your God ask of you but to fear the LORD your

*a*15 Or *And I had the two tablets of the covenant with me, one in each hand*   *b*1 That is, an ark

Count the Ways

Read: Deuteronomy 10:12-22

MOTHERS UNCONDITIONALLY LOVE their children long before their child can return that love in tangible ways. Who can measure the power of the moment when a child first utters, "I love you, Mommy"?

Just as a mom longs to hear her child utter those four simple words, God, who loves us far more than any human mother, wants to hear us say that we love him. A simple, "I love you, God" will do.

But moms know that children must also show their love in tangible ways. Moms start by asking for obedience to simple commands like, "Hold Mommy's hand while we cross the street" and "Pick up your toys and put them away." These simple acts of obedience speak volumes.

It's much the same with God. He asks us to walk in his ways, to hold his hand as we walk through life. He wants us to take time to be with him, conversing or just sitting in silence with him. We show him we love him by living at peace with our brothers and sisters and by showing love to all his children. Simple acts of kindness show God that we love him as he loves us—sacrificially.

Children should also develop a healthy fear and respect for their moms. They know if they do something wrong, there will be consequences, such as a time-out. God's children should have a reverential awe of him too. He is the great and mighty Lord of lords. His presence makes kings and armies tremble. And he is loving enough to discipline those he loves. If God has told you to take a personal time-out to reflect and repent, it's important that you take time to sit at his feet and pour out your heart.

A good mother wouldn't feed her children junk food or put her children into dangerous situations. She wants her children to grow strong and healthy, so they'll live long lives. So, too, a child of God learns to discipline her spirit, mind and body, so as to become more Christlike. To avoid what he forbids so that she can stay strong. To eat what is good for her body and take in that which feeds her mind and spirit.

Loving God is a choice that grows through continued acts of obedience. Katherine Anne Porter observed, "Love must be learned again and again; there is no end to it." Choosing to love will please God, and it will bring joy to your life.

Deuteronomy 10:12–13

And now, O Israel, what does the LORD your God ask of you but to fear the LORD your God, to walk in all his ways, to love him, to serve the LORD your God with all your heart and with all your soul, and to observe the LORD's commands and decrees that I am giving you today for your own good?

reflection

1 When was the last time you told God you love him?

2 When was the last time you served another out of love for God?

3 Can you think of a benefit you've enjoyed because you obeyed a specific command of God?

RELATED READINGS

Psalm 63:1–11;
Micah 6:6–8;
Mark 12:28–34

Wednesday

God, to walk in all his ways, to love him, to serve the LORD your God with all your heart and with all your soul, **13**and to observe the LORD's commands and decrees that I am giving you today for your own good?

14To the LORD your God belong the heavens, even the highest heavens, the earth and everything in it. **15**Yet the LORD set his affection on your forefathers and loved them, and he chose you, their descendants, above all the nations, as it is today. **16**Circumcise your hearts, therefore, and do not be stiff-necked any longer. **17**For the LORD your God is God of gods and Lord of lords, the great God, mighty and awesome, who shows no partiality and accepts no bribes. **18**He defends the cause of the fatherless and the widow, and loves the alien, giving him food and clothing. **19**And you are to love those who are aliens, for you yourselves were aliens in Egypt. **20**Fear the LORD your God and serve him. Hold fast to him and take your oaths in his name. **21**He is your praise; he is your God, who performed for you those great and awesome wonders you saw with your own eyes. **22**Your forefathers who went down into Egypt were seventy in all, and now the LORD your God has made you as numerous as the stars in the sky.

Love and Obey the LORD

11 Love the LORD your God and keep his requirements, his decrees, his laws and his commands always. **2**Remember today that your children were not the ones who saw and experienced the discipline of the LORD your God: his majesty, his mighty hand, his outstretched arm; **3**the signs he performed and the things he did in the heart of Egypt, both to Pharaoh king of Egypt and to his whole country; **4**what he did to the Egyptian army, to its horses and chariots, how he overwhelmed them with the waters of the Red Sea*a* as they were pursuing you, and how the LORD brought lasting ruin on them. **5**It was not your children

who saw what he did for you in the desert until you arrived at this place, **6**and what he did to Dathan and Abiram, sons of Eliab the Reubenite, when the earth opened its mouth right in the middle of all Israel and swallowed them up with their households, their tents and every living thing that belonged to them. **7**But it was your own eyes that saw all these great things the LORD has done.

8Observe therefore all the commands I am giving you today, so that you may have the strength to go in and take over the land that you are crossing the Jordan to possess, **9**and so that you may live long in the land that the LORD swore to your forefathers to give to them and their descendants, a land flowing with milk and honey. **10**The land you are entering to take over is not like the land of Egypt, from which you have come, where you planted your seed and irrigated it by foot as in a vegetable garden. **11**But the land you are crossing the Jordan to take possession of is a land of mountains and valleys that drinks rain from heaven. **12**It is a land the LORD your God cares for; the eyes of the LORD your God are continually on it from the beginning of the year to its end.

13So if you faithfully obey the commands I am giving you today—to love the LORD your God and to serve him with all your heart and with all your soul— **14**then I will send rain on your land in its season, both autumn and spring rains, so that you may gather in your grain, new wine and oil. **15**I will provide grass in the fields for your cattle, and you will eat and be satisfied.

16Be careful, or you will be enticed to turn away and worship other gods and bow down to them. **17**Then the LORD's anger will burn against you, and he will shut the heavens so that it will not rain and the ground will yield no produce, and you will soon perish from the good land the LORD is giving you. **18**Fix these words of mine in your hearts and minds; tie them as symbols on your hands and bind them

Deuteronomy 10:17

God Is Impartial

For the LORD your God is God of gods and Lord of lords, the great God, mighty and awesome, who shows no partiality and accepts no bribes.

---

*a*4 Hebrew *Yam Suph*; that is, Sea of Reeds

on your foreheads. ¹⁹Teach them to your children, talking about them when you sit at home and when you walk along the road, when you lie down and when you get up. ²⁰Write them on the doorframes of your houses and on your gates, ²¹so that your days and the days of your children may be many in the land that the Lord swore to give your forefathers, as many as the days that the heavens are above the earth.

²²If you carefully observe all these commands I am giving you to follow—to love the Lord your God, to walk in all his ways and to hold fast to him— ²³then the Lord will drive out all these nations before you, and you will dispossess nations larger and stronger than you. ²⁴Every place where you set your foot will be yours: Your territory will extend from the desert to Lebanon, and from the Euphrates River to the western sea.ᵃ ²⁵No man will be able to stand against you. The Lord your God, as he promised you, will put the terror and fear of you on the whole land, wherever you go.

²⁶See, I am setting before you today a blessing and a curse— ²⁷the blessing if you obey the commands of the Lord your God that I am giving you today; ²⁸the curse if you disobey the commands of the Lord your God and turn from the way that I command you today by following other gods, which you have not known. ²⁹When the Lord your God has brought you into the land you are entering to possess, you are to proclaim on Mount Gerizim the blessings, and on Mount Ebal the curses. ³⁰As you know, these mountains are across the Jordan, west of the road,ᵇ toward the setting sun, near the great trees of Moreh, in the territory of those Canaanites living in the Arabah in the vicinity of Gilgal. ³¹You are about to cross the Jordan to enter and take possession of the land the Lord your God is giving you. When you have taken it over and are living there, ³²be sure that you obey all the decrees and laws I am setting before you today.

The One Place of Worship

12 These are the decrees and laws you must be careful to follow in the land that the Lord, the God of your fathers, has given you to possess—as long as you live in the

land. ²Destroy completely all the places on the high mountains and on the hills and under every spreading tree where the nations you are dispossessing worship their gods. ³Break down their altars, smash their sacred stones and burn their Asherah poles in the fire; cut down the idols of their gods and wipe out their names from those places.

⁴You must not worship the Lord your God in their way. ⁵But you are to seek the place the Lord your God will choose from among all your tribes to put his Name there for his dwelling. To that place you must go; ⁶there bring your burnt offerings and sacrifices, your tithes and special gifts, what you have vowed to give and your freewill offerings, and the firstborn of your herds and flocks. ⁷There, in the presence of the Lord your God, you and your families shall eat and shall rejoice in everything you have put your hand to, because the Lord your God has blessed you.

⁸You are not to do as we do here today, everyone as he sees fit, ⁹since you have not yet reached the resting place and the inheritance the Lord your God is giving you. ¹⁰But you will cross the Jordan and settle in the land the Lord your God is giving you as an inheritance, and he will give you rest from all your enemies around you so that you will live in safety. ¹¹Then to the place the Lord your God will choose as a dwelling for his Name—there you are to bring everything I command you: your burnt offerings and sacrifices, your tithes and special gifts, and all the choice possessions you have vowed to the Lord. ¹²And there rejoice before the Lord your God, you, your sons and daughters, your menservants and maidservants, and the Levites from your towns, who have no allotment or inheritance of their own. ¹³Be careful not to sacrifice your burnt offerings anywhere you please. ¹⁴Offer them only at the place the Lord will choose in one of your tribes, and there observe everything I command you.

¹⁵Nevertheless, you may slaughter your animals in any of your towns and eat as much of the meat as you want, as if it were gazelle or deer, according to the blessing the Lord your God gives you. Both the ceremonially unclean and the clean may eat it. ¹⁶But you must not eat

---

ᵃ24 That is, the Mediterranean   ᵇ30 Or *Jordan, westward*

the blood; pour it out on the ground like water. ¹⁷You must not eat in your own towns the tithe of your grain and new wine and oil, or the first-born of your herds and flocks, or whatever you have vowed to give, or your freewill offerings or special gifts. ¹⁸Instead, you are to eat them in the presence of the LORD your God at the place the LORD your God will choose—you, your sons and daughters, your menservants and maidservants, and the Levites from your towns—and you are to rejoice before the LORD your God in everything you put your hand to. ¹⁹Be careful not to neglect the Levites as long as you live in your land.

²⁰When the LORD your God has enlarged your territory as he promised you, and you crave meat and say, "I would like some meat," then you may eat as much of it as you want. ²¹If the place where the LORD your God chooses to put his Name is too far away from you, you may slaughter animals from the herds and flocks the LORD has given you, as I have commanded you, and in your own towns you may eat as much of them as you want. ²²Eat them as you would gazelle or deer. Both the ceremonially unclean and the clean may eat. ²³But be sure you do not eat the blood, because the blood is the life, and you must not eat the life with the meat. ²⁴You must not eat the blood; pour it out on the ground like water. ²⁵Do not eat it, so that it may go well with you and your children after you, because you will be doing what is right in the eyes of the LORD.

²⁶But take your consecrated things and whatever you have vowed to give, and go to the place the LORD will choose. ²⁷Present your burnt offerings on the altar of the LORD your God, both the meat and the blood. The blood of your sacrifices must be poured beside the altar of the LORD your God, but you may eat the meat. ²⁸Be careful to obey all these regulations I am giving you, so that it may always go well with you and your children after you, because you will be doing what is good and right in the eyes of the LORD your God.

²⁹The LORD your God will cut off before you the nations you are about to invade and dispossess. But when you have driven them out and settled in their land, ³⁰and after they have been destroyed before you, be careful not to be ensnared by inquiring about their gods, saying, "How do these nations serve their gods? We will do the same." ³¹You must not worship the LORD your God in their way, because in worshiping their gods, they do all kinds of detestable things the LORD hates. They even burn their sons and daughters in the fire as sacrifices to their gods.

³²See that you do all I command you; do not add to it or take away from it.

Worshiping Other Gods

13 If a prophet, or one who foretells by dreams, appears among you and announces to you a miraculous sign or wonder, ²and if the sign or wonder of which he has spoken takes place, and he says, "Let us follow other gods" (gods you have not known) "and let us worship them," ³you must not listen to the words of that prophet or dreamer. The LORD your God is testing you to find out whether you love him with all your heart and with all your soul. ⁴It is the LORD your God you must follow, and him you must revere. Keep his commands and obey him; serve him and hold fast to him. ⁵That prophet or dreamer must be put to death, because he preached rebellion against the LORD your God, who brought you out of Egypt, redeemed you from the land of slavery; he has tried to turn you from the way the LORD your God commanded you to follow. You must purge the evil from among you.

Deuteronomy 13:3

God Tests Our Love

The LORD your God is testing you to find out whether you love him with all your heart and with all your soul.

⁶If your very own brother, or your son or daughter, or the wife you love, or your closest friend secretly entices you, saying, "Let us go and worship other gods" (gods that neither you nor your fathers have known, ⁷gods of the peoples around you, whether near or far, from one end of the land to the other), ⁸do not yield to

him or listen to him. Show him no pity. Do not spare him or shield him. 9You must certainly put him to death. Your hand must be the first in putting him to death, and then the hands of all the people. 10Stone him to death, because he tried to turn you away from the LORD your God, who brought you out of Egypt, out of the land of slavery. 11Then all Israel will hear and be afraid, and no one among you will do such an evil thing again.

12If you hear it said about one of the towns the LORD your God is giving you to live in 13that wicked men have arisen among you and have led the people of their town astray, saying, "Let us go and worship other gods" (gods you have not known), 14then you must inquire, probe and investigate it thoroughly. And if it is true and it has been proved that this detestable thing has been done among you, 15you must certainly put to the sword all who live in that town. Destroy it completely,*a* both its people and its livestock. 16Gather all the plunder of the town into the middle of the public square and completely burn the town and all its plunder as a whole burnt offering to the LORD your God. It is to remain a ruin forever, never to be rebuilt. 17None of those condemned things*a* shall be found in your hands, so that the LORD will turn from his fierce anger; he will show you mercy, have compassion on you, and increase your numbers, as he promised on oath to your forefathers, 18because you obey the LORD your God, keeping all his commands that I am giving you today and doing what is right in his eyes.

Clean and Unclean Food

14 You are the children of the LORD your God. Do not cut yourselves or shave the front of your heads for the dead, 2for you are a people holy to the LORD your God. Out of all the peoples on the face of the earth, the LORD has chosen you to be his treasured possession.

3Do not eat any detestable thing. 4These are the animals you may eat: the ox, the sheep, the goat, 5the deer, the gazelle, the roe deer, the wild goat, the ibex, the antelope and the mountain sheep.*b* 6You may eat any animal that has

a split hoof divided in two and that chews the cud. 7However, of those that chew the cud or that have a split hoof completely divided you may not eat the camel, the rabbit or the coney.*c* Although they chew the cud, they do not have a split hoof; they are ceremonially unclean for you. 8The pig is also unclean; although it has a split hoof, it does not chew the cud. You are not to eat their meat or touch their carcasses.

9Of all the creatures living in the water, you may eat any that has fins and scales. 10But anything that does not have fins and scales you may not eat; for you it is unclean.

11You may eat any clean bird. 12But these you may not eat: the eagle, the vulture, the black vulture, 13the red kite, the black kite, any kind of falcon, 14any kind of raven, 15the horned owl, the screech owl, the gull, any kind of hawk, 16the little owl, the great owl, the white owl, 17the desert owl, the osprey, the cormorant, 18the stork, any kind of heron, the hoopoe and the bat.

19All flying insects that swarm are unclean to you; do not eat them. 20But any winged creature that is clean you may eat.

21Do not eat anything you find already dead. You may give it to an alien living in any of your towns, and he may eat it, or you may sell it to a foreigner. But you are a people holy to the LORD your God.

Do not cook a young goat in its mother's milk.

Tithes

22Be sure to set aside a tenth of all that your fields produce each year. 23Eat the tithe of your grain, new wine and oil, and the firstborn of your herds and flocks in the presence of the LORD your God at the place he will choose as a dwelling for his Name, so that you may learn to revere the LORD your God always. 24But if that place is too distant and you have been blessed by the LORD your God and cannot carry your tithe (because the place where the LORD will choose to put his Name is so far away), 25then exchange your tithe for silver, and take the silver with you and go to the place the LORD your God will choose. 26Use the silver to buy whatever you like: cattle, sheep, wine or other

---

*a*15,17 The Hebrew term refers to the irrevocable giving over of things or persons to the LORD, often by totally destroying them.   *b*5 The precise identification of some of the birds and animals in this chapter is uncertain.   *c*7 That is, the hyrax or rock badger fermented drink, or anything you wish. Then you and your household shall eat there in the presence of the LORD your God and rejoice. ²⁷And do not neglect the Levites living in your towns, for they have no allotment or inheritance of their own.

²⁸At the end of every three years, bring all the tithes of that year's produce and store it in your towns, ²⁹so that the Levites (who have no allotment or inheritance of their own) and the aliens, the fatherless and the widows who live in your towns may come and eat and be satisfied, and so that the LORD your God may bless you in all the work of your hands.

The Year for Canceling Debts

15 At the end of every seven years you must cancel debts. ²This is how it is to be done: Every creditor shall cancel the loan he has made to his fellow Israelite. He shall not require payment from his fellow Israelite or brother, because the LORD's time for canceling debts has been proclaimed. ³You may require payment from a foreigner, but you must cancel any debt your brother owes you. ⁴However, there should be no poor among you, for in the land the LORD your God is giving you to possess as your inheritance, he will richly bless you, ⁵if only you fully obey the LORD your God and are careful to follow all these commands I am giving you today. ⁶For the LORD your God will bless you as he has promised, and you will lend to many nations but will borrow from none. You will rule over many nations but none will rule over you.

⁷If there is a poor man among your brothers in any of the towns of the land that the LORD your God is giving you, do not be hardhearted or tightfisted toward your poor brother. ⁸Rather be openhanded and freely lend him whatever he needs. ⁹Be careful not to harbor this wicked thought: "The seventh year, the year for canceling debts, is near," so that you do not show ill will toward your needy brother

and give him nothing. He may then appeal to the LORD against you, and you will be found guilty of sin. ¹⁰Give generously to him and do so without a grudging heart; then because of this the LORD your God will bless you in all your work and in everything you put your hand to. ¹¹There will always be poor people in the land. Therefore I command you to be openhanded toward your brothers and toward the poor and needy in your land.

Freeing Servants

¹²If a fellow Hebrew, a man or a woman, sells himself to you and serves you six years, in the seventh year you must let him go free. ¹³And when you release him, do not send him away empty-handed. ¹⁴Supply him liberally from your flock, your threshing floor and your winepress. Give to him as the LORD your God has blessed you. ¹⁵Remember that you were slaves in Egypt and the LORD your God redeemed you. That is why I give you this command today.

¹⁶But if your servant says to you, "I do not want to leave you," because he loves you and your family and is well off with you, ¹⁷then take an awl and push it through his ear lobe into the door, and he will become your servant for life. Do the same for your maidservant. ¹⁸Do not consider it a hardship to set your servant free, because his service to you these six years has been worth twice as much as that of a hired hand. And the LORD your God will bless you in everything you do.

The Firstborn Animals

¹⁹Set apart for the LORD your God every firstborn male of your herds and flocks. Do not put the firstborn of your oxen to work, and do not shear the firstborn of your sheep. ²⁰Each year you and your family are to eat them in the presence of the LORD your God at the place he will choose. ²¹If an animal has a defect, is lame or blind, or has any serious flaw, you must not sacrifice it to the LORD your God. ²²You are to eat it in your own towns. Both the ceremonially

---

Deuteronomy 15:10

God Blesses Us

Give generously to him and do so without a grudging heart; then because of this the LORD your God will bless you in all your work and in everything you put your hand to.

Openhearted and Openhanded

Read: Deuteronomy 15:1–11

THERE IS MUCH SUFFERING in the world—very much. Material suffering is suffering from hunger, suffering from homelessness, from all kinds of disease, but I still think that the greatest suffering is being lonely, feeling unloved, just having no one. I have come more and more to realize that it is being unwanted that is the worst disease that any human being can ever experience. In these times of development, the whole world runs and is hurried. But there are some who fall down on the way and have no strength to go ahead. These are the ones we must care about.

Let us be very sincere in our dealings with each other and have the courage to accept each other as we are. Do not be surprised at or become preoccupied with each other's failure; rather see and find the good in each other, for each one of us is created in the image of God. Jesus has said it beautifully: "I am the vine, you are the branches." The life-giving sap that flows from the vine through each of the branches is the same.

Be kind in your actions. Do not think that you are the only one who can do efficient work, work worth showing. This makes you harsh in your judgment of others who may not have the same talents. Do your best and trust that others do their best. And be faithful in small things because it is in them that your strength lies.

In loving one another through our works we bring an increase of grace and a growth in divine love.

> Be the living expression of God's kindness:
> kindness in your face,
> kindness in your eyes,
> kindness in your smile,
> kindness in your warm greeting.
> — Mother Teresa

Deuteronomy 15:7–8

If there is a poor man among your brothers in any of the towns of the land that the LORD your God is giving you, do not be hardhearted or tightfisted toward your poor brother. Rather be openhanded and freely lend him whatever he needs.

reflection

1 Whom do you have trouble accepting? Are there people that you find yourself judging?

2 How have you shown that you care for the downtrodden?

3 List three practical ways you will follow Mother Teresa's example of loving others by being openhanded to those less fortunate than you.

RELATED READINGS

Psalm 72:12–14;
Isaiah 61:1–3;
Luke 6:37–38

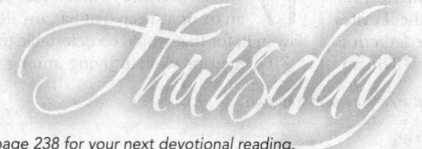

Go to page 238 for your next devotional reading.

unclean and the clean may eat it, as if it were gazelle or deer. 23But you must not eat the blood; pour it out on the ground like water.

Passover

16 Observe the month of Abib and celebrate the Passover of the LORD your God, because in the month of Abib he brought you out of Egypt by night. 2Sacrifice as the Passover to the LORD your God an animal from your flock or herd at the place the LORD will choose as a dwelling for his Name. 3Do not eat it with bread made with yeast, but for seven days eat unleavened bread, the bread of affliction, because you left Egypt in haste—so that all the days of your life you may remember the time of your departure from Egypt. 4Let no yeast be found in your possession in all your land for seven days. Do not let any of the meat you sacrifice on the evening of the first day remain until morning.

5You must not sacrifice the Passover in any town the LORD your God gives you 6except in the place he will choose as a dwelling for his Name. There you must sacrifice the Passover in the evening, when the sun goes down, on the anniversary[a] of your departure from Egypt. 7Roast it and eat it at the place the LORD your God will choose. Then in the morning return to your tents. 8For six days eat unleavened bread and on the seventh day hold an assembly to the LORD your God and do no work.

Feast of Weeks

9Count off seven weeks from the time you begin to put the sickle to the standing grain. 10Then celebrate the Feast of Weeks to the LORD your God by giving a freewill offering in proportion to the blessings the LORD your God has given you. 11And rejoice before the LORD your God at the place he will choose as a dwelling for his Name—you, your sons and daughters, the menservants and maidservants, the Levites in your towns, and the aliens, the fatherless and the widows living among you. 12Remember that you were slaves in Egypt, and follow carefully these decrees.

Feast of Tabernacles

13Celebrate the Feast of Tabernacles for seven days after you have gathered the produce of your threshing floor and your winepress. 14Be joyful at your Feast—you, your sons and daughters, your menservants and maidservants, and the Levites, the aliens, the fatherless and the widows who live in your towns. 15For seven days celebrate the Feast to the LORD your God at the place the LORD will choose. For the LORD your God will bless you in all your harvest and in all the work of your hands, and your joy will be complete.

16Three times a year all your men must appear before the LORD your God at the place he will choose: at the Feast of Unleavened Bread, the Feast of Weeks and the Feast of Tabernacles. No man should appear before the LORD empty-handed: 17Each of you must bring a gift in proportion to the way the LORD your God has blessed you.

Judges

18Appoint judges and officials for each of your tribes in every town the LORD your God is giving you, and they shall judge the people fairly. 19Do not pervert justice or show partiality. Do not accept a bribe, for a bribe blinds the eyes of the wise and twists the words of the righteous. 20Follow justice and justice alone, so that you may live and possess the land the LORD your God is giving you.

Worshiping Other Gods

21Do not set up any wooden Asherah pole[b] beside the altar you build to the LORD your God, 22and do not erect a sacred stone, for these the LORD your God hates.

17 Do not sacrifice to the LORD your God an ox or a sheep that has any defect or flaw in it, for that would be detestable to him.

2If a man or woman living among you in

> **Deuteronomy 16:20**
>
> *God Loves Justice*
>
> Follow justice and justice alone, so that you may live and possess the land the LORD your God is giving you.

---

[a]6 Or *down, at the time of day*   [b]21 Or *Do not plant any tree dedicated to Asherah*

one of the towns the LORD gives you is found doing evil in the eyes of the LORD your God in violation of his covenant, ³and contrary to my command has worshiped other gods, bowing down to them or to the sun or the moon or the stars of the sky, ⁴and this has been brought to your attention, then you must investigate it thoroughly. If it is true and it has been proved that this detestable thing has been done in Israel, ⁵take the man or woman who has done this evil deed to your city gate and stone that person to death. ⁶On the testimony of two or three witnesses a man shall be put to death, but no one shall be put to death on the testimony of only one witness. ⁷The hands of the witnesses must be the first in putting him to death, and then the hands of all the people. You must purge the evil from among you.

Law Courts

⁸If cases come before your courts that are too difficult for you to judge—whether bloodshed, lawsuits or assaults—take them to the place the LORD your God will choose. ⁹Go to the priests, who are Levites, and to the judge who is in office at that time. Inquire of them and they will give you the verdict. ¹⁰You must act according to the decisions they give you at the place the LORD will choose. Be careful to do everything they direct you to do. ¹¹Act according to the law they teach you and the decisions they give you. Do not turn aside from what they tell you, to the right or to the left. ¹²The man who shows contempt for the judge or for the priest who stands ministering there to the LORD your God must be put to death. You must purge the evil from Israel. ¹³All the people will hear and be afraid, and will not be contemptuous again.

The King

¹⁴When you enter the land the LORD your God is giving you and have taken possession of it and settled in it, and you say, "Let us set a king over us like all the nations around us," ¹⁵be sure to appoint over you the king the LORD your God chooses. He must be from among your own brothers. Do not place a foreigner over you, one who is not a brother Israelite. ¹⁶The king, moreover, must not acquire great numbers of horses for himself or make the people

return to Egypt to get more of them, for the LORD has told you, "You are not to go back that way again." ¹⁷He must not take many wives, or his heart will be led astray. He must not accumulate large amounts of silver and gold.

¹⁸When he takes the throne of his kingdom, he is to write for himself on a scroll a copy of this law, taken from that of the priests, who are Levites. ¹⁹It is to be with him, and he is to read it all the days of his life so that he may learn to revere the LORD his God and follow carefully all the words of this law and these decrees ²⁰and not consider himself better than his brothers and turn from the law to the right or to the left. Then he and his descendants will reign a long time over his kingdom in Israel.

Offerings for Priests and Levites

18 The priests, who are Levites—indeed the whole tribe of Levi—are to have no allotment or inheritance with Israel. They shall live on the offerings made to the LORD by fire, for that is their inheritance. ²They shall have no inheritance among their brothers; the LORD is their inheritance, as he promised them.

³This is the share due the priests from the people who sacrifice a bull or a sheep: the shoulder, the jowls and the inner parts. ⁴You are to give them the firstfruits of your grain, new wine and oil, and the first wool from the shearing of your sheep, ⁵for the LORD your God has chosen them and their descendants out of all your tribes to stand and minister in the LORD's name always.

⁶If a Levite moves from one of your towns anywhere in Israel where he is living, and comes in all earnestness to the place the LORD will choose, ⁷he may minister in the name of the LORD his God like all his fellow Levites who serve there in the presence of the LORD. ⁸He is to share equally in their benefits, even though he has received money from the sale of family possessions.

Detestable Practices

⁹When you enter the land the LORD your God is giving you, do not learn to imitate the detestable ways of the nations there. ¹⁰Let no one be found among you who sacrifices his son or daughter in*a* the fire, who practices divination

a 10 Or *who makes his son or daughter pass through*

233

or sorcery, interprets omens, engages in witchcraft, ¹¹or casts spells, or who is a medium or spiritist or who consults the dead. ¹²Anyone who does these things is detestable to the LORD, and because of these detestable practices the LORD your God will drive out those nations before you. ¹³You must be blameless before the LORD your God.

The Prophet

¹⁴The nations you will dispossess listen to those who practice sorcery or divination. But as for you, the LORD your God has not permitted you to do so. ¹⁵The LORD your God will raise up for you a prophet like me from among your own brothers. You must listen to him. ¹⁶For this is what you asked of the LORD your God at Horeb on the day of the assembly when you said, "Let us not hear the voice of the LORD our God nor see this great fire anymore, or we will die."

¹⁷The LORD said to me: "What they say is good. ¹⁸I will raise up for them a prophet like you from among their brothers; I will put my words in his mouth, and he will tell them everything I command him. ¹⁹If anyone does not listen to my words that the prophet speaks in my name, I myself will call him to account. ²⁰But a prophet who presumes to speak in my name anything I have not commanded him to say, or a prophet who speaks in the name of other gods, must be put to death."

²¹You may say to yourselves, "How can we know when a message has not been spoken by the LORD?" ²²If what a prophet proclaims in the name of the LORD does not take place or come true, that is a message the LORD has not spoken. That prophet has spoken presumptuously. Do not be afraid of him.

Cities of Refuge

19 When the LORD your God has destroyed the nations whose land he is giving you, and when you have driven them out and settled in their towns and houses, ²then set aside for yourselves three cities centrally located in the land the LORD your God is giving you to possess. ³Build roads to them and divide into three parts the land the LORD your God is giving you as an inheritance, so that anyone who kills a man may flee there.

⁴This is the rule concerning the man who kills another and flees there to save his life—one who kills his neighbor unintentionally, without malice aforethought. ⁵For instance, a man may go into the forest with his neighbor to cut wood, and as he swings his ax to fell a tree, the head may fly off and hit his neighbor and kill him. That man may flee to one of these cities and save his life. ⁶Otherwise, the avenger of blood might pursue him in a rage, overtake him if the distance is too great, and kill him even though he is not deserving of death, since he did it to his neighbor without malice aforethought. ⁷This is why I command you to set aside for yourselves three cities.

⁸If the LORD your God enlarges your territory, as he promised on oath to your forefathers, and gives you the whole land he promised them, ⁹because you carefully follow all these laws I command you today—to love the LORD your God and to walk always in his ways—then you are to set aside three more cities. ¹⁰Do this so that innocent blood will not be shed in your land, which the LORD your God is giving you as your inheritance, and so that you will not be guilty of bloodshed.

¹¹But if a man hates his neighbor and lies in wait for him, assaults and kills him, and then flees to one of these cities, ¹²the elders of his town shall send for him, bring him back from the city, and hand him over to the avenger of blood to die. ¹³Show him no pity. You must purge from Israel the guilt of shedding innocent blood, so that it may go well with you.

¹⁴Do not move your neighbor's boundary stone set up by your predecessors in the inheritance you receive in the land the LORD your God is giving you to possess.

Witnesses

¹⁵One witness is not enough to convict a man accused of any crime or offense he may have committed. A matter must be established by the testimony of two or three witnesses.

¹⁶If a malicious witness takes the stand to accuse a man of a crime, ¹⁷the two men involved in the dispute must stand in the presence of the LORD before the priests and the judges who are in office at the time. ¹⁸The judges must make a thorough investigation, and if the witness proves to be a liar, giving false testimony against

his brother, **19**then do to him as he intended to do to his brother. You must purge the evil from among you. **20**The rest of the people will hear of this and be afraid, and never again will such an evil thing be done among you. **21**Show no pity: life for life, eye for eye, tooth for tooth, hand for hand, foot for foot.

Going to War

20 When you go to war against your enemies and see horses and chariots and an army greater than yours, do not be afraid of them, because the LORD your God, who brought you up out of Egypt, will be with you. **2**When you are about to go into battle, the priest shall come forward and address the army. **3**He shall say: "Hear, O Israel, today you are going into battle against your enemies. Do not be fainthearted or afraid; do not be terrified or give way to panic before them. **4**For the LORD your God is the one who goes with you to fight for you against your enemies to give you victory."

5The officers shall say to the army: "Has anyone built a new house and not dedicated it? Let him go home, or he may die in battle and someone else may dedicate it. **6**Has anyone planted a vineyard and not begun to enjoy it? Let him go home, or he may die in battle and someone else enjoy it. **7**Has anyone become pledged to a woman and not married her? Let him go home, or he may die in battle and someone else marry her." **8**Then the officers shall add, "Is any man afraid or fainthearted? Let him go home so that his brothers will not become disheartened too." **9**When the officers have finished speaking to the army, they shall appoint commanders over it.

10When you march up to attack a city, make its people an offer of peace. **11**If they accept and open their gates, all the people in it shall be subject to forced labor and shall work for you. **12**If they refuse to make peace and they engage you in battle, lay siege to that city. **13**When the LORD

your God delivers it into your hand, put to the sword all the men in it. **14**As for the women, the children, the livestock and everything else in the city, you may take these as plunder for yourselves. And you may use the plunder the LORD your God gives you from your enemies. **15**This is how you are to treat all the cities that are at a distance from you and do not belong to the nations nearby.

16However, in the cities of the nations the LORD your God is giving you as an inheritance, do not leave alive anything that breathes. **17**Completely destroy*a* them—the Hittites, Amorites, Canaanites, Perizzites, Hivites and Jebusites—as the LORD your God has commanded you. **18**Otherwise, they will teach you to follow all the detestable things they do in worshiping their gods, and you will sin against the LORD your God.

19When you lay siege to a city for a long time, fighting against it to capture it, do not destroy its trees by putting an ax to them, because you can eat their fruit. Do not cut them down. Are the trees of the field people, that you should besiege them?*b* **20**However, you may cut down trees that you know are not fruit trees and use them to build siege works until the city at war with you falls.

Atonement for an Unsolved Murder

21 If a man is found slain, lying in a field in the land the LORD your God is giving you to possess, and it is not known who killed him, **2**your elders and judges shall go out and measure the distance from the body to the neighboring towns. **3**Then the elders of the town nearest the body shall take a heifer that has never been worked and has never worn a yoke **4**and lead her down to a valley that has not been plowed or planted and where there is a flowing stream. There in the valley they are to break the heifer's neck. **5**The priests, the sons of Levi, shall step forward, for the LORD your God has chosen them to minister and to

---

> **Deuteronomy 20:4**
>
> *God Gives*
> *Victories*
>
> "For the LORD your God
> is the one who goes
> with you to fight for you
> against your enemies
> to give you victory."

---

a **17** The Hebrew term refers to the irrevocable giving over of things or persons to the LORD, often by totally destroying them.   *b* **19** Or *down to use in the siege, for the fruit trees are for the benefit of man.*

pronounce blessings in the name of the LORD and to decide all cases of dispute and assault. 6Then all the elders of the town nearest the body shall wash their hands over the heifer whose neck was broken in the valley, 7and they shall declare: "Our hands did not shed this blood, nor did our eyes see it done. 8Accept this atonement for your people Israel, whom you have redeemed, O LORD, and do not hold your people guilty of the blood of an innocent man." And the bloodshed will be atoned for. 9So you will purge from yourselves the guilt of shedding innocent blood, since you have done what is right in the eyes of the LORD.

Marrying a Captive Woman

10When you go to war against your enemies and the LORD your God delivers them into your hands and you take captives, 11if you notice among the captives a beautiful woman and are attracted to her, you may take her as your wife. 12Bring her into your home and have her shave her head, trim her nails 13and put aside the clothes she was wearing when captured. After she has lived in your house and mourned her father and mother for a full month, then you may go to her and be her husband and she shall be your wife. 14If you are not pleased with her, let her go wherever she wishes. You must not sell her or treat her as a slave, since you have dishonored her.

The Right of the Firstborn

15If a man has two wives, and he loves one but not the other, and both bear him sons but the firstborn is the son of the wife he does not love, 16when he wills his property to his sons, he must not give the rights of the firstborn to the son of the wife he loves in preference to his actual firstborn, the son of the wife he does not love. 17He must acknowledge the son of his unloved wife as the firstborn by giving him a double share of all he has. That son is the first sign of his father's strength. The right of the firstborn belongs to him.

A Rebellious Son

18If a man has a stubborn and rebellious son who does not obey his father and mother and will not listen to them when they discipline

him, 19his father and mother shall take hold of him and bring him to the elders at the gate of his town. 20They shall say to the elders, "This son of ours is stubborn and rebellious. He will not obey us. He is a profligate and a drunkard." 21Then all the men of his town shall stone him to death. You must purge the evil from among you. All Israel will hear of it and be afraid.

Various Laws

22If a man guilty of a capital offense is put to death and his body is hung on a tree, 23you must not leave his body on the tree overnight. Be sure to bury him that same day, because anyone who is hung on a tree is under God's curse. You must not desecrate the land the LORD your God is giving you as an inheritance.

22 If you see your brother's ox or sheep straying, do not ignore it but be sure to take it back to him. 2If the brother does not live near you or if you do not know who he is, take it home with you and keep it until he comes looking for it. Then give it back to him. 3Do the same if you find your brother's donkey or his cloak or anything he loses. Do not ignore it.

4If you see your brother's donkey or his ox fallen on the road, do not ignore it. Help him get it to its feet.

5A woman must not wear men's clothing, nor a man wear women's clothing, for the LORD your God detests anyone who does this.

6If you come across a bird's nest beside the road, either in a tree or on the ground, and the mother is sitting on the young or on the eggs, do not take the mother with the young. 7You may take the young, but be sure to let the mother go, so that it may go well with you and you may have a long life.

8When you build a new house, make a parapet around your roof so that you may not bring the guilt of bloodshed on your house if someone falls from the roof.

9Do not plant two kinds of seed in your vineyard; if you do, not only the crops you plant but also the fruit of the vineyard will be defiled.[a]

10Do not plow with an ox and a donkey yoked together.

11Do not wear clothes of wool and linen woven together.

---

a9 Or be forfeited to the sanctuary

[12]Make tassels on the four corners of the cloak you wear.

Marriage Violations

[13]If a man takes a wife and, after lying with her, dislikes her [14]and slanders her and gives her a bad name, saying, "I married this woman, but when I approached her, I did not find proof of her virginity," [15]then the girl's father and mother shall bring proof that she was a virgin to the town elders at the gate. [16]The girl's father will say to the elders, "I gave my daughter in marriage to this man, but he dislikes her. [17]Now he has slandered her and said, 'I did not find your daughter to be a virgin.' But here is the proof of my daughter's virginity." Then her parents shall display the cloth before the elders of the town, [18]and the elders shall take the man and punish him. [19]They shall fine him a hundred shekels of silver[a] and give them to the girl's father, because this man has given an Israelite virgin a bad name. She shall continue to be his wife; he must not divorce her as long as he lives.

[20]If, however, the charge is true and no proof of the girl's virginity can be found, [21]she shall be brought to the door of her father's house and there the men of her town shall stone her to death. She has done a disgraceful thing in Israel by being promiscuous while still in her father's house. You must purge the evil from among you.

[22]If a man is found sleeping with another man's wife, both the man who slept with her and the woman must die. You must purge the evil from Israel.

[23]If a man happens to meet in a town a virgin pledged to be married and he sleeps with her, [24]you shall take both of them to the gate of that town and stone them to death—the girl because she was in a town and did not scream for help, and the man because he violated another man's wife. You must purge the evil from among you.

[25]But if out in the country a man happens to meet a girl pledged to be married and rapes her, only the man who has done this shall die. [26]Do nothing to the girl; she has committed no sin deserving death. This case is like that of someone who attacks and murders his neighbor, [27]for the man found the girl out in the country, and though the betrothed girl screamed, there was no one to rescue her.

[28]If a man happens to meet a virgin who is not pledged to be married and rapes her and they are discovered, [29]he shall pay the girl's father fifty shekels of silver.[b] He must marry the girl, for he has violated her. He can never divorce her as long as he lives.

[30]A man is not to marry his father's wife; he must not dishonor his father's bed.

Exclusion From the Assembly

23 No one who has been emasculated by crushing or cutting may enter the assembly of the LORD.

[2]No one born of a forbidden marriage[c] nor any of his descendants may enter the assembly of the LORD, even down to the tenth generation.

[3]No Ammonite or Moabite or any of his descendants may enter the assembly of the LORD, even down to the tenth generation. [4]For they did not come to meet you with bread and water on your way when you came out of Egypt, and they hired Balaam son of Beor from Pethor in Aram Naharaim[d] to pronounce a curse on you. [5]However, the LORD your God would not listen to Balaam but turned the curse into a blessing for you, because the LORD your God loves you. [6]Do not seek a treaty of friendship with them as long as you live.

[7]Do not abhor an Edomite, for he is your brother. Do not abhor an Egyptian, because you lived as an alien in his country. [8]The third generation of children born to them may enter the assembly of the LORD.

Uncleanness in the Camp

[9]When you are encamped against your enemies, keep away from everything impure. [10]If one of your men is unclean because of a nocturnal emission, he is to go outside the camp and stay there. [11]But as evening approaches he is to wash himself, and at sunset he may return to the camp.

[12]Designate a place outside the camp where you can go to relieve yourself. [13]As part of your

---

[a]19 That is, about 2 1/2 pounds (about 1 kilogram)   [b]29 That is, about 1 1/4 pounds (about 0.6 kilogram)   [c]2 Or *one of illegitimate birth*
[d]4 That is, Northwest Mesopotamia

Sexual Honor

Deuteronomy 22:22

If a man is found sleeping with another man's wife, both the man who slept with her and the woman must die. You must purge the evil from Israel.

reflection

1 In what ways do you think your views of sexuality and morality have been shaped by our culture?

2 What feelings come to mind when you think about your past and present sexual behavior? Have you asked Jesus to cleanse you of any dishonorable actions? Have you accepted his forgiveness?

3 How are you instilling and upholding God's principles of sexual honor in your children's lives?

RELATED READINGS

Matthew 5:27–28;
1 Corinthians 6:19–20;
1 Thessalonians 4:3–7;
Hebrews 13:4

Read: Deuteronomy 22:13–30

IN THE HELL OF DANTE'S *INFERNO*, the poet reserves the lowest pit for the traitors. There rests Judas Iscariot among other treacherous friends. Dante imagined that the worst of sins sent the perpetrators to the worst of punishment. Breach of trust, dishonoring intimate friendship, carried the harshest sentence: eternal freezing.

Though Dante rooted his poetry in allegory more than Scripture, God's severe punishment for betrayal can be seen throughout the book of Deuteronomy. And what human betrayal surpasses that of a wife against her husband or vice versa? God instituted a sexual union between man and woman from the beginning of time. Sex was integral to God's plan. Marriage would be a blessing, honorable in every way.

However, what God intended for honor, we often pervert into dishonorable, selfish acts. The enormous capacity for sex to bind two people together also carries an equal capacity to destroy lives when practiced outside God's purpose. The harsh penalties for sexual misconduct confirm the grave importance God placed on sexual intimacy.

Jesus did not abandon God's best intentions for human sexuality but brought forgiveness and grace, especially to those who were the most sexually powerless. In John's Gospel, we see Jesus respond practically and lovingly to two women. He did not join those condemning the adulterous woman to death by stoning (see John 8:3–11). Instead, he forgave her, instructing her not to sin again. To the woman at the well, married five times and living with a man, Jesus offered "living water" to wash her clean (see John 4:7–26). Without condoning her sexual history, Jesus graciously offered forgiveness and new life.

What many term as "sexual freedom" comes at a very high price; those who pursue it can reap consequences, such as sexually transmitted diseases, emotional wounds, guilt, broken relationships and more. But we can be free of a painful sexual history by asking Christ for forgiveness.

If past sexual sin still harrows your soul, accept the love and forgiveness he offers. If you feel guilty for a marital collapse, know that Jesus knows all about it and offers a clean slate. God created you as a beautifully sexual human being. Celebrate that fact, but honor him with it.

---

equipment have something to dig with, and when you relieve yourself, dig a hole and cover up your excrement. **14**For the LORD your God moves about in your camp to protect you and to deliver your enemies to you. Your camp must be holy, so that he will not see among you anything indecent and turn away from you.

Miscellaneous Laws

15If a slave has taken refuge with you, do not hand him over to his master. **16**Let him live among you wherever he likes and in whatever town he chooses. Do not oppress him.

17No Israelite man or woman is to become a shrine prostitute. **18**You must not bring the earnings of a female prostitute or of a male prostitute*a* into the house of the LORD your God to pay any vow, because the LORD your God detests them both.

19Do not charge your brother interest, whether on money or food or anything else that may earn interest. **20**You may charge a foreigner interest, but not a brother Israelite, so that the LORD your God may bless you in everything you put your hand to in the land you are entering to possess.

21If you make a vow to the LORD your God, do not be slow to pay it, for the LORD your God will certainly demand it of you and you will be guilty of sin. **22**But if you refrain from making a vow, you will not be guilty. **23**Whatever your lips utter you must be sure to do, because you made your vow freely to the LORD your God with your own mouth.

24If you enter your neighbor's vineyard, you may eat all the grapes you want, but do not put any in your basket. **25**If you enter your neighbor's grainfield, you may pick kernels with your hands, but you must not put a sickle to his standing grain.

24 If a man marries a woman who becomes displeasing to him because he finds something indecent about her, and he writes her a certificate of divorce, gives it to her and sends her from his house, **2**and if after she leaves his house she becomes the wife of another man, **3**and her second husband dislikes her and writes her a certificate of divorce, gives it to her and sends her from his house, or if he dies, **4**then her first husband, who divorced her, is not allowed to marry her again after she has been defiled. That would be detestable in the eyes of the LORD. Do not bring sin upon the land the LORD your God is giving you as an inheritance.

5If a man has recently married, he must not be sent to war or have any other duty laid on him. For one year he is to be free to stay at home and bring happiness to the wife he has married.

6Do not take a pair of millstones—not even the upper one—as security for a debt, because that would be taking a man's livelihood as security.

7If a man is caught kidnapping one of his brother Israelites and treats him as a slave or sells him, the kidnapper must die. You must purge the evil from among you.

8In cases of leprous*b* diseases be very careful to do exactly as the priests, who are Levites, instruct you. You must follow carefully what I have commanded them. **9**Remember what the LORD your God did to Miriam along the way after you came out of Egypt.

10When you make a loan of any kind to your neighbor, do not go into his house to get what he is offering as a pledge. **11**Stay outside and let the man to whom you are making the loan bring the pledge out to you. **12**If the man is poor, do not go to sleep with his pledge in your possession. **13**Return his cloak to him by sunset so that he may sleep in it. Then he will thank you, and it will be regarded as a righteous act in the sight of the LORD your God.

14Do not take advantage of a hired man who is poor and needy, whether he is a brother Israelite or an alien living in one of your towns. **15**Pay him his wages each day before sunset, because he is poor and is counting on

> ### Deuteronomy 23:14
> *God Defends Us*
>
> For the LORD your God moves about in your camp to protect you and to deliver your enemies to you.

---

*a***18** Hebrew *of a dog*   *b***8** The Hebrew word was used for various diseases affecting the skin—not necessarily leprosy.

it. Otherwise he may cry to the LORD against you, and you will be guilty of sin.

¹⁶Fathers shall not be put to death for their children, nor children put to death for their fathers; each is to die for his own sin.

¹⁷Do not deprive the alien or the fatherless of justice, or take the cloak of the widow as a pledge. ¹⁸Remember that you were slaves in Egypt and the LORD your God redeemed you from there. That is why I command you to do this.

¹⁹When you are harvesting in your field and you overlook a sheaf, do not go back to get it. Leave it for the fatherless and the widow, so that the LORD your God may bless you in all the work of your hands. ²⁰When you beat the olives from your trees, do not go over the branches a second time. Leave what remains for the alien, the fatherless and the widow. ²¹When you harvest the grapes in your vineyard, do not go over the vines again. Leave what remains for the alien, the fatherless and the widow. ²²Remember that you were slaves in Egypt. That is why I command you to do this.

25 When men have a dispute, they are to take it to court and the judges will decide the case, acquitting the innocent and condemning the guilty. ²If the guilty man deserves to be beaten, the judge shall make him lie down and have him flogged in his presence with the number of lashes his crime deserves, ³but he must not give him more than forty lashes. If he is flogged more than that, your brother will be degraded in your eyes.

⁴Do not muzzle an ox while it is treading out the grain.

⁵If brothers are living together and one of them dies without a son, his widow must not marry outside the family. Her husband's brother shall take her and marry her and fulfill the duty of a brother-in-law to her. ⁶The first son she bears shall carry on the name of the dead brother so that his name will not be blotted out from Israel.

⁷However, if a man does not want to marry his brother's wife, she shall go to the elders at the town gate and say, "My husband's brother refuses to carry on his brother's name in Israel. He will not fulfill the duty of a brother-in-law to me." ⁸Then the elders of his town shall summon him and talk to him. If he persists in saying, "I do not want to marry her," ⁹his brother's widow shall go up to him in the presence of the elders, take off one of his sandals, spit in his face and say, "This is what is done to the man who will not build up his brother's family line." ¹⁰That man's line shall be known in Israel as the Family of the Unsandaled.

¹¹If two men are fighting and the wife of one of them comes to rescue her husband from his assailant, and she reaches out and seizes him by his private parts, ¹²you shall cut off her hand. Show her no pity.

¹³Do not have two differing weights in your bag—one heavy, one light. ¹⁴Do not have two differing measures in your house—one large, one small. ¹⁵You must have accurate and honest weights and measures, so that you may live long in the land the LORD your God is giving you. ¹⁶For the LORD your God detests anyone who does these things, anyone who deals dishonestly.

¹⁷Remember what the Amalekites did to you along the way when you came out of Egypt. ¹⁸When you were weary and worn out, they met you on your journey and cut off all who were lagging behind; they had no fear of God. ¹⁹When the LORD your God gives you rest from all the enemies around you in the land he is giving you to possess as an inheritance, you shall blot out the memory of Amalek from under heaven. Do not forget!

Firstfruits and Tithes

26 When you have entered the land the LORD your God is giving you as an inheritance and have taken possession of it and settled in it, ²take some of the firstfruits of all that you produce from the soil of the land the LORD your God is giving you and put them in a basket. Then go to the place the LORD your

---

Deuteronomy 24:19

God Is Generous

When you are harvesting in your field and you overlook a sheaf, do not go back to get it. Leave it for the alien, the fatherless and the widow.

God will choose as a dwelling for his Name ³and say to the priest in office at the time, "I declare today to the LORD your God that I have come to the land the LORD swore to our forefathers to give us." ⁴The priest shall take the basket from your hands and set it down in front of the altar of the LORD your God. ⁵Then you shall declare before the LORD your God: "My father was a wandering Aramean, and he went down into Egypt with a few people and lived there and became a great nation, powerful and numerous. ⁶But the Egyptians mistreated us and made us suffer, putting us to hard labor. ⁷Then we cried out to the LORD, the God of our fathers, and the LORD heard our voice and saw our misery, toil and oppression. ⁸So the LORD brought us out of Egypt with a mighty hand and an outstretched arm, with great terror and with miraculous signs and wonders. ⁹He brought us to this place and gave us this land, a land flowing with milk and honey; ¹⁰and now I bring the firstfruits of the soil that you, O LORD, have given me." Place the basket before the LORD your God and bow down before him. ¹¹And you and the Levites and the aliens among you shall rejoice in all the good things the LORD your God has given to you and your household.

¹²When you have finished setting aside a tenth of all your produce in the third year, the year of the tithe, you shall give it to the Levite, the alien, the fatherless and the widow, so that they may eat in your towns and be satisfied. ¹³Then say to the LORD your God: "I have removed from my house the sacred portion and have given it to the Levite, the alien, the fatherless and the widow, according to all you commanded. I have not turned aside from your commands nor have I forgotten any of them. ¹⁴I have not eaten any of the sacred portion while I was in mourning, nor have I removed any of it while I was unclean, nor have I offered any of it to the dead. I have obeyed the LORD my God; I have done everything you

commanded me. ¹⁵Look down from heaven, your holy dwelling place, and bless your people Israel and the land you have given us as you promised on oath to our forefathers, a land flowing with milk and honey."

Follow the LORD's Commands

¹⁶The LORD your God commands you this day to follow these decrees and laws; carefully observe them with all your heart and with all your soul. ¹⁷You have declared this day that the LORD is your God and that you will walk in his ways, that you will keep his decrees, commands and laws, and that you will obey him. ¹⁸And the LORD has declared this day that you are his people, his treasured possession as he promised, and that you are to keep all his commands. ¹⁹He has declared that he will set you in praise, fame and honor high above all the nations he has made and that you will be a people holy to the LORD your God, as he promised.

The Altar on Mount Ebal

27 Moses and the elders of Israel commanded the people: "Keep all these commands that I give you today. ²When you have crossed the Jordan into the land the LORD your God is giving you, set up some large stones and coat them with plaster. ³Write on them all the words of this law when you have crossed over to enter the land the LORD your God is giving you, a land flowing with milk and honey, just as the LORD, the God of your fathers, promised you. ⁴And when you have crossed the Jordan, set up these stones on Mount Ebal, as I command you today, and coat them with plaster. ⁵Build there an altar to the LORD your God, an altar of stones. Do not use any iron tool upon them. ⁶Build the altar of the LORD your God with fieldstones and offer burnt offerings on it to the LORD your God. ⁷Sacrifice fellowship offerings*a* there, eating them and rejoicing in the presence of the LORD your God. ⁸And you shall write very clearly all the words of this law on these stones you have set up."

> ### Deuteronomy 26:18
>
> *God Treasures Us*
>
> And the LORD has declared this day that you are his people, his treasured possession as he promised, and that you are to keep all his commands.

a 7 Traditionally *peace offerings*

Curses From Mount Ebal

⁹Then Moses and the priests, who are Levites, said to all Israel, "Be silent, O Israel, and listen! You have now become the people of the LORD your God. ¹⁰Obey the LORD your God and follow his commands and decrees that I give you today."

¹¹On the same day Moses commanded the people:

¹²When you have crossed the Jordan, these tribes shall stand on Mount Gerizim to bless the people: Simeon, Levi, Judah, Issachar, Joseph and Benjamin. ¹³And these tribes shall stand on Mount Ebal to pronounce curses: Reuben, Gad, Asher, Zebulun, Dan and Naphtali.

¹⁴The Levites shall recite to all the people of Israel in a loud voice:

¹⁵"Cursed is the man who carves an image or casts an idol—a thing detestable to the LORD, the work of the craftsman's hands—and sets it up in secret."

Then all the people shall say, "Amen!"

¹⁶"Cursed is the man who dishonors his father or his mother."

Then all the people shall say, "Amen!"

¹⁷"Cursed is the man who moves his neighbor's boundary stone."

Then all the people shall say, "Amen!"

¹⁸"Cursed is the man who leads the blind astray on the road."

Then all the people shall say, "Amen!"

¹⁹"Cursed is the man who withholds justice from the alien, the fatherless or the widow."

Then all the people shall say, "Amen!"

²⁰"Cursed is the man who sleeps with his father's wife, for he dishonors his father's bed."

Then all the people shall say, "Amen!"

²¹"Cursed is the man who has sexual relations with any animal."

Then all the people shall say, "Amen!"

²²"Cursed is the man who sleeps with his sister, the daughter of his father or the daughter of his mother."

Then all the people shall say, "Amen!"

²³"Cursed is the man who sleeps with his mother-in-law."

Then all the people shall say, "Amen!"

²⁴"Cursed is the man who kills his neighbor secretly."

Then all the people shall say, "Amen!"

²⁵"Cursed is the man who accepts a bribe to kill an innocent person."

Then all the people shall say, "Amen!"

²⁶"Cursed is the man who does not uphold the words of this law by carrying them out."

Then all the people shall say, "Amen!"

Blessings for Obedience

28 If you fully obey the LORD your God and carefully follow all his commands I give you today, the LORD your God will set you high above all the nations on earth. ²All these blessings will come upon you and accompany you if you obey the LORD your God:

³You will be blessed in the city and blessed in the country.

⁴The fruit of your womb will be blessed, and the crops of your land and the young of your livestock—the calves of your herds and the lambs of your flocks.

⁵Your basket and your kneading trough will be blessed.

⁶You will be blessed when you come in and blessed when you go out.

⁷The LORD will grant that the enemies who rise up against you will be defeated before you. They will come at you from one direction but flee from you in seven.

⁸The LORD will send a blessing on your barns and on everything you put your hand to. The LORD your God will bless you in the land he is giving you.

⁹The LORD will establish you as his holy people, as he promised you on oath, if you keep the commands of the LORD your God and walk in his ways. ¹⁰Then all the peoples on earth will see that you are called by the name of the LORD, and they will fear you. ¹¹The LORD will grant you abundant prosperity—in the fruit of your womb, the young of your livestock and the crops of your ground—in the land he swore to your forefathers to give you.

¹²The LORD will open the heavens, the storehouse of his bounty, to send rain on your land in season and to bless all the work of your hands. You will lend to many nations but will

Two

DINAH

DINAH REMEMBERED BEING LOVED by two men. One had tickled her ears with whispered words of affection. He made her heart flutter with his promises—she'd never heard a man be so vulnerable with a woman. She'd caught him staring at her when they talked, almost transfixed. And his boyish eyes seemed to ask, almost plead with her, to be his forever.

His words were tender and gentle, but not his touch.

No, his touch seemed to be that of another man altogether. A demanding, self-centered man who roughed her face with his beard; whose fingertips were more like talons, securing her so she could not get away. This man did not listen to her cries. He only thought about what he wanted.

But what did Dinah want? It hadn't seemed to matter. Her name floated among the tall grass in the fields in a discussion among the two families—as casually as if they were negotiating a business deal, not a marriage.

"My son Shechem has his heart set on your daughter," his father had told her father and brothers. The man who had violated her was now talking about his heart? Were we now back to the other man with the winsome words?

"I'll pay whatever you ask me . . . Only give me the girl as my wife."

Devoted and sacrificial, *this* man spoke the language of love fluently. *This* man said what every girl her age wanted to hear. She could have loved *that* man, she would often think to herself years later. The events from that summer traipsed across her mind at the oddest times. Washing clothes. Walking to market. Whenever her mind grew still enough to remember what her heart could not forget.

Did the man with the velvety words ever really exist? Perhaps she simply wanted to believe he existed to assuage her misplaced guilt. However, she could not deny the memory of the other man who haunted her dreams. Two men had loved Dinah. But they shared one name.

She had been sure time would heal her wounds. Yet here she was, years later, not yet over either one.

—Prayer—

"O Lord, hear my voice. Let your ears be attentive to my cry for mercy" (Psalm 130:2).

When Shechem . . . saw her, he took her and violated her. His heart was drawn to Dinah daughter of Jacob, and he loved the girl and spoke tenderly to her.

Genesis 34:2–3

ASSIGNED READING:

Genesis 34

Weekend

Go to page 248 for your next devotional reading.

borrow from none. [13]The LORD will make you the head, not the tail. If you pay attention to the commands of the LORD your God that I give you this day and carefully follow them, you will always be at the top, never at the bottom. [14]Do not turn aside from any of the commands I give you today, to the right or to the left, following other gods and serving them.

Curses for Disobedience

[15]However, if you do not obey the LORD your God and do not carefully follow all his commands and decrees I am giving you today, all these curses will come upon you and overtake you:

[16]You will be cursed in the city and cursed in the country.

[17]Your basket and your kneading trough will be cursed.

[18]The fruit of your womb will be cursed, and the crops of your land, and the calves of your herds and the lambs of your flocks.

[19]You will be cursed when you come in and cursed when you go out.

[20]The LORD will send on you curses, confusion and rebuke in everything you put your hand to, until you are destroyed and come to sudden ruin because of the evil you have done in forsaking him.[a] [21]The LORD will plague you with diseases until he has destroyed you from the land you are entering to possess. [22]The LORD will strike you with wasting disease, with fever and inflammation, with scorching heat and drought, with blight and mildew, which will plague you until you perish. [23]The sky over your head will be bronze, the ground beneath you iron. [24]The LORD will turn the rain of your country into dust and powder; it will come down from the skies until you are destroyed.

[25]The LORD will cause you to be defeated before your enemies. You will come at them from one direction but flee from them in seven, and you will become a thing of horror to all the kingdoms on earth. [26]Your carcasses will be food for all the birds of the air and the beasts of the earth, and there will be no one to frighten them away. [27]The LORD will afflict you with the boils of Egypt and with tumors, festering sores and the itch, from which you cannot be cured. [28]The LORD will afflict you with madness, blindness and confusion of mind. [29]At midday you will grope about like a blind man in the dark. You will be unsuccessful in everything you do; day after day you will be oppressed and robbed, with no one to rescue you.

[30]You will be pledged to be married to a woman, but another will take her and ravish her. You will build a house, but you will not live in it. You will plant a vineyard, but you will not even begin to enjoy its fruit. [31]Your ox will be slaughtered before your eyes, but you will eat none of it. Your donkey will be forcibly taken from you and will not be returned. Your sheep will be given to your enemies, and no one will rescue them. [32]Your sons and daughters will be given to another nation, and you will wear out your eyes watching for them day after day, powerless to lift a hand. [33]A people that you do not know will eat what your land and labor produce, and you will have nothing but cruel oppression all your days. [34]The sights you see will drive you mad. [35]The LORD will afflict your knees and legs with painful boils that cannot be cured, spreading from the soles of your feet to the top of your head.

[36]The LORD will drive you and the king you set over you to a nation unknown to you or your fathers. There you will worship other gods, gods of wood and stone. [37]You will become a thing of horror and an object of scorn and ridicule to all the nations where the LORD will drive you.

[38]You will sow much seed in the field but you will harvest little, because locusts will devour it. [39]You will plant vineyards and cultivate them but you will not drink the wine or gather the grapes, because worms will eat them. [40]You will have olive trees throughout your country but you will not use the oil, because the olives will drop off. [41]You will have sons and daughters but you will not keep them, because they will go into captivity. [42]Swarms of locusts will take over all your trees and the crops of your land.

[43]The alien who lives among you will rise above you higher and higher, but you will sink

---

[a]20 Hebrew *me*

lower and lower. **44**He will lend to you, but you will not lend to him. He will be the head, but you will be the tail.

45All these curses will come upon you. They will pursue you and overtake you until you are destroyed, because you did not obey the LORD your God and observe the commands and decrees he gave you. **46**They will be a sign and a wonder to you and your descendants forever. **47**Because you did not serve the LORD your God joyfully and gladly in the time of prosperity, **48**therefore in hunger and thirst, in nakedness and dire poverty, you will serve the enemies the LORD sends against you. He will put an iron yoke on your neck until he has destroyed you.

49The LORD will bring a nation against you from far away, from the ends of the earth, like an eagle swooping down, a nation whose language you will not understand, **50**a fierce-looking nation without respect for the old or pity for the young. **51**They will devour the young of your livestock and the crops of your land until you are destroyed. They will leave you no grain, new wine or oil, nor any calves of your herds or lambs of your flocks until you are ruined. **52**They will lay siege to all the cities throughout your land until the high fortified walls in which you trust fall down. They will besiege all the cities throughout the land the LORD your God is giving you.

53Because of the suffering that your enemy will inflict on you during the siege, you will eat the fruit of the womb, the flesh of the sons and daughters the LORD your God has given you. **54**Even the most gentle and sensitive man among you will have no compassion on his own brother or the wife he loves or his surviving children, **55**and he will not give to one of them any of the flesh of his children that he is eating. It will be all he has left because of the suffering your enemy will inflict on you during the siege of all your cities. **56**The most gentle and sensitive woman among you—so sensitive and gentle that she would not venture to touch the ground with the sole of her foot—will begrudge the husband she loves and her own son or daughter **57**the afterbirth from her womb and the children she bears. For she intends to eat them secretly during the siege and in the

distress that your enemy will inflict on you in your cities.

58If you do not carefully follow all the words of this law, which are written in this book, and do not revere this glorious and awesome name—the LORD your God— **59**the LORD will send fearful plagues on you and your descendants, harsh and prolonged disasters, and severe and lingering illnesses. **60**He will bring upon you all the diseases of Egypt that you dreaded, and they will cling to you. **61**The LORD will also bring on you every kind of sickness and disaster not recorded in this Book of the Law, until you are destroyed. **62**You who were as numerous as the stars in the sky will be left but few in number, because you did not obey the LORD your God. **63**Just as it pleased the LORD to make you prosper and increase in number, so it will please him to ruin and destroy you. You will be uprooted from the land you are entering to possess.

64Then the LORD will scatter you among all nations, from one end of the earth to the other. There you will worship other gods—gods of wood and stone, which neither you nor your fathers have known. **65**Among those nations you will find no repose, no resting place for the sole of your foot. There the LORD will give you an anxious mind, eyes weary with longing, and a despairing heart. **66**You will live in constant suspense, filled with dread both night and day, never sure of your life. **67**In the morning you will say, "If only it were evening!" and in the evening, "If only it were morning!"—because of the terror that will fill your hearts and the sights that your eyes will see. **68**The LORD will send you back in ships to Egypt on a journey I said you should never make again. There you will offer yourselves for sale to your enemies as male and female slaves, but no one will buy you.

Renewal of the Covenant

29 These are the terms of the covenant the LORD commanded Moses to make with the Israelites in Moab, in addition to the covenant he had made with them at Horeb.

2Moses summoned all the Israelites and said to them:

Your eyes have seen all that the LORD did in Egypt to Pharaoh, to all his officials and to all his land. ³With your own eyes you saw those great trials, those miraculous signs and great wonders. ⁴But to this day the Lord has not given you a mind that understands or eyes that see or ears that hear. ⁵During the forty years that I led you through the desert, your clothes did not wear out, nor did the sandals on your feet. ⁶You ate no bread and drank no wine or other fermented drink. I did this so that you might know that I am the Lord your God.

⁷When you reached this place, Sihon king of Heshbon and Og king of Bashan came out to fight against us, but we defeated them. ⁸We took their land and gave it as an inheritance to the Reubenites, the Gadites and the half-tribe of Manasseh.

⁹Carefully follow the terms of this covenant, so that you may prosper in everything you do. ¹⁰All of you are standing today in the presence of the Lord your God—your leaders and chief men, your elders and officials, and all the other men of Israel, ¹¹together with your children and your wives, and the aliens living in your camps who chop your wood and carry your water. ¹²You are standing here in order to enter into a covenant with the Lord your God, a covenant the Lord is making with you this day and sealing with an oath, ¹³to confirm you this day as his people, that he may be your God as he promised you and as he swore to your fathers, Abraham, Isaac and Jacob. ¹⁴I am making this covenant, with its oath, not only with you ¹⁵who are standing here with us today in the presence of the Lord our God but also with those who are not here today.

¹⁶You yourselves know how we lived in Egypt and how we passed through the countries on the way here. ¹⁷You saw among them their detestable images and idols of wood and stone, of silver and gold. ¹⁸Make sure there is no man or woman, clan or tribe among you today whose heart turns away from the Lord our God to go and worship the gods of those nations; make sure there is no root among you that produces such bitter poison.

¹⁹When such a person hears the words of this oath, he invokes a blessing on himself and therefore thinks, "I will be safe, even though I persist in going my own way." This will bring disaster on the watered land as well as the dry.ᵃ ²⁰The Lord will never be willing to forgive him; his wrath and zeal will burn against that man. All the curses written in this book will fall upon him, and the Lord will blot out his name from under heaven. ²¹The Lord will single him out from all the tribes of Israel for disaster, according to all the curses of the covenant written in this Book of the Law.

²²Your children who follow you in later generations and foreigners who come from distant lands will see the calamities that have fallen on the land and the diseases with which the Lord has afflicted it. ²³The whole land will be a burning waste of salt and sulfur—nothing planted, nothing sprouting, no vegetation growing on it. It will be like the destruction of Sodom and Gomorrah, Admah and Zeboiim, which the Lord overthrew in fierce anger. ²⁴All the nations will ask: "Why has the Lord done this to this land? Why this fierce, burning anger?"

²⁵And the answer will be: "It is because this people abandoned the covenant of the Lord, the God of their fathers, the covenant he made with them when he brought them out of Egypt. ²⁶They went off and worshiped other gods and bowed down to them, gods they did not know, gods he had not given them. ²⁷Therefore the Lord's anger burned against this land, so that he brought on it all the curses written in this book. ²⁸In furious anger and in great wrath the Lord uprooted them from their land and thrust them into another land, as it is now."

²⁹The secret things belong to the Lord our God, but the things revealed belong to us and to our children forever, that we may follow all the words of this law.

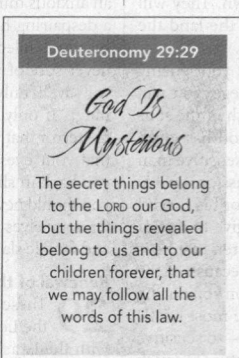

Deuteronomy 29:29

God Is Mysterious

The secret things belong to the Lord our God, but the things revealed belong to us and to our children forever, that we may follow all the words of this law.

ᵃ 19 Or way, in order to add drunkenness to thirst."

Prosperity After Turning to the LORD

30 When all these blessings and curses I have set before you come upon you and you take them to heart wherever the LORD your God disperses you among the nations, ²and when you and your children return to the LORD your God and obey him with all your heart and with all your soul according to everything I command you today, ³then the LORD your God will restore your fortunes[a] and have compassion on you and gather you again from all the nations where he scattered you. ⁴Even if you have been banished to the most distant land under the heavens, from there the LORD your God will gather you and bring you back. ⁵He will bring you to the land that belonged to your fathers, and you will take possession of it. He will make you more prosperous and numerous than your fathers. ⁶The LORD your God will circumcise your hearts and the hearts of your descendants, so that you may love him with all your heart and with all your soul, and live. ⁷The LORD your God will put all these curses on your enemies who hate and persecute you. ⁸You will again obey the LORD and follow all his commands I am giving you today. ⁹Then the LORD your God will make you most prosperous in all the work of your hands and in the fruit of your womb, the young of your livestock and the crops of your land. The LORD will again delight in you and make you prosperous, just as he delighted in your fathers, ¹⁰if you obey the LORD your God and keep his commands and decrees that are written in this Book of the Law and turn to the LORD your God with all your heart and all your soul.

The Offer of Life or Death

¹¹Now what I am commanding you today is not too difficult for you or beyond your reach. ¹²It is not up in heaven, so that you have to ask, "Who will ascend into heaven to get it and proclaim it to us so we may obey it?" ¹³Nor is it beyond the sea, so that you have to ask, "Who will cross the sea to get it and proclaim it to us so we may obey it?" ¹⁴No, the word is very near you; it is in your mouth and in your heart so you may obey it.

¹⁵See, I set before you today life and prosperity, death and destruction. ¹⁶For I command you today to love the LORD your God, to walk in his ways, and to keep his commands, decrees and laws; then you will live and increase, and the LORD your God will bless you in the land you are entering to possess.

¹⁷But if your heart turns away and you are not obedient, and if you are drawn away to bow down to other gods and worship them, ¹⁸I declare to you this day that you will certainly be destroyed. You will not live long in the land you are crossing the Jordan to enter and possess.

¹⁹This day I call heaven and earth as witnesses against you that I have set before you life and death, blessings and curses. Now choose life, so that you and your children may live ²⁰and that you may love the LORD your God, listen to his voice, and hold fast to him. For the LORD is your life, and he will give you many years in the land he swore to give to your fathers, Abraham, Isaac and Jacob.

Deuteronomy 30:20

God Is Life

And that you may love the LORD your God, listen to his voice, and hold fast to him. For the LORD is your life, and he will give you many years in the land he swore to give to your fathers, Abraham, Isaac and Jacob.

Joshua to Succeed Moses

31 Then Moses went out and spoke these words to all Israel: ²"I am now a hundred and twenty years old and I am no longer able to lead you. The LORD has said to me, 'You shall not cross the Jordan.' ³The LORD your God himself will cross over ahead of you. He will destroy these nations before you, and you will take possession of their land. Joshua also will cross over ahead of you, as the LORD said. ⁴And the LORD will do to them what he did to Sihon and Og, the kings of the Amorites, whom he destroyed along with their land. ⁵The LORD will deliver them to you, and you must do to them all that I have commanded you.

---

a3 Or *will bring you back from captivity*

Who's the Boss?

Now what I am commanding you today is not too difficult for you or beyond your reach.

reflection

1 Do you ever find yourself offering excuses for failing to follow God's commandments?

2 In what ways have you benefited by obeying God's rules of conduct?

3 How quick are you to obey the voice of your Master—instantly, hesitantly, occasionally? What does this tell you about your relationship with him?

RELATED READINGS

Exodus 20:2–17;
Philippians 2:12–13;
1 Thessalonians 5:24

Read: Deuteronomy 30:11–20

IN HIS AUTOBIOGRAPHY, *A Life in Our Times*, historian John Kenneth Galbraith wrote admiringly of his family's housekeeper, Emily Gloria Wilson. "It had been a wearying day, and I asked Emily to hold all telephone calls while I had a nap. Shortly thereafter the phone rang. Lyndon Johnson was calling from the White House."

"Get me Ken Galbraith. This is Lyndon Johnson."

"He is sleeping, Mr. President. He said not to disturb him."

"Well, wake him up. I want to talk to him."

"No, Mr. President," Emily replied firmly. "I work for him, not you." She refused to wake her employer.

When Ken returned the president's call later, he reported that LBJ could scarcely control his pleasure. "Tell that woman I want her here in the White House!"

Ken's instructions to his housekeeper had been clear, and Emily Wilson followed them faithfully. Another might have been tempted to cave in to the demands of the caller, but Emily had her orders and she followed them to the letter. She knew for whom she worked.

When God gave his commandments to the nation of Israel, he was very clear. He stipulated laws and rules of conduct for the well-being and prosperity of his beloved people. Their job was to simply obey.

In the book of Deuteronomy (often referred to as the book of the Law) God reminds the people of what he has done on their behalf. He also reassures them that obedience is not beyond their reach. His standards are not impossibly high or patronizingly low. Instead, God has clearly revealed his will through his Word. He has even written it on their hearts! Their response is to obey.

Do you find yourself offering excuses for breaking God's laws? Are you tempted to regard the Ten Commandments as the "Ten Suggestions"? Do the demands of others drown out the voice of your Creator?

Emily Wilson was able to say "no" to a president because her instructions from her master were clear. Do you listen to the voice of your Master?

Monday

Go to page 254 for your next devotional reading.

⁶Be strong and courageous. Do not be afraid or terrified because of them, for the LORD your God goes with you; he will never leave you nor forsake you."

⁷Then Moses summoned Joshua and said to him in the presence of all Israel, "Be strong and courageous, for you must go with this people into the land that the LORD swore to their forefathers to give them, and you must divide it among them as their inheritance. ⁸The LORD himself goes before you and will be with you; he will never leave you nor forsake you. Do not be afraid; do not be discouraged."

The Reading of the Law

⁹So Moses wrote down this law and gave it to the priests, the sons of Levi, who carried the ark of the covenant of the LORD, and to all the elders of Israel. ¹⁰Then Moses commanded them: "At the end of every seven years, in the year for canceling debts, during the Feast of Tabernacles, ¹¹when all Israel comes to appear before the LORD your God at the place he will choose, you shall read this law before them in their hearing. ¹²Assemble the people—men, women and children, and the aliens living in your towns—so they can listen and learn to fear the LORD your God and follow carefully all the words of this law. ¹³Their children, who do not know this law, must hear it and learn to fear the LORD your God as long as you live in the land you are crossing the Jordan to possess."

Israel's Rebellion Predicted

¹⁴The LORD said to Moses, "Now the day of your death is near. Call Joshua and present yourselves at the Tent of Meeting, where I will commission him." So Moses and Joshua came and presented themselves at the Tent of Meeting.

¹⁵Then the LORD appeared at the Tent in a pillar of cloud, and the cloud stood over the entrance to the Tent. ¹⁶And the LORD said to Moses: "You are going to rest with your fathers, and these people will soon prostitute themselves to the foreign gods of the land they are entering. They will forsake me and break the covenant I made with them. ¹⁷On that day I will become angry with them and forsake them; I will hide my face from them, and they will be destroyed. Many disasters and difficulties will come upon them, and on that day they will ask, 'Have not

these disasters come upon us because our God is not with us?' ¹⁸And I will certainly hide my face on that day because of all their wickedness in turning to other gods.

¹⁹"Now write down for yourselves this song and teach it to the Israelites and have them sing it, so that it may be a witness for me against them. ²⁰When I have brought them into the land flowing with milk and honey, the land I promised on oath to their forefathers, and when they eat their fill and thrive, they will turn to other gods and worship them, rejecting me and breaking my covenant. ²¹And when many disasters and difficulties come upon them, this song will testify against them, because it will not be forgotten by their descendants. I know what they are disposed to do, even before I bring them into the land I promised them on oath." ²²So Moses wrote down this song that day and taught it to the Israelites.

²³The LORD gave this command to Joshua son of Nun: "Be strong and courageous, for you will bring the Israelites into the land I promised them on oath, and I myself will be with you."

²⁴After Moses finished writing in a book the words of this law from beginning to end, ²⁵he gave this command to the Levites who carried the ark of the covenant of the LORD: ²⁶"Take this Book of the Law and place it beside the ark of the covenant of the LORD your God. There it will remain as a witness against you. ²⁷For I know how rebellious and stiff-necked you are. If you have been rebellious against the LORD while I am still alive and with you, how much more will you rebel after I die! ²⁸Assemble before me all the elders of your tribes and all your officials, so that I can speak these words in their hearing and call heaven and earth to testify against them. ²⁹For I know that after my death you are sure to become utterly corrupt and to turn from the way I have commanded you. In days to come, disaster will fall upon you because you will do evil in the sight of the LORD and provoke him to anger by what your hands have made."

The Song of Moses

³⁰And Moses recited the words of this song from beginning to end in the hearing of the whole assembly of Israel:

32 Listen, O heavens, and I will speak;
hear, O earth, the words of my
mouth.
2 Let my teaching fall like rain
and my words descend like dew,
like showers on new grass,
like abundant rain on tender plants.

3 I will proclaim the name of the LORD.
Oh, praise the greatness of our God!
4 He is the Rock, his works
are perfect,
and all his ways are just.
A faithful God who does no
wrong,
upright and just is he.

5 They have acted corruptly
toward him;
to their shame they
are no longer his
children,
but a warped and
crooked
generation.ᵃ
6 Is this the way you repay
the LORD,
O foolish and unwise people?
Is he not your Father, your Creator,ᵇ
who made you and formed you?

7 Remember the days of old;
consider the generations long past.
Ask your father and he will tell you,
your elders, and they will explain to you.
8 When the Most High gave the nations
their inheritance,
when he divided all mankind,
he set up boundaries for the peoples
according to the number of the sons of
Israel.ᶜ
9 For the LORD's portion is his people,
Jacob his allotted inheritance.

10 In a desert land he found him,
in a barren and howling waste.
He shielded him and cared for him;
he guarded him as the apple of his eye,
11 like an eagle that stirs up its nest
and hovers over its young,

that spreads its wings to catch them
and carries them on its pinions.
12 The LORD alone led him;
no foreign god was with him.

13 He made him ride on the heights of the land
and fed him with the fruit of the fields.
He nourished him with honey from the
rock,
and with oil from the
flinty crag,
14 with curds and milk from
herd and flock
and with fattened lambs
and goats,
with choice rams of Bashan
and the finest kernels of
wheat.
You drank the foaming
blood of the grape.

15 Jeshurunᵈ grew fat and
kicked;
filled with food, he
became heavy and
sleek.
He abandoned the God who made him
and rejected the Rock his Savior.
16 They made him jealous with their foreign
gods
and angered him with their detestable
idols.
17 They sacrificed to demons, which are not
God—
gods they had not known,
gods that recently appeared,
gods your fathers did not fear.
18 You deserted the Rock, who fathered you;
you forgot the God who gave you birth.

19 The LORD saw this and rejected them
because he was angered by his sons and
daughters.
20 "I will hide my face from them," he said,
"and see what their end will be;
for they are a perverse generation,
children who are unfaithful.
21 They made me jealous by what is no god
and angered me with their worthless
idols.

Deuteronomy 32:4

God Is Resolute

He is the Rock,
his works are perfect,
and all his ways are just.
A faithful God who
does no wrong,
upright and just is he.

ᵃ5 Or *Corrupt are they and not his children, / a generation warped and twisted to their shame*   ᵇ6 Or *Father, who bought you*
ᶜ8 Masoretic Text; Dead Sea Scrolls (see also Septuagint) *sons of God*   ᵈ15 *Jeshurun* means *the upright one,* that is, Israel.

I will make them envious by those who are
not a people;
I will make them angry by a nation that
has no understanding.
²² For a fire has been kindled by my wrath,
one that burns to the realm of death*a*
below.
It will devour the earth and its harvests
and set afire the foundations of the
mountains.

²³ "I will heap calamities upon them
and spend my arrows against them.
²⁴ I will send wasting famine against them,
consuming pestilence and deadly
plague;
I will send against them the fangs of wild
beasts,
the venom of vipers that glide in the dust.
²⁵ In the street the sword will make them
childless;
in their homes terror will reign.
Young men and young women will perish,
infants and gray-haired men.
²⁶ I said I would scatter them
and blot out their memory from
mankind,
²⁷ but I dreaded the taunt of the enemy,
lest the adversary misunderstand
and say, 'Our hand has triumphed;
the LORD has not done all this.'"

²⁸ They are a nation without sense,
there is no discernment in them.
²⁹ If only they were wise and would
understand this
and discern what their end will be!
³⁰ How could one man chase a thousand,
or two put ten thousand to flight,
unless their Rock had sold them,
unless the LORD had given them up?
³¹ For their rock is not like our Rock,
as even our enemies concede.
³² Their vine comes from the vine of Sodom
and from the fields of Gomorrah.
Their grapes are filled with poison,
and their clusters with bitterness.
³³ Their wine is the venom of serpents,
the deadly poison of cobras.

³⁴ "Have I not kept this in reserve
and sealed it in my vaults?
³⁵ It is mine to avenge; I will repay.
In due time their foot will slip;
their day of disaster is near
and their doom rushes upon them."

³⁶ The LORD will judge his people
and have compassion on his servants
when he sees their strength is gone
and no one is left, slave or free.
³⁷ He will say: "Now where are their gods,
the rock they took refuge in,
³⁸ the gods who ate the fat of their sacrifices
and drank the wine of their drink
offerings?
Let them rise up to help you!
Let them give you shelter!

³⁹ "See now that I myself am He!
There is no god besides me.
I put to death and I bring to life,
I have wounded and I will heal,
and no one can deliver out of my
hand.
⁴⁰ I lift my hand to heaven and declare:
As surely as I live forever,
⁴¹ when I sharpen my flashing sword
and my hand grasps it in judgment,
I will take vengeance on my adversaries
and repay those who hate me.
⁴² I will make my arrows drunk with blood,
while my sword devours flesh:
the blood of the slain and the captives,
the heads of the enemy leaders."

⁴³ Rejoice, O nations, with his people,*b,c*
for he will avenge the blood of his
servants;
he will take vengeance on his enemies
and make atonement for his land and
people.

⁴⁴ Moses came with Joshua*d* son of Nun and
spoke all the words of this song in the hearing
of the people. ⁴⁵ When Moses finished reciting
all these words to all Israel, ⁴⁶ he said to them,
"Take to heart all the words I have solemnly
declared to you this day, so that you may command your children to obey carefully all the

---

*a*22 Hebrew *to Sheol*   *b*43 Or *Make his people rejoice, O nations*   *c*43 Masoretic Text; Dead Sea Scrolls (see also Septuagint) *people, / and
let all the angels worship him /*   *d*44 Hebrew *Hoshea*, a variant of *Joshua*

words of this law. ⁴⁷They are not just idle words for you—they are your life. By them you will live long in the land you are crossing the Jordan to possess."

Moses to Die on Mount Nebo

⁴⁸On that same day the LORD told Moses, ⁴⁹"Go up into the Abarim Range to Mount Nebo in Moab, across from Jericho, and view Canaan, the land I am giving the Israelites as their own possession. ⁵⁰There on the mountain that you have climbed you will die and be gathered to your people, just as your brother Aaron died on Mount Hor and was gathered to his people. ⁵¹This is because both of you broke faith with me in the presence of the Israelites at the waters of Meribah Kadesh in the Desert of Zin and because you did not uphold my holiness among the Israelites. ⁵²Therefore, you will see the land only from a distance; you will not enter the land I am giving to the people of Israel."

Moses Blesses the Tribes

33 This is the blessing that Moses the man of God pronounced on the Israelites before his death. ²He said:

"The LORD came from Sinai
  and dawned over them from Seir;
  he shone forth from Mount Paran.
He came withᵃ myriads of
    holy ones
  from the south, from his
    mountain slopes.ᵇ
³ Surely it is you who love the
    people;
  all the holy ones are in
    your hand.
At your feet they all bow
    down,
  and from you receive
    instruction,
⁴ the law that Moses gave us,
  the possession of the
    assembly of Jacob.
⁵ He was king over Jeshurunᶜ
  when the leaders of the
    people assembled,
  along with the tribes of Israel.

⁶ "Let Reuben live and not die,
  norᵈ his men be few."

⁷ And this he said about Judah:

"Hear, O LORD, the cry of Judah;
  bring him to his people.
With his own hands he defends his cause.
  Oh, be his help against his foes!"

⁸ About Levi he said:

"Your Thummim and Urim belong
  to the man you favored.
You tested him at Massah;
  you contended with him at the waters of
    Meribah.
⁹ He said of his father and mother,
  'I have no regard for them.'
He did not recognize his brothers
  or acknowledge his own children,
but he watched over your word
  and guarded your covenant.
¹⁰ He teaches your precepts to Jacob
  and your law to Israel.
He offers incense before you
  and whole burnt offerings on your altar.
¹¹ Bless all his skills, O LORD,
  and be pleased with the work of his hands.
Smite the loins of those who rise up against
    him;
    strike his foes till they
      rise no more."

¹² About Benjamin he said:

"Let the beloved of the LORD
    rest secure in him,
  for he shields him all day
    long,
  and the one the LORD
    loves rests between
    his shoulders."

¹³ About Joseph he said:

"May the LORD bless his
    land
  with the precious dew
    from heaven above
and with the deep waters that lie below;

Deuteronomy 33:12

God Shields Us

About Benjamin he said:
"Let the beloved of the
LORD rest secure in him,
for he shields him
all day long,
and the one the LORD
loves rests between
his shoulders."

ᵃ2 Or *from* ᵇ2 The meaning of the Hebrew for this phrase is uncertain. ᶜ5 *Jeshurun* means *the upright one,* that is, Israel; also in verse 26. ᵈ6 Or *but let*

¹⁴with the best the sun brings forth
and the finest the moon can yield;
¹⁵with the choicest gifts of the ancient
mountains
and the fruitfulness of the everlasting
hills;
¹⁶with the best gifts of the earth and its
fullness
and the favor of him who dwelt in the
burning bush.
Let all these rest on the head of Joseph,
on the brow of the prince among^a his
brothers.
¹⁷In majesty he is like a firstborn bull;
his horns are the horns of a wild ox.
With them he will gore the nations,
even those at the ends of the earth.
Such are the ten thousands of Ephraim;
such are the thousands of Manasseh."

¹⁸About Zebulun he said:

"Rejoice, Zebulun, in your going out,
and you, Issachar, in your tents.
¹⁹They will summon peoples to the
mountain
and there offer sacrifices of
righteousness;
they will feast on the abundance of the
seas,
on the treasures hidden in the sand."

²⁰About Gad he said:

"Blessed is he who enlarges Gad's
domain!
Gad lives there like a lion,
tearing at arm or head.
²¹He chose the best land for himself;
the leader's portion was kept for him.
When the heads of the people assembled,
he carried out the LORD's righteous will,
and his judgments concerning Israel."

²²About Dan he said:

"Dan is a lion's cub,
springing out of Bashan."

²³About Naphtali he said:

"Naphtali is abounding with the favor of
the LORD

and is full of his blessing;
he will inherit southward to the lake."

²⁴About Asher he said:

"Most blessed of sons is Asher;
let him be favored by his brothers,
and let him bathe his feet in oil.
²⁵The bolts of your gates will be iron and
bronze,
and your strength will equal your days.

²⁶"There is no one like the God of
Jeshurun,
who rides on the heavens to help you
and on the clouds in his majesty.
²⁷The eternal God is your refuge,
and underneath are the everlasting
arms.
He will drive out your enemy before you,
saying, 'Destroy him!'
²⁸So Israel will live in safety alone;
Jacob's spring is secure
in a land of grain and new wine,
where the heavens drop dew.
²⁹Blessed are you, O Israel!
Who is like you,
a people saved by the LORD?
He is your shield and helper
and your glorious sword.
Your enemies will cower before you,
and you will trample down their high
places.^b"

The Death of Moses

34 Then Moses climbed Mount Nebo
from the plains of Moab to the top of
Pisgah, across from Jericho. There the LORD
showed him the whole land—from Gilead to
Dan, ²all of Naphtali, the territory of Ephraim
and Manasseh, all the land of Judah as far as the
western sea,^c ³the Negev and the whole region
from the Valley of Jericho, the City of Palms,
as far as Zoar. ⁴Then the LORD said to him,
"This is the land I promised on oath to Abraham, Isaac and Jacob when I said, 'I will give it
to your descendants.' I have let you see it with
your eyes, but you will not cross over into it."

⁵And Moses the servant of the LORD died
there in Moab, as the LORD had said. ⁶He buried him^d in Moab, in the valley opposite Beth

^a16 Or *of the one separated from*   ^b29 Or *will tread upon their bodies*   ^c2 That is, the Mediterranean   ^d6 Or *He was buried*

Deuteronomy 34:4–5

Then the LORD said to him, "This is the land I promised on oath to Abraham, Isaac and Jacob when I said, 'I will give it to your descendants.' I have let you see it with your eyes, but you will not cross over into it." And Moses the servant of the LORD died there in Moab, as the LORD had said.

reflection

1 Put yourself in Moses' shoes. Do you think he was satisfied with his legacy? Why or why not?

2 Who are you responsible for leading at home, work or church?

3 Pray that you will leave a spiritual legacy in your wake—that those who follow after you will tell others about Jesus Christ.

RELATED READINGS

Genesis 12:1–2;
Hebrews 10:39—12:2

Read: Deuteronomy 34:1–12

ONE FEBRUARY DAY in Ireland in the 1800s, John D'Esterre was killed in a duel, leaving an 18-year-old widow named Jane. With little money and past due bills, the bailiffs came to seize their property and threatened to return to sell her husband's body to the mortuary. Jane took her husband's body and buried it in an unmarked grave. Then she fled to a village on the Scottish-English border.

One day, feeling despondent, Jane sat beside the river and contemplated suicide. Just then, Jane heard whistling. A young ploughman, known as a "hymn-whistler," had begun work in the fields. Jane was touched. She thought of her two small children who needed her. She was healthy and had her whole life before her. If a man plowing fields could whistle, she could keep going. So she returned to Dublin. Shortly afterward, she attended St. George's Church and trusted Jesus Christ as her Savior. God gave her an unusual burden: to pray earnestly for her children and the 12 generations to follow, desiring to leave a spiritual legacy.

Jane later married a wealthy man named Captain John Guinness and continued in prayer. Her son, Grattan, became a minister. His preaching helped trigger the 1859 Irish revival where up to 100,000 people came to Christ in one year. Generations later, Dr. Os Guinness, son of Chinese missionaries, gained worldwide acclaim as Christ's spokesman. Though she didn't live to see all the results of her many prayers, Jane left an incredible legacy.

For 40 years, Moses faithfully served God. He nurtured the promise planted centuries earlier that his people would live in their own land and worship the one true God. Though Moses had a moment of defiance when he struck the rock, he was still allowed to see the promised land. His legacy? He recorded God's laws for posterity; he led God's people to freedom—all the way to the brink of the promised land.

You may not be a Moses leading a nation out of bondage, but, like Jane Guinness, you can leave a spiritual heritage. The most powerful instrument at your disposal is prayer. No matter what your situation in life, no matter what your gifts or talents, you can pray for others. You can leave a beautiful legacy, asking God that those who follow after you will impact the world for Christ.

Tuesday

Peor, but to this day no one knows where his grave is. **7**Moses was a hundred and twenty years old when he died, yet his eyes were not weak nor his strength gone. **8**The Israelites grieved for Moses in the plains of Moab thirty days, until the time of weeping and mourning was over.

9Now Joshua son of Nun was filled with the spirit*ᵃ* of wisdom because Moses had laid his hands on him. So the Israelites lis-tened to him and did what the LORD had commanded Moses.

10Since then, no prophet has risen in Israel like Moses, whom the LORD knew face to face, **11**who did all those miraculous signs and won-ders the LORD sent him to do in Egypt—to Pharaoh and to all his officials and to his whole land. **12**For no one has ever shown the mighty power or performed the awesome deeds that Moses did in the sight of all Israel.

Joshua

Author:
Joshua.

Audience:
The Israelites who settled
in the promised land.

Date:
Late 1300s B.C., with ad-
ditions and edits at later
dates, possibly during the
early monarchy of Israel.

Setting:
Crossing the Jordan River
and entering the promised
land, also called Canaan.

Verse to Remember:
"Be strong and coura-
geous, because you will
lead these people to
inherit the land I swore
to their forefathers to
give them." (1:6)

After 40 years of wandering, it was time for the children of Israel to conquer the promised land. The book of Joshua begins with several exhortations to their new leader, Joshua, to "be strong and courageous." *God was ready to fight for his people.* In some of the many battles they faced, the people disobeyed God or failed to trust him—with disastrous results. But when they obeyed God, *they experienced grand victories,* and the nations learned to fear them. The book of Joshua covers Israel's history from the crossing of the Jordan River to the successful division of the land by tribes, including cities of refuge and towns for the Levites.

The LORD Commands Joshua

1 After the death of Moses the servant of the LORD, the LORD said to Joshua son of Nun, Moses' aide: ²"Moses my servant is dead. Now then, you and all these people, get ready to cross the Jordan River into the land I am about to give to them—to the Israelites. ³I will give you every place where you set your foot, as I promised Moses. ⁴Your territory will extend from the desert to Lebanon, and from the great river, the Euphrates—all the Hittite country—to the Great Sea*a* on the west. ⁵No one will be able to stand up against you all the days of your life. As I was with Moses, so I will be with you; I will never leave you nor forsake you.

⁶"Be strong and courageous, because you will lead these people to inherit the land I swore to their forefathers to give them. ⁷Be strong and

*a*4 That is, the Mediterranean

very courageous. Be careful to obey all the law my servant Moses gave you; do not turn from it to the right or to the left, that you may be successful wherever you go. **8**Do not let this Book of the Law depart from your mouth; meditate on it day and night, so that you may be careful to do everything written in it. Then you will be prosperous and successful. **9**Have I not commanded you? Be strong and courageous. Do not be terrified; do not be discouraged, for the LORD your God will be with you wherever you go."

10So Joshua ordered the officers of the people: **11**"Go through the camp and tell the people, 'Get your supplies ready. Three days from now you will cross the Jordan here to go in and take possession of the land the LORD your God is giving you for your own.'"

12But to the Reubenites, the Gadites and the half-tribe of Manasseh, Joshua said, **13**"Remember the command that Moses the servant of the LORD gave you: 'The LORD your God is giving you rest and has granted you this land.' **14**Your wives, your children and your livestock may stay in the land that Moses gave you east of the Jordan, but all your fighting men, fully armed, must cross over ahead of your brothers. You are to help your brothers **15**until the LORD gives them rest, as he has done for you, and until they too have taken possession of the land that the LORD your God is giving them. After that, you may go back and occupy your own land, which Moses the servant of the LORD gave you east of the Jordan toward the sunrise."

16Then they answered Joshua, "Whatever you have commanded us we will do, and wherever you send us we will go. **17**Just as we fully obeyed Moses, so we will obey you. Only may the LORD your God be with you as he was with Moses. **18**Whoever rebels against your word and does not obey your words, whatever you may command them, will be put to death. Only be strong and courageous!"

Joshua 1:9

God Is With Us

"Have I not commanded you? Be strong and courageous. Do not be terrified; do not be discouraged, for the LORD your God will be with you wherever you go."

Rahab and the Spies

2 Then Joshua son of Nun secretly sent two spies from Shittim. "Go, look over the land," he said, "especially Jericho." So they went and entered the house of a prostitute[a] named Rahab and stayed there.

2The king of Jericho was told, "Look! Some of the Israelites have come here tonight to spy out the land." **3**So the king of Jericho sent this message to Rahab: "Bring out the men who came to you and entered your house, because they have come to spy out the whole land."

4But the woman had taken the two men and hidden them. She said, "Yes, the men came to me, but I did not know where they had come from. **5**At dusk, when it was time to close the city gate, the men left. I don't know which way they went. Go after them quickly. You may catch up with them." **6**(But she had taken them up to the roof and hidden them under the stalks of flax she had laid out on the roof.) **7**So the men set out in pursuit of the spies on the road that leads to the fords of the Jordan, and as soon as the pursuers had gone out, the gate was shut.

8Before the spies lay down for the night, she went up on the roof **9**and said to them, "I know that the LORD has given this land to you and that a great fear of you has fallen on us, so that all who live in this country are melting in fear because of you. **10**We have heard how the LORD dried up the water of the Red Sea[b] for you when you came out of Egypt, and what you did to Sihon and Og, the two kings of the Amorites east of the Jordan, whom you completely destroyed.[c] **11**When we heard of it, our hearts melted and everyone's courage failed because of you, for the LORD your God is God in heaven above and on the earth below. **12**Now then, please swear to me by the LORD that you will show kindness to my family, because I have shown kindness to you. Give me a sure sign **13**that you will spare the lives of my

*a*1 Or possibly *an innkeeper*   *b*10 Hebrew *Yam Suph*; that is, Sea of Reeds   *c*10 The Hebrew term refers to the irrevocable giving over of things or persons to the LORD, often by totally destroying them.

father and mother, my brothers and sisters, and all who belong to them, and that you will save us from death."

¹⁴"Our lives for your lives!" the men assured her. "If you don't tell what we are doing, we will treat you kindly and faithfully when the LORD gives us the land."

¹⁵So she let them down by a rope through the window, for the house she lived in was part of the city wall. ¹⁶Now she had said to them, "Go to the hills so the pursuers will not find you. Hide yourselves there three days until they return, and then go on your way."

¹⁷The men said to her, "This oath you made us swear will not be binding on us ¹⁸unless, when we enter the land, you have tied this scarlet cord in the window through which you let us down, and unless you have brought your father and mother, your brothers and all your family into your house. ¹⁹If anyone goes outside your house into the street, his blood will be on his own head; we will not be responsible. As for anyone who is in the house with you, his blood will be on our head if a hand is laid on him. ²⁰But if you tell what we are doing, we will be released from the oath you made us swear."

²¹"Agreed," she replied. "Let it be as you say." So she sent them away and they departed. And she tied the scarlet cord in the window.

²²When they left, they went into the hills and stayed there three days, until the pursuers had searched all along the road and returned without finding them. ²³Then the two men started back. They went down out of the hills, forded the river and came to Joshua son of Nun and told him everything that had happened to them. ²⁴They said to Joshua, "The LORD has surely given the whole land into our hands; all the people are melting in fear because of us."

Crossing the Jordan

3 Early in the morning Joshua and all the Israelites set out from Shittim and went to the Jordan, where they camped before cross-ing over. ²After three days the officers went throughout the camp, ³giving orders to the people: "When you see the ark of the covenant of the LORD your God, and the priests, who are Levites, carrying it, you are to move out from your positions and follow it. ⁴Then you will know which way to go, since you have never been this way before. But keep a distance of about a thousand yards*ᵃ* between you and the ark; do not go near it."

⁵Joshua told the people, "Consecrate yourselves, for to-morrow the LORD will do amaz-ing things among you."

⁶Joshua said to the priests, "Take up the ark of the covenant and pass on ahead of the people." So they took it up and went ahead of them.

⁷And the LORD said to Joshua, "Today I will begin to exalt you in the eyes of all Israel, so they may know that I am with you as I was with Moses. ⁸Tell the priests who carry the ark of the covenant: 'When you reach the edge of the Jordan's waters, go and stand in the river.'"

⁹Joshua said to the Israelites, "Come here and listen to the words of the LORD your God. ¹⁰This is how you will know that the living God is among you and that he will certainly drive out before you the Canaanites, Hittites, Hivites, Perizzites, Girgashites, Amorites and Jebusites. ¹¹See, the ark of the covenant of the Lord of all the earth will go into the Jordan ahead of you. ¹²Now then, choose twelve men from the tribes of Israel, one from each tribe. ¹³And as soon as the priests who carry the ark of the LORD—the Lord of all the earth—set foot in the Jordan, its waters flowing downstream will be cut off and stand up in a heap."

¹⁴So when the people broke camp to cross the Jordan, the priests carrying the ark of the covenant went ahead of them. ¹⁵Now the Jordan is at flood stage all during harvest. Yet as soon as the priests who carried the ark reached the Jordan and their feet touched the water's edge, ¹⁶the water from upstream stopped flow-ing. It piled up in a heap a great distance away,

---

Joshua 3:5

God Is Amazing

Joshua told the people, "Consecrate yourselves, for tomorrow the LORD will do amazing things among you."

---

*ᵃ*4 Hebrew *about two thousand cubits* (about 900 meters)

Dry Ground

Read: Joshua 3:1–17

I BELIEVE THAT, in guiding us, God deals with us as He dealt with the Israelites as He led them out of Egypt.

The first crossing of the sea was made very easy.

The guidance could not have been simpler: The east wind blew and divided the sea before the people had to cross. Not so much as a foot was wet, except perhaps by a wind-driven spray. Moreover, it was impossible, as it were, to disobey, since they were pursued by Pharaoh's chariots and horsemen (Exodus 14).

But how different it was on the second occasion. The priests had to walk into the strong current of a flooded river and stand still there. An order to scoff at, and what a sight it would pose to other men! But it was not until they obeyed—without a particle of visible proof that they were doing right—and carried the ark right into the river, that the water rolled back before them (Joshua 3).

So it may be for us, as we go on with God. You and I may be called again and again to walk right into our own "rivers," whatever they may be—to wet our feet in them. We may be called to do what nobody understands except those to whom the word of guidance is given—and with it, His promise too.

But understand this: The word must come first, and also His promise. You and I must be sure of what we are called to do, with an inward conviction that absolutely nothing can shake. In my own case, again and again, I have had to wet my feet in the water . . . Only God and those who have to walk in that path know how hard this kind of faith-life can be. But He does know.

If only the next step is clear, then the one thing to do is take it! Don't pledge your Lord or yourself to any steps beyond what you know. You don't see them yet.

Once when I was climbing at night, in a forest before there was a made path, I learned what was meant by the words of Psalm 119:105: Your word is a lamp to my feet, and a light for my path.

I had only a lantern, and had to hold it very low or I would certainly have slipped on those rough rocks.

We don't walk spiritually by electric light, but by a hand-held lantern. And a lantern shows only the next step—not several steps ahead.

—Amy Carmichael

Joshua 3:17

The priests who carried the ark of the covenant of the LORD stood firm on dry ground in the middle of the Jordan, while all Israel passed by until the whole nation had completed the crossing on dry ground.

reflection

1 Why do you suppose God saw fit to repeat this miracle for a new generation?

2 Why did God direct the Israelites through such a difficult path?

3 When have you sensed God's guidance leading you in a difficult direction?

RELATED READINGS

Exodus 13:17—14:31;
Psalm 106:1–12

Wednesday

Go to page 261 for your next devotional reading.

259

at a town called Adam in the vicinity of Zarethan, while the water flowing down to the Sea of the Arabah (the Salt Sea[a]) was completely cut off. So the people crossed over opposite Jericho. [17]The priests who carried the ark of the covenant of the LORD stood firm on dry ground in the middle of the Jordan, while all Israel passed by until the whole nation had completed the crossing on dry ground.

4 When the whole nation had finished crossing the Jordan, the LORD said to Joshua, [2]"Choose twelve men from among the people, one from each tribe, [3]and tell them to take up twelve stones from the middle of the Jordan from right where the priests stood and to carry them over with you and put them down at the place where you stay tonight."

[4]So Joshua called together the twelve men he had appointed from the Israelites, one from each tribe, [5]and said to them, "Go over before the ark of the LORD your God into the middle of the Jordan. Each of you is to take up a stone on his shoulder, according to the number of the tribes of the Israelites, [6]to serve as a sign among you. In the future, when your children ask you, 'What do these stones mean?' [7]tell them that the flow of the Jordan was cut off before the ark of the covenant of the LORD. When it crossed the Jordan, the waters of the Jordan were cut off. These stones are to be a memorial to the people of Israel forever."

[8]So the Israelites did as Joshua commanded them. They took twelve stones from the middle of the Jordan, according to the number of the tribes of the Israelites, as the LORD had told Joshua; and they carried them over with them to their camp, where they put them down. [9]Joshua set up the twelve stones that had been[b] in the middle of the Jordan at the spot where the priests who carried the ark of the covenant had stood. And they are there to this day.

[10]Now the priests who carried the ark remained standing in the middle of the Jordan until everything the LORD had commanded Joshua was done by the people, just as Moses had directed Joshua. The people hurried over, [11]and as soon as all of them had crossed, the ark of the LORD and the priests came to the other side while the people watched. [12]The men of Reuben, Gad and the half-tribe of Manasseh crossed over, armed, in front of the Israelites, as Moses had directed them. [13]About forty thousand armed for battle crossed over before the LORD to the plains of Jericho for war.

[14]That day the LORD exalted Joshua in the sight of all Israel; and they revered him all the days of his life, just as they had revered Moses.

[15]Then the LORD said to Joshua, [16]"Command the priests carrying the ark of the Testimony to come up out of the Jordan."

[17]So Joshua commanded the priests, "Come up out of the Jordan."

[18]And the priests came up out of the river carrying the ark of the covenant of the LORD. No sooner had they set their feet on the dry ground than the waters of the Jordan returned to their place and ran at flood stage as before.

[19]On the tenth day of the first month the people went up from the Jordan and camped at Gilgal on the eastern border of Jericho. [20]And Joshua set up at Gilgal the twelve stones they had taken out of the Jordan. [21]He said to the Israelites, "In the future when your descendants ask their fathers, 'What do these stones mean?' [22]tell them, 'Israel crossed the Jordan on dry ground.' [23]For the LORD your God dried up the Jordan before you until you had crossed over. The LORD your God did to the Jordan just what he had done to the Red Sea[c] when he dried it up before us until we had crossed over. [24]He did this so that all the peoples of the earth might know that the hand of the LORD is powerful and so that you might always fear the LORD your God."

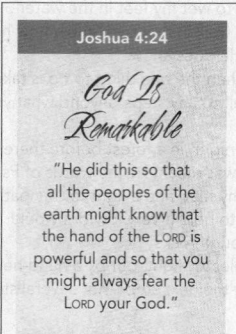

Joshua 4:24

God Is Remarkable

"He did this so that all the peoples of the earth might know that the hand of the LORD is powerful and so that you might always fear the LORD your God."

---

[a]16 That is, the Dead Sea   [b]9 Or *Joshua also set up twelve stones*   [c]23 Hebrew *Yam Suph*; that is, Sea of Reeds

Memorial Stones

Read: Joshua 4:1–7

FROM BIRTHSTONES TO GRAVESTONES, diamond rings to marble statues, humankind has used stones from time immemorial to mark significant life passages: births, deaths, engagements, victory in war, monuments to great people. What is it that makes stones such perfect material for the job? They're durable, slow to age, solid and often very beautiful. Stones symbolize a permanence reaching beyond our short human life spans.

God knows that we need tangible reminders of our encounters with him. No matter how life-changing an event may be, our memories cannot always retain the impact. We forget. And we forget to tell our children. A spiritual heritage can be washed away. This is why God instructed Joshua, Israel's leader, to build a memorial of stones when God piled up the waters of the Jordan so that the Israelites could walk across the dry riverbed, just as he had parted the waters of the Red Sea. The memorial was to be a visible reminder that he would lead their children across a sea of obstacles for generations to come.

Consider where God directed Joshua to get the stones from—not the river shallows or banks, but from the middle of the Jordan where the priests stood with the ark of the covenant. It was a picture of the presence of God in the depths, among his people. Once-submerged stones were brought to the riverbank and set up as a memorial.

What are you facing today? Whatever the challenge, do you believe that God can part the deep and flowing waters? Take a moment and ask God to reveal his presence and power. Then find some sort of "stone" (something concrete—a literal rock, a photograph, a note from a friend) to serve as a visual reminder of God's power to intervene in your journey. Build a monument in your yard or in your house or on your desk—and in your heart. Use this monument as a reminder of this moment, both for you and for generations to come. God cares deeply that you remember his goodness and pass those memories on to the next generation.

Joshua 4:5–7

"Go over before the ark of the LORD your God into the middle of the Jordan. Each of you is to take up a stone on his shoulder, according to the number of the tribes of the Israelites, to serve as a sign among you. In the future, when your children ask you, 'What do these stones mean?' tell them that the flow of the Jordan was cut off before the ark of the covenant of the LORD."

reflection

1 Recall one instance in which God miraculously cleared the way for you.

2 What memory "stone" can you save to remind you of God's work?

3 Whether or not you are a mother, children probably live in your community or extended family. Choose a child in your life to tell this story to. Who will you share this memory with and how might it glorify God?

RELATED READINGS

Exodus 3:14–15;
Psalms 77:11–12; 78:5–8;
145:4–5

Thursday

Go to page 263 for your next devotional reading.

Circumcision at Gilgal

5 Now when all the Amorite kings west of the Jordan and all the Canaanite kings along the coast heard how the LORD had dried up the Jordan before the Israelites until we had crossed over, their hearts melted and they no longer had the courage to face the Israelites.

²At that time the LORD said to Joshua, "Make flint knives and circumcise the Israelites again." ³So Joshua made flint knives and circumcised the Israelites at Gibeath Haaraloth.*ᵃ*

⁴Now this is why he did so: All those who came out of Egypt—all the men of military age—died in the desert on the way after leaving Egypt. ⁵All the people that came out had been circumcised, but all the people born in the desert during the journey from Egypt had not. ⁶The Israelites had moved about in the desert forty years until all the men who were of military age when they left Egypt had died, since they had not obeyed the LORD. For the LORD had sworn to them that they would not see the land that he had solemnly promised their fathers to give us, a land flowing with milk and honey. ⁷So he raised up their sons in their place, and these were the ones Joshua circumcised. They were still uncircumcised because they had not been circumcised on the way. ⁸And after the whole nation had been circumcised, they remained where they were in camp until they were healed.

⁹Then the LORD said to Joshua, "Today I have rolled away the reproach of Egypt from you." So the place has been called Gilgal*ᵇ* to this day.

¹⁰On the evening of the fourteenth day of the month, while camped at Gilgal on the plains of Jericho, the Israelites celebrated the Passover. ¹¹The day after the Passover, that very day, they ate some of the produce of the land: unleavened bread and roasted grain. ¹²The manna stopped the day after*ᶜ* they ate this food from the land; there was no longer any manna for the Israelites, but that year they ate of the produce of Canaan.

The Fall of Jericho

¹³Now when Joshua was near Jericho, he looked up and saw a man standing in front of him with a drawn sword in his hand. Joshua went up to him and asked, "Are you for us or for our enemies?"

¹⁴"Neither," he replied, "but as commander of the army of the LORD I have now come." Then Joshua fell facedown to the ground in reverence, and asked him, "What message does my Lord*ᵈ* have for his servant?"

¹⁵The commander of the LORD's army replied, "Take off your sandals, for the place where you are standing is holy." And Joshua did so.

6 Now Jericho was tightly shut up because of the Israelites. No one went out and no one came in.

²Then the LORD said to Joshua, "See, I have delivered Jericho into your hands, along with its king and its fighting men. ³March around the city once with all the armed men. Do this for six days. ⁴Have seven priests carry trumpets of rams' horns in front of the ark. On the seventh day, march around the city seven times, with the priests blowing the trumpets. ⁵When you hear them sound a long blast on the trumpets, have all the people give a loud shout; then the wall of the city will collapse and the people will go up, every man straight in."

⁶So Joshua son of Nun called the priests and said to them, "Take up the ark of the covenant of the LORD and have seven priests carry trumpets in front of it." ⁷And he ordered the people, "Advance! March around the city, with the armed guard going ahead of the ark of the LORD."

⁸When Joshua had spoken to the people, the seven priests carrying the seven trumpets before the LORD went forward, blowing their trumpets, and the ark of the LORD's covenant followed them. ⁹The armed guard marched ahead of the priests who blew the trumpets, and the rear guard followed the ark. All this time the trumpets were sounding. ¹⁰But Joshua had commanded the people, "Do not give a war cry, do not raise your voices, do not say a word until the day I tell you to shout. Then shout!" ¹¹So he had the ark of the LORD carried around the city, circling it once. Then the people returned to camp and spent the night there.

¹²Joshua got up early the next morning and

ᵃ3 Gibeath Haaraloth means hill of foreskins.   *ᵇ9 Gilgal sounds like the Hebrew for roll.*   *ᶜ12 Or the day*   *ᵈ14 Or lord*

Victory Cry

Read: Joshua 6:1–20

PICTURE YOURSELF at your niece's final soccer game of the season. If they win, they will be in the playoffs. The team has been behind the entire game, and they look exhausted. But just in the last few minutes they've tied the score. Now the seconds are ticking away. The game is almost over. The parents are white-knuckled. The fans are holding their breath. Your niece makes a great move and takes the ball down the field. You're shouting at the top of your lungs, "Go, go!" She makes a an incredible pass across the field. You know this is it . . . just one goal away from victory.

The Israelites had waited 40 years to shout the victory cry. Now they're at the goal. For six days they had followed God's commands and had marched silently around Jericho. Now it was the seventh day. Imagine the suspense . . . the eerie quiet building up for six long days. Would God himself appear to tear down the walls? Would the inhabitants of Jericho surrender without a fight? Would the Israelites make the right play? Then God gave the go-ahead: Sound the trumpets; shout for victory, and the walls of the city will collapse. Just as God promised, "the trumpets sounded, the people shouted," and victory was theirs. The Israelites conquered the city of Jericho, finally claiming their rightful place in the promised land.

The Israelites must have felt so relieved to claim a victory after so many years of waiting and preparing. Can you relate? Have you been feeling that you are in a holding pattern, that your circumstances are not changing? Do you long to have resolution, to have even a small victory? God is working even while you are waiting. Think of this time of waiting as a process that will eventually culminate in a victory. In the meantime, remain faithful and know that God is there with you, preparing you for the battles, goals and victories to come.

Go to page 269 for your next devotional reading.

Joshua 6:20

When the trumpets sounded, the people shouted, and at the sound of the trumpet, when the people gave a loud shout, the wall collapsed; so every man charged straight in, and they took the city.

reflection

1 Is there an area in your life in which you are waiting for a change? What is God teaching you as you wait?

2 What is your attitude when you are forced into waiting for something? What can you learn from the Israelites' experiences in the desert and then in the promised land?

3 Have you recently experienced a victory in your life? Who can you encourage by sharing your story?

RELATED READINGS

Numbers 14:6–9;
Joshua 2:1–24;
2 Corinthians 4:16–18

Friday

the priests took up the ark of the LORD. 13The seven priests carrying the seven trumpets went forward, marching before the ark of the LORD and blowing the trumpets. The armed men went ahead of them and the rear guard followed the ark of the LORD, while the trumpets kept sounding. 14So on the second day they marched around the city once and returned to the camp. They did this for six days.

15On the seventh day, they got up at daybreak and marched around the city seven times in the same manner, except that on that day they circled the city seven times. 16The seventh time around, when the priests sounded the trumpet blast, Joshua commanded the people, "Shout! For the LORD has given you the city! 17The city and all that is in it are to be devoted*a* to the LORD. Only Rahab the prostitute*b* and all who are with her in her house shall be spared, because she hid the spies we sent. 18But keep away from the devoted things, so that you will not bring about your own destruction by taking any of them. Otherwise you will make the camp of Israel liable to destruction and bring trouble on it. 19All the silver and gold and the articles of bronze and iron are sacred to the LORD and must go into his treasury."

20When the trumpets sounded, the people shouted, and at the sound of the trumpet, when the people gave a loud shout, the wall collapsed; so every man charged straight in, and they took the city. 21They devoted the city to the LORD and destroyed with the sword every living thing in it—men and women, young and old, cattle, sheep and donkeys.

22Joshua said to the two men who had spied out the land, "Go into the prostitute's house and bring her out and all who belong to her, in accordance with your oath to her." 23So the young men who had done the spying went in and brought out Rahab, her father and mother and brothers and all who belonged to her. They brought out her entire family and put them in a place outside the camp of Israel.

24Then they burned the whole city and everything in it, but they put the silver and gold and the articles of bronze and iron into the trea-

sury of the LORD's house. 25But Joshua spared Rahab the prostitute, with her family and all who belonged to her, because she hid the men Joshua had sent as spies to Jericho—and she lives among the Israelites to this day.

26At that time Joshua pronounced this solemn oath: "Cursed before the LORD is the man who undertakes to rebuild this city, Jericho:

"At the cost of his firstborn son
    will he lay its foundations;
at the cost of his youngest
    will he set up its gates."

27So the LORD was with Joshua, and his fame spread throughout the land.

Achan's Sin

7 But the Israelites acted unfaithfully in regard to the devoted things*c*; Achan son of Carmi, the son of Zimri,*d* the son of Zerah, of the tribe of Judah, took some of them. So the LORD's anger burned against Israel.

2Now Joshua sent men from Jericho to Ai, which is near Beth Aven to the east of Bethel, and told them, "Go up and spy out the region." So the men went up and spied out Ai.

3When they returned to Joshua, they said, "Not all the people will have to go up against Ai. Send two or three thousand men to take it and do not weary all the people, for only a few men are there." 4So about three thousand men went up; but they were routed by the men of Ai, 5who killed about thirty-six of them. They chased the Israelites from the city gate as far as the stone quarries*e* and struck them down on the slopes. At this the hearts of the people melted and became like water.

6Then Joshua tore his clothes and fell facedown to the ground before the ark of the LORD, remaining there till evening. The elders of Israel did the same, and sprinkled dust on their heads. 7And Joshua said, "Ah, Sovereign LORD, why did you ever bring this people across the Jordan to deliver us into the hands of the Amorites to destroy us? If only we had been content to stay on the other side of the Jordan! 8O Lord, what can I say, now that Israel has

---

a17 The Hebrew term refers to the irrevocable giving over of things or persons to the LORD, often by totally destroying them; also in verses 18 and 21.   *b17* Or possibly *innkeeper*; also in verses 22 and 25   *c1* The Hebrew term refers to the irrevocable giving over of things or persons to the LORD, often by totally destroying them; also in verses 11, 12, 13 and 15.   *d1* See Septuagint and 1 Chron. 2:6; Hebrew *Zabdi*; also in verses 17 and 18.   *e5* Or *as far as Shebarim* been routed by its enemies? ⁹The Canaanites and the other people of the country will hear about this and they will surround us and wipe out our name from the earth. What then will you do for your own great name?"

¹⁰The Lord said to Joshua, "Stand up! What are you doing down on your face? ¹¹Israel has sinned; they have violated my covenant, which I commanded them to keep. They have taken some of the devoted things; they have stolen, they have lied, they have put them with their own possessions. ¹²That is why the Israelites cannot stand against their enemies; they turn their backs and run because they have been made liable to destruction. I will not be with you anymore unless you destroy whatever among you is devoted to destruction.

¹³"Go, consecrate the people. Tell them, 'Consecrate yourselves in preparation for tomorrow; for this is what the Lord, the God of Israel, says: That which is devoted is among you, O Israel. You cannot stand against your enemies until you remove it.

¹⁴"'In the morning, present yourselves tribe by tribe. The tribe that the Lord takes shall come forward clan by clan; the clan that the Lord takes shall come forward family by family; and the family that the Lord takes shall come forward man by man. ¹⁵He who is caught with the devoted things shall be destroyed by fire, along with all that belongs to him. He has violated the covenant of the Lord and has done a disgraceful thing in Israel!'"

¹⁶Early the next morning Joshua had Israel come forward by tribes, and Judah was taken. ¹⁷The clans of Judah came forward, and he took the Zerahites. He had the clan of the Zerahites come forward by families, and Zimri was taken. ¹⁸Joshua had his family come forward man by man, and Achan son of Carmi, the son of Zimri, the son of Zerah, of the tribe of Judah, was taken.

Joshua 7:7
God Is Sovereign
And Joshua said, "Ah, Sovereign Lord, why did you ever bring this people across the Jordan to deliver us into the hands of the Amorites to destroy us?"

¹⁹Then Joshua said to Achan, "My son, give glory to the Lord,ᵃ the God of Israel, and give him the praise.ᵇ Tell me what you have done; do not hide it from me."

²⁰Achan replied, "It is true! I have sinned against the Lord, the God of Israel. This is what I have done: ²¹When I saw in the plunder a beautiful robe from Babylonia,ᶜ two hundred shekelsᵈ of silver and a wedge of gold weighing fifty shekels,ᵉ I coveted them and took them. They are hidden in the ground inside my tent, with the silver underneath."

²²So Joshua sent messengers, and they ran to the tent, and there it was, hidden in his tent, with the silver underneath. ²³They took the things from the tent, brought them to Joshua and all the Israelites and spread them out before the Lord.

²⁴Then Joshua, together with all Israel, took Achan son of Zerah, the silver, the robe, the gold wedge, his sons and daughters, his cattle, donkeys and sheep, his tent and all that he had, to the Valley of Achor. ²⁵Joshua said, "Why have you brought this trouble on us? The Lord will bring trouble on you today."

Then all Israel stoned him, and after they had stoned the rest, they burned them. ²⁶Over Achan they heaped up a large pile of rocks, which remains to this day. Then the Lord turned from his fierce anger. Therefore that place has been called the Valley of Achorᶠ ever since.

Ai Destroyed

8 Then the Lord said to Joshua, "Do not be afraid; do not be discouraged. Take the whole army with you, and go up and attack Ai. For I have delivered into your hands the king of Ai, his people, his city and his land. ²You shall do to Ai and its king as you did to Jericho and its king, except that you may carry off their plunder and livestock for yourselves. Set an ambush behind the city."

ᵃ**19** A solemn charge to tell the truth ᵇ**19** Or *and confess to him* ᶜ**21** Hebrew *Shinar* ᵈ**21** That is, about 5 pounds (about 2.3 kilograms) ᵉ**21** That is, about 1 1/4 pounds (about 0.6 kilogram) ᶠ**26** *Achor* means *trouble.*

³So Joshua and the whole army moved out to attack Ai. He chose thirty thousand of his best fighting men and sent them out at night ⁴with these orders: "Listen carefully. You are to set an ambush behind the city. Don't go very far from it. All of you be on the alert. ⁵I and all those with me will advance on the city, and when the men come out against us, as they did before, we will flee from them. ⁶They will pursue us until we have lured them away from the city, for they will say, 'They are running away from us as they did before.' So when we flee from them, ⁷you are to rise up from ambush and take the city. The LORD your God will give it into your hand. ⁸When you have taken the city, set it on fire. Do what the LORD has commanded. See to it; you have my orders."

⁹Then Joshua sent them off, and they went to the place of ambush and lay in wait between Bethel and Ai, to the west of Ai—but Joshua spent that night with the people.

¹⁰Early the next morning Joshua mustered his men, and he and the leaders of Israel marched before them to Ai. ¹¹The entire force that was with him marched up and approached the city and arrived in front of it. They set up camp north of Ai, with the valley between them and the city. ¹²Joshua had taken about five thousand men and set them in ambush between Bethel and Ai, to the west of the city. ¹³They had the soldiers take up their positions—all those in the camp to the north of the city and the ambush to the west of it. That night Joshua went into the valley.

¹⁴When the king of Ai saw this, he and all the men of the city hurried out early in the morning to meet Israel in battle at a certain place overlooking the Arabah. But he did not know that an ambush had been set against him behind the city. ¹⁵Joshua and all Israel let themselves be driven back before them, and they fled toward the desert. ¹⁶All the men of Ai were called to pursue them, and they pur-

sued Joshua and were lured away from the city. ¹⁷Not a man remained in Ai or Bethel who did not go after Israel. They left the city open and went in pursuit of Israel.

¹⁸Then the LORD said to Joshua, "Hold out toward Ai the javelin that is in your hand, for into your hand I will deliver the city." So Joshua held out his javelin toward Ai. ¹⁹As soon as he did this, the men in the ambush rose quickly from their position and rushed forward. They entered the city and captured it and quickly set it on fire.

²⁰The men of Ai looked back and saw the smoke of the city rising against the sky, but they had no chance to escape in any direction, for the Israelites who had been fleeing toward the desert had turned back against their pursuers. ²¹For when Joshua and all Israel saw that the ambush had taken the city and that smoke was going up from the city, they turned around and attacked the men of Ai. ²²The men of the ambush also came out of the city against them, so that they were caught in the middle, with Israelites on both sides. Israel cut them down, leaving them neither survivors nor fugitives. ²³But they took the king of Ai alive and brought him to Joshua.

²⁴When Israel had finished killing all the men of Ai in the fields and in the desert where they had chased them, and when every one of them had been put to the sword, all the Israelites returned to Ai and killed those who were in it. ²⁵Twelve thousand men and women fell that day—all the people of Ai. ²⁶For Joshua did not draw back the hand that held out his javelin until he had destroyed[a] all who lived in Ai. ²⁷But Israel did carry off for themselves the livestock and plunder of this city, as the LORD had instructed Joshua.

²⁸So Joshua burned Ai and made it a permanent heap of ruins, a desolate place to this day. ²⁹He hung the king of Ai on a tree and left him there until evening. At sunset, Joshua ordered them to take his body from the tree and throw

---

Joshua 8:18

God Is a Deliverer

Then the LORD said to Joshua, "Hold out toward Ai the javelin that is in your hand, for into your hand I will deliver the city." So Joshua held out his javelin toward Ai.

---

[a]26 The Hebrew term refers to the irrevocable giving over of things or persons to the LORD, often by totally destroying them.

it down at the entrance of the city gate. And they raised a large pile of rocks over it, which remains to this day.

The Covenant Renewed at Mount Ebal

³⁰Then Joshua built on Mount Ebal an altar to the LORD, the God of Israel, ³¹as Moses the servant of the LORD had commanded the Israelites. He built it according to what is written in the Book of the Law of Moses—an altar of uncut stones, on which no iron tool had been used. On it they offered to the LORD burnt offerings and sacrificed fellowship offerings.*ᵃ* ³²There, in the presence of the Israelites, Joshua copied on stones the law of Moses, which he had written. ³³All Israel, aliens and citizens alike, with their elders, officials and judges, were standing on both sides of the ark of the covenant of the LORD, facing those who carried it—the priests, who were Levites. Half of the people stood in front of Mount Gerizim and half of them in front of Mount Ebal, as Moses the servant of the LORD had formerly commanded when he gave instructions to bless the people of Israel.

³⁴Afterward, Joshua read all the words of the law—the blessings and the curses—just as it is written in the Book of the Law. ³⁵There was not a word of all that Moses had commanded that Joshua did not read to the whole assembly of Israel, including the women and children, and the aliens who lived among them.

The Gibeonite Deception

9 Now when all the kings west of the Jordan heard about these things—those in the hill country, in the western foothills, and along the entire coast of the Great Sea*ᵇ* as far as Lebanon (the kings of the Hittites, Amorites, Canaanites, Perizzites, Hivites and Jebusites)— ²they came together to make war against Joshua and Israel.

³However, when the people of Gibeon heard what Joshua had done to Jericho and Ai, ⁴they resorted to a ruse: They went as a delegation whose donkeys were loaded*ᶜ* with worn-out sacks and old wineskins, cracked and mended. ⁵The men put worn and patched sandals on their feet and wore old clothes. All the bread of their food supply was dry and moldy. ⁶Then

they went to Joshua in the camp at Gilgal and said to him and the men of Israel, "We have come from a distant country; make a treaty with us."

⁷The men of Israel said to the Hivites, "But perhaps you live near us. How then can we make a treaty with you?"

⁸"We are your servants," they said to Joshua.

But Joshua asked, "Who are you and where do you come from?"

⁹They answered: "Your servants have come from a very distant country because of the fame of the LORD your God. For we have heard reports of him: all that he did in Egypt, ¹⁰and all that he did to the two kings of the Amorites east of the Jordan—Sihon king of Heshbon, and Og king of Bashan, who reigned in Ashtaroth. ¹¹And our elders and all those living in our country said to us, 'Take provisions for your journey; go and meet them and say to them, "We are your servants; make a treaty with us."' ¹²This bread of ours was warm when we packed it at home on the day we left to come to you. But now see how dry and moldy it is. ¹³And these wineskins that we filled were new, but see how cracked they are. And our clothes and sandals are worn out by the very long journey."

¹⁴The men of Israel sampled their provisions but did not inquire of the LORD. ¹⁵Then Joshua made a treaty of peace with them to let them live, and the leaders of the assembly ratified it by oath.

¹⁶Three days after they made the treaty with the Gibeonites, the Israelites heard that they were neighbors, living near them. ¹⁷So the Israelites set out and on the third day came to their cities: Gibeon, Kephirah, Beeroth and Kiriath Jearim. ¹⁸But the Israelites did not attack them, because the leaders of the assembly had sworn an oath to them by the LORD, the God of Israel.

The whole assembly grumbled against the leaders, ¹⁹but all the leaders answered, "We have given them our oath by the LORD, the God of Israel, and we cannot touch them now. ²⁰This is what we will do to them: We will let them

---

ᵃ31 Traditionally peace offerings   ᵇ1 That is, the Mediterranean   ᶜ4 Most Hebrew manuscripts; some Hebrew manuscripts, Vulgate and Syriac (see also Septuagint) They prepared provisions and loaded their donkeys live, so that wrath will not fall on us for breaking the oath we swore to them." [21]They continued, "Let them live, but let them be woodcutters and water carriers for the entire community." So the leaders' promise to them was kept.

[22]Then Joshua summoned the Gibeonites and said, "Why did you deceive us by saying, 'We live a long way from you,' while actually you live near us? [23]You are now under a curse: You will never cease to serve as woodcutters and water carriers for the house of my God."

[24]They answered Joshua, "Your servants were clearly told how the LORD your God had commanded his servant Moses to give you the whole land and to wipe out all its inhabitants from before you. So we feared for our lives because of you, and that is why we did this. [25]We are now in your hands. Do to us whatever seems good and right to you."

[26]So Joshua saved them from the Israelites, and they did not kill them. [27]That day he made the Gibeonites woodcutters and water carriers for the community and for the altar of the LORD at the place the LORD would choose. And that is what they are to this day.

The Sun Stands Still

10 Now Adoni-Zedek king of Jerusalem heard that Joshua had taken Ai and totally destroyed[a] it, doing to Ai and its king as he had done to Jericho and its king, and that the people of Gibeon had made a treaty of peace with Israel and were living near them. [2]He and his people were very much alarmed at this, because Gibeon was an important city, like one of the royal cities; it was larger than Ai, and all its men were good fighters. [3]So Adoni-Zedek king of Jerusalem appealed to Hoham king of Hebron, Piram king of Jarmuth, Japhia king of Lachish and Debir king of Eglon. [4]"Come up and help me attack Gibeon," he said, "because it has made peace with Joshua and the Israelites."

[5]Then the five kings of the Amorites—the kings of Jerusalem, Hebron, Jarmuth, Lachish and Eglon—joined forces. They moved up with all their troops and took up positions against Gibeon and attacked it.

[6]The Gibeonites then sent word to Joshua in the camp at Gilgal: "Do not abandon your servants. Come up to us quickly and save us! Help us, because all the Amorite kings from the hill country have joined forces against us."

[7]So Joshua marched up from Gilgal with his entire army, including all the best fighting men. [8]The LORD said to Joshua, "Do not be afraid of them; I have given them into your hand. Not one of them will be able to withstand you."

[9]After an all-night march from Gilgal, Joshua took them by surprise. [10]The LORD threw them into confusion before Israel, who defeated them in a great victory at Gibeon. Israel pursued them along the road going up to Beth Horon and cut them down all the way to Azekah and Makkedah. [11]As they fled before Israel on the road down from Beth Horon to Azekah, the LORD hurled large hailstones down on them from the sky, and more of them died from the hailstones than were killed by the swords of the Israelites.

[12]On the day the LORD gave the Amorites over to Israel, Joshua said to the LORD in the presence of Israel:

Joshua 10:14

God Fights for Us

There has never been a day like it before or since, a day when the LORD listened to a man. Surely the LORD was fighting for Israel!

"O sun, stand still over
                Gibeon,
    O moon, over the Valley
                of Aijalon."
[13]So the sun stood still,
    and the moon stopped,
        till the nation avenged
            itself on[b] its
                enemies,

as it is written in the Book of Jashar.

The sun stopped in the middle of the sky and delayed going down about a full day. [14]There has never been a day like it before or since, a day when the LORD listened to a man. Surely the LORD was fighting for Israel!

---

[a]1 The Hebrew term refers to the irrevocable giving over of things or persons to the LORD, often by totally destroying them; also in verses 28, 35, 37, 39 and 40. [b]13 Or *nation triumphed over*

It's Time

SHIPHRAH AND PUAH

"COME QUICKLY! It's almost time."

Gathering the folds of her long robe in her well-worn hands, Shiphrah hurried through the door. Her eyes narrowed and adjusted to the relative darkness inside the home. Light from a small oil lantern cast the shadow of two women on the wall. One squatted in a corner, knees bent, as another woman hunched beside her.

"A fresh cloth, Shiphrah!" one of the shadows barked. "I can see the head."

Puah always was the bossier of the two women. They were midwives by training and friends by choice. Shiphrah obediently brought the strips of cloth to Puah.

It was an ordinary day. Women birthed babies into the world all the time. But today was different. This baby was different; it was a boy. The king of Egypt made his order clear: If it is a girl, let her live. If it is a boy, kill him. The strength of the Hebrews threatened Pharaoh and intimidated him. He would quell their numbers with his murderous plot and keep their supposed rebellion at bay. But if the women obeyed him, what would that make them? Murderers?

Shiphrah and Puah did not discuss Pharaoh's orders openly. Silently they worked alongside each other, except for the routine bedside manner required at each birth. However, every time, when it became clear they would have to make a decision, their minds raced through their options.

To disobey the highest authority meant certain death. Pharaoh was willing to slaughter innocent children; two midwives were nothing to him. If they did their job, someone would die, but they would live another day. The dilemma tugged at their hearts each time they pondered their duties. The God of the Hebrews had made himself real to them in ways they could not explain. They feared Pharaoh, but they revered God.

Just then, an agonized scream, followed by a loud sigh, snapped both women to attention. It was time.

"Push! Push!" they responded in unison.

—*Prayer*—

My awesome God, I serve you alone, not the world. Help me to be strong against outside influences and keep me focused on your commands.

The midwives, however, feared God and did not do what the king of Egypt had told them to do; they let the boys live.

Exodus 1:17

ASSIGNED READING:

Exodus 1:15–21

Weekend

Go to page 273 for your next devotional reading.

¹⁵Then Joshua returned with all Israel to the camp at Gilgal.

Five Amorite Kings Killed

¹⁶Now the five kings had fled and hidden in the cave at Makkedah. ¹⁷When Joshua was told that the five kings had been found hiding in the cave at Makkedah, ¹⁸he said, "Roll large rocks up to the mouth of the cave, and post some men there to guard it. ¹⁹But don't stop! Pursue your enemies, attack them from the rear and don't let them reach their cities, for the LORD your God has given them into your hand."

²⁰So Joshua and the Israelites destroyed them completely—almost to a man—but the few who were left reached their fortified cities. ²¹The whole army then returned safely to Joshua in the camp at Makkedah, and no one uttered a word against the Israelites.

²²Joshua said, "Open the mouth of the cave and bring those five kings out to me." ²³So they brought the five kings out of the cave—the kings of Jerusalem, Hebron, Jarmuth, Lachish and Eglon. ²⁴When they had brought these kings to Joshua, he summoned all the men of Israel and said to the army commanders who had come with him, "Come here and put your feet on the necks of these kings." So they came forward and placed their feet on their necks.

²⁵Joshua said to them, "Do not be afraid; do not be discouraged. Be strong and courageous. This is what the LORD will do to all the enemies you are going to fight." ²⁶Then Joshua struck and killed the kings and hung them on five trees, and they were left hanging on the trees until evening.

²⁷At sunset Joshua gave the order and they took them down from the trees and threw them into the cave where they had been hiding. At the mouth of the cave they placed large rocks, which are there to this day.

²⁸That day Joshua took Makkedah. He put the city and its king to the sword and totally destroyed everyone in it. He left no survivors. And he did to the king of Makkedah as he had done to the king of Jericho.

Southern Cities Conquered

²⁹Then Joshua and all Israel with him moved on from Makkedah to Libnah and attacked it. ³⁰The LORD also gave that city and its king into Israel's hand. The city and everyone in it Joshua put to the sword. He left no survivors there. And he did to its king as he had done to the king of Jericho.

³¹Then Joshua and all Israel with him moved on from Libnah to Lachish; he took up positions against it and attacked it. ³²The LORD handed Lachish over to Israel, and Joshua took it on the second day. The city and everyone in it he put to the sword, just as he had done to Libnah. ³³Meanwhile, Horam king of Gezer had come up to help Lachish, but Joshua defeated him and his army—until no survivors were left.

³⁴Then Joshua and all Israel with him moved on from Lachish to Eglon; they took up positions against it and attacked it. ³⁵They captured it that same day and put it to the sword and totally destroyed everyone in it, just as they had done to Lachish.

³⁶Then Joshua and all Israel with him went up from Eglon to Hebron and attacked it. ³⁷They took the city and put it to the sword, together with its king, its villages and everyone in it. They left no survivors. Just as at Eglon, they totally destroyed it and everyone in it.

³⁸Then Joshua and all Israel with him turned around and attacked Debir. ³⁹They took the city, its king and its villages, and put them to the sword. Everyone in it they totally destroyed. They left no survivors. They did to Debir and its king as they had done to Libnah and its king and to Hebron.

⁴⁰So Joshua subdued the whole region, including the hill country, the Negev, the western foothills and the mountain slopes, together with all their kings. He left no survivors. He totally destroyed all who breathed, just as the LORD, the God of Israel, had commanded. ⁴¹Joshua subdued them from Kadesh Barnea to Gaza and from the whole region of Goshen to Gibeon. ⁴²All these kings and their lands Joshua conquered in one campaign, because the LORD, the God of Israel, fought for Israel.

⁴³Then Joshua returned with all Israel to the camp at Gilgal.

Northern Kings Defeated

11 When Jabin king of Hazor heard of this, he sent word to Jobab king of Madon, to the kings of Shimron and Acshaph,

[2] and to the northern kings who were in the mountains, in the Arabah south of Kinnereth, in the western foothills and in Naphoth Dor[a] on the west; [3] to the Canaanites in the east and west; to the Amorites, Hittites, Perizzites and Jebusites in the hill country; and to the Hivites below Hermon in the region of Mizpah. [4] They came out with all their troops and a large number of horses and chariots—a huge army, as numerous as the sand on the seashore. [5] All these kings joined forces and made camp together at the Waters of Merom, to fight against Israel.

[6] The Lord said to Joshua, "Do not be afraid of them, because by this time tomorrow I will hand all of them over to Israel, slain. You are to hamstring their horses and burn their chariots."

[7] So Joshua and his whole army came against them suddenly at the Waters of Merom and attacked them, [8] and the Lord gave them into the hand of Israel. They defeated them and pursued them all the way to Greater Sidon, to Misrephoth Maim, and to the Valley of Mizpah on the east, until no survivors were left. [9] Joshua did to them as the Lord had directed: He hamstrung their horses and burned their chariots.

[10] At that time Joshua turned back and captured Hazor and put its king to the sword. (Hazor had been the head of all these kingdoms.) [11] Everyone in it they put to the sword. They totally destroyed[b] them, not sparing anything that breathed, and he burned up Hazor itself.

[12] Joshua took all these royal cities and their kings and put them to the sword. He totally destroyed them, as Moses the servant of the Lord had commanded. [13] Yet Israel did not burn any of the cities built on their mounds—except Hazor, which Joshua burned. [14] The Israelites carried off for themselves all the plunder and livestock of these cities, but all the people they put to the sword until they completely destroyed them, not sparing anyone that breathed. [15] As the Lord commanded his servant Moses, so Moses commanded Joshua, and Joshua did it; he left nothing undone of all that the Lord commanded Moses.

[16] So Joshua took this entire land: the hill country, all the Negev, the whole region of Go-

shen, the western foothills, the Arabah and the mountains of Israel with their foothills, [17] from Mount Halak, which rises toward Seir, to Baal Gad in the Valley of Lebanon below Mount Hermon. He captured all their kings and struck them down, putting them to death. [18] Joshua waged war against all these kings for a long time. [19] Except for the Hivites living in Gibeon, not one city made a treaty of peace with the Israelites, who took them all in battle. [20] For it was the Lord himself who hardened their hearts to wage war against Israel, so that he might destroy them totally, exterminating them without mercy, as the Lord had commanded Moses.

[21] At that time Joshua went and destroyed the Anakites from the hill country: from Hebron, Debir and Anab, from all the hill country of Judah, and from all the hill country of Israel. Joshua totally destroyed them and their towns. [22] No Anakites were left in Israelite territory; only in Gaza, Gath and Ashdod did any survive. [23] So Joshua took the entire land, just as the Lord had directed Moses, and he gave it as an inheritance to Israel according to their tribal divisions.

Then the land had rest from war.

List of Defeated Kings

12 These are the kings of the land whom the Israelites had defeated and whose territory they took over east of the Jordan, from the Arnon Gorge to Mount Hermon, including all the eastern side of the Arabah:

[2] Sihon king of the Amorites,
    who reigned in Heshbon. He ruled from Aroer on the rim of the Arnon Gorge— from the middle of the gorge—to the Jabbok River, which is the border of the Ammonites. This included half of Gilead. [3] He also ruled over the eastern Arabah from the Sea of Kinnereth[c] to the Sea of the Arabah (the Salt Sea[d]), to Beth Jeshimoth, and then southward below the slopes of Pisgah.

[4] And the territory of Og king of Bashan,
    one of the last of the Rephaites, who reigned in Ashtaroth and Edrei. [5] He ruled over Mount Hermon, Salecah, all

a 2 Or *in the heights of Dor*   b 11 The Hebrew term refers to the irrevocable giving over of things or persons to the Lord, often by totally destroying them; also in verses 12, 20 and 21.   c 3 That is, Galilee   d 3 That is, the Dead Sea of Bashan to the border of the people of Geshur and Maacah, and half of Gilead to the border of Sihon king of Heshbon.

⁶Moses, the servant of the LORD, and the Israelites conquered them. And Moses the servant of the LORD gave their land to the Reubenites, the Gadites and the half-tribe of Manasseh to be their possession.

⁷These are the kings of the land that Joshua and the Israelites conquered on the west side of the Jordan, from Baal Gad in the Valley of Lebanon to Mount Halak, which rises toward Seir (their lands Joshua gave as an inheritance to the tribes of Israel according to their tribal divisions— ⁸the hill country, the western foothills, the Arabah, the mountain slopes, the desert and the Negev—the lands of the Hittites, Amorites, Canaanites, Perizzites, Hivites and Jebusites):

⁹ the king of Jericho	one
the king of Ai (near Bethel)	one
¹⁰ the king of Jerusalem	one
the king of Hebron	one
¹¹ the king of Jarmuth	one
the king of Lachish	one
¹² the king of Eglon	one
the king of Gezer	one
¹³ the king of Debir	one
the king of Geder	one
¹⁴ the king of Hormah	one
the king of Arad	one
¹⁵ the king of Libnah	one
the king of Adullam	one
¹⁶ the king of Makkedah	one
the king of Bethel	one
¹⁷ the king of Tappuah	one
the king of Hepher	one
¹⁸ the king of Aphek	one
the king of Lasharon	one
¹⁹ the king of Madon	one
the king of Hazor	one
²⁰ the king of Shimron Meron	one
the king of Acshaph	one
²¹ the king of Taanach	one
the king of Megiddo	one
²² the king of Kedesh	one
the king of Jokneam in Carmel	one
²³ the king of Dor (in Naphoth Dor[a])	one
the king of Goyim in Gilgal	one
²⁴ the king of Tirzah	one
thirty-one kings in all.	

Land Still to Be Taken

13 When Joshua was old and well advanced in years, the LORD said to him, "You are very old, and there are still very large areas of land to be taken over.

²"This is the land that remains: all the regions of the Philistines and Geshurites: ³from the Shihor River on the east of Egypt to the territory of Ekron on the north, all of it counted as Canaanite (the territory of the five Philistine rulers in Gaza, Ashdod, Ashkelon, Gath and Ekron—that of the Avvites); ⁴from the south, all the land of the Canaanites, from Arah of the Sidonians as far as Aphek, the region of the Amorites, ⁵the area of the Gebalites[b]; and all Lebanon to the east, from Baal Gad below Mount Hermon to Lebo[c] Hamath.

⁶"As for all the inhabitants of the mountain regions from Lebanon to Misrephoth Maim, that is, all the Sidonians, I myself will drive them out before the Israelites. Be sure to allocate this land to Israel for an inheritance, as I have instructed you, ⁷and divide it as an inheritance among the nine tribes and half of the tribe of Manasseh."

Division of the Land East of the Jordan

⁸The other half of Manasseh,[d] the Reubenites and the Gadites had received the inheritance that Moses had given them east of the Jordan, as he, the servant of the LORD, had assigned it to them.

⁹It extended from Aroer on the rim of the Arnon Gorge, and from the town in the middle of the gorge, and included the whole plateau of Medeba as far as Dibon, ¹⁰and all the towns of Sihon king of the Amorites, who ruled in Heshbon, out to the border of the Ammonites. ¹¹It also included Gilead, the territory of the people of Geshur and Maacah, all of Mount

---

a23 Or *in the heights of Dor*   *b5* That is, the area of Byblos   *c5* Or *to the entrance to*   *d8* Hebrew *With it* (that is, with the other half of Manasseh)

Never Too Old

IN THE EARLY 1900s, a desperate father prayed for his sick daughter: "God, spare her life and I'll serve you with mine." Miraculously, the girl recovered. The grateful father quit his job, packed his large family (along with a cow and some chickens) and moved to Texas for seminary. In his mid-30s, he became an evangelist who held tent revivals in Texas and Oklahoma.

For many years, the pastor faithfully preached the gospel. Even after reaching the century mark, he'd rise every day and don a three-piece suit. Despite shaky legs and cataract-clouded eyes, he'd wait for his son-in-law, married to the daughter who had nearly died so many years ago, to guide him downtown for coffee. A newcomer asked, "Why do you get so dressed up?" The aged pastor replied, "I never know when I'll lead someone to the Lord. By the way, son, do you know Jesus?" Reverend A. F. Whitlock understood a simple truth: You're never too old to serve God.

As a young man, Joshua was sent to spy out the promised land. Only he and Caleb believed the Israelites could conquer the enemies living there. So the people wandered 40 years until the exodus generation perished—save the two spies. Then, succeeding Moses, Joshua led Israel into the promised land. Though he was about 80, Joshua captained Israel to victory over six nations and 31 kings.

Fast-forward 20 years. Joshua 13:1 somewhat understates, "Joshua was old and well advanced in years." It is estimated he was around 100 years old. Joshua might have expected God to send him on vacation: go float atop the Dead Sea or fish in the Lake of Galilee. But God didn't offer Joshua a retirement plan. Instead he said, "There are still very large areas of land to be taken over." Joshua's next task was to divide the land.

Maybe you think you're too old to keep serving God. You've offered your tithes, taught Sunday school, led women's ministry and sung in the choir. What's left? There are always "lands" left to conquer. There are children to tell stories to, younger women who would love to hear about your history, sick people to visit, prayers to pray, people who have yet to hear the Good News. You're never too old to tell others about God's love.

Go to page 285 for your next devotional reading.

Joshua 13:1

When Joshua was old and well advanced in years, the LORD said to him, "You are very old, and there are still very large areas of land to be taken over."

reflection

1 How has your age affected your ability to serve God (perhaps people don't take you seriously because you're younger or overlook you due to advanced age)?

2 What areas has God placed before you to "conquer" (neighborhood, work, family, etc.)?

3 Explain how Joshua's story encourages you to continue serving God regardless of your age—young or old.

RELATED READINGS

Numbers 13:16—14:10;
Psalm 71:18;
Proverbs 16:31; 20:29;
Isaiah 46:3–4

"I've discovered, to my delight, that spiritual gifts don't age."

Jill Briscoe

273

Hermon and all Bashan as far as Sale-cah— ¹²that is, the whole kingdom of Og in Bashan, who had reigned in Ashtaroth and Edrei and had survived as one of the last of the Rephaites. Moses had defeated them and taken over their land. ¹³But the Israelites did not drive out the people of Geshur and Maacah, so they continue to live among the Israelites to this day.

¹⁴But to the tribe of Levi he gave no inheritance, since the offerings made by fire to the LORD, the God of Israel, are their inheritance, as he promised them.

¹⁵This is what Moses had given to the tribe of Reuben, clan by clan:

¹⁶The territory from Aroer on the rim of the Arnon Gorge, and from the town in the middle of the gorge, and the whole plateau past Medeba ¹⁷to Heshbon and all its towns on the plateau, including Dibon, Bamoth Baal, Beth Baal Meon, ¹⁸Jahaz, Kedemoth, Mephaath, ¹⁹Kiriathaim, Sibmah, Zereth Shahar on the hill in the valley, ²⁰Beth Peor, the slopes of Pisgah, and Beth Jeshimoth— ²¹all the towns on the plateau and the entire realm of Sihon king of the Amorites, who ruled at Heshbon. Moses had defeated him and the Midianite chiefs, Evi, Rekem, Zur, Hur and Reba—princes allied with Sihon—who lived in that country. ²²In addition to those slain in battle, the Israelites had put to the sword Balaam son of Beor, who practiced divination. ²³The boundary of the Reubenites was the bank of the Jordan. These towns and their villages were the inheritance of the Reubenites, clan by clan.

²⁴This is what Moses had given to the tribe of Gad, clan by clan:

²⁵The territory of Jazer, all the towns of Gilead and half the Ammonite country as far as Aroer, near Rabbah; ²⁶and from Heshbon to Ramath Mizpah and Betonim, and from Mahanaim to the territory of Debir; ²⁷and in the valley, Beth Haram,

Beth Nimrah, Succoth and Zaphon with the rest of the realm of Sihon king of Heshbon (the east side of the Jordan, the territory up to the end of the Sea of Kinnereth[a]). ²⁸These towns and their villages were the inheritance of the Gadites, clan by clan.

²⁹This is what Moses had given to the half-tribe of Manasseh, that is, to half the family of the descendants of Manasseh, clan by clan:

³⁰The territory extending from Mahanaim and including all of Bashan, the entire realm of Og king of Bashan—all the settlements of Jair in Bashan, sixty towns, ³¹half of Gilead, and Ashtaroth and Edrei (the royal cities of Og in Bashan). This was for the descendants of Makir son of Manasseh—for half of the sons of Makir, clan by clan.

³²This is the inheritance Moses had given when he was in the plains of Moab across the Jordan east of Jericho. ³³But to the tribe of Levi, Moses had given no inheritance; the LORD, the God of Israel, is their inheritance, as he promised them.

Division of the Land West of the Jordan

14 Now these are the areas the Israelites received as an inheritance in the land of Canaan, which Eleazar the priest, Joshua son of Nun and the heads of the tribal clans of Israel allotted to them. ²Their inheritances were assigned by lot to the nine-and-a-half tribes, as the LORD had commanded through Moses. ³Moses had granted the two-and-a-half tribes their inheritance east of the Jordan but had not granted the Levites an inheritance among the rest, ⁴for the sons of Joseph had become two tribes—Manasseh and Ephraim. The Levites received no share of the land but only towns to live in, with pasturelands for their flocks and herds. ⁵So the Israelites divided the land, just as the LORD had commanded Moses.

Hebron Given to Caleb

⁶Now the men of Judah approached Joshua at Gilgal, and Caleb son of Jephunneh the Kenizzite said to him, "You know what the LORD

---

[a] 27 That is, Galilee

said to Moses the man of God at Kadesh Barnea about you and me. [7]I was forty years old when Moses the servant of the LORD sent me from Kadesh Barnea to explore the land. And I brought him back a report according to my convictions, [8]but my brothers who went up with me made the hearts of the people melt with fear. I, however, followed the LORD my God wholeheartedly. [9]So on that day Moses swore to me, 'The land on which your feet have walked will be your inheritance and that of your children forever, because you have followed the LORD my God wholeheartedly.'[a]

[10]"Now then, just as the LORD promised, he has kept me alive for forty-five years since the time he said this to Moses, while Israel moved about in the desert. So here I am today, eighty-five years old! [11]I am still as strong today as the day Moses sent me out; I'm just as vigorous to go out to battle now as I was then. [12]Now give me this hill country that the LORD promised me that day. You yourself heard then that the Anakites were there and their cities were large and fortified, but, the LORD helping me, I will drive them out just as he said."

[13]Then Joshua blessed Caleb son of Jephunneh and gave him Hebron as his inheritance. [14]So Hebron has belonged to Caleb son of Jephunneh the Kenizzite ever since, because he followed the LORD, the God of Israel, wholeheartedly. [15](Hebron used to be called Kiriath Arba after Arba, who was the greatest man among the Anakites.)

Then the land had rest from war.

Allotment for Judah

15

The allotment for the tribe of Judah, clan by clan, extended down to the territory of Edom, to the Desert of Zin in the extreme south.

[2]Their southern boundary started from the bay at the southern end of the Salt Sea,[b] [3]crossed south of Scorpion[c] Pass, continued on to Zin and went over to the south of Kadesh Barnea. Then it ran past Hezron up to Addar and curved around to Karka. [4]It then passed along to Azmon and joined the Wadi of Egypt, ending at the sea. This is their[d] southern boundary.

[5]The eastern boundary is the Salt Sea as far as the mouth of the Jordan.

The northern boundary started from the bay of the sea at the mouth of the Jordan, [6]went up to Beth Hoglah and continued north of Beth Arabah to the Stone of Bohan son of Reuben. [7]The boundary then went up to Debir from the Valley of Achor and turned north to Gilgal, which faces the Pass of Adummim south of the gorge. It continued along to the waters of En Shemesh and came out at En Rogel. [8]Then it ran up the Valley of Ben Hinnom along the southern slope of the Jebusite city (that is, Jerusalem). From there it climbed to the top of the hill west of the Hinnom Valley at the northern end of the Valley of Rephaim. [9]From the hilltop the boundary headed toward the spring of the waters of Nephtoah, came out at the towns of Mount Ephron and went down toward Baalah (that is, Kiriath Jearim). [10]Then it curved westward from Baalah to Mount Seir, ran along the northern slope of Mount Jearim (that is, Kesalon), continued down to Beth Shemesh and crossed to Timnah. [11]It went to the northern slope of Ekron, turned toward Shikkeron, passed along to Mount Baalah and reached Jabneel. The boundary ended at the sea.

[12]The western boundary is the coastline of the Great Sea.[e] These are the boundaries around the people of Judah by their clans.

[13]In accordance with the LORD's command to him, Joshua gave to Caleb son of Jephunneh a portion in Judah—Kiriath Arba, that is, Hebron. (Arba was the forefather of Anak.) [14]From Hebron Caleb drove out the three Anakites—Sheshai, Ahiman and Talmai—descendants of Anak. [15]From there he marched against the people living in Debir (formerly called Kiriath Sepher). [16]And Caleb said, "I will give my daughter Acsah in marriage to the man who attacks and captures Kiriath Sepher."

---

[a]9 Deut. 1:36   [b]2 That is, the Dead Sea; also in verse 5   [c]3 Hebrew *Akrabbim*   [d]4 Hebrew *your*   [e]12 That is, the Mediterranean; also in verse 47

17Othniel son of Kenaz, Caleb's brother, took it; so Caleb gave his daughter Acsah to him in marriage.

18One day when she came to Othniel, she urged him*a* to ask her father for a field. When she got off her donkey, Caleb asked her, "What can I do for you?"

19She replied, "Do me a special favor. Since you have given me land in the Negev, give me also springs of water." So Caleb gave her the upper and lower springs.

20This is the inheritance of the tribe of Judah, clan by clan:

21The southernmost towns of the tribe of Judah in the Negev toward the boundary of Edom were:

Kabzeel, Eder, Jagur, 22Kinah, Dimonah, Adadah, 23Kedesh, Hazor, Ithnan, 24Ziph, Telem, Bealoth, 25Hazor Hadattah, Kerioth Hezron (that is, Hazor), 26Amam, Shema, Moladah, 27Hazar Gaddah, Heshmon, Beth Pelet, 28Hazar Shual, Beersheba, Biziothiah, 29Baalah, Iim, Ezem, 30Eltolad, Kesil, Hormah, 31Ziklag, Madmannah, Sansannah, 32Lebaoth, Shilhim, Ain and Rimmon—a total of twenty-nine towns and their villages.

33In the western foothills:

Eshtaol, Zorah, Ashnah, 34Zanoah, En Gannim, Tappuah, Enam, 35Jarmuth, Adullam, Socoh, Azekah, 36Shaaraim, Adithaim and Gederah (or Gederothaim)*b*—fourteen towns and their villages.

37Zenan, Hadashah, Migdal Gad, 38Dilean, Mizpah, Joktheel, 39Lachish, Bozkath, Eglon, 40Cabbon, Lahmas, Kitlish, 41Gederoth, Beth Dagon, Naamah and Makkedah—sixteen towns and their villages.

42Libnah, Ether, Ashan, 43Iphtah, Ashnah, Nezib, 44Keilah, Aczib and Mareshah—nine towns and their villages.

45Ekron, with its surrounding settlements and villages; 46west of Ekron, all that were in the vicinity of Ashdod,

together with their villages; 47Ashdod, its surrounding settlements and villages; and Gaza, its settlements and villages, as far as the Wadi of Egypt and the coastline of the Great Sea.

48In the hill country:

Shamir, Jattir, Socoh, 49Dannah, Kiriath Sannah (that is, Debir), 50Anab, Eshtemoh, Anim, 51Goshen, Holon and Giloh—eleven towns and their villages.

52Arab, Dumah, Eshan, 53Janim, Beth Tappuah, Aphekah, 54Humtah, Kiriath Arba (that is, Hebron) and Zior—nine towns and their villages.

55Maon, Carmel, Ziph, Juttah, 56Jezreel, Jokdeam, Zanoah, 57Kain, Gibeah and Timnah—ten towns and their villages.

58Halhul, Beth Zur, Gedor, 59Maarath, Beth Anoth and Eltekon—six towns and their villages.

60Kiriath Baal (that is, Kiriath Jearim) and Rabbah—two towns and their villages.

61In the desert:

Beth Arabah, Middin, Secacah, 62Nibshan, the City of Salt and En Gedi—six towns and their villages.

63Judah could not dislodge the Jebusites, who were living in Jerusalem; to this day the Jebusites live there with the people of Judah.

Allotment for Ephraim and Manasseh

16 The allotment for Joseph began at the Jordan of Jericho,*c* east of the waters of Jericho, and went up from there through the desert into the hill country of Bethel. 2It went on from Bethel (that is, Luz),*d* crossed over to the territory of the Arkites in Ataroth, 3descended westward to the territory of the Japhletites as far as the region of Lower Beth Horon and on to Gezer, ending at the sea.

4So Manasseh and Ephraim, the descendants of Joseph, received their inheritance.

5This was the territory of Ephraim, clan by clan:

---

*a***18** Hebrew and some Septuagint manuscripts; other Septuagint manuscripts (see also note at Judges 1:14) *Othniel, he urged her*   *b***36** Or *Gederah and Gederothaim*   *c***1** *Jordan of Jericho* was possibly an ancient name for the Jordan River.   *d***2** Septuagint; Hebrew *Bethel to Luz*

The boundary of their inheritance went from Ataroth Addar in the east to Upper Beth Horon ⁶and continued to the sea. From Micmethath on the north it curved eastward to Taanath Shiloh, passing by it to Janoah on the east. ⁷Then it went down from Janoah to Ataroth and Naarah, touched Jericho and came out at the Jordan. ⁸From Tappuah the border went west to the Kanah Ravine and ended at the sea. This was the inheritance of the tribe of the Ephraimites, clan by clan. ⁹It also included all the towns and their villages that were set aside for the Ephraimites within the inheritance of the Manassites.

¹⁰They did not dislodge the Canaanites living in Gezer; to this day the Canaanites live among the people of Ephraim but are required to do forced labor.

17 This was the allotment for the tribe of Manasseh as Joseph's firstborn, that is, for Makir, Manasseh's firstborn. Makir was the ancestor of the Gileadites, who had received Gilead and Bashan because the Makirites were great soldiers. ²So this allotment was for the rest of the people of Manasseh—the clans of Abiezer, Helek, Asriel, Shechem, Hepher and Shemida. These are the other male descendants of Manasseh son of Joseph by their clans.

³Now Zelophehad son of Hepher, the son of Gilead, the son of Makir, the son of Manasseh, had no sons but only daughters, whose names were Mahlah, Noah, Hoglah, Milcah and Tirzah. ⁴They went to Eleazar the priest, Joshua son of Nun, and the leaders and said, "The LORD commanded Moses to give us an inheritance among our brothers." So Joshua gave them an inheritance along with the brothers of their father, according to the LORD's command. ⁵Manasseh's share consisted of ten tracts of land besides Gilead and Bashan east of the Jordan, ⁶because the daughters of the tribe of Manasseh received an inheritance among the sons. The land of Gilead belonged to the rest of the descendants of Manasseh.

⁷The territory of Manasseh extended from Asher to Micmethath east of Shechem. The boundary ran southward from there to include the people living at En Tappuah. ⁸(Manasseh had the land of Tappuah, but Tappuah itself, on the boundary of Manasseh, belonged to the Ephraimites.) ⁹Then the boundary continued south to the Kanah Ravine. There were towns belonging to Ephraim lying among the towns of Manasseh, but the boundary of Manasseh was the northern side of the ravine and ended at the sea. ¹⁰On the south the land belonged to Ephraim, on the north to Manasseh. The territory of Manasseh reached the sea and bordered Asher on the north and Issachar on the east.

¹¹Within Issachar and Asher, Manasseh also had Beth Shan, Ibleam and the people of Dor, Endor, Taanach and Megiddo, together with their surrounding settlements (the third in the list is Naphoth*a*).

¹²Yet the Manassites were not able to occupy these towns, for the Canaanites were determined to live in that region. ¹³However, when the Israelites grew stronger, they subjected the Canaanites to forced labor but did not drive them out completely.

¹⁴The people of Joseph said to Joshua, "Why have you given us only one allotment and one portion for an inheritance? We are a numerous people and the LORD has blessed us abundantly."

¹⁵"If you are so numerous," Joshua answered, "and if the hill country of Ephraim is too small for you, go up into the forest and clear land for yourselves there in the land of the Perizzites and Rephaites."

¹⁶The people of Joseph replied, "The hill country is not enough for us, and all the Canaanites who live in the plain have iron

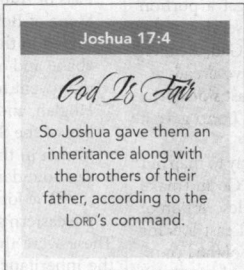

Joshua 17:4

God Is Fair

So Joshua gave them an inheritance along with the brothers of their father, according to the LORD's command.

---

a 11 That is, Naphoth Dor

chariots, both those in Beth Shan and its settlements and those in the Valley of Jezreel."

17But Joshua said to the house of Joseph—to Ephraim and Manasseh—"You are numerous and very powerful. You will have not only one allotment 18but the forested hill country as well. Clear it, and its farthest limits will be yours; though the Canaanites have iron chariots and though they are strong, you can drive them out."

Division of the Rest of the Land

18 The whole assembly of the Israelites gathered at Shiloh and set up the Tent of Meeting there. The country was brought under their control, 2but there were still seven Israelite tribes who had not yet received their inheritance.

3So Joshua said to the Israelites: "How long will you wait before you begin to take possession of the land that the LORD, the God of your fathers, has given you? 4Appoint three men from each tribe. I will send them out to make a survey of the land and to write a description of it, according to the inheritance of each. Then they will return to me. 5You are to divide the land into seven parts. Judah is to remain in its territory on the south and the house of Joseph in its territory on the north. 6After you have written descriptions of the seven parts of the land, bring them here to me and I will cast lots for you in the presence of the LORD our God. 7The Levites, however, do not get a portion among you, because the priestly service of the LORD is their inheritance. And Gad, Reuben and the half-tribe of Manasseh have already received their inheritance on the east side of the Jordan. Moses the servant of the LORD gave it to them."

8As the men started on their way to map out the land, Joshua instructed them, "Go and make a survey of the land and write a description of it. Then return to me, and I will cast lots for you here at Shiloh in the presence of the LORD." 9So the men left and went through the land. They wrote its description on a scroll, town by town, in seven parts, and returned to Joshua in the camp at Shiloh. 10Joshua then cast lots for them in Shiloh in the presence of the LORD,

and there he distributed the land to the Israelites according to their tribal divisions.

Allotment for Benjamin

11The lot came up for the tribe of Benjamin, clan by clan. Their allotted territory lay between the tribes of Judah and Joseph:

12On the north side their boundary began at the Jordan, passed the northern slope of Jericho and headed west into the hill country, coming out at the desert of Beth Aven. 13From there it crossed to the south slope of Luz (that is, Bethel) and went down to Ataroth Addar on the hill south of Lower Beth Horon.

14From the hill facing Beth Horon on the south the boundary turned south along the western side and came out at Kiriath Baal (that is, Kiriath Jearim), a town of the people of Judah. This was the western side.

15The southern side began at the outskirts of Kiriath Jearim on the west, and the boundary came out at the spring of the waters of Nephtoah. 16The boundary went down to the foot of the hill facing the Valley of Ben Hinnom, north of the Valley of Rephaim. It continued down the Hinnom Valley along the southern slope of the Jebusite city and so to En Rogel. 17It then curved north, went to En Shemesh, continued to Geliloth, which faces the Pass of Adummim, and ran down to the Stone of Bohan son of Reuben. 18It continued to the northern slope of Beth Arabah*a* and on down into the Arabah. 19It then went to the northern slope of Beth Hoglah and came out at the northern bay of the Salt Sea,*b* at the mouth of the Jordan in the south. This was the southern boundary.

20The Jordan formed the boundary on the eastern side.

These were the boundaries that marked out the inheritance of the clans of Benjamin on all sides.

21The tribe of Benjamin, clan by clan, had the following cities:

Jericho, Beth Hoglah, Emek Keziz,

---

*a*18 Septuagint; Hebrew *slope facing the Arabah*   *b*19 That is, the Dead Sea

²²Beth Arabah, Zemaraim, Bethel, ²³Avvim, Parah, Ophrah, ²⁴Kephar Ammoni, Ophni and Geba—twelve towns and their villages.

²⁵Gibeon, Ramah, Beeroth, ²⁶Mizpah, Kephirah, Mozah, ²⁷Rekem, Irpeel, Taralah, ²⁸Zelah, Haeleph, the Jebusite city (that is, Jerusalem), Gibeah and Kiriath—fourteen towns and their villages.

This was the inheritance of Benjamin for its clans.

Allotment for Simeon

19 The second lot came out for the tribe of Simeon, clan by clan. Their inheritance lay within the territory of Judah. ²It included:

Beersheba (or Sheba),ᵃ Moladah, ³Hazar Shual, Balah, Ezem, ⁴Eltolad, Bethul, Hormah, ⁵Ziklag, Beth Marcaboth, Hazar Susah, ⁶Beth Lebaoth and Sharuhen—thirteen towns and their villages;

⁷Ain, Rimmon, Ether and Ashan—four towns and their villages— ⁸and all the villages around these towns as far as Baalath Beer (Ramah in the Negev).

This was the inheritance of the tribe of the Simeonites, clan by clan. ⁹The inheritance of the Simeonites was taken from the share of Judah, because Judah's portion was more than they needed. So the Simeonites received their inheritance within the territory of Judah.

Allotment for Zebulun

¹⁰The third lot came up for Zebulun, clan by clan:

The boundary of their inheritance went as far as Sarid. ¹¹Going west it ran to Maralah, touched Dabbesheth, and extended to the ravine near Jokneam. ¹²It turned east from Sarid to the sunrise to the territory of Kisloth Tabor and went on to Daberath and up to Japhia. ¹³Then it continued eastward to Gath Hepher and Eth Kazin; it came out at Rimmon and turned toward Neah. ¹⁴There the boundary went around on the north to Hannathon and ended at the Valley of Iphtah El. ¹⁵Included were Kattath, Nahalal, Shimron, Idalah and Bethlehem. There were twelve towns and their villages.

¹⁶These towns and their villages were the inheritance of Zebulun, clan by clan.

Allotment for Issachar

¹⁷The fourth lot came out for Issachar, clan by clan. ¹⁸Their territory included:

Jezreel, Kesulloth, Shunem, ¹⁹Hapharaim, Shion, Anaharath, ²⁰Rabbith, Kishion, Ebez, ²¹Remeth, En Gannim, En Haddah and Beth Pazzez. ²²The boundary touched Tabor, Shahazumah and Beth Shemesh, and ended at the Jordan. There were sixteen towns and their villages.

²³These towns and their villages were the inheritance of the tribe of Issachar, clan by clan.

Allotment for Asher

²⁴The fifth lot came out for the tribe of Asher, clan by clan. ²⁵Their territory included:

Helkath, Hali, Beten, Acshaph, ²⁶Allammelech, Amad and Mishal. On the west the boundary touched Carmel and Shihor Libnath. ²⁷It then turned east toward Beth Dagon, touched Zebulun and the Valley of Iphtah El, and went north to Beth Emek and Neiel, passing Cabul on the left. ²⁸It went to Abdon,ᵇ Rehob, Hammon and Kanah, as far as Greater Sidon. ²⁹The boundary then turned back toward Ramah and went to the fortified city of Tyre, turned toward Hosah and came out at the sea in the region of Aczib, ³⁰Ummah, Aphek and Rehob. There were twenty-two towns and their villages.

³¹These towns and their villages were the inheritance of the tribe of Asher, clan by clan.

Allotment for Naphtali

³²The sixth lot came out for Naphtali, clan by clan:

³³Their boundary went from Heleph and the large tree in Zaanannim, passing Adami Nekeb and Jabneel to Lakkum and ending at the Jordan. ³⁴The boundary ran west through Aznoth Tabor and came out at Hukkok. It touched Zebulun on the south, Asher on the west and the Jordanᶜ

ᵃ2 Or *Beersheba, Sheba;* 1 Chron. 4:28 does not have *Sheba.* ᵇ28 Some Hebrew manuscripts (see also Joshua 21:30); most Hebrew manuscripts *Ebron* ᶜ34 Septuagint; Hebrew *west, and Judah, the Jordan,* on the east. 35 The fortified cities were Ziddim, Zer, Hammath, Rakkath, Kinnereth, 36 Adamah, Ramah, Hazor, 37 Kedesh, Edrei, En Hazor, 38 Iron, Migdal El, Horem, Beth Anath and Beth Shemesh. There were nineteen towns and their villages.

39 These towns and their villages were the inheritance of the tribe of Naphtali, clan by clan.

Allotment for Dan

40 The seventh lot came out for the tribe of Dan, clan by clan. 41 The territory of their inheritance included:

Zorah, Eshtaol, Ir Shemesh, 42 Shaalabbin, Aijalon, Ithlah, 43 Elon, Timnah, Ekron, 44 Eltekeh, Gibbethon, Baalath, 45 Jehud, Bene Berak, Gath Rimmon, 46 Me Jarkon and Rakkon, with the area facing Joppa.

47 (But the Danites had difficulty taking possession of their territory, so they went up and attacked Leshem, took it, put it to the sword and occupied it. They settled in Leshem and named it Dan after their forefather.)

48 These towns and their villages were the inheritance of the tribe of Dan, clan by clan.

Allotment for Joshua

49 When they had finished dividing the land into its allotted portions, the Israelites gave Joshua son of Nun an inheritance among them, 50 as the LORD had commanded. They gave him the town he asked for—Timnath Serah*a* in the hill country of Ephraim. And he built up the town and settled there.

51 These are the territories that Eleazar the priest, Joshua son of Nun and the heads of the tribal clans of Israel assigned by lot at Shiloh in the presence of the LORD at the entrance to the Tent of Meeting. And so they finished dividing the land.

Cities of Refuge

20 Then the LORD said to Joshua: 2 "Tell the Israelites to designate the cities of refuge, as I instructed you through Moses, 3 so that anyone who kills a person accidentally and unintentionally may flee there and find protection from the avenger of blood.

4 "When he flees to one of these cities, he is to stand in the entrance of the city gate and state his case before the elders of that city. Then they are to admit him into their city and give him a place to live with them. 5 If the avenger of blood pursues him, they must not surrender the one accused, because he killed his neighbor unintentionally and without malice aforethought. 6 He is to stay in that city until he has stood trial before the assembly and until the death of the high priest who is serving at that time. Then he may go back to his own home in the town from which he fled."

7 So they set apart Kedesh in Galilee in the hill country of Naphtali, Shechem in the hill country of Ephraim, and Kiriath Arba (that is, Hebron) in the hill country of Judah. 8 On the east side of the Jordan of Jericho*b* they designated Bezer in the desert on the plateau in the tribe of Reuben, Ramoth in Gilead in the tribe of Gad, and Golan in Bashan in the tribe of Manasseh. 9 Any of the Israelites or any alien living among them who killed someone accidentally could flee to these designated cities and not be killed by the avenger of blood prior to standing trial before the assembly.

Towns for the Levites

21 Now the family heads of the Levites approached Eleazar the priest, Joshua son of Nun, and the heads of the other tribal families of Israel 2 at Shiloh in Canaan and said to them, "The LORD commanded through Moses that you give us towns to live in, with pasturelands for our livestock." 3 So, as the LORD had commanded, the Israelites gave the Levites the following towns and pasturelands out of their own inheritance:

4 The first lot came out for the Kohathites, clan by clan. The Levites who were descendants of Aaron the priest were allotted thirteen towns from the tribes of Judah, Simeon and Benjamin. 5 The rest of Kohath's descendants were allotted ten towns from the clans of the tribes of Ephraim, Dan and half of Manasseh.

6 The descendants of Gershon were allotted thirteen towns from the clans of the tribes of Issachar, Asher, Naphtali and the half-tribe of Manasseh in Bashan.

7 The descendants of Merari, clan by clan, re-

---

*a*50 Also known as *Timnath Heres* (see Judges 2:9)   *b*8 *Jordan of Jericho* was possibly an ancient name for the Jordan River.

ceived twelve towns from the tribes of Reuben, Gad and Zebulun.

⁸So the Israelites allotted to the Levites these towns and their pasturelands, as the LORD had commanded through Moses.

⁹From the tribes of Judah and Simeon they allotted the following towns by name ¹⁰(these towns were assigned to the descendants of Aaron who were from the Kohathite clans of the Levites, because the first lot fell to them):

¹¹They gave them Kiriath Arba (that is, Hebron), with its surrounding pastureland, in the hill country of Judah. (Arba was the forefather of Anak.) ¹²But the fields and villages around the city they had given to Caleb son of Jephunneh as his possession.

¹³So to the descendants of Aaron the priest they gave Hebron (a city of refuge for one accused of murder), Libnah, ¹⁴Jattir, Eshtemoa, ¹⁵Holon, Debir, ¹⁶Ain, Juttah and Beth Shemesh, together with their pasturelands—nine towns from these two tribes.

¹⁷And from the tribe of Benjamin they gave them Gibeon, Geba, ¹⁸Anathoth and Almon, together with their pasturelands—four towns.

¹⁹All the towns for the priests, the descendants of Aaron, were thirteen, together with their pasturelands.

²⁰The rest of the Kohathite clans of the Levites were allotted towns from the tribe of Ephraim:

²¹In the hill country of Ephraim were given Shechem (a city of refuge for one accused of murder) and Gezer, ²²Kibzaim and Beth Horon, together with their pasturelands—four towns.

²³Also from the tribe of Dan they received Eltekeh, Gibbethon, ²⁴Aijalon and Gath Rimmon, together with their pasturelands—four towns.

²⁵From half the tribe of Manasseh they received Taanach and Gath Rimmon, together with their pasturelands—two towns.

²⁶All these ten towns and their pasturelands were given to the rest of the Kohathite clans.

²⁷The Levite clans of the Gershonites were given:

from the half-tribe of Manasseh, Golan in Bashan (a city of refuge for one accused of murder) and Be Eshtarah, together with their pasturelands—two towns;

²⁸from the tribe of Issachar, Kishion, Daberath, ²⁹Jarmuth and En Gannim, together with their pasturelands—four towns;

³⁰from the tribe of Asher, Mishal, Abdon, ³¹Helkath and Rehob, together with their pasturelands—four towns;

³²from the tribe of Naphtali, Kedesh in Galilee (a city of refuge for one accused of murder), Hammoth Dor and Kartan, together with their pasturelands—three towns.

³³All the towns of the Gershonite clans were thirteen, together with their pasturelands.

³⁴The Merarite clans (the rest of the Levites) were given:

from the tribe of Zebulun, Jokneam, Kartah, ³⁵Dimnah and Nahalal, together with their pasturelands—four towns;

³⁶from the tribe of Reuben, Bezer, Jahaz, ³⁷Kedemoth and Mephaath, together with their pasturelands—four towns;

³⁸from the tribe of Gad, Ramoth in Gilead (a city of refuge for one accused of murder), Mahanaim, ³⁹Heshbon and Jazer, together with their pasturelands—four towns in all.

⁴⁰All the towns allotted to the Merarite clans, who were the rest of the Levites, were twelve.

⁴¹The towns of the Levites in the territory held by the Israelites were forty-eight in all, together with their pasturelands. ⁴²Each of these towns had pasturelands surrounding it; this was true for all these towns.

⁴³So the LORD gave Israel all the land he had sworn to give their forefathers, and they took possession of it and settled there. ⁴⁴The LORD gave them rest on every side, just as he had sworn to their forefathers. Not one of their

enemies withstood them; the LORD handed all their enemies over to them. 45 Not one of all the LORD's good promises to the house of Israel failed; every one was fulfilled.

Eastern Tribes Return Home

22 Then Joshua summoned the Reubenites, the Gadites and the half-tribe of Manasseh 2 and said to them, "You have done all that Moses the servant of the LORD commanded, and you have obeyed me in everything I commanded. 3 For a long time now—to this very day—you have not deserted your brothers but have carried out the mission the LORD your God gave you. 4 Now that the LORD your God has given your brothers rest as he promised, return to your homes in the land that Moses the servant of the LORD gave you on the other side of the Jordan. 5 But be very careful to keep the commandment and the law that Moses the servant of the LORD gave you: to love the LORD your God, to walk in all his ways, to obey his commands, to hold fast to him and to serve him with all your heart and all your soul."

6 Then Joshua blessed them and sent them away, and they went to their homes. 7 (To the half-tribe of Manasseh Moses had given land in Bashan, and to the other half of the tribe Joshua gave land on the west side of the Jordan with their brothers.) When Joshua sent them home, he blessed them, 8 saying, "Return to your homes with your great wealth—with large herds of livestock, with silver, gold, bronze and iron, and a great quantity of clothing—and divide with your brothers the plunder from your enemies."

9 So the Reubenites, the Gadites and the half-tribe of Manasseh left the Israelites at Shiloh in Canaan to return to Gilead, their own land, which they had acquired in accordance with the command of the LORD through Moses.

10 When they came to Geliloth near the Jordan in the land of Canaan, the Reubenites, the Gadites and the half-tribe of Manasseh built an

imposing altar there by the Jordan. 11 And when the Israelites heard that they had built the altar on the border of Canaan at Geliloth near the Jordan on the Israelite side, 12 the whole assembly of Israel gathered at Shiloh to go to war against them.

13 So the Israelites sent Phinehas son of Eleazar, the priest, to the land of Gilead—to Reuben, Gad and the half-tribe of Manasseh. 14 With him they sent ten of the chief men, one for each of the tribes of Israel, each the head of a family division among the Israelite clans.

15 When they went to Gilead—to Reuben, Gad and the half-tribe of Manasseh—they said to them: 16 "The whole assembly of the LORD says: 'How could you break faith with the God of Israel like this? How could you turn away from the LORD and build yourselves an altar in rebellion against him now? 17 Was not the sin of Peor enough for us? Up to this very day we have not cleansed ourselves from that sin, even though a plague fell on the community of the LORD! 18 And are you now turning away from the LORD?

"'If you rebel against the LORD today, tomorrow he will be angry with the whole community of Israel. 19 If the land you possess is defiled, come over to the LORD's land, where the LORD's tabernacle stands, and share the land with us. But do not rebel against the LORD or against us by building an altar for yourselves, other than the altar of the LORD our God. 20 When Achan son of Zerah acted unfaithfully regarding the devoted things,*a* did not wrath come upon the whole community of Israel? He was not the only one who died for his sin.'"

21 Then Reuben, Gad and the half-tribe of Manasseh replied to the heads of the clans of Israel: 22 "The Mighty One, God, the LORD! The Mighty One, God, the LORD! He knows! And let Israel know! If this has been in rebellion or disobedience to the LORD, do not spare us this day. 23 If we have built our own altar to turn away from the LORD and to offer burnt offerings and grain offerings, or to sacrifice fellow-

---

Joshua 21:45

God Delivers on His Promises

"Not one of all the LORD's good promises to the house of Israel failed; every one was fulfilled."

---

a 20 The Hebrew term refers to the irrevocable giving over of things or persons to the LORD, often by totally destroying them.

ship offerings[a] on it, may the LORD himself call us to account.

24"No! We did it for fear that some day your descendants might say to ours, 'What do you have to do with the LORD, the God of Israel? 25The LORD has made the Jordan a boundary between us and you—you Reubenites and Gadites! You have no share in the LORD.' So your descendants might cause ours to stop fearing the LORD.

26"That is why we said, 'Let us get ready and build an altar—but not for burnt offerings or sacrifices.' 27On the contrary, it is to be a witness between us and you and the generations that follow, that we will worship the LORD at his sanctuary with our burnt offerings, sacrifices and fellowship offerings. Then in the future your descendants will not be able to say to ours, 'You have no share in the LORD.'

28"And we said, 'If they ever say this to us, or to our descendants, we will answer: Look at the replica of the LORD's altar, which our fathers built, not for burnt offerings and sacrifices, but as a witness between us and you.'

29"Far be it from us to rebel against the LORD and turn away from him today by building an altar for burnt offerings, grain offerings and sacrifices, other than the altar of the LORD our God that stands before his tabernacle."

30When Phinehas the priest and the leaders of the community—the heads of the clans of the Israelites—heard what Reuben, Gad and Manasseh had to say, they were pleased. 31And Phinehas son of Eleazar, the priest, said to Reuben, Gad and Manasseh, "Today we know that the LORD is with us, because you have not acted unfaithfully toward the LORD in this matter. Now you have rescued the Israelites from the LORD's hand."

32Then Phinehas son of Eleazar, the priest, and the leaders returned to Canaan from their meeting with the Reubenites and Gadites in Gilead and reported to the Israelites. 33They were glad to hear the report and praised God.

And they talked no more about going to war against them to devastate the country where the Reubenites and the Gadites lived.

34And the Reubenites and the Gadites gave the altar this name: A Witness Between Us that the LORD is God.

Joshua 22:22

God Is Mighty

"The Mighty One, God, the LORD! The Mighty One, God, the LORD! He knows! And let Israel know! If this has been in rebellion or disobedience to the LORD, do not spare us this day."

Joshua's Farewell to the Leaders

23 After a long time had passed and the LORD had given Israel rest from all their enemies around them, Joshua, by then old and well advanced in years, 2summoned all Israel—their elders, leaders, judges and officials—and said to them: "I am old and well advanced in years. 3You yourselves have seen everything the LORD your God has done to all these nations for your sake; it was the LORD your God who fought for you. 4Remember how I have allotted as an inheritance for your tribes all the land of the nations that remain—the nations I conquered—between the Jordan and the Great Sea[b] in the west. 5The LORD your God himself will drive them out of your way. He will push them out before you, and you will take possession of their land, as the LORD your God promised you.

6"Be very strong; be careful to obey all that is written in the Book of the Law of Moses, without turning aside to the right or to the left. 7Do not associate with these nations that remain among you; do not invoke the names of their gods or swear by them. You must not serve them or bow down to them. 8But you are to hold fast to the LORD your God, as you have until now.

9"The LORD has driven out before you great and powerful nations; to this day no one has been able to withstand you. 10One of you routs a thousand, because the LORD your God fights for you, just as he promised. 11So be very careful to love the LORD your God.

12"But if you turn away and ally yourselves with the survivors of these nations that remain

---

[a]23 Traditionally peace offerings; also in verse 27   [b]4 That is, the Mediterranean

among you and if you intermarry with them and associate with them, **13**then you may be sure that the LORD your God will no longer drive out these nations before you. Instead, they will become snares and traps for you, whips on your backs and thorns in your eyes, until you perish from this good land, which the LORD your God has given you.

14"Now I am about to go the way of all the earth. You know with all your heart and soul that not one of all the good promises the LORD your God gave you has failed. Every promise has been fulfilled; not one has failed. **15**But just as every good promise of the LORD your God has come true, so the LORD will bring on you all the evil he has threatened, until he has destroyed you from this good land he has given you. **16**If you violate the covenant of the LORD your God, which he commanded you, and go and serve other gods and bow down to them, the LORD's anger will burn against you, and you will quickly perish from the good land he has given you."

The Covenant Renewed at Shechem

24 Then Joshua assembled all the tribes of Israel at Shechem. He summoned the elders, leaders, judges and officials of Israel, and they presented themselves before God.

2Joshua said to all the people, "This is what the LORD, the God of Israel, says: 'Long ago your forefathers, including Terah the father of Abraham and Nahor, lived beyond the River[a] and worshiped other gods. **3**But I took your father Abraham from the land beyond the River and led him throughout Canaan and gave him many descendants. I gave him Isaac, **4**and to Isaac I gave Jacob and Esau. I assigned the hill country of Seir to Esau, but Jacob and his sons went down to Egypt.

5"'Then I sent Moses and Aaron, and I afflicted the Egyptians by what I did there, and I brought you out. **6**When I brought your fathers out of Egypt, you came to the sea, and the Egyptians pursued them with chariots and horsemen[b] as far as the Red Sea.[c] **7**But they cried to the LORD for help, and he put darkness between you and the Egyptians; he brought the sea over them and covered them. You saw with your own eyes what I did to the Egyptians. Then you lived in the desert for a long time.

8"'I brought you to the land of the Amorites who lived east of the Jordan. They fought against you, but I gave them into your hands. I destroyed them from before you, and you took possession of their land. **9**When Balak son of Zippor, the king of Moab, prepared to fight against Israel, he sent for Balaam son of Beor to put a curse on you. **10**But I would not listen to Balaam, so he blessed you again and again, and I delivered you out of his hand.

11"'Then you crossed the Jordan and came to Jericho. The citizens of Jericho fought against you, as did also the Amorites, Perizzites, Canaanites, Hittites, Girgashites, Hivites and Jebusites, but I gave them into your hands. **12**I sent the hornet ahead of you, which drove them out before you—also the two Amorite kings. You did not do it with your own sword and bow. **13**So I gave you a land on which you did not toil and cities you did not build; and you live in them and eat from vineyards and olive groves that you did not plant.'

14"Now fear the LORD and serve him with all faithfulness. Throw away the gods your forefathers worshiped beyond the River and in Egypt, and serve the LORD. **15**But if serving the LORD seems undesirable to you, then choose for yourselves this day whom you will serve, whether the gods your forefathers served beyond the River, or the gods of the Amorites, in whose land you are living. But as for me and my household, we will serve the LORD."

16Then the people answered, "Far be it from us to forsake the LORD to serve other gods! **17**It was the LORD our God himself who brought us and our fathers up out of Egypt, from that land

Joshua 23:10

God Brings Success

"One of you routs a thousand, because the LORD your God fights for you, just as he promised."

---

*a***2** That is, the Euphrates; also in verses 3, 14 and 15   *b***6** Or *charioteers*   *c***6** Hebrew *Yam Suph*; that is, Sea of Reeds

Choose Wisely

Read: Joshua 24:14–24

JOSHUA HAD FAITHFULLY led the Israelites into the promised land. Yet the time had come for the new nation to move forward. So he gave his farewell address, urging the people to choose wisely whom they would serve. He challenged them to make a conscious decision not to become entangled with the old gods but to serve the one true God. Knowing that the best leaders lead by example, he told the people that he and his household would "serve the LORD."

If you read the story of Susannah Wesley's life, you realize that her farewell address might have sounded very similar to Joshua's. Her son John Wesley, the eighteenth-century evangelist and co-founder of Methodism, wrote how she had wisely chosen to impact her household for the Lord. In *The Journal of John Wesley* he remembered, "The mother of the Wesleys was a remarkable woman, though cast in a mold not much to our minds nowadays. She had nineteen children and greatly prided herself on having taught them, one after another, by frequent chastisements to— what do you think? to cry softly. She had theories of education and strength of will, and of arm too, to carry them out . . . The mother of the Wesleys thought more of her children's souls than of their bodies . . . Coming . . . as he did of a theological stock, having a saint for a father and a notable devout woman for a mother, Wesley from his early days learned to regard religion as the business." Susannah Wesley's wise choice to train her children in the ways of the Lord helped pave the way for a spiritual revival in England.

It has been said that a choice repeated becomes a habit; a habit develops your character; and your character determines your destiny. Joshua's choices led to a destiny of faithful leadership and a family of faith. Susannah Wesley's wise choices led to a family of faith and a spiritual heritage that has stood the test of time. You are faced with the same choices today: to lead your household in serving the Lord or to serve the gods of the world. Will you choose wisely?

Joshua 24:15

"But if serving the LORD seems undesirable to you, then choose for yourselves this day whom you will serve, whether the gods your forefathers served beyond the River, or the gods of the Amorites, in whose land you are living. But as for me and my household, we will serve the LORD."

reflection

1 Who makes up your "house" (it could be extended family, friends, coworkers, etc.)?

2 How have you chosen to serve the Lord by serving them?

3 Pray that God will show you some creative ways to impact others for the Lord. Pray that you can choose wisely as you make decisions for those in your "household" of influence.

RELATED READINGS

Deuteronomy 30:15–19;
1 Kings 18:20–21;
2 Timothy 3:14–15

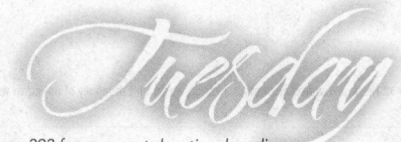

Tuesday

Go to page 292 for your next devotional reading.

of slavery, and performed those great signs before our eyes. He protected us on our entire journey and among all the nations through which we traveled. **18** And the LORD drove out before us all the nations, including the Amorites, who lived in the land. We too will serve the LORD, because he is our God."

19 Joshua said to the people, "You are not able to serve the LORD. He is a holy God; he is a jealous God. He will not forgive your rebellion and your sins. **20** If you forsake the LORD and serve foreign gods, he will turn and bring disaster on you and make an end of you, after he has been good to you."

21 But the people said to Joshua, "No! We will serve the LORD."

22 Then Joshua said, "You are witnesses against yourselves that you have chosen to serve the LORD."

"Yes, we are witnesses," they replied.

23 "Now then," said Joshua, "throw away the foreign gods that are among you and yield your hearts to the LORD, the God of Israel."

24 And the people said to Joshua, "We will serve the LORD our God and obey him."

25 On that day Joshua made a covenant for the people, and there at Shechem he drew up for them decrees and laws. **26** And Joshua recorded these things in the Book of the Law of God. Then he took a large stone and set it up there under the oak near the holy place of the LORD.

27 "See!" he said to all the people. "This stone will be a witness against us. It has heard all the words the LORD has said to us. It will be a witness against you if you are untrue to your God."

Buried in the Promised Land

28 Then Joshua sent the people away, each to his own inheritance.

29 After these things, Joshua son of Nun, the servant of the LORD, died at the age of a hundred and ten. **30** And they buried him in the land of his inheritance, at Timnath Serah[a] in the hill country of Ephraim, north of Mount Gaash.

31 Israel served the LORD throughout the lifetime of Joshua and of the elders who outlived him and who had experienced everything the LORD had done for Israel.

32 And Joseph's bones, which the Israelites had brought up from Egypt, were buried at Shechem in the tract of land that Jacob bought for a hundred pieces of silver[b] from the sons of Hamor, the father of Shechem. This became the inheritance of Joseph's descendants.

33 And Eleazar son of Aaron died and was buried at Gibeah, which had been allotted to his son Phinehas in the hill country of Ephraim.

---

[a]30 Also known as *Timnath Heres* (see Judges 2:9)   [b]32 Hebrew *hundred kesitahs*; a kesitah was a unit of money of unknown weight and value.

Judges

It never takes long to fall. In the generation following Joshua's spectacular conquest of Canaan, the people succumbed to *complacency and outright rebellion.* The people who were to worship only God strayed and began to worship the pagan deities of their neighbors. It was an affront that God could not ignore. He brought judgment by means of other nations that swept in and attacked Israel. But even in his judgment, God never lost his love for them. *He gave them judges,* people who would lead them and save them from their enemies. And so began the cycle: When the people were in distress, *they cried out to God.* When God helped them and all was well again, they slipped right back into their idol worship.

Author:
Likely Samuel.

Audience:
The Israelites living in the promised land.

Date:
Around 1000 B.C.

Setting:
Israel's ups and (mostly) downs after the time of Joshua.

Verse to Remember:
After that whole generation had been gathered to their fathers, another generation grew up, who knew neither the LORD nor what he had done for Israel. (2:10)

Israel Fights the Remaining Canaanites

1 After the death of Joshua, the Israelites asked the LORD, "Who will be the first to go up and fight for us against the Canaanites?"

2 The LORD answered, "Judah is to go; I have given the land into their hands."

3 Then the men of Judah said to the Simeonites their brothers, "Come up with us into the territory allotted to us, to fight against the Canaanites. We in turn will go with you into yours." So the Simeonites went with them.

4 When Judah attacked, the LORD gave the Canaanites and Perizzites into their hands and they struck down ten thousand men at Bezek. 5 It was there that they found Adoni-Bezek and fought against him, putting to rout the Canaanites and Perizzites. 6 Adoni-Bezek fled, but they chased him and caught him, and cut off his thumbs and big toes.

7 Then Adoni-Bezek said, "Seventy kings with their thumbs and big toes cut off have picked up scraps under my table. Now God

has paid me back for what I did to them." They brought him to Jerusalem, and he died there.

⁸The men of Judah attacked Jerusalem also and took it. They put the city to the sword and set it on fire.

⁹After that, the men of Judah went down to fight against the Canaanites living in the hill country, the Negev and the western foothills. ¹⁰They advanced against the Canaanites living in Hebron (formerly called Kiriath Arba) and defeated Sheshai, Ahiman and Talmai.

¹¹From there they advanced against the people living in Debir (formerly called Kiriath Sepher). ¹²And Caleb said, "I will give my daughter Acsah in marriage to the man who attacks and captures Kiriath Sepher." ¹³Othniel son of Kenaz, Caleb's younger brother, took it; so Caleb gave his daughter Acsah to him in marriage.

¹⁴One day when she came to Othniel, she urged him*a* to ask her father for a field. When she got off her donkey, Caleb asked her, "What can I do for you?"

¹⁵She replied, "Do me a special favor. Since you have given me land in the Negev, give me also springs of water." Then Caleb gave her the upper and lower springs.

¹⁶The descendants of Moses' father-in-law, the Kenite, went up from the City of Palms*b* with the men of Judah to live among the people of the Desert of Judah in the Negev near Arad.

¹⁷Then the men of Judah went with the Simeonites their brothers and attacked the Canaanites living in Zephath, and they totally destroyed*c* the city. Therefore it was called Hormah.*d* ¹⁸The men of Judah also took*e* Gaza, Ashkelon and Ekron—each city with its territory.

¹⁹The LORD was with the men of Judah. They took possession of the hill country, but they were unable to drive the people from the plains, because they had iron chariots. ²⁰As Moses had promised, Hebron was given to Caleb, who drove from it the three sons of Anak. ²¹The Benjamites, however, failed to dislodge the Jebusites, who were living in Jerusalem; to this day the Jebusites live there with the Benjamites.

²²Now the house of Joseph attacked Bethel, and the LORD was with them. ²³When they sent men to spy out Bethel (formerly called Luz), ²⁴the spies saw a man coming out of the city and they said to him, "Show us how to get into the city and we will see that you are treated well." ²⁵So he showed them, and they put the city to the sword but spared the man and his whole family. ²⁶He then went to the land of the Hittites, where he built a city and called it Luz, which is its name to this day.

²⁷But Manasseh did not drive out the people of Beth Shan or Taanach or Dor or Ibleam or Megiddo and their surrounding settlements, for the Canaanites were determined to live in that land. ²⁸When Israel became strong, they pressed the Canaanites into forced labor but never drove them out completely. ²⁹Nor did Ephraim drive out the Canaanites living in Gezer, but the Canaanites continued to live there among them. ³⁰Neither did Zebulun drive out the Canaanites living in Kitron or Nahalol, who remained among them; but they did subject them to forced labor. ³¹Nor did Asher drive out those living in Acco or Sidon or Ahlab or Aczib or Helbah or Aphek or Rehob, ³²and because of this the people of Asher lived among the Canaanite inhabitants of the land. ³³Neither did Naphtali drive out those living in Beth Shemesh or Beth Anath; but the Naphtalites too lived among the Canaanite inhabitants of the land, and those living in Beth Shemesh and Beth Anath became forced laborers for them. ³⁴The Amorites confined the Danites to the hill country, not allowing them to come down into the plain. ³⁵And the Amorites were determined also to hold out in Mount Heres, Aijalon and Shaalbim, but when the power of the house of Joseph increased, they too were pressed into forced labor. ³⁶The boundary of the Amorites was from Scorpion*f* Pass to Sela and beyond.

The Angel of the LORD at Bokim

2 The angel of the LORD went up from Gilgal to Bokim and said, "I brought you up out of Egypt and led you into the land that I swore to give to your forefathers. I said, 'I will never break my covenant with you, ²and you

---

*a*14 Hebrew; Septuagint and Vulgate *Othniel, he urged her*   *b*16 That is, Jericho   *c*17 The Hebrew term refers to the irrevocable giving over of things or persons to the LORD, often by totally destroying them.   *d*17 *Hormah* means *destruction.*   *e*18 Hebrew; Septuagint *Judah did not take*   *f*36 Hebrew *Akrabbim* shall not make a covenant with the people of this land, but you shall break down their altars.' Yet you have disobeyed me. Why have you done this? ³Now therefore I tell you that I will not drive them out before you; they will be thorns in your sides and their gods will be a snare to you."

⁴When the angel of the LORD had spoken these things to all the Israelites, the people wept aloud, ⁵and they called that place Bokim.ᵃ There they offered sacrifices to the LORD.

Disobedience and Defeat

⁶After Joshua had dismissed the Israelites, they went to take possession of the land, each to his own inheritance. ⁷The people served the LORD throughout the lifetime of Joshua and of the elders who outlived him and who had seen all the great things the LORD had done for Israel.

⁸Joshua son of Nun, the servant of the LORD, died at the age of a hundred and ten. ⁹And they buried him in the land of his inheritance, at Timnath Heresᵇ in the hill country of Ephraim, north of Mount Gaash.

¹⁰After that whole generation had been gathered to their fathers, another generation grew up, who knew neither the LORD nor what he had done for Israel. ¹¹Then the Israelites did evil in the eyes of the LORD and served the Baals. ¹²They forsook the LORD, the God of their fathers, who had brought them out of Egypt. They followed and worshiped various gods of the peoples around them. They provoked the LORD to anger ¹³because they forsook him and served Baal and the Ashtoreths. ¹⁴In his anger against Israel the LORD handed them over to raiders who plundered them. He sold them to their enemies all around, whom they were no longer able to resist. ¹⁵Whenever Israel went out to fight, the hand of the LORD was against them to defeat them, just as he had sworn to them. They were in great distress.

¹⁶Then the LORD raised up judges,ᶜ who

saved them out of the hands of these raiders. ¹⁷Yet they would not listen to their judges but prostituted themselves to other gods and worshiped them. Unlike their fathers, they quickly turned from the way in which their fathers had walked, the way of obedience to the LORD's commands. ¹⁸Whenever the LORD raised up a judge for them, he was with the judge and saved them out of the hands of their enemies as long as the judge lived; for the LORD had compassion on them as they groaned under those who oppressed and afflicted them. ¹⁹But when the judge died, the people returned to ways even more corrupt than those of their fathers, following other gods and serving and worshiping them. They refused to give up their evil practices and stubborn ways.

²⁰Therefore the LORD was very angry with Israel and said, "Because this nation has violated the covenant that I laid down for their forefathers and has not listened to me, ²¹I will no longer drive out before them any of the nations Joshua left when he died. ²²I will use them to test Israel and see whether they will keep the way of the LORD and walk in it as their forefathers did." ²³The LORD had allowed those nations to remain; he did not drive them out at once by giving them into the hands of Joshua.

3 These are the nations the LORD left to test all those Israelites who had not experienced any of the wars in Canaan ²(he did this only to teach warfare to the descendants of the Israelites who had not had previous battle experience): ³the five rulers of the Philistines, all the Canaanites, the Sidonians, and the Hivites living in the Lebanon mountains from Mount Baal Hermon to Leboᵈ Hamath. ⁴They were left to test the Israelites to see whether they would obey the LORD's commands, which he had given their forefathers through Moses.

⁵The Israelites lived among the Canaanites, Hittites, Amorites, Perizzites, Hivites and

Judges 2:18

God Is Compassionate

Whenever the LORD raised up a judge for them, he was with the judge and saved them out of the hands of their enemies as long as the judge lived.

ᵃ5 *Bokim* means *weepers.*   ᵇ9 Also known as *Timnath Serah* (see Joshua 19:50 and 24:30)   ᶜ16 Or *leaders*; similarly in verses 17–19   ᵈ3 Or *to the entrance to*

Jebusites. ⁶They took their daughters in marriage and gave their own daughters to their sons, and served their gods.

Othniel

⁷The Israelites did evil in the eyes of the LORD; they forgot the LORD their God and served the Baals and the Asherahs. ⁸The anger of the LORD burned against Israel so that he sold them into the hands of Cushan-Rishathaim king of Aram Naharaim,ᵃ to whom the Israelites were subject for eight years. ⁹But when they cried out to the LORD, he raised up for them a deliverer, Othniel son of Kenaz, Caleb's younger brother, who saved them. ¹⁰The Spirit of the LORD came upon him, so that he became Israel's judgeᵇ and went to war. The LORD gave Cushan-Rishathaim king of Aram into the hands of Othniel, who overpowered him. ¹¹So the land had peace for forty years, until Othniel son of Kenaz died.

Ehud

¹²Once again the Israelites did evil in the eyes of the LORD, and because they did this evil the LORD gave Eglon king of Moab power over Israel. ¹³Getting the Ammonites and Amalekites to join him, Eglon came and attacked Israel, and they took possession of the City of Palms.ᶜ ¹⁴The Israelites were subject to Eglon king of Moab for eighteen years.

¹⁵Again the Israelites cried out to the LORD, and he gave them a deliverer—Ehud, a left-handed man, the son of Gera the Benjamite. The Israelites sent him with tribute to Eglon king of Moab. ¹⁶Now Ehud had made a double-edged sword about a foot and a halfᵈ long, which he strapped to his right thigh under his clothing. ¹⁷He presented the tribute to Eglon king of Moab, who was a very fat man. ¹⁸After Ehud had presented the tribute, he sent on their way the men who had carried it. ¹⁹At the idolsᵉ near Gilgal he himself turned back and said, "I have a secret message for you, O king."

The king said, "Quiet!" And all his attendants left him.

²⁰Ehud then approached him while he was sitting alone in the upper room of his summer palaceᶠ and said, "I have a message from God for you." As the king rose from his seat, ²¹Ehud reached with his left hand, drew the sword from his right thigh and plunged it into the king's belly. ²²Even the handle sank in after the blade, which came out his back. Ehud did not pull the sword out, and the fat closed in over it. ²³Then Ehud went out to the porchᵍ; he shut the doors of the upper room behind him and locked them.

²⁴After he had gone, the servants came and found the doors of the upper room locked. They said, "He must be relieving himself in the inner room of the house." ²⁵They waited to the point of embarrassment, but when he did not open the doors of the room, they took a key and unlocked them. There they saw their lord fallen to the floor, dead.

²⁶While they waited, Ehud got away. He passed by the idols and escaped to Seirah. ²⁷When he arrived there, he blew a trumpet in the hill country of Ephraim, and the Israelites went down with him from the hills, with him leading them.

²⁸"Follow me," he ordered, "for the LORD has given Moab, your enemy, into your hands." So they followed him down and, taking possession of the fords of the Jordan that led to Moab, they allowed no one to cross over. ²⁹At that time they struck down about ten thousand Moabites, all vigorous and strong; not a man escaped. ³⁰That day Moab was made subject to Israel, and the land had peace for eighty years.

Shamgar

³¹After Ehud came Shamgar son of Anath, who struck down six hundred Philistines with an oxgoad. He too saved Israel.

> ### Judges 3:8
>
> ### *God Hates Sin*
>
> The anger of the LORD burned against Israel so that he sold them into the hands of Cushan-Rishathaim king of Aram Naharaim, to whom the Israelites were subject for eight years.

ᵃ8 That is, Northwest Mesopotamia   ᵇ10 Or *leader*   ᶜ13 That is, Jericho   ᵈ16 Hebrew *a cubit* (about 0.5 meter)   ᵉ19 Or *the stone quarries*; also in verse 26   ᶠ20 The meaning of the Hebrew for this phrase is uncertain.   ᵍ23 The meaning of the Hebrew for this word is uncertain.

Deborah

4 After Ehud died, the Israelites once again did evil in the eyes of the Lord. ²So the Lord sold them into the hands of Jabin, a king of Canaan, who reigned in Hazor. The commander of his army was Sisera, who lived in Harosheth Haggoyim. ³Because he had nine hundred iron chariots and had cruelly oppressed the Israelites for twenty years, they cried to the Lord for help.

⁴Deborah, a prophetess, the wife of Lappidoth, was leading*ᵃ* Israel at that time. ⁵She held court under the Palm of Deborah between Ramah and Bethel in the hill country of Ephraim, and the Israelites came to her to have their disputes decided. ⁶She sent for Barak son of Abinoam from Kedesh in Naphtali and said to him, "The Lord, the God of Israel, commands you: 'Go, take with you ten thousand men of Naphtali and Zebulun and lead the way to Mount Tabor. ⁷I will lure Sisera, the commander of Jabin's army, with his chariots and his troops to the Kishon River and give him into your hands.'"

⁸Barak said to her, "If you go with me, I will go; but if you don't go with me, I won't go."

⁹"Very well," Deborah said, "I will go with you. But because of the way you are going about this,*ᵇ* the honor will not be yours, for the Lord will hand Sisera over to a woman." So Deborah went with Barak to Kedesh, ¹⁰where he summoned Zebulun and Naphtali. Ten thousand men followed him, and Deborah also went with him.

¹¹Now Heber the Kenite had left the other Kenites, the descendants of Hobab, Moses' brother-in-law,*ᶜ* and pitched his tent by the great tree in Zaanannim near Kedesh.

¹²When they told Sisera that Barak son of Abinoam had gone up to Mount Tabor, ¹³Sisera gathered together his nine hundred iron chariots and all the men with him, from Harosheth Haggoyim to the Kishon River.

¹⁴Then Deborah said to Barak, "Go! This is the day the Lord has given Sisera into your hands. Has not the Lord gone ahead of you?" So Barak went down Mount Tabor, followed by ten thousand men. ¹⁵At Barak's advance, the Lord routed Sisera and all his chariots and army by the sword, and Sisera abandoned his chariot and fled on foot. ¹⁶But Barak pursued the chariots and army as far as Harosheth Haggoyim. All the troops of Sisera fell by the sword; not a man was left.

¹⁷Sisera, however, fled on foot to the tent of Jael, the wife of Heber the Kenite, because there were friendly relations between Jabin king of Hazor and the clan of Heber the Kenite.

¹⁸Jael went out to meet Sisera and said to him, "Come, my lord, come right in. Don't be afraid." So he entered her tent, and she put a covering over him.

¹⁹"I'm thirsty," he said. "Please give me some water." She opened a skin of milk, gave him a drink, and covered him up.

²⁰"Stand in the doorway of the tent," he told her. "If someone comes by and asks you, 'Is anyone here?' say 'No.'"

²¹But Jael, Heber's wife, picked up a tent peg and a hammer and went quietly to him while he lay fast asleep, exhausted. She drove the peg through his temple into the ground, and he died.

²²Barak came by in pursuit of Sisera, and Jael went out to meet him. "Come," she said, "I will show you the man you're looking for." So he went in with her, and there lay Sisera with the tent peg through his temple—dead.

²³On that day God subdued Jabin, the Canaanite king, before the Israelites. ²⁴And the hand of the Israelites grew stronger and stronger against Jabin, the Canaanite king, until they destroyed him.

The Song of Deborah

5 On that day Deborah and Barak son of Abinoam sang this song:

² "When the princes in Israel take the lead,
    when the people willingly offer
        themselves—
    praise the Lord!

³ "Hear this, you kings! Listen, you rulers!
    I will sing to*ᵈ* the Lord, I will sing;
    I will make music to*ᵉ* the Lord, the God
        of Israel.

ᵃ4 Traditionally judging   ᵇ9 Or But on the expedition you are undertaking   ᶜ11 Or father-in-law   ᵈ3 Or of   ᵉ3 Or / with song I will praise

Deborah the Sabra

Judges 4:4–5
Deborah, a prophetess,
the wife of Lappidoth,
was leading Israel at
that time. She held
court under the Palm
of Deborah between
Ramah and Bethel in the
hill country of Ephraim,
and the Israelites came
to her to have their
disputes decided.

reflection

1 Who among your friends is most like the prickly pear Penny described?

2 In what ways are you sometimes sharp on the outside yet sweet on the inside?

3 Spend some time praying that God would soften your edges. Pray for the friends in your life, asking God to strengthen them when necessary and sweeten them when needed.

RELATED READINGS

Exodus 15:20–21;
Isaiah 51:3;
Ephesians 6:18

SOMETIMES LIFE ON EARTH can seem like a wilderness in which we must learn to thrive under sometimes harsh conditions. But walking in the world's wilderness, I've discovered some beautiful desert plants growing in my garden of friends.

One of my desert plant friends is a prickly pear cactus. Prickly pears are covered with spikes, but when they bloom their flowers are big and brilliant. Today in Israel, people born in the land are called *sabras*, because they are tough on the outside and sweet on the inside. That's like my friend Pia, who grew up in the tough streets of New York and learned to stick up for herself because she grew up in a single-parent household and her mother was at work all day, leaving Pia as the family protector . . . The first time we met, she slapped down one of my ideas for a women's retreat. Later, however, she called to give me a Scripture as encouragement. I've learned that I can bring Pia my troubles and she will blossom into a prayer warrior . . .

I think of Deborah as a prickly pear cactus. Though she was female, Deborah was given the responsibility of judging the wayward Israelites. Scripture tells us "[she held court under the Palm of Deborah between Ramah and Bethel in the hill country of Ephraim, and the Israelites came up to her to have their disputes decided]" (Judges 4:5). To understand her personality, you need to understand her name. Deborah literally means wasp and her story reveals that she was willing to sting if need be, even leading an army to war if the Lord led. She was uncompromising in her zeal for the Lord, singing, "[So may all your enemies perish, O Lord! But may they who love you be like the sun when it rises in its strength]" (Judges 5:31). This godly woman could be prickly, but she also blessed those who followed the Lord . . .

Perhaps you know someone who is as prickly as a cactus. The care of prickly pears is quite simple: Put them in the sun and don't overwater them. You can care for your prickly friends the same way. Make sure you place them in the Son by praying for them often. And don't saturate them with too much attention. That's when you might get stung.

— *Penny Pierce Rose*

 Go to page 294 for your next devotional reading.

4 "O Lord, when you went out from Seir,
    when you marched from the land of
        Edom,
  the earth shook, the heavens poured,
    the clouds poured down water.
5 The mountains quaked
        before the Lord, the
        One of Sinai,
    before the Lord, the God
        of Israel.

6 "In the days of Shamgar
        son of Anath,
    in the days of Jael,
        the roads were
        abandoned;
    travelers took to winding
        paths.
7 Village life^a in Israel
        ceased,
    ceased until I,^b Deborah,
        arose,
    arose a mother in Israel.
8 When they chose new gods,
    war came to the city gates,
  and not a shield or spear was seen
    among forty thousand in Israel.
9 My heart is with Israel's princes,
    with the willing volunteers among the
        people.
    Praise the Lord!

10 "You who ride on white donkeys,
    sitting on your saddle blankets,
    and you who walk along the road,
  consider 11 the voice of the singers^c at the
        watering places.
    They recite the righteous acts of the Lord,
    the righteous acts of his warriors^d in
        Israel.

  "Then the people of the Lord
        went down to the city gates.
12 'Wake up, wake up, Deborah!
    Wake up, wake up, break out in song!
  Arise, O Barak!
    Take captive your captives, O son of
        Abinoam.'

13 "Then the men who were left
    came down to the nobles;

the people of the Lord
    came to me with the mighty.
14 Some came from Ephraim, whose roots
    were in Amalek;
        Benjamin was with
            the people who
            followed you.
    From Makir captains came
        down,
        from Zebulun those who
            bear a commander's
            staff.
15 The princes of Issachar
        were with Deborah;
    yes, Issachar was with
        Barak,
    rushing after him into
        the valley.
  In the districts of Reuben
        there was much
        searching of heart.
16 Why did you stay among the campfires^e
    to hear the whistling for the flocks?
  In the districts of Reuben
    there was much searching of heart.
17 Gilead stayed beyond the Jordan.
    And Dan, why did he linger by the
        ships?
  Asher remained on the coast
    and stayed in his coves.
18 The people of Zebulun risked their very
        lives;
    so did Naphtali on the heights of the
        field.

19 "Kings came, they fought;
    the kings of Canaan fought
  at Taanach by the waters of Megiddo,
    but they carried off no silver, no plunder.
20 From the heavens the stars fought,
    from their courses they fought against
        Sisera.
21 The river Kishon swept them away,
    the age-old river, the river Kishon.
    March on, my soul; be strong!
22 Then thundered the horses' hoofs—
    galloping, galloping go his mighty
        steeds.
23 'Curse Meroz,' said the angel of the Lord.

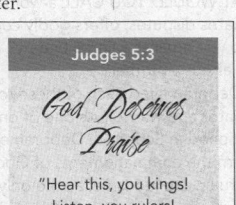

Judges 5:3

God Deserves
Praise

"Hear this, you kings!
Listen, you rulers!
I will sing to the Lord,
    I will sing;
I will make music to the
Lord, the God of Israel."

---

a 7 Or *Warriors*   b 7 Or *you*   c 11 Or *archers*; the meaning of the Hebrew for this word is uncertain.   d 11 Or *villagers*   e 16 Or *saddlebags*

Spiritual Motherhood

Village life in Israel
ceased, ceased until I,
Deborah, arose, arose
a mother in Israel.

reflection

1 What are some specific ways in which you can become a spiritual mother to someone else?

2 How does the story of Deborah encourage you in your various leadership roles?

3 Whom do you think God may have placed in your life to nurture or encourage?

RELATED READINGS

Proverbs 31:10–31;
Titus 2:3–8

Read: Judges 4–5

WHAT WOULD YOU CALL a woman who sits under a palm tree, mediates disputes, offers godly counsel and takes up weapons to go to war against a fierce enemy? A madwoman? A multitasker? How about a mother?

Deborah filled each of these roles. She was a prophetess, ruler, mediator and warrior. As one of only a handful of prophetesses mentioned in Scripture, Deborah exercised the divine ability to discern the commandments of God and declare them to others. As a ruler, she led Israel as the only female judge. As a mediator, Deborah conducted arbitration and settled disputes. As a warrior, she went to battle on behalf of her extended family, the children of Israel.

A woman this gifted at multitasking could be called many things, but Deborah designated one title for herself: mother. Although her husband is named in Scripture, there is no record that she had children. However, rather than referring to herself as a judge or prophetess she instead called herself "I, Deborah . . . a mother in Israel."

The Biblical record of this highly respected leader is a case study in spiritual motherhood. Deborah was leading Israel at a time when the country needed protection from the domination of the Canaanites, ruled by King Jabin and his military commander Sisera. God told her to instruct an Israelite warrior named Barak to take ten thousand troops into battle against Sisera. God promised victory if Barak followed his directions. Barak, however, refused to go unless Deborah went with him.

Although Deborah warned Barak that his honor would suffer as a result of his lack of faith, she agreed to accompany him into battle. Rather than holding his timidity against him, Deborah decided to do what was best for her nation: She fought the enemy like a mother bear.

We do not have to carry, adopt or raise children in order to qualify as spiritual mothers. Instead, we only need to display a willingness to use the gifts that God has entrusted to us in order to nurture others and strengthen others in their faith. Deborah was such a woman. Are you willing to let God use you?

Go to page 298 for your next devotional reading.

'Curse its people bitterly,
because they did not come to help the
Lord,
to help the Lord against the mighty.'

24 "Most blessed of women be Jael,
the wife of Heber the Kenite,
most blessed of tent-dwelling women.
25 He asked for water, and she gave him milk;
in a bowl fit for nobles she brought him
curdled milk.
26 Her hand reached for the tent peg,
her right hand for the workman's
hammer.
She struck Sisera, she crushed his head,
she shattered and pierced his temple.
27 At her feet he sank,
he fell; there he lay.
At her feet he sank, he fell;
where he sank, there he fell—dead.

28 "Through the window peered Sisera's
mother;
behind the lattice she cried out,
'Why is his chariot so long in coming?
Why is the clatter of his chariots
delayed?'
29 The wisest of her ladies answer her;
indeed, she keeps saying to herself,
30 'Are they not finding and dividing the
spoils:
a girl or two for each man,
colorful garments as plunder for Sisera,
colorful garments embroidered,
highly embroidered garments for my
neck—
all this as plunder?'

31 "So may all your enemies perish, O Lord!
But may they who love you be like the
sun
when it rises in its strength."

Then the land had peace forty years.

Gideon

6 Again the Israelites did evil in the eyes
of the Lord, and for seven years he gave
them into the hands of the Midianites. 2 Because the power of Midian was so oppressive,

the Israelites prepared shelters for themselves
in mountain clefts, caves and strongholds.
3 Whenever the Israelites planted their crops,
the Midianites, Amalekites and other eastern
peoples invaded the country. 4 They camped
on the land and ruined the crops all the way to
Gaza and did not spare a living thing for Israel,
neither sheep nor cattle nor donkeys. 5 They
came up with their livestock and their tents
like swarms of locusts. It was impossible to
count the men and their camels; they invaded
the land to ravage it. 6 Midian so impoverished
the Israelites that they cried out to the Lord
for help.

7 When the Israelites cried to the Lord because of Midian, 8 he sent them a prophet, who
said, "This is what the Lord, the God of Israel,
says: I brought you up out of Egypt, out of the
land of slavery. 9 I snatched you from the power
of Egypt and from the hand of all your oppressors. I drove them from before you and gave
you their land. 10 I said to you, 'I am the Lord
your God; do not worship the gods of the Amorites, in whose land you live.' But you have not
listened to me."

11 The angel of the Lord came and sat down
under the oak in Ophrah that belonged to Joash the Abiezrite, where his son Gideon was
threshing wheat in a winepress to keep it from
the Midianites. 12 When the angel of the Lord
appeared to Gideon, he said, "The Lord is with
you, mighty warrior."

13 "But sir," Gideon replied, "if the Lord
is with us, why has all this happened to us?
Where are all his wonders that our fathers told
us about when they said, 'Did not the Lord
bring us up out of Egypt?' But now the Lord
has abandoned us and put us into the hand of
Midian."

14 The Lord turned to him and said, "Go
in the strength you have and save Israel out of
Midian's hand. Am I not sending you?"

15 "But Lord,ᵃ" Gideon asked, "how can I
save Israel? My clan is the weakest in Manasseh, and I am the least in my family."

16 The Lord answered, "I will be with you,
and you will strike down all the Midianites
together."

17 Gideon replied, "If now I have found favor

ᵃ15 Or sir

in your eyes, give me a sign that it is really you talking to me. **18**Please do not go away until I come back and bring my offering and set it before you."

And the LORD said, "I will wait until you return."

19Gideon went in, prepared a young goat, and from an ephah*a* of flour he made bread without yeast. Putting the meat in a basket and its broth in a pot, he brought them out and offered them to him under the oak.

20The angel of God said to him, "Take the meat and the unleavened bread, place them on this rock, and pour out the broth." And Gideon did so. **21**With the tip of the staff that was in his hand, the angel of the LORD touched the meat and the unleavened bread. Fire flared from the rock, consuming the meat and the bread. And the angel of the LORD disappeared. **22**When Gideon realized that it was the angel of the LORD, he exclaimed, "Ah, Sovereign LORD! I have seen the angel of the LORD face to face!"

23But the LORD said to him, "Peace! Do not be afraid. You are not going to die."

24So Gideon built an altar to the LORD there and called it The LORD is Peace. To this day it stands in Ophrah of the Abiezrites.

25That same night the LORD said to him, "Take the second bull from your father's herd, the one seven years old.*b* Tear down your father's altar to Baal and cut down the Asherah pole*c* beside it. **26**Then build a proper kind of*d* altar to the LORD your God on the top of this height. Using the wood of the Asherah pole that you cut down, offer the second*e* bull as a burnt offering."

27So Gideon took ten of his servants and did as the LORD told him. But because he was afraid of his family and the men of the town, he did it at night rather than in the daytime.

28In the morning when the men of the town got up, there was Baal's altar, demolished, with the Asherah pole beside it cut down and the second bull sacrificed on the newly built altar!

29They asked each other, "Who did this?"

When they carefully investigated, they were told, "Gideon son of Joash did it."

30The men of the town demanded of Joash, "Bring out your son. He must die, because he has broken down Baal's altar and cut down the Asherah pole beside it."

31But Joash replied to the hostile crowd around him, "Are you going to plead Baal's cause? Are you trying to save him? Whoever fights for him shall be put to death by morning! If Baal really is a god, he can defend himself when someone breaks down his altar." **32**So that day they called Gideon "Jerub-Baal,*f*" saying, "Let Baal contend with him," because he broke down Baal's altar.

33Now all the Midianites, Amalekites and other eastern peoples joined forces and crossed over the Jordan and camped in the Valley of Jezreel. **34**Then the Spirit of the LORD came upon Gideon, and he blew a trumpet, summoning the Abiezrites to follow him. **35**He sent messengers throughout Manasseh, calling them to arms, and also into Asher, Zebulun and Naphtali, so that they too went up to meet them.

36Gideon said to God, "If you will save Israel by my hand as you have promised— **37**look, I will place a wool fleece on the threshing floor. If there is dew only on the fleece and all the ground is dry, then I will know that you will save Israel by my hand, as you said." **38**And that is what happened. Gideon rose early the next day; he squeezed the fleece and wrung out the dew—a bowlful of water.

39Then Gideon said to God, "Do not be angry with me. Let me make just one more request. Allow me one more test with the fleece. This time make the fleece dry and the ground covered with dew." **40**That night God did so. Only the fleece was dry; all the ground was covered with dew.

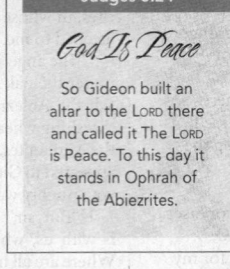

Judges 6:24

God Is Peace

So Gideon built an altar to the LORD there and called it The LORD is Peace. To this day it stands in Ophrah of the Abiezrites.

---

*a***19** That is, probably about 3/5 bushel (about 22 liters) *b***25** Or *Take a full-grown, mature bull from your father's herd* *c***25** That is, a symbol of the goddess Asherah; here and elsewhere in Judges *d***26** Or *build with layers of stone an* *e***26** Or *full-grown*; also in verse 28 *f***32** Jerub-Baal means *let Baal contend.*

Gideon Defeats the Midianites

7 Early in the morning, Jerub-Baal (that is, Gideon) and all his men camped at the spring of Harod. The camp of Midian was north of them in the valley near the hill of Moreh. ²The LORD said to Gideon, "You have too many men for me to deliver Midian into their hands. In order that Israel may not boast against me that her own strength has saved her, ³announce now to the people, 'Anyone who trembles with fear may turn back and leave Mount Gilead.'" So twenty-two thousand men left, while ten thousand remained.

⁴But the LORD said to Gideon, "There are still too many men. Take them down to the water, and I will sift them for you there. If I say, 'This one shall go with you,' he shall go; but if I say, 'This one shall not go with you,' he shall not go."

⁵So Gideon took the men down to the water. There the LORD told him, "Separate those who lap the water with their tongues like a dog from those who kneel down to drink." ⁶Three hundred men lapped with their hands to their mouths. All the rest got down on their knees to drink.

⁷The LORD said to Gideon, "With the three hundred men that lapped I will save you and give the Midianites into your hands. Let all the other men go, each to his own place." ⁸So Gideon sent the rest of the Israelites to their tents but kept the three hundred, who took over the provisions and trumpets of the others.

Now the camp of Midian lay below him in the valley. ⁹During that night the LORD said to Gideon, "Get up, go down against the camp, because I am going to give it into your hands. ¹⁰If you are afraid to attack, go down to the camp with your servant Purah ¹¹and listen to what they are saying. Afterward, you will be encouraged to attack the camp." So he and Purah his servant went down to the outposts of the camp. ¹²The Midianites, the Amalekites and all the other eastern peoples had settled in the valley, thick as locusts. Their camels could no more be counted than the sand on the seashore.

¹³Gideon arrived just as a man was telling a friend his dream. "I had a dream," he was saying. "A round loaf of barley bread came tumbling into the Midianite camp. It struck the tent with such force that the tent overturned and collapsed."

¹⁴His friend responded, "This can be nothing other than the sword of Gideon son of Joash, the Israelite. God has given the Midianites and the whole camp into his hands."

¹⁵When Gideon heard the dream and its interpretation, he worshiped God. He returned to the camp of Israel and called out, "Get up! The LORD has given the Midianite camp into your hands." ¹⁶Dividing the three hundred men into three companies, he placed trumpets and empty jars in the hands of all of them, with torches inside.

¹⁷"Watch me," he told them. "Follow my lead. When I get to the edge of the camp, do exactly as I do. ¹⁸When I and all who are with me blow our trumpets, then from all around the camp blow yours and shout, 'For the LORD and for Gideon.'"

¹⁹Gideon and the hundred men with him reached the edge of the camp at the beginning of the middle watch, just after they had changed the guard. They blew their trumpets and broke the jars that were in their hands. ²⁰The three companies blew the trumpets and smashed the jars. Grasping the torches in their left hands and holding in their right hands the trumpets they were to blow, they shouted, "A sword for the LORD and for Gideon!" ²¹While each man held his position around the camp, all the Midianites ran, crying out as they fled.

²²When the three hundred trumpets sounded, the LORD caused the men throughout the camp to turn on each other with their swords. The army fled to Beth Shittah toward Zererah as far as the border of Abel Meholah near Tabbath. ²³Israelites from Naphtali, Asher and all Manasseh were called out, and they pursued the Midianites. ²⁴Gideon sent messengers throughout the hill country of Ephraim, saying, "Come down against the Midianites and seize the waters of the Jordan ahead of them as far as Beth Barah."

So all the men of Ephraim were called out and they took the waters of the Jordan as far as Beth Barah. ²⁵They also captured two of the Midianite leaders, Oreb and Zeeb. They killed Oreb at the rock of Oreb, and Zeeb at the winepress of Zeeb. They pursued the Midianites and

Is the Battle Too Big?

Read: Judges 7:1–22

Judges 7:9

During that night the LORD said to Gideon, "Get up, go down against the camp, because I am going to give it into your hands."

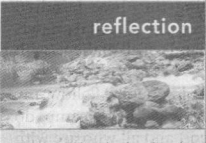

reflection

1 Describe the last battle you faced.

2 Did you rely on your own power or the power of God?

3 After reading this Scripture passage, how will you face your next battle?

RELATED READINGS

1 Samuel 17:32–50;
2 Chronicles 20:5–15;
1 Timothy 6:11–12

HAVE YOU EVER TURNED AWAY from a battle you knew you should fight to its conclusion? Lynn desperately wanted to run from her battle. But she didn't.

When the phone rang at her house, she picked it up at the same time as her husband. She started to say something, but stopped when she overheard a female voice on the line. Lynn bit her quivering lip as she overheard evidence of her husband's affair. After a confrontation, her husband moved into the woman's house. Deeply depressed, she found herself unable to face her neighbors and friends.

One day Maggie, one of Lynn's friends, insisted on dropping by. Maggie took one look at Lynn's tear-streaked face and the defeated slump of her shoulders and sent Lynn to bed. That night Maggie stayed by her bedside, praying. Every time Lynn awoke from her restless sleep, she saw her friend's lips moving, pleading with God. The next morning, Maggie made Lynn get up, shower and dress. She helped her brush her hair, then prepared breakfast. Afterward, they prayed together about Lynn's situation.

Gideon was brave, but he knew the enemy was strong. So God came to Gideon and promised him victory. He instructed Gideon to battle the massive army of the Midianites with only 300 men. Imagine how Gideon felt. He faced a battle in which he was significantly outnumbered. But Gideon battled the enemy using the weapons God had chosen: blaring trumpets and glowing torches.

Through the help and support of many friends, God gave Lynn the spiritual strength and courage to talk to her husband. Regardless of the outcome of her heartbreaking situation, she knew that she had to face the battle head-on. She couldn't lock herself in her house and wish it all away. Lynn had to fight.

What do you do when you face a battle? Do you run away? Do you hope it will go away? Or do you stand and fight, leaning on God for support?

Perhaps for you it's the dawn of a battle: a difficult discussion with your spouse, a confrontation with a coworker, a meeting with a school principal. Take a few deep breaths and then ask God to go with you and give you *his* weapons for the battle. Though you may feel small and powerless, God will be mighty and powerful. He will equip you to do what is required of you.

brought the heads of Oreb and Zeeb to Gideon, who was by the Jordan.

Zebah and Zalmunna

8 Now the Ephraimites asked Gideon, "Why have you treated us like this? Why didn't you call us when you went to fight Midian?" And they criticized him sharply.

²But he answered them, "What have I accomplished compared to you? Aren't the gleanings of Ephraim's grapes better than the full grape harvest of Abiezer? ³God gave Oreb and Zeeb, the Midianite leaders, into your hands. What was I able to do compared to you?" At this, their resentment against him subsided.

⁴Gideon and his three hundred men, exhausted yet keeping up the pursuit, came to the Jordan and crossed it. ⁵He said to the men of Succoth, "Give my troops some bread; they are worn out, and I am still pursuing Zebah and Zalmunna, the kings of Midian."

⁶But the officials of Succoth said, "Do you already have the hands of Zebah and Zalmunna in your possession? Why should we give bread to your troops?"

⁷Then Gideon replied, "Just for that, when the LORD has given Zebah and Zalmunna into my hand, I will tear your flesh with desert thorns and briers."

⁸From there he went up to Peniel*a* and made the same request of them, but they answered as the men of Succoth had. ⁹So he said to the men of Peniel, "When I return in triumph, I will tear down this tower."

¹⁰Now Zebah and Zalmunna were in Karkor with a force of about fifteen thousand men, all that were left of the armies of the eastern peoples; a hundred and twenty thousand swordsmen had fallen. ¹¹Gideon went up by the route of the nomads east of Nobah and Jogbehah and fell upon the unsuspecting army. ¹²Zebah and Zalmunna, the two kings of Midian, fled, but he pursued them and captured them, routing their entire army.

¹³Gideon son of Joash then returned from the battle by the Pass of Heres. ¹⁴He caught a young man of Succoth and questioned him, and the young man wrote down for him the names of the seventy-seven officials of Succoth, the elders of the town. ¹⁵Then Gideon came and said to the men of Succoth, "Here are Zebah and Zalmunna, about whom you taunted me by saying, 'Do you already have the hands of Zebah and Zalmunna in your possession? Why should we give bread to your exhausted men?'" ¹⁶He took the elders of the town and taught the men of Succoth a lesson by punishing them with desert thorns and briers. ¹⁷He also pulled down the tower of Peniel and killed the men of the town.

¹⁸Then he asked Zebah and Zalmunna, "What kind of men did you kill at Tabor?"

"Men like you," they answered, "each one with the bearing of a prince."

¹⁹Gideon replied, "Those were my brothers, the sons of my own mother. As surely as the LORD lives, if you had spared their lives, I would not kill you." ²⁰Turning to Jether, his oldest son, he said, "Kill them!" But Jether did not draw his sword, because he was only a boy and was afraid.

²¹Zebah and Zalmunna said, "Come, do it yourself. 'As is the man, so is his strength.'" So Gideon stepped forward and killed them, and took the ornaments off their camels' necks.

Gideon's Ephod

²²The Israelites said to Gideon, "Rule over us—you, your son and your grandson—because you have saved us out of the hand of Midian."

²³But Gideon told them, "I will not rule over you, nor will my son rule over you. The LORD will rule over you." ²⁴And he said, "I do have one request, that each of you give me an earring from your share of the plunder." (It was the custom of the Ishmaelites to wear gold earrings.)

²⁵They answered, "We'll be glad to give them." So they spread out a garment, and each man threw a ring from his plunder onto it. ²⁶The weight of

> **Judges 8:23**
>
> *God Is Our Ruler*
>
> But Gideon told them,
> "I will not rule over you,
> nor will my son rule over
> you. The LORD will
> rule over you."

---

*a*8 Hebrew *Penuel*, a variant of *Peniel*; also in verses 9 and 17 the gold rings he asked for came to seventeen hundred shekels,[a] not counting the ornaments, the pendants and the purple garments worn by the kings of Midian or the chains that were on their camels' necks. 27Gideon made the gold into an ephod, which he placed in Ophrah, his town. All Israel prostituted themselves by worshiping it there, and it became a snare to Gideon and his family.

Gideon's Death

28Thus Midian was subdued before the Israelites and did not raise its head again. During Gideon's lifetime, the land enjoyed peace forty years.

29Jerub-Baal son of Joash went back home to live. 30He had seventy sons of his own, for he had many wives. 31His concubine, who lived in Shechem, also bore him a son, whom he named Abimelech. 32Gideon son of Joash died at a good old age and was buried in the tomb of his father Joash in Ophrah of the Abiezrites.

33No sooner had Gideon died than the Israelites again prostituted themselves to the Baals. They set up Baal-Berith as their god and 34did not remember the LORD their God, who had rescued them from the hands of all their enemies on every side. 35They also failed to show kindness to the family of Jerub-Baal (that is, Gideon) for all the good things he had done for them.

Abimelech

9 Abimelech son of Jerub-Baal went to his mother's brothers in Shechem and said to them and to all his mother's clan, 2"Ask all the citizens of Shechem, 'Which is better for you: to have all seventy of Jerub-Baal's sons rule over you, or just one man?' Remember, I am your flesh and blood."

3When the brothers repeated all this to the citizens of Shechem, they were inclined to follow Abimelech, for they said, "He is our brother." 4They gave him seventy shekels[b] of silver from the temple of Baal-Berith, and Abimelech used it to hire reckless adventurers, who became his followers. 5He went to his father's home in Ophrah and on one stone murdered his seventy brothers, the sons of Jerub-Baal. But Jotham, the youngest son of Jerub-Baal, escaped by hiding. 6Then all the citizens of Shechem and Beth Millo gathered beside the great tree at the pillar in Shechem to crown Abimelech king.

7When Jotham was told about this, he climbed up on the top of Mount Gerizim and shouted to them, "Listen to me, citizens of Shechem, so that God may listen to you. 8One day the trees went out to anoint a king for themselves. They said to the olive tree, 'Be our king.'

9"But the olive tree answered, 'Should I give up my oil, by which both gods and men are honored, to hold sway over the trees?'

10"Next, the trees said to the fig tree, 'Come and be our king.'

11"But the fig tree replied, 'Should I give up my fruit, so good and sweet, to hold sway over the trees?'

12"Then the trees said to the vine, 'Come and be our king.'

13"But the vine answered, 'Should I give up my wine, which cheers both gods and men, to hold sway over the trees?'

14"Finally all the trees said to the thornbush, 'Come and be our king.'

15"The thornbush said to the trees, 'If you really want to anoint me king over you, come and take refuge in my shade; but if not, then let fire come out of the thornbush and consume the cedars of Lebanon!'

16"Now if you have acted honorably and in good faith when you made Abimelech king, and if you have been fair to Jerub-Baal and his family, and if you have treated him as he deserves— 17and to think that my father fought for you, risked his life to rescue you from the hand of Midian 18(but today you have revolted against my father's family, murdered his seventy sons on a single stone, and made Abimelech, the son of his slave girl, king over the citizens of Shechem because he is your brother)— 19if then you have acted honorably and in good faith toward Jerub-Baal and his family today, may Abimelech be your joy, and may you be his, too! 20But if you have not, let fire come out from Abimelech and consume you, citizens of Shechem and Beth Millo, and let fire come out from you, citizens of Shechem and Beth Millo, and consume Abimelech!"

21Then Jotham fled, escaping to Beer, and

---

[a]26 That is, about 43 pounds (about 19.5 kilograms)   [b]4 That is, about 1 3/4 pounds (about 0.8 kilogram)

he lived there because he was afraid of his brother Abimelech.

²²After Abimelech had governed Israel three years, ²³God sent an evil spirit between Abimelech and the citizens of Shechem, who acted treacherously against Abimelech. ²⁴God did this in order that the crime against Jerub-Baal's seventy sons, the shedding of their blood, might be avenged on their brother Abimelech and on the citizens of Shechem, who had helped him murder his brothers. ²⁵In opposition to him these citizens of Shechem set men on the hilltops to ambush and rob everyone who passed by, and this was reported to Abimelech.

²⁶Now Gaal son of Ebed moved with his brothers into Shechem, and its citizens put their confidence in him. ²⁷After they had gone out into the fields and gathered the grapes and trodden them, they held a festival in the temple of their god. While they were eating and drinking, they cursed Abimelech. ²⁸Then Gaal son of Ebed said, "Who is Abimelech, and who is Shechem, that we should be subject to him? Isn't he Jerub-Baal's son, and isn't Zebul his deputy? Serve the men of Hamor, Shechem's father! Why should we serve Abimelech? ²⁹If only this people were under my command! Then I would get rid of him. I would say to Abimelech, 'Call out your whole army!'"ᵃ

³⁰When Zebul the governor of the city heard what Gaal son of Ebed said, he was very angry. ³¹Under cover he sent messengers to Abimelech, saying, "Gaal son of Ebed and his brothers have come to Shechem and are stirring up the city against you. ³²Now then, during the night you and your men should come and lie in wait in the fields. ³³In the morning at sunrise, advance against the city. When Gaal and his men come out against you, do whatever your hand finds to do."

³⁴So Abimelech and all his troops set out by night and took up concealed positions near Shechem in four companies. ³⁵Now Gaal son of Ebed had gone out and was standing at the entrance to the city gate just as Abimelech and his soldiers came out from their hiding place.

³⁶When Gaal saw them, he said to Zebul, "Look, people are coming down from the tops of the mountains!"

Zebul replied, "You mistake the shadows of the mountains for men."

³⁷But Gaal spoke up again: "Look, people are coming down from the center of the land, and a company is coming from the direction of the soothsayers' tree."

³⁸Then Zebul said to him, "Where is your big talk now, you who said, 'Who is Abimelech that we should be subject to him?' Aren't these the men you ridiculed? Go out and fight them!"

³⁹So Gaal led outᵇ the citizens of Shechem and fought Abimelech. ⁴⁰Abimelech chased him, and many fell wounded in the flight—all the way to the entrance to the gate. ⁴¹Abimelech stayed in Arumah, and Zebul drove Gaal and his brothers out of Shechem.

⁴²The next day the people of Shechem went out to the fields, and this was reported to Abimelech. ⁴³So he took his men, divided them into three companies and set an ambush in the fields. When he saw the people coming out of the city, he rose to attack them. ⁴⁴Abimelech and the companies with him rushed forward to a position at the entrance to the city gate. Then two companies rushed upon those in the fields and struck them down. ⁴⁵All that day Abimelech pressed his attack against the city until he had captured it and killed its people. Then he destroyed the city and scattered salt over it.

⁴⁶On hearing this, the citizens in the tower of Shechem went into the stronghold of the temple of El-Berith. ⁴⁷When Abimelech heard that they had assembled there, ⁴⁸he and all his men went up Mount Zalmon. He took an ax and cut off some branches, which he lifted to his shoulders. He ordered the men with him, "Quick! Do what you have seen me do!" ⁴⁹So all the men cut branches and followed Abimelech. They piled them against the stronghold and set it on fire over the people inside. So all the people in the tower of Shechem, about a thousand men and women, also died.

⁵⁰Next Abimelech went to Thebez and besieged it and captured it. ⁵¹Inside the city, however, was a strong tower, to which all the men and women—all the people of the city—fled. They locked themselves in and climbed up on the tower roof. ⁵²Abimelech went to the tower and stormed it. But as he approached

ᵃ29 Septuagint; Hebrew *him.*" Then he said to Abimelech, "Call out your whole army!"   ᵇ39 Or *Gaal went out in the sight of* the entrance to the tower to set it on fire, 53a woman dropped an upper millstone on his head and cracked his skull.

54Hurriedly he called to his armor-bearer, "Draw your sword and kill me, so that they can't say, 'A woman killed him.'" So his servant ran him through, and he died. 55When the Israelites saw that Abimelech was dead, they went home.

56Thus God repaid the wickedness that Abimelech had done to his father by murdering his seventy brothers. 57God also made the men of Shechem pay for all their wickedness. The curse of Jotham son of Jerub-Baal came on them.

Tola

10 After the time of Abimelech a man of Issachar, Tola son of Puah, the son of Dodo, rose to save Israel. He lived in Shamir, in the hill country of Ephraim. 2He leda Israel twenty-three years; then he died, and was buried in Shamir.

Jair

3He was followed by Jair of Gilead, who led Israel twenty-two years. 4He had thirty sons, who rode thirty donkeys. They controlled thirty towns in Gilead, which to this day are called Havvoth Jair.b 5When Jair died, he was buried in Kamon.

Jephthah

6Again the Israelites did evil in the eyes of the LORD. They served the Baals and the Ashtoreths, and the gods of Aram, the gods of Sidon, the gods of Moab, the gods of the Ammonites and the gods of the Philistines. And because the Israelites forsook the LORD and no longer served him, 7he became angry with them. He sold them into the hands of the Philistines and the Ammonites, 8who that year shattered and crushed them. For eighteen years they oppressed all the Israelites on the east side of the Jordan in Gilead, the land of the Amorites. 9The Ammonites also crossed the Jordan to

fight against Judah, Benjamin and the house of Ephraim; and Israel was in great distress. 10Then the Israelites cried out to the LORD, "We have sinned against you, forsaking our God and serving the Baals."

11The LORD replied, "When the Egyptians, the Amorites, the Ammonites, the Philistines, 12the Sidonians, the Amalekites and the Maonitesc oppressed you and you cried to me for help, did I not save you from their hands? 13But you have forsaken me and served other gods, so I will no longer save you. 14Go and cry out to the gods you have chosen. Let them save you when you are in trouble!"

15But the Israelites said to the LORD, "We have sinned. Do with us whatever you think best, but please rescue us now." 16Then they got rid of the foreign gods among them and served the LORD. And he could bear Israel's misery no longer.

17When the Ammonites were called to arms and camped in Gilead, the Israelites assembled and camped at Mizpah. 18The leaders of the people of Gilead said to each other, "Whoever will launch the attack against the Ammonites will be the head of all those living in Gilead."

11 Jephthah the Gileadite was a mighty warrior. His father was Gilead; his mother was a prostitute. 2Gilead's wife also bore him sons, and when they were grown up, they drove Jephthah away. "You are not going to get any inheritance in our family," they said, "because you are the son of another woman." 3So Jephthah fled from his brothers and settled in the land of Tob, where a group of adventurers gathered around him and followed him.

4Some time later, when the Ammonites made war on Israel, 5the elders of Gilead went to get Jephthah from the land of Tob. 6"Come," they said, "be our commander, so we can fight the Ammonites."

7Jephthah said to them, "Didn't you hate me and drive me from my father's house? Why do you come to me now, when you're in trouble?"

Judges 10:16

God Is Merciful

Then they got rid of the foreign gods among them and served the LORD. And he could bear Israel's misery no longer.

---

a2 Traditionally *judged*; also in verse 3   b4 Or *called the settlements of Jair*   c12 Hebrew; some Septuagint manuscripts *Midianites*

8The elders of Gilead said to him, "Nevertheless, we are turning to you now; come with us to fight the Ammonites, and you will be our head over all who live in Gilead."

9Jephthah answered, "Suppose you take me back to fight the Ammonites and the LORD gives them to me—will I really be your head?"

10The elders of Gilead replied, "The LORD is our witness; we will certainly do as you say." **11**So Jephthah went with the elders of Gilead, and the people made him head and commander over them. And he repeated all his words before the LORD in Mizpah.

12Then Jephthah sent messengers to the Ammonite king with the question: "What do you have against us that you have attacked our country?"

13The king of the Ammonites answered Jephthah's messengers, "When Israel came up out of Egypt, they took away my land from the Arnon to the Jabbok, all the way to the Jordan. Now give it back peaceably."

14Jephthah sent back messengers to the Ammonite king, **15**saying:

"This is what Jephthah says: Israel did not take the land of Moab or the land of the Ammonites. **16**But when they came up out of Egypt, Israel went through the desert to the Red Sea[a] and on to Kadesh. **17**Then Israel sent messengers to the king of Edom, saying, 'Give us permission to go through your country,' but the king of Edom would not listen. They sent also to the king of Moab, and he refused. So Israel stayed at Kadesh.

18"Next they traveled through the desert, skirted the lands of Edom and Moab, passed along the eastern side of the country of Moab, and camped on the other side of the Arnon. They did not enter the territory of Moab, for the Arnon was its border.

19"Then Israel sent messengers to Sihon king of the Amorites, who ruled in Heshbon, and said to him, 'Let us pass through your country to our own place.' **20**Sihon, however, did not trust Israel[b] to pass through his territory. He mustered all his men and encamped at Jahaz and fought with Israel.

21"Then the LORD, the God of Israel, gave Sihon and all his men into Israel's hands, and they defeated them. Israel took over all the land of the Amorites who lived in that country, **22**capturing all of it from the Arnon to the Jabbok and from the desert to the Jordan.

23"Now since the LORD, the God of Israel, has driven the Amorites out before his people Israel, what right have you to take it over? **24**Will you not take what your god Chemosh gives you? Likewise, whatever the LORD our God has given us, we will possess. **25**Are you better than Balak son of Zippor, king of Moab? Did he ever quarrel with Israel or fight with them? **26**For three hundred years Israel occupied Heshbon, Aroer, the surrounding settlements and all the towns along the Arnon. Why didn't you retake them during that time? **27**I have not wronged you, but you are doing me wrong by waging war against me. Let the LORD, the Judge,[c] decide the dispute this day between the Israelites and the Ammonites."

28The king of Ammon, however, paid no attention to the message Jephthah sent him.

29Then the Spirit of the LORD came upon Jephthah. He crossed Gilead and Manasseh, passed through Mizpah of Gilead, and from there he advanced against the Ammonites. **30**And Jephthah made a vow to the LORD: "If you give the Ammonites into my hands, **31**whatever comes out of the door of my house to meet me when I return in triumph from the Ammonites will be the LORD's, and I will sacrifice it as a burnt offering."

32Then Jephthah went over to fight the Ammonites, and the LORD gave them into his hands. **33**He devastated twenty towns from Aroer to the vicinity of Minnith, as far as Abel Keramim. Thus Israel subdued Ammon.

34When Jephthah returned to his home in Mizpah, who should come out to meet him but his daughter, dancing to the sound of tambourines! She was an only child. Except for her

---

[a]16 Hebrew *Yam Suph*; that is, Sea of Reeds   [b]20 Or *however, would not make an agreement for Israel*   [c]27 Or *Ruler*

Steps of Faith

MIRIAM

But the Israelites went through the sea on dry ground, with a wall of water on their right and on their left.

Exodus 14:29

"OUCH!" INSTINCTIVELY, SHE nursed her finger in her mouth.

The blade of a reed grass had grazed her finger as she hurriedly joined her mother near the riverbank.

"Shh, be quiet darling," her mother whispered. Although her mother spoke calmly, she'd never seen her look so preoccupied. Her face seemed heavy, almost stone-like, burdened with emotion that Miriam couldn't quite pinpoint.

What was it Mother felt . . . fear . . . worry . . . distress? Miriam decided that whatever it was, it frightened her.

Of course, Miriam had been scared before—hearing strange sounds at night or a sudden clap of thunder. But what she saw on her mother's face ushered in her first experience of cold-blooded fear. A strange, raw energy channeled like currents of lightning between them as they huddled together near the shore.

"What if the princess doesn't find my brother nestled in the curve of the shallow embankment? What if she becomes angry with me because he is a Hebrew boy? What if she wants to kill us?" Miriam's mind raced with anxiety.

She cast one last worried glance over her shoulder at her mother before stepping into the shallow water along the shoreline and making her way toward the princess. Moving forward in faith in the midst of fear, she began a strange dance step she would dance again later in her life.

And now, years later as an adult woman, standing at the shore of the Red Sea after fleeing from slavery in Egypt, she felt that same fear in the core of her being—that same adrenaline-laced, metallic sensation in her mouth. The two days were like bookends in her mind, full of similarities: risk, uncertainty, limited options.

"What if Pharaoh's army reaches the shore before we all cross over? What if one of our carts breaks down or a child falls in the sea? What if . . ."

But something was different this time as an adult. She could call upon the same faith in the midst of fear that she'd practiced as a child. It would strengthen her to step forward and do what must be done once more. Miriam cast another glance over her shoulder at the approaching Egyptian army before confidently and resolutely striding into the shallow water.

ASSIGNED READING:

Exodus 2:1–10; 13:17—15:21

—*Prayer*—
Savior, I can and will, with your help, overcome my fears.

Weekend

he had neither son nor daughter. ³⁵When he saw her, he tore his clothes and cried, "Oh! My daughter! You have made me miserable and wretched, because I have made a vow to the LORD that I cannot break."

³⁶"My father," she replied, "you have given your word to the LORD. Do to me just as you promised, now that the LORD has avenged you of your enemies, the Ammonites. ³⁷But grant me this one request," she said. "Give me two months to roam the hills and weep with my friends, because I will never marry."

³⁸"You may go," he said. And he let her go for two months. She and the girls went into the hills and wept because she would never marry. ³⁹After the two months, she returned to her father and he did to her as he had vowed. And she was a virgin.

From this comes the Israelite custom ⁴⁰that each year the young women of Israel go out for four days to commemorate the daughter of Jephthah the Gileadite.

Jephthah and Ephraim

12 The men of Ephraim called out their forces, crossed over to Zaphon and said to Jephthah, "Why did you go to fight the Ammonites without calling us to go with you? We're going to burn down your house over your head."

²Jephthah answered, "I and my people were engaged in a great struggle with the Ammonites, and although I called, you didn't save me out of their hands. ³When I saw that you wouldn't help, I took my life in my hands and crossed over to fight the Ammonites, and the LORD gave me the victory over them. Now why have you come up today to fight me?"

⁴Jephthah then called together the men of Gilead and fought against Ephraim. The Gileadites struck them down because the Ephraimites had said, "You Gileadites are renegades from Ephraim and Manasseh." ⁵The Gileadites captured the fords of the Jordan leading to Ephraim, and whenever a survivor of Ephraim said, "Let me cross over," the men of Gilead asked him, "Are you an Ephraimite?" If he replied, "No," ⁶they said, "All right, say 'Shibboleth.'" If he said, "Sibboleth," because he could

not pronounce the word correctly, they seized him and killed him at the fords of the Jordan. Forty-two thousand Ephraimites were killed at that time.

⁷Jephthah led*a* Israel six years. Then Jephthah the Gileadite died, and was buried in a town in Gilead.

Ibzan, Elon and Abdon

⁸After him, Ibzan of Bethlehem led Israel. ⁹He had thirty sons and thirty daughters. He gave his daughters away in marriage to those outside his clan, and for his sons he brought in thirty young women as wives from outside his clan. Ibzan led Israel seven years. ¹⁰Then Ibzan died, and was buried in Bethlehem.

¹¹After him, Elon the Zebulunite led Israel ten years. ¹²Then Elon died, and was buried in Aijalon in the land of Zebulun.

¹³After him, Abdon son of Hillel, from Pirathon, led Israel. ¹⁴He had forty sons and thirty grandsons, who rode on seventy donkeys. He led Israel eight years. ¹⁵Then Abdon son of Hillel died, and was buried at Pirathon in Ephraim, in the hill country of the Amalekites.

The Birth of Samson

13 Again the Israelites did evil in the eyes of the LORD, so the LORD delivered them into the hands of the Philistines for forty years.

²A certain man of Zorah, named Manoah, from the clan of the Danites, had a wife who was sterile and remained childless. ³The angel of the LORD appeared to her and said, "You are sterile and childless, but you are going to conceive and have a son. ⁴Now see to it that you drink no wine or other fermented drink and that you do not eat anything unclean, ⁵because you will conceive and give birth to a son. No razor may be used on his head, because the boy is to be a Nazirite, set apart to God from birth, and he will begin the deliverance of Israel from the hands of the Philistines."

⁶Then the woman went to her husband and told him, "A man of God came to me. He looked like an angel of God, very awesome. I didn't ask him where he came from, and he didn't tell me his name. ⁷But he said to me, 'You will conceive and give birth to a son. Now then,

*a*7 Traditionally *judged*; also in verses 8–14

drink no wine or other fermented drink and do not eat anything unclean, because the boy will be a Nazirite of God from birth until the day of his death.' "

⁸Then Manoah prayed to the LORD: "O Lord, I beg you, let the man of God you sent to us come again to teach us how to bring up the boy who is to be born."

⁹God heard Manoah, and the angel of God came again to the woman while she was out in the field; but her husband Manoah was not with her. ¹⁰The woman hurried to tell her husband, "He's here! The man who appeared to me the other day!"

¹¹Manoah got up and followed his wife. When he came to the man, he said, "Are you the one who talked to my wife?"

"I am," he said.

¹²So Manoah asked him, "When your words are fulfilled, what is to be the rule for the boy's life and work?"

¹³The angel of the LORD answered, "Your wife must do all that I have told her. ¹⁴She must not eat anything that comes from the grapevine, nor drink any wine or other fermented drink nor eat anything unclean. She must do everything I have commanded her."

¹⁵Manoah said to the angel of the LORD, "We would like you to stay until we prepare a young goat for you."

¹⁶The angel of the LORD replied, "Even though you detain me, I will not eat any of your food. But if you prepare a burnt offering, offer it to the LORD." (Manoah did not realize that it was the angel of the LORD.)

¹⁷Then Manoah inquired of the angel of the LORD, "What is your name, so that we may honor you when your word comes true?"

¹⁸He replied, "Why do you ask my name? It is beyond understanding.[a]"

¹⁹Then Manoah took a young goat, together with the grain offering, and sacrificed it on a rock to the LORD. And the LORD did an amazing thing while Manoah and his wife watched: ²⁰As the flame blazed up from the altar toward heaven, the angel of the LORD ascended in the flame. Seeing this, Manoah and his wife fell with their faces to the ground. ²¹When the angel of the LORD did not show himself again to Manoah and his wife, Manoah realized that it was the angel of the LORD.

²²"We are doomed to die!" he said to his wife. "We have seen God!"

²³But his wife answered, "If the LORD had meant to kill us, he would not have accepted a burnt offering and grain offering from our hands, nor shown us all these things or now told us this."

²⁴The woman gave birth to a boy and named him Samson. He grew and the LORD blessed him, ²⁵and the Spirit of the LORD began to stir him while he was in Mahaneh Dan, between Zorah and Eshtaol.

Samson's Marriage

14 Samson went down to Timnah and saw there a young Philistine woman. ²When he returned, he said to his father and mother, "I have seen a Philistine woman in Timnah; now get her for me as my wife."

³His father and mother replied, "Isn't there an acceptable woman among your relatives or among all our people? Must you go to the uncircumcised Philistines to get a wife?"

But Samson said to his father, "Get her for me. She's the right one for me." ⁴(His parents did not know that this was from the LORD, who was seeking an occasion to confront the Philistines; for at that time they were ruling over Israel.) ⁵Samson went down to Timnah together with his father and mother. As they approached the vineyards of Timnah, suddenly a young lion came roaring toward him. ⁶The Spirit of the LORD came upon him in power so that he tore the lion apart with his bare hands as he might have torn a young goat. But he told neither his father nor his mother what he had done. ⁷Then he went down and talked with the woman, and he liked her.

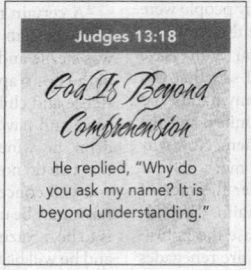

Judges 13:18

God Is Beyond Comprehension

He replied, "Why do you ask my name? It is beyond understanding."

ª 18 Or *is wonderful*

8Some time later, when he went back to marry her, he turned aside to look at the lion's carcass. In it was a swarm of bees and some honey, 9which he scooped out with his hands and ate as he went along. When he rejoined his parents, he gave them some, and they too ate it. But he did not tell them that he had taken the honey from the lion's carcass.

10Now her father went down to see the woman. And Samson made a feast there, as was customary for bridegrooms. 11When he appeared, he was given thirty companions.

12"Let me tell you a riddle," Samson said to them. "If you can give me the answer within the seven days of the feast, I will give you thirty linen garments and thirty sets of clothes. 13If you can't tell me the answer, you must give me thirty linen garments and thirty sets of clothes."

"Tell us your riddle," they said. "Let's hear it."

14He replied,

"Out of the eater, something to eat;
    out of the strong, something sweet."

For three days they could not give the answer.

15On the fourth*a* day, they said to Samson's wife, "Coax your husband into explaining the riddle for us, or we will burn you and your father's household to death. Did you invite us here to rob us?"

16Then Samson's wife threw herself on him, sobbing, "You hate me! You don't really love me. You've given my people a riddle, but you haven't told me the answer."

"I haven't even explained it to my father or mother," he replied, "so why should I explain it to you?" 17She cried the whole seven days of the feast. So on the seventh day he finally told her, because she continued to press him. She in turn explained the riddle to her people.

18Before sunset on the seventh day the men of the town said to him,

"What is sweeter than honey?
    What is stronger than a lion?"

Samson said to them,

"If you had not plowed with my heifer,
    you would not have solved my riddle."

19Then the Spirit of the LORD came upon him in power. He went down to Ashkelon, struck down thirty of their men, stripped them of their belongings and gave their clothes to those who had explained the riddle. Burning with anger, he went up to his father's house. 20And Samson's wife was given to the friend who had attended him at his wedding.

Samson's Vengeance on the Philistines

15 Later on, at the time of wheat harvest, Samson took a young goat and went to visit his wife. He said, "I'm going to my wife's room." But her father would not let him go in.

2"I was so sure you thoroughly hated her," he said, "that I gave her to your friend. Isn't her younger sister more attractive? Take her instead."

3Samson said to them, "This time I have a right to get even with the Philistines; I will really harm them." 4So he went out and caught three hundred foxes and tied them tail to tail in pairs. He then fastened a torch to every pair of tails, 5lit the torches and let the foxes loose in the standing grain of the Philistines. He burned up the shocks and standing grain, together with the vineyards and olive groves.

6When the Philistines asked, "Who did this?" they were told, "Samson, the Timnite's son-in-law, because his wife was given to his friend."

So the Philistines went up and burned her and her father to death. 7Samson said to them, "Since you've acted like this, I won't stop until I get my revenge on you." 8He attacked them viciously and slaughtered many of them. Then he went down and stayed in a cave in the rock of Etam.

9The Philistines went up and camped in Judah, spreading out near Lehi. 10The men of Judah asked, "Why have you come to fight us?"

"We have come to take Samson prisoner," they answered, "to do to him as he did to us."

11Then three thousand men from Judah went down to the cave in the rock of Etam and said to Samson, "Don't you realize that the Philistines are rulers over us? What have you done to us?"

He answered, "I merely did to them what they did to me."

*a*15 Some Septuagint manuscripts and Syriac; Hebrew *seventh*

¹²They said to him, "We've come to tie you up and hand you over to the Philistines."

Samson said, "Swear to me that you won't kill me yourselves."

¹³"Agreed," they answered. "We will only tie you up and hand you over to them. We will not kill you." So they bound him with two new ropes and led him up from the rock. ¹⁴As he approached Lehi, the Philistines came toward him shouting. The Spirit of the LORD came upon him in power. The ropes on his arms became like charred flax, and the bindings dropped from his hands. ¹⁵Finding a fresh jawbone of a donkey, he grabbed it and struck down a thousand men.

¹⁶Then Samson said,

"With a donkey's jawbone
    I have made donkeys of them.ᵃ
With a donkey's jawbone
    I have killed a thousand men."

¹⁷When he finished speaking, he threw away the jawbone; and the place was called Ramath Lehi.ᵇ

¹⁸Because he was very thirsty, he cried out to the LORD, "You have given your servant this great victory. Must I now die of thirst and fall into the hands of the uncircumcised?" ¹⁹Then God opened up the hollow place in Lehi, and water came out of it. When Samson drank, his strength returned and he revived. So the spring was called En Hakkore,ᶜ and it is still there in Lehi.

²⁰Samson ledᵈ Israel for twenty years in the days of the Philistines.

Samson and Delilah

16 One day Samson went to Gaza, where he saw a prostitute. He went in to spend the night with her. ²The people of Gaza were told, "Samson is here!" So they surrounded the place and lay in wait for him all night at the city gate. They made no move during the night, saying, "At dawn we'll kill him."

³But Samson lay there only until the middle of the night. Then he got up and took hold of the doors of the city gate, together with the two posts, and tore them loose, bar and all. He lifted them to his shoulders and carried them to the top of the hill that faces Hebron.

⁴Some time later, he fell in love with a woman in the Valley of Sorek whose name was Delilah. ⁵The rulers of the Philistines went to her and said, "See if you can lure him into showing you the secret of his great strength and how we can overpower him so we may tie him up and subdue him. Each one of us will give you eleven hundred shekelsᵉ of silver."

⁶So Delilah said to Samson, "Tell me the secret of your great strength and how you can be tied up and subdued."

⁷Samson answered her, "If anyone ties me with seven fresh thongsᶠ that have not been dried, I'll become as weak as any other man."

⁸Then the rulers of the Philistines brought her seven fresh thongs that had not been dried, and she tied him with them. ⁹With men hidden in the room, she called to him, "Samson, the Philistines are upon you!" But he snapped the thongs as easily as a piece of string snaps when it comes close to a flame. So the secret of his strength was not discovered.

¹⁰Then Delilah said to Samson, "You have made a fool of me; you lied to me. Come now, tell me how you can be tied."

¹¹He said, "If anyone ties me securely with new ropes that have never been used, I'll become as weak as any other man."

¹²So Delilah took new ropes and tied him with them. Then, with men hidden in the room, she called to him, "Samson, the Philistines are upon you!" But he snapped the ropes off his arms as if they were threads.

¹³Delilah then said to Samson, "Until now, you have been making a fool of me and lying to me. Tell me how you can be tied."

He replied, "If you weave the seven braids of my head into the fabric ˌon the loomˌ and tighten it with the pin, I'll become as weak as any other man." So while he was sleeping, Delilah took the seven braids of his head, wove them into the fabric ¹⁴andᵍ tightened it with the pin.

Again she called to him, "Samson, the Phi-

ᵃ16 Or *made a heap or two;* the Hebrew for *donkey* sounds like the Hebrew for *heap.*   ᵇ17 *Ramath Lehi* means *jawbone hill.*   ᶜ19 *En Hakkore* means *caller's spring.*   ᵈ20 Traditionally *judged*   ᵉ5 That is, about 28 pounds (about 13 kilograms)   ᶠ7 Or *bowstrings;* also in verses 8 and 9   ᵍ13,14 Some Septuagint manuscripts; Hebrew *"I can if you weave the seven braids of my head into the fabric ˌon the loom."*   ¹⁴*So she*

Femme Fatales

Read: Judges 16:4–22

A FEMME FATALE IS A WOMAN who uses the powers of seduction to lure a man into a dangerous or compromising situation. One woman infamous for her influence was Mata Hari. At the turn of the twentieth century in Paris, Mata Hari created a fictitious persona and performed exotic Indian dance to great acclaim. Although her background was fabricated, Parisian society embraced her . . . and men were beguiled by her. Her sensuous dance seduced powerful men in influential positions. Many believe she used feminine guile to extract military secrets. Ultimately, the French tried Mata Hari and executed her as a double agent in World War I. At her trial she said, "Harlot, yes. But traitor? Never!"

In the Bible, we meet another woman who used her feminine allure to affect the destiny of a man. During the time of the judges, Delilah used her influence to discover the secrets of one of Israel's judges, Samson. Three different times Delilah begged him to give her information about the source of his strength. Three times he resisted. Each time Delilah proved herself false, calling for the Philistines to subdue the strong man. More stunning is that Delilah used the same method over and over again . . . and Samson allowed himself to be tricked each time. Ultimately, Delilah discovered the truth about Samson's strength and turned him over to her countrymen.

Delilah's story shows how men can be swayed by women's wiles and their own desires. Delilah used her sexual attraction and her cunning to bring a man down—for a price. She relentlessly manipulated Samson in order to get the information she needed. When he finally revealed the truth, she rushed to the Philistine rulers to gather her reward. In a heartbeat, Samson lost not just his strength, but the divine gift God had bestowed upon him.

We think it would be great to be able to get our husbands, boyfriends, coworkers, etc. to do what we want. And perhaps, sometimes, we *do* use feminine wiles, manipulation and nagging to get our way. But are such methods honest? Are they loving? Wouldn't it be better to be the kind of woman others can trust? How much better to employ honesty, kindness and patience to build up the men we love, rather than trample them in the pursuit of our selfish desires

Judges 16:15–16

Then she said to him,
"How can you say,
'I love you,' when you
won't confide in me?
This is the third time
you have made a fool of
me and haven't told me
the secret of your great
strength." With such
nagging she prodded
him day after day until he
was tired to death.

reflection

1 Have you ever nagged, manipulated or tricked a man in order to get your way?

2 How did it make you feel? How do you think it made him feel?

3 What words will you use to build up the men in your life?

RELATED READINGS

Proverbs 14:1; 19:13; 31:11–12; 1 Peter 3:1–6

Monday

Go to page 316 for your next devotional reading.

listines are upon you!" He awoke from his sleep and pulled up the pin and the loom, with the fabric.

¹⁵Then she said to him, "How can you say, 'I love you,' when you won't confide in me? This is the third time you have made a fool of me and haven't told me the secret of your great strength." ¹⁶With such nagging she prodded him day after day until he was tired to death.

¹⁷So he told her everything. "No razor has ever been used on my head," he said, "because I have been a Nazirite set apart to God since birth. If my head were shaved, my strength would leave me, and I would become as weak as any other man."

¹⁸When Delilah saw that he had told her everything, she sent word to the rulers of the Philistines, "Come back once more; he has told me everything." So the rulers of the Philistines returned with the silver in their hands. ¹⁹Having put him to sleep on her lap, she called a man to shave off the seven braids of his hair, and so began to subdue him.*ᵃ* And his strength left him.

²⁰Then she called, "Samson, the Philistines are upon you!"

He awoke from his sleep and thought, "I'll go out as before and shake myself free." But he did not know that the LORD had left him.

²¹Then the Philistines seized him, gouged out his eyes and took him down to Gaza. Binding him with bronze shackles, they set him to grinding in the prison. ²²But the hair on his head began to grow again after it had been shaved.

The Death of Samson

²³Now the rulers of the Philistines assembled to offer a great sacrifice to Dagon their god and to celebrate, saying, "Our god has delivered Samson, our enemy, into our hands."

²⁴When the people saw him, they praised their god, saying,

"Our god has delivered our enemy
into our hands,
the one who laid waste our land
and multiplied our slain."

²⁵While they were in high spirits, they shouted, "Bring out Samson to entertain us." So they called Samson out of the prison, and he performed for them.

When they stood him among the pillars, ²⁶Samson said to the servant who held his hand, "Put me where I can feel the pillars that support the temple, so that I may lean against them." ²⁷Now the temple was crowded with men and women; all the rulers of the Philistines were there, and on the roof were about three thousand men and women watching Samson perform. ²⁸Then Samson prayed to the LORD, "O Sovereign LORD, remember me. O God, please strengthen me just once more, and let me with one blow get revenge on the Philistines for my two eyes." ²⁹Then Samson reached toward the two central pillars on which the temple stood. Bracing himself against them, his right hand on the one and his left hand on the other, ³⁰Samson said, "Let me die with the Philistines!" Then he pushed with all his might, and down came the temple on the rulers and all the people in it. Thus he killed many more when he died than while he lived.

³¹Then his brothers and his father's whole family went down to get him. They brought him back and buried him between Zorah and Eshtaol in the tomb of Manoah his father. He had led*ᵇ* Israel twenty years.

Micah's Idols

17 Now a man named Micah from the hill country of Ephraim ²said to his mother, "The eleven hundred shekels*ᶜ* of silver that were taken from you and about which I heard you utter a curse—I have that silver with me; I took it."

Judges 16:28

God Remembers His Children

Then Samson prayed to the LORD, "O Sovereign LORD, remember me. O God, please strengthen me just once more, and let me with one blow get revenge on the Philistines for my two eyes."

---

*ᵃ19 Hebrew; some Septuagint manuscripts *and he began to weaken* 13 kilograms)* *ᵇ31 Traditionally *judged* *ᶜ2 That is, about 28 pounds (about 13 kilograms)

Then his mother said, "The LORD bless you, my son!"

3 When he returned the eleven hundred shekels of silver to his mother, she said, "I solemnly consecrate my silver to the LORD for my son to make a carved image and a cast idol. I will give it back to you."

4 So he returned the silver to his mother, and she took two hundred shekels*a* of silver and gave them to a silversmith, who made them into the image and the idol. And they were put in Micah's house.

5 Now this man Micah had a shrine, and he made an ephod and some idols and installed one of his sons as his priest. **6** In those days Israel had no king; everyone did as he saw fit.

7 A young Levite from Bethlehem in Judah, who had been living within the clan of Judah, **8** left that town in search of some other place to stay. On his way*b* he came to Micah's house in the hill country of Ephraim.

9 Micah asked him, "Where are you from?"

"I'm a Levite from Bethlehem in Judah," he said, "and I'm looking for a place to stay."

10 Then Micah said to him, "Live with me and be my father and priest, and I'll give you ten shekels*c* of silver a year, your clothes and your food." **11** So the Levite agreed to live with him, and the young man was to him like one of his sons. **12** Then Micah installed the Levite, and the young man became his priest and lived in his house. **13** And Micah said, "Now I know that the LORD will be good to me, since this Levite has become my priest."

Danites Settle in Laish

18 In those days Israel had no king.

And in those days the tribe of the Danites was seeking a place of their own where they might settle, because they had not yet come into an inheritance among the tribes of Israel. **2** So the Danites sent five warriors from Zorah and Eshtaol to spy out the land and explore it. These men represented all their clans. They told them, "Go, explore the land."

The men entered the hill country of Ephraim and came to the house of Micah, where they spent the night. **3** When they were near Micah's house, they recognized the voice of the young Levite; so they turned in there and asked him, "Who brought you here? What are you doing in this place? Why are you here?"

4 He told them what Micah had done for him, and said, "He has hired me and I am his priest."

5 Then they said to him, "Please inquire of God to learn whether our journey will be successful."

6 The priest answered them, "Go in peace. Your journey has the LORD's approval."

7 So the five men left and came to Laish, where they saw that the people were living in safety, like the Sidonians, unsuspecting and secure. And since their land lacked nothing, they were prosperous.*d* Also, they lived a long way from the Sidonians and had no relationship with anyone else.*e*

8 When they returned to Zorah and Eshtaol, their brothers asked them, "How did you find things?"

9 They answered, "Come on, let's attack them! We have seen that the land is very good. Aren't you going to do something? Don't hesitate to go there and take it over. **10** When you get there, you will find an unsuspecting people and a spacious land that God has put into your hands, a land that lacks nothing whatever."

11 Then six hundred men from the clan of the Danites, armed for battle, set out from Zorah and Eshtaol. **12** On their way they set up camp near Kiriath Jearim in Judah. This is why the place west of Kiriath Jearim is called Mahaneh Dan*f* to this day. **13** From there they went on to the hill country of Ephraim and came to Micah's house.

14 Then the five men who had spied out the land of Laish said to their brothers, "Do you know that one of these houses has an ephod, other household gods, a carved image and a cast idol? Now you know what to do." **15** So they turned in there and went to the house of the young Levite at Micah's place and greeted him. **16** The six hundred Danites, armed for battle, stood at the entrance to the gate. **17** The five men who had spied out the land went

---

*a*4 That is, about 5 pounds (about 2.3 kilograms)   *b*8 Or *To carry on his profession*   *c*10 That is, about 4 ounces (about 110 grams)   *d*7 The meaning of the Hebrew for this clause is uncertain.   *e*7 Hebrew; some Septuagint manuscripts *with the Arameans*   *f*12 Mahaneh Dan means *Dan's camp*.

inside and took the carved image, the ephod, the other household gods and the cast idol while the priest and the six hundred armed men stood at the entrance to the gate.

¹⁸When these men went into Micah's house and took the carved image, the ephod, the other household gods and the cast idol, the priest said to them, "What are you doing?"

¹⁹They answered him, "Be quiet! Don't say a word. Come with us, and be our father and priest. Isn't it better that you serve a tribe and clan in Israel as priest rather than just one man's household?" ²⁰Then the priest was glad. He took the ephod, the other household gods and the carved image and went along with the people. ²¹Putting their little children, their livestock and their possessions in front of them, they turned away and left.

²²When they had gone some distance from Micah's house, the men who lived near Micah were called together and overtook the Danites. ²³As they shouted after them, the Danites turned and said to Micah, "What's the matter with you that you called out your men to fight?"

²⁴He replied, "You took the gods I made, and my priest, and went away. What else do I have? How can you ask, 'What's the matter with you?'"

²⁵The Danites answered, "Don't argue with us, or some hot-tempered men will attack you, and you and your family will lose your lives." ²⁶So the Danites went their way, and Micah, seeing that they were too strong for him, turned around and went back home.

²⁷Then they took what Micah had made, and his priest, and went on to Laish, against a peaceful and unsuspecting people. They attacked them with the sword and burned down their city. ²⁸There was no one to rescue them because they lived a long way from Sidon and had no relationship with anyone else. The city was in a valley near Beth Rehob.

The Danites rebuilt the city and settled there. ²⁹They named it Dan after their forefather Dan, who was born to Israel—though the city used to be called Laish. ³⁰There the Danites set up for themselves the idols, and Jonathan son of Gershom, the son of Moses,ª and his sons

were priests for the tribe of Dan until the time of the captivity of the land. ³¹They continued to use the idols Micah had made, all the time the house of God was in Shiloh.

A Levite and His Concubine

19 In those days Israel had no king.

Now a Levite who lived in a remote area in the hill country of Ephraim took a concubine from Bethlehem in Judah. ²But she was unfaithful to him. She left him and went back to her father's house in Bethlehem, Judah. After she had been there four months, ³her husband went to her to persuade her to return. He had with him his servant and two donkeys. She took him into her father's house, and when her father saw him, he gladly welcomed him. ⁴His father-in-law, the girl's father, prevailed upon him to stay; so he remained with him three days, eating and drinking, and sleeping there.

⁵On the fourth day they got up early and he prepared to leave, but the girl's father said to his son-in-law, "Refresh yourself with something to eat; then you can go." ⁶So the two of them sat down to eat and drink together. Afterward the girl's father said, "Please stay tonight and enjoy yourself." ⁷And when the man got up to go, his father-in-law persuaded him, so he stayed there that night. ⁸On the morning of the fifth day, when he rose to go, the girl's father said, "Refresh yourself. Wait till afternoon!" So the two of them ate together.

⁹Then when the man, with his concubine and his servant, got up to leave, his father-in-law, the girl's father, said, "Now look, it's almost evening. Spend the night here; the day is nearly over. Stay and enjoy yourself. Early tomorrow morning you can get up and be on your way home." ¹⁰But, unwilling to stay another night, the man left and went toward Jebus (that is, Jerusalem), with his two saddled donkeys and his concubine.

¹¹When they were near Jebus and the day was almost gone, the servant said to his master, "Come, let's stop at this city of the Jebusites and spend the night."

¹²His master replied, "No. We won't go into an alien city, whose people are not Israelites. We will go on to Gibeah." ¹³He added, "Come,

---

ª30 An ancient Hebrew scribal tradition, some Septuagint manuscripts and Vulgate; Masoretic Text *Manasseh* let's try to reach Gibeah or Ramah and spend the night in one of those places." ¹⁴So they went on, and the sun set as they neared Gibeah in Benjamin. ¹⁵There they stopped to spend the night. They went and sat in the city square, but no one took them into his home for the night.

¹⁶That evening an old man from the hill country of Ephraim, who was living in Gibeah (the men of the place were Benjamites), came in from his work in the fields. ¹⁷When he looked and saw the traveler in the city square, the old man asked, "Where are you going? Where did you come from?"

¹⁸He answered, "We are on our way from Bethlehem in Judah to a remote area in the hill country of Ephraim where I live. I have been to Bethlehem in Judah and now I am going to the house of the LORD. No one has taken me into his house. ¹⁹We have both straw and fodder for our donkeys and bread and wine for ourselves your servants—me, your maidservant, and the young man with us. We don't need anything."

²⁰"You are welcome at my house," the old man said. "Let me supply whatever you need. Only don't spend the night in the square." ²¹So he took him into his house and fed his donkeys. After they had washed their feet, they had something to eat and drink.

²²While they were enjoying themselves, some of the wicked men of the city surrounded the house. Pounding on the door, they shouted to the old man who owned the house, "Bring out the man who came to your house so we can have sex with him."

²³The owner of the house went outside and said to them, "No, my friends, don't be so vile. Since this man is my guest, don't do this disgraceful thing. ²⁴Look, here is my virgin daughter, and his concubine. I will bring them out to you now, and you can use them and do to them whatever you wish. But to this man, don't do such a disgraceful thing."

²⁵But the men would not listen to him. So the man took his concubine and sent her outside to them, and they raped her and abused her throughout the night, and at dawn they let her go. ²⁶At daybreak the woman went back to the house where her master was staying, fell down at the door and lay there until daylight.

²⁷When her master got up in the morning and opened the door of the house and stepped out to continue on his way, there lay his concubine, fallen in the doorway of the house, with her hands on the threshold. ²⁸He said to her, "Get up; let's go." But there was no answer. Then the man put her on his donkey and set out for home.

²⁹When he reached home, he took a knife and cut up his concubine, limb by limb, into twelve parts and sent them into all the areas of Israel. ³⁰Everyone who saw it said, "Such a thing has never been seen or done, not since the day the Israelites came up out of Egypt. Think about it! Consider it! Tell us what to do!"

Israelites Fight the Benjamites

20 Then all the Israelites from Dan to Beersheba and from the land of Gilead came out as one man and assembled before the LORD in Mizpah. ²The leaders of all the people of the tribes of Israel took their places in the assembly of the people of God, four hundred thousand soldiers armed with swords. ³(The Benjamites heard that the Israelites had gone up to Mizpah.) Then the Israelites said, "Tell us how this awful thing happened."

⁴So the Levite, the husband of the murdered woman, said, "I and my concubine came to Gibeah in Benjamin to spend the night. ⁵During the night the men of Gibeah came after me and surrounded the house, intending to kill me. They raped my concubine, and she died. ⁶I took my concubine, cut her into pieces and sent one piece to each region of Israel's inheritance, because they committed this lewd and disgraceful act in Israel. ⁷Now, all you Israelites, speak up and give your verdict."

⁸All the people rose as one man, saying, "None of us will go home. No, not one of us will return to his house. ⁹But now this is what we'll do to Gibeah: We'll go up against it as the lot directs. ¹⁰We'll take ten men out of every hundred from all the tribes of Israel, and a hundred from a thousand, and a thousand from ten thousand, to get provisions for the army. Then, when the army arrives at Gibeah*a* in Benjamin, it can give them what they deserve for all this vileness done in Israel." ¹¹So all the men

---

*a*10 One Hebrew manuscript; most Hebrew manuscripts *Geba,* a variant of *Gibeah* of Israel got together and united as one man against the city.

¹²The tribes of Israel sent men throughout the tribe of Benjamin, saying, "What about this awful crime that was committed among you? ¹³Now surrender those wicked men of Gibeah so that we may put them to death and purge the evil from Israel."

But the Benjamites would not listen to their fellow Israelites. ¹⁴From their towns they came together at Gibeah to fight against the Israelites. ¹⁵At once the Benjamites mobilized twenty-six thousand swordsmen from their towns, in addition to seven hundred chosen men from those living in Gibeah. ¹⁶Among all these soldiers there were seven hundred chosen men who were left-handed, each of whom could sling a stone at a hair and not miss.

¹⁷Israel, apart from Benjamin, mustered four hundred thousand swordsmen, all of them fighting men.

¹⁸The Israelites went up to Bethel[a] and inquired of God. They said, "Who of us shall go first to fight against the Benjamites?"

The LORD replied, "Judah shall go first."

¹⁹The next morning the Israelites got up and pitched camp near Gibeah. ²⁰The men of Israel went out to fight the Benjamites and took up battle positions against them at Gibeah. ²¹The Benjamites came out of Gibeah and cut down twenty-two thousand Israelites on the battlefield that day. ²²But the men of Israel encouraged one another and again took up their positions where they had stationed themselves the first day. ²³The Israelites went up and wept before the LORD until evening, and they inquired of the LORD. They said, "Shall we go up again to battle against the Benjamites, our brothers?"

The LORD answered, "Go up against them."

²⁴Then the Israelites drew near to Benjamin the second day. ²⁵This time, when the Benjamites came out from Gibeah to oppose them,

they cut down another eighteen thousand Israelites, all of them armed with swords.

²⁶Then the Israelites, all the people, went up to Bethel, and there they sat weeping before the LORD. They fasted that day until evening and presented burnt offerings and fellowship offerings[b] to the LORD. ²⁷And the Israelites inquired of the LORD. (In those days the ark of the covenant of God was there, ²⁸with Phinehas son of Eleazar, the son of Aaron, ministering before it.) They asked, "Shall we go up again to battle with Benjamin our brother, or not?"

The LORD responded, "Go, for tomorrow I will give them into your hands."

Judges 20:28

God Comes Through

The LORD responded, "Go, for tomorrow I will give them into your hands."

²⁹Then Israel set an ambush around Gibeah. ³⁰They went up against the Benjamites on the third day and took up positions against Gibeah as they had done before. ³¹The Benjamites came out to meet them and were drawn away from the city. They began to inflict casualties on the Israelites as before, so that about thirty men fell in the open field and on the roads—the one leading to Bethel and the other to Gibeah.

³²While the Benjamites were saying, "We are defeating them as before," the Israelites were saying, "Let's retreat and draw them away from the city to the roads."

³³All the men of Israel moved from their places and took up positions at Baal Tamar, and the Israelite ambush charged out of its place on the west[c] of Gibeah.[d] ³⁴Then ten thousand of Israel's finest men made a frontal attack on Gibeah. The fighting was so heavy that the Benjamites did not realize how near disaster was. ³⁵The LORD defeated Benjamin before Israel, and on that day the Israelites struck down 25,100 Benjamites, all armed with swords. ³⁶Then the Benjamites saw that they were beaten.

Now the men of Israel had given way before Benjamin, because they relied on the ambush they had set near Gibeah. ³⁷The men who had been in ambush made a sudden dash into Gibeah, spread out and put the whole city to

---

a 18 Or *to the house of God*; also in verse 26   *b* 26 Traditionally *peace offerings*   *c* 33 Some Septuagint manuscripts and Vulgate; the meaning of the Hebrew for this word is uncertain.   *d* 33 Hebrew *Geba*, a variant of *Gibeah* the sword. [38]The men of Israel had arranged with the ambush that they should send up a great cloud of smoke from the city, [39]and then the men of Israel would turn in the battle.

The Benjamites had begun to inflict casualties on the men of Israel (about thirty), and they said, "We are defeating them as in the first battle." [40]But when the column of smoke began to rise from the city, the Benjamites turned and saw the smoke of the whole city going up into the sky. [41]Then the men of Israel turned on them, and the men of Benjamin were terrified, because they realized that disaster had come upon them. [42]So they fled before the Israelites in the direction of the desert, but they could not escape the battle. And the men of Israel who came out of the towns cut them down there. [43]They surrounded the Benjamites, chased them and easily[a] overran them in the vicinity of Gibeah on the east. [44]Eighteen thousand Benjamites fell, all of them valiant fighters. [45]As they turned and fled toward the desert to the rock of Rimmon, the Israelites cut down five thousand men along the roads. They kept pressing after the Benjamites as far as Gidom and struck down two thousand more.

[46]On that day twenty-five thousand Benjamite swordsmen fell, all of them valiant fighters. [47]But six hundred men turned and fled into the desert to the rock of Rimmon, where they stayed four months. [48]The men of Israel went back to Benjamin and put all the towns to the sword, including the animals and everything else they found. All the towns they came across they set on fire.

Wives for the Benjamites

21 The men of Israel had taken an oath at Mizpah: "Not one of us will give his daughter in marriage to a Benjamite."

[2]The people went to Bethel,[b] where they sat before God until evening, raising their voices and weeping bitterly. [3]"O LORD, the God of Israel," they cried, "why has this happened to Israel? Why should one tribe be missing from Israel today?"

[4]Early the next day the people built an altar and presented burnt offerings and fellowship offerings.[c]

[5]Then the Israelites asked, "Who from all the tribes of Israel has failed to assemble before the LORD?" For they had taken a solemn oath that anyone who failed to assemble before the LORD at Mizpah should certainly be put to death.

[6]Now the Israelites grieved for their brothers, the Benjamites. "Today one tribe is cut off from Israel," they said. [7]"How can we provide wives for those who are left, since we have taken an oath by the LORD not to give them any of our daughters in marriage?" [8]Then they asked, "Which one of the tribes of Israel failed to assemble before the LORD at Mizpah?" They discovered that no one from Jabesh Gilead had come to the camp for the assembly. [9]For when they counted the people, they found that none of the people of Jabesh Gilead were there.

[10]So the assembly sent twelve thousand fighting men with instructions to go to Jabesh Gilead and put to the sword those living there, including the women and children. [11]"This is what you are to do," they said. "Kill every male and every woman who is not a virgin." [12]They found among the people living in Jabesh Gilead four hundred young women who had never slept with a man, and they took them to the camp at Shiloh in Canaan.

[13]Then the whole assembly sent an offer of peace to the Benjamites at the rock of Rimmon. [14]So the Benjamites returned at that time and were given the women of Jabesh Gilead who had been spared. But there were not enough for all of them.

[15]The people grieved for Benjamin, because the LORD had made a gap in the tribes of Israel. [16]And the elders of the assembly said, "With the women of Benjamin destroyed, how shall we provide wives for the men who are left? [17]The Benjamite survivors must have heirs," they said, "so that a tribe of Israel will not be wiped out. [18]We can't give them our daughters as wives, since we Israelites have taken this oath: 'Cursed be anyone who gives a wife to a Benjamite.' [19]But look, there is the annual festival of the LORD in Shiloh, to the north of Bethel, and east of the road that goes from Bethel to Shechem, and to the south of Lebonah."

[20]So they instructed the Benjamites, saying,

---

[a]43 The meaning of the Hebrew for this word is uncertain.   [b]2 Or *to the house of God*   [c]4 Traditionally *peace offerings*

Read: Judges 21:1–25

I USED TO HAVE AN ANSWER for most problems in life. I had a lot to say on almost any subject. I now have fewer answers, and might be reduced to the simple phrase, God is faithful. I don't say that lightly or without thought; I say it because I know it is true, and I have discovered that it is true no matter what is happening in my life. With confidence, I add these words to the end of the worst statements in the world: My child is sick and I don't know what to do . . . but God is faithful; I lost my job and I don't know how I will pay my bills . . . but God is faithful; my husband has left me and my heart is torn in two . . . but God is faithful.

I don't mean that he will wave a magic wand and everything will fall into place; far from it. What I mean is that if in the darkest times in our lives we will learn to keep turning our face toward him, he is faithful. Faithful to be with us, faithful to watch over us, faithful to work in us to make us the men and women we are called to be . . .

Think of your own life. Stop for a moment and reflect on any situation where it seemed as if you were on your own, that it was hopeless, that you were forgotten. Remember how you could never have anticipated God showing up, but he did, with flying colors—even if it seemed like he left you dangling just a little too long for comfort!

I don't know what the circumstances of your life are right now, or how fast you feel you're falling, or whether you're frozen on the bar, afraid to let go and grab hold of God's hands. What I can tell you is that he is here, right now, and he won't let you go. He will catch you in midair. The net of his faithful love will cushion you when you free-fall.

—Sheila Walsh

reflection

1 From your experiences in life, what do you know to be true about God?

2 How has God shown himself to be faithful in the past? How does this give you confidence for the future?

3 Follow Sheila's suggestion and spend some time turning your face in trust toward God, even if things seem dark right now. Ask God to turn you into a faithful woman serving a faithful God.

RELATED READINGS

Deuteronomy 7:7–9;
Joshua 18:11–21;
Acts 13:16–25

Go to page 320 for your next devotional reading.

"Go and hide in the vineyards ²¹and watch. When the girls of Shiloh come out to join in the dancing, then rush from the vineyards and each of you seize a wife from the girls of Shiloh and go to the land of Benjamin. ²²When their fathers or brothers complain to us, we will say to them, 'Do us a kindness by helping them, because we did not get wives for them during the war, and you are innocent, since you did not give your daughters to them.'"

²³So that is what the Benjamites did. While the girls were dancing, each man caught one and carried her off to be his wife. Then they returned to their inheritance and rebuilt the towns and settled in them.

²⁴At that time the Israelites left that place and went home to their tribes and clans, each to his own inheritance.

²⁵In those days Israel had no king; everyone did as he saw fit.

Ruth

Author:
Unknown.

Audience:
The people of Israel.

Date:
Around 1000 B.C.

Setting:
The story is set sometime during the time of the judges when Israel and Moab were at peace.

Verse to Remember:
"Don't urge me to leave you or to turn back from you. Where you go I will go, and where you stay I will stay. Your people will be my people and your God my God." (1:16)

The book of Ruth is an ancient story that follows the journey of *one Jewish family's struggle* for survival. Escaping famine, Elimelech traveled to Moab with his wife, Naomi, and two sons. But ten years later, we find *Naomi in mourning* at the loss of both her husband and two sons. She is left alone in a foreign land with two Moabite daughters-in-law and no hope of future happiness . . . or so it seems. Naomi is a woman who forgot her dream, but *God had not forgotten her.* Through an unlikely chain of events, God restored her joy through her foreigner daughter-in-law and a kind, wealthy relative.

Naomi and Ruth

1 In the days when the judges ruled,[a] there was a famine in the land, and a man from Bethlehem in Judah, together with his wife and two sons, went to live for a while in the country of Moab. ²The man's name was Elimelech, his wife's name Naomi, and the names of his two sons were Mahlon and Kilion. They were Ephrathites from Bethlehem, Judah. And they went to Moab and lived there.

³Now Elimelech, Naomi's husband, died, and she was left with her two sons. ⁴They married Moabite women, one named Orpah and the other Ruth. After they had lived there about ten years, ⁵both Mahlon and Kilion also died, and Naomi was left without her two sons and her husband.

⁶When she heard in Moab that the LORD had come to the aid of his people by providing food for them, Naomi and her daughters-in-law pre-

[a]1 Traditionally *judged*

pared to return home from there. ⁷With her two daughters-in-law she left the place where she had been living and set out on the road that would take them back to the land of Judah.

⁸Then Naomi said to her two daughters-in-law, "Go back, each of you, to your mother's home. May the LORD show kindness to you, as you have shown to your dead and to me. ⁹May the LORD grant that each of you will find rest in the home of another husband."

Then she kissed them and they wept aloud ¹⁰and said to her, "We will go back with you to your people."

¹¹But Naomi said, "Return home, my daughters. Why would you come with me? Am I going to have any more sons, who could become your husbands? ¹²Return home, my daughters; I am too old to have another husband. Even if I thought there was still hope for me—even if I had a husband tonight and then gave birth to sons— ¹³would you wait until they grew up? Would you remain unmarried for them? No, my daughters. It is more bitter for me than for you, because the LORD's hand has gone out against me!"

¹⁴At this they wept again. Then Orpah kissed her mother-in-law good-by, but Ruth clung to her.

¹⁵"Look," said Naomi, "your sister-in-law is going back to her people and her gods. Go back with her."

¹⁶But Ruth replied, "Don't urge me to leave you or to turn back from you. Where you go I will go, and where you stay I will stay. Your people will be my people and your God my God. ¹⁷Where you die I will die, and there I will be buried. May the LORD deal with me, be it ever so severely, if anything but death separates you and me." ¹⁸When Naomi realized that Ruth was determined to go with her, she stopped urging her.

¹⁹So the two women went on until they came to Bethlehem. When they arrived in Beth-

lehem, the whole town was stirred because of them, and the women exclaimed, "Can this be Naomi?"

²⁰"Don't call me Naomi,ᵃ" she told them. "Call me Mara,ᵇ because the Almightyᶜ has made my life very bitter. ²¹I went away full, but the LORD has brought me back empty. Why call me Naomi? The LORD has afflictedᵈ me; the Almighty has brought misfortune upon me."

²²So Naomi returned from Moab accompanied by Ruth the Moabitess, her daughter-in-law, arriving in Bethlehem as the barley harvest was beginning.

Ruth Meets Boaz

2 Now Naomi had a relative on her husband's side, from the clan of Elimelech, a man of standing, whose name was Boaz.

²And Ruth the Moabitess said to Naomi, "Let me go to the fields and pick up the leftover grain behind anyone in whose eyes I find favor."

Naomi said to her, "Go ahead, my daughter." ³So she went out and began to glean in the fields behind the harvesters. As it turned out, she found herself working in a field belonging to Boaz, who was from the clan of Elimelech.

⁴Just then Boaz arrived from Bethlehem and greeted the harvesters, "The LORD be with you!"

"The LORD bless you!" they called back.

⁵Boaz asked the foreman of his harvesters, "Whose young woman is that?"

⁶The foreman replied, "She is the Moabitess who came back from Moab with Naomi. ⁷She said, 'Please let me glean and gather among the sheaves behind the harvesters.' She went into the field and has worked steadily from morning till now, except for a short rest in the shelter."

⁸So Boaz said to Ruth, "My daughter, listen to me. Don't go and glean in another field and

Ruth 1:16

God Adopts His Followers

But Ruth replied, "Don't urge me to leave you or to turn back from you. Where you go I will go, and where you stay I will stay. Your people will be my people and your God my God."

ᵃ**20** *Naomi* means *pleasant*; also in verse 21. ᵇ**20** *Mara* means *bitter*. ᶜ**20** Hebrew *Shaddai*; also in verse 21 ᵈ**21** Or *has testified against*

From Death to New Life

Read: Ruth 1:1–22

Ruth 1:16

But Ruth replied, "Don't urge me to leave you or to turn back from you. Where you go I will go, and where you stay I will stay. Your people will be my people and your God my God.

reflection

1 How has death touched your life?

2 How has God used death to resurrect your hope?

3 Can you help someone you know who is struggling with loss? Share your journey with her and encourage her from your own experiences.

RELATED READINGS

Jeremiah 29:11–14;
Romans 6:4–10;
Philippians 3:7–14;
1 Peter 1:3–7

"The ability to find joy in the world of sorrow and hope at the edge of despair is a woman's witness to courage and her gift of new life to all."

Miriam Theresa Winter

IN 1942, VIOLETTE SZABO'S HUSBAND, Lieutenant Etienne Szabo of the Free French Forces, died in action. Violette could easily have retired from sight. Their marriage had lasted barely two years. Etienne would never meet their daughter. But shortly after Etienne's death, 21-year-old Violette faced a choice: remain in the relative safety of England or go behind enemy lines as a spy in occupied France. She chose to venture courageously into her husband's country.

Ruth faced a similar decision when her husband died. Her mother-in-law, Naomi, had decided to return to Bethlehem. When Naomi urged Ruth and her sister-in-law to stay in Moab, Orpah chose to stay among her people and pagan gods. She disappeared into the land and from the Scriptural record. Ruth, however, chose to follow her mother-in-law to the land of Judah.

So, with Naomi, Ruth journeyed to the promised land, where she found new hope, a new husband and a place in the genealogy of the Messiah. Her story illustrates a paradox of faith: New life can come from the tragedy of death (see John 12:24).

Not all of us have experienced the death of a spouse as Violette or Ruth did, but we have all experienced death in some form. Some of us have lost someone dear, leaving emptiness in our hearts. We go on, but we ache for their presence.

What do you do in the face of death? Do you blame God, as Naomi did? Do you stay put in nowhere land, as Orpah stayed in Moab? Or do you let God weave your grief into a new story, as Ruth did?

On Violette Szabo's second mission in France, a German patrol ambushed and wounded her. She insisted her French guide save himself and escape, which he did. During her capture and imprisonment, her fellow prisoners would remember her incredible generosity and courage. In the winter of 1945, Madame Szabo gave her life aiding in the effort to free her husband's homeland.

Our faith promises new life. God knows the "deaths" you've experienced. His plans for you are good, though they may look different than you expected. Rest in the knowledge that God uses every circumstance to strengthen your faith in him. When you think that life as you knew it is over, remember the One who said "I am making everything new" (Revelation 21:5).

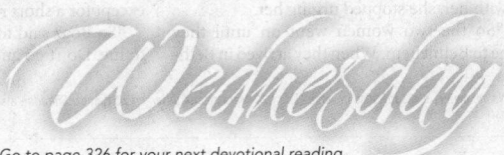

don't go away from here. Stay here with my servant girls. ⁹Watch the field where the men are harvesting, and follow along after the girls. I have told the men not to touch you. And whenever you are thirsty, go and get a drink from the water jars the men have filled."

¹⁰At this, she bowed down with her face to the ground. She exclaimed, "Why have I found such favor in your eyes that you notice me—a foreigner?"

¹¹Boaz replied, "I've been told all about what you have done for your mother-in-law since the death of your husband—how you left your father and mother and your homeland and came to live with a people you did not know before. ¹²May the LORD repay you for what you have done. May you be richly rewarded by the LORD, the God of Israel, under whose wings you have come to take refuge."

¹³"May I continue to find favor in your eyes, my lord," she said. "You have given me comfort and have spoken kindly to your servant—though I do not have the standing of one of your servant girls."

¹⁴At mealtime Boaz said to her, "Come over here. Have some bread and dip it in the wine vinegar."

When she sat down with the harvesters, he offered her some roasted grain. She ate all she wanted and had some left over. ¹⁵As she got up to glean, Boaz gave orders to his men, "Even if she gathers among the sheaves, don't embarrass her. ¹⁶Rather, pull out some stalks for her from the bundles and leave them for her to pick up, and don't rebuke her."

¹⁷So Ruth gleaned in the field until evening. Then she threshed the barley she had gathered, and it amounted to about an ephah.ᵃ ¹⁸She carried it back to town, and her mother-in-law saw how much she had gathered. Ruth also brought out and gave her what she had left over after she had eaten enough.

¹⁹Her mother-in-law asked her, "Where did you glean today? Where did you work? Blessed be the man who took notice of you!"

Then Ruth told her mother-in-law about the one at whose place she had been working. "The name of the man I worked with today is Boaz," she said.

²⁰"The LORD bless him!" Naomi said to her daughter-in-law. "He has not stopped showing his kindness to the living and the dead." She added, "That man is our close relative; he is one of our kinsman-redeemers."

²¹Then Ruth the Moabitess said, "He even said to me, 'Stay with my workers until they finish harvesting all my grain.'"

²²Naomi said to Ruth her daughter-in-law, "It will be good for you, my daughter, to go with his girls, because in someone else's field you might be harmed."

²³So Ruth stayed close to the servant girls of Boaz to glean until the barley and wheat harvests were finished. And she lived with her mother-in-law.

Ruth and Boaz at the Threshing Floor

3 One day Naomi her mother-in-law said to her, "My daughter, should I not try to find a homeᵇ for you, where you will be well provided for? ²Is not Boaz, with whose servant girls you have been, a kinsman of ours? Tonight he will be winnowing barley on the threshing floor. ³Wash and perfume yourself, and put on your best clothes. Then go down to the threshing floor, but don't let him know you are there until he has finished eating and drinking. ⁴When he lies down, note the place where he is lying. Then go and uncover his feet and lie down. He will tell you what to do."

⁵"I will do whatever you say," Ruth answered. ⁶So she went down to the threshing floor and did everything her mother-in-law told her to do.

⁷When Boaz had finished eating and drinking and was in good spirits, he went over to lie down at the far end of the grain pile. Ruth approached quietly, uncovered his feet and lay down. ⁸In the middle of the night something startled the man, and he turned and discovered a woman lying at his feet.

⁹"Who are you?" he asked.

"I am your servant Ruth," she said. "Spread the corner of your garment over me, since you are a kinsman-redeemer."

¹⁰"The LORD bless you, my daughter," he replied. "This kindness is greater than that which you showed earlier: You have not run after the

---

ᵃ17 That is, probably about 3/5 bushel (about 22 liters)   ᵇ1 Hebrew *find rest* (see Ruth 1:9) younger men, whether rich or poor. ¹¹And now, my daughter, don't be afraid. I will do for you all you ask. All my fellow townsmen know that you are a woman of noble character. ¹²Although it is true that I am near of kin, there is a kinsman-redeemer nearer than I. ¹³Stay here for the night, and in the morning if he wants to redeem, good; let him redeem. But if he is not willing, as surely as the LORD lives I will do it. Lie here until morning."

¹⁴So she lay at his feet until morning, but got up before anyone could be recognized; and he said, "Don't let it be known that a woman came to the threshing floor."

¹⁵He also said, "Bring me the shawl you are wearing and hold it out." When she did so, he poured into it six measures of barley and put it on her. Then he*a* went back to town.

¹⁶When Ruth came to her mother-in-law, Naomi asked, "How did it go, my daughter?"

Then she told her everything Boaz had done for her ¹⁷and added, "He gave me these six measures of barley, saying, 'Don't go back to your mother-in-law empty-handed.' "

¹⁸Then Naomi said, "Wait, my daughter, until you find out what happens. For the man will not rest until the matter is settled today."

Boaz Marries Ruth

4 Meanwhile Boaz went up to the town gate and sat there. When the kinsman-redeemer he had mentioned came along, Boaz said, "Come over here, my friend, and sit down." So he went over and sat down. ²Boaz took ten of the elders of the town and said, "Sit here," and they did so. ³Then he said to the kinsman-redeemer, "Naomi, who has come back from Moab, is selling the piece of land that belonged to our brother Elimelech. ⁴I thought I should bring the matter to your attention and suggest that you buy it in the presence of these seated here and in the presence of the elders of my people. If you will redeem it, do so.

But if you*b* will not, tell me, so I will know. For no one has the right to do it except you, and I am next in line."

"I will redeem it," he said.

⁵Then Boaz said, "On the day you buy the land from Naomi and from Ruth the Moabitess, you acquire*c* the dead man's widow, in order to maintain the name of the dead with his property."

⁶At this, the kinsman-redeemer said, "Then I cannot redeem it because I might endanger my own estate. You redeem it yourself. I cannot do it."

⁷(Now in earlier times in Israel, for the redemption and transfer of property to become final, one party took off his sandal and gave it to the other. This was the method of legalizing transactions in Israel.)

⁸So the kinsman-redeemer said to Boaz, "Buy it yourself." And he removed his sandal.

⁹Then Boaz announced to the elders and all the people, "Today you are witnesses that I have bought from Naomi all the property of Elimelech, Kilion and Mahlon. ¹⁰I have also acquired Ruth the Moabitess, Mahlon's widow, as my wife, in order to maintain the name of the dead with his property, so that his name will not disappear from among his family or from the town records. Today you are witnesses!"

¹¹Then the elders and all those at the gate said, "We are witnesses. May the LORD make the woman who is coming into your home like Rachel and Leah, who together built up the house of Israel. May you have standing in Ephrathah and be famous in Bethlehem. ¹²Through the offspring the LORD gives you by this young woman, may your family be like that of Perez, whom Tamar bore to Judah."

The Genealogy of David

¹³So Boaz took Ruth and she became his wife. Then he went to her, and the LORD enabled her to conceive, and she gave birth to a son. ¹⁴The women said to Naomi: "Praise be to

Ruth 4:14

God Meets Our Needs

The women said to Naomi: "Praise be to the LORD, who this day has not left you without a kinsman-redeemer. May he become famous throughout Israel!"

---

*a*15 Most Hebrew manuscripts; many Hebrew manuscripts, Vulgate and Syriac *she* *b*4 Many Hebrew manuscripts, Septuagint, Vulgate and Syriac; most Hebrew manuscripts *he* *c*5 Hebrew; Vulgate and Syriac *Naomi, you acquire Ruth the Moabitess,* the LORD, who this day has not left you without a kinsman-redeemer. May he become famous throughout Israel! ¹⁵He will renew your life and sustain you in your old age. For your daughter-in-law, who loves you and who is better to you than seven sons, has given him birth."

¹⁶Then Naomi took the child, laid him in her lap and cared for him. ¹⁷The women living there said, "Naomi has a son." And they named him Obed. He was the father of Jesse, the father of David.

¹⁸This, then, is the family line of Perez:

Perez was the father of Hezron,
¹⁹Hezron the father of Ram,
Ram the father of Amminadab,
²⁰Amminadab the father of Nahshon,
Nahshon the father of Salmon,[a]
²¹Salmon the father of Boaz,
Boaz the father of Obed,
²²Obed the father of Jesse,
and Jesse the father of David.

---

^a20 A few Hebrew manuscripts, some Septuagint manuscripts and Vulgate (see also verse 21 and Septuagint of 1 Chron. 2:11); most Hebrew manuscripts *Salma*

1 Samuel

First Samuel is one of the *most action-packed* books in the Bible. It marks a crucial turn in Israel's history when the people shifted from being ruled by theocracy (rule by God) and led by judges to a monarchy (rule by a king). This turn forever *alters the course of history,* and around the bend lie battles, allegiances, valor, cowardice, enemies and the truest of friends.

Samuel presided over Israel during this time of transition as both prophet and judge. He anointed two kings during his lifetime—*Saul and David.* He loved both men and believed in their abilities as leaders, and yet he watched one fail and the other flourish. Each man had choices to make, and each had consequences to live with as a result of those choices. They faced personal and national crises, and as we watch them work their way through those challenges, we see both what happens when we follow what seems best to our human reasoning and what happens when we entrust ourselves to *God's care and timing.*

Author:
Unknown.

Audience:
The people of Israel.

Date:
Sometime after the division of Israel into the northern and southern kingdoms, around 930 B.C.

Setting:
The people of Israel want to shift from a theocracy to a monarchy.

Verse to Remember:
"Does the LORD delight in burnt offerings and sacrifices as much as in obeying the voice of the LORD? To obey is better than sacrifice, and to heed is better than the fat of rams." (15:22)

The Birth of Samuel

1 There was a certain man from Ramathaim, a Zuphite[a] from the hill country of Ephraim, whose name was Elkanah son of Jeroham, the son of Elihu, the son of Tohu, the son of Zuph, an Ephraimite. ²He had two wives; one was called Hannah and the other Peninnah. Peninnah had children, but Hannah had none.

³Year after year this man went up from his town to worship and sacrifice to the LORD Almighty at Shiloh, where Hophni and Phinehas, the two sons of Eli, were priests of the LORD. ⁴Whenever the day came for Elkanah to sacrifice, he would give portions of the meat to his wife Peninnah and to all her sons and daughters. ⁵But to Hannah he gave a double portion

---

a 1 Or *from Ramathaim Zuphim*

because he loved her, and the LORD had closed her womb. [6]And because the LORD had closed her womb, her rival kept provoking her in order to irritate her. [7]This went on year after year. Whenever Hannah went up to the house of the LORD, her rival provoked her till she wept and would not eat. [8]Elkanah her husband would say to her, "Hannah, why are you weeping? Why don't you eat? Why are you downhearted? Don't I mean more to you than ten sons?"

[9]Once when they had finished eating and drinking in Shiloh, Hannah stood up. Now Eli the priest was sitting on a chair by the doorpost of the LORD's temple.[a] [10]In bitterness of soul Hannah wept much and prayed to the LORD. [11]And she made a vow, saying, "O LORD Almighty, if you will only look upon your servant's misery and remember me, and not forget your servant but give her a son, then I will give him to the LORD for all the days of his life, and no razor will ever be used on his head."

[12]As she kept on praying to the LORD, Eli observed her mouth. [13]Hannah was praying in her heart, and her lips were moving but her voice was not heard. Eli thought she was drunk [14]and said to her, "How long will you keep on getting drunk? Get rid of your wine."

[15]"Not so, my lord," Hannah replied, "I am a woman who is deeply troubled. I have not been drinking wine or beer; I was pouring out my soul to the LORD. [16]Do not take your servant for a wicked woman; I have been praying here out of my great anguish and grief."

[17]Eli answered, "Go in peace, and may the God of Israel grant you what you have asked of him."

[18]She said, "May your servant find favor in your eyes." Then she went her way and ate something, and her face was no longer downcast.

[19]Early the next morning they arose and worshiped before the LORD and then went back to their home at Ramah. Elkanah lay with Hannah his wife, and the LORD remembered her. [20]So in the course of time Hannah conceived and gave birth to a son. She named him Samuel,[b] saying, "Because I asked the LORD for him."

Hannah Dedicates Samuel

[21]When the man Elkanah went up with all his family to offer the annual sacrifice to the LORD and to fulfill his vow, [22]Hannah did not go. She said to her husband, "After the boy is weaned, I will take him and present him before the LORD, and he will live there always."

[23]"Do what seems best to you," Elkanah her husband told her. "Stay here until you have weaned him; only may the LORD make good his[c] word." So the woman stayed at home and nursed her son until she had weaned him.

[24]After he was weaned, she took the boy with her, young as he was, along with a three-year-old bull,[d] an ephah[e] of flour and a skin of wine, and brought him to the house of the LORD at Shiloh. [25]When they had slaughtered the bull, they brought the boy to Eli, [26]and she said to him, "As surely as you live, my lord, I am the woman who stood here beside you praying to the LORD. [27]I prayed for this child, and the LORD has granted me what I asked of him. [28]So now I give him to the LORD. For his whole life he will be given over to the LORD." And he worshiped the LORD there.

Hannah's Prayer

2 Then Hannah prayed and said:

"My heart rejoices in the LORD;
    in the LORD my horn[f] is lifted high.
My mouth boasts over my enemies,
    for I delight in your deliverance.

[2] "There is no one holy[g] like the LORD;
    there is no one besides you;
    there is no Rock like our God.

---

[a]9 That is, tabernacle [b]20 *Samuel* sounds like the Hebrew for *heard of God*. [c]23 Masoretic Text; Dead Sea Scrolls, Septuagint and Syriac *your* [d]24 Dead Sea Scrolls, Septuagint and Syriac; Masoretic Text *with three bulls* [e]24 That is, probably about 3/5 bushel (about 22 liters) [f]1 *Horn* here symbolizes strength; also in verse 10. [g]2 Or *no Holy One*

---

1 Samuel 1:20

God Answers Prayer

So in the course of time Hannah conceived and gave birth to a son. She named him Samuel, saying, "Because I asked the LORD for him."

Ultimate Surrender

1 Samuel 1:28

"So now I give him to the LORD. For his whole life he will be given over to the LORD."

reflection

1 What one thing are you holding back from God?

2 What would happen if you released it?

3 Why does God insist we sometimes give up things that seem to bring us joy?

RELATED READINGS

Genesis 22:1–19;
Matthew 6:19–34

PROBABLY THE HARDEST THING for me to surrender to God—and this may sound silly because you may be expecting me to say, "My children"—was the huge, five-bedroom home I purchased five years after my divorce. I knew that my home belonged to God and that I was simply a steward of what he had entrusted to me, but that didn't keep it from becoming an idol. My wonderful house in its expensive zip code supplied status. I couldn't imagine giving it up, especially if God wanted me to live somewhere I didn't like.

I eventually realized I was supposed to sell that house, but for a full year I dug in my heels and refused to do it. What a nightmare I lived trying to untangle God's best for my life while still continuing to weave in my stubborn wishes. But God was persistent. He kept reminding me of his desire through the wise counsel of my brother Paul and sister Cathy. He continued to impress on me the need to downsize and simplify my life.

I finally came to the point where I knew I simply needed to obey God and sell the house. When I moved into a smaller home, I suddenly had much more time and energy. I found that I could focus more earnestly on my writing, which was something I had not been able to do previously with all the repairs, chores and decorating.

As terrible as it sounds, it was easier for me to surrender my children to God than it was to trust him with my home. Sad, huh? But I knew in my heart that my children would be in better hands with God than with me. While it was still excruciatingly hard to turn my children's lives over to him, I released them to his loving care by saying a simple, heartfelt prayer to that effect. Actually, I had to say that prayer many times. It seemed to take me forever to be able to voice words that were not a lie. Though I did not drop off my kids at the local temple to be raised by a holy man, like Hannah did with her son Samuel, I did choose to trust that God would love them and guide their lives better than I could.

—Katie Brazelton

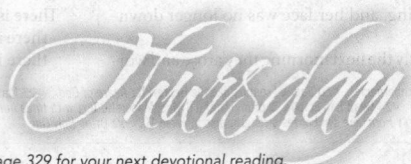

Go to page 329 for your next devotional reading.

3 "Do not keep talking so proudly
    or let your mouth speak such arrogance,
for the LORD is a God who knows,
    and by him deeds are weighed.

4 "The bows of the warriors
        are broken,
    but those who stumbled
        are armed with
        strength.
5 Those who were full hire
        themselves out for
        food,
    but those who were
        hungry hunger no
        more.
She who was barren
        has borne seven
        children,
    but she who has had
        many sons pines away.

6 "The LORD brings death and makes alive;
    he brings down to the grave[a] and raises
        up.
7 The LORD sends poverty and wealth;
    he humbles and he exalts.
8 He raises the poor from the dust
        and lifts the needy from the ash heap;
    he seats them with princes
        and has them inherit a throne of honor.

"For the foundations of the earth are the
        LORD's;
    upon them he has set the world.
9 He will guard the feet of his saints,
    but the wicked will be silenced in
        darkness.

"It is not by strength that one prevails;
10   those who oppose the LORD will be
        shattered.
He will thunder against them from heaven;
    the LORD will judge the ends of the
        earth.

"He will give strength to his king
    and exalt the horn of his anointed."

11 Then Elkanah went home to Ramah, but
the boy ministered before the LORD under Eli
the priest.

Eli's Wicked Sons

12 Eli's sons were wicked men; they had no
regard for the LORD. 13 Now it was the practice
of the priests with the people that whenever
anyone offered a sacrifice
and while the meat was being
boiled, the servant of the priest
would come with a three-
pronged fork in his hand. 14 He
would plunge it into the pan or
kettle or caldron or pot, and
the priest would take for himself whatever the fork brought
up. This is how they treated all
the Israelites who came to Shiloh. 15 But even before the fat
was burned, the servant of the
priest would come and say to
the man who was sacrificing,
"Give the priest some meat to roast; he won't
accept boiled meat from you, but only raw."

16 If the man said to him, "Let the fat be
burned up first, and then take whatever you
want," the servant would then answer, "No,
hand it over now; if you don't, I'll take it
by force."

17 This sin of the young men was very great
in the LORD's sight, for they[b] were treating the
LORD's offering with contempt.

18 But Samuel was ministering before the
LORD—a boy wearing a linen ephod. 19 Each
year his mother made him a little robe and took
it to him when she went up with her husband
to offer the annual sacrifice. 20 Eli would bless
Elkanah and his wife, saying, "May the LORD
give you children by this woman to take the
place of the one she prayed for and gave to the
LORD." Then they would go home. 21 And the
LORD was gracious to Hannah; she conceived
and gave birth to three sons and two daughters.
Meanwhile, the boy Samuel grew up in the presence of the LORD.

22 Now Eli, who was very old, heard about
everything his sons were doing to all Israel and
how they slept with the women who served at
the entrance to the Tent of Meeting. 23 So he
said to them, "Why do you do such things? I
hear from all the people about these wicked
deeds of yours. 24 No, my sons; it is not a good

---

1 Samuel 2:2

God Is Holy

"There is no one holy
like the LORD;
there is no one
besides you;
there is no Rock
like our God."

---

[a]6 Hebrew *Sheol*   [b]17 Or *men*

report that I hear spreading among the Lord's people. ²⁵If a man sins against another man, God*a* may mediate for him; but if a man sins against the Lord, who will intercede for him?" His sons, however, did not listen to their father's rebuke, for it was the Lord's will to put them to death.

²⁶And the boy Samuel continued to grow in stature and in favor with the Lord and with men.

Prophecy Against the House of Eli

²⁷Now a man of God came to Eli and said to him, "This is what the Lord says: 'Did I not clearly reveal myself to your father's house when they were in Egypt under Pharaoh? ²⁸I chose your father out of all the tribes of Israel to be my priest, to go up to my altar, to burn incense, and to wear an ephod in my presence. I also gave your father's house all the offerings made with fire by the Israelites. ²⁹Why do you*b* scorn my sacrifice and offering that I prescribed for my dwelling? Why do you honor your sons more than me by fattening yourselves on the choice parts of every offering made by my people Israel?'

³⁰"Therefore the Lord, the God of Israel, declares: 'I promised that your house and your father's house would minister before me forever.' But now the Lord declares: 'Far be it from me! Those who honor me I will honor, but those who despise me will be disdained. ³¹The time is coming when I will cut short your strength and the strength of your father's house, so that there will not be an old man in your family line ³²and you will see distress in my dwelling. Although good will be done to Israel, in your family line there will never be an old man. ³³Every one of you that I do not cut off from my altar will be spared only to blind your eyes with tears and to grieve your heart, and all your descendants will die in the prime of life.

³⁴" 'And what happens to your two sons, Hophni and Phinehas, will be a sign to you—they will both die on the same day. ³⁵I will raise up for myself a faithful priest, who will do according to what is in my heart and mind. I will firmly establish his house, and he will minister before my anointed one always. ³⁶Then every-

one left in your family line will come and bow down before him for a piece of silver and a crust of bread and plead, "Appoint me to some priestly office so I can have food to eat." ' "

The Lord Calls Samuel

3 The boy Samuel ministered before the Lord under Eli. In those days the word of the Lord was rare; there were not many visions.

²One night Eli, whose eyes were becoming so weak that he could barely see, was lying down in his usual place. ³The lamp of God had not yet gone out, and Samuel was lying down in the temple*c* of the Lord, where the ark of God was. ⁴Then the Lord called Samuel.

Samuel answered, "Here I am." ⁵And he ran to Eli and said, "Here I am; you called me."

But Eli said, "I did not call; go back and lie down." So he went and lay down.

⁶Again the Lord called, "Samuel!" And Samuel got up and went to Eli and said, "Here I am; you called me."

"My son," Eli said, "I did not call; go back and lie down."

⁷Now Samuel did not yet know the Lord: The word of the Lord had not yet been revealed to him.

⁸The Lord called Samuel a third time, and Samuel got up and went to Eli and said, "Here I am; you called me."

Then Eli realized that the Lord was calling the boy. ⁹So Eli told Samuel, "Go and lie down, and if he calls you, say, 'Speak, Lord, for your servant is listening.' " So Samuel went and lay down in his place.

¹⁰The Lord came and stood there, calling as at the other times, "Samuel! Samuel!"

Then Samuel said, "Speak, for your servant is listening."

¹¹And the Lord said to Samuel: "See, I am about to do something in Israel that will make the ears of everyone who hears of it tingle. ¹²At that time I will carry out against Eli everything I spoke against his family—from beginning to end. ¹³For I told him that I would judge his family forever because of the sin he knew about; his sons made themselves contemptible,*d* and he failed to restrain them.

---

*a*25 Or *the judges*   *b*29 The Hebrew is plural.   *c*3 That is, tabernacle   *d*13 Masoretic Text; an ancient Hebrew scribal tradition and Septuagint *sons blasphemed God*

Are You Listening?

WHEN WAS THE LAST TIME you heard from God? Think about it. Has God's still, small voice been drowned out by the hum of too much noise from work, family, church and friends?

The adolescent boy Samuel was lying in the temple. It was still night because "the lamp of God had not yet gone out" (the lamp would not have been allowed to go out before morning). Samuel was probably lonely, having been separated from his family and dedicated by his mother Hannah to work for the old, blind priest Eli in the temple. It seems to have been a discouraging time to work there: "The word of the LORD was rare; there were not many visions." But as Samuel drowsed on his pallet, the sound of his name cut through the flickering dimness.

"Samuel!"

Naturally, Samuel thought Eli had called. "Here I am," replied the boy. Again, "Samuel!" Again, "Here I am." Samuel listened keenly, but the summons didn't come from Eli. God himself called Samuel that evening, and Eli taught the boy the right response: "Speak, for your servant is listening."

What made Samuel so ready to hear God's voice? For one thing, he was a faithful and obedient servant. He was ready to respond to his master, and his willingness made him ready to respond to God as well. He was being faithful in the small things of his everyday life and was therefore entrusted with a great thing, to be a prophet of God and to restore the priesthood's honor.

Samuel was also in the right place to listen. Are you? His posture *invited* God to speak to him: *faithful, obedient, humble, waiting, receptive.* His willingness to respond became instrumental in restoring holiness to the land: "[God] revealed himself to Samuel through his word. And Samuel's word came to all Israel."

If you want to hear God speak, do what you can to be ready. Be prepared when you're in a place of outward silence and sanctuary: as you lay awake in the early hours of the morning, while you wait in your car for your children to get out of school, when you walk the dog in the evening. Seek an inner silence and sanctuary also: Let go of mental noise and emotional confusion. Take deep breaths in and out until your heart and respiration rate slow. Humbly and receptively invite God to speak to you, and wait with faithful and obedient readiness. When God calls your name, respond, "Speak, Lord, for your servant is listening."

1 Samuel 3:10

The LORD came and stood there, calling as at the other times, "Samuel! Samuel!" Then Samuel said, "Speak, for your servant is listening."

reflection

1 What are some things that drown out God's voice for you? What makes it difficult for you to be still in God's presence?

2 Are personal sins blocking you from hearing God's voice? Take time to confess any wrongs you've committed and ask God to cleanse you.

3 Read Psalm 84 to prepare you to spend time in God's presence.

RELATED READINGS

Psalms 84:1–12; 86:1–17; Matthew 5:8; John 10:1–6

Friday

Go to page 334 for your next devotional reading.

14Therefore, I swore to the house of Eli, 'The guilt of Eli's house will never be atoned for by sacrifice or offering.'"

15Samuel lay down until morning and then opened the doors of the house of the LORD. He was afraid to tell Eli the vision, 16but Eli called him and said, "Samuel, my son."

Samuel answered, "Here I am."

17"What was it he said to you?" Eli asked. "Do not hide it from me. May God deal with you, be it ever so severely, if you hide from me anything he told you." 18So Samuel told him everything, hiding nothing from him. Then Eli said, "He is the LORD; let him do what is good in his eyes."

19The LORD was with Samuel as he grew up, and he let none of his words fall to the ground. 20And all Israel from Dan to Beersheba recognized that Samuel was attested as a prophet of the LORD. 21The LORD continued to appear at Shiloh, and there he revealed himself to Samuel through his word.

4 And Samuel's word came to all Israel.

The Philistines Capture the Ark

Now the Israelites went out to fight against the Philistines. The Israelites camped at Ebenezer, and the Philistines at Aphek. 2The Philistines deployed their forces to meet Israel, and as the battle spread, Israel was defeated by the Philistines, who killed about four thousand of them on the battlefield. 3When the soldiers returned to camp, the elders of Israel asked, "Why did the LORD bring defeat upon us today before the Philistines? Let us bring the ark of the LORD's covenant from Shiloh, so that it*a* may go with us and save us from the hand of our enemies."

4So the people sent men to Shiloh, and they brought back the ark of the covenant of the LORD Almighty, who is enthroned between the cherubim. And Eli's two sons, Hophni and Phinehas, were there with the ark of the covenant of God.

5When the ark of the LORD's covenant came into the camp, all Israel raised such a great shout that the ground shook. 6Hearing the uproar, the Philistines asked, "What's all this shouting in the Hebrew camp?"

When they learned that the ark of the LORD had come into the camp, 7the Philistines were afraid. "A god has come into the camp," they said. "We're in trouble! Nothing like this has happened before. 8Woe to us! Who will deliver us from the hand of these mighty gods? They are the gods who struck the Egyptians with all kinds of plagues in the desert. 9Be strong, Philistines! Be men, or you will be subject to the Hebrews, as they have been to you. Be men, and fight!"

10So the Philistines fought, and the Israelites were defeated and every man fled to his tent. The slaughter was very great; Israel lost thirty thousand foot soldiers. 11The ark of God was captured, and Eli's two sons, Hophni and Phinehas, died.

Death of Eli

12That same day a Benjamite ran from the battle line and went to Shiloh, his clothes torn and dust on his head. 13When he arrived, there was Eli sitting on his chair by the side of the road, watching, because his heart feared for the ark of God. When the man entered the town and told what had happened, the whole town sent up a cry.

14Eli heard the outcry and asked, "What is the meaning of this uproar?"

The man hurried over to Eli, 15who was ninety-eight years old and whose eyes were set so that he could not see. 16He told Eli, "I have just come from the battle line; I fled from it this very day."

Eli asked, "What happened, my son?"

17The man who brought the news replied, "Israel fled before the Philistines, and the army has suffered heavy losses. Also your two sons, Hophni and Phinehas, are dead, and the ark of God has been captured."

18When he mentioned the ark of God, Eli fell backward off his chair by the side of the gate. His neck was broken and he died, for he was an old man and heavy. He had led*b* Israel forty years.

19His daughter-in-law, the wife of Phinehas, was pregnant and near the time of delivery. When she heard the news that the ark of God had been captured and that her father-in-law

*a3 Or he *b18 Traditionally *judged*

and her husband were dead, she went into labor and gave birth, but was overcome by her labor pains. ²⁰As she was dying, the women attending her said, "Don't despair; you have given birth to a son." But she did not respond or pay any attention.

²¹She named the boy Ichabod,ᵃ saying, "The glory has departed from Israel"—because of the capture of the ark of God and the deaths of her father-in-law and her husband. ²²She said, "The glory has departed from Israel, for the ark of God has been captured."

The Ark in Ashdod and Ekron

5 After the Philistines had captured the ark of God, they took it from Ebenezer to Ashdod. ²Then they carried the ark into Dagon's temple and set it beside Dagon. ³When the people of Ashdod rose early the next day, there was Dagon, fallen on his face on the ground before the ark of the Lord! They took Dagon and put him back in his place. ⁴But the following morning when they rose, there was Dagon, fallen on his face on the ground before the ark of the Lord! His head and hands had been broken off and were lying on the threshold; only his body remained. ⁵That is why to this day neither the priests of Dagon nor any others who enter Dagon's temple at Ashdod step on the threshold.

⁶The Lord's hand was heavy upon the people of Ashdod and its vicinity; he brought devastation upon them and afflicted them with tumors.ᵇ ⁷When the men of Ashdod saw what was happening, they said, "The ark of the god of Israel must not stay here with us, because his hand is heavy upon us and upon Dagon our god." ⁸So they called together all the rulers of the Philistines and asked them, "What shall we do with the ark of the god of Israel?"

They answered, "Have the ark of the god of Israel moved to Gath." So they moved the ark of the God of Israel.

⁹But after they had moved it, the Lord's hand was against that city, throwing it into a great panic. He afflicted the people of the city, both young and old, with an outbreak of tumors.ᶜ ¹⁰So they sent the ark of God to Ekron.

As the ark of God was entering Ekron, the people of Ekron cried out, "They have brought the ark of the god of Israel around to us to kill us and our people." ¹¹So they called together all the rulers of the Philistines and said, "Send the ark of the god of Israel away; let it go back to its own place, or itᵈ will kill us and our people." For death had filled the city with panic; God's hand was very heavy upon it. ¹²Those who did not die were afflicted with tumors, and the outcry of the city went up to heaven.

The Ark Returned to Israel

6 When the ark of the Lord had been in Philistine territory seven months, ²the Philistines called for the priests and the diviners and said, "What shall we do with the ark of the Lord? Tell us how we should send it back to its place."

³They answered, "If you return the ark of the god of Israel, do not send it away empty, but by all means send a guilt offering to him. Then you will be healed, and you will know why his hand has not been lifted from you."

⁴The Philistines asked, "What guilt offering should we send to him?"

They replied, "Five gold tumors and five gold rats, according to the number of the Philistine rulers, because the same plague has struck both you and your rulers. ⁵Make models of the tumors and of the rats that are destroying the country, and pay honor to Israel's god. Perhaps he will lift his hand from you and your gods and your land. ⁶Why do you harden your hearts as the Egyptians and Pharaoh did? When heᵉ treated them harshly, did they not send the Israelites out so they could go on their way? ⁷"Now then, get a new cart ready, with two

1 Samuel 5:4

God Is Supreme

But the following morning when they rose, there was Dagon, fallen on his face on the ground before the ark of the Lord! His head and hands had been broken off and were lying on the threshold; only his body remained.

ᵃ21 *Ichabod* means *no glory.* ᵇ6 Hebrew; Septuagint and Vulgate *tumors. And rats appeared in their land, and death and destruction were throughout the city* ᶜ9 Or *with tumors in the groin* (see Septuagint) ᵈ11 Or *he* ᵉ6 That is, God cows that have calved and have never been yoked. Hitch the cows to the cart, but take their calves away and pen them up. **8** Take the ark of the LORD and put it on the cart, and in a chest beside it put the gold objects you are sending back to him as a guilt offering. Send it on its way, **9** but keep watching it. If it goes up to its own territory, toward Beth Shemesh, then the LORD has brought this great disaster on us. But if it does not, then we will know that it was not his hand that struck us and that it happened to us by chance."

10 So they did this. They took two such cows and hitched them to the cart and penned up their calves. **11** They placed the ark of the LORD on the cart and along with it the chest containing the gold rats and the models of the tumors. **12** Then the cows went straight up toward Beth Shemesh, keeping on the road and lowing all the way; they did not turn to the right or to the left. The rulers of the Philistines followed them as far as the border of Beth Shemesh.

13 Now the people of Beth Shemesh were harvesting their wheat in the valley, and when they looked up and saw the ark, they rejoiced at the sight. **14** The cart came to the field of Joshua of Beth Shemesh, and there it stopped beside a large rock. The people chopped up the wood of the cart and sacrificed the cows as a burnt offering to the LORD. **15** The Levites took down the ark of the LORD, together with the chest containing the gold objects, and placed them on the large rock. On that day the people of Beth Shemesh offered burnt offerings and made sacrifices to the LORD. **16** The five rulers of the Philistines saw all this and then returned that same day to Ekron.

17 These are the gold tumors the Philistines sent as a guilt offering to the LORD—one each for Ashdod, Gaza, Ashkelon, Gath and Ekron. **18** And the number of the gold rats was according to the number of Philistine towns belonging to the five rulers—the fortified towns with their country villages. The large rock, on which[a] they set the ark of the LORD, is a witness to this day in the field of Joshua of Beth Shemesh.

19 But God struck down some of the men of Beth Shemesh, putting seventy[b] of them to death because they had looked into the ark of the LORD. The people mourned because of the heavy blow the LORD had dealt them, **20** and the men of Beth Shemesh asked, "Who can stand in the presence of the LORD, this holy God? To whom will the ark go up from here?"

21 Then they sent messengers to the people of Kiriath Jearim, saying, "The Philistines have returned the ark of the LORD. Come down and **7** take it up to your place." **1** So the men of Kiriath Jearim came and took up the ark of the LORD. They took it to Abinadab's house on the hill and consecrated Eleazar his son to guard the ark of the LORD.

Samuel Subdues the Philistines at Mizpah

2 It was a long time, twenty years in all, that the ark remained at Kiriath Jearim, and all the people of Israel mourned and sought after the LORD. **3** And Samuel said to the whole house of Israel, "If you are returning to the LORD with all your hearts, then rid yourselves of the foreign gods and the Ashtoreths and commit yourselves to the LORD and serve him only, and he will deliver you out of the hand of the Philistines." **4** So the Israelites put away their Baals and Ashtoreths, and served the LORD only.

5 Then Samuel said, "Assemble all Israel at Mizpah and I will intercede with the LORD for you." **6** When they had assembled at Mizpah, they drew water and poured it out before the LORD. On that day they fasted and there they confessed, "We have sinned against the LORD." And Samuel was leader[c] of Israel at Mizpah.

7 When the Philistines heard that Israel had assembled at Mizpah, the rulers of the Philistines came up to attack them. And when the Israelites heard of it, they were afraid because of the Philistines. **8** They said to Samuel, "Do

---

1 Samuel 6:20

God Is Holy

And the men of Beth Shemesh asked, "Who can stand in the presence of the LORD, this holy God? To whom will the ark go up from here?"

---

[a] 18 A few Hebrew manuscripts (see also Septuagint); most Hebrew manuscripts *villages as far as Greater Abel, where* [b] 19 A few Hebrew manuscripts; most Hebrew manuscripts and Septuagint *50,070* [c] 6 Traditionally *judge*

not stop crying out to the LORD our God for us, that he may rescue us from the hand of the Philistines." ⁹Then Samuel took a suckling lamb and offered it up as a whole burnt offering to the LORD. He cried out to the LORD on Israel's behalf, and the LORD answered him.

¹⁰While Samuel was sacrificing the burnt offering, the Philistines drew near to engage Israel in battle. But that day the LORD thundered with loud thunder against the Philistines and threw them into such a panic that they were routed before the Israelites. ¹¹The men of Israel rushed out of Mizpah and pursued the Philistines, slaughtering them along the way to a point below Beth Car. ¹²Then Samuel took a stone and set it up between Mizpah and Shen. He named it Ebenezer,ᵃ saying, "Thus far has the LORD helped us." ¹³So the Philistines were subdued and did not invade Israelite territory again.

Throughout Samuel's lifetime, the hand of the LORD was against the Philistines. ¹⁴The towns from Ekron to Gath that the Philistines had captured from Israel were restored to her, and Israel delivered the neighboring territory from the power of the Philistines. And there was peace between Israel and the Amorites.

¹⁵Samuel continued as judge over Israel all the days of his life. ¹⁶From year to year he went on a circuit from Bethel to Gilgal to Mizpah, judging Israel in all those places. ¹⁷But he always went back to Ramah, where his home was, and there he also judged Israel. And he built an altar there to the LORD.

Israel Asks for a King

8 When Samuel grew old, he appointed his sons as judges for Israel. ²The name of his firstborn was Joel and the name of his second was Abijah, and they served at Beersheba. ³But his sons did not walk in his ways. They turned aside after dishonest gain and accepted bribes and perverted justice.

⁴So all the elders of Israel gathered together and came to Samuel at Ramah. ⁵They said to him, "You are old, and your sons do not walk in your ways; now appoint a king to leadᵇ us, such as all the other nations have."

⁶But when they said, "Give us a king to lead us," this displeased Samuel; so he prayed to the LORD. ⁷And the LORD told him: "Listen to all that the people are saying to you; it is not you they have rejected, but they have rejected me as their king. ⁸As they have done from the day I brought them up out of Egypt until this day, forsaking me and serving other gods, so they are doing to you. ⁹Now listen to them; but warn them solemnly and let them know what the king who will reign over them will do."

¹⁰Samuel told all the words of the LORD to the people who were asking him for a king. ¹¹He said, "This is what the king who will reign over you will do: He will take your sons and make them serve with his chariots and horses, and they will run in front of his chariots. ¹²Some he will assign to be commanders of thousands and commanders of fifties, and others to plow his ground and reap his harvest, and still others to make weapons of war and equipment for his chariots. ¹³He will take your daughters to be perfumers and cooks and bakers. ¹⁴He will take the best of your fields and vineyards and olive groves and give them to his attendants. ¹⁵He will take a tenth of your grain and of your vintage and give it to his officials and attendants. ¹⁶Your menservants and maidservants and the best of your cattleᶜ and donkeys he will take for his own use. ¹⁷He will take a tenth of your flocks, and you yourselves will become his slaves. ¹⁸When that day comes, you will cry out for relief from the king you have chosen, and the LORD will not answer you in that day."

¹⁹But the people refused to listen to Samuel. "No!" they said. "We want a king over us. ²⁰Then we will be like all the other nations, with a king to lead us and to go out before us and fight our battles."

---

1 Samuel 7:10

God Thunders

That day the LORD thundered with loud thunder against the Philistines and threw them into such a panic that they were routed before the Israelites.

ᵃ12 *Ebenezer* means *stone of help.*   ᵇ5 Traditionally *judge;* also in verses 6 and 20   ᶜ16 Septuagint; Hebrew *young men*

JOCHEBED

By faith Moses'
parents hid him
for three months
after he was
born, because
they saw he was
no ordinary child,
and they were
not afraid of the
king's edict.

Hebrews 11:23

"SO SORRY YOU CAN'T STAY LONGER," Jochebed said to her friend and stood pointedly by the door. The warmth of the afternoon sun streamed onto their timeworn faces.

A neighbor had dropped by for the afternoon. Jochebed liked her well enough, and she enjoyed the welcome break during the day's routine. But Jochebed carried a secret no one outside of her immediate family could know. And if the woman stayed much longer late in the day like this, her mystery would be found out.

Jochebed had been privy to many secrets herself over the years—things most anyone keeps secret: a friend's envy, a neighbor's indiscretion. However, those secrets were nothing like this; nothing like a matter of life and death. And so it was well worth it to appear rude to her neighbor, to be a little more reclusive than she'd been before, to find creative ways to time her trips to the market.

What she did, she did in faith. Simple faith.

Faith: The hope that what she was doing was for the right reason, at the right time. That God had bestowed her with a sense of timing that was beyond human reasoning. *Faith:* The knowledge that there was no guarantee for the future, but there was grace for the day. Each evening gave her strength to continue her mission the next day. *Faith:* A tiny seed that she nurtured faithfully; a seed that grew delicate tendrils of courage to keep going despite the risks. *Faith:* The assurance that the God-given hunch, the slightest suspicion and the dream burrowed deep within the heart are not one's own doing, but the very evidence of God at work

Jochebed pondered these thoughts and watched her neighbor amble down the street. Just then, her little secret awoke from his nap.

—Prayer—
Father in heaven, help me to live out my faith in tangible ways today and every day.

ASSIGNED READING:

Exodus
2:1–10;
6:1—7:6

Weekend

Go to page 343 for your next devotional reading.

²¹When Samuel heard all that the people said, he repeated it before the Lord. ²²The Lord answered, "Listen to them and give them a king."

Then Samuel said to the men of Israel, "Everyone go back to his town."

Samuel Anoints Saul

9 There was a Benjamite, a man of standing, whose name was Kish son of Abiel, the son of Zeror, the son of Becorath, the son of Aphiah of Benjamin. ²He had a son named Saul, an impressive young man without equal among the Israelites—a head taller than any of the others.

³Now the donkeys belonging to Saul's father Kish were lost, and Kish said to his son Saul, "Take one of the servants with you and go and look for the donkeys." ⁴So he passed through the hill country of Ephraim and through the area around Shalisha, but they did not find them. They went on into the district of Shaalim, but the donkeys were not there. Then he passed through the territory of Benjamin, but they did not find them.

⁵When they reached the district of Zuph, Saul said to the servant who was with him, "Come, let's go back, or my father will stop thinking about the donkeys and start worrying about us."

⁶But the servant replied, "Look, in this town there is a man of God; he is highly respected, and everything he says comes true. Let's go there now. Perhaps he will tell us what way to take."

⁷Saul said to his servant, "If we go, what can we give the man? The food in our sacks is gone. We have no gift to take to the man of God. What do we have?"

⁸The servant answered him again. "Look," he said, "I have a quarter of a shekel*ᵃ* of silver. I will give it to the man of God so that he will tell us what way to take." ⁹(Formerly in Israel, if a man went to inquire of God, he would say, "Come, let us go to the seer," because the prophet of today used to be called a seer.)

¹⁰"Good," Saul said to his servant. "Come, let's go." So they set out for the town where the man of God was.

¹¹As they were going up the hill to the town, they met some girls coming out to draw water, and they asked them, "Is the seer here?"

¹²"He is," they answered. "He's ahead of you. Hurry now; he has just come to our town today, for the people have a sacrifice at the high place. ¹³As soon as you enter the town, you will find him before he goes up to the high place to eat. The people will not begin eating until he comes, because he must bless the sacrifice; afterward, those who are invited will eat. Go up now; you should find him about this time."

¹⁴They went up to the town, and as they were entering it, there was Samuel, coming toward them on his way up to the high place.

¹⁵Now the day before Saul came, the Lord had revealed this to Samuel: ¹⁶"About this time tomorrow I will send you a man from the land of Benjamin. Anoint him leader over my people Israel; he will deliver my people from the hand of the Philistines. I have looked upon my people, for their cry has reached me."

¹⁷When Samuel caught sight of Saul, the Lord said to him, "This is the man I spoke to you about; he will govern my people."

¹⁸Saul approached Samuel in the gateway and asked, "Would you please tell me where the seer's house is?"

¹⁹"I am the seer," Samuel replied. "Go up ahead of me to the high place, for today you are to eat with me, and in the morning I will let you go and will tell you all that is in your heart. ²⁰As for the donkeys you lost three days ago, do not worry about them; they have been found. And to whom is all the desire of Israel turned, if not to you and all your father's family?"

²¹Saul answered, "But am I not a Benjamite, from the smallest tribe of Israel, and is not my clan the least of all the clans of the tribe of Benjamin? Why do you say such a thing to me?"

²²Then Samuel brought Saul and his servant into the hall and seated them at the head of those who were invited—about thirty in number. ²³Samuel said to the cook, "Bring the piece of meat I gave you, the one I told you to lay aside."

²⁴So the cook took up the leg with what was on it and set it in front of Saul. Samuel said, "Here is what has been kept for you. Eat,

---

*ᵃ*8 That is, about 1/10 ounce (about 3 grams)

because it was set aside for you for this occasion, from the time I said, 'I have invited guests.'" And Saul dined with Samuel that day.

²⁵After they came down from the high place to the town, Samuel talked with Saul on the roof of his house. ²⁶They rose about daybreak and Samuel called to Saul on the roof, "Get ready, and I will send you on your way." When Saul got ready, he and Samuel went outside together. ²⁷As they were going down to the edge of the town, Samuel said to Saul, "Tell the servant to go on ahead of us"—and the servant did so—"but you stay here awhile, so that I may give you a message from God."

10 Then Samuel took a flask of oil and poured it on Saul's head and kissed him, saying, "Has not the LORD anointed you leader over his inheritance?ᵃ ²When you leave me today, you will meet two men near Rachel's tomb, at Zelzah on the border of Benjamin. They will say to you, 'The donkeys you set out to look for have been found. And now your father has stopped thinking about them and is worried about you. He is asking, "What shall I do about my son?"'

³"Then you will go on from there until you reach the great tree of Tabor. Three men going up to God at Bethel will meet you there. One will be carrying three young goats, another three loaves of bread, and another a skin of wine. ⁴They will greet you and offer you two loaves of bread, which you will accept from them.

⁵"After that you will go to Gibeah of God, where there is a Philistine outpost. As you approach the town, you will meet a procession of prophets coming down from the high place with lyres, tambourines, flutes and harps being played before them, and they will be prophesying. ⁶The Spirit of the LORD will come upon you in power, and you will prophesy with them; and you will be changed into a different person. ⁷Once these signs are

fulfilled, do whatever your hand finds to do, for God is with you.

⁸"Go down ahead of me to Gilgal. I will surely come down to you to sacrifice burnt offerings and fellowship offerings,ᵇ but you must wait seven days until I come to you and tell you what you are to do."

Saul Made King

⁹As Saul turned to leave Samuel, God changed Saul's heart, and all these signs were fulfilled that day. ¹⁰When they arrived at Gibeah, a procession of prophets met him; the Spirit of God came upon him in power, and he joined in their prophesying. ¹¹When all those who had formerly known him saw him prophesying with the prophets, they asked each other, "What is this that has happened to the son of Kish? Is Saul also among the prophets?"

¹²A man who lived there answered, "And who is their father?" So it became a saying: "Is Saul also among the prophets?" ¹³After Saul stopped prophesying, he went to the high place.

¹⁴Now Saul's uncle asked him and his servant, "Where have you been?"

"Looking for the donkeys," he said. "But when we saw they were not to be found, we went to Samuel."

¹⁵Saul's uncle said, "Tell me what Samuel said to you."

¹⁶Saul replied, "He assured us that the donkeys had been found." But he did not tell his uncle what Samuel had said about the kingship.

¹⁷Samuel summoned the people of Israel to the LORD at Mizpah ¹⁸and said to them, "This is what the LORD, the God of Israel, says: 'I brought Israel up out of Egypt, and I delivered you from the power of Egypt and all the kingdoms that oppressed you.' ¹⁹But you have now rejected your God, who saves you out of all your calamities and distresses. And you have said, 'No, set a king over us.' So now

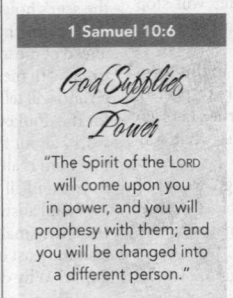

1 Samuel 10:6

God Supplies Power

"The Spirit of the LORD will come upon you in power, and you will prophesy with them; and you will be changed into a different person."

ᵃ1 Hebrew; Septuagint and Vulgate *over his people Israel? You will reign over the LORD's people and save them from the power of their enemies round about. And this will be a sign to you that the LORD has anointed you leader over his inheritance:* ᵇ8 Traditionally *peace offerings* present yourselves before the LORD by your tribes and clans."

²⁰When Samuel brought all the tribes of Israel near, the tribe of Benjamin was chosen. ²¹Then he brought forward the tribe of Benjamin, clan by clan, and Matri's clan was chosen. Finally Saul son of Kish was chosen. But when they looked for him, he was not to be found. ²²So they inquired further of the LORD, "Has the man come here yet?"

And the LORD said, "Yes, he has hidden himself among the baggage."

²³They ran and brought him out, and as he stood among the people he was a head taller than any of the others. ²⁴Samuel said to all the people, "Do you see the man the LORD has chosen? There is no one like him among all the people."

Then the people shouted, "Long live the king!"

²⁵Samuel explained to the people the regulations of the kingship. He wrote them down on a scroll and deposited it before the LORD. Then Samuel dismissed the people, each to his own home.

²⁶Saul also went to his home in Gibeah, accompanied by valiant men whose hearts God had touched. ²⁷But some troublemakers said, "How can this fellow save us?" They despised him and brought him no gifts. But Saul kept silent.

Saul Rescues the City of Jabesh

11 Nahash the Ammonite went up and besieged Jabesh Gilead. And all the men of Jabesh said to him, "Make a treaty with us, and we will be subject to you."

²But Nahash the Ammonite replied, "I will make a treaty with you only on the condition that I gouge out the right eye of every one of you and so bring disgrace on all Israel."

³The elders of Jabesh said to him, "Give us seven days so we can send messengers throughout Israel; if no one comes to rescue us, we will surrender to you."

⁴When the messengers came to Gibeah of Saul and reported these terms to the people, they all wept aloud. ⁵Just then Saul was returning from the fields, behind his oxen, and he asked, "What is wrong with the people? Why are they weeping?" Then they repeated to him what the men of Jabesh had said.

⁶When Saul heard their words, the Spirit of God came upon him in power, and he burned with anger. ⁷He took a pair of oxen, cut them into pieces, and sent the pieces by messengers throughout Israel, proclaiming, "This is what will be done to the oxen of anyone who does not follow Saul and Samuel." Then the terror of the LORD fell on the people, and they turned out as one man. ⁸When Saul mustered them at Bezek, the men of Israel numbered three hundred thousand and the men of Judah thirty thousand.

⁹They told the messengers who had come, "Say to the men of Jabesh Gilead, 'By the time the sun is hot tomorrow, you will be delivered.'" When the messengers went and reported this to the men of Jabesh, they were elated. ¹⁰They said to the Ammonites, "Tomorrow we will surrender to you, and you can do to us whatever seems good to you."

¹¹The next day Saul separated his men into three divisions; during the last watch of the night they broke into the camp of the Ammonites and slaughtered them until the heat of the day. Those who survived were scattered, so that no two of them were left together.

Saul Confirmed as King

¹²The people then said to Samuel, "Who was it that asked, 'Shall Saul reign over us?' Bring these men to us and we will put them to death."

¹³But Saul said, "No one shall be put to death today, for this day the LORD has rescued Israel."

¹⁴Then Samuel said to the people, "Come, let us go to Gilgal and there reaffirm the kingship." ¹⁵So all the people went to Gilgal and confirmed Saul as king in the presence of the LORD. There they sacrificed fellowship offerings*a* before the LORD, and Saul and all the Israelites held a great celebration.

Samuel's Farewell Speech

12 Samuel said to all Israel, "I have listened to everything you said to me and have set a king over you. ²Now you have a king as

---

*a*15 Traditionally *peace offerings*

your leader. As for me, I am old and gray, and my sons are here with you. I have been your leader from my youth until this day. **3**Here I stand. Testify against me in the presence of the LORD and his anointed. Whose ox have I taken? Whose donkey have I taken? Whom have I cheated? Whom have I oppressed? From whose hand have I accepted a bribe to make me shut my eyes? If I have done any of these, I will make it right."

4"You have not cheated or oppressed us," they replied. "You have not taken anything from anyone's hand."

5Samuel said to them, "The LORD is witness against you, and also his anointed is witness this day, that you have not found anything in my hand."

"He is witness," they said.

6Then Samuel said to the people, "It is the LORD who appointed Moses and Aaron and brought your forefathers up out of Egypt. **7**Now then, stand here, because I am going to confront you with evidence before the LORD as to all the righteous acts performed by the LORD for you and your fathers.

8"After Jacob entered Egypt, they cried to the LORD for help, and the LORD sent Moses and Aaron, who brought your forefathers out of Egypt and settled them in this place.

9"But they forgot the LORD their God; so he sold them into the hand of Sisera, the commander of the army of Hazor, and into the hands of the Philistines and the king of Moab, who fought against them. **10**They cried out to the LORD and said, 'We have sinned; we have forsaken the LORD and served the Baals and the Ashtoreths. But now deliver us from the hands of our enemies, and we will serve you.' **11**Then the LORD sent Jerub-Baal,*a* Barak,*b* Jephthah and Samuel,*c* and he delivered you from the hands of your enemies on every side, so that you lived securely.

12"But when you saw that Nahash king of the Ammonites was moving against you, you said to me, 'No, we want a king to rule over us'—even though the LORD your God was your king. **13**Now here is the king you have chosen, the one you asked for; see, the LORD has set a king over you. **14**If you fear the LORD and serve and obey him and do not rebel against his commands, and if both you and the king who reigns over you follow the LORD your God—good! **15**But if you do not obey the LORD, and if you rebel against his commands, his hand will be against you, as it was against your fathers.

16"Now then, stand still and see this great thing the LORD is about to do before your eyes! **17**Is it not wheat harvest now? I will call upon the LORD to send thunder and rain. And you will realize what an evil thing you did in the eyes of the LORD when you asked for a king."

18Then Samuel called upon the LORD, and that same day the LORD sent thunder and rain. So all the people stood in awe of the LORD and of Samuel.

19The people all said to Samuel, "Pray to the LORD your God for your servants so that we will not die, for we have added to all our other sins the evil of asking for a king."

20"Do not be afraid," Samuel replied. "You have done all this evil; yet do not turn away from the LORD, but serve the LORD with all your heart. **21**Do not turn away after useless idols. They can do you no good, nor can they rescue you, because they are useless. **22**For the sake of his great name the LORD will not reject his people, because the LORD was pleased to make you his own. **23**As for me, far be it from me that I should sin against the LORD by failing to pray for you. And I will teach you the way that is good and right. **24**But be sure to fear the LORD and serve him faithfully with all your heart; consider what great things he has done for you. **25**Yet if you persist in doing evil, both you and your king will be swept away."

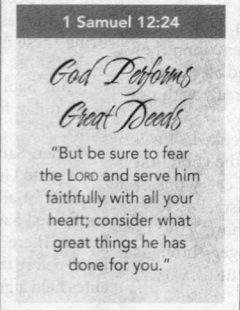

1 Samuel 12:24

God Performs Great Deeds

"But be sure to fear the LORD and serve him faithfully with all your heart; consider what great things he has done for you."

*a*11 Also called *Gideon*   *b*11 Some Septuagint manuscripts and Syriac; Hebrew *Bedan*   *c*11 Hebrew; some Septuagint manuscripts and Syriac *Samson*

Samuel Rebukes Saul

13 Saul was thirty[a] years old when he became king, and he reigned over Israel forty-[b] two years.

[2] Saul[c] chose three thousand men from Israel; two thousand were with him at Micmash and in the hill country of Bethel, and a thousand were with Jonathan at Gibeah in Benjamin. The rest of the men he sent back to their homes.

[3] Jonathan attacked the Philistine outpost at Geba, and the Philistines heard about it. Then Saul had the trumpet blown throughout the land and said, "Let the Hebrews hear!" [4] So all Israel heard the news: "Saul has attacked the Philistine outpost, and now Israel has become a stench to the Philistines." And the people were summoned to join Saul at Gilgal.

[5] The Philistines assembled to fight Israel, with three thousand[d] chariots, six thousand charioteers, and soldiers as numerous as the sand on the seashore. They went up and camped at Micmash, east of Beth Aven. [6] When the men of Israel saw that their situation was critical and that their army was hard pressed, they hid in caves and thickets, among the rocks, and in pits and cisterns. [7] Some Hebrews even crossed the Jordan to the land of Gad and Gilead.

Saul remained at Gilgal, and all the troops with him were quaking with fear. [8] He waited seven days, the time set by Samuel; but Samuel did not come to Gilgal, and Saul's men began to scatter. [9] So he said, "Bring me the burnt offering and the fellowship offerings.[e]" And Saul offered up the burnt offering. [10] Just as he finished making the offering, Samuel arrived, and Saul went out to greet him.

[11] "What have you done?" asked Samuel.

Saul replied, "When I saw that the men were scattering, and that you did not come at the set time, and that the Philistines were assembling at Micmash, [12] I thought, 'Now the Philistines will come down against me at Gilgal, and I have not sought the LORD's favor.' So I felt compelled to offer the burnt offering."

[13] "You acted foolishly," Samuel said. "You have not kept the command the LORD your God gave you; if you had, he would have established your kingdom over Israel for all time. [14] But now your kingdom will not endure; the LORD has sought out a man after his own heart and appointed him leader of his people, because you have not kept the LORD's command."

[15] Then Samuel left Gilgal[f] and went up to Gibeah in Benjamin, and Saul counted the men who were with him. They numbered about six hundred.

Israel Without Weapons

[16] Saul and his son Jonathan and the men with them were staying in Gibeah[g] in Benjamin, while the Philistines camped at Micmash. [17] Raiding parties went out from the Philistine camp in three detachments. One turned toward Ophrah in the vicinity of Shual, [18] another toward Beth Horon, and the third toward the borderland overlooking the Valley of Zeboim facing the desert.

[19] Not a blacksmith could be found in the whole land of Israel, because the Philistines had said, "Otherwise the Hebrews will make swords or spears!" [20] So all Israel went down to the Philistines to have their plowshares, mattocks, axes and sickles[h] sharpened. [21] The price was two thirds of a shekel[i] for sharpening plowshares and mattocks, and a third of a shekel[j] for sharpening forks and axes and for repointing goads.

[22] So on the day of the battle not a soldier with Saul and Jonathan had a sword or spear in his hand; only Saul and his son Jonathan had them.

Jonathan Attacks the Philistines

[23] Now a detachment of Philistines had gone out to the pass at Micmash. **14** [1] One day Jonathan son of Saul said to the young man bearing his armor, "Come, let's go over to the Philistine outpost on the other side." But he did not tell his father.

[2] Saul was staying on the outskirts of Gibeah under a pomegranate tree in Migron. With him were about six hundred men, [3] among

---

[a]1 A few late manuscripts of the Septuagint; Hebrew does not have *thirty*.   [b]1 See the round number in Acts 13:21; Hebrew does not have *forty-*.   [c]1,2 Or *and when he had reigned over Israel two years*, [2] *he*   [d]5 Some Septuagint manuscripts and Syriac; Hebrew *thirty thousand*   [e]9 Traditionally *peace offerings*   [f]15 Hebrew; Septuagint *Gilgal and went his way; the rest of the people went after Saul to meet the army, and they went out of Gilgal*   [g]16 Two Hebrew manuscripts; most Hebrew manuscripts *Geba*, a variant of *Gibeah*   [h]20 Septuagint; Hebrew *plowshares*   [i]21 Hebrew *pim*; that is, about 1/4 ounce (about 8 grams)   [j]21 That is, about 1/8 ounce (about 4 grams)

whom was Ahijah, who was wearing an ephod. He was a son of Ichabod's brother Ahitub son of Phinehas, the son of Eli, the LORD's priest in Shiloh. No one was aware that Jonathan had left.

⁴On each side of the pass that Jonathan intended to cross to reach the Philistine outpost was a cliff; one was called Bozez, and the other Seneh. ⁵One cliff stood to the north toward Micmash, the other to the south toward Geba.

⁶Jonathan said to his young armor-bearer, "Come, let's go over to the outpost of those uncircumcised fellows. Perhaps the LORD will act in our behalf. Nothing can hinder the LORD from saving, whether by many or by few."

⁷"Do all that you have in mind," his armor-bearer said. "Go ahead; I am with you heart and soul."

⁸Jonathan said, "Come, then; we will cross over toward the men and let them see us. ⁹If they say to us, 'Wait there until we come to you,' we will stay where we are and not go up to them. ¹⁰But if they say, 'Come up to us,' we will climb up, because that will be our sign that the LORD has given them into our hands."

¹¹So both of them showed themselves to the Philistine outpost. "Look!" said the Philistines. "The Hebrews are crawling out of the holes they were hiding in." ¹²The men of the outpost shouted to Jonathan and his armor-bearer, "Come up to us and we'll teach you a lesson."

So Jonathan said to his armor-bearer, "Climb up after me; the LORD has given them into the hand of Israel."

¹³Jonathan climbed up, using his hands and feet, with his armor-bearer right behind him. The Philistines fell before Jonathan, and his armor-bearer followed and killed behind him. ¹⁴In that first attack Jonathan and his armor-bearer killed some twenty men in an area of about half an acre.ᵃ

Israel Routs the Philistines

¹⁵Then panic struck the whole army—those in the camp and field, and those in the outposts and raiding parties—and the ground shook. It was a panic sent by God.ᵇ

¹⁶Saul's lookouts at Gibeah in Benjamin saw the army melting away in all directions. ¹⁷Then Saul said to the men who were with him, "Muster the forces and see who has left us." When they did, it was Jonathan and his armor-bearer who were not there.

¹⁸Saul said to Ahijah, "Bring the ark of God." (At that time it was with the Israelites.)ᶜ ¹⁹While Saul was talking to the priest, the tumult in the Philistine camp increased more and more. So Saul said to the priest, "Withdraw your hand."

²⁰Then Saul and all his men assembled and went to the battle. They found the Philistines in total confusion, striking each other with their swords. ²¹Those Hebrews who had previously been with the Philistines and had gone up with them to their camp went over to the Israelites who were with Saul and Jonathan. ²²When all the Israelites who had hidden in the hill country of Ephraim heard that the Philistines were on the run, they joined the battle in hot pursuit. ²³So the LORD rescued Israel that day, and the battle moved on beyond Beth Aven.

Jonathan Eats Honey

²⁴Now the men of Israel were in distress that day, because Saul had bound the people under an oath, saying, "Cursed be any man who eats food before evening comes, before I have avenged myself on my enemies!" So none of the troops tasted food.

²⁵The entire armyᵈ entered the woods, and there was honey on the ground. ²⁶When they went into the woods, they saw the honey oozing out, yet no one put his hand to his mouth, because they feared the oath. ²⁷But Jonathan had not heard that his father had bound the people with the oath, so he reached out the end of the staff that was in his hand and dipped it into the honeycomb. He raised his hand to his mouth, and his eyes brightened.ᵉ ²⁸Then one of the soldiers told him, "Your father bound the army under a strict oath, saying, 'Cursed be any man who eats food today!' That is why the men are faint."

²⁹Jonathan said, "My father has made trouble for the country. See how my eyes brightenedᶠ when I tasted a little of this honey.

ᵃ14 Hebrew half a yoke; a "yoke" was the land plowed by a yoke of oxen in one day. ᵇ15 Or a terrible panic ᶜ18 Hebrew; Septuagint "Bring the ephod." (At that time he wore the ephod before the Israelites.) ᵈ25 Or Now all the people of the land ᵉ27 Or his strength was renewed ᶠ29 Or my strength was renewed

³⁰How much better it would have been if the men had eaten today some of the plunder they took from their enemies. Would not the slaughter of the Philistines have been even greater?"

³¹That day, after the Israelites had struck down the Philistines from Micmash to Aijalon, they were exhausted. ³²They pounced on the plunder and, taking sheep, cattle and calves, they butchered them on the ground and ate them, together with the blood. ³³Then someone said to Saul, "Look, the men are sinning against the LORD by eating meat that has blood in it."

"You have broken faith," he said. "Roll a large stone over here at once." ³⁴Then he said, "Go out among the men and tell them, 'Each of you bring me your cattle and sheep, and slaughter them here and eat them. Do not sin against the LORD by eating meat with blood still in it.'"

So everyone brought his ox that night and slaughtered it there. ³⁵Then Saul built an altar to the LORD; it was the first time he had done this.

³⁶Saul said, "Let us go down after the Philistines by night and plunder them till dawn, and let us not leave one of them alive."

"Do whatever seems best to you," they replied.

But the priest said, "Let us inquire of God here."

³⁷So Saul asked God, "Shall I go down after the Philistines? Will you give them into Israel's hand?" But God did not answer him that day.

³⁸Saul therefore said, "Come here, all you who are leaders of the army, and let us find out what sin has been committed today. ³⁹As surely as the LORD who rescues Israel lives, even if it lies with my son Jonathan, he must die." But not one of the men said a word.

⁴⁰Saul then said to all the Israelites, "You stand over there; I and Jonathan my son will stand over here."

"Do what seems best to you," the men replied.

⁴¹Then Saul prayed to the LORD, the God of Israel, "Give me the right answer."ᵃ And Jonathan and Saul were taken by lot, and the men were cleared. ⁴²Saul said, "Cast the lot between

me and Jonathan my son." And Jonathan was taken.

⁴³Then Saul said to Jonathan, "Tell me what you have done."

So Jonathan told him, "I merely tasted a little honey with the end of my staff. And now must I die?"

⁴⁴Saul said, "May God deal with me, be it ever so severely, if you do not die, Jonathan."

⁴⁵But the men said to Saul, "Should Jonathan die—he who has brought about this great deliverance in Israel? Never! As surely as the LORD lives, not a hair of his head will fall to the ground, for he did this today with God's help." So the men rescued Jonathan, and he was not put to death.

⁴⁶Then Saul stopped pursuing the Philistines, and they withdrew to their own land.

⁴⁷After Saul had assumed rule over Israel, he fought against their enemies on every side: Moab, the Ammonites, Edom, the kingsᵇ of Zobah, and the Philistines. Wherever he turned, he inflicted punishment on them.ᶜ ⁴⁸He fought valiantly and defeated the Amalekites, delivering Israel from the hands of those who had plundered them.

Saul's Family

⁴⁹Saul's sons were Jonathan, Ishvi and Malki-Shua. The name of his older daughter was Merab, and that of the younger was Michal. ⁵⁰His wife's name was Ahinoam daughter of Ahimaaz. The name of the commander of Saul's army was Abner son of Ner, and Ner was Saul's uncle. ⁵¹Saul's father Kish and Abner's father Ner were sons of Abiel.

⁵²All the days of Saul there was bitter war with the Philistines, and whenever Saul saw a mighty or brave man, he took him into his service.

The LORD Rejects Saul as King

15 Samuel said to Saul, "I am the one the LORD sent to anoint you king over his people Israel; so listen now to the message from the LORD. ²This is what the LORD Almighty says: 'I will punish the Amalekites for what they did to Israel when they waylaid them as they came up from Egypt. ³Now go, attack

---

ᵃ41 Hebrew; Septuagint *"Why have you not answered your servant today? If the fault is in me or my son Jonathan, respond with Urim, but if the men of Israel are at fault, respond with Thummim."*   ᵇ47 Masoretic Text; Dead Sea Scrolls and Septuagint *king*   ᶜ47 Hebrew; Septuagint *he was victorious* the Amalekites and totally destroy[a] everything that belongs to them. Do not spare them; put to death men and women, children and infants, cattle and sheep, camels and donkeys.' "

4So Saul summoned the men and mustered them at Telaim—two hundred thousand foot soldiers and ten thousand men from Judah. 5Saul went to the city of Amalek and set an ambush in the ravine. 6Then he said to the Kenites, "Go away, leave the Amalekites so that I do not destroy you along with them; for you showed kindness to all the Israelites when they came up out of Egypt." So the Kenites moved away from the Amalekites.

7Then Saul attacked the Amalekites all the way from Havilah to Shur, to the east of Egypt. 8He took Agag king of the Amalekites alive, and all his people he totally destroyed with the sword. 9But Saul and the army spared Agag and the best of the sheep and cattle, the fat calves[b] and lambs—everything that was good. These they were unwilling to destroy completely, but everything that was despised and weak they totally destroyed.

10Then the word of the LORD came to Samuel: 11"I am grieved that I have made Saul king, because he has turned away from me and has not carried out my instructions." Samuel was troubled, and he cried out to the LORD all that night.

12Early in the morning Samuel got up and went to meet Saul, but he was told, "Saul has gone to Carmel. There he has set up a monument in his own honor and has turned and gone on down to Gilgal."

13When Samuel reached him, Saul said, "The LORD bless you! I have carried out the LORD's instructions."

14But Samuel said, "What then is this bleating of sheep in my ears? What is this lowing of cattle that I hear?"

15Saul answered, "The soldiers brought them from the Amalekites; they spared the best of the sheep and cattle to sacrifice to the LORD your God, but we totally destroyed the rest."

16"Stop!" Samuel said to Saul. "Let me tell you what the LORD said to me last night."

"Tell me," Saul replied.

17Samuel said, "Although you were once small in your own eyes, did you not become the head of the tribes of Israel? The LORD anointed you king over Israel. 18And he sent you on a mission, saying, 'Go and completely destroy those wicked people, the Amalekites; make war on them until you have wiped them out.' 19Why did you not obey the LORD? Why did you pounce on the plunder and do evil in the eyes of the LORD?"

20"But I did obey the LORD," Saul said. "I went on the mission the LORD assigned me. I completely destroyed the Amalekites and brought back Agag their king. 21The soldiers took sheep and cattle from the plunder, the best of what was devoted to God, in order to sacrifice them to the LORD your God at Gilgal."

22But Samuel replied:

"Does the LORD delight in burnt offerings
    and sacrifices
  as much as in obeying the voice of the
    LORD?
To obey is better than sacrifice,
  and to heed is better than the fat of
    rams.
23For rebellion is like the sin of divination,
  and arrogance like the evil of
    idolatry.
Because you have rejected the word of the
    LORD,
  he has rejected you as king."

24Then Saul said to Samuel, "I have sinned. I violated the LORD's command and your instructions. I was afraid of the people and so I gave in to them. 25Now I beg you, forgive my sin and come back with me, so that I may worship the LORD."

26But Samuel said to him, "I will not go back with you. You have rejected the word of the LORD, and the LORD has rejected you as king over Israel!"

27As Samuel turned to leave, Saul caught hold of the hem of his robe, and it tore. 28Samuel said to him, "The LORD has torn the kingdom of Israel from you today and has given it to one of your neighbors—to one better than you. 29He who is the Glory of Israel does not

---

[a]3 The Hebrew term refers to the irrevocable giving over of things or persons to the LORD, often by totally destroying them; also in verses 8, 9, 15, 18, 20 and 21.   [b]9 Or *the grown bulls*; the meaning of the Hebrew for this phrase is uncertain.

But, Lord!

Read: 1 Samuel 15:1–23

"YES, MOM, I HEAR YOU! I'll get my homework done and unload the dishwasher before I watch TV." Brent looked his mom straight in the eyes and repeated her instructions. Marlene had to work the third shift this week, and she wouldn't be around when Brent got home from school. Later, when she inspected her son's work, she realized he hadn't followed all of her directions. When she confronted him, Brent rolled his eyes and said, "But, Mom, I didn't think you meant all of it!" Walking away in disgust, she muttered, "Where did I go wrong?"

Marlene sounds a little like Samuel when he expressed God's grief over Saul's misbehavior: "I am grieved that I have made Saul king." Samuel, God's messenger on earth, had given Saul clear instructions: Wipe out all of the Amalekites and take no plunder. No exceptions.

But Saul's actions revealed his self-willed heart: "But, Lord, I didn't think you meant all of them!" God's commands didn't fit Saul's plans, so he tweaked them to fit his convenience.

We're all a little like Saul. We all fall into the "but, Lord" trap.

I know your grace is sufficient, but, Lord, I think I'll take the easy way out.

But, Lord, why can't I tell five of my best friends about what happened?

But, Lord, surely flirting isn't cheating.

But, Lord, this chat room helps me escape my boring life.

But, Lord, overeating isn't hurting anyone else, is it?

We dig ourselves in deeper when, instead of squelching temptation, we turn toward it. The turn starts when, like Saul, we respond to God's promptings within us with "*But, Lord . . .*" and "[reject] the word of the LORD." The more frequently we make that turn, the more we fool ourselves that we are innocent.

Our daily lives present us with ample opportunity to choose God's leading or to reject it. Saul chose to disobey, and it cost him the kingdom. Jesus chose to obey, and he gained the keys to the kingdom of heaven. The only "but" believers should utter is the one Christ taught us to pray, "Not as I will, *but* as you will" (Matthew 26:39, emphasis added).

Go to page 347 for your next devotional reading.

1 Samuel 15:11

"I am grieved that I have made Saul king, because he has turned away from me and has not carried out my instructions." Samuel was troubled, and he cried out to the LORD all that night.

reflection

1 How is "*but, Lord*" a phrase that creeps into your vocabulary?

2 In what ways have you tweaked God's instructions to suit your convenience?

3 What are some practical ways you can turn from a temptation in your life? Make a commitment today to take whatever steps you must to obey God with no *ifs*, *ands* or *buts*.

RELATED READINGS

Proverbs 4:20–27;
Matthew 26:36–46;
1 John 3:21–24

Monday

lie or change his mind; for he is not a man, that he should change his mind."

³⁰Saul replied, "I have sinned. But please honor me before the elders of my people and before Israel; come back with me, so that I may worship the LORD your God." ³¹So Samuel went back with Saul, and Saul worshiped the LORD.

³²Then Samuel said, "Bring me Agag king of the Amalekites."

Agag came to him confidently,ᵃ thinking, "Surely the bitterness of death is past."

³³But Samuel said,

"As your sword has made
        women childless,
    so will your mother be childless among
        women."

And Samuel put Agag to death before the LORD at Gilgal.

³⁴Then Samuel left for Ramah, but Saul went up to his home in Gibeah of Saul. ³⁵Until the day Samuel died, he did not go to see Saul again, though Samuel mourned for him. And the LORD was grieved that he had made Saul king over Israel.

Samuel Anoints David

16 The LORD said to Samuel, "How long will you mourn for Saul, since I have rejected him as king over Israel? Fill your horn with oil and be on your way; I am sending you to Jesse of Bethlehem. I have chosen one of his sons to be king."

²But Samuel said, "How can I go? Saul will hear about it and kill me."

The LORD said, "Take a heifer with you and say, 'I have come to sacrifice to the LORD.' ³Invite Jesse to the sacrifice, and I will show you what to do. You are to anoint for me the one I indicate."

⁴Samuel did what the LORD said. When he arrived at Bethlehem, the elders of the town trembled when they met him. They asked, "Do you come in peace?"

⁵Samuel replied, "Yes, in peace; I have come to sacrifice to the LORD. Consecrate yourselves and come to the sacrifice with me." Then he consecrated Jesse and his sons and invited them to the sacrifice.

⁶When they arrived, Samuel saw Eliab and thought, "Surely the LORD's anointed stands here before the LORD."

⁷But the LORD said to Samuel, "Do not consider his appearance or his height, for I have rejected him. The LORD does not look at the things man looks at. Man looks at the outward appearance, but the LORD looks at the heart."

⁸Then Jesse called Abinadab and had him pass in front of Samuel. But Samuel said, "The LORD has not chosen this one either." ⁹Jesse then had Shammah pass by, but Samuel said, "Nor has the LORD chosen this one." ¹⁰Jesse had seven of his sons pass before Samuel, but Samuel said to him, "The LORD has not chosen these." ¹¹So he asked Jesse, "Are these all the sons you have?"

"There is still the youngest," Jesse answered, "but he is tending the sheep."

Samuel said, "Send for him; we will not sit downᵇ until he arrives."

¹²So he sent and had him brought in. He was ruddy, with a fine appearance and handsome features.

Then the LORD said, "Rise and anoint him; he is the one."

¹³So Samuel took the horn of oil and anointed him in the presence of his brothers, and from that day on the Spirit of the LORD came upon David in power. Samuel then went to Ramah.

David in Saul's Service

¹⁴Now the Spirit of the LORD had departed from Saul, and an evilᶜ spirit from the LORD tormented him.

¹⁵Saul's attendants said to him, "See, an evil spirit from God is tormenting you. ¹⁶Let our lord command his servants here to search for someone who can play the harp. He will play when the evil spirit from God comes upon you, and you will feel better."

1 Samuel 15:29

God Is Resolute

"He who is the Glory of Israel does not lie or change his mind; for he is not a man, that he should change his mind."

ᵃ32 Or *him trembling, yet*   ᵇ11 Some Septuagint manuscripts; Hebrew *not gather around*   ᶜ14 Or *injurious*; also in verses 15, 16 and 23

¹⁷So Saul said to his attendants, "Find someone who plays well and bring him to me."

¹⁸One of the servants answered, "I have seen a son of Jesse of Bethlehem who knows how to play the harp. He is a brave man and a warrior. He speaks well and is a fine-looking man. And the Lord is with him."

¹⁹Then Saul sent messengers to Jesse and said, "Send me your son David, who is with the sheep." ²⁰So Jesse took a donkey loaded with bread, a skin of wine and a young goat and sent them with his son David to Saul.

²¹David came to Saul and entered his service. Saul liked him very much, and David became one of his armor-bearers. ²²Then Saul sent word to Jesse, saying, "Allow David to remain in my service, for I am pleased with him."

²³Whenever the spirit from God came upon Saul, David would take his harp and play. Then relief would come to Saul; he would feel better, and the evil spirit would leave him.

David and Goliath

17 Now the Philistines gathered their forces for war and assembled at Socoh in Judah. They pitched camp at Ephes Dammim, between Socoh and Azekah. ²Saul and the Israelites assembled and camped in the Valley of Elah and drew up their battle line to meet the Philistines. ³The Philistines occupied one hill and the Israelites another, with the valley between them.

⁴A champion named Goliath, who was from Gath, came out of the Philistine camp. He was over nine feet*a* tall. ⁵He had a bronze helmet on his head and wore a coat of scale armor of bronze weighing five thousand shekels*b*; ⁶on his legs he wore bronze greaves, and a bronze javelin was slung on his back. ⁷His spear shaft was like a weaver's rod, and its iron point weighed six hundred shekels.*c* His shield bearer went ahead of him.

⁸Goliath stood and shouted to the ranks of Israel, "Why do you come out and line up for battle? Am I not a Philistine, and are you not the servants of Saul? Choose a man and have him come down to me. ⁹If he is able to fight and kill me, we will become your subjects; but if I over-

come him and kill him, you will become our subjects and serve us." ¹⁰Then the Philistine said, "This day I defy the ranks of Israel! Give me a man and let us fight each other." ¹¹On hearing the Philistine's words, Saul and all the Israelites were dismayed and terrified.

¹²Now David was the son of an Ephrathite named Jesse, who was from Bethlehem in Judah. Jesse had eight sons, and in Saul's time he was old and well advanced in years. ¹³Jesse's three oldest sons had followed Saul to the war: The firstborn was Eliab; the second, Abinadab; and the third, Shammah. ¹⁴David was the youngest. The three oldest followed Saul, ¹⁵but David went back and forth from Saul to tend his father's sheep at Bethlehem.

¹⁶For forty days the Philistine came forward every morning and evening and took his stand.

¹⁷Now Jesse said to his son David, "Take this ephah*d* of roasted grain and these ten loaves of bread for your brothers and hurry to their camp. ¹⁸Take along these ten cheeses to the commander of their unit.*e* See how your brothers are and bring back some assurance*f* from them. ¹⁹They are with Saul and all the men of Israel in the Valley of Elah, fighting against the Philistines."

²⁰Early in the morning David left the flock with a shepherd, loaded up and set out, as Jesse had directed. He reached the camp as the army was going out to its battle positions, shouting the war cry. ²¹Israel and the Philistines were drawing up their lines facing each other. ²²David left his things with the keeper of supplies, ran to the battle lines and greeted his brothers. ²³As he was talking with them, Goliath, the Philistine champion from Gath, stepped out from his lines and shouted his usual defiance, and David heard it. ²⁴When the Israelites saw the man, they all ran from him in great fear.

²⁵Now the Israelites had been saying, "Do you see how this man keeps coming out? He comes out to defy Israel. The king will give great wealth to the man who kills him. He will also give him his daughter in marriage and will exempt his father's family from taxes in Israel."

²⁶David asked the men standing near

---

*a*4 Hebrew *was six cubits and a span* (about 3 meters)   *b*5 That is, about 125 pounds (about 57 kilograms)   *c*7 That is, about 15 pounds (about 7 kilograms)   *d*17 That is, probably about 3/5 bushel (about 22 liters)   *e*18 Hebrew *thousand*   *f*18 Or *some token*; or *some pledge of spoils*

345

him, "What will be done for the man who kills this Philistine and removes this disgrace from Israel? Who is this uncircumcised Philistine that he should defy the armies of the living God?"

27They repeated to him what they had been saying and told him, "This is what will be done for the man who kills him."

28When Eliab, David's oldest brother, heard him speaking with the men, he burned with anger at him and asked, "Why have you come down here? And with whom did you leave those few sheep in the desert? I know how conceited you are and how wicked your heart is; you came down only to watch the battle."

29"Now what have I done?" said David. "Can't I even speak?" 30He then turned away to someone else and brought up the same matter, and the men answered him as before. 31What David said was overheard and reported to Saul, and Saul sent for him.

32David said to Saul, "Let no one lose heart on account of this Philistine; your servant will go and fight him."

33Saul replied, "You are not able to go out against this Philistine and fight him; you are only a boy, and he has been a fighting man from his youth."

34But David said to Saul, "Your servant has been keeping his father's sheep. When a lion or a bear came and carried off a sheep from the flock, 35I went after it, struck it and rescued the sheep from its mouth. When it turned on me, I seized it by its hair, struck it and killed it. 36Your servant has killed both the lion and the bear; this uncircumcised Philistine will be like one of them, because he has defied the armies of the living God. 37The LORD who delivered me from the paw of the lion and the paw of the bear will deliver me from the hand of this Philistine."

Saul said to David, "Go, and the LORD be with you."

38Then Saul dressed David in his own tunic. He put a coat of armor on him and a bronze helmet on his head. 39David fastened on his sword over the tunic and tried walking around, because he was not used to them.

"I cannot go in these," he said to Saul, "because I am not used to them." So he took them off. 40Then he took his staff in his hand, chose five smooth stones from the stream, put them in the pouch of his shepherd's bag and, with his sling in his hand, approached the Philistine.

41Meanwhile, the Philistine, with his shield bearer in front of him, kept coming closer to David. 42He looked David over and saw that he was only a boy, ruddy and handsome, and he despised him. 43He said to David, "Am I a dog, that you come at me with sticks?" And the Philistine cursed David by his gods. 44"Come here," he said, "and I'll give your flesh to the birds of the air and the beasts of the field!"

45David said to the Philistine, "You come against me with sword and spear and javelin, but I come against you in the name of the LORD Almighty, the God of the armies of Israel, whom you have defied. 46This day the LORD will hand you over to me, and I'll strike you down and cut off your head. Today I will give the carcasses of the Philistine army to the birds of the air and the beasts of the earth, and the whole world will know that there is a God in Israel. 47All those gathered here will know that it is not by sword or spear that the LORD's saves; for the battle is the LORD's, and he will give all of you into our hands."

1 Samuel 17:47

God Saves His Own

"All those gathered here will know that it is not by sword or spear that the LORD saves; for the battle is the LORD's, and he will give all of you into our hands."

48As the Philistine moved closer to attack him, David ran quickly toward the battle line to meet him. 49Reaching into his bag and taking out a stone, he slung it and struck the Philistine on the forehead. The stone sank into his forehead, and he fell facedown on the ground.

50So David triumphed over the Philistine with a sling and a stone; without a sword in his hand he struck down the Philistine and killed him.

51David ran and stood over him. He took

No Underdogs

Read: 1 Samuel 17:32–51

LONG REVILED AND FEARED by humans, due in part to their unearthly cackle, hyenas stand up to virtually any other animal. They are scrappy underdogs willing to fight enormous predators and staggering odds. The female hyena stays with and cares for her young longer than any other carnivore. Mothers will battle other bands of hyenas, and have even been known to face nearly certain death at the fangs of lions, when fighting for their young.

David, hardly more than a boy himself, defended something even more dear than an offspring: his people's God. God delights in calling those who are small and weak. It's a picture of God granting his people strength and power, equipping them to accomplish amazing things for his good purpose. We see the principle—God empowering the weak to conquer the strong—demonstrated throughout the Bible: The stories of Moses standing before Pharaoh, Elijah standing against the prophets of Baal, and Gideon fighting the Midianites all display the power of God working through weak human beings. And the principle doesn't stop there. When we look around in our churches, we see the same thing happening today on both large and small scales. Women pray together to battle for their families and marriages. Sunday school teachers work tirelessly to instill the knowledge of God in young hearts. Families provide food for those who have little. Missionary attorneys battle slavery and other injustices all over the world.

What hulking giant swaggers and struts through your territory, trying to keep you from moving forward? Do you have a monstrous fear of rejection? Do you harbor huge questions about your faith? Does the complexity of society's mammoth problems cause you to doubt God's strength?

Perhaps God is calling *you* to move from defense to offense, to count the importance of *who* you're defending before assessing the odds. For a female hyena, her young always trump physical danger, however big the predator. Perhaps, like David, God has called you to the battlefield. Before you go, carefully don the armor of God (see Ephesians 6:10–18). Then, when the giant tries to intimidate you, pick out your stone of faith and take aim. And cover your ears, because when you fight in the power of God through Jesus Christ, the crash will be deafening when the giant falls.

1 Samuel 17:45

David said to the Philistine, "You come against me with sword and spear and javelin, but I come against you in the name of the LORD Almighty, the God of the armies of Israel, whom you have defied."

reflection

1 Why do you think God used a shepherd boy rather than an entire army to bring down Goliath?

2 How does it encourage you to see how God empowers ordinary people to accomplish his purposes?

3 In which of your battles do you particularly need God's strength? Take the time to ask him to arm you head to toe. Ask him to transform your tiny pebble of faith into a powerful missile.

RELATED READINGS

1 Samuel 16:6–13;
Isaiah 41:10;
Ephesians 6:10–18

Tuesday

Go to page 351 for your next devotional reading.

hold of the Philistine's sword and drew it from the scabbard. After he killed him, he cut off his head with the sword.

When the Philistines saw that their hero was dead, they turned and ran. ⁵²Then the men of Israel and Judah surged forward with a shout and pursued the Philistines to the entrance of Gath[a] and to the gates of Ekron. Their dead were strewn along the Shaaraim road to Gath and Ekron. ⁵³When the Israelites returned from chasing the Philistines, they plundered their camp. ⁵⁴David took the Philistine's head and brought it to Jerusalem, and he put the Philistine's weapons in his own tent.

⁵⁵As Saul watched David going out to meet the Philistine, he said to Abner, commander of the army, "Abner, whose son is that young man?"

Abner replied, "As surely as you live, O king, I don't know."

⁵⁶The king said, "Find out whose son this young man is."

⁵⁷As soon as David returned from killing the Philistine, Abner took him and brought him before Saul, with David still holding the Philistine's head.

⁵⁸"Whose son are you, young man?" Saul asked him.

David said, "I am the son of your servant Jesse of Bethlehem."

Saul's Jealousy of David

18 After David had finished talking with Saul, Jonathan became one in spirit with David, and he loved him as himself. ²From that day Saul kept David with him and did not let him return to his father's house. ³And Jonathan made a covenant with David because he loved him as himself. ⁴Jonathan took off the robe he was wearing and gave it to David, along with his tunic, and even his sword, his bow and his belt.

⁵Whatever Saul sent him to do, David did it so successfully[b] that Saul gave him a high rank in the army. This pleased all the people, and Saul's officers as well.

⁶When the men were returning home after David had killed the Philistine, the women came out from all the towns of Israel to meet King Saul with singing and dancing, with joyful songs and with tambourines and lutes. ⁷As they danced, they sang:

"Saul has slain his thousands,
   and David his tens of thousands."

⁸Saul was very angry; this refrain galled him. "They have credited David with tens of thousands," he thought, "but me with only thousands. What more can he get but the kingdom?" ⁹And from that time on Saul kept a jealous eye on David.

¹⁰The next day an evil[c] spirit from God came forcefully upon Saul. He was prophesying in his house, while David was playing the harp, as he usually did. Saul had a spear in his hand ¹¹and he hurled it, saying to himself, "I'll pin David to the wall." But David eluded him twice.

¹²Saul was afraid of David, because the LORD was with David but had left Saul. ¹³So he sent David away from him and gave him command over a thousand men, and David led the troops in their campaigns. ¹⁴In everything he did he had great success,[d] because the LORD was with him. ¹⁵When Saul saw how successful[e] he was, he was afraid of him. ¹⁶But all Israel and Judah loved David, because he led them in their campaigns.

¹⁷Saul said to David, "Here is my older daughter Merab. I will give her to you in marriage; only serve me bravely and fight the battles of the LORD." For Saul said to himself, "I will not raise a hand against him. Let the Philistines do that!"

¹⁸But David said to Saul, "Who am I, and what is my family or my father's clan in Israel, that I should become the king's son-in-law?" ¹⁹So[f] when the time came for Merab, Saul's daughter, to be given to David, she was given in marriage to Adriel of Meholah.

²⁰Now Saul's daughter Michal was in love with David, and when they told Saul about it, he was pleased. ²¹"I will give her to him," he thought, "so that she may be a snare to him and so that the hand of the Philistines may be against him." So Saul said to David, "Now you have a second opportunity to become my son-in-law."

---

[a]52 Some Septuagint manuscripts; Hebrew *a valley*   [b]5 Or *wisely*   [c]10 Or *injurious*   [d]14 Or *he was very wise*   [e]15 Or *wise*   [f]19 Or *However,*

²²Then Saul ordered his attendants: "Speak to David privately and say, 'Look, the king is pleased with you, and his attendants all like you; now become his son-in-law.'"

²³They repeated these words to David. But David said, "Do you think it is a small matter to become the king's son-in-law? I'm only a poor man and little known."

²⁴When Saul's servants told him what David had said, ²⁵Saul replied, "Say to David, 'The king wants no other price for the bride than a hundred Philistine foreskins, to take revenge on his enemies.'" Saul's plan was to have David fall by the hands of the Philistines.

²⁶When the attendants told David these things, he was pleased to become the king's son-in-law. So before the allotted time elapsed, ²⁷David and his men went out and killed two hundred Philistines. He brought their foreskins and presented the full number to the king so that he might become the king's son-in-law. Then Saul gave him his daughter Michal in marriage.

²⁸When Saul realized that the LORD was with David and that his daughter Michal loved David, ²⁹Saul became still more afraid of him, and he remained his enemy the rest of his days.

³⁰The Philistine commanders continued to go out to battle, and as often as they did, David met with more success*a* than the rest of Saul's officers, and his name became well known.

Saul Tries to Kill David

19 Saul told his son Jonathan and all the attendants to kill David. But Jonathan was very fond of David ²and warned him, "My father Saul is looking for a chance to kill you. Be on your guard tomorrow morning; go into hiding and stay there. ³I will go out and stand with my father in the field where you are. I'll speak to him about you and will tell you what I find out."

⁴Jonathan spoke well of David to Saul his father and said to him, "Let not the king do wrong to his servant David; he has not wronged you, and what he has done has benefited you greatly. ⁵He took his life in his hands when he killed the Philistine. The LORD won a great victory for all Israel, and you saw it and were glad. Why then would you do wrong to an innocent man like David by killing him for no reason?"

⁶Saul listened to Jonathan and took this oath: "As surely as the LORD lives, David will not be put to death."

⁷So Jonathan called David and told him the whole conversation. He brought him to Saul, and David was with Saul as before.

⁸Once more war broke out, and David went out and fought the Philistines. He struck them with such force that they fled before him.

⁹But an evil*b* spirit from the LORD came upon Saul as he was sitting in his house with his spear in his hand. While David was playing the harp, ¹⁰Saul tried to pin him to the wall with his spear, but David eluded him as Saul drove the spear into the wall. That night David made good his escape.

¹¹Saul sent men to David's house to watch it and to kill him in the morning. But Michal, David's wife, warned him, "If you don't run for your life tonight, tomorrow you'll be killed." ¹²So Michal let David down through a window, and he fled and escaped. ¹³Then Michal took an idol*c* and laid it on the bed, covering it with a garment and putting some goats' hair at the head.

¹⁴When Saul sent the men to capture David, Michal said, "He is ill."

¹⁵Then Saul sent the men back to see David and told them, "Bring him up to me in his bed so that I may kill him." ¹⁶But when the men entered, there was the idol in the bed, and at the head was some goats' hair.

¹⁷Saul said to Michal, "Why did you deceive me like this and send my enemy away so that he escaped?"

Michal told him, "He said to me, 'Let me get away. Why should I kill you?'"

¹⁸When David had fled and made his escape, he went to Samuel at Ramah and told him all that Saul had done to him. Then he and Samuel went to Naioth and stayed there. ¹⁹Word came to Saul: "David is in Naioth at Ramah"; ²⁰so he sent men to capture him. But when they saw a group of prophets prophesying, with Samuel standing there as their leader, the Spirit of God came upon Saul's men and they also prophesied. ²¹Saul was told about it, and he sent more

---

*a*30 Or *David acted more wisely*   *b*9 Or *injurious*   *c*13 Hebrew *teraphim*; also in verse 16 men, and they prophesied too. Saul sent men a third time, and they also prophesied. **22**Finally, he himself left for Ramah and went to the great cistern at Secu. And he asked, "Where are Samuel and David?"

"Over in Naioth at Ramah," they said.

23So Saul went to Naioth at Ramah. But the Spirit of God came even upon him, and he walked along prophesying until he came to Naioth. **24**He stripped off his robes and also prophesied in Samuel's presence. He lay that way all that day and night. This is why people say, "Is Saul also among the prophets?"

David and Jonathan

20 Then David fled from Naioth at Ramah and went to Jonathan and asked, "What have I done? What is my crime? How have I wronged your father, that he is trying to take my life?"

2"Never!" Jonathan replied. "You are not going to die! Look, my father doesn't do anything, great or small, without confiding in me. Why would he hide this from me? It's not so!"

3But David took an oath and said, "Your father knows very well that I have found favor in your eyes, and he has said to himself, 'Jonathan must not know this or he will be grieved.' Yet as surely as the LORD lives and as you live, there is only a step between me and death."

4Jonathan said to David, "Whatever you want me to do, I'll do for you."

5So David said, "Look, tomorrow is the New Moon festival, and I am supposed to dine with the king; but let me go and hide in the field until the evening of the day after tomorrow. **6**If your father misses me at all, tell him, 'David earnestly asked my permission to hurry to Bethlehem, his hometown, because an annual sacrifice is being made there for his whole clan.' **7**If he says, 'Very well,' then your servant is safe. But if he loses his temper, you can be sure that he is determined to harm me. **8**As for you, show kindness to your servant, for you have brought him into a covenant with you before the LORD. If I am guilty, then kill me yourself! Why hand me over to your father?"

9"Never!" Jonathan said. "If I had the least inkling that my father was determined to harm you, wouldn't I tell you?"

10David asked, "Who will tell me if your father answers you harshly?"

11"Come," Jonathan said, "let's go out into the field." So they went there together.

12Then Jonathan said to David: "By the LORD, the God of Israel, I will surely sound out my father by this time the day after tomorrow! If he is favorably disposed toward you, will I not send you word and let you know? **13**But if my father is inclined to harm you, may the LORD deal with me, be it ever so severely, if I do not let you know and send you away safely. May the LORD be with you as he has been with my father. **14**But show me unfailing kindness like that of the LORD as long as I live, so that I may not be killed, **15**and do not ever cut off your kindness from my family—not even when the LORD has cut off every one of David's enemies from the face of the earth."

16So Jonathan made a covenant with the house of David, saying, "May the LORD call David's enemies to account." **17**And Jonathan had David reaffirm his oath out of love for him, because he loved him as he loved himself.

18Then Jonathan said to David: "Tomorrow is the New Moon festival. You will be missed, because your seat will be empty. **19**The day after tomorrow, toward evening, go to the place where you hid when this trouble began, and wait by the stone Ezel. **20**I will shoot three arrows to the side of it, as though I were shooting at a target. **21**Then I will send a boy and say, 'Go, find the arrows.' If I say to him, 'Look, the arrows are on this side of you; bring them here,' then come, because, as surely as the LORD lives, you are safe; there is no danger. **22**But if I say to the boy, 'Look, the arrows are beyond you,' then you must go, because the LORD has sent you away. **23**And about the matter you and I discussed—remember, the LORD is witness between you and me forever."

24So David hid in the field, and when the New Moon festival came, the king sat down to eat. **25**He sat in his customary place by the wall, opposite Jonathan,*a* and Abner sat next to Saul, but David's place was empty. **26**Saul said nothing that day, for he thought, "Something must have happened to David to make him ceremonially unclean—surely he is unclean." **27**But the next

---

*a*25 Septuagint; Hebrew *wall. Jonathan arose*

Friends

Read: 1 Samuel 20:1–42

A BRITISH PUBLICATION once offered a prize for the best definition of a friend. Among the thousands of answers mailed in, the top five were:

5) "One who multiplies joys, divides grief, and whose honesty is inviolable."

4) "One who understands our silence."

3) "A volume of sympathy bound in cloth."

2) "A watch that beats true for all time and never runs down."

The winning definition simply read:

1) "A friend is the one who comes in when the whole world has gone out."

David and Jonathan perfectly fit these definitions of a true friend. Jonathan had become "one in spirit with David, and he loved him as himself," and the two had made a covenant of friendship (1 Samuel 18:1,3). When Samuel anointed David to succeed Jonathan's father as king, Saul erupted in unbridled anger and forced David from the land. But Jonathan swore loyalty to God's chosen heir to the throne.

David and Jonathan's deep friendship was based not on family ties or warm, fuzzy feelings; they were bound by dedication to God and steadfast commitment to one another. Rather than being jealous of David for usurping his potential place as king, Jonathan accepted God's plan to make David king, sacrificially stepping down and supporting his friend.

And David reciprocated by remaining loyal to Jonathan and Jonathan's family. Even after Jonathan's death, David kept his vow of loyalty to his dear friend. He made sure that Jonathan and Saul were buried with royal honors. He invited Jonathan's disabled son, Mephibosheth, into his home and treated him like a prince.

In our culture, it seems more common to hear of women who have close friendships than men who do, so we're surprised that one of the most beautiful portraits of friendship in Scripture is the bond between these two warriors, who we might be inclined to think of as unemotional and detached. But we, as women, can model David and Jonathan's friendship. When our friendships are based on our common love for God and our desire for God's best for each other, then our friendships can be as tough and true and deep as the one between David and Jonathan.

---

1 Samuel 20:42

Jonathan said to David, "Go in peace, for we have sworn friendship with each other in the name of the LORD, saying, 'The LORD is witness between you and me, and between your descendants and my descendants forever.'" Then David left, and Jonathan went back to the town.

reflection

1 Which of your friends will "come in even if the world goes out"?

2 With whom do you share a covenant friendship, and how has this person shown herself to be a godly friend?

3 How has Jesus proved to be your *best* friend?

RELATED READINGS

Ruth 1:3–17; Proverbs 17:17; 18:24; Ecclesiastes 4:9–10; John 3:27–30

"The impulse of love that leads us to the doorway of a friend is the voice of God within and we need not be afraid to follow it."

Agnes Sanford

351

day, the second day of the month, David's place was empty again. Then Saul said to his son Jonathan, "Why hasn't the son of Jesse come to the meal, either yesterday or today?"

28 Jonathan answered, "David earnestly asked me for permission to go to Bethlehem. 29 He said, 'Let me go, because our family is observing a sacrifice in the town and my brother has ordered me to be there. If I have found favor in your eyes, let me get away to see my brothers.' That is why he has not come to the king's table."

30 Saul's anger flared up at Jonathan and he said to him, "You son of a perverse and rebellious woman! Don't I know that you have sided with the son of Jesse to your own shame and to the shame of the mother who bore you? 31 As long as the son of Jesse lives on this earth, neither you nor your kingdom will be established. Now send and bring him to me, for he must die!"

32 "Why should he be put to death? What has he done?" Jonathan asked his father. 33 But Saul hurled his spear at him to kill him. Then Jonathan knew that his father intended to kill David.

34 Jonathan got up from the table in fierce anger; on that second day of the month he did not eat, because he was grieved at his father's shameful treatment of David.

35 In the morning Jonathan went out to the field for his meeting with David. He had a small boy with him, 36 and he said to the boy, "Run and find the arrows I shoot." As the boy ran, he shot an arrow beyond him. 37 When the boy came to the place where Jonathan's arrow had fallen, Jonathan called out after him, "Isn't the arrow beyond you?" 38 Then he shouted, "Hurry! Go quickly! Don't stop!" The boy picked up the arrow and returned to his master. 39 (The boy knew nothing of all this; only Jonathan and David knew.) 40 Then Jonathan gave his weapons to the boy and said, "Go, carry them back to town."

41 After the boy had gone, David got up from the south side of the stone and bowed down before Jonathan three times, with his face to the ground. Then they kissed each other and wept together—but David wept the most.

42 Jonathan said to David, "Go in peace, for we have sworn friendship with each other in the name of the LORD, saying, 'The LORD is witness between you and me, and between your descendants and my descendants forever.'" Then David left, and Jonathan went back to the town.

1 Samuel 20:42

God Cements Friendships

Jonathan said to David, "Go in peace, for we have sworn friendship with each other in the name of the LORD."

David at Nob

21 David went to Nob, to Ahimelech the priest. Ahimelech trembled when he met him, and asked, "Why are you alone? Why is no one with you?"

2 David answered Ahimelech the priest, "The king charged me with a certain matter and said to me, 'No one is to know anything about your mission and your instructions.' As for my men, I have told them to meet me at a certain place. 3 Now then, what do you have on hand? Give me five loaves of bread, or whatever you can find."

4 But the priest answered David, "I don't have any ordinary bread on hand; however, there is some consecrated bread here—provided the men have kept themselves from women."

5 David replied, "Indeed women have been kept from us, as usual whenever[a] I set out. The men's things[b] are holy even on missions that are not holy. How much more so today!" 6 So the priest gave him the consecrated bread, since there was no bread there except the bread of the Presence that had been removed from before the LORD and replaced by hot bread on the day it was taken away.

7 Now one of Saul's servants was there that day, detained before the LORD; he was Doeg the Edomite, Saul's head shepherd.

8 David asked Ahimelech, "Don't you have a spear or a sword here? I haven't brought my sword or any other weapon, because the king's business was urgent."

---

[a] 5 Or from us in the past few days since   [b] 5 Or bodies

9The priest replied, "The sword of Goliath the Philistine, whom you killed in the Valley of Elah, is here; it is wrapped in a cloth behind the ephod. If you want it, take it; there is no sword here but that one."

David said, "There is none like it; give it to me."

David at Gath

10That day David fled from Saul and went to Achish king of Gath. 11But the servants of Achish said to him, "Isn't this David, the king of the land? Isn't he the one they sing about in their dances:

> "'Saul has slain his thousands,
>   and David his tens of thousands'?"

12David took these words to heart and was very much afraid of Achish king of Gath. 13So he pretended to be insane in their presence; and while he was in their hands he acted like a madman, making marks on the doors of the gate and letting saliva run down his beard.

14Achish said to his servants, "Look at the man! He is insane! Why bring him to me? 15Am I so short of madmen that you have to bring this fellow here to carry on like this in front of me? Must this man come into my house?"

David at Adullam and Mizpah

22 David left Gath and escaped to the cave of Adullam. When his brothers and his father's household heard about it, they went down to him there. 2All those who were in distress or in debt or discontented gathered around him, and he became their leader. About four hundred men were with him.

3From there David went to Mizpah in Moab and said to the king of Moab, "Would you let my father and mother come and stay with you until I learn what God will do for me?" 4So he left them with the king of Moab, and they stayed with him as long as David was in the stronghold.

5But the prophet Gad said to David, "Do not stay in the stronghold. Go into the land of Judah." So David left and went to the forest of Hereth.

Saul Kills the Priests of Nob

6Now Saul heard that David and his men had been discovered. And Saul, spear in hand, was seated under the tamarisk tree on the hill at Gibeah, with all his officials standing around him. 7Saul said to them, "Listen, men of Benjamin! Will the son of Jesse give all of you fields and vineyards? Will he make all of you commanders of thousands and commanders of hundreds? 8Is that why you have all conspired against me? No one tells me when my son makes a covenant with the son of Jesse. None of you is concerned about me or tells me that my son has incited my servant to lie in wait for me, as he does today."

9But Doeg the Edomite, who was standing with Saul's officials, said, "I saw the son of Jesse come to Ahimelech son of Ahitub at Nob. 10Ahimelech inquired of the LORD for him; he also gave him provisions and the sword of Goliath the Philistine."

11Then the king sent for the priest Ahimelech son of Ahitub and his father's whole family, who were the priests at Nob, and they all came to the king. 12Saul said, "Listen now, son of Ahitub."

"Yes, my lord," he answered.

13Saul said to him, "Why have you conspired against me, you and the son of Jesse, giving him bread and a sword and inquiring of God for him, so that he has rebelled against me and lies in wait for me, as he does today?"

14Ahimelech answered the king, "Who of all your servants is as loyal as David, the king's son-in-law, captain of your bodyguard and highly respected in your household? 15Was that day the first time I inquired of God for him? Of course not! Let not the king accuse your servant or any of his father's family, for your servant knows nothing at all about this whole affair."

16But the king said, "You will surely die, Ahimelech, you and your father's whole family."

17Then the king ordered the guards at his side: "Turn and kill the priests of the LORD, because they too have sided with David. They knew he was fleeing, yet they did not tell me."

But the king's officials were not willing to raise a hand to strike the priests of the LORD.

18The king then ordered Doeg, "You turn and strike down the priests." So Doeg the Edomite turned and struck them down. That day he killed eighty-five men who wore the linen ephod. 19He also put to the sword Nob, the town of the priests, with its men and women, its children and infants, and its cattle, donkeys and sheep.

20But Abiathar, a son of Ahimelech son of Ahitub, escaped and fled to join David. 21He told David that Saul had killed the priests of the LORD. 22Then David said to Abiathar: "That day, when Doeg the Edomite was there, I knew he would be sure to tell Saul. I am responsible for the death of your father's whole family. 23Stay with me; don't be afraid; the man who is seeking your life is seeking mine also. You will be safe with me."

David Saves Keilah

23 When David was told, "Look, the Philistines are fighting against Keilah and are looting the threshing floors," 2he inquired of the LORD, saying, "Shall I go and attack these Philistines?"

The LORD answered him, "Go, attack the Philistines and save Keilah."

3But David's men said to him, "Here in Judah we are afraid. How much more, then, if we go to Keilah against the Philistine forces!"

4Once again David inquired of the LORD, and the LORD answered him, "Go down to Keilah, for I am going to give the Philistines into your hand." 5So David and his men went to Keilah, fought the Philistines and carried off their livestock. He inflicted heavy losses on the Philistines and saved the people of Keilah. 6(Now Abiathar son of Ahimelech had brought the ephod down with him when he fled to David at Keilah.)

Saul Pursues David

7Saul was told that David had gone to Keilah, and he said, "God has handed him over to me, for David has imprisoned himself by entering a town with gates and bars." 8And Saul called up all his forces for battle, to go down to Keilah to besiege David and his men.

9When David learned that Saul was plotting against him, he said to Abiathar the priest,

"Bring the ephod." 10David said, "O LORD, God of Israel, your servant has heard definitely that Saul plans to come to Keilah and destroy the town on account of me. 11Will the citizens of Keilah surrender me to him? Will Saul come down, as your servant has heard? O LORD, God of Israel, tell your servant."

And the LORD said, "He will."

12Again David asked, "Will the citizens of Keilah surrender me and my men to Saul?"

And the LORD said, "They will."

13So David and his men, about six hundred in number, left Keilah and kept moving from place to place. When Saul was told that David had escaped from Keilah, he did not go there.

14David stayed in the desert strongholds and in the hills of the Desert of Ziph. Day after day Saul searched for him, but God did not give David into his hands.

15While David was at Horesh in the Desert of Ziph, he learned that Saul had come out to take his life. 16And Saul's son Jonathan went to David at Horesh and helped him find strength in God. 17"Don't be afraid," he said. "My father Saul will not lay a hand on you. You will be king over Israel, and I will be second to you. Even my father Saul knows this." 18The two of them made a covenant before the LORD. Then Jonathan went home, but David remained at Horesh.

19The Ziphites went up to Saul at Gibeah and said, "Is not David hiding among us in the strongholds at Horesh, on the hill of Hakilah, south of Jeshimon? 20Now, O king, come down whenever it pleases you to do so, and we will be responsible for handing him over to the king."

21Saul replied, "The LORD bless you for your concern for me. 22Go and make further preparation. Find out where David usually goes and who has seen him there. They tell me he is very crafty. 23Find out about all the hiding places he uses and come back to me with definite information.a Then I will go with you; if he is in the area, I will track him down among all the clans of Judah."

---

1 Samuel 23:16

God Gives Strength

And Saul's son Jonathan went to David at Horesh and helped him find strength in God.

---

a23 Or me at Nacon

²⁴So they set out and went to Ziph ahead of Saul. Now David and his men were in the Desert of Maon, in the Arabah south of Jeshimon. ²⁵Saul and his men began the search, and when David was told about it, he went down to the rock and stayed in the Desert of Maon. When Saul heard this, he went into the Desert of Maon in pursuit of David.

²⁶Saul was going along one side of the mountain, and David and his men were on the other side, hurrying to get away from Saul. As Saul and his forces were closing in on David and his men to capture them, ²⁷a messenger came to Saul, saying, "Come quickly! The Philistines are raiding the land." ²⁸Then Saul broke off his pursuit of David and went to meet the Philistines. That is why they call this place Sela Hammahlekoth.ᵃ ²⁹And David went up from there and lived in the strongholds of En Gedi.

David Spares Saul's Life

24 After Saul returned from pursuing the Philistines, he was told, "David is in the Desert of En Gedi." ²So Saul took three thousand chosen men from all Israel and set out to look for David and his men near the Crags of the Wild Goats.

³He came to the sheep pens along the way; a cave was there, and Saul went in to relieve himself. David and his men were far back in the cave. ⁴The men said, "This is the day the LORD spoke of when he saidᵇ to you, 'I will give your enemy into your hands for you to deal with as you wish.'" Then David crept up unnoticed and cut off a corner of Saul's robe.

⁵Afterward, David was conscience-stricken for having cut off a corner of his robe. ⁶He said to his men, "The LORD forbid that I should do such a thing to my master, the LORD's anointed, or lift my hand against him; for he is the anointed of the LORD." ⁷With these words David rebuked his men and did not allow them to attack Saul. And Saul left the cave and went his way.

⁸Then David went out of the cave and called out to Saul, "My lord the king!" When Saul looked behind him, David bowed down and prostrated himself with his face to the ground. ⁹He said to Saul, "Why do you listen when men say, 'David is bent on harming you'? ¹⁰This day you have seen with your own eyes how the LORD delivered you into my hands in the cave. Some urged me to kill you, but I spared you; I said, 'I will not lift my hand against my master, because he is the LORD's anointed.' ¹¹See, my father, look at this piece of your robe in my hand! I cut off the corner of your robe but did not kill you. Now understand and recognize that I am not guilty of wrongdoing or rebellion. I have not wronged you, but you are hunting me down to take my life. ¹²May the LORD judge between you and me. And may the LORD avenge the wrongs you have done to me, but my hand will not touch you. ¹³As the old saying goes, 'From evildoers come evil deeds,' so my hand will not touch you.

¹⁴"Against whom has the king of Israel come out? Whom are you pursuing? A dead dog? A flea? ¹⁵May the LORD be our judge and decide between us. May he consider my cause and uphold it; may he vindicate me by delivering me from your hand."

¹⁶When David finished saying this, Saul asked, "Is that your voice, David my son?" And he wept aloud. ¹⁷"You are more righteous than I," he said. "You have treated me well, but I have treated you badly. ¹⁸You have just now told me of the good you did to me; the LORD delivered me into your hands, but you did not kill me. ¹⁹When a man finds his enemy, does he let him get away unharmed? May the LORD reward you well for the way you treated me today. ²⁰I know that you will surely be king and that the kingdom of Israel will be established in your hands. ²¹Now swear to me by the LORD that you will not cut off my descendants or wipe out my name from my father's family."

²²So David gave his oath to Saul. Then Saul returned home, but David and his men went up to the stronghold.

David, Nabal and Abigail

25 Now Samuel died, and all Israel assembled and mourned for him; and they buried him at his home in Ramah.

Then David moved down into the Desert of Maon.ᶜ ²A certain man in Maon, who had property there at Carmel, was very wealthy.

ᵃ28 Sela Hammahlekoth means *rock of parting.*   ᵇ4 Or *"Today the LORD is saying*   ᶜ1 Some Septuagint manuscripts; Hebrew *Paran*

1 Samuel 24:6

"The LORD forbid that I should do such a thing to my master, the LORD's anointed, or lift my hand against him; for he is the anointed of the LORD."

reflection

1 In what ways have you been mistreated or misunderstood for doing the right thing?

2 What opportunities have you had to retaliate? How can you respond with blessing instead?

3 Who are the people in your life that misunderstand or persecute you? Pray that you will learn to walk in the footsteps of David and Jesus, learning to forgive and bless others who hurt you.

RELATED READINGS

Proverbs 8:12–21;
Matthew 5:38–48;
Romans 12:17–21;
1 Timothy 2:1–8

" Snuggle in God's arms. When you are hurting, when you feel lonely, left out, let him cradle you, comfort you, reassure you of his all-sufficient power and love."

Kay Arthur

Being Misunderstood

Read: 1 Samuel 24:1–7

CLARA BARTON, dubbed "the angel of the battlefield," had a reputation for refusing to hold a grudge against anyone. As founder of the Red Cross, people labeled her leadership style as authoritarian and used Congress's charter as a lever against her to force her to resign from her own organization. Once, a friend tried to get her to recall a cruel thing that had happened to her years before, but Clara claimed to have forgotten the incident. "Don't you remember the wrong that was done you?" the friend hounded. Clara answered calmly, "No, I distinctly remember forgetting that."

We've all been misunderstood or mistreated. No matter how hard we work at doing things right, there may be someone who doesn't see things the way we do or like the way we do things. Maybe it's a husband, child, coworker, parent or friend. They may not hear what we're trying to tell them, see what we're trying to show them or appreciate the intentions behind our actions. The philosopher Goethe said, "So long as you live and work, you will be misunderstood." But Clara Barton's philosophy is helpful: Choose to forget the insults and wrongs.

David seemed to live by this philosophy too. He didn't deserve to be persecuted by King Saul. He had served the king well. Yet here we find the two men at odds in a desert oasis, meeting unexpectedly in the back of a cold, damp cave. With a single, well-placed thrust of his sword, David could have killed Saul. But he recognized that Saul was God's anointed, so David chose to forget Saul's wrongs and not lay a hand against him.

How do you respond when you've been misunderstood? Can you leave matters in God's hands and choose to forget? Or will you take a bit of vengeance here and a slice of repayment there? Can you be content to wait for God to set things right . . . on his timetable rather than yours?

The next time you feel misunderstood or mistreated, remember that you're following in some pretty big footsteps. King David was persecuted for doing God's bidding and did not retaliate when he was attacked. Jesus, the sinless God-man, was persecuted and died for our sins, yet he willingly forgave from the cross those who had tormented him. What will you do the next time you're wronged?

Thursday

Go to page 358 for your next devotional reading.

He had a thousand goats and three thousand sheep, which he was shearing in Carmel. ³His name was Nabal and his wife's name was Abigail. She was an intelligent and beautiful woman, but her husband, a Calebite, was surly and mean in his dealings.

⁴While David was in the desert, he heard that Nabal was shearing sheep. ⁵So he sent ten young men and said to them, "Go up to Nabal at Carmel and greet him in my name. ⁶Say to him: 'Long life to you! Good health to you and your household! And good health to all that is yours!

⁷"'Now I hear that it is sheep-shearing time. When your shepherds were with us, we did not mistreat them, and the whole time they were at Carmel nothing of theirs was missing. ⁸Ask your own servants and they will tell you. Therefore be favorable toward my young men, since we come at a festive time. Please give your servants and your son David whatever you can find for them.'"

⁹When David's men arrived, they gave Nabal this message in David's name. Then they waited.

¹⁰Nabal answered David's servants, "Who is this David? Who is this son of Jesse? Many servants are breaking away from their masters these days. ¹¹Why should I take my bread and water, and the meat I have slaughtered for my shearers, and give it to men coming from who knows where?"

¹²David's men turned around and went back. When they arrived, they reported every word. ¹³David said to his men, "Put on your swords!" So they put on their swords, and David put on his. About four hundred men went up with David, while two hundred stayed with the supplies.

¹⁴One of the servants told Nabal's wife Abigail: "David sent messengers from the desert to give our master his greetings, but he hurled insults at them. ¹⁵Yet these men were very good to us. They did not mistreat us, and the whole time we were out in the fields near them nothing was missing. ¹⁶Night and day they were a wall around us all the time we were herding our sheep near them. ¹⁷Now think it over and see what you can do, because disaster is hang-

ing over our master and his whole household. He is such a wicked man that no one can talk to him."

¹⁸Abigail lost no time. She took two hundred loaves of bread, two skins of wine, five dressed sheep, five seahs*a* of roasted grain, a hundred cakes of raisins and two hundred cakes of pressed figs, and loaded them on donkeys. ¹⁹Then she told her servants, "Go on ahead; I'll follow you." But she did not tell her husband Nabal.

²⁰As she came riding her donkey into a mountain ravine, there were David and his men descending toward her, and she met them. ²¹David had just said, "It's been useless—all my watching over this fellow's property in the desert so that nothing of his was missing. He has paid me back evil for good. ²²May God deal with David,*b* be it ever so severely, if by morning I leave alive one male of all who belong to him!"

²³When Abigail saw David, she quickly got off her donkey and bowed down before David with her face to the ground. ²⁴She fell at his feet and said: "My lord, let the blame be on me alone. Please let your servant speak to you; hear what your servant has to say. ²⁵May my lord pay no attention to that wicked man Nabal. He is just like his name—his name is Fool, and folly goes with him. But as for me, your servant, I did not see the men my master sent.

²⁶"Now since the LORD has kept you, my master, from bloodshed and from avenging yourself with your own hands, as surely as the LORD lives and as you live, may your enemies and all who intend to harm my master be like Nabal. ²⁷And let this gift, which your servant has brought to my master, be given to the men who follow you. ²⁸Please forgive your servant's offense, for the LORD will certainly make a lasting dynasty for my master, because he fights the LORD's battles. Let no wrongdoing be found in you as long as you live. ²⁹Even though someone is pursuing you to take your life, the life of my master will be bound securely in the bundle of the living by the LORD your God. But the lives of your enemies he will hurl away as from the pocket of a sling. ³⁰When the LORD has done for my master every good thing he promised

---

*a*18 That is, probably about a bushel (about 37 liters)   *b*22 Some Septuagint manuscripts; Hebrew *with David's enemies*

A Woman of Discernment

1 Samuel 25:32–33

David said to Abigail, "Praise be to the LORD, the God of Israel, who has sent you today to meet me. May you be blessed for your good judgment and for keeping me from bloodshed this day and from avenging myself with my own hands."

reflection

1 Whom did David credit with Abigail's actions?

2 How have you seen a "gentle answer [turn] away wrath" (Proverbs 15:1)?

3 Whom could use your peaceful intervention right now? What situation calls for you to pray, offer gentle words or even invite warring parties to share a meal?

RELATED READINGS

1 Chronicles 3:1;
Psalm 141:3–4;
Proverbs 15:1–4;
Philemon 1–25

"The purpose of all prayer is to find God's will and to make that will our prayer."

Catherine Marshall

Read: 1 Samuel 25:1–42

MANY ANCIENT SOCIETIES protected the guest-host relationship as a sacred covenant, with grave consequences should an individual choose to disregard it. The Greeks called this hospitality bond *xenia*, and fought one of the most famous wars of antiquity, the Trojan War, over a breech of *xenia*. Paris kidnapped King Menelaus' wife, Helen, while a guest in the king's household. He was transgressing the sacred obligations of the *xenos*, the guest-friend within their gates, and his entire nation would pay.

Failure to return hospitality carried serious implications in Biblical times. Foolish, alcohol-abusing Nabal had insulted David by refusing to offer him and his men the typical Eastern courtesy: a share in the bounty of his household at sheep-shearing time. In so doing, Nabal put his wife and entire household at risk of retaliation. When Abigail heard about the situation, she could have responded by criticizing her husband or cursing his stupidity. She did neither. Instead, Abigail carried courage in one hand and provisions in the other. She restored peace on behalf of her household. Her discernment and tact calmed David's anger and honored God.

Abigail offered hospitality in the face of hostility. David was grateful that her wise intervention stopped him from committing murder. Ultimately, Nabal died of "natural" causes, brought about when Abigail told him of the crisis that had been averted. His heart turned to stone—God dealt with this hard-hearted man in his own way.

Hannah Hurnard says an intercessor is "one who is in such vital contact with God and with his fellowmen that he is like a live wire closing the gap between the saving power of God and the sinful men who have been cut off from that power."

While your community may not punish rudeness or slander with actual warfare, you're probably very familiar with the damage that smoldering hostility or gossip can bring to a family, a workplace or a church. When you become aware of an escalating crisis, ask God to give you the discernment to think quickly and act decisively. Then intervene with kindness on your lips and grace in your heart. Be more concerned with what you *can* offer than with what you cannot. Like Abigail, use the resources that God has placed at your disposal to help find a peaceful solution to a possibly explosive situation.

Go to page 366 for your next devotional reading.

concerning him and has appointed him leader over Israel, [31]my master will not have on his conscience the staggering burden of needless bloodshed or of having avenged himself. And when the LORD has brought my master success, remember your servant."

[32]David said to Abigail, "Praise be to the LORD, the God of Israel, who has sent you today to meet me. [33]May you be blessed for your good judgment and for keeping me from bloodshed this day and from avenging myself with my own hands. [34]Otherwise, as surely as the LORD, the God of Israel, lives, who has kept me from harming you, if you had not come quickly to meet me, not one male belonging to Nabal would have been left alive by daybreak."

[35]Then David accepted from her hand what she had brought him and said, "Go home in peace. I have heard your words and granted your request."

[36]When Abigail went to Nabal, he was in the house holding a banquet like that of a king. He was in high spirits and very drunk. So she told him nothing until daybreak. [37]Then in the morning, when Nabal was sober, his wife told him all these things, and his heart failed him and he became like a stone. [38]About ten days later, the LORD struck Nabal and he died.

[39]When David heard that Nabal was dead, he said, "Praise be to the LORD, who has upheld my cause against Nabal for treating me with contempt. He has kept his servant from doing wrong and has brought Nabal's wrongdoing down on his own head."

Then David sent word to Abigail, asking her to become his wife. [40]His servants went to Carmel and said to Abigail, "David has sent us to you to take you to become his wife."

[41]She bowed down with her face to the ground and said, "Here is your maidservant, ready to serve you and wash the feet of my master's servants." [42]Abigail quickly got on a donkey and, attended by her five maids, went with David's messengers and became his wife. [43]David had also married Ahinoam of Jezreel, and they both were his wives. [44]But Saul had given his daughter Michal, David's wife, to Paltiel[a] son of Laish, who was from Gallim.

David Again Spares Saul's Life

26 The Ziphites went to Saul at Gibeah and said, "Is not David hiding on the hill of Hakilah, which faces Jeshimon?"

[2]So Saul went down to the Desert of Ziph, with his three thousand chosen men of Israel, to search there for David. [3]Saul made his camp beside the road on the hill of Hakilah facing Jeshimon, but David stayed in the desert. When he saw that Saul had followed him there, [4]he sent out scouts and learned that Saul had definitely arrived.[b]

[5]Then David set out and went to the place where Saul had camped. He saw where Saul and Abner son of Ner, the commander of the army, had lain down. Saul was lying inside the camp, with the army encamped around him.

[6]David then asked Ahimelech the Hittite and Abishai son of Zeruiah, Joab's brother, "Who will go down into the camp with me to Saul?"

"I'll go with you," said Abishai.

[7]So David and Abishai went to the army by night, and there was Saul, lying asleep inside the camp with his spear stuck in the ground near his head. Abner and the soldiers were lying around him.

[8]Abishai said to David, "Today God has delivered your enemy into your hands. Now let me pin him to the ground with one thrust of my spear; I won't strike him twice."

[9]But David said to Abishai, "Don't destroy him! Who can lay a hand on the LORD's anointed and be guiltless? [10]As surely as the LORD lives," he said, "the LORD himself will strike him; either his time will come and he will die, or he will go into battle and perish. [11]But the LORD forbid that I should lay a hand on the LORD's anointed. Now get the spear and water jug that are near his head, and let's go."

[12]So David took the spear and water jug near Saul's head, and they left. No one saw or knew about it, nor did anyone wake up. They were all sleeping, because the LORD had put them into a deep sleep.

[13]Then David crossed over to the other side and stood on top of the hill some distance away; there was a wide space between them. [14]He called out to the army and to Abner son of Ner, "Aren't you going to answer me, Abner?"

---

[a]44 Hebrew *Palti*, a variant of *Paltiel*   [b]4 Or *had come to Nacon*

Abner replied, "Who are you who calls to the king?"

15David said, "You're a man, aren't you? And who is like you in Israel? Why didn't you guard your lord the king? Someone came to destroy your lord the king. 16What you have done is not good. As surely as the LORD lives, you and your men deserve to die, because you did not guard your master, the LORD's anointed. Look around you. Where are the king's spear and water jug that were near his head?"

17Saul recognized David's voice and said, "Is that your voice, David my son?"

David replied, "Yes it is, my lord the king." 18And he added, "Why is my lord pursuing his servant? What have I done, and what wrong am I guilty of? 19Now let my lord the king listen to his servant's words. If the LORD has incited you against me, then may he accept an offering. If, however, men have done it, may they be cursed before the LORD! They have now driven me from my share in the LORD's inheritance and have said, 'Go, serve other gods.' 20Now do not let my blood fall to the ground far from the presence of the LORD. The king of Israel has come out to look for a flea—as one hunts a partridge in the mountains."

21Then Saul said, "I have sinned. Come back, David my son. Because you considered my life precious today, I will not try to harm you again. Surely I have acted like a fool and have erred greatly."

22"Here is the king's spear," David answered. "Let one of your young men come over and get it. 23The LORD rewards every man for his righteousness and faithfulness. The LORD delivered you into my hands today, but I would not lay a hand on the LORD's anointed. 24As surely as I valued your life today, so may the LORD value my life and deliver me from all trouble."

25Then Saul said to David, "May you be blessed, my son David; you will do great things and surely triumph."

So David went on his way, and Saul returned home.

1 Samuel 26:23

God Rewards Faithfulness

"The LORD rewards every man for his righteousness and faithfulness. The LORD delivered you into my hands today, but I would not lay a hand on the LORD's anointed."

David Among the Philistines

27 But David thought to himself, "One of these days I will be destroyed by the hand of Saul. The best thing I can do is to escape to the land of the Philistines. Then Saul will give up searching for me anywhere in Israel, and I will slip out of his hand."

2So David and the six hundred men with him left and went over to Achish son of Maoch king of Gath. 3David and his men settled in Gath with Achish. Each man had his family with him, and David had his two wives: Ahinoam of Jezreel and Abigail of Carmel, the widow of Nabal. 4When Saul was told that David had fled to Gath, he no longer searched for him.

5Then David said to Achish, "If I have found favor in your eyes, let a place be assigned to me in one of the country towns, that I may live there. Why should your servant live in the royal city with you?"

6So on that day Achish gave him Ziklag, and it has belonged to the kings of Judah ever since. 7David lived in Philistine territory a year and four months.

8Now David and his men went up and raided the Geshurites, the Girzites and the Amalekites. (From ancient times these peoples had lived in the land extending to Shur and Egypt.) 9Whenever David attacked an area, he did not leave a man or woman alive, but took sheep and cattle, donkeys and camels, and clothes. Then he returned to Achish.

10When Achish asked, "Where did you go raiding today?" David would say, "Against the Negev of Judah" or "Against the Negev of Jerahmeel" or "Against the Negev of the Kenites." 11He did not leave a man or woman alive to be brought to Gath, for he thought, "They might inform on us and say, 'This is what David did.'" And such was his practice as long as he lived in Philistine territory. 12Achish trusted David and said to himself, "He has become so odious to his people, the Israelites, that he will be my servant forever."

Saul and the Witch of Endor

28 In those days the Philistines gathered their forces to fight against Israel. Achish said to David, "You must understand that you and your men will accompany me in the army."

² David said, "Then you will see for yourself what your servant can do."

Achish replied, "Very well, I will make you my bodyguard for life."

³ Now Samuel was dead, and all Israel had mourned for him and buried him in his own town of Ramah. Saul had expelled the mediums and spiritists from the land.

⁴ The Philistines assembled and came and set up camp at Shunem, while Saul gathered all the Israelites and set up camp at Gilboa. ⁵ When Saul saw the Philistine army, he was afraid; terror filled his heart. ⁶ He inquired of the LORD, but the LORD did not answer him by dreams or Urim or prophets. ⁷ Saul then said to his attendants, "Find me a woman who is a medium, so I may go and inquire of her."

"There is one in Endor," they said.

⁸ So Saul disguised himself, putting on other clothes, and at night he and two men went to the woman. "Consult a spirit for me," he said, "and bring up for me the one I name."

⁹ But the woman said to him, "Surely you know what Saul has done. He has cut off the mediums and spiritists from the land. Why have you set a trap for my life to bring about my death?"

¹⁰ Saul swore to her by the LORD, "As surely as the LORD lives, you will not be punished for this."

¹¹ Then the woman asked, "Whom shall I bring up for you?"

"Bring up Samuel," he said.

¹² When the woman saw Samuel, she cried out at the top of her voice and said to Saul, "Why have you deceived me? You are Saul!"

¹³ The king said to her, "Don't be afraid. What do you see?"

The woman said, "I see a spirit*a* coming up out of the ground."

¹⁴ "What does he look like?" he asked.

"An old man wearing a robe is coming up," she said.

Then Saul knew it was Samuel, and he bowed down and prostrated himself with his face to the ground.

¹⁵ Samuel said to Saul, "Why have you disturbed me by bringing me up?"

"I am in great distress," Saul said. "The Philistines are fighting against me, and God has turned away from me. He no longer answers me, either by prophets or by dreams. So I have called on you to tell me what to do."

¹⁶ Samuel said, "Why do you consult me, now that the LORD has turned away from you and become your enemy? ¹⁷ The LORD has done what he predicted through me. The LORD has torn the kingdom out of your hands and given it to one of your neighbors—to David. ¹⁸ Because you did not obey the LORD or carry out his fierce wrath against the Amalekites, the LORD has done this to you today. ¹⁹ The LORD will hand over both Israel and you to the Philistines, and tomorrow you and your sons will be with me. The LORD will also hand over the army of Israel to the Philistines."

²⁰ Immediately Saul fell full length on the ground, filled with fear because of Samuel's words. His strength was gone, for he had eaten nothing all that day and night.

²¹ When the woman came to Saul and saw that he was greatly shaken, she said, "Look, your maidservant has obeyed you. I took my life in my hands and did what you told me to do. ²² Now please listen to your servant and let me give you some food so you may eat and have the strength to go on your way."

²³ He refused and said, "I will not eat."

But his men joined the woman in urging him, and he listened to them. He got up from the ground and sat on the couch.

²⁴ The woman had a fattened calf at the house, which she butchered at once. She took some flour, kneaded it and baked bread without yeast. ²⁵ Then she set it before Saul and his men, and they ate. That same night they got up and left.

Achish Sends David Back to Ziklag

29 The Philistines gathered all their forces at Aphek, and Israel camped by the spring in Jezreel. ² As the Philistine rulers marched with their units of hundreds and

---

*a*13 Or *see spirits*; or *see gods*

thousands, David and his men were marching at the rear with Achish. ³The commanders of the Philistines asked, "What about these Hebrews?"

Achish replied, "Is this not David, who was an officer of Saul king of Israel? He has already been with me for over a year, and from the day he left Saul until now, I have found no fault in him."

⁴But the Philistine commanders were angry with him and said, "Send the man back, that he may return to the place you assigned him. He must not go with us into battle, or he will turn against us during the fighting. How better could he regain his master's favor than by taking the heads of our own men? ⁵Isn't this the David they sang about in their dances:

"'Saul has slain his
thousands,
and David his tens of
thousands'?"

⁶So Achish called David and said to him, "As surely as the LORD lives, you have been reliable, and I would be pleased to have you serve with me in the army. From the day you came to me until now, I have found no fault in you, but the rulers don't approve of you. ⁷Turn back and go in peace; do nothing to displease the Philistine rulers."

⁸"But what have I done?" asked David. "What have you found against your servant from the day I came to you until now? Why can't I go and fight against the enemies of my lord the king?"

⁹Achish answered, "I know that you have been as pleasing in my eyes as an angel of God; nevertheless, the Philistine commanders have said, 'He must not go up with us into battle.' ¹⁰Now get up early, along with your master's servants who have come with you, and leave in the morning as soon as it is light."

¹¹So David and his men got up early in the morning to go back to the land of the Philistines, and the Philistines went up to Jezreel.

David Destroys the Amalekites

30 David and his men reached Ziklag on the third day. Now the Amalekites had raided the Negev and Ziklag. They had attacked Ziklag and burned it, ²and had taken captive the women and all who were in it, both young and old. They killed none of them, but carried them off as they went on their way.

³When David and his men came to Ziklag, they found it destroyed by fire and their wives and sons and daughters taken captive. ⁴So David and his men wept aloud until they had no strength left to weep. ⁵David's two wives had been captured—Ahinoam of Jezreel and Abigail, the widow of Nabal of Carmel. ⁶David was greatly distressed because the men were talking of stoning him; each one was bitter in spirit because of his sons and daughters. But David found strength in the LORD his God.

⁷Then David said to Abiathar the priest, the son of Ahimelech, "Bring me the ephod." Abiathar brought it to him, ⁸and David inquired of the LORD, "Shall I pursue this raiding party? Will I overtake them?"

"Pursue them," he answered. "You will certainly overtake them and succeed in the rescue."

⁹David and the six hundred men with him came to the Besor Ravine, where some stayed behind, ¹⁰for two hundred men were too exhausted to cross the ravine. But David and four hundred men continued the pursuit.

¹¹They found an Egyptian in a field and brought him to David. They gave him water to drink and food to eat— ¹²part of a cake of pressed figs and two cakes of raisins. He ate and was revived, for he had not eaten any food or drunk any water for three days and three nights.

¹³David asked him, "To whom do you belong, and where do you come from?"

He said, "I am an Egyptian, the slave of an Amalekite. My master abandoned me when I

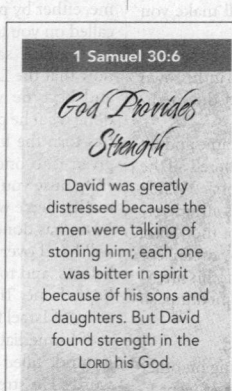

1 Samuel 30:6

God Provides Strength

David was greatly distressed because the men were talking of stoning him; each one was bitter in spirit because of his sons and daughters. But David found strength in the LORD his God.

became ill three days ago. ¹⁴We raided the Negev of the Kerethites and the territory belonging to Judah and the Negev of Caleb. And we burned Ziklag."

¹⁵David asked him, "Can you lead me down to this raiding party?"

He answered, "Swear to me before God that you will not kill me or hand me over to my master, and I will take you down to them."

¹⁶He led David down, and there they were, scattered over the countryside, eating, drinking and reveling because of the great amount of plunder they had taken from the land of the Philistines and from Judah. ¹⁷David fought them from dusk until the evening of the next day, and none of them got away, except four hundred young men who rode off on camels and fled. ¹⁸David recovered everything the Amalekites had taken, including his two wives. ¹⁹Nothing was missing: young or old, boy or girl, plunder or anything else they had taken. David brought everything back. ²⁰He took all the flocks and herds, and his men drove them ahead of the other livestock, saying, "This is David's plunder."

²¹Then David came to the two hundred men who had been too exhausted to follow him and who were left behind at the Besor Ravine. They came out to meet David and the people with him. As David and his men approached, he greeted them. ²²But all the evil men and troublemakers among David's followers said, "Because they did not go out with us, we will not share with them the plunder we recovered. However, each man may take his wife and children and go."

²³David replied, "No, my brothers, you must not do that with what the LORD has given us. He has protected us and handed over to us the forces that came against us. ²⁴Who will listen to what you say? The share of the man who stayed with the supplies is to be the same as that of him who went down to the battle. All will share alike." ²⁵David made this a statute and ordinance for Israel from that day to this.

²⁶When David arrived in Ziklag, he sent some of the plunder to the elders of Judah, who were his friends, saying, "Here is a present for you from the plunder of the LORD's enemies."

²⁷He sent it to those who were in Bethel, Ramoth Negev and Jattir; ²⁸to those in Aroer, Siphmoth, Eshtemoa ²⁹and Racal; to those in the towns of the Jerahmeelites and the Kenites; ³⁰to those in Hormah, Bor Ashan, Athach ³¹and Hebron; and to those in all the other places where David and his men had roamed.

Saul Takes His Life

31 Now the Philistines fought against Israel; the Israelites fled before them, and many fell slain on Mount Gilboa. ²The Philistines pressed hard after Saul and his sons, and they killed his sons Jonathan, Abinadab and Malki-Shua. ³The fighting grew fierce around Saul, and when the archers overtook him, they wounded him critically.

⁴Saul said to his armor-bearer, "Draw your sword and run me through, or these uncircumcised fellows will come and run me through and abuse me."

But his armor-bearer was terrified and would not do it; so Saul took his own sword and fell on it. ⁵When the armor-bearer saw that Saul was dead, he too fell on his sword and died with him. ⁶So Saul and his three sons and his armor-bearer and all his men died together that same day.

⁷When the Israelites along the valley and those across the Jordan saw that the Israelite army had fled and that Saul and his sons had died, they abandoned their towns and fled. And the Philistines came and occupied them.

⁸The next day, when the Philistines came to strip the dead, they found Saul and his three sons fallen on Mount Gilboa. ⁹They cut off his head and stripped off his armor, and they sent messengers throughout the land of the Philistines to proclaim the news in the temple of their idols and among their people. ¹⁰They put his armor in the temple of the Ashtoreths and fastened his body to the wall of Beth Shan.

¹¹When the people of Jabesh Gilead heard of what the Philistines had done to Saul, ¹²all their valiant men journeyed through the night to Beth Shan. They took down the bodies of Saul and his sons from the wall of Beth Shan and went to Jabesh, where they burned them. ¹³Then they took their bones and buried them under a tamarisk tree at Jabesh, and they fasted seven days.

Samuel

Author:
Unknown.

Audience:
The people of Israel.

Date:
Sometime after the division of Israel into the northern and southern kingdoms, around 930 B.C.

Setting:
Saul has proven to be a bad king. David is poised to begin his reign.

Verse to Remember:
And David knew that the LORD had established him as king over Israel and had exalted his kingdom for the sake of his people Israel. (5:12)

Nothing in the *life of King David* was boring. Giant killer, psalm writer, vagabond, king, adulterer, murderer, warrior . . . and founder of the dynasty that led to the greatest King of all. David's life had great highs and great lows. *But his love for God was deep* and sincere. He was open to God's redirection. He was humble and repentant before his own King. His worship was heartfelt and selfless. The story of David is the story of how God can work through someone who loves him.

Scripture presents an untouched portrait of its greatest human king. The picture comes complete with human failure. But *David relied upon God,* trusted God, loved God and submitted to God—and those attitudes deepened his relationship and friendship with his God.

David Hears of Saul's Death

1 After the death of Saul, David returned from defeating the Amalekites and stayed in Ziklag two days. **2**On the third day a man arrived from Saul's camp, with his clothes torn and with dust on his head. When he came to David, he fell to the ground to pay him honor.

3"Where have you come from?" David asked him.

He answered, "I have escaped from the Israelite camp."

4"What happened?" David asked. "Tell me."

He said, "The men fled from the battle. Many of them fell and died. And Saul and his son Jonathan are dead."

5Then David said to the young man who brought him the report, "How do you know that Saul and his son Jonathan are dead?"

6"I happened to be on Mount Gilboa," the young man said, "and there was Saul, leaning on his spear, with the chariots and riders almost upon him. **7**When he turned around and saw me, he called out to me, and I said, 'What can I do?'

⁸"He asked me, 'Who are you?'

"'An Amalekite,' I answered.

⁹"Then he said to me, 'Stand over me and kill me! I am in the throes of death, but I'm still alive.'

¹⁰"So I stood over him and killed him, because I knew that after he had fallen he could not survive. And I took the crown that was on his head and the band on his arm and have brought them here to my lord."

¹¹Then David and all the men with him took hold of their clothes and tore them. ¹²They mourned and wept and fasted till evening for Saul and his son Jonathan, and for the army of the Lord and the house of Israel, because they had fallen by the sword.

¹³David said to the young man who brought him the report, "Where are you from?"

"I am the son of an alien, an Amalekite," he answered.

¹⁴David asked him, "Why were you not afraid to lift your hand to destroy the Lord's anointed?"

¹⁵Then David called one of his men and said, "Go, strike him down!" So he struck him down, and he died. ¹⁶For David had said to him, "Your blood be on your own head. Your own mouth testified against you when you said, 'I killed the Lord's anointed.'"

David's Lament for Saul and Jonathan

¹⁷David took up this lament concerning Saul and his son Jonathan, ¹⁸and ordered that the men of Judah be taught this lament of the bow (it is written in the Book of Jashar):

¹⁹"Your glory, O Israel, lies slain on your
        heights.
    How the mighty have fallen!

²⁰"Tell it not in Gath,
        proclaim it not in the streets of
            Ashkelon,
    lest the daughters of the Philistines be
            glad,
        lest the daughters of the uncircumcised
            rejoice.

²¹"O mountains of Gilboa,
        may you have neither dew nor rain,

    nor fields that yield offerings of grain.
    For there the shield of the mighty was
            defiled,
        the shield of Saul—no longer rubbed
            with oil.

²²From the blood of the slain,
        from the flesh of the mighty,
    the bow of Jonathan did not turn back,
        the sword of Saul did not return
            unsatisfied.

²³"Saul and Jonathan—
        in life they were loved and gracious,
            and in death they were not parted.
    They were swifter than eagles,
        they were stronger than lions.

²⁴"O daughters of Israel,
        weep for Saul,
    who clothed you in scarlet and finery,
        who adorned your garments with
            ornaments of gold.

²⁵"How the mighty have fallen in battle!
        Jonathan lies slain on your heights.
²⁶I grieve for you, Jonathan my brother;
        you were very dear to me.
    Your love for me was wonderful,
        more wonderful than that of women.

²⁷"How the mighty have fallen!
        The weapons of war have perished!"

David Anointed King Over Judah

2 In the course of time, David inquired of the Lord. "Shall I go up to one of the towns of Judah?" he asked.

The Lord said, "Go up."

David asked, "Where shall I go?"

"To Hebron," the Lord answered.

²So David went up there with his two wives, Ahinoam of Jezreel and Abigail, the widow of Nabal of Carmel. ³David also took the men who were with him, each with his family, and they settled in Hebron and its towns. ⁴Then the men of Judah came to Hebron and there they anointed David king over the house of Judah.

When David was told that it was the men of Jabesh Gilead who had buried Saul, ⁵he sent messengers to the men of Jabesh Gilead to say to them, "The Lord bless you for showing this kindness to Saul your master by burying him. ⁶May the Lord now show you kindness and

A Thread of Faith

RAHAB

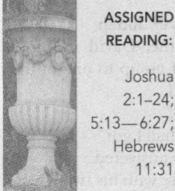

ASSIGNED READING:

Joshua
2:1–24;
5:13—6:27;
Hebrews
11:31

ALL HER HOPES AND DREAMS were fluttering in the wind outside her window. A tattered cord of scarlet material was all that separated certain death and the possibility of new life. Cart-bearing oxen lazily trudged through the city gate amid sounds of clattering wheels and lively street chatter. Sheepherders prodded their lumbering animals on their daily trip to market. Children played games directly underneath her window, barely noticing the scarlet cord now flapping against the city wall in a gentle wind.

Rahab's modest home was built into the city wall—prominently positioned, but vulnerable to the skillful soldiers she knew would soon advance on her city. Days earlier, when two enemy spies had made a pact with her to protect her home, she'd hung a scarlet cord outside her window as a sign, identifying her address to would-be attackers.

It was an unspoken symbol of agreement between three strangers. More than that, it was a powerful statement of faith—a testament of trust in a God she barely knew. A pagan by birth, Rahab had nothing more than a fledgling belief that the stories she'd heard about the miraculous power of the God of the Hebrews were true.

In the tension-filled days that followed, did she question herself? "Is your faith enough for you? Enough to stake everything on?" But she'd made up her mind. And hanging from her house was her testament to her resolution. She was making her stand, issuing her statement, identifying herself with a group of God-followers she'd never encountered and committing her life to a God she'd never seen.

And yet now, just days before the battle, the significance of the scarlet emblem went largely unnoticed by the men and women traveling the dusty streets of the walled city of Jericho. Her neighbors were unaware. However, Rahab knew that her decision had changed everything.

Time crept slowly by. She didn't know when the battle would occur. In the meantime, she anxiously checked and rechecked to be sure the cord was still there. The solitary strand reminded her in no uncertain terms that faith was now all she had. And that turned out to be all she needed.

—Prayer—
God, you are my powerful protector. Thank you for your care in my life.

Weekend

Go to page 371 for your next devotional reading.

faithfulness, and I too will show you the same favor because you have done this. ⁷Now then, be strong and brave, for Saul your master is dead, and the house of Judah has anointed me king over them."

War Between the Houses of David and Saul

⁸Meanwhile, Abner son of Ner, the commander of Saul's army, had taken Ish-Bosheth son of Saul and brought him over to Mahanaim. ⁹He made him king over Gilead, Ashuri[a] and Jezreel, and also over Ephraim, Benjamin and all Israel.

¹⁰Ish-Bosheth son of Saul was forty years old when he became king over Israel, and he reigned two years. The house of Judah, however, followed David. ¹¹The length of time David was king in Hebron over the house of Judah was seven years and six months.

¹²Abner son of Ner, together with the men of Ish-Bosheth son of Saul, left Mahanaim and went to Gibeon. ¹³Joab son of Zeruiah and David's men went out and met them at the pool of Gibeon. One group sat down on one side of the pool and one group on the other side.

¹⁴Then Abner said to Joab, "Let's have some of the young men get up and fight hand to hand in front of us."

"All right, let them do it," Joab said.

¹⁵So they stood up and were counted off—twelve men for Benjamin and Ish-Bosheth son of Saul, and twelve for David. ¹⁶Then each man grabbed his opponent by the head and thrust his dagger into his opponent's side, and they fell down together. So that place in Gibeon was called Helkath Hazzurim.[b]

¹⁷The battle that day was very fierce, and Abner and the men of Israel were defeated by David's men.

¹⁸The three sons of Zeruiah were there: Joab, Abishai and Asahel. Now Asahel was as fleet-footed as a wild gazelle. ¹⁹He chased Abner, turning neither to the right nor to the left as he pursued him. ²⁰Abner looked behind him and asked, "Is that you, Asahel?"

"It is," he answered.

²¹Then Abner said to him, "Turn aside to

the right or to the left; take on one of the young men and strip him of his weapons." But Asahel would not stop chasing him.

²²Again Abner warned Asahel, "Stop chasing me! Why should I strike you down? How could I look your brother Joab in the face?"

²³But Asahel refused to give up the pursuit; so Abner thrust the butt of his spear into Asahel's stomach, and the spear came out through his back. He fell there and died on the spot. And every man stopped when he came to the place where Asahel had fallen and died.

²⁴But Joab and Abishai pursued Abner, and as the sun was setting, they came to the hill of Ammah, near Giah on the way to the wasteland of Gibeon. ²⁵Then the men of Benjamin rallied behind Abner. They formed themselves into a group and took their stand on top of a hill.

²⁶Abner called out to Joab, "Must the sword devour forever? Don't you realize that this will end in bitterness? How long before you order your men to stop pursuing their brothers?"

²⁷Joab answered, "As surely as God lives, if you had not spoken, the men would have continued the pursuit of their brothers until morning.[c]

²⁸So Joab blew the trumpet, and all the men came to a halt; they no longer pursued Israel, nor did they fight anymore.

²⁹All that night Abner and his men marched through the Arabah. They crossed the Jordan, continued through the whole Bithron[d] and came to Mahanaim.

³⁰Then Joab returned from pursuing Abner and assembled all his men. Besides Asahel, nineteen of David's men were found missing. ³¹But David's men had killed three hundred and sixty Benjamites who were with Abner. ³²They took Asahel and buried him in his father's tomb at Bethlehem. Then Joab and his men marched all night and arrived at Hebron by daybreak.

3 The war between the house of Saul and the house of David lasted a long time. David grew stronger and stronger, while the house of Saul grew weaker and weaker.

²Sons were born to David in Hebron:

---

[a]9 Or Asher   [b]16 Helkath Hazzurim means field of daggers or field of hostilities.   [c]27 Or spoken this morning, the men would not have taken up the pursuit of their brothers; or spoken, the men would have given up the pursuit of their brothers by morning   [d]29 Or morning; or ravine; the meaning of the Hebrew for this word is uncertain.

His firstborn was Amnon the son of
Ahinoam of Jezreel;

³ his second, Kileab the son of Abigail
the widow of Nabal of Carmel;

the third, Absalom the son of Maacah
daughter of Talmai king of Geshur;

⁴ the fourth, Adonijah the son of Haggith;

the fifth, Shephatiah the son of Abital;

⁵ and the sixth, Ithream the son of David's wife Eglah.

These were born to David in Hebron.

Abner Goes Over to David

⁶ During the war between the house of
Saul and the house of David, Abner had been
strengthening his own position in the house of
Saul. ⁷ Now Saul had had a concubine named
Rizpah daughter of Aiah. And Ish-Bosheth
said to Abner, "Why did you sleep with my father's concubine?"

⁸ Abner was very angry because of what Ish-Bosheth said and he answered, "Am I a dog's
head—on Judah's side? This very day I am
loyal to the house of your father Saul and to his
family and friends. I haven't handed you over
to David. Yet now you accuse me of an offense
involving this woman! ⁹ May God deal with
Abner, be it ever so severely, if I do not do for
David what the LORD promised him on oath
¹⁰ and transfer the kingdom from the house of
Saul and establish David's throne over Israel
and Judah from Dan to Beersheba." ¹¹ Ish-Bosheth did not dare to say another word to Abner, because he was afraid of him.

¹² Then Abner sent messengers on his behalf
to say to David, "Whose land is it? Make an
agreement with me, and I will help you bring
all Israel over to you."

¹³ "Good," said David. "I will make an agreement with you. But I demand one thing of you:
Do not come into my presence unless you bring
Michal daughter of Saul when you come to see
me." ¹⁴ Then David sent messengers to Ish-Bosheth son of Saul, demanding, "Give me my
wife Michal, whom I betrothed to myself for
the price of a hundred Philistine foreskins."

¹⁵ So Ish-Bosheth gave orders and had her
taken away from her husband Paltiel son of Laish. ¹⁶ Her husband, however, went with her,
weeping behind her all the way to Bahurim.

Then Abner said to him, "Go back home!" So
he went back.

¹⁷ Abner conferred with the elders of Israel
and said, "For some time you have wanted to
make David your king. ¹⁸ Now do it! For the
LORD promised David, 'By my servant David
I will rescue my people Israel from the hand
of the Philistines and from the hand of all
their enemies.'"

¹⁹ Abner also spoke to the Benjamites in
person. Then he went to Hebron to tell David
everything that Israel and the whole house of
Benjamin wanted to do. ²⁰ When Abner, who
had twenty men with him, came to David at
Hebron, David prepared a feast for him and his
men. ²¹ Then Abner said to David, "Let me go
at once and assemble all Israel for my lord the
king, so that they may make a compact with
you, and that you may rule over all that your
heart desires." So David sent Abner away, and
he went in peace.

Joab Murders Abner

²² Just then David's men and Joab returned
from a raid and brought with them a great deal
of plunder. But Abner was no longer with David in Hebron, because David had sent him
away, and he had gone in peace. ²³ When Joab
and all the soldiers with him arrived, he was
told that Abner son of Ner had come to the
king and that the king had sent him away and
that he had gone in peace.

²⁴ So Joab went to the king and said, "What
have you done? Look, Abner came to you. Why
did you let him go? Now he is gone! ²⁵ You
know Abner son of Ner; he came to deceive
you and observe your movements and find out
everything you are doing."

²⁶ Joab then left David and sent messengers
after Abner, and they brought him back from
the well of Sirah. But David did not know it.
²⁷ Now when Abner returned to Hebron, Joab
took him aside into the gateway, as though to
speak with him privately. And there, to avenge
the blood of his brother Asahel, Joab stabbed
him in the stomach, and he died.

²⁸ Later, when David heard about this, he
said, "I and my kingdom are forever innocent
before the LORD concerning the blood of Abner son of Ner. ²⁹ May his blood fall upon the
head of Joab and upon all his father's house!

May Joab's house never be without someone who has a running sore or leprosy[a] or who leans on a crutch or who falls by the sword or who lacks food."

³⁰(Joab and his brother Abishai murdered Abner because he had killed their brother Asahel in the battle at Gibeon.)

³¹Then David said to Joab and all the people with him, "Tear your clothes and put on sackcloth and walk in mourning in front of Abner." King David himself walked behind the bier. ³²They buried Abner in Hebron, and the king wept aloud at Abner's tomb. All the people wept also.

³³The king sang this lament for Abner:

"Should Abner have died as the lawless die?

³⁴   Your hands were not bound,
        your feet were not fettered.
    You fell as one falls before wicked men."

And all the people wept over him again.

³⁵Then they all came and urged David to eat something while it was still day; but David took an oath, saying, "May God deal with me, be it ever so severely, if I taste bread or anything else before the sun sets!"

³⁶All the people took note and were pleased; indeed, everything the king did pleased them. ³⁷So on that day all the people and all Israel knew that the king had no part in the murder of Abner son of Ner.

³⁸Then the king said to his men, "Do you not realize that a prince and a great man has fallen in Israel this day? ³⁹And today, though I am the anointed king, I am weak, and these sons of Zeruiah are too strong for me. May the LORD repay the evildoer according to his evil deeds!"

Ish-Bosheth Murdered

4 When Ish-Bosheth son of Saul heard that Abner had died in Hebron, he lost courage, and all Israel became alarmed. ²Now Saul's son had two men who were leaders of raiding bands. One was named Baanah and the other Recab; they were sons of Rimmon the Beerothite from the tribe of Benjamin—Beeroth is considered part of Benjamin, ³because the people

of Beeroth fled to Gittaim and have lived there as aliens to this day.

⁴(Jonathan son of Saul had a son who was lame in both feet. He was five years old when the news about Saul and Jonathan came from Jezreel. His nurse picked him up and fled, but as she hurried to leave, he fell and became crippled. His name was Mephibosheth.)

⁵Now Recab and Baanah, the sons of Rimmon the Beerothite, set out for the house of Ish-Bosheth, and they arrived there in the heat of the day while he was taking his noonday rest. ⁶They went into the inner part of the house as if to get some wheat, and they stabbed him in the stomach. Then Recab and his brother Baanah slipped away.

⁷They had gone into the house while he was lying on the bed in his bedroom. After they stabbed and killed him, they cut off his head. Taking it with them, they traveled all night by way of the Arabah. ⁸They brought the head of Ish-Bosheth to David at Hebron and said to the king, "Here is the head of Ish-Bosheth son of Saul, your enemy, who tried to take your life. This day the LORD has avenged my lord the king against Saul and his offspring."

⁹David answered Recab and his brother Baanah, the sons of Rimmon the Beerothite, "As surely as the LORD lives, who has delivered me out of all trouble, ¹⁰when a man told me, 'Saul is dead,' and thought he was bringing good news, I seized him and put him to death in Ziklag. That was the reward I gave him for his news! ¹¹How much more—when wicked men have killed an innocent man in his own house and on his own bed—should I not now demand his blood from your hand and rid the earth of you!"

¹²So David gave an order to his men, and they cut off their hands and feet and hung the bodies by the pool in Hebron. But they took the head of Ish-Bosheth and buried it in Abner's tomb at Hebron.

David Becomes King Over Israel

5 All the tribes of Israel came to David at Hebron and said, "We are your own flesh and blood. ²In the past, while Saul was king over us, you were the one who led Israel on their

---

[a]29 The Hebrew word was used for various diseases affecting the skin—not necessarily leprosy.

military campaigns. And the LORD said to you, 'You will shepherd my people Israel, and you will become their ruler.'"

³When all the elders of Israel had come to King David at Hebron, the king made a compact with them at Hebron before the LORD, and they anointed David king over Israel.

⁴David was thirty years old when he became king, and he reigned forty years. ⁵In Hebron he reigned over Judah seven years and six months, and in Jerusalem he reigned over all Israel and Judah thirty-three years.

David Conquers Jerusalem

⁶The king and his men marched to Jerusalem to attack the Jebusites, who lived there. The Jebusites said to David, "You will not get in here; even the blind and the lame can ward you off." They thought, "David cannot get in here." ⁷Nevertheless, David captured the fortress of Zion, the City of David.

⁸On that day, David said, "Anyone who conquers the Jebusites will have to use the water shaft*ᵃ* to reach those 'lame and blind' who are David's enemies.*ᵇ*" That is why they say, "The 'blind and lame' will not enter the palace."

⁹David then took up residence in the fortress and called it the City of David. He built up the area around it, from the supporting terraces*ᶜ* inward. ¹⁰And he became more and more powerful, because the LORD God Almighty was with him.

¹¹Now Hiram king of Tyre sent messengers to David, along with cedar logs and carpenters and stonemasons, and they built a palace for David. ¹²And David knew that the LORD had established him as king over Israel and had exalted his kingdom for the sake of his people Israel.

¹³After he left Hebron, David took more concubines and wives in Jerusalem, and more sons and daughters were born to him. ¹⁴These are the names of the children born to him there: Shammua, Shobab, Nathan, Solomon, ¹⁵Ibhar, Elishua, Nepheg, Japhia, ¹⁶Elishama, Eliada and Eliphelet.

David Defeats the Philistines

¹⁷When the Philistines heard that David had been anointed king over Israel, they went up in full force to search for him, but David heard about it and went down to the stronghold. ¹⁸Now the Philistines had come and spread out in the Valley of Rephaim; ¹⁹so David inquired of the LORD, "Shall I go and attack the Philistines? Will you hand them over to me?"

The LORD answered him, "Go, for I will surely hand the Philistines over to you."

²⁰So David went to Baal Perazim, and there he defeated them. He said, "As waters break out, the LORD has broken out against my enemies before me." So that place was called Baal Perazim.*ᵈ* ²¹The Philistines abandoned their idols there, and David and his men carried them off.

²²Once more the Philistines came up and spread out in the Valley of Rephaim; ²³so David inquired of the LORD, and he answered, "Do not go straight up, but circle around behind them and attack them in front of the balsam trees. ²⁴As soon as you hear the sound of marching in the tops of the balsam trees, move quickly, because that will mean the LORD has gone out in front of you to strike the Philistine army." ²⁵So David did as the LORD commanded him, and he struck down the Philistines all the way from Gibeon*ᵉ* to Gezer.

The Ark Brought to Jerusalem

6 David again brought together out of Israel chosen men, thirty thousand in all. ²He and all his men set out from Baalah of Judah*ᶠ* to bring up from there the ark of God, which is called by the Name,*ᵍ* the name of the LORD Almighty, who is enthroned between the cherubim that are on the ark. ³They set the ark of God on a new cart and brought it from the house of Abinadab, which was on the hill.

2 Samuel 5:12

God Is in Control

And David knew that the LORD had established him as king over Israel and had exalted his kingdom for the sake of his people Israel.

ᵃ8 Or use scaling hooks ᵇ8 Or are hated by David ᶜ9 Or the Millo ᵈ20 Baal Perazim means the lord who breaks out. ᵉ25 Septuagint (see also 1 Chron. 14:16); Hebrew Geba ᶠ2 That is, Kiriath Jearim; Hebrew Baale Judah, a variant of Baalah of Judah ᵍ2 Hebrew; Septuagint and Vulgate do not have the Name.

Celebrate!

Read: 2 Samuel 6:1–23

IMAGINE THE QUEEN OF ENGLAND or the first lady of the United States leaping and dancing in her underclothes, shaking tambourines through the streets of London or Washington, crying, "Celebrate God!" Soon drums and cymbals join the merriment. Shocked bystanders raise their eyebrows; tongues wag and flashbulbs pop at such undignified decorum. The tabloids have a heyday.

Such would have been the scene if we today would have seen King David bringing the ark of the covenant back to Jerusalem. We might have been shocked that David and other dignitaries came into the city leaping, shouting and dancing through the streets. We read that at least one person was more than shocked; she was angry. Michal, David's wife, "despised him in her heart." David, however, didn't care what others thought, even if the disapproval came from one of his wives, Saul's daughter. He told her, "I will celebrate before the LORD. I will become even more undignified than this" (2 Samuel 6:21–22).

David rejoiced because the ark of the covenant, Israel's most sacred object of worship, had been reclaimed from the Philistines. David had every reason to dance for joy: The ark was back in Jerusalem, ready to regain its proper place in the Most Holy Place. David's exuberance spilled over in uninhibited public praise.

We all celebrate births and birthdays, weddings and anniversaries, graduations, promotions, holidays and winning seasons. But do we ever, like King David, celebrate God's blessings without concern for what others may think? Do we rejoice over the beauty of his creation or give him unrestrained praise for his loving-kindness and faithfulness?

We don't have to shake tambourines to exhibit hearts of worship. Our rejoicing may be outwardly exuberant or quietly subdued. Our praise may be either public or private. But when our hearts are filled with gratitude, outward expressions of praise will naturally overflow.

As women of God, we have every reason to dance with joy that the Lord is among us. If we choose to raise our hands or bend our knees in true worship, it's not undignified; it's a genuine expression of praise. Let's celebrate God by caring more about what God thinks than about what others think.

Go to page 375 for your next devotional reading.

2 Samuel 6:14–15

David . . . danced before the LORD with all his might, while he and the entire house of Israel brought up the ark of the LORD with shouts and the sound of trumpets.

reflection

1 How does your personality affect the way you praise God?

2 How do you react to others' behavior during worship? Have you ever pursed your lips or raised your eyebrows when someone was overly exuberant? Based on the Related Readings, what do you think is a good balance in worship?

3 What are some recent blessings that God has given you? Make a list of those blessings and sing a song of praise to God . . . and dance if you feel like it!

RELATED READINGS

Psalms 68:3–4; 150:1–6;
1 Corinthians 14:39–40;
James 5:13

Monday

Uzzah and Ahio, sons of Abinadab, were guiding the new cart [4]with the ark of God on it,[a] and Ahio was walking in front of it. [5]David and the whole house of Israel were celebrating with all their might before the LORD, with songs[b] and with harps, lyres, tambourines, sistrums and cymbals.

[6]When they came to the threshing floor of Nacon, Uzzah reached out and took hold of the ark of God, because the oxen stumbled. [7]The LORD's anger burned against Uzzah because of his irreverent act; therefore God struck him down and he died there beside the ark of God.

[8]Then David was angry because the LORD's wrath had broken out against Uzzah, and to this day that place is called Perez Uzzah.[c]

[9]David was afraid of the LORD that day and said, "How can the ark of the LORD ever come to me?" [10]He was not willing to take the ark of the LORD to be with him in the City of David. Instead, he took it aside to the house of Obed-Edom the Gittite. [11]The ark of the LORD remained in the house of Obed-Edom the Gittite for three months, and the LORD blessed him and his entire household.

[12]Now King David was told, "The LORD has blessed the household of Obed-Edom and everything he has, because of the ark of God." So David went down and brought up the ark of God from the house of Obed-Edom to the City of David with rejoicing. [13]When those who were carrying the ark of the LORD had taken six steps, he sacrificed a bull and a fattened calf. [14]David, wearing a linen ephod, danced before the LORD with all his might, [15]while he and the entire house of Israel brought up the ark of the LORD with shouts and the sound of trumpets.

[16]As the ark of the LORD was entering the City of David, Michal daughter of Saul watched from a window. And when she saw King David leaping and dancing before the LORD, she despised him in her heart.

[17]They brought the ark of the LORD and set it in its place inside the tent that David had pitched for it, and David sacrificed burnt offerings and fellowship offerings[d] before the LORD. [18]After he had finished sacrificing the burnt offerings and fellowship offerings, he blessed the people in the name of the LORD Almighty. [19]Then he gave a loaf of bread, a cake of dates and a cake of raisins to each person in the whole crowd of Israelites, both men and women. And all the people went to their homes.

[20]When David returned home to bless his household, Michal daughter of Saul came out to meet him and said, "How the king of Israel has distinguished himself today, disrobing in the sight of the slave girls of his servants as any vulgar fellow would!"

[21]David said to Michal, "It was before the LORD, who chose me rather than your father or anyone from his house when he appointed me ruler over the LORD's people Israel—I will celebrate before the LORD. [22]I will become even more undignified than this, and I will be humiliated in my own eyes. But by these slave girls you spoke of, I will be held in honor."

[23]And Michal daughter of Saul had no children to the day of her death.

God's Promise to David

7 After the king was settled in his palace and the LORD had given him rest from all his enemies around him, [2]he said to Nathan the prophet, "Here I am, living in a palace of cedar, while the ark of God remains in a tent."

[3]Nathan replied to the king, "Whatever you have in mind, go ahead and do it, for the LORD is with you."

[4]That night the word of the LORD came to Nathan, saying:

[5]"Go and tell my servant David, 'This is what the LORD says: Are you the one to build me a house to dwell in? [6]I have not dwelt in a house from the day I brought the Israelites up out of Egypt to this day. I have been moving from place to place with a tent as my dwelling. [7]Wherever I have moved with all the Israelites, did I ever say to any of their rulers whom I commanded to shepherd my people Israel, "Why have you not built me a house of cedar?"'

[8]"Now then, tell my servant David, 'This is what the LORD Almighty says: I

---

[a] 3,4 Dead Sea Scrolls and some Septuagint manuscripts; Masoretic Text *cart* [4] *and they brought it with the ark of God from the house of Abinadab, which was on the hill* [b] 5 See Dead Sea Scrolls, Septuagint and 1 Chronicles 13:8; Masoretic Text *celebrating before the LORD with all kinds of instruments made of pine.* [c] 8 *Perez Uzzah* means *outbreak against Uzzah.* [d] 17 Traditionally *peace offerings*; also in verse 18

took you from the pasture and from following the flock to be ruler over my people Israel. ⁹I have been with you wherever you have gone, and I have cut off all your enemies from before you. Now I will make your name great, like the names of the greatest men of the earth. ¹⁰And I will provide a place for my people Israel and will plant them so that they can have a home of their own and no longer be disturbed. Wicked people will not oppress them anymore, as they did at the beginning ¹¹and have done ever since the time I appointed leaders*ᵃ* over my people Israel. I will also give you rest from all your enemies.

"'The LORD declares to you that the LORD himself will establish a house for you: ¹²When your days are over and you rest with your fathers, I will raise up your offspring to succeed you, who will come from your own body, and I will establish his kingdom. ¹³He is the one who will build a house for my Name, and I will establish the throne of his kingdom forever. ¹⁴I will be his father, and he will be my son. When he does wrong, I will punish him with the rod of men, with floggings inflicted by men. ¹⁵But my love will never be taken away from him, as I took it away from Saul, whom I removed from before you. ¹⁶Your house and your kingdom will endure forever before me*ᵇ*; your throne will be established forever.'"

¹⁷Nathan reported to David all the words of this entire revelation.

David's Prayer

¹⁸Then King David went in and sat before the LORD, and he said:

"Who am I, O Sovereign LORD, and what is my family, that you have brought me this far? ¹⁹And as if this were not enough in your sight, O Sovereign LORD, you have also spoken about the future of the house of your servant. Is this your usual way of dealing with man, O Sovereign LORD?

²⁰"What more can David say to you? For you know your servant, O Sovereign LORD. ²¹For the sake of your word and according to your will, you have done this great thing and made it known to your servant.

²²"How great you are, O Sovereign LORD! There is no one like you, and there is no God but you, as we have heard with our own ears. ²³And who is like your people Israel—the one nation on earth that God went out to redeem as a people for himself, and to make a name for himself, and to perform great and awesome wonders by driving out nations and their gods from before your people, whom you redeemed from Egypt?*ᶜ* ²⁴You have established your people Israel as your very own forever, and you, O LORD, have become their God.

²⁵"And now, LORD God, keep forever the promise you have made concerning your servant and his house. Do as you promised, ²⁶so that your name will be great forever. Then men will say, 'The LORD Almighty is God over Israel!' And the house of your servant David will be established before you.

²⁷"O LORD Almighty, God of Israel, you have revealed this to your servant, saying, 'I will build a house for you.' So your servant has found courage to offer you this prayer. ²⁸O Sovereign LORD, you are God! Your words are trustworthy, and you have promised these good things to your servant. ²⁹Now be pleased to bless the house of your servant, that it may continue forever in your sight; for you,

2 Samuel 7:28

God Is Dependable

"O Sovereign LORD, you are God! Your words are trustworthy, and you have promised these good things to your servant."

---

*ᵃ*11 Traditionally *judges*   *ᵇ*16 Some Hebrew manuscripts and Septuagint; most Hebrew manuscripts *you*   *ᶜ*23 See Septuagint and 1 Chron. 17:21; Hebrew *wonders for your land and before your people, whom you redeemed from Egypt, from the nations and their gods.*

O Sovereign LORD, have spoken, and with your blessing the house of your servant will be blessed forever."

David's Victories

8 In the course of time, David defeated the Philistines and subdued them, and he took Metheg Ammah from the control of the Philistines.

²David also defeated the Moabites. He made them lie down on the ground and measured them off with a length of cord. Every two lengths of them were put to death, and the third length was allowed to live. So the Moabites became subject to David and brought tribute.

³Moreover, David fought Hadadezer son of Rehob, king of Zobah, when he went to restore his control along the Euphrates River. ⁴David captured a thousand of his chariots, seven thousand charioteers[a] and twenty thousand foot soldiers. He hamstrung all but a hundred of the chariot horses.

⁵When the Arameans of Damascus came to help Hadadezer king of Zobah, David struck down twenty-two thousand of them. ⁶He put garrisons in the Aramean kingdom of Damascus, and the Arameans became subject to him and brought tribute. The LORD gave David victory wherever he went.

⁷David took the gold shields that belonged to the officers of Hadadezer and brought them to Jerusalem. ⁸From Tebah[b] and Berothai, towns that belonged to Hadadezer, King David took a great quantity of bronze.

⁹When Tou[c] king of Hamath heard that David had defeated the entire army of Hadadezer, ¹⁰he sent his son Joram[d] to King David to greet him and congratulate him on his victory in battle over Hadadezer, who had been at war with Tou. Joram brought with him articles of silver and gold and bronze.

¹¹King David dedicated these articles to the LORD, as he had done with the silver and gold from all the nations he had subdued: ¹²Edom[e] and Moab, the Ammonites and the Philistines, and Amalek. He also dedicated the plunder taken from Hadadezer son of Rehob, king of Zobah.

¹³And David became famous after he returned from striking down eighteen thousand Edomites[f] in the Valley of Salt.

¹⁴He put garrisons throughout Edom, and all the Edomites became subject to David. The LORD gave David victory wherever he went.

---

2 Samuel 8:14

God Gives Victories

He put garrisons throughout Edom, and all the Edomites became subject to David. The LORD gave David victory wherever he went.

David's Officials

¹⁵David reigned over all Israel, doing what was just and right for all his people. ¹⁶Joab son of Zeruiah was over the army; Jehoshaphat son of Ahilud was recorder; ¹⁷Zadok son of Ahitub and Ahimelech son of Abiathar were priests; Seraiah was secretary; ¹⁸Benaiah son of Jehoiada was over the Kerethites and Pelethites; and David's sons were royal advisers.[g]

David and Mephibosheth

9 David asked, "Is there anyone still left of the house of Saul to whom I can show kindness for Jonathan's sake?"

²Now there was a servant of Saul's household named Ziba. They called him to appear before David, and the king said to him, "Are you Ziba?"

"Your servant," he replied.

³The king asked, "Is there no one still left of the house of Saul to whom I can show God's kindness?"

Ziba answered the king, "There is still a son of Jonathan; he is crippled in both feet."

⁴"Where is he?" the king asked.

Ziba answered, "He is at the house of Makir son of Ammiel in Lo Debar."

---

a 4 Septuagint (see also Dead Sea Scrolls and 1 Chron. 18:4); Masoretic Text captured seventeen hundred of his charioteers   b 8 See some Septuagint manuscripts (see also 1 Chron. 18:8); Hebrew Betah.   c 9 Hebrew Toi, a variant of Tou; also in verse 10   d 10 A variant of Hadoram   e 12 Some Hebrew manuscripts, Septuagint and Syriac (see also 1 Chron. 18:11); most Hebrew manuscripts Aram   f 13 A few Hebrew manuscripts, Septuagint and Syriac (see also 1 Chron. 18:12); most Hebrew manuscripts Aram (that is, Arameans)   g 18 Or were priests

Finding Sanctuary

Read: 2 Samuel 9:1–13

CLAIMING SANCTUARY IN A CHURCH dates to Britain in A.D. 600. Though the practice was formally abandoned in the seventeenth century, people seeking asylum still flee to churches today, clinging to the idea that into God's house no violence may enter. Do you long for a place of sanctuary when you sense imminent judgment? Maybe you've told a lie and stand before the wronged party. Perhaps you're innocent, but face a relative's creditors. We can all relate to the desire to crawl underground and disappear. Prince Mephibosheth certainly trembled at what King David would do to him.

After all, Mephibosheth was the last survivor in the line of his grandfather King Saul. In ancient Eastern culture, that position usually meant death, especially because Saul had repeatedly attempted to murder David. But David had no intention of handing down a death sentence. Instead he offered Mephibosheth sanctuary in his own palace. Because of Mephibosheth's relationship to David's dear friend Jonathan, the king welcomed him as an honored guest at his own table.

We all long for sanctuary. Crippled by sin, we enter God's presence with death hanging over our heads. But when we accept Jesus Christ's offer of eternal friendship, we receive eternal sanctuary at the King's table. At this feast, we will be given white robes to wear, and we will bow down in praise and adoration before the Prince of Peace.

Does an invitation to the King's palace fill you with fear or excitement? You may think that everything about you—your background, your body's condition, your emotional state, your past sins—should keep you away from the King's table. But none of that matters to God. Regardless of how unworthy you feel, you can know that you have been made worthy because you are a child of God.

Today, as you ponder the surprise of finding sanctuary instead of judgment, consider how you will live like a guest who carries an invitation to the King's table. Awake each day in anticipation of Christ's royal summons and walk tall, nurturing a longing for the day when you will sit before the King at the wedding supper of the Lamb.

2 Samuel 9:7–8

"Don't be afraid," David said to him, "for I will surely show you kindness for the sake of your father Jonathan. I will restore to you all the land that belonged to your grandfather Saul, and you will always eat at my table." Mephibosheth bowed down and said, "What is your servant, that you should notice a dead dog like me?"

reflection

1 Think about sitting at the King's table. What does this mean to you?

2 Read Matthew 22:1–14. What is the invitation? Is there anything that keeps you from fully accepting God's gift of grace? If so, what is it?

3 Read Revelation 7:9–17. What is your reaction to this passage?

RELATED READINGS

1 Samuel 20:12–17;
2 Samuel 4:4–6

Tuesday

Go to page 379 for your next devotional reading.

⁵So King David had him brought from Lo Debar, from the house of Makir son of Ammiel.

⁶When Mephibosheth son of Jonathan, the son of Saul, came to David, he bowed down to pay him honor.

David said, "Mephibosheth!"

"Your servant," he replied.

⁷"Don't be afraid," David said to him, "for I will surely show you kindness for the sake of your father Jonathan. I will restore to you all the land that belonged to your grandfather Saul, and you will always eat at my table."

⁸Mephibosheth bowed down and said, "What is your servant, that you should notice a dead dog like me?"

⁹Then the king summoned Ziba, Saul's servant, and said to him, "I have given your master's grandson everything that belonged to Saul and his family. ¹⁰You and your sons and your servants are to farm the land for him and bring in the crops, so that your master's grandson may be provided for. And Mephibosheth, grandson of your master, will always eat at my table." (Now Ziba had fifteen sons and twenty servants.)

¹¹Then Ziba said to the king, "Your servant will do whatever my lord the king commands his servant to do." So Mephibosheth ate at David's*a* table like one of the king's sons.

¹²Mephibosheth had a young son named Mica, and all the members of Ziba's household were servants of Mephibosheth. ¹³And Mephibosheth lived in Jerusalem, because he always ate at the king's table, and he was crippled in both feet.

David Defeats the Ammonites

10 In the course of time, the king of the Ammonites died, and his son Hanun succeeded him as king. ²David thought, "I will show kindness to Hanun son of Nahash, just as his father showed kindness to me." So David sent a delegation to express his sympathy to Hanun concerning his father.

When David's men came to the land of the Ammonites, ³the Ammonite nobles said to Hanun their lord, "Do you think David is honoring your father by sending men to you to express sympathy? Hasn't David sent them to you to explore the city and spy it out and overthrow it?" ⁴So Hanun seized David's men, shaved off half of each man's beard, cut off their garments in the middle at the buttocks, and sent them away.

⁵When David was told about this, he sent messengers to meet the men, for they were greatly humiliated. The king said, "Stay at Jericho till your beards have grown, and then come back."

⁶When the Ammonites realized that they had become a stench in David's nostrils, they hired twenty thousand Aramean foot soldiers from Beth Rehob and Zobah, as well as the king of Maacah with a thousand men, and also twelve thousand men from Tob.

⁷On hearing this, David sent Joab out with the entire army of fighting men. ⁸The Ammonites came out and drew up in battle formation at the entrance to their city gate, while the Arameans of Zobah and Rehob and the men of Tob and Maacah were by themselves in the open country.

⁹Joab saw that there were battle lines in front of him and behind him; so he selected some of the best troops in Israel and deployed them against the Arameans. ¹⁰He put the rest of the men under the command of Abishai his brother and deployed them against the Ammonites. ¹¹Joab said, "If the Arameans are too strong for me, then you are to come to my rescue; but if the Ammonites are too strong for you, then I will come to rescue you. ¹²Be strong and let us fight bravely for our people and the cities of our God. The Lord will do what is good in his sight."

¹³Then Joab and the troops with him advanced to fight the Arameans, and they fled before him. ¹⁴When the Ammonites saw that the Arameans were fleeing, they fled before Abishai and went inside the city. So Joab re-

2 Samuel 10:12

God Is Good

"Be strong and let us fight bravely for our people and the cities of our God. The Lord will do what is good in his sight."

---

a 11 Septuagint; Hebrew *my*

turned from fighting the Ammonites and came to Jerusalem.

15 After the Arameans saw that they had been routed by Israel, they regrouped. 16 Hadadezer had Arameans brought from beyond the River[a]; they went to Helam, with Shobach the commander of Hadadezer's army leading them.

17 When David was told of this, he gathered all Israel, crossed the Jordan and went to Helam. The Arameans formed their battle lines to meet David and fought against him. 18 But they fled before Israel, and David killed seven hundred of their charioteers and forty thousand of their foot soldiers.[b] He also struck down Shobach the commander of their army, and he died there. 19 When all the kings who were vassals of Hadadezer saw that they had been defeated by Israel, they made peace with the Israelites and became subject to them.

So the Arameans were afraid to help the Ammonites anymore.

David and Bathsheba

11 In the spring, at the time when kings go off to war, David sent Joab out with the king's men and the whole Israelite army. They destroyed the Ammonites and besieged Rabbah. But David remained in Jerusalem.

2 One evening David got up from his bed and walked around on the roof of the palace. From the roof he saw a woman bathing. The woman was very beautiful, 3 and David sent someone to find out about her. The man said, "Isn't this Bathsheba, the daughter of Eliam and the wife of Uriah the Hittite?" 4 Then David sent messengers to get her. She came to him, and he slept with her. (She had purified herself from her uncleanness.) Then[c] she went back home. 5 The woman conceived and sent word to David, saying, "I am pregnant."

6 So David sent this word to Joab: "Send me Uriah the Hittite." And Joab sent him to David. 7 When Uriah came to him, David asked him how Joab was, how the soldiers were and how the war was going. 8 Then David said to Uriah, "Go down to your house and wash your feet." So Uriah left the palace, and a gift from the king was sent after him. 9 But Uriah slept at the entrance to the palace with all his master's servants and did not go down to his house.

10 When David was told, "Uriah did not go home," he asked him, "Haven't you just come from a distance? Why didn't you go home?"

11 Uriah said to David, "The ark and Israel and Judah are staying in tents, and my master Joab and my lord's men are camped in the open fields. How could I go to my house to eat and drink and lie with my wife? As surely as you live, I will not do such a thing!"

12 Then David said to him, "Stay here one more day, and tomorrow I will send you back." So Uriah remained in Jerusalem that day and the next. 13 At David's invitation, he ate and drank with him, and David made him drunk. But in the evening Uriah went out to sleep on his mat among his master's servants; he did not go home.

14 In the morning David wrote a letter to Joab and sent it with Uriah. 15 In it he wrote, "Put Uriah in the front line where the fighting is fiercest. Then withdraw from him so he will be struck down and die."

16 So while Joab had the city under siege, he put Uriah at a place where he knew the strongest defenders were. 17 When the men of the city came out and fought against Joab, some of the men in David's army fell; moreover, Uriah the Hittite died.

18 Joab sent David a full account of the battle. 19 He instructed the messenger: "When you have finished giving the king this account of the battle, 20 the king's anger may flare up, and he may ask you, 'Why did you get so close to the city to fight? Didn't you know they would shoot arrows from the wall? 21 Who killed Abimelech son of Jerub-Besheth[d]? Didn't a woman throw an upper millstone on him from the wall, so that he died in Thebez? Why did you get so close to the wall?' If he asks you this, then say to him, 'Also, your servant Uriah the Hittite is dead.'"

22 The messenger set out, and when he arrived he told David everything Joab had sent him to say. 23 The messenger said to David, "The men overpowered us and came out against us in the open, but we drove them back to the entrance

---

[a]16 That is, the Euphrates   [b]18 Some Septuagint manuscripts (see also 1 Chron. 19:18); Hebrew *horsemen*   [c]4 Or *with her. When she purified herself from her uncleanness,*   [d]21 Also known as *Jerub-Baal* (that is, Gideon)

to the city gate. ²⁴Then the archers shot arrows at your servants from the wall, and some of the king's men died. Moreover, your servant Uriah the Hittite is dead."

²⁵David told the messenger, "Say this to Joab: 'Don't let this upset you; the sword devours one as well as another. Press the attack against the city and destroy it.' Say this to encourage Joab."

²⁶When Uriah's wife heard that her husband was dead, she mourned for him. ²⁷After the time of mourning was over, David had her brought to his house, and she became his wife and bore him a son. But the thing David had done displeased the LORD.

Nathan Rebukes David

12 The LORD sent Nathan to David. When he came to him, he said, "There were two men in a certain town, one rich and the other poor. ²The rich man had a very large number of sheep and cattle, ³but the poor man had nothing except one little ewe lamb he had bought. He raised it, and it grew up with him and his children. It shared his food, drank from his cup and even slept in his arms. It was like a daughter to him.

⁴"Now a traveler came to the rich man, but the rich man refrained from taking one of his own sheep or cattle to prepare a meal for the traveler who had come to him. Instead, he took the ewe lamb that belonged to the poor man and prepared it for the one who had come to him."

⁵David burned with anger against the man and said to Nathan, "As surely as the LORD lives, the man who did this deserves to die! ⁶He must pay for that lamb four times over, because he did such a thing and had no pity."

⁷Then Nathan said to David, "You are the man! This is what the LORD, the God of Israel, says: 'I anointed you king over Israel, and I delivered you from the hand of Saul. ⁸I gave you your master's house to you, and your master's wives into your arms. I gave you the house of Israel

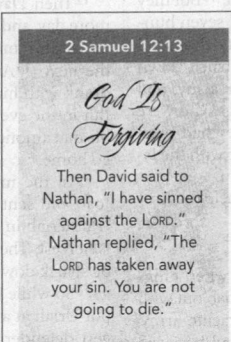

2 Samuel 12:13

God Is Forgiving

Then David said to Nathan, "I have sinned against the LORD." Nathan replied, "The LORD has taken away your sin. You are not going to die."

and Judah. And if all this had been too little, I would have given you even more. ⁹Why did you despise the word of the LORD by doing what is evil in his eyes? You struck down Uriah the Hittite with the sword and took his wife to be your own. You killed him with the sword of the Ammonites. ¹⁰Now, therefore, the sword will never depart from your house, because you despised me and took the wife of Uriah the Hittite to be your own.'

¹¹"This is what the LORD says: 'Out of your own household I am going to bring calamity upon you. Before your very eyes I will take your wives and give them to one who is close to you, and he will lie with your wives in broad daylight. ¹²You did it in secret, but I will do this thing in broad daylight before all Israel.'"

¹³Then David said to Nathan, "I have sinned against the LORD."

Nathan replied, "The LORD has taken away your sin. You are not going to die. ¹⁴But because by doing this you have made the enemies of the LORD show utter contempt,ᵃ the son born to you will die."

¹⁵After Nathan had gone home, the LORD struck the child that Uriah's wife had borne to David, and he became ill. ¹⁶David pleaded with God for the child. He fasted and went into his house and spent the nights lying on the ground. ¹⁷The elders of his household stood beside him to get him up from the ground, but he refused, and he would not eat any food with them.

¹⁸On the seventh day the child died. David's servants were afraid to tell him that the child was dead, for they thought, "While the child was still living, we spoke to David but he would not listen to us. How can we tell him the child is dead? He may do something desperate."

¹⁹David noticed that his servants were whispering among themselves and he realized the child was dead. "Is the child dead?" he asked.

"Yes," they replied, "he is dead."

ᵃ14 Masoretic Text; an ancient Hebrew scribal tradition *this you have shown utter contempt for the LORD*

Cleansed by the Light

Read: 2 Samuel 12:1–15

WHERE DO YOU GO when you feel flawed? Where do you find healing when you know you are sick?

For me, the only place to go was to the feet of the only One who is perfect, the only One who fully understands how flawed I am and yet who loves me completely.

Jesus said, "Come to me, all you who are weary and burdened, and I will give you rest" (Matthew 11:28). When our Lord was being brutally executed, he was taking upon himself all the filth and decay of a diseased world. He knew that we could not make it on our own, so he took our place. Wherever he encountered darkness, he brought light. When he met people who were in hiding, he called them out. Whether it was a "scarlet woman" or a little man hiding up a tree, his words were words of healing and hope and freedom. Isaiah told us, "The people walking in darkness have seen a great light; on those living in the land of the shadow of death a light has dawned" (Isaiah 9:2).

I have a friend who is a missionary on the border between Thailand and Cambodia. One of his concerns is for people suffering from leprosy in the refugee camps. He and his colleagues began to spend time with those men and women, doing what they could to aid them physically and spiritually. Eventually a church was born, right there in the middle of a leper camp. During one of their services, a man who had been among the first to make a commitment to following Christ said, "One of the most wonderful things that has happened to me since I met Jesus is that now I can look you in the face. I was too ashamed before because of my disfigurement, but if Jesus loves me so much, then I think that I can hold my head up high."

That is how it is supposed to be for us all. Jesus has restored our dignity. What we sold so cheaply in Eden, he has bought back for us at a great price. We all struggle with our humanity, with our selfishness, but cleansing is not found in the shadows; it is found in the burning light.

—Sheila Walsh

Go to page 389 for your next devotional reading.

2 Samuel 12:13

Then David said to Nathan, "I have sinned against the LORD." Nathan replied, "The LORD has taken away your sin. You are not going to die."

reflection

1 The man in the story felt ashamed before he met Jesus. Do you struggle with negative feelings?

2 How does it make you feel to know that you are completely loved?

3 Follow Sheila's advice (and David's example) and bring your sin into the burning light by offering a prayer of confession and repentance. Thank God for sending his Son to restore your dignity.

RELATED READINGS

Psalm 51:1–19;
John 8:12;
1 Corinthians 6:19–20

"As long as we are meddling with any part of sin, we shall never see clearly the blissful countenance of our Lord."

Julian of Norwich

20Then David got up from the ground. After he had washed, put on lotions and changed his clothes, he went into the house of the Lord and worshiped. Then he went to his own house, and at his request they served him food, and he ate.

21His servants asked him, "Why are you acting this way? While the child was alive, you fasted and wept, but now that the child is dead, you get up and eat!"

22He answered, "While the child was still alive, I fasted and wept. I thought, 'Who knows? The Lord may be gracious to me and let the child live.' 23But now that he is dead, why should I fast? Can I bring him back again? I will go to him, but he will not return to me."

24Then David comforted his wife Bathsheba, and he went to her and lay with her. She gave birth to a son, and they named him Solomon. The Lord loved him; 25and because the Lord loved him, he sent word through Nathan the prophet to name him Jedidiah.a

26Meanwhile Joab fought against Rabbah of the Ammonites and captured the royal citadel. 27Joab then sent messengers to David, saying, "I have fought against Rabbah and taken its water supply. 28Now muster the rest of the troops and besiege the city and capture it. Otherwise I will take the city, and it will be named after me."

29So David mustered the entire army and went to Rabbah, and attacked and captured it. 30He took the crown from the head of their kingb—its weight was a talentc of gold, and it was set with precious stones—and it was placed on David's head. He took a great quantity of plunder from the city 31and brought out the people who were there, consigning them to labor with saws and with iron picks and axes, and he made them work at brickmaking.d He did this to all the Ammonite towns. Then David and his entire army returned to Jerusalem.

Amnon and Tamar

13 In the course of time, Amnon son of David fell in love with Tamar, the beautiful sister of Absalom son of David.

2Amnon became frustrated to the point of illness on account of his sister Tamar, for she was a virgin, and it seemed impossible for him to do anything to her.

3Now Amnon had a friend named Jonadab son of Shimeah, David's brother. Jonadab was a very shrewd man. 4He asked Amnon, "Why do you, the king's son, look so haggard morning after morning? Won't you tell me?"

Amnon said to him, "I'm in love with Tamar, my brother Absalom's sister."

5"Go to bed and pretend to be ill," Jonadab said. "When your father comes to see you, say to him, 'I would like my sister Tamar to come and give me something to eat. Let her prepare the food in my sight so I may watch her and then eat it from her hand.'"

6So Amnon lay down and pretended to be ill. When the king came to see him, Amnon said to him, "I would like my sister Tamar to come and make some special bread in my sight, so I may eat from her hand."

7David sent word to Tamar at the palace: "Go to the house of your brother Amnon and prepare some food for him." 8So Tamar went to the house of her brother Amnon, who was lying down. She took some dough, kneaded it, made the bread in his sight and baked it. 9Then she took the pan and served him the bread, but he refused to eat.

"Send everyone out of here," Amnon said. So everyone left him. 10Then Amnon said to Tamar, "Bring the food here into my bedroom so I may eat from your hand." And Tamar took the bread she had prepared and brought it to her brother Amnon in his bedroom. 11But when she took it to him to eat, he grabbed her and said, "Come to bed with me, my sister."

12"Don't, my brother!" she said to him. "Don't force me. Such a thing should not be done in Israel! Don't do this wicked thing. 13What about me? Where could I get rid of my disgrace? And what about you? You would be like one of the wicked fools in Israel. Please speak to the king; he will not keep me from being married to you." 14But he refused to listen to her, and since he was stronger than she, he raped her.

15Then Amnon hated her with intense hatred. In fact, he hated her more than he had

---

a25 *Jedidiah* means *loved by the Lord.*   b30 Or *of Milcom* (that is, Molech)   c30 That is, about 75 pounds (about 34 kilograms)
d31 The meaning of the Hebrew for this clause is uncertain.

loved her. Amnon said to her, "Get up and get out!"

¹⁶"No!" she said to him. "Sending me away would be a greater wrong than what you have already done to me."

But he refused to listen to her. ¹⁷He called his personal servant and said, "Get this woman out of here and bolt the door after her." ¹⁸So his servant put her out and bolted the door after her. She was wearing a richly ornamented[a] robe, for this was the kind of garment the virgin daughters of the king wore. ¹⁹Tamar put ashes on her head and tore the ornamented[b] robe she was wearing. She put her hand on her head and went away, weeping aloud as she went.

²⁰Her brother Absalom said to her, "Has that Amnon, your brother, been with you? Be quiet now, my sister; he is your brother. Don't take this thing to heart." And Tamar lived in her brother Absalom's house, a desolate woman.

²¹When King David heard all this, he was furious. ²²Absalom never said a word to Amnon, either good or bad; he hated Amnon because he had disgraced his sister Tamar.

Absalom Kills Amnon

²³Two years later, when Absalom's sheepshearers were at Baal Hazor near the border of Ephraim, he invited all the king's sons to come there. ²⁴Absalom went to the king and said, "Your servant has had shearers come. Will the king and his officials please join me?"

²⁵"No, my son," the king replied. "All of us should not go; we would only be a burden to you." Although Absalom urged him, he still refused to go, but gave him his blessing.

²⁶Then Absalom said, "If not, please let my brother Amnon come with us."

The king asked him, "Why should he go with you?" ²⁷But Absalom urged him, so he sent with him Amnon and the rest of the king's sons.

²⁸Absalom ordered his men, "Listen! When Amnon is in high spirits from drinking wine and I say to you, 'Strike Amnon down,' then kill him. Don't be afraid. Have not I given you this order? Be strong and brave." ²⁹So Absalom's men did to Amnon what Absalom had or-

dered. Then all the king's sons got up, mounted their mules and fled.

³⁰While they were on their way, the report came to David: "Absalom has struck down all the king's sons; not one of them is left." ³¹The king stood up, tore his clothes and lay down on the ground; and all his servants stood by with their clothes torn.

³²But Jonadab son of Shimeah, David's brother, said, "My lord should not think that they killed all the princes; only Amnon is dead. This has been Absalom's expressed intention ever since the day Amnon raped his sister Tamar. ³³My lord the king should not be concerned about the report that all the king's sons are dead. Only Amnon is dead."

³⁴Meanwhile, Absalom had fled.

Now the man standing watch looked up and saw many people on the road west of him, coming down the side of the hill. The watchman went and told the king, "I see men in the direction of Horonaim, on the side of the hill."[c]

³⁵Jonadab said to the king, "See, the king's sons are here; it has happened just as your servant said."

³⁶As he finished speaking, the king's sons came in, wailing loudly. The king, too, and all his servants wept very bitterly.

³⁷Absalom fled and went to Talmai son of Ammihud, the king of Geshur. But King David mourned for his son every day.

³⁸After Absalom fled and went to Geshur, he stayed there three years. ³⁹And the spirit of the king[d] longed to go to Absalom, for he was consoled concerning Amnon's death.

Absalom Returns to Jerusalem

14 Joab son of Zeruiah knew that the king's heart longed for Absalom. ²So Joab sent someone to Tekoa and had a wise woman brought from there. He said to her, "Pretend you are in mourning. Dress in mourning clothes, and don't use any cosmetic lotions. Act like a woman who has spent many days grieving for the dead. ³Then go to the king and speak these words to him." And Joab put the words in her mouth.

⁴When the woman from Tekoa went[e] to the

---

[a]18 The meaning of the Hebrew for this phrase is uncertain.   [b]19 The meaning of the Hebrew for this word is uncertain.   [c]34 Septuagint; Hebrew does not have this sentence.   [d]39 Dead Sea Scrolls and some Septuagint manuscripts; Masoretic Text *But ¸the spirit of David the king*   [e]4 Many Hebrew manuscripts, Septuagint, Vulgate and Syriac; most Hebrew manuscripts *spoke*

king, she fell with her face to the ground to pay him honor, and she said, "Help me, O king!"

⁵The king asked her, "What is troubling you?"

She said, "I am indeed a widow; my husband is dead. ⁶I your servant had two sons. They got into a fight with each other in the field, and no one was there to separate them. One struck the other and killed him. ⁷Now the whole clan has risen up against your servant; they say, 'Hand over the one who struck his brother down, so that we may put him to death for the life of his brother whom he killed; then we will get rid of the heir as well.' They would put out the only burning coal I have left, leaving my husband neither name nor descendant on the face of the earth."

⁸The king said to the woman, "Go home, and I will issue an order in your behalf."

⁹But the woman from Tekoa said to him, "My lord the king, let the blame rest on me and on my father's family, and let the king and his throne be without guilt."

¹⁰The king replied, "If anyone says anything to you, bring him to me, and he will not bother you again."

¹¹She said, "Then let the king invoke the LORD his God to prevent the avenger of blood from adding to the destruction, so that my son will not be destroyed."

"As surely as the LORD lives," he said, "not one hair of your son's head will fall to the ground."

¹²Then the woman said, "Let your servant speak a word to my lord the king."

"Speak," he replied.

¹³The woman said, "Why then have you devised a thing like this against the people of God? When the king says this, does he not convict himself, for the king has not brought back his banished son? ¹⁴Like water spilled on the ground, which cannot be recovered, so we must die. But God does not take away life; instead, he devises ways so that a banished person may not remain estranged from him.

2 Samuel 14:14

God Seeks Us

But God does not take away life; instead, he devises ways so that a banished person may not remain estranged from him.

¹⁵"And now I have come to say this to my lord the king because the people have made me afraid. Your servant thought, 'I will speak to the king; perhaps he will do what his servant asks. ¹⁶Perhaps the king will agree to deliver his servant from the hand of the man who is trying to cut off both me and my son from the inheritance God gave us.'

¹⁷"And now your servant says, 'May the word of my lord the king bring me rest, for my lord the king is like an angel of God in discerning good and evil. May the LORD your God be with you.'"

¹⁸Then the king said to the woman, "Do not keep from me the answer to what I am going to ask you."

"Let my lord the king speak," the woman said.

¹⁹The king asked, "Isn't the hand of Joab with you in all this?"

The woman answered, "As surely as you live, my lord the king, no one can turn to the right or to the left from anything my lord the king says. Yes, it was your servant Joab who instructed me to do this and who put all these words into the mouth of your servant. ²⁰Your servant Joab did this to change the present situation. My lord has wisdom like that of an angel of God—he knows everything that happens in the land."

²¹The king said to Joab, "Very well, I will do it. Go, bring back the young man Absalom."

²²Joab fell with his face to the ground to pay him honor, and he blessed the king. Joab said, "Today your servant knows that he has found favor in your eyes, my lord the king, because the king has granted his servant's request."

²³Then Joab went to Geshur and brought Absalom back to Jerusalem. ²⁴But the king said, "He must go to his own house; he must not see my face." So Absalom went to his own house and did not see the face of the king.

²⁵In all Israel there was not a man so highly praised for his handsome appearance as Absa-

lom. From the top of his head to the sole of his foot there was no blemish in him. [26]Whenever he cut the hair of his head—he used to cut his hair from time to time when it became too heavy for him—he would weigh it, and its weight was two hundred shekels[a] by the royal standard.

[27]Three sons and a daughter were born to Absalom. The daughter's name was Tamar, and she became a beautiful woman.

[28]Absalom lived two years in Jerusalem without seeing the king's face. [29]Then Absalom sent for Joab in order to send him to the king, but Joab refused to come to him. So he sent a second time, but he refused to come. [30]Then he said to his servants, "Look, Joab's field is next to mine, and he has barley there. Go and set it on fire." So Absalom's servants set the field on fire.

[31]Then Joab did go to Absalom's house and he said to him, "Why have your servants set my field on fire?"

[32]Absalom said to Joab, "Look, I sent word to you and said, 'Come here so I can send you to the king to ask, "Why have I come from Geshur? It would be better for me if I were still there!"' Now then, I want to see the king's face, and if I am guilty of anything, let him put me to death."

[33]So Joab went to the king and told him this. Then the king summoned Absalom, and he came in and bowed down with his face to the ground before the king. And the king kissed Absalom.

Absalom's Conspiracy

15 In the course of time, Absalom provided himself with a chariot and horses and with fifty men to run ahead of him. [2]He would get up early and stand by the side of the road leading to the city gate. Whenever anyone came with a complaint to be placed before the king for a decision, Absalom would call out to him, "What town are you from?" He would answer, "Your servant is from one of the tribes of Israel." [3]Then Absalom would say to him, "Look, your claims are valid and proper, but there is no representative of the king to hear you." [4]And Absalom would add, "If only I were

appointed judge in the land! Then everyone who has a complaint or case could come to me and I would see that he gets justice."

[5]Also, whenever anyone approached him to bow down before him, Absalom would reach out his hand, take hold of him and kiss him. [6]Absalom behaved in this way toward all the Israelites who came to the king asking for justice, and so he stole the hearts of the men of Israel.

[7]At the end of four[b] years, Absalom said to the king, "Let me go to Hebron and fulfill a vow I made to the LORD. [8]While your servant was living at Geshur in Aram, I made this vow: 'If the LORD takes me back to Jerusalem, I will worship the LORD in Hebron.[c]'"

[9]The king said to him, "Go in peace." So he went to Hebron.

[10]Then Absalom sent secret messengers throughout the tribes of Israel to say, "As soon as you hear the sound of the trumpets, then say, 'Absalom is king in Hebron.'" [11]Two hundred men from Jerusalem had accompanied Absalom. They had been invited as guests and went quite innocently, knowing nothing about the matter. [12]While Absalom was offering sacrifices, he also sent for Ahithophel the Gilonite, David's counselor, to come from Giloh, his hometown. And so the conspiracy gained strength, and Absalom's following kept on increasing.

David Flees

[13]A messenger came and told David, "The hearts of the men of Israel are with Absalom."

[14]Then David said to all his officials who were with him in Jerusalem, "Come! We must flee, or none of us will escape from Absalom. We must leave immediately, or he will move quickly to overtake us and bring ruin upon us and put the city to the sword."

[15]The king's officials answered him, "Your servants are ready to do whatever our lord the king chooses."

[16]The king set out, with his entire household following him; but he left ten concubines to take care of the palace. [17]So the king set out, with all the people following him, and they halted at a place some distance away. [18]All his

---

[a]26 That is, about 5 pounds (about 2.3 kilograms)   [b]7 Some Septuagint manuscripts, Syriac and Josephus; Hebrew *forty*   [c]8 Some Septuagint manuscripts; Hebrew does not have *in Hebron*.

men marched past him, along with all the Kerethites and Pelethites; and all the six hundred Gittites who had accompanied him from Gath marched before the king.

¹⁹The king said to Ittai the Gittite, "Why should you come along with us? Go back and stay with King Absalom. You are a foreigner, an exile from your homeland. ²⁰You came only yesterday. And today shall I make you wander about with us, when I do not know where I am going? Go back, and take your countrymen. May kindness and faithfulness be with you."

²¹But Ittai replied to the king, "As surely as the LORD lives, and as my lord the king lives, wherever my lord the king may be, whether it means life or death, there will your servant be."

²²David said to Ittai, "Go ahead, march on." So Ittai the Gittite marched on with all his men and the families that were with him.

²³The whole countryside wept aloud as all the people passed by. The king also crossed the Kidron Valley, and all the people moved on toward the desert.

²⁴Zadok was there, too, and all the Levites who were with him were carrying the ark of the covenant of God. They set down the ark of God, and Abiathar offered sacrifices*a* until all the people had finished leaving the city.

²⁵Then the king said to Zadok, "Take the ark of God back into the city. If I find favor in the LORD's eyes, he will bring me back and let me see it and his dwelling place again. ²⁶But if he says, 'I am not pleased with you,' then I am ready; let him do to me whatever seems good to him."

²⁷The king also said to Zadok the priest, "Aren't you a seer? Go back to the city in peace, with your son Ahimaaz and Jonathan son of Abiathar. You and Abiathar take your two sons with you. ²⁸I will wait at the fords in the desert until word comes from you to inform me." ²⁹So Zadok and Abiathar took the ark of God back to Jerusalem and stayed there.

³⁰But David continued up the Mount of Olives, weeping as he went; his head was covered and he was barefoot. All the people with him covered their heads too and were weeping as they went up. ³¹Now David had been told,

"Ahithophel is among the conspirators with Absalom." So David prayed, "O LORD, turn Ahithophel's counsel into foolishness."

³²When David arrived at the summit, where people used to worship God, Hushai the Arkite was there to meet him, his robe torn and dust on his head. ³³David said to him, "If you go with me, you will be a burden to me. ³⁴But if you return to the city and say to Absalom, 'I will be your servant, O king; I was your father's servant in the past, but now I will be your servant,' then you can help me by frustrating Ahithophel's advice. ³⁵Won't the priests Zadok and Abiathar be there with you? Tell them anything you hear in the king's palace. ³⁶Their two sons, Ahimaaz son of Zadok and Jonathan son of Abiathar, are there with them. Send them to me with anything you hear."

³⁷So David's friend Hushai arrived at Jerusalem as Absalom was entering the city.

David and Ziba

16 When David had gone a short distance beyond the summit, there was Ziba, the steward of Mephibosheth, waiting to meet him. He had a string of donkeys saddled and loaded with two hundred loaves of bread, a hundred cakes of raisins, a hundred cakes of figs and a skin of wine.

²The king asked Ziba, "Why have you brought these?"

Ziba answered, "The donkeys are for the king's household to ride on, the bread and fruit are for the men to eat, and the wine is to refresh those who become exhausted in the desert."

³The king then asked, "Where is your master's grandson?"

Ziba said to him, "He is staying in Jerusalem, because he thinks, 'Today the house of Israel will give me back my grandfather's kingdom.'"

⁴Then the king said to Ziba, "All that belonged to Mephibosheth is now yours."

"I humbly bow," Ziba said. "May I find favor in your eyes, my lord the king."

Shimei Curses David

⁵As King David approached Bahurim, a man from the same clan as Saul's family came out from there. His name was Shimei son of Gera, and he cursed as he came out. ⁶He pelted

---

a24 Or Abiathar went up

David and all the king's officials with stones, though all the troops and the special guard were on David's right and left. [7]As he cursed, Shimei said, "Get out, get out, you man of blood, you scoundrel! [8]The LORD has repaid you for all the blood you shed in the household of Saul, in whose place you have reigned. The LORD has handed the kingdom over to your son Absalom. You have come to ruin because you are a man of blood!"

[9]Then Abishai son of Zeruiah said to the king, "Why should this dead dog curse my lord the king? Let me go over and cut off his head."

[10]But the king said, "What do you and I have in common, you sons of Zeruiah? If he is cursing because the LORD said to him, 'Curse David,' who can ask, 'Why do you do this?'"

[11]David then said to Abishai and all his officials, "My son, who is of my own flesh, is trying to take my life. How much more, then, this Benjamite! Leave him alone; let him curse, for the LORD has told him to. [12]It may be that the LORD will see my distress and repay me with good for the cursing I am receiving today."

[13]So David and his men continued along the road while Shimei was going along the hillside opposite him, cursing as he went and throwing stones at him and showering him with dirt. [14]The king and all the people with him arrived at their destination exhausted. And there he refreshed himself.

The Advice of Ahithophel and Hushai

[15]Meanwhile, Absalom and all the men of Israel came to Jerusalem, and Ahithophel was with him. [16]Then Hushai the Arkite, David's friend, went to Absalom and said to him, "Long live the king! Long live the king!"

[17]Absalom asked Hushai, "Is this the love you show your friend? Why didn't you go with your friend?"

[18]Hushai said to Absalom, "No, the one chosen by the LORD, by these people, and by all the men of Israel—his I will be, and I will remain with him. [19]Furthermore, whom should I serve? Should I not serve the son? Just as I served your father, so I will serve you."

[20]Absalom said to Ahithophel, "Give us your advice. What should we do?"

[21]Ahithophel answered, "Lie with your father's concubines whom he left to take care of the palace. Then all Israel will hear that you have made yourself a stench in your father's nostrils, and the hands of everyone with you will be strengthened." [22]So they pitched a tent for Absalom on the roof, and he lay with his father's concubines in the sight of all Israel.

[23]Now in those days the advice Ahithophel gave was like that of one who inquires of God. That was how both David and Absalom regarded all of Ahithophel's advice.

17 Ahithophel said to Absalom, "I would[a] choose twelve thousand men and set out tonight in pursuit of David. [2]I would[b] attack him while he is weary and weak. I would[b] strike him with terror, and then all the people with him will flee. I would[b] strike down only the king [3]and bring all the people back to you. The death of the man you seek will mean the return of all; all the people will be unharmed." [4]This plan seemed good to Absalom and to all the elders of Israel.

[5]But Absalom said, "Summon also Hushai the Arkite, so we can hear what he has to say." [6]When Hushai came to him, Absalom said, "Ahithophel has given this advice. Should we do what he says? If not, give us your opinion."

[7]Hushai replied to Absalom, "The advice Ahithophel has given is not good this time. [8]You know your father and his men; they are fighters, and as fierce as a wild bear robbed of her cubs. Besides, your father is an experienced fighter; he will not spend the night with the troops. [9]Even now, he is hidden in a cave or some other place. If he should attack your troops first,[c] whoever hears about it will say, 'There has been a slaughter among the troops who follow Absalom.' [10]Then even the bravest soldier, whose heart is like the heart of a lion, will melt with fear, for all Israel knows that your father is a fighter and that those with him are brave.

[11]"So I advise you: Let all Israel, from Dan to Beersheba—as numerous as the sand on the seashore—be gathered to you, with you yourself leading them into battle. [12]Then we will attack him wherever he may be found, and we will fall on him as dew settles on the ground.

---

[a]1 Or *Let me*   [b]2 Or *will*   [c]9 Or *When some of the men fall at the first attack*

Neither he nor any of his men will be left alive. **13**If he withdraws into a city, then all Israel will bring ropes to that city, and we will drag it down to the valley until not even a piece of it can be found."

14Absalom and all the men of Israel said, "The advice of Hushai the Arkite is better than that of Ahithophel." For the LORD had determined to frustrate the good advice of Ahithophel in order to bring disaster on Absalom.

15Hushai told Zadok and Abiathar, the priests, "Ahithophel has advised Absalom and the elders of Israel to do such and such, but I have advised them to do so and so. **16**Now send a message immediately and tell David, 'Do not spend the night at the fords in the desert; cross over without fail, or the king and all the people with him will be swallowed up.'"

17Jonathan and Ahimaaz were staying at En Rogel. A servant girl was to go and inform them, and they were to go and tell King David, for they could not risk being seen entering the city. **18**But a young man saw them and told Absalom. So the two of them left quickly and went to the house of a man in Bahurim. He had a well in his courtyard, and they climbed down into it. **19**His wife took a covering and spread it out over the opening of the well and scattered grain over it. No one knew anything about it.

20When Absalom's men came to the woman at the house, they asked, "Where are Ahimaaz and Jonathan?"

The woman answered them, "They crossed over the brook."[a] The men searched but found no one, so they returned to Jerusalem.

21After the men had gone, the two climbed out of the well and went to inform King David. They said to him, "Set out and cross the river at once; Ahithophel has advised such and such against you." **22**So David and all the people with him set out and crossed the Jordan. By daybreak, no one was left who had not crossed the Jordan.

23When Ahithophel saw that his advice had not been followed, he saddled his donkey and set out for his house in his hometown. He put

his house in order and then hanged himself. So he died and was buried in his father's tomb.

24David went to Mahanaim, and Absalom crossed the Jordan with all the men of Israel. **25**Absalom had appointed Amasa over the army in place of Joab. Amasa was the son of a man named Jether,[b] an Israelite[c] who had married Abigail,[d] the daughter of Nahash and sister of Zeruiah the mother of Joab. **26**The Israelites and Absalom camped in the land of Gilead.

27When David came to Mahanaim, Shobi son of Nahash from Rabbah of the Ammonites, and Makir son of Ammiel from Lo Debar, and Barzillai the Gileadite from Rogelim **28**brought bedding and bowls and articles of pottery. They also brought wheat and barley, flour and roasted grain, beans and lentils,[e] **29**honey and curds, sheep, and cheese from cows' milk for David and his people to eat. For they said, "The people have become hungry and tired and thirsty in the desert."

Absalom's Death

18 David mustered the men who were with him and appointed over them commanders of thousands and commanders of hundreds. **2**David sent the troops out—a third under the command of Joab, a third under Joab's brother Abishai son of Zeruiah, and a third under Ittai the Gittite. The king told the troops, "I myself will surely march out with you."

3But the men said, "You must not go out; if we are forced to flee, they won't care about us. Even if half of us die, they won't care; but you are worth ten thousand of us.[f] It would be better now for you to give us support from the city."

4The king answered, "I will do whatever seems best to you."

So the king stood beside the gate while all the men marched out in units of hundreds and of thousands. **5**The king commanded Joab, Abishai and Ittai, "Be gentle with the young man Absalom for my sake." And all the troops heard the king giving orders concerning Absalom to each of the commanders.

6The army marched into the field to fight

---

[a]20 Or *"They passed by the sheep pen toward the water."* [b]25 Hebrew *Ithra,* a variant of *Jether* [c]25 Hebrew and some Septuagint manuscripts; other Septuagint manuscripts (see also 1 Chron. 2:17) *Ishmaelite* or *Jezreelite* [d]25 Hebrew *Abigal,* a variant of *Abigail* [e]28 Most Septuagint manuscripts and Syriac; Hebrew *lentils, and roasted grain* [f]3 Two Hebrew manuscripts, some Septuagint manuscripts and Vulgate; most Hebrew manuscripts *care; for now there are ten thousand like us*

Israel, and the battle took place in the forest of Ephraim. ⁷There the army of Israel was defeated by David's men, and the casualties that day were great—twenty thousand men. ⁸The battle spread out over the whole countryside, and the forest claimed more lives that day than the sword.

⁹Now Absalom happened to meet David's men. He was riding his mule, and as the mule went under the thick branches of a large oak, Absalom's head got caught in the tree. He was left hanging in midair, while the mule he was riding kept on going.

¹⁰When one of the men saw this, he told Joab, "I just saw Absalom hanging in an oak tree."

¹¹Joab said to the man who had told him this, "What! You saw him? Why didn't you strike him to the ground right there? Then I would have had to give you ten shekels*a* of silver and a warrior's belt."

¹²But the man replied, "Even if a thousand shekels*b* were weighed out into my hands, I would not lift my hand against the king's son. In our hearing the king commanded you and Abishai and Ittai, 'Protect the young man Absalom for my sake.'*c* ¹³And if I had put my life in jeopardy*d*—and nothing is hidden from the king—you would have kept your distance from me."

¹⁴Joab said, "I'm not going to wait like this for you." So he took three javelins in his hand and plunged them into Absalom's heart while Absalom was still alive in the oak tree. ¹⁵And ten of Joab's armor-bearers surrounded Absalom, struck him and killed him.

¹⁶Then Joab sounded the trumpet, and the troops stopped pursuing Israel, for Joab halted them. ¹⁷They took Absalom, threw him into a big pit in the forest and piled up a large heap of rocks over him. Meanwhile, all the Israelites fled to their homes.

¹⁸During his lifetime Absalom had taken a pillar and erected it in the King's Valley as a monument to himself, for he thought, "I have no son to carry on the memory of my name." He named the pillar after himself, and it is called Absalom's Monument to this day.

David Mourns

¹⁹Now Ahimaaz son of Zadok said, "Let me run and take the news to the king that the LORD has delivered him from the hand of his enemies."

²⁰"You are not the one to take the news today," Joab told him. "You may take the news another time, but you must not do so today, because the king's son is dead."

²¹Then Joab said to a Cushite, "Go, tell the king what you have seen." The Cushite bowed down before Joab and ran off.

²²Ahimaaz son of Zadok again said to Joab, "Come what may, please let me run behind the Cushite."

But Joab replied, "My son, why do you want to go? You don't have any news that will bring you a reward."

²³He said, "Come what may, I want to run."

So Joab said, "Run!" Then Ahimaaz ran by way of the plain*e* and outran the Cushite.

²⁴While David was sitting between the inner and outer gates, the watchman went up to the roof of the gateway by the wall. As he looked out, he saw a man running alone. ²⁵The watchman called out to the king and reported it.

The king said, "If he is alone, he must have good news." And the man came closer and closer.

²⁶Then the watchman saw another man running, and he called down to the gatekeeper, "Look, another man running alone!"

The king said, "He must be bringing good news, too."

²⁷The watchman said, "It seems to me that the first one runs like Ahimaaz son of Zadok."

"He's a good man," the king said. "He comes with good news."

²⁸Then Ahimaaz called out to the king, "All is well!" He bowed down before the king with his face to the ground and said, "Praise be to the LORD your God! He has delivered up the men who lifted their hands against my lord the king."

²⁹The king asked, "Is the young man Absalom safe?"

Ahimaaz answered, "I saw great confusion just as Joab was about to send the king's servant

---

a11 That is, about 4 ounces (about 115 grams)   *b12* That is, about 25 pounds (about 11 kilograms)   *c12* A few Hebrew manuscripts, Septuagint, Vulgate and Syriac; most Hebrew manuscripts may be translated *Absalom, whoever you may be.*   *d13* Or *Otherwise, if I had acted treacherously toward him*   *e23* That is, the plain of the Jordan and me, your servant, but I don't know what it was."

[30]The king said, "Stand aside and wait here." So he stepped aside and stood there.

[31]Then the Cushite arrived and said, "My lord the king, hear the good news! The LORD has delivered you today from all who rose up against you."

[32]The king asked the Cushite, "Is the young man Absalom safe?"

The Cushite replied, "May the enemies of my lord the king and all who rise up to harm you be like that young man."

[33]The king was shaken. He went up to the room over the gateway and wept. As he went, he said: "O my son Absalom! My son, my son Absalom! If only I had died instead of you— O Absalom, my son, my son!"

19 Joab was told, "The king is weeping and mourning for Absalom." [2]And for the whole army the victory that day was turned into mourning, because on that day the troops heard it said, "The king is grieving for his son." [3]The men stole into the city that day as men steal in who are ashamed when they flee from battle. [4]The king covered his face and cried aloud, "O my son Absalom! O Absalom, my son, my son!"

[5]Then Joab went into the house to the king and said, "Today you have humiliated all your men, who have just saved your life and the lives of your sons and daughters and the lives of your wives and concubines. [6]You love those who hate you and hate those who love you. You have made it clear today that the commanders and their men mean nothing to you. I see that you would be pleased if Absalom were alive today and all of us were dead. [7]Now go out and encourage your men. I swear by the LORD that if you don't go out, not a man will be left with you by nightfall. This will be worse for you than all the calamities that have come upon you from your youth till now."

[8]So the king got up and took his seat in the gateway. When the men were told, "The king is sitting in the gateway," they all came before him.

David Returns to Jerusalem

Meanwhile, the Israelites had fled to their homes. [9]Throughout the tribes of Israel, the people were all arguing with each other, saying, "The king delivered us from the hand of our enemies; he is the one who rescued us from the hand of the Philistines. But now he has fled the country because of Absalom; [10]and Absalom, whom we anointed to rule over us, has died in battle. So why do you say nothing about bringing the king back?"

[11]King David sent this message to Zadok and Abiathar, the priests: "Ask the elders of Judah, 'Why should you be the last to bring the king back to his palace, since what is being said throughout Israel has reached the king at his quarters? [12]You are my brothers, my own flesh and blood. So why should you be the last to bring back the king?' [13]And say to Amasa, 'Are you not my own flesh and blood? May God deal with me, be it ever so severely, if from now on you are not the commander of my army in place of Joab.'"

[14]He won over the hearts of all the men of Judah as though they were one man. They sent word to the king, "Return, you and all your men." [15]Then the king returned and went as far as the Jordan.

Now the men of Judah had come to Gilgal to go out and meet the king and bring him across the Jordan. [16]Shimei son of Gera, the Benjamite from Bahurim, hurried down with the men of Judah to meet King David. [17]With him were a thousand Benjamites, along with Ziba, the steward of Saul's household, and his fifteen sons and twenty servants. They rushed to the Jordan, where the king was. [18]They crossed at the ford to take the king's household over and to do whatever he wished.

When Shimei son of Gera crossed the Jordan, he fell prostrate before the king [19]and said to him, "May my lord not hold me guilty. Do not remember how your servant did wrong on the day my lord the king left Jerusalem. May the king put it out of his mind. [20]For I your servant know that I have sinned, but today I have come here as the first of the whole house of Joseph to come down and meet my lord the king."

[21]Then Abishai son of Zeruiah said, "Shouldn't Shimei be put to death for this? He cursed the LORD's anointed."

[22]David replied, "What do you and I have in common, you sons of Zeruiah? This day you

Overwhelmed With Grief

Read: 2 Samuel 19:1–8

HAVE YOU EVER TRIED to comfort someone who refused to be comforted? Or maybe you were the one whose sorrow was so deep that no words or actions could penetrate your grief. We've all seen or experienced the gut-wrenching sorrow that causes us to want to deny the pain and turn back the hands of time. Sometimes all we can do is utter the name of the person we've lost.

Such was David's grief when he heard of Absalom's death. He stopped everything and, in true Eastern fashion, wailed for his rebellious son, even though Absalom was killed in a coup to steal his father's kingdom. Nevertheless, David was so grief-stricken that he was unable to cope with the responsibilities of reclaiming the kingdom. In fact, his grief was so debilitating that his closest aides warned him that if he didn't pull himself together and rejoice that his armies had conquered his enemies (including his son), his subjects would grow disheartened. As a father, David had every right to feel grief. However, as the leader of a nation, King David had to rise above his grief and carry on for the sake of his people.

The death of a child is beyond tragic. It is the deepest grief and sorrow. And there are other losses worth grieving: the death of a marriage, the end of a friendship or the loss of your health. Then comes the anguish. You want to blank out the present and look to the past. You deeply want to turn back the clock and reverse what has happened. You can't eat, sleep or work. In the freshness of the pain, it might seem you can never again function.

Maybe you are overwhelmed by a devastating grief right now or are trying to encourage someone else in a similar situation. Maybe you need to think about what David did. Embrace your personal grief, but remember your responsibilities to others, even though it may be the hardest thing to do.

God has not promised immunity from sorrow, but he has promised that he will be present with us through it: "Blessed are those who mourn, for they will be comforted" (Matthew 5:4).

2 Samuel 19:4

The king covered his face and cried aloud, "O my son Absalom! O Absalom, my son, my son!"

reflection

1 What event or events in your life have nearly overwhelmed you with grief? Describe what happened.

2 What responsibilities forced you to face your pain and function again?

3 How did God come alongside to comfort and strengthen you in your sorrow?

RELATED READINGS

Genesis 37:35;
Psalms 116:1–19;
126:5–6

"The risk of love is loss, and the price of loss is grief."

Hilary Stanton Zunin

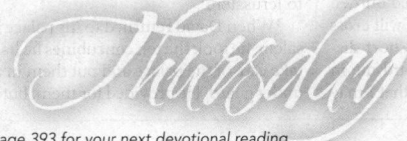

Thursday

Go to page 393 for your next devotional reading.

have become my adversaries! Should anyone be put to death in Israel today? Do I not know that today I am king over Israel?" ²³So the king said to Shimei, "You shall not die." And the king promised him on oath.

²⁴Mephibosheth, Saul's grandson, also went down to meet the king. He had not taken care of his feet or trimmed his mustache or washed his clothes from the day the king left until the day he returned safely. ²⁵When he came from Jerusalem to meet the king, the king asked him, "Why didn't you go with me, Mephibosheth?"

²⁶He said, "My lord the king, since I your servant am lame, I said, 'I will have my donkey saddled and will ride on it, so I can go with the king.' But Ziba my servant betrayed me. ²⁷And he has slandered your servant to my lord the king. My lord the king is like an angel of God; so do whatever pleases you. ²⁸All my grandfather's descendants deserved nothing but death from my lord the king, but you gave your servant a place among those who eat at your table. So what right do I have to make any more appeals to the king?"

²⁹The king said to him, "Why say more? I order you and Ziba to divide the fields."

³⁰Mephibosheth said to the king, "Let him take everything, now that my lord the king has arrived home safely."

³¹Barzillai the Gileadite also came down from Rogelim to cross the Jordan with the king and to send him on his way from there. ³²Now Barzillai was a very old man, eighty years of age. He had provided for the king during his stay in Mahanaim, for he was a very wealthy man. ³³The king said to Barzillai, "Cross over with me and stay with me in Jerusalem, and I will provide for you."

³⁴But Barzillai answered the king, "How many more years will I live, that I should go up to Jerusalem with the king? ³⁵I am now eighty years old. Can I tell the difference between what is good and what is not? Can your servant taste what he eats and drinks? Can I still hear the voices of men and women singers? Why should your servant be an added burden to my lord the king? ³⁶Your servant will cross over the Jordan with the king for a short distance, but why should the king reward me in this way? ³⁷Let your servant return, that I may die in my own town near the tomb of my father and mother. But here is your servant Kimham. Let him cross over with my lord the king. Do for him whatever pleases you."

³⁸The king said, "Kimham shall cross over with me, and I will do for him whatever pleases you. And anything you desire from me I will do for you."

³⁹So all the people crossed the Jordan, and then the king crossed over. The king kissed Barzillai and gave him his blessing, and Barzillai returned to his home.

⁴⁰When the king crossed over to Gilgal, Kimham crossed with him. All the troops of Judah and half the troops of Israel had taken the king over.

⁴¹Soon all the men of Israel were coming to the king and saying to him, "Why did our brothers, the men of Judah, steal the king away and bring him and his household across the Jordan, together with all his men?"

⁴²All the men of Judah answered the men of Israel, "We did this because the king is closely related to us. Why are you angry about it? Have we eaten any of the king's provisions? Have we taken anything for ourselves?"

⁴³Then the men of Israel answered the men of Judah, "We have ten shares in the king; and besides, we have a greater claim on David than you have. So why do you treat us with contempt? Were we not the first to speak of bringing back our king?"

But the men of Judah responded even more harshly than the men of Israel.

Sheba Rebels Against David

20 Now a troublemaker named Sheba son of Bicri, a Benjamite, happened to be there. He sounded the trumpet and shouted,

"We have no share in David,
no part in Jesse's son!
Every man to his tent, O Israel!"

²So all the men of Israel deserted David to follow Sheba son of Bicri. But the men of Judah stayed by their king all the way from the Jordan to Jerusalem.

³When David returned to his palace in Jerusalem, he took the ten concubines he had left to take care of the palace and put them in a house under guard. He provided for them, but did not

lie with them. They were kept in confinement till the day of their death, living as widows.

⁴Then the king said to Amasa, "Summon the men of Judah to come to me within three days, and be here yourself." ⁵But when Amasa went to summon Judah, he took longer than the time the king had set for him.

⁶David said to Abishai, "Now Sheba son of Bicri will do us more harm than Absalom did. Take your master's men and pursue him, or he will find fortified cities and escape from us." ⁷So Joab's men and the Kerethites and Pelethites and all the mighty warriors went out under the command of Abishai. They marched out from Jerusalem to pursue Sheba son of Bicri.

⁸While they were at the great rock in Gibeon, Amasa came to meet them. Joab was wearing his military tunic, and strapped over it at his waist was a belt with a dagger in its sheath. As he stepped forward, it dropped out of its sheath.

⁹Joab said to Amasa, "How are you, my brother?" Then Joab took Amasa by the beard with his right hand to kiss him. ¹⁰Amasa was not on his guard against the dagger in Joab's hand, and Joab plunged it into his belly, and his intestines spilled out on the ground. Without being stabbed again, Amasa died. Then Joab and his brother Abishai pursued Sheba son of Bicri.

¹¹One of Joab's men stood beside Amasa and said, "Whoever favors Joab, and whoever is for David, let him follow Joab!" ¹²Amasa lay wallowing in his blood in the middle of the road, and the man saw that all the troops came to a halt there. When he realized that everyone who came up to Amasa stopped, he dragged him from the road into a field and threw a garment over him. ¹³After Amasa had been removed from the road, all the men went on with Joab to pursue Sheba son of Bicri.

¹⁴Sheba passed through all the tribes of Israel to Abel Beth Maacah[a] and through the entire region of the Berites, who gathered together and followed him. ¹⁵All the troops with Joab came and besieged Sheba in Abel Beth Maacah. They built a siege ramp up to the city, and it stood against the outer fortifications. While they were battering the wall to bring it down,

¹⁶a wise woman called from the city, "Listen! Listen! Tell Joab to come here so I can speak to him." ¹⁷He went toward her, and she asked, "Are you Joab?"

"I am," he answered.

She said, "Listen to what your servant has to say."

"I'm listening," he said.

¹⁸She continued, "Long ago they used to say, 'Get your answer at Abel,' and that settled it. ¹⁹We are the peaceful and faithful in Israel. You are trying to destroy a city that is a mother in Israel. Why do you want to swallow up the LORD's inheritance?"

²⁰"Far be it from me!" Joab replied, "Far be it from me to swallow up or destroy! ²¹That is not the case. A man named Sheba son of Bicri, from the hill country of Ephraim, has lifted up his hand against the king, against David. Hand over this one man, and I'll withdraw from the city."

The woman said to Joab, "His head will be thrown to you from the wall."

²²Then the woman went to all the people with her wise advice, and they cut off the head of Sheba son of Bicri and threw it to Joab. So he sounded the trumpet, and his men dispersed from the city, each returning to his home. And Joab went back to the king in Jerusalem.

²³Joab was over Israel's entire army; Benaiah son of Jehoiada was over the Kerethites and Pelethites; ²⁴Adoniram[b] was in charge of forced labor; Jehoshaphat son of Ahilud was recorder; ²⁵Sheva was secretary; Zadok and Abiathar were priests; ²⁶and Ira the Jairite was David's priest.

The Gibeonites Avenged

21 During the reign of David, there was a famine for three successive years; so David sought the face of the LORD. The LORD said, "It is on account of Saul and his bloodstained house; it is because he put the Gibeonites to death."

²The king summoned the Gibeonites and spoke to them. (Now the Gibeonites were not a part of Israel but were survivors of the Amorites; the Israelites had sworn to spare them, but Saul in his zeal for Israel and Judah had

---

*a*14 Or *Abel, even Beth Maacah*; also in verse 15   *b*24 Some Septuagint manuscripts (see also 1 Kings 4:6 and 5:14); Hebrew *Adoram* tried to annihilate them.) ³David asked the Gibeonites, "What shall I do for you? How shall I make amends so that you will bless the LORD's inheritance?"

⁴The Gibeonites answered him, "We have no right to demand silver or gold from Saul or his family, nor do we have the right to put anyone in Israel to death."

"What do you want me to do for you?" David asked.

⁵They answered the king, "As for the man who destroyed us and plotted against us so that we have been decimated and have no place anywhere in Israel, ⁶let seven of his male descendants be given to us to be killed and exposed before the LORD at Gibeah of Saul—the LORD's chosen one."

So the king said, "I will give them to you."

⁷The king spared Mephibosheth son of Jonathan, the son of Saul, because of the oath before the LORD between David and Jonathan son of Saul. ⁸But the king took Armoni and Mephibosheth, the two sons of Aiah's daughter Rizpah, whom she had borne to Saul, together with the five sons of Saul's daughter Merab,ᵃ whom she had borne to Adriel son of Barzillai the Meholathite. ⁹He handed them over to the Gibeonites, who killed and exposed them on a hill before the LORD. All seven of them fell together; they were put to death during the first days of the harvest, just as the barley harvest was beginning.

¹⁰Rizpah daughter of Aiah took sackcloth and spread it out for herself on a rock. From the beginning of the harvest till the rain poured down from the heavens on the bodies, she did not let the birds of the air touch them by day or the wild animals by night. ¹¹When David was told what Aiah's daughter Rizpah, Saul's concubine, had done, ¹²he went and took the bones of Saul and his son Jonathan from the citizens of Jabesh Gilead. (They had taken them secretly from the public square at Beth Shan, where the Philistines had hung them after they struck Saul down on Gilboa.) ¹³David brought *the bones of Saul and his* son Jonathan from there, and the bones of those who had been killed and exposed were gathered up.

¹⁴They buried the bones of Saul and his son Jonathan in the tomb of Saul's father Kish, at Zela in Benjamin, and did everything the king commanded. After that, God answered prayer in behalf of the land.

Wars Against the Philistines

¹⁵Once again there was a battle between the Philistines and Israel. David went down with his men to fight against the Philistines, and he became exhausted. ¹⁶And Ishbi-Benob, one of the descendants of Rapha, whose bronze spearhead weighed three hundred shekelsᵇ and who was armed with a new ˌswordˌ said he would kill David. ¹⁷But Abishai son of Zeruiah came to David's rescue; he struck the Philistine down and killed him. Then David's men swore to him, saying, "Never again will you go out with us to battle, so that the lamp of Israel will not be extinguished."

¹⁸In the course of time, there was another battle with the Philistines, at Gob. At that time Sibbecai the Hushathite killed Saph, one of the descendants of Rapha.

¹⁹In another battle with the Philistines at Gob, Elhanan son of Jaare-Oregimᶜ the Bethlehemite killed Goliathᵈ the Gittite, who had a spear with a shaft like a weaver's rod.

²⁰In still another battle, which took place at Gath, there was a huge man with six fingers on each hand and six toes on each foot—twenty-four in all. He also was descended from Rapha. ²¹When he taunted Israel, Jonathan son of Shimeah, David's brother, killed him.

²²These four were descendants of Rapha in Gath, and they fell at the hands of David and his men.

David's Song of Praise

22 David sang to the LORD the words of this song when the LORD delivered him from the hand of all his enemies and from the hand of Saul. ²He said:

"The LORD is my rock, my fortress and my
      deliverer;
³   my God is my rock, in whom I take
      refuge,
      my shield and the hornᵉ of my salvation.

ᵃ8 Two Hebrew manuscripts, some Septuagint manuscripts and Syriac (see also 1 Samuel 18:19); most Hebrew and Septuagint manuscripts Michal   ᵇ16 That is, about 7 1/2 pounds (about 3.5 kilograms)   ᶜ19 Or son of Jair the weaver   ᵈ19 Hebrew and Septuagint; 1 Chron. 20:5 son of Jair killed Lahmi the brother of Goliath   ᵉ3 Horn here symbolizes strength.

Lifted Up

Read: 2 Samuel 22:1–51

GERALDINE SINGLETON FACED an unusual enemy. Her body waged war against her. She survived breast cancer and a mastectomy. Less than a decade later, the insidious disease returned as a brain tumor that spread to her bones. USA Today reports: "She has since weathered a car accident; a house fire; three 'mini strokes'; and hardest of all, the death of a brother and two sisters." Amazingly, Singleton doesn't feel downcast. She reports, "God has chosen to 'lift her up.' " Singleton now educates other cancer victims and has joined a choir of other breast cancer survivors who "sing through our storm."

You may not have experienced the same type of tempest as Geraldine Singleton, but life sends all kinds of storms: Financial struggles. Wayward children. The death of a loved one. Broken relationships. These events whip through our lives with gale force winds and leave us feeling shattered, powerless and adrift like victims of a mighty tempest.

Engulfed by the floods of life and surrounded by his enemies, David was in a vulnerable place. But he remained strong because he knew the One who could bring triumph out of tragedy and victory from defeat. David trusted his mighty Savior because their relationship rested on a rock-solid, centuries-old covenant that could not be swayed. Like a small child enveloped by his parents' love, David expected God to intervene. Based on what he knew of God's character and his covenant promise to his people, David expected redemption. His hopes were not in vain. God reached down and pulled David up from the depths.

The One who rescued David still waits for his people to call on him during whatever trials they face. The God who lifted David to new heights and gave him a song to sing wants to reach down from on high to lift your spirits and help you rise above your circumstances.

What can you do when the storm breaks? Where do you turn when your world seems to crumble around you? You're not in this alone! Follow David's lead and run to God, who wants to be your strong tower. Look to God to regenerate your strength. Just as David did, and as cancer survivors and survivors of other catastrophes do, cry out to the Lord for help. Then sing his praises when he reaches down to lift you up.

2 Samuel 22:17

"He reached down from on high and took hold of me; he drew me out of deep waters."

reflection

1 What storm are you currently weathering?

2 In what ways have you seen God lift you up in the past? Sing a song of praise to the Lord for his mighty works in the past, trusting that he will continue to work in the present.

3 What have you learned in the midst of your own storm to help lift up others?

RELATED READINGS

Psalms 18:1–50;
59:16–17;
Jonah 2:1–9

Go to page 398 for your next devotional reading.

He is my stronghold, my refuge and my
savior—
from violent men you save me.
⁴ I call to the LORD, who is worthy of praise,
and I am saved from my enemies.

⁵ "The waves of death swirled about me;
the torrents of destruction overwhelmed
me.
⁶ The cords of the grave*a* coiled around me;
the snares of death confronted me.
⁷ In my distress I called to the LORD;
I called out to my God.
From his temple he heard my voice;
my cry came to his ears.

⁸ "The earth trembled and quaked,
the foundations of the heavens*b* shook;
they trembled because he was angry.
⁹ Smoke rose from his nostrils;
consuming fire came from his mouth,
burning coals blazed out of it.
¹⁰ He parted the heavens and came down;
dark clouds were under his feet.
¹¹ He mounted the cherubim and flew;
he soared*c* on the wings of the wind.
¹² He made darkness his canopy around
him—
the dark*d* rain clouds of the sky.
¹³ Out of the brightness of his presence
bolts of lightning blazed forth.
¹⁴ The LORD thundered from heaven;
the voice of the Most High resounded.
¹⁵ He shot arrows and scattered the
enemies,
bolts of lightning and routed them.
¹⁶ The valleys of the sea were exposed
and the foundations of the earth laid
bare
at the rebuke of the LORD,
at the blast of breath from his nostrils.

¹⁷ "He reached down from on high and took
hold of me;
he drew me out of deep waters.
¹⁸ He rescued me from my powerful enemy,
from my foes, who were too strong for
me.

¹⁹ They confronted me in the day of my
disaster,
but the LORD was my support.
²⁰ He brought me out into a spacious place;
he rescued me because he delighted in me.

²¹ "The LORD has dealt with me according to
my righteousness;
according to the cleanness of my hands
he has rewarded me.
²² For I have kept the ways of the LORD;
I have not done evil by turning from my
God.
²³ All his laws are before me;
I have not turned away from his decrees.
²⁴ I have been blameless before him
and have kept myself from sin.
²⁵ The LORD has rewarded me according to
my righteousness,
according to my cleanness*e* in his sight.

²⁶ "To the faithful you show yourself faithful,
to the blameless you show yourself
blameless,
²⁷ to the pure you show yourself pure,
but to the crooked you show yourself
shrewd.
²⁸ You save the humble,
but your eyes are on the haughty to
bring them low.
²⁹ You are my lamp, O LORD;
the LORD turns my darkness into light.
³⁰ With your help I can advance against a
troop*f*;
with my God I can scale a wall.

³¹ "As for God, his way is perfect;
the word of the LORD is flawless.
He is a shield
for all who take refuge in him.
³² For who is God besides the LORD?
And who is the Rock except our God?
³³ It is God who arms me with strength*g*
and makes my way perfect.
³⁴ He makes my feet like the feet of a deer;
he enables me to stand on the heights.
³⁵ He trains my hands for battle;
my arms can bend a bow of bronze.

---

*a*6 Hebrew *Sheol* *b*8 Hebrew; Vulgate and Syriac (see also Psalm 18:7) *mountains* *c*11 Many Hebrew manuscripts (see also Psalm 18:10); most Hebrew manuscripts *appeared* *d*12 Septuagint and Vulgate (see also Psalm 18:11); Hebrew *massed* *e*25 Hebrew; Septuagint and Vulgate (see also Psalm 18:24) *to the cleanness of my hands* *f*30 Or *can run through a barricade* *g*33 Dead Sea Scrolls, some Septuagint manuscripts, Vulgate and Syriac (see also Psalm 18:32); Masoretic Text *who is my strong refuge*

³⁶You give me your shield of victory;
  you stoop down to make me great.
³⁷You broaden the path beneath me,
  so that my ankles do not turn.

³⁸"I pursued my enemies and crushed them;
  I did not turn back till they were
    destroyed.
³⁹I crushed them completely, and they could
    not rise;
  they fell beneath my feet.
⁴⁰You armed me with strength for battle;
  you made my adversaries bow at my feet.
⁴¹You made my enemies turn their backs in
    flight,
  and I destroyed my foes.
⁴²They cried for help, but there was no one to
    save them—
  to the LORD, but he did
    not answer.
⁴³I beat them as fine as the
    dust of the earth;
  I pounded and trampled
    them like mud in
    the streets.

⁴⁴"You have delivered me
    from the attacks of
    my people;
  you have preserved me as
    the head of nations.
  People I did not know are
    subject to me,
⁴⁵ and foreigners come cringing to me;
  as soon as they hear me, they obey me.
⁴⁶They all lose heart;
  they come trembling*a* from their
    strongholds.

⁴⁷"The LORD lives! Praise be to my Rock!
  Exalted be God, the Rock, my Savior!
⁴⁸He is the God who avenges me,
  who puts the nations under me,
⁴⁹ who sets me free from my enemies.
  You exalted me above my foes;
  from violent men you rescued me.
⁵⁰Therefore I will praise you, O LORD,
    among the nations;
  I will sing praises to your name.

⁵¹He gives his king great victories;
  he shows unfailing kindness to his
    anointed,
  to David and his descendants forever."

The Last Words of David

23 These are the last words of David:

"The oracle of David son of Jesse,
  the oracle of the man exalted by the
    Most High,
  the man anointed by the God of Jacob,
  Israel's singer of songs*b*:

²"The Spirit of the LORD spoke through me;
  his word was on my tongue.
³The God of Israel spoke,
    the Rock of Israel said
      to me:
  'When one rules over men
      in righteousness,
    when he rules in the fear
      of God,
⁴he is like the light of
      morning at sunrise
    on a cloudless morning,
    like the brightness after
      rain
    that brings the grass
      from the earth.'

⁵"Is not my house right with
      God?
  Has he not made with me an everlasting
    covenant,
  arranged and secured in every part?
  Will he not bring to fruition my salvation
    and grant me my every desire?
⁶But evil men are all to be cast aside like
    thorns,
  which are not gathered with the hand.
⁷Whoever touches thorns
  uses a tool of iron or the shaft of a spear;
  they are burned up where they lie."

David's Mighty Men

⁸These are the names of David's mighty
men:

Josheb-Basshebeth,*c* a Tahkemonite,*d* was

---

2 Samuel 23:4

God Is Light

"He is like the light of
morning at sunrise
on a cloudless morning,
like the brightness
after rain
that brings the grass
from the earth."

---

*a46 Some Septuagint manuscripts and Vulgate (see also Psalm 18:45); Masoretic Text *they arm themselves.*   *b1 Or *Israel's beloved singer*
*c8 Hebrew; some Septuagint manuscripts suggest *Ish-Bosheth,* that is, *Esh-Baal* (see also 1 Chron. 11:11 *Jashobeam*).   *d8 Probably a variant of *Hacmonite* (see 1 Chron. 11:11)

chief of the Three; he raised his spear against eight hundred men, whom he killed*a* in one encounter.

⁹Next to him was Eleazar son of Dodai the Ahohite. As one of the three mighty men, he was with David when they taunted the Philistines gathered at Pas Dammim,*b* for battle. Then the men of Israel retreated, ¹⁰but he stood his ground and struck down the Philistines till his hand grew tired and froze to the sword. The LORD brought about a great victory that day. The troops returned to Eleazar, but only to strip the dead.

¹¹Next to him was Shammah son of Agee the Hararite. When the Philistines banded together at a place where there was a field full of lentils, Israel's troops fled from them. ¹²But Shammah took his stand in the middle of the field. He defended it and struck the Philistines down, and the LORD brought about a great victory.

¹³During harvest time, three of the thirty chief men came down to David at the cave of Adullam, while a band of Philistines was encamped in the Valley of Rephaim. ¹⁴At that time David was in the stronghold, and the Philistine garrison was at Bethlehem. ¹⁵David longed for water and said, "Oh, that someone would get me a drink of water from the well near the gate of Bethlehem!" ¹⁶So the three mighty men broke through the Philistine lines, drew water from the well near the gate of Bethlehem and carried it back to David. But he refused to drink it; instead, he poured it out before the LORD. ¹⁷"Far be it from me, O LORD, to do this!" he said. "Is it not the blood of men who went at the risk of their lives?" And David would not drink it.

Such were the exploits of the three mighty men.

¹⁸Abishai the brother of Joab son of Zeruiah was chief of the Three.*c* He raised his spear against three hundred men, whom he killed, and so he became as famous as the Three. ¹⁹Was he not held in greater honor than the Three? He became their commander, even though he was not included among them.

²⁰Benaiah son of Jehoiada was a valiant fighter from Kabzeel, who performed great exploits. He struck down two of Moab's best men. He also went down into a pit on a snowy day and killed a lion. ²¹And he struck down a huge Egyptian. Although the Egyptian had a spear in his hand, Benaiah went against him with a club. He snatched the spear from the Egyptian's hand and killed him with his own spear. ²²Such were the exploits of Benaiah son of Jehoiada; he too was as famous as the three mighty men. ²³He was held in greater honor than any of the Thirty, but he was not included among the Three. And David put him in charge of his bodyguard.

²⁴ Among the Thirty were:

Asahel the brother of Joab,
Elhanan son of Dodo from Bethlehem,
²⁵ Shammah the Harodite,
Elika the Harodite,
²⁶ Helez the Paltite,
Ira son of Ikkesh from Tekoa,
²⁷ Abiezer from Anathoth,
Mebunnai*d* the Hushathite,
²⁸ Zalmon the Ahohite,
Maharai the Netophathite,
²⁹ Heled*e* son of Baanah the Netophathite,
Ithai son of Ribai from Gibeah in Benjamin,
³⁰ Benaiah the Pirathonite,
Hiddai*f* from the ravines of Gaash,
³¹ Abi-Albon the Arbathite,
Azmaveth the Barhumite,
³² Eliahba the Shaalbonite,
the sons of Jashen,
Jonathan ³³son of*g* Shammah the Hararite,
Ahiam son of Sharar*h* the Hararite,
³⁴ Eliphelet son of Ahasbai the Maacathite,
Eliam son of Ahithophel the Gilonite,
³⁵ Hezro the Carmelite,

---

*a*8 Some Septuagint manuscripts (see also 1 Chron. 11:11); Hebrew and other Septuagint manuscripts *Three; it was Adino the Eznite who killed eight hundred men*   *b*9 See 1 Chron. 11:13; Hebrew *gathered there.*   *c*18 Most Hebrew manuscripts (see also 1 Chron. 11:20); two Hebrew manuscripts and Syriac *Thirty*   *d*27 Hebrew; some Septuagint manuscripts (see also 1 Chron. 11:29) *Sibbecai*   *e*29 Some Hebrew manuscripts and Vulgate (see also 1 Chron. 11:30); most Hebrew manuscripts *Heleb*   *f*30 Hebrew; some Septuagint manuscripts (see also 1 Chron. 11:32) *Hurai*   *g*33 Some Septuagint manuscripts (see also 1 Chron. 11:34); Hebrew does not have *son of.*   *h*33 Hebrew; some Septuagint manuscripts (see also 1 Chron. 11:35) *Sacar*

Paarai the Arbite,
36 Igal son of Nathan from Zobah,
the son of Hagri,[a]
37 Zelek the Ammonite,
Naharai the Beerothite, the armor-bearer of Joab son of Zeruiah,
38 Ira the Ithrite,
Gareb the Ithrite
39 and Uriah the Hittite.
There were thirty-seven in all.

David Counts the Fighting Men

24 Again the anger of the LORD burned against Israel, and he incited David against them, saying, "Go and take a census of Israel and Judah."

2 So the king said to Joab and the army commanders[b] with him, "Go throughout the tribes of Israel from Dan to Beersheba and enroll the fighting men, so that I may know how many there are."

3 But Joab replied to the king, "May the LORD your God multiply the troops a hundred times over, and may the eyes of my lord the king see it. But why does my lord the king want to do such a thing?"

4 The king's word, however, overruled Joab and the army commanders; so they left the presence of the king to enroll the fighting men of Israel.

5 After crossing the Jordan, they camped near Aroer, south of the town in the gorge, and then went through Gad and on to Jazer. 6 They went to Gilead and the region of Tahtim Hodshi, and on to Dan Jaan and around toward Sidon. 7 Then they went toward the fortress of Tyre and all the towns of the Hivites and Canaanites. Finally, they went on to Beersheba in the Negev of Judah.

8 After they had gone through the entire land, they came back to Jerusalem at the end of nine months and twenty days.

9 Joab reported the number of the fighting men to the king: In Israel there were eight hundred thousand able-bodied men who could handle a sword, and in Judah five hundred thousand.

10 David was conscience-stricken after he had counted the fighting men, and he said to the LORD, "I have sinned greatly in what I have done. Now, O LORD, I beg you, take away the guilt of your servant. I have done a very foolish thing."

11 Before David got up the next morning, the word of the LORD had come to Gad the prophet, David's seer: 12 "Go and tell David, 'This is what the LORD says: I am giving you three options. Choose one of them for me to carry out against you.'"

13 So Gad went to David and said to him, "Shall there come upon you three[c] years of famine in your land? Or three months of fleeing from your enemies while they pursue you? Or three days of plague in your land? Now then, think it over and decide how I should answer the one who sent me."

14 David said to Gad, "I am in deep distress. Let us fall into the hands of the LORD, for his mercy is great; but do not let me fall into the hands of men."

15 So the LORD sent a plague on Israel from that morning until the end of the time designated, and seventy thousand of the people from Dan to Beersheba died. 16 When the angel stretched out his hand to destroy Jerusalem, the LORD was grieved because of the calamity and said to the angel who was afflicting the people, "Enough! Withdraw your hand." The angel of the LORD was then at the threshing floor of Araunah the Jebusite.

17 When David saw the angel who was striking down the people, he said to the LORD, "I am the one who has sinned and done wrong. These are but sheep. What have they done? Let your hand fall upon me and my family."

David Builds an Altar

18 On that day Gad went to David and said to him, "Go up and build an altar to the LORD on the threshing floor of Araunah the Jebusite." 19 So David went up, as the LORD had commanded through Gad. 20 When Araunah looked and saw the king and his men coming toward him, he went out and bowed down before the king with his face to the ground.

21 Araunah said, "Why has my lord the king come to his servant?"

"To buy your threshing floor," David

---

a36 Some Septuagint manuscripts (see also 1 Chron. 11:38); Hebrew *Haggadi*   b2 Septuagint (see also verse 4 and 1 Chron. 21:2); Hebrew *Joab the army commander*   c13 Septuagint (see also 1 Chron. 21:12); Hebrew *seven*

The Other Side of Decision

JAEL

Sisera, however, fled on foot to the tent of Jael, the wife of Heber the Kenite.

Judges 4:17

JAEL HAD HEARD THE RUMORS. There was talk about her husband, Heber. People said that he was the one who had most likely betrayed the Israelites to the commander of the Canaanite army, Sisera. Although they were Kenites, loyal descendants of Moses' brother-in-law, Jael knew more than most that one could never tell where Heber's loyalty lay. "He has a mind of his own," Jael had reminded herself many times when she didn't understand her husband's decisions.

She remembered the time Heber decided to take the family and split off from the rest of his tribespeople—the Kenites (who supported Israel)—in favor of a home closer to Kedesh. He had come home one day all excited, saying something about a gigantic tree he'd seen near Zaanannim that would make a great tent site. The next thing she knew, Jael was pacing the property line of her new home, nailing pegs in the ground and pitching the tent.

Jael, like many in her clan, had never had an occasion for testing her own decision-making abilities. They were nomads, and nomads were generally "go with the flow" folk who preferred to stay out of controversy. Taking a stand leads to putting down roots, which means making a decision. She remembered the times her leather-skinned grandmother had taken her face in her wrinkled hands and touted the family philosophy: "When times get tough, the tough get going." Somewhere. Anywhere. Wherever the problems couldn't follow you.

ASSIGNED READING:

Judges 4:11—5:31

So, when the opportunity came to cast a decisive vote in favor of Israel, an unexpected chance to go her own way, Jael faced a dilemma on several fronts. On the other side of her decision lay a number of unanswerable questions. Her husband had made his intentions rather clear—and they were *not* pro-Israel. How would he react if she killed Israel's greatest enemy? Her tribespeople—all of the influential people in her life—had exemplified passivity to an extreme. Would she be remembered as a hero? A traitor? As a crazy, peg-wielding warrior?

She took a deep breath and made her decision. Later, whenever Deborah's song was sung in her presence, she always smiled and looked away in embarrassment at the lyrics, "Most blessed of women be Jael . . ."

---Prayer---

Jesus, give me the courage and resolution to stay true to what I know is right!

Weekend

Go to page 405 for your next devotional reading.

answered, "so I can build an altar to the LORD, that the plague on the people may be stopped."

²²Araunah said to David, "Let my lord the king take whatever pleases him and offer it up. Here are oxen for the burnt offering, and here are threshing sledges and ox yokes for the wood. ²³O king, Araunah gives all this to the king." Araunah also said to him, "May the LORD your God accept you."

2 Samuel 24:25

God Answers Prayer

Then the LORD answered prayer in behalf of the land, and the plague on Israel was stopped.

²⁴But the king replied to Araunah, "No, I insist on paying you for it. I will not sacrifice to the LORD my God burnt offerings that cost me nothing."

So David bought the threshing floor and the oxen and paid fifty shekels[a] of silver for them. ²⁵David built an altar to the LORD there and sacrificed burnt offerings and fellowship offerings.[b] Then the LORD answered prayer in behalf of the land, and the plague on Israel was stopped.

---

[a]24 That is, about 1 1/4 pounds (about 0.6 kilogram)   [b]25 Traditionally *peace offerings*

1 Kings

Author:
Unknown.

Audience:
The people of Israel.

Date:
Originally, 1 and 2 Kings were one book, probably written during the Israelites' Babylonian exile, sometime between 560 and 550 B.C.

Setting:
David's faithful rule is the model for Israel's future kings.

Verse to Remember:
"May he turn our hearts to him, to walk in all his ways and to keep the commands, decrees and regulations he gave our fathers." (8:58)

The record of Israel's kings reads not as a "who's who," but rather as a *"who did and who didn't."* The measure of these men who led God's people, first as one nation and then as a divided kingdom, is based on one thing only: whether or not they did what was right in the eyes of the Lord. *Their lives set the standard* for the nation, and when they set the bar high, the people rose to it. But more often than not, they set a low standard, and the people stooped to it.

When the standard seemed to be at its lowest, *an intriguing man stepped onto the scene.* Elijah traveled the sin-soaked land with a message condemning idolatry and the miracles to back it up. He had a stubborn audience, but *he found open hearts* in unlikely places. In the worst of times, there will always be those who seek to do what is right in the eyes of the Lord, and those are the very people whom God still seeks today.

Adonijah Sets Himself Up as King

1 When King David was old and well advanced in years, he could not keep warm even when they put covers over him. ²So his servants said to him, "Let us look for a young virgin to attend the king and take care of him. She can lie beside him so that our lord the king may keep warm."

³Then they searched throughout Israel for a beautiful girl and found Abishag, a Shunammite, and brought her to the king. ⁴The girl was very beautiful; she took care of the king and waited on him, but the king had no intimate relations with her.

⁵Now Adonijah, whose mother was Haggith, put himself forward and said, "I will be king." So he got chariots and horses*a* ready, with fifty men to run ahead of him. ⁶(His fa-

*a*5 Or *charioteers*

ther had never interfered with him by asking, "Why do you behave as you do?" He was also very handsome and was born next after Absalom.)

7 Adonijah conferred with Joab son of Zeruiah and with Abiathar the priest, and they gave him their support. 8 But Zadok the priest, Benaiah son of Jehoiada, Nathan the prophet, Shimei and Rei*a* and David's special guard did not join Adonijah.

9 Adonijah then sacrificed sheep, cattle and fattened calves at the Stone of Zoheleth near En Rogel. He invited all his brothers, the king's sons, and all the men of Judah who were royal officials, 10 but he did not invite Nathan the prophet or Benaiah or the special guard or his brother Solomon.

11 Then Nathan asked Bathsheba, Solomon's mother, "Have you not heard that Adonijah, the son of Haggith, has become king without our lord David's knowing it? 12 Now then, let me advise you how you can save your own life and the life of your son Solomon. 13 Go in to King David and say to him, 'My lord the king, did you not swear to me your servant: "Surely Solomon your son shall be king after me, and he will sit on my throne"? Why then has Adonijah become king?' 14 While you are still there talking to the king, I will come in and confirm what you have said."

15 So Bathsheba went to see the aged king in his room, where Abishag the Shunammite was attending him. 16 Bathsheba bowed low and knelt before the king.

"What is it you want?" the king asked.

17 She said to him, "My lord, you yourself swore to me your servant by the LORD your God: 'Solomon your son shall be king after me, and he will sit on my throne.' 18 But now Adonijah has become king, and you, my lord the king, do not know about it. 19 He has sacrificed great numbers of cattle, fattened calves, and sheep, and has invited all the king's sons, Abiathar the priest and Joab the commander of the army, but he has not invited Solomon your servant. 20 My lord the king, the eyes of all Israel are on you, to learn from you who will sit on the throne of my lord the king after him. 21 Otherwise, as soon as my lord the king is laid

to rest with his fathers, I and my son Solomon will be treated as criminals."

22 While she was still speaking with the king, Nathan the prophet arrived. 23 And they told the king, "Nathan the prophet is here." So he went before the king and bowed with his face to the ground.

24 Nathan said, "Have you, my lord the king, declared that Adonijah shall be king after you, and that he will sit on your throne? 25 Today he has gone down and sacrificed great numbers of cattle, fattened calves, and sheep. He has invited all the king's sons, the commanders of the army and Abiathar the priest. Right now they are eating and drinking with him and saying, 'Long live King Adonijah!' 26 But me your servant, and Zadok the priest, and Benaiah son of Jehoiada, and your servant Solomon he did not invite. 27 Is this something my lord the king has done without letting his servants know who should sit on the throne of my lord the king after him?"

David Makes Solomon King

28 Then King David said, "Call in Bathsheba." So she came into the king's presence and stood before him.

29 The king then took an oath: "As surely as the LORD lives, who has delivered me out of every trouble, 30 I will surely carry out today what I swore to you by the LORD, the God of Israel: Solomon your son shall be king after me, and he will sit on my throne in my place."

31 Then Bathsheba bowed low with her face to the ground and, kneeling before the king, said, "May my lord King David live forever!"

32 King David said, "Call in Zadok the priest, Nathan the prophet and Benaiah son of Jehoiada." When they came before the king, 33 he said to them: "Take your lord's servants with you and set Solomon my son on my own mule and take him down to Gihon. 34 There have Zadok the priest and Nathan the prophet anoint him king over Israel. Blow the trumpet and shout, 'Long live King Solomon!' 35 Then you are to go up with him, and he is to come and sit on my throne and reign in my place. I have appointed him ruler over Israel and Judah."

a8 Or and his friends

³⁶Benaiah son of Jehoiada answered the king, "Amen! May the LORD, the God of my lord the king, so declare it. ³⁷As the LORD was with my lord the king, so may he be with Solomon to make his throne even greater than the throne of my lord King David!"

³⁸So Zadok the priest, Nathan the prophet, Benaiah son of Jehoiada, the Kerethites and the Pelethites went down and put Solomon on King David's mule and escorted him to Gihon. ³⁹Zadok the priest took the horn of oil from the sacred tent and anointed Solomon. Then they sounded the trumpet and all the people shouted, "Long live King Solomon!" ⁴⁰And all the people went up after him, playing flutes and rejoicing greatly, so that the ground shook with the sound.

⁴¹Adonijah and all the guests who were with him heard it as they were finishing their feast. On hearing the sound of the trumpet, Joab asked, "What's the meaning of all the noise in the city?"

⁴²Even as he was speaking, Jonathan son of Abiathar the priest arrived. Adonijah said, "Come in. A worthy man like you must be bringing good news."

⁴³"Not at all!" Jonathan answered. "Our lord King David has made Solomon king. ⁴⁴The king has sent with him Zadok the priest, Nathan the prophet, Benaiah son of Jehoiada, the Kerethites and the Pelethites, and they have put him on the king's mule, ⁴⁵and Zadok the priest and Nathan the prophet have anointed him king at Gihon. From there they have gone up cheering, and the city resounds with it. That's the noise you hear. ⁴⁶Moreover, Solomon has taken his seat on the royal throne. ⁴⁷Also, the royal officials have come to congratulate our lord King David, saying, 'May your God make Solomon's name more famous than yours and his throne greater than yours!' And the king bowed in worship on his bed ⁴⁸and said, 'Praise be to the LORD, the God of Israel, who

has allowed my eyes to see a successor on my throne today.'"

⁴⁹At this, all Adonijah's guests rose in alarm and dispersed. ⁵⁰But Adonijah, in fear of Solomon, went and took hold of the horns of the altar. ⁵¹Then Solomon was told, "Adonijah is afraid of King Solomon and is clinging to the horns of the altar. He says, 'Let King Solomon swear to me today that he will not put his servant to death with the sword.'"

⁵²Solomon replied, "If he shows himself to be a worthy man, not a hair of his head will fall to the ground; but if evil is found in him, he will die." ⁵³Then King Solomon sent men, and they brought him down from the altar. And Adonijah came and bowed down to King Solomon, and Solomon said, "Go to your home."

1 Kings 1:37

God Establishes Rulers

"As the LORD was with my lord the king, so may he be with Solomon to make his throne even greater than the throne of my lord King David!"

David's Charge to Solomon

2 When the time drew near for David to die, he gave a charge to Solomon his son.

²"I am about to go the way of all the earth," he said. "So be strong, show yourself a man, ³and observe what the LORD your God requires: Walk in his ways, and keep his decrees and commands, his laws and requirements, as written in the Law of Moses, so that you may prosper in all you do and wherever you go, ⁴and that the LORD may keep his promise to me: 'If your descendants watch how they live, and if they walk faithfully before me with all their heart and soul, you will never fail to have a man on the throne of Israel.'

⁵"Now you yourself know what Joab son of Zeruiah did to me—what he did to the two commanders of Israel's armies, Abner son of Ner and Amasa son of Jether. He killed them, shedding their blood in peacetime as if in battle, and with that blood stained the belt around his waist and the sandals on his feet. ⁶Deal with him according to your wisdom, but do not let his gray head go down to the grave*ᵃ* in peace.

⁷"But show kindness to the sons of Barzillai of Gilead and let them be among those who

---

ᵃ6 Hebrew Sheol; *also in verse 9*

eat at your table. They stood by me when I fled from your brother Absalom.

⁸"And remember, you have with you Shimei son of Gera, the Benjamite from Bahurim, who called down bitter curses on me the day I went to Mahanaim. When he came down to meet me at the Jordan, I swore to him by the LORD: 'I will not put you to death by the sword.' ⁹But now, do not consider him innocent. You are a man of wisdom; you will know what to do to him. Bring his gray head down to the grave in blood."

¹⁰Then David rested with his fathers and was buried in the City of David. ¹¹He had reigned forty years over Israel—seven years in Hebron and thirty-three in Jerusalem. ¹²So Solomon sat on the throne of his father David, and his rule was firmly established.

Solomon's Throne Established

¹³Now Adonijah, the son of Haggith, went to Bathsheba, Solomon's mother. Bathsheba asked him, "Do you come peacefully?"

He answered, "Yes, peacefully." ¹⁴Then he added, "I have something to say to you."

"You may say it," she replied.

¹⁵"As you know," he said, "the kingdom was mine. All Israel looked to me as their king. But things changed, and the kingdom has gone to my brother; for it has come to him from the LORD. ¹⁶Now I have one request to make of you. Do not refuse me."

"You may make it," she said.

¹⁷So he continued, "Please ask King Solomon—he will not refuse you—to give me Abishag the Shunammite as my wife."

¹⁸"Very well," Bathsheba replied, "I will speak to the king for you."

¹⁹When Bathsheba went to King Solomon to speak to him for Adonijah, the king stood up to meet her, bowed down to her and sat down on his throne. He had a throne brought for the king's mother, and she sat down at his right hand.

²⁰"I have one small request to make of you," she said. "Do not refuse me."

The king replied, "Make it, my mother; I will not refuse you."

²¹So she said, "Let Abishag the Shunammite be given in marriage to your brother Adonijah."

²²King Solomon answered his mother, "Why do you request Abishag the Shunammite for Adonijah? You might as well request the kingdom for him—after all, he is my older brother—yes, for him and for Abiathar the priest and Joab son of Zeruiah!"

²³Then King Solomon swore by the LORD: "May God deal with me, be it ever so severely, if Adonijah does not pay with his life for this request! ²⁴And now, as surely as the LORD lives—he who has established me securely on the throne of my father David and has founded a dynasty for me as he promised—Adonijah shall be put to death today!" ²⁵So King Solomon gave orders to Benaiah son of Jehoiada, and he struck down Adonijah and he died.

²⁶To Abiathar the priest the king said, "Go back to your fields in Anathoth. You deserve to die, but I will not put you to death now, because you carried the ark of the Sovereign LORD before my father David and shared all my father's hardships." ²⁷So Solomon removed Abiathar from the priesthood of the LORD, fulfilling the word the LORD had spoken at Shiloh about the house of Eli.

²⁸When the news reached Joab, who had conspired with Adonijah though not with Absalom, he fled to the tent of the LORD and took hold of the horns of the altar. ²⁹King Solomon was told that Joab had fled to the tent of the LORD and was beside the altar. Then Solomon ordered Benaiah son of Jehoiada, "Go, strike him down!"

³⁰So Benaiah entered the tent of the LORD and said to Joab, "The king says, 'Come out!'"

But he answered, "No, I will die here."

---

1 Kings 2:3

God Blesses Obedience

"And observe what the LORD your God requires: Walk in his ways, and keep his decrees and commands, his laws and requirements, as written in the Law of Moses, so that you may prosper in all you do and wherever you go."

Benaiah reported to the king, "This is how Joab answered me."

³¹Then the king commanded Benaiah, "Do as he says. Strike him down and bury him, and so clear me and my father's house of the guilt of the innocent blood that Joab shed. ³²The LORD will repay him for the blood he shed, because without the knowledge of my father David he attacked two men and killed them with the sword. Both of them—Abner son of Ner, commander of Israel's army, and Amasa son of Jether, commander of Judah's army—were better men and more upright than he. ³³May the guilt of their blood rest on the head of Joab and his descendants forever. But on David and his descendants, his house and his throne, may there be the LORD's peace forever."

³⁴So Benaiah son of Jehoiada went up and struck down Joab and killed him, and he was buried on his own land[a] in the desert. ³⁵The king put Benaiah son of Jehoiada over the army in Joab's position and replaced Abiathar with Zadok the priest.

³⁶Then the king sent for Shimei and said to him, "Build yourself a house in Jerusalem and live there, but do not go anywhere else. ³⁷The day you leave and cross the Kidron Valley, you can be sure you will die; your blood will be on your own head."

³⁸Shimei answered the king, "What you say is good. Your servant will do as my lord the king has said." And Shimei stayed in Jerusalem for a long time.

³⁹But three years later, two of Shimei's slaves ran off to Achish son of Maacah, king of Gath, and Shimei was told, "Your slaves are in Gath." ⁴⁰At this, he saddled his donkey and went to Achish at Gath in search of his slaves. So Shimei went away and brought the slaves back from Gath.

⁴¹When Solomon was told that Shimei had gone from Jerusalem to Gath and had returned, ⁴²the king summoned Shimei and said to him, "Did I not make you swear by the LORD and warn you, 'On the day you leave to go anywhere else, you can be sure you will die'? At that time you said to me, 'What you say is good. I will obey.' ⁴³Why then did you not keep your oath to the LORD and obey the command I gave you?"

⁴⁴The king also said to Shimei, "You know in your heart all the wrong you did to my father David. Now the LORD will repay you for your wrongdoing. ⁴⁵But King Solomon will be blessed, and David's throne will remain secure before the LORD forever."

⁴⁶Then the king gave the order to Benaiah son of Jehoiada, and he went out and struck Shimei down and killed him.

The kingdom was now firmly established in Solomon's hands.

Solomon Asks for Wisdom

3 Solomon made an alliance with Pharaoh king of Egypt and married his daughter. He brought her to the City of David until he finished building his palace and the temple of the LORD, and the wall around Jerusalem. ²The people, however, were still sacrificing at the high places, because a temple had not yet been built for the Name of the LORD. ³Solomon showed his love for the LORD by walking according to the statutes of his father David, except that he offered sacrifices and burned incense on the high places.

⁴The king went to Gibeon to offer sacrifices, for that was the most important high place, and Solomon offered a thousand burnt offerings on that altar. ⁵At Gibeon the LORD appeared to Solomon during the night in a dream, and God said, "Ask for whatever you want me to give you."

⁶Solomon answered, "You have shown great kindness to your servant, my father David, because he was faithful to you and righteous and upright in heart. You have continued this great kindness to him and have given him a son to sit on his throne this very day.

⁷"Now, O LORD my God, you have made your servant king in place of my father David. But I am only a little child and do not know how to carry out my duties. ⁸Your servant is here among the people you have chosen, a great people, too numerous to count or number. ⁹So give your servant a discerning heart to govern your people and to distinguish between right and wrong. For who is able to govern this great people of yours?"

¹⁰The Lord was pleased that Solomon had

---

[a]34 Or *buried in his tomb*

Worship and Wisdom

Read: 1 Kings 3:4–15

DARK CLOUDS SLIP between the guardian mountain peaks and scurry across the empty skies above Death Valley in California. Heat waves tremble over the parched earth as cloud shadows nibble at the eroded badlands and salt pans. Thunder rumbles in the distance. By late afternoon, the rain-gorged sky swings low. Suddenly the heavens burst! Fat raindrops jump like marbles on the hard-packed earth. Gradually the thirsty brown clods drink in water, softening to soak in more. A curtain of silver rain hangs between the churning sky and muddy valley floor. In a few weeks, Death Valley will explode to life in an astonishing feast of wildflowers.

Upon ascending to the throne, young Solomon traveled ten miles northwest to the hills of Gibeon to offer an extravagant sacrifice—a thousand burnt offerings. This was the same place where the sun stood still for Joshua and where twelve of David's strong men defeated twelve of Saul's men (see Joshua 10:1–14; 2 Samuel 2:12–17). In the middle of the night, God burst through to Solomon in a dream. Solomon could have requested anything in all the earth. Through time spent in worship, Solomon realized that wisdom was the greatest of all God's gifts.

Worship is like the rains that prepare the earth for God's blessings. The story of the youthful Solomon preparing to take the throne is a beautiful reminder to us of the importance of worship. The story of God granting him the gift of wisdom opens with a swell of costly and reverent worship. For us, too, worship creates a context for us to encounter God; it sets our souls in motion in an upward spiral by which we pursue God, and he gladly responds.

Worship book-ended the exchange between the Sovereign God and the new sovereign of Israel. Solomon returned from his heavenly encounter and again made an offering to the God of Israel in Jerusalem before the ark of the covenant.

Like a gathering cloud, worship encircles and protects God's people. It softens the soil of our hearts like nourishing rain. When we've been in a dark place and long for colorful beauty to replace the hardness that has settled into our scorched souls, simple acts of worship can prepare the way for God's words of wisdom to permeate our hearts. If your life seems parched, won't you allow God to paint a palette of colorful joy by spending time worshiping your Lord?

Go to page 412 for your next devotional reading.

1 Kings 3:5,15

At Gibeon the LORD appeared to Solomon during the night in a dream, and God said, "Ask for whatever you want me to give you." . . . He returned to Jerusalem, stood before the ark of the Lord's covenant and sacrificed burnt offerings and fellowship offerings.

reflection

1 Why is worship so important to God?

2 What kinds of extravagant (or at least consistent) worship characterize your life?

3 If God offered you anything you wish, what would you ask for? Has it changed having read this passage?

RELATED READINGS

Psalms 29; 100;
Proverbs 3:13–24;
Isaiah 55:10–12

405

asked for this. **11**So God said to him, "Since you have asked for this and not for long life or wealth for yourself, nor have asked for the death of your enemies but for discernment in administering justice, **12**I will do what you have asked. I will give you a wise and discerning heart, so that there will never have been anyone like you, nor will there ever be. **13**Moreover, I will give you what you have not asked for—both riches and honor—so that in your lifetime you will have no equal among kings. **14**And if you walk in my ways and obey my statutes and commands as David your father did, I will give you a long life." **15**Then Solomon awoke—and he realized it had been a dream.

He returned to Jerusalem, stood before the ark of the Lord's covenant and sacrificed burnt offerings and fellowship offerings.*a* Then he gave a feast for all his court.

A Wise Ruling

16Now two prostitutes came to the king and stood before him. **17**One of them said, "My lord, this woman and I live in the same house. I had a baby while she was there with me. **18**The third day after my child was born, this woman also had a baby. We were alone; there was no one in the house but the two of us.

19"During the night this woman's son died because she lay on him. **20**So she got up in the middle of the night and took my son from my side while I your servant was asleep. She put him by her breast and put her dead son by my breast. **21**The next morning, I got up to nurse my son—and he was dead! But when I looked at him closely in the morning light, I saw that it wasn't the son I had borne."

22The other woman said, "No! The living one is my son; the dead one is yours."

But the first one insisted, "No! The dead one is yours; the living one is mine." And so they argued before the king.

23The king said, "This one says, 'My son is alive and your son is dead,' while that one says, 'No! Your son is dead and mine is alive.'"

24Then the king said, "Bring me a sword." So they brought a sword for the king. **25**He then gave an order: "Cut the living child in two and give half to one and half to the other."

26The woman whose son was alive was filled with compassion for her son and said to the king, "Please, my lord, give her the living baby! Don't kill him!"

But the other said, "Neither I nor you shall have him. Cut him in two!"

27Then the king gave his ruling: "Give the living baby to the first woman. Do not kill him; she is his mother."

28When all Israel heard the verdict the king had given, they held the king in awe, because they saw that he had wisdom from God to administer justice.

Solomon's Officials and Governors

4 So King Solomon ruled over all Israel. **2**And these were his chief officials:

Azariah son of Zadok—the priest;
3 Elihoreph and Ahijah, sons of Shisha—secretaries;
Jehoshaphat son of Ahilud—recorder;
4 Benaiah son of Jehoiada—commander in chief;
Zadok and Abiathar—priests;
5 Azariah son of Nathan—in charge of the district officers;
Zabud son of Nathan—a priest and personal adviser to the king;
6 Ahishar—in charge of the palace;
Adoniram son of Abda—in charge of forced labor.

7Solomon also had twelve district governors over all Israel, who supplied provisions for the king and the royal household. Each one had to provide supplies for one month in the year. **8**These are their names:

Ben-Hur—in the hill country of Ephraim;
9 Ben-Deker—in Makaz, Shaalbim, Beth Shemesh and Elon Bethhanan;
10 Ben-Hesed—in Arubboth (Socoh and all the land of Hepher were his);
11 Ben-Abinadab—in Naphoth Dor*b* (he was married to Taphath daughter of Solomon);
12 Baana son of Ahilud—in Taanach and Megiddo, and in all of Beth Shan next to Zarethan below Jezreel, from Beth Shan to Abel Meholah across to Jokmeam;

---

*a*15 Traditionally *peace offerings*   *b*11 Or *in the heights of Dor*

¹³ Ben-Geber—in Ramoth Gilead (the settlements of Jair son of Manasseh in Gilead were his, as well as the district of Argob in Bashan and its sixty large walled cities with bronze gate bars);

¹⁴ Ahinadab son of Iddo—in Mahanaim;

¹⁵ Ahimaaz—in Naphtali (he had married Basemath daughter of Solomon);

¹⁶ Baana son of Hushai—in Asher and in Aloth;

¹⁷ Jehoshaphat son of Paruah—in Issachar;

¹⁸ Shimei son of Ela—in Benjamin;

¹⁹ Geber son of Uri—in Gilead (the country of Sihon king of the Amorites and the country of Og king of Bashan). He was the only governor over the district.

Solomon's Daily Provisions

²⁰ The people of Judah and Israel were as numerous as the sand on the seashore; they ate, they drank and they were happy. ²¹ And Solomon ruled over all the kingdoms from the River^a to the land of the Philistines, as far as the border of Egypt. These countries brought tribute and were Solomon's subjects all his life.

²² Solomon's daily provisions were thirty cors^b of fine flour and sixty cors^c of meal, ²³ ten head of stall-fed cattle, twenty of pasture-fed cattle and a hundred sheep and goats, as well as deer, gazelles, roebucks and choice fowl. ²⁴ For he ruled over all the kingdoms west of the River, from Tiphsah to Gaza, and had peace on all sides. ²⁵ During Solomon's lifetime Judah and Israel, from Dan to Beersheba, lived in safety, each man under his own vine and fig tree.

²⁶ Solomon had four^d thousand stalls for chariot horses, and twelve thousand horses.^e

²⁷ The district officers, each in his month, supplied provisions for King Solomon and all who came to the king's table. They saw to it that nothing was lacking. ²⁸ They also brought to the proper place their quotas of barley and straw for the chariot horses and the other horses.

Solomon's Wisdom

²⁹ God gave Solomon wisdom and very great insight, and a breadth of understanding as measureless as the sand on the seashore. ³⁰ Solomon's wisdom was greater than the wisdom of all the men of the East, and greater than all the wisdom of Egypt. ³¹ He was wiser than any other man, including Ethan the Ezrahite—wiser than Heman, Calcol and Darda, the sons of Mahol. And his fame spread to all the surrounding nations. ³² He spoke three thousand proverbs and his songs numbered a thousand and five. ³³ He described plant life, from the cedar of Lebanon to the hyssop that grows out of walls. He also taught about animals and birds, reptiles and fish. ³⁴ Men of all nations came to listen to Solomon's wisdom, sent by all the kings of the world, who had heard of his wisdom.

---

1 Kings 4:29

God Gives Wisdom

God gave Solomon wisdom and very great insight, and a breadth of understanding as measureless as the sand on the seashore.

Preparations for Building the Temple

5 When Hiram king of Tyre heard that Solomon had been anointed king to succeed his father David, he sent his envoys to Solomon, because he had always been on friendly terms with David. ² Solomon sent back this message to Hiram:

> ³ "You know that because of the wars waged against my father David from all sides, he could not build a temple for the Name of the LORD his God until the LORD put his enemies under his feet. ⁴ But now the LORD my God has given me rest on every side, and there is no adversary or disaster. ⁵ I intend, therefore, to build a temple for the Name of the LORD my God, as the LORD told my father David, when he said, 'Your son whom I will put on the throne in your place will build the temple for my Name.'
>
> ⁶ "So give orders that cedars of Lebanon be cut for me. My men will work with yours, and I will pay you for your men

---

^a21 That is, the Euphrates; also in verse 24   ^b22 That is, probably about 185 bushels (about 6.6 kiloliters)   ^c22 That is, probably about 375 bushels (about 13.2 kiloliters)   ^d26 Some Septuagint manuscripts (see also 2 Chron. 9:25); Hebrew *forty*   ^e26 Or *charioteers* whatever wages you set. You know that we have no one so skilled in felling timber as the Sidonians."

⁷When Hiram heard Solomon's message, he was greatly pleased and said, "Praise be to the LORD today, for he has given David a wise son to rule over this great nation."

⁸So Hiram sent word to Solomon:

"I have received the message you sent me and will do all you want in providing the cedar and pine logs. ⁹My men will haul them down from Lebanon to the sea, and I will float them in rafts by sea to the place you specify. There I will separate them and you can take them away. And you are to grant my wish by providing food for my royal household."

¹⁰In this way Hiram kept Solomon supplied with all the cedar and pine logs he wanted, ¹¹and Solomon gave Hiram twenty thousand cors*a* of wheat as food for his household, in addition to twenty thousand baths*b,c* of pressed olive oil. Solomon continued to do this for Hiram year after year. ¹²The LORD gave Solomon wisdom, just as he had promised him. There were peaceful relations between Hiram and Solomon, and the two of them made a treaty.

¹³King Solomon conscripted laborers from all Israel—thirty thousand men. ¹⁴He sent them off to Lebanon in shifts of ten thousand a month, so that they spent one month in Lebanon and two months at home. Adoniram was in charge of the forced labor. ¹⁵Solomon had seventy thousand carriers and eighty thousand stonecutters in the hills, ¹⁶as well as thirty-three hundred*d* foremen who supervised the project and directed the workmen. ¹⁷At the king's command they removed from the quarry large blocks of quality stone to provide a foundation of dressed stone for the temple. ¹⁸The craftsmen of Solomon and Hiram and the men of Gebal*e* cut and prepared the timber and stone for the building of the temple.

Solomon Builds the Temple

6 In the four hundred and eightieth*f* year after the Israelites had come out of Egypt, in the fourth year of Solomon's reign over Israel, in the month of Ziv, the second month, he began to build the temple of the LORD.

²The temple that King Solomon built for the LORD was sixty cubits long, twenty wide and thirty high.*g* ³The portico at the front of the main hall of the temple extended the width of the temple, that is twenty cubits,*h* and projected ten cubits*i* from the front of the temple. ⁴He made narrow clerestory windows in the temple. ⁵Against the walls of the main hall and inner sanctuary he built a structure around the building, in which there were side rooms. ⁶The lowest floor was five cubits*j* wide, the middle floor six cubits*k* and the third floor seven.*l* He made offset ledges around the outside of the temple so that nothing would be inserted into the temple walls.

⁷In building the temple, only blocks dressed at the quarry were used, and no hammer, chisel or any other iron tool was heard at the temple site while it was being built.

⁸The entrance to the lowest*m* floor was on the south side of the temple; a stairway led up to the middle level and from there to the third. ⁹So he built the temple and completed it, roofing it with beams and cedar planks. ¹⁰And he built the side rooms all along the temple. The height of each was five cubits, and they were attached to the temple by beams of cedar.

¹¹The word of the LORD came to Solomon: ¹²"As for this temple you are building, if you follow my decrees, carry out my regulations and keep all my commands and obey them, I will fulfill through you the promise I gave to David your father. ¹³And I will live among the Israelites and will not abandon my people Israel."

¹⁴So Solomon built the temple and completed it. ¹⁵He lined its interior walls with cedar boards, paneling them from the floor of the temple to the ceiling, and covered the floor of the temple with planks of pine. ¹⁶He parti-

*a*11 That is, probably about 125,000 bushels (about 4,400 kiloliters)   *b*11 Septuagint (see also 2 Chron. 2:10); Hebrew *twenty cors*
*c*11 That is, about 115,000 gallons (about 440 kiloliters)   *d*16 Hebrew; some Septuagint manuscripts (see also 2 Chron. 2:2,18) *thirty-six hundred*   *e*18 That is, Byblos   *f*1 Hebrew; Septuagint *four hundred and fortieth*   *g*2 That is, about 90 feet (about 27 meters) long and 30 feet (about 9 meters) wide and 45 feet (about 13.5 meters) high   *h*3 That is, about 30 feet (about 9 meters)   *i*3 That is, about 15 feet (about 4.5 meters)   *j*6 That is, about 7 1/2 feet (about 2.3 meters); also in verses 10 and 24   *k*6 That is, about 9 feet (about 2.7 meters)
*l*6 That is, about 10 1/2 feet (about 3.1 meters)   *m*8 Septuagint; Hebrew *middle*

tioned off twenty cubits[a] at the rear of the temple with cedar boards from floor to ceiling to form within the temple an inner sanctuary, the Most Holy Place. [17]The main hall in front of this room was forty cubits[b] long. [18]The inside of the temple was cedar, carved with gourds and open flowers. Everything was cedar; no stone was to be seen.

[19]He prepared the inner sanctuary within the temple to set the ark of the covenant of the LORD there. [20]The inner sanctuary was twenty cubits long, twenty wide and twenty high.[c] He overlaid the inside with pure gold, and he also overlaid the altar of cedar. [21]Solomon covered the inside of the temple with pure gold, and he extended gold chains across the front of the inner sanctuary, which was overlaid with gold. [22]So he overlaid the whole interior with gold. He also overlaid with gold the altar that belonged to the inner sanctuary.

[23]In the inner sanctuary he made a pair of cherubim of olive wood, each ten cubits[d] high. [24]One wing of the first cherub was five cubits long, and the other wing five cubits—ten cubits from wing tip to wing tip. [25]The second cherub also measured ten cubits, for the two cherubim were identical in size and shape. [26]The height of each cherub was ten cubits. [27]He placed the cherubim inside the innermost room of the temple, with their wings spread out. The wing of one cherub touched one wall, while the wing of the other touched the other wall, and their wings touched each other in the middle of the room. [28]He overlaid the cherubim with gold.

[29]On the walls all around the temple, in both the inner and outer rooms, he carved cherubim, palm trees and open flowers. [30]He also covered the floors of both the inner and outer rooms of the temple with gold.

[31]For the entrance of the inner sanctuary he made doors of olive wood with five-sided jambs. [32]And on the two olive wood doors he carved cherubim, palm trees and open flowers, and overlaid the cherubim and palm trees with beaten gold. [33]In the same way he made four-sided jambs of olive wood for the entrance to the main hall. [34]He also made two pine doors, each having two leaves that turned in sockets. [35]He carved cherubim, palm trees and open flowers on them and overlaid them with gold hammered evenly over the carvings.

[36]And he built the inner courtyard of three courses of dressed stone and one course of trimmed cedar beams.

[37]The foundation of the temple of the LORD was laid in the fourth year, in the month of Ziv. [38]In the eleventh year in the month of Bul, the eighth month, the temple was finished in all its details according to its specifications. He had spent seven years building it.

1 Kings 6:13

God Refuses to Abandon Us

"And I will live among the Israelites and will not abandon my people Israel."

Solomon Builds His Palace

7 It took Solomon thirteen years, however, to complete the construction of his palace. [2]He built the Palace of the Forest of Lebanon a hundred cubits long, fifty wide and thirty high,[e] with four rows of cedar columns supporting trimmed cedar beams. [3]It was roofed with cedar above the beams that rested on the columns—forty-five beams, fifteen to a row. [4]Its windows were placed high in sets of three, facing each other. [5]All the doorways had rectangular frames; they were in the front part in sets of three, facing each other.[f]

[6]He made a colonnade fifty cubits long and thirty wide.[g] In front of it was a portico, and in front of that were pillars and an overhanging roof.

[7]He built the throne hall, the Hall of Justice, where he was to judge, and he covered it with cedar from floor to ceiling.[h] [8]And the palace in which he was to live, set farther back, was similar in design. Solomon also made a palace like this hall for Pharaoh's daughter, whom he had married.

---

[a]16 That is, about 30 feet (about 9 meters) [b]17 That is, about 60 feet (about 18 meters) [c]20 That is, about 30 feet (about 9 meters) long, wide and high [d]23 That is, about 15 feet (about 4.5 meters) [e]2 That is, about 150 feet (about 46 meters) long, 75 feet (about 23 meters) wide and 45 feet (about 13.5 meters) high [f]5 The meaning of the Hebrew for this verse is uncertain. [g]6 That is, about 75 feet (about 23 meters) long and 45 feet (about 13.5 meters) wide [h]7 Vulgate and Syriac; Hebrew *floor*

9All these structures, from the outside to the great courtyard and from foundation to eaves, were made of blocks of high-grade stone cut to size and trimmed with a saw on their inner and outer faces. 10The foundations were laid with large stones of good quality, some measuring ten cubits*a* and some eight.*b* 11Above were high-grade stones, cut to size, and cedar beams. 12The great courtyard was surrounded by a wall of three courses of dressed stone and one course of trimmed cedar beams, as was the inner courtyard of the temple of the LORD with its portico.

The Temple's Furnishings

13King Solomon sent to Tyre and brought Huram,*c* 14whose mother was a widow from the tribe of Naphtali and whose father was a man of Tyre and a craftsman in bronze. Huram was highly skilled and experienced in all kinds of bronze work. He came to King Solomon and did all the work assigned to him.

15He cast two bronze pillars, each eighteen cubits high and twelve cubits around,*d* by line. 16He also made two capitals of cast bronze to set on the tops of the pillars; each capital was five cubits*e* high. 17A network of interwoven chains festooned the capitals on top of the pillars, seven for each capital. 18He made pomegranates in two rows*f* encircling each network to decorate the capitals on top of the pillars.*g* He did the same for each capital. 19The capitals on top of the pillars in the portico were in the shape of lilies, four cubits*h* high. 20On the capitals of both pillars, above the bowl-shaped part next to the network, were the two hundred pomegranates in rows all around. 21He erected the pillars at the portico of the temple. The pillar to the south he named Jakin*i* and the one to the north Boaz.*j* 22The capitals on top were in the shape of lilies. And so the work on the pillars was completed.

23He made the Sea of cast metal, circular in shape, measuring ten cubits*a* from rim to rim and five cubits high. It took a line of thirty cubits*k* to measure around it. 24Below the rim, gourds encircled it—ten to a cubit. The gourds were cast in two rows in one piece with the Sea.

25The Sea stood on twelve bulls, three facing north, three facing west, three facing south and three facing east. The Sea rested on top of them, and their hindquarters were toward the center. 26It was a handbreadth*l* in thickness, and its rim was like the rim of a cup, like a lily blossom. It held two thousand baths.*m*

27He also made ten movable stands of bronze; each was four cubits long, four wide and three high.*n* 28This is how the stands were made: They had side panels attached to uprights. 29On the panels between the uprights were lions, bulls and cherubim—and on the uprights as well. Above and below the lions and bulls were wreaths of hammered work. 30Each stand had four bronze wheels with bronze axles, and each had a basin resting on four supports, cast with wreaths on each side. 31On the inside of the stand there was an opening that had a circular frame one cubit*o* deep. This opening was round, and with its basework it measured a cubit and a half.*p* Around its opening there was engraving. The panels of the stands were square, not round. 32The four wheels were under the panels, and the axles of the wheels were attached to the stand. The diameter of each wheel was a cubit and a half. 33The wheels were made like chariot wheels; the axles, rims, spokes and hubs were all of cast metal.

34Each stand had four handles, one on each corner, projecting from the stand. 35At the top of the stand there was a circular band half a cubit*q* deep. The supports and panels were attached to the top of the stand. 36He engraved cherubim, lions and palm trees on the surfaces of the supports and on the panels, in every available space, with wreaths all around. 37This is the way he made the ten stands. They were all

---

a10,23 That is, about 15 feet (about 4.5 meters)   *b10* That is, about 12 feet (about 3.6 meters)   *c13* Hebrew *Hiram,* a variant of *Huram;* also in verses 40 and 45   *d15* That is, about 27 feet (about 8.1 meters) high and 18 feet (about 5.4 meters) around   *e16* That is, about 7 1/2 feet (about 2.3 meters); also in verse 23   *f18* Two Hebrew manuscripts and Septuagint; most Hebrew manuscripts *made the pillars, and there were two rows*   *g18* Many Hebrew manuscripts and Syriac; most Hebrew manuscripts *pomegranates*   *h19* That is, about 6 feet (about 1.8 meters); also in verse 38   *i21* *Jakin* probably means *he establishes.*   *j21* *Boaz* probably means *in him is strength.*   *k23* That is, about 45 feet (about 13.5 meters)   *l26* That is, about 3 inches (about 8 centimeters)   *m26* That is, probably about 11,500 gallons (about 44 kiloliters); the Septuagint does not have this sentence.   *n27* That is, about 6 feet (about 1.8 meters) long and wide and about 4 1/2 feet (about 1.3 meters) high   *o31* That is, about 1 1/2 feet (about 0.5 meter)   *p31* That is, about 2 1/4 feet (about 0.7 meter); also in verse 32   *q35* That is, about 3/4 foot (about 0.2 meter) cast in the same molds and were identical in size and shape.

38 He then made ten bronze basins, each holding forty baths[a] and measuring four cubits across, one basin to go on each of the ten stands. **39** He placed five of the stands on the south side of the temple and five on the north. He placed the Sea on the south side, at the southeast corner of the temple. He also made the basins and shovels and sprinkling bowls.

So Huram finished all the work he had undertaken for King Solomon in the temple of the Lord:

41 the two pillars;

the two bowl-shaped capitals on top of the pillars;

the two sets of network decorating the two bowl-shaped capitals on top of the pillars;

42 the four hundred pomegranates for the two sets of network (two rows of pomegranates for each network, decorating the bowl-shaped capitals on top of the pillars);

43 the ten stands with their ten basins;

44 the Sea and the twelve bulls under it;

45 the pots, shovels and sprinkling bowls.

All these objects that Huram made for King Solomon for the temple of the Lord were of burnished bronze. **46** The king had them cast in clay molds in the plain of the Jordan between Succoth and Zarethan. **47** Solomon left all these things unweighed, because there were so many; the weight of the bronze was not determined.

48 Solomon also made all the furnishings that were in the Lord's temple:

the golden altar;

the golden table on which was the bread of the Presence;

49 the lampstands of pure gold (five on the right and five on the left, in front of the inner sanctuary);

the gold floral work and lamps and tongs;

50 the pure gold basins, wick trimmers, sprinkling bowls, dishes and censers;

and the gold sockets for the doors of the

innermost room, the Most Holy Place, and also for the doors of the main hall of the temple.

51 When all the work King Solomon had done for the temple of the Lord was finished, he brought in the things his father David had dedicated—the silver and gold and the furnishings—and he placed them in the treasuries of the Lord's temple.

The Ark Brought to the Temple

8 Then King Solomon summoned into his presence at Jerusalem the elders of Israel, all the heads of the tribes and the chiefs of the Israelite families, to bring up the ark of the Lord's covenant from Zion, the City of David. **2** All the men of Israel came together to King Solomon at the time of the festival in the month of Ethanim, the seventh month.

3 When all the elders of Israel had arrived, the priests took up the ark, **4** and they brought up the ark of the Lord and the Tent of Meeting and all the sacred furnishings in it. The priests and Levites carried them up, **5** and King Solomon and the entire assembly of Israel that had gathered about him were before the ark, sacrificing so many sheep and cattle that they could not be recorded or counted.

6 The priests then brought the ark of the Lord's covenant to its place in the inner sanctuary of the temple, the Most Holy Place, and put it beneath the wings of the cherubim. **7** The cherubim spread their wings over the place of the ark and overshadowed the ark and its carrying poles. **8** These poles were so long that their ends could be seen from the Holy Place in front of the inner sanctuary, but not from outside the Holy Place; and they are still there today. **9** There was nothing in the ark except the two stone tablets that Moses had placed in it at Horeb, where the Lord made a covenant with the Israelites after they came out of Egypt.

10 When the priests withdrew from the Holy Place, the cloud filled the temple of the Lord. **11** And the priests could not perform their service because of the cloud, for the glory of the Lord filled his temple.

12 Then Solomon said, "The Lord has said that he would dwell in a dark cloud; **13** I have

a **38** That is, about 230 gallons (about 880 liters)

1 Kings 8:57–58

"May the LORD our God be with us as he was with our fathers; may he never leave us nor forsake us. May he turn our hearts to him, to walk in all his ways and to keep the commands, decrees and regulations he gave our fathers."

reflection

1 What does it mean to you to know that God dwells in you?

2 What is your reaction to the quote by J. Oswald Sanders? How intimate with God do you choose to be? What price would you pay to be closer to God?

3 When was the last time you were in awe of God or felt overwhelmed by his presence?

RELATED READINGS

Ezekiel 11:16–20;
Romans 6:12–14;
Ephesians 4:30;
Hebrews 8:8–12

"God is above, presiding; beneath, sustaining; within, filling."

Hildebert of Lavardin

Fit for His Dwelling

Read: 1 Kings 8:1–66

THE GRANDEUR OF OUR CITIES, the comforts of our homes, the conveniences of modern life saturate our consciousness. Unlike the Israelites, most of us do not lead a nomadic life, worshiping God in a tent designed for transience, by nature impermanent. We take for granted that the Holy Spirit now calls us the temple in which he resides. But consider what the temple meant to a people who longed for a lasting dwelling place for their God, a place of beauty where his presence would rest. Imagine the excitement when Solomon's magnificent temple was finally complete. As God's Spirit entered the completed sanctuary, it's likely that a reverential awe fell over the crowd.

Thousands of years have passed since that unforgettable day, and Solomon's temple is gone. But God continues to reside among us. He lives among us through his Holy Spirit and in each of us within the temple of our bodies. The God who could not be contained by the heavens has chosen his followers as the vessel of his presence.

But if God lives in us, why does it sometimes seem like he's far away? Solomon's prayer and blessing provide the answer: We lose our sense of God when our lives are not completely oriented to him. Verse 61 states: "But your hearts must be fully committed to the LORD." J. Oswald Sanders notes: "We are at this moment as close to God as we really choose to be. True, there are times when we would like to know a deeper intimacy, but when it comes to the point, we are not prepared to pay the price involved."

Solomon also recognized that we can't *force* God to dwell within us. The good things we do are never enough. In the end we are completely dependent upon God to make us fit for his dwelling, but if we invite him in, he will live with us. Jesus promised us this Spirit of truth, this Counselor, "If you love me, you will obey what I command. And I will ask the Father, and he will give you another Counselor to be with you forever—the Spirit of truth" (John 14:15–17). And Paul tells us that if the Spirit dwells in us, we will bear its harvest: "The fruit of the Spirit is love, joy, peace, patience, kindness, goodness, faithfulness, gentleness and self-control" (Galatians 5:22–23).

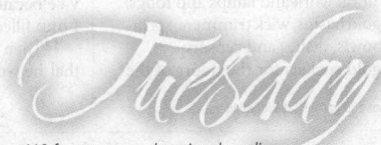

Tuesday

Go to page 418 for your next devotional reading.

indeed built a magnificent temple for you, a place for you to dwell forever."

¹⁴While the whole assembly of Israel was standing there, the king turned around and blessed them. ¹⁵Then he said:

"Praise be to the LORD, the God of Israel, who with his own hand has fulfilled what he promised with his own mouth to my father David. For he said, ¹⁶'Since the day I brought my people Israel out of Egypt, I have not chosen a city in any tribe of Israel to have a temple built for my Name to be there, but I have chosen David to rule my people Israel.'

¹⁷"My father David had it in his heart to build a temple for the Name of the LORD, the God of Israel. ¹⁸But the LORD said to my father David, 'Because it was in your heart to build a temple for my Name, you did well to have this in your heart. ¹⁹Nevertheless, you are not the one to build the temple, but your son, who is your own flesh and blood—he is the one who will build the temple for my Name.'

²⁰"The LORD has kept the promise he made: I have succeeded David my father and now I sit on the throne of Israel, just as the LORD promised, and I have built the temple for the Name of the LORD, the God of Israel. ²¹I have provided a place there for the ark, in which is the covenant of the LORD that he made with our fathers when he brought them out of Egypt."

Solomon's Prayer of Dedication

²²Then Solomon stood before the altar of the LORD in front of the whole assembly of Israel, spread out his hands toward heaven ²³and said:

"O LORD, God of Israel, there is no God like you in heaven above or on earth below—you who keep your covenant of love with your servants who continue wholeheartedly in your way. ²⁴You have kept your promise to your servant David my father; with your mouth you have promised—and with your hand you have fulfilled it—as it is today.

²⁵"Now LORD, God of Israel, keep for your servant David my father the promises you made to him when you said, 'You shall never fail to have a man to sit before me on the throne of Israel, if only your sons are careful in all they do to walk before me as you have done.' ²⁶And now, O God of Israel, let your word that you promised your servant David my father come true.

²⁷"But will God really dwell on earth? The heavens, even the highest heaven, cannot contain you. How much less this temple I have built! ²⁸Yet give attention to your servant's prayer and his plea for mercy, O LORD my God. Hear the cry and the prayer that your servant is praying in your presence this day. ²⁹May your eyes be open toward this temple night and day, this place of which you said, 'My Name shall be there,' so that you will hear the prayer your servant prays toward this place. ³⁰Hear the supplication of your servant and of your people Israel when they pray toward this place. Hear from heaven, your dwelling place, and when you hear, forgive.

³¹"When a man wrongs his neighbor and is required to take an oath and he comes and swears the oath before your altar in this temple, ³²then hear from heaven and act. Judge between your servants, condemning the guilty and bringing down on his own head what he has done. Declare the innocent not guilty, and so establish his innocence.

³³"When your people Israel have been defeated by an enemy because they have sinned against you, and when they turn back to you and confess your name, praying and making supplication to you in this temple, ³⁴then hear from heaven and forgive the sin of your people Israel and bring them back to the land you gave to their fathers.

³⁵"When the heavens are shut up and there is no rain because your people have sinned against you, and when they pray toward this place and confess your name and turn from their sin because you have afflicted them, ³⁶then hear from heaven and forgive the sin of your servants, your

people Israel. Teach them the right way to live, and send rain on the land you gave your people for an inheritance.

37"When famine or plague comes to the land, or blight or mildew, locusts or grasshoppers, or when an enemy besieges them in any of their cities, whatever disaster or disease may come, 38and when a prayer or plea is made by any of your people Israel—each one aware of the afflictions of his own heart, and spreading out his hands toward this temple— 39then hear from heaven, your dwelling place. Forgive and act; deal with each man according to all he does, since you know his heart (for you alone know the hearts of all men), 40so that they will fear you all the time they live in the land you gave our fathers.

41"As for the foreigner who does not belong to your people Israel but has come from a distant land because of your name— 42for men will hear of your great name and your mighty hand and your outstretched arm—when he comes and prays toward this temple, 43then hear from heaven, your dwelling place, and do whatever the foreigner asks of you, so that all the peoples of the earth may know your name and fear you, as do your own people Israel, and may know that this house I have built bears your Name.

44"When your people go to war against their enemies, wherever you send them, and when they pray to the LORD toward the city you have chosen and the temple I have built for your Name, 45then hear from heaven their prayer and their plea, and uphold their cause.

46"When they sin against you—for there is no one who does not sin—and you become angry with them and give them over to the enemy, who takes them captive to his own land, far away or near; 47and if they have a change

of heart in the land where they are held captive, and repent and plead with you in the land of their conquerors and say, 'We have sinned, we have done wrong, we have acted wickedly'; 48and if they turn back to you with all their heart and soul in the land of their enemies who took them captive, and pray to you toward the land you gave their fathers, toward the city you have chosen and the temple I have built for your Name; 49then from heaven, your dwelling place, hear their prayer and their plea, and uphold their cause. 50And forgive your people, who have sinned against you; forgive all the offenses they have committed against you, and cause their conquerors to show them mercy; 51for they are your people and your inheritance, whom you brought out of Egypt, out of that iron-smelting furnace.

52"May your eyes be open to your servant's plea and to the plea of your people Israel, and may you listen to them whenever they cry out to you. 53For you singled them out from all the nations of the world to be your own inheritance, just as you declared through your servant Moses when you, O Sovereign LORD, brought our fathers out of Egypt."

54When Solomon had finished all these prayers and supplications to the LORD, he rose from before the altar of the LORD, where he had been kneeling with his hands spread out toward heaven. 55He stood and blessed the whole assembly of Israel in a loud voice, saying:

56"Praise be to the LORD, who has given rest to his people Israel just as he promised. Not one word has failed of all the good promises he gave through his servant Mo-

1 Kings 8:56

God Gives Rest

"Praise be to the LORD, who has given rest to his people Israel just as he promised. Not one word has failed of all the good promises he gave through his servant Moses."

ses. 57May the LORD our God be with us as he was with our fathers; may he never leave us nor forsake us. 58May he turn our hearts to him, to walk in all his ways and to keep the commands, decrees and regulations he gave our fathers. ⁵⁹And may these words of mine, which I have prayed before the LORD, be near to the LORD our God day and night, that he may uphold the cause of his servant and the cause of his people Israel according to each day's need, ⁶⁰so that all the peoples of the earth may know that the LORD is God and that there is no other. ⁶¹But your hearts must be fully committed to the LORD our God, to live by his decrees and obey his commands, as at this time."

The Dedication of the Temple

⁶²Then the king and all Israel with him offered sacrifices before the LORD. ⁶³Solomon offered a sacrifice of fellowship offerings*a* to the LORD: twenty-two thousand cattle and a hundred and twenty thousand sheep and goats. So the king and all the Israelites dedicated the temple of the LORD.

⁶⁴On that same day the king consecrated the middle part of the courtyard in front of the temple of the LORD, and there he offered burnt offerings, grain offerings and the fat of the fellowship offerings, because the bronze altar before the LORD was too small to hold the burnt offerings, the grain offerings and the fat of the fellowship offerings.

⁶⁵So Solomon observed the festival at that time, and all Israel with him—a vast assembly, people from Lebo*b* Hamath to the Wadi of Egypt. They celebrated it before the LORD our God for seven days and seven days more, fourteen days in all. ⁶⁶On the following day he sent the people away. They blessed the king and then went home, joyful and glad in heart for all the good things the LORD had done for his servant David and his people Israel.

The LORD Appears to Solomon

9 When Solomon had finished building the temple of the LORD and the royal palace, and had achieved all he had desired to do, ²the LORD appeared to him a second time, as he had appeared to him at Gibeon. ³The LORD said to him:

"I have heard the prayer and plea you have made before me; I have consecrated this temple, which you have built, by putting my Name there forever. My eyes and my heart will always be there.

⁴"As for you, if you walk before me in integrity of heart and uprightness, as David your father did, and do all I command and observe my decrees and laws, ⁵I will establish your royal throne over Israel forever, as I promised David your father when I said, 'You shall never fail to have a man on the throne of Israel.'

⁶"But if you*c* or your sons turn away from me and do not observe the commands and decrees I have given you*c* and go off to serve other gods and worship them, ⁷then I will cut off Israel from the land I have given them and will reject this temple I have consecrated for my Name. Israel will then become a byword and an object of ridicule among all peoples. ⁸And though this temple is now imposing, all who pass by will be appalled and will scoff and say, 'Why has the LORD done such a thing to this land and to this temple?' ⁹People will answer, 'Because they have forsaken the LORD their God, who brought their fathers out of Egypt, and have embraced other gods, worshiping and serving them—that is why the LORD brought all this disaster on them.'"

Solomon's Other Activities

¹⁰At the end of twenty years, during which Solomon built these two buildings—the temple of the LORD and the royal palace— ¹¹King Solomon gave twenty towns in Galilee to Hiram king of Tyre, because Hiram had supplied him with all the cedar and pine and gold he wanted. ¹²But when Hiram went from Tyre to see the towns that Solomon had given him, he was not pleased with them. ¹³"What kind of towns are these you have given me, my brother?" he asked. And he called them the Land of Cabul,*d* a name they have to this day. ¹⁴Now Hiram had sent to the king 120 talents*e* of gold.

¹⁵Here is the account of the forced labor King Solomon conscripted to build the LORD's

---

a63 Traditionally *peace offerings*; also in verse 64   *b65* Or *from the entrance to*   *c6* The Hebrew is plural.   *d13* *Cabul* sounds like the Hebrew for *good-for-nothing*.   *e14* That is, about 4 1/2 tons (about 4 metric tons) temple, his own palace, the supporting terraces,[a] the wall of Jerusalem, and Hazor, Megiddo and Gezer. [16](Pharaoh king of Egypt had attacked and captured Gezer. He had set it on fire. He killed its Canaanite inhabitants and then gave it as a wedding gift to his daughter, Solomon's wife. [17]And Solomon rebuilt Gezer.) He built up Lower Beth Horon, [18]Baalath, and Tadmor[b] in the desert, within his land, [19]as well as all his store cities and the towns for his chariots and for his horses[c]—whatever he desired to build in Jerusalem, in Lebanon and throughout all the territory he ruled.

[20]All the people left from the Amorites, Hittites, Perizzites, Hivites and Jebusites (these peoples were not Israelites), [21]that is, their descendants remaining in the land, whom the Israelites could not exterminate[d]—these Solomon conscripted for his slave labor force, as it is to this day. [22]But Solomon did not make slaves of any of the Israelites; they were his fighting men, his government officials, his officers, his captains, and the commanders of his chariots and charioteers. [23]They were also the chief officials in charge of Solomon's projects—550 officials supervising the men who did the work.

[24]After Pharaoh's daughter had come up from the City of David to the palace Solomon had built for her, he constructed the supporting terraces.

[25]Three times a year Solomon sacrificed burnt offerings and fellowship offerings[e] on the altar he had built for the LORD, burning incense before the LORD along with them, and so fulfilled the temple obligations.

[26]King Solomon also built ships at Ezion Geber, which is near Elath in Edom, on the shore of the Red Sea.[f] [27]And Hiram sent his men—sailors who knew the sea—to serve in the fleet with Solomon's men. [28]They sailed to Ophir and brought back 420 talents[g] of gold, which they delivered to King Solomon.

The Queen of Sheba Visits Solomon

10 When the queen of Sheba heard about the fame of Solomon and his relation to the name of the LORD, she came to test him with hard questions. [2]Arriving at Jerusalem with a very great caravan—with camels carrying spices, large quantities of gold, and precious stones—she came to Solomon and talked with him about all that she had on her mind. [3]Solomon answered all her questions; nothing was too hard for the king to explain to her. [4]When the queen of Sheba saw all the wisdom of Solomon and the palace he had built, [5]the food on his table, the seating of his officials, the attending servants in their robes, his cupbearers, and the burnt offerings he made at[h] the temple of the LORD, she was overwhelmed.

[6]She said to the king, "The report I heard in my own country about your achievements and your wisdom is true. [7]But I did not believe these things until I came and saw with my own eyes. Indeed, not even half was told me; in wisdom and wealth you have far exceeded the report I heard. [8]How happy your men must be! How happy your officials, who continually stand before you and hear your wisdom! [9]Praise be to the LORD your God, who has delighted in you and placed you on the throne of Israel. Because of the LORD's eternal love for Israel, he has made you king, to maintain justice and righteousness."

[10]And she gave the king 120 talents[i] of gold, large quantities of spices, and precious stones. Never again were so many spices brought in as those the queen of Sheba gave to King Solomon.

[11](Hiram's ships brought gold from Ophir; and from there they brought great cargoes of almugwood[j] and precious stones. [12]The king used the almugwood to make supports for the temple of the LORD and for the royal palace, and to make harps and lyres for the musicians. So much almugwood has never been imported or seen since that day.)

[13]King Solomon gave the queen of Sheba all she desired and asked for, besides what he had given her out of his royal bounty. Then she left and returned with her retinue to her own country.

Solomon's Splendor

[14]The weight of the gold that Solomon received yearly was 666 talents,[k] [15]not including

---

[a]15 Or *the Millo*; also in verse 24 [b]18 The Hebrew may also be read *Tamar.* [c]19 Or *charioteers* [d]21 The Hebrew term refers to the irrevocable giving over of things or persons to the LORD, often by totally destroying them. [e]25 Traditionally *peace offerings* [f]26 Hebrew *Yam Suph*; that is, Sea of Reeds [g]28 That is, about 16 tons (about 14.5 metric tons) [h]5 Or *the ascent by which he went up to* [i]10 That is, about 4 1/2 tons (about 4 metric tons) [j]11 Probably a variant of *algumwood*; also in verse 12 [k]14 That is, about 25 tons (about 23 metric tons)

the revenues from merchants and traders and from all the Arabian kings and the governors of the land.

¹⁶King Solomon made two hundred large shields of hammered gold; six hundred bekas[a] of gold went into each shield. ¹⁷He also made three hundred small shields of hammered gold, with three minas[b] of gold in each shield. The king put them in the Palace of the Forest of Lebanon.

¹⁸Then the king made a great throne inlaid with ivory and overlaid with fine gold. ¹⁹The throne had six steps, and its back had a rounded top. On both sides of the seat were armrests, with a lion standing beside each of them. ²⁰Twelve lions stood on the six steps, one at either end of each step. Nothing like it had ever been made for any other kingdom. ²¹All King Solomon's goblets were gold, and all the household articles in the Palace of the Forest of Lebanon were pure gold. Nothing was made of silver, because silver was considered of little value in Solomon's days. ²²The king had a fleet of trading ships[c] at sea along with the ships of Hiram. Once every three years it returned, carrying gold, silver and ivory, and apes and baboons.

²³King Solomon was greater in riches and wisdom than all the other kings of the earth. ²⁴The whole world sought audience with Solomon to hear the wisdom God had put in his heart. ²⁵Year after year, everyone who came brought a gift—articles of silver and gold, robes, weapons and spices, and horses and mules.

²⁶Solomon accumulated chariots and horses; he had fourteen hundred chariots and twelve thousand horses,[d] which he kept in the chariot cities and also with him in Jerusalem. ²⁷The king made silver as common in Jerusalem as stones, and cedar as plentiful as sycamore-fig trees in the foothills. ²⁸Solomon's horses were imported from Egypt[e] and from Kue[f]—the royal merchants purchased them from Kue. ²⁹They imported a chariot from Egypt for six hundred shekels[g] of silver, and a horse for a hundred and fifty.[b] They also exported them to all the kings of the Hittites and of the Arameans.

Solomon's Wives

11 King Solomon, however, loved many foreign women besides Pharaoh's daughter—Moabites, Ammonites, Edomites, Sidonians and Hittites. ²They were from nations about which the LORD had told the Israelites, "You must not intermarry with them, because they will surely turn your hearts after their gods." Nevertheless, Solomon held fast to them in love. ³He had seven hundred wives of royal birth and three hundred concubines, and his wives led him astray. ⁴As Solomon grew old, his wives turned his heart after other gods, and his heart was not fully devoted to the LORD his God, as the heart of David his father had been. ⁵He followed Ashtoreth the goddess of the Sidonians, and Molech[h] the detestable god of the Ammonites. ⁶So Solomon did evil in the eyes of the LORD; he did not follow the LORD completely, as David his father had done.

⁷On a hill east of Jerusalem, Solomon built a high place for Chemosh the detestable god of Moab, and for Molech the detestable god of the Ammonites. ⁸He did the same for all his foreign wives, who burned incense and offered sacrifices to their gods.

⁹The LORD became angry with Solomon because his heart had turned away from the LORD, the God of Israel, who had appeared to him twice. ¹⁰Although he had forbidden Solomon to follow other gods, Solomon did not keep the LORD's command. ¹¹So the LORD said to Solomon, "Since this is your attitude and you have not kept my covenant and my decrees, which I commanded you, I will most certainly tear the kingdom away from you and give it to one of your subordinates. ¹²Nevertheless, for the sake of David your father, I will not do it during your lifetime. I will tear it out of the hand of your son. ¹³Yet I will not tear the whole kingdom from him, but will give him one tribe for the sake of David my servant and for the sake of Jerusalem, which I have chosen."

Solomon's Adversaries

¹⁴Then the LORD raised up against Solomon an adversary, Hadad the Edomite, from the royal line of Edom. ¹⁵Earlier when David was

---

*a*16 That is, about 7 1/2 pounds (about 3.5 kilograms) *b*17,29 That is, about 3 3/4 pounds (about 1.7 kilograms) *c*22 Hebrew *of ships of Tarshish* *d*26 Or *charioteers* *e*28 Or possibly *Muzur*, a region in Cilicia; also in verse 29 *f*28 Probably *Cilicia* *g*29 That is, about 15 pounds (about 7 kilograms) *h*5 Hebrew *Milcom*; also in verse 33

The Woman Who Had Everything

Read: 1 Kings 10:1–29

1 Kings 10:1

When the queen of Sheba heard about the fame of Solomon and his relation to the name of the LORD, she came to test him with hard questions.

reflection

1 List some of the "hard questions" you'd bring to the wisest man on earth.

2 As you've grown in your faith, have some of your hard questions or seeming contradictions grown less important to you? Why or why not?

3 Spend some time telling God all that you have on your mind. Then listen to what he has on his.

RELATED READINGS
Psalm 72:1–17;
Matthew 12:39–42

WHAT DO YOU ASK FOR if you are a queen? New jewels, a bigger palace or more servants? Maybe you look for wisdom. Here in 1 Kings 10 we meet the exotic queen of Sheba who had heard of King Solomon and the wisdom he possessed. So this woman, the ruler of a great empire in southern Arabia, ordered her servants to pack up her belongings and caravanned by camel to see the king. But she didn't come empty-handed. Like the Magi visiting Jesus, she came bearing gifts: spices, gold and precious stones. As a politician, she could have come to Solomon seeking a new trade route or asking for a peace treaty. But her purpose in making the long, grueling journey was clear: "She came to test him with hard questions" (1 Kings 10:1). The queen was on a spiritual quest, wanting to learn about Solomon's God. So she "talked with him about all that she had on her mind" (verse 2).

Do you have questions for God that you think he cannot or will not answer? Maybe you wonder about the origins of the universe. Perhaps you have questions about the apparent contradictions found in Scripture. It could be you have reservations about whether God even exists . . . or if you believe in his existence, you question whether he cares about the circumstances of your life.

Rest assured that God is not offended when you come to him with your candid questions. He knows that wisdom is more valuable than any treasure on earth. You don't need to be the queen of a nation or travel to a distant land to seek the answers to your heartfelt questions; you simply need to open the pages of God's Word and go to him in prayer. Solomon wrote, "Choose [God's] instruction instead of silver, knowledge rather than choice gold, for wisdom is more precious than rubies, and nothing you desire can compare with her" (Proverbs 8:10–11).

The woman who seemingly had everything the world had to offer knew she needed God's wisdom and went out of her way to obtain it. What lengths will you go to obtain the wisdom more valuable than jewels?

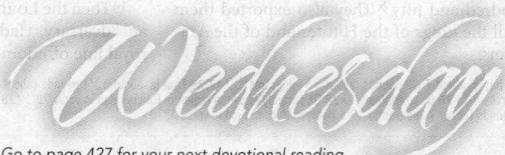

Wednesday

Go to page 427 for your next devotional reading.

fighting with Edom, Joab the commander of the army, who had gone up to bury the dead, had struck down all the men in Edom. [16]Joab and all the Israelites stayed there for six months, until they had destroyed all the men in Edom. [17]But Hadad, still only a boy, fled to Egypt with some Edomite officials who had served his father. [18]They set out from Midian and went to Paran. Then taking men from Paran with them, they went to Egypt, to Pharaoh king of Egypt, who gave Hadad a house and land and provided him with food.

[19]Pharaoh was so pleased with Hadad that he gave him a sister of his own wife, Queen Tahpenes, in marriage. [20]The sister of Tahpenes bore him a son named Genubath, whom Tahpenes brought up in the royal palace. There Genubath lived with Pharaoh's own children.

[21]While he was in Egypt, Hadad heard that David rested with his fathers and that Joab the commander of the army was also dead. Then Hadad said to Pharaoh, "Let me go, that I may return to my own country."

[22]"What have you lacked here that you want to go back to your own country?" Pharaoh asked.

"Nothing," Hadad replied, "but do let me go!"

[23]And God raised up against Solomon another adversary, Rezon son of Eliada, who had fled from his master, Hadadezer king of Zobah. [24]He gathered men around him and became the leader of a band of rebels when David destroyed the forces[a] of Zobah; the rebels went to Damascus, where they settled and took control. [25]Rezon was Israel's adversary as long as Solomon lived, adding to the trouble caused by Hadad. So Rezon ruled in Aram and was hostile toward Israel.

Jeroboam Rebels Against Solomon

[26]Also, Jeroboam son of Nebat rebelled against the king. He was one of Solomon's officials, an Ephraimite from Zeredah, and his mother was a widow named Zeruah.

[27]Here is the account of how he rebelled against the king: Solomon had built the supporting terraces[b] and had filled in the gap in the wall of the city of David his father. [28]Now Jeroboam was a man of standing, and when Solomon saw how well the young man did his work, he put him in charge of the whole labor force of the house of Joseph.

[29]About that time Jeroboam was going out of Jerusalem, and Ahijah the prophet of Shiloh met him on the way, wearing a new cloak. The two of them were alone out in the country, [30]and Ahijah took hold of the new cloak he was wearing and tore it into twelve pieces. [31]Then he said to Jeroboam, "Take ten pieces for yourself, for this is what the LORD, the God of Israel, says: 'See, I am going to tear the kingdom out of Solomon's hand and give you ten tribes. [32]But for the sake of my servant David and the city of Jerusalem, which I have chosen out of all the tribes of Israel, he will have one tribe. [33]I will do this because they have[c] forsaken me and worshiped Ashtoreth the goddess of the Sidonians, Chemosh the god of the Moabites, and Molech the god of the Ammonites, and have not walked in my ways, nor done what is right in my eyes, nor kept my statutes and laws as David, Solomon's father, did.

[34]"'But I will not take the whole kingdom out of Solomon's hand; I have made him ruler all the days of his life for the sake of David my servant, whom I chose and who observed my commands and statutes. [35]I will take the kingdom from his son's hands and give you ten tribes. [36]I will give one tribe to his son so that David my servant may always have a lamp before me in Jerusalem, the city where I chose to put my Name. [37]However, as for you, I will take you, and you will rule over all that your heart desires; you will be king over Israel. [38]If you do whatever I command you and walk in my ways and do what is right in my eyes by keeping my statutes and commands, as David my servant did, I will be with you. I will build you a dynasty as enduring as the one I built for David and will give Israel to you. [39]I will humble David's descendants because of this, but not forever.'"

[40]Solomon tried to kill Jeroboam, but Jeroboam fled to Egypt, to Shishak the king, and stayed there until Solomon's death.

Solomon's Death

[41]As for the other events of Solomon's reign—all he did and the wisdom he displayed—are they not written in the book of

---

*a*24 Hebrew *destroyed them*   *b*27 Or *the Millo*   *c*33 Hebrew; Septuagint, Vulgate and Syriac *because he has* the annals of Solomon? ⁴²Solomon reigned in Jerusalem over all Israel forty years. ⁴³Then he rested with his fathers and was buried in the city of David his father. And Rehoboam his son succeeded him as king.

Israel Rebels Against Rehoboam

12 Rehoboam went to Shechem, for all the Israelites had gone there to make him king. ²When Jeroboam son of Nebat heard this (he was still in Egypt, where he had fled from King Solomon), he returned from^a Egypt. ³So they sent for Jeroboam, and he and the whole assembly of Israel went to Rehoboam and said to him: ⁴"Your father put a heavy yoke on us, but now lighten the harsh labor and the heavy yoke he put on us, and we will serve you."

⁵Rehoboam answered, "Go away for three days and then come back to me." So the people went away.

⁶Then King Rehoboam consulted the elders who had served his father Solomon during his lifetime. "How would you advise me to answer these people?" he asked.

⁷They replied, "If today you will be a servant to these people and serve them and give them a favorable answer, they will always be your servants."

⁸But Rehoboam rejected the advice the elders gave him and consulted the young men who had grown up with him and were serving him. ⁹He asked them, "What is your advice? How should we answer these people who say to me, 'Lighten the yoke your father put on us'?"

¹⁰The young men who had grown up with him replied, "Tell these people who have said to you, 'Your father put a heavy yoke on us, but make our yoke lighter'—tell them, 'My little finger is thicker than my father's waist. ¹¹My father laid on you a heavy yoke; I will make it even heavier. My father scourged you with whips; I will scourge you with scorpions.'"

¹²Three days later Jeroboam and all the people returned to Rehoboam, as the king had said, "Come back to me in three days." ¹³The king answered the people harshly. Rejecting the advice given him by the elders, ¹⁴he followed the advice of the young men and said, "My father made your yoke heavy; I will make it even heavier. My father scourged you with whips; I will scourge you with scorpions." ¹⁵So the king did not listen to the people, for this turn of events was from the LORD, to fulfill the word the LORD had spoken to Jeroboam son of Nebat through Ahijah the Shilonite.

¹⁶When all Israel saw that the king refused to listen to them, they answered the king:

"What share do we have in David,
  what part in Jesse's son?
To your tents, O Israel!
  Look after your own house, O David!"

So the Israelites went home. ¹⁷But as for the Israelites who were living in the towns of Judah, Rehoboam still ruled over them.

¹⁸King Rehoboam sent out Adoniram,^b who was in charge of forced labor, but all Israel stoned him to death. King Rehoboam, however, managed to get into his chariot and escape to Jerusalem. ¹⁹So Israel has been in rebellion against the house of David to this day.

²⁰When all the Israelites heard that Jeroboam had returned, they sent and called him to the assembly and made him king over all Israel. Only the tribe of Judah remained loyal to the house of David.

²¹When Rehoboam arrived in Jerusalem, he mustered the whole house of Judah and the tribe of Benjamin—a hundred and eighty thousand fighting men—to make war against the house of Israel and to regain the kingdom for Rehoboam son of Solomon.

²²But this word of God came to Shemaiah the man of God: ²³"Say to Rehoboam son of Solomon king of Judah, to the whole house of Judah and Benjamin, and to the rest of the people, ²⁴'This is what the LORD says: Do not go up to fight against your brothers, the Israelites. Go home, every one of you, for this is my doing.'" So they obeyed the word of the LORD and went home again, as the LORD had ordered.

Golden Calves at Bethel and Dan

²⁵Then Jeroboam fortified Shechem in the hill country of Ephraim and lived there. From there he went out and built up Peniel.^c

²⁶Jeroboam thought to himself, "The kingdom will now likely revert to the house of

---

^a2 Or *he remained in*   ^b18 Some Septuagint manuscripts and Syriac (see also 1 Kings 4:6 and 5:14); Hebrew *Adoram*   ^c25 Hebrew *Penuel*, a variant of *Peniel*

David. ²⁷If these people go up to offer sacrifices at the temple of the LORD in Jerusalem, they will again give their allegiance to their lord, Rehoboam king of Judah. They will kill me and return to King Rehoboam."

²⁸After seeking advice, the king made two golden calves. He said to the people, "It is too much for you to go up to Jerusalem. Here are your gods, O Israel, who brought you up out of Egypt." ²⁹One he set up in Bethel, and the other in Dan. ³⁰And this thing became a sin; the people went even as far as Dan to worship the one there.

³¹Jeroboam built shrines on high places and appointed priests from all sorts of people, even though they were not Levites. ³²He instituted a festival on the fifteenth day of the eighth month, like the festival held in Judah, and offered sacrifices on the altar. This he did in Bethel, sacrificing to the calves he had made. And at Bethel he also installed priests at the high places he had made. ³³On the fifteenth day of the eighth month, a month of his own choosing, he offered sacrifices on the altar he had built at Bethel. So he instituted the festival for the Israelites and went up to the altar to make offerings.

The Man of God From Judah

13 By the word of the LORD a man of God came from Judah to Bethel, as Jeroboam was standing by the altar to make an offering. ²He cried out against the altar by the word of the LORD: "O altar, altar! This is what the LORD says: 'A son named Josiah will be born to the house of David. On you he will sacrifice the priests of the high places who now make offerings here, and human bones will be burned on you.'" ³That same day the man of God gave a sign: "This is the sign the LORD has declared: The altar will be split apart, and the ashes on it will be poured out.'"

⁴When King Jeroboam heard what the man of God cried out against the altar at Bethel, he

stretched out his hand from the altar and said, "Seize him!" But the hand he stretched out toward the man shriveled up, so that he could not pull it back. ⁵Also, the altar was split apart and its ashes poured out according to the sign given by the man of God by the word of the LORD.

⁶Then the king said to the man of God, "Intercede with the LORD your God and pray for me that my hand may be restored." So the man of God interceded with the LORD, and the king's hand was restored and became as it was before.

⁷The king said to the man of God, "Come home with me and have something to eat, and I will give you a gift."

⁸But the man of God answered the king, "Even if you were to give me half your possessions, I would not go with you, nor would I eat bread or drink water here. ⁹For I was commanded by the word of the LORD: 'You must not eat bread or drink water or return by the way you came.'" ¹⁰So he took another road and did not return by the way he had come to Bethel.

¹¹Now there was a certain old prophet living in Bethel, whose sons came and told him all that the man of God had done there that day. They also told their father what he had said to the king. ¹²Their father asked them, "Which way did he go?" And his sons showed him which road the man of God from Judah had taken. ¹³So he said to his sons, "Saddle the donkey for me." And when they had saddled the donkey for him, he mounted it ¹⁴and rode after the man of God. He found him sitting under an oak tree and asked, "Are you the man of God who came from Judah?"

"I am," he replied.

¹⁵So the prophet said to him, "Come home with me and eat."

¹⁶The man of God said, "I cannot turn back and go with you, nor can I eat bread or drink water with you in this place. ¹⁷I have been told by the word of the LORD: 'You must not

---

1 Kings 13:6

God Answers Prayer

Then the king said . . . "Intercede with the LORD your God and pray for me that my hand may be restored." So the man of God interceded with the LORD, and the king's hand was restored and became as it was before.

---

eat bread or drink water there or return by the way you came.'"

¹⁸The old prophet answered, "I too am a prophet, as you are. And an angel said to me by the word of the LORD: 'Bring him back with you to your house so that he may eat bread and drink water.'" (But he was lying to him.) ¹⁹So the man of God returned with him and ate and drank in his house.

²⁰While they were sitting at the table, the word of the LORD came to the old prophet who had brought him back. ²¹He cried out to the man of God who had come from Judah, "This is what the LORD says: 'You have defied the word of the LORD and have not kept the command the LORD your God gave you. ²²You came back and ate bread and drank water in the place where he told you not to eat or drink. Therefore your body will not be buried in the tomb of your fathers.'"

²³When the man of God had finished eating and drinking, the prophet who had brought him back saddled his donkey for him. ²⁴As he went on his way, a lion met him on the road and killed him, and his body was thrown down on the road, with both the donkey and the lion standing beside it. ²⁵Some people who passed by saw the body thrown down there, with the lion standing beside the body, and they went and reported it in the city where the old prophet lived.

²⁶When the prophet who had brought him back from his journey heard of it, he said, "It is the man of God who defied the word of the LORD. The LORD has given him over to the lion, which has mauled him and killed him, as the word of the LORD had warned him."

²⁷The prophet said to his sons, "Saddle the donkey for me," and they did so. ²⁸Then he went out and found the body thrown down on the road, with the donkey and the lion standing beside it. The lion had neither eaten the body nor mauled the donkey. ²⁹So the prophet picked up the body of the man of God, laid it on the donkey, and brought it back to his own city to mourn for him and bury him. ³⁰Then he laid the body in his own tomb, and they mourned over him and said, "Oh, my brother!"

³¹After burying him, he said to his sons, "When I die, bury me in the grave where the man of God is buried; lay my bones beside his bones. ³²For the message he declared by the word of the LORD against the altar in Bethel and against all the shrines on the high places in the towns of Samaria will certainly come true."

³³Even after this, Jeroboam did not change his evil ways, but once more appointed priests for the high places from all sorts of people. Anyone who wanted to become a priest he consecrated for the high places. ³⁴This was the sin of the house of Jeroboam that led to its downfall and to its destruction from the face of the earth.

Ahijah's Prophecy Against Jeroboam

14 At that time Abijah son of Jeroboam became ill, ²and Jeroboam said to his wife, "Go, disguise yourself, so you won't be recognized as the wife of Jeroboam. Then go to Shiloh. Ahijah the prophet is there—the one who told me I would be king over this people. ³Take ten loaves of bread with you, some cakes and a jar of honey, and go to him. He will tell you what will happen to the boy." ⁴So Jeroboam's wife did what he said and went to Ahijah's house in Shiloh.

Now Ahijah could not see; his sight was gone because of his age. ⁵But the LORD had told Ahijah, "Jeroboam's wife is coming to ask you about her son, for he is ill, and you are to give her such and such an answer. When she arrives, she will pretend to be someone else."

⁶So when Ahijah heard the sound of her footsteps at the door, he said, "Come in, wife of Jeroboam. Why this pretense? I have been sent to you with bad news. ⁷Go, tell Jeroboam that this is what the LORD, the God of Israel, says: 'I raised you up from among the people and made you a leader over my people Israel. ⁸I tore the kingdom away from the house of David and gave it to you, but you have not been like my servant David, who kept my commands and followed me with all his heart, doing only what was right in my eyes. ⁹You have done more evil than all who lived before you. You have made for yourself other gods, idols made of metal; you have provoked me to anger and thrust me behind your back.

¹⁰"'Because of this, I am going to bring disaster on the house of Jeroboam. I will cut off

from Jeroboam every last male in Israel—slave or free. I will burn up the house of Jeroboam as one burns dung, until it is all gone. [11]Dogs will eat those belonging to Jeroboam who die in the city, and the birds of the air will feed on those who die in the country. The LORD has spoken!'

[12]"As for you, go back home. When you set foot in your city, the boy will die. [13]All Israel will mourn for him and bury him. He is the only one belonging to Jeroboam who will be buried, because he is the only one in the house of Jeroboam in whom the LORD, the God of Israel, has found anything good.

[14]"The LORD will raise up for himself a king over Israel who will cut off the family of Jeroboam. This is the day! What? Yes, even now.[a] [15]And the LORD will strike Israel, so that it will be like a reed swaying in the water. He will uproot Israel from this good land that he gave to their forefathers and scatter them beyond the River,[b] because they provoked the LORD to anger by making Asherah poles.[c] [16]And he will give Israel up because of the sins Jeroboam has committed and has caused Israel to commit."

[17]Then Jeroboam's wife got up and left and went to Tirzah. As soon as she stepped over the threshold of the house, the boy died. [18]They buried him, and all Israel mourned for him, as the LORD had said through his servant the prophet Ahijah.

[19]The other events of Jeroboam's reign, his wars and how he ruled, are written in the book of the annals of the kings of Israel. [20]He reigned for twenty-two years and then rested with his fathers. And Nadab his son succeeded him as king.

Rehoboam King of Judah

[21]Rehoboam son of Solomon was king in Judah. He was forty-one years old when he be-

came king, and he reigned seventeen years in Jerusalem, the city the LORD had chosen out of all the tribes of Israel in which to put his Name. His mother's name was Naamah; she was an Ammonite.

[22]Judah did evil in the eyes of the LORD. By the sins they committed they stirred up his jealous anger more than their fathers had done. [23]They also set up for themselves high places, sacred stones and Asherah poles on every high hill and under every spreading tree. [24]There were even male shrine prostitutes in the land; the people engaged in all the detestable practices of the nations the LORD had driven out before the Israelites.

[25]In the fifth year of King Rehoboam, Shishak king of Egypt attacked Jerusalem. [26]He carried off the treasures of the temple of the LORD and the treasures of the royal palace. He took everything, including all the gold shields Solomon had made. [27]So King Rehoboam made bronze shields to replace them and assigned these to the commanders of the guard on duty at the entrance to the royal palace. [28]Whenever the king went to the LORD's temple, the guards bore the shields, and afterward they returned them to the guardroom.

[29]As for the other events of Rehoboam's reign, and all he did, are they not written in the book of the annals of the kings of Judah? [30]There was continual warfare between Rehoboam and Jeroboam. [31]And Rehoboam rested with his fathers and was buried with them in the City of David. His mother's name was Naamah; she was an Ammonite. And Abijah[d] his son succeeded him as king.

Abijah King of Judah

15 In the eighteenth year of the reign of Jeroboam son of Nebat, Abijah[e] became king of Judah, [2]and he reigned in

---

> ### 1 Kings 14:9
>
> *God Desires Worship*
>
> "You have done more evil than all who lived before you. You have made for yourself other gods, idols made of metal; you have provoked me to anger and thrust me behind your back."

---

[a]14 The meaning of the Hebrew for this sentence is uncertain.   [b]15 That is, the Euphrates   [c]15 That is, symbols of the goddess Asherah; here and elsewhere in 1 Kings   [d]31 Some Hebrew manuscripts and Septuagint (see also 2 Chron. 12:16); most Hebrew manuscripts *Abijam*   [e]1 Some Hebrew manuscripts and Septuagint (see also 2 Chron. 12:16); most Hebrew manuscripts *Abijam*; also in verses 7 and 8

Jerusalem three years. His mother's name was Maacah daughter of Abishalom.ᵃ

³He committed all the sins his father had done before him; his heart was not fully devoted to the LORD his God, as the heart of David his forefather had been. ⁴Nevertheless, for David's sake the LORD his God gave him a lamp in Jerusalem by raising up a son to succeed him and by making Jerusalem strong. ⁵For David had done what was right in the eyes of the LORD and had not failed to keep any of the LORD's commands all the days of his life—except in the case of Uriah the Hittite.

⁶There was war between Rehoboamᵇ and Jeroboam throughout Abijah's lifetime. ⁷As for the other events of Abijah's reign, and all he did, are they not written in the book of the annals of the kings of Judah? There was war between Abijah and Jeroboam. ⁸And Abijah rested with his fathers and was buried in the City of David. And Asa his son succeeded him as king.

Asa King of Judah

⁹In the twentieth year of Jeroboam king of Israel, Asa became king of Judah, ¹⁰and he reigned in Jerusalem forty-one years. His grandmother's name was Maacah daughter of Abishalom.

¹¹Asa did what was right in the eyes of the LORD, as his father David had done. ¹²He expelled the male shrine prostitutes from the land and got rid of all the idols his fathers had made. ¹³He even deposed his grandmother Maacah from her position as queen mother, because she had made a repulsive Asherah pole. Asa cut the pole down and burned it in the Kidron Valley. ¹⁴Although he did not remove the high places, Asa's heart was fully committed to the LORD all his life. ¹⁵He brought into the temple of the LORD the silver and gold and the articles that he and his father had dedicated.

¹⁶There was war between Asa and Baasha king of Israel throughout their reigns. ¹⁷Baasha king of Israel went up against Judah and fortified Ramah to prevent anyone from leaving or entering the territory of Asa king of Judah. ¹⁸Asa then took all the silver and gold that was left in the treasuries of the LORD's temple

and of his own palace. He entrusted it to his officials and sent them to Ben-Hadad son of Tabrimmon, the son of Hezion, the king of Aram, who was ruling in Damascus. ¹⁹"Let there be a treaty between me and you," he said, "as there was between my father and your father. See, I am sending you a gift of silver and gold. Now break your treaty with Baasha king of Israel so he will withdraw from me."

²⁰Ben-Hadad agreed with King Asa and sent the commanders of his forces against the towns of Israel. He conquered Ijon, Dan, Abel Beth Maacah and all Kinnereth in addition to Naphtali. ²¹When Baasha heard this, he stopped building Ramah and withdrew to Tirzah. ²²Then King Asa issued an order to all Judah—no one was exempt—and they carried away from Ramah the stones and timber Baasha had been using there. With them King Asa built up Geba in Benjamin, and also Mizpah.

²³As for all the other events of Asa's reign, all his achievements, all he did and the cities he built, are they not written in the book of the annals of the kings of Judah? In his old age, however, his feet became diseased. ²⁴Then Asa rested with his fathers and was buried with them in the city of his father David. And Jehoshaphat his son succeeded him as king.

Nadab King of Israel

²⁵Nadab son of Jeroboam became king of Israel in the second year of Asa king of Judah, and he reigned over Israel two years. ²⁶He did evil in the eyes of the LORD, walking in the ways of his father and in his sin, which he had caused Israel to commit.

²⁷Baasha son of Ahijah of the house of Issachar plotted against him, and he struck him down at Gibbethon, a Philistine town, while Nadab and all Israel were besieging it. ²⁸Baasha killed Nadab in the third year of Asa king of Judah and succeeded him as king.

²⁹As soon as he began to reign, he killed Jeroboam's whole family. He did not leave Jeroboam anyone that breathed, but destroyed them all, according to the word of the LORD given through his servant Ahijah the Shilonite— ³⁰because of the sins Jeroboam had committed and had caused Israel to commit,

ᵃ 2 A variant of *Absalom*; also in verse 10 ᵇ 6 Most Hebrew manuscripts; some Hebrew manuscripts and Syriac *Abijam* (that is, Abijah) and because he provoked the LORD, the God of Israel, to anger.

³¹As for the other events of Nadab's reign, and all he did, are they not written in the book of the annals of the kings of Israel? ³²There was war between Asa and Baasha king of Israel throughout their reigns.

Baasha King of Israel

³³In the third year of Asa king of Judah, Baasha son of Ahijah became king of all Israel in Tirzah, and he reigned twenty-four years. ³⁴He did evil in the eyes of the LORD, walking in the ways of Jeroboam and in his sin, which he had caused Israel to commit.

16 Then the word of the LORD came to Jehu son of Hanani against Baasha: ²"I lifted you up from the dust and made you leader of my people Israel, but you walked in the ways of Jeroboam and caused my people Israel to sin and to provoke me to anger by their sins. ³So I am about to consume Baasha and his house, and I will make your house like that of Jeroboam son of Nebat. ⁴Dogs will eat those belonging to Baasha who die in the city, and the birds of the air will feed on those who die in the country."

⁵As for the other events of Baasha's reign, what he did and his achievements, are they not written in the book of the annals of the kings of Israel? ⁶Baasha rested with his fathers and was buried in Tirzah. And Elah his son succeeded him as king.

⁷Moreover, the word of the LORD came through the prophet Jehu son of Hanani to Baasha and his house, because of all the evil he had done in the eyes of the LORD, provoking him to anger by the things he did, and becoming like the house of Jeroboam—and also because he destroyed it.

Elah King of Israel

⁸In the twenty-sixth year of Asa king of Judah, Elah son of Baasha became king of Israel, and he reigned in Tirzah two years.

⁹Zimri, one of his officials, who had command of half his chariots, plotted against him. Elah was in Tirzah at the time, getting drunk in the home of Arza, the man in charge of the palace at Tirzah. ¹⁰Zimri came in, struck him down and killed him in the twenty-seventh year of Asa king of Judah. Then he succeeded him as king.

¹¹As soon as he began to reign and was seated on the throne, he killed off Baasha's whole family. He did not spare a single male, whether relative or friend. ¹²So Zimri destroyed the whole family of Baasha, in accordance with the word of the LORD spoken against Baasha through the prophet Jehu— ¹³because of all the sins Baasha and his son Elah had committed and had caused Israel to commit, so that they provoked the LORD, the God of Israel, to anger by their worthless idols.

¹⁴As for the other events of Elah's reign, and all he did, are they not written in the book of the annals of the kings of Israel?

Zimri King of Israel

¹⁵In the twenty-seventh year of Asa king of Judah, Zimri reigned in Tirzah seven days. The army was encamped near Gibbethon, a Philistine town. ¹⁶When the Israelites in the camp heard that Zimri had plotted against the king and murdered him, they proclaimed Omri, the commander of the army, king over Israel that very day there in the camp. ¹⁷Then Omri and all the Israelites with him withdrew from Gibbethon and laid siege to Tirzah. ¹⁸When Zimri saw that the city was taken, he went into the citadel of the royal palace and set the palace on fire around him. So he died, ¹⁹because of the sins he had committed, doing evil in the eyes of the LORD and walking in the ways of Jeroboam and in the sin he had committed and had caused Israel to commit.

²⁰As for the other events of Zimri's reign, and the rebellion he carried out, are they not written in the book of the annals of the kings of Israel?

Omri King of Israel

²¹Then the people of Israel were split into two factions; half supported Tibni son of Ginath for king, and the other half supported Omri. ²²But Omri's followers proved stronger than those of Tibni son of Ginath. So Tibni died and Omri became king.

²³In the thirty-first year of Asa king of Judah, Omri became king of Israel, and he reigned twelve years, six of them in Tirzah. ²⁴He bought the hill of Samaria from Shemer

for two talents[a] of silver and built a city on the hill, calling it Samaria, after Shemer, the name of the former owner of the hill.

25 But Omri did evil in the eyes of the LORD and sinned more than all those before him. 26 He walked in all the ways of Jeroboam son of Nebat and in his sin, which he had caused Israel to commit, so that they provoked the LORD, the God of Israel, to anger by their worthless idols.

27 As for the other events of Omri's reign, what he did and the things he achieved, are they not written in the book of the annals of the kings of Israel? 28 Omri rested with his fathers and was buried in Samaria. And Ahab his son succeeded him as king.

Ahab Becomes King of Israel

29 In the thirty-eighth year of Asa king of Judah, Ahab son of Omri became king of Israel, and he reigned in Samaria over Israel twenty-two years. 30 Ahab son of Omri did more evil in the eyes of the LORD than any of those before him. 31 He not only considered it trivial to commit the sins of Jeroboam son of Nebat, but he also married Jezebel daughter of Ethbaal king of the Sidonians, and began to serve Baal and worship him. 32 He set up an altar for Baal in the temple of Baal that he built in Samaria. 33 Ahab also made an Asherah pole and did more to provoke the LORD, the God of Israel, to anger than did all the kings of Israel before him.

34 In Ahab's time, Hiel of Bethel rebuilt Jericho. He laid its foundations at the cost of his firstborn son Abiram, and he set up its gates at the cost of his youngest son Segub, in accordance with the word of the LORD spoken by Joshua son of Nun.

Elijah Fed by Ravens

17 Now Elijah the Tishbite, from Tishbe[b] in Gilead, said to Ahab, "As the LORD, the God of Israel, lives, whom I serve, there will be neither dew nor rain in the next few years except at my word."

2 Then the word of the LORD came to Elijah: 3 "Leave here, turn eastward and hide in the Kerith Ravine, east of the Jordan. 4 You will drink from the brook, and I have ordered the ravens to feed you there."

5 So he did what the LORD had told him. He went to the Kerith Ravine, east of the Jordan, and stayed there. 6 The ravens brought him bread and meat in the morning and bread and meat in the evening, and he drank from the brook.

The Widow at Zarephath

7 Some time later the brook dried up because there had been no rain in the land. 8 Then the word of the LORD came to him: 9 "Go at once to Zarephath of Sidon and stay there. I have commanded a widow in that place to supply you with food." 10 So he went to Zarephath. When he came to the town gate, a widow was there gathering sticks. He called to her and asked, "Would you bring me a little water in a jar so I may have a drink?" 11 As she was going to get it, he called, "And bring me, please, a piece of bread."

12 "As surely as the LORD your God lives," she replied, "I don't have any bread—only a handful of flour in a jar and a little oil in a jug. I am gathering a few sticks to take home and make a meal for myself and my son, that we may eat it—and die."

13 Elijah said to her, "Don't be afraid. Go home and do as you have said. But first make a small cake of bread for me from what you have and bring it to me, and then make something for yourself and your son. 14 For this is what the LORD, the God of Israel, says: 'The jar of flour will not be used up and the jug of oil will not run dry until the day the LORD gives rain on the land.'"

15 She went away and did as Elijah had told her. So there was food every day for Elijah and for the woman and her family. 16 For the jar of flour was not used up and the jug of oil did not run dry, in keeping with the word of the LORD spoken by Elijah.

17 Some time later the son of the woman who owned the house became ill. He grew worse and worse, and finally stopped breathing. 18 She said to Elijah, "What do you have against me, man of God? Did you come to remind me of my sin and kill my son?"

19 "Give me your son," Elijah replied. He took him from her arms, carried him to the

---

a 24 That is, about 150 pounds (about 70 kilograms)   *b* 1 Or *Tishbite, of the settlers*

Nothing's Impossible

Read: 1 Kings 17:7–24

"FAITH SEES THE INVISIBLE, believes the unbelievable and receives the impossible." It may be easy to say these words when times are good and food is plenty. But these words were spoken by Corrie ten Boom, who, along with her sister Betsie, suffered horribly at the hands of Nazi guards at the Ravensbruck concentration camp. They were imprisoned for providing a hiding place for persecuted Jews from Hitler's murderous Nazis.

With Betsie sick, Corrie tried to hoard a tiny brown bottle of liquid vitamins, but other women burned with fever, their teeth chattered with chill. She wanted to save the small amount left for the weakest inmates—but the numbers grew, reaching as many as 25. Corrie knew that sharing the drops would mean she'd have none left for her sister, but Betsie was emphatic that God would provide.

Amazingly, every time Corrie tilted the bottle for a sick inmate, one drop would pour out. When there couldn't possibly be any more, another dose was dispensed. When a guard smuggled in some vitamins for the prisoners, Corrie was elated. But first she determined to finish the drops in the bottle. She tipped it over, but no matter how hard she shook, no more came out.

Elijah was not in a prison camp, but the land was suffering from God's judgment of drought and famine. When he was hiding from King Ahab and he found refuge with a widow and her son, their jar of flour and jug of oil never ran dry. God faithfully supplied for his prophet and the people who harbored him during their time of need.

It may seem impossible to you that God would supply you with such basic things as flour and vitamins, but these stories are about the Savior who is the same yesterday, today and forever. What do you need from God? Is the paycheck barely enough to cover the bills? Do the clothes seem as though they won't last another season? Do you feel you can't handle another day in your present circumstances? Ask God to provide everything you need to live. He will multiply his grace toward you in your times of trouble. He sees you in your hiding place and will find a way to meet your needs. Believe it. All things are possible with God.

1 Kings 17:16

For the jar of flour was not used up and the jug of oil did not run dry, in keeping with the word of the LORD spoken by Elijah.

reflection

1 Describe a time in your life when your faith was running dry and you needed God to come through.

2 How did God provide?

3 Are you in need of anything from God right now? If you are in want, ask God to multiply what you have to meet your needs.

RELATED READINGS

Psalm 37:23–26;
John 6:1–13;
Philippians 4:10–12

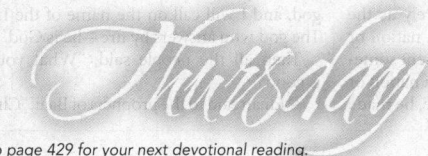

Thursday

Go to page 429 for your next devotional reading.

427

upper room where he was staying, and laid him on his bed. **20**Then he cried out to the LORD, "O LORD my God, have you brought tragedy also upon this widow I am staying with, by causing her son to die?" **21**Then he stretched himself out on the boy three times and cried to the LORD, "O LORD my God, let this boy's life return to him!"

22The LORD heard Elijah's cry, and the boy's life returned to him, and he lived. **23**Elijah picked up the child and carried him down from the room into the house. He gave him to his mother and said, "Look, your son is alive!"

24Then the woman said to Elijah, "Now I know that you are a man of God and that the word of the LORD from your mouth is the truth."

Elijah and Obadiah

18 After a long time, in the third year, the word of the LORD came to Elijah: "Go and present yourself to Ahab, and I will send rain on the land." **2**So Elijah went to present himself to Ahab.

Now the famine was severe in Samaria, **3**and Ahab had summoned Obadiah, who was in charge of his palace. (Obadiah was a devout believer in the LORD. **4**While Jezebel was killing off the LORD's prophets, Obadiah had taken a hundred prophets and hidden them in two caves, fifty in each, and had supplied them with food and water.) **5**Ahab had said to Obadiah, "Go through the land to all the springs and valleys. Maybe we can find some grass to keep the horses and mules alive so we will not have to kill any of our animals." **6**So they divided the land they were to cover, Ahab going in one direction and Obadiah in another.

7As Obadiah was walking along, Elijah met him. Obadiah recognized him, bowed down to the ground, and said, "Is it really you, my lord Elijah?"

8"Yes," he replied. "Go tell your master, 'Elijah is here.' "

9"What have I done wrong," asked Obadiah, "that you are handing your servant over to Ahab to be put to death? **10**As surely as the LORD your God lives, there is not a nation or kingdom where my master has not sent someone to look for you. And whenever a nation or kingdom claimed you were not there, he made

them swear they could not find you. **11**But now you tell me to go to my master and say, 'Elijah is here.' **12**I don't know where the Spirit of the LORD may carry you when I leave you. If I go and tell Ahab and he doesn't find you, he will kill me. Yet I your servant have worshiped the LORD since my youth. **13**Haven't you heard, my lord, what I did while Jezebel was killing the prophets of the LORD? I hid a hundred of the LORD's prophets in two caves, fifty in each, and supplied them with food and water. **14**And now you tell me to go to my master and say, 'Elijah is here.' He will kill me!"

15Elijah said, "As the LORD Almighty lives, whom I serve, I will surely present myself to Ahab today."

Elijah on Mount Carmel

16So Obadiah went to meet Ahab and told him, and Ahab went to meet Elijah. **17**When he saw Elijah, he said to him, "Is that you, you troubler of Israel?"

18"I have not made trouble for Israel," Elijah replied. "But you and your father's family have. You have abandoned the LORD's commands and have followed the Baals. **19**Now summon the people from all over Israel to meet me on Mount Carmel. And bring the four hundred and fifty prophets of Baal and the four hundred prophets of Asherah, who eat at Jezebel's table."

20So Ahab sent word throughout all Israel and assembled the prophets on Mount Carmel. **21**Elijah went before the people and said, "How long will you waver between two opinions? If the LORD is God, follow him; but if Baal is God, follow him."

But the people said nothing.

22Then Elijah said to them, "I am the only one of the LORD's prophets left, but Baal has four hundred and fifty prophets. **23**Get two bulls for us. Let them choose one for themselves, and let them cut it into pieces and put it on the wood but not set fire to it. I will prepare the other bull and put it on the wood but not set fire to it. **24**Then you call on the name of your god, and I will call on the name of the LORD. The god who answers by fire—he is God."

Then all the people said, "What you say is good."

25Elijah said to the prophets of Baal, "Choose

Caught in the Act

Read: 1 Kings 18:16–40

HAVE YOU EVER PRETENDED to think one thing while really believing something else? At one time or another most of us have tacitly agreed with a persuasive person simply by failing to disagree. Or we've looked the other way or nodded knowingly while a red flag went up in our minds. It's a difficult and even dangerous balancing act attempting to please people on both sides of a controversial fence. The only remedy for avoiding such a precarious position is to decide which side of the fence really matters and then get down from the fence and take a stand.

The prophet Elijah confronted the people of his day and demanded they choose whom they would serve—the true God of Israel or the false gods of the pagan nations surrounding them. He basically challenged them, "Get off the fence! You can't have it both ways. Either live your lives in a way that is pleasing to the one true God . . . or not."

Most of us have never been put in a position in which we had to choose between worshiping the true God or bowing down to statues made of wood or stone. Yet we often find ourselves tempted to try that balancing act while living in a spiritually and morally bankrupt culture. We may compromise our lifestyles, going to places or doing things we really know we shouldn't. We may even justify our behavior by saying we don't want to offend anyone. Or we neglect to say the things we know we should and then excuse ourselves by saying we will let our faith be seen in our actions rather than heard in our words. At times these may be legitimate claims, but at other times they may be nothing more than convenient excuses so we don't have to risk rejection.

Elijah wasn't concerned with rejection when he challenged the false prophets and called the people to serve the true God. He put it all on the line—even his life. The prophet refused to compromise or put himself in the precarious position of riding the fence; as a result, God vindicated him in the sight of his enemies. He was caught in the act of standing up for God. Can that be said of you?

1 Kings 18:21

Elijah went before the people and said, "How long will you waver between two opinions? If the LORD is God, follow him; but if Baal is God, follow him."

reflection

1 How have you been caught up in the balancing act of compromise?

2 Why do you sometimes compromise?

3 In what ways can you stand up for righteousness?

RELATED READINGS

Deuteronomy 30:15–20;
Joshua 24:14–19;
Matthew 10:32–39

Friday

Go to page 431 for your next devotional reading.

one of the bulls and prepare it first, since there are so many of you. Call on the name of your god, but do not light the fire." ²⁶So they took the bull given them and prepared it.

Then they called on the name of Baal from morning till noon. "O Baal, answer us!" they shouted. But there was no response; no one answered. And they danced around the altar they had made.

²⁷At noon Elijah began to taunt them. "Shout louder!" he said. "Surely he is a god! Perhaps he is deep in thought, or busy, or traveling. Maybe he is sleeping and must be awakened." ²⁸So they shouted louder and slashed themselves with swords and spears, as was their custom, until their blood flowed. ²⁹Midday passed, and they continued their frantic prophesying until the time for the evening sacrifice. But there was no response, no one answered, no one paid attention.

³⁰Then Elijah said to all the people, "Come here to me." They came to him, and he repaired the altar of the LORD, which was in ruins. ³¹Elijah took twelve stones, one for each of the tribes descended from Jacob, to whom the word of the LORD had come, saying, "Your name shall be Israel." ³²With the stones he built an altar in the name of the LORD, and he dug a trench around it large enough to hold two seahs*a* of seed. ³³He arranged the wood, cut the bull into pieces and laid it on the wood. Then he said to them, "Fill four large jars with water and pour it on the offering and on the wood."

³⁴"Do it again," he said, and they did it again.

"Do it a third time," he ordered, and they did it the third time. ³⁵The water ran down around the altar and even filled the trench.

³⁶At the time of sacrifice, the prophet Elijah stepped forward and prayed: "O LORD, God of Abraham, Isaac and Israel, let it be known today that you are God in Israel and that I am your servant and have done all these things at your command. ³⁷Answer me, O LORD, answer me, so these people will know that you, O LORD, are God, and that you are turning their hearts back again."

³⁸Then the fire of the LORD fell and burned up the sacrifice, the wood, the stones and the soil, and also licked up the water in the trench.

³⁹When all the people saw this, they fell prostrate and cried, "The LORD—he is God! The LORD—he is God!"

⁴⁰Then Elijah commanded them, "Seize the prophets of Baal. Don't let anyone get away!" They seized them, and Elijah had them brought down to the Kishon Valley and slaughtered there.

⁴¹And Elijah said to Ahab, "Go, eat and drink, for there is the sound of a heavy rain." ⁴²So Ahab went off to eat and drink, but Elijah climbed to the top of Carmel, bent down to the ground and put his face between his knees.

⁴³"Go and look toward the sea," he told his servant. And he went up and looked.

"There is nothing there," he said.

Seven times Elijah said, "Go back."

⁴⁴The seventh time the servant reported, "A cloud as small as a man's hand is rising from the sea."

So Elijah said, "Go and tell Ahab, 'Hitch up your chariot and go down before the rain stops you.'"

⁴⁵Meanwhile, the sky grew black with clouds, the wind rose, a heavy rain came on and Ahab rode off to Jezreel. ⁴⁶The power of the LORD came upon Elijah and, tucking his cloak into his belt, he ran ahead of Ahab all the way to Jezreel.

1 Kings 18:46

God Gives Energy

The power of the LORD came upon Elijah and, tucking his cloak into his belt, he ran ahead of Ahab all the way to Jezreel.

Elijah Flees to Horeb

19 Now Ahab told Jezebel everything Elijah had done and how he had killed all the prophets with the sword. ²So Jezebel sent a messenger to Elijah to say, "May the gods deal with me, be it ever so severely, if by this time tomorrow I do not make your life like that of one of them."

³Elijah was afraid*b* and ran for his life. When

---

*a*32 That is, probably about 13 quarts (about 15 liters) *b*3 Or *Elijah saw*

Legendary Leadership

DEBORAH

EACH NIGHT IT WAS THE SAME ROUTINE: rinse teeth, change clothes and off to bed—but never to sleep without a story first. Her children especially loved to hear her tell "Deborah stories" about their hero. The family favorite? The story of Barak and Sisera.

"Sometimes," she whispered, as she tucked them in, "I even think I saw her smiling." It was a long time ago, but she remembered her hero as if it were yesterday. She grew up near the Palm of Deborah, during a time when her family lived in oppression and fear. Those were dark days . . . until Deborah. Now when she recounted the stories to her boys, she tried to remember everything just as it was: The slight curl at the corners of Judge Deborah's lips that formed whenever she was deep in thought. Deborah's serious concentration when Barak breathlessly announced Sisera's encroaching ironclad army. She remembered how Deborah got a faraway look in her eyes; it was almost as if her mind were somewhere else altogether—drawing perspective, honing her instincts, receiving a wise word.

"She was a prophet!" her youngest Reuben gasped and tugged at his blanket.

"A prophetess," she corrected him kindly.

"What happened next?"

Of course, her boys knew what happened next—they could even tell the stories themselves, like any Israelite child could do. They were enamored with the legendary heroism, battle, treachery and victory surrounding the story of Deborah, Barak, Sisera and Jael.

She smiled as she found her place in the story again. This was the most exciting story about Deborah, but she recalled the simple acts of leadership that Deborah had provided in those first days of turmoil after the death of Sisera. She had observed Her Honor up close. She respected her work ethic, admired her utter dependence on God for strength and marveled at her wisdom.

"Can we sing the song?" Reuben's voice interrupted and whispered in the darkness. "Just the last part?"

"Just once," she smiled. "You start . . ."

"So . . . may . . . all . . ." he started slowly.

"Your enemies perish, O LORD!" big brother joined in.

"But may they who love you be like the sun . . ."

Before they had finished the last verse together, both boys were asleep. She continued contentedly singing softly to herself, trimmed the lamp and tiptoed out of their room.

—Prayer—
Lord, as you provided wisdom for Deborah, give me wisdom in all my decisions and responsibilities.

> *"Village life in Israel ceased, ceased until I, Deborah, arose, arose a mother in Israel."*
>
> **Judges 5:7**

ASSIGNED READING:

Judges 4–5

Weekend

Go to page 437 for your next devotional reading.

he came to Beersheba in Judah, he left his servant there, **4**while he himself went a day's journey into the desert. He came to a broom tree, sat down under it and prayed that he might die. "I have had enough, LORD," he said. "Take my life; I am no better than my ancestors." **5**Then he lay down under the tree and fell asleep.

All at once an angel touched him and said, "Get up and eat." **6**He looked around, and there by his head was a cake of bread baked over hot coals, and a jar of water. He ate and drank and then lay down again.

7The angel of the LORD came back a second time and touched him and said, "Get up and eat, for the journey is too much for you." **8**So he got up and ate and drank. Strengthened by that food, he traveled forty days and forty nights until he reached Horeb, the mountain of God. **9**There he went into a cave and spent the night.

The LORD Appears to Elijah

And the word of the LORD came to him: "What are you doing here, Elijah?"

10He replied, "I have been very zealous for the LORD God Almighty. The Israelites have rejected your covenant, broken down your altars, and put your prophets to death with the sword. I am the only one left, and now they are trying to kill me too."

11The LORD said, "Go out and stand on the mountain in the presence of the LORD, for the LORD is about to pass by."

Then a great and powerful wind tore the mountains apart and shattered the rocks before the LORD, but the LORD was not in the wind. After the wind there was an earthquake, but the LORD was not in the earthquake. **12**After the earthquake came a fire, but the LORD was not in the fire. And after the fire came a gentle whisper. **13**When Elijah heard it, he pulled his cloak over his face and went out and stood at the mouth of the cave.

Then a voice said to him, "What are you doing here, Elijah?"

14He replied, "I have been very zealous for the LORD God Almighty. The Israelites have rejected your covenant, broken down your altars, and put your prophets to death with the sword. I am the only one left, and now they are trying to kill me too."

15The LORD said to him, "Go back the way you came, and go to the Desert of Damascus. When you get there, anoint Hazael king over Aram. **16**Also, anoint Jehu son of Nimshi king over Israel, and anoint Elisha son of Shaphat from Abel Meholah to succeed you as prophet. **17**Jehu will put to death any who escape the sword of Hazael, and Elisha will put to death any who escape the sword of Jehu. **18**Yet I reserve seven thousand in Israel—all whose knees have not bowed down to Baal and all whose mouths have not kissed him."

The Call of Elisha

19So Elijah went from there and found Elisha son of Shaphat. He was plowing with twelve yoke of oxen, and he himself was driving the twelfth pair. Elijah went up to him and threw his cloak around him. **20**Elisha then left his oxen and ran after Elijah. "Let me kiss my father and mother good-by," he said, "and then I will come with you."

"Go back," Elijah replied. "What have I done to you?"

21So Elisha left him and went back. He took his yoke of oxen and slaughtered them. He burned the plowing equipment to cook the meat and gave it to the people, and they ate. Then he set out to follow Elijah and became his attendant.

Ben-Hadad Attacks Samaria

20 Now Ben-Hadad king of Aram mustered his entire army. Accompanied by thirty-two kings with their horses and chariots, he went up and besieged Samaria and attacked it. **2**He sent messengers into the city to Ahab king of Israel, saying, "This is what Ben-Hadad says: **3**'Your silver and gold are mine, and the best of your wives and children are mine.'"

4The king of Israel answered, "Just as you say, my lord the king. I and all I have are yours."

1 Kings 19:11

God Is Near

The LORD said, "Go out and stand on the mountain in the presence of the LORD, for the LORD is about to pass by."

⁵The messengers came again and said, "This is what Ben-Hadad says: 'I sent to demand your silver and gold, your wives and your children. ⁶But about this time tomorrow I am going to send my officials to search your palace and the houses of your officials. They will seize everything you value and carry it away.'"

⁷The king of Israel summoned all the elders of the land and said to them, "See how this man is looking for trouble! When he sent for my wives and my children, my silver and my gold, I did not refuse him."

⁸The elders and the people all answered, "Don't listen to him or agree to his demands."

⁹So he replied to Ben-Hadad's messengers, "Tell my lord the king, 'Your servant will do all you demanded the first time, but this demand I cannot meet.'" They left and took the answer back to Ben-Hadad.

¹⁰Then Ben-Hadad sent another message to Ahab: "May the gods deal with me, be it ever so severely, if enough dust remains in Samaria to give each of my men a handful."

¹¹The king of Israel answered, "Tell him: 'One who puts on his armor should not boast like one who takes it off.'"

¹²Ben-Hadad heard this message while he and the kings were drinking in their tents,ᵃ and he ordered his men: "Prepare to attack." So they prepared to attack the city.

Ahab Defeats Ben-Hadad

¹³Meanwhile a prophet came to Ahab king of Israel and announced, "This is what the LORD says: 'Do you see this vast army? I will give it into your hand today, and then you will know that I am the LORD.'"

¹⁴"But who will do this?" asked Ahab.

The prophet replied, "This is what the LORD says: 'The young officers of the provincial commanders will do it.'"

"And who will start the battle?" he asked.

The prophet answered, "You will."

¹⁵So Ahab summoned the young officers of the provincial commanders, 232 men. Then he assembled the rest of the Israelites, 7,000 in all. ¹⁶They set out at noon while Ben-Hadad and the 32 kings allied with him were in their tents getting drunk. ¹⁷The young officers of the provincial commanders went out first.

Now Ben-Hadad had dispatched scouts, who reported, "Men are advancing from Samaria."

¹⁸He said, "If they have come out for peace, take them alive; if they have come out for war, take them alive."

¹⁹The young officers of the provincial commanders marched out of the city with the army behind them ²⁰and each one struck down his opponent. At that, the Arameans fled, with the Israelites in pursuit. But Ben-Hadad king of Aram escaped on horseback with some of his horsemen. ²¹The king of Israel advanced and overpowered the horses and chariots and inflicted heavy losses on the Arameans.

²²Afterward, the prophet came to the king of Israel and said, "Strengthen your position and see what must be done, because next spring the king of Aram will attack you again."

²³Meanwhile, the officials of the king of Aram advised him, "Their gods are gods of the hills. That is why they were too strong for us. But if we fight them on the plains, surely we will be stronger than they. ²⁴Do this: Remove all the kings from their commands and replace them with other officers. ²⁵You must also raise an army like the one you lost—horse for horse and chariot for chariot—so we can fight Israel on the plains. Then surely we will be stronger than they." He agreed with them and acted accordingly.

²⁶The next spring Ben-Hadad mustered the Arameans and went up to Aphek to fight against Israel. ²⁷When the Israelites were also mustered and given provisions, they marched out to meet them. The Israelites camped opposite them like two small flocks of goats, while the Arameans covered the countryside.

²⁸The man of God came up and told the king of Israel, "This is what the LORD says: 'Because the Arameans think the LORD is a god of the hills and not a god of the valleys, I will deliver this vast army into your hands, and you will know that I am the LORD.'"

²⁹For seven days they camped opposite each other, and on the seventh day the battle was joined. The Israelites inflicted a hundred thousand casualties on the Aramean foot soldiers in one day. ³⁰The rest of them escaped to the city of Aphek, where the wall collapsed on

ᵃ12 Or *in Succoth*; also in verse 16

twenty-seven thousand of them. And Ben-Hadad fled to the city and hid in an inner room.

31His officials said to him, "Look, we have heard that the kings of the house of Israel are merciful. Let us go to the king of Israel with sackcloth around our waists and ropes around our heads. Perhaps he will spare your life."

32Wearing sackcloth around their waists and ropes around their heads, they went to the king of Israel and said, "Your servant Ben-Hadad says: 'Please let me live.'"

The king answered, "Is he still alive? He is my brother."

33The men took this as a good sign and were quick to pick up his word. "Yes, your brother Ben-Hadad!" they said.

"Go and get him," the king said. When Ben-Hadad came out, Ahab had him come up into his chariot.

34"I will return the cities my father took from your father," Ben-Hadad offered. "You may set up your own market areas in Damascus, as my father did in Samaria."

⌊Ahab said,⌋ "On the basis of a treaty I will set you free." So he made a treaty with him, and let him go.

A Prophet Condemns Ahab

35By the word of the LORD one of the sons of the prophets said to his companion, "Strike me with your weapon," but the man refused.

36So the prophet said, "Because you have not obeyed the LORD, as soon as you leave me a lion will kill you." And after the man went away, a lion found him and killed him.

37The prophet found another man and said, "Strike me, please." So the man struck him and wounded him. **38**Then the prophet went and stood by the road waiting for the king. He disguised himself with his headband down over his eyes. **39**As the king passed by, the prophet called out to him, "Your servant went into the thick of the battle, and someone came to me with a captive and said, 'Guard this man. If he is missing, it will be your life for his life, or you must pay a talent*a* of silver.' **40**While your servant was busy here and there, the man disappeared."

"That is your sentence," the king of Israel said. "You have pronounced it yourself."

41Then the prophet quickly removed the headband from his eyes, and the king of Israel recognized him as one of the prophets. **42**He said to the king, "This is what the LORD says: 'You have set free a man I had determined should die.*b* Therefore it is your life for his life, your people for his people.'" **43**Sullen and angry, the king of Israel went to his palace in Samaria.

Naboth's Vineyard

21 Some time later there was an incident involving a vineyard belonging to Naboth the Jezreelite. The vineyard was in Jezreel, close to the palace of Ahab king of Samaria. **2**Ahab said to Naboth, "Let me have your vineyard to use for a vegetable garden, since it is close to my palace. In exchange I will give you a better vineyard or, if you prefer, I will pay you whatever it is worth."

3But Naboth replied, "The LORD forbid that I should give you the inheritance of my fathers."

4So Ahab went home, sullen and angry because Naboth the Jezreelite had said, "I will not give you the inheritance of my fathers." He lay on his bed sulking and refused to eat.

5His wife Jezebel came in and asked him, "Why are you so sullen? Why won't you eat?"

6He answered her, "Because I said to Naboth the Jezreelite, 'Sell me your vineyard; or if you prefer, I will give you another vineyard in its place.' But he said, 'I will not give you my vineyard.'"

7Jezebel his wife said, "Is this how you act as king over Israel? Get up and eat! Cheer up. I'll get you the vineyard of Naboth the Jezreelite."

8So she wrote letters in Ahab's name, placed his seal on them, and sent them to the elders and nobles who lived in Naboth's city with him. **9**In those letters she wrote:

> "Proclaim a day of fasting and seat Naboth in a prominent place among the people. **10**But seat two scoundrels opposite him and have them testify that he has cursed both God and the king. Then take him out and stone him to death."

11So the elders and nobles who lived in Naboth's city did as Jezebel directed in the letters she had written to them. **12**They proclaimed

---

*a39 That is, about 75 pounds (about 34 kilograms)   *b42 The Hebrew term refers to the irrevocable giving over of things or persons to the LORD, often by totally destroying them.

a fast and seated Naboth in a prominent place among the people. ¹³Then two scoundrels came and sat opposite him and brought charges against Naboth before the people, saying, "Naboth has cursed both God and the king." So they took him outside the city and stoned him to death. ¹⁴Then they sent word to Jezebel: "Naboth has been stoned and is dead."

¹⁵As soon as Jezebel heard that Naboth had been stoned to death, she said to Ahab, "Get up and take possession of the vineyard of Naboth the Jezreelite that he refused to sell you. He is no longer alive, but dead." ¹⁶When Ahab heard that Naboth was dead, he got up and went down to take possession of Naboth's vineyard.

¹⁷Then the word of the LORD came to Elijah the Tishbite: ¹⁸"Go down to meet Ahab king of Israel, who rules in Samaria. He is now in Naboth's vineyard, where he has gone to take possession of it. ¹⁹Say to him, 'This is what the LORD says: Have you not murdered a man and seized his property?' Then say to him, 'This is what the LORD says: In the place where dogs licked up Naboth's blood, dogs will lick up your blood—yes, yours!'"

²⁰Ahab said to Elijah, "So you have found me, my enemy!"

"I have found you," he answered, "because you have sold yourself to do evil in the eyes of the LORD. ²¹'I am going to bring disaster on you. I will consume your descendants and cut off from Ahab every last male in Israel—slave or free. ²²I will make your house like that of Jeroboam son of Nebat and that of Baasha son of Ahijah, because you have provoked me to anger and have caused Israel to sin.'

²³"And also concerning Jezebel the LORD says: 'Dogs will devour Jezebel by the wall of ᵃ Jezreel.'

²⁴"Dogs will eat those belonging to Ahab who die in the city, and the birds of the air will feed on those who die in the country."

²⁵(There was never a man like Ahab, who sold himself to do evil in the eyes of the LORD, urged on by Jezebel his wife. ²⁶He behaved in the vilest manner by going after idols, like the Amorites the LORD drove out before Israel.)

²⁷When Ahab heard these words, he tore his clothes, put on sackcloth and fasted. He lay in sackcloth and went around meekly.

²⁸Then the word of the LORD came to Elijah the Tishbite: ²⁹"Have you noticed how Ahab has humbled himself before me? Because he has humbled himself, I will not bring this disaster in his day, but I will bring it on his house in the days of his son."

> **1 Kings 21:28–29**
>
> *God Is Merciful*
>
> Then the word of the LORD came to Elijah the Tishbite: "Have you noticed how Ahab has humbled himself before me? Because he has humbled himself, I will not bring this disaster in his day."

Micaiah Prophesies Against Ahab

22 For three years there was no war between Aram and Israel. ²But in the third year Jehoshaphat king of Judah went down to see the king of Israel. ³The king of Israel had said to his officials, "Don't you know that Ramoth Gilead belongs to us and yet we are doing nothing to retake it from the king of Aram?"

⁴So he asked Jehoshaphat, "Will you go with me to fight against Ramoth Gilead?"

Jehoshaphat replied to the king of Israel, "I am as you are, my people as your people, my horses as your horses." ⁵But Jehoshaphat also said to the king of Israel, "First seek the counsel of the LORD."

⁶So the king of Israel brought together the prophets—about four hundred men—and asked them, "Shall I go to war against Ramoth Gilead, or shall I refrain?"

"Go," they answered, "for the Lord will give it into the king's hand."

⁷But Jehoshaphat asked, "Is there not a prophet of the LORD here whom we can inquire of?"

⁸The king of Israel answered Jehoshaphat, "There is still one man through whom we can inquire of the LORD, but I hate him because he

ᵃ23 Most Hebrew manuscripts; a few Hebrew manuscripts, Vulgate and Syriac (see also 2 Kings 9:26) *the plot of ground at* never prophesies anything good about me, but always bad. He is Micaiah son of Imlah."

"The king should not say that," Jehoshaphat replied.

⁹So the king of Israel called one of his officials and said, "Bring Micaiah son of Imlah at once."

¹⁰Dressed in their royal robes, the king of Israel and Jehoshaphat king of Judah were sitting on their thrones at the threshing floor by the entrance of the gate of Samaria, with all the prophets prophesying before them. ¹¹Now Zedekiah son of Kenaanah had made iron horns and he declared, "This is what the LORD says: 'With these you will gore the Arameans until they are destroyed.'"

¹²All the other prophets were prophesying the same thing. "Attack Ramoth Gilead and be victorious," they said, "for the LORD will give it into the king's hand."

¹³The messenger who had gone to summon Micaiah said to him, "Look, as one man the other prophets are predicting success for the king. Let your word agree with theirs, and speak favorably."

¹⁴But Micaiah said, "As surely as the LORD lives, I can tell him only what the LORD tells me."

¹⁵When he arrived, the king asked him, "Micaiah, shall we go to war against Ramoth Gilead, or shall I refrain?"

"Attack and be victorious," he answered, "for the LORD will give it into the king's hand."

¹⁶The king said to him, "How many times must I make you swear to tell me nothing but the truth in the name of the LORD?"

¹⁷Then Micaiah answered, "I saw all Israel scattered on the hills like sheep without a shepherd, and the LORD said, 'These people have no master. Let each one go home in peace.'"

¹⁸The king of Israel said to Jehoshaphat, "Didn't I tell you that he never prophesies anything good about me, but only bad?"

¹⁹Micaiah continued, "Therefore hear the word of the LORD: I saw the LORD sitting on his throne with all the host of heaven standing around him on his right and on his left. ²⁰And the LORD said, 'Who will entice Ahab into attacking Ramoth Gilead and going to his death there?'

"One suggested this, and another that. ²¹Finally, a spirit came forward, stood before the LORD and said, 'I will entice him.'

²²"'By what means?' the LORD asked.

"'I will go out and be a lying spirit in the mouths of all his prophets,' he said.

"'You will succeed in enticing him,' said the LORD. 'Go and do it.'

²³"So now the LORD has put a lying spirit in the mouths of all these prophets of yours. The LORD has decreed disaster for you."

²⁴Then Zedekiah son of Kenaanah went up and slapped Micaiah in the face. "Which way did the spirit from*a* the LORD go when he went from me to speak to you?" he asked.

²⁵Micaiah replied, "You will find out on the day you go to hide in an inner room."

²⁶The king of Israel then ordered, "Take Micaiah and send him back to Amon the ruler of the city and to Joash the king's son ²⁷and say, 'This is what the king says: Put this fellow in prison and give him nothing but bread and water until I return safely.'"

²⁸Micaiah declared, "If you ever return safely, the LORD has not spoken through me." Then he added, "Mark my words, all you people!"

Ahab Killed at Ramoth Gilead

²⁹So the king of Israel and Jehoshaphat king of Judah went up to Ramoth Gilead. ³⁰The king of Israel said to Jehoshaphat, "I will enter the battle in disguise, but you wear your royal robes." So the king of Israel disguised himself and went into battle.

---

1 Kings 22:19

God Is King of All

Micaiah continued, "Therefore hear the word of the LORD: I saw the LORD sitting on his throne with all the host of heaven standing around him on his right and on his left."

---

a24 Or Spirit of

Family Resemblance

Read: 1 Kings 22:41–53

MOST CHILDREN RESEMBLE their parents in some way. Sometimes the resemblance is physical: They're born with their mother's eyes or father's grin. Other times, the likeness relates to personality traits: They've inherited a hot temper from papa or a sweet disposition from mama. For Christian parents, the most important thing is not whether our kids inherit dad's curly hair or mom's way with words. The most important trait we long to pass on is our love for the Lord. We want our children to be members of the family of faith. Parents who love God want to give their children every opportunity to learn what that means.

The Bible doesn't describe Jehoshaphat's physical appearance, but it does reveal that he bore a strong family resemblance to his father Asa, who was known for opposing idolatry and worshiping God. Like father, like son. Jehoshaphat was a good and godly king who reigned over Judah for 25 years. His epitaph could be summed up in a few poignant words: "Jehoshaphat, who sought the LORD with all his heart" (2 Chronicles 22:9). By following in his godly father's footsteps, King Jehoshaphat pleased God.

It's been well said that God has no grandchildren, only children. Each and every individual has to decide whether or not to accept redemption through Jesus Christ. Children who are brought up in Christian homes have the benefit of the teaching and influence of their parents, although it's their decision to follow their parents' example or walk away. But it's a great advantage to grow up with godly role models. Just look at young Timothy, who was commended for his "sincere faith, which first lived in [his] grandmother Lois and [his] mother Eunice" (2 Timothy 1:5).

Not everyone has had the benefit of a Christian upbringing, but that in no way excludes them from the family of God. God has a way of adopting some of the most unlikely spiritual orphans. He wants you and me and others in the family to adopt them too! We can show them how to live in a holy way just as Asa showed Jehoshaphat. You may or may not have kids who have inherited your eyes and ears, but you can help others develop eyes to see God and ears to hear the gospel. Encourage those in your sphere of influence to cultivate a strong family resemblance to their heavenly Father.

1 Kings 22:42–43

Jehoshaphat was thirty-five years old when he became king, and he reigned in Jerusalem twenty-five years. His mother's name was Azubah daughter of Shilhi. In everything he walked in the ways of his father Asa and did not stray from them; he did what was right in the eyes of the LORD.

reflection

1 How did you come into God's family?

2 How have you grown to "look like" God since you joined his family?

3 Which of God's traits would you like to model to your children or your "faith children"?

RELATED READINGS

1 Kings 15:11–15;
2 Chronicles 17:3–6;
22:7–9

Monday

Go to page 441 for your next devotional reading.

³¹Now the king of Aram had ordered his thirty-two chariot commanders, "Do not fight with anyone, small or great, except the king of Israel." ³²When the chariot commanders saw Jehoshaphat, they thought, "Surely this is the king of Israel." So they turned to attack him, but when Jehoshaphat cried out, ³³the chariot commanders saw that he was not the king of Israel and stopped pursuing him.

³⁴But someone drew his bow at random and hit the king of Israel between the sections of his armor. The king told his chariot driver, "Wheel around and get me out of the fighting. I've been wounded." ³⁵All day long the battle raged, and the king was propped up in his chariot facing the Arameans. The blood from his wound ran onto the floor of the chariot, and that evening he died. ³⁶As the sun was setting, a cry spread through the army: "Every man to his town; everyone to his land!"

³⁷So the king died and was brought to Samaria, and they buried him there. ³⁸They washed the chariot at a pool in Samaria (where the prostitutes bathed),ᵃ and the dogs licked up his blood, as the word of the LORD had declared.

³⁹As for the other events of Ahab's reign, including all he did, the palace he built and inlaid with ivory, and the cities he fortified, are they not written in the book of the annals of the kings of Israel? ⁴⁰Ahab rested with his fathers. And Ahaziah his son succeeded him as king.

Jehoshaphat King of Judah

⁴¹Jehoshaphat son of Asa became king of Judah in the fourth year of Ahab king of Israel. ⁴²Jehoshaphat was thirty-five years old when he became king, and he reigned in Jerusalem twenty-five years. His mother's name was Azubah daughter of Shilhi. ⁴³In everything he walked in the ways of his father Asa and did not stray from them; he did what was right in the eyes of the LORD. The high places, however, were not removed, and the people continued to offer sacrifices and burn incense there. ⁴⁴Jehoshaphat was also at peace with the king of Israel.

⁴⁵As for the other events of Jehoshaphat's reign, the things he achieved and his military exploits, are they not written in the book of the annals of the kings of Judah? ⁴⁶He rid the land of the rest of the male shrine prostitutes who remained there even after the reign of his father Asa. ⁴⁷There was then no king in Edom; a deputy ruled.

⁴⁸Now Jehoshaphat built a fleet of trading shipsᵇ to go to Ophir for gold, but they never set sail—they were wrecked at Ezion Geber. ⁴⁹At that time Ahaziah son of Ahab said to Jehoshaphat, "Let my men sail with your men," but Jehoshaphat refused.

⁵⁰Then Jehoshaphat rested with his fathers and was buried with them in the city of David his father. And Jehoram his son succeeded him.

Ahaziah King of Israel

⁵¹Ahaziah son of Ahab became king of Israel in Samaria in the seventeenth year of Jehoshaphat king of Judah, and he reigned over Israel two years. ⁵²He did evil in the eyes of the LORD, because he walked in the ways of his father and mother and in the ways of Jeroboam son of Nebat, who caused Israel to sin. ⁵³He served and worshiped Baal and provoked the LORD, the God of Israel, to anger, just as his father had done.

ᵃ38 Or *Samaria and cleaned the weapons*   ᵇ48 Hebrew *of ships of Tarshish*

2 Kings

Second Kings continues the *stories of the kings* of Israel and Judah. Much of its storyline focuses on Elijah's successor, Elisha. Elijah's public confrontations with King Ahab are replaced with Elisha's *quieter miracles* of mercy. The ministries of several other prophets, including Isaiah, are also covered in this book. But mostly it looks at the kings—most of them forgettable.

As you read of the different kings and prophets, notice how *God used various personalities* with assorted gifts—if the leaders chose to follow him. Those who looked to God for leadership were worthy leaders to their own people, but those who tried to lead without him inevitably failed.

Author:
Unknown.

Audience:
The people of Israel.

Date:
Between 560 and 550 B.C.

Setting:
One kingdom has divided into two.

Verse to Remember:
The LORD warned Israel and Judah through all his prophets and seers: "Turn from your evil ways. Observe my commands and decrees, in accordance with the entire Law that I commanded your fathers to obey and that I delivered to you through my servants the prophets." (17:13)

The LORD's Judgment on Ahaziah

1 After Ahab's death, Moab rebelled against Israel. ²Now Ahaziah had fallen through the lattice of his upper room in Samaria and injured himself. So he sent messengers, saying to them, "Go and consult Baal-Zebub, the god of Ekron, to see if I will recover from this injury."

³But the angel of the LORD said to Elijah the Tishbite, "Go up and meet the messengers of the king of Samaria and ask them, 'Is it because there is no God in Israel that you are going off to consult Baal-Zebub, the god of Ekron?' ⁴Therefore this is what the LORD says: 'You will not leave the bed you are lying on. You will certainly die!'" So Elijah went.

⁵When the messengers returned to the king, he asked them, "Why have you come back?"

⁶"A man came to meet us," they replied. "And he said to us, 'Go back to the king who sent you and tell him, "This is what the LORD says: Is it because there is no God in Israel that you are sending men to consult Baal-Zebub, the god of Ekron? Therefore you will not leave the bed you are lying on. You will certainly die!"'"

⁷The king asked them, "What kind of man was it who came to meet you and told you this?"

⁸They replied, "He was a man with a garment of hair and with a leather belt around his waist."

The king said, "That was Elijah the Tishbite."

⁹Then he sent to Elijah a captain with his company of fifty men. The captain went up to Elijah, who was sitting on the top of a hill, and said to him, "Man of God, the king says, 'Come down!'"

¹⁰Elijah answered the captain, "If I am a man of God, may fire come down from heaven and consume you and your fifty men!" Then fire fell from heaven and consumed the captain and his men.

¹¹At this the king sent to Elijah another captain with his fifty men. The captain said to him, "Man of God, this is what the king says, 'Come down at once!'"

¹²"If I am a man of God," Elijah replied, "may fire come down from heaven and consume you and your fifty men!" Then the fire of God fell from heaven and consumed him and his fifty men.

¹³So the king sent a third captain with his fifty men. This third captain went up and fell on his knees before Elijah. "Man of God," he begged, "please have respect for my life and the lives of these fifty men, your servants! ¹⁴See, fire has fallen from heaven and consumed the first two captains and all their men. But now have respect for my life!"

¹⁵The angel of the LORD said to Elijah, "Go down with him; do not be afraid of him." So Elijah got up and went down with him to the king.

¹⁶He told the king, "This is what the LORD says: Is it because there is no God in Israel for you to consult that you have sent messengers to consult Baal-Zebub, the god of Ekron? Because you have done this, you will never leave the bed you are lying on. You will certainly die!" ¹⁷So he died, according to the word of the LORD that Elijah had spoken.

Because Ahaziah had no son, Joram[a] succeeded him as king in the second year of Jehoram son of Jehoshaphat king of Judah. ¹⁸As for all the other events of Ahaziah's reign, and what he did, are they not written in the book of the annals of the kings of Israel?

Elijah Taken Up to Heaven

2 When the LORD was about to take Elijah up to heaven in a whirlwind, Elijah and Elisha were on their way from Gilgal. ²Elijah said to Elisha, "Stay here; the LORD has sent me to Bethel."

But Elisha said, "As surely as the LORD lives and as you live, I will not leave you." So they went down to Bethel.

³The company of the prophets at Bethel came out to Elisha and asked, "Do you know that the LORD is going to take your master from you today?"

"Yes, I know," Elisha replied, "but do not speak of it."

⁴Then Elijah said to him, "Stay here, Elisha; the LORD has sent me to Jericho."

And he replied, "As surely as the LORD lives and as you live, I will not leave you." So they went to Jericho.

⁵The company of the prophets at Jericho went up to Elisha and asked him, "Do you know that the LORD is going to take your master from you today?"

"Yes, I know," he replied, "but do not speak of it."

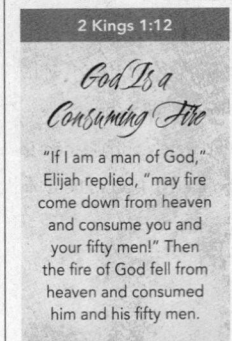

2 Kings 1:12

God Is a Consuming Fire

"If I am a man of God," Elijah replied, "may fire come down from heaven and consume you and your fifty men!" Then the fire of God fell from heaven and consumed him and his fifty men.

ᵃ17 Hebrew *Jehoram*, a variant of *Joram*

Stay With Me

Read: 2 Kings 2:1–15

WHERE HAVE ALL the mentors gone? Where are the older, wiser women who once taught younger women to bake bread, sew clothing and keep their kitchens spotless? Where are the women who once gathered in homes for coffee and encouragement? They haven't disappeared. They can be found in the church, in homes, offices, neighborhoods and schools. Their focus may have changed, but they are still there for the younger women who have much to learn from them.

Some of today's mentors are much like Elijah, who was faithfully carrying on in his role as God's prophet when he saw Elisha working in his father's fields. He saw the potential in this young man, so he threw his mantle on Elisha's shoulders, symbolically passing the leadership to the next generation. Elisha then said good-bye to his old life and moved forward, following Elijah and learning from the older man.

That's where we find the prophetic pair now: at Bethel, the house of God. Elisha had steadfastly stayed with his mentor Elijah. Even when Elijah commanded Elisha to remain in Bethel, Elisha refused, saying he would never leave the older prophet's side. Thus, Elisha expressed his love and faithfulness not only to Elijah, but also to God. Elisha vowed never to leave Elijah, and he didn't until he had gleaned everything he needed to know from this godly man, until he received the blessing of his mentor, until he watched his mentor vanish in a heavenly whirlwind.

We all need mentors like Elijah: women who have faced challenges and overcome; women who have grown through struggle and perseverance; women who have seen God perform miracles; women who have gone through hard times and experienced God's presence with them. These are the women who can pass on the news that God's Word is still active and dynamic among us. These are the ones who can place the mantle on our shoulders and confirm that we're ready to move on to greater tasks.

Who are the godly women walking along the roads in your life, willing to pass on the knowledge they've gained? Who has watched you as you've worked in your Bible study, your volunteer position or at your job? Who has seen your gifts and your potential? Try being like Elisha. Follow her and glean from her knowledge of the living God concerning how to best serve him.

2 Kings 2:2

Elijah said to Elisha, "Stay here; the LORD has sent me to Bethel." But Elisha said, "As surely as the LORD lives and as you live, I will not leave you." So they went down to Bethel.

reflection

1 Who do you see as an Elijah, faithfully serving God in your community?

2 What do you need to do to become more available to learn from a godly mentor?

3 In what ways could you become a mentor to another woman? Think of someone you know who could use a godly mentor to come alongside her in her work.

RELATED READINGS

1 Kings 19:19–21; Titus 2:1–5

Go to page 446 for your next devotional reading.

6Then Elijah said to him, "Stay here; the LORD has sent me to the Jordan."

And he replied, "As surely as the LORD lives and as you live, I will not leave you." So the two of them walked on.

7Fifty men of the company of the prophets went and stood at a distance, facing the place where Elijah and Elisha had stopped at the Jordan. 8Elijah took his cloak, rolled it up and struck the water with it. The water divided to the right and to the left, and the two of them crossed over on dry ground.

9When they had crossed, Elijah said to Elisha, "Tell me, what can I do for you before I am taken from you?"

"Let me inherit a double portion of your spirit," Elisha replied.

10"You have asked a difficult thing," Elijah said, "yet if you see me when I am taken from you, it will be yours—otherwise not."

11As they were walking along and talking together, suddenly a chariot of fire and horses of fire appeared and separated the two of them, and Elijah went up to heaven in a whirlwind. 12Elisha saw this and cried out, "My father! My father! The chariots and horsemen of Israel!" And Elisha saw him no more. Then he took hold of his own clothes and tore them apart.

13He picked up the cloak that had fallen from Elijah and went back and stood on the bank of the Jordan. 14Then he took the cloak that had fallen from him and struck the water with it. "Where now is the LORD, the God of Elijah?" he asked. When he struck the water, it divided to the right and to the left, and he crossed over.

15The company of the prophets from Jericho, who were watching, said, "The spirit of Elijah is resting on Elisha." And they went to meet him and bowed to the ground before him. 16"Look," they said, "we your servants have fifty able men. Let them go and look for your master. Perhaps the Spirit of the LORD has picked him up and set him down on some mountain or in some valley."

"No," Elisha replied, "do not send them."

17But they persisted until he was too ashamed to refuse. So he said, "Send them." And they sent fifty men, who searched for three days but did not find him. 18When they returned to Elisha, who was staying in Jericho, he said to them, "Didn't I tell you not to go?"

Healing of the Water

19The men of the city said to Elisha, "Look, our lord, this town is well situated, as you can see, but the water is bad and the land is unproductive."

20"Bring me a new bowl," he said, "and put salt in it." So they brought it to him.

21Then he went out to the spring and threw the salt into it, saying, "This is what the LORD says: 'I have healed this water. Never again will it cause death or make the land unproductive.'" 22And the water has remained wholesome to this day, according to the word Elisha had spoken.

Elisha Is Jeered

23From there Elisha went up to Bethel. As he was walking along the road, some youths came out of the town and jeered at him. "Go on up, you baldhead!" they said. "Go on up, you baldhead!" 24He turned around, looked at them and called down a curse on them in the name of the LORD. Then two bears came out of the woods and mauled forty-two of the youths. 25And he went on to Mount Carmel and from there returned to Samaria.

Moab Revolts

3 Joram[a] son of Ahab became king of Israel in Samaria in the eighteenth year of Jehoshaphat king of Judah, and he reigned twelve years. 2He did evil in the eyes of the LORD, but not as his father and mother had done. He got rid of the sacred stone of Baal that his father had made. 3Nevertheless he clung to the sins of Jeroboam son of Nebat, which he had caused Israel to commit; he did not turn away from them.

4Now Mesha king of Moab raised sheep, and he had to supply the king of Israel with a hundred thousand lambs and with the wool of a hundred thousand rams. 5But after Ahab died, the king of Moab rebelled against the king of Israel. 6So at that time King Joram set out from Samaria and mobilized all Israel. 7He also sent this message to Jehoshaphat king of Judah:

a1 Hebrew *Jehoram*, a variant of *Joram*; also in verse 6

"The king of Moab has rebelled against me. Will you go with me to fight against Moab?"

"I will go with you," he replied. "I am as you are, my people as your people, my horses as your horses."

⁸"By what route shall we attack?" he asked.

"Through the Desert of Edom," he answered.

⁹So the king of Israel set out with the king of Judah and the king of Edom. After a roundabout march of seven days, the army had no more water for themselves or for the animals with them.

¹⁰"What!" exclaimed the king of Israel. "Has the Lord called us three kings together only to hand us over to Moab?"

¹¹But Jehoshaphat asked, "Is there no prophet of the Lord here, that we may inquire of the Lord through him?"

An officer of the king of Israel answered, "Elisha son of Shaphat is here. He used to pour water on the hands of Elijah.ᵃ"

¹²Jehoshaphat said, "The word of the Lord is with him." So the king of Israel and Jehoshaphat and the king of Edom went down to him.

¹³Elisha said to the king of Israel, "What do we have to do with each other? Go to the prophets of your father and the prophets of your mother."

"No," the king of Israel answered, "because it was the Lord who called us three kings together to hand us over to Moab."

¹⁴Elisha said, "As surely as the Lord Almighty lives, whom I serve, if I did not have respect for the presence of Jehoshaphat king of Judah, I would not look at you or even notice you. ¹⁵But now bring me a harpist."

While the harpist was playing, the hand of the Lord came upon Elisha ¹⁶and he said, "This is what the Lord says: Make this valley full of ditches. ¹⁷For this is what the Lord says: You will see neither wind nor rain, yet this valley will be filled with water, and you, your cattle and your other animals will drink. ¹⁸This is an easy thing in the eyes of the Lord; he will also hand Moab over to you. ¹⁹You will overthrow every fortified city and every major town. You will cut down every good tree, stop up all the springs, and ruin every good field with stones."

²⁰The next morning, about the time for offering the sacrifice, there it was—water flowing from the direction of Edom! And the land was filled with water.

²¹Now all the Moabites had heard that the kings had come to fight against them; so every man, young and old, who could bear arms was called up and stationed on the border. ²²When they got up early in the morning, the sun was shining on the water. To the Moabites across the way, the water looked red—like blood. ²³"That's blood!" they said. "Those kings must have fought and slaughtered each other. Now to the plunder, Moab!"

²⁴But when the Moabites came to the camp of Israel, the Israelites rose up and fought them until they fled. And the Israelites invaded the land and slaughtered the Moabites. ²⁵They destroyed the towns, and each man threw a stone on every good field until it was covered. They stopped up all the springs and cut down every good tree. Only Kir Hareseth was left with its stones in place, but men armed with slings surrounded it and attacked it as well.

²⁶When the king of Moab saw that the battle had gone against him, he took with him seven hundred swordsmen to break through to the king of Edom, but they failed. ²⁷Then he took his firstborn son, who was to succeed him as king, and offered him as a sacrifice on the city wall. The fury against Israel was great; they withdrew and returned to their own land.

The Widow's Oil

4 The wife of a man from the company of the prophets cried out to Elisha, "Your servant my husband is dead, and you know that he revered the Lord. But now his creditor is coming to take my two boys as his slaves."

²Elisha replied to her, "How can I help you? Tell me, what do you have in your house?"

"Your servant has nothing there at all," she said, "except a little oil."

³Elisha said, "Go around and ask all your neighbors for empty jars. Don't ask for just a few. ⁴Then go inside and shut the door behind you and your sons. Pour oil into all the jars, and as each is filled, put it to one side."

⁵She left him and afterward shut the door

ᵃ11 That is, he was Elijah's personal servant.

behind her and her sons. They brought the jars to her and she kept pouring. **6**When all the jars were full, she said to her son, "Bring me another one."

But he replied, "There is not a jar left." Then the oil stopped flowing.

7She went and told the man of God, and he said, "Go, sell the oil and pay your debts. You and your sons can live on what is left."

The Shunammite's Son Restored to Life

8One day Elisha went to Shunem. And a well-to-do woman was there, who urged him to stay for a meal. So whenever he came by, he stopped there to eat. **9**She said to her husband, "I know that this man who often comes our way is a holy man of God. **10**Let's make a small room on the roof and put in it a bed and a table, a chair and a lamp for him. Then he can stay there whenever he comes to us."

11One day when Elisha came, he went up to his room and lay down there. **12**He said to his servant Gehazi, "Call the Shunammite." So he called her, and she stood before him. **13**Elisha said to him, "Tell her, 'You have gone to all this trouble for us. Now what can be done for you? Can we speak on your behalf to the king or the commander of the army?'"

She replied, "I have a home among my own people."

14"What can be done for her?" Elisha asked.

Gehazi said, "Well, she has no son and her husband is old."

15Then Elisha said, "Call her." So he called her, and she stood in the doorway. **16**"About this time next year," Elisha said, "you will hold a son in your arms."

"No, my lord," she objected. "Don't mislead your servant, O man of God!"

17But the woman became pregnant, and the next year about that same time she gave birth to a son, just as Elisha had told her.

18The child grew, and one day he went out to his father, who was with the reapers. **19**"My head! My head!" he said to his father.

His father told a servant, "Carry him to his mother." **20**After the servant had lifted him up and carried him to his mother, the boy sat on her lap until noon, and then he died. **21**She went up and laid him on the bed of the man of God, then shut the door and went out.

22She called her husband and said, "Please send me one of the servants and a donkey so I can go to the man of God quickly and return."

23"Why go to him today?" he asked. "It's not the New Moon or the Sabbath."

"It's all right," she said.

24She saddled the donkey and said to her servant, "Lead on; don't slow down for me unless I tell you." **25**So she set out and came to the man of God at Mount Carmel.

When he saw her in the distance, the man of God said to his servant Gehazi, "Look! There's the Shunammite! **26**Run to meet her and ask her, 'Are you all right? Is your husband all right? Is your child all right?'"

"Everything is all right," she said.

27When she reached the man of God at the mountain, she took hold of his feet. Gehazi came over to push her away, but the man of God said, "Leave her alone! She is in bitter distress, but the LORD has hidden it from me and has not told me why."

28"Did I ask you for a son, my lord?" she said. "Didn't I tell you, 'Don't raise my hopes'?"

29Elisha said to Gehazi, "Tuck your cloak into your belt, take my staff in your hand and run. If you meet anyone, do not greet him, and if anyone greets you, do not answer. Lay my staff on the boy's face."

30But the child's mother said, "As surely as the LORD lives and as you live, I will not leave you." So he got up and followed her.

31Gehazi went on ahead and laid the staff on the boy's face, but there was no sound or response. So Gehazi went back to meet Elisha and told him, "The boy has not awakened."

32When Elisha reached the house, there was the boy lying dead on his couch. **33**He went in, shut the door on the two of them and prayed to the LORD. **34**Then he got on the bed and lay upon the boy, mouth to mouth, eyes to eyes, hands to hands. As he stretched himself out upon him, the boy's body grew warm. **35**Elisha turned away and walked back and forth in the room and then got on the bed and stretched out upon him once more. The boy sneezed seven times and opened his eyes.

36Elisha summoned Gehazi and said, "Call the Shunammite." And he did. When she came, he said, "Take your son." **37**She came in, fell at his feet and bowed to the ground. Then she took her son and went out.

Death in the Pot

38Elisha returned to Gilgal and there was a famine in that region. While the company of the prophets was meeting with him, he said to his servant, "Put on the large pot and cook some stew for these men."

39One of them went out into the fields to gather herbs and found a wild vine. He gathered some of its gourds and filled the fold of his cloak. When he returned, he cut them up into the pot of stew, though no one knew what they were. **40**The stew was poured out for the men, but as they began to eat it, they cried out, "O man of God, there is death in the pot!" And they could not eat it.

41Elisha said, "Get some flour." He put it into the pot and said, "Serve it to the people to eat." And there was nothing harmful in the pot.

Feeding of a Hundred

42A man came from Baal Shalishah, bringing the man of God twenty loaves of barley bread baked from the first ripe grain, along with some heads of new grain. "Give it to the people to eat," Elisha said.

43"How can I set this before a hundred men?" his servant asked.

But Elisha answered, "Give it to the people to eat. For this is what the LORD says: 'They will eat and have some left over.'" **44**Then he set it before them, and they ate and had some left over, according to the word of the LORD.

Naaman Healed of Leprosy

5 Now Naaman was commander of the army of the king of Aram. He was a great man in the sight of his master and highly regarded, because through him the LORD had given victory to Aram. He was a valiant soldier, but he had leprosy.[a]

2Now bands from Aram had gone out and

had taken captive a young girl from Israel, and she served Naaman's wife. **3**She said to her mistress, "If only my master would see the prophet who is in Samaria! He would cure him of his leprosy."

4Naaman went to his master and told him what the girl from Israel had said. **5**"By all means, go," the king of Aram replied. "I will send a letter to the king of Israel." So Naaman left, taking with him ten talents[b] of silver, six thousand shekels[c] of gold and ten sets of clothing. **6**The letter that he took to the king of Israel read: "With this letter I am sending my servant Naaman to you so that you may cure him of his leprosy."

7As soon as the king of Israel read the letter, he tore his robes and said, "Am I God? Can I kill and bring back to life? Why does this fellow send someone to me to be cured of his leprosy? See how he is trying to pick a quarrel with me!"

8When Elisha the man of God heard that the king of Israel had torn his robes, he sent him this message: "Why have you torn your robes? Have the man come to me and he will know that there is a prophet in Israel." **9**So Naaman went with his horses and chariots and stopped at the door of Elisha's house. **10**Elisha sent a messenger to say to him, "Go, wash yourself seven times in the Jordan, and your flesh will be restored and you will be cleansed."

11But Naaman went away angry and said, "I thought that he would surely come out to me and stand and call on the name of the LORD his God, wave his hand over the spot and cure me of my leprosy. **12**Are not Abana and Pharpar, the rivers of Damascus, better than any of the waters of Israel? Couldn't I wash in them and be cleansed?" So he turned and went off in a rage.

13Naaman's servants went to him and said,

2 Kings 4:43

God Provides Abundantly

"How can I set this before a hundred men?" his servant asked. Elisha answered, "Give it to the people to eat. For this is what the LORD says: 'They will eat and have some left over.' "

---

*a*1 The Hebrew word was used for various diseases affecting the skin—not necessarily leprosy; also in verses 3, 6, 7, 11 and 27.
*b*5 That is, about 750 pounds (about 340 kilograms)   *c*5 That is, about 150 pounds (about 70 kilograms)

Those Exceptions of Life

Read: 2 Kings 5:1–14

2 Kings 5:1

Now Naaman was com-
mander of the army of
the king of Aram.
He was a great man in
the sight of his master
and highly regarded,
because through him the
LORD had given victory
to Aram. He was a valiant
soldier, but
he had leprosy.

reflection

1 What *except* has dis-
rupted your life?

2 How have you handled
your exception? How
has this story lent some
perspective on your own
situation?

3 What step has God
asked you to take that
you are reluctant to try?

RELATED READINGS

Luke 4:24–27;
John 9:1–11

IS YOUR LIFE HAPPY . . . *except* for one thing? Perhaps you enjoy
a loving marriage, a beautiful home and financial ease . . . *except* you suffer from infertility. Maybe you have graduated with a
master's degree, founded a business and are in top physical condition . . . *except* your parents are getting divorced. If you compiled
a list of all the positives in your life, what would you include? *I have
great friends; I'm an accomplished pianist; I've inherited a green
thumb.* But what disrupts your sense of well-being? All of us possess at least one *except* that gets in the way of our happiness.

An unnamed slave girl experienced some poignant *excepts* in
her young life. She was one of God's chosen people. She had faith
in God . . . *except* she was a captive of war in a foreign land. The
good news: She found herself in the household of a commander
of the army.

Naaman, the commander, also experienced some significant
excepts. He had great authority and was highly regarded by the
king. Although he was a Gentile, he found favor with the God of
Israel and was granted military victory. *Except* one thing plagued
him: leprosy. If only he could find a cure, his life would be complete.

The slave girl and Naaman had choices to make concerning
life's exceptions. Would they let the exceptions rule their lives?
Or would they let God rule without exception? The slave girl
could have let her situation make her bitter. Instead, she chose to
help the man who was her master. And Naaman chose to take the
advice of a servant girl, not allowing his pride to stand in the way
of her help.

Is God asking you to take one step of obedience that may
bring help and healing to another person? Perhaps it's as simple
as taking up a pen and beginning a note of apology even though
you're still hurting from what *they* did to *you?* Maybe you need to
carve out time for the one thing you've been dreading to do.
It could be you're compelled to take one act of firm discipline for
the unruly child you love. That first step of obedience can bring
your exception into a different light when you learn step by step
what it means to trust God without exceptions.

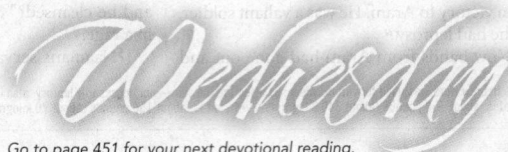

Go to page 451 for your next devotional reading.

"My father, if the prophet had told you to do some great thing, would you not have done it? How much more, then, when he tells you, 'Wash and be cleansed'!" ¹⁴So he went down and dipped himself in the Jordan seven times, as the man of God had told him, and his flesh was restored and became clean like that of a young boy.

¹⁵Then Naaman and all his attendants went back to the man of God. He stood before him and said, "Now I know that there is no God in all the world except in Israel. Please accept now a gift from your servant."

¹⁶The prophet answered, "As surely as the LORD lives, whom I serve, I will not accept a thing." And even though Naaman urged him, he refused.

¹⁷"If you will not," said Naaman, "please let me, your servant, be given as much earth as a pair of mules can carry, for your servant will never again make burnt offerings and sacrifices to any other god but the LORD. ¹⁸But may the LORD forgive your servant for this one thing: When my master enters the temple of Rimmon to bow down and he is leaning on my arm and I bow there also—when I bow down in the temple of Rimmon, may the LORD forgive your servant for this."

¹⁹"Go in peace," Elisha said.

After Naaman had traveled some distance, ²⁰Gehazi, the servant of Elisha the man of God, said to himself, "My master was too easy on Naaman, this Aramean, by not accepting from him what he brought. As surely as the LORD lives, I will run after him and get something from him."

²¹So Gehazi hurried after Naaman. When Naaman saw him running toward him, he got down from the chariot to meet him. "Is everything all right?" he asked.

²²"Everything is all right," Gehazi answered. "My master sent me to say, 'Two young men from the company of the prophets have just come to me from the hill country of Ephraim. Please give them a talent*a* of silver and two sets of clothing.'"

²³"By all means, take two talents," said Naaman. He urged Gehazi to accept them, and then tied up the two talents of silver in two bags, with two sets of clothing. He gave them to two of his servants, and they carried them ahead of Gehazi. ²⁴When Gehazi came to the hill, he took the things from the servants and put them away in the house. He sent the men away and they left. ²⁵Then he went in and stood before his master Elisha.

"Where have you been, Gehazi?" Elisha asked.

"Your servant didn't go anywhere," Gehazi answered.

²⁶But Elisha said to him, "Was not my spirit with you when the man got down from his chariot to meet you? Is this the time to take money, or to accept clothes, olive groves, vineyards, flocks, herds, or menservants and maidservants? ²⁷Naaman's leprosy will cling to you and to your descendants forever." Then Gehazi went from Elisha's presence and he was leprous, as white as snow.

An Axhead Floats

6 The company of the prophets said to Elisha, "Look, the place where we meet with you is too small for us. ²Let us go to the Jordan, where each of us can get a pole; and let us build a place there for us to live."

And he said, "Go."

³Then one of them said, "Won't you please come with your servants?"

"I will," Elisha replied. ⁴And he went with them.

They went to the Jordan and began to cut down trees. ⁵As one of them was cutting down a tree, the iron axhead fell into the water. "Oh, my lord," he cried out, "it was borrowed!"

⁶The man of God asked, "Where did it fall?" When he showed him the place, Elisha cut a stick and threw it there, and made the iron float. ⁷"Lift it out," he said. Then the man reached out his hand and took it.

Elisha Traps Blinded Arameans

⁸Now the king of Aram was at war with Israel. After conferring with his officers, he said, "I will set up my camp in such and such a place."

⁹The man of God sent word to the king of Israel: "Beware of passing that place, because the Arameans are going down there." ¹⁰So the

a22 That is, about 75 pounds (about 34 kilograms)

king of Israel checked on the place indicated by the man of God. Time and again Elisha warned the king, so that he was on his guard in such places.

¹¹This enraged the king of Aram. He summoned his officers and demanded of them, "Will you not tell me which of us is on the side of the king of Israel?"

¹²"None of us, my lord the king," said one of his officers, "but Elisha, the prophet who is in Israel, tells the king of Israel the very words you speak in your bedroom."

¹³"Go, find out where he is," the king ordered, "so I can send men and capture him." The report came back: "He is in Dothan."

¹⁴Then he sent horses and chariots and a strong force there. They went by night and surrounded the city.

¹⁵When the servant of the man of God got up and went out early the next morning, an army with horses and chariots had surrounded the city. "Oh, my lord, what shall we do?" the servant asked.

¹⁶"Don't be afraid," the prophet answered. "Those who are with us are more than those who are with them."

¹⁷And Elisha prayed, "O LORD, open his eyes so he may see." Then the LORD opened the servant's eyes, and he looked and saw the hills full of horses and chariots of fire all around Elisha.

¹⁸As the enemy came down toward him, Elisha prayed to the LORD, "Strike these people with blindness." So he struck them with blindness, as Elisha had asked.

¹⁹Elisha told them, "This is not the road and this is not the city. Follow me, and I will lead you to the man you are looking for." And he led them to Samaria.

²⁰After they entered the city, Elisha said, "LORD, open the eyes of these men so they can see." Then the LORD opened their eyes and they looked, and there they were, inside Samaria.

²¹When the king of Israel saw them, he asked Elisha, "Shall I kill them, my father? Shall I kill them?"

²²"Do not kill them," he answered. "Would you kill men you have captured with your own sword or bow? Set food and water before them so that they may eat and drink and then go back to their master." ²³So he prepared a great feast for them, and after they had finished eating and drinking, he sent them away, and they returned to their master. So the bands from Aram stopped raiding Israel's territory.

Famine in Besieged Samaria

²⁴Some time later, Ben-Hadad king of Aram mobilized his entire army and marched up and laid siege to Samaria. ²⁵There was a great famine in the city; the siege lasted so long that a donkey's head sold for eighty shekels*a* of silver, and a quarter of a cab*b* of seed pods*c* for five shekels.*d*

²⁶As the king of Israel was passing by on the wall, a woman cried to him, "Help me, my lord the king!"

²⁷The king replied, "If the LORD does not help you, where can I get help for you? From the threshing floor? From the winepress?" ²⁸Then he asked her, "What's the matter?"

She answered, "This woman said to me, 'Give up your son so we may eat him today, and tomorrow we'll eat my son.' ²⁹So we cooked my son and ate him. The next day I said to her, 'Give up your son so we may eat him,' but she had hidden him."

³⁰When the king heard the woman's words, he tore his robes. As he went along the wall, the people looked, and there, underneath, he had sackcloth on his body. ³¹He said, "May God deal with me, be it ever so severely, if the head of Elisha son of Shaphat remains on his shoulders today!"

³²Now Elisha was sitting in his house, and the elders were sitting with him. The king sent a messenger ahead, but before he arrived, Elisha said to the elders, "Don't you see how this

---

2 Kings 6:16

God Is Greater

"Don't be afraid," the prophet answered. "Those who are with us are more than those who are with them."

---

*a25 That is, about 2 pounds (about 1 kilogram) *b25 That is, probably about 1/2 pint (about 0.3 liter) *c25 Or of doves' dung
*d25 That is, about 2 ounces (about 55 grams)

murderer is sending someone to cut off my head? Look, when the messenger comes, shut the door and hold it shut against him. Is not the sound of his master's footsteps behind him?"

[33]While he was still talking to them, the messenger came down to him. And the king said, "This disaster is from the LORD. Why should I wait for the LORD any longer?"

7 Elisha said, "Hear the word of the LORD. This is what the LORD says: About this time tomorrow, a seah[a] of flour will sell for a shekel[b] and two seahs[c] of barley for a shekel at the gate of Samaria."

[2]The officer on whose arm the king was leaning said to the man of God, "Look, even if the LORD should open the floodgates of the heavens, could this happen?"

"You will see it with your own eyes," answered Elisha, "but you will not eat any of it!"

The Siege Lifted

[3]Now there were four men with leprosy[d] at the entrance of the city gate. They said to each other, "Why stay here until we die? [4]If we say, 'We'll go into the city'—the famine is there, and we will die. And if we stay here, we will die. So let's go over to the camp of the Arameans and surrender. If they spare us, we live; if they kill us, then we die."

[5]At dusk they got up and went to the camp of the Arameans. When they reached the edge of the camp, not a man was there, [6]for the Lord had caused the Arameans to hear the sound of chariots and horses and a great army, so that they said to one another, "Look, the king of Israel has hired the Hittite and Egyptian kings to attack us!" [7]So they got up and fled in the dusk and abandoned their tents and their horses and donkeys. They left the camp as it was and ran for their lives.

[8]The men who had leprosy reached the edge of the camp and entered one of the tents. They ate and drank, and carried away silver, gold and clothes, and went off and hid them. They returned and entered another tent and took some things from it and hid them also.

[9]Then they said to each other, "We're not doing right. This is a day of good news and we are keeping it to ourselves. If we wait until daylight, punishment will overtake us. Let's go at once and report this to the royal palace."

[10]So they went and called out to the city gatekeepers and told them, "We went into the Aramean camp and not a man was there—not a sound of anyone—only tethered horses and donkeys, and the tents left just as they were." [11]The gatekeepers shouted the news, and it was reported within the palace.

[12]The king got up in the night and said to his officers, "I will tell you what the Arameans have done to us. They know we are starving; so they have left the camp to hide in the countryside, thinking, 'They will surely come out, and then we will take them alive and get into the city.'"

[13]One of his officers answered, "Have some men take five of the horses that are left in the city. Their plight will be like that of all the Israelites left here—yes, they will only be like all these Israelites who are doomed. So let us send them to find out what happened."

[14]So they selected two chariots with their horses, and the king sent them after the Aramean army. He commanded the drivers, "Go and find out what has happened." [15]They followed them as far as the Jordan, and they found the whole road strewn with the clothing and equipment the Arameans had thrown away in their headlong flight. So the messengers returned and reported to the king. [16]Then the people went out and plundered the camp of the Arameans. So a seah of flour sold for a shekel, and two seahs of barley sold for a shekel, as the LORD had said.

[17]Now the king had put the officer on whose arm he leaned in charge of the gate, and the people trampled him in the gateway, and he died, just as the man of God had foretold when the king came down to his house. [18]It happened as the man of God had said to the king: "About this time tomorrow, a seah of flour will sell for a shekel and two seahs of barley for a shekel at the gate of Samaria."

[19]The officer had said to the man of God, "Look, even if the LORD should open the floodgates of the heavens, could this happen?" The man of God had replied, "You will see it with

---

[a]1 That is, probably about 7 quarts (about 7.3 liters); also in verses 16 and 18   [b]1 That is, about 2/5 ounce (about 11 grams); also in verses 16 and 18   [c]1 That is, probably about 13 quarts (about 15 liters); also in verses 16 and 18   [d]3 The Hebrew word is used for various diseases affecting the skin—not necessarily leprosy; also in verse 8.

your own eyes, but you will not eat any of it!" [20]And that is exactly what happened to him, for the people trampled him in the gateway, and he died.

The Shunammite's Land Restored

8 Now Elisha had said to the woman whose son he had restored to life, "Go away with your family and stay for a while wherever you can, because the LORD has decreed a famine in the land that will last seven years." [2]The woman proceeded to do as the man of God said. She and her family went away and stayed in the land of the Philistines seven years.

[3]At the end of the seven years she came back from the land of the Philistines and went to the king to beg for her house and land. [4]The king was talking to Gehazi, the servant of the man of God, and had said, "Tell me about all the great things Elisha has done." [5]Just as Gehazi was telling the king how Elisha had restored the dead to life, the woman whose son Elisha had brought back to life came to beg the king for her house and land.

Gehazi said, "This is the woman, my lord the king, and this is her son whom Elisha restored to life." [6]The king asked the woman about it, and she told him.

Then he assigned an official to her case and said to him, "Give back everything that belonged to her, including all the income from her land from the day she left the country until now."

Hazael Murders Ben-Hadad

[7]Elisha went to Damascus, and Ben-Hadad king of Aram was ill. When the king was told, "The man of God has come all the way up here," [8]he said to Hazael, "Take a gift with you and go to meet the man of God. Consult the LORD through him; ask him, 'Will I recover from this illness?'"

[9]Hazael went to meet Elisha, taking with him as a gift forty camel-loads of all the finest wares of Damascus. He went in and stood before him, and said, "Your son Ben-Hadad king of Aram has sent me to ask, 'Will I recover from this illness?'"

[10]Elisha answered, "Go and say to him,

'You will certainly recover'; but[a] the LORD has revealed to me that he will in fact die." [11]He stared at him with a fixed gaze until Hazael felt ashamed. Then the man of God began to weep.

[12]"Why is my lord weeping?" asked Hazael.

"Because I know the harm you will do to the Israelites," he answered. "You will set fire to their fortified places, kill their young men with the sword, dash their little children to the ground, and rip open their pregnant women."

[13]Hazael said, "How could your servant, a mere dog, accomplish such a feat?"

"The LORD has shown me that you will become king of Aram," answered Elisha.

[14]Then Hazael left Elisha and returned to his master. When Ben-Hadad asked, "What did Elisha say to you?" Hazael replied, "He told me that you would certainly recover." [15]But the next day he took a thick cloth, soaked it in water and spread it over the king's face, so that he died. Then Hazael succeeded him as king.

Jehoram King of Judah

[16]In the fifth year of Joram son of Ahab king of Israel, when Jehoshaphat was king of Judah, Jehoram son of Jehoshaphat began his reign as king of Judah. [17]He was thirty-two years old when he became king, and he reigned in Jerusalem eight years. [18]He walked in the ways of the kings of Israel, as the house of Ahab had done, for he married a daughter of Ahab. He did evil in the eyes of the LORD. [19]Nevertheless, for the sake of his servant David, the LORD was not willing to destroy Judah. He had promised to maintain a lamp for David and his descendants forever.

[20]In the time of Jehoram, Edom rebelled against Judah and set up its own king. [21]So Jehoram[b] went to Zair with all his chariots. The Edomites surrounded him and his chariot commanders, but he rose up and broke through by night; his army, however, fled back home. [22]To this day Edom has been in rebellion against Judah. Libnah revolted at the same time.

[23]As for the other events of Jehoram's reign, and all he did, are they not written in the book of the annals of the kings of Judah? [24]Jehoram rested with his fathers and was buried with

---

*a*10 The Hebrew may also be read *Go and say, 'You will certainly not recover,' for.*   *b*21 Hebrew *Joram*, a variant of *Jehoram*; also in verses 23 and 24

When God Promises

Read: 2 Kings 8:16–24

THE STORY IS TOLD of a 91-year-old woman who said, "I spend about one hour each day with my Lord, reading my Bible and Christian literature. When people ask what good all my reading does if I can't remember what I've read, my answer is always the same: 'I'm in pretty good health, have a roof over my head and have plenty of food to eat. I also have two sons and one grandson who love me dearly. My cup runneth over.' I am not concerned about my memory. I just do my reading and God does the remembering."

God doesn't forget his promises; he remembers them regardless of how much time passes. King Jehoram, Judah's fifth king, reigned for eight years. Unlike his faithful father, Jehoshaphat, who worshiped the Lord, Jehoram "did evil in the eyes of the LORD" (2 Kings 8:18) and incurred God's anger. God allowed the Philistines, Arabians and Cushites to invade and plunder the land. Jehoram died a painful death and was denied burial in the tomb of the kings (see 2 Chronicles 21:16–20).

Because of Jehoram's evil actions, his reign ended painfully and abruptly. But God allowed Jehoram's grandson to survive. God remembered his promise to King David that he would preserve a godly remnant so that a Savior, his only Son, could be born through the tribe of Judah.

The people waited years for the Messiah. There were good kings and bad kings, captivity and foreign occupation. But through it all, God was mindful of his promise to send a Savior through the line of Judah. Roughly 600 years after the final book in the Old Testament was written, God kept his promise by sending Jesus in his perfect time, in his perfect way.

The sad truth is that people *do* break promises. They fail to keep their word. And this breaks our hearts. But no matter how many promises have been broken, no matter how many people have let us down, God never will. He is faithful . . . even if his promises take time to come to fruition. As the apostle Paul says, "For no matter how many promises God has made, they are 'Yes' in Christ. And so through him the 'Amen' is spoken by us to the glory of God" (2 Corinthians 1:20).

2 Kings 8:19

Nevertheless, for the sake of his servant David, the LORD was not willing to destroy Judah. He had promised to maintain a lamp for David and his descendants forever.

reflection

1 What promise have you been waiting for God to keep?

2 How have people's broken promises made it difficult for you to trust in God's promises?

3 How does it comfort you to know that God always keeps his promises? How does it challenge you to know that sometimes his promises take time to be fulfilled?

RELATED READINGS

2 Samuel 7:4–16;
Psalm 89:1–52;
2 Peter 3:8–9

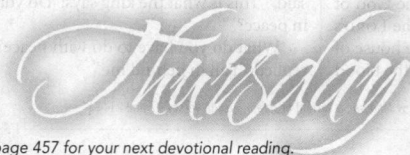

Go to page 457 for your next devotional reading.

451

them in the City of David. And Ahaziah his son succeeded him as king.

Ahaziah King of Judah

²⁵In the twelfth year of Joram son of Ahab king of Israel, Ahaziah son of Jehoram king of Judah began to reign. ²⁶Ahaziah was twenty-two years old when he became king, and he reigned in Jerusalem one year. His mother's name was Athaliah, a granddaughter of Omri king of Israel. ²⁷He walked in the ways of the house of Ahab and did evil in the eyes of the LORD, as the house of Ahab had done, for he was related by marriage to Ahab's family.

²⁸Ahaziah went with Joram son of Ahab to war against Hazael king of Aram at Ramoth Gilead. The Arameans wounded Joram; ²⁹so King Joram returned to Jezreel to recover from the wounds the Arameans had inflicted on him at Ramoth*ᵃ* in his battle with Hazael king of Aram.

Then Ahaziah son of Jehoram king of Judah went down to Jezreel to see Joram son of Ahab, because he had been wounded.

Jehu Anointed King of Israel

9 The prophet Elisha summoned a man from the company of the prophets and said to him, "Tuck your cloak into your belt, take this flask of oil with you and go to Ramoth Gilead. ²When you get there, look for Jehu son of Jehoshaphat, the son of Nimshi. Go to him, get him away from his companions and take him into an inner room. ³Then take the flask and pour the oil on his head and declare, 'This is what the LORD says: I anoint you king over Israel.' Then open the door and run; don't delay!"

⁴So the young man, the prophet, went to Ramoth Gilead. ⁵When he arrived, he found the army officers sitting together. "I have a message for you, commander," he said.

"For which of us?" asked Jehu.

"For you, commander," he replied.

⁶Jehu got up and went into the house. Then the prophet poured the oil on Jehu's head and declared, "This is what the LORD, the God of Israel, says: 'I anoint you king over the LORD's people Israel. ⁷You are to destroy the house of Ahab your master, and I will avenge the blood

of my servants the prophets and the blood of all the LORD's servants shed by Jezebel. ⁸The whole house of Ahab will perish. I will cut off from Ahab every last male in Israel—slave or free. ⁹I will make the house of Ahab like the house of Jeroboam son of Nebat and like the house of Baasha son of Ahijah. ¹⁰As for Jezebel, dogs will devour her on the plot of ground at Jezreel, and no one will bury her.'" Then he opened the door and ran.

¹¹When Jehu went out to his fellow officers, one of them asked him, "Is everything all right? Why did this madman come to you?"

"You know the man and the sort of things he says," Jehu replied.

¹²"That's not true!" they said. "Tell us."

Jehu said, "Here is what he told me: 'This is what the LORD says: I anoint you king over Israel.'"

¹³They hurried and took their cloaks and spread them under him on the bare steps. Then they blew the trumpet and shouted, "Jehu is king!"

Jehu Kills Joram and Ahaziah

¹⁴So Jehu son of Jehoshaphat, the son of Nimshi, conspired against Joram. (Now Joram and all Israel had been defending Ramoth Gilead against Hazael king of Aram, ¹⁵but King Joram*ᵇ* had returned to Jezreel to recover from the wounds the Arameans had inflicted on him in the battle with Hazael king of Aram.) Jehu said, "If this is the way you feel, don't let anyone slip out of the city to go and tell the news in Jezreel." ¹⁶Then he got into his chariot and rode to Jezreel, because Joram was resting there and Ahaziah king of Judah had gone down to see him.

¹⁷When the lookout standing on the tower in Jezreel saw Jehu's troops approaching, he called out, "I see some troops coming."

"Get a horseman," Joram ordered. "Send him to meet them and ask, 'Do you come in peace?'"

¹⁸The horseman rode off to meet Jehu and said, "This is what the king says: 'Do you come in peace?'"

"What do you have to do with peace?" Jehu replied. "Fall in behind me."

ᵃ29 Hebrew *Ramah*, a variant of *Ramoth*   *ᵇ15* Hebrew *Jehoram*, a variant of *Joram*; also in verses 17 and 21–24

The lookout reported, "The messenger has reached them, but he isn't coming back."

19 So the king sent out a second horseman. When he came to them he said, "This is what the king says: 'Do you come in peace?'"

Jehu replied, "What do you have to do with peace? Fall in behind me."

20 The lookout reported, "He has reached them, but he isn't coming back either. The driving is like that of Jehu son of Nimshi—he drives like a madman."

21 "Hitch up my chariot," Joram ordered. And when it was hitched up, Joram king of Israel and Ahaziah king of Judah rode out, each in his own chariot, to meet Jehu. They met him at the plot of ground that had belonged to Naboth the Jezreelite. 22 When Joram saw Jehu he asked, "Have you come in peace, Jehu?"

"How can there be peace," Jehu replied, "as long as all the idolatry and witchcraft of your mother Jezebel abound?"

23 Joram turned about and fled, calling out to Ahaziah, "Treachery, Ahaziah!"

24 Then Jehu drew his bow and shot Joram between the shoulders. The arrow pierced his heart and he slumped down in his chariot. 25 Jehu said to Bidkar, his chariot officer, "Pick him up and throw him on the field that belonged to Naboth the Jezreelite. Remember how you and I were riding together in chariots behind Ahab his father when the LORD made this prophecy about him: 26 'Yesterday I saw the blood of Naboth and the blood of his sons, declares the LORD, and I will surely make you pay for it on this plot of ground, declares the LORD.'[a] Now then, pick him up and throw him on that plot, in accordance with the word of the LORD."

27 When Ahaziah king of Judah saw what had happened, he fled up the road to Beth Haggan.[b] Jehu chased him, shouting, "Kill him too!" They wounded him in his chariot on the way up to Gur near Ibleam, but he escaped to Megiddo and died there. 28 His servants took him by chariot to Jerusalem and buried him with his fathers in his tomb in the City of David. 29 (In the eleventh year of Joram son of Ahab, Ahaziah had become king of Judah.)

Jezebel Killed

30 Then Jehu went to Jezreel. When Jezebel heard about it, she painted her eyes, arranged her hair and looked out of a window. 31 As Jehu entered the gate, she asked, "Have you come in peace, Zimri, you murderer of your master?"[c]

32 He looked up at the window and called out, "Who is on my side? Who?" Two or three eunuchs looked down at him. 33 "Throw her down!" Jehu said. So they threw her down, and some of her blood spattered the wall and the horses as they trampled her underfoot.

34 Jehu went in and ate and drank. "Take care of that cursed woman," he said, "and bury her, for she was a king's daughter." 35 But when they went out to bury her, they found nothing except her skull, her feet and her hands. 36 They went back and told Jehu, who said, "This is the word of the LORD that he spoke through his servant Elijah the Tishbite: On the plot of ground at Jezreel dogs will devour Jezebel's flesh.[d] 37 Jezebel's body will be like refuse on the ground in the plot at Jezreel, so that no one will be able to say, 'This is Jezebel.'"

Ahab's Family Killed

10 Now there were in Samaria seventy sons of the house of Ahab. So Jehu wrote letters and sent them to Samaria: to the officials of Jezreel,[e] to the elders and to the guardians of Ahab's children. He said, 2 "As soon as this letter reaches you, since your master's sons are with you and you have chariots and horses, a fortified city and weapons, 3 choose the best and most worthy of your master's sons and set him on his father's throne. Then fight for your master's house."

4 But they were terrified and said, "If two kings could not resist him, how can we?"

5 So the palace administrator, the city governor, the elders and the guardians sent this message to Jehu: "We are your servants and we will do anything you say. We will not appoint anyone as king; you do whatever you think best."

6 Then Jehu wrote them a second letter, saying, "If you are on my side and will obey me, take the heads of your master's sons and come to me in Jezreel by this time tomorrow."

Now the royal princes, seventy of them, were

---

*a*26 See 1 Kings 21:19.   *b*27 Or *fled by way of the garden house*   *c*31 Or *"Did Zimri have peace, who murdered his master?"*
*d*36 See 1 Kings 21:23.   *e*1 Hebrew; some Septuagint manuscripts and Vulgate *of the city*

with the leading men of the city, who were rearing them. ⁷When the letter arrived, these men took the princes and slaughtered all seventy of them. They put their heads in baskets and sent them to Jehu in Jezreel. ⁸When the messenger arrived, he told Jehu, "They have brought the heads of the princes."

Then Jehu ordered, "Put them in two piles at the entrance of the city gate until morning."

⁹The next morning Jehu went out. He stood before all the people and said, "You are innocent. It was I who conspired against my master and killed him, but who killed all these? ¹⁰Know then, that not a word the LORD has spoken against the house of Ahab will fail. The LORD has done what he promised through his servant Elijah." ¹¹So Jehu killed everyone in Jezreel who remained of the house of Ahab, as well as all his chief men, his close friends and his priests, leaving him no survivor.

¹²Jehu then set out and went toward Samaria. At Beth Eked of the Shepherds, ¹³he met some relatives of Ahaziah king of Judah and asked, "Who are you?"

They said, "We are relatives of Ahaziah, and we have come down to greet the families of the king and of the queen mother."

¹⁴"Take them alive!" he ordered. So they took them alive and slaughtered them by the well of Beth Eked—forty-two men. He left no survivor.

¹⁵After he left there, he came upon Jehonadab son of Recab, who was on his way to meet him. Jehu greeted him and said, "Are you in accord with me, as I am with you?"

"I am," Jehonadab answered.

"If so," said Jehu, "give me your hand." So he did, and Jehu helped him up into the chariot. ¹⁶Jehu said, "Come with me and see my zeal for the LORD." Then he had him ride along in his chariot.

¹⁷When Jehu came to Samaria, he killed all who were left there of Ahab's family; he destroyed them, according to the word of the LORD spoken to Elijah.

Ministers of Baal Killed

¹⁸Then Jehu brought all the people together and said to them, "Ahab served Baal a little; Jehu will serve him much. ¹⁹Now summon all the prophets of Baal, all his ministers and all his priests. See that no one is missing, because I am going to hold a great sacrifice for Baal. Anyone who fails to come will no longer live." But Jehu was acting deceptively in order to destroy the ministers of Baal.

²⁰Jehu said, "Call an assembly in honor of Baal." So they proclaimed it. ²¹Then he sent word throughout Israel, and all the ministers of Baal came; not one stayed away. They crowded into the temple of Baal until it was full from one end to the other. ²²And Jehu said to the keeper of the wardrobe, "Bring robes for all the ministers of Baal." So he brought out robes for them.

²³Then Jehu and Jehonadab son of Recab went into the temple of Baal. Jehu said to the ministers of Baal, "Look around and see that no servants of the LORD are here with you— only ministers of Baal." ²⁴So they went in to make sacrifices and burnt offerings. Now Jehu had posted eighty men outside with this warning: "If one of you lets any of the men I am placing in your hands escape, it will be your life for his life."

²⁵As soon as Jehu had finished making the burnt offering, he ordered the guards and officers: "Go in and kill them; let no one escape." So they cut them down with the sword. The guards and officers threw the bodies out and then entered the inner shrine of the temple of Baal. ²⁶They brought the sacred stone out of the temple of Baal and burned it. ²⁷They demolished the sacred stone of Baal and tore down the temple of Baal, and people have used it for a latrine to this day.

²⁸So Jehu destroyed Baal worship in Israel. ²⁹However, he did not turn away from the sins of Jeroboam son of Nebat, which he had caused Israel to commit—the worship of the golden calves at Bethel and Dan.

³⁰The LORD said to Jehu, "Because you have done well in accomplishing what is right in my eyes and have done to the house of Ahab all I had in mind to do, your descendants will sit on the throne of Israel to the fourth generation." ³¹Yet Jehu was not careful to keep the law of the LORD, the God of Israel, with all his heart. He did not turn away from the sins of Jeroboam, which he had caused Israel to commit.

³²In those days the LORD began to reduce the size of Israel. Hazael overpowered the Isra-

elites throughout their territory [33]east of the Jordan in all the land of Gilead (the region of Gad, Reuben and Manasseh), from Aroer by the Arnon Gorge through Gilead to Bashan. [34]As for the other events of Jehu's reign, all he did, and all his achievements, are they not written in the book of the annals of the kings of Israel?

[35]Jehu rested with his fathers and was buried in Samaria. And Jehoahaz his son succeeded him as king. [36]The time that Jehu reigned over Israel in Samaria was twenty-eight years.

Athaliah and Joash

11 When Athaliah the mother of Ahaziah saw that her son was dead, she proceeded to destroy the whole royal family. [2]But Jehosheba, the daughter of King Jehoram[a] and sister of Ahaziah, took Joash son of Ahaziah and stole him away from among the royal princes, who were about to be murdered. She put him and his nurse in a bedroom to hide him from Athaliah; so he was not killed. [3]He remained hidden with his nurse at the temple of the LORD for six years while Athaliah ruled the land.

[4]In the seventh year Jehoiada sent for the commanders of units of a hundred, the Carites and the guards and had them brought to him at the temple of the LORD. He made a covenant with them and put them under oath at the temple of the LORD. Then he showed them the king's son. [5]He commanded them, saying, "This is what you are to do: You who are in the three companies that are going on duty on the Sabbath—a third of you guarding the royal palace, [6]a third at the Sur Gate, and a third at the gate behind the guard, who take turns guarding the temple— [7]and you who are in the other two companies that normally go off Sabbath duty are all to guard the temple for the king. [8]Station yourselves around the king, each man with his weapon in his hand. Anyone who approaches your ranks[b] must be put to death. Stay close to the king wherever he goes."

2 Kings 10:30

God Rewards Obedience

The LORD said to Jehu, "Because you have done well in accomplishing what is right in my eyes and have done to the house of Ahab all I had in mind to do, your descendants will sit on the throne of Israel to the fourth generation."

[9]The commanders of units of a hundred did just as Jehoiada the priest ordered. Each one took his men—those who were going on duty on the Sabbath and those who were going off duty—and came to Jehoiada the priest. [10]Then he gave the commanders the spears and shields that had belonged to King David and that were in the temple of the LORD. [11]The guards, each with his weapon in his hand, stationed themselves around the king—near the altar and the temple, from the south side to the north side of the temple.

[12]Jehoiada brought out the king's son and put the crown on him; he presented him with a copy of the covenant and proclaimed him king. They anointed him, and the people clapped their hands and shouted, "Long live the king!"

[13]When Athaliah heard the noise made by the guards and the people, she went to the people at the temple of the LORD. [14]She looked and there was the king, standing by the pillar, as the custom was. The officers and the trumpeters were beside the king, and all the people of the land were rejoicing and blowing trumpets. Then Athaliah tore her robes and called out, "Treason! Treason!"

[15]Jehoiada the priest ordered the commanders of units of a hundred, who were in charge of the troops: "Bring her out between the ranks[c] and put to the sword anyone who follows her." For the priest had said, "She must not be put to death in the temple of the LORD." [16]So they seized her as she reached the place where the horses enter the palace grounds, and there she was put to death.

[17]Jehoiada then made a covenant between the LORD and the king and people that they would be the LORD's people. He also made a covenant between the king and the people. [18]All the people of the land went to the temple of Baal and tore it down. They smashed the altars and idols to pieces and killed Mattan the priest of Baal in front of the altars.

---

*a*2 Hebrew *Joram,* a variant of *Jehoram*   *b*8 Or *approaches the precincts*   *c*15 Or *out from the precincts*

Then Jehoiada the priest posted guards at the temple of the LORD. ¹⁹He took with him the commanders of hundreds, the Carites, the guards and all the people of the land, and together they brought the king down from the temple of the LORD and went into the palace, entering by way of the gate of the guards. The king then took his place on the royal throne, ²⁰and all the people of the land rejoiced. And the city was quiet, because Athaliah had been slain with the sword at the palace.

²¹Joash*ᵃ* was seven years old when he began to reign.

Joash Repairs the Temple

12 In the seventh year of Jehu, Joash*ᵇ* became king, and he reigned in Jerusalem forty years. His mother's name was Zibiah; she was from Beersheba. ²Joash did what was right in the eyes of the LORD all the years Jehoiada the priest instructed him. ³The high places, however, were not removed; the people continued to offer sacrifices and burn incense there.

⁴Joash said to the priests, "Collect all the money that is brought as sacred offerings to the temple of the LORD—the money collected in the census, the money received from personal vows and the money brought voluntarily to the temple. ⁵Let every priest receive the money from one of the treasurers, and let it be used to repair whatever damage is found in the temple."

⁶But by the twenty-third year of King Joash the priests still had not repaired the temple. ⁷Therefore King Joash summoned Jehoiada the priest and the other priests and asked them, "Why aren't you repairing the damage done to the temple? Take no more money from your treasurers, but hand it over for repairing the temple." ⁸The priests agreed that they would not collect any more money from the people and that they would not repair the temple themselves.

⁹Jehoiada the priest took a chest and bored a hole in its lid. He placed it beside the altar, on the right side as one enters the temple of the LORD. The priests who guarded the entrance put into the chest all the money that was brought to the temple of the LORD. ¹⁰Whenever they saw that there was a large amount of money in the chest,

the royal secretary and the high priest came, counted the money that had been brought into the temple of the LORD and put it into bags. ¹¹When the amount had been determined, they gave the money to the men appointed to supervise the work on the temple. With it they paid those who worked on the temple of the LORD—the carpenters and builders, ¹²the masons and stonecutters. They purchased timber and dressed stone for the repair of the temple of the LORD, and met all the other expenses of restoring the temple.

¹³The money brought into the temple was not spent for making silver basins, wick trimmers, sprinkling bowls, trumpets or any other articles of gold or silver for the temple of the LORD; ¹⁴it was paid to the workmen, who used it to repair the temple. ¹⁵They did not require an accounting from those to whom they gave the money to pay the workers, because they acted with complete honesty. ¹⁶The money from the guilt offerings and sin offerings was not brought into the temple of the LORD; it belonged to the priests.

¹⁷About this time Hazael king of Aram went up and attacked Gath and captured it. Then he turned to attack Jerusalem. ¹⁸But Joash king of Judah took all the sacred objects dedicated by his fathers—Jehoshaphat, Jehoram and Ahaziah, the kings of Judah—and the gifts he himself had dedicated and all the gold found in the treasuries of the temple of the LORD and of the royal palace, and he sent them to Hazael king of Aram, who then withdrew from Jerusalem.

¹⁹As for the other events of the reign of Joash, and all he did, are they not written in the book of the annals of the kings of Judah? ²⁰His officials conspired against him and assassinated him at Beth Millo, on the road down to Silla. ²¹The officials who murdered him were Jozabad son of Shimeath and Jehozabad son of Shomer. He died and was buried with his fathers in the City of David. And Amaziah his son succeeded him as king.

Jehoahaz King of Israel

13 In the twenty-third year of Joash son of Ahaziah king of Judah, Jehoahaz son of Jehu became king of Israel in Samaria,

ᵃ21 Hebrew Jehoash, a variant of Joash   ᵇ1 Hebrew Jehoash, a variant of Joash; also in verses 2, 4, 6, 7 and 18

The Truth Will Come Out

Read: 2 Kings 12:1–21

EARLY GREEK TRAGEDIANS obsessed over deception. Reading the plays of Sophocles and Euripides, one might conclude that they lived in societies paranoid that a web of half-truths and lies prevailed. Their mythical figures spoke in riddles; those who tried to evade prophecies unwittingly played into the hands of fate. When the truth did finally come to light, it often appeared only when calamity had already struck. We may feel this way about various aspects of our lives. Paranoia may plague our opinions on politics, our neighbors, even our family. Honesty once broken takes a long time to rebuild. Thus, scrupulous honesty in our dealings with others is one of our most valuable assets.

The workers described in 2 Kings 12 realized the value of trustworthiness. They were so well known for their complete honesty that they weren't required to give an account for how they spent the vast amounts of money allotted for the temple's reconstruction.

How different that scene in 2 Kings is from the scene in Genesis 3, where God confronted Adam and Eve and demanded an accounting from them after their fateful encounter with the serpent. For the first time in this first couple's lives—which had been perfect, stress-free and marked by an ongoing, intimate relationship with their Creator—the two garden-dwellers were asked to account for their actions to God himself. Why? Because they had listened to the serpent's lies, compromised what they knew to be the truth of God's Word and allowed sin to invade paradise.

Can you relate? Maybe your lies don't seem serpent-sized, but even so-called white lies can open the door to compromise and sin. Maybe you don't tell the whole truth about the money you've spent or about why you can't take on a project or about the company supplies you took home. But even the Greek tragedians knew that lies don't stay hidden forever. When a lie is discovered, we risk losing the trust of those we most value.

Wouldn't it be better to live like the straightforward workers in this story? Their reputation for "complete honesty" went before them, gaining them the respect of their superiors and even the king.

2 Kings 12:15

They did not require an accounting from those to whom they gave the money to pay the workers, because they acted with complete honesty.

reflection

1 Have you compromised the truth and gotten caught up in "little white lies"? What was the outcome?

2 What do you want your reputation to look like? Ask God to help you become a person known for her complete honesty.

3 Can you think of any situation in which it would be right and necessary to hide the truth? (Hint: Read 2 Kings 11:1–3.)

RELATED READINGS

Genesis 3:1–24;
Proverbs 16:11;
Isaiah 59:12–15;
Acts 5:1–11

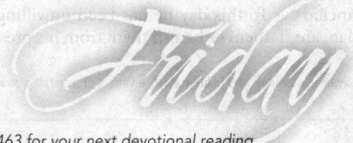

Friday

Go to page 463 for your next devotional reading.

457

and he reigned seventeen years. ²He did evil in the eyes of the LORD by following the sins of Jeroboam son of Nebat, which he had caused Israel to commit, and he did not turn away from them. ³So the LORD's anger burned against Israel, and for a long time he kept them under the power of Hazael king of Aram and Ben-Hadad his son.

⁴Then Jehoahaz sought the LORD's favor, and the LORD listened to him, for he saw how severely the king of Aram was oppressing Israel. ⁵The LORD provided a deliverer for Israel, and they escaped from the power of Aram. So the Israelites lived in their own homes as they had before. ⁶But they did not turn away from the sins of the house of Jeroboam, which he had caused Israel to commit; they continued in them. Also, the Asherah pole*a* remained standing in Samaria.

⁷Nothing had been left of the army of Jehoahaz except fifty horsemen, ten chariots and ten thousand foot soldiers, for the king of Aram had destroyed the rest and made them like the dust at threshing time.

⁸As for the other events of the reign of Jehoahaz, all he did and his achievements, are they not written in the book of the annals of the kings of Israel? ⁹Jehoahaz rested with his fathers and was buried in Samaria. And Jehoash*b* his son succeeded him as king.

Jehoash King of Israel

¹⁰In the thirty-seventh year of Joash king of Judah, Jehoash son of Jehoahaz became king of Israel in Samaria, and he reigned sixteen years. ¹¹He did evil in the eyes of the LORD and did not turn away from any of the sins of Jeroboam son of Nebat, which he had caused Israel to commit; he continued in them.

¹²As for the other events of the reign of Jehoash, all he did and his achievements, including his war against Amaziah king of Judah, are

they not written in the book of the annals of the kings of Israel? ¹³Jehoash rested with his fathers, and Jeroboam succeeded him on the throne. Jehoash was buried in Samaria with the kings of Israel.

¹⁴Now Elisha was suffering from the illness from which he died. Jehoash king of Israel went down to see him and wept over him. "My father! My father!" he cried. "The chariots and horsemen of Israel!"

¹⁵Elisha said, "Get a bow and some arrows," and he did so. ¹⁶"Take the bow in your hands," he said to the king of Israel. When he had taken it, Elisha put his hands on the king's hands.

¹⁷"Open the east window," he said, and he opened it. "Shoot!" Elisha said, and he shot. "The LORD's arrow of victory, the arrow of victory over Aram!" Elisha declared. "You will completely destroy the Arameans at Aphek."

¹⁸Then he said, "Take the arrows," and the king took them. Elisha told him, "Strike the ground." He struck it three times and stopped. ¹⁹The man of God was angry with him and said, "You should have struck the ground five or six times; then you would have defeated Aram and completely destroyed it. But now you will defeat it only three times."

²⁰Elisha died and was buried.

Now Moabite raiders used to enter the country every spring. ²¹Once while some Israelites were burying a man, suddenly they saw a band of raiders; so they threw the man's body into Elisha's tomb. When the body touched Elisha's bones, the man came to life and stood up on his feet.

²²Hazael king of Aram oppressed Israel throughout the reign of Jehoahaz. ²³But the LORD was gracious to them and had compassion and showed concern for them because of his covenant with Abraham, Isaac and Jacob. To this day he has been unwilling to destroy them or banish them from his presence.

2 Kings 13:23

God Is Compassionate

But the LORD was gracious to them and had compassion and showed concern for them . . . To this day he has been unwilling to destroy them or banish them from his presence.

---

*a*6 That is, a symbol of the goddess Asherah; here and elsewhere in 2 Kings and 25   *b*9 Hebrew *Joash,* a variant of *Jehoash;* also in verses 12–14

²⁴Hazael king of Aram died, and Ben-Hadad his son succeeded him as king. ²⁵Then Jehoash son of Jehoahaz recaptured from Ben-Hadad son of Hazael the towns he had taken in battle from his father Jehoahaz. Three times Jehoash defeated him, and so he recovered the Israelite towns.

Amaziah King of Judah

14 In the second year of Jehoash*a* son of Jehoahaz king of Israel, Amaziah son of Joash king of Judah began to reign. ²He was twenty-five years old when he became king, and he reigned in Jerusalem twenty-nine years. His mother's name was Jehoaddin; she was from Jerusalem. ³He did what was right in the eyes of the LORD, but not as his father David had done. In everything he followed the example of his father Joash. ⁴The high places, however, were not removed; the people continued to offer sacrifices and burn incense there.

⁵After the kingdom was firmly in his grasp, he executed the officials who had murdered his father the king. ⁶Yet he did not put the sons of the assassins to death, in accordance with what is written in the Book of the Law of Moses where the LORD commanded: "Fathers shall not be put to death for their children, nor children put to death for their fathers; each is to die for his own sins."*b*

⁷He was the one who defeated ten thousand Edomites in the Valley of Salt and captured Sela in battle, calling it Joktheel, the name it has to this day.

⁸Then Amaziah sent messengers to Jehoash son of Jehoahaz, the son of Jehu, king of Israel, with the challenge: "Come, meet me face to face."

⁹But Jehoash king of Israel replied to Amaziah king of Judah: "A thistle in Lebanon sent a message to a cedar in Lebanon, 'Give your daughter to my son in marriage.' Then a wild beast in Lebanon came along and trampled the thistle underfoot. ¹⁰You have indeed defeated Edom and now you are arrogant. Glory in your victory, but stay at home! Why ask for trouble and cause your own downfall and that of Judah also?"

¹¹Amaziah, however, would not listen, so Je-

hoash king of Israel attacked. He and Amaziah king of Judah faced each other at Beth Shemesh in Judah. ¹²Judah was routed by Israel, and every man fled to his home. ¹³Jehoash king of Israel captured Amaziah king of Judah, the son of Joash, the son of Ahaziah, at Beth Shemesh. Then Jehoash went to Jerusalem and broke down the wall of Jerusalem from the Ephraim Gate to the Corner Gate—a section about six hundred feet long.*c* ¹⁴He took all the gold and silver and all the articles found in the temple of the LORD and in the treasuries of the royal palace. He also took hostages and returned to Samaria.

¹⁵As for the other events of the reign of Jehoash, what he did and his achievements, including his war against Amaziah king of Judah, are they not written in the book of the annals of the kings of Israel? ¹⁶Jehoash rested with his fathers and was buried in Samaria with the kings of Israel. And Jeroboam his son succeeded him as king.

¹⁷Amaziah son of Joash king of Judah lived for fifteen years after the death of Jehoash son of Jehoahaz king of Israel. ¹⁸As for the other events of Amaziah's reign, are they not written in the book of the annals of the kings of Judah?

¹⁹They conspired against him in Jerusalem, and he fled to Lachish, but they sent men after him to Lachish and killed him there. ²⁰He was brought back by horse and was buried in Jerusalem with his fathers, in the City of David.

²¹Then all the people of Judah took Azariah,*d* who was sixteen years old, and made him king in place of his father Amaziah. ²²He was the one who rebuilt Elath and restored it to Judah after Amaziah rested with his fathers.

Jeroboam II King of Israel

²³In the fifteenth year of Amaziah son of Joash king of Judah, Jeroboam son of Jehoash king of Israel became king in Samaria, and he reigned forty-one years. ²⁴He did evil in the eyes of the LORD and did not turn away from any of the sins of Jeroboam son of Nebat, which he had caused Israel to commit. ²⁵He was the one who restored the boundaries of Israel from Lebo*e* Hamath to the Sea of the Arabah,*f* in

---

*a*1 Hebrew *Joash*, a variant of *Jehoash*; also in verses 13, 23 and 27 *b*6 Deut. 24:16 *c*13 Hebrew *four hundred cubits* (about 180 meters) *d*21 Also called *Uzziah* *e*25 Or *from the entrance to* *f*25 That is, the Dead Sea accordance with the word of the LORD, the God of Israel, spoken through his servant Jonah son of Amittai, the prophet from Gath Hepher.

26The LORD had seen how bitterly everyone in Israel, whether slave or free, was suffering; there was no one to help them. 27And since the LORD had not said he would blot out the name of Israel from under heaven, he saved them by the hand of Jeroboam son of Jehoash.

28As for the other events of Jeroboam's reign, all he did, and his military achievements, including how he recovered for Israel both Damascus and Hamath, which had belonged to Yaudi,*a* are they not written in the book of the annals of the kings of Israel? 29Jeroboam rested with his fathers, the kings of Israel. And Zechariah his son succeeded him as king.

Azariah King of Judah

15 In the twenty-seventh year of Jeroboam king of Israel, Azariah son of Amaziah king of Judah began to reign. 2He was sixteen years old when he became king, and he reigned in Jerusalem fifty-two years. His mother's name was Jecoliah; she was from Jerusalem. 3He did what was right in the eyes of the LORD, just as his father Amaziah had done. 4The high places, however, were not removed; the people continued to offer sacrifices and burn incense there.

5The LORD afflicted the king with leprosy*b* until the day he died, and he lived in a separate house.*c* Jotham the king's son had charge of the palace and governed the people of the land.

6As for the other events of Azariah's reign, and all he did, are they not written in the book of the annals of the kings of Judah? 7Azariah rested with his fathers and was buried near them in the City of David. And Jotham his son succeeded him as king.

Zechariah King of Israel

8In the thirty-eighth year of Azariah king of Judah, Zechariah son of Jeroboam became king of Israel in Samaria, and he reigned six months. 9He did evil in the eyes of the LORD, as his fathers had done. He did not turn away from the sins of Jeroboam son of Nebat, which he had caused Israel to commit.

10Shallum son of Jabesh conspired against Zechariah. He attacked him in front of the people,*d* assassinated him and succeeded him as king. 11The other events of Zechariah's reign are written in the book of the annals of the kings of Israel. 12So the word of the LORD spoken to Jehu was fulfilled: "Your descendants will sit on the throne of Israel to the fourth generation."*e*

Shallum King of Israel

13Shallum son of Jabesh became king in the thirty-ninth year of Uzziah king of Judah, and he reigned in Samaria one month. 14Then Menahem son of Gadi went from Tirzah up to Samaria. He attacked Shallum son of Jabesh in Samaria, assassinated him and succeeded him as king.

15The other events of Shallum's reign, and the conspiracy he led, are written in the book of the annals of the kings of Israel.

16At that time Menahem, starting out from Tirzah, attacked Tiphsah and everyone in the city and its vicinity, because they refused to open their gates. He sacked Tiphsah and ripped open all the pregnant women.

Menahem King of Israel

17In the thirty-ninth year of Azariah king of Judah, Menahem son of Gadi became king of Israel, and he reigned in Samaria ten years. 18He did evil in the eyes of the LORD. During his entire reign he did not turn away from the sins of Jeroboam son of Nebat, which he had caused Israel to commit.

19Then Pul*f* king of Assyria invaded the land, and Menahem gave him a thousand talents*g* of silver to gain his support and strengthen his own hold on the kingdom.

---

2 Kings 14:27

God Saves

And since the LORD had not said he would blot out the name of Israel from under heaven, he saved them by the hand of Jeroboam son of Jehoash.

---

*a***28** Or *Judah*   *b***5** The Hebrew word was used for various diseases affecting the skin—not necessarily leprosy.   *c***5** Or *in a house where he was relieved of responsibility*   *d***10** Hebrew; some Septuagint manuscripts *in Ibleam*   *e***12** 2 Kings 10:30   *f***19** Also called *Tiglath-Pileser*   *g***19** That is, about 37 tons (about 34 metric tons)

²⁰Menahem exacted this money from Israel. Every wealthy man had to contribute fifty shekels[a] of silver to be given to the king of Assyria. So the king of Assyria withdrew and stayed in the land no longer.

²¹As for the other events of Menahem's reign, and all he did, are they not written in the book of the annals of the kings of Israel? ²²Menahem rested with his fathers. And Pekahiah his son succeeded him as king.

Pekahiah King of Israel

²³In the fiftieth year of Azariah king of Judah, Pekahiah son of Menahem became king of Israel in Samaria, and he reigned two years. ²⁴Pekahiah did evil in the eyes of the LORD. He did not turn away from the sins of Jeroboam son of Nebat, which he had caused Israel to commit. ²⁵One of his chief officers, Pekah son of Remaliah, conspired against him. Taking fifty men of Gilead with him, he assassinated Pekahiah, along with Argob and Arieh, in the citadel of the royal palace at Samaria. So Pekah killed Pekahiah and succeeded him as king.

²⁶The other events of Pekahiah's reign, and all he did, are written in the book of the annals of the kings of Israel.

Pekah King of Israel

²⁷In the fifty-second year of Azariah king of Judah, Pekah son of Remaliah became king of Israel in Samaria, and he reigned twenty years. ²⁸He did evil in the eyes of the LORD. He did not turn away from the sins of Jeroboam son of Nebat, which he had caused Israel to commit.

²⁹In the time of Pekah king of Israel, Tiglath-Pileser king of Assyria came and took Ijon, Abel Beth Maacah, Janoah, Kedesh and Hazor. He took Gilead and Galilee, including all the land of Naphtali, and deported the people to Assyria. ³⁰Then Hoshea son of Elah conspired against Pekah son of Remaliah. He attacked and assassinated him, and then succeeded him as king in the twentieth year of Jotham son of Uzziah.

³¹As for the other events of Pekah's reign, and all he did, are they not written in the book of the annals of the kings of Israel?

Jotham King of Judah

³²In the second year of Pekah son of Remaliah king of Israel, Jotham son of Uzziah king of Judah began to reign. ³³He was twenty-five years old when he became king, and he reigned in Jerusalem sixteen years. His mother's name was Jerusha daughter of Zadok. ³⁴He did what was right in the eyes of the LORD, just as his father Uzziah had done. ³⁵The high places, however, were not removed; the people continued to offer sacrifices and burn incense there. Jotham rebuilt the Upper Gate of the temple of the LORD.

³⁶As for the other events of Jotham's reign, and what he did, are they not written in the book of the annals of the kings of Judah? ³⁷(In those days the LORD began to send Rezin king of Aram and Pekah son of Remaliah against Judah.) ³⁸Jotham rested with his fathers and was buried with them in the City of David, the city of his father. And Ahaz his son succeeded him as king.

Ahaz King of Judah

16 In the seventeenth year of Pekah son of Remaliah, Ahaz son of Jotham king of Judah began to reign. ²Ahaz was twenty years old when he became king, and he reigned in Jerusalem sixteen years. Unlike David his father, he did not do what was right in the eyes of the LORD his God. ³He walked in the ways of the kings of Israel and even sacrificed his son in[b] the fire, following the detestable ways of the nations the LORD had driven out before the Israelites. ⁴He offered sacrifices and burned incense at the high places, on the hilltops and under every spreading tree.

⁵Then Rezin king of Aram and Pekah son of Remaliah king of Israel marched up to fight against Jerusalem and besieged Ahaz, but they could not overpower him. ⁶At that time, Rezin king of Aram recovered Elath for Aram by driving out the men of Judah. Edomites then moved into Elath and have lived there to this day.

⁷Ahaz sent messengers to say to Tiglath-Pileser king of Assyria, "I am your servant and vassal. Come up and save me out of the hand of the king of Aram and of the king of Israel, who are attacking me." ⁸And Ahaz took the silver and gold found in the temple of the LORD and

---

[a]20 That is, about 1 1/4 pounds (about 0.6 kilogram)   [b]3 Or even made his son pass through

in the treasuries of the royal palace and sent it as a gift to the king of Assyria. ⁹The king of Assyria complied by attacking Damascus and capturing it. He deported its inhabitants to Kir and put Rezin to death.

¹⁰Then King Ahaz went to Damascus to meet Tiglath-Pileser king of Assyria. He saw an altar in Damascus and sent to Uriah the priest a sketch of the altar, with detailed plans for its construction. ¹¹So Uriah the priest built an altar in accordance with all the plans that King Ahaz had sent from Damascus and finished it before King Ahaz returned. ¹²When the king came back from Damascus and saw the altar, he approached it and presented offerings*a* on it. ¹³He offered up his burnt offering and grain offering, poured out his drink offering, and sprinkled the blood of his fellowship offerings*b* on the altar. ¹⁴The bronze altar that stood before the LORD he brought from the front of the temple—from between the new altar and the temple of the LORD—and put it on the north side of the new altar.

¹⁵King Ahaz then gave these orders to Uriah the priest: "On the large new altar, offer the morning burnt offering and the evening grain offering, the king's burnt offering and his grain offering, and the burnt offering of all the people of the land, and their grain offering and their drink offering. Sprinkle on the altar all the blood of the burnt offerings and sacrifices. But I will use the bronze altar for seeking guidance." ¹⁶And Uriah the priest did just as King Ahaz had ordered.

¹⁷King Ahaz took away the side panels and removed the basins from the movable stands. He removed the Sea from the bronze bulls that supported it and set it on a stone base. ¹⁸He took away the Sabbath canopy*c* that had been built at the temple and removed the royal entryway outside the temple of the LORD, in deference to the king of Assyria.

¹⁹As for the other events of the reign of Ahaz, and what he did, are they not written in the book of the annals of the kings of Judah? ²⁰Ahaz rested with his fathers and was buried with them in the City of David. And Hezekiah his son succeeded him as king.

Hoshea Last King of Israel

17 In the twelfth year of Ahaz king of Judah, Hoshea son of Elah became king of Israel in Samaria, and he reigned nine years. ²He did evil in the eyes of the LORD, but not like the kings of Israel who preceded him.

³Shalmaneser king of Assyria came up to attack Hoshea, who had been Shalmaneser's vassal and had paid him tribute. ⁴But the king of Assyria discovered that Hoshea was a traitor, for he had sent envoys to So*d* king of Egypt, and he no longer paid tribute to the king of Assyria, as he had done year by year. Therefore Shalmaneser seized him and put him in prison. ⁵The king of Assyria invaded the entire land, marched against Samaria and laid siege to it for three years. ⁶In the ninth year of Hoshea, the king of Assyria captured Samaria and deported the Israelites to Assyria. He settled them in Halah, in Gozan on the Habor River and in the towns of the Medes.

Israel Exiled Because of Sin

⁷All this took place because the Israelites had sinned against the LORD their God, who had brought them up out of Egypt from under the power of Pharaoh king of Egypt. They worshiped other gods ⁸and followed the practices of the nations the LORD had driven out before them, as well as the practices that the kings of Israel had introduced. ⁹The Israelites secretly did things against the LORD their God that were not right. From watchtower to fortified city they built themselves high places in all their towns. ¹⁰They set up sacred stones and Asherah poles on every high hill and under every spreading tree. ¹¹At every high place they burned incense, as the nations whom the LORD had driven out before them had done. They did wicked things that provoked the LORD to anger. ¹²They worshiped idols, though the LORD had said, "You shall not do this."*e* ¹³The LORD warned Israel and Judah through all his prophets and seers: "Turn from your evil ways. Observe my commands and decrees, in accordance with the entire Law that I commanded your fathers to obey and that I delivered to you through my servants the prophets."

¹⁴But they would not listen and were as

*a*12 Or *and went up*   *b*13 Traditionally *peace offerings*   *c*18 Or *the dais of his throne* (see Septuagint)   *d*4 Or *to Sais, to the*; *So* is possibly an abbreviation for *Osorkon.*   *e*12 Exodus 20:4,5

Beyond Understanding

MOTHER OF SAMSON

IT WAS BEYOND UNDERSTANDING.

She had been a faithful wife to Manoah for many years—a good wife. And although the two of them made a happy family together, they longed for the joy of raising a child. Yet for some reason, God had not entrusted her with a baby. She endured all the hurtful inquiries from insensitive neighbors and nosy relatives. When she could, she skillfully dodged questions that left her open to comments and criticisms. But sometimes the pain was inescapable. *What's wrong with me? Would I really be such a bad mother? Can God not trust me with a baby?*

So, when she heard what the man in front of her was saying, she could not take it in. *A child? A son?* One moment she was busy filling skins with water. The next, a man appeared out of nowhere, telling her the best news of her life. Not only that, but he said this child would be no ordinary child. He would be . . . *what had he said?* He would be *"set apart to God from birth"*?

It was beyond understanding.

She had a difficult time trying to explain it to Manoah that night. Even when the angel appeared to her a second time, it didn't get any easier. Thankfully, Manoah was there to talk to the man this time, but it still seemed unbelievable. When her husband asked for the angel's name, his reply struck a familiar chord within her heart.

"My name? It is beyond understanding."

Yes, it was all beyond her understanding. Why had God chosen her? Why had he allowed her to cry all those tears all those many nights? Why was he coming to her now? Why?

It was, as it was supposed to be, beyond understanding.

—*Prayer*—
Lord, allow me to rejoice in your perfect timing—especially when I don't understand it.

> God heard Manoah, and the angel of God came again to the woman while she was out in the field.
>
> **Judges 13:9**

ASSIGNED READING:
Judges 13:1–24

Weekend

Go to page 467 for your next devotional reading.

stiff-necked as their fathers, who did not trust in the LORD their God. **15**They rejected his decrees and the covenant he had made with their fathers and the warnings he had given them. They followed worthless idols and themselves became worthless. They imitated the nations around them although the LORD had ordered them, "Do not do as they do," and they did the things the LORD had forbidden them to do.

16They forsook all the commands of the LORD their God and made for themselves two idols cast in the shape of calves, and an Asherah pole. They bowed down to all the starry hosts, and they worshiped Baal. **17**They sacrificed their sons and daughters in*a* the fire. They practiced divination and sorcery and sold themselves to do evil in the eyes of the LORD, provoking him to anger.

18So the LORD was very angry with Israel and removed them from his presence. Only the tribe of Judah was left, **19**and even Judah did not keep the commands of the LORD their God. They followed the practices Israel had introduced. **20**Therefore the LORD rejected all the people of Israel; he afflicted them and gave them into the hands of plunderers, until he thrust them from his presence.

21When he tore Israel away from the house of David, they made Jeroboam son of Nebat their king. Jeroboam enticed Israel away from following the LORD and caused them to commit a great sin. **22**The Israelites persisted in all the sins of Jeroboam and did not turn away from them **23**until the LORD removed them from his presence, as he had warned through all his servants the prophets. So the people of Israel were taken from their homeland into exile in Assyria, and they are still there.

Samaria Resettled

24The king of Assyria brought people from Babylon, Cuthah, Avva, Hamath and Sepharvaim and settled them in the towns of Samaria to replace the Israelites. They took over Samaria and lived in its towns. **25**When they first lived there, they did not worship the LORD; so he sent lions among them and they killed some of the people. **26**It was reported to the king of Assyria: "The people you deported and resettled in the towns of Samaria do not know what the god of that country requires. He has sent lions among them, which are killing them off, because the people do not know what he requires."

27Then the king of Assyria gave this order: "Have one of the priests you took captive from Samaria go back to live there and teach the people what the god of the land requires." **28**So one of the priests who had been exiled from Samaria came to live in Bethel and taught them how to worship the LORD.

29Nevertheless, each national group made its own gods in the several towns where they settled, and set them up in the shrines the people of Samaria had made at the high places. **30**The men from Babylon made Succoth Benoth, the men from Cuthah made Nergal, and the men from Hamath made Ashima; **31**the Avvites made Nibhaz and Tartak, and the Sepharvites burned their children in the fire as sacrifices to Adrammelech and Anammelech, the gods of Sepharvaim. **32**They worshiped the LORD, but they also appointed all sorts of their own people to officiate for them as priests in the shrines at the high places. **33**They worshiped the LORD, but they also served their own gods in accordance with the customs of the nations from which they had been brought.

34To this day they persist in their former practices. They neither worship the LORD nor adhere to the decrees and ordinances, the laws and commands that the LORD gave the descendants of Jacob, whom he named Israel. **35**When the LORD made a covenant with the Israelites, he commanded them: "Do not worship any other gods or bow down

2 Kings 17:23

God Disciplines

The LORD removed them from his presence, as he had warned through all his servants the prophets. So the people of Israel were taken from their homeland into exile in Assyria, and they are still there.

a **17** Or *They made their sons and daughters pass through* to them, serve them or sacrifice to them. 36But the LORD, who brought you up out of Egypt with mighty power and outstretched arm, is the one you must worship. To him you shall bow down and to him offer sacrifices. 37You must always be careful to keep the decrees and ordinances, the laws and commands he wrote for you. Do not worship other gods. 38Do not forget the covenant I have made with you, and do not worship other gods. 39Rather, worship the LORD your God; it is he who will deliver you from the hand of all your enemies."

40They would not listen, however, but persisted in their former practices. 41Even while these people were worshiping the LORD, they were serving their idols. To this day their children and grandchildren continue to do as their fathers did.

Hezekiah King of Judah

18 In the third year of Hoshea son of Elah king of Israel, Hezekiah son of Ahaz king of Judah began to reign. 2He was twenty-five years old when he became king, and he reigned in Jerusalem twenty-nine years. His mother's name was Abijah*a* daughter of Zechariah. 3He did what was right in the eyes of the LORD, just as his father David had done. 4He removed the high places, smashed the sacred stones and cut down the Asherah poles. He broke into pieces the bronze snake Moses had made, for up to that time the Israelites had been burning incense to it. (It was called*b* Nehushtan.*c*)

5Hezekiah trusted in the LORD, the God of Israel. There was no one like him among all the kings of Judah, either before him or after him. 6He held fast to the LORD and did not cease to follow him; he kept the commands the LORD had given Moses. 7And the LORD was with him; he was successful in whatever he undertook. He rebelled against the king of Assyria and did not serve him. 8From watchtower to fortified city, he defeated the Philistines, as far as Gaza and its territory.

9In King Hezekiah's fourth year, which was the seventh year of Hoshea son of Elah king of Israel, Shalmaneser king of Assyria marched against Samaria and laid siege to it. 10At the

end of three years the Assyrians took it. So Samaria was captured in Hezekiah's sixth year, which was the ninth year of Hoshea king of Israel. 11The king of Assyria deported Israel to Assyria and settled them in Halah, in Gozan on the Habor River and in towns of the Medes. 12This happened because they had not obeyed the LORD their God, but had violated his covenant—all that Moses the servant of the LORD commanded. They neither listened to the commands nor carried them out.

13In the fourteenth year of King Hezekiah's reign, Sennacherib king of Assyria attacked all the fortified cities of Judah and captured them. 14So Hezekiah king of Judah sent this message to the king of Assyria at Lachish: "I have done wrong. Withdraw from me, and I will pay whatever you demand of me." The king of Assyria exacted from Hezekiah king of Judah three hundred talents*d* of silver and thirty talents*e* of gold. 15So Hezekiah gave him all the silver that was found in the temple of the LORD and in the treasuries of the royal palace.

16At this time Hezekiah king of Judah stripped off the gold with which he had covered the doors and doorposts of the temple of the LORD, and gave it to the king of Assyria.

Sennacherib Threatens Jerusalem

17The king of Assyria sent his supreme commander, his chief officer and his field commander with a large army, from Lachish to King Hezekiah at Jerusalem. They came up to Jerusalem and stopped at the aqueduct of the Upper Pool, on the road to the Washerman's Field. 18They called for the king; and Eliakim son of Hilkiah the palace administrator, Shebna the secretary, and Joah son of Asaph the recorder went out to them.

19The field commander said to them, "Tell Hezekiah:

"'This is what the great king, the king of Assyria, says: On what are you basing this confidence of yours? 20You say you have strategy and military strength—but you speak only empty words. On whom are you depending, that you rebel against me? 21Look now, you are depending on

---

*a*2 Hebrew *Abi,* a variant of *Abijah*   *b*4 Or *He called it*   *c*4 *Nehushtan* sounds like the Hebrew for *bronze* and *snake* and *unclean thing.*
*d*14 That is, about 11 tons (about 10 metric tons)   *e*14 That is, about 1 ton (about 1 metric ton)

Egypt, that splintered reed of a staff, which pierces a man's hand and wounds him if he leans on it! Such is Pharaoh king of Egypt to all who depend on him. ²²And if you say to me, "We are depending on the LORD our God"—isn't he the one whose high places and altars Hezekiah removed, saying to Judah and Jerusalem, "You must worship before this altar in Jerusalem"?

²³"'Come now, make a bargain with my master, the king of Assyria: I will give you two thousand horses—if you can put riders on them! ²⁴How can you repulse one officer of the least of my master's officials, even though you are depending on Egypt for chariots and horsemen*a*? ²⁵Furthermore, have I come to attack and destroy this place without word from the LORD? The LORD himself told me to march against this country and destroy it.'"

²⁶Then Eliakim son of Hilkiah, and Shebna and Joah said to the field commander, "Please speak to your servants in Aramaic, since we understand it. Don't speak to us in Hebrew in the hearing of the people on the wall."

²⁷But the commander replied, "Was it only to your master and you that my master sent me to say these things, and not to the men sitting on the wall—who, like you, will have to eat their own filth and drink their own urine?"

²⁸Then the commander stood and called out in Hebrew: "Hear the word of the great king, the king of Assyria! ²⁹This is what the king says: Do not let Hezekiah deceive you. He cannot deliver you from my hand. ³⁰Do not let Hezekiah persuade you to trust in the LORD when he says, 'The LORD will surely deliver us; this city will not be given into the hand of the king of Assyria.'

³¹"Do not listen to Hezekiah. This is what the king of Assyria says: Make peace with me and come out to me. Then every one of you will eat from his own vine and fig tree and drink water from his own cistern, ³²until I come and take you to a land like your own, a land of grain and new wine, a land of bread and vineyards, a land of olive trees and honey. Choose life and not death!

"Do not listen to Hezekiah, for he is misleading you when he says, 'The LORD will deliver us.' ³³Has the god of any nation ever delivered his land from the hand of the king of Assyria? ³⁴Where are the gods of Hamath and Arpad? Where are the gods of Sepharvaim, Hena and Ivvah? Have they rescued Samaria from my hand? ³⁵Who of all the gods of these countries has been able to save his land from me? How then can the LORD deliver Jerusalem from my hand?"

³⁶But the people remained silent and said nothing in reply, because the king had commanded, "Do not answer him."

³⁷Then Eliakim son of Hilkiah the palace administrator, Shebna the secretary and Joah son of Asaph the recorder went to Hezekiah, with their clothes torn, and told him what the field commander had said.

Jerusalem's Deliverance Foretold

19 When King Hezekiah heard this, he tore his clothes and put on sackcloth and went into the temple of the LORD. ²He sent Eliakim the palace administrator, Shebna the secretary and the leading priests, all wearing sackcloth, to the prophet Isaiah son of Amoz. ³They told him, "This is what Hezekiah says: This day is a day of distress and rebuke and disgrace, as when children come to the point of birth and there is no strength to deliver them. ⁴It may be that the LORD your God will hear all the words of the field commander, whom his master, the king of Assyria, has sent to ridicule the living God, and that he will rebuke him for the words the LORD your God has heard. Therefore pray for the remnant that still survives."

⁵When King Hezekiah's officials came to Isaiah, ⁶Isaiah said to them, "Tell your master, 'This is what the LORD says: Do not be afraid of what you have heard—those words with which the underlings of the king of Assyria have blasphemed me. ⁷Listen! I am going to put such a spirit in him that when he hears a certain report, he will return to his own country, and there I will have him cut down with the sword.'"

⁸When the field commander heard that the king of Assyria had left Lachish, he withdrew and found the king fighting against Libnah.

---

a24 Or charioteers

Never-Fail Disaster Plan

Read: 2 Kings 18:19—19:19

ON SEVERAL OCCASIONS, Pastor Isaac Raju was beaten by Hindu neighbors who objected to the church meetings in his home. Then, when Pastor Raju's mother-in-law died, their house was surrounded by Hindu neighbors insisting that she, a Christian, be cremated according to Hindu tradition. The pastor and his wife were held against their will on the upper level of their own home as a Hindu priest chanted funeral rites on the ground floor.

A month later, in the wake of one of the most terrible tsunamis in Southeast Asia's history, the Christians reached out to their persecutors. Filled with compassion, Pastor Isaac Raju and his 25 congregants helped bury bodies and provide food and clothing for the tsunami survivors. Pastor Raju reminded his congregation, "Nothing happens without the knowledge of God. Everything is in his hands." He wanted his church to show love to their neighbors by providing physical needs like clothing, rice and cooking pots and by telling them about the love of God.

For years, Indian Christians have been marked as one of the most persecuted groups on the planet. They suffer torture, persecution and constant threats from their Hindu neighbors. Yet they didn't look away when disaster struck. They moved among the hungry, hurt and mourning, friends and enemies alike, offering fresh water and bowls of steaming rice . . . just as they knew Jesus would have done.

King Hezekiah, one of Judah's godly kings, also endured taunts and intimidation at the hands of his enemies. When a letter came from the Assyrian King Sennacherib threatening that he would conquer Judah, Hezekiah had his own disaster plan. He laid out the letter before the Lord and prayed. In his faithfulness, God listened and delivered the Israelites.

What do you do when you encounter a terrible scenario that seems to have no solution? When tragedy roars down on you like a tsunami? When something or someone truly terrifying marches your way? Do you curl up in retreat? Do you strike back in retaliation? Or do you lay the situation out before God and trust him to show you what to do?

Wouldn't it be wonderful if down the road everyone who looks at the end of your story has reason to exclaim, "Who is a God like yours!"

Go to page 472 for your next devotional reading.

2 Kings 19:19

"Now, O LORD our God, deliver us from [Sennacherib's] hand, so that all kingdoms on earth may know that you alone, O LORD, are God."

reflection

1 When have you felt trapped or persecuted for your faith?

2 What are some ways you can tangibly show Christ's love to those who have hurt you?

3 What specific situation are you facing in which you require God's help and protection? Follow Hezekiah's lead and lay your problems before the Lord in prayer.

RELATED READINGS

Psalm 115:1–8;
Matthew 5:10–12;
Luke 6:27–36

Monday

⁹Now Sennacherib received a report that Tirhakah, the Cushite*ᵃ* king of Egypt, was marching out to fight against him. So he again sent messengers to Hezekiah with this word: ¹⁰"Say to Hezekiah king of Judah: Do not let the god you depend on deceive you when he says, 'Jerusalem will not be handed over to the king of Assyria.' ¹¹Surely you have heard what the kings of Assyria have done to all the countries, destroying them completely. And will you be delivered? ¹²Did the gods of the nations that were destroyed by my forefathers deliver them: the gods of Gozan, Haran, Rezeph and the people of Eden who were in Tel Assar? ¹³Where is the king of Hamath, the king of Arpad, the king of the city of Sepharvaim, or of Hena or Ivvah?"

Hezekiah's Prayer

¹⁴Hezekiah received the letter from the messengers and read it. Then he went up to the temple of the LORD and spread it out before the LORD. ¹⁵And Hezekiah prayed to the LORD: "O LORD, God of Israel, enthroned between the cherubim, you alone are God over all the kingdoms of the earth. You have made heaven and earth. ¹⁶Give ear, O LORD, and hear; open your eyes, O LORD, and see; listen to the words Sennacherib has sent to insult the living God.

¹⁷"It is true, O LORD, that the Assyrian kings have laid waste these nations and their lands. ¹⁸They have thrown their gods into the fire and destroyed them, for they were not gods but only wood and stone, fashioned by men's hands. ¹⁹Now, O LORD our God, deliver us from his hand, so that all kingdoms on earth may know that you alone, O LORD, are God."

Isaiah Prophesies Sennacherib's Fall

²⁰Then Isaiah son of Amoz sent a message to Hezekiah: "This is what the LORD, the God of Israel, says: I have heard your prayer concerning Sennacherib king of Assyria. ²¹This is the word that the LORD has spoken against him:

"'The Virgin Daughter of Zion
   despises you and mocks you.
The Daughter of Jerusalem
   tosses her head as you flee.

²²Who is it you have insulted and
      blasphemed?
   Against whom have you raised your
      voice
and lifted your eyes in pride?
   Against the Holy One of Israel!
²³By your messengers
   you have heaped insults on the Lord.
And you have said,
   "With my many chariots
I have ascended the heights of the
      mountains,
   the utmost heights of Lebanon.
I have cut down its tallest cedars,
   the choicest of its pines.
I have reached its remotest parts,
   the finest of its forests.
²⁴I have dug wells in foreign lands
   and drunk the water there.
With the soles of my feet
   I have dried up all the streams of Egypt."

²⁵"'Have you not heard?
   Long ago I ordained it.
In days of old I planned it;
   now I have brought it to pass,
that you have turned fortified cities
   into piles of stone.
²⁶Their people, drained of power,
   are dismayed and put to shame.
They are like plants in the field,
   like tender green shoots,
like grass sprouting on the roof,
   scorched before it grows up.

²⁷"'But I know where you stay
   and when you come and go
   and how you rage against me.
²⁸Because you rage against me
   and your insolence has reached my ears,
I will put my hook in your nose
   and my bit in your mouth,
and I will make you return
   by the way you came.'

²⁹"This will be the sign for you, O Hezekiah:

"This year you will eat what grows by itself,
   and the second year what springs from
      that.

ᵃ9 That is, from the upper Nile region

But in the third year sow and reap,
plant vineyards and eat their fruit.
30 Once more a remnant of the house of
Judah
will take root below and bear fruit
above.
31 For out of Jerusalem will come a remnant,
and out of Mount Zion a band of
survivors.

The zeal of the LORD Almighty will accomplish this.

32 "Therefore this is what the LORD says concerning the king of Assyria:

"He will not enter this city
or shoot an arrow here.
He will not come before it with shield
or build a siege ramp against it.
33 By the way that he came he
will return;
he will not enter this city,
declares the LORD.
34 I will defend this city and
save it,
for my sake and for the
sake of David my
servant."

35 That night the angel of
the LORD went out and put to
death a hundred and eighty-
five thousand men in the Assyrian camp. When the people
got up the next morning—there were all the
dead bodies! 36 So Sennacherib king of Assyria
broke camp and withdrew. He returned to Nineveh and stayed there.

37 One day, while he was worshiping in the
temple of his god Nisroch, his sons Adrammelech and Sharezer cut him down with the
sword, and they escaped to the land of Ararat. And Esarhaddon his son succeeded him
as king.

Hezekiah's Illness

20 In those days Hezekiah became ill and
was at the point of death. The prophet
Isaiah son of Amoz went to him and said,
"This is what the LORD says: Put your house
in order, because you are going to die; you will
not recover."

2 Hezekiah turned his face to the wall and
prayed to the LORD, 3 "Remember, O LORD,
how I have walked before you faithfully and
with wholehearted devotion and have done
what is good in your eyes." And Hezekiah wept
bitterly.

4 Before Isaiah had left the middle court, the
word of the LORD came to him: 5 "Go back and
tell Hezekiah, the leader of my people, 'This is
what the LORD, the God of your father David,
says: I have heard your prayer and seen your
tears; I will heal you. On the third day from
now you will go up to the temple of the LORD.
6 I will add fifteen years to your life. And I will
deliver you and this city from the hand of the
king of Assyria. I will defend this city for my
sake and for the sake of my servant David.' "

7 Then Isaiah said, "Prepare a poultice of
figs." They did so and applied it
to the boil, and he recovered.

8 Hezekiah had asked Isaiah,
"What will be the sign that
the LORD will heal me and
that I will go up to the temple
of the LORD on the third day
from now?"

9 Isaiah answered, "This is
the LORD's sign to you that
the LORD will do what he has
promised: Shall the shadow go
forward ten steps, or shall it go
back ten steps?"

10 "It is a simple matter
for the shadow to go forward ten steps," said
Hezekiah. "Rather, have it go back ten steps."

11 Then the prophet Isaiah called upon the
LORD, and the LORD made the shadow go back
the ten steps it had gone down on the stairway
of Ahaz.

Envoys From Babylon

12 At that time Merodach-Baladan son of Baladan king of Babylon sent Hezekiah letters and
a gift, because he had heard of Hezekiah's illness. 13 Hezekiah received the messengers and
showed them all that was in his storehouses—
the silver, the gold, the spices and the fine
oil—his armory and everything found among
his treasures. There was nothing in his palace
or in all his kingdom that Hezekiah did not
show them.

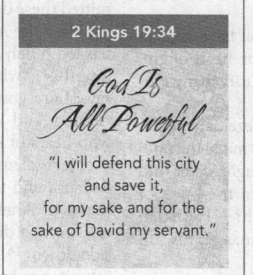

2 Kings 19:34

*God Is
All Powerful*

"I will defend this city
and save it,
for my sake and for the
sake of David my servant."

¹⁴Then Isaiah the prophet went to King Hezekiah and asked, "What did those men say, and where did they come from?"

"From a distant land," Hezekiah replied. "They came from Babylon."

¹⁵The prophet asked, "What did they see in your palace?"

"They saw everything in my palace," Hezekiah said. "There is nothing among my treasures that I did not show them."

¹⁶Then Isaiah said to Hezekiah, "Hear the word of the LORD: ¹⁷The time will surely come when everything in your palace, and all that your fathers have stored up until this day, will be carried off to Babylon. Nothing will be left, says the LORD. ¹⁸And some of your descendants, your own flesh and blood, that will be born to you, will be taken away, and they will become eunuchs in the palace of the king of Babylon."

¹⁹"The word of the LORD you have spoken is good," Hezekiah replied. For he thought, "Will there not be peace and security in my lifetime?"

²⁰As for the other events of Hezekiah's reign, all his achievements and how he made the pool and the tunnel by which he brought water into the city, are they not written in the book of the annals of the kings of Judah? ²¹Hezekiah rested with his fathers. And Manasseh his son succeeded him as king.

Manasseh King of Judah

21 Manasseh was twelve years old when he became king, and he reigned in Jerusalem fifty-five years. His mother's name was Hephzibah. ²He did evil in the eyes of the LORD, following the detestable practices of the nations the LORD had driven out before the Israelites. ³He rebuilt the high places his father Hezekiah had destroyed; he also erected altars to Baal and made an Asherah pole, as Ahab king of Israel had done. He bowed down to all the starry hosts and worshiped them. ⁴He built altars in the temple of the LORD, of which the LORD had said, "In Jerusalem I will put my Name." ⁵In both courts of the temple of the LORD, he built altars to all the starry hosts. ⁶He sacrificed his own son in^a the fire, practiced sorcery and divination, and consulted mediums and spiritists. He did much evil in the eyes of the LORD, provoking him to anger.

⁷He took the carved Asherah pole he had made and put it in the temple, of which the LORD had said to David and to his son Solomon, "In this temple and in Jerusalem, which I have chosen out of all the tribes of Israel, I will put my Name forever. ⁸I will not again make the feet of the Israelites wander from the land I gave their forefathers, if only they will be careful to do everything I commanded them and will keep the whole Law that my servant Moses gave them." ⁹But the people did not listen. Manasseh led them astray, so that they did more evil than the nations the LORD had destroyed before the Israelites.

¹⁰The LORD said through his servants the prophets: ¹¹"Manasseh king of Judah has committed these detestable sins. He has done more evil than the Amorites who preceded him and has led Judah into sin with his idols. ¹²Therefore this is what the LORD, the God of Israel, says: I am going to bring such disaster on Jerusalem and Judah that the ears of everyone who hears of it will tingle. ¹³I will stretch out over Jerusalem the measuring line used against Samaria and the plumb line used against the house of Ahab. I will wipe out Jerusalem as one wipes a dish, wiping it and turning it upside down. ¹⁴I will forsake the remnant of my inheritance and hand them over to their enemies. They will be looted and plundered by all their foes, ¹⁵because they have done evil in my eyes and have provoked me to anger from the day their forefathers came out of Egypt until this day."

¹⁶Moreover, Manasseh also shed so much innocent blood that he filled Jerusalem from end to end—besides the sin that he had caused Judah to commit, so that they did evil in the eyes of the LORD.

¹⁷As for the other events of Manasseh's reign, and all he did, including the sin he committed, are they not written in the book of the annals of the kings of Judah? ¹⁸Manasseh rested with his fathers and was buried in his palace garden, the garden of Uzza. And Amon his son succeeded him as king.

^a6 Or *He made his own son pass through*

Amon King of Judah

¹⁹Amon was twenty-two years old when he became king, and he reigned in Jerusalem two years. His mother's name was Meshullemeth daughter of Haruz; she was from Jotbah. ²⁰He did evil in the eyes of the LORD, as his father Manasseh had done. ²¹He walked in all the ways of his father; he worshiped the idols his father had worshiped, and bowed down to them. ²²He forsook the LORD, the God of his fathers, and did not walk in the way of the LORD.

²³Amon's officials conspired against him and assassinated the king in his palace. ²⁴Then the people of the land killed all who had plotted against King Amon, and they made Josiah his son king in his place.

²⁵As for the other events of Amon's reign, and what he did, are they not written in the book of the annals of the kings of Judah? ²⁶He was buried in his grave in the garden of Uzza. And Josiah his son succeeded him as king.

The Book of the Law Found

22 Josiah was eight years old when he became king, and he reigned in Jerusalem thirty-one years. His mother's name was Jedidah daughter of Adaiah; she was from Bozkath. ²He did what was right in the eyes of the LORD and walked in all the ways of his father David, not turning aside to the right or to the left.

³In the eighteenth year of his reign, King Josiah sent the secretary, Shaphan son of Azaliah, the son of Meshullam, to the temple of the LORD. He said: ⁴"Go up to Hilkiah the high priest and have him get ready the money that has been brought into the temple of the LORD, which the doorkeepers have collected from the people. ⁵Have them entrust it to the men appointed to supervise the work on the temple. And have these men pay the workers who repair the temple of the LORD— ⁶the carpenters, the builders and the masons. Also have them purchase timber and dressed stone to repair the temple. ⁷But they need not account for the money entrusted to them, because they are acting faithfully."

⁸Hilkiah the high priest said to Shaphan the secretary, "I have found the Book of the Law in the temple of the LORD." He gave it to Shaphan, who read it. ⁹Then Shaphan the secretary went to the king and reported to him: "Your officials have paid out the money that was in the temple of the LORD and have entrusted it to the workers and supervisors at the temple." ¹⁰Then Shaphan the secretary informed the king, "Hilkiah the priest has given me a book." And Shaphan read from it in the presence of the king.

¹¹When the king heard the words of the Book of the Law, he tore his robes. ¹²He gave these orders to Hilkiah the priest, Ahikam son of Shaphan, Acbor son of Micaiah, Shaphan the secretary and Asaiah the king's attendant: ¹³"Go and inquire of the LORD for me and for the people and for all Judah about what is written in this book that has been found. Great is the LORD's anger that burns against us because our fathers have not obeyed the words of this book; they have not acted in accordance with all that is written concerning us."

¹⁴Hilkiah the priest, Ahikam, Acbor, Shaphan and Asaiah went to speak to the prophetess Huldah, who was the wife of Shallum son of Tikvah, the son of Harhas, keeper of the wardrobe. She lived in Jerusalem, in the Second District.

¹⁵She said to them, "This is what the LORD, the God of Israel, says: Tell the man who sent you to me, ¹⁶'This is what the LORD says: I am going to bring disaster on this place and its people, according to everything written in the book the king of Judah has read. ¹⁷Because they have forsaken me and burned incense to other gods and provoked me to anger by all the idols their hands have made,^a my anger will burn against this place and will not be quenched.' ¹⁸Tell the king of Judah, who sent you to inquire of the LORD, 'This is what the LORD, the God of Israel, says concerning the words you heard: ¹⁹Because your heart was responsive and you humbled yourself before the LORD when you heard what I have spoken against this place and its people, that they would become accursed and laid waste, and because you tore your robes and wept in my presence, I have heard you, declares the LORD. ²⁰Therefore I will gather you to your fathers, and you will be buried in peace. Your eyes will not see all the disaster I am going to bring on this place.'"

So they took her answer back to the king.

^a17 Or *by everything they have done*

Life Condensed

2 Kings 22:2

[Josiah] did what was right in the eyes of the Lord and walked in all the ways of his father David, not turning aside to the right or to the left.

reflection

1 How would you describe your character when it comes to following God's ways? Write a one-sentence summary of your current life, starting with "I walk in the way of . . ."

2 What might God want to change in your life so that your life summary will be different?

3 What steps will you take today to walk in God's ways?

RELATED READINGS

2 Kings 23:8–25;
Psalm 26:1–3;
Isaiah 30:19–26;
Galatians 5:25

CONDENSED SOUP. CONDENSED MILK. Condensed books. We like all sorts of things that are condensed, consolidated, compressed, abridged or abbreviated. Make it short. Make it quick. Whatever saves time. Whatever gets us to the bottom line.

The condensed version of King Josiah's life is found in a single sentence. Thirty-one words in one verse sum up the essence of his entire life: "He did what was right in the eyes of the Lord and walked in all the ways of his father David, not turning aside to the right or to the left." Amazing! Concise! Josiah walked the path of righteousness without swerving.

Josiah became king at age 8 and reigned until his death at 39. His father and grandfather both reigned over Judah before him. Both "did evil in the eyes of the Lord" (2 Kings 21:20). Despite his evil legacy, Josiah turned his heart toward God. And although Judah, the nation he ruled, had turned to worship false gods, Josiah did not waver in his allegiance to the one true God. No other king before or after him stayed on course like Josiah.

If your life were condensed into a short synopsis—one brief sentence—what would be said of you? How our lives are summarized depends on the choices we make each day. We have the tendency to become distracted with the cares and responsibilities of life. Laundry piles up. Bills need to be paid. Children get sick. As we care for our families and do our work, it's easy to become sidetracked from our primary purpose: pleasing God. It is easier to give lip service to spiritual things than to stay on course, keeping in step with the Spirit (see Galatians 5:25).

How will you be remembered? Eventually, someone will write your obituary or eulogy. Your life will be abridged into a few brief sentences and paragraphs. What will be said of you? More important, how will God summarize your life?

Let it be said of you, "_____ [fill in your name] did what was right in the eyes of the Lord and walked in the way of truth, not turning aside to the right or to the left."

Tuesday

Go to page 485 for your next devotional reading.

Josiah Renews the Covenant

23 Then the king called together all the elders of Judah and Jerusalem. ²He went up to the temple of the LORD with the men of Judah, the people of Jerusalem, the priests and the prophets—all the people from the least to the greatest. He read in their hearing all the words of the Book of the Covenant, which had been found in the temple of the LORD. ³The king stood by the pillar and renewed the covenant in the presence of the LORD—to follow the LORD and keep his commands, regulations and decrees with all his heart and all his soul, thus confirming the words of the covenant written in this book. Then all the people pledged themselves to the covenant.

⁴The king ordered Hilkiah the high priest, the priests next in rank and the doorkeepers to remove from the temple of the LORD all the articles made for Baal and Asherah and all the starry hosts. He burned them outside Jerusalem in the fields of the Kidron Valley and took the ashes to Bethel. ⁵He did away with the pagan priests appointed by the kings of Judah to burn incense on the high places of the towns of Judah and on those around Jerusalem—those who burned incense to Baal, to the sun and moon, to the constellations and to all the starry hosts. ⁶He took the Asherah pole from the temple of the LORD to the Kidron Valley outside Jerusalem and burned it there. He ground it to powder and scattered the dust over the graves of the common people. ⁷He also tore down the quarters of the male shrine prostitutes, which were in the temple of the LORD and where women did weaving for Asherah.

⁸Josiah brought all the priests from the towns of Judah and desecrated the high places, from Geba to Beersheba, where the priests had burned incense. He broke down the shrines*a* at the gates—at the entrance to the Gate of Joshua, the city governor, which is on the left of the city gate. ⁹Although the priests of the high places did not serve at the altar of the LORD in Jerusalem, they ate unleavened bread with their fellow priests.

¹⁰He desecrated Topheth, which was in the Valley of Ben Hinnom, so no one could use it to sacrifice his son or daughter in*b* the fire

to Molech. ¹¹He removed from the entrance to the temple of the LORD the horses that the kings of Judah had dedicated to the sun. They were in the court near the room of an official named Nathan-Melech. Josiah then burned the chariots dedicated to the sun.

¹²He pulled down the altars the kings of Judah had erected on the roof near the upper room of Ahaz, and the altars Manasseh had built in the two courts of the temple of the LORD. He removed them from there, smashed them to pieces and threw the rubble into the Kidron Valley. ¹³The king also desecrated the high places that were east of Jerusalem on the south of the Hill of Corruption—the ones Solomon king of Israel had built for Ashtoreth the vile goddess of the Sidonians, for Chemosh the vile god of Moab, and for Molech*c* the detestable god of the people of Ammon. ¹⁴Josiah smashed the sacred stones and cut down the Asherah poles and covered the sites with human bones.

¹⁵Even the altar at Bethel, the high place made by Jeroboam son of Nebat, who had caused Israel to sin—even that altar and high place he demolished. He burned the high place and ground it to powder, and burned the Asherah pole also. ¹⁶Then Josiah looked around, and when he saw the tombs that were there on the hillside, he had the bones removed from them and burned on the altar to defile it, in accordance with the word of the LORD proclaimed by the man of God who foretold these things.

¹⁷The king asked, "What is that tombstone I see?"

The men of the city said, "It marks the tomb of the man of God who came from Judah and pronounced against the altar of Bethel the very things you have done to it."

¹⁸"Leave it alone," he said. "Don't let anyone disturb his bones." So they spared his bones and those of the prophet who had come from Samaria.

¹⁹Just as he had done at Bethel, Josiah removed and defiled all the shrines at the high places that the kings of Israel had built in the towns of Samaria that had provoked the LORD to anger. ²⁰Josiah slaughtered all the priests

---

a8 Or *high places*   *b10* Or *to make his son or daughter pass through*   *c13* Hebrew *Milcom* of those high places on the altars and burned human bones on them. Then he went back to Jerusalem.

21The king gave this order to all the people: "Celebrate the Passover to the LORD your God, as it is written in this Book of the Covenant." 22Not since the days of the judges who led Israel, nor throughout the days of the kings of Israel and the kings of Judah, had any such Passover been observed. 23But in the eighteenth year of King Josiah, this Passover was celebrated to the LORD in Jerusalem.

24Furthermore, Josiah got rid of the mediums and spiritists, the household gods, the idols and all the other detestable things seen in Judah and Jerusalem. This he did to fulfill the requirements of the law written in the book that Hilkiah the priest had discovered in the temple of the LORD. 25Neither before nor after Josiah was there a king like him who turned to the LORD as he did—with all his heart and with all his soul and with all his strength, in accordance with all the Law of Moses.

26Nevertheless, the LORD did not turn away from the heat of his fierce anger, which burned against Judah because of all that Manasseh had done to provoke him to anger. 27So the LORD said, "I will remove Judah also from my presence as I removed Israel, and I will reject Jerusalem, the city I chose, and this temple, about which I said, 'There shall my Name be.'a"

28As for the other events of Josiah's reign, and all he did, are they not written in the book of the annals of the kings of Judah?

29While Josiah was king, Pharaoh Neco king of Egypt went up to the Euphrates River to help the king of Assyria. King Josiah marched out to meet him in battle, but Neco faced him and killed him at Megiddo. 30Josiah's servants brought his body in a chariot from Megiddo to Jerusalem and buried him in his own tomb. And the people of the land took Jehoahaz son of Josiah and anointed him and made him king in place of his father.

Jehoahaz King of Judah

31Jehoahaz was twenty-three years old when he became king, and he reigned in Jerusalem three months. His mother's name was Hamu-

tal daughter of Jeremiah; she was from Libnah. 32He did evil in the eyes of the LORD, just as his fathers had done. 33Pharaoh Neco put him in chains at Riblah in the land of Hamathb so that he might not reign in Jerusalem, and he imposed on Judah a levy of a hundred talentsc of silver and a talentd of gold. 34Pharaoh Neco made Eliakim son of Josiah king in place of his father Josiah and changed Eliakim's name to Jehoiakim. But he took Jehoahaz and carried him off to Egypt, and there he died. 35Jehoiakim paid Pharaoh Neco the silver and gold he demanded. In order to do so, he taxed the land and exacted the silver and gold from the people of the land according to their assessments.

Jehoiakim King of Judah

36Jehoiakim was twenty-five years old when he became king, and he reigned in Jerusalem eleven years. His mother's name was Zebidah daughter of Pedaiah; she was from Rumah. 37And he did evil in the eyes of the LORD, just as his fathers had done.

24 During Jehoiakim's reign, Nebuchadnezzar king of Babylon invaded the land, and Jehoiakim became his vassal for three years. But then he changed his mind and rebelled against Nebuchadnezzar. 2The LORD sent Babylonian,e Aramean, Moabite and Ammonite raiders against him. He sent them to destroy Judah, in accordance with the word of the LORD proclaimed by his servants the prophets. 3Surely these things happened to Judah according to the LORD's command, in order to remove them from his presence because of the sins of Manasseh and all he had done, 4including the shedding of innocent blood. For he had filled Jerusalem with innocent blood, and the LORD was not willing to forgive.

5As for the other events of Jehoiakim's reign, and all he did, are they not written in the book of the annals of the kings of Judah? 6Jehoiakim rested with his fathers. And Jehoiachin his son succeeded him as king.

7The king of Egypt did not march out from his own country again, because the king of Babylon had taken all his territory, from the Wadi of Egypt to the Euphrates River.

---

a27 1 Kings 8:29 b33 Hebrew; Septuagint (see also 2 Chron. 36:3) *Neco at Riblah in Hamath removed him* c33 That is, about 3 3/4 tons (about 3.4 metric tons) d33 That is, about 75 pounds (about 34 kilograms) e2 Or *Chaldean*

Jehoiachin King of Judah

8 Jehoiachin was eighteen years old when he became king, and he reigned in Jerusalem three months. His mother's name was Nehushta daughter of Elnathan; she was from Jerusalem. **9** He did evil in the eyes of the LORD, just as his father had done.

10 At that time the officers of Nebuchadnezzar king of Babylon advanced on Jerusalem and laid siege to it, **11** and Nebuchadnezzar himself came up to the city while his officers were besieging it. **12** Jehoiachin king of Judah, his mother, his attendants, his nobles and his officials all surrendered to him.

In the eighth year of the reign of the king of Babylon, he took Jehoiachin prisoner. **13** As the LORD had declared, Nebuchadnezzar removed all the treasures from the temple of the LORD and from the royal palace, and took away all the gold articles that Solomon king of Israel had made for the temple of the LORD. **14** He carried into exile all Jerusalem: all the officers and fighting men, and all the craftsmen and artisans—a total of ten thousand. Only the poorest people of the land were left.

15 Nebuchadnezzar took Jehoiachin captive to Babylon. He also took from Jerusalem to Babylon the king's mother, his wives, his officials and the leading men of the land. **16** The king of Babylon also deported to Babylon the entire force of seven thousand fighting men, strong and fit for war, and a thousand craftsmen and artisans. **17** He made Mattaniah, Jehoiachin's uncle, king in his place and changed his name to Zedekiah.

Zedekiah King of Judah

18 Zedekiah was twenty-one years old when he became king, and he reigned in Jerusalem eleven years. His mother's name was Hamutal daughter of Jeremiah; she was from Libnah. **19** He did evil in the eyes of the LORD, just as Jehoiakim had done. **20** It was because of the LORD's anger that all this happened to Jerusa-

2 Kings 24:13

God Is Sovereign

As the LORD had declared, Nebuchadnezzar removed all the treasures from the temple of the LORD and from the royal palace, and took away all the gold articles that Solomon king of Israel had made for the temple of the LORD.

lem and Judah, and in the end he thrust them from his presence.

The Fall of Jerusalem

Now Zedekiah rebelled against the king of Babylon.

25 So in the ninth year of Zedekiah's reign, on the tenth day of the tenth month, Nebuchadnezzar king of Babylon marched against Jerusalem with his whole army. He encamped outside the city and built siege works all around it. **2** The city was kept under siege until the eleventh year of King Zedekiah. **3** By the ninth day of the fourth,^{a} month the famine in the city had become so severe that there was no food for the people to eat. **4** Then the city wall was broken through, and the whole army fled at night through the gate between the two walls near the king's garden, though the Babylonians^b were surrounding the city. They fled toward the Arabah,^{c} **5** but the Babylonian^d army pursued the king and overtook him in the plains of Jericho. All his soldiers were separated from him and scattered, **6** and he was captured. He was taken to the king of Babylon at Riblah, where sentence was pronounced on him. **7** They killed the sons of Zedekiah before his eyes. Then they put out his eyes, bound him with bronze shackles and took him to Babylon.

8 On the seventh day of the fifth month, in the nineteenth year of Nebuchadnezzar king of Babylon, Nebuzaradan commander of the imperial guard, an official of the king of Babylon, came to Jerusalem. **9** He set fire to the temple of the LORD, the royal palace and all the houses of Jerusalem. Every important building he burned down. **10** The whole Babylonian army, under the commander of the imperial guard, broke down the walls around Jerusalem. **11** Nebuzaradan the commander of the guard carried into exile the people who remained in the city, along with the rest of the populace and those who had gone over to the king of

^{a}3 See Jer. 52:6. ^{b}4 Or *Chaldeans*; also in verses 13, 25 and 26 ^{c}4 Or *the Jordan Valley* ^{d}5 Or *Chaldean*; also in verses 10 and 24

Babylon. ¹²But the commander left behind some of the poorest people of the land to work the vineyards and fields.

¹³The Babylonians broke up the bronze pillars, the movable stands and the bronze Sea that were at the temple of the LORD and they carried the bronze to Babylon. ¹⁴They also took away the pots, shovels, wick trimmers, dishes and all the bronze articles used in the temple service. ¹⁵The commander of the imperial guard took away the censers and sprinkling bowls—all that were made of pure gold or silver.

¹⁶The bronze from the two pillars, the Sea and the movable stands, which Solomon had made for the temple of the LORD, was more than could be weighed. ¹⁷Each pillar was twenty-seven feet[a] high. The bronze capital on top of one pillar was four and a half feet[b] high and was decorated with a network and pomegranates of bronze all around. The other pillar, with its network, was similar.

¹⁸The commander of the guard took as prisoners Seraiah the chief priest, Zephaniah the priest next in rank and the three doorkeepers. ¹⁹Of those still in the city, he took the officer in charge of the fighting men and five royal advisers. He also took the secretary who was chief officer in charge of conscripting the people of the land and sixty of his men who were found in the city. ²⁰Nebuzaradan the commander took them all and brought them to the king of Babylon at Riblah. ²¹There at Riblah, in the land of Hamath, the king had them executed.

So Judah went into captivity, away from her land.

²²Nebuchadnezzar king of Babylon appointed Gedaliah son of Ahikam, the son of Shaphan, to be over the people he had left behind in Judah. ²³When all the army officers and their men heard that the king of Babylon had appointed Gedaliah as governor, they came to Gedaliah at Mizpah—Ishmael son of Nethaniah, Johanan son of Kareah, Seraiah son of Tanhumeth the Netophathite, Jaazaniah the son of the Maacathite, and their men. ²⁴Gedaliah took an oath to reassure them and their men. "Do not be afraid of the Babylonian officials," he said. "Settle down in the land and serve the king of Babylon, and it will go well with you."

²⁵In the seventh month, however, Ishmael son of Nethaniah, the son of Elishama, who was of royal blood, came with ten men and assassinated Gedaliah and also the men of Judah and the Babylonians who were with him at Mizpah. ²⁶At this, all the people from the least to the greatest, together with the army officers, fled to Egypt for fear of the Babylonians.

Jehoiachin Released

²⁷In the thirty-seventh year of the exile of Jehoiachin king of Judah, in the year Evil-Merodach[c] became king of Babylon, he released Jehoiachin from prison on the twenty-seventh day of the twelfth month. ²⁸He spoke kindly to him and gave him a seat of honor higher than those of the other kings who were with him in Babylon. ²⁹So Jehoiachin put aside his prison clothes and for the rest of his life ate regularly at the king's table. ³⁰Day by day the king gave Jehoiachin a regular allowance as long as he lived.

---

a 17 Hebrew *eighteen cubits* (about 8.1 meters)   *b 17* Hebrew *three cubits* (about 1.3 meters)   *c 27* Also called *Amel-Marduk*

1 Chronicles

The Chronicles were *written for a people* in the process of rebuilding—rebuilding their walls, their temple, their country, their lives. Judgment and exile were their most recent memories, and even at this point they were still subject to Persia. *They had once been God's people,* but now, with the exile over and the time for rebuilding begun, would he take them back? Would he even want them back?

"Remember," the Chronicler seems to say. Remember your past. These people in your family tree are more than just dusty old names. *They are a part of you.* Their choices are what created your history, and it is your history that shapes your present. *You would do well to learn from them.* You would do well to learn all you possibly can.

Author:
Unknown, but possibly Ezra.

Audience:
All Israel.

Date:
About 430 B.C.

Setting:
The book begins with Israel's genealogical records and then focuses on King David's reign, paralleling many of the events recorded in 2 Samuel.

Verse to Remember:
"You made your people Israel your very own forever, and you, O LORD, have become their God." (17:22)

Historical Records From Adam to Abraham

To Noah's Sons

1 Adam, Seth, Enosh, **2**Kenan, Mahalalel, Jared, **3**Enoch, Methuselah, Lamech, Noah.

4 The sons of Noah:*a*
Shem, Ham and Japheth.

The Japhethites

5 The sons*b* of Japheth:
Gomer, Magog, Madai, Javan, Tubal, Meshech and Tiras.

6 The sons of Gomer:
Ashkenaz, Riphath*c* and Togarmah.

7 The sons of Javan:
Elishah, Tarshish, the Kittim and the Rodanim.

---

*a*4 Septuagint; Hebrew does not have this line.   *b*5 *Sons* may mean *descendants* or *successors* or *nations*; also in verses 6–10, 17 and 20.
*c*6 Many Hebrew manuscripts and Vulgate (see also Septuagint and Gen. 10:3); most Hebrew manuscripts *Diphath*

The Hamites

8 The sons of Ham:

Cush, Mizraim,[a] Put and Canaan.

9 The sons of Cush:

Seba, Havilah, Sabta, Raamah and Sabteca.

The sons of Raamah:

Sheba and Dedan.

10 Cush was the father[b] of

Nimrod, who grew to be a mighty warrior on earth.

11 Mizraim was the father of

the Ludites, Anamites, Lehabites, Naphtuhites, **12** Pathrusites, Casluhites (from whom the Philistines came) and Caphtorites.

13 Canaan was the father of

Sidon his firstborn,[c] and of the Hittites, **14** Jebusites, Amorites, Girgashites, **15** Hivites, Arkites, Sinites, **16** Arvadites, Zemarites and Hamathites.

The Semites

17 The sons of Shem:

Elam, Asshur, Arphaxad, Lud and Aram.

The sons of Aram:[d]

Uz, Hul, Gether and Meshech.

18 Arphaxad was the father of Shelah,

and Shelah the father of Eber.

19 Two sons were born to Eber:

One was named Peleg,[e] because in his time the earth was divided; his brother was named Joktan.

20 Joktan was the father of

Almodad, Sheleph, Hazarmaveth, Jerah, **21** Hadoram, Uzal, Diklah, **22** Obal,[f] Abimael, Sheba, **23** Ophir, Havilah and Jobab. All these were sons of Joktan.

24 Shem, Arphaxad,[g] Shelah,

25 Eber, Peleg, Reu,

26 Serug, Nahor, Terah

27 and Abram (that is, Abraham).

The Family of Abraham

28 The sons of Abraham:

Isaac and Ishmael.

Descendants of Hagar

29 These were their descendants:

Nebaioth the firstborn of Ishmael, Kedar, Adbeel, Mibsam, **30** Mishma, Dumah, Massa, Hadad, Tema, **31** Jetur, Naphish and Kedemah. These were the sons of Ishmael.

Descendants of Keturah

32 The sons born to Keturah, Abraham's concubine:

Zimran, Jokshan, Medan, Midian, Ishbak and Shuah.

The sons of Jokshan:

Sheba and Dedan.

33 The sons of Midian:

Ephah, Epher, Hanoch, Abida and Eldaah.

All these were descendants of Keturah.

Descendants of Sarah

34 Abraham was the father of Isaac.

The sons of Isaac:

Esau and Israel.

Esau's Sons

35 The sons of Esau:

Eliphaz, Reuel, Jeush, Jalam and Korah.

36 The sons of Eliphaz:

Teman, Omar, Zepho,[h] Gatam and Kenaz;

by Timna: Amalek.[i]

37 The sons of Reuel:

Nahath, Zerah, Shammah and Mizzah.

The People of Seir in Edom

38 The sons of Seir:

Lotan, Shobal, Zibeon, Anah, Dishon, Ezer and Dishan.

39 The sons of Lotan:

Hori and Homam. Timna was Lotan's sister.

---

a 8 That is, Egypt; also in verse 11   *b* 10 *Father* may mean *ancestor* or *predecessor* or *founder*; also in verses 11, 13, 18 and 20.   *c* 13 Or *of the Sidonians, the foremost*   *d* 17 One Hebrew manuscript and some Septuagint manuscripts (see also Gen. 10:23); most Hebrew manuscripts do not have this line.   *e* 19 *Peleg* means *division.*   *f* 22 Some Hebrew manuscripts and Syriac (see also Gen. 10:28); most Hebrew manuscripts *Ebal*   *g* 24 Hebrew; some Septuagint manuscripts *Arphaxad, Cainan* (see also note at Gen. 11:10)   *h* 36 Many Hebrew manuscripts, some Septuagint manuscripts and Syriac (see also Gen. 36:11); most Hebrew manuscripts *Zephi*   *i* 36 Some Septuagint manuscripts (see also Gen. 36:12); Hebrew *Gatam, Kenaz, Timna and Amalek*

40 The sons of Shobal:

Alvan,[a] Manahath, Ebal, Shepho and Onam.

The sons of Zibeon:

Aiah and Anah.

41 The son of Anah:

Dishon.

The sons of Dishon:

Hemdan,[b] Eshban, Ithran and Keran.

42 The sons of Ezer:

Bilhan, Zaavan and Akan.[c]

The sons of Dishan[d]:

Uz and Aran.

The Rulers of Edom

43 These were the kings who reigned in Edom before any Israelite king reigned[e]:

Bela son of Beor, whose city was named Dinhabah.

44 When Bela died, Jobab son of Zerah from Bozrah succeeded him as king.

45 When Jobab died, Husham from the land of the Temanites succeeded him as king.

46 When Husham died, Hadad son of Bedad, who defeated Midian in the country of Moab, succeeded him as king. His city was named Avith.

47 When Hadad died, Samlah from Masrekah succeeded him as king.

48 When Samlah died, Shaul from Rehoboth on the river[f] succeeded him as king.

49 When Shaul died, Baal-Hanan son of Acbor succeeded him as king.

50 When Baal-Hanan died, Hadad succeeded him as king. His city was named Pau,[g] and his wife's name was Mehetabel daughter of Matred, the daughter of Me-Zahab. **51** Hadad also died.

The chiefs of Edom were:

Timna, Alvah, Jetheth, **52**Oholibamah, Elah, Pinon, **53**Kenaz, Teman, Mibzar, **54**Magdiel and Iram. These were the chiefs of Edom.

Israel's Sons

2 These were the sons of Israel:

Reuben, Simeon, Levi, Judah, Issachar, Zebulun, **2**Dan, Joseph, Benjamin, Naphtali, Gad and Asher.

Judah

To Hezron's Sons

3 The sons of Judah:

Er, Onan and Shelah. These three were born to him by a Canaanite woman, the daughter of Shua. Er, Judah's firstborn, was wicked in the LORD's sight; so the LORD put him to death. **4**Tamar, Judah's daughter-in-law, bore him Perez and Zerah. Judah had five sons in all.

5 The sons of Perez:

Hezron and Hamul.

6 The sons of Zerah:

Zimri, Ethan, Heman, Calcol and Darda[h]—five in all.

7 The son of Carmi:

Achar,[i] who brought trouble on Israel by violating the ban on taking devoted things.[j]

8 The son of Ethan:

Azariah.

9 The sons born to Hezron were:

Jerahmeel, Ram and Caleb.[k]

From Ram Son of Hezron

10 Ram was the father of

Amminadab, and Amminadab the father of Nahshon, the leader of the people of Judah. **11**Nahshon was the father of Salmon,[l] Salmon the father of Boaz, **12**Boaz the father of Obed and Obed the father of Jesse.

13 Jesse was the father of

Eliab his firstborn; the second son was Abinadab, the third Shimea, **14**the fourth Nethanel, the fifth Raddai, **15**the sixth Ozem and the seventh David. **16**Their sisters were Zeruiah and

*a*40 Many Hebrew manuscripts and some Septuagint manuscripts (see also Gen. 36:23); most Hebrew manuscripts *Alian*   *b*41 Many Hebrew manuscripts and some Septuagint manuscripts (see also Gen. 36:26); most Hebrew manuscripts *Hamran*   *c*42 Many Hebrew and Septuagint manuscripts (see also Gen. 36:27); most Hebrew manuscripts *Zaavan, Jaakan*   *d*42 Hebrew *Dishon*, a variant of *Dishan*   *e*43 Or *before an Israelite king reigned over them*   *f*48 Possibly the Euphrates   *g*50 Many Hebrew manuscripts, some Septuagint manuscripts, Vulgate and Syriac (see also Gen. 36:39); most Hebrew manuscripts *Pai*   *h*6 Many Hebrew manuscripts, some Septuagint manuscripts and Syriac (see also 1 Kings 4:31); most Hebrew manuscripts *Dara*   *i*7 *Achar* means *trouble; Achar* is called *Achan* in Joshua.   *j*7 The Hebrew term refers to the irrevocable giving over of things or persons to the LORD, often by totally destroying them.   *k*9 Hebrew *Kelubai*, a variant of *Caleb*   *l*11 Septuagint (see also Ruth 4:21); Hebrew *Salma*

Abigail. Zeruiah's three sons were Abishai, Joab and Asahel. **17** Abigail was the mother of Amasa, whose father was Jether the Ishmaelite.

Caleb Son of Hezron

18 Caleb son of Hezron had children by his wife Azubah (and by Jerioth). These were her sons: Jesher, Shobab and Ardon. **19** When Azubah died, Caleb married Ephrath, who bore him Hur. **20** Hur was the father of Uri, and Uri the father of Bezalel.

21 Later, Hezron lay with the daughter of Makir the father of Gilead (he had married her when he was sixty years old), and she bore him Segub. **22** Segub was the father of Jair, who controlled twenty-three towns in Gilead. **23** (But Geshur and Aram captured Havvoth Jair,*a* as well as Kenath with its surrounding settlements—sixty towns.) All these were descendants of Makir the father of Gilead.

24 After Hezron died in Caleb Ephrathah, Abijah the wife of Hezron bore him Ashhur the father*b* of Tekoa.

Jerahmeel Son of Hezron

25 The sons of Jerahmeel the firstborn of Hezron:
Ram his firstborn, Bunah, Oren, Ozem and*c* Ahijah. **26** Jerahmeel had another wife, whose name was Atarah; she was the mother of Onam.

27 The sons of Ram the firstborn of Jerahmeel:
Maaz, Jamin and Eker.

28 The sons of Onam:
Shammai and Jada.
The sons of Shammai:
Nadab and Abishur.

29 Abishur's wife was named Abihail, who bore him Ahban and Molid.

30 The sons of Nadab:
Seled and Appaim. Seled died without children.

31 The son of Appaim:
Ishi, who was the father of Sheshan.

Sheshan was the father of Ahlai.

32 The sons of Jada, Shammai's brother:
Jether and Jonathan. Jether died without children.

33 The sons of Jonathan:
Peleth and Zaza.
These were the descendants of Jerahmeel.

34 Sheshan had no sons—only daughters.
He had an Egyptian servant named Jarha. **35** Sheshan gave his daughter in marriage to his servant Jarha, and she bore him Attai.

36 Attai was the father of Nathan,
Nathan the father of Zabad,

37 Zabad the father of Ephlal,
Ephlal the father of Obed,

38 Obed the father of Jehu,
Jehu the father of Azariah,

39 Azariah the father of Helez,
Helez the father of Eleasah,

40 Eleasah the father of Sismai,
Sismai the father of Shallum,

41 Shallum the father of Jekamiah,
and Jekamiah the father of Elishama.

The Clans of Caleb

42 The sons of Caleb the brother of Jerahmeel:
Mesha his firstborn, who was the father of Ziph, and his son Mareshah,*d* who was the father of Hebron.

43 The sons of Hebron:
Korah, Tappuah, Rekem and Shema. **44** Shema was the father of Raham, and Raham the father of Jorkeam. Rekem was the father of Shammai. **45** The son of Shammai was Maon, and Maon was the father of Beth Zur.

46 Caleb's concubine Ephah was the mother of Haran, Moza and Gazez. Haran was the father of Gazez.

47 The sons of Jahdai:
Regem, Jotham, Geshan, Pelet, Ephah and Shaaph.

48 Caleb's concubine Maacah was the mother of Sheber and Tirhanah. **49** She also gave birth to Shaaph the father of Madmannah and to Sheva the father of Macbenah and Gibea. Caleb's daughter was

---

a23 Or *captured the settlements of Jair*   *b24 Father* may mean *civic leader* or *military leader;* also in verses 42, 45, 49–52 and possibly elsewhere.   *c25* Or *Oren and Ozem, by*   *d42* The meaning of the Hebrew for this phrase is uncertain.

Acsah. ⁵⁰These were the descendants of Caleb.

The sons of Hur the firstborn of Ephrathah:

Shobal the father of Kiriath Jearim,
⁵¹Salma the father of Bethlehem, and Hareph the father of Beth Gader.
⁵²The descendants of Shobal the father of Kiriath Jearim were:

Haroeh, half the Manahathites, ⁵³and the clans of Kiriath Jearim: the Ithrites, Puthites, Shumathites and Mishraites. From these descended the Zorathites and Eshtaolites.
⁵⁴The descendants of Salma:

Bethlehem, the Netophathites, Atroth Beth Joab, half the Manahathites, the Zorites, ⁵⁵and the clans of scribes*a* who lived at Jabez: the Tirathites, Shimeathites and Sucathites. These are the Kenites who came from Hammath, the father of the house of Recab.*b*

The Sons of David

3 These were the sons of David born to him in Hebron:

The firstborn was Amnon the son of Ahinoam of Jezreel;
the second, Daniel the son of Abigail of Carmel;
²the third, Absalom the son of Maacah daughter of Talmai king of Geshur;
the fourth, Adonijah the son of Haggith;
³the fifth, Shephatiah the son of Abital;
and the sixth, Ithream, by his wife Eglah.
⁴These six were born to David in Hebron, where he reigned seven years and six months.

David reigned in Jerusalem thirty-three years, ⁵and these were the children born to him there:

Shammua,*c* Shobab, Nathan and Solomon. These four were by Bathsheba*d* daughter of Ammiel. ⁶There were also

Ibhar, Elishua,*e* Eliphelet, ⁷Nogah, Nepheg, Japhia, ⁸Elishama, Eliada and Eliphelet—nine in all. ⁹All these were the sons of David, besides his sons by his concubines. And Tamar was their sister.

The Kings of Judah

¹⁰Solomon's son was Rehoboam,
Abijah his son,
Asa his son,
Jehoshaphat his son,
¹¹Jehoram*f* his son,
Ahaziah his son,
Joash his son,
¹²Amaziah his son,
Azariah his son,
Jotham his son,
¹³Ahaz his son,
Hezekiah his son,
Manasseh his son,
¹⁴Amon his son,
Josiah his son.
¹⁵The sons of Josiah:
Johanan the firstborn,
Jehoiakim the second son,
Zedekiah the third,
Shallum the fourth.
¹⁶The successors of Jehoiakim:
Jehoiachin*g* his son,
and Zedekiah.

The Royal Line After the Exile

¹⁷The descendants of Jehoiachin the captive:

Shealtiel his son, ¹⁸Malkiram, Pedaiah, Shenazzar, Jekamiah, Hoshama and Nedabiah.
¹⁹The sons of Pedaiah:
Zerubbabel and Shimei.
The sons of Zerubbabel:
Meshullam and Hananiah.
Shelomith was their sister.
²⁰There were also five others:
Hashubah, Ohel, Berekiah, Hasadiah and Jushab-Hesed.
²¹The descendants of Hananiah:
Pelatiah and Jeshaiah, and the sons of

---

*a*55 Or *of the Sopherites*   *b*55 Or *father of Beth Recab*   *c*5 Hebrew *Shimea*, a variant of *Shammua*   *d*5 One Hebrew manuscript and Vulgate (see also Septuagint and 2 Samuel 11:3); most Hebrew manuscripts *Bathshua*   *e*6 Two Hebrew manuscripts (see also 2 Samuel 5:15 and 1 Chron. 14:5); most Hebrew manuscripts *Elishama*   *f*11 Hebrew *Joram*, a variant of *Jehoram*   *g*16 Hebrew *Jeconiah*, a variant of *Jehoiachin*; also in verse 17

Rephaiah, of Arnan, of Obadiah and of Shecaniah.

22 The descendants of Shecaniah:

Shemaiah and his sons:

Hattush, Igal, Bariah, Neariah and Shaphat—six in all.

23 The sons of Neariah:

Elioenai, Hizkiah and Azrikam—three in all.

24 The sons of Elioenai:

Hodaviah, Eliashib, Pelaiah, Akkub, Johanan, Delaiah and Anani—seven in all.

Other Clans of Judah

4 The descendants of Judah:

Perez, Hezron, Carmi, Hur and Shobal.

2 Reaiah son of Shobal was the father of Jahath, and Jahath the father of Ahumai and Lahad. These were the clans of the Zorathites.

3 These were the sons[a] of Etam:

Jezreel, Ishma and Idbash. Their sister was named Hazzelelponi. 4 Penuel was the father of Gedor, and Ezer the father of Hushah.

These were the descendants of Hur, the firstborn of Ephrathah and father[b] of Bethlehem.

5 Ashhur the father of Tekoa had two wives, Helah and Naarah.

6 Naarah bore him Ahuzzam, Hepher, Temeni and Haahashtari. These were the descendants of Naarah.

7 The sons of Helah:

Zereth, Zohar, Ethnan, 8 and Koz, who was the father of Anub and Hazzobebah and of the clans of Aharhel son of Harum.

9 Jabez was more honorable than his brothers. His mother had named him Jabez,[c] saying, "I gave birth to him in pain." 10 Jabez cried out to the God of Israel, "Oh, that you would bless

me and enlarge my territory! Let your hand be with me, and keep me from harm so that I will be free from pain." And God granted his request.

1 Chronicles 4:10

God Blesses Faith

Jabez cried out to the God of Israel, "Oh, that you would bless me and enlarge my territory! Let your hand be with me, and keep me from harm so that I will be free from pain." And God granted his request.

11 Kelub, Shuhah's brother, was the father of Mehir, who was the father of Eshton. 12 Eshton was the father of Beth Rapha, Paseah and Tehinnah the father of Ir Nahash.[d] These were the men of Recah.

13 The sons of Kenaz:

Othniel and Seraiah.

The sons of Othniel:

Hathath and Meonothai.[e] 14 Meonothai was the father of Ophrah.

Seraiah was the father of Joab,

the father of Ge Harashim.[f] It was called this because its people were craftsmen.

15 The sons of Caleb son of Jephunneh:

Iru, Elah and Naam.

The son of Elah:

Kenaz.

16 The sons of Jehallelel:

Ziph, Ziphah, Tiria and Asarel.

17 The sons of Ezrah:

Jether, Mered, Epher and Jalon. One of Mered's wives gave birth to Miriam, Shammai and Ishbah the father of Eshtemoa. 18 (His Judean wife gave birth to Jered the father of Gedor, Heber the father of Soco, and Jekuthiel the father of Zanoah.) These were the children of Pharaoh's daughter Bithiah, whom Mered had married.

19 The sons of Hodiah's wife, the sister of Naham:

the father of Keilah the Garmite, and Eshtemoa the Maacathite.

20 The sons of Shimon:

Amnon, Rinnah, Ben-Hanan and Tilon.

---

a3 Some Septuagint manuscripts (see also Vulgate); Hebrew *father*   b4 *Father* may mean *civic leader* or *military leader*; also in verses 12, 14, 17, 18 and possibly elsewhere.   c9 *Jabez* sounds like the Hebrew for *pain*.   d12 Or *of the city of Nahash*   e13 Some Septuagint manuscripts and Vulgate; Hebrew does not have *and Meonothai*.   f14 *Ge Harashim* means *valley of craftsmen*.

The descendants of Ishi:
Zoheth and Ben-Zoheth.

²¹ The sons of Shelah son of Judah:
Er the father of Lecah, Laadah the father of Mareshah and the clans of the linen workers at Beth Ashbea, ²² Jokim, the men of Cozeba, and Joash and Saraph, who ruled in Moab and Jashubi Lehem. (These records are from ancient times.) ²³ They were the potters who lived at Netaim and Gederah; they stayed there and worked for the king.

Simeon

²⁴ The descendants of Simeon:
Nemuel, Jamin, Jarib, Zerah and Shaul;
²⁵ Shallum was Shaul's son, Mibsam his son and Mishma his son.
²⁶ The descendants of Mishma:
Hammuel his son, Zaccur his son and Shimei his son.
²⁷ Shimei had sixteen sons and six daughters, but his brothers did not have many children; so their entire clan did not become as numerous as the people of Judah. ²⁸ They lived in Beersheba, Moladah, Hazar Shual, ²⁹ Bilhah, Ezem, Tolad, ³⁰ Bethuel, Hormah, Ziklag, ³¹ Beth Marcaboth, Hazar Susim, Beth Biri and Shaaraim. These were their towns until the reign of David. ³² Their surrounding villages were Etam, Ain, Rimmon, Token and Ashan—five towns— ³³ and all the villages around these towns as far as Baalath.ᵃ These were their settlements. And they kept a genealogical record.

³⁴ Meshobab, Jamlech, Joshah son of Amaziah, ³⁵ Joel, Jehu son of Joshibiah, the son of Seraiah, the son of Asiel, ³⁶ also Elioenai, Jaakobah, Jeshohaiah, Asaiah, Adiel, Jesimiel, Benaiah, ³⁷ and Ziza son of Shiphi, the son of Allon, the son of Jedaiah, the son of Shimri, the son of Shemaiah.

³⁸ The men listed above by name were leaders of their clans. Their families increased greatly, ³⁹ and they went to the outskirts of Gedor to the east of the valley in search of pasture for their flocks. ⁴⁰ They found rich, good pasture, and the land was spacious, peaceful and quiet. Some Hamites had lived there formerly.

⁴¹ The men whose names were listed came in the days of Hezekiah king of Judah. They attacked the Hamites in their dwellings and also the Meunites who were there and completely destroyedᵇ them, as is evident to this day. Then they settled in their place, because there was pasture for their flocks. ⁴² And five hundred of these Simeonites, led by Pelatiah, Neariah, Rephaiah and Uzziel, the sons of Ishi, invaded the hill country of Seir. ⁴³ They killed the remaining Amalekites who had escaped, and they have lived there to this day.

Reuben

5 The sons of Reuben the firstborn of Israel (he was the firstborn, but when he defiled his father's marriage bed, his rights as firstborn were given to the sons of Joseph son of Israel; so he could not be listed in the genealogical record in accordance with his birthright, ² and though Judah was the strongest of his brothers and a ruler came from him, the rights of the firstborn belonged to Joseph)— ³ the sons of Reuben the firstborn of Israel:
Hanoch, Pallu, Hezron and Carmi.

⁴ The descendants of Joel:
Shemaiah his son, Gog his son,
Shimei his son, ⁵ Micah his son,
Reaiah his son, Baal his son,
⁶ and Beerah his son, whom Tiglath-Pileserᶜ king of Assyria took into exile.
Beerah was a leader of the Reubenites.
⁷ Their relatives by clans, listed according to their genealogical records:
Jeiel the chief, Zechariah, ⁸ and Bela son of Azaz, the son of Shema, the son of Joel. They settled in the area from Aroer to Nebo and Baal Meon. ⁹ To the east they occupied the land up to the edge of the desert that extends to the Euphrates River, because their livestock had increased in Gilead.
¹⁰ During Saul's reign they waged war against the Hagrites, who were defeated at their hands; they occupied the dwellings of the Hagrites throughout the entire region east of Gilead.

ᵃ33 Some Septuagint manuscripts (see also Joshua 19:8); Hebrew *Baal*   ᵇ41 The Hebrew term refers to the irrevocable giving over of things or persons to the Lᴏʀᴅ, often by totally destroying them.   ᶜ6 Hebrew *Tilgath-Pilneser*, a variant of *Tiglath-Pileser*; also in verse 26

Gad

11 The Gadites lived next to them in Bashan, as far as Salecah:

12 Joel was the chief, Shapham the second, then Janai and Shaphat, in Bashan.

13 Their relatives, by families, were:

Michael, Meshullam, Sheba, Jorai, Jacan, Zia and Eber—seven in all.

14 These were the sons of Abihail son of Huri, the son of Jaroah, the son of Gilead, the son of Michael, the son of Jeshishai, the son of Jahdo, the son of Buz.

15 Ahi son of Abdiel, the son of Guni, was head of their family.

16 The Gadites lived in Gilead, in Bashan and its outlying villages, and on all the pasturelands of Sharon as far as they extended.

17 All these were entered in the genealogical records during the reigns of Jotham king of Judah and Jeroboam king of Israel.

18 The Reubenites, the Gadites and the half-tribe of Manasseh had 44,760 men ready for military service—able-bodied men who could handle shield and sword, who could use a bow, and who were trained for battle. 19 They waged war against the Hagrites, Jetur, Naphish and Nodab. 20 They were helped in fighting them, and God handed the Hagrites and all their allies over to them, because they cried out to him during the battle. He answered their prayers, because they trusted in him. 21 They seized the livestock of the Hagrites—fifty thousand camels, two hundred fifty thousand sheep and two thousand donkeys. They also took one hundred thousand people captive, 22 and many others fell slain, because the battle was God's. And they occupied the land until the exile.

The Half-Tribe of Manasseh

23 The people of the half-tribe of Manasseh were numerous; they settled in the land from Bashan to Baal Hermon, that is, to Senir (Mount Hermon).

24 These were the heads of their families: Epher, Ishi, Eliel, Azriel, Jeremiah, Hodaviah and Jahdiel. They were brave warriors, famous men, and heads of their families. 25 But they were unfaithful to the God of their fathers and prostituted themselves to the gods of the peoples of the land, whom God had destroyed before them. 26 So the God of Israel stirred up the spirit of Pul king of Assyria (that is, Tiglath-Pileser king of Assyria), who took the Reubenites, the Gadites and the half-tribe of Manasseh into exile. He took them to Halah, Habor, Hara and the river of Gozan, where they are to this day.

Levi

6 The sons of Levi:

Gershon, Kohath and Merari.

2 The sons of Kohath:

Amram, Izhar, Hebron and Uzziel.

3 The children of Amram:

Aaron, Moses and Miriam.

The sons of Aaron:

Nadab, Abihu, Eleazar and Ithamar.

4 Eleazar was the father of Phinehas,

Phinehas the father of Abishua,

5 Abishua the father of Bukki,

Bukki the father of Uzzi,

6 Uzzi the father of Zerahiah,

Zerahiah the father of Meraioth,

7 Meraioth the father of Amariah,

Amariah the father of Ahitub,

8 Ahitub the father of Zadok,

Zadok the father of Ahimaaz,

9 Ahimaaz the father of Azariah,

Azariah the father of Johanan,

10 Johanan the father of Azariah (it was he who served as priest in the temple Solomon built in Jerusalem),

11 Azariah the father of Amariah,

Amariah the father of Ahitub,

12 Ahitub the father of Zadok,

Zadok the father of Shallum,

13 Shallum the father of Hilkiah,

Hilkiah the father of Azariah,

14 Azariah the father of Seraiah,

and Seraiah the father of Jehozadak.

15 Jehozadak was deported when the LORD sent Judah and Jerusalem into exile by the hand of Nebuchadnezzar.

16 The sons of Levi:

Gershon,[a] Kohath and Merari.

17 These are the names of the sons of Gershon:

---

a16 Hebrew Gershom, a variant of Gershon; also in verses 17, 20, 43, 62 and 71

Our Secret Weapon

Read: 1 Chronicles 5:18–22

IMAGINE RANKS OF WARRIORS stretching as far as the eye can see. Their weapons glinting in the morning sunlight, spread over the villages and pastures of the land God had given them. Nearly 45,000 strapping young men—weapon-savvy, war-hungry and expertly trained—fingering their bows and sword hilts impatiently. They had trained for this battle.

In the silence you could have heard a horse snort, a fish jump in the Jordan, a scabbard ring hollow against a shield. But as the battle got underway and the screams tore at their eardrums, you could hear something else: the cries of the warriors calling out to God for help. He was the secret weapon in the battle. And they trusted him for the victory.

Let's face it; life is more a battlefield than a playground. Every day we face enemies we can't even see. We are at war "against the powers of this dark world and against the spiritual forces of evil in the heavenly realms" (Ephesians 6:12). We fight battles within ourselves—against insecurity, anxiety, depression. We fight for spiritual territory rather than for plots of land. We fight against the fallen things in this world: materialism, greed, selfishness, addiction, violence, apathy, prejudice, injustice . . . and the list goes on. Daunting enemies, indeed.

As soldiers in God's army we are called to do battle with evil by putting on the armor of God (see Ephesians 6:10–18). Every morning, picture yourself donning each piece like a modern-day Joan of Arc: the belt of God's truth, the breastplate of righteousness, the gospel of peace. Take up your shield of faith, the helmet of salvation and the sword of the Spirit. And then, like the Israelites, employ your "secret weapon": prayer. Ask God for help, "pray[ing] in the Spirit . . . with all kinds of prayers and requests" (Ephesians 6:18). One commentator said, "Satan trembles when he sees the weakest saint upon his knees." Don't hesitate to utilize your secret weapon by praying to the Lord of hosts, and trust him to hear your prayers. He's the one who will lead you to win your battle because he has already won the war.

Go to page 493 for your next devotional reading.

1 Chronicles 5:20

They were helped in fighting them, and God handed the Hagrites and all their allies over to them, because they cried out to him during the battle. He answered their prayers, because they trusted in him.

reflection

1 Are most of your battles fought against "inward" or "outward" foes?

2 What weapons are you finding most effective against your foe?

3 How often do you utilize your "secret weapon" (prayer)?

RELATED READINGS

Psalm 24:1–10;
Philippians 4:6;
James 4:1–8;
1 Peter 3:10–16

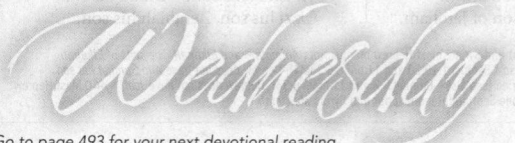

Wednesday

Libni and Shimei.

18 The sons of Kohath:

Amram, Izhar, Hebron and Uzziel.

19 The sons of Merari:

Mahli and Mushi.

These are the clans of the Levites listed according to their fathers:

20 Of Gershon:

Libni his son, Jehath his son,
Zimmah his son, 21 Joah his son,
Iddo his son, Zerah his son
and Jeatherai his son.

22 The descendants of Kohath:

Amminadab his son, Korah his son,
Assir his son, 23 Elkanah his son,
Ebiasaph his son, Assir his son,

24 Tahath his son, Uriel his son,
Uzziah his son and Shaul his son.

25 The descendants of Elkanah:

Amasai, Ahimoth,

26 Elkanah his son,a Zophai his son,
Nahath his son, 27 Eliab his son,
Jeroham his son, Elkanah his son
and Samuel his son.b

28 The sons of Samuel:

Joelc the firstborn
and Abijah the second son.

29 The descendants of Merari:

Mahli, Libni his son,
Shimei his son, Uzzah his son,

30 Shimea his son, Haggiah his son
and Asaiah his son.

The Temple Musicians

31 These are the men David put in charge of the music in the house of the LORD after the ark came to rest there. 32 They ministered with music before the tabernacle, the Tent of Meeting, until Solomon built the temple of the LORD in Jerusalem. They performed their duties according to the regulations laid down for them.

33 Here are the men who served, together with their sons:

From the Kohathites:

Heman, the musician,
the son of Joel, the son of Samuel,

34 the son of Elkanah, the son of Jeroham,

the son of Eliel, the son of Toah,

35 the son of Zuph, the son of Elkanah,
the son of Mahath, the son of Amasai,

36 the son of Elkanah, the son of Joel,
the son of Azariah, the son of Zephaniah,

37 the son of Tahath, the son of Assir,
the son of Ebiasaph, the son of Korah,

38 the son of Izhar, the son of Kohath,
the son of Levi, the son of Israel;

39 and Heman's associate Asaph, who served at his right hand:

Asaph son of Berekiah, the son of Shimea,

40 the son of Michael, the son of Baaseiah,d
the son of Malkijah, 41 the son of Ethni,
the son of Zerah, the son of Adaiah,

42 the son of Ethan, the son of Zimmah,
the son of Shimei, 43 the son of Jahath,
the son of Gershon, the son of Levi;

44 and from their associates, the Merarites, at his left hand:

Ethan son of Kishi, the son of Abdi,
the son of Malluch, 45 the son of Hashabiah,
the son of Amaziah, the son of Hilkiah,

46 the son of Amzi, the son of Bani,
the son of Shemer, 47 the son of Mahli,
the son of Mushi, the son of Merari,
the son of Levi.

48 Their fellow Levites were assigned to all the other duties of the tabernacle, the house of God. 49 But Aaron and his descendants were the ones who presented offerings on the altar of burnt offering and on the altar of incense in connection with all that was done in the Most Holy Place, making atonement for Israel, in accordance with all that Moses the servant of God had commanded.

50 These were the descendants of Aaron:

Eleazar his son, Phinehas his son,
Abishua his son, 51 Bukki his son,
Uzzi his son, Zerahiah his son,

---

a26 Some Hebrew manuscripts, Septuagint and Syriac; most Hebrew manuscripts Ahimoth 26 and Elkanah. The sons of Elkanah: b27 Some Septuagint manuscripts (see also 1 Samuel 1:19,20 and 1 Chron. 6:33,34); Hebrew does not have and Samuel his son. c28 Some Septuagint manuscripts and Syriac (see also 1 Samuel 8:2 and 1 Chron. 6:33); Hebrew does not have Joel. d40 Most Hebrew manuscripts; some Hebrew manuscripts, one Septuagint manuscript and Syriac Maaseiah

⁵²Meraioth his son, Amariah his son, Ahitub his son, ⁵³Zadok his son and Ahimaaz his son.

⁵⁴These were the locations of their settlements allotted as their territory (they were assigned to the descendants of Aaron who were from the Kohathite clan, because the first lot was for them): ⁵⁵They were given Hebron in Judah with its surrounding pasturelands. ⁵⁶But the fields and villages around the city were given to Caleb son of Jephunneh.

⁵⁷So the descendants of Aaron were given Hebron (a city of refuge), and Libnah,ᵃ Jattir, Eshtemoa, ⁵⁸Hilen, Debir, ⁵⁹Ashan, Juttahᵇ and Beth Shemesh, together with their pasturelands. ⁶⁰And from the tribe of Benjamin they were given Gibeon,ᶜ Geba, Alemeth and Anathoth, together with their pasturelands.

These towns, which were distributed among the Kohathite clans, were thirteen in all.

⁶¹The rest of Kohath's descendants were allotted ten towns from the clans of half the tribe of Manasseh.

⁶²The descendants of Gershon, clan by clan, were allotted thirteen towns from the tribes of Issachar, Asher and Naphtali, and from the part of the tribe of Manasseh that is in Bashan.

⁶³The descendants of Merari, clan by clan, were allotted twelve towns from the tribes of Reuben, Gad and Zebulun.

⁶⁴So the Israelites gave the Levites these towns and their pasturelands. ⁶⁵From the tribes of Judah, Simeon and Benjamin they allotted the previously named towns.

⁶⁶Some of the Kohathite clans were given as their territory towns from the tribe of Ephraim.

---

1 Chronicles 6:49

God Requires Payment for Sin

But Aaron and his descendants were the ones who presented offerings on the altar of burnt offering and on the altar of incense in connection with all that was done in the Most Holy Place, making atonement for Israel.

---

⁶⁷In the hill country of Ephraim they were given Shechem (a city of refuge), and Gezer,ᵈ ⁶⁸Jokmeam, Beth Horon, ⁶⁹Aijalon and Gath Rimmon, together with their pasturelands.

⁷⁰And from half the tribe of Manasseh the Israelites gave Aner and Bileam, together with their pasturelands, to the rest of the Kohathite clans.

⁷¹The Gershonites received the following:

From the clan of the half-tribe of Manasseh
    they received Golan in Bashan and also Ashtaroth, together with their pasturelands;
⁷²from the tribe of Issachar
    they received Kedesh, Daberath, ⁷³Ramoth and Anem, together with their pasturelands;
⁷⁴from the tribe of Asher
    they received Mashal, Abdon, ⁷⁵Hukok and Rehob, together with their pasturelands;
⁷⁶and from the tribe of Naphtali
    they received Kedesh in Galilee, Hammon and Kiriathaim, together with their pasturelands.

⁷⁷The Merarites (the rest of the Levites) received the following:

From the tribe of Zebulun
    they received Jokneam, Kartah,ᵉ Rimmono and Tabor, together with their pasturelands;
⁷⁸from the tribe of Reuben across the Jordan east of Jericho
    they received Bezer in the desert, Jahzah, ⁷⁹Kedemoth and Mephaath, together with their pasturelands;
⁸⁰and from the tribe of Gad
    they received Ramoth in Gilead,

ᵃ57 See Joshua 21:13; Hebrew *given the cities of refuge: Hebron, Libnah.*   ᵇ59 Syriac (see also Septuagint and Joshua 21:16); Hebrew does not have *Juttah.*   ᶜ60 See Joshua 21:17; Hebrew does not have *Gibeon.*   ᵈ67 See Joshua 21:21; Hebrew *given the cities of refuge: Shechem, Gezer.*   ᵉ77 See Septuagint and Joshua 21:34; Hebrew does not have *Jokneam, Kartah.*

Mahanaim, 81Heshbon and Jazer, together with their pasturelands.

Issachar

7 The sons of Issachar:
Tola, Puah, Jashub and Shimron—four in all.

2 The sons of Tola:
Uzzi, Rephaiah, Jeriel, Jahmai, Ibsam and Samuel—heads of their families. During the reign of David, the descendants of Tola listed as fighting men in their genealogy numbered 22,600.

3 The son of Uzzi:
Izrahiah.

The sons of Izrahiah:
Michael, Obadiah, Joel and Isshiah. All five of them were chiefs. 4According to their family genealogy, they had 36,000 men ready for battle, for they had many wives and children.

5 The relatives who were fighting men belonging to all the clans of Issachar, as listed in their genealogy, were 87,000 in all.

Benjamin

6 Three sons of Benjamin:
Bela, Beker and Jediael.

7 The sons of Bela:
Ezbon, Uzzi, Uzziel, Jerimoth and Iri, heads of families—five in all. Their genealogical record listed 22,034 fighting men.

8 The sons of Beker:
Zemirah, Joash, Eliezer, Elioenai, Omri, Jeremoth, Abijah, Anathoth and Alemeth. All these were the sons of Beker. 9Their genealogical record listed the heads of families and 20,200 fighting men.

10 The son of Jediael:
Bilhan.

The sons of Bilhan:
Jeush, Benjamin, Ehud, Kenaanah, Zethan, Tarshish and Ahishahar. 11All these sons of Jediael were heads of families. There were 17,200 fighting men ready to go out to war.

12 The Shuppites and Huppites were the descendants of Ir, and the Hushites the descendants of Aher.

Naphtali

13 The sons of Naphtali:
Jahziel, Guni, Jezer and Shillem*a*—the descendants of Bilhah.

Manasseh

14 The descendants of Manasseh:
Asriel was his descendant through his Aramean concubine. She gave birth to Makir the father of Gilead. 15Makir took a wife from among the Huppites and Shuppites. His sister's name was Maacah.

Another descendant was named Zelophehad, who had only daughters.

16Makir's wife Maacah gave birth to a son and named him Peresh. His brother was named Sheresh, and his sons were Ulam and Rakem.

17 The son of Ulam:
Bedan.

These were the sons of Gilead son of Makir, the son of Manasseh. 18His sister Hammoleketh gave birth to Ishhod, Abiezer and Mahlah.

19 The sons of Shemida were:
Ahian, Shechem, Likhi and Aniam.

Ephraim

20 The descendants of Ephraim:
Shuthelah, Bered his son,
Tahath his son, Eleadah his son,
Tahath his son, 21Zabad his son
and Shuthelah his son.

Ezer and Elead were killed by the native-born men of Gath, when they went down to seize their livestock. 22Their father Ephraim mourned for them many days, and his relatives came to comfort him. 23Then he lay with his wife again, and she became pregnant and gave birth to a son. He named him Beriah,*b* because there had been misfortune in his family. 24His daughter was Sheerah, who built Lower and Upper Beth Horon as well as Uzzen Sheerah.

25 Rephah was his son, Resheph his son,*c*

a13 Some Hebrew and Septuagint manuscripts (see also Gen. 46:24 and Num. 26:49); most Hebrew manuscripts *Shallum*   *b23 Beriah* sounds like the Hebrew for *misfortune*.   *c25* Some Septuagint manuscripts; Hebrew does not have *his son*.

Telah his son, Tahan his son,
26 Ladan his son, Ammihud his son,
Elishama his son, 27 Nun his son
and Joshua his son.

28 Their lands and settlements included Bethel and its surrounding villages, Naaran to the east, Gezer and its villages to the west, and Shechem and its villages all the way to Ayyah and its villages. 29 Along the borders of Manasseh were Beth Shan, Taanach, Megiddo and Dor, together with their villages. The descendants of Joseph son of Israel lived in these towns.

Asher

30 The sons of Asher:
Imnah, Ishvah, Ishvi and Beriah. Their sister was Serah.
31 The sons of Beriah:
Heber and Malkiel, who was the father of Birzaith.
32 Heber was the father of Japhlet, Shomer and Hotham and of their sister Shua.
33 The sons of Japhlet:
Pasach, Bimhal and Ashvath.
These were Japhlet's sons.
34 The sons of Shomer:
Ahi, Rohgah,[a] Hubbah and Aram.
35 The sons of his brother Helem:
Zophah, Imna, Shelesh and Amal.
36 The sons of Zophah:
Suah, Harnepher, Shual, Beri, Imrah, 37 Bezer, Hod, Shamma, Shilshah, Ithran[b] and Beera.
38 The sons of Jether:
Jephunneh, Pispah and Ara.
39 The sons of Ulla:
Arah, Hanniel and Rizia.

40 All these were descendants of Asher—heads of families, choice men, brave warriors and outstanding leaders. The number of men ready for battle, as listed in their genealogy, was 26,000.

The Genealogy of Saul the Benjamite

8 Benjamin was the father of Bela his firstborn,
Ashbel the second son, Aharah the third,

2 Nohah the fourth and Rapha the fifth.
3 The sons of Bela were:
Addar, Gera, Abihud,[c] 4 Abishua, Naaman, Ahoah, 5 Gera, Shephuphan and Huram.

6 These were the descendants of Ehud, who were heads of families of those living in Geba and were deported to Manahath:
7 Naaman, Ahijah, and Gera, who deported them and who was the father of Uzza and Ahihud.

8 Sons were born to Shaharaim in Moab after he had divorced his wives Hushim and Baara. 9 By his wife Hodesh he had Jobab, Zibia, Mesha, Malcam, 10 Jeuz, Sakia and Mirmah. These were his sons, heads of families. 11 By Hushim he had Abitub and Elpaal.

12 The sons of Elpaal:
Eber, Misham, Shemed (who built Ono and Lod with its surrounding villages), 13 and Beriah and Shema, who were heads of families of those living in Aijalon and who drove out the inhabitants of Gath.

14 Ahio, Shashak, Jeremoth, 15 Zebadiah, Arad, Eder, 16 Michael, Ishpah and Joha were the sons of Beriah.

17 Zebadiah, Meshullam, Hizki, Heber, 18 Ishmerai, Izliah and Jobab were the sons of Elpaal.

19 Jakim, Zicri, Zabdi, 20 Elienai, Zillethai, Eliel, 21 Adaiah, Beraiah and Shimrath were the sons of Shimei.

22 Ishpan, Eber, Eliel, 23 Abdon, Zicri, Hanan, 24 Hananiah, Elam, Anthothijah, 25 Iphdeiah and Penuel were the sons of Shashak.

26 Shamsherai, Shehariah, Athaliah, 27 Jaareshiah, Elijah and Zicri were the sons of Jeroham.

28 All these were heads of families, chiefs as listed in their genealogy, and they lived in Jerusalem.

29 Jeiel[d] the father[e] of Gibeon lived in Gibeon.
His wife's name was Maacah, 30 and his firstborn son was Abdon, followed by

---

[a]34 Or *of his brother Shomer: Rohgah*   [b]37 Possibly a variant of *Jether*   [c]3 Or *Gera the father of Ehud*   [d]29 Some Septuagint manuscripts (see also 1 Chron. 9:35); Hebrew does not have *Jeiel.*   [e]29 *Father* may mean *civic leader* or *military leader.*

Zur, Kish, Baal, Ner,[a] Nadab, 31Gedor, Ahio, Zeker 32and Mikloth, who was the father of Shimeah. They too lived near their relatives in Jerusalem.

33 Ner was the father of Kish, Kish the father of Saul, and Saul the father of Jonathan, Malki-Shua, Abinadab and Esh-Baal.[b]

34 The son of Jonathan:

Merib-Baal,[c] who was the father of Micah.

35 The sons of Micah:

Pithon, Melech, Tarea and Ahaz.

36 Ahaz was the father of Jehoaddah, Jehoaddah was the father of Alemeth, Azmaveth and Zimri, and Zimri was the father of Moza. 37Moza was the father of Binea; Raphah was his son, Eleasah his son and Azel his son.

38 Azel had six sons, and these were their names:

Azrikam, Bokeru, Ishmael, Sheariah, Obadiah and Hanan. All these were the sons of Azel.

39 The sons of his brother Eshek:

Ulam his firstborn, Jeush the second son and Eliphelet the third. 40The sons of Ulam were brave warriors who could handle the bow. They had many sons and grandsons—150 in all.

All these were the descendants of Benjamin.

9 All Israel was listed in the genealogies recorded in the book of the kings of Israel.

The People in Jerusalem

The people of Judah were taken captive to Babylon because of their unfaithfulness. 2Now the first to resettle on their own property in their own towns were some Israelites, priests, Levites and temple servants.

3 Those from Judah, from Benjamin, and from Ephraim and Manasseh who lived in Jerusalem were:

4 Uthai son of Ammihud, the son of Omri, the son of Imri, the son of Bani, a descendant of Perez son of Judah.

5 Of the Shilonites:

Asaiah the firstborn and his sons.

6 Of the Zerahites:

Jeuel.

The people from Judah numbered 690.

7 Of the Benjamites:

Sallu son of Meshullam, the son of Hodaviah, the son of Hassenuah;

8 Ibneiah son of Jeroham; Elah son of Uzzi, the son of Micri; and Meshullam son of Shephatiah, the son of Reuel, the son of Ibnijah.

9 The people from Benjamin, as listed in their genealogy, numbered 956. All these men were heads of their families.

10 Of the priests:

Jedaiah; Jehoiarib; Jakin;

11 Azariah son of Hilkiah, the son of Meshullam, the son of Zadok, the son of Meraioth, the son of Ahitub, the official in charge of the house of God;

12 Adaiah son of Jeroham, the son of Pashhur, the son of Malkijah; and Maasai son of Adiel, the son of Jahzerah, the son of Meshullam, the son of Meshillemith, the son of Immer.

13 The priests, who were heads of families, numbered 1,760. They were able men, responsible for ministering in the house of God.

14 Of the Levites:

Shemaiah son of Hasshub, the son of Azrikam, the son of Hashabiah, a Merarite; 15Bakbakkar, Heresh, Galal and Mattaniah son of Mica, the son of Zicri, the son of Asaph; 16Obadiah son of Shemaiah, the son of Galal, the son of Jeduthun; and Berekiah son of Asa, the son of Elkanah, who lived in the villages of the Netophathites.

17 The gatekeepers:

Shallum, Akkub, Talmon, Ahiman and their brothers, Shallum their chief 18being stationed at the King's Gate on the east, up to the present time. These were the gatekeepers belonging to the camp of the Levites. 19Shallum son of Kore, the son of Ebiasaph, the son of Korah, and his fellow gatekeepers from

---

[a]30 Some Septuagint manuscripts (see also 1 Chron. 9:36); Hebrew does not have *Ner.*   [b]33 Also known as *Ish-Bosheth*   [c]34 Also known as *Mephibosheth*

his family (the Korahites) were responsible for guarding the thresholds of the Tent[a] just as their fathers had been responsible for guarding the entrance to the dwelling of the LORD. [20]In earlier times Phinehas son of Eleazar was in charge of the gatekeepers, and the LORD was with him. [21]Zechariah son of Meshelemiah was the gatekeeper at the entrance to the Tent of Meeting.

[22]Altogether, those chosen to be gatekeepers at the thresholds numbered 212. They were registered by genealogy in their villages. The gatekeepers had been assigned to their positions of trust by David and Samuel the seer. [23]They and their descendants were in charge of guarding the gates of the house of the LORD—the house called the Tent. [24]The gatekeepers were on the four sides: east, west, north and south. [25]Their brothers in their villages had to come from time to time and share their duties for seven-day periods. [26]But the four principal gatekeepers, who were Levites, were entrusted with the responsibility for the rooms and treasuries in the house of God. [27]They would spend the night stationed around the house of God, because they had to guard it; and they had charge of the key for opening it each morning.

[28]Some of them were in charge of the articles used in the temple service; they counted them when they were brought in and when they were taken out. [29]Others were assigned to take care of the furnishings and all the other articles of the sanctuary, as well as the flour and wine, and the oil, incense and spices. [30]But some of the priests took care of mixing the spices. [31]A Levite named Mattithiah, the firstborn son of Shallum the Korahite, was entrusted with the responsibility for baking the offering bread. [32]Some of their Kohathite brothers were in charge of preparing for every Sabbath the bread set out on the table.

[33]Those who were musicians, heads of Levite families, stayed in the rooms of the temple and were exempt from other duties because they were responsible for the work day and night.

[34]All these were heads of Levite families, chiefs as listed in their genealogy, and they lived in Jerusalem.

The Genealogy of Saul

[35]Jeiel the father[b] of Gibeon lived in Gibeon.

His wife's name was Maacah, [36]and his firstborn son was Abdon, followed by Zur, Kish, Baal, Ner, Nadab, [37]Gedor, Ahio, Zechariah and Mikloth. [38]Mikloth was the father of Shimeam. They too lived near their relatives in Jerusalem.

[39]Ner was the father of Kish, Kish the father of Saul, and Saul the father of Jonathan, Malki-Shua, Abinadab and Esh-Baal.[c]

[40]The son of Jonathan:

Merib-Baal,[d] who was the father of Micah.

[41]The sons of Micah:

Pithon, Melech, Tahrea and Ahaz.[e]

[42]Ahaz was the father of Jadah, Jadah[f] was the father of Alemeth, Azmaveth and Zimri, and Zimri was the father of Moza. [43]Moza was the father of Binea; Rephaiah was his son, Eleasah his son and Azel his son.

[44]Azel had six sons, and these were their names:

Azrikam, Bokeru, Ishmael, Sheariah, Obadiah and Hanan. These were the sons of Azel.

Saul Takes His Life

10 Now the Philistines fought against Israel; the Israelites fled before them, and many fell slain on Mount Gilboa. [2]The Philistines pressed hard after Saul and his sons, and they killed his sons Jonathan, Abinadab and Malki-Shua. [3]The fighting grew fierce around Saul, and when the archers overtook him, they wounded him.

[4]Saul said to his armor-bearer, "Draw your sword and run me through, or these uncircumcised fellows will come and abuse me."

But his armor-bearer was terrified and would not do it; so Saul took his own sword and fell on it. [5]When the armor-bearer saw that Saul

---

[a]19 That is, the temple; also in verses 21 and 23   [b]35 *Father* may mean *civic leader* or *military leader.*   [c]39 Also known as *Ish-Bosheth*
[d]40 Also known as *Mephibosheth*   [e]41 Vulgate and Syriac (see also Septuagint and 1 Chron. 8:35); Hebrew does not have *and Ahaz.*
[f]42 Some Hebrew manuscripts and Septuagint (see also 1 Chron. 8:36); most Hebrew manuscripts *Jarah, Jarah*

was dead, he too fell on his sword and died. ⁶So Saul and his three sons died, and all his house died together.

⁷When all the Israelites in the valley saw that the army had fled and that Saul and his sons had died, they abandoned their towns and fled. And the Philistines came and occupied them.

⁸The next day, when the Philistines came to strip the dead, they found Saul and his sons fallen on Mount Gilboa. ⁹They stripped him and took his head and his armor, and sent messengers throughout the land of the Philistines to proclaim the news among their idols and their people. ¹⁰They put his armor in the temple of their gods and hung up his head in the temple of Dagon.

¹¹When all the inhabitants of Jabesh Gilead heard of everything the Philistines had done to Saul, ¹²all their valiant men went and took the bodies of Saul and his sons and brought them to Jabesh. Then they buried their bones under the great tree in Jabesh, and they fasted seven days.

¹³Saul died because he was unfaithful to the Lord; he did not keep the word of the Lord and even consulted a medium for guidance, ¹⁴and did not inquire of the Lord. So the Lord put him to death and turned the kingdom over to David son of Jesse.

David Becomes King Over Israel

11 All Israel came together to David at Hebron and said, "We are your own flesh and blood. ²In the past, even while Saul was king, you were the one who led Israel on their military campaigns. And the Lord your God said to you, 'You will shepherd my people Israel, and you will become their ruler.'"

³When all the elders of Israel had come to King David at Hebron, he made a compact with them at Hebron before the Lord, and they anointed David king over Israel, as the Lord had promised through Samuel.

David Conquers Jerusalem

⁴David and all the Israelites marched to Jerusalem (that is, Jebus). The Jebusites who lived there ⁵said to David, "You will not get in here." Nevertheless, David captured the fortress of Zion, the City of David.

⁶David had said, "Whoever leads the attack on the Jebusites will become commander-in-chief." Joab son of Zeruiah went up first, and so he received the command.

⁷David then took up residence in the fortress, and so it was called the City of David. ⁸He built up the city around it, from the supporting terraces*a* to the surrounding wall, while Joab restored the rest of the city. ⁹And David became more and more powerful, because the Lord Almighty was with him.

David's Mighty Men

¹⁰These were the chiefs of David's mighty men—they, together with all Israel, gave his kingship strong support to extend it over the whole land, as the Lord had promised— ¹¹this is the list of David's mighty men:

Jashobeam,*b* a Hacmonite, was chief of the officers*c*; he raised his spear against three hundred men, whom he killed in one encounter.

¹²Next to him was Eleazar son of Dodai the Ahohite, one of the three mighty men. ¹³He was with David at Pas Dammim when the Philistines gathered there for battle. At a place where there was a field full of barley, the troops fled from the Philistines. ¹⁴But they took their stand in the middle of the field. They defended it and struck the Philistines down, and the Lord brought about a great victory.

¹⁵Three of the thirty chiefs came down to David to the rock at the cave of Adullam, while a band of Philistines was encamped in the Valley of Rephaim. ¹⁶At that time David was in the stronghold, and the Philistine garrison was at Bethlehem. ¹⁷David longed for water and said, "Oh, that someone would get me a drink of

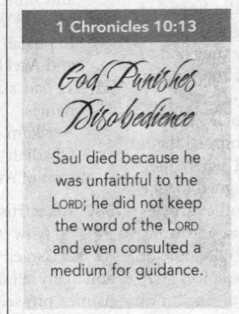

1 Chronicles 10:13

God Punishes Disobedience

Saul died because he was unfaithful to the Lord; he did not keep the word of the Lord and even consulted a medium for guidance.

---

*a*8 Or *the Millo*   *b*11 Possibly a variant of *Jashob-Baal*   *c*11 Or *Thirty*; some Septuagint manuscripts *Three* (see also 2 Samuel 23:8)

Perfect Timing

Read: 1 Chronicles 11:1–19

DO YOU EVER GET TIRED of waiting for God to keep his promises? "Lord, I know one day you're coming to bring justice, but right now there's such corruption in my city!" "God, I know Jesus is coming to judge evildoers, but some of them just broke my windshield!" "Father, you promise someday we'll all live in perfect health, but my body's failing." For those of us who long for everything to finally be all right, our heart's desire is, "Come quickly, Lord Jesus!"

The people of Israel must have felt impatience and frustration when David was anointed king by Samuel. At that time the land faced years under the rule of the unstable King Saul, from whom the Spirit of the Lord had departed because of Saul's sinful choices. The people had watched Saul disobey God by taking on the role of a priest, though he wasn't a Levite. Then he failed to kill the king of the Amalekites as he had been told. Playing politics, he fought jealously against his own warrior, David. He even had the audacity to seek advice from a medium at Endor. Surely it was time for a new king! Must they wait forever?

In time Saul died and God raised up a new king. Good-looking, strong and powerful, David was anointed king by the elders of Israel, just as Samuel had promised. Best of all, here was a king who loved God and would lead the nation back to worshiping him.

The prophets and New Testament writers have promised that the King of kings, Jesus Christ, is coming again to establish his perfect kingdom. So what is he waiting for? Haven't things gotten bad enough? Isn't there enough pain, sorrow, corruption and cruelty in the world?

When you grow weary of waiting for Christ's return, remember that God is willing to wait because he is so merciful. Peter said, "The Lord is not slow in keeping his promise, as some understand slowness. He is patient with you, not wanting anyone to perish, but everyone to come to repentance" (2 Peter 3:9). He is waiting for everyone who will to come to saving faith. When that time comes, he will keep his promise, just as he said.

Go to page 497 for your next devotional reading.

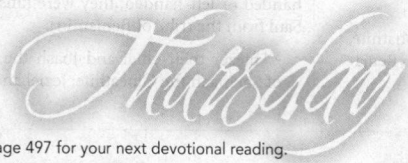

---

1 Chronicles 11:3

When all the elders of Israel had come to King David at Hebron, he made a compact with them at Hebron before the LORD, and they anointed David king over Israel, as the LORD had promised through Samuel.

reflection

1 When in your life has God patiently waited for you to respond to him?

2 Do you know someone who still needs to know Jesus? How can you pray for that person? What can you say to him or her?

3 What does 2 Peter 3:11–14 say about being ready for the day of the Lord? How can you pray in order to be ready?

RELATED READINGS

1 Samuel 16:1–13; 28:1–25; Acts 1:7–8; 1 Thessalonians 4:15–17

"He who loves the coming of the Lord is not he who affirms it is far off, nor is it he who says it is near. It is he who, whether it be far or near, awaits it with sincere faith, steadfast hope and fervent love."

Saint Augustine

493

water from the well near the gate of Bethlehem!" ¹⁸So the Three broke through the Philistine lines, drew water from the well near the gate of Bethlehem and carried it back to David. But he refused to drink it; instead, he poured it out before the LORD. ¹⁹"God forbid that I should do this!" he said. "Should I drink the blood of these men who went at the risk of their lives?" Because they risked their lives to bring it back, David would not drink it.

Such were the exploits of the three mighty men.

²⁰Abishai the brother of Joab was chief of the Three. He raised his spear against three hundred men, whom he killed, and so he became as famous as the Three. ²¹He was doubly honored above the Three and became their commander, even though he was not included among them.

²²Benaiah son of Jehoiada was a valiant fighter from Kabzeel, who performed great exploits. He struck down two of Moab's best men. He also went down into a pit on a snowy day and killed a lion. ²³And he struck down an Egyptian who was seven and a half feet[a] tall. Although the Egyptian had a spear like a weaver's rod in his hand, Benaiah went against him with a club. He snatched the spear from the Egyptian's hand and killed him with his own spear. ²⁴Such were the exploits of Benaiah son of Jehoiada; he too was as famous as the three mighty men. ²⁵He was held in greater honor than any of the Thirty, but he was not included among the Three. And David put him in charge of his bodyguard.

²⁶The mighty men were:

Asahel the brother of Joab,
Elhanan son of Dodo from Bethlehem,
²⁷Shammoth the Harorite,
Helez the Pelonite,
²⁸Ira son of Ikkesh from Tekoa,
Abiezer from Anathoth,
²⁹Sibbecai the Hushathite,
Ilai the Ahohite,
³⁰Maharai the Netophathite,
Heled son of Baanah the Netophathite,
³¹Ithai son of Ribai from Gibeah in Benjamin,

Benaiah the Pirathonite,
³²Hurai from the ravines of Gaash,
Abiel the Arbathite,
³³Azmaveth the Baharumite,
Eliahba the Shaalbonite,
³⁴the sons of Hashem the Gizonite,
Jonathan son of Shagee the Hararite,
³⁵Ahiam son of Sacar the Hararite,
Eliphal son of Ur,
³⁶Hepher the Mekerathite,
Ahijah the Pelonite,
³⁷Hezro the Carmelite,
Naarai son of Ezbai,
³⁸Joel the brother of Nathan,
Mibhar son of Hagri,
³⁹Zelek the Ammonite,
Naharai the Berothite, the armorbearer of Joab son of Zeruiah,
⁴⁰Ira the Ithrite,
Gareb the Ithrite,
⁴¹Uriah the Hittite,
Zabad son of Ahlai,
⁴²Adina son of Shiza the Reubenite, who was chief of the Reubenites, and the thirty with him,
⁴³Hanan son of Maacah,
Joshaphat the Mithnite,
⁴⁴Uzzia the Ashterathite,
Shama and Jeiel the sons of Hotham the Aroerite,
⁴⁵Jediael son of Shimri,
his brother Joha the Tizite,
⁴⁶Eliel the Mahavite,
Jeribai and Joshaviah the sons of Elnaam,
Ithmah the Moabite,
⁴⁷Eliel, Obed and Jaasiel the Mezobaite.

Warriors Join David

12 These were the men who came to David at Ziklag, while he was banished from the presence of Saul son of Kish (they were among the warriors who helped him in battle; ²they were armed with bows and were able to shoot arrows or to sling stones right-handed or left-handed; they were kinsmen of Saul from the tribe of Benjamin):

³Ahiezer their chief and Joash the sons of Shemaah the Gibeathite; Jeziel and Pe-

a23 Hebrew five cubits (about 2.3 meters)

let the sons of Azmaveth; Beracah, Jehu the Anathothite, [4]and Ishmaiah the Gibeonite, a mighty man among the Thirty, who was a leader of the Thirty; Jeremiah, Jahaziel, Johanan, Jozabad the Gederathite, [5]Eluzai, Jerimoth, Bealiah, Shemariah and Shephatiah the Haruphite; [6]Elkanah, Isshiah, Azarel, Joezer and Jashobeam the Korahites; [7]and Joelah and Zebadiah the sons of Jeroham from Gedor.

[8]Some Gadites defected to David at his stronghold in the desert. They were brave warriors, ready for battle and able to handle the shield and spear. Their faces were the faces of lions, and they were as swift as gazelles in the mountains.

[9]Ezer was the chief,
Obadiah the second in command, Eliab the third,
[10]Mishmannah the fourth, Jeremiah the fifth,
[11]Attai the sixth, Eliel the seventh,
[12]Johanan the eighth, Elzabad the ninth,
[13]Jeremiah the tenth and Macbannai the eleventh.

[14]These Gadites were army commanders; the least was a match for a hundred, and the greatest for a thousand. [15]It was they who crossed the Jordan in the first month when it was overflowing all its banks, and they put to flight everyone living in the valleys, to the east and to the west.

[16]Other Benjamites and some men from Judah also came to David in his stronghold. [17]David went out to meet them and said to them, "If you have come to me in peace, to help me, I am ready to have you unite with me. But if you have come to betray me to my enemies when my hands are free from violence, may the God of our fathers see it and judge you."

[18]Then the Spirit came upon Amasai, chief of the Thirty, and he said:

"We are yours, O David!
We are with you, O son of Jesse!
Success, success to you,
and success to those who help you,
for your God will help you."

So David received them and made them leaders of his raiding bands.

[19]Some of the men of Manasseh defected to David when he went with the Philistines to fight against Saul. (He and his men did not help the Philistines because, after consultation, their rulers sent him away. They said, "It will cost us our heads if he deserts to his master Saul.") [20]When David went to Ziklag, these were the men of Manasseh who defected to him: Adnah, Jozabad, Jediael, Michael, Jozabad, Elihu and Zillethai, leaders of units of a thousand in Manasseh. [21]They helped David against raiding bands, for all of them were brave warriors, and they were commanders in his army. [22]Day after day men came to help David, until he had a great army, like the army of God.[a]

Others Join David at Hebron

[23]These are the numbers of the men armed for battle who came to David at Hebron to turn Saul's kingdom over to him, as the LORD had said:

[24]men of Judah, carrying shield and spear—6,800 armed for battle;
[25]men of Simeon, warriors ready for battle—7,100;
[26]men of Levi—4,600, [27]including Jehoiada, leader of the family of Aaron, with 3,700 men, [28]and Zadok, a brave young warrior, with 22 officers from his family;
[29]men of Benjamin, Saul's kinsmen—3,000, most of whom had remained loyal to Saul's house until then;
[30]men of Ephraim, brave warriors, famous in their own clans—20,800;
[31]men of half the tribe of Manasseh, designated by name to come and make David king—18,000;
[32]men of Issachar, who understood the times and knew what Israel should do—200 chiefs, with all their relatives under their command;
[33]men of Zebulun, experienced soldiers prepared for battle with every type of weapon, to help David with undivided loyalty—50,000;
[34]men of Naphtali—1,000 officers, together

[a]22 Or *a great and mighty army*

495

with 37,000 men carrying shields and spears;

[35] men of Dan, ready for battle—28,600;

[36] men of Asher, experienced soldiers prepared for battle—40,000;

[37] and from east of the Jordan, men of Reuben, Gad and the half-tribe of Manasseh, armed with every type of weapon—120,000.

[38] All these were fighting men who volunteered to serve in the ranks. They came to Hebron fully determined to make David king over all Israel. All the rest of the Israelites were also of one mind to make David king. [39] The men spent three days there with David, eating and drinking, for their families had supplied provisions for them. [40] Also, their neighbors from as far away as Issachar, Zebulun and Naphtali came bringing food on donkeys, camels, mules and oxen. There were plentiful supplies of flour, fig cakes, raisin cakes, wine, oil, cattle and sheep, for there was joy in Israel.

Bringing Back the Ark

13 David conferred with each of his officers, the commanders of thousands and commanders of hundreds. [2] He then said to the whole assembly of Israel, "If it seems good to you and if it is the will of the LORD our God, let us send word far and wide to the rest of our brothers throughout the territories of Israel, and also to the priests and Levites who are with them in their towns and pasturelands, to come and join us. [3] Let us bring the ark of our God back to us, for we did not inquire of[a] it[b] during the reign of Saul." [4] The whole assembly agreed to do this, because it seemed right to all the people.

[5] So David assembled all the Israelites, from the Shihor River in Egypt to Lebo[c] Hamath, to bring the ark of God from Kiriath Jearim. [6] David and all the Israelites with him went to Baalah of Judah (Kiriath Jearim) to bring up from there the ark of God the LORD, who is enthroned between the cherubim—the ark that is *called by the Name.*

[7] They moved the ark of God from Abinadab's house on a new cart, with Uzzah and Ahio guiding it. [8] David and all the Israelites were celebrating with all their might before God, with songs and with harps, lyres, tambourines, cymbals and trumpets.

[9] When they came to the threshing floor of Kidon, Uzzah reached out his hand to steady the ark, because the oxen stumbled. [10] The LORD's anger burned against Uzzah, and he struck him down because he had put his hand on the ark. So he died there before God.

[11] Then David was angry because the LORD's wrath had broken out against Uzzah, and to this day that place is called Perez Uzzah.[d]

[12] David was afraid of God that day and asked, "How can I ever bring the ark of God to me?" [13] He did not take the ark to be with him in the City of David. Instead, he took it aside to the house of Obed-Edom the Gittite. [14] The ark of God remained with the family of Obed-Edom in his house for three months, and the LORD blessed his household and everything he had.

David's House and Family

14 Now Hiram king of Tyre sent messengers to David, along with cedar logs, stonemasons and carpenters to build a palace for him. [2] And David knew that the LORD had established him as king over Israel and that his kingdom had been highly exalted for the sake of his people Israel.

[3] In Jerusalem David took more wives and became the father of more sons and daughters. [4] These are the names of the children born to him there: Shammua, Shobab, Nathan, Solomon, [5] Ibhar, Elishua, Elpelet, [6] Nogah, Nepheg, Japhia, [7] Elishama, Beeliada[e] and Eliphelet.

David Defeats the Philistines

[8] When the Philistines heard that David had been anointed king over all Israel, they went up in full force to search for him, but David heard about it and went out to meet them. [9] Now the Philistines had come and raided the Valley of Rephaim; [10] so David inquired of God: "Shall I go and attack the Philistines? Will you hand them over to me?"

The LORD answered him, "Go, I will hand them over to you."

[11] So David and his men went up to Baal Perazim, and there he defeated them. He said, "As

---

a3 Or *we neglected*   *b3* Or *him*   *c5* Or *to the entrance to*   *d11* *Perez Uzzah* means *outbreak against Uzzah.*   *e7* A variant of *Eliada*

Thinking About God

Read: 1 Chronicles 13:1–6

DRIVING TO THE GROCERY STORE after a blizzard, a woman listened on her radio to the Christian announcer say, "Our mission is to help you think more about God today than you did yesterday."

Hmmm, the woman thought, *I don't think I even thought about God yesterday.*

She remembered waking up to snow swirling outside. She'd made hot chocolate and kept the kids entertained all day until the electricity went off. Then she gathered sleeping bags and flashlights for the night. She'd watched the thermometer in the house drop and worried about staying warm through the night. She remembered feeling relieved when the electricity came back on hours later. *But, did I pray? Did I think about God?* She couldn't remember consciously giving God a thought during that busy day.

After David assumed the throne of Israel, he recognized that the people had been remiss in thinking about God. Their leader, King Saul, had been unfaithful to God and hadn't sought God's guidance for some time. So David's first royal act was to bring the ark of the covenant to Jerusalem, back to its place at the center of worship among the people of God as a physical reminder of God's presence, sovereignty and faithfulness.

Physical reminders of God can help us take time to talk to him and to listen to him. Many of the great cathedrals of Europe were built at the center of towns, the hub of people's business and worship life. Our churches today are also physical reminders of God. When we step into our church buildings, we're reminded that we meet God there.

We are also reminded of God through his people. Take a moment to express your love and thanksgiving to God for encircling you with loving friends and family.

And if we develop eyes to see, God will give us glimpses of himself through the beauty of nature: a blooming rose bush, a glorious sunset, a soft snowfall. Take time to whisper a prayer of adoration.

You can also place reminders around your home or office to trigger thoughts of God: your favorite Bible sitting by the chair; books, music and artwork placed in prominent positions. Don't let a day go by after which you wonder, *Did I think about God today?*

1 Chronicles 13:2–3

He then said to the whole assembly of Israel, "If it seems good to you and if it is the will of the LORD our God . . . let us bring the ark of our God back to us, for we did not inquire of it during the reign of Saul."

reflection

1 Are there stretches of time when you don't think about God? How do those times affect you?

2 What brings you back to God after a time away?

3 What physical reminders do you use to prompt you to think about God? Can you think of other ways to keep God in the forefront of your mind?

RELATED READINGS

Deuteronomy 8:10–18;
1 Chronicles 10:1–14;
Acts 17:27–28

"Build yourself a cell in your heart and retire there to pray."

Catherine of Siena

Go to page 499 for your next devotional reading.

waters break out, God has broken out against my enemies by my hand." So that place was called Baal Perazim.[a] 12 The Philistines had abandoned their gods there, and David gave orders to burn them in the fire.

13 Once more the Philistines raided the valley; 14 so David inquired of God again, and God answered him, "Do not go straight up, but circle around them and attack them in front of the balsam trees. 15 As soon as you hear the sound of marching in the tops of the balsam trees, move out to battle, because that will mean God has gone out in front of you to strike the Philistine army." 16 So David did as God commanded him, and they struck down the Philistine army, all the way from Gibeon to Gezer.

17 So David's fame spread throughout every land, and the LORD made all the nations fear him.

The Ark Brought to Jerusalem

15 After David had constructed buildings for himself in the City of David, he prepared a place for the ark of God and pitched a tent for it. 2 Then David said, "No one but the Levites may carry the ark of God, because the LORD chose them to carry the ark of the LORD and to minister before him forever."

3 David assembled all Israel in Jerusalem to bring up the ark of the LORD to the place he had prepared for it. 4 He called together the descendants of Aaron and the Levites:

5 From the descendants of Kohath,
   Uriel the leader and 120 relatives;
6 from the descendants of Merari,
   Asaiah the leader and 220 relatives;
7 from the descendants of Gershon,[b]
   Joel the leader and 130 relatives;
8 from the descendants of Elizaphan,
   Shemaiah the leader and 200 relatives;
9 from the descendants of Hebron,
   Eliel the leader and 80 relatives;
10 from the descendants of Uzziel,
   Amminadab the leader and 112 relatives.

11 Then David summoned Zadok and Abiathar the priests, and Uriel, Asaiah, Joel, Shemaiah, Eliel and Amminadab the Levites. 12 He

said to them, "You are the heads of the Levitical families; you and your fellow Levites are to consecrate yourselves and bring up the ark of the LORD, the God of Israel, to the place I have prepared for it. 13 It was because you, the Levites, did not bring it up the first time that the LORD our God broke out in anger against us. We did not inquire of him about how to do it in the prescribed way." 14 So the priests and Levites consecrated themselves in order to bring up the ark of the LORD, the God of Israel. 15 And the Levites carried the ark of God with the poles on their shoulders, as Moses had commanded in accordance with the word of the LORD.

16 David told the leaders of the Levites to appoint their brothers as singers to sing joyful songs, accompanied by musical instruments: lyres, harps and cymbals.

17 So the Levites appointed Heman son of Joel; from his brothers, Asaph son of Berekiah; and from their brothers the Merarites, Ethan son of Kushaiah; 18 and with them their brothers next in rank: Zechariah,[c] Jaaziel, Shemiramoth, Jehiel, Unni, Eliab, Benaiah, Maaseiah, Mattithiah, Eliphelehu, Mikneiah, Obed-Edom and Jeiel,[d] the gatekeepers.

19 The musicians Heman, Asaph and Ethan were to sound the bronze cymbals; 20 Zechariah, Aziel, Shemiramoth, Jehiel, Unni, Eliab, Maaseiah and Benaiah were to play the lyres according to alamoth,[e] 21 and Mattithiah, Eliphelehu, Mikneiah, Obed-Edom, Jeiel and Azaziah were to play the harps, directing according to sheminith.[e] 22 Kenaniah the head Levite was in charge of the singing; that was his responsibility because he was skillful at it.

23 Berekiah and Elkanah were to be doorkeepers for the ark. 24 Shebaniah, Joshaphat, Nethanel, Amasai, Zechariah, Benaiah and Eliezer the priests were to blow trumpets before the ark of God. Obed-Edom and Jehiah were also to be doorkeepers for the ark.

25 So David and the elders of Israel and the commanders of units of a thousand went to bring up the ark of the covenant of the LORD from the house of Obed-Edom, with rejoicing. 26 Because God had helped the Levites who were carrying the ark of the covenant of the

a 11 *Baal Perazim* means *the lord who breaks out.*   *b* 7 Hebrew *Gershom,* a variant of *Gershon*   *c* 18 Three Hebrew manuscripts and most Septuagint manuscripts (see also verse 20 and 1 Chron. 16:5); most Hebrew manuscripts *Zechariah son and* or *Zechariah, Ben and*   *d* 18 Hebrew; Septuagint (see also verse 21) *Jeiel and Azaziah*   *e* 20,21 Probably a musical term

Love Is Blind

DELILAH

DEAR DIARY:

If I hear one more story about how cute Samson and Delilah are together, I'm going to be sick. Ever since the two of them fell in "love" (questionable in my mind), that's all my friends talk about. They go from trying to guess when they'll marry to figuring out when they'll have a baby.

"I think it'll be a boy for sure."

"No, a girl. My mom says beautiful women always have girls first."

"What if it's twins?"

"Boy twins! Imagine two Samson hunks!"

All their squealing—as if this is the romance of the century—I just can't take it anymore.

Although he's definitely not my type, I admit he's kind of cute. Handsome, really. And all Delilah can do is toy with him like a cat playing with a mouse before she devours it. Why is it that bad girls like her always get the good guys to fall for them? She's manipulative, bossy, and when she doesn't get her way, she whines. It's so irritating.

What does Samson see in her anyway? Well, there's the obvious. But I think he even considers her little tantrums cute. Almost endearing. And that's why he continues to tease her every night, leading her on with stories about this and that. Whenever she pouts, he just calls her over and starts whispering in her ear until soon the two of them are laughing and chatting again. Sickening.

Can't he see what she's doing to him?

This week, I overheard some people in town talking about Delilah, something about money and betrayal. It figures. She always finds a way to get all the attention around here. Well maybe this little scheme will backfire. I guess we'll just have to wait and see.

—Prayer—
God, help me to learn from this story to be honest in all my relationships, to look to you only for my fulfillment and to live my life without envy or discontent.

Some time later, he fell in love with a woman in the Valley of Sorek whose name was Delilah.

Judges 16:4

ASSIGNED READING:

Judges 16:1–31

Weekend

LORD, seven bulls and seven rams were sacrificed. **27**Now David was clothed in a robe of fine linen, as were all the Levites who were carrying the ark, and as were the singers, and Kenaniah, who was in charge of the singing of the choirs. David also wore a linen ephod. **28**So all Israel brought up the ark of the covenant of the LORD with shouts, with the sounding of rams' horns and trumpets, and of cymbals, and the playing of lyres and harps.

29As the ark of the covenant of the LORD was entering the City of David, Michal daughter of Saul watched from a window. And when she saw King David dancing and celebrating, she despised him in her heart.

16

They brought the ark of God and set it inside the tent that David had pitched for it, and they presented burnt offerings and fellowship offerings*a* before God. **2**After David had finished sacrificing the burnt offerings and fellowship offerings, he blessed the people in the name of the LORD. **3**Then he gave a loaf of bread, a cake of dates and a cake of raisins to each Israelite man and woman.

4He appointed some of the Levites to minister before the ark of the LORD, to make petition, to give thanks, and to praise the LORD, the God of Israel: **5**Asaph was the chief, Zechariah second, then Jeiel, Shemiramoth, Jehiel, Mattithiah, Eliab, Benaiah, Obed-Edom and Jeiel. They were to play the lyres and harps, Asaph was to sound the cymbals, **6**and Benaiah and Jahaziel the priests were to blow the trumpets regularly before the ark of the covenant of God.

David's Psalm of Thanks

7That day David first committed to Asaph and his associates this psalm of thanks to the LORD:

8Give thanks to the LORD,
   call on his name;
make known among the nations what he
   has done.
9Sing to him, sing praise to him;

tell of all his wonderful acts.
10Glory in his holy name;
   let the hearts of those who seek the
      LORD rejoice.
11Look to the LORD and his strength;
   seek his face always.
12Remember the wonders he has done,
   his miracles, and the judgments he
      pronounced,
13O descendants of Israel his servant,
   O sons of Jacob, his chosen ones.

14He is the LORD our God;
   his judgments are in all the earth.
15He remembers*b* his covenant forever,
   the word he commanded, for a thousand
      generations,
16the covenant he made with Abraham,
   the oath he swore to Isaac.
17He confirmed it to Jacob as a decree,
   to Israel as an everlasting covenant:
18"To you I will give the land of Canaan
   as the portion you will inherit."

19When they were but few in number,
   few indeed, and strangers in it,
20they*c* wandered from nation to nation,
   from one kingdom to another.
21He allowed no man to oppress them;
   for their sake he rebuked kings:
22"Do not touch my anointed ones;
   do my prophets no harm."

23Sing to the LORD, all the
      earth;
   proclaim his salvation
      day after day.
24Declare his glory among
      the nations,
   his marvelous deeds
      among all
      peoples.

25For great is the LORD and
      most worthy of
      praise;
   he is to be feared above
      all gods.
26For all the gods of the nations are idols,
   but the LORD made the heavens.

1 Chronicles 16:26

God Is the True God

For all the gods of the
nations are idols,
but the LORD made
the heavens.

---

*a***1** Traditionally *peace offerings*; also in verse 2   *b***15** Some Septuagint manuscripts (see also Psalm 105:8); Hebrew *Remember*   *c***18–20** One Hebrew manuscript, Septuagint and Vulgate (see also Psalm 105:12); most Hebrew manuscripts *inherit,* / **19***though you are but few in number,* / *few indeed, and strangers in it."* / **20***They*

A Glorious Outpouring

Read: 1 Chronicles 16:7–36

WE OFTEN THINK of gratitude in terms of gain: Someone gives you a ride to work. A neighbor cooks a meal when you've had surgery. Your boss notices your hard work and gives you a raise. Of course you're grateful. And if you remember your mother's upbringing, you promptly write a thank-you note.

It's more astonishing to witness people overcome with an attitude of thanksgiving in dire circumstances. Think of the parents of a terminally ill child who praise God for each day of their daughter's life. You might be baffled by a family's ability to be thankful in the midst of disaster, weeping with joy that even though their house and possessions have been destroyed by flood, fire or earthquake, their family has survived.

Even deeper than gratitude for a favor or thankfulness in the midst of misery, thanksgiving can be viewed as a testament to an enduring quality in someone we admire and respect. For instance, David celebrated God's divine attributes with a heart of pure thanksgiving. With great fanfare, the ark of the covenant had finally arrived in Jerusalem and taken its place into the tent David had prepared for it. After the offerings were made and the feast was over, David's gladness spilled over into a great song of jubilant thanksgiving.

Consider the countless reasons you have to be grateful. Has something brought great joy to your life? Consider the attributes of those you love: your husband's faithfulness, your friends' trustworthiness, your parents' goodness, your child's tender heart.

Today is the perfect time to "give thanks to the LORD, for he is good." Start by expressing thanks for some of the things David included in his prayer:

- "[God's] wonderful acts . . ." (verse 9)
- "His miracles . . ." (verse 12)
- "His salvation . . ." (verse 23)
- "His glory . . ." (verse 24)
- "His marvelous deeds among all peoples . . ." (verse 24)
- "His holiness . . ." (verse 29)

Everything about God is worthy of our praise. Let us not allow anyone or anything to rob us of the gift of a thankful heart. We can sing with David, "Let the heavens rejoice, let the earth be glad; let them say among the nations, 'The LORD reigns!'" (verse 31).

1 Chronicles 16:34

Give thanks to the LORD, for he is good; his love endures forever.

reflection

1 Do you think your friends and family would characterize you as a grateful person? Why or why not?

2 What are the characteristics of God for which you are thankful?

3 How often do you remember to thank God for his work in your life and in the world around you? Spend some time thanking God for his qualities listed in today's devotions.

RELATED READINGS

Psalms 100:1–5;
136:1–26;
Colossians 3:16–17

"Thou who hast given so much to me, give me one more thing—a grateful heart!"

George Herbert

Monday

Go to page 505 for your next devotional reading.

27 Splendor and majesty are before him;
strength and joy in his dwelling place.
28 Ascribe to the LORD, O families of nations,
ascribe to the LORD glory and strength,
29   ascribe to the LORD the glory due his
name.
Bring an offering and come before him;
worship the LORD in the splendor of his*a*
holiness.
30 Tremble before him, all the earth!
The world is firmly established; it cannot
be moved.
31 Let the heavens rejoice, let the earth be
glad;
let them say among the nations, "The
LORD reigns!"
32 Let the sea resound, and all that is in it;
let the fields be jubilant, and everything
in them!
33 Then the trees of the forest will sing,
they will sing for joy before the LORD,
for he comes to judge the earth.

34 Give thanks to the LORD, for he is good;
his love endures forever.
35 Cry out, "Save us, O God our Savior;
gather us and deliver us from the
nations,
that we may give thanks to your holy
name,
that we may glory in your praise."
36 Praise be to the LORD, the God of Israel,
from everlasting to everlasting.

Then all the people said "Amen" and "Praise
the LORD."

37 David left Asaph and his associates before
the ark of the covenant of the LORD to minister there regularly, according to each day's requirements. 38 He also left Obed-Edom and his
sixty-eight associates to minister with them.
Obed-Edom son of Jeduthun, and also Hosah,
were gatekeepers.

39 David left Zadok the priest and his fellow
priests before the tabernacle of the LORD at the
high place in Gibeon 40 to present burnt offerings to the LORD on the altar of burnt offering
regularly, morning and evening, in accordance
with everything written in the Law of the LORD,
which he had given Israel. 41 With them were

Heman and Jeduthun and the rest of those chosen and designated by name to give thanks to
the LORD, "for his love endures forever." 42 Heman and Jeduthun were responsible for the
sounding of the trumpets and cymbals and for
the playing of the other instruments for sacred
song. The sons of Jeduthun were stationed at
the gate.

43 Then all the people left, each for his own
home, and David returned home to bless his
family.

God's Promise to David

17 After David was settled in his palace,
he said to Nathan the prophet, "Here I
am, living in a palace of cedar, while the ark of
the covenant of the LORD is under a tent."

2 Nathan replied to David, "Whatever you
have in mind, do it, for God is with you."

3 That night the word of God came to Nathan, saying:

4 "Go and tell my servant David, 'This is
what the LORD says: You are not the one to
build me a house to dwell in. 5 I have not
dwelt in a house from the day I brought
Israel up out of Egypt to this day. I have
moved from one tent site to another, from
one dwelling place to another. 6 Wherever
I have moved with all the Israelites, did I
ever say to any of their leaders*b* whom I
commanded to shepherd my people, "Why
have you not built me a house of cedar?"'

7 "Now then, tell my servant David,
'This is what the LORD Almighty says: I
took you from the pasture and from following the flock, to be ruler over my people Israel. 8 I have been with you wherever
you have gone, and I have cut off all your
enemies from before you. Now I will
make your name like the names of the
greatest men of the earth. 9 And I will provide a place for my people Israel and will
plant them so that they can have a home
of their own and no longer be disturbed.
Wicked people will not oppress them anymore, as they did at the beginning 10 and
have done ever since the time I appointed
leaders over my people Israel. I will also
subdue all your enemies.

*a*29 Or LORD with the splendor of   *b*6 Traditionally judges; also in verse 10

" 'I declare to you that the LORD will build a house for you: ¹¹When your days are over and you go to be with your fathers, I will raise up your offspring to succeed you, one of your own sons, and I will establish his kingdom. ¹²He is the one who will build a house for me, and I will establish his throne forever. ¹³I will be his father, and he will be my son. I will never take my love away from him, as I took it away from your predecessor. ¹⁴I will set him over my house and my kingdom forever; his throne will be established forever.' "

¹⁵Nathan reported to David all the words of this entire revelation.

David's Prayer

¹⁶Then King David went in and sat before the LORD, and he said:

"Who am I, O LORD God, and what is my family, that you have brought me this far? ¹⁷And as if this were not enough in your sight, O God, you have spoken about the future of the house of your servant. You have looked on me as though I were the most exalted of men, O LORD God.

¹⁸"What more can David say to you for honoring your servant? For you know your servant, ¹⁹O LORD. For the sake of your servant and according to your will, you have done this great thing and made known all these great promises.

²⁰"There is no one like you, O LORD, and there is no God but you, as we have heard with our own ears. ²¹And who is like your people Israel—the one nation on earth whose God went out to redeem a people for himself, and to make a name for yourself, and to perform great and awesome wonders by driving out nations from before your people, whom you redeemed from Egypt? ²²You made your people Israel your very own

forever, and you, O LORD, have become their God.

²³"And now, LORD, let the promise you have made concerning your servant and his house be established forever. Do as you promised, ²⁴so that it will be established and that your name will be great forever. Then men will say, 'The LORD Almighty, the God over Israel, is Israel's God!' And the house of your servant David will be established before you.

²⁵"You, my God, have revealed to your servant that you will build a house for him. So your servant has found courage to pray to you. ²⁶O LORD, you are God! You have promised these good things to your servant. ²⁷Now you have been pleased to bless the house of your servant, that it may continue forever in your sight; for you, O LORD, have blessed it, and it will be blessed forever."

David's Victories

18 In the course of time, David defeated the Philistines and subdued them, and he took Gath and its surrounding villages from the control of the Philistines.

²David also defeated the Moabites, and they became subject to him and brought tribute.

³Moreover, David fought Hadadezer king of Zobah, as far as Hamath, when he went to establish his control along the Euphrates River. ⁴David captured a thousand of his chariots, seven thousand charioteers and twenty thousand foot soldiers. He hamstrung all but a hundred of the chariot horses.

⁵When the Arameans of Damascus came to help Hadadezer king of Zobah, David struck down twenty-two thousand of them. ⁶He put garrisons in the Aramean kingdom of Damascus, and the Arameans became subject to him and brought tribute. The LORD gave David victory everywhere he went.

⁷David took the gold shields carried by the officers of Hadadezer and brought them to Jerusalem. ⁸From Tebah*ᵃ*

1 Chronicles 17:20

God Is Unsurpassed

"There is no one like you, O LORD, and there is no God but you, as we have heard with our own ears."

ᵃ8 Hebrew Tibhath, *a variant of* Tebah

and Cun, towns that belonged to Hadadezer, David took a great quantity of bronze, which Solomon used to make the bronze Sea, the pillars and various bronze articles.

⁹When Tou king of Hamath heard that David had defeated the entire army of Hadadezer king of Zobah, ¹⁰he sent his son Hadoram to King David to greet him and congratulate him on his victory in battle over Hadadezer, who had been at war with Tou. Hadoram brought all kinds of articles of gold and silver and bronze.

¹¹King David dedicated these articles to the LORD, as he had done with the silver and gold he had taken from all these nations: Edom and Moab, the Ammonites and the Philistines, and Amalek.

¹²Abishai son of Zeruiah struck down eighteen thousand Edomites in the Valley of Salt. ¹³He put garrisons in Edom, and all the Edomites became subject to David. The LORD gave David victory everywhere he went.

David's Officials

¹⁴David reigned over all Israel, doing what was just and right for all his people. ¹⁵Joab son of Zeruiah was over the army; Jehoshaphat son of Ahilud was recorder; ¹⁶Zadok son of Ahitub and Ahimelech*a* son of Abiathar were priests; Shavsha was secretary; ¹⁷Benaiah son of Jehoiada was over the Kerethites and Pelethites; and David's sons were chief officials at the king's side.

The Battle Against the Ammonites

19 In the course of time, Nahash king of the Ammonites died, and his son succeeded him as king. ²David thought, "I will show kindness to Hanun son of Nahash, because his father showed kindness to me." So David sent a delegation to express his sympathy to Hanun concerning his father.

When David's men came to Hanun in the land of the Ammonites to express sympathy to him, ³the Ammonite nobles said to Hanun, "Do you think David is honoring your father by sending men to you to express sympathy? Haven't his men come to you to explore and spy out the country and overthrow it?" ⁴So Hanun seized David's men, shaved them, cut off

their garments in the middle at the buttocks, and sent them away.

⁵When someone came and told David about the men, he sent messengers to meet them, for they were greatly humiliated. The king said, "Stay at Jericho till your beards have grown, and then come back."

⁶When the Ammonites realized that they had become a stench in David's nostrils, Hanun and the Ammonites sent a thousand talents*b* of silver to hire chariots and charioteers from Aram Naharaim,*c* Aram Maacah and Zobah. ⁷They hired thirty-two thousand chariots and charioteers, as well as the king of Maacah with his troops, who came and camped near Medeba, while the Ammonites were mustered from their towns and moved out for battle.

⁸On hearing this, David sent Joab out with the entire army of fighting men. ⁹The Ammonites came out and drew up in battle formation at the entrance to their city, while the kings who had come were by themselves in the open country.

¹⁰Joab saw that there were battle lines in front of him and behind him; so he selected some of the best troops in Israel and deployed them against the Arameans. ¹¹He put the rest of the men under the command of Abishai his brother, and they were deployed against the Ammonites. ¹²Joab said, "If the Arameans are too strong for me, then you are to rescue me; but if the Ammonites are too strong for you, then I will rescue you. ¹³Be strong and let us fight bravely for our people and the cities of our God. The LORD will do what is good in his sight."

¹⁴Then Joab and the troops with him advanced to fight the Arameans, and they fled before him. ¹⁵When the Ammonites saw that the Arameans were fleeing, they too fled before his brother Abishai and went inside the city. So Joab went back to Jerusalem.

¹⁶After the Arameans saw that they had been routed by Israel, they sent messengers and had Arameans brought from beyond the River,*d* with Shophach the commander of Hadadezer's army leading them.

¹⁷When David was told of this, he gathered all Israel and crossed the Jordan; he advanced

---

*a*16 Some Hebrew manuscripts, Vulgate and Syriac (see also 2 Samuel 8:17); most Hebrew manuscripts *Abimelech*   *b*6 That is, about 37 tons (about 34 metric tons)   *c*6 That is, Northwest Mesopotamia   *d*16 That is, the Euphrates

Acts of Kindness

Read: 1 Chronicles 19:1–19

MOST OF US REMEMBER where we were on September 11, 2001, when four commercial airliners became missiles in the hands of terrorists. We were at work, home or school when we got the urgent call, "Turn on the television!" We watched replays of the plane hitting Tower One of the World Trade Center in New York City. Time stood still as we watched another plane strike Tower Two. We willed the towers to stand . . . but they crumbled before our eyes. Even the seemingly impregnable Pentagon was a target. The horrifying marks of the crash site in a lonely Pennsylvania field pay homage to the passengers who bravely fought back. The death toll of this atrocity rose to almost 3,000 people.

America was stunned at this attack on its own soil. Some were amazed that people immediately responded with kindness and compassion. *USA Today* reported, "In New York, people literally took the shirts off their backs and bandaged the injured." Furthermore, tens of thousands of people lined up to donate blood at hospitals and blood banks. Solemn candlelight vigils were held throughout the world. "Miss Manners," Judith Martin, reported a shocking return to civility. "Please, please, let's make it last," she exhorted. But shouldn't acts of kindness be our ordinary response, not an extraordinary reaction to a catastrophic event?

Nahash, the Ammonite king, had rendered some memorable service to King David. When he died, David responded by acting kindly toward Hanun, Nahash's son. However, David's kindness was misinterpreted. The men sent by David to express sympathy over Nahash's death were humiliated and accused of spying. War ensued, though it was certainly not the intended outcome of David's gesture.

Just as God unreservedly extends kindness to us, we are called to "clothe [ourselves] with compassion, kindness, humility, gentleness and patience" (Colossians 3:12). We are to reflect God's kindness to others, regardless of how they choose to respond.

Don't wait for a crisis to extend loving-kindness. Take the time to ponder who is suffering from a recent heartbreak. Maybe they could use a listening ear or a shoulder to cry on. Who feels discouraged in your circle of friends? Maybe they need to hear an encouraging word. Who might feel alone? Perhaps you could pick up the phone to tell them that you care . . . and then leave the outcome to God.

Go to page 515 for your next devotional reading.

---

1 Chronicles 19:2

David thought, "I will show kindness to Hanun son of Nahash, because his father showed kindness to me." So David sent a delegation to express his sympathy to Hanun concerning his father.

reflection

1 Who has recently shown you kindness in words or actions? How did you respond?

2 Has there ever been a time when your kindness was misinterpreted? How did that make you feel?

3 What kindness is God prompting you to show toward someone today?

RELATED READINGS

Proverbs 11:16–17;
Hosea 11:1–4;
John 15:1–5;
Galatians 5:22–26

against them and formed his battle lines opposite them. David formed his lines to meet the Arameans in battle, and they fought against him. [18]But they fled before Israel, and David killed seven thousand of their charioteers and forty thousand of their foot soldiers. He also killed Shophach the commander of their army.

[19]When the vassals of Hadadezer saw that they had been defeated by Israel, they made peace with David and became subject to him.

So the Arameans were not willing to help the Ammonites anymore.

The Capture of Rabbah

20 In the spring, at the time when kings go off to war, Joab led out the armed forces. He laid waste the land of the Ammonites and went to Rabbah and besieged it, but David remained in Jerusalem. Joab attacked Rabbah and left it in ruins. [2]David took the crown from the head of their king[a]—its weight was found to be a talent[b] of gold, and it was set with precious stones—and it was placed on David's head. He took a great quantity of plunder from the city [3]and brought out the people who were there, consigning them to labor with saws and with iron picks and axes. David did this to all the Ammonite towns. Then David and his entire army returned to Jerusalem.

War With the Philistines

[4]In the course of time, war broke out with the Philistines, at Gezer. At that time Sibbecai the Hushathite killed Sippai, one of the descendants of the Rephaites, and the Philistines were subjugated.

[5]In another battle with the Philistines, Elhanan son of Jair killed Lahmi the brother of Goliath the Gittite, who had a spear with a shaft like a weaver's rod.

[6]In still another battle, which took place at Gath, there was a huge man with six fingers on each hand and six toes on each foot—twenty-four in all. He also was descended from Rapha. [7]When he taunted Israel, Jonathan son of Shimea, David's brother, killed him.

[8]These were descendants of Rapha in Gath, and they fell at the hands of David and his men.

David Numbers the Fighting Men

21 Satan rose up against Israel and incited David to take a census of Israel. [2]So David said to Joab and the commanders of the troops, "Go and count the Israelites from Beersheba to Dan. Then report back to me so that I may know how many there are."

[3]But Joab replied, "May the LORD multiply his troops a hundred times over. My lord the king, are they not all my lord's subjects? Why does my lord want to do this? Why should he bring guilt on Israel?"

[4]The king's word, however, overruled Joab; so Joab left and went throughout Israel and then came back to Jerusalem. [5]Joab reported the number of the fighting men to David: In all Israel there were one million one hundred thousand men who could handle a sword, including four hundred and seventy thousand in Judah.

[6]But Joab did not include Levi and Benjamin in the numbering, because the king's command was repulsive to him. [7]This command was also evil in the sight of God; so he punished Israel.

[8]Then David said to God, "I have sinned greatly by doing this. Now, I beg you, take away the guilt of your servant. I have done a very foolish thing."

[9]The LORD said to Gad, David's seer, [10]"Go and tell David, 'This is what the LORD says: I am giving you three options. Choose one of them for me to carry out against you.'"

[11]So Gad went to David and said to him, "This is what the LORD says: 'Take your choice: [12]three years of famine, three months of being swept away[c] before your enemies, with their swords overtaking you, or three days of the sword of the LORD—days of plague in the land, with the angel of the LORD ravaging every part of Israel.' Now then, decide how I should answer the one who sent me."

[13]David said to Gad, "I am in deep distress. Let me fall into the hands of the LORD, for his mercy is very great; but do not let me fall into the hands of men."

[14]So the LORD sent a plague on Israel, and seventy thousand men of Israel fell dead. [15]And God sent an angel to destroy Jerusalem.

*a*2 Or *of Milcom*, that is, Molech   *b*2 That is, about 75 pounds (about 34 kilograms)   *c*12 Hebrew; Septuagint and Vulgate (see also 2 Samuel 24:13) *of fleeing*

But as the angel was doing so, the LORD saw it and was grieved because of the calamity and said to the angel who was destroying the people, "Enough! Withdraw your hand." The angel of the LORD was then standing at the threshing floor of Araunah[a] the Jebusite.

16David looked up and saw the angel of the LORD standing between heaven and earth, with a drawn sword in his hand extended over Jerusalem. Then David and the elders, clothed in sackcloth, fell facedown.

17David said to God, "Was it not I who ordered the fighting men to be counted? I am the one who has sinned and done wrong. These are but sheep. What have they done? O LORD my God, let your hand fall upon me and my family, but do not let this plague remain on your people."

18Then the angel of the LORD ordered Gad to tell David to go up and build an altar to the LORD on the threshing floor of Araunah the Jebusite. 19So David went up in obedience to the word that Gad had spoken in the name of the LORD.

20While Araunah was threshing wheat, he turned and saw the angel; his four sons who were with him hid themselves. 21Then David approached, and when Araunah looked and saw him, he left the threshing floor and bowed down before David with his face to the ground.

22David said to him, "Let me have the site of your threshing floor so I can build an altar to the LORD, that the plague on the people may be stopped. Sell it to me at the full price."

23Araunah said to David, "Take it! Let my lord the king do whatever pleases him. Look, I will give the oxen for the burnt offerings, the threshing sledges for the wood, and the wheat for the grain offering. I will give all this."

24But King David replied to Araunah, "No, I insist on paying the full price. I will not take for the LORD what is yours, or sacrifice a burnt offering that costs me nothing."

25So David paid Araunah six hundred shekels[b] of gold for the site. 26David built an altar to the LORD there and sacrificed burnt offerings and fellowship offerings.[c] He called on the LORD, and the LORD answered him with fire from heaven on the altar of burnt offering.

27Then the LORD spoke to the angel, and he put his sword back into its sheath. 28At that time, when David saw that the LORD had answered him on the threshing floor of Araunah the Jebusite, he offered sacrifices there. 29The tabernacle of the LORD, which Moses had made in the desert, and the altar of burnt offering were at that time on the high place at Gibeon. 30But David could not go before it to inquire of God, because he was afraid of the sword of the angel of the LORD.

22 Then David said, "The house of the LORD God is to be here, and also the altar of burnt offering for Israel."

Preparations for the Temple

2So David gave orders to assemble the aliens living in Israel, and from among them he appointed stonecutters to prepare dressed stone for building the house of God. 3He provided a large amount of iron to make nails for the doors of the gateways and for the fittings, and more bronze than could be weighed. 4He also provided more cedar logs than could be counted, for the Sidonians and Tyrians had brought large numbers of them to David.

5David said, "My son Solomon is young and inexperienced, and the house to be built for the LORD should be of great magnificence and fame and splendor in the sight of all the nations. Therefore I will make preparations for it." So David made extensive preparations before his death.

6Then he called for his son Solomon and charged him to build a house for the LORD, the God of Israel. 7David said to Solomon: "My son, I had it in my heart to build a house for the Name of the LORD my God. 8But this word of the LORD came to me: 'You have shed much blood and have fought many wars. You are not to build a house for my Name, because you have shed much blood on the earth in my sight. 9But you will have a son who will be a man of peace and rest, and I will give him rest from all his enemies on every side. His name will be Solomon,[d] and I will grant Israel peace and quiet during his reign. 10He is the one who

---

[a]15 Hebrew *Ornan,* a variant of *Araunah;* also in verses 18–28   [b]25 That is, about 15 pounds (about 7 kilograms)   [c]26 Traditionally peace offerings   [d]9 *Solomon* sounds like and may be derived from the Hebrew for *peace.*

will build a house for my Name. He will be my son, and I will be his father. And I will establish the throne of his kingdom over Israel forever."

¹¹"Now, my son, the LORD be with you, and may you have success and build the house of the LORD your God, as he said you would. ¹²May the LORD give you discretion and understanding when he puts you in command over Israel, so that you may keep the law of the LORD your God. ¹³Then you will have success if you are careful to observe the decrees and laws that the LORD gave Moses for Israel. Be strong and courageous. Do not be afraid or discouraged.

¹⁴"I have taken great pains to provide for the temple of the LORD a hundred thousand talents[a] of gold, a million talents[b] of silver, quantities of bronze and iron too great to be weighed, and wood and stone. And you may add to them. ¹⁵You have many workmen: stonecutters, masons and carpenters, as well as men skilled in every kind of work ¹⁶in gold and silver, bronze and iron—craftsmen beyond number. Now begin the work, and the LORD be with you."

¹⁷Then David ordered all the leaders of Israel to help his son Solomon. ¹⁸He said to them, "Is not the LORD your God with you? And has he not granted you rest on every side? For he has handed the inhabitants of the land over to me, and the land is subject to the LORD and to his people. ¹⁹Now devote your heart and soul to seeking the LORD your God. Begin to build the sanctuary of the LORD God, so that you may bring the ark of the covenant of the LORD and the sacred articles belonging to God into the temple that will be built for the Name of the LORD."

The Levites

23 When David was old and full of years, he made his son Solomon king over Israel.

²He also gathered together all the leaders of

---

1 Chronicles 22:11

God Is With Us

"Now, my son, the LORD be with you, and may you have success and build the house of the LORD your God, as he said you would."

Israel, as well as the priests and Levites. ³The Levites thirty years old or more were counted, and the total number of men was thirty-eight thousand. ⁴David said, "Of these, twenty-four thousand are to supervise the work of the temple of the LORD and six thousand are to be officials and judges. ⁵Four thousand are to be gatekeepers and four thousand are to praise the LORD with the musical instruments I have provided for that purpose."

⁶David divided the Levites into groups corresponding to the sons of Levi: Gershon, Kohath and Merari.

Gershonites

⁷Belonging to the Gershonites:
Ladan and Shimei.

⁸The sons of Ladan:
Jehiel the first, Zetham and Joel—three in all.

⁹The sons of Shimei:
Shelomoth, Haziel and Haran—three in all.

These were the heads of the families of Ladan.

¹⁰And the sons of Shimei:
Jahath, Ziza,[c] Jeush and Beriah.

These were the sons of Shimei—four in all.

¹¹Jahath was the first and Ziza the second, but Jeush and Beriah did not have many sons; so they were counted as one family with one assignment.

Kohathites

¹²The sons of Kohath:
Amram, Izhar, Hebron and Uzziel—four in all.

¹³The sons of Amram:
Aaron and Moses.

Aaron was set apart, he and his descendants forever, to consecrate the most holy things, to offer sacrifices before the LORD, to minister before him and

---

a14 That is, about 3,750 tons (about 3,450 metric tons)   *b14* That is, about 37,500 tons (about 34,500 metric tons)   *c10* One Hebrew manuscript, Septuagint and Vulgate (see also verse 11); most Hebrew manuscripts *Zina* to pronounce blessings in his name forever. [14] The sons of Moses the man of God were counted as part of the tribe of Levi.

[15] The sons of Moses:
Gershom and Eliezer.
[16] The descendants of Gershom:
Shubael was the first.
[17] The descendants of Eliezer:
Rehabiah was the first.
Eliezer had no other sons, but the sons of Rehabiah were very numerous.
[18] The sons of Izhar:
Shelomith was the first.
[19] The sons of Hebron:
Jeriah the first, Amariah the second, Jahaziel the third and Jekameam the fourth.
[20] The sons of Uzziel:
Micah the first and Isshiah the second.

Merarites
[21] The sons of Merari:
Mahli and Mushi.
The sons of Mahli:
Eleazar and Kish.
[22] Eleazar died without having sons: he had only daughters. Their cousins, the sons of Kish, married them.
[23] The sons of Mushi:
Mahli, Eder and Jerimoth—three in all.

[24] These were the descendants of Levi by their families—the heads of families as they were registered under their names and counted individually, that is, the workers twenty years old or more who served in the temple of the LORD. [25] For David had said, "Since the LORD, the God of Israel, has granted rest to his people and has come to dwell in Jerusalem forever, [26] the Levites no longer need to carry the tabernacle or any of the articles used in its service." [27] According to the last instructions of David, the Levites were counted from those twenty years old or more.

[28] The duty of the Levites was to help Aaron's descendants in the service of the temple of the LORD: to be in charge of the courtyards, the side rooms, the purification of all sacred things and the performance of other duties at the house of God. [29] They were in charge of the bread set out on the table, the flour for the grain offerings, the unleavened wafers, the baking and the mixing, and all measurements of quantity and size. [30] They were also to stand every morning to thank and praise the LORD. They were to do the same in the evening [31] and whenever burnt offerings were presented to the LORD on Sabbaths and at New Moon festivals and at appointed feasts. They were to serve before the LORD regularly in the proper number and in the way prescribed for them.

[32] And so the Levites carried out their responsibilities for the Tent of Meeting, for the Holy Place and, under their brothers the descendants of Aaron, for the service of the temple of the LORD.

The Divisions of Priests

24 These were the divisions of the sons of Aaron:

The sons of Aaron were Nadab, Abihu, Eleazar and Ithamar. [2] But Nadab and Abihu died before their father did, and they had no sons; so Eleazar and Ithamar served as the priests. [3] With the help of Zadok a descendant of Eleazar and Ahimelech a descendant of Ithamar, David separated them into divisions for their appointed order of ministering. [4] A larger number of leaders were found among Eleazar's descendants than among Ithamar's, and they were divided accordingly: sixteen heads of families from Eleazar's descendants and eight heads of families from Ithamar's descendants. [5] They divided them impartially by drawing lots, for there were officials of the sanctuary and officials of God among the descendants of both Eleazar and Ithamar.

[6] The scribe Shemaiah son of Nethanel, a Levite, recorded their names in the presence of the king and of the officials: Zadok the priest, Ahimelech son of Abiathar and the heads of families of the priests and of the Levites—one

---

1 Chronicles 23:30

God Is Worthy of Praise

They were also to stand every morning to thank and praise the LORD. They were to do the same in the evening.

---

family being taken from Eleazar and then one from Ithamar.

[7] The first lot fell to Jehoiarib,
the second to Jedaiah,
[8] the third to Harim,
the fourth to Seorim,
[9] the fifth to Malkijah,
the sixth to Mijamin,
[10] the seventh to Hakkoz,
the eighth to Abijah,
[11] the ninth to Jeshua,
the tenth to Shecaniah,
[12] the eleventh to Eliashib,
the twelfth to Jakim,
[13] the thirteenth to Huppah,
the fourteenth to Jeshebeab,
[14] the fifteenth to Bilgah,
the sixteenth to Immer,
[15] the seventeenth to Hezir,
the eighteenth to Happizzez,
[16] the nineteenth to Pethahiah,
the twentieth to Jehezkel,
[17] the twenty-first to Jakin,
the twenty-second to Gamul,
[18] the twenty-third to Delaiah
and the twenty-fourth to Maaziah.

[19] This was their appointed order of ministering when they entered the temple of the LORD, according to the regulations prescribed for them by their forefather Aaron, as the LORD, the God of Israel, had commanded him.

The Rest of the Levites

[20] As for the rest of the descendants of Levi:
from the sons of Amram: Shubael;
from the sons of Shubael: Jehdeiah.
[21] As for Rehabiah, from his sons:
Isshiah was the first.
[22] From the Izharites: Shelomoth;
from the sons of Shelomoth: Jahath.
[23] The sons of Hebron: Jeriah the first,[a]
Amariah the second, Jahaziel the third
and Jekameam the fourth.
[24] The son of Uzziel: Micah;
from the sons of Micah: Shamir.
[25] The brother of Micah: Isshiah;
from the sons of Isshiah: Zechariah.

[26] The sons of Merari: Mahli and Mushi.
The son of Jaaziah: Beno.
[27] The sons of Merari:
from Jaaziah: Beno, Shoham, Zaccur
and Ibri.
[28] From Mahli: Eleazar, who had no sons.
[29] From Kish: the son of Kish:
Jerahmeel.
[30] And the sons of Mushi: Mahli, Eder
and Jerimoth.

These were the Levites, according to their families. [31] They also cast lots, just as their brothers the descendants of Aaron did, in the presence of King David and of Zadok, Ahimelech, and the heads of families of the priests and of the Levites. The families of the oldest brother were treated the same as those of the youngest.

The Singers

25 David, together with the commanders of the army, set apart some of the sons of Asaph, Heman and Jeduthun for the ministry of prophesying, accompanied by harps, lyres and cymbals. Here is the list of the men who performed this service:

[2] From the sons of Asaph:
Zaccur, Joseph, Nethaniah and Asarelah.
The sons of Asaph were under the supervision of Asaph, who prophesied under the king's supervision.
[3] As for Jeduthun, from his sons:
Gedaliah, Zeri, Jeshaiah, Shimei,[b] Hashabiah and Mattithiah, six in all, under the supervision of their father Jeduthun, who prophesied, using the harp in thanking and praising the LORD.
[4] As for Heman, from his sons:
Bukkiah, Mattaniah, Uzziel, Shubael and Jerimoth; Hananiah, Hanani, Eliathah, Giddalti and Romamti-Ezer; Joshbekashah, Mallothi, Hothir and Mahazioth.
[5] All these were sons of Heman the king's seer. They were given him through the promises of God to exalt him.[c] God gave Heman fourteen sons and three daughters.

---

[a]23 Two Hebrew manuscripts and some Septuagint manuscripts (see also 1 Chron. 23:19); most Hebrew manuscripts *The sons of Jeriah:*
[b]3 One Hebrew manuscript and some Septuagint manuscripts (see also verse 17); most Hebrew manuscripts do not have *Shimei.*
[c]5 Hebrew *exalt the horn*

⁶All these men were under the supervision of their fathers for the music of the temple of the LORD, with cymbals, lyres and harps, for the ministry at the house of God. Asaph, Jeduthun and Heman were under the supervision of the king. ⁷Along with their relatives—all of them trained and skilled in music for the LORD—they numbered 288. ⁸Young and old alike, teacher as well as student, cast lots for their duties.

⁹The first lot, which was for Asaph, fell
   to Joseph,
   his sons and relatives,ᵃ   12ᵇ
the second to Gedaliah,
   he and his relatives and sons,   12
¹⁰the third to Zaccur,
   his sons and relatives,   12
¹¹the fourth to Izri,ᶜ
   his sons and relatives,   12
¹²the fifth to Nethaniah,
   his sons and relatives,   12
¹³the sixth to Bukkiah,
   his sons and relatives,   12
¹⁴the seventh to Jesarelah,ᵈ
   his sons and relatives,   12
¹⁵the eighth to Jeshaiah,
   his sons and relatives,   12
¹⁶the ninth to Mattaniah,
   his sons and relatives,   12
¹⁷the tenth to Shimei,
   his sons and relatives,   12
¹⁸the eleventh to Azarel,ᵉ
   his sons and relatives,   12
¹⁹the twelfth to Hashabiah,
   his sons and relatives,   12
²⁰the thirteenth to Shubael,
   his sons and relatives,   12
²¹the fourteenth to Mattithiah,
   his sons and relatives,   12
²²the fifteenth to Jerimoth,
   his sons and relatives,   12
²³the sixteenth to Hananiah,
   his sons and relatives,   12
²⁴the seventeenth to Joshbekashah,
   his sons and relatives,   12
²⁵the eighteenth to Hanani,
   his sons and relatives,   12
²⁶the nineteenth to Mallothi,
   his sons and relatives,   12
²⁷the twentieth to Eliathah,
   his sons and relatives,   12
²⁸the twenty-first to Hothir,
   his sons and relatives,   12
²⁹the twenty-second to Giddalti,
   his sons and relatives,   12
³⁰the twenty-third to Mahazioth,
   his sons and relatives,   12
³¹the twenty-fourth to Romamti-Ezer,
   his sons and relatives,   12

The Gatekeepers

26

The divisions of the gatekeepers:

From the Korahites: Meshelemiah son of Kore, one of the sons of Asaph.

²Meshelemiah had sons:
   Zechariah the firstborn,
   Jediael the second,
   Zebadiah the third,
   Jathniel the fourth,
³   Elam the fifth,
   Jehohanan the sixth
   and Eliehoenai the seventh.
⁴Obed-Edom also had sons:
   Shemaiah the firstborn,
   Jehozabad the second,
   Joah the third,
   Sacar the fourth,
   Nethanel the fifth,
⁵   Ammiel the sixth,
   Issachar the seventh
   and Peullethai the eighth.
   (For God had blessed Obed-Edom.)

⁶His son Shemaiah also had sons, who were leaders in their father's family because they were very capable men. ⁷The sons of Shemaiah: Othni, Rephael, Obed and Elzabad; his relatives Elihu and Semakiah were also able men. ⁸All these were descendants of Obed-Edom; they and their sons and their relatives were capable men with the strength to do the work—descendants of Obed-Edom, 62 in all.

⁹Meshelemiah had sons and relatives, who were able men—18 in all.

ᵃ9 See Septuagint; Hebrew does not have *his sons and relatives.*   ᵇ9 See the total in verse 7; Hebrew does not have *twelve.*
ᶜ11 A variant of *Zeri*   ᵈ14 A variant of *Asarelah*   ᵉ18 A variant of *Uzziel*

¹⁰Hosah the Merarite had sons: Shimri the first (although he was not the firstborn, his father had appointed him the first), ¹¹Hilkiah the second, Tabaliah the third and Zechariah the fourth. The sons and relatives of Hosah were 13 in all.

¹²These divisions of the gatekeepers, through their chief men, had duties for ministering in the temple of the LORD, just as their relatives had. ¹³Lots were cast for each gate, according to their families, young and old alike.

¹⁴The lot for the East Gate fell to Shelemiah.ᵃ Then lots were cast for his son Zechariah, a wise counselor, and the lot for the North Gate fell to him. ¹⁵The lot for the South Gate fell to Obed-Edom, and the lot for the storehouse fell to his sons. ¹⁶The lots for the West Gate and the Shalleketh Gate on the upper road fell to Shuppim and Hosah.

Guard was alongside of guard: ¹⁷There were six Levites a day on the east, four a day on the north, four a day on the south and two at a time at the storehouse. ¹⁸As for the court to the west, there were four at the road and two at the court itself.

¹⁹These were the divisions of the gatekeepers who were descendants of Korah and Merari.

The Treasurers and Other Officials

²⁰Their fellow Levites wereᵇ in charge of the treasuries of the house of God and the treasuries for the dedicated things.

²¹The descendants of Ladan, who were Gershonites through Ladan and who were heads of families belonging to Ladan the Gershonite, were Jehieli, ²²the sons of Jehieli, Zetham and his brother Joel. They were in charge of the treasuries of the temple of the LORD.

²³From the Amramites, the Izharites, the Hebronites and the Uzzielites:

²⁴Shubael, a descendant of Gershom son of Moses, was the officer in charge of the treasuries. ²⁵His relatives through Eliezer: Rehabiah his son, Jeshaiah his son, Joram his son, Zicri his son and Shelomith his son. ²⁶Shelomith and his relatives were in charge of all the treasuries for the things dedicated by King David, by the heads of families who were the commanders of thousands and commanders of hundreds, and by the other army commanders. ²⁷Some of the plunder taken in battle they dedicated for the repair of the temple of the LORD. ²⁸And everything dedicated by Samuel the seer and by Saul son of Kish, Abner son of Ner and Joab son of Zeruiah, and all the other dedicated things were in the care of Shelomith and his relatives.

²⁹From the Izharites: Kenaniah and his sons were assigned duties away from the temple, as officials and judges over Israel.

³⁰From the Hebronites: Hashabiah and his relatives—seventeen hundred able men—were responsible in Israel west of the Jordan for all the work of the LORD and for the king's service. ³¹As for the Hebronites, Jeriah was their chief according to the genealogical records of their families. In the fortieth year of David's reign a search was made in the records, and capable men among the Hebronites were found at Jazer in Gilead. ³²Jeriah had twenty-seven hundred relatives, who were able men and heads of families, and King David put them in charge of the Reubenites, the Gadites and the half-tribe of Manasseh for every matter pertaining to God and for the affairs of the king.

Army Divisions

27 This is the list of the Israelites—heads of families, commanders of thousands and commanders of hundreds, and their officers, who served the king in all that concerned the army divisions that were on duty month by month throughout the year. Each division consisted of 24,000 men.

²In charge of the first division, for the first month, was Jashobeam son of Zabdiel. There were 24,000 men in his division. ³He was a descendant of Perez and chief of all the army officers for the first month. ⁴In charge of the division for the second month was Dodai the Ahohite; Mikloth

---

ᵃ14 A variant of *Meshelemiah*   ᵇ20 Septuagint; Hebrew *As for the Levites, Ahijah was*

was the leader of his division. There were 24,000 men in his division.

5 The third army commander, for the third month, was Benaiah son of Jehoiada the priest. He was chief and there were 24,000 men in his division. 6 This was the Benaiah who was a mighty man among the Thirty and was over the Thirty. His son Ammizabad was in charge of his division.

7 The fourth, for the fourth month, was Asahel the brother of Joab; his son Zebadiah was his successor. There were 24,000 men in his division.

8 The fifth, for the fifth month, was the commander Shamhuth the Izrahite. There were 24,000 men in his division.

9 The sixth, for the sixth month, was Ira the son of Ikkesh the Tekoite. There were 24,000 men in his division.

10 The seventh, for the seventh month, was Helez the Pelonite, an Ephraimite. There were 24,000 men in his division.

11 The eighth, for the eighth month, was Sibbecai the Hushathite, a Zerahite. There were 24,000 men in his division.

12 The ninth, for the ninth month, was Abiezer the Anathothite, a Benjamite. There were 24,000 men in his division.

13 The tenth, for the tenth month, was Maharai the Netophathite, a Zerahite. There were 24,000 men in his division.

14 The eleventh, for the eleventh month, was Benaiah the Pirathonite, an Ephraimite. There were 24,000 men in his division.

15 The twelfth, for the twelfth month, was Heldai the Netophathite, from the family of Othniel. There were 24,000 men in his division.

Officers of the Tribes

16 The officers over the tribes of Israel:

over the Reubenites: Eliezer son of Zicri;
over the Simeonites: Shephatiah son of Maacah;
17 over Levi: Hashabiah son of Kemuel;
over Aaron: Zadok;
18 over Judah: Elihu, a brother of David;
over Issachar: Omri son of Michael;
19 over Zebulun: Ishmaiah son of Obadiah;

over Naphtali: Jerimoth son of Azriel;
20 over the Ephraimites: Hoshea son of Azaziah;
over half the tribe of Manasseh: Joel son of Pedaiah;
21 over the half-tribe of Manasseh in Gilead: Iddo son of Zechariah;
over Benjamin: Jaasiel son of Abner;
22 over Dan: Azarel son of Jeroham.

These were the officers over the tribes of Israel.

23 David did not take the number of the men twenty years old or less, because the LORD had promised to make Israel as numerous as the stars in the sky. 24 Joab son of Zeruiah began to count the men but did not finish. Wrath came on Israel on account of this numbering, and the number was not entered in the book[a] of the annals of King David.

The King's Overseers

25 Azmaveth son of Adiel was in charge of the royal storehouses.

Jonathan son of Uzziah was in charge of the storehouses in the outlying districts, in the towns, the villages and the watchtowers.

26 Ezri son of Kelub was in charge of the field workers who farmed the land.

27 Shimei the Ramathite was in charge of the vineyards.

Zabdi the Shiphmite was in charge of the produce of the vineyards for the wine vats.

28 Baal-Hanan the Gederite was in charge of the olive and sycamore-fig trees in the western foothills.

Joash was in charge of the supplies of olive oil.

29 Shitrai the Sharonite was in charge of the herds grazing in Sharon.

Shaphat son of Adlai was in charge of the herds in the valleys.

30 Obil the Ishmaelite was in charge of the camels.

Jehdeiah the Meronothite was in charge of the donkeys.

31 Jaziz the Hagrite was in charge of the flocks.

All these were the officials in charge of King David's property.

a 24 Septuagint; Hebrew number

³²Jonathan, David's uncle, was a counselor, a man of insight and a scribe. Jehiel son of Hacmoni took care of the king's sons.

³³Ahithophel was the king's counselor.

Hushai the Arkite was the king's friend. ³⁴Ahithophel was succeeded by Jehoiada son of Benaiah and by Abiathar.

Joab was the commander of the royal army.

David's Plans for the Temple

28 David summoned all the officials of Israel to assemble at Jerusalem: the officers over the tribes, the commanders of the divisions in the service of the king, the commanders of thousands and commanders of hundreds, and the officials in charge of all the property and livestock belonging to the king and his sons, together with the palace officials, the mighty men and all the brave warriors.

1 Chronicles 28:9

God Can Be Found

"The LORD searches every heart and understands every motive behind the thoughts. If you seek him, he will be found by you; but if you forsake him, he will reject you forever."

²King David rose to his feet and said: "Listen to me, my brothers and my people. I had it in my heart to build a house as a place of rest for the ark of the covenant of the LORD, for the footstool of our God, and I made plans to build it. ³But God said to me, 'You are not to build a house for my Name, because you are a warrior and have shed blood.'

⁴"Yet the LORD, the God of Israel, chose me from my whole family to be king over Israel forever. He chose Judah as leader, and from the house of Judah he chose my family, and from my father's sons he was pleased to make me king over all Israel. ⁵Of all my sons—and the LORD has given me many—he has chosen my son Solomon to sit on the throne of the kingdom of the LORD over Israel. ⁶He said to me: 'Solomon your son is the one who will build my house and my courts, for I have chosen him to be my son, and I will be his father. ⁷I will establish his kingdom forever if he is unswerving in carrying out my commands and laws, as is being done at this time.'

⁸"So now I charge you in the sight of all Israel and of the assembly of the LORD, and in the hearing of our God: Be careful to follow all the commands of the LORD your God, that you may possess this good land and pass it on as an inheritance to your descendants forever.

⁹"And you, my son Solomon, acknowledge the God of your father, and serve him with wholehearted devotion and with a willing mind, for the LORD searches every heart and understands every motive behind the thoughts. If you seek him, he will be found by you; but if you forsake him, he will reject you forever. ¹⁰Consider now, for the LORD has chosen you to build a temple as a sanctuary. Be strong and do the work."

¹¹Then David gave his son Solomon the plans for the portico of the temple, its buildings, its storerooms, its upper parts, its inner rooms and the place of atonement. ¹²He gave him the plans of all that the Spirit had put in his mind for the courts of the temple of the LORD and all the surrounding rooms, for the treasuries of the temple of God and for the treasuries for the dedicated things. ¹³He gave him instructions for the divisions of the priests and Levites, and for all the work of serving in the temple of the LORD, as well as for all the articles to be used in its service. ¹⁴He designated the weight of gold for all the gold articles to be used in various kinds of service, and the weight of silver for all the silver articles to be used in various kinds of service: ¹⁵the weight of gold for the gold lampstands and their lamps, with the weight for each lampstand and its lamps; and the weight of silver for each silver lampstand and its lamps, according to the use of each lampstand; ¹⁶the weight of gold for each table for consecrated bread; the weight of silver for the silver tables; ¹⁷the weight of pure gold for the forks, sprinkling bowls and pitchers; the weight of gold for each gold dish; the weight of silver for each silver dish; ¹⁸and the weight of the refined gold for the altar of incense. He also gave him the plan for the chariot, that is, the cherubim of gold

Big Plans

Read: 1 Chronicles 28:1–21

GOD HAD BIG PLANS for Solomon. He wanted him to build the temple. Solomon's dad, King David, had completed the plans and handed the task over to his son. Some parents might have said, "Be careful to follow the blueprints." Others might have said, "Be wise about the budget." But David commanded, "Be strong and courageous, and do the work." At least 30 times in Scripture God's people are told, "Be strong." Why? Because human beings are so easily discouraged. When we encounter a big task, we tend to lose courage, lose heart and sometimes even lose faith.

You might be thinking, *David had to fight giants. What kind of courage did Solomon need to build a temple?* But imagine the emotional pressure of trying to create a home for the Creator of the universe. Who wouldn't need courage to build a home beautiful enough for God? And take a moment to imagine the spiritual opposition Solomon faced. Those who don't believe in God or who don't understand the importance of God's work will always oppose it. Surely there were naysayers who objected to the cost of the materials. No doubt they grumbled about Solomon's focus on the temple at the expense of their agendas for the nation. It takes a brave leader to follow God's commands rather than collapse under the weight of criticism.

God has plans for you too. He has transformed your heart into a temple for his Holy Spirit. It takes courage to be a godly woman. There will be people who oppose God's work in your life. There will be naysayers who may try to convince you that the cost of serving God is too high or that the time and attention you pay to his Word is too great. There may be those who say you can cut corners, that you can hedge on God's intentions for the way you live. Don't believe it. The same God who helped David fight giants is the same God who enabled Solomon to build the most magnificent temple the people had ever seen. That God is *your* God, and he inhabits your heart. Therefore, "Be strong and courageous, and do the work." God was faithful to stay with Solomon and complete the work of the temple. He'll be faithful to complete the good work he began in you too.

1 Chronicles 28:20

David also said to Solomon his son, "Be strong and courageous, and do the work. Do not be afraid or discouraged, for the LORD God, my God, is with you. He will not fail you or forsake you until all the work for the service of the temple of the LORD is finished."

reflection

1 What type of construction is God doing in your "temple" right now?

2 How does the command to "be strong and courageous" encourage you?

3 Are there any naysayers in your life? Pray for the wisdom and courage to follow God's leading rather than be discouraged by their criticism.

RELATED READINGS

Joshua 1:6–9;
1 Kings 5:1–6;
Philippians 1:6

"Courage is fear that has said its prayers."

Dorothy Bernard

Wednesday

Go to page 520 for your next devotional reading.

that spread their wings and shelter the ark of the covenant of the LORD.

¹⁹"All this," David said, "I have in writing from the hand of the LORD upon me, and he gave me understanding in all the details of the plan."

²⁰David also said to Solomon his son, "Be strong and courageous, and do the work. Do not be afraid or discouraged, for the LORD God, my God, is with you. He will not fail you or forsake you until all the work for the service of the temple of the LORD is finished. ²¹The divisions of the priests and Levites are ready for all the work on the temple of God, and every willing man skilled in any craft will help you in all the work. The officials and all the people will obey your every command."

Gifts for Building the Temple

29 Then King David said to the whole assembly: "My son Solomon, the one whom God has chosen, is young and inexperienced. The task is great, because this palatial structure is not for man but for the LORD God. ²With all my resources I have provided for the temple of my God—gold for the gold work, silver for the silver, bronze for the bronze, iron for the iron and wood for the wood, as well as onyx for the settings, turquoise,ᵃ stones of various colors, and all kinds of fine stone and marble—all of these in large quantities. ³Besides, in my devotion to the temple of my God I now give my personal treasures of gold and silver for the temple of my God, over and above everything I have provided for this holy temple: ⁴three thousand talentsᵇ of gold (gold of Ophir) and seven thousand talentsᶜ of refined silver, for the overlaying of the walls of the buildings, ⁵for the gold work and the silver work, and for all the work to be done by the craftsmen. Now, who is willing to consecrate himself today to the LORD?"

⁶Then the leaders of families, the officers of the tribes of Israel, the commanders of thousands and commanders of hundreds, and the officials in charge of the king's work gave willingly. ⁷They gave toward the work on the temple of God five thousand talentsᵈ and ten thousand daricsᵉ of gold, ten thousand talentsᶠ of silver, eighteen thousand talentsᵍ of bronze and a hundred thousand talentsʰ of iron. ⁸Any who had precious stones gave them to the treasury of the temple of the LORD in the custody of Jehiel the Gershonite. ⁹The people rejoiced at the willing response of their leaders, for they had given freely and wholeheartedly to the LORD. David the king also rejoiced greatly.

David's Prayer

¹⁰David praised the LORD in the presence of the whole assembly, saying,

"Praise be to you, O LORD,
   God of our father Israel,
   from everlasting to everlasting.
¹¹ Yours, O LORD, is the greatness and the power
   and the glory and the majesty and the splendor,
      for everything in heaven
         and earth is yours.
      Yours, O LORD, is the kingdom;
         you are exalted as head
            over all.
¹² Wealth and honor come
         from you;
      you are the ruler of all
         things.
      In your hands are strength
         and power
      to exalt and give strength
         to all.
¹³ Now, our God, we give you
         thanks,
      and praise your glorious
         name.

1 Chronicles 29:12

God Gives Strength and Honor

"Wealth and honor come from you;
you are the ruler of all things.
In your hands are strength and power
to exalt and give strength to all."

¹⁴"But who am I, and who are my people, that we should be able to give as generously as

---

ᵃ2 The meaning of the Hebrew for this word is uncertain.   ᵇ4 That is, about 110 tons (about 100 metric tons)   ᶜ4 That is, about 260 tons (about 240 metric tons)   ᵈ7 That is, about 190 tons (about 170 metric tons)   ᵉ7 That is, about 185 pounds (about 84 kilograms)   ᶠ7 That is, about 375 tons (about 345 metric tons)   ᵍ7 That is, about 675 tons (about 610 metric tons)   ʰ7 That is, about 3,750 tons (about 3,450 metric tons) this? Everything comes from you, and we have given you only what comes from your hand. [15]We are aliens and strangers in your sight, as were all our forefathers. Our days on earth are like a shadow, without hope. [16]O LORD our God, as for all this abundance that we have provided for building you a temple for your Holy Name, it comes from your hand, and all of it belongs to you. [17]I know, my God, that you test the heart and are pleased with integrity. All these things have I given willingly and with honest intent. And now I have seen with joy how willingly your people who are here have given to you. [18]O LORD, God of our fathers Abraham, Isaac and Israel, keep this desire in the hearts of your people forever, and keep their hearts loyal to you. [19]And give my son Solomon the wholehearted devotion to keep your commands, requirements and decrees and to do everything to build the palatial structure for which I have provided."

[20]Then David said to the whole assembly, "Praise the LORD your God." So they all praised the LORD, the God of their fathers; they bowed low and fell prostrate before the LORD and the king.

Solomon Acknowledged as King

[21]The next day they made sacrifices to the LORD and presented burnt offerings to him: a thousand bulls, a thousand rams and a thousand male lambs, together with their drink offerings, and other sacrifices in abundance for all Israel. [22]They ate and drank with great joy in the presence of the LORD that day.

Then they acknowledged Solomon son of David as king a second time, anointing him before the LORD to be ruler and Zadok to be priest. [23]So Solomon sat on the throne of the LORD as king in place of his father David. He prospered and all Israel obeyed him. [24]All the officers and mighty men, as well as all of King David's sons, pledged their submission to King Solomon.

[25]The LORD highly exalted Solomon in the sight of all Israel and bestowed on him royal splendor such as no king over Israel ever had before.

The Death of David

[26]David son of Jesse was king over all Israel. [27]He ruled over Israel forty years—seven in Hebron and thirty-three in Jerusalem. [28]He died at a good old age, having enjoyed long life, wealth and honor. His son Solomon succeeded him as king.

[29]As for the events of King David's reign, from beginning to end, they are written in the records of Samuel the seer, the records of Nathan the prophet and the records of Gad the seer, [30]together with the details of his reign and power, and the circumstances that surrounded him and Israel and the kingdoms of all the other lands.

2 Chronicles

Author:
Unknown,
but possibly Ezra.

Audience:
All Israel.

Date:
About 430 B.C.

Setting:
The book covers the time
from Solomon's reign
(970 B.C.) to the Babylonian
exile (586 B.C.), paralleling many of the events of
1 and 2 Kings.

Verse to Remember:
"If my people, who are
called by my name, will
humble themselves and
pray and seek my face
and turn from their wicked
ways, then will I hear from
heaven and will forgive
their sin and will heal
their land." (7:14)

David's son Solomon is firmly established as king, and his rule starts out strong. There is one thing he desires from God more than anything else: *wisdom.* Solomon receives that gift, but by the end of his life he is often turning his back on it.

As the book goes through the roll call of various kings of Judah, good kings alternate with bad until the *Law of God is found* when Josiah becomes king—implying that at some point God's Law had actually been lost!

As illustrated by Solomon and a few other kings, it is possible to start life dedicated to God and end it distracted by false gods and wrong priorities. Even the kings of *God's own people were not immune* to the lure of self-centered desires and false gods.

Solomon Asks for Wisdom

1 Solomon son of David established him-self firmly over his kingdom, for the LORD his God was with him and made him exceedingly great.

2 Then Solomon spoke to all Israel—to the commanders of thousands and commanders of hundreds, to the judges and to all the leaders in Israel, the heads of families— 3 and Solomon and the whole assembly went to the high place at Gibeon, for God's Tent of Meeting was there, which Moses the LORD's servant had made in the desert. 4 Now David had brought up the ark of God from Kiriath Jearim to the place he had

prepared for it, because he had pitched a tent for it in Jerusalem. ⁵But the bronze altar that Bezalel son of Uri, the son of Hur, had made was in Gibeon in front of the tabernacle of the LORD; so Solomon and the assembly inquired of him there. ⁶Solomon went up to the bronze altar before the LORD in the Tent of Meeting and offered a thousand burnt offerings on it.

⁷That night God appeared to Solomon and said to him, "Ask for whatever you want me to give you."

⁸Solomon answered God, "You have shown great kindness to David my father and have made me king in his place. ⁹Now, LORD God, let your promise to my father David be confirmed, for you have made me king over a people who are as numerous as the dust of the earth. ¹⁰Give me wisdom and knowledge, that I may lead this people, for who is able to govern this great people of yours?"

¹¹God said to Solomon, "Since this is your heart's desire and you have not asked for wealth, riches or honor, nor for the death of your enemies, and since you have not asked for a long life but for wisdom and knowledge to govern my people over whom I have made you king, ¹²therefore wisdom and knowledge will be given you. And I will also give you wealth, riches and honor, such as no king who was before you ever had and none after you will have."

¹³Then Solomon went to Jerusalem from the high place at Gibeon, from before the Tent of Meeting. And he reigned over Israel.

¹⁴Solomon accumulated chariots and horses; he had fourteen hundred chariots and twelve thousand horses,ᵃ which he kept in the chariot cities and also with him in Jerusalem. ¹⁵The king made silver and gold as common in Jerusalem as stones, and cedar as plentiful as sycamore-fig trees in the foothills. ¹⁶Solomon's horses were imported from Egyptᵇ and from Kueᶜ—the royal merchants purchased them from Kue. ¹⁷They imported a chariot from Egypt for six hundred shekelsᵈ of silver, and a horse for a hundred and fifty.ᵉ They also exported them to all the kings of the Hittites and of the Arameans.

Preparations for Building the Temple

2 Solomon gave orders to build a temple for the Name of the LORD and a royal palace for himself. ²He conscripted seventy thousand men as carriers and eighty thousand as stonecutters in the hills and thirty-six hundred as foremen over them.

³Solomon sent this message to Hiramᶠ king of Tyre:

"Send me cedar logs as you did for my father David when you sent him cedar to build a palace to live in. ⁴Now I am about to build a temple for the Name of the LORD my God and to dedicate it to him for burning fragrant incense before him, for setting out the consecrated bread regularly, and for making burnt offerings every morning and evening and on Sabbaths and New Moons and at the appointed feasts of the LORD our God. This is a lasting ordinance for Israel.

⁵"The temple I am going to build will be great, because our God is greater than all other gods. ⁶But who is able to build a temple for him, since the heavens, even the highest heavens, cannot contain him? Who then am I to build a temple for him, except as a place to burn sacrifices before him?

⁷"Send me, therefore, a man skilled to work in gold and silver, bronze and iron, and in purple, crimson and blue yarn, and experienced in the art of engraving, to work in Judah and Jerusalem with my skilled craftsmen, whom my father David provided.

2 Chronicles 2:6

God Is Unfathomable

"But who is able to build a temple for him, since the heavens, even the highest heavens, cannot contain him? Who then am I to build a temple for him, except as a place to burn sacrifices before him?"

ᵃ14 Or *charioteers*   ᵇ16 Or possibly *Muzur*, a region in Cilicia; also in verse 17   ᶜ16 Probably Cilicia   ᵈ17 That is, about 15 pounds (about 7 kilograms)   ᵉ17 That is, about 3 3/4 pounds (about 1.7 kilograms)   ᶠ3 Hebrew *Huram*, a variant of *Hiram*; also in verses 11 and 12

Something Beautiful for God

2 Chronicles 2:1

Solomon gave orders to build a temple for the Name of the LORD and a royal palace for himself.

reflection

1 What problems could you foresee in constructing a building for God? What satisfactions?

2 How much of your time and possessions do you dedicate to God? Is it a fair percentage?

3 What gifts or resources has God blessed you with? How can you use something of yourself to give back to God?

RELATED READINGS

Mark 14:3–9;
Acts 7:44–50

"(Work) is, or should be, the full expression of the worker's faculties, the thing in which he finds spiritual, mental and bodily satisfaction, and the medium in which he offers himself to God."

Dorothy Lee Sayers

Read: 2 Chronicles 2:1–6

IT'S NOT WRONG to want something for yourself—as long as you don't cling too tightly to it. When it comes to sharing, the fair split goes, "One for you, one for me."

Solomon had plenty of possessions, and he was generous and played fair. A temple for God, a palace for himself. Do you know someone who's done the same? They have the money to build a nice house for themselves, and they also fund a church project or a center for the homeless. We can be encouraged by their example and by Solomon's example: He knew that the most worthy God of the universe deserves the best workmanship, the finest materials and the choicest offerings.

What a daring project: building a house for Almighty God! Solomon understood the irony—that he, a mortal man, would do such a thing. He insisted that nothing be slipshod. He endeavored for seven years to produce the most magnificent temple possible, using gold, silver, precious stones, marble and cedar—most of it collected for years by his father, David, and the rest of it donated by the people of Israel. Even so, would it pass muster for Yahweh's majesty? Would it cause visitors and worshipers to think great and high thoughts of the God of Israel? Would it reflect God's beauty and grandeur?

God doesn't need our things. But he ordains our work and endows us with creativity and talent. He designed us to be busy about the business of doing things for him, of making all kinds of things that reflect his regenerating grace and that glorify him.

In what beautiful enterprise might God be directing you to be involved? It could be people or projects, aptitudes or art. You may have the ability to create something that reveals and reflects some of his greatness. If so, ask him to provide the resources. Find the helpers and materials needed to accomplish the goal. Go ahead and enjoy the process and the fruit of your labor, like Solomon did. But give fairly and generously to the author of your gifts and talents. Do a God-sized work for him.

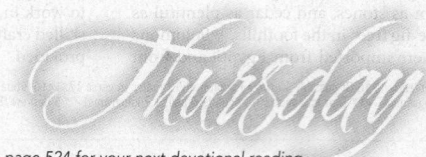

Thursday

Go to page 524 for your next devotional reading.

[8]"Send me also cedar, pine and algum[a] logs from Lebanon, for I know that your men are skilled in cutting timber there. My men will work with yours [9]to provide me with plenty of lumber, because the temple I build must be large and magnificent. [10]I will give your servants, the woodsmen who cut the timber, twenty thousand cors[b] of ground wheat, twenty thousand cors of barley, twenty thousand baths[c] of wine and twenty thousand baths of olive oil."

[11]Hiram king of Tyre replied by letter to Solomon:

"Because the LORD loves his people, he has made you their king."

[12]And Hiram added:

"Praise be to the LORD, the God of Israel, who made heaven and earth! He has given King David a wise son, endowed with intelligence and discernment, who will build a temple for the LORD and a palace for himself.

[13]"I am sending you Huram-Abi, a man of great skill, [14]whose mother was from Dan and whose father was from Tyre. He is trained to work in gold and silver, bronze and iron, stone and wood, and with purple and blue and crimson yarn and fine linen. He is experienced in all kinds of engraving and can execute any design given to him. He will work with your craftsmen and with those of my lord, David your father.

[15]"Now let my lord send his servants the wheat and barley and the olive oil and wine he promised, [16]and we will cut all the logs from Lebanon that you need and will float them in rafts by sea down to Joppa. You can then take them up to Jerusalem."

[17]Solomon took a census of all the aliens who were in Israel, after the census his father David had taken; and they were found to be 153,600. [18]He assigned 70,000 of them to be carriers and 80,000 to be stonecutters in the hills, with 3,600 foremen over them to keep the people working.

Solomon Builds the Temple

3 Then Solomon began to build the temple of the LORD in Jerusalem on Mount Moriah, where the LORD had appeared to his father David. It was on the threshing floor of Araunah[d] the Jebusite, the place provided by David. [2]He began building on the second day of the second month in the fourth year of his reign.

[3]The foundation Solomon laid for building the temple of God was sixty cubits long and twenty cubits wide[e] (using the cubit of the old standard). [4]The portico at the front of the temple was twenty cubits[f] long across the width of the building and twenty cubits[g] high.

He overlaid the inside with pure gold. [5]He paneled the main hall with pine and covered it with fine gold and decorated it with palm tree and chain designs. [6]He adorned the temple with precious stones. And the gold he used was gold of Parvaim. [7]He overlaid the ceiling beams, doorframes, walls and doors of the temple with gold, and he carved cherubim on the walls.

[8]He built the Most Holy Place, its length corresponding to the width of the temple—twenty cubits long and twenty cubits wide. He overlaid the inside with six hundred talents[h] of fine gold. [9]The gold nails weighed fifty shekels.[i] He also overlaid the upper parts with gold.

[10]In the Most Holy Place he made a pair of sculptured cherubim and overlaid them with gold. [11]The total wingspan of the cherubim was twenty cubits. One wing of the first cherub was five cubits[j] long and touched the temple wall, while its other wing, also five cubits long, touched the wing of the other cherub. [12]Similarly one wing of the second cherub was five cubits long and touched the other temple wall, and its other wing, also five cubits long, touched the wing of the first cherub. [13]The wings of these cherubim extended twenty cubits. They stood on their feet, facing the main hall.[k]

---

[a]8 Probably a variant of *almug*; possibly juniper   [b]10 That is, probably about 125,000 bushels (about 4,400 kiloliters)   [c]10 That is, probably about 115,000 gallons (about 440 kiloliters)   [d]1 Hebrew *Ornan*, a variant of *Araunah*   [e]3 That is, about 90 feet (about 27 meters) long and 30 feet (about 9 meters) wide   [f]4 That is, about 30 feet (about 9 meters); also in verses 8, 11 and 13   [g]4 Some Septuagint and Syriac manuscripts; Hebrew *and a hundred and twenty*   [h]8 That is, about 23 tons (about 21 metric tons)   [i]9 That is, about 1 1/4 pounds (about 0.6 kilogram)   [j]11 That is, about 7 1/2 feet (about 2.3 meters); also in verse 15   [k]13 Or *facing inward*

[14]He made the curtain of blue, purple and crimson yarn and fine linen, with cherubim worked into it.

[15]In the front of the temple he made two pillars, which together were thirty-five cubits[a] long, each with a capital on top measuring five cubits. [16]He made interwoven chains[b] and put them on top of the pillars. He also made a hundred pomegranates and attached them to the chains. [17]He erected the pillars in the front of the temple, one to the south and one to the north. The one to the south he named Jakin[c] and the one to the north Boaz.[d]

The Temple's Furnishings

4 He made a bronze altar twenty cubits long, twenty cubits wide and ten cubits high.[e] [2]He made the Sea of cast metal, circular in shape, measuring ten cubits from rim to rim and five cubits[f] high. It took a line of thirty cubits[g] to measure around it. [3]Below the rim, figures of bulls encircled it—ten to a cubit.[h] The bulls were cast in two rows in one piece with the Sea.

[4]The Sea stood on twelve bulls, three facing north, three facing west, three facing south and three facing east. The Sea rested on top of them, and their hindquarters were toward the center. [5]It was a handbreadth[i] in thickness, and its rim was like the rim of a cup, like a lily blossom. It held three thousand baths.[j]

[6]He then made ten basins for washing and placed five on the south side and five on the north. In them the things to be used for the burnt offerings were rinsed, but the Sea was to be used by the priests for washing.

[7]He made ten gold lampstands according to the specifications for them and placed them in the temple, five on the south side and five on the north.

[8]He made ten tables and placed them in the temple, five on the south side and five on the north. He also made a hundred gold sprinkling bowls.

[9]He made the courtyard of the priests, and the large court and the doors for the court, and overlaid the doors with bronze. [10]He placed the Sea on the south side, at the southeast corner.

[11]He also made the pots and shovels and sprinkling bowls.

So Huram finished the work he had undertaken for King Solomon in the temple of God:

[12]the two pillars;

the two bowl-shaped capitals on top of the pillars;

the two sets of network decorating the two bowl-shaped capitals on top of the pillars;

[13]the four hundred pomegranates for the two sets of network (two rows of pomegranates for each network, decorating the bowl-shaped capitals on top of the pillars);

[14]the stands with their basins;

[15]the Sea and the twelve bulls under it;

[16]the pots, shovels, meat forks and all related articles.

All the objects that Huram-Abi made for King Solomon for the temple of the LORD were of polished bronze. [17]The king had them cast in clay molds in the plain of the Jordan between Succoth and Zarethan.[k] [18]All these things that Solomon made amounted to so much that the weight of the bronze was not determined.

[19]Solomon also made all the furnishings that were in God's temple:

the golden altar;

the tables on which was the bread of the Presence;

[20]the lampstands of pure gold with their lamps, to burn in front of the inner sanctuary as prescribed;

[21]the gold floral work and lamps and tongs (they were solid gold);

[22]the pure gold wick trimmers, sprinkling bowls, dishes and censers; and the gold doors of the temple: the inner doors to the Most Holy Place and the doors of the main hall.

5 When all the work Solomon had done for the temple of the LORD was finished, he brought in the things his father David had

---

[a]15 That is, about 52 feet (about 16 meters)   [b]16 Or possibly *made chains in the inner sanctuary*; the meaning of the Hebrew for this phrase is uncertain.   [c]17 *Jakin* probably means *he establishes.*   [d]17 *Boaz* probably means *in him is strength.*   [e]1 That is, about 30 feet (about 9 meters) long and wide, and about 15 feet (about 4.5 meters) high   [f]2 That is, about 7 1/2 feet (about 2.3 meters) high   [g]2 That is, about 45 feet (about 13.5 meters)   [h]3 That is, about 1 1/2 feet (about 0.5 meter)   [i]5 That is, about 3 inches (about 8 centimeters)   [j]5 That is, about 17,500 gallons (about 66 kiloliters)   [k]17 Hebrew *Zeredatha,* a variant of *Zarethan*

dedicated—the silver and gold and all the furnishings—and he placed them in the treasuries of God's temple.

The Ark Brought to the Temple

2 Then Solomon summoned to Jerusalem the elders of Israel, all the heads of the tribes and the chiefs of the Israelite families, to bring up the ark of the LORD's covenant from Zion, the City of David. **3** And all the men of Israel came together to the king at the time of the festival in the seventh month.

4 When all the elders of Israel had arrived, the Levites took up the ark, **5** and they brought up the ark and the Tent of Meeting and all the sacred furnishings in it. The priests, who were Levites, carried them up; **6** and King Solomon and the entire assembly of Israel that had gathered about him were before the ark, sacrificing so many sheep and cattle that they could not be recorded or counted.

7 The priests then brought the ark of the LORD's covenant to its place in the inner sanctuary of the temple, the Most Holy Place, and put it beneath the wings of the cherubim. **8** The cherubim spread their wings over the place of the ark and covered the ark and its carrying poles. **9** These poles were so long that their ends, extending from the ark, could be seen from in front of the inner sanctuary, but not from outside the Holy Place; and they are still there today. **10** There was nothing in the ark except the two tablets that Moses had placed in it at Horeb, where the LORD made a covenant with the Israelites after they came out of Egypt.

11 The priests then withdrew from the Holy Place. All the priests who were there had consecrated themselves, regardless of their divisions. **12** All the Levites who were musicians—Asaph, Heman, Jeduthun and their sons and relatives—stood on the east side of the altar, dressed in fine linen and playing cymbals, harps and lyres. They were accompanied by 120 priests sounding trumpets. **13** The trumpeters and singers joined in unison, as with one voice, to give praise and thanks to the LORD. Accompanied by trumpets, cymbals and other

instruments, they raised their voices in praise to the LORD and sang:

> "He is good;
> his love endures forever."

> 2 Chronicles 5:13
>
> *God Is Good*
>
> "He is good;
> his love endures forever."

Then the temple of the LORD was filled with a cloud, **14** and the priests could not perform their service because of the cloud, for the glory of the LORD filled the temple of God.

6 Then Solomon said, "The LORD has said that he would dwell in a dark cloud; **2** I have built a magnificent temple for you, a place for you to dwell forever."

3 While the whole assembly of Israel was standing there, the king turned around and blessed them. **4** Then he said:

"Praise be to the LORD, the God of Israel, who with his hands has fulfilled what he promised with his mouth to my father David. For he said, **5** 'Since the day I brought my people out of Egypt, I have not chosen a city in any tribe of Israel to have a temple built for my Name to be there, nor have I chosen anyone to be the leader over my people Israel. **6** But now I have chosen Jerusalem for my Name to be there, and I have chosen David to rule my people Israel.'

7 "My father David had it in his heart to build a temple for the Name of the LORD, the God of Israel. **8** But the LORD said to my father David, 'Because it was in your heart to build a temple for my Name, you did well to have this in your heart. **9** Nevertheless, you are not the one to build the temple, but your son, who is your own flesh and blood—he is the one who will build the temple for my Name.'

10 "The LORD has kept the promise he made. I have succeeded David my father and now I sit on the throne of Israel, just as the LORD promised, and I have built the temple for the Name of the LORD, the God of Israel. **11** There I have placed the ark, in which is the covenant of the LORD that he made with the people of Israel."

2 Chronicles 6:9

"Nevertheless, you are
not the one to build the
temple, but your son,
who is your own flesh
and blood—he is the one
who will build the temple
for my Name."

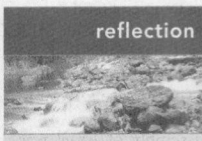

reflection

1 What loose ends have
you picked up and be-
gun working on?

2 What loose ends are
you leaving for others
to pick up and leave their
personal touch on?

3 How does considering
both those who have
gone before you and those
who will come after you
impact the work you are
doing today?

RELATED READINGS

1 Chronicles 28:2–3,
11–19;
1 Corinthians 3:10–15

Read: 2 Chronicles 6:1–10

GOD TOLD DAVID that he wouldn't be the one to finish what he
started. Abraham was promised descendents, but he would never
bounce all of them on his knees. The prophets were promised a
Messiah, but they didn't live to see him in the flesh.

We can't always finish what we start. That idea often runs
counter to our sensibilities as women. Of course we have to finish.
We have calendar planners. We have to-do lists. We have people
depending on us. We hate loose ends. We have every intention
of completing what we begin. But sometimes we're supposed to
leave some loose ends dangling.

King David knew a thing or two about loose ends. He had the
noble ambition of building a temple for God. He drew the blueprints according to God's specifications. He gathered the supplies.
But he never set a single stone in place. He had been a warrior and
had shed blood. So God had in mind a different man for the job:
David's son Solomon. When Solomon became king, he picked up
the loose ends his father had left and went to work. The plans were
David's, but the work of constructing the temple belonged to King
Solomon.

Think about it. Even King Solomon said, "There is nothing new
under the sun" (Ecclesiastes 1:9). Much of the work we do for God
is a continuation of what another person began. We teach a class
that someone else started. We mentor a woman that someone
else brought to faith. We paint walls that someone else erected.
When we're gone, new voices will fill that classroom. New mentors
will emerge. New hands will paint church walls. And that's as it
should be.

If David had pressed ahead with constructing the temple, not
only would he have been disobedient, but he also would have
deprived his son of a unique opportunity to use his wisdom, gifts
and talents to serve God.

Is there a task or position you are clinging to that God is asking
you to release? The simple truth is that loose ends leave room
for someone else to come along and continue the work in new
and unique ways. And God may want you to move forward to a
different phase of life. Leaving room for loose ends allows God's
kingdom to extend beyond our influence and reach into eternity.

Solomon's Prayer of Dedication

12Then Solomon stood before the altar of the LORD in front of the whole assembly of Israel and spread out his hands. **13**Now he had made a bronze platform, five cubits*a* long, five cubits wide and three cubits*b* high, and had placed it in the center of the outer court. He stood on the platform and then knelt down before the whole assembly of Israel and spread out his hands toward heaven. **14**He said:

"O LORD, God of Israel, there is no God like you in heaven or on earth—you who keep your covenant of love with your servants who continue wholeheartedly in your way. **15**You have kept your promise to your servant David my father; with your mouth you have promised and with your hand you have fulfilled it—as it is today.

16"Now LORD, God of Israel, keep for your servant David my father the promises you made to him when you said, 'You shall never fail to have a man to sit before me on the throne of Israel, if only your sons are careful in all they do to walk before me according to my law, as you have done.' **17**And now, O LORD, God of Israel, let your word that you promised your servant David come true.

18"But will God really dwell on earth with men? The heavens, even the highest heavens, cannot contain you. How much less this temple I have built! **19**Yet give attention to your servant's prayer and his plea for mercy, O LORD my God. Hear the cry and the prayer that your servant is praying in your presence. **20**May your eyes be open toward this temple day and night, this place of which you said you would put your Name there. May you hear the prayer your servant prays toward this place. **21**Hear the supplications of your servant and of your people Israel when they pray toward this place. Hear from heaven, your dwelling place; and when you hear, forgive.

22"When a man wrongs his neighbor and is required to take an oath and he comes and swears the oath before your altar in this temple, **23**then hear from heaven and act. Judge between your servants, repaying the guilty by bringing down on his own head what he has done. Declare the innocent not guilty and so establish his innocence.

24"When your people Israel have been defeated by an enemy because they have sinned against you and when they turn back and confess your name, praying and making supplication before you in this temple, **25**then hear from heaven and forgive the sin of your people Israel and bring them back to the land you gave to them and their fathers.

26"When the heavens are shut up and there is no rain because your people have sinned against you, and when they pray toward this place and confess your name and turn from their sin because you have afflicted them, **27**then hear from heaven and forgive the sin of your servants, your people Israel. Teach them the right way to live, and send rain on the land you gave your people for an inheritance.

28"When famine or plague comes to the land, or blight or mildew, locusts or grasshoppers, or when enemies besiege them in any of their cities, whatever disaster or disease may come, **29**and when a prayer or plea is made by any of your people Israel—each one aware of his afflictions and pains, and spreading out his hands toward this temple— **30**then hear from heaven, your dwelling place. Forgive, and deal with each man according to all he does, since you know his heart (for you alone know the hearts of men), **31**so that they will fear you and walk in your ways all the time they live in the land you gave our fathers.

32"As for the foreigner who does not belong to your people Israel but has come from a distant land because of your great name and your mighty hand and your outstretched arm—when he comes and prays toward this temple, **33**then hear from heaven, your dwelling place, and

*a*13 That is, about 7 1/2 feet (about 2.3 meters) *b*13 That is, about 4 1/2 feet (about 1.3 meters) do whatever the foreigner asks of you, so that all the peoples of the earth may know your name and fear you, as do your own people Israel, and may know that this house I have built bears your Name.

³⁴"When your people go to war against their enemies, wherever you send them, and when they pray to you toward this city you have chosen and the temple I have built for your Name, ³⁵then hear from heaven their prayer and their plea, and uphold their cause.

³⁶"When they sin against you—for there is no one who does not sin—and you become angry with them and give them over to the enemy, who takes them captive to a land far away or near; ³⁷and if they have a change of heart in the land where they are held captive, and repent and plead with you in the land of their captivity and say, 'We have sinned, we have done wrong and acted wickedly'; ³⁸and if they turn back to you with all their heart and soul in the land of their captivity where they were taken, and pray toward the land you gave their fathers, toward the city you have chosen and toward the temple I have built for your Name; ³⁹then from heaven, your dwelling place, hear their prayer and their pleas, and uphold their cause. And forgive your people, who have sinned against you.

⁴⁰"Now, my God, may your eyes be open and your ears attentive to the prayers offered in this place.

⁴¹"Now arise, O LORD God, and come to
　　your resting place,
　　you and the ark of your might.
May your priests, O LORD God, be
　　clothed with salvation,
　　may your saints rejoice in your
　　goodness.
⁴²O LORD God, do not reject your
　　anointed one.

2 Chronicles 6:39

God Hears Us

"Hear their prayer and their pleas, and uphold their cause. And forgive your people, who have sinned against you."

Remember the great love promised to David your servant."

The Dedication of the Temple

7 When Solomon finished praying, fire came down from heaven and consumed the burnt offering and the sacrifices, and the glory of the LORD filled the temple. ²The priests could not enter the temple of the LORD because the glory of the LORD filled it. ³When all the Israelites saw the fire coming down and the glory of the LORD above the temple, they knelt on the pavement with their faces to the ground, and they worshiped and gave thanks to the LORD, saying,

"He is good;
　　his love endures forever."

⁴Then the king and all the people offered sacrifices before the LORD. ⁵And King Solomon offered a sacrifice of twenty-two thousand head of cattle and a hundred and twenty thousand sheep and goats. So the king and all the people dedicated the temple of God. ⁶The priests took their positions, as did the Levites with the LORD's musical instruments, which King David had made for praising the LORD and which were used when he gave thanks, saying, "His love endures forever." Opposite the Levites, the priests blew their trumpets, and all the Israelites were standing.

⁷Solomon consecrated the middle part of the courtyard in front of the temple of the LORD, and there he offered burnt offerings and the fat of the fellowship offerings,*ᵃ* because the bronze altar he had made could not hold the burnt offerings, the grain offerings and the fat portions.

⁸So Solomon observed the festival at that time for seven days, and all Israel with him—a vast assembly, people from Lebo*ᵇ* Hamath to the Wadi of Egypt. ⁹On the eighth day they held an assembly, for they had celebrated the dedication of the altar for seven days and the festival for seven days more. ¹⁰On the twenty-third day of the seventh month he sent the

ᵃ7 Traditionally peace offerings   ᵇ8 Or from the entrance to

Learning to Wait

NAOMI

"HOW DID IT GO, my daughter?" Naomi asked her daughter-in-law Ruth.

Ruth had just returned from spending an evening with Boaz. Like a schoolgirl describing her first experience falling in love, the words tumbled out of her.

The way her daughter-in-law smiled and mindlessly fingered a lock of her hair whenever she said Boaz' name reminded Naomi of an earlier time: a time when the very thought of her former husband, Elimelech, "Eli" as he liked to call him, sent a chill of excitement through her.

But that was before—before their hometown of Bethlehem became a poorhouse, before the famine, before the move to Moab, before immeasurable heartache and loss. When she lost her husband and then both sons, she was sure life would never be the same. And it never was. When she decided to return to Bethlehem, her friends even paid tribute to that fact.

She remembered the surprise on their faces. The words they didn't bother to whisper: "Can this be Naomi?" they wondered aloud, staring at the shadow of the woman they'd known.

Naomi had scoffed at the irony. Her mother had named her "Pleasant." What was pleasant about her life now? Instead of joy there was suffering; bitterness was her only destiny now.

However, from the ruddy soil of her sorrow, seeds of hope sprouted from one small word: *wait.*

Wait for God's timing. Bethlehem, the "house of bread," would again be filled with a luscious aroma.

Wait for God's provision. Boaz, the one-in-a-million man, would soon marry Ruth.

Wait for God's blessing. Jesus, the direct descendant of Boaz and Ruth, was coming.

So, today, when her daughter-in-law (now practically a daughter) came to her, she saw uncertainty in her eyes. She knew there were questions, unpredictable situations. Would Ruth have a chance at happiness again? Was there hope? There was no way to know for sure. But Naomi offered Ruth the best advice she could—something she'd learned the hard way.

"Wait. Wait, my daughter, until you find out what happens . . ." Just wait.

"Wait, my daughter, until you find out what happens. For the man will not rest until the matter is settled today."

Ruth 3:18

ASSIGNED READING:

Ruth 2–4

—Prayer—
Great Savior, take away the impatience in my soul so I can better see your good plans for me.

Weekend

Go to page 530 for your next devotional reading.

people to their homes, joyful and glad in heart for the good things the LORD had done for David and Solomon and for his people Israel.

The LORD Appears to Solomon

¹¹When Solomon had finished the temple of the LORD and the royal palace, and had succeeded in carrying out all he had in mind to do in the temple of the LORD and in his own palace, ¹²the LORD appeared to him at night and said:

"I have heard your prayer and have chosen this place for myself as a temple for sacrifices.

¹³"When I shut up the heavens so that there is no rain, or command locusts to devour the land or send a plague among my people, ¹⁴if my people, who are called by my name, will humble themselves and pray and seek my face and turn from their wicked ways, then will I hear from heaven and will forgive their sin and will heal their land. ¹⁵Now my eyes will be open and my ears attentive to the prayers offered in this place. ¹⁶I have chosen and consecrated this temple so that my Name may be there forever. My eyes and my heart will always be there.

¹⁷"As for you, if you walk before me as David your father did, and do all I command, and observe my decrees and laws, ¹⁸I will establish your royal throne, as I covenanted with David your father when I said, 'You shall never fail to have a man to rule over Israel.'

¹⁹"But if you[a] turn away and forsake the decrees and commands I have given you[a] and go off to serve other gods and worship them, ²⁰then I will uproot Israel from my land, which I have given them, and will reject this temple I have consecrated for my Name. I will make it a byword and an object of ridicule among all peoples. ²¹And though this temple is now so imposing, all who pass by will be appalled and say, 'Why has the LORD done such a thing to this land and to this temple?' ²²People will answer, 'Because they have forsaken the LORD, the God of their fathers, who brought them out of Egypt, and have embraced other gods, worshiping and serving them—that is why he brought all this disaster on them.'"

Solomon's Other Activities

8 At the end of twenty years, during which Solomon built the temple of the LORD and his own palace, ²Solomon rebuilt the villages that Hiram[b] had given him, and settled Israelites in them. ³Solomon then went to Hamath Zobah and captured it. ⁴He also built up Tadmor in the desert and all the store cities he had built in Hamath. ⁵He rebuilt Upper Beth Horon and Lower Beth Horon as fortified cities, with walls and with gates and bars, ⁶as well as Baalath and all his store cities, and all the cities for his chariots and for his horses[c]—whatever he desired to build in Jerusalem, in Lebanon and throughout all the territory he ruled.

⁷All the people left from the Hittites, Amorites, Perizzites, Hivites and Jebusites (these peoples were not Israelites), ⁸that is, their descendants remaining in the land, whom the Israelites had not destroyed—these Solomon conscripted for his slave labor force, as it is to this day. ⁹But Solomon did not make slaves of the Israelites for his work; they were his fighting men, commanders of his captains, and commanders of his chariots and charioteers. ¹⁰They were also King Solomon's chief officials—two hundred and fifty officials supervising the men.

¹¹Solomon brought Pharaoh's daughter up from the City of David to the palace he had built for her, for he said, "My wife must not live in the palace of David king of Israel, because

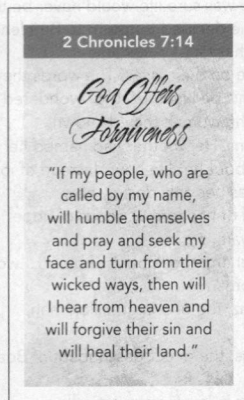

2 Chronicles 7:14

God Offers Forgiveness

"If my people, who are called by my name, will humble themselves and pray and seek my face and turn from their wicked ways, then will I hear from heaven and will forgive their sin and will heal their land."

---

[a]19 The Hebrew is plural.   [b]2 Hebrew *Huram*, a variant of *Hiram*; also in verse 18   [c]6 Or *charioteers*

the places the ark of the Lord has entered are holy."

¹²On the altar of the Lord that he had built in front of the portico, Solomon sacrificed burnt offerings to the Lord, ¹³according to the daily requirement for offerings commanded by Moses for Sabbaths, New Moons and the three annual feasts—the Feast of Unleavened Bread, the Feast of Weeks and the Feast of Tabernacles. ¹⁴In keeping with the ordinance of his father David, he appointed the divisions of the priests for their duties, and the Levites to lead the praise and to assist the priests according to each day's requirement. He also appointed the gatekeepers by divisions for the various gates, because this was what David the man of God had ordered. ¹⁵They did not deviate from the king's commands to the priests or to the Levites in any matter, including that of the treasuries.

¹⁶All Solomon's work was carried out, from the day the foundation of the temple of the Lord was laid until its completion. So the temple of the Lord was finished.

¹⁷Then Solomon went to Ezion Geber and Elath on the coast of Edom. ¹⁸And Hiram sent him ships commanded by his own officers, men who knew the sea. These, with Solomon's men, sailed to Ophir and brought back four hundred and fifty talents*a* of gold, which they delivered to King Solomon.

The Queen of Sheba Visits Solomon

9 When the queen of Sheba heard of Solomon's fame, she came to Jerusalem to test him with hard questions. Arriving with a very great caravan—with camels carrying spices, large quantities of gold, and precious stones—she came to Solomon and talked with him about all she had on her mind. ²Solomon answered all her questions; nothing was too hard for him to explain to her. ³When the queen of Sheba saw the wisdom of Solomon, as well as the palace he had built, ⁴the food on his table, the seating of his officials, the attending servants in their robes, the cupbearers in their robes and the burnt offerings he made at*b* the temple of the Lord, she was overwhelmed.

⁵She said to the king, "The report I heard in my own country about your achievements and your wisdom is true. ⁶But I did not believe what they said until I came and saw with my own eyes. Indeed, not even half the greatness of your wisdom was told me; you have far exceeded the report I heard. ⁷How happy your men must be! How happy your officials, who continually stand before you and hear your wisdom! ⁸Praise be to the Lord your God, who has delighted in you and placed you on his throne as king to rule for the Lord your God. Because of the love of your God for Israel and his desire to uphold them forever, he has made you king over them, to maintain justice and righteousness."

⁹Then she gave the king 120 talents*c* of gold, large quantities of spices, and precious stones. There had never been such spices as those the queen of Sheba gave to King Solomon.

¹⁰(The men of Hiram and the men of Solomon brought gold from Ophir; they also brought algumwood*d* and precious stones. ¹¹The king used the algumwood to make steps for the temple of the Lord and for the royal palace, and to make harps and lyres for the musicians. Nothing like them had ever been seen in Judah.)

¹²King Solomon gave the queen of Sheba all she desired and asked for; he gave her more than she had brought to him. Then she left and returned with her retinue to her own country.

Solomon's Splendor

¹³The weight of the gold that Solomon received yearly was 666 talents,*e* ¹⁴not including the revenues brought in by merchants and traders. Also all the kings of Arabia and the governors of the land brought gold and silver to Solomon.

¹⁵King Solomon made two hundred large shields of hammered gold; six hundred bekas*f* of hammered gold went into each shield. ¹⁶He also made three hundred small shields of hammered gold, with three hundred bekas*g* of gold in each shield. The king put them in the Palace of the Forest of Lebanon.

---

*a***18** That is, about 17 tons (about 16 metric tons)   *b***4** Or *the ascent by which he went up to*   *c***9** That is, about 4 1/2 tons (about 4 metric tons)   *d***10** Probably a variant of *almugwood*   *e***13** That is, about 25 tons (about 23 metric tons)   *f***15** That is, about 7 1/2 pounds (about 3.5 kilograms)   *g***16** That is, about 3 3/4 pounds (about 1.7 kilograms)

2 Chronicles 8:11

Solomon brought Pharaoh's daughter up from the City of David to the palace he had built for her, for he said, "My wife must not live in the palace of David king of Israel, because the places the ark of the LORD has entered are holy."

reflection

1 How do your unbelieving friends and family affect your attitude toward God?

2 What are some concrete ways you can keep holy what is holy, while still honoring and respecting the unbelievers you love?

3 Think about the burden you feel toward a spouse or loved one who wants nothing to do with the Lord. Spend time in prayer, giving your anxieties and grief about them to God.

RELATED READINGS

1 Kings 7:1–8; 11:1–13; Philippians 4:4–7; 1 Peter 3:1–6

Read: 2 Chronicles 8:1–11

DO YOU LIVE with an unbelieving husband, longing to someday witness his change of heart? Have you grown discouraged at how easily he picks apart your imperfections or the obvious faults he sees in "God's people"? Maybe it's not your husband but a parent, coworker or good friend who wants nothing to do with your faith. So you continue to suffer in silence. How can you live a life that honors God and cling to what is holy when those around you feel ambivalent, at best, or openly hostile, at worst, toward the God you love?

Solomon would have empathized with your plight. Second Chronicles 8 tells us that he married an Egyptian princess. Pharaoh's daughter was an ironic choice for the wisest man on earth. Was his memory so short that he did not recall the Israelites' miraculous escape from bondage to his wife's ancestors? And even if his wife was a believer in the true God, surely she had servants who worshiped Egyptian gods. Solomon recognized that God's holiness must take precedence over his wife's comfort, so he moved her and her household to the outskirts of Jerusalem. He separated her from God's holy place.

The princess must have known why she was being relocated. Did she resent this separation? Did she try to undermine Solomon's efforts to remain faithful to God? The Scriptural record does not say. We do learn later that in his old age, Solomon's heart was divided by the gods of his many wives. Ultimately, he could not keep his faith from being corrupted by the influence of those closest to him.

God knows the agony of loving those who, at present, want nothing to do with him. Think of all the people he created who openly reject him. Yet he still loves them and shows by example that his "kindness . . . leads [them] toward repentance" (Romans 2:4). In your own circumstances, follow God's example by being kind but firm. Be faithful to keep yourself wholly holy. By doing this you can help win your spouse, parent, child, colleague or friend to true belief. Be encouraged by Peter's words, "If any of them do not believe the word, they may be won over without words by [your] behavior" (1 Peter 3:1). You can rest in the knowledge that they are in God's loving hands . . . and so are you.

Monday

Go to page 535 for your next devotional reading.

17Then the king made a great throne inlaid with ivory and overlaid with pure gold. 18The throne had six steps, and a footstool of gold was attached to it. On both sides of the seat were armrests, with a lion standing beside each of them. 19Twelve lions stood on the six steps, one at either end of each step. Nothing like it had ever been made for any other kingdom. 20All King Solomon's goblets were gold, and all the household articles in the Palace of the Forest of Lebanon were pure gold. Nothing was made of silver, because silver was considered of little value in Solomon's day. 21The king had a fleet of trading ships*a* manned by Hiram's*b* men. Once every three years it returned, carrying gold, silver and ivory, and apes and baboons.

22King Solomon was greater in riches and wisdom than all the other kings of the earth. 23All the kings of the earth sought audience with Solomon to hear the wisdom God had put in his heart. 24Year after year, everyone who came brought a gift—articles of silver and gold, and robes, weapons and spices, and horses and mules.

25Solomon had four thousand stalls for horses and chariots, and twelve thousand horses,*c* which he kept in the chariot cities and also with him in Jerusalem. 26He ruled over all the kings from the River*d* to the land of the Philistines, as far as the border of Egypt. 27The king made silver as common in Jerusalem as stones, and cedar as plentiful as sycamore-fig trees in the foothills. 28Solomon's horses were imported from Egypt*e* and from all other countries.

Solomon's Death

29As for the other events of Solomon's reign, from beginning to end, are they not written in the records of Nathan the prophet, in the prophecy of Ahijah the Shilonite and in the visions of Iddo the seer concerning Jeroboam son of Nebat? 30Solomon reigned in Jerusalem over all Israel forty years. 31Then he rested with his fathers and was buried in the city of David his father. And Rehoboam his son succeeded him as king.

Israel Rebels Against Rehoboam

10 Rehoboam went to Shechem, for all the Israelites had gone there to make him king. 2When Jeroboam son of Nebat heard this (he was in Egypt, where he had fled from King Solomon), he returned from Egypt. 3So they sent for Jeroboam, and he and all Israel went to Rehoboam and said to him: 4"Your father put a heavy yoke on us, but now lighten the harsh labor and the heavy yoke he put on us, and we will serve you."

5Rehoboam answered, "Come back to me in three days." So the people went away.

6Then King Rehoboam consulted the elders who had served his father Solomon during his lifetime. "How would you advise me to answer these people?" he asked.

7They replied, "If you will be kind to these people and please them and give them a favorable answer, they will always be your servants."

8But Rehoboam rejected the advice the elders gave him and consulted the young men who had grown up with him and were serving him. 9He asked them, "What is your advice? How should we answer these people who say to me, 'Lighten the yoke your father put on us'?"

10The young men who had grown up with him replied, "Tell the people who have said to you, 'Your father put a heavy yoke on us, but make our yoke lighter'—tell them, 'My little finger is thicker than my father's waist. 11My father laid on you a heavy yoke; I will make it even heavier. My father scourged you with whips; I will scourge you with scorpions.'"

12Three days later Jeroboam and all the people returned to Rehoboam, as the king had said, "Come back to me in three days." 13The king answered them harshly. Rejecting the advice of the elders, 14he followed the advice of the young men and said, "My father made your yoke heavy; I will make it even heavier. My father scourged you with whips; I will scourge you with scorpions." 15So the king did not listen to the people, for this turn of events was from God, to fulfill the word the LORD had spoken to Jeroboam son of Nebat through Ahijah the Shilonite.

*a*21 Hebrew *of ships that could go to Tarshish*   *b*21 Hebrew *Huram,* a variant of *Hiram*   *c*25 Or *charioteers*   *d*26 That is, the Euphrates
*e*28 Or possibly *Muzur,* a region in Cilicia

¹⁶When all Israel saw that the king refused to listen to them, they answered the king:

"What share do we have in David,
    what part in Jesse's son?
To your tents, O Israel!
    Look after your own house, O David!"

So all the Israelites went home. ¹⁷But as for the Israelites who were living in the towns of Judah, Rehoboam still ruled over them.

¹⁸King Rehoboam sent out Adoniram,ᵃ who was in charge of forced labor, but the Israelites stoned him to death. King Rehoboam, however, managed to get into his chariot and escape to Jerusalem. ¹⁹So Israel has been in rebellion against the house of David to this day.

11 When Rehoboam arrived in Jerusalem, he mustered the house of Judah and Benjamin—a hundred and eighty thousand fighting men—to make war against Israel and to regain the kingdom for Rehoboam.

²But this word of the LORD came to Shemaiah the man of God: ³"Say to Rehoboam son of Solomon king of Judah and to all the Israelites in Judah and Benjamin, ⁴'This is what the LORD says: Do not go up to fight against your brothers. Go home, every one of you, for this is my doing.'" So they obeyed the words of the LORD and turned back from marching against Jeroboam.

Rehoboam Fortifies Judah

⁵Rehoboam lived in Jerusalem and built up towns for defense in Judah: ⁶Bethlehem, Etam, Tekoa, ⁷Beth Zur, Soco, Adullam, ⁸Gath, Mareshah, Ziph, ⁹Adoraim, Lachish, Azekah, ¹⁰Zorah, Aijalon and Hebron. These were fortified cities in Judah and Benjamin. ¹¹He strengthened their defenses and put commanders in them, with supplies of food, olive oil and wine. ¹²He put shields and spears in all the cities, and made them very strong. So Judah and Benjamin were his.

¹³The priests and Levites from all their districts throughout Israel sided with him. ¹⁴The Levites even abandoned their pasturelands and property, and came to Judah and Jerusalem because Jeroboam and his sons had rejected them as priests of the LORD. ¹⁵And he appointed his own priests for the high places and for the goat and calf idols he had made. ¹⁶Those from every tribe of Israel who set their hearts on seeking the LORD, the God of Israel, followed the Levites to Jerusalem to offer sacrifices to the LORD, the God of their fathers. ¹⁷They strengthened the kingdom of Judah and supported Rehoboam son of Solomon three years, walking in the ways of David and Solomon during this time.

Rehoboam's Family

¹⁸Rehoboam married Mahalath, who was the daughter of David's son Jerimoth and of Abihail, the daughter of Jesse's son Eliab. ¹⁹She bore him sons: Jeush, Shemariah and Zaham. ²⁰Then he married Maacah daughter of Absalom, who bore him Abijah, Attai, Ziza and Shelomith. ²¹Rehoboam loved Maacah daughter of Absalom more than any of his other wives and concubines. In all, he had eighteen wives and sixty concubines, twenty-eight sons and sixty daughters.

²²Rehoboam appointed Abijah son of Maacah to be the chief prince among his brothers, in order to make him king. ²³He acted wisely, dispersing some of his sons throughout the districts of Judah and Benjamin, and to all the fortified cities. He gave them abundant provisions and took many wives for them.

Shishak Attacks Jerusalem

12 After Rehoboam's position as king was established and he had become strong, he and all Israelᵇ with him abandoned the law of the LORD. ²Because they had been unfaithful to the LORD, Shishak king of Egypt attacked Jerusalem in the fifth year of King Rehoboam. ³With twelve hundred chariots and sixty thousand horsemen and the innumerable troops of Libyans, Sukkites and Cushitesᶜ that came with him from Egypt, ⁴he captured the fortified cities of Judah and came as far as Jerusalem.

⁵Then the prophet Shemaiah came to Rehoboam and to the leaders of Judah who had assembled in Jerusalem for fear of Shishak, and he said to them, "This is what the LORD says, 'You have abandoned me; therefore, I now abandon you to Shishak.'"

ᵃ18 Hebrew *Hadoram*, a variant of *Adoniram*   ᵇ1 That is, Judah, as frequently in 2 Chronicles   ᶜ3 That is, people from the upper Nile region

⁶The leaders of Israel and the king humbled themselves and said, "The LORD is just."

⁷When the LORD saw that they humbled themselves, this word of the LORD came to Shemaiah: "Since they have humbled themselves, I will not destroy them but will soon give them deliverance. My wrath will not be poured out on Jerusalem through Shishak. ⁸They will, however, become subject to him, so that they may learn the difference between serving me and serving the kings of other lands."

⁹When Shishak king of Egypt attacked Jerusalem, he carried off the treasures of the temple of the LORD and the treasures of the royal palace. He took everything, including the gold shields Solomon had made. ¹⁰So King Rehoboam made bronze shields to replace them and assigned these to the commanders of the guard on duty at the entrance to the royal palace. ¹¹Whenever the king went to the LORD's temple, the guards went with him, bearing the shields, and afterward they returned them to the guardroom.

¹²Because Rehoboam humbled himself, the LORD's anger turned from him, and he was not totally destroyed. Indeed, there was some good in Judah.

¹³King Rehoboam established himself firmly in Jerusalem and continued as king. He was forty-one years old when he became king, and he reigned seventeen years in Jerusalem, the city the LORD had chosen out of all the tribes of Israel in which to put his Name. His mother's name was Naamah; she was an Ammonite. ¹⁴He did evil because he had not set his heart on seeking the LORD.

¹⁵As for the events of Rehoboam's reign, from beginning to end, are they not written in the records of Shemaiah the prophet and of Iddo the seer that deal with genealogies? There was continual warfare between Rehoboam and Jeroboam. ¹⁶Rehoboam rested with his fathers and was buried in the City of David. And Abijah his son succeeded him as king.

Abijah King of Judah

13 In the eighteenth year of the reign of Jeroboam, Abijah became king of Judah, ²and he reigned in Jerusalem three years. His mother's name was Maacah,ᵃ a daughterᵇ of Uriel of Gibeah.

There was war between Abijah and Jeroboam. ³Abijah went into battle with a force of four hundred thousand able fighting men, and Jeroboam drew up a battle line against him with eight hundred thousand able troops.

⁴Abijah stood on Mount Zemaraim, in the hill country of Ephraim, and said, "Jeroboam and all Israel, listen to me! ⁵Don't you know that the LORD, the God of Israel, has given the kingship of Israel to David and his descendants forever by a covenant of salt? ⁶Yet Jeroboam son of Nebat, an official of Solomon son of David, rebelled against his master. ⁷Some worthless scoundrels gathered around him and opposed Rehoboam son of Solomon when he was young and indecisive and not strong enough to resist them.

⁸"And now you plan to resist the kingdom of the LORD, which is in the hands of David's descendants. You are indeed a vast army and have with you the golden calves that Jeroboam made to be your gods. ⁹But didn't you drive out the priests of the LORD, the sons of Aaron, and the Levites, and make priests of your own as the peoples of other lands do? Whoever comes to consecrate himself with a young bull and seven rams may become a priest of what are not gods.

¹⁰"As for us, the LORD is our God, and we have not forsaken him. The priests who serve the LORD are sons of Aaron, and the Levites assist them. ¹¹Every morning and evening they present burnt offerings and fragrant incense to the LORD. They set out the bread on the ceremonially clean table and light the lamps on the gold lampstand every evening. We are observing the requirements of the LORD our God. But you have forsaken him. ¹²God is with us; he is our leader. His priests with their trumpets will sound the battle cry against you. Men of Israel, do not fight against the LORD, the God of your fathers, for you will not succeed."

¹³Now Jeroboam had sent troops around to the rear, so that while he was in front of Judah the ambush was behind them. ¹⁴Judah turned and saw that they were being attacked at both front and rear. Then they cried out to the LORD.

ᵃ2 Most Septuagint manuscripts and Syriac (see also 2 Chron. 11:20 and 1 Kings 15:2); Hebrew *Micaiah*   ᵇ2 Or *granddaughter*

The priests blew their trumpets ¹⁵and the men of Judah raised the battle cry. At the sound of their battle cry, God routed Jeroboam and all Israel before Abijah and Judah. ¹⁶The Israelites fled before Judah, and God delivered them into their hands. ¹⁷Abijah and his men inflicted heavy losses on them, so that there were five hundred thousand casualties among Israel's able men. ¹⁸The men of Israel were subdued on that occasion, and the men of Judah were victorious because they relied on the LORD, the God of their fathers.

¹⁹Abijah pursued Jeroboam and took from him the towns of Bethel, Jeshanah and Ephron, with their surrounding villages. ²⁰Jeroboam did not regain power during the time of Abijah. And the LORD struck him down and he died.

²¹But Abijah grew in strength. He married fourteen wives and had twenty-two sons and sixteen daughters.

²²The other events of Abijah's reign, what he did and what he said, are written in the annotations of the prophet Iddo.

14 And Abijah rested with his fathers and was buried in the City of David. Asa his son succeeded him as king, and in his days the country was at peace for ten years.

Asa King of Judah

²Asa did what was good and right in the eyes of the LORD his God. ³He removed the foreign altars and the high places, smashed the sacred stones and cut down the Asherah poles.ᵃ ⁴He commanded Judah to seek the LORD, the God of their fathers, and to obey his laws and commands. ⁵He removed the high places and incense altars in every town in Judah, and the kingdom was at peace under him. ⁶He built up the fortified cities of Judah, since the land was at peace. No one was at war with him during those years, for the LORD gave him rest.

⁷"Let us build up these towns," he said to Judah, "and put walls around them, with towers, gates and bars. The land is still ours, because we have sought the LORD our God; we sought him and he has given us rest on every side." So they built and prospered.

⁸Asa had an army of three hundred thousand men from Judah, equipped with large shields and with spears, and two hundred and eighty thousand from Benjamin, armed with small shields and with bows. All these were brave fighting men.

⁹Zerah the Cushite marched out against them with a vast armyᵇ and three hundred chariots, and came as far as Mareshah. ¹⁰Asa went out to meet him, and they took up battle positions in the Valley of Zephathah near Mareshah.

¹¹Then Asa called to the LORD his God and said, "LORD, there is no one like you to help the powerless against the mighty. Help us, O LORD our God, for we rely on you, and in your name we have come against this vast army. O LORD, you are our God; do not let man prevail against you."

¹²The LORD struck down the Cushites before Asa and Judah. The Cushites fled, ¹³and Asa and his army pursued them as far as Gerar. Such a great number of Cushites fell that they could not recover; they were crushed before the LORD and his forces. The men of Judah carried off a large amount of plunder. ¹⁴They destroyed all the villages around Gerar, for the terror of the LORD had fallen upon them. They plundered all these villages, since there was much booty there. ¹⁵They also attacked the camps of the herdsmen and carried off droves of sheep and goats and camels. Then they returned to Jerusalem.

Asa's Reform

15 The Spirit of God came upon Azariah son of Oded. ²He went out to meet Asa and said to him, "Listen to me, Asa and all Judah and Benjamin. The LORD is with you when you are with him. If you seek him, he will

2 Chronicles 14:11

God Helps the Powerless

Then Asa called to the LORD his God and said, "LORD, there is no one like you to help the powerless against the mighty."

ᵃ3 That is, symbols of the goddess Asherah; here and elsewhere in 2 Chronicles   ᵇ9 Hebrew *with an army of a thousand thousands* or *with an army of thousands upon thousands*

Good and Right

Read: 2 Chronicles 14:1–15

WHEN SHE WAS 11 years old, Victoria, the girl who would be queen, saw a royal family tree and supposedly remarked, "I am nearer to the throne than I thought." Then, according to her governess, she vowed, "I will be good." Queen Victoria's January 23, 1901, obituary in the New York Times said, "It was never quite so true as in her time that the British Empire was one on which the sun never set." Not only was Victoria a good queen, she was a godly queen. Engraved above the door at the Frogmore Royal Mausoleum where she lies buried beside her beloved Prince Albert are the inspiring words, "Farewell best beloved, here at last I shall rest with thee, with thee in Christ I shall rise again."

The day will come when our obituaries will be written. Others will review our lives and summarize what they saw in a few short words. We will have left our mark, and it will be too late to change it. The challenge now is to live so as to be remembered as good and godly women.

The chroniclers who wrote these books in the Bible were in large part eulogists, evaluating the lives of the kings of Israel. They recorded the good and bad history in black and white for us to read many years later. In the list of so many kings who did evil, King Asa stands out for doing what was good and right. He stepped up to a throne in a kingdom that was in spiritual disarray, and he made a deliberate choice: He and his people would seek the Lord and obey his laws.

In later days, when people reminisce about your life, what will they remember? Will they remember a woman who did what was good and right in the eyes of the Lord despite the cost? Will they remember a woman who continued to do God's work until her last days? What will your close friends remember? What about your husband, children, siblings, coworkers? As long as you draw breath, your mark on this world is still being made. It doesn't become indelible until after you're gone. There is still time to be remembered as someone who sought God and did her best to do what was "good and right."

2 Chronicles 14:2

Asa did what was good and right in the eyes of the Lord his God.

reflection

1 What kind of legacy are you leaving for those around you?

2 How can you make pleasing God the main desire of your heart? Insert your name in verse 2: "_____ does what is good and right in the eyes of the Lord her God."

3 Think of one or two people you want to be at your funeral. What do you want them to remember about you?

RELATED READINGS

Ephesians 2:6–10;
Colossians 3:23–25

Tuesday

Go to page 543 for your next devotional reading.

be found by you, but if you forsake him, he will forsake you. ³For a long time Israel was without the true God, without a priest to teach and without the law. ⁴But in their distress they turned to the LORD, the God of Israel, and sought him, and he was found by them. ⁵In those days it was not safe to travel about, for all the inhabitants of the lands were in great turmoil. ⁶One nation was being crushed by another and one city by another, because God was troubling them with every kind of distress. ⁷But as for you, be strong and do not give up, for your work will be rewarded."

⁸When Asa heard these words and the prophecy of Azariah son of ᵃ Oded the prophet, he took courage. He removed the detestable idols from the whole land of Judah and Benjamin and from the towns he had captured in the hills of Ephraim. He repaired the altar of the LORD that was in front of the portico of the LORD's temple.

⁹Then he assembled all Judah and Benjamin and the people from Ephraim, Manasseh and Simeon who had settled among them, for large numbers had come over to him from Israel when they saw that the LORD his God was with him.

¹⁰They assembled at Jerusalem in the third month of the fifteenth year of Asa's reign. ¹¹At that time they sacrificed to the LORD seven hundred head of cattle and seven thousand sheep and goats from the plunder they had brought back. ¹²They entered into a covenant to seek the LORD, the God of their fathers, with all their heart and soul. ¹³All who would not seek the LORD, the God of Israel, were to be put to death, whether small or great, man or woman. ¹⁴They took an oath to the LORD with loud acclamation, with shouting and with trumpets and horns. ¹⁵All Judah rejoiced about the oath because they had sworn it wholeheartedly. They sought God eagerly, and he was found by them. So the LORD gave them rest on every side.

¹⁶King Asa also deposed his grandmother Maacah from her position as queen mother, because she had made a repulsive Asherah pole. Asa cut the pole down, broke it up and burned it in the Kidron Valley. ¹⁷Although he did not remove the high places from Israel, Asa's heart was fully committed ₍to the LORD₎ all his life. ¹⁸He brought into the temple of God the silver and gold and the articles that he and his father had dedicated.

¹⁹There was no more war until the thirty-fifth year of Asa's reign.

Asa's Last Years

16 In the thirty-sixth year of Asa's reign Baasha king of Israel went up against Judah and fortified Ramah to prevent anyone from leaving or entering the territory of Asa king of Judah.

²Asa then took the silver and gold out of the treasuries of the LORD's temple and of his own palace and sent it to Ben-Hadad king of Aram, who was ruling in Damascus. ³"Let there be a treaty between me and you," he said, "as there was between my father and your father. See, I am sending you silver and gold. Now break your treaty with Baasha king of Israel so he will withdraw from me."

⁴Ben-Hadad agreed with King Asa and sent the commanders of his forces against the towns of Israel. They conquered Ijon, Dan, Abel Maimᵇ and all the store cities of Naphtali. ⁵When Baasha heard this, he stopped building Ramah and abandoned his work. ⁶Then King Asa brought all the men of Judah, and they carried away from Ramah the stones and timber Baasha had been using. With them he built up Geba and Mizpah.

⁷At that time Hanani the seer came to Asa king of Judah and said to him: "Because you relied on the king of Aram and not on the LORD your God, the army of the king of Aram has escaped from your hand. ⁸Were not the Cushitesᶜ and Libyans a mighty army with great numbers of chariots and horsemenᵈ? Yet when you relied on the LORD, he delivered them into your hand. ⁹For the eyes of the LORD range throughout the

> **2 Chronicles 15:7**
>
> *God Rewards*
>
> "But as for you, be strong and do not give up, for your work will be rewarded."

ᵃ8 Vulgate and Syriac (see also Septuagint and verse 1); Hebrew does not have *Azariah son of.* ᵇ4 Also known as *Abel Beth Maacah* ᶜ8 That is, people from the upper Nile region ᵈ8 Or *charioteers* earth to strengthen those whose hearts are fully committed to him. You have done a foolish thing, and from now on you will be at war."

¹⁰Asa was angry with the seer because of this; he was so enraged that he put him in prison. At the same time Asa brutally oppressed some of the people.

¹¹The events of Asa's reign, from beginning to end, are written in the book of the kings of Judah and Israel. ¹²In the thirty-ninth year of his reign Asa was afflicted with a disease in his feet. Though his disease was severe, even in his illness he did not seek help from the LORD, but only from the physicians. ¹³Then in the forty-first year of his reign Asa died and rested with his fathers. ¹⁴They buried him in the tomb that he had cut out for himself in the City of David. They laid him on a bier covered with spices and various blended perfumes, and they made a huge fire in his honor.

Jehoshaphat King of Judah

17 Jehoshaphat his son succeeded him as king and strengthened himself against Israel. ²He stationed troops in all the fortified cities of Judah and put garrisons in Judah and in the towns of Ephraim that his father Asa had captured.

³The LORD was with Jehoshaphat because in his early years he walked in the ways his father David had followed. He did not consult the Baals ⁴but sought the God of his father and followed his commands rather than the practices of Israel. ⁵The LORD established the kingdom under his control; and all Judah brought gifts to Jehoshaphat, so that he had great wealth and honor. ⁶His heart was devoted to the ways of the LORD; furthermore, he removed the high places and the Asherah poles from Judah.

⁷In the third year of his reign he sent his officials Ben-Hail, Obadiah, Zechariah, Nethanel and Micaiah to teach in the towns of Judah. ⁸With them were certain Levites—Shemaiah, Nethaniah, Zebadiah, Asahel, Shemiramoth, Jehonathan, Adonijah, Tobijah and Tob-Adonijah—and the priests Elishama and Jehoram.

⁹They taught throughout Judah, taking with them the Book of the Law of the LORD; they went around to all the towns of Judah and taught the people.

¹⁰The fear of the LORD fell on all the kingdoms of the lands surrounding Judah, so that they did not make war with Jehoshaphat. ¹¹Some Philistines brought Jehoshaphat gifts and silver as tribute, and the Arabs brought him flocks: seven thousand seven hundred rams and seven thousand seven hundred goats.

¹²Jehoshaphat became more and more powerful; he built forts and store cities in Judah ¹³and had large supplies in the towns of Judah. He also kept experienced fighting men in Jerusalem. ¹⁴Their enrollment by families was as follows:

From Judah, commanders of units of 1,000:
Adnah the commander, with 300,000 fighting men;
¹⁵next, Jehohanan the commander, with 280,000;
¹⁶next, Amasiah son of Zicri, who volunteered himself for the service of the LORD, with 200,000.
¹⁷From Benjamin:
Eliada, a valiant soldier, with 200,000 men armed with bows and shields;
¹⁸next, Jehozabad, with 180,000 men armed for battle.

¹⁹These were the men who served the king, besides those he stationed in the fortified cities throughout Judah.

Micaiah Prophesies Against Ahab

18 Now Jehoshaphat had great wealth and honor, and he allied himself with Ahab by marriage. ²Some years later he went down to visit Ahab in Samaria. Ahab slaughtered many sheep and cattle for him and the people with him and urged him to attack Ramoth Gilead. ³Ahab king of Israel asked Jehoshaphat king of Judah, "Will you go with me against Ramoth Gilead?"

---

2 Chronicles 16:9

God Wants Committed Women

For the eyes of the LORD range throughout the earth to strengthen those whose hearts are fully committed to him.

Jehoshaphat replied, "I am as you are, and my people as your people; we will join you in the war." **4**But Jehoshaphat also said to the king of Israel, "First seek the counsel of the LORD."

5So the king of Israel brought together the prophets—four hundred men—and asked them, "Shall we go to war against Ramoth Gilead, or shall I refrain?"

"Go," they answered, "for God will give it into the king's hand."

6But Jehoshaphat asked, "Is there not a prophet of the LORD here whom we can inquire of?"

7The king of Israel answered Jehoshaphat, "There is still one man through whom we can inquire of the LORD, but I hate him because he never prophesies anything good about me, but always bad. He is Micaiah son of Imlah."

"The king should not say that," Jehoshaphat replied.

8So the king of Israel called one of his officials and said, "Bring Micaiah son of Imlah at once."

9Dressed in their royal robes, the king of Israel and Jehoshaphat king of Judah were sitting on their thrones at the threshing floor by the entrance to the gate of Samaria, with all the prophets prophesying before them. **10**Now Zedekiah son of Kenaanah had made iron horns, and he declared, "This is what the LORD says: 'With these you will gore the Arameans until they are destroyed.'"

11All the other prophets were prophesying the same thing. "Attack Ramoth Gilead and be victorious," they said, "for the LORD will give it into the king's hand."

12The messenger who had gone to summon Micaiah said to him, "Look, as one man the other prophets are predicting success for the king. Let your word agree with theirs, and speak favorably."

13But Micaiah said, "As surely as the LORD lives, I can tell him only what my God says."

14When he arrived, the king asked him, "Micaiah, shall we go to war against Ramoth Gilead, or shall I refrain?"

"Attack and be victorious," he answered, "for they will be given into your hand."

15The king said to him, "How many times must I make you swear to tell me nothing but the truth in the name of the LORD?"

16Then Micaiah answered, "I saw all Israel scattered on the hills like sheep without a shepherd, and the LORD said, 'These people have no master. Let each one go home in peace.'"

17The king of Israel said to Jehoshaphat, "Didn't I tell you that he never prophesies anything good about me, but only bad?"

18Micaiah continued, "Therefore hear the word of the LORD: I saw the LORD sitting on his throne with all the host of heaven standing on his right and on his left. **19**And the LORD said, 'Who will entice Ahab king of Israel into attacking Ramoth Gilead and going to his death there?'

"One suggested this, and another that. **20**Finally, a spirit came forward, stood before the LORD and said, 'I will entice him.'

"'By what means?' the LORD asked.

21"'I will go and be a lying spirit in the mouths of all his prophets,' he said.

"'You will succeed in enticing him,' said the LORD. 'Go and do it.'

22"So now the LORD has put a lying spirit in the mouths of these prophets of yours. The LORD has decreed disaster for you."

23Then Zedekiah son of Kenaanah went up and slapped Micaiah in the face. "Which way did the spirit from*a* the LORD go when he went from me to speak to you?" he asked.

24Micaiah replied, "You will find out on the day you go to hide in an inner room."

25The king of Israel then ordered, "Take Micaiah and send him back to Amon the ruler of the city and to Joash the king's son, **26**and say, 'This is what the king says: Put this fellow in prison and give him nothing but bread and water until I return safely.'"

27Micaiah declared, "If you ever return safely, the LORD has not spoken through me." Then he added, "Mark my words, all you people!"

Ahab Killed at Ramoth Gilead

28So the king of Israel and Jehoshaphat king of Judah went up to Ramoth Gilead. **29**The king of Israel said to Jehoshaphat, "I will enter the battle in disguise, but you wear your royal

a23 Or Spirit of

robes." So the king of Israel disguised himself and went into battle.

³⁰Now the king of Aram had ordered his chariot commanders, "Do not fight with anyone, small or great, except the king of Israel." ³¹When the chariot commanders saw Jehoshaphat, they thought, "This is the king of Israel." So they turned to attack him, but Jehoshaphat cried out, and the LORD helped him. God drew them away from him, ³²for when the chariot commanders saw that he was not the king of Israel, they stopped pursuing him.

³³But someone drew his bow at random and hit the king of Israel between the sections of his armor. The king told the chariot driver, "Wheel around and get me out of the fighting. I've been wounded." ³⁴All day long the battle raged, and the king of Israel propped himself up in his chariot facing the Arameans until evening. Then at sunset he died.

19 When Jehoshaphat king of Judah returned safely to his palace in Jerusalem, ²Jehu the seer, the son of Hanani, went out to meet him and said to the king, "Should you help the wicked and love*ᵃ* those who hate the LORD? Because of this, the wrath of the LORD is upon you. ³There is, however, some good in you, for you have rid the land of the Asherah poles and have set your heart on seeking God."

Jehoshaphat Appoints Judges

⁴Jehoshaphat lived in Jerusalem, and he went out again among the people from Beersheba to the hill country of Ephraim and turned them back to the LORD, the God of their fathers. ⁵He appointed judges in the land, in each of the fortified cities of Judah. ⁶He told them, "Consider carefully what you do, because you are not judging for man but for the LORD, who is with you whenever you give a verdict. ⁷Now let the fear of the LORD be upon you. Judge carefully, for with the LORD our God there is no injustice or partiality or bribery."

⁸In Jerusalem also, Jehoshaphat appointed some of the Levites, priests and heads of Israelite families to administer the law of the LORD and to settle disputes. And they lived in Jerusalem. ⁹He gave them these orders: "You must serve faithfully and wholeheartedly in the fear of the LORD. ¹⁰In every case that comes before you from your fellow countrymen who live in the cities—whether bloodshed or other concerns of the law, commands, decrees or ordinances —you are to warn them not to sin against the LORD; otherwise his wrath will come on you and your brothers. Do this, and you will not sin.

¹¹"Amariah the chief priest will be over you in any matter concerning the LORD, and Zebadiah son of Ishmael, the leader of the tribe of Judah, will be over you in any matter concerning the king, and the Levites will serve as officials before you. Act with courage, and may the LORD be with those who do well."

Jehoshaphat Defeats Moab and Ammon

20 After this, the Moabites and Ammonites with some of the Meunites*ᵇ* came to make war on Jehoshaphat.

²Some men came and told Jehoshaphat, "A vast army is coming against you from Edom,*ᶜ* from the other side of the Sea.*ᵈ* It is already in Hazazon Tamar" (that is, En Gedi). ³Alarmed, Jehoshaphat resolved to inquire of the LORD, and he proclaimed a fast for all Judah. ⁴The people of Judah came together to seek help from the LORD; indeed, they came from every town in Judah to seek him.

⁵Then Jehoshaphat stood up in the assembly of Judah and Jerusalem at the temple of the LORD in the front of the new courtyard ⁶and said:

"O LORD, God of our fathers, are you not the God who is in heaven? You rule over all the kingdoms of the nations. Power and might are in your hand, and no one can withstand you. ⁷O our God, did you not drive out the inhabitants of this

2 Chronicles 19:7

God Is Impartial

Now let the fear of the LORD be upon you. Judge carefully, for with the LORD our God there is no injustice or partiality or bribery.

---

*ᵃ*2 Or *and make alliances with*   *ᵇ*1 Some Septuagint manuscripts; Hebrew *Ammonites*   *ᶜ*2 One Hebrew manuscript; most Hebrew manuscripts, Septuagint and Vulgate *Aram*   *ᵈ*2 That is, the Dead Sea land before your people Israel and give it forever to the descendants of Abraham your friend? [8]They have lived in it and have built in it a sanctuary for your Name, saying, [9]'If calamity comes upon us, whether the sword of judgment, or plague or famine, we will stand in your presence before this temple that bears your Name and will cry out to you in our distress, and you will hear us and save us.'

[10]"But now here are men from Ammon, Moab and Mount Seir, whose territory you would not allow Israel to invade when they came from Egypt; so they turned away from them and did not destroy them. [11]See how they are repaying us by coming to drive us out of the possession you gave us as an inheritance. [12]O our God, will you not judge them? For we have no power to face this vast army that is attacking us. We do not know what to do, but our eyes are upon you."

[13]All the men of Judah, with their wives and children and little ones, stood there before the LORD.

[14]Then the Spirit of the LORD came upon Jahaziel son of Zechariah, the son of Benaiah, the son of Jeiel, the son of Mattaniah, a Levite and descendant of Asaph, as he stood in the assembly.

[15]He said: "Listen, King Jehoshaphat and all who live in Judah and Jerusalem! This is what the LORD says to you: 'Do not be afraid or discouraged because of this vast army. For the battle is not yours, but God's. [16]Tomorrow march down against them. They will be climbing up by the Pass of Ziz, and you will find them at the end of the gorge in the Desert of Jeruel. [17]You will not have to fight this battle. Take up your positions; stand firm and see the deliverance the LORD will give you, O Judah and Jerusalem. Do not be afraid; do not be discouraged. Go out to face them tomorrow, and the LORD will be with you.'"

[18]Jehoshaphat bowed with his face to the ground, and all the people of Judah and Jerusalem fell down in worship before the LORD. [19]Then some Levites from the Kohathites and

Korahites stood up and praised the LORD, the God of Israel, with a very loud voice.

[20]Early in the morning they left for the Desert of Tekoa. As they set out, Jehoshaphat stood and said, "Listen to me, Judah and people of Jerusalem! Have faith in the LORD your God and you will be upheld; have faith in his prophets and you will be successful." [21]After consulting the people, Jehoshaphat appointed men to sing to the LORD and to praise him for the splendor of his[a] holiness as they went out at the head of the army, saying:

"Give thanks to the LORD,
    for his love endures forever."

[22]As they began to sing and praise, the LORD set ambushes against the men of Ammon and Moab and Mount Seir who were invading Judah, and they were defeated. [23]The men of Ammon and Moab rose up against the men from Mount Seir to destroy and annihilate them. After they finished slaughtering the men from Seir, they helped to destroy one another.

[24]When the men of Judah came to the place that overlooks the desert and looked toward the vast army, they saw only dead bodies lying on the ground; no one had escaped. [25]So Jehoshaphat and his men went to carry off their plunder, and they found among them a great amount of equipment and clothing[b] and also articles of value—more than they could take away. There was so much plunder that it took three days to collect it. [26]On the fourth day they assembled in the Valley of Beracah, where they praised the LORD. This is why it is called the Valley of Beracah[c] to this day.

[27]Then, led by Jehoshaphat, all the men of Judah and Jerusalem returned joyfully to Jerusalem, for the LORD had given them cause to rejoice over their enemies. [28]They entered Jerusalem and went to the temple of the LORD with harps and lutes and trumpets.

[29]The fear of God came upon all the kingdoms of the countries when they heard how the LORD had fought against the enemies of Israel. [30]And the kingdom of Jehoshaphat was at peace, for his God had given him rest on every side.

---

[a]21 Or *him with the splendor of*   [b]25 Some Hebrew manuscripts and Vulgate; most Hebrew manuscripts *corpses*   [c]26 *Beracah* means *praise*.

The End of Jehoshaphat's Reign

³¹So Jehoshaphat reigned over Judah. He was thirty-five years old when he became king of Judah, and he reigned in Jerusalem twenty-five years. His mother's name was Azubah daughter of Shilhi. ³²He walked in the ways of his father Asa and did not stray from them; he did what was right in the eyes of the LORD. ³³The high places, however, were not removed, and the people still had not set their hearts on the God of their fathers.

³⁴The other events of Jehoshaphat's reign, from beginning to end, are written in the annals of Jehu son of Hanani, which are recorded in the book of the kings of Israel.

³⁵Later, Jehoshaphat king of Judah made an alliance with Ahaziah king of Israel, who was guilty of wickedness. ³⁶He agreed with him to construct a fleet of trading ships.ᵃ After these were built at Ezion Geber, ³⁷Eliezer son of Dodavahu of Mareshah prophesied against Jehoshaphat, saying, "Because you have made an alliance with Ahaziah, the LORD will destroy what you have made." The ships were wrecked and were not able to set sail to trade.ᵇ

21 Then Jehoshaphat rested with his fathers and was buried with them in the City of David. And Jehoram his son succeeded him as king. ²Jehoram's brothers, the sons of Jehoshaphat, were Azariah, Jehiel, Zechariah, Azariahu, Michael and Shephatiah. All these were sons of Jehoshaphat king of Israel.ᶜ ³Their father had given them many gifts of silver and gold and articles of value, as well as fortified cities in Judah, but he had given the kingdom to Jehoram because he was his firstborn son.

Jehoram King of Judah

⁴When Jehoram established himself firmly over his father's kingdom, he put all his brothers to the sword along with some of the princes of Israel. ⁵Jehoram was thirty-two years old when he became king, and he reigned in Jeru-

---

2 Chronicles 20:29

God Fights for His People

The fear of God came upon all the kingdoms of the countries when they heard how the LORD had fought against the enemies of Israel.

---

salem eight years. ⁶He walked in the ways of the kings of Israel, as the house of Ahab had done, for he married a daughter of Ahab. He did evil in the eyes of the LORD. ⁷Nevertheless, because of the covenant the LORD had made with David, the LORD was not willing to destroy the house of David. He had promised to maintain a lamp for him and his descendants forever.

⁸In the time of Jehoram, Edom rebelled against Judah and set up its own king. ⁹So Jehoram went there with his officers and all his chariots. The Edomites surrounded him and his chariot commanders, but he rose up and broke through by night. ¹⁰To this day Edom has been in rebellion against Judah.

Libnah revolted at the same time, because Jehoram had forsaken the LORD, the God of his fathers. ¹¹He had also built high places on the hills of Judah and had caused the people of Jerusalem to prostitute themselves and had led Judah astray.

¹²Jehoram received a letter from Elijah the prophet, which said:

"This is what the LORD, the God of your father David, says: 'You have not walked in the ways of your father Jehoshaphat or of Asa king of Judah. ¹³But you have walked in the ways of the kings of Israel, and you have led Judah and the people of Jerusalem to prostitute themselves, just as the house of Ahab did. You have also murdered your own brothers, members of your father's house, men who were better than you. ¹⁴So now the LORD is about to strike your people, your sons, your wives and everything that is yours, with a heavy blow. ¹⁵You yourself will be very ill with a lingering disease of the bowels, until the disease causes your bowels to come out.'"

¹⁶The LORD aroused against Jehoram the hostility of the Philistines and of the Arabs who lived near the Cushites. ¹⁷They attacked

---

ᵃ36 Hebrew *of ships that could go to Tarshish*   ᵇ37 Hebrew *sail for Tarshish*   ᶜ2 That is, Judah, as frequently in 2 Chronicles

Judah, invaded it and carried off all the goods found in the king's palace, together with his sons and wives. Not a son was left to him except Ahaziah,*a* the youngest.

¹⁸After all this, the LORD afflicted Jehoram with an incurable disease of the bowels. ¹⁹In the course of time, at the end of the second year, his bowels came out because of the disease, and he died in great pain. His people made no fire in his honor, as they had for his fathers.

²⁰Jehoram was thirty-two years old when he became king, and he reigned in Jerusalem eight years. He passed away, to no one's regret, and was buried in the City of David, but not in the tombs of the kings.

Ahaziah King of Judah

22 The people of Jerusalem made Ahaziah, Jehoram's youngest son, king in his place, since the raiders, who came with the Arabs into the camp, had killed all the older sons. So Ahaziah son of Jehoram king of Judah began to reign.

²Ahaziah was twenty-two*b* years old when he became king, and he reigned in Jerusalem one year. His mother's name was Athaliah, a granddaughter of Omri.

³He too walked in the ways of the house of Ahab, for his mother encouraged him in doing wrong. ⁴He did evil in the eyes of the LORD, as the house of Ahab had done, for after his father's death they became his advisers, to his undoing. ⁵He also followed their counsel when he went with Joram*c* son of Ahab king of Israel to war against Hazael king of Aram at Ramoth Gilead. The Arameans wounded Joram; ⁶so he returned to Jezreel to recover from the wounds they had inflicted on him at Ramoth*d* in his battle with Hazael king of Aram.

Then Ahaziah*e* son of Jehoram king of Judah went down to Jezreel to see Joram son of Ahab because he had been wounded.

⁷Through Ahaziah's visit to Joram, God brought about Ahaziah's downfall. When Ahaziah arrived, he went out with Joram to meet Jehu son of Nimshi, whom the LORD had anointed to destroy the house of Ahab. ⁸While

Jehu was executing judgment on the house of Ahab, he found the princes of Judah and the sons of Ahaziah's relatives, who had been attending Ahaziah, and he killed them. ⁹He then went in search of Ahaziah, and his men captured him while he was hiding in Samaria. He was brought to Jehu and put to death. They buried him, for they said, "He was a son of Jehoshaphat, who sought the LORD with all his heart." So there was no one in the house of Ahaziah powerful enough to retain the kingdom.

Athaliah and Joash

¹⁰When Athaliah the mother of Ahaziah saw that her son was dead, she proceeded to destroy the whole royal family of the house of Judah. ¹¹But Jehosheba,*f* the daughter of King Jehoram, took Joash son of Ahaziah and stole him away from among the royal princes who were about to be murdered and put him and his nurse in a bedroom. Because Jehosheba,*f* the daughter of King Jehoram and wife of the priest Jehoiada, was Ahaziah's sister, she hid the child from Athaliah so she could not kill him. ¹²He remained hidden with them at the temple of God for six years while Athaliah ruled the land.

23 In the seventh year Jehoiada showed his strength. He made a covenant with the commanders of units of a hundred: Azariah son of Jeroham, Ishmael son of Jehohanan, Azariah son of Obed, Maaseiah son of Adaiah, and Elishaphat son of Zicri. ²They went throughout Judah and gathered the Levites and the heads of Israelite families from all the towns. When they came to Jerusalem, ³the whole assembly made a covenant with the king at the temple of God.

Jehoiada said to them, "The king's son shall reign, as the LORD promised concerning the descendants of David. ⁴Now this is what you are to do: A third of you priests and Levites who are going on duty on the Sabbath are to keep watch at the doors, ⁵a third of you at the royal palace and a third at the Foundation Gate, and all the other men are to be in the courtyards of the temple of the LORD. ⁶No one is to enter the

---

*a*17 Hebrew *Jehoahaz*, a variant of *Ahaziah*   *b*2 Some Septuagint manuscripts and Syriac (see also 2 Kings 8:26); Hebrew *forty-two*   *c*5 Hebrew *Jehoram*, a variant of *Joram*; also in verses 6 and 7   *d*6 Hebrew *Ramah*, a variant of *Ramoth*   *e*6 Some Hebrew manuscripts, Septuagint, Vulgate and Syriac (see also 2 Kings 8:29); most Hebrew manuscripts *Azariah*   *f*11 Hebrew *Jehoshabeath*, a variant of *Jehosheba*

Make a Difference

Read: 2 Chronicles 22:10–12

CAN ONE WOMAN really make a difference in a community? What about in an entire nation? You might think the answer is no. But think again. When you read the story of Jehosheba in 2 Chronicles, you'll realize that the answer is a wholehearted yes.

When Jehosheba realized that Athaliah was determined to destroy the royal line of Judah, she bravely hid her nephew Joash in the temple until he was old enough to succeed to the throne. When Joash was seven years old, he ascended to the throne and later repaired the temple and tore down the altars to Baal. More important, he preserved the Messianic line. Jehosheba made a difference in the life of another person; but she also made decisions that affected the outcome of a nation, and ultimately, it made a difference for all of humanity. Because of Jehosheba's courage at this time in history, "our Lord descended from Judah" (Hebrews 7:14).

In the eleventh century, a woman of noble birth impacted a nation. Princess Margaret was exiled with her family when the Danes overran England. Educated in Hungary, she returned to England during the reign of her great-uncle, Edward the Confessor. As one of the last remaining members of the Saxon royal family, she fled north to the Royal Scots Court during the Norman Conquest. Beautiful, intelligent and devout, Margaret won the heart of the Scottish king, Malcolm Canmore, and married him in 1069. She is credited with instigating the reform of the Church of Scotland, which had reached a low point in its history. In her private life, Margaret avidly prayed and gave lavishly to the poor. Her position allowed her to free many Anglo-Saxon prisoners.

You may not see yourself as a woman of influence. You may feel shy about sharing your faith with your kids, friends, family or coworkers. But there are many ways you can make a difference. You can refuse to give in to peer pressure or refuse to give up on a prodigal. You can speak out in the voting booth or on the editorial page. When you stand up for God's standards, you might be surprised—like a small pebble thrown into a large body of water, your words, actions and prayers can ripple outward if you muster up the courage to take a stand.

2 Chronicles 22:11

But Jehosheba, the daughter of King Jehoram, took Joash son of Ahaziah and stole him away from among the royal princes who were about to be murdered and put him and his nurse in a bedroom. Because Jehosheba, the daughter of King Jehoram and wife of the priest Jehoiada, was Ahaziah's sister, she hid the child from Athaliah so she could not kill him.

reflection

1 What women in your community are having a great impact?

2 Over whom do you have the most influence?

3 As you reflect on Jehosheba and Queen Margaret, determine how you can inspire those around you for the kingdom of God.

RELATED READINGS

Exodus 1:15–17;
Matthew 10:32–33;
1 Peter 2:9–10

Wednesday

Go to page 548 for your next devotional reading.

temple of the LORD except the priests and Levites on duty; they may enter because they are consecrated, but all the other men are to guard what the LORD has assigned to them.[a] 7The Levites are to station themselves around the king, each man with his weapons in his hand. Anyone who enters the temple must be put to death. Stay close to the king wherever he goes."

8The Levites and all the men of Judah did just as Jehoiada the priest ordered. Each one took his men—those who were going on duty on the Sabbath and those who were going off duty—for Jehoiada the priest had not released any of the divisions. 9Then he gave the commanders of units of a hundred the spears and the large and small shields that had belonged to King David and that were in the temple of God. 10He stationed all the men, each with his weapon in his hand, around the king—near the altar and the temple, from the south side to the north side of the temple.

11Jehoiada and his sons brought out the king's son and put the crown on him; they presented him with a copy of the covenant and proclaimed him king. They anointed him and shouted, "Long live the king!"

12When Athaliah heard the noise of the people running and cheering the king, she went to them at the temple of the LORD. 13She looked, and there was the king, standing by his pillar at the entrance. The officers and the trumpeters were beside the king, and all the people of the land were rejoicing and blowing trumpets, and singers with musical instruments were leading the praises. Then Athaliah tore her robes and shouted, "Treason! Treason!"

14Jehoiada the priest sent out the commanders of units of a hundred, who were in charge of the troops, and said to them: "Bring her out between the ranks[b] and put to the sword anyone who follows her." For the priest had said, "Do not put her to death at the temple of the LORD." 15So they seized her as she reached the entrance of the Horse Gate on the palace grounds, and there they put her to death.

16Jehoiada then made a covenant that he and the people and the king[c] would be the LORD's people. 17All the people went to the temple of Baal and tore it down. They smashed the altars and idols and killed Mattan the priest of Baal in front of the altars.

18Then Jehoiada placed the oversight of the temple of the LORD in the hands of the priests, who were Levites, to whom David had made assignments in the temple, to present the burnt offerings of the LORD as written in the Law of Moses, with rejoicing and singing, as David had ordered. 19He also stationed doorkeepers at the gates of the LORD's temple so that no one who was in any way unclean might enter.

20He took with him the commanders of hundreds, the nobles, the rulers of the people and all the people of the land and brought the king down from the temple of the LORD. They went into the palace through the Upper Gate and seated the king on the royal throne, 21and all the people of the land rejoiced. And the city was quiet, because Athaliah had been slain with the sword.

Joash Repairs the Temple

24 Joash was seven years old when he became king, and he reigned in Jerusalem forty years. His mother's name was Zibiah; she was from Beersheba. 2Joash did what was right in the eyes of the LORD all the years of Jehoiada the priest. 3Jehoiada chose two wives for him, and he had sons and daughters.

4Some time later Joash decided to restore the temple of the LORD. 5He called together the priests and Levites and said to them, "Go to the towns of Judah and collect the money due annually from all Israel, to repair the temple of your God. Do it now." But the Levites did not act at once.

6Therefore the king summoned Jehoiada the chief priest and said to him, "Why haven't you required the Levites to bring in from Judah and Jerusalem the tax imposed by Moses the servant of the LORD and by the assembly of Israel for the Tent of the Testimony?"

7Now the sons of that wicked woman Athaliah had broken into the temple of God and had used even its sacred objects for the Baals.

8At the king's command, a chest was made and placed outside, at the gate of the temple of the LORD. 9A proclamation was then issued in

---

[a]6 Or to observe the LORD's command not to enter, [b]14 Or out from the precincts [c]16 Or covenant between the LORD and the people and the king that they (see 2 Kings 11:17)

Judah and Jerusalem that they should bring to the LORD the tax that Moses the servant of God had required of Israel in the desert. [10]All the officials and all the people brought their contributions gladly, dropping them into the chest until it was full. [11]Whenever the chest was brought in by the Levites to the king's officials and they saw that there was a large amount of money, the royal secretary and the officer of the chief priest would come and empty the chest and carry it back to its place. They did this regularly and collected a great amount of money. [12]The king and Jehoiada gave it to the men who carried out the work required for the temple of the LORD. They hired masons and carpenters to restore the LORD's temple, and also workers in iron and bronze to repair the temple.

[13]The men in charge of the work were diligent, and the repairs progressed under them. They rebuilt the temple of God according to its original design and reinforced it. [14]When they had finished, they brought the rest of the money to the king and Jehoiada, and with it were made articles for the LORD's temple: articles for the service and for the burnt offerings, and also dishes and other objects of gold and silver. As long as Jehoiada lived, burnt offerings were presented continually in the temple of the LORD.

[15]Now Jehoiada was old and full of years, and he died at the age of a hundred and thirty. [16]He was buried with the kings in the City of David, because of the good he had done in Israel for God and his temple.

The Wickedness of Joash

[17]After the death of Jehoiada, the officials of Judah came and paid homage to the king, and he listened to them. [18]They abandoned the temple of the LORD, the God of their fathers, and worshiped Asherah poles and idols. Because of their guilt, God's anger came upon Judah and Jerusalem. [19]Although the LORD sent prophets to the people to bring them back to him, and though they testified against them, they would not listen.

> **2 Chronicles 24:19**
>
> *God Sends People to Speak for Him*
>
> Although the LORD sent prophets to the people to bring them back to him, and though they testified against them, they would not listen.

[20]Then the Spirit of God came upon Zechariah son of Jehoiada the priest. He stood before the people and said, "This is what God says: 'Why do you disobey the LORD's commands? You will not prosper. Because you have forsaken the LORD, he has forsaken you.'"

[21]But they plotted against him, and by order of the king they stoned him to death in the courtyard of the LORD's temple. [22]King Joash did not remember the kindness Zechariah's father Jehoiada had shown him but killed his son, who said as he lay dying, "May the LORD see this and call you to account."

[23]At the turn of the year,[a] the army of Aram marched against Joash; it invaded Judah and Jerusalem and killed all the leaders of the people. They sent all the plunder to their king in Damascus. [24]Although the Aramean army had come with only a few men, the LORD delivered into their hands a much larger army. Because Judah had forsaken the LORD, the God of their fathers, judgment was executed on Joash. [25]When the Arameans withdrew, they left Joash severely wounded. His officials conspired against him for murdering the son of Jehoiada the priest, and they killed him in his bed. So he died and was buried in the City of David, but not in the tombs of the kings.

[26]Those who conspired against him were Zabad,[b] son of Shimeath an Ammonite woman, and Jehozabad, son of Shimrith[c] a Moabite woman. [27]The account of his sons, the many prophecies about him, and the record of the restoration of the temple of God are written in the annotations on the book of the kings. And Amaziah his son succeeded him as king.

Amaziah King of Judah

25 Amaziah was twenty-five years old when he became king, and he reigned in Jerusalem twenty-nine years. His mother's

---

[a]23 Probably in the spring   [b]26 A variant of *Jozabad*   [c]26 A variant of *Shomer*

name was Jehoaddin[a]; she was from Jerusalem. ²He did what was right in the eyes of the LORD, but not wholeheartedly. ³After the kingdom was firmly in his control, he executed the officials who had murdered his father the king. ⁴Yet he did not put their sons to death, but acted in accordance with what is written in the Law, in the Book of Moses, where the LORD commanded: "Fathers shall not be put to death for their children, nor children put to death for their fathers; each is to die for his own sins."[b]

⁵Amaziah called the people of Judah together and assigned them according to their families to commanders of thousands and commanders of hundreds for all Judah and Benjamin. He then mustered those twenty years old or more and found that there were three hundred thousand men ready for military service, able to handle the spear and shield. ⁶He also hired a hundred thousand fighting men from Israel for a hundred talents[c] of silver.

⁷But a man of God came to him and said, "O king, these troops from Israel must not march with you, for the LORD is not with Israel—not with any of the people of Ephraim. ⁸Even if you go and fight courageously in battle, God will overthrow you before the enemy, for God has the power to help or to overthrow."

⁹Amaziah asked the man of God, "But what about the hundred talents I paid for these Israelite troops?"

The man of God replied, "The LORD can give you much more than that."

¹⁰So Amaziah dismissed the troops who had come to him from Ephraim and sent them home. They were furious with Judah and left for home in a great rage.

¹¹Amaziah then marshaled his strength and led his army to the Valley of Salt, where he killed ten thousand men of Seir. ¹²The army of Judah also captured ten thousand men alive, took them to the top of a cliff and threw them down so that all were dashed to pieces.

2 Chronicles 25:9

God Has Unlimited Wealth

Amaziah asked the man of God, "But what about the hundred talents I paid for these Israelite troops?" The man of God replied, "The LORD can give you much more than that."

¹³Meanwhile the troops that Amaziah had sent back and had not allowed to take part in the war raided Judean towns from Samaria to Beth Horon. They killed three thousand people and carried off great quantities of plunder.

¹⁴When Amaziah returned from slaughtering the Edomites, he brought back the gods of the people of Seir. He set them up as his own gods, bowed down to them and burned sacrifices to them. ¹⁵The anger of the LORD burned against Amaziah, and he sent a prophet to him, who said, "Why do you consult this people's gods, which could not save their own people from your hand?"

¹⁶While he was still speaking, the king said to him, "Have we appointed you an adviser to the king? Stop! Why be struck down?"

So the prophet stopped but said, "I know that God has determined to destroy you, because you have done this and have not listened to my counsel."

¹⁷After Amaziah king of Judah consulted his advisers, he sent this challenge to Jehoash[d] son of Jehoahaz, the son of Jehu, king of Israel: "Come, meet me face to face."

¹⁸But Jehoash king of Israel replied to Amaziah king of Judah: "A thistle in Lebanon sent a message to a cedar in Lebanon, 'Give your daughter to my son in marriage.' Then a wild beast in Lebanon came along and trampled the thistle underfoot. ¹⁹You say to yourself that you have defeated Edom, and now you are arrogant and proud. But stay at home! Why ask for trouble and cause your own downfall and that of Judah also?"

²⁰Amaziah, however, would not listen, for God so worked that he might hand them over to ₁Jehoash₁, because they sought the gods of Edom. ²¹So Jehoash king of Israel attacked. He and Amaziah king of Judah faced each other at Beth Shemesh in Judah. ²²Judah was routed by Israel, and every man fled to his home. ²³Jehoash king of Israel cap-

---

*a*1 Hebrew *Jehoaddan*, a variant of *Jehoaddin*   *b*4 Deut. 24:16   *c*6 That is, about 3 3/4 tons (about 3.4 metric tons); also in verse 9   *d*17 Hebrew *Joash*, a variant of *Jehoash*; also in verses 18, 21, 23 and 25 tured Amaziah king of Judah, the son of Joash, the son of Ahaziah,[a] at Beth Shemesh. Then Jehoash brought him to Jerusalem and broke down the wall of Jerusalem from the Ephraim Gate to the Corner Gate—a section about six hundred feet[b] long. 24He took all the gold and silver and all the articles found in the temple of God that had been in the care of Obed-Edom, together with the palace treasures and the hostages, and returned to Samaria.

25Amaziah son of Joash king of Judah lived for fifteen years after the death of Jehoash son of Jehoahaz king of Israel. 26As for the other events of Amaziah's reign, from beginning to end, are they not written in the book of the kings of Judah and Israel? 27From the time that Amaziah turned away from following the Lord, they conspired against him in Jerusalem and he fled to Lachish, but they sent men after him to Lachish and killed him there. 28He was brought back by horse and was buried with his fathers in the City of Judah.

Uzziah King of Judah

26 Then all the people of Judah took Uzziah,[c] who was sixteen years old, and made him king in place of his father Amaziah. 2He was the one who rebuilt Elath and restored it to Judah after Amaziah rested with his fathers.

3Uzziah was sixteen years old when he became king, and he reigned in Jerusalem fifty-two years. His mother's name was Jecoliah; she was from Jerusalem. 4He did what was right in the eyes of the Lord, just as his father Amaziah had done. 5He sought God during the days of Zechariah, who instructed him in the fear[d] of God. As long as he sought the Lord, God gave him success.

6He went to war against the Philistines and broke down the walls of Gath, Jabneh and Ashdod. He then rebuilt towns near Ashdod and elsewhere among the Philistines. 7God helped him against the Philistines and against the Arabs who lived in Gur Baal and against the Meunites. 8The Ammonites brought tribute to Uzziah, and his fame spread as far as the border of Egypt, because he had become very powerful.

9Uzziah built towers in Jerusalem at the Corner Gate, at the Valley Gate and at the angle of the wall, and he fortified them. 10He also built towers in the desert and dug many cisterns, because he had much livestock in the foothills and in the plain. He had people working his fields and vineyards in the hills and in the fertile lands, for he loved the soil.

11Uzziah had a well-trained army, ready to go out by divisions according to their numbers as mustered by Jeiel the secretary and Maaseiah the officer under the direction of Hananiah, one of the royal officials. 12The total number of family leaders over the fighting men was 2,600. 13Under their command was an army of 307,500 men trained for war, a powerful force to support the king against his enemies. 14Uzziah provided shields, spears, helmets, coats of armor, bows and slingstones for the entire army. 15In Jerusalem he made machines designed by skillful men for use on the towers and on the corner defenses to shoot arrows and hurl large stones. His fame spread far and wide, for he was greatly helped until he became powerful.

16But after Uzziah became powerful, his pride led to his downfall. He was unfaithful to the Lord his God, and entered the temple of the Lord to burn incense on the altar of incense. 17Azariah the priest with eighty other courageous priests of the Lord followed him in. 18They confronted him and said, "It is not right for you, Uzziah, to burn incense to the Lord. That is for the priests, the descendants of Aaron, who have been consecrated to burn incense. Leave the sanctuary, for you have been unfaithful; and you will not be honored by the Lord God."

19Uzziah, who had a censer in his hand ready to burn incense, became angry. While he was raging at the priests in their presence before the incense altar in the Lord's temple, leprosy[e] broke out on his forehead. 20When Azariah the chief priest and all the other priests looked at him, they saw that he had leprosy on his forehead, so they hurried him out. Indeed, he himself was eager to leave, because the Lord had afflicted him.

---

[a]23 Hebrew *Jehoahaz*, a variant of *Ahaziah*   [b]23 Hebrew *four hundred cubits* (about 180 meters)   [c]1 Also called *Azariah*   [d]5 Many Hebrew manuscripts, Septuagint and Syriac; other Hebrew manuscripts *vision*   [e]19 The Hebrew word was used for various diseases affecting the skin—not necessarily leprosy; also in verses 20, 21 and 23.

The Good and Bad of Pride

2 Chronicles 26:16

But after Uzziah became
powerful, his pride led
to his downfall.

reflection

1 What are the things
you take a healthy pride
in (for example, your abilities, children, etc.)? Do you
have trouble acknowledg-
ing that you do some things
well?

2 What things has God
done in and through
your life that you can boast
about?

3 How does God's work
in your life cause you to
feel less proud and more
humble?

RELATED READINGS

Psalm 10:4–18;
Proverbs 16:18–20; 22:4;
James 3:13–16

Read: 2 Chronicles 26:1–23

IT'S INTERESTING HOW one simple word can conjure up two
opposing connotations. For example, when you hear the word
food, do you respond by feeling grateful for the nutritional elements of food or are you plagued with guilt for indulging in less
than healthy choices? Some foods can build up your health; other
foods tear it down.

The word *pride* also has two connotations. In the context of
self-respect and dignity, pride motivates us to tend to our health
and general well-being and to appreciate our God-given talents
and strengths. We don't often talk about this kind of pride.

The flip side of pride offers a warning—with good reason. The
evil inclination of pride contains self-centeredness that leads downward. Rather than building spiritual health, the other side of pride
carves out a path of destruction: arrogance, conceit and egotism.

Crowned king at the tender age of 16, Uzziah knew success
as long as he sought God. But his career as king careened out of
control when pride clouded his vision of himself and of God. Within
this chapter, we observe how a once good king spiritually declined
to a leprous and isolated man. What a prime example of the
adage, "Power corrupts." King Uzziah's power and fame inflated
the evil inclinations of his pride, which ultimately led to
his downfall.

Have you ever witnessed the downfall of another person? Have
you watched someone make a horrible choice when you knew they
should stop and turn around? Maybe you watched your parents
divorce, and nothing you said made a difference. Maybe right now
you're watching a child that you love turn prodigal, and your heart
is breaking because she's choosing not to listen to you or God.

So how do we cultivate the right kind of pride in our lives?
Just as a healthy diet requires the right balance of foods, the right
kind of pride requires balancing humility with a right relationship
with God. When we understand that the positive and wonderful
gifts he's given us come directly from him, we learn to cultivate
healthy pride, not in ourselves, but in the Lord who has given us
everything. As Paul wrote, "Let him who boasts boast in the Lord"
(2 Corinthians 10:17).

Thursday

Go to page 551 for your next devotional reading.

²¹King Uzziah had leprosy until the day he died. He lived in a separate house*ᵃ*—leprous, and excluded from the temple of the LORD. Jotham his son had charge of the palace and governed the people of the land.

²²The other events of Uzziah's reign, from beginning to end, are recorded by the prophet Isaiah son of Amoz. ²³Uzziah rested with his fathers and was buried near them in a field for burial that belonged to the kings, for people said, "He had leprosy." And Jotham his son succeeded him as king.

Jotham King of Judah

27 Jotham was twenty-five years old when he became king, and he reigned in Jerusalem sixteen years. His mother's name was Jerusha daughter of Zadok. ²He did what was right in the eyes of the LORD, just as his father Uzziah had done, but unlike him he did not enter the temple of the LORD. The people, however, continued their corrupt practices. ³Jotham rebuilt the Upper Gate of the temple of the LORD and did extensive work on the wall at the hill of Ophel. ⁴He built towns in the Judean hills and forts and towers in the wooded areas.

⁵Jotham made war on the king of the Ammonites and conquered them. That year the Ammonites paid him a hundred talents*ᵇ* of silver, ten thousand cors*ᶜ* of wheat and ten thousand cors of barley. The Ammonites brought him the same amount also in the second and third years.

⁶Jotham grew powerful because he walked steadfastly before the LORD his God.

⁷The other events in Jotham's reign, including all his wars and the other things he did, are written in the book of the kings of Israel and Judah. ⁸He was twenty-five years old when he became king, and he reigned in Jerusalem sixteen years. ⁹Jotham rested with his fathers and was buried in the City of David. And Ahaz his son succeeded him as king.

Ahaz King of Judah

28 Ahaz was twenty years old when he became king, and he reigned in Jerusalem sixteen years. Unlike David his father, he did not do what was right in the eyes of the LORD. ²He walked in the ways of the kings of Israel and also made cast idols for worshiping the Baals. ³He burned sacrifices in the Valley of Ben Hinnom and sacrificed his sons in the fire, following the detestable ways of the nations the LORD had driven out before the Israelites. ⁴He offered sacrifices and burned incense at the high places, on the hilltops and under every spreading tree.

⁵Therefore the LORD his God handed him over to the king of Aram. The Arameans defeated him and took many of his people as prisoners and brought them to Damascus.

He was also given into the hands of the king of Israel, who inflicted heavy casualties on him. ⁶In one day Pekah son of Remaliah killed a hundred and twenty thousand soldiers in Judah—because Judah had forsaken the LORD, the God of their fathers. ⁷Zicri, an Ephraimite warrior, killed Maaseiah the king's son, Azrikam the officer in charge of the palace, and Elkanah, second to the king. ⁸The Israelites took captive from their kinsmen two hundred thousand wives, sons and daughters. They also took a great deal of plunder, which they carried back to Samaria.

⁹But a prophet of the LORD named Oded was there, and he went out to meet the army when it returned to Samaria. He said to them, "Because the LORD, the God of your fathers, was angry with Judah, he gave them into your hand. But you have slaughtered them in a rage that reaches to heaven. ¹⁰And now you intend to make the men and women of Judah and Jerusalem your slaves. But aren't you also guilty of sins against the LORD your God? ¹¹Now listen to me! Send back your fellow countrymen you have taken as prisoners, for the LORD's fierce anger rests on you."

¹²Then some of the leaders in Ephraim—Azariah son of Jehohanan, Berekiah son of Meshillemoth, Jehizkiah son of Shallum, and Amasa son of Hadlai—confronted those who were arriving from the war. ¹³"You must not bring those prisoners here," they said, "or we will be guilty before the LORD. Do you intend to add to our sin and guilt? For our guilt is

---

*ᵃ*21 Or *in a house where he was relieved of responsibilities*   *ᵇ*5 That is, about 3 3/4 tons (about 3.4 metric tons)   *ᶜ*5 That is, probably about 62,000 bushels (about 2,200 kiloliters) already great, and his fierce anger rests on Israel."

14 So the soldiers gave up the prisoners and plunder in the presence of the officials and all the assembly. 15 The men designated by name took the prisoners, and from the plunder they clothed all who were naked. They provided them with clothes and sandals, food and drink, and healing balm. All those who were weak they put on donkeys. So they took them back to their fellow countrymen at Jericho, the City of Palms, and returned to Samaria.

16 At that time King Ahaz sent to the king[a] of Assyria for help. 17 The Edomites had again come and attacked Judah and carried away prisoners, 18 while the Philistines had raided towns in the foothills and in the Negev of Judah. They captured and occupied Beth Shemesh, Aijalon and Gederoth, as well as Soco, Timnah and Gimzo, with their surrounding villages. 19 The LORD had humbled Judah because of Ahaz king of Israel,[b] for he had promoted wickedness in Judah and had been most unfaithful to the LORD. 20 Tiglath-Pileser[c] king of Assyria came to him, but he gave him trouble instead of help. 21 Ahaz took some of the things from the temple of the LORD and from the royal palace and from the princes and presented them to the king of Assyria, but that did not help him.

22 In his time of trouble King Ahaz became even more unfaithful to the LORD. 23 He offered sacrifices to the gods of Damascus, who had defeated him; for he thought, "Since the gods of the kings of Aram have helped them, I will sacrifice to them so they will help me." But they were his downfall and the downfall of all Israel.

24 Ahaz gathered together the furnishings from the temple of God and took them away.[d] He shut the doors of the LORD's temple and set up altars at every street corner in Jerusalem. 25 In every town in Judah he built high places to burn sacrifices to other gods and provoked the LORD, the God of his fathers, to anger.

26 The other events of his reign and all his ways, from beginning to end, are written in the book of the kings of Judah and Israel. 27 Ahaz rested with his fathers and was buried in the city of Jerusalem, but he was not placed in the tombs of the kings of Israel. And Hezekiah his son succeeded him as king.

Hezekiah Purifies the Temple

29 Hezekiah was twenty-five years old when he became king, and he reigned in Jerusalem twenty-nine years. His mother's name was Abijah daughter of Zechariah. 2 He did what was right in the eyes of the LORD, just as his father David had done.

3 In the first month of the first year of his reign, he opened the doors of the temple of the LORD and repaired them. 4 He brought in the priests and the Levites, assembled them in the square on the east side 5 and said: "Listen to me, Levites! Consecrate yourselves now and consecrate the temple of the LORD, the God of your fathers. Remove all defilement from the sanctuary. 6 Our fathers were unfaithful; they did evil in the eyes of the LORD our God and forsook him. They turned their faces away from the LORD's dwelling place and turned their backs on him. 7 They also shut the doors of the portico and put out the lamps. They did not burn incense or present any burnt offerings at the sanctuary to the God of Israel. 8 Therefore, the anger of the LORD has fallen on Judah and Jerusalem; he has made them an object of dread and horror and scorn, as you can see with your own eyes. 9 This is why our fathers have fallen by the sword and why our sons and daughters and our wives are in captivity. 10 Now I intend to make a covenant with the LORD, the God of Israel, so that his fierce anger will turn away from us. 11 My sons, do not be negligent now, for the LORD has

2 Chronicles 29:10

God Withholds His Wrath

"Now I intend to make a covenant with the LORD, the God of Israel, so that his fierce anger will turn away from us."

---

[a]16 One Hebrew manuscript, Septuagint and Vulgate (see also 2 Kings 16:7); most Hebrew manuscripts *kings*   [b]19 That is, Judah, as frequently in 2 Chronicles   [c]20 Hebrew *Tilgath-Pilneser*, a variant of *Tiglath-Pileser*   [d]24 Or *and cut them up*

First Things First

Read: 2 Chronicles 29:1–11

WHAT WOULD YOU do if you were elected president of the world? What would be the first thing on your official to-do list? Eliminate world hunger? Disarm all nuclear weapons? Wipe out poverty?

Hezekiah was only 25 years old when he became king of Judah. His first priority was to repair the temple and reestablish worship, helping the people reconnect with God. In 2 Kings we're told that "Hezekiah trusted in the LORD, the God of Israel. There was no one like him among all the kings of Judah, either before him or after him . . . And the LORD was with him; he was successful in whatever he undertook" (2 Kings 18:5,7). Hezekiah's most notable accomplishment in his 29-year reign was drawing his people back to God.

Most likely you will not be chosen to rule a country, but you are the queen of your castle—your home. So what is the first thing on your to-do list each day? What is your number one priority? Eliminate your kids' hunger? Disarm family disputes? Tackle the budget? Or when you get up, do you put your house in order by first putting your heart in order? The best way to run a home, a business or a country is from your knees in prayer.

Take a cue from Hezekiah . . . and from David and Jesus. Each of them gave their relationship with God top priority. David wrote, "The LORD has heard my cry for mercy; the LORD accepts my prayer" (Psalm 6:9). "Jesus got up, left the house and went off to a solitary place, where he prayed" (Mark 1:35). They both put first things first by spending time with God even in the midst of other pressing needs.

Like Hezekiah, we have only a short time to make a difference to those in our small kingdoms. We cannot afford not to avail ourselves of God's wisdom and strength. Open the doors of your heart's temple and keep them open as you go about your day, submitting your thoughts and actions to God. Think of Jesus sitting beside you while you drive, in your office, at the kitchen table—and talk to him as you would a friend. And whenever possible, schedule extended prayer times into your life when you can choose "what is better" (Luke 10:42) by sitting at his feet and listening to him.

---

2 Chronicles 29:3

In the first month of the first year of his reign, he opened the doors of the temple of the LORD and repaired them.

reflection

1 You really are the "queen of your house." What things need your attention each day?

2 What do you see as important in your life?

3 How is God asking you to adjust your priorities to put first things first?

RELATED READINGS

2 Chronicles 7:12–16;
Psalm 5:1–3;
Luke 10:38–42;
1 Thessalonians 5:16–18

"If God is not first in our thoughts and efforts in the morning, he will be in the last place the remainder of the day."

E. M. Bounds

Go to page 564 for your next devotional reading.

chosen you to stand before him and serve him, to minister before him and to burn incense."

12 Then these Levites set to work:

from the Kohathites,

Mahath son of Amasai and Joel son of Azariah;

from the Merarites,

Kish son of Abdi and Azariah son of Jehallelel;

from the Gershonites,

Joah son of Zimmah and Eden son of Joah;

13 from the descendants of Elizaphan,

Shimri and Jeiel;

from the descendants of Asaph,

Zechariah and Mattaniah;

14 from the descendants of Heman,

Jehiel and Shimei;

from the descendants of Jeduthun,

Shemaiah and Uzziel.

15 When they had assembled their brothers and consecrated themselves, they went in to purify the temple of the LORD, as the king had ordered, following the word of the LORD. 16 The priests went into the sanctuary of the LORD to purify it. They brought out to the courtyard of the LORD's temple everything unclean that they found in the temple of the LORD. The Levites took it and carried it out to the Kidron Valley. 17 They began the consecration on the first day of the first month, and by the eighth day of the month they reached the portico of the LORD. For eight more days they consecrated the temple of the LORD itself, finishing on the sixteenth day of the first month.

18 Then they went in to King Hezekiah and reported: "We have purified the entire temple of the LORD, the altar of burnt offering with all its utensils, and the table for setting out the consecrated bread, with all its articles. 19 We have prepared and consecrated all the articles that King Ahaz removed in his unfaithfulness while he was king. They are now in front of the LORD's altar."

20 Early the next morning King Hezekiah gathered the city officials together and went up to the temple of the LORD. 21 They brought seven bulls, seven rams, seven male lambs and seven male goats as a sin offering for the kingdom, for the sanctuary and for Judah. The king commanded the priests, the descendants of Aaron, to offer these on the altar of the LORD. 22 So they slaughtered the bulls, and the priests took the blood and sprinkled it on the altar; next they slaughtered the rams and sprinkled their blood on the altar; then they slaughtered the lambs and sprinkled their blood on the altar. 23 The goats for the sin offering were brought before the king and the assembly, and they laid their hands on them. 24 The priests then slaughtered the goats and presented their blood on the altar for a sin offering to atone for all Israel, because the king had ordered the burnt offering and the sin offering for all Israel.

25 He stationed the Levites in the temple of the LORD with cymbals, harps and lyres in the way prescribed by David and Gad the king's seer and Nathan the prophet; this was commanded by the LORD through his prophets. 26 So the Levites stood ready with David's instruments, and the priests with their trumpets.

27 Hezekiah gave the order to sacrifice the burnt offering on the altar. As the offering began, singing to the LORD began also, accompanied by trumpets and the instruments of David king of Israel. 28 The whole assembly bowed in worship, while the singers sang and the trumpeters played. All this continued until the sacrifice of the burnt offering was completed.

29 When the offerings were finished, the king and everyone present with him knelt down and worshiped. 30 King Hezekiah and his officials ordered the Levites to praise the LORD with the words of David and of Asaph the seer. So they sang praises with gladness and bowed their heads and worshiped.

31 Then Hezekiah said, "You have now dedicated yourselves to the LORD. Come and bring sacrifices and thank offerings to the temple of the LORD." So the assembly brought sacrifices and thank offerings, and all whose hearts were willing brought burnt offerings.

32 The number of burnt offerings the assembly brought was seventy bulls, a hundred rams and two hundred male lambs—all of them for burnt offerings to the LORD. 33 The animals consecrated as sacrifices amounted to six hundred bulls and three thousand sheep and goats. 34 The priests, however, were too few to skin all the burnt offerings; so their kinsmen the Le-

vites helped them until the task was finished and until other priests had been consecrated, for the Levites had been more conscientious in consecrating themselves than the priests had been. ³⁵There were burnt offerings in abundance, together with the fat of the fellowship offerings*a* and the drink offerings that accompanied the burnt offerings.

So the service of the temple of the LORD was reestablished. ³⁶Hezekiah and all the people rejoiced at what God had brought about for his people, because it was done so quickly.

Hezekiah Celebrates the Passover

30 Hezekiah sent word to all Israel and Judah and also wrote letters to Ephraim and Manasseh, inviting them to come to the temple of the LORD in Jerusalem and celebrate the Passover to the LORD, the God of Israel. ²The king and his officials and the whole assembly in Jerusalem decided to celebrate the Passover in the second month. ³They had not been able to celebrate it at the regular time because not enough priests had consecrated themselves and the people had not assembled in Jerusalem. ⁴The plan seemed right both to the king and to the whole assembly. ⁵They decided to send a proclamation throughout Israel, from Beersheba to Dan, calling the people to come to Jerusalem and celebrate the Passover to the LORD, the God of Israel. It had not been celebrated in large numbers according to what was written.

⁶At the king's command, couriers went throughout Israel and Judah with letters from the king and from his officials, which read:

"People of Israel, return to the LORD, the God of Abraham, Isaac and Israel, that he may return to you who are left, who have escaped from the hand of the kings of Assyria. ⁷Do not be like your fathers and brothers, who were unfaithful to the LORD, the God of their fathers, so that he

made them an object of horror, as you see. ⁸Do not be stiff-necked, as your fathers were; submit to the LORD. Come to the sanctuary, which he has consecrated forever. Serve the LORD your God, so that his fierce anger will turn away from you. ⁹If you return to the LORD, then your brothers and your children will be shown compassion by their captors and will come back to this land, for the LORD your God is gracious and compassionate. He will not turn his face from you if you return to him."

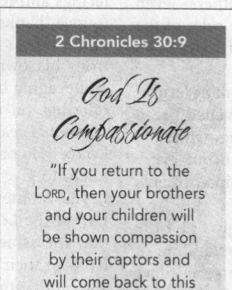

2 Chronicles 30:9

God Is Compassionate

"If you return to the LORD, then your brothers and your children will be shown compassion by their captors and will come back to this land, for the LORD your God is gracious and compassionate."

¹⁰The couriers went from town to town in Ephraim and Manasseh, as far as Zebulun, but the people scorned and ridiculed them. ¹¹Nevertheless, some men of Asher, Manasseh and Zebulun humbled themselves and went to Jerusalem. ¹²Also in Judah the hand of God was on the people to give them unity of mind to carry out what the king and his officials had ordered, following the word of the LORD.

¹³A very large crowd of people assembled in Jerusalem to celebrate the Feast of Unleavened Bread in the second month. ¹⁴They removed the altars in Jerusalem and cleared away the incense altars and threw them into the Kidron Valley.

¹⁵They slaughtered the Passover lamb on the fourteenth day of the second month. The priests and the Levites were ashamed and consecrated themselves and brought burnt offerings to the temple of the LORD. ¹⁶Then they took up their regular positions as prescribed in the Law of Moses the man of God. The priests sprinkled the blood handed to them by the Levites. ¹⁷Since many in the crowd had not consecrated themselves, the Levites had to kill the Passover lambs for all those who were not ceremonially clean and could not consecrate their lambs to the LORD. ¹⁸Although most of the many people who came from Ephraim, Manasseh, Issachar and Zebulun had not purified

*a*35 Traditionally *peace offerings*

themselves, yet they ate the Passover, contrary to what was written. But Hezekiah prayed for them, saying, "May the LORD, who is good, pardon everyone **19**who sets his heart on seeking God—the LORD, the God of his fathers—even if he is not clean according to the rules of the sanctuary." **20**And the LORD heard Hezekiah and healed the people.

21The Israelites who were present in Jerusalem celebrated the Feast of Unleavened Bread for seven days with great rejoicing, while the Levites and priests sang to the LORD every day, accompanied by the LORD's instruments of praise.*a*

22Hezekiah spoke encouragingly to all the Levites, who showed good understanding of the service of the LORD. For the seven days they ate their assigned portion and offered fellowship offerings*b* and praised the LORD, the God of their fathers.

23The whole assembly then agreed to celebrate the festival seven more days; so for another seven days they celebrated joyfully. **24**Hezekiah king of Judah provided a thousand bulls and seven thousand sheep and goats for the assembly, and the officials provided them with a thousand bulls and ten thousand sheep and goats. A great number of priests consecrated themselves. **25**The entire assembly of Judah rejoiced, along with the priests and Levites and all who had assembled from Israel, including the aliens who had come from Israel and those who lived in Judah. **26**There was great joy in Jerusalem, for since the days of Solomon son of David king of Israel there had been nothing like this in Jerusalem. **27**The priests and the Levites stood to bless the people, and God heard them, for their prayer reached heaven, his holy dwelling place.

31 When all this had ended, the Israelites who were there went out to the towns of Judah, smashed the sacred stones and cut down the Asherah poles. They destroyed the high places and the altars throughout Judah and Benjamin and in Ephraim and Manasseh. After they had destroyed all of them, the Israelites returned to their own towns and to their own property.

Contributions for Worship

2Hezekiah assigned the priests and Levites to divisions—each of them according to their duties as priests or Levites—to offer burnt offerings and fellowship offerings,*b* to minister, to give thanks and to sing praises at the gates of the LORD's dwelling. **3**The king contributed from his own possessions for the morning and evening burnt offerings and for the burnt offerings on the Sabbaths, New Moons and appointed feasts as written in the Law of the LORD. **4**He ordered the people living in Jerusalem to give the portion due the priests and Levites so they could devote themselves to the Law of the LORD. **5**As soon as the order went out, the Israelites generously gave the firstfruits of their grain, new wine, oil and honey and all that the fields produced. They brought a great amount, a tithe of everything. **6**The men of Israel and Judah who lived in the towns of Judah also brought a tithe of their herds and flocks and a tithe of the holy things dedicated to the LORD their God, and they piled them in heaps. **7**They began doing this in the third month and finished in the seventh month. **8**When Hezekiah and his officials came and saw the heaps, they praised the LORD and blessed his people Israel.

9Hezekiah asked the priests and Levites about the heaps; **10**and Azariah the chief priest, from the family of Zadok, answered, "Since the people began to bring their contributions to the temple of the LORD, we have had enough to eat and plenty to spare, because the LORD has blessed his people, and this great amount is left over."

11Hezekiah gave orders to prepare storerooms in the temple of the LORD, and this was done. **12**Then they faithfully brought in the contributions, tithes and dedicated gifts. Conaniah, a Levite, was in charge of these things, and his brother Shimei was next in rank. **13**Jehiel, Azaziah, Nahath, Asahel, Jerimoth, Jozabad, Eliel, Ismakiah, Mahath and Benaiah were supervisors under Conaniah and Shimei his brother, by appointment of King Hezekiah and Azariah the official in charge of the temple of God.

14Kore son of Imnah the Levite, keeper of

---

*a*21 Or *priests praised the LORD every day with resounding instruments belonging to the LORD*   *b*22,2 Traditionally *peace offerings* the East Gate, was in charge of the freewill offerings given to God, distributing the contributions made to the LORD and also the consecrated gifts. ¹⁵Eden, Miniamin, Jeshua, Shemaiah, Amariah and Shecaniah assisted him faithfully in the towns of the priests, distributing to their fellow priests according to their divisions, old and young alike.

¹⁶In addition, they distributed to the males three years old or more whose names were in the genealogical records—all who would enter the temple of the LORD to perform the daily duties of their various tasks, according to their responsibilities and their divisions. ¹⁷And they distributed to the priests enrolled by their families in the genealogical records and likewise to the Levites twenty years old or more, according to their responsibilities and their divisions. ¹⁸They included all the little ones, the wives, and the sons and daughters of the whole community listed in these genealogical records. For they were faithful in consecrating themselves.

¹⁹As for the priests, the descendants of Aaron, who lived on the farm lands around their towns or in any other towns, men were designated by name to distribute portions to every male among them and to all who were recorded in the genealogies of the Levites.

²⁰This is what Hezekiah did throughout Judah, doing what was good and right and faithful before the LORD his God. ²¹In everything that he undertook in the service of God's temple and in obedience to the law and the commands, he sought his God and worked wholeheartedly. And so he prospered.

Sennacherib Threatens Jerusalem

32 After all that Hezekiah had so faithfully done, Sennacherib king of Assyria came and invaded Judah. He laid siege to the fortified cities, thinking to conquer them for himself. ²When Hezekiah saw that Sennacherib had come and that he intended to make war on Jerusalem, ³he consulted with his officials and military staff about blocking off the water from the springs outside the city, and they helped him. ⁴A large force of men assembled, and they blocked all the springs and the stream that flowed through the land. "Why should the kings*ᵃ* of Assyria come and find plenty of water?" they said. ⁵Then he worked hard repairing all the broken sections of the wall and building towers on it. He built another wall outside that one and reinforced the supporting terraces*ᵇ* of the City of David. He also made large numbers of weapons and shields.

⁶He appointed military officers over the people and assembled them before him in the square at the city gate and encouraged them with these words: ⁷"Be strong and courageous. Do not be afraid or discouraged because of the king of Assyria and the vast army with him, for there is a greater power with us than with him. ⁸With him is only the arm of flesh, but with us is the LORD our God to help us and to fight our battles." And the people gained confidence from what Hezekiah the king of Judah said.

2 Chronicles 32:8

God Aids His People

"With him is only the arm of flesh, but with us is our God to help us and to fight our battles."

⁹Later, when Sennacherib king of Assyria and all his forces were laying siege to Lachish, he sent his officers to Jerusalem with this message for Hezekiah king of Judah and for all the people of Judah who were there:

¹⁰"This is what Sennacherib king of Assyria says: On what are you basing your confidence, that you remain in Jerusalem under siege? ¹¹When Hezekiah says, 'The LORD our God will save us from the hand of the king of Assyria,' he is misleading you, to let you die of hunger and thirst. ¹²Did not Hezekiah himself remove this god's high places and altars, saying to Judah and Jerusalem, 'You must worship before one altar and burn sacrifices on it'?

¹³"Do you not know what I and my fathers have done to all the peoples of the other lands? Were the gods of those nations ever able to deliver their land from my hand? ¹⁴Who of all the gods of these

---

*ᵃ*4 Hebrew; Septuagint and Syriac *king* *ᵇ*5 Or *the Millo* nations that my fathers destroyed has been able to save his people from me? How then can your god deliver you from my hand? ¹⁵Now do not let Hezekiah deceive you and mislead you like this. Do not believe him, for no god of any nation or kingdom has been able to deliver his people from my hand or the hand of my fathers. How much less will your god deliver you from my hand!"

¹⁶Sennacherib's officers spoke further against the LORD God and against his servant Hezekiah. ¹⁷The king also wrote letters insulting the LORD, the God of Israel, and saying this against him: "Just as the gods of the peoples of the other lands did not rescue their people from my hand, so the god of Hezekiah will not rescue his people from my hand." ¹⁸Then they called out in Hebrew to the people of Jerusalem who were on the wall, to terrify them and make them afraid in order to capture the city. ¹⁹They spoke about the God of Jerusalem as they did about the gods of the other peoples of the world—the work of men's hands.

²⁰King Hezekiah and the prophet Isaiah son of Amoz cried out in prayer to heaven about this. ²¹And the LORD sent an angel, who annihilated all the fighting men and the leaders and officers in the camp of the Assyrian king. So he withdrew to his own land in disgrace. And when he went into the temple of his god, some of his sons cut him down with the sword.

²²So the LORD saved Hezekiah and the people of Jerusalem from the hand of Sennacherib king of Assyria and from the hand of all others. He took care of them^a on every side. ²³Many brought offerings to Jerusalem for the LORD and valuable gifts for Hezekiah king of Judah. From then on he was highly regarded by all the nations.

Hezekiah's Pride, Success and Death

²⁴In those days Hezekiah became ill and was at the point of death. He prayed to the LORD, who answered him and gave him a miraculous sign. ²⁵But Hezekiah's heart was proud and he did not respond to the kindness shown him; therefore the LORD's wrath was on him and

on Judah and Jerusalem. ²⁶Then Hezekiah repented of the pride of his heart, as did the people of Jerusalem; therefore the LORD's wrath did not come upon them during the days of Hezekiah.

²⁷Hezekiah had very great riches and honor, and he made treasuries for his silver and gold and for his precious stones, spices, shields and all kinds of valuables. ²⁸He also made buildings to store the harvest of grain, new wine and oil; and he made stalls for various kinds of cattle, and pens for the flocks. ²⁹He built villages and acquired great numbers of flocks and herds, for God had given him very great riches.

³⁰It was Hezekiah who blocked the upper outlet of the Gihon spring and channeled the water down to the west side of the City of David. He succeeded in everything he undertook. ³¹But when envoys were sent by the rulers of Babylon to ask him about the miraculous sign that had occurred in the land, God left him to test him and to know everything that was in his heart.

³²The other events of Hezekiah's reign and his acts of devotion are written in the vision of the prophet Isaiah son of Amoz in the book of the kings of Judah and Israel. ³³Hezekiah rested with his fathers and was buried on the hill where the tombs of David's descendants are. All Judah and the people of Jerusalem honored him when he died. And Manasseh his son succeeded him as king.

Manasseh King of Judah

33 Manasseh was twelve years old when he became king, and he reigned in Jerusalem fifty-five years. ²He did evil in the eyes of the LORD, following the detestable practices of the nations the LORD had driven out before the Israelites. ³He rebuilt the high places his father Hezekiah had demolished; he also erected altars to the Baals and made Asherah poles. He bowed down to all the starry hosts and worshiped them. ⁴He built altars in the temple of the LORD, of which the LORD had said, "My Name will remain in Jerusalem forever." ⁵In both courts of the temple of the LORD, he built altars to all the starry hosts. ⁶He sacrificed his sons in^b the fire in the Valley of Ben Hinnom,

---

^a22 Hebrew; Septuagint and Vulgate *He gave them rest*   ^b6 Or *He made his sons pass through*

practiced sorcery, divination and witchcraft, and consulted mediums and spiritists. He did much evil in the eyes of the LORD, provoking him to anger.

7He took the carved image he had made and put it in God's temple, of which God had said to David and to his son Solomon, "In this temple and in Jerusalem, which I have chosen out of all the tribes of Israel, I will put my Name forever. 8I will not again make the feet of the Israelites leave the land I assigned to your forefathers, if only they will be careful to do everything I commanded them concerning all the laws, decrees and ordinances given through Moses." 9But Manasseh led Judah and the people of Jerusalem astray, so that they did more evil than the nations the LORD had destroyed before the Israelites.

10The LORD spoke to Manasseh and his people, but they paid no attention. 11So the LORD brought against them the army commanders of the king of Assyria, who took Manasseh prisoner, put a hook in his nose, bound him with bronze shackles and took him to Babylon. 12In his distress he sought the favor of the LORD his God and humbled himself greatly before the God of his fathers. 13And when he prayed to him, the LORD was moved by his entreaty and listened to his plea; so he brought him back to Jerusalem and to his kingdom. Then Manasseh knew that the LORD is God.

14Afterward he rebuilt the outer wall of the City of David, west of the Gihon spring in the valley, as far as the entrance of the Fish Gate and encircling the hill of Ophel; he also made it much higher. He stationed military commanders in all the fortified cities in Judah.

15He got rid of the foreign gods and removed the image from the temple of the LORD, as well as all the altars he had built on the temple hill and in Jerusalem; and he threw them out of the city. 16Then he restored the altar of the LORD and sacrificed fellowship offerings[a] and thank offerings on it, and told Judah to serve the LORD, the God of Israel. 17The people, however, continued to sacrifice at the high places, but only to the LORD their God.

18The other events of Manasseh's reign, including his prayer to his God and the words the seers spoke to him in the name of the LORD, the God of Israel, are written in the annals of the kings of Israel.[b] 19His prayer and how God was moved by his entreaty, as well as all his sins and unfaithfulness, and the sites where he built high places and set up Asherah poles and idols before he humbled himself—all are written in the records of the seers.[c] 20Manasseh rested with his fathers and was buried in his palace. And Amon his son succeeded him as king.

Amon King of Judah

21Amon was twenty-two years old when he became king, and he reigned in Jerusalem two years. 22He did evil in the eyes of the LORD, as his father Manasseh had done. Amon worshiped and offered sacrifices to all the idols Manasseh had made. 23But unlike his father Manasseh, he did not humble himself before the LORD; Amon increased his guilt.

24Amon's officials conspired against him and assassinated him in his palace. 25Then the people of the land killed all who had plotted against King Amon, and they made Josiah his son king in his place.

Josiah's Reforms

34 Josiah was eight years old when he became king, and he reigned in Jerusalem thirty-one years. 2He did what was right in the eyes of the LORD and walked in the ways of his father David, not turning aside to the right or to the left.

3In the eighth year of his reign, while he was still young, he began to seek the God of his father David. In his twelfth year he began to purge Judah and Jerusalem of high places, Asherah poles, carved idols and cast images. 4Under his direction the altars of the Baals were torn down; he cut to pieces the incense altars that were above them, and smashed the Asherah poles, the idols and the images. These he broke to pieces and scattered over the graves of those who had sacrificed to them. 5He burned the bones of the priests on their altars, and so he purged Judah and Jerusalem. 6In the towns of Manasseh, Ephraim and Simeon, as far as Naphtali, and in the ruins around them, 7he

---

[a]16 Traditionally *peace offerings*   [b]18 That is, Judah, as frequently in 2 Chronicles   [c]19 One Hebrew manuscript and Septuagint; most Hebrew manuscripts *of Hozai*

tore down the altars and the Asherah poles and crushed the idols to powder and cut to pieces all the incense altars throughout Israel. Then he went back to Jerusalem.

8In the eighteenth year of Josiah's reign, to purify the land and the temple, he sent Shaphan son of Azaliah and Maaseiah the ruler of the city, with Joah son of Joahaz, the recorder, to repair the temple of the LORD his God.

9They went to Hilkiah the high priest and gave him the money that had been brought into the temple of God, which the Levites who were the doorkeepers had collected from the people of Manasseh, Ephraim and the entire remnant of Israel and from all the people of Judah and Benjamin and the inhabitants of Jerusalem. 10Then they entrusted it to the men appointed to supervise the work on the LORD's temple. These men paid the workers who repaired and restored the temple. 11They also gave money to the carpenters and builders to purchase dressed stone, and timber for joists and beams for the buildings that the kings of Judah had allowed to fall into ruin.

12The men did the work faithfully. Over them to direct them were Jahath and Obadiah, Levites descended from Merari, and Zechariah and Meshullam, descended from Kohath. The Levites—all who were skilled in playing musical instruments— 13had charge of the laborers and supervised all the workers from job to job. Some of the Levites were secretaries, scribes and doorkeepers.

The Book of the Law Found

14While they were bringing out the money that had been taken into the temple of the LORD, Hilkiah the priest found the Book of the Law of the LORD that had been given through Moses. 15Hilkiah said to Shaphan the secretary, "I have found the Book of the Law in the temple of the LORD." He gave it to Shaphan.

16Then Shaphan took the book to the king and reported to him: "Your officials are doing everything that has been committed to them. 17They have paid out the money that was in the temple of the LORD and have entrusted it to the supervisors and workers." 18Then Shaphan the secretary informed the king, "Hilkiah the priest has given me a book." And Shaphan read from it in the presence of the king.

19When the king heard the words of the Law, he tore his robes. 20He gave these orders to Hilkiah, Ahikam son of Shaphan, Abdon son of Micah,[a] Shaphan the secretary and Asaiah the king's attendant: 21"Go and inquire of the LORD for me and for the remnant in Israel and Judah about what is written in this book that has been found. Great is the LORD's anger that is poured out on us because our fathers have not kept the word of the LORD; they have not acted in accordance with all that is written in this book."

22Hilkiah and those the king had sent with him[b] went to speak to the prophetess Huldah, who was the wife of Shallum son of Tokhath,[c] the son of Hasrah,[d] keeper of the wardrobe. She lived in Jerusalem, in the Second District.

23She said to them, "This is what the LORD, the God of Israel, says: Tell the man who sent you to me, 24'This is what the LORD says: I am going to bring disaster on this place and its people—all the curses written in the book that has been read in the presence of the king of Judah. 25Because they have forsaken me and burned incense to other gods and provoked me to anger by all that their hands have made,[e] my anger will be poured out on this place and will not be quenched.' 26Tell the king of Judah, who sent you to inquire of the LORD, 'This is what the LORD, the God of Israel, says concerning the words you heard: 27Because your heart was responsive and you humbled yourself before God when you heard what he spoke against this place and its people, and because

2 Chronicles 34:27

God Hears Humble People

"Because your heart was responsive and you humbled yourself before God...I have heard you, declares the LORD."

---

a20 Also called *Acbor son of Micaiah*   b22 One Hebrew manuscript, Vulgate and Syriac; most Hebrew manuscripts do not have *had sent with him.*   c22 Also called *Tikvah*   d22 Also called *Harhas*   e25 Or *by everything they have done* you humbled yourself before me and tore your robes and wept in my presence, I have heard you, declares the LORD. ²⁸Now I will gather you to your fathers, and you will be buried in peace. Your eyes will not see all the disaster I am going to bring on this place and on those who live here.'"

So they took her answer back to the king.

²⁹Then the king called together all the elders of Judah and Jerusalem. ³⁰He went up to the temple of the LORD with the men of Judah, the people of Jerusalem, the priests and the Levites—all the people from the least to the greatest. He read in their hearing all the words of the Book of the Covenant, which had been found in the temple of the LORD. ³¹The king stood by his pillar and renewed the covenant in the presence of the LORD—to follow the LORD and keep his commands, regulations and decrees with all his heart and all his soul, and to obey the words of the covenant written in this book.

³²Then he had everyone in Jerusalem and Benjamin pledge themselves to it; the people of Jerusalem did this in accordance with the covenant of God, the God of their fathers.

³³Josiah removed all the detestable idols from all the territory belonging to the Israelites, and he had all who were present in Israel serve the LORD their God. As long as he lived, they did not fail to follow the LORD, the God of their fathers.

Josiah Celebrates the Passover

35 Josiah celebrated the Passover to the LORD in Jerusalem, and the Passover lamb was slaughtered on the fourteenth day of the first month. ²He appointed the priests to their duties and encouraged them in the service of the LORD's temple. ³He said to the Levites, who instructed all Israel and who had been consecrated to the LORD: "Put the sacred ark in the temple that Solomon son of David king of Israel built. It is not to be carried about on your shoulders. Now serve the LORD your God and his people Israel. ⁴Prepare yourselves by families in your divisions, according to the directions written by David king of Israel and by his son Solomon.

⁵"Stand in the holy place with a group of Levites for each subdivision of the families of your fellow countrymen, the lay people. ⁶Slaughter the Passover lambs, consecrate yourselves and prepare the lambs for your fellow countrymen, doing what the LORD commanded through Moses."

⁷Josiah provided for all the lay people who were there a total of thirty thousand sheep and goats for the Passover offerings, and also three thousand cattle—all from the king's own possessions.

⁸His officials also contributed voluntarily to the people and the priests and Levites. Hilkiah, Zechariah and Jehiel, the administrators of God's temple, gave the priests twenty-six hundred Passover offerings and three hundred cattle. ⁹Also Conaniah along with Shemaiah and Nethanel, his brothers, and Hashabiah, Jeiel and Jozabad, the leaders of the Levites, provided five thousand Passover offerings and five hundred head of cattle for the Levites.

¹⁰The service was arranged and the priests stood in their places with the Levites in their divisions as the king had ordered. ¹¹The Passover lambs were slaughtered, and the priests sprinkled the blood handed to them, while the Levites skinned the animals. ¹²They set aside the burnt offerings to give them to the subdivisions of the families of the people to offer to the LORD, as is written in the Book of Moses. They did the same with the cattle. ¹³They roasted the Passover animals over the fire as prescribed, and boiled the holy offerings in pots, caldrons and pans and served them quickly to all the people. ¹⁴After this, they made preparations for themselves and for the priests, because the priests, the descendants of Aaron, were sacrificing the burnt offerings and the fat portions until nightfall. So the Levites made preparations for themselves and for the Aaronic priests.

¹⁵The musicians, the descendants of Asaph, were in the places prescribed by David, Asaph, Heman and Jeduthun the king's seer. The gatekeepers at each gate did not need to leave their posts, because their fellow Levites made the preparations for them.

¹⁶So at that time the entire service of the LORD was carried out for the celebration of the Passover and the offering of burnt offerings on the altar of the LORD, as King Josiah

had ordered. [17]The Israelites who were present celebrated the Passover at that time and observed the Feast of Unleavened Bread for seven days. [18]The Passover had not been observed like this in Israel since the days of the prophet Samuel; and none of the kings of Israel had ever celebrated such a Passover as did Josiah, with the priests, the Levites and all Judah and Israel who were there with the people of Jerusalem. [19]This Passover was celebrated in the eighteenth year of Josiah's reign.

The Death of Josiah

[20]After all this, when Josiah had set the temple in order, Neco king of Egypt went up to fight at Carchemish on the Euphrates, and Josiah marched out to meet him in battle. [21]But Neco sent messengers to him, saying, "What quarrel is there between you and me, O king of Judah? It is not you I am attacking at this time, but the house with which I am at war. God has told me to hurry; so stop opposing God, who is with me, or he will destroy you."

[22]Josiah, however, would not turn away from him, but disguised himself to engage him in battle. He would not listen to what Neco had said at God's command but went to fight him on the plain of Megiddo.

[23]Archers shot King Josiah, and he told his officers, "Take me away; I am badly wounded." [24]So they took him out of his chariot, put him in the other chariot he had and brought him to Jerusalem, where he died. He was buried in the tombs of his fathers, and all Judah and Jerusalem mourned for him.

[25]Jeremiah composed laments for Josiah, and to this day all the men and women singers commemorate Josiah in the laments. These became a tradition in Israel and are written in the Laments.

[26]The other events of Josiah's reign and his acts of devotion, according to what is written in the Law of the LORD— [27]all the events, from beginning to end, are written in the book of the

36 kings of Israel and Judah. [1]And the people of the land took Jehoahaz son of Josiah and made him king in Jerusalem in place of his father.

Jehoahaz King of Judah

[2]Jehoahaz[a] was twenty-three years old when he became king, and he reigned in Jerusalem three months. [3]The king of Egypt dethroned him in Jerusalem and imposed on Judah a levy of a hundred talents[b] of silver and a talent[c] of gold. [4]The king of Egypt made Eliakim, a brother of Jehoahaz, king over Judah and Jerusalem and changed Eliakim's name to Jehoiakim. But Neco took Eliakim's brother Jehoahaz and carried him off to Egypt.

Jehoiakim King of Judah

[5]Jehoiakim was twenty-five years old when he became king, and he reigned in Jerusalem eleven years. He did evil in the eyes of the LORD his God. [6]Nebuchadnezzar king of Babylon attacked him and bound him with bronze shackles to take him to Babylon. [7]Nebuchadnezzar also took to Babylon articles from the temple of the LORD and put them in his temple[d] there.

[8]The other events of Jehoiakim's reign, the detestable things he did and all that was found against him, are written in the book of the kings of Israel and Judah. And Jehoiachin his son succeeded him as king.

Jehoiachin King of Judah

[9]Jehoiachin was eighteen[e] years old when he became king, and he reigned in Jerusalem three months and ten days. He did evil in the eyes of the LORD. [10]In the spring, King Nebuchadnezzar sent for him and brought him to Babylon, together with articles of value from the temple of the LORD, and he made Jehoiachin's uncle,[f] Zedekiah, king over Judah and Jerusalem.

Zedekiah King of Judah

[11]Zedekiah was twenty-one years old when he became king, and he reigned in Jerusalem eleven years. [12]He did evil in the eyes of the LORD his God and did not humble himself before Jeremiah the prophet, who spoke the word of the LORD. [13]He also rebelled against King Nebuchadnezzar, who had made him take an oath in God's name. He became stiff-necked and hardened his heart and would not turn to the LORD, the God of Israel. [14]Furthermore, all the leaders of the priests and the people

*a*2 Hebrew *Joahaz*, a variant of *Jehoahaz*; also in verse 4   *b*3 That is, about 3 3/4 tons (about 3.4 metric tons)   *c*3 That is, about 75 pounds (about 34 kilograms)   *d*7 Or *palace*   *e*9 One Hebrew manuscript, some Septuagint manuscripts and Syriac (see also 2 Kings 24:8); most Hebrew manuscripts *eight*   *f*10 Hebrew *brother*, that is, relative (see 2 Kings 24:17) became more and more unfaithful, following all the detestable practices of the nations and defiling the temple of the LORD, which he had consecrated in Jerusalem.

The Fall of Jerusalem

[15] The LORD, the God of their fathers, sent word to them through his messengers again and again, because he had pity on his people and on his dwelling place. [16] But they mocked God's messengers, despised his words and scoffed at his prophets until the wrath of the LORD was aroused against his people and there was no remedy. [17] He brought up against them the king of the Babylonians,[a] who killed their young men with the sword in the sanctuary, and spared neither young man nor young woman, old man or aged. God handed all of them over to Nebuchadnezzar. [18] He carried to Babylon all the articles from the temple of God, both large and small, and the treasures of the LORD's temple and the treasures of the king and his officials. [19] They set fire to God's temple and broke down the wall of Jerusalem; they burned all the palaces and destroyed everything of value there.

[20] He carried into exile to Babylon the remnant, who escaped from the sword, and they became servants to him and his sons until the kingdom of Persia came to power. [21] The land enjoyed its sabbath rests; all the time of its desolation it rested, until the seventy years were completed in fulfillment of the word of the LORD spoken by Jeremiah.

[22] In the first year of Cyrus king of Persia, in order to fulfill the word of the LORD spoken by Jeremiah, the LORD moved the heart of Cyrus king of Persia to make a proclamation throughout his realm and to put it in writing:

[23] "This is what Cyrus king of Persia says:

"'The LORD, the God of heaven, has given me all the kingdoms of the earth and he has appointed me to build a temple for him at Jerusalem in Judah. Anyone of his people among you—may the LORD his God be with him, and let him go up.'"

[a] 17 Or *Chaldeans*

Ezra

Author:
Unknown, but possibly Ezra. (Note: There are portions written in the first person by Ezra. The author of the third person parts is debatable.)

Audience:
All Israel.

Date:
Around 440 B.C.

Setting:
The homecoming of the exiles from Babylon who will start rebuilding God's temple.

Verse to Remember:
"Though we are slaves, our God has not deserted us in our bondage. He has shown us kindness in the sight of the kings of Persia: He has granted us new life to rebuild the house of our God and repair its ruins, and he has given us a wall of protection in Judah and Jerusalem." (9:9)

A second chance is a remarkable gift. It's never deserved; it is a sheer *act of grace*. And it is precisely what God gave to his people. The same hands that brought judgment, destruction and 70 years of exile led those exiles back to the *land of promise* to start over again.

When the people reached their homeland, they made *a great beginning*. They gave freely; they offered sacrifices; they celebrated the feasts; they began rebuilding the temple—they did all the things the people of God should do. But in any work we do for God, there is opposition. For the returning exiles, it came on two fronts: *outside enemies and old tendencies*. As is often the case, the old tendencies were by far the greater threat. But greater than any enemy from within or without is a sovereign God who moves the hearts of people and who is willing to give second chances. He did both for the Israelites in Ezra's day, and *he still does both for us today*.

Cyrus Helps the Exiles to Return

1 In the first year of Cyrus king of Persia, in order to fulfill the word of the LORD spoken by Jeremiah, the LORD moved the heart of Cyrus king of Persia to make a proclamation throughout his realm and to put it in writing:

2"This is what Cyrus king of Persia says:

"'The LORD, the God of heaven, has given me all the kingdoms of the earth and he has appointed me to build a temple for him at Jerusalem in Judah. ³Anyone of his people among you—may his God be with him, and let him go up to Jerusalem in Judah and build the temple of the LORD, the God of Israel, the God who is in Jerusalem. ⁴And the people of any place where survivors may now be living are to provide him with silver and gold, with goods and livestock, and with freewill offerings for the temple of God in Jerusalem.'"

⁵Then the family heads of Judah and Benjamin, and the priests and Levites—everyone whose heart God had moved—prepared to go up and build the house of the LORD in Jerusalem. ⁶All their neighbors assisted them with articles of silver and gold, with goods and livestock, and with valuable gifts, in addition to all the freewill offerings. ⁷Moreover, King Cyrus brought out the articles belonging to the temple of the LORD, which Nebuchadnezzar had carried away from Jerusalem and had placed in the temple of his god.ᵃ ⁸Cyrus king of Persia had them brought by Mithredath the treasurer, who counted them out to Sheshbazzar the prince of Judah.

⁹This was the inventory:

gold dishes	30
silver dishes	1,000
silver pansᵇ	29
¹⁰ gold bowls	30
matching silver bowls	410
other articles	1,000

¹¹In all, there were 5,400 articles of gold and of silver. Sheshbazzar brought all these along when the exiles came up from Babylon to Jerusalem.

The List of the Exiles Who Returned

2 Now these are the people of the province who came up from the captivity of the exiles, whom Nebuchadnezzar king of Babylon had taken captive to Babylon (they returned to Jerusalem and Judah, each to his own town, ²in company with Zerubbabel, Jeshua, Nehemiah, Seraiah, Reelaiah, Mordecai, Bilshan, Mispar, Bigvai, Rehum and Baanah):

The list of the men of the people of Israel:

³ the descendants of Parosh	2,172
⁴ of Shephatiah	372
⁵ of Arah	775
⁶ of Pahath-Moab (through the line of Jeshua and Joab)	2,812
⁷ of Elam	1,254
⁸ of Zattu	945
⁹ of Zaccai	760
¹⁰ of Bani	642
¹¹ of Bebai	623
¹² of Azgad	1,222
¹³ of Adonikam	666
¹⁴ of Bigvai	2,056
¹⁵ of Adin	454
¹⁶ of Ater (through Hezekiah)	98
¹⁷ of Bezai	323
¹⁸ of Jorah	112
¹⁹ of Hashum	223
²⁰ of Gibbar	95
²¹ the men of Bethlehem	123
²² of Netophah	56
²³ of Anathoth	128
²⁴ of Azmaveth	42
²⁵ of Kiriath Jearim,ᶜ Kephirah and Beeroth	743
²⁶ of Ramah and Geba	621
²⁷ of Micmash	122
²⁸ of Bethel and Ai	223
²⁹ of Nebo	52
³⁰ of Magbish	156
³¹ of the other Elam	1,254
³² of Harim	320
³³ of Lod, Hadid and Ono	725
³⁴ of Jericho	345
³⁵ of Senaah	3,630

³⁶The priests:

the descendants of Jedaiah (through the family of Jeshua)	973
³⁷ of Immer	1,052
³⁸ of Pashhur	1,247
³⁹ of Harim	1,017

ᵃ7 Or gods   ᵇ9 The meaning of the Hebrew for this word is uncertain.   ᶜ25 See Septuagint (see also Neh. 7:29); Hebrew Kiriath Arim.

RUTH DIDN'T BLAME ORPAH.

Not for returning to life in Moab and not for leaving Naomi.

She knew how Orpah felt. They were both young widows in the prime of their lives. In such a situation, it would be smart to stay near the familiar and enjoy the protection of family.

If that's what one wanted.

Ruth just wasn't so sure it was worth wanting.

At the same time, what was so promising or even the least bit intriguing about accompanying a withered woman to a foreign land? Ruth couldn't say for certain. Whatever it was, Orpah certainly didn't see it, couldn't see it. But Ruth saw it. Something Ruth saw in Naomi inspired her to take the greatest gamble of her young life up to that point and move to Bethlehem.

She had seen it in her father-in-law's name, "My God is King." Who was this God, and would he really rule as a righteous king? She wondered.

She had observed it in her deceased husband's godly heritage, and it touched her deep inside.

She had witnessed it in Naomi's inner strength.

Everything had been taken from her mother-in-law, and many nights Ruth had heard her crying bitter tears. Still, trouble could not completely extinguish Naomi's flicker of hope. When Naomi decided to return home to Bethlehem, instead of leaving her faith in a foreign land, she accepted her pain and determined to see what God would do. To Ruth, it spoke of perseverance, of an unconquered spirit.

Most of all, it spoke to the emptiness in Ruth's own soul. Growing up among the pagan religion of her land, she found herself unimpressed with the gods of her childhood. The brief time with Naomi's family had shown her something different. Her own "religion" had left her cold. Naomi's God, whoever he was, seemed to leave her heart strangely warmed.

If Ruth's gamble to accompany Naomi to Bethlehem didn't pay off, she might have a lifetime of loneliness to regret it. But if it did . . . well, it would change everything.

—*Prayer*—
"When I called you, you answered me" (Psalm 138:3).

> "Your people will
> be my people
> and your God
> my God."
>
> **Ruth 1:16**

ASSIGNED READING:

Ruth 1:1–22

Weekend

⁴⁰The Levites:

the descendants of Jeshua and Kadmiel
(through the line of Hodaviah)   74

⁴¹The singers:

the descendants of Asaph   128

⁴²The gatekeepers of the temple:

the descendants of
Shallum, Ater, Talmon,
Akkub, Hatita and Shobai   139

⁴³The temple servants:

the descendants of
Ziha, Hasupha, Tabbaoth,
⁴⁴Keros, Siaha, Padon,
⁴⁵Lebanah, Hagabah, Akkub,
⁴⁶Hagab, Shalmai, Hanan,
⁴⁷Giddel, Gahar, Reaiah,
⁴⁸Rezin, Nekoda, Gazzam,
⁴⁹Uzza, Paseah, Besai,
⁵⁰Asnah, Meunim, Nephusim,
⁵¹Bakbuk, Hakupha, Harhur,
⁵²Bazluth, Mehida, Harsha,
⁵³Barkos, Sisera, Temah,
⁵⁴Neziah and Hatipha

⁵⁵The descendants of the servants of Solomon:

the descendants of
Sotai, Hassophereth, Peruda,
⁵⁶Jaala, Darkon, Giddel,
⁵⁷Shephatiah, Hattil,
Pokereth-Hazzebaim and Ami

⁵⁸The temple servants and the
descendants of the servants
of Solomon   392

⁵⁹The following came up from the towns of Tel Melah, Tel Harsha, Kerub, Addon and Immer, but they could not show that their families were descended from Israel:

⁶⁰The descendants of
Delaiah, Tobiah and Nekoda   652

⁶¹And from among the priests:

The descendants of
Hobaiah, Hakkoz and Barzillai (a
man who had married a daughter of Barzillai the Gileadite and was called by that name).

⁶²These searched for their family records, but they could not find them and so were excluded from the priesthood as unclean. ⁶³The governor ordered them not to eat any of the most sacred food until there was a priest ministering with the Urim and Thummim.

⁶⁴The whole company numbered 42,360, ⁶⁵besides their 7,337 menservants and maidservants; and they also had 200 men and women singers. ⁶⁶They had 736 horses, 245 mules, ⁶⁷435 camels and 6,720 donkeys.

⁶⁸When they arrived at the house of the Lord in Jerusalem, some of the heads of the families gave freewill offerings toward the rebuilding of the house of God on its site. ⁶⁹According to their ability they gave to the treasury for this work 61,000 drachmas*a* of gold, 5,000 minas*b* of silver and 100 priestly garments.

⁷⁰The priests, the Levites, the singers, the gatekeepers and the temple servants settled in their own towns, along with some of the other people, and the rest of the Israelites settled in their towns.

Rebuilding the Altar

3 When the seventh month came and the Israelites had settled in their towns, the people assembled as one man in Jerusalem. ²Then Jeshua son of Jozadak and his fellow priests and Zerubbabel son of Shealtiel and his associates began to build the altar of the God of Israel to sacrifice burnt offerings on it, in accordance with what is written in the Law of Moses the man of God. ³Despite their fear of the peoples around them, they built the altar on its foundation and sacrificed burnt offerings on it to the Lord, both the morning and evening sacrifices. ⁴Then in accordance with what is written, they celebrated the Feast of Tabernacles with the required number of burnt offerings prescribed for each day. ⁵After that, they presented the regular burnt offerings, the New Moon sacrifices and the sacrifices for all the appointed sacred

---

*a*69 That is, about 1,100 pounds (about 500 kilograms)   *b*69 That is, about 3 tons (about 2.9 metric tons) feasts of the LORD, as well as those brought as freewill offerings to the LORD. ⁶On the first day of the seventh month they began to offer burnt offerings to the LORD, though the foundation of the LORD's temple had not yet been laid.

Rebuilding the Temple

⁷Then they gave money to the masons and carpenters, and gave food and drink and oil to the people of Sidon and Tyre, so that they would bring cedar logs by sea from Lebanon to Joppa, as authorized by Cyrus king of Persia.

⁸In the second month of the second year after their arrival at the house of God in Jerusalem, Zerubbabel son of Shealtiel, Jeshua son of Jozadak and the rest of their brothers (the priests and the Levites and all who had returned from the captivity to Jerusalem) began the work, appointing Levites twenty years of age and older to supervise the building of the house of the LORD. ⁹Jeshua and his sons and brothers and Kadmiel and his sons (descendants of Hodaviah[a]) and the sons of Henadad and their sons and brothers—all Levites—joined together in supervising those working on the house of God.

¹⁰When the builders laid the foundation of the temple of the LORD, the priests in their vestments and with trumpets, and the Levites (the sons of Asaph) with cymbals, took their places to praise the LORD, as prescribed by David king of Israel. ¹¹With praise and thanksgiving they sang to the LORD:

"He is good;
  his love to Israel endures
  forever."

And all the people gave a great shout of praise to the LORD, because the foundation of the house of the LORD was laid. ¹²But many of the older priests and Levites and family heads, who had seen the former temple, wept aloud when they saw the foundation of this temple being laid, while many others shouted for joy. ¹³No one could distinguish the sound of the shouts of joy from the sound of weeping, because the people made so much noise. And the sound was heard far away.

Opposition to the Rebuilding

4 When the enemies of Judah and Benjamin heard that the exiles were building a temple for the LORD, the God of Israel, ²they came to Zerubbabel and to the heads of the families and said, "Let us help you build because, like you, we seek your God and have been sacrificing to him since the time of Esarhaddon king of Assyria, who brought us here."

³But Zerubbabel, Jeshua and the rest of the heads of the families of Israel answered, "You have no part with us in building a temple to our God. We alone will build it for the LORD, the God of Israel, as King Cyrus, the king of Persia, commanded us."

⁴Then the peoples around them set out to discourage the people of Judah and make them afraid to go on building.[b] ⁵They hired counselors to work against them and frustrate their plans during the entire reign of Cyrus king of Persia and down to the reign of Darius king of Persia.

Later Opposition Under Xerxes and Artaxerxes

⁶At the beginning of the reign of Xerxes,[c] they lodged an accusation against the people of Judah and Jerusalem.

⁷And in the days of Artaxerxes king of Persia, Bishlam, Mithredath, Tabeel and the rest of his associates wrote a letter to Artaxerxes. The letter was written in Aramaic script and in the Aramaic language.[d,e]

⁸Rehum the commanding officer and Shimshai the secretary wrote a letter against Jerusalem to Artaxerxes the king as follows:

⁹Rehum the commanding officer and Shimshai the secretary, together with the rest of their associates—the judges and officials over the men from

Ezra 3:11

God's Love Endures

With praise and thanksgiving they sang to the LORD: "He is good; his love to Israel endures forever."

---

[a]9 Hebrew *Yehudah*, probably a variant of *Hodaviah* [b]4 Or *and troubled them as they built* [c]6 Hebrew *Ahasuerus*, a variant of Xerxes' Persian name [d]7 Or *written in Aramaic and translated* [e]7 The text of Ezra 4:8—6:18 is in Aramaic.

Tripolis, Persia,*a* Erech and Babylon, the Elamites of Susa, **10**and the other people whom the great and honorable Ashurbanipal*b* deported and settled in the city of Samaria and elsewhere in Trans-Euphrates.

11(This is a copy of the letter they sent him.)

To King Artaxerxes,

From your servants, the men of Trans-Euphrates:

12The king should know that the Jews who came up to us from you have gone to Jerusalem and are rebuilding that rebellious and wicked city. They are restoring the walls and repairing the foundations. **13**Furthermore, the king should know that if this city is built and its walls are restored, no more taxes, tribute or duty will be paid, and the royal revenues will suffer. **14**Now since we are under obligation to the palace and it is not proper for us to see the king dishonored, we are sending this message to inform the king, **15**so that a search may be made in the archives of your predecessors. In these records you will find that this city is a rebellious city, troublesome to kings and provinces, a place of rebellion from ancient times. That is why this city was destroyed. **16**We inform the king that if this city is built and its walls are restored, you will be left with nothing in Trans-Euphrates.

17The king sent this reply:

To Rehum the commanding officer, Shimshai the secretary and the rest of their associates living in Samaria and elsewhere in Trans-Euphrates:

Greetings.

18The letter you sent us has been read and translated in my presence. **19**I issued an order and a search was made, and it was found that this city has a long history of revolt against kings and has been a place of rebellion and sedition. **20**Jerusalem has

had powerful kings ruling over the whole of Trans-Euphrates, and taxes, tribute and duty were paid to them. **21**Now issue an order to these men to stop work, so that this city will not be rebuilt until I so order. **22**Be careful not to neglect this matter. Why let this threat grow, to the detriment of the royal interests?

23As soon as the copy of the letter of King Artaxerxes was read to Rehum and Shimshai the secretary and their associates, they went immediately to the Jews in Jerusalem and compelled them by force to stop.

24Thus the work on the house of God in Jerusalem came to a standstill until the second year of the reign of Darius king of Persia.

Tattenai's Letter to Darius

5 Now Haggai the prophet and Zechariah the prophet, a descendant of Iddo, prophesied to the Jews in Judah and Jerusalem in the name of the God of Israel, who was over them. **2**Then Zerubbabel son of Shealtiel and Jeshua son of Jozadak set to work to rebuild the house of God in Jerusalem. And the prophets of God were with them, helping them.

3At that time Tattenai, governor of Trans-Euphrates, and Shethar-Bozenai and their associates went to them and asked, "Who authorized you to rebuild this temple and restore this structure?" **4**They also asked, "What are the names of the men constructing this building?"*c* **5**But the eye of their God was watching over the elders of the Jews, and they were not stopped until a report could go to Darius and his written reply was received.

6This is a copy of the letter that Tattenai, governor of Trans-Euphrates, and Shethar-Bozenai and their associates, the officials of Trans-Euphrates, sent to King Darius. **7**The report they sent him read as follows:

To King Darius:

Cordial greetings.

8The king should know that we went to the district of Judah, to the temple of the great God. The people are building it with

---

*a*9 Or *officials, magistrates and governors over the men from*   *b*10 Aramaic *Osnappar,* a variant of *Ashurbanipal*   *c*4 See Septuagint; Aramaic *We told them the names of the men constructing this building.*

large stones and placing the timbers in the walls. The work is being carried on with diligence and is making rapid progress under their direction.

⁹We questioned the elders and asked them, "Who authorized you to rebuild this temple and restore this structure?" ¹⁰We also asked them their names, so that we could write down the names of their leaders for your information.

¹¹This is the answer they gave us:

"We are the servants of the God of heaven and earth, and we are rebuilding the temple that was built many years ago, one that a great king of Israel built and finished. ¹²But because our fathers angered the God of heaven, he handed them over to Nebuchadnezzar the Chaldean, king of Babylon, who destroyed this temple and deported the people to Babylon.

¹³"However, in the first year of Cyrus king of Babylon, King Cyrus issued a decree to rebuild this house of God. ¹⁴He even removed from the temple*ᵃ* of Babylon the gold and silver articles of the house of God, which Nebuchadnezzar had taken from the temple in Jerusalem and brought to the temple*ᵃ* in Babylon.

"Then King Cyrus gave them to a man named Sheshbazzar, whom he had appointed governor, ¹⁵and he told him, 'Take these articles and go and deposit them in the temple in Jerusalem. And rebuild the house of God on its site.' ¹⁶So this Sheshbazzar came and laid the foundations of the house of God in Jerusalem. From that day to the present it has been under construction but is not yet finished."

¹⁷Now if it pleases the king, let a search be made in the royal archives of Babylon to see if King Cyrus did in fact issue a decree to rebuild this house of God in Jerusalem. Then let the king send us his decision in this matter.

The Decree of Darius

6 King Darius then issued an order, and they searched in the archives stored in the treasury at Babylon. ²A scroll was found in the citadel of Ecbatana in the province of Media, and this was written on it:

Memorandum:

³In the first year of King Cyrus, the king issued a decree concerning the temple of God in Jerusalem:

Let the temple be rebuilt as a place to present sacrifices, and let its foundations be laid. It is to be ninety feet*ᵇ* high and ninety feet wide, ⁴with three courses of large stones and one of timbers. The costs are to be paid by the royal treasury. ⁵Also, the gold and silver articles of the house of God, which Nebuchadnezzar took from the temple in Jerusalem and brought to Babylon, are to be returned to their places in the temple in Jerusalem; they are to be deposited in the house of God.

⁶Now then, Tattenai, governor of Trans-Euphrates, and Shethar-Bozenai and you, their fellow officials of that province, stay away from there. ⁷Do not interfere with the work on this temple of God. Let the governor of the Jews and the Jewish elders rebuild this house of God on its site.

⁸Moreover, I hereby decree what you are to do for these elders of the Jews in the construction of this house of God:

The expenses of these men are to be fully paid out of the royal treasury, from the revenues of Trans-Euphrates, so that the work will not stop. ⁹Whatever is needed—young bulls, rams, male lambs for burnt offerings to the God of heaven, and wheat, salt, wine and oil, as requested by the priests in Jerusalem—must be given them daily without fail, ¹⁰so that they may offer sacrifices pleasing to the God of heaven and pray for the well-being of the king and his sons.

¹¹Furthermore, I decree that if anyone changes this edict, a beam is to be pulled from his house and he is to be lifted up and impaled on it. And for this crime his house is to be made a pile of rubble. ¹²May God, who has caused his Name to dwell there, overthrow any king or people

ᵃ14 Or palace   ᵇ3 Aramaic sixty cubits (about 27 meters) who lifts a hand to change this decree or to destroy this temple in Jerusalem.

I, Darius, have decreed it. Let it be carried out with diligence.

Completion and Dedication of the Temple

¹³Then, because of the decree King Darius had sent, Tattenai, governor of Trans-Euphrates, and Shethar-Bozenai and their associates carried it out with diligence. ¹⁴So the elders of the Jews continued to build and prosper under the preaching of Haggai the prophet and Zechariah, a descendant of Iddo. They finished building the temple according to the command of the God of Israel and the decrees of Cyrus, Darius and Artaxerxes, kings of Persia. ¹⁵The temple was completed on the third day of the month Adar, in the sixth year of the reign of King Darius.

¹⁶Then the people of Israel—the priests, the Levites and the rest of the exiles—celebrated the dedication of the house of God with joy. ¹⁷For the dedication of this house of God they offered a hundred bulls, two hundred rams, four hundred male lambs and, as a sin offering for all Israel, twelve male goats, one for each of the tribes of Israel. ¹⁸And they installed the priests in their divisions and the Levites in their groups for the service of God at Jerusalem, according to what is written in the Book of Moses.

The Passover

¹⁹On the fourteenth day of the first month, the exiles celebrated the Passover. ²⁰The priests and Levites had purified themselves and were all ceremonially clean. The Levites slaughtered the Passover lamb for all the exiles, for their brothers the priests and for themselves. ²¹So the Israelites who had returned from the exile ate it, together with all who had separated themselves from the unclean practices of their Gentile neighbors in order to seek the LORD, the God of Israel. ²²For seven days they celebrated

with joy the Feast of Unleavened Bread, because the LORD had filled them with joy by changing the attitude of the king of Assyria, so that he assisted them in the work on the house of God, the God of Israel.

Ezra Comes to Jerusalem

7 After these things, during the reign of Artaxerxes king of Persia, Ezra son of Seraiah, the son of Azariah, the son of Hilkiah, ²the son of Shallum, the son of Zadok, the son of Ahitub, ³the son of Amariah, the son of Azariah, the son of Meraioth, ⁴the son of Zerahiah, the son of Uzzi, the son of Bukki, ⁵the son of Abishua, the son of Phinehas, the son of Eleazar, the son of Aaron the chief priest— ⁶this Ezra came up from Babylon. He was a teacher well versed in the Law of Moses, which the LORD, the God of Israel, had given. The king had granted him everything he asked, for the hand of the LORD his God was on him. ⁷Some of the Israelites, including priests, Levites, singers, gatekeepers and temple servants, also came up to Jerusalem in the seventh year of King Artaxerxes.

⁸Ezra arrived in Jerusalem in the fifth month of the seventh year of the king. ⁹He had begun his journey from Babylon on the first day of the first month, and he arrived in Jerusalem on the first day of the fifth month, for the gracious hand of his God was on him. ¹⁰For Ezra had devoted himself to the study and observance of the Law of the LORD, and to teaching its decrees and laws in Israel.

King Artaxerxes' Letter to Ezra

¹¹This is a copy of the letter King Artaxerxes had given to Ezra the priest and teacher, a man learned in matters concerning the commands and decrees of the LORD for Israel:

¹²ᵃArtaxerxes, king of kings,

To Ezra the priest, a teacher of the Law of the God of heaven:

Ezra 6:12

God Reigns Over All

May God, who has caused his Name to dwell there, overthrow any king or people who lifts a hand to change this decree or to destroy this temple in Jerusalem.

ᵃ12 The text of Ezra 7:12–26 is in Aramaic.

Greetings.

13 Now I decree that any of the Israelites in my kingdom, including priests and Levites, who wish to go to Jerusalem with you, may go. 14 You are sent by the king and his seven advisers to inquire about Judah and Jerusalem with regard to the Law of your God, which is in your hand. 15 Moreover, you are to take with you the silver and gold that the king and his advisers have freely given to the God of Israel, whose dwelling is in Jerusalem, 16 together with all the silver and gold you may obtain from the province of Babylon, as well as the freewill offerings of the people and priests for the temple of their God in Jerusalem. 17 With this money be sure to buy bulls, rams and male lambs, together with their grain offerings and drink offerings, and sacrifice them on the altar of the temple of your God in Jerusalem.

18 You and your brother Jews may then do whatever seems best with the rest of the silver and gold, in accordance with the will of your God. 19 Deliver to the God of Jerusalem all the articles entrusted to you for worship in the temple of your God. 20 And anything else needed for the temple of your God that you may have occasion to supply, you may provide from the royal treasury.

21 Now I, King Artaxerxes, order all the treasurers of Trans-Euphrates to provide with diligence whatever Ezra the priest, a teacher of the Law of the God of heaven, may ask of you— 22 up to a hundred talents[a] of silver, a hundred cors[b] of wheat, a hundred baths[c] of wine, a hundred baths[c] of olive oil, and salt without limit. 23 Whatever the God of heaven has prescribed, let it be done with diligence for the temple of the God of heaven. Why

should there be wrath against the realm of the king and of his sons? 24 You are also to know that you have no authority to impose taxes, tribute or duty on any of the priests, Levites, singers, gatekeepers, temple servants or other workers at this house of God.

25 And you, Ezra, in accordance with the wisdom of your God, which you possess, appoint magistrates and judges to administer justice to all the people of Trans-Euphrates—all who know the laws of your God. And you are to teach any who do not know them. 26 Whoever does not obey the law of your God and the law of the king must surely be punished by death, banishment, confiscation of property, or imprisonment.

27 Praise be to the LORD, the God of our fathers, who has put it into the king's heart to bring honor to the house of the LORD in Jerusalem in this way 28 and who has extended his good favor to me before the king and his advisers and all the king's powerful officials. Because the hand of the LORD my God was on me, I took courage and gathered leading men from Israel to go up with me.

Ezra 7:27

God Realigns Others' Plans

Praise be to the LORD, the God of our fathers, who has put it into the king's heart to bring honor to the house of the LORD in Jerusalem in this way.

List of the Family Heads Returning With Ezra

8 These are the family heads and those registered with them who came up with me from Babylon during the reign of King Artaxerxes:

2 of the descendants of Phinehas, Gershom;

of the descendants of Ithamar, Daniel;

of the descendants of David, Hattush 3 of the descendants of Shecaniah;

of the descendants of Parosh, Zechariah, and with him were registered 150 men;

[a]22 That is, about 3 3/4 tons (about 3.4 metric tons) *[b]22 That is, probably about 600 bushels (about 22 kiloliters)* *[c]22 That is, probably about 600 gallons (about 2.2 kiloliters)*

⁴of the descendants of Pahath-Moab, Elie-hoenai son of Zerahiah, and with him 200 men;

⁵of the descendants of Zattu,ᵃ Shecaniah son of Jahaziel, and with him 300 men;

⁶of the descendants of Adin, Ebed son of Jonathan, and with him 50 men;

⁷of the descendants of Elam, Jeshaiah son of Athaliah, and with him 70 men;

⁸of the descendants of Shephatiah, Zeb-adiah son of Michael, and with him 80 men;

⁹of the descendants of Joab, Obadiah son of Jehiel, and with him 218 men;

¹⁰of the descendants of Bani,ᵇ Shelomith son of Josiphiah, and with him 160 men;

¹¹of the descendants of Bebai, Zechariah son of Bebai, and with him 28 men;

¹²of the descendants of Azgad, Johanan son of Hakkatan, and with him 110 men;

¹³of the descendants of Adonikam, the last ones, whose names were Eliphelet, Jeuel and Shemaiah, and with them 60 men;

¹⁴of the descendants of Bigvai, Uthai and Zaccur, and with them 70 men.

The Return to Jerusalem

¹⁵I assembled them at the canal that flows toward Ahava, and we camped there three days. When I checked among the people and the priests, I found no Levites there. ¹⁶So I summoned Eliezer, Ariel, Shemaiah, Elna-than, Jarib, Elnathan, Nathan, Zechariah and Meshullam, who were leaders, and Joiarib and Elnathan, who were men of learning, ¹⁷and I sent them to Iddo, the leader in Casiphia. I told them what to say to Iddo and his kinsmen, the temple servants in Casiphia, so that they might bring attendants to us for the house of our God. ¹⁸Because the gracious hand of our God was on us, they brought us Sherebiah, a capable man, from the descendants of Mahli son of Levi, the son of Israel, and Sherebiah's sons and brothers, 18 men; ¹⁹and Hashabiah, together with Jeshaiah from the descendants of Merari, and his brothers and nephews, 20 men. ²⁰They also brought 220 of the temple servants—a body that David and the officials had established to assist the Levites. All were registered by name.

²¹There, by the Ahava Canal, I proclaimed a fast, so that we might humble ourselves be-fore our God and ask him for a safe journey for us and our children, with all our possessions. ²²I was ashamed to ask the king for soldiers and horsemen to protect us from enemies on the road, because we had told the king, "The gracious hand of our God is on everyone who looks to him, but his great anger is against all who forsake him." ²³So we fasted and peti-tioned our God about this, and he answered our prayer.

²⁴Then I set apart twelve of the leading priests, together with Sherebiah, Hashabiah and ten of their brothers, ²⁵and I weighed out to them the offering of silver and gold and the articles that the king, his advisers, his officials and all Israel present there had donated for the house of our God. ²⁶I weighed out to them 650 talentsᶜ of silver, silver articles weighing 100 tal-ents,ᵈ 100 talentsᵈ of gold, ²⁷20 bowls of gold valued at 1,000 darics,ᵉ and two fine articles of polished bronze, as precious as gold.

²⁸I said to them, "You as well as these arti-cles are consecrated to the LORD. The silver and gold are a freewill offering to the LORD, the God of your fathers. ²⁹Guard them carefully until you weigh them out in the chambers of the house of the LORD in Jerusalem before the leading priests and the Levites and the family heads of Israel." ³⁰Then the priests and Levites received the silver and gold and sacred articles that had been weighed out to be taken to the house of our God in Jerusalem.

³¹On the twelfth day of the first month we set out from the Ahava Canal to go to Jerusa-lem. The hand of our God was on us, and he protected us from enemies and bandits along the way. ³²So we arrived in Jerusalem, where we rested three days.

³³On the fourth day, in the house of our God, we weighed out the silver and gold and the sacred articles into the hands of Meremoth son of Uriah, the priest. Eleazar son of Phine-has was with him, and so were the Levites Joza-bad son of Jeshua and Noadiah son of Binnui.

ᵃ5 Some Septuagint manuscripts (also 1 Esdras 8:32); Hebrew does not have *Zattu*.   ᵇ10 Some Septuagint manuscripts (also 1 Esdras 8:36); Hebrew does not have *Bani*.   ᶜ26 That is, about 25 tons (about 22 metric tons)   ᵈ26 That is, about 3 3/4 tons (about 3.4 metric tons)   ᵉ27 That is, about 19 pounds (about 8.5 kilograms)

Total Dependence

Read: Ezra 8:21-34

Ezra 8:22-23

I was ashamed to ask the king for soldiers and horsemen to protect us from enemies on the road, because we had told the king, "The gracious hand of our God is on everyone who looks to him, but his great anger is against all who forsake him." So we fasted and petitioned our God about this, and he answered our prayer.

reflection

1 How have you found that your reason sometimes interferes with your faith?

2 What makes it difficult for you to depend on God?

3 How can prioritizing prayer in your life make a difference in preparing you for your faith journey?

RELATED READINGS

Proverbs 3:5-6;
Isaiah 58:6-9;
Hebrews 11:1-2

LISA REALIZED SHE needed to depend on God when she discovered she was pregnant. She was excited and happy—but the timing wasn't perfect. Her husband had two years until he finished his degree. She was supporting both of them by working two jobs. Whenever she thought about the future, she broke out in a cold sweat. How would they make the rent? Would she have to quit one of her jobs? Would her husband have to quit school? She decided that the best course was to pray for God to show them the way.

Ezra sets a great example for anyone facing an unknown future. Before he and a group of returning exiles began their 900-mile trek back to Jerusalem, they all fasted and prayed for a safe journey—literally, a "straight way." They prayed for God's favor and protection and trusted "God's gracious hand" would guide them.

God is also with you to guide you, regardless of your circumstances. Perhaps you're venturing out, depending on God for the first time. Take a step of faith and follow where he leads. He will surely guide you to the next step . . . and the next. You'll discover that faith will lead you where reason may not.

Faith and reason have been compared to two travelers. Think of Faith as a woman who can walk 20 or 30 miles at a time without flagging, while Reason is a child who can only muster the strength to go two or three miles. One day Reason said to Faith, "Oh, Faith, let me walk with you." But Faith replied, "Oh, Reason, you can never walk with me!" Nevertheless, they set out together. When they came to a deep river, Reason said, "I can never ford this," but Faith waded through it, singing. When they reached a high mountain, Reason despaired. But Faith carried Reason on her back. The writer of this old tale said, "Oh, how dependent upon Faith is Reason!"

Why has God made faith the indispensable ingredient in our journey of faith? Perhaps so that we will become totally dependent upon him. Reason tells us to stay put. Faith calls us to step out, reassuring us that "nothing is impossible with God" (Luke 1:37).

Monday

Go to page 577 for your next devotional reading.

³⁴Everything was accounted for by number and weight, and the entire weight was recorded at that time.

³⁵Then the exiles who had returned from captivity sacrificed burnt offerings to the God of Israel: twelve bulls for all Israel, ninety-six rams, seventy-seven male lambs and, as a sin offering, twelve male goats. All this was a burnt offering to the LORD. ³⁶They also delivered the king's orders to the royal satraps and to the governors of Trans-Euphrates, who then gave assistance to the people and to the house of God.

Ezra's Prayer About Intermarriage

9 After these things had been done, the leaders came to me and said, "The people of Israel, including the priests and the Levites, have not kept themselves separate from the neighboring peoples with their detestable practices, like those of the Canaanites, Hittites, Perizzites, Jebusites, Ammonites, Moabites, Egyptians and Amorites. ²They have taken some of their daughters as wives for themselves and their sons, and have mingled the holy race with the peoples around them. And the leaders and officials have led the way in this unfaithfulness."

³When I heard this, I tore my tunic and cloak, pulled hair from my head and beard and sat down appalled. ⁴Then everyone who trembled at the words of the God of Israel gathered around me because of this unfaithfulness of the exiles. And I sat there appalled until the evening sacrifice.

⁵Then, at the evening sacrifice, I rose from my self-abasement, with my tunic and cloak torn, and fell on my knees with my hands spread out to the LORD my God ⁶and prayed:

"O my God, I am too ashamed and disgraced to lift up my face to you, my God, because our sins are higher than our heads and our guilt has reached to the heavens. ⁷From the days of our forefathers until now, our guilt has been great. Because of our sins, we and our kings and our priests have been subjected to the sword and captivity, to pillage and humiliation at the hand of foreign kings, as it is today.

⁸"But now, for a brief moment, the LORD our God has been gracious in leaving us a remnant and giving us a firm place in his sanctuary, and so our God gives light to our eyes and a little relief in our bondage. ⁹Though we are slaves, our God has not deserted us in our bondage. He has shown us kindness in the sight of the kings of Persia: He has granted us new life to rebuild the house of our God and repair its ruins, and he has given us a wall of protection in Judah and Jerusalem.

¹⁰"But now, O our God, what can we say after this? For we have disregarded the commands ¹¹you gave through your servants the prophets when you said: 'The land you are entering to possess is a land polluted by the corruption of its peoples. By their detestable practices they have filled it with their impurity from one end to the other. ¹²Therefore, do not give your daughters in marriage to their sons or take their daughters for your sons. Do not seek a treaty of friendship with them at any time, that you may be strong and eat the good things of the land and leave it to your children as an everlasting inheritance.'

¹³"What has happened to us is a result of our evil deeds and our great guilt, and yet, our God, you have punished us less than our sins have deserved and have given us a remnant like this. ¹⁴Shall we again break your commands and intermarry with the peoples who commit such detestable practices? Would you not be angry enough with us to destroy us, leaving us no remnant or survivor? ¹⁵O LORD, God of Israel, you are righteous! We are left this day as a remnant. Here we are before you in our guilt, though because of it not one of us can stand in your presence."

Ezra 9:15

God Is Righteous

"O LORD, God of Israel, you are righteous! We are left this day as a remnant. Here we are before you in our guilt, though because of it not one of us can stand in your presence."

The People's Confession of Sin

10 While Ezra was praying and confessing, weeping and throwing himself down before the house of God, a large crowd of Israelites—men, women and children—gathered around him. They too wept bitterly. ²Then Shecaniah son of Jehiel, one of the descendants of Elam, said to Ezra, "We have been unfaithful to our God by marrying foreign women from the peoples around us. But in spite of this, there is still hope for Israel. ³Now let us make a covenant before our God to send away all these women and their children, in accordance with the counsel of my lord and of those who fear the commands of our God. Let it be done according to the Law. ⁴Rise up; this matter is in your hands. We will support you, so take courage and do it."

⁵So Ezra rose up and put the leading priests and Levites and all Israel under oath to do what had been suggested. And they took the oath. ⁶Then Ezra withdrew from before the house of God and went to the room of Jehohanan son of Eliashib. While he was there, he ate no food and drank no water, because he continued to mourn over the unfaithfulness of the exiles.

⁷A proclamation was then issued throughout Judah and Jerusalem for all the exiles to assemble in Jerusalem. ⁸Anyone who failed to appear within three days would forfeit all his property, in accordance with the decision of the officials and elders, and would himself be expelled from the assembly of the exiles.

⁹Within the three days, all the men of Judah and Benjamin had gathered in Jerusalem. And on the twentieth day of the ninth month, all the people were sitting in the square before the house of God, greatly distressed by the occasion and because of the rain. ¹⁰Then Ezra the priest stood up and said to them, "You have been unfaithful; you have married foreign women, adding to Israel's guilt. ¹¹Now make confession to the LORD, the God of your fathers, and do his will. Separate yourselves from the peoples around you and from your foreign wives."

¹²The whole assembly responded with a loud voice: "You are right! We must do as you say. ¹³But there are many people here and it is the rainy season; so we cannot stand outside. Besides, this matter cannot be taken care of in a day or two, because we have sinned greatly in this thing. ¹⁴Let our officials act for the whole assembly. Then let everyone in our towns who has married a foreign woman come at a set time, along with the elders and judges of each town, until the fierce anger of our God in this matter is turned away from us." ¹⁵Only Jonathan son of Asahel and Jahzeiah son of Tikvah, supported by Meshullam and Shabbethai the Levite, opposed this.

¹⁶So the exiles did as was proposed. Ezra the priest selected men who were family heads, one from each family division, and all of them designated by name. On the first day of the tenth month they sat down to investigate the cases, ¹⁷and by the first day of the first month they finished dealing with all the men who had married foreign women.

Those Guilty of Intermarriage

¹⁸Among the descendants of the priests, the following had married foreign women:

From the descendants of Jeshua son of Jozadak, and his brothers: Maaseiah, Eliezer, Jarib and Gedaliah. ¹⁹(They all gave their hands in pledge to put away their wives, and for their guilt they each presented a ram from the flock as a guilt offering.)

²⁰From the descendants of Immer:
Hanani and Zebadiah.

²¹From the descendants of Harim:
Maaseiah, Elijah, Shemaiah, Jehiel and Uzziah.

²²From the descendants of Pashhur:
Elioenai, Maaseiah, Ishmael, Nethanel, Jozabad and Elasah.

²³Among the Levites:

Jozabad, Shimei, Kelaiah (that is, Kelita), Pethahiah, Judah and Eliezer.

²⁴From the singers:
Eliashib.
From the gatekeepers:
Shallum, Telem and Uri.

²⁵And among the other Israelites:

From the descendants of Parosh:
Ramiah, Izziah, Malkijah, Mijamin, Eleazar, Malkijah and Benaiah.

26 From the descendants of Elam:
  Mattaniah, Zechariah, Jehiel, Abdi, Jeremoth and Elijah.
27 From the descendants of Zattu:
  Elioenai, Eliashib, Mattaniah, Jeremoth, Zabad and Aziza.
28 From the descendants of Bebai:
  Jehohanan, Hananiah, Zabbai and Athlai.
29 From the descendants of Bani:
  Meshullam, Malluch, Adaiah, Jashub, Sheal and Jeremoth.
30 From the descendants of Pahath-Moab:
  Adna, Kelal, Benaiah, Maaseiah, Mattaniah, Bezalel, Binnui and Manasseh.
31 From the descendants of Harim:
  Eliezer, Ishijah, Malkijah, Shemaiah, Shimeon, 32 Benjamin, Malluch and Shemariah.

33 From the descendants of Hashum:
  Mattenai, Mattattah, Zabad, Eliphelet, Jeremai, Manasseh and Shimei.
34 From the descendants of Bani:
  Maadai, Amram, Uel, 35 Benaiah, Bedeiah, Keluhi, 36 Vaniah, Meremoth, Eliashib, 37 Mattaniah, Mattenai and Jaasu.
38 From the descendants of Binnui:a
  Shimei, 39 Shelemiah, Nathan, Adaiah, 40 Macnadebai, Shashai, Sharai, 41 Azarel, Shelemiah, Shemariah, 42 Shallum, Amariah and Joseph.
43 From the descendants of Nebo:
  Jeiel, Mattithiah, Zabad, Zebina, Jaddai, Joel and Benaiah.

44 All these had married foreign women, and some of them had children by these wives.b

---

a 37,38 See Septuagint (also 1 Esdras 9:34); Hebrew *Jaasu* 38 *and Bani and Binnui,*   b 44 Or *and they sent them away with their children*

Nehemiah

Author:
Unknown, but possibly
Ezra or Nehemiah.

Audience:
All Israel.

Date:
Around 430 B.C.

Setting:
Battling harsh opposition,
the exiles rebuild the
city wall of Jerusalem.

Verse to Remember:
So the wall was completed
on the twenty-fifth of Elul,
in fifty-two days. When all
our enemies heard about
this, all the surrounding
nations were afraid and
lost their self-confidence,
because they realized that
this work had been done
with the help of our God.
(6:15–16)

The city of Jerusalem had been the seat of King David and Solomon. In its glory days, it was a beacon to surrounding nations of how the great *God of Israel protected his people*. But the people were disobedient, and in judgment, they were marched away to exile by their Babylonian captors. The city's glory turned to ruin and shame. After decades, many of the exiles had returned to Jerusalem, but it was still vulnerable to the violence and scorn of its enemies. The walls and gates remained in ruins. When Nehemiah, cupbearer to King Artaxerxes, heard of the city's shame, he was devastated. He knew they had to rebuild the wall to offer protection to the people and to demonstrate *God's glory once again*.

Nehemiah prayed before he spoke with the king. He prayed on the journey. He prayed when he encountered resistance. *Look for his prayers* scattered throughout the book and see what you can learn. Nehemiah also demonstrated what it means to be a godly leader, and through his leadership there was powerful unity among God's people.

Nehemiah's Prayer

1 The words of Nehemiah son of Hacaliah:

In the month of Kislev in the twentieth year, while I was in the citadel of Susa, **2** Hanani, one of my brothers, came from Judah with some other men, and I questioned them about the Jewish remnant that survived the exile, and also about Jerusalem.

3 They said to me, "Those who survived the exile and are back in the province are in great trouble and disgrace. The wall of Jerusalem is broken down, and its gates have been burned with fire."

A Pattern for Prayer

Read: Nehemiah 1:1–11

IN 1960s SOUTHERN CALIFORNIA, the beaches were littered with hippies searching for the meaning of life through free love, psychedelic drugs and communal living. One day, a pastor's wife went to the beach and was distressed to see the aimless kids and began to weep. Kay Smith determined to do something, so she gathered several of her friends and, as she puts it, "saturated the air with prayer." She asked her husband, Pastor Chuck Smith, to open his church to this generation. Many people were shocked when the hippies showed up, barefoot and bedraggled, and sat on the floor rather than in the pews. But the Smiths embraced them. Their ministry was a vital part of the "Jesus Movement" that swept the country. It can be said that true revival begins with heartfelt tears but finds its voice in prayer.

Nehemiah, one of the most powerful Jews in Babylon, broke down in tears when he heard of Jerusalem's miserable condition. He mourned for God's holy city and scattered people. His compassion compelled him to pray and fast for them. His prayer reflected his heart's passion and also offers a pattern for our prayers.

First, Nehemiah acknowledged who God is: "the great and awesome God." When we focus on who God is, it helps to put our own problems into proper perspective.

Next Nehemiah acknowledged who he himself was: God's servant. When we maintain an attitude of humility toward our heavenly Father, we are reminded of our dependence on God.

Then Nehemiah confessed his own sins and the sins of the Israelites. He didn't gloss over the transgressions but stated them in honest repentance. Repentance freed him—and can free us—to make the next step in prayer.

Awed, humbled and forgiven—Nehemiah reminded God of his promises to his people. He recounted God's promises to the children of Israel and interceded for his people, asking God to hear his prayer and favor him.

What situation has brought you to tears? If it is enough to touch your heart, it's enough to bring you to your knees. Follow Nehemiah's pattern: Acknowledge who God is and who you are, confess your sins and remind God of his promises. When you do these things, you can come to God knowing that "he hears the prayer of the righteous" (Proverbs 15:29).

Go to page 579 for your next devotional reading.

Nehemiah 1:4

When I heard these things, I sat down and wept. For some days I mourned and fasted and prayed before the God of heaven.

reflection

1 When was the last time you wept in prayer for someone who needed God's help?

2 What word best describes Nehemiah's heart? Ask God to give you a heart of compassion like Nehemiah's.

3 Follow Nehemiah's pattern and pray for a person or situation causing you to grieve.

RELATED READINGS

Psalm 89:5–8;
Isaiah 25:1–9;
Matthew 6:9–13

Tuesday

⁴When I heard these things, I sat down and wept. For some days I mourned and fasted and prayed before the God of heaven. ⁵Then I said:

"O Lᴏʀᴅ, God of heaven, the great and awesome God, who keeps his covenant of love with those who love him and obey his commands, ⁶let your ear be attentive and your eyes open to hear the prayer your servant is praying before you day and night for your servants, the people of Israel. I confess the sins we Israelites, including myself and my father's house, have committed against you. ⁷We have acted very wickedly toward you. We have not obeyed the commands, decrees and laws you gave your servant Moses.

⁸"Remember the instruction you gave your servant Moses, saying, 'If you are unfaithful, I will scatter you among the nations, ⁹but if you return to me and obey my commands, then even if your exiled people are at the farthest horizon, I will gather them from there and bring them to the place I have chosen as a dwelling for my Name.'

¹⁰"They are your servants and your people, whom you redeemed by your great strength and your mighty hand. ¹¹O Lord, let your ear be attentive to the prayer of this your servant and to the prayer of your servants who delight in revering your name. Give your servant success today by granting him favor in the presence of this man."

I was cupbearer to the king.

Artaxerxes Sends Nehemiah to Jerusalem

2 In the month of Nisan in the twentieth year of King Artaxerxes, when wine was brought for him, I took the wine and gave it to the king. I had not been sad in his presence before; ²so the king asked me, "Why does your

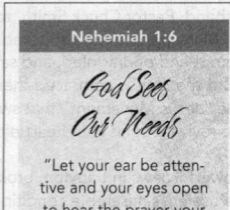

Nehemiah 1:6

God Sees Our Needs

"Let your ear be attentive and your eyes open to hear the prayer your servant is praying before you day and night for your servants, the people of Israel."

face look so sad when you are not ill? This can be nothing but sadness of heart."

I was very much afraid, ³but I said to the king, "May the king live forever! Why should my face not look sad when the city where my fathers are buried lies in ruins, and its gates have been destroyed by fire?"

⁴The king said to me, "What is it you want?"

Then I prayed to the God of heaven, ⁵and I answered the king, "If it pleases the king and if your servant has found favor in his sight, let him send me to the city in Judah where my fathers are buried so that I can rebuild it."

⁶Then the king, with the queen sitting beside him, asked me, "How long will your journey take, and when will you get back?" It pleased the king to send me; so I set a time.

⁷I also said to him, "If it pleases the king, may I have letters to the governors of Trans-Euphrates, so that they will provide me safe-conduct until I arrive in Judah? ⁸And may I have a letter to Asaph, keeper of the king's forest, so he will give me timber to make beams for the gates of the citadel by the temple and for the city wall and for the residence I will occupy?" And because the gracious hand of my God was upon me, the king granted my requests. ⁹So I went to the governors of Trans-Euphrates and gave them the king's letters. The king had also sent army officers and cavalry with me.

¹⁰When Sanballat the Horonite and Tobiah the Ammonite official heard about this, they were very much disturbed that someone had come to promote the welfare of the Israelites.

Nehemiah Inspects Jerusalem's Walls

¹¹I went to Jerusalem, and after staying there three days ¹²I set out during the night with a few men. I had not told anyone what my God had put in my heart to do for Jerusalem. There were no mounts with me except the one I was riding on.

¹³By night I went out through the Valley Gate toward the Jackalᵃ Well and the Dung

ᵃ13 Or Serpent or Fig

Help!

Read: Nehemiah 2:1-18

HOW WOULD YOU complete this sentence: "When I am afraid, I _____"? When things heat up do you run in the opposite direction, hide your true feelings or stick your head in the proverbial sand? Chances are you've done all three at one time or another. But here's another option: pray . . . fast!

Nehemiah faced a potentially terrifying situation. Four months before, he had discovered that the walls of Jerusalem had been destroyed and the gates burned with fire. The Jewish remnant had returned from exile, but their city was in ruins with no walls to protect them from enemy attacks and wild animals. Nehemiah longed to return to Jerusalem and help rebuild the walls, but as the king's cupbearer he was expected to be cheerful and keep his personal problems to himself. Any other response could mean death.

But Nehemiah couldn't hide his concern for God's city and people. The king noticed his servant's downcast countenance. "Why does your face look so sad?" he asked. "What do you want?"

Time must have stood still for Nehemiah. *This is what I've longed for, prayed about, dreamed of,* he may have thought. Or maybe he thought, *Oh no! This is what I feared!* But as the knot formed in Nehemiah's stomach and the lump rose in his throat, we see one of the most beautiful, spontaneous prayers in the Bible, "Then I prayed to the God of heaven."

All through the day we are faced with decisions great and small. Some require extended periods of prayer, such as Nehemiah experienced in chapter 1. Others prompt spontaneous prayers that come as easily and naturally as our very breath . . . *Help!*

What do you face today? What decisions do you have to make? You may not face a life-or-death situation like Nehemiah, but the God of heaven and earth longs to hear your simple, spontaneous prayers. *Help . . . now!*

Nehemiah 2:2,4

I was very much afraid . . . Then I prayed to the God of heaven.

reflection

1 How do you normally handle fearful situations?

2 How can you apply Nehemiah's prayer strategy to your life?

3 Have you experienced a time when God answered your specific prayer? Think of someone with whom you can share your story.

RELATED READINGS

Psalms 27:1–14; 55:16–23; 91:1–16; 1 Thessalonians 5:17

"Never be afraid to trust an unknown future to a known God."

Corrie ten Boom

Go to page 582 for your next devotional reading.

Gate, examining the walls of Jerusalem, which had been broken down, and its gates, which had been destroyed by fire. ¹⁴Then I moved on toward the Fountain Gate and the King's Pool, but there was not enough room for my mount to get through; ¹⁵so I went up the valley by night, examining the wall. Finally, I turned back and reentered through the Valley Gate. ¹⁶The officials did not know where I had gone or what I was doing, because as yet I had said nothing to the Jews or the priests or nobles or officials or any others who would be doing the work.

¹⁷Then I said to them, "You see the trouble we are in: Jerusalem lies in ruins, and its gates have been burned with fire. Come, let us rebuild the wall of Jerusalem, and we will no longer be in disgrace." ¹⁸I also told them about the gracious hand of my God upon me and what the king had said to me.

They replied, "Let us start rebuilding." So they began this good work.

¹⁹But when Sanballat the Horonite, Tobiah the Ammonite official and Geshem the Arab heard about it, they mocked and ridiculed us. "What is this you are doing?" they asked. "Are you rebelling against the king?"

²⁰I answered them by saying, "The God of heaven will give us success. We his servants will start rebuilding, but as for you, you have no share in Jerusalem or any claim or historic right to it."

Builders of the Wall

3 Eliashib the high priest and his fellow priests went to work and rebuilt the Sheep Gate. They dedicated it and set its doors in place, building as far as the Tower of the Hundred, which they dedicated, and as far as the Tower of Hananel. ²The men of Jericho built the adjoining section, and Zaccur son of Imri built next to them.

³The Fish Gate was rebuilt by the sons of Hassenaah. They laid its beams and put its doors and bolts and bars in place. ⁴Meremoth son of Uriah, the son of Hakkoz, repaired the next section. Next to him Meshullam son of Berekiah, the son of Meshezabel, made repairs, and next to him Zadok son of Baana also

made repairs. ⁵The next section was repaired by the men of Tekoa, but their nobles would not put their shoulders to the work under their supervisors.^a

⁶The Jeshanah^b Gate was repaired by Joiada son of Paseah and Meshullam son of Besodeiah. They laid its beams and put its doors and bolts and bars in place. ⁷Next to them, repairs were made by men from Gibeon and Mizpah—Melatiah of Gibeon and Jadon of Meronoth—places under the authority of the governor of Trans-Euphrates. ⁸Uzziel son of Harhaiah, one of the goldsmiths, repaired the next section; and Hananiah, one of the perfume-makers, made repairs next to that. They restored^c Jerusalem as far as the Broad Wall. ⁹Rephaiah son of Hur, ruler of a half-district of Jerusalem, repaired the next section. ¹⁰Adjoining this, Jedaiah son of Harumaph made repairs opposite his house, and Hattush son of Hashabneiah made repairs next to him. ¹¹Malkijah son of Harim and Hasshub son of Pahath-Moab repaired another section and the Tower of the Ovens. ¹²Shallum son of Hallohesh, ruler of a half-district of Jerusalem, repaired the next section with the help of his daughters.

¹³The Valley Gate was repaired by Hanun and the residents of Zanoah. They rebuilt it and put its doors and bolts and bars in place. They also repaired five hundred yards^d of the wall as far as the Dung Gate.

¹⁴The Dung Gate was repaired by Malkijah son of Recab, ruler of the district of Beth Hakkerem. He rebuilt it and put its doors and bolts and bars in place.

¹⁵The Fountain Gate was repaired by Shallun son of Col-Hozeh, ruler of the district of Mizpah. He rebuilt it, roofing it over and putting its doors and bolts and bars in place. He also repaired the wall of the Pool of Siloam,^e by the King's Garden, as far as the steps going down from the City of David. ¹⁶Beyond him, Nehemiah son of Azbuk, ruler of a half-district of Beth Zur, made repairs up to a point opposite the tombs^f of David, as far as the artificial pool and the House of the Heroes.

---

^a5 Or *their Lord* or *the governor*   ^b6 Or *Old*   ^c8 Or *They left out part of*   ^d13 Hebrew *a thousand cubits* (about 450 meters)   ^e15 Hebrew *Shelah*, a variant of *Shiloah*, that is, Siloam   ^f16 Hebrew; Septuagint, some Vulgate manuscripts and Syriac *tomb*

¹⁷Next to him, the repairs were made by the Levites under Rehum son of Bani. Beside him, Hashabiah, ruler of half the district of Keilah, carried out repairs for his district. ¹⁸Next to him, the repairs were made by their countrymen under Binnuiª son of Henadad, ruler of the other half-district of Keilah. ¹⁹Next to him, Ezer son of Jeshua, ruler of Mizpah, repaired another section, from a point facing the ascent to the armory as far as the angle. ²⁰Next to him, Baruch son of Zabbai zealously repaired another section, from the angle to the entrance of the house of Eliashib the high priest. ²¹Next to him, Meremoth son of Uriah, the son of Hakkoz, repaired another section, from the entrance of Eliashib's house to the end of it.

²²The repairs next to him were made by the priests from the surrounding region. ²³Beyond them, Benjamin and Hasshub made repairs in front of their house; and next to them, Azariah son of Maaseiah, the son of Ananiah, beside his house. ²⁴Next to him, Binnui son of Henadad repaired another section, from Azariah's house to the angle and the corner, ²⁵and Palal son of Uzai worked opposite the angle and the tower projecting from the upper palace near the court of the guard. Next to him, Pedaiah son of Parosh ²⁶and the temple servants living on the hill of Ophel made repairs up to a point opposite the Water Gate toward the east and the projecting tower. ²⁷Next to them, the men of Tekoa repaired another section, from the great projecting tower to the wall of Ophel.

²⁸Above the Horse Gate, the priests made repairs, each in front of his own house. ²⁹Next to them, Zadok son of Immer made repairs opposite his house. Next to him, Shemaiah son of Shecaniah, the guard at the East Gate, made repairs. ³⁰Next to him, Hananiah son of Shelemiah, and Hanun, the sixth son of Zalaph, repaired another section. Next to them, Meshullam son of Berekiah made repairs opposite his living quarters. ³¹Next to him, Malkijah, one of the goldsmiths, made repairs as far as the house of the temple servants and the merchants, opposite the Inspection Gate, and as far as the room above the corner; ³²and between the room above the corner and the Sheep Gate the goldsmiths and merchants made repairs.

Opposition to the Rebuilding

4 When Sanballat heard that we were rebuilding the wall, he became angry and was greatly incensed. He ridiculed the Jews, ²and in the presence of his associates and the army of Samaria, he said, "What are those feeble Jews doing? Will they restore their wall? Will they offer sacrifices? Will they finish in a day? Can they bring the stones back to life from those heaps of rubble—burned as they are?"

³Tobiah the Ammonite, who was at his side, said, "What they are building—if even a fox climbed up on it, he would break down their wall of stones!"

⁴Hear us, O our God, for we are despised. Turn their insults back on their own heads. Give them over as plunder in a land of captivity. ⁵Do not cover up their guilt or blot out their sins from your sight, for they have thrown insults in the face ofᵇ the builders.

⁶So we rebuilt the wall till all of it reached half its height, for the people worked with all their heart.

⁷But when Sanballat, Tobiah, the Arabs, the Ammonites and the men of Ashdod heard that the repairs to Jerusalem's walls had gone ahead and that the gaps were being closed, they were very angry. ⁸They all plotted together to come and fight against Jerusalem and stir up trouble against it. ⁹But we prayed to our God and posted a guard day and night to meet this threat.

¹⁰Meanwhile, the people in Judah said, "The strength of the laborers is giving out, and

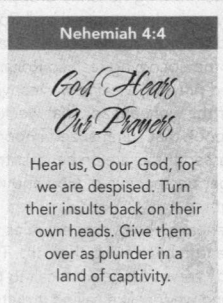

Nehemiah 4:4

God Hears Our Prayers

Hear us, O our God, for we are despised. Turn their insults back on their own heads. Give them over as plunder in a land of captivity.

ª18 Two Hebrew manuscripts and Syriac (see also Septuagint and verse 24); most Hebrew manuscripts *Bavvai*   ᵇ5 Or *have provoked you to anger before*

Persistence Prays

Nehemiah 4:8–10

They all plotted together to come and fight against Jerusalem and stir up trouble against it. But we prayed to our God and posted a guard day and night to meet this threat. Meanwhile, the people in Judah said, "The strength of the laborers is giving out, and there is so much rubble that we cannot rebuild the wall."

reflection

1 What task seems too big or too daunting for you to finish?

2 Who could you ask to come alongside you in prayer?

3 Write down some good things that might result if you do complete your task. Ask God to give you the persistence to finish what you've started.

RELATED READINGS

Isaiah 40:1–31;
2 Timothy 4:6–8;
Hebrews 12:1–13

WHEN THE JEWS listened to the taunts and insults of their enemies, they felt their strength dissipating and even felt like giving up. It took the watchful eyes of Nehemiah to see the deeper spiritual realities—that God was greater than the enemy and that he would strengthen his people so that they could finish building the wall.

Maxine recalled a time when discouragement nearly won a victory in her life. She had returned to college at midlife to get her teaching certification in English. She was overwhelmed at the thought of taking the National Teacher's Examination in English, which consisted of comprehensive questions about literature titles, authors and characters—all only fuzzy memories from her young-adult college days. A friend had taken the exam twice and failed, and Maxine dreaded that possibility.

One morning Roxanne dropped by Maxine's home. "I'm not exactly sure why I stopped by," Roxanne said. "I felt a tug to come by and see how you're doing." Maxine related her apprehensions about the upcoming test, so Roxanne prayed with her. When they finished praying, Maxine was convinced that God would strengthen her for the work ahead. That week she began studying a thousand-page book that summarized important literature. Two months later she passed the exam on her first try. Through prayer, she regained a proper perspective of God and was able to find renewed strength.

Nehemiah knew that enemies were plotting, so he summoned up strength by seeking the Lord. The simple phrase "but we prayed" serves as a clarion call to prayer when the work seems too hard and we feel like calling it quits. Think about it. If Nehemiah had given up, the walls of Jerusalem would not have been rebuilt. If Maxine had given up, students might have been robbed of a godly teacher. What if Jesus had given up? We would not have a Savior to forgive our sins. Thankfully, he finished what he started.

Through prayer, you can carry on too, knowing that "he who began a good work in you will carry it on to completion until the day of Christ Jesus" (Philippians 1:6).

Go to page 587 for your next devotional reading.

there is so much rubble that we cannot rebuild the wall."

¹¹Also our enemies said, "Before they know it or see us, we will be right there among them and will kill them and put an end to the work."

¹²Then the Jews who lived near them came and told us ten times over, "Wherever you turn, they will attack us."

¹³Therefore I stationed some of the people behind the lowest points of the wall at the exposed places, posting them by families, with their swords, spears and bows. ¹⁴After I looked things over, I stood up and said to the nobles, the officials and the rest of the people, "Don't be afraid of them. Remember the Lord, who is great and awesome, and fight for your brothers, your sons and your daughters, your wives and your homes."

¹⁵When our enemies heard that we were aware of their plot and that God had frustrated it, we all returned to the wall, each to his own work.

¹⁶From that day on, half of my men did the work, while the other half were equipped with spears, shields, bows and armor. The officers posted themselves behind all the people of Judah ¹⁷who were building the wall. Those who carried materials did their work with one hand and held a weapon in the other, ¹⁸and each of the builders wore his sword at his side as he worked. But the man who sounded the trumpet stayed with me.

¹⁹Then I said to the nobles, the officials and the rest of the people, "The work is extensive and spread out, and we are widely separated from each other along the wall. ²⁰Wherever you hear the sound of the trumpet, join us there. Our God will fight for us!"

²¹So we continued the work with half the men holding spears, from the first light of dawn till the stars came out. ²²At that time I also said to the people, "Have every man and his helper stay inside Jerusalem at night, so they can serve us as guards by night and workmen by day." ²³Neither I nor my brothers nor my men nor the guards with me took off our clothes; each had his weapon, even when he went for water.ᵃ

ᵃ23 The meaning of the Hebrew for this clause is uncertain.

Nehemiah Helps the Poor

5 Now the men and their wives raised a great outcry against their Jewish brothers. ²Some were saying, "We and our sons and daughters are numerous; in order for us to eat and stay alive, we must get grain."

³Others were saying, "We are mortgaging our fields, our vineyards and our homes to get grain during the famine."

⁴Still others were saying, "We have had to borrow money to pay the king's tax on our fields and vineyards. ⁵Although we are of the same flesh and blood as our countrymen and though our sons are as good as theirs, yet we have to subject our sons and daughters to slavery. Some of our daughters have already been enslaved, but we are powerless, because our fields and our vineyards belong to others."

⁶When I heard their outcry and these charges, I was very angry. ⁷I pondered them in my mind and then accused the nobles and officials. I told them, "You are exacting usury from your own countrymen!" So I called together a large meeting to deal with them ⁸and said: "As far as possible, we have bought back our Jewish brothers who were sold to the Gentiles. Now you are selling your brothers, only for them to be sold back to us!" They kept quiet, because they could find nothing to say.

⁹So I continued, "What you are doing is not right. Shouldn't you walk in the fear of our God to avoid the reproach of our Gentile enemies? ¹⁰I and my brothers and my men are also lending the people money and grain. But let the exacting of usury stop! ¹¹Give back to them immediately their fields, vineyards, olive groves and houses, and also the usury you are charging them—the hundredth part of the money, grain, new wine and oil."

¹²"We will give it back," they said. "And we will not demand anything more from them. We will do as you say."

Then I summoned the priests and made the nobles and officials take an oath to do what they had promised. ¹³I also shook out the folds of my robe and said, "In this way may God shake out of his house and possessions every man who does not keep this promise. So may such a man be shaken out and emptied!"

At this the whole assembly said, "Amen," and praised the LORD. And the people did as they had promised.

14Moreover, from the twentieth year of King Artaxerxes, when I was appointed to be their governor in the land of Judah, until his thirty-second year—twelve years—neither I nor my brothers ate the food allotted to the governor. 15But the earlier governors—those preceding me—placed a heavy burden on the people and took forty shekels*a* of silver from them in addition to food and wine. Their assistants also lorded it over the people. But out of reverence for God I did not act like that. 16Instead, I devoted myself to the work on this wall. All my men were assembled there for the work; we*b* did not acquire any land.

17Furthermore, a hundred and fifty Jews and officials ate at my table, as well as those who came to us from the surrounding nations. 18Each day one ox, six choice sheep and some poultry were prepared for me, and every ten days an abundant supply of wine of all kinds. In spite of all this, I never demanded the food allotted to the governor, because the demands were heavy on these people.

19Remember me with favor, O my God, for all I have done for these people.

Further Opposition to the Rebuilding

6 When word came to Sanballat, Tobiah, Geshem the Arab and the rest of our enemies that I had rebuilt the wall and not a gap was left in it—though up to that time I had not set the doors in the gates— 2Sanballat and Geshem sent me this message: "Come, let us meet together in one of the villages*c* on the plain of Ono."

But they were scheming to harm me; 3so I sent messengers to them with this reply: "I am carrying on a great project and cannot go down. Why should the work stop while I leave it and go down to you?" 4Four times they sent me the same message, and each time I gave them the same answer.

5Then, the fifth time, Sanballat sent his aide to me with the same message, and in his hand was an unsealed letter 6in which was written:

"It is reported among the nations—and Geshem*d* says it is true—that you and the Jews are plotting to revolt, and therefore you are building the wall. Moreover, according to these reports you are about to become their king 7and have even appointed prophets to make this proclamation about you in Jerusalem: 'There is a king in Judah!' Now this report will get back to the king; so come, let us confer together."

8I sent him this reply: "Nothing like what you are saying is happening; you are just making it up out of your head."

9They were all trying to frighten us, thinking, "Their hands will get too weak for the work, and it will not be completed."

But I prayed, "Now strengthen my hands."

10One day I went to the house of Shemaiah son of Delaiah, the son of Mehetabel, who was shut in at his home. He said, "Let us meet in the house of God, inside the temple, and let us close the temple doors, because men are coming to kill you—by night they are coming to kill you."

11But I said, "Should a man like me run away? Or should one like me go into the temple to save his life? I will not go!" 12I realized that God had not sent him, but that he had prophesied against me because Tobiah and Sanballat had hired him. 13He had been hired to intimidate me so that I would commit a sin by doing this, and then they would give me a bad name to discredit me.

14Remember Tobiah and Sanballat, O my God, because of what they have done; remember also the prophetess Noadiah and the rest of the prophets who have been trying to intimidate me.

The Completion of the Wall

15So the wall was completed on the twenty-fifth of Elul, in fifty-two days. 16When all our enemies heard about this, all the surrounding nations were afraid and lost their self-confidence, because they realized that this work had been done with the help of our God.

17Also, in those days the nobles of Judah

---

*a*15 That is, about 1 pound (about 0.5 kilogram)   *b*16 Most Hebrew manuscripts; some Hebrew manuscripts, Septuagint, Vulgate and Syriac *I*   *c*2 Or *in Kephirim*   *d*6 Hebrew *Gashmu*, a variant of *Geshem* were sending many letters to Tobiah, and replies from Tobiah kept coming to them. 18For many in Judah were under oath to him, since he was son-in-law to Shecaniah son of Arah, and his son Jehohanan had married the daughter of Meshullam son of Berekiah. 19Moreover, they kept reporting to me his good deeds and then telling him what I said. And Tobiah sent letters to intimidate me.

7 After the wall had been rebuilt and I had set the doors in place, the gatekeepers and the singers and the Levites were appointed. 2I put in charge of Jerusalem my brother Hanani, along with*a* Hananiah the commander of the citadel, because he was a man of integrity and feared God more than most men do. 3I said to them, "The gates of Jerusalem are not to be opened until the sun is hot. While the gatekeepers are still on duty, have them shut the doors and bar them. Also appoint residents of Jerusalem as guards, some at their posts and some near their own houses."

The List of the Exiles Who Returned

4Now the city was large and spacious, but there were few people in it, and the houses had not yet been rebuilt. 5So my God put it into my heart to assemble the nobles, the officials and the common people for registration by families. I found the genealogical record of those who had been the first to return. This is what I found written there:

6These are the people of the province who came up from the captivity of the exiles whom Nebuchadnezzar king of Babylon had taken captive (they returned to Jerusalem and Judah, each to his own town, 7in company with Zerubbabel, Jeshua, Nehemiah, Azariah, Raamiah, Nahamani, Mordecai, Bilshan, Mispereth, Bigvai, Nehum and Baanah):

The list of the men of Israel:

8the descendants of Parosh	2,172
9of Shephatiah	372
10of Arah	652
11of Pahath-Moab (through the line of Jeshua and Joab)	2,818
12of Elam	1,254
13of Zattu	845
14of Zaccai	760
15of Binnui	648
16of Bebai	628
17of Azgad	2,322
18of Adonikam	667
19of Bigvai	2,067
20of Adin	655
21of Ater (through Hezekiah)	98
22of Hashum	328
23of Bezai	324
24of Hariph	112
25of Gibeon	95
26the men of Bethlehem and Netophah	188
27of Anathoth	128
28of Beth Azmaveth	42
29of Kiriath Jearim, Kephirah and Beeroth	743
30of Ramah and Geba	621
31of Micmash	122
32of Bethel and Ai	123
33of the other Nebo	52
34of the other Elam	1,254
35of Harim	320
36of Jericho	345
37of Lod, Hadid and Ono	721
38of Senaah	3,930

39The priests:

the descendants of Jedaiah (through the family of Jeshua)	973
40of Immer	1,052
41of Pashhur	1,247
42of Harim	1,017

43The Levites:

the descendants of Jeshua (through Kadmiel through the line of Hodaviah)	74

44The singers:

the descendants of Asaph	148

45The gatekeepers:

the descendants of Shallum, Ater, Talmon, Akkub, Hatita and Shobai	138

a2 Or *Hanani, that is,*

46 The temple servants:

the descendants of
    Ziha, Hasupha, Tabbaoth,
47 Keros, Sia, Padon,
48 Lebana, Hagaba, Shalmai,
49 Hanan, Giddel, Gahar,
50 Reaiah, Rezin, Nekoda,
51 Gazzam, Uzza, Paseah,
52 Besai, Meunim, Nephusim,
53 Bakbuk, Hakupha, Harhur,
54 Bazluth, Mehida, Harsha,
55 Barkos, Sisera, Temah,
56 Neziah and Hatipha

57 The descendants of the servants of Solomon:

the descendants of
    Sotai, Sophereth, Perida,
58 Jaala, Darkon, Giddel,
59 Shephatiah, Hattil,
    Pokereth-Hazzebaim and Amon

60 The temple servants and the
    descendants of the servants
    of Solomon   392

61 The following came up from the towns of Tel Melah, Tel Harsha, Kerub, Addon and Immer, but they could not show that their families were descended from Israel:

62 the descendants of
    Delaiah, Tobiah and Nekoda   642

63 And from among the priests:

the descendants of
    Hobaiah, Hakkoz and Barzillai (a
    man who had married a daughter of
    Barzillai the Gileadite and was called
    by that name).

64 These searched for their family records, but they could not find them and so were excluded from the priesthood as unclean. 65 The governor, therefore, ordered them not to eat any of the most sacred food until there should be a priest ministering with the Urim and Thummim.

66 The whole company numbered 42,360, 67 besides their 7,337 menservants and maidservants; and they also had 245 men and women singers. 68 There were 736 horses, 245 mules,*a* 69 435 camels and 6,720 donkeys.

70 Some of the heads of the families contributed to the work. The governor gave to the treasury 1,000 drachmas*b* of gold, 50 bowls and 530 garments for priests. 71 Some of the heads of the families gave to the treasury for the work 20,000 drachmas*c* of gold and 2,200 minas*d* of silver. 72 The total given by the rest of the people was 20,000 drachmas of gold, 2,000 minas*e* of silver and 67 garments for priests.

73 The priests, the Levites, the gatekeepers, the singers and the temple servants, along with certain of the people and the rest of the Israelites, settled in their own towns.

Ezra Reads the Law

8 When the seventh month came and the Israelites had settled in their towns, 1 all the people assembled as one man in the square before the Water Gate. They told Ezra the scribe to bring out the Book of the Law of Moses, which the LORD had commanded for Israel.

2 So on the first day of the seventh month Ezra the priest brought the Law before the assembly, which was made up of men and women and all who were able to understand. 3 He read it aloud from daybreak till noon as he faced the square before the Water Gate in the presence of the men, women and others who could understand. And all the people listened attentively to the Book of the Law.

4 Ezra the scribe stood on a high wooden platform built for the occasion. Beside him on his right stood Mattithiah, Shema, Anaiah, Uriah, Hilkiah and Maaseiah; and on his left were Pedaiah, Mishael, Malkijah, Hashum, Hashbaddanah, Zechariah and Meshullam.

5 Ezra opened the book. All the people could see him because he was standing above them; and as he opened it, the people all stood up.

a68 Some Hebrew manuscripts (see also Ezra 2:66); most Hebrew manuscripts do not have this verse.   *b70* That is, about 19 pounds (about 8.5 kilograms)   *c71* That is, about 375 pounds (about 170 kilograms); also in verse 72   *d71* That is, about 1 1/3 tons (about 1.2 metric tons)   *e72* That is, about 1 1/4 tons (about 1.1 metric tons)

Unlimited Source of Joy

Read: Nehemiah 8:1–12

WHAT A GLORIOUS DAY! The people are finally celebrating the completion of their dream—the rebuilding of the wall around Jerusalem. Yet, upon hearing the reading of God's laws, the people are cut to the heart, grieved by their sin. Nehemiah tells the people to put away their mourning, "For the joy of the LORD is your strength." How could they have joy in the face of their guilt and sorrow? How could they experience joy even when they had neglected God's ways?

Let's bring this into our own lives. Can we experience joy even in the midst of realizing how broken and needy we are? In the midst of our disappointment and struggles? Yes, we can! The joy available to us—like the joy that was available to the people of Jerusalem—is not dependent upon us or on our circumstances. It's not dependent on our temperament or hormone levels. This joy does not come from "having it all together," or from everything going well, accomplishing our goals or overcoming obstacles. No, this joy is "of the LORD."

Joy—true joy—originates from God and from living in close connection with God, not from our immediate situation or emotional state. Joy is always accessible to us because God has given us his Holy Spirit (see Galatians 5:22–23). Not only do we have constant access to the Spirit of joy, but this joy is also, according to Nehemiah, our very strength; and it is available now! The enemy tries to deceive us into believing we cannot experience joy—at least not just yet. We buy into the thinking that says, "When this is over, when I finish this, when I obtain that, when I've resolved this . . . then I can experience joy."

Yet God wants us to know his joy *now*. Not tomorrow, not when we're healed, not when sorrow has passed, not when we've become successful, not when our child or spouse changes, not when we've lost ten pounds, not when we've paid off our debt, received a promotion or bought a bigger home, but *now*—this day!

Lasting joy does not reside in God's blessings, God's favor, God's gifts or God's people, but in God *himself*. Take time this day to seek the Lord and draw upon him to find your joy—your strength.

Nehemiah 8:10

"Do not grieve, for the joy of the LORD is your strength."

reflection

1 What's the difference between joy and feeling happy?

2 What or whom do you tend to look to first as your source of joy?

3 What are you waiting to overcome, obtain or get rid of before experiencing God's joy?

RELATED READINGS

Psalms 43:1–5; 51:1–12; 118:24; John 15:9–17

Go to page 598 for your next devotional reading.

⁶Ezra praised the LORD, the great God; and all the people lifted their hands and responded, "Amen! Amen!" Then they bowed down and worshiped the LORD with their faces to the ground.

⁷The Levites—Jeshua, Bani, Sherebiah, Jamin, Akkub, Shabbethai, Hodiah, Maaseiah, Kelita, Azariah, Jozabad, Hanan and Pelaiah—instructed the people in the Law while the people were standing there. ⁸They read from the Book of the Law of God, making it clear*ᵃ* and giving the meaning so that the people could understand what was being read.

⁹Then Nehemiah the governor, Ezra the priest and scribe, and the Levites who were instructing the people said to them all, "This day is sacred to the LORD your God. Do not mourn or weep." For all the people had been weeping as they listened to the words of the Law.

¹⁰Nehemiah said, "Go and enjoy choice food and sweet drinks, and send some to those who have nothing prepared. This day is sacred to our Lord. Do not grieve, for the joy of the LORD is your strength."

¹¹The Levites calmed all the people, saying, "Be still, for this is a sacred day. Do not grieve."

¹²Then all the people went away to eat and drink, to send portions of food and to celebrate with great joy, because they now understood the words that had been made known to them.

¹³On the second day of the month, the heads of all the families, along with the priests and the Levites, gathered around Ezra the scribe to give attention to the words of the Law. ¹⁴They found written in the Law, which the LORD had commanded through Moses, that the Israelites were to live in booths during the feast of the seventh month ¹⁵and that they should *proclaim this* word and spread it throughout their towns and in Jerusalem: "Go out into the hill country and bring back branches from olive and wild olive trees, and from myrtles, palms and shade trees, to make booths"—as it is written.*ᵇ*

¹⁶So the people went out and brought back branches and built themselves booths on their own roofs, in their courtyards, in the courts of the house of God and in the square by the Water Gate and the one by the Gate of Ephraim. ¹⁷The whole company that had returned from exile built booths and lived in them. From the days of Joshua son of Nun until that day, the Israelites had not celebrated it like this. And their joy was very great.

¹⁸Day after day, from the first day to the last, Ezra read from the Book of the Law of God. They celebrated the feast for seven days, and on the eighth day, in accordance with the regulation, there was an assembly.

The Israelites Confess Their Sins

9 On the twenty-fourth day of the same month, the Israelites gathered together, fasting and wearing sackcloth and having dust on their heads. ²Those of Israelite descent had separated themselves from all foreigners. They stood in their places and confessed their sins and the wickedness of their fathers. ³They stood where they were and read from the Book of the Law of the LORD their God for a quarter of the day, and spent another quarter in confession and in worshiping the LORD their God. ⁴Standing on the stairs were the Levites—Jeshua, Bani, Kadmiel, Shebaniah, Bunni, Sherebiah, Bani and Kenani—who called with loud voices to the LORD their God. ⁵And the Levites—Jeshua, Kadmiel, Bani, Hashabneiah, Sherebiah, Hodiah, Shebaniah and Pethahiah—said: "Stand up and praise the LORD your God, who is from everlasting to everlasting.*ᶜ*"

"Blessed be your glorious name, and may it be exalted above all blessing and praise. ⁶You alone are the LORD. You

Nehemiah 9:6

God Gives Life

"You alone are the LORD. You made the heavens, even the highest heavens, and all their starry host, the earth and all that is on it, the seas and all that is in them. You give life to everything, and the multitudes of heaven worship you."

---

*ᵃ*8 Or *God, translating it*   *ᵇ*15 See Lev. 23:37–40.   *ᶜ*5 Or *God for ever and ever* made the heavens, even the highest heavens, and all their starry host, the earth and all that is on it, the seas and all that is in them. You give life to everything, and the multitudes of heaven worship you.

7"You are the LORD God, who chose Abram and brought him out of Ur of the Chaldeans and named him Abraham. 8You found his heart faithful to you, and you made a covenant with him to give to his descendants the land of the Canaanites, Hittites, Amorites, Perizzites, Jebusites and Girgashites. You have kept your promise because you are righteous.

9"You saw the suffering of our forefathers in Egypt; you heard their cry at the Red Sea.*a* 10You sent miraculous signs and wonders against Pharaoh, against all his officials and all the people of his land, for you knew how arrogantly the Egyptians treated them. You made a name for yourself, which remains to this day. 11You divided the sea before them, so that they passed through it on dry ground, but you hurled their pursuers into the depths, like a stone into mighty waters. 12By day you led them with a pillar of cloud, and by night with a pillar of fire to give them light on the way they were to take.

13"You came down on Mount Sinai; you spoke to them from heaven. You gave them regulations and laws that are just and right, and decrees and commands that are good. 14You made known to them your holy Sabbath and gave them commands, decrees and laws through your servant Moses. 15In their hunger you gave them bread from heaven and in their thirst you brought them water from the rock; you told them to go in and take possession of the land you had sworn with uplifted hand to give them.

16"But they, our forefathers, became arrogant and stiff-necked, and did not obey your commands. 17They refused to listen and failed to remember the miracles you performed among them. They became stiff-necked and in their rebellion

appointed a leader in order to return to their slavery. But you are a forgiving God, gracious and compassionate, slow to anger and abounding in love. Therefore you did not desert them, 18even when they cast for themselves an image of a calf and said, 'This is your god, who brought you up out of Egypt,' or when they committed awful blasphemies.

19"Because of your great compassion you did not abandon them in the desert. By day the pillar of cloud did not cease to guide them on their path, nor the pillar of fire by night to shine on the way they were to take. 20You gave your good Spirit to instruct them. You did not withhold your manna from their mouths, and you gave them water for their thirst. 21For forty years you sustained them in the desert; they lacked nothing, their clothes did not wear out nor did their feet become swollen.

22"You gave them kingdoms and nations, allotting to them even the remotest frontiers. They took over the country of Sihon*b* king of Heshbon and the country of Og king of Bashan. 23You made their sons as numerous as the stars in the sky, and you brought them into the land that you told their fathers to enter and possess. 24Their sons went in and took possession of the land. You subdued before them the Canaanites, who lived in the land; you handed the Canaanites over to them, along with their kings and the peoples of the land, to deal with them as they pleased. 25They captured fortified cities and fertile land; they took possession of houses filled with all kinds of good things, wells already dug, vineyards, olive groves and fruit trees in abundance. They ate to the full and were well-nourished; they reveled in your great goodness.

26"But they were disobedient and rebelled against you; they put your law behind their backs. They killed your prophets, who had admonished them in order to turn them back to you; they committed awful blasphemies. 27So you

---

*a*9 Hebrew *Yam Suph*; that is, Sea of Reeds *b*22 One Hebrew manuscript and Septuagint; most Hebrew manuscripts *Sihon, that is, the country of the* handed them over to their enemies, who oppressed them. But when they were oppressed they cried out to you. From heaven you heard them, and in your great compassion you gave them deliverers, who rescued them from the hand of their enemies.

28"But as soon as they were at rest, they again did what was evil in your sight. Then you abandoned them to the hand of their enemies so that they ruled over them. And when they cried out to you again, you heard from heaven, and in your compassion you delivered them time after time.

29"You warned them to return to your law, but they became arrogant and disobeyed your commands. They sinned against your ordinances, by which a man will live if he obeys them. Stubbornly they turned their backs on you, became stiff-necked and refused to listen. 30For many years you were patient with them. By your Spirit you admonished them through your prophets. Yet they paid no attention, so you handed them over to the neighboring peoples. 31But in your great mercy you did not put an end to them or abandon them, for you are a gracious and merciful God.

32"Now therefore, O our God, the great, mighty and awesome God, who keeps his covenant of love, do not let all this hardship seem trifling in your eyes—the hardship that has come upon us, upon our kings and leaders, upon our priests and prophets, upon our fathers and all your people, from the days of the kings of Assyria until today. 33In all that has happened to us, you have been just; you have acted faithfully, while we did wrong. 34Our kings, our leaders, our priests and our fathers did not follow your law; they did not pay attention to your commands or the warnings you gave them. 35Even while they were in their kingdom, enjoying your great goodness to them in the spacious and fertile land you gave them, they did not serve you or turn from their evil ways.

36"But see, we are slaves today, slaves in the land you gave our forefathers so they could eat its fruit and the other good things it produces. 37Because of our sins, its abundant harvest goes to the kings you have placed over us. They rule over our bodies and our cattle as they please. We are in great distress.

The Agreement of the People

38"In view of all this, we are making a binding agreement, putting it in writing, and our leaders, our Levites and our priests are affixing their seals to it."

10 Those who sealed it were:

Nehemiah the governor, the son of Hacaliah.

Zedekiah, 2Seraiah, Azariah, Jeremiah, 3Pashhur, Amariah, Malkijah, 4Hattush, Shebaniah, Malluch, 5Harim, Meremoth, Obadiah, 6Daniel, Ginnethon, Baruch, 7Meshullam, Abijah, Mijamin, 8Maaziah, Bilgai and Shemaiah. These were the priests.

9The Levites:

Jeshua son of Azaniah, Binnui of the sons of Henadad, Kadmiel, 10and their associates: Shebaniah, Hodiah, Kelita, Pelaiah, Hanan, 11Mica, Rehob, Hashabiah, 12Zaccur, Sherebiah, Shebaniah, 13Hodiah, Bani and Beninu.

14The leaders of the people:

Parosh, Pahath-Moab, Elam, Zattu, Bani, 15Bunni, Azgad, Bebai, 16Adonijah, Bigvai, Adin, 17Ater, Hezekiah, Azzur, 18Hodiah, Hashum, Bezai, 19Hariph, Anathoth, Nebai, 20Magpiash, Meshullam, Hezir, 21Meshezabel, Zadok, Jaddua, 22Pelatiah, Hanan, Anaiah, 23Hoshea, Hananiah, Hasshub, 24Hallohesh, Pilha, Shobek, 25Rehum, Hashabnah, Maaseiah, 26Ahiah, Hanan, Anan, 27Malluch, Harim and Baanah.

28 "The rest of the people—priests, Levites, gatekeepers, singers, temple servants and all who separated themselves from the neighboring peoples for the sake of the Law of God, together with their wives and all their sons and daughters who are able to understand— 29 all these now join their brothers the nobles, and bind themselves with a curse and an oath to follow the Law of God given through Moses the servant of God and to obey carefully all the commands, regulations and decrees of the LORD our Lord.

30 "We promise not to give our daughters in marriage to the peoples around us or take their daughters for our sons.

31 "When the neighboring peoples bring merchandise or grain to sell on the Sabbath, we will not buy from them on the Sabbath or on any holy day. Every seventh year we will forgo working the land and will cancel all debts.

32 "We assume the responsibility for carrying out the commands to give a third of a shekel[a] each year for the service of the house of our God: 33 for the bread set out on the table; for the regular grain offerings and burnt offerings; for the offerings on the Sabbaths, New Moon festivals and appointed feasts; for the holy offerings; for sin offerings to make atonement for Israel; and for all the duties of the house of our God.

34 "We—the priests, the Levites and the people—have cast lots to determine when each of our families is to bring to the house of our God at set times each year a contribution of wood to burn on the altar of the LORD our God, as it is written in the Law.

35 "We also assume responsibility for bringing to the house of the LORD each year the firstfruits of our crops and of every fruit tree.

36 "As it is also written in the Law, we will bring the firstborn of our sons and of our cattle, of our herds and of our flocks to the house of our God, to the priests ministering there.

37 "Moreover, we will bring to the storerooms of the house of our God, to the priests, the first of our ground meal, of our ˻grain˼ offerings, of the fruit of all our trees and of our new wine and oil. And we will bring a tithe of our crops to the Levites, for it is the Levites who collect the tithes in all the towns where we work. 38 A priest descended from Aaron is to accompany the Levites when they receive the tithes, and the Levites are to bring a tenth of the tithes up to the house of our God, to the storerooms of the treasury. 39 The people of Israel, including the Levites, are to bring their contributions of grain, new wine and oil to the storerooms where the articles for the sanctuary are kept and where the ministering priests, the gatekeepers and the singers stay.

"We will not neglect the house of our God."

The New Residents of Jerusalem

11 Now the leaders of the people settled in Jerusalem, and the rest of the people cast lots to bring one out of every ten to live in Jerusalem, the holy city, while the remaining nine were to stay in their own towns. 2 The people commended all the men who volunteered to live in Jerusalem.

3 These are the provincial leaders who settled in Jerusalem (now some Israelites, priests, Levites, temple servants and descendants of Solomon's servants lived in the towns of Judah, each on his own property in the various towns, 4 while other people from both Judah and Benjamin lived in Jerusalem):

From the descendants of Judah:

Athaiah son of Uzziah, the son of Zechariah, the son of Amariah, the son of Shephatiah, the son of Mahalalel, a descendant of Perez; 5 and Maaseiah son of Baruch, the son of Col-Hozeh, the son of Hazaiah, the son of Adaiah, the son of Joiarib, the son of Zechariah, a descendant of Shelah. 6 The descendants of Perez who lived in Jerusalem totaled 468 able men.

a32 That is, about 1/8 ounce (about 4 grams)

7From the descendants of Benjamin:

Sallu son of Meshullam, the son of Joed, the son of Pedaiah, the son of Kolaiah, the son of Maaseiah, the son of Ithiel, the son of Jeshaiah, 8and his followers, Gabbai and Sallai—928 men. 9Joel son of Zicri was their chief officer, and Judah son of Hassenuah was over the Second District of the city.

10From the priests:

Jedaiah; the son of Joiarib; Jakin; 11Seraiah son of Hilkiah, the son of Meshullam, the son of Zadok, the son of Meraioth, the son of Ahitub, supervisor in the house of God, 12and their associates, who carried on work for the temple—822 men; Adaiah son of Jeroham, the son of Pelaliah, the son of Amzi, the son of Zechariah, the son of Pashhur, the son of Malkijah, 13and his associates, who were heads of families—242 men; Amashsai son of Azarel, the son of Ahzai, the son of Meshillemoth, the son of Immer, 14and his*a* associates, who were able men—128. Their chief officer was Zabdiel son of Haggedolim.

15From the Levites:

Shemaiah son of Hasshub, the son of Azrikam, the son of Hashabiah, the son of Bunni; 16Shabbethai and Jozabad, two of the heads of the Levites, who had charge of the outside work of the house of God; 17Mattaniah son of Mica, the son of Zabdi, the son of Asaph, the director who led in thanksgiving and prayer; Bakbukiah, second among his associates; and Abda son of Shammua, the son of Galal, the son of Jeduthun. 18The Levites in the holy city totaled 284.

19The gatekeepers:

Akkub, Talmon and their associates, who kept watch at the gates—172 men.

20The rest of the Israelites, with the priests and Levites, were in all the towns of Judah, each on his ancestral property.

21The temple servants lived on the hill of Ophel, and Ziha and Gishpa were in charge of them.

22The chief officer of the Levites in Jerusalem was Uzzi son of Bani, the son of Hashabiah, the son of Mattaniah, the son of Mica. Uzzi was one of Asaph's descendants, who were the singers responsible for the service of the house of God. 23The singers were under the king's orders, which regulated their daily activity.

24Pethahiah son of Meshezabel, one of the descendants of Zerah son of Judah, was the king's agent in all affairs relating to the people.

25As for the villages with their fields, some of the people of Judah lived in Kiriath Arba and its surrounding settlements, in Dibon and its settlements, in Jekabzeel and its villages, 26in Jeshua, in Moladah, in Beth Pelet, 27in Hazar Shual, in Beersheba and its settlements, 28in Ziklag, in Meconah and its settlements, 29in En Rimmon, in Zorah, in Jarmuth, 30Zanoah, Adullam and their villages, in Lachish and its fields, and in Azekah and its settlements. So they were living all the way from Beersheba to the Valley of Hinnom.

31The descendants of the Benjamites from Geba lived in Micmash, Aija, Bethel and its settlements, 32in Anathoth, Nob and Ananiah, 33in Hazor, Ramah and Gittaim, 34in Hadid, Zeboim and Neballat, 35in Lod and Ono, and in the Valley of the Craftsmen.

36Some of the divisions of the Levites of Judah settled in Benjamin.

Priests and Levites

12 These were the priests and Levites who returned with Zerubbabel son of Shealtiel and with Jeshua:

Seraiah, Jeremiah, Ezra,
2 Amariah, Malluch, Hattush,
3 Shecaniah, Rehum, Meremoth,
4 Iddo, Ginnethon,*b* Abijah,
5 Mijamin,*c* Moadiah, Bilgah,
6 Shemaiah, Joiarib, Jedaiah,
7 Sallu, Amok, Hilkiah and Jedaiah.

These were the leaders of the priests and their associates in the days of Jeshua.

8The Levites were Jeshua, Binnui, Kadmiel, Sherebiah, Judah, and also Mattaniah, who,

---

*a*14 Most Septuagint manuscripts; Hebrew *their*   *b*4 Many Hebrew manuscripts and Vulgate (see also Neh. 12:16); most Hebrew manuscripts *Ginnethoi*   *c*5 A variant of *Miniamin* together with his associates, was in charge of the songs of thanksgiving. ⁹Bakbukiah and Unni, their associates, stood opposite them in the services.

¹⁰Jeshua was the father of Joiakim, Joiakim the father of Eliashib, Eliashib the father of Joiada, ¹¹Joiada the father of Jonathan, and Jonathan the father of Jaddua.

¹²In the days of Joiakim, these were the heads of the priestly families:

of Seraiah's family, Meraiah;

of Jeremiah's, Hananiah;

¹³ of Ezra's, Meshullam;

of Amariah's, Jehohanan;

¹⁴ of Malluch's, Jonathan;

of Shecaniah's,ᵃ Joseph;

¹⁵ of Harim's, Adna;

of Meremoth's,ᵇ Helkai;

¹⁶ of Iddo's, Zechariah;

of Ginnethon's, Meshullam;

¹⁷ of Abijah's, Zicri;

of Miniamin's and of Moadiah's, Piltai;

¹⁸ of Bilgah's, Shammua;

of Shemaiah's, Jehonathan;

¹⁹ of Joiarib's, Mattenai;

of Jedaiah's, Uzzi;

²⁰ of Sallu's, Kallai;

of Amok's, Eber;

²¹ of Hilkiah's, Hashabiah;

of Jedaiah's, Nethanel.

²²The family heads of the Levites in the days of Eliashib, Joiada, Johanan and Jaddua, as well as those of the priests, were recorded in the reign of Darius the Persian. ²³The family heads among the descendants of Levi up to the time of Johanan son of Eliashib were recorded in the book of the annals. ²⁴And the leaders of the Levites were Hashabiah, Sherebiah, Jeshua son of Kadmiel, and their associates, who stood opposite them to give praise and thanksgiving, one section responding to the other, as prescribed by David the man of God.

²⁵Mattaniah, Bakbukiah, Obadiah, Meshullam, Talmon and Akkub were gatekeepers who guarded the storerooms at the gates. ²⁶They served in the days of Joiakim son of Jeshua, the son of Jozadak, and in the days of Nehemiah the governor and of Ezra the priest and scribe.

Dedication of the Wall of Jerusalem

²⁷At the dedication of the wall of Jerusalem, the Levites were sought out from where they lived and were brought to Jerusalem to celebrate joyfully the dedication with songs of thanksgiving and with the music of cymbals, harps and lyres. ²⁸The singers also were brought together from the region around Jerusalem—from the villages of the Netophathites, ²⁹from Beth Gilgal, and from the area of Geba and Azmaveth, for the singers had built villages for themselves around Jerusalem. ³⁰When the priests and Levites had purified themselves ceremonially, they purified the people, the gates and the wall.

³¹I had the leaders of Judah go up on topᶜ of the wall. I also assigned two large choirs to give thanks. One was to proceed on topᵈ of the wall to the right, toward the Dung Gate. ³²Hoshaiah and half the leaders of Judah followed them, ³³along with Azariah, Ezra, Meshullam, ³⁴Judah, Benjamin, Shemaiah, Jeremiah, ³⁵as well as some priests with trumpets, and also Zechariah son of Jonathan, the son of Shemaiah, the son of Mattaniah, the son of Micaiah, the son of Zaccur, the son of Asaph, ³⁶and his associates—Shemaiah, Azarel, Milalai, Gilalai, Maai, Nethanel, Judah and Hanani—with musical instruments ⌜prescribed by⌝ David the man of God. Ezra the scribe led the procession. ³⁷At the Fountain Gate they continued directly up the steps of the City of David on the ascent to the wall and passed above the house of David to the Water Gate on the east.

³⁸The second choir proceeded in the opposite direction. I followed them on topᵉ of the wall, together with half the people—past the Tower of the Ovens to the Broad Wall, ³⁹over the Gate of Ephraim, the Jeshanahᶠ Gate, the Fish Gate, the Tower of Hananel and the Tower of the Hundred, as far as the Sheep Gate. At the Gate of the Guard they stopped.

⁴⁰The two choirs that gave thanks then took their places in the house of God; so did I, together with half the officials, ⁴¹as well as the priests—Eliakim, Maaseiah, Miniamin, Micaiah, Elioenai, Zechariah and Hananiah with their trumpets— ⁴²and also Maaseiah,

---

ᵃ14 Very many Hebrew manuscripts, some Septuagint manuscripts and Syriac (see also Neh. 12:3); most Hebrew manuscripts *Shebaniah's*   ᵇ15 Some Septuagint manuscripts (see also Neh. 12:3); Hebrew *Meraioth's*   ᶜ31 Or *go alongside*   ᵈ31 Or *proceed alongside*   ᵉ38 Or *them alongside*   ᶠ39 Or *Old*

Shemaiah, Eleazar, Uzzi, Jehohanan, Malkijah, Elam and Ezer. The choirs sang under the direction of Jezrahiah. ⁴³And on that day they offered great sacrifices, rejoicing because God had given them great joy. The women and children also rejoiced. The sound of rejoicing in Jerusalem could be heard far away.

⁴⁴At that time men were appointed to be in charge of the storerooms for the contributions, firstfruits and tithes. From the fields around the towns they were to bring into the storerooms the portions required by the Law for the priests and the Levites, for Judah was pleased with the ministering priests and Levites. ⁴⁵They performed the service of their God and the service of purification, as did also the singers and gatekeepers, according to the commands of David and his son Solomon. ⁴⁶For long ago, in the days of David and Asaph, there had been directors for the singers and for the songs of praise and thanksgiving to God. ⁴⁷So in the days of Zerubbabel and of Nehemiah, all Israel contributed the daily portions for the singers and gatekeepers. They also set aside the portion for the other Levites, and the Levites set aside the portion for the descendants of Aaron.

Nehemiah's Final Reforms

13 On that day the Book of Moses was read aloud in the hearing of the people and there it was found written that no Ammonite or Moabite should ever be admitted into the assembly of God, ²because they had not met the Israelites with food and water but had hired Balaam to call a curse down on them. (Our God, however, turned the curse into a blessing.) ³When the people heard this law, they excluded from Israel all who were of foreign descent.

⁴Before this, Eliashib the priest had been put in charge of the storerooms of the house of our God. He was closely associated with Tobiah, ⁵and he had provided him with a large room formerly used to store the grain offerings and incense and temple articles, and also the tithes of grain, new wine and oil prescribed for the Levites, singers and gatekeepers, as well as the contributions for the priests.

⁶But while all this was going on, I was not in Jerusalem, for in the thirty-second year of Artaxerxes king of Babylon I had returned to the king. Some time later I asked his permission ⁷and came back to Jerusalem. Here I learned about the evil thing Eliashib had done in providing Tobiah a room in the courts of the house of God. ⁸I was greatly displeased and threw all Tobiah's household goods out of the room. ⁹I gave orders to purify the rooms, and then I put back into them the equipment of the house of God, with the grain offerings and the incense.

¹⁰I also learned that the portions assigned to the Levites had not been given to them, and that all the Levites and singers responsible for the service had gone back to their own fields. ¹¹So I rebuked the officials and asked them, "Why is the house of God neglected?" Then I called them together and stationed them at their posts.

¹²All Judah brought the tithes of grain, new wine and oil into the storerooms. ¹³I put Shelemiah the priest, Zadok the scribe, and a Levite named Pedaiah in charge of the storerooms and made Hanan son of Zaccur, the son of Mattaniah, their assistant, because these men were considered trustworthy. They were made responsible for distributing the supplies to their brothers.

¹⁴Remember me for this, O my God, and do not blot out what I have so faithfully done for the house of my God and its services.

¹⁵In those days I saw men in Judah treading winepresses on the Sabbath and bringing in grain and loading it on donkeys, together with wine, grapes, figs and all other kinds of loads. And they were bringing all this into Jerusalem on the Sabbath. Therefore I warned them against selling food on that day. ¹⁶Men from

---

Nehemiah 12:43

God Gives Joy

And on that day they offered great sacrifices, rejoicing because God had given them great joy. The women and children also rejoiced. The sound of rejoicing in Jerusalem could be heard far away.

Tyre who lived in Jerusalem were bringing in fish and all kinds of merchandise and selling them in Jerusalem on the Sabbath to the people of Judah. [17]I rebuked the nobles of Judah and said to them, "What is this wicked thing you are doing—desecrating the Sabbath day? [18]Didn't your forefathers do the same things, so that our God brought all this calamity upon us and upon this city? Now you are stirring up more wrath against Israel by desecrating the Sabbath."

[19]When evening shadows fell on the gates of Jerusalem before the Sabbath, I ordered the doors to be shut and not opened until the Sabbath was over. I stationed some of my own men at the gates so that no load could be brought in on the Sabbath day. [20]Once or twice the merchants and sellers of all kinds of goods spent the night outside Jerusalem. [21]But I warned them and said, "Why do you spend the night by the wall? If you do this again, I will lay hands on you." From that time on they no longer came on the Sabbath. [22]Then I commanded the Levites to purify themselves and go and guard the gates in order to keep the Sabbath day holy.

Remember me for this also, O my God, and show mercy to me according to your great love.

[23]Moreover, in those days I saw men of Judah who had married women from Ashdod, Ammon and Moab. [24]Half of their children spoke the language of Ashdod or the language of one of the other peoples, and did not know how to speak the language of Judah. [25]I rebuked them and called curses down on them. I beat some of the men and pulled out their hair. I made them take an oath in God's name and said: "You are not to give your daughters in marriage to their sons, nor are you to take their daughters in marriage for your sons or for yourselves. [26]Was it not because of marriages like these that Solomon king of Israel sinned? Among the many nations there was no king like him. He was loved by his God, and God made him king over all Israel, but even he was led into sin by foreign women. [27]Must we hear now that you too are doing all this terrible wickedness and are being unfaithful to our God by marrying foreign women?"

[28]One of the sons of Joiada son of Eliashib the high priest was son-in-law to Sanballat the Horonite. And I drove him away from me.

[29]Remember them, O my God, because they defiled the priestly office and the covenant of the priesthood and of the Levites.

[30]So I purified the priests and the Levites of everything foreign, and assigned them duties, each to his own task. [31]I also made provision for contributions of wood at designated times, and for the firstfruits.

Remember me with favor, O my God.

Esther

Author:
Unknown.

Audience:
All Israel.

Date:
Written in hindsight, after the events described in the book. About 460 B.C.

Setting:
Susa, the capital of the Persian Empire, during a turbulent time for the Jews.

Verse to Remember:
"And who knows but that you have come to royal position for such a time as this?" (4:14)

Silence. Utter, complete silence. We read the pages of Scripture expecting to hear God's voice, but when we turn to the book of Esther, we find only silence. Nowhere in these pages is God's name mentioned. No direct words. No prophecies. No prayers. The nation of Israel was in exile, living in subjection to a pagan king. *God was silent, but he was not absent.*

It is there, in heaven's stillness, that a young woman enters the scene. Esther is a Jew, but she finds herself upon the stage of the Persian court with all its foreign customs and intrigues. And God has a purpose for her, right where she is. As Esther's story unfolds, *watch for God's providence.* You will not see his hand, but you can see his fingerprints all over the situation.

Queen Vashti Deposed

1 This is what happened during the time of Xerxes,[a] the Xerxes who ruled over 127 provinces stretching from India to Cush[b]: ²At that time King Xerxes reigned from his royal throne in the citadel of Susa, ³and in the third year of his reign he gave a banquet for all his nobles and officials. The military leaders of Persia and Media, the princes, and the nobles of the provinces were present.

⁴For a full 180 days he displayed the vast wealth of his kingdom and the splendor and glory of his majesty. ⁵When these days were over, the king gave a banquet, lasting seven days, in the enclosed garden of the king's palace, for all the people from the least to the

---

ᵃ1 Hebrew *Ahasuerus*, a variant of Xerxes' Persian name; here and throughout Esther   ᵇ1 That is, the upper Nile region greatest, who were in the citadel of Susa. ⁶The garden had hangings of white and blue linen, fastened with cords of white linen and purple material to silver rings on marble pillars. There were couches of gold and silver on a mosaic pavement of porphyry, marble, mother-of-pearl and other costly stones. ⁷Wine was served in goblets of gold, each one different from the other, and the royal wine was abundant, in keeping with the king's liberality. ⁸By the king's command each guest was allowed to drink in his own way, for the king instructed all the wine stewards to serve each man what he wished.

⁹Queen Vashti also gave a banquet for the women in the royal palace of King Xerxes.

¹⁰On the seventh day, when King Xerxes was in high spirits from wine, he commanded the seven eunuchs who served him—Mehuman, Biztha, Harbona, Bigtha, Abagtha, Zethar and Carcas— ¹¹to bring before him Queen Vashti, wearing her royal crown, in order to display her beauty to the people and nobles, for she was lovely to look at. ¹²But when the attendants delivered the king's command, Queen Vashti refused to come. Then the king became furious and burned with anger.

¹³Since it was customary for the king to consult experts in matters of law and justice, he spoke with the wise men who understood the times ¹⁴and were closest to the king—Carshena, Shethar, Admatha, Tarshish, Meres, Marsena and Memucan, the seven nobles of Persia and Media who had special access to the king and were highest in the kingdom.

¹⁵"According to law, what must be done to Queen Vashti?" he asked. "She has not obeyed the command of King Xerxes that the eunuchs have taken to her."

¹⁶Then Memucan replied in the presence of the king and the nobles, "Queen Vashti has done wrong, not only against the king but also against all the nobles and the peoples of all the provinces of King Xerxes. ¹⁷For the queen's conduct will become known to all the women, and so they will despise their husbands and say, 'King Xerxes commanded Queen Vashti to be brought before him, but she would not come.' ¹⁸This very day the Persian and Median

women of the nobility who have heard about the queen's conduct will respond to all the king's nobles in the same way. There will be no end of disrespect and discord.

¹⁹"Therefore, if it pleases the king, let him issue a royal decree and let it be written in the laws of Persia and Media, which cannot be repealed, that Vashti is never again to enter the presence of King Xerxes. Also let the king give her royal position to someone else who is better than she. ²⁰Then when the king's edict is proclaimed throughout all his vast realm, all the women will respect their husbands, from the least to the greatest."

²¹The king and his nobles were pleased with this advice, so the king did as Memucan proposed. ²²He sent dispatches to all parts of the kingdom, to each province in its own script and to each people in its own language, proclaiming in each people's tongue that every man should be ruler over his own household.

Esther Made Queen

2 Later when the anger of King Xerxes had subsided, he remembered Vashti and what she had done and what he had decreed about her. ²Then the king's personal attendants proposed, "Let a search be made for beautiful young virgins for the king. ³Let the king appoint commissioners in every province of his realm to bring all these beautiful girls into the harem at the citadel of Susa. Let them be placed under the care of Hegai, the king's eunuch, who is in charge of the women; and let beauty treatments be given to them. ⁴Then let the girl who pleases the king be queen instead of Vashti." This advice appealed to the king, and he followed it.

⁵Now there was in the citadel of Susa a Jew of the tribe of Benjamin, named Mordecai son of Jair, the son of Shimei, the son of Kish, ⁶who had been carried into exile from Jerusalem by Nebuchadnezzar king of Babylon, among those taken captive with Jehoiachin*a* king of Judah. ⁷Mordecai had a cousin named Hadassah, whom he had brought up because she had neither father nor mother. This girl, who was also known as Esther, was lovely in form and features, and Mordecai had taken her as his own daughter when her father and mother died.

*a*6 Hebrew *Jeconiah*, a variant of *Jehoiachin*

A Rival and a Wife

PENINNAH

Because the
LORD had closed
her womb, her
rival kept provok-
ing her in order
to irritate her.
This went on year
after year.

1 Samuel 1:6–7

**ASSIGNED
READING:**

1 Samuel
1:1–28

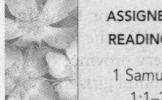

"MY FATHER MADE IT FOR THE *BAAABY*." Peninnah held a small wooden toy in her hands.

Her voice inflection rose on the last part of that sentence, stretching out the word as long as she possibly could. Peninnah was always doing that to Hannah—endlessly talking about babies, children, runny noses and nursing. Peninnah had a special knack for turning every occasion into an opportunity to make a dig at Hannah's infertility.

"Do you *like* it, Hannah?" She pushed just a little more.

Hannah didn't respond. She busied herself with that day's list of household chores. Peninnah turned away. *Score!* she thought to herself gleefully. And for a minute, she felt good.

It was hard living under the same roof 24/7. Peninnah and Hannah shared living quarters, meals, household chores and the love of a husband. Well, they sort of shared that, Peninnah thought with a pang. She recalled the way Elkanah spoke with tenderness to Hannah, how he showered her with gifts, how he always made sure she had everything she wanted—and how he *looked* at her. Peninnah saw that look. And he never looked at *her* that way. She had given Elkanah sons and daughters; he should have doted on her and loved her beyond reason for her gifts to him. Oh, he was kind to her. Nice. Pleasant. And he loved the kids. But that look. He *never* looked at *her* that way.

It was so unfair. According to the culture of that day, Peninnah was the superior wife. Any woman who remained childless was seen as a blight on society, a misfit. Hannah should have been unloved. Not Peninnah and her many sons and daughters. She knew she was better, more valuable. And she made certain Hannah never, ever, not even for one second, forgot it.

Peninnah gloated and planned her next slight. This time she'd mention something in front of Elkanah. Her children were proof that she was better than Hannah. Now, if only she could *feel* that way.

—Prayer—
Lord, sometimes in my quest to fulfill my own needs, I trample on those around me. Forgive me, and help me to treat others with love.

Weekend

8When the king's order and edict had been proclaimed, many girls were brought to the citadel of Susa and put under the care of Hegai. Esther also was taken to the king's palace and entrusted to Hegai, who had charge of the harem. 9The girl pleased him and won his favor. Immediately he provided her with her beauty treatments and special food. He assigned to her seven maids selected from the king's palace and moved her and her maids into the best place in the harem.

10Esther had not revealed her nationality and family background, because Mordecai had forbidden her to do so. 11Every day he walked back and forth near the courtyard of the harem to find out how Esther was and what was happening to her.

12Before a girl's turn came to go in to King Xerxes, she had to complete twelve months of beauty treatments prescribed for the women, six months with oil of myrrh and six with perfumes and cosmetics. 13And this is how she would go to the king: Anything she wanted was given her to take with her from the harem to the king's palace. 14In the evening she would go there and in the morning return to another part of the harem to the care of Shaashgaz, the king's eunuch who was in charge of the concubines. She would not return to the king unless he was pleased with her and summoned her by name.

15When the turn came for Esther (the girl Mordecai had adopted, the daughter of his uncle Abihail) to go to the king, she asked for nothing other than what Hegai, the king's eunuch who was in charge of the harem, suggested. And Esther won the favor of everyone who saw her. 16She was taken to King Xerxes in the royal residence in the tenth month, the month of Tebeth, in the seventh year of his reign.

17Now the king was attracted to Esther more than to any of the other women, and she won his favor and approval more than any of the other virgins. So he set a royal crown on her head and made her queen instead of Vashti. 18And the king gave a great banquet, Esther's banquet, for all his nobles and officials. He proclaimed a holiday throughout the provinces and distributed gifts with royal liberality.

Mordecai Uncovers a Conspiracy

19When the virgins were assembled a second time, Mordecai was sitting at the king's gate. 20But Esther had kept secret her family background and nationality just as Mordecai had told her to do, for she continued to follow Mordecai's instructions as she had done when he was bringing her up.

21During the time Mordecai was sitting at the king's gate, Bigthana[a] and Teresh, two of the king's officers who guarded the doorway, became angry and conspired to assassinate King Xerxes. 22But Esther found out about the plot and told Queen Esther, who in turn reported it to the king, giving credit to Mordecai. 23And when the report was investigated and found to be true, the two officials were hanged on a gallows.[b] All this was recorded in the book of the annals in the presence of the king.

Haman's Plot to Destroy the Jews

3 After these events, King Xerxes honored Haman son of Hammedatha, the Agagite, elevating him and giving him a seat of honor higher than that of all the other nobles. 2All the royal officials at the king's gate knelt down and paid honor to Haman, for the king had commanded this concerning him. But Mordecai would not kneel down or pay him honor.

3Then the royal officials at the king's gate asked Mordecai, "Why do you disobey the king's command?" 4Day after day they spoke to him but he refused to comply. Therefore they told Haman about it to see whether Mordecai's behavior would be tolerated, for he had told them he was a Jew.

5When Haman saw that Mordecai would not kneel down or pay him honor, he was enraged. 6Yet having learned who Mordecai's people were, he scorned the idea of killing only Mordecai. Instead Haman looked for a way to destroy all Mordecai's people, the Jews, throughout the whole kingdom of Xerxes.

7In the twelfth year of King Xerxes, in the first month, the month of Nisan, they cast the pur (that is, the lot) in the presence of Haman to select a day and month. And the lot fell on[c] the twelfth month, the month of Adar.

---

a21 Hebrew Bigthan, a variant of Bigthana   b23 Or were hung (or impaled) on poles; similarly elsewhere in Esther   c7 Septuagint; Hebrew does not have And the lot fell on.

⁸Then Haman said to King Xerxes, "There is a certain people dispersed and scattered among the peoples in all the provinces of your kingdom whose customs are different from those of all other people and who do not obey the king's laws; it is not in the king's best interest to tolerate them. ⁹If it pleases the king, let a decree be issued to destroy them, and I will put ten thousand talents*a* of silver into the royal treasury for the men who carry out this business."

¹⁰So the king took his signet ring from his finger and gave it to Haman son of Hammedatha, the Agagite, the enemy of the Jews. ¹¹"Keep the money," the king said to Haman, "and do with the people as you please."

¹²Then on the thirteenth day of the first month the royal secretaries were summoned. They wrote out in the script of each province and in the language of each people all Haman's orders to the king's satraps, the governors of the various provinces and the nobles of the various peoples. These were written in the name of King Xerxes himself and sealed with his own ring. ¹³Dispatches were sent by couriers to all the king's provinces with the order to destroy, kill and annihilate all the Jews—young and old, women and little children—on a single day, the thirteenth day of the twelfth month, the month of Adar, and to plunder their goods. ¹⁴A copy of the text of the edict was to be issued as law in every province and made known to the people of every nationality so they would be ready for that day.

¹⁵Spurred on by the king's command, the couriers went out, and the edict was issued in the citadel of Susa. The king and Haman sat down to drink, but the city of Susa was bewildered.

Mordecai Persuades Esther to Help

4 When Mordecai learned of all that had been done, he tore his clothes, put on sackcloth and ashes, and went out into the city, wailing loudly and bitterly. ²But he went only as far as the king's gate, because no one clothed in sackcloth was allowed to enter it. ³In every province to which the edict and order of the king came, there was great mourning among the Jews, with fasting, weeping and wailing. Many lay in sackcloth and ashes.

⁴When Esther's maids and eunuchs came and told her about Mordecai, she was in great distress. She sent clothes for him to put on instead of his sackcloth, but he would not accept them. ⁵Then Esther summoned Hathach, one of the king's eunuchs assigned to attend her, and ordered him to find out what was troubling Mordecai and why.

⁶So Hathach went out to Mordecai in the open square of the city in front of the king's gate. ⁷Mordecai told him everything that had happened to him, including the exact amount of money Haman had promised to pay into the royal treasury for the destruction of the Jews. ⁸He also gave him a copy of the text of the edict for their annihilation, which had been published in Susa, to show to Esther and explain it to her, and he told him to urge her to go into the king's presence to beg for mercy and plead with him for her people.

⁹Hathach went back and reported to Esther what Mordecai had said. ¹⁰Then she instructed him to say to Mordecai, ¹¹"All the king's officials and the people of the royal provinces know that for any man or woman who approaches the king in the inner court without being summoned the king has but one law: that he be put to death. The only exception to this is for the king to extend the gold scepter to him and spare his life. But thirty days have passed since I was called to go to the king."

¹²When Esther's words were reported to Mordecai, ¹³he sent back this answer: "Do not think that because you are in the king's house you alone of all the Jews will escape. ¹⁴For if you remain silent at this time, relief and deliverance for the Jews will arise from another place, but you and your father's family will perish. And who knows but

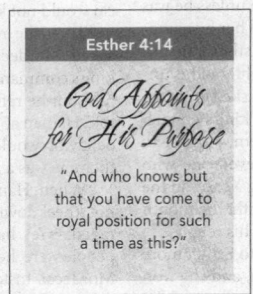

Esther 4:14

God Appoints for His Purpose

"And who knows but that you have come to royal position for such a time as this?"

---

a9 That is, about 375 tons (about 345 metric tons)

that you have come to royal position for such a time as this?"

¹⁵Then Esther sent this reply to Mordecai: ¹⁶"Go, gather together all the Jews who are in Susa, and fast for me. Do not eat or drink for three days, night or day. I and my maids will fast as you do. When this is done, I will go to the king, even though it is against the law. And if I perish, I perish."

¹⁷So Mordecai went away and carried out all of Esther's instructions.

Esther's Request to the King

5 On the third day Esther put on her royal robes and stood in the inner court of the palace, in front of the king's hall. The king was sitting on his royal throne in the hall, facing the entrance. ²When he saw Queen Esther standing in the court, he was pleased with her and held out to her the gold scepter that was in his hand. So Esther approached and touched the tip of the scepter.

³Then the king asked, "What is it, Queen Esther? What is your request? Even up to half the kingdom, it will be given you."

⁴"If it pleases the king," replied Esther, "let the king, together with Haman, come today to a banquet I have prepared for him."

⁵"Bring Haman at once," the king said, "so that we may do what Esther asks."

So the king and Haman went to the banquet Esther had prepared. ⁶As they were drinking wine, the king again asked Esther, "Now what is your petition? It will be given you. And what is your request? Even up to half the kingdom, it will be granted."

⁷Esther replied, "My petition and my request is this: ⁸If the king regards me with favor and if it pleases the king to grant my petition and fulfill my request, let the king and Haman come tomorrow to the banquet I will prepare for them. Then I will answer the king's question."

Haman's Rage Against Mordecai

⁹Haman went out that day happy and in high spirits. But when he saw Mordecai at the king's gate and observed that he neither rose nor showed fear in his presence, he was filled with rage against Mordecai. ¹⁰Nevertheless, Haman restrained himself and went home.

Calling together his friends and Zeresh, his wife, ¹¹Haman boasted to them about his vast wealth, his many sons, and all the ways the king had honored him and how he had elevated him above the other nobles and officials. ¹²"And that's not all," Haman added. "I'm the only person Queen Esther invited to accompany the king to the banquet she gave. And she has invited me along with the king tomorrow. ¹³But all this gives me no satisfaction as long as I see that Jew Mordecai sitting at the king's gate."

¹⁴His wife Zeresh and all his friends said to him, "Have a gallows built, seventy-five feet*a* high, and ask the king in the morning to have Mordecai hanged on it. Then go with the king to the dinner and be happy." This suggestion delighted Haman, and he had the gallows built.

Mordecai Honored

6 That night the king could not sleep; so he ordered the book of the chronicles, the record of his reign, to be brought in and read to him. ²It was found recorded there that Mordecai had exposed Bigthana and Teresh, two of the king's officers who guarded the doorway, who had conspired to assassinate King Xerxes.

³"What honor and recognition has Mordecai received for this?" the king asked.

"Nothing has been done for him," his attendants answered.

⁴The king said, "Who is in the court?" Now Haman had just entered the outer court of the palace to speak to the king about hanging Mordecai on the gallows he had erected for him.

⁵His attendants answered, "Haman is standing in the court."

"Bring him in," the king ordered.

⁶When Haman entered, the king asked him, "What should be done for the man the king delights to honor?"

Now Haman thought to himself, "Who is there that the king would rather honor than me?" ⁷So he answered the king, "For the man the king delights to honor, ⁸have them bring a royal robe the king has worn and a horse the king has ridden, one with a royal crest

---

a14 Hebrew fifty cubits (about 23 meters)

placed on its head. ⁹Then let the robe and horse be entrusted to one of the king's most noble princes. Let them robe the man the king delights to honor, and lead him on the horse through the city streets, proclaiming before him, 'This is what is done for the man the king delights to honor!'"

¹⁰"Go at once," the king commanded Haman. "Get the robe and the horse and do just as you have suggested for Mordecai the Jew, who sits at the king's gate. Do not neglect anything you have recommended."

¹¹So Haman got the robe and the horse. He robed Mordecai, and led him on horseback through the city streets, proclaiming before him, "This is what is done for the man the king delights to honor!"

¹²Afterward Mordecai returned to the king's gate. But Haman rushed home, with his head covered in grief, ¹³and told Zeresh his wife and all his friends everything that had happened to him.

His advisers and his wife Zeresh said to him, "Since Mordecai, before whom your downfall has started, is of Jewish origin, you cannot stand against him—you will surely come to ruin!" ¹⁴While they were still talking with him, the king's eunuchs arrived and hurried Haman away to the banquet Esther had prepared.

Haman Hanged

7 So the king and Haman went to dine with Queen Esther, ²and as they were drinking wine on that second day, the king again asked, "Queen Esther, what is your petition? It will be given you. What is your request? Even up to half the kingdom, it will be granted."

³Then Queen Esther answered, "If I have found favor with you, O king, and if it pleases your majesty, grant me my life—this is my petition. And spare my people—this is my request. ⁴For I and my people have been sold for destruction and slaughter and annihilation. If we had merely been sold as male and female slaves, I would have kept quiet, because no such distress would justify disturbing the king.ᵃ"

⁵King Xerxes asked Queen Esther, "Who is he? Where is the man who has dared to do such a thing?"

⁶Esther said, "The adversary and enemy is this vile Haman."

Then Haman was terrified before the king and queen. ⁷The king got up in a rage, left his wine and went out into the palace garden. But Haman, realizing that the king had already decided his fate, stayed behind to beg Queen Esther for his life.

⁸Just as the king returned from the palace garden to the banquet hall, Haman was falling on the couch where Esther was reclining.

The king exclaimed, "Will he even molest the queen while she is with me in the house?"

As soon as the word left the king's mouth, they covered Haman's face. ⁹Then Harbona, one of the eunuchs attending the king, said, "A gallows seventy-five feetᵇ high stands by Haman's house. He had it made for Mordecai, who spoke up to help the king."

The king said, "Hang him on it!" ¹⁰So they hanged Haman on the gallows he had prepared for Mordecai. Then the king's fury subsided.

The King's Edict in Behalf of the Jews

8 That same day King Xerxes gave Queen Esther the estate of Haman, the enemy of the Jews. And Mordecai came into the presence of the king, for Esther had told how he was related to her. ²The king took off his signet ring, which he had reclaimed from Haman, and presented it to Mordecai. And Esther appointed him over Haman's estate.

³Esther again pleaded with the king, falling at his feet and weeping. She begged him to put an end to the evil plan of Haman the Agagite, which he had devised against the Jews. ⁴Then the king extended the gold scepter to Esther and she arose and stood before him.

⁵"If it pleases the king," she said, "and if he regards me with favor and thinks it the right thing to do, and if he is pleased with me, let an order be written overruling the dispatches that Haman son of Hammedatha, the Agagite, devised and wrote to destroy the Jews in all the king's provinces. ⁶For how can I bear to see disaster fall on my people? How can I bear to see the destruction of my family?"

⁷King Xerxes replied to Queen Esther and to Mordecai the Jew, "Because Haman attacked

---

ᵃ4 Or quiet, but the compensation our adversary offers cannot be compared with the loss the king would suffer   ᵇ9 Hebrew fifty cubits (about 23 meters)

Too Tired?

Read: Esther 7:1–10

ROSA LOUISE PARKS was tired. The petite African American woman sat quietly, grateful to find a seat on the bus after spending most of the day on her feet. When a white passenger demanded she give up her seat, Rosa looked up. Segregation was the law in Montgomery, Alabama, in 1955. Blacks were expected to yield their seats on public transportation to whites. To refuse meant arrest. Rosa stayed seated, and her actions helped change the landscape of the United States. Years later, Rosa wrote that it wasn't physical weariness that gave her such inner strength. She said, "Our mistreatment was just not right, and I was tired of it."

Centuries earlier, another woman was faced with a decision. Like Rosa, Esther had two strikes against her in the Persian Empire: She was female and a member of an oppressed people, the Jews. Although King Xerxes had chosen Esther to be queen, she was forbidden to approach the powerful king without an invitation. And an evil prime minister named Haman was plotting to annihilate the Jews. Esther's cousin Mordecai's plea to intervene meant risking her own life. It took courage for Queen Esther to take a stand, just as it took courage for Rosa Parks to remain seated. Both women's actions opened the door to freedom for their people.

Many of us may think we're safe from the type of persecution Rosa Parks and Esther faced. But Christians are being persecuted throughout the world in places like China, the Sudan and North Korea. Every day people die for the privilege of worshiping Jesus. It is estimated that more Christians died for their faith in the twentieth century than all the previous 19 centuries combined, and the numbers appear to be rising in the twenty-first century. Even in places where there is no outright persecution, many people think Christians are naive and out of touch with so-called reality. Some people do not really know or understand the person and mission of Jesus and will take every opportunity to slander his followers.

Wherever God has placed you, he can use you to speak his truth—words of love, justice and faith to a lost world—even if it means being misunderstood or ridiculed. Yes, it may be difficult and you may be weary; but, sister, "never tire of doing what is right" (2 Thessalonians 3:13).

Esther 7:3–4

Then Queen Esther answered, "If I have found favor with you, O king, and if it pleases your majesty, grant me my life—this is my petition. And spare my people—this is my request. For I and my people have been sold for destruction and slaughter and annihilation. If we had merely been sold as male and female slaves, I would have kept quiet, because no such distress would justify disturbing the king."

reflection

1 How did reading about Rosa Parks and Queen Esther inspire you?

2 Have you ever felt God nudging you to speak up about a situation? What happened?

3 What do you need to take a stand on in your home, neighborhood or in the political arena?

RELATED READINGS

Psalm 118:6–9;
Luke 21:5–19;
2 Timothy 3:10–17

Go to page 607 for your next devotional reading.

the Jews, I have given his estate to Esther, and they have hanged him on the gallows. ⁸Now write another decree in the king's name in behalf of the Jews as seems best to you, and seal it with the king's signet ring—for no document written in the king's name and sealed with his ring can be revoked."

⁹At once the royal secretaries were summoned—on the twenty-third day of the third month, the month of Sivan. They wrote out all Mordecai's orders to the Jews, and to the satraps, governors and nobles of the 127 provinces stretching from India to Cush.*ᵃ* These orders were written in the script of each province and the language of each people and also to the Jews in their own script and language. ¹⁰Mordecai wrote in the name of King Xerxes, sealed the dispatches with the king's signet ring, and sent them by mounted couriers, who rode fast horses especially bred for the king.

¹¹The king's edict granted the Jews in every city the right to assemble and protect themselves; to destroy, kill and annihilate any armed force of any nationality or province that might attack them and their women and children; and to plunder the property of their enemies. ¹²The day appointed for the Jews to do this in all the provinces of King Xerxes was the thirteenth day of the twelfth month, the month of Adar. ¹³A copy of the text of the edict was to be issued as law in every province and made known to the people of every nationality so that the Jews would be ready on that day to avenge themselves on their enemies.

¹⁴The couriers, riding the royal horses, raced out, spurred on by the king's command. And the edict was also issued in the citadel of Susa.

¹⁵Mordecai left the king's presence wearing royal garments of blue and white, a large crown of gold and a purple robe of fine linen. And the city of Susa held a joyous celebration. ¹⁶For the Jews it was a time of happiness and joy, gladness and honor. ¹⁷In every province and in every city, wherever the edict of the king went, there was joy and gladness among the Jews, with feasting and celebrating. And many people of other nationalities became Jews because fear of the Jews had seized them.

Triumph of the Jews

9 On the thirteenth day of the twelfth month, the month of Adar, the edict commanded by the king was to be carried out. On this day the enemies of the Jews had hoped to overpower them, but now the tables were turned and the Jews got the upper hand over those who hated them. ²The Jews assembled in their cities in all the provinces of King Xerxes to attack those seeking their destruction. No one could stand against them, because the people of all the other nationalities were afraid of them. ³And all the nobles of the provinces, the satraps, the governors and the king's administrators helped the Jews, because fear of Mordecai had seized them. ⁴Mordecai was prominent in the palace; his reputation spread throughout the provinces, and he became more and more powerful.

⁵The Jews struck down all their enemies with the sword, killing and destroying them, and they did what they pleased to those who hated them. ⁶In the citadel of Susa, the Jews killed and destroyed five hundred men. ⁷They also killed Parshandatha, Dalphon, Aspatha, ⁸Poratha, Adalia, Aridatha, ⁹Parmashta, Arisai, Aridai and Vaizatha, ¹⁰the ten sons of Haman son of Hammedatha, the enemy of the Jews. But they did not lay their hands on the plunder.

¹¹The number of those slain in the citadel of Susa was reported to the king that same day. ¹²The king said to Queen Esther, "The Jews have killed and destroyed five hundred men and the ten sons of Haman in the citadel of Susa. What have they done in the rest of the king's provinces? Now what is your petition? It will be given you. What is your request? It will also be granted."

¹³"If it pleases the king," Esther answered, "give the Jews in Susa permission to carry out this day's edict tomorrow also, and let Haman's ten sons be hanged on gallows."

¹⁴So the king commanded that this be done. An edict was issued in Susa, and they hanged the ten sons of Haman. ¹⁵The Jews in Susa came together on the fourteenth day of the month of Adar, and they put to death in Susa three hundred men, but they did not lay their hands on the plunder.

---

*ᵃ*9 That is, the upper Nile region

¹⁶Meanwhile, the remainder of the Jews who were in the king's provinces also assembled to protect themselves and get relief from their enemies. They killed seventy-five thousand of them but did not lay their hands on the plunder. ¹⁷This happened on the thirteenth day of the month of Adar, and on the fourteenth they rested and made it a day of feasting and joy.

Purim Celebrated

¹⁸The Jews in Susa, however, had assembled on the thirteenth and fourteenth, and then on the fifteenth they rested and made it a day of feasting and joy.

¹⁹That is why rural Jews—those living in villages—observe the fourteenth of the month of Adar as a day of joy and feasting, a day for giving presents to each other.

²⁰Mordecai recorded these events, and he sent letters to all the Jews throughout the provinces of King Xerxes, near and far, ²¹to have them celebrate annually the fourteenth and fifteenth days of the month of Adar ²²as the time when the Jews got relief from their enemies, and as the month when their sorrow was turned into joy and their mourning into a day of celebration. He wrote them to observe the days as days of feasting and joy and giving presents of food to one another and gifts to the poor.

²³So the Jews agreed to continue the celebration they had begun, doing what Mordecai had written to them. ²⁴For Haman son of Hammedatha, the Agagite, the enemy of all the Jews, had plotted against the Jews to destroy them and had cast the *pur* (that is, the lot) for their ruin and destruction. ²⁵But when the plot came to the king's attention,[a] he issued written orders that the evil scheme Haman had devised against the Jews should come back onto his own head, and that he and his sons should be hanged on the gallows. ²⁶(Therefore these days

were called Purim, from the word *pur*.) Because of everything written in this letter and because of what they had seen and what had happened to them, ²⁷the Jews took it upon themselves to establish the custom that they and their descendants and all who join them should without fail observe these two days every year, in the way prescribed and at the time appointed. ²⁸These days should be remembered and observed in every generation by every family, and in every province and in every city. And these days of Purim should never cease to be celebrated by the Jews, nor should the memory of them die out among their descendants.

²⁹So Queen Esther, daughter of Abihail, along with Mordecai the Jew, wrote with full authority to confirm this second letter concerning Purim. ³⁰And Mordecai sent letters to all the Jews in the 127 provinces of the kingdom of Xerxes—words of goodwill and assurance— ³¹to establish these days of Purim at their designated times, as Mordecai the Jew and Queen Esther had decreed for them, and as they had established for themselves and their descendants in regard to their times of fasting and lamentation. ³²Esther's decree confirmed these regulations about Purim, and it was written down in the records.

The Greatness of Mordecai

10 King Xerxes imposed tribute throughout the empire, to its distant shores. ²And all his acts of power and might, together with a full account of the greatness of Mordecai to which the king had raised him, are they not written in the book of the annals of the kings of Media and Persia? ³Mordecai the Jew was second in rank to King Xerxes, preeminent among the Jews, and held in high esteem by his many fellow Jews, because he worked for the good of his people and spoke up for the welfare of all the Jews.

Esther 9:22

God Relieves Sorrow

The Jews got relief from their enemies, and . . . their sorrow was turned into joy and their mourning into a day of celebration.

ᵃ25 Or when Esther came before the king

Job

Author:
Unknown.

Audience:
God's people.

Date:
Unknown B.C.

Setting:
Job lived in Uz, east of Canaan. His story is one of personal tragedy.

Verse to Remember:
"Naked I came from my mother's womb, and naked I will depart. The LORD gave and the LORD has taken away; may the name of the LORD be praised."
(1:21)

One of the best-known stories in Scripture, the book of Job *demonstrates God's providence in a believer's suffering.* Satan challenged God that Job was righteous only because of his wealth. Job's friends insisted that his suffering proved he was guilty of hidden sin and that God was displeased with him. Then God himself showed up with a long list of questions, demonstrating how *his creation reveals* his majesty and mystery—a mystery hidden from Job until he saw God himself and submitted before him. At the end of the story, Job's wealth was restored and his family grew. But more than that, *Job had seen God* and *knew God's goodness* even in suffering.

Prologue

1 In the land of Uz there lived a man whose name was Job. This man was blameless and upright; he feared God and shunned evil. ²He had seven sons and three daughters, ³and he owned seven thousand sheep, three thousand camels, five hundred yoke of oxen and five hundred donkeys, and had a large number of servants. He was the greatest man among all the people of the East.

⁴His sons used to take turns holding feasts in their homes, and they would invite their three sisters to eat and drink with them. ⁵When a

period of feasting had run its course, Job would send and have them purified. Early in the morning he would sacrifice a burnt offering for each of them, thinking, "Perhaps my children have sinned and cursed God in their hearts." This was Job's regular custom.

Job's First Test

⁶One day the angels*ᵃ* came to present themselves before the LORD, and Satan*ᵇ* also came with them. ⁷The LORD said to Satan, "Where have you come from?"

Satan answered the LORD, "From roaming

ᵃ6 Hebrew the sons of God   *ᵇ6* Satan *means* accuser.

To Know God Is to Trust God

Read: Job 1:1–22

IMAGINE THAT YOUR NEIGHBOR calls you at work, telling you the terrible news that your house and vehicles have been destroyed by fire, and while that person is still speaking, you learn that you've been fired from your job. While those words are still coming out of your employer's mouth, your husband calls: your kids and all their families have been killed while they were vacationing together.

These are the unimaginable circumstances Job encountered. Devastating messages assaulted him again and again—each one coming while the messenger "was still speaking." Who can even begin to comprehend his sheer horror at learning that all ten of his children were dead?

What did Job do? What was his initial response upon hearing of the loss of all he owned and of all he held dear? First, he grieved. He physically responded in the Eastern mode of grief by tearing his robe and shaving his head to display his deep sorrow. Yet no outward sign of grief could capture the inward torture Job felt.

Job's next step demonstrates faithfulness toward God. He fell to the ground and worshiped. That's right—he didn't berate God or ask "Why me?" or "Why them?" Instead, he acknowledged that everything comes from God, and he praised the name of the Lord. Try envisioning that scene. It will take your breath away. Picture this man, deep in the throes of grief, praising God. In light of the horrific blows dealt to him, how did he do that?

Only one answer suffices: Job knew God—*really* knew him with an uncommon intimacy. His close communion with God had taught him that God was the only one who could give him any kind of real comfort. Job's knowledge yielded a deep trust in an infallible Lord—a trust that enabled Job's heart to keep beating even in the face of overwhelming heartbreak. It enabled him to respond to horrible pain with worship and praise.

Yes, times of seeking for answers and grappling for understanding followed that day of destruction, but Job's initial response reflected a heart that knew and trusted God. What an amazing and beautiful image!

Job 1:20–21

Then he fell to the ground in worship and said: "Naked I came from my mother's womb, and naked I will depart. The LORD gave and the LORD has taken away; may the name of the LORD be praised."

reflection

1 How have you responded to bad news in the past? With praise? Anger? Despair? Confusion?

2 Job knew God well enough to turn to him in grief. How deep does your knowledge of God go? How close is your heart attuned to his?

3 How might going through tough times or experiencing pain and grief help someone know God?

RELATED READINGS

Deuteronomy 32:36–39; Psalms 42:1–11; 86:1–17

Tuesday

Go to page 609 for your next devotional reading.

through the earth and going back and forth in it."

⁸Then the LORD said to Satan, "Have you considered my servant Job? There is no one on earth like him; he is blameless and upright, a man who fears God and shuns evil."

⁹"Does Job fear God for nothing?" Satan replied. ¹⁰"Have you not put a hedge around him and his household and everything he has? You have blessed the work of his hands, so that his flocks and herds are spread throughout the land. ¹¹But stretch out your hand and strike everything he has, and he will surely curse you to your face."

¹²The LORD said to Satan, "Very well, then, everything he has is in your hands, but on the man himself do not lay a finger."

Then Satan went out from the presence of the LORD.

¹³One day when Job's sons and daughters were feasting and drinking wine at the oldest brother's house, ¹⁴a messenger came to Job and said, "The oxen were plowing and the donkeys were grazing nearby, ¹⁵and the Sabeans attacked and carried them off. They put the servants to the sword, and I am the only one who has escaped to tell you!"

¹⁶While he was still speaking, another messenger came and said, "The fire of God fell from the sky and burned up the sheep and the servants, and I am the only one who has escaped to tell you!"

¹⁷While he was still speaking, another messenger came and said, "The Chaldeans formed three raiding parties and swept down on your camels and carried them off. They put the servants to the sword, and I am the only one who has escaped to tell you!"

¹⁸While he was still speaking, yet another messenger came and said, "Your sons and daughters were feasting and drinking wine at the oldest brother's house, ¹⁹when suddenly a mighty wind swept in from the desert and struck the four corners of the house. It collapsed on them and they are dead, and I am the only one who has escaped to tell you!"

²⁰At this, Job got up and tore his robe and shaved his head. Then he fell to the ground in worship ²¹and said:

> "Naked I came from my
>   mother's womb,
>   and naked I will depart.ᵃ
> The LORD gave and the
>   LORD has taken
>   away;
>   may the name of the
>   LORD be praised."

²²In all this, Job did not sin by charging God with wrongdoing.

Job's Second Test

2 On another day the angelsᵇ came to present themselves before the LORD, and Satan also came with them to present himself before him. ²And the LORD said to Satan, "Where have you come from?"

Satan answered the LORD, "From roaming through the earth and going back and forth in it."

³Then the LORD said to Satan, "Have you considered my servant Job? There is no one on earth like him; he is blameless and upright, a man who fears God and shuns evil. And he still maintains his integrity, though you incited me against him to ruin him without any reason."

⁴"Skin for skin!" Satan replied. "A man will give all he has for his own life. ⁵But stretch out your hand and strike his flesh and bones, and he will surely curse you to your face."

⁶The LORD said to Satan, "Very well, then, he is in your hands; but you must spare his life."

⁷So Satan went out from the presence of the LORD and afflicted Job with painful sores from the soles of his feet to the top of his head. ⁸Then Job took a piece of broken pottery and scraped himself with it as he sat among the ashes.

⁹His wife said to him, "Are you still holding on to your integrity? Curse God and die!"

Job 1:21

God Gives and Takes Away

"Naked I came from my mother's womb, and naked I will depart. The LORD gave and the LORD has taken away; may the name of the LORD be praised."

ᵃ21 Or *will return there*   ᵇ1 Hebrew *the sons of God*

Silence Is Golden

Read: Job 2:9–13

THERE'S NO "HOW-TO" MANUAL describing what to say or do for someone who has suffered a great loss. A mother loses her child to disease, a wife loses her husband to divorce, a family loses their home to fire. What do you say?

Job was suffering. All of his children, servants, flocks and herds were gone. His health and well-being were decimated. Job's wife bitterly responded, "Curse God and die!" As much as she, too, must have been suffering, Job's wife talked too much and too soon.

When Job's three friends, Eliphaz, Bildad and Zophar, came to see him, the Bible tells us that Job had been disfigured by grief. Job's friends wept aloud, tore their robes and threw dust into the air—the ancient mourning rituals for death or tragic loss. For seven days and nights they did not utter a word. They simply sat beside him in silence.

Later on, Job's friends tried to explain away his misfortunes and wrongly blamed Job. But at the beginning, they got it right by recognizing that nothing they could say could assuage his grief. Here, they offered him not words but the comfort of their presence.

When we encounter friends who have suffered great loss, it is easy to drop off a casserole, send a sympathy card or say, "Call me if you need anything." We often rely on pat answers: "God knows best; all things work together for good." Sometimes we speak too much or too soon. Maybe we're fearful in the presence of others' pain, so we babble about meaningless things. Sometimes we're fearful of the roiling emotions lurking below the surface, so we don't even make contact.

Perhaps Job's friends stumbled onto one key to mourning with those who mourn: Have the wisdom to know when to talk and when to stay silent. Solomon said, "There is a time for everything . . . a time to weep and time to laugh . . . a time to be silent and a time to speak" (Ecclesiastes 3:1,4,7). You can pray for the wisdom to realize when your presence will speak louder than words. Your presence says, "I'm here for you. I love you. I am walking through this valley with you."

The next time you find yourself eye-to-eye with someone in grief, don't worry about what you will say. God will give you words to speak and the wisdom to know when to keep silent.

Job 2:13

Then they sat on the ground with him for seven days and seven nights. No one said a word to him, because they saw how great his suffering was.

reflection

1 Has there ever been a time when you were grieving or struggling and someone's advice or comments were like pouring salt on a wound? How did it affect you?

2 What was the most helpful thing that anyone has ever done for you during a time of loss or great struggle?

3 How can you show support to someone you know who is struggling?

RELATED READINGS

Proverbs 20:15; 25:20; Romans 12:15; 2 Corinthians 1:3–11

Wednesday

Go to page 615 for your next devotional reading.

¹⁰He replied, "You are talking like a foolish*a* woman. Shall we accept good from God, and not trouble?"

In all this, Job did not sin in what he said.

Job's Three Friends

¹¹When Job's three friends, Eliphaz the Temanite, Bildad the Shuhite and Zophar the Naamathite, heard about all the troubles that had come upon him, they set out from their homes and met together by agreement to go and sympathize with him and comfort him. ¹²When they saw him from a distance, they could hardly recognize him; they began to weep aloud, and they tore their robes and sprinkled dust on their heads. ¹³Then they sat on the ground with him for seven days and seven nights. No one said a word to him, because they saw how great his suffering was.

Job Speaks

3 After this, Job opened his mouth and cursed the day of his birth. ²He said:

³ "May the day of my birth perish,
    and the night it was said, 'A boy is born!'
⁴ That day—may it turn to darkness;
    may God above not care about it;
    may no light shine upon it.
⁵ May darkness and deep shadow*b* claim it once more;
    may a cloud settle over it;
    may blackness overwhelm its light.
⁶ That night—may thick darkness seize it;
    may it not be included among the days of the year
    nor be entered in any of the months.
⁷ May that night be barren;
    may no shout of joy be heard in it.
⁸ May those who curse days*c* curse that day,
    those who are ready to rouse Leviathan.
⁹ May its morning stars become dark;
    may it wait for daylight in vain
    and not see the first rays of dawn,
¹⁰ for it did not shut the doors of the womb on me
    to hide trouble from my eyes.

¹¹ "Why did I not perish at birth,
    and die as I came from the womb?
¹² Why were there knees to receive me
    and breasts that I might be nursed?
¹³ For now I would be lying down in peace;
    I would be asleep and at rest
¹⁴ with kings and counselors of the earth,
    who built for themselves places now lying in ruins,
¹⁵ with rulers who had gold,
    who filled their houses with silver.
¹⁶ Or why was I not hidden in the ground like a stillborn child,
    like an infant who never saw the light of day?
¹⁷ There the wicked cease from turmoil,
    and there the weary are at rest.
¹⁸ Captives also enjoy their ease;
    they no longer hear the slave driver's shout.
¹⁹ The small and the great are there,
    and the slave is freed from his master.

²⁰ "Why is light given to those in misery,
    and life to the bitter of soul,
²¹ to those who long for death that does not come,
    who search for it more than for hidden treasure,
²² who are filled with gladness
    and rejoice when they reach the grave?
²³ Why is life given to a man
    whose way is hidden,
    whom God has hedged in?
²⁴ For sighing comes to me instead of food;
    my groans pour out like water.
²⁵ What I feared has come upon me;
    what I dreaded has happened to me.
²⁶ I have no peace, no quietness;
    I have no rest, but only turmoil."

Eliphaz

4 Then Eliphaz the Temanite replied:

² "If someone ventures a word with you, will you be impatient?
    But who can keep from speaking?
³ Think how you have instructed many,
    how you have strengthened feeble hands.
⁴ Your words have supported those who stumbled;
    you have strengthened faltering knees.

---

*a*10 The Hebrew word rendered *foolish* denotes moral deficiency.   *b*5 Or *and the shadow of death*   *c*8 Or *the sea*

⁵ But now trouble comes to you, and you are
        discouraged;
    it strikes you, and you are dismayed.
⁶ Should not your piety be your confidence
    and your blameless ways your hope?

⁷ "Consider now: Who, being innocent, has
        ever perished?
    Where were the upright ever destroyed?
⁸ As I have observed, those who plow evil
    and those who sow trouble reap it.
⁹ At the breath of God they are destroyed;
    at the blast of his anger they perish.
¹⁰ The lions may roar and growl,
    yet the teeth of the great lions are
        broken.
¹¹ The lion perishes for lack of prey,
    and the cubs of the lioness are scattered.

¹² "A word was secretly brought to me,
    my ears caught a whisper of it.
¹³ Amid disquieting dreams in the night,
    when deep sleep falls on men,
¹⁴ fear and trembling seized me
    and made all my bones shake.
¹⁵ A spirit glided past my face,
    and the hair on my body stood on end.
¹⁶ It stopped,
    but I could not tell what it was.
    A form stood before my
        eyes,
    and I heard a hushed
        voice:
¹⁷ 'Can a mortal be more
        righteous than
        God?
    Can a man be more pure
        than his Maker?
¹⁸ If God places no trust in his
        servants,
    if he charges his angels
        with error,
¹⁹ how much more those who live in houses
        of clay,
    whose foundations are in the dust,
    who are crushed more readily than a
        moth!
²⁰ Between dawn and dusk they are broken to
        pieces;
    unnoticed, they perish forever.

²¹ Are not the cords of their tent pulled up,
    so that they die without wisdom?'ᵃ

5 "Call if you will, but who will answer
        you?
    To which of the holy ones will you turn?
² Resentment kills a fool,
    and envy slays the simple.
³ I myself have seen a fool taking root,
    but suddenly his house was cursed.
⁴ His children are far from safety,
    crushed in court without a defender.
⁵ The hungry consume his harvest,
    taking it even from among thorns,
    and the thirsty pant after his wealth.
⁶ For hardship does not spring from the
        soil,
    nor does trouble sprout from the
        ground.
⁷ Yet man is born to trouble
    as surely as sparks fly upward.

⁸ "But if it were I, I would appeal to God;
    I would lay my cause before him.
⁹ He performs wonders that cannot be
        fathomed,
    miracles that cannot be counted.
¹⁰ He bestows rain on the earth;
    he sends water upon the countryside.
¹¹ The lowly he sets on high,
    and those who mourn
        are lifted to safety.
¹² He thwarts the plans of the
        crafty,
    so that their hands
        achieve no success.
¹³ He catches the wise in their
        craftiness,
    and the schemes of the
        wily are swept away.
¹⁴ Darkness comes upon
        them in the
        daytime;
    at noon they grope as in the night.
¹⁵ He saves the needy from the sword in their
        mouth;
    he saves them from the clutches of the
        powerful.
¹⁶ So the poor have hope,
    and injustice shuts its mouth.

> **Job 4:17**
>
> *God Is Pure*
>
> "Can a mortal be more
> righteous than God?
> Can a man be more pure
> than his Maker?"

ᵃ21 Some interpreters end the quotation after verse 17.

17 "Blessed is the man whom God corrects;
   so do not despise the discipline of the
      Almighty.ᵃ
18 For he wounds, but he also
      binds up;
   he injures, but his hands
      also heal.
19 From six calamities he will
      rescue you;
   in seven no harm will
      befall you.
20 In famine he will ransom
      you from death,
   and in battle from the
      stroke of the sword.
21 You will be protected from
      the lash of the
      tongue,
   and need not fear when
      destruction comes.
22 You will laugh at destruction and famine,
   and need not fear the beasts of the earth.
23 For you will have a covenant with the
      stones of the field,
   and the wild animals will be at peace
      with you.
24 You will know that your tent is secure;
   you will take stock of your property and
      find nothing missing.
25 You will know that your children will be
      many,
   and your descendants like the grass of
      the earth.
26 You will come to the grave in full vigor,
   like sheaves gathered in season.

27 "We have examined this, and it is true.
   So hear it and apply it to yourself."

Job

6

Then Job replied:

2 "If only my anguish could be weighed
   and all my misery be placed on the
      scales!
3 It would surely outweigh the sand of the
      seas—
   no wonder my words have been
      impetuous.
4 The arrows of the Almighty are in me,

Job 5:17

God Disciplines Us

"Blessed is the man
whom God corrects;
so do not despise
the discipline of the
Almighty."

---

   my spirit drinks in their poison;
   God's terrors are marshaled against me.
5 Does a wild donkey bray when it has grass,
   or an ox bellow when it
      has fodder?
6 Is tasteless food eaten
      without salt,
   or is there flavor in the
      white of an eggᵇ?
7 I refuse to touch it;
   such food makes me ill.

8 "Oh, that I might have my
      request,
   that God would grant
      what I hope for,
9 that God would be willing
      to crush me,
   to let loose his hand and
      cut me off!
10 Then I would still have this consolation—
   my joy in unrelenting pain—
   that I had not denied the words of the
      Holy One.

11 "What strength do I have, that I should
      still hope?
   What prospects, that I should be
      patient?
12 Do I have the strength of stone?
   Is my flesh bronze?
13 Do I have any power to help myself,
   now that success has been driven from
      me?

14 "A despairing man should have the
      devotion of his friends,
   even though he forsakes the fear of the
      Almighty.
15 But my brothers are as undependable as
      intermittent streams,
   as the streams that overflow
16 when darkened by thawing ice
   and swollen with melting snow,
17 but that cease to flow in the dry season,
   and in the heat vanish from their
      channels.
18 Caravans turn aside from their routes;
   they go up into the wasteland and
      perish.
19 The caravans of Tema look for water,

ᵃ17 Hebrew *Shaddai*; here and throughout Job   ᵇ6 The meaning of the Hebrew for this phrase is uncertain.

the traveling merchants of Sheba look
in hope.
20 They are distressed, because they had been
confident;
they arrive there, only to be
disappointed.
21 Now you too have proved to be of no help;
you see something dreadful and are
afraid.
22 Have I ever said, 'Give something on my
behalf,
pay a ransom for me from your wealth,
23 deliver me from the hand of the enemy,
ransom me from the clutches of the
ruthless'?

24 "Teach me, and I will be quiet;
show me where I have been wrong.
25 How painful are honest words!
But what do your arguments prove?
26 Do you mean to correct what I say,
and treat the words of a despairing man
as wind?
27 You would even cast lots for the fatherless
and barter away your friend.

28 "But now be so kind as to look at me.
Would I lie to your face?
29 Relent, do not be unjust;
reconsider, for my integrity is at stake.[a]
30 Is there any wickedness on my lips?
Can my mouth not discern malice?

7 "Does not man have hard service on
earth?
Are not his days like
those of a hired
man?
2 Like a slave longing for the
evening shadows,
or a hired man waiting
eagerly for his
wages,
3 so I have been allotted
months of futility,
and nights of misery
have been assigned
to me.
4 When I lie down I think,
'How long before I get up?'

The night drags on, and I toss till dawn.
5 My body is clothed with worms and scabs,
my skin is broken and festering.

6 "My days are swifter than a weaver's
shuttle,
and they come to an end without hope.
7 Remember, O God, that my life is but a
breath;
my eyes will never see happiness again.
8 The eye that now sees me will see me no
longer;
you will look for me, but I will be no
more.
9 As a cloud vanishes and is gone,
so he who goes down to the grave[b] does
not return.
10 He will never come to his house again;
his place will know him no more.

11 "Therefore I will not keep silent;
I will speak out in the anguish of my
spirit,
I will complain in the bitterness of my
soul.
12 Am I the sea, or the monster of the deep,
that you put me under guard?
13 When I think my bed will comfort me
and my couch will ease my complaint,
14 even then you frighten me with dreams
and terrify me with visions,
15 so that I prefer strangling and death,
rather than this body of mine.
16 I despise my life; I would not live forever.
Let me alone; my days
have no meaning.

17 "What is man that you
make so much of
him,
that you give him so
much attention,
18 that you examine him
every morning
and test him every
moment?
19 Will you never look away
from me,
or let me alone even for
an instant?

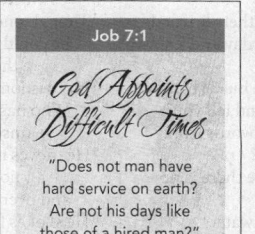

Job 7:1

*God Appoints
Difficult Times*

"Does not man have
hard service on earth?
Are not his days like
those of a hired man?"

---

20 If I have sinned, what have I done to you,
    O watcher of men?
  Why have you made me your target?
    Have I become a burden to you?[a]
21 Why do you not pardon my offenses
    and forgive my sins?
  For I will soon lie down in the dust;
    you will search for me, but I will be no
      more."

Bildad

8 Then Bildad the Shuhite replied:

2 "How long will you say such things?
    Your words are a
      blustering wind.
3 Does God pervert justice?
    Does the Almighty
      pervert what is
      right?
4 When your children sinned
      against him,
  he gave them over to the
    penalty of their sin.
5 But if you will look to God
    and plead with the
      Almighty,
6 if you are pure and upright,
    even now he will rouse
      himself on your behalf
  and restore you to your rightful place.
7 Your beginnings will seem humble,
    so prosperous will your future be.

8 "Ask the former generations
    and find out what their fathers learned,
9 for we were born only yesterday and know
      nothing,
  and our days on earth are but a shadow.
10 Will they not instruct you and tell you?
    Will they not bring forth words from
      their understanding?
11 Can papyrus grow tall where there is no
      marsh?
    Can reeds thrive without water?
12 While still growing and uncut,
    they wither more quickly than grass.
13 Such is the destiny of all who forget God;
    so perishes the hope of the godless.

14 What he trusts in is fragile[b];
    what he relies on is a spider's web.
15 He leans on his web, but it gives way;
    he clings to it, but it does not hold.
16 He is like a well-watered plant in the
      sunshine,
    spreading its shoots over the garden;
17 it entwines its roots around a pile of rocks
    and looks for a place among the stones.
18 But when it is torn from its spot,
    that place disowns it and says, 'I never
      saw you.'
19 Surely its life withers away,
    and[c] from the soil other plants grow.

20 "Surely God does not reject
    a blameless man
  or strengthen the hands
    of evildoers.
21 He will yet fill your mouth
    with laughter
  and your lips with shouts
    of joy.
22 Your enemies will be
    clothed in shame,
  and the tents of the
    wicked will be no
      more."

Job

9 Then Job replied:

2 "Indeed, I know that this is true.
    But how can a mortal be righteous
      before God?
3 Though one wished to dispute with him,
    he could not answer him one time out of
      a thousand.
4 His wisdom is profound, his power is vast.
    Who has resisted him and come out
      unscathed?
5 He moves mountains without their
      knowing it
    and overturns them in his anger.
6 He shakes the earth from its place
    and makes its pillars tremble.
7 He speaks to the sun and it does not shine;
    he seals off the light of the stars.
8 He alone stretches out the heavens

---

a20 A few manuscripts of the Masoretic Text, an ancient Hebrew scribal tradition and Septuagint; most manuscripts of the Masoretic Text
I have become a burden to myself. *b14* The meaning of the Hebrew for this word is uncertain. *c19* Or *Surely all the joy it has / is that*

Job 8:3

God's Judgment Is Right

"Does God pervert justice?
Does the Almighty pervert what is right?"

Beyond the Questions

Read: Job 9:1–35

ZELIE GUERIN MARTIN could have chosen to believe that God was not fair. She was born in 1831 in Alencon, France, and described her childhood as "dismal," recounting how she received little love or affection from her parents. After she married her husband, Louis, she began what started as a happy life as a wife and mother. But tragedy soon struck when four of her nine children died within three years of one another. She lamented, "I haven't a penny's worth of courage." She could have questioned God's love and goodness in the midst of such raw pain. Instead, she looked beyond her present suffering toward a hopeful eternity. The book of Job says, "Man born of woman is of few days and full of trouble" (Job 14:1). Zelie echoed Job's outlook when her life was derailed by death: "My children were not lost forever; life is short and full of miseries, and we shall find our little ones again up above."

The death of Job's children and the loss of all he possessed were inexplicable from a human perspective. It just didn't seem fair. Job longed to argue with God and plead his case, but he realized that God "is not a man like me that I might answer him" (Job 9:32). He longed for someone to "arbitrate" between them.

As mere mortals, it's simply not possible to look beyond heaven's veil to see why God allows things to happen as they do. The simple truth is that God is God, and we are not. And let's face it: Sometimes the things that happen don't seem fair. But thankfully, God *has* sent an arbitrator in the form of his Son, Jesus Christ, to mediate between humans and our holy God. The Bible tells us that Jesus "is able to save completely those who come to God through him, because he always lives to intercede for them" (Hebrews 7:25).

Though we may suffer temporarily on this earth—and no one is denying the intense grief we experience as human beings—through faith in Christ, we can rest assured of an eternity where "there will be no more death or mourning or crying or pain" (Revelation 21:4).

Job 9:32–33

"He is not a man like me that I might answer him, that we might confront each other in court. If only there were someone to arbitrate between us, to lay his hand upon us both."

reflection

1 Describe a time when you wanted to question God. What did you want to dispute or ask?

2 Do you feel closer to God or farther away from him when you question the unfairness of life?

3 Have you asked Jesus to be your arbitrator so that you can enter eternity? If you have not, will you do so now, so you can rest assured of an eternal life in Christ?

RELATED READINGS

Isaiah 55:8–11;
Romans 8:31–39;
James 5:7–11

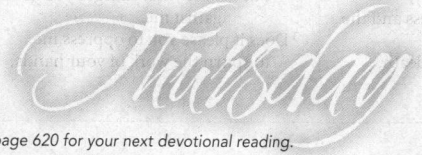

Thursday

Go to page 620 for your next devotional reading.

and treads on the waves of the sea.
9 He is the Maker of the Bear and Orion,
   the Pleiades and the constellations of the
   south.
10 He performs wonders that cannot be
   fathomed,
   miracles that cannot be counted.
11 When he passes me, I cannot see him;
   when he goes by, I cannot perceive him.
12 If he snatches away, who can stop him?
   Who can say to him, 'What are you
   doing?'
13 God does not restrain his anger;
   even the cohorts of Rahab cowered at
   his feet.

14 "How then can I dispute with him?
   How can I find words to argue with
   him?
15 Though I were innocent, I
   could not answer
   him;
   I could only plead with
   my Judge for mercy.
16 Even if I summoned him
   and he responded,
   I do not believe he would
   give me a hearing.
17 He would crush me with a
   storm
   and multiply my wounds
   for no reason.
18 He would not let me regain
   my breath
   but would overwhelm me with misery.
19 If it is a matter of strength, he is mighty!
   And if it is a matter of justice, who will
   summon him*a*?
20 Even if I were innocent, my mouth would
   condemn me;
   if I were blameless, it would pronounce
   me guilty.

21 "Although I am blameless,
   I have no concern for myself;
   I despise my own life.
22 It is all the same; that is why I say,
   'He destroys both the blameless and the
   wicked.'
23 When a scourge brings sudden death,

he mocks the despair of the innocent.
24 When a land falls into the hands of the
   wicked,
   he blindfolds its judges.
   If it is not he, then who is it?

25 "My days are swifter than a runner;
   they fly away without a glimpse of joy.
26 They skim past like boats of papyrus,
   like eagles swooping down on their prey.
27 If I say, 'I will forget my complaint,
   I will change my expression, and smile,'
28 I still dread all my sufferings,
   for I know you will not hold me
   innocent.
29 Since I am already found guilty,
   why should I struggle in vain?
30 Even if I washed myself with soap*b*
   and my hands with
   washing soda,
31 you would plunge me into a
   slime pit
   so that even my clothes
   would detest me.

32 "He is not a man like me
   that I might answer
   him,
   that we might confront
   each other in court.
33 If only there were someone
   to arbitrate between
   us,
   to lay his hand upon us both,
34 someone to remove God's rod from me,
   so that his terror would frighten me no
   more.
35 Then I would speak up without fear of him,
   but as it now stands with me, I cannot.

10

"I loathe my very life;
   therefore I will give free rein to my
   complaint
   and speak out in the bitterness of my
   soul.
2 I will say to God: Do not condemn me,
   but tell me what charges you have
   against me.
3 Does it please you to oppress me,
   to spurn the work of your hands,

Job 9:32

God Is Superior to Humans

"He is not a man like me
that I might answer him,
that we might confront
each other in court."

---

*a*19 See Septuagint; Hebrew *me*. *b*30 Or *snow*

while you smile on the schemes of the wicked?
4 Do you have eyes of flesh?
Do you see as a mortal sees?
5 Are your days like those of a mortal
or your years like those of a man,
6 that you must search out my faults
and probe after my sin—
7 though you know that I am not guilty
and that no one can rescue me from your hand?

8 "Your hands shaped me and made me.
Will you now turn and destroy me?
9 Remember that you molded me like clay.
Will you now turn me to dust again?
10 Did you not pour me out like milk
and curdle me like cheese,
11 clothe me with skin and flesh
and knit me together with bones and sinews?
12 You gave me life and showed me kindness,
and in your providence watched over my spirit.

13 "But this is what you concealed in your heart,
and I know that this was in your mind:
14 If I sinned, you would be watching me
and would not let my offense go unpunished.
15 If I am guilty—woe to me!
Even if I am innocent, I cannot lift my head,
for I am full of shame
and drowned in*a* my affliction.
16 If I hold my head high, you stalk me like a lion
and again display your awesome power against me.
17 You bring new witnesses against me
and increase your anger toward me;
your forces come against me wave upon wave.

18 "Why then did you bring me out of the womb?
I wish I had died before any eye saw me.
19 If only I had never come into being,
or had been carried straight from the womb to the grave!
20 Are not my few days almost over?
Turn away from me so I can have a moment's joy
21 before I go to the place of no return,
to the land of gloom and deep shadow,*b*
22 to the land of deepest night,
of deep shadow and disorder,
where even the light is like darkness."

Zophar

11 Then Zophar the Naamathite replied:

2 "Are all these words to go unanswered?
Is this talker to be vindicated?
3 Will your idle talk reduce men to silence?
Will no one rebuke you when you mock?
4 You say to God, 'My beliefs are flawless
and I am pure in your sight.'
5 Oh, how I wish that God would speak,
that he would open his lips against you
6 and disclose to you the secrets of wisdom,
for true wisdom has two sides.
Know this: God has even forgotten some of your sin.

7 "Can you fathom the mysteries of God?
Can you probe the limits of the Almighty?
8 They are higher than the heavens—what can you do?
They are deeper than the depths of the grave*c*—what can you know?
9 Their measure is longer than the earth
and wider than the sea.

10 "If he comes along and confines you in prison
and convenes a court, who can oppose him?

Job 11:7

God Is Mysterious

"Can you fathom the mysteries of God?
Can you probe the limits of the Almighty?"

---

*a*15 Or *and aware of* *b*21 Or *and the shadow of death; also in verse 22* *c*8 Hebrew *than Sheol*

11 Surely he recognizes deceitful men;
  and when he sees evil, does he not take
    note?
12 But a witless man can no more become
    wise
  than a wild donkey's colt can be born a
    man.*a*

13 "Yet if you devote your heart to him
  and stretch out your hands to him,
14 if you put away the sin that is in your hand
  and allow no evil to dwell in your tent,
15 then you will lift up your face without
    shame;
  you will stand firm and without fear.
16 You will surely forget your trouble,
  recalling it only as waters gone by.
17 Life will be brighter than noonday,
  and darkness will become like morning.
18 You will be secure, because there is hope;
  you will look about you and take your
    rest in safety.
19 You will lie down, with no one to make
    you afraid,
  and many will court your favor.
20 But the eyes of the wicked will fail,
  and escape will elude them;
    their hope will become a dying gasp."

Job

12

Then Job replied:

2 "Doubtless you are the people,
  and wisdom will die with you!
3 But I have a mind as well as you;
  I am not inferior to you.
  Who does not know all these things?

4 "I have become a laughingstock to my
    friends,
  though I called upon God and he
    answered—
  a mere laughingstock, though righteous
    and blameless!
5 Men at ease have contempt for misfortune
  as the fate of those whose feet are
    slipping.
6 The tents of marauders are undisturbed,
  and those who provoke God are
    secure—

those who carry their god in their
  hands.*b*

7 "But ask the animals, and they will teach
    you,
  or the birds of the air, and they will tell
    you;
8 or speak to the earth, and it will teach you,
  or let the fish of the sea inform you.
9 Which of all these does not know
  that the hand of the LORD has done this?
10 In his hand is the life of every creature
  and the breath of all mankind.
11 Does not the ear test words
  as the tongue tastes food?
12 Is not wisdom found among the aged?
  Does not long life bring understanding?

13 "To God belong wisdom and power;
  counsel and understanding are his.
14 What he tears down cannot be rebuilt;
  the man he imprisons cannot be
    released.
15 If he holds back the waters, there is
    drought;
  if he lets them loose, they devastate the
    land.
16 To him belong strength and victory;
  both deceived and deceiver are his.
17 He leads counselors away stripped
  and makes fools of judges.
18 He takes off the shackles put on by kings
  and ties a loincloth*c* around their waist.
19 He leads priests away stripped
  and overthrows men long established.
20 He silences the lips of trusted advisers
  and takes away the discernment of elders.
21 He pours contempt on nobles
  and disarms the mighty.
22 He reveals the deep things of darkness
  and brings deep shadows into the light.
23 He makes nations great, and destroys
    them;
  he enlarges nations, and disperses them.
24 He deprives the leaders of the earth of their
    reason;
  he sends them wandering through a
    trackless waste.
25 They grope in darkness with no light;
  he makes them stagger like drunkards.

*a*12 Or *wild donkey can be born tame*   *b*6 Or *secure / in what God's hand brings them*   *c*18 Or *shackles of kings / and ties a belt*

13

¹ "My eyes have seen all this,
  my ears have heard and understood
    it.
² What you know, I also know;
  I am not inferior to you.
³ But I desire to speak to the Almighty
  and to argue my case with God.
⁴ You, however, smear me with lies;
  you are worthless physicians, all of you!
⁵ If only you would be altogether silent!
  For you, that would be wisdom.
⁶ Hear now my argument;
  listen to the plea of my lips.
⁷ Will you speak wickedly on God's behalf?
  Will you speak deceitfully for him?
⁸ Will you show him partiality?
  Will you argue the case for God?
⁹ Would it turn out well if he examined you?
  Could you deceive him as you might
    deceive men?
¹⁰ He would surely rebuke you
  if you secretly showed partiality.
¹¹ Would not his splendor terrify you?
  Would not the dread of him fall on
    you?
¹² Your maxims are proverbs of ashes;
  your defenses are defenses of clay.

¹³ "Keep silent and let me speak;
  then let come to me what may.
¹⁴ Why do I put myself in
    jeopardy
  and take my life in my
    hands?
¹⁵ Though he slay me, yet will
    I hope in him;
  I will surely[a] defend my
    ways to his face.
¹⁶ Indeed, this will turn out
    for my deliverance,
  for no godless man
    would dare come
    before him!
¹⁷ Listen carefully to my
    words;
  let your ears take in what I say.
¹⁸ Now that I have prepared my case,
  I know I will be vindicated.
¹⁹ Can anyone bring charges against me?
  If so, I will be silent and die.

²⁰ "Only grant me these two things, O God,
  and then I will not hide from you:
²¹ Withdraw your hand far from me,
  and stop frightening me with your
    terrors.
²² Then summon me and I will answer,
  or let me speak, and you reply.
²³ How many wrongs and sins have I
    committed?
  Show me my offense and my sin.
²⁴ Why do you hide your face
  and consider me your enemy?
²⁵ Will you torment a windblown leaf?
  Will you chase after dry chaff?
²⁶ For you write down bitter things against
    me
  and make me inherit the sins of my
    youth.
²⁷ You fasten my feet in shackles;
  you keep close watch on all my paths
  by putting marks on the soles of my feet.

²⁸ "So man wastes away like something
    rotten,
  like a garment eaten by moths.

14

¹ "Man born of woman
  is of few days and full of trouble.
² He springs up like a flower and withers
    away;
      like a fleeting shadow, he
        does not endure.
³ Do you fix your eye on such
        a one?
  Will you bring him[b]
        before you for
        judgment?
⁴ Who can bring what is
        pure from the
        impure?
  No one!
⁵ Man's days are determined;
      you have decreed the
        number of his
        months
  and have set limits he cannot exceed.
⁶ So look away from him and let him
    alone,
  till he has put in his time like a hired
    man.

Job 13:15

God Is Trustworthy

"Though he slay me, yet
will I hope in him;
I will surely defend my
ways to his face."

ᵃ15 Or *He will surely slay me; I have no hope — / yet I will*   ᵇ3 Septuagint, Vulgate and Syriac; Hebrew *me*

Job 13:15

"Though he slay me, yet will I hope in him."

reflection

1 Have you ever wondered if suffering is the result of sinfulness?

2 Has this devotional caused you to rethink your position? Why or why not?

3 Make Job's proclamation personal to your situation: "Though he _____, yet will I hope in him." (For example: "Though he allows breast cancer, yet will I hope in him.")

RELATED READINGS

Job 1:1–22;
Romans 5:1–5;
2 Corinthians 12:7–10

Read: Job 13:1–28

CARING FOR A PARENT with Alzheimer's disease takes what Carolyn Sherman calls "the patience of Job." Carolyn and Sandy Sherman have cared for both their mothers for ten years. For two of those years the two older women lived at home with the Shermans. Carolyn says she prayed many times for the patience and strength to see this through. "You do get irritated. You do lose it sometimes," said Carolyn. "I never realized that it would take so much time and so much patience." Carolyn went on to say that she had prayed many times for the ability to see it through.

Even well-intentioned people, like Job's foolish counselors, believe that all suffering or sickness is the direct result of sin. Throughout the book of Job we've seen Job's friends try to convince him that he had done something to displease God, that somehow Job was responsible for the horrible things that had happened to him. But this could not be further from the truth. Everyone suffers—the righteous and the unrighteous—including Job, who "was blameless and upright; he feared God and shunned evil" (Job 1:1). For some reason God chose to use Job as an example of patience in the midst of great suffering.

When something tragic happens, we often scramble to figure out why. Did I sin? Did they sin? If we didn't sin, then who sinned? Like Job's friends, we just want to affix blame so we can make some kind of sense out of the seemingly senseless. But not all suffering is the direct result of sin. Paul's thorn in the flesh was not given to him because he was such a sinner, but because God wanted him to understand something important about suffering. God said, "My grace is sufficient for you, for my power is made perfect in weakness" (2 Corinthians 12:9).

The simple truth is that God is not constrained to tell us *why* bad things happen to us. But he will let us know *how* to walk through them . . . with patience and hope. Yes, Job had some questions he wanted God to answer. But despite his questions Job could still faithfully proclaim, "Though he slay me, yet will I hope in him." Can the same be said of you?

Friday

Go to page 630 for your next devotional reading.

7 "At least there is hope for a tree:
   If it is cut down, it will sprout again,
   and its new shoots will not fail.
8 Its roots may grow old in the ground
   and its stump die in the soil,
9 yet at the scent of water it will bud
   and put forth shoots like a plant.
10 But man dies and is laid low;
   he breathes his last and is no more.
11 As water disappears from the sea
   or a riverbed becomes parched and dry,
12 so man lies down and does not rise;
   till the heavens are no more, men will
      not awake
   or be roused from their sleep.

13 "If only you would hide me in the grave*a*
   and conceal me till your anger has
      passed!
   If only you would set me a time
   and then remember me!
14 If a man dies, will he live again?
   All the days of my hard service
   I will wait for my renewal*b* to come.
15 You will call and I will answer you;
   you will long for the creature your hands
      have made.
16 Surely then you will count my steps
   but not keep track of my sin.
17 My offenses will be sealed up in a bag;
   you will cover over my sin.

18 "But as a mountain erodes and crumbles
   and as a rock is moved from its place,
19 as water wears away stones
   and torrents wash away the soil,
   so you destroy man's hope.
20 You overpower him once for all, and he is
      gone;
   you change his countenance and send
      him away.
21 If his sons are honored, he does not know it;
   if they are brought low, he does not see it.
22 He feels but the pain of his own body
   and mourns only for himself."

Eliphaz

15

Then Eliphaz the Temanite replied:

2 "Would a wise man answer with empty
   notions

---

or fill his belly with the hot east wind?
3 Would he argue with useless words,
   with speeches that have no value?
4 But you even undermine piety
   and hinder devotion to God.
5 Your sin prompts your mouth;
   you adopt the tongue of the crafty.
6 Your own mouth condemns you, not mine;
   your own lips testify against you.

7 "Are you the first man ever born?
   Were you brought forth before the hills?
8 Do you listen in on God's council?
   Do you limit wisdom to yourself?
9 What do you know that we do not know?
   What insights do you have that we do
      not have?
10 The gray-haired and the aged are on our
      side,
   men even older than your father.
11 Are God's consolations not enough for
      you,
   words spoken gently to you?
12 Why has your heart carried you away,
   and why do your eyes flash,
13 so that you vent your rage against God
   and pour out such words from your
      mouth?

14 "What is man, that he could be pure,
   or one born of woman, that he could be
      righteous?
15 If God places no trust in his holy ones,
   if even the heavens are not pure in his
      eyes,
16 how much less man, who is vile and
      corrupt,
   who drinks up evil like water!

17 "Listen to me and I will explain to you;
   let me tell you what I have seen,
18 what wise men have declared,
   hiding nothing received from their
      fathers
19 (to whom alone the land was given
   when no alien passed among them):
20 All his days the wicked man suffers
      torment,
   the ruthless through all the years stored
      up for him.
21 Terrifying sounds fill his ears;

---

*a*13 Hebrew *Sheol*   *b*14 Or *release*

when all seems well, marauders attack
    him.
²²He despairs of escaping the darkness;
    he is marked for the sword.
²³He wanders about—food for vultures[a];
    he knows the day of darkness is at
        hand.
²⁴Distress and anguish fill him with terror;
    they overwhelm him, like a king poised
        to attack,
²⁵because he shakes his fist at God
    and vaunts himself against the
        Almighty,
²⁶defiantly charging against him
    with a thick, strong shield.

²⁷"Though his face is covered with fat
    and his waist bulges with flesh,
²⁸he will inhabit ruined towns
    and houses where no one lives,
    houses crumbling to rubble.
²⁹He will no longer be rich and his wealth
        will not endure,
    nor will his possessions spread over the
        land.
³⁰He will not escape the darkness;
    a flame will wither his shoots,
    and the breath of God's mouth will
        carry him away.
³¹Let him not deceive himself by trusting
        what is worthless,
    for he will get nothing in return.
³²Before his time he will be paid in full,
    and his branches will not flourish.
³³He will be like a vine stripped of its unripe
        grapes,
    like an olive tree shedding its blossoms.
³⁴For the company of the godless will be
        barren,
    and fire will consume the tents of those
        who love bribes.
³⁵They conceive trouble and give birth to
        evil;
    their womb fashions deceit."

Job

16

Then Job replied:

²"I have heard many things like these;
    miserable comforters are you all!

³Will your long-winded speeches never
        end?
    What ails you that you keep on arguing?
⁴I also could speak like you,
    if you were in my place;
    I could make fine speeches against you
        and shake my head at you.
⁵But my mouth would encourage you;
    comfort from my lips would bring you
        relief.

⁶"Yet if I speak, my pain is not relieved;
    and if I refrain, it does not go away.
⁷Surely, O God, you have worn me out;
    you have devastated my entire
        household.
⁸You have bound me—and it has become a
        witness;
    my gauntness rises up and testifies
        against me.
⁹God assails me and tears me in his anger
        and gnashes his teeth at me;
    my opponent fastens on me his piercing
        eyes.
¹⁰Men open their mouths to jeer at me;
    they strike my cheek in scorn
    and unite together against me.
¹¹God has turned me over to evil men
    and thrown me into the clutches of the
        wicked.
¹²All was well with me, but he shattered me;
    he seized me by the neck and crushed
        me.
    He has made me his target;
¹³   his archers surround me.
    Without pity, he pierces my kidneys
        and spills my gall on the ground.
¹⁴Again and again he bursts upon me;
    he rushes at me like a warrior.

¹⁵"I have sewed sackcloth over my skin
    and buried my brow in the dust.
¹⁶My face is red with weeping,
    deep shadows ring my eyes;
¹⁷yet my hands have been free of violence
        and my prayer is pure.

¹⁸"O earth, do not cover my blood;
    may my cry never be laid to rest!
¹⁹Even now my witness is in heaven;

---

[a]23 Or about, looking for food

my advocate is on high.
²⁰ My intercessor is my friend[a]
as my eyes pour out tears
to God;
²¹ on behalf of a man he
pleads with God
as a man pleads for his
friend.

²² "Only a few years will pass
before I go on the
journey of no
return.

17 ¹ My spirit is broken,
my days are cut short,
the grave awaits me.
² Surely mockers surround
me;
my eyes must dwell on their hostility.

³ "Give me, O God, the pledge you demand.
Who else will put up security for me?
⁴ You have closed their minds to
understanding;
therefore you will not let them triumph.
⁵ If a man denounces his friends for reward,
the eyes of his children will fail.

⁶ "God has made me a byword to everyone,
a man in whose face people spit.
⁷ My eyes have grown dim with grief;
my whole frame is but a shadow.
⁸ Upright men are appalled at this;
the innocent are aroused against the
ungodly.
⁹ Nevertheless, the righteous will hold to
their ways,
and those with clean hands will grow
stronger.

¹⁰ "But come on, all of you, try again!
I will not find a wise man among you.
¹¹ My days have passed, my plans are
shattered,
and so are the desires of my heart.
¹² These men turn night into day;
in the face of darkness they say, 'Light
is near.'
¹³ If the only home I hope for is the grave,[b]
if I spread out my bed in darkness,
¹⁴ if I say to corruption, 'You are my father,'

Job 16:19

God Is Our Advocate

"Even now my witness
is in heaven;
my advocate is on high."

and to the worm, 'My mother' or 'My
sister,'
¹⁵ where then is my hope?
Who can see any hope
for me?
¹⁶ Will it go down to the gates
of death[b]?
Will we descend together
into the dust?"

Bildad

18 Then Bildad the Shuhite replied:

² "When will you end these
speeches?
Be sensible, and then we
can talk.
³ Why are we regarded as cattle
and considered stupid in your sight?
⁴ You who tear yourself to pieces in your
anger,
is the earth to be abandoned for your
sake?
Or must the rocks be moved from their
place?

⁵ "The lamp of the wicked is snuffed out;
the flame of his fire stops burning.
⁶ The light in his tent becomes dark;
the lamp beside him goes out.
⁷ The vigor of his step is weakened;
his own schemes throw him down.
⁸ His feet thrust him into a net
and he wanders into its mesh.
⁹ A trap seizes him by the heel;
a snare holds him fast.
¹⁰ A noose is hidden for him on the ground;
a trap lies in his path.
¹¹ Terrors startle him on every side
and dog his every step.
¹² Calamity is hungry for him;
disaster is ready for him when he falls.
¹³ It eats away parts of his skin;
death's firstborn devours his limbs.
¹⁴ He is torn from the security of his tent
and marched off to the king of terrors.
¹⁵ Fire resides[c] in his tent;
burning sulfur is scattered over his
dwelling.
¹⁶ His roots dry up below

---

[a]20 Or *My friends treat me with scorn*   [b]13,16 Hebrew *Sheol*   [c]15 Or *Nothing he had remains*

and his branches wither above.
¹⁷ The memory of him perishes from the earth;
    he has no name in the land.
¹⁸ He is driven from light into darkness
    and is banished from the world.
¹⁹ He has no offspring or descendants among his people,
    no survivor where once he lived.
²⁰ Men of the west are appalled at his fate;
    men of the east are seized with horror.
²¹ Surely such is the dwelling of an evil man;
    such is the place of one who knows not God."

Job

19

Then Job replied:

² "How long will you torment me
    and crush me with words?
³ Ten times now you have reproached me;
    shamelessly you attack me.
⁴ If it is true that I have gone astray,
    my error remains my concern alone.
⁵ If indeed you would exalt yourselves above me
    and use my humiliation against me,
⁶ then know that God has wronged me
    and drawn his net around me.

⁷ "Though I cry, 'I've been wronged!' I get no response;
    though I call for help, there is no justice.
⁸ He has blocked my way so I cannot pass;
    he has shrouded my paths in darkness.
⁹ He has stripped me of my honor
    and removed the crown from my head.
¹⁰ He tears me down on every side till I am gone;
    he uproots my hope like a tree.
¹¹ His anger burns against me;
    he counts me among his enemies.

¹² His troops advance in force;
    they build a siege ramp against me
    and encamp around my tent.

¹³ "He has alienated my brothers from me;
    my acquaintances are completely estranged from me.
¹⁴ My kinsmen have gone away;
    my friends have forgotten me.
¹⁵ My guests and my maidservants count me a stranger;
    they look upon me as an alien.
¹⁶ I summon my servant, but he does not answer,
    though I beg him with my own mouth.
¹⁷ My breath is offensive to my wife;
    I am loathsome to my own brothers.
¹⁸ Even the little boys scorn me;
    when I appear, they ridicule me.
¹⁹ All my intimate friends detest me;
    those I love have turned against me.
²⁰ I am nothing but skin and bones;
    I have escaped with only the skin of my teeth.ᵃ

²¹ "Have pity on me, my friends, have pity,
    for the hand of God has struck me.
²² Why do you pursue me as God does?
    Will you never get enough of my flesh?

²³ "Oh, that my words were recorded,
    that they were written on a scroll,
²⁴ that they were inscribed with an iron tool on ᵇ lead,
    or engraved in rock forever!
²⁵ I know that my Redeemer ᶜ lives,
    and that in the end he will stand upon the earth.ᵈ
²⁶ And after my skin has been destroyed,
    yet ᵉ in ᶠ my flesh I will see God;
²⁷ I myself will see him
    with my own eyes—I, and not another.
    How my heart yearns within me!

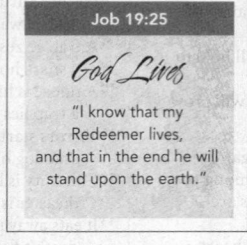

Job 19:25

God Lives

"I know that my Redeemer lives, and that in the end he will stand upon the earth."

ᵃ 20 Or *only my gums* ᵇ 24 Or *and* ᶜ 25 Or *defender* ᵈ 25 Or *upon my grave* ᵉ 26 Or *And after I awake, / though this body has been destroyed, / then* ᶠ 26 Or *apart from*

28 "If you say, 'How we will hound him,
    since the root of the trouble lies in
        him,^{a}'
29 you should fear the sword yourselves;
    for wrath will bring punishment by the
        sword,
    and then you will know that there is
        judgment.^{b}"

Zophar

20 Then Zophar the Naamathite replied:

2 "My troubled thoughts prompt me to
        answer
    because I am greatly disturbed.
3 I hear a rebuke that dishonors me,
    and my understanding inspires me to
        reply.

4 "Surely you know how it has been from of
        old,
    ever since man^c was placed on the
        earth,
5 that the mirth of the wicked is brief,
    the joy of the godless lasts but a
        moment.
6 Though his pride reaches to the heavens
    and his head touches the clouds,
7 he will perish forever, like his own dung;
    those who have seen him will say,
        'Where is he?'
8 Like a dream he flies away, no more to be
        found,
    banished like a vision of the night.
9 The eye that saw him will not see him
        again;
    his place will look on him no more.
10 His children must make amends to the
        poor;
    his own hands must give back his
        wealth.
11 The youthful vigor that fills his bones
    will lie with him in the dust.

12 "Though evil is sweet in his mouth
    and he hides it under his tongue,
13 though he cannot bear to let it go
    and keeps it in his mouth,
14 yet his food will turn sour in his
        stomach;

it will become the venom of serpents
        within him.
15 He will spit out the riches he swallowed;
    God will make his stomach vomit them
        up.
16 He will suck the poison of serpents;
    the fangs of an adder will kill him.
17 He will not enjoy the streams,
    the rivers flowing with honey and
        cream.
18 What he toiled for he must give back
        uneaten;
    he will not enjoy the profit from his
        trading.
19 For he has oppressed the poor and left
        them destitute;
    he has seized houses he did not build.

20 "Surely he will have no respite from his
        craving;
    he cannot save himself by his
        treasure.
21 Nothing is left for him to devour;
    his prosperity will not endure.
22 In the midst of his plenty, distress will
        overtake him;
    the full force of misery will come upon
        him.
23 When he has filled his belly,
    God will vent his burning anger against
        him
    and rain down his blows upon him.
24 Though he flees from an iron weapon,
    a bronze-tipped arrow pierces him.
25 He pulls it out of his back,
    the gleaming point out of his liver.
    Terrors will come over him;
26   total darkness lies in wait for his
        treasures.
    A fire unfanned will consume him
    and devour what is left in his tent.
27 The heavens will expose his guilt;
    the earth will rise up against him.
28 A flood will carry off his house,
    rushing waters^d on the day of God's
        wrath.
29 Such is the fate God allots the wicked,
    the heritage appointed for them by
        God."

---

^{a}28 Many Hebrew manuscripts, Septuagint and Vulgate; most Hebrew manuscripts me ^{b}29 Or / that you may come to know the Almighty
^{c}4 Or Adam ^{d}28 Or The possessions in his house will be carried off, / washed away

Job

21

Then Job replied:

2 "Listen carefully to my words;
  let this be the consolation you give me.
3 Bear with me while I speak,
  and after I have spoken, mock on.

4 "Is my complaint directed to man?
  Why should I not be impatient?
5 Look at me and be astonished;
  clap your hand over your mouth.
6 When I think about this, I am terrified;
  trembling seizes my body.
7 Why do the wicked live on,
  growing old and increasing in power?
8 They see their children established around
    them,
  their offspring before their eyes.
9 Their homes are safe and free from fear;
  the rod of God is not upon them.
10 Their bulls never fail to breed;
  their cows calve and do not miscarry.
11 They send forth their children as a flock;
  their little ones dance about.
12 They sing to the music of tambourine and
    harp;
  they make merry to the sound of the
    flute.
13 They spend their years in prosperity
  and go down to the grave*a* in peace.*b*
14 Yet they say to God, 'Leave us alone!
  We have no desire to know your ways.
15 Who is the Almighty, that we should serve
    him?
  What would we gain by praying to him?'
16 But their prosperity is not in their own
    hands,
  so I stand aloof from the counsel of the
    wicked.

17 "Yet how often is the lamp of the wicked
    snuffed out?
  How often does calamity come upon
    them,
  the fate God allots in his anger?
18 How often are they like straw before the
    wind,
  like chaff swept away by a gale?

19 It is said, 'God stores up a man's
    punishment for his sons.'
  Let him repay the man himself, so that
    he will know it!
20 Let his own eyes see his destruction;
  let him drink of the wrath of the
    Almighty.*c*
21 For what does he care about the family he
    leaves behind
  when his allotted months come to an
    end?

22 "Can anyone teach knowledge to God,
  since he judges even the highest?
23 One man dies in full vigor,
  completely secure and at ease,
24 his body*d* well nourished,
  his bones rich with marrow.
25 Another man dies in bitterness of soul,
  never having enjoyed anything good.
26 Side by side they lie in the dust,
  and worms cover them both.

27 "I know full well what you are thinking,
  the schemes by which you would wrong
    me.
28 You say, 'Where now is the great man's
    house,
  the tents where wicked men lived?'
29 Have you never questioned those who
    travel?
  Have you paid no regard to their
    accounts—
30 that the evil man is spared from the day of
    calamity,
  that he is delivered from*e* the day of
    wrath?
31 Who denounces his conduct to his face?
  Who repays him for what he has done?
32 He is carried to the grave,
  and watch is kept over his tomb.
33 The soil in the valley is sweet to him;
  all men follow after him,
  and a countless throng goes*f* before him.

34 "So how can you console me with your
    nonsense?
  Nothing is left of your answers but
    falsehood!"

---

*a*13 Hebrew *Sheol* *b*13 Or *in an instant* *c*17–20 Verses 17 and 18 may be taken as exclamations and 19 and 20 as declarations.
*d*24 The meaning of the Hebrew for this word is uncertain. *e*30 Or *man is reserved for the day of calamity, / that he is brought forth to*
*f*33 Or / *as a countless throng went*

Eliphaz

22

Then Eliphaz the Temanite replied:

2 "Can a man be of benefit to God?
  Can even a wise man benefit him?
3 What pleasure would it give the Almighty
      if you were righteous?
  What would he gain if your ways were
      blameless?

4 "Is it for your piety that he rebukes you
      and brings charges against you?
5 Is not your wickedness great?
  Are not your sins endless?
6 You demanded security from your
      brothers for no reason;
  you stripped men of their clothing,
      leaving them naked.
7 You gave no water to the weary
      and you withheld food from the hungry,
8 though you were a powerful man, owning
      land—
  an honored man, living on it.
9 And you sent widows away empty-handed
      and broke the strength of the fatherless.
10 That is why snares are all around you,
      why sudden peril terrifies you,
11 why it is so dark you cannot see,
      and why a flood of water covers you.

12 "Is not God in the heights of heaven?
  And see how lofty are the highest stars!
13 Yet you say, 'What does God know?
  Does he judge through such darkness?
14 Thick clouds veil him, so he does not see us
      as he goes about in the vaulted heavens.'
15 Will you keep to the old path
      that evil men have trod?
16 They were carried off before their time,
      their foundations washed away by a
      flood.
17 They said to God, 'Leave us alone!
  What can the Almighty do to us?'
18 Yet it was he who filled their houses with
      good things,
  so I stand aloof from the counsel of the
      wicked.

19 "The righteous see their ruin and rejoice;
  the innocent mock them, saying,

20 'Surely our foes are destroyed,
      and fire devours their wealth.'

21 "Submit to God and be at peace with him;
  in this way prosperity will come to you.
22 Accept instruction from his mouth
      and lay up his words in your heart.
23 If you return to the Almighty, you will be
      restored:
  If you remove wickedness far from your
      tent
24 and assign your nuggets to the dust,
      your gold of Ophir to the rocks in the
      ravines,
25 then the Almighty will be your gold,
      the choicest silver for you.
26 Surely then you will find delight in the
      Almighty
  and will lift up your face to God.
27 You will pray to him, and he will hear you,
      and you will fulfill your vows.
28 What you decide on will be done,
      and light will shine on your ways.
29 When men are brought low and you say,
      'Lift them up!'
  then he will save the downcast.
30 He will deliver even one who is not
      innocent,
  who will be delivered through the
      cleanness of your hands."

Job

23

Then Job replied:

2 "Even today my complaint is bitter;
  his hand[a] is heavy in spite of[b] my
      groaning.
3 If only I knew where to find him;
      if only I could go to his dwelling!
4 I would state my case before him
      and fill my mouth with arguments.
5 I would find out what he would answer me,
      and consider what he would say.
6 Would he oppose me with great power?
  No, he would not press charges against
      me.
7 There an upright man could present his
      case before him,
  and I would be delivered forever from
      my judge.

---

a 2 Septuagint and Syriac; Hebrew / the hand on me   b 2 Or heavy on me in

8 "But if I go to the east, he is not there;
   if I go to the west, I do not find him.
9 When he is at work in the north, I do not
      see him;
   when he turns to the south, I catch no
      glimpse of him.
10 But he knows the way that I take;
   when he has tested me, I will come forth
      as gold.
11 My feet have closely followed his steps;
   I have kept to his way without turning
      aside.
12 I have not departed from the commands of
      his lips;
   I have treasured the words of his mouth
      more than my daily bread.

13 "But he stands alone, and who can oppose
      him?
   He does whatever he pleases.
14 He carries out his decree against me,
   and many such plans he still has in
      store.
15 That is why I am terrified
      before him;
   when I think of all this, I
      fear him.
16 God has made my heart
      faint;
   the Almighty has
      terrified me.
17 Yet I am not silenced by the
      darkness,
   by the thick darkness
      that covers my face.

24 "Why does the
      Almighty not set times for
      judgment?
   Why must those who know him look in
      vain for such days?
2 Men move boundary stones;
   they pasture flocks they have stolen.
3 They drive away the orphan's donkey
   and take the widow's ox in pledge.
4 They thrust the needy from the path
   and force all the poor of the land into
      hiding.
5 Like wild donkeys in the desert,

the poor go about their labor of foraging
      food;
   the wasteland provides food for their
      children.
6 They gather fodder in the fields
   and glean in the vineyards of the
      wicked.
7 Lacking clothes, they spend the night
      naked;
   they have nothing to cover themselves in
      the cold.
8 They are drenched by mountain rains
   and hug the rocks for lack of shelter.
9 The fatherless child is snatched from the
      breast;
   the infant of the poor is seized for a debt.
10 Lacking clothes, they go about naked;
   they carry the sheaves, but still go
      hungry.
11 They crush olives among the terraces[a];
   they tread the winepresses, yet suffer
      thirst.

Job 23:13

God Is Unchangeable

"But he stands alone, and
who can oppose him?
He does whatever
he pleases."

12 The groans of the dying
      rise from the city,
   and the souls of the
      wounded cry out
      for help.
   But God charges no one
      with wrongdoing.

13 "There are those who rebel
      against the light,
   who do not know its
      ways
   or stay in its paths.
14 When daylight is gone, the
      murderer rises up
   and kills the poor and needy;
   in the night he steals forth like a thief.
15 The eye of the adulterer watches for dusk;
   he thinks, 'No eye will see me,'
   and he keeps his face concealed.
16 In the dark, men break into houses,
   but by day they shut themselves in;
   they want nothing to do with the light.
17 For all of them, deep darkness is their
      morning[b];
   they make friends with the terrors of
      darkness.[c]

---

[a]11 Or *olives between the millstones*; the meaning of the Hebrew for this word is uncertain.   [b]17 Or *them, their morning is like the shadow of death*   [c]17 Or *of the shadow of death*

18 "Yet they are foam on the surface of the
water;
their portion of the land is cursed,
so that no one goes to the vineyards.
19 As heat and drought snatch away the
melted snow,
so the grave[a] snatches away those who
have sinned.
20 The womb forgets them,
the worm feasts on them;
evil men are no longer remembered
but are broken like a tree.
21 They prey on the barren and childless
woman,
and to the widow show no kindness.
22 But God drags away the
mighty by his
power;
though they become
established, they
have no assurance
of life.
23 He may let them rest in a
feeling of security,
but his eyes are on their
ways.
24 For a little while they are
exalted, and then
they are gone;
they are brought low and
gathered up like all
others;
they are cut off like heads of grain.

25 "If this is not so, who can prove me false
and reduce my words to nothing?"

Bildad

25

Then Bildad the Shuhite replied:

2 "Dominion and awe belong to God;
he establishes order in the heights of
heaven.
3 Can his forces be numbered?
Upon whom does his light not rise?
4 How then can a man be righteous before
God?
How can one born of woman be pure?
5 If even the moon is not bright
and the stars are not pure in his eyes,

6 how much less man, who is but a maggot—
a son of man, who is only a worm!"

Job

26

Then Job replied:

2 "How you have helped the powerless!
How you have saved the arm that is
feeble!
3 What advice you have offered to one
without wisdom!
And what great insight you have
displayed!
4 Who has helped you utter these words?
And whose spirit spoke from your
mouth?

5 "The dead are in deep
anguish,
those beneath the waters
and all that live in
them.
6 Death[a] is naked before
God;
Destruction[b] lies
uncovered.
7 He spreads out the
northern ⌊skies⌋ over
empty space;
he suspends the earth
over nothing.
8 He wraps up the waters in
his clouds,
yet the clouds do not burst under their
weight.
9 He covers the face of the full moon,
spreading his clouds over it.
10 He marks out the horizon on the face of
the waters
for a boundary between light and
darkness.
11 The pillars of the heavens quake,
aghast at his rebuke.
12 By his power he churned up the sea;
by his wisdom he cut Rahab to pieces.
13 By his breath the skies became fair;
his hand pierced the gliding serpent.
14 And these are but the outer fringe of his
works;
how faint the whisper we hear of him!"

> ### Job 26:7
>
> *God Sustains the World*
>
> "He spreads out the
> northern skies over
> empty space;
> he suspends the earth
> over nothing."

---

[a] 19,6 Hebrew *Sheol*   [b] 6 Hebrew *Abaddon*

Release

HANNAH

O LORD

Almighty, if you
will only look upon
your servant's
misery and
remember me,
and not forget
your servant but
give her a son,
then I will give
him to the LORD
for all the days
of his life, and no
razor will ever be
used on his head.

1 Samuel 1:11

**ASSIGNED
READING:**

1 Samuel
1–2

SHE DIDN'T NEED THREE WISHES.

She only needed one. What she most wanted in life could be summed up in a single wish. For so many years, she'd thought about it to the point where realizing that dream became an all-consuming pursuit. Waking and sleeping, it was her primary focus. It preoccupied her mind like background noise—a constant loop reminding her over and over again that what she wanted most she couldn't have.

"Have you tried some herbs from the midwife? I hear they can really help."

"Did you offer a sacrifice? God will answer you."

"Have you talked with your husband about it?"

"Have you . . ."

Her friends were only trying to help, but they just served to remind Hannah that they'd likely never wanted something as badly as she had. *Of course* she'd tried everything. She'd been down every route imaginable, many times; and still nothing.

Until, one day, she realized something.

She wanted this one wish so much that she was willing to release it in order to receive it.

It went against every fiber of her being, but she knew it was the right thing to do. When God answered her prayer, and she finally possessed what she desired, she knew that she would have to give it back to him. The ability to do that came from him too. Only God could help her do this, to understand that she was to hold her precious gift loosely, open-palmed, so that in God's time, when he received it back from her, he would not have to pry away her fingers.

For the first time in a long time, she felt release and a sense of peace when she quietly prayed, "I will give him to the LORD for all the days of his life."

—Prayer—
Gracious God, thank you for the wisdom and grace to make tough decisions in your name.

Weekend

Go to page 635 for your next devotional reading.

Who then can understand the thunder
of his power?"

27

And Job continued his discourse:

² "As surely as God lives, who has denied me
justice,
the Almighty, who has made me taste
bitterness of soul,
³ as long as I have life within me,
the breath of God in my nostrils,
⁴ my lips will not speak wickedness,
and my tongue will utter no deceit.
⁵ I will never admit you are in the right;
till I die, I will not deny my integrity.
⁶ I will maintain my righteousness and
never let go of it;
my conscience will not reproach me as
long as I live.

⁷ "May my enemies be like the wicked,
my adversaries like the unjust!
⁸ For what hope has the godless when he is
cut off,
when God takes away his life?
⁹ Does God listen to his cry
when distress comes upon him?
¹⁰ Will he find delight in the Almighty?
Will he call upon God at all times?

¹¹ "I will teach you about the power of God;
the ways of the Almighty I will not
conceal.
¹² You have all seen this yourselves.
Why then this meaningless talk?

¹³ "Here is the fate God allots to the wicked,
the heritage a ruthless man receives
from the Almighty:
¹⁴ However many his children, their fate is
the sword;
his offspring will never have enough to
eat.
¹⁵ The plague will bury those who survive
him,
and their widows will not weep for
them.
¹⁶ Though he heaps up silver like dust
and clothes like piles of clay,
¹⁷ what he lays up the righteous will wear,
and the innocent will divide his silver.

¹⁸ The house he builds is like a moth's
cocoon,
like a hut made by a watchman.
¹⁹ He lies down wealthy, but will do so no
more;
when he opens his eyes, all is gone.
²⁰ Terrors overtake him like a flood;
a tempest snatches him away in the
night.
²¹ The east wind carries him off, and he is
gone;
it sweeps him out of his place.
²² It hurls itself against him without mercy
as he flees headlong from its power.
²³ It claps its hands in derision
and hisses him out of his place.

28

"There is a mine for silver
and a place where gold is refined.
² Iron is taken from the earth,
and copper is smelted from ore.
³ Man puts an end to the darkness;
he searches the farthest recesses
for ore in the blackest darkness.
⁴ Far from where people dwell he cuts a
shaft,
in places forgotten by the foot of man;
far from men he dangles and sways.
⁵ The earth, from which food comes,
is transformed below as by fire;
⁶ sapphires^a come from its rocks,
and its dust contains nuggets of gold.
⁷ No bird of prey knows that hidden path,
no falcon's eye has seen it.
⁸ Proud beasts do not set foot on it,
and no lion prowls there.
⁹ Man's hand assaults the flinty rock
and lays bare the roots of the mountains.
¹⁰ He tunnels through the rock;
his eyes see all its treasures.
¹¹ He searches^b the sources of the rivers
and brings hidden things to light.

¹² "But where can wisdom be found?
Where does understanding dwell?
¹³ Man does not comprehend its worth;
it cannot be found in the land of the
living.
¹⁴ The deep says, 'It is not in me';
the sea says, 'It is not with me.'

---

^a6 Or *lapis lazuli*; also in verse 16   ^b11 Septuagint, Aquila and Vulgate; Hebrew *He dams up*

¹⁵ It cannot be bought with the finest gold,
nor can its price be weighed in silver.
¹⁶ It cannot be bought with the gold of Ophir,
with precious onyx or sapphires.
¹⁷ Neither gold nor crystal can compare with it,
nor can it be had for jewels of gold.
¹⁸ Coral and jasper are not worthy of mention;
the price of wisdom is beyond rubies.
¹⁹ The topaz of Cush cannot compare with it;
it cannot be bought with pure gold.

²⁰ "Where then does wisdom come from?
Where does understanding dwell?
²¹ It is hidden from the eyes of every living thing,
concealed even from the birds of the air.
²² Destruction*a* and Death say,
'Only a rumor of it has reached our ears.'
²³ God understands the way to it
and he alone knows where it dwells,
²⁴ for he views the ends of the earth
and sees everything under the heavens.
²⁵ When he established the force of the wind
and measured out the waters,
²⁶ when he made a decree for the rain
and a path for the thunderstorm,
²⁷ then he looked at wisdom and appraised it;
he confirmed it and tested it.
²⁸ And he said to man,
'The fear of the Lord—
that is wisdom,
and to shun evil is
understanding.'"

29

Job continued his discourse:

² "How I long for the months gone by,
for the days when God watched over me,
³ when his lamp shone upon my head
and by his light I walked through darkness!
⁴ Oh, for the days when I was in my prime,

when God's intimate friendship blessed my house,
⁵ when the Almighty was still with me
and my children were around me,
⁶ when my path was drenched with cream
and the rock poured out for me streams of olive oil.

⁷ "When I went to the gate of the city
and took my seat in the public square,
⁸ the young men saw me and stepped aside
and the old men rose to their feet;
⁹ the chief men refrained from speaking
and covered their mouths with their hands;
¹⁰ the voices of the nobles were hushed,
and their tongues stuck to the roof of their mouths.
¹¹ Whoever heard me spoke well of me,
and those who saw me commended me,
¹² because I rescued the poor who cried for help,
and the fatherless who had none to assist him.
¹³ The man who was dying blessed me;
I made the widow's heart sing.
¹⁴ I put on righteousness as my clothing;
justice was my robe and my turban.
¹⁵ I was eyes to the blind
and feet to the lame.
¹⁶ I was a father to the needy;
I took up the case of the stranger.
¹⁷ I broke the fangs of the wicked
and snatched the victims from their teeth.

¹⁸ "I thought, 'I will die in my own house,
my days as numerous as the grains of sand.
¹⁹ My roots will reach to the water,
and the dew will lie all night on my branches.
²⁰ My glory will remain fresh in me,
the bow ever new in my hand.'

> **Job 28:28**
>
> *God Is to Be Revered*
>
> "And he said to man,
> 'The fear of the Lord—
> that is wisdom,
> and to shun evil is
> understanding.'"

---

*a*22 Hebrew *Abaddon*

²¹"Men listened to me expectantly,
  waiting in silence for my counsel.
²²After I had spoken, they spoke no more;
  my words fell gently on their ears.
²³They waited for me as for showers
  and drank in my words as the spring
    rain.
²⁴When I smiled at them, they scarcely
    believed it;
  the light of my face was precious to
    them.^a
²⁵I chose the way for them and sat as their
    chief;
  I dwelt as a king among his troops;
  I was like one who comforts mourners.

30

"But now they mock me,
  men younger than I,
  whose fathers I would have disdained
    to put with my sheep dogs.
²Of what use was the strength of their
    hands to me,
  since their vigor had gone from them?
³Haggard from want and hunger,
  they roamed^b the parched land
    in desolate wastelands at night.
⁴In the brush they gathered salt herbs,
  and their food^c was the root of the
    broom tree.
⁵They were banished from their fellow men,
  shouted at as if they were thieves.
⁶They were forced to live in the dry stream
    beds,
  among the rocks and in holes in the
    ground.
⁷They brayed among the bushes
  and huddled in the undergrowth.
⁸A base and nameless brood,
  they were driven out of the land.

⁹"And now their sons mock me in song;
  I have become a byword among them.
¹⁰They detest me and keep their distance;
  they do not hesitate to spit in my face.
¹¹Now that God has unstrung my bow and
    afflicted me,
  they throw off restraint in my presence.
¹²On my right the tribe^d attacks;
  they lay snares for my feet,

  they build their siege ramps against me.
¹³They break up my road;
  they succeed in destroying me—
    without anyone's helping them.^e
¹⁴They advance as through a gaping breach;
  amid the ruins they come rolling in.
¹⁵Terrors overwhelm me;
  my dignity is driven away as by the
    wind,
  my safety vanishes like a cloud.

¹⁶"And now my life ebbs away;
  days of suffering grip me.
¹⁷Night pierces my bones;
  my gnawing pains never rest.
¹⁸In his great power God becomes like
    clothing to me^f;
  he binds me like the neck of my
    garment.
¹⁹He throws me into the mud,
  and I am reduced to dust and ashes.

²⁰"I cry out to you, O God, but you do not
    answer;
  I stand up, but you merely look at me.
²¹You turn on me ruthlessly;
  with the might of your hand you attack
    me.
²²You snatch me up and drive me before the
    wind;
  you toss me about in the storm.
²³I know you will bring me down to death,
  to the place appointed for all the living.

²⁴"Surely no one lays a hand on a broken
    man
  when he cries for help in his distress.
²⁵Have I not wept for those in trouble?
  Has not my soul grieved for the poor?
²⁶Yet when I hoped for good, evil came;
  when I looked for light, then came
    darkness.
²⁷The churning inside me never stops;
  days of suffering confront me.
²⁸I go about blackened, but not by the sun;
  I stand up in the assembly and cry for
    help.
²⁹I have become a brother of jackals,
  a companion of owls.
³⁰My skin grows black and peels;

---

^a24 The meaning of the Hebrew for this clause is uncertain. ^b3 Or gnawed ^c4 Or fuel ^d12 The meaning of the Hebrew for this word is uncertain. ^e13 Or me. / 'No one can help him,' they say. ^f18 Hebrew; Septuagint God grasps my clothing

my body burns with fever.
³¹ My harp is tuned to mourning,
and my flute to the sound of wailing.

31

"I made a covenant with my eyes
not to look lustfully at a girl.
² For what is man's lot from God above,
his heritage from the Almighty on high?
³ Is it not ruin for the wicked,
disaster for those who do
wrong?
⁴ Does he not see my ways
and count my every step?

Job 31:4

God Sees All

"Does he not see my ways
and count my
every step?"

---

⁵ "If I have walked in
falsehood
or my foot has hurried
after deceit—
⁶ let God weigh me in honest
scales
and he will know that I
am blameless—
⁷ if my steps have turned from the path,
if my heart has been led by my eyes,
or if my hands have been defiled,
⁸ then may others eat what I have sown,
and may my crops be uprooted.

⁹ "If my heart has been enticed by a woman,
or if I have lurked at my neighbor's door,
¹⁰ then may my wife grind another man's
grain,
and may other men sleep with her.
¹¹ For that would have been shameful,
a sin to be judged.
¹² It is a fire that burns to Destruction*a*;
it would have uprooted my harvest.

¹³ "If I have denied justice to my menservants
and maidservants
when they had a grievance against me,
¹⁴ what will I do when God confronts me?
What will I answer when called to
account?
¹⁵ Did not he who made me in the womb
make them?
Did not the same one form us both
within our mothers?

¹⁶ "If I have denied the desires of the poor
or let the eyes of the widow grow weary,
¹⁷ if I have kept my bread to myself,
not sharing it with the fatherless—
¹⁸ but from my youth I reared him as would a
father,
and from my birth I guided the widow—
¹⁹ if I have seen anyone perishing for lack of
clothing,
or a needy man without a garment,
²⁰ and his heart did not bless
me
for warming him with
the fleece from my
sheep,
²¹ if I have raised my hand
against the
fatherless,
knowing that I had
influence in court,
²² then let my arm fall from
the shoulder,
let it be broken off at the joint.
²³ For I dreaded destruction from God,
and for fear of his splendor I could not
do such things.

²⁴ "If I have put my trust in gold
or said to pure gold, 'You are my
security,'
²⁵ if I have rejoiced over my great wealth,
the fortune my hands had gained,
²⁶ if I have regarded the sun in its radiance
or the moon moving in splendor,
²⁷ so that my heart was secretly enticed
and my hand offered them a kiss of
homage,
²⁸ then these also would be sins to be
judged,
for I would have been unfaithful to God
on high.

²⁹ "If I have rejoiced at my enemy's
misfortune
or gloated over the trouble that came to
him—
³⁰ I have not allowed my mouth to sin
by invoking a curse against his life—
³¹ if the men of my household have never
said,
'Who has not had his fill of Job's
meat?'—

---

a 12 Hebrew *Abaddon*

Hanging on to Hope

Read: Job 31:1–40

"SOMETIMES FAITH IS just hanging on in the dark." These words, spoken by a wise woman, were offered as solace to a suffering friend. Sometimes things just don't make sense. Sometimes we simply can't see beyond the pain. Sometimes we can't even manage to utter a prayer.

In those dark nights—when life seems to suffocate us with sorrow—faith compels us to hang on. We've seen that Job, who suffered great losses, felt that way. Job 31 records the final words of Job's defense before God after his three friends filled the air with their empty explanations of why Job had suffered so greatly.

Think about it. We know the conversation God had with Satan at the beginning of this account, yet we are still appalled by the tragic events of Job's life. Job had no idea Satan was tempting him because God was allowing his faith to be tested. No wonder Job reeled from his losses and grasped for answers. We can feel the pain and desperation in his voice when he cried, "Oh, that I had someone to hear me!" But throughout his trial, throughout his test, Job knew the Almighty was listening.

Have you ever felt that way? Perhaps your heart's cry surfaced in a winter season of your life—cold, dark and endless. Did your winter only worsen when you received heartless indictments from your "friends" rather than warm words of understanding and consolation? You may be in that barren season even now, with no one to offer you comfort or relief. Allow Job's words to comfort you as a fellow traveler on your journey: "Let the Almighty answer me."

Job recounted his actions based on his heart for God, although he never knew what had happened in heaven to instigate his suffering. While we may learn God's reasons later (sometimes only in eternity), for now all that is required is for us to "hang on in the dark" until God's light illumines the way again.

Job 31:35

"Oh, that I had someone to hear me! I sign now my defense—let the Almighty answer me; let my accuser put his indictment in writing."

reflection

1 What have been the darkest days of your life?

2 In what ways did God shine hope through your darkness?

3 Do you know someone who is echoing Job's plea to be heard? Try offering the warmth of comfort and a listening ear.

RELATED READINGS

Isaiah 55:6–13;
Lamentations 3:18–26;
Micah 7:1–9

Monday

Go to page 640 for your next devotional reading.

³²but no stranger had to spend the night in
  the street,
    for my door was always open to the
    traveler—
³³if I have concealed my sin as men do,ᵃ
    by hiding my guilt in my heart
³⁴because I so feared the crowd
    and so dreaded the contempt of the
    clans
      that I kept silent and would not go
      outside

³⁵("Oh, that I had someone to hear me!
    I sign now my defense—let the
    Almighty answer me;
      let my accuser put his indictment in
      writing.
³⁶Surely I would wear it on my shoulder,
    I would put it on like a crown.
³⁷I would give him an account of my every
  step;
    like a prince I would approach him.)—

³⁸"if my land cries out against me
    and all its furrows are wet with tears,
³⁹if I have devoured its yield without
  payment
    or broken the spirit of its tenants,
⁴⁰then let briers come up instead of wheat
    and weeds instead of barley."

The words of Job are ended.

Elihu

32 So these three men stopped answering Job, because he was righteous in
his own eyes. ²But Elihu son of Barakel the
Buzite, of the family of Ram, became very angry with Job for justifying himself rather than
God. ³He was also angry with the three friends,
because they had found no way to refute Job,
and yet had condemned him.ᵇ ⁴Now Elihu
had waited before speaking to Job because they
were older than he. ⁵But when he saw that the
three men had nothing more to say, his anger
was aroused.

⁶So Elihu son of Barakel the Buzite said:

"I am young in years,
  and you are old;
    that is why I was fearful,
      not daring to tell you what I know.
⁷I thought, 'Age should speak;
    advanced years should teach wisdom.'
⁸But it is the spiritᶜ in a man,
    the breath of the Almighty, that gives
    him understanding.
⁹It is not only the oldᵈ who are wise,
    not only the aged who understand what
    is right.

¹⁰"Therefore I say: Listen to me;
    I too will tell you what I know.
¹¹I waited while you spoke,
    I listened to your reasoning;
      while you were searching for words,
¹²   I gave you my full attention.
    But not one of you has proved Job wrong;
      none of you has answered his
      arguments.
¹³Do not say, 'We have found wisdom;
    let God refute him, not man.'
¹⁴But Job has not marshaled his words
  against me,
    and I will not answer him with your
    arguments.

¹⁵"They are dismayed and have no more to
  say;
    words have failed them.
¹⁶Must I wait, now that they are silent,
    now that they stand there with no reply?
¹⁷I too will have my say;
    I too will tell what I know.
¹⁸For I am full of words,
    and the spirit within me compels me;
¹⁹inside I am like bottled-up wine,
    like new wineskins ready to burst.
²⁰I must speak and find relief;
    I must open my lips and reply.
²¹I will show partiality to no one,
    nor will I flatter any man;
²²for if I were skilled in flattery,
    my Maker would soon take me away.

33 "But now, Job, listen to my words;
    pay attention to everything I say.
²I am about to open my mouth;
    my words are on the tip of my tongue.
³My words come from an upright heart;
    my lips sincerely speak what I know.

ᵃ33 Or *as Adam did*   ᵇ3 Masoretic Text; an ancient Hebrew scribal tradition *Job, and so had condemned God*   ᶜ8 Or *Spirit*; also in
verse 18   ᵈ9 Or *many; or great*

4 The Spirit of God has made me;
  the breath of the Almighty gives me life.
5 Answer me then, if you can;
  prepare yourself and confront me.
6 I am just like you before God;
  I too have been taken from clay.
7 No fear of me should alarm you,
  nor should my hand be heavy upon you.

8 "But you have said in my hearing—
  I heard the very words—
9 'I am pure and without sin;
  I am clean and free from guilt.
10 Yet God has found fault with me;
  he considers me his enemy.
11 He fastens my feet in shackles;
  he keeps close watch on all my paths.'

12 "But I tell you, in this you are not right,
  for God is greater than man.
13 Why do you complain to him
  that he answers none of man's words[a]?
14 For God does speak—now one way, now another—
  though man may not perceive it.
15 In a dream, in a vision of the night,
  when deep sleep falls on men
  as they slumber in their beds,
16 he may speak in their ears
  and terrify them with warnings,
17 to turn man from wrongdoing
  and keep him from pride,
18 to preserve his soul from the pit,[b]
  his life from perishing by the sword.[c]
19 Or a man may be chastened on a bed of pain
  with constant distress in his bones,
20 so that his very being finds food repulsive
  and his soul loathes the choicest meal.
21 His flesh wastes away to nothing,
  and his bones, once hidden, now stick out.
22 His soul draws near to the pit,[d]
  and his life to the messengers of death.[e]

23 "Yet if there is an angel on his side
  as a mediator, one out of a thousand,
  to tell a man what is right for him,
24 to be gracious to him and say,
  'Spare him from going down to the pit[f];
  I have found a ransom for him'—
25 then his flesh is renewed like a child's;
  it is restored as in the days of his youth.
26 He prays to God and finds favor with him,
  he sees God's face and shouts for joy;
  he is restored by God to his righteous state.
27 Then he comes to men and says,
  'I sinned, and perverted what was right,
  but I did not get what I deserved.
28 He redeemed my soul from going down to the pit,[g]
  and I will live to enjoy the light.'

29 "God does all these things to a man—
  twice, even three times—
30 to turn back his soul from the pit,[h]
  that the light of life may shine on him.

31 "Pay attention, Job, and listen to me;
  be silent, and I will speak.
32 If you have anything to say, answer me;
  speak up, for I want you to be cleared.
33 But if not, then listen to me;
  be silent, and I will teach you wisdom."

34 Then Elihu said:

2 "Hear my words, you wise men;
  listen to me, you men of learning.
3 For the ear tests words
  as the tongue tastes food.
4 Let us discern for ourselves what is right;
  let us learn together what is good.

5 "Job says, 'I am innocent,
  but God denies me justice.
6 Although I am right,
  I am considered a liar;

Job 33:4

God Created Us

"The Spirit of God
has made me;
the breath of the
Almighty gives me life."

---

a13 Or *that he does not answer for any of his actions*   b18 Or *preserve him from the grave*   c18 Or *from crossing the River*   d22 Or *He draws near to the grave*   e22 Or *to the dead*   f24 Or *grave*   g28 Or *redeemed me from going down to the grave*   h30 Or *turn him back from the grave*

although I am guiltless,
his arrow inflicts an incurable wound.'
7 What man is like Job,
who drinks scorn like water?
8 He keeps company with evildoers;
he associates with wicked men.
9 For he says, 'It profits a man nothing
when he tries to please God.'

10 "So listen to me, you men of
understanding.
Far be it from God to do evil,
from the Almighty to do wrong.
11 He repays a man for what he has done;
he brings upon him what his conduct
deserves.
12 It is unthinkable that God would do
wrong,
that the Almighty would pervert justice.
13 Who appointed him over the earth?
Who put him in charge of the whole
world?
14 If it were his intention
and he withdrew his spirit*a* and breath,
15 all mankind would perish together
and man would return to the dust.

16 "If you have understanding, hear this;
listen to what I say.
17 Can he who hates justice govern?
Will you condemn the just and mighty
One?
18 Is he not the One who says to kings, 'You
are worthless,'
and to nobles, 'You are wicked,'
19 who shows no partiality to princes
and does not favor the rich over the
poor,
for they are all the work of his hands?
20 They die in an instant, in the middle of the
night;
the people are shaken and they pass
away;
the mighty are removed without human
hand.

21 "His eyes are on the ways of men;
he sees their every step.
22 There is no dark place, no deep shadow,
where evildoers can hide.

23 God has no need to examine men further,
that they should come before him for
judgment.
24 Without inquiry he shatters the mighty
and sets up others in their place.
25 Because he takes note of their deeds,
he overthrows them in the night and
they are crushed.
26 He punishes them for their wickedness
where everyone can see them,
27 because they turned from following him
and had no regard for any of his ways.
28 They caused the cry of the poor to come
before him,
so that he heard the cry of the needy.
29 But if he remains silent, who can condemn
him?
If he hides his face, who can see him?
Yet he is over man and nation alike,
30 to keep a godless man from ruling,
from laying snares for the people.

31 "Suppose a man says to God,
'I am guilty but will offend no more.
32 Teach me what I cannot see;
if I have done wrong, I will not do so
again.'
33 Should God then reward you on your
terms,
when you refuse to repent?
You must decide, not I;
so tell me what you know.

34 "Men of understanding declare,
wise men who hear me say to me,
35 'Job speaks without knowledge;
his words lack insight.'
36 Oh, that Job might be tested to the utmost
for answering like a wicked man!
37 To his sin he adds rebellion;
scornfully he claps his hands among us
and multiplies his words against God."

35

Then Elihu said:

2 "Do you think this is just?
You say, 'I will be cleared by God.*b*'
3 Yet you ask him, 'What profit is it to me,*c*
and what do I gain by not sinning?'

4 "I would like to reply to you

---

*a*14 Or *Spirit*   *b*2 Or *My righteousness is more than God's*   *c*3 Or *you*

and to your friends with you.
⁵ Look up at the heavens and see;
  gaze at the clouds so high above you.
⁶ If you sin, how does that
    affect him?
  If your sins are many,
    what that do
    to him?
⁷ If you are righteous, what
    do you give to him,
  or what does he receive
    from your hand?
⁸ Your wickedness affects
    only a man like
    yourself,
  and your righteousness
    only the sons of
    men.

⁹ "Men cry out under a load of oppression;
  they plead for relief from the arm of the
    powerful.
¹⁰ But no one says, 'Where is God my Maker,
  who gives songs in the night,
¹¹ who teaches more to us than toᵃ the beasts
    of the earth
  and makes us wiser thanᵇ the birds of
    the air?'
¹² He does not answer when men cry out
  because of the arrogance of the wicked.
¹³ Indeed, God does not listen to their empty
    plea;
  the Almighty pays no attention to it.
¹⁴ How much less, then, will he listen
  when you say that you do not see him,
  that your case is before him
  and you must wait for him,
¹⁵ and further, that his anger never punishes
  and he does not take the least notice of
    wickedness.ᶜ
¹⁶ So Job opens his mouth with empty talk;
  without knowledge he multiplies words."

36 Elihu continued:

² "Bear with me a little longer and I will
    show you
  that there is more to be said in God's
    behalf.

³ I get my knowledge from afar;
  I will ascribe justice to my Maker.
⁴ Be assured that my words are not false;
    one perfect in knowledge
      is with you.

⁵ "God is mighty, but does
      not despise men;
  he is mighty, and firm in
      his purpose.
⁶ He does not keep the
      wicked alive
  but gives the afflicted
      their rights.
⁷ He does not take his eyes
      off the righteous;
  he enthrones them with
      kings
  and exalts them forever.

⁸ But if men are bound in chains,
  held fast by cords of affliction,
⁹ he tells them what they have done—
  that they have sinned arrogantly.
¹⁰ He makes them listen to correction
  and commands them to repent of their
    evil.
¹¹ If they obey and serve him,
  they will spend the rest of their days in
    prosperity
  and their years in contentment.
¹² But if they do not listen,
  they will perish by the swordᵈ
  and die without knowledge.

¹³ "The godless in heart harbor resentment;
  even when he fetters them, they do not
    cry for help.
¹⁴ They die in their youth,
  among male prostitutes of the shrines.
¹⁵ But those who suffer he delivers in their
    suffering;
  he speaks to them in their affliction.

¹⁶ "He is wooing you from the jaws of
    distress
  to a spacious place free from restriction,
  to the comfort of your table laden with
    choice food.
¹⁷ But now you are laden with the judgment
    due the wicked;

> ### Job 35:7
>
> *God Is
> Self-Sufficient*
>
> "If you are righteous,
> what do you give to him,
> or what does he receive
> from your hand?"

ᵃ11 Or *teaches us by* ᵇ11 Or *us wise by* ᶜ15 Symmachus, Theodotion and Vulgate; the meaning of the Hebrew for this word is uncertain.
ᵈ12 Or *will cross the River*

Job 36:27–28

"He draws up the drops
of water, which distill as
rain to the streams;
the clouds pour down
their moisture and
abundant showers fall
on mankind."

reflection

1 What circumstances can
only God change? Do
you trust him to do that?

2 Do you have trouble
believing that nothing
is too difficult for God?
Why or why not?

3 Take some time to reflect on God's names
mentioned in today's devotional. Which of his names
are the most meaningful to
you in your present circumstances?

RELATED READINGS

Psalms 24:1–2; 104:1–35;
Isaiah 40:28–31;
Hebrews 11:1–3

Read: Job 36:21–33

METEOROLOGISTS HAVE STUDIED weather patterns to discover
the what, when, where and how of rain, thunder, lightning, hail,
drought and monsoons. They have pondered why deserts receive
less than an inch of rain per year, while India's monsoons pour
down over 400 inches annually. Why does lightning strike? What
causes hail? How can we predict hurricanes?

While great strides have been made in observing, predicting
and understanding the weather, no one has been able to change it.
Why? Because while human beings have studied the what, when,
where and how, they often have forgotten to ask the most important question of all: *Who?*

Job's friend, Elihu, didn't subscribe to the weather channel
or own a farmer's almanac. He understood, however, that God
controls it all: "He draws up the drops of water, which distill as rain
to the streams; the clouds pour down their moisture and abundant
showers fall on mankind." He could have said, "I don't understand
the process of condensation and precipitation, but I do understand
that God is in control."

The first words in the Bible are, "In the beginning God." While
we might not understand all the intricate details and secrets of life,
we can hold on to this: *God set the universe in motion and sustains
it.* Paul wrote, "He is before all things, and in him [Jesus Christ]
all things hold together" (Colossians 1:17). "Sovereign LORD, you
have made the heavens and the earth by your great power and
outstretched arm. Nothing is too hard for you" (Jeremiah 32:17).

Are you going through a difficult situation in your life right
now? Are there circumstances that you cannot understand? Instead
of trying to fix it or control it, rather than trying to figure out the
what, when, where and why of your struggle, focus instead on
Who:

God is *Elohim*—the Creator, who made you for a purpose.

God is *El Elyon*—God Most High, whose ways are higher than
your ways.

God is *El Roi*—the God who sees and knows where you are
and how you feel.

God is *El Shaddai*—the Lord God Almighty, the one who can
change you or walk with you through your circumstances as surely
as he can send rain from heaven.

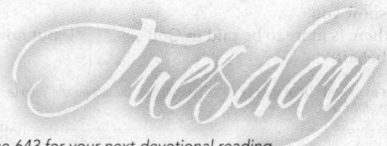

Go to page 643 for your next devotional reading.

judgment and justice have taken hold of you.

¹⁸ Be careful that no one entices you by riches;
do not let a large bribe turn you aside.
¹⁹ Would your wealth
or even all your mighty efforts
sustain you so you would not be in distress?
²⁰ Do not long for the night,
to drag people away from their homes.ᵃ
²¹ Beware of turning to evil,
which you seem to prefer to affliction.

²² "God is exalted in his power.
Who is a teacher like him?
²³ Who has prescribed his ways for him,
or said to him, 'You have done wrong'?
²⁴ Remember to extol his work,
which men have praised in song.
²⁵ All mankind has seen it;
men gaze on it from afar.
²⁶ How great is God—beyond our understanding!
The number of his years is past finding out.

²⁷ "He draws up the drops of water,
which distill as rain to the streamsᵇ;
²⁸ the clouds pour down their moisture
and abundant showers fall on mankind.
²⁹ Who can understand how he spreads out the clouds,
how he thunders from his pavilion?
³⁰ See how he scatters his lightning about him,
bathing the depths of the sea.
³¹ This is the way he governsᶜ the nations
and provides food in abundance.
³² He fills his hands with lightning
and commands it to strike its mark.
³³ His thunder announces the coming storm;
even the cattle make known its approach.ᵈ

37 "At this my heart pounds
and leaps from its place.
² Listen! Listen to the roar of his voice,
to the rumbling that comes from his mouth.
³ He unleashes his lightning beneath the whole heaven
and sends it to the ends of the earth.
⁴ After that comes the sound of his roar;
he thunders with his majestic voice.
When his voice resounds,
he holds nothing back.
⁵ God's voice thunders in marvelous ways;
he does great things beyond our understanding.
⁶ He says to the snow, 'Fall on the earth,'
and to the rain shower, 'Be a mighty downpour.'
⁷ So that all men he has made may know his work,
he stops every man from his labor.ᵉ
⁸ The animals take cover;
they remain in their dens.
⁹ The tempest comes out from its chamber,
the cold from the driving winds.
¹⁰ The breath of God produces ice,
and the broad waters become frozen.
¹¹ He loads the clouds with moisture;
he scatters his lightning through them.
¹² At his direction they swirl around
over the face of the whole earth
to do whatever he commands them.
¹³ He brings the clouds to punish men,
or to water his earthᶠ and show his love.

¹⁴ "Listen to this, Job;
stop and consider God's wonders.
¹⁵ Do you know how God controls the clouds
and makes his lightning flash?
¹⁶ Do you know how the clouds hang poised,
those wonders of him who is perfect in knowledge?

> **Job 36:26**
>
> *God Is Past Comprehension*
>
> "How great is God—beyond our understanding! The number of his years is past finding out."

ᵃ20 The meaning of the Hebrew for verses 18–20 is uncertain.   ᵇ27 Or *distill from the mist as rain*   ᶜ31 Or *nourishes*
ᵈ33 Or *announces his coming— / the One zealous against evil*   ᵉ7 Or / *he fills all men with fear by his power*   ᶠ13 Or *to favor them*

17 You who swelter in your clothes
  when the land lies hushed under the
    south wind,
18 can you join him in spreading out the
    skies,
  hard as a mirror of cast bronze?

19 "Tell us what we should say to him;
  we cannot draw up our case because of
    our darkness.
20 Should he be told that I want to speak?
  Would any man ask to be swallowed up?
21 Now no one can look at the sun,
  bright as it is in the skies
  after the wind has swept
    them clean.
22 Out of the north he comes
    in golden splendor;
  God comes in awesome
    majesty.
23 The Almighty is beyond
    our reach and
    exalted in power;
  in his justice and great
    righteousness, he
    does not oppress.
24 Therefore, men revere him,
  for does he not have
    regard for all the wise in heart?*a*"

The Lord Speaks

38 Then the Lord answered Job out of the
storm. He said:

2 "Who is this that darkens my counsel
  with words without knowledge?
3 Brace yourself like a man;
  I will question you,
  and you shall answer me.

4 "Where were you when I laid the earth's
    foundation?
  Tell me, if you understand.
5 Who marked off its dimensions? Surely
    you know!
  Who stretched a measuring line across
    it?
6 On what were its footings set,
  or who laid its cornerstone—
7 while the morning stars sang together
  and all the angels*b* shouted for joy?

8 "Who shut up the sea behind doors
  when it burst forth from the womb,
9 when I made the clouds its garment
  and wrapped it in thick darkness,
10 when I fixed limits for it
  and set its doors and bars in place,
11 when I said, 'This far you may come and
    no farther;
  here is where your proud waves halt'?

12 "Have you ever given orders to the
    morning,
  or shown the dawn its place,
13 that it might take the earth
    by the edges
  and shake the wicked out
    of it?
14 The earth takes shape like
    clay under a seal;
  its features stand out like
    those of a garment.
15 The wicked are denied their
    light,
  and their upraised arm is
    broken.

16 "Have you journeyed to the
    springs of the sea
  or walked in the recesses of the deep?
17 Have the gates of death been shown to you?
  Have you seen the gates of the shadow
    of death*c*?
18 Have you comprehended the vast expanses
    of the earth?
  Tell me, if you know all this.

19 "What is the way to the abode of light?
  And where does darkness reside?
20 Can you take them to their places?
  Do you know the paths to their
    dwellings?
21 Surely you know, for you were already born!
  You have lived so many years!

22 "Have you entered the storehouses of the
    snow
  or seen the storehouses of the hail,
23 which I reserve for times of trouble,
  for days of war and battle?
24 What is the way to the place where the
    lightning is dispersed,

> **Job 37:23**
>
> *God Is Righteous*
>
> The Almighty is beyond
> our reach and exalted
> in power;
> in his justice and great
> righteousness, he does
> not oppress.

*a*24 Or *for he does not have regard for any who think they are wise.*   *b*7 Hebrew *the sons of God*   *c*17 Or *gates of deep shadows*

God Speaks

Read: Job 38:1-41

FOR 37 CHAPTERS Job and his friends have grappled with the question of suffering. Why do people suffer? Is it because God isn't there? Because God doesn't care? Because the one suffering has done something to displease God? Job and his friends have gone around and around and still come up empty. Finally God "answered Job out of the storm" (Job 38:1).

God didn't deign to tell Job the reason for Job's suffering, but he did remind Job that he is the mighty God who marked the dimensions of the earth, fixed the limits of the sea and blanketed the sky with clouds. This is the God whom Job and his friends dared to question. The audacity of trying to bring God down to their level! But when God spoke, he showed them how much bigger and more magnificent were his ways than their ways.

In the midst of God's glory, Job gained a proper perspective on his suffering. The same is true for us. When we hear God speak and remember his glory, we know our suffering is not in vain. Henry Gariepy wrote, "Many who have trod the path of suffering and sensed the Presence on the road will share the sentiment of the unknown poet":

> I walked a mile with Pleasure,
> She chatted all the way,
> But left me none the wiser
> For all she had to say.
>
> I walked a mile with Sorrow,
> And ne'r a word said she,
> But, oh, the thing I learned from her
> When Sorrow walked with me!

Have you been grappling with pain and suffering? Are you trying to figure out why God has allowed sorrow and trouble to come into your life? The best solution isn't to talk endlessly with your friends and try to figure out the reasons for your suffering. Wait for God, the one who gave "orders to the morning" (Job 38:12), to speak with you in the midst of the storm.

Go to page 646 for your next devotional reading.

Job 38:1

Then the LORD answered Job out of the storm.

reflection

1 When you suffer, whom do you tend to talk to?

2 Has any human philosopher, speaker or writer been able to comfort you when you've suffered?

3 Does it comfort you to know that while God is powerful enough to create the vast universe, he is interested enough to speak to you personally?

RELATED READINGS

Nahum 1:3-5;
2 Peter 1:16-21

"Absolutely everything that can happen to us—good, bad or indifferent —God knows and cares about."

Thelma Wells

643

or the place where the east winds are
scattered over the earth?
25 Who cuts a channel for the torrents of rain,
and a path for the thunderstorm,
26 to water a land where no man lives,
a desert with no one in it,
27 to satisfy a desolate wasteland
and make it sprout with grass?
28 Does the rain have a father?
Who fathers the drops of dew?
29 From whose womb comes the ice?
Who gives birth to the frost from the
heavens
30 when the waters become hard as stone,
when the surface of the deep is frozen?

31 "Can you bind the beautiful*a* Pleiades?
Can you loose the cords of Orion?
32 Can you bring forth the constellations in
their seasons*b*
or lead out the Bear*c* with its cubs?
33 Do you know the laws of the heavens?
Can you set up ⌊God's*d*⌋ dominion over
the earth?

34 "Can you raise your voice to the clouds
and cover yourself with a flood of water?
35 Do you send the lightning bolts on their
way?
Do they report to you, 'Here we are'?
36 Who endowed the heart*e* with wisdom
or gave understanding to the mind*e*?
37 Who has the wisdom to count the clouds?
Who can tip over the water jars of the
heavens
38 when the dust becomes hard
and the clods of earth stick together?

39 "Do you hunt the prey for the lioness
and satisfy the hunger of the lions
40 when they crouch in their dens
or lie in wait in a thicket?
41 Who provides food for the raven
when its young cry out to God
and wander about for lack of food?

39 "Do you know when the mountain
goats give birth?
Do you watch when the doe bears her
fawn?

2 Do you count the months till they bear?
Do you know the time they give birth?
3 They crouch down and bring forth their
young;
their labor pains are ended.
4 Their young thrive and grow strong in the
wilds;
they leave and do not return.

5 "Who let the wild donkey go free?
Who untied his ropes?
6 I gave him the wasteland as his home,
the salt flats as his habitat.
7 He laughs at the commotion in the town;
he does not hear a driver's shout.
8 He ranges the hills for his pasture
and searches for any green thing.

9 "Will the wild ox consent to serve you?
Will he stay by your manger at night?
10 Can you hold him to the furrow with a
harness?
Will he till the valleys behind you?
11 Will you rely on him for his great
strength?
Will you leave your heavy work to him?
12 Can you trust him to bring in your grain
and gather it to your threshing floor?

13 "The wings of the ostrich flap joyfully,
but they cannot compare with the
pinions and feathers of the stork.
14 She lays her eggs on the ground
and lets them warm in the sand,
15 unmindful that a foot may crush them,
that some wild animal may trample
them.
16 She treats her young harshly, as if they
were not hers;
she cares not that her labor was in vain,
17 for God did not endow her with wisdom
or give her a share of good sense.
18 Yet when she spreads her feathers to run,
she laughs at horse and rider.

19 "Do you give the horse his strength
or clothe his neck with a flowing mane?
20 Do you make him leap like a locust,
striking terror with his proud snorting?
21 He paws fiercely, rejoicing in his strength,

---

*a*31 Or *the twinkling;* or *the chains of the*   *b*32 Or *the morning star in its season*   *c*32 Or *out Leo*   *d*33 Or *his;* or *their*
*e*36 The meaning of the Hebrew for this word is uncertain.

and charges into the fray.
²² He laughs at fear, afraid of nothing;
he does not shy away from the sword.
²³ The quiver rattles against his side,
along with the flashing spear and lance.
²⁴ In frenzied excitement he eats up the
ground;
he cannot stand still when the trumpet
sounds.
²⁵ At the blast of the trumpet he snorts, 'Aha!'
He catches the scent of battle from afar,
the shout of commanders and the battle
cry.

²⁶ "Does the hawk take flight by your wisdom
and spread his wings toward the south?
²⁷ Does the eagle soar at your command
and build his nest on high?
²⁸ He dwells on a cliff and stays there at night;
a rocky crag is his stronghold.
²⁹ From there he seeks out his food;
his eyes detect it from afar.
³⁰ His young ones feast on blood,
and where the slain are, there is he."

40

The LORD said to Job:

² "Will the one who contends with the
Almighty correct him?
Let him who accuses God answer him!"

³ Then Job answered the LORD:

⁴ "I am unworthy—how can I reply to you?
I put my hand over my mouth.
⁵ I spoke once, but I have no answer—
twice, but I will say no more."

⁶ Then the LORD spoke to Job out of the
storm:

⁷ "Brace yourself like a man;
I will question you,
and you shall answer me.

⁸ "Would you discredit my justice?
Would you condemn me to justify
yourself?
⁹ Do you have an arm like God's,
and can your voice thunder like his?
¹⁰ Then adorn yourself with glory and
splendor,

and clothe yourself in honor and
majesty.
¹¹ Unleash the fury of your wrath,
look at every proud man and bring him
low,
¹² look at every proud man and humble him,
crush the wicked where they stand.
¹³ Bury them all in the dust together;
shroud their faces in the grave.
¹⁴ Then I myself will admit to you
that your own right hand can save you.

¹⁵ "Look at the behemoth,ᵃ
which I made along with you
and which feeds on grass like an ox.
¹⁶ What strength he has in his loins,
what power in the muscles of his belly!
¹⁷ His tailᵇ sways like a cedar;
the sinews of his thighs are close-knit.
¹⁸ His bones are tubes of bronze,
his limbs like rods of iron.
¹⁹ He ranks first among the works of God,
yet his Maker can approach him with
his sword.
²⁰ The hills bring him their produce,
and all the wild animals play nearby.
²¹ Under the lotus plants he lies,
hidden among the reeds in the marsh.
²² The lotuses conceal him in their shadow;
the poplars by the stream surround him.
²³ When the river rages, he is not alarmed;
he is secure, though the Jordan should
surge against his mouth.
²⁴ Can anyone capture him by the eyes,ᶜ
or trap him and pierce his nose?

41

"Can you pull in the leviathanᵈ with
a fishhook
or tie down his tongue with a rope?
² Can you put a cord through his nose
or pierce his jaw with a hook?
³ Will he keep begging you for mercy?
Will he speak to you with gentle words?
⁴ Will he make an agreement with you
for you to take him as your slave for life?
⁵ Can you make a pet of him like a bird
or put him on a leash for your girls?
⁶ Will traders barter for him?
Will they divide him up among the
merchants?

ᵃ15 Possibly the hippopotamus or the elephant   ᵇ17 Possibly trunk   ᶜ24 Or *by a water hole*   ᵈ1 Possibly the crocodile

Job 40:3–5

Then Job answered the
LORD: "I am unworthy—
how can I reply to you?
I put my hand over my
mouth. I spoke once, but
I have no answer—twice,
but I will say no more."

reflection

1 Think of a time when
you have wondered,
Why, God? What was the
situation?

2 In what ways do you
need to be quiet, to
repent and to humbly bow
before God as Job did?

3 What have you learned
about God through
your difficult experiences?

RELATED READINGS

Psalm 46:8–10;
Zephaniah 3:17;
Romans 8:18–39;
1 Peter 4:12–19

Read: Job 40:1–14

WHO HASN'T WANTED to shake her fist at God and scream,
"Why?"

The question catches in your throat when you visit your friend
who is barely recognizable, ravaged by chemotherapy. It comes
to mind when a friend's baby dies or a spouse has an affair. *Why?
Why did my baby die? Why did my husband leave me? Why did we
lose all our savings in a bad investment?* These questions wrack our
thoughts and challenge our faith. How can a loving God allow so
much pain?

When we consider the mystery of suffering, the story of Job
inevitably comes to mind. At this point in the story, Job has suffered horribly, and he has boldly questioned God, protesting that
he didn't deserve to lose his family, his health and his possessions. Well-intentioned friends have come alongside him, offering
unhelpful explanations and pat answers. Job has cried out to God,
and God has answered him with amazing words and unfathomable questions. The Lord challenged him with questions that reveal
Job's limitations. No, Job does not have power like God's. He
cannot adorn himself with glory and splendor. He cannot judge the
wicked. Only God is sovereign. Job is merely human. Job began
to understand and bowed in silence to the Creator of the universe,
saying, "I am unworthy . . . I will say no more" (Job 40:4–5).

But notice something else. God loved Job enough to be with
him in his suffering—and that made all the difference. Job didn't
need to keep asking the questions because he had discovered that
God himself was the answer. He didn't need the specifics; he finally
rested in the truth that God is God . . . and that was enough.

Sometimes, when we reach the end of ourselves, when we
reach the end of the tears and the rage and the questions, when
we are quiet, we hear him say, "I am God. I am here."

Thursday

Go to page 650 for your next devotional reading.

⁷Can you fill his hide with harpoons
　or his head with fishing spears?
⁸If you lay a hand on him,
　you will remember the struggle and
　never do it again!
⁹Any hope of subduing him is false;
　the mere sight of him is overpowering.
¹⁰No one is fierce enough to rouse him.
　Who then is able to stand against me?
¹¹Who has a claim against me that I must
　pay?
　Everything under heaven belongs to me.

¹²"I will not fail to speak of his limbs,
　his strength and his graceful form.
¹³Who can strip off his outer coat?
　Who would approach him with a bridle?
¹⁴Who dares open the doors of his mouth,
　ringed about with his fearsome teeth?
¹⁵His back has*ᵃ* rows of shields
　tightly sealed together;
¹⁶each is so close to the next
　that no air can pass between.
¹⁷They are joined fast to one another;
　they cling together and cannot be
　parted.
¹⁸His snorting throws out flashes of light;
　his eyes are like the rays of dawn.
¹⁹Firebrands stream from his
　mouth;
　sparks of fire shoot out.
²⁰Smoke pours from his
　nostrils
　as from a boiling pot
　over a fire of reeds.
²¹His breath sets coals ablaze,
　and flames dart from his
　mouth.
²²Strength resides in his
　neck;
　dismay goes before him.
²³The folds of his flesh are
　tightly joined;
　they are firm and immovable.
²⁴His chest is hard as rock,
　hard as a lower millstone.
²⁵When he rises up, the mighty are terrified;
　they retreat before his thrashing.
²⁶The sword that reaches him has no effect,

　nor does the spear or the dart or the
　javelin.
²⁷Iron he treats like straw
　and bronze like rotten wood.
²⁸Arrows do not make him flee;
　slingstones are like chaff to him.
²⁹A club seems to him but a piece of straw;
　he laughs at the rattling of the lance.
³⁰His undersides are jagged potsherds,
　leaving a trail in the mud like a
　threshing sledge.
³¹He makes the depths churn like a boiling
　caldron
　and stirs up the sea like a pot of
　ointment.
³²Behind him he leaves a glistening wake;
　one would think the deep had white
　hair.
³³Nothing on earth is his equal—
　a creature without fear.
³⁴He looks down on all that are haughty;
　he is king over all that are proud."

Job

42

Then Job replied to the LORD:

²"I know that you can do all things;
　no plan of yours can be thwarted.
³You asked, ⌊'Who is this
　that obscures my
　counsel without
　knowledge?'⌋
　Surely I spoke of things I
　did not understand,
　things too wonderful for
　me to know.

⁴⌊"You said,⌋ 'Listen now,
　and I will speak;
　I will question you,
　and you shall answer me.'
⁵My ears had heard of you
　but now my eyes have
　seen you.
⁶Therefore I despise myself
　and repent in dust and ashes."

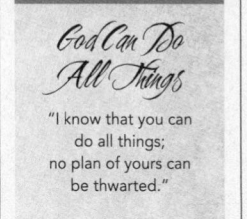

Job 42:2

God Can Do All Things

"I know that you can
do all things;
no plan of yours can
be thwarted."

Epilogue

⁷After the LORD had said these things to
Job, he said to Eliphaz the Temanite, "I am

ᵃ15 Or *His pride is his*

angry with you and your two friends, because you have not spoken of me what is right, as my servant Job has. **8**So now take seven bulls and seven rams and go to my servant Job and sacrifice a burnt offering for yourselves. My servant Job will pray for you, and I will accept his prayer and not deal with you according to your folly. You have not spoken of me what is right, as my servant Job has." **9**So Eliphaz the Temanite, Bildad the Shuhite and Zophar the Naamathite did what the LORD told them; and the LORD accepted Job's prayer.

10After Job had prayed for his friends, the LORD made him prosperous again and gave him twice as much as he had before. **11**All his brothers and sisters and everyone who had known him before came and ate with him in his house. They comforted and consoled him over all the trouble the LORD had brought upon him, and each one gave him a piece of silver[a] and a gold ring.

12The LORD blessed the latter part of Job's life more than the first. He had fourteen thousand sheep, six thousand camels, a thousand yoke of oxen and a thousand donkeys. **13**And he also had seven sons and three daughters. **14**The first daughter he named Jemimah, the second Keziah and the third Keren-Happuch. **15**Nowhere in all the land were there found women as beautiful as Job's daughters, and their father granted them an inheritance along with their brothers.

16After this, Job lived a hundred and forty years; he saw his children and their children to the fourth generation. **17**And so he died, old and full of years.

---

a 11 Hebrew *him a kesitah*; a kesitah was a unit of money of unknown weight and value.

Psalms

Every congregation needs a songbook, for it is our songs that unite us in one voice and one purpose: *worshiping God.* The musical meters for the psalms collected here have been lost to time, but the words remain, striking chords of their own with their vivid language, beautiful artistry and startling honesty.

We find in the psalms *a mirror to our human existence.* There are psalms that overflow with praise and adoration and others that are heavy with grief and sorrow. There are psalms expressing frustration that God is not helping or even listening, and there are psalms of wide-eyed wonder about who we are in relation to this omniscient, omnipotent God.

The psalms are songs and poems, but they are also prayers. In reading them we learn to pray from the heart, to lay ourselves open before *a God who already knows the depths* of what lurks within us, who gives us freedom to bring those depths to the light, and who loves us still.

Author:
David, Asaph, the sons of Korah, Solomon, Heman, Ethan and Moses.

Audience:
All Israel.

Date:
Written between the time of Moses (about 1440 B.C.) and the time following the Babylonian captivity (after 538 B.C.).

Setting:
Picture a passionate worship service in God's temple with God's people.

Verse to Remember:
Your word is a lamp to my feet and a light for my path. (119:105)

BOOK I
Psalms 1–41

Psalm 1

1 Blessed is the man
who does not walk in the counsel of the wicked
or stand in the way of sinners
or sit in the seat of mockers.
2 But his delight is in the law of the LORD,
and on his law he meditates day and night.
3 He is like a tree planted by streams of water,
which yields its fruit in season
and whose leaf does not wither.
Whatever he does prospers.

Like a Tree

Read: Psalm 1:1–6

Psalm 1:2–3

But his delight is in the law of the LORD, and on his law he meditates day and night. He is like a tree planted by streams of water, which yields its fruit in season and whose leaf does not wither. Whatever he does prospers.

reflection

1 What three adjectives would describe your interest in the Scriptures? Is "delightful" on your list?

2 Does the idea of delighting in God's Word attract you to the Bible? What other things motivate you to spend time in God's Word?

3 How is your spiritual life growing like a prosperous fruit tree? Find a picture of a beautiful tree to use as a bookmark to remind you of Psalm 1.

RELATED READINGS

Psalms 112:1–10;
119:9–16;
Jeremiah 17:7–8;
John 7:38;
Revelation 7:17

WHAT GIVES YOU DELIGHT? You know, that sense of unparalleled joy, that amazing degree of enjoyment and pleasure, even to the point of rapture. That's how the dictionary defines delight. But how do you define delight? Is it playing with your baby, reading a good book, walking on the beach at sunset or working on scrapbook pages? Maybe you delight in running through rain-washed streets in the early morning or hiking in the mountains on a sunny autumn day. Maybe your delight is getting lost in playing games or listening to music.

The psalmist defines delight as immersing oneself in the law of the Lord. He sings of the person who finds joy in listening to God's voice in Scripture, who discovers with pleasure "the riches of the wisdom and knowledge of God" (Romans 11:33). For this person, meditating on the Scriptures is not a duty that fulfills a certain obligation, but it is willingly devoting spare time, staying up late into the night immersed in the Bible.

And what is the result of this constant delight in God's Word? One becomes like a tree planted by a river. You've seen them— tall, vital trees, well-watered because they are rooted deep in the stream. This tree is resplendent with foliage in rich shades of green. It's a tree that can withstand biting frost, harsh winds and blazing sun.

A person who delights in God's Word will prosper and have integrity, will speak truthfully and exhibit stability and strength. This is the person who will reflect the face of God like a river reflects the sun in dappled waves. This one is truly blessed.

The book of Psalms is a wonderful place to introduce yourself to the idea of delighting in God's Word. The poetic music of the psalms is rich in metaphors and images that let your imagination soar with the grandeur, majesty, wisdom and unsurpassing love of God. You will see him as a rock, a fortress, a strong tower, a nurturing mother and so much more. He rides on the wind and shows himself in the starry heavens. Delight yourself in singing along with the psalmist and plant your roots deep in the nourishing living water of God's Word.

Go to page 654 for your next devotional reading.

⁴ Not so the wicked!
    They are like chaff
    that the wind blows away.
⁵ Therefore the wicked will not stand in the
        judgment,
    nor sinners in the
        assembly of the
        righteous.

⁶ For the LORD watches
    over the way of the
        righteous,
    but the way of the wicked
        will perish.

Psalm 2

¹ Why do the nations
    conspire*ᵃ*
    and the peoples plot in
        vain?
² The kings of the earth take
        their stand
    and the rulers gather together
        against the LORD
    and against his Anointed One.*ᵇ*
³ "Let us break their chains," they say,
    "and throw off their fetters."

⁴ The One enthroned in heaven laughs;
    the Lord scoffs at them.
⁵ Then he rebukes them in his anger
    and terrifies them in his wrath, saying,
⁶ "I have installed my King*ᶜ*
    on Zion, my holy hill."

⁷ I will proclaim the decree of the LORD:

He said to me, "You are my Son*ᵈ*;
    today I have become your Father.*ᵉ*
⁸ Ask of me,
    and I will make the nations your
        inheritance,
    the ends of the earth your possession.
⁹ You will rule them with an iron scepter*ᶠ*;
    you will dash them to pieces like
        pottery."

¹⁰ Therefore, you kings, be wise;
    be warned, you rulers of the earth.
¹¹ Serve the LORD with fear
    and rejoice with trembling.

¹² Kiss the Son, lest he be angry
    and you be destroyed in your way,
    for his wrath can flare up in a moment.
    Blessed are all who take refuge in him.

Psalm 3

A psalm of David. When he fled
    from his son Absalom.

¹ O LORD, how many are my
        foes!
    How many rise up
        against me!
² Many are saying of me,
    "God will not deliver
        him."   *Selah*ᵍ

³ But you are a shield around
        me, O LORD;
    you bestow glory on
        me and lift*ʰ* up my
        head.

⁴ To the LORD I cry aloud,
    and he answers me from his holy
        hill.   *Selah*

⁵ I lie down and sleep;
    I wake again, because the LORD sustains
        me.
⁶ I will not fear the tens of thousands
    drawn up against me on every side.

⁷ Arise, O LORD!
    Deliver me, O my God!
    Strike all my enemies on the jaw;
    break the teeth of the wicked.

⁸ From the LORD comes deliverance.
    May your blessing be on your
        people.   *Selah*

Psalm 4

For the director of music. With stringed
    instruments. A psalm of David.

¹ Answer me when I call to you,
    O my righteous God.
    Give me relief from my distress;
    be merciful to me and hear my
        prayer.

² How long, O men, will you turn my glory
    into shame*ⁱ*?

> **Psalm 1:6**
>
> *God Watches*
> *Over Us*
>
> For the LORD watches
> over the way of
> the righteous,
> but the way of the
> wicked will perish.

---

*ᵃ*1 Hebrew; Septuagint *rage*   *ᵇ*2 Or *anointed one*   *ᶜ*6 Or *king*   *ᵈ*7 Or *son; also in verse 12*   *ᵉ*7 Or *have begotten you*   *ᶠ*9 Or *will break them with a rod of iron*   *ᵍ*2 A word of uncertain meaning, occurring frequently in the Psalms; possibly a musical term   *ʰ*3 Or LORD, / *my Glorious One, who lifts*   *ⁱ*2 Or *you dishonor my Glorious One*

How long will you love delusions and
seek false gods[a]? *Selah*
[3] Know that the LORD has set apart the
godly for himself;
the LORD will hear when I call to him.

[4] In your anger do not sin;
when you are on your beds,
search your hearts and be silent. *Selah*
[5] Offer right sacrifices
and trust in the LORD.

[6] Many are asking, "Who can
show us any good?"
Let the light of your
face shine upon us,
O LORD.
[7] You have filled my heart
with greater joy
than when their grain
and new wine
abound.
[8] I will lie down and sleep in
peace,
for you alone, O LORD,
make me dwell in safety.

Psalm 5
For the director of music. For flutes.
A psalm of David.

[1] Give ear to my words, O LORD,
consider my sighing.
[2] Listen to my cry for help,
my King and my God,
for to you I pray.
[3] In the morning, O LORD, you hear my
voice;
in the morning I lay my requests before
you
and wait in expectation.

[4] You are not a God who takes pleasure in
evil;
with you the wicked cannot dwell.
[5] The arrogant cannot stand in your presence;
you hate all who do wrong.
[6] You destroy those who tell lies;
bloodthirsty and deceitful men
the LORD abhors.
[7] But I, by your great mercy,
will come into your house;

in reverence will I bow down
toward your holy temple.
[8] Lead me, O LORD, in your righteousness
because of my enemies—
make straight your way before me.

[9] Not a word from their mouth can be
trusted;
their heart is filled with destruction.
Their throat is an open grave;
with their tongue they
speak deceit.
[10] Declare them guilty,
O God!
Let their intrigues be
their downfall.
Banish them for their
many sins,
for they have rebelled
against you.

[11] But let all who take refuge
in you be glad;
let them ever sing for joy.
Spread your protection
over them,
that those who love your name may
rejoice in you.
[12] For surely, O LORD, you bless the
righteous;
you surround them with your favor as
with a shield.

Psalm 6
For the director of music. With stringed
instruments. According to *sheminith.*[b]
A psalm of David.

[1] O LORD, do not rebuke me in your
anger
or discipline me in your wrath.
[2] Be merciful to me, LORD, for I am faint;
O LORD, heal me, for my bones are in
agony.
[3] My soul is in anguish.
How long, O LORD, how long?

[4] Turn, O LORD, and deliver me;
save me because of your unfailing
love.
[5] No one remembers you when he is dead.
Who praises you from the grave[c]?

Psalm 5:11

God Offers Refuge

But let all who take
refuge in you be glad;
let them ever sing for joy.
Spread your protection
over them,
that those who love your
name may rejoice in you.

---

[a] 2 Or *seek lies*   [b] Title: Probably a musical term   [c] 5 Hebrew *Sheol*

⁶I am worn out from groaning;
 all night long I flood my bed with
  weeping
 and drench my couch with tears.
⁷My eyes grow weak with sorrow;
 they fail because of all my foes.

⁸Away from me, all you who do evil,
 for the LORD has heard my weeping.
⁹The LORD has heard my cry for mercy;
 the LORD accepts my prayer.
¹⁰All my enemies will be ashamed and
  dismayed;
 they will turn back in sudden disgrace.

Psalm 7

*A shiggaion[a] of David, which he sang to the LORD
concerning Cush, a Benjamite.*

¹O LORD my God, I take refuge in you;
 save and deliver me from
  all who pursue me,
²or they will tear me like a
  lion
 and rip me to pieces with
  no one to rescue me.

³O LORD my God, if I have
  done this
 and there is guilt on my
  hands—
⁴if I have done evil to him
  who is at peace
  with me
 or without cause have
  robbed my foe—
⁵then let my enemy pursue and overtake
  me;
 let him trample my life to the ground
 and make me sleep in the dust. *Selah*

⁶Arise, O LORD, in your anger;
 rise up against the rage of my enemies.
 Awake, my God; decree justice.
⁷Let the assembled peoples gather around
  you.
 Rule over them from on high;
⁸ let the LORD judge the peoples.
Judge me, O LORD, according to my
  righteousness,
 according to my integrity, O Most High.

⁹O righteous God,
 who searches minds and hearts,
 bring to an end the violence of the wicked
 and make the righteous secure.

¹⁰My shield[b] is God Most High,
 who saves the upright in heart.
¹¹God is a righteous judge,
 a God who expresses his wrath every
  day.
¹²If he does not relent,
 he[c] will sharpen his sword;
 he will bend and string his bow.
¹³He has prepared his deadly weapons;
 he makes ready his flaming arrows.
¹⁴He who is pregnant with evil
 and conceives trouble gives birth to
  disillusionment.
¹⁵He who digs a hole and
  scoops it out
 falls into the pit he has
  made.
¹⁶The trouble he causes
  recoils on himself;
 his violence comes down
  on his own head.

¹⁷I will give thanks to the
  LORD because of his
  righteousness
 and will sing praise to
  the name of the
  LORD Most High.

Psalm 7:17

God Is Righteous

I will give thanks to
the LORD because of
his righteousness
and will sing praise
to the name of the
LORD Most High.

Psalm 8

For the director of music. According to gittith.[d]
A psalm of David.

¹O LORD, our Lord,
 how majestic is your name in all the
  earth!

You have set your glory
 above the heavens.
²From the lips of children and infants
 you have ordained praise[e]
because of your enemies,
 to silence the foe and the avenger.

³When I consider your heavens,
 the work of your fingers,

---

*a Title: Probably a literary or musical term   b 10 Or sovereign   c 12 Or If a man does not repent, / God   d Title: Probably a musical term
e 2 Or strength*

Love Gone Wrong

MICHAL

And Michal daughter of Saul had no children to the day of her death.

2 Samuel 6:23

ASSIGNED READING:

1 Samuel
18:1—
19:17; 25:44;
2 Samuel 3:6–21;
6:1–23

MICHAL HATED TO REHASH an old event, but she always found herself powerless against the tug of her memories.

She remembered it had started out so well. Boy meets girl. Girl falls for boy. Soon, rumors were circulating throughout the kingdom that something was afoot between a princess and a warrior. Michal remembered how the women, busy with their daily chores in the market or at the wells, could not keep from chattering.

"I heard the princess has a crush on David."

"That's so yesterday. I heard they're in love. And Saul wants them to be married as soon as possible."

"Not only that, I heard the groom is giving the bride's father a really strange wedding gift . . ."

(Whispers) "A hundred what?"

She recalled how the excitement brewing back in those days had made the kingdom seem electric. Of course, there were those who tried to tell her that it would not be easy to love a headstrong soldier: the long nights away from home, the constant danger, the family allegiances and betrayals. But in the innocent throes of love, she didn't want to imagine how difficult her relationship with David might turn out to be.

She found herself falling more in love with David with each passing day, but her father Saul only grew increasingly jealous. David held full sway over her allegiance, and her father couldn't stand it. So, he did what only the king could do: He sent her away and even forced her to marry someone else.

Even though she made her way back to David in time, it was never the same. Their love, if it had ever truly existed, had completely unraveled. To Michal, it felt as if resuming her place as David's wife was now only a business arrangement, an attempt to fulfill an obligation. No longer in love, they stayed together for the kingdom's sake.

Whenever she allowed the memories to surface, they always ended the same way. She was left with only a cruel snapshot of love gone wrong—a miserable, spiteful woman and a man ready to move on.

—Prayer—
God, things don't always work out the way I want them to. Give me wisdom and grace to accept life's disappointments.

Weekend

Go to page 658 for your next devotional reading.

the moon and the stars,
which you have set in place,
[4] what is man that you are mindful of him,
the son of man that you care for him?
[5] You made him a little lower than the
heavenly beings[a]
and crowned him with glory and honor.

[6] You made him ruler over the works of your
hands;
you put everything under his feet:
[7] all flocks and herds,
and the beasts of the field,
[8] the birds of the air,
and the fish of the sea,
all that swim the paths of the seas.

[9] O LORD, our Lord,
how majestic is your name in all the
earth!

Psalm 9[b]

For the director of music. To the tune of, "The
Death of the Son." A psalm of David.

[1] I will praise you, O LORD, with all my
heart;
I will tell of all your wonders.
[2] I will be glad and rejoice in you;
I will sing praise to your name, O Most
High.

[3] My enemies turn back;
they stumble and perish before you.
[4] For you have upheld my right and my
cause;
you have sat on your throne, judging
righteously.
[5] You have rebuked the nations and
destroyed the wicked;
you have blotted out their name for ever
and ever.
[6] Endless ruin has overtaken the enemy,
you have uprooted their cities;
even the memory of them has perished.

[7] The LORD reigns forever;
he has established his throne for
judgment.
[8] He will judge the world in righteousness;
he will govern the peoples with justice.
[9] The LORD is a refuge for the oppressed,

a stronghold in times of trouble.
[10] Those who know your name will trust in
you,
for you, LORD, have never forsaken those
who seek you.

[11] Sing praises to the LORD, enthroned in
Zion;
proclaim among the nations what he has
done.
[12] For he who avenges blood remembers;
he does not ignore the cry of the
afflicted.

[13] O LORD, see how my enemies persecute
me!
Have mercy and lift me up from the
gates of death,
[14] that I may declare your praises
in the gates of the Daughter of Zion
and there rejoice in your salvation.

[15] The nations have fallen into the pit they
have dug;
their feet are caught in the net they have
hidden.
[16] The LORD is known by his justice;
the wicked are ensnared by the work of
their hands. *Higgaion.[c] Selah*
[17] The wicked return to the grave,[d]
all the nations that forget God.
[18] But the needy will not always be forgotten,
nor the hope of the afflicted ever perish.

[19] Arise, O LORD, let not man triumph;
let the nations be judged in your
presence.
[20] Strike them with terror, O LORD;
let the nations know they are but
men. *Selah*

Psalm 10[b]

[1] Why, O LORD, do you stand far off?
Why do you hide yourself in times of
trouble?

[2] In his arrogance the wicked man hunts
down the weak,
who are caught in the schemes he devises.
[3] He boasts of the cravings of his heart;
he blesses the greedy and reviles the
LORD.

---

[a]5 Or *than God*   [b]Psalms 9 and 10 may have been originally a single acrostic poem, the stanzas of which begin with the successive letters
of the Hebrew alphabet. In the Septuagint they constitute one psalm.   [c]16 Or *Meditation*; possibly a musical notation   [d]17 Hebrew *Sheol*

⁴ In his pride the wicked does not seek him;
  in all his thoughts there is no room for
    God.
⁵ His ways are always prosperous;
  he is haughty and your laws are far from
    him;
  he sneers at all his enemies.
⁶ He says to himself, "Nothing will shake
    me;
  I'll always be happy and never have
    trouble."
⁷ His mouth is full of curses
    and lies and threats;
  trouble and evil are
    under his tongue.
⁸ He lies in wait near the
    villages;
  from ambush he murders
    the innocent,
  watching in secret for his
    victims.
⁹ He lies in wait like a lion in
    cover;
  he lies in wait to catch
    the helpless;
  he catches the helpless
    and drags them off in his net.
¹⁰ His victims are crushed, they collapse;
  they fall under his strength.
¹¹ He says to himself, "God has forgotten;
  he covers his face and never sees."

¹² Arise, Lord! Lift up your hand, O God.
  Do not forget the helpless.
¹³ Why does the wicked man revile God?
  Why does he say to himself,
    "He won't call me to account"?
¹⁴ But you, O God, do see trouble and grief;
  you consider it to take it in hand.
  The victim commits himself to you;
  you are the helper of the fatherless.
¹⁵ Break the arm of the wicked and evil
    man;
  call him to account for his wickedness
    that would not be found out.

¹⁶ The Lord is King for ever and ever;
  the nations will perish from his land.
¹⁷ You hear, O Lord, the desire of the
    afflicted;

you encourage them, and you listen to
    their cry,
¹⁸ defending the fatherless and the
    oppressed,
  in order that man, who is of the earth,
    may terrify no more.

Psalm 11
For the director of music. Of David.

¹ In the Lord I take refuge.
  How then can you say to me:
    "Flee like a bird to your
      mountain.
² For look, the wicked bend
      their bows;
    they set their arrows
      against the strings
    to shoot from the
      shadows
    at the upright in heart.
³ When the foundations are
      being destroyed,
    what can the righteous
      do*a*?"

⁴ The Lord is in his holy
    temple;
  the Lord is on his heavenly throne.
  He observes the sons of men;
    his eyes examine them.
⁵ The Lord examines the righteous,
  but the wicked*b* and those who love
    violence
    his soul hates.
⁶ On the wicked he will rain
    fiery coals and burning sulfur;
  a scorching wind will be their lot.

⁷ For the Lord is righteous,
  he loves justice;
  upright men will see his face.

Psalm 12
For the director of music. According to *sheminith*.*c*
A psalm of David.

¹ Help, Lord, for the godly are no more;
  the faithful have vanished from among
    men.
² Everyone lies to his neighbor;
  their flattering lips speak with
    deception.

> ### Psalm 10:17
> ## God Encourages the Afflicted
>
> You hear, O Lord, the
> desire of the afflicted;
> you encourage them,
> and you listen
> to their cry.

---

*a*3 Or *what is the Righteous One doing*   *b*5 Or *The Lord, the Righteous One, examines the wicked, /*   *c*Title: Probably a musical term

³ May the LORD cut off all flattering lips
  and every boastful tongue
⁴ that says, "We will triumph with our
  tongues;
  we own our lips*a*—who is our master?"

⁵ "Because of the oppression
    of the weak
  and the groaning of the
    needy,
  I will now arise," says the
    LORD.
  "I will protect them from
    those who malign
    them."
⁶ And the words of the LORD
  are flawless,
  like silver refined in a
    furnace of clay,
  purified seven times.

⁷ O LORD, you will keep us safe
  and protect us from such people forever.
⁸ The wicked freely strut about
  when what is vile is honored among
    men.

Psalm 13
For the director of music. A psalm of David.

¹ How long, O LORD? Will you forget me
  forever?
  How long will you hide your face from me?
² How long must I wrestle with my thoughts
  and every day have sorrow in my heart?
  How long will my enemy triumph over
    me?

³ Look on me and answer, O LORD my God.
  Give light to my eyes, or I will sleep in
    death;
⁴ my enemy will say, "I have overcome him,"
  and my foes will rejoice when I fall.

⁵ But I trust in your unfailing love;
  my heart rejoices in your salvation.
⁶ I will sing to the LORD,
  for he has been good to me.

Psalm 14
For the director of music. Of David.

¹ The fool*b* says in his heart,
  "There is no God."

They are corrupt, their deeds are vile;
  there is no one who does good.

² The LORD looks down from heaven
    on the sons of men
  to see if there are any who understand,
    any who seek God.
³ All have turned aside,
    they have together
      become corrupt;
  there is no one who does
    good,
  not even one.

⁴ Will evildoers never
    learn—
  those who devour my
    people as men eat
    bread
  and who do not call on
    the LORD?
⁵ There they are, overwhelmed with dread,
  for God is present in the company of the
    righteous.
⁶ You evildoers frustrate the plans of the poor,
  but the LORD is their refuge.

⁷ Oh, that salvation for Israel would come
    out of Zion!
  When the LORD restores the fortunes of
    his people,
  let Jacob rejoice and Israel be glad!

Psalm 15
A psalm of David.

¹ LORD, who may dwell in your sanctuary?
  Who may live on your holy hill?

² He whose walk is blameless
    and who does what is righteous,
  who speaks the truth from his heart
³   and has no slander on his tongue,
  who does his neighbor no wrong
    and casts no slur on his fellowman,
⁴ who despises a vile man
    but honors those who fear the LORD,
  who keeps his oath
    even when it hurts,
⁵ who lends his money without usury
    and does not accept a bribe against the
      innocent.

> **Psalm 12:6**
>
> *God Is Truthful*
>
> And the words of the
> LORD are flawless,
> like silver refined in
> a furnace of clay,
> purified seven times.

---

*a*4 Or / *our lips are our plowshares*   *b*1 The Hebrew words rendered *fool* in Psalms denote one who is morally deficient.

Never Alone

Psalm 13:5

But I trust in your
unfailing love;
my heart rejoices in
your salvation.

reflection

1 Have you experienced
a time when you
couldn't feel God's pres-
ence? When?

2 How did you respond?
What did you do?

3 Based on your under-
standing of Psalm 13,
what will you do next time
you find yourself feeling
this way?

RELATED READINGS

Deuteronomy 31:1–6;
Isaiah 54:1–17;
Lamentations 3:31–33

AT AGE 46, PETER MARSHALL, chaplain of the United States
Senate, died of a heart attack. Soon after he died, his wife,
Catherine Marshall, stood beside his body. Later she wrote how
the presence of God comforted her:

"As I opened the door," she wrote, "there was the instanta-
neous awareness that I was not alone. Yet the man I loved was
not in the still form on the bed. I knew that Peter was near and
alive. And beside him was another presence of transcendent glory,
the Lord he had served through long years." God stood beside
Catherine to comfort her in her deepest grief.

In this psalm, the writer found himself feeling so alone, so
seemingly abandoned by God, that he was plunged into a deep
depression and despair that took him to the edge of death. He was
wrestling with his thoughts. His sorrow was overwhelming.

Perhaps you can relate to such feelings. Perhaps you know
what it's like when your thoughts are whirling around in aching
confusion. You may know what it's like to plead with God for light,
for peace, for an alternative to the spiritual death you think is
imminent.

Then comes the "*but.*" The psalmist, even as he was suffering
terribly, stopped himself with that little word. David chose to trust
in God's goodness even when his heart was failing and grieving.
Because he knew God, he chose to trust in God's unfailing love and
rejoice even in the midst of sorrow.

Did you get that? He said, "But . . . I will" (verses 5–6). The
psalmist made a choice. He made a conscious decision to trust in
God's love even when the dark clouds of terror and depression hid
God's face.

David knew this as a fact. And you can know it too: You are
never alone. God is always nearby . . . even when you can't see his
face or feel his presence. When you feel alone, call out to him. No
matter how you feel, the fact remains: He is here. He is everywhere.
And he hears your cries.

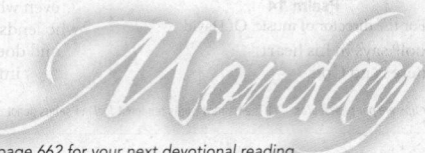

Monday

Go to page 662 for your next devotional reading.

He who does these things
will never be shaken.

Psalm 16

A *miktam*[a] of David.

[1] Keep me safe, O God,
for in you I take refuge.

[2] I said to the LORD, "You are my Lord;
apart from you I have no good thing."
[3] As for the saints who are in the land,
they are the glorious ones in whom is all
my delight.[b]
[4] The sorrows of those will increase
who run after other gods.
I will not pour out their
libations of blood
or take up their names
on my lips.

[5] LORD, you have assigned
me my portion and
my cup;
you have made my lot
secure.
[6] The boundary lines have
fallen for me in
pleasant places;
surely I have a delightful
inheritance.

[7] I will praise the LORD, who
counsels me;
even at night my heart instructs me.
[8] I have set the LORD always before me.
Because he is at my right hand,
I will not be shaken.

[9] Therefore my heart is glad and my tongue
rejoices;
my body also will rest secure,
[10] because you will not abandon me to the
grave,[c]
nor will you let your Holy One[d] see
decay.
[11] You have made[e] known to me the path of
life;
you will fill me with joy in your
presence,
with eternal pleasures at your right
hand.

Psalm 17

A prayer of David.

[1] Hear, O LORD, my righteous plea;
listen to my cry.
Give ear to my prayer—
it does not rise from deceitful lips.
[2] May my vindication come from you;
may your eyes see what is right.

[3] Though you probe my heart and examine
me at night,
though you test me, you will find
nothing;
I have resolved that my
mouth will not sin.
[4] As for the deeds of men—
by the word of your lips
I have kept myself
from the ways of the
violent.
[5] My steps have held to your
paths;
my feet have not slipped.

[6] I call on you, O God, for
you will answer me;
give ear to me and hear
my prayer.
[7] Show the wonder of your
great love,
you who save by your
right hand
those who take refuge in you from their
foes.

[8] Keep me as the apple of your eye;
hide me in the shadow of your
wings
[9] from the wicked who assail me,
from my mortal enemies who surround
me.

[10] They close up their callous hearts,
and their mouths speak with
arrogance.
[11] They have tracked me down, they now
surround me,
with eyes alert, to throw me to the
ground.
[12] They are like a lion hungry for prey,
like a great lion crouching in cover.

Psalm 16:5

God Offers Security

LORD, you have assigned
me my portion
and my cup;
you have made
my lot secure.

---

[a] Title: Probably a literary or musical term   [b] 3 Or *As for the pagan priests who are in the land / and the nobles in whom all delight, I said:*
[c] 10 Hebrew *Sheol*   [d] 10 Or *your faithful one*   [e] 11 Or *You will make*

13 Rise up, O LORD, confront them, bring
      them down;
   rescue me from the wicked by your
      sword.
14 O LORD, by your hand save
      me from such men,
   from men of this world
      whose reward is in
      this life.

   You still the hunger of
      those you cherish;
   their sons have plenty,
      and they store up wealth
      for their children.
15 And I—in righteousness I
      will see your face;
   when I awake, I will be
      satisfied with seeing
      your likeness.

Psalm 18

For the director of music. Of David the servant
of the LORD. He sang to the LORD the words of
this song when the LORD delivered him from the
hand of all his enemies and from the hand of Saul.
He said:

1 I love you, O LORD, my strength.

2 The LORD is my rock, my fortress and my
      deliverer;
   my God is my rock, in whom I take
      refuge.
   He is my shield and the horn[a] of my
      salvation, my stronghold.
3 I call to the LORD, who is worthy of praise,
   and I am saved from my enemies.

4 The cords of death entangled me;
   the torrents of destruction overwhelmed
      me.
5 The cords of the grave[b] coiled around me;
   the snares of death confronted me.
6 In my distress I called to the LORD;
   I cried to my God for help.
   From his temple he heard my voice;
   my cry came before him, into his ears.

7 The earth trembled and quaked,
   and the foundations of the mountains
      shook;

they trembled because he was angry.
8 Smoke rose from his nostrils;
   consuming fire came from his mouth,
   burning coals blazed out of it.
9 He parted the heavens and
      came down;
   dark clouds were under
      his feet.
10 He mounted the cherubim
      and flew;
   he soared on the wings
      of the wind.
11 He made darkness his
      covering, his
      canopy around
      him—
   the dark rain clouds of
      the sky.
12 Out of the brightness of
      his presence clouds
      advanced,
   with hailstones and bolts of lightning.
13 The LORD thundered from heaven;
   the voice of the Most High resounded.[c]
14 He shot his arrows and scattered the
      enemies,
   great bolts of lightning and routed
      them.
15 The valleys of the sea were exposed
   and the foundations of the earth laid
      bare
   at your rebuke, O LORD,
   at the blast of breath from your nostrils.

16 He reached down from on high and took
      hold of me;
   he drew me out of deep waters.
17 He rescued me from my powerful enemy,
   from my foes, who were too strong for
      me.
18 They confronted me in the day of my
      disaster,
   but the LORD was my support.
19 He brought me out into a spacious place;
   he rescued me because he delighted in
      me.
20 The LORD has dealt with me according to
      my righteousness;

> **Psalm 17:15**
>
> *God Provides Satisfaction*
>
> And I—in righteousness
> I will see your face;
> when I awake, I will be
> satisfied with seeing
> your likeness.

---

a2 Horn here symbolizes strength. b5 Hebrew Sheol c13 Some Hebrew manuscripts and Septuagint (see also 2 Samuel 22:14); most Hebrew manuscripts resounded, / amid hailstones and bolts of lightning

according to the cleanness of my hands
he has rewarded me.
21 For I have kept the ways of the Lord;
I have not done evil by turning from my
God.
22 All his laws are before me;
I have not turned away from his decrees.
23 I have been blameless before him
and have kept myself from sin.
24 The Lord has rewarded me according to
my righteousness,
according to the cleanness of my hands
in his sight.

25 To the faithful you show yourself faithful,
to the blameless you show yourself
blameless,
26 to the pure you show yourself pure,
but to the crooked you show yourself
shrewd.
27 You save the humble
but bring low those whose eyes are
haughty.
28 You, O Lord, keep my lamp burning;
my God turns my darkness into light.
29 With your help I can advance against a
troop*a*;
with my God I can scale a wall.

30 As for God, his way is perfect;
the word of the Lord is flawless.
He is a shield
for all who take refuge in him.
31 For who is God besides the Lord?
And who is the Rock except our God?
32 It is God who arms me with strength
and makes my way perfect.
33 He makes my feet like the feet of a deer;
he enables me to stand on the heights.
34 He trains my hands for battle;
my arms can bend a bow of bronze.
35 You give me your shield of victory,
and your right hand sustains me;
you stoop down to make me great.
36 You broaden the path beneath me,
so that my ankles do not turn.

37 I pursued my enemies and overtook them;
I did not turn back till they were
destroyed.
38 I crushed them so that they could not rise;
they fell beneath my feet.
39 You armed me with strength for battle;
you made my adversaries bow at my feet.
40 You made my enemies turn their backs in
flight,
and I destroyed my foes.
41 They cried for help, but there was no one to
save them—
to the Lord, but he did not answer.
42 I beat them as fine as dust borne on the
wind;
I poured them out like mud in the
streets.

43 You have delivered me from the attacks of
the people;
you have made me the head of nations;
people I did not know are subject to me.
44 As soon as they hear me, they obey me;
foreigners cringe before me.
45 They all lose heart;
they come trembling from their
strongholds.

46 The Lord lives! Praise be to my Rock!
Exalted be God my Savior!
47 He is the God who avenges me,
who subdues nations under me,
48 who saves me from my enemies.
You exalted me above my foes;
from violent men you rescued me.
49 Therefore I will praise you among the
nations, O Lord;
I will sing praises to your name.
50 He gives his king great victories;
he shows unfailing kindness to his
anointed,
to David and his descendants forever.

Psalm 19

For the director of music. A psalm of David.

1 The heavens declare the glory of God;
the skies proclaim the work of his
hands.
2 Day after day they pour forth speech;
night after night they display
knowledge.
3 There is no speech or language
where their voice is not heard.*b*

---

*a*29 Or *can run through a barricade*   *b*3 Or *They have no speech, there are no words; / no sound is heard from them*

An Articulate Creation

Read: Psalm 19:1–14

Psalm 19:1

The heavens declare the glory of God; the skies proclaim the work of his hands.

reflection

1 Which aspects of nature resonate with you? Perhaps you enjoy a beautiful sunset or bird watching; whatever the particular expression, think about how you can incorporate worship or prayer into the time you spend appreciating the natural world.

2 How can you reconcile the importance of worshiping the Creator with the responsibility of stewardship of God's creation?

3 Think about the last time nature made a strong impression on you—good or bad. How can you subject your emotional responses to the cosmos to the psalmist's idea that the creation proclaims God's invisible qualities?

RELATED READINGS

Job 38:1–41;
Isaiah 65:17–25;
Romans 8:18–27

WE LIVE IN TUMULTUOUS TIMES of natural disaster. The news carries stories of devastating earthquakes, floods and tropical storms that career along coastlines and cause massive losses of property and life in the cities, towns and individual households they invade. Amidst screaming natural forces it may be easy to forget that even the winds and rains submit to God's voice. Although the natural world does not glorify itself, the booming truths pounding in the surf and soaring through the skies fall on many a deaf ear. But nature's voice "goes out into all the earth" proclaiming the articulate truth that God is in his heaven and watching over his creation.

In an urban setting, where smog blankets the sky and artificial light dulls the stars, seeing God's imprint may be difficult. Natural disasters may strike us more as an example of nature's random savagery than the handiwork of our all-powerful God. Certainly the creation groans under the curse of sin, just as we do. We cannot pretend to understand the reasons for earthquakes, floods or fires, but we do know the One who controls the universe, and we can cling to him amidst the rising waters.

The next time you witness a flower growing between the sidewalk cracks, a raging thunderstorm or a magnificent sunset, remember that creation acts as a signpost, pointing to Someone greater than "Mother Nature." It reveals the God who wants all people of all nations to recognize his majesty, to worship the One whose infinite creativity and power produced the spectacular displays found in the natural world.

The natural world is a testimony to God's magnificent creatorship and also should be the object of our diligent stewardship. However, we must flee the two extremes—either fearing nature's power or worshiping creation and not the Creator. Even today, the creation is God's universal proclamation of his nature, underpinning his special revelation through Christ and the Scriptures. As women who love and appreciate the beauty of the world, may we always remember to listen closely to the deeper truths of God's goodness and grandeur that whisper from the rushing stream or shout from the thunderclap.

Tuesday

⁴ Their voice*ᵃ* goes out into all the earth,
  their words to the ends of the world.

  In the heavens he has pitched a tent for the
    sun,
⁵   which is like a bridegroom coming forth
    from his pavilion,
  like a champion rejoicing to run his
    course.
⁶ It rises at one end of the heavens
  and makes its circuit to the other;
    nothing is hidden from its heat.

⁷ The law of the Lᴏʀᴅ is perfect,
  reviving the soul.
  The statutes of the Lᴏʀᴅ are trustworthy,
    making wise the simple.
⁸ The precepts of the Lᴏʀᴅ are right,
  giving joy to the heart.
  The commands of the Lᴏʀᴅ are radiant,
    giving light to the eyes.
⁹ The fear of the Lᴏʀᴅ is pure,
  enduring forever.
  The ordinances of the Lᴏʀᴅ are sure
    and altogether righteous.
¹⁰ They are more precious than gold,
  than much pure gold;
  they are sweeter than honey,
    than honey from the comb.
¹¹ By them is your servant warned;
  in keeping them there is great reward.

¹² Who can discern his errors?
  Forgive my hidden faults.
¹³ Keep your servant also from willful sins;
  may they not rule over me.
  Then will I be blameless,
    innocent of great transgression.

¹⁴ May the words of my mouth and the
    meditation of my heart
  be pleasing in your sight,
  O Lᴏʀᴅ, my Rock and my Redeemer.

Psalm 20
For the director of music. A psalm of David.

¹ May the Lᴏʀᴅ answer you when you are in
    distress;
  may the name of the God of Jacob
    protect you.
² May he send you help from the sanctuary

and grant you support from Zion.
³ May he remember all your sacrifices
  and accept your burnt offerings.   *Selah*

⁴ May he give you the desire of your heart
  and make all your plans succeed.
⁵ We will shout for joy when you are
    victorious
  and will lift up our banners in the name
    of our God.

  May the Lᴏʀᴅ grant all your requests.

⁶ Now I know that the Lᴏʀᴅ saves his
    anointed;
  he answers him from his holy heaven
  with the saving power of his right
    hand.
⁷ Some trust in chariots and some in
    horses,
  but we trust in the name of the Lᴏʀᴅ
    our God.
⁸ They are brought to their knees and fall,
  but we rise up and stand firm.

⁹ O Lᴏʀᴅ, save the king!
  Answerᵇ us when we call!

Psalm 21
For the director of music. A psalm of David.

¹ O Lᴏʀᴅ, the king rejoices in your strength.
  How great is his joy in the victories you
    give!
² You have granted him the desire of his
    heart
  and have not withheld the request of his
    lips.   *Selah*
³ You welcomed him with rich blessings
  and placed a crown of pure gold on his
    head.
⁴ He asked you for life, and you gave it to
    him—
  length of days, for ever and ever.
⁵ Through the victories you gave, his glory is
    great;
  you have bestowed on him splendor and
    majesty.
⁶ Surely you have granted him eternal
    blessings
  and made him glad with the joy of your
    presence.
⁷ For the king trusts in the Lᴏʀᴅ;

ᵃ4 Septuagint, Jerome and Syriac; Hebrew line   *ᵇ9 Or save! / O King, answer*

through the unfailing love of the Most
High
he will not be shaken.

8 Your hand will lay hold on all your enemies;
your right hand will seize your foes.
9 At the time of your appearing
you will make them like a fiery furnace.
In his wrath the LORD will swallow them
up,
and his fire will consume them.
10 You will destroy their descendants from
the earth,
their posterity from mankind.
11 Though they plot evil against you
and devise wicked schemes, they cannot
succeed;
12 for you will make them turn their backs
when you aim at them with drawn bow.

13 Be exalted, O LORD, in your strength;
we will sing and praise your might.

Psalm 22

For the director of music. To ˌthe tune of˛ "The Doe
of the Morning." A psalm of David.

1 My God, my God, why have you forsaken
me?
Why are you so far from saving me,
so far from the words of my groaning?
2 O my God, I cry out by day, but you do not
answer,
by night, and am not
silent.

3 Yet you are enthroned as
the Holy One;
you are the praise of
Israel.ᵃ
4 In you our fathers put their
trust;
they trusted and you
delivered them.
5 They cried to you and were
saved;
in you they trusted and were not
disappointed.

6 But I am a worm and not a man,
scorned by men and despised by the
people.

7 All who see me mock me;
they hurl insults, shaking their heads:
8 "He trusts in the LORD;
let the LORD rescue him.
Let him deliver him,
since he delights in him."

9 Yet you brought me out of the womb;
you made me trust in you
even at my mother's breast.
10 From birth I was cast upon you;
from my mother's womb you have been
my God.
11 Do not be far from me,
for trouble is near
and there is no one to help.

12 Many bulls surround me;
strong bulls of Bashan encircle me.
13 Roaring lions tearing their prey
open their mouths wide against me.
14 I am poured out like water,
and all my bones are out of joint.
My heart has turned to wax;
it has melted away within me.
15 My strength is dried up like a potsherd,
and my tongue sticks to the roof of my
mouth;
you lay meᵇ in the dust of death.
16 Dogs have surrounded me;
a band of evil men has encircled me,
they have piercedᶜ my
hands and my
feet.
17 I can count all my bones;
people stare and gloat
over me.
18 They divide my garments
among them
and cast lots for my
clothing.

19 But you, O LORD, be not far
off;
O my Strength, come
quickly to help me.
20 Deliver my life from the sword,
my precious life from the power of the
dogs.
21 Rescue me from the mouth of the lions;

Psalm 22:3

God Is Holy

Yet you are enthroned
as the Holy One;
you are the praise
of Israel.

ᵃ3 Or *Yet you are holy, / enthroned on the praises of Israel* ᵇ15 Or *I am laid* ᶜ16 Some Hebrew manuscripts, Septuagint and Syriac;
most Hebrew manuscripts / *like the lion,*

save^a me from the horns of the wild
oxen.

²² I will declare your name to my brothers;
in the congregation I will praise you.
²³ You who fear the LORD, praise him!
All you descendants of Jacob, honor him!
Revere him, all you descendants of
Israel!
²⁴ For he has not despised or disdained
the suffering of the afflicted one;
he has not hidden his face from him
but has listened to his cry for help.

²⁵ From you comes the theme of my praise in
the great assembly;
before those who fear you^b will I fulfill
my vows.
²⁶ The poor will eat and be satisfied;
they who seek the LORD will praise
him—
may your hearts live forever!
²⁷ All the ends of the earth
will remember and turn to the LORD,
and all the families of the nations
will bow down before him,
²⁸ for dominion belongs to the LORD
and he rules over the
nations.

²⁹ All the rich of the earth will
feast and worship;
all who go down to the
dust will kneel
before him—
those who cannot keep
themselves alive.
³⁰ Posterity will serve him;
future generations will
be told about the
Lord.
³¹ They will proclaim his
righteousness
to a people yet unborn—
for he has done it.

Psalm 23
A psalm of David.

¹ The LORD is my shepherd, I shall not be in
want.

² He makes me lie down in green
pastures,
he leads me beside quiet waters,
³ he restores my soul.
He guides me in paths of righteousness
for his name's sake.
⁴ Even though I walk
through the valley of the shadow of
death,^c
I will fear no evil,
for you are with me;
your rod and your staff,
they comfort me.

⁵ You prepare a table before me
in the presence of my enemies.
You anoint my head with oil;
my cup overflows.
⁶ Surely goodness and love will follow me
all the days of my life,
and I will dwell in the house of the LORD
forever.

Psalm 24
Of David. A psalm.

¹ The earth is the LORD's, and everything
in it,
the world, and all who
live in it;
² for he founded it upon the
seas
and established it upon
the waters.

³ Who may ascend the hill of
the LORD?
Who may stand in his
holy place?
⁴ He who has clean hands
and a pure heart,
who does not lift up his
soul to an idol
or swear by what is false.^d
⁵ He will receive blessing from the LORD
and vindication from God his Savior.
⁶ Such is the generation of those who seek
him,
who seek your face, O God of
Jacob.^e   *Selah*

> **Psalm 24:1**
>
> *God Owns Everything*
>
> The earth is the LORD's,
> and everything in it,
> the world, and all
> who live in it.

---

^a21 Or / you have heard   ^b25 Hebrew him   ^c4 Or through the darkest valley   ^d4 Or swear falsely   ^e6 Two Hebrew manuscripts and Syriac (see also Septuagint); most Hebrew manuscripts face, Jacob

7 Lift up your heads, O you gates;
    be lifted up, you ancient doors,
    that the King of glory may come in.
8 Who is this King of glory?
    The LORD strong and mighty,
    the LORD mighty in battle.
9 Lift up your heads, O you gates;
    lift them up, you ancient doors,
    that the King of glory may come in.
10 Who is he, this King of glory?
    The LORD Almighty—
    he is the King of glory. *Selah*

Psalm 25[a]
Of David.

1 To you, O LORD, I lift up my soul;
2   in you I trust, O my God.
    Do not let me be put to shame,
    nor let my enemies triumph over me.
3 No one whose hope is in you
    will ever be put to shame,
    but they will be put to shame
    who are treacherous without excuse.

4 Show me your ways, O LORD,
    teach me your paths;
5 guide me in your truth and teach me,
    for you are God my Savior,
    and my hope is in you all day long.
6 Remember, O LORD, your great mercy and
        love,
    for they are from of old.
7 Remember not the sins of my youth
    and my rebellious ways;
    according to your love remember me,
    for you are good, O LORD.

8 Good and upright is the LORD;
    therefore he instructs sinners in his ways.
9 He guides the humble in what is right
    and teaches them his way.
10 All the ways of the LORD are loving and
        faithful
    for those who keep the demands of his
        covenant.
11 For the sake of your name, O LORD,
    forgive my iniquity, though it is great.
12 Who, then, is the man that fears the LORD?
    He will instruct him in the way chosen
        for him.

13 He will spend his days in prosperity,
    and his descendants will inherit the
        land.
14 The LORD confides in those who fear him;
    he makes his covenant known to them.
15 My eyes are ever on the LORD,
    for only he will release my feet from the
        snare.

16 Turn to me and be gracious to me,
    for I am lonely and afflicted.
17 The troubles of my heart have multiplied;
    free me from my anguish.
18 Look upon my affliction and my distress
    and take away all my sins.
19 See how my enemies have increased
    and how fiercely they hate me!
20 Guard my life and rescue me;
    let me not be put to shame,
    for I take refuge in you.
21 May integrity and uprightness protect me,
    because my hope is in you.

22 Redeem Israel, O God,
    from all their troubles!

Psalm 26
Of David.

1 Vindicate me, O LORD,
    for I have led a blameless life;
    I have trusted in the LORD
    without wavering.
2 Test me, O LORD, and try me,
    examine my heart and my mind;
3 for your love is ever before me,
    and I walk continually in your truth.
4 I do not sit with deceitful men,
    nor do I consort with hypocrites;
5 I abhor the assembly of evildoers
    and refuse to sit with the wicked.
6 I wash my hands in innocence,
    and go about your altar, O LORD,
7 proclaiming aloud your praise
    and telling of all your wonderful deeds.
8 I love the house where you live, O LORD,
    the place where your glory dwells.

9 Do not take away my soul along with
        sinners,
    my life with bloodthirsty men,
10 in whose hands are wicked schemes,

---

*a This psalm is an acrostic poem, the verses of which begin with the successive letters of the Hebrew alphabet.

666

Coming Clean

Read: Psalm 24:1–10

THE VIENNA MATERNITY HOSPITAL was the largest maternity hospital in the world in the middle of the nineteenth century. It was considered a safer place to deliver a child than a home. Yet the mortality rates for mothers giving birth were alarming. Studies done from 1839 to 1847 revealed that women attended by medical students were dying at nearly triple the rate of those attended by midwives. The cause? Unwashed hands. Doctors would routinely conduct post-mortems and then proceed directly to the maternity wards to deliver babies. Finally, a Hungarian doctor named Ignaz Phillip Semmelweis introduced the doctors to hand washing with a chlorine solution between procedures. Only then did the mortality rates of mothers of newborns drop dramatically.

Today we understand to a far greater degree the role of bacteria in producing and spreading disease. Medical personnel and restaurant workers alike are required to wash their hands regularly. And how often do we hear mothers urge their children, "Wash your hands before you come to the table!"

Just as external cleanliness promotes physical health, having "clean hands" before God promotes spiritual health. Scrubbing up spiritually involves repentance—confessing our sins, coming clean—before God so that we can experience spiritual well-being. The psalmist pleaded, "Create in me a pure heart, O God, and renew a steadfast spirit within me" (Psalm 51:10).

In her book *With My Whole Heart*, author Karen Mains writes, "Spiritual awakening always begins with cleansing. It begins in the heart of the individual who suddenly says to herself, 'I'm dirty.' And that is painful, particularly if we've been pretending all along to be clean."

If you long for greater intimacy with God, ask him to examine your heart to see if there are any areas in which you need to come clean before him. Confession, in its most elemental form, simply means agreeing with God that you've departed from his ways and fallen short of his standards. Admit to him—and to yourself—that you are in need of a spiritual bath. Be prepared, like a little child, to squirm a little when he reminds you to wash behind your ears. But, oh, the joy of coming clean!

Psalm 24:3–4

Who may ascend the hill of the LORD? Who may stand in his holy place? He who has clean hands and a pure heart.

reflection

1 When was the last time you "washed your hands" by spending time in confession to God?

2 Ask God to bring things to mind that you need to confess to him today.

3 Spend some time asking God to forgive you of those things that displease him. Thank him that "if we confess our sins, he is faithful and just and will forgive us our sins and purify us from all unrighteousness" (1 John 1:9).

RELATED READINGS

2 Samuel 12:1–13;
Psalm 51:1–19;
Matthew 5:8

Go to page 669 for your next devotional reading.

whose right hands are full of bribes.
¹¹ But I lead a blameless life;
    redeem me and be merciful to me.

¹² My feet stand on level ground;
    in the great assembly I will praise the
        LORD.

Psalm 27
Of David.

¹ The LORD is my light and my salvation—
    whom shall I fear?
The LORD is the stronghold
        of my life—
    of whom shall I be
        afraid?
² When evil men advance
        against me
    to devour my flesh,ᵃ
    when my enemies and my
        foes attack me,
    they will stumble and
        fall.
³ Though an army besiege
        me,
    my heart will not fear;
    though war break out
        against me,
    even then will I be
        confident.

⁴ One thing I ask of the LORD,
    this is what I seek:
    that I may dwell in the house of the LORD
        all the days of my life,
    to gaze upon the beauty of the LORD
        and to seek him in his temple.
⁵ For in the day of trouble
    he will keep me safe in his dwelling;
    he will hide me in the shelter of his
        tabernacle
    and set me high upon a rock.
⁶ Then my head will be exalted
        above the enemies who surround me;
    at his tabernacle will I sacrifice with shouts
        of joy;
    I will sing and make music to the LORD.

⁷ Hear my voice when I call, O LORD;
    be merciful to me and answer me.
⁸ My heart says of you, "Seek hisᵇ face!"

Your face, LORD, I will seek.
⁹ Do not hide your face from me,
    do not turn your servant away in anger;
    you have been my helper.
Do not reject me or forsake me,
    O God my Savior.
¹⁰ Though my father and mother forsake me,
    the LORD will receive me.
¹¹ Teach me your way, O LORD;
    lead me in a straight path
        because of my oppressors.
    ¹² Do not turn me over to the
            desire of my foes,
        for false witnesses rise up
            against me,
        breathing out violence.

¹³ I am still confident of this:
    I will see the goodness of
        the LORD
    in the land of the living.
¹⁴ Wait for the LORD;
    be strong and take heart
    and wait for the LORD.

Psalm 28
Of David.

¹ To you I call, O LORD my
        Rock;
    do not turn a deaf ear
        to me.
For if you remain silent,
    I will be like those who have gone down
        to the pit.
² Hear my cry for mercy
    as I call to you for help,
    as I lift up my hands
        toward your Most Holy Place.

³ Do not drag me away with the wicked,
    with those who do evil,
    who speak cordially with their neighbors
        but harbor malice in their hearts.
⁴ Repay them for their deeds
    and for their evil work;
    repay them for what their hands have done
        and bring back upon them what they
            deserve.
⁵ Since they show no regard for the works of
        the LORD
    and what his hands have done,

Psalm 27:1

God Is My Salvation

The LORD is my light
and my salvation—
whom shall I fear?
The LORD is the
stronghold of my life—
of whom shall
I be afraid?

ᵃ2 Or *to slander me*   ᵇ8 Or *To you, O my heart, he has said, "Seek my*

Fearless

Read: Psalm 27:1–14

WHOM DO YOU FEAR? Let's face it: It's a scary world out there. All kinds of people may do us harm—from the stranger lurking on the corner to the terrorist lurking behind a computer somewhere, from a drunken driver to a corrupt investment firm.

Sometimes we fear people who may harm us in more personal ways—the boss who has it out for us or the woman who dislikes us. We may find ourselves working harder when the boss is around or walking on eggshells around the neighborhood gossip. We may violate our own consciences so we don't offend those who make sure their opinions are heard. We are afraid of those peers who like to put pressure on us.

David, who wrote this psalm, had many enemies chasing him at one time or another. He was no stranger to danger. But he also knew that God was powerful and knowledgeable enough to thwart the plans others might have to harm him. He knew that God could intervene on his behalf. He knew that God had plans for him. He knew that God had his best interests at heart. So in this ringing statement of trust, he put his fate in the hands of God who would be his "stronghold" (Psalm 27:1).

We can learn from David one key to facing our fears. David escaped the pressure of fear and warfare by retreating into God's holy presence in the tabernacle. He proclaimed, "I will sing and make music to the LORD" (verse 6). Praise and worship can help to take our minds off of our fears by placing our thoughts on our powerful God.

David also reminds us to "wait for the LORD; be strong and take heart and wait for the LORD" (verse 14). Though God's answer may not come when or how we expect it, we can trust that he is more faithful than even a parent. Even if our boss fires us, our best friend gossips behind our back or our retirement fund is drained, God will surround us with his love. In spite of anything that can happen, God will be there for us. Ultimately, we who trust in him find safety for our souls. Since that is the case, whom on earth should we fear?

Psalm 27:1

The LORD is my light and my salvation— whom shall I fear? The LORD is the stronghold of my life—of whom shall I be afraid?

reflection

1 Whom do you fear and why?

2 How has God shielded you when you have been in a frightening situation?

3 How do you reconcile this psalm and its implications with the realization that some faithful people do come to physical harm?

RELATED READINGS

Joshua 1:5–9; Luke 12:4–7; Romans 8:35–39; 1 John 4:14–18

"Where are the men and women who love God supremely and fear nothing and no one but God?"

Nancy Leigh DeMoss

Go to page 676 for your next devotional reading.

he will tear them down
 and never build them up again.

6 Praise be to the LORD,
 for he has heard my cry for mercy.
7 The LORD is my strength and my shield;
 my heart trusts in him, and I am helped.
 My heart leaps for joy
 and I will give thanks to him in song.

8 The LORD is the strength of his people,
 a fortress of salvation for his anointed
 one.
9 Save your people and bless your
 inheritance;
 be their shepherd and carry them
 forever.

Psalm 29
A psalm of David.

1 Ascribe to the LORD, O mighty ones,
 ascribe to the LORD glory and strength.
2 Ascribe to the LORD the glory due his
 name;
 worship the LORD in the splendor of his*a*
 holiness.

3 The voice of the LORD is over the waters;
 the God of glory thunders,
 the LORD thunders over the mighty
 waters.
4 The voice of the LORD is powerful;
 the voice of the LORD is majestic.
5 The voice of the LORD breaks the cedars;
 the LORD breaks in pieces the cedars of
 Lebanon.
6 He makes Lebanon skip like a calf,
 Sirion*b* like a young wild ox.
7 The voice of the LORD strikes
 with flashes of lightning.
8 The voice of the LORD shakes the desert;
 the LORD shakes the Desert of Kadesh.
9 The voice of the LORD twists the oaks*c*
 and strips the forests bare.
 And in his temple all cry, "Glory!"

10 The LORD sits*d* enthroned over the flood;
 the LORD is enthroned as King forever.
11 The LORD gives strength to his people;
 the LORD blesses his people with peace.

Psalm 30
A psalm. A song. For the dedication of the temple.*e*
Of David.

1 I will exalt you, O LORD,
 for you lifted me out of the depths
 and did not let my enemies gloat over
 me.
2 O LORD my God, I called to you for help
 and you healed me.
3 O LORD, you brought me up from the
 grave*f*;
 you spared me from going down into
 the pit.

4 Sing to the LORD, you saints of his;
 praise his holy name.
5 For his anger lasts only a moment,
 but his favor lasts a lifetime;
 weeping may remain for a night,
 but rejoicing comes in the morning.

6 When I felt secure, I said,
 "I will never be shaken."
7 O LORD, when you favored me,
 you made my mountain*g* stand firm;
 but when you hid your face,
 I was dismayed.

8 To you, O LORD, I called;
 to the Lord I cried for mercy:
9 "What gain is there in my destruction,*h*
 in my going down into the pit?
 Will the dust praise you?
 Will it proclaim your faithfulness?
10 Hear, O LORD, and be merciful to me;
 O LORD, be my help."

11 You turned my wailing into dancing;
 you removed my sackcloth and clothed
 me with joy,
12 that my heart may sing to you and not be
 silent.
 O LORD my God, I will give you thanks
 forever.

Psalm 31
For the director of music. A psalm of David.

1 In you, O LORD, I have taken refuge;
 let me never be put to shame;
 deliver me in your righteousness.
2 Turn your ear to me,

---

*a*2 Or *LORD with the splendor of*   *b*6 That is, Mount Hermon   *c*9 Or *LORD makes the deer give birth*   *d*10 Or *sat*   *e*Title: Or *palace*
*f*3 Hebrew *Sheol*   *g*7 Or *hill country*   *h*9 Or *there if I am silenced*

come quickly to my rescue;
be my rock of refuge,
a strong fortress to save me.
³ Since you are my rock and my fortress,
for the sake of your name lead and guide
me.
⁴ Free me from the trap that is set for me,
for you are my refuge.
⁵ Into your hands I commit
my spirit;
redeem me, O Lord, the
God of truth.

⁶ I hate those who cling to
worthless idols;
I trust in the Lord.
⁷ I will be glad and rejoice in
your love,
for you saw my affliction
and knew the anguish of
my soul.
⁸ You have not handed me
over to the enemy
but have set my feet in a
spacious place.

⁹ Be merciful to me, O Lord, for I am in
distress;
my eyes grow weak with sorrow,
my soul and my body with grief.
¹⁰ My life is consumed by anguish
and my years by groaning;
my strength fails because of my affliction,ᵃ
and my bones grow weak.
¹¹ Because of all my enemies,
I am the utter contempt of my
neighbors;
I am a dread to my friends—
those who see me on the street flee from
me.
¹² I am forgotten by them as though I were
dead;
I have become like broken pottery.
¹³ For I hear the slander of many;
there is terror on every side;
they conspire against me
and plot to take my life.
¹⁴ But I trust in you, O Lord;
I say, "You are my God."

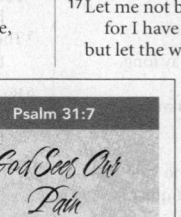

Psalm 31:7

God Sees Our Pain

I will be glad and
rejoice in your love,
for you saw my affliction
and knew the anguish
of my soul.

¹⁵ My times are in your hands;
deliver me from my enemies
and from those who pursue me.
¹⁶ Let your face shine on your servant;
save me in your unfailing love.
¹⁷ Let me not be put to shame, O Lord,
for I have cried out to you;
but let the wicked be put to shame
and lie silent in the
grave.ᵇ
¹⁸ Let their lying lips be
silenced,
for with pride and
contempt
they speak arrogantly
against the
righteous.

¹⁹ How great is your
goodness,
which you have stored
up for those who
fear you,
which you bestow in the
sight of men
on those who take refuge in you.
²⁰ In the shelter of your presence you hide
them
from the intrigues of men;
in your dwelling you keep them safe
from accusing tongues.

²¹ Praise be to the Lord,
for he showed his wonderful love to me
when I was in a besieged city.
²² In my alarm I said,
"I am cut off from your sight!"
Yet you heard my cry for mercy
when I called to you for help.

²³ Love the Lord, all his saints!
The Lord preserves the faithful,
but the proud he pays back in full.
²⁴ Be strong and take heart,
all you who hope in the Lord.

Psalm 32
Of David. A *maskil*.ᶜ

¹ Blessed is he
whose transgressions are forgiven,

ᵃ10 Or *guilt*   ᵇ17 Hebrew *Sheol*   ᶜTitle: Probably a literary or musical term

whose sins are covered.
²Blessed is the man
whose sin the LORD does not count
against him
and in whose spirit is no deceit.

³When I kept silent,
my bones wasted away
through my groaning all day long.
⁴For day and night
your hand was heavy upon me;
my strength was sapped
as in the heat of summer. *Selah*

⁵Then I acknowledged my sin to you
and did not cover up my iniquity.
I said, "I will confess
my transgressions to the LORD"—
and you forgave
the guilt of my
sin. *Selah*

⁶Therefore let everyone who
is godly pray to you
while you may be found;
surely when the mighty
waters rise,
they will not reach him.
⁷You are my hiding place;
you will protect me from
trouble
and surround me with
songs of deliverance. *Selah*

⁸I will instruct you and teach you in the way
you should go;
I will counsel you and watch over you.
⁹Do not be like the horse or the mule,
which have no understanding
but must be controlled by bit and bridle
or they will not come to you.
¹⁰Many are the woes of the wicked,
but the LORD's unfailing love
surrounds the man who trusts in him.

¹¹Rejoice in the LORD and be glad, you
righteous;
sing, all you who are upright in heart!

Psalm 33

¹Sing joyfully to the LORD, you righteous;
it is fitting for the upright to praise him.
²Praise the LORD with the harp;

make music to him on the ten-stringed
lyre.
³Sing to him a new song;
play skillfully, and shout for joy.

⁴For the word of the LORD is right and true;
he is faithful in all he does.
⁵The LORD loves righteousness and justice;
the earth is full of his unfailing love.

⁶By the word of the LORD were the heavens
made,
their starry host by the breath of his
mouth.
⁷He gathers the waters of the sea into jars[a];
he puts the deep into storehouses.
⁸Let all the earth fear the LORD;
let all the people of the
world revere him.
⁹For he spoke, and it came
to be;
he commanded, and it
stood firm.
¹⁰The LORD foils the plans of
the nations;
he thwarts the purposes
of the peoples.
¹¹But the plans of the LORD
stand firm forever,
the purposes of his
heart through all
generations.

¹²Blessed is the nation whose God is the
LORD,
the people he chose for his inheritance.
¹³From heaven the LORD looks down
and sees all mankind;
¹⁴from his dwelling place he watches
all who live on earth—
¹⁵he who forms the hearts of all,
who considers everything they do.
¹⁶No king is saved by the size of his army;
no warrior escapes by his great strength.
¹⁷A horse is a vain hope for deliverance;
despite all its great strength it cannot
save.
¹⁸But the eyes of the LORD are on those who
fear him,
on those whose hope is in his unfailing
love,

> **Psalm 32:8**
>
> *God Counsels Us*
>
> I will instruct you and
> teach you in the way
> you should go;
> I will counsel you and
> watch over you.

---

[a]7 Or *sea as into a heap*

¹⁹ to deliver them from death
 and keep them alive in famine.

²⁰ We wait in hope for the LORD;
 he is our help and our shield.
²¹ In him our hearts rejoice,
 for we trust in his holy name.
²² May your unfailing love rest upon us,
 O LORD,
 even as we put our hope in you.

Psalm 34[a]

Of David. When he pretended to be insane before
Abimelech, who drove him away, and he left.

¹ I will extol the LORD at all times;
 his praise will always be on my lips.
² My soul will boast in the LORD;
 let the afflicted hear and rejoice.
³ Glorify the LORD with me;
 let us exalt his name together.

⁴ I sought the LORD, and he answered me;
 he delivered me from all my fears.
⁵ Those who look to him are radiant;
 their faces are never covered with shame.
⁶ This poor man called, and the LORD heard
 him;
 he saved him out of all his troubles.
⁷ The angel of the LORD encamps around
 those who fear him,
 and he delivers them.

⁸ Taste and see that the LORD is good;
 blessed is the man who takes refuge in
 him.
⁹ Fear the LORD, you his saints,
 for those who fear him lack nothing.
¹⁰ The lions may grow weak and hungry,
 but those who seek the LORD lack no
 good thing.

¹¹ Come, my children, listen to me;
 I will teach you the fear of the LORD.
¹² Whoever of you loves life
 and desires to see many good days,
¹³ keep your tongue from evil
 and your lips from speaking lies.
¹⁴ Turn from evil and do good;
 seek peace and pursue it.

¹⁵ The eyes of the LORD are on the righteous
 and his ears are attentive to their cry;

¹⁶ the face of the LORD is against those who
 do evil,
 to cut off the memory of them from the
 earth.

¹⁷ The righteous cry out, and the LORD hears
 them;
 he delivers them from all their troubles.
¹⁸ The LORD is close to the brokenhearted
 and saves those who are crushed in
 spirit.

¹⁹ A righteous man may have many troubles,
 but the LORD delivers him from them
 all;
²⁰ he protects all his bones,
 not one of them will be broken.

²¹ Evil will slay the wicked;
 the foes of the righteous will be
 condemned.
²² The LORD redeems his servants;
 no one will be condemned who takes
 refuge in him.

Psalm 35

Of David.

¹ Contend, O LORD, with those who contend
 with me;
 fight against those who fight against me.
² Take up shield and buckler;
 arise and come to my aid.
³ Brandish spear and javelin[b]
 against those who pursue me.
 Say to my soul,
 "I am your salvation."

⁴ May those who seek my life
 be disgraced and put to shame;
 may those who plot my ruin
 be turned back in dismay.
⁵ May they be like chaff before the wind,
 with the angel of the LORD driving them
 away;
⁶ may their path be dark and slippery,
 with the angel of the LORD pursuing
 them.
⁷ Since they hid their net for me without
 cause
 and without cause dug a pit for me,
⁸ may ruin overtake them by surprise—

---

[a] This psalm is an acrostic poem, the verses of which begin with the successive letters of the Hebrew alphabet.   [b] 3 Or *and block the way*

may the net they hid entangle them,
    may they fall into the pit, to their ruin.
9 Then my soul will rejoice in the LORD
    and delight in his salvation.
10 My whole being will exclaim,
    "Who is like you, O LORD?
    You rescue the poor from those too strong
        for them,
    the poor and needy from those who rob
        them."

11 Ruthless witnesses come forward;
    they question me on things I know
        nothing about.
12 They repay me evil for good
    and leave my soul forlorn.
13 Yet when they were ill, I put on sackcloth
    and humbled myself with fasting.
    When my prayers returned to me
        unanswered,
14   I went about mourning
        as though for my friend or brother.
    I bowed my head in grief
        as though weeping for my mother.
15 But when I stumbled, they gathered in
        glee;
    attackers gathered against me when I
        was unaware.
    They slandered me without ceasing.
16 Like the ungodly they maliciously
        mocked[a];
    they gnashed their teeth at me.
17 O Lord, how long will you look on?
    Rescue my life from their ravages,
    my precious life from these lions.
18 I will give you thanks in the great
        assembly;
    among throngs of people I will praise
        you.

19 Let not those gloat over me
    who are my enemies without cause;
    let not those who hate me without reason
        maliciously wink the eye.
20 They do not speak peaceably,
    but devise false accusations
        against those who live quietly in the
            land.
21 They gape at me and say, "Aha! Aha!
    With our own eyes we have seen it."

22 O LORD, you have seen this; be not silent.
    Do not be far from me, O Lord.
23 Awake, and rise to my defense!
    Contend for me, my God and Lord.
24 Vindicate me in your righteousness,
        O LORD my God;
    do not let them gloat over me.
25 Do not let them think, "Aha, just what we
        wanted!"
    or say, "We have swallowed him up."

26 May all who gloat over my distress
    be put to shame and confusion;
    may all who exalt themselves over me
    be clothed with shame and disgrace.
27 May those who delight in my vindication
    shout for joy and gladness;
    may they always say, "The LORD be exalted,
    who delights in the well-being of his
        servant."
28 My tongue will speak of your
        righteousness
    and of your praises all day long.

Psalm 36

For the director of music. Of David the servant of
the LORD.

1 An oracle is within my heart
    concerning the sinfulness of the
        wicked:[b]
    There is no fear of God
    before his eyes.
2 For in his own eyes he flatters himself
    too much to detect or hate his sin.
3 The words of his mouth are wicked and
        deceitful;
    he has ceased to be wise and to do good.
4 Even on his bed he plots evil;
    he commits himself to a sinful course
    and does not reject what is wrong.

5 Your love, O LORD, reaches to the heavens,
    your faithfulness to the skies.
6 Your righteousness is like the mighty
        mountains,
    your justice like the great deep.
    O LORD, you preserve both man and
        beast.
7   How priceless is your unfailing love!
    Both high and low among men

---

[a]16 Septuagint; Hebrew may mean *ungodly circle of mockers.* [b]1 Or *heart: / Sin proceeds from the wicked.*

find[a] refuge in the shadow of your wings.
8 They feast on the abundance of your house;
you give them drink
from your river of
delights.
9 For with you is the fountain
of life;
in your light we see light.

10 Continue your love to those
who know you,
your righteousness to the
upright in heart.
11 May the foot of the proud
not come against
me,
nor the hand of the
wicked drive me away.
12 See how the evildoers lie fallen—
thrown down, not able to rise!

Psalm 37[b]
Of David.

1 Do not fret because of evil men
or be envious of those who do wrong;
2 for like the grass they will soon wither,
like green plants they will soon die away.

3 Trust in the LORD and do good;
dwell in the land and enjoy safe pasture.
4 Delight yourself in the LORD
and he will give you the desires of your
heart.

5 Commit your way to the LORD;
trust in him and he will do this:
6 He will make your righteousness shine like
the dawn,
the justice of your cause like the
noonday sun.

7 Be still before the LORD and wait patiently
for him;
do not fret when men succeed in their
ways,
when they carry out their wicked
schemes.

8 Refrain from anger and turn from wrath;
do not fret—it leads only to evil.
9 For evil men will be cut off,

but those who hope in the LORD will
inherit the land.

10 A little while, and the
wicked will be no
more;
though you look for
them, they will not
be found.
11 But the meek will inherit
the land
and enjoy great peace.

12 The wicked plot against the
righteous
and gnash their teeth at
them;
13 but the Lord laughs at the wicked,
for he knows their day is coming.

14 The wicked draw the sword
and bend the bow
to bring down the poor and needy,
to slay those whose ways are upright.
15 But their swords will pierce their own
hearts,
and their bows will be broken.

16 Better the little that the righteous have
than the wealth of many wicked;
17 for the power of the wicked will be
broken,
but the LORD upholds the righteous.

18 The days of the blameless are known to the
LORD,
and their inheritance will endure
forever.
19 In times of disaster they will not wither;
in days of famine they will enjoy
plenty.

20 But the wicked will perish:
The LORD's enemies will be like the
beauty of the fields,
they will vanish—vanish like smoke.

21 The wicked borrow and do not repay,
but the righteous give generously;
22 those the LORD blesses will inherit the
land,
but those he curses will be cut off.

Psalm 36:5

God Offers Loyalty

Your love, O LORD,
reaches to the heavens,
your faithfulness
to the skies.

---

[a]7 Or *love, O God! / Men find*; or *love! / Both heavenly beings and men / find*   [b]This psalm is an acrostic poem, the stanzas of which begin with the successive letters of the Hebrew alphabet.

Psalm 37:1–2

Do not fret because of
evil men or be envious
of those who do wrong;
for like the grass they
will soon wither,
like green plants they
will soon die away.

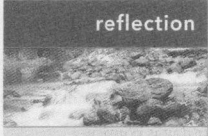

reflection

1 When have you suffered from injustice?

2 How did you react to the situation?

3 What do you need to do to learn to trust God more?

RELATED READINGS

Genesis 50:15–21;
Psalm 1:1–6;
Romans 8:18–28

Read: Psalm 37:1–11

BEING THE VICTIM OF INJUSTICE can test the very roots of our faith. Lori discovered this when her husband, Sam, was accused of animal abuse the winter several of his cattle died in a blizzard. Although autopsies revealed the animals had been well fed, a key defense witness wasn't allowed to testify and important evidence was not submitted. Still, Lori and Sam trusted the jury to sift through the case and find him innocent. Instead, he was convicted and sentenced to five years probation and a large fine. They could have allowed bitterness and anger to cloud their lives, but instead they chose to hang on to the promises of God that David describes in Psalm 37.

Almost everyone at one time or another has experienced a situation where they find themselves saying, "That's not fair!" The psalmist faced such a situation when he saw his enemies prosper while he suffered. David, however, turned his focus to God; he found hope in knowing that God would set things right. What was the path David took to finding peace in the midst of injustice?

♦ "Trust in the LORD." Every event in our lives—good and bad—is filtered through God's sovereign hands. We can trust God to use for our good anything that others intend as evil.

♦ "Do good." Whatever happens, despite the injustices that we suffer, we are to choose the higher path that demonstrates God's Spirit within us.

♦ "Dwell in the land." Though we may feel like running away from conflict or trying to hide from challenges, doing so robs us of experiencing how God can provide a place of rest and safety: "I will lie down and sleep in peace, for you alone, O LORD, make me dwell in safety" (Psalm 4:8).

♦ "Delight yourself in the LORD." Rather than getting depressed about our tough situation, turning our thoughts to God's presence and singing his praise songs will lift our spirits.

♦ "Commit your way to the LORD." We can decide to follow God, regardless of what others do or say.

♦ "Be still before the LORD." We can afford a lifetime of patience, for we know that God will make things right. He is a just God who will one day rule and reign with complete fairness and impartiality.

Go to page 679 for your next devotional reading.

23 If the LORD delights in a man's way,
  he makes his steps firm;
24 though he stumble, he will not fall,
  for the LORD upholds him with his
    hand.

25 I was young and now I am old,
  yet I have never seen the righteous
    forsaken
  or their children begging bread.
26 They are always generous and lend freely;
  their children will be blessed.

27 Turn from evil and do good;
  then you will dwell in the land forever.
28 For the LORD loves the just
  and will not forsake his faithful ones.

  They will be protected forever,
    but the offspring of the wicked will be
      cut off;
29 the righteous will inherit the land
  and dwell in it forever.

30 The mouth of the righteous man utters
    wisdom,
  and his tongue speaks what is just.
31 The law of his God is in his heart;
  his feet do not slip.

32 The wicked lie in wait for the righteous,
  seeking their very lives;
33 but the LORD will not leave
    them in their power
  or let them be
    condemned when
    brought to trial.

34 Wait for the LORD
    and keep his way.
  He will exalt you to inherit
    the land;
  when the wicked are cut
    off, you will see it.

35 I have seen a wicked and
    ruthless man
  flourishing like a green
    tree in its native soil,
36 but he soon passed away and was no more;
  though I looked for him, he could not
    be found.

37 Consider the blameless, observe the
    upright;
  there is a future[a] for the man of peace.
38 But all sinners will be destroyed;
  the future[b] of the wicked will be cut off.

39 The salvation of the righteous comes from
    the LORD;
  he is their stronghold in time of trouble.
40 The LORD helps them and delivers them;
  he delivers them from the wicked and
    saves them,
  because they take refuge in him.

Psalm 38

A psalm of David. A petition.

1 O LORD, do not rebuke me in your anger
  or discipline me in your wrath.
2 For your arrows have pierced me,
  and your hand has come down upon me.
3 Because of your wrath there is no health in
    my body;
  my bones have no soundness because of
    my sin.
4 My guilt has overwhelmed me
  like a burden too heavy to bear.

5 My wounds fester and are loathsome
  because of my sinful folly.
6 I am bowed down and brought very low;
  all day long I go about mourning.
7 My back is filled with
    searing pain;
  there is no health in my
    body.
8 I am feeble and utterly
    crushed;
  I groan in anguish of
    heart.

9 All my longings lie open
    before you, O Lord;
  my sighing is not hidden
    from you.
10 My heart pounds, my
    strength fails me;
  even the light has gone
    from my eyes.
11 My friends and companions avoid me
    because of my wounds;
  my neighbors stay far away.

Psalm 38:9

God Knows Our Desires

All my longings lie open
before you, O LORD;
my sighing is not hidden
from you.

---

a 37 Or there will be posterity   b 38 Or posterity

¹²Those who seek my life set their traps,
  those who would harm me talk of my
    ruin;
  all day long they plot deception.

¹³I am like a deaf man, who cannot hear,
  like a mute, who cannot open his
    mouth;
¹⁴I have become like a man who does not
    hear,
  whose mouth can offer no reply.

¹⁵I wait for you, O Lord;
  you will answer, O Lord my God.
¹⁶For I said, "Do not let them gloat
  or exalt themselves over me when my
    foot slips."

¹⁷For I am about to fall,
  and my pain is ever with me.
¹⁸I confess my iniquity;
  I am troubled by my sin.
¹⁹Many are those who are my vigorous
    enemies;
  those who hate me
    without reason are
    numerous.
²⁰Those who repay my good
    with evil
  slander me when I
    pursue what is
    good.

²¹O Lord, do not forsake me;
  be not far from me, O my
    God.
²²Come quickly to help me,
  O Lord my Savior.

Psalm 39

For the director of music. For Jeduthun. A psalm
of David.

¹I said, "I will watch my ways
  and keep my tongue from sin;
  I will put a muzzle on my mouth
    as long as the wicked are in my
    presence."
²But when I was silent and still,
  not even saying anything good,
  my anguish increased.
³My heart grew hot within me,
  and as I meditated, the fire burned;
  then I spoke with my tongue:

⁴"Show me, O Lord, my life's end
  and the number of my days;
  let me know how fleeting is my life.
⁵You have made my days a mere
    handbreadth;
  the span of my years is as nothing before
    you.
  Each man's life is but a breath.   *Selah*
⁶Man is a mere phantom as he goes to and
    fro:
  He bustles about, but only in vain;
  he heaps up wealth, not knowing who
    will get it.

⁷"But now, Lord, what do I look for?
  My hope is in you.
⁸Save me from all my transgressions;
  do not make me the scorn of fools.
⁹I was silent; I would not open my mouth,
  for you are the one who has done this.
¹⁰Remove your scourge from me;
  I am overcome by the blow of your
    hand.
¹¹You rebuke and discipline
    men for their sin;
  you consume their
    wealth like a
    moth—
  each man is but a breath.
                      Selah

¹²"Hear my prayer, O Lord,
    listen to my cry for help;
    be not deaf to my
    weeping.
  For I dwell with you as an
    alien,
  a stranger, as all my fathers were.
¹³Look away from me, that I may rejoice
    again
  before I depart and am no more."

> ### Psalm 39:12
>
> *God Knows Our Needs*
>
> Hear my prayer, O Lord,
> listen to my cry for help;
> be not deaf to
> my weeping.

Psalm 40

For the director of music. Of David. A psalm.

¹I waited patiently for the Lord;
  he turned to me and heard my cry.
²He lifted me out of the slimy pit,
  out of the mud and mire;
  he set my feet on a rock
    and gave me a firm place to stand.
³He put a new song in my mouth,
  a hymn of praise to our God.

A Second Chance at Love

ABIGAIL

"HOW DID A SMART WOMAN like you end up with a man like Nabal?"

It wasn't the first time Abigail had heard a question like that. Even when people didn't have the nerve to ask it outright, Abigail knew what they were thinking. And she agreed. A brash, outspoken nitwit, Nabal was not exactly a perfect match for her.

Where he was quick to anger, she thought of herself as more of a slow boil. Whereas he reacted, she preferred to patiently contemplate her next move. No one ever had to guess what Nabal was thinking. His mouth ran ahead of his thoughts on a regular basis. Not Abigail. She liked choosing her words carefully—which is why it was so frustrating that his indiscretions always landed both of them in trouble.

"I don't know how you remain so patient," said her friends, looking at her with pity.

"Couldn't you just kill him when he acts like that?" inquired others sarcastically.

Even when Nabal insulted David, and she could have allowed him to suffer for his actions, she wouldn't let herself do it. She couldn't, even though she knew many women would have been happy to sit back and watch their husbands reap the consequences of their actions. But there were too many other issues at stake, too many other people whose lives depended on her husband. She gathered up her supplies and rushed to her donkey.

It wasn't the first time she'd had to clean up after him—something an outspoken neighbor rudely emphasized as Abigail rushed to meet David with a peace offering to cover Nabal's latest offense. "And it won't be the *last* time either . . ." she added as Abigail made her way down the pathway.

But it was.

—Prayer—
Help me to be faithful, Lord, wherever you've called me to be.

May my lord pay no attention to that wicked man Nabal. He is just like his name— his name is Fool, and folly goes with him.

1 Samuel 25:25

ASSIGNED READING:

1 Samuel 25:1–44

Go to page 682 for your next devotional reading.

Weekend

Many will see and fear
and put their trust in the Lord.

4 Blessed is the man
who makes the Lord his trust,
who does not look to the proud,
to those who turn aside to false gods.*a*

5 Many, O Lord my God,
are the wonders you have done.
The things you planned for us
no one can recount to you;
were I to speak and tell of them,
they would be too many to declare.

6 Sacrifice and offering you did not desire,
but my ears you have pierced*b,c*;
burnt offerings and sin offerings
you did not require.

7 Then I said, "Here I am, I have come—
it is written about me in the scroll.*d*

8 I desire to do your will, O my God;
your law is within my heart."

9 I proclaim righteousness in the great
assembly;
I do not seal my lips,
as you know, O Lord.

10 I do not hide your righteousness in my
heart;
I speak of your faithfulness and
salvation.
I do not conceal your love and your truth
from the great assembly.

11 Do not withhold your mercy from me,
O Lord;
may your love and your truth always
protect me.

12 For troubles without number surround me;
my sins have overtaken me, and I
cannot see.
They are more than the hairs of my head,
and my heart fails within me.

13 Be pleased, O Lord, to save me;
O Lord, come quickly to help me.

14 May all who seek to take my life
be put to shame and confusion;
may all who desire my ruin
be turned back in disgrace.

15 May those who say to me, "Aha! Aha!"

be appalled at their own shame.

16 But may all who seek you
rejoice and be glad in you;
may those who love your salvation always
say,
"The Lord be exalted!"

17 Yet I am poor and needy;
may the Lord think of me.
You are my help and my deliverer;
O my God, do not delay.

Psalm 41
For the director of music. A psalm of David.

1 Blessed is he who has regard for the weak;
the Lord delivers him in times of
trouble.

2 The Lord will protect him and preserve
his life;
he will bless him in the land
and not surrender him to the desire of
his foes.

3 The Lord will sustain him on his sickbed
and restore him from his bed of illness.

4 I said, "O Lord, have mercy on me;
heal me, for I have sinned against you."

5 My enemies say of me in malice,
"When will he die and his name
perish?"

6 Whenever one comes to see me,
he speaks falsely, while his heart gathers
slander;
then he goes out and spreads it abroad.

7 All my enemies whisper together against
me;
they imagine the worst for me, saying,

8 "A vile disease has beset him;
he will never get up from the place
where he lies."

9 Even my close friend, whom I trusted,
he who shared my bread,
has lifted up his heel against me.

10 But you, O Lord, have mercy on me;
raise me up, that I may repay them.

11 I know that you are pleased with me,
for my enemy does not triumph over me.

12 In my integrity you uphold me
and set me in your presence forever.

---

*a*4 Or *to falsehood*   *b*6 Hebrew; Septuagint *but a body you have prepared for me* (see also Symmachus and Theodotion)   *c*6 Or *opened*
*d*7 Or *come / with the scroll written for me*

13 Praise be to the LORD, the God of Israel,
　from everlasting to everlasting.
　　Amen and Amen.

BOOK II
Psalms 42–72

Psalm 42[a]
For the director of music.
A *maskil*[b] of the Sons of Korah.

1 As the deer pants for streams of water,
　so my soul pants for you, O God.
2 My soul thirsts for God, for the living God.
　When can I go and meet
　　with God?
3 My tears have been my food
　　day and night,
　while men say to me all day
　　long,
　　"Where is your God?"
4 These things I remember
　as I pour out my soul:
how I used to go with the
　　multitude,
　leading the procession to
　　the house of God,
with shouts of joy and
　　thanksgiving
　　among the festive
　　throng.

5 Why are you downcast, O my soul?
　Why so disturbed within me?
Put your hope in God,
　for I will yet praise him,
　my Savior and 6my God.

My[c] soul is downcast within me;
　therefore I will remember you
from the land of the Jordan,
　the heights of Hermon—from Mount
　　Mizar.
7 Deep calls to deep
　in the roar of your waterfalls;
all your waves and breakers
　have swept over me.

8 By day the LORD directs his love,
　at night his song is with me—
　a prayer to the God of my life.

9 I say to God my Rock,
　"Why have you forgotten me?
Why must I go about mourning,
　oppressed by the enemy?"
10 My bones suffer mortal agony
　as my foes taunt me,
saying to me all day long,
　"Where is your God?"

11 Why are you downcast, O my soul?
　Why so disturbed within me?
Put your hope in God,
　for I will yet praise him,
　my Savior and my God.

Psalm 43[a]
1 Vindicate me, O God,
　and plead my cause
　　against an ungodly
　　nation;
　rescue me from deceitful
　　and wicked men.
2 You are God my
　　stronghold.
　Why have you rejected
　　me?
Why must I go about
　　mourning,
　oppressed by the enemy?
3 Send forth your light and
　　your truth,
　let them guide me;
let them bring me to your holy mountain,
　to the place where you dwell.
4 Then will I go to the altar of God,
　to God, my joy and my delight.
I will praise you with the harp,
　O God, my God.

5 Why are you downcast, O my soul?
　Why so disturbed within me?
Put your hope in God,
　for I will yet praise him,
　my Savior and my God.

Psalm 44
For the director of music. Of the Sons of Korah.
A *maskil*.[b]

1 We have heard with our ears, O God;
　our fathers have told us

Psalm 43:3

God Brings Us to Him

Send forth your light
and your truth,
let them guide me;
let them bring me to
your holy mountain,
to the place where
you dwell.

---

a In many Hebrew manuscripts Psalms 42 and 43 constitute one psalm.　b Title: Probably a literary or musical term
c 5,6 A few Hebrew manuscripts, Septuagint and Syriac; most Hebrew manuscripts *praise him for his saving help.* / 6 O my God, my

From Despair to Hope

Psalm 42:5

Why are you downcast,
O my soul? Why so
disturbed within me?
Put your hope in God,
for I will yet praise him,
my Savior and my God.

reflection

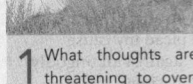

1 What thoughts are threatening to overflow and leave you feeling hopeless?

2 What words does your soul need to hear right now?

3 What are some specific reasons why you can hope in God? Spend some time meditating on God's loving-kindness, goodness, power, faithfulness and mercy. Practice sitting quietly in his presence.

RELATED READINGS

Psalm 27:13–14; 43:1–5;
84:1–12;
Hebrews 6:13–20

Read: Psalm 42:1–11

THROUGHOUT THE DAY, many thoughts flow through our minds—from what we will cook for dinner to wondering if our friend's struggling marriage will survive. In the midst of our thinking, an undercurrent of despair can creep in while we watch the nightly news, hear of a cancer diagnosis, sort out a misunderstanding or deal with whatever we're facing that day.

Exiled north to Jordan and overflowing with a longing to return to Jerusalem, the psalmist voiced his deep sadness. Rather than denying or minimizing his pain, he clearly identified his sorrow and proclaimed his thirst for God.

Then what? The psalmist spoke to his soul! Was he mad? Did he have a personality disorder? No! He practiced the secret to overcoming hopelessness—the hopelessness that can trickle into our hearts and minds until we find ourselves in the rushing current, tumbling toward a waterfall of despair. Three times in Psalms 42 and 43, the psalmist admonishes his soul to "hope in God, for I will yet praise him!"

The psalmist encouraged his soul to praise God—in other words, to acknowledge, affirm and adore God's character, even when he was feeling downcast in spirit or disturbed in heart. Our souls need similar encouragement. When we choose to dwell upon God's character, we always have something to praise him about: his loving-kindness, goodness, power, faithfulness and mercy. If we want to bolster our souls with hope, we can start by filling our mouths with praise. When we choose to dwell on God's light and truth, our souls can overflow with the comfort of being guided by God (see Psalm 43:3). When we choose to live close to God's heart, we overflow with delight and joy (see verse 4).

If you are submerged in pain, sorrow, despair or confusion, maybe you need to give your soul a good talking to. What will you say?

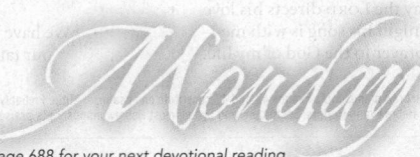

Monday

Go to page 688 for your next devotional reading.

what you did in their days,
  in days long ago.
2 With your hand you drove out the nations
    and planted our fathers;
  you crushed the peoples
    and made our fathers flourish.
3 It was not by their sword that they won the
    land,
  nor did their arm bring them victory;
  it was your right hand, your arm,
    and the light of your face, for you loved
      them.

4 You are my King and my God,
    who decrees*a* victories for Jacob.
5 Through you we push back our enemies;
    through your name we trample our foes.
6 I do not trust in my bow,
    my sword does not bring me victory;
7 but you give us victory over our enemies,
    you put our adversaries to shame.
8 In God we make our boast all day long,
    and we will praise your name
      forever.   *Selah*

9 But now you have rejected and humbled
    us;
  you no longer go out with our armies.
10 You made us retreat before the enemy,
    and our adversaries have plundered us.
11 You gave us up to be devoured like sheep
    and have scattered us among the nations.
12 You sold your people for a pittance,
    gaining nothing from their sale.

13 You have made us a reproach to our
    neighbors,
  the scorn and derision of those around
    us.
14 You have made us a byword among the
    nations;
  the peoples shake their heads at us.
15 My disgrace is before me all day long,
    and my face is covered with shame
16 at the taunts of those who reproach and
    revile me,
  because of the enemy, who is bent on
    revenge.

17 All this happened to us,
    though we had not forgotten you

or been false to your covenant.
18 Our hearts had not turned back;
    our feet had not strayed from your path.
19 But you crushed us and made us a haunt
    for jackals
  and covered us over with deep darkness.

20 If we had forgotten the name of our God
    or spread out our hands to a foreign god,
21 would not God have discovered it,
    since he knows the secrets of the heart?
22 Yet for your sake we face death all day
    long;
  we are considered as sheep to be
    slaughtered.

23 Awake, O Lord! Why do you sleep?
    Rouse yourself! Do not reject us forever.
24 Why do you hide your face
    and forget our misery and oppression?

25 We are brought down to the dust;
    our bodies cling to the ground.
26 Rise up and help us;
    redeem us because of your unfailing
      love.

Psalm 45

For the director of music. To the tune of, "Lilies."
Of the Sons of Korah. A *maskil.b* A wedding song.

1 My heart is stirred by a noble theme
    as I recite my verses for the king;
  my tongue is the pen of a skillful
    writer.

2 You are the most excellent of men
    and your lips have been anointed with
      grace,
  since God has blessed you forever.
3 Gird your sword upon your side, O mighty
    one;
  clothe yourself with splendor and
    majesty.
4 In your majesty ride forth victoriously
    in behalf of truth, humility and
      righteousness;
  let your right hand display awesome
    deeds.
5 Let your sharp arrows pierce the hearts of
    the king's enemies;
  let the nations fall beneath your feet.

---

*a*4 Septuagint, Aquila and Syriac; Hebrew *King, O God; / command* *b*Title: Probably a literary or musical term

⁶ Your throne, O God, will last for ever and
ever;
a scepter of justice will be the scepter of
your kingdom.
⁷ You love righteousness and hate
wickedness;
therefore God, your God, has set
you above your
companions
by anointing you with
the oil of joy.
⁸ All your robes are fragrant
with myrrh and
aloes and cassia;
from palaces adorned
with ivory
the music of the strings
makes you glad.
⁹ Daughters of kings are
among your
honored women;
at your right hand is the
royal bride in gold of Ophir.

¹⁰ Listen, O daughter, consider and give ear:
Forget your people and your father's
house.
¹¹ The king is enthralled by your beauty;
honor him, for he is your lord.
¹² The Daughter of Tyre will come with a
gift,ᵃ
men of wealth will seek your favor.

¹³ All glorious is the princess within her
chamber;
her gown is interwoven with gold.
¹⁴ In embroidered garments she is led to the
king;
her virgin companions follow her
and are brought to you.
¹⁵ They are led in with joy and gladness;
they enter the palace of the king.

¹⁶ Your sons will take the place of your fathers;
you will make them princes throughout
the land.
¹⁷ I will perpetuate your memory through all
generations;
therefore the nations will praise you for
ever and ever.

Psalm 46:1

*God Is Our
Strength*

God is our refuge
and strength,
an ever-present help
in trouble.

Psalm 46

For the director of music. Of the Sons of Korah.
According to *alamoth*.ᵇ A song.

¹ God is our refuge and strength,
an ever-present help in trouble.
² Therefore we will not fear, though the
earth give way
and the mountains fall
into the heart of the
sea,
³ though its waters roar and
foam
and the mountains
quake with their
surging.   *Selah*

⁴ There is a river whose
streams make glad
the city of God,
the holy place where the
Most High dwells.
⁵ God is within her, she will
not fall;
God will help her at break of day.
⁶ Nations are in uproar, kingdoms fall;
he lifts his voice, the earth melts.

⁷ The LORD Almighty is with us;
the God of Jacob is our fortress.   *Selah*

⁸ Come and see the works of the LORD,
the desolations he has brought on the
earth.
⁹ He makes wars cease to the ends of the
earth;
he breaks the bow and shatters the
spear,
he burns the shieldsᶜ with fire.
¹⁰ "Be still, and know that I am God;
I will be exalted among the nations,
I will be exalted in the earth."

¹¹ The LORD Almighty is with us;
the God of Jacob is our fortress.   *Selah*

Psalm 47

For the director of music. Of the Sons of Korah.
A psalm.

¹ Clap your hands, all you nations;
shout to God with cries of joy.
² How awesome is the LORD Most High,

ᵃ12 Or *A Tyrian robe is among the gifts*   ᵇTitle: Probably a musical term   ᶜ9 Or *chariots*

the great King over all the earth!
³ He subdued nations under us,
    peoples under our feet.
⁴ He chose our inheritance for us,
    the pride of Jacob, whom he
        loved.   *Selah*

⁵ God has ascended amid shouts of joy,
    the LORD amid the sounding of
        trumpets.
⁶ Sing praises to God, sing praises;
    sing praises to our King, sing praises.

⁷ For God is the King of all
        the earth;
    sing to him a psalm*ᵃ* of
        praise.
⁸ God reigns over the
        nations;
    God is seated on his holy
        throne.
⁹ The nobles of the nations
        assemble
    as the people of the God
        of Abraham,
for the kings*ᵇ* of the earth
    belong to God;
    he is greatly exalted.

Psalm 48

A song. A psalm of the Sons of Korah.

¹ Great is the LORD, and most worthy of
        praise,
    in the city of our God, his holy mountain.
² It is beautiful in its loftiness,
        the joy of the whole earth.
    Like the utmost heights of Zaphon*ᶜ* is
        Mount Zion,
    the*ᵈ* city of the Great King.
³ God is in her citadels;
    he has shown himself to be her fortress.

⁴ When the kings joined forces,
    when they advanced together,
⁵ they saw her and were astounded;
    they fled in terror.
⁶ Trembling seized them there,
    pain like that of a woman in labor.
⁷ You destroyed them like ships of Tarshish
    shattered by an east wind.

⁸ As we have heard,
    so have we seen
in the city of the LORD Almighty,
    in the city of our God:
    God makes her secure forever.   *Selah*

⁹ Within your temple, O God,
    we meditate on your unfailing love.
¹⁰ Like your name, O God,
    your praise reaches to the ends of the
        earth;
    your right hand is filled with
        righteousness.
¹¹ Mount Zion rejoices,
    the villages of Judah are
        glad
    because of your
        judgments.

¹² Walk about Zion, go
        around her,
    count her towers,
¹³ consider well her ramparts,
    view her citadels,
    that you may tell of
        them to the next
        generation.

¹⁴ For this God is our God for ever and ever;
    he will be our guide even to the end.

Psalm 49

For the director of music. Of the Sons of Korah.
A psalm.

¹ Hear this, all you peoples;
    listen, all who live in this world,
² both low and high,
    rich and poor alike:
³ My mouth will speak words of wisdom;
    the utterance from my heart will give
        understanding.
⁴ I will turn my ear to a proverb;
    with the harp I will expound my riddle:

⁵ Why should I fear when evil days come,
    when wicked deceivers surround me—
⁶ those who trust in their wealth
    and boast of their great riches?
⁷ No man can redeem the life of another
    or give to God a ransom for him—
⁸ the ransom for a life is costly,

> ### Psalm 48:14
>
> *God Provides Guidance*
>
> For this God is our God
> for ever and ever;
> he will be our guide
> even to the end.

---

*ᵃ*7 Or *a maskil* (probably a literary or musical term)   *ᵇ*9 Or *shields*   *ᶜ*2 *Zaphon* can refer to a sacred mountain or the direction north.
*ᵈ*2 Or *earth, / Mount Zion, on the northern side / of the*

no payment is ever enough—
9 that he should live on forever
and not see decay.

10 For all can see that wise men die;
the foolish and the senseless alike perish
and leave their wealth to others.
11 Their tombs will remain their houses*a*
forever,
their dwellings for endless generations,
though they had*b* named lands after
themselves.

12 But man, despite his riches, does not
endure;
he is*c* like the beasts that perish.

13 This is the fate of those who trust in
themselves,
and of their followers, who approve their
sayings.   *Selah*
14 Like sheep they are destined for the grave,*d*
and death will feed on them.
The upright will rule over them in the
morning;
their forms will decay in the grave,*d*
far from their princely mansions.
15 But God will redeem my life*e* from the
grave;
he will surely take me to himself. *Selah*

16 Do not be overawed when a man grows
rich,
when the splendor of his house increases;
17 for he will take nothing with him when he
dies,
his splendor will not descend with him.
18 Though while he lived he counted himself
blessed—
and men praise you when you prosper—
19 he will join the generation of his fathers,
who will never see the light ⸤of life⸥.

20 A man who has riches without
understanding
is like the beasts that perish.

Psalm 50
A psalm of Asaph.

1 The Mighty One, God, the LORD,
speaks and summons the earth

from the rising of the sun to the place
where it sets.
2 From Zion, perfect in beauty,
God shines forth.
3 Our God comes and will not be silent;
a fire devours before him,
and around him a tempest rages.
4 He summons the heavens above,
and the earth, that he may judge his
people:
5 "Gather to me my consecrated ones,
who made a covenant with me by
sacrifice."
6 And the heavens proclaim his
righteousness,
for God himself is judge.   *Selah*

7 "Hear, O my people, and I will speak,
O Israel, and I will testify against you:
I am God, your God.
8 I do not rebuke you for your sacrifices
or your burnt offerings, which are ever
before me.
9 I have no need of a bull from your stall
or of goats from your pens,
10 for every animal of the forest is mine,
and the cattle on a thousand hills.
11 I know every bird in the mountains,
and the creatures of the field are mine.
12 If I were hungry I would not tell you,
for the world is mine, and all that is in it.
13 Do I eat the flesh of bulls
or drink the blood of goats?
14 Sacrifice thank offerings to God,
fulfill your vows to the Most High,
15 and call upon me in the day of trouble;
I will deliver you, and you will honor
me."

16 But to the wicked, God says:

"What right have you to recite my laws
or take my covenant on your lips?
17 You hate my instruction
and cast my words behind you.
18 When you see a thief, you join with him;
you throw in your lot with adulterers.
19 You use your mouth for evil
and harness your tongue to deceit.
20 You speak continually against your brother

---

*a*11 Septuagint and Syriac; Hebrew *In their thoughts their houses will remain*   *b*11 Or */ for they have*   *c*12 Hebrew; Septuagint and Syriac read verse 12 the same as verse 20.   *d*14 Hebrew *Sheol*; also in verse 15   *e*15 Or *soul*

and slander your own mother's son.
21 These things you have done and I kept silent;
     you thought I was altogether[a] like you.
But I will rebuke you
     and accuse you to your face.

22 "Consider this, you who forget God,
     or I will tear you to pieces, with none to rescue:
23 He who sacrifices thank offerings honors me,
     and he prepares the way
     so that I may show him[b] the salvation of God."

Psalm 51

For the director of music. A psalm of David. When the prophet Nathan came to him after David had committed adultery with Bathsheba.

1 Have mercy on me, O God,
     according to your unfailing love;
according to your great compassion
     blot out my transgressions.
2 Wash away all my iniquity
     and cleanse me from my sin.

3 For I know my transgressions,
     and my sin is always before me.
4 Against you, you only, have I sinned
     and done what is evil in your sight,
so that you are proved right when you speak
     and justified when you judge.
5 Surely I was sinful at birth,
     sinful from the time my mother conceived me.
6 Surely you desire truth in the inner parts[c];
     you teach[d] me wisdom in the inmost place.

7 Cleanse me with hyssop, and I will be clean;
     wash me, and I will be whiter than snow.
8 Let me hear joy and gladness;
     let the bones you have crushed rejoice.
9 Hide your face from my sins
     and blot out all my iniquity.

10 Create in me a pure heart, O God,
     and renew a steadfast spirit within me.

11 Do not cast me from your presence
     or take your Holy Spirit from me.
12 Restore to me the joy of your salvation
     and grant me a willing spirit, to sustain me.

13 Then I will teach transgressors your ways,
     and sinners will turn back to you.
14 Save me from bloodguilt, O God,
     the God who saves me,
     and my tongue will sing of your righteousness.
15 O Lord, open my lips,
     and my mouth will declare your praise.
16 You do not delight in sacrifice, or I would bring it;
     you do not take pleasure in burnt offerings.
17 The sacrifices of God are[e] a broken spirit;
     a broken and contrite heart,
     O God, you will not despise.

18 In your good pleasure make Zion prosper;
     build up the walls of Jerusalem.
19 Then there will be righteous sacrifices,
     whole burnt offerings to delight you;
     then bulls will be offered on your altar.

Psalm 52

For the director of music. A maskil[f] of David. When Doeg the Edomite had gone to Saul and told him: "David has gone to the house of Ahimelech."

1 Why do you boast of evil, you mighty man?
     Why do you boast all day long,
     you who are a disgrace in the eyes of God?
2 Your tongue plots destruction;
     it is like a sharpened razor,
     you who practice deceit.
3 You love evil rather than good,
     falsehood rather than speaking the truth.   Selah
4 You love every harmful word,
     O you deceitful tongue!

5 Surely God will bring you down to everlasting ruin:
     He will snatch you up and tear you from your tent;

---

a21 Or thought the 'I AM' was   b23 Or and to him who considers his way / I will show   c6 The meaning of the Hebrew for this phrase is uncertain.   d6 Or you desired...; / you taught   e17 Or My sacrifice, O God, is   fTitle: Probably a literary or musical term

O God, Have Mercy

Read: Psalm 51:1–19

Psalm 51:1

Have mercy on me,
O God, according to
your unfailing love;
according to your great
compassion blot out
my transgressions.

reflection

1 What excuses have
you recently made to
God, others and yourself
for your sin?

2 How have you re-
named your sin to
make it sound better?

3 How does it comfort
you that God doesn't
forgive excuses but that he
does forgive sin?

RELATED READINGS

2 Samuel 11:1—12:25;
Psalm 103:8–18;
Romans 3:21–24

*"If we cover our sin,
God will expose it.
If we expose our sin,
God will cover it."*

Unknown

WE EXCUSE OURSELVES so easily. I was tired. He started it. That's
the way I was raised. Everyone else does it. The woman you put
here with me—she gave me some fruit from the tree, and I ate it.
It's his fault. It's her fault. Maybe it's even God's fault. But surely it's
not my fault!

O God, have mercy.

Until we stop making excuses, we aren't ready to be forgiven.
Whether we think we're above the law (as David apparently
thought when he chose to send for the married Bathsheba) or
that our action is okay if others started it (as Adam thought in the
garden) or that it isn't really worth God's notice (as Ananias and
Sapphira may have thought when they lied about their offering to
the church), our excuses cover us as poorly as Adam and Eve's fig
leaves in the Garden of Eden.

Sometimes we change the name to cover our sin: It's not
gossip; it's sharing. It's not coveting; it's admiring. It's not lying; it's
explaining. David even planned to have his lover's husband killed
in war to make the object of his lust a widow, thinking that would
redefine adultery. But God didn't buy it.

O God, have mercy.

God doesn't forgive excuses. But God *does* forgive sin. He's
waiting for us to call it what he calls it: sin. When we acknowledge
our sin and repent, God removes sin as far as the east is from the
west. Picture a globe in your mind. No matter how far you go,
you'll never discover west by traveling east. That's how far God is
willing to cleanse, forgive and make us new.

When the prophet Nathan confronted King David about his
sin, David's repentance was deep and real. In Psalm 51 he put
his feelings into words. He cried out for God's mercy, asking
God to cleanse him of his sin, to teach him wisdom and to heal
his conscience and his emotions. David's song of confession and
restoration can give us courage to confess our wrongs, no matter
how great our wrongdoings seem to us and no matter how far
away from God we feel.

Repentance frees us. Honesty renews us. God's mercy
cleanses us.

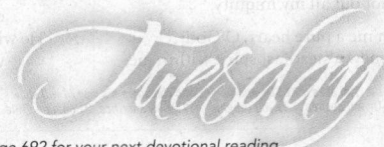

he will uproot you from the land of the
living.   *Selah*
⁶ The righteous will see and fear;
they will laugh at him, saying,
⁷ "Here now is the man
who did not make God his stronghold
but trusted in his great wealth
and grew strong by destroying others!"

⁸ But I am like an olive tree
flourishing in the house of God;
I trust in God's unfailing love
for ever and ever.
⁹ I will praise you forever for what you have
done;
in your name I will hope, for your name
is good.
I will praise you in the presence of your
saints.

Psalm 53

For the director of music. According to *mahalath.*ᵃ
A *maskil*ᵇ of David.

¹ The fool says in his heart,
"There is no God."
They are corrupt, and their
ways are vile;
there is no one who does
good.

² God looks down from
heaven
on the sons of men
to see if there are any who
understand,
any who seek God.
³ Everyone has turned away,
they have together
become corrupt;
there is no one who does
good,
not even one.

⁴ Will the evildoers never learn—
those who devour my people as men eat
bread
and who do not call on God?
⁵ There they were, overwhelmed with dread,
where there was nothing to dread.
God scattered the bones of those who
attacked you;

Psalm 53:1

*God Can Be
Known*

The fool says in his heart,
"There is no God."
They are corrupt, and
their ways are vile;
there is no one who
does good.

---

you put them to shame, for God
despised them.

⁶ Oh, that salvation for Israel would come
out of Zion!
When God restores the fortunes of his
people,
let Jacob rejoice and Israel be glad!

Psalm 54

For the director of music. With stringed
instruments. A *maskil*ᵇ of David. When the
Ziphites had gone to Saul and said, "Is not David
hiding among us?"

¹ Save me, O God, by your name;
vindicate me by your might.
² Hear my prayer, O God;
listen to the words of my mouth.

³ Strangers are attacking me;
ruthless men seek my life—
men without regard for God.   *Selah*

⁴ Surely God is my help;
the Lord is the one who sustains me.

⁵ Let evil recoil on those who
slander me;
in your faithfulness
destroy them.

⁶ I will sacrifice a freewill
offering to you;
I will praise your name,
O LORD,
for it is good.
⁷ For he has delivered
me from all my
troubles,
and my eyes have looked
in triumph on my
foes.

Psalm 55

For the director of music. With stringed
instruments. A *maskil*ᵇ of David.

¹ Listen to my prayer, O God,
do not ignore my plea;
²   hear me and answer me.
My thoughts trouble me and I am
distraught
³   at the voice of the enemy,
at the stares of the wicked;

ᵃTitle: Probably a musical term   ᵇTitle: Probably a literary or musical term

for they bring down suffering upon me
and revile me in their anger.

4 My heart is in anguish within me;
the terrors of death assail me.
5 Fear and trembling have beset me;
horror has overwhelmed me.
6 I said, "Oh, that I had the wings of a dove!
I would fly away and be at rest—
7 I would flee far away
and stay in the desert;   *Selah*
8 I would hurry to my place of shelter,
far from the tempest and storm."

9 Confuse the wicked, O Lord, confound
their speech,
for I see violence and strife in the city.
10 Day and night they prowl about on its
walls;
malice and abuse are within it.
11 Destructive forces are at work in the city;
threats and lies never leave its streets.

12 If an enemy were insulting me,
I could endure it;
if a foe were raising himself against me,
I could hide from him.
13 But it is you, a man like myself,
my companion, my close friend,
14 with whom I once enjoyed sweet fellowship
as we walked with the throng at the
house of God.

15 Let death take my enemies by surprise;
let them go down alive to the grave,[a]
for evil finds lodging among them.

16 But I call to God,
and the LORD saves me.
17 Evening, morning and noon
I cry out in distress,
and he hears my voice.
18 He ransoms me unharmed
from the battle waged against me,
even though many oppose me.
19 God, who is enthroned forever,
will hear them and afflict them— *Selah*
men who never change their ways
and have no fear of God.

20 My companion attacks his friends;
he violates his covenant.

21 His speech is smooth as butter,
yet war is in his heart;
his words are more soothing than oil,
yet they are drawn swords.

22 Cast your cares on the LORD
and he will sustain you;
he will never let the righteous fall.
23 But you, O God, will bring down the
wicked
into the pit of corruption;
bloodthirsty and deceitful men
will not live out half their days.

But as for me, I trust in you.

Psalm 56

For the director of music. To ˌthe tune of˴ "A Dove
on Distant Oaks." Of David. A *miktam*.[b] When the
Philistines had seized him in Gath.

1 Be merciful to me, O God, for men hotly
pursue me;
all day long they press their attack.
2 My slanderers pursue me all day long;
many are attacking me in their pride.

3 When I am afraid,
I will trust in you.
4 In God, whose word I praise,
in God I trust; I will not be afraid.
What can mortal man do to me?

5 All day long they twist my words;
they are always plotting to harm me.
6 They conspire, they lurk,
they watch my steps,
eager to take my life.

7 On no account let them escape;
in your anger, O God, bring down the
nations.
8 Record my lament;
list my tears on your scroll[c]—
are they not in your record?

9 Then my enemies will turn back
when I call for help.
By this I will know that God is for me.
10 In God, whose word I praise,
in the LORD, whose word I praise—
11 in God I trust; I will not be afraid.
What can man do to me?

---

[a]15 Hebrew *Sheol*   [b]Title: Probably a literary or musical term   [c]8 Or / *put my tears in your wineskin*

¹² I am under vows to you, O God;
  I will present my thank offerings to you.
¹³ For you have delivered me*a* from death
  and my feet from stumbling,
 that I may walk before God
  in the light of life.*b*

Psalm 57

For the director of music. ⌞To the tune of⌟ "Do Not
Destroy." Of David. A *miktam.c* When he had fled
from Saul into the cave.

¹ Have mercy on me, O God, have mercy on
  me,
  for in you my soul takes refuge.
 I will take refuge in the shadow of your
  wings
 until the disaster has passed.

² I cry out to God Most High,
  to God, who fulfills ⌞his⌟
  purpose⌟ for me.
³ He sends from heaven and
  saves me,
  rebuking those who
  hotly pursue me;
          Selah
 God sends his love and
  his faithfulness.

⁴ I am in the midst of lions;
  I lie among ravenous
  beasts—
 men whose teeth are spears
  and arrows,
 whose tongues are sharp swords.

⁵ Be exalted, O God, above the heavens;
  let your glory be over all the earth.

⁶ They spread a net for my feet—
  I was bowed down in distress.
 They dug a pit in my path—
  but they have fallen into it themselves.
          Selah

⁷ My heart is steadfast, O God,
  my heart is steadfast;
  I will sing and make music.
⁸ Awake, my soul!
  Awake, harp and lyre!
  I will awaken the dawn.

> ### Psalm 57:3
>
> *God Shelters Us*
>
> He sends from heaven
> and saves me,
> rebuking those who
> hotly pursue me;
> God sends his love and
> his faithfulness.

⁹ I will praise you, O Lord, among the
  nations;
  I will sing of you among the peoples.
¹⁰ For great is your love, reaching to the
  heavens;
 your faithfulness reaches to the
  skies.

¹¹ Be exalted, O God, above the heavens;
  let your glory be over all the earth.

Psalm 58

For the director of music. ⌞To the tune of⌟ "Do Not
Destroy." Of David. A *miktam.c*

¹ Do you rulers indeed speak justly?
  Do you judge uprightly among men?
² No, in your heart you devise injustice,
  and your hands mete
  out violence on the
  earth.
³ Even from birth the wicked
  go astray;
 from the womb they are
  wayward and speak
  lies.
⁴ Their venom is like the
  venom of a snake,
 like that of a cobra that
  has stopped its ears,
⁵ that will not heed the tune
  of the charmer,
 however skillful the
  enchanter may be.

⁶ Break the teeth in their mouths, O God;
  tear out, O Lord, the fangs of the lions!
⁷ Let them vanish like water that flows
  away;
 when they draw the bow, let their arrows
  be blunted.
⁸ Like a slug melting away as it moves along,
  like a stillborn child, may they not see
  the sun.

⁹ Before your pots can feel ⌞the heat of⌟ the
  thorns—
 whether they are green or dry—the
  wicked will be swept away.*d*
¹⁰ The righteous will be glad when they are
  avenged,

---

a13 Or *my soul* *b13* Or *the land of the living* *c*Title: Probably a literary or musical term *d9* The meaning of the Hebrew for this verse is
uncertain.

Light in a Dark Cave

Read: Psalm 57:1–11

Psalm 57:2–3

I cry out to God Most High, to God, who fulfills his purpose for me. He sends from heaven and saves me, rebuking those who hotly pursue me; God sends his love and his faithfulness.

reflection

1 Have you ever found yourself in a dark cave? Describe it.

2 What can you learn from David regarding worshiping God even in the midst of hard times? Spend some time working through the four steps from worry to worship found in Psalm 57. Write them down, personalizing them if you can.

3 Read Psalm 57 aloud as a praise song to God.

RELATED READINGS

1 Samuel 24:1–22;
Luke 1:69–75;
Acts 16:22–34;
1 Peter 3:13–16

DAVID FOUND HIMSELF in a lonely, dark cave at En Gedi. He was hiding from King Saul, in fear for his life and pursued by thousands of his own countrymen.

How did David climb out from his soul's dark hiding place? We find some clues in Psalm 57, penned while David lived in the cave. This page from David's songbook reflects the roller coaster of emotions he experienced. You might recognize some of his feelings: fear turned to faith, panic rolled toward hope, terror shifted to trust, dependence circled to dread. Up and down, around and around, back and forth . . . but David always returned to God—worshiping him even in a dark cave.

In his grotto hiding place, David cried out to God for help, "Have mercy on me, O God" (verse 1). What a great place to start when we're in a dark place. Then, he wrote what he knew to be true about his God, saying, "God sends his love and his faithfulness" (verse 3). Recounting God's character traits helps to take our focus off ourselves and place our focus rightly on him. Next, David verbalized his fears, saying, "I am in the midst of lions" (verse 4). Naming our fears can make our enemies seem smaller in the context of the Creator of the universe. Finally, he relinquished his circumstances to God's glory, saying, "Be exalted, O God, above the heavens" (verse 5). Like Jesus during his dark night in the garden of Gethsemane, David sought God's will above his own. This progression toward trusting God lit David's way from a place of worry to one of worship; he chose to hide in the shadow of God's wings, whether he lived in a cave or in a palace. When Saul came to En Gedi and entered the cave, David had the courage to do the right thing: He spared the life of the king God had anointed, and he sought reconciliation with Saul, even though it might mean death for him.

If you're in the dark, follow David's steps and walk toward the light: (1) Cry out for mercy. (2) Remember God's love and faithfulness. (3) Verbalize your fears. (4) Pray that God's will be accomplished in your life for his glory. Then choose to worship God wherever you may be.

Go to page 701 for your next devotional reading.

when they bathe their feet in the blood
of the wicked.
[11] Then men will say,
"Surely the righteous still are rewarded;
surely there is a God who
judges the earth."

Psalm 59

For the director of music. To the
tune of "Do Not Destroy." Of
David. A *miktam.ᵃ* When Saul
had sent men to watch David's
house in order to kill him.

[1] Deliver me from my
enemies, O God;
protect me from those
who rise up against
me.
[2] Deliver me from evildoers
and save me from
bloodthirsty men.

[3] See how they lie in wait for me!
Fierce men conspire against me
for no offense or sin of mine, O LORD.
[4] I have done no wrong, yet they are ready to
attack me.
Arise to help me; look on my plight!
[5] O LORD God Almighty, the God of Israel,
rouse yourself to punish all the nations;
show no mercy to wicked traitors. *Selah*

[6] They return at evening,
snarling like dogs,
and prowl about the city.
[7] See what they spew from their mouths—
they spew out swords from their lips,
and they say, "Who can hear us?"
[8] But you, O LORD, laugh at them;
you scoff at all those nations.

[9] O my Strength, I watch for you;
you, O God, are my fortress, [10]my
loving God.

God will go before me
and will let me gloat over those who
slander me.
[11] But do not kill them, O Lord our shield,ᵇ
or my people will forget.
In your might make them wander about,

and bring them down.
[12] For the sins of their mouths,
for the words of their lips,
let them be caught in their pride.
For the curses and lies they
utter,
[13] consume them in wrath,
consume them till they
are no more.
Then it will be known
to the ends of the
earth
that God rules over
Jacob. *Selah*

[14] They return at evening,
snarling like dogs,
and prowl about the city.
[15] They wander about for food
and howl if not satisfied.

[16] But I will sing of your strength,
in the morning I will sing of your love;
for you are my fortress,
my refuge in times of trouble.

[17] O my Strength, I sing praise to you;
you, O God, are my fortress, my loving
God.

Psalm 58:11

*God Rewards
the Righteous*

Then men will say,
"Surely the righteous still
are rewarded;
surely there is a God who
judges the earth."

Psalm 60

For the director of music. To the tune of, "The
Lily of the Covenant." A *miktamᵃ* of David. For
teaching. When he fought Aram Naharaimᶜ
and Aram Zobah,ᵈ and when Joab returned and
struck down twelve thousand Edomites in the
Valley of Salt.

[1] You have rejected us, O God, and burst
forth upon us;
you have been angry—now restore us!
[2] You have shaken the land and torn it open;
mend its fractures, for it is quaking.
[3] You have shown your people desperate
times;
you have given us wine that makes us
stagger.

[4] But for those who fear you, you have raised
a banner
to be unfurled against the bow. *Selah*

[5] Save us and help us with your right hand,

ᵃTitle: Probably a literary or musical term   ᵇ11 Or *sovereign*   ᶜTitle: That is, Arameans of Northwest Mesopotamia   ᵈTitle: That is,
Arameans of central Syria

that those you love may be delivered.
6 God has spoken from his sanctuary:
"In triumph I will parcel out Shechem
and measure off the Valley of Succoth.
7 Gilead is mine, and Manasseh is mine;
Ephraim is my helmet,
Judah my scepter.
8 Moab is my washbasin,
upon Edom I toss my sandal;
over Philistia I shout in triumph."

9 Who will bring me to the fortified city?
Who will lead me to Edom?
10 Is it not you, O God, you who have
rejected us
and no longer go out with our armies?
11 Give us aid against the enemy,
for the help of man is worthless.
12 With God we will gain the victory,
and he will trample down our enemies.

Psalm 61
For the director of music. With stringed
instruments. Of David.

1 Hear my cry, O God;
listen to my prayer.

2 From the ends of the earth
I call to you,
I call as my heart grows
faint;
lead me to the rock that
is higher than I.
3 For you have been my
refuge,
a strong tower against
the foe.

4 I long to dwell in your tent
forever
and take refuge in the
shelter of your wings.   *Selah*
5 For you have heard my vows, O God;
you have given me the heritage of those
who fear your name.

6 Increase the days of the king's life,
his years for many generations.
7 May he be enthroned in God's presence
forever;
appoint your love and faithfulness to
protect him.

8 Then will I ever sing praise to your name
and fulfill my vows day after day.

Psalm 62
For the director of music. For Jeduthun.
A psalm of David.

1 My soul finds rest in God alone;
my salvation comes from him.
2 He alone is my rock and my salvation;
he is my fortress, I will never be
shaken.

3 How long will you assault a man?
Would all of you throw him down—
this leaning wall, this tottering fence?
4 They fully intend to topple him
from his lofty place;
they take delight in lies.
With their mouths they bless,
but in their hearts they curse.   *Selah*

5 Find rest, O my soul, in God alone;
my hope comes from him.
6 He alone is my rock and my salvation;
he is my fortress, I will not be shaken.
7 My salvation and my honor
depend on God[a];
he is my mighty rock, my
refuge.
8 Trust in him at all times,
O people;
pour out your hearts to
him,
for God is our refuge.   *Selah*

9 Lowborn men are but a
breath,
the highborn are but
a lie;
if weighed on a balance,
they are nothing;
together they are only a breath.
10 Do not trust in extortion
or take pride in stolen goods;
though your riches increase,
do not set your heart on them.

11 One thing God has spoken,
two things have I heard:
that you, O God, are strong,
12   and that you, O Lord, are loving.

> ### Psalm 61:3
>
> *God Is a Strong Tower*
>
> For you have been
> my refuge,
> a strong tower against
> the foe.

---

a7 Or / God Most High is my salvation and my honor

Surely you will reward each person
  according to what he has done.

Psalm 63

A psalm of David. When he was in the Desert
of Judah.

[1] O God, you are my God,
  earnestly I seek you;
my soul thirsts for you,
  my body longs for you,
in a dry and weary land
  where there is no water.

[2] I have seen you in the sanctuary
  and beheld your power and your glory.
[3] Because your love is better than life,
  my lips will glorify you.
[4] I will praise you as long as I live,
  and in your name I will lift up my
    hands.
[5] My soul will be satisfied as with the richest
    of foods;
  with singing lips my mouth will praise
    you.

[6] On my bed I remember you;
  I think of you through the watches of
    the night.
[7] Because you are my help,
  I sing in the shadow of your wings.
[8] My soul clings to you;
  your right hand upholds me.

[9] They who seek my life will be destroyed;
  they will go down to the depths of the
    earth.
[10] They will be given over to the sword
  and become food for jackals.

[11] But the king will rejoice in God;
  all who swear by God's name will praise
    him,
  while the mouths of liars will be silenced.

Psalm 64

For the director of music. A psalm of David.

[1] Hear me, O God, as I voice my complaint;
  protect my life from the threat of the
    enemy.
[2] Hide me from the conspiracy of the
    wicked,
  from that noisy crowd of evildoers.

[3] They sharpen their tongues like swords
  and aim their words like deadly arrows.
[4] They shoot from ambush at the innocent
    man;
  they shoot at him suddenly, without fear.

[5] They encourage each other in evil plans,
  they talk about hiding their snares;
  they say, "Who will see them[a]?"
[6] They plot injustice and say,
  "We have devised a perfect plan!"
  Surely the mind and heart of man are
    cunning.

[7] But God will shoot them with arrows;
  suddenly they will be struck down.
[8] He will turn their own tongues against
    them
  and bring them to ruin;
  all who see them will shake their heads
    in scorn.

[9] All mankind will fear;
  they will proclaim the works of God
  and ponder what he has done.
[10] Let the righteous rejoice in the LORD
  and take refuge in him;
  let all the upright in heart praise him!

Psalm 65

For the director of music. A psalm of David.
A song.

[1] Praise awaits[b] you, O God, in Zion;
  to you our vows will be fulfilled.
[2] O you who hear prayer,
  to you all men will come.
[3] When we were overwhelmed by sins,
  you forgave[c] our transgressions.
[4] Blessed are those you choose
  and bring near to live in your courts!
We are filled with the good things of your
    house,
  of your holy temple.

[5] You answer us with awesome deeds of
    righteousness,
  O God our Savior,
the hope of all the ends of the earth
  and of the farthest seas,
[6] who formed the mountains by your power,
  having armed yourself with strength,

---

*a*5 Or *us*   *b*1 Or *befits*; the meaning of the Hebrew for this word is uncertain.   *c*3 Or *made atonement for*

7 who stilled the roaring of the seas,
    the roaring of their waves,
    and the turmoil of the nations.
8 Those living far away fear your wonders;
    where morning dawns and evening
        fades
    you call forth songs of joy.

9 You care for the land and water it;
    you enrich it abundantly.
  The streams of God are filled with water
    to provide the people with grain,
    for so you have ordained it.[a]
10 You drench its furrows
    and level its ridges;
  you soften it with showers
    and bless its crops.
11 You crown the year with your bounty,
    and your carts overflow with
        abundance.
12 The grasslands of the desert overflow;
    the hills are clothed with gladness.
13 The meadows are covered with flocks
    and the valleys are mantled with grain;
    they shout for joy and sing.

Psalm 66
For the director of music. A song. A psalm.

1 Shout with joy to God, all the earth!
2   Sing the glory of his name;
    make his praise glorious!
3 Say to God, "How awesome are your
        deeds!
    So great is your power
    that your enemies cringe before you.
4 All the earth bows down to you;
    they sing praise to you,
    they sing praise to your name."   Selah

5 Come and see what God has done,
    how awesome his works in man's behalf!
6 He turned the sea into dry land,
    they passed through the waters on foot—
    come, let us rejoice in him.
7 He rules forever by his power,
    his eyes watch the nations—
    let not the rebellious rise up against
        him.   Selah

8 Praise our God, O peoples,
    let the sound of his praise be heard;

9 he has preserved our lives
    and kept our feet from slipping.
10 For you, O God, tested us;
    you refined us like silver.
11 You brought us into prison
    and laid burdens on our backs.
12 You let men ride over our heads;
    we went through fire and water,
    but you brought us to a place of
        abundance.

13 I will come to your temple with burnt
        offerings
    and fulfill my vows to you—
14 vows my lips promised and my mouth
        spoke
    when I was in trouble.
15 I will sacrifice fat animals to you
    and an offering of rams;
    I will offer bulls and goats.   Selah

16 Come and listen, all you who fear God;
    let me tell you what he has done for
        me.
17 I cried out to him with my mouth;
    his praise was on my tongue.
18 If I had cherished sin in my heart,
    the Lord would not have listened;
19 but God has surely listened
    and heard my voice in prayer.
20 Praise be to God,
    who has not rejected my prayer
    or withheld his love from me!

Psalm 67
For the director of music. With stringed
instruments. A psalm. A song.

1 May God be gracious to us and bless us
    and make his face shine upon us,
                                        Selah
2 that your ways may be known on earth,
    your salvation among all nations.

3 May the peoples praise you, O God;
    may all the peoples praise you.
4 May the nations be glad and sing for joy,
    for you rule the peoples justly
    and guide the nations of the earth.
                                        Selah
5 May the peoples praise you, O God;
    may all the peoples praise you.

a9 Or for that is how you prepare the land

6 Then the land will yield its harvest,
	and God, our God, will bless us.
7 God will bless us,
	and all the ends of the earth will fear
		him.

Psalm 68

For the director of music. Of David. A psalm.
A song.

1 May God arise, may his enemies be
		scattered;
	may his foes flee before him.
2 As smoke is blown away by the wind,
	may you blow them away;
as wax melts before the fire,
	may the wicked perish before God.
3 But may the righteous be
			glad
	and rejoice before God;
	may they be happy and
		joyful.

4 Sing to God, sing praise to
		his name,
	extol him who rides on
		the clouds*a*—
his name is the Lord—
	and rejoice before him.
5 A father to the fatherless, a
		defender of widows,
	is God in his holy
		dwelling.
6 God sets the lonely in families,*b*
	he leads forth the prisoners with singing;
	but the rebellious live in a sun-scorched
		land.

7 When you went out before your people,
		O God,
	when you marched through the
		wasteland,				*Selah*
8 the earth shook,
	the heavens poured down rain,
	before God, the One of Sinai,
	before God, the God of Israel.
9 You gave abundant showers, O God;
	you refreshed your weary inheritance.
10 Your people settled in it,
	and from your bounty, O God, you
		provided for the poor.

11 The Lord announced the word,
	and great was the company of those who
		proclaimed it:
12 "Kings and armies flee in haste;
	in the camps men divide the plunder.
13 Even while you sleep among the
		campfires,*c*
	the wings of my dove are sheathed with
		silver,
	its feathers with shining gold."
14 When the Almighty*d* scattered the kings
		in the land,
	it was like snow fallen on Zalmon.

15 The mountains of Bashan are majestic
		mountains;
	rugged are the
		mountains of
		Bashan.
16 Why gaze in envy,
		O rugged
		mountains,
	at the mountain where
		God chooses to
		reign,
	where the Lord himself
		will dwell forever?
17 The chariots of God are
		tens of thousands
		and thousands of
		thousands;
	the Lord has come from Sinai into his
		sanctuary.
18 When you ascended on high,
	you led captives in your train;
	you received gifts from men,
even from*e* the rebellious—
	that you,*f* O Lord God, might dwell
		there.

19 Praise be to the Lord, to God our Savior,
	who daily bears our burdens.		*Selah*
20 Our God is a God who saves;
	from the Sovereign Lord comes escape
		from death.
21 Surely God will crush the heads of his
		enemies,
	the hairy crowns of those who go on in
		their sins.

Psalm 68:4
God Is Majestic
Sing to God, sing praise to his name, extol him who rides on the clouds— his name is the Lord— and rejoice before him.

---

*a*4 Or / prepare the way for him who rides through the deserts   *b*6 Or the desolate in a homeland   *c*13 Or saddlebags   *d*14 Hebrew Shaddai   *e*18 Or gifts for men, / even   *f*18 Or they

22 The Lord says, "I will bring them from
    Bashan;
  I will bring them from the depths of the
    sea,
23 that you may plunge your feet in the blood
    of your foes,
  while the tongues of your dogs have
    their share."

24 Your procession has come into view,
    O God,
  the procession of my God and King into
    the sanctuary.
25 In front are the singers, after them the
    musicians;
  with them are the maidens playing
    tambourines.
26 Praise God in the great congregation;
  praise the LORD in the assembly of
    Israel.
27 There is the little tribe of Benjamin,
    leading them,
  there the great throng of Judah's
    princes,
  and there the princes of Zebulun and of
    Naphtali.

28 Summon your power, O God[a];
  show us your strength, O God, as you
    have done before.
29 Because of your temple at Jerusalem
  kings will bring you gifts.
30 Rebuke the beast among the reeds,
  the herd of bulls among the calves of the
    nations.
  Humbled, may it bring bars of silver.
  Scatter the nations who delight in
    war.
31 Envoys will come from Egypt;
  Cush[b] will submit herself to God.

32 Sing to God, O kingdoms of the earth,
  sing praise to the Lord,   Selah
33 to him who rides the ancient skies above,
  who thunders with mighty voice.
34 Proclaim the power of God,
  whose majesty is over Israel,
  whose power is in the skies.
35 You are awesome, O God, in your
    sanctuary;

the God of Israel gives power and
    strength to his people.

Praise be to God!

Psalm 69

For the director of music. To the tune of, "Lilies."
Of David.

1 Save me, O God,
  for the waters have come up to my neck.
2 I sink in the miry depths,
  where there is no foothold.
  I have come into the deep waters;
  the floods engulf me.
3 I am worn out calling for help;
  my throat is parched.
  My eyes fail,
  looking for my God.
4 Those who hate me without reason
  outnumber the hairs of my head;
  many are my enemies without cause,
  those who seek to destroy me.
  I am forced to restore
  what I did not steal.

5 You know my folly, O God;
  my guilt is not hidden from you.

6 May those who hope in you
  not be disgraced because of me,
  O Lord, the LORD Almighty;
  may those who seek you
  not be put to shame because of me,
  O God of Israel.
7 For I endure scorn for your sake,
  and shame covers my face.
8 I am a stranger to my brothers,
  an alien to my own mother's sons;
9 for zeal for your house consumes me,
  and the insults of those who insult you
    fall on me.
10 When I weep and fast,
  I must endure scorn;
11 when I put on sackcloth,
  people make sport of me.
12 Those who sit at the gate mock me,
  and I am the song of the drunkards.

13 But I pray to you, O LORD,
  in the time of your favor;
  in your great love, O God,

a28 Many Hebrew manuscripts, Septuagint and Syriac; most Hebrew manuscripts *Your God has summoned power for you*   b31 That is, the
upper Nile region

answer me with your sure salvation.
14 Rescue me from the mire,
    do not let me sink;
    deliver me from those who hate me,
    from the deep waters.
15 Do not let the floodwaters engulf me
    or the depths swallow me up
    or the pit close its mouth over me.
16 Answer me, O LORD, out of the goodness
    of your love;
    in your great mercy turn to me.
17 Do not hide your face from your servant;
    answer me quickly, for I am in trouble.
18 Come near and rescue me;
    redeem me because of my foes.

19 You know how I am scorned, disgraced
    and shamed;
    all my enemies are before you.
20 Scorn has broken my heart
    and has left me helpless;
    I looked for sympathy, but there was
    none,
    for comforters, but I found none.
21 They put gall in my food
    and gave me vinegar for my thirst.

22 May the table set before them become a
    snare;
    may it become retribution and*a* a trap.
23 May their eyes be darkened so they cannot
    see,
    and their backs be bent
    forever.
24 Pour out your wrath on
    them;
    let your fierce anger
    overtake them.
25 May their place be deserted;
    let there be no one to
    dwell in their tents.
26 For they persecute those
    you wound
    and talk about the pain
    of those you hurt.
27 Charge them with crime
    upon crime;
    do not let them share in your salvation.
28 May they be blotted out of the book of life
    and not be listed with the righteous.

*a*22 Or snare / and their fellowship become

29 I am in pain and distress;
    may your salvation, O God, protect me.

30 I will praise God's name in song
    and glorify him with thanksgiving.
31 This will please the LORD more than an ox,
    more than a bull with its horns and hoofs.
32 The poor will see and be glad—
    you who seek God, may your hearts live!
33 The LORD hears the needy
    and does not despise his captive people.

34 Let heaven and earth praise him,
    the seas and all that move in them,
35 for God will save Zion
    and rebuild the cities of Judah.
    Then people will settle there and possess it;
36   the children of his servants will inherit
    it,
    and those who love his name will dwell
    there.

Psalm 70

For the director of music. Of David. A petition.

1 Hasten, O God, to save me;
    O LORD, come quickly to help me.
2 May those who seek my life
    be put to shame and confusion;
    may all who desire my ruin
    be turned back in disgrace.
3 May those who say to me, "Aha! Aha!"
    turn back because of
    their shame.
4 But may all who seek you
    rejoice and be glad in
    you;
    may those who love your
    salvation always say,
    "Let God be exalted!"

5 Yet I am poor and needy;
    come quickly to me,
    O God.
    You are my help and my
    deliverer;
    O LORD, do not delay.

Psalm 70:5

God Rescues Us

Yet I am poor and needy;
come quickly to me,
O God.
You are my help and
my deliverer;
O LORD, do not delay.

Psalm 71

1 In you, O LORD, I have taken refuge;
    let me never be put to shame.
2 Rescue me and deliver me in your
    righteousness;

turn your ear to me and save me.
³ Be my rock of refuge,
  to which I can always go;
give the command to save me,
  for you are my rock and my fortress.

⁴ Deliver me, O my God,
    from the hand of
    the wicked,
  from the grasp of evil
    and cruel men.

⁵ For you have been my hope,
    O Sovereign LORD,
  my confidence since my
    youth.
⁶ From birth I have relied on
    you;
  you brought me forth
    from my mother's
    womb.
  I will ever praise you.
⁷ I have become like a portent to many,
  but you are my strong refuge.
⁸ My mouth is filled with your praise,
  declaring your splendor all day long.

⁹ Do not cast me away when I am old;
  do not forsake me when my strength is
    gone.
¹⁰ For my enemies speak against me;
  those who wait to kill me conspire
    together.
¹¹ They say, "God has forsaken him;
  pursue him and seize him,
  for no one will rescue him."
¹² Be not far from me, O God;
  come quickly, O my God, to help me.
¹³ May my accusers perish in shame;
  may those who want to harm me
  be covered with scorn and disgrace.

¹⁴ But as for me, I will always have hope;
  I will praise you more and more.
¹⁵ My mouth will tell of your righteousness,
  of your salvation all day long,
  though I know not its measure.
¹⁶ I will come and proclaim your *mighty acts*,
    O Sovereign LORD;
  I will proclaim your righteousness,
    yours alone.

Psalm 71:5

God Inspires Confidence

For you have been my
hope, O Sovereign LORD,
my confidence since
my youth.

¹⁷ Since my youth, O God, you have taught
    me,
  and to this day I declare your marvelous
    deeds.
¹⁸ Even when I am old and gray,
      do not forsake me,
      O God,
  till I declare your power to
      the next generation,
    your might to all who are
      to come.

¹⁹ Your righteousness reaches
    to the skies, O God,
  you who have done great
    things.
    Who, O God, is like you?
²⁰ Though you have made me
      see troubles, many
      and bitter,
  you will restore my life again;
  from the depths of the earth
    you will again bring me up.
²¹ You will increase my honor
  and comfort me once again.

²² I will praise you with the harp
    for your faithfulness, O my God;
  I will sing praise to you with the lyre,
    O Holy One of Israel.
²³ My lips will shout for joy
    when I sing praise to you—
  I, whom you have redeemed.
²⁴ My tongue will tell of your righteous acts
    all day long,
  for those who wanted to harm me
    have been put to shame and confusion.

Psalm 72
Of Solomon.

¹ Endow the king with your justice, O God,
  the royal son with your righteousness.
² He will[a] judge your people in
    righteousness,
  your afflicted ones with justice.
³ The mountains will bring prosperity to the
    people,
  the hills the fruit of righteousness.
⁴ He will defend the afflicted among the
    people

a 2 Or *May he*; similarly in verses 3–11 and 17

Unshakable Confidence

Read: Psalm 71:1–24

WHAT DO YOU RELY ON to give you confidence? Your skills, your degrees, your accomplishments? What about when you sense a call to do a task for which you feel unqualified? Have you ever found yourself wondering, "Who am I to _____ [lead this group, start this ministry, supervise these employees, organize this fundraiser, teach these children . . .]?" Have you ever thought, "You picked the wrong woman for this job, Lord"?

If we rely on ourselves, we will *not* be qualified for that which God calls us. In fact, throughout Scripture we see that God often chose people who felt unqualified for the tasks God laid before them: Abraham, Sarah, Moses, David, Esther and Mary all felt unequal to the task. But if God can use a roaming Bedouin to birth a nation, a stuttering speaker to confront Egypt's pharaoh, a shepherd boy to lead a nation, an exiled Jewish girl to rescue her people and a timid teenager to bear the Son of God, then God can use us! The critical question isn't, "Can I do this?" The better question is, "Can God do this through me?" The answer is a resounding "Yes!"

When the psalmist asked God to be a refuge and rescuer in Psalm 71, he boldly proclaimed his dependence upon the Sovereign Lord. The psalmist knew that every breath he had taken had occurred because God had given it. Throughout his lifetime he had been dependent on God.

When we feel weak-kneed and lack confidence, we are most open to relying on God. The Bible gives us affirmation after affirmation of God's strength in the face of our limited ability: "I can do everything through him who gives me strength" (Philippians 4:13). "Nothing is impossible with God" (Luke 1:37). "Nothing is too hard for [the Lord]" (Jeremiah 32:17). "In all these things we are more than conquerors through him who loved us" (Romans 8:37). "My grace is sufficient for you, for my power is made perfect in weakness" (2 Corinthians 12:9). Nothing silences the voice of timidity as powerfully as the voice of Scripture.

So if you find yourself in a new situation today, make sure you don't rely on your own limited talents or skills, but that you place your unshakable confidence in the limitless God.

Go to page 712 for your next devotional reading.

Psalm 71:5–6

For you have been my hope, O Sovereign LORD, my confidence since my youth. From birth I have relied on you.

reflection

1 On what or on whom do you tend to rely when feeling out of your comfort zone?

2 Is there an area in your life in which God might be calling you to move out in faith? What fears do you have about that situation?

3 How does the psalmist's reliance on God in Psalm 71 encourage you and renew your confidence in God's ability to help you?

RELATED READINGS

Exodus 3:1–15;
Joshua 1:1–9;
Luke 1:26–38;
2 Corinthians 3:4–6;
2 Timothy 1:7–12

and save the children of the needy;
he will crush the oppressor.

⁵ He will endure[a] as long as the sun,
as long as the moon, through all
generations.
⁶ He will be like rain falling on a mown
field,
like showers watering the earth.
⁷ In his days the righteous will flourish;
prosperity will abound till the moon is
no more.

⁸ He will rule from sea to sea
and from the River[b] to the ends of the
earth.[c]
⁹ The desert tribes will bow before him
and his enemies will lick the dust.
¹⁰ The kings of Tarshish and of distant shores
will bring tribute to him;
the kings of Sheba and Seba
will present him gifts.
¹¹ All kings will bow down to him
and all nations will serve him.

¹² For he will deliver the needy who cry out,
the afflicted who have no one to help.
¹³ He will take pity on the weak and the needy
and save the needy from death.
¹⁴ He will rescue them from oppression and
violence,
for precious is their blood in his sight.

¹⁵ Long may he live!
May gold from Sheba be given him.
May people ever pray for him
and bless him all day long.
¹⁶ Let grain abound throughout the land;
on the tops of the hills may it sway.
Let its fruit flourish like Lebanon;
let it thrive like the grass of the field.
¹⁷ May his name endure forever;
may it continue as long as the sun.

All nations will be blessed through him,
and they will call him blessed.

¹⁸ Praise be to the LORD God, the God of
Israel,
who alone does marvelous deeds.

¹⁹ Praise be to his glorious name forever;
may the whole earth be filled with his
glory.
Amen and Amen.

²⁰ This concludes the prayers of David son of
Jesse.

BOOK III
Psalms 73–89

Psalm 73
A psalm of Asaph.

¹ Surely God is good to Israel,
to those who are pure in heart.

² But as for me, my feet had almost slipped;
I had nearly lost my foothold.
³ For I envied the arrogant
when I saw the prosperity of the wicked.

⁴ They have no struggles;
their bodies are healthy and strong.[d]
⁵ They are free from the burdens common to
man;
they are not plagued by human ills.
⁶ Therefore pride is their necklace;
they clothe themselves with violence.
⁷ From their callous hearts comes iniquity[e]
the evil conceits of their minds know no
limits.
⁸ They scoff, and speak with malice;
in their arrogance they threaten
oppression.
⁹ Their mouths lay claim to heaven,
and their tongues take possession of the
earth.
¹⁰ Therefore their people turn to them
and drink up waters in abundance.[f]
¹¹ They say, "How can God know?
Does the Most High have knowledge?"

¹² This is what the wicked are like—
always carefree, they increase in wealth.

¹³ Surely in vain have I kept my heart pure;
in vain have I washed my hands in
innocence.
¹⁴ All day long I have been plagued;
I have been punished every morning.

---

[a]5 Septuagint; Hebrew *You will be feared*   [b]8 That is, the Euphrates   [c]8 Or *the end of the land*   [d]4 With a different word division of the Hebrew; Masoretic Text *struggles at their death; / their bodies are healthy*   [e]7 Syriac (see also Septuagint); Hebrew *Their eyes bulge with fat*   [f]10 The meaning of the Hebrew for this verse is uncertain.

15 If I had said, "I will speak thus,"
    I would have betrayed your children.
16 When I tried to understand all this,
    it was oppressive to me
17 till I entered the sanctuary of God;
    then I understood their final destiny.

18 Surely you place them on slippery
        ground;
    you cast them down to ruin.
19 How suddenly are they destroyed,
    completely swept away by terrors!
20 As a dream when one awakes,
    so when you arise, O Lord,
    you will despise them as fantasies.

21 When my heart was grieved
    and my spirit embittered,
22 I was senseless and ignorant;
    I was a brute beast before you.

23 Yet I am always with you;
    you hold me by my right hand.
24 You guide me with your counsel,
    and afterward you will take me into
        glory.
25 Whom have I in heaven but you?
    And earth has nothing I desire besides
        you.
26 My flesh and my heart may fail,
    but God is the strength of my heart
    and my portion forever.

27 Those who are far from you will perish;
    you destroy all who are unfaithful to
        you.
28 But as for me, it is good to be near God.
    I have made the Sovereign LORD my
        refuge;
    I will tell of all your deeds.

Psalm 74
A *maskil*[a] of Asaph.

1 Why have you rejected us forever, O God?
    Why does your anger smolder against
        the sheep of your pasture?
2 Remember the people you purchased of
        old,
    the tribe of your inheritance, whom you
        redeemed—
    Mount Zion, where you dwelt.

3 Turn your steps toward these everlasting
        ruins,
    all this destruction the enemy has
        brought on the sanctuary.

4 Your foes roared in the place where you
        met with us;
    they set up their standards as signs.
5 They behaved like men wielding axes
    to cut through a thicket of trees.
6 They smashed all the carved paneling
    with their axes and hatchets.
7 They burned your sanctuary to the
        ground;
    they defiled the dwelling place of your
        Name.
8 They said in their hearts, "We will crush
        them completely!"
    They burned every place where God was
        worshiped in the land.
9 We are given no miraculous signs;
    no prophets are left,
    and none of us knows how long this will
        be.

10 How long will the enemy mock you,
        O God?
    Will the foe revile your name forever?
11 Why do you hold back your hand, your
        right hand?
    Take it from the folds of your garment
        and destroy them!

12 But you, O God, are my king from of
        old;
    you bring salvation upon the earth.
13 It was you who split open the sea by your
        power;
    you broke the heads of the monster in
        the waters.
14 It was you who crushed the heads of
        Leviathan
    and gave him as food to the creatures of
        the desert.
15 It was you who opened up springs and
        streams;
    you dried up the ever flowing rivers.
16 The day is yours, and yours also the
        night;
    you established the sun and moon.

[a]Title: Probably a literary or musical term

17 It was you who set all the boundaries of the earth;
   you made both summer and winter.

18 Remember how the enemy has mocked you, O LORD,
   how foolish people have reviled your name.

19 Do not hand over the life of your dove to wild beasts;
   do not forget the lives of your afflicted people forever.

20 Have regard for your covenant,
   because haunts of violence fill the dark places of the land.

21 Do not let the oppressed retreat in disgrace;
   may the poor and needy praise your name.

22 Rise up, O God, and defend your cause;
   remember how fools mock you all day long.

23 Do not ignore the clamor of your adversaries,
   the uproar of your enemies, which rises continually.

Psalm 75

For the director of music. To the tune of, "Do Not Destroy." A psalm of Asaph. A song.

1 We give thanks to you,
     O God,
   we give thanks, for your Name is near;
   men tell of your wonderful deeds.

2 You say, "I choose the appointed time;
   it is I who judge uprightly.

3 When the earth and all its people quake,
   it is I who hold its pillars firm.   *Selah*

4 To the arrogant I say, 'Boast no more,'
   and to the wicked, 'Do not lift up your horns.

5 Do not lift your horns against heaven;
   do not speak with outstretched neck.'"

6 No one from the east or the west
   or from the desert can exalt a man.

7 But it is God who judges:
   He brings one down, he exalts another.

8 In the hand of the LORD is a cup
   full of foaming wine mixed with spices;
   he pours it out, and all the wicked of the earth
   drink it down to its very dregs.

9 As for me, I will declare this forever;
   I will sing praise to the God of Jacob.

10 I will cut off the horns of all the wicked,
   but the horns of the righteous will be lifted up.

Psalm 76

For the director of music. With stringed instruments. A psalm of Asaph. A song.

1 In Judah God is known;
   his name is great in Israel.

2 His tent is in Salem,
   his dwelling place in Zion.

3 There he broke the flashing arrows,
   the shields and the swords, the weapons of war.   *Selah*

4 You are resplendent with light,
   more majestic than mountains rich with game.

5 Valiant men lie plundered,
   they sleep their last sleep;
   not one of the warriors can lift his hands.

6 At your rebuke, O God of Jacob,
   both horse and chariot lie still.

7 You alone are to be feared.
   Who can stand before you when you are angry?

8 From heaven you pronounced judgment,
   and the land feared and was quiet—

9 when you, O God, rose up to judge,
   to save all the afflicted of the land.   *Selah*

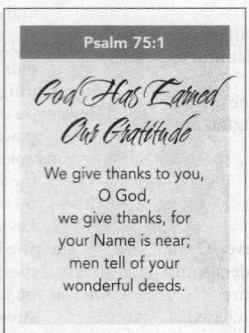

Psalm 75:1

God Has Earned Our Gratitude

We give thanks to you,
   O God,
we give thanks, for
   your Name is near;
men tell of your
   wonderful deeds.

¹⁰Surely your wrath against men brings you
    praise,
  and the survivors of your wrath are
    restrained.*ᵃ*

¹¹Make vows to the Lᴏʀᴅ your God and
    fulfill them;
  let all the neighboring lands
  bring gifts to the One to be feared.
¹²He breaks the spirit of rulers;
  he is feared by the kings of the earth.

Psalm 77
For the director of music. For Jeduthun. Of Asaph.
A psalm.

¹I cried out to God for help;
  I cried out to God to hear me.
²When I was in distress, I sought the Lord;
  at night I stretched out untiring hands
  and my soul refused to be comforted.

³I remembered you, O God, and I groaned;
  I mused, and my spirit grew faint.
        Selah

⁴You kept my eyes from closing;
  I was too troubled to speak.
⁵I thought about the former days,
  the years of long ago;
⁶I remembered my songs in the night.
  My heart mused and my spirit inquired:

⁷"Will the Lord reject
    forever?
  Will he never show his
    favor again?
⁸Has his unfailing love
    vanished forever?
  Has his promise failed
    for all time?
⁹Has God forgotten to be
    merciful?
  Has he in anger withheld
    his compassion?"
        Selah

¹⁰Then I thought, "To this I
    will appeal:
  the years of the right
    hand of the Most
    High."
¹¹I will remember the deeds of the Lᴏʀᴅ;

yes, I will remember your miracles of
    long ago.
¹²I will meditate on all your works
  and consider all your mighty deeds.

¹³Your ways, O God, are holy.
  What god is so great as our God?
¹⁴You are the God who performs miracles;
  you display your power among the
    peoples.
¹⁵With your mighty arm you redeemed your
    people,
  the descendants of Jacob and Joseph.
        Selah

¹⁶The waters saw you, O God,
  the waters saw you and writhed;
  the very depths were convulsed.
¹⁷The clouds poured down water,
  the skies resounded with thunder;
  your arrows flashed back and forth.
¹⁸Your thunder was heard in the whirlwind,
  your lightning lit up the world;
  the earth trembled and quaked.
¹⁹Your path led through the sea,
  your way through the mighty waters,
  though your footprints were not seen.

²⁰You led your people like a flock
  by the hand of Moses and Aaron.

Psalm 78
A maskilᵇ of Asaph.

¹O my people, hear my
    teaching;
  listen to the words of my
    mouth.
²I will open my mouth in
    parables,
  I will utter hidden
    things, things from
    of old—
³what we have heard and
    known,
  what our fathers have
    told us.
⁴We will not hide them
    from their children;
  we will tell the next
    generation

Psalm 78:4

God Is Praiseworthy

We will not hide them
from their children;
we will tell the
next generation
the praiseworthy deeds
of the Lᴏʀᴅ,
his power, and the
wonders he has done.

---

*ᵃ*10 Or *Surely the wrath of men brings you praise, / and with the remainder of wrath you arm yourself*   *ᵇ*Title: Probably a literary or musical term

the praiseworthy deeds of the Lord,
his power, and the wonders he has done.
⁵ He decreed statutes for Jacob
and established the law in Israel,
which he commanded our forefathers
to teach their children,
⁶ so the next generation would know them,
even the children yet to be born,
and they in turn would tell their
children.
⁷ Then they would put their trust in God
and would not forget his deeds
but would keep his commands.
⁸ They would not be like their forefathers—
a stubborn and rebellious generation,
whose hearts were not loyal to God,
whose spirits were not faithful to him.

⁹ The men of Ephraim, though armed with
bows,
turned back on the day of battle;
¹⁰ they did not keep God's covenant
and refused to live by his law.
¹¹ They forgot what he had done,
the wonders he had shown them.
¹² He did miracles in the sight of their fathers
in the land of Egypt, in the region of
Zoan.
¹³ He divided the sea and led them through;
he made the water stand firm like a wall.
¹⁴ He guided them with the cloud by day
and with light from the fire all night.
¹⁵ He split the rocks in the desert
and gave them water as abundant as the
seas;
¹⁶ he brought streams out of a rocky crag
and made water flow down like rivers.

¹⁷ But they continued to sin against him,
rebelling in the desert against the Most
High.
¹⁸ They willfully put God to the test
by demanding the food they craved.
¹⁹ They spoke against God, saying,
"Can God spread a table in the desert?
²⁰ When he struck the rock, water gushed out,
and streams flowed abundantly.
But can he also give us food?
Can he supply meat for his people?"
²¹ When the Lord heard them, he was very
angry;

his fire broke out against Jacob,
and his wrath rose against Israel,
²² for they did not believe in God
or trust in his deliverance.
²³ Yet he gave a command to the skies above
and opened the doors of the heavens;
²⁴ he rained down manna for the people to
eat,
he gave them the grain of heaven.
²⁵ Men ate the bread of angels;
he sent them all the food they could eat.
²⁶ He let loose the east wind from the heavens
and led forth the south wind by his
power.
²⁷ He rained meat down on them like dust,
flying birds like sand on the seashore.
²⁸ He made them come down inside their
camp,
all around their tents.
²⁹ They ate till they had more than enough,
for he had given them what they craved.
³⁰ But before they turned from the food they
craved,
even while it was still in their mouths,
³¹ God's anger rose against them;
he put to death the sturdiest among
them,
cutting down the young men of Israel.

³² In spite of all this, they kept on sinning;
in spite of his wonders, they did not
believe.
³³ So he ended their days in futility
and their years in terror.
³⁴ Whenever God slew them, they would seek
him;
they eagerly turned to him again.
³⁵ They remembered that God was their
Rock,
that God Most High was their
Redeemer.
³⁶ But then they would flatter him with their
mouths,
lying to him with their tongues;
³⁷ their hearts were not loyal to him,
they were not faithful to his covenant.
³⁸ Yet he was merciful;
he forgave their iniquities
and did not destroy them.
Time after time he restrained his anger
and did not stir up his full wrath.

³⁹ He remembered that they were but flesh,
a passing breeze that does not return.

⁴⁰ How often they rebelled against him in the desert
and grieved him in the wasteland!
⁴¹ Again and again they put God to the test;
they vexed the Holy One of Israel.
⁴² They did not remember his power—
the day he redeemed them from the oppressor,
⁴³ the day he displayed his miraculous signs in Egypt,
his wonders in the region of Zoan.
⁴⁴ He turned their rivers to blood;
they could not drink from their streams.
⁴⁵ He sent swarms of flies that devoured them,
and frogs that devastated them.
⁴⁶ He gave their crops to the grasshopper,
their produce to the locust.
⁴⁷ He destroyed their vines with hail
and their sycamore-figs with sleet.
⁴⁸ He gave over their cattle to the hail,
their livestock to bolts of lightning.
⁴⁹ He unleashed against them his hot anger,
his wrath, indignation and hostility—
a band of destroying angels.
⁵⁰ He prepared a path for his anger;
he did not spare them from death
but gave them over to the plague.
⁵¹ He struck down all the firstborn of Egypt,
the firstfruits of manhood in the tents of Ham.
⁵² But he brought his people out like a flock;
he led them like sheep through the desert.
⁵³ He guided them safely, so they were unafraid;
but the sea engulfed their enemies.
⁵⁴ Thus he brought them to the border of his holy land,
to the hill country his right hand had taken.
⁵⁵ He drove out nations before them
and allotted their lands to them as an inheritance;
he settled the tribes of Israel in their homes.

⁵⁶ But they put God to the test
and rebelled against the Most High;

they did not keep his statutes.
⁵⁷ Like their fathers they were disloyal and faithless,
as unreliable as a faulty bow.
⁵⁸ They angered him with their high places;
they aroused his jealousy with their idols.
⁵⁹ When God heard them, he was very angry;
he rejected Israel completely.
⁶⁰ He abandoned the tabernacle of Shiloh,
the tent he had set up among men.
⁶¹ He sent the ark of his might into captivity,
his splendor into the hands of the enemy.
⁶² He gave his people over to the sword;
he was very angry with his inheritance.
⁶³ Fire consumed their young men,
and their maidens had no wedding songs;
⁶⁴ their priests were put to the sword,
and their widows could not weep.

⁶⁵ Then the Lord awoke as from sleep,
as a man wakes from the stupor of wine.
⁶⁶ He beat back his enemies;
he put them to everlasting shame.
⁶⁷ Then he rejected the tents of Joseph,
he did not choose the tribe of Ephraim;
⁶⁸ but he chose the tribe of Judah,
Mount Zion, which he loved.
⁶⁹ He built his sanctuary like the heights,
like the earth that he established forever.
⁷⁰ He chose David his servant
and took him from the sheep pens;
⁷¹ from tending the sheep he brought him
to be the shepherd of his people Jacob,
of Israel his inheritance.
⁷² And David shepherded them with integrity of heart;
with skillful hands he led them.

Psalm 79

A psalm of Asaph.

¹ O God, the nations have invaded your inheritance;
they have defiled your holy temple,
they have reduced Jerusalem to rubble.
² They have given the dead bodies of your servants
as food to the birds of the air,

the flesh of your saints to the beasts of
the earth.
³ They have poured out blood like water
all around Jerusalem,
and there is no one to bury the dead.
⁴ We are objects of reproach to our
neighbors,
of scorn and derision to those around
us.

⁵ How long, O LORD? Will you be angry
forever?
How long will your jealousy burn like
fire?
⁶ Pour out your wrath on the nations
that do not acknowledge you,
on the kingdoms
that do not call on your name;
⁷ for they have devoured Jacob
and destroyed his homeland.
⁸ Do not hold against us the sins of the
fathers;
may your mercy come quickly to meet
us,
for we are in desperate need.

⁹ Help us, O God our Savior,
for the glory of your name;
deliver us and forgive our sins
for your name's sake.
¹⁰ Why should the nations say,
"Where is their God?"
Before our eyes, make known among the
nations
that you avenge the outpoured blood of
your servants.
¹¹ May the groans of the prisoners come
before you;
by the strength of your arm
preserve those condemned to die.

¹² Pay back into the laps of our neighbors
seven times
the reproach they have hurled at you,
O Lord.
¹³ Then we your people, the sheep of your
pasture,
will praise you forever;
from generation to generation
we will recount your praise.

Psalm 80

For the director of music. To the tune of "The
Lilies of the Covenant." Of Asaph. A psalm.

¹ Hear us, O Shepherd of Israel,
you who lead Joseph like a flock;
you who sit enthroned between the
cherubim, shine forth
² before Ephraim, Benjamin and
Manasseh.
Awaken your might;
come and save us.

³ Restore us, O God;
make your face shine upon us,
that we may be saved.

⁴ O LORD God Almighty,
how long will your anger smolder
against the prayers of your people?
⁵ You have fed them with the bread of tears;
you have made them drink tears by the
bowlful.
⁶ You have made us a source of contention to
our neighbors,
and our enemies mock us.

⁷ Restore us, O God Almighty;
make your face shine upon us,
that we may be saved.

⁸ You brought a vine out of Egypt;
you drove out the nations and planted it.
⁹ You cleared the ground for it,
and it took root and filled the land.
¹⁰ The mountains were covered with its
shade,
the mighty cedars with its branches.
¹¹ It sent out its boughs to the Sea,ᵃ
its shoots as far as the River.ᵇ

¹² Why have you broken down its walls
so that all who pass by pick its grapes?
¹³ Boars from the forest ravage it
and the creatures of the field feed on it.
¹⁴ Return to us, O God Almighty!
Look down from heaven and see!
Watch over this vine,
¹⁵ the root your right hand has planted,
the sonᶜ you have raised up for yourself.

¹⁶ Your vine is cut down, it is burned with
fire;

ᵃ11 Probably the Mediterranean   ᵇ11 That is, the Euphrates   ᶜ15 Or branch

at your rebuke your people perish.
¹⁷ Let your hand rest on the man at your
right hand,
the son of man you have raised up for
yourself.
¹⁸ Then we will not turn away from you;
revive us, and we will call on your name.

¹⁹ Restore us, O LORD God Almighty;
make your face shine upon us,
that we may be saved.

Psalm 81

For the director of music. According to *gittith*.[a]
Of Asaph.

¹ Sing for joy to God our strength;
shout aloud to the God
of Jacob!
² Begin the music, strike the
tambourine,
play the melodious harp
and lyre.

³ Sound the ram's horn at the
New Moon,
and when the moon is
full, on the day of
our Feast;
⁴ this is a decree for Israel,
an ordinance of the God
of Jacob.
⁵ He established it as a statute for Joseph
when he went out against Egypt,
where we heard a language we did not
understand.[b]

⁶ He says, "I removed the burden from their
shoulders;
their hands were set free from the
basket.
⁷ In your distress you called and I rescued
you,
I answered you out of a thundercloud;
I tested you at the waters of Meribah.
Selah

⁸ "Hear, O my people, and I will warn you—
if you would but listen to me, O Israel!
⁹ You shall have no foreign god among you;
you shall not bow down to an alien god.
¹⁰ I am the LORD your God,

who brought you up out of Egypt.
Open wide your mouth and I will fill it.

¹¹ "But my people would not listen to me;
Israel would not submit to me.
¹² So I gave them over to their stubborn
hearts
to follow their own devices.

¹³ "If my people would but listen to me,
if Israel would follow my ways,
¹⁴ how quickly would I subdue their enemies
and turn my hand against their foes!
¹⁵ Those who hate the LORD would cringe
before him,
and their punishment would last forever.
¹⁶ But you would be fed with
the finest of wheat;
with honey from the
rock I would satisfy
you."

Psalm 82

A psalm of Asaph.

¹ God presides in the great
assembly;
he gives judgment
among the "gods":

² "How long will you[c] defend
the unjust
and show partiality to the wicked? *Selah*
³ Defend the cause of the weak and
fatherless;
maintain the rights of the poor and
oppressed.
⁴ Rescue the weak and needy;
deliver them from the hand of the wicked.

⁵ "They know nothing, they understand
nothing.
They walk about in darkness;
all the foundations of the earth are
shaken.

⁶ "I said, 'You are "gods";
you are all sons of the Most High.'
⁷ But you will die like mere men;
you will fall like every other ruler."

⁸ Rise up, O God, judge the earth,
for all the nations are your inheritance.

Psalm 81:1

God Is Strong

Sing for joy to God
our strength;
shout aloud to the
God of Jacob!

---

a Title: Probably a musical term   *b* 5 Or *I and we heard a voice we had not known*   *c* 2 The Hebrew is plural.

Psalm 83

A song. A psalm of Asaph.

¹ O God, do not keep silent;
  be not quiet, O God, be not still.
² See how your enemies are astir,
  how your foes rear their heads.
³ With cunning they conspire against your
    people;
  they plot against those you cherish.
⁴ "Come," they say, "let us destroy them as a
    nation,
  that the name of Israel be remembered
    no more."

⁵ With one mind they plot together;
  they form an alliance against you—
⁶ the tents of Edom and the Ishmaelites,
  of Moab and the Hagrites,
⁷ Gebal,ᵃ Ammon and Amalek,
  Philistia, with the people of Tyre.
⁸ Even Assyria has joined them
  to lend strength to the descendants of
    Lot.   Selah

⁹ Do to them as you did to Midian,
  as you did to Sisera and Jabin at the river
    Kishon,
¹⁰ who perished at Endor
  and became like refuse on the ground.
¹¹ Make their nobles like Oreb and Zeeb,
  all their princes like Zebah and
    Zalmunna,
¹² who said, "Let us take possession
  of the pasturelands of God."

¹³ Make them like tumbleweed, O my God,
  like chaff before the wind.
¹⁴ As fire consumes the forest
  or a flame sets the mountains ablaze,
¹⁵ so pursue them with your tempest
  and terrify them with your storm.
¹⁶ Cover their faces with shame
  so that men will seek your name,
    O Lord.

¹⁷ May they ever be ashamed and dismayed;
  may they perish in disgrace.
¹⁸ Let them know that you, whose name is
    the Lord—
  that you alone are the Most High over
    all the earth.

Psalm 84

For the director of music. According to *gittith*.ᵇ
Of the Sons of Korah. A psalm.

¹ How lovely is your dwelling place,
  O Lord Almighty!
² My soul yearns, even faints,
  for the courts of the Lord;
  my heart and my flesh cry out
  for the living God.

³ Even the sparrow has found a home,
  and the swallow a nest for herself,
  where she may have her young—
  a place near your altar,
  O Lord Almighty, my King and my
    God.
⁴ Blessed are those who dwell in your house;
  they are ever praising you.   Selah

⁵ Blessed are those whose strength is in you,
  who have set their hearts on pilgrimage.
⁶ As they pass through the Valley of Baca,
  they make it a place of springs;
  the autumn rains also cover it with
    pools.ᶜ
⁷ They go from strength to strength,
  till each appears before God in Zion.

⁸ Hear my prayer, O Lord God Almighty;
  listen to me, O God of Jacob.   Selah
⁹ Look upon our shield,ᵈ O God;
  look with favor on your anointed one.

¹⁰ Better is one day in your courts
  than a thousand elsewhere;
  I would rather be a doorkeeper in the
    house of my God
  than dwell in the tents of the wicked.
¹¹ For the Lord God is a sun and shield;
  the Lord bestows favor and honor;
  no good thing does he withhold
  from those whose walk is blameless.

¹² O Lord Almighty,
  blessed is the man who trusts in you.

Psalm 85

For the director of music. Of the Sons of Korah.
A psalm.

¹ You showed favor to your land, O Lord;
  you restored the fortunes of Jacob.
² You forgave the iniquity of your people

ᵃ7 That is, Byblos   ᵇTitle: Probably a musical term   ᶜ6 Or *blessings*   ᵈ9 Or *sovereign*

and covered all their sins. *Selah*

³ You set aside all your wrath
and turned from your fierce anger.

⁴ Restore us again, O God our Savior,
and put away your displeasure toward
us.

⁵ Will you be angry with us forever?
Will you prolong your anger through all
generations?

⁶ Will you not revive us again,
that your people may rejoice in you?

⁷ Show us your unfailing love, O LORD,
and grant us your salvation.

⁸ I will listen to what God the
LORD will say;
he promises peace to his
people, his saints—
but let them not return
to folly.

⁹ Surely his salvation is near
those who fear him,
that his glory may dwell
in our land.

¹⁰ Love and faithfulness meet
together;
righteousness and peace
kiss each other.

¹¹ Faithfulness springs forth
from the earth,
and righteousness looks down from
heaven.

¹² The LORD will indeed give what is good,
and our land will yield its harvest.

¹³ Righteousness goes before him
and prepares the way for his steps.

Psalm 86
A prayer of David.

¹ Hear, O LORD, and answer me,
for I am poor and needy.

² Guard my life, for I am devoted to you.
You are my God; save your servant
who trusts in you.

³ Have mercy on me, O Lord,
for I call to you all day long.

⁴ Bring joy to your servant,
for to you, O Lord,
I lift up my soul.

⁵ You are forgiving and good, O Lord,
abounding in love to all who call to you.

⁶ Hear my prayer, O LORD;
listen to my cry for mercy.

⁷ In the day of my trouble I will call to you,
for you will answer me.

⁸ Among the gods there is none like you,
O Lord;
no deeds can compare with yours.

⁹ All the nations you have made
will come and worship before you,
O Lord;
they will bring glory to your name.

¹⁰ For you are great and do
marvelous deeds;
you alone are God.

¹¹ Teach me your way,
O LORD,
and I will walk in your
truth;
give me an undivided
heart,
that I may fear your
name.

¹² I will praise you, O Lord
my God, with all
my heart;
I will glorify your name
forever.

¹³ For great is your love toward me;
you have delivered me from the depths
of the grave.ᵃ

¹⁴ The arrogant are attacking me, O God;
a band of ruthless men seeks my life—
men without regard for you.

¹⁵ But you, O Lord, are a compassionate and
gracious God,
slow to anger, abounding in love and
faithfulness.

¹⁶ Turn to me and have mercy on me;
grant your strength to your servant
and save the son of your maidservant.ᵇ

¹⁷ Give me a sign of your goodness,
that my enemies may see it and be put
to shame,
for you, O LORD, have helped me and
comforted me.

Psalm 85:8

God Promises Peace

I will listen to what God
the LORD will say;
he promises peace to his
people, his saints—
but let them not
return to folly.

ᵃ13 Hebrew *Sheol*   ᵇ16 Or *save your faithful son*

Will the Real God Please Stand Up?

Psalm 86:15

But you, O Lord, are a compassionate and gracious God, slow to anger, abounding in love and faithfulness.

Read: Psalm 86:1–17

reflection

1 What false images of God do you have that keep you from coming boldly before his throne?

2 How has a parent shaped your image of God, positively or negatively? How have other relationships in your life shaped your image of God?

3 Choose one character trait of God's that is listed in this psalm and meditate on it today. What new insights do you gain?

RELATED READINGS

Psalms 103:1–22;
145:1–21;
Lamentations 3:22–23;
John 4:24

WHEN YOU APPROACH GOD in prayer, what are the "givens" you believe about him? That he hears you, forgives you and loves you with a steadfast love? That's how the psalmist describes God. But do you sometimes secretly picture him as an unmerciful judge, wondering if he really will forgive *this* sin—the one you find yourself repeatedly battling? Or does God seem like an absentee parent who is unresponsive to your needs rather than a loving Father who understands your pain? When you've blown it again, do you sense that God has a scowl of disappointment on his face rather than open, welcoming arms?

Sometimes without realizing it, we project upon God images of our own making—a demanding taskmaster for whom we never can do enough, an exacting parent we can never quite please, a short-tempered boss we easily anger. Yet, this is not the God of the Bible, the God of David, and this is not the real God.

Listen to David's description of the God he knew so intimately: "You are . . . abounding in love to all who call to you" (verse 5). God is not an unmerciful, cruel master but a "forgiving and good" heavenly Father. He is not skimpy with his love, and he does not play favorites. He is not a God who gives love conditionally. No, this God—our God—is overflowing with love. Even when he was poor, weak, needy and in trouble, David proclaimed, "Great is your love toward me" (verse 13).

Who is this God we serve? This is no impotent God: "You are great and do marvelous deeds" (verse 10). This is no uncaring, unaware, neglectful God who tells us, "Get over it." Rather, he is a "compassionate and gracious God" (verse 15) who comforts us in our tears. He is not a temperamental, grumpy, quick-to-anger God, but one who is "slow to anger" (verse 15). He is not an unpredictable, fickle, unreliable God, but one "abounding in . . . faithfulness" (verse 15). There is no God like him!

When you find yourself hesitant to come before God or to wholly trust him, consider what image of God you're holding onto. Is it the real God of Scripture or an impostor? Worship the real God, in spirit and in truth.

Psalm 87

Of the Sons of Korah. A psalm. A song.

1 He has set his foundation on the holy
    mountain;
2   the LORD loves the gates of Zion
    more than all the dwellings of Jacob.
3 Glorious things are said of you,
    O city of God: *Selah*

4 "I will record Rahab*a* and Babylon
    among those who acknowledge me—
    Philistia too, and Tyre, along with Cush*b*—
    and will say, 'This*c* one was born in Zion.' "

5 Indeed, of Zion it will be said,
    "This one and that one were born in her,
    and the Most High himself will establish
        her."
6 The LORD will write in the register of the
        peoples:
    "This one was born in Zion."   *Selah*
7 As they make music they will sing,
    "All my fountains are in you."

Psalm 88

A song. A psalm of the Sons of Korah. For the
director of music. According to *mahalath
leannoth.d* A *maskilе* of Heman the Ezrahite.

1 O LORD, the God who saves me,
    day and night I cry out before you.
2 May my prayer come before you;
    turn your ear to my cry.

3 For my soul is full of trouble
    and my life draws near the grave.*f*
4 I am counted among those
        who go down to the
        pit;
    I am like a man without
        strength.
5 I am set apart with the dead,
    like the slain who lie in
        the grave,
    whom you remember no
        more,
    who are cut off from
        your care.

6 You have put me in the
        lowest pit,
    in the darkest depths.

7 Your wrath lies heavily upon me;
    you have overwhelmed me with all your
        waves.   *Selah*
8 You have taken from me my closest friends
    and have made me repulsive to them.
    I am confined and cannot escape;
9   my eyes are dim with grief.

    I call to you, O LORD, every day;
    I spread out my hands to you.
10 Do you show your wonders to the dead?
    Do those who are dead rise up and
        praise you?   *Selah*
11 Is your love declared in the grave,
    your faithfulness in Destruction*g*?
12 Are your wonders known in the place of
        darkness,
    or your righteous deeds in the land of
        oblivion?

13 But I cry to you for help, O LORD;
    in the morning my prayer comes before
        you.
14 Why, O LORD, do you reject me
    and hide your face from me?

15 From my youth I have been afflicted and
        close to death;
    I have suffered your terrors and am in
        despair.
16 Your wrath has swept over me;
    your terrors have destroyed me.
17 All day long they surround me like a flood;
    they have completely engulfed me.
18   You have taken my
        companions and
        loved ones from me;
    the darkness is my
        closest friend.

Psalm 89

A *maskilе* of Ethan the Ezrahite.

1 I will sing of the LORD's
        great love forever;
    with my mouth I
        will make your
        faithfulness
        known through all
        generations.

Psalm 89:1

God Is Faithful

I will sing of the LORD's
great love forever;
with my mouth I will
make your faithfulness
known through all
generations.

*a4 A poetic name for Egypt   b4 That is, the upper Nile region   c4 Or "O Rahab and Babylon, / Philistia, Tyre and Cush, / I will record
concerning those who acknowledge me: / 'This   d Title: Possibly a tune, "The Suffering of Affliction"   е Title: Probably a literary or musical
term   f3 Hebrew Sheol   g11 Hebrew Abaddon*

² I will declare that your love stands firm
forever,
that you established your faithfulness in
heaven itself.

³ You said, "I have made a covenant with my
chosen one,
I have sworn to David my servant,
⁴ 'I will establish your line forever
and make your throne firm through all
generations.'"   *Selah*

⁵ The heavens praise your wonders, O LORD,
your faithfulness too, in the assembly of
the holy ones.
⁶ For who in the skies above can compare
with the LORD?
Who is like the LORD among the
heavenly beings?
⁷ In the council of the holy ones God is
greatly feared;
he is more awesome than all who
surround him.
⁸ O LORD God Almighty, who is like you?
You are mighty, O LORD, and your
faithfulness surrounds you.

⁹ You rule over the surging sea;
when its waves mount up, you still them.
¹⁰ You crushed Rahab like one of the slain;
with your strong arm you scattered your
enemies.
¹¹ The heavens are yours, and yours also the
earth;
you founded the world and all that is
in it.
¹² You created the north and the south;
Tabor and Hermon sing for joy at your
name.
¹³ Your arm is endued with power;
your hand is strong, your right hand
exalted.

¹⁴ Righteousness and justice are the
foundation of your throne;
love and faithfulness go before you.
¹⁵ Blessed are those who have learned to
acclaim you,
who walk in the light of your presence,
O LORD.
¹⁶ They rejoice in your name all day long;

they exult in your righteousness.
¹⁷ For you are their glory and strength,
and by your favor you exalt our horn.ᵃ
¹⁸ Indeed, our shieldᵇ belongs to the LORD,
our king to the Holy One of Israel.

¹⁹ Once you spoke in a vision,
to your faithful people you said:
"I have bestowed strength on a warrior;
I have exalted a young man from among
the people.
²⁰ I have found David my servant;
with my sacred oil I have anointed him.
²¹ My hand will sustain him;
surely my arm will strengthen him.
²² No enemy will subject him to tribute;
no wicked man will oppress him.
²³ I will crush his foes before him
and strike down his adversaries.
²⁴ My faithful love will be with him,
and through my name his hornᶜ will be
exalted.
²⁵ I will set his hand over the sea,
his right hand over the rivers.
²⁶ He will call out to me, 'You are my
Father,
my God, the Rock my Savior.'
²⁷ I will also appoint him my firstborn,
the most exalted of the kings of the
earth.
²⁸ I will maintain my love to him forever,
and my covenant with him will never
fail.
²⁹ I will establish his line forever,
his throne as long as the heavens
endure.

³⁰ "If his sons forsake my law
and do not follow my statutes,
³¹ if they violate my decrees
and fail to keep my commands,
³² I will punish their sin with the rod,
their iniquity with flogging;
³³ but I will not take my love from him,
nor will I ever betray my faithfulness.
³⁴ I will not violate my covenant
or alter what my lips have uttered.
³⁵ Once for all, I have sworn by my holiness—
and I will not lie to David—
³⁶ that his line will continue forever

ᵃ17 *Horn* here symbolizes strong one.   ᵇ18 Or *sovereign*   ᶜ24 *Horn* here symbolizes strength.

and his throne endure before me like
the sun;

³⁷ it will be established forever like the moon,
the faithful witness in the sky."   *Selah*

³⁸ But you have rejected, you have spurned,
you have been very angry with your
anointed one.

³⁹ You have renounced the covenant with
your servant
and have defiled his crown in the dust.

⁴⁰ You have broken through all his walls
and reduced his strongholds to ruins.

⁴¹ All who pass by have plundered him;
he has become the scorn of his
neighbors.

⁴² You have exalted the right hand of his foes;
you have made all his enemies rejoice.

⁴³ You have turned back the edge of his
sword
and have not supported him in battle.

⁴⁴ You have put an end to his splendor
and cast his throne to the ground.

⁴⁵ You have cut short the days of his youth;
you have covered him with a mantle of
shame.   *Selah*

⁴⁶ How long, O LORD? Will you hide yourself
forever?
How long will your wrath burn like fire?

⁴⁷ Remember how fleeting is my life.
For what futility you have created all
men!

⁴⁸ What man can live and not see death,
or save himself from the power of the
grave^a?   *Selah*

⁴⁹ O Lord, where is your former great love,
which in your faithfulness you swore to
David?

⁵⁰ Remember, Lord, how your servant has^b
been mocked,
how I bear in my heart the taunts of all
the nations,

⁵¹ the taunts with which your enemies have
mocked, O LORD,
with which they have mocked every step
of your anointed one.

⁵² Praise be to the LORD forever!
Amen and Amen.

BOOK IV
Psalms 90–106

Psalm 90
A prayer of Moses the man of God.

¹ Lord, you have been our dwelling place
throughout all generations.

² Before the mountains were born
or you brought forth the earth and the
world,
from everlasting to everlasting you are
God.

³ You turn men back to dust,
saying, "Return to dust, O sons of men."

⁴ For a thousand years in your sight
are like a day that has just gone by,
or like a watch in the night.

⁵ You sweep men away in the sleep of
death;
they are like the new grass of the
morning—

⁶ though in the morning it springs up new,
by evening it is dry and withered.

⁷ We are consumed by your anger
and terrified by your indignation.

⁸ You have set our iniquities before you,
our secret sins in the light of your
presence.

⁹ All our days pass away under your wrath;
we finish our years with a moan.

¹⁰ The length of our days is seventy years—
or eighty, if we have the strength;
yet their span^c is but trouble and sorrow,
for they quickly pass, and we fly away.

¹¹ Who knows the power of your anger?
For your wrath is as great as the fear that
is due you.

¹² Teach us to number our days aright,
that we may gain a heart of wisdom.

¹³ Relent, O LORD! How long will it be?
Have compassion on your servants.

¹⁴ Satisfy us in the morning with your
unfailing love,
that we may sing for joy and be glad all
our days.

¹⁵ Make us glad for as many days as you have
afflicted us,

---

^a48 Hebrew *Sheol*   ^b50 Or *your servants have*   ^c10 Or *yet the best of them*

Unthinkable

BATHSHEBA

David pleaded with God for the child. He fasted and went into his house and spent the nights lying on the ground.

2 Samuel 12:16

ASSIGNED READING:

2 Samuel 11:1—12:25;
1 Kings 1–2;
Psalm 51:1–19

"THE SON BORN to you will die."

As David recounted what the prophet had told him, Bathsheba shuddered. Her breath froze in her lungs so that she could neither inhale nor exhale. Like a wounded animal, an involuntary moan escaped her lips. She felt her face flush as she reached out to steady herself on David's arm.

David, too, was visibly shaken. His bloodshot eyes stared into hers.

"No. It couldn't be . . ." Her first thoughts denied the truth. Their baby boy, barely a week old, had been the picture of health just that morning. But now, with David's words ringing in her ears, she gathered the hem of her dress and ran down the palace hallway to his room. His elderly nanny met her at the doorway, frantic with concern.

"Your Highness . . . the baby . . ." her words swam together in confusion. "Something is wrong."

Bathsheba rushed to where he lay, scooping the limp figure into her arms. His breathing was shallow and ragged. Her perfectly healthy boy, their son, was now dying.

She sank to her knees in a crumpled heap and pushed back her hair with her palms. *This couldn't be happening.* First her husband, Uriah, and now the unthinkable. How much more could she take?

She realized what the prophet said regarding sin, but who could think about blame at a time like this? The overwhelming pain of losing a child eclipsed everything else. And watching David suffer heightened her agony. For the next few days, she watched helplessly as grief threatened to drown her husband. He wouldn't eat. He wouldn't sleep.

If they had lost their child suddenly in an accident, perhaps it wouldn't hurt so badly. But she was sure that this relentless swell of heartache upon heartache each passing day was much worse.

Finally, at the end of the week, the tide receded. And what remained, mingled with the pain and heartache, was the strangest sensation of peace and relief.

—Prayer—
Gracious Lord, forgive my sin, heal my heart and give me peace.

Weekend

for as many years as we have seen
trouble.
¹⁶May your deeds be shown to your servants,
your splendor to their children.

¹⁷May the favor[a] of the Lord our God rest
upon us;
establish the work of our hands for us—
yes, establish the work of our hands.

Psalm 91

¹He who dwells in the shelter of the Most
High
will rest in the shadow of the Almighty.[b]
²I will say[c] of the Lord, "He is my refuge
and my fortress,
my God, in whom I trust."

³Surely he will save you from the fowler's
snare
and from the deadly pestilence.
⁴He will cover you with his feathers,
and under his wings you will find
refuge;
his faithfulness will be your shield and
rampart.
⁵You will not fear the terror of night,
nor the arrow that flies
by day,
⁶nor the pestilence that
stalks in the
darkness,
nor the plague that
destroys at midday.
⁷A thousand may fall at your
side,
ten thousand at your
right hand,
but it will not come near
you.
⁸You will only observe with
your eyes
and see the punishment of the wicked.

⁹If you make the Most High your
dwelling—
even the Lord, who is my refuge—
¹⁰then no harm will befall you,
no disaster will come near your tent.
¹¹For he will command his angels
concerning you

to guard you in all your ways;
¹²they will lift you up in their hands,
so that you will not strike your foot
against a stone.
¹³You will tread upon the lion and the cobra;
you will trample the great lion and the
serpent.

¹⁴"Because he loves me," says the Lord, "I
will rescue him;
I will protect him, for he acknowledges
my name.
¹⁵He will call upon me, and I will answer
him;
I will be with him in trouble,
I will deliver him and honor him.
¹⁶With long life will I satisfy him
and show him my salvation."

Psalm 92

A psalm. A song. For the Sabbath day.

¹It is good to praise the Lord
and make music to your name, O Most
High,
²to proclaim your love in the morning
and your faithfulness at night,
³to the music of the ten-
stringed lyre
and the melody of the
harp.

⁴For you make me glad
by your deeds,
O Lord;
I sing for joy at the works
of your hands.
⁵How great are your works,
O Lord,
how profound your
thoughts!
⁶The senseless man does not
know,
fools do not understand,
⁷that though the wicked spring up like grass
and all evildoers flourish,
they will be forever destroyed.

⁸But you, O Lord, are exalted forever.

⁹For surely your enemies, O Lord,
surely your enemies will perish;

Psalm 91:4

God Shields Us

He will cover you with
his feathers,
and under his wings
you will find refuge;
his faithfulness will be
your shield and rampart.

^a17 Or beauty ^b1 Hebrew Shaddai ^c2 Or He says

717

All Creation Praises Him

Psalm 92:1–2

It is good to praise the LORD and make music to your name, O Most High, to proclaim your love in the morning and your faithfulness at night.

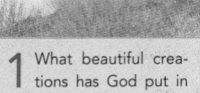

reflection

1 What beautiful creations has God put in your neighborhood or hometown for which you can praise him?

2 How has God surprised you with his love and creativity?

3 What are five things you can praise God for today?

RELATED READINGS

Psalms 19:1–14; 96:1–13; 148:1–14; Luke 19:28–40

> "What an inexpressible joy for me, to look up through the apple blossoms and the fluttering leaves, and to see God's love there."
>
> Elizabeth Charles

INSTEAD OF GREETING the morning with a grunt and a cup of coffee, birds wake up singing. Every morning around daybreak neighborhoods fill with birdsong. Referred to by bird-watchers as "the dawn chorus," the daily songfest marks a bird's territory and communicates to our ears a sound of reckless, warbling joy. True, birdsong is glorious, but only human beings sing words of praise. And our God who filled his universe with all sorts of wonderful extras *wants* our praise. He wants *our* praise. Why? Because God is worthy. Jesus said that if his followers "keep quiet, the stones will cry out" (Luke 19:40).

God, who gave the crow his harsh caw and dark plumage, also granted the cardinal his lovely song and a coat that can be seen half a block away. The God who created broccoli also surprises us with the taste of watermelon in the season we need it most. The Creator sprinkled the world with butterflies and fireflies and gave us noisy, refreshing creeks and waterfalls. He hid treasures of gold and copper, diamonds and rubies inside his mountains. And he gave us voices and even rounded up psalmists to write some of the words we can sing.

In Psalm 92 the psalmist recites several reasons why "it is good to praise the LORD":

♦ For who God is—exalted, the Most High, upright, a Rock, loving and faithful

♦ For what he does—great works and profound thoughts, judges the wicked, defeats enemies

This God deserves the praises of all his creatures: people, birds—and even the stones of the field. Whether our instrument is a flute, a guitar or our own off-key singing voices, God wants our praise. Declaring his love and faithfulness morning, noon and night is good. The ability to praise our Maker in song and words is a gift that only humans have. Use that gift and lift up a chorus of praise today.

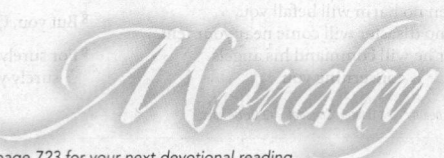

Monday

Go to page 723 for your next devotional reading.

all evildoers will be scattered.
¹⁰ You have exalted my horn^a like that of a
wild ox;
fine oils have been poured upon me.
¹¹ My eyes have seen the defeat of my
adversaries;
my ears have heard the rout of my
wicked foes.

¹² The righteous will flourish like a palm tree,
they will grow like a cedar of Lebanon;
¹³ planted in the house of the LORD,
they will flourish in the courts of our
God.
¹⁴ They will still bear fruit in old age,
they will stay fresh and green,
¹⁵ proclaiming, "The LORD is upright;
he is my Rock, and there is no
wickedness in him."

Psalm 93

¹ The LORD reigns, he is robed in majesty;
the LORD is robed in majesty
and is armed with strength.
The world is firmly established;
it cannot be moved.
² Your throne was established long ago;
you are from all eternity.

³ The seas have lifted up,
O LORD,
the seas have lifted up
their voice;
the seas have lifted up
their pounding
waves.
⁴ Mightier than the thunder
of the great waters,
mightier than the
breakers of the
sea—
the LORD on high is
mighty.

⁵ Your statutes stand firm;
holiness adorns your house
for endless days, O LORD.

Psalm 94

¹ O LORD, the God who avenges,
O God who avenges, shine forth.

² Rise up, O Judge of the earth;
pay back to the proud what they deserve.
³ How long will the wicked, O LORD,
how long will the wicked be jubilant?

⁴ They pour out arrogant words;
all the evildoers are full of boasting.
⁵ They crush your people, O LORD;
they oppress your inheritance.
⁶ They slay the widow and the alien;
they murder the fatherless.
⁷ They say, "The LORD does not see;
the God of Jacob pays no heed."

⁸ Take heed, you senseless ones among the
people;
you fools, when will you become wise?
⁹ Does he who implanted the ear not hear?
Does he who formed the eye not see?
¹⁰ Does he who disciplines nations not
punish?
Does he who teaches man lack
knowledge?
¹¹ The LORD knows the thoughts of man;
he knows that they are futile.

¹² Blessed is the man you discipline, O LORD,
the man you teach from your law;
¹³ you grant him relief from days of trouble,
till a pit is dug for the
wicked.
¹⁴ For the LORD will not reject
his people;
he will never forsake his
inheritance.
¹⁵ Judgment will again
be founded on
righteousness,
and all the upright in
heart will follow it.

¹⁶ Who will rise up for me
against the wicked?
Who will take a stand
for me against
evildoers?
¹⁷ Unless the LORD had given me help,
I would soon have dwelt in the silence
of death.
¹⁸ When I said, "My foot is slipping,"
your love, O LORD, supported me.

> **Psalm 94:14**
>
> *God Keeps His People*
>
> For the LORD will not
> reject his people;
> he will never forsake
> his inheritance.

---

^a 10 *Horn* here symbolizes strength.

19 When anxiety was great within me,
  your consolation brought joy to my soul.

20 Can a corrupt throne be allied with you—
  one that brings on misery by its decrees?
21 They band together against the righteous
  and condemn the innocent to death.
22 But the LORD has become my fortress,
  and my God the rock in whom I take
  refuge.
23 He will repay them for their sins
  and destroy them for their wickedness;
  the LORD our God will destroy them.

Psalm 95

1 Come, let us sing for joy to the LORD;
  let us shout aloud to the Rock of our
  salvation.
2 Let us come before him with thanksgiving
  and extol him with music and song.

3 For the LORD is the great God,
  the great King above all gods.
4 In his hand are the depths of the earth,
  and the mountain peaks belong to him.
5 The sea is his, for he made it,
  and his hands formed the dry land.

6 Come, let us bow down in worship,
  let us kneel before the LORD our Maker;
7 for he is our God
  and we are the people of his pasture,
  the flock under his care.

  Today, if you hear his voice,
8 do not harden your hearts as you did at
  Meribah,*a*
  as you did that day at Massah*b* in the
  desert,
9 where your fathers tested and tried me,
  though they had seen what I did.
10 For forty years I was angry with that
  generation;
  I said, "They are a people whose hearts
  go astray,
  and they have not known my ways."
11 So I declared on oath in my anger,
  "They shall never enter my rest."

Psalm 96

1 Sing to the LORD a new song;
  sing to the LORD, all the earth.

2 Sing to the LORD, praise his name;
  proclaim his salvation day after day.
3 Declare his glory among the nations,
  his marvelous deeds among all peoples.

4 For great is the LORD and most worthy of
  praise;
  he is to be feared above all gods.
5 For all the gods of the nations are idols,
  but the LORD made the heavens.
6 Splendor and majesty are before him;
  strength and glory are in his sanctuary.

7 Ascribe to the LORD, O families of nations,
  ascribe to the LORD glory and strength.
8 Ascribe to the LORD the glory due his
  name;
  bring an offering and come into his
  courts.
9 Worship the LORD in the splendor of his*c*
  holiness;
  tremble before him, all the earth.

10 Say among the nations, "The LORD reigns."
  The world is firmly established, it cannot
  be moved;
  he will judge the peoples with equity.
11 Let the heavens rejoice, let the earth be
  glad;
  let the sea resound, and all that is in it;
12 let the fields be jubilant, and everything
  in them.
  Then all the trees of the forest will sing for
  joy;
13 they will sing before the LORD, for he
  comes,
  he comes to judge the earth.
  He will judge the world in righteousness
  and the peoples in his truth.

Psalm 97

1 The LORD reigns, let the earth be glad;
  let the distant shores rejoice.

2 Clouds and thick darkness surround him;
  righteousness and justice are the
  foundation of his throne.
3 Fire goes before him
  and consumes his foes on every side.
4 His lightning lights up the world;
  the earth sees and trembles.

---

a8 Meribah means *quarreling.* *b8 Massah* means *testing.* *c9* Or LORD *with the splendor of*

5 The mountains melt like wax before the
    LORD,
  before the Lord of all the earth.
6 The heavens proclaim his righteousness,
    and all the peoples see his glory.

7 All who worship images are put to shame,
    those who boast in idols—
  worship him, all you gods!

8 Zion hears and rejoices
    and the villages of Judah are glad
  because of your judgments, O LORD.
9 For you, O LORD, are the Most High over
    all the earth;
  you are exalted far above all gods.

10 Let those who love the
    LORD hate evil,
  for he guards the lives of
    his faithful ones
  and delivers them from
    the hand of the
    wicked.
11 Light is shed upon the
    righteous
  and joy on the upright in
    heart.
12 Rejoice in the LORD, you
    who are righteous,
  and praise his holy name.

Psalm 98

A psalm.

1 Sing to the LORD a new song,
    for he has done marvelous things;
  his right hand and his holy arm
    have worked salvation for him.
2 The LORD has made his salvation known
    and revealed his righteousness to the
      nations.
3 He has remembered his love
    and his faithfulness to the house of
      Israel;
  all the ends of the earth have seen
    the salvation of our God.

4 Shout for joy to the LORD, all the earth,
    burst into jubilant song with music;
5 make music to the LORD with the harp,
    with the harp and the sound of singing,

6 with trumpets and the blast of the ram's
    horn—
  shout for joy before the LORD, the King.

7 Let the sea resound, and everything in it,
    the world, and all who live in it.
8 Let the rivers clap their hands,
    let the mountains sing together for joy;
9 let them sing before the LORD,
    for he comes to judge the earth.
  He will judge the world in righteousness
    and the peoples with equity.

Psalm 99

1 The LORD reigns,
    let the nations tremble;
  he sits enthroned between the cherubim,
    let the earth shake.
2 Great is the LORD in Zion;
    he is exalted over all the
      nations.
3 Let them praise your great
    and awesome
      name—
  he is holy.

4 The King is mighty, he
    loves justice—
  you have established
    equity;
  in Jacob you have done
    what is just and right.
5 Exalt the LORD our God
  and worship at his footstool;
  he is holy.

6 Moses and Aaron were among his priests,
    Samuel was among those who called on
      his name;
  they called on the LORD
    and he answered them.
7 He spoke to them from the pillar of
    cloud;
  they kept his statutes and the decrees he
    gave them.

8 O LORD our God,
    you answered them;
  you were to Israel[a] a forgiving God,
    though you punished their misdeeds.[b]
9 Exalt the LORD our God

Psalm 99:1

God Rules All Nations

The LORD reigns,
let the nations tremble;
he sits enthroned
between the cherubim,
let the earth shake.

---

a8 Hebrew *them*   b8 Or / *an avenger of the wrongs done to them*

and worship at his holy mountain,
for the LORD our God is holy.

Psalm 100

A psalm. For giving thanks.

1 Shout for joy to the LORD, all the earth.
2 Worship the LORD with gladness;
  come before him with joyful songs.
3 Know that the LORD is God.
  It is he who made us, and we are his*a*;
  we are his people, the sheep of his
    pasture.

4 Enter his gates with thanksgiving
  and his courts with praise;
  give thanks to him and praise his name.
5 For the LORD is good and his love endures
    forever;
  his faithfulness continues through all
    generations.

Psalm 101

Of David. A psalm.

1 I will sing of your love and justice;
  to you, O LORD, I will sing praise.
2 I will be careful to lead a blameless life—
  when will you come to me?

  I will walk in my house
  with blameless heart.
3 I will set before my eyes
  no vile thing.

  The deeds of faithless men I hate;
  they will not cling to me.
4 Men of perverse heart shall be far from me;
  I will have nothing to do with evil.

5 Whoever slanders his neighbor in secret,
  him will I put to silence;
  whoever has haughty eyes and a proud
    heart,
  him will I not endure.

6 My eyes will be on the faithful in the land,
  that they may dwell with me;
  he whose walk is blameless
  will minister to me.

7 No one who practices deceit
  will dwell in my house;
  no one who speaks falsely
  will stand in my presence.

8 Every morning I will put to silence
  all the wicked in the land;
  I will cut off every evildoer
  from the city of the LORD.

Psalm 102

A prayer of an afflicted man. When he is faint
and pours out his lament before the LORD.

1 Hear my prayer, O LORD;
  let my cry for help come to you.
2 Do not hide your face from me
  when I am in distress.
  Turn your ear to me;
  when I call, answer me quickly.

3 For my days vanish like smoke;
  my bones burn like glowing embers.
4 My heart is blighted and withered like
    grass;
  I forget to eat my food.
5 Because of my loud groaning
  I am reduced to skin and bones.
6 I am like a desert owl,
  like an owl among the ruins.
7 I lie awake; I have become
  like a bird alone on a roof.
8 All day long my enemies taunt me;
  those who rail against me use my name
    as a curse.
9 For I eat ashes as my food
  and mingle my drink with tears
10 because of your great wrath,
  for you have taken me up and thrown
    me aside.
11 My days are like the evening shadow;
  I wither away like grass.

12 But you, O LORD, sit enthroned forever;
  your renown endures through all
    generations.
13 You will arise and have compassion on
    Zion,
  for it is time to show favor to her;
  the appointed time has come.
14 For her stones are dear to your servants;
  her very dust moves them to pity.
15 The nations will fear the name of the
    LORD,
  all the kings of the earth will revere your
    glory.
16 For the LORD will rebuild Zion

a3 Or and not we ourselves

The Wow in Worship

Read: Psalm 100:1–5

SOMETIMES WE LACK THE *WOW* in our worship. Psalm 100 offers us a spiritual pick-me-up. It reveals that the more you know about God's nature, the more you'll express your love for him. Information leads to adoration. When the psalmist reflected on the Lord as God, Creator and Shepherd, it resulted in worship, gladness and joyful songs. It's true; to know him is to love him.

Knowing that "the Lord is God" (verse 3) identifies him as the only true God. He exists before all, after all and above all. He possesses power unlimited, knowledge unfathomable and a presence unavoidable. He is indescribable, indispensable and indisputable. God is big!

A little girl listened as her father read family devotions. She seemed awed by her parents' talk of God's limitless power. "Daddy," she asked, "how big is God?" Her father answered, "Honey, he is always a lot bigger than what you need." Believing that God is bigger than your situation produces passion in your praise.

Knowing that "it is he who made us" (verse 3) reveals him as Creator, the One who fashioned us into his very image (see Genesis 1:27). He displays his creativity through forming humans who are diverse yet distinct. But why did God create us? The psalmist says we were created to become his people—those of his highest priority. Your value lies not in *who* you are but in *whose* you are. Belonging to God adds awe to your adoration.

Knowing that "we are . . . the sheep of his pasture" (verse 3) can help us understand the tender care God shows his people. Shepherds are responsible for every aspect of their flock's well-being and take these responsibilities very seriously. They make sure their sheep have protection, guidance, pasture, sustenance and rest. Your Good Shepherd is like that. He leads his sheep to "green pastures" (Psalm 23:2), "calls his own sheep by name" (John 10:3) and "lays down his life for the sheep" (John 10:11). Showing gratitude to your Shepherd can engender gladness in your heart.

Understanding that the Lord is bigger than any of your needs, that he is *your* Creator—you belong to him—can't help but put the wow back into your worship!

Psalm 100:2–3

Worship the Lord with gladness; come before him with joyful songs. Know that the Lord is God. It is he who made us, and we are his; we are his people, the sheep of his pasture.

reflection

1 On a scale of one to ten, how would you rank the intensity of your worship?

2 List some of the attributes of God. In what ways has he revealed himself to you?

3 How does knowing the nature of God affect how you praise him? Now take some time to enter his gates with a joyful song that celebrates his character.

RELATED READINGS

Psalm 23:1–6;
Isaiah 42:5–6;
Romans 9:25–26;
Colossians 1:16–17

Tuesday

Go to page 726 for your next devotional reading.

and appear in his glory.
17 He will respond to the prayer of the
destitute;
he will not despise their plea.

18 Let this be written for a future generation,
that a people not yet created may praise
the LORD:
19 "The LORD looked down from his
sanctuary on high,
from heaven he viewed the earth,
20 to hear the groans of the prisoners
and release those condemned to death."
21 So the name of the LORD will be declared
in Zion
and his praise in Jerusalem
22 when the peoples and the kingdoms
assemble to worship the LORD.

23 In the course of my life[a] he
broke my strength;
he cut short my days.
24 So I said:
"Do not take me away,
O my God, in the
midst of my days;
your years go on through
all generations.
25 In the beginning you laid
the foundations of
the earth,
and the heavens are the
work of your hands.
26 They will perish, but you
remain;
they will all wear out like a garment.
Like clothing you will change them
and they will be discarded.
27 But you remain the same,
and your years will never end.
28 The children of your servants will live in
your presence;
their descendants will be established
before you."

Psalm 103
Of David.

1 Praise the LORD, O my soul;
all my inmost being, praise his holy
name.

---

[a]23 Or By his power

2 Praise the LORD, O my soul,
and forget not all his benefits—
3 who forgives all your sins
and heals all your diseases,
4 who redeems your life from the pit
and crowns you with love and
compassion,
5 who satisfies your desires with good
things
so that your youth is renewed like the
eagle's.

6 The LORD works righteousness
and justice for all the oppressed.

7 He made known his ways to Moses,
his deeds to the people of Israel:
8 The LORD is compassionate and gracious,
slow to anger, abounding in love.
9 He will not always accuse,
nor will he harbor his
anger forever;
10 he does not treat us as our
sins deserve
or repay us according to
our iniquities.
11 For as high as the heavens
are above the earth,
so great is his love for
those who fear him;
12 as far as the east is from the
west,
so far has he removed
our transgressions
from us.

13 As a father has compassion on his
children,
so the LORD has compassion on those
who fear him;
14 for he knows how we are formed,
he remembers that we are dust.
15 As for man, his days are like grass,
he flourishes like a flower of the field;
16 the wind blows over it and it is gone,
and its place remembers it no more.
17 But from everlasting to everlasting
the LORD's love is with those who fear
him,
and his righteousness with their
children's children—

Psalm 102:25

God Made Everything

In the beginning you laid
the foundations
of the earth,
and the heavens are the
work of your hands.

---

18 with those who keep his covenant
and remember to obey his precepts.

19 The LORD has established his throne in
heaven,
and his kingdom rules over all.

20 Praise the LORD, you his angels,
you mighty ones who do his bidding,
who obey his word.
21 Praise the LORD, all his heavenly hosts,
you his servants who do his will.
22 Praise the LORD, all his works
everywhere in his dominion.

Praise the LORD, O my soul.

Psalm 104

1 Praise the LORD, O my soul.

O LORD my God, you are very great;
you are clothed with splendor and
majesty.
2 He wraps himself in light as with a
garment;
he stretches out the heavens like a tent
3 and lays the beams of his upper
chambers on their waters.
He makes the clouds his chariot
and rides on the wings of the wind.
4 He makes winds his messengers,*a*
flames of fire his servants.

5 He set the earth on its foundations;
it can never be moved.
6 You covered it with the deep as with a
garment;
the waters stood above the mountains.
7 But at your rebuke the waters fled,
at the sound of your thunder they took
to flight;
8 they flowed over the mountains,
they went down into the valleys,
to the place you assigned for them.
9 You set a boundary they cannot cross;
never again will they cover the earth.

10 He makes springs pour water into the
ravines;
it flows between the mountains.
11 They give water to all the beasts of the field;
the wild donkeys quench their thirst.
12 The birds of the air nest by the waters;

they sing among the branches.
13 He waters the mountains from his upper
chambers;
the earth is satisfied by the fruit of his
work.
14 He makes grass grow for the cattle,
and plants for man to cultivate—
bringing forth food from the earth:
15 wine that gladdens the heart of man,
oil to make his face shine,
and bread that sustains his heart.
16 The trees of the LORD are well watered,
the cedars of Lebanon that he planted.
17 There the birds make their nests;
the stork has its home in the pine trees.
18 The high mountains belong to the wild
goats;
the crags are a refuge for the coneys.*b*

19 The moon marks off the seasons,
and the sun knows when to go down.
20 You bring darkness, it becomes night,
and all the beasts of the forest prowl.
21 The lions roar for their prey
and seek their food from God.
22 The sun rises, and they steal away;
they return and lie down in their dens.
23 Then man goes out to his work,
to his labor until evening.

24 How many are your works, O LORD!
In wisdom you made them all;
the earth is full of your creatures.
25 There is the sea, vast and spacious,
teeming with creatures beyond
number—
living things both large and small.
26 There the ships go to and fro,
and the leviathan, which you formed to
frolic there.

27 These all look to you
to give them their food at the proper
time.
28 When you give it to them,
they gather it up;
when you open your hand,
they are satisfied with good things.
29 When you hide your face,
they are terrified;
when you take away their breath,

*a*4 Or *angels*   *b*18 That is, the hyrax or rock badger

Grow Up, Not Old

Read: Psalm 103:1–22

Psalm 103:15–16

As for man, his days are like grass, he flourishes like a flower of the field; the wind blows over it and it is gone, and its place remembers it no more.

1 How has your culture's view of aging affected your self-image?

2 How does knowing that God views you as lovely make you feel?

3 As you've grown older, how has your wisdom increased?

RELATED READINGS

Psalm 71:17–21;
Proverbs 16:31;
Isaiah 46:3–4

"By focusing our heart's desire on Christ and letting the Holy Spirit transform us from the inside out, we are indeed becoming beautiful where it really counts."

Debra Evans

"I USED TO BE CUTE, BUT NOW I feel invisible," said the 50-something lady as she laughed nervously, but her eyes glistened with tears. A 30-something woman expressed the same feelings, saying, "When I was in my 20s, I turned a few heads, but now, hey, I'm a mom of four. What do I expect?" Both women are attractive . . . some might even say they're beautiful. But they each struggle with their self-image because our culture is not kind to aging women. Physical beauty and glamorized sexuality are prized above character and inner loveliness. God's view—the Biblical view—of growing older makes the world's view of beauty seem silly and nonsensical. But it takes mental discipline to focus on God's standards of worth and beauty when so many media outlets suggest that anyone over 30 is past their prime.

God doesn't pretend that growing older is easy. He acknowledges that our days are as fleeting as the grass growing in the field. We all realize that our outward beauty will fade away like a flower that blooms for a season and then disappears. Thankfully, our heavenly Father values the inner beauty that will never perish, an eternal beauty that comes from a heart radiating with God's love.

Yes, aging is hard. For most of us, getting older means losing our youthful beauty and experiencing the breakdown of our bodies. But God tells us that there is a loveliness that comes with maturity. When we know Jesus as our Savior, we are more aware that each day brings us closer to that place where there will be no more tears, no more sorrow, no more death. Growing older for the child of God does not mean feeling useless and ugly. It means growing up and maturing into a person who looks like God—exhibiting his qualities of compassion, abounding love and mercy. The truth is, you're getting older every day. Embrace aging as your pathway to being ever growing, ever green with an eternal purpose.

Wednesday

Go to page 734 for your next devotional reading.

they die and return to the dust.
³⁰ When you send your Spirit,
 they are created,
 and you renew the face of the earth.

³¹ May the glory of the LORD endure forever;
 may the LORD rejoice in his works—
³² he who looks at the earth, and it trembles,
 who touches the mountains, and they
 smoke.

³³ I will sing to the LORD all my life;
 I will sing praise to my God as long as
 I live.
³⁴ May my meditation be pleasing to him,
 as I rejoice in the LORD.
³⁵ But may sinners vanish from the earth
 and the wicked be no more.

Praise the LORD, O my soul.

Praise the LORD.^a

Psalm 105

¹ Give thanks to the LORD, call on his name;
 make known among the nations what he
 has done.
² Sing to him, sing praise to him;
 tell of all his wonderful acts.
³ Glory in his holy name;
 let the hearts of those who seek the
 LORD rejoice.
⁴ Look to the LORD and his strength;
 seek his face always.

⁵ Remember the wonders he
 has done,
 his miracles, and the
 judgments he
 pronounced,
⁶ O descendants of Abraham
 his servant,
 O sons of Jacob, his
 chosen ones.
⁷ He is the LORD our God;
 his judgments are in all
 the earth.

⁸ He remembers his covenant
 forever,
 the word he commanded, for a thousand
 generations,
⁹ the covenant he made with Abraham,

the oath he swore to Isaac.
¹⁰ He confirmed it to Jacob as a decree,
 to Israel as an everlasting covenant:
¹¹ "To you I will give the land of Canaan
 as the portion you will inherit."

¹² When they were but few in number,
 few indeed, and strangers in it,
¹³ they wandered from nation to nation,
 from one kingdom to another.
¹⁴ He allowed no one to oppress them;
 for their sake he rebuked kings:
¹⁵ "Do not touch my anointed ones;
 do my prophets no harm."

¹⁶ He called down famine on the land
 and destroyed all their supplies of
 food;
¹⁷ and he sent a man before them—
 Joseph, sold as a slave.
¹⁸ They bruised his feet with shackles,
 his neck was put in irons,
¹⁹ till what he foretold came to pass,
 till the word of the LORD proved him
 true.
²⁰ The king sent and released him,
 the ruler of peoples set him free.
²¹ He made him master of his household,
 ruler over all he possessed,
²² to instruct his princes as he pleased
 and teach his elders wisdom.

²³ Then Israel entered Egypt;
 Jacob lived as an alien in
 the land of Ham.
²⁴ The LORD made his people
 very fruitful;
 he made them too
 numerous for their
 foes,
²⁵ whose hearts he turned to
 hate his people,
 to conspire against his
 servants.
²⁶ He sent Moses his servant,
 and Aaron, whom he
 had chosen.
²⁷ They performed his miraculous signs
 among them,
 his wonders in the land of Ham.

Psalm 105:8

God Remembers His Promises

He remembers his covenant forever, the word he commanded, for a thousand generations.

---

^a35 Hebrew *Hallelu Yah*; in the Septuagint this line stands at the beginning of Psalm 105.

28 He sent darkness and made the land
         dark—
      for had they not rebelled against his
         words?
29 He turned their waters into blood,
      causing their fish to die.
30 Their land teemed with frogs,
      which went up into the bedrooms of
         their rulers.
31 He spoke, and there came swarms of
         flies,
      and gnats throughout their country.
32 He turned their rain into hail,
      with lightning throughout their land;
33 he struck down their vines and fig trees
      and shattered the trees of their country.
34 He spoke, and the locusts came,
      grasshoppers without number;
35 they ate up every green thing in their land,
      ate up the produce of their soil.
36 Then he struck down all the firstborn in
         their land,
      the firstfruits of all their manhood.

37 He brought out Israel, laden with silver
         and gold,
      and from among their tribes no one
         faltered.
38 Egypt was glad when they left,
      because dread of Israel had fallen on
         them.
39 He spread out a cloud as a covering,
      and a fire to give light at night.
40 They asked, and he brought them quail
      and satisfied them with the bread of
         heaven.
41 He opened the rock, and water gushed out;
      like a river it flowed in the desert.

42 For he remembered his holy promise
      given to his servant Abraham.
43 He brought out his people with rejoicing,
      his chosen ones with shouts of joy;
44 he gave them the lands of the nations,
      and they fell heir to what others had
         toiled for—
45 that they might keep his precepts
      and observe his laws.

      Praise the LORD.[a]

Psalm 106

1 Praise the LORD.[b]

      Give thanks to the LORD, for he is good;
         his love endures forever.
2 Who can proclaim the mighty acts of the
         LORD
      or fully declare his praise?
3 Blessed are they who maintain justice,
      who constantly do what is right.

4 Remember me, O LORD, when you show
      favor to your people,
      come to my aid when you save them,
5 that I may enjoy the prosperity of your
         chosen ones,
      that I may share in the joy of your nation
      and join your inheritance in giving
         praise.

6 We have sinned, even as our fathers did;
      we have done wrong and acted wickedly.
7 When our fathers were in Egypt,
      they gave no thought to your miracles;
      they did not remember your many
         kindnesses,
      and they rebelled by the sea, the Red
         Sea.[c]
8 Yet he saved them for his name's sake,
      to make his mighty power known.
9 He rebuked the Red Sea, and it dried up;
      he led them through the depths as
         through a desert.
10 He saved them from the hand of the foe;
      from the hand of the enemy he
         redeemed them.
11 The waters covered their adversaries;
      not one of them survived.
12 Then they believed his promises
      and sang his praise.

13 But they soon forgot what he had done
      and did not wait for his counsel.
14 In the desert they gave in to their craving;
      in the wasteland they put God to the
         test.
15 So he gave them what they asked for,
      but sent a wasting disease upon them.

16 In the camp they grew envious of Moses
      and of Aaron, who was consecrated to
         the LORD.

a45 Hebrew Hallelu Yah   b1 Hebrew Hallelu Yah; also in verse 48   c7 Hebrew Yam Suph; that is, Sea of Reeds; also in verses 9 and 22

17 The earth opened up and swallowed
  Dathan;
  it buried the company of Abiram.
18 Fire blazed among their followers;
  a flame consumed the wicked.

19 At Horeb they made a calf
  and worshiped an idol cast from metal.
20 They exchanged their Glory
  for an image of a bull, which eats grass.
21 They forgot the God who saved them,
  who had done great things in Egypt,
22 miracles in the land of Ham
  and awesome deeds by the Red Sea.
23 So he said he would destroy them—
  had not Moses, his chosen one,
  stood in the breach before him
  to keep his wrath from destroying them.

24 Then they despised the pleasant land;
  they did not believe his promise.
25 They grumbled in their tents
  and did not obey the LORD.
26 So he swore to them with uplifted hand
  that he would make them fall in the
    desert,
27 make their descendants fall among the
    nations
  and scatter them throughout the lands.

28 They yoked themselves to the Baal of Peor
  and ate sacrifices offered to lifeless gods;
29 they provoked the LORD to anger by their
    wicked deeds,
  and a plague broke out among them.
30 But Phinehas stood up and intervened,
  and the plague was checked.
31 This was credited to him as righteousness
  for endless generations to come.

32 By the waters of Meribah they angered the
    LORD,
  and trouble came to Moses because of
    them;
33 for they rebelled against the Spirit of God,
  and rash words came from Moses' lips.[a]

34 They did not destroy the peoples
  as the LORD had commanded them,
35 but they mingled with the nations
  and adopted their customs.

36 They worshiped their idols,
  which became a snare to them.
37 They sacrificed their sons
  and their daughters to demons.
38 They shed innocent blood,
  the blood of their sons and daughters,
  whom they sacrificed to the idols of
    Canaan,
  and the land was desecrated by their
    blood.
39 They defiled themselves by what they did;
  by their deeds they prostituted
    themselves.

40 Therefore the LORD was angry with his
    people
  and abhorred his inheritance.
41 He handed them over to the nations,
  and their foes ruled over them.
42 Their enemies oppressed them
  and subjected them to their power.
43 Many times he delivered them,
  but they were bent on rebellion
  and they wasted away in their sin.

44 But he took note of their distress
  when he heard their cry;
45 for their sake he remembered his covenant
  and out of his great love he relented.
46 He caused them to be pitied
  by all who held them captive.

47 Save us, O LORD our God,
  and gather us from the nations,
  that we may give thanks to your holy name
  and glory in your praise.

48 Praise be to the LORD, the God of Israel,
  from everlasting to everlasting.
  Let all the people say, "Amen!"

  Praise the LORD.

BOOK V
Psalms 107–150

Psalm 107
1 Give thanks to the LORD, for he is good;
  his love endures forever.
2 Let the redeemed of the LORD say this—
  those he redeemed from the hand of the
    foe,

---

[a]33 Or *against his spirit, / and rash words came from his lips*

3 those he gathered from the lands,
from east and west, from north and
south.*a*

4 Some wandered in desert wastelands,
finding no way to a city where they
could settle.
5 They were hungry and thirsty,
and their lives ebbed away.
6 Then they cried out to the LORD in their
trouble,
and he delivered them from their
distress.
7 He led them by a straight way
to a city where they
could settle.
8 Let them give thanks to
the LORD for his
unfailing love
and his wonderful deeds
for men,
9 for he satisfies the thirsty
and fills the hungry with
good things.

10 Some sat in darkness and
the deepest gloom,
prisoners suffering in
iron chains,
11 for they had rebelled
against the words of God
and despised the counsel of the Most
High.
12 So he subjected them to bitter labor;
they stumbled, and there was no one to
help.
13 Then they cried to the LORD in their
trouble,
and he saved them from their
distress.
14 He brought them out of darkness and the
deepest gloom
and broke away their chains.
15 Let them give thanks to the LORD for his
unfailing love
and his wonderful deeds for men,
16 for he breaks down gates of bronze
and cuts through bars of iron.

17 Some became fools through their
rebellious ways

a3 Hebrew north and the sea

730

and suffered affliction because of their
iniquities.
18 They loathed all food
and drew near the gates of death.
19 Then they cried to the LORD in their
trouble,
and he saved them from their distress.
20 He sent forth his word and healed them;
he rescued them from the grave.
21 Let them give thanks to the LORD for his
unfailing love
and his wonderful deeds for men.
22 Let them sacrifice thank offerings
and tell of his works with
songs of joy.

23 Others went out on the sea
in ships;
they were merchants on
the mighty waters.
24 They saw the works of the
LORD,
his wonderful deeds in
the deep.
25 For he spoke and stirred up
a tempest
that lifted high the waves.
26 They mounted up to the
heavens and went
down to the depths;
in their peril their courage melted away.
27 They reeled and staggered like drunken
men;
they were at their wits' end.
28 Then they cried out to the LORD in their
trouble,
and he brought them out of their
distress.
29 He stilled the storm to a whisper;
the waves of the sea were hushed.
30 They were glad when it grew calm,
and he guided them to their desired
haven.
31 Let them give thanks to the LORD for his
unfailing love
and his wonderful deeds for men.
32 Let them exalt him in the assembly of the
people
and praise him in the council of the
elders.

Psalm 107:8

*God Gives
Unfailing Love*

Let them give thanks
to the LORD for his
unfailing love
and his wonderful
deeds for men.

³³He turned rivers into a desert,
  flowing springs into thirsty ground,
³⁴and fruitful land into a salt waste,
  because of the wickedness of those who
  lived there.
³⁵He turned the desert into pools of water
  and the parched ground into flowing
  springs;
³⁶there he brought the hungry to live,
  and they founded a city where they
  could settle.
³⁷They sowed fields and planted vineyards
  that yielded a fruitful harvest;
³⁸he blessed them, and their numbers greatly
  increased,
  and he did not let their herds diminish.

³⁹Then their numbers decreased, and they
  were humbled
  by oppression, calamity and sorrow;
⁴⁰he who pours contempt on nobles
  made them wander in a trackless waste.
⁴¹But he lifted the needy out of their
  affliction
  and increased their families like flocks.
⁴²The upright see and rejoice,
  but all the wicked shut their mouths.

⁴³Whoever is wise, let him heed these things
  and consider the great love of the LORD.

Psalm 108
A song. A psalm of David.

¹My heart is steadfast, O God;
  I will sing and make music with all my
  soul.
²Awake, harp and lyre!
  I will awaken the dawn.
³I will praise you, O LORD, among the
  nations;
  I will sing of you among the peoples.
⁴For great is your love, higher than the
  heavens;
  your faithfulness reaches to the skies.
⁵Be exalted, O God, above the heavens,
  and let your glory be over all the earth.

⁶Save us and help us with your right hand,
  that those you love may be delivered.
⁷God has spoken from his sanctuary:

"In triumph I will parcel out Shechem
  and measure off the Valley of Succoth.
⁸Gilead is mine, Manasseh is mine;
  Ephraim is my helmet,
  Judah my scepter.
⁹Moab is my washbasin,
  upon Edom I toss my sandal;
  over Philistia I shout in triumph."

¹⁰Who will bring me to the fortified city?
  Who will lead me to Edom?
¹¹Is it not you, O God, you who have
  rejected us
  and no longer go out with our armies?
¹²Give us aid against the enemy,
  for the help of man is worthless.
¹³With God we will gain the victory,
  and he will trample down our enemies.

Psalm 109
For the director of music. Of David. A psalm.

¹O God, whom I praise,
  do not remain silent,
²for wicked and deceitful men
  have opened their mouths against me;
  they have spoken against me with lying
  tongues.
³With words of hatred they surround me;
  they attack me without cause.
⁴In return for my friendship they accuse
  me,
  but I am a man of prayer.
⁵They repay me evil for good,
  and hatred for my friendship.

⁶Appoint*ᵃ* an evil man*ᵇ* to oppose him;
  let an accuser*ᶜ* stand at his right hand.
⁷When he is tried, let him be found guilty,
  and may his prayers condemn him.
⁸May his days be few;
  may another take his place of leadership.
⁹May his children be fatherless
  and his wife a widow.
¹⁰May his children be wandering beggars;
  may they be driven*ᵈ* from their ruined
  homes.
¹¹May a creditor seize all he has;
  may strangers plunder the fruits of his
  labor.
¹²May no one extend kindness to him

ᵃ6 Or They say, "Appoint (with quotation marks at the end of verse 19)   ᵇ6 Or the Evil One   ᶜ6 Or let Satan   ᵈ10 Septuagint; Hebrew sought

or take pity on his fatherless children.
¹³ May his descendants be cut off,
 their names blotted out from the next
  generation.
¹⁴ May the iniquity of his fathers be
  remembered before the LORD;
 may the sin of his mother never be
  blotted out.
¹⁵ May their sins always remain before the
  LORD,
 that he may cut off the memory of them
  from the earth.

¹⁶ For he never thought of doing a kindness,
 but hounded to death the poor
  and the needy and the brokenhearted.
¹⁷ He loved to pronounce a curse—
 may it[a] come on him;
 he found no pleasure in blessing—
 may it be[b] far from him.
¹⁸ He wore cursing as his garment;
 it entered into his body like water,
  into his bones like oil.
¹⁹ May it be like a cloak wrapped about him,
 like a belt tied forever around him.
²⁰ May this be the LORD's payment to my
  accusers,
 to those who speak evil of me.

²¹ But you, O Sovereign LORD,
 deal well with me for your name's sake;
 out of the goodness of your love, deliver
  me.
²² For I am poor and needy,
 and my heart is wounded within me.
²³ I fade away like an evening shadow;
 I am shaken off like a locust.
²⁴ My knees give way from fasting;
 my body is thin and gaunt.
²⁵ I am an object of scorn to my accusers;
 when they see me, they shake their heads.

²⁶ Help me, O LORD my God;
 save me in accordance with your love.
²⁷ Let them know that it is your hand,
 that you, O LORD, have done it.
²⁸ They may curse, but you will bless;
 when they attack they will be put to
  shame,

but your servant will rejoice.
²⁹ My accusers will be clothed with disgrace
 and wrapped in shame as in a cloak.

³⁰ With my mouth I will greatly extol the
  LORD;
 in the great throng I will praise him.
³¹ For he stands at the right hand of the
  needy one,
 to save his life from those who condemn
  him.

Psalm 110
Of David. A psalm.

¹ The LORD says to my Lord:
 "Sit at my right hand
 until I make your enemies
  a footstool for your feet."

² The LORD will extend your mighty scepter
  from Zion;
 you will rule in the midst of your
  enemies.
³ Your troops will be willing
 on your day of battle.
 Arrayed in holy majesty,
  from the womb of the dawn
  you will receive the dew of your youth.[c]

⁴ The LORD has sworn
 and will not change his mind:
 "You are a priest forever,
  in the order of Melchizedek."

⁵ The Lord is at your right hand;
 he will crush kings on the day of his
  wrath.
⁶ He will judge the nations, heaping up the
  dead
 and crushing the rulers of the whole
  earth.
⁷ He will drink from a brook beside the
  way[d];
 therefore he will lift up his head.

Psalm 111[e]

¹ Praise the LORD.[f]

 I will extol the LORD with all my heart
 in the council of the upright and in the
  assembly.

---

a17 Or *curse, / and it has* *b17* Or *blessing, / and it is* *c3* Or / *your young men will come to you like the dew* *d7* Or / *The One who grants succession will set him in authority* *e*This psalm is an acrostic poem, the lines of which begin with the successive letters of the Hebrew alphabet. *f1* Hebrew *Hallelu Yah*

2 Great are the works of the LORD;
   they are pondered by all who delight in
      them.
3 Glorious and majestic are his deeds,
   and his righteousness endures forever.
4 He has caused his wonders to be
      remembered;
   the LORD is gracious and compassionate.
5 He provides food for those who fear him;
   he remembers his covenant forever.
6 He has shown his people the power of his
      works,
   giving them the lands of other nations.
7 The works of his hands are faithful and
      just;
   all his precepts are trustworthy.
8 They are steadfast for ever and ever,
   done in faithfulness and
      uprightness.
9 He provided redemption
   for his people;
   he ordained his covenant
      forever—
   holy and awesome is his
      name.
10 The fear of the LORD is
      the beginning of
      wisdom;
   all who follow his
      precepts have good
      understanding.
   To him belongs eternal
      praise.

Psalm 112[a]
1 Praise the LORD.[b]

Blessed is the man who fears the LORD,
   who finds great delight in his
      commands.
2 His children will be mighty in the land;
   the generation of the upright will be
      blessed.
3 Wealth and riches are in his house,
   and his righteousness endures forever.
4 Even in darkness light dawns for the
      upright,

for the gracious and compassionate and
   righteous man.[c]
5 Good will come to him who is generous
   and lends freely,
   who conducts his affairs with justice.
6 Surely he will never be shaken;
   a righteous man will be remembered
      forever.
7 He will have no fear of bad news;
   his heart is steadfast, trusting in the
      LORD.
8 His heart is secure, he will have no fear;
   in the end he will look in triumph on
      his foes.
9 He has scattered abroad his gifts to the
      poor,
         his righteousness
            endures forever;
         his horn[d] will be lifted
            high in honor.

10 The wicked man will see
      and be vexed,
   he will gnash his teeth
      and waste away;
   the longings of the
      wicked will come to
         nothing.

Psalm 113
1 Praise the LORD.[e]

Praise, O servants of the
      LORD,
   praise the name of the
      LORD.
2 Let the name of the LORD
   be praised,
both now and forevermore.
3 From the rising of the sun to the place
      where it sets,
   the name of the LORD is to be praised.

4 The LORD is exalted over all the nations,
   his glory above the heavens.
5 Who is like the LORD our God,
   the One who sits enthroned on high,
6 who stoops down to look
   on the heavens and the earth?

> **Psalm 111:10**
>
> *God Gives Wisdom*
>
> The fear of the LORD is
> the beginning
> of wisdom;
> all who follow his
> precepts have good
> understanding.
> To him belongs
> eternal praise.

---

[a] This psalm is an acrostic poem, the lines of which begin with the successive letters of the Hebrew alphabet.   [b] 1 Hebrew *Hallelu Yah*
[c] 4 Or / *for the LORD is gracious and compassionate and righteous*   [d] 9 *Horn* here symbolizes dignity.   [e] 1 Hebrew *Hallelu Yah*; also in
verse 9

A Checklist of Delight

Read: Psalm 112:1–10

Psalm 112:1

Praise the LORD. Blessed is the man who fears the LORD, who finds great delight in his commands.

reflection

1 What keeps you from acknowledging God's gifts to you?

2 What could you do to live a more mindful and thankful life?

3 Why does God tell you to praise him? What will you praise him for today?

RELATED READINGS

1 Chronicles 29:20;
Psalms 65:1–13;
103:1–22; 104:1–35

"Celebrating each new day helps us develop the ability to be grateful for all new moments and for the God who is in each one."

Karen Burton Mains

LIFE. CHECK. *OXYGEN.* CHECK. *Food.* Check. *Ability to read.* Check.

How long has it been since you listed the good things God has given you? He created a beautiful world full of all you need: air, water, thousands of varieties of food and much more. In giving you your family, your ability to smell and your sense of humor, God has given you precious gifts. From telling Old Testament tales of his long-suffering to letting you see behind the scenes of his Son's trip to Earth, his Word is an extra-special love gift.

The psalms give many examples of praise and list many good reasons for thanksgiving. *Give thanks in all circumstances?* Check. Even in the midst of trials, praise is appropriate because God is keeping track of your enemies while you sleep. *Give praise for dark times?* Check. Even in darkness his light dawns. *Thank him for family?* Check. God will meet your needs and watch over your children. *Delight in God's commands?* Check. Even God's commands are counted among his gracious blessings, for they bring us life.

Scripture never promises believers a trial-free life. But God's Word does promise a life of purpose, direction and blessing under his watchful care. It does promise that the one who trusts God is secure.

Have you thanked God for gravity lately? For clouds that shade you from the summer sun, provide the rain and glow at sunrise? For your ears, your nose, your eyes? For giving humankind the ability to create penicillin, the electric light, the telephone, the means of preserving food? For loving you enough to claim you as his child? For watching over you even when you are busy or distracted and you forget him? For protecting you and giving you purpose and hope? Make your own checklist. He is worthy of your praise.

734

Go to page 738 for your next devotional reading.

7 He raises the poor from the dust
  and lifts the needy from the ash heap;
8 he seats them with princes,
  with the princes of their people.
9 He settles the barren woman in her home
  as a happy mother of children.

Praise the LORD.

Psalm 114

1 When Israel came out of Egypt,
  the house of Jacob from a people of
      foreign tongue,
2 Judah became God's sanctuary,
  Israel his dominion.

3 The sea looked and fled,
  the Jordan turned back;
4 the mountains skipped like rams,
  the hills like lambs.

5 Why was it, O sea, that you fled,
  O Jordan, that you turned back,
6 you mountains, that you skipped like
      rams,
  you hills, like lambs?

7 Tremble, O earth, at the presence of the
      Lord,
  at the presence of the God of Jacob,
8 who turned the rock into a pool,
  the hard rock into springs of water.

Psalm 115

1 Not to us, O LORD, not to us
  but to your name be the glory,
  because of your love and faithfulness.

2 Why do the nations say,
  "Where is their God?"
3 Our God is in heaven;
  he does whatever pleases him.
4 But their idols are silver and gold,
  made by the hands of men.
5 They have mouths, but cannot speak,
  eyes, but they cannot see;
6 they have ears, but cannot hear,
  noses, but they cannot smell;
7 they have hands, but cannot feel,
  feet, but they cannot walk;
  nor can they utter a sound with their
      throats.

8 Those who make them will be like them,
  and so will all who trust in them.

9 O house of Israel, trust in the LORD—
  he is their help and shield.
10 O house of Aaron, trust in the LORD—
  he is their help and shield.
11 You who fear him, trust in the LORD—
  he is their help and shield.

12 The LORD remembers us and will bless us:
  He will bless the house of Israel,
  he will bless the house of Aaron,
13 he will bless those who fear the LORD—
  small and great alike.

14 May the LORD make you increase,
  both you and your children.
15 May you be blessed by the LORD,
  the Maker of heaven and earth.

16 The highest heavens belong to the LORD,
  but the earth he has given to man.
17 It is not the dead who praise the LORD,
  those who go down to silence;
18 it is we who extol the LORD,
  both now and forevermore.

Praise the LORD.*a*

Psalm 116

1 I love the LORD, for he heard my voice;
  he heard my cry for mercy.
2 Because he turned his ear to me,
  I will call on him as long as I live.

3 The cords of death entangled me,
  the anguish of the grave*b* came upon
      me;
  I was overcome by trouble and sorrow.
4 Then I called on the name of the LORD:
  "O LORD, save me!"

5 The LORD is gracious and righteous;
  our God is full of compassion.
6 The LORD protects the simplehearted;
  when I was in great need, he saved me.

7 Be at rest once more, O my soul,
  for the LORD has been good to you.

8 For you, O LORD, have delivered my soul
      from death,
  my eyes from tears,

a 18 Hebrew *Hallelu Yah*   *b* 3 Hebrew *Sheol*

my feet from stumbling,
⁹ that I may walk before the LORD
   in the land of the living.
¹⁰ I believed; therefore*a* I said,
   "I am greatly afflicted."
¹¹ And in my dismay I said,
   "All men are liars."

¹² How can I repay the LORD
   for all his goodness to me?
¹³ I will lift up the cup of salvation
   and call on the name of
      the LORD.
¹⁴ I will fulfill my vows to the
      LORD
   in the presence of all his
      people.

¹⁵ Precious in the sight of the
      LORD
   is the death of his saints.
¹⁶ O LORD, truly I am your
      servant;
   I am your servant,
      the son of your
      maidservant*b*;
   you have freed me from my chains.

¹⁷ I will sacrifice a thank offering to you
   and call on the name of the LORD.
¹⁸ I will fulfill my vows to the LORD
   in the presence of all his people,
¹⁹ in the courts of the house of the LORD—
   in your midst, O Jerusalem.

Praise the LORD.*c*

Psalm 117

¹ Praise the LORD, all you nations;
   extol him, all you peoples.
² For great is his love toward us,
   and the faithfulness of the LORD
      endures forever.

Praise the LORD.*c*

Psalm 118

¹ Give thanks to the LORD, for he is good;
   his love endures forever.

² Let Israel say:
   "His love endures forever."
³ Let the house of Aaron say:

"His love endures forever."
⁴ Let those who fear the LORD say:
   "His love endures forever."

⁵ In my anguish I cried to the LORD,
   and he answered by setting me free.
⁶ The LORD is with me; I will not be afraid.
   What can man do to me?
⁷ The LORD is with me; he is my helper.
   I will look in triumph on my enemies.

⁸ It is better to take refuge in the LORD
   than to trust in man.
⁹ It is better to take refuge in
      the LORD
   than to trust in princes.

¹⁰ All the nations surrounded
      me,
   but in the name of the
      LORD I cut them off.
¹¹ They surrounded me on
      every side,
   but in the name of the
      LORD I cut them off.
¹² They swarmed around me
      like bees,
   but they died out as quickly as burning
      thorns;
   in the name of the LORD I cut them off.

¹³ I was pushed back and about to fall,
   but the LORD helped me.
¹⁴ The LORD is my strength and my song;
   he has become my salvation.

¹⁵ Shouts of joy and victory
   resound in the tents of the righteous:
   "The LORD's right hand has done mighty
      things!
¹⁶   The LORD's right hand is lifted high;
   the LORD's right hand has done mighty
      things!"

¹⁷ I will not die but live,
   and will proclaim what the LORD has
      done.
¹⁸ The LORD has chastened me severely,
   but he has not given me over to death.
¹⁹ Open for me the gates of righteousness;
   I will enter and give thanks to the LORD.

> **Psalm 116:15**
>
> ## God Welcomes Us to Heaven
>
> Precious in the sight
> of the LORD
> is the death of his saints.

---

a 10 Or *believed even when*   *b* 16 Or *servant, your faithful son*   *c* 19,2 Hebrew *Hallelu Yah*

²⁰This is the gate of the LORD
  through which the righteous may enter.
²¹I will give you thanks, for you answered
    me;
  you have become my salvation.

²²The stone the builders rejected
  has become the capstone;
²³the LORD has done this,
  and it is marvelous in our eyes.
²⁴This is the day the LORD has made;
  let us rejoice and be glad in it.

²⁵O LORD, save us;
  O LORD, grant us success.
²⁶Blessed is he who comes in the name of the
    LORD.
  From the house of the LORD we bless
    you.^a
²⁷The LORD is God,
  and he has made his light shine upon us.
  With boughs in hand, join in the festal
    procession
  up^b to the horns of the altar.

²⁸You are my God, and I will give you
    thanks;
  you are my God, and I will exalt you.

²⁹Give thanks to the LORD, for he is good;
  his love endures forever.

Psalm 119^c

א Aleph

¹Blessed are they whose ways are
    blameless,
  who walk according to the law of the
    LORD.
²Blessed are they who keep his statutes
  and seek him with all their heart.
³They do nothing wrong;
  they walk in his ways.
⁴You have laid down precepts
  that are to be fully obeyed.
⁵Oh, that my ways were steadfast
  in obeying your decrees!
⁶Then I would not be put to shame
  when I consider all your commands.
⁷I will praise you with an upright heart
  as I learn your righteous laws.

⁸I will obey your decrees;
  do not utterly forsake me.

ב Beth

⁹How can a young man keep his way pure?
  By living according to your word.
¹⁰I seek you with all my heart;
  do not let me stray from your
    commands.
¹¹I have hidden your word in my heart
  that I might not sin against you.
¹²Praise be to you, O LORD;
  teach me your decrees.
¹³With my lips I recount
  all the laws that come from your
    mouth.
¹⁴I rejoice in following your statutes
  as one rejoices in great riches.
¹⁵I meditate on your precepts
  and consider your ways.
¹⁶I delight in your decrees;
  I will not neglect your word.

ג Gimel

¹⁷Do good to your servant, and I will live;
  I will obey your word.
¹⁸Open my eyes that I may see
  wonderful things in your law.
¹⁹I am a stranger on earth;
  do not hide your commands from me.
²⁰My soul is consumed with longing
  for your laws at all times.
²¹You rebuke the arrogant, who are cursed
  and who stray from your commands.
²²Remove from me scorn and contempt,
  for I keep your statutes.
²³Though rulers sit together and slander me,
  your servant will meditate on your
    decrees.
²⁴Your statutes are my delight;
  they are my counselors.

ד Daleth

²⁵I am laid low in the dust;
  preserve my life according to your word.
²⁶I recounted my ways and you answered
    me;
  teach me your decrees.

^a26 The Hebrew is plural. ^b27 Or *Bind the festal sacrifice with ropes / and take it* ^cThis psalm is an acrostic poem; the verses of each stanza begin with the same letter of the Hebrew alphabet.

It's Later Than You Think

Read: Psalm 118:1–29

Psalm 118:24

This is the day the LORD has made; let us rejoice and be glad in it.

reflection

1 How can you relate to Luci's thoughts on how we strive to save time, but in the process, we're missing out on something?

2 How will you follow her suggestion to take the time to do something beautifully?

3 Memorize Psalm 118:24, "This is the day the LORD has made; let us rejoice and be glad in it." Whenever you find yourself in a hurry, bring this Scripture to mind, and rejoice in the Lord!

RELATED READINGS

Romans 5:1–5;
Philippians 4:4–7

WHEN I WAS A CHILD, our family had a chiming clock that had been handed down through the generations and was a well-loved treasure. On the hour, of course, it would chime out the time, and by it we kept on schedule with meals and departures and awakening and bedtime. Many nights, from our respective bedrooms, each of us would call out the number of chimes until the last one stopped.

One night, after we had all gone to bed about midnight, the clock began to gong and we started our audible ritual: "Nine . . . ten . . . eleven . . . twelve." Just as we closed our mouths after shouting out TWELVE! the clock struck thirteen. We could hardly believe our ears. Where did that come from? I wondered, as we all laughed heartily from our beds. Then, almost in perfect unison, we called out: "It's later than you think!"

For most of us, that's the problem: Our greatest fear is running out of time. So we hurry through life trying desperately to get everything done: working overtime, eating fast food in the car, racing down the freeway. We've gone from The One Minute Manager to The One Minute Mother to One Minute Wisdom. Life itself encourages us to hurry. I can do my laundry twice as fast as my grandmother did; I can travel coast to coast faster than my father ever could; I can handle correspondence that took my mother hours with a few keystrokes and mouse clicks. And yet, I seem to have less time than they did. What has happened?

In our quest to save time, we're losing something. I thought the other day about how my grandparents valued time. They always had time for my parents and my brothers and me; they had time for music in their home (each of them was a competent musician); they emphasized beautifully served meals, family reunions and long conversations. It seemed they had time for everything in life that was important, because they took time to live . . .

Today, this very day, why don't you think of something that takes a bit of extra time to do and do it. Do it for yourself. Do it for a family member. Do it for a neighbor or friend. Do it for the Lord . . . Don't wait for another time. Rejoice in this day and be glad! Tonight, your clock could strike thirteen.

—*Luci Swindoll*

---

²⁷ Let me understand the teaching of your
    precepts;
    then I will meditate on your wonders.
²⁸ My soul is weary with sorrow;
    strengthen me according to your word.
²⁹ Keep me from deceitful ways;
    be gracious to me through your law.
³⁰ I have chosen the way of truth;
    I have set my heart on your laws.
³¹ I hold fast to your statutes, O LORD;
    do not let me be put to shame.
³² I run in the path of your commands,
    for you have set my heart free.

ה He

³³ Teach me, O LORD, to follow your decrees;
    then I will keep them to the end.
³⁴ Give me understanding, and I will keep
    your law
    and obey it with all my heart.
³⁵ Direct me in the path of your commands,
    for there I find delight.
³⁶ Turn my heart toward your statutes
    and not toward selfish gain.
³⁷ Turn my eyes away from worthless things;
    preserve my life according to your
    word.ᵃ
³⁸ Fulfill your promise to your servant,
    so that you may be feared.
³⁹ Take away the disgrace I dread,
    for your laws are good.
⁴⁰ How I long for your precepts!
    Preserve my life in your righteousness.

ו Waw

⁴¹ May your unfailing love come to me,
    O LORD,
    your salvation according to your promise;
⁴² then I will answer the one who taunts me,
    for I trust in your word.
⁴³ Do not snatch the word of truth from my
    mouth,
    for I have put my hope in your laws.
⁴⁴ I will always obey your law,
    for ever and ever.
⁴⁵ I will walk about in freedom,
    for I have sought out your precepts.
⁴⁶ I will speak of your statutes before kings
    and will not be put to shame,

⁴⁷ for I delight in your commands
    because I love them.
⁴⁸ I lift up my hands toᵇ your commands,
    which I love,
    and I meditate on your decrees.

ז Zayin

⁴⁹ Remember your word to your servant,
    for you have given me hope.
⁵⁰ My comfort in my suffering is this:
    Your promise preserves my life.
⁵¹ The arrogant mock me without restraint,
    but I do not turn from your law.
⁵² I remember your ancient laws, O LORD,
    and I find comfort in them.
⁵³ Indignation grips me because of the
    wicked,
    who have forsaken your law.
⁵⁴ Your decrees are the theme of my song
    wherever I lodge.
⁵⁵ In the night I remember your name,
    O LORD,
    and I will keep your law.
⁵⁶ This has been my practice:
    I obey your precepts.

ח Heth

⁵⁷ You are my portion, O LORD;
    I have promised to obey your words.
⁵⁸ I have sought your face with all my heart;
    be gracious to me according to your
    promise.
⁵⁹ I have considered my ways
    and have turned my steps to your
    statutes.
⁶⁰ I will hasten and not delay
    to obey your commands.
⁶¹ Though the wicked bind me with ropes,
    I will not forget your law.
⁶² At midnight I rise to give you thanks
    for your righteous laws.
⁶³ I am a friend to all who fear you,
    to all who follow your precepts.
⁶⁴ The earth is filled with your love, O LORD;
    teach me your decrees.

ט Teth

⁶⁵ Do good to your servant
    according to your word, O LORD.

ᵃ37 Two manuscripts of the Masoretic Text and Dead Sea Scrolls; most manuscripts of the Masoretic Text *life in your way*   ᵇ48 Or *for*

66 Teach me knowledge and good judgment,
    for I believe in your commands.
67 Before I was afflicted I went astray,
    but now I obey your word.
68 You are good, and what you do is good;
    teach me your decrees.
69 Though the arrogant have smeared me
      with lies,
    I keep your precepts with all my heart.
70 Their hearts are callous and unfeeling,
    but I delight in your law.
71 It was good for me to be afflicted
    so that I might learn your decrees.
72 The law from your mouth is more precious
      to me
    than thousands of pieces of silver and
      gold.

י Yodh

73 Your hands made me and formed me;
    give me understanding to learn your
      commands.
74 May those who fear you rejoice when they
      see me,
    for I have put my hope in your word.
75 I know, O LORD, that your laws are
      righteous,
    and in faithfulness you have afflicted
      me.
76 May your unfailing love be my comfort,
    according to your promise to your
      servant.
77 Let your compassion come to me that I
      may live,
    for your law is my delight.
78 May the arrogant be put to shame for
      wronging me without cause;
    but I will meditate on your precepts.
79 May those who fear you turn to me,
    those who understand your statutes.
80 May my heart be blameless toward your
      decrees,
    that I may not be put to shame.

כ Kaph

81 My soul faints with longing for your
      salvation,
    but I have put my hope in your word.
82 My eyes fail, looking for your promise;
    I say, "When will you comfort me?"

83 Though I am like a wineskin in the
      smoke,
    I do not forget your decrees.
84 How long must your servant wait?
    When will you punish my persecutors?
85 The arrogant dig pitfalls for me,
    contrary to your law.
86 All your commands are trustworthy;
    help me, for men persecute me without
      cause.
87 They almost wiped me from the earth,
    but I have not forsaken your precepts.
88 Preserve my life according to your love,
    and I will obey the statutes of your
      mouth.

ל Lamedh

89 Your word, O LORD, is eternal;
    it stands firm in the heavens.
90 Your faithfulness continues through all
      generations;
    you established the earth, and it
      endures.
91 Your laws endure to this day,
    for all things serve you.
92 If your law had not been my delight,
    I would have perished in my affliction.
93 I will never forget your precepts,
    for by them you have preserved my life.
94 Save me, for I am yours;
    I have sought out your precepts.
95 The wicked are waiting to destroy me,
    but I will ponder your statutes.
96 To all perfection I see a limit;
    but your commands are boundless.

מ Mem

97 Oh, how I love your law!
    I meditate on it all day long.
98 Your commands make me wiser than
      my enemies,
    for they are ever with me.
99 I have more insight than all my teachers,
    for I meditate on your statutes.
100 I have more understanding than
      the elders,
    for I obey your precepts.
101 I have kept my feet from every evil path
    so that I might obey your word.
102 I have not departed from your laws,

for you yourself have taught me.
103 How sweet are your words to my taste,
sweeter than honey to my mouth!
104 I gain understanding from your precepts;
therefore I hate every wrong path.

נ Nun

105 Your word is a lamp to my feet
and a light for my path.
106 I have taken an oath and
confirmed it,
that I will follow your
righteous laws.
107 I have suffered much;
preserve my life,
O LORD, according
to your word.
108 Accept, O LORD, the
willing praise of
my mouth,
and teach me your laws.
109 Though I constantly take
my life in my hands,
I will not forget your law.
110 The wicked have set a snare for me,
but I have not strayed from your
precepts.
111 Your statutes are my heritage forever;
they are the joy of my heart.
112 My heart is set on keeping your decrees
to the very end.

ס Samekh

113 I hate double-minded men,
but I love your law.
114 You are my refuge and my shield;
I have put my hope in your word.
115 Away from me, you evildoers,
that I may keep the commands of my
God!
116 Sustain me according to your promise,
and I will live;
do not let my hopes be dashed.
117 Uphold me, and I will be delivered;
I will always have regard for your
decrees.
118 You reject all who stray from your decrees,
for their deceitfulness is in vain.
119 All the wicked of the earth you discard
like dross;

therefore I love your statutes.
120 My flesh trembles in fear of you;
I stand in awe of your laws.

ע Ayin

121 I have done what is righteous and just;
do not leave me to my oppressors.
122 Ensure your servant's well-being;
let not the arrogant
oppress me.
123 My eyes fail, looking for
your salvation,
looking for your
righteous promise.
124 Deal with your servant
according to
your love
and teach me your
decrees.
125 I am your servant; give
me discernment
that I may understand
your statutes.
126 It is time for you to act, O LORD;
your law is being broken.
127 Because I love your commands
more than gold, more than pure gold,
128 and because I consider all your
precepts right,
I hate every wrong path.

פ Pe

129 Your statutes are wonderful;
therefore I obey them.
130 The unfolding of your words gives light;
it gives understanding to the simple.
131 I open my mouth and pant,
longing for your commands.
132 Turn to me and have mercy on me,
as you always do to those who love
your name.
133 Direct my footsteps according to
your word;
let no sin rule over me.
134 Redeem me from the oppression of men,
that I may obey your precepts.
135 Make your face shine upon your servant
and teach me your decrees.
136 Streams of tears flow from my eyes,
for your law is not obeyed.

Psalm 119:105

*God Gives
Instruction*

Your word is a lamp
to my feet
and a light for my path.

צ Tsadhe

137 Righteous are you, O LORD,
and your laws are right.
138 The statutes you have laid down
are righteous;
they are fully trustworthy.
139 My zeal wears me out,
for my enemies ignore your words.
140 Your promises have been
thoroughly tested,
and your servant loves them.
141 Though I am lowly and despised,
I do not forget your precepts.
142 Your righteousness is everlasting
and your law is true.
143 Trouble and distress have come upon me,
but your commands are my delight.
144 Your statutes are forever right;
give me understanding that I may live.

ק Qoph

145 I call with all my heart; answer me,
O LORD,
and I will obey your decrees.
146 I call out to you; save me
and I will keep your statutes.
147 I rise before dawn and cry for help;
I have put my hope in your word.
148 My eyes stay open through the watches of
the night,
that I may meditate on your promises.
149 Hear my voice in accordance with
your love;
preserve my life, O LORD, according to
your laws.
150 Those who devise wicked schemes
are near,
but they are far from your law.
151 Yet you are near, O LORD,
and all your commands are true.
152 Long ago I learned from your statutes
that you established them to last forever.

ר Resh

153 Look upon my suffering and deliver me,
for I have not forgotten your law.
154 Defend my cause and redeem me;
preserve my life according to your
promise.
155 Salvation is far from the wicked,
for they do not seek out your decrees.
156 Your compassion is great, O LORD;
preserve my life according to your laws.
157 Many are the foes who persecute me,
but I have not turned from your statutes.
158 I look on the faithless with loathing,
for they do not obey your word.
159 See how I love your precepts;
preserve my life, O LORD, according to
your love.
160 All your words are true;
all your righteous laws are eternal.

שׁ Sin and Shin

161 Rulers persecute me without cause,
but my heart trembles at your word.
162 I rejoice in your promise
like one who finds great spoil.
163 I hate and abhor falsehood
but I love your law.
164 Seven times a day I praise you
for your righteous laws.
165 Great peace have they who love your law,
and nothing can make them stumble.
166 I wait for your salvation, O LORD,
and I follow your commands.
167 I obey your statutes,
for I love them greatly.
168 I obey your precepts and your statutes,
for all my ways are known to you.

ת Taw

169 May my cry come before you, O LORD;
give me understanding according to
your word.
170 May my supplication come before you;
deliver me according to your promise.
171 May my lips overflow with praise,
for you teach me your decrees.
172 May my tongue sing of your word,
for all your commands are righteous.
173 May your hand be ready to help me,
for I have chosen your precepts.
174 I long for your salvation, O LORD,
and your law is my delight.
175 Let me live that I may praise you,
and may your laws sustain me.
176 I have strayed like a lost sheep.
Seek your servant,
for I have not forgotten your commands.

Psalm 120
A song of ascents.

1 I call on the LORD in my distress,
   and he answers me.
2 Save me, O LORD, from lying lips
   and from deceitful tongues.

3 What will he do to you,
   and what more besides, O deceitful
      tongue?
4 He will punish you with a warrior's sharp
      arrows,
   with burning coals of the broom tree.

5 Woe to me that I dwell in Meshech,
   that I live among the tents of Kedar!
6 Too long have I lived
   among those who hate peace.
7 I am a man of peace;
   but when I speak, they are for war.

Psalm 121
A song of ascents.

1 I lift up my eyes to the hills—
   where does my help come from?
2 My help comes from the LORD,
   the Maker of heaven and
      earth.

3 He will not let your foot
      slip—
   he who watches over you
      will not slumber;
4 indeed, he who watches
      over Israel
   will neither slumber nor
      sleep.

5 The LORD watches over
      you—
   the LORD is your shade at
      your right hand;
6 the sun will not harm you by day,
   nor the moon by night.

7 The LORD will keep you from all harm—
   he will watch over your life;
8 the LORD will watch over your coming and
      going
   both now and forevermore.

Psalm 122
A song of ascents. Of David.

1 I rejoiced with those who said to me,
   "Let us go to the house of the LORD."
2 Our feet are standing
   in your gates, O Jerusalem.

3 Jerusalem is built like a city
   that is closely compacted together.
4 That is where the tribes go up,
   the tribes of the LORD,
   to praise the name of the LORD
   according to the statute given to Israel.
5 There the thrones for judgment stand,
   the thrones of the house of David.

6 Pray for the peace of Jerusalem:
   "May those who love you be secure.
7 May there be peace within your walls
   and security within your citadels."
8 For the sake of my brothers and friends,
   I will say, "Peace be within you."
9 For the sake of the house of the LORD our
      God,
   I will seek your prosperity.

Psalm 123
A song of ascents.

1 I lift up my eyes to you,
   to you whose throne is in
      heaven.
2 As the eyes of slaves look
   to the hand of their
      master,
   as the eyes of a maid look
   to the hand of her
      mistress,
   so our eyes look to the
      LORD our God,
   till he shows us his
      mercy.

3 Have mercy on us, O LORD,
   have mercy on us,
   for we have endured much contempt.
4 We have endured much ridicule from the
      proud,
   much contempt from the arrogant.

Psalm 124
A song of ascents. Of David.

1 If the LORD had not been on our side—
   let Israel say—
2 if the LORD had not been on our side
   when men attacked us,
3 when their anger flared against us,

Psalm 121:2

God Is Our Help

My help comes from
the LORD,
the Maker of heaven
and earth.

they would have swallowed us alive;
⁴ the flood would have engulfed us,
   the torrent would have swept over us,
⁵ the raging waters
   would have swept us away.

⁶ Praise be to the LORD,
   who has not let us be torn by their teeth.
⁷ We have escaped like a bird
   out of the fowler's snare;
  the snare has been broken,
   and we have escaped.
⁸ Our help is in the name of the LORD,
   the Maker of heaven and earth.

Psalm 125
A song of ascents.

¹ Those who trust in the LORD are like
   Mount Zion,
  which cannot be shaken
   but endures forever.
² As the mountains surround
   Jerusalem,
  so the LORD surrounds
   his people
  both now and
   forevermore.

³ The scepter of the wicked
   will not remain
  over the land allotted to
   the righteous,
for then the righteous might use
   their hands to do evil.

⁴ Do good, O LORD, to those who are good,
   to those who are upright in heart.
⁵ But those who turn to crooked ways
   the LORD will banish with the
    evildoers.

Peace be upon Israel.

Psalm 126
A song of ascents.

¹ When the LORD brought back the captives
   to*ᵃ* Zion,
  we were like men who dreamed.*ᵇ*
² Our mouths were filled with laughter,
   our tongues with songs of joy.
  Then it was said among the nations,

"The LORD has done great things for
   them."
³ The LORD has done great things for us,
   and we are filled with joy.

⁴ Restore our fortunes,*ᶜ* O LORD,
   like streams in the Negev.
⁵ Those who sow in tears
   will reap with songs of joy.
⁶ He who goes out weeping,
   carrying seed to sow,
  will return with songs of joy,
   carrying sheaves with him.

Psalm 127
A song of ascents. Of Solomon.

¹ Unless the LORD builds the house,
   its builders labor in vain.

> **Psalm 127:1**
>
> *God Offers Firm Foundations*
>
> Unless the LORD builds
> the house,
> its builders labor in vain.

      Unless the LORD watches
        over the city,
      the watchmen stand
        guard in vain.
² In vain you rise early
   and stay up late,
  toiling for food to eat—
   for he grants sleep to*ᵈ*
    those he loves.

³ Sons are a heritage from
   the LORD,
  children a reward from
   him.
⁴ Like arrows in the hands of a warrior
   are sons born in one's youth.
⁵ Blessed is the man
   whose quiver is full of them.
  They will not be put to shame
   when they contend with their enemies
    in the gate.

Psalm 128
A song of ascents.

¹ Blessed are all who fear the LORD,
   who walk in his ways.
² You will eat the fruit of your labor;
   blessings and prosperity will be yours.
³ Your wife will be like a fruitful vine
   within your house;
  your sons will be like olive shoots
   around your table.

---

*ᵃ*1 Or LORD *restored the fortunes of*   *ᵇ*1 Or *men restored to health*   *ᶜ*4 Or *Bring back our captives*   *ᵈ*2 Or *eat— / for while they sleep he provides for*

What Might Have Been

TAMAR

THINGS WERE NOT as they should have been.

For one thing, Tamar now lived with her brother, isolated from her other virgin sisters. She could no longer call the house they had shared her "home." She was different from all of them, tainted. Her change of address seemed to mirror her change in life. She could never go back. Her home was not, nor would it ever be, as it should have been.

Secondly, the richly ornamented robe she used to wear so proudly was now merely a shredded scrap, a visible symbol that her personality and purity were forever altered. Her view of herself, as well as the way others looked at her, was altered and would never be as it once had been.

On top of all that, she would never marry. *What man would have her?* she wondered. Who could see beauty in a crushed rose? One day, she was a young woman with her whole life ahead of her. The next day, all of that changed. Her options were no longer as they once had been.

She would never have children. She was, after all, "damaged goods," "used." Imaginary adjectives swirled around her in a dark cloud, publicly labeling her disgrace. Her future would never be as it should have been.

Her father overlooked it. Her brother downplayed it. Those who should have been her avengers were, instead, passive. It shouldn't have been that way.

The stronger took advantage of the weaker.

Evil overcame good.

She was innocent but somehow made to feel guilty.

Nothing, *nothing*, is as it should be in a fallen world. Not for Tamar; and, really, not for any woman before or since.

What happened to Tamar wasn't something that should have happened. And she had to find a way to go on.

—**Prayer**—
Loving Savior, I pray for healing of the painful experiences in my life, and in the lives of those around me.

> "What about me? Where could I get rid of my disgrace?"
>
> 2 Samuel 13:13

ASSIGNED READING:
2 Samuel 13:1–39

Weekend

Go to page 749 for your next devotional reading.

4 Thus is the man blessed
    who fears the LORD.

5 May the LORD bless you from Zion
    all the days of your life;
  may you see the prosperity of Jerusalem,
6   and may you live to see your children's
    children.

  Peace be upon Israel.

Psalm 129

A song of ascents.

1 They have greatly oppressed me from my
    youth—
    let Israel say—
2 they have greatly oppressed me from my
    youth,
  but they have not gained the victory
    over me.
3 Plowmen have plowed my back
    and made their furrows long.
4 But the LORD is righteous;
    he has cut me free from the cords of the
    wicked.

5 May all who hate Zion
    be turned back in shame.
6 May they be like grass on the roof,
    which withers before it can grow;
7 with it the reaper cannot fill his hands,
    nor the one who gathers fill his arms.
8 May those who pass by not say,
    "The blessing of the LORD be upon
    you;
  we bless you in the name of the LORD."

Psalm 130

A song of ascents.

1 Out of the depths I cry to you, O LORD;
2   O Lord, hear my voice.
  Let your ears be attentive
    to my cry for mercy.

3 If you, O LORD, kept a record of sins,
    O Lord, who could stand?
4 But with you there is forgiveness;
    therefore you are feared.

5 I wait for the LORD, my soul waits,
    and in his word I put my hope.
6 My soul waits for the Lord

more than watchmen wait for the
    morning,
  more than watchmen wait for the
    morning.
7 O Israel, put your hope in the LORD,
    for with the LORD is unfailing love
    and with him is full redemption.
8 He himself will redeem Israel
    from all their sins.

Psalm 131

A song of ascents. Of David.

1 My heart is not proud, O LORD,
    my eyes are not haughty;
  I do not concern myself with great matters
    or things too wonderful for me.
2 But I have stilled and quieted my soul;
    like a weaned child with its mother,
    like a weaned child is my soul within me.

3 O Israel, put your hope in the LORD
    both now and forevermore.

Psalm 132

A song of ascents.

1 O LORD, remember David
    and all the hardships he endured.

2 He swore an oath to the LORD
    and made a vow to the Mighty One of
    Jacob:
3 "I will not enter my house
    or go to my bed—
4 I will allow no sleep to my eyes,
    no slumber to my eyelids,
5 till I find a place for the LORD,
    a dwelling for the Mighty One of Jacob."

6 We heard it in Ephrathah,
    we came upon it in the fields of Jaar:*ᵃ;ᵇ*
7 "Let us go to his dwelling place;
    let us worship at his footstool—
8 arise, O LORD, and come to your resting
    place,
    you and the ark of your might.
9 May your priests be clothed with
    righteousness;
    may your saints sing for joy."

10 For the sake of David your servant,
    do not reject your anointed one.

ᵃ6 That is, Kiriath Jearim   ᵇ6 Or heard of it in Ephrathah, / we found it in the fields of Jaar. (And no quotes around verses 7–9)

11 The LORD swore an oath to David,
  a sure oath that he will not revoke:
"One of your own descendants
  I will place on your throne—
12 if your sons keep my covenant
  and the statutes I teach them,
then their sons will sit
  on your throne for ever and ever."

13 For the LORD has chosen Zion,
  he has desired it for his dwelling:
14 "This is my resting place for ever and
  ever;
  here I will sit enthroned, for I have
  desired it—
15 I will bless her with abundant provisions;
  her poor will I satisfy with food.
16 I will clothe her priests with salvation,
  and her saints will ever
  sing for joy.

17 "Here I will make a horn[a]
  grow for David
  and set up a lamp for my
  anointed one.
18 I will clothe his enemies
  with shame,
  but the crown on
  his head will be
  resplendent."

Psalm 133

A song of ascents. Of David.

1 How good and pleasant it is
  when brothers live
  together in unity!
2 It is like precious oil poured on the head,
  running down on the beard,
  running down on Aaron's beard,
  down upon the collar of his robes.
3 It is as if the dew of Hermon
  were falling on Mount Zion.
For there the LORD bestows his blessing,
  even life forevermore.

Psalm 134

A song of ascents.

1 Praise the LORD, all you servants of the
  LORD
who minister by night in the house of
  the LORD.

2 Lift up your hands in the sanctuary
  and praise the LORD.

3 May the LORD, the Maker of heaven and
  earth,
  bless you from Zion.

Psalm 135

1 Praise the LORD.[b]

Praise the name of the LORD;
  praise him, you servants of the LORD,
2 you who minister in the house of the
  LORD,
  in the courts of the house of our God.

3 Praise the LORD, for the LORD is good;
  sing praise to his name, for that is
  pleasant.
4 For the LORD has chosen
  Jacob to be his
  own,
  Israel to be his treasured
  possession.
5 I know that the LORD is
  great,
  that our Lord is greater
  than all gods.
6 The LORD does whatever
  pleases him,
  in the heavens and on
  the earth,
  in the seas and all their
  depths.
7 He makes clouds rise from
  the ends of the
  earth;
he sends lightning with the rain
  and brings out the wind from his
  storehouses.

8 He struck down the firstborn of Egypt,
  the firstborn of men and animals.
9 He sent his signs and wonders into your
  midst, O Egypt,
  against Pharaoh and all his servants.
10 He struck down many nations
  and killed mighty kings—
11 Sihon king of the Amorites,
  Og king of Bashan
  and all the kings of Canaan—

Psalm 135:6

God Answers to Himself

The LORD does whatever
pleases him,
in the heavens and
on the earth,
in the seas and all
their depths.

---

[a]17 *Horn* here symbolizes strong one, that is, king.   [b]1 Hebrew *Hallelu Yah*; also in verses 3 and 21

¹²and he gave their land as an inheritance,
an inheritance to his people Israel.

¹³Your name, O LORD, endures forever,
your renown, O LORD, through all
generations.

¹⁴For the LORD will vindicate his people
and have compassion on his servants.

¹⁵The idols of the nations are silver and gold,
made by the hands of men.

¹⁶They have mouths, but cannot speak,
eyes, but they cannot see;

¹⁷they have ears, but cannot hear,
nor is there breath in their mouths.

¹⁸Those who make them will be like them,
and so will all who trust in them.

¹⁹O house of Israel, praise the LORD;
O house of Aaron, praise the LORD;

²⁰O house of Levi, praise the LORD;
you who fear him, praise the LORD.

²¹Praise be to the LORD from Zion,
to him who dwells in Jerusalem.

Praise the LORD.

Psalm 136

¹Give thanks to the LORD, for he is good.
His love endures forever.

²Give thanks to the God of gods.
His love endures forever.

³Give thanks to the Lord of lords:
His love endures forever.

⁴to him who alone does great wonders,
His love endures forever.

⁵who by his understanding made the
heavens,
His love endures forever.

⁶who spread out the earth upon the waters,
His love endures forever.

⁷who made the great lights—
His love endures forever.

⁸the sun to govern the day,
His love endures forever.

⁹the moon and stars to govern the night;
His love endures forever.

¹⁰to him who struck down the firstborn of
Egypt
His love endures forever.

¹¹and brought Israel out from among them
His love endures forever.

¹²with a mighty hand and outstretched arm;
His love endures forever.

¹³to him who divided the Red Sea^a asunder
His love endures forever.

¹⁴and brought Israel through the midst of it,
His love endures forever.

¹⁵but swept Pharaoh and his army into the
Red Sea;
His love endures forever.

¹⁶to him who led his people through the
desert,
His love endures forever.

¹⁷who struck down great kings,
His love endures forever.

¹⁸and killed mighty kings—
His love endures forever.

¹⁹Sihon king of the Amorites
His love endures forever.

²⁰and Og king of Bashan—
His love endures forever.

²¹and gave their land as an inheritance,
His love endures forever.

²²an inheritance to his servant Israel;
His love endures forever.

²³to the One who remembered us in our low
estate
His love endures forever.

²⁴and freed us from our enemies,
His love endures forever.

²⁵and who gives food to every creature.
His love endures forever.

²⁶Give thanks to the God of heaven.
His love endures forever.

Psalm 137

¹By the rivers of Babylon we sat and wept
when we remembered Zion.

²There on the poplars
we hung our harps,

³for there our captors asked us for songs,
our tormentors demanded songs of joy;
they said, "Sing us one of the songs of
Zion!"

⁴How can we sing the songs of the LORD
while in a foreign land?

---

^a13 Hebrew *Yam Suph*; that is, Sea of Reeds; also in verse 15

Enduring, Endearing Love

Read: Psalm 136:1–26

"DIAMONDS ARE FOREVER"—at least that's what the jewelry industry hopes enamored couples everywhere will believe. One advertiser boasted, "Since diamonds last forever, a diamond engagement ring tells your sweetheart that your love for her will be unwavering on into eternity." Unfortunately, a diamond often outlasts the marriage it was meant to symbolize. Human love is not flawless.

So, where can you find flawless and eternal love? Psalm 136 asserts repeatedly that God's love "endures forever." This antiphonal song served as an anthem or pledge of mutual love between God and his people. Old Testament priests sang the first phrase in these verses while the congregation answered with the refrain: "His love endures forever." It was much like an exchange of wedding vows between God and his bride, the nation of Israel (see Isaiah 62:5).

God desires the closeness of such a relationship with each of us for eternity. And his love lasts beyond a lifetime. Not only does God offer us *enduring* love, he also extends to us *endearing* love, a strong affection that lifts one higher or increases the value of the one beloved. *Enduring* speaks of the *quantity* of God's love while *endearing* portrays the *quality*. The psalmist says that God is "the One who remembered us in our low estate" (verse 23). We are nothing. But God loved us before we were lovely. We are his diamonds in the rough.

In the rough, a diamond looks like a common pebble. The stone must undergo a finishing process to bring out its full radiance. It is then held against a large grinding wheel to cut and polish the stone. Many meticulous hours are spent perfecting it.

Like the nation of Israel, God has lifted you out of the rubble of a worthless life. He is polishing and chiseling you into a jewel of great beauty. You are his diamond. You are like a bride being prepared for the bridegroom. *And his love endures forever.*

Go to page 755 for your next devotional reading.

Psalm 136:1,23

Give thanks . . . to the One who remembered us in our low estate . . . *His love endures forever.*

reflection

1 In what ways has the human love you've experienced been flawed and temporary?

2 In what ways have you experienced God's enduring love personally?

3 How does it make you feel to know that God values you as a priceless diamond? How does it make you feel to know that he is chiseling and polishing you into a jewel of great beauty?

RELATED READINGS

Isaiah 62:1–5;
Zechariah 9:14–17;
Revelation 19:5–10

⁵ If I forget you, O Jerusalem,
  may my right hand forget ⸢its skill⸣.
⁶ May my tongue cling to the roof of my
    mouth
  if I do not remember you,
  if I do not consider Jerusalem
    my highest joy.

⁷ Remember, O LORD, what
    the Edomites did
  on the day Jerusalem fell.
"Tear it down," they cried,
  "tear it down to its
    foundations!"

⁸ O Daughter of Babylon,
    doomed to
    destruction,
  happy is he who repays
    you
  for what you have done
    to us—
⁹ he who seizes your infants
  and dashes them against
    the rocks.

Psalm 138
Of David.

¹ I will praise you, O LORD, with all my
    heart;
  before the "gods" I will sing your praise.
² I will bow down toward your holy temple
  and will praise your name
  for your love and your faithfulness,
  for you have exalted above all things
    your name and your word.
³ When I called, you answered me;
  you made me bold and stouthearted.

⁴ May all the kings of the earth praise you,
    O LORD,
  when they hear the words of your
    mouth.
⁵ May they sing of the ways of the LORD,
  for the glory of the LORD is great.

⁶ Though the LORD is on high, he looks
    upon the lowly,
  but the proud he knows from afar.
⁷ Though I walk in the midst of trouble,
  you preserve my life;

you stretch out your hand against the
    anger of my foes,
  with your right hand you save me.
⁸ The LORD will fulfill ⸢his purpose⸣ for me;
  your love, O LORD, endures forever—
  do not abandon the works of your
    hands.

Psalm 138:8

*God Has
a Purpose*

The LORD will fulfill
his purpose for me;
your love, O LORD,
endures forever—
do not abandon the
works of your hands.

Psalm 139
For the director of music.
Of David. A psalm.

¹ O LORD, you have
    searched me
  and you know me.
² You know when I sit and
    when I rise;
  you perceive my
    thoughts from afar.
³ You discern my going out
    and my lying down;
  you are familiar with all
    my ways.
⁴ Before a word is on my
    tongue
  you know it completely, O LORD.

⁵ You hem me in—behind and before;
  you have laid your hand upon me.
⁶ Such knowledge is too wonderful for me,
  too lofty for me to attain.

⁷ Where can I go from your Spirit?
  Where can I flee from your presence?
⁸ If I go up to the heavens, you are there;
  if I make my bed in the depths,ᵃ you are
    there.
⁹ If I rise on the wings of the dawn,
  if I settle on the far side of the sea,
¹⁰ even there your hand will guide me,
  your right hand will hold me fast.

¹¹ If I say, "Surely the darkness will hide me
  and the light become night around me,"
¹² even the darkness will not be dark to
    you;
  the night will shine like the day,
  for darkness is as light to you.

¹³ For you created my inmost being;
  you knit me together in my mother's
    womb.

ᵃ8 Hebrew *Sheol*

[14] I praise you because I am fearfully and
      wonderfully made;
   your works are wonderful,
   I know that full well.
[15] My frame was not hidden from you
   when I was made in the secret place.
   When I was woven together in the depths
      of the earth,
[16] your eyes saw my unformed body.
   All the days ordained for me
   were written in your book
   before one of them came to be.

[17] How precious to[a] me are your thoughts,
      O God!
   How vast is the sum of them!
[18] Were I to count them,
   they would outnumber the grains of sand.
   When I awake,
   I am still with you.

[19] If only you would slay the wicked, O God!
   Away from me, you bloodthirsty men!
[20] They speak of you with evil intent;
   your adversaries misuse your name.
[21] Do I not hate those who hate you, O LORD,
   and abhor those who rise up against
      you?
[22] I have nothing but hatred for them;
   I count them my enemies.

[23] Search me, O God, and know my heart;
   test me and know my anxious thoughts.
[24] See if there is any offensive way in me,
   and lead me in the way everlasting.

Psalm 140
For the director of music. A psalm of David.

[1] Rescue me, O LORD, from evil men;
   protect me from men of violence,
[2] who devise evil plans in their hearts
   and stir up war every day.
[3] They make their tongues as sharp as a
      serpent's;
   the poison of vipers is on their lips.
                                        Selah

[4] Keep me, O LORD, from the hands of the
      wicked;
   protect me from men of violence
   who plan to trip my feet.

[5] Proud men have hidden a snare for me;
   they have spread out the cords of their
      net
   and have set traps for me along my path.
                                        Selah

[6] O LORD, I say to you, "You are my God."
   Hear, O LORD, my cry for mercy.
[7] O Sovereign LORD, my strong deliverer,
   who shields my head in the day of
      battle—
[8] do not grant the wicked their desires,
      O LORD;
   do not let their plans succeed,
   or they will become proud.   *Selah*

[9] Let the heads of those who surround me
   be covered with the trouble their lips
      have caused.
[10] Let burning coals fall upon them;
   may they be thrown into the fire,
   into miry pits, never to rise.
[11] Let slanderers not be established in the
      land;
   may disaster hunt down men of violence.

[12] I know that the LORD secures justice for
      the poor
   and upholds the cause of the needy.
[13] Surely the righteous will praise your name
   and the upright will live before you.

Psalm 141
A psalm of David.

[1] O LORD, I call to you; come quickly to me.
   Hear my voice when I call to you.
[2] May my prayer be set before you like
      incense;
   may the lifting up of my hands be like
      the evening sacrifice.

[3] Set a guard over my mouth, O LORD;
   keep watch over the door of my lips.
[4] Let not my heart be drawn to what is evil,
   to take part in wicked deeds
   with men who are evildoers;
   let me not eat of their delicacies.

[5] Let a righteous man[b] strike me—it is a
      kindness;
   let him rebuke me—it is oil on my head.
   My head will not refuse it.

[a]17 Or *concerning*   [b]5 Or *Let the Righteous One*

Yet my prayer is ever against the deeds of
evildoers;
6 their rulers will be thrown down from
the cliffs,
and the wicked will learn that my words
were well spoken.
7 They will say, "As one plows and breaks
up the earth,
so our bones have been scattered at the
mouth of the grave.*a*"

8 But my eyes are fixed on you, O Sovereign
LORD;
in you I take refuge—do not give me
over to death.
9 Keep me from the snares they have laid for
me,
from the traps set by evildoers.
10 Let the wicked fall into their own nets,
while I pass by in safety.

Psalm 142
A *maskil*b of David. When he was in the cave.
A prayer.

1 I cry aloud to the LORD;
I lift up my voice to the LORD for
mercy.
2 I pour out my complaint before him;
before him I tell my trouble.

3 When my spirit grows faint within me,
it is you who know my way.
In the path where I walk
men have hidden a snare for me.
4 Look to my right and see;
no one is concerned for me.
I have no refuge;
no one cares for my life.

5 I cry to you, O LORD;
I say, "You are my refuge,
my portion in the land of the living."
6 Listen to my cry,
for I am in desperate need;
rescue me from those who pursue me,
for they are too strong for me.
7 Set me free from my prison,
that I may praise your name.

Then the righteous will gather about me
because of your goodness to me.

Psalm 143
A psalm of David.

1 O LORD, hear my prayer,
listen to my cry for mercy;
in your faithfulness and righteousness
come to my relief.
2 Do not bring your servant into judgment,
for no one living is righteous before
you.

3 The enemy pursues me,
he crushes me to the ground;
he makes me dwell in darkness
like those long dead.
4 So my spirit grows faint within me;
my heart within me is dismayed.

5 I remember the days of long ago;
I meditate on all your works
and consider what your hands have
done.
6 I spread out my hands to you;
my soul thirsts for you like a parched
land.   *Selah*

7 Answer me quickly, O LORD;
my spirit fails.
Do not hide your face from me
or I will be like those who go down to
the pit.
8 Let the morning bring me word of your
unfailing love,
for I have put my trust in you.
Show me the way I should go,
for to you I lift up my soul.
9 Rescue me from my enemies, O LORD,
for I hide myself in you.
10 Teach me to do your will,
for you are my God;
may your good Spirit
lead me on level ground.

11 For your name's sake, O LORD, preserve
my life;
in your righteousness, bring me out of
trouble.
12 In your unfailing love, silence my
enemies;
destroy all my foes,
for I am your servant.

---

*a*7 Hebrew *Sheol*   *b*Title: Probably a literary or musical term

Psalm 144

Of David.

1 Praise be to the LORD my Rock,
    who trains my hands for war,
    my fingers for battle.
2 He is my loving God and my fortress,
    my stronghold and my deliverer,
  my shield, in whom I take refuge,
    who subdues peoples*a* under me.

3 O LORD, what is man that you care for
        him,
    the son of man that you think of him?
4 Man is like a breath;
    his days are like a fleeting shadow.

5 Part your heavens, O LORD, and come
        down;
    touch the mountains, so that they
        smoke.
6 Send forth lightning and scatter the
        enemies ;
    shoot your arrows and rout them.
7 Reach down your hand from on high;
    deliver me and rescue me
  from the mighty waters,
    from the hands of foreigners
8 whose mouths are full of lies,
    whose right hands are deceitful.

9 I will sing a new song to you, O God;
    on the ten-stringed lyre I will make
        music to you,
10 to the One who gives victory to kings,
    who delivers his servant David from the
        deadly sword.

11 Deliver me and rescue me
    from the hands of
        foreigners
  whose mouths are full of
        lies,
    whose right hands are
        deceitful.

12 Then our sons in their
        youth
    will be like well-nurtured
        plants,

and our daughters will be like pillars
    carved to adorn a palace.
13 Our barns will be filled
    with every kind of provision.
Our sheep will increase by thousands,
    by tens of thousands in our fields;
14   our oxen will draw heavy loads.*b*
There will be no breaching of walls,
    no going into captivity,
    no cry of distress in our streets.

15 Blessed are the people of whom this is true;
    blessed are the people whose God is the
        LORD.

Psalm 145*c*

A psalm of praise. Of David.

1 I will exalt you, my God the King;
    I will praise your name for ever and
        ever.
2 Every day I will praise you
    and extol your name for ever and ever.

3 Great is the LORD and most worthy of
        praise;
    his greatness no one can fathom.
4 One generation will commend your works
        to another;
    they will tell of your mighty acts.
5 They will speak of the glorious splendor of
        your majesty,
    and I will meditate on your wonderful
        works.*d*
6 They will tell of the power of your awesome
        works,
        and I will proclaim your
            great deeds.
7 They will celebrate your
        abundant goodness
    and joyfully sing of your
        righteousness.

8 The LORD is gracious and
        compassionate,
    slow to anger and rich
        in love.
9 The LORD is good to all;
    he has compassion on all
        he has made.

Psalm 145:8

God Is Enduring

The LORD is gracious and
compassionate,
slow to anger and
rich in love.

---

*a*2 Many manuscripts of the Masoretic Text, Dead Sea Scrolls, Aquila, Jerome and Syriac; most manuscripts of the Masoretic Text *subdues my people*   *b*14 Or *our chieftains will be firmly established*   *c*This psalm is an acrostic poem, the verses of which (including verse 13b) begin with the successive letters of the Hebrew alphabet.   *d*5 Dead Sea Scrolls and Syriac (see also Septuagint); Masoretic Text *On the glorious splendor of your majesty / and on your wonderful works I will meditate*

¹⁰ All you have made will praise you,
O Lord;
your saints will extol you.
¹¹ They will tell of the glory of your
kingdom
and speak of your might,
¹² so that all men may know of your mighty
acts
and the glorious splendor of your
kingdom.
¹³ Your kingdom is an everlasting kingdom,
and your dominion endures through all
generations.

The Lord is faithful to all his promises
and loving toward all he has made.ᵃ
¹⁴ The Lord upholds all those who fall
and lifts up all who are bowed down.
¹⁵ The eyes of all look to you,
and you give them their food at the
proper time.
¹⁶ You open your hand
and satisfy the desires of every living
thing.

¹⁷ The Lord is righteous in all his ways
and loving toward all he has made.
¹⁸ The Lord is near to all who call on him,
to all who call on him in truth.
¹⁹ He fulfills the desires of those who fear
him;
he hears their cry and saves them.
²⁰ The Lord watches over all who love
him,
but all the wicked he will
destroy.

²¹ My mouth will speak in
praise of the Lord.
Let every creature praise
his holy name
for ever and ever.

Psalm 146

¹ Praise the Lord.ᵇ

Praise the Lord, O my
soul.
² I will praise the Lord all my life;
I will sing praise to my God as long as
I live.

³ Do not put your trust in princes,
in mortal men, who cannot save.
⁴ When their spirit departs, they return to
the ground;
on that very day their plans come to
nothing.

⁵ Blessed is he whose help is the God of
Jacob,
whose hope is in the Lord his God,
⁶ the Maker of heaven and earth,
the sea, and everything in them—
the Lord, who remains faithful forever.
⁷ He upholds the cause of the oppressed
and gives food to the hungry.
The Lord sets prisoners free,
⁸ the Lord gives sight to the blind,
the Lord lifts up those who are bowed
down,
the Lord loves the righteous.
⁹ The Lord watches over the alien
and sustains the fatherless and the
widow,
but he frustrates the ways of the
wicked.

¹⁰ The Lord reigns forever,
your God, O Zion, for all generations.

Praise the Lord.

Psalm 147

¹ Praise the Lord.ᶜ

How good it is to sing praises to our God,
how pleasant and fitting
to praise him!

² The Lord builds up
Jerusalem;
he gathers the exiles of
Israel.
³ He heals the brokenhearted
and binds up their
wounds.

⁴ He determines the number
of the stars
and calls them each by
name.
⁵ Great is our Lord and mighty in power;
his understanding has no limit.

Psalm 147:5

God Is Limitless

Great is our Lord and
mighty in power;
his understanding
has no limit.

ᵃ13 One manuscript of the Masoretic Text, Dead Sea Scrolls and Syriac (see also Septuagint); most manuscripts of the Masoretic Text do not have the last two lines of verse 13.   ᵇ1 Hebrew *Hallelu Yah*; also in verse 10   ᶜ1 Hebrew *Hallelu Yah*; also in verse 20

God in Your Brag Book

Read: Psalm 145:1–21

WHOM DO YOU BRAG ABOUT? Do your friends hear about your brilliant daughter, your generous sister, your adorable puppy? Have you in turn seen every photo of a friend's grandchild, heard about every new word, every tooth and every step?

How often do you brag about God? People in your life need to hear from you about him—your children, nieces and nephews, godchildren, neighborhood kids, everyone. They will someday have their own stories of how their prayers were answered. They will learn about God's faithfulness as they go through hard times. God will bless them with delightful surprises. They will experience God's mercy and tenderness for themselves. But until they have their own stories, they need to hear *yours*. Your stories will "prime the pump" as it were and alert them to watch for God as they "live and move and have [their] being" in him (Acts 17:28).

Scripture tells us that God is gracious and compassionate, patient and merciful. King David knew this from his own experience. God protected him from many who would have killed him, including his own king and father-in-law, King Saul, and later his son Absalom, who wanted to be king himself. David knew God as the only King who is always righteous. David also knew God as the One who forgives, who washes away devastating sins instead of killing the sinner. David knew God in a surprisingly intimate way. The shepherd knew God as his Shepherd. The king called God his own King.

It's easy to complain about inefficient checkout clerks, dangerous drivers and ungrateful relatives. It's natural to tell our stories of financial hardship and illness and slights from our friends. It's great to have funny stories to tell about what has happened to us. But it's so much sweeter and deeper to bless others with stories about the good things, the true things, the beautiful and enduring things that we've experienced with God. It's so rewarding to look for opportunities to praise God and to remember how he has been good to us. It's so wonderfully fun to brag about God.

Go to page 759 for your next devotional reading.

Tuesday

Psalm 145:4

One generation will commend your works to another; they will tell of your mighty acts.

reflection

1 Why do you think David spent so much time praising God?

2 What special reasons do you have to praise God?

3 How can you brag about God to someone today?

RELATED READINGS

Deuteronomy 6:1–9;
Psalm 105:1–5;
Philippians 4:4–9

⁶ The LORD sustains the humble
  but casts the wicked to the ground.

⁷ Sing to the LORD with thanksgiving;
  make music to our God on the harp.

⁸ He covers the sky with clouds;
  he supplies the earth with rain
  and makes grass grow on the hills.

⁹ He provides food for the cattle
  and for the young ravens when they call.

¹⁰ His pleasure is not in the strength of the
  horse,
  nor his delight in the legs of a man;

¹¹ the LORD delights in those who fear him,
  who put their hope in his unfailing love.

¹² Extol the LORD, O Jerusalem;
  praise your God, O Zion,

¹³ for he strengthens the bars of your gates
  and blesses your people within you.

¹⁴ He grants peace to your borders
  and satisfies you with the finest of wheat.

¹⁵ He sends his command to the earth;
  his word runs swiftly.

¹⁶ He spreads the snow like wool
  and scatters the frost like ashes.

¹⁷ He hurls down his hail like pebbles.
  Who can withstand his icy blast?

¹⁸ He sends his word and melts them;
  he stirs up his breezes, and the waters
  flow.

¹⁹ He has revealed his word to Jacob,
  his laws and decrees to Israel.

²⁰ He has done this for no other nation;
  they do not know his laws.

  Praise the LORD.

Psalm 148

¹ Praise the LORD.ᵃ

  Praise the LORD from the heavens,
  praise him in the heights above.

² Praise him, all his angels,
  praise him, all his heavenly hosts.

³ Praise him, sun and moon,
  praise him, all you shining stars.

⁴ Praise him, you highest heavens
  and you waters above the skies.

⁵ Let them praise the name of the LORD,

  for he commanded and they were
  created.

⁶ He set them in place for ever and ever;
  he gave a decree that will never pass
  away.

⁷ Praise the LORD from the earth,
  you great sea creatures and all ocean
  depths,

⁸ lightning and hail, snow and clouds,
  stormy winds that do his bidding,

⁹ you mountains and all hills,
  fruit trees and all cedars,

¹⁰ wild animals and all cattle,
  small creatures and flying birds,

¹¹ kings of the earth and all nations,
  you princes and all rulers on earth,

¹² young men and maidens,
  old men and children.

¹³ Let them praise the name of the LORD,
  for his name alone is exalted;
  his splendor is above the earth and the
  heavens.

¹⁴ He has raised up for his people a horn,ᵇ
  the praise of all his saints,
  of Israel, the people close to his heart.

  Praise the LORD.

Psalm 149

¹ Praise the LORD.ᶜ

  Sing to the LORD a new song,
  his praise in the assembly of the saints.

² Let Israel rejoice in their Maker;
  let the people of Zion be glad in their
  King.

³ Let them praise his name with dancing
  and make music to him with
  tambourine and harp.

⁴ For the LORD takes delight in his people;
  he crowns the humble with salvation.

⁵ Let the saints rejoice in this honor
  and sing for joy on their beds.

⁶ May the praise of God be in their mouths
  and a double-edged sword in their
  hands,

⁷ to inflict vengeance on the nations
  and punishment on the peoples,

ᵃ1 Hebrew *Hallelu Yah*; also in verse 14   ᵇ14 *Horn* here symbolizes strong one, that is, king.   ᶜ1 Hebrew *Hallelu Yah*; also in verse 9

[8] to bind their kings with fetters,
their nobles with shackles of iron,
[9] to carry out the sentence written against
them.
This is the glory of all his saints.

Praise the LORD.

Psalm 150

[1] Praise the LORD.[a]

Praise God in his sanctuary;
praise him in his mighty heavens.
[2] Praise him for his acts of power;
praise him for his surpassing greatness.
[3] Praise him with the sounding of the
trumpet,
praise him with the harp and lyre,
[4] praise him with tambourine and dancing,
praise him with the strings and flute,
[5] praise him with the clash of cymbals,
praise him with resounding cymbals.

[6] Let everything that has breath praise the
LORD.

Praise the LORD.

---

[a]1 Hebrew *Hallelu Yah*; also in verse 6

Proverbs

Author:
Primarily King Solomon.

Audience:
All Israel.

Date:
Solomon wrote most of the proverbs during his reign (970 to 930 B.C.), but the book wasn't fully compiled until around 700 B.C.

Setting:
Written during Solomon's wiser days. Solomon had great wisdom, but he gave in to temptation later on in his life.

Verse to Remember:
The fear of the LORD is the beginning of knowledge, but fools despise wisdom and discipline. (1:7)

Wisdom is at the heart of Proverbs. Most of the book was written by King Solomon, whom *God blessed with the gift* of great wisdom. Delving into subjects as varied as money, relationships, folly, adultery, child-rearing, contentment and choosing good companions, the book is a treasure trove of advice. *Godly wisdom* is one of life's most important and valuable pursuits, *worth much more* than material wealth. Many people choose to read this book monthly, one chapter each day, to be sure to keep the lessons learned at the front of their minds.

Prologue: Purpose and Theme

1 The proverbs of Solomon son of David, king of Israel:

2 for attaining wisdom and discipline;
   for understanding words of insight;
3 for acquiring a disciplined and prudent life,
   doing what is right and just and fair;
4 for giving prudence to the simple,
   knowledge and discretion to the young—
5 let the wise listen and add to their learning,
   and let the discerning get guidance—
6 for understanding proverbs and parables,
   the sayings and riddles of the wise.

7 The fear of the LORD is the beginning of knowledge,

Perpetual Puberty

Read: Proverbs 1:1–33

JUNIOR HIGH. The place where we transitioned to adolescence with pimply faces and few social skills. A time when it was uncool to listen to authority. When sarcasm and spite peppered our speech. We thought we knew it all. Now—after 20, 30 or 40 years—many of us look back with regret on some of the choices we made then. We still wince when we remember the wounds we received from cutting words; we still wince when we remember the wounds we inflicted on others. What was missing during that season of life? Could it have been wisdom?

Actually, wisdom was there all the time, but we probably ignored it. When we allow wisdom to go unheeded, we're like a teenager stuck in perpetual puberty. In Proverbs 1, Solomon describes the unwise as those who "delight in mockery" (verse 22), reject help (verse 24) and ignore advice (verse 25). It sounds like Solomon knew more than a few spiritual adolescents, doesn't it?

He goes on to say that those who reject God's knowledge will "eat the fruit of their ways and be filled with the fruit of their schemes" (verse 31). In other words, we will reap what we sow, or in popular jargon, "we'll get what we deserve." Wisdom's warning is appropriate for all of us, regardless of our age.

Where are you on your spiritual journey? Are you stuck in perpetual spiritual puberty? Here are a few signs: You constantly worry about what others think of you. You overreact to stressful situations. You're too proud or stubborn to listen to those older and wiser. You stay with one group and ridicule others. If you've found yourself in perpetual puberty, then seek wisdom.

God's wisdom isn't reserved for a few scholars; it's available to everyone. Wisdom is found in the book that holds eternal truth—God's Word. According to Solomon, wisdom comes from listening to God (one of the most frequent commands in the Old Testament) and obeying him. Wisdom comes from letting the Holy Spirit live within you. Wisdom grows when, "like newborn babies, [you] crave pure spiritual milk, so that by it you may grow up in your salvation, now that you have tasted that the Lord is good" (1 Peter 2:2–3). If you're stuck in spiritual adolescence, listen, learn and grow spiritually mature.

Proverbs 1:24–25

You rejected me when I called and no one gave heed when I stretched out my hand . . . You ignored all my advice and would not accept my rebuke.

reflection

1 When you think back to your junior high years, what feelings do you experience?

2 Describe a time when you disregarded wisdom. What was the result?

3 How will you go about growing more and seeking wisdom?

RELATED READINGS

Psalm 81:8–16;
Jeremiah 13:15–17;
Galatians 6:6–10

Go to page 765 for your next devotional reading.

but fools[a] despise wisdom and
discipline.

Exhortations to Embrace Wisdom

Warning Against Enticement

8 Listen, my son, to your father's instruction
and do not forsake your mother's
teaching.
9 They will be a garland to grace your head
and a chain to adorn your neck.

10 My son, if sinners entice you,
do not give in to them.
11 If they say, "Come along with us;
let's lie in wait for someone's blood,
let's waylay some harmless soul;
12 let's swallow them alive, like the grave,[b]
and whole, like those who go down to
the pit;
13 we will get all sorts of valuable things
and fill our houses with plunder;
14 throw in your lot with us,
and we will share a common purse"—
15 my son, do not go along with them,
do not set foot on their paths;
16 for their feet rush into sin,
they are swift to shed blood.
17 How useless to spread a net
in full view of all the birds!
18 These men lie in wait for their own blood;
they waylay only themselves!
19 Such is the end of all who go after
ill-gotten gain;
it takes away the lives of those who get it.

Warning Against Rejecting Wisdom

20 Wisdom calls aloud in the street,
she raises her voice in the public
squares;
21 at the head of the noisy streets[c] she cries
out,
in the gateways of the city she makes her
speech:

22 "How long will you simple ones[d] love your
simple ways?
How long will mockers delight in
mockery
and fools hate knowledge?

23 If you had responded to my rebuke,
I would have poured out my heart to you
and made my thoughts known to you.
24 But since you rejected me when I called
and no one gave heed when I stretched
out my hand,
25 since you ignored all my advice
and would not accept my rebuke,
26 I in turn will laugh at your disaster;
I will mock when calamity overtakes
you—
27 when calamity overtakes you like a storm,
when disaster sweeps over you like a
whirlwind,
when distress and trouble overwhelm
you.

28 "Then they will call to me but I will not
answer;
they will look for me but will not find
me.
29 Since they hated knowledge
and did not choose to fear the LORD,
30 since they would not accept my advice
and spurned my rebuke,
31 they will eat the fruit of their ways
and be filled with the fruit of their
schemes.
32 For the waywardness of the simple will kill
them,
and the complacency of fools will
destroy them;
33 but whoever listens to me will live in safety
and be at ease, without fear of harm."

Moral Benefits of Wisdom

2 My son, if you accept my words
and store up my commands within you,
2 turning your ear to wisdom
and applying your heart to
understanding,
3 and if you call out for insight
and cry aloud for understanding,
4 and if you look for it as for silver
and search for it as for hidden treasure,
5 then you will understand the fear of the
LORD
and find the knowledge of God.
6 For the LORD gives wisdom,

---

*a*7 The Hebrew words rendered *fool* in Proverbs, and often elsewhere in the Old Testament, denote one who is morally deficient.
*b*12 Hebrew *Sheol* *c*21 Hebrew; Septuagint / *on the tops of the walls* *d*22 The Hebrew word rendered *simple* in Proverbs generally
denotes one without moral direction and inclined to evil.

and from his mouth come knowledge
and understanding.
⁷ He holds victory in store for the upright,
he is a shield to those whose walk is
blameless,
⁸ for he guards the course of the just
and protects the way of his faithful ones.

⁹ Then you will understand what is right and
just
and fair—every good
path.
¹⁰ For wisdom will enter your
heart,
and knowledge will be
pleasant to your
soul.
¹¹ Discretion will protect you,
and understanding will
guard you.

¹² Wisdom will save you from
the ways of wicked
men,
from men whose words are perverse,
¹³ who leave the straight paths
to walk in dark ways,
¹⁴ who delight in doing wrong
and rejoice in the perverseness of evil,
¹⁵ whose paths are crooked
and who are devious in their ways.

¹⁶ It will save you also from the adulteress,
from the wayward wife with her
seductive words,
¹⁷ who has left the partner of her youth
and ignored the covenant she made
before God.^a
¹⁸ For her house leads down to death
and her paths to the spirits of the dead.
¹⁹ None who go to her return
or attain the paths of life.

²⁰ Thus you will walk in the ways of good
men
and keep to the paths of the righteous.
²¹ For the upright will live in the land,
and the blameless will remain in it;
²² but the wicked will be cut off from the
land,
and the unfaithful will be torn from it.

Further Benefits of Wisdom

3 My son, do not forget my teaching,
but keep my commands in your heart,
² for they will prolong your life many years
and bring you prosperity.

³ Let love and faithfulness never leave you;
bind them around your neck,
write them on the tablet of your heart.
⁴ Then you will win favor
and a good name
in the sight of God and
man.

⁵ Trust in the LORD with all
your heart
and lean not on your
own understanding;
⁶ in all your ways
acknowledge him,
and he will make your
paths straight.^b

⁷ Do not be wise in your own
eyes;
fear the LORD and shun evil.
⁸ This will bring health to your body
and nourishment to your bones.

⁹ Honor the LORD with your wealth,
with the firstfruits of all your crops;
¹⁰ then your barns will be filled to
overflowing,
and your vats will brim over with new
wine.

¹¹ My son, do not despise the LORD's
discipline
and do not resent his rebuke,
¹² because the LORD disciplines those he
loves,
as a father^c the son he delights in.

¹³ Blessed is the man who finds wisdom,
the man who gains understanding,
¹⁴ for she is more profitable than silver
and yields better returns than gold.
¹⁵ She is more precious than rubies;
nothing you desire can compare with
her.
¹⁶ Long life is in her right hand;
in her left hand are riches and honor.

Proverbs 3:6

*God Gives
Guidance*

In all your ways
acknowledge him,
and he will make your
paths straight.

---

^a17 Or *covenant of her God*   ^b6 Or *will direct your paths*   ^c12 Hebrew; Septuagint / *and he punishes*

17 Her ways are pleasant ways,
and all her paths are peace.
18 She is a tree of life to those who embrace
her;
those who lay hold of her will be blessed.

19 By wisdom the LORD laid the earth's
foundations,
by understanding he set the heavens in
place;
20 by his knowledge the deeps were divided,
and the clouds let drop the dew.

21 My son, preserve sound judgment and
discernment,
do not let them out of your sight;
22 they will be life for you,
an ornament to grace your neck.
23 Then you will go on your way in safety,
and your foot will not stumble;
24 when you lie down, you will not be afraid;
when you lie down, your sleep will be
sweet.
25 Have no fear of sudden disaster
or of the ruin that overtakes the wicked,
26 for the LORD will be your confidence
and will keep your foot from being
snared.

27 Do not withhold good from those who
deserve it,
when it is in your power to act.
28 Do not say to your neighbor,
"Come back later; I'll give it
tomorrow"—
when you now have it with you.

29 Do not plot harm against your neighbor,
who lives trustfully near you.
30 Do not accuse a man for no reason—
when he has done you no harm.

31 Do not envy a violent man
or choose any of his ways,
32 for the LORD detests a perverse man
but takes the upright into his
confidence.

33 The LORD's curse is on the house of the
wicked,
but he blesses the home of the righteous.
34 He mocks proud mockers

but gives grace to the humble.
35 The wise inherit honor,
but fools he holds up to shame.

Wisdom Is Supreme

4 Listen, my sons, to a father's instruction;
pay attention and gain understanding.
2 I give you sound learning,
so do not forsake my teaching.
3 When I was a boy in my father's house,
still tender, and an only child of my
mother,
4 he taught me and said,
"Lay hold of my words with all your
heart;
keep my commands and you will live.
5 Get wisdom, get understanding;
do not forget my words or swerve from
them.
6 Do not forsake wisdom, and she will
protect you;
love her, and she will watch over you.
7 Wisdom is supreme; therefore get wisdom.
Though it cost all you have,^{a} get
understanding.
8 Esteem her, and she will exalt you;
embrace her, and she will honor you.
9 She will set a garland of grace on your head
and present you with a crown of
splendor."

10 Listen, my son, accept what I say,
and the years of your life will be many.
11 I guide you in the way of wisdom
and lead you along straight paths.
12 When you walk, your steps will not be
hampered;
when you run, you will not stumble.
13 Hold on to instruction, do not let it go;
guard it well, for it is your life.
14 Do not set foot on the path of the wicked
or walk in the way of evil men.
15 Avoid it, do not travel on it;
turn from it and go on your way.
16 For they cannot sleep till they do evil;
they are robbed of slumber till they
make someone fall.
17 They eat the bread of wickedness
and drink the wine of violence.

^{a}7 Or Whatever else you get

18 The path of the righteous is like the first
    gleam of dawn,
    shining ever brighter till the full light
        of day.
19 But the way of the wicked is like deep
    darkness;
    they do not know what makes them
        stumble.

20 My son, pay attention to what I say;
    listen closely to my words.
21 Do not let them out of your sight,
    keep them within your heart;
22 for they are life to those who find them
    and health to a man's whole body.
23 Above all else, guard your heart,
    for it is the wellspring of life.
24 Put away perversity from your mouth;
    keep corrupt talk far from your lips.
25 Let your eyes look straight ahead,
    fix your gaze directly before you.
26 Make level*a* paths for your feet
    and take only ways that are firm.
27 Do not swerve to the right or the left;
    keep your foot from evil.

Warning Against Adultery

5 My son, pay attention to my wisdom,
    listen well to my words of insight,
2 that you may maintain discretion
    and your lips may preserve knowledge.
3 For the lips of an adulteress
    drip honey,
    and her speech is
        smoother than oil;
4 but in the end she is bitter
    as gall,
    sharp as a double-edged
        sword.
5 Her feet go down to death;
    her steps lead straight to
        the grave.*b*
6 She gives no thought to the
        way of life;
    her paths are crooked,
        but she knows it
        not.

7 Now then, my sons, listen to me;
    do not turn aside from what I say.

8 Keep to a path far from her,
    do not go near the door of her house,
9 lest you give your best strength to
        others
    and your years to one who is cruel,
10 lest strangers feast on your wealth
    and your toil enrich another man's
        house.
11 At the end of your life you will groan,
    when your flesh and body are
        spent.
12 You will say, "How I hated discipline!
    How my heart spurned correction!
13 I would not obey my teachers
    or listen to my instructors.
14 I have come to the brink of utter ruin
    in the midst of the whole assembly."

15 Drink water from your own cistern,
    running water from your own well.
16 Should your springs overflow in the
        streets,
    your streams of water in the public
        squares?
17 Let them be yours alone,
    never to be shared with strangers.
18 May your fountain be blessed,
    and may you rejoice in the wife of your
        youth.
19 A loving doe, a graceful deer—
    may her breasts satisfy
        you always,
    may you ever be
        captivated by her
        love.
20 Why be captivated, my son,
    by an adulteress?
    Why embrace the bosom
        of another man's
        wife?

21 For a man's ways are in full
        view of the LORD,
    and he examines all his
        paths.
22 The evil deeds of a wicked
        man ensnare him;
    the cords of his sin hold him fast.
23 He will die for lack of discipline,
    led astray by his own great folly.

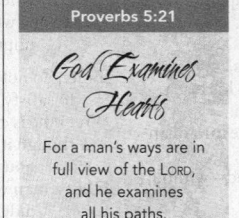

Proverbs 5:21

God Examines Hearts

For a man's ways are in
full view of the LORD,
and he examines
all his paths.

---

*a***26** Or *Consider the*   *b***5** Hebrew *Sheol*

Warnings Against Folly

6 My son, if you have put up security for
your neighbor,
    if you have struck hands in pledge for
another,
² if you have been trapped by what you said,
    ensnared by the words of your mouth,
³ then do this, my son, to free yourself,
    since you have fallen into your
        neighbor's hands:
  Go and humble yourself;
    press your plea with your neighbor!
⁴ Allow no sleep to your eyes,
    no slumber to your eyelids.
⁵ Free yourself, like a gazelle from the hand
    of the hunter,
    like a bird from the snare of the fowler.

⁶ Go to the ant, you sluggard;
    consider its ways and be wise!
⁷ It has no commander,
    no overseer or ruler,
⁸ yet it stores its provisions in summer
    and gathers its food at harvest.

⁹ How long will you lie there, you sluggard?
    When will you get up from your sleep?
¹⁰ A little sleep, a little slumber,
    a little folding of the hands to rest—
¹¹ and poverty will come on you like a bandit
    and scarcity like an armed man.ᵃ

¹² A scoundrel and villain,
    who goes about with a corrupt mouth,
¹³   who winks with his eye,
    signals with his feet
    and motions with his fingers,
¹⁴   who plots evil with deceit in his heart—
    he always stirs up dissension.
¹⁵ Therefore disaster will overtake him in an
    instant;
    he will suddenly be destroyed—without
        remedy.

¹⁶ There are six things the LORD hates,
    seven that are detestable to him:
¹⁷   haughty eyes,
    a lying tongue,
    hands that shed innocent blood,
¹⁸   a heart that devises wicked schemes,
    feet that are quick to rush into evil,
¹⁹   a false witness who pours out lies
    and a man who stirs up dissension
        among brothers.

Warning Against Adultery

²⁰ My son, keep your father's commands
    and do not forsake your mother's
        teaching.
²¹ Bind them upon your heart forever;
    fasten them around your neck.
²² When you walk, they will guide you;
    when you sleep, they will watch over
        you;
    when you awake, they will speak to you.
²³ For these commands are a lamp,
    this teaching is a light,
  and the corrections of discipline
    are the way to life,
²⁴ keeping you from the immoral woman,
    from the smooth tongue of the wayward
        wife.
²⁵ Do not lust in your heart after her beauty
    or let her captivate you with her eyes,
²⁶ for the prostitute reduces you to a loaf of
    bread,
    and the adulteress preys upon your very
        life.
²⁷ Can a man scoop fire into his lap
    without his clothes being burned?
²⁸ Can a man walk on hot coals
    without his feet being scorched?
²⁹ So is he who sleeps with another man's
    wife;
    no one who touches her will go
        unpunished.

³⁰ Men do not despise a thief if he steals
    to satisfy his hunger when he is starving.
³¹ Yet if he is caught, he must pay sevenfold,
    though it costs him all the wealth of his
        house.
³² But a man who commits adultery lacks
    judgment;
    whoever does so destroys himself.
³³ Blows and disgrace are his lot,
    and his shame will never be wiped away;
³⁴ for jealousy arouses a husband's fury,
    and he will show no mercy when he
        takes revenge.
³⁵ He will not accept any compensation;

ᵃ11 Or *like a vagrant / and scarcity like a beggar*

Things God Hates

Read: Proverbs 6:16–19

HATE IS A SEVERE WORD. It expresses an intense hostility or extreme dislike. Many children use the word without thought, and most parents admonish them, "We don't use the word *hate*." But inevitably the harsh word slips out: "I hate vegetables!" "I hate my little brother!" Many adults aren't much better, and the word slips out all too easily: "I hate it when the pastor's wife gets all the glory." "I hate that man's singing." "I hate skinny models." "I hate to cook dinner."

What do you hate? What things do you avoid at all costs? For some the thought of a certain activity causes intense agitation. Perhaps your first auto accident occurred during a blizzard. To this day, you hate getting behind the steering wheel when the fluffy flakes appear. Everybody hates something. And strange as it may seem, the Bible says that even the all-loving God hates some things.

It may seem strange to us to read the words "hate" and "God" in the same sentence. If God is love, then what does he hate? Solomon lists the top seven things God hates: (1) a prideful sneer, (2) fraud, (3) bloodshed, (4) conspiracy, (5) evil intent, (6) perjury and (7) inciting division among God's people. Bible commentator Matthew Henry wrote, "God hates sin; he hates every sin; he can never be reconciled to it; he hates nothing but sin," but apparently these sins are especially repugnant to him.

This list possesses a common thread; it includes sins particularly harmful to others. Since human beings are God's special creation, he is exceptionally sensitive to sins that cause grief for others. The list also crescendos: the first six sins place emphasis on the seventh. It's bad for you to sin, but it is "detestable" to start a chain reaction—causing others to sin too.

What are the top seven things you hate? The psalmist said, "Let those who love the LORD hate evil" (Psalm 97:10). To love God is to hate what he hates. Instead of despising veggies or hating to drive on icy roads, go a little deeper. Really think about what's on God's "hate" list. Then banish those things from your house and your heart.

Proverbs 6:16

There are six things the LORD hates, seven that are detestable to him.

reflection

1 What on God's list of things to hate surprises you?

2 Ask God to show you if you have ever practiced anything on this list. If so, what? (Be honest.)

3 How will you banish the things on God's list from your life?

RELATED READINGS

Psalm 101:1–8;
Proverbs 8:13;
Romans 1:18–20

Thursday

Go to page 769 for your next devotional reading.

he will refuse the bribe, however great
it is.

Warning Against the Adulteress

7 My son, keep my words
and store up my commands within you.
² Keep my commands and you will live;
guard my teachings as the apple of your
eye.
³ Bind them on your fingers;
write them on the tablet of your heart.
⁴ Say to wisdom, "You are my sister,"
and call understanding your kinsman;
⁵ they will keep you from the adulteress,
from the wayward wife with her
seductive words.

⁶ At the window of my house
I looked out through the lattice.
⁷ I saw among the simple,
I noticed among the young men,
a youth who lacked judgment.
⁸ He was going down the street near her
corner,
walking along in the direction of her
house
⁹ at twilight, as the day was fading,
as the dark of night set in.

¹⁰ Then out came a woman to meet him,
dressed like a prostitute and with crafty
intent.
¹¹ (She is loud and defiant,
her feet never stay at home;
¹² now in the street, now in the squares,
at every corner she lurks.)
¹³ She took hold of him and kissed him
and with a brazen face she said:

¹⁴ "I have fellowship offerings[a] at home;
today I fulfilled my vows.
¹⁵ So I came out to meet you;
I looked for you and have found you!
¹⁶ I have covered my bed
with colored linens from Egypt.
¹⁷ I have perfumed my bed
with myrrh, aloes and cinnamon.
¹⁸ Come, let's drink deep of love till morning;
let's enjoy ourselves with love!
¹⁹ My husband is not at home;

he has gone on a long journey.
²⁰ He took his purse filled with money
and will not be home till full moon."

²¹ With persuasive words she led him astray;
she seduced him with her smooth talk.
²² All at once he followed her
like an ox going to the slaughter,
like a deer[b] stepping into a noose[c]
²³ till an arrow pierces his liver,
like a bird darting into a snare,
little knowing it will cost him his life.

²⁴ Now then, my sons, listen to me;
pay attention to what I say.
²⁵ Do not let your heart turn to her ways
or stray into her paths.
²⁶ Many are the victims she has brought
down;
her slain are a mighty throng.
²⁷ Her house is a highway to the grave,[d]
leading down to the chambers of death.

Wisdom's Call

8 Does not wisdom call out?
Does not understanding raise her voice?
² On the heights along the way,
where the paths meet, she takes her
stand;
³ beside the gates leading into the city,
at the entrances, she cries aloud:
⁴ "To you, O men, I call out;
I raise my voice to all mankind.
⁵ You who are simple, gain prudence;
you who are foolish, gain
understanding.
⁶ Listen, for I have worthy things to say;
I open my lips to speak what is right.
⁷ My mouth speaks what is true,
for my lips detest wickedness.
⁸ All the words of my mouth are just;
none of them is crooked or perverse.
⁹ To the discerning all of them are right;
they are faultless to those who have
knowledge.
¹⁰ Choose my instruction instead of silver,
knowledge rather than choice gold,
¹¹ for wisdom is more precious than rubies,
and nothing you desire can compare
with her.

---

a14 Traditionally *peace offerings*   *b22* Syriac (see also Septuagint); Hebrew *fool*   *c22* The meaning of the Hebrew for this line is
uncertain.   *d27* Hebrew *Sheol*

¹²"I, wisdom, dwell together with prudence;
    I possess knowledge and discretion.
¹³To fear the LORD is to hate evil;
    I hate pride and arrogance,
    evil behavior and perverse speech.
¹⁴Counsel and sound judgment are mine;
    I have understanding and power.
¹⁵By me kings reign
    and rulers make laws that are just;
¹⁶by me princes govern,
    and all nobles who rule on earth.ᵃ
¹⁷I love those who love me,
    and those who seek me find me.
¹⁸With me are riches and honor,
    enduring wealth and prosperity.
¹⁹My fruit is better than fine gold;
    what I yield surpasses choice silver.
²⁰I walk in the way of righteousness,
    along the paths of justice,
²¹bestowing wealth on those who love me
    and making their treasuries full.

²²"The LORD brought me forth as the first of
        his works,ᵇ,ᶜ
    before his deeds of old;
²³I was appointedᵈ from eternity,
    from the beginning, before the world
        began.
²⁴When there were no oceans, I was given
        birth,
    when there were no springs abounding
        with water;
²⁵before the mountains were settled in place,
    before the hills, I was given birth,
²⁶before he made the earth or its fields
    or any of the dust of the world.
²⁷I was there when he set the heavens in
        place,
    when he marked out the horizon on the
        face of the deep,
²⁸when he established the clouds above
    and fixed securely the fountains of the
        deep,
²⁹when he gave the sea its boundary
    so the waters would not overstep his
        command,
    and when he marked out the foundations
        of the earth.
³⁰   Then I was the craftsman at his side.

I was filled with delight day after day,
    rejoicing always in his presence,
³¹rejoicing in his whole world
    and delighting in mankind.

³²"Now then, my sons, listen to me;
    blessed are those who keep my ways.
³³Listen to my instruction and be wise;
    do not ignore it.
³⁴Blessed is the man who listens to me,
    watching daily at my doors,
    waiting at my doorway.
³⁵For whoever finds me finds life
    and receives favor from the LORD.
³⁶But whoever fails to find me harms
        himself;
    all who hate me love death."

Invitations of Wisdom and of Folly

9 Wisdom has built her house;
    she has hewn out its seven pillars.
² She has prepared her meat and mixed her
        wine;
    she has also set her table.
³ She has sent out her maids, and she calls
    from the highest point of the city.
⁴ "Let all who are simple come in here!"
    she says to those who lack judgment.
⁵ "Come, eat my food
    and drink the wine I have mixed.
⁶ Leave your simple ways and you will live;
    walk in the way of understanding.

⁷ "Whoever corrects a mocker invites insult;
    whoever rebukes a wicked man incurs
        abuse.
⁸ Do not rebuke a mocker or he will hate
        you;
    rebuke a wise man and he will love you.
⁹ Instruct a wise man and he will be wiser
        still;
    teach a righteous man and he will add to
        his learning.

¹⁰ "The fear of the LORD is the beginning of
        wisdom,
    and knowledge of the Holy One is
        understanding.
¹¹ For through me your days will be many,
    and years will be added to your life.

ᵃ16 Many Hebrew manuscripts and Septuagint; most Hebrew manuscripts *and nobles—all righteous rulers*   ᵇ22 Or *way*; or *dominion*
ᶜ22 Or *The LORD possessed me at the beginning of his work*; or *The LORD brought me forth at the beginning of his work*   ᵈ23 Or *fashioned*

12 If you are wise, your wisdom will reward
  you;
    if you are a mocker, you alone will
      suffer."

13 The woman Folly is loud;
    she is undisciplined and without
      knowledge.
14 She sits at the door of her house,
    on a seat at the highest point of the city,
15 calling out to those who pass by,
    who go straight on their way.
16 "Let all who are simple come in here!"
    she says to those who lack judgment.
17 "Stolen water is sweet;
    food eaten in secret is delicious!"
18 But little do they know that the dead are
      there,
    that her guests are in the depths of the
      grave.[a]

Proverbs of Solomon

10

The proverbs of Solomon:

A wise son brings joy to his father,
    but a foolish son grief to his mother.

2 Ill-gotten treasures are of no value,
    but righteousness delivers from death.

3 The LORD does not let the righteous go
      hungry
    but he thwarts the craving of the
      wicked.

4 Lazy hands make a man poor,
    but diligent hands bring wealth.

5 He who gathers crops in summer is a wise
      son,
    but he who sleeps during harvest is a
      disgraceful son.

6 Blessings crown the head of the righteous,
    but violence overwhelms the mouth of
      the wicked.[b]

7 The memory of the righteous will be a
      blessing,
    but the name of the wicked will rot.

8 The wise in heart accept commands,
    but a chattering fool comes to ruin.

9 The man of integrity walks securely,
    but he who takes crooked paths will be
      found out.

10 He who winks maliciously causes grief,
    and a chattering fool comes to ruin.

11 The mouth of the righteous is a fountain of
      life,
    but violence overwhelms the mouth of
      the wicked.

12 Hatred stirs up dissension,
    but love covers over all wrongs.

13 Wisdom is found on the lips of the
      discerning,
    but a rod is for the back of him who
      lacks judgment.

14 Wise men store up knowledge,
    but the mouth of a fool invites ruin.

15 The wealth of the rich is their fortified city,
    but poverty is the ruin of the poor.

16 The wages of the righteous bring them
      life,
    but the income of the wicked brings
      them punishment.

17 He who heeds discipline shows the way to
      life,
    but whoever ignores correction leads
      others astray.

18 He who conceals his hatred has lying lips,
    and whoever spreads slander is a fool.

19 When words are many, sin is not absent,
    but he who holds his tongue is wise.

20 The tongue of the righteous is choice
      silver,
    but the heart of the wicked is of little
      value.

21 The lips of the righteous nourish many,
    but fools die for lack of judgment.

22 The blessing of the LORD brings wealth,
    and he adds no trouble to it.

23 A fool finds pleasure in evil conduct,
    but a man of understanding delights in
      wisdom.

a 18 Hebrew *Sheol*   b 6 Or *but the mouth of the wicked conceals violence*; also in verse 11

Nourishing Words

Read: Proverbs 10:16–22

DURING WORLD WAR II the Office of War developed a media campaign called "Loose lips sink ships!" to help the citizenry maintain a code of silence. With Japanese and German submarines patrolling the coastlines of the United States, those leading the Office of War realized that silence meant security. One of their most memorable posters depicted a fiery ship sinking into the ocean.

Such urgent statements may have invited skepticism, but, to the soldier on the ground, stray comments presented very present dangers. A careless word could cost lives. King Solomon would not have laughed at such dire warnings. The sagacious king understood the power words have to destroy. In Proverbs 10 he reminds us we have the power to raise or sink the spirits of the people around us with our words.

Take a moment to think about your recent conversations. Have you felt nourished by someone's encouraging words? How did those words lift you up? How did you respond? Or perhaps you remember when someone's language wounded your spirit. Maybe you were torpedoed by a thoughtless comment from a neighbor or struck down by a destructive argument with a family member or friend. We have all experienced the withering force of cruel words. But consider the effects of good and kind speech. Just as foolish talk can bring death, truth spoken with love can lift the discouraged soul, restore dignity to the oppressed and heal the brokenhearted. God places great importance on our words. The apostle Paul did too. He said, "Let your conversation be always full of grace, seasoned with salt, so that you may know how to answer everyone" (Colossians 4:6).

Your words have the power of life or death. You can wound another's spirit or protect another's dignity by the words you speak. Choose your words wisely. Kindly nourish and uplift those around you.

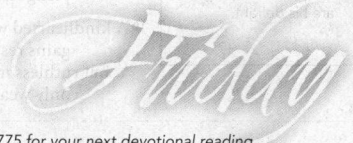

Go to page 775 for your next devotional reading.

Proverbs 10:21

The lips of the righteous nourish many, but fools die for lack of judgment.

reflection

1. Describe a time when your words wounded someone's spirit or nourished someone's spirit.

2. What has been the tone of the words coming out of your mouth today? How do they reflect what's in your heart?

3. How has God's Word proven to have power in your life?

RELATED READINGS

Ecclesiastes 5:2–3;
10:12–14;
James 3:1–12

²⁴ What the wicked dreads will overtake him;
  what the righteous desire will be
    granted.

²⁵ When the storm has swept by, the wicked
    are gone,
  but the righteous stand firm forever.

²⁶ As vinegar to the teeth and smoke to the
    eyes,
  so is a sluggard to those who send him.

²⁷ The fear of the Lord adds length to life,
  but the years of the wicked are cut short.

²⁸ The prospect of the righteous is joy,
  but the hopes of the wicked come to
    nothing.

²⁹ The way of the Lord is a refuge for the
    righteous,
  but it is the ruin of those who do evil.

³⁰ The righteous will never be uprooted,
  but the wicked will not remain in the
    land.

³¹ The mouth of the righteous brings forth
    wisdom,
  but a perverse tongue will be cut out.

³² The lips of the righteous know what is
    fitting,
  but the mouth of the wicked only what
    is perverse.

11 The Lord abhors dishonest scales,
      but accurate weights are his delight.

² When pride comes, then comes disgrace,
  but with humility comes
    wisdom.

³ The integrity of the upright
    guides them,
  but the unfaithful are
    destroyed by their
    duplicity.

⁴ Wealth is worthless in the
    day of wrath,
  but righteousness
    delivers from death.

⁵ The righteousness of the
    blameless makes a
    straight way for them,

but the wicked are brought down by
    their own wickedness.

⁶ The righteousness of the upright delivers
    them,
  but the unfaithful are trapped by evil
    desires.

⁷ When a wicked man dies, his hope
    perishes;
  all he expected from his power comes to
    nothing.

⁸ The righteous man is rescued from
    trouble,
  and it comes on the wicked instead.

⁹ With his mouth the godless destroys his
    neighbor,
  but through knowledge the righteous
    escape.

¹⁰ When the righteous prosper, the city
    rejoices;
  when the wicked perish, there are shouts
    of joy.

¹¹ Through the blessing of the upright a city
    is exalted,
  but by the mouth of the wicked it is
    destroyed.

¹² A man who lacks judgment derides his
    neighbor,
  but a man of understanding holds his
    tongue.

¹³ A gossip betrays a confidence,
  but a trustworthy man keeps a secret.

¹⁴ For lack of guidance a
    nation falls,
  but many advisers make
    victory sure.

¹⁵ He who puts up security for
    another will surely
    suffer,
  but whoever refuses
    to strike hands in
    pledge is safe.

¹⁶ A kindhearted woman
    gains respect,
  but ruthless men gain
    only wealth.

Proverbs 11:1

God Loves Honesty

The Lord abhors
dishonest scales,
but accurate weights
are his delight.

---

17 A kind man benefits himself,
    but a cruel man brings trouble on
        himself.

18 The wicked man earns deceptive wages,
    but he who sows righteousness reaps a
        sure reward.

19 The truly righteous man attains life,
    but he who pursues evil goes to his
        death.

20 The LORD detests men of
        perverse heart
    but he delights in those
        whose ways are
        blameless.

21 Be sure of this: The
        wicked will not go
        unpunished,
    but those who are
        righteous will go
        free.

22 Like a gold ring in a pig's
        snout
    is a beautiful woman
        who shows no discretion.

23 The desire of the righteous ends only in
        good,
    but the hope of the wicked only in wrath.

24 One man gives freely, yet gains even more;
    another withholds unduly, but comes to
        poverty.

25 A generous man will prosper;
    he who refreshes others will himself be
        refreshed.

26 People curse the man who hoards grain,
    but blessing crowns him who is willing
        to sell.

27 He who seeks good finds goodwill,
    but evil comes to him who searches
        for it.

28 Whoever trusts in his riches will fall,
    but the righteous will thrive like a green
        leaf.

29 He who brings trouble on his family will
        inherit only wind,

and the fool will be servant to the wise.

30 The fruit of the righteous is a tree of life,
    and he who wins souls is wise.

31 If the righteous receive their due on earth,
    how much more the ungodly and the
        sinner!

12 Whoever loves discipline loves
        knowledge,
    but he who hates correction is stupid.

2 A good man obtains favor
        from the LORD,
    but the LORD condemns
        a crafty man.

3 A man cannot be
        established through
        wickedness,
    but the righteous cannot
        be uprooted.

4 A wife of noble character
        is her husband's
        crown,
    but a disgraceful wife
        is like decay in his
        bones.

5 The plans of the righteous are just,
    but the advice of the wicked is deceitful.

6 The words of the wicked lie in wait for
        blood,
    but the speech of the upright rescues
        them.

7 Wicked men are overthrown and are no
        more,
    but the house of the righteous stands
        firm.

8 A man is praised according to his
        wisdom,
    but men with warped minds are
        despised.

9 Better to be a nobody and yet have a
        servant
    than pretend to be somebody and have
        no food.

10 A righteous man cares for the needs of his
        animal,

Proverbs 12:2

God Hates Deceit

A good man obtains
favor from the LORD,
but the LORD condemns
a crafty man.

but the kindest acts of the wicked are
cruel.

11 He who works his land will have abundant
food,
but he who chases fantasies lacks
judgment.

12 The wicked desire the plunder of evil men,
but the root of the righteous flourishes.

13 An evil man is trapped by his sinful talk,
but a righteous man escapes trouble.

14 From the fruit of his lips a man is filled
with good things
as surely as the work of his hands
rewards him.

15 The way of a fool seems right to him,
but a wise man listens to advice.

16 A fool shows his annoyance at once,
but a prudent man overlooks an insult.

17 A truthful witness gives honest testimony,
but a false witness tells lies.

18 Reckless words pierce like a sword,
but the tongue of the wise brings healing.

19 Truthful lips endure forever,
but a lying tongue lasts only a moment.

20 There is deceit in the hearts of those who
plot evil,
but joy for those who promote peace.

21 No harm befalls the righteous,
but the wicked have their fill of trouble.

22 The LORD detests lying lips,
but he delights in men who are truthful.

23 A prudent man keeps his knowledge to
himself,
but the heart of fools blurts out folly.

24 Diligent hands will rule,
but laziness ends in slave labor.

25 An anxious heart weighs a man down,
but a kind word cheers him up.

26 A righteous man is cautious in friendship,[a]
but the way of the wicked leads them
astray.

27 The lazy man does not roast[b] his game,
but the diligent man prizes his
possessions.

28 In the way of righteousness there is life;
along that path is immortality.

13 A wise son heeds his father's
instruction,
but a mocker does not listen to rebuke.

2 From the fruit of his lips a man enjoys
good things,
but the unfaithful have a craving for
violence.

3 He who guards his lips guards his life,
but he who speaks rashly will come to
ruin.

4 The sluggard craves and gets nothing,
but the desires of the diligent are fully
satisfied.

5 The righteous hate what is false,
but the wicked bring shame and
disgrace.

6 Righteousness guards the man of
integrity,
but wickedness overthrows the sinner.

7 One man pretends to be rich, yet has
nothing;
another pretends to be poor, yet has
great wealth.

8 A man's riches may ransom his life,
but a poor man hears no threat.

9 The light of the righteous shines brightly,
but the lamp of the wicked is snuffed
out.

10 Pride only breeds quarrels,
but wisdom is found in those who take
advice.

11 Dishonest money dwindles away,
but he who gathers money little by little
makes it grow.

12 Hope deferred makes the heart sick,
but a longing fulfilled is a tree of life.

13 He who scorns instruction will pay for it,

---

a26 Or *man is a guide to his neighbor*   *b27* The meaning of the Hebrew for this word is uncertain.

but he who respects a command is
rewarded.

¹⁴ The teaching of the wise is a fountain of
life,
turning a man from the snares of death.

¹⁵ Good understanding wins favor,
but the way of the unfaithful is hard.ᵃ

¹⁶ Every prudent man acts out of knowledge,
but a fool exposes his folly.

¹⁷ A wicked messenger falls into trouble,
but a trustworthy envoy brings
healing.

¹⁸ He who ignores discipline comes to
poverty and shame,
but whoever heeds correction is
honored.

¹⁹ A longing fulfilled is sweet to the soul,
but fools detest turning from evil.

²⁰ He who walks with the wise grows wise,
but a companion of fools suffers harm.

²¹ Misfortune pursues the sinner,
but prosperity is the reward of the
righteous.

²² A good man leaves an inheritance for his
children's children,
but a sinner's wealth is stored up for the
righteous.

²³ A poor man's field may produce abundant
food,
but injustice sweeps it away.

²⁴ He who spares the rod hates his son,
but he who loves him is careful to
discipline him.

²⁵ The righteous eat to their hearts' content,
but the stomach of the wicked goes
hungry.

14 The wise woman builds her house,
but with her own hands the foolish
one tears hers down.

² He whose walk is upright fears the LORD,
but he whose ways are devious despises
him.

³ A fool's talk brings a rod to his back,
but the lips of the wise protect them.

⁴ Where there are no oxen, the manger is
empty,
but from the strength of an ox comes an
abundant harvest.

⁵ A truthful witness does not deceive,
but a false witness pours out lies.

⁶ The mocker seeks wisdom and finds none,
but knowledge comes easily to the
discerning.

⁷ Stay away from a foolish man,
for you will not find knowledge on his
lips.

⁸ The wisdom of the prudent is to give
thought to their ways,
but the folly of fools is deception.

⁹ Fools mock at making amends for sin,
but goodwill is found among the
upright.

¹⁰ Each heart knows its own bitterness,
and no one else can share its joy.

¹¹ The house of the wicked will be destroyed,
but the tent of the upright will flourish.

¹² There is a way that seems right to a man,
but in the end it leads to death.

¹³ Even in laughter the heart may ache,
and joy may end in grief.

¹⁴ The faithless will be fully repaid for their
ways,
and the good man rewarded for his.

¹⁵ A simple man believes anything,
but a prudent man gives thought to his
steps.

¹⁶ A wise man fears the LORD and shuns evil,
but a fool is hotheaded and reckless.

¹⁷ A quick-tempered man does foolish things,
and a crafty man is hated.

¹⁸ The simple inherit folly,
but the prudent are crowned with
knowledge.

ᵃ15 Or *unfaithful does not endure*

¹⁹Evil men will bow down in the presence of
the good,
and the wicked at the gates of the
righteous.

²⁰The poor are shunned even by their
neighbors,
but the rich have many friends.

²¹He who despises his neighbor sins,
but blessed is he who is kind to the
needy.

²²Do not those who plot evil go astray?
But those who plan what is good find^a
love and faithfulness.

²³All hard work brings a profit,
but mere talk leads only to poverty.

²⁴The wealth of the wise is their crown,
but the folly of fools yields folly.

²⁵A truthful witness saves
lives,
but a false witness is
deceitful.

²⁶He who fears the LORD has
a secure fortress,
and for his children it
will be a refuge.

²⁷The fear of the LORD is a
fountain of life,
turning a man from the
snares of death.

²⁸A large population is a
king's glory,
but without subjects a prince is ruined.

²⁹A patient man has great understanding,
but a quick-tempered man displays folly.

³⁰A heart at peace gives life to the body,
but envy rots the bones.

³¹He who oppresses the poor shows
contempt for their Maker,
but whoever is kind to the needy honors
God.

³²When calamity comes, the wicked are
brought down,
but even in death the righteous have a
refuge.

³³Wisdom reposes in the heart of the
discerning
and even among fools she lets herself be
known.^b

³⁴Righteousness exalts a nation,
but sin is a disgrace to any people.

³⁵A king delights in a wise servant,
but a shameful servant incurs his wrath.

15 A gentle answer turns away wrath,
but a harsh word stirs up anger.

²The tongue of the wise commends
knowledge,
but the mouth of the fool gushes folly.

³The eyes of the LORD are everywhere,
keeping watch on the wicked and the
good.

⁴The tongue that brings
healing is a tree of
life,
but a deceitful tongue
crushes the spirit.

⁵A fool spurns his father's
discipline,
but whoever heeds
correction shows
prudence.

⁶The house of the righteous
contains great
treasure,
but the income of the wicked brings
them trouble.

⁷The lips of the wise spread knowledge;
not so the hearts of fools.

⁸The LORD detests the sacrifice of the wicked,
but the prayer of the upright pleases him.

⁹The LORD detests the way of the wicked
but he loves those who pursue
righteousness.

¹⁰Stern discipline awaits him who leaves the
path;
he who hates correction will die.

> **Proverbs 14:26**
>
> *God Gives Security*
>
> He who fears the LORD
> has a secure fortress,
> and for his children it
> will be a refuge.

^a22 Or *show* ^b33 Hebrew; Septuagint and Syriac / *but in the heart of fools she is not known*

Life's Questions

QUEEN OF SHEBA

SHE HAD QUESTIONS. And she didn't think twice about traveling 1500 miles, one way, to get answers.

Over the years, her wise, elderly subjects often told her that the longer she lived, the more mysterious life would seem. "Life brings all kinds of questions our way," they would say. "Live long enough and you'll find this to be truer by the day."

All she knew was that she'd already lived long enough and seen enough of the world to have questions—lots of them. *Why does poverty exist? Why do the innocent suffer? What is the meaning of life? Is this all there is?*

She came to Jerusalem with much on her mind, determined to leave with a sense of satisfaction. And Solomon did not disappoint. To her delight, not only did Solomon answer all of her questions, he also explained them in a way that made sense to her.

She enjoyed the challenge of bringing her strictly pagan viewpoint into conversation with the God-fearing Solomon. She loved that he didn't blindly agree with her every thought—a welcome relief from the palace back home, where no one dared oppose her. Posing her pagan perspective against his faith lent itself to lively discussion in their late-night talks, afternoon debates and intellectual jousts.

"Naturally," she would later tell her people back home, "there were some questions Solomon didn't have to answer." *Was the God of Israel as great as he claimed? Does he really bless those who serve him? Is there no end to his resources and might?* The evidence, she concluded, spoke for itself. She merely had to look around for the answer. Forty thousand horses, expansive borders and a palace dripping with gold and silver spoke more than words ever could.

"Not the half has been told," she would often recall of her time with Solomon. "Not the half."

—Prayer—
Great God, I have many questions. Grant me the wisdom to see your truth all around me.

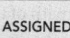

She came to Solomon and talked with him about all that she had on her mind.

1 Kings 10:2

ASSIGNED READING:

1 Kings 10:1–29;
2 Chronicles 9:1–28

Weekend

11 Death and Destruction[a] lie open before the LORD—
how much more the hearts of men!

12 A mocker resents correction;
he will not consult the wise.

13 A happy heart makes the face cheerful,
but heartache crushes the spirit.

14 The discerning heart seeks knowledge,
but the mouth of a fool feeds on folly.

15 All the days of the oppressed are wretched,
but the cheerful heart has a continual feast.

16 Better a little with the fear of the LORD
than great wealth with turmoil.

17 Better a meal of vegetables where there is love
than a fattened calf with hatred.

18 A hot-tempered man stirs up dissension,
but a patient man calms a quarrel.

19 The way of the sluggard is blocked with thorns,
but the path of the upright is a highway.

20 A wise son brings joy to his father,
but a foolish man despises his mother.

21 Folly delights a man who lacks judgment,
but a man of understanding keeps a straight course.

22 Plans fail for lack of counsel,
but with many advisers they succeed.

23 A man finds joy in giving an apt reply—
and how good is a timely word!

24 The path of life leads upward for the wise
to keep him from going down to the grave.[b]

25 The LORD tears down the proud man's house

but he keeps the widow's boundaries intact.

26 The LORD detests the thoughts of the wicked,
but those of the pure are pleasing to him.

27 A greedy man brings trouble to his family,
but he who hates bribes will live.

28 The heart of the righteous weighs its answers,
but the mouth of the wicked gushes evil.

29 The LORD is far from the wicked
but he hears the prayer of the righteous.

30 A cheerful look brings joy to the heart,
and good news gives health to the bones.

31 He who listens to a life-giving rebuke
will be at home among the wise.

32 He who ignores discipline despises himself,
but whoever heeds correction gains understanding.

33 The fear of the LORD teaches a man wisdom,[c]
and humility comes before honor.

16 To man belong the plans of the heart,
but from the LORD comes the reply of the tongue.

2 All a man's ways seem innocent to him,
but motives are weighed by the LORD.

3 Commit to the LORD whatever you do,
and your plans will succeed.

4 The LORD works out everything for his own ends—
even the wicked for a day of disaster.

5 The LORD detests all the proud of heart.
Be sure of this: They will not go unpunished.

Proverbs 16:1

God Gives Us Words

To man belong the plans of the heart, but from the LORD comes the reply of the tongue.

---

⁶Through love and faithfulness sin is atoned for;
   through the fear of the LORD a man avoids evil.

⁷When a man's ways are pleasing to the LORD,
   he makes even his enemies live at peace with him.

⁸Better a little with righteousness
   than much gain with injustice.

⁹In his heart a man plans his course,
   but the LORD determines his steps.

¹⁰The lips of a king speak as an oracle,
   and his mouth should not betray justice.

¹¹Honest scales and balances are from the LORD;
   all the weights in the bag are of his making.

¹²Kings detest wrongdoing,
   for a throne is established through righteousness.

¹³Kings take pleasure in honest lips;
   they value a man who speaks the truth.

¹⁴A king's wrath is a messenger of death,
   but a wise man will appease it.

¹⁵When a king's face brightens, it means life;
   his favor is like a rain cloud in spring.

¹⁶How much better to get wisdom than gold,
   to choose understanding rather than silver!

¹⁷The highway of the upright avoids evil;
   he who guards his way guards his life.

¹⁸Pride goes before destruction,
   a haughty spirit before a fall.

¹⁹Better to be lowly in spirit and among the oppressed
   than to share plunder with the proud.

²⁰Whoever gives heed to instruction prospers,
   and blessed is he who trusts in the LORD.

²¹The wise in heart are called discerning,
   and pleasant words promote instruction.ᵃ

²²Understanding is a fountain of life to those who have it,
   but folly brings punishment to fools.

²³A wise man's heart guides his mouth,
   and his lips promote instruction.ᵇ

²⁴Pleasant words are a honeycomb,
   sweet to the soul and healing to the bones.

²⁵There is a way that seems right to a man,
   but in the end it leads to death.

²⁶The laborer's appetite works for him;
   his hunger drives him on.

²⁷A scoundrel plots evil,
   and his speech is like a scorching fire.

²⁸A perverse man stirs up dissension,
   and a gossip separates close friends.

²⁹A violent man entices his neighbor
   and leads him down a path that is not good.

³⁰He who winks with his eye is plotting perversity;
   he who purses his lips is bent on evil.

³¹Gray hair is a crown of splendor;
   it is attained by a righteous life.

³²Better a patient man than a warrior,
   a man who controls his temper than one who takes a city.

³³The lot is cast into the lap,
   but its every decision is from the LORD.

17 Better a dry crust with peace and quiet
   than a house full of feasting,ᶜ with strife.

²A wise servant will rule over a disgraceful son,
   and will share the inheritance as one of the brothers.

³The crucible for silver and the furnace for gold,
   but the LORD tests the heart.

⁴A wicked man listens to evil lips;
   a liar pays attention to a malicious tongue.

ᵃ21 Or words make a man persuasive   ᵇ23 Or mouth / and makes his lips persuasive   ᶜ1 Hebrew sacrifices

5 He who mocks the poor shows contempt
    for their Maker;
  whoever gloats over disaster will not go
    unpunished.

6 Children's children are a crown to the
    aged,
  and parents are the pride of their
    children.

7 Arrogant*a* lips are unsuited to a fool—
  how much worse lying lips to a ruler!

8 A bribe is a charm to the one who gives it;
  wherever he turns, he succeeds.

9 He who covers over an offense promotes
    love,
  but whoever repeats the matter separates
    close friends.

10 A rebuke impresses a man of discernment
  more than a hundred lashes a fool.

11 An evil man is bent only on rebellion;
  a merciless official will be sent against
    him.

12 Better to meet a bear robbed of her cubs
  than a fool in his folly.

13 If a man pays back evil for good,
  evil will never leave his house.

14 Starting a quarrel is like breaching a dam;
  so drop the matter before a dispute
    breaks out.

15 Acquitting the guilty and condemning the
    innocent—
  the LORD detests them both.

16 Of what use is money in the hand of a fool,
  since he has no desire to get wisdom?

17 A friend loves at all times,
  and a brother is born for adversity.

18 A man lacking in judgment strikes hands
    in pledge
  and puts up security for his neighbor.

19 He who loves a quarrel loves sin;
  he who builds a high gate invites
    destruction.

20 A man of perverse heart does not prosper;
  he whose tongue is deceitful falls into
    trouble.

21 To have a fool for a son brings grief;
  there is no joy for the father of a fool.

22 A cheerful heart is good medicine,
  but a crushed spirit dries up the bones.

23 A wicked man accepts a bribe in secret
  to pervert the course of justice.

24 A discerning man keeps wisdom in view,
  but a fool's eyes wander to the ends of
    the earth.

25 A foolish son brings grief to his father
  and bitterness to the one who bore him.

26 It is not good to punish an innocent man,
  or to flog officials for their integrity.

27 A man of knowledge uses words with
    restraint,
  and a man of understanding is even-
    tempered.

28 Even a fool is thought wise if he keeps
    silent,
  and discerning if he holds his tongue.

18 An unfriendly man pursues selfish
    ends;
  he defies all sound judgment.

2 A fool finds no pleasure in understanding
  but delights in airing his own opinions.

3 When wickedness comes, so does
    contempt,
  and with shame comes disgrace.

4 The words of a man's mouth are deep
    waters,
  but the fountain of wisdom is a bubbling
    brook.

5 It is not good to be partial to the wicked
  or to deprive the innocent of justice.

6 A fool's lips bring him strife,
  and his mouth invites a beating.

7 A fool's mouth is his undoing,
  and his lips are a snare to his soul.

a7 Or Eloquent

778

⁸ The words of a gossip are like choice morsels;
    they go down to a man's inmost parts.

⁹ One who is slack in his work
    is brother to one who destroys.

¹⁰ The name of the LORD is a
       strong tower;
    the righteous run to it
       and are safe.

¹¹ The wealth of the rich is
       their fortified city;
    they imagine it an
       unscalable wall.

¹² Before his downfall a man's
       heart is proud,
    but humility comes
       before honor.

¹³ He who answers before
       listening—
    that is his folly and his shame.

¹⁴ A man's spirit sustains him in sickness,
    but a crushed spirit who can bear?

¹⁵ The heart of the discerning acquires
       knowledge;
    the ears of the wise seek it out.

¹⁶ A gift opens the way for the giver
    and ushers him into the presence of the
       great.

¹⁷ The first to present his case seems right,
    till another comes forward and
       questions him.

¹⁸ Casting the lot settles disputes
    and keeps strong opponents apart.

¹⁹ An offended brother is more unyielding
       than a fortified city,
    and disputes are like the barred gates of
       a citadel.

²⁰ From the fruit of his mouth a man's
       stomach is filled;
    with the harvest from his lips he is
       satisfied.

²¹ The tongue has the power of life and death,
    and those who love it will eat its fruit.

²² He who finds a wife finds what is good
    and receives favor from the LORD.

²³ A poor man pleads for mercy,
    but a rich man answers harshly.

²⁴ A man of many
       companions may
       come to ruin,
    but there is a friend who
       sticks closer than a
       brother.

19 Better a poor man
       whose walk is
       blameless
    than a fool whose lips are
       perverse.

² It is not good to have zeal
       without knowledge,
    nor to be hasty and miss
       the way.

³ A man's own folly ruins his life,
    yet his heart rages against the LORD.

⁴ Wealth brings many friends,
    but a poor man's friend deserts him.

⁵ A false witness will not go unpunished,
    and he who pours out lies will not go
       free.

⁶ Many curry favor with a ruler,
    and everyone is the friend of a man who
       gives gifts.

⁷ A poor man is shunned by all his
       relatives—
    how much more do his friends avoid
       him!
   Though he pursues them with pleading,
    they are nowhere to be found.ᵃ

⁸ He who gets wisdom loves his own soul;
    he who cherishes understanding
       prospers.

⁹ A false witness will not go unpunished,
    and he who pours out lies will perish.

¹⁰ It is not fitting for a fool to live in luxury—
    how much worse for a slave to rule over
       princes!

> **Proverbs 18:24**
>
> *God Is a
> Lasting Friend*
>
> A man of many
> companions may
> come to ruin,
> but there is a friend
> who sticks closer
> than a brother.

ᵃ7 The meaning of the Hebrew for this sentence is uncertain.

11 A man's wisdom gives him patience;
   it is to his glory to overlook an offense.

12 A king's rage is like the roar of a lion,
   but his favor is like dew on the grass.

13 A foolish son is his father's ruin,
   and a quarrelsome wife is like a constant
      dripping.

14 Houses and wealth are inherited from
      parents,
   but a prudent wife is from the LORD.

15 Laziness brings on deep sleep,
   and the shiftless man goes hungry.

16 He who obeys instructions guards his life,
   but he who is contemptuous of his ways
      will die.

17 He who is kind to the poor lends to the
      LORD,
   and he will reward him for what he has
      done.

18 Discipline your son, for in that there is
      hope;
   do not be a willing party to his death.

19 A hot-tempered man must pay the penalty;
   if you rescue him, you will have to do it
      again.

20 Listen to advice and accept instruction,
   and in the end you will be wise.

21 Many are the plans in a man's heart,
   but it is the LORD's purpose that prevails.

22 What a man desires is
      unfailing love[a];
   better to be poor than
      a liar.

23 The fear of the LORD leads
      to life:
   Then one rests content,
      untouched by
      trouble.

24 The sluggard buries his
      hand in the dish;
   he will not even bring it
      back to his mouth!

25 Flog a mocker, and the simple will learn
      prudence;
   rebuke a discerning man, and he will
      gain knowledge.

26 He who robs his father and drives out his
      mother
   is a son who brings shame and
      disgrace.

27 Stop listening to instruction, my son,
   and you will stray from the words of
      knowledge.

28 A corrupt witness mocks at justice,
   and the mouth of the wicked gulps
      down evil.

29 Penalties are prepared for mockers,
   and beatings for the backs of fools.

20 Wine is a mocker and beer a
      brawler;
   whoever is led astray by them is not
      wise.

2 A king's wrath is like the roar of a lion;
   he who angers him forfeits his life.

3 It is to a man's honor to avoid strife,
   but every fool is quick to quarrel.

4 A sluggard does not plow in season;
   so at harvest time he looks but finds
      nothing.

5 The purposes of a man's heart are deep
      waters,
   but a man of understanding draws them
      out.

Proverbs 19:21

God Prevails in His Plans

Many are the plans in
a man's heart,
but it is the LORD's
purpose that prevails.

6 Many a man claims to have
      unfailing love,
   but a faithful man who
      can find?

7 The righteous man leads a
      blameless life;
   blessed are his children
      after him.

8 When a king sits on his
      throne to judge,
   he winnows out all evil
      with his eyes.

[a] 22 Or A man's greed is his shame

Paybacks

Read: Proverbs 20:1–22

REVENGE ISN'T SWEET; instead, it makes us sour. Studies have shown an association between negative emotions such as anger and revenge with a variety of destructive physical symptoms, including headaches, backaches, allergic disorders, ulcers, nausea, high blood pressure and heart attacks. Sadly, while vengeful people plot another's demise, they themselves often develop a painful health problem. Paybacks have a way of paying us back.

Revenge is an outward manifestation of an underlying problem: anger. Anger left unchecked will deepen into bitter roots of resentment or jealousy. And when these unbiblical attitudes are full-grown, the desire for revenge springs up. Revenge opposes the Golden Rule: "Do to others what you would have them do to you" (Matthew 7:12). Instead of taking things into our own hands, this proverb encourages us to let go and let God deal with our enemies. Because God is just, those who are wicked will eventually get their "just desserts."

Louis XII of France is said to have treated his enemies in an unexpected manner after ascending to the throne. Before coming to power, he had been cast into prison and kept in chains. Later when he did become king, he was urged to seek revenge on those who had opposed him, but he refused. Instead, he prepared a scroll on which he listed all who had perpetrated crimes against him. Behind every man's name he placed a cross in red ink. When the guilty heard about this, they feared for their lives and fled. Then the king explained, "The cross which I drew beside each name was not a sign of punishment, but a pledge of forgiveness extended for the sake of the crucified Savior, who upon His cross forgave His enemies and prayed for them."

Getting revenge may get us even with our enemies, but forgiveness places us above them. In fact, we are never more like God than when we turn the other cheek. In the Lord's Prayer, the only petition that is conditional is forgiveness: "Forgive us our debts, as we also have forgiven our debtors" (Matthew 6:12). Why can we forego revenge and offer forgiveness? Because we have been forgiven by God. To issue payback is human, but to pardon is divine.

Proverbs 20:22

Do not say, "I'll pay you back for this wrong!" Wait for the LORD, and he will deliver you.

reflection

1 Have you been contemplating a payback? Are you experiencing any painful physical, emotional or spiritual consequences?

2 What are some of the things God has forgiven you for?

3 How does reviewing how you've been forgiven help you let go of revenge and let God handle the paybacks?

RELATED READINGS

Matthew 6:12–15;
Luke 6:27–36;
Romans 12:14–21

"Forgiveness is the key that unlocks the door of resentment and the handcuffs of hate. It is a power that breaks the chains of bitterness and the shackles of selfishness."

Corrie ten Boom

Monday

Go to page 784 for your next devotional reading.

9 Who can say, "I have kept my heart pure;
   I am clean and without sin"?

10 Differing weights and differing
      measures—
   the LORD detests them both.

11 Even a child is known by
      his actions,
   by whether his conduct is
      pure and right.

12 Ears that hear and eyes that
      see—
   the LORD has made them
      both.

13 Do not love sleep or you
      will grow poor;
   stay awake and you will
      have food to spare.

14 "It's no good, it's no good!" says the buyer;
   then off he goes and boasts about his
      purchase.

15 Gold there is, and rubies in abundance,
   but lips that speak knowledge are a rare
      jewel.

16 Take the garment of one who puts up
      security for a stranger;
   hold it in pledge if he does it for a
      wayward woman.

17 Food gained by fraud tastes sweet to a
      man,
   but he ends up with a mouth full of
      gravel.

18 Make plans by seeking advice;
   if you wage war, obtain guidance.

19 A gossip betrays a confidence;
   so avoid a man who talks too much.

20 If a man curses his father or mother,
   his lamp will be snuffed out in pitch
      darkness.

21 An inheritance quickly gained at the
      beginning
   will not be blessed at the end.

22 Do not say, "I'll pay you back for this
      wrong!"

a27 Or *The spirit of man is the Lord's lamp*

782

   Wait for the LORD, and he will deliver
   you.

23 The LORD detests differing weights,
   and dishonest scales do not please him.

24 A man's steps are directed
      by the LORD.
   How then can anyone
      understand his own
      way?

25 It is a trap for a man to
      dedicate something
      rashly
   and only later to consider
      his vows.

26 A wise king winnows out
      the wicked;
   he drives the threshing
      wheel over them.

27 The lamp of the LORD searches the spirit of
      a man[a];
   it searches out his inmost being.

28 Love and faithfulness keep a king safe;
   through love his throne is made
      secure.

29 The glory of young men is their
      strength,
   gray hair the splendor of the old.

30 Blows and wounds cleanse away evil,
   and beatings purge the inmost
      being.

21 The king's heart is in the hand of the
      LORD;
   he directs it like a watercourse wherever
      he pleases.

2 All a man's ways seem right to him,
   but the LORD weighs the heart.

3 To do what is right and just
   is more acceptable to the LORD than
      sacrifice.

4 Haughty eyes and a proud heart,
   the lamp of the wicked, are sin!

5 The plans of the diligent lead to profit
   as surely as haste leads to poverty.

Proverbs 20:24

*God
Directs Steps*

A man's steps are
directed by the LORD.
How then can anyone
understand his own way?

6 A fortune made by a lying tongue
  is a fleeting vapor and a deadly snare.[a]

7 The violence of the wicked will drag them
      away,
  for they refuse to do what is right.

8 The way of the guilty is devious,
  but the conduct of the innocent is
      upright.

9 Better to live on a corner of the roof
  than share a house with a quarrelsome
      wife.

10 The wicked man craves evil;
  his neighbor gets no mercy from him.

11 When a mocker is punished, the simple
      gain wisdom;
  when a wise man is instructed, he gets
      knowledge.

12 The Righteous One[b] takes note of the
      house of the wicked
  and brings the wicked to ruin.

13 If a man shuts his ears to the cry of the
      poor,
  he too will cry out and not be answered.

14 A gift given in secret soothes anger,
  and a bribe concealed in the cloak
      pacifies great wrath.

15 When justice is done, it brings joy to the
      righteous
  but terror to evildoers.

16 A man who strays from the path of
      understanding
  comes to rest in the company of the
      dead.

17 He who loves pleasure will become poor;
  whoever loves wine and oil will never
      be rich.

18 The wicked become a ransom for the
      righteous,
  and the unfaithful for the upright.

19 Better to live in a desert
  than with a quarrelsome and ill-
      tempered wife.

20 In the house of the wise are stores of choice
      food and oil,
  but a foolish man devours all he has.

21 He who pursues righteousness and love
  finds life, prosperity[c] and honor.

22 A wise man attacks the city of the mighty
  and pulls down the stronghold in which
      they trust.

23 He who guards his mouth and his tongue
  keeps himself from calamity.

24 The proud and arrogant man—"Mocker" is
      his name;
  he behaves with overweening pride.

25 The sluggard's craving will be the death of
      him,
  because his hands refuse to work.

26 All day long he craves for more,
  but the righteous give without sparing.

27 The sacrifice of the wicked is detestable—
  how much more so when brought with
      evil intent!

28 A false witness will perish,
  and whoever listens to him will be
      destroyed forever.[d]

29 A wicked man puts up a bold front,
  but an upright man gives thought to his
      ways.

30 There is no wisdom, no insight, no plan
  that can succeed against the LORD.

31 The horse is made ready for the day of
      battle,
  but victory rests with the LORD.

22 A good name is more desirable than
  great riches;
  to be esteemed is better than silver or
      gold.

2 Rich and poor have this in common:
  The LORD is the Maker of them all.

3 A prudent man sees danger and takes
      refuge,
  but the simple keep going and suffer
      for it.

*a***6** Some Hebrew manuscripts, Septuagint and Vulgate; most Hebrew manuscripts *vapor for those who seek death*   *b***12** Or *The righteous man*   *c***21** Or *righteousness*   *d***28** Or / *but the words of an obedient man will live on*

Investments of the Heart

Read: Proverbs 22:1–11

Proverbs 22:4

Humility and the fear of the LORD bring wealth and honor and life.

reflection

1 How do you define wealth? How does God?

2 What, in your own life, does it look like to "fear God"?

3 How do you invest the riches you've been given by God (your money, time, talents, etc.)?

RELATED READINGS

Psalm 37:1–6;
Proverbs 3:1–10;
Mark 12:43–44;
1 Timothy 6:17–19

IF DR. SEUSS HAD ENDED UP on Wall Street instead of Mulberry Street, perhaps his book titles may have sounded something like this: Great Day for the Dow! Horton Hears a Hedge and a High Index; Green Backs and Pork. The growth of investment companies and of commercialism demonstrates the continuing deification of the almighty dollar.

We all know that money can't buy love, happiness or redemption. So why does the book of Proverbs imply that wealth, honor and life will come to those who are humble and fear the Lord? There are Christians who are not wealthy by any stretch of the imagination, just as there are wealthy Christians who don't seem humble. Just what is the principle behind this proverb?

First, God's definition of "wealth" isn't the same as the world's definition. King Solomon's riches were legendary; his yearly income amounted to 25 tons of gold, not counting outside revenues from merchants and traders (see 1 Kings 10:14–15). In terms of finance, King Solomon was clearly qualified to write about wealth and prosperity. But the king soon discovered that God's inheritance isn't about quarterly dividends, accelerated land accumulation or a vast collection of chariots and horses. Rather, it is about the heart. In God's eyes, spiritual riches are acquired by being rich toward him—by exhibiting a humble reverence for his awesome holiness. Spiritual wealth is laced with integrity, bejeweled by honor and polished for eternity. Spiritual riches will pay dividends in prudence, humility, honor, discipline, generosity, purity and graciousness.

This proverb is not a guide for earning wealth but a general principle for living wisely. Although this is not a guarantee that God will make us rich, spiritual riches can help reap financial stability (see Proverbs 21:20). Prudence will teach us to save for a rainy day rather than spend heedlessly. Disciplined giving can benefit us financially as well as spiritually. God delights in giving to the giver. Jesus said, "Give, and it will be given to you. A good measure, pressed down, shaken together and running over, will be poured into your lap" (Luke 6:38). But more important than financial wealth is the richness of living a godly life. We may not live on Wall Street, but we can make investments every day that will yield the benefits of humility, the fear of the Lord, honor and eternal life.

Go to page 788 for your next devotional reading.

⁴ Humility and the fear of the LORD
  bring wealth and honor and life.

⁵ In the paths of the wicked lie thorns and
    snares,
  but he who guards his soul stays far
    from them.

⁶ Train*a* a child in the way he should go,
  and when he is old he will not turn
    from it.

⁷ The rich rule over the poor,
  and the borrower is servant to the lender.

⁸ He who sows wickedness reaps trouble,
  and the rod of his fury will be destroyed.

⁹ A generous man will himself be blessed,
  for he shares his food with the poor.

¹⁰ Drive out the mocker, and out goes strife;
  quarrels and insults are ended.

¹¹ He who loves a pure heart and whose
    speech is gracious
  will have the king for his friend.

¹² The eyes of the LORD keep watch over
    knowledge,
  but he frustrates the words of the
    unfaithful.

¹³ The sluggard says, "There is a lion outside!"
  or, "I will be murdered in the streets!"

¹⁴ The mouth of an adulteress is a deep pit;
  he who is under the LORD's wrath will
    fall into it.

¹⁵ Folly is bound up in the heart of a child,
  but the rod of discipline will drive it far
    from him.

¹⁶ He who oppresses the poor to increase his
    wealth
  and he who gives gifts to the rich—both
    come to poverty.

Sayings of the Wise

¹⁷ Pay attention and listen to the sayings of
    the wise;
  apply your heart to what I teach,
¹⁸ for it is pleasing when you keep them in
    your heart

and have all of them ready on your lips.
¹⁹ So that your trust may be in the LORD,
  I teach you today, even you.
²⁰ Have I not written thirty*b* sayings for you,
  sayings of counsel and knowledge,
²¹ teaching you true and reliable words,
  so that you can give sound answers
    to him who sent you?

²² Do not exploit the poor because they are
    poor
  and do not crush the needy in court,
²³ for the LORD will take up their case
  and will plunder those who plunder
    them.

²⁴ Do not make friends with a hot-tempered
    man,
  do not associate with one easily angered,
²⁵ or you may learn his ways
  and get yourself ensnared.

²⁶ Do not be a man who strikes hands in
    pledge
  or puts up security for debts;
²⁷ if you lack the means to pay,
  your very bed will be snatched from
    under you.

²⁸ Do not move an ancient boundary stone
  set up by your forefathers.

²⁹ Do you see a man skilled in his work?
  He will serve before kings;
  he will not serve before obscure men.

23 When you sit to dine with a ruler,
    note well what*c* is before you,
² and put a knife to your throat
  if you are given to gluttony.
³ Do not crave his delicacies,
  for that food is deceptive.

⁴ Do not wear yourself out to get rich;
  have the wisdom to show restraint.
⁵ Cast but a glance at riches, and they are
    gone,
  for they will surely sprout wings
  and fly off to the sky like an eagle.

⁶ Do not eat the food of a stingy man,
  do not crave his delicacies;
⁷ for he is the kind of man

a6 Or Start b20 Or not formerly written; or not written excellent c1 Or who

who is always thinking about the cost.[a]
"Eat and drink," he says to you,
but his heart is not with you.
8 You will vomit up the little you have
eaten
and will have wasted your compliments.

9 Do not speak to a fool,
for he will scorn the wisdom of your
words.

10 Do not move an ancient boundary stone
or encroach on the fields of the
fatherless,
11 for their Defender is strong;
he will take up their case against you.

12 Apply your heart to instruction
and your ears to words of knowledge.

13 Do not withhold discipline from a child;
if you punish him with the rod, he will
not die.
14 Punish him with the rod
and save his soul from death.[b]

15 My son, if your heart is wise,
then my heart will be glad;
16 my inmost being will rejoice
when your lips speak what is right.

17 Do not let your heart envy sinners,
but always be zealous for the fear of the
LORD.
18 There is surely a future hope for you,
and your hope will not be cut off.

19 Listen, my son, and be wise,
and keep your heart on the right path.
20 Do not join those who drink too much
wine
or gorge themselves on meat,
21 for drunkards and gluttons become poor,
and drowsiness clothes them in rags.

22 Listen to your father, who gave you life,
and do not despise your mother when
she is old.
23 Buy the truth and do not sell it;
get wisdom, discipline and
understanding.
24 The father of a righteous man has great joy;
he who has a wise son delights in him.

25 May your father and mother be glad;
may she who gave you birth rejoice!

26 My son, give me your heart
and let your eyes keep to my ways,
27 for a prostitute is a deep pit
and a wayward wife is a narrow well.
28 Like a bandit she lies in wait,
and multiplies the unfaithful among
men.

29 Who has woe? Who has sorrow?
Who has strife? Who has complaints?
Who has needless bruises? Who has
bloodshot eyes?
30 Those who linger over wine,
who go to sample bowls of mixed wine.
31 Do not gaze at wine when it is red,
when it sparkles in the cup,
when it goes down smoothly!
32 In the end it bites like a snake
and poisons like a viper.
33 Your eyes will see strange sights
and your mind imagine confusing
things.
34 You will be like one sleeping on the high
seas,
lying on top of the rigging.
35 "They hit me," you will say, "but I'm not
hurt!
They beat me, but I don't feel it!
When will I wake up
so I can find another drink?"

24

Do not envy wicked men,
do not desire their company;
2 for their hearts plot violence,
and their lips talk about making
trouble.

3 By wisdom a house is built,
and through understanding it is
established;
4 through knowledge its rooms are filled
with rare and beautiful treasures.

5 A wise man has great power,
and a man of knowledge increases
strength;
6 for waging war you need guidance,
and for victory many advisers.

---

[a]7 Or for as he thinks within himself, / so he is; or for as he puts on a feast, / so he is   [b]14 Hebrew Sheol

7 Wisdom is too high for a fool;
   in the assembly at the gate he has
      nothing to say.

8 He who plots evil
   will be known as a schemer.
9 The schemes of folly are sin,
   and men detest a mocker.

10 If you falter in times of trouble,
   how small is your strength!

11 Rescue those being led away to death;
   hold back those staggering toward
      slaughter.
12 If you say, "But we knew nothing about this,"
   does not he who weighs the heart
      perceive it?
   Does not he who guards your life know it?
   Will he not repay each person according
      to what he has done?

13 Eat honey, my son, for it is good;
   honey from the comb is sweet to your
      taste.
14 Know also that wisdom is sweet to your
      soul;
   if you find it, there is a future hope for
      you,
   and your hope will not be cut off.

15 Do not lie in wait like an outlaw against a
      righteous man's house,
   do not raid his dwelling place;
16 for though a righteous man falls seven
      times, he rises again,
   but the wicked are brought down by
      calamity.

17 Do not gloat when your enemy falls;
   when he stumbles, do not let your heart
      rejoice,
18 or the LORD will see and disapprove
   and turn his wrath away from him.

19 Do not fret because of evil men
   or be envious of the wicked,
20 for the evil man has no future hope,
   and the lamp of the wicked will be
      snuffed out.

21 Fear the LORD and the king, my son,
   and do not join with the rebellious,

22 for those two will send sudden destruction
      upon them,
   and who knows what calamities they
      can bring?

Further Sayings of the Wise

23 These also are sayings of the wise:

To show partiality in judging is not good:
24 Whoever says to the guilty, "You are
      innocent"—
   peoples will curse him and nations
      denounce him.
25 But it will go well with those who convict
      the guilty,
   and rich blessing will come upon them.

26 An honest answer
   is like a kiss on the lips.

27 Finish your outdoor work
   and get your fields ready;
   after that, build your house.

28 Do not testify against your neighbor
      without cause,
   or use your lips to deceive.
29 Do not say, "I'll do to him as he has done to
      me;
   I'll pay that man back for what he did."

30 I went past the field of the sluggard,
   past the vineyard of the man who lacks
      judgment;
31 thorns had come up everywhere,
   the ground was covered with weeds,
   and the stone wall was in ruins.
32 I applied my heart to what I observed
   and learned a lesson from what I saw:
33 A little sleep, a little slumber,
   a little folding of the hands to rest—
34 and poverty will come on you like a bandit
   and scarcity like an armed man.[a]

More Proverbs of Solomon

25 These are more proverbs of Solomon,
copied by the men of Hezekiah king
of Judah:

2 It is the glory of God to conceal a matter;
   to search out a matter is the glory of
      kings.

---

a 34 Or like a vagrant / and scarcity like a beggar

Proverbs 25:11

A word aptly spoken
is like apples of gold
in settings of silver.

Apples of Gold

Read: Proverbs 25:1–15

reflection

1 How have you been affected negatively by hurtful words? In what ways are you guilty of hurting others with your words?

2 Can you think of a time when you have been on the receiving end of positive and encouraging words? How did they affect you?

3 Ask God to show you someone to whisper words of encouragement to today.

RELATED READINGS

Proverbs 12:25;
Colossians 3:12–14;
1 Timothy 4:12;
1 Peter 3:9–12

"If I can enjoy a joke at the expense of another; if I can in any way slight another in conversation, or even in thought, then I know nothing of Calvary's love."

Amy Carmichael

IN THE 1950s, Mary grew up knowing she was different from other kids . . . and she hated it. Because she had a cleft palate, she had learned to steel herself against the jokes and stares of children who teased her about her misshapen lip, crooked nose and garbled speech. Mary was convinced that no one outside her family could ever love her . . . until she entered Mrs. Leonard's class. Mrs. Leonard had a warm smile, a round face and beautiful brown hair. All of the children liked Mrs. Leonard, but Mary grew to love her.

In those days, teachers administered a hearing test in the classroom. Unfortunately, Mary not only had a speech impediment due to her cleft palate, she was also partially deaf in one ear. Determined not to let the children have something else to tease her about, she thought of a way to cheat on the hearing test: She could pass the "whisper test" by covering her bad ear and turning her good ear toward her teacher. On the day of the dreaded hearing test, surely God put seven words in Mrs. Leonard's mouth that changed Mary's life forever. When it was time for Mary's "whisper test," she clearly heard the words: "I wish you were my little girl."

Solomon called these kinds of words "apples of gold in settings of silver." They are words that can erase years of pain and sorrow. They are words filled with love and acceptance. They are words that are priceless to those who hear them.

If someone listened in on your conversations, would their lives be changed for better or worse? Would they hear you speaking about the character flaws of others as if they were physical defects or would they hear that you consider others as beautiful in God's eyes? Ask yourself if your words build up or tear down. Do your words push others away from you or draw others near? Most important, do they draw others to God?

It's never too late to dispense apples of gold in settings of silver. Seek someone who is downcast and whisper a word of encouragement. You never know who needs to hear the words, "I wish you were my friend."

³ As the heavens are high and the earth is
    deep,
    so the hearts of kings are unsearchable.

⁴ Remove the dross from the silver,
    and out comes material for[a] the
        silversmith;
⁵ remove the wicked from the king's
        presence,
    and his throne will be established
        through righteousness.

⁶ Do not exalt yourself in the king's
        presence,
    and do not claim a place among great
        men;
⁷ it is better for him to say to you, "Come up
        here,"
    than for him to humiliate you before a
        nobleman.

What you have seen with your eyes
⁸   do not bring[b] hastily to court,
    for what will you do in the end
        if your neighbor puts you to shame?

⁹ If you argue your case with a neighbor,
    do not betray another man's confidence,
¹⁰ or he who hears it may shame you
    and you will never lose your bad
        reputation.

¹¹ A word aptly spoken
    is like apples of gold in settings of silver.

¹² Like an earring of gold or an ornament of
        fine gold
    is a wise man's rebuke to a listening ear.

¹³ Like the coolness of snow at harvest time
    is a trustworthy messenger to those who
        send him;
    he refreshes the spirit of his masters.

¹⁴ Like clouds and wind without rain
    is a man who boasts of gifts he does not
        give.

¹⁵ Through patience a ruler can be
        persuaded,
    and a gentle tongue can break a bone.

¹⁶ If you find honey, eat just enough—
    too much of it, and you will vomit.

¹⁷ Seldom set foot in your neighbor's
        house—
    too much of you, and he will hate you.

¹⁸ Like a club or a sword or a sharp arrow
    is the man who gives false testimony
        against his neighbor.

¹⁹ Like a bad tooth or a lame foot
    is reliance on the unfaithful in times of
        trouble.

²⁰ Like one who takes away a garment on a
        cold day,
    or like vinegar poured on soda,
    is one who sings songs to a heavy
        heart.

²¹ If your enemy is hungry, give him food to
        eat;
    if he is thirsty, give him water to drink.

²² In doing this, you will heap burning coals
        on his head,
    and the LORD will reward you.

²³ As a north wind brings rain,
    so a sly tongue brings angry looks.

²⁴ Better to live on a corner of the roof
    than share a house with a quarrelsome
        wife.

²⁵ Like cold water to a weary soul
    is good news from a distant land.

²⁶ Like a muddied spring or a polluted well
    is a righteous man who gives way to the
        wicked.

²⁷ It is not good to eat too much honey,
    nor is it honorable to seek one's own
        honor.

²⁸ Like a city whose walls are broken down
    is a man who lacks self-control.

26

Like snow in summer or rain in
    harvest,
    honor is not fitting for a fool.

² Like a fluttering sparrow or a darting
        swallow,
    an undeserved curse does not come to
        rest.

ᵃ4 Or *comes a vessel from*   ᵇ7,8 Or *nobleman / on whom you had set your eyes.* / ⁸ Do not go

3 A whip for the horse, a halter for the
    donkey,
  and a rod for the backs of fools!

4 Do not answer a fool according to his folly,
  or you will be like him yourself.

5 Answer a fool according to his folly,
  or he will be wise in his own eyes.

6 Like cutting off one's feet or drinking
    violence
  is the sending of a message by the hand
    of a fool.

7 Like a lame man's legs that hang limp
  is a proverb in the mouth of a fool.

8 Like tying a stone in a sling
  is the giving of honor to a fool.

9 Like a thornbush in a drunkard's hand
  is a proverb in the mouth of a fool.

10 Like an archer who wounds at random
  is he who hires a fool or any passer-by.

11 As a dog returns to its vomit,
  so a fool repeats his folly.

12 Do you see a man wise in his own eyes?
  There is more hope for a fool than for
    him.

13 The sluggard says, "There is a lion in the
    road,
  a fierce lion roaming the streets!"

14 As a door turns on its hinges,
  so a sluggard turns on
    his bed.

15 The sluggard buries his
    hand in the dish;
  he is too lazy to bring it
    back to his mouth.

16 The sluggard is wiser in his
    own eyes
  than seven men who
    answer discreetly.

17 Like one who seizes a dog
    by the ears
  is a passer-by who
    meddles in a quarrel not his own.

18 Like a madman shooting
    firebrands or deadly arrows
19 is a man who deceives his neighbor
  and says, "I was only joking!"

20 Without wood a fire goes out;
  without gossip a quarrel dies down.

21 As charcoal to embers and as wood to fire,
  so is a quarrelsome man for kindling
    strife.

22 The words of a gossip are like choice
    morsels;
  they go down to a man's inmost parts.

23 Like a coating of glaze[a] over earthenware
  are fervent lips with an evil heart.

24 A malicious man disguises himself with
    his lips,
  but in his heart he harbors deceit.

25 Though his speech is charming, do not
    believe him,
  for seven abominations fill his heart.

26 His malice may be concealed by
    deception,
  but his wickedness will be exposed in
    the assembly.

27 If a man digs a pit, he will fall into it;
  if a man rolls a stone, it will roll back on
    him.

28 A lying tongue hates those it hurts,
  and a flattering mouth works ruin.

27 Do not boast about
    tomorrow,
  for you do not know
    what a day may
    bring forth.

2 Let another praise you,
  and not your own
    mouth;
  someone else, and not
    your own lips.

3 Stone is heavy and sand a
    burden,
  but provocation by a
    fool is heavier than
    both.

Proverbs 27:2

**God Commends
Humility**

Let another praise you,
and not your own mouth;
someone else, and
not your own lips.

---

a 23 With a different word division of the Hebrew; Masoretic Text *of silver dross*

⁴ Anger is cruel and fury overwhelming,
  but who can stand before jealousy?

⁵ Better is open rebuke
  than hidden love.

⁶ Wounds from a friend can be trusted,
  but an enemy multiplies kisses.

⁷ He who is full loathes honey,
  but to the hungry even what is bitter
    tastes sweet.

⁸ Like a bird that strays from its nest
  is a man who strays from his home.

⁹ Perfume and incense bring joy to the heart,
  and the pleasantness of one's friend
    springs from his earnest counsel.

¹⁰ Do not forsake your friend and the friend
    of your father,
  and do not go to your brother's house
    when disaster strikes you—
  better a neighbor nearby than a brother
    far away.

¹¹ Be wise, my son, and bring joy to my heart;
  then I can answer anyone who treats me
    with contempt.

¹² The prudent see danger and take refuge,
  but the simple keep going and suffer
    for it.

¹³ Take the garment of one who puts up
    security for a stranger;
  hold it in pledge if he does it for a
    wayward woman.

¹⁴ If a man loudly blesses his neighbor early
    in the morning,
  it will be taken as a curse.

¹⁵ A quarrelsome wife is like
  a constant dripping on a rainy day;
¹⁶ restraining her is like restraining the wind
  or grasping oil with the hand.

¹⁷ As iron sharpens iron,
  so one man sharpens another.

¹⁸ He who tends a fig tree will eat its fruit,
  and he who looks after his master will be
    honored.

¹⁹ As water reflects a face,
  so a man's heart reflects the man.

²⁰ Death and Destruction[a] are never satisfied,
  and neither are the eyes of man.

²¹ The crucible for silver and the furnace for
    gold,
  but man is tested by the praise he
    receives.

²² Though you grind a fool in a mortar,
  grinding him like grain with a pestle,
  you will not remove his folly from him.

²³ Be sure you know the condition of your
    flocks,
  give careful attention to your herds;
²⁴ for riches do not endure forever,
  and a crown is not secure for all
    generations.
²⁵ When the hay is removed and new growth
    appears
  and the grass from the hills is gathered
    in,
²⁶ the lambs will provide you with clothing,
  and the goats with the price of a field.
²⁷ You will have plenty of goats' milk
  to feed you and your family
  and to nourish your servant girls.

28 The wicked man flees though no one
    pursues,
  but the righteous are as bold as a lion.

² When a country is rebellious, it has many
    rulers,
  but a man of understanding and
    knowledge maintains order.

³ A ruler[b] who oppresses the poor
  is like a driving rain that leaves no crops.

⁴ Those who forsake the law praise the
    wicked,
  but those who keep the law resist them.

⁵ Evil men do not understand justice,
  but those who seek the Lord
    understand it fully.

⁶ Better a poor man whose walk is blameless
  than a rich man whose ways are
    perverse.

---

a 20 Hebrew *Sheol and Abaddon*   *b* 3 Or *A poor man*

⁷ He who keeps the law is a discerning son,
  but a companion of gluttons disgraces
    his father.

⁸ He who increases his wealth by exorbitant
    interest
  amasses it for another, who will be kind
    to the poor.

⁹ If anyone turns a deaf ear to the law,
  even his prayers are detestable.

¹⁰ He who leads the upright along an evil
    path
  will fall into his own trap,
  but the blameless will receive a good
    inheritance.

¹¹ A rich man may be wise in his own eyes,
  but a poor man who has discernment
    sees through him.

¹² When the righteous triumph, there is great
    elation;
  but when the wicked rise to power, men
    go into hiding.

¹³ He who conceals his sins does not prosper,
  but whoever confesses and renounces
    them finds mercy.

¹⁴ Blessed is the man who always fears the
    LORD,
  but he who hardens his heart falls into
    trouble.

¹⁵ Like a roaring lion or a charging bear
  is a wicked man ruling over a helpless
    people.

¹⁶ A tyrannical ruler lacks judgment,
  but he who hates ill-gotten gain will
    enjoy a long life.

¹⁷ A man tormented by the guilt of murder
  will be a fugitive till death;
  let no one support him.

¹⁸ He whose walk is blameless is kept safe,
  but he whose ways are perverse will
    suddenly fall.

¹⁹ He who works his land will have abundant
    food,
  but the one who chases fantasies will
    have his fill of poverty.

²⁰ A faithful man will be richly blessed,
  but one eager to get rich will not go
    unpunished.

²¹ To show partiality is not good—
  yet a man will do wrong for a piece of
    bread.

²² A stingy man is eager to get rich
  and is unaware that poverty awaits him.

²³ He who rebukes a man will in the end gain
    more favor
  than he who has a flattering tongue.

²⁴ He who robs his father or mother
  and says, "It's not wrong"—
  he is partner to him who destroys.

²⁵ A greedy man stirs up dissension,
  but he who trusts in the LORD will
    prosper.

²⁶ He who trusts in himself is a fool,
  but he who walks in wisdom is kept
    safe.

²⁷ He who gives to the poor will lack nothing,
  but he who closes his eyes to them
    receives many curses.

²⁸ When the wicked rise to power, people go
    into hiding;
  but when the wicked perish, the
    righteous thrive.

29 A man who remains stiff-necked
    after many rebukes
  will suddenly be destroyed—without
    remedy.

² When the righteous thrive, the people
    rejoice;
  when the wicked rule, the people groan.

³ A man who loves wisdom brings joy to his
    father,
  but a companion of prostitutes
    squanders his wealth.

⁴ By justice a king gives a country stability,
  but one who is greedy for bribes tears it
    down.

⁵ Whoever flatters his neighbor
  is spreading a net for his feet.

⁶ An evil man is snared by his own sin,
  but a righteous one can sing and be glad.

⁷ The righteous care about justice for the
    poor,
  but the wicked have no such concern.

⁸ Mockers stir up a city,
  but wise men turn away anger.

⁹ If a wise man goes to court with a fool,
  the fool rages and scoffs, and there is no
    peace.

¹⁰ Bloodthirsty men hate a man of integrity
  and seek to kill the upright.

¹¹ A fool gives full vent to his anger,
  but a wise man keeps himself under
    control.

¹² If a ruler listens to lies,
  all his officials become wicked.

¹³ The poor man and the oppressor have this
    in common:
  The LORD gives sight to the eyes of both.

¹⁴ If a king judges the poor with fairness,
  his throne will always be secure.

¹⁵ The rod of correction imparts wisdom,
  but a child left to himself disgraces his
    mother.

¹⁶ When the wicked thrive, so does sin,
  but the righteous will see their downfall.

¹⁷ Discipline your son, and he
    will give you peace;
  he will bring delight to
    your soul.

¹⁸ Where there is no
    revelation, the
    people cast off
    restraint;
  but blessed is he who
    keeps the law.

¹⁹ A servant cannot be
    corrected by mere
    words;
  though he understands,
    he will not respond.

²⁰ Do you see a man who speaks in haste?
  There is more hope for a fool than for
    him.

²¹ If a man pampers his servant from youth,
  he will bring grief *ᵃ* in the end.

²² An angry man stirs up dissension,
  and a hot-tempered one commits many
    sins.

²³ A man's pride brings him low,
  but a man of lowly spirit gains honor.

²⁴ The accomplice of a thief is his own
    enemy;
  he is put under oath and dare not testify.

²⁵ Fear of man will prove to be a snare,
  but whoever trusts in the LORD is kept
    safe.

²⁶ Many seek an audience with a ruler,
  but it is from the LORD that man gets
    justice.

²⁷ The righteous detest the dishonest;
  the wicked detest the upright.

Sayings of Agur

30 The sayings of Agur son of Jakeh—
    an oracle*ᵇ*:

This man declared to Ithiel,
  to Ithiel and to Ucal:*ᶜ*

² "I am the most ignorant of
      men;
    I do not have a man's
      understanding.
  ³ I have not learned wisdom,
    nor have I knowledge of
      the Holy One.
  ⁴ Who has gone up to heaven
      and come down?
    Who has gathered up the
      wind in the hollow
      of his hands?
  Who has wrapped up the
      waters in his cloak?
    Who has established
      all the ends of the
      earth?

Proverbs 29:18

*God Blesses
His Followers*

Where there is no
revelation, the people
cast off restraint;
but blessed is he who
keeps the law.

---

*ᵃ*21 The meaning of the Hebrew for this word is uncertain. *ᵇ*1 Or *Jakeh of Massa* *ᶜ*1 Masoretic Text; with a different word division of the Hebrew *declared,* "I am weary, O God; / I am weary, O God, and faint.

What is his name, and the name of his
son?
Tell me if you know!

5 "Every word of God is
flawless;
he is a shield to those
who take refuge in
him.
6 Do not add to his words,
or he will rebuke you and
prove you a liar.

7 "Two things I ask of you,
O LORD;
do not refuse me before
I die:
8 Keep falsehood and lies far
from me;
give me neither poverty nor riches,
but give me only my daily bread.
9 Otherwise, I may have too much and
disown you
and say, 'Who is the LORD?'
Or I may become poor and steal,
and so dishonor the name of my God.

10 "Do not slander a servant to his master,
or he will curse you, and you will pay
for it.

11 "There are those who curse their fathers
and do not bless their mothers;
12 those who are pure in their own eyes
and yet are not cleansed of their filth;
13 those whose eyes are ever so haughty,
whose glances are so disdainful;
14 those whose teeth are swords
and whose jaws are set with knives
to devour the poor from the earth,
the needy from among mankind.

15 "The leech has two daughters.
'Give! Give!' they cry.

"There are three things that are never
satisfied,
four that never say, 'Enough!':
16 the grave,a the barren womb,
land, which is never satisfied with water,
and fire, which never says, 'Enough!'

17 "The eye that mocks a father,
that scorns obedience to a mother,
will be pecked out by the ravens of the
valley,
will be eaten by the
vultures.

18 "There are three things that
are too amazing for
me,
four that I do not
understand:
19 the way of an eagle in the
sky,
the way of a snake on a
rock,
the way of a ship on the
high seas,
and the way of a man
with a maiden.

20 "This is the way of an adulteress:
She eats and wipes her mouth
and says, 'I've done nothing wrong.'

21 "Under three things the earth trembles,
under four it cannot bear up:
22 a servant who becomes king,
a fool who is full of food,
23 an unloved woman who is married,
and a maidservant who displaces her
mistress.

24 "Four things on earth are small,
yet they are extremely wise:
25 Ants are creatures of little strength,
yet they store up their food in the
summer;
26 coneysb are creatures of little power,
yet they make their home in the
crags;
27 locusts have no king,
yet they advance together in ranks;
28 a lizard can be caught with the hand,
yet it is found in kings' palaces.

29 "There are three things that are stately in
their stride,
four that move with stately bearing:
30 a lion, mighty among beasts,
who retreats before nothing;

> ## Proverbs 30:5
>
> ### God Is Flawless
>
> Every word of God
> is flawless;
> he is a shield to those
> who take refuge in him.

---

a16 Hebrew Sheol   b26 That is, the hyrax or rock badger

You Gotta Laugh

Read: Proverbs 31:10–31

OH, THE UNIQUE CHALLENGES awaiting the woman approaching middle age! Imagine waking up one morning to find your face sort of lying in a pool beside you. Your once tight abs have been replaced with something rather squishy that has to be gathered up (starting somewhere around the knees) and tucked into industrial–strength, control-top pantyhose. Imagine suddenly realizing that your thighs almost create sparks when you walk. Your biceps are so deflated that in a strong breeze you worry that they might actually make a flapping sound. Maybe you don't have to imagine it. Maybe you're living it.

God might have knit these bodies together out of a more "permanent press" kind of fabric. He could have built in a kind of stretch that wouldn't lose its elasticity around middle age. But he didn't. And through our aging and all the challenges we live through, he teaches us what's really important.

The Proverbs 31 "virtuous woman" got in on that teaching. She could "laugh at the days to come" (verse 25). Her future held flabby abs and combustible thighs too. But she could laugh. Why?

The passage describes a woman who seems just about perfect. Many Bible teachers call her the "virtuous woman," and she makes Martha Stewart look like a novice. She keeps her husband happy; she works eagerly; she gets up early and stays up late. She gives to others generously, makes her own clothes, is an eloquent teacher, and her kids love her. A woman like this "who can find," indeed! She is a formidable pattern, an intimidating example.

But look past the outward layer. Look deeper. You'll see a woman of wisdom who fully understood what was really important. She understood what it meant to work hard and to serve God with her whole heart. She understood that everything of consequence was wrapped up in him. Serving others came as a natural extension of serving him.

There's only one metamorphosis that matters—and it will keep every woman eternally beautiful. It's a metamorphosis of the heart. The Scripture says, "Therefore, if anyone is in Christ, he is a new creation; the old has gone, the new has come!" (2 Corinthians 5:17). Having a heart of unselfish service that has been transformed by Christ—that's what's important. And that is what gives us the ability to laugh at the future . . . even if it involves flabby thighs.

Proverbs 31:25,30

She is clothed with strength and dignity; she can laugh at the days to come . . . Charm is deceptive, and beauty is fleeting; but a woman who fears the LORD is to be praised.

reflection

1 When your attention to appearance gets out of whack and your focus is more on looks than on eternal things, how might "fearing the Lord" turn your focus back to where it needs to be?

2 What are some of the ways the woman in Proverbs 31:10–31 served others?

3 How many different types of people did her daily life and ministry touch? How might you underestimate the many lives you touch each day?

RELATED READINGS

Psalm 139:1–24;
Romans 12:1–12;
Galatians 6:9–10;
1 Peter 3:1–6

Go to page 799 for your next devotional reading.

³¹a strutting rooster, a he-goat,
and a king with his army around him.ᵃ

³²"If you have played the fool and exalted
yourself,
or if you have planned evil,
clap your hand over your mouth!
³³For as churning the milk produces butter,
and as twisting the nose produces blood,
so stirring up anger produces strife."

Sayings of King Lemuel

31 The sayings of King Lemuel—an ora-
cleᵇ his mother taught him:

²"O my son, O son of my womb,
O son of my vows,ᶜ
³do not spend your strength on women,
your vigor on those who ruin kings.

⁴"It is not for kings, O Lemuel—
not for kings to drink wine,
not for rulers to crave beer,
⁵lest they drink and forget what the law
decrees,
and deprive all the oppressed of their
rights.
⁶Give beer to those who are perishing,
wine to those who are in anguish;
⁷let them drink and forget their poverty
and remember their misery no more.

⁸"Speak up for those who cannot speak for
themselves,
for the rights of all who are destitute.
⁹Speak up and judge fairly;
defend the rights of the poor and needy."

Epilogue: The Wife of Noble Character

¹⁰ᵈA wife of noble character who can find?
She is worth far more than rubies.
¹¹Her husband has full confidence in her
and lacks nothing of value.
¹²She brings him good, not harm,
all the days of her life.
¹³She selects wool and flax
and works with eager hands.
¹⁴She is like the merchant ships,
bringing her food from afar.
¹⁵She gets up while it is still dark;
she provides food for her family
and portions for her servant girls.
¹⁶She considers a field and buys it;
out of her earnings she plants a
vineyard.
¹⁷She sets about her work vigorously;
her arms are strong for her tasks.
¹⁸She sees that her trading is profitable,
and her lamp does not go out at night.
¹⁹In her hand she holds the distaff
and grasps the spindle with her fingers.
²⁰She opens her arms to the poor
and extends her hands to the needy.
²¹When it snows, she has no fear for her
household;
for all of them are clothed in scarlet.
²²She makes coverings for her bed;
she is clothed in fine linen and purple.
²³Her husband is respected at the city gate,
where he takes his seat among the elders
of the land.
²⁴She makes linen garments and sells them,
and supplies the merchants with sashes.
²⁵She is clothed with strength and dignity;
she can laugh at the days to come.
²⁶She speaks with wisdom,
and faithful instruction is on her
tongue.
²⁷She watches over the affairs of her
household
and does not eat the bread of idleness.
²⁸Her children arise and call her blessed;
her husband also, and he praises her:
²⁹"Many women do noble things,
but you surpass them all."
³⁰Charm is deceptive, and beauty is fleeting;
but a woman who fears the LORD is to be
praised.
³¹Give her the reward she has earned,
and let her works bring her praise at the
city gate.

ᵃ31 Or *king secure against revolt*   ᵇ1 Or *of Lemuel king of Massa, which*   ᶜ2 Or */ the answer to my prayers*   ᵈ10 Verses 10–31 are an acrostic, each verse beginning with a successive letter of the Hebrew alphabet.

Ecclesiastes

The book of Ecclesiastes takes the reader along on the *adventurous quest for meaning in life.* It's a search we are all on to some degree or another as we live our lives each day. We want to spend our time and energy on what is meaningful and on what will last. But finding those things— *that's the challenge.*

As we follow the Teacher's trail, we find that he's already looked for meaning in most places we would try. Wisdom—a good place to start—he's already plumbed. Pleasures and work and money and getting ahead—he's been there. Even madness and folly—he's tried those too. He's lived long and seen much, and he's found little that has meaning. But the meaning *is* there. *There is treasure at the end of the quest,* and along the way are insights, truths and intriguing ways of looking at life from someone who has examined it from every angle.

Author:
The Teacher, who was probably King Solomon.

Audience:
All Israel.

Date:
Most likely near the end of Solomon's life, 930 B.C.

Setting:
In the twilight of his life, the wise Teacher reflects on human existence.

Verse to Remember:
Now all has been heard; here is the conclusion of the matter: Fear God and keep his commandments, for this is the whole duty of man. (12:13)

Everything Is Meaningless

1 The words of the Teacher,*a* son of David, king in Jerusalem:

2 "Meaningless! Meaningless!"
　　says the Teacher.

"Utterly meaningless!
　　Everything is meaningless."

3 What does man gain from all his labor
　　at which he toils under the sun?
4 Generations come and generations go,

*a*1 Or *leader of the assembly;* also in verses 2 and 12

797

but the earth remains forever.
5 The sun rises and the sun sets,
    and hurries back to where it rises.
6 The wind blows to the south
    and turns to the north;
round and round it goes,
    ever returning on its course.
7 All streams flow into the sea,
    yet the sea is never full.
To the place the streams come from,
    there they return again.
8 All things are wearisome,
    more than one can say.
The eye never has enough of seeing,
    nor the ear its fill of hearing.
9 What has been will be again,
    what has been done will be done again;
    there is nothing new under the sun.
10 Is there anything of which one can say,
    "Look! This is something new"?
It was here already, long ago;
    it was here before our time.
11 There is no remembrance of men of old,
    and even those who are yet to come
will not be remembered
    by those who follow.

Wisdom Is Meaningless

12 I, the Teacher, was king over Israel in Jerusalem. 13 I devoted myself to study and to explore by wisdom all that is done under heaven. What a heavy burden God has laid on men! 14 I have seen all the things that are done under the sun; all of them are meaningless, a chasing after the wind.

15 What is twisted cannot be straightened;
    what is lacking cannot be counted.

16 I thought to myself, "Look, I have grown and increased in wisdom more than anyone who has ruled over Jerusalem before me; I have experienced much of wisdom and knowledge." 17 Then I applied myself to the understanding of wisdom, and also of madness and folly, but I learned that this, too, is a chasing after the wind.

18 For with much wisdom comes much sorrow;
    the more knowledge, the more grief.

Pleasures Are Meaningless

2 I thought in my heart, "Come now, I will test you with pleasure to find out what is good." But that also proved to be meaningless. 2 "Laughter," I said, "is foolish. And what does pleasure accomplish?" 3 I tried cheering myself with wine, and embracing folly—my mind still guiding me with wisdom. I wanted to see what was worthwhile for men to do under heaven during the few days of their lives.

4 I undertook great projects: I built houses for myself and planted vineyards. 5 I made gardens and parks and planted all kinds of fruit trees in them. 6 I made reservoirs to water groves of flourishing trees. 7 I bought male and female slaves and had other slaves who were born in my house. I also owned more herds and flocks than anyone in Jerusalem before me. 8 I amassed silver and gold for myself, and the treasure of kings and provinces. I acquired men and women singers, and a harem*a* as well—the delights of the heart of man. 9 I became greater by far than anyone in Jerusalem before me. In all this my wisdom stayed with me.

10 I denied myself nothing my eyes desired;
    I refused my heart no pleasure.
My heart took delight in all my work,
    and this was the reward for all my labor.
11 Yet when I surveyed all that my hands had done
    and what I had toiled to achieve,
everything was meaningless, a chasing
        after the wind;
    nothing was gained under the sun.

Wisdom and Folly Are Meaningless

12 Then I turned my thoughts to consider wisdom,
    and also madness and folly.
What more can the king's successor do
    than what has already been done?
13 I saw that wisdom is better than folly,
    just as light is better than darkness.
14 The wise man has eyes in his head,
    while the fool walks in the darkness;
but I came to realize
    that the same fate overtakes them both.

15 Then I thought in my heart,

---

a8 The meaning of the Hebrew for this phrase is uncertain.

Wind Catchers

Read: Ecclesiastes 2:1-11

HAVE YOU EVER TRIED to catch the wind? Perhaps you once launched a kite on a passing breeze or trimmed your sails to harness the swirling air currents to propel your sailboat forward. But did you honestly catch the wind—or did it catch you? Wind is elusive. It is intangible. Chimes or catchers hanging on your back porch may detect its presence or point out its direction, but they'll never contain it.

Solomon discovered that finding pleasure is as elusive as catching the wind. He pursued everything imaginable to achieve lasting bliss. But the smartest man alive still had a restless mind. The richest man in the world couldn't buy happiness. The most powerful person in the kingdom was unable to satisfy his own heart. And although he had 700 wives and 300 concubines, he never found true love. His conclusion? These pursuits were meaningless, completely unsatisfying.

Securing happiness on our own is like trying to catch the wind. We can try to chase it, but it will always remain just out of reach. The Bible teaches us that instead of searching for happiness, we should allow God's joy and peace to reign in our hearts. Instead of striving for the things we think will satisfy, we can learn to find true contentment by looking to God, whatever our circumstance.

The Bible often uses the word *blessed*, which means "oh, how happy." To God, blessed people are happy people and happy people are blessed. Solomon's father, King David, said blessed are those whose sins are forgiven (see Psalm 32:1), who trust in the Lord (see Psalm 40:4) and who draw near to God (see Psalm 65:4). The true source of pleasure is God. Don't waste your time trying to catch the wind; instead, find true happiness by laying hold of the Wind Maker.

Ecclesiastes 2:11

Yet when I surveyed all that my hands had done and what I had toiled to achieve, everything was meaningless, a chasing after the wind; nothing was gained under the sun.

reflection

1 In what ways have you chased after something but found it meaningless?

2 What are some things "in your own backyard" that bring you joy?

3 When have you experienced a time of real contentment?

RELATED READINGS

Psalms 68:3; 84:1–12;
John 3:5–8;
1 Timothy 6:6–10

"*Many persons have a wrong idea of what constitutes true happiness. It is not attained through self-gratification but through fidelity to a worthy purpose.*"

Helen Adams Keller

Go to page 801 for your next devotional reading.

"The fate of the fool will overtake me
    also.
    What then do I gain by being wise?"
I said in my heart,
    "This too is meaningless."
16 For the wise man, like the fool, will not be
    long remembered;
    in days to come both will be forgotten.
Like the fool, the wise man too must die!

Toil Is Meaningless

17 So I hated life, because the work that is done under the sun was grievous to me. All of it is meaningless, a chasing after the wind. 18 I hated all the things I had toiled for under the sun, because I must leave them to the one who comes after me. 19 And who knows whether he will be a wise man or a fool? Yet he will have control over all the work into which I have poured my effort and skill under the sun. This too is meaningless. 20 So my heart began to despair over all my toilsome labor under the sun. 21 For a man may do his work with wisdom, knowledge and skill, and then he must leave all he owns to someone who has not worked for it. This too is meaningless and a great misfortune. 22 What does a man get for all the toil and anxious striving with which he labors under the sun? 23 All his days his work is pain and grief; even at night his mind does not rest. This too is meaningless.

24 A man can do nothing better than to eat and drink and find satisfaction in his work. This too, I see, is from the hand of God, 25 for without him, who can eat or find enjoyment? 26 To the man who pleases him, God gives wisdom, knowledge and happiness, but to the sinner he gives the task of gathering and storing up wealth to hand it over to the one who pleases God. This too is meaningless, a chasing after the wind.

A Time for Everything

3 There is a time for everything,
    and a season for every activity under
        heaven:

2   a time to be born and a time to die,
    a time to plant and a time to uproot,
3   a time to kill and a time to heal,
    a time to tear down and a time to build,
4   a time to weep and a time to laugh,
    a time to mourn and a time to dance,
5   a time to scatter stones and a time to
        gather them,
    a time to embrace and a time to refrain,
6   a time to search and a time to give up,
    a time to keep and a time to throw away,
7   a time to tear and a time to mend,
    a time to be silent and a time to speak,
8   a time to love and a time to hate,
    a time for war and a time for peace.

9 What does the worker gain from his toil? 10 I have seen the burden God has laid on men. 11 He has made everything beautiful in its time. He has also set eternity in the hearts of men; yet they cannot fathom what God has done from beginning to end. 12 I know that there is nothing better for men than to be happy and do good while they live. 13 That everyone may eat and drink, and find satisfaction in all his toil—this is the gift of God. 14 I know that everything God does will endure forever; nothing can be added to it and nothing taken from it. God does it so that men will revere him.

15 Whatever is has already
        been,
    and what will be has
        been before;
    and God will call the
        past to account.[a]

16 And I saw something else under the sun:
    In the place of judgment—
        wickedness was
        there,
    in the place of justice—
        wickedness was
        there.

17 I thought in my heart,

"God will bring to judgment
    both the righteous and the wicked,
for there will be a time for every activity,
    a time for every deed."

Ecclesiastes 2:24

God Provides Satisfaction

A man can do nothing better than to eat and drink and find satisfaction in his work. This too, I see, is from the hand of God.

---

[a] 15 Or *God calls back the past*

Power of Persuasion

JEZEBEL

"WHO'S GOING TO STOP ME?"

She didn't really expect anyone to respond. She already knew the answer. Sure, her husband was technically king. But all she had to do was make one comment, quip a phrase or even raise one of her pointed eyebrows, and she had his ear. Everyone in the palace, from the lowest servant to the highest official, knew who wore the royal pants in the family. She wasn't the most powerful woman in the land for nothing.

Keeping her husband in line was easy. In fact, with her persuasive talents, she wielded control over an entire kingdom to serve her religious ideals. She motivated some 850 pagan priests to do her bidding and ever-increase her influence. She came to be known as a woman who always got her way—and a woman dedicated to expanding the worship of Baal. Throughout her reign in the northern kingdom of Israel, she ensured that Baal worship flourished. She even convinced her husband to build a temple to Baal in Samaria, the capital.

However, her reign did not go unchallenged. "Those cursed God-fearing Israelites drive me mad," she would often say. Despite her many supporters, the opposition (no matter how small compared to her supporters) irritated her to no end. If someone questioned her, she had them arrested. If someone spoke against her, she silenced them. Permanently. Still, despite the numbers she persecuted, it seemed like more opponents cropped up every day. She heard rumors that there were those who had never worshiped Baal—and did not intend to.

Toward the end, she might have sensed her days were numbered and so became even more ravenously devoted to her cause, driven by a devilish force she may not have fully understood. And ironically, although she devoted herself to making an indelible impression on others for the sake of her cause, within moments of her death, not an earthly remnant of her remained.

—Prayer—

Jesus, give me strength to stand against evil. Give me wisdom to keep my heart pure.

There was never a man like Ahab, who sold himself to do evil in the eyes of the LORD, urged on by Jezebel his wife.

1 Kings 21:25

ASSIGNED READING:

1 Kings
16:29–33;
18:1—19:18;
21:1–29;
2 Kings 9:1–37

Weekend

Go to page 805 for your next devotional reading.

¹⁸I also thought, "As for men, God tests them so that they may see that they are like the animals. ¹⁹Man's fate is like that of the animals; the same fate awaits them both: As one dies, so dies the other. All have the same breath*a*; man has no advantage over the animal. Everything is meaningless. ²⁰All go to the same place; all come from dust, and to dust all return. ²¹Who knows if the spirit of man rises upward and if the spirit of the animal*b* goes down into the earth?"

²²So I saw that there is nothing better for a man than to enjoy his work, because that is his lot. For who can bring him to see what will happen after him?

Oppression, Toil, Friendlessness

4 Again I looked and saw all the oppression that was taking place under the sun:

I saw the tears of the oppressed—
    and they have no comforter;
power was on the side of their
        oppressors—
    and they have no comforter.
² And I declared that the dead,
    who had already died,
are happier than the living,
    who are still alive.
³ But better than both
    is he who has not yet been,
who has not seen the evil
    that is done under the sun.

⁴And I saw that all labor and all achievement spring from man's envy of his neighbor. This too is meaningless, a chasing after the wind.

⁵ The fool folds his hands
    and ruins himself.
⁶ Better one handful with tranquillity
    than two handfuls with toil
    and chasing after the wind.

⁷Again I saw something meaningless under the sun:

⁸ There was a man all alone;
    he had neither son nor brother.
There was no end to his toil,
    yet his eyes were not content with his
        wealth.

"For whom am I toiling," he asked,
    "and why am I depriving myself of
        enjoyment?"
This too is meaningless—
    a miserable business!

⁹ Two are better than one,
    because they have a good return for
        their work:
¹⁰ If one falls down,
    his friend can help him up.
But pity the man who falls
    and has no one to help him up!
¹¹ Also, if two lie down together, they will
        keep warm.
    But how can one keep warm alone?
¹² Though one may be overpowered,
    two can defend themselves.
A cord of three strands is not quickly
        broken.

Advancement Is Meaningless

¹³Better a poor but wise youth than an old but foolish king who no longer knows how to take warning. ¹⁴The youth may have come from prison to the kingship, or he may have been born in poverty within his kingdom. ¹⁵I saw that all who lived and walked under the sun followed the youth, the king's successor. ¹⁶There was no end to all the people who were before them. But those who came later were not pleased with the successor. This too is meaningless, a chasing after the wind.

Stand in Awe of God

5 Guard your steps when you go to the house of God. Go near to listen rather than to offer the sacrifice of fools, who do not know that they do wrong.

² Do not be quick with your mouth,
    do not be hasty in your heart
    to utter anything before God.
God is in heaven
    and you are on earth,
    so let your words be few.
³ As a dream comes when there are many
        cares,
    so the speech of a fool when there are
        many words.

a19 Or *spirit*   *b21* Or *Who knows the spirit of man, which rises upward, or the spirit of the animal, which*

⁴When you make a vow to God, do not delay in fulfilling it. He has no pleasure in fools; fulfill your vow. ⁵It is better not to vow than to make a vow and not fulfill it. ⁶Do not let your mouth lead you into sin. And do not protest to the temple messenger, "My vow was a mistake." Why should God be angry at what you say and destroy the work of your hands? ⁷Much dreaming and many words are meaningless. Therefore stand in awe of God.

Riches Are Meaningless

⁸If you see the poor oppressed in a district, and justice and rights denied, do not be surprised at such things; for one official is eyed by a higher one, and over them both are others higher still. ⁹The increase from the land is taken by all; the king himself profits from the fields.

¹⁰Whoever loves money never has money
    enough;
    whoever loves wealth is never satisfied
      with his income.
    This too is meaningless.

¹¹As goods increase,
    so do those who consume them.
    And what benefit are they to the owner
      except to feast his eyes on them?

¹²The sleep of a laborer is sweet,
    whether he eats little or much,
    but the abundance of a rich man
      permits him no sleep.

¹³I have seen a grievous evil under the sun:

wealth hoarded to the harm of its owner,
¹⁴   or wealth lost through some misfortune,
so that when he has a son
    there is nothing left for him.
¹⁵Naked a man comes from his mother's
    womb,
    and as he comes, so he departs.
He takes nothing from his labor
    that he can carry in his hand.

¹⁶This too is a grievous evil:

As a man comes, so he departs,
    and what does he gain,
    since he toils for the wind?
¹⁷All his days he eats in darkness,
    with great frustration, affliction and
    anger.

¹⁸Then I realized that it is good and proper for a man to eat and drink, and to find satisfaction in his toilsome labor under the sun during the few days of life God has given him—for this is his lot. ¹⁹Moreover, when God gives any man wealth and possessions, and enables him to enjoy them, to accept his lot and be happy in his work—this is a gift of God. ²⁰He seldom reflects on the days of his life, because God keeps him occupied with gladness of heart.

6 I have seen another evil under the sun, and it weighs heavily on men: ²God gives a man wealth, possessions and honor, so that he lacks nothing his heart desires, but God does not enable him to enjoy them, and a stranger enjoys them instead. This is meaningless, a grievous evil.

³A man may have a hundred children and live many years; yet no matter how long he lives, if he cannot enjoy his prosperity and does not receive proper burial, I say that a stillborn child is better off than he. ⁴It comes without meaning, it departs in darkness, and in darkness its name is shrouded. ⁵Though it never saw the sun or knew anything, it has more rest than does that man— ⁶even if he lives a thousand years twice over but fails to enjoy his prosperity. Do not all go to the same place?

⁷All man's efforts are for his mouth,
    yet his appetite is never satisfied.
⁸What advantage has a wise man
    over a fool?
What does a poor man gain
    by knowing how to conduct himself
      before others?
⁹Better what the eye sees
    than the roving of the appetite.
This too is meaningless,
    a chasing after the wind.

¹⁰Whatever exists has already been named,
    and what man is has been known;
no man can contend
    with one who is stronger than he.
¹¹The more the words,
    the less the meaning,
    and how does that profit anyone?

¹²For who knows what is good for a man in life, during the few and meaningless days he passes through like a shadow? Who can tell him what will happen under the sun after he is gone?

Wisdom

7 A good name is better
than fine perfume,
and the day of death
better than the day
of birth.
² It is better to go to a house
of mourning
than to go to a house of
feasting,
for death is the destiny of
every man;
the living should take
this to heart.
³ Sorrow is better than laughter,
because a sad face is good for the heart.
⁴ The heart of the wise is in the house of
mourning,
but the heart of fools is in the house of
pleasure.
⁵ It is better to heed a wise man's rebuke
than to listen to the song of fools.
⁶ Like the crackling of thorns under the pot,
so is the laughter of fools.
This too is meaningless.

⁷ Extortion turns a wise man into a fool,
and a bribe corrupts the heart.

⁸ The end of a matter is better than its
beginning,
and patience is better than pride.
⁹ Do not be quickly provoked in your spirit,
for anger resides in the lap of fools.

¹⁰ Do not say, "Why were the old days better
than these?"
For it is not wise to ask such questions.

¹¹ Wisdom, like an inheritance, is a good
thing
and benefits those who see the sun.
¹² Wisdom is a shelter
as money is a shelter,
but the advantage of knowledge is this:

that wisdom preserves the life of its
possessor.

¹³ Consider what God has done:

Who can straighten
what he has made
crooked?
¹⁴ When times are good, be
happy;
but when times are bad,
consider:
God has made the one
as well as the other.
Therefore, a man cannot
discover
anything about his
future.

¹⁵ In this meaningless life of
mine I have seen
both of these:

a righteous man perishing in his
righteousness,
and a wicked man living long in his
wickedness.
¹⁶ Do not be overrighteous,
neither be overwise—
why destroy yourself?
¹⁷ Do not be overwicked,
and do not be a fool—
why die before your time?
¹⁸ It is good to grasp the one
and not let go of the other.
The man who fears God will avoid all
extremes.ᵃ

¹⁹ Wisdom makes one wise man more
powerful
than ten rulers in a city.

²⁰ There is not a righteous man on earth
who does what is right and never sins.

²¹ Do not pay attention to every word people
say,
or you may hear your servant cursing
you—
²² for you know in your heart
that many times you yourself have
cursed others.

Ecclesiastes 7:13

God Is Omnipotent

Consider what God
has done:
Who can straighten
what he has made
crooked?

ᵃ 18 Or will follow them both

Remember the Good Ol' Days?

Read: Ecclesiastes 7:2–14

IT'S EASY TO THINK THE PAST was better than today. Most of us have selective memories. We only remember what we want to remember. We reminisce about our fun-loving college days but forget how we stayed up all night to study, subsisting on Ramen noodles and completely stressing out because no one had asked us to the upcoming party. We remember being single—enjoying the freedom to have ice cream for dinner—but forget how lonely we felt eating by ourselves. We recall our children as darling babies but don't remember how frustrated we were when the "terrible twos" hit.

You could make the case that it's good to forget the bad. However, when we look at the past through rose-colored glasses, we run the risk of being ungrateful for what we have right now. Rather than seeing today's gifts, we yearn for yesterday's fun and games, conveniently glossing over the past's difficulties.

Our days, months and years are made up of both good times and bad. The tapestry of life's events makes up the very essence of who we are. Think about today and the difficulties you are encountering: The laundry is piling up. The roof needs fixing. Your kids aren't listening to you. Now consider some of the memories you're making today: Your baby took his first steps. Your daughter graduated from kindergarten, high school or college. You got that big promotion. You finally started your own business.

Thank God for all your wonderful memories. Take the difficult things to God in prayer. Ask him what he wants you to learn from your present situation. God doesn't waste any of our experiences. He can use the good ol' days, as well as the not-so-great days, to benefit us, if we let him. The key is to remember things as they really were, to be content with things as they really are and to trust God to take care of the future.

Ecclesiastes 7:10,14

Do not say, "Why were the old days better than these?" For it is not wise to ask such questions...When times are good, be happy; but when times are bad, consider: God has made the one as well as the other. Therefore, a man cannot discover anything about his future.

reflection

1 Name some difficulties you've faced in the past. What good came out of them?

2 What difficulties are you facing right now? How might God use them for your good or the good of someone else?

3 Name some of the women you know who have used their difficulties to help others. How have they glorified God?

RELATED READINGS

Exodus 16:1–8;
Isaiah 40:28–31;
43:18–19

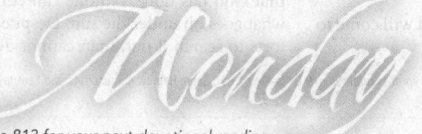

Go to page 813 for your next devotional reading.

23 All this I tested by wisdom and I said,

"I am determined to be wise"—
but this was beyond me.
24 Whatever wisdom may be,
it is far off and most profound—
who can discover it?
25 So I turned my mind to understand,
to investigate and to search out wisdom
and the scheme of things
and to understand the stupidity of
wickedness
and the madness of folly.

26 I find more bitter than death
the woman who is a snare,
whose heart is a trap
and whose hands are chains.
The man who pleases God will escape her,
but the sinner she will ensnare.

27 "Look," says the Teacher,[a] "this is what I
have discovered:

"Adding one thing to another to discover
the scheme of things—
28 while I was still searching
but not finding—
I found one upright man among a
thousand,
but not one upright woman among
them all.
29 This only have I found:
God made mankind upright,
but men have gone in search of many
schemes."

8 Who is like the wise man?
Who knows the explanation of things?
Wisdom brightens a man's face
and changes its hard appearance.

Obey the King

2 Obey the king's command, I say, because
you took an oath before God. 3 Do not be in a
hurry to leave the king's presence. Do not stand
up for a bad cause, for he will do whatever he
pleases. 4 Since a king's word is supreme, who
can say to him, "What are you doing?"

5 Whoever obeys his command will come to
no harm,

and the wise heart will know the proper
time and procedure.
6 For there is a proper time and procedure
for every matter,
though a man's misery weighs heavily
upon him.

7 Since no man knows the future,
who can tell him what is to come?
8 No man has power over the wind to
contain it[b];
so no one has power over the day of his
death.
As no one is discharged in time of war,
so wickedness will not release those who
practice it.

9 All this I saw, as I applied my mind to everything done under the sun. There is a time when
a man lords it over others to his own[c] hurt.
10 Then too, I saw the wicked buried—those
who used to come and go from the holy place
and receive praise[d] in the city where they did
this. This too is meaningless.

11 When the sentence for a crime is not
quickly carried out, the hearts of the people are
filled with schemes to do wrong. 12 Although
a wicked man commits a hundred crimes and
still lives a long time, I know that it will go better with God-fearing men, who are reverent before God. 13 Yet because the wicked do not fear
God, it will not go well with them, and their
days will not lengthen like a shadow.

14 There is something else meaningless that
occurs on earth: righteous men who get what
the wicked deserve, and wicked men who get
what the righteous deserve. This too, I say, is
meaningless. 15 So I commend the enjoyment
of life, because nothing is better for a man under the sun than to eat and drink and be glad.
Then joy will accompany him in his work all
the days of the life God has given him under
the sun.

16 When I applied my mind to know wisdom
and to observe man's labor on earth—his eyes
not seeing sleep day or night— 17 then I saw all
that God has done. No one can comprehend
what goes on under the sun. Despite all his efforts to search it out, man cannot discover its

---

a 27 Or leader of the assembly   b 8 Or over his spirit to retain it   c 9 Or to their   d 10 Some Hebrew manuscripts and Septuagint (Aquila);
most Hebrew manuscripts and are forgotten

meaning. Even if a wise man claims he knows, he cannot really comprehend it.

A Common Destiny for All

9 So I reflected on all this and concluded that the righteous and the wise and what they do are in God's hands, but no man knows whether love or hate awaits him. ²All share a common destiny—the righteous and the wicked, the good and the bad,*ᵃ* the clean and the unclean, those who offer sacrifices and those who do not.

As it is with the good man,
    so with the sinner;
as it is with those who take oaths,
    so with those who are afraid to take
        them.

³This is the evil in everything that happens under the sun: The same destiny overtakes all. The hearts of men, moreover, are full of evil and there is madness in their hearts while they live, and afterward they join the dead. ⁴Anyone who is among the living has hope*ᵇ*—even a live dog is better off than a dead lion!

⁵ For the living know that they will die,
    but the dead know nothing;
they have no further reward,
    and even the memory of them is
        forgotten.
⁶ Their love, their hate
    and their jealousy have long since
        vanished;
never again will they have a part
    in anything that happens under the sun.

⁷Go, eat your food with gladness, and drink your wine with a joyful heart, for it is now that God favors what you do. ⁸Always be clothed in white, and always anoint your head with oil. ⁹Enjoy life with your wife, whom you love, all the days of this meaningless life that God has given you under the sun—all your meaningless days. For this is your lot in life and in your toilsome labor under the sun. ¹⁰Whatever your hand finds to do, do it with all your might, for in the grave,*ᶜ* where you are going, there is neither working nor planning nor knowledge nor wisdom.

¹¹I have seen something else under the sun:

The race is not to the swift
    or the battle to the strong,
nor does food come to the wise
    or wealth to the brilliant
    or favor to the learned;
but time and chance happen to them all.

¹²Moreover, no man knows when his hour will come:

As fish are caught in a cruel net,
    or birds are taken in a snare,
so men are trapped by evil times
    that fall unexpectedly upon them.

Wisdom Better Than Folly

¹³I also saw under the sun this example of wisdom that greatly impressed me: ¹⁴There was once a small city with only a few people in it. And a powerful king came against it, surrounded it and built huge siegeworks against it. ¹⁵Now there lived in that city a man poor but wise, and he saved the city by his wisdom. But nobody remembered that poor man. ¹⁶So I said, "Wisdom is better than strength." But the poor man's wisdom is despised, and his words are no longer heeded.

¹⁷The quiet words of the wise are more to be
        heeded
    than the shouts of a ruler of fools.
¹⁸Wisdom is better than weapons of war,
    but one sinner destroys much good.

10 As dead flies give perfume a bad
        smell,
    so a little folly outweighs wisdom and
        honor.
²The heart of the wise inclines to the right,
    but the heart of the fool to the left.
³Even as he walks along the road,
    the fool lacks sense
    and shows everyone how stupid he is.
⁴If a ruler's anger rises against you,
    do not leave your post;
    calmness can lay great errors to rest.

⁵There is an evil I have seen under the sun,
    the sort of error that arises from a ruler:
⁶Fools are put in many high positions,

ᵃ2 Septuagint (Aquila), Vulgate and Syriac; Hebrew does not have *and the bad.*   *ᵇ4* Or *What then is to be chosen? With all who live, there is hope*   *ᶜ10* Hebrew *Sheol*

while the rich occupy the low ones.
⁷ I have seen slaves on horseback,
while princes go on foot like slaves.

⁸ Whoever digs a pit may fall into it;
whoever breaks through a wall may be
bitten by a snake.
⁹ Whoever quarries stones may be injured
by them;
whoever splits logs may be endangered
by them.

¹⁰ If the ax is dull
and its edge unsharpened,
more strength is needed
but skill will bring success.

¹¹ If a snake bites before it is charmed,
there is no profit for the charmer.

¹² Words from a wise man's mouth are
gracious,
but a fool is consumed by his own lips.
¹³ At the beginning his words are folly;
at the end they are wicked madness—
¹⁴ and the fool multiplies words.

No one knows what is coming—
who can tell him what will happen after
him?

¹⁵ A fool's work wearies him;
he does not know the way to town.

¹⁶ Woe to you, O land whose king was a
servant[a]
and whose princes feast in the morning.
¹⁷ Blessed are you, O land whose king is of
noble birth
and whose princes eat at a proper time—
for strength and not for drunkenness.

¹⁸ If a man is lazy, the rafters sag;
if his hands are idle, the house leaks.

¹⁹ A feast is made for laughter,
and wine makes life merry,
but money is the answer for everything.

²⁰ Do not revile the king even in your
thoughts,
or curse the rich in your bedroom,
because a bird of the air may carry your
words,

and a bird on the wing may report what
you say.

Bread Upon the Waters

11 Cast your bread upon the waters,
for after many days you will find it
again.
² Give portions to seven, yes to eight,
for you do not know what disaster may
come upon the land.

³ If clouds are full of water,
they pour rain upon the earth.
Whether a tree falls to the south or to the
north,
in the place where it falls, there will it lie.
⁴ Whoever watches the wind will not plant;
whoever looks at the clouds will not
reap.

⁵ As you do not know the path of the wind,
or how the body is formed[b] in a
mother's womb,
so you cannot understand the work of
God,
the Maker of all things.

⁶ Sow your seed in the morning,
and at evening let not your hands be
idle,
for you do not know which will succeed,
whether this or that,
or whether both will do equally well.

Remember Your Creator While Young

⁷ Light is sweet,
and it pleases the eyes to see the sun.
⁸ However many years a man may live,
let him enjoy them all.
But let him remember the days of
darkness,
for they will be many.
Everything to come is meaningless.

⁹ Be happy, young man, while you are
young,
and let your heart give you joy in the
days of your youth.
Follow the ways of your heart
and whatever your eyes see,
but know that for all these things
God will bring you to judgment.

---

a16 Or *king is a child*   *b5* Or *know how life* (or *the spirit*) / *enters the body being formed*

¹⁰So then, banish anxiety from your heart
   and cast off the troubles of your body,
   for youth and vigor are meaningless.

12 Remember your Creator
      in the days of your youth,
   before the days of trouble come
   and the years approach when you will
      say,
   "I find no pleasure in them"—
²before the sun and the light
   and the moon and the stars grow dark,
   and the clouds return after the rain;
³when the keepers of the house tremble,
   and the strong men stoop,
   when the grinders cease because they are
      few,
   and those looking through the windows
      grow dim;
⁴when the doors to the street are closed
   and the sound of grinding fades;
   when men rise up at the sound of birds,
   but all their songs grow faint;
⁵when men are afraid of heights
   and of dangers in the
      streets;
   when the almond tree
      blossoms
   and the grasshopper
      drags himself along
   and desire no longer is
      stirred.
   Then man goes to his
      eternal home
   and mourners go about
      the streets.

⁶Remember him—before
   the silver cord is
   severed,

or the golden bowl is broken;
   before the pitcher is shattered at the
      spring,
   or the wheel broken at the well,
⁷and the dust returns to the ground it
      came from,
   and the spirit returns to God who
      gave it.

⁸"Meaningless! Meaningless!" says the
      Teacher.*a*
   "Everything is meaningless!"

The Conclusion of the Matter

⁹Not only was the Teacher wise, but also
he imparted knowledge to the people. He pondered and searched out and set in order many
proverbs. ¹⁰The Teacher searched to find just
the right words, and what he wrote was upright
and true.

¹¹The words of the wise are like goads, their
collected sayings like firmly embedded nails—
given by one Shepherd. ¹²Be warned, my son,
of anything in addition to them.

   Of making many books
there is no end, and much
study wearies the body.

¹³Now all has been heard;
      here is the conclusion of
      the matter:
   Fear God and keep his
      commandments,
   for this is the whole
      ˻duty˼ of man.
¹⁴For God will bring every
      deed into judgment,
      including every hidden
      thing,
   whether it is good or evil.

Ecclesiastes 12:14

*God Exposes
Secrets*

For God will bring every
deed into judgment,
including every
hidden thing,
whether it is good or evil.

---

a8 Or the leader of the assembly; also in verses 9 and 10

Song of Songs

Author:
Probably King Solomon.

Audience:
All Israel.

Date:
Most likely early in Solomon's reign, around 965 B.C.

Setting:
Storybook romance and steamy dialogue between two God-fearing, passionate lovers.

Verse to Remember:
Many waters cannot quench love; rivers cannot wash it away. If one were to give all the wealth of his house for love, it would be utterly scorned. (8:7)

What's *that* book doing in the Bible? Song of Songs is anything but the typical book of Scripture. A love song that ranges from the softly romantic to the wildly erotic, *Song of Songs celebrates the gift* of marital love. Readers are cautioned not to "arouse or awaken love" too early. But for this husband and wife, much joy is to be found in their private, tender love. They kiss and caress and whisper to each other. They belong to each other, rejoice in each other and brag on each other. Many of the metaphors for the lovers' beauty are agricultural and may sound unusual to our ears, but the love and desire translate into any culture.

Not only did God create marriage, but the inclusion of this book in Scripture says that he rejoices in married love and wants his people to rejoice in it too.

---

1 Solomon's Song of Songs.

Beloved[a]

2 Let him kiss me with the kisses of his mouth—
    for your love is more delightful than wine.
3 Pleasing is the fragrance of your perfumes;
    your name is like perfume poured out.
    No wonder the maidens love you!
4 Take me away with you—let us hurry!
    Let the king bring me into his chambers.

Friends

    We rejoice and delight in you[b];
    we will praise your love more than wine.

[a]Primarily on the basis of the gender of the Hebrew pronouns used, male and female speakers are indicated in the margins by the captions *Lover* and *Beloved* respectively. The words of others are marked *Friends*. In some instances the divisions and their captions are debatable.
[b]4 The Hebrew is masculine singular.

Beloved

How right they are to adore you!

5 Dark am I, yet lovely,
  O daughters of Jerusalem,
  dark like the tents of Kedar,
  like the tent curtains of Solomon.*a*

6 Do not stare at me because I am dark,
  because I am darkened by the sun.
  My mother's sons were angry with me
  and made me take care of the vineyards;
  my own vineyard I have neglected.

7 Tell me, you whom I love, where you graze
    your flock
  and where you rest your sheep at midday.
  Why should I be like a veiled woman
  beside the flocks of your friends?

Friends

8 If you do not know, most beautiful of
    women,
  follow the tracks of the sheep
  and graze your young goats
  by the tents of the shepherds.

Lover

9 I liken you, my darling, to a mare
  harnessed to one of the chariots of
    Pharaoh.

10 Your cheeks are beautiful with earrings,
  your neck with strings of jewels.

11 We will make you earrings of gold,
  studded with silver.

Beloved

12 While the king was at his table,
  my perfume spread its fragrance.

13 My lover is to me a sachet of myrrh
  resting between my breasts.

14 My lover is to me a cluster of henna
    blossoms
  from the vineyards of En Gedi.

Lover

15 How beautiful you are, my darling!
  Oh, how beautiful!
  Your eyes are doves.

Beloved

16 How handsome you are, my lover!
  Oh, how charming!
  And our bed is verdant.

Lover

17 The beams of our house are cedars;
  our rafters are firs.

Belovedb

2 I am a rose*c* of Sharon,
  a lily of the valleys.

Lover

2 Like a lily among thorns
  is my darling among the maidens.

Beloved

3 Like an apple tree among the trees of the
    forest
  is my lover among the young men.
  I delight to sit in his shade,
  and his fruit is sweet to my taste.

4 He has taken me to the banquet hall,
  and his banner over me is love.

5 Strengthen me with raisins,
  refresh me with apples,
  for I am faint with love.

6 His left arm is under my head,
  and his right arm embraces me.

7 Daughters of Jerusalem, I charge you
  by the gazelles and by the does of the
    field:
  Do not arouse or awaken love
  until it so desires.

8 Listen! My lover!
  Look! Here he comes,
  leaping across the mountains,
  bounding over the hills.

9 My lover is like a gazelle or a young stag.
  Look! There he stands behind our wall,
  gazing through the windows,
  peering through the lattice.

10 My lover spoke and said to me,
  "Arise, my darling,
  my beautiful one, and come with me.

11 See! The winter is past;
  the rains are over and gone.

12 Flowers appear on the earth;
  the season of singing has come,
  the cooing of doves
  is heard in our land.

13 The fig tree forms its early fruit;
  the blossoming vines spread their
    fragrance.

---

*a*5 Or *Salma* *b*Or *Lover* *c*1 Possibly a member of the crocus family

Arise, come, my darling;
  my beautiful one, come with me."

Lover

14 My dove in the clefts of the rock,
    in the hiding places on the
      mountainside,
  show me your face,
    let me hear your voice;
  for your voice is sweet,
    and your face is lovely.
15 Catch for us the foxes,
    the little foxes
  that ruin the vineyards,
    our vineyards that are in bloom.

Beloved

16 My lover is mine and I am
    his;
  he browses among the
    lilies.
17 Until the day breaks
    and the shadows flee,
  turn, my lover,
    and be like a gazelle
  or like a young stag
    on the rugged hills.*a*

3 All night long on my bed
    I looked for the one my
      heart loves;
  I looked for him but did not find him.
2 I will get up now and go about the city,
    through its streets and squares;
  I will search for the one my heart loves.
  So I looked for him but did not find him.
3 The watchmen found me
    as they made their rounds in the city.
  "Have you seen the one my heart loves?"
4 Scarcely had I passed them
    when I found the one my heart loves.
  I held him and would not let him go
    till I had brought him to my mother's
      house,
    to the room of the one who conceived
      me.
5 Daughters of Jerusalem, I charge you
    by the gazelles and by the does of the
      field:
  Do not arouse or awaken love
    until it so desires.

6 Who is this coming up from the desert
    like a column of smoke,
  perfumed with myrrh and incense
    made from all the spices of the
      merchant?
7 Look! It is Solomon's carriage,
    escorted by sixty warriors,
    the noblest of Israel,
8 all of them wearing the sword,
    all experienced in battle,
  each with his sword at his side,
    prepared for the terrors of the night.
9 King Solomon made for himself the
    carriage;
  he made it of wood from Lebanon.
10 Its posts he made of silver,
      its base of gold.
    Its seat was upholstered
      with purple,
    its interior lovingly
      inlaid
    by*b* the daughters of
      Jerusalem.
11 Come out, you daughters of
      Zion,
    and look at King
      Solomon wearing
      the crown,
  the crown with which his mother
    crowned him
  on the day of his wedding,
    the day his heart rejoiced.

Lover

4 How beautiful you are, my darling!
    Oh, how beautiful!
  Your eyes behind your veil are doves.
  Your hair is like a flock of goats
    descending from Mount Gilead.
2 Your teeth are like a flock of sheep just
    shorn,
    coming up from the washing.
  Each has its twin;
    not one of them is alone.
3 Your lips are like a scarlet ribbon;
    your mouth is lovely.
  Your temples behind your veil
    are like the halves of a pomegranate.
4 Your neck is like the tower of David,
    built with elegance*c*;

Song of Songs 2:16

*God Has
Affection for Us*

My lover is mine
and I am his.

---

*a*17 Or *the hills of Bether*   *b*10 Or *its inlaid interior a gift of love / from*   *c*4 The meaning of the Hebrew for this word is uncertain.

Picture Perfect Bride

Read: Song of Songs 4:1–16

OURS WAS A WEDDING unlike any other, I'm sure . . .

When the organ music began, I wheeled toward the door, stopping for a moment in front of a full-length mirror. I looked a little like a float in the Rose Parade.

The glass doors of the sanctuary opened, and I positioned myself at the top of the aisle, breathing deeply to steady my nerves. Daddy looked resplendent in his gray morning suit and a Windsor cravat. I'd never seen him so formally attired, nor he me. He smiled in a way that told me, *You're not my little pal anymore, not my cowgirl. And I'm glad.*

I leaned toward his ear, and above the organ music I explained in a loud whisper that I would wheel slowly so he could keep up with me. He handed Judy one of his crutches and held onto the armrest of my chair for support.

"You're marrying a good one, honey-girl," he told me . . .

Just before the wedding march began, I looked down at my gown. *Aaugh!* I groaned—I had wheeled over the hem and left a huge, greasy tire mark. It didn't help that my dress hung clumped and uneven. And even though my chair was spiffed up, the wheels and gears were still visible through the wire mesh. My bouquet of daisies was off center on my lap, because my hands couldn't hold them. I was not a picture perfect bride.

As my last bridesmaid finished her walk, the organ pipes crescendoed, and I inched my chair closer to the last pew, wanting to catch a glimpse of Ken. Suddenly, I spotted him down front, standing at attention and looking tall and elegant in his tuxedo. I looked down, my face hot and my heart pounding. It was a flush of nerves I'd never felt before. When I looked up again, I saw him craning to look up the aisle, to find me. Our eyes met, and—it was amazing—from that point, everything changed.

How I looked no longer mattered. I forgot all about my wheelchair. Grease stains? Flowers? No longer did I feel ugly or unworthy. The love in Ken's eyes washed it all away. I was the pure and perfect bride—his bride. That's what he saw, and that's what changed me.

—Joni Eareckson Tada

Song of Songs 4:9

You have stolen my heart, my sister, my bride; you have stolen my heart with one glance of your eyes, with one jewel of your necklace.

reflection

1 Think about a wedding you witnessed. How did everything else fade away once the bride and groom saw one another face-to-face?

2 Does it surprise you that God takes such delight in marriages? Why or why not?

3 What especially moved you about Joni's story? How have you felt ugly or unworthy in your life? How has the love of another person (a friend, relative, child or spouse) changed that? How has God's love changed your life?

RELATED READINGS

Genesis 2:18–25;
1 Corinthians 13:1–13;
Ephesians 5:21–33

Go to page 817 for your next devotional reading.

on it hang a thousand shields,
    all of them shields of warriors.
⁵ Your two breasts are like two fawns,
    like twin fawns of a gazelle
    that browse among the lilies.
⁶ Until the day breaks
    and the shadows flee,
  I will go to the mountain of myrrh
    and to the hill of incense.
⁷ All beautiful you are, my darling;
    there is no flaw in you.

⁸ Come with me from Lebanon, my bride,
    come with me from Lebanon.
  Descend from the crest of Amana,
    from the top of Senir, the summit of
        Hermon,
  from the lions' dens
    and the mountain haunts of the
        leopards.
⁹ You have stolen my heart, my sister, my
        bride;
    you have stolen my heart
  with one glance of your eyes,
    with one jewel of your necklace.
¹⁰ How delightful is your love, my sister, my
        bride!
    How much more pleasing is your love
        than wine,
    and the fragrance of your perfume than
        any spice!
¹¹ Your lips drop sweetness as the
        honeycomb, my bride;
    milk and honey are under your tongue.
  The fragrance of your garments is like
        that of Lebanon.
¹² You are a garden locked up, my sister, my
        bride;
    you are a spring enclosed, a sealed
        fountain.
¹³ Your plants are an orchard of
        pomegranates
    with choice fruits,
    with henna and nard,
¹⁴   nard and saffron,
    calamus and cinnamon,
  with every kind of incense tree,
    with myrrh and aloes
    and all the finest spices.

¹⁵ You are[a] a garden fountain,
    a well of flowing water
    streaming down from Lebanon.

Beloved
¹⁶ Awake, north wind,
    and come, south wind!
  Blow on my garden,
    that its fragrance may spread abroad.
  Let my lover come into his garden
    and taste its choice fruits.

Lover
5 I have come into my garden, my sister,
        my bride;
    I have gathered my myrrh with my
        spice.
  I have eaten my honeycomb and my honey;
    I have drunk my wine and my milk.

Friends
  Eat, O friends, and drink;
    drink your fill, O lovers.

Beloved
² I slept but my heart was awake.
    Listen! My lover is knocking:
  "Open to me, my sister, my darling,
    my dove, my flawless one.
  My head is drenched with dew,
    my hair with the dampness of the
        night."
³ I have taken off my robe—
    must I put it on again?
  I have washed my feet—
    must I soil them again?
⁴ My lover thrust his hand through the
        latch-opening;
    my heart began to pound for him.
⁵ I arose to open for my lover,
    and my hands dripped with myrrh,
  my fingers with flowing myrrh,
    on the handles of the lock.
⁶ I opened for my lover,
    but my lover had left; he was gone.
    My heart sank at his departure.[b]
  I looked for him but did not find him.
    I called him but he did not answer.
⁷ The watchmen found me
    as they made their rounds in the city.
  They beat me, they bruised me;

---

*a*15 Or *I am* (spoken by the *Beloved*)   *b*6 Or *heart had gone out to him when he spoke*

they took away my cloak,
those watchmen of the walls!
⁸ O daughters of Jerusalem, I charge you—
if you find my lover,
what will you tell him?
Tell him I am faint with love.

Friends

⁹ How is your beloved better than others,
most beautiful of women?
How is your beloved better than others,
that you charge us so?

Beloved

¹⁰ My lover is radiant and ruddy,
outstanding among ten thousand.
¹¹ His head is purest gold;
his hair is wavy
and black as a raven.
¹² His eyes are like doves
by the water streams,
washed in milk,
mounted like jewels.
¹³ His cheeks are like beds of spice
yielding perfume.
His lips are like lilies
dripping with myrrh.
¹⁴ His arms are rods of gold
set with chrysolite.
His body is like polished ivory
decorated with sapphires.ᵃ
¹⁵ His legs are pillars of marble
set on bases of pure gold.
His appearance is like Lebanon,
choice as its cedars.
¹⁶ His mouth is sweetness itself;
he is altogether lovely.
This is my lover, this my friend,
O daughters of Jerusalem.

Friends

6 Where has your lover gone,
most beautiful of women?
Which way did your lover turn,
that we may look for him with you?

Beloved

² My lover has gone down to his garden,
to the beds of spices,
to browse in the gardens
and to gather lilies.

³ I am my lover's and my lover is mine;
he browses among the lilies.

Lover

⁴ You are beautiful, my darling, as Tirzah,
lovely as Jerusalem,
majestic as troops with banners.
⁵ Turn your eyes from me;
they overwhelm me.
Your hair is like a flock of goats
descending from Gilead.
⁶ Your teeth are like a flock of sheep
coming up from the washing.
Each has its twin,
not one of them is alone.
⁷ Your temples behind your veil
are like the halves of a pomegranate.
⁸ Sixty queens there may be,
and eighty concubines,
and virgins beyond number;
⁹ but my dove, my perfect one, is unique,
the only daughter of her mother,
the favorite of the one who bore her.
The maidens saw her and called her blessed;
the queens and concubines praised her.

Friends

¹⁰ Who is this that appears like the dawn,
fair as the moon, bright as the sun,
majestic as the stars in procession?

Lover

¹¹ I went down to the grove of nut trees
to look at the new growth in the valley,
to see if the vines had budded
or the pomegranates were in bloom.
¹² Before I realized it,
my desire set me among the royal
chariots of my people.ᵇ

Friends

¹³ Come back, come back, O Shulammite;
come back, come back, that we may gaze
on you!

Lover

Why would you gaze on the Shulammite
as on the dance of Mahanaim?

7 How beautiful your sandaled feet,
O prince's daughter!
Your graceful legs are like jewels,

ᵃ14 Or *lapis lazuli* ᵇ12 Or *among the chariots of Amminadab; or among the chariots of the people of the prince*

the work of a craftsman's hands.
² Your navel is a rounded goblet
that never lacks blended wine.
Your waist is a mound of wheat
encircled by lilies.
³ Your breasts are like two fawns,
twins of a gazelle.
⁴ Your neck is like an ivory tower.
Your eyes are the pools of Heshbon
by the gate of Bath Rabbim.
Your nose is like the tower of Lebanon
looking toward Damascus.
⁵ Your head crowns you like Mount Carmel.
Your hair is like royal tapestry;
the king is held captive by its tresses.
⁶ How beautiful you are and how pleasing,
O love, with your delights!
⁷ Your stature is like that of the palm,
and your breasts like clusters of fruit.
⁸ I said, "I will climb the palm tree;
I will take hold of its fruit."
May your breasts be like the clusters of the
vine,
the fragrance of your
breath like apples,
⁹ and your mouth like the
best wine.

Beloved

May the wine go straight to
my lover,
flowing gently over lips
and teeth.ᵃ
¹⁰ I belong to my lover,
and his desire is for me.
¹¹ Come, my lover, let us go to
the countryside,
let us spend the night in
the villages.ᵇ
¹² Let us go early to the
vineyards
to see if the vines have budded,
if their blossoms have opened,
and if the pomegranates are in bloom—
there I will give you my love.
¹³ The mandrakes send out their fragrance,
and at our door is every delicacy,
both new and old,
that I have stored up for you, my lover.

8 If only you were to me like a brother,
who was nursed at my mother's breasts!
Then, if I found you outside,
I would kiss you,
and no one would despise me.
² I would lead you
and bring you to my mother's house—
she who has taught me.
I would give you spiced wine to drink,
the nectar of my pomegranates.
³ His left arm is under my head
and his right arm embraces me.
⁴ Daughters of Jerusalem, I charge you:
Do not arouse or awaken love
until it so desires.

Friends

⁵ Who is this coming up from the desert
leaning on her lover?

Beloved

Under the apple tree I roused you;
there your mother conceived you,
there she who was in
labor gave you
birth.
⁶ Place me like a seal over
your heart,
like a seal on your arm;
for love is as strong as
death,
its jealousyᶜ unyielding
as the grave.ᵈ
It burns like blazing fire,
like a mighty flame.ᵉ
⁷ Many waters cannot
quench love;
rivers cannot wash it
away.
If one were to give
all the wealth of his
house for love,
itᶠ would be utterly scorned.

Friends

⁸ We have a young sister,
and her breasts are not yet grown.
What shall we do for our sister
for the day she is spoken for?
⁹ If she is a wall,

> **Song of Songs 8:6**
>
> *God Gives*
> *Unyielding Love*
>
> For love is as strong
> as death,
> its jealousy unyielding
> as the grave.
> It burns like
> blazing fire,
> like a mighty flame.

ᵃ9 Septuagint, Aquila, Vulgate and Syriac; Hebrew *lips of sleepers*   ᵇ11 Or *henna bushes*   ᶜ6 Or *ardor*   ᵈ6 Hebrew *Sheol*   ᵉ6 Or / *like the very flame of the* LORD   ᶠ7 Or *he*

The Strongest Love

Read: Song of Songs 8:1–7

FROM *ROMEO AND JULIET* to the movie *Titanic*, books, films and stories tell us that there is a love that is great enough to die for. Many women would say their greatest earthly desire is for true intimacy with a man—not a vague commitment or wishy-washy affection. Some might say they want a love worth dying for. Maybe you feel the same way. In fact, if you are honest, on many days you long more for the affirmation and passion of a husband or boyfriend than you ache for the love of God.

God is love—even your desire for love points to him as the source of all love. The love between a man and a woman is a beautiful reflection of God's love, but you only desire that kind of love because God has placed that desire in you.

The Song of Songs presents a picture of love between a man and a woman that reflects the love of God. God doesn't love you at a distance or remember you as an afterthought. Look at the words used to express his love: *seal, strong, unyielding, blazing* and *unquenchable*. He loves everything about you, the way you walk, talk, laugh and brush your hair. He loves you in more ways than you can ever know because he knows you through and through. He knows your thoughts, when you sit, when you rise and when you lie down (see Psalm 139).

God wants you to believe that he loves you! He doesn't put conditions on his love. He only asks that you respond to his love: "Place me like a seal over your heart." Imagine God saying to you, "*I love you so much that I want to be with you intimately, at all times.*" God loves you with the strongest love imaginable—a love that is as strong as death. In fact, he proved his love through Christ's sacrifice on the cross. This ultimate gift showed us that his love for us was, in fact, a love worth dying for.

Song of Songs 8:6

Place me like a seal over your heart, like a seal on your arm; for love is as strong as death, its jealousy unyielding as the grave. It burns like blazing fire, like a mighty flame.

reflection

1 What keeps you from believing and fully accepting God's love?

2 How would your thoughts and actions be different this week if you fully believed that God loved you?

3 Read Psalm 139. Memorize as much of it as you can. How does it change your view of yourself to realize how intimately God knows you and loves you?

RELATED READINGS

Psalm 136:1–26;
Ephesians 3:14–19;
1 John 4:7–12

"There is no need to plead that the love of God shall fill our heart as though he were unwilling to fill us. He is willing as light is willing to flood a room that is opened to its brightness."

Amy Carmichael

Go to page 826 for your next devotional reading.

we will build towers of silver on her.
If she is a door,
we will enclose her with panels of cedar.

Beloved

10 I am a wall,
and my breasts are like towers.
Thus I have become in his eyes
like one bringing contentment.
11 Solomon had a vineyard in Baal Hamon;
he let out his vineyard to tenants.
Each was to bring for its fruit
a thousand shekels[a] of silver.
12 But my own vineyard is mine to give;

the thousand shekels are for you,
O Solomon,
and two hundred[b] are for those who
tend its fruit.

Lover

13 You who dwell in the gardens
with friends in attendance,
let me hear your voice!

Beloved

14 Come away, my lover,
and be like a gazelle
or like a young stag
on the spice-laden mountains.

---

[a] 11 That is, about 25 pounds (about 11.5 kilograms); also in verse 12   [b] 12 That is, about 5 pounds (about 2.3 kilograms)

Isaiah

When God chose Israel to be his own people, he told them plainly that *they were to worship him alone*. But the people failed to obey. They worshiped false gods, and though God repeatedly warned them to return to him, they stubbornly clung to their idols and pagan alliances.

Isaiah paints in bold strokes the sins of a people who had *denied their allegiance to God*. In equally bold strokes is the response that God's holiness demands. But the picture is not painted in black and white. It is in full color, complete with shadings and depths that reach far into the future. Yes, *God would judge* his people. But he would do more than that. He would redeem them. In the darkest place of judgment, *the light of a Redeemer still shines through*.

The book of Isaiah has been described as a condensed version of the Bible, for it captures the essence of both the Old and New Testaments. Through Isaiah's poetic words we see that God is both loving and just, a shepherd and a warrior. And above all, he is a holy God who loves his people and *will go to any lengths to redeem them*.

Author:
Isaiah.

Audience:
Judah, Israel, surrounding pagan nations.

Date:
Between 701 and 681 B.C.

Setting:
Judgment is on the horizon for Judah as the Assyrians threaten to overtake them.

Verse to Remember:
"Though the mountains be shaken and the hills be removed, yet my unfailing love for you will not be shaken nor my covenant of peace be removed," says the LORD, who has compassion on you. (54:10)

1

The vision concerning Judah and Jerusalem that Isaiah son of Amoz saw during the reigns of Uzziah, Jotham, Ahaz and Hezekiah, kings of Judah.

A Rebellious Nation

² Hear, O heavens! Listen, O earth!
  For the LORD has spoken:
"I reared children and brought them up,

but they have rebelled against me.
³ The ox knows his master,
  the donkey his owner's manger,
but Israel does not know,
  my people do not understand."

⁴ Ah, sinful nation,
  a people loaded with guilt,
a brood of evildoers,
  children given to corruption!
They have forsaken the Lord;
  they have spurned the Holy One of
    Israel
  and turned their backs on him.

⁵ Why should you be beaten anymore?
  Why do you persist in rebellion?
Your whole head is injured,
  your whole heart afflicted.
⁶ From the sole of your foot to the top of
    your head
  there is no soundness—
only wounds and welts
  and open sores,
not cleansed or bandaged
  or soothed with oil.

⁷ Your country is desolate,
  your cities burned with fire;
your fields are being stripped by foreigners
  right before you,
  laid waste as when overthrown by
    strangers.
⁸ The Daughter of Zion is left
  like a shelter in a vineyard,
like a hut in a field of melons,
  like a city under siege.
⁹ Unless the Lord Almighty
  had left us some survivors,
we would have become like Sodom,
  we would have been like Gomorrah.

¹⁰ Hear the word of the Lord,
  you rulers of Sodom;
listen to the law of our God,
  you people of Gomorrah!
¹¹ "The multitude of your sacrifices—
  what are they to me?" says the Lord.
"I have more than enough of burnt
    offerings,
  of rams and the fat of fattened animals;

I have no pleasure
  in the blood of bulls and lambs and
    goats.
¹² When you come to appear before me,
  who has asked this of you,
  this trampling of my courts?
¹³ Stop bringing meaningless offerings!
  Your incense is detestable to me.
New Moons, Sabbaths and convocations—
  I cannot bear your evil assemblies.
¹⁴ Your New Moon festivals and your
    appointed feasts
  my soul hates.
They have become a burden to me;
  I am weary of bearing them.
¹⁵ When you spread out your hands in prayer,
  I will hide my eyes from you;
even if you offer many prayers,
  I will not listen.
Your hands are full of blood;
¹⁶   wash and make yourselves clean.
Take your evil deeds
  out of my sight!
Stop doing wrong,
¹⁷   learn to do right!
Seek justice,
  encourage the oppressed.ᵃ
Defend the cause of the fatherless,
  plead the case of the widow.

¹⁸ "Come now, let us reason together,"
  says the Lord.
"Though your sins are like scarlet,
  they shall be as white as snow;
though they are red as crimson,
  they shall be like wool.
¹⁹ If you are willing and obedient,
  you will eat the best from the land;
²⁰ but if you resist and rebel,
  you will be devoured by the sword."
    For the mouth of the Lord has spoken.

²¹ See how the faithful city
  has become a harlot!
She once was full of justice;
  righteousness used to dwell in her—
  but now murderers!
²² Your silver has become dross,
  your choice wine is diluted with water.
²³ Your rulers are rebels,

ᵃ17 Or / rebuke the oppressor

companions of thieves;
they all love bribes
and chase after gifts.
They do not defend the cause of the
fatherless;
the widow's case does not come before
them.
24 Therefore the Lord, the LORD Almighty,
the Mighty One of Israel, declares:
"Ah, I will get relief from my foes
and avenge myself on my enemies.
25 I will turn my hand against you;
I will thoroughly purge away your dross
and remove all your impurities.
26 I will restore your judges as in days of old,
your counselors as at the beginning.
Afterward you will be called
the City of Righteousness,
the Faithful City."

27 Zion will be redeemed with justice,
her penitent ones with righteousness.
28 But rebels and sinners will both be broken,
and those who forsake the LORD will
perish.

29 "You will be ashamed because of the sacred
oaks
in which you have delighted;
you will be disgraced because of the
gardens
that you have chosen.
30 You will be like an oak with
fading leaves,
like a garden without
water.
31 The mighty man will
become tinder
and his work a spark;
both will burn together,
with no one to quench
the fire."

The Mountain of the LORD

2 This is what Isaiah son of Amoz saw concerning Judah and Jerusalem:

2 In the last days

the mountain of the LORD's temple will be
established

as chief among the mountains;
it will be raised above the hills,
and all nations will stream to it.

3 Many peoples will come and say,

"Come, let us go up to the mountain of the
LORD,
to the house of the God of Jacob.
He will teach us his ways,
so that we may walk in his paths."
The law will go out from Zion,
the word of the LORD from Jerusalem.
4 He will judge between the nations
and will settle disputes for many peoples.
They will beat their swords into plowshares
and their spears into pruning hooks.
Nation will not take up sword against
nation,
nor will they train for war anymore.

5 Come, O house of Jacob,
let us walk in the light of the LORD.

The Day of the LORD

6 You have abandoned your people,
the house of Jacob.
They are full of superstitions from the East;
they practice divination like the
Philistines
and clasp hands with
pagans.
7 Their land is full of silver
and gold;
there is no end to their
treasures.
Their land is full of horses;
there is no end to their
chariots.
8 Their land is full of idols;
they bow down to the
work of their hands,
to what their fingers have
made.

Isaiah 2:10

God Is Majestic

Go into the rocks,
hide in the ground
from dread of the LORD
and the splendor
of his majesty!

9 So man will be brought low
and mankind humbled—
do not forgive them.[a]

10 Go into the rocks,
hide in the ground
from dread of the LORD

---

a 9 Or not raise them up

and the splendor of his majesty!
¹¹ The eyes of the arrogant man will be
humbled
and the pride of men brought low;
the LORD alone will be exalted in that day.

¹² The LORD Almighty has a day in store
for all the proud and lofty,
for all that is exalted
(and they will be humbled),
¹³ for all the cedars of Lebanon, tall and lofty,
and all the oaks of Bashan,
¹⁴ for all the towering mountains
and all the high hills,
¹⁵ for every lofty tower
and every fortified wall,
¹⁶ for every trading ship*a*
and every stately vessel.
¹⁷ The arrogance of man will be brought low
and the pride of men humbled;
the LORD alone will be exalted in that day,
¹⁸ and the idols will totally disappear.

¹⁹ Men will flee to caves in the rocks
and to holes in the ground
from dread of the LORD
and the splendor of his majesty,
when he rises to shake the earth.
²⁰ In that day men will throw away
to the rodents and bats
their idols of silver and idols of gold,
which they made to worship.
²¹ They will flee to caverns in the rocks
and to the overhanging crags
from dread of the LORD
and the splendor of his majesty,
when he rises to shake the earth.

²² Stop trusting in man,
who has but a breath in his nostrils.
Of what account is he?

Judgment on Jerusalem and Judah

3 See now, the Lord,
the LORD Almighty,
is about to take from Jerusalem and Judah
both supply and support:
all supplies of food and all supplies of
water,
² the hero and warrior,
the judge and prophet,

the soothsayer and elder,
³ the captain of fifty and man of rank,
the counselor, skilled craftsman and
clever enchanter.

⁴ I will make boys their officials;
mere children will govern them.
⁵ People will oppress each other—
man against man, neighbor against
neighbor.
The young will rise up against the old,
the base against the honorable.

⁶ A man will seize one of his brothers
at his father's home, and say,
"You have a cloak, you be our leader;
take charge of this heap of ruins!"
⁷ But in that day he will cry out,
"I have no remedy.
I have no food or clothing in my house;
do not make me the leader of the
people."

⁸ Jerusalem staggers,
Judah is falling;
their words and deeds are against the LORD,
defying his glorious presence.
⁹ The look on their faces testifies against
them;
they parade their sin like Sodom;
they do not hide it.
Woe to them!
They have brought disaster upon
themselves.

¹⁰ Tell the righteous it will be well with them,
for they will enjoy the fruit of their
deeds.
¹¹ Woe to the wicked! Disaster is upon them!
They will be paid back for what their hands
have done.

¹² Youths oppress my people,
women rule over them.
O my people, your guides lead you astray;
they turn you from the path.

¹³ The LORD takes his place in court;
he rises to judge the people.
¹⁴ The LORD enters into judgment
against the elders and leaders of his
people:

a16 Hebrew *every ship of Tarshish*

"It is you who have ruined my vineyard;
    the plunder from the poor is in your
      houses.
15 What do you mean by crushing my people
    and grinding the faces of the poor?"
      declares the Lord, the Lord Almighty.

16 The Lord says,
"The women of Zion are haughty,
    walking along with outstretched necks,
    flirting with their eyes,
tripping along with mincing steps,
    with ornaments jingling on their
      ankles.
17 Therefore the Lord will bring sores on the
    heads of the women of Zion;
    the Lord will make their scalps bald."

18 In that day the Lord will snatch away their finery: the bangles and headbands and crescent necklaces, 19 the earrings and bracelets and veils, 20 the headdresses and ankle chains and sashes, the perfume bottles and charms, 21 the signet rings and nose rings, 22 the fine robes and the capes and cloaks, the purses 23 and mirrors, and the linen garments and tiaras and shawls.

24 Instead of fragrance there will be a stench;
    instead of a sash, a rope;
instead of well-dressed hair, baldness;
    instead of fine clothing, sackcloth;
    instead of beauty, branding.
25 Your men will fall by the sword,
    your warriors in battle.
26 The gates of Zion will lament and mourn;
    destitute, she will sit on the ground.

4 ¹ In that day seven women
    will take hold of one man
and say, "We will eat our own food
    and provide our own clothes;
only let us be called by your name.
    Take away our disgrace!"

The Branch of the Lord

2 In that day the Branch of the Lord will be beautiful and glorious, and the fruit of the land will be the pride and glory of the survivors in Israel. 3 Those who are left in Zion, who remain in Jerusalem, will be called holy, all who are recorded among the living in Jerusalem. 4 The Lord will wash away the filth of the women of Zion; he will cleanse the bloodstains from Jerusalem by a spirit[a] of judgment and a spirit[a] of fire. 5 Then the Lord will create over all of Mount Zion and over those who assemble there a cloud of smoke by day and a glow of flaming fire by night; over all the glory will be a canopy. 6 It will be a shelter and shade from the heat of the day, and a refuge and hiding place from the storm and rain.

The Song of the Vineyard

5 I will sing for the one I love
    a song about his vineyard:
My loved one had a vineyard
    on a fertile hillside.
2 He dug it up and cleared it of stones
    and planted it with the choicest vines.
He built a watchtower in it
    and cut out a winepress as well.
Then he looked for a crop of good grapes,
    but it yielded only bad fruit.

3 "Now you dwellers in Jerusalem and men
      of Judah,
    judge between me and my vineyard.
4 What more could have been done for my
      vineyard
    than I have done for it?
When I looked for good grapes,
    why did it yield only bad?
5 Now I will tell you
    what I am going to do to my vineyard:
I will take away its hedge,
    and it will be destroyed;
I will break down its wall,
    and it will be trampled.
6 I will make it a wasteland,
    neither pruned nor cultivated,
    and briers and thorns will grow there.
I will command the clouds
    not to rain on it."

7 The vineyard of the Lord Almighty
    is the house of Israel,
and the men of Judah
    are the garden of his delight.
And he looked for justice, but saw
      bloodshed;
for righteousness, but heard cries of
      distress.

a4 Or the Spirit

Woes and Judgments

⁸ Woe to you who add house to house
　　and join field to field
till no space is left
　　and you live alone in the land.

⁹ The LORD Almighty has declared in my hearing:

"Surely the great houses will become desolate,
　　the fine mansions left without occupants.
¹⁰ A ten-acre^a vineyard will produce only a bath^b of wine,
　　a homer^c of seed only an ephah^d of grain."

¹¹ Woe to those who rise early in the morning
　　to run after their drinks,
who stay up late at night
　　till they are inflamed with wine.
¹² They have harps and lyres at their banquets,
　　tambourines and flutes and wine,
but they have no regard for the deeds of the LORD,
　　no respect for the work of his hands.
¹³ Therefore my people will go into exile
　　for lack of understanding;
their men of rank will die
　　of hunger
and their masses will be
　　parched with thirst.
¹⁴ Therefore the grave^e
　　enlarges its appetite
and opens its mouth
　　without limit;
into it will descend their
　　nobles and masses
with all their brawlers
　　and revelers.
¹⁵ So man will be brought low
　　and mankind humbled,
the eyes of the arrogant
　　humbled.
¹⁶ But the LORD Almighty will be exalted by his justice,

and the holy God will show himself holy
　　by his righteousness.
¹⁷ Then sheep will graze as in their own pasture;
　　lambs will feed^f among the ruins of the rich.

¹⁸ Woe to those who draw sin along with cords of deceit,
　　and wickedness as with cart ropes,
¹⁹ to those who say, "Let God hurry,
　　let him hasten his work
so we may see it.
Let it approach,
　　let the plan of the Holy One of Israel come,
so we may know it."

²⁰ Woe to those who call evil good
　　and good evil,
who put darkness for light
　　and light for darkness,
who put bitter for sweet
　　and sweet for bitter.

²¹ Woe to those who are wise in their own eyes
　　and clever in their own sight.

²² Woe to those who are heroes at drinking wine
　　and champions at mixing drinks,
²³ who acquit the guilty for a bribe,
　　but deny justice to the innocent.
²⁴ Therefore, as tongues of fire
　　lick up straw
and as dry grass sinks
　　down in the flames,
so their roots will decay
　　and their flowers blow
　　away like dust;
for they have rejected the
　　law of the LORD
　　Almighty
and spurned the word
　　of the Holy One of
　　Israel.
²⁵ Therefore the LORD's anger burns against his people;

Isaiah 5:16

God Is Just

But the LORD Almighty will be exalted by his justice, and the holy God will show himself holy by his righteousness.

---

^a10 Hebrew *ten-yoke*, that is, the land plowed by 10 yoke of oxen in one day　　^b10 That is, probably about 6 gallons (about 22 liters)
^c10 That is, probably about 6 bushels (about 220 liters)　　^d10 That is, probably about 3/5 bushel (about 22 liters)　　^e14 Hebrew *Sheol*
^f17 Septuagint; Hebrew / *strangers will eat*

his hand is raised and he strikes them
down.
The mountains shake,
and the dead bodies are like refuse in
the streets.

Yet for all this, his anger is not turned
away,
his hand is still upraised.

²⁶ He lifts up a banner for the distant
nations,
he whistles for those at the ends of the
earth.
Here they come,
swiftly and speedily!
²⁷ Not one of them grows tired or stumbles,
not one slumbers or sleeps;
not a belt is loosened at the waist,
not a sandal thong is broken.
²⁸ Their arrows are sharp,
all their bows are strung;
their horses' hoofs seem like flint,
their chariot wheels like a whirlwind.
²⁹ Their roar is like that of the lion,
they roar like young lions;
they growl as they seize their prey
and carry it off with no one to rescue.
³⁰ In that day they will roar over it
like the roaring of the sea.
And if one looks at the land,
he will see darkness and distress;
even the light will be darkened by the
clouds.

Isaiah's Commission

6 In the year that King Uzziah died, I saw
the Lord seated on a throne, high and
exalted, and the train of his robe filled the
temple. ²Above him were seraphs, each with
six wings: With two they covered their
faces, with two they covered their feet, and
with two they were flying. ³And they were calling to one another:

"Holy, holy, holy is the Lord Almighty;
the whole earth is full of his glory."

⁴At the sound of their voices the doorposts
and thresholds shook and the temple was filled
with smoke.

⁵"Woe to me!" I cried. "I am ruined! For I
am a man of unclean lips, and I live among a
people of unclean lips, and my eyes have seen
the King, the Lord Almighty."

⁶Then one of the seraphs flew to me with a
live coal in his hand, which he had taken with
tongs from the altar. ⁷With it he touched my
mouth and said, "See, this has touched your
lips; your guilt is taken away and your sin
atoned for."

⁸Then I heard the voice of the Lord saying,
"Whom shall I send? And who will go for us?"
And I said, "Here am I. Send me!"
⁹He said, "Go and tell this people:

"'Be ever hearing, but never
understanding;
be ever seeing, but never perceiving.'

¹⁰ Make the heart of this people calloused;
make their ears dull
and close their eyes.ᵃ
Otherwise they might see with their eyes,
hear with their ears,
understand with their hearts,
and turn and be healed."

¹¹ Then I said, "For how long, O Lord?"
And he answered:

"Until the cities lie ruined
and without inhabitant,
until the houses are left deserted
and the fields ruined and ravaged,
¹² until the Lord has sent everyone far away
and the land is utterly forsaken.
¹³ And though a tenth remains in the land,
it will again be laid waste.
But as the terebinth and oak
leave stumps when they are cut down,
so the holy seed will be the stump in the
land."

The Sign of Immanuel

7 When Ahaz son of Jotham, the son of
Uzziah, was king of Judah, King Rezin of
Aram and Pekah son of Remaliah king of Israel
marched up to fight against Jerusalem, but they
could not overpower it.

²Now the house of David was told, "Aram
has allied itself withᵇ Ephraim"; so the hearts of

ᵃ9,10 Hebrew; Septuagint 'You will be ever hearing, but never understanding; / you will be ever seeing, but never perceiving.' / ¹⁰This
people's heart has become calloused; / they hardly hear with their ears, / and they have closed their eyes   ᵇ2 Or has set up camp in

Isaiah 6:8

Then I heard the voice of the Lord saying, "Whom shall I send? And who will go for us?" And I said, "Here am I. Send me!"

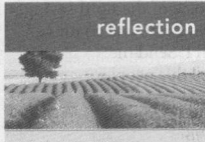

reflection

1 In what ways has worship sustained and encouraged you in the past?

2 What difficult task is God calling you to now? Will you say, like Isaiah, "Here am I, send me"?

3 Take some time to sit quietly and think about God. Let yourself think of his holiness, his majesty, his power, his love. Be still and know that he is God.

RELATED READINGS

1 Kings 17:1–6;
Isaiah 50:4–10;
Hebrews 13:20–21

Read: Isaiah 6:1–8

WHO LIKES TO TAKE ON TROUBLE? Worse yet, to do so single-handedly? The task Isaiah faced was a difficult and undesirable one. The Israelites were in a mess—again. They were suffering because of their sinful ways. The problem was so immense and overwhelming that no one seemed able or even available to help.

God himself asked the question, "Whom shall I send? And who will go for us?" Isaiah answered, "Here am I. Send me!"

Wait a minute. What made Isaiah run to the problem rather than following the instinct to avoid conflict and personal danger? Isaiah wasn't a damage-control expert or a crisis-management counselor. He was a lone prophet. So how was he equipped to intervene?

What prompted Isaiah to step forward and offer himself to God was an experience in worship that altered him forever. Isaiah saw God seated on his throne in heaven. His senses were overwhelmed with the magnificence of God's presence. He heard the antiphonal singing of the seraphs, whose voices shook the doorposts and thresholds. Smoke filled the sanctuary. Isaiah was humbled and awestruck.

Everything pointed the prophet beyond the current task to the eternal glory of God. The weight of coming face-to-face with God was so intense that it nearly crushed Isaiah. Yet at the same time it revived and rejuvenated him. Seeing God in all his glory and splendor and worshiping him equipped Isaiah to serve God.

Has God called you to a task for which you feel completely inadequate? Perhaps you're parenting a child with a disability, disciplining a rebellious son, caring for an elderly parent, battling to preserve a broken marriage. The key to taking on the extraordinary challenge is to worship God, to spend time in his presence meditating on just how awesome he is. When we praise God's holiness and majesty, when we focus on his strength and wisdom, then we are assured of the courage and vigor he makes available to us—the power to go one more mile, to endure one more day, to love one more hour, to forgive one more time. Like Isaiah, we can face these hard assignments with confidence that if God has called us, he will equip us.

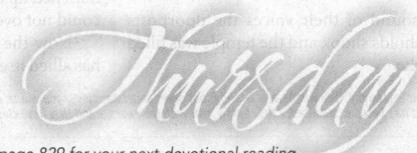

Go to page 829 for your next devotional reading.

Ahaz and his people were shaken, as the trees of the forest are shaken by the wind.

³Then the LORD said to Isaiah, "Go out, you and your son Shear-Jashub,ᵃ to meet Ahaz at the end of the aqueduct of the Upper Pool, on the road to the Washerman's Field. ⁴Say to him, 'Be careful, keep calm and don't be afraid. Do not lose heart because of these two smoldering stubs of firewood—because of the fierce anger of Rezin and Aram and of the son of Remaliah. ⁵Aram, Ephraim and Remaliah's son have plotted your ruin, saying, ⁶"Let us invade Judah; let us tear it apart and divide it among ourselves, and make the son of Tabeel king over it." ⁷Yet this is what the Sovereign LORD says:

> " 'It will not take place,
>   it will not happen,
> ⁸ for the head of Aram is Damascus,
>   and the head of Damascus is only Rezin.
>   Within sixty-five years
>   Ephraim will be too shattered to be a
>   people.
> ⁹ The head of Ephraim is Samaria,
>   and the head of Samaria is only
>   Remaliah's son.
>   If you do not stand firm in your faith,
>   you will not stand at all.' "

¹⁰Again the LORD spoke to Ahaz, ¹¹"Ask the LORD your God for a sign, whether in the deepest depths or in the highest heights."

¹²But Ahaz said, "I will not ask; I will not put the LORD to the test."

¹³Then Isaiah said, "Hear now, you house of David! Is it not enough to try the patience of men? Will you try the patience of my God also? ¹⁴Therefore the Lord himself will give youᵇ a sign: The virgin will be with child and will give birth to a son, andᶜ will call him Immanuel.ᵈ ¹⁵He will eat curds and honey when he knows enough to reject the wrong and choose the right. ¹⁶But before the boy knows enough to reject the wrong and choose the right, the land of the two kings you dread will be laid waste. ¹⁷The LORD will bring on you and on your people and on the house of your father a time unlike any since Ephraim broke away from Judah—he will bring the king of Assyria."

¹⁸In that day the LORD will whistle for flies from the distant streams of Egypt and for bees from the land of Assyria. ¹⁹They will all come and settle in the steep ravines and in the crevices in the rocks, on all the thornbushes and at all the water holes. ²⁰In that day the Lord will use a razor hired from beyond the Riverᵉ—the king of Assyria—to shave your head and the hair of your legs, and to take off your beards also. ²¹In that day, a man will keep alive a young cow and two goats. ²²And because of the abundance of the milk they give, he will have curds to eat. All who remain in the land will eat curds and honey. ²³In that day, in every place where there were a thousand vines worth a thousand silver shekels,ᶠ there will be only briers and thorns. ²⁴Men will go there with bow and arrow, for the land will be covered with briers and thorns. ²⁵As for all the hills once cultivated by the hoe, you will no longer go there for fear of the briers and thorns; they will become places where cattle are turned loose and where sheep run.

Assyria, the LORD's Instrument

8 The LORD said to me, "Take a large scroll and write on it with an ordinary pen: Maher-Shalal-Hash-Baz.ᵍ ²And I will call in Uriah the priest and Zechariah son of Jeberekiah as reliable witnesses for me."

³Then I went to the prophetess, and she conceived and gave birth to a son. And the LORD said to me, "Name him Maher-Shalal-Hash-Baz. ⁴Before the boy knows how to say 'My father' or 'My mother,' the wealth of Damascus and the plunder of Samaria will be carried off by the king of Assyria."

⁵The LORD spoke to me again:

> ⁶ "Because this people has rejected
>   the gently flowing waters of Shiloah
>   and rejoices over Rezin
>   and the son of Remaliah,
> ⁷ therefore the Lord is about to bring against
>   them
>   the mighty floodwaters of the Riverᵉ—
>   the king of Assyria with all his pomp.
>   It will overflow all its channels,
>   run over all its banks
> ⁸ and sweep on into Judah, swirling over it,

ᵃ3 *Shear-Jashub* means *a remnant will return.*   ᵇ14 The Hebrew is plural.   ᶜ14 Masoretic Text; Dead Sea Scrolls *and he* or *and they*   ᵈ14 *Immanuel* means *God with us.*   ᵉ20,7 That is, the Euphrates   ᶠ23 That is, about 25 pounds (about 11.5 kilograms)   ᵍ1 *Maher-Shalal-Hash-Baz* means *quick to the plunder, swift to the spoil*; also in verse 3.

passing through it and reaching up to
the neck.
Its outspread wings will cover the breadth
of your land,
O Immanuel[a]!"

[9] Raise the war cry,[b] you nations, and be
shattered!
Listen, all you distant lands.
Prepare for battle, and be shattered!
Prepare for battle, and be shattered!
[10] Devise your strategy, but it will be
thwarted;
propose your plan, but it will not stand,
for God is with us.[c]

Fear God

[11] The LORD spoke to me with his strong
hand upon me, warning me not to follow the
way of this people. He said:

[12] "Do not call conspiracy
everything that these people call
conspiracy[d];
do not fear what they fear,
and do not dread it.
[13] The LORD Almighty is
the one you are to
regard as holy,
he is the one you are to
fear,
he is the one you are to
dread,
[14] and he will be a sanctuary;
but for both houses of
Israel he will be
a stone that causes men to
stumble
and a rock that makes
them fall.
And for the people of
Jerusalem he will be
a trap and a snare.
[15] Many of them will stumble;
they will fall and be broken,
they will be snared and captured."

[16] Bind up the testimony
and seal up the law among my disciples.
[17] I will wait for the LORD,

who is hiding his face from the house of
Jacob.
I will put my trust in him.

[18] Here am I, and the children the LORD
has given me. We are signs and symbols in
Israel from the LORD Almighty, who dwells on
Mount Zion.

[19] When men tell you to consult mediums
and spiritists, who whisper and mutter, should
not a people inquire of their God? Why consult the dead on behalf of the living? [20] To the
law and to the testimony! If they do not speak
according to this word, they have no light of
dawn. [21] Distressed and hungry, they will roam
through the land; when they are famished, they
will become enraged and, looking upward, will
curse their king and their God. [22] Then they
will look toward the earth and see only distress
and darkness and fearful gloom, and they will
be thrust into utter darkness.

To Us a Child Is Born

9 Nevertheless, there will be no more gloom
for those who were in distress. In the past
he humbled the land of Zebulun and the land
of Naphtali, but in the future
he will honor Galilee of the
Gentiles, by the way of the sea,
along the Jordan—

[2] The people walking in
darkness
have seen a great light;
on those living in the land
of the shadow of
death[e]
a light has dawned.
[3] You have enlarged the
nation
and increased their joy;
they rejoice before you
as people rejoice at the harvest,
as men rejoice
when dividing the plunder.
[4] For as in the day of Midian's defeat,
you have shattered
the yoke that burdens them,
the bar across their shoulders,
the rod of their oppressor.

Isaiah 8:13

God Is Holy

"The LORD Almighty is
the one you are to
regard as holy,
he is the one you
are to fear,
he is the one you
are to dread."

---

[a]8 *Immanuel* means *God with us.*   [b]9 Or *Do your worst*   [c]10 Hebrew *Immanuel*   [d]12 Or *Do not call for a treaty / every time these people*
call for a treaty   [e]2 Or *land of darkness*

A King by Any Other Name

Read: Isaiah 9:2–7

ACCORDING TO THE SOCIAL SECURITY ADMINISTRATION, Minnie, Ida and Bertha were just a few of the top ten girls' names in the 1880s. Today those names have given way to names such as Kaitlyn, Sarah, Emily and Natalie.

Names are important. Expectant parents spend hours choosing the perfect name for their baby, speaking the names aloud and looking up the meanings. They imagine what their child's name will communicate and how others will respond when they hear the name. Names can shape the child's life in many ways.

God gave his Son Jesus many names when Isaiah recorded this prophecy. The Messiah was to come as a dawning light for the people of God who were living in the darkness of their sins. He was to be a Wonderful Counselor, Mighty God, Everlasting Father and Prince of Peace.

We sometimes don't really think about these names because they are so familiar to us. Speak them slowly aloud. Concentrate on absorbing the meaning of each one.

When Isaiah spoke each of these names to the people of Judah and Israel, he proclaimed the reality of the coming Messiah and of all he would mean to the nation—a nation that was crying out for direction, deliverance and light. The Messiah's names indicate all that he would be to them: One who would listen and guide, One who would rescue them, One who was timeless, One who would care for them like a parent, One who would bring justice and peace to their land.

Which of these names of Jesus holds the most meaning for you today? Do you most need a Wonderful Counselor? Are you most aware of the Mighty God? Perhaps you seek the direction of an Everlasting Father or crave the presence of the Prince of Peace. Whatever name you choose, write it on your daily calendar or put it on a sticky note on your fridge. Throughout the day, think about that name. Ask God to show you how he fulfills all the promise his name holds out to you.

Isaiah 9:6

For to us a child is born,
to us a son is given,
and the government
will be on his shoulders.
And he will be called
Wonderful Counselor,
Mighty God, Everlasting
Father, Prince of Peace.

reflection

1 Which of God's attributes are reflected in the names for Christ given in this passage? Pray and ask God to reveal all that they can mean to you personally.

2 What name do you commonly use to refer to Jesus? How might referring to his various names affect the way you approach times of prayer and solitude with him?

3 How can these names of Jesus be useful in telling others about him?

RELATED READINGS

Exodus 3:13–15;
Luke 1:31–33;
John 8:58

Friday

Go to page 833 for your next devotional reading.

⁵ Every warrior's boot used in battle
  and every garment rolled in blood
will be destined for burning,
  will be fuel for the fire.
⁶ For to us a child is born,
  to us a son is given,
  and the government will
    be on his shoulders.
And he will be called
  Wonderful Counselor,[a]
    Mighty God,
  Everlasting Father,
    Prince of Peace.
⁷ Of the increase of his
    government and
    peace
  there will be no end.
He will reign on David's
    throne
  and over his kingdom,
establishing and upholding
    it
  with justice and
    righteousness
  from that time on and forever.
The zeal of the LORD Almighty
  will accomplish this.

The LORD's Anger Against Israel

⁸ The Lord has sent a message against Jacob;
  it will fall on Israel.
⁹ All the people will know it—
  Ephraim and the inhabitants of
    Samaria—
who say with pride
  and arrogance of heart,
¹⁰ "The bricks have fallen down,
  but we will rebuild with dressed stone;
the fig trees have been felled,
  but we will replace them with cedars."
¹¹ But the LORD has strengthened Rezin's foes
    against them
  and has spurred their enemies on.
¹² Arameans from the east and Philistines
    from the west
  have devoured Israel with open mouth.

Yet for all this, his anger is not turned
    away,
  his hand is still upraised.

¹³ But the people have not returned to him
    who struck them,
  nor have they sought the LORD
    Almighty.
¹⁴ So the LORD will cut off
    from Israel both
    head and tail,
  both palm branch and
    reed in a single day;
¹⁵ the elders and prominent
    men are the head,
  the prophets who teach
    lies are the tail.
¹⁶ Those who guide this
    people mislead
    them,
  and those who are
    guided are led
    astray.
¹⁷ Therefore the Lord will
    take no pleasure in
    the young men,
  nor will he pity the
    fatherless and
    widows,
for everyone is ungodly and wicked,
  every mouth speaks vileness.

Yet for all this, his anger is not turned
    away,
  his hand is still upraised.

¹⁸ Surely wickedness burns like a fire;
  it consumes briers and thorns,
it sets the forest thickets ablaze,
  so that it rolls upward in a column of
    smoke.
¹⁹ By the wrath of the LORD Almighty
    the land will be scorched
  and the people will be fuel for the fire;
    no one will spare his brother.
²⁰ On the right they will devour,
    but still be hungry;
  on the left they will eat,
    but not be satisfied.
Each will feed on the flesh of his own
    offspring[b]:
²¹   Manasseh will feed on Ephraim, and
    Ephraim on Manasseh;
  together they will turn against Judah.

Isaiah 9:6

God Gives Us Hope

For to us a child is born,
to us a son is given,
and the government will
be on his shoulders.
And he will be called
Wonderful Counselor,
Mighty God,
Everlasting Father,
Prince of Peace.

ᵃ6 Or *Wonderful, Counselor*   ᵇ20 Or *arm*

Yet for all this, his anger is not turned
away,
his hand is still upraised.

10 Woe to those who make unjust laws,
to those who issue oppressive
decrees,
² to deprive the poor of their rights
and withhold justice from the oppressed
of my people,
making widows their prey
and robbing the fatherless.
³ What will you do on the day of reckoning,
when disaster comes from afar?
To whom will you run for help?
Where will you leave your riches?
⁴ Nothing will remain but to cringe among
the captives
or fall among the slain.

Yet for all this, his anger is not turned
away,
his hand is still upraised.

God's Judgment on Assyria

⁵ "Woe to the Assyrian, the rod of my anger,
in whose hand is the club of my wrath!
⁶ I send him against a godless nation,
I dispatch him against a people who
anger me,
to seize loot and snatch plunder,
and to trample them down like mud in
the streets.
⁷ But this is not what he intends,
this is not what he has in mind;
his purpose is to destroy,
to put an end to many nations.
⁸ 'Are not my commanders all kings?' he
says.
⁹ 'Has not Calno fared like Carchemish?
Is not Hamath like Arpad,
and Samaria like Damascus?
¹⁰ As my hand seized the kingdoms of the
idols,
kingdoms whose images excelled those
of Jerusalem and Samaria—
¹¹ shall I not deal with Jerusalem and her
images
as I dealt with Samaria and her idols?'"

¹²When the Lord has finished all his work
against Mount Zion and Jerusalem, he will say,
"I will punish the king of Assyria for the willful
pride of his heart and the haughty look in his
eyes. ¹³For he says:

"'By the strength of my hand I have done
this,
and by my wisdom, because I have
understanding.
I removed the boundaries of nations,
I plundered their treasures;
like a mighty one I subdued*a* their kings.
¹⁴As one reaches into a nest,
so my hand reached for the wealth of the
nations;
as men gather abandoned eggs,
so I gathered all the countries;
not one flapped a wing,
or opened its mouth to chirp.'"

¹⁵Does the ax raise itself above him who
swings it,
or the saw boast against him who uses
it?
As if a rod were to wield him who lifts it
up,
or a club brandish him who is not wood!
¹⁶Therefore, the Lord, the LORD Almighty,
will send a wasting disease upon his
sturdy warriors;
under his pomp a fire will be kindled
like a blazing flame.
¹⁷The Light of Israel will become a fire,
their Holy One a flame;
in a single day it will burn and consume
his thorns and his briers.
¹⁸The splendor of his forests and fertile fields
it will completely destroy,
as when a sick man wastes away.
¹⁹And the remaining trees of his forests will
be so few
that a child could write them down.

The Remnant of Israel

²⁰In that day the remnant of Israel,
the survivors of the house of Jacob,
will no longer rely on him
who struck them down
but will truly rely on the LORD,

a 13 Or I subdued the mighty,

the Holy One of Israel.
²¹ A remnant will return,ᵃ a remnant of Jacob
will return to the Mighty God.
²² Though your people, O Israel, be like the sand by the sea,
only a remnant will return.
Destruction has been decreed,
overwhelming and righteous.
²³ The Lord, the LORD Almighty, will carry out
the destruction decreed upon the whole land.

²⁴ Therefore, this is what the Lord, the LORD Almighty, says:

"O my people who live in Zion,
do not be afraid of the Assyrians,
who beat you with a rod
and lift up a club against you, as Egypt did.
²⁵ Very soon my anger against you will end
and my wrath will be directed to their destruction."

²⁶ The LORD Almighty will lash them with a whip,
as when he struck down Midian at the rock of Oreb;
and he will raise his staff over the waters,
as he did in Egypt.
²⁷ In that day their burden will be lifted from your shoulders,
their yoke from your neck;
the yoke will be broken
because you have grown so fat.ᵇ

²⁸ They enter Aiath;
they pass through Migron;
they store supplies at Micmash.
²⁹ They go over the pass, and say,
"We will camp overnight at Geba."
Ramah trembles;
Gibeah of Saul flees.
³⁰ Cry out, O Daughter of Gallim!

Listen, O Laishah!
Poor Anathoth!
³¹ Madmenah is in flight;
the people of Gebim take cover.
³² This day they will halt at Nob;
they will shake their fist
at the mount of the Daughter of Zion,
at the hill of Jerusalem.

³³ See, the Lord, the LORD Almighty,
will lop off the boughs with great power.
The lofty trees will be felled,
the tall ones will be brought low.
³⁴ He will cut down the forest thickets with an ax;
Lebanon will fall before the Mighty One.

The Branch From Jesse

11 A shoot will come up from the stump of Jesse;
from his roots a Branch will bear fruit.
² The Spirit of the LORD will rest on him—
the Spirit of wisdom and of understanding,
the Spirit of counsel and of power,
the Spirit of knowledge and of the fear of the LORD—
³ and he will delight in the fear of the LORD.

He will not judge by what he sees with his eyes,
or decide by what he hears with his ears;
⁴ but with righteousness he will judge the needy,
with justice he will give decisions for the poor of the earth.
He will strike the earth with the rod of his mouth;
with the breath of his lips he will slay the wicked.
⁵ Righteousness will be his belt
and faithfulness the sash around his waist.

⁶ The wolf will live with the lamb,
the leopard will lie down with the goat,

Isaiah 11:4

God Is Righteous

But with righteousness he will judge the needy, with justice he will give decisions for the poor of the earth.

ᵃ**21** Hebrew *shear-jashub*; also in verse 22   ᵇ**27** Hebrew; Septuagint *broken / from your shoulders*

Perfect Timing

NAAMAN'S WIFE'S SERVANT GIRL

IT WAS A SIMPLE CASE of being in the wrong place at the wrong time. Or was it?

After all, she hadn't signed up to be his household servant. The fact was that she had been kidnapped to serve in Aram (also known as Syria). If anyone had a right to be angry, it was her. She remembered the day the Aramean rabble-rousers crossed her path as if it were yesterday.

She had simply been minding her own business in her homeland of Israel (just southwest of Aram). Sure, she'd heard the stories about the Arameans taking children away from their families. After all, the two countries had several generations of animosity between them. Under King David's rule, Aram had actually paid tribute to Israel. But now Aram had become a powerful threat, and their surprise raids occurred more frequently. All the village mothers warned their children not to linger too long at the well or play outside after dark. *But nothing would happen to her, would it?*

But something did happen to her. She ended up in the enemy's lair—destined to grow up as a servant in a strange land. Wrong place, wrong time. Right?

Right, except the evidence spoke otherwise.

"If it weren't for me," she reasoned, "my master, Naaman, would never have seen Elisha for a cure." And if he hadn't seen Elisha and experienced miraculous healing, he would never have been witness to the power of God. He would never have become the unmistakable, living proof for Israel's God among the very people who'd kidnapped her.

So, was she in the wrong place at the wrong time? "Yes and no," she would later conclude when telling the story to the neighborhood children. It was the worst thing that had ever happened to her, but it was also a great thing that changed the lives of many people.

Certainly, she would have rather stayed near her home in Israel. But God gave her a chance to speak just the right thing, at just the right time, in just the place where God could use her.

—Prayer—
I open myself to your leading, Father. I will be ready when I hear your call, ready to answer in a way that is pleasing to you.

> *She said to her mistress, "If only my master would see the prophet who is in Samaria! He would cure him of his leprosy."*
>
> **2 Kings 5:3**

ASSIGNED READING:

2 Kings 5:1–27

Go to page 840 for your next devotional reading.

Weekend

the calf and the lion and the yearling[a]
together;
and a little child will lead them.
⁷ The cow will feed with the bear,
their young will lie down together,
and the lion will eat straw like the ox.
⁸ The infant will play near the hole of the
cobra,
and the young child put his hand into
the viper's nest.
⁹ They will neither harm nor destroy
on all my holy mountain,
for the earth will be full of the knowledge
of the LORD
as the waters cover the sea.

¹⁰In that day the Root of Jesse will stand as a banner for the peoples; the nations will rally to him, and his place of rest will be glorious. ¹¹In that day the Lord will reach out his hand a second time to reclaim the remnant that is left of his people from Assyria, from Lower Egypt, from Upper Egypt,[b] from Cush,[c] from Elam, from Babylonia,[d] from Hamath and from the islands of the sea.

¹² He will raise a banner for
the nations
and gather the exiles of
Israel;
he will assemble the
scattered people of
Judah
from the four quarters of the earth.
¹³ Ephraim's jealousy will vanish,
and Judah's enemies[e] will be cut off;
Ephraim will not be jealous of Judah,
nor Judah hostile toward Ephraim.
¹⁴ They will swoop down on the slopes of
Philistia to the west;
together they will plunder the people to
the east.
They will lay hands on Edom and Moab,
and the Ammonites will be subject to
them.

¹⁵ The LORD will dry up
the gulf of the Egyptian sea;
with a scorching wind he will sweep his
hand
over the Euphrates River.[f]
He will break it up into seven streams
so that men can cross over in sandals.
¹⁶ There will be a highway for the remnant of
his people
that is left from Assyria,
as there was for Israel
when they came up from Egypt.

Songs of Praise

12 In that day you will say:

"I will praise you, O LORD.
Although you were angry with me,
your anger has turned
away
and you have comforted
me.
² Surely God is my salvation;
I will trust and not be
afraid.
The LORD, the LORD, is my
strength and my
song;
he has become my
salvation."
³ With joy you will draw
water
from the wells of
salvation.

⁴In that day you will say:

"Give thanks to the LORD, call on his
name;
make known among the nations what he
has done,
and proclaim that his name is
exalted.
⁵ Sing to the LORD, for he has done glorious
things;
let this be known to all the world.
⁶ Shout aloud and sing for joy, people of
Zion,
for great is the Holy One of Israel among
you."

Isaiah 12:2

God Is Our Salvation

"Surely God is my
salvation;
I will trust and not
be afraid.
The LORD, the LORD, is my
strength and my song;
he has become
my salvation."

ᵃ6 Hebrew; Septuagint *lion will feed* ᵇ11 Hebrew *from Pathros* ᶜ11 That is, the upper Nile region ᵈ11 Hebrew *Shinar* ᵉ13 Or *hostility*
ᶠ15 Hebrew *the River*

A Prophecy Against Babylon

13 An oracle concerning Babylon that Isaiah son of Amoz saw:

² Raise a banner on a bare hilltop,
  shout to them;
beckon to them
  to enter the gates of the nobles.
³ I have commanded my holy ones;
  I have summoned my warriors to carry
    out my wrath—
  those who rejoice in my triumph.

⁴ Listen, a noise on the mountains,
  like that of a great multitude!
Listen, an uproar among the kingdoms,
  like nations massing together!
The LORD Almighty is mustering
  an army for war.
⁵ They come from faraway lands,
  from the ends of the heavens—
the LORD and the weapons of his wrath—
  to destroy the whole country.

⁶ Wail, for the day of the LORD is near;
  it will come like destruction from the
    Almighty.ᵃ
⁷ Because of this, all hands will go limp,
  every man's heart will
    melt.
⁸ Terror will seize them,
  pain and anguish will
    grip them;
  they will writhe like a
    woman in labor.
They will look aghast at
  each other,
  their faces aflame.

⁹ See, the day of the LORD is
    coming
  —a cruel day, with wrath
    and fierce anger—
to make the land desolate
  and destroy the sinners
    within it.
¹⁰ The stars of heaven and
    their constellations
  will not show their light.
The rising sun will be darkened
  and the moon will not give its light.

¹¹ I will punish the world for its evil,
  the wicked for their sins.
I will put an end to the arrogance of the
    haughty
  and will humble the pride of the
    ruthless.
¹² I will make man scarcer than pure gold,
  more rare than the gold of Ophir.
¹³ Therefore I will make the heavens tremble;
  and the earth will shake from its place
at the wrath of the LORD Almighty,
  in the day of his burning anger.

¹⁴ Like a hunted gazelle,
  like sheep without a shepherd,
each will return to his own people,
  each will flee to his native land.
¹⁵ Whoever is captured will be thrust
    through;
  all who are caught will fall by the sword.
¹⁶ Their infants will be dashed to pieces
    before their eyes;
  their houses will be looted and their
    wives ravished.

¹⁷ See, I will stir up against them the Medes,
  who do not care for silver
    and have no delight in
      gold.
¹⁸ Their bows will strike
    down the young
      men;
  they will have no mercy
    on infants
  nor will they look with
    compassion on
      children.
¹⁹ Babylon, the jewel of
    kingdoms,
  the glory of the
    Babylonians'ᵇ pride,
will be overthrown by God
  like Sodom and
    Gomorrah.
²⁰ She will never be inhabited
    or lived in through all
      generations;
  no Arab will pitch his tent
    there,
no shepherd will rest his flocks there.

Isaiah 13:9

God Will Exercise His Wrath

See, the day of the
LORD is coming
—a cruel day, with wrath
and fierce anger—
to make the land
desolate
and destroy the sinners
within it.

ᵃ6 Hebrew *Shaddai*   ᵇ19 Or *Chaldeans'*

²¹But desert creatures will lie there,
  jackals will fill her houses;
there the owls will dwell,
  and there the wild goats will leap about.
²²Hyenas will howl in her strongholds,
  jackals in her luxurious palaces.
Her time is at hand,
  and her days will not be prolonged.

14 The LORD will have compassion on
  Jacob;
  once again he will choose Israel
  and will settle them in their own land.
Aliens will join them
  and unite with the house of Jacob.
²Nations will take them
  and bring them to their own place.
And the house of Israel will possess the
  nations
  as menservants and maidservants in the
  LORD's land.
They will make captives of their captors
  and rule over their oppressors.

³On the day the LORD gives you relief from
suffering and turmoil and cruel bondage, ⁴you
will take up this taunt against the king of Babylon:

How the oppressor has come to an end!
  How his fury*ᵃ* has ended!
⁵The LORD has broken the rod of the
  wicked,
  the scepter of the rulers,
⁶which in anger struck down peoples
  with unceasing blows,
and in fury subdued nations
  with relentless aggression.
⁷All the lands are at rest and at peace;
  they break into singing.
⁸Even the pine trees and the cedars of
  Lebanon
  exult over you and say,
"Now that you have been laid low,
  no woodsman comes to cut us down."

⁹The grave*ᵇ* below is all astir
  to meet you at your coming;
it rouses the spirits of the departed to greet
  you—

all those who were leaders in the
  world;
it makes them rise from their thrones—
  all those who were kings over the
  nations.
¹⁰They will all respond,
  they will say to you,
"You also have become weak, as we are;
  you have become like us."
¹¹All your pomp has been brought down to
  the grave,
  along with the noise of your harps;
maggots are spread out beneath you
  and worms cover you.

¹²How you have fallen from heaven,
  O morning star, son of the dawn!
You have been cast down to the earth,
  you who once laid low the nations!
¹³You said in your heart,
  "I will ascend to heaven;
I will raise my throne
  above the stars of God;
I will sit enthroned on the mount of
  assembly,
  on the utmost heights of the sacred
  mountain.*ᶜ*
¹⁴I will ascend above the tops of the clouds;
  I will make myself like the Most High."
¹⁵But you are brought down to the grave,
  to the depths of the pit.

¹⁶Those who see you stare at you,
  they ponder your fate:
"Is this the man who shook the earth
  and made kingdoms tremble,
¹⁷the man who made the world a desert,
  who overthrew its cities
  and would not let his captives go home?"
¹⁸All the kings of the nations lie in state,
  each in his own tomb.
¹⁹But you are cast out of your tomb
  like a rejected branch;
you are covered with the slain,
  with those pierced by the sword,
  those who descend to the stones of the
  pit.
Like a corpse trampled underfoot,
²⁰ you will not join them in burial,

ᵃ4 Dead Sea Scrolls, Septuagint and Syriac; the meaning of the word in the Masoretic Text is uncertain.   *ᵇ9* Hebrew *Sheol*; also in verses 11 and 15   *ᶜ13* Or *the north*; Hebrew *Zaphon*

for you have destroyed your land
and killed your people.

The offspring of the wicked
will never be mentioned again.
21 Prepare a place to slaughter his sons
for the sins of their forefathers;
they are not to rise to inherit the land
and cover the earth with their cities.

22 "I will rise up against them,"
declares the LORD Almighty.
"I will cut off from Babylon her name and
survivors,
her offspring and descendants,"
declares the LORD.
23 "I will turn her into a place for owls
and into swampland;
I will sweep her with the broom of
destruction,"
declares the LORD Almighty.

A Prophecy Against Assyria
24 The LORD Almighty has sworn,

"Surely, as I have planned, so it will be,
and as I have purposed, so it will stand.
25 I will crush the Assyrian in my land;
on my mountains I will trample him
down.
His yoke will be taken from my people,
and his burden removed from their
shoulders."

26 This is the plan determined for the whole
world;
this is the hand stretched out over all
nations.
27 For the LORD Almighty has purposed, and
who can thwart him?
His hand is stretched out, and who can
turn it back?

A Prophecy Against the Philistines
28 This oracle came in the year King Ahaz
died:

29 Do not rejoice, all you Philistines,
that the rod that struck you is broken;
from the root of that snake will spring up
a viper,
its fruit will be a darting, venomous
serpent.

30 The poorest of the poor will find pasture,
and the needy will lie down in safety.
But your root I will destroy by famine;
it will slay your survivors.

31 Wail, O gate! Howl, O city!
Melt away, all you Philistines!
A cloud of smoke comes from the north,
and there is not a straggler in its ranks.
32 What answer shall be given
to the envoys of that nation?
"The LORD has established Zion,
and in her his afflicted people will find
refuge."

A Prophecy Against Moab

15
An oracle concerning Moab:

Ar in Moab is ruined,
destroyed in a night!
Kir in Moab is ruined,
destroyed in a night!
2 Dibon goes up to its temple,
to its high places to weep;
Moab wails over Nebo and Medeba.
Every head is shaved
and every beard cut off.
3 In the streets they wear sackcloth;
on the roofs and in the public squares
they all wail,
prostrate with weeping.
4 Heshbon and Elealeh cry out,
their voices are heard all the way to
Jahaz.
Therefore the armed men of Moab cry out,
and their hearts are faint.

5 My heart cries out over Moab;
her fugitives flee as far as Zoar,
as far as Eglath Shelishiyah.
They go up the way to Luhith,
weeping as they go;
on the road to Horonaim
they lament their destruction.
6 The waters of Nimrim are dried up
and the grass is withered;
the vegetation is gone
and nothing green is left.
7 So the wealth they have acquired and
stored up
they carry away over the Ravine of the
Poplars.

⁸Their outcry echoes along the border of
    Moab;
  their wailing reaches as far as Eglaim,
  their lamentation as far as Beer Elim.
⁹Dimon's*a* waters are full of blood,
  but I will bring still more upon
    Dimon*a*—
a lion upon the fugitives of Moab
  and upon those who remain in the land.

16

Send lambs as tribute
  to the ruler of the land,
from Sela, across the desert,
  to the mount of the Daughter of Zion.
²Like fluttering birds
  pushed from the nest,
so are the women of Moab
  at the fords of the Arnon.

³"Give us counsel,
  render a decision.
Make your shadow like night—
  at high noon.
Hide the fugitives,
  do not betray the refugees.
⁴Let the Moabite fugitives stay with you;
  be their shelter from the destroyer."

The oppressor will come to an end,
  and destruction will cease;
  the aggressor will vanish from the land.
⁵In love a throne will be established;
  in faithfulness a man will sit on it—
  one from the house*b* of David—
one who in judging seeks justice
  and speeds the cause of righteousness.

⁶We have heard of Moab's pride—
  her overweening pride and conceit,
her pride and her insolence—
  but her boasts are empty.
⁷Therefore the Moabites wail,
  they wail together for Moab.
Lament and grieve
  for the men*c* of Kir Hareseth.
⁸The fields of Heshbon wither,
  the vines of Sibmah also.
The rulers of the nations
  have trampled down the choicest vines,
  which once reached Jazer

and spread toward the desert.
Their shoots spread out
  and went as far as the sea.
⁹So I weep, as Jazer weeps,
  for the vines of Sibmah.
O Heshbon, O Elealeh,
  I drench you with tears!
The shouts of joy over your ripened fruit
  and over your harvests have been stilled.
¹⁰Joy and gladness are taken away from the
    orchards;
  no one sings or shouts in the vineyards;
no one treads out wine at the presses,
  for I have put an end to the shouting.
¹¹My heart laments for Moab like a harp,
  my inmost being for Kir Hareseth.
¹²When Moab appears at her high place,
  she only wears herself out;
when she goes to her shrine to pray,
  it is to no avail.

¹³This is the word the LORD has already spoken concerning Moab. ¹⁴But now the LORD says: "Within three years, as a servant bound by contract would count them, Moab's splendor and all her many people will be despised, and her survivors will be very few and feeble."

An Oracle Against Damascus

17

An oracle concerning Damascus:

"See, Damascus will no longer be a city
  but will become a heap of ruins.
²The cities of Aroer will be deserted
  and left to flocks, which will lie down,
  with no one to make them afraid.
³The fortified city will disappear from
    Ephraim,
  and royal power from Damascus;
the remnant of Aram will be
  like the glory of the Israelites,"
      declares the LORD Almighty.

⁴"In that day the glory of Jacob will fade;
  the fat of his body will waste away.
⁵It will be as when a reaper gathers the
    standing grain
  and harvests the grain with his arm—
as when a man gleans heads of grain
  in the Valley of Rephaim.

---

a9 Masoretic Text; Dead Sea Scrolls, some Septuagint manuscripts and Vulgate *Dibon*   *b5* Hebrew *tent*   *c7* Or "*raisin cakes,*" a wordplay

⁶Yet some gleanings will remain,
  as when an olive tree is beaten,
leaving two or three olives on the topmost
    branches,
  four or five on the fruitful boughs,"
    declares the LORD, the God of Israel.

⁷In that day men will look to their Maker
  and turn their eyes to the Holy One of
    Israel.
⁸They will not look to the
      altars,
  the work of their hands,
and they will have no
      regard for the
      Asherah poles*a*
  and the incense altars
    their fingers have
    made.

⁹In that day their strong cities, which they left because of
the Israelites, will be like places
abandoned to thickets and undergrowth. And all will be desolation.

¹⁰You have forgotten God your Savior;
  you have not remembered the Rock,
    your fortress.
Therefore, though you set out the finest
    plants
  and plant imported vines,
¹¹though on the day you set them out, you
    make them grow,
  and on the morning when you plant
    them, you bring them to bud,
yet the harvest will be as nothing
  in the day of disease and incurable pain.

¹²Oh, the raging of many nations—
  they rage like the raging sea!
Oh, the uproar of the peoples—
  they roar like the roaring of great
    waters!
¹³Although the peoples roar like the roar of
    surging waters,
  when he rebukes them they flee far away,
driven before the wind like chaff on the
    hills,
  like tumbleweed before a gale.

¹⁴In the evening, sudden terror!
  Before the morning, they are gone!
This is the portion of those who loot us,
  the lot of those who plunder us.

A Prophecy Against Cush

18 Woe to the land of whirring wings*b*
    along the rivers of Cush,*c*
²which sends envoys by sea
      in papyrus boats over the
      water.

Go, swift messengers,
  to a people tall and
      smooth-skinned,
  to a people feared far and
      wide,
an aggressive nation of
      strange speech,
  whose land is divided by
      rivers.

³All you people of the world,
    you who live on the
      earth,
when a banner is raised on the mountains,
  you will see it,
and when a trumpet sounds,
  you will hear it.
⁴This is what the LORD says to me:
  "I will remain quiet and will look on
    from my dwelling place,
like shimmering heat in the sunshine,
  like a cloud of dew in the heat of
    harvest."
⁵For, before the harvest, when the blossom
    is gone
  and the flower becomes a ripening
    grape,
he will cut off the shoots with pruning
    knives,
  and cut down and take away the
    spreading branches.
⁶They will all be left to the mountain birds
    of prey
  and to the wild animals;
the birds will feed on them all summer,
  the wild animals all winter.

⁷At that time gifts will be brought to the
LORD Almighty

> **Isaiah 17:7**
>
> *God Is Our Maker*
>
> In that day men will look
> to their Maker
> and turn their eyes to the
> Holy One of Israel.

---

*a*8 That is, symbols of the goddess Asherah   *b*1 Or *of locusts*   *c*1 That is, the upper Nile region

Isaiah 17:10–11

You have forgotten God your Savior; you have not remembered the Rock, your fortress. Therefore, though you set out the finest plants and plant imported vines, though on the day you set them out, you make them grow, and on the morning when you plant them, you bring them to bud, yet the harvest will be as nothing in the day of disease and incurable pain.

reflection

1 Think about a moment when you were especially aware of God's presence in your life. What did that feel like?

2 What do you have in your home that can be your morning and evening reminder of God's presence and power?

3 What difference does it make in your day when you are mindful of God's presence?

RELATED READINGS

Deuteronomy 4:5–9;
Psalm 42:1–2;
Proverbs 3:1–6

Read: Isaiah 17:7–14

IT IS AMAZING THAT we can inhabit creation on this marvelous planet—in the midst of the changing seasons, with natural wonders surrounding us—and not always be aware of our Creator. Yet it happens. The momentum of life picks up, the to-do lists lengthen, the needs around us scream for attention, and before we know it, we have forgotten what is most important.

It's not a new problem. Throughout the Old Testament, God used prophets like Isaiah to confront his people about this very thing. God reminded the people to be mindful of him, to remember their history, to keep their priorities in line—but they had trouble listening. Therefore, their efforts came up empty. They spent time doing what they thought was important, but they harvested only unexpected suffering. Anything they planted and nurtured without consulting the Gardener would come to ruin and disease. Isaiah prophesied that when they forgot that God was their source of life, they would harvest only dead vines and shriveled fruit.

Centuries later, Jesus brought this same metaphor home to his disciples: "I am the true vine, and my Father is the gardener . . . I am the vine; you are the branches. If a man remains in me and I in him, he will bear much fruit; apart from me you can do nothing" (John 15:1,5).

No matter what we do, whether it's planting a vineyard, starting a business, raising children or running a ministry, if we do not consult God, if we are not connected to the Vine, we will not yield a harvest.

It's essential to remember that God is the One who causes us to bear fruit. When life is off kilter, what reminders can you plant in your life to bring you into his presence? Ancient Jews practiced several reminders of God's presence. Their daily rituals and yearly feasts symbolized and celebrated their history with God.

It's important to practice daily and weekly habits that remind us of God's presence. Simple things can help us grow in our faith life: meditating on God's goodness while in the car-pool line, posting a Scripture verse in the kitchen, listening to worship music while getting ready in the morning or taking a prayer walk each day. Be creative in the ways you find to stay connected to the Vine.

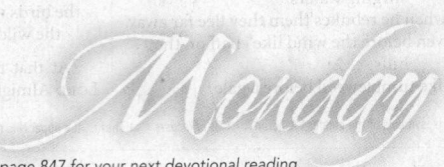

Monday

Go to page 847 for your next devotional reading.

from a people tall and smooth-skinned,
from a people feared far and wide,
an aggressive nation of strange speech,
whose land is divided by rivers—

the gifts will be brought to Mount Zion, the place of the Name of the LORD Almighty.

A Prophecy About Egypt

19 An oracle concerning Egypt:

See, the LORD rides on a swift cloud
and is coming to Egypt.
The idols of Egypt tremble before him,
and the hearts of the Egyptians melt
within them.

² "I will stir up Egyptian against Egyptian—
brother will fight against brother,
neighbor against neighbor,
city against city,
kingdom against kingdom.
³ The Egyptians will lose heart,
and I will bring their plans to nothing;
they will consult the idols and the spirits of
the dead,
the mediums and the spiritists.
⁴ I will hand the Egyptians over
to the power of a cruel master,
and a fierce king will rule over them,"
declares the Lord, the LORD Almighty.

⁵ The waters of the river will dry up,
and the riverbed will be parched and
dry.
⁶ The canals will stink;
the streams of Egypt will dwindle and
dry up.
The reeds and rushes will wither,
⁷ also the plants along the Nile,
at the mouth of the river.
Every sown field along the Nile
will become parched, will blow away
and be no more.
⁸ The fishermen will groan and lament,
all who cast hooks into the Nile;
those who throw nets on the water
will pine away.
⁹ Those who work with combed flax will
despair,

the weavers of fine linen will lose hope.
¹⁰ The workers in cloth will be dejected,
and all the wage earners will be sick at
heart.

¹¹ The officials of Zoan are nothing but fools;
the wise counselors of Pharaoh give
senseless advice.
How can you say to Pharaoh,
"I am one of the wise men,
a disciple of the ancient kings"?

¹² Where are your wise men now?
Let them show you and make known
what the LORD Almighty
has planned against Egypt.
¹³ The officials of Zoan have become fools,
the leaders of Memphis*a* are deceived;
the cornerstones of her peoples
have led Egypt astray.
¹⁴ The LORD has poured into them
a spirit of dizziness;
they make Egypt stagger in all that she does,
as a drunkard staggers around in his
vomit.
¹⁵ There is nothing Egypt can do—
head or tail, palm branch or reed.

¹⁶ In that day the Egyptians will be like women. They will shudder with fear at the uplifted hand that the LORD Almighty raises against them. ¹⁷ And the land of Judah will bring terror to the Egyptians; everyone to whom Judah is mentioned will be terrified, because of what the LORD Almighty is planning against them.

¹⁸ In that day five cities in Egypt will speak the language of Canaan and swear allegiance to the LORD Almighty. One of them will be called the City of Destruction.*b*

¹⁹ In that day there will be an altar to the LORD in the heart of Egypt, and a monument to the LORD at its border. ²⁰ It will be a sign and witness to the LORD Almighty in the land of Egypt. When they cry out to the LORD because of their oppressors, he will send them a savior and defender, and he will rescue them. ²¹ So the LORD will make himself known to the Egyptians, and in that day they will acknowledge the LORD. They will worship with sacrifices and

---

*a*13 Hebrew *Noph*   *b*18 Most manuscripts of the Masoretic Text; some manuscripts of the Masoretic Text, Dead Sea Scrolls and Vulgate *City of the Sun* (that is, Heliopolis) grain offerings; they will make vows to the LORD and keep them. ²²The LORD will strike Egypt with a plague; he will strike them and heal them. They will turn to the LORD, and he will respond to their pleas and heal them.

²³In that day there will be a highway from Egypt to Assyria. The Assyrians will go to Egypt and the Egyptians to Assyria. The Egyptians and Assyrians will worship together. ²⁴In that day Israel will be the third, along with Egypt and Assyria, a blessing on the earth. ²⁵The LORD Almighty will bless them, saying, "Blessed be Egypt my people, Assyria my handiwork, and Israel my inheritance."

A Prophecy Against Egypt and Cush

20 In the year that the supreme commander, sent by Sargon king of Assyria, came to Ashdod and attacked and captured it— ²at that time the LORD spoke through Isaiah son of Amoz. He said to him, "Take off the sackcloth from your body and the sandals from your feet." And he did so, going around stripped and barefoot.

³Then the LORD said, "Just as my servant Isaiah has gone stripped and barefoot for three years, as a sign and portent against Egypt and Cush,ᵃ ⁴so the king of Assyria will lead away stripped and barefoot the Egyptian captives and Cushite exiles, young and old, with buttocks bared—to Egypt's shame. ⁵Those who trusted in Cush and boasted in Egypt will be afraid and put to shame. ⁶In that day the people who live on this coast will say, 'See what has happened to those we relied on, those we fled to for help and deliverance from the king of Assyria! How then can we escape?'"

A Prophecy Against Babylon

21 An oracle concerning the Desert by the Sea:

Like whirlwinds sweeping through the
        southland,
    an invader comes from the desert,
        from a land of terror.

² A dire vision has been shown to me:
    The traitor betrays, the looter takes loot.
    Elam, attack! Media, lay siege!
    I will bring to an end all the groaning
        she caused.

³ At this my body is racked with pain,
    pangs seize me, like those of a woman
        in labor;
I am staggered by what I hear,
    I am bewildered by what I see.
⁴ My heart falters,
    fear makes me tremble;
the twilight I longed for
    has become a horror to me.

⁵ They set the tables,
    they spread the rugs,
    they eat, they drink!
Get up, you officers,
    oil the shields!

⁶ This is what the Lord says to me:

"Go, post a lookout
    and have him report what he sees.
⁷ When he sees chariots
    with teams of horses,
riders on donkeys
    or riders on camels,
let him be alert,
    fully alert."

⁸ And the lookoutᵇ shouted,

"Day after day, my lord, I stand on the
        watchtower;
every night I stay at my post.
⁹ Look, here comes a man in a chariot
    with a team of horses.
And he gives back the answer:
    'Babylon has fallen, has fallen!
All the images of its gods
    lie shattered on the ground!'"

¹⁰ O my people, crushed on the threshing
        floor,
    I tell you what I have heard
from the LORD Almighty,
    from the God of Israel.

A Prophecy Against Edom

¹¹ An oracle concerning Dumahᶜ:

Someone calls to me from Seir,
    "Watchman, what is left of the night?

ᵃ3 That is, the upper Nile region; also in verse 5   ᵇ8 Dead Sea Scrolls and Syriac; Masoretic Text A lion   ᶜ11 Dumah means silence or stillness, a wordplay on Edom.

Watchman, what is left of the night?"
¹²The watchman replies,
  "Morning is coming, but also the night.
If you would ask, then ask;
  and come back yet again."

A Prophecy Against Arabia

¹³An oracle concerning Arabia:

You caravans of Dedanites,
  who camp in the thickets of Arabia,
¹⁴ bring water for the thirsty;
you who live in Tema,
  bring food for the fugitives.
¹⁵They flee from the sword,
  from the drawn sword,
from the bent bow
  and from the heat of battle.

¹⁶This is what the Lord says to me: "Within one year, as a servant bound by contract would count it, all the pomp of Kedar will come to an end. ¹⁷The survivors of the bowmen, the warriors of Kedar, will be few." The LORD, the God of Israel, has spoken.

A Prophecy About Jerusalem

22 An oracle concerning the Valley of Vision:

What troubles you now,
  that you have all gone up on the roofs,
²O town full of commotion,
  O city of tumult and revelry?
Your slain were not killed by the sword,
  nor did they die in battle.
³All your leaders have fled together;
  they have been captured without using
    the bow.
All you who were caught were taken
    prisoner together,
  having fled while the enemy was still far
    away.
⁴Therefore I said, "Turn away from me;
  let me weep bitterly.
Do not try to console me
  over the destruction of my people."

⁵The Lord, the LORD Almighty, has a day
  of tumult and trampling and terror
  in the Valley of Vision,
a day of battering down walls
  and of crying out to the mountains.

⁶Elam takes up the quiver,
  with her charioteers and horses;
  Kir uncovers the shield.
⁷Your choicest valleys are full of chariots,
  and horsemen are posted at the city
    gates;
⁸ the defenses of Judah are stripped away.

And you looked in that day
  to the weapons in the Palace of the
    Forest;
⁹you saw that the City of David
  had many breaches in its defenses;
you stored up water
  in the Lower Pool.
¹⁰You counted the buildings in Jerusalem
  and tore down houses to strengthen the
    wall.
¹¹You built a reservoir between the two walls
  for the water of the Old Pool,
but you did not look to the One who made
    it,
  or have regard for the One who planned
    it long ago.

¹²The Lord, the LORD Almighty,
  called you on that day
to weep and to wail,
  to tear out your hair and put on
    sackcloth.
¹³But see, there is joy and revelry,
  slaughtering of cattle and killing of
    sheep,
  eating of meat and drinking of wine!
"Let us eat and drink," you say,
  "for tomorrow we die!"

¹⁴The LORD Almighty has revealed this in my hearing: "Till your dying day this sin will not be atoned for," says the Lord, the LORD Almighty.

¹⁵This is what the Lord, the LORD Almighty, says:

"Go, say to this steward,
  to Shebna, who is in charge of the palace:
¹⁶What are you doing here and who gave you
    permission
  to cut out a grave for yourself here,
hewing your grave on the height
  and chiseling your resting place in the
    rock?

17 "Beware, the LORD is about to take firm
          hold of you
     and hurl you away, O you mighty man.
18 He will roll you up tightly like a ball
     and throw you into a large country.
   There you will die
     and there your splendid chariots will
          remain—
   you disgrace to your master's house!
19 I will depose you from your office,
     and you will be ousted from your
          position.

20 "In that day I will summon my servant, Eliakim son of Hilkiah. 21 I will clothe him with
your robe and fasten your sash around him and
hand your authority over to him. He will be a
father to those who live in Jerusalem and to the
house of Judah. 22 I will place on his shoulder
the key to the house of David; what he opens
no one can shut, and what he shuts no one can
open. 23 I will drive him like a peg into a firm
place; he will be a seat[a] of honor for the house
of his father. 24 All the glory of his family will
hang on him: its offspring and offshoots—all
its lesser vessels, from the bowls to all the jars.

25 "In that day," declares the LORD Almighty,
"the peg driven into the firm place will give
way; it will be sheared off and will fall, and the
load hanging on it will be cut
down." The LORD has spoken.

A Prophecy About Tyre

23 An oracle concerning
Tyre:

   Wail, O ships of Tarshish!
     For Tyre is destroyed
          and left without house or
               harbor.
   From the land of Cyprus[b]
     word has come to them.

2 Be silent, you people of the
          island
     and you merchants of
          Sidon,
   whom the seafarers have
          enriched.

3 On the great waters
     came the grain of the Shihor;
   the harvest of the Nile[c] was the revenue of
          Tyre,
     and she became the marketplace of the
          nations.

4 Be ashamed, O Sidon, and you, O fortress
          of the sea,
     for the sea has spoken:
   "I have neither been in labor nor given
          birth;
     I have neither reared sons nor brought
          up daughters."
5 When word comes to Egypt,
     they will be in anguish at the report
          from Tyre.

6 Cross over to Tarshish;
     wail, you people of the island.
7 Is this your city of revelry,
     the old, old city,
   whose feet have taken her
     to settle in far-off lands?
8 Who planned this against Tyre,
     the bestower of crowns,
   whose merchants are princes,
     whose traders are renowned in the
          earth?
9 The LORD Almighty planned it,
          to bring low the pride of
               all glory
          and to humble all who
               are renowned on
               the earth.

10 Till[d] your land as along the
               Nile,
          O Daughter of Tarshish,
     for you no longer have a
          harbor.
11 The LORD has stretched out
     his hand over the
          sea
     and made its kingdoms
          tremble.
   He has given an order
          concerning
          Phoenicia[e]

Isaiah 23:11

God Surpasses All

The LORD has stretched
out his hand over the sea
and made its kingdoms
tremble.
He has given an order
concerning Phoenicia
that her fortresses
be destroyed.

---

[a]23 Or *throne*   [b]1 Hebrew *Kittim*   [c]2,3 Masoretic Text; one Dead Sea Scroll *Sidon, / who cross over the sea; / your envoys [3]are on the great waters. / The grain of the Shihor, / the harvest of the Nile,*   [d]10 Dead Sea Scrolls and some Septuagint manuscripts; Masoretic Text *Go through*   [e]11 Hebrew *Canaan*

that her fortresses be destroyed.
12 He said, "No more of your reveling,
O Virgin Daughter of Sidon, now crushed!

"Up, cross over to Cyprus[a];
even there you will find no rest."
13 Look at the land of the Babylonians,[b]
this people that is now of no account!
The Assyrians have made it
a place for desert creatures;
they raised up their siege towers,
they stripped its fortresses bare
and turned it into a ruin.

14 Wail, you ships of Tarshish;
your fortress is destroyed!

15 At that time Tyre will be forgotten for seventy years, the span of a king's life. But at the end of these seventy years, it will happen to Tyre as in the song of the prostitute:

16 "Take up a harp, walk through the city,
O prostitute forgotten;
play the harp well, sing many a song,
so that you will be remembered."

17 At the end of seventy years, the LORD will deal with Tyre. She will return to her hire as a prostitute and will ply her trade with all the kingdoms on the face of the earth. 18 Yet her profit and her earnings will be set apart for the LORD; they will not be stored up or hoarded. Her profits will go to those who live before the LORD, for abundant food and fine clothes.

The LORD's Devastation of the Earth

24 See, the LORD is going to lay waste the earth
and devastate it;
he will ruin its face
and scatter its inhabitants—
2 it will be the same
for priest as for people,
for master as for servant,
for mistress as for maid,
for seller as for buyer,
for borrower as for lender,
for debtor as for creditor.
3 The earth will be completely laid waste
and totally plundered.
The LORD has spoken this word.

4 The earth dries up and withers,
the world languishes and withers,
the exalted of the earth languish.
5 The earth is defiled by its people;
they have disobeyed the laws,
violated the statutes
and broken the everlasting covenant.
6 Therefore a curse consumes the earth;
its people must bear their guilt.
Therefore earth's inhabitants are burned
up,
and very few are left.
7 The new wine dries up and the vine
withers;
all the merrymakers groan.
8 The gaiety of the tambourines is stilled,
the noise of the revelers has stopped,
the joyful harp is silent.
9 No longer do they drink wine with a song;
the beer is bitter to its drinkers.
10 The ruined city lies desolate;
the entrance to every house is barred.
11 In the streets they cry out for wine;
all joy turns to gloom,
all gaiety is banished from the earth.
12 The city is left in ruins,
its gate is battered to pieces.
13 So will it be on the earth
and among the nations,
as when an olive tree is beaten,
or as when gleanings are left after the
grape harvest.

14 They raise their voices, they shout for joy;
from the west they acclaim the LORD's
majesty.
15 Therefore in the east give glory to the
LORD;
exalt the name of the LORD, the God of
Israel,
in the islands of the sea.
16 From the ends of the earth we hear
singing:
"Glory to the Righteous One."

But I said, "I waste away, I waste away!
Woe to me!
The treacherous betray!
With treachery the treacherous betray!"
17 Terror and pit and snare await you,

a 12 Hebrew *Kittim* b 13 Or *Chaldeans*

O people of the earth.
18 Whoever flees at the sound of terror
will fall into a pit;
whoever climbs out of the pit
will be caught in a snare.

The floodgates of the heavens are opened,
the foundations of the earth shake.
19 The earth is broken up,
the earth is split asunder,
the earth is thoroughly shaken.
20 The earth reels like a drunkard,
it sways like a hut in the wind;
so heavy upon it is the guilt of its rebellion
that it falls—never to rise again.

21 In that day the LORD will punish
the powers in the heavens above
and the kings on the earth below.
22 They will be herded together
like prisoners bound in a dungeon;
they will be shut up in prison
and be punished[a] after many days.
23 The moon will be abashed, the sun
ashamed;
for the LORD Almighty will reign
on Mount Zion and in Jerusalem,
and before its elders, gloriously.

Praise to the LORD

25 O LORD, you are my God;
I will exalt you and
praise your name,
for in perfect faithfulness
you have done marvelous
things,
things planned long ago.
2 You have made the city a
heap of rubble,
the fortified town a ruin,
the foreigners' stronghold a
city no more;
it will never be rebuilt.
3 Therefore strong peoples
will honor you;
cities of ruthless nations
will revere you.
4 You have been a refuge for
the poor,
a refuge for the needy in his distress,

a shelter from the storm
and a shade from the heat.
For the breath of the ruthless
is like a storm driving against a wall
5 and like the heat of the desert.
You silence the uproar of foreigners;
as heat is reduced by the shadow of a
cloud,
so the song of the ruthless is stilled.

6 On this mountain the LORD Almighty will
prepare
a feast of rich food for all peoples,
a banquet of aged wine—
the best of meats and the finest of wines.
7 On this mountain he will destroy
the shroud that enfolds all peoples,
the sheet that covers all nations;
8 he will swallow up death forever.
The Sovereign LORD will wipe away the
tears
from all faces;
he will remove the disgrace of his people
from all the earth.
The LORD has spoken.

9 In that day they will say,

"Surely this is our God;
we trusted in him, and he saved us.
This is the LORD, we trusted in him;
let us rejoice and be glad
in his salvation."

10 The hand of the LORD
will rest on this
mountain;
but Moab will be
trampled under
him
as straw is trampled
down in the
manure.
11 They will spread out their
hands in it,
as a swimmer spreads
out his hands to
swim.
God will bring down their
pride
despite the cleverness[b] of their hands.

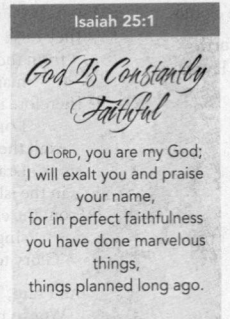

Isaiah 25:1

*God Is Constantly
Faithful*

O LORD, you are my God;
I will exalt you and praise
your name,
for in perfect faithfulness
you have done marvelous
things,
things planned long ago.

---

a22 Or *released*   b11 The meaning of the Hebrew for this word is uncertain.

Thank You!

Read: Isaiah 25:1–9

DESPITE ALL THE PROMISES and reminders, sometimes the stain of my sin seems so repugnant and the gift of His grace seems so extravagant that I can hardly believe He bestows it on us ruined sinners so freely. But He does. His Word tells us, "If we confess our sins, he is faithful and just and will forgive us our sins and purify us from all unrighteousness."

Still, I sometimes find myself asking, *Lord, did we hear You right? Did You say all* unrighteousness? *Do You mean all my sin, past, present, and future? Even if it's sin I consider little and insignificant, like gossip; or medium-sized, like losing my temper; or great big, like murder and adultery and stealing? Did You really mean all my sin is forgiven?*

Then I hear Him whispering to my heart—listen, and you may hear him too: "Anne, the blood of Jesus . . . purifies you from all sin . . . In him you have redemption through his blood, the forgiveness of sins, in accordance with the riches of God's grace . . . Because it is impossible for the blood of bulls and goats to take away your sins . . . Christ came into the world . . . You have been made holy through the sacrifice of the body of Jesus Christ once for all . . . The Holy Spirit also testifies to you about this . . . Your sins and lawless acts I will remember no more."

Hearing these words in my heart, I cry out in gratitude, *Thank You! Thank You! Thank You, dear Jesus, for cleansing me and washing me by Your blood! Based on Your Word, I know I am clean and forgiven. Amen.*

Whew! I feel better. Like I've had a shower after a strenuous work-out! Now . . . now, I'm finally ready to *really* talk to Him. And I sense that He is waiting, listening, gently inviting: *Therefore, Anne, since you have confidence to enter the Most Holy Place by the blood of Jesus, by a new and living way opened for you through the curtain, that is, his body, and since you have a great priest over the house of God, draw near to God with a sincere heart in full assurance, having your heart sprinkled to cleanse you from a guilty conscience* [see Hebrews 10:19–22].

—Anne Graham Lotz

Isaiah 25:9

In that day they will say, "Surely this is our God; we trusted in him, and he saved us. This is the LORD, we trusted in him; let us rejoice and be glad in his salvation."

reflection

1 Do you, like Anne Graham Lotz, have a difficult time believing that God can forgive you of *all* unrighteousness?

2 Take a few moments to meditate on today's devotional passage. Listen for the voice of assurance in your heart that you have, indeed, been forgiven if you've accepted Christ's sacrifice.

3 Now take the time to "rejoice and be glad in his salvation" (Isaiah 25:9).

RELATED READINGS

Psalms 32:1–2;
103:11–12;
Micah 7:19;
Mark 2:1–12

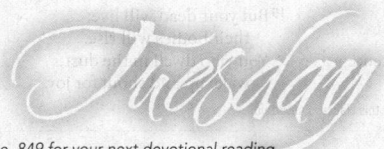

¹²He will bring down your high fortified
walls
and lay them low;
he will bring them down to the ground,
to the very dust.

A Song of Praise

26 In that day this song will be sung in the
land of Judah:

We have a strong city;
God makes salvation
its walls and ramparts.
²Open the gates
that the righteous nation
may enter,
the nation that keeps
faith.
³You will keep in perfect
peace
him whose mind is
steadfast,
because he trusts in you.
⁴Trust in the LORD forever,
for the LORD, the LORD,
is the Rock eternal.
⁵He humbles those who
dwell on high,
he lays the lofty city low;
he levels it to the ground
and casts it down to the dust.
⁶Feet trample it down—
the feet of the oppressed,
the footsteps of the poor.

⁷The path of the righteous is level;
O upright One, you make the way of the
righteous smooth.
⁸Yes, LORD, walking in the way of your
laws,[a]
we wait for you;
your name and renown
are the desire of our hearts.
⁹My soul yearns for you in the night;
in the morning my spirit longs for you.
When your judgments come upon the
earth,
the people of the world learn
righteousness.
¹⁰Though grace is shown to the wicked,
they do not learn righteousness;

even in a land of uprightness they go on
doing evil
and regard not the majesty of the LORD.
¹¹O LORD, your hand is lifted high,
but they do not see it.
Let them see your zeal for your people and
be put to shame;
let the fire reserved for your enemies
consume them.

¹²LORD, you establish peace for us;
all that we have accomplished you have
done for us.

¹³O LORD, our God, other
lords besides you
have ruled over us,
but your name alone do
we honor.
¹⁴They are now dead, they
live no more;
those departed spirits do
not rise.
You punished them and
brought them to
ruin;
you wiped out all
memory of them.
¹⁵You have enlarged the
nation, O LORD;
you have enlarged the nation.
You have gained glory for yourself;
you have extended all the borders of the
land.

¹⁶LORD, they came to you in their distress;
when you disciplined them,
they could barely whisper a prayer.[b]
¹⁷As a woman with child and about to give
birth
writhes and cries out in her pain,
so were we in your presence, O LORD.
¹⁸We were with child, we writhed in pain,
but we gave birth to wind.
We have not brought salvation to the earth;
we have not given birth to people of the
world.

¹⁹But your dead will live;
their bodies will rise.
You who dwell in the dust,
wake up and shout for joy.

Isaiah 26:3

*God Brings
Peace*

You will keep in
perfect peace
him whose mind
is steadfast,
because he trusts in you.

---

[a]8 Or *judgments*   [b]16 The meaning of the Hebrew for this clause is uncertain.

Traveling Heavenward

Read: Isaiah 26:1–21

MARKIE, WHO WAS FIVE YEARS OLD, seemed unusually fixated on heaven because so many people he loved were already there. "Why would anyone rather stay on earth when heaven is such a great place?" he often asked.

"Grammy, I want to go to heaven today!" said Markie.

Grandma laughed and agreed, "Me, too, Markie!"

"Let's go!" he yelled.

She sighed before responding, "Mark, only Jesus can decide when it's time for us to go to heaven."

He paused before asking, "Well, why won't he let us go today?"

"We can't leave earth until our work is done."

The boy processed that thought. Then he noticed the piles of Christmas packages and wrapping paper supplies and exclaimed, "Okay, Grammy, let's get these packages wrapped so we can get our work done, and then Jesus will let us go to heaven."

"Well, he might have other tasks for us to do, too, before our work is over."

Satisfied with that answer, they tackled the packages and talked about what other "jobs" God might have for them that day.

Markie is not the first person to feel the tension of longing for heaven while still living here on earth. The prophet Isaiah spoke for generations of believers who have God's promise that this life is not all there is. There is life after death, and one day we'll wake up in heaven. Our time here is only a tiny dash in the line that stretches toward eternity.

We have the rest of our lives to look forward to, and yet we must focus on the rest of today first. We're headed for home, but we're still on the journey.

Isaiah 26:19

But your dead will live; their bodies will rise. You who dwell in the dust, wake up and shout for joy. Your dew is like the dew of the morning; the earth will give birth to her dead.

reflection

1 What work does God have for you today?

2 How would seeing each day in the context of heaven deepen your desire for intimacy with Jesus?

3 What would happen if, before getting out of bed tomorrow morning, you asked yourself, "How will I travel heavenward today?"

RELATED READINGS

Psalm 84:1–7;
1 Thessalonians 4:13–18;
Hebrews 11:1–40

Wednesday

Go to page 852 for your next devotional reading.

Your dew is like the dew of the morning;
　　the earth will give birth to her dead.

²⁰Go, my people, enter your rooms
　　and shut the doors behind you;
hide yourselves for a little while
　　until his wrath has passed by.
²¹See, the LORD is coming out of his
　　　dwelling
　　to punish the people of the earth for
　　　their sins.
The earth will disclose the blood shed
　　　upon her;
　　she will conceal her slain no longer.

Deliverance of Israel

27 In that day,

the LORD will punish with his sword,
　　his fierce, great and powerful sword,
Leviathan the gliding serpent,
　　Leviathan the coiling serpent;
he will slay the monster of the sea.

²In that day—

"Sing about a fruitful vineyard:
³ I, the LORD, watch over it;
　　I water it continually.
I guard it day and night
　　so that no one may harm it.
⁴ I am not angry.
If only there were briers and thorns
　　　confronting me!
　　I would march against them in battle;
　　I would set them all on fire.
⁵Or else let them come to me for refuge;
　　let them make peace with me,
　　yes, let them make peace with me."

⁶In days to come Jacob will take root,
　　Israel will bud and blossom
　　and fill all the world with fruit.

⁷Has ˌthe LORDˌ struck her
　　as he struck down those who struck her?
Has she been killed
　　as those were killed who killed her?
⁸By warfare[a] and exile you contend with
　　　her—
　　with his fierce blast he drives her out,
　　as on a day the east wind blows.

⁹By this, then, will Jacob's guilt be atoned
　　　for,
　　and this will be the full fruitage of the
　　　removal of his sin:
When he makes all the altar stones
　　to be like chalk stones crushed to pieces,
no Asherah poles[b] or incense altars
　　will be left standing.
¹⁰The fortified city stands desolate,
　　an abandoned settlement, forsaken like
　　　the desert;
there the calves graze,
　　there they lie down;
　　they strip its branches bare.
¹¹When its twigs are dry, they are broken off
　　and women come and make fires with
　　　them.
For this is a people without understanding;
　　so their Maker has no compassion on
　　　them,
　　and their Creator shows them no favor.

¹²In that day the LORD will thresh from
the flowing Euphrates[c] to the Wadi of Egypt,
and you, O Israelites, will be gathered up one
by one. ¹³And in that day a great trumpet will
sound. Those who were perishing in Assyria
and those who were exiled in Egypt will come
and worship the LORD on the holy mountain
in Jerusalem.

Woe to Ephraim

28 Woe to that wreath, the pride of
　　Ephraim's drunkards,
　　to the fading flower, his glorious beauty,
set on the head of a fertile valley—
　　to that city, the pride of those laid low
　　　by wine!
²See, the Lord has one who is powerful and
　　　strong.
　　Like a hailstorm and a destructive wind,
like a driving rain and a flooding
　　　downpour,
　　he will throw it forcefully to the ground.
³That wreath, the pride of Ephraim's
　　　drunkards,
　　will be trampled underfoot.
⁴That fading flower, his glorious beauty,
　　set on the head of a fertile valley,
　　will be like a fig ripe before harvest—

ᵃ8 See Septuagint; the meaning of the Hebrew for this word is uncertain.　　ᵇ9 That is, symbols of the goddess Asherah　　ᶜ12 Hebrew *River*

as soon as someone sees it and takes it in
    his hand,
  he swallows it.

5 In that day the LORD Almighty
  will be a glorious crown,
a beautiful wreath
  for the remnant of his people.
6 He will be a spirit of justice
  to him who sits in judgment,
a source of strength
  to those who turn back the battle at the
    gate.

7 And these also stagger from wine
  and reel from beer:
Priests and prophets stagger from beer
  and are befuddled with wine;
they reel from beer,
  they stagger when seeing visions,
  they stumble when rendering decisions.
8 All the tables are covered with vomit
  and there is not a spot without filth.

9 "Who is it he is trying to teach?
  To whom is he explaining his message?
To children weaned from their milk,
  to those just taken from the breast?
10 For it is:
  Do and do, do and do,
  rule on rule, rule on rule[a];
  a little here, a little there."

11 Very well then, with foreign lips and
    strange tongues
  God will speak to this people,
12 to whom he said,
  "This is the resting place, let the weary
    rest";
and, "This is the place of repose"—
  but they would not listen.
13 So then, the word of the LORD to them will
    become:
  Do and do, do and do,
  rule on rule, rule on rule;
  a little here, a little there—
so that they will go and fall backward,
  be injured and snared and captured.

14 Therefore hear the word of the LORD, you
    scoffers

who rule this people in Jerusalem.
15 You boast, "We have entered into a
    covenant with death,
  with the grave[b] we have made an
    agreement.
When an overwhelming scourge sweeps by,
  it cannot touch us,
for we have made a lie our refuge
  and falsehood[c] our hiding place."

16 So this is what the Sovereign LORD says:

"See, I lay a stone in Zion,
  a tested stone,
a precious cornerstone for a sure
    foundation;
  the one who trusts will never be
    dismayed.
17 I will make justice the measuring line
  and righteousness the plumb line;
hail will sweep away your refuge, the lie,
  and water will overflow your hiding
    place.
18 Your covenant with death will be annulled;
  your agreement with the grave will not
    stand.
When the overwhelming scourge sweeps
    by,
  you will be beaten down by it.
19 As often as it comes it will carry you away;
  morning after morning, by day and by
    night,
  it will sweep through."

The understanding of this message
  will bring sheer terror.
20 The bed is too short to stretch out on,
  the blanket too narrow to wrap around
    you.
21 The LORD will rise up as he did at Mount
    Perazim,
  he will rouse himself as in the Valley of
    Gibeon—
to do his work, his strange work,
  and perform his task, his alien task.
22 Now stop your mocking,
  or your chains will become heavier;
the Lord, the LORD Almighty, has told me
  of the destruction decreed against the
    whole land.

*a*10 Hebrew / *sav lasav sav lasav / kav lakav kav lakav* (possibly meaningless sounds; perhaps a mimicking of the prophet's words); also
in verse 13 *b*15 Hebrew *Sheol*; also in verse 18 *c*15 Or *false gods*

Crowned With Hope

Isaiah 28:5

In that day the LORD Almighty will be a glorious crown, a beautiful wreath for the remnant of his people.

reflection

1 Who do you know who is an example of hope amid dark circumstances? How do you feel when you're around that person?

2 When your surroundings seem dismal, how does God's presence give you renewed hope?

3 God's presence in your life can shine as a beacon to others. Think of a relationship or circumstance in your life that needs an infusion of light today. Pray for God's presence in that situation.

RELATED READINGS

Leviticus 25:35–43;
Isaiah 61:1—62:5;
Jonah 3:1–10;
Romans 8:18–39

Read: Isaiah 28:1–6

IN THE MIDDLE OF A GRAY TENEMENT BUILDING, there is a cheerful wreath brightening a doorway. Among the broken bottles and litter in a run-down neighborhood, there is a carefully tended garden of flowers. These surprises stand out like beacons, saying, "In this house, hope flourishes. In this house, we believe, even in the midst of deferred dreams and dismal surroundings." Think about a woman you know whose home life you certainly don't envy, yet she holds her head up with dignity and grace. She always imparts a word of encouragement and joy. God encircles her life like a golden crown. She stands out like a beacon of God's presence.

Ephraim, the northern kingdom of Israel, was facing a dismal future as it slid into idolatry. Its wreath of glory was fading fast. Amid Isaiah's prophecy of doom, however, there was a gleam of hope. God had a remnant of faithful people, and God promised to encircle their lives like a glorious crown of strength and hope.

We all can sympathize with the feeling of being trapped in dismal or destructive situations. Perhaps you work with people who see nothing wrong with dishonesty, and you're waging what feels like a losing battle for the truth. Maybe your husband does nothing but discourage or criticize, and you feel yourself fading daily beneath the weight of his words. To those hoping in the darkness, God promises to adorn us with his glory, to encircle our bowed and tired heads with a magnificent wreath: his presence.

God has a special place in his heart for the downtrodden. In reality, we're all beaten back by the world at some point in our day or week. When you feel discouraged or oppressed, picture God's presence, like a lovely wreath, resting on you and strengthening you. Then stand out like a beacon that shines in a world badly in need of hope.

Thursday

---

23 Listen and hear my voice;
    pay attention and hear what I say.
24 When a farmer plows for planting, does he
        plow continually?
    Does he keep on breaking up and
        harrowing the soil?
25 When he has leveled the surface,
        does he not sow caraway and scatter
        cummin?
    Does he not plant wheat in its place,[a]
        barley in its plot,[a]
        and spelt in its field?
26 His God instructs him
    and teaches him the right way.

27 Caraway is not threshed with a sledge,
    nor is a cartwheel rolled over cummin;
    caraway is beaten out with a rod,
        and cummin with a stick.
28 Grain must be ground to make bread;
    so one does not go on threshing it
        forever.
    Though he drives the wheels of his
        threshing cart over it,
    his horses do not grind it.
29 All this also comes from the LORD
        Almighty,
    wonderful in counsel and magnificent
        in wisdom.

Woe to David's City

29 Woe to you, Ariel, Ariel,
    the city where David settled!
    Add year to year
    and let your cycle of festivals go on.
2 Yet I will besiege Ariel;
    she will mourn and lament,
    she will be to me like an altar hearth.[b]
3 I will encamp against you all around;
    I will encircle you with towers
    and set up my siege works against you.
4 Brought low, you will speak from the
        ground;
    your speech will mumble out of the dust.
    Your voice will come ghostlike from the
        earth;
    out of the dust your speech will whisper.

5 But your many enemies will become like
    fine dust,

    the ruthless hordes like blown chaff.
Suddenly, in an instant,
6   the LORD Almighty will come
    with thunder and earthquake and great
        noise,
    with windstorm and tempest and flames
        of a devouring fire.
7 Then the hordes of all the nations that fight
        against Ariel,
    that attack her and her fortress and
        besiege her,
    will be as it is with a dream,
    with a vision in the night—
8 as when a hungry man dreams that he is
        eating,
    but he awakens, and his hunger
        remains;
    as when a thirsty man dreams that he is
        drinking,
    but he awakens faint, with his thirst
        unquenched.
So will it be with the hordes of all the
        nations
    that fight against Mount Zion.

9 Be stunned and amazed,
    blind yourselves and be sightless;
    be drunk, but not from wine,
    stagger, but not from beer.
10 The LORD has brought over you a deep
        sleep:
    He has sealed your eyes (the prophets);
    he has covered your heads (the seers).

11 For you this whole vision is nothing but
words sealed in a scroll. And if you give the
scroll to someone who can read, and say to him,
"Read this, please," he will answer, "I can't; it is
sealed." 12 Or if you give the scroll to someone
who cannot read, and say, "Read this, please,"
he will answer, "I don't know how to read."

13 The Lord says:

"These people come near to me with their
        mouth
    and honor me with their lips,
    but their hearts are far from me.
Their worship of me
    is made up only of rules taught by men.[c]

---

[a]25 The meaning of the Hebrew for this word is uncertain.   [b]2 The Hebrew for *altar hearth* sounds like the Hebrew for *Ariel*.   [c]13 Hebrew;
Septuagint *They worship me in vain; / their teachings are but rules taught by men*

¹⁴Therefore once more I will astound these
people
with wonder upon wonder;
the wisdom of the wise will perish,
the intelligence of the intelligent will
vanish."

¹⁵Woe to those who go to
great depths
to hide their plans from
the LORD,
who do their work in
darkness and think,
"Who sees us? Who will
know?"

¹⁶You turn things upside
down,
as if the potter were
thought to be like
the clay!
Shall what is formed say to
him who formed it,
"He did not make me"?
Can the pot say of the
potter,
"He knows nothing"?

¹⁷In a very short time, will not Lebanon be
turned into a fertile field
and the fertile field seem like a forest?
¹⁸In that day the deaf will hear the words of
the scroll,
and out of gloom and darkness
the eyes of the blind will see.
¹⁹Once more the humble will rejoice in the
LORD;
the needy will rejoice in the Holy One
of Israel.
²⁰The ruthless will vanish,
the mockers will disappear,
and all who have an eye for evil will be
cut down—
²¹those who with a word make a man out to
be guilty,
who ensnare the defender in court
and with false testimony deprive the
innocent of justice.

²²Therefore this is what the LORD, who redeemed Abraham, says to the house of Jacob:

"No longer will Jacob be ashamed;
no longer will their faces grow pale.

²³When they see among them their children,
the work of my hands,
they will keep my name holy;
they will acknowledge the holiness of
the Holy One of Jacob,
and will stand in awe of
the God of Israel.
²⁴Those who are wayward
in spirit will gain
understanding;
those who complain will
accept instruction."

Woe to the Obstinate Nation

30 "Woe to the obstinate
children,"
declares the LORD,
"to those who carry out
plans that are not
mine,
forming an alliance, but
not by my Spirit,
heaping sin upon sin;
²who go down to Egypt
without consulting me;
who look for help to Pharaoh's protection,
to Egypt's shade for refuge.
³But Pharaoh's protection will be to your
shame,
Egypt's shade will bring you disgrace.
⁴Though they have officials in Zoan
and their envoys have arrived in
Hanes,
⁵everyone will be put to shame
because of a people useless to them,
who bring neither help nor advantage,
but only shame and disgrace."

⁶An oracle concerning the animals of the
Negev:

Through a land of hardship and distress,
of lions and lionesses,
of adders and darting snakes,
the envoys carry their riches on donkeys'
backs,
their treasures on the humps of camels,
to that unprofitable nation,
⁷ to Egypt, whose help is utterly useless.
Therefore I call her
Rahab the Do-Nothing.

Isaiah 29:15

God Knows All Plans

Woe to those who go to
great depths
to hide their plans
from the LORD,
who do their work in
darkness and think,
"Who sees us? Who
will know?"

---

⁸Go now, write it on a tablet for them,
    inscribe it on a scroll,
that for the days to come
    it may be an everlasting witness.
⁹These are rebellious people, deceitful
        children,
    children unwilling to listen to the
        LORD's instruction.
¹⁰They say to the seers,
    "See no more visions!"
and to the prophets,
    "Give us no more visions of what is
        right!
Tell us pleasant things,
    prophesy illusions.
¹¹Leave this way,
    get off this path,
and stop confronting us
    with the Holy One of Israel!"

¹²Therefore, this is what the Holy One of
Israel says:

"Because you have rejected this message,
    relied on oppression
    and depended on deceit,
¹³this sin will become for you
    like a high wall, cracked and bulging,
    that collapses suddenly, in an instant.
¹⁴It will break in pieces like pottery,
    shattered so mercilessly
that among its pieces not
        a fragment will be
        found
    for taking coals from a
        hearth
    or scooping water out of
        a cistern."

¹⁵This is what the Sover-
eign LORD, the Holy One of
Israel, says:

"In repentance and rest is
        your salvation,
    in quietness and trust is
        your strength,
    but you would have none
        of it.
¹⁶You said, 'No, we will flee on horses.'
    Therefore you will flee!
You said, 'We will ride off on swift horses.'
    Therefore your pursuers will be swift!
¹⁷A thousand will flee
    at the threat of one;
at the threat of five
    you will all flee away,
till you are left
    like a flagstaff on a mountaintop,
    like a banner on a hill."

¹⁸Yet the LORD longs to be gracious to you;
    he rises to show you compassion.
For the LORD is a God of justice.
    Blessed are all who wait for him!

¹⁹O people of Zion, who live in Jerusalem,
you will weep no more. How gracious he will
be when you cry for help! As soon as he hears,
he will answer you. ²⁰Although the Lord gives
you the bread of adversity and the water of
affliction, your teachers will be hidden no
more; with your own eyes you will see them.
²¹Whether you turn to the right or to the left,
your ears will hear a voice behind you, saying,
"This is the way; walk in it." ²²Then you will
defile your idols overlaid with silver and your
images covered with gold; you will throw them
away like a menstrual cloth and say to them,
"Away with you!"

²³He will also send you rain for the seed you
sow in the ground, and the food that comes
from the land will be rich and
plentiful. In that day your cattle will graze in broad meadows. ²⁴The oxen and donkeys
that work the soil will eat fodder and mash, spread out with
fork and shovel. ²⁵In the day
of great slaughter, when the
towers fall, streams of water
will flow on every high mountain and every lofty hill. ²⁶The
moon will shine like the sun,
and the sunlight will be seven
times brighter, like the light of
seven full days, when the LORD
binds up the bruises of his people and heals the wounds he
inflicted.

²⁷See, the Name of the LORD comes from
    afar,

Isaiah 30:27

God Is a Consuming Fire

See, the Name of the
LORD comes from afar,
with burning anger and
dense clouds of smoke;
his lips are full of wrath,
and his tongue is a
consuming fire.

with burning anger and dense clouds of
smoke;
his lips are full of wrath,
and his tongue is a consuming fire.
28 His breath is like a rushing torrent,
rising up to the neck.
He shakes the nations in the sieve of
destruction;
he places in the jaws of the peoples
a bit that leads them astray.
29 And you will sing
as on the night you celebrate a holy
festival;
your hearts will rejoice
as when people go up with flutes
to the mountain of the LORD,
to the Rock of Israel.
30 The LORD will cause men to hear his
majestic voice
and will make them see his arm coming
down
with raging anger and consuming fire,
with cloudburst, thunderstorm and hail.
31 The voice of the LORD will shatter Assyria;
with his scepter he will strike them
down.
32 Every stroke the LORD lays on them
with his punishing rod
will be to the music of tambourines and
harps,
as he fights them in battle with the blows
of his arm.
33 Topheth has long been prepared;
it has been made ready for the king.
Its fire pit has been made deep and wide,
with an abundance of fire and wood;
the breath of the LORD,
like a stream of burning sulfur,
sets it ablaze.

Woe to Those Who Rely on Egypt

31 Woe to those who go down to Egypt
for help,
who rely on horses,
who trust in the multitude of their chariots
and in the great strength of their
horsemen,
but do not look to the Holy One of Israel,
or seek help from the LORD.
2 Yet he too is wise and can bring disaster;
he does not take back his words.

He will rise up against the house of the
wicked,
against those who help evildoers.
3 But the Egyptians are men and not God;
their horses are flesh and not spirit.
When the LORD stretches out his hand,
he who helps will stumble,
he who is helped will fall;
both will perish together.

4 This is what the LORD says to me:

"As a lion growls,
a great lion over his prey—
and though a whole band of shepherds
is called together against him,
he is not frightened by their shouts
or disturbed by their clamor—
so the LORD Almighty will come down
to do battle on Mount Zion and on its
heights.
5 Like birds hovering overhead,
the LORD Almighty will shield
Jerusalem;
he will shield it and deliver it,
he will 'pass over' it and will rescue it."

6 Return to him you have so greatly revolted
against, O Israelites. 7 For in that day every one
of you will reject the idols of silver and gold
your sinful hands have made.

8 "Assyria will fall by a sword that is not of
man;
a sword, not of mortals, will devour
them.
They will flee before the sword
and their young men will be put to
forced labor.
9 Their stronghold will fall because of terror;
at sight of the battle standard their
commanders will panic,"
declares the LORD,
whose fire is in Zion,
whose furnace is in Jerusalem.

The Kingdom of Righteousness

32 See, a king will reign in
righteousness
and rulers will rule with justice.
2 Each man will be like a shelter from the
wind
and a refuge from the storm,

like streams of water in the desert
   and the shadow of a great rock in a
      thirsty land.

³ Then the eyes of those who see will no
      longer be closed,
   and the ears of those who hear will
      listen.
⁴ The mind of the rash will know and
      understand,
   and the stammering tongue will be
      fluent and clear.
⁵ No longer will the fool be called noble
   nor the scoundrel be highly respected.
⁶ For the fool speaks folly,
   his mind is busy with evil:
He practices ungodliness
   and spreads error concerning the LORD;
the hungry he leaves empty
   and from the thirsty he withholds
      water.
⁷ The scoundrel's methods are wicked,
   he makes up evil schemes
to destroy the poor with lies,
   even when the plea of the needy is just.
⁸ But the noble man makes noble plans,
   and by noble deeds he stands.

The Women of Jerusalem

⁹ You women who are so complacent,
   rise up and listen to me;
you daughters who feel secure,
   hear what I have to say!
¹⁰ In little more than a year
   you who feel secure will
      tremble;
the grape harvest will fail,
   and the harvest of fruit
      will not come.
¹¹ Tremble, you complacent
      women;
   shudder, you daughters
      who feel secure!
Strip off your clothes,
   put sackcloth around
      your waists.
¹² Beat your breasts for the
      pleasant fields,
   for the fruitful vines
¹³ and for the land of my
      people,

a land overgrown with thorns and
      briers—
yes, mourn for all houses of merriment
   and for this city of revelry.
¹⁴ The fortress will be abandoned,
   the noisy city deserted;
citadel and watchtower will become a
      wasteland forever,
   the delight of donkeys, a pasture for
      flocks,
¹⁵ till the Spirit is poured upon us from on
      high,
   and the desert becomes a fertile field,
   and the fertile field seems like a forest.
¹⁶ Justice will dwell in the desert
   and righteousness live in the fertile
      field.
¹⁷ The fruit of righteousness will be peace;
   the effect of righteousness will be
      quietness and confidence forever.
¹⁸ My people will live in peaceful dwelling
      places,
   in secure homes,
   in undisturbed places of rest.
¹⁹ Though hail flattens the forest
   and the city is leveled completely,
²⁰ how blessed you will be,
   sowing your seed by every stream,
   and letting your cattle and donkeys
      range free.

Distress and Help

33 Woe to you, O destroyer,
      you who have not been destroyed!
   Woe to you, O traitor,
      you who have not been
         betrayed!
   When you stop destroying,
      you will be destroyed;
   when you stop betraying,
      you will be betrayed.

² O LORD, be gracious to us;
      we long for you.
   Be our strength every
         morning,
      our salvation in time of
         distress.
³ At the thunder of your
         voice, the peoples
            flee;

Isaiah 33:2

*God Gives
Daily Strength*

O LORD, be gracious
   to us;
we long for you.
Be our strength
   every morning,
our salvation in time
   of distress.

Security

Isaiah 32:9

You women who are so complacent, rise up and listen to me; you daughters who feel secure, hear what I have to say!

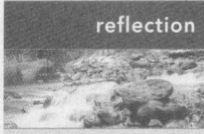

reflection

1 What source of false security might be the cause of complacency in your life?

2 What distracts you from placing all your trust in God?

3 Write a prayer today that expresses your desire to trust in God as your "soul" security.

RELATED READINGS

Isaiah 31:1–3; 65:17–25;
Jeremiah 9:23–24;
Haggai 1:3–11;
Revelation 21:1–5

"The center of God's will is our only safety."

Betsie ten Boom

Read: Isaiah 32:9–20

SURELY ISAIAH IS ADDRESSING rich women with time to lounge around in opulent comfort, isn't he? Yes, but the complacent women Isaiah describes are nevertheless some of God's chosen and beloved people. Instead of staying true to their covenant with God, they grew accustomed to their easy, luxurious lives and content with empty, religious rituals. Instead of finding their security in God, the strength and resources of their circumstances had sidetracked their loyalty. As a result, Isaiah used them as an example of how the people of Jerusalem had let their values become skewed, and now he had to warn them of an impending disaster.

"In little more than a year you who feel secure will tremble" (verse 10). Why? Because the Assyrians, the most brutal army on the planet, would soon invade their land. Their fields would be trampled, their children viciously slaughtered and the rest of the people taken into captivity. Every ounce of smugness would be shattered; every strain of security, obliterated.

Who has the luxury to be complacent? We've got careers, kids and cleaning to manage. But Isaiah could just as easily be addressing many of us today. External things and relationships so easily distract us from finding our security in God. We all have different methods of trying to find our security outside of God. Some of us try to find security in our looks, while others are affirmation junkies—always looking for one more accolade. Some look for security in a savings account or stock portfolio, having their kids in the "best" schools or living in a safe neighborhood. They have a job, insurance, a healthy body and a healthy checking account. They vacation twice a year and drive a new car. What more could they need?

While some of us may allow these things to lull us into a false sense of security, any one of them could be gone in a moment. Beauty fades, stocks tumble, houses deteriorate and people disappoint us. Hurricanes hit, terrorists strike and cancer can be only a few multiplying cells away. The fact is there is no real security while we live on this earth. It's a frightening fact, but true. God does not want us to live in fear because he promises to be with his people. But only he can provide "secure homes," "peaceful dwelling places," "fertile fields," "quietness and confidence" and "undisturbed places of rest" (verses 15–18).

when you rise up, the nations scatter.
⁴ Your plunder, O nations, is harvested as
by young locusts;
like a swarm of locusts men pounce
on it.

⁵ The Lord is exalted, for he dwells on high;
he will fill Zion with justice and
righteousness.
⁶ He will be the sure foundation for your
times,
a rich store of salvation and wisdom and
knowledge;
the fear of the Lord is the key to this
treasure.ᵃ

⁷ Look, their brave men cry aloud in the
streets;
the envoys of peace weep bitterly.
⁸ The highways are deserted,
no travelers are on the roads.
The treaty is broken,
its witnessesᵇ are despised,
no one is respected.
⁹ The land mournsᶜ and wastes away,
Lebanon is ashamed and withers;
Sharon is like the Arabah,
and Bashan and Carmel drop their
leaves.

¹⁰ "Now will I arise," says the Lord.
"Now will I be exalted;
now will I be lifted up.
¹¹ You conceive chaff,
you give birth to straw;
your breath is a fire that consumes you.
¹² The peoples will be burned as if to lime;
like cut thornbushes they will be set
ablaze."

¹³ You who are far away, hear what I have
done;
you who are near, acknowledge my
power!
¹⁴ The sinners in Zion are terrified;
trembling grips the godless:
"Who of us can dwell with the consuming
fire?
Who of us can dwell with everlasting
burning?"
¹⁵ He who walks righteously

and speaks what is right,
who rejects gain from extortion
and keeps his hand from accepting
bribes,
who stops his ears against plots of murder
and shuts his eyes against contemplating
evil—
¹⁶ this is the man who will dwell on the
heights,
whose refuge will be the mountain
fortress.
His bread will be supplied,
and water will not fail him.

¹⁷ Your eyes will see the king in his beauty
and view a land that stretches afar.
¹⁸ In your thoughts you will ponder the
former terror:
"Where is that chief officer?
Where is the one who took the revenue?
Where is the officer in charge of the
towers?"
¹⁹ You will see those arrogant people no
more,
those people of an obscure speech,
with their strange, incomprehensible
tongue.

²⁰ Look upon Zion, the city of our festivals;
your eyes will see Jerusalem,
a peaceful abode, a tent that will not be
moved;
its stakes will never be pulled up,
nor any of its ropes broken.
²¹ There the Lord will be our Mighty One.
It will be like a place of broad rivers and
streams.
No galley with oars will ride them,
no mighty ship will sail them.
²² For the Lord is our judge,
the Lord is our lawgiver,
the Lord is our king;
it is he who will save us.
²³ Your rigging hangs loose:
The mast is not held secure,
the sail is not spread.
Then an abundance of spoils will be
divided
and even the lame will carry off plunder.

ᵃ6 Or *is a treasure from him*   ᵇ8 Dead Sea Scrolls; Masoretic Text / *the cities*   ᶜ9 Or *dries up*

²⁴ No one living in Zion will say, "I am ill";
　　and the sins of those who dwell there
　　　will be forgiven.

Judgment Against the Nations

34 Come near, you nations, and listen;
　　pay attention, you peoples!
　Let the earth hear, and all that is in it,
　　the world, and all that comes out of it!
² The Lᴏʀᴅ is angry with all nations;
　　his wrath is upon all their armies.
　He will totally destroy[a] them,
　　he will give them over to slaughter.
³ Their slain will be thrown out,
　　their dead bodies will send up a stench;
　the mountains will be soaked with their
　　　blood.
⁴ All the stars of the heavens will be
　　　dissolved
　　and the sky rolled up like a scroll;
　all the starry host will fall
　　like withered leaves from the vine,
　　like shriveled figs from the fig tree.

⁵ My sword has drunk its fill in the
　　　heavens;
　　see, it descends in judgment on Edom,
　　the people I have totally destroyed.
⁶ The sword of the Lᴏʀᴅ is bathed in blood,
　　it is covered with fat—
　the blood of lambs and goats,
　　fat from the kidneys of rams.
　For the Lᴏʀᴅ has a sacrifice in Bozrah
　　and a great slaughter in Edom.
⁷ And the wild oxen will fall with them,
　　the bull calves and the great bulls.
　Their land will be drenched with blood,
　　and the dust will be soaked with fat.

⁸ For the Lᴏʀᴅ has a day of vengeance,
　　a year of retribution, to uphold Zion's
　　　cause.
⁹ Edom's streams will be turned into pitch,
　　her dust into burning sulfur;
　　her land will become blazing pitch!
¹⁰ It will not be quenched night and day;
　　its smoke will rise forever.
　From generation to generation it will lie
　　　desolate;
　　no one will ever pass through it again.

¹¹ The desert owl[b] and screech owl[b] will
　　　possess it;
　　the great owl[b] and the raven will nest
　　　there.
　God will stretch out over Edom
　　the measuring line of chaos
　　and the plumb line of desolation.
¹² Her nobles will have nothing there to be
　　　called a kingdom,
　　all her princes will vanish away.
¹³ Thorns will overrun her citadels,
　　nettles and brambles her strongholds.
　She will become a haunt for jackals,
　　a home for owls.
¹⁴ Desert creatures will meet with hyenas,
　　and wild goats will bleat to each other;
　there the night creatures will also repose
　　and find for themselves places of rest.
¹⁵ The owl will nest there and lay eggs,
　　she will hatch them, and care for her
　　　young under the shadow of her
　　　wings;
　there also the falcons will gather,
　　each with its mate.

¹⁶ Look in the scroll of the Lᴏʀᴅ and read:

None of these will be missing,
　not one will lack her mate.
For it is his mouth that has given the order,
　and his Spirit will gather them together.
¹⁷ He allots their portions;
　his hand distributes them by measure.
　They will possess it forever
　　and dwell there from generation to
　　　generation.

Joy of the Redeemed

35 The desert and the parched land will
　　be glad;
　the wilderness will rejoice and blossom.
　Like the crocus, ² it will burst into bloom;
　　it will rejoice greatly and shout for joy.
　The glory of Lebanon will be given to it,
　　the splendor of Carmel and Sharon;
　they will see the glory of the Lᴏʀᴅ,
　　the splendor of our God.

³ Strengthen the feeble hands,
　　steady the knees that give way;

ᵃ2 The Hebrew term refers to the irrevocable giving over of things or persons to the Lᴏʀᴅ, often by totally destroying them; also in verse 5.　ᵇ11 The precise identification of these birds is uncertain.

Family Ties

ATHALIAH

LIKE ANY BRIDE, she made sure her wedding day was all she had dreamed of. But unlike other brides, she intended for her marriage to go down in history—for all the wrong reasons.

On the groom's side of the family: Jehoram, the firstborn son of King Jehoshaphat, king of Judah—a bold leader with a wicked weakness for nepotism. And on the bride's? King Ahab, renowned for his Baal worship and evil choices. Athaliah and her betrothed had been anticipating this day for a long time, the day they would be joined in a partnership that would advance their mutual agendas: reigning with a singleminded focus and making sure there was no one left alive to make a counterclaim to the throne.

But if Athaliah was going to make history, she would have to surpass someone she had known and watched throughout her formative years: Queen Jezebel, King Ahab's infamous wife. Jezebel was considered as one of the most ruthless rulers in the history of Israel. And growing up in the palace, Athaliah had seen Jezebel persecute the opposition without mercy.

With her eye on her goal, it didn't take long for her treachery to trump that of her murderous family. Instead of grieving her son's tragic death, she seized the moment. She nonchalantly killed all of his children—her own grandchildren—in order to solidify her position as queen. Therefore, nothing stood in the way as she seized power. Athaliah finally put all that she'd learned into practice. And then some. In her mind, she was unstoppable.

Just like Jezebel had once thought too.

—Prayer—

"A good name is more desirable than great riches; to be esteemed is better than silver or gold" (Proverbs 22:1).

All the people of the land rejoiced. And the city was quiet, because Athaliah had been slain with the sword.

2 Chronicles 23:21

ASSIGNED READING:

2 Kings 8:25—11:20;
2 Chronicles 22:10–12; 24:1–8

Weekend

⁴say to those with fearful hearts,
  "Be strong, do not fear;
your God will come,
  he will come with vengeance;
with divine retribution
  he will come to save you."

⁵Then will the eyes of the blind be opened
  and the ears of the deaf unstopped.
⁶Then will the lame leap like a deer,
  and the mute tongue shout for joy.
Water will gush forth in the wilderness
  and streams in the desert.
⁷The burning sand will become a pool,
  the thirsty ground bubbling springs.
In the haunts where jackals once lay,
  grass and reeds and papyrus will grow.

⁸And a highway will be there;
  it will be called the Way of Holiness.
The unclean will not journey on it;
  it will be for those who walk in that
    Way;
  wicked fools will not go about on it.ᵃ
⁹No lion will be there,
  nor will any ferocious
    beast get up on it;
  they will not be found
    there.
But only the redeemed will
    walk there,
10   and the ransomed of the
    LORD will return.
They will enter Zion with
    singing;
  everlasting joy will
    crown their heads.
Gladness and joy will
    overtake them,
  and sorrow and sighing
    will flee away.

Sennacherib Threatens Jerusalem

36 In the fourteenth year of King Hezekiah's reign, Sennacherib king of Assyria attacked all the fortified cities of Judah and captured them. ²Then the king of Assyria sent his field commander with a large army from Lachish to King Hezekiah at Jerusalem. When the commander stopped at the aqueduct of the Upper Pool, on the road to the Washerman's Field, ³Eliakim son of Hilkiah the palace administrator, Shebna the secretary, and Joah son of Asaph the recorder went out to him.

⁴The field commander said to them, "Tell Hezekiah,

"'This is what the great king, the king of Assyria, says: On what are you basing this confidence of yours? ⁵You say you have strategy and military strength—but you speak only empty words. On whom are you depending, that you rebel against me? ⁶Look now, you are depending on Egypt, that splintered reed of a staff, which pierces a man's hand and wounds him if he leans on it! Such is Pharaoh king of Egypt to all who depend on him. ⁷And if you say to me, "We are depending on the LORD our God"—isn't he the one whose high places and altars Hezekiah removed, saying to Judah and Jerusalem, "You must worship before this altar"?

⁸"'Come now, make a bargain with my master, the king of Assyria: I will give you two thousand horses—if you can put riders on them! ⁹How then can you repulse one officer of the least of my master's officials, even though you are depending on Egypt for chariots and horsemen? ¹⁰Furthermore, have I come to attack and destroy this land without the LORD? The LORD himself told me to march against this country and destroy it.'"

¹¹Then Eliakim, Shebna and Joah said to the field commander, "Please speak to your servants in Aramaic, since we understand it. Don't speak to us in Hebrew in the hearing of the people on the wall."

¹²But the commander replied, "Was it only to your master and you that my master sent me to say these things, and not to the men sitting

Isaiah 35:10

God Extends Everlasting Joy

And the ransomed of the LORD will return. They will enter Zion with singing; everlasting joy will crown their heads.

ᵃ8 Or / the simple will not stray from it

Are We There Yet?

Read: Isaiah 35:1–10

ANYONE WHO HAS EVER TAKEN a road trip with small children can anticipate the question. Kids seldom understand the concept of time and distance. It might be many miles yet to Grandma's house, but restless children pepper their parents with questions before they've even reached the turnpike. "Are we there yet?"

Scripture often describes our lives in terms of a spiritual journey. "Therefore, strengthen your feeble arms and weak knees. Make level paths for your feet," wrote the author of Hebrews (Hebrews 12:12–13). The prophet Jeremiah gave this travel advisory: "Set up road signs; put up guideposts. Take note of the highway, the road that you take" (Jeremiah 31:21).

Some stretches of our spiritual roadway are straight and smooth; others are marred by a habitual sin, a time of distance from God or another difficulty that makes our path "rocky." Isaiah wrote of a different kind of highway: a highway of holiness. In Biblical times, certain roads between temples could only be used by those who were ceremonially clean; therefore, "the Way of Holiness" refers to an actual, literal road.

Spiritually speaking, we are on a path that is leading somewhere. How do we know if we are on the highway of holiness in our own journeys? The book of Romans contains signposts often referred to as the "Roman Road," and the direction they point concludes with this promise: "If you confess with your mouth, 'Jesus is Lord,' and believe in your heart that God raised him from the dead, you will be saved" (Romans 10:9). When it comes to our final destination, none of us is "there yet," but we have God's Word to lead us in the right direction. Author and speaker Patsy Clairmont wrote, "I don't know where the long and winding road is leading you, but I do know this: if you remember passing Calvary, you are on the right road."

Isaiah 35:8

And a highway will be there; it will be called the Way of Holiness. The unclean will not journey on it; it will be for those who walk in that Way; wicked fools will not go about on it.

reflection

1 What does the concept of a "highway of holiness" mean to you personally?

2 How do you reconcile the disparity between God's holiness and your own imperfections?

3 Take a look at Romans 3–10 and identify the various signposts of faith on "the Roman Road."

RELATED READINGS

Isaiah 40:3–5;
Romans 3:23; 5:8; 6:23;
10:9–13

"We have ample evidence that the Lord is able to guide."

Elisabeth Elliot

Monday

Go to page 868 for your next devotional reading.

on the wall—who, like you, will have to eat their own filth and drink their own urine?"

¹³Then the commander stood and called out in Hebrew, "Hear the words of the great king, the king of Assyria! ¹⁴This is what the king says: Do not let Hezekiah deceive you. He cannot deliver you! ¹⁵Do not let Hezekiah persuade you to trust in the LORD when he says, 'The LORD will surely deliver us; this city will not be given into the hand of the king of Assyria.'

¹⁶"Do not listen to Hezekiah. This is what the king of Assyria says: Make peace with me and come out to me. Then every one of you will eat from his own vine and fig tree and drink water from his own cistern, ¹⁷until I come and take you to a land like your own—a land of grain and new wine, a land of bread and vineyards.

¹⁸"Do not let Hezekiah mislead you when he says, 'The LORD will deliver us.' Has the god of any nation ever delivered his land from the hand of the king of Assyria? ¹⁹Where are the gods of Hamath and Arpad? Where are the gods of Sepharvaim? Have they rescued Samaria from my hand? ²⁰Who of all the gods of these countries has been able to save his land from me? How then can the LORD deliver Jerusalem from my hand?"

²¹But the people remained silent and said nothing in reply, because the king had commanded, "Do not answer him."

²²Then Eliakim son of Hilkiah the palace administrator, Shebna the secretary, and Joah son of Asaph the recorder went to Hezekiah, with their clothes torn, and told him what the field commander had said.

Jerusalem's Deliverance Foretold

37 When King Hezekiah heard this, he tore his clothes and put on sackcloth and went into the temple of the LORD. ²He sent Eliakim the palace administrator, Shebna the secretary, and the leading priests, all wearing sackcloth, to the prophet Isaiah son of Amoz. ³They told him, "This is what Hezekiah says: This day is a day of distress and rebuke and disgrace, as when children come to the point of birth and there is no strength to deliver them. ⁴It may be that the LORD your God will hear the words of the field commander, whom his master, the king of Assyria, has sent to ridicule the living God, and that he will rebuke him for the words the LORD your God has heard. Therefore pray for the remnant that still survives."

⁵When King Hezekiah's officials came to Isaiah, ⁶Isaiah said to them, "Tell your master, 'This is what the LORD says: Do not be afraid of what you have heard—those words with which the underlings of the king of Assyria have blasphemed me. ⁷Listen! I am going to put a spirit in him so that when he hears a certain report, he will return to his own country, and there I will have him cut down with the sword.'"

⁸When the field commander heard that the king of Assyria had left Lachish, he withdrew and found the king fighting against Libnah.

⁹Now Sennacherib received a report that Tirhakah, the Cushite[a] king of Egypt, was marching out to fight against him. When he heard it, he sent messengers to Hezekiah with this word: ¹⁰"Say to Hezekiah king of Judah: Do not let the god you depend on deceive you when he says, 'Jerusalem will not be handed over to the king of Assyria.' ¹¹Surely you have heard what the kings of Assyria have done to all the countries, destroying them completely. And will you be delivered? ¹²Did the gods of the nations that were destroyed by my forefathers deliver them—the gods of Gozan, Haran, Rezeph and the people of Eden who were in Tel Assar? ¹³Where is the king of Hamath, the king of Arpad, the king of the city of Sepharvaim, or of Hena or Ivvah?"

Hezekiah's Prayer

¹⁴Hezekiah received the letter from the messengers and read it. Then he went up to the temple of the LORD and spread it out before the LORD. ¹⁵And Hezekiah prayed to the LORD: ¹⁶"O LORD Almighty, God of Israel, enthroned between the cherubim, you alone are God over all the kingdoms of the earth. You have made heaven and earth. ¹⁷Give ear, O LORD, and hear; open your eyes, O LORD, and see; listen to all the words Sennacherib has sent to insult the living God.

¹⁸"It is true, O LORD, that the Assyrian kings have laid waste all these peoples and their lands. ¹⁹They have thrown their gods into the fire and destroyed them, for they were not gods

a9 That is, from the upper Nile region

but only wood and stone, fashioned by human hands. **20**Now, O LORD our God, deliver us from his hand, so that all kingdoms on earth may know that you alone, O LORD, are God.*a*"

Sennacherib's Fall

21Then Isaiah son of Amoz sent a message to Hezekiah: "This is what the LORD, the God of Israel, says: Because you have prayed to me concerning Sennacherib king of Assyria, **22**this is the word the LORD has spoken against him:

"The Virgin Daughter of Zion
despises and mocks you.
The Daughter of Jerusalem
tosses her head as you flee.
23Who is it you have insulted and
blasphemed?
Against whom have you raised your
voice
and lifted your eyes in pride?
Against the Holy One of Israel!
24By your messengers
you have heaped insults on the Lord.
And you have said,
'With my many chariots
I have ascended the heights of the
mountains,
the utmost heights of Lebanon.
I have cut down its tallest cedars,
the choicest of its pines.
I have reached its remotest heights,
the finest of its forests.
25I have dug wells in foreign lands*b*
and drunk the water there.
With the soles of my feet
I have dried up all the streams of
Egypt.'

26"Have you not heard?
Long ago I ordained it.
In days of old I planned it;
now I have brought it to pass,
that you have turned fortified cities
into piles of stone.
27Their people, drained of power,
are dismayed and put to shame.
They are like plants in the field,
like tender green shoots,

like grass sprouting on the roof,
scorched*c* before it grows up.

28"But I know where you stay
and when you come and go
and how you rage against me.
29Because you rage against me
and because your insolence has reached
my ears,
I will put my hook in your nose
and my bit in your mouth,
and I will make you return
by the way you came.

30"This will be the sign for you, O Hezekiah:

"This year you will eat what grows by itself,
and the second year what springs from
that.
But in the third year sow and reap,
plant vineyards and eat their fruit.
31Once more a remnant of the house of
Judah
will take root below and bear fruit
above.
32For out of Jerusalem will come a remnant,
and out of Mount Zion a band of
survivors.
The zeal of the LORD Almighty
will accomplish this.

33"Therefore this is what the LORD says concerning the king of Assyria:

"He will not enter this city
or shoot an arrow here.
He will not come before it with shield
or build a siege ramp against it.
34By the way that he came he will return;
he will not enter this city,"
declares the LORD.
35"I will defend this city and save it,
for my sake and for the sake of David
my servant!"

36Then the angel of the LORD went out and put to death a hundred and eighty-five thousand men in the Assyrian camp. When the people got up the next morning—there were all the dead bodies! **37**So Sennacherib king of Assyria

---

*a*20 Dead Sea Scrolls (see also 2 Kings 19:19); Masoretic Text *alone are the LORD*   *b*25 Dead Sea Scrolls (see also 2 Kings 19:24); Masoretic Text does not have *in foreign lands.*   *c*27 Some manuscripts of the Masoretic Text, Dead Sea Scrolls and some Septuagint manuscripts (see also 2 Kings 19:26); most manuscripts of the Masoretic Text *roof / and terraced fields* broke camp and withdrew. He returned to Nineveh and stayed there.

38One day, while he was worshiping in the temple of his god Nisroch, his sons Adrammelech and Sharezer cut him down with the sword, and they escaped to the land of Ararat. And Esarhaddon his son succeeded him as king.

Hezekiah's Illness

38 In those days Hezekiah became ill and was at the point of death. The prophet Isaiah son of Amoz went to him and said, "This is what the LORD says: Put your house in order, because you are going to die; you will not recover."

²Hezekiah turned his face to the wall and prayed to the LORD, ³"Remember, O LORD, how I have walked before you faithfully and with wholehearted devotion and have done what is good in your eyes." And Hezekiah wept bitterly.

⁴Then the word of the LORD came to Isaiah: ⁵"Go and tell Hezekiah, 'This is what the LORD, the God of your father David, says: I have heard your prayer and seen your tears; I will add fifteen years to your life. ⁶And I will deliver you and this city from the hand of the king of Assyria. I will defend this city.

⁷"'This is the LORD's sign to you that the LORD will do what he has promised: ⁸I will make the shadow cast by the sun go back the ten steps it has gone down on the stairway of Ahaz.'" So the sunlight went back the ten steps it had gone down.

⁹A writing of Hezekiah king of Judah after his illness and recovery:

¹⁰I said, "In the prime of my life
    must I go through the gates of death*ᵃ*
    and be robbed of the rest of my years?"
¹¹I said, "I will not again see the LORD,
    the LORD, in the land of the living;
    no longer will I look on mankind,

    or be with those who now dwell in this world.*ᵇ*
¹²Like a shepherd's tent my house
    has been pulled down and taken from me.
Like a weaver I have rolled up my life,
    and he has cut me off from the loom;
    day and night you made an end of me.
¹³I waited patiently till dawn,
    but like a lion he broke all my bones;
    day and night you made an end of me.
¹⁴I cried like a swift or thrush,
    I moaned like a mourning dove.
My eyes grew weak as I looked to the heavens.
    I am troubled; O Lord, come to my aid!"

¹⁵But what can I say?
    He has spoken to me, and he himself has done this.
I will walk humbly all my years
    because of this anguish of my soul.
¹⁶Lord, by such things men live;
    and my spirit finds life in them too.
You restored me to health
    and let me live.
¹⁷Surely it was for my benefit
    that I suffered such anguish.
In your love you kept me
    from the pit of destruction;
you have put all my sins
        behind your back.
¹⁸For the grave*ᵃ* cannot
        praise you,
    death cannot sing your
        praise;
    those who go down to the
        pit
    cannot hope for your
        faithfulness.
¹⁹The living, the living—they
        praise you,
    as I am doing today;
    fathers tell their children
        about your faithfulness.

²⁰The LORD will save me,
    and we will sing with stringed instruments

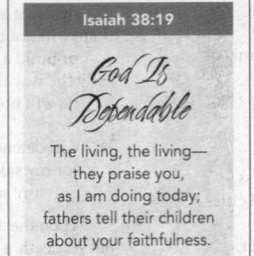

Isaiah 38:19

God Is Dependable

The living, the living—
they praise you,
as I am doing today;
fathers tell their children
about your faithfulness.

---

*ᵃ*10,18 Hebrew *Sheol*   *ᵇ*11 A few Hebrew manuscripts; most Hebrew manuscripts *in the place of cessation*

all the days of our lives
   in the temple of the Lord.

²¹Isaiah had said, "Prepare a poultice of figs and apply it to the boil, and he will recover." ²²Hezekiah had asked, "What will be the sign that I will go up to the temple of the Lord?"

Envoys From Babylon

39 At that time Merodach-Baladan son of Baladan king of Babylon sent Hezekiah letters and a gift, because he had heard of his illness and recovery. ²Hezekiah received the envoys gladly and showed them what was in his storehouses—the silver, the gold, the spices, the fine oil, his entire armory and everything found among his treasures. There was nothing in his palace or in all his kingdom that Hezekiah did not show them.

³Then Isaiah the prophet went to King Hezekiah and asked, "What did those men say, and where did they come from?"

"From a distant land," Hezekiah replied. "They came to me from Babylon."

⁴The prophet asked, "What did they see in your palace?"

"They saw everything in my palace," Hezekiah said. "There is nothing among my treasures that I did not show them."

⁵Then Isaiah said to Hezekiah, "Hear the word of the Lord Almighty: ⁶The time will surely come when everything in your palace, and all that your fathers have stored up until this day, will be carried off to Babylon. Nothing will be left, says the Lord. ⁷And some of your descendants, your own flesh and blood who will be born to you, will be taken away, and they will become eunuchs in the palace of the king of Babylon."

⁸"The word of the Lord you have spoken is good," Hezekiah replied. For he thought, "There will be peace and security in my lifetime."

Comfort for God's People

40 Comfort, comfort my people, says your God.
² Speak tenderly to Jerusalem,
   and proclaim to her
that her hard service has been completed,
   that her sin has been paid for,

that she has received from the Lord's hand
   double for all her sins.

³ A voice of one calling:
"In the desert prepare
   the way for the Lord*ª*;
make straight in the wilderness
   a highway for our God.*ᵇ*
⁴ Every valley shall be raised up,
   every mountain and hill made low;
the rugged ground shall become level,
   the rugged places a plain.
⁵ And the glory of the Lord will be revealed,
   and all mankind together will see it.
      For the mouth of the Lord
         has spoken."

⁶ A voice says, "Cry out."
   And I said, "What shall I cry?"

"All men are like grass,
   and all their glory is like the flowers of
      the field.
⁷ The grass withers and the flowers fall,
   because the breath of the Lord blows
      on them.
   Surely the people are grass.
⁸ The grass withers and the flowers fall,
   but the word of our God stands forever."

⁹ You who bring good tidings to Zion,
   go up on a high mountain.
You who bring good tidings to Jerusalem,*ᶜ*
   lift up your voice with a shout,
lift it up, do not be afraid;
   say to the towns of Judah,
   "Here is your God!"
¹⁰ See, the Sovereign Lord comes with
      power,
   and his arm rules for him.
See, his reward is with him,
   and his recompense accompanies him.
¹¹ He tends his flock like a shepherd:
   He gathers the lambs in his arms
and carries them close to his heart;
   he gently leads those that have young.

¹² Who has measured the waters in the
      hollow of his hand,
   or with the breadth of his hand marked
      off the heavens?

ª3 Or *A voice of one calling in the desert: / "Prepare the way for the Lord* *ᵇ3* Hebrew; Septuagint *make straight the paths of our God*
ᶜ9 Or *O Zion, bringer of good tidings, / go up on a high mountain. / O Jerusalem, bringer of good tidings*

The God of All Comfort

Isaiah 40:1–2

Comfort, comfort my people, says your God. Speak tenderly to Jerusalem, and proclaim to her that her hard service has been completed, that her sin has been paid for, that she has received from the LORD's hand double for all her sins.

reflection

1 Read through this chapter again. What phrases give you great comfort?

2 What painful sins do you need forgiveness and comfort for? Meditate on the mystery of comfort from a God you have wronged.

3 Where can you reflect the gift of God's righteousness today?

RELATED READINGS

Lamentations 3:19–26;
Hosea 2:14–23;
John 1:19–28;
2 Corinthians 1:3–4

HUMANS CRAVE COMFORT. From infancy, we cry for our mother's arms. When we are hurt, we long for tenderness; even hardened criminals weep for compassion in the isolation of a prison cell.

Though Israel didn't yet realize it, Isaiah was envisioning a day when its people would long for comfort like they longed for their next breath. Isaiah repeatedly warned them that sorrow and degradation awaited them because of their sin, and the outlook didn't look good. They would be exiled to Babylon because of their rebellion, and compassion would seem far from reach.

Even in the midst of their pain, though, God promised his people lavish solace: "Comfort, comfort my people," he said. Remarkable, isn't he? It's one thing to comfort someone who has been wronged, to nurse their wounds and soothe their pain. But what if that person has *done* wrong and is suffering for it? Justice says that they deserve what they get. But God spoke these gracious and merciful words through Isaiah: God will comfort those who have wronged *him*.

Isaiah's prophecy not only looked forward to a time when God would restore Israel, but it also looked ahead to the time when John the Baptist would announce the coming of Jesus, whom God would send as the ultimate comfort. Jesus would offer himself as a final sacrifice—the Lamb of God—and he would take on himself the pain of sin on behalf of those who believe in him.

Through Isaiah, a glorious love song radiates hope to a people caught up in the current of sin. Though justice says we deserve to suffer, God's compassionate grace says, "Comfort, comfort my people." The God of all comfort longs to take us in his arms and comfort us.

Who has held the dust of the earth in a
    basket,
    or weighed the mountains on the scales
    and the hills in a balance?
¹³ Who has understood the mind[a] of the
    LORD,
    or instructed him as his counselor?
¹⁴ Whom did the LORD consult to enlighten
    him,
    and who taught him the right way?
Who was it that taught him knowledge
    or showed him the path of
    understanding?

¹⁵ Surely the nations are like a drop in a
    bucket;
    they are regarded as dust on the scales;
he weighs the islands as though they
    were fine dust.
¹⁶ Lebanon is not sufficient for altar fires,
    nor its animals enough for burnt
    offerings.
¹⁷ Before him all the nations are as nothing;
    they are regarded by him as worthless
    and less than nothing.

¹⁸ To whom, then, will you compare God?
    What image will you compare him to?
¹⁹ As for an idol, a craftsman casts it,
    and a goldsmith overlays it with gold
    and fashions silver chains for it.
²⁰ A man too poor to present such an offering
    selects wood that will not rot.
He looks for a skilled craftsman
    to set up an idol that will not topple.

²¹ Do you not know?
    Have you not heard?
Has it not been told you from the beginning?
    Have you not understood since the earth
        was founded?
²² He sits enthroned above the circle of the
    earth,
    and its people are like grasshoppers.
He stretches out the heavens like a canopy,
    and spreads them out like a tent to live
        in.
²³ He brings princes to naught
    and reduces the rulers of this world to
        nothing.

²⁴ No sooner are they planted,
    no sooner are they sown,
    no sooner do they take root in the
        ground,
than he blows on them and they wither,
    and a whirlwind sweeps them away like
        chaff.

²⁵ "To whom will you compare me?
    Or who is my equal?" says the Holy One.
²⁶ Lift your eyes and look to the heavens:
    Who created all these?
He who brings out the starry host one by
    one,
    and calls them each by name.
Because of his great power and mighty
    strength,
    not one of them is missing.

²⁷ Why do you say, O Jacob,
    and complain, O Israel,
"My way is hidden from the LORD;
    my cause is disregarded by my God"?
²⁸ Do you not know?
    Have you not heard?
The LORD is the everlasting God,
    the Creator of the ends of the earth.
He will not grow tired or weary,
    and his understanding no one can
        fathom.
²⁹ He gives strength to the weary
    and increases the power of the weak.
³⁰ Even youths grow tired and weary,
    and young men stumble and fall;
³¹ but those who hope in the LORD
    will renew their strength.
They will soar on wings like eagles;
    they will run and not grow weary,
    they will walk and not be faint.

The Helper of Israel

41 "Be silent before me, you islands!
    Let the nations renew their strength!
Let them come forward and speak;
    let us meet together at the place of
        judgment.

² "Who has stirred up one from the east,
    calling him in righteousness to his
        service[b]?
He hands nations over to him

---

[a]13 Or *Spirit*; or *spirit*   [b]2 Or / *whom victory meets at every step*

and subdues kings before him.
He turns them to dust with his sword,
to windblown chaff with his bow.
³ He pursues them and moves on unscathed,
by a path his feet have not traveled
before.
⁴ Who has done this and carried it through,
calling forth the generations from the
beginning?
I, the LORD—with the first of them
and with the last—I am he."

⁵ The islands have seen it and fear;
the ends of the earth tremble.
They approach and come forward;
6   each helps the other
and says to his brother, "Be strong!"
⁷ The craftsman encourages the goldsmith,
and he who smooths with the hammer
spurs on him who strikes the anvil.
He says of the welding, "It is good."
He nails down the idol so it will not
topple.

⁸ "But you, O Israel, my servant,
Jacob, whom I have chosen,
you descendants of Abraham my
friend,
⁹ I took you from the ends of the earth,
from its farthest corners I called you.
I said, 'You are my servant';
I have chosen you and
have not rejected
you.
¹⁰ So do not fear, for I am with
you;
do not be dismayed, for I
am your God.
I will strengthen you and
help you;
I will uphold you with
my righteous right
hand.

¹¹ "All who rage against you
will surely be ashamed
and disgraced;
those who oppose you
will be as nothing and
perish.
¹² Though you search for your enemies,
you will not find them.

Those who wage war against you
will be as nothing at all.
¹³ For I am the LORD, your God,
who takes hold of your right hand
and says to you, Do not fear;
I will help you.
¹⁴ Do not be afraid, O worm Jacob,
O little Israel,
for I myself will help you," declares the
LORD,
your Redeemer, the Holy One of Israel.
¹⁵ "See, I will make you into a threshing
sledge,
new and sharp, with many teeth.
You will thresh the mountains and crush
them,
and reduce the hills to chaff.
¹⁶ You will winnow them, the wind will pick
them up,
and a gale will blow them away.
But you will rejoice in the LORD
and glory in the Holy One of Israel.

¹⁷ "The poor and needy search for water,
but there is none;
their tongues are parched with thirst.
But I the LORD will answer them;
I, the God of Israel, will not forsake
them.
¹⁸ I will make rivers flow on barren heights,
and springs within the
valleys.
I will turn the desert into
pools of water,
and the parched ground
into springs.
¹⁹ I will put in the desert
the cedar and the acacia,
the myrtle and the
olive.
I will set pines in the
wasteland,
the fir and the cypress
together,
²⁰ so that people may see and
know,
may consider and
understand,
that the hand of the LORD
has done this,
that the Holy One of Israel has created it.

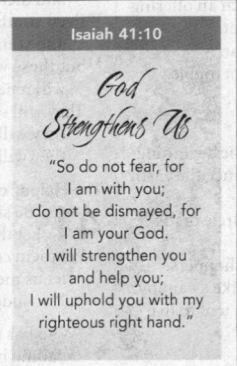

Isaiah 41:10

God
Strengthens Us

"So do not fear, for
I am with you;
do not be dismayed, for
I am your God.
I will strengthen you
and help you;
I will uphold you with my
righteous right hand."

21 "Present your case," says the LORD.
   "Set forth your arguments," says Jacob's
      King.
22 "Bring in your idols to tell us
   what is going to happen.
 Tell us what the former things were,
   so that we may consider them
   and know their final outcome.
 Or declare to us the things to come,
23   tell us what the future holds,
   so we may know that you are gods.
 Do something, whether good or bad,
   so that we will be dismayed and filled
      with fear.
24 But you are less than nothing
   and your works are utterly worthless;
   he who chooses you is detestable.

25 "I have stirred up one from the north, and
      he comes—
   one from the rising sun who calls on my
      name.
 He treads on rulers as if they were mortar,
   as if he were a potter treading the clay.
26 Who told of this from the beginning, so we
      could know,
   or beforehand, so we could say, 'He was
      right'?
 No one told of this,
   no one foretold it,
   no one heard any words from you.
27 I was the first to tell Zion, 'Look, here they
      are!'
   I gave to Jerusalem a messenger of good
      tidings.
28 I look but there is no one—
   no one among them to give counsel,
   no one to give answer when I ask them.
29 See, they are all false!
   Their deeds amount to nothing;
   their images are but wind and
      confusion.

The Servant of the LORD

42 "Here is my servant, whom I uphold,
   my chosen one in whom I delight;
 I will put my Spirit on him
   and he will bring justice to the nations.
2 He will not shout or cry out,
   or raise his voice in the streets.
3 A bruised reed he will not break,

and a smoldering wick he will not snuff
   out.
 In faithfulness he will bring forth
      justice;
4   he will not falter or be discouraged
 till he establishes justice on earth.
   In his law the islands will put their
      hope."

5 This is what God the LORD says—
 he who created the heavens and stretched
      them out,
   who spread out the earth and all that
      comes out of it,
 who gives breath to its people,
   and life to those who walk on it:
6 "I, the LORD, have called you in
      righteousness;
   I will take hold of your hand.
 I will keep you and will make you
   to be a covenant for the people
   and a light for the Gentiles,
7 to open eyes that are blind,
   to free captives from prison
   and to release from the dungeon those
      who sit in darkness.

8 "I am the LORD; that is my name!
   I will not give my glory to another
   or my praise to idols.
9 See, the former things have taken place,
   and new things I declare;
 before they spring into being
   I announce them to you."

Song of Praise to the LORD

10 Sing to the LORD a new song,
   his praise from the ends of the earth,
 you who go down to the sea, and all that
      is in it,
   you islands, and all who live in them.
11 Let the desert and its towns raise their
      voices;
   let the settlements where Kedar lives
      rejoice.
 Let the people of Sela sing for joy;
   let them shout from the mountaintops.
12 Let them give glory to the LORD
   and proclaim his praise in the islands.
13 The LORD will march out like a mighty
      man,
   like a warrior he will stir up his zeal;

with a shout he will raise the battle cry
  and will triumph over his enemies.

14 "For a long time I have kept silent,
  I have been quiet and held myself back.
But now, like a woman in childbirth,
  I cry out, I gasp and pant.
15 I will lay waste the mountains and hills
  and dry up all their vegetation;
I will turn rivers into islands
  and dry up the pools.
16 I will lead the blind by ways they have not
    known,
  along unfamiliar paths I will guide
    them;
I will turn the darkness into light before
    them
  and make the rough places smooth.
These are the things I will do;
  I will not forsake them.
17 But those who trust in idols,
  who say to images, 'You are our gods,'
  will be turned back in utter shame.

Israel Blind and Deaf

18 "Hear, you deaf;
  look, you blind, and see!
19 Who is blind but my
      servant,
  and deaf like the
      messenger I send?
Who is blind like the one
      committed to me,
  blind like the servant of
      the LORD?
20 You have seen many things,
      but have paid no
      attention;
  your ears are open, but
      you hear nothing."
21 It pleased the LORD
  for the sake of his
      righteousness
  to make his law great and glorious.
22 But this is a people plundered and
      looted,
  all of them trapped in pits
  or hidden away in prisons.
They have become plunder,
  with no one to rescue them;

they have been made loot,
  with no one to say, "Send them back."

23 Which of you will listen to this
  or pay close attention in time to come?
24 Who handed Jacob over to become loot,
  and Israel to the plunderers?
Was it not the LORD,
  against whom we have sinned?
For they would not follow his ways;
  they did not obey his law.
25 So he poured out on them his burning
      anger,
  the violence of war.
It enveloped them in flames, yet they did
      not understand;
  it consumed them, but they did not take
    it to heart.

Israel's Only Savior

43 But now, this is what the LORD says—
  he who created you, O Jacob,
  he who formed you, O Israel:
      "Fear not, for I have
        redeemed you;
      I have summoned you by
        name; you are mine.
2 When you pass through the
        waters,
  I will be with you;
and when you pass
        through the rivers,
  they will not sweep over
        you.
When you walk through
        the fire,
  you will not be burned;
  the flames will not set
        you ablaze.
3 For I am the LORD, your
        God,
  the Holy One of Israel,
        your Savior;
I give Egypt for your ransom,
  Cush[a] and Seba in your stead.
4 Since you are precious and honored in my
      sight,
  and because I love you,
I will give men in exchange for you,
  and people in exchange for your life.

Isaiah 43:1

God Created Us

But now, this is what
the LORD says—
he who created you,
O Jacob,
he who formed you,
O Israel:
"Fear not, for I have
redeemed you;
I have summoned you by
name; you are mine."

a3 That is, the upper Nile region

⁵ Do not be afraid, for I am with you;
    I will bring your children from the east
    and gather you from the west.
⁶ I will say to the north, 'Give them up!'
    and to the south, 'Do not hold them
        back.'
  Bring my sons from afar
    and my daughters from the ends of the
        earth—
⁷ everyone who is called by my name,
    whom I created for my glory,
    whom I formed and made."

⁸ Lead out those who have eyes but are
        blind,
    who have ears but are deaf.
⁹ All the nations gather together
    and the peoples assemble.
  Which of them foretold this
    and proclaimed to us the former things?
  Let them bring in their witnesses to prove
        they were right,
    so that others may hear and say, "It is
        true."
¹⁰ "You are my witnesses," declares the LORD,
    "and my servant whom I have chosen,
  so that you may know and believe me
    and understand that I am he.
  Before me no god was formed,
    nor will there be one after me.
¹¹ I, even I, am the LORD,
    and apart from me there is no savior.
¹² I have revealed and saved and
        proclaimed—
    I, and not some foreign god among you.
  You are my witnesses," declares the LORD,
    "that I am God.
¹³   Yes, and from ancient days I am he.
  No one can deliver out of my hand.
    When I act, who can reverse it?"

God's Mercy and Israel's Unfaithfulness

¹⁴ This is what the LORD says—
    your Redeemer, the Holy One of Israel:
  "For your sake I will send to Babylon
    and bring down as fugitives all the
        Babylonians,ᵃ
    in the ships in which they took pride.
¹⁵ I am the LORD, your Holy One,
    Israel's Creator, your King."

¹⁶ This is what the LORD says—
    he who made a way through the sea,
    a path through the mighty waters,
¹⁷ who drew out the chariots and horses,
    the army and reinforcements together,
  and they lay there, never to rise again,
    extinguished, snuffed out like a wick:
¹⁸ "Forget the former things;
    do not dwell on the past.
¹⁹ See, I am doing a new thing!
    Now it springs up; do you not perceive
        it?
  I am making a way in the desert
    and streams in the wasteland.
²⁰ The wild animals honor me,
    the jackals and the owls,
  because I provide water in the desert
    and streams in the wasteland,
  to give drink to my people, my chosen,
²¹   the people I formed for myself
    that they may proclaim my praise.

²² "Yet you have not called upon me,
        O Jacob,
    you have not wearied yourselves for me,
        O Israel.
²³ You have not brought me sheep for burnt
        offerings,
    nor honored me with your sacrifices.
  I have not burdened you with grain
        offerings
    nor wearied you with demands for
        incense.
²⁴ You have not bought any fragrant calamus
        for me,
    or lavished on me the fat of your
        sacrifices.
  But you have burdened me with your sins
    and wearied me with your offenses.

²⁵ "I, even I, am he who blots out
    your transgressions, for my own sake,
    and remembers your sins no more.
²⁶ Review the past for me,
    let us argue the matter together;
    state the case for your innocence.
²⁷ Your first father sinned;
    your spokesmen rebelled against me.
²⁸ So I will disgrace the dignitaries of your
        temple,

ᵃ 14 Or *Chaldeans*

and I will consign Jacob to destruction[a]
and Israel to scorn.

Israel the Chosen

44 "But now listen, O Jacob, my servant,
Israel, whom I have chosen.
[2] This is what the LORD says—
he who made you, who formed you in
the womb,
and who will help you:
Do not be afraid, O Jacob, my servant,
Jeshurun, whom I have chosen.
[3] For I will pour water on the thirsty land,
and streams on the dry ground;
I will pour out my Spirit on your offspring,
and my blessing on your descendants.
[4] They will spring up like grass in a meadow,
like poplar trees by flowing streams.
[5] One will say, 'I belong to the LORD';
another will call himself by the name of
Jacob;
still another will write on his hand, 'The
LORD's,'
and will take the name Israel.

The LORD, Not Idols

[6] "This is what the LORD says—
Israel's King and Redeemer, the LORD
Almighty:
I am the first and I am the last;
apart from me there is no God.
[7] Who then is like me? Let him proclaim it.
Let him declare and lay out before me
what has happened since I established my
ancient people,
and what is yet to come—
yes, let him foretell what will come.
[8] Do not tremble, do not be afraid.
Did I not proclaim this and foretell it
long ago?
You are my witnesses. Is there any God
besides me?
No, there is no other Rock; I know not
one."

[9] All who make idols are nothing,
and the things they treasure are
worthless.
Those who would speak up for them are
blind;

they are ignorant, to their own shame.
[10] Who shapes a god and casts an idol,
which can profit him nothing?
[11] He and his kind will be put to shame;
craftsmen are nothing but men.
Let them all come together and take their
stand;
they will be brought down to terror and
infamy.

[12] The blacksmith takes a tool
and works with it in the coals;
he shapes an idol with hammers,
he forges it with the might of his arm.
He gets hungry and loses his strength;
he drinks no water and grows faint.
[13] The carpenter measures with a line
and makes an outline with a marker;
he roughs it out with chisels
and marks it with compasses.
He shapes it in the form of man,
of man in all his glory,
that it may dwell in a shrine.
[14] He cut down cedars,
or perhaps took a cypress or oak.
He let it grow among the trees of the forest,
or planted a pine, and the rain made it
grow.
[15] It is man's fuel for burning;
some of it he takes and warms himself,
he kindles a fire and bakes bread.
But he also fashions a god and worships it;
he makes an idol and bows down to it.
[16] Half of the wood he burns in the fire;
over it he prepares his meal,
he roasts his meat and eats his fill.
He also warms himself and says,
"Ah! I am warm; I see the fire."
[17] From the rest he makes a god, his idol;
he bows down to it and worships.
He prays to it and says,
"Save me; you are my god."
[18] They know nothing, they understand
nothing;
their eyes are plastered over so they
cannot see,
and their minds closed so they cannot
understand.
[19] No one stops to think,

---

[a]28 The Hebrew term refers to the irrevocable giving over of things or persons to the LORD, often by totally destroying them.

no one has the knowledge or
understanding to say,
"Half of it I used for fuel;
I even baked bread over its coals,
I roasted meat and I ate.
Shall I make a detestable thing from what
is left?
Shall I bow down to a block of wood?"
20 He feeds on ashes, a deluded heart
misleads him;
he cannot save himself, or say,
"Is not this thing in my right hand a
lie?"

21 "Remember these things, O Jacob,
for you are my servant, O Israel.
I have made you, you are my servant;
O Israel, I will not forget you.
22 I have swept away your offenses like a
cloud,
your sins like the morning mist.
Return to me,
for I have redeemed you."

23 Sing for joy, O heavens, for the LORD has
done this;
shout aloud, O earth beneath.
Burst into song, you mountains,
you forests and all your trees,
for the LORD has redeemed Jacob,
he displays his glory in Israel.

Jerusalem to Be Inhabited

24 "This is what the LORD says—
your Redeemer, who formed you in the
womb:

I am the LORD,
who has made all things,
who alone stretched out the heavens,
who spread out the earth by myself,

25 who foils the signs of false prophets
and makes fools of diviners,
who overthrows the learning of the wise
and turns it into nonsense,
26 who carries out the words of his servants
and fulfills the predictions of his
messengers,

who says of Jerusalem, 'It shall be
inhabited,'

of the towns of Judah, 'They shall be
built,'
and of their ruins, 'I will restore them,'
27 who says to the watery deep, 'Be dry,
and I will dry up your streams,'
28 who says of Cyrus, 'He is my shepherd
and will accomplish all that I please;
he will say of Jerusalem, "Let it be
rebuilt,"
and of the temple, "Let its foundations
be laid." '

45 "This is what the LORD says to his
anointed,
to Cyrus, whose right hand I take
hold of
to subdue nations before him
and to strip kings of their armor,
to open doors before him
so that gates will not be shut:
2 I will go before you
and will level the mountains*a*;
I will break down gates of bronze
and cut through bars of iron.
3 I will give you the treasures of darkness,
riches stored in secret places,
so that you may know that I am the LORD,
the God of Israel, who summons you by
name.
4 For the sake of Jacob my servant,
of Israel my chosen,
I summon you by name
and bestow on you a title of honor,
though you do not acknowledge me.
5 I am the LORD, and there is no other;
apart from me there is no God.
I will strengthen you,
though you have not acknowledged me,
6 so that from the rising of the sun
to the place of its setting
men may know there is none besides me.
I am the LORD, and there is no other.
7 I form the light and create darkness,
I bring prosperity and create disaster;
I, the LORD, do all these things.

8 "You heavens above, rain down
righteousness;
let the clouds shower it down.

*a*2 Dead Sea Scrolls and Septuagint; the meaning of the word in the Masoretic Text is uncertain.

Let the earth open wide,
  let salvation spring up,
let righteousness grow with it;
  I, the LORD, have created it.

9 "Woe to him who quarrels with his Maker,
  to him who is but a potsherd among the
    potsherds on the ground.
Does the clay say to the potter,
  'What are you making?'
Does your work say,
  'He has no hands'?
10 Woe to him who says to his father,
  'What have you begotten?'
or to his mother,
  'What have you brought to birth?'

11 "This is what the LORD says—
  the Holy One of Israel, and its Maker:
Concerning things to come,
  do you question me about my children,
  or give me orders about the work of my
    hands?
12 It is I who made the earth
  and created mankind upon it.
My own hands stretched out the heavens;
  I marshaled their starry hosts.
13 I will raise up Cyrus[a] in my
    righteousness:
  I will make all his ways straight.
He will rebuild my city
  and set my exiles free,
but not for a price or reward,
  says the LORD Almighty."

14 This is what the LORD says:

"The products of Egypt and
    the merchandise of
    Cush,[b]
  and those tall Sabeans—
they will come over to you
  and will be yours;
they will trudge behind
    you,
  coming over to you in
    chains.
They will bow down before
    you
  and plead with you,
    saying,

'Surely God is with you, and there is no
    other;
  there is no other god.'"

15 Truly you are a God who hides himself,
  O God and Savior of Israel.
16 All the makers of idols will be put to shame
    and disgraced;
  they will go off into disgrace together.
17 But Israel will be saved by the LORD
  with an everlasting salvation;
you will never be put to shame or disgraced,
  to ages everlasting.

18 For this is what the LORD says—
  he who created the heavens,
  he is God;
he who fashioned and made the earth,
  he founded it;
he did not create it to be empty,
  but formed it to be inhabited—
he says:
"I am the LORD,
  and there is no other.
19 I have not spoken in secret,
  from somewhere in a land of darkness;
I have not said to Jacob's descendants,
  'Seek me in vain.'
I, the LORD, speak the truth;
  I declare what is right.

20 "Gather together and come;
  assemble, you fugitives from the nations.
Ignorant are those who carry about idols
    of wood,
  who pray to gods that cannot save.
21 Declare what is to be,
    present it—
  let them take counsel
    together.
Who foretold this long ago,
  who declared it from the
    distant past?
Was it not I, the LORD?
  And there is no God
    apart from me,
a righteous God and a
    Savior;
  there is none but me.

22 "Turn to me and be saved,

Isaiah 45:22

God Offers Salvation

"Turn to me and be saved,
all you ends of the earth;
for I am God, and
there is no other."

---

[a] 13 Hebrew *him*   [b] 14 That is, the upper Nile region

all you ends of the earth;
for I am God, and there is no other.
23 By myself I have sworn,
my mouth has uttered in all integrity
a word that will not be revoked:
Before me every knee will bow;
by me every tongue will swear.
24 They will say of me, 'In the LORD alone
are righteousness and strength.'"
All who have raged against him
will come to him and be put to shame.
25 But in the LORD all the descendants of Israel
will be found righteous and will exult.

Gods of Babylon

46 Bel bows down, Nebo stoops low;
their idols are borne by beasts of
burden.[a]
The images that are carried about are
burdensome,
a burden for the weary.
2 They stoop and bow down together;
unable to rescue the burden,
they themselves go off into captivity.

3 "Listen to me, O house of Jacob,
all you who remain of the house of Israel,
you whom I have upheld since you were
conceived,
and have carried since your birth.
4 Even to your old age and gray hairs
I am he, I am he who will sustain you.
I have made you and I will carry you;
I will sustain you and I will rescue you.

5 "To whom will you compare me or count
me equal?
To whom will you liken me that we may
be compared?
6 Some pour out gold from their bags
and weigh out silver on the scales;
they hire a goldsmith to make it into a god,
and they bow down and worship it.
7 They lift it to their shoulders and carry it;
they set it up in its place, and there it
stands.
From that spot it cannot move.
Though one cries out to it, it does not
answer;
it cannot save him from his troubles.

8 "Remember this, fix it in mind,
take it to heart, you rebels.
9 Remember the former things, those of long
ago;
I am God, and there is no other;
I am God, and there is none like me.
10 I make known the end from the beginning,
from ancient times, what is still to come.
I say: My purpose will stand,
and I will do all that I please.
11 From the east I summon a bird of prey;
from a far-off land, a man to fulfill my
purpose.
What I have said, that will I bring about;
what I have planned, that will I do.
12 Listen to me, you stubborn-hearted,
you who are far from righteousness.
13 I am bringing my righteousness near,
it is not far away;
and my salvation will not be delayed.
I will grant salvation to Zion,
my splendor to Israel.

The Fall of Babylon

47 "Go down, sit in the dust,
Virgin Daughter of Babylon;
sit on the ground without a throne,
Daughter of the Babylonians.[b]
No more will you be called
tender or delicate.
2 Take millstones and grind flour;
take off your veil.
Lift up your skirts, bare your legs,
and wade through the streams.
3 Your nakedness will be exposed
and your shame uncovered.
I will take vengeance;
I will spare no one."

4 Our Redeemer—the LORD Almighty is his
name—
is the Holy One of Israel.

5 "Sit in silence, go into darkness,
Daughter of the Babylonians;
no more will you be called
queen of kingdoms.
6 I was angry with my people
and desecrated my inheritance;
I gave them into your hand,

---

[a]1 Or *are but beasts and cattle*   [b]1 Or *Chaldeans*; also in verse 5

and you showed them no mercy.
Even on the aged
you laid a very heavy yoke.
7 You said, 'I will continue forever—
the eternal queen!'
But you did not consider these things
or reflect on what might happen.

8 "Now then, listen, you wanton creature,
lounging in your security
and saying to yourself,
'I am, and there is none besides me.
I will never be a widow
or suffer the loss of children.'
9 Both of these will overtake you
in a moment, on a single day:
loss of children and widowhood.
They will come upon you in full measure,
in spite of your many sorceries
and all your potent spells.
10 You have trusted in your wickedness
and have said, 'No one sees me.'
Your wisdom and knowledge mislead you
when you say to yourself,
'I am, and there is none besides me.'
11 Disaster will come upon you,
and you will not know how to conjure
it away.
A calamity will fall upon you
that you cannot ward off with a ransom;
a catastrophe you cannot foresee
will suddenly come upon you.

12 "Keep on, then, with your magic spells
and with your many sorceries,
which you have labored at since
childhood.
Perhaps you will succeed,
perhaps you will cause terror.
13 All the counsel you have received has only
worn you out!
Let your astrologers come forward,
those stargazers who make predictions
month by month,
let them save you from what is coming
upon you.
14 Surely they are like stubble;
the fire will burn them up.
They cannot even save themselves
from the power of the flame.
Here are no coals to warm anyone;

here is no fire to sit by.
15 That is all they can do for you—
these you have labored with
and trafficked with since childhood.
Each of them goes on in his error;
there is not one that can save you.

Stubborn Israel

48 "Listen to this, O house of Jacob,
you who are called by the name of
Israel
and come from the line of Judah,
you who take oaths in the name of the
LORD
and invoke the God of Israel—
but not in truth or righteousness—
2 you who call yourselves citizens of the holy
city
and rely on the God of Israel—
the LORD Almighty is his name:
3 I foretold the former things long ago,
my mouth announced them and I made
them known;
then suddenly I acted, and they came
to pass.
4 For I knew how stubborn you were;
the sinews of your neck were iron,
your forehead was bronze.
5 Therefore I told you these things long ago;
before they happened I announced them
to you
so that you could not say,
'My idols did them;
my wooden image and metal god
ordained them.'
6 You have heard these things; look at them
all.
Will you not admit them?

"From now on I will tell you of new things,
of hidden things unknown to you.
7 They are created now, and not long ago;
you have not heard of them before
today.
So you cannot say,
'Yes, I knew of them.'
8 You have neither heard nor understood;
from of old your ear has not been open.
Well do I know how treacherous you are;
you were called a rebel from birth.
9 For my own name's sake I delay my wrath;

for the sake of my praise I hold it back
from you,
so as not to cut you off.

¹⁰ See, I have refined you, though not as
silver;
I have tested you in the
furnace of affliction.

¹¹ For my own sake, for my
own sake, I do this.
How can I let myself be
defamed?
I will not yield my glory
to another.

Israel Freed

¹² "Listen to me, O Jacob,
Israel, whom I have
called:
I am he;
I am the first and I am
the last.

¹³ My own hand laid the foundations of the
earth,
and my right hand spread out the
heavens;
when I summon them,
they all stand up together.

¹⁴ "Come together, all of you, and listen:
Which of the idols has foretold these
things?
The LORD's chosen ally
will carry out his purpose against
Babylon;
his arm will be against the
Babylonians.ᵃ

¹⁵ I, even I, have spoken;
yes, I have called him.
I will bring him,
and he will succeed in his mission.

¹⁶ "Come near me and listen to this:

"From the first announcement I have not
spoken in secret;
at the time it happens, I am there."

And now the Sovereign LORD has sent me,
with his Spirit.

¹⁷ This is what the LORD says—
your Redeemer, the Holy One of Israel:

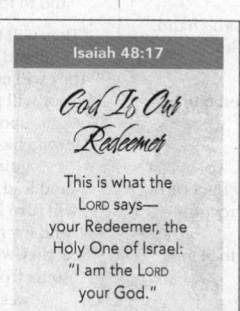

Isaiah 48:17

God Is Our Redeemer

This is what the
LORD says—
your Redeemer, the
Holy One of Israel:
"I am the LORD
your God."

"I am the LORD your God,
who teaches you what is best for you,
who directs you in the way you should
go.

¹⁸ If only you had paid
attention to my
commands,
your peace would have
been like a river,
your righteousness like
the waves of the
sea.

¹⁹ Your descendants would
have been like the
sand,
your children like its
numberless grains;
their name would never be
cut off
nor destroyed from
before me."

²⁰ Leave Babylon,
flee from the Babylonians!
Announce this with shouts of joy
and proclaim it.
Send it out to the ends of the earth;
say, "The LORD has redeemed his
servant Jacob."

²¹ They did not thirst when he led them
through the deserts;
he made water flow for them from the
rock;
he split the rock
and water gushed out.

²² "There is no peace," says the LORD, "for the
wicked."

The Servant of the LORD

49 Listen to me, you islands;
hear this, you distant nations:
Before I was born the LORD called me;
from my birth he has made mention of
my name.

² He made my mouth like a sharpened
sword,
in the shadow of his hand he hid me;
he made me into a polished arrow
and concealed me in his quiver.

³ He said to me, "You are my servant,

ᵃ 14 Or *Chaldeans*; also in verse 20

Israel, in whom I will display my
splendor."
4 But I said, "I have labored to no purpose;
I have spent my strength in vain and for
nothing.
Yet what is due me is in the LORD's hand,
and my reward is with my God."

5 And now the LORD says—
he who formed me in the womb to be
his servant
to bring Jacob back to him
and gather Israel to himself,
for I am honored in the eyes of the LORD
and my God has been my strength—
6 he says:
"It is too small a thing for you to be my
servant
to restore the tribes of Jacob
and bring back those of Israel I have
kept.
I will also make you a light for the
Gentiles,
that you may bring my salvation to the
ends of the earth."

7 This is what the LORD
says—
the Redeemer and Holy
One of Israel—
to him who was despised
and abhorred by the
nation,
to the servant of rulers:
"Kings will see you and
rise up,
princes will see and bow
down,
because of the LORD, who is
faithful,
the Holy One of Israel,
who has chosen
you."

Restoration of Israel

8 This is what the LORD says:

"In the time of my favor I will answer you,
and in the day of salvation I will help
you;
I will keep you and will make you

to be a covenant for the people,
to restore the land
and to reassign its desolate inheritances,
9 to say to the captives, 'Come out,'
and to those in darkness, 'Be free!'

"They will feed beside the roads
and find pasture on every barren hill.
10 They will neither hunger nor thirst,
nor will the desert heat or the sun beat
upon them.
He who has compassion on them will
guide them
and lead them beside springs of water.
11 I will turn all my mountains into roads,
and my highways will be raised up.
12 See, they will come from afar—
some from the north, some from the
west,
some from the region of Aswan.ᵃ"

13 Shout for joy, O heavens;
rejoice, O earth;
burst into song, O mountains!
For the LORD comforts his people
and will have
compassion on his
afflicted ones.

14 But Zion said, "The LORD
has forsaken me,
the Lord has forgotten
me."

15 "Can a mother forget the
baby at her breast
and have no compassion
on the child she has
borne?
Though she may forget,
I will not forget you!
16 See, I have engraved you
on the palms of my
hands;
your walls are ever before me.
17 Your sons hasten back,
and those who laid you waste depart
from you.
18 Lift up your eyes and look around;
all your sons gather and come to you.
As surely as I live," declares the LORD,

Isaiah 49:15

God Doesn't Forget Us

"Can a mother forget the
baby at her breast
and have no compassion
on the child she
has borne?
Though she may forget,
I will not forget you!"

ᵃ12 Dead Sea Scrolls; Masoretic Text *Sinim*

"you will wear them all as ornaments;
    you will put them on, like a bride.

19 "Though you were ruined and made
        desolate
    and your land laid waste,
now you will be too small for your people,
    and those who devoured you will be far
        away.
20 The children born during your
        bereavement
    will yet say in your hearing,
'This place is too small for us;
    give us more space to live in.'
21 Then you will say in your heart,
    'Who bore me these?
I was bereaved and barren;
    I was exiled and rejected.
    Who brought these up?
I was left all alone,
    but these—where have they come
        from?'"

22 This is what the Sovereign LORD says:

"See, I will beckon to the Gentiles,
    I will lift up my banner to the peoples;
they will bring your sons in their arms
    and carry your daughters on their
        shoulders.
23 Kings will be your foster fathers,
    and their queens your nursing mothers.
They will bow down before you with their
        faces to the ground;
    they will lick the dust at your feet.
Then you will know that I am the LORD;
    those who hope in me will not be
        disappointed."

24 Can plunder be taken from warriors,
    or captives rescued from the fierce[a]?

25 But this is what the LORD says:

"Yes, captives will be taken from warriors,
    and plunder retrieved from the fierce;
I will contend with those who contend
        with you,
    and your children I will save.
26 I will make your oppressors eat their own
        flesh;

they will be drunk on their own blood,
    as with wine.
Then all mankind will know
    that I, the LORD, am your Savior,
    your Redeemer, the Mighty One of
        Jacob."

Israel's Sin and the Servant's Obedience

50 This is what the LORD says:

"Where is your mother's certificate of
        divorce
    with which I sent her away?
Or to which of my creditors
    did I sell you?
Because of your sins you were sold;
    because of your transgressions your
        mother was sent away.
2 When I came, why was there no one?
    When I called, why was there no one to
        answer?
Was my arm too short to ransom you?
    Do I lack the strength to rescue you?
By a mere rebuke I dry up the sea,
    I turn rivers into a desert;
their fish rot for lack of water
    and die of thirst.
3 I clothe the sky with darkness
    and make sackcloth its covering."

4 The Sovereign LORD has given me an
        instructed tongue,
    to know the word that sustains the
        weary.
He wakens me morning by morning,
    wakens my ear to listen like one being
        taught.
5 The Sovereign LORD has opened my ears,
    and I have not been rebellious;
    I have not drawn back.
6 I offered my back to those who beat me,
    my cheeks to those who pulled out my
        beard;
I did not hide my face
    from mocking and spitting.
7 Because the Sovereign LORD helps me,
    I will not be disgraced.
Therefore have I set my face like flint,
    and I know I will not be put to shame.
8 He who vindicates me is near.

---

a24 Dead Sea Scrolls, Vulgate and Syriac (see also Septuagint and verse 25); Masoretic Text *righteous*

Who then will bring charges against
    me?
  Let us face each other!
  Who is my accuser?
  Let him confront me!
⁹ It is the Sovereign LORD who helps me.
  Who is he that will condemn me?
  They will all wear out like a garment;
  the moths will eat them up.

¹⁰ Who among you fears the LORD
  and obeys the word of his servant?
  Let him who walks in the dark,
  who has no light,
  trust in the name of the LORD
  and rely on his God.
¹¹ But now, all you who light fires
  and provide yourselves with flaming
    torches,
  go, walk in the light of your fires
  and of the torches you have set ablaze.
  This is what you shall receive from my
    hand:
  You will lie down in torment.

Everlasting Salvation for Zion

51 "Listen to me, you who pursue
    righteousness
  and who seek the LORD:
  Look to the rock from which you were cut
  and to the quarry from which you were
    hewn;
² look to Abraham, your father,
  and to Sarah, who gave you birth.
  When I called him he was but one,
  and I blessed him and made him many.
³ The LORD will surely comfort Zion
  and will look with compassion on all her
    ruins;
  he will make her deserts like Eden,
  her wastelands like the garden of the
    LORD.
  Joy and gladness will be found in her,
  thanksgiving and the sound of singing.

⁴ "Listen to me, my people;
  hear me, my nation:
  The law will go out from me;
  my justice will become a light to the
    nations.
⁵ My righteousness draws near speedily,
  my salvation is on the way,

  and my arm will bring justice to the
    nations.
  The islands will look to me
  and wait in hope for my arm.
⁶ Lift up your eyes to the heavens,
  look at the earth beneath;
  the heavens will vanish like smoke,
  the earth will wear out like a garment
  and its inhabitants die like flies.
  But my salvation will last forever,
  my righteousness will never fail.

⁷ "Hear me, you who know what is right,
  you people who have my law in your
    hearts:
  Do not fear the reproach of men
  or be terrified by their insults.
⁸ For the moth will eat them up like a
    garment;
  the worm will devour them like wool.
  But my righteousness will last forever,
  my salvation through all generations."

⁹ Awake, awake! Clothe yourself with
    strength,
  O arm of the LORD;
  awake, as in days gone by,
  as in generations of old.
  Was it not you who cut Rahab to pieces,
  who pierced that monster through?
¹⁰ Was it not you who dried up the sea,
  the waters of the great deep,
  who made a road in the depths of the sea
  so that the redeemed might cross over?
¹¹ The ransomed of the LORD will return.
  They will enter Zion with singing;
  everlasting joy will crown their heads.
  Gladness and joy will overtake them,
  and sorrow and sighing will flee away.

¹² "I, even I, am he who comforts you.
  Who are you that you fear mortal men,
  the sons of men, who are but grass,
¹³ that you forget the LORD your Maker,
  who stretched out the heavens
  and laid the foundations of the earth,
  that you live in constant terror every day
  because of the wrath of the oppressor,
  who is bent on destruction?
  For where is the wrath of the oppressor?
¹⁴   The cowering prisoners will soon be set
    free;

they will not die in their dungeon,
  nor will they lack bread.
¹⁵For I am the LORD your God,
  who churns up the sea so that its waves
    roar—
  the LORD Almighty is his name.
¹⁶I have put my words in your mouth
  and covered you with the shadow of my
    hand—
I who set the heavens in place,
  who laid the foundations of the
    earth,
  and who say to Zion, 'You are my
    people.'"

The Cup of the LORD's Wrath

¹⁷Awake, awake!
  Rise up, O Jerusalem,
you who have drunk from the hand of the
    LORD
  the cup of his wrath,
you who have drained to its dregs
  the goblet that makes men stagger.
¹⁸Of all the sons she bore
  there was none to guide her;
of all the sons she reared
  there was none to take her by the
    hand.
¹⁹These double calamities have come upon
    you—
  who can comfort you?—
ruin and destruction,
    famine and sword—
  who can[a] console you?
²⁰Your sons have fainted;
  they lie at the head of
    every street,
  like antelope caught in
    a net.
They are filled with the
    wrath of the LORD
  and the rebuke of your
    God.

²¹Therefore hear this, you
    afflicted one,
  made drunk, but not
    with wine.
²²This is what your Sovereign LORD says,
  your God, who defends his people:

"See, I have taken out of your hand
  the cup that made you stagger;
from that cup, the goblet of my
    wrath,
  you will never drink again.
²³I will put it into the hands of your
    tormentors,
  who said to you,
  'Fall prostrate that we may walk over
    you.'
And you made your back like the
    ground,
  like a street to be walked over."

52

Awake, awake, O Zion,
  clothe yourself with strength.
Put on your garments of splendor,
  O Jerusalem, the holy city.
The uncircumcised and defiled
  will not enter you again.
²Shake off your dust;
  rise up, sit enthroned, O Jerusalem.
Free yourself from the chains on your
    neck,
  O captive Daughter of Zion.

³For this is what the LORD says:

"You were sold for nothing,
  and without money you will be
    redeemed."

⁴For this is what the Sovereign LORD says:

"At first my people went
    down to Egypt to
    live;
  lately, Assyria has
    oppressed them.

⁵"And now what do I have
here?" declares the LORD.

"For my people have been
    taken away for
    nothing,
  and those who rule them
    mock,[b]"
    declares the LORD.

"And all day long
  my name is constantly blasphemed.

Isaiah 51:12

God Comforts His People

"I, even I, am he who
comforts you.
Who are you that you
fear mortal men,
the sons of men, who
are but grass?"

ᵃ19 Dead Sea Scrolls, Septuagint, Vulgate and Syriac; Masoretic Text / how can I   ᵇ5 Dead Sea Scrolls and Vulgate; Masoretic Text wail

⁶ Therefore my people will know my name;
    therefore in that day they will know
that it is I who foretold it.
    Yes, it is I."

⁷ How beautiful on the mountains
    are the feet of those who bring good
        news,
who proclaim peace,
    who bring good tidings,
    who proclaim salvation,
who say to Zion,
    "Your God reigns!"
⁸ Listen! Your watchmen lift
        up their voices;
    together they shout for
        joy.
When the LORD returns to
        Zion,
    they will see it with their
        own eyes.
⁹ Burst into songs of joy
        together,
    you ruins of Jerusalem,
for the LORD has comforted
        his people,
    he has redeemed Jerusalem.
¹⁰ The LORD will lay bare his holy arm
    in the sight of all the nations,
and all the ends of the earth will see
    the salvation of our God.

¹¹ Depart, depart, go out from there!
    Touch no unclean thing!
Come out from it and be pure,
    you who carry the vessels of the LORD.
¹² But you will not leave in haste
    or go in flight;
for the LORD will go before you,
    the God of Israel will be your rear guard.

The Suffering and Glory of the Servant
¹³ See, my servant will act wisely[a];
    he will be raised and lifted up and
        highly exalted.
¹⁴ Just as there were many who were appalled
    at him[b]—
    his appearance was so disfigured beyond
        that of any man
    and his form marred beyond human
        likeness—

¹⁵ so will he sprinkle many nations,[c]
    and kings will shut their mouths
        because of him.
For what they were not told, they will see,
    and what they have not heard, they will
        understand.

53

Who has believed our message
and to whom has the arm of the
LORD been revealed?
² He grew up before him like
        a tender shoot,
    and like a root out of dry
        ground.
He had no beauty or
        majesty to attract us
        to him,
    nothing in his
        appearance that we
        should desire him.
³ He was despised and
        rejected by men,
    a man of sorrows, and
        familiar with
        suffering.
Like one from whom men hide their faces
    he was despised, and we esteemed him
        not.

⁴ Surely he took up our infirmities
    and carried our sorrows,
yet we considered him stricken by God,
    smitten by him, and afflicted.
⁵ But he was pierced for our transgressions,
    he was crushed for our iniquities;
the punishment that brought us peace was
        upon him,
    and by his wounds we are healed.
⁶ We all, like sheep, have gone astray,
    each of us has turned to his own way;
and the LORD has laid on him
    the iniquity of us all.

⁷ He was oppressed and afflicted,
    yet he did not open his mouth;
he was led like a lamb to the slaughter,
    and as a sheep before her shearers is
        silent,
so he did not open his mouth.
⁸ By oppression[d] and judgment he was taken
        away.

Isaiah 52:7

God Reigns Over the World

How beautiful on the
mountains
are the feet of those who
bring good news . . .
"Your God reigns!"

---

[a]13 Or *will prosper*   [b]14 Hebrew *you*   [c]15 Hebrew; Septuagint *so will many nations marvel at him*   [d]8 Or *From arrest*

Rejoice in Suffering?

Read: Isaiah 53:1–12

DID YOU WONDER IF you read that Scripture verse right? God *willed* for Jesus to suffer. Those are difficult words to understand. We don't want to believe it. After all, if God intended for Jesus to suffer, he might want us to suffer too. And we're not sure we're up for that calling.

"Isn't God loving?" we reason. "If so, why would he want us to suffer? It doesn't make sense. Shouldn't God want his children to live in a world with no difficulties, disease or death?"

Ah, but God *did* create the world perfect and without suffering in a garden long ago. We all have an Eden-like yearning because God created us to live there. But we sinned, and suffering was the penalty for sin. Therefore, in this life, we will experience suffering and death. In fact, as the Isaiah passage reveals, God actually *intended* for Jesus to suffer during his earthly life so that we could be saved.

In Romans, Paul tells us to expect suffering on earth—and even to rejoice in it. Why rejoice? Because God uses it to produce perseverance, character and hope. God doesn't waste any suffering we experience. He uses it for our good if we let him.

However, God isn't callous to our suffering. He cares deeply. Jesus showed us that when he came to earth. He healed those who were suffering. He wept because people were suffering. And now he has conquered suffering. He is seated at the right hand of God. We will suffer on earth, but the story doesn't end there. Go back to Isaiah 53:11: "After the suffering of his soul, he will see the light of life." That was true for Jesus, and it's true for all those who believe Jesus is Lord. Your suffering is not the end of the story. If you're a believer, you will one day live in a perfect place: "Then I saw a new heaven and a new earth . . . There will be no more death or mourning or crying or pain, for the old order of things has passed away" (Revelation 21:1,4).

Isaiah 53:10–11

Yet it was the LORD's will to crush him and cause him to suffer, and though the LORD makes his life a guilt offering, he will see his offspring and prolong his days, and the will of the LORD will prosper in his hand. After the suffering of his soul, he will see the light of life and be satisfied; by his knowledge my righteous servant will justify many, and he will bear their iniquities.

reflection

1 Where do you see suffering today?

2 Can you give examples of how God has comforted you during a time of suffering or has brought you through a trial?

3 Think of someone you can encourage who is suffering. Which of God's promises can you share?

RELATED READINGS

Exodus 3:7–9;
Romans 5:3–8; 8:17–25;
James 1:2–4

Go to page 894 for your next devotional reading.

And who can speak of his descendants?
For he was cut off from the land of the
living;
for the transgression of my people he
was stricken.[a]

9 He was assigned a grave with the wicked,
and with the rich in his death,
though he had done no violence,
nor was any deceit in his mouth.

10 Yet it was the LORD's will to crush him and
cause him to suffer,
and though the LORD makes[b] his life a
guilt offering,
he will see his offspring and prolong his
days,
and the will of the LORD will prosper in
his hand.

11 After the suffering of his soul,
he will see the light of life[c] and be
satisfied[d];
by his knowledge[e] my righteous servant
will justify many,
and he will bear their iniquities.

12 Therefore I will give him a portion among
the great,[f]
and he will divide the spoils with the
strong,[g]
because he poured out his life unto death,
and was numbered with the
transgressors.
For he bore the sin of many,
and made intercession for the
transgressors.

The Future Glory of Zion

54 "Sing, O barren woman,
you who never bore a child;
burst into song, shout for joy,
you who were never in labor;
because more are the children of the
desolate woman
than of her who has a husband,"
says the LORD.

2 "Enlarge the place of your tent,
stretch your tent curtains wide,
do not hold back;
lengthen your cords,

strengthen your stakes.
3 For you will spread out to the right and to
the left;
your descendants will dispossess nations
and settle in their desolate cities.

4 "Do not be afraid; you will not suffer
shame.
Do not fear disgrace; you will not be
humiliated.
You will forget the shame of your youth
and remember no more the reproach of
your widowhood.
5 For your Maker is your husband—
the LORD Almighty is his name—
the Holy One of Israel is your Redeemer;
he is called the God of all the earth.
6 The LORD will call you back
as if you were a wife deserted and
distressed in spirit—
a wife who married young,
only to be rejected," says your God.
7 "For a brief moment I abandoned you,
but with deep compassion I will bring
you back.
8 In a surge of anger
I hid my face from you for a moment,
but with everlasting kindness
I will have compassion on you,"
says the LORD your Redeemer.

9 "To me this is like the days of Noah,
when I swore that the waters of Noah
would never again cover the
earth.
So now I have sworn not to be angry with
you,
never to rebuke you again.
10 Though the mountains be shaken
and the hills be removed,
yet my unfailing love for you will not be
shaken
nor my covenant of peace be removed,"
says the LORD, who has compassion on
you.

11 "O afflicted city, lashed by storms and not
comforted,

---

a8 Or away. / Yet who of his generation considered / that he was cut off from the land of the living / for the transgression of my people, / to whom the blow was due? b10 Hebrew though you make c11 Dead Sea Scrolls (see also Septuagint); Masoretic Text does not have the light of life. d11 Or (with Masoretic Text) He will see the result of the suffering of his soul / and be satisfied e11 Or by knowledge of him f12 Or many g12 Or numerous

I will build you with stones of
    turquoise,*a*
your foundations with sapphires.*b*
¹² I will make your battlements of rubies,
    your gates of sparkling jewels,
    and all your walls of precious stones.
¹³ All your sons will be taught by the LORD,
    and great will be your children's peace.
¹⁴ In righteousness you will be established:
    Tyranny will be far from you;
    you will have nothing to fear.
Terror will be far removed;
    it will not come near you.
¹⁵ If anyone does attack you, it will not be my
    doing;
whoever attacks you will surrender to
    you.

¹⁶ "See, it is I who created the blacksmith
    who fans the coals into flame
    and forges a weapon fit for its work.
And it is I who have created the destroyer
    to work havoc;
¹⁷   no weapon forged against you will
    prevail,
    and you will refute every tongue that
    accuses you.
This is the heritage of the servants of the
    LORD,
and this is their
         vindication from
         me,"
         declares the LORD.

Invitation to the Thirsty

55 "Come, all you who
    are thirsty,
come to the waters;
and you who have no
    money,
come, buy and eat!
Come, buy wine and milk
    without money and
    without cost.
² Why spend money on what
    is not bread,
and your labor on what
    does not satisfy?
Listen, listen to me, and eat
    what is good,

and your soul will delight in the richest
    of fare.
³ Give ear and come to me;
    hear me, that your soul may live.
I will make an everlasting covenant with
    you,
    my faithful love promised to David.
⁴ See, I have made him a witness to the
    peoples,
    a leader and commander of the peoples.
⁵ Surely you will summon nations you know
    not,
    and nations that do not know you will
      hasten to you,
because of the LORD your God,
    the Holy One of Israel,
    for he has endowed you with splendor."

⁶ Seek the LORD while he may be found;
    call on him while he is near.
⁷ Let the wicked forsake his way
    and the evil man his thoughts.
Let him turn to the LORD, and he will have
    mercy on him,
    and to our God, for he will freely
      pardon.

⁸ "For my thoughts are not your thoughts,
    neither are your ways my ways,"
         declares the LORD.
⁹ "As the heavens are higher
        than the earth,
    so are my ways higher
        than your ways
    and my thoughts than
        your thoughts.
¹⁰ As the rain and the snow
    come down from heaven,
    and do not return to it
      without watering the
      earth
and making it bud and
      flourish,
    so that it yields seed for
      the sower and bread
      for the eater,
¹¹ so is my word that goes out
    from my mouth:
It will not return to me
    empty,

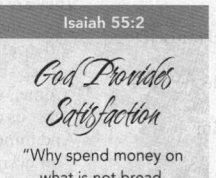

Isaiah 55:2

*God Provides
Satisfaction*

"Why spend money on
what is not bread,
and your labor on what
does not satisfy?
Listen, listen to me, and
eat what is good,
and your soul will delight
in the richest of fare."

---

*a*11 The meaning of the Hebrew for this word is uncertain.   *b*11 Or *lapis lazuli*

but will accomplish what I desire
    and achieve the purpose for which I
        sent it.
¹²You will go out in joy
    and be led forth in peace;
the mountains and hills
    will burst into song before you,
and all the trees of the field
    will clap their hands.
¹³Instead of the thornbush will grow the
        pine tree,
    and instead of briers the myrtle will
        grow.
This will be for the LORD's renown,
    for an everlasting sign,
    which will not be destroyed."

Salvation for Others

56 This is what the LORD says:

"Maintain justice
    and do what is right,
for my salvation is close at hand
    and my righteousness will soon be
        revealed.
²Blessed is the man who does this,
    the man who holds it fast,
who keeps the Sabbath without desecrating
        it,
    and keeps his hand from doing any
        evil."

³Let no foreigner who has bound himself to
        the LORD say,
    "The LORD will surely exclude me from
        his people."
And let not any eunuch complain,
    "I am only a dry tree."

⁴For this is what the LORD says:

"To the eunuchs who keep my Sabbaths,
    who choose what pleases me
    and hold fast to my covenant—
⁵to them I will give within my temple and
        its walls
    a memorial and a name
    better than sons and daughters;
I will give them an everlasting name
    that will not be cut off.
⁶And foreigners who bind themselves to the
        LORD

to serve him,
to love the name of the LORD,
    and to worship him,
all who keep the Sabbath without
        desecrating it
    and who hold fast to my covenant—
⁷these I will bring to my holy mountain
    and give them joy in my house of
        prayer.
Their burnt offerings and sacrifices
    will be accepted on my altar;
for my house will be called
    a house of prayer for all nations."
⁸The Sovereign LORD declares—
    he who gathers the exiles of Israel:
"I will gather still others to them
    besides those already gathered."

God's Accusation Against the Wicked

⁹Come, all you beasts of the field,
    come and devour, all you beasts of the
        forest!
¹⁰Israel's watchmen are blind,
    they all lack knowledge;
they are all mute dogs,
    they cannot bark;
they lie around and dream,
    they love to sleep.
¹¹They are dogs with mighty appetites;
    they never have enough.
They are shepherds who lack
        understanding;
    they all turn to their own way,
    each seeks his own gain.
¹²"Come," each one cries, "let me get wine!
    Let us drink our fill of beer!
And tomorrow will be like today,
    or even far better."

57 The righteous perish,
    and no one ponders it in his heart;
devout men are taken away,
    and no one understands
that the righteous are taken away
    to be spared from evil.
²Those who walk uprightly
    enter into peace;
    they find rest as they lie in death.

³"But you—come here, you sons of a
        sorceress,

you offspring of adulterers and
    prostitutes!
⁴ Whom are you mocking?
    At whom do you sneer
    and stick out your tongue?
Are you not a brood of rebels,
    the offspring of liars?
⁵ You burn with lust among the oaks
    and under every spreading tree;
you sacrifice your children in the ravines
    and under the overhanging crags.
⁶ The idols among the smooth stones of the
        ravines are your portion;
    they, they are your lot.
Yes, to them you have poured out drink
        offerings
    and offered grain offerings.
    In the light of these things, should I
        relent?
⁷ You have made your bed on a high and
        lofty hill;
    there you went up to offer your
        sacrifices.
⁸ Behind your doors and your doorposts
    you have put your pagan symbols.
    Forsaking me, you uncovered your bed,
        you climbed into it and opened it wide;
you made a pact with those whose beds
        you love,
    and you looked on their nakedness.
⁹ You went to Molech*a* with olive oil
    and increased your perfumes.
You sent your ambassadors*b* far away;
    you descended to the grave*c* itself!
¹⁰ You were wearied by all your ways,
    but you would not say, 'It is hopeless.'
You found renewal of your strength,
    and so you did not faint.

¹¹ "Whom have you so dreaded and feared
    that you have been false to me,
and have neither remembered me
    nor pondered this in your hearts?
Is it not because I have long been silent
    that you do not fear me?
¹² I will expose your righteousness and your
        works,
    and they will not benefit you.
¹³ When you cry out for help,

let your collection of idols save you!
The wind will carry all of them off,
    a mere breath will blow them away.
But the man who makes me his refuge
    will inherit the land
    and possess my holy mountain."

Comfort for the Contrite
¹⁴ And it will be said:

"Build up, build up, prepare the road!
    Remove the obstacles out of the way of
        my people."
¹⁵ For this is what the high and lofty One
        says—
    he who lives forever, whose name is
        holy:
"I live in a high and holy place,
    but also with him who is contrite and
        lowly in spirit,
to revive the spirit of the lowly
    and to revive the heart of the contrite.
¹⁶ I will not accuse forever,
    nor will I always be angry,
for then the spirit of man would grow faint
        before me—
    the breath of man that I have created.
¹⁷ I was enraged by his sinful greed;
    I punished him, and hid my face in
        anger,
    yet he kept on in his willful ways.
¹⁸ I have seen his ways, but I will heal him;
    I will guide him and restore comfort to
        him,
¹⁹   creating praise on the lips of the
        mourners in Israel.
Peace, peace, to those far and near,"
    says the Lᴏʀᴅ. "And I will heal them."
²⁰ But the wicked are like the tossing sea,
    which cannot rest,
    whose waves cast up mire and mud.
²¹ "There is no peace," says my God, "for the
        wicked."

True Fasting
58 "Shout it aloud, do not hold back.
    Raise your voice like a trumpet.
Declare to my people their rebellion
    and to the house of Jacob their sins.
² For day after day they seek me out;

---

*a*9 Or *to the king*   *b*9 Or *idols*   *c*9 Hebrew *Sheol*

they seem eager to know my ways,
as if they were a nation that does what is
          right
    and has not forsaken the commands of
          its God.
They ask me for just decisions
    and seem eager for God to come near
          them.
³ 'Why have we fasted,' they say,
    'and you have not seen it?
Why have we humbled ourselves,
    and you have not noticed?'

"Yet on the day of your fasting, you do as
          you please
    and exploit all your workers.
⁴ Your fasting ends in quarreling and strife,
    and in striking each
          other with wicked
          fists.
You cannot fast as you do
          today
    and expect your voice to
          be heard on high.
⁵ Is this the kind of fast I
          have chosen,
    only a day for a man to
          humble himself?
Is it only for bowing one's
          head like a reed
    and for lying on
          sackcloth and
          ashes?
Is that what you call a fast,
    a day acceptable to the LORD?

⁶ "Is not this the kind of fasting I have
          chosen:
    to loose the chains of injustice
          and untie the cords of the yoke,
    to set the oppressed free
          and break every yoke?
⁷ Is it not to share your food with the hungry
    and to provide the poor wanderer with
          shelter—
when you see the naked, to clothe him,
    and *not* to turn away from your own
          flesh and blood?
⁸ Then your light will break forth like the
          dawn,

and your healing will quickly appear;
then your righteousness*a* will go before
          you,
    and the glory of the LORD will be your
          rear guard.
⁹ Then you will call, and the LORD will
          answer;
    you will cry for help, and he will say:
          Here am I.

"If you do away with the yoke of oppression,
    with the pointing finger and malicious
          talk,
¹⁰ and if you spend yourselves in behalf of the
          hungry
    and satisfy the needs of the oppressed,
          then your light will rise in
                the darkness,
          and your night will
                become like the
                noonday.
¹¹ The LORD will guide you
                always;
          he will satisfy your needs
                in a sun-scorched
                land
          and will strengthen your
                frame.
You will be like a well-
                watered garden,
          like a spring whose
                waters never fail.
¹² Your people will rebuild
                the ancient ruins
    and will raise up the age-old
          foundations;
you will be called Repairer of Broken
          Walls,
    Restorer of Streets with Dwellings.

¹³ "If you keep your feet from breaking the
          Sabbath
    and from doing as you please on my
          holy day,
if you call the Sabbath a delight
    and the LORD's holy day honorable,
and if you honor it by not going your own
          way
    and not doing as you please or speaking
          idle words,

Isaiah 58:11

God Carries Us Through

"The LORD will guide
you always;
he will satisfy your needs
in a sun-scorched land
and will strengthen
your frame."

---

a8 Or your righteous One

¹⁴ then you will find your joy in the LORD,
  and I will cause you to ride on the
    heights of the land
  and to feast on the inheritance of your
    father Jacob."
    The mouth of the LORD has spoken.

Sin, Confession and Redemption

59 Surely the arm of the LORD is not too
      short to save,
  nor his ear too dull to hear.
² But your iniquities have separated
    you from your God;
  your sins have hidden his face from you,
    so that he will not hear.
³ For your hands are stained with blood,
    your fingers with guilt.
  Your lips have spoken lies,
    and your tongue mutters wicked things.
⁴ No one calls for justice;
    no one pleads his case with integrity.
  They rely on empty arguments and speak
    lies;
    they conceive trouble and give birth to
      evil.
⁵ They hatch the eggs of vipers
    and spin a spider's web.
  Whoever eats their eggs will die,
    and when one is broken, an adder is
      hatched.
⁶ Their cobwebs are useless for clothing;
    they cannot cover themselves with what
      they make.
  Their deeds are evil deeds,
    and acts of violence are in their hands.
⁷ Their feet rush into sin;
    they are swift to shed innocent blood.
  Their thoughts are evil thoughts;
    ruin and destruction mark their ways.
⁸ The way of peace they do not know;
    there is no justice in their paths.
  They have turned them into crooked roads;
    no one who walks in them will know
      peace.

⁹ So justice is far from us,
    and righteousness does not reach us.
  We look for light, but all is darkness;
    for brightness, but we walk in deep
      shadows.

¹⁰ Like the blind we grope along the wall,
    feeling our way like men without eyes.
  At midday we stumble as if it were twilight;
    among the strong, we are like the dead.
¹¹ We all growl like bears;
    we moan mournfully like doves.
  We look for justice, but find none;
    for deliverance, but it is far away.

¹² For our offenses are many in your sight,
    and our sins testify against us.
  Our offenses are ever with us,
    and we acknowledge our iniquities:
¹³ rebellion and treachery against the LORD,
    turning our backs on our God,
  fomenting oppression and revolt,
    uttering lies our hearts have conceived.
¹⁴ So justice is driven back,
    and righteousness stands at a distance;
  truth has stumbled in the streets,
    honesty cannot enter.
¹⁵ Truth is nowhere to be found,
    and whoever shuns evil becomes a prey.

  The LORD looked and was displeased
    that there was no justice.
¹⁶ He saw that there was no one,
    he was appalled that there was no one to
      intervene;
  so his own arm worked salvation for him,
    and his own righteousness sustained
      him.
¹⁷ He put on righteousness as his breastplate,
    and the helmet of salvation on his head;
  he put on the garments of vengeance
    and wrapped himself in zeal as in a
      cloak.
¹⁸ According to what they have done,
    so will he repay
  wrath to his enemies
    and retribution to his foes;
  he will repay the islands their due.
¹⁹ From the west, men will fear the name of
    the LORD,
  and from the rising of the sun, they will
    revere his glory.
  For he will come like a pent-up flood
    that the breath of the LORD drives
      along.ᵃ

ᵃ **19** Or *When the enemy comes in like a flood, / the Spirit of the LORD will put him to flight*

20 "The Redeemer will come to Zion,
   to those in Jacob who repent of their
      sins,"
                      declares the LORD.

21 "As for me, this is my covenant with them,"
says the LORD. "My Spirit, who is on you, and
my words that I have put in your mouth will not
depart from your mouth, or from the mouths
of your children, or from the mouths of their
descendants from this time on and forever,"
says the LORD.

The Glory of Zion

60 "Arise, shine, for your light has
   come,
      and the glory of the LORD rises upon
         you.
2 See, darkness covers the earth
      and thick darkness is over the peoples,
   but the LORD rises upon you
      and his glory appears over you.
3 Nations will come to your light,
      and kings to the brightness of your
         dawn.

4 "Lift up your eyes and look about you:
      All assemble and come to you;
   your sons come from afar,
      and your daughters are carried on the
         arm.
5 Then you will look and be radiant,
      your heart will throb and swell with joy;
   the wealth on the seas will be brought to
         you,
      to you the riches of the nations will
         come.
6 Herds of camels will cover your land,
      young camels of Midian and Ephah.
   And all from Sheba will come,
      bearing gold and incense
      and proclaiming the praise of the LORD.
7 All Kedar's flocks will be gathered to you,
      the rams of Nebaioth will serve you;
   they will be accepted as offerings on my
         altar,
      and I will adorn my glorious temple.

8 "Who are these that fly along like clouds,
      like doves to their nests?
9 Surely the islands look to me;

in the lead are the ships of Tarshish,[a]
   bringing your sons from afar,
      with their silver and gold,
   to the honor of the LORD your God,
      the Holy One of Israel,
      for he has endowed you with splendor.

10 "Foreigners will rebuild your walls,
      and their kings will serve you.
   Though in anger I struck you,
      in favor I will show you compassion.
11 Your gates will always stand open,
      they will never be shut, day or night,
   so that men may bring you the wealth of
         the nations—
      their kings led in triumphal procession.
12 For the nation or kingdom that will not
         serve you will perish;
      it will be utterly ruined.

13 "The glory of Lebanon will come to you,
      the pine, the fir and the cypress together,
   to adorn the place of my sanctuary;
      and I will glorify the place of my feet.
14 The sons of your oppressors will come
         bowing before you;
      all who despise you will bow down at
         your feet
   and will call you the City of the LORD,
      Zion of the Holy One of Israel.

15 "Although you have been forsaken and
         hated,
      with no one traveling through,
   I will make you the everlasting pride
      and the joy of all generations.
16 You will drink the milk of nations
      and be nursed at royal breasts.
   Then you will know that I, the LORD, am
         your Savior,
      your Redeemer, the Mighty One of
         Jacob.
17 Instead of bronze I will bring you gold,
      and silver in place of iron.
   Instead of wood I will bring you bronze,
      and iron in place of stones.
   I will make peace your governor
      and righteousness your ruler.
18 No longer will violence be heard in your
         land,

---

a 9 Or the trading ships

nor ruin or destruction within your
    borders,
but you will call your walls Salvation
    and your gates Praise.
19 The sun will no more be your light by day,
    nor will the brightness of the moon
        shine on you,
for the LORD will be your everlasting light,
    and your God will be your glory.
20 Your sun will never set again,
    and your moon will wane no more;
the LORD will be your everlasting light,
    and your days of sorrow will end.
21 Then will all your people be righteous
    and they will possess the land forever.
They are the shoot I have planted,
    the work of my hands,
    for the display of my splendor.
22 The least of you will become a thousand,
    the smallest a mighty nation.
I am the LORD;
    in its time I will do this swiftly."

The Year of the LORD's Favor

61 The Spirit of the Sovereign LORD is
        on me,
    because the LORD has anointed me
    to preach good news to the poor.
He has sent me to bind up the
        brokenhearted,
    to proclaim freedom for the captives
    and release from
        darkness for the
        prisoners,*a*
2 to proclaim the year of the
        LORD's favor
    and the day of vengeance
        of our God,
    to comfort all who mourn,
3   and provide for those
        who grieve in
        Zion—
    to bestow on them a crown
        of beauty
    instead of ashes,
    the oil of gladness
        instead of mourning,
    and a garment of praise
        instead of a spirit of despair.
They will be called oaks of righteousness,

*a*1 Hebrew; Septuagint *the blind*

a planting of the LORD
    for the display of his splendor.

4 They will rebuild the ancient ruins
    and restore the places long devastated;
they will renew the ruined cities
    that have been devastated for
        generations.
5 Aliens will shepherd your flocks;
    foreigners will work your fields and
        vineyards.
6 And you will be called priests of the LORD,
    you will be named ministers of our God.
You will feed on the wealth of nations,
    and in their riches you will boast.

7 Instead of their shame
    my people will receive a double portion,
    and instead of disgrace
    they will rejoice in their inheritance;
and so they will inherit a double portion in
        their land,
    and everlasting joy will be theirs.

8 "For I, the LORD, love justice;
    I hate robbery and iniquity.
In my faithfulness I will reward them
    and make an everlasting covenant with
        them.
9 Their descendants will be known among
        the nations
    and their offspring among the peoples.
All who see them will
        acknowledge
    that they are a people the
        LORD has blessed."

10 I delight greatly in the
        LORD;
    my soul rejoices in my
        God.
For he has clothed me
    with garments of
        salvation
    and arrayed me in a robe
        of righteousness,
as a bridegroom adorns his
    head like a priest,
and as a bride adorns herself with her
    jewels.
11 For as the soil makes the sprout come up

Isaiah 61:10

God Saves

I delight greatly in
    the LORD . . .
For he has clothed
me with garments of
    salvation
and arrayed me in a robe
    of righteousness.

Read: Isaiah 61:1–6

Isaiah 61:3

[He will] provide for those who grieve in Zion—to bestow on them a crown of beauty instead of ashes, the oil of gladness instead of mourning, and a garment of praise instead of a spirit of despair. They will be called oaks of righteousness, a planting of the LORD for the display of his splendor.

reflection

1 How does this passage bring hope to your times of misery?

2 How does God's ability to transform your grief into joy demonstrate his power?

3 How might God be planning to display his splendor through your current difficult circumstance?

RELATED READINGS

Psalm 92:12–13;
Isaiah 44:23;
Jeremiah 31:13;
1 Peter 4:12–13

MARY WAS BORN INTO A DIRTY and crowded working-class district in Scotland in 1848. Her father sometimes threw her out on the streets when he arrived home drunk, and by age 14 she was working ten-hour shifts at the textile mill to support her family.

But God exchanged Mary Slessor's misery for something better when she began working at a city mission in Dundee. While there, she was inspired to sail to West Africa as a missionary to Calabar. Mary was no richer in Africa than she had been in Scotland—in fact, she now made her home in a mud hut. Throughout her 39 years in Africa, she never married. She was not even always in good health: Malaria and boils plagued her.

Yet, despite the pain she suffered, God displayed his splendor through Mary and her work. She found joy in rescuing children from ritual murder. She discovered pleasure and purpose serving as a peacemaker with the Okoyong people. And she adopted a family. "If anyone may testify as to the reality of his presence and power, it is surely this unworthy servant," she wrote to a friend. "He and his Word are a living bright reality for sure . . . I mean to glorify him and to magnify his grace."

The Israelites also had their share of misery. The Assyrians swept them from their homeland, destroying all they loved and everything familiar. However, their story, like Mary's, didn't end in misery. In fact, Isaiah predicted joy was ahead. God planned to exchange their mourning and despair for gladness and praise. Why? So that once rescued, God's people would be living demonstrations of his splendor.

We each suffer our own miseries, and we think things will never change. Perhaps you've experienced burdensome memories, a scarring divorce or a difficult diagnosis. However, can you sense any hope? Can you see God on the march, gradually transforming the pain into something you can endure? You never know; up ahead you just might see the possibility of joy. Like the Jews in exile, and like Mary Slessor in Scotland, you can trust that, despite the present pain, God has plans for your future. He is able to use whatever you go through today to display his splendor through you tomorrow.

Thursday

and a garden causes seeds to grow,
so the Sovereign LORD will make
righteousness and praise
spring up before all nations.

Zion's New Name

62 For Zion's sake I will not keep silent,
for Jerusalem's sake I will not remain
quiet,
till her righteousness shines out like the
dawn,
her salvation like a blazing torch.
² The nations will see your righteousness,
and all kings your glory;
you will be called by a new name
that the mouth of the LORD will
bestow.
³ You will be a crown of splendor in the
LORD's hand,
a royal diadem in the hand of your
God.
⁴ No longer will they call you Deserted,
or name your land Desolate.
But you will be called Hephzibah,*
and your land Beulah*;
for the LORD will take delight in you,
and your land will be married.
⁵ As a young man marries a maiden,
so will your sons* marry you;
as a bridegroom rejoices over his bride,
so will your God rejoice over you.

⁶ I have posted watchmen on your walls,
O Jerusalem;
they will never be silent day or night.
You who call on the LORD,
give yourselves no rest,
⁷ and give him no rest till he establishes
Jerusalem
and makes her the praise of the earth.

⁸ The LORD has sworn by his right hand
and by his mighty arm:
"Never again will I give your grain
as food for your enemies,
and never again will foreigners drink the
new wine
for which you have toiled;
⁹ but those who harvest it will eat it
and praise the LORD,

and those who gather the grapes will
drink it
in the courts of my sanctuary."

¹⁰ Pass through, pass through the gates!
Prepare the way for the people.
Build up, build up the highway!
Remove the stones.
Raise a banner for the nations.

¹¹ The LORD has made proclamation
to the ends of the earth:
"Say to the Daughter of Zion,
'See, your Savior comes!
See, his reward is with him,
and his recompense accompanies him.'"
¹² They will be called the Holy People,
the Redeemed of the LORD;
and you will be called Sought After,
the City No Longer Deserted.

God's Day of Vengeance and Redemption

63 Who is this coming from Edom,
from Bozrah, with his garments
stained crimson?
Who is this, robed in splendor,
striding forward in the greatness of his
strength?

"It is I, speaking in righteousness,
mighty to save."

² Why are your garments red,
like those of one treading the winepress?

³ "I have trodden the winepress alone;
from the nations no one was with me.
I trampled them in my anger
and trod them down in my wrath;
their blood spattered my garments,
and I stained all my clothing.
⁴ For the day of vengeance was in my heart,
and the year of my redemption has
come.
⁵ I looked, but there was no one to help,
I was appalled that no one gave support;
so my own arm worked salvation for me,
and my own wrath sustained me.
⁶ I trampled the nations in my anger;
in my wrath I made them drunk
and poured their blood on the ground."

---

⁴ Hephzibah means *my delight is in her.*   *⁴ Beulah* means *married.*   *⁵ Or Builder*

Praise and Prayer

7 I will tell of the kindnesses of the Lord,
    the deeds for which he is to be praised,
    according to all the Lord has done for
        us—
yes, the many good things he has done
    for the house of Israel,
    according to his compassion and many
        kindnesses.
8 He said, "Surely they are my people,
    sons who will not be false to me";
    and so he became their Savior.
9 In all their distress he too was distressed,
    and the angel of his presence saved
        them.
In his love and mercy he redeemed them;
    he lifted them up and carried them
    all the days of old.
10 Yet they rebelled
    and grieved his Holy Spirit.
So he turned and became their enemy
    and he himself fought against them.

11 Then his people recalled*a* the days of old,
    the days of Moses and his people—
where is he who brought them through
        the sea,
    with the shepherd of his flock?
Where is he who set
    his Holy Spirit among them,
12 who sent his glorious arm
        of power
    to be at Moses' right
        hand,
who divided the waters
        before them,
    to gain for himself
        everlasting renown,
13 who led them through the
        depths?
Like a horse in open
        country,
    they did not stumble;
14 like cattle that go down to
        the plain,
    they were given rest by the Spirit of the
        Lord.
This is how you guided your people
    to make for yourself a glorious name.

15 Look down from heaven and see
    from your lofty throne, holy and
        glorious.
Where are your zeal and your might?
    Your tenderness and compassion are
        withheld from us.
16 But you are our Father,
    though Abraham does not know us
    or Israel acknowledge us;
you, O Lord, are our Father,
    our Redeemer from of old is your name.
17 Why, O Lord, do you make us wander
        from your ways
    and harden our hearts so we do not
        revere you?
Return for the sake of your servants,
    the tribes that are your inheritance.
18 For a little while your people possessed
        your holy place,
    but now our enemies have trampled
        down your sanctuary.
19 We are yours from of old;
    but you have not ruled over them,
    they have not been called by your
        name.*b*

64 Oh, that you would rend the heavens
        and come down,
    that the mountains would tremble
        before you!
2 As when fire sets twigs
        ablaze
    and causes water to boil,
come down to make your
        name known to
        your enemies
    and cause the nations to
        quake before you!
3 For when you did awesome
        things that we did
        not expect,
    you came down, and
        the mountains
        trembled before
        you.
4 Since ancient times no one has heard,
    no ear has perceived,
    no eye has seen any God besides you,

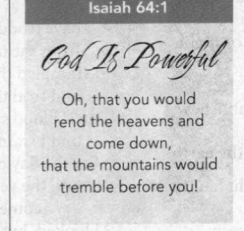

Isaiah 64:1

God Is Powerful

Oh, that you would
rend the heavens
and come down,
that the mountains would
tremble before you!

---

a 11 Or *But may he recall*   *b* 19 Or *We are like those you have never ruled, / like those never called by your name*

who acts on behalf of those who wait
    for him.
⁵ You come to the help of those who gladly
    do right,
    who remember your ways.
But when we continued to sin against
    them,
    you were angry.
    How then can we be saved?
⁶ All of us have become like one who is
    unclean,
    and all our righteous acts are like filthy
    rags;
we all shrivel up like a leaf,
    and like the wind our sins sweep us
    away.
⁷ No one calls on your name
    or strives to lay hold of you;
for you have hidden your face from us
    and made us waste away because of our
    sins.

⁸ Yet, O LORD, you are our Father.
    We are the clay, you are the potter;
    we are all the work of your hand.
⁹ Do not be angry beyond measure, O LORD;
    do not remember our sins forever.
    Oh, look upon us, we pray,
    for we are all your people.
¹⁰ Your sacred cities have become a desert;
    even Zion is a desert, Jerusalem a
    desolation.
¹¹ Our holy and glorious temple, where our
    fathers praised you,
    has been burned with fire,
    and all that we treasured lies in ruins.
¹² After all this, O LORD, will you hold
    yourself back?
    Will you keep silent and punish us
    beyond measure?

Judgment and Salvation

65 "I revealed myself to those who did
    not ask for me;
    I was found by those who did not seek
    me.
To a nation that did not call on my name,
    I said, 'Here am I, here am I.'
² All day long I have held out my hands
    to an obstinate people,
    who walk in ways not good,

pursuing their own imaginations—
³ a people who continually provoke me
    to my very face,
offering sacrifices in gardens
    and burning incense on altars of brick;
⁴ who sit among the graves
    and spend their nights keeping secret
    vigil;
who eat the flesh of pigs,
    and whose pots hold broth of unclean
    meat;
⁵ who say, 'Keep away; don't come near me,
    for I am too sacred for you!'
Such people are smoke in my nostrils,
    a fire that keeps burning all day.

⁶ "See, it stands written before me:
    I will not keep silent but will pay back
    in full;
    I will pay it back into their laps—
⁷ both your sins and the sins of your
    fathers,"
    says the LORD.
"Because they burned sacrifices on the
    mountains
    and defied me on the hills,
I will measure into their laps
    the full payment for their former deeds."

⁸ This is what the LORD says:

"As when juice is still found in a cluster of
    grapes
    and men say, 'Don't destroy it,
    there is yet some good in it,'
so will I do in behalf of my servants;
    I will not destroy them all.
⁹ I will bring forth descendants from Jacob,
    and from Judah those who will possess
    my mountains;
my chosen people will inherit them,
    and there will my servants live.
¹⁰ Sharon will become a pasture for flocks,
    and the Valley of Achor a resting place
    for herds,
    for my people who seek me.

¹¹ "But as for you who forsake the LORD
    and forget my holy mountain,
who spread a table for Fortune
    and fill bowls of mixed wine for Destiny,
¹² I will destine you for the sword,

and you will all bend down for the
slaughter;
for I called but you did not answer,
I spoke but you did not listen.
You did evil in my sight
and chose what displeases me."

13 Therefore this is what the Sovereign
Lord says:

"My servants will eat,
but you will go hungry;
my servants will drink,
but you will go thirsty;
my servants will rejoice,
but you will be put to shame.
14 My servants will sing
out of the joy of their hearts,
but you will cry out
from anguish of heart
and wail in brokenness
of spirit.
15 You will leave your name
to my chosen ones as a
curse;
the Sovereign Lord will
put you to death,
but to his servants he will
give another name.
16 Whoever invokes a blessing
in the land
will do so by the God of
truth;
he who takes an oath in the
land
will swear by the God of truth.
For the past troubles will be forgotten
and hidden from my eyes.

New Heavens and a New Earth

17 "Behold, I will create
new heavens and a new earth.
The former things will not be remembered,
nor will they come to mind.
18 But be glad and rejoice forever
in what I will create,
for I will create Jerusalem to be a delight
and its people a joy.
19 I will rejoice over Jerusalem
and take delight in my people;

the sound of weeping and of crying
will be heard in it no more.

20 "Never again will there be in it
an infant who lives but a few days,
or an old man who does not live out his
years;
he who dies at a hundred
will be thought a mere youth;
he who fails to reach[a] a hundred
will be considered accursed.
21 They will build houses and dwell in them;
they will plant vineyards and eat their
fruit.
22 No longer will they build houses and
others live in them,
or plant and others eat.
For as the days of a tree,
so will be the days of my people;
my chosen ones will long
enjoy
the works of their hands.
23 They will not toil in vain
or bear children doomed
to misfortune;
for they will be a people
blessed by the
Lord,
they and their
descendants with
them.
24 Before they call I will
answer;
while they are still
speaking I will hear.
25 The wolf and the lamb will feed together,
and the lion will eat straw like the ox,
but dust will be the serpent's food.
They will neither harm nor destroy
on all my holy mountain,"
says the Lord.

> **Isaiah 65:24**
>
> *God Has
> Quick Answers*
>
> "Before they call
> I will answer;
> while they are still
> speaking I will hear."

Judgment and Hope

66

This is what the Lord says:

"Heaven is my throne,
and the earth is my footstool.
Where is the house you will build for me?
Where will my resting place be?
2 Has not my hand made all these things,

---

[a] 20 Or / the sinner who reaches

and so they came into being?"
declares the LORD.

"This is the one I esteem:
he who is humble and contrite in spirit,
and trembles at my word.
³ But whoever sacrifices a bull
is like one who kills a man,
and whoever offers a lamb,
like one who breaks a dog's neck;
whoever makes a grain offering
is like one who presents pig's blood,
and whoever burns memorial incense,
like one who worships an idol.
They have chosen their own ways,
and their souls delight in their
abominations;
⁴ so I also will choose harsh treatment for
them
and will bring upon them what they
dread.
For when I called, no one answered,
when I spoke, no one listened.
They did evil in my sight
and chose what displeases me."

⁵ Hear the word of the LORD,
you who tremble at his word:
"Your brothers who hate you,
and exclude you because of my name,
have said,
'Let the LORD be glorified,
that we may see your joy!'
Yet they will be put to shame.
⁶ Hear that uproar from the city,
hear that noise from the temple!
It is the sound of the LORD
repaying his enemies all they deserve.

⁷ "Before she goes into labor,
she gives birth;
before the pains come upon her,
she delivers a son.
⁸ Who has ever heard of such a thing?
Who has ever seen such things?
Can a country be born in a day
or a nation be brought forth in a
moment?
Yet no sooner is Zion in labor
than she gives birth to her children.

⁹ Do I bring to the moment of birth
and not give delivery?" says the LORD.
"Do I close up the womb
when I bring to delivery?" says your
God.
¹⁰ "Rejoice with Jerusalem and be glad for
her,
all you who love her;
rejoice greatly with her,
all you who mourn over her.
¹¹ For you will nurse and be satisfied
at her comforting breasts;
you will drink deeply
and delight in her overflowing
abundance."

¹² For this is what the LORD says:

"I will extend peace to her like a river,
and the wealth of nations like a flooding
stream;
you will nurse and be carried on her arm
and dandled on her knees.
¹³ As a mother comforts her child,
so will I comfort you;
and you will be comforted over
Jerusalem."

¹⁴ When you see this, your heart will rejoice
and you will flourish like grass;
the hand of the LORD will be made known
to his servants,
but his fury will be shown to his foes.
¹⁵ See, the LORD is coming with fire,
and his chariots are like a whirlwind;
he will bring down his anger with fury,
and his rebuke with flames of fire.
¹⁶ For with fire and with his sword
the LORD will execute judgment upon
all men,
and many will be those slain by the
LORD.

¹⁷ "Those who consecrate and purify themselves to go into the gardens, following the
one in the midst of*ᵃ* those who eat the flesh of
pigs and rats and other abominable things—
they will meet their end together," declares
the LORD.
¹⁸ "And I, because of their actions and their
imaginations, am about to come*ᵇ* and gather

ᵃ 17 Or *gardens behind one of your temples, and*   ᵇ 18 The meaning of the Hebrew for this clause is uncertain.

all nations and tongues, and they will come and see my glory.

19"I will set a sign among them, and I will send some of those who survive to the nations—to Tarshish, to the Libyans[a] and Lydians (famous as archers), to Tubal and Greece, and to the distant islands that have not heard of my fame or seen my glory. They will proclaim my glory among the nations. 20And they will bring all your brothers, from all the nations, to my holy mountain in Jerusalem as an offering to the LORD—on horses, in chariots and wagons, and on mules and camels," says the LORD. "They will bring them, as the Israelites bring their grain offerings, to the temple of the LORD in ceremonially clean vessels. 21And I will select some of them also to be priests and Levites," says the LORD.

22"As the new heavens and the new earth that I make will endure before me," declares the LORD, "so will your name and descendants endure. 23From one New Moon to another and from one Sabbath to another, all mankind will come and bow down before me," says the LORD. 24"And they will go out and look upon the dead bodies of those who rebelled against me; their worm will not die, nor will their fire be quenched, and they will be loathsome to all mankind."

Jeremiah

The people of Jerusalem used to love God with the love of a new bride for her husband; now even the priests, lawmakers, leaders and prophets have begun to worship Baal and other false gods. God has warned the people for 23 years, and *now his patience* is coming to an end. Judah is about to go into exile for 70 years. They had broken God's covenant, and now they would suffer the consequences.

Even in the prediction of doom, *there is hope.* The time of exile will not last forever; God's people will be restored. God's prophet, Jeremiah, is to buy a field to emphasize that point. But notice how Jeremiah and his message were received. Yet Jeremiah is obedient to God, and *God is faithful to his promises.*

Author:
Jeremiah.

Audience:
Jerusalem—Judah's capital city.

Date:
Jeremiah wrote from 626 B.C. through sometime after the fall of Jerusalem in 586 B.C.

Setting:
Jeremiah's message is Judah's last hope before God allows Babylon to sweep the country away.

Verse to Remember:
"My people have committed two sins: They have forsaken me, the spring of living water, and have dug their own cisterns, broken cisterns that cannot hold water." (2:13)

1 The words of Jeremiah son of Hilkiah, one of the priests at Anathoth in the territory of Benjamin. ²The word of the LORD came to him in the thirteenth year of the reign of Josiah son of Amon king of Judah, ³and through the reign of Jehoiakim son of Josiah king of Judah, down to the fifth month of the eleventh year of Zedekiah son of Josiah king of Judah, when the people of Jerusalem went into exile.

The Call of Jeremiah

⁴The word of the LORD came to me, saying,

⁵"Before I formed you in the womb I knew[a] you,

ᵃ5 Or *chose*

before you were born I set you apart;
I appointed you as a prophet to the
 nations."

⁶"Ah, Sovereign Lord," I said, "I do not
know how to speak; I am only a child."

⁷But the Lord said to me, "Do not say, 'I am
only a child.' You must go to everyone I send
you to and say whatever I command you. ⁸Do
not be afraid of them, for I am with you and
will rescue you," declares the Lord.

⁹Then the Lord reached out his hand and
touched my mouth and said to me, "Now, I
have put my words in your mouth. ¹⁰See, today
I appoint you over nations and kingdoms to uproot and tear down, to destroy and overthrow,
to build and to plant."

¹¹The word of the Lord came to me: "What
do you see, Jeremiah?"

"I see the branch of an almond tree," I replied.

¹²The Lord said to me, "You have seen
correctly, for I am watching*a* to see that my
word is fulfilled."

¹³The word of the Lord came to me again:
"What do you see?"

"I see a boiling pot, tilting away from the
north," I answered.

¹⁴The Lord said to me, "From the north disaster will be poured out on all who live in the
land. ¹⁵I am about to summon all the peoples
of the northern kingdoms," declares the Lord.

"Their kings will come and set up their
 thrones
 in the entrance of the gates of
 Jerusalem;
they will come against all her surrounding
 walls
 and against all the towns of Judah.
¹⁶I will pronounce my judgments on my
 people
 because of their wickedness in forsaking
 me,
in burning incense to other gods
 and in worshiping what their hands
 have made.

¹⁷"Get yourself ready! Stand up and say to
them whatever I command you. Do not be
terrified by them, or I will terrify you before

them. ¹⁸Today I have made you a fortified city,
an iron pillar and a bronze wall to stand against
the whole land—against the kings of Judah, its
officials, its priests and the people of the land.
¹⁹They will fight against you but will not overcome you, for I am with you and will rescue
you," declares the Lord.

Israel Forsakes God

2 The word of the Lord came to me: ²"Go
and proclaim in the hearing of Jerusalem:

"'I remember the devotion of your youth,
 how as a bride you loved me
and followed me through the desert,
 through a land not sown.
³Israel was holy to the Lord,
 the firstfruits of his harvest;
all who devoured her were held guilty,
 and disaster overtook them,'"
                            declares the Lord.

⁴Hear the word of the Lord, O house of
 Jacob,
 all you clans of the house of Israel.

⁵This is what the Lord says:

"What fault did your fathers find in me,
 that they strayed so far from me?
They followed worthless idols
 and became worthless themselves.
⁶They did not ask, 'Where is the Lord,
 who brought us up out of Egypt
and led us through the barren
 wilderness,
 through a land of deserts and rifts,
a land of drought and darkness,*b*
 a land where no one travels and no one
 lives?'
⁷I brought you into a fertile land
 to eat its fruit and rich produce.
But you came and defiled my land
 and made my inheritance detestable.
⁸The priests did not ask,
 'Where is the Lord?'
Those who deal with the law did not know
 me;
 the leaders rebelled against me.
The prophets prophesied by Baal,
 following worthless idols.

---

*a*12 The Hebrew for *watching* sounds like the Hebrew for *almond tree.*   *b*6 Or *and the shadow of death*

9 "Therefore I bring charges against you
     again,"
                              declares the LORD.
   "And I will bring charges against your
     children's children.
10 Cross over to the coasts of Kittim*a* and
     look,
   send to Kedar*b* and observe closely;
   see if there has ever been anything like
     this:
11 Has a nation ever changed its gods?
   (Yet they are not gods at all.)
   But my people have exchanged their*c* Glory
     for worthless idols.
12 Be appalled at this, O heavens,
   and shudder with great horror,"
                              declares the LORD.
13 "My people have committed two sins:
   They have forsaken me,
     the spring of living water,
   and have dug their own
     cisterns,
   broken cisterns that
     cannot hold water.
14 Is Israel a servant, a slave by
     birth?
   Why then has he become
     plunder?
15 Lions have roared;
   they have growled at him.
   They have laid waste his
     land;
   his towns are burned and
     deserted.
16 Also, the men of Memphis*d*
     and Tahpanhes
   have shaved the crown of your head.*e*
17 Have you not brought this on yourselves
   by forsaking the LORD your God
   when he led you in the way?
18 Now why go to Egypt
   to drink water from the Shihor*f*?
   And why go to Assyria
   to drink water from the River*g*?
19 Your wickedness will punish you;
   your backsliding will rebuke you.
   Consider then and realize
   how evil and bitter it is for you

when you forsake the LORD your God
   and have no awe of me,"
               declares the Lord, the LORD Almighty.

20 "Long ago you broke off your yoke
   and tore off your bonds;
   you said, 'I will not serve you!'
   Indeed, on every high hill
   and under every spreading tree
   you lay down as a prostitute.
21 I had planted you like a choice vine
   of sound and reliable stock.
   How then did you turn against me
   into a corrupt, wild vine?
22 Although you wash yourself with soda
   and use an abundance of soap,
   the stain of your guilt is still before me,"
               declares the Sovereign LORD.
23 "How can you say, 'I am not defiled;
   I have not run after the
     Baals'?
   See how you behaved in the
     valley;
   consider what you have
     done.
   You are a swift she-camel
     running here and there,
24 a wild donkey accustomed
     to the desert,
   sniffing the wind in her
     craving—
   in her heat who can
     restrain her?
   Any males that pursue
     her need not tire
     themselves;
   at mating time they will find her.
25 Do not run until your feet are bare
   and your throat is dry.
   But you said, 'It's no use!
   I love foreign gods,
   and I must go after them.'

26 "As a thief is disgraced when he is caught,
   so the house of Israel is disgraced—
   they, their kings and their officials,
   their priests and their prophets.
27 They say to wood, 'You are my father,'
   and to stone, 'You gave me birth.'

Jeremiah 2:13

God Is a Spring of Life

"My people have
committed two sins:
They have forsaken me,
the spring of living water,
and have dug their
own cisterns."

---

*a*10 That is, Cyprus and western coastlands   *b*10 The home of Bedouin tribes in the Syro-Arabian desert   *c*11 Masoretic Text; an ancient
Hebrew scribal tradition *my*   *d*16 Hebrew *Noph*   *e*16 Or *have cracked your skull*   *f*18 That is, a branch of the Nile   *g*18 That is, the
Euphrates

They have turned their backs to me
  and not their faces;
yet when they are in trouble, they say,
  'Come and save us!'
28 Where then are the gods you made for
    yourselves?
  Let them come if they can save you
    when you are in trouble!
For you have as many gods
  as you have towns, O Judah.

29 "Why do you bring charges against me?
  You have all rebelled against me,"
              declares the LORD.
30 "In vain I punished your people;
  they did not respond to correction.
Your sword has devoured your prophets
  like a ravening lion.

31 "You of this generation, consider the word
of the LORD:

  "Have I been a desert to Israel
    or a land of great darkness?
  Why do my people say, 'We are free to
      roam;
    we will come to you no more'?
32 Does a maiden forget her jewelry,
    a bride her wedding ornaments?
  Yet my people have forgotten me,
    days without number.
33 How skilled you are at pursuing love!
    Even the worst of women can learn from
      your ways.
34 On your clothes men find
    the lifeblood of the innocent poor,
    though you did not catch them
      breaking in.
  Yet in spite of all this
35   you say, 'I am innocent;
    he is not angry with me.'
  But I will pass judgment on you
    because you say, 'I have not sinned.'
36 Why do you go about so much,
    changing your ways?
  You will be disappointed by Egypt
    as you were by Assyria.
37 You will also leave that place
    with your hands on your head,
  for the LORD has rejected those you trust;
    you will not be helped by them.

3 "If a man divorces his wife
    and she leaves him and marries another
      man,
  should he return to her again?
    Would not the land be completely
      defiled?
But you have lived as a prostitute with
    many lovers—
  would you now return to me?"
                  declares the LORD.
2 "Look up to the barren heights and see.
    Is there any place where you have not
      been ravished?
  By the roadside you sat waiting for lovers,
    sat like a nomad[a] in the desert.
  You have defiled the land
    with your prostitution and wickedness.
3 Therefore the showers have been withheld,
    and no spring rains have fallen.
  Yet you have the brazen look of a
      prostitute;
    you refuse to blush with shame.
4 Have you not just called to me:
    'My Father, my friend from my youth,
5 will you always be angry?
    Will your wrath continue forever?'
  This is how you talk,
    but you do all the evil you can."

Unfaithful Israel

6 During the reign of King Josiah, the LORD
said to me, "Have you seen what faithless Israel
has done? She has gone up on every high hill
and under every spreading tree and has committed adultery there. 7 I thought that after she
had done all this she would return to me but
she did not, and her unfaithful sister Judah saw
it. 8 I gave faithless Israel her certificate of divorce and sent her away because of all her adulteries. Yet I saw that her unfaithful sister Judah
had no fear; she also went out and committed
adultery. 9 Because Israel's immorality mattered
so little to her, she defiled the land and committed adultery with stone and wood. 10 In spite
of all this, her unfaithful sister Judah did not
return to me with all her heart, but only in pretense," declares the LORD.

11 The LORD said to me, "Faithless Israel is
more righteous than unfaithful Judah. 12 Go,
proclaim this message toward the north:

Inside Out

Read: Jeremiah 2:32–33

LIKE MANY WOMEN each morning, perhaps you wake up, pour yourself a cup of caffeine, take a shower and then get ready to meet the world. You pick out an outfit (preferably one that makes you look five to ten pounds lighter), do your hair and put on makeup. Finally, you add jewelry, a belt and maybe a purse. Voilà! You're ready to meet the day.

The care involved in our routines begs the question: How much time do we spend getting ready *spiritually* each morning? Do we take any time at all to ask God to guide us during our day? Do we read the Scriptures, meditate or pray so that we can be more patient, kind and loving with our spouse and children? Or do we worry more about getting out the door than about the condition of our hearts?

Caring for our outward appearance is not wrong . . . as long as we don't neglect focusing on our inner thoughts and attitudes too. The prophet Jeremiah noted that women are unlikely to forget their accessories, but God's people are prone to forget him. If we're honest, we'll admit that we are much like the Israelites. In the midst of our busy lives, God often gets pushed to the bottom of our to-do lists. But spiritual growth happens from the inside out.

Try this: Tomorrow as you shower, praise God for the cleansing that Jesus' forgiveness provides. As you're getting dressed, thank God for clothing you with Christ's righteousness. When you put on your moisturizer, ask God to soften your heart to his leading throughout the day. As you apply your makeup, thank him for being the foundation of your life. When you put in your contacts, ask God to give you eyes to see his workings in the world. And as you put on your earrings, thank him for beautifying your life with the fruits of the Spirit.

Who knows? After talking to God throughout the morning, you might not even need caffeine!

Jeremiah 2:32

"Does a maiden forget her jewelry, a bride her wedding ornaments? Yet my people have forgotten me, days without number."

reflection

1. What "enemies of the soul" (busyness, etc.) cause you to sometimes forget to take time with God?

2. How much time do you spend daily in prayer and Bible study, preparing your heart for the day?

3. What are some ways you can become more balanced in your life?

RELATED READINGS

Psalm 5:1–3;
Proverbs 31:30;
Romans 12:1–2;
Ephesians 4:21–24;
1 Peter 3:3–6

"Help me, God, to slow down, to be silent, so I can hear You and do Your will and not mine."

Marian Wright Edelman

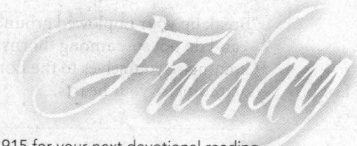

Go to page 915 for your next devotional reading.

" 'Return, faithless Israel,' declares the LORD,
  'I will frown on you no longer,
for I am merciful,' declares the LORD,
  'I will not be angry forever.
¹³ Only acknowledge your guilt—
  you have rebelled against the LORD your
    God,
you have scattered your favors to foreign
    gods
  under every spreading tree,
  and have not obeyed me,' "
                          declares the LORD.

¹⁴ "Return, faithless people," declares the
LORD, "for I am your husband. I will choose
you—one from a town and two from a clan—
and bring you to Zion. ¹⁵ Then
I will give you shepherds after
my own heart, who will lead
you with knowledge and understanding. ¹⁶ In those days, when
your numbers have increased
greatly in the land," declares
the LORD, "men will no longer
say, 'The ark of the covenant of
the LORD.' It will never enter
their minds or be remembered;
it will not be missed, nor will
another one be made. ¹⁷ At that
time they will call Jerusalem
The Throne of the LORD, and
all nations will gather in Jerusalem to honor the name of the LORD. No longer
will they follow the stubbornness of their evil
hearts. ¹⁸ In those days the house of Judah will
join the house of Israel, and together they will
come from a northern land to the land I gave
your forefathers as an inheritance.

¹⁹ "I myself said,

" 'How gladly would I treat you like sons
    and give you a desirable land,
  the most beautiful inheritance of any
    nation.'
I thought you would call me 'Father'
  and not turn away from following me.
²⁰ But like a woman unfaithful to her
    husband,
  so you have been unfaithful to me,
    O house of Israel,"
                          declares the LORD.

²¹ A cry is heard on the barren heights,
  the weeping and pleading of the people
    of Israel,
because they have perverted their ways
  and have forgotten the LORD their God.

²² "Return, faithless people;
  I will cure you of backsliding."

"Yes, we will come to you,
  for you are the LORD our God.
²³ Surely the idolatrous commotion on the
    hills
  and mountains is a deception;
surely in the LORD our God
  is the salvation of Israel.
²⁴ From our youth shameful
    gods have
    consumed
  the fruits of our fathers'
    labor—
  their flocks and herds,
    their sons and daughters.
²⁵ Let us lie down in our
    shame,
  and let our disgrace
    cover us.
We have sinned against the
    LORD our God,
  both we and our fathers;
from our youth till this day
  we have not obeyed the
    LORD our God."

Jeremiah 3:15

*God Commissions
Caretakers*

"Then I will give you
shepherds after my own
heart, who will lead you
with knowledge and
understanding."

4 "If you will return, O Israel,
      return to me,"
                          declares the LORD.
"If you put your detestable idols out of my
    sight
  and no longer go astray,
² and if in a truthful, just and righteous way
    you swear, 'As surely as the LORD lives,'
then the nations will be blessed by him
  and in him they will glory."

³ This is what the LORD says to the men of
Judah and to Jerusalem:

"Break up your unplowed ground
  and do not sow among thorns.
⁴ Circumcise yourselves to the LORD,
  circumcise your hearts,

you men of Judah and people of
    Jerusalem,
or my wrath will break out and burn like
    fire
    because of the evil you have done—
    burn with no one to quench it.

Disaster From the North

5 "Announce in Judah and proclaim in
        Jerusalem and say:
    'Sound the trumpet throughout the
        land!'
    Cry aloud and say:
    'Gather together!
        Let us flee to the fortified cities!'
6 Raise the signal to go to Zion!
        Flee for safety without delay!
    For I am bringing disaster from the north,
        even terrible destruction."

7 A lion has come out of his lair;
        a destroyer of nations has set out.
    He has left his place
        to lay waste your land.
    Your towns will lie in ruins
        without inhabitant.
8 So put on sackcloth,
        lament and wail,
    for the fierce anger of the LORD
        has not turned away from us.

9 "In that day," declares the LORD,
    "the king and the officials will lose
        heart,
    the priests will be horrified,
        and the prophets will be appalled."

10 Then I said, "Ah, Sovereign LORD, how
completely you have deceived this people and
Jerusalem by saying, 'You will have peace,'
when the sword is at our throats."

11 At that time this people and Jerusalem
will be told, "A scorching wind from the barren heights in the desert blows toward my people, but not to winnow or cleanse; 12 a wind
too strong for that comes from me.ᵃ Now I pronounce my judgments against them."

13 Look! He advances like the clouds,
        his chariots come like a whirlwind,
    his horses are swifter than eagles.
        Woe to us! We are ruined!

14 O Jerusalem, wash the evil from your heart
        and be saved.
    How long will you harbor wicked
        thoughts?
15 A voice is announcing from Dan,
        proclaiming disaster from the hills of
        Ephraim.
16 "Tell this to the nations,
        proclaim it to Jerusalem:
    'A besieging army is coming from a distant
        land,
    raising a war cry against the cities of
        Judah.
17 They surround her like men guarding a
        field,
    because she has rebelled against me,' "
                            declares the LORD.
18 "Your own conduct and actions
        have brought this upon you.
    This is your punishment.
        How bitter it is!
        How it pierces to the heart!"

19 Oh, my anguish, my anguish!
        I writhe in pain.
    Oh, the agony of my heart!
        My heart pounds within me,
        I cannot keep silent.
    For I have heard the sound of the trumpet;
        I have heard the battle cry.
20 Disaster follows disaster;
        the whole land lies in ruins.
    In an instant my tents are destroyed,
        my shelter in a moment.
21 How long must I see the battle standard
        and hear the sound of the trumpet?

22 "My people are fools;
        they do not know me.
    They are senseless children;
        they have no understanding.
    They are skilled in doing evil;
        they know not how to do good."

23 I looked at the earth,
        and it was formless and empty;
    and at the heavens,
        and their light was gone.
24 I looked at the mountains,
        and they were quaking;
    all the hills were swaying.

ᵃ12 Or comes at my command

²⁵ I looked, and there were no people;
  every bird in the sky had flown away.
²⁶ I looked, and the fruitful land was a desert;
  all its towns lay in ruins
  before the LORD, before his fierce anger.

²⁷ This is what the LORD says:

"The whole land will be ruined,
  though I will not destroy it completely.
²⁸ Therefore the earth will mourn
  and the heavens above grow dark,
because I have spoken and will not relent,
  I have decided and will not turn back."

²⁹ At the sound of horsemen and archers
  every town takes to flight.
Some go into the thickets;
  some climb up among the rocks.
All the towns are deserted;
  no one lives in them.

³⁰ What are you doing, O devastated one?
  Why dress yourself in scarlet
  and put on jewels of gold?
Why shade your eyes with paint?
  You adorn yourself in vain.
Your lovers despise you;
  they seek your life.

³¹ I hear a cry as of a woman in labor,
  a groan as of one bearing her first child—
the cry of the Daughter of Zion gasping for
    breath,
  stretching out her hands and saying,
"Alas! I am fainting;
  my life is given over to murderers."

Not One Is Upright

5 "Go up and down the streets of
    Jerusalem,
  look around and consider,
  search through her squares.
If you can find but one person
  who deals honestly and seeks the truth,
  I will forgive this city.
² Although they say, 'As surely as the LORD
    lives,'
  still they are swearing falsely."

³ O LORD, do not your eyes look for truth?
  You struck them, but they felt no pain;
  you crushed them, but they refused
    correction.
They made their faces harder than stone
  and refused to repent.
⁴ I thought, "These are only the poor;
  they are foolish,
for they do not know the way of the LORD,
  the requirements of their God.
⁵ So I will go to the leaders
  and speak to them;
surely they know the way of the LORD,
  the requirements of their God."
But with one accord they too had broken
    off the yoke
  and torn off the bonds.
⁶ Therefore a lion from the forest will attack
    them,
  a wolf from the desert will ravage them,
a leopard will lie in wait near their towns
  to tear to pieces any who venture out,
for their rebellion is great
  and their backslidings many.

⁷ "Why should I forgive you?
  Your children have forsaken me
  and sworn by gods that are not gods.
I supplied all their needs,
  yet they committed adultery
  and thronged to the houses of
    prostitutes.
⁸ They are well-fed, lusty stallions,
  each neighing for another man's wife.
⁹ Should I not punish them for this?"
  declares the LORD.
"Should I not avenge myself
  on such a nation as this?

¹⁰ "Go through her vineyards and ravage
    them,
  but do not destroy them completely.
Strip off her branches,
  for these people do not belong to the
    LORD.
¹¹ The house of Israel and the house of Judah
  have been utterly unfaithful to me,"
                        declares the LORD.

¹² They have lied about the LORD;
  they said, "He will do nothing!
No harm will come to us;
  we will never see sword or famine.
¹³ The prophets are but wind
  and the word is not in them;
  so let what they say be done to them."

¹⁴Therefore this is what the LORD God Almighty says:

"Because the people have spoken these words,
  I will make my words in your mouth a fire
  and these people the wood it consumes.
¹⁵O house of Israel," declares the LORD,
  "I am bringing a distant nation against you—
an ancient and enduring nation,
  a people whose language you do not know,
  whose speech you do not understand.
¹⁶Their quivers are like an open grave;
  all of them are mighty warriors.
¹⁷They will devour your harvests and food,
  devour your sons and daughters;
they will devour your flocks and herds,
  devour your vines and fig trees.
With the sword they will destroy
  the fortified cities in which you trust.

¹⁸"Yet even in those days," declares the LORD, "I will not destroy you completely. ¹⁹And when the people ask, 'Why has the LORD our God done all this to us?' you will tell them, 'As you have forsaken me and served foreign gods in your own land, so now you will serve foreigners in a land not your own.'

²⁰"Announce this to the house of Jacob
  and proclaim it in Judah:
²¹Hear this, you foolish and senseless people,
  who have eyes but do not see,
  who have ears but do not hear:
²²Should you not fear me?" declares the LORD.
  "Should you not tremble in my presence?
I made the sand a boundary for the sea,
  an everlasting barrier it cannot cross.
The waves may roll, but they cannot prevail;
  they may roar, but they cannot cross it.
²³But these people have stubborn and rebellious hearts;

they have turned aside and gone away.
²⁴They do not say to themselves,
  'Let us fear the LORD our God,
who gives autumn and spring rains in season,
  who assures us of the regular weeks of harvest.'
²⁵Your wrongdoings have kept these away;
  your sins have deprived you of good.

²⁶"Among my people are wicked men
  who lie in wait like men who snare birds
  and like those who set traps to catch men.
²⁷Like cages full of birds,
  their houses are full of deceit;
they have become rich and powerful
²⁸ and have grown fat and sleek.
  Their evil deeds have no limit;
  they do not plead the case of the fatherless to win it,
  they do not defend the rights of the poor.
²⁹Should I not punish them for this?"
  declares the LORD.
  "Should I not avenge myself
  on such a nation as this?
³⁰"A horrible and shocking thing
  has happened in the land:
³¹The prophets prophesy lies,
  the priests rule by their own authority,
and my people love it this way.
  But what will you do in the end?

Jerusalem Under Siege

6 "Flee for safety, people of Benjamin!
  Flee from Jerusalem!
Sound the trumpet in Tekoa!
  Raise the signal over Beth Hakkerem!
For disaster looms out of the north,
  even terrible destruction.
²I will destroy the Daughter of Zion,
  so beautiful and delicate.
³Shepherds with their flocks will come against her;

Jeremiah 5:18

God Shows Mercy

"Yet even in those days,"
declares the LORD,
"I will not destroy you
completely."

they will pitch their tents around her,
each tending his own portion."

4 "Prepare for battle against her!
   Arise, let us attack at noon!
But, alas, the daylight is fading,
   and the shadows of evening grow long.
5 So arise, let us attack at night
   and destroy her fortresses!"

6 This is what the LORD Almighty says:

"Cut down the trees
   and build siege ramps against Jerusalem.
This city must be punished;
   it is filled with oppression.
7 As a well pours out its water,
   so she pours out her wickedness.
Violence and destruction resound in her;
   her sickness and wounds are ever before
      me.
8 Take warning, O Jerusalem,
   or I will turn away from you
and make your land desolate
   so no one can live in it."

9 This is what the LORD Almighty says:

"Let them glean the remnant of Israel
   as thoroughly as a vine;
pass your hand over the branches again,
   like one gathering grapes."

10 To whom can I speak and give warning?
   Who will listen to me?
Their ears are closed[a]
   so they cannot hear.
The word of the LORD is offensive to them;
   they find no pleasure in it.
11 But I am full of the wrath of the LORD,
   and I cannot hold it in.

"Pour it out on the children in the street
   and on the young men gathered
      together;
both husband and wife will be caught in it,
   and the old, those weighed down with
      years.
12 Their houses will be turned over to others,
   together with their fields and their
      wives,
when I stretch out my hand

against those who live in the land,"
         declares the LORD.
13 "From the least to the greatest,
   all are greedy for gain;
prophets and priests alike,
   all practice deceit.
14 They dress the wound of my people
   as though it were not serious.
'Peace, peace,' they say,
   when there is no peace.
15 Are they ashamed of their loathsome
      conduct?
   No, they have no shame at all;
   they do not even know how to blush.
So they will fall among the fallen;
   they will be brought down when I
      punish them,"
            says the LORD.

16 This is what the LORD says:

"Stand at the crossroads and look;
   ask for the ancient paths,
ask where the good way is, and walk in it,
   and you will find rest for your souls.
But you said, 'We will not walk in it.'
17 I appointed watchmen over you and said,
   'Listen to the sound of the trumpet!'
But you said, 'We will not listen.'
18 Therefore hear, O nations;
   observe, O witnesses,
   what will happen to them.
19 Hear, O earth:
I am bringing disaster on this people,
   the fruit of their schemes,
because they have not listened to my
      words
   and have rejected my law.
20 What do I care about incense from Sheba
   or sweet calamus from a distant land?
Your burnt offerings are not acceptable;
   your sacrifices do not please me."

21 Therefore this is what the LORD says:

"I will put obstacles before this people.
   Fathers and sons alike will stumble over
      them;
   neighbors and friends will perish."

22 This is what the LORD says:

---

a 10 Hebrew uncircumcised

"Look, an army is coming
    from the land of the north;
a great nation is being stirred up
    from the ends of the earth.
²³They are armed with bow and spear;
    they are cruel and show no mercy.
They sound like the roaring sea
    as they ride on their horses;
they come like men in battle formation
    to attack you, O Daughter of Zion."

²⁴We have heard reports about them,
    and our hands hang limp.
Anguish has gripped us,
    pain like that of a woman in labor.
²⁵Do not go out to the fields
    or walk on the roads,
for the enemy has a sword,
    and there is terror on every side.
²⁶O my people, put on sackcloth
    and roll in ashes;
mourn with bitter wailing
    as for an only son,
for suddenly the destroyer
    will come upon us.

²⁷"I have made you a tester of metals
    and my people the ore,
that you may observe
    and test their ways.
²⁸They are all hardened rebels,
    going about to slander.
They are bronze and iron;
    they all act corruptly.
²⁹The bellows blow fiercely
    to burn away the lead with fire,
but the refining goes on in vain;
    the wicked are not purged out.
³⁰They are called rejected silver,
    because the LORD has rejected them."

False Religion Worthless

7 This is the word that came to Jeremiah from the LORD: ²"Stand at the gate of the LORD's house and there proclaim this message:

"'Hear the word of the LORD, all you people of Judah who come through these gates to worship the LORD. ³This is what the LORD Almighty, the God of Israel, says: Reform your ways and your actions, and I will let you live in this place. ⁴Do not trust in deceptive words

ᵃ9 Or and swear by false gods

and say, "This is the temple of the LORD, the temple of the LORD, the temple of the LORD!" ⁵If you really change your ways and your actions and deal with each other justly, ⁶if you do not oppress the alien, the fatherless or the widow and do not shed innocent blood in this place, and if you do not follow other gods to your own harm, ⁷then I will let you live in this place, in the land I gave your forefathers for ever and ever. ⁸But look, you are trusting in deceptive words that are worthless.

⁹"'Will you steal and murder, commit adultery and perjury,ᵃ burn incense to Baal and follow other gods you have not known, ¹⁰and then come and stand before me in this house, which bears my Name, and say, "We are safe"— safe to do all these detestable things? ¹¹Has this house, which bears my Name, become a den of robbers to you? But I have been watching! declares the LORD.

¹²"'Go now to the place in Shiloh where I first made a dwelling for my Name, and see what I did to it because of the wickedness of my people Israel. ¹³While you were doing all these things, declares the LORD, I spoke to you again and again, but you did not listen; I called you, but you did not answer. ¹⁴Therefore, what I did to Shiloh I will now do to the house that bears my Name, the temple you trust in, the place I gave to you and your fathers. ¹⁵I will thrust you from my presence, just as I did all your brothers, the people of Ephraim.'

¹⁶"So do not pray for this people nor offer any plea or petition for them; do not plead with me, for I will not listen to you. ¹⁷Do you not see what they are doing in the towns of Judah and in the streets of Jerusalem? ¹⁸The children gather wood, the fathers light the fire, and the women knead the dough and make cakes of bread for the Queen of Heaven. They pour out drink offerings to other gods to provoke me to anger. ¹⁹But am I the one they are provoking? declares the LORD. Are they not rather harming themselves, to their own shame?

²⁰"'Therefore this is what the Sovereign LORD says: My anger and my wrath will be poured out on this place, on man and beast, on the trees of the field and on the fruit of the ground, and it will burn and not be quenched.

²¹"'This is what the LORD Almighty, the God of Israel, says: Go ahead, add your burnt offerings to your other sacrifices and eat the meat yourselves! ²²For when I brought your forefathers out of Egypt and spoke to them, I did not just give them commands about burnt offerings and sacrifices, ²³but I gave them this command: Obey me, and I will be your God and you will be my people. Walk in all the ways I command you, that it may go well with you. ²⁴But they did not listen or pay attention; instead, they followed the stubborn inclinations of their evil hearts. They went backward and not forward. ²⁵From the time your forefathers left Egypt until now, day after day, again and again I sent you my servants the prophets. ²⁶But they did not listen to me or pay attention. They were stiff-necked and did more evil than their forefathers.'

²⁷"When you tell them all this, they will not listen to you; when you call to them, they will not answer. ²⁸Therefore say to them, 'This is the nation that has not obeyed the LORD its God or responded to correction. Truth has perished; it has vanished from their lips. ²⁹Cut off your hair and throw it away; take up a lament on the barren heights, for the LORD has rejected and abandoned this generation that is under his wrath.

The Valley of Slaughter

³⁰"'The people of Judah have done evil in my eyes, declares the LORD. They have set up their detestable idols in the house that bears my Name and have defiled it. ³¹They have built the high places of Topheth in the Valley of Ben Hinnom to burn their sons and daughters in the fire—something I did not command, nor did it enter my mind. ³²So beware, the days are coming, declares the LORD, when people will no longer call it Topheth or the Valley of Ben Hinnom, but the Valley of Slaughter, for they will bury the dead in Topheth until there is no more room. ³³Then the carcasses of this people will become food for the birds of the air and the beasts of the earth, and there will be no one to frighten them away. ³⁴I will bring an end to the sounds of joy and gladness and to the voices of bride and bridegroom in the towns of Judah and the streets of Jerusalem, for the land will become desolate.

8 "'At that time, declares the LORD, the bones of the kings and officials of Judah, the bones of the priests and prophets, and the bones of the people of Jerusalem will be removed from their graves. ²They will be exposed to the sun and the moon and all the stars of the heavens, which they have loved and served and which they have followed and consulted and worshiped. They will not be gathered up or buried, but will be like refuse lying on the ground. ³Wherever I banish them, all the survivors of this evil nation will prefer death to life, declares the LORD Almighty.'

Sin and Punishment

⁴"Say to them, 'This is what the LORD says:

"'When men fall down, do they not
        get up?
    When a man turns away, does he not
        return?
⁵ Why then have these people turned away?
    Why does Jerusalem always turn away?
They cling to deceit;
    they refuse to return.
⁶ I have listened attentively,
    but they do not say what is right.
No one repents of his wickedness,
    saying, "What have I done?"
Each pursues his own course
    like a horse charging into battle.
⁷ Even the stork in the sky
    knows her appointed seasons,
and the dove, the swift and the thrush
    observe the time of their migration.
But my people do not know
    the requirements of the LORD.

⁸ "'How can you say, "We are wise,
    for we have the law of the LORD,"
when actually the lying pen of the scribes
    has handled it falsely?
⁹ The wise will be put to shame;
    they will be dismayed and trapped.
Since they have rejected the word of the
        LORD,
    what kind of wisdom do they have?
¹⁰ Therefore I will give their wives to other
        men
    and their fields to new owners.
From the least to the greatest,
    all are greedy for gain;

prophets and priests alike,
all practice deceit.
11 They dress the wound of my people
as though it were not serious.
"Peace, peace," they say,
when there is no peace.
12 Are they ashamed of their
loathsome conduct?
No, they have no shame
at all;
they do not even know
how to blush.
So they will fall among the
fallen;
they will be brought
down when they are
punished,
says the LORD.

13 " 'I will take away their
harvest,
declares the LORD.
There will be no grapes on the vine.
There will be no figs on the tree,
and their leaves will wither.
What I have given them
will be taken from them.ᵃ' "

14 "Why are we sitting here?
Gather together!
Let us flee to the fortified cities
and perish there!
For the LORD our God has doomed us to
perish
and given us poisoned water to
drink,
because we have sinned against him.
15 We hoped for peace
but no good has come,
for a time of healing
but there was only terror.
16 The snorting of the enemy's horses
is heard from Dan;
at the neighing of their stallions
the whole land trembles.
They have come to devour
the land and everything in it,
the city and all who live there."

17 "See, I will send venomous snakes among
you,

vipers that cannot be charmed,
and they will bite you,"
declares the LORD.

18 O my Comforterᵃ in sorrow,
my heart is faint within
me.
19 Listen to the cry of my
people
from a land far away:
"Is the LORD not in Zion?
Is her King no longer
there?"

"Why have they provoked
me to anger with
their images,
with their worthless
foreign idols?"

20 "The harvest is past,
the summer has ended,
and we are not saved."

21 Since my people are crushed, I am
crushed;
I mourn, and horror grips me.
22 Is there no balm in Gilead?
Is there no physician there?
Why then is there no healing
for the wound of my people?

9 ¹Oh, that my head were a spring of water
and my eyes a fountain of tears!
I would weep day and night
for the slain of my people.
² Oh, that I had in the desert
a lodging place for travelers,
so that I might leave my people
and go away from them;
for they are all adulterers,
a crowd of unfaithful people.

³ "They make ready their tongue
like a bow, to shoot lies;
it is not by truth
that they triumphᵇ in the land.
They go from one sin to another;
they do not acknowledge me,"
declares the LORD.

⁴ "Beware of your friends;
do not trust your brothers.
For every brother is a deceiver,ᶜ

Jeremiah 8:18
God Is Our Comforter
O my Comforter in sorrow, my heart is faint within me.

ᵃ13,18 The meaning of the Hebrew for this sentence is uncertain.   ᵇ3 Or lies; / they are not valiant for truth   ᶜ4 Or a deceiving Jacob

and every friend a slanderer.
⁵ Friend deceives friend,
    and no one speaks the truth.
They have taught their tongues to lie;
    they weary themselves with sinning.
⁶ You[a] live in the midst of deception;
    in their deceit they refuse to
        acknowledge me,"
                declares the LORD.

⁷ Therefore this is what the LORD Almighty says:

"See, I will refine and test them,
    for what else can I do
    because of the sin of my people?
⁸ Their tongue is a deadly arrow;
    it speaks with deceit.
With his mouth each speaks cordially to
        his neighbor,
    but in his heart he sets a trap for him.
⁹ Should I not punish them for this?"
    declares the LORD.
"Should I not avenge myself
    on such a nation as this?"

¹⁰ I will weep and wail for the mountains
    and take up a lament concerning the
        desert pastures.
They are desolate and untraveled,
    and the lowing of cattle is not heard.
The birds of the air have fled
    and the animals are gone.

¹¹ "I will make Jerusalem a heap of ruins,
    a haunt of jackals;
and I will lay waste the towns of Judah
    so no one can live there."

¹² What man is wise enough to understand this? Who has been instructed by the LORD and can explain it? Why has the land been ruined and laid waste like a desert that no one can cross?

¹³ The LORD said, "It is because they have forsaken my law, which I set before them; they have not obeyed me or followed my law. ¹⁴ Instead, they have followed the stubbornness of their hearts; they have followed the Baals, as their fathers taught them." ¹⁵ Therefore, this is what the LORD Almighty, the God of Israel, says: "See, I will make this people eat bitter food

and drink poisoned water. ¹⁶ I will scatter them among nations that neither they nor their fathers have known, and I will pursue them with the sword until I have destroyed them."

¹⁷ This is what the LORD Almighty says:

"Consider now! Call for the wailing
        women to come;
    send for the most skillful of them.
¹⁸ Let them come quickly
    and wail over us
till our eyes overflow with tears
    and water streams from our eyelids.
¹⁹ The sound of wailing is heard from Zion:
    'How ruined we are!
    How great is our shame!
We must leave our land
    because our houses are in ruins.'"

²⁰ Now, O women, hear the word of the
        LORD;
    open your ears to the words of his
        mouth.
Teach your daughters how to wail;
    teach one another a lament.
²¹ Death has climbed in through our
        windows
    and has entered our fortresses;
it has cut off the children from the streets
    and the young men from the public
        squares.

²² Say, "This is what the LORD declares:

"'The dead bodies of men will lie
    like refuse on the open field,
like cut grain behind the reaper,
    with no one to gather them.'"

²³ This is what the LORD says:

"Let not the wise man boast of his wisdom
    or the strong man boast of his strength
    or the rich man boast of his riches,
²⁴ but let him who boasts boast about this:
    that he understands and knows me,
that I am the LORD, who exercises
        kindness,
    justice and righteousness on earth,
    for in these I delight,"
                declares the LORD.

[a]6 That is, Jeremiah (the Hebrew is singular)

Staying Spiritually Sage

HULDAH

READY IN A PINCH. That was Huldah, a prophetess in Judah. The thing about being one of God's messengers was that people usually didn't turn to her until it was a time of crisis. When the people needed to hear a word from God, then they turned to the resident prophetess for answers.

It didn't rattle her, this last-minute urgency. It came with the territory.

"I guess I'm used to it by now," she mused, as she patiently listened to the king's officials recount how they made the exciting discovery. Although she could name several male prophets in her people's history, only two other women knew her particular job stress. She shared her esteemed title of "prophetess" with Miriam (see Exodus 15:20) and Deborah (see Judges 4:4). With a reputation for integrity, truthfulness and spiritual discernment, she was the natural choice to handle such sensitive information related to the newly rediscovered Book of the Law.

Unlike her friends who worked in the fields or the market, she didn't keep office hours. "I never know when someone will need me," she often said.

She never knew when she would need to share a word of wisdom or petition the Lord on the people's behalf, so she had to stay prepared. She couldn't slack off, spiritually speaking. She drew strength by reminding herself that she couldn't afford to miss an opportunity to be available and useful to God. And on this day, she was able to deliver the timely and sensitive message that God wanted Judah to hear.

"You never know when someone will show up on your doorstep seeking spiritual wisdom," Huldah would often say. "Sometimes, it's your friend or neighbor. Sometimes it's the king. No matter who shows up, God has a word for them. And it's good to be prepared."

—*Prayer*—
Gracious God, keep me prepared so that I may be of service to others in need. Give me the wisdom and discernment to find the right words to help where I can.

Hilkiah the priest, Ahikam, Acbor, Shaphan and Asaiah went to speak to the prophetess Huldah.

2 Kings 22:14

ASSIGNED READING:

2 Kings 22:14–20

Weekend

25 "The days are coming," declares the LORD, "when I will punish all who are circumcised only in the flesh— **26** Egypt, Judah, Edom, Ammon, Moab and all who live in the desert in distant places.*a* For all these nations are really uncircumcised, and even the whole house of Israel is uncircumcised in heart."

God and Idols

10 Hear what the LORD says to you, O house of Israel. **2** This is what the LORD says:

> "Do not learn the ways of the nations
>   or be terrified by signs in the sky,
>   though the nations are terrified by them.
> **3** For the customs of the peoples are
>   worthless;
>   they cut a tree out of the forest,
>   and a craftsman shapes it with his chisel.
> **4** They adorn it with silver and gold;
>   they fasten it with hammer and nails
>   so it will not totter.
> **5** Like a scarecrow in a melon patch,
>   their idols cannot speak;
>   they must be carried
>   because they cannot walk.
> Do not fear them;
>   they can do no harm
>   nor can they do any
>   good."

6 No one is like you, O LORD;
    you are great,
    and your name is mighty
        in power.
7 Who should not revere you,
        O King of the nations?
    This is your due.
Among all the wise men of
        the nations
    and in all their
        kingdoms,
    there is no one like you.
8 They are all senseless and foolish;
    they are taught by worthless wooden
        idols.
9 Hammered silver is brought from Tarshish
    and gold from Uphaz.
What the craftsman and goldsmith have
        made

is then dressed in blue and purple—
    all made by skilled workers.
10 But the LORD is the true God;
    he is the living God, the eternal King.
When he is angry, the earth trembles;
    the nations cannot endure his wrath.

11 "Tell them this: 'These gods, who did not make the heavens and the earth, will perish from the earth and from under the heavens.'*b*

12 But God made the earth by his power;
    he founded the world by his wisdom
    and stretched out the heavens by his
        understanding.
13 When he thunders, the waters in the
        heavens roar;
    he makes clouds rise from the ends of
        the earth.
He sends lightning with the rain
    and brings out the wind from his
        storehouses.

14 Everyone is senseless and without
        knowledge;
    every goldsmith is shamed by his idols.
His images are a fraud;
    they have no breath in them.
15 They are worthless, the
        objects of
        mockery;
    when their judgment
        comes, they will
        perish.
16 He who is the Portion of
        Jacob is not like
        these,
    for he is the Maker of all
        things,
    including Israel, the tribe
        of his inheritance—
    the LORD Almighty is his
        name.

Jeremiah 10:7

God Is King of the Nations

"Who should not revere you, O King of the nations?"

Coming Destruction

17 Gather up your belongings to leave the
        land,
    you who live under siege.
18 For this is what the LORD says:
> "At this time I will hurl out
>   those who live in this land;

---

a **26** Or *desert and who clip the hair by their foreheads*   *b* **11** The text of this verse is in Aramaic.

I will bring distress on them
    so that they may be captured."

19 Woe to me because of my injury!
    My wound is incurable!
Yet I said to myself,
    "This is my sickness, and I must endure
      it."
20 My tent is destroyed;
    all its ropes are snapped.
My sons are gone from me and are no more;
    no one is left now to pitch my tent
    or to set up my shelter.
21 The shepherds are senseless
    and do not inquire of the LORD;
so they do not prosper
    and all their flock is scattered.
22 Listen! The report is coming—
    a great commotion from the land of the
      north!
It will make the towns of Judah desolate,
    a haunt of jackals.

Jeremiah's Prayer

23 I know, O LORD, that a man's life is not his
    own;
    it is not for man to direct his steps.
24 Correct me, LORD, but only with justice—
    not in your anger,
    lest you reduce me to nothing.
25 Pour out your wrath on the nations
    that do not acknowledge you,
    on the peoples who do not call on your
      name.
For they have devoured Jacob;
    they have devoured him completely
    and destroyed his homeland.

The Covenant Is Broken

11 This is the word that came to Jeremiah from the LORD: 2 "Listen to the terms of this covenant and tell them to the people of Judah and to those who live in Jerusalem. 3 Tell them that this is what the LORD, the God of Israel, says: 'Cursed is the man who does not obey the terms of this covenant— 4 the terms I commanded your forefathers when I brought them out of Egypt, out of the iron-smelting furnace.' I said, 'Obey me and do everything I command you, and you will be my people, and

I will be your God. 5 Then I will fulfill the oath I swore to your forefathers, to give them a land flowing with milk and honey'—the land you possess today."

I answered, "Amen, LORD."

6 The LORD said to me, "Proclaim all these words in the towns of Judah and in the streets of Jerusalem: 'Listen to the terms of this covenant and follow them. 7 From the time I brought your forefathers up from Egypt until today, I warned them again and again, saying, "Obey me." 8 But they did not listen or pay attention; instead, they followed the stubbornness of their evil hearts. So I brought on them all the curses of the covenant I had commanded them to follow but that they did not keep.' "

9 Then the LORD said to me, "There is a conspiracy among the people of Judah and those who live in Jerusalem. 10 They have returned to the sins of their forefathers, who refused to listen to my words. They have followed other gods to serve them. Both the house of Israel and the house of Judah have broken the covenant I made with their forefathers. 11 Therefore this is what the LORD says: 'I will bring on them a disaster they cannot escape. Although they cry out to me, I will not listen to them. 12 The towns of Judah and the people of Jerusalem will go and cry out to the gods to whom they burn incense, but they will not help them at all when disaster strikes. 13 You have as many gods as you have towns, O Judah; and the altars you have set up to burn incense to that shameful god Baal are as many as the streets of Jerusalem.'

14 "Do not pray for this people nor offer any plea or petition for them, because I will not listen when they call to me in the time of their distress.

15 "What is my beloved doing in my temple
    as she works out her evil schemes with
      many?
    Can consecrated meat avert ⌊your
      punishment⌋?
When you engage in your wickedness,
    then you rejoice.[a]"

16 The LORD called you a thriving olive tree
    with fruit beautiful in form.

---

a 15 Or Could consecrated meat avert your punishment? / Then you would rejoice

But with the roar of a mighty storm
    he will set it on fire,
    and its branches will be broken.

¹⁷The LORD Almighty, who planted you, has decreed disaster for you, because the house of Israel and the house of Judah have done evil and provoked me to anger by burning incense to Baal.

Plot Against Jeremiah

¹⁸Because the LORD revealed their plot to me, I knew it, for at that time he showed me what they were doing. ¹⁹I had been like a gentle lamb led to the slaughter; I did not realize that they had plotted against me, saying,

"Let us destroy the tree and its fruit;
    let us cut him off from the land of the
        living,
    that his name be remembered no more."

²⁰But, O LORD Almighty, you who judge
        righteously
    and test the heart and mind,
    let me see your vengeance upon them,
        for to you I have committed my cause.

²¹"Therefore this is what the LORD says about the men of Anathoth who are seeking your life and saying, 'Do not prophesy in the name of the LORD or you will die by our hands'— ²²therefore this is what the LORD Almighty says: 'I will punish them. Their young men will die by the sword, their sons and daughters by famine. ²³Not even a remnant will be left to them, because I will bring disaster on the men of Anathoth in the year of their punishment.'"

Jeremiah's Complaint

12 You are always righteous, O LORD,
        when I bring a case before you.
    Yet I would speak with you about your
        justice:
    Why does the way of the wicked
        prosper?
    Why do all the faithless live at ease?
² You have planted them, and they have
        taken root;
    they grow and bear fruit.
    You are always on their lips
        but far from their hearts.
³ Yet you know me, O LORD;

you see me and test my thoughts about
        you.
    Drag them off like sheep to be butchered!
    Set them apart for the day of slaughter!
⁴ How long will the land lie parched[a]
    and the grass in every field be withered?
    Because those who live in it are wicked,
        the animals and birds have perished.
    Moreover, the people are saying,
        "He will not see what happens to us."

God's Answer

⁵ "If you have raced with men on foot
        and they have worn you out,
    how can you compete with horses?
    If you stumble in safe country,[b]
        how will you manage in the thickets by[c]
            the Jordan?
⁶ Your brothers, your own family—
        even they have betrayed you;
    they have raised a loud cry against you.
    Do not trust them,
        though they speak well of you.

⁷ "I will forsake my house,
        abandon my inheritance;
    I will give the one I love
        into the hands of her enemies.
⁸ My inheritance has become to me
        like a lion in the forest.
    She roars at me;
        therefore I hate her.
⁹ Has not my inheritance become to me
        like a speckled bird of prey
    that other birds of prey surround and
            attack?
    Go and gather all the wild beasts;
        bring them to devour.
¹⁰ Many shepherds will ruin my vineyard
        and trample down my field;
    they will turn my pleasant field
        into a desolate wasteland.
¹¹ It will be made a wasteland,
        parched and desolate before me;
    the whole land will be laid waste
        because there is no one who cares.
¹² Over all the barren heights in the desert
        destroyers will swarm,
    for the sword of the LORD will devour
        from one end of the land to the other;

ᵃ4 Or *land mourn* ᵇ5 Or *If you put your trust in a land of safety* ᶜ5 Or *the flooding of*

Why Do the Wicked Prosper?

Read: Jeremiah 12:1–17

WE'VE ALL ASKED QUESTIONS similar to Jeremiah's at least once:

Why does she get the promotion even though she makes unethical decisions?

Why did her children turn out better than mine even though she seemed to neglect them?

Why do they have what they need and more when they don't know what it *means* to tithe?

It's hard to understand why God appears to sanction those who openly disregard him. In Jeremiah's case, it was people in his own hometown he was trying to help who had turned against him. They even plotted to kill him!

Sometimes we may feel that God has given a greater measure of his protection and provision to people who don't live upright lives. It's hard to reconcile God's nature when we see injustice all around us. We wonder why he doesn't intervene immediately to punish those who make sinful choices.

If you sometimes question God's actions, you're in good company. Throughout history, God's people have wrestled with the same issues. We look at martyrs, missionaries and others serving God who experience horrible suffering and pain. Why do evildoers often seem to have the easiest lives, while people of faith struggle? Shouldn't it be the other way around? This side of heaven, we may never be able to answer such questions.

Even so, we know our God knows the hearts and motives of all people. He sees when innocents are harmed and the upright are dealt injustice. And he does care. It may look like he isn't intervening now, but a time is coming when each person must account for his or her life. As Jesus said, "Will not God bring about justice for his chosen ones, who cry out to him day and night? Will he keep putting them off? I tell you, he will see that they get justice, and quickly. However, when the Son of Man comes, will he find faith on the earth?" (Luke 18:7–8).

While we may not understand God's ways, we know that he is all-wise, all-knowing and just. He watches over us and will make everything right in its time. The key is for each of us to remain faithful to him until then.

Jeremiah 12:1–2

You are always righteous, O LORD, when I bring a case before you. Yet I would speak with you about your justice: Why does the way of the wicked prosper? Why do all the faithless live at ease? You have planted them, and they have taken root; they grow and bear fruit. You are always on their lips but far from their hearts.

reflection

1 What situation has caused you to wonder why the wicked prosper?

2 When you're tempted to question God's actions, what steps can you take to remember his wisdom?

3 What assurance do you have that God will render his justice one day?

RELATED READINGS

Job 21:7–21;
Psalms 73:1–28;
145:17–20;
Proverbs 11:21–23

Go to page 924 for your next devotional reading.

no one will be safe.
13 They will sow wheat but reap thorns;
 they will wear themselves out but gain
 nothing.
So bear the shame of your harvest
 because of the LORD's fierce anger."

14 This is what the LORD says: "As for all my wicked neighbors who seize the inheritance I gave my people Israel, I will uproot them from their lands and I will uproot the house of Judah from among them. 15 But after I uproot them, I will again have compassion and will bring each of them back to his own inheritance and his own country. 16 And if they learn well the ways of my people and swear by my name, saying, 'As surely as the LORD lives'—even as they once taught my people to swear by Baal—then they will be established among my people. 17 But if any nation does not listen, I will completely uproot and destroy it," declares the LORD.

A Linen Belt

13 This is what the LORD said to me: "Go and buy a linen belt and put it around your waist, but do not let it touch water." 2 So I bought a belt, as the LORD directed, and put it around my waist.

3 Then the word of the LORD came to me a second time: 4 "Take the belt you bought and are wearing around your waist, and go now to Perath[a] and hide it there in a crevice in the rocks." 5 So I went and hid it at Perath, as the LORD told me.

6 Many days later the LORD said to me, "Go now to Perath and get the belt I told you to hide there." 7 So I went to Perath and dug up the belt and took it from the place where I had hidden it, but now it was ruined and completely useless.

8 Then the word of the LORD came to me: 9 "This is what the LORD says: 'In the same way I will ruin the pride of Judah and the great pride of Jerusalem. 10 These wicked people, who refuse to listen to my words, who follow the stubbornness of their hearts and go after

other gods to serve and worship them, will be like this belt—completely useless! 11 For as a belt is bound around a man's waist, so I bound the whole house of Israel and the whole house of Judah to me,' declares the LORD, 'to be my people for my renown and praise and honor. But they have not listened.'

Wineskins

12 "Say to them: 'This is what the LORD, the God of Israel, says: Every wineskin should be filled with wine.' And if they say to you, 'Don't we know that every wineskin should be filled with wine?' 13 then tell them, 'This is what the LORD says: I am going to fill with drunkenness all who live in this land, including the kings who sit on David's throne, the priests, the prophets and all those living in Jerusalem. 14 I will smash them one against the other, fathers and sons alike, declares the LORD. I will allow no pity or mercy or compassion to keep me from destroying them.' "

Threat of Captivity

15 Hear and pay attention,
 do not be arrogant,
 for the LORD has spoken.
16 Give glory to the LORD
 your God
 before he brings the
 darkness,
 before your feet stumble
 on the darkening hills.
You hope for light,
 but he will turn it to
 thick darkness
 and change it to deep
 gloom.
17 But if you do not listen,
 I will weep in secret
 because of your pride;
 my eyes will weep bitterly,
 overflowing with tears,
 because the LORD's flock
 will be taken captive.

18 Say to the king and to the queen mother,
 "Come down from your thrones,
 for your glorious crowns
 will fall from your heads."
19 The cities in the Negev will be shut up,

Jeremiah 13:16

God Is Worthy of Praise

Give glory to the LORD
your God
before he brings
the darkness,
before your feet stumble
on the darkening hills.

---

a 4 Or possibly *the Euphrates*; also in verses 5–7

and there will be no one to open them.
All Judah will be carried into exile,
    carried completely away.

20 Lift up your eyes and see
    those who are coming from the north.
Where is the flock that was entrusted to
    you,
    the sheep of which you boasted?
21 What will you say when the LORD sets
    over you
those you cultivated as your special allies?
Will not pain grip you
    like that of a woman in labor?
22 And if you ask yourself,
    "Why has this happened to me?"—
it is because of your many sins
    that your skirts have been torn off
    and your body mistreated.
23 Can the Ethiopian[a] change his skin
    or the leopard its spots?
Neither can you do good
    who are accustomed to
        doing evil.

24 "I will scatter you like chaff
    driven by the desert
        wind.
25 This is your lot,
    the portion I have
        decreed for you,"
            declares the LORD,
"because you have
    forgotten me
    and trusted in false gods.
26 I will pull up your skirts
    over your face
    that your shame may be
        seen—
27 your adulteries and lustful neighings,
    your shameless prostitution!
I have seen your detestable acts
    on the hills and in the fields.
Woe to you, O Jerusalem!
    How long will you be unclean?"

Drought, Famine, Sword

14 This is the word of the LORD to Jeremiah concerning the drought:

2 "Judah mourns,

a 23 Hebrew *Cushite* (probably a person from the upper Nile region)

her cities languish;
they wail for the land,
    and a cry goes up from Jerusalem.
3 The nobles send their servants for water;
    they go to the cisterns
    but find no water.
They return with their jars unfilled;
    dismayed and despairing,
    they cover their heads.
4 The ground is cracked
    because there is no rain in the land;
the farmers are dismayed
    and cover their heads.
5 Even the doe in the field
    deserts her newborn fawn
    because there is no grass.
6 Wild donkeys stand on the barren
        heights
    and pant like jackals;
        their eyesight fails
        for lack of pasture."

7 Although our sins testify
        against us,
    O LORD, do something
        for the sake of your
        name.
For our backsliding is
        great;
    we have sinned against
        you.
8 O Hope of Israel,
    its Savior in times of
        distress,
why are you like a
        stranger in the
        land,
    like a traveler who stays
        only a night?
9 Why are you like a man taken by surprise,
    like a warrior powerless to save?
You are among us, O LORD,
    and we bear your name;
    do not forsake us!

10 This is what the LORD says about this
people:

"They greatly love to wander;
    they do not restrain their feet.
So the LORD does not accept them;

> **Jeremiah 14:7**
>
> *God Honors His Name*
>
> "Although our sins
> testify against us,
> O LORD, do something for
> the sake of your name.
> For our backsliding
> is great;
> we have sinned
> against you."

he will now remember their wickedness
and punish them for their sins."

¹¹Then the LORD said to me, "Do not pray
for the well-being of this people. ¹²Although
they fast, I will not listen to their cry; though
they offer burnt offerings and grain offerings,
I will not accept them. Instead, I will destroy
them with the sword, famine and plague."

¹³But I said, "Ah, Sovereign LORD, the prophets keep telling them, 'You will not see the
sword or suffer famine. Indeed, I will give you
lasting peace in this place.'"

¹⁴Then the LORD said to me, "The prophets are prophesying lies in my name. I have
not sent them or appointed them or spoken
to them. They are prophesying to you false
visions, divinations, idolatries*a* and the delusions of their own minds. ¹⁵Therefore, this is
what the LORD says about the prophets who
are prophesying in my name: I did not send
them, yet they are saying, 'No sword or famine
will touch this land.' Those same prophets will
perish by sword and famine. ¹⁶And the people
they are prophesying to will be thrown out into
the streets of Jerusalem because of the famine
and sword. There will be no one to bury them
or their wives, their sons or their daughters.
I will pour out on them the calamity they deserve.

¹⁷"Speak this word to them:

"'Let my eyes overflow with tears
    night and day without ceasing;
for my virgin daughter—my people—
    has suffered a grievous wound,
    a crushing blow.
¹⁸If I go into the country,
    I see those slain by the sword;
if I go into the city,
    I see the ravages of famine.
Both prophet and priest
    have gone to a land they know not.'"

¹⁹Have you rejected Judah completely?
    Do you despise Zion?
Why have you afflicted us
    so that we cannot be healed?
We hoped for peace
    but no good has come,

for a time of healing
    but there is only terror.
²⁰O LORD, we acknowledge our wickedness
    and the guilt of our fathers;
    we have indeed sinned against you.
²¹For the sake of your name do not despise
        us;
    do not dishonor your glorious throne.
Remember your covenant with us
    and do not break it.
²²Do any of the worthless idols of the nations
        bring rain?
    Do the skies themselves send down
        showers?
No, it is you, O LORD our God.
    Therefore our hope is in you,
    for you are the one who does all this.

15 Then the LORD said to me: "Even if
Moses and Samuel were to stand be-
fore me, my heart would not go out to this people. Send them away from my presence! Let
them go! ²And if they ask you, 'Where shall we
go?' tell them, 'This is what the LORD says:

"'Those destined for death, to death;
    those for the sword, to the sword;
    those for starvation, to starvation;
    those for captivity, to captivity.'

³"I will send four kinds of destroyers against
them," declares the LORD, "the sword to kill and
the dogs to drag away and the birds of the air
and the beasts of the earth to devour and destroy. ⁴I will make them abhorrent to all the
kingdoms of the earth because of what Manasseh son of Hezekiah king of Judah did in Jerusalem.

⁵"Who will have pity on you, O Jerusalem?
    Who will mourn for you?
    Who will stop to ask how you are?
⁶You have rejected me," declares the LORD.
    "You keep on backsliding.
So I will lay hands on you and destroy you;
    I can no longer show compassion.
⁷I will winnow them with a winnowing fork
    at the city gates of the land.
I will bring bereavement and destruction
        on my people,
    for they have not changed their ways.

a 14 Or visions, worthless divinations

8 I will make their widows more numerous
   than the sand of the sea.
At midday I will bring a destroyer
   against the mothers of their young men;
suddenly I will bring down on them
   anguish and terror.
9 The mother of seven will grow faint
   and breathe her last.
Her sun will set while it is still day;
   she will be disgraced and humiliated.
I will put the survivors to the sword
   before their enemies,"
                          declares the LORD.

10 Alas, my mother, that you gave me birth,
   a man with whom the whole land strives
      and contends!
I have neither lent nor borrowed,
   yet everyone curses me.

11 The LORD said,

"Surely I will deliver you for a good
      purpose;
   surely I will make your enemies plead
      with you
   in times of disaster and times of distress.

12 "Can a man break iron—
   iron from the north—or bronze?
13 Your wealth and your treasures
   I will give as plunder, without charge,
because of all your sins
   throughout your country.
14 I will enslave you to your enemies
   in[a] a land you do not know,
for my anger will kindle a fire
   that will burn against you."

15 You understand, O LORD;
   remember me and care for me.
   Avenge me on my persecutors.
You are long-suffering—do not take me
      away;
   think of how I suffer reproach for your
      sake.
16 When your words came, I ate them;
   they were my joy and my heart's delight,
for I bear your name,
   O LORD God Almighty.
17 I never sat in the company of revelers,
   never made merry with them;
I sat alone because your hand was on me
   and you had filled me with indignation.
18 Why is my pain unending
   and my wound grievous and incurable?
Will you be to me like a deceptive brook,
   like a spring that fails?

19 Therefore this is what the LORD says:

"If you repent, I will restore you
   that you may serve me;
if you utter worthy, not worthless, words,
   you will be my spokesman.
Let this people turn to you,
   but you must not turn to them.
20 I will make you a wall to this people,
   a fortified wall of bronze;
they will fight against you
   but will not overcome you,
for I am with you
   to rescue and save you,"
                          declares the LORD.
21 "I will save you from the hands of the
      wicked
   and redeem you from the grasp of the
      cruel."

Day of Disaster

16 Then the word of the LORD came to
me: 2 "You must not marry and have
sons or daughters in this place." 3 For this is
what the LORD says about the sons and daughters born in this land and about the women
who are their mothers and the men who are
their fathers: 4 "They will die of deadly diseases.
They will not be mourned or buried but will be
like refuse lying on the ground. They will perish by sword and famine, and their dead bodies
will become food for the birds of the air and the
beasts of the earth."

5 For this is what the LORD says: "Do not enter a house where there is a funeral meal; do
not go to mourn or show sympathy, because
I have withdrawn my blessing, my love and
my pity from this people," declares the LORD.
6 "Both high and low will die in this land. They
will not be buried or mourned, and no one
will cut himself or shave his head for them.
7 No one will offer food to comfort those who

---

[a]14 Some Hebrew manuscripts, Septuagint and Syriac (see also Jer. 17:4); most Hebrew manuscripts *I will cause your enemies to bring you / into*

Intimate Doubt

Why is my pain unend-
ing and my wound
grievous and incurable?
Will you be to me like
a deceptive brook, like
a spring that fails?

reflection

1 Describe the most
discouraging job or
task that you've ever un-
dertaken. What made it
difficult? What were your
complaints?

2 What feels impossible
and discouraging to
you right now? How is it
affecting you?

3 Write out your "in-
timate doubts" and
express your needs to
God. When you are fin-
ished, reclaim his promise
to be with you as you follow him.

RELATED READINGS

Jeremiah 1:4–8;
12:1–3; 20:7–12;
Jude 22

Read: Jeremiah 15:1–21

HELP WANTED:

Who: An ordained spokesperson who is passionate, committed, can endure criticism and perhaps even personal injury and
imprisonment. Must be willing to look ridiculous and bear the scorn
of peers. Personal characteristics: introverted, unmarried, childless
and prone to melancholy. Can be a person who cries easily.

What: Tell the people of Judah that their revival is superficial
and unpleasing to the Lord and that God will therefore judge them.

When: Starts immediately—never mind the economic, political
and social collapse of Judah.

Pay: None

Any takers? Didn't think so.

No wonder no prophet ever chose his job. Being a prophet
was, no doubt, the most discouraging job on the planet. However,
that doesn't mean that God is a cosmic taskmaster who doles out
difficult assignments to teach people like Jeremiah to trust him
more.

Instead, God gave Jeremiah the freedom to express his
doubts. Jeremiah did so on several occasions, and the audacity in
Jeremiah's words reveals his intimacy with God. They're the kind of
words one might hear in a lover's quarrel: "Don't you care? Aren't
you going to notice me? I feel so alone." We don't speak that
way to a stranger or even an acquaintance; words like this we only
speak to someone we love. In this case, doubt is not an indication
of failure. It's an indication of intimacy.

In turn, the Lord responded to Jeremiah with firm grace: "If
you repent, I will restore you that you may [continue to] serve me"
(verse 19). In other words, there is a time to express doubt; but
there is also a point at which we must return to our senses before
we forget who God is and what he's called us to do. Talk to God
about your doubts and your questions, but don't go so far that you
begin to lose focus of who you are and who God is.

Are you in the middle of a seemingly impossible assignment?
Are you wondering if God really knows how much you can take?
God knows your limits; he realizes that he calls flawed people to
enormous tasks. Yet his promise is forever the same: "I am with you
always, to the very end of the age" (Matthew 28:20).

Go to page 927 for your next devotional reading.

mourn for the dead—not even for a father or a mother—nor will anyone give them a drink to console them.

8"And do not enter a house where there is feasting and sit down to eat and drink. 9For this is what the LORD Almighty, the God of Israel, says: Before your eyes and in your days I will bring an end to the sounds of joy and gladness and to the voices of bride and bridegroom in this place.

10"When you tell these people all this and they ask you, 'Why has the LORD decreed such a great disaster against us? What wrong have we done? What sin have we committed against the LORD our God?' 11then say to them, 'It is because your fathers forsook me,' declares the LORD, 'and followed other gods and served and worshiped them. They forsook me and did not keep my law. 12But you have behaved more wickedly than your fathers. See how each of you is following the stubbornness of his evil heart instead of obeying me. 13So I will throw you out of this land into a land neither you nor your fathers have known, and there you will serve other gods day and night, for I will show you no favor.'

14"However, the days are coming," declares the LORD, "when men will no longer say, 'As surely as the LORD lives, who brought the Israelites up out of Egypt,' 15but they will say, 'As surely as the LORD lives, who brought the Israelites up out of the land of the north and out of all the countries where he had banished them.' For I will restore them to the land I gave their forefathers.

16"But now I will send for many fishermen," declares the LORD, "and they will catch them. After that I will send for many hunters, and they will hunt them down on every mountain and hill and from the crevices of the rocks. 17My eyes are on all their ways; they are not hidden from me, nor is their sin concealed from my eyes. 18I will repay them double for their wickedness and their sin, because they have defiled my land with the lifeless forms of their vile images and have filled my inheritance with their detestable idols."

19O LORD, my strength and my fortress,
    my refuge in time of distress,
to you the nations will come
    from the ends of the earth and say,
"Our fathers possessed nothing but false
        gods,
    worthless idols that did
        them no good.
20Do men make their own
        gods?
    Yes, but they are not
        gods!"

21"Therefore I will teach
        them—
    this time I will teach
        them
    my power and might.
Then they will know
    that my name is the
        LORD.

Jeremiah 16:21

God Teaches Us

"Therefore I will teach them—this time I will teach them my power and might. Then they will know that my name is the LORD."

17 "Judah's sin is engraved with an iron
        tool,
    inscribed with a flint point,
on the tablets of their hearts
    and on the horns of their altars.
2Even their children remember
    their altars and Asherah poles[a]
beside the spreading trees
    and on the high hills.
3My mountain in the land
    and your[b] wealth and all your treasures
I will give away as plunder,
    together with your high places,
    because of sin throughout your
        country.
4Through your own fault you will lose
    the inheritance I gave you.
I will enslave you to your enemies
    in a land you do not know,
for you have kindled my anger,
    and it will burn forever."

5This is what the LORD says:

"Cursed is the one who trusts in man,
    who depends on flesh for his strength

a2 That is, symbols of the goddess Asherah   b2,3 Or hills /3 and the mountains of the land. / Your

and whose heart turns away from the
LORD.
⁶ He will be like a bush in the wastelands;
he will not see prosperity when it comes.
He will dwell in the parched places of the
desert,
in a salt land where no one lives.

⁷ "But blessed is the man who trusts in the
LORD,
whose confidence is in him.
⁸ He will be like a tree planted by the water
that sends out its roots by the stream.
It does not fear when heat comes;
its leaves are always green.
It has no worries in a year of drought
and never fails to bear fruit."

⁹ The heart is deceitful above all things
and beyond cure.
Who can understand it?

¹⁰ "I the LORD search the heart
and examine the mind,
to reward a man according to his conduct,
according to what his deeds deserve."

¹¹ Like a partridge that hatches eggs it did not
lay
is the man who gains riches by unjust
means.
When his life is half gone, they will desert
him,
and in the end he will prove to be a fool.

¹² A glorious throne, exalted from the
beginning,
is the place of our sanctuary.
¹³ O LORD, the hope of Israel,
all who forsake you will be put to shame.
Those who turn away from you will be
written in the dust
because they have forsaken the LORD,
the spring of living water.

¹⁴ Heal me, O LORD, and I will be healed;
save me and I will be saved,
for you are the one I praise.
¹⁵ They keep saying to me,
"Where is the word of the LORD?
Let it now be fulfilled!"
¹⁶ I have not run away from being your
shepherd;

you know I have not desired the day of
despair.
What passes my lips is open before you.
¹⁷ Do not be a terror to me;
you are my refuge in the day of disaster.
¹⁸ Let my persecutors be put to shame,
but keep me from shame;
let them be terrified,
but keep me from terror.
Bring on them the day of disaster;
destroy them with double destruction.

Keeping the Sabbath Holy

¹⁹ This is what the LORD said to me: "Go
and stand at the gate of the people, through
which the kings of Judah go in and out; stand
also at all the other gates of Jerusalem. ²⁰ Say
to them, 'Hear the word of the LORD, O kings
of Judah and all people of Judah and everyone
living in Jerusalem who come through these
gates. ²¹ This is what the LORD says: Be careful not to carry a load on the Sabbath day or
bring it through the gates of Jerusalem. ²² Do
not bring a load out of your houses or do any
work on the Sabbath, but keep the Sabbath day
holy, as I commanded your forefathers. ²³ Yet
they did not listen or pay attention; they were
stiff-necked and would not listen or respond to
discipline. ²⁴ But if you are careful to obey me,
declares the LORD, and bring no load through
the gates of this city on the Sabbath, but keep
the Sabbath day holy by not doing any work on
it, ²⁵ then kings who sit on David's throne will
come through the gates of this city with their
officials. They and their officials will come riding in chariots and on horses, accompanied by
the men of Judah and those living in Jerusalem,
and this city will be inhabited forever. ²⁶ People
will come from the towns of Judah and the
villages around Jerusalem, from the territory
of Benjamin and the western foothills, from
the hill country and the Negev, bringing burnt
offerings and sacrifices, grain offerings, incense
and thank offerings to the house of the LORD.
²⁷ But if you do not obey me to keep the Sabbath day holy by not carrying any load as you
come through the gates of Jerusalem on the
Sabbath day, then I will kindle an unquenchable fire in the gates of Jerusalem that will consume her fortresses.' "

Saving a Terminal Heart

Read: Jeremiah 17:5–14

WHEN YOU HEAR THE WORDS "heart failure," a pang of panic, regret or sorrow may surge through you. Many women have lost parents, friends or a husband to a weakly pumping heart. Maybe you suffer from heart disease. But even if your physical heart is healthy, your spiritual heart is a terminal case. The prophet Jeremiah described it this way: "The heart is . . . beyond cure."

Maybe you believe your own spiritual heart works just fine, thank you. Your own efforts will cure you—or so you think. "Go with your heart," the world says. What do you believe? Do you agree with Jeremiah's assessment or are you feeling that the world is right on this point?

To determine the state of your heart you need the help of a professional. Better than any doctor's diagnosis, God probes the inner workings of our hearts. Just as a woman with a feeble heart can only guess at the true condition of her ventricles without an expert exam, so each of us must rely on God's perfect knowledge of our soul. When you have to choose between your own assessment of your heart and God's, do you believe your prognosis or do you listen to the One with the power to heal?

Most of us would use any means possible to halt progressive heart failure, but we still face the temptation to doubt the doctor's orders. Maybe we're told to eat right and exercise, but it seems too hard to keep on living a healthy lifestyle. In the same way, we might disbelieve that God's searching eyes can see the areas of our hearts we try to hide. Or we tell ourselves that what is wrong won't likely kill us—at least today. So we ignore it. Not doing what we need to do to heal our physical heart will allow the damage to progress. Disregard of our spiritual health is just as devastating.

The bad news: You have a broken heart. The good news: God can cure the incurable.

Jeremiah 17:9–10

The heart is deceitful above all things and beyond cure. Who can understand it? "I the LORD search the heart and examine the mind, to reward a man according to his conduct, according to what his deeds deserve."

reflection

1 In what areas of your life do you suffer from spiritual heart disease?

2 What keeps you from following the Great Physician's orders?

3 In what ways can you entrust your *whole* heart to God's care?

RELATED READINGS

Isaiah 58:6–14;
Matthew 15:18;
Acts 15:8–9;
Hebrews 4:12–13

Wednesday

Go to page 929 for your next devotional reading.

At the Potter's House

18 This is the word that came to Jeremiah from the LORD: [2]"Go down to the potter's house, and there I will give you my message." [3]So I went down to the potter's house, and I saw him working at the wheel. [4]But the pot he was shaping from the clay was marred in his hands; so the potter formed it into another pot, shaping it as seemed best to him.

[5]Then the word of the LORD came to me: [6]"O house of Israel, can I not do with you as this potter does?" declares the LORD. "Like clay in the hand of the potter, so are you in my hand, O house of Israel. [7]If at any time I announce that a nation or kingdom is to be uprooted, torn down and destroyed, [8]and if that nation I warned repents of its evil, then I will relent and not inflict on it the disaster I had planned. [9]And if at another time I announce that a nation or kingdom is to be built up and planted, [10]and if it does evil in my sight and does not obey me, then I will reconsider the good I had intended to do for it.

[11]"Now therefore say to the people of Judah and those living in Jerusalem, 'This is what the LORD says: Look! I am preparing a disaster for you and devising a plan against you. So turn from your evil ways, each one of you, and reform your ways and your actions.' [12]But they will reply, 'It's no use. We will continue with our own plans; each of us will follow the stubbornness of his evil heart.'"

[13]Therefore this is what the LORD says:

"Inquire among the nations:
　Who has ever heard anything like this?
A most horrible thing has been done
　by Virgin Israel.
[14]Does the snow of Lebanon
　ever vanish from its rocky slopes?
Do its cool waters from distant sources
　ever cease to flow?[a]
[15]Yet my people have forgotten me;
　they burn incense to worthless idols,
which made them stumble in their ways
　and in the ancient paths.
They made them walk in bypaths
　and on roads not built up.
[16]Their land will be laid waste,
　an object of lasting scorn;
all who pass by will be appalled
　and will shake their heads.
[17]Like a wind from the east,
　I will scatter them before their enemies;
I will show them my back and not my face
　in the day of their disaster."

[18]They said, "Come, let's make plans against Jeremiah; for the teaching of the law by the priest will not be lost, nor will counsel from the wise, nor the word from the prophets. So come, let's attack him with our tongues and pay no attention to anything he says."

[19]Listen to me, O LORD;
　hear what my accusers
　　are saying!
[20]Should good be repaid with
　evil?
　Yet they have dug a pit
　　for me.
Remember that I stood before you
　and spoke in their behalf
to turn your wrath away from them.
[21]So give their children over to famine;
　hand them over to the power of the
　　sword.
Let their wives be made childless and
　widows;
　let their men be put to death,
　their young men slain by the sword in
　　battle.
[22]Let a cry be heard from their houses
　when you suddenly bring invaders
　　against them,
for they have dug a pit to capture me
　and have hidden snares for my feet.
[23]But you know, O LORD,
　all their plots to kill me.
Do not forgive their crimes
　or blot out their sins from your sight.

Jeremiah 18:6

God Shapes Us

"O house of Israel, can I not do with you as this potter does?" declares the LORD. "Like clay in the hand of the potter, so are you in my hand, O house of Israel."

---

[a]14 The meaning of the Hebrew for this sentence is uncertain.

928

Pain at the Potter's Wheel

Read: Jeremiah 18:1–10

HAVE YOU SEEN A POTTER at the wheel lately? As modern-day thinkers, we might wonder why God sent Jeremiah down to the potter's house. We may not know much about pottery, except that it's beautiful and expensive. But in Jeremiah's day, pottery was essential for everyday living. Seeing a potter at work was probably as common then as seeing an office worker at a keyboard today.

So when God sent Jeremiah to the potter's wheel, he drew on an image that was very familiar to the Israelites in order to highlight the difference between the Creator and the created being, the sovereign versus the subject. The potter is highly skilled, imaginative and purposefully intent upon the outcome of his creation. In contrast, the clay is crude and unformed, misshapen and useless without the intervention of the master potter. By observing a potter at work, it becomes clear who is doing the shaping and who is being shaped.

How odd it would be for the clay to call out to the potter, "Hey, ease up there. Not so rough!" It's ridiculous to envision. And yet, Jeremiah's lesson of the potter still resonates with us. It is often painful to be the clay. At times we are pressed, pushed, molded and remolded. Our Potter may crush us from time to time when he encounters residual clumps that need smoothing over.

However, our master Potter knows his business far better than we do. We are a marred and messy mixture of clay and water. In the hands of our skilled Potter, the outcome is a beautiful and unique work of art.

This week try to remember the picture of a potter and his clay. Consider the difference between the Creator and the creation. It may help to remember that our wise and loving God knows the beautiful vessel he alone is capable of fashioning.

Jeremiah 18:4

But the pot he was shaping from the clay was marred in his hands; so the potter formed it into another pot, shaping it as seemed best to him.

reflection

1 How do you feel about the analogy of being made and shaped by the Potter?

2 Describe a time when you were in need of reshaping by God. In what ways has God proven himself a trustworthy Potter?

3 What do you think God is trying to create in your life right now?

RELATED READINGS

Isaiah 45:9–12; 64:8;
Romans 9:20–21

Thursday

Let them be overthrown before you;
  deal with them in the time of your
    anger.

19 This is what the LORD says: "Go and buy a clay jar from a potter. Take along some of the elders of the people and of the priests ²and go out to the Valley of Ben Hinnom, near the entrance of the Potsherd Gate. There proclaim the words I tell you, ³and say, 'Hear the word of the LORD, O kings of Judah and people of Jerusalem. This is what the LORD Almighty, the God of Israel, says: Listen! I am going to bring a disaster on this place that will make the ears of everyone who hears of it tingle. ⁴For they have forsaken me and made this a place of foreign gods; they have burned sacrifices in it to gods that neither they nor their fathers nor the kings of Judah ever knew, and they have filled this place with the blood of the innocent. ⁵They have built the high places of Baal to burn their sons in the fire as offerings to Baal—something I did not command or mention, nor did it enter my mind. ⁶So beware, the days are coming, declares the LORD, when people will no longer call this place Topheth or the Valley of Ben Hinnom, but the Valley of Slaughter.

⁷"'In this place I will ruin*ᵃ* the plans of Judah and Jerusalem. I will make them fall by the sword before their enemies, at the hands of those who seek their lives, and I will give their carcasses as food to the birds of the air and the beasts of the earth. ⁸I will devastate this city and make it an object of scorn; all who pass by will be appalled and will scoff because of all its wounds. ⁹I will make them eat the flesh of their sons and daughters, and they will eat one another's flesh during the stress of the siege imposed on them by the enemies who seek their lives.'

¹⁰"Then break the jar while those who go with you are watching, ¹¹and say to them, 'This is what the LORD Almighty says: I will smash this nation and this city just as this potter's jar is smashed and cannot be repaired. They will bury the dead in Topheth until there is no more room. ¹²This is what I will do to this place and to those who live here, declares the LORD. I will make this city like Topheth. ¹³The houses in Je-

rusalem and those of the kings of Judah will be defiled like this place, Topheth—all the houses where they burned incense on the roofs to all the starry hosts and poured out drink offerings to other gods.'"

¹⁴Jeremiah then returned from Topheth, where the LORD had sent him to prophesy, and stood in the court of the LORD's temple and said to all the people, ¹⁵"This is what the LORD Almighty, the God of Israel, says: 'Listen! I am going to bring on this city and the villages around it every disaster I pronounced against them, because they were stiff-necked and would not listen to my words.'"

Jeremiah and Pashhur

20 When the priest Pashhur son of Immer, the chief officer in the temple of the LORD, heard Jeremiah prophesying these things, ²he had Jeremiah the prophet beaten and put in the stocks at the Upper Gate of Benjamin at the LORD's temple. ³The next day, when Pashhur released him from the stocks, Jeremiah said to him, "The LORD's name for you is not Pashhur, but Magor-Missabib.*ᵇ* ⁴For this is what the LORD says: 'I will make you a terror to yourself and to all your friends; with your own eyes you will see them fall by the sword of their enemies. I will hand all Judah over to the king of Babylon, who will carry them away to Babylon or put them to the sword. ⁵I will hand over to their enemies all the wealth of this city—all its products, all its valuables and all the treasures of the kings of Judah. They will take it away as plunder and carry it off to Babylon. ⁶And you, Pashhur, and all who live in your house will go into exile to Babylon. There you will die and be buried, you and all your friends to whom you have prophesied lies.'"

Jeremiah's Complaint

⁷O LORD, you deceived*ᶜ* me, and I was
    deceived*ᶜ*;
  you overpowered me and prevailed.
I am ridiculed all day long;
  everyone mocks me.
⁸Whenever I speak, I cry out
  proclaiming violence and destruction.
So the word of the LORD has brought me

ᵃ7 The Hebrew for *ruin* sounds like the Hebrew for *jar* (see verses 1 and 10).   *ᵇ3* *Magor-Missabib* means *terror on every side*.
ᶜ7 Or *persuaded*

insult and reproach all day long.
⁹But if I say, "I will not mention him
    or speak any more in his name,"
his word is in my heart like a fire,
    a fire shut up in my bones.
I am weary of holding it in;
    indeed, I cannot.
¹⁰I hear many whispering,
    "Terror on every side!
    Report him! Let's report him!"
All my friends
    are waiting for me to slip, saying,
"Perhaps he will be deceived;
    then we will prevail over him
    and take our revenge on him."

¹¹But the LORD is with me like a mighty
        warrior;
    so my persecutors will stumble and not
        prevail.
They will fail and be thoroughly disgraced;
    their dishonor will never be forgotten.
¹²O LORD Almighty, you who examine the
        righteous
    and probe the heart and mind,
let me see your vengeance
        upon them,
    for to you I have
        committed my
        cause.

¹³Sing to the LORD!
    Give praise to the LORD!
He rescues the life of the
        needy
    from the hands of the
        wicked.

¹⁴Cursed be the day I was
        born!
    May the day my mother
        bore me not be blessed!
¹⁵Cursed be the man who brought my father
        the news,
    who made him very glad, saying,
    "A child is born to you—a son!"
¹⁶May that man be like the towns
        the LORD overthrew without pity.
    May he hear wailing in the morning,
        a battle cry at noon.

¹⁷For he did not kill me in the womb,
    with my mother as my grave,
    her womb enlarged forever.
¹⁸Why did I ever come out of the womb
    to see trouble and sorrow
    and to end my days in shame?

God Rejects Zedekiah's Request

21 The word came to Jeremiah from the LORD when King Zedekiah sent to him Pashhur son of Malkijah and the priest Zephaniah son of Maaseiah. They said: ²"Inquire now of the LORD for us because Nebuchadnezzar[a] king of Babylon is attacking us. Perhaps the LORD will perform wonders for us as in times past so that he will withdraw from us."

³But Jeremiah answered them, "Tell Zedekiah, ⁴'This is what the LORD, the God of Israel, says: I am about to turn against you the weapons of war that are in your hands, which you are using to fight the king of Babylon and the Babylonians[b] who are outside the wall besieging you. And I will gather them inside this city. ⁵I myself will fight against you with an outstretched hand and a mighty arm in anger and fury and great wrath. ⁶I will strike down those who live in this city—both men and animals—and they will die of a terrible plague. ⁷After that, declares the LORD, I will hand over Zedekiah king of Judah, his officials and the people in this city who survive the plague, sword and famine, to Nebuchadnezzar king of Babylon and to their enemies who seek their lives. He will put them to the sword; he will show them no mercy or pity or compassion.'

⁸"Furthermore, tell the people, 'This is what the LORD says: See, I am setting before you the way of life and the way of death. ⁹Whoever stays in this city will die by the sword, famine or plague. But whoever goes out and surrenders to the Babylonians who are besieging you will live; he will escape with his life. ¹⁰I have determined to do this city harm and not good,

Jeremiah 20:13

God Rescues

Sing to the LORD!
Give praise to the LORD!
He rescues the life
of the needy
from the hands
of the wicked.

ᵃ2 Hebrew *Nebuchadrezzar*, of which *Nebuchadnezzar* is a variant; here and often in Jeremiah and Ezekiel ᵇ4 Or *Chaldeans*; also in verse 9 declares the LORD. It will be given into the hands of the king of Babylon, and he will destroy it with fire.'

11"Moreover, say to the royal house of Judah, 'Hear the word of the LORD; 12O house of David, this is what the LORD says:

> "'Administer justice every morning;
>   rescue from the hand of his oppressor
>   the one who has been robbed,
> or my wrath will break out and burn like
>   fire
> because of the evil you have done—
>   burn with no one to quench it.
> 13I am against you, Jerusalem,
>   you who live above this valley
>   on the rocky plateau,
>   declares the LORD—
> you who say, "Who can come against us?
>   Who can enter our refuge?"
> 14I will punish you as your deeds deserve,
>   declares the LORD.
> I will kindle a fire in your forests
>   that will consume everything around
>   you.'"

Judgment Against Evil Kings

22 This is what the LORD says: "Go down to the palace of the king of Judah and proclaim this message there: 2'Hear the word of the LORD, O king of Judah, you who sit on David's throne—you, your officials and your people who come through these gates. 3This is what the LORD says: Do what is just and right. Rescue from the hand of his oppressor the one who has been robbed. Do no wrong or violence to the alien, the fatherless or the widow, and do not shed innocent blood in this place. 4For if you are careful to carry out these commands, then kings who sit on David's throne will come through the gates of this palace, riding in chariots and on horses, accompanied by their officials and their people. 5But if you do not obey these commands, declares the LORD, I swear by myself that this palace will become a ruin.'"

6For this is what the LORD says about the palace of the king of Judah:

> "Though you are like Gilead to me,
>   like the summit of Lebanon,
> I will surely make you like a desert,

> like towns not inhabited.
> 7I will send destroyers against you,
>   each man with his weapons,
> and they will cut up your fine cedar beams
>   and throw them into the fire.

8"People from many nations will pass by this city and will ask one another, 'Why has the LORD done such a thing to this great city?' 9And the answer will be: 'Because they have forsaken the covenant of the LORD their God and have worshiped and served other gods.'"

> 10Do not weep for the dead king, or mourn
>   his loss;
> rather, weep bitterly for him who is
>   exiled,
> because he will never return
>   nor see his native land again.

11For this is what the LORD says about Shallum[a] son of Josiah, who succeeded his father as king of Judah but has gone from this place: "He will never return. 12He will die in the place where they have led him captive; he will not see this land again."

> 13"Woe to him who builds his palace by
>   unrighteousness,
>   his upper rooms by injustice,
> making his countrymen work for nothing,
>   not paying them for their labor.
> 14He says, 'I will build myself a great palace
>   with spacious upper rooms.'
> So he makes large windows in it,
>   panels it with cedar
>   and decorates it in red.

> 15"Does it make you a king
>   to have more and more cedar?
> Did not your father have food and drink?
>   He did what was right and just,
>   so all went well with him.
> 16He defended the cause of the poor and
>   needy,
>   and so all went well.
> Is that not what it means to know me?"
>   declares the LORD.
> 17"But your eyes and your heart
>   are set only on dishonest gain,
> on shedding innocent blood
>   and on oppression and extortion."

a11 Also called *Jehoahaz*

What God Values

Read: Jeremiah 22:1–5

IN THE MIDDLE OF A TUMULTUOUS TIME in American history, an activist arose who did what was right for the oppressed. Coretta Scott, a vivacious young woman studying voice and violin at the New England Conservatory, met a charismatic young doctoral student in Boston who shared her passions. She swept Martin Luther King Jr. off his feet. They married and became partners in a tireless fight for social justice and the civil rights of all Americans.

For 38 years following her husband's tragic death, Mrs. King traveled the world, speaking out against all manner of injustice and oppression, received by heads of state and even preaching in St. Paul's Cathedral in Rome. With her passing in 2006, Coretta Scott King left a rich living legacy of welcoming the alien, caring for the widow and orphan, and fighting for the freedom of all people regardless of race, creed or culture. She cared about what God cared about.

The kingdom of Judah was corrupt and rebellious, and in response, God was sending judgment. Jeremiah had an urgent message from God that would save the kingdom. Was it to build up their armies? Was it to build a new city wall? Was it to go to war? No. Jeremiah said, "Do what is right. Rescue the oppressed. If you do, then the kingdom will last; if you don't, then the kingdom will end in ruins." But the people didn't listen. They didn't care about what God valued. And it cost them everything.

Fast-forward several centuries to scenes of our world, and things haven't changed all that much. The world today doesn't care much about what God cares about. It's easy to talk about justice, but it's another thing to do what is just and right. It's easy to remain comfortable and complacent, but it's hard to move out of our comfort zone. But loving God means loving what he values. And God cares about those who suffer injustice and oppression.

Jeremiah 22:3

"This is what the LORD says: Do what is just and right. Rescue from the hand of his oppressor the one who has been robbed. Do no wrong or violence to the alien, the fatherless or the widow, and do not shed innocent blood in this place."

reflection

1 As we become women after God's own heart and learn to value what he values, our awareness of the needs around us increases. What injustices do you witness around you, and what can you do to help the situation?

2 How does the gospel provide an answer to the suffering endured by so many in this world?

3 What steps can you take to serve someone who is oppressed politically, socially, economically or spiritually?

RELATED READINGS

Isaiah 58:6–14;
James 2:14–26

Go to page 935 for your next devotional reading.

¹⁸Therefore this is what the LORD says about Jehoiakim son of Josiah king of Judah:

"They will not mourn for him:
  'Alas, my brother! Alas, my sister!'
They will not mourn for him:
  'Alas, my master! Alas, his splendor!'
¹⁹He will have the burial of a donkey—
    dragged away and thrown
    outside the gates of Jerusalem."

²⁰"Go up to Lebanon and cry out,
    let your voice be heard in Bashan,
cry out from Abarim,
    for all your allies are crushed.
²¹I warned you when you felt secure,
    but you said, 'I will not listen!'
This has been your way from your youth;
    you have not obeyed me.
²²The wind will drive all your shepherds
      away,
    and your allies will go into exile.
Then you will be ashamed and disgraced
    because of all your wickedness.
²³You who live in 'Lebanon,'ᵃ
    who are nestled in cedar buildings,
how you will groan when pangs come
      upon you,
    pain like that of a woman in labor!

²⁴"As surely as I live," declares the LORD, "even if you, Jehoiachinᵇ son of Jehoiakim king of Judah, were a signet ring on my right hand, I would still pull you off. ²⁵I will hand you over to those who seek your life, those you fear—to Nebuchadnezzar king of Babylon and to the Babylonians.ᶜ ²⁶I will hurl you and the mother who gave you birth into another country, where neither of you was born, and there you both will die. ²⁷You will never come back to the land you long to return to."

²⁸Is this man Jehoiachin a despised, broken
      pot,
    an object no one wants?
Why will he and his children be hurled
      out,
    cast into a land they do not know?
²⁹O land, land, land,
    hear the word of the LORD!

³⁰This is what the LORD says:
"Record this man as if childless,
    a man who will not prosper in his
      lifetime,
for none of his offspring will prosper,
    none will sit on the throne of David
    or rule anymore in Judah."

The Righteous Branch

23 "Woe to the shepherds who are destroying and scattering the sheep of my pasture!" declares the LORD. ²Therefore this is what the LORD, the God of Israel, says to the shepherds who tend my people: "Because you have scattered my flock and driven them away and have not bestowed care on them, I will bestow punishment on you for the evil you have done," declares the LORD. ³"I myself will gather the remnant of my flock out of all the countries where I have driven them and will bring them back to their pasture, where they will be fruitful and increase in number. ⁴I will place shepherds over them who will tend them, and they will no longer be afraid or terrified, nor will any be missing," declares the LORD.

⁵"The days are coming," declares the LORD,
    "when I will raise up to Davidᵈ a
      righteous Branch,
a King who will reign wisely
    and do what is just and right in the land.
⁶In his days Judah will be saved
    and Israel will live in safety.
This is the name by which he will be called:
    The LORD Our Righteousness.

⁷"So then, the days are coming," declares the LORD, "when people will no longer say, 'As surely as the LORD lives, who brought the Israelites up out of Egypt,' ⁸but they will say, 'As surely as the LORD lives, who brought the descendants of Israel up out of the land of the north and out of all the countries where he had banished them.' Then they will live in their own land."

Lying Prophets

⁹Concerning the prophets:

My heart is broken within me;
    all my bones tremble.

ᵃ23 That is, the palace in Jerusalem (see 1 Kings 7:2) ᵇ24 Hebrew *Coniah*, a variant of *Jehoiachin*; also in verse 28 ᶜ25 Or *Chaldeans* ᵈ5 Or *up from David's line*

More Than a Pretty Face

ESTHER

SHE BREATHED A SIGH of relief. He hadn't forgotten.

In the midst of scheduling important meetings, summoning officials and juggling all of his other kingly duties, King Xerxes had not allowed his wife's request to go unnoticed. In fact, she'd seen how his eyes darted her way throughout the banquet that night as he spoke to his guest, Haman, and quietly directed the royal stewards throughout the meal.

Esther was aware of the allure of her beauty. She knew garnering the king's eye was rarely an issue. She was, after all, ravishing—among a thousand women in the land, she was indisputably the most beautiful. Ever since she was a little girl, she'd realized there was something special about her. Women in the marketplace would point to her and smile softly, admiring the length of her rich hair or her sculpted features. Whenever strangers lathered compliments on her, her family beamed with joy, and Esther blushed on more than one occasion.

However, what she had to do tonight would require more than her looks. When Mordecai sought her out for the sake of their people, he wasn't necessarily addressing Esther, the beauty. He was summoning something he'd seen deep inside her that others, so taken with her outward appearance, had hardly noticed. It would take more than a pretty face to convince the king to reverse his order against her people, the Jews. It would exact from Esther the whole of who she was—her mind, her heart and her strength.

As King Xerxes raised the sweet-tasting wine to his lips, he spoke to her. "Queen Esther, what is your petition? It will be given you. What is your request?"

At that moment, Esther did not think about the style of her hair. She did not wonder if her face looked radiant or her lips plump. She did not inwardly debate whether her thighs were too big or her hips too wide. She looked deep within herself, called up her courage, engaged her mind and made her request.

—Prayer—

Thank you, God, for equipping women like Esther to be examples of strength and courage for women throughout the years.

> *Then Queen Esther answered, "If I have found favor with you, O king, and if it pleases your majesty, grant me my life—this is my petition."*
>
> Esther 7:3

ASSIGNED READING:

Esther

Go to page 941 for your next devotional reading.

Weekend

I am like a drunken man,
    like a man overcome by wine,
because of the LORD
    and his holy words.
¹⁰The land is full of adulterers;
    because of the curse*a* the land lies
        parched*b*
    and the pastures in the desert are
        withered.
The prophets follow an evil course
    and use their power unjustly.

¹¹ "Both prophet and priest are godless;
    even in my temple I find their
        wickedness,"

                                declares the LORD.

¹² "Therefore their path will become slippery;
    they will be banished to darkness
        and there they will fall.
I will bring disaster on them
    in the year they are punished,"

                                declares the LORD.

¹³ "Among the prophets of Samaria
    I saw this repulsive thing:
They prophesied by Baal
    and led my people Israel astray.
¹⁴And among the prophets of Jerusalem
    I have seen something horrible:
They commit adultery and live a lie.
    They strengthen the hands of evildoers,
so that no one turns from his
        wickedness.
They are all like Sodom to
        me;
    the people of Jerusalem
        are like Gomorrah."

¹⁵Therefore, this is what the
LORD Almighty says concerning the prophets:

"I will make them eat bitter
        food
    and drink poisoned
        water,
because from the prophets
        of Jerusalem
    ungodliness has spread
        throughout the
            land."

¹⁶This is what the LORD Almighty says:

"Do not listen to what the prophets are
        prophesying to you;
    they fill you with false hopes.
They speak visions from their own minds,
    not from the mouth of the LORD.
¹⁷They keep saying to those who despise me,
    'The LORD says: You will have peace.'
And to all who follow the stubbornness of
        their hearts
    they say, 'No harm will come to you.'
¹⁸But which of them has stood in the council
        of the LORD
    to see or to hear his word?
    Who has listened and heard his word?
¹⁹See, the storm of the LORD
    will burst out in wrath,
a whirlwind swirling down
    on the heads of the wicked.
²⁰The anger of the LORD will not turn back
    until he fully accomplishes
    the purposes of his heart.
In days to come
    you will understand it clearly.
²¹I did not send these prophets,
    yet they have run with their message;
I did not speak to them,
    yet they have prophesied.
²²But if they had stood in my council,
    they would have proclaimed my words
        to my people
    and would have turned
        them from their evil
            ways
        and from their evil
            deeds.

²³ "Am I only a God nearby,"
            declares the LORD,
    "and not a God far away?
²⁴Can anyone hide in secret
        places
    so that I cannot see him?"
            declares the LORD.
"Do not I fill heaven and
        earth?"
            declares the LORD.

Jeremiah 23:24

God Sees Everything

"Can anyone hide in
secret places
so that I cannot
see him?"
declares the LORD.

²⁵ "I have heard what the prophets say who
prophesy lies in my name. They say, 'I had a

---

*a*10 Or *because of these things*   *b*10 Or *land mourns* dream! I had a dream!' 26How long will this continue in the hearts of these lying prophets, who prophesy the delusions of their own minds? 27They think the dreams they tell one another will make my people forget my name, just as their fathers forgot my name through Baal worship. 28Let the prophet who has a dream tell his dream, but let the one who has my word speak it faithfully. For what has straw to do with grain?" declares the LORD. 29"Is not my word like fire," declares the LORD, "and like a hammer that breaks a rock in pieces?

30"Therefore," declares the LORD, "I am against the prophets who steal from one another words supposedly from me. 31Yes," declares the LORD, "I am against the prophets who wag their own tongues and yet declare, 'The LORD declares.' 32Indeed, I am against those who prophesy false dreams," declares the LORD. "They tell them and lead my people astray with their reckless lies, yet I did not send or appoint them. They do not benefit these people in the least," declares the LORD.

False Oracles and False Prophets

33"When these people, or a prophet or a priest, ask you, 'What is the oracle*a* of the LORD?' say to them, 'What oracle?*b* I will forsake you, declares the LORD.' 34If a prophet or a priest or anyone else claims, 'This is the oracle of the LORD,' I will punish that man and his household. 35This is what each of you keeps on saying to his friend or relative: 'What is the LORD's answer?' or 'What has the LORD spoken?' 36But you must not mention 'the oracle of the LORD' again, because every man's own word becomes his oracle and so you distort the words of the living God, the LORD Almighty, our God. 37This is what you keep saying to a prophet: 'What is the LORD's answer to you?' or 'What has the LORD spoken?' 38Although you claim, 'This is the oracle of the LORD,' this is what the LORD says: You used the words, 'This is the oracle of the LORD,' even though I told you that you must not claim, 'This is the oracle of the LORD.' 39Therefore, I will surely forget you and cast you out of my presence along with the city I gave to you and your fathers. 40I will bring upon you everlasting

disgrace—everlasting shame that will not be forgotten."

Two Baskets of Figs

24 After Jehoiachin*c* son of Jehoiakim king of Judah and the officials, the craftsmen and the artisans of Judah were carried into exile from Jerusalem to Babylon by Nebuchadnezzar king of Babylon, the LORD showed me two baskets of figs placed in front of the temple of the LORD. 2One basket had very good figs, like those that ripen early; the other basket had very poor figs, so bad they could not be eaten.

3Then the LORD asked me, "What do you see, Jeremiah?"

"Figs," I answered. "The good ones are very good, but the poor ones are so bad they cannot be eaten."

4Then the word of the LORD came to me: 5"This is what the LORD, the God of Israel, says: 'Like these good figs, I regard as good the exiles from Judah, whom I sent away from this place to the land of the Babylonians.*d* 6My eyes will watch over them for their good, and I will bring them back to this land. I will build them up and not tear them down; I will plant them and not uproot them. 7I will give them a heart to know me, that I am the LORD. They will be my people, and I will be their God, for they will return to me with all their heart.

8"'But like the poor figs, which are so bad they cannot be eaten,' says the LORD, 'so will I deal with Zedekiah king of Judah, his officials and the survivors from Jerusalem, whether they remain in this land or live in Egypt. 9I will make them abhorrent and an offense to all the kingdoms of the earth, a reproach and a byword, an object of ridicule and cursing, wherever I banish them. 10I will send the sword, famine and plague against them until they are destroyed from the land I gave to them and their fathers.'"

Seventy Years of Captivity

25 The word came to Jeremiah concerning all the people of Judah in the fourth year of Jehoiakim son of Josiah king of Judah, which was the first year of

---

*a*33 Or *burden* (see Septuagint and Vulgate)   *b*33 Hebrew; Septuagint and Vulgate *'You are the burden.* (The Hebrew for *oracle* and *burden* is the same.)   *c*1 Hebrew *Jeconiah*, a variant of *Jehoiachin*   *d*5 Or *Chaldeans*

Nebuchadnezzar king of Babylon. ²So Jeremiah the prophet said to all the people of Judah and to all those living in Jerusalem: ³For twenty-three years—from the thirteenth year of Josiah son of Amon king of Judah until this very day—the word of the LORD has come to me and I have spoken to you again and again, but you have not listened.

⁴And though the LORD has sent all his servants the prophets to you again and again, you have not listened or paid any attention. ⁵They said, "Turn now, each of you, from your evil ways and your evil practices, and you can stay in the land the LORD gave to you and your fathers for ever and ever. ⁶Do not follow other gods to serve and worship them; do not provoke me to anger with what your hands have made. Then I will not harm you."

⁷"But you did not listen to me," declares the LORD, "and you have provoked me with what your hands have made, and you have brought harm to yourselves."

⁸Therefore the LORD Almighty says this: "Because you have not listened to my words, ⁹I will summon all the peoples of the north and my servant Nebuchadnezzar king of Babylon," declares the LORD, "and I will bring them against this land and its inhabitants and against all the surrounding nations. I will completely destroy*a* them and make them an object of horror and scorn, and an everlasting ruin. ¹⁰I will banish from them the sounds of joy and gladness, the voices of bride and bridegroom, the sound of millstones and the light of the lamp. ¹¹This whole country will become a desolate wasteland, and these nations will serve the king of Babylon seventy years.

¹²"But when the seventy years are fulfilled, I will punish the king of Babylon and his nation, the land of the Babylonians,*b* for their guilt," declares the LORD, "and will make it desolate forever. ¹³I will bring upon that land all the things I have spoken against it, all that are written in this book and prophesied by Jeremiah against all the nations. ¹⁴They themselves will be enslaved by many nations and great kings; I will repay them according to their deeds and the work of their hands."

The Cup of God's Wrath

¹⁵This is what the LORD, the God of Israel, said to me: "Take from my hand this cup filled with the wine of my wrath and make all the nations to whom I send you drink it. ¹⁶When they drink it, they will stagger and go mad because of the sword I will send among them."

¹⁷So I took the cup from the LORD's hand and made all the nations to whom he sent me drink it: ¹⁸Jerusalem and the towns of Judah, its kings and officials, to make them a ruin and an object of horror and scorn and cursing, as they are today; ¹⁹Pharaoh king of Egypt, his attendants, his officials and all his people, ²⁰and all the foreign people there; all the kings of Uz; all the kings of the Philistines (those of Ashkelon, Gaza, Ekron, and the people left at Ashdod); ²¹Edom, Moab and Ammon; ²²all the kings of Tyre and Sidon; the kings of the coastlands across the sea; ²³Dedan, Tema, Buz and all who are in distant places*c*; ²⁴all the kings of Arabia and all the kings of the foreign people who live in the desert; ²⁵all the kings of Zimri, Elam and Media; ²⁶and all the kings of the north, near and far, one after the other—all the kingdoms on the face of the earth. And after all of them, the king of Sheshach*d* will drink it too.

²⁷"Then tell them, 'This is what the LORD Almighty, the God of Israel, says: Drink, get drunk and vomit, and fall to rise no more because of the sword I will send among you.' ²⁸But if they refuse to take the cup from your hand and drink, tell them, 'This is what the LORD Almighty says: You must drink it! ²⁹See, I am beginning to bring disaster on the city that bears my Name, and will you indeed go unpunished? You will not go unpunished, for I am calling down a sword upon all who live on the earth, declares the LORD Almighty.'

³⁰"Now prophesy all these words against them and say to them:

" 'The LORD will roar from on high;
    he will thunder from his holy dwelling
    and roar mightily against his land.
He will shout like those who tread the
      grapes,
    shout against all who live on the earth.

---

*a*9 The Hebrew term refers to the irrevocable giving over of things or persons to the LORD, often by totally destroying them.   *b*12 Or *Chaldeans*   *c*23 Or *who clip the hair by their foreheads*   *d*26 *Sheshach* is a cryptogram for Babylon.

³¹ The tumult will resound to the ends of the
earth,
for the LORD will bring charges against
the nations;
he will bring judgment on
all mankind
and put the wicked to the
sword,"
declares the LORD.

³² This is what the LORD Almighty says:

"Look! Disaster is
spreading
from nation to nation;
a mighty storm is rising
from the ends of the
earth."

³³ At that time those slain by
the LORD will be everywhere—
from one end of the earth to
the other. They will not be mourned or gathered up or buried, but will be like refuse lying
on the ground.

³⁴ Weep and wail, you shepherds;
roll in the dust, you leaders of the flock.
For your time to be slaughtered has come;
you will fall and be shattered like fine
pottery.
³⁵ The shepherds will have nowhere to flee,
the leaders of the flock no place to
escape.
³⁶ Hear the cry of the shepherds,
the wailing of the leaders of the flock,
for the LORD is destroying their pasture.
³⁷ The peaceful meadows will be laid waste
because of the fierce anger of the LORD.
³⁸ Like a lion he will leave his lair,
and their land will become desolate
because of the sword*a* of the oppressor
and because of the LORD's fierce anger.

Jeremiah Threatened With Death

26 Early in the reign of Jehoiakim son of
Josiah king of Judah, this word came
from the LORD: ²"This is what the LORD says:
Stand in the courtyard of the LORD's house and
speak to all the people of the towns of Judah
who come to worship in the house of the LORD.

Tell them everything I command you; do not
omit a word. ³ Perhaps they will listen and each
will turn from his evil way. Then I will relent
and not bring on them the di-
saster I was planning because
of the evil they have done. ⁴ Say
to them, 'This is what the LORD
says: If you do not listen to me
and follow my law, which I
have set before you, ⁵ and if
you do not listen to the words
of my servants the prophets,
whom I have sent to you again
and again (though you have
not listened), ⁶ then I will make
this house like Shiloh and this
city an object of cursing among
all the nations of the earth.'"

⁷ The priests, the proph-
ets and all the people heard
Jeremiah speak these words in
the house of the LORD. ⁸ But as soon as Jeremiah
finished telling all the people everything the
LORD had commanded him to say, the priests,
the prophets and all the people seized him and
said, "You must die! ⁹ Why do you prophesy in
the LORD's name that this house will be like Shiloh and this city will be desolate and deserted?"
And all the people crowded around Jeremiah
in the house of the LORD.

¹⁰ When the officials of Judah heard about
these things, they went up from the royal palace to the house of the LORD and took their
places at the entrance of the New Gate of the
LORD's house. ¹¹ Then the priests and the prophets said to the officials and all the people, "This
man should be sentenced to death because he
has prophesied against this city. You have heard
it with your own ears!"

¹² Then Jeremiah said to all the officials and
all the people: "The LORD sent me to prophesy
against this house and this city all the things
you have heard. ¹³ Now reform your ways and
your actions and obey the LORD your God.
Then the LORD will relent and not bring the disaster he has pronounced against you. ¹⁴ As for
me, I am in your hands; do with me whatever
you think is good and right. ¹⁵ Be assured,
however, that if you put me to death, you will

> ### Jeremiah 26:3
>
> *God Withholds
> His Wrath*
>
> "Perhaps they will listen
> and each will turn from
> his evil way. Then I will
> relent and not bring on
> them the disaster I was
> planning because of the
> evil they have done."

---

*a*38 Some Hebrew manuscripts and Septuagint (see also Jer. 46:16 and 50:16); most Hebrew manuscripts *anger* bring the guilt of innocent blood on yourselves and on this city and on those who live in it, for in truth the LORD has sent me to you to speak all these words in your hearing."

16Then the officials and all the people said to the priests and the prophets, "This man should not be sentenced to death! He has spoken to us in the name of the LORD our God."

17Some of the elders of the land stepped forward and said to the entire assembly of people, 18"Micah of Moresheth prophesied in the days of Hezekiah king of Judah. He told all the people of Judah, 'This is what the LORD Almighty says:

"'Zion will be plowed like
    a field,
Jerusalem will become a
    heap of rubble,
the temple hill a mound
    overgrown with
    thickets.'*a*

19"Did Hezekiah king of Judah or anyone else in Judah put him to death? Did not Hezekiah fear the LORD and seek his favor? And did not the LORD relent, so that he did not bring the disaster he pronounced against them? We are about to bring a terrible disaster on ourselves!"

20(Now Uriah son of Shemaiah from Kiriath Jearim was another man who prophesied in the name of the LORD; he prophesied the same things against this city and this land as Jeremiah did. 21When King Jehoiakim and all his officers and officials heard his words, the king sought to put him to death. But Uriah heard of it and fled in fear to Egypt. 22King Jehoiakim, however, sent Elnathan son of Acbor to Egypt, along with some other men. 23They brought Uriah out of Egypt and took him to King Jehoiakim, who had him struck down with a sword and his body thrown into the burial place of the common people.)

24Furthermore, Ahikam son of Shaphan supported Jeremiah, and so he was not handed over to the people to be put to death.

Judah to Serve Nebuchadnezzar

27 Early in the reign of Zedekiah*b* son of Josiah king of Judah, this word came to Jeremiah from the LORD: 2This is what the LORD said to me: "Make a yoke out of straps and crossbars and put it on your neck. 3Then send word to the kings of Edom, Moab, Ammon, Tyre and Sidon through the envoys who have come to Jerusalem to Zedekiah king of Judah. 4Give them a message for their masters and say, 'This is what the LORD Almighty, the God of Israel, says: "Tell this to your masters: 5With my great power and outstretched arm I made the earth and its people and the animals that are on it, and I give it to anyone I please. 6Now I will hand all your countries over to my servant Nebuchadnezzar king of Babylon; I will make even the wild animals subject to him. 7All nations will serve him and his son and his grandson until the time for his land comes; then many nations and great kings will subjugate him.

8"'"If, however, any nation or kingdom will not serve Nebuchadnezzar king of Babylon or bow its neck under his yoke, I will punish that nation with the sword, famine and plague, declares the LORD, until I destroy it by his hand. 9So do not listen to your prophets, your diviners, your interpreters of dreams, your mediums or your sorcerers who tell you, 'You will not serve the king of Babylon.' 10They prophesy lies to you that will only serve to remove you far from your lands; I will banish you and you will perish. 11But if any nation will bow its neck under the yoke of the king of Babylon and serve him, I will let that nation remain in its own land to till it and to live there, declares the LORD." '"

12I gave the same message to Zedekiah king of Judah. I said, "Bow your neck under the yoke of the king of Babylon; serve him and his people, and you will live. 13Why will you and your people die by the sword, famine and plague

---

Jeremiah 27:5

God Gives at His Discretion

"With my great power and outstretched arm I made the earth and its people and the animals that are on it, and I give it to anyone I please."

---

*a*18 Micah 3:12 *b*1 A few Hebrew manuscripts and Syriac (see also Jer. 27:3, 12 and 28:1); most Hebrew manuscripts *Jehoiakim* (Most Septuagint manuscripts do not have this verse.)

Primary Source

Read: Jeremiah 27:1–22

IN THE INFORMATION AGE, there is no shortage of perspectives. Newscasts, blogs, radio, movies, television and opinion polls constantly assail us with how we should feel and think about all kinds of issues. However, when believers need perspective, where do we turn? Whose voice echoes in our ears?

We like to say that we turn to God and to the Scriptures. But if we're truthful, we're a lot like the children of Israel. Instead of getting information from the primary source, they sought out false prophets. If they had listened to Jeremiah, they would have known God was saying just the opposite of what they were hearing.

Today, it's unlikely that a believer would seek out mediums or psychics for advice on life—although they are readily available. However, a number of other sources influence our thoughts and decisions, and not all of them are godly. From social trends to cultural mores, other people greatly affect how we see life. And Satan is aware of just how much "airtime" is available to influence us throughout our day.

Case in point: What are you worried about today? Headlines like terrorism, war, financial collapse? If those threats don't concern you, perhaps daytime television has convinced you that your children might be on meth or that your husband might be having an affair. And we wonder why we sometimes live with a vague sense of dread much of the time! Maybe instead of turning to God for perspective, we've been turning elsewhere.

It's normal to be concerned about our lives and our loved ones . . . but if we're not careful, anxiety can all too quickly imprison us. When you feel the cords of anxiety and worry tightening around you, think about the Lord's promises, his sovereignty and his goodness. Why not start by reading less of the newspaper and more of God's Word? Try turning off the television and tuning into praise music. You don't need to completely hide from the world, but try spending as much time hearing from God as you do hearing from other sources. The more you dwell on God's faithfulness, the less likely you'll view life from the wrong perspective. Go to the primary source for wisdom and insight.

Jeremiah 27:9

"So do not listen to your prophets, your diviners, your interpreters of dreams, your mediums or your sorcerers who tell you, 'You will not serve the king of Babylon.' "

reflection

1 What "voices" are you listening to each day?

2 In what ways do you struggle with worry and fear? Be specific.

3 Think of three ways you can dwell on God's promises—instead of what you fear—today.

RELATED READINGS

2 Kings 24:8–17;
Psalms 27:1–3; 94:19;
Philippians 4:4–9

"How do we find the peace and simplicity we crave in our lives? I think the answer lies in patience and prayer."

Ellyn Sanna

Monday

Go to page 944 for your next devotional reading.

with which the LORD has threatened any nation that will not serve the king of Babylon? ¹⁴Do not listen to the words of the prophets who say to you, 'You will not serve the king of Babylon,' for they are prophesying lies to you. ¹⁵'I have not sent them,' declares the LORD. 'They are prophesying lies in my name. Therefore, I will banish you and you will perish, both you and the prophets who prophesy to you.'"

¹⁶Then I said to the priests and all these people, "This is what the LORD says: Do not listen to the prophets who say, 'Very soon now the articles from the LORD's house will be brought back from Babylon.' They are prophesying lies to you. ¹⁷Do not listen to them. Serve the king of Babylon, and you will live. Why should this city become a ruin? ¹⁸If they are prophets and have the word of the LORD, let them plead with the LORD Almighty that the furnishings remaining in the house of the LORD and in the palace of the king of Judah and in Jerusalem not be taken to Babylon. ¹⁹For this is what the LORD Almighty says about the pillars, the Sea, the movable stands and the other furnishings that are left in this city, ²⁰which Nebuchadnezzar king of Babylon did not take away when he carried Jehoiachin*ᵃ* son of Jehoiakim king of Judah into exile from Jerusalem to Babylon, along with all the nobles of Judah and Jerusalem— ²¹yes, this is what the LORD Almighty, the God of Israel, says about the things that are left in the house of the LORD and in the palace of the king of Judah and in Jerusalem: ²²'They will be taken to Babylon and there they will remain until the day I come for them,' declares the LORD. 'Then I will bring them back and restore them to this place.'"

The False Prophet Hananiah

28 In the fifth month of that same year, the fourth year, early in the reign of Zedekiah king of Judah, the prophet Hananiah son of Azzur, who was from Gibeon, said to me in the house of the LORD in the presence of the priests and all the people: ²"This is what the LORD Almighty, the God of Israel, says: 'I will break the yoke of the king of Babylon. ³Within two years I will bring back to this place all the articles of the LORD's house that Nebuchadnez-

zar king of Babylon removed from here and took to Babylon. ⁴I will also bring back to this place Jehoiachin*ᵃ* son of Jehoiakim king of Judah and all the other exiles from Judah who went to Babylon,' declares the LORD, 'for I will break the yoke of the king of Babylon.'"

⁵Then the prophet Jeremiah replied to the prophet Hananiah before the priests and all the people who were standing in the house of the LORD. ⁶He said, "Amen! May the LORD do so! May the LORD fulfill the words you have prophesied by bringing the articles of the LORD's house and all the exiles back to this place from Babylon. ⁷Nevertheless, listen to what I have to say in your hearing and in the hearing of all the people: ⁸From early times the prophets who preceded you and me have prophesied war, disaster and plague against many countries and great kingdoms. ⁹But the prophet who prophesies peace will be recognized as one truly sent by the LORD only if his prediction comes true."

¹⁰Then the prophet Hananiah took the yoke off the neck of the prophet Jeremiah and broke it, ¹¹and he said before all the people, "This is what the LORD says: 'In the same way will I break the yoke of Nebuchadnezzar king of Babylon off the neck of all the nations within two years.'" At this, the prophet Jeremiah went on his way.

¹²Shortly after the prophet Hananiah had broken the yoke off the neck of the prophet Jeremiah, the word of the LORD came to Jeremiah: ¹³"Go and tell Hananiah, 'This is what the LORD says: You have broken a wooden yoke, but in its place you will get a yoke of iron. ¹⁴This is what the LORD Almighty, the God of Israel, says: I will put an iron yoke on the necks of all these nations to make them serve Nebuchadnezzar king of Babylon, and they will serve him. I will even give him control over the wild animals.'"

¹⁵Then the prophet Jeremiah said to Hananiah the prophet, "Listen, Hananiah! The LORD has not sent you, yet you have persuaded this nation to trust in lies. ¹⁶Therefore, this is what the LORD says: 'I am about to remove you from the face of the earth. This very year you are going to die, because you have preached rebellion against the LORD.'"

ᵃ20,4 Hebrew *Jeconiah,* a variant of *Jehoiachin*

¹⁷In the seventh month of that same year, Hananiah the prophet died.

A Letter to the Exiles

29 This is the text of the letter that the prophet Jeremiah sent from Jerusalem to the surviving elders among the exiles and to the priests, the prophets and all the other people Nebuchadnezzar had carried into exile from Jerusalem to Babylon. ²(This was after King Jehoiachin*a* and the queen mother, the court officials and the leaders of Judah and Jerusalem, the craftsmen and the artisans had gone into exile from Jerusalem.) ³He entrusted the letter to Elasah son of Shaphan and to Gemariah son of Hilkiah, whom Zedekiah king of Judah sent to King Nebuchadnezzar in Babylon. It said:

⁴This is what the LORD Almighty, the God of Israel, says to all those I carried into exile from Jerusalem to Babylon: ⁵"Build houses and settle down; plant gardens and eat what they produce. ⁶Marry and have sons and daughters; find wives for your sons and give your daughters in marriage, so that they too may have sons and daughters. Increase in number there; do not decrease. ⁷Also, seek the peace and prosperity of the city to which I have carried you into exile. Pray to the LORD for it, because if it prospers, you too will prosper." ⁸Yes, this is what the LORD Almighty, the God of Israel, says: "Do not let the prophets and diviners among you deceive you. Do not listen to the dreams you encourage them to have. ⁹They are prophesying lies to you in my name. I have not sent them," declares the LORD.

¹⁰This is what the LORD says: "When seventy years are completed for Babylon, I will come to you and fulfill my gracious promise to bring you back to this place. ¹¹For I know the plans I have for you," declares the LORD, "plans to prosper you and not

to harm you, plans to give you hope and a future. ¹²Then you will call upon me and come and pray to me, and I will listen to you. ¹³You will seek me and find me when you seek me with all your heart. ¹⁴I will be found by you," declares the LORD, "and will bring you back from captivity.*b* I will gather you from all the nations and places where I have banished you," declares the LORD, "and will bring you back to the place from which I carried you into exile."

¹⁵You may say, "The LORD has raised up prophets for us in Babylon," ¹⁶but this is what the LORD says about the king who sits on David's throne and all the people who remain in this city, your countrymen who did not go with you into exile— ¹⁷yes, this is what the LORD Almighty says: "I will send the sword, famine and plague against them and I will make them like poor figs that are so bad they cannot be eaten. ¹⁸I will pursue them with the sword, famine and plague and will make them abhorrent to all the kingdoms of the earth and an object of cursing and horror, of scorn and reproach, among all the nations where I drive them. ¹⁹For they have not listened to my words," declares the LORD, "words that I sent to them again and again by my servants the prophets. And you exiles have not listened either," declares the LORD.

²⁰Therefore, hear the word of the LORD, all you exiles whom I have sent away from Jerusalem to Babylon. ²¹This is what the LORD Almighty, the God of Israel, says about Ahab son of Kolaiah and Zedekiah son of Maaseiah, who are prophesying lies to you in my name: "I will hand them over to Nebuchadnezzar king of Babylon, and he will put them to death before your very eyes. ²²Because of them, all the exiles from Judah who are in Babylon

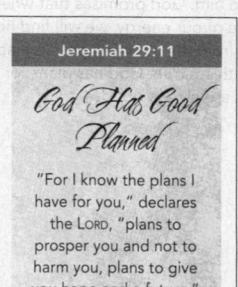

Jeremiah 29:11

God Has Good Planned

"For I know the plans I have for you," declares the LORD, "plans to prosper you and not to harm you, plans to give you hope and a future."

---

*a*2 Hebrew *Jeconiah*, a variant of *Jehoiachin*   *b*14 Or *will restore your fortunes*

God Owns Time

Read: Jeremiah 29:4-14

Jeremiah 29:11-14

"I know the plans I have for you," declares the LORD, "plans to prosper you and not to harm you, plans to give you hope and a future. Then you will call upon me and come and pray to me, and I will listen to you. You will seek me and find me when you seek me with all your heart. I will be found by you," declares the LORD, "and will bring you back from captivity."

reflection

1 When was a time you felt surrounded by darkness?

2 How can knowing that God owns time give you perspective on a difficult situation?

3 If you're in a tough place right now, spend some time crying out to God. Ask him for renewed hope, for the strength to lean on him and for the wisdom to know what to ask for.

RELATED READINGS

2 Chronicles 7:12–16;
Psalm 40:1–17;
Isaiah 55:1–13

IT'S SO HARD TO LOOK beyond our circumstances. For the Jews in the time of Jeremiah, it seemed impossible. The Babylonians had whisked them from their homes and settled them in enemy territory. Into this depressing scene, God sent Jeremiah, the anguished prophet of judgment. But his message this time was one of hope. In essence, he said, "Though your circumstances look bleak, your confinement will be limited. So settle in and make a home away from home for yourselves. As incredible as it sounds, look for and enjoy the moments of joy, even in this place. It won't be long before the worst will be over."

Today endless darkness may seem to surround you, just as the Israelites experienced. Maybe it is hard to remember the last time you felt free or comfortable. You've watched your business struggle, your friend fight disease or a child disown you. And you may have lived in this place for such a long time that you consider it a second home.

Whether or not the darkness is of your own making, and whether or not you can see its end, remember this: God owns time. Though he rarely shares his reasons with us, he knows why he allows the pain to continue. And he also knows the date—the day, the hour and the precise minute—when the agony will end. Not only that, but he also knows what he has in store for us when it's over.

Through Jeremiah, God invited the exiles to look to him, to call to him. God promises that when we search for him with every ounce of our energy, we will find him. In his time, he will bring us back from the dark and hostile places. As difficult as it is to imagine now, this is true: God has plans for us. And because he's God, his plans are always good.

Tuesday

will use this curse: 'The LORD treat you like Zedekiah and Ahab, whom the king of Babylon burned in the fire.' ²³For they have done outrageous things in Israel; they have committed adultery with their neighbors' wives and in my name have spoken lies, which I did not tell them to do. I know it and am a witness to it," declares the LORD.

Message to Shemaiah

²⁴Tell Shemaiah the Nehelamite, ²⁵"This is what the LORD Almighty, the God of Israel, says: You sent letters in your own name to all the people in Jerusalem, to Zephaniah son of Maaseiah the priest, and to all the other priests. You said to Zephaniah, ²⁶'The LORD has appointed you priest in place of Jehoiada to be in charge of the house of the LORD; you should put any madman who acts like a prophet into the stocks and neck-irons. ²⁷So why have you not reprimanded Jeremiah from Anathoth, who poses as a prophet among you? ²⁸He has sent this message to us in Babylon: It will be a long time. Therefore build houses and settle down; plant gardens and eat what they produce.'"

²⁹Zephaniah the priest, however, read the letter to Jeremiah the prophet. ³⁰Then the word of the LORD came to Jeremiah: ³¹"Send this message to all the exiles: 'This is what the LORD says about Shemaiah the Nehelamite: Because Shemaiah has prophesied to you, even though I did not send him, and has led you to believe a lie, ³²this is what the LORD says: I will surely punish Shemaiah the Nehelamite and his descendants. He will have no one left among this people, nor will he see the good things I will do for my people, declares the LORD, because he has preached rebellion against me.'"

Restoration of Israel

30 This is the word that came to Jeremiah from the LORD: ²"This is what the LORD, the God of Israel, says: 'Write in a book

*a*3 Or *will restore the fortunes of my people Israel and Judah*

all the words I have spoken to you. ³The days are coming,' declares the LORD, 'when I will bring my people Israel and Judah back from captivity*a* and restore them to the land I gave their forefathers to possess,' says the LORD."

⁴These are the words the LORD spoke concerning Israel and Judah: ⁵"This is what the LORD says:

"'Cries of fear are heard—
    terror, not peace.
⁶ Ask and see:
    Can a man bear children?
Then why do I see every strong man
    with his hands on his stomach like a
        woman in labor,
    every face turned deathly pale?
⁷ How awful that day will be!
    None will be like it.
It will be a time of trouble for Jacob,
    but he will be saved out of it.

⁸ "'In that day,' declares the LORD Almighty,
    'I will break the yoke off their necks
and will tear off their bonds;
    no longer will foreigners enslave them.
⁹ Instead, they will serve the LORD their
        God
    and David their king,
    whom I will raise up for them.

¹⁰ "'So do not fear, O Jacob
        my servant;
    do not be dismayed,
        O Israel,'
            declares the LORD.
    'I will surely save you out
        of a distant place,
    your descendants from
        the land of their
            exile.
Jacob will again have peace
        and security,
    and no one will make
        him afraid.
¹¹ I am with you and will save you,'
        declares the LORD.
    'Though I completely destroy all the
        nations
    among which I scatter you,
    I will not completely destroy you.

Jeremiah 30:11

God Saves His People

"I am with you and will save you," declares the LORD.

I will discipline you but only with justice;
    I will not let you go entirely
        unpunished.'

¹²"This is what the LORD says:

"'Your wound is incurable,
    your injury beyond healing.
¹³ There is no one to plead your cause,
    no remedy for your sore,
    no healing for you.
¹⁴ All your allies have forgotten you;
    they care nothing for you.
I have struck you as an enemy would
    and punished you as would the cruel,
because your guilt is so great
    and your sins so many.
¹⁵ Why do you cry out over your wound,
    your pain that has no cure?
Because of your great guilt and many sins
    I have done these things to you.

¹⁶ "'But all who devour you will be devoured;
    all your enemies will go into exile.
Those who plunder you will be plundered;
    all who make spoil of you I will despoil.
¹⁷ But I will restore you to health
    and heal your wounds,
                    declares the LORD,
'because you are called an outcast,
    Zion for whom no one cares.'

¹⁸ "This is what the LORD says:

"'I will restore the fortunes of Jacob's tents
    and have compassion on his dwellings;
the city will be rebuilt on her ruins,
    and the palace will stand in its proper
        place.
¹⁹ From them will come songs of
        thanksgiving
    and the sound of rejoicing.
I will add to their numbers,
    and they will not be decreased;
I will bring them honor,
    and they will not be disdained.
²⁰ Their children will be as in days of old,
    and their community will be established
        before me;
I will punish all who oppress them.
²¹ Their leader will be one of their own;
    their ruler will arise from among them.

---

*a*3 Or *LORD has appeared to us from afar*

I will bring him near and he will come
        close to me,
    for who is he who will devote himself
        to be close to me?'
                    declares the LORD.
²² "'So you will be my people,
    and I will be your God.'"

²³ See, the storm of the LORD
    will burst out in wrath,
a driving wind swirling down
    on the heads of the wicked.
²⁴ The fierce anger of the LORD will not turn
        back
    until he fully accomplishes
        the purposes of his heart.
In days to come
    you will understand this.

31

"At that time," declares the LORD, "I
will be the God of all the clans of Israel,
and they will be my people."

² This is what the LORD says:

"The people who survive the sword
    will find favor in the desert;
    I will come to give rest to Israel."

³ The LORD appeared to us in the past,*a* saying:

"I have loved you with an everlasting love;
    I have drawn you with loving-kindness.
⁴ I will build you up again
    and you will be rebuilt, O Virgin Israel.
Again you will take up your tambourines
    and go out to dance with the joyful.
⁵ Again you will plant vineyards
    on the hills of Samaria;
the farmers will plant them
    and enjoy their fruit.
⁶ There will be a day when watchmen cry
        out
    on the hills of Ephraim,
'Come, let us go up to Zion,
    to the LORD our God.'"

⁷ This is what the LORD says:

"Sing with joy for Jacob;
    shout for the foremost of the nations.
Make your praises heard, and say,
    'O LORD, save your people,

the remnant of Israel.'

8 See, I will bring them from the land of the
north
and gather them from the ends of the
earth.
Among them will be the blind and the
lame,
expectant mothers and women in labor;
a great throng will return.
9 They will come with weeping;
they will pray as I bring them back.
I will lead them beside streams of water
on a level path where they will not
stumble,
because I am Israel's father,
and Ephraim is my firstborn son.

10 "Hear the word of the LORD, O nations;
proclaim it in distant coastlands:
'He who scattered Israel will gather them
and will watch over his flock like a
shepherd.'
11 For the LORD will ransom Jacob
and redeem them from the hand of
those stronger than they.
12 They will come and shout for joy on the
heights of Zion;
they will rejoice in the bounty of the
LORD—
the grain, the new wine and the oil,
the young of the flocks and herds.
They will be like a well-watered garden,
and they will sorrow no more.
13 Then maidens will dance and be glad,
young men and old as well.
I will turn their mourning into gladness;
I will give them comfort and joy instead
of sorrow.
14 I will satisfy the priests with abundance,
and my people will be filled with my
bounty,"
declares the LORD.

15 This is what the LORD says:

"A voice is heard in Ramah,
mourning and great weeping,
Rachel weeping for her children
and refusing to be comforted,
because her children are no more."

16 This is what the LORD says:

"Restrain your voice from weeping
and your eyes from tears,
for your work will be rewarded,"
declares the LORD.
"They will return from the land of the
enemy.
17 So there is hope for your future,"
declares the LORD.
"Your children will return to their own
land.

18 "I have surely heard Ephraim's moaning:
'You disciplined me like an unruly calf,
and I have been disciplined.
Restore me, and I will return,
because you are the LORD my God.
19 After I strayed,
I repented;
after I came to understand,
I beat my breast.
I was ashamed and humiliated
because I bore the disgrace of my youth.'
20 Is not Ephraim my dear son,
the child in whom I delight?
Though I often speak against him,
I still remember him.
Therefore my heart yearns for him;
I have great compassion for him,"
declares the LORD.

21 "Set up road signs;
put up guideposts.
Take note of the highway,
the road that you take.
Return, O Virgin Israel,
return to your towns.
22 How long will you wander,
O unfaithful daughter?
The LORD will create a new thing on
earth—
a woman will surround[a] a man."

23 This is what the LORD Almighty, the God
of Israel, says: "When I bring them back from
captivity,[b] the people in the land of Judah and
in its towns will once again use these words:
'The LORD bless you, O righteous dwelling,
O sacred mountain.' 24 People will live together
in Judah and all its towns—farmers and those

---

[a]22 Or *will go about seeking*; or *will protect*   [b]23 Or *I restore their fortunes*

who move about with their flocks. ²⁵I will refresh the weary and satisfy the faint."

²⁶At this I awoke and looked around. My sleep had been pleasant to me.

²⁷"The days are coming," declares the LORD, "when I will plant the house of Israel and the house of Judah with the offspring of men and of animals. ²⁸Just as I watched over them to uproot and tear down, and to overthrow, destroy and bring disaster, so I will watch over them to build and to plant," declares the LORD. ²⁹"In those days people will no longer say,

'The fathers have eaten sour grapes,
    and the children's teeth are set on edge.'

³⁰Instead, everyone will die for his own sin; whoever eats sour grapes—his own teeth will be set on edge.

³¹"The time is coming," declares the LORD,
    "when I will make a new covenant
with the house of Israel
    and with the house of Judah.
³²It will not be like the covenant
    I made with their forefathers
when I took them by the hand
    to lead them out of Egypt,
because they broke my covenant,
    though I was a husband to*a* them,*b*"
                    declares the LORD.
³³"This is the covenant I will make with the
        house of Israel
    after that time," declares the LORD.
"I will put my law in their minds
    and write it on their hearts.
I will be their God,
    and they will be my people.
³⁴No longer will a man teach his neighbor,
    or a man his brother, saying, 'Know the
        LORD,'
because they will all know me,
    from the least of them to the greatest,"
                    declares the LORD.
"For I will forgive their wickedness
    and will remember their sins no more."

³⁵This is what the LORD says,

he who appoints the sun
    to shine by day,

who decrees the moon and stars
    to shine by night,
who stirs up the sea
    so that its waves roar—
    the LORD Almighty is his name:
³⁶"Only if these decrees vanish from my
        sight,"
    declares the LORD,
"will the descendants of Israel ever cease
    to be a nation before me."

³⁷This is what the LORD says:

"Only if the heavens above can be
        measured
    and the foundations of the earth below
        be searched out
will I reject all the descendants of Israel
    because of all they have done,"
                    declares the LORD.

³⁸"The days are coming," declares the LORD, "when this city will be rebuilt for me from the Tower of Hananel to the Corner Gate. ³⁹The measuring line will stretch from there straight to the hill of Gareb and then turn to Goah. ⁴⁰The whole valley where dead bodies and ashes are thrown, and all the terraces out to the Kidron Valley on the east as far as the corner of the Horse Gate, will be holy to the LORD. The city will never again be uprooted or demolished."

Jeremiah Buys a Field

32 This is the word that came to Jeremiah from the LORD in the tenth year of Zedekiah king of Judah, which was the eighteenth year of Nebuchadnezzar. ²The army of the king of Babylon was then besieging Jerusalem, and Jeremiah the prophet was confined in the courtyard of the guard in the royal palace of Judah.

³Now Zedekiah king of Judah had imprisoned him there, saying, "Why do you prophesy as you do? You say, 'This is what the LORD says: I am about to hand this city over to the king of Babylon, and he will capture it. ⁴Zedekiah king of Judah will not escape out of the hands of the Babylonians*c* but will certainly be handed over to the king of Babylon, and will speak with him

---

*a*32 Hebrew; Septuagint and Syriac / *and I turned away from*   *b*32 Or *was their master*   *c*4 Or *Chaldeans*; also in verses 5, 24, 25, 28, 29 and 43

Written on Our Hearts

Read: Jeremiah 31:31–37

OUR DAYS ARE FILLED with juggling and struggling. We struggle to get the kids to school on time, to get to the office on time and then to get back home on time. We contend with our schedules to get the house clean, the project done, the meals made and the mortgage paid. We juggle returning e-mails and phone calls to our friends. We may even have the same approach in our relationship with God. In the midst of the tumult and pressure, it's hard to fit it all in.

The reality is, we don't always "want" God enough to fit him into our schedule. We will never get closer to God if we rely on our effort and willpower alone. Jeremiah reminds us of a life-changing truth: God *wants* to be near us. You may know that on some level already. But when it comes to reading the Bible when you are exhausted at the end of the day, do you feel *desired*? When it comes to prayer, do you believe God is tired of your mumblings or that he is still eager to hear your voice? Is it hard to imagine that you could commit a thousand sins today and still be confident that God wants to be with you as much as he would if you had lived perfectly?

God wants to be with you. God wants you to know him. He wants you to live a life full of freedom and abundance (see John 10:10; Hebrews 2:14–15). He wants to give you good things. He wants this so much that he took the initiative to write his laws in your heart and mind so you would never be without them.

In the midst of your working, pushing and hurrying, the God of the universe isn't waiting for an opening in your schedule. He has already come to you. What does it look like to respond to his desire for intimacy? It might mean simply acknowledging his presence, recognizing the truth already written on your heart. It might mean enjoying the freedom that comes when you quit striving and working and rest in the power of his presence and forgiveness.

No matter how you respond, know that he is there waiting for you.

Go to page 955 for your next devotional reading.

Jeremiah 31:33–34

"This is the covenant I will make with the house of Israel after that time," declares the LORD. "I will put my law in their minds and write it on their hearts. I will be their God, and they will be my people. No longer will a man teach his neighbor, or a man his brother, saying, 'Know the LORD,' because they will all know me, from the least of them to the greatest," declares the LORD. "For I will forgive their wickedness and will remember their sins no more."

reflection

1 Why is it important to remember that God took the initiative in his relationship with you?

2 In what ways does the pace of your days affect your relationship with God?

3 Do you like the idea of God wanting you? How do you respond to the measures God takes to seek you and find you?

RELATED READINGS

Psalm 62:1–8;
Isaiah 65:1–3,17–25;
Hosea 11:1–8

face to face and see him with his own eyes. [5]He will take Zedekiah to Babylon, where he will remain until I deal with him, declares the LORD. If you fight against the Babylonians, you will not succeed.'"

[6]Jeremiah said, "The word of the LORD came to me: [7]Hanamel son of Shallum your uncle is going to come to you and say, 'Buy my field at Anathoth, because as nearest relative it is your right and duty to buy it.'

[8]"Then, just as the LORD had said, my cousin Hanamel came to me in the courtyard of the guard and said, 'Buy my field at Anathoth in the territory of Benjamin. Since it is your right to redeem it and possess it, buy it for yourself.'

"I knew that this was the word of the LORD; [9]so I bought the field at Anathoth from my cousin Hanamel and weighed out for him seventeen shekels[a] of silver. [10]I signed and sealed the deed, had it witnessed, and weighed out the silver on the scales. [11]I took the deed of purchase—the sealed copy containing the terms and conditions, as well as the unsealed copy— [12]and I gave this deed to Baruch son of Neriah, the son of Mahseiah, in the presence of my cousin Hanamel and of the witnesses who had signed the deed and of all the Jews sitting in the courtyard of the guard.

[13]"In their presence I gave Baruch these instructions: [14]'This is what the LORD Almighty, the God of Israel, says: Take these documents, both the sealed and unsealed copies of the deed of purchase, and put them in a clay jar so they will last a long time. [15]For this is what the LORD Almighty, the God of Israel, says: Houses, fields and vineyards will again be bought in this land.'

[16]"After I had given the deed of purchase to Baruch son of Neriah, I prayed to the LORD:

[17]"Ah, Sovereign LORD, you have made the heavens and the earth by your great power and outstretched arm. Nothing is too hard for you. [18]You show love to thousands but bring the punishment for the fathers' sins into the laps of their children after them. O great and powerful God, whose name is the LORD Almighty, [19]great are your purposes and mighty are your deeds. Your eyes are open to all the ways of men; you reward everyone according to his conduct and as his deeds deserve. [20]You performed miraculous signs and wonders in Egypt and have continued them to this day, both in Israel and among all mankind, and have gained the renown that is still yours. [21]You brought your people Israel out of Egypt with signs and wonders, by a mighty hand and an outstretched arm and with great terror. [22]You gave them this land you had sworn to give their forefathers, a land flowing with milk and honey. [23]They came in and took possession of it, but they did not obey you or follow your law; they did not do what you commanded them to do. So you brought all this disaster upon them.

[24]"See how the siege ramps are built up to take the city. Because of the sword, famine and plague, the city will be handed over to the Babylonians who are attacking it. What you said has happened, as you now see. [25]And though the city will be handed over to the Babylonians, you, O Sovereign LORD, say to me, 'Buy the field with silver and have the transaction witnessed.'"

[26]Then the word of the LORD came to Jeremiah: [27]"I am the LORD, the God of all mankind. Is anything too hard for me? [28]Therefore, this is what the LORD says: I am about to hand this city over to the Babylonians and to Nebuchadnezzar king of Babylon, who will capture it. [29]The Babylonians who are attacking this city will come in and set it on fire; they will burn it down, along with the houses where the people provoked me to anger by burning incense on the roofs to Baal and by pouring out drink offerings to other gods.

Jeremiah 32:17

God Is Sovereign

"Ah, Sovereign LORD, you have made the heavens and the earth by your great power and outstretched arm. Nothing is too hard for you."

[a]9 That is, about 7 ounces (about 200 grams)

³⁰"The people of Israel and Judah have done nothing but evil in my sight from their youth; indeed, the people of Israel have done nothing but provoke me with what their hands have made, declares the LORD. ³¹From the day it was built until now, this city has so aroused my anger and wrath that I must remove it from my sight. ³²The people of Israel and Judah have provoked me by all the evil they have done—they, their kings and officials, their priests and prophets, the men of Judah and the people of Jerusalem. ³³They turned their backs to me and not their faces; though I taught them again and again, they would not listen or respond to discipline. ³⁴They set up their abominable idols in the house that bears my Name and defiled it. ³⁵They built high places for Baal in the Valley of Ben Hinnom to sacrifice their sons and daughters[a] to Molech, though I never commanded, nor did it enter my mind, that they should do such a detestable thing and so make Judah sin.

³⁶"You are saying about this city, 'By the sword, famine and plague it will be handed over to the king of Babylon'; but this is what the LORD, the God of Israel, says: ³⁷I will surely gather them from all the lands where I banish them in my furious anger and great wrath; I will bring them back to this place and let them live in safety. ³⁸They will be my people, and I will be their God. ³⁹I will give them singleness of heart and action, so that they will always fear me for their own good and the good of their children after them. ⁴⁰I will make an everlasting covenant with them: I will never stop doing good to them, and I will inspire them to fear me, so that they will never turn away from me. ⁴¹I will rejoice in doing them good and will assuredly plant them in this land with all my heart and soul.

⁴²"This is what the LORD says: As I have brought all this great calamity on this people, so I will give them all the prosperity I have promised them. ⁴³Once more fields will be bought in this land of which you say, 'It is a des-

olate waste, without men or animals, for it has been handed over to the Babylonians.' ⁴⁴Fields will be bought for silver, and deeds will be signed, sealed and witnessed in the territory of Benjamin, in the villages around Jerusalem, in the towns of Judah and in the towns of the hill country, of the western foothills and of the Negev, because I will restore their fortunes,[b] declares the LORD."

Promise of Restoration

33 While Jeremiah was still confined in the courtyard of the guard, the word of the LORD came to him a second time: ²"This is what the LORD says, he who made the earth, the LORD who formed it and established it—the LORD is his name: ³'Call to me and I will answer you and tell you great and unsearchable things you do not know.' ⁴For this is what the LORD, the God of Israel, says about the houses in this city and the royal palaces of Judah that have been torn down to be used against the siege ramps and the sword ⁵in the fight with the Babylonians[c]: 'They will be filled with the dead bodies of the men I will slay in my anger and wrath. I will hide my face from this city because of all its wickedness.

⁶"'Nevertheless, I will bring health and healing to it; I will heal my people and will let them enjoy abundant peace and security. ⁷I will bring Judah and Israel back from captivity[d] and will rebuild them as they were before. ⁸I will cleanse them from all the sin they have committed against me and will forgive all their sins of rebellion against me. ⁹Then this city will bring me renown, joy, praise and honor before all nations on earth that hear of all the good things I do for it; and they will be in awe and will tremble at the abundant prosperity and peace I provide for it.'

¹⁰"This is what the LORD says: 'You say about this place, "It is a desolate waste, without men or animals." Yet in the towns of Judah and the streets of Jerusalem that are deserted, inhabited

---

Jeremiah 33:3

God Answers Prayers

"Call to me and I will answer you and tell you great and unreachable things you do not know."

---

[a]35 Or *to make their sons and daughters pass through the fire* [b]44 Or *will bring them back from captivity* [c]5 Or *Chaldeans*
[d]7 Or *will restore the fortunes of Judah and Israel*

951

by neither men nor animals, there will be heard once more **11** the sounds of joy and gladness, the voices of bride and bridegroom, and the voices of those who bring thank offerings to the house of the LORD, saying,

"Give thanks to the LORD Almighty,
  for the LORD is good;
  his love endures forever."

For I will restore the fortunes of the land as they were before,' says the LORD.

12 "This is what the LORD Almighty says: 'In this place, desolate and without men or animals—in all its towns there will again be pastures for shepherds to rest their flocks. **13** In the towns of the hill country, of the western foothills and of the Negev, in the territory of Benjamin, in the villages around Jerusalem and in the towns of Judah, flocks will again pass under the hand of the one who counts them,' says the LORD.

14 "'The days are coming,' declares the LORD, 'when I will fulfill the gracious promise I made to the house of Israel and to the house of Judah.

15 "'In those days and at that time
  I will make a righteous Branch sprout
    from David's line;
  he will do what is just and right in the
    land.
16 In those days Judah will be saved
  and Jerusalem will live in safety.
This is the name by which it[a] will be called:
  The LORD Our Righteousness.'

17 For this is what the LORD says: 'David will never fail to have a man to sit on the throne of the house of Israel, **18** nor will the priests, who are Levites, ever fail to have a man to stand before me continually to offer burnt offerings, to burn grain offerings and to present sacrifices.'"

19 The word of the LORD came to Jeremiah: **20** "This is what the LORD says: 'If you can break my covenant with the day and my covenant with the night, so that day and night no longer come at their appointed time, **21** then my covenant with David my servant—and my covenant with the Levites who are priests ministering before me—can be broken and David will no longer have a descendant to reign on his throne. **22** I will make the descendants of David my servant and the Levites who minister before me as countless as the stars of the sky and as measureless as the sand on the seashore.'"

23 The word of the LORD came to Jeremiah: **24** "Have you not noticed that these people are saying, 'The LORD has rejected the two kingdoms[b] he chose'? So they despise my people and no longer regard them as a nation. **25** This is what the LORD says: 'If I have not established my covenant with day and night and the fixed laws of heaven and earth, **26** then I will reject the descendants of Jacob and David my servant and will not choose one of his sons to rule over the descendants of Abraham, Isaac and Jacob. For I will restore their fortunes[c] and have compassion on them.'"

Warning to Zedekiah

34 While Nebuchadnezzar king of Babylon and all his army and all the kingdoms and peoples in the empire he ruled were fighting against Jerusalem and all its surrounding towns, this word came to Jeremiah from the LORD: **2** "This is what the LORD, the God of Israel, says: Go to Zedekiah king of Judah and tell him, 'This is what the LORD says: I am about to hand this city over to the king of Babylon, and he will burn it down. **3** You will not escape from his grasp but will surely be captured and handed over to him. You will see the king of Babylon with your own eyes, and he will speak with you face to face. And you will go to Babylon.

4 "'Yet hear the promise of the LORD, O Zedekiah king of Judah. This is what the LORD says concerning you: You will not die by the sword; **5** you will die peacefully. As people made a funeral fire in honor of your fathers, the former kings who preceded you, so they will make a fire in your honor and lament, "Alas, O master!" I myself make this promise, declares the LORD.'"

6 Then Jeremiah the prophet told all this to Zedekiah king of Judah, in Jerusalem, **7** while the army of the king of Babylon was fighting against Jerusalem and the other cities of Judah

a16 Or *he*   b24 Or *families*   c26 Or *will bring them back from captivity* that were still holding out—Lachish and Azekah. These were the only fortified cities left in Judah.

Freedom for Slaves

[8]The word came to Jeremiah from the LORD after King Zedekiah had made a covenant with all the people in Jerusalem to proclaim freedom for the slaves. [9]Everyone was to free his Hebrew slaves, both male and female; no one was to hold a fellow Jew in bondage. [10]So all the officials and people who entered into this covenant agreed that they would free their male and female slaves and no longer hold them in bondage. They agreed, and set them free. [11]But afterward they changed their minds and took back the slaves they had freed and enslaved them again.

[12]Then the word of the LORD came to Jeremiah: [13]"This is what the LORD, the God of Israel, says: I made a covenant with your forefathers when I brought them out of Egypt, out of the land of slavery. I said, [14]'Every seventh year each of you must free any fellow Hebrew who has sold himself to you. After he has served you six years, you must let him go free.'[a] Your fathers, however, did not listen to me or pay attention to me. [15]Recently you repented and did what is right in my sight: Each of you proclaimed freedom to his countrymen. You even made a covenant before me in the house that bears my Name. [16]But now you have turned around and profaned my name; each of you has taken back the male and female slaves you had set free to go where they wished. You have forced them to become your slaves again.

[17]"Therefore, this is what the LORD says: You have not obeyed me; you have not proclaimed freedom for your fellow countrymen. So I now proclaim 'freedom' for you, declares the LORD—'freedom' to fall by the sword, plague and famine. I will make you abhorrent to all the kingdoms of the earth. [18]The men who have violated my covenant and have not fulfilled the terms of the covenant they made before me, I will treat like the calf they cut in two and then walked between its pieces. [19]The leaders of Judah and Jerusalem, the court officials, the priests and all the people of the land who walked between the pieces of the calf, [20]I

will hand over to their enemies who seek their lives. Their dead bodies will become food for the birds of the air and the beasts of the earth.

[21]"I will hand Zedekiah king of Judah and his officials over to their enemies who seek their lives, to the army of the king of Babylon, which has withdrawn from you. [22]I am going to give the order, declares the LORD, and I will bring them back to this city. They will fight against it, take it and burn it down. And I will lay waste the towns of Judah so no one can live there."

The Recabites

35 This is the word that came to Jeremiah from the LORD during the reign of Jehoiakim son of Josiah king of Judah: [2]"Go to the Recabite family and invite them to come to one of the side rooms of the house of the LORD and give them wine to drink."

[3]So I went to get Jaazaniah son of Jeremiah, the son of Habazziniah, and his brothers and all his sons—the whole family of the Recabites. [4]I brought them into the house of the LORD, into the room of the sons of Hanan son of Igdaliah the man of God. It was next to the room of the officials, which was over that of Maaseiah son of Shallum the doorkeeper. [5]Then I set bowls full of wine and some cups before the men of the Recabite family and said to them, "Drink some wine."

[6]But they replied, "We do not drink wine, because our forefather Jonadab son of Recab gave us this command: 'Neither you nor your descendants must ever drink wine. [7]Also you must never build houses, sow seed or plant vineyards; you must never have any of these things, but must always live in tents. Then you will live a long time in the land where you are nomads.' [8]We have obeyed everything our forefather Jonadab son of Recab commanded us. Neither we nor our wives nor our sons and daughters have ever drunk wine [9]or built houses to live in or had vineyards, fields or crops. [10]We have lived in tents and have fully obeyed everything our forefather Jonadab commanded us. [11]But when Nebuchadnezzar king of Babylon invaded this land, we said, 'Come, we must go to Jerusalem to escape the Babylonian[b] and Aramean armies.' So we have remained in Jerusalem."

[12]Then the word of the LORD came to

[a]14 Deut. 15:12   [b]11 Or *Chaldean*

Jeremiah, saying: ¹³"This is what the LORD Almighty, the God of Israel, says: Go and tell the men of Judah and the people of Jerusalem, 'Will you not learn a lesson and obey my words?' declares the LORD. ¹⁴'Jonadab son of Recab ordered his sons not to drink wine and this command has been kept. To this day they do not drink wine, because they obey their forefather's command. But I have spoken to you again and again, yet you have not obeyed me. ¹⁵Again and again I sent all my servants the prophets to you. They said, "Each of you must turn from your wicked ways and reform your actions; do not follow other gods to serve them. Then you will live in the land I have given to you and your fathers." But you have not paid attention or listened to me. ¹⁶The descendants of Jonadab son of Recab have carried out the command their forefather gave them, but these people have not obeyed me.'

¹⁷"Therefore, this is what the LORD God Almighty, the God of Israel, says: 'Listen! I am going to bring on Judah and on everyone living in Jerusalem every disaster I pronounced against them. I spoke to them, but they did not listen; I called to them, but they did not answer.'"

¹⁸Then Jeremiah said to the family of the Recabites, "This is what the LORD Almighty, the God of Israel, says: 'You have obeyed the command of your forefather Jonadab and have followed all his instructions and have done everything he ordered.' ¹⁹Therefore, this is what the LORD Almighty, the God of Israel, says: 'Jonadab son of Recab will never fail to have a man to serve me.'"

Jehoiakim Burns Jeremiah's Scroll

36 In the fourth year of Jehoiakim son of Josiah king of Judah, this word came to Jeremiah from the LORD: ²"Take a scroll and write on it all the words I have spoken to you concerning Israel, Judah and all the other nations from the time I began speaking to you in the reign of Josiah till now. ³Perhaps when the people of Judah hear about every disaster I plan to inflict on them, each of them will turn from his wicked way; then I will forgive their wickedness and their sin."

⁴So Jeremiah called Baruch son of Neriah, and while Jeremiah dictated all the words the LORD had spoken to him, Baruch wrote them

on the scroll. ⁵Then Jeremiah told Baruch, "I am restricted; I cannot go to the LORD's temple. ⁶So you go to the house of the LORD on a day of fasting and read to the people from the scroll the words of the LORD that you wrote as I dictated. Read them to all the people of Judah who come in from their towns. ⁷Perhaps they will bring their petition before the LORD, and each will turn from his wicked ways, for the anger and wrath pronounced against this people by the LORD are great."

⁸Baruch son of Neriah did everything Jeremiah the prophet told him to do; at the LORD's temple he read the words of the LORD from the scroll. ⁹In the ninth month of the fifth year of Jehoiakim son of Josiah king of Judah, a time of fasting before the LORD was proclaimed for all the people in Jerusalem and those who had come from the towns of Judah. ¹⁰From the room of Gemariah son of Shaphan the secretary, which was in the upper courtyard at the entrance of the New Gate of the temple, Baruch read to all the people at the LORD's temple the words of Jeremiah from the scroll.

¹¹When Micaiah son of Gemariah, the son of Shaphan, heard all the words of the LORD from the scroll, ¹²he went down to the secretary's room in the royal palace, where all the officials were sitting: Elishama the secretary, Delaiah son of Shemaiah, Elnathan son of Acbor, Gemariah son of Shaphan, Zedekiah son of Hananiah, and all the other officials. ¹³After Micaiah told them everything he had heard Baruch read to the people from the scroll, ¹⁴all the officials sent Jehudi son of Nethaniah, the son of Shelemiah, the son of Cushi, to say to Baruch, "Bring the scroll from which you have read to the people and come." So Baruch son of Neriah went to them with the scroll in his hand. ¹⁵They said to him, "Sit down, please, and read it to us."

So Baruch read it to them. ¹⁶When they heard all these words, they looked at each other in fear and said to Baruch, "We must report all these words to the king." ¹⁷Then they asked Baruch, "Tell us, how did you come to write all this? Did Jeremiah dictate it?"

¹⁸"Yes," Baruch replied, "he dictated all these words to me, and I wrote them in ink on the scroll."

Personal Delivery

Read: Jeremiah 36:1–32

"PUT IT IN WRITING."

Those four words get results. Have a complaint? Put it in writing. Have a deal? Put it in writing. Need to clarify something? Put it in writing. And so when God wanted to get someone's attention, that's exactly what he did: He put it in writing.

Through the prophet Jeremiah and his faithful scribe, Baruch, God dictated a personal message to King Jehoiakim and his people: "Dear Jehoiakim: Here is the word of the Lord . . ." While we don't know exactly what part of Jeremiah's prophecy was written down for the king, we know this much: The king didn't like it. In fact, not only did the king refuse to comply, but he treated God's words with contempt by burning the scroll piece by piece—an unthinkable, unspeakable atrocity. No one in his right mind would treat the words of God in such a way, right?

And yet, have you ever disrespected God's Word? Think about it. You may not torch its pages, but have you ever just ignored it? You may not outwardly rebel, but have you refused to let the words of the Bible touch your life? God has put his love story in writing for us to enjoy. Yet we so often ignore it, downplay it or even entirely forget about it in the course of our daily lives.

"Dear _____: Here are my words for you . . ."

Put your name in the blank. Think of his story as a first-class letter addressed to you. Think of his words as intimate and deeply personal—something he wants you to know, something straight from his heart. When God had something important to say, he could have used a number of means to communicate it. But he chose to put it in writing.

Every day this week, carve out a few quiet minutes, find a cozy corner and open his "letter." Find out what he wants to say to you personally.

Go to page 960 for your next devotional reading.

Jeremiah 36:2–3

"Take a scroll and write on it all the words I have spoken to you concerning Israel, Judah and all the other nations from the time I began speaking to you in the reign of Josiah till now. Perhaps when the people of Judah hear about every disaster I plan to inflict on them, each of them will turn from his wicked way; then I will forgive their wickedness and their sin."

reflection

1 Why do you think King Jehoiakim reacted with so much hostility to God's words?

2 What is your favorite part of God's "letter" to you, the Bible? Why?

3 How does it make you feel to know God wrote this letter with you in mind?

RELATED READINGS

2 Kings 23:36 — 24:6;
John 16:12–16;
2 Thessalonians 1:5–10;
2 Peter 1:19–21

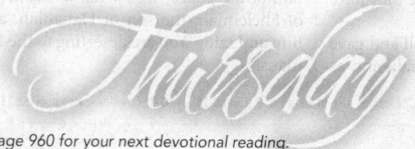

¹⁹Then the officials said to Baruch, "You and Jeremiah, go and hide. Don't let anyone know where you are."

²⁰After they put the scroll in the room of Elishama the secretary, they went to the king in the courtyard and reported everything to him. ²¹The king sent Jehudi to get the scroll, and Jehudi brought it from the room of Elishama the secretary and read it to the king and all the officials standing beside him. ²²It was the ninth month and the king was sitting in the winter apartment, with a fire burning in the firepot in front of him. ²³Whenever Jehudi had read three or four columns of the scroll, the king cut them off with a scribe's knife and threw them into the firepot, until the entire scroll was burned in the fire. ²⁴The king and all his attendants who heard all these words showed no fear, nor did they tear their clothes. ²⁵Even though Elnathan, Delaiah and Gemariah urged the king not to burn the scroll, he would not listen to them. ²⁶Instead, the king commanded Jerahmeel, a son of the king, Seraiah son of Azriel and Shelemiah son of Abdeel to arrest Baruch the scribe and Jeremiah the prophet. But the LORD had hidden them.

²⁷After the king burned the scroll containing the words that Baruch had written at Jeremiah's dictation, the word of the LORD came to Jeremiah: ²⁸"Take another scroll and write on it all the words that were on the first scroll, which Jehoiakim king of Judah burned up. ²⁹Also tell Jehoiakim king of Judah, 'This is what the LORD says: You burned that scroll and said, "Why did you write on it that the king of Babylon would certainly come and destroy this land and cut off both men and animals from it?" ³⁰Therefore, this is what the LORD says about Jehoiakim king of Judah: He will have no one to sit on the throne of David; his body will be thrown out and exposed to the heat by day and the frost by night. ³¹I will punish him and his children and his attendants for their wickedness; I will bring on them and those living in Jerusalem and the people of Judah every disaster I pronounced against them, because they have not listened.'"

³²So Jeremiah took another scroll and gave it to the scribe Baruch son of Neriah, and as Jeremiah dictated, Baruch wrote on it all the words of the scroll that Jehoiakim king of Judah had burned in the fire. And many similar words were added to them.

Jeremiah in Prison

37 Zedekiah son of Josiah was made king of Judah by Nebuchadnezzar king of Babylon; he reigned in place of Jehoiachin[a] son of Jehoiakim. ²Neither he nor his attendants nor the people of the land paid any attention to the words the LORD had spoken through Jeremiah the prophet.

³King Zedekiah, however, sent Jehucal son of Shelemiah with the priest Zephaniah son of Maaseiah to Jeremiah the prophet with this message: "Please pray to the LORD our God for us."

⁴Now Jeremiah was free to come and go among the people, for he had not yet been put in prison. ⁵Pharaoh's army had marched out of Egypt, and when the Babylonians[b] who were besieging Jerusalem heard the report about them, they withdrew from Jerusalem.

⁶Then the word of the LORD came to Jeremiah the prophet: ⁷"This is what the LORD, the God of Israel, says: Tell the king of Judah, who sent you to inquire of me, 'Pharaoh's army, which has marched out to support you, will go back to its own land, to Egypt. ⁸Then the Babylonians will return and attack this city; they will capture it and burn it down.'

⁹"This is what the LORD says: Do not deceive yourselves, thinking, 'The Babylonians will surely leave us.' They will not! ¹⁰Even if you were to defeat the entire Babylonian[c] army that is attacking you and only wounded men were left in their tents, they would come out and burn this city down."

¹¹After the Babylonian army had withdrawn from Jerusalem because of Pharaoh's army, ¹²Jeremiah started to leave the city to go to the territory of Benjamin to get his share of the property among the people there. ¹³But when he reached the Benjamin Gate, the captain of the guard, whose name was Irijah son of Shelemiah, the son of Hananiah, arrested him and said, "You are deserting to the Babylonians!"

---

*a*1 Hebrew *Coniah*, a variant of *Jehoiachin* *b*5 Or *Chaldeans*; also in verses 8, 9, 13 and 14 *c*10 Or *Chaldean*; also in verse 11

14"That's not true!" Jeremiah said. "I am not deserting to the Babylonians." But Irijah would not listen to him; instead, he arrested Jeremiah and brought him to the officials. 15They were angry with Jeremiah and had him beaten and imprisoned in the house of Jonathan the secretary, which they had made into a prison.

16Jeremiah was put into a vaulted cell in a dungeon, where he remained a long time. 17Then King Zedekiah sent for him and had him brought to the palace, where he asked him privately, "Is there any word from the LORD?"

"Yes," Jeremiah replied, "you will be handed over to the king of Babylon."

18Then Jeremiah said to King Zedekiah, "What crime have I committed against you or your officials or this people, that you have put me in prison? 19Where are your prophets who prophesied to you, 'The king of Babylon will not attack you or this land'? 20But now, my lord the king, please listen. Let me bring my petition before you: Do not send me back to the house of Jonathan the secretary, or I will die there."

21King Zedekiah then gave orders for Jeremiah to be placed in the courtyard of the guard and given bread from the street of the bakers each day until all the bread in the city was gone. So Jeremiah remained in the courtyard of the guard.

Jeremiah Thrown Into a Cistern

38 Shephatiah son of Mattan, Gedaliah son of Pashhur, Jehucal[a] son of Shelemiah, and Pashhur son of Malkijah heard what Jeremiah was telling all the people when he said, 2"This is what the LORD says: 'Whoever stays in this city will die by the sword, famine or plague, but whoever goes over to the Babylonians[b] will live. He will escape with his life; he will live.' 3And this is what the LORD says: 'This city will certainly be handed over to the army of the king of Babylon, who will capture it.'"

4Then the officials said to the king, "This man should be put to death. He is discouraging the soldiers who are left in this city, as well as all the people, by the things he is saying to them. This man is not seeking the good of these people but their ruin."

5"He is in your hands," King Zedekiah answered. "The king can do nothing to oppose you."

6So they took Jeremiah and put him into the cistern of Malkijah, the king's son, which was in the courtyard of the guard. They lowered Jeremiah by ropes into the cistern; it had no water in it, only mud, and Jeremiah sank down into the mud.

7But Ebed-Melech, a Cushite,[c] an official[d] in the royal palace, heard that they had put Jeremiah into the cistern. While the king was sitting in the Benjamin Gate, 8Ebed-Melech went out of the palace and said to him, 9"My lord the king, these men have acted wickedly in all they have done to Jeremiah the prophet. They have thrown him into a cistern, where he will starve to death when there is no longer any bread in the city."

10Then the king commanded Ebed-Melech the Cushite, "Take thirty men from here with you and lift Jeremiah the prophet out of the cistern before he dies."

11So Ebed-Melech took the men with him and went to a room under the treasury in the palace. He took some old rags and worn-out clothes from there and let them down with ropes to Jeremiah in the cistern. 12Ebed-Melech the Cushite said to Jeremiah, "Put these old rags and worn-out clothes under your arms to pad the ropes." Jeremiah did so, 13and they pulled him up with the ropes and lifted him out of the cistern. And Jeremiah remained in the courtyard of the guard.

Zedekiah Questions Jeremiah Again

14Then King Zedekiah sent for Jeremiah the prophet and had him brought to the third entrance to the temple of the LORD. "I am going to ask you something," the king said to Jeremiah. "Do not hide anything from me."

15Jeremiah said to Zedekiah, "If I give you an answer, will you not kill me? Even if I did give you counsel, you would not listen to me."

16But King Zedekiah swore this oath secretly to Jeremiah: "As surely as the LORD lives, who has given us breath, I will neither kill you nor hand you over to those who are seeking your life."

17Then Jeremiah said to Zedekiah, "This

---

*a*1 Hebrew *Jucal,* a variant of *Jehucal*   *b*2 Or *Chaldeans*; also in verses 18, 19 and 23   *c*7 Probably from the upper Nile region   *d*7 Or *a eunuch* is what the LORD God Almighty, the God of Israel, says: 'If you surrender to the officers of the king of Babylon, your life will be spared and this city will not be burned down; you and your family will live. **18**But if you will not surrender to the officers of the king of Babylon, this city will be handed over to the Babylonians and they will burn it down; you yourself will not escape from their hands.' "

19King Zedekiah said to Jeremiah, "I am afraid of the Jews who have gone over to the Babylonians, for the Babylonians may hand me over to them and they will mistreat me."

20"They will not hand you over," Jeremiah replied. "Obey the LORD by doing what I tell you. Then it will go well with you, and your life will be spared. **21**But if you refuse to surrender, this is what the LORD has revealed to me: **22**All the women left in the palace of the king of Judah will be brought out to the officials of the king of Babylon. Those women will say to you:

"'They misled you and overcame you—
those trusted friends of yours.
Your feet are sunk in the mud;
your friends have deserted you.'

23"All your wives and children will be brought out to the Babylonians. You yourself will not escape from their hands but will be captured by the king of Babylon; and this city will[a] be burned down."

24Then Zedekiah said to Jeremiah, "Do not let anyone know about this conversation, or you may die. **25**If the officials hear that I talked with you, and they come to you and say, 'Tell us what you said to the king and what the king said to you; do not hide it from us or we will kill you,' **26**then tell them, 'I was pleading with the king not to send me back to Jonathan's house to die there.' "

27All the officials did come to Jeremiah and question him, and he told them everything the king had ordered him to say. So they said no more to him, for no one had heard his conversation with the king.

28And Jeremiah remained in the courtyard of the guard until the day Jerusalem was captured.

The Fall of Jerusalem

39 This is how Jerusalem was taken: **1**In the ninth year of Zedekiah king of Judah, in the tenth month, Nebuchadnezzar king of Babylon marched against Jerusalem with his whole army and laid siege to it. **2**And on the ninth day of the fourth month of Zedekiah's eleventh year, the city wall was broken through. **3**Then all the officials of the king of Babylon came and took seats in the Middle Gate: Nergal-Sharezer of Samgar, Nebo-Sarsekim[b] a chief officer, Nergal-Sharezer a high official and all the other officials of the king of Babylon. **4**When Zedekiah king of Judah and all the soldiers saw them, they fled; they left the city at night by way of the king's garden, through the gate between the two walls, and headed toward the Arabah.[c]

5But the Babylonian[d] army pursued them and overtook Zedekiah in the plains of Jericho. They captured him and took him to Nebuchadnezzar king of Babylon at Riblah in the land of Hamath, where he pronounced sentence on him. **6**There at Riblah the king of Babylon slaughtered the sons of Zedekiah before his eyes and also killed all the nobles of Judah. **7**Then he put out Zedekiah's eyes and bound him with bronze shackles to take him to Babylon.

8The Babylonians[e] set fire to the royal palace and the houses of the people and broke down the walls of Jerusalem. **9**Nebuzaradan commander of the imperial guard carried into exile to Babylon the people who remained in the city, along with those who had gone over to him, and the rest of the people. **10**But Nebuzaradan the commander of the guard left behind in the land of Judah some of the poor people, who owned nothing; and at that time he gave them vineyards and fields.

11Now Nebuchadnezzar king of Babylon had given these orders about Jeremiah through Nebuzaradan commander of the imperial guard: **12**"Take him and look after him; don't harm him but do for him whatever he asks." **13**So Nebuzaradan the commander of the guard, Nebushazban a chief officer, Nergal-Sharezer a high official and all the other officers of the king of Babylon **14**sent and had Jeremiah taken

---

*a*23 Or *and you will cause this city to*   *b*3 Or *Nergal-Sharezer, Samgar-Nebo, Sarsekim*   *c*4 Or *the Jordan Valley*   *d*5 Or *Chaldean*
*e*8 Or *Chaldeans*

out of the courtyard of the guard. They turned him over to Gedaliah son of Ahikam, the son of Shaphan, to take him back to his home. So he remained among his own people.

¹⁵While Jeremiah had been confined in the courtyard of the guard, the word of the LORD came to him: ¹⁶"Go and tell Ebed-Melech the Cushite, 'This is what the LORD Almighty, the God of Israel, says: I am about to fulfill my words against this city through disaster, not prosperity. At that time they will be fulfilled before your eyes. ¹⁷But I will rescue you on that day, declares the LORD; you will not be handed over to those you fear. ¹⁸I will save you; you will not fall by the sword but will escape with your life, because you trust in me, declares the LORD.'"

Jeremiah 39:18

God Saves Those Who Trust

"I will save you; you will not fall by the sword but will escape with your life, because you trust in me, declares the LORD."

Jeremiah Freed

40 The word came to Jeremiah from the LORD after Nebuzaradan commander of the imperial guard had released him at Ramah. He had found Jeremiah bound in chains among all the captives from Jerusalem and Judah who were being carried into exile to Babylon. ²When the commander of the guard found Jeremiah, he said to him, "The LORD your God decreed this disaster for this place. ³And now the LORD has brought it about; he has done just as he said he would. All this happened because you people sinned against the LORD and did not obey him. ⁴But today I am freeing you from the chains on your wrists. Come with me to Babylon, if you like, and I will look after you; but if you do not want to, then don't come. Look, the whole country lies before you; go wherever you please." ⁵However, before Jeremiah turned to go,ᵃ Nebuzaradan added, "Go back to Gedaliah son of Ahikam, the son of Shaphan, whom the king of Babylon has appointed over the towns of Judah, and live with him among the people, or go anywhere else you please."

Then the commander gave him provisions and a present and let him go. ⁶So Jeremiah went to Gedaliah son of Ahikam at Mizpah

and stayed with him among the people who were left behind in the land.

Gedaliah Assassinated

⁷When all the army officers and their men who were still in the open country heard that the king of Babylon had appointed Gedaliah son of Ahikam as governor over the land and had put him in charge of the men, women and children who were the poorest in the land and who had not been carried into exile to Babylon, ⁸they came to Gedaliah at Mizpah—Ishmael son of Nethaniah, Johanan and Jonathan the sons of Kareah, Seraiah son of Tanhumeth, the sons of Ephai the Netophathite, and Jaazaniahᵇ the son of the Maacathite, and their men. ⁹Gedaliah son of Ahikam, the son of Shaphan, took an oath to reassure them and their men. "Do not be afraid to serve the Babylonians,ᶜ" he said. "Settle down in the land and serve the king of Babylon, and it will go well with you. ¹⁰I myself will stay at Mizpah to represent you before the Babylonians who come to us, but you are to harvest the wine, summer fruit and oil, and put them in your storage jars, and live in the towns you have taken over."

¹¹When all the Jews in Moab, Ammon, Edom and all the other countries heard that the king of Babylon had left a remnant in Judah and had appointed Gedaliah son of Ahikam, the son of Shaphan, as governor over them, ¹²they all came back to the land of Judah, to Gedaliah at Mizpah, from all the countries where they had been scattered. And they harvested an abundance of wine and summer fruit.

¹³Johanan son of Kareah and all the army officers still in the open country came to Gedaliah at Mizpah ¹⁴and said to him, "Don't you know that Baalis king of the Ammonites has sent Ishmael son of Nethaniah to take your life?" But Gedaliah son of Ahikam did not believe them.

¹⁵Then Johanan son of Kareah said privately to Gedaliah in Mizpah, "Let me go and kill

---

ᵃ5 Or *Jeremiah answered*   ᵇ8 Hebrew *Jezaniah*, a variant of *Jaazaniah*   ᶜ9 Or *Chaldeans*; also in verse 10

Queen of Denial

Jeremiah 40:2–3

When the commander of the guard found Jeremiah, he said to him, "The LORD your God decreed this disaster for this place. And now the LORD has brought it about; he has done just as he said he would. All this happened because you people sinned against the LORD and did not obey him."

reflection

1 When have you specifically ignored warning signs and faced a consequence as a result?

2 In what ways has God spoken to you when you strayed off the path he set out for you?

3 What area related to obedience do you struggle with the most?

RELATED READINGS

Deuteronomy 30:1–10;
Psalm 94:12;
Isaiah 55:6–7;
Hebrews 12:5–6

Read: Jeremiah 40:1–6

HAVE YOU EVER IGNORED specific warnings and then faced the consequences? You should have seen it coming—in fact, you did. But you just drifted along on your raft of denial, like a complacent Queen Cleopatra drifting on her barge down the Nile. Before you knew it, it was too late.

Jeremiah's hometown was in ruins—Jerusalem had fallen, just as God said it would. The most important religious symbols of the Jews had been desecrated. Everything Jeremiah's nation stood for was devastated. And according to the commander of the guard who released Jeremiah from his chains, even Israel's enemies knew that Jerusalem's destruction was because of the people's disobedience.

For generations, God had warned the Israelites that if they let themselves slide spiritually, they would suffer as a nation. He called them back to himself as king after king led the people further away from their spiritual roots. He sent prophets like Jeremiah with messages that were both harsh and hopeful. Through these prophets, God practically begged his people to repent.

They had seen it coming, but it was too late now.

There is hope after this kind of judgment, but the road back is long and hard. The citizens of Jerusalem did return—70 years later. Those who had been carried away as children were old by the time they began to rebuild their country.

What warnings about tomorrow are you not heeding today? What river of denial are you white-water rafting on? Are you thinking God will overlook your trifling with his commands? God *will* discipline us because he loves us. He would no more let us get away with our destructive behavior than good parents would overlook rebellion.

Don't let complacency keep you from action. More than likely, something in your life—a thought pattern, an attitude or an action—needs adjustment today so that you can stay on the path God has for you. You've been thinking about addressing it, wondering if it was God's voice you were hearing. Don't stay in denial. Respond today to avoid repercussions tomorrow.

Friday

Go to page 964 for your next devotional reading.

Ishmael son of Nethaniah, and no one will know it. Why should he take your life and cause all the Jews who are gathered around you to be scattered and the remnant of Judah to perish?"

¹⁶But Gedaliah son of Ahikam said to Johanan son of Kareah, "Don't do such a thing! What you are saying about Ishmael is not true."

41 In the seventh month Ishmael son of Nethaniah, the son of Elishama, who was of royal blood and had been one of the king's officers, came with ten men to Gedaliah son of Ahikam at Mizpah. While they were eating together there, ²Ishmael son of Nethaniah and the ten men who were with him got up and struck down Gedaliah son of Ahikam, the son of Shaphan, with the sword, killing the one whom the king of Babylon had appointed as governor over the land. ³Ishmael also killed all the Jews who were with Gedaliah at Mizpah, as well as the Babylonian*a* soldiers who were there.

⁴The day after Gedaliah's assassination, before anyone knew about it, ⁵eighty men who had shaved off their beards, torn their clothes and cut themselves came from Shechem, Shiloh and Samaria, bringing grain offerings and incense with them to the house of the LORD. ⁶Ishmael son of Nethaniah went out from Mizpah to meet them, weeping as he went. When he met them, he said, "Come to Gedaliah son of Ahikam." ⁷When they went into the city, Ishmael son of Nethaniah and the men who were with him slaughtered them and threw them into a cistern. ⁸But ten of them said to Ishmael, "Don't kill us! We have wheat and barley, oil and honey, hidden in a field." So he let them alone and did not kill them with the others. ⁹Now the cistern where he threw all the bodies of the men he had killed along with Gedaliah was the one King Asa had made as part of his defense against Baasha king of Israel. Ishmael son of Nethaniah filled it with the dead.

¹⁰Ishmael made captives of all the rest of the people who were in Mizpah—the king's daughters along with all the others who were left there, over whom Nebuzaradan commander of the imperial guard had appointed Gedaliah

son of Ahikam. Ishmael son of Nethaniah took them captive and set out to cross over to the Ammonites.

¹¹When Johanan son of Kareah and all the army officers who were with him heard about all the crimes Ishmael son of Nethaniah had committed, ¹²they took all their men and went to fight Ishmael son of Nethaniah. They caught up with him near the great pool in Gibeon. ¹³When all the people Ishmael had with him saw Johanan son of Kareah and the army officers who were with him, they were glad. ¹⁴All the people Ishmael had taken captive at Mizpah turned and went over to Johanan son of Kareah. ¹⁵But Ishmael son of Nethaniah and eight of his men escaped from Johanan and fled to the Ammonites.

Flight to Egypt

¹⁶Then Johanan son of Kareah and all the army officers who were with him led away all the survivors from Mizpah whom he had recovered from Ishmael son of Nethaniah after he had assassinated Gedaliah son of Ahikam: the soldiers, women, children and court officials he had brought from Gibeon. ¹⁷And they went on, stopping at Geruth Kimham near Bethlehem on their way to Egypt ¹⁸to escape the Babylonians.*b* They were afraid of them because Ishmael son of Nethaniah had killed Gedaliah son of Ahikam, whom the king of Babylon had appointed as governor over the land.

42 Then all the army officers, including Johanan son of Kareah and Jezaniah*c* son of Hoshaiah, and all the people from the least to the greatest approached ²Jeremiah the prophet and said to him, "Please hear our petition and pray to the LORD your God for this entire remnant. For as you now see, though we were once many, now only a few are left. ³Pray that the LORD your God will tell us where we should go and what we should do."

⁴"I have heard you," replied Jeremiah the prophet. "I will certainly pray to the LORD your God as you have requested; I will tell you everything the LORD says and will keep nothing back from you."

⁵Then they said to Jeremiah, "May the LORD be a true and faithful witness against us if we

---

*a*3 Or *Chaldean*   *b*18 Or *Chaldeans*   *c*1 Hebrew; Septuagint (see also 43:2) *Azariah* do not act in accordance with everything the LORD your God sends you to tell us. ⁶Whether it is favorable or unfavorable, we will obey the LORD our God, to whom we are sending you, so that it will go well with us, for we will obey the LORD our God."

⁷Ten days later the word of the LORD came to Jeremiah. ⁸So he called together Johanan son of Kareah and all the army officers who were with him and all the people from the least to the greatest. ⁹He said to them, "This is what the LORD, the God of Israel, to whom you sent me to present your petition, says: ¹⁰'If you stay in this land, I will build you up and not tear you down; I will plant you and not uproot you, for I am grieved over the disaster I have inflicted on you. ¹¹Do not be afraid of the king of Babylon, whom you now fear. Do not be afraid of him, declares the LORD, for I am with you and will save you and deliver you from his hands. ¹²I will show you compassion so that he will have compassion on you and restore you to your land.'

¹³"However, if you say, 'We will not stay in this land,' and so disobey the LORD your God, ¹⁴and if you say, 'No, we will go and live in Egypt, where we will not see war or hear the trumpet or be hungry for bread,' ¹⁵then hear the word of the LORD, O remnant of Judah. This is what the LORD Almighty, the God of Israel, says: 'If you are determined to go to Egypt and you do go to settle there, ¹⁶then the sword you fear will overtake you there, and the famine you dread will follow you into Egypt, and there you will die. ¹⁷Indeed, all who are determined to go to Egypt to settle there will die by the sword, famine and plague; not one of them will survive or escape the disaster I will bring on them.' ¹⁸This is what the LORD Almighty, the God of Israel, says: 'As my anger and wrath have been poured out on those who lived in Jerusalem, so will my wrath be poured out on you when you go to Egypt. You will be an object of cursing and horror, of condem-

Jeremiah 42:6

God Seeks Obedience

"Whether it is favorable or unfavorable, we will obey the LORD our God, to whom we are sending you, so that it will go well with us, for we will obey the LORD our God."

nation and reproach; you will never see this place again.'

¹⁹"O remnant of Judah, the LORD has told you, 'Do not go to Egypt.' Be sure of this: I warn you today ²⁰that you made a fatal mistake*ᵃ* when you sent me to the LORD your God and said, 'Pray to the LORD our God for us; tell us everything he says and we will do it.' ²¹I have told you today, but you still have not obeyed the LORD your God in all he sent me to tell you. ²²So now, be sure of this: You will die by the sword, famine and plague in the place where you want to go to settle."

43 When Jeremiah finished telling the people all the words of the LORD their God—everything the LORD had sent him to tell them— ²Azariah son of Hoshaiah and Johanan son of Kareah and all the arrogant men said to Jeremiah, "You are lying! The LORD our God has not sent you to say, 'You must not go to Egypt to settle there.' ³But Baruch son of Neriah is inciting you against us to hand us over to the Babylonians,*ᵇ* so they may kill us or carry us into exile to Babylon."

⁴So Johanan son of Kareah and all the army officers and all the people disobeyed the LORD's command to stay in the land of Judah. ⁵Instead, Johanan son of Kareah and all the army officers led away all the remnant of Judah who had come back to live in the land of Judah from all the nations where they had been scattered. ⁶They also led away all the men, women and children and the king's daughters whom Nebuzaradan commander of the imperial guard had left with Gedaliah son of Ahikam, the son of Shaphan, and Jeremiah the prophet and Baruch son of Neriah. ⁷So they entered Egypt in disobedience to the LORD and went as far as Tahpanhes.

⁸In Tahpanhes the word of the LORD came to Jeremiah: ⁹"While the Jews are watching, take some large stones with you and bury them in clay in the brick pavement at the entrance

ᵃ20 Or you erred in your hearts   *ᵇ3 Or Chaldeans*

to Pharaoh's palace in Tahpanhes. ¹⁰Then say to them, 'This is what the LORD Almighty, the God of Israel, says: I will send for my servant Nebuchadnezzar king of Babylon, and I will set his throne over these stones I have buried here; he will spread his royal canopy above them. ¹¹He will come and attack Egypt, bringing death to those destined for death, captivity to those destined for captivity, and the sword to those destined for the sword. ¹²He*ᵃ* will set fire to the temples of the gods of Egypt; he will burn their temples and take their gods captive. As a shepherd wraps his garment around him, so will he wrap Egypt around himself and depart from there unscathed. ¹³There in the temple of the sun*ᵇ* in Egypt he will demolish the sacred pillars and will burn down the temples of the gods of Egypt.'"

Disaster Because of Idolatry

44 This word came to Jeremiah concerning all the Jews living in Lower Egypt—in Migdol, Tahpanhes and Memphis*ᶜ*—and in Upper Egypt*ᵈ*: ²"This is what the LORD Almighty, the God of Israel, says: You saw the great disaster I brought on Jerusalem and on all the towns of Judah. Today they lie deserted and in ruins ³because of the evil they have done. They provoked me to anger by burning incense and by worshiping other gods that neither they nor you nor your fathers ever knew. ⁴Again and again I sent my servants the prophets, who said, 'Do not do this detestable thing that I hate!' ⁵But they did not listen or pay attention; they did not turn from their wickedness or stop burning incense to other gods. ⁶Therefore, my fierce anger was poured out; it raged against the towns of Judah and the streets of Jerusalem and made them the desolate ruins they are today.

⁷"Now this is what the LORD God Almighty, the God of Israel, says: Why bring such great disaster on yourselves by cutting off from Judah the men and women, the children and infants, and so leave yourselves without a remnant? ⁸Why provoke me to anger with what your hands have made, burning incense to other gods in Egypt, where you have come to live? You will destroy yourselves and make yourselves an object of cursing and reproach among all the nations on earth. ⁹Have you forgotten the wickedness committed by your fathers and by the kings and queens of Judah and the wickedness committed by you and your wives in the land of Judah and the streets of Jerusalem? ¹⁰To this day they have not humbled themselves or shown reverence, nor have they followed my law and the decrees I set before you and your fathers.

¹¹"Therefore, this is what the LORD Almighty, the God of Israel, says: I am determined to bring disaster on you and to destroy all Judah. ¹²I will take away the remnant of Judah who were determined to go to Egypt to settle there. They will all perish in Egypt; they will fall by the sword or die from famine. From the least to the greatest, they will die by sword or famine. They will become an object of cursing and horror, of condemnation and reproach. ¹³I will punish those who live in Egypt with the sword, famine and plague, as I punished Jerusalem. ¹⁴None of the remnant of Judah who have gone to live in Egypt will escape or survive to return to the land of Judah, to which they long to return and live; none will return except a few fugitives."

¹⁵Then all the men who knew that their wives were burning incense to other gods, along with all the women who were present—a large assembly—and all the people living in Lower and Upper Egypt,*ᵉ* said to Jeremiah, ¹⁶"We will not listen to the message you have spoken to us in the name of the LORD! ¹⁷We will certainly do everything we said we would: We will burn incense to the Queen of Heaven and will pour out drink offerings to her just as we and our fathers, our kings and our officials did in the towns of Judah and in the streets of Jerusalem. At that time we had plenty of food and were well off and suffered no harm. ¹⁸But ever since we stopped burning incense to the Queen of Heaven and pouring out drink offerings to her, we have had nothing and have been perishing by sword and famine."

¹⁹The women added, "When we burned incense to the Queen of Heaven and poured out drink offerings to her, did not our husbands know that we were making cakes like her image and pouring out drink offerings to her?"

²⁰Then Jeremiah said to all the people, both

*ᵃ*12 Or I   *ᵇ*13 Or in Heliopolis   *ᶜ*1 Hebrew Noph   *ᵈ*1 Hebrew in Pathros   *ᵉ*15 Hebrew in Egypt and Pathros

Quit!

JOB'S WIFE

SHE WAS AT HER WIT'S END.

Emotionally depleted from her grievous losses, Job's wife had nothing left to give to her husband. She'd wept so much in such a short time that she was sure she'd cried her last tear. Life seemed hopeless and, worse yet, she felt like God did not seem to care. Everything she'd cherished was now nothing but a memory.

And even the memories were starting to blur. One day, she had the frightening experience of suddenly not being able to picture her loved ones' faces in her mind—her sons and daughters, their spouses. What did they look like? Could she remember clearly? Under the stress of her situation, she suffered untold emotional and psychological distress, digressing into symptoms of physical pain. She wasn't eating. She wasn't sleeping.

So, perhaps it's not that surprising that the day she saw her husband covered in boils and scraping himself with a shard of pottery, she just lost it. Job's wife fell to pieces emotionally and spiritually.

Her tirade may have been a long time in coming—it's unclear from the details in the story. Maybe she had resented Job's piety and devotion to God for a while. On the other hand, maybe she had actually been on the same level spiritually as her husband before her tragic loss and was simply responding under stress in exactly the way some of us might in a similar situation. Only in her instance, her breakdown was recorded for posterity.

We know Job was a righteous man—but, the truth is, we don't know if his wife ever got back on track with God. We can't say with certainty if she ever returned to faith in him (if she'd ever had faith at all). What we do know about her story is that life hurts sometimes. And if we all really spoke our mind during the times when it hurts us the most, we might sound more like her than we care to admit.

—Prayer—
Heavenly Father, life is so difficult sometimes. Help me to remember to turn to you when I need support and encouragement.

> *His wife said to him, "Are you still holding on to your integrity? Curse God and die!"*
>
> Job 2:9

ASSIGNED READING:

Job 1:1—2:10

Weekend

Go to page 982 for your next devotional reading.

men and women, who were answering him, [21]"Did not the LORD remember and think about the incense burned in the towns of Judah and the streets of Jerusalem by you and your fathers, your kings and your officials and the people of the land? [22]When the LORD could no longer endure your wicked actions and the detestable things you did, your land became an object of cursing and a desolate waste without inhabitants, as it is today. [23]Because you have burned incense and have sinned against the LORD and have not obeyed him or followed his law or his decrees or his stipulations, this disaster has come upon you, as you now see."

[24]Then Jeremiah said to all the people, including the women, "Hear the word of the LORD, all you people of Judah in Egypt. [25]This is what the LORD Almighty, the God of Israel, says: You and your wives have shown by your actions what you promised when you said, 'We will certainly carry out the vows we made to burn incense and pour out drink offerings to the Queen of Heaven.'

"Go ahead then, do what you promised! Keep your vows! [26]But hear the word of the LORD, all Jews living in Egypt: 'I swear by my great name,' says the LORD, 'that no one from Judah living anywhere in Egypt will ever again invoke my name or swear, "As surely as the Sovereign LORD lives." [27]For I am watching over them for harm, not for good; the Jews in Egypt will perish by sword and famine until they are all destroyed. [28]Those who escape the sword and return to the land of Judah from Egypt will be very few. Then the whole remnant of Judah who came to live in Egypt will know whose word will stand—mine or theirs.

[29]"'This will be the sign to you that I will punish you in this place,' declares the LORD, 'so that you will know that my threats of harm against you will surely stand.' [30]This is what the LORD says: 'I am going to hand Pharaoh Hophra king of Egypt over to his enemies who seek his life, just as I handed Zedekiah king of Judah over to Nebuchadnezzar king of Babylon, the enemy who was seeking his life.'"

A Message to Baruch

45 This is what Jeremiah the prophet told Baruch son of Neriah in the fourth year of Jehoiakim son of Josiah king of Judah, after Baruch had written on a scroll the words Jeremiah was then dictating: [2]"This is what the LORD, the God of Israel, says to you, Baruch: [3]You said, 'Woe to me! The LORD has added sorrow to my pain; I am worn out with groaning and find no rest.'"

[4]The LORD said, "Say this to him: 'This is what the LORD says: I will overthrow what I have built and uproot what I have planted, throughout the land. [5]Should you then seek great things for yourself? Seek them not. For I will bring disaster on all people, declares the LORD, but wherever you go I will let you escape with your life.'"

A Message About Egypt

46 This is the word of the LORD that came to Jeremiah the prophet concerning the nations:

[2]Concerning Egypt:

This is the message against the army of Pharaoh Neco king of Egypt, which was defeated at Carchemish on the Euphrates River by Nebuchadnezzar king of Babylon in the fourth year of Jehoiakim son of Josiah king of Judah:

[3] "Prepare your shields, both large and
small,
and march out for battle!
[4] Harness the horses,
mount the steeds!
Take your positions
with helmets on!
Polish your spears,
put on your armor!
[5] What do I see?
They are terrified,
they are retreating,
their warriors are defeated.
They flee in haste
without looking back,
and there is terror on every side,"
declares the LORD.
[6] "The swift cannot flee
nor the strong escape.
In the north by the River Euphrates
they stumble and fall.

[7] "Who is this that rises like the Nile,
like rivers of surging waters?

⁸Egypt rises like the Nile,
　like rivers of surging waters.
She says, 'I will rise and cover the earth;
　I will destroy cities and their people.'
⁹Charge, O horses!
　Drive furiously, O charioteers!
March on, O warriors—
　men of Cush*a* and Put who carry
　　shields,
　men of Lydia who draw the bow.
¹⁰But that day belongs to the Lord, the LORD
　　Almighty—
　a day of vengeance, for vengeance on
　　his foes.
The sword will devour till it is satisfied,
　till it has quenched its thirst with blood.
For the Lord, the LORD Almighty, will
　　offer sacrifice
　in the land of the north by the River
　　Euphrates.

¹¹"Go up to Gilead and get balm,
　O Virgin Daughter of Egypt.
But you multiply remedies in vain;
　there is no healing for you.
¹²The nations will hear of your shame;
　your cries will fill the earth.
One warrior will stumble over another;
　both will fall down together."

¹³This is the message the LORD spoke to
Jeremiah the prophet about the coming of Nebuchadnezzar king of Babylon to attack Egypt:

¹⁴"Announce this in Egypt, and proclaim it
　　in Migdol;
　proclaim it also in Memphis*b* and
　　Tahpanhes:
'Take your positions and get ready,
　for the sword devours those around
　　you.'
¹⁵Why will your warriors be laid low?
　They cannot stand, for the LORD will
　　push them down.
¹⁶They will stumble repeatedly;
　they will fall over each other.
They will say, 'Get up, let us go back
　to our own people and our native lands,
　away from the sword of the oppressor.'
¹⁷There they will exclaim,

'Pharaoh king of Egypt is only a loud
　　noise;
　he has missed his opportunity.'

¹⁸"As surely as I live," declares the King,
　whose name is the LORD Almighty,
"one will come who is like Tabor among
　　the mountains,
　like Carmel by the sea.
¹⁹Pack your belongings for exile,
　you who live in Egypt,
for Memphis will be laid waste
　and lie in ruins without inhabitant.

²⁰"Egypt is a beautiful heifer,
　but a gadfly is coming
　　against her from the north.
²¹The mercenaries in her ranks
　are like fattened calves.
They too will turn and flee together,
　they will not stand their ground,
for the day of disaster is coming upon
　　them,
　the time for them to be punished.
²²Egypt will hiss like a fleeing serpent
　as the enemy advances in force;
they will come against her with axes,
　like men who cut down trees.
²³They will chop down her forest,
　　　　　　　declares the LORD,
　"dense though it be.
They are more numerous than locusts,
　they cannot be counted.
²⁴The Daughter of Egypt will be put to
　　shame,
　handed over to the people of the north."

²⁵The LORD Almighty, the God of Israel, says:
"I am about to bring punishment on Amon god
of Thebes,*c* on Pharaoh, on Egypt and her gods
and her kings, and on those who rely on Pharaoh. ²⁶I will hand them over to those who seek
their lives, to Nebuchadnezzar king of Babylon
and his officers. Later, however, Egypt will be
inhabited as in times past," declares the LORD.

²⁷"Do not fear, O Jacob my servant;
　do not be dismayed, O Israel.
I will surely save you out of a distant place,
　your descendants from the land of their
　　exile.

---

a9 That is, the upper Nile region　　*b14* Hebrew *Noph*; also in verse 19　　*c25* Hebrew *No*

Jacob will again have peace and security,
and no one will make him afraid.
28 Do not fear, O Jacob my servant,
for I am with you,"
declares the LORD.
"Though I completely
destroy all the
nations
among which I scatter
you,
I will not completely
destroy you.
I will discipline you but
only with justice;
I will not let you
go entirely
unpunished."

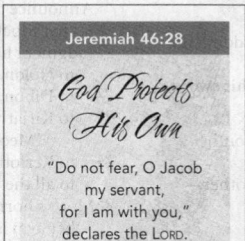

Jeremiah 46:28

God Protects His Own

"Do not fear, O Jacob
my servant,
for I am with you,"
declares the LORD.

A Message About the Philistines

47 This is the word of the LORD that came
to Jeremiah the prophet concerning
the Philistines before Pharaoh attacked Gaza:

2 This is what the LORD says:

"See how the waters are rising in the north;
they will become an overflowing torrent.
They will overflow the land and everything
in it,
the towns and those who live in them.
The people will cry out;
all who dwell in the land will wail
3 at the sound of the hoofs of galloping
steeds,
at the noise of enemy chariots
and the rumble of their wheels.
Fathers will not turn to help their children;
their hands will hang limp.
4 For the day has come
to destroy all the Philistines
and to cut off all survivors
who could help Tyre and Sidon.
The LORD is about to destroy the
Philistines,
the remnant from the coasts of
Caphtor.[a]
5 Gaza will shave her head in mourning;
Ashkelon will be silenced.
O remnant on the plain,
how long will you cut yourselves?

6 "'Ah, sword of the LORD,' you cry,
'how long till you rest?
Return to your scabbard;
cease and be still.'
7 But how can it rest
when the LORD has
commanded it,
when he has ordered it
to attack Ashkelon and
the coast?"

A Message About Moab

48 Concerning Moab:

This is what the LORD Al-
mighty, the God of Israel, says:

"Woe to Nebo, for it will be
ruined.
Kiriathaim will be disgraced and
captured;
the stronghold[b] will be disgraced and
shattered.
2 Moab will be praised no more;
in Heshbon[c] men will plot her downfall:
'Come, let us put an end to that nation.'
You too, O Madmen,[d] will be silenced;
the sword will pursue you.
3 Listen to the cries from Horonaim,
cries of great havoc and destruction.
4 Moab will be broken;
her little ones will cry out.[e]
5 They go up the way to Luhith,
weeping bitterly as they go;
on the road down to Horonaim
anguished cries over the destruction are
heard.
6 Flee! Run for your lives;
become like a bush[f] in the desert.
7 Since you trust in your deeds and riches,
you too will be taken captive,
and Chemosh will go into exile,
together with his priests and officials.
8 The destroyer will come against every
town,
and not a town will escape.
The valley will be ruined
and the plateau destroyed,
because the LORD has spoken.

a4 That is, Crete   b1 Or / Misgab   c2 The Hebrew for Heshbon sounds like the Hebrew for plot.   d2 The name of the Moabite town
Madmen sounds like the Hebrew for be silenced.   e4 Hebrew; Septuagint / proclaim it to Zoar   f6 Or like Aroer

⁹ Put salt on Moab,
    for she will be laid waste*a*;
her towns will become desolate,
    with no one to live in them.

¹⁰ "A curse on him who is lax in doing the
    Lord's work!
A curse on him who keeps his sword
    from bloodshed!

¹¹ "Moab has been at rest from youth,
    like wine left on its dregs,
not poured from one jar to another—
    she has not gone into exile.
So she tastes as she did,
    and her aroma is unchanged.
¹² But days are coming,"
    declares the Lord,
"when I will send men who pour from jars,
    and they will pour her out;
they will empty her jars
    and smash her jugs.
¹³ Then Moab will be ashamed of Chemosh,
    as the house of Israel was ashamed
when they trusted in Bethel.

¹⁴ "How can you say, 'We are warriors,
    men valiant in battle'?
¹⁵ Moab will be destroyed and her towns
    invaded;
her finest young men will go down in
    the slaughter,"
    declares the King, whose name is the
    Lord Almighty.
¹⁶ "The fall of Moab is at hand;
    her calamity will come quickly.
¹⁷ Mourn for her, all who live around her,
    all who know her fame;
say, 'How broken is the mighty scepter,
    how broken the glorious staff!'

¹⁸ "Come down from your glory
    and sit on the parched ground,
O inhabitants of the Daughter of Dibon,
for he who destroys Moab
    will come up against you
    and ruin your fortified cities.
¹⁹ Stand by the road and watch,
    you who live in Aroer.
Ask the man fleeing and the woman
    escaping,

ask them, 'What has happened?'
²⁰ Moab is disgraced, for she is shattered.
    Wail and cry out!
Announce by the Arnon
    that Moab is destroyed.
²¹ Judgment has come to the plateau—
    to Holon, Jahzah and Mephaath,
²²   to Dibon, Nebo and Beth Diblathaim,
²³   to Kiriathaim, Beth Gamul and Beth
        Meon,
²⁴   to Kerioth and Bozrah—
    to all the towns of Moab, far and near.
²⁵ Moab's horn*b* is cut off;
    her arm is broken,"
                      declares the Lord.

²⁶ "Make her drunk,
    for she has defied the Lord.
Let Moab wallow in her vomit;
    let her be an object of ridicule.
²⁷ Was not Israel the object of your ridicule?
    Was she caught among thieves,
that you shake your head in scorn
    whenever you speak of her?
²⁸ Abandon your towns and dwell among the
    rocks,
    you who live in Moab.
Be like a dove that makes its nest
    at the mouth of a cave.

²⁹ "We have heard of Moab's pride—
    her overweening pride and conceit,
her pride and arrogance
    and the haughtiness of her heart.
³⁰ I know her insolence but it is futile,"
                      declares the Lord,
    "and her boasts accomplish nothing.
³¹ Therefore I wail over Moab,
    for all Moab I cry out,
I moan for the men of Kir Hareseth.
³² I weep for you, as Jazer weeps,
    O vines of Sibmah.
Your branches spread as far as the sea;
    they reached as far as the sea of Jazer.
The destroyer has fallen
    on your ripened fruit and grapes.
³³ Joy and gladness are gone
    from the orchards and fields of Moab.
I have stopped the flow of wine from the
    presses;

---

a 9 Or *Give wings to Moab, / for she will fly away*   *b* 25 *Horn* here symbolizes strength.

no one treads them with shouts of joy.
Although there are shouts,
they are not shouts of joy.

34 "The sound of their cry rises
from Heshbon to Elealeh and Jahaz,
from Zoar as far as Horonaim and Eglath
Shelishiyah,
for even the waters of Nimrim are
dried up.
35 In Moab I will put an end
to those who make offerings on the high
places
and burn incense to their gods,"
declares the LORD.
36 "So my heart laments for Moab like a flute;
it laments like a flute for the men of Kir
Haraseth.
The wealth they acquired is gone.
37 Every head is shaved
and every beard cut off;
every hand is slashed
and every waist is covered with
sackcloth.
38 On all the roofs in Moab
and in the public squares
there is nothing but mourning,
for I have broken Moab
like a jar that no one wants,"
declares the LORD.
39 "How shattered she is! How they wail!
How Moab turns her back in shame!
Moab has become an object of ridicule,
an object of horror to all those around
her."

40 This is what the LORD says:

"Look! An eagle is swooping down,
spreading its wings over Moab.
41 Kerioth[a] will be captured
and the strongholds taken.
In that day the hearts of Moab's warriors
will be like the heart of a woman in
labor.
42 Moab will be destroyed as a nation
because she defied the LORD.
43 Terror and pit and snare await you,
O people of Moab,"
declares the LORD.

44 "Whoever flees from the terror
will fall into a pit,
whoever climbs out of the pit
will be caught in a snare;
for I will bring upon Moab
the year of her punishment,"
declares the LORD.

45 "In the shadow of Heshbon
the fugitives stand helpless,
for a fire has gone out from Heshbon,
a blaze from the midst of Sihon;
it burns the foreheads of Moab,
the skulls of the noisy boasters.
46 Woe to you, O Moab!
The people of Chemosh are destroyed;
your sons are taken into exile
and your daughters into captivity.

47 "Yet I will restore the fortunes of Moab
in days to come,"
declares the LORD.

Here ends the judgment on Moab.

A Message About Ammon

49 Concerning the Ammonites:

This is what the LORD says:

"Has Israel no sons?
Has she no heirs?
Why then has Molech[b] taken possession
of Gad?
Why do his people live in its towns?
2 But the days are coming,"
declares the LORD,
"when I will sound the battle cry
against Rabbah of the Ammonites;
it will become a mound of ruins,
and its surrounding villages will be set
on fire.
Then Israel will drive out
those who drove her out,"
says the LORD.
3 "Wail, O Heshbon, for Ai is destroyed!
Cry out, O inhabitants of Rabbah!
Put on sackcloth and mourn;
rush here and there inside the walls,
for Molech will go into exile,
together with his priests and officials.

---

a 41 Or *The cities*   *b* 1 Or *their king*; Hebrew *malcam*; also in verse 3

⁴ Why do you boast of your valleys,
    boast of your valleys so fruitful?
O unfaithful daughter,
    you trust in your riches and say,
    'Who will attack me?'
⁵ I will bring terror on you
    from all those around you,"
        declares the Lord, the LORD Almighty.
"Every one of you will be driven away,
    and no one will gather the fugitives.

⁶ "Yet afterward, I will restore the fortunes
    of the Ammonites,"
        declares the LORD.

A Message About Edom

⁷ Concerning Edom:

This is what the LORD Almighty says:

"Is there no longer wisdom in Teman?
    Has counsel perished from the prudent?
    Has their wisdom decayed?
⁸ Turn and flee, hide in deep caves,
    you who live in Dedan,
for I will bring disaster on Esau
    at the time I punish him.
⁹ If grape pickers came to you,
    would they not leave a few grapes?
If thieves came during the night,
    would they not steal only as much as
        they wanted?
¹⁰ But I will strip Esau bare;
    I will uncover his hiding places,
    so that he cannot conceal himself.
His children, relatives and neighbors will
        perish,
    and he will be no more.
¹¹ Leave your orphans; I will protect their
        lives.
    Your widows too can trust in me."

¹² This is what the LORD says: "If those who
do not deserve to drink the cup must drink it,
why should you go unpunished? You will not
go unpunished, but must drink it. ¹³ I swear by
myself," declares the LORD, "that Bozrah will
become a ruin and an object of horror, of reproach and of cursing; and all its towns will be
in ruins forever."

¹⁴ I have heard a message from the LORD:

An envoy was sent to the nations to say,
    "Assemble yourselves to attack it!
    Rise up for battle!"

¹⁵ "Now I will make you small among the
        nations,
    despised among men.
¹⁶ The terror you inspire
    and the pride of your heart have
        deceived you,
you who live in the clefts of the rocks,
    who occupy the heights of the hill.
Though you build your nest as high as the
        eagle's,
    from there I will bring you down,"
        declares the LORD.
¹⁷ "Edom will become an object of horror;
    all who pass by will be appalled and will
        scoff
    because of all its wounds.
¹⁸ As Sodom and Gomorrah were
        overthrown,
    along with their neighboring towns,"
        says the LORD,
"so no one will live there;
    no man will dwell in it.

¹⁹ "Like a lion coming up from Jordan's
        thickets
    to a rich pastureland,
I will chase Edom from its land in an
        instant.
    Who is the chosen one I will appoint for
        this?
Who is like me and who can challenge me?
    And what shepherd can stand against
        me?"
²⁰ Therefore, hear what the LORD has planned
        against Edom,
    what he has purposed against those who
        live in Teman:
The young of the flock will be dragged
        away;
    he will completely destroy their pasture
        because of them.
²¹ At the sound of their fall the earth will
        tremble;
    their cry will resound to the Red Sea.ᵃ
²² Look! An eagle will soar and swoop down,
    spreading its wings over Bozrah.

ᵃ21 Hebrew *Yam Suph*; that is, Sea of Reeds

In that day the hearts of Edom's warriors
will be like the heart of a woman in
labor.

A Message About Damascus

23Concerning Damascus:

"Hamath and Arpad are dismayed,
for they have heard bad news.
They are disheartened,
troubled like[a] the restless sea.
24Damascus has become feeble,
she has turned to flee
and panic has gripped her;
anguish and pain have seized her,
pain like that of a woman in labor.
25Why has the city of renown not been
abandoned,
the town in which I delight?
26Surely, her young men will fall in the
streets;
all her soldiers will be silenced in that
day,"
declares the LORD Almighty.
27"I will set fire to the walls of Damascus;
it will consume the fortresses of Ben-
Hadad."

A Message About Kedar and Hazor

28Concerning Kedar and the kingdoms of
Hazor, which Nebuchadnezzar king of Babylon
attacked:

This is what the LORD says:

"Arise, and attack Kedar
and destroy the people of the East.
29Their tents and their flocks will be taken;
their shelters will be carried off
with all their goods and camels.
Men will shout to them,
'Terror on every side!'
30"Flee quickly away!
Stay in deep caves, you who live in Hazor,"
declares the LORD.
"Nebuchadnezzar king of Babylon has
plotted against you;
he has devised a plan against you.

31"Arise and attack a nation at ease,
which lives in confidence,"
declares the LORD,

"a nation that has neither gates nor bars;
its people live alone.
32Their camels will become plunder,
and their large herds will be booty.
I will scatter to the winds those who are in
distant places[b]
and will bring disaster on them from
every side,"
declares the LORD.
33"Hazor will become a haunt of jackals,
a desolate place forever.
No one will live there;
no man will dwell in it."

A Message About Elam

34This is the word of the LORD that came to
Jeremiah the prophet concerning Elam, early
in the reign of Zedekiah king of Judah:

35This is what the LORD Almighty says:

"See, I will break the bow of Elam,
the mainstay of their might.
36I will bring against Elam the four winds
from the four quarters of the heavens;
I will scatter them to the four winds,
and there will not be a nation
where Elam's exiles do not go.
37I will shatter Elam before their foes,
before those who seek their lives;
I will bring disaster upon them,
even my fierce anger,"
declares the LORD.
"I will pursue them with the sword
until I have made an end of them.
38I will set my throne in Elam
and destroy her king and officials,"
declares the LORD.

39"Yet I will restore the fortunes of Elam
in days to come,"
declares the LORD.

A Message About Babylon

50 This is the word the LORD spoke
through Jeremiah the prophet concerning Babylon and the land of the Babylonians[c]:

2"Announce and proclaim among the
nations,
lift up a banner and proclaim it;
keep nothing back, but say,

---

*a*23 Hebrew *on* or *by* *b*32 Or *who clip the hair by their foreheads* *c*1 Or *Chaldeans;* also in verses 8, 25, 35 and 45

'Babylon will be captured;
    Bel will be put to shame,
    Marduk filled with terror.
Her images will be put to shame
    and her idols filled with terror.'
³ A nation from the north will attack her
    and lay waste her land.
No one will live in it;
    both men and animals will flee away.

⁴ "In those days, at that time,"
    declares the Lord,
"the people of Israel and the people of
        Judah together
    will go in tears to seek the Lord their God.
⁵ They will ask the way to Zion
    and turn their faces toward it.
They will come and bind themselves to the
        Lord
    in an everlasting covenant
    that will not be forgotten.

⁶ "My people have been lost sheep;
    their shepherds have led them astray
    and caused them to roam on the
        mountains.
They wandered over mountain and hill
    and forgot their own resting place.
⁷ Whoever found them devoured them;
    their enemies said, 'We are not guilty,
for they sinned against the Lord, their
        true pasture,
    the Lord, the hope of their fathers.'

⁸ "Flee out of Babylon;
    leave the land of the Babylonians,
    and be like the goats that lead the flock.
⁹ For I will stir up and bring against Babylon
    an alliance of great nations from the
        land of the north.
They will take up their positions against
        her,
    and from the north she will be captured.
Their arrows will be like skilled warriors
    who do not return empty-handed.
¹⁰ So Babylonia^a will be plundered;
    all who plunder her will have their fill,"
            declares the Lord.

¹¹ "Because you rejoice and are glad,
    you who pillage my inheritance,
because you frolic like a heifer threshing
        grain
    and neigh like stallions,
¹² your mother will be greatly ashamed;
    she who gave you birth will be
        disgraced.
She will be the least of the nations—
    a wilderness, a dry land, a desert.
¹³ Because of the Lord's anger she will not be
        inhabited
    but will be completely desolate.
All who pass Babylon will be horrified and
        scoff
    because of all her wounds.

¹⁴ "Take up your positions around Babylon,
    all you who draw the bow.
Shoot at her! Spare no arrows,
    for she has sinned against the Lord.
¹⁵ Shout against her on every side!
    She surrenders, her towers fall,
    her walls are torn down.
Since this is the vengeance of the Lord,
    take vengeance on her;
    do to her as she has done to others.
¹⁶ Cut off from Babylon the sower,
    and the reaper with his sickle at harvest.
Because of the sword of the oppressor
    let everyone return to his own people,
    let everyone flee to his own land.

¹⁷ "Israel is a scattered flock
    that lions have chased away.
The first to devour him
    was the king of Assyria;
the last to crush his bones
    was Nebuchadnezzar king of Babylon."

¹⁸ Therefore this is what the Lord Almighty,
the God of Israel, says:

"I will punish the king of Babylon and his
        land
    as I punished the king of Assyria.
¹⁹ But I will bring Israel back to his own
        pasture
    and he will graze on Carmel and
        Bashan;
his appetite will be satisfied
    on the hills of Ephraim and Gilead.
²⁰ In those days, at that time,"

---

^a 10 Or *Chaldea*

declares the LORD,
"search will be made for Israel's guilt,
but there will be none,
and for the sins of Judah,
but none will be found,
for I will forgive the
remnant I spare.

21 "Attack the land of
Merathaim
and those who live in
Pekod.
Pursue, kill and completely
destroy[a] them,"
declares the LORD.
"Do everything I have
commanded you.
22 The noise of battle is in the
land,
the noise of great
destruction!
23 How broken and shattered
is the hammer of the
whole earth!
How desolate is Babylon
among the nations!
24 I set a trap for you, O Babylon,
and you were caught before you knew it;
you were found and captured
because you opposed the LORD.
25 The LORD has opened his arsenal
and brought out the weapons of his wrath,
for the Sovereign LORD Almighty has work
to do
in the land of the Babylonians.
26 Come against her from afar.
Break open her granaries;
pile her up like heaps of grain.
Completely destroy her
and leave her no remnant.
27 Kill all her young bulls;
let them go down to the slaughter!
Woe to them! For their day has come,
the time for them to be punished.
28 Listen to the fugitives and refugees from
Babylon
declaring in Zion
how the LORD our God has taken
vengeance,
vengeance for his temple.

Jeremiah 50:20

God Forgives His People

"In those days, at
that time,"
declares the LORD,
"search will be made
for Israel's guilt,
but there will be none,
and for the sins of Judah,
but none will be found,
for I will forgive the
remnant I spare."

29 "Summon archers against Babylon,
all those who draw the bow.
Encamp all around her;
let no one escape.
Repay her for her deeds;
do to her as she has done.
For she has defied the
LORD,
the Holy One of Israel.
30 Therefore, her young men
will fall in the
streets;
all her soldiers will be
silenced in that
day,"
declares the LORD.
31 "See, I am against you,
O arrogant one,"
declares the Lord, the
LORD Almighty,
"for your day has come,
the time for you to be
punished.
32 The arrogant one will stumble and fall
and no one will help her up;
I will kindle a fire in her towns
that will consume all who are around
her."

33 This is what the LORD Almighty says:

"The people of Israel are oppressed,
and the people of Judah as well.
All their captors hold them fast,
refusing to let them go.
34 Yet their Redeemer is strong;
the LORD Almighty is his name.
He will vigorously defend their cause
so that he may bring rest to their land,
but unrest to those who live in Babylon.

35 "A sword against the Babylonians!"
declares the LORD—
"against those who live in Babylon
and against her officials and wise men!
36 A sword against her false prophets!
They will become fools.
A sword against her warriors!
They will be filled with terror.
37 A sword against her horses and chariots
and all the foreigners in her ranks!

---

[a]21 The Hebrew term refers to the irrevocable giving over of things or persons to the LORD, often by totally destroying them; also in verse 26.

They will become women.
A sword against her treasures!
They will be plundered.
³⁸ A drought on[a] her waters!
They will dry up.
For it is a land of idols,
idols that will go mad with terror.

³⁹ "So desert creatures and hyenas will live
there,
and there the owl will dwell.
It will never again be inhabited
or lived in from generation to
generation.
⁴⁰ As God overthrew Sodom and Gomorrah
along with their neighboring towns,"
declares the LORD,
"so no one will live there;
no man will dwell in it.

⁴¹ "Look! An army is coming from the north;
a great nation and many kings
are being stirred up from the ends of the
earth.
⁴² They are armed with bows and spears;
they are cruel and without mercy.
They sound like the roaring sea
as they ride on their horses;
they come like men in battle formation
to attack you, O Daughter of Babylon.
⁴³ The king of Babylon has heard reports
about them,
and his hands hang limp.
Anguish has gripped him,
pain like that of a woman in labor.
⁴⁴ Like a lion coming up from Jordan's
thickets
to a rich pastureland,
I will chase Babylon from its land in an
instant.
Who is the chosen one I will appoint for
this?
Who is like me and who can challenge me?
And what shepherd can stand against
me?"
⁴⁵ Therefore, hear what the LORD has planned
against Babylon,
what he has purposed against the land
of the Babylonians:

The young of the flock will be dragged
away;
he will completely destroy their pasture
because of them.
⁴⁶ At the sound of Babylon's capture the earth
will tremble;
its cry will resound among the nations.

51

This is what the LORD says:

"See, I will stir up the spirit of a destroyer
against Babylon and the people of Leb
Kamai.[b]
² I will send foreigners to Babylon
to winnow her and to devastate her land;
they will oppose her on every side
in the day of her disaster.
³ Let not the archer string his bow,
nor let him put on his armor.
Do not spare her young men;
completely destroy[c] her army.
⁴ They will fall down slain in Babylon,[d]
fatally wounded in her streets.
⁵ For Israel and Judah have not been
forsaken
by their God, the LORD Almighty,
though their land[e] is full of guilt
before the Holy One of Israel.

⁶ "Flee from Babylon!
Run for your lives!
Do not be destroyed because of her sins.
It is time for the LORD's vengeance;
he will pay her what she deserves.
⁷ Babylon was a gold cup in the LORD's
hand;
she made the whole earth drunk.
The nations drank her wine;
therefore they have now gone mad.
⁸ Babylon will suddenly fall and be broken.
Wail over her!
Get balm for her pain;
perhaps she can be healed.

⁹ "'We would have healed Babylon,
but she cannot be healed;
let us leave her and each go to his own land,
for her judgment reaches to the skies,
it rises as high as the clouds.'

---

^a38 Or *A sword against*   ^b1 *Leb Kamai* is a cryptogram for Chaldea, that is, Babylonia.   ^c3 The Hebrew term refers to the irrevocable giving over of things or persons to the LORD, often by totally destroying them.   ^d4 Or *Chaldea*   ^e5 Or *I and the land of the Babylonians*

10 "'The LORD has vindicated us;
    come, let us tell in Zion
    what the LORD our God has done.'

11 "Sharpen the arrows,
    take up the shields!
The LORD has stirred up the kings of the
        Medes,
    because his purpose is to destroy
        Babylon.
The LORD will take vengeance,
    vengeance for his temple.
12 Lift up a banner against the walls of
        Babylon!
    Reinforce the guard,
station the watchmen,
    prepare an ambush!
The LORD will carry out his purpose,
    his decree against the people of Babylon.
13 You who live by many waters
    and are rich in treasures,
your end has come,
    the time for you to be cut off.
14 The LORD Almighty has
        sworn by himself:
    I will surely fill you with
        men, as with a
        swarm of locusts,
    and they will shout in
        triumph over you.

15 "He made the earth by his
        power;
    he founded the world by
        his wisdom
    and stretched out the
        heavens by his
        understanding.
16 When he thunders, the
        waters in the
        heavens roar;
    he makes clouds rise from the ends of
        the earth.
He sends lightning with the rain
    and brings out the wind from his
        storehouses.
17 "Every man is senseless and without
        knowledge;
    every goldsmith is shamed by his idols.
His images are a fraud;

they have no breath in them.
18 They are worthless, the objects of mockery;
    when their judgment comes, they will
        perish.
19 He who is the Portion of Jacob is not like
        these,
    for he is the Maker of all things,
including the tribe of his inheritance—
    the LORD Almighty is his name.

20 "You are my war club,
    my weapon for battle—
with you I shatter nations,
    with you I destroy kingdoms,
21 with you I shatter horse and rider,
    with you I shatter chariot and driver,
22 with you I shatter man and woman,
    with you I shatter old man and youth,
    with you I shatter young man and
        maiden,
23 with you I shatter shepherd and flock,
    with you I shatter farmer and oxen,
        with you I shatter
            governors and
            officials.

24 "Before your eyes I will repay Babylon and all who live in Babylonia[a] for all the wrong they have done in Zion," declares the LORD.

25 "I am against you,
        O destroying
            mountain,
    you who destroy the
        whole earth,"
        declares the LORD.
"I will stretch out my hand
        against you,
    roll you off the cliffs,
    and make you a burned-
        out mountain.
26 No rock will be taken from you for a
        cornerstone,
    nor any stone for a foundation,
    for you will be desolate forever,"
        declares the LORD.

27 "Lift up a banner in the land!
    Blow the trumpet among the nations!

Jeremiah 51:15

God Created the World

"He made the earth
by his power;
he founded the world
by his wisdom
and stretched out
the heavens by his
understanding."

---

[a]24 Or Chaldea; also in verse 35

Prepare the nations for battle against her;
  summon against her these kingdoms:
    Ararat, Minni and Ashkenaz.
Appoint a commander against her;
  send up horses like a swarm of locusts.
28 Prepare the nations for battle against her—
  the kings of the Medes,
their governors and all their officials,
  and all the countries they rule.
29 The land trembles and writhes,
  for the LORD's purposes against Babylon
    stand—
to lay waste the land of Babylon
  so that no one will live there.
30 Babylon's warriors have stopped fighting;
  they remain in their strongholds.
Their strength is exhausted;
  they have become like women.
Her dwellings are set on fire;
  the bars of her gates are broken.
31 One courier follows another
  and messenger follows messenger
to announce to the king of Babylon
  that his entire city is captured,
32 the river crossings seized,
  the marshes set on fire,
  and the soldiers terrified."

33 This is what the LORD Almighty, the God
of Israel, says:

"The Daughter of Babylon is like a
    threshing floor
  at the time it is trampled;
the time to harvest her will soon come."

34 "Nebuchadnezzar king of Babylon has
    devoured us,
  he has thrown us into confusion,
  he has made us an empty jar.
Like a serpent he has swallowed us
  and filled his stomach with our
    delicacies,
  and then has spewed us out.
35 May the violence done to our flesh[a] be
    upon Babylon,"
  say the inhabitants of Zion.
"May our blood be on those who live in
    Babylonia,"
  says Jerusalem.

36 Therefore, this is what the LORD says:

"See, I will defend your cause
  and avenge you;
I will dry up her sea
  and make her springs dry.
37 Babylon will be a heap of ruins,
  a haunt of jackals,
an object of horror and scorn,
  a place where no one lives.
38 Her people all roar like young lions,
  they growl like lion cubs.
39 But while they are aroused,
  I will set out a feast for them
  and make them drunk,
so that they shout with laughter—
  then sleep forever and not awake,"
                    declares the LORD.
40 "I will bring them down
  like lambs to the slaughter,
  like rams and goats.

41 "How Sheshach[b] will be captured,
  the boast of the whole earth seized!
What a horror Babylon will be
  among the nations!
42 The sea will rise over Babylon;
  its roaring waves will cover her.
43 Her towns will be desolate,
  a dry and desert land,
a land where no one lives,
  through which no man travels.
44 I will punish Bel in Babylon
  and make him spew out what he has
    swallowed.
The nations will no longer stream to him.
  And the wall of Babylon will fall.

45 "Come out of her, my people!
  Run for your lives!
  Run from the fierce anger of the LORD.
46 Do not lose heart or be afraid
  when rumors are heard in the land;
one rumor comes this year, another the
    next,
  rumors of violence in the land
  and of ruler against ruler.
47 For the time will surely come
  when I will punish the idols of
    Babylon;
  her whole land will be disgraced

---

a35 Or done to us and to our children   b41 Sheshach is a cryptogram for Babylon.

and her slain will all lie fallen within her.
⁴⁸Then heaven and earth and all that is in
them
will shout for joy over Babylon,
for out of the north
destroyers will attack her,"
declares the LORD.

⁴⁹"Babylon must fall because of Israel's slain,
just as the slain in all the earth
have fallen because of Babylon.
⁵⁰You who have escaped the sword,
leave and do not linger!
Remember the LORD in a distant land,
and think on Jerusalem."

⁵¹"We are disgraced,
for we have been insulted
and shame covers our faces,
because foreigners have entered
the holy places of the LORD's house."

⁵²"But days are coming," declares the LORD,
"when I will punish her idols,
and throughout her land
the wounded will groan.
⁵³Even if Babylon reaches the sky
and fortifies her lofty stronghold,
I will send destroyers against her,"
declares the LORD.

⁵⁴"The sound of a cry comes from Babylon,
the sound of great destruction
from the land of the Babylonians.ᵃ
⁵⁵The LORD will destroy Babylon;
he will silence her noisy din.
Waves of enemies will rage like great
waters;
the roar of their voices will resound.
⁵⁶A destroyer will come against Babylon;
her warriors will be captured,
and their bows will be broken.
For the LORD is a God of retribution;
he will repay in full.
⁵⁷I will make her officials and wise men
drunk,
her governors, officers and warriors as
well;
they will sleep forever and not awake,"
declares the King, whose name is the
LORD Almighty.

⁵⁸This is what the LORD Almighty says:

"Babylon's thick wall will be leveled
and her high gates set on fire;
the peoples exhaust themselves for
nothing,
the nations' labor is only fuel for the
flames."

⁵⁹This is the message Jeremiah gave to the
staff officer Seraiah son of Neriah, the son of
Mahseiah, when he went to Babylon with
Zedekiah king of Judah in the fourth year of
his reign. ⁶⁰Jeremiah had written on a scroll
about all the disasters that would come upon
Babylon—all that had been recorded concerning Babylon. ⁶¹He said to Seraiah, "When
you get to Babylon, see that you read all these
words aloud. ⁶²Then say, 'O LORD, you have
said you will destroy this place, so that neither
man nor animal will live in it; it will be desolate
forever.' ⁶³When you finish reading this scroll,
tie a stone to it and throw it into the Euphrates. ⁶⁴Then say, 'So will Babylon sink to rise no
more because of the disaster I will bring upon
her. And her people will fall.'"

The words of Jeremiah end here.

The Fall of Jerusalem

52 Zedekiah was twenty-one years old
when he became king, and he reigned
in Jerusalem eleven years. His mother's name
was Hamutal daughter of Jeremiah; she was
from Libnah. ²He did evil in the eyes of the
LORD, just as Jehoiakim had done. ³It was
because of the LORD's anger that all this happened to Jerusalem and Judah, and in the end
he thrust them from his presence.

Now Zedekiah rebelled against the king
of Babylon.

⁴So in the ninth year of Zedekiah's reign, on
the tenth day of the tenth month, Nebuchadnezzar king of Babylon marched against Jerusalem with his whole army. They camped outside
the city and built siege works all around it. ⁵The
city was kept under siege until the eleventh year
of King Zedekiah.

⁶By the ninth day of the fourth month
the famine in the city had become so severe
that there was no food for the people to eat.

ᵃ54 Or *Chaldeans*

⁷Then the city wall was broken through, and the whole army fled. They left the city at night through the gate between the two walls near the king's garden, though the Babylonians*a* were surrounding the city. They fled toward the Arabah,*b* ⁸but the Babylonian*c* army pursued King Zedekiah and overtook him in the plains of Jericho. All his soldiers were separated from him and scattered, ⁹and he was captured.

He was taken to the king of Babylon at Riblah in the land of Hamath, where he pronounced sentence on him. ¹⁰There at Riblah the king of Babylon slaughtered the sons of Zedekiah before his eyes; he also killed all the officials of Judah. ¹¹Then he put out Zedekiah's eyes, bound him with bronze shackles and took him to Babylon, where he put him in prison till the day of his death.

¹²On the tenth day of the fifth month, in the nineteenth year of Nebuchadnezzar king of Babylon, Nebuzaradan commander of the imperial guard, who served the king of Babylon, came to Jerusalem. ¹³He set fire to the temple of the LORD, the royal palace and all the houses of Jerusalem. Every important building he burned down. ¹⁴The whole Babylonian army under the commander of the imperial guard broke down all the walls around Jerusalem. ¹⁵Nebuzaradan the commander of the guard carried into exile some of the poorest people and those who remained in the city, along with the rest of the craftsmen*d* and those who had gone over to the king of Babylon. ¹⁶But Nebuzaradan left behind the rest of the poorest people of the land to work the vineyards and fields.

¹⁷The Babylonians broke up the bronze pillars, the movable stands and the bronze Sea that were at the temple of the LORD and they carried all the bronze to Babylon. ¹⁸They also took away the pots, shovels, wick trimmers, sprinkling bowls, dishes and all the bronze articles used in the temple service. ¹⁹The commander of the imperial guard took away the basins, censers, sprinkling bowls, pots, lampstands, dishes and bowls used for drink offerings—all that were made of pure gold or silver.

²⁰The bronze from the two pillars, the Sea and the twelve bronze bulls under it, and the movable stands, which King Solomon had made for the temple of the LORD, was more than could be weighed. ²¹Each of the pillars was eighteen cubits high and twelve cubits in circumference*e*; each was four fingers thick, and hollow. ²²The bronze capital on top of the one pillar was five cubits*f* high and was decorated with a network and pomegranates of bronze all around. The other pillar, with its pomegranates, was similar. ²³There were ninety-six pomegranates on the sides; the total number of pomegranates above the surrounding network was a hundred.

²⁴The commander of the guard took as prisoners Seraiah the chief priest, Zephaniah the priest next in rank and the three doorkeepers. ²⁵Of those still in the city, he took the officer in charge of the fighting men, and seven royal advisers. He also took the secretary who was chief officer in charge of conscripting the people of the land and sixty of his men who were found in the city. ²⁶Nebuzaradan the commander took them all and brought them to the king of Babylon at Riblah. ²⁷There at Riblah, in the land of Hamath, the king had them executed.

So Judah went into captivity, away from her land. ²⁸This is the number of the people Nebuchadnezzar carried into exile:

in the seventh year, 3,023 Jews;

²⁹in Nebuchadnezzar's eighteenth year,
832 people from Jerusalem;

³⁰in his twenty-third year,
745 Jews taken into exile by Nebuzaradan the commander of the imperial guard.

There were 4,600 people in all.

Jehoiachin Released

³¹In the thirty-seventh year of the exile of Jehoiachin king of Judah, in the year Evil-Merodach*g* became king of Babylon, he released Jehoiachin king of Judah and freed him from prison on the twenty-fifth day of the twelfth month. ³²He spoke kindly to him and gave him a seat of honor higher than those of the

---

*a*7 Or *Chaldeans*; also in verse 17   *b*7 Or *the Jordan Valley*   *c*8 Or *Chaldean*; also in verse 14   *d*15 Or *populace*   *e*21 That is, about 27 feet (about 8.1 meters) high and 18 feet (about 5.4 meters) in circumference   *f*22 That is, about 7 1/2 feet (about 2.3 meters)   *g*31 Also called *Amel-Marduk* other kings who were with him in Babylon. ³³So Jehoiachin put aside his prison clothes and for the rest of his life ate regularly at the king's table. ³⁴Day by day the king of Babylon gave Jehoiachin a regular allowance as long as he lived, till the day of his death.

Lamentations

Author:
Anonymous
(possibly Jeremiah).

Audience:
All who mourned
Jerusalem's destruction.

Date:
Shortly after the fall of
Jerusalem in 586 B.C.

Setting:
The Babylonians had
destroyed God's holy city
of Jerusalem. Those who
weren't killed or tortured
were taken as prisoners.

Verse to Remember:
How deserted lies the city,
once so full of people!
How like a widow is she,
who once was great
among the nations! She
who was queen among the
provinces has now
become a slave. (1:1)

Jerusalem has been destroyed. The beautiful city with its glorious temple representing God's presence has been nearly leveled, with most of its people killed or taken prisoner. The few people left in the city are destitute, hopeless and frightened.

The book of Lamentations is a series of poems—five stanzas of 22 or 66 verses each. Each poem is a lament, and in chapter 5, the climax of the book, *all joy is gone,* and the author pleads for God to return to his people. Other places in Scripture make clear that *God shared the sorrow* of his prophets and his people as they lamented the destruction of Jerusalem and the hard times its people were facing.

---

1 ^a How deserted lies the city,
   once so full of people!
How like a widow is she,
   who once was great among the nations!
She who was queen among the provinces
   has now become a slave.

² Bitterly she weeps at night,
   tears are upon her cheeks.
Among all her lovers
   there is none to comfort her.
All her friends have betrayed her;
   they have become her enemies.

^aThis chapter is an acrostic poem, the verses of which begin with the successive letters of the Hebrew alphabet.

³ After affliction and harsh labor,
　　Judah has gone into exile.
She dwells among the nations;
　　she finds no resting place.
All who pursue her have overtaken her
　　in the midst of her distress.

⁴ The roads to Zion mourn,
　　for no one comes to her appointed
　　　　feasts.
All her gateways are desolate,
　　her priests groan,
her maidens grieve,
　　and she is in bitter anguish.

⁵ Her foes have become her masters;
　　her enemies are at ease.
The LORD has brought her grief
　　because of her many sins.
Her children have gone into exile,
　　captive before the foe.

⁶ All the splendor has departed
　　from the Daughter of Zion.
Her princes are like deer
　　that find no pasture;
in weakness they have fled
　　before the pursuer.

⁷ In the days of her affliction and wandering
　　Jerusalem remembers all the treasures
　　that were hers in days of old.
When her people fell into enemy hands,
　　there was no one to help her.
Her enemies looked at her
　　and laughed at her destruction.

⁸ Jerusalem has sinned greatly
　　and so has become unclean.
All who honored her despise her,
　　for they have seen her nakedness;
she herself groans
　　and turns away.

⁹ Her filthiness clung to her skirts;
　　she did not consider her future.
Her fall was astounding;
　　there was none to comfort her.
"Look, O LORD, on my affliction,
　　for the enemy has triumphed."

¹⁰ The enemy laid hands
　　on all her treasures;

she saw pagan nations
　　enter her sanctuary—
those you had forbidden
　　to enter your assembly.

¹¹ All her people groan
　　as they search for bread;
they barter their treasures for food
　　to keep themselves alive.
"Look, O LORD, and consider,
　　for I am despised."

¹² "Is it nothing to you, all you who pass by?
　　Look around and see.
Is any suffering like my suffering
　　that was inflicted on me,
that the LORD brought on me
　　in the day of his fierce anger?

¹³ "From on high he sent fire,
　　sent it down into my bones.
He spread a net for my feet
　　and turned me back.
He made me desolate,
　　faint all the day long.

¹⁴ "My sins have been bound into a yoke*a*;
　　by his hands they were woven together.
They have come upon my neck
　　and the Lord has sapped my strength.
He has handed me over
　　to those I cannot withstand.

¹⁵ "The Lord has rejected
　　all the warriors in my midst;
he has summoned an army against me
　　to*b* crush my young men.
In his winepress the Lord has trampled
　　the Virgin Daughter of Judah.

¹⁶ "This is why I weep
　　and my eyes overflow with tears.
No one is near to comfort me,
　　no one to restore my spirit.
My children are destitute
　　because the enemy has prevailed."

¹⁷ Zion stretches out her hands,
　　but there is no one to comfort her.
The LORD has decreed for Jacob
　　that his neighbors become his foes;
Jerusalem has become
　　an unclean thing among them.

a 14 Most Hebrew manuscripts; Septuagint *He kept watch over my sins*　*b* 15 Or *has set a time for me / when he will*

Brought to Grief

Lamentations 1:5

The Lord has brought her grief because of her many sins.

reflection

1 When was the last time you wept over sin—in your life or in the lives of others?

2 Why does grief accompany sin?

3 Is there a friend or family member who needs your prayers? How can you pray for them? How can you help them in their grief?

RELATED READINGS

Psalm 30:4–5;
Jeremiah 13:16–17;
29:11–14;
Joel 2:25–26;
Micah 7:18–20;
1 John 1:8–9

Read: Lamentations 1:1–11

CAROL DIDN'T WANT to believe her daughter's news.

Rachel had always been a good kid who went to church every Sunday. She had vowed to remain sexually pure until marriage. She didn't even have a boyfriend. So Carol was surprised when Rachel called from a friend's house at 3:00 A.M. in tears. In between her sobs, it sounded as if Rachel said she was pregnant.

Carol felt a rush of feelings all at once—disbelief, fear, anger, helplessness. All she could do for the moment was cry with her daughter. And just as Rachel had to face the consequences of her sin, so did her mother. Grief overwhelmed them both.

In Lamentations, Jeremiah felt overwhelmed too. He wept over the consequences of Judah's sin. The Babylonian army destroyed the beautiful temple, killed most of the people of Jerusalem and captured the rest. Jeremiah groaned over the people's suffering and their broken relationship with God. He longed for them to repent, so God would restore them.

Likewise, Carol, with lots of tears, prayed for her daughter's restoration to God. The road seemed long at the time, but she kept praying. When finally Rachel's selfish tears turned into repentance, God welcomed her warmly. He lavished forgiveness upon her and began to bless her obedience.

Carol walked her own journey with God during those tough nine months, and she came out of it with a new ministry. She now volunteers each week with the local Crisis Pregnancy Center where she gives practical and spiritual help to young women just like Rachel.

While sin brings regret and consequences we cannot change, God is still good. He forgives us, restores us and renews us in ways we never thought possible.

Monday

Go to page 986 for your next devotional reading.

¹⁸ "The LORD is righteous,
      yet I rebelled against his command.
   Listen, all you peoples;
      look upon my suffering.
   My young men and maidens
      have gone into exile.

¹⁹ "I called to my allies
      but they betrayed me.
   My priests and my elders
      perished in the city
   while they searched for food
      to keep themselves alive.

²⁰ "See, O LORD, how
         distressed I am!
      I am in torment within,
   and in my heart I am
         disturbed,
      for I have been most
         rebellious.
   Outside, the sword
         bereaves;
      inside, there is only
         death.

²¹ "People have heard my
         groaning,
      but there is no one to comfort me.
   All my enemies have heard of my distress;
      they rejoice at what you have done.
   May you bring the day you have announced
      so they may become like me.

²² "Let all their wickedness come before you;
      deal with them
   as you have dealt with me
      because of all my sins.
   My groans are many
      and my heart is faint."

2ᵃ How the Lord has covered the
         Daughter of Zion
      with the cloud of his angerᵇ!
   He has hurled down the splendor of Israel
      from heaven to earth;
   he has not remembered his footstool
      in the day of his anger.

² Without pity the Lord has swallowed up
      all the dwellings of Jacob;

in his wrath he has torn down
      the strongholds of the Daughter of
         Judah.
   He has brought her kingdom and its
         princes
      down to the ground in dishonor.

³ In fierce anger he has cut off
      every hornᶜ of Israel.
   He has withdrawn his right hand
      at the approach of the enemy.
   He has burned in Jacob
         like a flaming fire
      that consumes
         everything around
            it.

⁴ Like an enemy he has
         strung his bow;
      his right hand is ready.
   Like a foe he has slain
      all who were pleasing to
         the eye;
   he has poured out his
         wrath like fire
      on the tent of the
         Daughter of Zion.

⁵ The Lord is like an enemy;
      he has swallowed up Israel.
   He has swallowed up all her palaces
      and destroyed her strongholds.
   He has multiplied mourning and
         lamentation
      for the Daughter of Judah.

⁶ He has laid waste his dwelling like a
         garden;
      he has destroyed his place of meeting.
   The LORD has made Zion forget
      her appointed feasts and her Sabbaths;
   in his fierce anger he has spurned
      both king and priest.

⁷ The Lord has rejected his altar
      and abandoned his sanctuary.
   He has handed over to the enemy
      the walls of her palaces;
   they have raised a shout in the house of the
         LORD
      as on the day of an appointed feast.

> **Lamentations 1:20**
>
> *God Sees Affliction*
>
> "See, O LORD, how
> distressed I am!
> I am in torment within,
> and in my heart
> I am disturbed."

ᵃThis chapter is an acrostic poem, the verses of which begin with the successive letters of the Hebrew alphabet.   ᵇ1 Or *How the Lord in his anger / has treated the Daughter of Zion with contempt*   ᶜ3 Or *all the strength*; or *every king*; horn here symbolizes strength.

8 The LORD determined to tear down
    the wall around the Daughter of Zion.
He stretched out a measuring line
    and did not withhold his hand from
        destroying.
He made ramparts and walls lament;
    together they wasted away.

9 Her gates have sunk into the ground;
    their bars he has broken and
        destroyed.
Her king and her princes are exiled among
        the nations,
    the law is no more,
and her prophets no longer find
    visions from the LORD.

10 The elders of the Daughter of Zion
    sit on the ground in silence;
they have sprinkled dust on
        their heads
    and put on sackcloth.
The young women of
        Jerusalem
    have bowed their heads
        to the ground.

11 My eyes fail from weeping,
    I am in torment within,
my heart is poured out on
        the ground
because my people are
        destroyed,
because children and
        infants faint
    in the streets of the city.

12 They say to their mothers,
    "Where is bread and wine?"
as they faint like wounded men
    in the streets of the city,
as their lives ebb away
    in their mothers' arms.

13 What can I say for you?
    With what can I compare you,
        O Daughter of Jerusalem?
To what can I liken you,
    that I may comfort you,
        O Virgin Daughter of Zion?
Your wound is as deep as the sea.
    Who can heal you?

14 The visions of your prophets
    were false and worthless;
they did not expose your sin
    to ward off your captivity.
The oracles they gave you
    were false and misleading.

15 All who pass your way
    clap their hands at you;
they scoff and shake their heads
    at the Daughter of Jerusalem:
"Is this the city that was called
    the perfection of beauty,
        the joy of the whole earth?"

16 All your enemies open their mouths
    wide against you;
they scoff and gnash their teeth
        and say, "We have
            swallowed her up.
This is the day we have
            waited for;
    we have lived to see it."

17 The LORD has done what he
        planned;
he has fulfilled his word,
    which he decreed long
        ago.
He has overthrown you
        without pity,
he has let the enemy
        gloat over you,
he has exalted the horn[a]
    of your foes.

18 The hearts of the people
    cry out to the Lord.
O wall of the Daughter of Zion,
    let your tears flow like a river
        day and night;
give yourself no relief,
    your eyes no rest.

19 Arise, cry out in the night,
    as the watches of the night begin;
pour out your heart like water
    in the presence of the Lord.
Lift up your hands to him
    for the lives of your children,
who faint from hunger
    at the head of every street.

Lamentations 2:17

God Does As He Planned

The LORD has done
what he planned;
he has fulfilled his word,
which he decreed
long ago.

---

[a] 17 *Horn* here symbolizes strength.

20 "Look, O LORD, and consider:
  Whom have you ever treated like this?
Should women eat their offspring,
  the children they have cared for?
Should priest and prophet be killed
  in the sanctuary of the Lord?

21 "Young and old lie together
  in the dust of the streets;
my young men and maidens
  have fallen by the sword.
You have slain them in the day of your
    anger;
  you have slaughtered them without pity.

22 "As you summon to a feast day,
  so you summoned against me terrors on
    every side.
In the day of the LORD's anger
  no one escaped or survived;
those I cared for and reared,
  my enemy has destroyed."

3 *a* I am the man who has seen affliction
    by the rod of his wrath.
2 He has driven me away and made me walk
  in darkness rather than light;
3 indeed, he has turned his
    hand against me
  again and again, all day
    long.

4 He has made my skin and
    my flesh grow old
  and has broken my
    bones.
5 He has besieged me and
    surrounded me
  with bitterness and
    hardship.
6 He has made me dwell in
    darkness
  like those long dead.

7 He has walled me in so I cannot escape;
  he has weighed me down with chains.
8 Even when I call out or cry for help,
  he shuts out my prayer.
9 He has barred my way with blocks of stone;
  he has made my paths crooked.

10 Like a bear lying in wait,
  like a lion in hiding,
11 he dragged me from the path and
    mangled me
  and left me without help.
12 He drew his bow
  and made me the target for his arrows.

13 He pierced my heart
  with arrows from his quiver.
14 I became the laughingstock of all my
    people;
  they mock me in song all day long.
15 He has filled me with bitter herbs
  and sated me with gall.

16 He has broken my teeth with gravel;
  he has trampled me in the dust.
17 I have been deprived of peace;
  I have forgotten what prosperity is.
18 So I say, "My splendor is gone
  and all that I had hoped from the LORD."

19 I remember my affliction and my wandering,
  the bitterness and the gall.
20 I well remember them,
  and my soul is downcast within me.
21 Yet this I call to mind
  and therefore I have hope:

22 Because of the LORD's great
    love we are not
      consumed,
  for his compassions
    never fail.
23 They are new every
    morning;
  great is your faithfulness.
24 I say to myself, "The LORD
    is my portion;
  therefore I will wait for
    him."

25 The LORD is good to those
    whose hope is in
      him,
  to the one who seeks him;
26 it is good to wait quietly
  for the salvation of the LORD.
27 It is good for a man to bear the yoke
  while he is young.

Lamentations 3:22

God Has Unfailing Compassion

Because of the LORD's great love we are not consumed, for his compassions never fail.

---

a This chapter is an acrostic poem; the verses of each stanza begin with the successive letters of the Hebrew alphabet, and the verses within each stanza begin with the same letter.

Lamentations 3:21–23

Yet this I call to mind
and therefore I have
hope: Because of the
LORD's great love we
are not consumed,
for his compassions
never fail. They are new
every morning; great
is your faithfulness.

reflection

1 Recall a time in your
life when you experi-
enced God's discipline for
disobedient choices. How
did you feel?

2 When you disobey
God, do you quickly
respond with repentance
and confession? Why or
why not?

3 In what way have you
experienced the ever-
new compassion of God?

RELATED READINGS

Jeremiah 3:12–13;
Zechariah 10:6;
Luke 15:3–24

Read: Lamentations 3:21–51

STARTING OVER. It's the second chance we didn't think we'd have.
It's a wave of relief that washes over our past mistakes. It is a gift
from God we don't deserve.

In the book of Lamentations, the prophet Jeremiah looks back
at the destruction of Jerusalem. God promised that his people
would face punishment for their sinful choices, and he was true to
his word. Their city had been ravaged, and they were now living in
exile. The temple was completely destroyed.

In the midst of Jeremiah's lament, however, he remembers the
mercy of God. Were it not for God's mercy, every one of God's
people would have perished. The judgment on them was painful, but God would not leave them ruined. Eventually, after they
acknowledged their disobedience and confessed their sin, God
would forgive and restore them. He would allow them to start over
once more. And he does the same for us.

Maybe you have experienced the discipline of God in your
own life. You have suffered painful consequences for sinful choices
you have made. Perhaps you feel that God has left you there. If so,
remember that although God is just, he is also full of mercy. His
compassions never fail. He promises to forgive us when we come
to him and confess what we have done or not done. No matter
how you have offended God, you can have hope because of his
great mercy. You can always have a fresh start with him because his
compassions are "new every morning."

Take some time to thank God for the specific ways he has acted mercifully toward you. Thank him for forgiving your sin. Express
gratitude to him for actively restoring you. You may even want to
sing or pray the words to the hymn, "Great Is Thy Faithfulness":

> "Pardon for sin and a peace that endureth
> Thine own dear presence to cheer and to guide;
> Strength for today and bright hope for tomorrow,
> Blessings all mine, with ten thousand beside!"

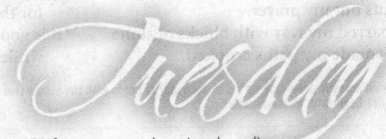

28 Let him sit alone in silence,
    for the LORD has laid it on him.
29 Let him bury his face in the dust—
    there may yet be hope.
30 Let him offer his cheek to one who would
        strike him,
    and let him be filled with disgrace.

31 For men are not cast off
    by the Lord forever.
32 Though he brings grief, he will show
        compassion,
    so great is his unfailing love.
33 For he does not willingly bring affliction
    or grief to the children of men.

34 To crush underfoot
    all prisoners in the land,
35 to deny a man his rights
    before the Most High,
36 to deprive a man of justice—
    would not the Lord see such things?

37 Who can speak and have it happen
    if the Lord has not decreed it?
38 Is it not from the mouth of the Most High
    that both calamities and good things
        come?
39 Why should any living man complain
    when punished for his sins?

40 Let us examine our ways and test them,
    and let us return to the LORD.
41 Let us lift up our hearts and our hands
    to God in heaven, and say:
42 "We have sinned and rebelled
    and you have not forgiven.

43 "You have covered yourself with anger and
        pursued us;
    you have slain without pity.
44 You have covered yourself with a cloud
    so that no prayer can get through.
45 You have made us scum and refuse
    among the nations.

46 "All our enemies have opened their mouths
    wide against us.
47 We have suffered terror and pitfalls,
    ruin and destruction."
48 Streams of tears flow from my eyes
    because my people are destroyed.

49 My eyes will flow unceasingly,
    without relief,
50 until the LORD looks down
    from heaven and sees.
51 What I see brings grief to my soul
    because of all the women of my city.

52 Those who were my enemies without cause
    hunted me like a bird.
53 They tried to end my life in a pit
    and threw stones at me;
54 the waters closed over my head,
    and I thought I was about to be cut off.

55 I called on your name, O LORD,
    from the depths of the pit.
56 You heard my plea: "Do not close your ears
    to my cry for relief."
57 You came near when I called you,
    and you said, "Do not fear."

58 O Lord, you took up my case;
    you redeemed my life.
59 You have seen, O LORD, the wrong done to
        me.
    Uphold my cause!
60 You have seen the depth of their
        vengeance,
    all their plots against me.

61 O LORD, you have heard their insults,
    all their plots against me—
62 what my enemies whisper and mutter
    against me all day long.
63 Look at them! Sitting or standing,
    they mock me in their songs.

64 Pay them back what they deserve,
        O LORD,
    for what their hands have done.
65 Put a veil over their hearts,
    and may your curse be on them!
66 Pursue them in anger and destroy them
    from under the heavens of the LORD.

4 *a* How the gold has lost its luster,
        the fine gold become dull!
    The sacred gems are scattered
        at the head of every street.

2 How the precious sons of Zion,
    once worth their weight in gold,

---

a This chapter is an acrostic poem, the verses of which begin with the successive letters of the Hebrew alphabet.

are now considered as pots of clay,
the work of a potter's hands!

3 Even jackals offer their breasts
to nurse their young,
but my people have become heartless
like ostriches in the desert.

4 Because of thirst the infant's tongue
sticks to the roof of its mouth;
the children beg for bread,
but no one gives it to them.

5 Those who once ate delicacies
are destitute in the streets.
Those nurtured in purple
now lie on ash heaps.

6 The punishment of my people
is greater than that of Sodom,
which was overthrown in a moment
without a hand turned to help her.

7 Their princes were brighter than snow
and whiter than milk,
their bodies more ruddy than rubies,
their appearance like sapphires.*a*

8 But now they are blacker than soot;
they are not recognized in the streets.
Their skin has shriveled on their bones;
it has become as dry as a stick.

9 Those killed by the sword are better off
than those who die of famine;
racked with hunger, they waste away
for lack of food from the field.

10 With their own hands compassionate
women
have cooked their own children,
who became their food
when my people were destroyed.

11 The LORD has given full vent to his wrath;
he has poured out his fierce anger.
He kindled a fire in Zion
that consumed her foundations.

12 The kings of the earth did not believe,
nor did any of the world's people,
that enemies and foes could enter
the gates of Jerusalem.

13 But it happened because of the sins of her
prophets
and the iniquities of her priests,
who shed within her
the blood of the righteous.

14 Now they grope through the streets
like men who are blind.
They are so defiled with blood
that no one dares to touch their
garments.

15 "Go away! You are unclean!" men cry to
them.
"Away! Away! Don't touch us!"
When they flee and wander about,
people among the nations say,
"They can stay here no longer."

16 The LORD himself has scattered them;
he no longer watches over them.
The priests are shown no honor,
the elders no favor.

17 Moreover, our eyes failed,
looking in vain for help;
from our towers we watched
for a nation that could not save us.

18 Men stalked us at every step,
so we could not walk in our streets.
Our end was near, our days were
numbered,
for our end had come.

19 Our pursuers were swifter
than eagles in the sky;
they chased us over the mountains
and lay in wait for us in the desert.

20 The LORD's anointed, our very life breath,
was caught in their traps.
We thought that under his shadow
we would live among the nations.

21 Rejoice and be glad, O Daughter of Edom,
you who live in the land of Uz.
But to you also the cup will be passed;
you will be drunk and stripped naked.

22 O Daughter of Zion, your punishment will
end;
he will not prolong your exile.

a7 Or *lapis lazuli*

But, O Daughter of Edom, he will punish
   your sin
   and expose your wickedness.

5 Remember, O LORD, what has happened
   to us;
   look, and see our disgrace.
2 Our inheritance has been turned over to
   aliens,
   our homes to foreigners.
3 We have become orphans and fatherless,
   our mothers like widows.
4 We must buy the water we drink;
   our wood can be had only at a price.
5 Those who pursue us are at our heels;
   we are weary and find no rest.
6 We submitted to Egypt and
   Assyria
   to get enough bread.
7 Our fathers sinned and are
   no more,
   and we bear their
   punishment.
8 Slaves rule over us,
   and there is none to free
   us from their hands.
9 We get our bread at the risk
   of our lives
   because of the sword in
   the desert.
10 Our skin is hot as an oven,
   feverish from hunger.
11 Women have been ravished in Zion,
   and virgins in the towns of Judah.
12 Princes have been hung up by their hands;
   elders are shown no respect.
13 Young men toil at the millstones;
   boys stagger under loads of wood.
14 The elders are gone from the city gate;
   the young men have stopped their
   music.
15 Joy is gone from our hearts;
   our dancing has turned to mourning.
16 The crown has fallen from our head.
   Woe to us, for we have sinned!
17 Because of this our hearts are faint,
   because of these things our eyes grow
   dim
18 for Mount Zion, which lies desolate,
   with jackals prowling
   over it.

19 You, O LORD, reign
   forever;
   your throne endures
   from generation to
   generation.
20 Why do you always forget
   us?
   Why do you forsake us
   so long?
21 Restore us to yourself,
   O LORD, that we
   may return;
   renew our days as of old
22 unless you have utterly rejected us
   and are angry with us beyond measure.

Lamentations 5:21

*God Can
Restore Us*

Restore us to yourself,
O LORD, that we
may return;
renew our days as of old.

989

Ezekiel

Author:
Ezekiel.

Audience:
Ezekiel's fellow
Jewish exiles
in Babylon.

Date:
Between 593
and 571 B.C.

Setting:
The priest Ezekiel
prophesied to his
fellow Jews, who
were taken as pris-
oners to Babylon
in 597 B.C.

Verse to Remember:
"I will give you a
new heart and put
a new spirit in you; I
will remove from you
your heart of stone
and give you a heart
of flesh." (36:26)

Throughout Israel's recorded history in the Old Testament, *God outlined the way to blessing.* But he also outlined the consequences that would result from disobedience. Enter Ezekiel. Ezekiel was a prophet who warned God's people of their impending judgment, often using creative and stark analogies. At the same time, he spoke of hope for the future restoration of Israel. He described a time when the people's hard hearts would be softened and God's Spirit would dwell within them.

From the first chapter of Ezekiel until the last, we see *portraits of the sovereignty of God.* He is in control over nature, people and history. At least 65 times in this one book, God says, "Then they will know that I am the LORD." He did not orchestrate the fall of Jerusalem, the destruction of the temple or the judgment of the nations without an end result in mind. His glory and honor are always at stake. What a joy as we turn the final pages of this book of judgment to see that *a plan for deliverance is always in God's mind*—a plan of ultimate revival, redemption and restoration.

The Living Creatures and the Glory of the LORD

1 In the*ᵃ* thirtieth year, in the fourth month on the fifth day, while I was among the exiles by the Kebar River, the heavens were opened and I saw visions of God.

²On the fifth of the month—it was the fifth year of the exile of King Jehoiachin— ³the word of the LORD came to Ezekiel the priest, the son of Buzi,*ᵇ* by the Kebar River in the land of the Babylonians.*ᶜ* There the hand of the LORD was upon him.

*ᵃ*1 Or *my*, *ᵇ*3 Or *Ezekiel son of Buzi the priest* *ᶜ*3 Or *Chaldeans*

⁴I looked, and I saw a windstorm coming out of the north—an immense cloud with flashing lightning and surrounded by brilliant light. The center of the fire looked like glowing metal, ⁵and in the fire was what looked like four living creatures. In appearance their form was that of a man, ⁶but each of them had four faces and four wings. ⁷Their legs were straight; their feet were like those of a calf and gleamed like burnished bronze. ⁸Under their wings on their four sides they had the hands of a man. All four of them had faces and wings, ⁹and their wings touched one another. Each one went straight ahead; they did not turn as they moved.

¹⁰Their faces looked like this: Each of the four had the face of a man, and on the right side each had the face of a lion, and on the left the face of an ox; each also had the face of an eagle. ¹¹Such were their faces. Their wings were spread out upward; each had two wings, one touching the wing of another creature on either side, and two wings covering its body. ¹²Each one went straight ahead. Wherever the spirit would go, they would go, without turning as they went. ¹³The appearance of the living creatures was like burning coals of fire or like torches. Fire moved back and forth among the creatures; it was bright, and lightning flashed out of it. ¹⁴The creatures sped back and forth like flashes of lightning.

¹⁵As I looked at the living creatures, I saw a wheel on the ground beside each creature with its four faces. ¹⁶This was the appearance and structure of the wheels: They sparkled like chrysolite, and all four looked alike. Each appeared to be made like a wheel intersecting a wheel. ¹⁷As they moved, they would go in any one of the four directions the creatures faced; the wheels did not turn about*a* as the creatures went. ¹⁸Their rims were high and awesome, and all four rims were full of eyes all around.

¹⁹When the living creatures moved, the wheels beside them moved; and when the living creatures rose from the ground, the wheels also rose. ²⁰Wherever the spirit would go, they would go, and the wheels would rise along with them, because the spirit of the living creatures was in the wheels. ²¹When the creatures moved, they also moved; when the creatures

stood still, they also stood still; and when the creatures rose from the ground, the wheels rose along with them, because the spirit of the living creatures was in the wheels.

²²Spread out above the heads of the living creatures was what looked like an expanse, sparkling like ice, and awesome. ²³Under the expanse their wings were stretched out one toward the other, and each had two wings covering its body. ²⁴When the creatures moved, I heard the sound of their wings, like the roar of rushing waters, like the voice of the Almighty,*b* like the tumult of an army. When they stood still, they lowered their wings.

²⁵Then there came a voice from above the expanse over their heads as they stood with lowered wings. ²⁶Above the expanse over their heads was what looked like a throne of sapphire,*c* and high above on the throne was a figure like that of a man. ²⁷I saw that from what appeared to be his waist up he looked like glowing metal, as if full of fire, and that from there down he looked like fire; and brilliant light surrounded him. ²⁸Like the appearance of a rainbow in the clouds on a rainy day, so was the radiance around him.

This was the appearance of the likeness of the glory of the LORD. When I saw it, I fell facedown, and I heard the voice of one speaking.

Ezekiel's Call

2 He said to me, "Son of man, stand up on your feet and I will speak to you." ²As he spoke, the Spirit came into me and raised me to my feet, and I heard him speaking to me.

³He said: "Son of man, I am sending you to the Israelites, to a rebellious nation that has rebelled against me; they and their fathers have been in revolt against me to this very day. ⁴The people to whom I am sending you are obstinate and stubborn. Say to them, 'This is what the Sovereign LORD says.' ⁵And whether they listen or fail to listen—for they are a rebellious house—they will know that a prophet has been among them. ⁶And you, son of man, do not be afraid of them or their words. Do not be afraid, though briers and thorns are all around you and you live among scorpions. Do not be afraid of what they say or terrified by them, though

---

a 17 Or *aside*   *b* 24 Hebrew *Shaddai*   *c* 26 Or *lapis lazuli*

Like the appearance of
a rainbow in the clouds
on a rainy day, so was
the radiance around him.
This was the appearance
of the likeness of the
glory of the LORD. When
I saw it, I fell facedown,
and I heard the voice
of one speaking.

reflection

1 Do you ever feel unin-
spired and unrewarded
in your ministry, task or
job?

2 Where do you usually
look for motivation?

3 How has God revealed
himself to you in a way
that has strengthened and
encouraged you?

RELATED READINGS

Isaiah 6:1–13;
Ezekiel 3:22–23;
8:1–4; 10:3–5;
Acts 9:1–9;
2 Corinthians 12:2–6

"*God is compelled to
conceal himself in
a measure from the
natural world, for
the divine illumina-
tion would blind the
eyes of mortal man
were it to shine upon
him in full strength.*"

L. S. Thornton

Wild Inspiration

Read: Ezekiel 1:1–28

DO YOU EVER READ Bible passages and just scratch your head
in confusion? For most non-scholarly Bible readers, the book of
Ezekiel is chock-full of kaleidoscopic visions that seem more like
Star Wars than Scripture. After reading Ezekiel 1, can you imagine
what fun Hollywood would have in creating their rendition of this
scene? Even animatronics wizards might struggle to come up with
a four-winged human being with four faces (that of a man, lion, ox
and eagle)—on wheels, no less. God is, indeed, more creative than
any human being's imagination.

Why would God give this wild vision to Ezekiel?

The answer might have to do with inspiration. It seems that
what enabled the prophet Ezekiel and his contemporaries to press
on in their difficult ministries was a powerful, majestic vision of
God. Ezekiel's particular vision left an indelible impression: God
was the absolute Sovereign over all of creation and history. The
prophet would remember this one-of-a-kind experience and return
to it all of his life.

Ezekiel could describe the cherubim in this vision with great
detail. However, when he saw "the appearance of the likeness of
the glory of the LORD," he groped for words and ultimately could
not respond. He could only fall facedown—awestruck by God's
holiness and glory.

Ezekiel, like most Biblical prophets, endured his share of shame
and often appeared foolish to his contemporaries. He did not have
a dream job . . . so he needed a vision. His visions of God sustained, encouraged, strengthened and directed him in an otherwise difficult and thankless task.

What is your vision of God? What keeps you staying with the
job God has called you to do? Is your motivation based on who
God has revealed himself to be? Whatever your task today, dare to
ask the wild, holy, Sovereign God of Ezekiel to reveal his majesty to
encourage and strengthen you.

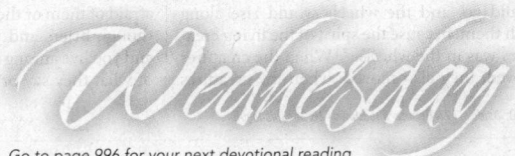

Wednesday

Go to page 996 for your next devotional reading.

they are a rebellious house. ⁷You must speak my words to them, whether they listen or fail to listen, for they are rebellious. ⁸But you, son of man, listen to what I say to you. Do not rebel like that rebellious house; open your mouth and eat what I give you."

⁹Then I looked, and I saw a hand stretched out to me. In it was a scroll, ¹⁰which he unrolled before me. On both sides of it were written words of lament and mourning and woe.

3 And he said to me, "Son of man, eat what is before you, eat this scroll; then go and speak to the house of Israel." ²So I opened my mouth, and he gave me the scroll to eat.

³Then he said to me, "Son of man, eat this scroll I am giving you and fill your stomach with it." So I ate it, and it tasted as sweet as honey in my mouth.

⁴He then said to me: "Son of man, go now to the house of Israel and speak my words to them. ⁵You are not being sent to a people of obscure speech and difficult language, but to the house of Israel— ⁶not to many peoples of obscure speech and difficult language, whose words you cannot understand. Surely if I had sent you to them, they would have listened to you. ⁷But the house of Israel is not willing to listen to you because they are not willing to listen to me, for the whole house of Israel is hardened and obstinate. ⁸But I will make you as unyielding and hardened as they are. ⁹I will make your forehead like the hardest stone, harder than flint. Do not be afraid of them or terrified by them, though they are a rebellious house."

¹⁰And he said to me, "Son of man, listen carefully and take to heart all the words I speak to you. ¹¹Go now to your countrymen in exile and speak to them. Say to them, 'This is what the Sovereign Lord says,' whether they listen or fail to listen."

¹²Then the Spirit lifted me up, and I heard behind me a loud rumbling sound—May the glory of the Lord be praised in his dwelling place!— ¹³the sound of the wings of the living creatures brushing against each other and the sound of the wheels beside them, a loud rumbling sound. ¹⁴The Spirit then lifted me up and took me away, and I went in bitterness and in the anger of my spirit, with the strong hand of the Lord upon me. ¹⁵I came to the exiles who lived at Tel Abib near the Kebar River. And there, where they were living, I sat among them for seven days—overwhelmed.

Warning to Israel

¹⁶At the end of seven days the word of the Lord came to me: ¹⁷"Son of man, I have made you a watchman for the house of Israel; so hear the word I speak and give them warning from me. ¹⁸When I say to a wicked man, 'You will surely die,' and you do not warn him or speak out to dissuade him from his evil ways in order to save his life, that wicked man will die forᵃ his sin, and I will hold you accountable for his blood. ¹⁹But if you do warn the wicked man and he does not turn from his wickedness or from his evil ways, he will die for his sin; but you will have saved yourself.

²⁰"Again, when a righteous man turns from his righteousness and does evil, and I put a stumbling block before him, he will die. Since you did not warn him, he will die for his sin. The righteous things he did will not be remembered, and I will hold you accountable for his blood. ²¹But if you do warn the righteous man not to sin and he does not sin, he will surely live because he took warning, and you will have saved yourself."

²²The hand of the Lord was upon me there, and he said to me, "Get up and go out to the plain, and there I will speak to you." ²³So I got up and went out to the plain. And the glory of the Lord was standing there, like the glory I had seen by the Kebar River, and I fell facedown.

Ezekiel 3:18

God Holds Us Accountable

"When I say to a wicked man, 'You will surely die,' and you do not warn him or speak out to dissuade him from his evil ways in order to save his life, that wicked man will die for his sin, and I will hold you accountable."

ᵃ18 Or *in*; also in verses 19 and 20

24Then the Spirit came into me and raised me to my feet. He spoke to me and said: "Go, shut yourself inside your house. 25And you, son of man, they will tie with ropes; you will be bound so that you cannot go out among the people. 26I will make your tongue stick to the roof of your mouth so that you will be silent and unable to rebuke them, though they are a rebellious house. 27But when I speak to you, I will open your mouth and you shall say to them, 'This is what the Sovereign LORD says.' Whoever will listen let him listen, and whoever will refuse let him refuse; for they are a rebellious house.

Siege of Jerusalem Symbolized

4 "Now, son of man, take a clay tablet, put it in front of you and draw the city of Jerusalem on it. 2Then lay siege to it: Erect siege works against it, build a ramp up to it, set up camps against it and put battering rams around it. 3Then take an iron pan, place it as an iron wall between you and the city and turn your face toward it. It will be under siege, and you shall besiege it. This will be a sign to the house of Israel.

4"Then lie on your left side and put the sin of the house of Israel upon yourself.a You are to bear their sin for the number of days you lie on your side. 5I have assigned you the same number of days as the years of their sin. So for 390 days you will bear the sin of the house of Israel.

6"After you have finished this, lie down again, this time on your right side, and bear the sin of the house of Judah. I have assigned you 40 days, a day for each year. 7Turn your face toward the siege of Jerusalem and with bared arm prophesy against her. 8I will tie you up with ropes so that you cannot turn from one side to the other until you have finished the days of your siege.

9"Take wheat and barley, beans and lentils, millet and spelt; put them in a storage jar and use them to make bread for yourself. You are to eat it during the 390 days you lie on your side. 10Weigh out twenty shekelsb of food to eat each day and eat it at set times. 11Also measure out a sixth of a hinc of water and drink it at set times.

12Eat the food as you would a barley cake; bake it in the sight of the people, using human excrement for fuel." 13The LORD said, "In this way the people of Israel will eat defiled food among the nations where I will drive them."

14Then I said, "Not so, Sovereign LORD! I have never defiled myself. From my youth until now I have never eaten anything found dead or torn by wild animals. No unclean meat has ever entered my mouth."

15"Very well," he said, "I will let you bake your bread over cow manure instead of human excrement."

16He then said to me: "Son of man, I will cut off the supply of food in Jerusalem. The people will eat rationed food in anxiety and drink rationed water in despair, 17for food and water will be scarce. They will be appalled at the sight of each other and will waste away because ofd their sin.

5 "Now, son of man, take a sharp sword and use it as a barber's razor to shave your head and your beard. Then take a set of scales and divide up the hair. 2When the days of your siege come to an end, burn a third of the hair with fire inside the city. Take a third and strike it with the sword all around the city. And scatter a third to the wind. For I will pursue them with drawn sword. 3But take a few strands of hair and tuck them away in the folds of your garment. 4Again, take a few of these and throw them into the fire and burn them up. A fire will spread from there to the whole house of Israel.

5"This is what the Sovereign LORD says: This is Jerusalem, which I have set in the center of the nations, with countries all around her. 6Yet in her wickedness she has rebelled against my laws and decrees more than the nations and countries around her. She has rejected my laws and has not followed my decrees.

7"Therefore this is what the Sovereign LORD says: You have been more unruly than the nations around you and have not followed my decrees or kept my laws. You have not evene conformed to the standards of the nations around you.

8"Therefore this is what the Sovereign LORD says: I myself am against you, Jerusalem, and

---

a4 Or your side   b10 That is, about 8 ounces (about 0.2 kilogram)   c11 That is, about 2/3 quart (about 0.6 liter)   d17 Or away in
e7 Most Hebrew manuscripts; some Hebrew manuscripts and Syriac You have

I will inflict punishment on you in the sight of the nations. ⁹Because of all your detestable idols, I will do to you what I have never done before and will never do again.

¹⁰Therefore in your midst fathers will eat their children, and children will eat their fathers. I will inflict punishment on you and will scatter all your survivors to the winds. ¹¹Therefore as surely as I live, declares the Sovereign LORD, because you have defiled my sanctuary with all your vile images and detestable practices, I myself will withdraw my favor; I will not look on you with pity or spare you. ¹²A third of your people will die of the plague or perish by famine inside you; a third will fall by the sword outside your walls; and a third I will scatter to the winds and pursue with drawn sword.

¹³"Then my anger will cease and my wrath against them will subside, and I will be avenged. And when I have spent my wrath upon them, they will know that I the LORD have spoken in my zeal.

¹⁴"I will make you a ruin and a reproach among the nations around you, in the sight of all who pass by. ¹⁵You will be a reproach and a taunt, a warning and an object of horror to the nations around you when I inflict punishment on you in anger and in wrath and with stinging rebuke. I the LORD have spoken. ¹⁶When I shoot at you with my deadly and destructive arrows of famine, I will shoot to destroy you. I will bring more and more famine upon you and cut off your supply of food. ¹⁷I will send famine and wild beasts against you, and they will leave you childless. Plague and bloodshed will sweep through you, and I will bring the sword against you. I the LORD have spoken."

A Prophecy Against the Mountains of Israel

6 The word of the LORD came to me: ²"Son of man, set your face against the mountains of Israel; prophesy against them ³and say: 'O mountains of Israel, hear the word of the Sovereign LORD. This is what the Sovereign LORD says to the mountains and hills, to the ravines and valleys: I am about to bring a sword against you, and I will destroy your high places. ⁴Your altars will be demolished and your incense altars will be smashed; and I will slay your people in front of your idols. ⁵I will lay the dead bodies of the Israelites in front of their idols, and I will scatter your bones around your altars. ⁶Wherever you live, the towns will be laid waste and the high places demolished, so that your altars will be laid waste and devastated, your idols smashed and ruined, your incense altars broken down, and what you have made wiped out. ⁷Your people will fall slain among you, and you will know that I am the LORD.

⁸"'But I will spare some, for some of you will escape the sword when you are scattered among the lands and nations. ⁹Then in the nations where they have been carried captive, those who escape will remember me—how I have been grieved by their adulterous hearts, which have turned away from me, and by their eyes, which have lusted after their idols. They will loathe themselves for the evil they have done and for all their detestable practices. ¹⁰And they will know that I am the LORD; I did not threaten in vain to bring this calamity on them.

¹¹"'This is what the Sovereign LORD says: Strike your hands together and stamp your feet and cry out "Alas!" because of all the wicked and detestable practices of the house of Israel, for they will fall by the sword, famine and plague. ¹²He that is far away will die of the plague, and he that is near will fall by the sword, and he that survives and is spared will die of famine. So will I spend my wrath upon them. ¹³And they will know that I am the LORD, when their people lie slain among their idols around their altars, on every high hill and on all the mountaintops, under every spreading tree and every leafy oak—places where they offered fragrant incense to all their idols. ¹⁴And I will stretch

---

Ezekiel 5:11

God Can Withdraw Favor

"Therefore as surely as I live, declares the Sovereign LORD, because you have defiled my sanctuary with all your vile images and detestable practices, I myself will withdraw my favor; I will not look on you with pity or spare you."

Renewal by Fire

Read: Ezekiel 6:1–14

Ezekiel 6:6

"Wherever you live, the towns will be laid waste and the high places demolished, so that your altars will be laid waste and devastated, your idols smashed and ruined, your incense altars broken down, and what you have made wiped out."

reflection

1 How about you? Do you have deadwood accumulating in your soul that needs God's renewing discipline?

2 Why is God's discipline a sign of his love?

3 How will you praise God for his "controlled burning" in your life?

RELATED READINGS

Exodus 32:1–35;
Judges 3:7–14;
Jeremiah 44:1–30;
Hebrews 12:4–11

NEARLY EIGHT MILLION ACRES of forest area burned across America in 2004. In the past, the common thought was that no fire was a good fire. But conservation experts tell us that forest fires actually contribute to the health and well-being of the forest.

Amid densely packed old-growth trees, leaves, branches and other debris constantly accumulate on the woodland floor. If not consumed in small, natural fires, this deadwood over time will continue to build and become susceptible to even larger, more intense fires that are more difficult to control.

In addition, trees such as the jack pine actually *require* a blaze to crack their seeds and begin the process of rebirth. Amidst the devastation wrought by wildfire, these hard seeds burst forth with new life as the forest slowly rebuilds. New growth provides a better habitat for many animals so that biodiversity improves. New initiatives for "controlled burning" have emerged to help forests return to their natural cycles of renewal through fire.

The prophet Ezekiel railed against people weighed down by some serious "deadwood"—disobedience and idolatry—that had accumulated over years. Ezekiel informed the people that God was enraged by their rebellion. God's anger, however, was not simply a punishment, but a necessary means by which their love and devotion to him would be renewed. How is that? God's judgment rejuvenated the hearts of his people from the damaging effects of apathy, just as forest fires cleanse the forest of stagnation and decay.

Discipline gets our attention. Consequences alert us that something is wrong. If God simply left us alone, negative attitudes would slowly accumulate in our hearts. Unchecked, we would become prime candidates for uncontrolled disaster.

Have you ever experienced a time when your sin resulted in painful consequences? Can you see how those consequences might have served to renew your relationship with God? Were there signs of renewal in your attitude toward him because you learned from your mistakes? Ezekiel understood the principle of renewal; he longed to see God's rebuke result in repentance for his people. Though God may choose to burn out the deadwood in your life, he does so for a good reason. Don't fight it. Learn from it.

Go to page 1000 for your next devotional reading.

out my hand against them and make the land a desolate waste from the desert to Diblah[a]—wherever they live. Then they will know that I am the LORD.'"

The End Has Come

7 The word of the LORD came to me: 2"Son of man, this is what the Sovereign LORD says to the land of Israel: The end! The end has come upon the four corners of the land. 3The end is now upon you and I will unleash my anger against you. I will judge you according to your conduct and repay you for all your detestable practices. 4I will not look on you with pity or spare you; I will surely repay you for your conduct and the detestable practices among you. Then you will know that I am the LORD.

5"This is what the Sovereign LORD says:

Disaster! An unheard-of[b] disaster is coming. 6The end has come! The end has come! It has roused itself against you. It has come! 7Doom has come upon you—you who dwell in the land. The time has come, the day is near; there is panic, not joy, upon the mountains. 8I am about to pour out my wrath on you and spend my anger against you; I will judge you according to your conduct and repay you for all your detestable practices. 9I will not look on you with pity or spare you; I will repay you in accordance with your conduct and the detestable practices among you. Then you will know that it is I the LORD who strikes the blow.

10"The day is here! It has come! Doom has burst forth, the rod has budded, arrogance has blossomed! 11Violence has grown into[c] a rod to punish wickedness; none of the people will be left, none of that crowd—no wealth, nothing of value. 12The time has come, the day has arrived. Let not the buyer rejoice nor the seller grieve, for wrath is upon the whole crowd. 13The seller will not recover the land he has sold as long as both of them live, for the vision concerning the whole crowd will not be reversed. Because of their sins, not one of them will preserve his life. 14Though they blow the trumpet and get everything ready, no one will go into battle, for my wrath is upon the whole crowd.

15"Outside is the sword, inside are plague and famine; those in the country will die by the sword, and those in the city will be devoured by famine and plague. 16All who survive and escape will be in the mountains, moaning like doves of the valleys, each because of his sins. 17Every hand will go limp, and every knee will become as weak as water. 18They will put on sackcloth and be clothed with terror. Their faces will be covered with shame and their heads will be shaved. 19They will throw their silver into the streets, and their gold will be an unclean thing. Their silver and gold will not be able to save them in the day of the LORD's wrath. They will not satisfy their hunger or fill their stomachs with it, for it has made them stumble into sin. 20They were proud of their beautiful jewelry and used it to make their detestable idols and vile images. Therefore I will turn these into an unclean thing for them. 21I will hand it all over as plunder to foreigners and as loot to the wicked of the earth, and they will defile it. 22I will turn my face away from them, and they will desecrate my treasured place; robbers will enter it and desecrate it.

23"Prepare chains, because the land is full of bloodshed and the city is full of violence. 24I will bring the most wicked of the nations to take possession of their houses; I will put an end to the pride of the mighty, and their sanctuaries will be desecrated. 25When terror comes, they will seek peace, but there will be none. 26Calamity upon calamity will come, and rumor upon rumor. They will try to get a vision from the prophet; the teaching of the law by the priest will be lost, as will the counsel of the elders. 27The king will mourn, the prince will be clothed with despair, and the hands of the people of the land will tremble. I will deal with them according to their conduct, and by their own standards I will judge them. Then they will know that I am the LORD."

Idolatry in the Temple

8 In the sixth year, in the sixth month on the fifth day, while I was sitting in my house and the elders of Judah were sitting before me, the hand of the Sovereign LORD came upon me there. 2I looked, and I saw a figure like that of a man.[d] From what appeared to be his waist down he was like fire, and from there up his

---

[a]14 Most Hebrew manuscripts; a few Hebrew manuscripts *Riblah*   [b]5 Most Hebrew manuscripts; some Hebrew manuscripts and Syriac *Disaster after*   [c]11 Or *The violent one has become*   [d]2 Or *saw a fiery figure*

appearance was as bright as glowing metal. ³He stretched out what looked like a hand and took me by the hair of my head. The Spirit lifted me up between earth and heaven and in visions of God he took me to Jerusalem, to the entrance to the north gate of the inner court, where the idol that provokes to jealousy stood. ⁴And there before me was the glory of the God of Israel, as in the vision I had seen in the plain.

⁵Then he said to me, "Son of man, look toward the north." So I looked, and in the entrance north of the gate of the altar I saw this idol of jealousy.

⁶And he said to me, "Son of man, do you see what they are doing—the utterly detestable things the house of Israel is doing here, things that will drive me far from my sanctuary? But you will see things that are even more detestable."

⁷Then he brought me to the entrance to the court. I looked, and I saw a hole in the wall. ⁸He said to me, "Son of man, now dig into the wall." So I dug into the wall and saw a doorway there.

⁹And he said to me, "Go in and see the wicked and detestable things they are doing here." ¹⁰So I went in and looked, and I saw portrayed all over the walls all kinds of crawling things and detestable animals and all the idols of the house of Israel. ¹¹In front of them stood seventy elders of the house of Israel, and Jaazaniah son of Shaphan was standing among them. Each had a censer in his hand, and a fragrant cloud of incense was rising.

¹²He said to me, "Son of man, have you seen what the elders of the house of Israel are doing in the darkness, each at the shrine of his own idol? They say, 'The LORD does not see us; the LORD has forsaken the land.'" ¹³Again, he said, "You will see them doing things that are even more detestable."

¹⁴Then he brought me to the entrance to the north gate of the house of the LORD, and I saw women sitting there, mourning for Tammuz. ¹⁵He said to me, "Do you see this, son of man? You will see things that are even more detestable than this."

¹⁶He then brought me into the inner court of the house of the LORD, and there at the entrance to the temple, between the portico and the altar, were about twenty-five men. With their backs toward the temple of the LORD and their faces toward the east, they were bowing down to the sun in the east.

¹⁷He said to me, "Have you seen this, son of man? Is it a trivial matter for the house of Judah to do the detestable things they are doing here? Must they also fill the land with violence and continually provoke me to anger? Look at them putting the branch to their nose! ¹⁸Therefore I will deal with them in anger; I will not look on them with pity or spare them. Although they shout in my ears, I will not listen to them."

Idolaters Killed

9 Then I heard him call out in a loud voice, "Bring the guards of the city here, each with a weapon in his hand." ²And I saw six men coming from the direction of the upper gate, which faces north, each with a deadly weapon in his hand. With them was a man clothed in linen who had a writing kit at his side. They came in and stood beside the bronze altar.

³Now the glory of the God of Israel went up from above the cherubim, where it had been, and moved to the threshold of the temple. Then the LORD called to the man clothed in linen who had the writing kit at his side ⁴and said to him, "Go throughout the city of Jerusalem and put a mark on the foreheads of those who grieve and lament over all the detestable things that are done in it."

⁵As I listened, he said to the others, "Follow him through the city and kill, without showing pity or compassion. ⁶Slaughter old men, young men and maidens, women and children, but do not touch anyone who has the mark. Begin at my sanctuary." So they began with the elders who were in front of the temple.

⁷Then he said to them, "Defile the temple and fill the courts with the slain. Go!" So they went out and began killing throughout the city. ⁸While they were killing and I was left alone, I fell facedown, crying out, "Ah, Sovereign LORD! Are you going to destroy the entire remnant of Israel in this outpouring of your wrath on Jerusalem?"

⁹He answered me, "The sin of the house of Israel and Judah is exceedingly great; the land is full of bloodshed and the city is full of injustice. They say, 'The LORD has forsaken the land; the

LORD does not see." [10]So I will not look on them with pity or spare them, but I will bring down on their own heads what they have done."

[11]Then the man in linen with the writing kit at his side brought back word, saying, "I have done as you commanded."

The Glory Departs From the Temple

10 I looked, and I saw the likeness of a throne of sapphire[a] above the expanse that was over the heads of the cherubim. [2]The LORD said to the man clothed in linen, "Go in among the wheels beneath the cherubim. Fill your hands with burning coals from among the cherubim and scatter them over the city." And as I watched, he went in.

[3]Now the cherubim were standing on the south side of the temple when the man went in, and a cloud filled the inner court. [4]Then the glory of the LORD rose from above the cherubim and moved to the threshold of the temple. The cloud filled the temple, and the court was full of the radiance of the glory of the LORD. [5]The sound of the wings of the cherubim could be heard as far away as the outer court, like the voice of God Almighty[b] when he speaks.

[6]When the LORD commanded the man in linen, "Take fire from among the wheels, from among the cherubim," the man went in and stood beside a wheel. [7]Then one of the cherubim reached out his hand to the fire that was among them. He took up some of it and put it into the hands of the man in linen, who took it and went out. [8](Under the wings of the cherubim could be seen what looked like the hands of a man.)

[9]I looked, and I saw beside the cherubim four wheels, one beside each of the cherubim; the wheels sparkled like chrysolite. [10]As for their appearance, the four of them looked alike; each was like a wheel intersecting a wheel. [11]As they moved, they would go in any one of the four directions the cherubim faced; the wheels

Ezekiel 10:4

God Is Radiant

Then the glory of the LORD rose from above the cherubim and moved to the threshold of the temple. The cloud filled the temple, and the court was full of the radiance of the glory of the LORD.

did not turn about[c] as the cherubim went. The cherubim went in whatever direction the head faced, without turning as they went. [12]Their entire bodies, including their backs, their hands and their wings, were completely full of eyes, as were their four wheels. [13]I heard the wheels being called "the whirling wheels." [14]Each of the cherubim had four faces: One face was that of a cherub, the second the face of a man, the third the face of a lion, and the fourth the face of an eagle.

[15]Then the cherubim rose upward. These were the living creatures I had seen by the Kebar River. [16]When the cherubim moved, the wheels beside them moved; and when the cherubim spread their wings to rise from the ground, the wheels did not leave their side. [17]When the cherubim stood still, they also stood still; and when the cherubim rose, they rose with them, because the spirit of the living creatures was in them.

[18]Then the glory of the LORD departed from over the threshold of the temple and stopped above the cherubim. [19]While I watched, the cherubim spread their wings and rose from the ground, and as they went, the wheels went with them. They stopped at the entrance to the east gate of the LORD's house, and the glory of the God of Israel was above them.

[20]These were the living creatures I had seen beneath the God of Israel by the Kebar River, and I realized that they were cherubim. [21]Each had four faces and four wings, and under their wings was what looked like the hands of a man. [22]Their faces had the same appearance as those I had seen by the Kebar River. Each one went straight ahead.

Judgment on Israel's Leaders

11 Then the Spirit lifted me up and brought me to the gate of the house of the LORD that faces east. There at the entrance to the gate were twenty-five men, and I saw among them Jaazaniah son of Azzur and

[a]1 Or *lapis lazuli* [b]5 Hebrew *El-Shaddai* [c]11 Or *aside*

Light the Way

Ezekiel 10:4

Then the glory of the Lord rose from above the cherubim and moved to the threshold of the temple. The cloud filled the temple, and the court was full of the radiance of the glory of the Lord.

reflection

1 How does it comfort you to know that God's glory radiates in heaven?

2 What are some of the lies that comprise the "dark darkness" described in today's devotional? How do these lies affect *your* life?

3 How will you glorify God by helping those who are sitting in darkness to see the light?

RELATED READINGS

Psalm 138:1–8;
Habakkuk 3:3–4;
John 1:6–9

Read: Ezekiel 10:1–22

GOD SPEAKS TO US of "light" and "dark" to help us to understand that we can make such terrible mistakes about what the world is, what the universe is, who we are ourselves, whether there is any life after we die, whether there is a place called heaven. We can make such terrible mistakes about whether God made the world or whether it came by chance. We can make such terrible mistakes about whom to believe, and just believe lies instead of the truth. God tells us that believing lies and making such mistakes about life is like sitting in dark darkness. Then He says that because people are in such dark darkness, one of three Persons, God the Son, came to be born as a baby, to grow up to teach and live so that people would have light to see and understand what mistakes they had made.

John did not talk about himself. He even called himself a "voice of one calling in the [desert]" (Luke 3:4)! Constantly he told people what terrible mistakes they had made, and what sinners they were in their rebellion against what is true, and against God who really exists. John told them that a Savior was coming to save them from the results of all this sin and rebellion. John told people that a "light" was coming to lighten their darkness, and to guide their feet into the true path. John told people the truth.

All this happened about two thousand years ago. Now it is history. But it is important to us because it is true history. You are a person. I am a person. We are people who have been born into the world, and we are alive today in this time of history. We need to know how we "fit in." We need to know about the past, and we need to know about what is coming in the future, but we need to know what we are meant to do right now. One thing we are meant to do is to give light to others sitting in darkness.

—Edith Schaeffer

Pelatiah son of Benaiah, leaders of the people. [2]The LORD said to me, "Son of man, these are the men who are plotting evil and giving wicked advice in this city. [3]They say, 'Will it not soon be time to build houses?[a] This city is a cooking pot, and we are the meat.' [4]Therefore prophesy against them; prophesy, son of man."

[5]Then the Spirit of the LORD came upon me, and he told me to say: "This is what the LORD says: That is what you are saying, O house of Israel, but I know what is going through your mind. [6]You have killed many people in this city and filled its streets with the dead.

[7]"Therefore this is what the Sovereign LORD says: The bodies you have thrown there are the meat and this city is the pot, but I will drive you out of it. [8]You fear the sword, and the sword is what I will bring against you, declares the Sovereign LORD. [9]I will drive you out of the city and hand you over to foreigners and inflict punishment on you. [10]You will fall by the sword, and I will execute judgment on you at the borders of Israel. Then you will know that I am the LORD. [11]This city will not be a pot for you, nor will you be the meat in it; I will execute judgment on you at the borders of Israel. [12]And you will know that I am the LORD, for you have not followed my decrees or kept my laws but have conformed to the standards of the nations around you."

[13]Now as I was prophesying, Pelatiah son of Benaiah died. Then I fell facedown and cried out in a loud voice, "Ah, Sovereign LORD! Will you completely destroy the remnant of Israel?"

[14]The word of the LORD came to me: [15]"Son of man, your brothers—your brothers who are your blood relatives[b]—and the whole house of Israel—are those of whom the people of Jerusalem have said, 'They are[c] far away from the LORD; this land was given to us as our possession.'

Promised Return of Israel

[16]"Therefore say: 'This is what the Sovereign LORD says: Although I sent them far away among the nations and scattered them among the countries, yet for a little while I have been a sanctuary for them in the countries where they have gone.'

[17]"Therefore say: 'This is what the Sovereign LORD says: I will gather you from the nations and bring you back from the countries where you have been scattered, and I will give you back the land of Israel again.'

[18]"They will return to it and remove all its vile images and detestable idols. [19]I will give them an undivided heart and put a new spirit in them; I will remove from them their heart of stone and give them a heart of flesh. [20]Then they will follow my decrees and be careful to keep my laws. They will be my people, and I will be their God. [21]But as for those whose hearts are devoted to their vile images and detestable idols, I will bring down on their own heads what they have done, declares the Sovereign LORD."

[22]Then the cherubim, with the wheels beside them, spread their wings, and the glory of the God of Israel was above them. [23]The glory of the LORD went up from within the city and stopped above the mountain east of it. [24]The Spirit lifted me up and brought me to the exiles in Babylonia[d] in the vision given by the Spirit of God.

Then the vision I had seen went up from me, [25]and I told the exiles everything the LORD had shown me.

The Exile Symbolized

12 The word of the LORD came to me: [2]"Son of man, you are living among a rebellious people. They have eyes to see but do not see and ears to hear but do not hear, for they are a rebellious people.

> ### Ezekiel 11:19
>
> *God Renews Hearts*
>
> "I will give them an undivided heart and put a new spirit in them; I will remove from them their heart of stone and give them a heart of flesh."

---

[a]3 Or *This is not the time to build houses.*   [b]15 Or *are in exile with you* (see Septuagint and Syriac)   [c]15 Or *those to whom the people of Jerusalem have said, 'Stay*   [d]24 Or *Chaldea*

Unfailing Love

GOMER

**ASSIGNED
READING:**

Hosea 1–3

"HOW DOES HE DO IT?"

"He's a fool for her, I tell you."

"Senseless. You tell him she's a tramp . . . a vixen . . . and it's as if he doesn't hear you at all."

"Somebody told me he's not even the father of those children."

The chatter in the marketplace among the women rose to a crescendo as they daily observed the strange and wonderful relationship between Gomer and her husband. She was strange, and he was wonderful—too wonderful for her.

"Why does he put up with her?" they all wanted to know. How could a prophet—a prophet of God—put up with the wandering eye and straying heart of an out-and-out adulteress and still claim unfailing love for her? It was a mystery to the townspeople.

And to Gomer.

It seemed no matter how deeply she wounded her husband, he would not give up on her. She habitually ran from the security of his love to find solace in the arms of strangers. She preferred the emotionless physicality of those she met on the street to his unfailing, undying love. Instead of loving the one who called her by name, she preferred the anonymity of someone with no name, no home and no family.

Gomer herself must have wondered sometimes about the contradictions. Did she ever stop to ask why Hosea so relentlessly and tenderly loved her? Or why she rejected his love? Did she ever doubt her own emotional stability since she proved incapable of commitment? Some say the definition of insanity is repeating the same action over and over again but expecting a different response. In Gomer's case, she was "crazy" to think that her loveless pursuits could satisfy the core needs for fulfillment and security that every woman has. However, it didn't keep her from running away from the very thing she desperately wanted to find—unfailing love.

—*Prayer*—

"Give thanks to the LORD, for he is good; his love endures forever" (1 Chronicles 16:34).

³"Therefore, son of man, pack your belongings for exile and in the daytime, as they watch, set out and go from where you are to another place. Perhaps they will understand, though they are a rebellious house. ⁴During the daytime, while they watch, bring out your belongings packed for exile. Then in the evening, while they are watching, go out like those who go into exile. ⁵While they watch, dig through the wall and take your belongings out through it. ⁶Put them on your shoulder as they are watching and carry them out at dusk. Cover your face so that you cannot see the land, for I have made you a sign to the house of Israel."

⁷So I did as I was commanded. During the day I brought out my things packed for exile. Then in the evening I dug through the wall with my hands. I took my belongings out at dusk, carrying them on my shoulders while they watched.

⁸In the morning the word of the LORD came to me: ⁹"Son of man, did not that rebellious house of Israel ask you, 'What are you doing?'

¹⁰"Say to them, 'This is what the Sovereign LORD says: This oracle concerns the prince in Jerusalem and the whole house of Israel who are there.' ¹¹Say to them, 'I am a sign to you.'

"As I have done, so it will be done to them. They will go into exile as captives.

¹²"The prince among them will put his things on his shoulder at dusk and leave, and a hole will be dug in the wall for him to go through. He will cover his face so that he cannot see the land. ¹³I will spread my net for him, and he will be caught in my snare; I will bring him to Babylonia, the land of the Chaldeans, but he will not see it, and there he will die. ¹⁴I will scatter to the winds all those around him—his staff and all his troops—and I will pursue them with drawn sword.

¹⁵"They will know that I am the LORD, when I disperse them among the nations and scatter them through the countries. ¹⁶But I will spare a few of them from the sword, famine and plague, so that in the nations where they go they may acknowledge all their detestable practices. Then they will know that I am the LORD."

¹⁷The word of the LORD came to me: ¹⁸"Son of man, tremble as you eat your food, and shudder in fear as you drink your water. ¹⁹Say to the people of the land: 'This is what the Sovereign LORD says about those living in Jerusalem and in the land of Israel: They will eat their food in anxiety and drink their water in despair, for their land will be stripped of everything in it because of the violence of all who live there. ²⁰The inhabited towns will be laid waste and the land will be desolate. Then you will know that I am the LORD.'"

²¹The word of the LORD came to me: ²²"Son of man, what is this proverb you have in the land of Israel: 'The days go by and every vision comes to nothing'? ²³Say to them, 'This is what the Sovereign LORD says: I am going to put an end to this proverb, and they will no longer quote it in Israel.' Say to them, 'The days are near when every vision will be fulfilled. ²⁴For there will be no more false visions or flattering divinations among the people of Israel. ²⁵But I the LORD will speak what I will, and it shall be fulfilled without delay. For in your days, you rebellious house, I will fulfill whatever I say, declares the Sovereign LORD.'"

²⁶The word of the LORD came to me: ²⁷"Son of man, the house of Israel is saying, 'The vision he sees is for many years from now, and he prophesies about the distant future.'

²⁸"Therefore say to them, 'This is what the Sovereign LORD says: None of my words will be delayed any longer; whatever I say will be fulfilled, declares the Sovereign LORD.'"

False Prophets Condemned

13 The word of the LORD came to me: ²"Son of man, prophesy against the prophets of Israel who are now prophesying. Say to those who prophesy out of their own imagination: 'Hear the word of the LORD! ³This is what the Sovereign LORD says: Woe to the foolish*ᵃ* prophets who follow their own spirit and have seen nothing! ⁴Your prophets, O Israel, are like jackals among ruins. ⁵You have not gone up to the breaks in the wall to repair it for the house of Israel so that it will stand firm in the battle on the day of the LORD. ⁶Their visions are false and their divinations a lie. They say, "The LORD declares," when the LORD has not sent them; yet they expect their words to be fulfilled. ⁷Have you not seen false

ᵃ3 Or wicked

Shelter in a Strange Land

Read: Ezekiel 11:16–25

Ezekiel 11:16

"Therefore say: 'This is what the Sovereign LORD says: Although I sent them far away among the nations and scattered them among the countries, yet for a little while I have been a sanctuary for them in the countries where they have gone.'"

reflection

1 How do you react to feelings of loneliness or isolation in your life?

2 Remembering that God provides you with sanctuary isn't always easy. During difficult times when you may not feel his presence, how can you practically remind yourself of this truth?

3 Spend some time praying for things that seem "far off"—family, friends, even a place you dearly miss. Ask the Lord to satisfy these longings in you. Ask him to ultimately satisfy you with himself.

RELATED READINGS

Isaiah 4:5–6;
Jeremiah 1:17–19;
Luke 18:28–30

THE PAST TWO CENTURIES have produced an unprecedented shrinking of time and distance. Journeys that once required days or weeks have now been reduced to hours with trains, automobiles and air travel—methods of transportation that would have seemed fantastical a hundred years ago. Yet the availability of these means of travel has also introduced a new level of fragmentation. Perhaps you've moved far from your parents; perhaps your job requires you to travel to a different city every day; perhaps your children or grandchildren live a long plane ride from you. As a result, you sometimes feel isolated from your friends and family. Though you long for closeness with others, you often find only loneliness.

The Israelites had slavery to add to their dislocation anxiety. God scattered them among foreign nations, fulfilling his promise to send them into captivity if they forgot to keep him first and foremost in their lives. In strange lands, far from temple life and the comfort of communal worship, God promised to be their sanctuary in the midst of their isolation. The abiding presence of the Lord would go with the scattered people into foreign lands.

We, too, long to be hidden in the presence of God. Following Christ can be a lonely journey in a hostile world. Many of us sit in silent agony at meetings as colleagues ridicule some aspect of our faith. Many of us can relate to feelings of abiding isolation not too different from the Israelites' alien existence as they groaned before God. They longed to return to their country from the foreign lands where everything seemed antagonistic to the faith they had earlier taken for granted.

God wants us to learn an important lesson from these seasons of loneliness: Our true citizenship is in heaven. When you feel like an outsider, remember that you are a citizen of heaven, and God promises to be your sanctuary in these foreign lands.

Go to page 1009 for your next devotional reading.

visions and uttered lying divinations when you say, "The LORD declares," though I have not spoken?

8 "Therefore this is what the Sovereign LORD says: Because of your false words and lying visions, I am against you, declares the Sovereign LORD. 9 My hand will be against the prophets who see false visions and utter lying divinations. They will not belong to the council of my people or be listed in the records of the house of Israel, nor will they enter the land of Israel. Then you will know that I am the Sovereign LORD.

10 "Because they lead my people astray, saying, "Peace," when there is no peace, and because, when a flimsy wall is built, they cover it with whitewash, 11 therefore tell those who cover it with whitewash that it is going to fall. Rain will come in torrents, and I will send hailstones hurtling down, and violent winds will burst forth. 12 When the wall collapses, will people not ask you, "Where is the whitewash you covered it with?"

13 "Therefore this is what the Sovereign LORD says: In my wrath I will unleash a violent wind, and in my anger hailstones and torrents of rain will fall with destructive fury. 14 I will tear down the wall you have covered with whitewash and will level it to the ground so that its foundation will be laid bare. When it*a* falls, you will be destroyed in it; and you will know that I am the LORD. 15 So I will spend my wrath against the wall and against those who covered it with whitewash. I will say to you, "The wall is gone and so are those who whitewashed it, 16 those prophets of Israel who prophesied to Jerusalem and saw visions of peace for her when there was no peace, declares the Sovereign LORD."

17 "Now, son of man, set your face against the daughters of your people who prophesy out of their own imagination. Prophesy against them 18 and say, 'This is what the Sovereign LORD says: Woe to the women who sew magic charms on all their wrists and make veils of various lengths for their heads in order to ensnare people. Will you ensnare the lives of my people but preserve your own? 19 You have profaned me among my people for a few handfuls of barley and scraps of bread. By lying to my people, who listen to lies, you have killed those who should not have died and have spared those who should not live.

20 "Therefore this is what the Sovereign LORD says: I am against your magic charms with which you ensnare people like birds and I will tear them from your arms; I will set free the people that you ensnare like birds. 21 I will tear off your veils and save my people from your hands, and they will no longer fall prey to your power. Then you will know that I am the LORD. 22 Because you disheartened the righteous with your lies, when I had brought them no grief, and because you encouraged the wicked not to turn from their evil ways and so save their lives, 23 therefore you will no longer see false visions or practice divination. I will save my people from your hands. And then you will know that I am the LORD.'"

Idolaters Condemned

14 Some of the elders of Israel came to me and sat down in front of me. 2 Then the word of the LORD came to me: 3 "Son of man, these men have set up idols in their hearts and put wicked stumbling blocks before their faces. Should I let them inquire of me at all? 4 Therefore speak to them and tell them, 'This is what the Sovereign LORD says: When any Israelite sets up idols in his heart and puts a wicked stumbling block before his face and then goes to a prophet, I the LORD will answer him myself in keeping with his great idolatry. 5 I will do this to recapture the hearts of the people of Israel, who have all deserted me for their idols.'

6 "Therefore say to the house of Israel, 'This is what the Sovereign LORD says: Repent! Turn from your idols and renounce all your detestable practices!

7 "When any Israelite or any alien living in Israel separates himself from me and sets up idols in his heart and puts a wicked stumbling block before his face and then goes to a prophet to inquire of me, I the LORD will answer him myself. 8 I will set my face against that man and make him an example and a byword. I will cut him off from my people. Then you will know that I am the LORD.

9 "And if the prophet is enticed to utter

a 14 Or *the city*

a prophecy, I the LORD have enticed that prophet, and I will stretch out my hand against him and destroy him from among my people Israel. 10They will bear their guilt—the prophet will be as guilty as the one who consults him. 11Then the people of Israel will no longer stray from me, nor will they defile themselves anymore with all their sins. They will be my people, and I will be their God, declares the Sovereign LORD.'"

Judgment Inescapable

12The word of the LORD came to me: 13"Son of man, if a country sins against me by being unfaithful and I stretch out my hand against it to cut off its food supply and send famine upon it and kill its men and their animals, 14even if these three men—Noah, Daniel*a* and Job—were in it, they could save only themselves by their righteousness, declares the Sovereign LORD.

15"Or if I send wild beasts through that country and they leave it childless and it becomes desolate so that no one can pass through it because of the beasts, 16as surely as I live, declares the Sovereign LORD, even if these three men were in it, they could not save their own sons or daughters. They alone would be saved, but the land would be desolate.

17"Or if I bring a sword against that country and say, 'Let the sword pass throughout the land,' and I kill its men and their animals, 18as surely as I live, declares the Sovereign LORD, even if these three men were in it, they could not save their own sons or daughters. They alone would be saved.

19"Or if I send a plague into that land and pour out my wrath upon it through bloodshed, killing its men and their animals, 20as surely as I live, declares the Sovereign LORD, even if Noah, Daniel and Job were in it, they could save neither son nor daughter. They would save only themselves by their righteousness.

21"For this is what the Sovereign LORD says: How much worse will it be when I send against Jerusalem my four dreadful judgments—sword and famine and wild beasts and plague—to kill its men and their animals! 22Yet there will be some survivors—sons and daughters who will be brought out of it. They will come to you, and when you see their conduct and their actions, you will be consoled regarding the disaster I have brought upon Jerusalem—every disaster I have brought upon it. 23You will be consoled when you see their conduct and their actions, for you will know that I have done nothing in it without cause, declares the Sovereign LORD."

Jerusalem, A Useless Vine

15 The word of the LORD came to me: 2"Son of man, how is the wood of a vine better than that of a branch on any of the trees in the forest? 3Is wood ever taken from it to make anything useful? Do they make pegs from it to hang things on? 4And after it is thrown on the fire as fuel and the fire burns both ends and chars the middle, is it then useful for anything? 5If it was not useful for anything when it was whole, how much less can it be made into something useful when the fire has burned it and it is charred?

6"Therefore this is what the Sovereign LORD says: As I have given the wood of the vine among the trees of the forest as fuel for the fire, so will I treat the people living in Jerusalem. 7I will set my face against them. Although they have come out of the fire, the fire will yet consume them. And when I set my face against them, you will know that I am the LORD. 8I will make the land desolate because they have been unfaithful, declares the Sovereign LORD."

An Allegory of Unfaithful Jerusalem

16 The word of the LORD came to me: 2"Son of man, confront Jerusalem with her detestable practices 3and say, 'This is what the Sovereign LORD says to Jerusalem: Your ancestry and birth were in the land of the Canaanites; your father was an Amorite and your mother a Hittite. 4On the day you were born your cord was not cut, nor were you washed with water to make you clean, nor were you rubbed with salt or wrapped in cloths. 5No one looked on you with pity or had compassion enough to do any of these things for you. Rather, you were thrown out into the open field, for on the day you were born you were despised.

6"'Then I passed by and saw you kicking about in your blood, and as you lay there in

*a14 Or *Danel*; the Hebrew spelling may suggest a person other than the prophet Daniel; also in verse 20.*

your blood I said to you, "Live!"[a] 7I made you grow like a plant of the field. You grew up and developed and became the most beautiful of jewels.[b] Your breasts were formed and your hair grew, you who were naked and bare.

8 "'Later I passed by, and when I looked at you and saw that you were old enough for love, I spread the corner of my garment over you and covered your nakedness. I gave you my solemn oath and entered into a covenant with you, declares the Sovereign LORD, and you became mine.

9 "'I bathed[c] you with water and washed the blood from you and put ointments on you. 10I clothed you with an embroidered dress and put leather sandals on you. I dressed you in fine linen and covered you with costly garments. 11I adorned you with jewelry: I put bracelets on your arms and a necklace around your neck, 12and I put a ring on your nose, earrings on your ears and a beautiful crown on your head. 13So you were adorned with gold and silver; your clothes were of fine linen and costly fabric and embroidered cloth. Your food was fine flour, honey and olive oil. You became very beautiful and rose to be a queen. 14And your fame spread among the nations on account of your beauty, because the splendor I had given you made your beauty perfect, declares the Sovereign LORD.

15 "'But you trusted in your beauty and used your fame to become a prostitute. You lavished your favors on anyone who passed by and your beauty became his.[d] 16You took some of your garments to make gaudy high places, where you carried on your prostitution. Such things should not happen, nor should they ever occur. 17You also took the fine jewelry I gave you, the jewelry made of my gold and silver, and you made for yourself male idols and engaged in prostitution with them. 18And you took your embroidered clothes to put on them, and you offered my oil and incense before them. 19Also the food I provided for you—the fine flour, olive oil and honey I gave you to eat—you offered as fragrant incense before them. That is what happened, declares the Sovereign LORD.

20 "'And you took your sons and daughters whom you bore to me and sacrificed them as food to the idols. Was your prostitution not enough? 21You slaughtered my children and sacrificed them[e] to the idols. 22In all your detestable practices and your prostitution you did not remember the days of your youth, when you were naked and bare, kicking about in your blood.

23 "'Woe! Woe to you, declares the Sovereign LORD. In addition to all your other wickedness, 24you built a mound for yourself and made a lofty shrine in every public square. 25At the head of every street you built your lofty shrines and degraded your beauty, offering your body with increasing promiscuity to anyone who passed by. 26You engaged in prostitution with the Egyptians, your lustful neighbors, and provoked me to anger with your increasing promiscuity. 27So I stretched out my hand against you and reduced your territory; I gave you over to the greed of your enemies, the daughters of the Philistines, who were shocked by your lewd conduct. 28You engaged in prostitution with the Assyrians too, because you were insatiable; and even after that, you still were not satisfied. 29Then you increased your promiscuity to include Babylonia,[f] a land of merchants, but even with this you were not satisfied.

30 "'How weak-willed you are, declares the Sovereign LORD, when you do all these things, acting like a brazen prostitute! 31When you built your mounds at the head of every street and made your lofty shrines in every public square, you were unlike a prostitute, because you scorned payment.

32 "'You adulterous wife! You prefer strangers to your own husband! 33Every prostitute receives a fee, but you give gifts to all your lovers, bribing them to come to you from everywhere for your illicit favors. 34So in your prostitution you are the opposite of others; no one runs after you for your favors. You are the very opposite, for you give payment and none is given to you.

35 "'Therefore, you prostitute, hear the word of the LORD! 36This is what the Sovereign LORD says: Because you poured out your wealth[g] and exposed your nakedness in your promiscuity

---

[a]6 A few Hebrew manuscripts, Septuagint and Syriac; most Hebrew manuscripts *"Live!" And as you lay there in your blood I said to you, "Live!"* [b]7 Or *became mature* [c]9 Or *I had bathed* [d]15 Most Hebrew manuscripts; one Hebrew manuscript (see some Septuagint manuscripts) *by. Such a thing should not happen* [e]21 Or *and made them pass through the fire* [f]29 Or *Chaldea* [g]36 Or *lust*

with your lovers, and because of all your detestable idols, and because you gave them your children's blood, 37therefore I am going to gather all your lovers, with whom you found pleasure, those you loved as well as those you hated. I will gather them against you from all around and will strip you in front of them, and they will see all your nakedness. 38I will sentence you to the punishment of women who commit adultery and who shed blood; I will bring upon you the blood vengeance of my wrath and jealous anger. 39Then I will hand you over to your lovers, and they will tear down your mounds and destroy your lofty shrines. They will strip you of your clothes and take your fine jewelry and leave you naked and bare. 40They will bring a mob against you, who will stone you and hack you to pieces with their swords. 41They will burn down your houses and inflict punishment on you in the sight of many women. I will put a stop to your prostitution, and you will no longer pay your lovers. 42Then my wrath against you will subside and my jealous anger will turn away from you; I will be calm and no longer angry.

43"'Because you did not remember the days of your youth but enraged me with all these things, I will surely bring down on your head what you have done, declares the Sovereign LORD. Did you not add lewdness to all your other detestable practices?

44"'Everyone who quotes proverbs will quote this proverb about you: "Like mother, like daughter." 45You are a true daughter of your mother, who despised her husband and her children; and you are a true sister of your sisters, who despised their husbands and their children. Your mother was a Hittite and your father an Amorite. 46Your older sister was Samaria, who lived to the north of you with her daughters; and your younger sister, who lived to the south of you with her daughters, was Sodom. 47You not only walked in their ways and copied their detestable practices, but in all your ways you soon became more depraved than they. 48As surely as I live, declares the Sovereign LORD, your sister Sodom and her daughters never did what you and your daughters have done.

49"'Now this was the sin of your sister Sodom: She and her daughters were arrogant, overfed and unconcerned; they did not help the poor and needy. 50They were haughty and did detestable things before me. Therefore I did away with them as you have seen. 51Samaria did not commit half the sins you did. You have done more detestable things than they, and have made your sisters seem righteous by all these things you have done. 52Bear your disgrace, for you have furnished some justification for your sisters. Because your sins were more vile than theirs, they appear more righteous than you. So then, be ashamed and bear your disgrace, for you have made your sisters appear righteous.

53"'However, I will restore the fortunes of Sodom and her daughters and of Samaria and her daughters, and your fortunes along with them, 54so that you may bear your disgrace and be ashamed of all you have done in giving them comfort. 55And your sisters, Sodom with her daughters and Samaria with her daughters, will return to what they were before; and you and your daughters will return to what you were before. 56You would not even mention your sister Sodom in the day of your pride, 57before your wickedness was uncovered. Even so, you are now scorned by the daughters of Edom[a] and all her neighbors and the daughters of the Philistines—all those around you who despise you. 58You will bear the consequences of your lewdness and your detestable practices, declares the LORD.

59"'This is what the Sovereign LORD says: I will deal with you as you deserve, because you have despised my oath by breaking the covenant. 60Yet I will remember the covenant I made with you in the days of your youth, and I will establish an everlasting covenant with you. 61Then you will remember your ways and be ashamed when you receive your sisters, both those who are older than you and those who are younger. I will give them to you as daughters, but not on the basis of my covenant with you. 62So I will establish my covenant with you, and you will know that I am the LORD. 63Then, when I make atonement for you for all you have done, you will remember and be

a 57 Many Hebrew manuscripts and Syriac; most Hebrew manuscripts, Septuagint and Vulgate Aram

Turn Around

Read: Ezekiel 16:1–63

CHOICES CAN DETERMINE the course of a life. They can establish the legacy of a family. And they can affect the destiny of a nation. Wise choices will bring blessing; foolish ones will bring destruction and pain. Some choices can cost us nearly everything.

This passage tells an allegory of how the people of Jerusalem betrayed God. The language paints a picture of a loving God who had compassion on people who had nothing of their own, who were alone and helpless. God's tender care is beautiful to see. But we are shocked as the story continues. The people betray God—they abandon their Savior and pursue other gods. God's love is spurned by the people's willful and selfish choices.

Maybe you've made some poor choices too. Have you chosen to walk your own road, going against what you know to be right? Has the allure of illicit love, personal ambition, intriguing philosophies or accumulating things or anything else caused you to overlook what is really important? Have you realized yet that God is not going to change the rules or make an exception for you? God will deal with you. There is no getting around that. He loves you too much to leave you to follow your own ways or the ways of the world.

The next choice you make could be the one that changes your life. Instead of going your own way, return to the Lover of your soul. Rather than making choices on a whim, think carefully and wisely. Be honest with God about the mistakes you've made. Let go of your self-centered ways—completely—and turn full-faced toward God. Be intentional. Deliberate. And choose to "offer your bodies as living sacrifices, holy and pleasing to God—this is your spiritual act of worship. Do not conform any longer to the pattern of this world, but be transformed by the renewing of your mind. Then you will be able to test and approve what God's will is—his good, pleasing and perfect will" (Romans 12:1–2).

Go to page 1012 for your next devotional reading.

Tuesday

Ezekiel 16:60–61

"Yet I will remember the covenant I made with you in the days of your youth, and I will establish an everlasting covenant with you. Then you will remember your ways and be ashamed."

reflection

1 How have the choices you have made, good and bad, affected the course of your life?

2 Is there an area of your life in which you need to turn from disobedience? If so, will you do so today?

3 What tangible steps will you take to turn toward God?

RELATED READINGS

Ezekiel 36:24–27;
Hebrews 12:14–29;
1 Peter 3:8–12

"Turn to God from idols. For the sword of His wrath that had been aimed at you has been sheathed into the heart of His Son...Because He has died for you, you were forgiven."

Paris Reidhead

ashamed and never again open your mouth because of your humiliation, declares the Sovereign LORD.'"

Two Eagles and a Vine

17 The word of the LORD came to me: 2"Son of man, set forth an allegory and tell the house of Israel a parable. 3Say to them, 'This is what the Sovereign LORD says: A great eagle with powerful wings, long feathers and full plumage of varied colors came to Lebanon. Taking hold of the top of a cedar, 4he broke off its topmost shoot and carried it away to a land of merchants, where he planted it in a city of traders.

5"'He took some of the seed of your land and put it in fertile soil. He planted it like a willow by abundant water, 6and it sprouted and became a low, spreading vine. Its branches turned toward him, but its roots remained under it. So it became a vine and produced branches and put out leafy boughs.

7"'But there was another great eagle with powerful wings and full plumage. The vine now sent out its roots toward him from the plot where it was planted and stretched out its branches to him for water. 8It had been planted in good soil by abundant water so that it would produce branches, bear fruit and become a splendid vine.'

9"Say to them, 'This is what the Sovereign LORD says: Will it thrive? Will it not be uprooted and stripped of its fruit so that it withers? All its new growth will wither. It will not take a strong arm or many people to pull it up by the roots. 10Even if it is transplanted, will it thrive? Will it not wither completely when the east wind strikes it—wither away in the plot where it grew?'"

11Then the word of the LORD came to me: 12"Say to this rebellious house, 'Do you not know what these things mean?' Say to them: 'The king of Babylon went to Jerusalem and carried off her king and her nobles, bringing them back with him to Babylon. 13Then he took a member of the royal family and made a treaty with him, putting him under oath. He also carried away the leading men of the land, 14so that the kingdom would be brought low, unable to rise again, surviving only by keeping his treaty. 15But the king rebelled against him by sending his envoys to Egypt to get horses and a large army. Will he succeed? Will he who does such things escape? Will he break the treaty and yet escape?

16"'As surely as I live, declares the Sovereign LORD, he shall die in Babylon, in the land of the king who put him on the throne, whose oath he despised and whose treaty he broke. 17Pharaoh with his mighty army and great horde will be of no help to him in war, when ramps are built and siege works erected to destroy many lives. 18He despised the oath by breaking the covenant. Because he had given his hand in pledge and yet did all these things, he shall not escape.

19"'Therefore this is what the Sovereign LORD says: As surely as I live, I will bring down on his head my oath that he despised and my covenant that he broke. 20I will spread my net for him, and he will be caught in my snare. I will bring him to Babylon and execute judgment upon him there because he was unfaithful to me. 21All his fleeing troops will fall by the sword, and the survivors will be scattered to the winds. Then you will know that I the LORD have spoken.

22"'This is what the Sovereign LORD says: I myself will take a shoot from the very top of a cedar and plant it; I will break off a tender sprig from its topmost shoots and plant it on a high and lofty mountain. 23On the mountain heights of Israel I will plant it; it will produce branches and bear fruit and become a splendid cedar. Birds of every kind will nest in it; they will find shelter in the shade of its branches. 24All the trees of the field will know that I the LORD bring down the tall tree and make the low tree grow tall. I dry up the green tree and make the dry tree flourish.

"'I the LORD have spoken, and I will do it.'"

The Soul Who Sins Will Die

18 The word of the LORD came to me: 2"What do you people mean by quoting this proverb about the land of Israel:

"'The fathers eat sour grapes,
    and the children's teeth are set on edge'?

3"As surely as I live, declares the Sovereign LORD, you will no longer quote this proverb in Israel. 4For every living soul belongs to me, the father as well as the son—both alike belong to me. The soul who sins is the one who will die.

⁵ "Suppose there is a
    righteous man
    who does what is just
        and right.
⁶ He does not eat at the
        mountain shrines
    or look to the idols of the
        house of Israel.
    He does not defile his
        neighbor's wife
    or lie with a woman
        during her period.
⁷ He does not oppress
        anyone,
    but returns what he took
        in pledge for a loan.
    He does not commit robbery
    but gives his food to the hungry
    and provides clothing for the naked.
⁸ He does not lend at usury
    or take excessive interest.ᵃ
    He withholds his hand from doing wrong
    and judges fairly between man and man.
⁹ He follows my decrees
    and faithfully keeps my laws.
    That man is righteous;
    he will surely live,
            declares the Sovereign LORD.

¹⁰ "Suppose he has a violent son, who sheds blood or does any of these other thingsᵇ ¹¹(though the father has done none of them):

    "He eats at the mountain shrines.
    He defiles his neighbor's wife.
¹² He oppresses the poor and needy.
    He commits robbery.
    He does not return what he took in pledge.
    He looks to the idols.
    He does detestable things.
¹³ He lends at usury and takes excessive
        interest.

Will such a man live? He will not! Because he has done all these detestable things, he will surely be put to death and his blood will be on his own head.

¹⁴ "But suppose this son has a son who sees

all the sins his father commits, and though he sees them, he does not do such things:

¹⁵ "He does not eat at the
        mountain shrines
    or look to the idols of the
        house of Israel.
    He does not defile his
        neighbor's wife.
¹⁶ He does not oppress
        anyone
    or require a pledge for a
        loan.
    He does not commit
        robbery
    but gives his food to the
        hungry
    and provides clothing for
        the naked.
¹⁷ He withholds his hand from sinᶜ
    and takes no usury or excessive interest.
    He keeps my laws and follows my decrees.

He will not die for his father's sin; he will surely live. ¹⁸But his father will die for his own sin, because he practiced extortion, robbed his brother and did what was wrong among his people.

¹⁹ "Yet you ask, 'Why does the son not share the guilt of his father?' Since the son has done what is just and right and has been careful to keep all my decrees, he will surely live. ²⁰The soul who sins is the one who will die. The son will not share the guilt of the father, nor will the father share the guilt of the son. The righteousness of the righteous man will be credited to him, and the wickedness of the wicked will be charged against him.

²¹ "But if a wicked man turns away from all the sins he has committed and keeps all my decrees and does what is just and right, he will surely live; he will not die. ²²None of the offenses he has committed will be remembered against him. Because of the righteous things he has done, he will live. ²³Do I take any pleasure in the death of the wicked? declares the Sovereign LORD. Rather, am I not pleased when they turn from their ways and live?

²⁴ "But if a righteous man turns from his righteousness and commits sin and does the same detestable things the wicked man does, will he

---

Ezekiel 18:4

God Is Over All

"For every living soul belongs to me, the father as well as the son—both alike belong to me. The soul who sins is the one who will die."

ᵃ8 Or *take interest*; similarly in verses 13 and 17   ᵇ10 Or *things to a brother*   ᶜ17 Septuagint (see also verse 8); Hebrew *from the poor*

1011

Ezekiel 18:18–19

"But his father will die
for his own sin, because
he practiced extortion,
robbed his brother and
did what was wrong
among his people. Yet
you ask, 'Why does the
son not share the guilt
of his father?' Since
the son has done what
is just and right and
has been careful to
keep all my decrees,
he will surely live."

reflection

1 What unhealthy behavioral patterns can you identify in past generations of your family?

2 How do these negative actions impact your life today?

3 How can you begin to establish a new spiritual legacy for yourself and your family?

RELATED READINGS

Leviticus 20:9–12;
Isaiah 58:12;
Matthew 16:27

Read: Ezekiel 18:1–18

SINGER AND AUTHOR STORMIE OMARTIAN has written candidly of the horrors she survived as a child. Stormie's abusive mother was mentally ill. As a result, Stormie was neglected and tragically abused. For much of her early childhood, Stormie remained locked in a closet by her unstable mother, and Stormie's father did nothing to intervene. As an adult, Stormie found hope and healing through her relationship with Jesus Christ. She chose to walk a different path than her parents and in faith guide her children down a godly path.

Perhaps you can relate to Stormie's story. Maybe you grew up in a dysfunctional, abusive or unbelieving home and are tempted to believe that you are destined to repeat the same unhealthy behaviors you witnessed there. Just as heart disease or breast cancer can run in a family, sometimes behavior modeled by certain influential family members can spread throughout the entire family. However, Scripture makes it clear that we are not doomed to repeat the mistakes of others. We can be liberated from the bondage of sin through the freedom found in the perfect role model, Jesus Christ. Jesus said, "So if the Son sets you free, you will be free indeed" (John 8:36). The key is to walk in freedom and faith, obedience and blessing.

While God does not *punish* us for the sins of our family members or caregivers, their sins may cause us to be more likely to make poor choices, exhibit unhealthy patterns or otherwise suffer from their actions. We must remember that we are not responsible for their wrongs. Although affected, we are not condemned because we grew up in an abusive or unbelieving home. Nor are we saved by the faith of godly parents. Each one of us is accountable before God for our own actions.

If someone's sins against you have resulted in fear, unforgiveness or despair, take courage from the fact that God's grace is greater than any wrong. Step into the freedom he has for you today.

Wednesday

 Go to page 1018 for your next devotional reading.

live? None of the righteous things he has done will be remembered. Because of the unfaithfulness he is guilty of and because of the sins he has committed, he will die.

25 "Yet you say, 'The way of the Lord is not just.' Hear, O house of Israel: Is my way unjust? Is it not your ways that are unjust? 26 If a righteous man turns from his righteousness and commits sin, he will die for it; because of the sin he has committed he will die. 27 But if a wicked man turns away from the wickedness he has committed and does what is just and right, he will save his life. 28 Because he considers all the offenses he has committed and turns away from them, he will surely live; he will not die. 29 Yet the house of Israel says, 'The way of the Lord is not just.' Are my ways unjust, O house of Israel? Is it not your ways that are unjust?

30 "Therefore, O house of Israel, I will judge you, each one according to his ways, declares the Sovereign Lord. Repent! Turn away from all your offenses; then sin will not be your downfall. 31 Rid yourselves of all the offenses you have committed, and get a new heart and a new spirit. Why will you die, O house of Israel? 32 For I take no pleasure in the death of anyone, declares the Sovereign Lord. Repent and live!

A Lament for Israel's Princes

19 "Take up a lament concerning the princes of Israel 2 and say:

"'What a lioness was your mother
    among the lions!
She lay down among the young lions
    and reared her cubs.
3 She brought up one of her cubs,
    and he became a strong lion.
He learned to tear the prey
    and he devoured men.
4 The nations heard about him,
    and he was trapped in their pit.
They led him with hooks
    to the land of Egypt.

5 "'When she saw her hope unfulfilled,
    her expectation gone,
she took another of her cubs
    and made him a strong lion.
6 He prowled among the lions,

for he was now a strong lion.
He learned to tear the prey
    and he devoured men.
7 He broke down[a] their strongholds
    and devastated their towns.
The land and all who were in it
    were terrified by his roaring.
8 Then the nations came against him,
    those from regions round about.
They spread their net for him,
    and he was trapped in their pit.
9 With hooks they pulled him into a cage
    and brought him to the king of Babylon.
They put him in prison,
    so his roar was heard no longer
    on the mountains of Israel.

10 "'Your mother was like a vine in your
        vineyard[b]
    planted by the water;
it was fruitful and full of branches
    because of abundant water.
11 Its branches were strong,
    fit for a ruler's scepter.
It towered high
    above the thick foliage,
conspicuous for its height
    and for its many branches.
12 But it was uprooted in fury
    and thrown to the ground.
The east wind made it shrivel,
    it was stripped of its fruit;
its strong branches withered
    and fire consumed them.
13 Now it is planted in the desert,
    in a dry and thirsty land.
14 Fire spread from one of its main[c] branches
    and consumed its fruit.
No strong branch is left on it
    fit for a ruler's scepter.'

This is a lament and is to be used as a lament."

Rebellious Israel

20 In the seventh year, in the fifth month on the tenth day, some of the elders of Israel came to inquire of the Lord, and they sat down in front of me.

2 Then the word of the Lord came to me: 3 "Son of man, speak to the elders of Israel

---

a 7 Targum (see Septuagint); Hebrew He knew   b 10 Two Hebrew manuscripts; most Hebrew manuscripts your blood   c 14 Or from under its and say to them, 'This is what the Sovereign LORD says: Have you come to inquire of me? As surely as I live, I will not let you inquire of me, declares the Sovereign LORD.'

⁴"Will you judge them? Will you judge them, son of man? Then confront them with the detestable practices of their fathers ⁵and say to them: 'This is what the Sovereign LORD says: On the day I chose Israel, I swore with uplifted hand to the descendants of the house of Jacob and revealed myself to them in Egypt. With uplifted hand I said to them, "I am the LORD your God." ⁶On that day I swore to them that I would bring them out of Egypt into a land I had searched out for them, a land flowing with milk and honey, the most beautiful of all lands. ⁷And I said to them, "Each of you, get rid of the vile images you have set your eyes on, and do not defile yourselves with the idols of Egypt. I am the LORD your God."

⁸"But they rebelled against me and would not listen to me; they did not get rid of the vile images they had set their eyes on, nor did they forsake the idols of Egypt. So I said I would pour out my wrath on them and spend my anger against them in Egypt. ⁹But for the sake of my name I did what would keep it from being profaned in the eyes of the nations they lived among and in whose sight I had revealed myself to the Israelites by bringing them out of Egypt. ¹⁰Therefore I led them out of Egypt and brought them into the desert. ¹¹I gave them my decrees and made known to them my laws, for the man who obeys them will live by them. ¹²Also I gave them my Sabbaths as a sign between us, so they would know that I the LORD made them holy.

¹³"Yet the people of Israel rebelled against me in the desert. They did not follow my decrees but rejected my laws—although the man who obeys them will live by them—and they utterly desecrated my Sabbaths. So I said I would pour out my wrath on them and destroy them in the desert. ¹⁴But for the sake of my name I

did what would keep it from being profaned in the eyes of the nations in whose sight I had brought them out. ¹⁵Also with uplifted hand I swore to them in the desert that I would not bring them into the land I had given them—a land flowing with milk and honey, most beautiful of all lands— ¹⁶because they rejected my laws and did not follow my decrees and desecrated my Sabbaths. For their hearts were devoted to their idols. ¹⁷Yet I looked on them with pity and did not destroy them or put an end to them in the desert. ¹⁸I said to their children in the desert, "Do not follow the statutes of your fathers or keep their laws or defile yourselves with their idols. ¹⁹I am the LORD your God; follow my decrees and be careful to keep my laws. ²⁰Keep my Sabbaths holy, that they may be a sign between us. Then you will know that I am the LORD your God."

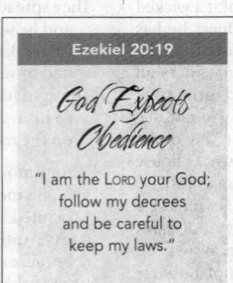

Ezekiel 20:19

God Expects Obedience

"I am the LORD your God; follow my decrees and be careful to keep my laws."

²¹"But the children rebelled against me: They did not follow my decrees, they were not careful to keep my laws—although the man who obeys them will live by them—and they desecrated my Sabbaths. So I said I would pour out my wrath on them and spend my anger against them in the desert. ²²But I withheld my hand, and for the sake of my name I did what would keep it from being profaned in the eyes of the nations in whose sight I had brought them out. ²³Also with uplifted hand I swore to them in the desert that I would disperse them among the nations and scatter them through the countries, ²⁴because they had not obeyed my laws but had rejected my decrees and desecrated my Sabbaths, and their eyes lusted after their fathers' idols. ²⁵I also gave them over to statutes that were not good and laws they could not live by; ²⁶I let them become defiled through their gifts—the sacrifice of every firstborn*a*—that I might fill them with horror so they would know that I am the LORD.'

²⁷"Therefore, son of man, speak to the people of Israel and say to them, 'This is what the Sovereign LORD says: In this also your fathers

---

a26 Or *—making every firstborn pass through the fire*

blasphemed me by forsaking me: ²⁸When I brought them into the land I had sworn to give them and they saw any high hill or any leafy tree, there they offered their sacrifices, made offerings that provoked me to anger, presented their fragrant incense and poured out their drink offerings. ²⁹Then I said to them: What is this high place you go to?'" (It is called Bamah^a to this day.)

Judgment and Restoration

³⁰"Therefore say to the house of Israel: 'This is what the Sovereign LORD says: Will you defile yourselves the way your fathers did and lust after their vile images? ³¹When you offer your gifts—the sacrifice of your sons in^b the fire—you continue to defile yourselves with all your idols to this day. Am I to let you inquire of me, O house of Israel? As surely as I live, declares the Sovereign LORD, I will not let you inquire of me.

³²"'You say, "We want to be like the nations, like the peoples of the world, who serve wood and stone." But what you have in mind will never happen. ³³As surely as I live, declares the Sovereign LORD, I will rule over you with a mighty hand and an outstretched arm and with outpoured wrath. ³⁴I will bring you from the nations and gather you from the countries where you have been scattered—with a mighty hand and an outstretched arm and with outpoured wrath. ³⁵I will bring you into the desert of the nations and there, face to face, I will execute judgment upon you. ³⁶As I judged your fathers in the desert of the land of Egypt, so I will judge you, declares the Sovereign LORD. ³⁷I will take note of you as you pass under my rod, and I will bring you into the bond of the covenant. ³⁸I will purge you of those who revolt and rebel against me. Although I will bring them out of the land where they are living, yet they will not enter the land of Israel. Then you will know that I am the LORD.

³⁹"'As for you, O house of Israel, this is what the Sovereign LORD says: Go and serve your idols, every one of you! But afterward you will surely listen to me and no longer profane my holy name with your gifts and idols. ⁴⁰For on my holy mountain, the high mountain of Israel, declares the Sovereign LORD, there in the land the entire house of Israel will serve me, and there I will accept them. There I will require your offerings and your choice gifts,^c along with all your holy sacrifices. ⁴¹I will accept you as fragrant incense when I bring you out from the nations and gather you from the countries where you have been scattered, and I will show myself holy among you in the sight of the nations. ⁴²Then you will know that I am the LORD, when I bring you into the land of Israel, the land I had sworn with uplifted hand to give to your fathers. ⁴³There you will remember your conduct and all the actions by which you have defiled yourselves, and you will loathe yourselves for all the evil you have done. ⁴⁴You will know that I am the LORD, when I deal with you for my name's sake and not according to your evil ways and your corrupt practices, O house of Israel, declares the Sovereign LORD.'"

Prophecy Against the South

⁴⁵The word of the LORD came to me: ⁴⁶"Son of man, set your face toward the south; preach against the south and prophesy against the forest of the southland. ⁴⁷Say to the southern forest: 'Hear the word of the LORD. This is what the Sovereign LORD says: I am about to set fire to you, and it will consume all your trees, both green and dry. The blazing flame will not be quenched, and every face from south to north will be scorched by it. ⁴⁸Everyone will see that I the LORD have kindled it; it will not be quenched.'"

⁴⁹Then I said, "Ah, Sovereign LORD! They are saying of me, 'Isn't he just telling parables?'"

Babylon, God's Sword of Judgment

21 The word of the LORD came to me: ²"Son of man, set your face against Jerusalem and preach against the sanctuary. Prophesy against the land of Israel ³and say to her: 'This is what the LORD says: I am against you. I will draw my sword from its scabbard and cut off from you both the righteous and the wicked. ⁴Because I am going to cut off the righteous and the wicked, my sword will be unsheathed against everyone from south to north. ⁵Then all people will know that I the

---

^a29 *Bamah* means *high place.*   ^b31 Or *—making your sons pass through*   ^c40 Or *and the gifts of your firstfruits*

Lᴏʀᴅ have drawn my sword from its scabbard; it will not return again.'

6"Therefore groan, son of man! Groan before them with broken heart and bitter grief. 7And when they ask you, 'Why are you groaning?' you shall say, 'Because of the news that is coming. Every heart will melt and every hand go limp; every spirit will become faint and every knee become as weak as water.' It is coming! It will surely take place, declares the Sovereign Lᴏʀᴅ."

8The word of the Lᴏʀᴅ came to me: 9"Son of man, prophesy and say, 'This is what the Lord says:

"'A sword, a sword,
    sharpened and polished—
10sharpened for the slaughter,
    polished to flash like lightning!

"'Shall we rejoice in the scepter of my son Judah ? The sword despises every such stick.

11"'The sword is appointed to be polished,
    to be grasped with the hand;
it is sharpened and polished,
    made ready for the hand of the slayer.
12Cry out and wail, son of man,
    for it is against my people;
it is against all the princes of Israel.
They are thrown to the sword
    along with my people.
Therefore beat your breast.

13"'Testing will surely come. And what if the scepter of Judah, which the sword despises, does not continue? declares the Sovereign Lᴏʀᴅ.'

14"So then, son of man, prophesy
    and strike your hands together.
Let the sword strike twice,
    even three times.
It is a sword for slaughter—
    a sword for great slaughter,
    closing in on them from every side.
15So that hearts may melt
    and the fallen be many,
I have stationed the sword for slaughter*a*
    at all their gates.
Oh! It is made to flash like lightning,

it is grasped for slaughter.
16O sword, slash to the right,
    then to the left,
    wherever your blade is turned.
17I too will strike my hands together,
    and my wrath will subside.
I the Lᴏʀᴅ have spoken."

18The word of the Lᴏʀᴅ came to me: 19"Son of man, mark out two roads for the sword of the king of Babylon to take, both starting from the same country. Make a signpost where the road branches off to the city. 20Mark out one road for the sword to come against Rabbah of the Ammonites and another against Judah and fortified Jerusalem. 21For the king of Babylon will stop at the fork in the road, at the junction of the two roads, to seek an omen: He will cast lots with arrows, he will consult his idols, he will examine the liver. 22Into his right hand will come the lot for Jerusalem, where he is to set up battering rams, to give the command to slaughter, to sound the battle cry, to set battering rams against the gates, to build a ramp and to erect siege works. 23It will seem like a false omen to those who have sworn allegiance to him, but he will remind them of their guilt and take them captive.

24"Therefore this is what the Sovereign Lᴏʀᴅ says: 'Because you people have brought to mind your guilt by your open rebellion, revealing your sins in all that you do—because you have done this, you will be taken captive.

25"'O profane and wicked prince of Israel, whose day has come, whose time of punishment has reached its climax, 26this is what the Sovereign Lᴏʀᴅ says: Take off the turban, remove the crown. It will not be as it was: The lowly will be exalted and the exalted will be brought low. 27A ruin! A ruin! I will make it a ruin! It will not be restored until he comes to whom it rightfully belongs; to him I will give it.'

28"And you, son of man, prophesy and say, 'This is what the Sovereign Lᴏʀᴅ says about the Ammonites and their insults:

"'A sword, a sword,
    drawn for the slaughter,
    polished to consume

a15 Septuagint; the meaning of the Hebrew for this word is uncertain.

and to flash like lightning!
²⁹ Despite false visions concerning you
    and lying divinations about you,
it will be laid on the necks
    of the wicked who are to be slain,
whose day has come,
    whose time of punishment has reached
      its climax.
³⁰ Return the sword to its scabbard.
    In the place where you were created,
in the land of your ancestry,
    I will judge you.
³¹ I will pour out my wrath upon you
    and breathe out my fiery
      anger against you;
I will hand you over to
    brutal men,
    men skilled in
      destruction.
³² You will be fuel for the fire,
    your blood will be shed
      in your land,
you will be remembered no
    more;
    for I the Lord have
      spoken.' "

Jerusalem's Sins

22 The word of the Lord came to me: ²"Son of man, will you judge her? Will you judge this city of bloodshed? Then confront her with all her detestable practices ³and say: 'This is what the Sovereign Lord says: O city that brings on herself doom by shedding blood in her midst and defiles herself by making idols, ⁴you have become guilty because of the blood you have shed and have become defiled by the idols you have made. You have brought your days to a close, and the end of your years has come. Therefore I will make you an object of scorn to the nations and a laughingstock to all the countries. ⁵Those who are near and those who are far away will mock you, O infamous city, full of turmoil.

⁶ "See how each of the princes of Israel who are in you uses his power to shed blood. ⁷In you they have treated father and mother with contempt; in you they have oppressed the alien and mistreated the fatherless and the widow. ⁸You have despised my holy things and desecrated my Sabbaths. ⁹In you are slanderous men bent on shedding blood; in you are those who eat at the mountain shrines and commit lewd acts. ¹⁰In you are those who dishonor their fathers' bed; in you are those who violate women during their period, when they are ceremonially unclean. ¹¹In you one man commits a detestable offense with his neighbor's wife, another shamefully defiles his daughter-in-law, and another violates his sister, his own father's daughter. ¹²In you men accept bribes to shed blood; you take usury and excessive interest*ᵃ* and make unjust gain from your neighbors by extortion. And you have forgotten me, declares the Sovereign Lord.

¹³ "I will surely strike my hands together at the unjust gain you have made and at the blood you have shed in your midst. ¹⁴Will your courage endure or your hands be strong in the day I deal with you? I the Lord have spoken, and I will do it. ¹⁵I will disperse you among the nations and scatter you through the countries; and I will put an end to your uncleanness. ¹⁶When you have been defiled*ᵇ* in the eyes of the nations, you will know that I am the Lord.' "

¹⁷ Then the word of the Lord came to me: ¹⁸"Son of man, the house of Israel has become dross to me; all of them are the copper, tin, iron and lead left inside a furnace. They are but the dross of silver. ¹⁹Therefore this is what the Sovereign Lord says: 'Because you have all become dross, I will gather you into Jerusalem. ²⁰As men gather silver, copper, iron, lead and tin into a furnace to melt it with a fiery blast, so will I gather you in my anger and my wrath and put you inside the city and melt you. ²¹I will gather you and I will blow on you with my fiery wrath, and you will be melted inside her. ²²As silver is melted in a furnace, so you will be melted inside her, and you will know that I the Lord have poured out my wrath upon you.' "

²³ Again the word of the Lord came to me: ²⁴"Son of man, say to the land, 'You are a land

Ezekiel 22:14

God Follows Through

"Will your courage endure or your hands be strong in the day I deal with you? I the Lord have spoken, and I will do it."

ᵃ 12 Or *usury and interest*   ᵇ 16 Or *When I have allotted you your inheritance*

Ezekiel 22:22

"As silver is melted in a
furnace, so you will be
melted inside her, and
you will know that I the
LORD have poured out
my wrath upon you."

reflection

1 How do you think suffering can strengthen
your relationship with
God?

2 Have you experienced
pain that drew you
closer to God?

3 What would it be like
for you to embrace the
difficult things of your life
today—physical pain, a
strained relationship or a
major disappointment—as
part of God's redemptive
work in you?

RELATED READINGS

Psalm 103:1–22;
Zechariah 7:8–14;
Revelation 20:1–4

*"Suffering is the
very best gift God
has to give us.
He gives it only to
his chosen friends."*

Therese of Liseux

Read: Ezekiel 22:17–22

HOW DO YOU EXPLAIN the presence of pain?

In his book *Celebrating the Wrath of God*, Jim McGuiggan
writes of a young Christian couple who longed to have a baby.
After years of prayer, they finally had a child, but the little one had
severe spina bifida and did not live long. How could God allow
such loss? McGuiggan writes that as long as we continue to think
of God as a warm and fuzzy deity, we will be unable to understand
the presence of pain in the world and the power of God to redeem
our pain.

It may seem easier to focus on the "nice" passages of Scripture
that speak clearly of God's love; however, to ignore the passages
about God's anger, vengeance and jealousy is to miss who God
is. In Ezekiel 22, the prophet speaks hard truth to the nation of
Israel. It may have been easier for Israel to hear of God's affection
for them, but that would have been counter to God's nature. God
hates anything and everything that destroys the people and the
world he created. He is angry with those who participate in that
destruction. He is jealous of anything that breaks his covenant of
love with his people. God loves what he created, and he will pour
out his righteous wrath as a reflection of that love. Read that again,
slowly.

Sin alters the created order so significantly that it leads to the
sickness, disease, sadness, stress and fatigue that we experience.
God hates all the sin and sorrow that causes suffering and has sent
the Messiah to redeem the world from it. The good news is that
suffering can point us to God's power to console and redeem.

Just as the Israelites in Ezekiel's time suffered, we, too, will
suffer . . . it's a Biblical promise: "It has been granted to you on behalf of Christ not only to believe on him, but also to suffer for him"
(Philippians 1:29). Sometimes suffering is the direct result of our
sin. Sometimes suffering is simply a consequence of the fact that
we are fragile human beings. Sometimes we suffer as the result of
other people's sins. But while we live on this earth, we will endure
pain and suffering. Won't you allow God to use your pain to draw
you closer to him?

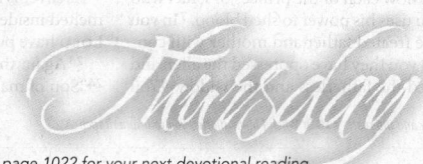
Thursday

Go to page 1022 for your next devotional reading.

that has had no rain or showers*a* in the day of wrath.' 25There is a conspiracy of her princes*b* within her like a roaring lion tearing its prey; they devour people, take treasures and precious things and make many widows within her. 26Her priests do violence to my law and profane my holy things; they do not distinguish between the holy and the common; they teach that there is no difference between the unclean and the clean; and they shut their eyes to the keeping of my Sabbaths, so that I am profaned among them. 27Her officials within her are like wolves tearing their prey; they shed blood and kill people to make unjust gain. 28Her prophets whitewash these deeds for them by false visions and lying divinations. They say, 'This is what the Sovereign LORD says'—when the LORD has not spoken. 29The people of the land practice extortion and commit robbery; they oppress the poor and needy and mistreat the alien, denying them justice.

30"I looked for a man among them who would build up the wall and stand before me in the gap on behalf of the land so I would not have to destroy it, but I found none. 31So I will pour out my wrath on them and consume them with my fiery anger, bringing down on their own heads all they have done, declares the Sovereign LORD."

Two Adulterous Sisters

23 The word of the LORD came to me: 2"Son of man, there were two women, daughters of the same mother. 3They became prostitutes in Egypt, engaging in prostitution from their youth. In that land their breasts were fondled and their virgin bosoms caressed. 4The older was named Oholah, and her sister was Oholibah. They were mine and gave birth to sons and daughters. Oholah is Samaria, and Oholibah is Jerusalem.

5"Oholah engaged in prostitution while she was still mine; and she lusted after her lovers, the Assyrians—warriors 6clothed in blue, governors and commanders, all of them handsome young men, and mounted horsemen. 7She gave herself as a prostitute to all the elite of the Assyrians and defiled herself with all the idols of everyone she lusted after. 8She did not give up the prostitution she began in Egypt, when during her youth men slept with her, caressed her virgin bosom and poured out their lust upon her.

9"Therefore I handed her over to her lovers, the Assyrians, for whom she lusted. 10They stripped her naked, took away her sons and daughters and killed her with the sword. She became a byword among women, and punishment was inflicted on her.

11"Her sister Oholibah saw this, yet in her lust and prostitution she was more depraved than her sister. 12She too lusted after the Assyrians—governors and commanders, warriors in full dress, mounted horsemen, all handsome young men. 13I saw that she too defiled herself; both of them went the same way.

14"But she carried her prostitution still further. She saw men portrayed on a wall, figures of Chaldeans*c* portrayed in red, 15with belts around their waists and flowing turbans on their heads; all of them looked like Babylonian chariot officers, natives of Chaldea.*d* 16As soon as she saw them, she lusted after them and sent messengers to them in Chaldea. 17Then the Babylonians came to her, to the bed of love, and in their lust they defiled her. After she had been defiled by them, she turned away from them in disgust. 18When she carried on her prostitution openly and exposed her nakedness, I turned away from her in disgust, just as I had turned away from her sister. 19Yet she became more and more promiscuous as she recalled the days of her youth, when she was a prostitute in Egypt. 20There she lusted after her lovers, whose genitals were like those of donkeys and whose emission was like that of horses. 21So you longed for the lewdness of your youth, when in Egypt your bosom was caressed and your young breasts fondled.*e*

22"Therefore, Oholibah, this is what the Sovereign LORD says: I will stir up your lovers against you, those you turned away from in disgust, and I will bring them against you from every side— 23the Babylonians and all the Chaldeans, the men of Pekod and Shoa and Koa, and all the Assyrians with them, handsome young men, all of them governors

---

*a*24 Septuagint; Hebrew *has not been cleansed or rained on*   *b*25 Septuagint; Hebrew *prophets*   *c*14 Or *Babylonians*   *d*15 Or *Babylonia*; also in verse 16   *e*21 Syriac (see also verse 3); Hebrew *caressed because of your young breasts* and commanders, chariot officers and men of high rank, all mounted on horses. [24]They will come against you with weapons,[a] chariots and wagons and with a throng of people; they will take up positions against you on every side with large and small shields and with helmets. I will turn you over to them for punishment, and they will punish you according to their standards. [25]I will direct my jealous anger against you, and they will deal with you in fury. They will cut off your noses and your ears, and those of you who are left will fall by the sword. They will take away your sons and daughters, and those of you who are left will be consumed by fire. [26]They will also strip you of your clothes and take your fine jewelry. [27]So I will put a stop to the lewdness and prostitution you began in Egypt. You will not look on these things with longing or remember Egypt anymore.

[28]"For this is what the Sovereign LORD says: I am about to hand you over to those you hate, to those you turned away from in disgust. [29]They will deal with you in hatred and take away everything you have worked for. They will leave you naked and bare, and the shame of your prostitution will be exposed. Your lewdness and promiscuity [30]have brought this upon you, because you lusted after the nations and defiled yourself with their idols. [31]You have gone the way of your sister; so I will put her cup into your hand.

[32]This is what the Sovereign LORD says:

> "You will drink your sister's cup,
> a cup large and deep;
> it will bring scorn and derision,
> for it holds so much.
> [33]You will be filled with drunkenness and
> sorrow,
> the cup of ruin and desolation,
> the cup of your sister Samaria.
> [34]You will drink it and drain it dry;
> you will dash it to pieces
> and tear your breasts.

I have spoken, declares the Sovereign LORD.

[35]"Therefore this is what the Sovereign LORD says: Since you have forgotten me and thrust me behind your back, you must bear the consequences of your lewdness and prostitution."

[36]The LORD said to me: "Son of man, will you judge Oholah and Oholibah? Then confront them with their detestable practices, [37]for they have committed adultery and blood is on their hands. They committed adultery with their idols; they even sacrificed their children, whom they bore to me,[b] as food for them. [38]They have also done this to me: At that same time they defiled my sanctuary and desecrated my Sabbaths. [39]On the very day they sacrificed their children to their idols, they entered my sanctuary and desecrated it. That is what they did in my house.

[40]"They even sent messengers for men who came from far away, and when they arrived you bathed yourself for them, painted your eyes and put on your jewelry. [41]You sat on an elegant couch, with a table spread before it on which you had placed the incense and oil that belonged to me.

[42]"The noise of a carefree crowd was around her; Sabeans[c] were brought from the desert along with men from the rabble, and they put bracelets on the arms of the woman and her sister and beautiful crowns on their heads. [43]Then I said about the one worn out by adultery, 'Now let them use her as a prostitute, for that is all she is.' [44]And they slept with her. As men sleep with a prostitute, so they slept with those lewd women, Oholah and Oholibah. [45]But righteous men will sentence them to the punishment of women who commit adultery and shed blood, because they are adulterous and blood is on their hands.

[46]"This is what the Sovereign LORD says: Bring a mob against them and give them over to terror and plunder. [47]The mob will stone them and cut them down with their swords; they will kill their sons and daughters and burn down their houses.

[48]"So I will put an end to lewdness in the land, that all women may take warning and not imitate you. [49]You will suffer the penalty for your lewdness and bear the consequences of your sins of idolatry. Then you will know that I am the Sovereign LORD."

---

[a]24 The meaning of the Hebrew for this word is uncertain.   [b]37 Or *even made the children they bore to me pass through the fire*,   [c]42 Or *drunkards*

The Cooking Pot

24 In the ninth year, in the tenth month on the tenth day, the word of the LORD came to me: **2**"Son of man, record this date, this very date, because the king of Babylon has laid siege to Jerusalem this very day. **3**Tell this rebellious house a parable and say to them: 'This is what the Sovereign LORD says:

"'Put on the cooking pot; put it on
    and pour water into it.
4 Put into it the pieces of meat,
    all the choice pieces—the leg and the
        shoulder.
Fill it with the best of these bones;
5   take the pick of the flock.
Pile wood beneath it for the bones;
    bring it to a boil
    and cook the bones in it.

6"'For this is what the Sovereign LORD says:

"'Woe to the city of bloodshed,
    to the pot now encrusted,
    whose deposit will not go away!
Empty it piece by piece
    without casting lots for them.

7"'For the blood she shed is in her midst:
    She poured it on the bare rock;
she did not pour it on the ground,
    where the dust would cover it.
8 To stir up wrath and take revenge
    I put her blood on the bare rock,
    so that it would not be covered.

9"'Therefore this is what the Sovereign LORD says:

"'Woe to the city of bloodshed!
    I, too, will pile the wood high.
10 So heap on the wood
    and kindle the fire.
Cook the meat well,
    mixing in the spices;
    and let the bones be charred.
11 Then set the empty pot on the coals
    till it becomes hot and its copper
        glows
so its impurities may be melted
    and its deposit burned away.
12 It has frustrated all efforts;

its heavy deposit has not been removed,
    not even by fire.

13"'Now your impurity is lewdness. Because I tried to cleanse you but you would not be cleansed from your impurity, you will not be clean again until my wrath against you has subsided.

14"'I the LORD have spoken. The time has come for me to act. I will not hold back; I will not have pity, nor will I relent. You will be judged according to your conduct and your actions, declares the Sovereign LORD.'"

Ezekiel's Wife Dies

15The word of the LORD came to me: **16**"Son of man, with one blow I am about to take away from you the delight of your eyes. Yet do not lament or weep or shed any tears. **17**Groan quietly; do not mourn for the dead. Keep your turban fastened and your sandals on your feet; do not cover the lower part of your face or eat the customary food ₍of mourners₎."

18So I spoke to the people in the morning, and in the evening my wife died. The next morning I did as I had been commanded.

19Then the people asked me, "Won't you tell us what these things have to do with us?"

20So I said to them, "The word of the LORD came to me: **21**Say to the house of Israel, 'This is what the Sovereign LORD says: I am about to desecrate my sanctuary—the stronghold in which you take pride, the delight of your eyes, the object of your affection. The sons and daughters you left behind will fall by the sword. **22**And you will do as I have done. You will not cover the lower part of your face or eat the customary food ₍of mourners₎. **23**You will keep your turbans on your heads and your sandals on your feet. You will not mourn or weep but will waste away because of *a* your sins and groan among yourselves. **24**Ezekiel will be a sign to you; you will do just as he has done. When this happens, you will know that I am the Sovereign LORD.'

25"And you, son of man, on the day I take away their stronghold, their joy and glory, the delight of their eyes, their heart's desire, and their sons and daughters as well— **26**on that day a fugitive will come to tell you the news.

*a*23 Or *away in*

Ezekiel 24:18

So I spoke to the people in the morning, and in the evening my wife died. The next morning I did as I had been commanded.

reflection

1 How do you think that Ezekiel was able to do what God asked?

2 What do you think the people learned from Ezekiel's actions?

3 What can others learn about God from watching how you handle life's challenges?

RELATED READINGS

Ezekiel 12:9–11;
Matthew 5:16;
Luke 11:30;
1 Timothy 4:15–16;
1 Peter 2:12

Read: Ezekiel 24:15–27

IMAGES OF JOHN F. KENNEDY'S assassination on November 22, 1963, are seared on many people's memories. We remember the Dallas motorcade, with the Camelot couple smiling and waving. We remember Jackie in her pink suit and pillbox hat. Then the shock of the shots from the Texas School Book Depository. Who can forget the dignified stance of Jacqueline Kennedy or the heart-wrenching icon of John Jr. standing at attention, saluting his father's flag-draped casket as it passed by on the horse-drawn caisson? Though the family's loss was very public, their grief was dignified and private.

When God told Ezekiel that his wife, whom he deeply loved, was going to die, it had the same sense of tragedy. And Ezekiel, too, was required to deal with his sorrow before a watching world.

God used Ezekiel's tragedy as a symbol that the Israelite people could learn from. His wife's death foreshadowed a time when the sanctuary would be desecrated and the people's children would be killed. God insisted that Ezekiel not grieve his loss publicly, only privately. When the people asked why Ezekiel was not grieving, he was able to explain God's prophecy: The people would not be able to publicly mourn their losses. Instead, they would privately grieve over their own sin that caused such destruction. Ezekiel's loss was altogether real, deep and painful. Yet God used that experience.

God used Ezekiel as a signpost to direct others to him and to help them know he was the Lord (verse 27). Ezekiel said, "I did as I had been commanded," and he turned his tragedy into a life that pointed to God. Our lives also have the potential to reveal who God is. While an entire nation might not be watching, those closest to us are key viewers when it comes to watching the drama of our lives unfold. How we handle a number of plots—loss, success, friendship, marriage, finances—gives others an opportunity to see the difference that being a disciple of Jesus makes.

²⁷At that time your mouth will be opened; you will speak with him and will no longer be silent. So you will be a sign to them, and they will know that I am the LORD."

A Prophecy Against Ammon

25 The word of the LORD came to me: ²"Son of man, set your face against the Ammonites and prophesy against them. ³Say to them, 'Hear the word of the Sovereign LORD. This is what the Sovereign LORD says: Because you said "Aha!" over my sanctuary when it was desecrated and over the land of Israel when it was laid waste and over the people of Judah when they went into exile, ⁴therefore I am going to give you to the people of the East as a possession. They will set up their camps and pitch their tents among you; they will eat your fruit and drink your milk. ⁵I will turn Rabbah into a pasture for camels and Ammon into a resting place for sheep. Then you will know that I am the LORD. ⁶For this is what the Sovereign LORD says: Because you have clapped your hands and stamped your feet, rejoicing with all the malice of your heart against the land of Israel, ⁷therefore I will stretch out my hand against you and give you as plunder to the nations. I will cut you off from the nations and exterminate you from the countries. I will destroy you, and you will know that I am the LORD.'

A Prophecy Against Moab

⁸"This is what the Sovereign LORD says: 'Because Moab and Seir said, "Look, the house of Judah has become like all the other nations," ⁹therefore I will expose the flank of Moab, beginning at its frontier towns—Beth Jeshimoth, Baal Meon and Kiriathaim—the glory of that land. ¹⁰I will give Moab along with the Ammonites to the people of the East as a possession, so that the Ammonites will not be remembered among the nations; ¹¹and I will inflict punishment on Moab. Then they will know that I am the LORD.'"

A Prophecy Against Edom

¹²"This is what the Sovereign LORD says: 'Because Edom took revenge on the house of Judah and became very guilty by doing so, ¹³therefore this is what the Sovereign LORD

says: I will stretch out my hand against Edom and kill its men and their animals. I will lay it waste, and from Teman to Dedan they will fall by the sword. ¹⁴I will take vengeance on Edom by the hand of my people Israel, and they will deal with Edom in accordance with my anger and my wrath; they will know my vengeance, declares the Sovereign LORD.'"

A Prophecy Against Philistia

¹⁵"This is what the Sovereign LORD says: 'Because the Philistines acted in vengeance and took revenge with malice in their hearts, and with ancient hostility sought to destroy Judah, ¹⁶therefore this is what the Sovereign LORD says: I am about to stretch out my hand against the Philistines, and I will cut off the Kerethites and destroy those remaining along the coast. ¹⁷I will carry out great vengeance on them and punish them in my wrath. Then they will know that I am the LORD, when I take vengeance on them.'"

A Prophecy Against Tyre

26 In the eleventh year, on the first day of the month, the word of the LORD came to me: ²"Son of man, because Tyre has said of Jerusalem, 'Aha! The gate to the nations is broken, and its doors have swung open to me; now that she lies in ruins I will prosper,' ³therefore this is what the Sovereign LORD says: I am against you, O Tyre, and I will bring many nations against you, like the sea casting up its waves. ⁴They will destroy the walls of Tyre and pull down her towers; I will scrape away her rubble and make her a bare rock. ⁵Out in the sea she will become a place to spread fishnets, for I have spoken, declares the Sovereign LORD. She will become plunder for the nations, ⁶and her settlements on the mainland will be ravaged by the sword. Then they will know that I am the LORD.

⁷"For this is what the Sovereign LORD says: From the north I am going to bring against Tyre Nebuchadnezzar[a] king of Babylon, king of kings, with horses and chariots, with horsemen and a great army. ⁸He will ravage your settlements on the mainland with the sword; he will set up siege works against you, build a ramp up to your walls and raise his shields against you.

---

[a]7 Hebrew *Nebuchadrezzar*, of which *Nebuchadnezzar* is a variant; here and often in Ezekiel and Jeremiah

⁹He will direct the blows of his battering rams against your walls and demolish your towers with his weapons. ¹⁰His horses will be so many that they will cover you with dust. Your walls will tremble at the noise of the war horses, wagons and chariots when he enters your gates as men enter a city whose walls have been broken through. ¹¹The hoofs of his horses will trample all your streets; he will kill your people with the sword, and your strong pillars will fall to the ground. ¹²They will plunder your wealth and loot your merchandise; they will break down your walls and demolish your fine houses and throw your stones, timber and rubble into the sea. ¹³I will put an end to your noisy songs, and the music of your harps will be heard no more. ¹⁴I will make you a bare rock, and you will become a place to spread fishnets. You will never be rebuilt, for I the LORD have spoken, declares the Sovereign LORD.

¹⁵"This is what the Sovereign LORD says to Tyre: Will not the coastlands tremble at the sound of your fall, when the wounded groan and the slaughter takes place in you? ¹⁶Then all the princes of the coast will step down from their thrones and lay aside their robes and take off their embroidered garments. Clothed with terror, they will sit on the ground, trembling every moment, appalled at you. ¹⁷Then they will take up a lament concerning you and say to you:

> "'How you are destroyed, O city of
>   renown,
>   peopled by men of the sea!
> You were a power on the seas,
>   you and your citizens;
> you put your terror
>   on all who lived there.
> ¹⁸Now the coastlands tremble
>   on the day of your fall;
> the islands in the sea
>   are terrified at your collapse.'

¹⁹"This is what the Sovereign LORD says: When I make you a desolate city, like cities no longer inhabited, and when I bring the ocean depths over you and its vast waters cover you, ²⁰then I will bring you down with those who go down to the pit, to the people of long ago. I will make you dwell in the earth below, as in ancient ruins, with those who go down to the pit, and you will not return or take your place*a* in the land of the living. ²¹I will bring you to a horrible end and you will be no more. You will be sought, but you will never again be found, declares the Sovereign LORD."

A Lament for Tyre

27 The word of the LORD came to me: ²"Son of man, take up a lament concerning Tyre. ³Say to Tyre, situated at the gateway to the sea, merchant of peoples on many coasts, 'This is what the Sovereign LORD says:

> "'You say, O Tyre,
>   "I am perfect in beauty."
> ⁴Your domain was on the high seas;
>   your builders brought your beauty to
>   perfection.
> ⁵They made all your timbers
>   of pine trees from Senir*b*;
> they took a cedar from Lebanon
>   to make a mast for you.
> ⁶Of oaks from Bashan
>   they made your oars;
> of cypress wood*c* from the coasts of
>   Cyprus*d*
>   they made your deck, inlaid with ivory.
> ⁷Fine embroidered linen from Egypt was
>   your sail
>   and served as your banner;
> your awnings were of blue and purple
>   from the coasts of Elishah.
> ⁸Men of Sidon and Arvad were your
>   oarsmen;
>   your skilled men, O Tyre, were aboard
>   as your seamen.
> ⁹Veteran craftsmen of Gebal*e* were on board
>   as shipwrights to caulk your seams.
> All the ships of the sea and their sailors
>   came alongside to trade for your wares.
>
> ¹⁰"'Men of Persia, Lydia and Put
>   served as soldiers in your army.
> They hung their shields and helmets on
>   your walls,
>   bringing you splendor.
> ¹¹Men of Arvad and Helech

---

*a*20 Septuagint; Hebrew *return, and I will give glory*   *b*5 That is, Hermon   *c*6 Targum; the Masoretic Text has a different division of the consonants.   *d*6 Hebrew *Kittim*   *e*9 That is, Byblos

manned your walls on every side;
men of Gammad
were in your towers.
They hung their shields around your walls;
they brought your beauty to perfection.

12 "'Tarshish did business with you because of your great wealth of goods; they exchanged silver, iron, tin and lead for your merchandise.

13 "'Greece, Tubal and Meshech traded with you; they exchanged slaves and articles of bronze for your wares.

14 "'Men of Beth Togarmah exchanged work horses, war horses and mules for your merchandise.

15 "'The men of Rhodes*a* traded with you, and many coastlands were your customers; they paid you with ivory tusks and ebony.

16 "'Aram*b* did business with you because of your many products; they exchanged turquoise, purple fabric, embroidered work, fine linen, coral and rubies for your merchandise.

17 "'Judah and Israel traded with you; they exchanged wheat from Minnith and confections,*c* honey, oil and balm for your wares.

18 "'Damascus, because of your many products and great wealth of goods, did business with you in wine from Helbon and wool from Zahar.

19 "'Danites and Greeks from Uzal bought your merchandise; they exchanged wrought iron, cassia and calamus for your wares.

20 "'Dedan traded in saddle blankets with you.

21 "'Arabia and all the princes of Kedar were your customers; they did business with you in lambs, rams and goats.

22 "'The merchants of Sheba and Raamah traded with you; for your merchandise they exchanged the finest of all kinds of spices and precious stones, and gold.

23 "'Haran, Canneh and Eden and merchants of Sheba, Asshur and Kilmad traded with you. 24 In your marketplace they traded with you beautiful garments, blue fabric, embroidered work and multicolored rugs with cords twisted and tightly knotted.

25 "'The ships of Tarshish serve
as carriers for your wares.

You are filled with heavy cargo
in the heart of the sea.
26 Your oarsmen take you
out to the high seas.
But the east wind will break you to pieces
in the heart of the sea.
27 Your wealth, merchandise and wares,
your mariners, seamen and shipwrights,
your merchants and all your soldiers,
and everyone else on board
will sink into the heart of the sea
on the day of your shipwreck.
28 The shorelands will quake
when your seamen cry out.
29 All who handle the oars
will abandon their ships;
the mariners and all the seamen
will stand on the shore.
30 They will raise their voice
and cry bitterly over you;
they will sprinkle dust on their heads
and roll in ashes.
31 They will shave their heads because of you
and will put on sackcloth.
They will weep over you with anguish of
soul
and with bitter mourning.
32 As they wail and mourn over you,
they will take up a lament concerning
you:
"Who was ever silenced like Tyre,
surrounded by the sea?"
33 When your merchandise went out on the
seas,
you satisfied many nations;
with your great wealth and your wares
you enriched the kings of the earth.
34 Now you are shattered by the sea
in the depths of the waters;
your wares and all your company
have gone down with you.
35 All who live in the coastlands
are appalled at you;
their kings shudder with horror
and their faces are distorted with fear.
36 The merchants among the nations hiss at
you;
you have come to a horrible end
and will be no more.'"

a 15 Septuagint; Hebrew *Dedan*   *b* 16 Most Hebrew manuscripts; some Hebrew manuscripts and Syriac *Edom*   *c* 17 The meaning of the Hebrew for this word is uncertain.

A Prophecy Against the King of Tyre

28 The word of the LORD came to me: ²"Son of man, say to the ruler of Tyre, 'This is what the Sovereign LORD says:

"'In the pride of your heart
    you say, "I am a god;
I sit on the throne of a god
    in the heart of the seas."
But you are a man and not a god,
    though you think you are as wise as a
        god.
³ Are you wiser than Daniel[a]?
    Is no secret hidden from you?
⁴ By your wisdom and understanding
    you have gained wealth for yourself
and amassed gold and silver
    in your treasuries.
⁵ By your great skill in trading
    you have increased your wealth,
and because of your wealth
    your heart has grown proud.

⁶"'Therefore this is what the Sovereign LORD says:

"'Because you think you are wise,
    as wise as a god,
⁷ I am going to bring foreigners against you,
    the most ruthless of nations;
they will draw their swords
    against your beauty
    and wisdom
    and pierce your shining
        splendor.
⁸ They will bring you down
        to the pit,
    and you will die a violent
        death
    in the heart of the seas.
⁹ Will you then say, "I am a
        god,"
    in the presence of those
        who kill you?
You will be but a man, not
        a god,
    in the hands of those who slay you.
¹⁰ You will die the death of the
        uncircumcised
    at the hands of foreigners.

I have spoken, declares the Sovereign LORD.'"

¹¹The word of the LORD came to me: ¹²"Son of man, take up a lament concerning the king of Tyre and say to him: 'This is what the Sovereign LORD says:

"'You were the model of perfection,
    full of wisdom and perfect in beauty.
¹³ You were in Eden,
    the garden of God;
every precious stone adorned you:
    ruby, topaz and emerald,
    chrysolite, onyx and jasper,
    sapphire,[b] turquoise and beryl.[c]
Your settings and mountings[d] were made
        of gold;
    on the day you were created they were
        prepared.
¹⁴ You were anointed as a guardian cherub,
    for so I ordained you.
You were on the holy mount of God;
    you walked among the fiery stones.
¹⁵ You were blameless in your ways
    from the day you were created
    till wickedness was found in you.
¹⁶ Through your widespread trade
    you were filled with violence,
    and you sinned.
So I drove you in disgrace
        from the mount of
        God,
    and I expelled you,
        O guardian cherub,
    from among the fiery
        stones.
¹⁷ Your heart became proud
        on account of your
        beauty,
    and you corrupted your
        wisdom
    because of your splendor.
So I threw you to the earth;
    I made a spectacle of you
        before kings.
¹⁸ By your many sins and dishonest trade
    you have desecrated your sanctuaries.
So I made a fire come out from you,
    and it consumed you,

Ezekiel 28:17

God Judges Pride

"Your heart became proud
on account of
your beauty,
and you corrupted
your wisdom
because of your
splendor."

---

[a]3 Or *Danel*; the Hebrew spelling may suggest a person other than the prophet Daniel.   [b]13 Or *lapis lazuli*   [c]13 The precise identification of some of these precious stones is uncertain.   [d]13 The meaning of the Hebrew for this phrase is uncertain.

and I reduced you to ashes on the ground
　in the sight of all who were watching.
19 All the nations who knew you
　are appalled at you;
you have come to a horrible end
　and will be no more.'"

A Prophecy Against Sidon

20 The word of the LORD came to me: **21** "Son
of man, set your face against Sidon; prophesy
against her **22** and say: 'This is what the Sovereign LORD says:

"'I am against you, O Sidon,
　and I will gain glory within you.
They will know that I am the LORD,
　when I inflict punishment on her
　and show myself holy within her.
23 I will send a plague upon her
　and make blood flow in her streets.
The slain will fall within her,
　with the sword against her on every side.
Then they will know that I am the LORD.

24 "'No longer will the people of Israel have
malicious neighbors who are painful briers and
sharp thorns. Then they will know that I am
the Sovereign LORD.

25 "'This is what the Sovereign LORD says:
When I gather the people of Israel from the
nations where they have been scattered, I will
show myself holy among them in the sight of
the nations. Then they will live in their own
land, which I gave to my servant Jacob. **26** They
will live there in safety and will build houses
and plant vineyards; they will live in safety
when I inflict punishment on all their neighbors who maligned them. Then they will know
that I am the LORD their God.'"

A Prophecy Against Egypt

29 In the tenth year, in the tenth month on
the twelfth day, the word of the LORD
came to me: **2** "Son of man, set your face against
Pharaoh king of Egypt and prophesy against
him and against all Egypt. **3** Speak to him and
say: 'This is what the Sovereign LORD says:

"'I am against you, Pharaoh king of Egypt,
　you great monster lying among your
　　streams.

You say, "The Nile is mine;
　I made it for myself."
4 But I will put hooks in your jaws
　and make the fish of your streams stick
　　to your scales.
I will pull you out from among your
　　streams,
　with all the fish sticking to your scales.
5 I will leave you in the desert,
　you and all the fish of your streams.
You will fall on the open field
　and not be gathered or picked up.
I will give you as food
　to the beasts of the earth and the birds
　　of the air.

6 Then all who live in Egypt will know that I
am the LORD.

"'You have been a staff of reed for the house
of Israel. **7** When they grasped you with their
hands, you splintered and you tore open their
shoulders; when they leaned on you, you broke
and their backs were wrenched.*a*

8 "'Therefore this is what the Sovereign
LORD says: I will bring a sword against you and
kill your men and their animals. **9** Egypt will
become a desolate wasteland. Then they will
know that I am the LORD.

"'Because you said, "The Nile is mine; I made
it," **10** therefore I am against you and against
your streams, and I will make the land of Egypt
a ruin and a desolate waste from Migdol to Aswan, as far as the border of Cush.*b* **11** No foot of
man or animal will pass through it; no one will
live there for forty years. **12** I will make the land
of Egypt desolate among devastated lands, and
her cities will lie desolate forty years among ruined cities. And I will disperse the Egyptians
among the nations and scatter them through
the countries.

13 "'Yet this is what the Sovereign LORD says:
At the end of forty years I will gather the Egyptians from the nations where they were scattered. **14** I will bring them back from captivity
and return them to Upper Egypt,*c* the land of
their ancestry. There they will be a lowly kingdom. **15** It will be the lowliest of kingdoms and
will never again exalt itself above the other

---

*a*7 Syriac (see also Septuagint and Vulgate); Hebrew *and you caused their backs to stand*　　*b*10 That is, the upper Nile region
*c*14 Hebrew *to Pathros*

nations. I will make it so weak that it will never again rule over the nations. ¹⁶Egypt will no longer be a source of confidence for the people of Israel but will be a reminder of their sin in turning to her for help. Then they will know that I am the Sovereign Lord.'"

¹⁷In the twenty-seventh year, in the first month on the first day, the word of the Lord came to me: ¹⁸"Son of man, Nebuchadnezzar king of Babylon drove his army in a hard campaign against Tyre; every head was rubbed bare and every shoulder made raw. Yet he and his army got no reward from the campaign he led against Tyre. ¹⁹Therefore this is what the Sovereign Lord says: I am going to give Egypt to Nebuchadnezzar king of Babylon, and he will carry off its wealth. He will loot and plunder the land as pay for his army. ²⁰I have given him Egypt as a reward for his efforts because he and his army did it for me, declares the Sovereign Lord. ²¹On that day I will make a horn[a] grow for the house of Israel, and I will open your mouth among them. Then they will know that I am the Lord."

A Lament for Egypt

30 The word of the Lord came to me: ²"Son of man, prophesy and say: 'This is what the Sovereign Lord says:

"'Wail and say,
    "Alas for that day!"
³ For the day is near,
    the day of the Lord is near—
a day of clouds,
    a time of doom for the nations.
⁴ A sword will come against Egypt,
    and anguish will come upon Cush.[b]
When the slain fall in Egypt,
    her wealth will be carried away
    and her foundations torn down.

⁵Cush and Put, Lydia and all Arabia, Libya[c] and the people of the covenant land will fall by the sword along with Egypt.

⁶"'This is what the Lord says:

"'The allies of Egypt will fall
    and her proud strength will fail.

From Migdol to Aswan
    they will fall by the sword within her,
        declares the Sovereign Lord.
⁷ "They will be desolate
    among desolate lands,
and their cities will lie
    among ruined cities.
⁸ Then they will know that I am the Lord,
    when I set fire to Egypt
    and all her helpers are crushed.

⁹"'On that day messengers will go out from me in ships to frighten Cush out of her complacency. Anguish will take hold of them on the day of Egypt's doom, for it is sure to come.

¹⁰ "This is what the Sovereign Lord says:

"'I will put an end to the hordes of Egypt
    by the hand of Nebuchadnezzar king of
        Babylon.
¹¹ He and his army—the most ruthless of
        nations—
    will be brought in to destroy the land.
They will draw their swords against Egypt
    and fill the land with the slain.
¹² I will dry up the streams of the Nile
    and sell the land to evil men;
by the hand of foreigners
    I will lay waste the land and everything
        in it.

I the Lord have spoken.

¹³ "This is what the Sovereign Lord says:

"'I will destroy the idols
    and put an end to the images in
        Memphis.[d]
No longer will there be a prince in Egypt,
    and I will spread fear throughout the
        land.
¹⁴ I will lay waste Upper Egypt,[e]
    set fire to Zoan
    and inflict punishment on Thebes.[f]
¹⁵ I will pour out my wrath on Pelusium,[g]
    the stronghold of Egypt,
    and cut off the hordes of Thebes.
¹⁶ I will set fire to Egypt;
    Pelusium will writhe in agony.

---

[a]21 *Horn* here symbolizes strength.   [b]4 That is, the upper Nile region; also in verses 5 and 9   [c]5 Hebrew *Cub*   [d]13 Hebrew *Noph*; also in verse 16   [e]14 Hebrew *waste Pathros*   [f]14 Hebrew *No*; also in verses 15 and 16   [g]15 Hebrew *Sin*; also in verse 16

Thebes will be taken by storm;
    Memphis will be in constant distress.
17 The young men of Heliopolis*a* and
        Bubastis*b*
    will fall by the sword,
    and the cities themselves will go into
        captivity.
18 Dark will be the day at Tahpanhes
        when I break the yoke of Egypt;
    there her proud strength will come to
        an end.
    She will be covered with clouds,
        and her villages will go into captivity.
19 So I will inflict punishment on Egypt,
        and they will know that I am the LORD.'"

20 In the eleventh year, in the first month on the seventh day, the word of the LORD came to me: 21 "Son of man, I have broken the arm of Pharaoh king of Egypt. It has not been bound up for healing or put in a splint so as to become strong enough to hold a sword. 22 Therefore this is what the Sovereign LORD says: I am against Pharaoh king of Egypt. I will break both his arms, the good arm as well as the broken one, and make the sword fall from his hand. 23 I will disperse the Egyptians among the nations and scatter them through the countries. 24 I will strengthen the arms of the king of Babylon and put my sword in his hand, but I will break the arms of Pharaoh, and he will groan before him like a mortally wounded man. 25 I will strengthen the arms of the king of Babylon, but the arms of Pharaoh will fall limp. Then they will know that I am the LORD, when I put my sword into the hand of the king of Babylon and he brandishes it against Egypt. 26 I will disperse the Egyptians among the nations and scatter them through the countries. Then they will know that I am the LORD."

A Cedar in Lebanon

31 In the eleventh year, in the third month on the first day, the word of the LORD came to me: 2 "Son of man, say to Pharaoh king of Egypt and to his hordes:

" 'Who can be compared with you in
        majesty?
3 Consider Assyria, once a cedar in
        Lebanon,

with beautiful branches overshadowing
        the forest;
    it towered on high,
        its top above the thick foliage.
4 The waters nourished it,
        deep springs made it grow tall;
    their streams flowed
        all around its base
    and sent their channels
        to all the trees of the field.
5 So it towered higher
        than all the trees of the field;
    its boughs increased
        and its branches grew long,
        spreading because of abundant waters.
6 All the birds of the air
        nested in its boughs,
    all the beasts of the field
        gave birth under its branches;
    all the great nations
        lived in its shade.
7 It was majestic in beauty,
        with its spreading boughs,
    for its roots went down
        to abundant waters.
8 The cedars in the garden of God
        could not rival it,
    nor could the pine trees
        equal its boughs,
    nor could the plane trees
        compare with its branches—
    no tree in the garden of God
        could match its beauty.
9 I made it beautiful
        with abundant branches,
    the envy of all the trees of Eden
        in the garden of God.

10 "Therefore this is what the Sovereign LORD says: Because it towered on high, lifting its top above the thick foliage, and because it was proud of its height, 11 I handed it over to the ruler of the nations, for him to deal with according to its wickedness. I cast it aside, 12 and the most ruthless of foreign nations cut it down and left it. Its boughs fell on the mountains and in all the valleys; its branches lay broken in all the ravines of the land. All the nations of the earth came out from under its shade and left it. 13 All the birds of the air settled on the fallen

a 17 Hebrew Awen (or On)   *b 17 Hebrew Pi Beseth*

tree, and all the beasts of the field were among its branches. [14]Therefore no other trees by the waters are ever to tower proudly on high, lifting their tops above the thick foliage. No other trees so well-watered are ever to reach such a height; they are all destined for death, for the earth below, among mortal men, with those who go down to the pit.

[15]"'This is what the Sovereign LORD says: On the day it was brought down to the grave[a] I covered the deep springs with mourning for it; I held back its streams, and its abundant waters were restrained. Because of it I clothed Lebanon with gloom, and all the trees of the field withered away. [16]I made the nations tremble at the sound of its fall when I brought it down to the grave with those who go down to the pit. Then all the trees of Eden, the choicest and best of Lebanon, all the trees that were well-watered, were consoled in the earth below. [17]Those who lived in its shade, its allies among the nations, had also gone down to the grave with it, joining those killed by the sword.

[18]"'Which of the trees of Eden can be compared with you in splendor and majesty? Yet you, too, will be brought down with the trees of Eden to the earth below; you will lie among the uncircumcised, with those killed by the sword.

"'This is Pharaoh and all his hordes, declares the Sovereign LORD.'"

A Lament for Pharaoh

32 In the twelfth year, in the twelfth month on the first day, the word of the LORD came to me: [2]"Son of man, take up a lament concerning Pharaoh king of Egypt and say to him:

"'You are like a lion among the nations;
    you are like a monster in the seas
thrashing about in your streams,
    churning the water with your feet
    and muddying the streams.

[3]"'This is what the Sovereign LORD says:

"'With a great throng of people
    I will cast my net over you,
    and they will haul you up in my net.
[4]I will throw you on the land

and hurl you on the open field.
I will let all the birds of the air settle on you
    and all the beasts of the earth gorge
        themselves on you.
[5]I will spread your flesh on the mountains
    and fill the valleys with your remains.
[6]I will drench the land with your flowing
        blood
    all the way to the mountains,
    and the ravines will be filled with your
        flesh.
[7]When I snuff you out, I will cover the
        heavens
    and darken their stars;
I will cover the sun with a cloud,
    and the moon will not give its light.
[8]All the shining lights in the heavens
    I will darken over you;
    I will bring darkness over your land,
        declares the Sovereign LORD.
[9]I will trouble the hearts of many peoples
    when I bring about your destruction
        among the nations,
    among[b] lands you have not known.
[10]I will cause many peoples to be appalled at
        you,
    and their kings will shudder with horror
        because of you
    when I brandish my sword before them.
On the day of your downfall
    each of them will tremble
    every moment for his life.

[11]"'For this is what the Sovereign LORD says:

"'The sword of the king of Babylon
    will come against you.
[12]I will cause your hordes to fall
    by the swords of mighty men—
    the most ruthless of all nations.
They will shatter the pride of Egypt,
    and all her hordes will be overthrown.
[13]I will destroy all her cattle
    from beside abundant waters
no longer to be stirred by the foot of man
    or muddied by the hoofs of cattle.
[14]Then I will let her waters settle
    and make her streams flow like oil,
        declares the Sovereign LORD.

---

[a]15 Hebrew *Sheol*; also in verses 16 and 17   [b]9 Hebrew; Septuagint *bring you into captivity among the nations, / to*

¹⁵When I make Egypt desolate
　　and strip the land of everything in it,
　when I strike down all who live there,
　　then they will know that I am the LORD.'

¹⁶"This is the lament they will chant for her. The daughters of the nations will chant it; for Egypt and all her hordes they will chant it, declares the Sovereign LORD."

¹⁷In the twelfth year, on the fifteenth day of the month, the word of the LORD came to me: ¹⁸"Son of man, wail for the hordes of Egypt and consign to the earth below both her and the daughters of mighty nations, with those who go down to the pit. ¹⁹Say to them, 'Are you more favored than others? Go down and be laid among the uncircumcised.' ²⁰They will fall among those killed by the sword. The sword is drawn; let her be dragged off with all her hordes. ²¹From within the grave*a* the mighty leaders will say of Egypt and her allies, 'They have come down and they lie with the uncircumcised, with those killed by the sword.'

²²"Assyria is there with her whole army; she is surrounded by the graves of all her slain, all who have fallen by the sword. ²³Their graves are in the depths of the pit and her army lies around her grave. All who had spread terror in the land of the living are slain, fallen by the sword.

²⁴"Elam is there, with all her hordes around her grave. All of them are slain, fallen by the sword. All who had spread terror in the land of the living went down uncircumcised to the earth below. They bear their shame with those who go down to the pit. ²⁵A bed is made for her among the slain, with all her hordes around her grave. All of them are uncircumcised, killed by the sword. Because their terror had spread in the land of the living, they bear their shame with those who go down to the pit; they are laid among the slain.

²⁶"Meshech and Tubal are there, with all their hordes around their graves. All of them are uncircumcised, killed by the sword because they spread their terror in the land of the living. ²⁷Do they not lie with the other uncircumcised warriors who have fallen, who went down to the grave with their weapons of war,

whose swords were placed under their heads? The punishment for their sins rested on their bones, though the terror of these warriors had stalked through the land of the living.

²⁸"You too, O Pharaoh, will be broken and will lie among the uncircumcised, with those killed by the sword.

²⁹"Edom is there, her kings and all her princes; despite their power, they are laid with those killed by the sword. They lie with the uncircumcised, with those who go down to the pit.

³⁰"All the princes of the north and all the Sidonians are there; they went down with the slain in disgrace despite the terror caused by their power. They lie uncircumcised with those killed by the sword and bear their shame with those who go down to the pit.

³¹"Pharaoh—he and all his army—will see them and he will be consoled for all his hordes that were killed by the sword, declares the Sovereign LORD. ³²Although I had him spread terror in the land of the living, Pharaoh and all his hordes will be laid among the uncircumcised, with those killed by the sword, declares the Sovereign LORD."

Ezekiel a Watchman

33 The word of the LORD came to me: ²"Son of man, speak to your countrymen and say to them: 'When I bring the sword against a land, and the people of the land choose one of their men and make him their watchman, ³and he sees the sword coming against the land and blows the trumpet to warn the people, ⁴then if anyone hears the trumpet but does not take warning and the sword comes and takes his life, his blood will be on his own head. ⁵Since he heard the sound of the trumpet but did not take warning, his blood will be on his own head. If he had taken warning, he would have saved himself. ⁶But if the watchman sees the sword coming and does not blow the trumpet to warn the people and the sword comes and takes the life of one of them, that man will be taken away because of his sin, but I will hold the watchman accountable for his blood.'

⁷"Son of man, I have made you a watchman

---

a21 Hebrew *Sheol*; also in verse 27

for the house of Israel; so hear the word I speak and give them warning from me. **8** When I say to the wicked, 'O wicked man, you will surely die,' and you do not speak out to dissuade him from his ways, that wicked man will die for[a] his sin, and I will hold you accountable for his blood. **9** But if you do warn the wicked man to turn from his ways and he does not do so, he will die for his sin, but you will have saved yourself.

10 "Son of man, say to the house of Israel, 'This is what you are saying: "Our offenses and sins weigh us down, and we are wasting away because of[b] them. How then can we live?" ' **11** Say to them, 'As surely as I live, declares the Sovereign Lord, I take no pleasure in the death of the wicked, but rather that they turn from their ways and live. Turn! Turn from your evil ways! Why will you die, O house of Israel?'

12 "Therefore, son of man, say to your countrymen, 'The righteousness of the righteous man will not save him when he disobeys, and the wickedness of the wicked man will not cause him to fall when he turns from it. The righteous man, if he sins, will not be allowed to live because of his former righteousness.' **13** If I tell the righteous man that he will surely live, but then he trusts in his righteousness and does evil, none of the righteous things he has done will be remembered; he will die for the evil he has done. **14** And if I say to the wicked man, 'You will surely die,' but he then turns away from his sin and does what is just and right— **15** if he gives back what he took in pledge for a loan, returns what he has stolen, follows the decrees that give life, and does no evil, he will surely live; he will not die. **16** None of the sins he has committed will be remembered against him. He has done what is just and right; he will surely live.

17 "Yet your countrymen say, 'The way of the Lord is not just.' But it is their way that is

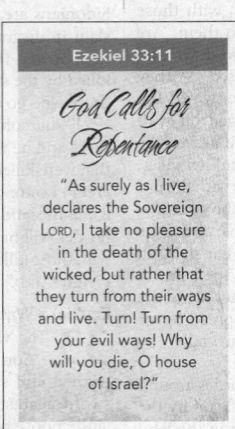

Ezekiel 33:11

God Calls for Repentance

"As surely as I live, declares the Sovereign Lord, I take no pleasure in the death of the wicked, but rather that they turn from their ways and live. Turn! Turn from your evil ways! Why will you die, O house of Israel?"

not just. **18** If a righteous man turns from his righteousness and does evil, he will die for it. **19** And if a wicked man turns away from his wickedness and does what is just and right, he will live by doing so. **20** Yet, O house of Israel, you say, 'The way of the Lord is not just.' But I will judge each of you according to his own ways."

Jerusalem's Fall Explained

21 In the twelfth year of our exile, in the tenth month on the fifth day, a man who had escaped from Jerusalem came to me and said, "The city has fallen!" **22** Now the evening before the man arrived, the hand of the Lord was upon me, and he opened my mouth before the man came to me in the morning. So my mouth was opened and I was no longer silent.

23 Then the word of the Lord came to me: **24** "Son of man, the people living in those ruins in the land of Israel are saying, 'Abraham was only one man, yet he possessed the land. But we are many; surely the land has been given to us as our possession.' **25** Therefore say to them, 'This is what the Sovereign Lord says: Since you eat meat with the blood still in it and look to your idols and shed blood, should you then possess the land? **26** You rely on your sword, you do detestable things, and each of you defiles his neighbor's wife. Should you then possess the land?'

27 "Say this to them: 'This is what the Sovereign Lord says: As surely as I live, those who are left in the ruins will fall by the sword, those out in the country I will give to the wild animals to be devoured, and those in strongholds and caves will die of a plague. **28** I will make the land a desolate waste, and her proud strength will come to an end, and the mountains of Israel will become desolate so that no one will cross them. **29** Then they will know that I am the Lord, when I have made the land a deso-

a 8 Or *in*; also in verse 9   *b* 10 Or *away in*

late waste because of all the detestable things they have done.'

³⁰"As for you, son of man, your countrymen are talking together about you by the walls and at the doors of the houses, saying to each other, 'Come and hear the message that has come from the LORD.' ³¹My people come to you, as they usually do, and sit before you to listen to your words, but they do not put them into practice. With their mouths they express devotion, but their hearts are greedy for unjust gain. ³²Indeed, to them you are nothing more than one who sings love songs with a beautiful voice and plays an instrument well, for they hear your words but do not put them into practice.

³³"When all this comes true—and it surely will—then they will know that a prophet has been among them."

Shepherds and Sheep

34 The word of the LORD came to me: ²"Son of man, prophesy against the shepherds of Israel; prophesy and say to them: 'This is what the Sovereign LORD says: Woe to the shepherds of Israel who only take care of themselves! Should not shepherds take care of the flock? ³You eat the curds, clothe yourselves with the wool and slaughter the choice animals, but you do not take care of the flock. ⁴You have not strengthened the weak or healed the sick or bound up the injured. You have not brought back the strays or searched for the lost. You have ruled them harshly and brutally. ⁵So they were scattered because there was no shepherd, and when they were scattered they became food for all the wild animals. ⁶My sheep wandered over all the mountains and on every high hill. They were scattered over the whole earth, and no one searched or looked for them.

⁷" 'Therefore, you shepherds, hear the word of the LORD: ⁸As surely as I live, declares the Sovereign LORD, because my flock lacks a shepherd and so has been plundered and has become food for all the wild animals, and because my shepherds did not search for my flock but cared for themselves rather than for my flock, ⁹therefore, O shepherds, hear the word of the LORD: ¹⁰This is what the Sovereign LORD says: I am against the shepherds and will hold them accountable for my flock. I will remove them from tending the flock so that the shepherds can no longer feed themselves. I will rescue my flock from their mouths, and it will no longer be food for them.

¹¹" 'For this is what the Sovereign LORD says: I myself will search for my sheep and look after them. ¹²As a shepherd looks after his scattered flock when he is with them, so will I look after my sheep. I will rescue them from all the places where they were scattered on a day of clouds and darkness. ¹³I will bring them out from the nations and gather them from the countries, and I will bring them into their own land. I will pasture them on the mountains of Israel, in the ravines and in all the settlements in the land. ¹⁴I will tend them in a good pasture, and the mountain heights of Israel will be their grazing land. There they will lie down in good grazing land, and there they will feed in a rich pasture on the mountains of Israel. ¹⁵I myself will tend my sheep and have them lie down, declares the Sovereign LORD. ¹⁶I will search for the lost and bring back the strays. I will bind up the injured and strengthen the weak, but the sleek and the strong I will destroy. I will shepherd the flock with justice.

¹⁷" 'As for you, my flock, this is what the Sovereign LORD says: I will judge between one sheep and another, and between rams and goats. ¹⁸Is it not enough for you to feed on the good pasture? Must you also trample the rest of your pasture with your feet? Is it not enough for you to drink clear water? Must you also muddy the rest with your feet? ¹⁹Must my flock feed on what you have trampled and drink what you have muddied with your feet?

²⁰" 'Therefore this is what the Sovereign LORD says to them: See, I myself will judge between the fat sheep and the lean sheep. ²¹Because you shove with flank and shoulder, butting all the weak sheep with your horns until you have driven them away, ²²I will save my flock, and they will no longer be plundered. I will judge between one sheep and another. ²³I will place over them one shepherd, my servant David, and he will tend them; he will tend them and be their shepherd. ²⁴I the LORD will be their God, and my servant David will be prince among them. I the LORD have spoken.

²⁵" 'I will make a covenant of peace with them and rid the land of wild beasts so that

MARY

But Mary treasured up all these things and pondered them in her heart.

Luke 2:19

ASSIGNED READING:

Luke 2:19, 21–40

"DID YOU HEAR ANYTHING I JUST SAID?"

Startled by the piercing tone of the market manager's voice, Mary blinked rapidly as if awakening from a deep dream. She quickly responded, "Yes . . . so sorry. That challah loaf there—that's fine. And these too," she added, clutching three heads of garlic in her hand. Mary quickly paid the manager his due and headed home before her young son awoke from his nap.

So much had happened in her life, she'd hardly taken time to think through all of it. At any given moment, her mind would suddenly float away to memories. Yet she could never grasp their full meaning.

As the afternoon sun cast the shadow of her small frame on the dirt path, various scenes surfaced: that first day in the temple; the look of rapture on the face of the prophetess Anna as she blessed Mary's child. And what did Simeon mean—something about a sword piercing her own soul someday?

Mary turned a corner and saw the familiar roofline of her home in the distance. Almost home. She smiled to herself, recalling the warm feeling of security that had washed over her when they had first seen the outline of the sleepy town of Nazareth. They had been so frightened, but Joseph felt God leading them there through his dreams. And now, though not his birthplace, their son would come to know it as "home." Jesus of Nazareth.

"You are to give him the name Jesus. He will be great and will be called the Son of the Most High" (Luke 1:31–32).

Like a thousand times before, her mind pondered the angel's words and the Magi's posture before her child—all as if for the first time. Mary stored each moment and memory surrounding her precious baby boy inside of her heart. Tucked away treasures, they were her comfort and her assurance. Most of all, they were hers and hers alone to ponder. No one else could share her chosen place—the earthly mother of the Son of God.

—Prayer—
You have chosen me to live in this place and time, Lord. May I live out my days for your glory.

Go to page 1038 for your next devotional reading.

they may live in the desert and sleep in the forests in safety. 26I will bless them and the places surrounding my hill.a I will send down showers in season; there will be showers of blessing. 27The trees of the field will yield their fruit and the ground will yield its crops; the people will be secure in their land. They will know that I am the LORD, when I break the bars of their yoke and rescue them from the hands of those who enslaved them. 28They will no longer be plundered by the nations, nor will wild animals devour them. They will live in safety, and no one will make them afraid. 29I will provide for them a land renowned for its crops, and they will no longer be victims of famine in the land or bear the scorn of the nations. 30Then they will know that I, the LORD their God, am with them and that they, the house of Israel, are my people, declares the Sovereign LORD. 31You my sheep, the sheep of my pasture, are people, and I am your God, declares the Sovereign LORD.'"

A Prophecy Against Edom

35 The word of the LORD came to me: 2"Son of man, set your face against Mount Seir; prophesy against it 3and say: 'This is what the Sovereign LORD says: I am against you, Mount Seir, and I will stretch out my hand against you and make you a desolate waste. 4I will turn your towns into ruins and you will be desolate. Then you will know that I am the LORD.

5"'Because you harbored an ancient hostility and delivered the Israelites over to the sword at the time of their calamity, the time their punishment reached its climax, 6therefore as surely as I live, declares the Sovereign LORD, I will give you over to bloodshed and it will pursue you. Since you did not hate bloodshed, bloodshed will pursue you. 7I will make Mount Seir a desolate waste and cut off from it all who come and go. 8I will fill your mountains with the slain; those killed by the sword will fall on your hills and in your valleys and in all your ravines. 9I will make you desolate forever; your towns will not be inhabited. Then you will know that I am the LORD.

10"'Because you have said, "These two nations and countries will be ours and we will take possession of them," even though I the LORD was there, 11therefore as surely as I live, declares the Sovereign LORD, I will treat you in accordance with the anger and jealousy you showed in your hatred of them and I will make myself known among them when I judge you. 12Then you will know that I the LORD have heard all the contemptible things you have said against the mountains of Israel. You said, "They have been laid waste and have been given over to us to devour." 13You boasted against me and spoke against me without restraint, and I heard it. 14This is what the Sovereign LORD says: While the whole earth rejoices, I will make you desolate. 15Because you rejoiced when the inheritance of the house of Israel became desolate, that is how I will treat you. You will be desolate, O Mount Seir, you and all of Edom. Then they will know that I am the LORD.'"

A Prophecy to the Mountains of Israel

36 "Son of man, prophesy to the mountains of Israel and say, 'O mountains of Israel, hear the word of the LORD. 2This is what the Sovereign LORD says: The enemy said of you, "Aha! The ancient heights have become our possession."' 3Therefore prophesy and say, 'This is what the Sovereign LORD says: Because they ravaged and hounded you from every side so that you became the possession of the rest of the nations and the object of people's malicious talk and slander, 4therefore, O mountains of Israel, hear the word of the Sovereign LORD: This is what the Sovereign LORD says to the mountains and hills, to the ravines and valleys, to the desolate ruins and the deserted towns that have been plundered and ridiculed by the rest of the nations around you— 5this is what the Sovereign LORD says: In my burning zeal I have spoken against the rest of the nations, and against all Edom, for with glee and with malice in their hearts they made my land their own possession so that they might plunder its pastureland.' 6Therefore prophesy concerning the land of Israel and say to the mountains and hills, to the ravines and valleys: 'This is what the Sovereign LORD says: I speak in my jealous wrath because you have suffered the scorn of the nations. 7Therefore this is what

---

a26 Or I will make them and the places surrounding my hill a blessing the Sovereign LORD says: I swear with uplifted hand that the nations around you will also suffer scorn.

8 "'But you, O mountains of Israel, will produce branches and fruit for my people Israel, for they will soon come home. 9 I am concerned for you and will look on you with favor; you will be plowed and sown, 10 and I will multiply the number of people upon you, even the whole house of Israel. The towns will be inhabited and the ruins rebuilt. 11 I will increase the number of men and animals upon you, and they will be fruitful and become numerous. I will settle people on you as in the past and will make you prosper more than before. Then you will know that I am the LORD. 12 I will cause people, my people Israel, to walk upon you. They will possess you, and you will be their inheritance; you will never again deprive them of their children.

13 "'This is what the Sovereign LORD says: Because people say to you, "You devour men and deprive your nation of its children," 14 therefore you will no longer devour men or make your nation childless, declares the Sovereign LORD. 15 No longer will I make you hear the taunts of the nations, and no longer will you suffer the scorn of the peoples or cause your nation to fall, declares the Sovereign LORD.'"

16 Again the word of the LORD came to me: 17 "Son of man, when the people of Israel were living in their own land, they defiled it by their conduct and their actions. Their conduct was like a woman's monthly uncleanness in my sight. 18 So I poured out my wrath on them because they had shed blood in the land and because they had defiled it with their idols. 19 I dispersed them among the nations, and they were scattered through the countries; I judged them according to their conduct and their actions. 20 And wherever they went among the nations they profaned my holy name, for it was said of them, 'These are the LORD's people, and yet they had to leave his land.' 21 I had concern for my holy name, which the house of Israel profaned among the nations where they had gone.

22 "Therefore say to the house of Israel, 'This is what the Sovereign LORD says: It is not for your sake, O house of Israel, that I am going to do these things, but for the sake of my holy name, which you have profaned among the nations where you have gone. 23 I will show the holiness of my great name, which has been profaned among the nations, the name you have profaned among them. Then the nations will know that I am the LORD, declares the Sovereign LORD, when I show myself holy through you before their eyes.

24 "'For I will take you out of the nations; I will gather you from all the countries and bring you back into your own land. 25 I will sprinkle clean water on you, and you will be clean; I will cleanse you from all your impurities and from all your idols. 26 I will give you a new heart and put a new spirit in you; I will remove from you your heart of stone and give you a heart of flesh. 27 And I will put my Spirit in you and move you to follow my decrees and be careful to keep my laws. 28 You will live in the land I gave your forefathers; you will be my people, and I will be your God. 29 I will save you from all your uncleanness. I will call for the grain and make it plentiful and will not bring famine upon you. 30 I will increase the fruit of the trees and the crops of the field, so that you will no longer suffer disgrace among the nations because of famine. 31 Then you will remember your evil ways and wicked deeds, and you will loathe yourselves for your sins and detestable practices. 32 I want you to know that I am not doing this for your sake, declares the Sovereign LORD. Be ashamed and disgraced for your conduct, O house of Israel!

33 "'This is what the Sovereign LORD says: On the day I cleanse you from all your sins, I will resettle your towns, and the ruins will be rebuilt. 34 The desolate land will be cultivated instead of lying desolate in the sight of all who pass through it. 35 They will say, "This land that was laid waste has become like the garden of Eden; the cities that were lying in ruins, desolate and destroyed, are now fortified and inhabited." 36 Then the nations around you that remain will know that I the LORD have rebuilt what was destroyed and have replanted what was desolate. I the LORD have spoken, and I will do it.'

37 "This is what the Sovereign LORD says: Once again I will yield to the plea of the house of Israel and do this for them: I will make their

people as numerous as sheep, [38]as numerous as the flocks for offerings at Jerusalem during her appointed feasts. So will the ruined cities be filled with flocks of people. Then they will know that I am the LORD."

The Valley of Dry Bones

37 The hand of the LORD was upon me, and he brought me out by the Spirit of the LORD and set me in the middle of a valley; it was full of bones. [2]He led me back and forth among them, and I saw a great many bones on the floor of the valley, bones that were very dry. [3]He asked me, "Son of man, can these bones live?"

I said, "O Sovereign LORD, you alone know."

[4]Then he said to me, "Prophesy to these bones and say to them, 'Dry bones, hear the word of the LORD! [5]This is what the Sovereign LORD says to these bones: I will make breath[a] enter you, and you will come to life. [6]I will attach tendons to you and make flesh come upon you and cover you with skin; I will put breath in you, and you will come to life. Then you will know that I am the LORD.'"

[7]So I prophesied as I was commanded. And as I was prophesying, there was a noise, a rattling sound, and the bones came together, bone to bone. [8]I looked, and tendons and flesh appeared on them and skin covered them, but there was no breath in them.

[9]Then he said to me, "Prophesy to the breath; prophesy, son of man, and say to it, 'This is what the Sovereign LORD says: Come from the four winds, O breath, and breathe into these slain, that they may live.'" [10]So I prophesied as he commanded me, and breath entered them; they came to life and stood up on their feet—a vast army.

[11]Then he said to me: "Son of man, these bones are the whole house of Israel. They say, 'Our bones are dried up and our hope is gone; we are cut off.' [12]Therefore prophesy and say to them: 'This is what the Sovereign LORD says:

O my people, I am going to open your graves and bring you up from them; I will bring you back to the land of Israel. [13]Then you, my people, will know that I am the LORD, when I open your graves and bring you up from them. [14]I will put my Spirit in you and you will live, and I will settle you in your own land. Then you will know that I the LORD have spoken, and I have done it, declares the LORD.'"

One Nation Under One King

[15]The word of the LORD came to me: [16]"Son of man, take a stick of wood and write on it, 'Belonging to Judah and the Israelites associated with him.' Then take another stick of wood, and write on it, 'Ephraim's stick, belonging to Joseph and all the house of Israel associated with him.' [17]Join them together into one stick so that they will become one in your hand.

[18]"When your countrymen ask you, 'Won't you tell us what you mean by this?' [19]say to them, 'This is what the Sovereign LORD says: I am going to take the stick of Joseph—which is in Ephraim's hand—and of the Israelite tribes associated with him, and join it to Judah's stick, making them a single stick of wood, and they will become one in my hand.' [20]Hold before their eyes the sticks you have written on [21]and say to them, 'This is what the Sovereign LORD says: I will take the Israelites out of the nations where they have gone. I will gather them from all around and bring them back into their own land. [22]I will make them one nation in the land, on the mountains of Israel. There will be one king over all of them and they will never again be two nations or be divided into two kingdoms. [23]They will no longer defile themselves with their idols and vile images or with any of their offenses, for I will save them from all their sinful backsliding,[b] and I will cleanse them. They will be my people, and I will be their God.

Ezekiel 36:36

God Rebuilds Lives

"Then the nations around you that remain will know that I the LORD have rebuilt what was destroyed and have replanted what was desolate. I the LORD have spoken, and I will do it."

---

[a]5 The Hebrew for this word can also mean *wind* or *spirit* (see verses 6–14).   [b]23 Many Hebrew manuscripts (see also Septuagint); most Hebrew manuscripts *all their dwelling places where they sinned*

Life From Death

Ezekiel 37:3–4

He asked me, "Son of man, can these bones live?" I said, "O Sovereign LORD, you alone know." Then he said to me, "Prophesy to these bones and say to them, 'Dry bones, hear the word of the LORD!' "

reflection

1 How far are you in the process of regeneration? Where is God continuing to work on you?

2 What keeps you from believing that God can restore the parts of your life that feel dead or broken?

3 What is the "something more" God may be calling you to?

RELATED READINGS

Genesis 2:7;
John 8:3–11;
Romans 6:3–4;
2 Corinthians 3:18

IN ONE OF THE MOST STRIKING parts of Ezekiel's prophecy, God gave him a vision right out of a fright night for middle schoolers— a valley of death full of skeletons so decayed they were just piles of bones.

Nevertheless, God's message wasn't about death; it was about life. It was about God's power to bring life from death. It doesn't matter if the body is in the ground—or if what's left of it is on the ground. It doesn't matter if the skeleton has come apart and is mixed in with other old bones. God has the power to bring life out of a valley of death.

We may be physically alive, but sometimes we feel as if we're wandering in that valley. We feel as spiritually, emotionally or even relationally as dead as an old pile of bones. Inside we may feel as useless as old skeletons. If we're stuck in our old patterns, we may feel that it's too late to change. If we've been waiting to serve God in a specific way, we may fear that we've waited too long. We are oh-so-certain that our chance to be all God wants us to be has passed us by. But Ezekiel's vision reminds us that nothing and no one is too far gone for God to regenerate. God is able to resurrect dead dreams, missed opportunities, dying marriages and terminal friendships. He is God, and he can do anything.

Instead of believing that your mistakes and regrets pose too much of an obstacle to him, do you believe God can energize you with new life and purpose? Can you look beyond the vulture-picked-over-dry-bones of your missteps, rebellions and outright mess-ups? Will you see that the hope of your life is wrapped up not in your own power to overcome your inertia and bad habits but in God's desire to renew you, to call you to something more?

Monday

Go to page 1046 for your next devotional reading.

²⁴"'My servant David will be king over them, and they will all have one shepherd. They will follow my laws and be careful to keep my decrees. ²⁵They will live in the land I gave to my servant Jacob, the land where your fathers lived. They and their children and their children's children will live there forever, and David my servant will be their prince forever. ²⁶I will make a covenant of peace with them; it will be an everlasting covenant. I will establish them and increase their numbers, and I will put my sanctuary among them forever. ²⁷My dwelling place will be with them; I will be their God, and they will be my people. ²⁸Then the nations will know that I the LORD make Israel holy, when my sanctuary is among them forever.'"

A Prophecy Against Gog

38 The word of the LORD came to me: ²"Son of man, set your face against Gog, of the land of Magog, the chief prince of*ᵃ* Meshech and Tubal; prophesy against him ³and say: 'This is what the Sovereign LORD says: I am against you, O Gog, chief prince of*ᵇ* Meshech and Tubal. ⁴I will turn you around, put hooks in your jaws and bring you out with your whole army—your horses, your horsemen fully armed, and a great horde with large and small shields, all of them brandishing their swords. ⁵Persia, Cush*ᶜ* and Put will be with them, all with shields and helmets, ⁶also Gomer with all its troops, and Beth Togarmah from the far north with all its troops—the many nations with you.

⁷"'Get ready; be prepared, you and all the hordes gathered about you, and take command of them. ⁸After many days you will be called to arms. In future years you will invade a land that has recovered from war, whose people were gathered from many nations to the mountains of Israel, which had long been desolate. They had been brought out from the nations, and now all of them live in safety. ⁹You and all your troops and the many nations with you will go up, advancing like a storm; you will be like a cloud covering the land.

¹⁰"'This is what the Sovereign LORD says: On that day thoughts will come into your mind and you will devise an evil scheme. ¹¹You will say, "I will invade a land of unwalled villages; I will attack a peaceful and unsuspecting people—all of them living without walls and without gates and bars. ¹²I will plunder and loot and turn my hand against the resettled ruins and the people gathered from the nations, rich in livestock and goods, living at the center of the land." ¹³Sheba and Dedan and the merchants of Tarshish and all her villages*ᵈ* will say to you, "Have you come to plunder? Have you gathered your hordes to loot, to carry off silver and gold, to take away livestock and goods and to seize much plunder?"'

¹⁴"Therefore, son of man, prophesy and say to Gog: 'This is what the Sovereign LORD says: In that day, when my people Israel are living in safety, will you not take notice of it? ¹⁵You will come from your place in the far north, you and many nations with you, all of them riding on horses, a great horde, a mighty army. ¹⁶You will advance against my people Israel like a cloud that covers the land. In days to come, O Gog, I will bring you against my land, so that the nations may know me when I show myself holy through you before their eyes.

¹⁷"'This is what the Sovereign LORD says: Are you not the one I spoke of in former days by my servants the prophets of Israel? At that time they prophesied for years that I would bring you against them. ¹⁸This is what will happen in that day: When Gog attacks the land of Israel, my hot anger will be aroused, declares the Sovereign LORD. ¹⁹In my zeal and fiery wrath I declare that at that time there shall be a great earthquake in the land of Israel. ²⁰The fish of the sea, the birds of the air, the beasts of the field, every creature that moves along the ground, and all the people on the face of the earth will tremble at my presence. The mountains will be overturned, the cliffs will crumble and every wall will fall to the ground. ²¹I will summon a sword against Gog on all my mountains, declares the Sovereign LORD. Every man's sword will be against his brother. ²²I will execute judgment upon him with plague and bloodshed; I will pour down torrents of rain, hailstones and burning sulfur on him and on his troops and on the many nations with him. ²³And so I will show my greatness and my

ᵃ2 Or *the prince of Rosh,* ᵇ3 Or *Gog, prince of Rosh,* ᶜ5 That is, the upper Nile region ᵈ13 Or *her strong lions* holiness, and I will make myself known in the sight of many nations. Then they will know that I am the LORD.'

39

"Son of man, prophesy against Gog and say: 'This is what the Sovereign LORD says: I am against you, O Gog, chief prince of[a] Meshech and Tubal. [2] I will turn you around and drag you along. I will bring you from the far north and send you against the mountains of Israel. [3] Then I will strike your bow from your left hand and make your arrows drop from your right hand. [4] On the mountains of Israel you will fall, you and all your troops and the nations with you. I will give you as food to all kinds of carrion birds and to the wild animals. [5] You will fall in the open field, for I have spoken, declares the Sovereign LORD. [6] I will send fire on Magog and on those who live in safety in the coastlands, and they will know that I am the LORD.

[7] "I will make known my holy name among my people Israel. I will no longer let my holy name be profaned, and the nations will know that I the LORD am the Holy One in Israel. [8] It is coming! It will surely take place, declares the Sovereign LORD. This is the day I have spoken of.

[9] "Then those who live in the towns of Israel will go out and use the weapons for fuel and burn them up—the small and large shields, the bows and arrows, the war clubs and spears. For seven years they will use them for fuel. [10] They will not need to gather wood from the fields or cut it from the forests, because they will use the weapons for fuel. And they will plunder those who plundered them and loot those who looted them, declares the Sovereign LORD.

[11] "On that day I will give Gog a burial place in Israel, in the valley of those who travel east toward[b] the Sea.[c] It will block the way of travelers, because Gog and all his hordes will be buried there. So it will be called the Valley of Hamon Gog.[d]

[12] "For seven months the house of Israel will be burying them in order to cleanse the land. [13] All the people of the land will bury them, and the day I am glorified will be a memorable day for them, declares the Sovereign LORD.

[14] "Men will be regularly employed to cleanse the land. Some will go throughout the land and, in addition to them, others will bury those that remain on the ground. At the end of the seven months they will begin their search. [15] As they go through the land and one of them sees a human bone, he will set up a marker beside it until the gravediggers have buried it in the Valley of Hamon Gog. [16] (Also a town called Hamonah[e] will be there.) And so they will cleanse the land.'

[17] "Son of man, this is what the Sovereign LORD says: Call out to every kind of bird and all the wild animals: 'Assemble and come together from all around to the sacrifice I am preparing for you, the great sacrifice on the mountains of Israel. There you will eat flesh and drink blood. [18] You will eat the flesh of mighty men and drink the blood of the princes of the earth as if they were rams and lambs, goats and bulls—all of them fattened animals from Bashan. [19] At the sacrifice I am preparing for you, you will eat fat till you are glutted and drink blood till you are drunk. [20] At my table you will eat your fill of horses and riders, mighty men and soldiers of every kind,' declares the Sovereign LORD.

[21] "I will display my glory among the nations, and all the nations will see the punishment I inflict and the hand I lay upon them. [22] From that day forward the house of Israel will know that I am the LORD their God. [23] And the nations will know that the people of Israel went into exile for their sin, because they were unfaithful to me. So I hid my face from them and handed them over to their enemies, and they all fell by the sword. [24] I dealt with them according to their uncleanness and their offenses, and I hid my face from them.

Ezekiel 38:23

God Reveals His Greatness

"And so I will show my greatness and my holiness, and I will make myself known in the sight of many nations. Then they will know that I am the LORD."

---

[a] 1 Or *Gog, prince of Rosh,*   [b] 11 Or *of*   [c] 11 That is, the Dead Sea   [d] 11 *Hamon Gog* means *hordes of Gog.*   [e] 16 *Hamonah* means *horde.*

²⁵"Therefore this is what the Sovereign LORD says: I will now bring Jacob back from captivity[a] and will have compassion on all the people of Israel, and I will be zealous for my holy name. ²⁶They will forget their shame and all the unfaithfulness they showed toward me when they lived in safety in their land with no one to make them afraid. ²⁷When I have brought them back from the nations and have gathered them from the countries of their enemies, I will show myself holy through them in the sight of many nations. ²⁸Then they will know that I am the LORD their God, for though I sent them into exile among the nations, I will gather them to their own land, not leaving any behind. ²⁹I will no longer hide my face from them, for I will pour out my Spirit on the house of Israel, declares the Sovereign LORD."

The New Temple Area

40 In the twenty-fifth year of our exile, at the beginning of the year, on the tenth of the month, in the fourteenth year after the fall of the city—on that very day the hand of the LORD was upon me and he took me there. ²In visions of God he took me to the land of Israel and set me on a very high mountain, on whose south side were some buildings that looked like a city. ³He took me there, and I saw a man whose appearance was like bronze; he was standing in the gateway with a linen cord and a measuring rod in his hand. ⁴The man said to me, "Son of man, look with your eyes and hear with your ears and pay attention to everything I am going to show you, for that is why you have been brought here. Tell the house of Israel everything you see."

The East Gate to the Outer Court

⁵I saw a wall completely surrounding the temple area. The length of the measuring rod

Ezekiel 39:25

God Protects His Reputation

"Therefore this is what the Sovereign LORD says: I will now bring Jacob back from captivity and will have compassion on all the people of Israel, and I will be zealous for my holy name."

in the man's hand was six long cubits, each of which was a cubit[b] and a handbreadth.[c] He measured the wall; it was one measuring rod thick and one rod high.

⁶Then he went to the gate facing east. He climbed its steps and measured the threshold of the gate; it was one rod deep.[d] ⁷The alcoves for the guards were one rod long and one rod wide, and the projecting walls between the alcoves were five cubits thick. And the threshold of the gate next to the portico facing the temple was one rod deep.

⁸Then he measured the portico of the gateway; ⁹it[e] was eight cubits deep and its jambs were two cubits thick. The portico of the gateway faced the temple.

¹⁰Inside the east gate were three alcoves on each side; the three had the same measurements, and the faces of the projecting walls on each side had the same measurements. ¹¹Then he measured the width of the entrance to the gateway; it was ten cubits and its length was thirteen cubits. ¹²In front of each alcove was a wall one cubit high, and the alcoves were six cubits square. ¹³Then he measured the gateway from the top of the rear wall of one alcove to the top of the opposite one; the distance was twenty-five cubits from one parapet opening to the opposite one. ¹⁴He measured along the faces of the projecting walls all around the inside of the gateway—sixty cubits. The measurement was up to the portico[f] facing the courtyard.[g] ¹⁵The distance from the entrance of the gateway to the far end of its portico was fifty cubits. ¹⁶The alcoves and the projecting walls inside the gateway were surmounted by narrow parapet openings all around, as was the portico; the openings all around faced inward. The faces of the projecting walls were decorated with palm trees.

---

[a]25 Or *now restore the fortunes of Jacob*   [b]5 The common cubit was about 1 1/2 feet (about 0.5 meter).   [c]5 That is, about 3 inches (about 8 centimeters)   [d]6 Septuagint; Hebrew *deep, the first threshold, one rod deep*   [e]8,9 Many Hebrew manuscripts, Septuagint, Vulgate and Syriac; most Hebrew manuscripts *gateway facing the temple; it was one rod deep.* ⁹*Then he measured the portico of the gateway; it*   [f]14 Septuagint; Hebrew *projecting wall*   [g]14 The meaning of the Hebrew for this verse is uncertain.

The Outer Court

17Then he brought me into the outer court. There I saw some rooms and a pavement that had been constructed all around the court; there were thirty rooms along the pavement. 18It abutted the sides of the gateways and was as wide as they were long; this was the lower pavement. 19Then he measured the distance from the inside of the lower gateway to the outside of the inner court; it was a hundred cubits on the east side as well as on the north.

The North Gate

20Then he measured the length and width of the gate facing north, leading into the outer court. 21Its alcoves—three on each side—its projecting walls and its portico had the same measurements as those of the first gateway. It was fifty cubits long and twenty-five cubits wide. 22Its openings, its portico and its palm tree decorations had the same measurements as those of the gate facing east. Seven steps led up to it, with its portico opposite them. 23There was a gate to the inner court facing the north gate, just as there was on the east. He measured from one gate to the opposite one; it was a hundred cubits.

The South Gate

24Then he led me to the south side and I saw a gate facing south. He measured its jambs and its portico, and they had the same measurements as the others. 25The gateway and its portico had narrow openings all around, like the openings of the others. It was fifty cubits long and twenty-five cubits wide. 26Seven steps led up to it, with its portico opposite them; it had palm tree decorations on the faces of the projecting walls on each side. 27The inner court also had a gate facing south, and he measured from this gate to the outer gate on the south side; it was a hundred cubits.

Gates to the Inner Court

28Then he brought me into the inner court through the south gate, and he measured the south gate; it had the same measurements as the others. 29Its alcoves, its projecting walls and its portico had the same measurements as the others. The gateway and its portico had openings all around. It was fifty cubits long and twenty-

five cubits wide. 30(The porticoes of the gateways around the inner court were twenty-five cubits wide and five cubits deep.) 31Its portico faced the outer court; palm trees decorated its jambs, and eight steps led up to it.

32Then he brought me to the inner court on the east side, and he measured the gateway; it had the same measurements as the others. 33Its alcoves, its projecting walls and its portico had the same measurements as the others. The gateway and its portico had openings all around. It was fifty cubits long and twenty-five cubits wide. 34Its portico faced the outer court; palm trees decorated the jambs on either side, and eight steps led up to it.

35Then he brought me to the north gate and measured it. It had the same measurements as the others, 36as did its alcoves, its projecting walls and its portico, and it had openings all around. It was fifty cubits long and twenty-five cubits wide. 37Its portico[a] faced the outer court; palm trees decorated the jambs on either side, and eight steps led up to it.

The Rooms for Preparing Sacrifices

38A room with a doorway was by the portico in each of the inner gateways, where the burnt offerings were washed. 39In the portico of the gateway were two tables on each side, on which the burnt offerings, sin offerings and guilt offerings were slaughtered. 40By the outside wall of the portico of the gateway, near the steps at the entrance to the north gateway were two tables, and on the other side of the steps were two tables. 41So there were four tables on one side of the gateway and four on the other—eight tables in all—on which the sacrifices were slaughtered. 42There were also four tables of dressed stone for the burnt offerings, each a cubit and a half long, a cubit and a half wide and a cubit high. On them were placed the utensils for slaughtering the burnt offerings and the other sacrifices. 43And double-pronged hooks, each a handbreadth long, were attached to the wall all around. The tables were for the flesh of the offerings.

Rooms for the Priests

44Outside the inner gate, within the inner court, were two rooms, one[b] at the side of the

---

a37 Septuagint (see also verses 31 and 34); Hebrew jambs   b44 Septuagint; Hebrew were rooms for singers, which were north gate and facing south, and another at the side of the south*a* gate and facing north. **45**He said to me, "The room facing south is for the priests who have charge of the temple, **46**and the room facing north is for the priests who have charge of the altar. These are the sons of Zadok, who are the only Levites who may draw near to the LORD to minister before him."

47Then he measured the court: It was square—a hundred cubits long and a hundred cubits wide. And the altar was in front of the temple.

The Temple

48He brought me to the portico of the temple and measured the jambs of the portico; they were five cubits wide on either side. The width of the entrance was fourteen cubits and its projecting walls were*b* three cubits wide on either side. **49**The portico was twenty cubits wide, and twelve*c* cubits from front to back. It was reached by a flight of stairs,*d* and there were pillars on each side of the jambs.

41 Then the man brought me to the outer sanctuary and measured the jambs; the width of the jambs was six cubits*e* on each side.*f* **2**The entrance was ten cubits wide, and the projecting walls on each side of it were five cubits wide. He also measured the outer sanctuary; it was forty cubits long and twenty cubits wide.

3Then he went into the inner sanctuary and measured the jambs of the entrance; each was two cubits wide. The entrance was six cubits wide, and the projecting walls on each side of it were seven cubits wide. **4**And he measured the length of the inner sanctuary; it was twenty cubits, and its width was twenty cubits across the end of the outer sanctuary. He said to me, "This is the Most Holy Place."

5Then he measured the wall of the temple; it was six cubits thick, and each side room around the temple was four cubits wide. **6**The side rooms were on three levels, one above another, thirty on each level. There were ledges all around the wall of the temple to serve as supports for the side rooms, so that the supports were not inserted into the wall of the temple.

7The side rooms all around the temple were wider at each successive level. The structure surrounding the temple was built in ascending stages, so that the rooms widened as one went upward. A stairway went up from the lowest floor to the top floor through the middle floor.

8I saw that the temple had a raised base all around it, forming the foundation of the side rooms. It was the length of the rod, six long cubits. **9**The outer wall of the side rooms was five cubits thick. The open area between the side rooms of the temple **10**and the ⸂priests'⸃ rooms was twenty cubits wide all around the temple. **11**There were entrances to the side rooms from the open area, one on the north and another on the south; and the base adjoining the open area was five cubits wide all around.

12The building facing the temple courtyard on the west side was seventy cubits wide. The wall of the building was five cubits thick all around, and its length was ninety cubits.

13Then he measured the temple; it was a hundred cubits long, and the temple courtyard and the building with its walls were also a hundred cubits long. **14**The width of the temple courtyard on the east, including the front of the temple, was a hundred cubits.

15Then he measured the length of the building facing the courtyard at the rear of the temple, including its galleries on each side; it was a hundred cubits.

The outer sanctuary, the inner sanctuary and the portico facing the court, **16**as well as the thresholds and the narrow windows and galleries around the three of them—everything beyond and including the threshold was covered with wood. The floor, the wall up to the windows, and the windows were covered. **17**In the space above the outside of the entrance to the inner sanctuary and on the walls at regular intervals all around the inner and outer sanctuary **18**were carved cherubim and palm trees. Palm trees alternated with cherubim. Each cherub had two faces: **19**the face of a man toward the palm tree on one side and the face of a lion toward the palm tree on the other. They were carved all around the whole temple. **20**From the floor to the area above the

---

*a*44 Septuagint; Hebrew *east*   *b*48 Septuagint; Hebrew *entrance was*   *c*49 Septuagint; Hebrew *eleven*   *d*49 Hebrew; Septuagint *Ten steps led up to it*   *e*1 The common cubit was about 1 1/2 feet (about 0.5 meter).   *f*1 One Hebrew manuscript and Septuagint; most Hebrew manuscripts *side, the width of the tent* entrance, cherubim and palm trees were carved on the wall of the outer sanctuary.

21The outer sanctuary had a rectangular doorframe, and the one at the front of the Most Holy Place was similar. 22There was a wooden altar three cubits high and two cubits square*a*; its corners, its base*b* and its sides were of wood. The man said to me, "This is the table that is before the LORD." 23Both the outer sanctuary and the Most Holy Place had double doors. 24Each door had two leaves—two hinged leaves for each door. 25And on the doors of the outer sanctuary were carved cherubim and palm trees like those carved on the walls, and there was a wooden overhang on the front of the portico. 26On the sidewalls of the portico were narrow windows with palm trees carved on each side. The side rooms of the temple also had overhangs.

Rooms for the Priests

42 Then the man led me northward into the outer court and brought me to the rooms opposite the temple courtyard and opposite the outer wall on the north side. 2The building whose door faced north was a hundred cubits*c* long and fifty cubits wide. 3Both in the section twenty cubits from the inner court and in the section opposite the pavement of the outer court, gallery faced gallery at the three levels. 4In front of the rooms was an inner passageway ten cubits wide and a hundred cubits*d* long. Their doors were on the north. 5Now the upper rooms were narrower, for the galleries took more space from them than from the rooms on the lower and middle floors of the building. 6The rooms on the third floor had no pillars, as the courts had; so they were smaller in floor space than those on the lower and middle floors. 7There was an outer wall parallel to the rooms and the outer court; it extended in front of the rooms for fifty cubits. 8While the row of rooms on the side next to the outer court was fifty cubits long, the row on the side nearest the sanctuary was a hundred cubits long. 9The lower rooms had an entrance on the east side as one enters them from the outer court.

10On the south side*e* along the length of the wall of the outer court, adjoining the temple courtyard and opposite the outer wall, were rooms 11with a passageway in front of them. These were like the rooms on the north; they had the same length and width, with similar exits and dimensions. Similar to the doorways on the north 12were the doorways of the rooms on the south. There was a doorway at the beginning of the passageway that was parallel to the corresponding wall extending eastward, by which one enters the rooms.

13Then he said to me, "The north and south rooms facing the temple courtyard are the priests' rooms, where the priests who approach the LORD will eat the most holy offerings. There they will put the most holy offerings—the grain offerings, the sin offerings and the guilt offerings—for the place is holy. 14Once the priests enter the holy precincts, they are not to go into the outer court until they leave behind the garments in which they minister, for these are holy. They are to put on other clothes before they go near the places that are for the people."

15When he had finished measuring what was inside the temple area, he led me out by the east gate and measured the area all around: 16He measured the east side with the measuring rod; it was five hundred cubits.*f* 17He measured the north side; it was five hundred cubits*g* by the measuring rod. 18He measured the south side; it was five hundred cubits by the measuring rod. 19Then he turned to the west side and measured; it was five hundred cubits by the measuring rod. 20So he measured the area on all four sides. It had a wall around it, five hundred cubits long and five hundred cubits wide, to separate the holy from the common.

The Glory Returns to the Temple

43 Then the man brought me to the gate facing east, 2and I saw the glory of the God of Israel coming from the east. His voice was like the roar of rushing waters, and the land was radiant with his glory. 3The vision I saw was like the vision I had seen when he*h* came to destroy the city and like the visions I had seen by the Kebar River, and I fell facedown. 4The

---

*a*22 Septuagint; Hebrew *long*   *b*22 Septuagint; Hebrew *length*   *c*2 The common cubit was about 1 1/2 feet (about 0.5 meter).   *d*4 Septuagint and Syriac; Hebrew *and one cubit*   *e*10 Septuagint; Hebrew *Eastward*   *f*16 See Septuagint of verse 17; Hebrew *rods*; also in verses 18 and 19.   *g*17 Septuagint; Hebrew *rods*   *h*3 Some Hebrew manuscripts and Vulgate; most Hebrew manuscripts *I* glory of the Lord entered the temple through the gate facing east. [5]Then the Spirit lifted me up and brought me into the inner court, and the glory of the Lord filled the temple.

[6]While the man was standing beside me, I heard someone speaking to me from inside the temple. [7]He said: "Son of man, this is the place of my throne and the place for the soles of my feet. This is where I will live among the Israelites forever. The house of Israel will never again defile my holy name—neither they nor their kings—by their prostitution[a] and the lifeless idols[b] of their kings at their high places. [8]When they placed their threshold next to my threshold and their doorposts beside my doorposts, with only a wall between me and them, they defiled my holy name by their detestable practices. So I destroyed them in my anger. [9]Now let them put away from me their prostitution and the lifeless idols of their kings, and I will live among them forever.

[10]"Son of man, describe the temple to the people of Israel, that they may be ashamed of their sins. Let them consider the plan, [11]and if they are ashamed of all they have done, make known to them the design of the temple—its arrangement, its exits and entrances—its whole design and all its regulations[c] and laws. Write these down before them so that they may be faithful to its design and follow all its regulations.

[12]"This is the law of the temple: All the surrounding area on top of the mountain will be most holy. Such is the law of the temple.

The Altar

[13]"These are the measurements of the altar in long cubits, that cubit being a cubit[d] and a handbreadth[e]: Its gutter is a cubit deep and a cubit wide, with a rim of one span[f] around the edge. And this is the height of the altar: [14]From the gutter on the ground up to the lower ledge

it is two cubits high and a cubit wide, and from the smaller ledge up to the larger ledge it is four cubits high and a cubit wide. [15]The altar hearth is four cubits high, and four horns project upward from the hearth. [16]The altar hearth is square, twelve cubits long and twelve cubits wide. [17]The upper ledge also is square, fourteen cubits long and fourteen cubits wide, with a rim of half a cubit and a gutter of a cubit all around. The steps of the altar face east."

[18]Then he said to me, "Son of man, this is what the Sovereign Lord says: These will be the regulations for sacrificing burnt offerings and sprinkling blood upon the altar when it is built: [19]You are to give a young bull as a sin offering to the priests, who are Levites, of the family of Zadok, who come near to minister before me, declares the Sovereign Lord. [20]You are to take some of its blood and put it on the four horns of the altar and on the four corners of the upper ledge and all around the rim, and so purify the altar and make atonement for it. [21]You are to take the bull for the sin offering and burn it in the designated part of the temple area outside the sanctuary.

[22]"On the second day you are to offer a male goat without defect for a sin offering, and the altar is to be purified as it was purified with the bull. [23]When you have finished purifying it, you are to offer a young bull and a ram from the flock, both without defect. [24]You are to offer them before the Lord, and the priests are to sprinkle salt on them and sacrifice them as a burnt offering to the Lord.

[25]"For seven days you are to provide a male goat daily for a sin offering; you are also to provide a young bull and a ram from the flock, both without defect. [26]For seven days they are to make atonement for the altar and cleanse it; thus they will dedicate it. [27]At the end of these days, from the eighth day on, the priests are to present your burnt offerings and fellowship

> Ezekiel 43:2
>
> *God Displays His Glory*
>
> And I saw the glory of the God of Israel coming from the east. His voice was like the roar of rushing waters, and the land was radiant with his glory.

---

[a]7 Or *their spiritual adultery*; also in verse 9   [b]7 Or *the corpses*; also in verse 9   [c]11 Some Hebrew manuscripts and Septuagint; most Hebrew manuscripts *regulations and its whole design*   [d]13 The common cubit was about 1 1/2 feet (about 0.5 meter).   [e]13 That is, about 3 inches (about 8 centimeters)   [f]13 That is, about 9 inches (about 22 centimeters)

God in You

Read: Ezekiel 43:1–12

Ezekiel 43:5

Then the Spirit lifted me up and brought me into the inner court, and the glory of the LORD filled the temple.

reflection

1 What sinful habit, if you allow it to continue, could destroy your temple?

2 How could you better care for your temple?

3 What does God's glory look like in your life? (For some help, see Galatians 5:22–23.)

RELATED READINGS

1 Kings 6:1–38;
8:57–61; 9:6–9;
John 2:18–22;
1 Corinthians 6:19–20

PICTURE A CONSUMING FIRE, a cumulus cloud, a rainbow on an overcast day. In the Old Testament, God gives us many compelling images of his glory. At that time, his glory dwelled in temples made by human hands. And one day, as Ezekiel's grandiose vision details, his glory will fill the temple once again.

The unifying theme of God's glory, in both the Old and New Testaments, is holiness: the purity of a consuming fire (Exodus 24:17), the stark contrast of a white cloud against the sky (Exodus 40:35), and the hope that a colorful rainbow inspires on a rainy day (Ezekiel 1:28). God's glory is another way to speak of his holiness.

While we wait for God's glory to fill the temple one day, the God of the universe makes his home in human hearts. When Jesus returned to heaven, he left the Holy Spirit to fill the hearts of his people. God resides within those who have invited him. Our bodies are temples of the Lord, says the apostle Paul in 1 Corinthians 6:19, so we must honor them by pursuing and practicing holiness.

We see a pattern through the Old and New Testaments of sin destroying the temple. The same thing happens today with our temples (bodies). Sin drives out holiness and destroys our fellowship with God.

Ezekiel's vision should challenge us to make a choice. We can fill our temple with sin or with God's glory . . . but there is not room for both. Either sin will fill our temple and destroy us body and soul, or God's holiness, the righteousness that comes from him, will find a home in our hearts.

Ezekiel's vision ultimately speaks of a time when the temple will no longer be defiled by sin. Instead, God's glory, his beauty, splendor and majesty will fill the temple.

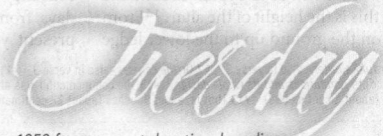

Go to page 1050 for your next devotional reading.

offerings[a] on the altar. Then I will accept you, declares the Sovereign LORD."

The Prince, the Levites, the Priests

44 Then the man brought me back to the outer gate of the sanctuary, the one facing east, and it was shut. ²The LORD said to me, "This gate is to remain shut. It must not be opened; no one may enter through it. It is to remain shut because the LORD, the God of Israel, has entered through it. ³The prince himself is the only one who may sit inside the gateway to eat in the presence of the LORD. He is to enter by way of the portico of the gateway and go out the same way."

⁴Then the man brought me by way of the north gate to the front of the temple. I looked and saw the glory of the LORD filling the temple of the LORD, and I fell facedown.

⁵The LORD said to me, "Son of man, look carefully, listen closely and give attention to everything I tell you concerning all the regulations regarding the temple of the LORD. Give attention to the entrance of the temple and all the exits of the sanctuary. ⁶Say to the rebellious house of Israel, 'This is what the Sovereign LORD says: Enough of your detestable practices, O house of Israel! ⁷In addition to all your other detestable practices, you brought foreigners uncircumcised in heart and flesh into my sanctuary, desecrating my temple while you offered me food, fat and blood, and you broke my covenant. ⁸Instead of carrying out your duty in regard to my holy things, you put others in charge of my sanctuary. ⁹This is what the Sovereign LORD says: No foreigner uncircumcised in heart and flesh is to enter my sanctuary, not even the foreigners who live among the Israelites.

¹⁰"'The Levites who went far from me when Israel went astray and who wandered from me after their idols must bear the consequences of their sin. ¹¹They may serve in my sanctuary, having charge of the gates of the temple and serving in it; they may slaughter the burnt offerings and sacrifices for the people and stand before the people and serve them. ¹²But because they served them in the presence of their idols and made the house of Israel fall into sin, therefore I have sworn with uplifted hand that they must bear the consequences of their sin, declares the Sovereign LORD. ¹³They are not to come near to serve me as priests or come near any of my holy things or my most holy offerings; they must bear the shame of their detestable practices. ¹⁴Yet I will put them in charge of the duties of the temple and all the work that is to be done in it.

¹⁵"'But the priests, who are Levites and descendants of Zadok and who faithfully carried out the duties of my sanctuary when the Israelites went astray from me, are to come near to minister before me; they are to stand before me to offer sacrifices of fat and blood, declares the Sovereign LORD. ¹⁶They alone are to enter my sanctuary; they alone are to come near my table to minister before me and perform my service.

¹⁷"'When they enter the gates of the inner court, they are to wear linen clothes; they must not wear any woolen garment while ministering at the gates of the inner court or inside the temple. ¹⁸They are to wear linen turbans on their heads and linen undergarments around their waists. They must not wear anything that makes them perspire. ¹⁹When they go out into the outer court where the people are, they are to take off the clothes they have been ministering in and are to leave them in the sacred rooms, and put on other clothes, so that they do not consecrate the people by means of their garments.

²⁰"'They must not shave their heads or let their hair grow long, but they are to keep the hair of their heads trimmed. ²¹No priest is to drink wine when he enters the inner court. ²²They must not marry widows or divorced women; they may marry only virgins of Israelite descent or widows of priests. ²³They are to teach my people the difference between the holy and the common and show them how to distinguish between the unclean and the clean.

²⁴"'In any dispute, the priests are to serve as judges and decide it according to my ordinances. They are to keep my laws and my decrees for all my appointed feasts, and they are to keep my Sabbaths holy.

---

[a]27 Traditionally *peace offerings*

²⁵ "'A priest must not defile himself by going near a dead person; however, if the dead person was his father or mother, son or daughter, brother or unmarried sister, then he may defile himself. ²⁶ After he is cleansed, he must wait seven days. ²⁷ On the day he goes into the inner court of the sanctuary to minister in the sanctuary, he is to offer a sin offering for himself, declares the Sovereign LORD.

²⁸ "'I am to be the only inheritance the priests have. You are to give them no possession in Israel; I will be their possession. ²⁹ They will eat the grain offerings, the sin offerings and the guilt offerings; and everything in Israel devoted[a] to the LORD will belong to them. ³⁰ The best of all the firstfruits and of all your special gifts will belong to the priests. You are to give them the first portion of your ground meal so that a blessing may rest on your household. ³¹ The priests must not eat anything, bird or animal, found dead or torn by wild animals.

Division of the Land

45 "'When you allot the land as an inheritance, you are to present to the LORD a portion of the land as a sacred district, 25,000 cubits long and 20,000[b] cubits wide; the entire area will be holy. ² Of this, a section 500 cubits square is to be for the sanctuary, with 50 cubits around it for open land. ³ In the sacred district, measure off a section 25,000 cubits[c] long and 10,000 cubits[d] wide. In it will be the sanctuary, the Most Holy Place. ⁴ It will be the sacred portion of the land for the priests, who minister in the sanctuary and who draw near to minister before the LORD. It will be a place for their houses as well as a holy place for the sanctuary. ⁵ An area 25,000 cubits long and 10,000 cubits wide will belong to the Levites, who serve in the temple, as their possession for towns to live in.[e]

⁶ "'You are to give the city as its property an area 5,000 cubits wide and 25,000 cubits long, adjoining the sacred portion; it will belong to the whole house of Israel.

⁷ "'The prince will have the land bordering each side of the area formed by the sacred district and the property of the city. It will extend westward from the west side and eastward from the east side, running lengthwise from the western to the eastern border parallel to one of the tribal portions. ⁸ This land will be his possession in Israel. And my princes will no longer oppress my people but will allow the house of Israel to possess the land according to their tribes.

⁹ "'This is what the Sovereign LORD says: You have gone far enough, O princes of Israel! Give up your violence and oppression and do what is just and right. Stop dispossessing my people, declares the Sovereign LORD. ¹⁰ You are to use accurate scales, an accurate ephah[f] and an accurate bath.[g] ¹¹ The ephah and the bath are to be the same size, the bath containing a tenth of a homer[h] and the ephah a tenth of a homer; the homer is to be the standard measure for both. ¹² The shekel[i] is to consist of twenty gerahs. Twenty shekels plus twenty-five shekels plus fifteen shekels equal one mina.[j]

Offerings and Holy Days

¹³ "'This is the special gift you are to offer: a sixth of an ephah from each homer of wheat and a sixth of an ephah from each homer of barley. ¹⁴ The prescribed portion of oil, measured by the bath, is a tenth of a bath from each cor (which consists of ten baths or one homer, for ten baths are equivalent to a homer). ¹⁵ Also one sheep is to be taken from every flock of two hundred from the well-watered pastures of Israel. These will be used for the grain offer-

---

Ezekiel 45:9

God Hates Oppression

"This is what the Sovereign LORD says: You have gone far enough, O princes of Israel! Give up your violence and oppression and do what is just and right. Stop dispossessing my people, declares the Sovereign LORD."

---

a29 The Hebrew term refers to the irrevocable giving over of things or persons to the LORD.   b1 Septuagint (see also verses 3 and 5 and 48:9); Hebrew 10,000   c3 That is, about 7 miles (about 12 kilometers)   d3 That is, about 3 miles (about 5 kilometers)   e5 Septuagint; Hebrew temple; they will have as their possession 20 rooms   f10 An ephah was a dry measure.   g10 A bath was a liquid measure. h11 A homer was a dry measure.   i12 A shekel weighed about 2/5 ounce (about 11.5 grams).   j12 That is, 60 shekels; the common mina was 50 shekels.

ings, burnt offerings and fellowship offerings[a] to make atonement for the people, declares the Sovereign LORD. [16]All the people of the land will participate in this special gift for the use of the prince in Israel. [17]It will be the duty of the prince to provide the burnt offerings, grain offerings and drink offerings at the festivals, the New Moons and the Sabbaths—at all the appointed feasts of the house of Israel. He will provide the sin offerings, grain offerings, burnt offerings and fellowship offerings to make atonement for the house of Israel.

[18]"'This is what the Sovereign LORD says: In the first month on the first day you are to take a young bull without defect and purify the sanctuary. [19]The priest is to take some of the blood of the sin offering and put it on the doorposts of the temple, on the four corners of the upper ledge of the altar and on the gateposts of the inner court. [20]You are to do the same on the seventh day of the month for anyone who sins unintentionally or through ignorance; so you are to make atonement for the temple.

[21]"'In the first month on the fourteenth day you are to observe the Passover, a feast lasting seven days, during which you shall eat bread made without yeast. [22]On that day the prince is to provide a bull as a sin offering for himself and for all the people of the land. [23]Every day during the seven days of the Feast he is to provide seven bulls and seven rams without defect as a burnt offering to the LORD, and a male goat for a sin offering. [24]He is to provide as a grain offering an ephah for each bull and an ephah for each ram, along with a hin[b] of oil for each ephah.

[25]"'During the seven days of the Feast, which begins in the seventh month on the fifteenth day, he is to make the same provision for sin offerings, burnt offerings, grain offerings and oil.

46

"'This is what the Sovereign LORD says: The gate of the inner court facing east is to be shut on the six working days, but on the Sabbath day and on the day of the New Moon it is to be opened. [2]The prince is to enter from the outside through the portico of the gateway and stand by the gatepost. The priests are to

sacrifice his burnt offering and his fellowship offerings.[c] He is to worship at the threshold of the gateway and then go out, but the gate will not be shut until evening. [3]On the Sabbaths and New Moons the people of the land are to worship in the presence of the LORD at the entrance to that gateway. [4]The burnt offering the prince brings to the LORD on the Sabbath day is to be six male lambs and a ram, all without defect. [5]The grain offering given with the ram is to be an ephah,[d] and the grain offering with the lambs is to be as much as he pleases, along with a hin[b] of oil for each ephah. [6]On the day of the New Moon he is to offer a young bull, six lambs and a ram, all without defect. [7]He is to provide as a grain offering one ephah with the bull, one ephah with the ram, and with the lambs as much as he wants to give, along with a hin of oil with each ephah. [8]When the prince enters, he is to go in through the portico of the gateway, and he is to come out the same way.

[9]"'When the people of the land come before the LORD at the appointed feasts, whoever enters by the north gate to worship is to go out the south gate; and whoever enters by the south gate is to go out the north gate. No one is to return through the gate by which he entered, but each is to go out the opposite gate. [10]The prince is to be among them, going in when they go in and going out when they go out.

[11]"'At the festivals and the appointed feasts, the grain offering is to be an ephah with a bull, an ephah with a ram, and with the lambs as much as one pleases, along with a hin of oil for each ephah. [12]When the prince provides a freewill offering to the LORD—whether a burnt offering or fellowship offerings—the gate facing east is to be opened for him. He shall offer his burnt offering or his fellowship offerings as he does on the Sabbath day. Then he shall go out, and after he has gone out, the gate will be shut.

[13]"'Every day you are to provide a year-old lamb without defect for a burnt offering to the LORD; morning by morning you shall provide it. [14]You are also to provide with it morning by morning a grain offering, consisting of a sixth of an ephah with a third of a hin of oil to

---

[a]15 Traditionally *peace offerings*; also in verse 17   [b]24,5 That is, probably about 4 quarts (about 4 liters)   [c]2 Traditionally *peace offerings*; also in verse 12   [d]5 That is, probably about 3/5 bushel (about 22 liters)

Once and for All

Read: Ezekiel 45:18–25

Ezekiel 45:22–23

"On that day the prince is to provide a bull as a sin offering for himself and for all the people of the land. Every day during the seven days of the Feast he is to provide seven bulls and seven rams without defect as a burnt offering to the LORD, and a male goat for a sin offering."

reflection

1 How does the sacrifice of Jesus reveal his love for you?

2 Whenever you struggle with feelings of guilt over confessed sin, what can you do to remind yourself that you are forgiven?

3 What action can you take today that will show that you believe that your sin is paid for?

RELATED READINGS

Psalm 103:11–12;
Hebrews 9:11–14;
10:1–14

IMAGINE YOUR CALENDAR reading something like this:

9:00 A.M.	Dentist
10:00 A.M.	Cleaners, bank
12:30 P.M.	Lunch meeting
2:30 P.M.	Pick up kids/goat
4:00 P.M.	Stop by altar for sacrifice
Note to self:	Make sacrifice third Tuesday of every month.

Are you nagged by guilty feelings over your sins? Do you replay mistakes in your head over and over? For the Israelites, sin must have been almost continually on their minds. Just when they finished one sacrifice, it was time for another. The Old Testament sacrificial system was extremely complex, with many dates and details to remember. Sacrifices were made again and again—for the same individuals. Because they could not permanently remove the sin of the people, the blood of countless animals spilled down the altar year after year.

Only one sacrifice has ever been sufficient to atone for people's sin once for all time. Through Jesus Christ's death on the cross we can receive forgiveness from sin—permanently. There is no additional sacrifice needed.

Maybe you have personally received Christ's gift of forgiveness, but you wrestle with guilt over past sins. If that is the case, you probably don't need a calendar like the Israelites' had to remind you of your sin; you may even have plenty of people in your life that won't let you forget it. Your thoughts constantly accuse you, and you feel that Christ's sacrifice wasn't enough to pay for your failures and mistakes.

These thoughts and feelings are not from God. Satan would like nothing more than to make us feel that we are not forgiven. Satan reminds us of our sins, holding them over our heads. But when we believe his lies, we deny the truth of what Christ accomplished.

The next time you feel guilt start to surface, recall the permanent and perfect sacrifice of Christ. He paid for your sin. All of it.

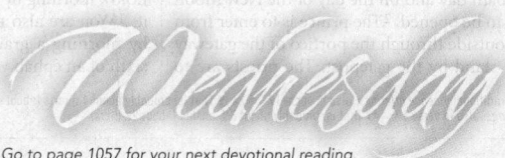

Wednesday

Go to page 1057 for your next devotional reading.

moisten the flour. The presenting of this grain offering to the LORD is a lasting ordinance. **15**So the lamb and the grain offering and the oil shall be provided morning by morning for a regular burnt offering.

16" 'This is what the Sovereign LORD says: If the prince makes a gift from his inheritance to one of his sons, it will also belong to his descendants; it is to be their property by inheritance. **17**If, however, he makes a gift from his inheritance to one of his servants, the servant may keep it until the year of freedom; then it will revert to the prince. His inheritance belongs to his sons only; it is theirs. **18**The prince must not take any of the inheritance of the people, driving them off their property. He is to give his sons their inheritance out of his own property, so that none of my people will be separated from his property.' "

19Then the man brought me through the entrance at the side of the gate to the sacred rooms facing north, which belonged to the priests, and showed me a place at the western end. **20**He said to me, "This is the place where the priests will cook the guilt offering and the sin offering and bake the grain offering, to avoid bringing them into the outer court and consecrating the people."

21He then brought me to the outer court and led me around to its four corners, and I saw in each corner another court. **22**In the four corners of the outer court were enclosed*a* courts, forty cubits long and thirty cubits wide; each of the courts in the four corners was the same size. **23**Around the inside of each of the four courts was a ledge of stone, with places for fire built all around under the ledge. **24**He said to me, "These are the kitchens where those who minister at the temple will cook the sacrifices of the people."

The River From the Temple

47 The man brought me back to the entrance of the temple, and I saw water coming out from under the threshold of the temple toward the east (for the temple faced east). The water was coming down from under the south side of the temple, south of the altar. **2**He then brought me out through the

north gate and led me around to the outside to the outer gate facing east, and the water was flowing from the south side.

3As the man went eastward with a measuring line in his hand, he measured off a thousand cubits*b* and then led me through water that was ankle-deep. **4**He measured off another thousand cubits and led me through water that was knee-deep. He measured off another thousand and led me through water that was up to the waist. **5**He measured off another thousand, but now it was a river that I could not cross, because the water had risen and was deep enough to swim in—a river that no one could cross. **6**He asked me, "Son of man, do you see this?"

Then he led me back to the bank of the river. **7**When I arrived there, I saw a great number of trees on each side of the river. **8**He said to me, "This water flows toward the eastern region and goes down into the Arabah,*c* where it enters the Sea.*d* When it empties into the Sea,*d* the water there becomes fresh. **9**Swarms of living creatures will live wherever the river flows. There will be large numbers of fish, because this water flows there and makes the salt water fresh; so where the river flows everything will live. **10**Fishermen will stand along the shore; from En Gedi to En Eglaim there will be places for spreading nets. The fish will be of many kinds—like the fish of the Great Sea.*e* **11**But the swamps and marshes will not become fresh; they will be left for salt. **12**Fruit trees of all kinds will grow on both banks of the river. Their leaves will not wither, nor will their fruit fail. Every month they will bear, because the water from the sanctuary flows to them. Their fruit will serve for food and their leaves for healing."

The Boundaries of the Land

13This is what the Sovereign LORD says: "These are the boundaries by which you are to divide the land for an inheritance among the twelve tribes of Israel, with two portions for Joseph. **14**You are to divide it equally among them. Because I swore with uplifted hand to give it to your forefathers, this land will become your inheritance.

---

*a*22 The meaning of the Hebrew for this word is uncertain.   *b*3 That is, about 1,500 feet (about 450 meters)   *c*8 Or *the Jordan Valley*   *d*8 That is, the Dead Sea   *e*10 That is, the Mediterranean; also in verses 15, 19 and 20

15 "This is to be the boundary of the land:

"On the north side it will run from the Great Sea by the Hethlon road past Lebo[a] Hamath to Zedad, 16 Berothah[b] and Sibraim (which lies on the border between Damascus and Hamath), as far as Hazer Hatticon, which is on the border of Hauran. 17 The boundary will extend from the sea to Hazar Enan,[c] along the northern border of Damascus, with the border of Hamath to the north. This will be the north boundary.

18 "On the east side the boundary will run between Hauran and Damascus, along the Jordan between Gilead and the land of Israel, to the eastern sea and as far as Tamar.[d] This will be the east boundary.

19 "On the south side it will run from Tamar as far as the waters of Meribah Kadesh, then along the Wadi of Egypt to the Great Sea. This will be the south boundary.

20 "On the west side, the Great Sea will be the boundary to a point opposite Lebo[e] Hamath. This will be the west boundary.

21 "You are to distribute this land among yourselves according to the tribes of Israel. 22 You are to allot it as an inheritance for yourselves and for the aliens who have settled among you and who have children. You are to consider them as native-born Israelites; along with you they are to be allotted an inheritance among the tribes of Israel. 23 In whatever tribe the alien settles, there you are to give him his inheritance," declares the Sovereign LORD.

The Division of the Land

48 "These are the tribes, listed by name: At the northern frontier, Dan will have one portion; it will follow the Hethlon road to Lebo[f] Hamath; Hazar Enan and the northern border of Damascus next to Hamath will be part of its border from the east side to the west side.

2 "Asher will have one portion; it will border the territory of Dan from east to west.

3 "Naphtali will have one portion; it will border the territory of Asher from east to west.

4 "Manasseh will have one portion; it will bor-

der the territory of Naphtali from east to west.

5 "Ephraim will have one portion; it will border the territory of Manasseh from east to west.

6 "Reuben will have one portion; it will border the territory of Ephraim from east to west.

7 "Judah will have one portion; it will border the territory of Reuben from east to west.

8 "Bordering the territory of Judah from east to west will be the portion you are to present as a special gift. It will be 25,000 cubits[g] wide, and its length from east to west will equal one of the tribal portions; the sanctuary will be in the center of it.

9 "The special portion you are to offer to the LORD will be 25,000 cubits long and 10,000 cubits[h] wide. 10 This will be the sacred portion for the priests. It will be 25,000 cubits long on the north side, 10,000 cubits wide on the west side, 10,000 cubits wide on the east side and 25,000 cubits long on the south side. In the center of it will be the sanctuary of the LORD. 11 This will be for the consecrated priests, the Zadokites, who were faithful in serving me and did not go astray as the Levites did when the Israelites went astray. 12 It will be a special gift to them from the sacred portion of the land, a most holy portion, bordering the territory of the Levites.

13 "Alongside the territory of the priests, the Levites will have an allotment 25,000 cubits long and 10,000 cubits wide. Its total length will be 25,000 cubits and its width 10,000 cubits. 14 They must not sell or exchange any of it. This is the best of the land and must not pass into other hands, because it is holy to the LORD.

15 "The remaining area, 5,000 cubits wide and 25,000 cubits long, will be for the common use of the city, for houses and for pastureland. The city will be in the center of it 16 and will have these measurements: the north side 4,500 cubits, the south side 4,500 cubits, the east side 4,500 cubits, and the west side 4,500 cubits. 17 The pastureland for the city will be 250 cubits on the north, 250 cubits on the south, 250 cubits on the east, and 250 cubits on the west. 18 What remains of the area, bordering on the sacred portion and running the length of it, will

---

*a*15 Or *past the entrance to*   *b*15,16 See Septuagint and Ezekiel 48:1; Hebrew *road to go into Zedad,* *16*Hamath, Berothah   *c*17 Hebrew *Enon,* a variant of *Enan*   *d*18 Septuagint and Syriac; Hebrew *Israel. You will measure to the eastern sea*   *e*20 Or *opposite the entrance to*   *f*1 Or *to the entrance to*   *g*8 That is, about 7 miles (about 12 kilometers)   *h*9 That is, about 3 miles (about 5 kilometers) be 10,000 cubits on the east side and 10,000 cubits on the west side. Its produce will supply food for the workers of the city. **19**The workers from the city who farm it will come from all the tribes of Israel. **20**The entire portion will be a square, 25,000 cubits on each side. As a special gift you will set aside the sacred portion, along with the property of the city.

21"What remains on both sides of the area formed by the sacred portion and the city property will belong to the prince. It will extend eastward from the 25,000 cubits of the sacred portion to the eastern border, and westward from the 25,000 cubits to the western border. Both these areas running the length of the tribal portions will belong to the prince, and the sacred portion with the temple sanctuary will be in the center of them. **22**So the property of the Levites and the property of the city will lie in the center of the area that belongs to the prince. The area belonging to the prince will lie between the border of Judah and the border of Benjamin.

23"As for the rest of the tribes: Benjamin will have one portion; it will extend from the east side to the west side.

24"Simeon will have one portion; it will border the territory of Benjamin from east to west.

25"Issachar will have one portion; it will border the territory of Simeon from east to west.

26"Zebulun will have one portion; it will border the territory of Issachar from east to west.

27"Gad will have one portion; it will border the territory of Zebulun from east to west.

28"The southern boundary of Gad will run south from Tamar to the waters of Meribah Kadesh, then along the Wadi of Egypt to the Great Sea.*a*

29"This is the land you are to allot as an inheritance to the tribes of Israel, and these will be their portions," declares the Sovereign LORD.

The Gates of the City

30"These will be the exits of the city: Beginning on the north side, which is 4,500 cubits long, **31**the gates of the city will be named after the tribes of Israel. The three gates on the north side will be the gate of Reuben, the gate of Judah and the gate of Levi.

32"On the east side, which is 4,500 cubits long, will be three gates: the gate of Joseph, the gate of Benjamin and the gate of Dan.

33"On the south side, which measures 4,500 cubits, will be three gates: the gate of Simeon, the gate of Issachar and the gate of Zebulun.

34"On the west side, which is 4,500 cubits long, will be three gates: the gate of Gad, the gate of Asher and the gate of Naphtali.

35"The distance all around will be 18,000 cubits.

"And the name of the city from that time on will be:

THE LORD IS THERE."

a28 That is, the Mediterranean

Daniel

Author: Daniel.	Time and eternity intertwine in this book written during the days of exile. There are backward glances at *past sins that need to be confessed.* There are present tests and challenges to be faced. And there are prophetic visions that reach far into the future. At a time when the people of Israel wondered if God's covenant with them had been destroyed along with the temple, we find God is not only present, *but he is actively working* on behalf of his people, both for Daniel's generation and for the generations to come.
Audience: Exiles in Babylon and all of God's people.	
Date: About 530 B.C.	
Setting: The Jews are taken into captivity by the Babylonians.	A window opens in this book, and we catch a *glimpse of the workings of heaven,* of angels delayed while they battle resistance, of visions that strike terror and of explanations that are only partially understood. *But we also see life on this earth,* specifically life in exile, away from the land of promise, away from home. And we see that this life is fraught with *challenges that lead us to make the choice* between saving our own skin or entrusting ourselves to God's protection.
Verses to Remember: "If we are thrown into the blazing furnace, the God we serve is able to save us from it, and he will rescue us from your hand, O king. But even if he does not, we want you to know, O king, that we will not serve your gods or worship the image of gold you have set up." (3:17–18)	

Daniel's Training in Babylon

1 In the third year of the reign of Jehoiakim king of Judah, Nebuchadnezzar king of Babylon came to Jerusalem and besieged it. ²And the Lord delivered Jehoiakim king of Judah into his hand, along with some of the arti-

cles from the temple of God. These he carried off to the temple of his god in Babylonia[a] and put in the treasure house of his god.

³Then the king ordered Ashpenaz, chief of his court officials, to bring in some of the Israelites from the royal family and the nobility—

---

[a]2 Hebrew *Shinar*

⁴young men without any physical defect, handsome, showing aptitude for every kind of learning, well informed, quick to understand, and qualified to serve in the king's palace. He was to teach them the language and literature of the Babylonians.ᵃ ⁵The king assigned them a daily amount of food and wine from the king's table. They were to be trained for three years, and after that they were to enter the king's service.

⁶Among these were some from Judah: Daniel, Hananiah, Mishael and Azariah. ⁷The chief official gave them new names: to Daniel, the name Belteshazzar; to Hananiah, Shadrach; to Mishael, Meshach; and to Azariah, Abednego.

⁸But Daniel resolved not to defile himself with the royal food and wine, and he asked the chief official for permission not to defile himself this way. ⁹Now God had caused the official to show favor and sympathy to Daniel, ¹⁰but the official told Daniel, "I am afraid of my lord the king, who has assigned yourᵇ food and drink. Why should he see you looking worse than the other young men your age? The king would then have my head because of you."

¹¹Daniel then said to the guard whom the chief official had appointed over Daniel, Hananiah, Mishael and Azariah, ¹²"Please test your servants for ten days: Give us nothing but vegetables to eat and water to drink. ¹³Then compare our appearance with that of the young men who eat the royal food, and treat your servants in accordance with what you see." ¹⁴So he agreed to this and tested them for ten days.

¹⁵At the end of the ten days they looked healthier and better nourished than any of the young men who ate the royal food. ¹⁶So the guard took away their choice food and the wine they were to drink and gave them vegetables instead.

¹⁷To these four young men God gave knowledge and understanding of all kinds of literature and learning. And Daniel could understand visions and dreams of all kinds.

¹⁸At the end of the time set by the king to bring them in, the chief official presented them to Nebuchadnezzar. ¹⁹The king talked with them, and he found none equal to Daniel, Hananiah, Mishael and Azariah; so they entered the king's service. ²⁰In every matter of wisdom and understanding about which the king questioned them, he found them ten times better than all the magicians and enchanters in his whole kingdom.

²¹And Daniel remained there until the first year of King Cyrus.

Nebuchadnezzar's Dream

2 In the second year of his reign, Nebuchadnezzar had dreams; his mind was troubled and he could not sleep. ²So the king summoned the magicians, enchanters, sorcerers and astrologersᶜ to tell him what he had dreamed. When they came in and stood before the king, ³he said to them, "I have had a dream that troubles me and I want to know what it means.ᵈ"

⁴Then the astrologers answered the king in Aramaic,ᵉ "O king, live forever! Tell your servants the dream, and we will interpret it."

⁵The king replied to the astrologers, "This is what I have firmly decided: If you do not tell me what my dream was and interpret it, I will have you cut into pieces and your houses turned into piles of rubble. ⁶But if you tell me the dream and explain it, you will receive from me gifts and rewards and great honor. So tell me the dream and interpret it for me."

⁷Once more they replied, "Let the king tell his servants the dream, and we will interpret it."

⁸Then the king answered, "I am certain that you are trying to gain time, because you realize that this is what I have firmly decided: ⁹If you do not tell me the dream, there is just one penalty for you. You have conspired to tell me misleading and wicked things, hoping the situation will change. So then, tell me the dream, and I will know that you can interpret it for me."

¹⁰The astrologers answered the king, "There is not a man on earth who can do what the king asks! No king, however great and mighty, has ever asked such a thing of any magician or enchanter or astrologer. ¹¹What the king asks too difficult. No one can reveal it to the king except the gods, and they do not live among men."

ᵃ4 Or Chaldeans   ᵇ10 The Hebrew for your and you in this verse is plural.   ᶜ2 Or Chaldeans; also in verses 4, 5 and 10   ᵈ3 Or was
ᵉ4 The text from here through chapter 7 is in Aramaic.

¹²This made the king so angry and furious that he ordered the execution of all the wise men of Babylon. ¹³So the decree was issued to put the wise men to death, and men were sent to look for Daniel and his friends to put them to death.

¹⁴When Arioch, the commander of the king's guard, had gone out to put to death the wise men of Babylon, Daniel spoke to him with wisdom and tact. ¹⁵He asked the king's officer, "Why did the king issue such a harsh decree?" Arioch then explained the matter to Daniel. ¹⁶At this, Daniel went in to the king and asked for time, so that he might interpret the dream for him.

¹⁷Then Daniel returned to his house and explained the matter to his friends Hananiah, Mishael and Azariah. ¹⁸He urged them to plead for mercy from the God of heaven concerning this mystery, so that he and his friends might not be executed with the rest of the wise men of Babylon. ¹⁹During the night the mystery was revealed to Daniel in a vision. Then Daniel praised the God of heaven ²⁰and said:

> "Praise be to the name of
>   God for ever and
>   ever;
>   wisdom and power are
>   his.
> ²¹He changes times and
>   seasons;
>   he sets up kings and deposes them.
> He gives wisdom to the wise
>   and knowledge to the discerning.
> ²²He reveals deep and hidden things;
>   he knows what lies in darkness,
>   and light dwells with him.
> ²³I thank and praise you, O God of my
>   fathers:
> You have given me wisdom and power,
>   you have made known to me what we
>   asked of you,
>   you have made known to us the dream
>   of the king."

Daniel Interprets the Dream

²⁴Then Daniel went to Arioch, whom the king had appointed to execute the wise men of Babylon, and said to him, "Do not execute the wise men of Babylon. Take me to the king, and I will interpret his dream for him."

²⁵Arioch took Daniel to the king at once and said, "I have found a man among the exiles from Judah who can tell the king what his dream means."

²⁶The king asked Daniel (also called Belteshazzar), "Are you able to tell me what I saw in my dream and interpret it?"

²⁷Daniel replied, "No wise man, enchanter, magician or diviner can explain to the king the mystery he has asked about, ²⁸but there is a God in heaven who reveals mysteries. He has shown King Nebuchadnezzar what will happen in days to come. Your dream and the visions that passed through your mind as you lay on your bed are these:

²⁹"As you were lying there, O king, your mind turned to things to come, and the revealer of mysteries showed you what is going to happen. ³⁰As for me, this mystery has been revealed to me, not because I have greater wisdom than other living men, but so that you, O king, may know the interpretation and that you may understand what went through your mind.

³¹"You looked, O king, and there before you stood a large statue—an enormous, dazzling statue, awesome in appearance. ³²The head of the statue was made of pure gold, its chest and arms of silver, its belly and thighs of bronze, ³³its legs of iron, its feet partly of iron and partly of baked clay. ³⁴While you were watching, a rock was cut out, but not by human hands. It struck the statue on its feet of iron and clay and smashed them. ³⁵Then the iron, the clay, the bronze, the silver and the gold were broken to pieces at the same time and became like chaff on a threshing floor in the summer. The wind

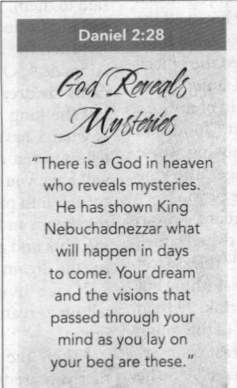

Daniel 2:28

God Reveals Mysteries

"There is a God in heaven who reveals mysteries. He has shown King Nebuchadnezzar what will happen in days to come. Your dream and the visions that passed through your mind as you lay on your bed are these."

Dream Weaver

Read: Daniel 2:24–47

AS YOU APPROACH THE KING'S THRONE, a swarm of whispers fills the room.

"Who does she think she is?" "She'll never be able to do it."

Striding steadily forward, and struggling with your own self-doubts, you wonder, "Will all these gawking eyes witness an execution or a miracle today?"

While these thoughts took place in your imagination, a similar situation occurred in Daniel's reality. He stood face-to-face with an unpredictable despot, King Nebuchadnezzar, who had murdered many of Daniel's family and friends during their exile to Babylon. Now Daniel's own life was in danger (along with all the other scholars and key advisers of the nation) unless someone—anyone—could interpret the king's strange dream. Daniel's life depended upon being able to do what no one had been able to do—not even the king's "wise men."

Talk about stress. Daniel faced a seemingly impossible and dangerous circumstance requiring the utmost wisdom and bravery. Not only had he been exiled to Babylon (modern-day Baghdad), but now he faced an even more pressing drama.

How did Daniel handle this super-dramatic, high-stress situation? He coped with it by cultivating a close relationship with God and depending on God for wisdom and power (verses 20–23). When the drama heated up, when asked if he could interpret Nebuchadnezzar's dream, Daniel did not talk himself up. He humbly responded, "No [one] can explain to the king the mystery he has asked about, but there is a God in heaven who reveals mysteries" (verses 27–28). Daniel invited God into his drama.

In the course of our lives, we're sometimes called to deal with stressful or uncomfortable situations. You may work as the only female in your church's leadership; you may care for your aging in-laws, who have never thought you were good enough for their son. No matter what the situation, the best way to handle it with grace and wisdom is to invite God to direct the circumstance. Let him weave your way through with his wisdom. Lean on his strength. Rely on his insights. You may not feel like you can handle the stress, but with God's help, you can.

Daniel 2:24

"Take me to the king, and I will interpret his dream for him."

reflection

1 What difficult circumstances are you facing right now?

2 How does your heart feel in the midst of your own drama? Small? Broken? Weak?

3 Share your feelings with a trusted friend and together invite the God of wisdom and power into the situation.

RELATED READINGS

Genesis 41:15–16;
Esther 3:12–15; 5:1–3;
Daniel 2:1–23

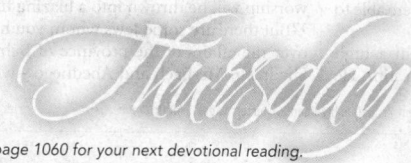

Thursday

Go to page 1060 for your next devotional reading.

swept them away without leaving a trace. But the rock that struck the statue became a huge mountain and filled the whole earth.

36"This was the dream, and now we will interpret it to the king. 37You, O king, are the king of kings. The God of heaven has given you dominion and power and might and glory; 38in your hands he has placed mankind and the beasts of the field and the birds of the air. Wherever they live, he has made you ruler over them all. You are that head of gold.

39"After you, another kingdom will rise, inferior to yours. Next, a third kingdom, one of bronze, will rule over the whole earth. 40Finally, there will be a fourth kingdom, strong as iron—for iron breaks and smashes everything—and as iron breaks things to pieces, so it will crush and break all the others. 41Just as you saw that the feet and toes were partly of baked clay and partly of iron, so this will be a divided kingdom; yet it will have some of the strength of iron in it, even as you saw iron mixed with clay. 42As the toes were partly iron and partly clay, so this kingdom will be partly strong and partly brittle. 43And just as you saw the iron mixed with baked clay, so the people will be a mixture and will not remain united, any more than iron mixes with clay.

44"In the time of those kings, the God of heaven will set up a kingdom that will never be destroyed, nor will it be left to another people. It will crush all those kingdoms and bring them to an end, but it will itself endure forever. 45This is the meaning of the vision of the rock cut out of a mountain, but not by human hands—a rock that broke the iron, the bronze, the clay, the silver and the gold to pieces.

"The great God has shown the king what will take place in the future. The dream is true and the interpretation is trustworthy."

46Then King Nebuchadnezzar fell prostrate before Daniel and paid him honor and ordered that an offering and incense be presented to him. 47The king said to Daniel, "Surely your God is the God of gods and the Lord of kings and a revealer of mysteries, for you were able to reveal this mystery."

48Then the king placed Daniel in a high position and lavished many gifts on him. He made him ruler over the entire province of Babylon and placed him in charge of all its wise men. 49Moreover, at Daniel's request the king appointed Shadrach, Meshach and Abednego administrators over the province of Babylon, while Daniel himself remained at the royal court.

The Image of Gold and the Fiery Furnace

3 King Nebuchadnezzar made an image of gold, ninety feet high and nine feet*a* wide, and set it up on the plain of Dura in the province of Babylon. 2He then summoned the satraps, prefects, governors, advisers, treasurers, judges, magistrates and all the other provincial officials to come to the dedication of the image he had set up. 3So the satraps, prefects, governors, advisers, treasurers, judges, magistrates and all the other provincial officials assembled for the dedication of the image that King Nebuchadnezzar had set up, and they stood before it.

4Then the herald loudly proclaimed, "This is what you are commanded to do, O peoples, nations and men of every language: 5As soon as you hear the sound of the horn, flute, zither, lyre, harp, pipes and all kinds of music, you must fall down and worship the image of gold that King Nebuchadnezzar has set up. 6Whoever does not fall down and worship will immediately be thrown into a blazing furnace."

7Therefore, as soon as they heard the sound of the horn, flute, zither, lyre, harp and all kinds of music, all the peoples, nations and men of every language fell down and worshiped the image of gold that King Nebuchadnezzar had set up.

8At this time some astrologers*b* came forward and denounced the Jews. 9They said to King Nebuchadnezzar, "O king, live forever! 10You have issued a decree, O king, that everyone who hears the sound of the horn, flute, zither, lyre, harp, pipes and all kinds of music must fall down and worship the image of gold, 11and that whoever does not fall down and worship will be thrown into a blazing furnace. 12But there are some Jews whom you have set over the affairs of the province of Babylon— Shadrach, Meshach and Abednego—who pay

*a*1 Aramaic *sixty cubits high and six cubits wide* (about 27 meters high and 2.7 meters wide)   *b*8 Or *Chaldeans* no attention to you, O king. They neither serve your gods nor worship the image of gold you have set up."

¹³Furious with rage, Nebuchadnezzar summoned Shadrach, Meshach and Abednego. So these men were brought before the king, ¹⁴and Nebuchadnezzar said to them, "Is it true, Shadrach, Meshach and Abednego, that you do not serve my gods or worship the image of gold I have set up? ¹⁵Now when you hear the sound of the horn, flute, zither, lyre, harp, pipes and all kinds of music, if you are ready to fall down and worship the image I made, very good. But if you do not worship it, you will be thrown immediately into a blazing furnace. Then what god will be able to rescue you from my hand?"

¹⁶Shadrach, Meshach and Abednego replied to the king, "O Nebuchadnezzar, we do not need to defend ourselves before you in this matter. ¹⁷If we are thrown into the blazing furnace, the God we serve is able to save us from it, and he will rescue us from your hand, O king. ¹⁸But even if he does not, we want you to know, O king, that we will not serve your gods or worship the image of gold you have set up."

¹⁹Then Nebuchadnezzar was furious with Shadrach, Meshach and Abednego, and his attitude toward them changed. He ordered the furnace heated seven times hotter than usual ²⁰and commanded some of the strongest soldiers in his army to tie up Shadrach, Meshach and Abednego and throw them into the blazing furnace. ²¹So these men, wearing their robes, trousers, turbans and other clothes, were bound and thrown into the blazing furnace. ²²The king's command was so urgent and the furnace so hot that the flames of the fire killed the soldiers who took up Shadrach, Meshach and Abednego, ²³and these three men, firmly tied, fell into the blazing furnace.

²⁴Then King Nebuchadnezzar leaped to his feet in amazement and asked his advisers, "Weren't there three men that we tied up and threw into the fire?"

They replied, "Certainly, O king."

²⁵He said, "Look! I see four men walking around in the fire, unbound and unharmed, and the fourth looks like a son of the gods."

²⁶Nebuchadnezzar then approached the opening of the blazing furnace and shouted, "Shadrach, Meshach and Abednego, servants of the Most High God, come out! Come here!"

So Shadrach, Meshach and Abednego came out of the fire, ²⁷and the satraps, prefects, governors and royal advisers crowded around them. They saw that the fire had not harmed their bodies, nor was a hair of their heads singed; their robes were not scorched, and there was no smell of fire on them.

²⁸Then Nebuchadnezzar said, "Praise be to the God of Shadrach, Meshach and Abednego, who has sent his angel and rescued his servants! They trusted in him and defied the king's command and were willing to give up their lives rather than serve or worship any god except their own God. ²⁹Therefore I decree that the people of any nation or language who say anything against the God of Shadrach, Meshach and Abednego be cut into pieces and their houses be turned into piles of rubble, for no other god can save in this way."

³⁰Then the king promoted Shadrach, Meshach and Abednego in the province of Babylon.

Nebuchadnezzar's Dream of a Tree

4 King Nebuchadnezzar,

To the peoples, nations and men of every language, who live in all the world:

May you prosper greatly!

²It is my pleasure to tell you about the miraculous signs and wonders that the Most High God has performed for me.

³How great are his signs,
  how mighty his wonders!
His kingdom is an eternal kingdom;
  his dominion endures from
    generation to generation.

⁴I, Nebuchadnezzar, was at home in my palace, contented and prosperous. ⁵I had a dream that made me afraid. As I was lying in my bed, the images and visions that passed through my mind terrified me. ⁶So I commanded that all the wise men of Babylon be brought before me to interpret the dream for me. ⁷When the magicians,

Able to Save

"If we are thrown into the blazing furnace, the God we serve is able to save us from it, and he will rescue us from your hand, O king. But even if he does not, we want you to know, O king, that we will not serve your gods or worship the image of gold you have set up."

reflection

1 What kind of persecution do you face for being a Christian? How do you deal with it?

2 What would it be like to face dire persecution like so many people around the world today?

3 What lessons have you learned from Perpetua and Daniel's three friends?

RELATED READINGS
Psalm 124:1–8;
Isaiah 43:1–13;
Matthew 5:11,44;
Luke 21:12–19

SHADRACH, MESHACH AND ABEDNEGO survived a close encounter with martyrdom. Because they defied the ruling authority, they were scheduled to be thrown into a furnace. But trusting God to honor their faithfulness, they vowed fidelity—even if it cost them their lives. While we know the end of the story (they lived), they had no certainty that they would survive the raging blaze of Nebuchadnezzar's furnace when they stood up for God. And though they were certain of God's power and willingness to protect them, they didn't demand that he save them.

Now consider this story that occurred centuries later: A judge summoned Perpetua, age 26, and commanded her to deny God or face certain death. Perpetua, with a newborn infant, faced a dilemma. North African Christians under Roman rule in A.D. 200 ran the risk of being put to death for openly acknowledging their faith. As her father looked on, urging her to save herself for her child cradled in his arms, still she would not do as she was commanded and sacrifice to idols.

Perpetua held fast in her conviction and faith in the living God. When the wild bull that was released to attack her and another believer failed to kill them, the Romans sent in the gladiators. A terrified young man approached her and made several ineffectual stabs. In a final act of mercy, she steered his sword into the lethal blow and died.

Many Christians face persecution today. At some point many more may have to make the choice to denounce God or risk everything they hold dear, including their lives. And many face such choices now, though with less threatening consequences: We may be ostracized from our families or passed over for promotions. We may be treated unjustly or misunderstood.

Have you ever thought about what you would do if you were faced with dire persecution? Are you willing to risk everything because you are convinced that loving God is worth whatever sacrifices you face? When faced with the choice to remain faithful or cave in to fear, think of the three young men in Babylon and Perpetua in North Africa who counted their own lives as nothing compared to the grace they had been given.

enchanters, astrologers[a] and diviners came, I told them the dream, but they could not interpret it for me. **8**Finally, Daniel came into my presence and I told him the dream. (He is called Belteshazzar, after the name of my god, and the spirit of the holy gods is in him.)

9I said, "Belteshazzar, chief of the magicians, I know that the spirit of the holy gods is in you, and no mystery is too difficult for you. Here is my dream; interpret it for me. **10**These are the visions I saw while lying in my bed: I looked, and there before me stood a tree in the middle of the land. Its height was enormous. **11**The tree grew large and strong and its top touched the sky; it was visible to the ends of the earth. **12**Its leaves were beautiful, its fruit abundant, and on it was food for all. Under it the beasts of the field found shelter, and the birds of the air lived in its branches; from it every creature was fed.

13"In the visions I saw while lying in my bed, I looked, and there before me was a messenger,[b] a holy one, coming down from heaven. **14**He called in a loud voice: 'Cut down the tree and trim off its branches; strip off its leaves and scatter its fruit. Let the animals flee from under it and the birds from its branches. **15**But let the stump and its roots, bound with iron and bronze, remain in the ground, in the grass of the field.

" 'Let him be drenched with the dew of heaven, and let him live with the animals among the plants of the earth. **16**Let his mind be changed from that of a man and let him be given the mind of an animal, till seven times[c] pass by for him.

17" 'The decision is announced by messengers, the holy ones declare the verdict, so that the living may know that the Most High is sovereign over the kingdoms of men and gives them to anyone he wishes and sets over them the lowliest of men.'

18"This is the dream that I, King Nebuchadnezzar, had. Now, Belteshazzar, tell me what it means, for none of the wise men in my kingdom can interpret it for me. But you can, because the spirit of the holy gods is in you."

Daniel Interprets the Dream

19Then Daniel (also called Belteshazzar) was greatly perplexed for a time, and his thoughts terrified him. So the king said, "Belteshazzar, do not let the dream or its meaning alarm you."

Belteshazzar answered, "My lord, if only the dream applied to your enemies and its meaning to your adversaries! **20**The tree you saw, which grew large and strong, with its top touching the sky, visible to the whole earth, **21**with beautiful leaves and abundant fruit, providing food for all, giving shelter to the beasts of the field, and having nesting places in its branches for the birds of the air— **22**you, O king, are that tree! You have become great and strong; your greatness has grown until it reaches the sky, and your dominion extends to distant parts of the earth.

23"You, O king, saw a messenger, a holy one, coming down from heaven and saying, 'Cut down the tree and destroy it, but leave the stump, bound with iron and bronze, in the grass of the field, while its roots remain in the ground. Let him be drenched with the dew of heaven; let him live like the wild animals, until seven times pass by for him.'

24"This is the interpretation, O king, and this is the decree the Most High has issued against my lord the king: **25**You will be driven away from people and will live with the wild animals; you will eat grass like cattle and be drenched with the dew of heaven. Seven times will pass by for you until you acknowledge that the Most High is sovereign over the kingdoms of men and gives them to anyone he wishes. **26**The command to leave the stump of the tree with its roots means that your kingdom will be restored to you when you acknowledge that Heaven rules. **27**Therefore, O king, be pleased to accept my advice: Renounce your sins by doing what is right, and your wickedness by being kind

---

a 7 Or *Chaldeans*   *b* 13 Or *watchman;* also in verses 17 and 23   *c* 16 Or *years;* also in verses 23, 25 and 32 to the oppressed. It may be that then your prosperity will continue."

The Dream Is Fulfilled

²⁸ All this happened to King Nebuchadnezzar. ²⁹ Twelve months later, as the king was walking on the roof of the royal palace of Babylon, ³⁰ he said, "Is not this the great Babylon I have built as the royal residence, by my mighty power and for the glory of my majesty?"

³¹ The words were still on his lips when a voice came from heaven, "This is what is decreed for you, King Nebuchadnezzar: Your royal authority has been taken from you. ³² You will be driven away from people and will live with the wild animals; you will eat grass like cattle. Seven times will pass by for you until you acknowledge that the Most High is sovereign over the kingdoms of men and gives them to anyone he wishes."

³³ Immediately what had been said about Nebuchadnezzar was fulfilled. He was driven away from people and ate grass like cattle. His body was drenched with the dew of heaven until his hair grew like the feathers of an eagle and his nails like the claws of a bird.

³⁴ At the end of that time, I, Nebuchadnezzar, raised my eyes toward heaven, and my sanity was restored. Then I praised the Most High; I honored and glorified him who lives forever.

His dominion is an eternal dominion;
his kingdom endures from generation to generation.
³⁵ All the peoples of the earth
are regarded as nothing.
He does as he pleases
with the powers of heaven
and the peoples of the earth.

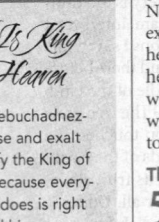

Daniel 4:37

God Is King of Heaven

Now I, Nebuchadnezzar, praise and exalt and glorify the King of heaven, because everything he does is right and all his ways are just. And those who walk in pride he is able to humble.

No one can hold back his hand
or say to him: "What have you done?"

³⁶ At the same time that my sanity was restored, my honor and splendor were returned to me for the glory of my kingdom. My advisers and nobles sought me out, and I was restored to my throne and became even greater than before. ³⁷ Now I, Nebuchadnezzar, praise and exalt and glorify the King of heaven, because everything he does is right and all his ways are just. And those who walk in pride he is able to humble.

The Writing on the Wall

5 King Belshazzar gave a great banquet for a thousand of his nobles and drank wine with them. ² While Belshazzar was drinking his wine, he gave orders to bring in the gold and silver goblets that Nebuchadnezzar his father*ᵃ* had taken from the temple in Jerusalem, so that the king and his nobles, his wives and his concubines might drink from them. ³ So they brought in the gold goblets that had been taken from the temple of God in Jerusalem, and the king and his nobles, his wives and his concubines drank from them. ⁴ As they drank the wine, they praised the gods of gold and silver, of bronze, iron, wood and stone.

⁵ Suddenly the fingers of a human hand appeared and wrote on the plaster of the wall, near the lampstand in the royal palace. The king watched the hand as it wrote. ⁶ His face turned pale and he was so frightened that his knees knocked together and his legs gave way.

⁷ The king called out for the enchanters, astrologers*ᵇ* and diviners to be brought and said to these wise men of Babylon, "Whoever reads this writing and tells me what it means will be clothed in purple and have a gold chain placed around his neck, and he will be made the third highest ruler in the kingdom."

⁸ Then all the king's wise men came in, but

ᵃ2 Or *ancestor;* or *predecessor;* also in verses 11, 13 and 18 *ᵇ7* Or *Chaldeans;* also in verse 11

Dear John

ELIZABETH

DEAREST JOHN:

I'm writing to you, my son, so you will always know how much your mother loved you. Before you were even a twinkle in your daddy's eye, we prayed for your arrival and safekeeping. True, we'd practically given up on having a child of our own. But how glad we are to finally say that you belong to us!

I remember when your father came home and "told" me the news that we were going to have a son. Of course, he couldn't speak a word of the wonderful message God's angel had delivered to him that day. But we managed to get it out of him anyway! My first thought was, *The Lord has done this for me.* Already, God determined that you would bring me so much happiness.

The next few months flew by. Son, I have to tell you that I was pretty nervous about being pregnant for the first time. Every woman I'd ever known had these horror stories about morning sickness. Of course, I would never tell them this, but I was strangely pleased to go through this rite of passage. Instead of dreading the nausea and queasiness, it reminded me that my body was undergoing wonderful changes to prepare a home for you to live in for the next few months. Every kick, every gurgle, reminded me that I was no longer alone. You were there with me, my son, throughout my day. And I would soon see you face-to-face!

Of course, your Aunt Mary and I were pregnant at about the same time. We couldn't have been happier! Apparently, you felt the same way about her baby boy. You won't remember this, but you leaped in my womb when the two of you first "met"! Mary and I couldn't believe it, and together we praised God for his two gracious gifts. That day, we agreed that we were the most blessed women on earth because we believed that God would do what he said he would do. My John, never forget that you are a miracle.

Love,
Mother

—Prayer—
Giving Father, thank you for the gift of love.

[Zechariah's] wife Elizabeth was also a descendant of Aaron. Both of them were upright in the sight of God, observing all the Lord's commandments and regulations blamelessly.

Luke 1:5–6

ASSIGNED READING:

Luke 1:5–80

Weekend

they could not read the writing or tell the king what it meant. **9**So King Belshazzar became even more terrified and his face grew more pale. His nobles were baffled.

10The queen,*a* hearing the voices of the king and his nobles, came into the banquet hall. "O king, live forever!" she said. "Don't be alarmed! Don't look so pale! **11**There is a man in your kingdom who has the spirit of the holy gods in him. In the time of your father he was found to have insight and intelligence and wisdom like that of the gods. King Nebuchadnezzar your father—your father the king, I say—appointed him chief of the magicians, enchanters, astrologers and diviners. **12**This man Daniel, whom the king called Belteshazzar, was found to have a keen mind and knowledge and understanding, and also the ability to interpret dreams, explain riddles and solve difficult problems. Call for Daniel, and he will tell you what the writing means."

13So Daniel was brought before the king, and the king said to him, "Are you Daniel, one of the exiles my father the king brought from Judah? **14**I have heard that the spirit of the gods is in you and that you have insight, intelligence and outstanding wisdom. **15**The wise men and enchanters were brought before me to read this writing and tell me what it means, but they could not explain it. **16**Now I have heard that you are able to give interpretations and to solve difficult problems. If you can read this writing and tell me what it means, you will be clothed in purple and have a gold chain placed around your neck, and you will be made the third highest ruler in the kingdom."

17Then Daniel answered the king, "You may keep your gifts for yourself and give your rewards to someone else. Nevertheless, I will read the writing for the king and tell him what it means.

18"O king, the Most High God gave your father Nebuchadnezzar sovereignty and greatness and glory and splendor. **19**Because of the high position he gave him, all the peoples and nations and men of every language dreaded and feared him. Those the king wanted to put to death, he put to death; those he wanted to spare, he spared; those he wanted to promote, he promoted; and those he wanted to humble, he humbled. **20**But when his heart became arrogant and hardened with pride, he was deposed from his royal throne and stripped of his glory. **21**He was driven away from people and given the mind of an animal; he lived with the wild donkeys and ate grass like cattle; and his body was drenched with the dew of heaven, until he acknowledged that the Most High God is sovereign over the kingdoms of men and sets over them anyone he wishes.

22"But you his son,*b* O Belshazzar, have not humbled yourself, though you knew all this. **23**Instead, you have set yourself up against the Lord of heaven. You had the goblets from his temple brought to you, and you and your nobles, your wives and your concubines drank wine from them. You praised the gods of silver and gold, of bronze, iron, wood and stone, which cannot see or hear or understand. But you did not honor the God who holds in his hand your life and all your ways. **24**Therefore he sent the hand that wrote the inscription.

25"This is the inscription that was written:

MENE, MENE, TEKEL, PARSIN*c*

26"This is what these words mean:

*Mene**d*: God has numbered the days of your reign and brought it to an end.

27 *Tekel**e*: You have been weighed on the scales and found wanting.

28 *Peres**f*: Your kingdom is divided and given to the Medes and Persians."

29Then at Belshazzar's command, Daniel was clothed in purple, a gold chain was placed around his neck, and he was proclaimed the third highest ruler in the kingdom.

30That very night Belshazzar, king of the Babylonians,*g* was slain, **31**and Darius the Mede took over the kingdom, at the age of sixty-two.

Daniel in the Den of Lions

6 It pleased Darius to appoint 120 satraps to rule throughout the kingdom, **2**with three administrators over them, one of whom

---

*a*10 Or *queen mother*   *b*22 Or *descendant; or successor*   *c*25 Aramaic *UPARSIN* (that is, *AND PARSIN*)   *d*26 *Mene* can mean *numbered* or *mina* (a unit of money).   *e*27 *Tekel* can mean *weighed* or *shekel.*   *f*28 *Peres* (the singular of *Parsin*) can mean *divided* or *Persia* or *a half mina* or *a half shekel.*   *g*30 Or *Chaldeans* was Daniel. The satraps were made accountable to them so that the king might not suffer loss. ³Now Daniel so distinguished himself among the administrators and the satraps by his exceptional qualities that the king planned to set him over the whole kingdom. ⁴At this, the administrators and the satraps tried to find grounds for charges against Daniel in his conduct of government affairs, but they were unable to do so. They could find no corruption in him, because he was trustworthy and neither corrupt nor negligent. ⁵Finally these men said, "We will never find any basis for charges against this man Daniel unless it has something to do with the law of his God."

⁶So the administrators and the satraps went as a group to the king and said: "O King Darius, live forever! ⁷The royal administrators, prefects, satraps, advisers and governors have all agreed that the king should issue an edict and enforce the decree that anyone who prays to any god or man during the next thirty days, except to you, O king, shall be thrown into the lions' den. ⁸Now, O king, issue the decree and put it in writing so that it cannot be altered—in accordance with the laws of the Medes and Persians, which cannot be repealed." ⁹So King Darius put the decree in writing.

¹⁰Now when Daniel learned that the decree had been published, he went home to his upstairs room where the windows opened toward Jerusalem. Three times a day he got down on his knees and prayed, giving thanks to his God, just as he had done before. ¹¹Then these men went as a group and found Daniel praying and asking God for help. ¹²So they went to the king and spoke to him about his royal decree: "Did you not publish a decree that during the next thirty days anyone who prays to any god or man except to you, O king, would be thrown into the lions' den?"

The king answered, "The decree stands—in accordance with the laws of the Medes and Persians, which cannot be repealed."

¹³Then they said to the king, "Daniel, who is one of the exiles from Judah, pays no attention to you, O king, or to the decree you put in writing. He still prays three times a day." ¹⁴When the king heard this, he was greatly distressed; he was determined to rescue Daniel and made every effort until sundown to save him.

¹⁵Then the men went as a group to the king and said to him, "Remember, O king, that according to the law of the Medes and Persians no decree or edict that the king issues can be changed."

¹⁶So the king gave the order, and they brought Daniel and threw him into the lions' den. The king said to Daniel, "May your God, whom you serve continually, rescue you!"

¹⁷A stone was brought and placed over the mouth of the den, and the king sealed it with his own signet ring and with the rings of his nobles, so that Daniel's situation might not be changed. ¹⁸Then the king returned to his palace and spent the night without eating and without any entertainment being brought to him. And he could not sleep.

¹⁹At the first light of dawn, the king got up and hurried to the lions' den. ²⁰When he came near the den, he called to Daniel in an anguished voice, "Daniel, servant of the living God, has your God, whom you serve continually, been able to rescue you from the lions?"

²¹Daniel answered, "O king, live forever! ²²My God sent his angel, and he shut the mouths of the lions. They have not hurt me, because I was found innocent in his sight. Nor have I ever done any wrong before you, O king."

²³The king was overjoyed and gave orders to lift Daniel out of the den. And when Daniel was lifted from the den, no wound was found on him, because he had trusted in his God.

²⁴At the king's command, the men who had falsely accused Daniel were brought in and thrown into the lions' den, along with their wives and children. And before they reached

Daniel 6:16

God Rescues His People

So the king gave the order, and they brought Daniel and threw him into the lions' den. The king said to Daniel, "May your God, whom you serve continually, rescue you!"

the floor of the den, the lions overpowered them and crushed all their bones.

²⁵ Then King Darius wrote to all the peoples, nations and men of every language throughout the land:

"May you prosper greatly!

²⁶ "I issue a decree that in every part of my kingdom people must fear and reverence the God of Daniel.

"For he is the living God
    and he endures forever;
his kingdom will not be destroyed,
    his dominion will never end.
²⁷ He rescues and he saves;
    he performs signs and wonders
    in the heavens and on the earth.
He has rescued Daniel
    from the power of the lions."

²⁸ So Daniel prospered during the reign of Darius and the reign of Cyrus[a] the Persian.

Daniel's Dream of Four Beasts

7 In the first year of Belshazzar king of Babylon, Daniel had a dream, and visions passed through his mind as he was lying on his bed. He wrote down the substance of his dream.

² Daniel said: "In my vision at night I looked, and there before me were the four winds of heaven churning up the great sea. ³ Four great beasts, each different from the others, came up out of the sea.

⁴ "The first was like a lion, and it had the wings of an eagle. I watched until its wings were torn off and it was lifted from the ground so that it stood on two feet like a man, and the heart of a man was given to it.

⁵ "And there before me was a second beast, which looked like a bear. It was raised up on one of its sides, and it had three ribs in its mouth between its teeth. It was told, 'Get up and eat your fill of flesh!'

⁶ "After that, I looked, and there before me was another beast, one that looked like a leopard. And on its back it had four wings like those of a bird. This beast had four heads, and it was given authority to rule.

⁷ "After that, in my vision at night I looked, and there before me was a fourth beast—terrifying and frightening and very powerful. It had large iron teeth; it crushed and devoured its victims and trampled underfoot whatever was left. It was different from all the former beasts, and it had ten horns.

⁸ "While I was thinking about the horns, there before me was another horn, a little one, which came up among them; and three of the first horns were uprooted before it. This horn had eyes like the eyes of a man and a mouth that spoke boastfully.

⁹ "As I looked,

"thrones were set in place,
    and the Ancient of Days took his seat.
His clothing was as white as snow;
    the hair of his head was white like wool.
His throne was flaming with fire,
    and its wheels were all ablaze.
¹⁰ A river of fire was flowing,
    coming out from before him.
Thousands upon thousands attended him;
    ten thousand times ten thousand stood
        before him.
The court was seated,
    and the books were opened.

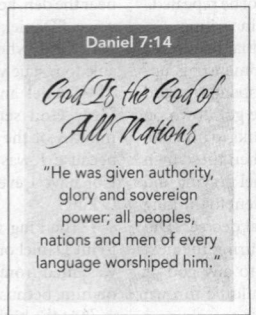

Daniel 7:14

God Is the God of All Nations

"He was given authority, glory and sovereign power; all peoples, nations and men of every language worshiped him."

¹¹ "Then I continued to watch because of the boastful words the horn was speaking. I kept looking until the beast was slain and its body destroyed and thrown into the blazing fire. ¹² (The other beasts had been stripped of their authority, but were allowed to live for a period of time.)

¹³ "In my vision at night I looked, and there before me was one like a son of man, coming with the clouds of heaven. He approached the Ancient of Days and was led into his presence. ¹⁴ He was given authority, glory and sovereign power; all

---

a28 Or *Darius, that is, the reign of Cyrus*

Princes of Pride

Read: Daniel 6:1–28

DON'T YOU HATE IT when someone "steals your thunder" or takes your job and performs it better than you did? Then perhaps you understand the 120 sneering satraps from Daniel 6, because that's exactly what Daniel did, much to their dismay.

The "satraps" (also translated "captains" or "princes") were politicians and possibly royalty. They were men of power, prestige and persuasion, and they were also prideful—and that's a deadly combination.

Through God's power, Daniel obtained the favor of the king and thereby received a much-coveted position of authority. The satraps' unchecked pride eventually festered into a full-blown contagion. In presenting their strategy to eliminate Daniel, they preyed upon the king's own sense of pride. And because Daniel failed to give in to their demands, he incurred the penalty of the king's decree.

Pride. Pride. Pride. It's everywhere in this story.

Except in the heart of Daniel, the second most powerful leader in the land. His answer is laden with humility; the credit to his survival goes to God alone. What a difference from those prideful princes. Daniel refused to be sucked into the princes' vortex of pride. Because that's what pride does; it draws others in, destroying everyone in its path.

Those who are slaves to pride do anything to maintain the illusion that they are more capable, more worthy and more significant than others. Pride prompts people to do any number of horrible acts to those they think are lesser beings than themselves. Pride is the original sin—it was Satan's sin in heaven and the sin he promotes among human beings (see Isaiah 14:13).

And pride before God is absurd as well as deadly. "The LORD sustains the humble but casts the wicked to the ground," says Psalm 147:6; and that's exactly what happened in this story. While Daniel lived on in the good graces of the king, the prideful satraps were thrown into the same hole they had dug for Daniel.

The cure for pride is cultivating humility. Humility is being honest about who we really are before God. Humility is recognizing who God is: the King of kings and Lord of lords. Being empty before God is the only way he can fill us with himself.

Daniel 6:22

"My God sent his angel, and he shut the mouths of the lions. They have not hurt me, because I was found innocent in his sight. Nor have I ever done any wrong before you, O king."

reflection

1 Why do you think God hates pride?

2 When was the last time you asked God to show you your pride?

3 How can you be more like Daniel and less like the prideful satraps?

RELATED READINGS

Proverbs 3:34; 11:2; 16:18;
Matthew 11:29;
Ephesians 4:2;
James 4:10

"Humility is strong—not bold; quiet—not speechless; sure—not arrogant."

Estelle Smith

Monday

Go to page 1077 for your next devotional reading.

peoples, nations and men of every language worshiped him. His dominion is an everlasting dominion that will not pass away, and his kingdom is one that will never be destroyed.

The Interpretation of the Dream

15"I, Daniel, was troubled in spirit, and the visions that passed through my mind disturbed me. **16**I approached one of those standing there and asked him the true meaning of all this.

"So he told me and gave me the interpretation of these things: **17**'The four great beasts are four kingdoms that will rise from the earth. **18**But the saints of the Most High will receive the kingdom and will possess it forever—yes, for ever and ever.'

19"Then I wanted to know the true meaning of the fourth beast, which was different from all the others and most terrifying, with its iron teeth and bronze claws—the beast that crushed and devoured its victims and trampled underfoot whatever was left. **20**I also wanted to know about the ten horns on its head and about the other horn that came up, before which three of them fell—the horn that looked more imposing than the others and that had eyes and a mouth that spoke boastfully. **21**As I watched, this horn was waging war against the saints and defeating them, **22**until the Ancient of Days came and pronounced judgment in favor of the saints of the Most High, and the time came when they possessed the kingdom.

23"He gave me this explanation: 'The fourth beast is a fourth kingdom that will appear on earth. It will be different from all the other kingdoms and will devour the whole earth, trampling it down and crushing it. **24**The ten horns are ten kings who will come from this kingdom. After them another king will arise, different from the earlier ones; he will subdue three kings. **25**He will speak against the Most High and oppress his saints and try to change the set times and the laws. The saints will be handed over to him for a time, times and half a time.*a*

26"'But the court will sit, and his power will be taken away and completely destroyed forever. **27**Then the sovereignty, power and greatness of the kingdoms under the whole heaven will be handed over to the saints, the people of the Most High. His kingdom will be an everlasting kingdom, and all rulers will worship and obey him.'

28"This is the end of the matter. I, Daniel, was deeply troubled by my thoughts, and my face turned pale, but I kept the matter to myself."

Daniel's Vision of a Ram and a Goat

8 In the third year of King Belshazzar's reign, I, Daniel, had a vision, after the one that had already appeared to me. **2**In my vision I saw myself in the citadel of Susa in the province of Elam; in the vision I was beside the Ulai Canal. **3**I looked up, and there before me was a ram with two horns, standing beside the canal, and the horns were long. One of the horns was longer than the other but grew up later. **4**I watched the ram as he charged toward the west and the north and the south. No animal could stand against him, and none could rescue from his power. He did as he pleased and became great.

5As I was thinking about this, suddenly a goat with a prominent horn between his eyes came from the west, crossing the whole earth without touching the ground. **6**He came toward the two-horned ram I had seen standing beside the canal and charged at him in great rage. **7**I saw him attack the ram furiously, striking the ram and shattering his two horns. The ram was powerless to stand against him; the goat knocked him to the ground and trampled on him, and none could rescue the ram from his power. **8**The goat became very great, but at the height of his power his large horn was broken off, and in its place four prominent horns grew up toward the four winds of heaven.

9Out of one of them came another horn, which started small but grew in power to the south and to the east and toward the Beautiful Land. **10**It grew until it reached the host of the heavens, and it threw some of the starry host down to the earth and trampled on them. **11**It set itself up to be as great as the Prince of the host; it took away the daily sacrifice from him, and the place of his sanctuary was brought low. **12**Because of rebellion, the host ⌊of the saints⌋*b*

---

a25 Or *for a year, two years and half a year*   *b12* Or *rebellion, the armies* and the daily sacrifice were given over to it. It prospered in everything it did, and truth was thrown to the ground.

¹³Then I heard a holy one speaking, and another holy one said to him, "How long will it take for the vision to be fulfilled—the vision concerning the daily sacrifice, the rebellion that causes desolation, and the surrender of the sanctuary and of the host that will be trampled underfoot?"

¹⁴He said to me, "It will take 2,300 evenings and mornings; then the sanctuary will be reconsecrated."

The Interpretation of the Vision

¹⁵While I, Daniel, was watching the vision and trying to understand it, there before me stood one who looked like a man. ¹⁶And I heard a man's voice from the Ulai calling, "Gabriel, tell this man the meaning of the vision."

¹⁷As he came near the place where I was standing, I was terrified and fell prostrate. "Son of man," he said to me, "understand that the vision concerns the time of the end."

¹⁸While he was speaking to me, I was in a deep sleep, with my face to the ground. Then he touched me and raised me to my feet.

¹⁹He said: "I am going to tell you what will happen later in the time of wrath, because the vision concerns the appointed time of the end.ᵃ ²⁰The two-horned ram that you saw represents the kings of Media and Persia. ²¹The shaggy goat is the king of Greece, and the large horn between his eyes is the first king. ²²The four horns that replaced the one that was broken off represent four kingdoms that will emerge from his nation but will not have the same power.

²³"In the latter part of their reign, when rebels have become completely wicked, a stern-faced king, a master of intrigue, will arise. ²⁴He will become very strong, but not by his own power. He will cause astounding devastation and will succeed in whatever he does. He will destroy the mighty men and the holy people. ²⁵He will cause deceit to prosper, and he will consider himself superior. When they feel secure, he will destroy many and take his stand against the Prince of princes. Yet he will be destroyed, but not by human power.

²⁶"The vision of the evenings and mornings that has been given you is true, but seal up the vision, for it concerns the distant future."

²⁷I, Daniel, was exhausted and lay ill for several days. Then I got up and went about the king's business. I was appalled by the vision; it was beyond understanding.

Daniel's Prayer

9 In the first year of Darius son of Xerxesᵇ (a Mede by descent), who was made ruler over the Babylonianᶜ kingdom— ²in the first year of his reign, I, Daniel, understood from the Scriptures, according to the word of the Lord given to Jeremiah the prophet, that the desolation of Jerusalem would last seventy years. ³So I turned to the Lord God and pleaded with him in prayer and petition, in fasting, and in sackcloth and ashes.

⁴I prayed to the Lord my God and confessed:

"O Lord, the great and awesome God, who keeps his covenant of love with all who love him and obey his commands, ⁵we have sinned and done wrong. We have been wicked and have rebelled; we have turned away from your commands and laws. ⁶We have not listened to your servants the prophets, who spoke in your name to our kings, our princes and our fathers, and to all the people of the land.

⁷"Lord, you are righteous, but this day we are covered with shame—the men of Judah and people of Jerusalem and all Israel, both near and far, in all the countries where you have scattered us because of our unfaithfulness to you. ⁸O Lord, we and our kings, our princes and our fathers are covered with shame because we have sinned against you. ⁹The Lord our God is merciful and forgiving, even though we have rebelled against him; ¹⁰we have not obeyed the Lord our God or kept the laws he gave us through his servants the prophets. ¹¹All Israel has transgressed your law and turned away, refusing to obey you.

"Therefore the curses and sworn judgments written in the Law of Moses, the servant of God, have been poured out on us,

---

ᵃ19 Or *because the end will be at the appointed time*   ᵇ1 Hebrew *Ahasuerus*   ᶜ1 Or *Chaldean* because we have sinned against you. [12]You have fulfilled the words spoken against us and against our rulers by bringing upon us great disaster. Under the whole heaven nothing has ever been done like what has been done to Jerusalem. [13]Just as it is written in the Law of Moses, all this disaster has come upon us, yet we have not sought the favor of the LORD our God by turning from our sins and giving attention to your truth. [14]The LORD did not hesitate to bring the disaster upon us, for the LORD our God is righteous in everything he does; yet we have not obeyed him.

[15]"Now, O Lord our God, who brought your people out of Egypt with a mighty hand and who made for yourself a name that endures to this day, we have sinned, we have done wrong. [16]O Lord, in keeping with all your righteous acts, turn away your anger and your wrath from Jerusalem, your city, your holy hill. Our sins and the iniquities of our fathers have made Jerusalem and your people an object of scorn to all those around us.

[17]"Now, our God, hear the prayers and petitions of your servant. For your sake, O Lord, look with favor on your desolate sanctuary. [18]Give ear, O God, and hear; open your eyes and see the desolation of the city that bears your Name. We do not make requests of you because we are righteous, but because of your great mercy. [19]O Lord, listen! O Lord, forgive! O Lord, hear and act! For your sake, O my God, do not delay, because your city and your people bear your Name."

The Seventy "Sevens"

[20]While I was speaking and praying, confessing my sin and the sin of my people Israel and making my request to the LORD my God for his holy hill— [21]while I was still in prayer, Gabriel, the man I had seen in the earlier vision, came to me in swift flight about the time of the evening sacrifice. [22]He instructed me and said to me, "Daniel, I have now come to

give you insight and understanding. [23]As soon as you began to pray, an answer was given, which I have come to tell you, for you are highly esteemed. Therefore, consider the message and understand the vision:

[24]"Seventy 'sevens'[a] are decreed for your people and your holy city to finish[b] transgression, to put an end to sin, to atone for wickedness, to bring in everlasting righteousness, to seal up vision and prophecy and to anoint the most holy.[c]

[25]"Know and understand this: From the issuing of the decree[d] to restore and rebuild Jerusalem until the Anointed One,[e] the ruler, comes, there will be seven 'sevens,' and sixty-two 'sevens.' It will be rebuilt with streets and a trench, but in times of trouble. [26]After the sixty-two 'sevens,' the Anointed One will be cut off and will have nothing.[f] The people of the ruler who will come will destroy the city and the sanctuary. The end will come like a flood: War will continue until the end, and desolations have been decreed. [27]He will confirm a covenant with many for one 'seven.'[g] In the middle of the 'seven'[g] he will put an end to sacrifice and offering. And on a wing of the temple he will set up an abomination that causes desolation, until the end that is decreed is poured out on him."[h]"[i]

Daniel's Vision of a Man

10 In the third year of Cyrus king of Persia, a revelation was given to Daniel (who was called Belteshazzar). Its message was true and it concerned a great war.[j] The understanding of the message came to him in a vision.

[2]At that time I, Daniel, mourned for three weeks. [3]I ate no choice food; no meat or wine touched my lips; and I used no lotions at all until the three weeks were over.

[4]On the twenty-fourth day of the first month, as I was standing on the bank of the great river, the Tigris, [5]I looked up and there before me was a man dressed in linen, with a belt of the finest gold around his waist. [6]His body was like chrysolite, his face like lightning,

---

[a]24 Or 'weeks'; also in verses 25 and 26   [b]24 Or restrain   [c]24 Or Most Holy Place; or most holy One   [d]25 Or word   [e]25 Or an anointed one; also in verse 26   [f]26 Or off and will have no one; or off, but not for himself   [g]27 Or 'week'   [h]27 Or it   [i]27 Or And one who causes desolation will come upon the pinnacle of the abominable temple, until the end that is decreed is poured out on the desolated city   [j]1 Or true and burdensome

his eyes like flaming torches, his arms and legs like the gleam of burnished bronze, and his voice like the sound of a multitude.

7I, Daniel, was the only one who saw the vision; the men with me did not see it, but such terror overwhelmed them that they fled and hid themselves. 8So I was left alone, gazing at this great vision; I had no strength left, my face turned deathly pale and I was helpless. 9Then I heard him speaking, and as I listened to him, I fell into a deep sleep, my face to the ground.

10A hand touched me and set me trembling on my hands and knees. 11He said, "Daniel, you who are highly esteemed, consider carefully the words I am about to speak to you, and stand up, for I have now been sent to you." And when he said this to me, I stood up trembling.

12Then he continued, "Do not be afraid, Daniel. Since the first day that you set your mind to gain understanding and to humble yourself before your God, your words were heard, and I have come in response to them. 13But the prince of the Persian kingdom resisted me twenty-one days. Then Michael, one of the chief princes, came to help me, because I was detained there with the king of Persia. 14Now I have come to explain to you what will happen to your people in the future, for the vision concerns a time yet to come."

15While he was saying this to me, I bowed with my face toward the ground and was speechless. 16Then one who looked like a man*a* touched my lips, and I opened my mouth and began to speak. I said to the one standing before me, "I am overcome with anguish because of the vision, my lord, and I am helpless. 17How can I, your servant, talk with you, my lord? My strength is gone and I can hardly breathe."

18Again the one who looked like a man touched me and gave me strength. 19"Do not be afraid, O man highly esteemed," he said. "Peace! Be strong now; be strong."

When he spoke to me, I was strengthened and said, "Speak, my lord, since you have given me strength."

20So he said, "Do you know why I have come to you? Soon I will return to fight against the prince of Persia, and when I go, the prince

of Greece will come; 21but first I will tell you what is written in the Book of Truth. (No one supports me against them except Michael, **11** your prince. 1And in the first year of Darius the Mede, I took my stand to support and protect him.)

The Kings of the South and the North

2"Now then, I tell you the truth: Three more kings will appear in Persia, and then a fourth, who will be far richer than all the others. When he has gained power by his wealth, he will stir up everyone against the kingdom of Greece. 3Then a mighty king will appear, who will rule with great power and do as he pleases. 4After he has appeared, his empire will be broken up and parceled out toward the four winds of heaven. It will not go to his descendants, nor will it have the power he exercised, because his empire will be uprooted and given to others.

5"The king of the South will become strong, but one of his commanders will become even stronger than he and will rule his own kingdom with great power. 6After some years, they will become allies. The daughter of the king of the South will go to the king of the North to make an alliance, but she will not retain her power, and he and his power*b* will not last. In those days she will be handed over, together with her royal escort and her father*c* and the one who supported her.

7"One from her family line will arise to take her place. He will attack the forces of the king of the North and enter his fortress; he will fight against them and be victorious. 8He will also seize their gods, their metal images and their valuable articles of silver and gold and carry them off to Egypt. For some years he will leave the king of the North alone. 9Then the king of the North will invade the realm of the king of the South but will retreat to his own country. 10His sons will prepare for war and assemble a great army, which will sweep on like an irresistible flood and carry the battle as far as his fortress.

11"Then the king of the South will march out in a rage and fight against the king of the North, who will raise a large army, but it will be defeated. 12When the army is carried off,

---

a16 Most manuscripts of the Masoretic Text; one manuscript of the Masoretic Text, Dead Sea Scrolls and Septuagint Then something that looked like a man's hand *b6 Or offspring c6 Or child (see Vulgate and Syriac)* the king of the South will be filled with pride and will slaughter many thousands, yet he will not remain triumphant. [13]For the king of the North will muster another army, larger than the first; and after several years, he will advance with a huge army fully equipped.

[14]"In those times many will rise against the king of the South. The violent men among your own people will rebel in fulfillment of the vision, but without success. [15]Then the king of the North will come and build up siege ramps and will capture a fortified city. The forces of the South will be powerless to resist; even their best troops will not have the strength to stand. [16]The invader will do as he pleases; no one will be able to stand against him. He will establish himself in the Beautiful Land and will have the power to destroy it. [17]He will determine to come with the might of his entire kingdom and will make an alliance with the king of the South. And he will give him a daughter in marriage in order to overthrow the kingdom, but his plans[a] will not succeed or help him. [18]Then he will turn his attention to the coastlands and will take many of them, but a commander will put an end to his insolence and will turn his insolence back upon him. [19]After this, he will turn back toward the fortresses of his own country but will stumble and fall, to be seen no more.

[20]"His successor will send out a tax collector to maintain the royal splendor. In a few years, however, he will be destroyed, yet not in anger or in battle.

[21]"He will be succeeded by a contemptible person who has not been given the honor of royalty. He will invade the kingdom when its people feel secure, and he will seize it through intrigue. [22]Then an overwhelming army will be swept away before him; both it and a prince of the covenant will be destroyed. [23]After coming to an agreement with him, he will act deceitfully, and with only a few people he will rise to power. [24]When the richest provinces feel secure, he will invade them and will achieve what neither his fathers nor his forefathers did. He will distribute plunder, loot and wealth among his followers. He will plot the overthrow of fortresses—but only for a time.

[25]"With a large army he will stir up his strength and courage against the king of the South. The king of the South will wage war with a large and very powerful army, but he will not be able to stand because of the plots devised against him. [26]Those who eat from the king's provisions will try to destroy him; his army will be swept away, and many will fall in battle. [27]The two kings, with their hearts bent on evil, will sit at the same table and lie to each other, but to no avail, because an end will still come at the appointed time. [28]The king of the North will return to his own country with great wealth, but his heart will be set against the holy covenant. He will take action against it and then return to his own country.

[29]"At the appointed time he will invade the South again, but this time the outcome will be different from what it was before. [30]Ships of the western coastlands[b] will oppose him, and he will lose heart. Then he will turn back and vent his fury against the holy covenant. He will return and show favor to those who forsake the holy covenant.

[31]"His armed forces will rise up to desecrate the temple fortress and will abolish the daily sacrifice. Then they will set up the abomination that causes desolation. [32]With flattery he will corrupt those who have violated the covenant, but the people who know their God will firmly resist him.

[33]"Those who are wise will instruct many, though for a time they will fall by the sword or be burned or captured or plundered. [34]When they fall, they will receive a little help, and many who are not sincere will join them. [35]Some of the wise will stumble, so that they may be refined, purified and made spotless until the time of the end, for it will still come at the appointed time.

The King Who Exalts Himself

[36]"The king will do as he pleases. He will exalt and magnify himself above every god and will say unheard-of things against the God of gods. He will be successful until the time of wrath is completed, for what has been determined must take place. [37]He will show no regard for the gods of his fathers or for the one desired by women, nor will he regard any god,

---

[a]17 Or *but she* [b]30 Hebrew *of Kittim*

but will exalt himself above them all. ³⁸Instead of them, he will honor a god of fortresses; a god unknown to his fathers he will honor with gold and silver, with precious stones and costly gifts. ³⁹He will attack the mightiest fortresses with the help of a foreign god and will greatly honor those who acknowledge him. He will make them rulers over many people and will distribute the land at a price.ᵃ

⁴⁰"At the time of the end the king of the South will engage him in battle, and the king of the North will storm out against him with chariots and cavalry and a great fleet of ships. He will invade many countries and sweep through them like a flood. ⁴¹He will also invade the Beautiful Land. Many countries will fall, but Edom, Moab and the leaders of Ammon will be delivered from his hand. ⁴²He will extend his power over many countries; Egypt will not escape. ⁴³He will gain control of the treasures of gold and silver and all the riches of Egypt, with the Libyans and Nubians in submission. ⁴⁴But reports from the east and the north will alarm him, and he will set out in a great rage to destroy and annihilate many. ⁴⁵He will pitch his royal tents between the seas atᵇ the beautiful holy mountain. Yet he will come to his end, and no one will help him.

The End Times

12 "At that time Michael, the great prince who protects your people, will arise. There will be a time of distress such as has not happened from the beginning of nations until then. But at that time your people—everyone whose name is found written in the book—will be delivered. ²Multitudes who sleep in the dust of the earth will awake: some to everlasting life, others to shame and everlasting contempt. ³Those

who are wiseᶜ will shine like the brightness of the heavens, and those who lead many to righteousness, like the stars for ever and ever. ⁴But you, Daniel, close up and seal the words of the scroll until the time of the end. Many will go here and there to increase knowledge."

⁵Then I, Daniel, looked, and there before me stood two others, one on this bank of the river and one on the opposite bank. ⁶One of them said to the man clothed in linen, who was above the waters of the river, "How long will it be before these astonishing things are fulfilled?"

⁷The man clothed in linen, who was above the waters of the river, lifted his right hand and his left hand toward heaven, and I heard him swear by him who lives forever, saying, "It will be for a time, times and half a time.ᵈ When the power of the holy people has been finally broken, all these things will be completed."

⁸I heard, but I did not understand. So I asked, "My lord, what will the outcome of all this be?"

⁹He replied, "Go your way, Daniel, because the words are closed up and sealed until the time of the end. ¹⁰Many will be purified, made spotless and refined, but the wicked will continue to be wicked. None of the wicked will understand, but those who are wise will understand.

¹¹"From the time that the daily sacrifice is abolished and the abomination that causes desolation is set up, there will be 1,290 days. ¹²Blessed is the one who waits for and reaches the end of the 1,335 days.

¹³"As for you, go your way till the end. You will rest, and then at the end of the days you will rise to receive your allotted inheritance."

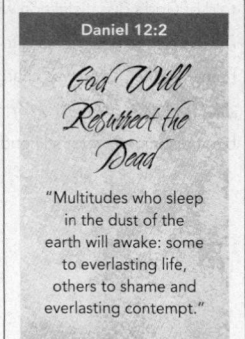

Daniel 12:2

God Will Resurrect the Dead

"Multitudes who sleep in the dust of the earth will awake: some to everlasting life, others to shame and everlasting contempt."

ᵃ39 Or *land for a reward*   ᵇ45 Or *the sea and*   ᶜ3 Or *who impart wisdom*   ᵈ7 Or *a year, two years and half a year*

Hosea

Author:
Hosea.

Audience:
The northern kingdom of Israel and all of God's people.

Date:
About 715 B.C.

Setting:
Hosea lived during the time of the end of the northern kingdom, which fell in 722 B.C.

Verse to Remember:
The LORD said to [Hosea], "Go, take to yourself an adulterous wife and children of unfaithfulness, because the land is guilty of the vilest adultery in departing from the LORD." (1:2)

God's prophets did more than give sermons warning of God's judgments. Sometimes their lives were the people's lessons. *God asked Hosea to do a difficult thing:* He was to marry a woman who would abuse his love. As the people of Israel prostituted themselves with false gods, so Hosea's wife, Gomer, would leave him for other men.

Each of Gomer's three children received a name that told of God's dissatisfaction with Israel's spiritual adultery. And as Hosea bought his wife and brought her back home, so the nation was charged *to return to God and be faithful to him.* God's yearning love had been disdained, yet it still endured.

1 The word of the LORD that came to Hosea son of Beeri during the reigns of Uzziah, Jotham, Ahaz and Hezekiah, kings of Judah, and during the reign of Jeroboam son of Jehoash[a] king of Israel:

[a] 1 Hebrew *Joash*, a variant of *Jehoash*

Hosea's Wife and Children

2When the LORD began to speak through Hosea, the LORD said to him, "Go, take to yourself an adulterous wife and children of unfaithfulness, because the land is guilty of the vilest adultery in departing from the LORD." ³So he married Gomer daughter of Diblaim, and she conceived and bore him a son.

⁴Then the LORD said to Hosea, "Call him Jezreel, because I will soon punish the house of Jehu for the massacre at Jezreel, and I will put an end to the kingdom of Israel. ⁵In that day I will break Israel's bow in the Valley of Jezreel."

⁶Gomer conceived again and gave birth to a daughter. Then the LORD said to Hosea, "Call her Lo-Ruhamah,ᵃ for I will no longer show love to the house of Israel, that I should at all forgive them. ⁷Yet I will show love to the house of Judah; and I will save them—not by bow, sword or battle, or by horses and horsemen, but by the LORD their God."

⁸After she had weaned Lo-Ruhamah, Gomer had another son. ⁹Then the LORD said, "Call him Lo-Ammi,ᵇ for you are not my people, and I am not your God.

¹⁰"Yet the Israelites will be like the sand on the seashore, which cannot be measured or counted. In the place where it was said to them, 'You are not my people,' they will be called 'sons of the living God.' ¹¹The people of Judah and the people of Israel will be reunited, and they will appoint one leader and will come up out of the land, for great will be the day of Jezreel.

2 "Say of your brothers, 'My people,' and of your sisters, 'My loved one.'

Israel Punished and Restored

² "Rebuke your mother, rebuke her,
    for she is not my wife,
    and I am not her husband.
Let her remove the adulterous look from
        her face
    and the unfaithfulness from between
        her breasts.
³ Otherwise I will strip her naked
    and make her as bare as on the day she
        was born;
I will make her like a desert,
    turn her into a parched land,

and slay her with thirst.
⁴ I will not show my love to her children,
    because they are the children of
        adultery.
⁵ Their mother has been unfaithful
    and has conceived them in disgrace.
She said, 'I will go after my lovers,
        who give me my food
        and my water,
    my wool and my linen,
        my oil and my
            drink.'
⁶ Therefore I will block
        her path with
        thornbushes;
    I will wall her in so that
        she cannot find her
            way.
⁷ She will chase after her
        lovers but not catch
            them;
    she will look for them
        but not find them.
Then she will say,
    'I will go back to my
        husband as at first,
    for then I was better off than now.'
⁸ She has not acknowledged that I was the
        one
    who gave her the grain, the new wine
        and oil,
    who lavished on her the silver and gold—
        which they used for Baal.

⁹ "Therefore I will take away my grain when
        it ripens,
    and my new wine when it is ready.
I will take back my wool and my linen,
    intended to cover her nakedness.
¹⁰ So now I will expose her lewdness
        before the eyes of her lovers;
    no one will take her out of my hands.
¹¹ I will stop all her celebrations:
    her yearly festivals, her New Moons,
    her Sabbath days—all her appointed
        feasts.
¹² I will ruin her vines and her fig trees,
    which she said were her pay from her
        lovers;
I will make them a thicket,

Hosea 1:7

God Demonstrates Love

"Yet I will show love to the house of Judah; and I will save them—not by bow, sword or battle, or by horses and horsemen, but by the LORD their God."

ᵃ6 *Lo-Ruhamah* means *not loved.*   ᵇ9 *Lo-Ammi* means *not my people.*

and wild animals will devour them.

¹³ I will punish her for the days
  she burned incense to the Baals;
she decked herself with rings and jewelry,
  and went after her lovers,
  but me she forgot,"
                    declares the LORD.

¹⁴ "Therefore I am now going to allure her;
  I will lead her into the desert
  and speak tenderly to her.
¹⁵ There I will give her back her vineyards,
  and will make the Valley of Achor*a* a
    door of hope.
There she will sing*b* as in the days of her
    youth,
  as in the day she came up out of Egypt.

¹⁶ "In that day," declares the LORD,
  "you will call me 'my husband';
  you will no longer call me 'my
    master.'*c*
¹⁷ I will remove the names of the Baals from
    her lips;
  no longer will their names be invoked.
¹⁸ In that day I will make a covenant for
    them
  with the beasts of the field and the birds
    of the air
  and the creatures that move along the
    ground.
  Bow and sword and battle
  I will abolish from the land,
  so that all may lie down in safety.
¹⁹ I will betroth you to me
    forever;
  I will betroth you in*d*
    righteousness and
    justice,
  in*e* love and compassion.
²⁰ I will betroth you in
    faithfulness,
  and you will
    acknowledge the
    LORD.

²¹ "In that day I will respond,"
  declares the LORD—
  "I will respond to the skies,

and they will respond to the earth;
²² and the earth will respond to the grain,
  the new wine and oil,
  and they will respond to Jezreel.*f*
²³ I will plant her for myself in the land;
  I will show my love to the one I called
    'Not my loved one.'*g*
  I will say to those called 'Not my people,'*h*
    'You are my people';
  and they will say, 'You are my God.'"

Hosea's Reconciliation With His Wife

3 The LORD said to me, "Go, show your love
to your wife again, though she is loved by
another and is an adulteress. Love her as the
LORD loves the Israelites, though they turn to
other gods and love the sacred raisin cakes."

² So I bought her for fifteen shekels*i* of silver and about a homer and a lethek*j* of barley.
³ Then I told her, "You are to live with*k* me many
days; you must not be a prostitute or be intimate with any man, and I will live with*k* you."

⁴ For the Israelites will live many days without king or prince, without sacrifice or sacred
stones, without ephod or idol. ⁵ Afterward the
Israelites will return and seek the LORD their
God and David their king. They will come
trembling to the LORD and to his blessings in
the last days.

The Charge Against Israel

4 Hear the word of the LORD, you
    Israelites,
  because the LORD has a charge to bring
    against you who live in
    the land:
  "There is no faithfulness,
    no love,
    no acknowledgment of
    God in the land.
² There is only cursing,*l* lying
    and murder,
  stealing and adultery;
  they break all bounds,
  and bloodshed follows
    bloodshed.
³ Because of this the land
    mourns,*m*
and all who live in it waste away;

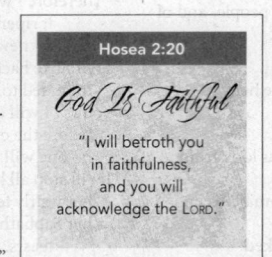

Hosea 2:20

God Is Faithful

"I will betroth you
in faithfulness,
and you will
acknowledge the LORD."

---

*a*15 *Achor* means *trouble.*   *b*15 Or *respond.*   *c*16 Hebrew *baal*   *d*19 Or *with;* also in verse 20   *e*19 Or *with*   *f*22 *Jezreel* means *God plants.*   *g*23 Hebrew *Lo-Ruhamah*   *h*23 Hebrew *Lo-Ammi*   *i*2 That is, about 6 ounces (about 170 grams)   *j*2 That is, probably about 10 bushels (about 330 liters)   *k*3 Or *wait for*   *l*2 That is, to pronounce a curse upon   *m*3 Or *dries up*

Real Joy

Read: Hosea 3:1-5

SEVERAL YEARS AGO I SPOKE at a women's retreat where their theme was "Experiencing the Joy!" I remember telling them that "real joy is knowing the depth of your sin and the extent of your idolatry." Until you believe with your whole being that, given the right set of circumstances, you are capable of committing any sin, and until you know that apart from Christ there is nothing that's naturally good in you, then you will never know real joy.

Real joy is knowing how bad I am and then comparing it to how much I have been forgiven. Jesus said it himself: Those who have been forgiven much, love much. Their gratitude spills over, and they find themselves crazy in love with God, falling at his feet, worshiping with abandon. They find themselves loving others extravagantly and forgiving others from the heart. For not only do those who have been forgiven much love much, but they forgive much too. As the Bible instructs, we are to "be kind and compassionate to one another, forgiving each other, just as in Christ God forgave you" (Ephesians 4:32).

Although some sins are more heinous than others—murder is more detrimental to society than entertaining lustful thoughts or stealing a packet of Sweet 'N Low—all sin is grievous to God. All sin separates us from him. All sin is serious . . .

Whenever my heart starts to grow cold, when I take comfort in being "not so bad" and seek satisfaction in feeling superior to others, all I need is to look at the cross of Christ. Then, once I see clearly that it was me who put Jesus there, I remember his words to another sinful woman: "Your sins are forgiven . . . Your faith has saved you; go in peace" (Luke 7:48,50).

—Nancy Kennedy

Hosea 3:1

The LORD said to me, "Go, show your love to your wife again, though she is loved by another and is an adulteress. Love her as the LORD loves the Israelites, though they turn to other gods and love the sacred raisin cakes."

reflection

1 Put yourself in Hosea's place. How do you think he felt when he was asked to take back an adulteress wife?

2 Now put yourself in Hosea's wife's place. How grateful do you think she was for Hosea's love? How does it make you feel to know that God is *always* willing to take you back—regardless of how "bad" you are?

3 Spend some time reflecting on the thought that real joy is knowing how much you've been forgiven. Thank your heavenly Husband for forgiving you and loving you enough to send his Son to provide perfect peace and joy.

RELATED READINGS

Psalm 103:8–12;
Isaiah 38:16–19;
Acts 3:19

Go to page 1080 for your next devotional reading.

the beasts of the field and the birds of the
air
and the fish of the sea are dying.

4 "But let no man bring a charge,
let no man accuse another,
for your people are like those
who bring charges against a priest.
5 You stumble day and night,
and the prophets stumble with you.
So I will destroy your mother—
6 my people are destroyed from lack of
knowledge.

"Because you have rejected knowledge,
I also reject you as my priests;
because you have ignored the law of your
God,
I also will ignore your children.
7 The more the priests increased,
the more they sinned against me;
they exchanged*a* their*b* Glory for
something disgraceful.
8 They feed on the sins of my people
and relish their wickedness.
9 And it will be: Like people, like priests.
I will punish both of them for their
ways
and repay them for their deeds.

10 "They will eat but not have enough;
they will engage in prostitution but not
increase,
because they have deserted the LORD
to give themselves 11 to prostitution,
to old wine and new,
which take away the understanding 12 of
my people.
They consult a wooden idol
and are answered by a stick of wood.
A spirit of prostitution leads them astray;
they are unfaithful to their God.
13 They sacrifice on the mountaintops
and burn offerings on the hills,
under oak, poplar and terebinth,
where the shade is pleasant.
Therefore your daughters turn to
prostitution
and your daughters-in-law to adultery.

14 "I will not punish your daughters
when they turn to prostitution,
nor your daughters-in-law
when they commit adultery,
because the men themselves consort with
harlots
and sacrifice with shrine prostitutes—
a people without understanding will
come to ruin!

15 "Though you commit adultery, O Israel,
let not Judah become guilty.

"Do not go to Gilgal;
do not go up to Beth Aven.*c*
And do not swear, 'As surely as the LORD
lives!'
16 The Israelites are stubborn,
like a stubborn heifer.
How then can the LORD pasture them
like lambs in a meadow?
17 Ephraim is joined to idols;
leave him alone!
18 Even when their drinks are gone,
they continue their prostitution;
their rulers dearly love shameful ways.
19 A whirlwind will sweep them away,
and their sacrifices will bring them
shame.

Judgment Against Israel

5 "Hear this, you priests!
Pay attention, you Israelites!
Listen, O royal house!
This judgment is against you:
You have been a snare at Mizpah,
a net spread out on Tabor.
2 The rebels are deep in slaughter.
I will discipline all of them.
3 I know all about Ephraim;
Israel is not hidden from me.
Ephraim, you have now turned to
prostitution;
Israel is corrupt.

4 "Their deeds do not permit them
to return to their God.
A spirit of prostitution is in their heart;
they do not acknowledge the LORD.
5 Israel's arrogance testifies against them;

---

*a*7 Syriac and an ancient Hebrew scribal tradition; Masoretic Text *I will exchange*   *b*7 Masoretic Text; an ancient Hebrew scribal tradition *my*   *c*15 *Beth Aven* means *house of wickedness* (a name for Bethel, which means *house of God*).

the Israelites, even Ephraim, stumble in
their sin;
Judah also stumbles with them.
⁶ When they go with their flocks and herds
to seek the LORD,
they will not find him;
he has withdrawn himself from them.
⁷ They are unfaithful to the LORD;
they give birth to illegitimate children.
Now their New Moon festivals
will devour them and their fields.

⁸ "Sound the trumpet in Gibeah,
the horn in Ramah.
Raise the battle cry in Beth Aven*ᵃ*;
lead on, O Benjamin.
⁹ Ephraim will be laid waste
on the day of reckoning.
Among the tribes of Israel
I proclaim what is certain.
¹⁰ Judah's leaders are like those
who move boundary stones.
I will pour out my wrath on them
like a flood of water.
¹¹ Ephraim is oppressed,
trampled in judgment,
intent on pursuing
idols.*ᵇ*
¹² I am like a moth to
Ephraim,
like rot to the people of
Judah.

¹³ "When Ephraim saw his
sickness,
and Judah his sores,
then Ephraim turned to
Assyria,
and sent to the great king
for help.
But he is not able to cure
you,
not able to heal your sores.
¹⁴ For I will be like a lion to Ephraim,
like a great lion to Judah.
I will tear them to pieces and go away;
I will carry them off, with no one to
rescue them.
¹⁵ Then I will go back to my place

until they admit their guilt.
And they will seek my face;
in their misery they will earnestly seek
me."

Israel Unrepentant

6 "Come, let us return to the LORD.
He has torn us to pieces
but he will heal us;
he has injured us
but he will bind up our wounds.
² After two days he will revive us;
on the third day he will restore us,
that we may live in his presence.
³ Let us acknowledge the LORD;
let us press on to acknowledge him.
As surely as the sun rises,
he will appear;
he will come to us like the winter rains,
like the spring rains that water the
earth."

⁴ "What can I do with you, Ephraim?
What can I do with you, Judah?
Your love is like the morning mist,
like the early dew that disappears.
⁵ Therefore I cut you in
pieces with my
prophets,
I killed you with the
words of my mouth;
my judgments flashed
like lightning upon
you.
⁶ For I desire mercy, not
sacrifice,
and acknowledgment
of God rather than
burnt offerings.
⁷ Like Adam,*ᶜ* they have
broken the
covenant—
they were unfaithful to me there.
⁸ Gilead is a city of wicked men,
stained with footprints of blood.
⁹ As marauders lie in ambush for a man,
so do bands of priests;
they murder on the road to Shechem,
committing shameful crimes.

Hosea 6:6

God Desires Obedience

"For I desire mercy,
not sacrifice,
and acknowledgment
of God rather than
burnt offerings."

ᵃ8 *Beth Aven* means *house of wickedness* (a name for Bethel, which means *house of God*). *ᵇ11* The meaning of the Hebrew for this word
is uncertain. *ᶜ7* Or *As at Adam;* or *Like men*

Hosea 6:1

"Come, let us return to the LORD. He has torn us to pieces but he will heal us; he has injured us but he will bind up our wounds."

reflection

1 How often do you recognize the Holy Spirit's voice when he nudges you to confess your sins?

2 Is anything holding you back from coming clean before God and others? Is it pride, shame, fear or something else?

3 Do you believe that God is ready to forgive you? Now, will you let him?

RELATED READINGS

Psalms 32:5–6; 130:3–8;
Romans 8:26–27;
Galatians 6:8;
Ephesians 4:30

SHERRY'S HUSBAND, RON, was out of town, and she ended up going out to dinner with a male coworker. But since the evening wasn't romantic, she decided not to tell Ron. After all, Sherry reasoned, he'd most likely be angry—and nothing had happened. But as she talked to Ron on the phone that night, a voice inside her whispered, *Come clean.*

Amelia's two boys were extremely rowdy at the restaurant. Since she was looking forward to having a long conversation with a friend who had come along, she was angrier than usual—and she yelled at the kids on the way home. As the boys slunk into the house, shoulders sagging, Amelia's conscience urged her to apologize. She ignored it, but she couldn't sleep that night.

A friend shares something confidential with you, and you tell some of your friends from church about it as a "prayer request." Immediately, you feel ashamed. Later, you want to confess your wrongdoing, but something inside you hesitates.

Human beings, every one, tend to be like the children of Israel. Time and time again God sent prophets to warn them of the consequences of their sins. Godly people like Hosea wept as they told the people that God longed for them to soften their hearts and come back to him like a wife would return to her husband. Sometimes they listened to the warnings, but usually they continued down the destructive vortex, making light of God's mercy and forgetting how he had always loved them.

Living in the new covenant, we don't fear the kind of destruction the Israelites faced—destruction at the hands of foreign oppressors and captivity in a foreign land. Jesus has already paid the whole bill for our sin. So shouldn't we be extra sensitive when we know that the Spirit of the living God is nudging us to come clean with our sin? Yet it's still a choice for each one of us. The Spirit can whisper our names and call us back, but we have to listen and be openhearted enough to hear his still, small voice. We can turn around and ask God (and others) to forgive us or risk grieving the Spirit and continue on a lonely and ultimately destructive path.

When the Spirit whispers, will you listen?

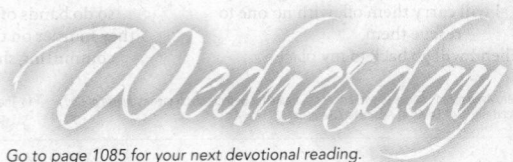

Wednesday

Go to page 1085 for your next devotional reading.

¹⁰ I have seen a horrible thing
in the house of Israel.
There Ephraim is given to prostitution
and Israel is defiled.

¹¹ "Also for you, Judah,
a harvest is appointed.

"Whenever I would restore the fortunes of
my people,
7 ¹ whenever I would heal Israel,
the sins of Ephraim are exposed
and the crimes of Samaria revealed.
They practice deceit,
thieves break into houses,
bandits rob in the streets;
² but they do not realize
that I remember all their evil deeds.
Their sins engulf them;
they are always before me.

³ "They delight the king with their
wickedness,
the princes with their lies.
⁴ They are all adulterers,
burning like an oven
whose fire the baker need not stir
from the kneading of the dough till it
rises.
⁵ On the day of the festival of our king
the princes become inflamed with
wine,
and he joins hands with the mockers.
⁶ Their hearts are like an oven;
they approach him with intrigue.
Their passion smolders all night;
in the morning it blazes like a flaming
fire.
⁷ All of them are hot as an oven;
they devour their rulers.
All their kings fall,
and none of them calls on me.

⁸ "Ephraim mixes with the nations;
Ephraim is a flat cake not turned over.
⁹ Foreigners sap his strength,
but he does not realize it.
His hair is sprinkled with gray,
but he does not notice.
¹⁰ Israel's arrogance testifies against him,
but despite all this

he does not return to the LORD his God
or search for him.

¹¹ "Ephraim is like a dove,
easily deceived and senseless—
now calling to Egypt,
now turning to Assyria.
¹² When they go, I will throw my net over
them;
I will pull them down like birds of the
air.
When I hear them flocking together,
I will catch them.
¹³ Woe to them,
because they have strayed from me!
Destruction to them,
because they have rebelled against me!
I long to redeem them
but they speak lies against me.
¹⁴ They do not cry out to me from their
hearts
but wail upon their beds.
They gather together*a* for grain and new
wine
but turn away from me.
¹⁵ I trained them and strengthened them,
but they plot evil against me.
¹⁶ They do not turn to the Most High;
they are like a faulty bow.
Their leaders will fall by the sword
because of their insolent words.
For this they will be ridiculed
in the land of Egypt.

Israel to Reap the Whirlwind

8 "Put the trumpet to your lips!
An eagle is over the house of the LORD
because the people have broken my
covenant
and rebelled against my law.
² Israel cries out to me,
'O our God, we acknowledge you!'
³ But Israel has rejected what is good;
an enemy will pursue him.
⁴ They set up kings without my consent;
they choose princes without my
approval.
With their silver and gold
they make idols for themselves
to their own destruction.

---

a 14 Most Hebrew manuscripts; some Hebrew manuscripts and Septuagint *They slash themselves*

5 Throw out your calf-idol, O Samaria!
  My anger burns against them.
  How long will they be incapable of purity?
6   They are from Israel!
  This calf—a craftsman has made it;
    it is not God.
  It will be broken in pieces,
    that calf of Samaria.

7 "They sow the wind
    and reap the whirlwind.
  The stalk has no head;
    it will produce no flour.
  Were it to yield grain,
    foreigners would swallow it up.
8 Israel is swallowed up;
    now she is among the nations
    like a worthless thing.
9 For they have gone up to Assyria
    like a wild donkey wandering alone.
  Ephraim has sold herself to lovers.
10 Although they have sold themselves
    among the nations,
  I will now gather them together.
  They will begin to waste away
    under the oppression of the mighty
      king.

11 "Though Ephraim built many altars for sin
    offerings,
  these have become altars for sinning.
12 I wrote for them the many things of my
    law,
  but they regarded them as something
    alien.
13 They offer sacrifices given to me
    and they eat the meat,
  but the LORD is not pleased with them.
  Now he will remember their wickedness
    and punish their sins:
  They will return to Egypt.
14 Israel has forgotten his Maker
    and built palaces;
  Judah has fortified many towns.
  But I will send fire upon their cities
    that will consume their fortresses."

Punishment for Israel

9 Do not rejoice, O Israel;
    do not be jubilant like the other nations.
  For you have been unfaithful to your God;

  you love the wages of a prostitute
    at every threshing floor.
2 Threshing floors and winepresses will not
    feed the people;
  the new wine will fail them.
3 They will not remain in the LORD's land;
  Ephraim will return to Egypt
    and eat unclean*a* food in Assyria.
4 They will not pour out wine offerings to
    the LORD,
  nor will their sacrifices please him.
  Such sacrifices will be to them like the
    bread of mourners;
  all who eat them will be unclean.
  This food will be for themselves;
    it will not come into the temple of the
      LORD.

5 What will you do on the day of your
    appointed feasts,
  on the festival days of the LORD?
6 Even if they escape from destruction,
    Egypt will gather them,
  and Memphis will bury them.
  Their treasures of silver will be taken over
    by briers,
  and thorns will overrun their tents.
7 The days of punishment are coming,
    the days of reckoning are at hand.
  Let Israel know this.
  Because your sins are so many
    and your hostility so great,
  the prophet is considered a fool,
    the inspired man a maniac.
8 The prophet, along with my God,
    is the watchman over Ephraim,*b*
  yet snares await him on all his paths,
    and hostility in the house of his God.
9 They have sunk deep into corruption,
    as in the days of Gibeah.
  God will remember their wickedness
    and punish them for their sins.

10 "When I found Israel,
    it was like finding grapes in the
      desert;
  when I saw your fathers,
    it was like seeing the early fruit on the
      fig tree.
  But when they came to Baal Peor,

---

*a*3 That is, ceremonially unclean   *b*8 Or *The prophet is the watchman over Ephraim, / the people of my God*

they consecrated themselves to that
shameful idol
and became as vile as the thing they
loved.
[11] Ephraim's glory will fly away like a bird—
no birth, no pregnancy, no conception.
[12] Even if they rear children,
I will bereave them of every one.
Woe to them
when I turn away from them!
[13] I have seen Ephraim, like Tyre,
planted in a pleasant place.
But Ephraim will bring out
their children to the slayer."
[14] Give them, O LORD—
what will you give them?
Give them wombs that miscarry
and breasts that are dry.
[15] "Because of all their wickedness in Gilgal,
I hated them there.
Because of their sinful deeds,
I will drive them out of my house.
I will no longer love them;
all their leaders are rebellious.
[16] Ephraim is blighted,
their root is withered,
they yield no fruit.
Even if they bear children,
I will slay their cherished offspring."
[17] My God will reject them
because they have not obeyed him;
they will be wanderers among the
nations.

10 Israel was a spreading vine;
he brought forth fruit for himself.
As his fruit increased,
he built more altars;
as his land prospered,
he adorned his sacred stones.
[2] Their heart is deceitful,
and now they must bear their guilt.
The LORD will demolish their altars
and destroy their sacred stones.

[3] Then they will say, "We have no king
because we did not revere the LORD.
But even if we had a king,

what could he do for us?"
[4] They make many promises,
take false oaths
and make agreements;
therefore lawsuits spring up
like poisonous weeds in a plowed field.
[5] The people who live in Samaria fear
for the calf-idol of Beth Aven.[a]
Its people will mourn over it,
and so will its idolatrous priests,
those who had rejoiced over its splendor,
because it is taken from them into exile.
[6] It will be carried to Assyria
as tribute for the great king.
Ephraim will be disgraced;
Israel will be ashamed of its wooden
idols.[b]
[7] Samaria and its king will float away
like a twig on the surface of the waters.
[8] The high places of wickedness[c] will be
destroyed—
it is the sin of Israel.
Thorns and thistles will grow up
and cover their altars.
Then they will say to the mountains,
"Cover us!"
and to the hills, "Fall on us!"
[9] "Since the days of Gibeah, you have
sinned, O Israel,
and there you have remained.[d]
Did not war overtake
the evildoers in Gibeah?
[10] When I please, I will punish them;
nations will be gathered against them
to put them in bonds for their double
sin.
[11] Ephraim is a trained heifer
that loves to thresh;
so I will put a yoke
on her fair neck.
I will drive Ephraim,
Judah must plow,
and Jacob must break up the ground.
[12] Sow for yourselves righteousness,
reap the fruit of unfailing love,
and break up your unplowed ground;
for it is time to seek the LORD,
until he comes

---

[a]5 *Beth Aven* means *house of wickedness* (a name for Bethel, which means *house of God*). [b]6 Or *its counsel* [c]8 Hebrew *aven*, a reference to Beth Aven (a derogatory name for Bethel) [d]9 Or *there a stand was taken*

and showers righteousness on you.
13 But you have planted wickedness,
  you have reaped evil,
  you have eaten the fruit of deception.
Because you have depended on your own
    strength
  and on your many warriors,
14 the roar of battle will rise against your
    people,
  so that all your fortresses will be
    devastated—
as Shalman devastated Beth Arbel on the
    day of battle,
  when mothers were dashed to the
    ground with their children.
15 Thus will it happen to you, O Bethel,
  because your wickedness is great.
When that day dawns,
  the king of Israel will be completely
    destroyed.

God's Love for Israel

11 "When Israel was a child, I loved
    him,
  and out of Egypt I called my son.
2 But the more I*a* called Israel,
  the further they went from me.*b*
They sacrificed to the Baals
  and they burned incense to images.
3 It was I who taught Ephraim to walk,
  taking them by the arms;
but they did not realize
  it was I who healed them.
4 I led them with cords of human kindness,
  with ties of love;
I lifted the yoke from their neck
  and bent down to feed them.

5 "Will they not return to Egypt
  and will not Assyria rule over them
  because they refuse to repent?
6 Swords will flash in their cities,
  will destroy the bars of their gates
  and put an end to their plans.
7 My people are determined to turn from me.
  Even if they call to the Most High,
  he will by no means exalt them.

8 "How can I give you up, Ephraim?
  How can I hand you over, Israel?

How can I treat you like Admah?
  How can I make you like Zeboiim?
My heart is changed within me;
  all my compassion is aroused.
9 I will not carry out my fierce anger,
  nor will I turn and devastate
    Ephraim.
For I am God, and not man—
  the Holy One among you.
I will not come in wrath.*c*
10 They will follow the LORD;
  he will roar like a lion.
When he roars,
  his children will come trembling from
    the west.
11 They will come trembling
  like birds from Egypt,
  like doves from Assyria.
I will settle them in their homes,"
  declares the LORD.

Israel's Sin

12 Ephraim has surrounded me with lies,
  the house of Israel with deceit.
And Judah is unruly against God,
  even against the faithful Holy One.

12 1 Ephraim feeds on the wind;
  he pursues the east wind all day
  and multiplies lies and violence.
He makes a treaty with Assyria
  and sends olive oil to Egypt.
2 The LORD has a charge to bring against
    Judah;
  he will punish Jacob*d* according to his
    ways
  and repay him according to his deeds.
3 In the womb he grasped his brother's heel;
  as a man he struggled with God.
4 He struggled with the angel and overcame
    him;
  he wept and begged for his favor.
He found him at Bethel
  and talked with him there—
5 the LORD God Almighty,
  the LORD is his name of renown!
6 But you must return to your God;
  maintain love and justice,
  and wait for your God always.

---

*a*2 Some Septuagint manuscripts; Hebrew *they*   *b*2 Septuagint; Hebrew *them*   *c*9 Or *come against any city*   *d*2 *Jacob* means *he grasps the heel* (figuratively, *he deceives*).

Stop Running Away

Read: Hosea 11:1–11

HE DIDN'T JUST WALK AWAY from God. He ran. After leaving home, the young North African pursued his study of philosophy—and his appetites—in Carthage, Rome and then Milan. Over time, he grew dissatisfied. Finally, in anguish in his Milan garden, he cried out to God. He then heard a child's voice singing what he understood to be a message from God: "Take up and read." He picked up a nearby copy of the apostle Paul's epistles. What he read changed his life.

Augustine would become the bishop of Hippo. His defense of the Christian faith would serve as a foundation for the church for the following one thousand years. "Go on, O Lord, and act," this sinner-turned-priest wrote. "Stir us up and call us back; inflame us and draw us to thee; stir us up and grow sweet to us; let us now love thee, let us run to thee."

Hosea likewise describes a God who leads his people and loves them like the perfect Father he is, a father who has every reason to be angry with his children when they run in the opposite direction, discounting the gifts he has given them, honoring everything and anything but him, and refusing to listen or to come home to him. Even so, God's "compassion is aroused," writes the prophet Hosea. Though the people deserve it, he "will not come in wrath." Instead, he comes to them in love.

Hosea reminds his people that it is time to stop running away and start running back into God's open arms. God will not give up. No, he cannot. His love constrains him. God's restraint allowed Augustine and the children of Israel the opportunity to stop being headstrong and run in the right direction—toward him.

No matter how many miles from home you feel, no matter how long it's been since you whispered a prayer or listened for God's voice, the journey back to where you belong is one step away. "Come trembling" to him like a dove, and he will settle you in his home (see verse 11).

Hosea 11:7–9

"My people are determined to turn from me. Even if they call to the Most High, he will by no means exalt them. How can I give you up, Ephraim? How can I hand you over, Israel? How can I treat you like Admah? How can I make you like Zeboiim? My heart is changed within me; all my compassion is aroused. I will not carry out my fierce anger, nor will I turn and devastate Ephraim. For I am God, and not man—the Holy One among you. I will not come in wrath."

Thursday

Go to page 1092 for your next devotional reading.

7 The merchant uses dishonest scales;
  he loves to defraud.
8 Ephraim boasts,
  "I am very rich; I have become wealthy.
With all my wealth they
    will not find in me
  any iniquity or sin."

9 "I am the LORD your God,
  ⌊who brought you⌋ out
    of*ª Egypt;
I will make you live in tents
    again,
  as in the days of your
    appointed feasts.
10 I spoke to the prophets,
  gave them many visions
  and told parables
    through them."

11 Is Gilead wicked?
  Its people are worthless!
Do they sacrifice bulls in
    Gilgal?
  Their altars will be like piles of stones
    on a plowed field.
12 Jacob fled to the country of Aramᵇ;
  Israel served to get a wife,
  and to pay for her he tended sheep.
13 The LORD used a prophet to bring Israel up
    from Egypt,
  by a prophet he cared for him.
14 But Ephraim has bitterly provoked him to
    anger;
  his Lord will leave upon him the guilt of
    his bloodshed
  and will repay him for his contempt.

The LORD's Anger Against Israel

13 When Ephraim spoke, men
    trembled;
  he was exalted in Israel.
But he became guilty of Baal worship
    and died.
2 Now they sin more and more;
  they make idols for themselves from
    their silver,
cleverly fashioned images,
  all of them the work of craftsmen.
It is said of these people,

"They offer human sacrifice
  and kissᶜ the calf-idols."
3 Therefore they will be like the morning
    mist,
  like the early dew that
    disappears,
  like chaff swirling from a
    threshing floor,
  like smoke escaping
    through a window.

> **Hosea 13:4**
>
> *God Is the Only God*
>
> "But I am the LORD your God, who brought you out of Egypt. You shall acknowledge no God but me, no Savior except me."

4 "But I am the LORD your
    God,
  ⌊who brought you⌋ out
    of*ª Egypt.
You shall acknowledge no
    God but me,
  no Savior except me.
5 I cared for you in the
    desert,
  in the land of burning
    heat.
6 When I fed them, they were satisfied;
  when they were satisfied, they became
    proud;
  then they forgot me.
7 So I will come upon them like a lion,
  like a leopard I will lurk by the path.
8 Like a bear robbed of her cubs,
  I will attack them and rip them open.
Like a lion I will devour them;
  a wild animal will tear them apart.

9 "You are destroyed, O Israel,
  because you are against me, against your
    helper.
10 Where is your king, that he may save
    you?
  Where are your rulers in all your
    towns,
of whom you said,
  'Give me a king and princes'?
11 So in my anger I gave you a king,
  and in my wrath I took him away.
12 The guilt of Ephraim is stored up,
  his sins are kept on record.
13 Pains as of a woman in childbirth come to
    him,
  but he is a child without wisdom;
  when the time arrives,

ª9,4 Or *God / ever since you were in*   ᵇ12 That is, Northwest Mesopotamia   ᶜ2 Or *"Men who sacrifice / kiss* he does not come to the opening of the womb.

14 "I will ransom them from the power of the grave[a];
　I will redeem them from death.
Where, O death, are your plagues?
　Where, O grave,[a] is your destruction?

"I will have no compassion,
15　even though he thrives among his brothers.
An east wind from the LORD will come,
　blowing in from the desert;
his spring will fail
　and his well dry up.
His storehouse will be plundered
　of all its treasures.
16 The people of Samaria must bear their guilt,
　because they have rebelled against their God.
They will fall by the sword;
　their little ones will be dashed to the ground,
　their pregnant women ripped open."

Repentance to Bring Blessing

14 Return, O Israel, to the LORD your God.
　Your sins have been your downfall!
2 Take words with you
　and return to the LORD.
Say to him:
　"Forgive all our sins
and receive us graciously,
　that we may offer the fruit of our lips.[b]

3 Assyria cannot save us;
　we will not mount war-horses.
We will never again say 'Our gods'
　to what our own hands have made,
　for in you the fatherless find compassion."

4 "I will heal their waywardness
　and love them freely,
　for my anger has turned away from them.
5 I will be like the dew to Israel;
　he will blossom like a lily.
Like a cedar of Lebanon
　he will send down his roots;
6　his young shoots will grow.
His splendor will be like an olive tree,
　his fragrance like a cedar of Lebanon.
7 Men will dwell again in his shade.
He will flourish like the grain.
He will blossom like a vine,
　and his fame will be like the wine from Lebanon.
8 O Ephraim, what more have I[c] to do with idols?
I will answer him and care for him.
I am like a green pine tree;
　your fruitfulness comes from me."

9 Who is wise? He will realize these things.
　Who is discerning? He will understand them.
The ways of the LORD are right;
　the righteous walk in them,
　but the rebellious stumble in them.

Hosea 14:9

God Does Right

The ways of the LORD are right;
the righteous walk in them,
but the rebellious stumble in them.

Joel

Author:
Joel.

Audience:
The southern kingdom (Judah) and all of God's people.

Date:
About 835 B.C.

Setting:
The people of Judah trusted in their great wealth, not in God.

Verse to Remember:
Rend your heart and not your garments. Return to the LORD your God, for he is gracious and compassionate, slow to anger and abounding in love, and he relents from sending calamity. (2:13)

The land of Judah lay in ruins. Locusts of many varieties had eaten every green thing. Every blade of grass, every ear of grain, every leaf off the trees. The cattle grew gaunt and bawled out their hunger. The sheep wandered in confusion. The people were also beginning to go hungry, and *their hearts were far from God.* And now maybe, just maybe, God could finally get their attention. After the devastation of the locusts, God stepped in through the prophet Joel's words: *"The day of the Lord is coming.* A day of great darkness and gloom and judgment." But God didn't stop there. "Repent, and *I will show pity.* Come to me with a right heart, rather than with sacrifices that you don't really want to give, and I will be gracious. And someday your children will know me too."

This brief book is packed with *the awesome reality of God's power* over all events—past, present and future. And it's also packed with the hope of God's great compassion and love for his people.

---

1 The word of the LORD that came to Joel son of Pethuel.

An Invasion of Locusts

² Hear this, you elders;
    listen, all who live in the land.
Has anything like this ever happened in
        your days
    or in the days of your forefathers?

³ Tell it to your children,
    and let your children tell it to their
        children,
    and their children to the next
        generation.
⁴ What the locust swarm has left
    the great locusts have eaten;
what the great locusts have left
    the young locusts have eaten;

what the young locusts have left
    other locusts*a* have eaten.

5 Wake up, you drunkards, and weep!
    Wail, all you drinkers of wine;
wail because of the new wine,
    for it has been snatched from your lips.
6 A nation has invaded my land,
    powerful and without number;
it has the teeth of a lion,
    the fangs of a lioness.
7 It has laid waste my vines
    and ruined my fig trees.
It has stripped off their bark
    and thrown it away,
    leaving their branches white.

8 Mourn like a virgin*b* in sackcloth
    grieving for the husband*c* of her youth.
9 Grain offerings and drink offerings
    are cut off from the house of the Lord.
The priests are in mourning,
    those who minister before the Lord.
10 The fields are ruined,
    the ground is dried up*d*;
the grain is destroyed,
    the new wine is dried up,
    the oil fails.
11 Despair, you farmers,
    wail, you vine growers;
grieve for the wheat and the barley,
    because the harvest of the field is
        destroyed.
12 The vine is dried up
    and the fig tree is withered;
the pomegranate, the palm and the apple
        tree—
    all the trees of the field—are dried up.
Surely the joy of mankind
    is withered away.

A Call to Repentance

13 Put on sackcloth, O priests, and mourn;
    wail, you who minister before the altar.
Come, spend the night in sackcloth,
    you who minister before my God;
for the grain offerings and drink offerings
    are withheld from the house of your
        God.
14 Declare a holy fast;

call a sacred assembly.
Summon the elders
    and all who live in the land
to the house of the Lord your God,
    and cry out to the Lord.

15 Alas for that day!
    For the day of the Lord is near;
    it will come like destruction from the
        Almighty.*e*

16 Has not the food been cut off
    before our very eyes—
joy and gladness
    from the house of our God?
17 The seeds are shriveled
    beneath the clods.*f*
The storehouses are in ruins,
    the granaries have been broken down,
    for the grain has dried up.
18 How the cattle moan!
    The herds mill about
because they have no pasture;
    even the flocks of sheep are suffering.

19 To you, O Lord, I call,
    for fire has devoured the open pastures
    and flames have burned up all the trees
        of the field.
20 Even the wild animals pant for you;
    the streams of water have dried up
    and fire has devoured the open pastures.

An Army of Locusts

2 Blow the trumpet in Zion;
    sound the alarm on my holy hill.
Let all who live in the land tremble,
    for the day of the Lord is coming.
It is close at hand—
2   a day of darkness and gloom,
        a day of clouds and blackness.
Like dawn spreading across the mountains
    a large and mighty army comes,
such as never was of old
    nor ever will be in ages to come.

3 Before them fire devours,
    behind them a flame blazes.
Before them the land is like the garden of
        Eden,
    behind them, a desert waste—

*a*4 The precise meaning of the four Hebrew words used here for locusts is uncertain.   *b*8 Or *young woman*   *c*8 Or *betrothed*
*d*10 Or *ground mourns*   *e*15 Hebrew *Shaddai*   *f*17 The meaning of the Hebrew for this word is uncertain.

nothing escapes them.
⁴ They have the appearance of horses;
they gallop along like
cavalry.
⁵ With a noise like that of
chariots
they leap over the
mountaintops,
like a crackling fire
consuming stubble,
like a mighty army
drawn up for battle.

⁶ At the sight of them,
nations are in
anguish;
every face turns pale.
⁷ They charge like warriors;
they scale walls like
soldiers.
They all march in line,
not swerving from their course.
⁸ They do not jostle each other;
each marches straight ahead.
They plunge through defenses
without breaking ranks.
⁹ They rush upon the city;
they run along the wall.
They climb into the houses;
like thieves they enter through the
windows.

¹⁰ Before them the earth shakes,
the sky trembles,
the sun and moon are darkened,
and the stars no longer shine.
¹¹ The Lord thunders
at the head of his army;
his forces are beyond number,
and mighty are those who obey his
command.
The day of the Lord is great;
it is dreadful.
Who can endure it?

Rend Your Heart
¹² "Even now," declares the Lord,
"return to me with all your heart,
with fasting and weeping and
mourning."

¹³ Rend your heart
and not your garments.
Return to the Lord your
God,
for he is gracious and
compassionate,
slow to anger and
abounding in love,
and he relents from
sending calamity.
¹⁴ Who knows? He may turn
and have pity
and leave behind a
blessing—
grain offerings and drink
offerings
for the Lord your God.

¹⁵ Blow the trumpet in Zion,
declare a holy fast,
call a sacred assembly.
¹⁶ Gather the people,
consecrate the assembly;
bring together the elders,
gather the children,
those nursing at the breast.
Let the bridegroom leave his room
and the bride her chamber.
¹⁷ Let the priests, who minister before the
Lord,
weep between the temple porch and the
altar.
Let them say, "Spare your people, O Lord.
Do not make your inheritance an object
of scorn,
a byword among the nations.
Why should they say among the peoples,
'Where is their God?'"

The Lord's Answer
¹⁸ Then the Lord will be jealous for his land
and take pity on his people.

¹⁹ The Lord will reply*a* to them:

"I am sending you grain, new wine and oil,
enough to satisfy you fully;
never again will I make you
an object of scorn to the nations.

²⁰ "I will drive the northern army far from
you,

Joel 2:13

God Is Slow to Anger

Return to the Lord
your God,
for he is gracious and
compassionate,
slow to anger and
abounding in love,
and he relents from
sending calamity.

---

*a*18,19 Or *Lord was jealous... / and took pity... / *19 *The Lord replied*

pushing it into a parched and barren
land,
with its front columns going into the
eastern sea[a]
and those in the rear into the western
sea.[b]
And its stench will go up;
its smell will rise."

Surely he has done great things.[c]
21   Be not afraid, O land;
be glad and rejoice.
Surely the LORD has done great things.
22   Be not afraid, O wild animals,
for the open pastures are becoming
green.
The trees are bearing their fruit;
the fig tree and the vine yield their riches.
23 Be glad, O people of Zion,
rejoice in the LORD your God,
for he has given you
the autumn rains in righteousness.[d]
He sends you abundant showers,
both autumn and spring rains, as before.
24 The threshing floors will be filled with
grain;
the vats will overflow with new wine
and oil.

25 "I will repay you for the years the locusts
have eaten—
the great locust and the young locust,
the other locusts and the locust
swarm[e]—
my great army that I sent among you.
26 You will have plenty to eat, until you are
full,
and you will praise the name of the
LORD your God,
who has worked wonders for you;
never again will my people be shamed.
27 Then you will know that I am in Israel,
that I am the LORD your God,
and that there is no other;
never again will my people be shamed.

The Day of the LORD

28 "And afterward,
I will pour out my Spirit on all people.

Your sons and daughters will prophesy,
your old men will dream dreams,
your young men will see visions.
29 Even on my servants, both men and
women,
I will pour out my Spirit in those days.
30 I will show wonders in the heavens
and on the earth,
blood and fire and billows of smoke.
31 The sun will be turned to darkness
and the moon to blood
before the coming of the great and
dreadful day of the LORD.
32 And everyone who calls
on the name of the LORD will be saved;
for on Mount Zion and in Jerusalem
there will be deliverance,
as the LORD has said,
among the survivors
whom the LORD calls.

The Nations Judged

3 "In those days and at that time,
when I restore the fortunes of Judah and
Jerusalem,
2 I will gather all nations
and bring them down to the Valley of
Jehoshaphat.[f]
There I will enter into judgment against
them
concerning my inheritance, my people
Israel,
for they scattered my people among the
nations
and divided up my land.
3 They cast lots for my people
and traded boys for prostitutes;
they sold girls for wine
that they might drink.

4 "Now what have you against me, O Tyre
and Sidon and all you regions of Philistia? Are
you repaying me for something I have done?
If you are paying me back, I will swiftly and
speedily return on your own heads what you
have done. 5 For you took my silver and my
gold and carried off my finest treasures to your
temples. 6 You sold the people of Judah and

---

[a]20 That is, the Dead Sea   [b]20 That is, the Mediterranean   [c]20 Or rise. / Surely it has done great things."   [d]23 Or / the teacher for
righteousness: [e]25 The precise meaning of the four Hebrew words used here for locusts is uncertain.   [f]2 Jehoshaphat means the LORD
judges; also in verse 12.

Joel 2:25,27

"I will repay you for the years the locusts have eaten—the great locust and the young locust, the other locusts and the locust swarm—my great army that I sent among you . . . Then you will know that I am in Israel, that I am the LORD your God, and that there is no other; never again will my people be shamed."

reflection

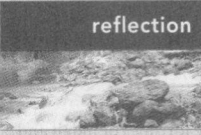

1 What area of your life seems lost or hopeless? Ask God for the strength to resist giving way to discouragement.

2 How does God's promise to "repay you for the years the locusts have eaten" give you hope?

3 How does the thought that what you are enduring is "but for a moment" in light of eternity bring you comfort?

RELATED READINGS

Psalm 103:1–22;
2 Corinthians 4:16–17;
Revelation 2:20–29

Read: Joel 2:1–32

AFTER THE WICKED KING LOUIS XIV OF FRANCE revoked the Edict of Nantes and condemned tens of thousands of the noblest men and women of France to torture and to death, many brave women were imprisoned in a huge tower called the Tour de Constance. The dungeon was a terrible place; its walls were 15 feet thick, and it was lighted only by narrow embrasures. The sister of a martyred minister lived for 36 years in that prison, and never gave way.

When at last the Huguenot women were released in 1768, someone found a word scored in the middle of the hard stone floor. The inscription is hardly readable, and to see it on a fine summer day, one has to kneel down and have a candle lighted; otherwise it is too dark. That one word is *Resist*. It is thought that some woman carved it, perhaps with a needle (the tracing is so faint), toiling at that word to help and strengthen herself and others, so that after she was gone they might be encouraged in their resolve to endure till the end. Surely the powers of endurance that God can give to the human soul are beyond our understanding. These women had not even the comfort of their Bibles. They had nothing, *nothing*—but God. Can the God who so gloriously nourished them with heavenly strength not feed us also, in our lesser needs, as we wait day by day upon Him?

When we think of suffering, such as myriads have endured in all ages, in all lands, and of the suffering, too, that many are enduring today, our own little troubles and difficulties seem too small to think about at all, and we can only find relief in praying for those who suffer. And yet, though this is so, sometimes our trifles can try us a good deal, and those words, "And even this shall pass," may perhaps bring comfort to some among us. At longest it is "but for a moment," and then . . . ?

—*Amy Carmichael*

Go to page 1097 for your next devotional reading.

Jerusalem to the Greeks, that you might send them far from their homeland.

7"See, I am going to rouse them out of the places to which you sold them, and I will return on your own heads what you have done. 8I will sell your sons and daughters to the people of Judah, and they will sell them to the Sabeans, a nation far away." The LORD has spoken.

9 Proclaim this among the
    nations:
    Prepare for war!
Rouse the warriors!
    Let all the fighting men draw near and
      attack.
10Beat your plowshares into swords
    and your pruning hooks into spears.
Let the weakling say,
    "I am strong!"
11Come quickly, all you nations from every
    side,
    and assemble there.

Bring down your warriors, O LORD!

12"Let the nations be roused;
    let them advance into the Valley of
      Jehoshaphat,
for there I will sit
    to judge all the nations on every side.
13Swing the sickle,
    for the harvest is ripe.
Come, trample the grapes,
    for the winepress is full
    and the vats overflow—
so great is their wickedness!"

14Multitudes, multitudes
    in the valley of decision!
For the day of the LORD is near

in the valley of decision.
15The sun and moon will be darkened,
    and the stars no longer
      shine.
16The LORD will roar from
    Zion
    and thunder from
      Jerusalem;
the earth and the sky
    will tremble.
But the LORD will be
    a refuge for his
      people,
    a stronghold for the
      people of Israel.

Joel 3:16

God Is a Powerful Refuge

But the LORD will be a refuge for his people, a stronghold for the people of Israel.

Blessings for God's People

17"Then you will know that I, the LORD your
    God,
    dwell in Zion, my holy hill.
Jerusalem will be holy;
    never again will foreigners invade her.

18"In that day the mountains will drip new
    wine,
    and the hills will flow with milk;
    all the ravines of Judah will run with
      water.
A fountain will flow out of the LORD's
    house
    and will water the valley of acacias.*a*
19But Egypt will be desolate,
    Edom a desert waste,
because of violence done to the people of
    Judah,
    in whose land they shed innocent blood.
20Judah will be inhabited forever
    and Jerusalem through all generations.
21Their bloodguilt, which I have not
    pardoned,
    I will pardon."

The LORD dwells in Zion!

---

a 18 Or *Valley of Shittim*

Amos

Author:
Amos.

Audience:
The northern kingdom (Israel) and all of God's people.

Date:
About 760–750 B.C.

Setting:
Wealthy people were oppressing the poor in Israel.

Verse to Remember:
Seek good, not evil, that you may live. Then the LORD God Almighty will be with you, just as you say he is. (5:14)

Being God's chosen people is a privileged position to hold. But it comes with certain risks, namely complacency. Israel was enjoying a season of prosperity when Amos came preaching his message of doom. The people had fancy clothes, fine houses (sometimes two of them), plenty to eat and drink—no one wanted to listen to tales of destruction. They felt quite secure in what they presumed was God's blessing.

Their prosperity, however, was a facade. They had bought it at the price of injustice. They oppressed the poor and cheated in the courts. Worst of all, they kept up their religious appearances, making the prescribed offerings and celebrating the designated feasts, thinking that doing so would keep God placated. *They thought if they performed the right rituals,* they could live however they wanted. But they were dead wrong.

Amos preaches a point–blank message: God cannot be manipulated. And God's message then is the same message for us today. *God isn't looking for the right rituals;* he is looking for right living. And right living begins with justice and fairness for those who are most vulnerable.

1 The words of Amos, one of the shepherds of Tekoa—what he saw concerning Israel two years before the earthquake, when Uzziah was king of Judah and Jeroboam son of Jehoash[a] was king of Israel.

²He said:

"The LORD roars from Zion
    and thunders from Jerusalem;
the pastures of the shepherds dry up,[b]
    and the top of Carmel withers."

Judgment on Israel's Neighbors

³This is what the LORD says:

"For three sins of Damascus,
    even for four, I will not turn back my
        wrath.
Because she threshed Gilead
    with sledges having iron teeth,
⁴I will send fire upon the house of
        Hazael
    that will consume the fortresses of Ben-
        Hadad.
⁵I will break down the gate of Damascus;
    I will destroy the king who is in[c] the
        Valley of Aven[d]
and the one who holds the scepter in Beth
        Eden.
    The people of Aram will go into exile
        to Kir,"
                        says the LORD.

⁶This is what the LORD says:

"For three sins of Gaza,
    even for four, I will not turn back my
        wrath.
Because she took captive whole
        communities
    and sold them to Edom,
⁷I will send fire upon the walls of Gaza
    that will consume her fortresses.
⁸I will destroy the king[e] of Ashdod
    and the one who holds the scepter in
        Ashkelon.
I will turn my hand against Ekron,
    till the last of the Philistines is dead,"
                    says the Sovereign LORD.

⁹This is what the LORD says:

"For three sins of Tyre,
    even for four, I will not turn back my
        wrath.
Because she sold whole communities of
        captives to Edom,
    disregarding a treaty of brotherhood,
¹⁰I will send fire upon the walls of Tyre
    that will consume her fortresses."

¹¹This is what the LORD says:

"For three sins of Edom,
    even for four, I will not turn back my
        wrath.
Because he pursued his brother with a
        sword,
    stifling all compassion,[f]
because his anger raged continually
    and his fury flamed unchecked,
¹²I will send fire upon Teman
    that will consume the fortresses of
        Bozrah."

¹³This is what the LORD says:

"For three sins of Ammon,
    even for four, I will not turn back my
        wrath.
Because he ripped open the pregnant
        women of Gilead
    in order to extend his borders,
¹⁴I will set fire to the walls of Rabbah
    that will consume her fortresses
amid war cries on the day of battle,
    amid violent winds on a stormy day.
¹⁵Her king[g] will go into exile,
    he and his officials together,"
                        says the LORD.

2 This is what the LORD says:

"For three sins of Moab,
    even for four, I will not turn back my
        wrath.
Because he burned, as if to lime,
    the bones of Edom's king,
²I will send fire upon Moab
    that will consume the fortresses of
        Kerioth.[h]
Moab will go down in great tumult

---

*a*1 Hebrew *Joash,* a variant of *Jehoash*   *b*2 Or *shepherds mourn*   *c*5 Or *the inhabitants of*   *d*5 *Aven* means *wickedness.*
*e*8 Or *inhabitants*   *f*11 Or *sword / and destroyed his allies*   *g*15 Or *I / Molech;* Hebrew *malcam*   *h*2 Or *of her cities*

amid war cries and the blast of the
trumpet.
³ I will destroy her ruler
and kill all her officials with him,"
says the Lord.

⁴ This is what the Lord says:

"For three sins of Judah,
even for four, I will not turn back my
wrath .
Because they have rejected the law of the
Lord
and have not kept his decrees,
because they have been led astray by false
gods,ᵃ
the godsᵇ their ancestors followed,
⁵ I will send fire upon Judah
that will consume the fortresses of
Jerusalem."

Judgment on Israel

⁶ This is what the Lord says:

"For three sins of Israel,
even for four, I will not turn back my
wrath .
They sell the righteous for silver,
and the needy for a pair of sandals.
⁷ They trample on the heads of the poor
as upon the dust of the ground
and deny justice to the oppressed.
Father and son use the same girl
and so profane my holy name.
⁸ They lie down beside every altar
on garments taken in pledge.
In the house of their god
they drink wine taken as fines.

⁹ "I destroyed the Amorite before them,
though he was tall as the cedars
and strong as the oaks.
I destroyed his fruit above
and his roots below.

¹⁰ "I brought you up out of Egypt,
and I led you forty years in the desert
to give you the land of the Amorites.
¹¹ I also raised up prophets from among your
sons
and Nazirites from among your young
men.

Is this not true, people of Israel?"
declares the Lord.
¹² "But you made the Nazirites drink wine
and commanded the prophets not to
prophesy.

¹³ "Now then, I will crush you
as a cart crushes when loaded with
grain.
¹⁴ The swift will not escape,
the strong will not muster their
strength,
and the warrior will not save his life.
¹⁵ The archer will not stand his ground,
the fleet-footed soldier will not get
away,
and the horseman will not save his life.
¹⁶ Even the bravest warriors
will flee naked on that day,"
declares the Lord.

Witnesses Summoned Against Israel

3 Hear this word the Lord has spoken
against you, O people of Israel—against
the whole family I brought up out of Egypt:

² "You only have I chosen
of all the families of the earth;
therefore I will punish you
for all your sins."

³ Do two walk together
unless they have agreed to do so?
⁴ Does a lion roar in the thicket
when he has no prey?
Does he growl in his den
when he has caught nothing?
⁵ Does a bird fall into a trap on the ground
where no snare has been set?
Does a trap spring up from the earth
when there is nothing to catch?
⁶ When a trumpet sounds in a city,
do not the people tremble?
When disaster comes to a city,
has not the Lord caused it?

⁷ Surely the Sovereign Lord does nothing
without revealing his plan
to his servants the prophets.

⁸ The lion has roared—
who will not fear?

ᵃ4 Or by lies ᵇ4 Or lies

Perfect Timing

ANNA

SHE'D WAITED A LIFETIME for this one moment. When she saw the baby, nestled in Simeon's arms, she gasped.

This is no ordinary child, she thought to herself.

She carefully watched from a distance as the three of them stood in the temple with the baby—mother, father and Simeon. Simeon's strong voice rang out as he blessed the child and his parents.

"My eyes have seen your salvation," Simeon exclaimed.

Anna felt the corners of her wrinkled lips curve as she drew a ragged breath and whispered, "As have mine."

Although she had worshiped at the temple day and night continually, she still marveled at the timing. An elderly widow, she had lived just long enough to see the Messiah with her own eyes. She realized she would likely never see him as an adult man or even as a young boy. But she saw in this tiny newborn a promise that extended the realm of time and into eternity.

When Simeon returned the baby to his mother, Anna raised a slender, shaky finger. She bid Mary to come closer. The child's face, plump and peaceful as he slept soundly on his mother's breast, made her smile. Mary watched Anna respond to him with a precious combination of grandmotherly affection and austere reverence. Looking into the face of the child-King, she probably didn't know at that moment whether to kiss his face or kneel at his feet.

Feeling as though she were in a dream, she took Jesus' delicate hand in her own and patted it softly, tracing his tiny nails and fingertips as she began a prayer of thanks. She exclaimed. She whispered. She gave thanks to God for this astonishing gift. When she finished, she smiled a knowing smile at his young mother who was, by now, beaming.

"Yes, this was a day worth waiting for," she concluded. The Messiah had made his journey from heaven to earth, and she had been among the first witnesses.

—Prayer—
God, thank you for the precious gift of your Son, Jesus.

Coming up to them at that very moment, she gave thanks to God and spoke about the child to all who were looking forward to the redemption of Jerusalem.

Luke 2:38

ASSIGNED READING:

Luke
2:36–38

Weekend

Go to page 1103 for your next devotional reading.

The Sovereign LORD has spoken—
who can but prophesy?

⁹ Proclaim to the fortresses of Ashdod
and to the fortresses of Egypt:
"Assemble yourselves on the mountains of
Samaria;
see the great unrest within her
and the oppression among her people."

¹⁰ "They do not know how to do right,"
declares the LORD,
"who hoard plunder and loot in their
fortresses."

¹¹ Therefore this is what the Sovereign
LORD says:

"An enemy will overrun the land;
he will pull down your strongholds
and plunder your fortresses."

¹² This is what the LORD says:

"As a shepherd saves from the lion's mouth
only two leg bones or a piece of an ear,
so will the Israelites be saved,
those who sit in Samaria
on the edge of their beds
and in Damascus on their couches.ᵃ"

¹³ "Hear this and testify against the house
of Jacob," declares the Lord, the LORD God Almighty.

¹⁴ "On the day I punish Israel for her sins,
I will destroy the altars of Bethel;
the horns of the altar will be cut off
and fall to the ground.
¹⁵ I will tear down the winter house
along with the summer house;
the houses adorned with ivory will be
destroyed
and the mansions will be demolished,"
declares the LORD.

Israel Has Not Returned to God

4 Hear this word, you cows of Bashan on
Mount Samaria,
you women who oppress the poor and
crush the needy
and say to your husbands, "Bring us
some drinks!"

² The Sovereign LORD has sworn by his
holiness:
"The time will surely come
when you will be taken away with hooks,
the last of you with fishhooks.
³ You will each go straight out
through breaks in the wall,
and you will be cast out toward
Harmon,ᵇ"
declares the LORD.

⁴ "Go to Bethel and sin;
go to Gilgal and sin yet more.
Bring your sacrifices every morning,
your tithes every three years.ᶜ
⁵ Burn leavened bread as a thank offering
and brag about your freewill
offerings—
boast about them, you Israelites,
for this is what you love to do,"
declares the Sovereign LORD.

⁶ "I gave you empty stomachsᵈ in every city
and lack of bread in every town,
yet you have not returned to me,"
declares the LORD.

⁷ "I also withheld rain from you
when the harvest was still three months
away.
I sent rain on one town,
but withheld it from another.
One field had rain;
another had none and dried up.
⁸ People staggered from town to town for
water
but did not get enough to drink,
yet you have not returned to me,"
declares the LORD.

⁹ "Many times I struck your gardens and
vineyards,
I struck them with blight and mildew.
Locusts devoured your fig and olive trees,
yet you have not returned to me,"
declares the LORD.

¹⁰ "I sent plagues among you
as I did to Egypt.
I killed your young men with the sword,
along with your captured horses.

ᵃ12 The meaning of the Hebrew for this line is uncertain.   ᵇ3 Masoretic Text; with a different word division of the Hebrew (see Septuagint)
out, O mountain of oppression   ᶜ4 Or tithes on the third day   ᵈ6 Hebrew you cleanness of teeth

I filled your nostrils with the stench of
your camps,
yet you have not returned to me,"
declares the LORD.

¹¹"I overthrew some of you
as I[a] overthrew Sodom and Gomorrah.
You were like a burning stick snatched
from the fire,
yet you have not returned to me,"
declares the LORD.

¹²"Therefore this is what I will do to you,
Israel,
and because I will do this to you,
prepare to meet your
God, O Israel."

¹³He who forms the
mountains,
creates the wind,
and reveals his thoughts
to man,
he who turns dawn to
darkness,
and treads the high
places of the earth—
the LORD God Almighty
is his name.

A Lament and Call to Repentance

5 Hear this word, O house of Israel, this lament I take up concerning you:

²"Fallen is Virgin Israel,
never to rise again,
deserted in her own land,
with no one to lift her up."

³This is what the Sovereign LORD says:

"The city that marches out a thousand
strong for Israel
will have only a hundred left;
the town that marches out a hundred
strong
will have only ten left."

⁴This is what the LORD says to the house of
Israel:

"Seek me and live;
⁵   do not seek Bethel,

Amos 4:13

God Is Almighty

He who forms the
mountains,
creates the wind . . .
the LORD God Almighty
is his name.

do not go to Gilgal,
do not journey to Beersheba.
For Gilgal will surely go into exile,
and Bethel will be reduced to nothing.[b]"
⁶Seek the LORD and live,
or he will sweep through the house of
Joseph like a fire;
it will devour,
and Bethel will have no one to quench it.

⁷You who turn justice into bitterness
and cast righteousness to the ground
⁸(he who made the Pleiades and Orion,
who turns blackness into dawn
and darkens day into night,
who calls for the waters of
the sea
and pours them out
over the face of the
land—
the LORD is his name—
⁹he flashes destruction on
the stronghold
and brings the fortified
city to ruin),
¹⁰you hate the one who
reproves in court
and despise him who
tells the truth.

¹¹You trample on the poor
and force him to give you grain.
Therefore, though you have built stone
mansions,
you will not live in them;
though you have planted lush vineyards,
you will not drink their wine.
¹²For I know how many are your offenses
and how great your sins.

You oppress the righteous and take bribes
and you deprive the poor of justice in
the courts.
¹³Therefore the prudent man keeps quiet in
such times,
for the times are evil.

¹⁴Seek good, not evil,
that you may live.
Then the LORD God Almighty will be with
you,

---

a 11 Hebrew God   *b 5 Or grief; or wickedness; Hebrew aven, a reference to Beth Aven (a derogatory name for Bethel)*

just as you say he is.
¹⁵ Hate evil, love good;
maintain justice in the courts.
Perhaps the LORD God
Almighty will have
mercy
on the remnant of
Joseph.

¹⁶ Therefore this is what the Lord, the LORD God Almighty, says:

"There will be wailing in all
the streets
and cries of anguish in
every public square.
The farmers will be
summoned to weep
and the mourners to wail.
¹⁷ There will be wailing in all the vineyards,
for I will pass through your midst,"
says the LORD.

The Day of the LORD

¹⁸ Woe to you who long
for the day of the LORD!
Why do you long for the day of the LORD?
That day will be darkness, not light.
¹⁹ It will be as though a man fled from a lion
only to meet a bear,
as though he entered his house
and rested his hand on the wall
only to have a snake bite him.
²⁰ Will not the day of the LORD be darkness, not light—
pitch-dark, without a ray of brightness?

²¹ "I hate, I despise your religious feasts;
I cannot stand your assemblies.
²² Even though you bring me burnt offerings
and grain offerings,
I will not accept them.
Though you bring choice fellowship
offerings,ᵃ
I will have no regard for them.
²³ Away with the noise of your songs!
I will not listen to the music of your
harps.

²⁴ But let justice roll on like a river,
righteousness like a never-failing
stream!

Amos 5:24

God Desires Justice

"But let justice roll
on like a river,
righteousness like a
never-failing stream!"

---

²⁵ "Did you bring me
sacrifices and
offerings
forty years in the desert,
O house of Israel?
²⁶ You have lifted up the
shrine of your king,
the pedestal of your
idols,
the star of your godᵇ—
which you made for
yourselves.
²⁷ Therefore I will send you
into exile beyond
Damascus,"
says the LORD, whose name is God
Almighty.

Woe to the Complacent

6 Woe to you who are complacent in Zion,
and to you who feel secure on Mount
Samaria,
you notable men of the foremost nation,
to whom the people of Israel come!
² Go to Calneh and look at it;
go from there to great Hamath,
and then go down to Gath in Philistia.
Are they better off than your two
kingdoms?
Is their land larger than yours?
³ You put off the evil day
and bring near a reign of terror.
⁴ You lie on beds inlaid with ivory
and lounge on your couches.
You dine on choice lambs
and fattened calves.
⁵ You strum away on your harps like David
and improvise on musical instruments.
⁶ You drink wine by the bowlful
and use the finest lotions,
but you do not grieve over the ruin of
Joseph.
⁷ Therefore you will be among the first to go
into exile;
your feasting and lounging will end.

ᵃ22 Traditionally *peace offerings*   ᵇ26 Or *lifted up Sakkuth your king / and Kaiwan your idols, / your star-gods*; Septuagint *lifted up the shrine of Molech / and the star of your god Rephan, / their idols*

The Lord Abhors the Pride of Israel

8The Sovereign Lord has sworn by himself—the Lord God Almighty declares:

"I abhor the pride of Jacob
  and detest his fortresses;
I will deliver up the city
  and everything in it."

9If ten men are left in one house, they too will die. **10**And if a relative who is to burn the bodies comes to carry them out of the house and asks anyone still hiding there, "Is anyone with you?" and he says, "No," then he will say, "Hush! We must not mention the name of the Lord."

11For the Lord has given the command,
  and he will smash the great house into pieces
  and the small house into bits.

12Do horses run on the rocky crags?
  Does one plow there with oxen?
But you have turned justice into poison
  and the fruit of righteousness into bitterness—
13you who rejoice in the conquest of Lo Debar*a*
  and say, "Did we not take Karnaim*b* by our own strength?"

14For the Lord God Almighty declares,
  "I will stir up a nation against you,
    O house of Israel,
  that will oppress you all the way
    from Lebo*c* Hamath to the valley of the Arabah."

Locusts, Fire and a Plumb Line

7 This is what the Sovereign Lord showed me: He was preparing swarms of locusts after the king's share had been harvested and just as the second crop was coming up. **2**When they had stripped the land clean, I cried out, "Sovereign Lord, forgive! How can Jacob survive? He is so small!"

3So the Lord relented.

"This will not happen," the Lord said.

4This is what the Sovereign Lord showed me: The Sovereign Lord was calling for judgment by fire; it dried up the great deep and devoured the land. **5**Then I cried out, "Sovereign Lord, I beg you, stop! How can Jacob survive? He is so small!"

6So the Lord relented.

"This will not happen either," the Sovereign Lord said.

7This is what he showed me: The Lord was standing by a wall that had been built true to plumb, with a plumb line in his hand. **8**And the Lord asked me, "What do you see, Amos?"

"A plumb line," I replied.

Then the Lord said, "Look, I am setting a plumb line among my people Israel; I will spare them no longer.

9"The high places of Isaac will be destroyed
  and the sanctuaries of Israel will be ruined;
  with my sword I will rise against the house of Jeroboam."

Amos and Amaziah

10Then Amaziah the priest of Bethel sent a message to Jeroboam king of Israel: "Amos is raising a conspiracy against you in the very heart of Israel. The land cannot bear all his words. **11**For this is what Amos is saying:

"'Jeroboam will die by the sword,
  and Israel will surely go into exile,
    away from their native land.'"

12Then Amaziah said to Amos, "Get out, you seer! Go back to the land of Judah. Earn your bread there and do your prophesying there. **13**Don't prophesy anymore at Bethel, because this is the king's sanctuary and the temple of the kingdom."

14Amos answered Amaziah, "I was neither a prophet nor a prophet's son, but I was a shepherd, and I also took care of sycamore-fig trees. **15**But the Lord took me from tending the flock and said to me, 'Go, prophesy to my people Israel.' **16**Now then, hear the word of the Lord. You say,

"'Do not prophesy against Israel,
  and stop preaching against the house of Isaac.'

17"Therefore this is what the Lord says:

*a*13 *Lo Debar* means *nothing.*   *b*13 *Karnaim* means *horns; horn* here symbolizes strength.   *c*14 Or *from the entrance to*

" 'Your wife will become a prostitute in the
city,
and your sons and daughters will fall by
the sword.
Your land will be measured and divided
up,
and you yourself will die in a pagan*a*
country.
And Israel will certainly go into exile,
away from their native land.' "

A Basket of Ripe Fruit

8 This is what the Sovereign LORD showed
me: a basket of ripe fruit. ²"What do you
see, Amos?" he asked.

"A basket of ripe fruit," I answered.

Then the LORD said to me, "The time is ripe
for my people Israel; I will spare them no longer.

³"In that day," declares the Sovereign LORD,
"the songs in the temple will turn to wailing.*b*
Many, many bodies—flung everywhere! Silence!"

⁴Hear this, you who trample the needy
and do away with the poor of the land,

⁵saying,

"When will the New Moon be over
that we may sell grain,
and the Sabbath be ended
that we may market wheat?"—
skimping the measure,
boosting the price
and cheating with dishonest scales,
⁶buying the poor with silver
and the needy for a pair of sandals,
selling even the sweepings with the wheat.

⁷The LORD has sworn by the Pride of Jacob:
"I will never forget anything they have done.

⁸"Will not the land tremble for this,
and all who live in it mourn?
The whole land will rise like the Nile;
it will be stirred up and then sink
like the river of Egypt.

⁹"In that day," declares the Sovereign LORD,

"I will make the sun go down at noon
and darken the earth in broad daylight.

¹⁰I will turn your religious feasts into
mourning
and all your singing into weeping.
I will make all of you wear sackcloth
and shave your heads.
I will make that time like mourning for an
only son
and the end of it like a bitter day.

¹¹"The days are coming," declares the
Sovereign LORD,
"when I will send a famine through the
land—
not a famine of food or a thirst for water,
but a famine of hearing the words of the
LORD.
¹²Men will stagger from sea to sea
and wander from north to east,
searching for the word of the LORD,
but they will not find it.

¹³"In that day

"the lovely young women and strong
young men
will faint because of thirst.
¹⁴They who swear by the shame*c* of Samaria,
or say, 'As surely as your god lives,
O Dan,'
or, 'As surely as the god*d* of Beersheba
lives'—
they will fall,
never to rise again."

Israel to Be Destroyed

9 I saw the Lord standing by the altar, and
he said:

"Strike the tops of the pillars
so that the thresholds shake.
Bring them down on the heads of all the
people;
those who are left I will kill with the
sword.
Not one will get away,
none will escape.
²Though they dig down to the depths of the
grave,*e*
from there my hand will take them.
Though they climb up to the heavens,
from there I will bring them down.

*a*17 Hebrew *an unclean*   *b*3 Or *"the temple singers will wail*   *c*14 Or *by Ashima; or by the idol*   *d*14 Or *power*   *e*2 Hebrew *to Sheol*

What About the Poor?

Read: Amos 8:1–14

ASK YOUR NEIGHBOR OR COWORKER to list the "top ten" sins, and you will probably hear a version of the Ten Commandments. Murder, stealing, lying and adultery would probably head the list.

But when God revealed to Amos that he was about to bring judgment upon his people, he cited Israel's treatment of the poor as cause for punishment. In startling imagery, God said Israel had "trampled" the needy and cheated the poor. The poor, the victims of Israel's greed and exploitation, had no recourse but to appeal to God. And God listened.

In the New Testament, Jesus repeatedly takes up the often-overlooked cause of the poor. When Jesus preached in the synagogue in Luke 4:16–21, the prophecy he chose to read to reveal who he was came from Isaiah 61:1–2: "The Spirit of the Lord is on me, because he has anointed me to preach good news to the poor." When Jesus described final judgment in Matthew 25:31–46, he evaluated how well people cared for the hungry, the thirsty, the stranger, the needy and the imprisoned. Jesus so identifies with the poor in this passage that he says that the good deeds done to the "least of these" were counted as being done to him!

How does the way you live reveal your concern for the poor? Are the poor an afterthought? A nuisance? A perplexing problem you've quit trying to solve? For many of us, Amos's message challenges us to serve the poverty stricken in ways besides simply giving money. Volunteering in a food pantry or rescue mission may be the first step to helping poor people with their immediate needs. Working directly with people who are poor helps us to put names and faces on poverty. When we do that, we can no longer objectify and ignore the needy. But are there ways to take our compassion one step further? How can we speak up to make sure the poor aren't exploited? How can we work to make sure our institutions don't make the problem worse? How can we vote for policies and practices that are equitable?

It is God's desire that we be willing to share what we have with those in need and help the poor whenever we can. When we do, our hearts beat in time with his.

Amos 8:4–5

Hear this, you who trample the needy and do away with the poor of the land, saying, "When will the New Moon be over that we may sell grain, and the Sabbath be ended that we may market wheat?"— skimping the measure, boosting the price and cheating with dishonest scales.

reflection

1 What are your assumptions about why someone might be poor?

2 Have you ever been without what you needed to live? What did you do?

3 Why do you think God identifies himself with the poor? What does that tell you about his character?

RELATED READINGS

Isaiah 61:1–3;
Matthew 25:31–46;
Luke 4:16–21

Monday

Go to page 1109 for your next devotional reading.

³ Though they hide themselves on the top of
Carmel,
　　there I will hunt them down and seize
　　　　them.
Though they hide from me at the bottom
of the sea,
　　there I will command the serpent to bite
　　　　them.
⁴ Though they are driven into exile by their
enemies,
　　there I will command the sword to slay
　　　　them.
I will fix my eyes upon them
　　for evil and not for good."

⁵ The Lord, the LORD Almighty,
　　he who touches the earth and it melts,
　　and all who live in it mourn—
the whole land rises like the Nile,
　　then sinks like the river of Egypt—
⁶ he who builds his lofty palace*a* in the
heavens
　　and sets its foundation*b* on the earth,
who calls for the waters of the sea
　　and pours them out over the face of the
　　　　land—
　　the LORD is his name.

⁷ "Are not you Israelites
　　the same to me as the Cushites*c*?"
　　　　　　　　　　declares the LORD.
"Did I not bring Israel up from Egypt,
　　the Philistines from Caphtor*d*
　　and the Arameans from Kir?

⁸ "Surely the eyes of the Sovereign LORD
　　are on the sinful kingdom.
I will destroy it
　　from the face of the earth—
yet I will not totally destroy
　　the house of Jacob,"
　　　　　　　　　　declares the LORD.

⁹ "For I will give the command,
　　and I will shake the house of Israel
　　among all the nations
as grain is shaken in a sieve,
　　and not a pebble will reach the ground.
¹⁰ All the sinners among my people
　　will die by the sword,
all those who say,
　　'Disaster will not overtake or meet us.'

Israel's Restoration

¹¹ "In that day I will restore
　　David's fallen tent.
I will repair its broken places,
　　restore its ruins,
　　and build it as it used to be,
¹² so that they may possess the remnant of
Edom
　　and all the nations that bear my name,*e*"
　　　　　　　　declares the LORD, who will
　　　　　　　　　　do these things.

¹³ "The days are coming," declares the
LORD,

"when the reaper will be overtaken by the
plowman
　　and the planter by the one treading
　　　　grapes.
New wine will drip from the mountains
　　and flow from all the hills.
¹⁴ I will bring back my exiled*f* people Israel;
　　they will rebuild the ruined cities and
　　　　live in them.
They will plant vineyards and drink their
wine;
　　they will make gardens and eat their
　　　　fruit.
¹⁵ I will plant Israel in their own land,
　　never again to be uprooted
　　from the land I have given them,"

　　　　　　　　　　says the LORD your God.

*a*6 The meaning of the Hebrew for this phrase is uncertain.　　*b*6 The meaning of the Hebrew for this word is uncertain.　　*c*7 That is, people from the upper Nile region　　*d*7 That is, Crete　　*e*12 Hebrew; Septuagint *so that the remnant of men / and all the nations that bear my name may seek the Lord*　　*f*14 Or *will restore the fortunes of my*

Obadiah

The people of Edom, descendants of Jacob's brother Esau, *forgot brotherly kindness.* God told them they were proud, but he would soon humble them. Since they lived on a mountain, they looked down on everyone else. Not only were they pleased when the people of Israel suffered at the hands of their enemies, but they also helped themselves to the plunder as the city was destroyed. But God would punish the Edomites and show his love to the Israelites by doing so.

Those who mess with God's people challenge God himself. *Our protection is a job he takes personally* because he takes affronts against his people seriously. He may not act when or how we want him to, but we can rest assured that he will act. Like the people of Israel, *we are under his protection and his lasting covenant of love.*

Author:
Obadiah.

Audience:
The Edomites, Judah and all of God's people.

Date:
Probably during the Babylonian attacks on Jerusalem (605–586 B.C.).

Setting:
The Edomites, who were descendants of Esau and related to the Israelites, were harassing the people of Israel.

Verse to Remember:
"Because of the violence against your brother Jacob, you will be covered with shame; you will be destroyed forever." (10)

---

¹The vision of Obadiah.

This is what the Sovereign LORD says about Edom—

We have heard a message from the LORD:
    An envoy was sent to the nations to say,
"Rise, and let us go against her for battle"—

² "See, I will make you small among the nations;
    you will be utterly despised.
³ The pride of your heart has deceived you,

you who live in the clefts of the rocks*a*
and make your home on the heights,
you who say to yourself,
‘Who can bring me down to the
ground?’
4 Though you soar like the eagle
and make your nest among the stars,
from there I will bring you down,”
declares the Lord.

5 “If thieves came to you,
if robbers in the night—
Oh, what a disaster awaits you—
would they not steal only as much as
they wanted?
If grape pickers came to you,
would they not leave a few grapes?
6 But how Esau will be ransacked,
his hidden treasures pillaged!
7 All your allies will force you to the border;
your friends will deceive and overpower
you;
those who eat your bread will set a trap for
you,*b*
but you will not detect it.

8 “In that day,” declares the Lord,
“will I not destroy the wise men of
Edom,
men of understanding in the mountains
of Esau?
9 Your warriors, O Teman, will be terrified,
and everyone in Esau’s mountains
will be cut down in the slaughter.
10 Because of the violence against your
brother Jacob,
you will be covered with shame;
you will be destroyed forever.
11 On the day you stood aloof
while strangers carried off his wealth
and foreigners entered his gates
and cast lots for Jerusalem,
you were like one of them.
12 You should not look down on your brother
in the day of his misfortune,
nor rejoice over the people of Judah
in the day of their destruction,
nor boast so much
in the day of their trouble.
13 You should not march through the gates of
my people

in the day of their disaster,
nor look down on them in their calamity
in the day of their disaster,
nor seize their wealth
in the day of their disaster.
14 You should not wait at the crossroads
to cut down their fugitives,
nor hand over their survivors
in the day of their trouble.

15 “The day of the Lord is near
for all nations.
As you have done, it will be done to you;
your deeds will return upon your own
head.
16 Just as you drank on my holy hill,
so all the nations will drink
continually;
they will drink and drink
and be as if they had never been.
17 But on Mount Zion will be deliverance;
it will be holy,
and the house of Jacob
will possess its inheritance.
18 The house of Jacob will be a fire
and the house of Joseph a flame;
the house of Esau will be stubble,
and they will set it on fire and consume
it.
There will be no survivors
from the house of Esau.”
The Lord has spoken.

19 People from the Negev will occupy
the mountains of Esau,
and people from the foothills will possess
the land of the Philistines.
They will occupy the fields of Ephraim and
Samaria,
and Benjamin will possess Gilead.
20 This company of Israelite exiles who are in
Canaan
will possess ⌊the land⌋ as far as
Zarephath;
the exiles from Jerusalem who are in
Sepharad
will possess the towns of the Negev.
21 Deliverers will go up on*c* Mount Zion
to govern the mountains of Esau.
And the kingdom will be the Lord’s.

*a*3 Or of *Sela* *b*7 The meaning of the Hebrew for this clause is uncertain. *c*21 Or *from*

Jonah

God's choice of workers rarely falls along the lines of human logic. God wanted to have his words preached in the capital city of Assyria. He wanted the people of Nineveh, who were pagans and also Israel's enemy, to humble themselves and repent. And so he picked a prejudiced, stubborn, complaining man to be his mouthpiece. Jonah didn't want the job from the start. *But God wanted Jonah,* and he pursued him when he could have washed his hands of him and chosen someone else.

Jonah's story illustrates *God's boundless love.* We see God reaching across the boundaries of Israel into enemy territory. We see him reaching into the depths of the sea to save a rebellious man. And we see him patiently working with Jonah, and working with him again, to help him understand something of that boundless love. Jonah may not be the most admirable prophet God used, but he is exceedingly human. *And it is humans, including women like you, that God uses to do his work.*

Author:
Jonah.

Audience:
Israel and all of God's people.

Date:
Probably about 785–750 B.C.

Setting:
God sends a reluctant Jonah to Nineveh, the capital city of the dreaded nation of Assyria, to preach repentance.

Verse to Remember:
"O LORD, is this not what I said when I was still at home? That is why I was so quick to flee to Tarshish. I knew that you are a gracious and compassionate God, slow to anger and abounding in love, a God who relents from sending calamity." (4:2)

Jonah Flees From the LORD

1 The word of the LORD came to Jonah son of Amittai: 2"Go to the great city of Nineveh and preach against it, because its wickedness has come up before me."

3But Jonah ran away from the LORD and headed for Tarshish. He went down to Joppa, where he found a ship bound for that port. After paying the fare, he went aboard and sailed for Tarshish to flee from the LORD.

⁴Then the LORD sent a great wind on the sea, and such a violent storm arose that the ship threatened to break up. ⁵All the sailors were afraid and each cried out to his own god. And they threw the cargo into the sea to lighten the ship.

But Jonah had gone below deck, where he lay down and fell into a deep sleep. ⁶The captain went to him and said, "How can you sleep? Get up and call on your god! Maybe he will take notice of us, and we will not perish."

⁷Then the sailors said to each other, "Come, let us cast lots to find out who is responsible for this calamity." They cast lots and the lot fell on Jonah.

⁸So they asked him, "Tell us, who is responsible for making all this trouble for us? What do you do? Where do you come from? What is your country? From what people are you?"

⁹He answered, "I am a Hebrew and I worship the LORD, the God of heaven, who made the sea and the land."

¹⁰This terrified them and they asked, "What have you done?" (They knew he was running away from the LORD, because he had already told them so.)

¹¹The sea was getting rougher and rougher. So they asked him, "What should we do to you to make the sea calm down for us?"

¹²"Pick me up and throw me into the sea," he replied, "and it will become calm. I know that it is my fault that this great storm has come upon you."

¹³Instead, the men did their best to row back to land. But they could not, for the sea grew even wilder than before. ¹⁴Then they cried to the LORD, "O LORD, please do not let us die for taking this man's life. Do not hold us accountable for killing an innocent man, for you, O LORD, have done as you pleased." ¹⁵Then they took Jonah and threw him overboard, and the raging sea grew calm. ¹⁶At this the men greatly feared the LORD, and they offered a sacrifice to the LORD and made vows to him.

¹⁷But the LORD provided a great fish to swallow Jonah, and Jonah was inside the fish three days and three nights.

Jonah's Prayer

2 From inside the fish Jonah prayed to the LORD his God. ²He said:

"In my distress I called to the LORD,
    and he answered me.
From the depths of the grave*ᵃ* I called for help,
    and you listened to my cry.
³ You hurled me into the deep,
    into the very heart of the seas,
    and the currents swirled about me;
all your waves and breakers
    swept over me.
⁴ I said, 'I have been banished
    from your sight;
yet I will look again
    toward your holy temple.'
⁵ The engulfing waters threatened me,*ᵇ*
    the deep surrounded me;
    seaweed was wrapped around my head.
⁶ To the roots of the mountains I sank down;
    the earth beneath barred me in forever.
But you brought my life up
    from the pit,
    O LORD my God.

⁷ "When my life was ebbing away,
    I remembered you,
    LORD,
and my prayer rose to you,
    to your holy temple.

⁸ "Those who cling to
    worthless idols
    forfeit the grace that
    could be theirs.
⁹ But I, with a song of
    thanksgiving,
    will sacrifice to you.
What I have vowed I will make good.
    Salvation comes from the LORD."

Jonah 2:7

God Hears Prayer

"When my life was ebbing away, I remembered you, LORD, and my prayer rose to you, to your holy temple."

---

*ᵃ*2 Hebrew *Sheol*   *ᵇ*5 Or *waters were at my throat*

Wishing Them Well

Read: Jonah 3:1–10

HAVE YOU EVER HAD A FRIEND or acquaintance who made a wrong choice for every right choice you made, yet in the end your friend seemed to face none of the consequences you faced? It's hard to take, watching someone come out smelling like roses when you know the stinky stuff they've been rooted in.

If you can relate, then you can empathize with Jonah when God told him to go to Nineveh. Now, that was not just *any* field of service for the ancient prophet. It was Israel's greatest national enemy. The Ninevites were citizens of Assyria, a brutal nation to the east, and Israel's greatest threat.

It's no wonder that when the people of Nineveh did clean up their act (for a while anyway), Jonah was distressed. How could God sanction the redemption of a country like that? It didn't seem fair. And in truth, at least from Jonah's perspective, it probably wasn't.

It's tough to just do what's asked of you and leave the fairness issue to God, isn't it? It's hard to see people receive good things when they've caused you (or someone you love) pain. Like when your ex-son-in-law remarries or when the disloyal secretary down the hall gets a promotion you deserved. It's even harder to facilitate their good fortune, like Jonah did. Jesus said to love our enemies, but when it comes right down to it, we'd rather not.

How do we get past our feelings and wish our enemies well? We grace them with the same kind of mercy with which God graced us without expectation of getting anything back in return (see Luke 6:35–36). We focus on God and on the good things he has given us and done for us. The key to countering the envy of another's fortune is to be grateful for our own. And when we do that, we let go of the part of God's job that we'd like to do—the finger-pointing. It's just too hard to do our own work and God's too. And he does it so much better! Since we don't have his insight into the hearts and minds of those people we'd like to judge and condemn, it's better for us to push aside our limited understanding of justice and just trust him instead.

Jonah 3:1–2

Then the word of the LORD came to Jonah a second time: "Go to the great city of Nineveh and proclaim to it the message I give you."

reflection

1 Think about the feelings you have toward people who live under a completely different set of values than you do. How do your feelings for them compare to the love God has for them?

2 When it comes to people you dislike, why is it difficult to "wish them well"?

3 What keeps you from being able to leave that person solely accountable to God? Fear? Anger? Jealousy?

RELATED READINGS

Psalm 3:1–8;
Matthew 5:43–47;
20:1–16

Tuesday

Go to page 1115 for your next devotional reading.

10And the LORD commanded the fish, and it vomited Jonah onto dry land.

Jonah Goes to Nineveh

3 Then the word of the LORD came to Jonah a second time: 2"Go to the great city of Nineveh and proclaim to it the message I give you."

3Jonah obeyed the word of the LORD and went to Nineveh. Now Nineveh was a very important city—a visit required three days. 4On the first day, Jonah started into the city. He proclaimed: "Forty more days and Nineveh will be overturned." 5The Ninevites believed God. They declared a fast, and all of them, from the greatest to the least, put on sackcloth.

6When the news reached the king of Nineveh, he rose from his throne, took off his royal robes, covered himself with sackcloth and sat down in the dust. 7Then he issued a proclamation in Nineveh:

"By the decree of the king and his nobles:

Do not let any man or beast, herd or flock, taste anything; do not let them eat or drink. 8But let man and beast be covered with sackcloth. Let everyone call urgently on God. Let them give up their evil ways and their violence. 9Who knows? God may yet relent and with compassion turn from his fierce anger so that we will not perish."

10When God saw what they did and how they turned from their evil ways, he had compassion and did not bring upon them the destruction he had threatened.

Jonah 4:2

God Is Gracious

"I knew that you are a gracious and compassionate God, slow to anger and abounding in love, a God who relents from sending calamity."

Jonah's Anger at the LORD's Compassion

4 But Jonah was greatly displeased and became angry. 2He prayed to the LORD, "O LORD, is this not what I said when I was still at home? That is why I was so quick to flee to Tarshish. I knew that you are a gracious and compassionate God, slow to anger and abounding in love, a God who relents from sending calamity. 3Now, O LORD, take away my life, for it is better for me to die than to live."

4But the LORD replied, "Have you any right to be angry?"

5Jonah went out and sat down at a place east of the city. There he made himself a shelter, sat in its shade and waited to see what would happen to the city. 6Then the LORD God provided a vine and made it grow up over Jonah to give shade for his head to ease his discomfort, and Jonah was very happy about the vine. 7But at dawn the next day God provided a worm, which chewed the vine so that it withered. 8When the sun rose, God provided a scorching east wind, and the sun blazed on Jonah's head so that he grew faint. He wanted to die, and said, "It would be better for me to die than to live."

9But God said to Jonah, "Do you have a right to be angry about the vine?"

"I do," he said. "I am angry enough to die."

10But the LORD said, "You have been concerned about this vine, though you did not tend it or make it grow. It sprang up overnight and died overnight. 11But Nineveh has more than a hundred and twenty thousand people who cannot tell their right hand from their left, and many cattle as well. Should I not be concerned about that great city?"

Micah

God is a God of mercy. But make no mistake about it; *he will not let the wicked go unpunished.* The book of Micah places us on a pendulum that swings from blessing to judgment. The prophet Micah is brokenhearted over the rebellion of God's chosen people, and he urges them *to turn their hearts back to God.* Micah prophesies the downfall of the rich and powerful. He draws attention to the plight of the poor. His warnings to the Israelites are not popular. The people don't want to hear that their actions will have disastrous consequences. Micah sees that the people's earthly riches will leave them spiritually and emotionally bankrupt, and he encourages them to return to *the only One who can bring true fulfillment and joy.* Like a loving but stern parent, Micah holds their faces in his hands and says, in effect, "Listen to me" (Micah 1:2; 3:1; 6:1), as he promises the people that God will forgive them if they turn back to him.

Author:
Micah.

Audience:
The southern kingdom (Judah) and northern kingdom (Israel).

Date:
Likely between 742 and 687 B.C., during the time of Isaiah and Hosea.

Setting:
Political mayhem has the kingdoms reeling from one bad king to another. Micah steps in to prophesy judgment.

Verse to Remember:
He has showed you, O man, what is good. And what does the LORD require of you? To act justly and to love mercy and to walk humbly with your God. (6:8)

1 The word of the LORD that came to Micah of Moresheth during the reigns of Jotham, Ahaz and Hezekiah, kings of Judah—the vision he saw concerning Samaria and Jerusalem.

² Hear, O peoples, all of you,
   listen, O earth and all who are in it,
that the Sovereign LORD may witness against you,
   the Lord from his holy temple.

Judgment Against Samaria and Jerusalem

³ Look! The LORD is coming from his dwelling place;

he comes down and treads the high
places of the earth.
⁴ The mountains melt beneath him
and the valleys split apart,
like wax before the fire,
like water rushing down a slope.
⁵ All this is because of Jacob's transgression,
because of the sins of the house of Israel.
What is Jacob's transgression?
Is it not Samaria?
What is Judah's high place?
Is it not Jerusalem?

⁶ "Therefore I will make Samaria a heap of
rubble,
a place for planting vineyards.
I will pour her stones into the valley
and lay bare her foundations.
⁷ All her idols will be broken to pieces;
all her temple gifts will be burned with
fire;
I will destroy all her images.
Since she gathered her gifts from the wages
of prostitutes,
as the wages of prostitutes they will
again be used."

Weeping and Mourning

⁸ Because of this I will weep and wail;
I will go about barefoot and naked.
I will howl like a jackal
and moan like an owl.
⁹ For her wound is incurable;
it has come to Judah.
It*a* has reached the very gate of my people,
even to Jerusalem itself.
¹⁰ Tell it not in Gath*b*;
weep not at all.*c*
In Beth Ophrah*d*
roll in the dust.
¹¹ Pass on in nakedness and shame,
you who live in Shaphir.*e*
Those who live in Zaanan*f*
will not come out.
Beth Ezel is in mourning;
its protection is taken from you.
¹² Those who live in Maroth*g* writhe in pain,
waiting for relief,

because disaster has come from the LORD,
even to the gate of Jerusalem.
¹³ You who live in Lachish,*h*
harness the team to the chariot.
You were the beginning of sin
to the Daughter of Zion,
for the transgressions of Israel
were found in you.
¹⁴ Therefore you will give parting gifts
to Moresheth Gath.
The town of Aczib*i* will prove deceptive
to the kings of Israel.
¹⁵ I will bring a conqueror against you
who live in Mareshah.*j*
He who is the glory of Israel
will come to Adullam.
¹⁶ Shave your heads in mourning
for the children in whom you delight;
make yourselves as bald as the vulture,
for they will go from you into exile.

Man's Plans and God's

2 Woe to those who plan iniquity,
to those who plot evil on their beds!
At morning's light they carry it out
because it is in their power to do it.
² They covet fields and seize them,
and houses, and take them.
They defraud a man of his home,
a fellowman of his inheritance.

³ Therefore, the LORD says:

"I am planning disaster against this
people,
from which you cannot save yourselves.
You will no longer walk proudly,
for it will be a time of calamity.
⁴ In that day men will ridicule you;
they will taunt you with this mournful
song:
'We are utterly ruined;
my people's possession is divided up.
He takes it from me!
He assigns our fields to traitors.'"

⁵ Therefore you will have no one in the
assembly of the LORD
to divide the land by lot.

---

a9 Or *He*   *b10 Gath* sounds like the Hebrew for *tell.*   *c10* Hebrew; Septuagint may suggest *not in Acco.* The Hebrew for *in Acco* sounds like
the Hebrew for *weep.*   *d10 Beth Ophrah* means *house of dust.*   *e11 Shaphir* means *pleasant.*   *f11 Zaanan* sounds like the Hebrew for
come out.   *g12 Maroth* sounds like the Hebrew for *bitter.*   *h13 Lachish* sounds like the Hebrew for *team.*   *i14 Aczib* means *deception.*
j15 Mareshah sounds like the Hebrew for *conqueror.*

False Prophets

6 "Do not prophesy," their prophets say.
    "Do not prophesy about these things;
        disgrace will not overtake us."
7 Should it be said, O house of Jacob:
    "Is the Spirit of the LORD angry?
        Does he do such things?"

    "Do not my words do good
        to him whose ways are upright?
8 Lately my people have risen up
        like an enemy.
    You strip off the rich robe
        from those who pass by
            without a care,
        like men returning from
            battle.
9 You drive the women of my
        people
    from their pleasant
        homes.
    You take away my blessing
        from their children
            forever.
10 Get up, go away!
    For this is not your
        resting place,
    because it is defiled,
        it is ruined, beyond all
            remedy.
11 If a liar and deceiver comes and says,
    'I will prophesy for you plenty of wine
        and beer,'
    he would be just the prophet for this
        people!

Deliverance Promised

12 "I will surely gather all of you, O Jacob;
    I will surely bring together the remnant
        of Israel.
    I will bring them together like sheep in a
        pen,
    like a flock in its pasture;
        the place will throng with people.
13 One who breaks open the way will go up
        before them;
    they will break through the gate and go
        out.
    Their king will pass through before
        them,
    the LORD at their head."

Leaders and Prophets Rebuked

3 Then I said,

    "Listen, you leaders of Jacob,
        you rulers of the house of Israel.
    Should you not know justice,
2   you who hate good and love evil;
    who tear the skin from my people
        and the flesh from their bones;
3 who eat my people's flesh,
        strip off their skin
            and break their bones in
                pieces;
    who chop them up like
            meat for the pan,
        like flesh for the pot?"

4 Then they will cry out to
        the LORD,
    but he will not answer
        them.
    At that time he will hide
        his face from them
    because of the evil they
        have done.

5 This is what the LORD says:

    "As for the prophets
        who lead my people
            astray,
    if one feeds them,
        they proclaim 'peace';
    if he does not,
        they prepare to wage war against him.
6 Therefore night will come over you,
        without visions,
    and darkness, without divination.
    The sun will set for the prophets,
        and the day will go dark for them.
7 The seers will be ashamed
        and the diviners disgraced.
    They will all cover their faces
        because there is no answer from God."

8 But as for me, I am filled with power,
        with the Spirit of the LORD,
    and with justice and might,
    to declare to Jacob his transgression,
        to Israel his sin.
9 Hear this, you leaders of the house of
        Jacob,

Micah 3:4

God Cannot Look on Evil

Then they will cry out
to the LORD,
but he will not
answer them.
At that time he will
hide his face from
them because of the
evil they have done.

you rulers of the house of Israel,
who despise justice
and distort all that is right;
¹⁰who build Zion with bloodshed,
and Jerusalem with wickedness.
¹¹Her leaders judge for a bribe,
her priests teach for a price,
and her prophets tell fortunes for
money.
Yet they lean upon the LORD and say,
"Is not the LORD among us?
No disaster will come upon us."
¹²Therefore because of you,
Zion will be plowed like a field,
Jerusalem will become a heap of rubble,
the temple hill a mound overgrown with
thickets.

The Mountain of the LORD

4 In the last days

the mountain of the LORD's temple will be
established
as chief among the mountains;
it will be raised above the hills,
and peoples will stream to it.

²Many nations will come and say,

"Come, let us go up to the mountain of the
LORD,
to the house of the God of Jacob.
He will teach us his ways,
so that we may walk in his paths."
The law will go out from Zion,
the word of the LORD from Jerusalem.
³He will judge between many peoples
and will settle disputes for strong
nations far and wide.
They will beat their swords into plowshares
and their spears into pruning hooks.
Nation will not take up sword against
nation,
nor will they train for war anymore.
⁴Every man will sit under his own vine
and under his own fig tree,
and no one will make them afraid,
for the LORD Almighty has spoken.
⁵All the nations may walk
in the name of their gods;

we will walk in the name of the LORD
our God for ever and ever.

The LORD's Plan

⁶"In that day," declares the LORD,

"I will gather the lame;
I will assemble the exiles
and those I have brought to grief.
⁷I will make the lame a remnant,
those driven away a strong nation.
The LORD will rule over them in Mount
Zion
from that day and forever.
⁸As for you, O watchtower of the flock,
O stronghold[a] of the Daughter of
Zion,
the former dominion will be restored to
you;
kingship will come to the Daughter of
Jerusalem."

⁹Why do you now cry aloud—
have you no king?
Has your counselor perished,
that pain seizes you like that of a woman
in labor?
¹⁰Writhe in agony, O Daughter of Zion,
like a woman in labor,
for now you must leave the city
to camp in the open field.
You will go to Babylon;
there you will be rescued.
There the LORD will redeem you
out of the hand of your enemies.

¹¹But now many nations
are gathered against you.
They say, "Let her be defiled,
let our eyes gloat over Zion!"
¹²But they do not know
the thoughts of the LORD;
they do not understand his plan,
he who gathers them like sheaves to the
threshing floor.

¹³"Rise and thresh, O Daughter of Zion,
for I will give you horns of iron;
I will give you hoofs of bronze
and you will break to pieces many
nations."

---

*a*8 Or *hill*

God's Better Way

Read: Micah 4:1–13

THINGS WEREN'T GOING LUCI'S WAY at work. She worked longer and harder than ever without recognition and with no promotion in sight.

Even though she didn't like change, she started looking for another job. The one most intriguing to her seemed like a long shot—way out of her league. However, just as she was getting ready to accept another offer, the long shot came in. She was the company's top pick.

It was a perfect match. Luci couldn't have dreamed of a better job. Looking back, she realized she would never have sought the job if things at her old company hadn't become difficult. She wouldn't have *chosen* to have things turn sour so she would want to leave. At the time, the thought of moving to a new job seemed impossible. And scary.

But God wanted her to experience more. He wanted the best for her. And she would never have found his best if she hadn't experienced trouble at work. God allowed the problems and ultimately used them for her good, even though at the time it had been a mystery to her. She did not "know the thoughts of the LORD" (verse 12). Many times, neither do we.

Micah spoke of a future time when Jerusalem would experience peace . . . a time when war would end. At the time, it seemed like a crazy message. Things were more than uncomfortable; they were downright horrible. The armies of Babylon had destroyed the temple, killed people and tortured many more. Yet Micah said peace was coming. It didn't seem possible.

Sometimes, the things God promises for our future don't seem at all likely in light of what we're experiencing today. From our limited perspective, we don't see the big picture, only a tiny thumbnail print. Like Luci, we may be experiencing something difficult or uncomfortable that will result in something better. It's important to remember that sometimes our troubles are only a momentary detour leading us to God's best for us.

Micah 4:12

But they do not know the thoughts of the LORD; they do not understand his plan, he who gathers them like sheaves to the threshing floor.

reflection

1 How has God used a difficult situation in your past for your good?

2 Is there a situation in your life right now that you can look at from a fresh perspective?

3 How can you share your experiences with someone else who needs encouragement today?

RELATED READINGS

Psalms 92:4–5; 94:11;
Isaiah 55:8–9;
1 Corinthians 3:18–20

Wednesday

Go to page 1118 for your next devotional reading.

You will devote their ill-gotten gains to the
LORD,
their wealth to the Lord of all the earth.

A Promised Ruler From Bethlehem

5 Marshal your troops, O city of troops,[a]
for a siege is laid against us.
They strike Israel's ruler
on the cheek with a rod.

2 "But you, Bethlehem
Ephrathah,
though you are small
among the clans[b] of
Judah,
out of you will come for me
one who will be ruler
over Israel,
whose origins[c] are from
of old,
from ancient times.[d]"

3 Therefore Israel will be
abandoned
until the time when she
who is in labor gives
birth
and the rest of his brothers
return
to join the Israelites.

4 He will stand and shepherd his flock
in the strength of the LORD,
in the majesty of the name of the LORD
his God.
And they will live securely, for then his
greatness
will reach to the ends of the earth.

5 And he will be their peace.

Deliverance and Destruction

When the Assyrian invades our land
and marches through our fortresses,
we will raise against him seven shepherds,
even eight leaders of men.

6 They will rule[e] the land of Assyria with the
sword,
the land of Nimrod with drawn sword.[f]
He will deliver us from the Assyrian
when he invades our land
and marches into our borders.

7 The remnant of Jacob will be
in the midst of many peoples
like dew from the LORD,
like showers on the grass,
which do not wait for man
or linger for mankind.

8 The remnant of Jacob will be among the
nations,
in the midst of many peoples,
like a lion among the
beasts of the forest,
like a young lion among
flocks of sheep,
which mauls and mangles
as it goes,
and no one can rescue.

9 Your hand will be lifted
up in triumph over
your enemies,
and all your foes will be
destroyed.

10 "In that day," declares the
LORD,

"I will destroy your horses
from among you
and demolish your
chariots.

11 I will destroy the cities of
your land
and tear down all your strongholds.

12 I will destroy your witchcraft
and you will no longer cast spells.

13 I will destroy your carved images
and your sacred stones from among you;
you will no longer bow down
to the work of your hands.

14 I will uproot from among you your
Asherah poles[g]
and demolish your cities.

15 I will take vengeance in anger and wrath
upon the nations that have not obeyed
me."

The LORD's Case Against Israel

6 Listen to what the LORD says:

"Stand up, plead your case before the
mountains;

> ### Micah 5:2
>
> *God Knows
> the Future*
>
> "But you, Bethlehem
> Ephrathah,
> though you are small
> among the clans
> of Judah,
> out of you will
> come for me
> one who will be ruler
> over Israel."

---

a1 Or *Strengthen your walls, O walled city* b2 Or *rulers* c2 Hebrew *goings out* d2 Or *from days of eternity* e6 Or *crush* f6 Or *Nimrod in its gates* g14 That is, symbols of the goddess Asherah

let the hills hear what you have to say.
² Hear, O mountains, the LORD's accusation;
  listen, you everlasting foundations of the
    earth.
For the LORD has a case against his
    people;
  he is lodging a charge against Israel.

³ "My people, what have I done to you?
  How have I burdened you? Answer me.
⁴ I brought you up out of Egypt
  and redeemed you from the land of
    slavery.
  I sent Moses to lead you,
    also Aaron and Miriam.
⁵ My people, remember
  what Balak king of Moab counseled
  and what Balaam son of Beor answered.
  Remember ⌊your journey⌋ from Shittim to
    Gilgal,
  that you may know the righteous acts of
    the LORD."

⁶ With what shall I come before the LORD
  and bow down before the exalted God?
Shall I come before him with burnt
    offerings,
  with calves a year old?
⁷ Will the LORD be pleased
    with thousands of
      rams,
    with ten thousand rivers
      of oil?
  Shall I offer my
    firstborn for my
      transgression,
    the fruit of my body for
      the sin of my soul?
⁸ He has showed you, O man,
    what is good.
  And what does the LORD
    require of you?
  To act justly and to love
    mercy
  and to walk humbly with
    your God.

Israel's Guilt and Punishment

⁹ Listen! The LORD is calling to the city—
  and to fear your name is wisdom—

"Heed the rod and the One who
    appointed it.^a
¹⁰ Am I still to forget, O wicked house,
  your ill-gotten treasures
  and the short ephah,^b which is accursed?
¹¹ Shall I acquit a man with dishonest scales,
  with a bag of false weights?
¹² Her rich men are violent;
  her people are liars
  and their tongues speak deceitfully.
¹³ Therefore, I have begun to destroy you,
  to ruin you because of your sins.
¹⁴ You will eat but not be satisfied;
  your stomach will still be empty.^c
  You will store up but save nothing,
    because what you save I will give to the
      sword.
¹⁵ You will plant but not harvest;
  you will press olives but not use the oil
    on yourselves,
  you will crush grapes but not drink the
    wine.
¹⁶ You have observed the statutes of Omri
  and all the practices of Ahab's house,
  and you have followed their traditions.
  Therefore I will give you over to ruin
  and your people to derision;
    you will bear the scorn
      of the nations.^d"

Israel's Misery

7 What misery is mine!
  I am like one who
    gathers summer
      fruit
  at the gleaning of the
    vineyard;
  there is no cluster of grapes
    to eat,
  none of the early figs that
    I crave.
² The godly have been swept
    from the land;
  not one upright man
    remains.
  All men lie in wait to shed
    blood;
  each hunts his brother with a net.
³ Both hands are skilled in doing evil;

> **Micah 6:8**
>
> *God Requires Humility*
>
> He has showed you,
> O man, what is good.
> And what does the LORD
> require of you?
> To act justly and to
> love mercy
> and to walk humbly
> with your God.

---

^a9 The meaning of the Hebrew for this line is uncertain.   ^b10 An ephah was a dry measure.   ^c14 The meaning of the Hebrew for this word is uncertain.   ^d16 Septuagint; Hebrew *scorn due my people*

Micah 6:8

He has showed you,
O man, what is good.
And what does the
LORD require of you?
To act justly and to
love mercy and to walk
humbly with your God.

reflection

1 What are some ways
you have tried to sacri-
fice to God without having
an obedient heart?

2 In what concrete way
can you extend justice
and mercy today?

3 What changes do you
need to make so that
you fulfill the call to walk
humbly with God?

RELATED READINGS

Deuteronomy 11:1;
1 Samuel 15:22–23;
Romans 12:1–3

*"The pearl of
justice is found in
the heart of mercy."*

Catherine of Siena

Read: Micah 6:1–9

PICTURE A COURTROOM. The judge enters the room, his long robe flowing. From your angle, you can't see his face. But when he sits down at the bench, his identity is finally revealed. God is the judge. And his people are on trial.

The charges are as follows: They have turned away from God. They have forgotten his merciful help and deliverance from the past. They have taken his blessings for granted.

What can they do to find favor with God? Is there a sacrifice they can make? What penance is required? The people have tried to pacify him with offerings, large and costly. But Micah reminds us that God sees the heart. He knows these are not genuine, humble expressions of repentance. He sees that the sacrifices are an attempt to replace approaching God honestly.

Look over the list of requirements in today's passage. Do you deal with people and situations in a fair and honest way? Do you extend mercy even when it hurts to do so? Thankfully, what God requires is not a catalog of regulations and sacrifices. Instead, he simply issues a call to live in relationship with him. Day by day.

Attempting to appease God with offerings doesn't work. Like the Israelites, we are so often tempted to go through the motions and "pay God off." Giving tithes, attending church regularly and teaching are all good things, but they cannot take the place of identifying so closely with God that we almost automatically do that which is closest to his heart: *Act justly, love mercy and walk humbly with God.* That's what obedience really is. And obedience, which can sound like a dutiful word, or a grudging business exchange, should be a joyful word. It becomes so when we stop calculating the cost of doing what God commands and instead respond with abandon to the One who loves us.

God sees the motives hidden behind our every word and action. He tells us to come humbly, as children. Stop hedging. Stop making excuses. Just listen and follow. Let him show you who he really is. Above all, love him. Simply love him most of all.

Thursday

the ruler demands gifts,
the judge accepts bribes,
  the powerful dictate what they desire—
they all conspire together.
4 The best of them is like a brier,
  the most upright worse than a thorn
    hedge.
The day of your watchmen has come,
  the day God visits you.
Now is the time of their confusion.
5 Do not trust a neighbor;
  put no confidence in a friend.
Even with her who lies in your embrace
  be careful of your words.
6 For a son dishonors his father,
  a daughter rises up against her mother,
a daughter-in-law against her mother-in-
    law—
  a man's enemies are the members of his
    own household.

7 But as for me, I watch in hope for the
    LORD,
  I wait for God my Savior;
  my God will hear me.

Israel Will Rise
8 Do not gloat over me, my enemy!
  Though I have fallen, I will rise.
Though I sit in darkness,
  the LORD will be my
    light.
9 Because I have sinned
    against him,
  I will bear the LORD's
    wrath,
until he pleads my case
  and establishes my right.
He will bring me out into
    the light;
  I will see his
    righteousness.
10 Then my enemy will see it
  and will be covered with shame,
she who said to me,
  "Where is the LORD your God?"
My eyes will see her downfall;
  even now she will be trampled
    underfoot
  like mire in the streets.

11 The day for building your walls will come,
  the day for extending your boundaries.
12 In that day people will come to you
  from Assyria and the cities of Egypt,
even from Egypt to the Euphrates
  and from sea to sea
  and from mountain to mountain.
13 The earth will become desolate because of
    its inhabitants,
  as the result of their deeds.

Prayer and Praise
14 Shepherd your people with your staff,
  the flock of your inheritance,
which lives by itself in a forest,
  in fertile pasturelands.[a]
Let them feed in Bashan and Gilead
  as in days long ago.

15 "As in the days when you came out of
    Egypt,
  I will show them my wonders."

16 Nations will see and be ashamed,
  deprived of all their power.
They will lay their hands on their mouths
  and their ears will become deaf.
17 They will lick dust like a snake,
  like creatures that crawl on the ground.
They will come trembling out of their dens;
  they will turn in fear to
    the LORD our God
  and will be afraid of you.
18 Who is a God like you,
  who pardons sin and
    forgives the
      transgression
  of the remnant of his
    inheritance?
You do not stay angry
    forever
  but delight to show
    mercy.
19 You will again have compassion on us;
  you will tread our sins underfoot
and hurl all our iniquities into the
    depths of the sea.
20 You will be true to Jacob,
  and show mercy to Abraham,
as you pledged on oath to our fathers
  in days long ago.

> **Micah 7:18**
>
> *God Pardons Sins*
>
> Who is a God like you,
> who pardons sin
> and forgives the
> transgression?

a 14 Or *in the middle of Carmel*

Nahum

Author:
Nahum.

Audience:
The residents of
Nineveh and Judah.

Date:
Likely written shortly
before the fall of
Nineveh in 612 B.C.

Setting:
Assyria had just con-
quered the Egyptian city
of Thebes in 663 B.C., and
Judah seemed to be next.
However, Assyria would
fall in 612 B.C.

Verse to Remember:
The LORD has given a
command concerning you,
Nineveh: "You will have no
descendants to bear your
name. I will destroy the
carved images and cast
idols that are in the temple
of your gods. I will prepare
your grave, for you
are vile." (1:14)

The people of Nineveh had had their chance.
A little over one hundred years earlier, the people of
Nineveh had been warned by the reluctant prophet Jonah
about impending judgment. The people repented and
turned from their evil ways. Now, however, those who
had heeded God's call to repentance had failed to pass
on their fear of the Lord to their descendants. And so
the wicked capital city of Assyria had returned to its vile,
violent ways.

God speaks hotly of the residents of Nineveh—they are
his enemies, his foes. They want to destroy God's people,
Judah, *but God will destroy them.* Nineveh was a
"city of blood, full of lies, full of plunder, never without victims" (Nahum 3:1). Now the violence was coming to them
instead, and they would be utterly ruined. *God would
break their pride.* Their destruction would cause the
neighboring nations to rejoice. God will not let evil go
unpunished. He will deal with it in his time.

1

An oracle concerning Nineveh. The book of the vision of Nahum the Elkoshite.

The Lord's Anger Against Nineveh

2 The Lord is a jealous and avenging God;
    the Lord takes vengeance and is filled
      with wrath.
  The Lord takes vengeance on his foes
    and maintains his wrath against his
      enemies.
3 The Lord is slow to anger and great in
      power;
    the Lord will not leave the guilty
      unpunished.
  His way is in the whirlwind and the storm,
    and clouds are the dust of his feet.
4 He rebukes the sea and dries it up;
    he makes all the rivers run dry.
  Bashan and Carmel wither
    and the blossoms of Lebanon fade.
5 The mountains quake before him
    and the hills melt away.
  The earth trembles at his presence,
    the world and all who live in it.
6 Who can withstand his indignation?
    Who can endure his fierce anger?
  His wrath is poured out
      like fire;
    the rocks are shattered
      before him.

7 The Lord is good,
    a refuge in times of
      trouble.
  He cares for those who
    trust in him,
8   but with an
      overwhelming flood
  he will make an end of
    ⌊Nineveh⌋;
  he will pursue his foes
    into darkness.

9 Whatever they plot against the Lord
    he[a] will bring to an end;
    trouble will not come a second time.
10 They will be entangled among thorns
    and drunk from their wine;
    they will be consumed like dry stubble.[b]
11 From you, ⌊O Nineveh,⌋ has one come forth

who plots evil against the Lord
    and counsels wickedness.

12 This is what the Lord says:

"Although they have allies and are
      numerous,
    they will be cut off and pass away.
  Although I have afflicted you, ⌊O Judah,⌋
    I will afflict you no more.
13 Now I will break their yoke from your
      neck
    and tear your shackles away."

14 The Lord has given a command
      concerning you, ⌊Nineveh⌋:
  "You will have no descendants to bear
      your name.
  I will destroy the carved images and cast
      idols
    that are in the temple of your gods.
  I will prepare your grave,
    for you are vile."

15 Look, there on the mountains,
    the feet of one who brings good news,
    who proclaims peace!
  Celebrate your festivals, O Judah,
    and fulfill your vows.
  No more will the wicked
      invade you;
    they will be completely
      destroyed.

Nineveh to Fall

2 An attacker advances
      against you,
    ⌊Nineveh⌋.
  Guard the fortress,
    watch the road,
    brace yourselves,
    marshal all your
      strength!

2 The Lord will restore the splendor of
      Jacob
    like the splendor of Israel,
  though destroyers have laid them waste
    and have ruined their vines.

3 The shields of his soldiers are red;
    the warriors are clad in scarlet.

Nahum 1:7

God Is a Refuge

The Lord is good,
a refuge in times
of trouble.
He cares for those who
trust in him.

---

a9 Or *What do you foes plot against the Lord? / He*   b10 The meaning of the Hebrew for this verse is uncertain.

Bullies

Nahum 1:3

The Lord is slow to anger and great in power; the Lord will not leave the guilty unpunished. His way is in the whirlwind and the storm, and clouds are the dust of his feet.

reflection

1 Do you have experience with being "bullied"? Describe what it feels like.

2 Describe what it is like to finally have someone stick up for you.

3 Who are the "big bullies" in your present circumstances? Ask God to deal with them and be your "refuge in times of trouble."

RELATED READINGS

Psalms 62:11–12;
77:14–20;
Jonah 1:1–3;
Nahum 3:1–3,10

Read: Nahum 1:1–15

EVERY SCHOOLYARD HAS THEM. They're the nemesis of every 43-pound weakling and pig-tailed girl with lunch money. They are the menaces of the playground. It seems they never get caught—and there are very few who can or will stand up to them.

At this time in history, the biggest bullies on Israel's block were the Assyrians. The Ninevites, who lived in the capital city of Assyria, were vicious and arrogant. Hearing their name made the Israelites cringe and whimper. One hundred years earlier, Jonah had tried to run away from them, and for good reason. Their war crimes were legendary.

And dear Nahum, whose name means, "comfort," brings Israel some good news: The big bully is finally going to get his due. And who will avenge them? God himself. Jonah had demonstrated God's compassion toward the bullies and had given them a chance to change. Now, a century after their short-lived revival, Nahum lets them have it.

Nahum draws a terrifying cosmic portrait of the God who can make short work of any bully, no matter how big and pushy. God is slow to anger; he is not impulsive. But when he has waited with infinite patience for the guilty to change, watch out! The most powerful forces of nature—the whirlwind, the storm, the earthquake and the flood—are but a shadow of God's awesome power; they are his tools, as a hammer is the tool of a worker. The real force is the strength behind the hammer. And this worker, Israel's God, has declared of the bullies, "They will be cut off and pass away" (verse 12).

But Nahum's portrait is a study in contrasts and mystery: God is also "good, a refuge in times of trouble. He cares for those who trust in him" (verse 7). God is both stern *and* kind, just *and* loving.

The world is full of bullies. Maybe they've never looked at Nahum's portrait of God. The sight should strike as much terror in their hearts as looking up into the eye of a whirlwind. But as for you, keep Nahum's portrait in mind the next time you face a bully. God sees injustice and, in his time, will avenge the helpless and the innocent. If Jonah's story reminds us that their day may not be today, then Nahum assures us that their day will certainly come.

Go to page 1127 for your next devotional reading.

The metal on the chariots flashes
  on the day they are made ready;
  the spears of pine are brandished.[a]
4 The chariots storm through the
    streets,
  rushing back and forth through the
    squares.
They look like flaming torches;
  they dart about like lightning.

5 He summons his picked troops,
  yet they stumble on their way.
They dash to the city wall;
  the protective shield is put in place.
6 The river gates are thrown open
  and the palace collapses.
7 It is decreed[b] that the city
  be exiled and carried away.
Its slave girls moan like doves
  and beat upon their breasts.
8 Nineveh is like a pool,
  and its water is draining away.
"Stop! Stop!" they cry,
  but no one turns back.
9 Plunder the silver!
  Plunder the gold!
The supply is endless,
  the wealth from all its treasures!
10 She is pillaged, plundered, stripped!
  Hearts melt, knees give way,
  bodies tremble, every face grows pale.

11 Where now is the lions' den,
  the place where they fed their
    young,
where the lion and lioness went,
  and the cubs, with nothing to fear?
12 The lion killed enough for his cubs
  and strangled the prey for his mate,
filling his lairs with the kill
  and his dens with the prey.

13 "I am against you,"
  declares the LORD Almighty.
"I will burn up your chariots in smoke,
  and the sword will devour your young
    lions.
  I will leave you no prey on the earth.
The voices of your messengers
  will no longer be heard."

Woe to Nineveh

3 Woe to the city of blood,
  full of lies,
full of plunder,
  never without victims!
2 The crack of whips,
  the clatter of wheels,
galloping horses
  and jolting chariots!
3 Charging cavalry,
  flashing swords
  and glittering spears!
Many casualties,
  piles of dead,
bodies without number,
  people stumbling over the corpses—
4 all because of the wanton lust of a harlot,
  alluring, the mistress of sorceries,
who enslaved nations by her prostitution
  and peoples by her witchcraft.

5 "I am against you," declares the LORD
    Almighty.
  "I will lift your skirts over your face.
I will show the nations your nakedness
  and the kingdoms your shame.
6 I will pelt you with filth,
  I will treat you with contempt
  and make you a spectacle.
7 All who see you will flee from you and say,
  'Nineveh is in ruins—who will mourn
    for her?'
  Where can I find anyone to comfort
    you?"

8 Are you better than Thebes,[c]
  situated on the Nile,
  with water around her?
The river was her defense,
  the waters her wall.
9 Cush[d] and Egypt were her boundless
    strength;
  Put and Libya were among her allies.
10 Yet she was taken captive
  and went into exile.
Her infants were dashed to pieces
  at the head of every street.
Lots were cast for her nobles,
  and all her great men were put in chains.

a3 Hebrew; Septuagint and Syriac / the horsemen rush to and fro   b7 The meaning of the Hebrew for this word is uncertain.   c8 Hebrew
No Amon   d9 That is, the upper Nile region

1123

11 You too will become drunk;
      you will go into hiding
      and seek refuge from the enemy.

12 All your fortresses are like fig trees
      with their first ripe fruit;
   when they are shaken,
      the figs fall into the mouth of the eater.
13 Look at your troops—
      they are all women!
   The gates of your land
      are wide open to your enemies;
      fire has consumed their bars.

14 Draw water for the siege,
      strengthen your defenses!
   Work the clay,
      tread the mortar,
      repair the brickwork!
15 There the fire will devour you;
      the sword will cut you down
      and, like grasshoppers, consume you.
   Multiply like grasshoppers,
      multiply like locusts!

16 You have increased the number of your
         merchants
      till they are more than the stars of the
         sky,
   but like locusts they strip the land
      and then fly away.
17 Your guards are like locusts,
      your officials like swarms of locusts
      that settle in the walls on a cold day—
   but when the sun appears they fly away,
      and no one knows where.

18 O king of Assyria, your shepherds*a*
         slumber;
      your nobles lie down to rest.
   Your people are scattered on the mountains
      with no one to gather them.
19 Nothing can heal your wound;
      your injury is fatal.
   Everyone who hears the news about you
      claps his hands at your fall,
   for who has not felt
      your endless cruelty?

*a*18 Or *rulers*

Habakkuk

While most prophets delivered a message from God to his people, *the book of Habakkuk is a conversation* between God and the prophet himself. During his lifetime, Habakkuk not only experienced the prosperity and promise of spiritual renewal in Judah, but he also witnessed its decline. The conversation recorded in his book was not delivered directly to Israel but instead was about Israel and its impending destruction by the violent Babylonians.

Habakkuk addresses two main questions to God: How can you let such evil run rampant in the land? How can you use such godless people as the Babylonians to exact judgment? God did not answer all of Habakkuk's questions, but he did assure Habakkuk that *he was in control and would triumph in the end.* In conclusion, Habakkuk made a decision. In so many words, he said, *"God, you are awesome.* I will praise you no matter what. You are my strength."

Author:
Habakkuk.

Audience:
The southern kingdom of Judah and all of God's people.

Date:
About 605 B.C.

Setting:
Babylon was about to destroy Judah.

Verse to Remember:
LORD, I have heard of your fame; I stand in awe of your deeds, O LORD. Renew them in our day, in our time make them known; in wrath remember mercy. (3:2)

1

The oracle that Habakkuk the prophet received.

Habakkuk's Complaint

2 How long, O LORD, must I call for help,
  but you do not listen?
Or cry out to you, "Violence!"
  but you do not save?
3 Why do you make me look at injustice?
  Why do you tolerate wrong?
Destruction and violence are before me;
  there is strife, and conflict abounds.
4 Therefore the law is paralyzed,
  and justice never prevails.
The wicked hem in the righteous,
  so that justice is perverted.

The Lord's Answer

5 "Look at the nations and watch—
  and be utterly amazed.
For I am going to do something in your
    days
  that you would not
    believe,
  even if you were told.
6 I am raising up the
    Babylonians,*a*
  that ruthless and
    impetuous people,
who sweep across the whole
    earth
  to seize dwelling places
    not their own.
7 They are a feared and
    dreaded people;
  they are a law to
    themselves
  and promote their own honor.
8 Their horses are swifter than leopards,
  fiercer than wolves at dusk.
  Their cavalry gallops headlong;
    their horsemen come from afar.
  They fly like a vulture swooping to devour;
9   they all come bent on violence.
  Their hordes*b* advance like a desert wind
    and gather prisoners like sand.
10 They deride kings
    and scoff at rulers.
  They laugh at all fortified cities;
    they build earthen ramps and capture
      them.
11 Then they sweep past like the wind and go
      on—
  guilty men, whose own strength is their
    god."

Habakkuk's Second Complaint

12 O Lord, are you not from everlasting?
  My God, my Holy One, we will not die.
  O Lord, you have appointed them to
    execute judgment;
  O Rock, you have ordained them to
    punish.
13 Your eyes are too pure to look on evil;
  you cannot tolerate wrong.
  Why then do you tolerate the treacherous?

Why are you silent while the wicked
  swallow up those more righteous than
    themselves?
14 You have made men like fish in the sea,
    like sea creatures that
      have no ruler.
15 The wicked foe pulls all
      of them up with
        hooks,
  he catches them in his
    net,
  he gathers them up in his
    dragnet;
  and so he rejoices and is
    glad.
16 Therefore he sacrifices to
    his net
  and burns incense to his
    dragnet,
  for by his net he lives in
    luxury
  and enjoys the choicest food.
17 Is he to keep on emptying his net,
  destroying nations without mercy?

2 I will stand at my watch
   and station myself on the ramparts;
  I will look to see what he will say to me,
    and what answer I am to give to this
      complaint.*c*

The Lord's Answer

2 Then the Lord replied:

"Write down the revelation
  and make it plain on tablets
  so that a herald*d* may run with it.
3 For the revelation awaits an appointed
    time;
  it speaks of the end
    and will not prove false.
  Though it linger, wait for it;
    it*e* will certainly come and will not
      delay.

4 "See, he is puffed up;
  his desires are not upright—
  but the righteous will live by his faith*f*—
5 indeed, wine betrays him;
  he is arrogant and never at rest.

---

*a*6 Or *Chaldeans* *b*9 The meaning of the Hebrew for this word is uncertain. *c*1 Or *and what to answer when I am rebuked* *d*2 Or *so that whoever reads it* *e*3 Or *Though he linger, wait for him; / he* *f*4 Or *faithfulness*

Deep Waters

SAMARITAN WOMAN

SHE WAS NOT USED TO THIS KIND of male attention. Usually, men were interested in her for what they could get from her: good times and a few laughs—and sex. And then they were gone.

This man was different, she realized.

It was the first time in her life that she ever felt appreciated —not for what she could do but for who she was. This Jewish stranger told her things about her past she'd never told any other person, not even her closest friend. His familiarity startled, but did not frighten, her. It drew her in like the warmth from a fire on a bitterly cold day. He—dare she say it—loved her. He did.

And she knew it from the moment she saw him sitting there by the well.

But he was a Jew and she was a Samaritan. Jews and Samaritans did not associate with each other. When this man asked her for something to drink, he was violating the laws of his people, going against the customs of the time. A Jew would become ceremonially unclean after touching a Samaritan's jar of water. She marveled at his boldness. They weren't supposed to be talking. They weren't supposed to have anything to do with each other. But yet there he sat, talking to her like she was a person. Like she mattered. Like she was someone worth loving. She was amazed at his love.

What she didn't know was that as he drew from the deep and mysterious waters of her own soul, he had also unearthed a reciprocal love for him. She discovered that, in the few moments they shared, he had produced a pool of pure love within her. A love that she'd always longed to give to someone but thought no one would want. Her lovers certainly hadn't wanted it. But here, on a random day in Sychar, she'd finally found someone who did. Rather, that someone had found her.

—Prayer—
Wonderful Savior, thank you for your great love for me. Let your love inspire me to show love to others.

"Sir," the woman said, "you have nothing to draw with and the well is deep. Where can you get this living water?"

John 4:11

ASSIGNED READING:

John 4:1–42

 (decorative script) Weekend

Go to page 1133 for your next devotional reading.

Because he is as greedy as the grave *a*
    and like death is never satisfied,
he gathers to himself all the nations
    and takes captive all the peoples.

⁶"Will not all of them taunt him with ridicule and scorn, saying,

  " 'Woe to him who piles up stolen goods
    and makes himself wealthy by extortion!
    How long must this go on?'
⁷Will not your debtors *b* suddenly arise?
    Will they not wake up and make you
      tremble?
    Then you will become their victim.
⁸Because you have plundered many nations,
    the peoples who are left will plunder
      you.
For you have shed man's blood;
    you have destroyed lands and cities and
      everyone in them.

⁹"Woe to him who builds his realm by
    unjust gain
  to set his nest on high,
  to escape the clutches of ruin!
¹⁰You have plotted the ruin of many peoples,
    shaming your own house
      and forfeiting your
      life.
¹¹The stones of the wall will
    cry out,
  and the beams of the
    woodwork will
    echo it.

¹²"Woe to him who builds a
    city with bloodshed
  and establishes a town by
    crime!
¹³Has not the LORD Almighty
    determined
that the people's labor is only fuel for
    the fire,
that the nations exhaust themselves for
    nothing?
¹⁴For the earth will be filled with the
    knowledge of the glory of the
    LORD,
    as the waters cover the sea.

¹⁵"Woe to him who gives drink to his
    neighbors,
  pouring it from the wineskin till they
    are drunk,
  so that he can gaze on their naked
    bodies.
¹⁶You will be filled with shame instead of
    glory.
  Now it is your turn! Drink and be
    exposed *c*!
The cup from the LORD's right hand is
    coming around to you,
  and disgrace will cover your glory.
¹⁷The violence you have done to Lebanon
    will overwhelm you,
  and your destruction of animals will
    terrify you.
For you have shed man's blood;
    you have destroyed lands and cities and
      everyone in them.

¹⁸"Of what value is an idol, since a man has
    carved it?
  Or an image that teaches lies?
For he who makes it trusts in his own
    creation;
    he makes idols that
      cannot speak.
¹⁹Woe to him who says to
    wood, 'Come to
    life!'
  Or to lifeless stone,
    'Wake up!'
Can it give guidance?
  It is covered with gold
    and silver;
  there is no breath in it.
²⁰But the LORD is in his holy
    temple;
  let all the earth be silent
    before him."

Habakkuk 2:20

God Deserves Respect

"But the LORD is in his holy temple; let all the earth be silent before him."

Habakkuk's Prayer

3 A prayer of Habakkuk the prophet. On *shigionoth.* *d*

²LORD, I have heard of your fame;
  I stand in awe of your deeds,
    O LORD.
Renew them in our day,

in our time make them known;
in wrath remember mercy.

³ God came from Teman,
the Holy One from Mount Paran.
*Selah*ᵃ

His glory covered the heavens
and his praise filled the earth.
⁴ His splendor was like the sunrise;
rays flashed from his hand,
where his power was hidden.
⁵ Plague went before him;
pestilence followed his steps.
⁶ He stood, and shook the earth;
he looked, and made the nations
tremble.

The ancient mountains crumbled
and the age-old hills collapsed.
His ways are eternal.
⁷ I saw the tents of Cushan in distress,
the dwellings of Midian in anguish.

⁸ Were you angry with the rivers, O LORD?
Was your wrath against the streams?
Did you rage against the sea
when you rode with your horses
and your victorious chariots?
⁹ You uncovered your bow,
you called for many arrows.   *Selah*
You split the earth with rivers;
¹⁰   the mountains saw you and writhed.
Torrents of water swept by;
the deep roared
and lifted its waves on high.

¹¹ Sun and moon stood still in the heavens
at the glint of your flying arrows,
at the lightning of your flashing spear.

¹² In wrath you strode through the earth
and in anger you threshed the nations.
¹³ You came out to deliver your people,
to save your anointed one.
You crushed the leader of the land of
wickedness,
you stripped him from head to foot.
Selah
¹⁴ With his own spear you pierced his head
when his warriors stormed out to scatter
us,
gloating as though about to devour
the wretched who were in hiding.
¹⁵ You trampled the sea with your horses,
churning the great waters.

¹⁶ I heard and my heart pounded,
my lips quivered at the sound;
decay crept into my bones,
and my legs trembled.
Yet I will wait patiently for the day of
calamity
to come on the nation invading us.
¹⁷ Though the fig tree does not bud
and there are no grapes on the vines,
though the olive crop fails
and the fields produce no food,
though there are no sheep in the pen
and no cattle in the stalls,
¹⁸ yet I will rejoice in the LORD,
I will be joyful in God my Savior.

¹⁹ The Sovereign LORD is my strength;
he makes my feet like the feet of a deer,
he enables me to go on the heights.

For the director of music. On my stringed
instruments.

ᵃ3 A word of uncertain meaning; possibly a musical term; also in verses 9 and 13

Zephaniah

Author:
Zephaniah.

Audience:
Judah and all nations.

Date:
Likely during the early years of the reign of King Josiah (640–609 B.C.).

Setting:
Zephaniah's prophecy encouraged King Josiah to bring spiritual reform to Judah.

Verse to Remember:
"The LORD your God is with you, he is mighty to save. He will take great delight in you, he will quiet you with his love, he will rejoice over you with singing."
(3:17)

When sin goes unchecked for any length of time, it's easy to grow complacent, to think that God will never do anything about it, that nothing will ever change. *Our tolerance for sin increases over time,* and what once seemed abhorrent becomes acceptable, or at least not worth bothering with.

Zephaniah preached his message during a time when sin and idolatry had become the comfortable norm in Judah. His message was both broad and dire: *Destruction is coming.* God will punish the nations, and Judah and Jerusalem will not be exempt. God will deal with sin. And it will be devastating.

But, Zephaniah said, the devastation will not last forever. One day the shame and disgrace will be lifted. And a quiet season of healing and restoration will begin.

It's easy to skip to the end of the book and read the words of comfort. It's much harder to trudge through the words of judgment. But the order is there for a reason. *First sin must be dealt with.* Then, and only then, is restoration possible.

---

1 The word of the LORD that came to Zephaniah son of Cushi, the son of Gedaliah, the son of Amariah, the son of Hezekiah, during the reign of Josiah son of Amon king of Judah:

Warning of Coming Destruction

2 "I will sweep away everything
from the face of the earth,"
declares the LORD.
3 "I will sweep away both men and animals;

I will sweep away the birds of the air
and the fish of the sea.
The wicked will have only heaps of rubble[a]
when I cut off man from the face of the
earth,"
declares the LORD.

Against Judah

[4] "I will stretch out my hand against Judah
and against all who live in Jerusalem.
I will cut off from this place every remnant
of Baal,
the names of the pagan and the
idolatrous priests—
[5] those who bow down on the roofs
to worship the starry host,
those who bow down and swear by the
LORD
and who also swear by Molech,[b]
[6] those who turn back from following the
LORD
and neither seek the LORD nor inquire
of him.

[7] Be silent before the Sovereign LORD,
for the day of the LORD is near.
The LORD has prepared a sacrifice;
he has consecrated those he has invited.

[8] On the day of the LORD's sacrifice
I will punish the princes
and the king's sons
and all those clad
in foreign clothes.
[9] On that day I will punish
all who avoid stepping on the threshold,[c]
who fill the temple of their gods
with violence and deceit.

[10] "On that day," declares the LORD,
"a cry will go up from the Fish Gate,
wailing from the New Quarter,
and a loud crash from the hills.
[11] Wail, you who live in the market district[d];
all your merchants will be wiped out,
all who trade with[e] silver will be ruined.

[12] At that time I will search Jerusalem with
lamps
and punish those who are complacent,
who are like wine left on its dregs,
who think, 'The LORD will do nothing,

either good or bad.'
[13] Their wealth will be plundered,
their houses demolished.
They will build houses
but not live in them;
they will plant vineyards
but not drink the wine.

The Great Day of the LORD

[14] "The great day of the LORD is near—
near and coming quickly.
Listen! The cry on the day of the LORD will
be bitter,
the shouting of the warrior there.
[15] That day will be a day of wrath,
a day of distress and anguish,
a day of trouble and ruin,
a day of darkness and gloom,
a day of clouds and blackness,
[16] a day of trumpet and battle cry
against the fortified cities
and against the corner towers.

[17] I will bring distress on the people
and they will walk like blind men,
because they have sinned against the
LORD.
Their blood will be poured out like dust
and their entrails like filth.
[18] Neither their silver nor their gold
will be able to save them
on the day of the LORD's wrath.
In the fire of his jealousy
the whole world will be consumed,
for he will make a sudden end
of all who live in the earth."

2 Gather together, gather together,
O shameful nation,
[2] before the appointed time arrives
and that day sweeps on like chaff,
before the fierce anger of the LORD comes
upon you,
before the day of the LORD's wrath
comes upon you.
[3] Seek the LORD, all you humble of the land,
you who do what he commands.
Seek righteousness, seek humility;
perhaps you will be sheltered
on the day of the LORD's anger.

---

*a*3 The meaning of the Hebrew for this line is uncertain.   *b*5 Hebrew *Malcam*, that is, Milcom   *c*9 See 1 Samuel 5:5.   *d*11 Or *the Mortar*
*e*11 Or *in*

Against Philistia

⁴Gaza will be abandoned
    and Ashkelon left in ruins.
At midday Ashdod will be emptied
    and Ekron uprooted.
⁵Woe to you who live by the sea,
    O Kerethite people;
the word of the LORD is against you,
    O Canaan, land of the Philistines.

"I will destroy you,
    and none will be left."

⁶The land by the sea, where the Kerethites*a*
    dwell,
will be a place for shepherds and sheep
    pens.
⁷It will belong to the remnant of the house
    of Judah;
    there they will find pasture.
In the evening they will lie down
    in the houses of Ashkelon.
The LORD their God will care for them;
    he will restore their fortunes.*b*

Against Moab and Ammon

⁸"I have heard the insults of Moab
    and the taunts of the Ammonites,
who insulted my people
    and made threats against their land.
⁹Therefore, as surely as I live,"
    declares the LORD Almighty, the God
        of Israel,
"surely Moab will become like Sodom,
    the Ammonites like Gomorrah—
a place of weeds and salt pits,
    a wasteland forever.
The remnant of my people will plunder
    them;
    the survivors of my nation will inherit
        their land."

¹⁰This is what they will get in return for their
    pride,
    for insulting and mocking the people of
        the LORD Almighty.
¹¹The LORD will be awesome to them
    when he destroys all the gods of the land.
The nations on every shore will worship
    him,
    every one in its own land.

Against Cush

¹²"You too, O Cushites,*c*
    will be slain by my sword."

Against Assyria

¹³He will stretch out his hand against the
    north
    and destroy Assyria,
leaving Nineveh utterly desolate
    and dry as the desert.
¹⁴Flocks and herds will lie down there,
    creatures of every kind.
The desert owl and the screech owl
    will roost on her columns.
Their calls will echo through the windows,
    rubble will be in the doorways,
    the beams of cedar will be exposed.
¹⁵This is the carefree city
    that lived in safety.
She said to herself,
    "I am, and there is none besides me."
What a ruin she has become,
    a lair for wild beasts!
All who pass by her scoff
    and shake their fists.

The Future of Jerusalem

3 Woe to the city of oppressors,
    rebellious and defiled!
²She obeys no one,
    she accepts no correction.
She does not trust in the LORD,
    she does not draw near to her God.
³Her officials are roaring lions,
    her rulers are evening wolves,
    who leave nothing for the morning.
⁴Her prophets are arrogant;
    they are treacherous men.
Her priests profane the sanctuary
    and do violence to the law.
⁵The LORD within her is righteous;
    he does no wrong.
Morning by morning he dispenses his
    justice,
    and every new day he does not fail,
    yet the unrighteous know no shame.

⁶"I have cut off nations;
    their strongholds are demolished.
I have left their streets deserted,

---

*a*6 The meaning of the Hebrew for this word is uncertain.   *b*7 Or *will bring back their captives*   *c*12 That is, people from the upper Nile region

Going Home

Read: Zephaniah 3:14–20

THE TWENTIETH CENTURY was the bloodiest century in history. Amid millions of lives lost to warfare and violent conflict, international homelessness reached its zenith. Ethnic and religious groups on the fringes of society, hated and destroyed by neighbors, did not merely live without four walls and a roof—they literally had no home. *Home* embodies a state of well-being to which many will never return.

Some of the displaced peoples even bear the marks of their nomadic past in their names. With a name that can be translated "wanderer," the *Csángó* trace their ancestry back to the nomadic Asians of the Carpathian Mountains. Straddling the modern Romanian-Moldavian border, the Csángó people have never known what it feels like to be "home."

Many of us can relate to the wandering of the Csángó people. While we may have the physical comforts of a house, we still experience an indefinable, heartsick longing for home. Even women who appear to lead the ideal life—a seemingly perfect family, a good job, honor and respect within the community—can suffer silently from feelings of alienation. It's possible to feel displaced instead of secure in the arms of those we love. At the end of the day, lying in bed, one can be safely home and still feel profoundly *lost*.

In truth, we are all outsiders and wanderers according to God. Imagine what it would mean for a Csángó woman, always the alien, to hear God's promise through Zephaniah: "*I will bring you home.*" Now imagine the hopeful imagery of the joyous homecoming awaiting all of us. We may never experience what it's like to find our home in an earthly sense. But then again, maybe that's just as God intended. That homesick feeling reminds us that we're not yet really home.

Whenever your heart swells with longings for security and rest, remember God's promise to one day bring you safely home to his house, where he has prepared a room for you (see John 14:1–4).

Zephaniah 3:19–20

"At that time I will deal with all who oppressed you; I will rescue the lame and gather those who have been scattered. I will give them praise and honor in every land where they were put to shame. At that time I will gather you; at that time I will bring you home. I will give you honor and praise among all the peoples of the earth when I restore your fortunes before your very eyes," says the LORD.

reflection

1 Zephaniah describes *home* in terms of gathering the scattered. In what areas of your life do you feel scattered instead of grounded?

2 Why do you think women are vulnerable to feeling emotionally homeless?

3 How does the future promise of home affect your life today?

RELATED READINGS

Psalm 61:1–5;
Micah 4:6–8;
Hebrews 11:8–9;
Revelation 7:9–17

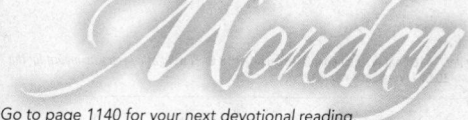

Go to page 1140 for your next devotional reading.

with no one passing through.
Their cities are destroyed;
    no one will be left—no one at all.
7 I said to the city,
    'Surely you will fear me
      and accept correction!'
Then her dwelling would not be cut off,
    nor all my punishments come upon her.
But they were still eager
    to act corruptly in all they did.
8 Therefore wait for me," declares the LORD,
    "for the day I will stand up to testify.[a]
I have decided to assemble the nations,
    to gather the kingdoms
and to pour out my wrath
    on them—
    all my fierce anger.
The whole world will be
    consumed
    by the fire of my jealous
    anger.

9 "Then will I purify the lips
    of the peoples,
that all of them may call
    on the name of the
    LORD
and serve him shoulder
    to shoulder.
10 From beyond the rivers of
    Cush[b]
my worshipers, my
    scattered people,
    will bring me offerings.
11 On that day you will not be put to shame
    for all the wrongs you have done to me,
because I will remove from this city
    those who rejoice in their pride.
Never again will you be haughty
    on my holy hill.
12 But I will leave within you
    the meek and humble,
    who trust in the name of the LORD.
13 The remnant of Israel will do no wrong;
    they will speak no lies,
    nor will deceit be found in their mouths.

They will eat and lie down
    and no one will make them afraid."

14 Sing, O Daughter of Zion;
    shout aloud, O Israel!
Be glad and rejoice with all your heart,
    O Daughter of Jerusalem!
15 The LORD has taken away your
    punishment,
    he has turned back your enemy.
The LORD, the King of Israel, is with you;
    never again will you fear any harm.
16 On that day they will say to Jerusalem,
    "Do not fear, O Zion;
    do not let your hands
    hang limp.
17 The LORD your God is with
    you,
    he is mighty to save.
He will take great delight
    in you,
    he will quiet you with his
    love,
    he will rejoice over you
    with singing."

18 "The sorrows for the
    appointed feasts
    I will remove from you;
    they are a burden and a
    reproach to you.[c]
19 At that time I will deal
    with all who oppressed
    you;
I will rescue the lame
    and gather those who have been
    scattered.
I will give them praise and honor
    in every land where they were put to
    shame.
20 At that time I will gather you;
    at that time I will bring you home.
I will give you honor and praise
    among all the peoples of the earth
when I restore your fortunes[d]
    before your very eyes,"
                says the LORD.

Zephaniah 3:17

God Rejoices Over Us

"The LORD your
God is with you,
he is mighty to save.
He will take great
delight in you,
he will quiet you
with his love,
he will rejoice over
you with singing."

---

[a]8 Septuagint and Syriac; Hebrew *will rise up to plunder*   [b]10 That is, the upper Nile region   [c]18 Or *"I will gather you who mourn for the appointed feasts; / your reproach is a burden to you*   [d]20 Or *I bring back your captives*

Haggai

Haggai, the second shortest book in the Old Testament, has one central theme: *What are you waiting for? Build God's house!* Throughout the Old Testament, having a place to worship God was of paramount importance. The Israelites built the tabernacle in the wilderness. Then Solomon built the magnificent temple in Jerusalem, which was destroyed by King Nebuchadnezzar when he conquered the land. In the book of Haggai, the exiled Israelites have returned to Jerusalem. *They start out with good intentions* to rebuild the temple, but their enthusiasm wanes as they face opposition and become distracted with building their own homes. Haggai speaks out, telling the Israelites to put aside their own personal agendas and finish the task set before them. *Make worshiping God a top priority,* he reminds them.

Author:
Haggai.

Audience:
The exiles who returned to Jerusalem.

Date:
520 B.C.

Setting:
The Persian king Cyrus allowed the Jews to return to Jerusalem to rebuild the temple. However, misplaced priorities and local opposition brought work to a halt.

Verse to Remember:
"You expected much, but see, it turned out to be little. What you brought home, I blew away. Why?" declares the LORD Almighty. "Because of my house, which remains a ruin, while each of you is busy with his own house." (1:9)

A Call to Build the House of the LORD

1 In the second year of King Darius, on the first day of the sixth month, the word of the LORD came through the prophet Haggai to Zerubbabel son of Shealtiel, governor of Judah, and to Joshua[a] son of Jehozadak, the high priest:

² This is what the LORD Almighty says: "These people say, 'The time has not yet come for the LORD's house to be built.'"

[a] 1 A variant of *Jeshua*; here and elsewhere in Haggai

³Then the word of the LORD came through the prophet Haggai: ⁴"Is it a time for you yourselves to be living in your paneled houses, while this house remains a ruin?"

⁵Now this is what the LORD Almighty says: "Give careful thought to your ways. ⁶You have planted much, but have harvested little. You eat, but never have enough. You drink, but never have your fill. You put on clothes, but are not warm. You earn wages, only to put them in a purse with holes in it."

⁷This is what the LORD Almighty says: "Give careful thought to your ways. ⁸Go up into the mountains and bring down timber and build the house, so that I may take pleasure in it and be honored," says the LORD. ⁹"You expected much, but see, it turned out to be little. What you brought home, I blew away. Why?" declares the LORD Almighty. "Because of my house, which remains a ruin, while each of you is busy with his own house. ¹⁰Therefore, because of you the heavens have withheld their dew and the earth its crops. ¹¹I called for a drought on the fields and the mountains, on the grain, the new wine, the oil and whatever the ground produces, on men and cattle, and on the labor of your hands."

¹²Then Zerubbabel son of Shealtiel, Joshua son of Jehozadak, the high priest, and the whole remnant of the people obeyed the voice of the LORD their God and the message of the prophet Haggai, because the LORD their God had sent him. And the people feared the LORD.

¹³Then Haggai, the LORD's messenger, gave this message of the LORD to the people: "I am with you," declares the LORD. ¹⁴So the LORD stirred up the spirit of Zerubbabel son of Shealtiel, governor of Judah, and the spirit of Joshua son of Jehozadak, the high priest, and the spirit of the whole remnant of the people. They came and began to work on the house of the LORD Almighty, their God, ¹⁵on the twenty-fourth day of the sixth month in the second year of King Darius.

The Promised Glory of the New House

2 On the twenty-first day of the seventh month, the word of the LORD came through the prophet Haggai: ²"Speak to Zerubbabel son of Shealtiel, governor of Judah, to Joshua son of Jehozadak, the high priest, and to the remnant of the people. Ask them, ³'Who of you is left who saw this house in its former glory? How does it look to you now? Does it not seem to you like nothing? ⁴But now be strong, O Zerubbabel,' declares the LORD. 'Be strong, O Joshua son of Jehozadak, the high priest. Be strong, all you people of the land,' declares the LORD, 'and work. For I am with you,' declares the LORD Almighty. ⁵'This is what I covenanted with you when you came out of Egypt. And my Spirit remains among you. Do not fear.'

⁶"This is what the LORD Almighty says: 'In a little while I will once more shake the heavens and the earth, the sea and the dry land. ⁷I will shake all nations, and the desired of all nations will come, and I will fill this house with glory,' says the LORD Almighty. ⁸'The silver is mine and the gold is mine,' declares the LORD Almighty. ⁹'The glory of this present house will be greater than the glory of the former house,' says the LORD Almighty. 'And in this place I will grant peace,' declares the LORD Almighty."

Blessings for a Defiled People

¹⁰On the twenty-fourth day of the ninth month, in the second year of Darius, the word of the LORD came to the prophet Haggai: ¹¹"This is what the LORD Almighty says: 'Ask the priests what the law says: ¹²If a person carries consecrated meat in the fold of his garment, and that fold touches some bread or stew, some wine, oil or other food, does it become consecrated?'"

The priests answered, "No."

¹³Then Haggai said, "If a person defiled by contact with a dead body touches one of these things, does it become defiled?"

"Yes," the priests replied, "it becomes defiled."

Haggai 1:13

God Is With Us

Then Haggai, the LORD's messenger, gave this message of the LORD to the people: "I am with you," declares the LORD.

[14]Then Haggai said, " 'So it is with this people and this nation in my sight,' declares the LORD. 'Whatever they do and whatever they offer there is defiled.

[15]" 'Now give careful thought to this from this day on[a]—consider how things were before one stone was laid on another in the LORD's temple. [16]When anyone came to a heap of twenty measures, there were only ten. When anyone went to a wine vat to draw fifty measures, there were only twenty. [17]I struck all the work of your hands with blight, mildew and hail, yet you did not turn to me,' declares the LORD. [18]'From this day on, from this twenty-fourth day of the ninth month, give careful thought to the day when the foundation of the LORD's temple was laid. Give careful thought: [19]Is there yet any seed left in the barn? Until now, the vine and the fig tree, the pomegranate and the olive tree have not borne fruit.

" 'From this day on I will bless you.' "

Zerubbabel the LORD's Signet Ring

[20]The word of the LORD came to Haggai a second time on the twenty-fourth day of the month: [21]"Tell Zerubbabel governor of Judah that I will shake the heavens and the earth. [22]I will overturn royal thrones and shatter the power of the foreign kingdoms. I will overthrow chariots and their drivers; horses and their riders will fall, each by the sword of his brother.

[23]" 'On that day,' declares the LORD Almighty, 'I will take you, my servant Zerubbabel son of Shealtiel,' declares the LORD, 'and I will make you like my signet ring, for I have chosen you,' declares the LORD Almighty."

_a_15 Or _to the days past_

Zechariah

Author:
Zechariah.

Audience:
The exiles who returned
to Jerusalem.

Date:
Between about
520 and 480 B.C.

Setting:
Zechariah, like Haggai,
encouraged the exiles
who had returned to
Jerusalem from Babylon to
complete the rebuilding
of the temple.

Verse to Remember:
Therefore tell the people:
This is what the LORD
Almighty says: "Return to
me," declares the LORD
Almighty, "and I will return
to you," says the LORD
Almighty. (1:3)

God's anger against his people will not last forever. At the end of the 70 years of Judah's captivity, *God sent messages of mercy to his people.* It was time to return and rebuild. The temple would be built again, and God would once again dwell among his people and make them prosper. In addition, God himself would judge their enemies. A series of *visions in Zechariah tell of cleansing and renewal*—of restored hope. The vision of the priest with filthy garments, reclothed by God in glistening, pure clothes, is a fitting image of the restoration of the people. And Zechariah's prophecies about the Messiah offered hope and inspiration to the people.

A Call to Return to the LORD

1 In the eighth month of the second year of Darius, the word of the LORD came to the prophet Zechariah son of Berekiah, the son of Iddo:

2 "The LORD was very angry with your forefathers. 3 Therefore tell the people: This is what the LORD Almighty says: 'Return to me,' declares the LORD Almighty, 'and I will return to you,' says the LORD Almighty. 4 Do not be like your forefathers, to whom the earlier prophets proclaimed: This is what the LORD Almighty says: 'Turn from your evil ways and your evil practices.' But they would not listen or pay attention to me, declares the LORD. 5 Where are your forefathers now? And the prophets, do

they live forever? **6**But did not my words and my decrees, which I commanded my servants the prophets, overtake your forefathers?

"Then they repented and said, 'The Lord Almighty has done to us what our ways and practices deserve, just as he determined to do.' "

The Man Among the Myrtle Trees

7On the twenty-fourth day of the eleventh month, the month of Shebat, in the second year of Darius, the word of the Lord came to the prophet Zechariah son of Berekiah, the son of Iddo.

8During the night I had a vision—and there before me was a man riding a red horse! He was standing among the myrtle trees in a ravine. Behind him were red, brown and white horses.

9I asked, "What are these, my lord?"

The angel who was talking with me answered, "I will show you what they are."

10Then the man standing among the myrtle trees explained, "They are the ones the Lord has sent to go throughout the earth."

11And they reported to the angel of the Lord, who was standing among the myrtle trees, "We have gone throughout the earth and found the whole world at rest and in peace."

12Then the angel of the Lord said, "Lord Almighty, how long will you withhold mercy from Jerusalem and from the towns of Judah, which you have been angry with these seventy years?" **13**So the Lord spoke kind and comforting words to the angel who talked with me.

14Then the angel who was speaking to me said, "Proclaim this word: This is what the Lord Almighty says: 'I am very jealous for Jerusalem and Zion, **15**but I am very angry with the nations that feel secure. I was only a little angry, but they added to the calamity.'

16"Therefore, this is what the Lord says: 'I will return to Jerusalem with mercy, and there my house will be rebuilt. And the measuring line will be stretched out over Jerusalem,' declares the Lord Almighty.

17"Proclaim further: This is what the Lord Almighty says: 'My towns will again overflow with prosperity, and the Lord will again comfort Zion and choose Jerusalem.' "

Four Horns and Four Craftsmen

18Then I looked up—and there before me were four horns! **19**I asked the angel who was speaking to me, "What are these?"

He answered me, "These are the horns that scattered Judah, Israel and Jerusalem."

20Then the Lord showed me four craftsmen. **21**I asked, "What are these coming to do?"

He answered, "These are the horns that scattered Judah so that no one could raise his head, but the craftsmen have come to terrify them and throw down these horns of the nations who lifted up their horns against the land of Judah to scatter its people."

A Man With a Measuring Line

2 Then I looked up—and there before me was a man with a measuring line in his hand! **2**I asked, "Where are you going?"

He answered me, "To measure Jerusalem, to find out how wide and how long it is."

3Then the angel who was speaking to me left, and another angel came to meet him **4**and said to him: "Run, tell that young man, 'Jerusalem will be a city without walls because of the great number of men and livestock in it. **5**And I myself will be a wall of fire around it,' declares the Lord, 'and I will be its glory within.'

6"Come! Come! Flee from the land of the north," declares the Lord, "for I have scattered you to the four winds of heaven," declares the Lord.

7"Come, O Zion! Escape, you who live in the Daughter of Babylon!" **8**For this is what the Lord Almighty says: "After he has honored me and has sent me against the nations that have plundered you—for whoever touches you touches the apple of his eye— **9**I will surely

---

Zechariah 1:3

God Calls Wayward People

"Therefore tell the people: This is what the Lord Almighty says: 'Return to me,' declares the Lord Almighty, 'and I will return to you,' says the Lord Almighty."

"Do not be like your
forefathers, to whom
the earlier prophets
proclaimed: This is what
the LORD Almighty says:
'Turn from your evil ways
and your evil practices.'
But they would not listen
or pay attention to me,
declares the LORD . . . But
did not my words and
my decrees, which I
commanded my servants
the prophets, overtake
your forefathers?"

reflection

1 Describe a time when
you felt desperate for
God's mercy. How did God
rescue you from the barren
place?

2 When did you know
that you belonged to
God? How does knowing
that your name is written
on his hand and in his book
of life comfort you?

3 In today's passage, the
Lord spoke of those
who would not listen to
him. Do you know people
like that? Spend time praying that they will begin to
hear God's voice and turn
or return to his Son.

RELATED READINGS

Isaiah 55:6–13;
Malachi 3:6–7;
1 Peter 2:22–24

Blessed Are the Desperate

Read: Zechariah 1:1–21

I'M A COLORFUL SINNER, and I've fallen woefully short of God's
glory. I'm desperate for divine help. We all are.

C.S. Lewis paints a vivid description of how we humans seem to
desecrate every good thing God does for us. In his book *Letters to
Malcolm*, Lewis writes, "We poison the wine as He decants it into
us; murder a melody He would play with us as the instrument. We
caricature the self-portrait He would paint. Hence all sin, whatever
else it is, is a sacrilege . . ."

Maybe you expect rejection from a perfect God because of
your less-than-perfect past. Or maybe you're spiritually crippled by
a sin that seems unforgivable. But the good news of the gospel is
that our heavenly Father loves us with an everlasting love . . .

We need to acknowledge the fact that we're crippled—that
there is nothing righteous in us, that we are desperate for His
mercy. And when the Spirit prompts us to recognize our need for
salvation, God provides a Savior through the sacrifice of His only
son, Jesus, who rescues us from barren places and gives us a seat
next to Him at the Lord's banquet table.

Because of God's mercy, our stained hearts have been
bleached by the blood of the Lamb. The God who spoke the universe into existence, who breathed life into Adam, who stretched
out the heavens and the necks of giraffes, has looked down, taken
our hand in His, and said, "Yep, she's Mine." Even though we're
crippled, we have been royally adopted by the King of Kings and
Lord of Lords. We are listed as His next of Kin. Our names are written on His hands and in His book of life. His love for us is based on
His character, not our performance. And it is greater than we could
ever hope for or imagine.

> He himself bore our sins in his body on the tree, so that we
> might die to sins and live for righteousness; by his wounds
> you have been healed. (1 Peter 2:24)

Blessed are the desperate.

—Lisa Harper

Go to page 1142 for your next devotional reading.

raise my hand against them so that their slaves will plunder them.[a] Then you will know that the LORD Almighty has sent me.

¹⁰"Shout and be glad, O Daughter of Zion. For I am coming, and I will live among you," declares the LORD. ¹¹"Many nations will be joined with the LORD in that day and will become my people. I will live among you and you will know that the LORD Almighty has sent me to you. ¹²The LORD will inherit Judah as his portion in the holy land and will again choose Jerusalem. ¹³Be still before the LORD, all mankind, because he has roused himself from his holy dwelling."

Clean Garments for the High Priest

3 Then he showed me Joshua[b] the high priest standing before the angel of the LORD, and Satan[c] standing at his right side to accuse him. ²The LORD said to Satan, "The LORD rebuke you, Satan! The LORD, who has chosen Jerusalem, rebuke you! Is not this man a burning stick snatched from the fire?"

³Now Joshua was dressed in filthy clothes as he stood before the angel. ⁴The angel said to those who were standing before him, "Take off his filthy clothes."

Then he said to Joshua, "See, I have taken away your sin, and I will put rich garments on you."

⁵Then I said, "Put a clean turban on his head." So they put a clean turban on his head and clothed him, while the angel of the LORD stood by.

⁶The angel of the LORD gave this charge to Joshua: ⁷"This is what the LORD Almighty says: 'If you will walk in my ways and keep my requirements, then you will govern my house and have charge of my courts, and I will give you a place among these standing here.

⁸"'Listen, O high priest Joshua and your associates seated before you, who are men symbolic of things to come: I am going to bring my servant, the Branch. ⁹See, the stone I have set in front of Joshua! There are seven eyes[d] on that one stone, and I will engrave an inscription on it,' says the LORD Almighty, 'and I will remove the sin of this land in a single day.

¹⁰"'In that day each of you will invite his neighbor to sit under his vine and fig tree,' declares the LORD Almighty."

The Gold Lampstand and the Two Olive Trees

4 Then the angel who talked with me returned and wakened me, as a man is wakened from his sleep. ²He asked me, "What do you see?"

I answered, "I see a solid gold lampstand with a bowl at the top and seven lights on it, with seven channels to the lights. ³Also there are two olive trees by it, one on the right of the bowl and the other on its left."

⁴I asked the angel who talked with me, "What are these, my lord?"

⁵He answered, "Do you not know what these are?"

"No, my lord," I replied.

⁶So he said to me, "This is the word of the LORD to Zerubbabel: 'Not by might nor by power, but by my Spirit,' says the LORD Almighty.

⁷"What[e] are you, O mighty mountain? Before Zerubbabel you will become level ground. Then he will bring out the capstone to shouts of 'God bless it! God bless it!'"

⁸Then the word of the LORD came to me: ⁹"The hands of Zerubbabel have laid the foundation of this temple; his hands will also complete it. Then you will know that the LORD Almighty has sent me to you.

¹⁰"Who despises the day of small things? Men will rejoice when they see the plumb line in the hand of Zerubbabel.

"(These seven are the eyes of the LORD, which range throughout the earth.)"

¹¹Then I asked the angel, "What are these two olive trees on the right and the left of the lampstand?"

Zechariah 4:6

God Is Spirit

So he said to me, "This is the word of the LORD to Zerubbabel: 'Not by might nor by power, but by my Spirit,' says the LORD Almighty."

---

[a] 8,9 Or *says after . . . eye:* ⁹ *"I . . . plunder them."*   [b] 1 A variant of *Jeshua*; here and elsewhere in Zechariah   [c] 1 *Satan* means *accuser.*
[d] 9 Or *facets*   [e] 7 Or *Who*

The Garments of Forgiveness

Zechariah 3:3–4

Now Joshua was dressed in filthy clothes as he stood before the angel. The angel said to those who were standing before him, "Take off his filthy clothes." Then he said to Joshua, "See, I have taken away your sin, and I will put rich garments on you."

reflection

1 What often holds women back from fully accepting God's forgiveness?

2 Why do we grow comfortable in the grungy clothes of sinful habits and patterns?

3 How would you look wearing God's beautiful garments of forgiveness?

RELATED READINGS

Psalms 51:2–7; 130:3–4;
Isaiah 1:18;
Jeremiah 33:6–8;
Revelation 7:9–14

Read: Zechariah 3:1–10

THERE'S NOTHING LIKE RETAIL THERAPY. Although not for everyone, a day spent perusing the latest fashions can do wonders for a litany of woes—at least temporarily. However much we like shopping for the new, in many ways we enjoy the old: the comfort of a ratty sweatshirt, the security of tradition, the familiarity of a well-traveled path.

Our sinful nature looks a lot like the comfort of a worn, old sweatshirt; it's familiar, well-fitted, and after a while we don't notice the rips and smudges. God, however, knows our desperate need for new clothes—not the materialistic, worldly kind; rather, the heavenly, eternal kind hemmed in heaven.

Our past mistakes and wrongs are like Joshua's dirty garments; they're stinky, stained and in need of a makeover. Zechariah's vision shows that instead of merely washing Joshua's clothing, God gives him an entire new outfit. That's retail therapy at its best.

Zechariah 3 reveals God's desire to remove Joshua's garments of sin and shame and to replace them—permanently. The new robes are perfectly pure, symbolizing cleansing and forgiveness. How strange it would be if Joshua refused the gift, only to cling to his filthy clothes. In this sense, rejecting God's forgiveness makes as much sense as a woman turning down a free shopping spree. And yet it happens every day. Rather than accepting God's gift of forgiveness, many individuals choose the familiarity of guilt and the comfort of self-condemnation.

God offers forgiveness to us free of charge. It's free because Jesus already paid the bill on the cross; Jesus' resurrection gives incalculable value to the robes of forgiveness. If he had not defeated death, the new clothes he offers would only be temporary. Because he lives, they will never fade or wear out.

Don't settle for grungy, old rags. Hand your "wardrobe" over, so God can give you a whole new look.

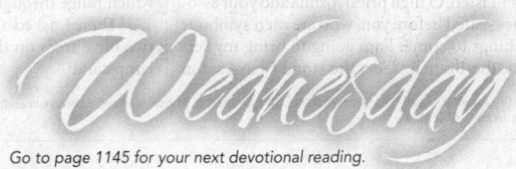

¹²Again I asked him, "What are these two olive branches beside the two gold pipes that pour out golden oil?"

¹³He replied, "Do you not know what these are?"

"No, my lord," I said.

¹⁴So he said, "These are the two who are anointed to*ᵃ* serve the Lord of all the earth."

The Flying Scroll

5 I looked again—and there before me was a flying scroll!

²He asked me, "What do you see?"

I answered, "I see a flying scroll, thirty feet long and fifteen feet wide."*ᵇ*

³And he said to me, "This is the curse that is going out over the whole land; for according to what it says on one side, every thief will be banished, and according to what it says on the other, everyone who swears falsely will be banished. ⁴The Lord Almighty declares, 'I will send it out, and it will enter the house of the thief and the house of him who swears falsely by my name. It will remain in his house and destroy it, both its timbers and its stones.'"

The Woman in a Basket

⁵Then the angel who was speaking to me came forward and said to me, "Look up and see what this is that is appearing."

⁶I asked, "What is it?"

He replied, "It is a measuring basket."*ᶜ* And he added, "This is the iniquity*ᵈ* of the people throughout the land."

⁷Then the cover of lead was raised, and there in the basket sat a woman! ⁸He said, "This is wickedness," and he pushed her back into the basket and pushed the lead cover down over its mouth.

⁹Then I looked up—and there before me were two women, with the wind in their wings! They had wings like those of a stork, and they lifted up the basket between heaven and earth.

¹⁰"Where are they taking the basket?" I asked the angel who was speaking to me.

¹¹He replied, "To the country of Babylonia*ᵉ* to build a house for it. When it is ready, the basket will be set there in its place."

Four Chariots

6 I looked up again—and there before me were four chariots coming out from between two mountains—mountains of bronze! ²The first chariot had red horses, the second black, ³the third white, and the fourth dappled—all of them powerful. ⁴I asked the angel who was speaking to me, "What are these, my lord?"

⁵The angel answered me, "These are the four spirits*ᶠ* of heaven, going out from standing in the presence of the Lord of the whole world. ⁶The one with the black horses is going toward the north country, the one with the white horses toward the west,*ᵍ* and the one with the dappled horses toward the south."

⁷When the powerful horses went out, they were straining to go throughout the earth. And he said, "Go throughout the earth!" So they went throughout the earth.

⁸Then he called to me, "Look, those going toward the north country have given my Spirit*ʰ* rest in the land of the north."

A Crown for Joshua

⁹The word of the Lord came to me: ¹⁰"Take silver and gold from the exiles Heldai, Tobijah and Jedaiah, who have arrived from Babylon. Go the same day to the house of Josiah son of Zephaniah. ¹¹Take the silver and gold and make a crown, and set it on the head of the high priest, Joshua son of Jehozadak. ¹²Tell him this is what the Lord Almighty says: 'Here is the man whose name is the Branch, and he will branch out from his place and build the temple of the Lord. ¹³It is he who will build the temple of the Lord, and he will be clothed with majesty and will sit and rule on his throne. And he will be a priest on his throne. And there will be harmony between the two.' ¹⁴The crown will be given to Heldai,*ⁱ* Tobijah, Jedaiah and Hen*ʲ* son of Zephaniah as a memorial in the temple of the Lord. ¹⁵Those who are far away will come and help to build the temple of the Lord, and you will know that the Lord Almighty has sent me to you. This will happen if you diligently obey the Lord your God."

---

*ᵃ*14 Or *two who bring oil and*   *ᵇ*2 Hebrew *twenty cubits long and ten cubits wide* (about 9 meters long and 4.5 meters wide)   *ᶜ*6 Hebrew *an ephah*; also in verses 7–11   *ᵈ*6 Or *appearance*   *ᵉ*11 Hebrew *Shinar*   *ᶠ*5 Or *winds*   *ᵍ*6 Or *horses after them*   *ʰ*8 Or *spirit*   *ⁱ*14 Syriac; Hebrew *Helem*   *ʲ*14 Or *and the gracious one, the*

Justice and Mercy, Not Fasting

7 In the fourth year of King Darius, the word of the LORD came to Zechariah on the fourth day of the ninth month, the month of Kislev. ²The people of Bethel had sent Sharezer and Regem-Melech, together with their men, to entreat the LORD ³by asking the priests of the house of the LORD Almighty and the prophets, "Should I mourn and fast in the fifth month, as I have done for so many years?"

⁴Then the word of the LORD Almighty came to me: ⁵"Ask all the people of the land and the priests, 'When you fasted and mourned in the fifth and seventh months for the past seventy years, was it really for me that you fasted? ⁶And when you were eating and drinking, were you not just feasting for yourselves? ⁷Are these not the words the LORD proclaimed through the earlier prophets when Jerusalem and its surrounding towns were at rest and prosperous, and the Negev and the western foothills were settled?'"

⁸And the word of the LORD came again to Zechariah: ⁹"This is what the LORD Almighty says: 'Administer true justice; show mercy and compassion to one another. ¹⁰Do not oppress the widow or the fatherless, the alien or the poor. In your hearts do not think evil of each other.'

¹¹"But they refused to pay attention; stubbornly they turned their backs and stopped up their ears. ¹²They made their hearts as hard as flint and would not listen to the law or to the words that the LORD Almighty had sent by his Spirit through the earlier prophets. So the LORD Almighty was very angry.

¹³"When I called, they did not listen; so when they called, I would not listen,' says the LORD Almighty. ¹⁴'I scattered them with a whirlwind among all the nations, where they were strangers. The land was left so desolate behind them that no one could come or go. This is how they made the pleasant land desolate.'"

The LORD Promises to Bless Jerusalem

8 Again the word of the LORD Almighty came to me. ²This is what the LORD Almighty says: "I am very jealous for Zion; I am burning with jealousy for her."

³This is what the LORD says: "I will return to Zion and dwell in Jerusalem. Then Jerusalem will be called the City of Truth, and the mountain of the LORD Almighty will be called the Holy Mountain."

⁴This is what the LORD Almighty says: "Once again men and women of ripe old age will sit in the streets of Jerusalem, each with cane in hand because of his age. ⁵The city streets will be filled with boys and girls playing there."

⁶This is what the LORD Almighty says: "It may seem marvelous to the remnant of this people at that time, but will it seem marvelous to me?" declares the LORD Almighty.

⁷This is what the LORD Almighty says: "I will save my people from the countries of the east and the west. ⁸I will bring them back to live in Jerusalem; they will be my people, and I will be faithful and righteous to them as their God."

⁹This is what the LORD Almighty says: "You who now hear these words spoken by the prophets who were there when the foundation was laid for the house of the LORD Almighty, let your hands be strong so that the temple may be built. ¹⁰Before that time there were no wages for man or beast. No one could go about his business safely because of his enemy, for I had turned every man against his neighbor. ¹¹But now I will not deal with the remnant of this people as I did in the past," declares the LORD Almighty.

¹²"The seed will grow well, the vine will yield its fruit, the ground will produce its crops, and the heavens will drop their dew. I will give all these things as an inheritance to the remnant of this people. ¹³As you have been an object of cursing among the nations, O Judah and Israel, so will I save you, and you will be a blessing. Do not be afraid, but let your hands be strong."

¹⁴This is what the LORD Almighty says: "Just as I had determined to bring disaster upon you and showed no pity when your fathers angered me," says the LORD Almighty, ¹⁵"so now I have determined to do good again to Jerusalem and Judah. Do not be afraid. ¹⁶These are the things you are to do: Speak the truth to each other, and render true and sound judgment in your courts; ¹⁷do not plot evil against your neighbor, and do not love to swear falsely. I hate all this," declares the LORD.

¹⁸Again the word of the LORD Almighty came to me. ¹⁹This is what the LORD Almighty

Failure to Communicate

Read: Zechariah 7:8–14

PERHAPS ONE OF THE MOST memorable movie lines of all times comes from the classic film *Cool Hand Luke* starring Paul Newman. A captain, played by Strother Martin, said these famous words, "What we've got here is failure to communicate. Some men you just can't reach, so you get what we had here last week which is the way he wants it. Well, he gets it." It's true, sometimes we get what we want.

The Israelites had a massive breakdown in communication with God. They did not listen when he called them. So when they finally called upon him, he would not listen to them. They got what they wanted.

The Lord had told his people to be truthful and just, merciful and compassionate, to care for each other and for strangers, and to think well of each other. They failed to listen to their God. Thus, Zechariah 7:13 is perhaps one of the saddest verses in Scripture. The Israelites did not avail themselves of the relationship God wanted with them. They thought they would avoid the consequences of miscommunication. Instead, God was unreachable for a time. They ended up in a land of desolation.

Desolation. A sorry sort of word. A sorry sort of life. We each know what that looks like. Not an inviting image. We don't really want to end up desolate and unheard, as the Israelites did, but how do we avoid it? How do we listen to God?

The Word of God is the framework from which we listen. When we know it and absorb it, it is dynamic and living. Scripture intersects with our thoughts, feelings and spirit. We create an open space for that to happen by dedicating time and attention to study and prayer. Out of love and respect for God, we concentrate on listening to him—as if he were the only other being in the universe. Listening means that we are receptive; like soft ground that soaks up the rain, so the Word can yield rich fruit in our lives. Listening to God, and heeding what God says, is the way to keep the "pleasant land" fruitful and to prevent it from becoming desolate (see verse 14). It's the only way to remain attuned to God and his voice.

Zechariah 7:13

" 'When I called, they did not listen; so when they called, I would not listen,' says the LORD Almighty."

reflection

1. Can you think of a time you listened to God and were blessed? How about a time when you didn't and suffered for it?

2. How can you remind yourself to listen to God?

3. What are some concrete ways you can love your Father by listening to him?

RELATED READINGS

Leviticus 26:14–28;
Psalm 81:8–16;
Matthew 13:13–23

Go to page 1153 for your next devotional reading.

says: "The fasts of the fourth, fifth, seventh and tenth months will become joyful and glad occasions and happy festivals for Judah. Therefore love truth and peace."

²⁰This is what the LORD Almighty says: "Many peoples and the inhabitants of many cities will yet come, ²¹and the inhabitants of one city will go to another and say, 'Let us go at once to entreat the LORD and seek the LORD Almighty. I myself am going.' ²²And many peoples and powerful nations will come to Jerusalem to seek the LORD Almighty and to entreat him."

²³This is what the LORD Almighty says: "In those days ten men from all languages and nations will take firm hold of one Jew by the hem of his robe and say, 'Let us go with you, because we have heard that God is with you.'"

Judgment on Israel's Enemies
An Oracle

9 The word of the LORD is against the land of Hadrach
and will rest upon Damascus—
for the eyes of men and all the tribes of Israel
are on the LORD—*a*
² and upon Hamath too, which borders on it,
and upon Tyre and Sidon, though they are very skillful.
³ Tyre has built herself a stronghold;
she has heaped up silver like dust,
and gold like the dirt of the streets.
⁴ But the Lord will take away her possessions
and destroy her power on the sea,
and she will be consumed by fire.
⁵ Ashkelon will see it and fear;
Gaza will writhe in agony,
and Ekron too, for her hope will wither.
Gaza will lose her king
and Ashkelon will be deserted.
⁶ Foreigners will occupy Ashdod,
and I will cut off the pride of the Philistines.
⁷ I will take the blood from their mouths,
the forbidden food from between their teeth.

Those who are left will belong to our God
and become leaders in Judah,
and Ekron will be like the Jebusites.
⁸ But I will defend my house
against marauding forces.
Never again will an oppressor overrun my people,
for now I am keeping watch.

The Coming of Zion's King
⁹ Rejoice greatly, O Daughter of Zion!
Shout, Daughter of Jerusalem!
See, your king*b* comes to you,
righteous and having salvation,
gentle and riding on a donkey,
on a colt, the foal of a donkey.
¹⁰ I will take away the chariots from Ephraim
and the war-horses from Jerusalem,
and the battle bow will be broken.
He will proclaim peace to the nations.
His rule will extend from sea to sea
and from the River*c* to the ends of the earth.*d*
¹¹ As for you, because of the blood of my covenant with you,
I will free your prisoners from the waterless pit.
¹² Return to your fortress, O prisoners of hope;
even now I announce that I will restore twice as much to you.
¹³ I will bend Judah as I bend my bow
and fill it with Ephraim.
I will rouse your sons, O Zion,
against your sons, O Greece,
and make you like a warrior's sword.

The LORD Will Appear
¹⁴ Then the LORD will appear over them;
his arrow will flash like lightning.
The Sovereign LORD will sound the trumpet;
he will march in the storms of the south,
¹⁵   and the LORD Almighty will shield them.
They will destroy
and overcome with slingstones.
They will drink and roar as with wine;
they will be full like a bowl

---

*a*1 Or *Damascus. / For the eye of the LORD is on all mankind, / as well as on the tribes of Israel*,   *b*9 Or *King*   *c*10 That is, the Euphrates
*d*10 Or *the end of the land*

used for sprinkling[a] the corners of the altar.

16 The LORD their God will save them on that day
as the flock of his people.
They will sparkle in his land
like jewels in a crown.

17 How attractive and beautiful they will be!
Grain will make the young men thrive,
and new wine the young women.

The LORD Will Care for Judah

10 Ask the LORD for rain in the springtime;
it is the LORD who makes the storm clouds.
He gives showers of rain to men,
and plants of the field to everyone.

2 The idols speak deceit,
diviners see visions that lie;
they tell dreams that are false,
they give comfort in vain.
Therefore the people wander like sheep
oppressed for lack of a shepherd.

3 "My anger burns against the shepherds,
and I will punish the leaders;
for the LORD Almighty will care
for his flock, the house of Judah,
and make them like
a proud horse in battle.

4 From Judah will come the cornerstone,
from him the tent peg,
from him the battle bow,
from him every ruler.

5 Together they[b] will be like mighty men
trampling the muddy streets in battle.
Because the LORD is with them,
they will fight and overthrow the horsemen.

6 "I will strengthen the house of Judah
and save the house of Joseph.
I will restore them

because I have compassion on them.
They will be as though
I had not rejected them,
for I am the LORD their God
and I will answer them.

7 The Ephraimites will become like mighty men,
and their hearts will be glad as with wine.
Their children will see it and be joyful;
their hearts will rejoice in the LORD.

8 I will signal for them
and gather them in.
Surely I will redeem them;
they will be as numerous as before.

9 Though I scatter them among the peoples,
yet in distant lands they will remember me.
They and their children will survive,
and they will return.

10 I will bring them back from Egypt
and gather them from Assyria.
I will bring them to Gilead and Lebanon,
and there will not be room enough for them.

11 They will pass through the sea of trouble;
the surging sea will be subdued
and all the depths of the Nile will dry up.
Assyria's pride will be brought down
and Egypt's scepter will pass away.

12 I will strengthen them in the LORD
and in his name they will walk,"
declares the LORD.

Zechariah 10:12

God Strengthens Us

"I will strengthen them in the LORD and in his name they will walk," declares the LORD.

---

11 Open your doors, O Lebanon,
so that fire may devour your cedars!

2 Wail, O pine tree, for the cedar has fallen;
the stately trees are ruined!
Wail, oaks of Bashan;
the dense forest has been cut down!

3 Listen to the wail of the shepherds;

---

their rich pastures are destroyed!
Listen to the roar of the lions;
the lush thicket of the Jordan is ruined!

Two Shepherds

[4] This is what the LORD my God says: "Pasture the flock marked for slaughter. [5] Their buyers slaughter them and go unpunished. Those who sell them say, 'Praise the LORD, I am rich!' Their own shepherds do not spare them. [6] For I will no longer have pity on the people of the land," declares the LORD. "I will hand everyone over to his neighbor and his king. They will oppress the land, and I will not rescue them from their hands."

[7] So I pastured the flock marked for slaughter, particularly the oppressed of the flock. Then I took two staffs and called one Favor and the other Union, and I pastured the flock. [8] In one month I got rid of the three shepherds.

The flock detested me, and I grew weary of them [9] and said, "I will not be your shepherd. Let the dying die, and the perishing perish. Let those who are left eat one another's flesh."

[10] Then I took my staff called Favor and broke it, revoking the covenant I had made with all the nations. [11] It was revoked on that day, and so the afflicted of the flock who were watching me knew it was the word of the LORD.

[12] I told them, "If you think it best, give me my pay; but if not, keep it." So they paid me thirty pieces of silver.

[13] And the LORD said to me, "Throw it to the potter"—the handsome price at which they priced me! So I took the thirty pieces of silver and threw them into the house of the LORD to the potter.

[14] Then I broke my second staff called Union, breaking the brotherhood between Judah and Israel.

[15] Then the LORD said to me, "Take again the equipment of a foolish shepherd. [16] For I am going to raise up a shepherd over the land who will not care for the lost, or seek the young, or heal the injured, or feed the healthy, but will eat the meat of the choice sheep, tearing off their hoofs.

[17] "Woe to the worthless shepherd,
who deserts the flock!

a 10 Or *the Spirit*   *b* 10 Or *to*

May the sword strike his arm and his right eye!
May his arm be completely withered,
his right eye totally blinded!"

Jerusalem's Enemies to Be Destroyed
An Oracle

12 This is the word of the LORD concerning Israel. The LORD, who stretches out the heavens, who lays the foundation of the earth, and who forms the spirit of man within him, declares: [2] "I am going to make Jerusalem a cup that sends all the surrounding peoples reeling. Judah will be besieged as well as Jerusalem. [3] On that day, when all the nations of the earth are gathered against her, I will make Jerusalem an immovable rock for all the nations. All who try to move it will injure themselves. [4] On that day I will strike every horse with panic and its rider with madness," declares the LORD. "I will keep a watchful eye over the house of Judah, but I will blind all the horses of the nations. [5] Then the leaders of Judah will say in their hearts, 'The people of Jerusalem are strong, because the LORD Almighty is their God.'

[6] "On that day I will make the leaders of Judah like a firepot in a woodpile, like a flaming torch among sheaves. They will consume right and left all the surrounding peoples, but Jerusalem will remain intact in her place.

[7] "The LORD will save the dwellings of Judah first, so that the honor of the house of David and of Jerusalem's inhabitants may not be greater than that of Judah. [8] On that day the LORD will shield those who live in Jerusalem, so that the feeblest among them will be like David, and the house of David will be like God, like the Angel of the LORD going before them. [9] On that day I will set out to destroy all the nations that attack Jerusalem.

Mourning for the One They Pierced

[10] "And I will pour out on the house of David and the inhabitants of Jerusalem a spirit*a* of grace and supplication. They will look on*b* me, the one they have pierced, and they will mourn for him as one mourns for an only child, and grieve bitterly for him as one grieves for a firstborn son. [11] On that day the weeping in Jerusalem will be great, like the weeping of Hadad

Rimmon in the plain of Megiddo. ¹²The land will mourn, each clan by itself, with their wives by themselves: the clan of the house of David and their wives, the clan of the house of Nathan and their wives, ¹³the clan of the house of Levi and their wives, the clan of Shimei and their wives, ¹⁴and all the rest of the clans and their wives.

Cleansing From Sin

13 "On that day a fountain will be opened to the house of David and the inhabitants of Jerusalem, to cleanse them from sin and impurity.

²"On that day, I will banish the names of the idols from the land, and they will be remembered no more," declares the LORD Almighty. "I will remove both the prophets and the spirit of impurity from the land. ³And if anyone still prophesies, his father and mother, to whom he was born, will say to him, 'You must die, because you have told lies in the LORD's name.' When he prophesies, his own parents will stab him.

⁴"On that day every prophet will be ashamed of his prophetic vision. He will not put on a prophet's garment of hair in order to deceive. ⁵He will say, 'I am not a prophet. I am a farmer; the land has been my livelihood since my youth.'ᵃ ⁶If someone asks him, 'What are these wounds on your bodyᵇ?' he will answer, 'The wounds I was given at the house of my friends.'

The Shepherd Struck, the Sheep Scattered

⁷"Awake, O sword, against
 my shepherd,
 against the man who is
 close to me!"
 declares the LORD
 Almighty.
"Strike the shepherd,
 and the sheep will be
 scattered,
 and I will turn my hand against the little
 ones.
⁸ In the whole land," declares the LORD,

"two-thirds will be struck down and
 perish;
 yet one-third will be left in it.
⁹ This third I will bring into the fire;
 I will refine them like silver
 and test them like gold.
They will call on my name
 and I will answer them;
 I will say, 'They are my people,'
 and they will say, 'The LORD is our
 God.'"

The LORD Comes and Reigns

14 A day of the LORD is coming when your plunder will be divided among you. ²I will gather all the nations to Jerusalem to fight against it; the city will be captured, the houses ransacked, and the women raped. Half of the city will go into exile, but the rest of the people will not be taken from the city. ³Then the LORD will go out and fight against those nations, as he fights in the day of battle. ⁴On that day his feet will stand on the Mount of Olives, east of Jerusalem, and the Mount of Olives will be split in two from east to west, forming a great valley, with half of the mountain moving north and half moving south. ⁵You will flee by my mountain valley, for it will extend to Azel. You will flee as you fled from the earthquakeᶜ in the days of Uzziah king of Judah. Then the LORD my God will come, and all the holy ones with him.

Zechariah 14:9

God Is One

The LORD will be king over the whole earth. On that day there will be one LORD, and his name the only name.

⁶On that day there will be no light, no cold or frost. ⁷It will be a unique day, without daytime or nighttime—a day known to the LORD. When evening comes, there will be light.

⁸On that day living water will flow out from Jerusalem, half to the eastern seaᵈ and half to the western sea,ᵉ in summer and in winter.

⁹The LORD will be king over the whole earth. On that day there will be one LORD, and his name the only name.

¹⁰The whole land, from Geba to Rimmon, south of Jerusalem, will become like the Arabah.

ᵃ5 Or *farmer; a man sold me in my youth* ᵇ6 Or *wounds between your hands* ᶜ5 Or *My mountain valley will be blocked and will extend to Azel. It will be blocked as it was blocked because of the earthquake* ᵈ8 That is, the Dead Sea ᵉ8 That is, the Mediterranean

But Jerusalem will be raised up and remain in its place, from the Benjamin Gate to the site of the First Gate, to the Corner Gate, and from the Tower of Hananel to the royal winepresses. ¹¹It will be inhabited; never again will it be destroyed. Jerusalem will be secure.

¹²This is the plague with which the LORD will strike all the nations that fought against Jerusalem: Their flesh will rot while they are still standing on their feet, their eyes will rot in their sockets, and their tongues will rot in their mouths. ¹³On that day men will be stricken by the LORD with great panic. Each man will seize the hand of another, and they will attack each other. ¹⁴Judah too will fight at Jerusalem. The wealth of all the surrounding nations will be collected—great quantities of gold and silver and clothing. ¹⁵A similar plague will strike the horses and mules, the camels and donkeys, and all the animals in those camps.

¹⁶Then the survivors from all the nations that have attacked Jerusalem will go up year after year to worship the King, the LORD Almighty, and to celebrate the Feast of Tabernacles. ¹⁷If any of the peoples of the earth do not go up to Jerusalem to worship the King, the LORD Almighty, they will have no rain. ¹⁸If the Egyptian people do not go up and take part, they will have no rain. The LORDᵃ will bring on them the plague he inflicts on the nations that do not go up to celebrate the Feast of Tabernacles. ¹⁹This will be the punishment of Egypt and the punishment of all the nations that do not go up to celebrate the Feast of Tabernacles.

²⁰On that day HOLY TO THE LORD will be inscribed on the bells of the horses, and the cooking pots in the LORD's house will be like the sacred bowls in front of the altar. ²¹Every pot in Jerusalem and Judah will be holy to the LORD Almighty, and all who come to sacrifice will take some of the pots and cook in them. And on that day there will no longer be a Canaaniteᵇ in the house of the LORD Almighty.

ᵃ18 Or part, then the LORD   ᵇ21 Or merchant

Malachi

Again and again God had shown his love for his people. Yet their love for him was sorely lacking. After returning to their homeland, the people embraced God's laws for a time, but they eventually became complacent. *Their worship involved merely following tradition*—and barely even that. The animals they sacrificed were ones they couldn't sell—crippled and blind animals. God's people, even the priests, were shortchanging him. They were even stealing from him in their refusal to give the tithe he had commanded. Then they had the gall to say, "It's futile to serve God," as though they resented what little they gave him. *"Come worship me when you mean it"* seems to be God's disgusted response.

Author:
Malachi.

Audience:
Jews in Jerusalem and all of God's people.

Date:
About 430 B.C.

Setting:
Although the temple in Jerusalem and the city walls had been rebuilt, the Jews languished in their worship.

Verse to Remember:
"My name will be great among the nations, from the rising to the setting of the sun. In every place incense and pure offerings will be brought to my name, because my name will be great among the nations," says the LORD Almighty. (1:11)

1 An oracle: The word of the LORD to Israel through Malachi.[a]

Jacob Loved, Esau Hated

2"I have loved you," says the LORD.

"But you ask, 'How have you loved us?'

"Was not Esau Jacob's brother?" the LORD says. "Yet I have loved Jacob, 3but Esau I have hated, and I have turned his mountains into a wasteland and left his inheritance to the desert jackals."

4Edom may say, "Though we have been crushed, we will rebuild the ruins."

But this is what the LORD Almighty says:

---

[a]1 *Malachi* means *my messenger.*

"They may build, but I will demolish. They will be called the Wicked Land, a people always under the wrath of the LORD. ⁵You will see it with your own eyes and say, 'Great is the LORD—even beyond the borders of Israel!'

Blemished Sacrifices

⁶"A son honors his father, and a servant his master. If I am a father, where is the honor due me? If I am a master, where is the respect due me?" says the LORD Almighty. "It is you, O priests, who show contempt for my name.

"But you ask, 'How have we shown contempt for your name?'

⁷"You place defiled food on my altar.

"But you ask, 'How have we defiled you?'

"By saying that the LORD's table is contemptible. ⁸When you bring blind animals for sacrifice, is that not wrong? When you sacrifice crippled or diseased animals, is that not wrong? Try offering them to your governor! Would he be pleased with you? Would he accept you?" says the LORD Almighty.

⁹"Now implore God to be gracious to us. With such offerings from your hands, will he accept you?"—says the LORD Almighty.

¹⁰"Oh, that one of you would shut the temple doors, so that you would not light useless fires on my altar! I am not pleased with you," says the LORD Almighty, "and I will accept no offering from your hands. ¹¹My name will be great among the nations, from the rising to the setting of the sun. In every place incense and pure offerings will be brought to my name, because my name will be great among the nations," says the LORD Almighty.

¹²"But you profane it by saying of the Lord's table, 'It is defiled,' and of its food, 'It is contemptible.' ¹³And you say, 'What a burden!' and you sniff at it contemptuously," says the LORD Almighty.

"When you bring injured, crippled or diseased animals and offer them as sacrifices, should I accept them from your hands?" says the LORD. ¹⁴"Cursed is the cheat who has an acceptable male in his flock and vows to give it, but then sacrifices a blemished animal to the Lord. For I am a great king," says the LORD Almighty, "and my name is to be feared among the nations.

Admonition for the Priests

2 "And now this admonition is for you, O priests. ²If you do not listen, and if you do not set your heart to honor my name," says the LORD Almighty, "I will send a curse upon you, and I will curse your blessings. Yes, I have already cursed them, because you have not set your heart to honor me.

³"Because of you I will rebuke*a* your descendants*b*; I will spread on your faces the offal from your festival sacrifices, and you will be carried off with it. ⁴And you will know that I have sent you this admonition so that my covenant with Levi may continue," says the LORD Almighty. ⁵"My covenant was with him, a covenant of life and peace, and I gave them to him; this called for reverence and he revered me and stood in awe of my name. ⁶True instruction was in his mouth and nothing false was found on his lips. He walked with me in peace and uprightness, and turned many from sin.

⁷"For the lips of a priest ought to preserve knowledge, and from his mouth men should seek instruction—because he is the messenger of the LORD Almighty. ⁸But you have turned from the way and by your teaching have caused many to stumble; you have violated the covenant with Levi," says the LORD Almighty. ⁹"So I have caused you to be despised and humiliated before all the people, because you have not followed my ways but have shown partiality in matters of the law."

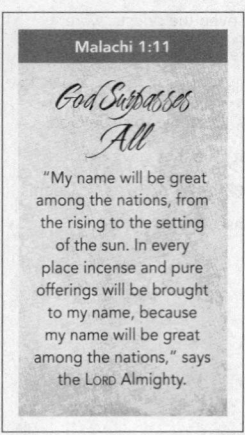

Malachi 1:11

God Surpasses All

"My name will be great among the nations, from the rising to the setting of the sun. In every place incense and pure offerings will be brought to my name, because my name will be great among the nations," says the LORD Almighty.

---

*a*3 Or *cut off* (see Septuagint)   *b*3 Or *will blight your grain*

Mine?

Read: Malachi 3:1–18

HAVE YOU EVER TRIED to take a toy from a toddler? If so, then you know it's hardly worth the effort. Even though the child probably doesn't know where the toy came from, the words *my* and *mine* repeatedly resound. It's hers and no one else's.

Mine. It's one of the first words we learn as children. No one has to teach us to be possessive. Hoarding comes naturally. Maybe we fear that we won't have what we need or that someone will take what we think rightfully belongs to us. Learning to share is so often the challenge.

God instituted the concept of tithing during Moses' time. Not only was it the way God provided for the Levites, but it was also a spiritual discipline to teach his people to rely on him. By giving God the first tenth of their produce, they acknowledged that all they had was from his hand. In this passage, God lamented that the people were robbing him by withholding their tithe. He asked them to "test" his generosity. And wow! God can pass *that* test, opening the floodgates of heaven and pouring out so much blessing that there will not be enough room for it.

With a return like that, who wouldn't want to give to God? But God doesn't ask us to give out of his own need or for what we receive in return. He asks us to give as a reflection of how generous he has been to us. He has, indeed, poured out mercy, forgiveness, provision and everything else we need. Jesus said, "Give, and it will be given to you. A good measure, pressed down, shaken together and running over, will be poured into your lap. For with the measure you use, it will be measured to you" (Luke 6:38). The Old Testament tithe was a requirement, but the New Testament offering is a test of the heart. Giving is not a duty but a joyous outpouring of gratitude. And giving is God's way of making us, his people, a conduit of his love to others.

We cannot receive God's gifts with closed fists. No, receiving requires open hands. What God pours into our hands, we pour out. And in God's kingdom, there is always more to spare.

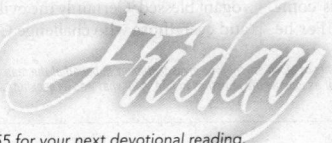

Go to page 1155 for your next devotional reading.

Malachi 3:10

"Bring the whole tithe into the storehouse, that there may be food in my house. Test me in this," says the LORD Almighty, "and see if I will not throw open the floodgates of heaven and pour out so much blessing that you will not have room enough for it."

reflection

1 Are your hands open or are you tightfisted, like a child with a toy?

2 Have you practiced the grace of generous giving? If so, what happened? How did giving affect you?

3 Why would giving to God in order to receive from God not be a good motive? What's wrong with this way of thinking?

RELATED READINGS

Proverbs 3:9–10;
Luke 21:1–4;
2 Corinthians 9:6–8

"Giving is a joy if we do it in the right spirit. It all depends on whether we think of it as 'What can I spare?' or as 'What can I share?'"

Esther York Burkholder

Judah Unfaithful

10Have we not all one Father[a]? Did not one God create us? Why do we profane the covenant of our fathers by breaking faith with one another?

11Judah has broken faith. A detestable thing has been committed in Israel and in Jerusalem: Judah has desecrated the sanctuary the LORD loves, by marrying the daughter of a foreign god. **12**As for the man who does this, whoever he may be, may the LORD cut him off from the tents of Jacob[b]—even though he brings offerings to the LORD Almighty.

13Another thing you do: You flood the LORD's altar with tears. You weep and wail because he no longer pays attention to your offerings or accepts them with pleasure from your hands. **14**You ask, "Why?" It is because the LORD is acting as the witness between you and the wife of your youth, because you have broken faith with her, though she is your partner, the wife of your marriage covenant.

15Has not the LORD made them one? In flesh and spirit they are his. And why one? Because he was seeking godly offspring.[c] So guard yourself in your spirit, and do not break faith with the wife of your youth.

16"I hate divorce," says the LORD God of Israel, "and I hate a man's covering himself[d] with violence as well as with his garment," says the LORD Almighty.

So guard yourself in your spirit, and do not break faith.

The Day of Judgment

17You have wearied the LORD with your words.

"How have we wearied him?" you ask.

By saying, "All who do evil are good in the eyes of the LORD, and he is pleased with them" or "Where is the God of justice?"

3 "See, I will send my messenger, who will prepare the way before me. Then suddenly the Lord you are seeking will come to his temple; the messenger of the covenant, whom you desire, will come," says the LORD Almighty.

2But who can endure the day of his coming? Who can stand when he appears? For he will be like a refiner's fire or a launderer's soap. **3**He will sit as a refiner and purifier of silver; he will purify the Levites and refine them like gold and silver. Then the LORD will have men who will bring offerings in righteousness, **4**and the offerings of Judah and Jerusalem will be acceptable to the LORD, as in days gone by, as in former years.

5"So I will come near to you for judgment. I will be quick to testify against sorcerers, adulterers and perjurers, against those who defraud laborers of their wages, who oppress the widows and the fatherless, and deprive aliens of justice, but do not fear me," says the LORD Almighty.

Robbing God

6"I the LORD do not change. So you, O descendants of Jacob, are not destroyed. **7**Ever since the time of your forefathers you have turned away from my decrees and have not kept them. Return to me, and I will return to you," says the LORD Almighty.

"But you ask, 'How are we to return?'

8"Will a man rob God? Yet you rob me.

"But you ask, 'How do we rob you?'

"In tithes and offerings. **9**You are under a curse—the whole nation of you—because you are robbing me. **10**Bring the whole tithe into the storehouse, that there may be food in my house. Test me in this," says the LORD Almighty, "and see if I will not throw open the floodgates of heaven and pour out so much blessing that you will not have room enough for it. **11**I will prevent pests from devouring your crops, and the vines in your fields will not cast their fruit," says the LORD Almighty. **12**"Then all the nations will call you blessed, for yours will be a delightful land," says the LORD Almighty.

13"You have said harsh things against me," says the LORD.

"Yet you ask, 'What have we said against you?'

14"You have said, 'It is futile to serve God. What did we gain by carrying out his requirements and going about like mourners before the LORD Almighty? **15**But now we call the arrogant blessed. Certainly the evildoers prosper, and even those who challenge God escape.'"

---

*a*10 Or *father*   *b*12 Or *12May the LORD cut off from the tents of Jacob anyone who gives testimony in behalf of the man who does this*   *c*15 Or *15But the one who is our father, did not do this, not as long as life remained in him. And what was he seeking? An offspring from God*   *d*16 Or *his wife*

Just a Touch

SUFFERING WOMAN

"IF I ONLY TOUCH HIS CLOAK, I will be healed." Her thoughts were single-focused; her intention was simple.

"If *I* only touch his cloak . . ."

No one could do it for her. She had to be the one who touched him. She had to draw on her fortitude to make her way through the crowd surrounding Jesus. She alone could summon the inner strength to step out in faith toward the Healer. Others had experienced healing, but no one could transfer the power to her. She had to encounter Jesus personally. She had suffered for 12 years alone. And she could not depend on anyone else to bring her to this moment. She had to do it herself.

"If I only *touch* his cloak . . ." How great was her faith in the Master! She surmised she only had to graze his power in order to be changed. She willingly believed that he would not require her to go to great lengths to receive what she needed. She did not intend to jump through hoops, recite a mantra or go through the motions to receive mercy. Her approach was simple and heartfelt. If reaching out to him in faith did not work, she had no other option.

"If I only touch *his* cloak . . ." She knew the source of the power. Those whom she'd sought assistance from before—doctors, priests, family and friends—had only let her down. None could give her relief. But when she saw Jesus and witnessed his miracles firsthand, she knew he was the One who would not disappoint. The disciples and the host of followers surrounding him may have intimidated her, but they did not distract her. She did not pull one of them aside and issue her request. She was laser-focused on the Father's Son.

"If I only touch his cloak, I will be *healed*." She did. And she was.

—*Prayer*—
God, give me faith like this woman . . . and heal me.

> Just then a woman who had been subject to bleeding for twelve years came up behind him and touched the edge of his cloak.
>
> **Matthew 9:20**

ASSIGNED READING:

Matthew 9:20–22;
Mark 5:25–34;
Luke 8:43–48

Weekend

16Then those who feared the LORD talked with each other, and the LORD listened and heard. A scroll of remembrance was written in his presence concerning those who feared the LORD and honored his name.

17"They will be mine," says the LORD Almighty, "in the day when I make up my treasured possession.a I will spare them, just as in compassion a man spares his son who serves him. 18And you will again see the distinction between the righteous and the wicked, between those who serve God and those who do not.

The Day of the LORD

4 "Surely the day is coming; it will burn like a furnace. All the arrogant and every evildoer will be stubble, and that day that is coming will set them on fire," says the LORD

Malachi 4:6

God Can Turn Hearts

"He will turn the hearts of the fathers to their children, and the hearts of the children to their fathers; or else I will come and strike the land with a curse."

Almighty. "Not a root or a branch will be left to them. 2But for you who revere my name, the sun of righteousness will rise with healing in its wings. And you will go out and leap like calves released from the stall. 3Then you will trample down the wicked; they will be ashes under the soles of your feet on the day when I do these things," says the LORD Almighty.

4"Remember the law of my servant Moses, the decrees and laws I gave him at Horeb for all Israel.

5"See, I will send you the prophet Elijah before that great and dreadful day of the LORD comes. 6He will turn the hearts of the fathers to their children, and the hearts of the children to their fathers; or else I will come and strike the land with a curse."

---

a17 Or Almighty, "my treasured possession, in the day when I act

The New Testament

Matthew

A silent interval of 400 years passed between the Old and New Testaments. Scripture says nothing of those years, but history tells us that they included times of peace and then *persecution for the people of God,* culminating with the oppression of the Roman Empire. It is to this Roman-ruled nation of Jews that Matthew primarily addresses his Gospel. A Jew himself, he was also a tax collector—a Roman puppet. Tax collectors were notorious cheaters, squeezing whatever they could out of their fellow citizens so they could skim a healthy profit off the top for themselves. But whatever Matthew once was, when he encountered Jesus, *he became a devoted disciple.*

This Gospel gives us an up-close-and-personal view of Jesus as teacher and healer, as well as a wide panoramic view showing how *Jesus fulfilled the ancient prophecies* that pointed to the promised King and Messiah. Jesus didn't just burst onto the scene. His life and his death were planned from the foundation of the world. Matthew shows us that *the whole of Scripture is one continuous story.*

Author:
Matthew, also called Levi.

Audience:
Followers of Jesus. Matthew wrote with a Jewish audience in mind.

Date:
Probably between A.D. 60 and 70.

Setting:
Matthew most likely wrote from Israel, though some believe he wrote from Syrian Antioch.

Verse to Remember:
This was to fulfill what was spoken through the prophet Isaiah: "He took up our infirmities and carried our diseases." (8:17)

The Genealogy of Jesus

1 A record of the genealogy of Jesus Christ the son of David, the son of Abraham:

² Abraham was the father of Isaac,
Isaac the father of Jacob,

Jacob the father of Judah and his brothers,
³ Judah the father of Perez and Zerah, whose mother was Tamar,
Perez the father of Hezron,

Hezron the father of Ram,

4 Ram the father of Amminadab,
Amminadab the father of Nahshon,
Nahshon the father of Salmon,

5 Salmon the father of Boaz, whose mother was Rahab,
Boaz the father of Obed, whose mother was Ruth,
Obed the father of Jesse,

6 and Jesse the father of King David.

David was the father of Solomon, whose mother had been Uriah's wife,

7 Solomon the father of Rehoboam,
Rehoboam the father of Abijah,
Abijah the father of Asa,

8 Asa the father of Jehoshaphat,
Jehoshaphat the father of Jehoram,
Jehoram the father of Uzziah,

9 Uzziah the father of Jotham,
Jotham the father of Ahaz,
Ahaz the father of Hezekiah,

10 Hezekiah the father of Manasseh,
Manasseh the father of Amon,
Amon the father of Josiah,

11 and Josiah the father of Jeconiah*a* and his brothers at the time of the exile to Babylon.

12 After the exile to Babylon:
Jeconiah was the father of Shealtiel,
Shealtiel the father of Zerubbabel,

13 Zerubbabel the father of Abiud,
Abiud the father of Eliakim,
Eliakim the father of Azor,

14 Azor the father of Zadok,
Zadok the father of Akim,
Akim the father of Eliud,

15 Eliud the father of Eleazar,
Eleazar the father of Matthan,
Matthan the father of Jacob,

16 and Jacob the father of Joseph, the husband of Mary, of whom was born Jesus, who is called Christ.

17 Thus there were fourteen generations in all from Abraham to David, fourteen from David to the exile to Babylon, and fourteen from the exile to the Christ.*b*

The Birth of Jesus Christ

18 This is how the birth of Jesus Christ came about: His mother Mary was pledged to be married to Joseph, but before they came together, she was found to be with child through the Holy Spirit. 19 Because Joseph her husband was a righteous man and did not want to expose her to public disgrace, he had in mind to divorce her quietly.

20 But after he had considered this, an angel of the Lord appeared to him in a dream and said, "Joseph son of David, do not be afraid to take Mary home as your wife, because what is conceived in her is from the Holy Spirit. 21 She will give birth to a son, and you are to give him the name Jesus,*c* because he will save his people from their sins."

22 All this took place to fulfill what the Lord had said through the prophet: 23 "The virgin will be with child and will give birth to a son, and they will call him Immanuel"*d*—which means, "God with us."

24 When Joseph woke up, he did what the angel of the Lord had commanded him and took Mary home as his wife. 25 But he had no union with her until she gave birth to a son. And he gave him the name Jesus.

The Visit of the Magi

2 After Jesus was born in Bethlehem in Judea, during the time of King Herod, Magi*e* from the east came to Jerusalem 2 and asked, "Where is the one who has been born king of the Jews? We saw his star in the east*f* and have come to worship him."

Matthew 1:21

God Reaches Out to Save

"She will give birth to a son, and you are to give him the name Jesus, because he will save his people from their sins."

---

*a*11 That is, Jehoiachin; also in verse 12   *b*17 Or *Messiah.* "The Christ" (Greek) and "the Messiah" (Hebrew) both mean "the Anointed One."   *c*21 *Jesus* is the Greek form of *Joshua,* which means *the Lord saves.*   *d*23 Isaiah 7:14   *e*1 Traditionally *Wise Men*   *f*2 Or *star when it rose*

Impossible Dream

Read: Matthew 1:18–25

FOR CENTURIES GOD'S PEOPLE had been waiting for the promised Messiah, each family hoping he would be born to them. Then in an "impossible" dream, Joseph received a revelation from heaven telling him that Mary, his betrothed, was going to bear God's son. An angel of the Lord instructed Joseph not to shame her, but to marry her and raise the Son of God as his own child. In this dream, God revealed that the coming baby was the promised one, the Messiah.

But was the dream really a nightmare for Joseph? Joseph must have wrestled with all that this news implied. For the rest of his life he might live with the whispers—whispers that he hadn't been able to wait until the marriage bed, or, worse, that he was raising another man's child. For a righteous man like Joseph, the prospect of living with this shame might have been just as impossible to understand as a pregnant virgin.

Joseph probably considered the weight of responsibility—and its impact on his fiancée, Mary. How could he teach God's Son anything? Would the Son of God want to play? Would he lead the Son of God in prayer? How would their own children feel? But Joseph put his doubts and questions aside and decided to accept the charge God had given him, regardless of the personal implications. And God blessed him, entrusting him with Jesus, who surely must have been a profound joy to have as his child.

You may have dreamed an impossible dream only to have it turn into a nightmare. Perhaps it was the dream of a perfect child who has turned into a challenging teenager. Maybe you dreamed of a new start but are now struggling to make a blended family work. Perhaps the whispers of others are shouting louder than their praise. You have a world of responsibilities sitting on your shoulders, and you're just not sure you can handle it all.

Do what Joseph did when facing the impossible. Bring Jesus into your home and invite him into your heart. He doesn't know the word *impossible* because with him all things are possible.

Matthew 1:24–25

When Joseph woke up, he did what the angel of the Lord had commanded him and took Mary home as his wife. But he had no union with her until she gave birth to a son. And he gave him the name Jesus.

reflection

1 What "impossible" news do you face?

2 What comfort do you find in the angel's words, "Do not be afraid"?

3 If you haven't asked Jesus to reside in your heart, say a prayer now, asking him to take up residence. Ask him to make the impossible possible by filling you with his Spirit and by giving you new life.

RELATED READINGS

Mark 10:26–29;
Luke 1:37;
Romans 8:28

Go to page 1168 for your next devotional reading.

³When King Herod heard this he was disturbed, and all Jerusalem with him. ⁴When he had called together all the people's chief priests and teachers of the law, he asked them where the Christ*ᵃ* was to be born. ⁵"In Bethlehem in Judea," they replied, "for this is what the prophet has written:

⁶"'But you, Bethlehem, in the land of Judah,
  are by no means least among the rulers
    of Judah;
for out of you will come a ruler
  who will be the shepherd of my people
    Israel.'*ᵇ*"

⁷Then Herod called the Magi secretly and found out from them the exact time the star had appeared. ⁸He sent them to Bethlehem and said, "Go and make a careful search for the child. As soon as you find him, report to me, so that I too may go and worship him."

⁹After they had heard the king, they went on their way, and the star they had seen in the east*ᶜ* went ahead of them until it stopped over the place where the child was. ¹⁰When they saw the star, they were overjoyed. ¹¹On coming to the house, they saw the child with his mother Mary, and they bowed down and worshiped him. Then they opened their treasures and presented him with gifts of gold and of incense and of myrrh. ¹²And having been warned in a dream not to go back to Herod, they returned to their country by another route.

The Escape to Egypt

¹³When they had gone, an angel of the Lord appeared to Joseph in a dream. "Get up," he said, "take the child and his mother and escape to Egypt. Stay there until I tell you, for Herod is going to search for the child to kill him."

¹⁴So he got up, took the child and his mother during the night and left for Egypt, ¹⁵where he stayed until the death of Herod. And so was fulfilled what the Lord had said through the prophet: "Out of Egypt I called my son."*ᵈ*

¹⁶When Herod realized that he had been outwitted by the Magi, he was furious, and he gave orders to kill all the boys in Bethlehem and its vicinity who were two years old and under, in accordance with the time he had learned from the Magi. ¹⁷Then what was said through the prophet Jeremiah was fulfilled:

¹⁸"A voice is heard in Ramah,
  weeping and great mourning,
Rachel weeping for her children
  and refusing to be comforted,
because they are no more."*ᵉ*

The Return to Nazareth

¹⁹After Herod died, an angel of the Lord appeared in a dream to Joseph in Egypt ²⁰and said, "Get up, take the child and his mother and go to the land of Israel, for those who were trying to take the child's life are dead."

²¹So he got up, took the child and his mother and went to the land of Israel. ²²But when he heard that Archelaus was reigning in Judea in place of his father Herod, he was afraid to go there. Having been warned in a dream, he withdrew to the district of Galilee, ²³and he went and lived in a town called Nazareth. So was fulfilled what was said through the prophets: "He will be called a Nazarene."

John the Baptist Prepares the Way

3 In those days John the Baptist came, preaching in the Desert of Judea ²and saying, "Repent, for the kingdom of heaven is near." ³This is he who was spoken of through the prophet Isaiah:

"A voice of one calling in the desert,
'Prepare the way for the Lord,
  make straight paths for him.'"*ᶠ*

⁴John's clothes were made of camel's hair, and he had a leather belt around his waist. His food was locusts and wild honey. ⁵People went out to him from Jerusalem and all Judea and the whole region of the Jordan. ⁶Confessing their sins, they were baptized by him in the Jordan River.

⁷But when he saw many of the Pharisees and Sadducees coming to where he was baptizing, he said to them: "You brood of vipers! Who warned you to flee from the coming wrath? ⁸Produce fruit in keeping with repentance. ⁹And do not think you can say to yourselves, 'We have Abraham as our father.' I tell you that out of these stones God can raise up children

---

*ᵃ*4 Or *Messiah*   *ᵇ*6 Micah 5:2   *ᶜ*9 Or *seen when it rose*   *ᵈ*15 Hosea 11:1   *ᵉ*18 Jer. 31:15   *ᶠ*3 Isaiah 40:3

for Abraham. **10**The ax is already at the root of the trees, and every tree that does not produce good fruit will be cut down and thrown into the fire.

11"I baptize you with*a* water for repentance. But after me will come one who is more powerful than I, whose sandals I am not fit to carry. He will baptize you with the Holy Spirit and with fire. **12**His winnowing fork is in his hand, and he will clear his threshing floor, gathering his wheat into the barn and burning up the chaff with unquenchable fire."

The Baptism of Jesus

13Then Jesus came from Galilee to the Jordan to be baptized by John. **14**But John tried to deter him, saying, "I need to be baptized by you, and do you come to me?"

15Jesus replied, "Let it be so now; it is proper for us to do this to fulfill all righteousness." Then John consented.

16As soon as Jesus was baptized, he went up out of the water. At that moment heaven was opened, and he saw the Spirit of God descending like a dove and lighting on him. **17**And a voice from heaven said, "This is my Son, whom I love; with him I am well pleased."

The Temptation of Jesus

4 Then Jesus was led by the Spirit into the desert to be tempted by the devil. **2**After fasting forty days and forty nights, he was hungry. **3**The tempter came to him and said, "If you are the Son of God, tell these stones to become bread."

4Jesus answered, "It is written: 'Man does not live on bread alone, but on every word that comes from the mouth of God.'*b*"

5Then the devil took him to the holy city and had him stand on the highest point of the temple. **6**"If you are the Son of God," he said, "throw yourself down. For it is written:

"'He will command his angels concerning you,
   and they will lift you up in their hands,
so that you will not strike your foot against a stone.'*c*"

7Jesus answered him, "It is also written: 'Do not put the Lord your God to the test.'*d*"

8Again, the devil took him to a very high mountain and showed him all the kingdoms of the world and their splendor. **9**"All this I will give you," he said, "if you will bow down and worship me."

10Jesus said to him, "Away from me, Satan! For it is written: 'Worship the Lord your God, and serve him only.'*e*"

11Then the devil left him, and angels came and attended him.

Jesus Begins to Preach

12When Jesus heard that John had been put in prison, he returned to Galilee. **13**Leaving Nazareth, he went and lived in Capernaum, which was by the lake in the area of Zebulun and Naphtali— **14**to fulfill what was said through the prophet Isaiah:

15"Land of Zebulun and land of Naphtali,
   the way to the sea, along the Jordan,
   Galilee of the Gentiles—
16the people living in darkness
   have seen a great light;
on those living in the land of the shadow of death
   a light has dawned."*f*

17From that time on Jesus began to preach, "Repent, for the kingdom of heaven is near."

The Calling of the First Disciples

18As Jesus was walking beside the Sea of Galilee, he saw two brothers, Simon called Peter and his brother Andrew. They were casting a net into the lake, for they were fishermen. **19**"Come, follow me," Jesus said, "and I will make you fishers of men." **20**At once they left their nets and followed him.

21Going on from there, he saw two other brothers, James son of Zebedee and his brother John. They were in a boat with their father Zebedee, preparing their nets. Jesus called them, **22**and immediately they left the boat and their father and followed him.

Jesus Heals the Sick

23Jesus went throughout Galilee, teaching in their synagogues, preaching the good news of the kingdom, and healing every disease and sickness among the people. **24**News about him

---

*a*11 Or *in*   *b*4 Deut. 8:3   *c*6 Psalm 91:11,12   *d*7 Deut. 6:16   *e*10 Deut. 6:13   *f*16 Isaiah 9:1,2 spread all over Syria, and people brought to him all who were ill with various diseases, those suffering severe pain, the demon-possessed, those having seizures, and the paralyzed, and he healed them. 25 Large crowds from Galilee, the Decapolis,*a* Jerusalem, Judea and the region across the Jordan followed him.

The Beatitudes

5 Now when he saw the crowds, he went up on a mountainside and sat down. His disciples came to him, 2 and he began to teach them, saying:

3 "Blessed are the poor in spirit,
  for theirs is the kingdom of heaven.
4 Blessed are those who mourn,
  for they will be comforted.
5 Blessed are the meek,
  for they will inherit the earth.
6 Blessed are those who hunger and thirst
    for righteousness,
  for they will be filled.
7 Blessed are the merciful,
  for they will be shown mercy.
8 Blessed are the pure in heart,
  for they will see God.
9 Blessed are the peacemakers,
  for they will be called sons of God.
10 Blessed are those who are persecuted
    because of righteousness,
  for theirs is the kingdom of heaven.

11 "Blessed are you when people insult you, persecute you and falsely say all kinds of evil against you because of me. 12 Rejoice and be glad, because great is your reward in heaven, for in the same way they persecuted the prophets who were before you.

Salt and Light

13 "You are the salt of the earth. But if the salt loses its saltiness, how can it be made salty again? It is no longer good for anything, except to be thrown out and trampled by men.

14 "You are the light of the world. A city on a hill cannot be hidden. 15 Neither do people light a lamp and put it under a bowl. Instead they put it on its stand, and it gives light to everyone in the house. 16 In the same way, let your light shine before men, that they may see your good deeds and praise your Father in heaven.

The Fulfillment of the Law

17 "Do not think that I have come to abolish the Law or the Prophets; I have not come to abolish them but to fulfill them. 18 I tell you the truth, until heaven and earth disappear, not the smallest letter, not the least stroke of a pen, will by any means disappear from the Law until everything is accomplished. 19 Anyone who breaks one of the least of these commandments and teaches others to do the same will be called least in the kingdom of heaven, but whoever practices and teaches these commands will be called great in the kingdom of heaven. 20 For I tell you that unless your righteousness surpasses that of the Pharisees and the teachers of the law, you will certainly not enter the kingdom of heaven.

Murder

21 "You have heard that it was said to the people long ago, 'Do not murder,*b* and anyone who murders will be subject to judgment.' 22 But I tell you that anyone who is angry with his brother*c* will be subject to judgment. Again, anyone who says to his brother, 'Raca,'*d* is answerable to the Sanhedrin. But anyone who says, 'You fool!' will be in danger of the fire of hell.

23 "Therefore, if you are offering your gift at the altar and there remember that your brother has something against you, 24 leave your gift there in front of the altar. First go and be reconciled to your brother; then come and offer your gift.

25 "Settle matters quickly with your adversary who is taking you to court. Do it while you are still with him on the way, or he may hand you over to the judge, and the judge may hand you over to the officer, and you may be thrown into prison. 26 I tell you the truth, you will not get out until you have paid the last penny.*e*

Adultery

27 "You have heard that it was said, 'Do not commit adultery.'*f* 28 But I tell you that anyone who looks at a woman lustfully has already committed adultery with her in his heart. 29 If your right eye causes you to sin, gouge it out

---

a 25 That is, the Ten Cities   *b* 21 Exodus 20:13   *c* 22 Some manuscripts *brother without cause*   *d* 22 An Aramaic term of contempt
e 26 Greek *kodrantes*   *f* 27 Exodus 20:14

and throw it away. It is better for you to lose one part of your body than for your whole body to be thrown into hell. ³⁰And if your right hand causes you to sin, cut it off and throw it away. It is better for you to lose one part of your body than for your whole body to go into hell.

Divorce

³¹"It has been said, 'Anyone who divorces his wife must give her a certificate of divorce.'ᵃ ³²But I tell you that anyone who divorces his wife, except for marital unfaithfulness, causes her to become an adulteress, and anyone who marries the divorced woman commits adultery.

Oaths

³³"Again, you have heard that it was said to the people long ago, 'Do not break your oath, but keep the oaths you have made to the Lord.' ³⁴But I tell you, Do not swear at all: either by heaven, for it is God's throne; ³⁵or by the earth, for it is his footstool; or by Jerusalem, for it is the city of the Great King. ³⁶And do not swear by your head, for you cannot make even one hair white or black. ³⁷Simply let your 'Yes' be 'Yes,' and your 'No,' 'No'; anything beyond this comes from the evil one.

An Eye for an Eye

³⁸"You have heard that it was said, 'Eye for eye, and tooth for tooth.'ᵇ ³⁹But I tell you, Do not resist an evil person. If someone strikes you on the right cheek, turn to him the other also. ⁴⁰And if someone wants to sue you and take your tunic, let him have your cloak as well. ⁴¹If someone forces you to go one mile, go with him two miles. ⁴²Give to the one who asks you, and do not turn away from the one who wants to borrow from you.

Love for Enemies

⁴³"You have heard that it was said, 'Love your neighborᶜ and hate your enemy.' ⁴⁴But I tell you: Love your enemiesᵈ and pray for those

who persecute you, ⁴⁵that you may be sons of your Father in heaven. He causes his sun to rise on the evil and the good, and sends rain on the righteous and the unrighteous. ⁴⁶If you love those who love you, what reward will you get? Are not even the tax collectors doing that? ⁴⁷And if you greet only your brothers, what are you doing more than others? Do not even pagans do that? ⁴⁸Be perfect, therefore, as your heavenly Father is perfect.

Giving to the Needy

6 "Be careful not to do your 'acts of righteousness' before men, to be seen by them. If you do, you will have no reward from your Father in heaven.

²"So when you give to the needy, do not announce it with trumpets, as the hypocrites do in the synagogues and on the streets, to be honored by men. I tell you the truth, they have received their reward in full. ³But when you give to the needy, do not let your left hand know what your right hand is doing, ⁴so that your giving may be in secret. Then your Father, who sees what is done in secret, will reward you.

Prayer

⁵"And when you pray, do not be like the hypocrites, for they love to pray standing in the synagogues and on the street corners to be seen by men. I tell you the truth, they have received their reward in full. ⁶But when you pray, go into your room, close the door and pray to your Father, who is unseen. Then your Father, who sees what is done in secret, will reward you. ⁷And when you pray, do not keep on babbling like pagans, for they think they will be heard because of their many words. ⁸Do not be like them, for your Father knows what you need before you ask him.

⁹"This, then, is how you should pray:

" 'Our Father in heaven,
hallowed be your name,
¹⁰your kingdom come,

Matthew 6:1

God Rewards Sincere Service

"Be careful not to do your 'acts of righteousness' before men, to be seen by them. If you do, you will have no reward from your Father in heaven."

ᵃ31 Deut. 24:1 ᵇ38 Exodus 21:24; Lev. 24:20; Deut. 19:21 ᶜ43 Lev. 19:18 ᵈ44 Some late manuscripts *enemies, bless those who curse you, do good to those who hate you*

your will be done
on earth as it is in heaven.
¹¹Give us today our daily bread.
¹²Forgive us our debts,
as we also have forgiven our debtors.
¹³And lead us not into temptation,
but deliver us from the evil one.ᵃ'

¹⁴For if you forgive men when they sin against you, your heavenly Father will also forgive you. ¹⁵But if you do not forgive men their sins, your Father will not forgive your sins.

Fasting

¹⁶"When you fast, do not look somber as the hypocrites do, for they disfigure their faces to show men they are fasting. I tell you the truth, they have received their reward in full. ¹⁷But when you fast, put oil on your head and wash your face, ¹⁸so that it will not be obvious to men that you are fasting, but only to your Father, who is unseen; and your Father, who sees what is done in secret, will reward you.

Treasures in Heaven

¹⁹"Do not store up for yourselves treasures on earth, where moth and rust destroy, and where thieves break in and steal. ²⁰But store up for yourselves treasures in heaven, where moth and rust do not destroy, and where thieves do not break in and steal. ²¹For where your treasure is, there your heart will be also.

²²"The eye is the lamp of the body. If your eyes are good, your whole body will be full of light. ²³But if your eyes are bad, your whole body will be full of darkness. If then the light within you is darkness, how great is that darkness!

²⁴"No one can serve two masters. Either he will hate the one and love the other, or he will be devoted to the one and despise the other. You cannot serve both God and Money.

Do Not Worry

²⁵"Therefore I tell you, do not worry about your life, what you will eat or drink; or about your body, what you will wear. Is not life more important than food, and the body more important than clothes? ²⁶Look at the birds of the air; they do not sow or reap or store away in barns, and yet your heavenly Father feeds them. Are you not much more valuable than they? ²⁷Who of you by worrying can add a single hour to his lifeᵇ?

²⁸"And why do you worry about clothes? See how the lilies of the field grow. They do not labor or spin. ²⁹Yet I tell you that not even Solomon in all his splendor was dressed like one of these. ³⁰If that is how God clothes the grass of the field, which is here today and tomorrow is thrown into the fire, will he not much more clothe you, O you of little faith? ³¹So do not worry, saying, 'What shall we eat?' or 'What shall we drink?' or 'What shall we wear?' ³²For the pagans run after all these things, and your heavenly Father knows that you need them. ³³But seek first his kingdom and his righteousness, and all these things will be given to you as well. ³⁴Therefore do not worry about tomorrow, for tomorrow will worry about itself. Each day has enough trouble of its own.

Judging Others

7 "Do not judge, or you too will be judged. ²For in the same way you judge others, you will be judged, and with the measure you use, it will be measured to you.

³"Why do you look at the speck of sawdust in your brother's eye and pay no attention to the plank in your own eye? ⁴How can you say to your brother, 'Let me take the speck out of your eye,' when all the time there is a plank in your own eye? ⁵You hypocrite, first take the plank out of your own eye, and then you will see clearly to remove the speck from your brother's eye.

⁶"Do not give dogs what is sacred; do not throw your pearls to pigs. If you do, they may trample them under their feet, and then turn and tear you to pieces.

Ask, Seek, Knock

⁷"Ask and it will be given to you; seek and you will find; knock and the door will be opened to you. ⁸For everyone who asks receives; he who seeks finds; and to him who knocks, the door will be opened.

⁹"Which of you, if his son asks for bread, will give him a stone? ¹⁰Or if he asks for a fish, will

---

ᵃ13 Or *from evil*; some late manuscripts *one, / for yours is the kingdom and the power and the glory forever. Amen.*   ᵇ27 Or *single cubit to his height* give him a snake? ¹¹If you, then, though you are evil, know how to give good gifts to your children, how much more will your Father in heaven give good gifts to those who ask him! ¹²So in everything, do to others what you would have them do to you, for this sums up the Law and the Prophets.

The Narrow and Wide Gates

¹³"Enter through the narrow gate. For wide is the gate and broad is the road that leads to destruction, and many enter through it. ¹⁴But small is the gate and narrow the road that leads to life, and only a few find it.

A Tree and Its Fruit

¹⁵"Watch out for false prophets. They come to you in sheep's clothing, but inwardly they are ferocious wolves. ¹⁶By their fruit you will recognize them. Do people pick grapes from thornbushes, or figs from thistles? ¹⁷Likewise every good tree bears good fruit, but a bad tree bears bad fruit. ¹⁸A good tree cannot bear bad fruit, and a bad tree cannot bear good fruit. ¹⁹Every tree that does not bear good fruit is cut down and thrown into the fire. ²⁰Thus, by their fruit you will recognize them.

²¹"Not everyone who says to me, 'Lord, Lord,' will enter the kingdom of heaven, but only he who does the will of my Father who is in heaven. ²²Many will say to me on that day, 'Lord, Lord, did we not prophesy in your name, and in your name drive out demons and perform many miracles?' ²³Then I will tell them plainly, 'I never knew you. Away from me, you evildoers!'

The Wise and Foolish Builders

²⁴"Therefore everyone who hears these words of mine and puts them into practice is like a wise man who built his house on the rock. ²⁵The rain came down, the streams rose, and the winds blew and beat against that house; yet it did not fall, because it had its foundation on the rock. ²⁶But everyone who hears these words of mine and does not put them into practice is like a foolish man who built his house on sand. ²⁷The rain came down, the streams rose, and the winds blew and beat against that house, and it fell with a great crash."

²⁸When Jesus had finished saying these things, the crowds were amazed at his teaching, ²⁹because he taught as one who had authority, and not as their teachers of the law.

The Man With Leprosy

8 When he came down from the mountainside, large crowds followed him. ²A man with leprosy[a] came and knelt before him and said, "Lord, if you are willing, you can make me clean."

³Jesus reached out his hand and touched the man. "I am willing," he said. "Be clean!" Immediately he was cured[b] of his leprosy. ⁴Then Jesus said to him, "See that you don't tell anyone. But go, show yourself to the priest and offer the gift Moses commanded, as a testimony to them."

The Faith of the Centurion

⁵When Jesus had entered Capernaum, a centurion came to him, asking for help. ⁶"Lord," he said, "my servant lies at home paralyzed and in terrible suffering."

⁷Jesus said to him, "I will go and heal him."

⁸The centurion replied, "Lord, I do not deserve to have you come under my roof. But just say the word, and my servant will be healed. ⁹For I myself am a man under authority, with soldiers under me. I tell this one, 'Go,' and he goes; and that one, 'Come,' and he comes. I say to my servant, 'Do this,' and he does it."

¹⁰When Jesus heard this, he was astonished and said to those following him, "I tell you the truth, I have not found anyone in Israel with such great faith. ¹¹I say to you that many will come from the east and the west, and will take their places at the feast with Abraham, Isaac and Jacob in the kingdom of heaven. ¹²But the subjects of the kingdom will be thrown outside, into the darkness, where there will be weeping and gnashing of teeth."

¹³Then Jesus said to the centurion, "Go! It will be done just as you believed it would." And his servant was healed at that very hour.

Jesus Heals Many

¹⁴When Jesus came into Peter's house, he saw Peter's mother-in-law lying in bed with a fever. ¹⁵He touched her hand and the fever

---

a2 The Greek word was used for various diseases affecting the skin—not necessarily leprosy.   *b3* Greek *made clean*

Matthew 7:11

"If you, then, though you are evil, know how to give good gifts to your children, how much more will your Father in heaven give good gifts to those who ask him!"

reflection

1 What is one good gift that God has offered you today? How have you embraced it?

2 In what ways do your memories of your earthly parents affect how you read this passage?

3 What spiritual gifts have you been given? Spend some time in prayer, asking your heavenly Father for gifts to build his body, the church.

RELATED READINGS

Romans 12:3–8;
1 Corinthians 12:4–31;
Ephesians 3:14–21;
James 1:17–18

"To remain a child before God is to recognize our nothingness, to expect everything from God as a little child expects everything from its father."

Therese of Liseux

Read: Matthew 7:7–29

ACCORDING TO RECENT STATISTICS, parents spend an average of $1,500 a year on clothes for their kids and $450 a year on furnishings for their kids' rooms. Children as young as elementary school age have cell phones, portable digital audio players, high-definition televisions and multiple video game platforms. Every year, parents in the United States spend tens of billions of dollars on Christmas gifts for their kids.

These statistics reflect more than rampant consumerism. They reflect the desire of parents to give gifts to their kids. Parents have always wanted their children to have good things.

Jesus used this universal truth to teach us of the power of prayer. It is a natural instinct to care for our child, to respond when our child asks for help or food or even a present. How much more will our heavenly Father give good gifts to his children!

Unlike earthly parents, God the Father gives *perfect* gifts because they are spiritual gifts uniquely suited to each of us. There's no such thing as a Christian who's been spoiled rotten with spiritual gifts. God gives us gifts that fit us perfectly, gifts that fill and complete us. How are we to respond to such generosity? By using those gifts to the utmost. Isn't that what every parent wants their child to do? We offer our children good things, so they'll know they are loved. But we want them to use their gifts often and take care of them.

And God wants us to *delight* in his good gifts. What parent wants a child to put a present back under the Christmas tree and walk away disappointed? We want to see joy on our child's face as she receives gifts from us. We want her to enjoy what we have given her. We know she loves her doll if she picks it up and hugs it. We're sure he loves his bike if he climbs on and rides it. Our heavenly Father longs for us to enjoy the gifts he gives, to wrap our arms around them and use them for his good pleasure. God's gifts are there for the taking . . . with pleasure.

Tuesday

Go to page 1171 for your next devotional reading.

left her, and she got up and began to wait on him.

¹⁶When evening came, many who were demon-possessed were brought to him, and he drove out the spirits with a word and healed all the sick. ¹⁷This was to fulfill what was spoken through the prophet Isaiah:

"He took up our infirmities
and carried our diseases."*a*

The Cost of Following Jesus

¹⁸When Jesus saw the crowd around him, he gave orders to cross to the other side of the lake. ¹⁹Then a teacher of the law came to him and said, "Teacher, I will follow you wherever you go."

²⁰Jesus replied, "Foxes have holes and birds of the air have nests, but the Son of Man has no place to lay his head."

²¹Another disciple said to him, "Lord, first let me go and bury my father."

²²But Jesus told him, "Follow me, and let the dead bury their own dead."

Jesus Calms the Storm

²³Then he got into the boat and his disciples followed him. ²⁴Without warning, a furious storm came up on the lake, so that the waves swept over the boat. But Jesus was sleeping. ²⁵The disciples went and woke him, saying, "Lord, save us! We're going to drown!"

²⁶He replied, "You of little faith, why are you so afraid?" Then he got up and rebuked the winds and the waves, and it was completely calm.

²⁷The men were amazed and asked, "What kind of man is this? Even the winds and the waves obey him!"

The Healing of Two Demon-possessed Men

²⁸When he arrived at the other side in the region of the Gadarenes,*b* two demon-possessed men coming from the tombs met him. They were so violent that no one could pass that way. ²⁹"What do you want with us, Son of God?"

they shouted. "Have you come here to torture us before the appointed time?"

³⁰Some distance from them a large herd of pigs was feeding. ³¹The demons begged Jesus, "If you drive us out, send us into the herd of pigs."

³²He said to them, "Go!" So they came out and went into the pigs, and the whole herd rushed down the steep bank into the lake and died in the water. ³³Those tending the pigs ran off, went into the town and reported all this, including what had happened to the demon-possessed men. ³⁴Then the whole town went out to meet Jesus. And when they saw him, they pleaded with him to leave their region.

Jesus Heals a Paralytic

9 Jesus stepped into a boat, crossed over and came to his own town. ²Some men brought to him a paralytic, lying on a mat. When Jesus saw their faith, he said to the paralytic, "Take heart, son; your sins are forgiven."

³At this, some of the teachers of the law said to themselves, "This fellow is blaspheming!"

⁴Knowing their thoughts, Jesus said, "Why do you entertain evil thoughts in your hearts? ⁵Which is easier: to say, 'Your sins are forgiven,' or to say, 'Get up and walk'? ⁶But so that you may know that the Son of Man has authority on earth to forgive sins…" Then he said to the paralytic, "Get up, take your mat and go home." ⁷And the man got up and went home. ⁸When the crowd saw this, they were filled with awe; and they praised God, who had given such authority to men.

Matthew 9:6

God Forgives Sins

"But so that you may know that the Son of Man has authority on earth to forgive sins . . ." Then he said to the paralytic, "Get up, take your mat and go home."

The Calling of Matthew

⁹As Jesus went on from there, he saw a man named Matthew sitting at the tax collector's booth. "Follow me," he told him, and Matthew got up and followed him.

¹⁰While Jesus was having dinner at Matthew's house, many tax collectors and "sinners"

a17 Isaiah 53:4   *b28* Some manuscripts *Gergesenes*; others *Gerasenes*

came and ate with him and his disciples.
¹¹When the Pharisees saw this, they asked his
disciples, "Why does your teacher eat with tax
collectors and 'sinners'?"

¹²On hearing this, Jesus said, "It is not the
healthy who need a doctor, but the sick. ¹³But
go and learn what this means: 'I desire mercy,
not sacrifice.'ᵃ For I have not come to call the
righteous, but sinners."

Jesus Questioned About Fasting

¹⁴Then John's disciples came and asked him,
"How is it that we and the Pharisees fast, but
your disciples do not fast?"

¹⁵Jesus answered, "How can the guests of
the bridegroom mourn while he is with them?
The time will come when the bridegroom will
be taken from them; then they will fast.

¹⁶"No one sews a patch of unshrunk cloth
on an old garment, for the patch will pull away
from the garment, making the tear worse. ¹⁷Nei-
ther do men pour new wine into old wineskins.
If they do, the skins will burst, the wine will run
out and the wineskins will be ruined. No, they
pour new wine into new wineskins, and both
are preserved."

A Dead Girl and a Sick Woman

¹⁸While he was saying this, a ruler came and
knelt before him and said, "My daughter has
just died. But come and put your hand on her,
and she will live." ¹⁹Jesus got up and went with
him, and so did his disciples.

²⁰Just then a woman who had been subject
to bleeding for twelve years came up behind
him and touched the edge of his cloak. ²¹She
said to herself, "If I only touch his cloak, I will
be healed."

²²Jesus turned and saw her. "Take heart,
daughter," he said, "your faith has healed you."
And the woman was healed from that moment.

²³When Jesus entered the ruler's house and
saw the flute players and the noisy crowd, ²⁴he
said, "Go away. The girl is not dead but asleep."
But they laughed at him. ²⁵After the crowd had
been put outside, he went in and took the girl
by the hand, and she got up. ²⁶News of this
spread through all that region.

Jesus Heals the Blind and Mute

²⁷As Jesus went on from there, two blind
men followed him, calling out, "Have mercy
on us, Son of David!"

²⁸When he had gone indoors, the blind men
came to him, and he asked them, "Do you believe that I am able to do this?"

"Yes, Lord," they replied.

²⁹Then he touched their eyes and said, "According to your faith will it be done to you";
³⁰and their sight was restored. Jesus warned
them sternly, "See that no one knows about
this." ³¹But they went out and spread the news
about him all over that region.

³²While they were going out, a man who
was demon-possessed and could not talk was
brought to Jesus. ³³And when the demon was
driven out, the man who had been mute spoke.
The crowd was amazed and said, "Nothing like
this has ever been seen in Israel."

³⁴But the Pharisees said, "It is by the prince
of demons that he drives out demons."

The Workers Are Few

³⁵Jesus went through all the towns and
villages, teaching in their synagogues, preaching the good news of the kingdom and healing
every disease and sickness. ³⁶When he saw the
crowds, he had compassion on them, because
they were harassed and helpless, like sheep without a shepherd. ³⁷Then he said to his disciples,
"The harvest is plentiful but the workers are
few. ³⁸Ask the Lord of the harvest, therefore,
to send out workers into his harvest field."

Jesus Sends Out the Twelve

10 He called his twelve disciples to him
and gave them authority to drive out
evilᵇ spirits and to heal every disease and sickness.

²These are the names of the twelve apostles: first, Simon (who is called Peter) and his
brother Andrew; James son of Zebedee, and
his brother John; ³Philip and Bartholomew;
Thomas and Matthew the tax collector; James
son of Alphaeus, and Thaddaeus; ⁴Simon the
Zealot and Judas Iscariot, who betrayed him.

⁵These twelve Jesus sent out with the following instructions: "Do not go among the Gentiles or enter any town of the Samaritans. ⁶Go

ᵃ13 Hosea 6:6   ᵇ1 Greek unclean

Press Toward Jesus

Read: Matthew 9:20–22

JOANNA LOOKED AT HERSELF in the mirror and sighed—a sigh of total, utter exhaustion. She felt much older than her 34 years. It felt as though she had been struggling with insomnia, muscle pain and fatigue forever. One doctor diagnosed her with Epstein Barr. Another with depression. Another simply said she didn't have a diagnosis. One seemed to hint that she was making up her symptoms.

Joanna knew God was in control, but it was hard to trust on days like this when all she wanted to do was crawl under the covers and sob. "God, where are you?" she cried. "How much longer do I have to go through this?" Joanna was desperate, so she leaned on Jesus. No, he didn't miraculously heal her. But he graciously helped her each and every day as she leaned on him for strength.

The woman who touched Jesus' cloak must have felt the same sort of desperation. The Bible says she had been bleeding for 12 years. Not only was she suffering physically, she was also probably suffering emotionally. In Jewish society, such a woman would have been labeled "unclean." Because of this status, she would have been considered an outcast. The loneliness and isolation must have felt overwhelming. No wonder she pressed through the multitude of people who were following the Messiah. She must have believed that touching him was her only hope.

Imagine her breathless expectation as she reached toward Jesus . . . and her overwhelming relief when she realized that he had, indeed, relieved her suffering. What joy must have flooded her the very instant she touched the hem of his cloak!

Are you feeling desperate like these two women? Do you cry for relief from a lingering illness? If so, take comfort in the fact that Jesus is near and that he is the Great Physician. Sometimes, he heals in an instant, as he did in this story. At other times, he heals over a period of years or he waits to heal, allowing us to press into him so that he can "strengthen [us] with power through his Spirit in [our] inner being" (Ephesians 3:16). At still other times, he does not heal. Then, like Paul, we learn that "[God's] power is made perfect in weakness" (2 Corinthians 12:9).

The ways in which God ministers to people are as varied as the people he touches—but he is *always* faithful to bring peace and joy, even in midst of our suffering. Today, press close to him. You'll experience his power.

Matthew 9:20–21

Just then a woman who had been subject to bleeding for twelve years came up behind him and touched the edge of his cloak. She said to herself, "If I only touch his cloak, I will be healed."

reflection

1 Describe an area of your life in which you feel truly desperate.

2 How have you felt isolated from others because of your circumstances?

3 Press into Jesus in prayer. Ask him to restore you to fellowship with him and fellowship with believers. Ask him to heal you physically, emotionally and spiritually. If he chooses not to heal you this day, ask him to strengthen you with his power instead.

RELATED READINGS

Luke 4:16–19;
2 Corinthians 12:7–9;
Hebrews 10:19–25

Wednesday

Go to page 1176 for your next devotional reading.

rather to the lost sheep of Israel. ⁷As you go, preach this message: 'The kingdom of heaven is near.' ⁸Heal the sick, raise the dead, cleanse those who have leprosy,ᵃ drive out demons. Freely you have received, freely give. ⁹Do not take along any gold or silver or copper in your belts; ¹⁰take no bag for the journey, or extra tunic, or sandals or a staff; for the worker is worth his keep.

¹¹"Whatever town or village you enter, search for some worthy person there and stay at his house until you leave. ¹²As you enter the home, give it your greeting. ¹³If the home is deserving, let your peace rest on it; if it is not, let your peace return to you. ¹⁴If anyone will not welcome you or listen to your words, shake the dust off your feet when you leave that home or town. ¹⁵I tell you the truth, it will be more bearable for Sodom and Gomorrah on the day of judgment than for that town. ¹⁶I am sending you out like sheep among wolves. Therefore be as shrewd as snakes and as innocent as doves.

¹⁷"Be on your guard against men; they will hand you over to the local councils and flog you in their synagogues. ¹⁸On my account you will be brought before governors and kings as witnesses to them and to the Gentiles. ¹⁹But when they arrest you, do not worry about what to say or how to say it. At that time you will be given what to say, ²⁰for it will not be you speaking, but the Spirit of your Father speaking through you.

²¹"Brother will betray brother to death, and a father his child; children will rebel against their parents and have them put to death. ²²All men will hate you because of me, but he who stands firm to the end will be saved. ²³When you are persecuted in one place, flee to another. I tell you the truth, you will not finish going through the cities of Israel before the Son of Man comes.

²⁴"A student is not above his teacher, nor a servant above his master. ²⁵It is enough for the student to be like his teacher, and the servant like his master. If the head of the house has been called Beelzebub,ᵇ how much more the members of his household!

²⁶"So do not be afraid of them. There is nothing concealed that will not be disclosed, or hidden that will not be made known. ²⁷What I tell you in the dark, speak in the daylight; what is whispered in your ear, proclaim from the roofs. ²⁸Do not be afraid of those who kill the body but cannot kill the soul. Rather, be afraid of the One who can destroy both soul and body in hell. ²⁹Are not two sparrows sold for a pennyᶜ? Yet not one of them will fall to the ground apart from the will of your Father. ³⁰And even the very hairs of your head are all numbered. ³¹So don't be afraid; you are worth more than many sparrows.

³²"Whoever acknowledges me before men, I will also acknowledge him before my Father in heaven. ³³But whoever disowns me before men, I will disown him before my Father in heaven.

³⁴"Do not suppose that I have come to bring peace to the earth. I did not come to bring peace, but a sword. ³⁵For I have come to turn

"'a man against his father,
     a daughter against her mother,
a daughter-in-law against her mother-in-law—
³⁶   a man's enemies will be the members of
          his own household.'ᵈ

³⁷"Anyone who loves his father or mother more than me is not worthy of me; anyone who loves his son or daughter more than me is not worthy of me; ³⁸and anyone who does not take his cross and follow me is not worthy of me. ³⁹Whoever finds his life will lose it, and whoever loses his life for my sake will find it.

⁴⁰"He who receives you receives me, and he who receives me receives the one who sent me.

Matthew 10:29

God Watches Over All

"Are not two sparrows sold for a penny? Yet not one of them will fall to the ground apart from the will of your Father."

ᵃ8 The Greek word was used for various diseases affecting the skin—not necessarily leprosy.   ᵇ25 Greek *Beezeboul* or *Beelzeboul*   ᶜ29 Greek *an assarion*   ᵈ36 Micah 7:6

41Anyone who receives a prophet because he is a prophet will receive a prophet's reward, and anyone who receives a righteous man because he is a righteous man will receive a righteous man's reward. 42And if anyone gives even a cup of cold water to one of these little ones because he is my disciple, I tell you the truth, he will certainly not lose his reward."

Jesus and John the Baptist

11 After Jesus had finished instructing his twelve disciples, he went on from there to teach and preach in the towns of Galilee.*a*

2When John heard in prison what Christ was doing, he sent his disciples 3to ask him, "Are you the one who was to come, or should we expect someone else?"

4Jesus replied, "Go back and report to John what you hear and see: 5The blind receive sight, the lame walk, those who have leprosy*b* are cured, the deaf hear, the dead are raised, and the good news is preached to the poor. 6Blessed is the man who does not fall away on account of me."

7As John's disciples were leaving, Jesus began to speak to the crowd about John: "What did you go out into the desert to see? A reed swayed by the wind? 8If not, what did you go out to see? A man dressed in fine clothes? No, those who wear fine clothes are in kings' palaces. 9Then what did you go out to see? A prophet? Yes, I tell you, and more than a prophet. 10This is the one about whom it is written:

"'I will send my messenger ahead of you,
who will prepare your way before you.'*c*

11I tell you the truth: Among those born of women there has not risen anyone greater than John the Baptist; yet he who is least in the kingdom of heaven is greater than he. 12From the days of John the Baptist until now, the kingdom of heaven has been forcefully advancing, and forceful men lay hold of it. 13For all the Prophets and the Law prophesied until John. 14And if you are willing to accept it, he is the Elijah who was to come. 15He who has ears, let him hear.

16"To what can I compare this generation? They are like children sitting in the marketplaces and calling out to others:

17"'We played the flute for you,
and you did not dance;
we sang a dirge,
and you did not mourn.'

18For John came neither eating nor drinking, and they say, 'He has a demon.' 19The Son of Man came eating and drinking, and they say, 'Here is a glutton and a drunkard, a friend of tax collectors and "sinners."' But wisdom is proved right by her actions."

Woe on Unrepentant Cities

20Then Jesus began to denounce the cities in which most of his miracles had been performed, because they did not repent. 21"Woe to you, Korazin! Woe to you, Bethsaida! If the miracles that were performed in you had been performed in Tyre and Sidon, they would have repented long ago in sackcloth and ashes. 22But I tell you, it will be more bearable for Tyre and Sidon on the day of judgment than for you. 23And you, Capernaum, will you be lifted up to the skies? No, you will go down to the depths.*d* If the miracles that were performed in you had been performed in Sodom, it would have remained to this day. 24But I tell you that it will be more bearable for Sodom on the day of judgment than for you."

Rest for the Weary

25At that time Jesus said, "I praise you, Father, Lord of heaven and earth, because you have hidden these things from the wise and learned, and revealed them to little children. 26Yes, Father, for this was your good pleasure.

27"All things have been committed to me by my Father. No one knows the Son except the Father, and no one knows the Father except the Son and those to whom the Son chooses to reveal him.

28"Come to me, all you who are weary and burdened, and I will give you rest. 29Take my yoke upon you and learn from me, for I am gentle and humble in heart, and you will find rest for your souls. 30For my yoke is easy and my burden is light."

*a*1 Greek *in their towns*   *b*5 The Greek word was used for various diseases affecting the skin—not necessarily leprosy.   *c*10 Mal. 3:1
*d*23 Greek *Hades*

Lord of the Sabbath

12 At that time Jesus went through the grainfields on the Sabbath. His disciples were hungry and began to pick some heads of grain and eat them. ²When the Pharisees saw this, they said to him, "Look! Your disciples are doing what is unlawful on the Sabbath."

³He answered, "Haven't you read what David did when he and his companions were hungry? ⁴He entered the house of God, and he and his companions ate the consecrated bread—which was not lawful for them to do, but only for the priests. ⁵Or haven't you read in the Law that on the Sabbath the priests in the temple desecrate the day and yet are innocent? ⁶I tell you that one*a* greater than the temple is here. ⁷If you had known what these words mean, 'I desire mercy, not sacrifice,'*b* you would not have condemned the innocent. ⁸For the Son of Man is Lord of the Sabbath."

⁹Going on from that place, he went into their synagogue, ¹⁰and a man with a shriveled hand was there. Looking for a reason to accuse Jesus, they asked him, "Is it lawful to heal on the Sabbath?"

¹¹He said to them, "If any of you has a sheep and it falls into a pit on the Sabbath, will you not take hold of it and lift it out? ¹²How much more valuable is a man than a sheep! Therefore it is lawful to do good on the Sabbath."

¹³Then he said to the man, "Stretch out your hand." So he stretched it out and it was completely restored, just as sound as the other. ¹⁴But the Pharisees went out and plotted how they might kill Jesus.

God's Chosen Servant

¹⁵Aware of this, Jesus withdrew from that place. Many followed him, and he healed all their sick, ¹⁶warning them not to tell who he was. ¹⁷This was to fulfill what was spoken through the prophet Isaiah:

¹⁸"Here is my servant whom I have chosen,
  the one I love, in whom I delight;
I will put my Spirit on him,

and he will proclaim justice to the
  nations.
¹⁹He will not quarrel or cry out;
  no one will hear his voice
    in the streets.
²⁰A bruised reed he will not
    break,
  and a smoldering wick
    he will not snuff
    out,
  till he leads justice to
    victory.
²¹ In his name the nations
    will put their
    hope."*c*

Matthew 11:28

God Gives Rest to the Weary

"Come to me, all you who are weary and burdened, and I will give you rest."

Jesus and Beelzebub

²²Then they brought him a demon-possessed man who was blind and mute, and Jesus healed him, so that he could both talk and see. ²³All the people were astonished and said, "Could this be the Son of David?"

²⁴But when the Pharisees heard this, they said, "It is only by Beelzebub,*d* the prince of demons, that this fellow drives out demons."

²⁵Jesus knew their thoughts and said to them, "Every kingdom divided against itself will be ruined, and every city or household divided against itself will not stand. ²⁶If Satan drives out Satan, he is divided against himself. How then can his kingdom stand? ²⁷And if I drive out demons by Beelzebub, by whom do your people drive them out? So then, they will be your judges. ²⁸But if I drive out demons by the Spirit of God, then the kingdom of God has come upon you.

²⁹"Or again, how can anyone enter a strong man's house and carry off his possessions unless he first ties up the strong man? Then he can rob his house.

³⁰"He who is not with me is against me, and he who does not gather with me scatters. ³¹And so I tell you, every sin and blasphemy will be forgiven men, but the blasphemy against the Spirit will not be forgiven. ³²Anyone who speaks a word against the Son of Man will be forgiven, but anyone who speaks against the Holy Spirit will not be forgiven, either in this age or in the age to come.

a6 Or something; also in verses 41 and 42 *b7 Hosea 6:6 c21 Isaiah 42:1–4 d24 Greek Beezeboul or Beelzeboul*; also in verse 27

33"Make a tree good and its fruit will be good, or make a tree bad and its fruit will be bad, for a tree is recognized by its fruit. 34You brood of vipers, how can you who are evil say anything good? For out of the overflow of the heart the mouth speaks. 35The good man brings good things out of the good stored up in him, and the evil man brings evil things out of the evil stored up in him. 36But I tell you that men will have to give account on the day of judgment for every careless word they have spoken. 37For by your words you will be acquitted, and by your words you will be condemned."

The Sign of Jonah

38Then some of the Pharisees and teachers of the law said to him, "Teacher, we want to see a miraculous sign from you."

39He answered, "A wicked and adulterous generation asks for a miraculous sign! But none will be given it except the sign of the prophet Jonah. 40For as Jonah was three days and three nights in the belly of a huge fish, so the Son of Man will be three days and three nights in the heart of the earth. 41The men of Nineveh will stand up at the judgment with this generation and condemn it; for they repented at the preaching of Jonah, and now one*a* greater than Jonah is here. 42The Queen of the South will rise at the judgment with this generation and condemn it; for she came from the ends of the earth to listen to Solomon's wisdom, and now one greater than Solomon is here.

43"When an evil*b* spirit comes out of a man, it goes through arid places seeking rest and does not find it. 44Then it says, 'I will return to the house I left.' When it arrives, it finds the house unoccupied, swept clean and put in order. 45Then it goes and takes with it seven other spirits more wicked than itself, and they go in and live there. And the final condition of that man is worse than the first. That is how it will be with this wicked generation."

Jesus' Mother and Brothers

46While Jesus was still talking to the crowd, his mother and brothers stood outside, wanting to speak to him. 47Someone told him, "Your mother and brothers are standing outside, wanting to speak to you."*c*

48He replied to him, "Who is my mother, and who are my brothers?" 49Pointing to his disciples, he said, "Here are my mother and my brothers. 50For whoever does the will of my Father in heaven is my brother and sister and mother."

The Parable of the Sower

13 That same day Jesus went out of the house and sat by the lake. 2Such large crowds gathered around him that he got into a boat and sat in it, while all the people stood on the shore. 3Then he told them many things in parables, saying: "A farmer went out to sow his seed. 4As he was scattering the seed, some fell along the path, and the birds came and ate it up. 5Some fell on rocky places, where it did not have much soil. It sprang up quickly, because the soil was shallow. 6But when the sun came up, the plants were scorched, and they withered because they had no root. 7Other seed fell among thorns, which grew up and choked the plants. 8Still other seed fell on good soil, where it produced a crop—a hundred, sixty or thirty times what was sown. 9He who has ears, let him hear."

10The disciples came to him and asked, "Why do you speak to the people in parables?"

11He replied, "The knowledge of the secrets of the kingdom of heaven has been given to you, but not to them. 12Whoever has will be given more, and he will have an abundance. Whoever does not have, even what he has will be taken from him. 13This is why I speak to them in parables:

"Though seeing, they do not see;
    though hearing, they do not hear or
        understand.

14In them is fulfilled the prophecy of Isaiah:

"'You will be ever hearing but never
        understanding;
    you will be ever seeing but never
        perceiving.
15For this people's heart has become
        calloused;
    they hardly hear with their ears,
    and they have closed their eyes.
Otherwise they might see with their eyes,

---

*a*41 Or *something*; also in verse 42   *b*43 Greek *unclean*   *c*47 Some manuscripts do not have verse 47.

Buried Treasure

Matthew 13:13

"This is why I speak to them in parables."

reflection

1 What Bible study tools or methods do you use on a daily basis?

2 Which of the following would you use to describe your time with God's Word: skimming the surface or digging for treasure?

3 What new treasure has God revealed to you lately? What could you do with that new insight?

RELATED READINGS

Psalm 78:1–4;
Proverbs 1:5–7; 2:3–5;
Mark 4:10–12;
Romans 11:33

Read: Matthew 13:1–58

ARE YOU DIGGING for buried treasure? If not, you should know that it's waiting there for you.

But wait. Don't reach for a shovel just yet. For this kind of digging, you need other kinds of tools: your Bible, a concordance and maybe a reliable commentary or two. And bring along your mind, heart, time and a bit of patience. You may ask, "What kind of treasure can I find with these tools?" The answer is profound. You'll find a wealth of God's wisdom that can only be found when you search for it as if you were digging for gold or silver buried beneath the earth's surface.

You may have noticed that if you read Scripture simply to check it off your to-do list, you don't gain much insight. But when you pray, when you compare one Scripture with another, when you meditate on verses, then you gain insight—then you find the golden nuggets of wisdom and truth that have been there all the time, buried beneath the surface.

In Matthew 11 and 12, Jesus had pronounced judgment on the unrepentant and especially the religious leaders who were uniting against him. But in Matthew 13, Jesus changed his approach in speaking to the crowds. He started teaching in parables—earthly stories with heavenly meanings. Only those who wanted to dig deep enough could understand what he was really saying. Others might pass Christ's teachings off as simple stories. But these "simple stories" were eternal stories—helping generations understand spiritual principles through physical metaphors. Rural folk could grasp the kingdom of heaven by looking at a farmer working in the fields. People in business could comprehend the kingdom of heaven through stories of faithful or evil servants. All could look forward to Christ's return via the story of a wedding and bridegroom. Simple stories—profound truth.

Jesus gladly answered his disciples' questions about his parables and gave them the interpretations. His hidden truths are an open secret for those who are really looking. When you ask the Holy Spirit to give you ears to hear and eyes to see, God will open his treasure house and give you fresh insight into his parables. Ask him for understanding, and he'll help you unearth buried treasure.

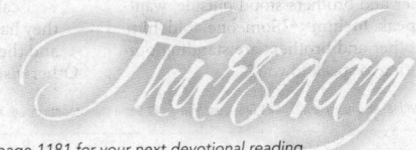

Thursday

Go to page 1181 for your next devotional reading.

hear with their ears,
understand with their hearts
and turn, and I would heal them.'[a]

16But blessed are your eyes because they see, and your ears because they hear. 17For I tell you the truth, many prophets and righteous men longed to see what you see but did not see it, and to hear what you hear but did not hear it.

18"Listen then to what the parable of the sower means: 19When anyone hears the message about the kingdom and does not understand it, the evil one comes and snatches away what was sown in his heart. This is the seed sown along the path. 20The one who received the seed that fell on rocky places is the man who hears the word and at once receives it with joy. 21But since he has no root, he lasts only a short time. When trouble or persecution comes because of the word, he quickly falls away. 22The one who received the seed that fell among the thorns is the man who hears the word, but the worries of this life and the deceitfulness of wealth choke it, making it unfruitful. 23But the one who received the seed that fell on good soil is the man who hears the word and understands it. He produces a crop, yielding a hundred, sixty or thirty times what was sown."

The Parable of the Weeds

24Jesus told them another parable: "The kingdom of heaven is like a man who sowed good seed in his field. 25But while everyone was sleeping, his enemy came and sowed weeds among the wheat, and went away. 26When the wheat sprouted and formed heads, then the weeds also appeared.

27"The owner's servants came to him and said, 'Sir, didn't you sow good seed in your field? Where then did the weeds come from?'

28" 'An enemy did this,' he replied.

"The servants asked him, 'Do you want us to go and pull them up?'

29" 'No,' he answered, 'because while you are pulling the weeds, you may root up the wheat with them. 30Let both grow together until the harvest. At that time I will tell the harvesters: First collect the weeds and tie them in bundles to be burned; then gather the wheat and bring it into my barn.' "

The Parables of the Mustard Seed and the Yeast

31He told them another parable: "The kingdom of heaven is like a mustard seed, which a man took and planted in his field. 32Though it is the smallest of all your seeds, yet when it grows, it is the largest of garden plants and becomes a tree, so that the birds of the air come and perch in its branches."

33He told them still another parable: "The kingdom of heaven is like yeast that a woman took and mixed into a large amount[b] of flour until it worked all through the dough."

34Jesus spoke all these things to the crowd in parables; he did not say anything to them without using a parable. 35So was fulfilled what was spoken through the prophet:

"I will open my mouth in parables,
    I will utter things hidden since the
        creation of the world."[c]

The Parable of the Weeds Explained

36Then he left the crowd and went into the house. His disciples came to him and said, "Explain to us the parable of the weeds in the field."

37He answered, "The one who sowed the good seed is the Son of Man. 38The field is the world, and the good seed stands for the sons of the kingdom. The weeds are the sons of the evil one, 39and the enemy who sows them is the devil. The harvest is the end of the age, and the harvesters are angels.

40"As the weeds are pulled up and burned in the fire, so it will be at the end of the age. 41The Son of Man will send out his angels, and they will weed out of his kingdom everything that causes sin and all who do evil. 42They will throw them into the fiery furnace, where there will be weeping and gnashing of teeth. 43Then the righteous will shine like the sun in the kingdom of their Father. He who has ears, let him hear.

The Parables of the Hidden Treasure and the Pearl

44"The kingdom of heaven is like treasure hidden in a field. When a man found it, he hid it again, and then in his joy went and sold all he had and bought that field.

[a]15 Isaiah 6:9,10   [b]33 Greek *three satas* (probably about 1/2 bushel or 22 liters)   [c]35 Psalm 78:2

45"Again, the kingdom of heaven is like a merchant looking for fine pearls. **46**When he found one of great value, he went away and sold everything he had and bought it.

The Parable of the Net

47"Once again, the kingdom of heaven is like a net that was let down into the lake and caught all kinds of fish. **48**When it was full, the fishermen pulled it up on the shore. Then they sat down and collected the good fish in baskets, but threw the bad away. **49**This is how it will be at the end of the age. The angels will come and separate the wicked from the righteous **50**and throw them into the fiery furnace, where there will be weeping and gnashing of teeth.

51"Have you understood all these things?" Jesus asked.

"Yes," they replied.

52He said to them, "Therefore every teacher of the law who has been instructed about the kingdom of heaven is like the owner of a house who brings out of his storeroom new treasures as well as old."

A Prophet Without Honor

53When Jesus had finished these parables, he moved on from there. **54**Coming to his hometown, he began teaching the people in their synagogue, and they were amazed. "Where did this man get this wisdom and these miraculous powers?" they asked. **55**"Isn't this the carpenter's son? Isn't his mother's name Mary, and aren't his brothers James, Joseph, Simon and Judas? **56**Aren't all his sisters with us? Where then did this man get all these things?" **57**And they took offense at him.

But Jesus said to them, "Only in his hometown and in his own house is a prophet without honor."

58And he did not do many miracles there because of their lack of faith.

John the Baptist Beheaded

14 At that time Herod the tetrarch heard the reports about Jesus, **2**and he said to his attendants, "This is John the Baptist; he has risen from the dead! That is why miraculous powers are at work in him."

3Now Herod had arrested John and bound him and put him in prison because of Herodias, his brother Philip's wife, **4**for John had been saying to him: "It is not lawful for you to have her." **5**Herod wanted to kill John, but he was afraid of the people, because they considered him a prophet.

6On Herod's birthday the daughter of Herodias danced for them and pleased Herod so much **7**that he promised with an oath to give her whatever she asked. **8**Prompted by her mother, she said, "Give me here on a platter the head of John the Baptist." **9**The king was distressed, but because of his oaths and his dinner guests, he ordered that her request be granted **10**and had John beheaded in the prison. **11**His head was brought in on a platter and given to the girl, who carried it to her mother. **12**John's disciples came and took his body and buried it. Then they went and told Jesus.

Jesus Feeds the Five Thousand

13When Jesus heard what had happened, he withdrew by boat privately to a solitary place. Hearing of this, the crowds followed him on foot from the towns. **14**When Jesus landed and saw a large crowd, he had compassion on them and healed their sick.

Matthew 14:14

God Has Compassion

When Jesus landed and saw a large crowd, he had compassion on them and healed their sick.

15As evening approached, the disciples came to him and said, "This is a remote place, and it's already getting late. Send the crowds away, so they can go to the villages and buy themselves some food."

16Jesus replied, "They do not need to go away. You give them something to eat."

17"We have here only five loaves of bread and two fish," they answered.

18"Bring them here to me," he said. **19**And he directed the people to sit down on the grass. Taking the five loaves and the two fish and looking up to heaven, he gave thanks and broke the loaves. Then he gave them to the disciples, and the disciples gave them to the people. **20**They all ate and were satisfied, and the disciples picked up twelve basketfuls of broken pieces that were left over. ²¹The number of those who ate was about five thousand men, besides women and children.

Jesus Walks on the Water

²²Immediately Jesus made the disciples get into the boat and go on ahead of him to the other side, while he dismissed the crowd. ²³After he had dismissed them, he went up on a mountainside by himself to pray. When evening came, he was there alone, ²⁴but the boat was already a considerable distance*ᵃ* from land, buffeted by the waves because the wind was against it.

²⁵During the fourth watch of the night Jesus went out to them, walking on the lake. ²⁶When the disciples saw him walking on the lake, they were terrified. "It's a ghost," they said, and cried out in fear.

²⁷But Jesus immediately said to them: "Take courage! It is I. Don't be afraid."

²⁸"Lord, if it's you," Peter replied, "tell me to come to you on the water."

²⁹"Come," he said.

Then Peter got down out of the boat, walked on the water and came toward Jesus. ³⁰But when he saw the wind, he was afraid and, beginning to sink, cried out, "Lord, save me!"

³¹Immediately Jesus reached out his hand and caught him. "You of little faith," he said, "why did you doubt?"

³²And when they climbed into the boat, the wind died down. ³³Then those who were in the boat worshiped him, saying, "Truly you are the Son of God."

³⁴When they had crossed over, they landed at Gennesaret. ³⁵And when the men of that place recognized Jesus, they sent word to all the surrounding country. People brought all their sick to him ³⁶and begged him to let the sick just touch the edge of his cloak, and all who touched him were healed.

Clean and Unclean

15 Then some Pharisees and teachers of the law came to Jesus from Jerusalem and asked, ²"Why do your disciples break the tradition of the elders? They don't wash their hands before they eat!"

³Jesus replied, "And why do you break the command of God for the sake of your tradition? ⁴For God said, 'Honor your father and mother'*ᵇ* and 'Anyone who curses his father or mother must be put to death.'*ᶜ* ⁵But you say that if a man says to his father or mother, 'Whatever help you might otherwise have received from me is a gift devoted to God,' ⁶he is not to 'honor his father*ᵈ*' with it. Thus you nullify the word of God for the sake of your tradition. ⁷You hypocrites! Isaiah was right when he prophesied about you:

⁸"'These people honor me with their lips,
    but their hearts are far from me.
⁹They worship me in vain;
    their teachings are but rules taught by
        men.'*ᵉ*"

¹⁰Jesus called the crowd to him and said, "Listen and understand. ¹¹What goes into a man's mouth does not make him 'unclean,' but what comes out of his mouth, that is what makes him 'unclean.'"

¹²Then the disciples came to him and asked, "Do you know that the Pharisees were offended when they heard this?"

¹³He replied, "Every plant that my heavenly Father has not planted will be pulled up by the roots. ¹⁴Leave them; they are blind guides.*ᶠ* If a blind man leads a blind man, both will fall into a pit."

¹⁵Peter said, "Explain the parable to us."

¹⁶"Are you still so dull?" Jesus asked them. ¹⁷"Don't you see that whatever enters the mouth goes into the stomach and then out of the body? ¹⁸But the things that come out of the mouth come from the heart, and these make a man 'unclean.' ¹⁹For out of the heart come evil thoughts, murder, adultery, sexual immorality, theft, false testimony, slander. ²⁰These are what make a man 'unclean'; but eating with unwashed hands does not make him 'unclean.'"

The Faith of the Canaanite Woman

²¹Leaving that place, Jesus withdrew to the region of Tyre and Sidon. ²²A Canaanite woman from that vicinity came to him, crying out, "Lord, Son of David, have mercy on me!

ᵃ24 Greek *many stadia*   *ᵇ4* Exodus 20:12; Deut. 5:16   *ᶜ4* Exodus 21:17; Lev. 20:9   *ᵈ6* Some manuscripts *father or his mother*
ᵉ9 Isaiah 29:13   *ᶠ14* Some manuscripts *guides of the blind*

My daughter is suffering terribly from demon-possession."

23 Jesus did not answer a word. So his disciples came to him and urged him, "Send her away, for she keeps crying out after us."

24 He answered, "I was sent only to the lost sheep of Israel."

25 The woman came and knelt before him. "Lord, help me!" she said.

26 He replied, "It is not right to take the children's bread and toss it to their dogs."

27 "Yes, Lord," she said, "but even the dogs eat the crumbs that fall from their masters' table."

28 Then Jesus answered, "Woman, you have great faith! Your request is granted." And her daughter was healed from that very hour.

Jesus Feeds the Four Thousand

29 Jesus left there and went along the Sea of Galilee. Then he went up on a mountainside and sat down. 30 Great crowds came to him, bringing the lame, the blind, the crippled, the mute and many others, and laid them at his feet; and he healed them. 31 The people were amazed when they saw the mute speaking, the crippled made well, the lame walking and the blind seeing. And they praised the God of Israel.

32 Jesus called his disciples to him and said, "I have compassion for these people; they have already been with me three days and have nothing to eat. I do not want to send them away hungry, or they may collapse on the way."

33 His disciples answered, "Where could we get enough bread in this remote place to feed such a crowd?"

34 "How many loaves do you have?" Jesus asked.

"Seven," they replied, "and a few small fish."

35 He told the crowd to sit down on the ground. 36 Then he took the seven loaves and the fish, and when he had given thanks, he broke them and gave them to the disciples, and they in turn to the people. 37 They all ate and were satisfied. Afterward the disciples picked up seven basketfuls of broken pieces that were left over. 38 The number of those who ate was four thousand, besides women and children.

39 After Jesus had sent the crowd away, he got into the boat and went to the vicinity of Magadan.

The Demand for a Sign

16 The Pharisees and Sadducees came to Jesus and tested him by asking him to show them a sign from heaven.

2 He replied,[a] "When evening comes, you say, 'It will be fair weather, for the sky is red,' 3 and in the morning, 'Today it will be stormy, for the sky is red and overcast.' You know how to interpret the appearance of the sky, but you cannot interpret the signs of the times. 4 A wicked and adulterous generation looks for a miraculous sign, but none will be given it except the sign of Jonah." Jesus then left them and went away.

The Yeast of the Pharisees and Sadducees

5 When they went across the lake, the disciples forgot to take bread. 6 "Be careful," Jesus said to them. "Be on your guard against the yeast of the Pharisees and Sadducees."

7 They discussed this among themselves and said, "It is because we didn't bring any bread."

8 Aware of their discussion, Jesus asked, "You of little faith, why are you talking among yourselves about having no bread? 9 Do you still not understand? Don't you remember the five loaves for the five thousand, and how many basketfuls you gathered? 10 Or the seven loaves for the four thousand, and how many basketfuls you gathered? 11 How is it you don't understand that I was not talking to you about bread? But be on your guard against the yeast of the Pharisees and Sadducees." 12 Then they understood that he was not telling them to guard against the yeast used in bread, but against the teaching of the Pharisees and Sadducees.

Peter's Confession of Christ

13 When Jesus came to the region of Caesarea Philippi, he asked his disciples, "Who do people say the Son of Man is?"

14 They replied, "Some say John the Baptist; others say Elijah; and still others, Jeremiah or one of the prophets."

a 2 Some early manuscripts do not have the rest of verse 2 and all of verse 3.

Jesus: Our Everything

Read: Matthew 16:13–26

"JESUS IS EVERYTHING." Mother Teresa's words were demonstrated by her selfless, Christlike actions—she was a friend to the poor, unabashedly loving society's rejects and giving hope to the hopeless in her adopted country of India. How broken her heart must have been every time she lifted an untouchable out of the gutter to die in her arms or she fed and bathed a hungry, dirty orphan.

Through her actions, this humble woman proved that Jesus was more than a good man, a brilliant teacher or even a prophet sent from God. She knew in her heart that Jesus is the Messiah, the Son of the living God, and that knowledge empowered her with enough love for a lifetime of service.

In Matthew 16, Jesus asked his disciples who they thought he was. Peter aced the pop quiz, calling him "the Son of the living God." We all know Peter wasn't perfect. He was the one who had the tendency to speak first and think later. He was the one who denied Christ three times at Jesus' trial. Yet at this key moment, he comprehended that Jesus was the Messiah God had promised for centuries. After Pentecost, Peter's boldness allowed him to proclaim Christ's identity whenever and wherever he could, regardless of the persecution and suffering it invited. Eventually, he was crucified for spreading the news that Jesus was God's Son. The ancient writer Origen records that Peter was crucified head down because he felt unworthy to die in the same manner as Jesus. To the apostle who had once denied him, Jesus was everything; in fact, Jesus was the only thing.

The One who lived among us was God's hands and feet. He gave us the very words of his Father. He taught us how to love. He taught us how to give. And he taught us to die as a grain of wheat dies, so that the seeds of life are multiplied (see John 12:24).

Mother Teresa and Simon Peter understood that with Jesus, there was no such thing as loving moderately. They showed others that Jesus was Lord of their lives by loving as he loved and serving as he served—continually, wholeheartedly and sacrificially.

Go to page 1184 for your next devotional reading.

Matthew 16:15–16

"But what about you?" he asked. "Who do you say I am?" Simon Peter answered, "You are the Christ, the Son of the living God."

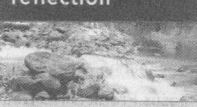

reflection

1 Fill in the blank with the words of your choice: Jesus is _____ _____.

2 How does your answer to the above question affect how you live?

3 On a scale of one to ten, how well are you loving others continually, wholeheartedly and sacrificially?

RELATED READINGS

John 11:25–27;
13:34–35;
1 John 3:1–3,16–24

¹⁵"But what about you?" he asked. "Who do you say I am?"

¹⁶Simon Peter answered, "You are the Christ,ᵃ the Son of the living God."

¹⁷Jesus replied, "Blessed are you, Simon son of Jonah, for this was not revealed to you by man, but by my Father in heaven. ¹⁸And I tell you that you are Peter,ᵇ and on this rock I will build my church, and the gates of Hadesᶜ will not overcome it.ᵈ ¹⁹I will give you the keys of the kingdom of heaven; whatever you bind on earth will beᵉ bound in heaven, and whatever you loose on earth will be ᵉ loosed in heaven." ²⁰Then he warned his disciples not to tell anyone that he was the Christ.

Jesus Predicts His Death

²¹From that time on Jesus began to explain to his disciples that he must go to Jerusalem and suffer many things at the hands of the elders, chief priests and teachers of the law, and that he must be killed and on the third day be raised to life.

²²Peter took him aside and began to rebuke him. "Never, Lord!" he said. "This shall never happen to you!"

²³Jesus turned and said to Peter, "Get behind me, Satan! You are a stumbling block to me; you do not have in mind the things of God, but the things of men."

²⁴Then Jesus said to his disciples, "If anyone would come after me, he must deny himself and take up his cross and follow me. ²⁵For whoever wants to save his lifeᶠ will lose it, but whoever loses his life for me will find it. ²⁶What good will it be for a man if he gains the whole world, yet forfeits his soul? Or what can a man give in exchange for his soul? ²⁷For the Son of Man is going to come in his Father's glory with his angels, and then he will reward each person according to what he has done. ²⁸I tell you the truth, some who are standing here will not taste death before they see the Son of Man coming in his kingdom."

Matthew 16:25

God Is Life

"For whoever wants to save his life will lose it, but whoever loses his life for me will find it."

The Transfiguration

17 After six days Jesus took with him Peter, James and John the brother of James, and led them up a high mountain by themselves. ²There he was transfigured before them. His face shone like the sun, and his clothes became as white as the light. ³Just then there appeared before them Moses and Elijah, talking with Jesus.

⁴Peter said to Jesus, "Lord, it is good for us to be here. If you wish, I will put up three shelters—one for you, one for Moses and one for Elijah."

⁵While he was still speaking, a bright cloud enveloped them, and a voice from the cloud said, "This is my Son, whom I love; with him I am well pleased. Listen to him!"

⁶When the disciples heard this, they fell facedown to the ground, terrified. ⁷But Jesus came and touched them. "Get up," he said. "Don't be afraid." ⁸When they looked up, they saw no one except Jesus.

⁹As they were coming down the mountain, Jesus instructed them, "Don't tell anyone what you have seen, until the Son of Man has been raised from the dead."

¹⁰The disciples asked him, "Why then do the teachers of the law say that Elijah must come first?"

¹¹Jesus replied, "To be sure, Elijah comes and will restore all things. ¹²But I tell you, Elijah has already come, and they did not recognize him, but have done to him everything they wished. In the same way the Son of Man is going to suffer at their hands." ¹³Then the disciples understood that he was talking to them about John the Baptist.

The Healing of a Boy With a Demon

¹⁴When they came to the crowd, a man approached Jesus and knelt before him. ¹⁵"Lord, have mercy on my son," he said. "He has seizures and is suffering greatly. He often falls into the fire or into the water. ¹⁶I brought him to your disciples, but they could not heal him."

ᵃ16 Or *Messiah*; also in verse 20   ᵇ18 *Peter* means *rock.*   ᶜ18 Or *hell*   ᵈ18 Or *not prove stronger than it*   ᵉ19 Or *have been*
ᶠ25 The Greek word means either *life* or *soul*; also in verse 26.

¹⁷"O unbelieving and perverse generation," Jesus replied, "how long shall I stay with you? How long shall I put up with you? Bring the boy here to me." ¹⁸Jesus rebuked the demon, and it came out of the boy, and he was healed from that moment.

¹⁹Then the disciples came to Jesus in private and asked, "Why couldn't we drive it out?"

²⁰He replied, "Because you have so little faith. I tell you the truth, if you have faith as small as a mustard seed, you can say to this mountain, 'Move from here to there' and it will move. Nothing will be impossible for you.ᵃ"

²²When they came together in Galilee, he said to them, "The Son of Man is going to be betrayed into the hands of men. ²³They will kill him, and on the third day he will be raised to life." And the disciples were filled with grief.

The Temple Tax

²⁴After Jesus and his disciples arrived in Capernaum, the collectors of the two-drachma tax came to Peter and asked, "Doesn't your teacher pay the temple taxᵇ?"

²⁵"Yes, he does," he replied.

When Peter came into the house, Jesus was the first to speak. "What do you think, Simon?" he asked. "From whom do the kings of the earth collect duty and taxes—from their own sons or from others?"

²⁶"From others," Peter answered.

"Then the sons are exempt," Jesus said to him. ²⁷"But so that we may not offend them, go to the lake and throw out your line. Take the first fish you catch; open its mouth and you will find a four-drachma coin. Take it and give it to them for my tax and yours."

The Greatest in the Kingdom of Heaven

18 At that time the disciples came to Jesus and asked, "Who is the greatest in the kingdom of heaven?"

²He called a little child and had him stand among them. ³And he said: "I tell you the truth, unless you change and become like little children, you will never enter the kingdom of heaven. ⁴Therefore, whoever humbles himself like this child is the greatest in the kingdom of heaven.

⁵"And whoever welcomes a little child like this in my name welcomes me. ⁶But if anyone causes one of these little ones who believe in me to sin, it would be better for him to have a large millstone hung around his neck and to be drowned in the depths of the sea.

⁷"Woe to the world because of the things that cause people to sin! Such things must come, but woe to the man through whom they come! ⁸If your hand or your foot causes you to sin, cut it off and throw it away. It is better for you to enter life maimed or crippled than to have two hands or two feet and be thrown into eternal fire. ⁹And if your eye causes you to sin, gouge it out and throw it away. It is better for you to enter life with one eye than to have two eyes and be thrown into the fire of hell.

The Parable of the Lost Sheep

¹⁰"See that you do not look down on one of these little ones. For I tell you that their angels in heaven always see the face of my Father in heaven.ᶜ

¹²"What do you think? If a man owns a hundred sheep, and one of them wanders away, will he not leave the ninety-nine on the hills and go to look for the one that wandered off? ¹³And if he finds it, I tell you the truth, he is happier about that one sheep than about the ninety-nine that did not wander off. ¹⁴In the same way your Father in heaven is not willing that any of these little ones should be lost.

A Brother Who Sins Against You

¹⁵"If your brother sins against you,ᵈ go and show him his fault, just between the two of you. If he listens to you, you have won your brother over. ¹⁶But if he will not listen, take one or two others along, so that 'every matter may be established by the testimony of two or three witnesses.'ᵉ ¹⁷If he refuses to listen to them, tell it to the church; and if he refuses to listen even to the church, treat him as you would a pagan or a tax collector.

¹⁸"I tell you the truth, whatever you bind on earth will beᶠ bound in heaven, and whatever you loose on earth will beᶠ loosed in heaven.

ᵃ20 Some manuscripts *you.* ²¹But this kind does not go out except by prayer and fasting.   ᵇ24 Greek *the two drachmas*   ᶜ10 Some manuscripts *heaven.* ¹¹The Son of Man came to save what was lost.   ᵈ15 Some manuscripts do not have *against you.*   ᵉ16 Deut. 19:15   ᶠ18 Or *have been*

Scorned

HERODIAS

So Herodias nursed a grudge against John and wanted to kill him.

Mark 6:19

"WHAT SHALL I ASK FOR?" asked her daughter, dressed in her beautiful dancing costume, as she stood impatiently before her mother.

Herodias paused a moment before answering. A thousand options came to mind. It wasn't every day that one had the chance to receive anything within a king's grasp. As queen, her own powers had limits. But this, this was an exceptional opportunity. And it required careful consideration.

Anything I ask for, I can receive . . . up to half of the kingdom . . . Herodias mused silently, mindlessly tapping her lips with her slender finger. *What should it be?*

Jewelry? Clothes? A statue in her honor?

Horses? Land? A new palace?

Amid a myriad of alternatives, suddenly she snapped to attention. She knew without a doubt what she wanted. It was something better than material objects, fame, riches or glory. It was something only the king could provide: revenge.

With it, she reasoned, maybe she could finally get a good night's sleep instead of laying awake at night thinking how one man named John had absolutely ruined her life.

With it, she hoped she could finally take the sting out of John's slanderous accusations. His judgmental attitude toward her constantly rang in her ears and gave her no peace.

With it, maybe this self-righteous know-it-all would stop haunting her thoughts and whipping her into such a frenzy that she could hardly think straight.

Yes, revenge was what she wanted.

And when it was served to her on a fine piece of dishware, she gloated. But only for a moment. As it turned out, her sleep from that night onward likely wasn't as restful as she'd hoped. The sting to her conscience wasn't any less painful; if she were truthful, it was actually much worse. And, though we can't be sure, one can guess that sometimes (if not every night) she still saw John in her dreams.

ASSIGNED READING:

Matthew 14:1–12;
Mark 6:14–29

—Prayer—
Lord God, teach me to handle my anger and hurt in a godly manner. Help me not to desire revenge, but help me to overcome evil with good.

Weekend

Go to page 1186 for your next devotional reading.

19"Again, I tell you that if two of you on earth agree about anything you ask for, it will be done for you by my Father in heaven. 20For where two or three come together in my name, there am I with them."

The Parable of the Unmerciful Servant

21Then Peter came to Jesus and asked, "Lord, how many times shall I forgive my brother when he sins against me? Up to seven times?"

22Jesus answered, "I tell you, not seven times, but seventy-seven times.*a*

23"Therefore, the kingdom of heaven is like a king who wanted to settle accounts with his servants. 24As he began the settlement, a man who owed him ten thousand talents*b* was brought to him. 25Since he was not able to pay, the master ordered that he and his wife and his children and all that he had be sold to repay the debt.

26"The servant fell on his knees before him. 'Be patient with me,' he begged, 'and I will pay back everything.' 27The servant's master took pity on him, canceled the debt and let him go.

28"But when that servant went out, he found one of his fellow servants who owed him a hundred denarii.*c* He grabbed him and began to choke him. 'Pay back what you owe me!' he demanded.

29"His fellow servant fell to his knees and begged him, 'Be patient with me, and I will pay you back.'

30"But he refused. Instead, he went off and had the man thrown into prison until he could pay the debt. 31When the other servants saw what had happened, they were greatly distressed and went and told their master everything that had happened.

32"Then the master called the servant in. 'You wicked servant,' he said, 'I canceled all that debt of yours because you begged me to. 33Shouldn't you have had mercy on your fellow servant just as I had on you?' 34In anger his master turned him over to the jailers to be tortured, until he should pay back all he owed.

35"This is how my heavenly Father will treat each of you unless you forgive your brother from your heart."

Divorce

19 When Jesus had finished saying these things, he left Galilee and went into the region of Judea to the other side of the Jordan. 2Large crowds followed him, and he healed them there.

3Some Pharisees came to him to test him. They asked, "Is it lawful for a man to divorce his wife for any and every reason?"

4"Haven't you read," he replied, "that at the beginning the Creator 'made them male and female,'*d* 5and said, 'For this reason a man will leave his father and mother and be united to his wife, and the two will become one flesh'*e*? 6So they are no longer two, but one. Therefore what God has joined together, let man not separate."

7"Why then," they asked, "did Moses command that a man give his wife a certificate of divorce and send her away?"

8Jesus replied, "Moses permitted you to divorce your wives because your hearts were hard. But it was not this way from the beginning. 9I tell you that anyone who divorces his wife, except for marital unfaithfulness, and marries another woman commits adultery."

10The disciples said to him, "If this is the situation between a husband and wife, it is better not to marry."

11Jesus replied, "Not everyone can accept this word, but only those to whom it has been given. 12For some are eunuchs because they were born that way; others were made that way by men; and others have renounced marriage*f* because of the kingdom of heaven. The one who can accept this should accept it."

The Little Children and Jesus

13Then little children were brought to Jesus for him to place his hands on them and pray for them. But the disciples rebuked those who brought them.

14Jesus said, "Let the little children come to me, and do not hinder them, for the kingdom of heaven belongs to such as these." 15When he had placed his hands on them, he went on from there.

---

*a*22 Or *seventy times seven*   *b*24 That is, millions of dollars   *c*28 That is, a few dollars   *d*4 Gen. 1:27   *e*5 Gen. 2:24   *f*12 Or *have made themselves eunuchs*

"Haven't you read . . . 'For this reason a man will leave his father and mother and be united to his wife, and the two will become one flesh'? So they are no longer two, but one. Therefore what God has joined together, let man not separate."

Superglue

Read: Matthew 19:1–12

SUPERGLUE WORKS. Once two items are glued together, separation becomes a painful, sticky mess. Paper tears and fabric frays if you divide the two pieces that have melded into one. Once separated, the original items are never the same—each inevitably retains fragments of the other. Think of two pieces of paper glued together—after they've been torn apart, each piece is ragged and weak. That's why superglue comes with a label advising the consumer to use extreme caution when handling it.

We might think of marriage as something like God's superglue because it weaves two lives intricately into one. After this blessed blending, attempts at separation cause irreparable damage. Hearts break, commitments crumble and families split. God's intertwining of husband and wife extends to children, friends and families related to the union. God's Word also provides a strong warning: "What God has joined together, let man not separate."

When Ruth Bell was a teenage girl, she left her childhood home in China to attend school in Korea. Her idea of the future? She fully intended to be an old maid missionary in Tibet. However, she did give the thought of a husband some serious consideration. So she wrote the following list of particulars:

"If I marry: He must be so tall that when he is on his knees, as one has said, he reaches all the way to heaven. His shoulders must be broad enough to bear the burden of a family. His lips must be strong enough to smile, firm enough to say no, and tender enough to kiss. Love must be so deep that it takes its stand in Christ and so wide that it takes the whole lost world in. He must be active enough to save souls. He must be big enough to be gentle and great enough to be thoughtful. His arms must be strong enough to carry a little child."

Ruth eventually found a man who fit her qualifications; she married evangelist Billy Graham. Ruth and Billy Graham realize that their marriage has endured the test of time not because they are perfect people, but because God is at the center of their relationship.

It takes supernatural empowerment and a determined effort on the part of both husband and wife to keep the bond of marriage strong. Only through God's strength can couples remain "superglued" together. As Solomon wisely said, "A cord of three strands is not quickly broken" (Ecclesiastes 4:12).

reflection

1 Have you ever tried to separate something that was superglued together? What was the result?

2 Think of someone—perhaps even yourself—who has experienced divorce. What were the residual effects? If you've been divorced, ask God to heal the hurts of your separation.

3 If you're married, list some practical ways you and your husband can stick together when the world tries to pull you apart.

RELATED READINGS

Genesis 2:19–25;
1 Corinthians 7:10–16;
Ephesians 5:21–33

"A good marriage is the union of two forgivers."

Ruth Graham

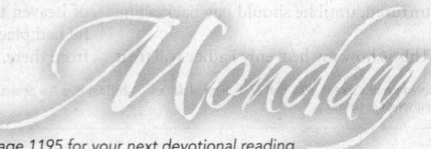

Monday

Go to page 1195 for your next devotional reading.

The Rich Young Man

¹⁶Now a man came up to Jesus and asked, "Teacher, what good thing must I do to get eternal life?"

¹⁷"Why do you ask me about what is good?" Jesus replied. "There is only One who is good. If you want to enter life, obey the commandments."

¹⁸"Which ones?" the man inquired.

Jesus replied, " 'Do not murder, do not commit adultery, do not steal, do not give false testimony, ¹⁹honor your father and mother,'[a] and 'love your neighbor as yourself.'[b]"

²⁰"All these I have kept," the young man said. "What do I still lack?"

²¹Jesus answered, "If you want to be perfect, go, sell your possessions and give to the poor, and you will have treasure in heaven. Then come, follow me."

²²When the young man heard this, he went away sad, because he had great wealth.

²³Then Jesus said to his disciples, "I tell you the truth, it is hard for a rich man to enter the kingdom of heaven. ²⁴Again I tell you, it is easier for a camel to go through the eye of a needle than for a rich man to enter the kingdom of God."

²⁵When the disciples heard this, they were greatly astonished and asked, "Who then can be saved?"

²⁶Jesus looked at them and said, "With man this is impossible, but with God all things are possible."

²⁷Peter answered him, "We have left everything to follow you! What then will there be for us?"

²⁸Jesus said to them, "I tell you the truth, at the renewal of all things, when the Son of Man sits on his glorious throne, you who have followed me will also sit on twelve thrones, judging the twelve tribes of Israel. ²⁹And everyone who has left houses or brothers or sisters or father or mother[c] or children or fields for my sake will receive a hundred times as much and will inherit eternal life.

³⁰But many who are first will be last, and many who are last will be first.

The Parable of the Workers in the Vineyard

20 "For the kingdom of heaven is like a landowner who went out early in the morning to hire men to work in his vineyard. ²He agreed to pay them a denarius for the day and sent them into his vineyard.

³"About the third hour he went out and saw others standing in the marketplace doing nothing. ⁴He told them, 'You also go and work in my vineyard, and I will pay you whatever is right.' ⁵So they went.

"He went out again about the sixth hour and the ninth hour and did the same thing. ⁶About the eleventh hour he went out and found still others standing around. He asked them, 'Why have you been standing here all day long doing nothing?'

⁷" 'Because no one has hired us,' they answered.

"He said to them, 'You also go and work in my vineyard.'

⁸"When evening came, the owner of the vineyard said to his foreman, 'Call the workers and pay them their wages, beginning with the last ones hired and going on to the first.'

⁹"The workers who were hired about the eleventh hour came and each received a denarius. ¹⁰So when those came who were hired first, they expected to receive more. But each one of them also received a denarius. ¹¹When they received it, they began to grumble against the landowner. ¹²'These men who were hired last worked only one hour,' they said, 'and you have made them equal to us who have borne the burden of the work and the heat of the day.'

¹³"But he answered one of them, 'Friend, I am not being unfair to you. Didn't you agree to work for a denarius? ¹⁴Take your pay and go. I want to give the man who was hired last the

Matthew 19:26

God Does the Impossible

Jesus looked at them and said, "With man this is impossible, but with God all things are possible."

---

[a]**19** Exodus 20:12–16; Deut. 5:16–20   [b]**19** Lev. 19:18   [c]**29** Some manuscripts *mother or wife*

same as I gave you. ¹⁵Don't have the right to do what I want with my own money? Or are you envious because I am generous?'

¹⁶"So the last will be first, and the first will be last."

Jesus Again Predicts His Death

¹⁷Now as Jesus was going up to Jerusalem, he took the twelve disciples aside and said to them, ¹⁸"We are going up to Jerusalem, and the Son of Man will be betrayed to the chief priests and the teachers of the law. They will condemn him to death ¹⁹and will turn him over to the Gentiles to be mocked and flogged and crucified. On the third day he will be raised to life!"

A Mother's Request

²⁰Then the mother of Zebedee's sons came to Jesus with her sons and, kneeling down, asked a favor of him.

²¹"What is it you want?" he asked.

She said, "Grant that one of these two sons of mine may sit at your right and the other at your left in your kingdom."

²²"You don't know what you are asking," Jesus said to them. "Can you drink the cup I am going to drink?"

"We can," they answered.

²³Jesus said to them, "You will indeed drink from my cup, but to sit at my right or left is not for me to grant. These places belong to those for whom they have been prepared by my Father."

²⁴When the ten heard about this, they were indignant with the two brothers. ²⁵Jesus called them together and said, "You know that the rulers of the Gentiles lord it over them, and their high officials exercise authority over them. ²⁶Not so with you. Instead, whoever wants to become great among you must be your servant, ²⁷and whoever wants to be first must be your slave— ²⁸just as the Son of Man did not come to be served, but to serve, and to give his life as a ransom for many."

Two Blind Men Receive Sight

²⁹As Jesus and his disciples were leaving Jericho, a large crowd followed him. ³⁰Two blind men were sitting by the roadside, and when they heard that Jesus was going by, they shouted, "Lord, Son of David, have mercy on us!"

³¹The crowd rebuked them and told them to be quiet, but they shouted all the louder, "Lord, Son of David, have mercy on us!"

³²Jesus stopped and called them. "What do you want me to do for you?" he asked.

³³"Lord," they answered, "we want our sight."

³⁴Jesus had compassion on them and touched their eyes. Immediately they received their sight and followed him.

The Triumphal Entry

21 As they approached Jerusalem and came to Bethphage on the Mount of Olives, Jesus sent two disciples, ²saying to them, "Go to the village ahead of you, and at once you will find a donkey tied there, with her colt by her. Untie them and bring them to me. ³If anyone says anything to you, tell him that the Lord needs them, and he will send them right away."

⁴This took place to fulfill what was spoken through the prophet:

⁵"Say to the Daughter of Zion,
  'See, your king comes to you,
gentle and riding on a donkey,
  on a colt, the foal of a donkey.'"^a

⁶The disciples went and did as Jesus had instructed them. ⁷They brought the donkey and the colt, placed their cloaks on them, and Jesus sat on them. ⁸A very large crowd spread their cloaks on the road, while others cut branches from the trees and spread them on the road. ⁹The crowds that went ahead of him and those that followed shouted,

"Hosanna^b to the Son of David!"

"Blessed is he who comes in the name of the Lord!"^c

"Hosanna^b in the highest!"

¹⁰When Jesus entered Jerusalem, the whole city was stirred and asked, "Who is this?"

¹¹The crowds answered, "This is Jesus, the prophet from Nazareth in Galilee."

<hr>

^a5 Zech. 9:9   ^b9 A Hebrew expression meaning "Save!" which became an exclamation of praise; also in verse 15   ^c9 Psalm 118:26

Jesus at the Temple

[12]Jesus entered the temple area and drove out all who were buying and selling there. He overturned the tables of the money changers and the benches of those selling doves. [13]"It is written," he said to them, "'My house will be called a house of prayer,'[a] but you are making it a 'den of robbers.'[b]"

[14]The blind and the lame came to him at the temple, and he healed them. [15]But when the chief priests and the teachers of the law saw the wonderful things he did and the children shouting in the temple area, "Hosanna to the Son of David," they were indignant.

[16]"Do you hear what these children are saying?" they asked him.

"Yes," replied Jesus, "have you never read,

"'From the lips of children and infants
you have ordained praise'[c]?"

[17]And he left them and went out of the city to Bethany, where he spent the night.

The Fig Tree Withers

[18]Early in the morning, as he was on his way back to the city, he was hungry. [19]Seeing a fig tree by the road, he went up to it but found nothing on it except leaves. Then he said to it, "May you never bear fruit again!" Immediately the tree withered.

[20]When the disciples saw this, they were amazed. "How did the fig tree wither so quickly?" they asked.

[21]Jesus replied, "I tell you the truth, if you have faith and do not doubt, not only can you do what was done to the fig tree, but also you can say to this mountain, 'Go, throw yourself into the sea,' and it will be done. [22]If you believe, you will receive whatever you ask for in prayer."

The Authority of Jesus Questioned

[23]Jesus entered the temple courts, and, while he was teaching, the chief priests and the elders of the people came to him. "By what authority are you doing these things?" they asked. "And who gave you this authority?"

[24]Jesus replied, "I will also ask you one question. If you answer me, I will tell you by what authority I am doing these things. [25]John's baptism—where did it come from? Was it from heaven, or from men?"

They discussed it among themselves and said, "If we say, 'From heaven,' he will ask, 'Then why didn't you believe him?' [26]But if we say, 'From men'—we are afraid of the people, for they all hold that John was a prophet."

[27]So they answered Jesus, "We don't know."

Then he said, "Neither will I tell you by what authority I am doing these things.

The Parable of the Two Sons

[28]"What do you think? There was a man who had two sons. He went to the first and said, 'Son, go and work today in the vineyard.'

[29]"'I will not,' he answered, but later he changed his mind and went.

[30]"Then the father went to the other son and said the same thing. He answered, 'I will, sir,' but he did not go.

[31]"Which of the two did what his father wanted?"

"The first," they answered.

Jesus said to them, "I tell you the truth, the tax collectors and the prostitutes are entering the kingdom of God ahead of you. [32]For John came to you to show you the way of righteousness, and you did not believe him, but the tax collectors and the prostitutes did. And even after you saw this, you did not repent and believe him.

The Parable of the Tenants

[33]"Listen to another parable: There was a landowner who planted a vineyard. He put a wall around it, dug a winepress in it and built a watchtower. Then he rented the vineyard to some farmers and went away on a journey. [34]When the harvest time approached, he sent his servants to the tenants to collect his fruit.

[35]"The tenants seized his servants; they beat one, killed another, and stoned a third. [36]Then he sent other servants to them, more than the first time, and the tenants treated them the same way. [37]Last of all, he sent his son to them. 'They will respect my son,' he said.

[38]"But when the tenants saw the son, they said to each other, 'This is the heir. Come, let's kill him and take his inheritance.' [39]So they took him and threw him out of the vineyard and killed him.

*a*13 Isaiah 56:7   *b*13 Jer. 7:11   *c*16 Psalm 8:2

40"Therefore, when the owner of the vineyard comes, what will he do to those tenants?"

41"He will bring those wretches to a wretched end," they replied, "and he will rent the vineyard to other tenants, who will give him his share of the crop at harvest time."

42Jesus said to them, "Have you never read in the Scriptures:

"'The stone the builders rejected
  has become the capstone*[a*];
the Lord has done this,
  and it is marvelous in our eyes'*[b]*?

43"Therefore I tell you that the kingdom of God will be taken away from you and given to a people who will produce its fruit. 44He who falls on this stone will be broken to pieces, but he on whom it falls will be crushed."*[c]*

45When the chief priests and the Pharisees heard Jesus' parables, they knew he was talking about them. 46They looked for a way to arrest him, but they were afraid of the crowd because the people held that he was a prophet.

The Parable of the Wedding Banquet

22 Jesus spoke to them again in parables, saying: 2"The kingdom of heaven is like a king who prepared a wedding banquet for his son. 3He sent his servants to those who had been invited to the banquet to tell them to come, but they refused to come.

4"Then he sent some more servants and said, 'Tell those who have been invited that I have prepared my dinner: My oxen and fattened cattle have been butchered, and everything is ready. Come to the wedding banquet.'

5"But they paid no attention and went off—one to his field, another to his business. 6The rest seized his servants, mistreated them and killed them. 7The king was enraged. He sent his army and destroyed those murderers and burned their city.

8"Then he said to his servants, 'The wedding banquet is ready, but those I invited did not deserve to come. 9Go to the street corners and invite to the banquet anyone you find.' 10So the servants went out into the streets and gathered all the people they could find, both good and bad, and the wedding hall was filled with guests.

11"But when the king came in to see the guests, he noticed a man there who was not wearing wedding clothes. 12'Friend,' he asked, 'how did you get in here without wedding clothes?' The man was speechless.

13"Then the king told the attendants, 'Tie him hand and foot, and throw him outside, into the darkness, where there will be weeping and gnashing of teeth.'

14"For many are invited, but few are chosen."

Paying Taxes to Caesar

15Then the Pharisees went out and laid plans to trap him in his words. 16They sent their disciples to him along with the Herodians. "Teacher," they said, "we know you are a man of integrity and that you teach the way of God in accordance with the truth. You aren't swayed by men, because you pay no attention to who they are. 17Tell us then, what is your opinion? Is it right to pay taxes to Caesar or not?"

18But Jesus, knowing their evil intent, said, "You hypocrites, why are you trying to trap me? 19Show me the coin used for paying the tax." They brought him a denarius, 20and he asked them, "Whose portrait is this? And whose inscription?"

21"Caesar's," they replied.

Then he said to them, "Give to Caesar what is Caesar's, and to God what is God's."

22When they heard this, they were amazed. So they left him and went away.

Marriage at the Resurrection

23That same day the Sadducees, who say there is no resurrection, came to him with a question. 24"Teacher," they said, "Moses told us that if a man dies without having children, his brother must marry the widow and have children for him. 25Now there were seven brothers among us. The first one married and died, and since he had no children, he left his wife to his brother. 26The same thing happened to the second and third brother, right on down to the seventh. 27Finally, the woman died. 28Now then, at the resurrection, whose wife will she be of the seven, since all of them were married to her?"

29Jesus replied, "You are in error because

*[a]*42 Or *cornerstone*   *[b]*42 Psalm 118:22,23   *[c]*44 Some manuscripts do not have verse 44.

you do not know the Scriptures or the power of God. 30At the resurrection people will neither marry nor be given in marriage; they will be like the angels in heaven. 31But about the resurrection of the dead—have you not read what God said to you, 32'I am the God of Abraham, the God of Isaac, and the God of Jacob'*a*? He is not the God of the dead but of the living."

33When the crowds heard this, they were astonished at his teaching.

The Greatest Commandment

34Hearing that Jesus had silenced the Sadducees, the Pharisees got together. 35One of them, an expert in the law, tested him with this question: 36"Teacher, which is the greatest commandment in the Law?"

37Jesus replied: "'Love the Lord your God with all your heart and with all your soul and with all your mind.'*b* 38This is the first and greatest commandment. 39And the second is like it: 'Love your neighbor as yourself.'*c* 40All the Law and the Prophets hang on these two commandments."

Whose Son Is the Christ?

41While the Pharisees were gathered together, Jesus asked them, 42"What do you think about the Christ*d*? Whose son is he?"

"The son of David," they replied.

43He said to them, "How is it then that David, speaking by the Spirit, calls him 'Lord'? For he says,

44"'The Lord said to my Lord:
  "Sit at my right hand
until I put your enemies
  under your feet." '*e*

45If then David calls him 'Lord,' how can he be his son?" 46No one could say a word in reply, and from that day on no one dared to ask him any more questions.

Seven Woes

23 Then Jesus said to the crowds and to his disciples: 2"The teachers of the law and the Pharisees sit in Moses' seat. 3So you must obey them and do everything they tell you. But do not do what they do, for they do not practice what they preach. 4They tie up heavy loads and put them on men's shoulders, but they themselves are not willing to lift a finger to move them.

5"Everything they do is done for men to see: They make their phylacteries*f* wide and the tassels on their garments long; 6they love the place of honor at banquets and the most important seats in the synagogues; 7they love to be greeted in the marketplaces and to have men call them 'Rabbi.'

8"But you are not to be called 'Rabbi,' for you have only one Master and you are all brothers. 9And do not call anyone on earth 'father,' for you have one Father, and he is in heaven. 10Nor are you to be called 'teacher,' for you have one Teacher, the Christ.*d* 11The greatest among you will be your servant. 12For whoever exalts himself will be humbled, and whoever humbles himself will be exalted.

13"Woe to you, teachers of the law and Pharisees, you hypocrites! You shut the kingdom of heaven in men's faces. You yourselves do not enter, nor will you let those enter who are trying to.*g*

15"Woe to you, teachers of the law and Pharisees, you hypocrites! You travel over land and sea to win a single convert, and when he becomes one, you make him twice as much a son of hell as you are.

16"Woe to you, blind guides! You say, 'If anyone swears by the temple, it means nothing; but if anyone swears by the gold of the temple, he is bound by his oath.' 17You blind fools! Which is greater: the gold, or the temple that makes the gold sacred? 18You also say, 'If anyone swears by the altar, it means nothing; but if anyone swears by the gift on it, he is bound by his oath.' 19You blind men! Which is greater: the gift, or the altar that makes the gift sacred? 20Therefore, he who swears by the altar swears by it and by everything on it. 21And he who swears by the temple swears by it and by the one who dwells in it. 22And he who swears by heaven swears by God's throne and by the one who sits on it.

23"Woe to you, teachers of the law and

---

*a*32 Exodus 3:6 *b*37 Deut. 6:5 *c*39 Lev. 19:18 *d*42,10 Or *Messiah* *e*44 Psalm 110:1 *f*5 That is, boxes containing Scripture verses, worn on forehead and arm *g*13 Some manuscripts *to.* 14*Woe to you, teachers of the law and Pharisees, you hypocrites! You devour widows' houses and for a show make lengthy prayers. Therefore you will be punished more severely.*

Pharisees, you hypocrites! You give a tenth of your spices—mint, dill and cummin. But you have neglected the more important matters of the law—justice, mercy and faithfulness. You should have practiced the latter, without neglecting the former. ²⁴You blind guides! You strain out a gnat but swallow a camel.

²⁵"Woe to you, teachers of the law and Pharisees, you hypocrites! You clean the outside of the cup and dish, but inside they are full of greed and self-indulgence. ²⁶Blind Pharisee! First clean the inside of the cup and dish, and then the outside also will be clean.

²⁷"Woe to you, teachers of the law and Pharisees, you hypocrites! You are like whitewashed tombs, which look beautiful on the outside but on the inside are full of dead men's bones and everything unclean. ²⁸In the same way, on the outside you appear to people as righteous but on the inside you are full of hypocrisy and wickedness.

²⁹"Woe to you, teachers of the law and Pharisees, you hypocrites! You build tombs for the prophets and decorate the graves of the righteous. ³⁰And you say, 'If we had lived in the days of our forefathers, we would not have taken part with them in shedding the blood of the prophets.' ³¹So you testify against yourselves that you are the descendants of those who murdered the prophets. ³²Fill up, then, the measure of the sin of your forefathers!

³³"You snakes! You brood of vipers! How will you escape being condemned to hell? ³⁴Therefore I am sending you prophets and wise men and teachers. Some of them you will kill and crucify; others you will flog in your synagogues and pursue from town to town. ³⁵And so upon you will come all the righteous blood that has been shed on earth, from the blood of righteous Abel to the blood of Zechariah son of Berekiah, whom you murdered between the temple and the altar. ³⁶I tell you the truth, all this will come upon this generation.

³⁷"O Jerusalem, Jerusalem, you who kill the prophets and stone those sent to you, how often I have longed to gather your children together, as a hen gathers her chicks under her wings, but you were not willing. ³⁸Look, your house is left to you desolate. ³⁹For I tell you, you will not

see me again until you say, 'Blessed is he who comes in the name of the Lord.'ᵃ"

Signs of the End of the Age

24 Jesus left the temple and was walking away when his disciples came up to him to call his attention to its buildings. ²"Do you see all these things?" he asked. "I tell you the truth, not one stone here will be left on another; every one will be thrown down."

³As Jesus was sitting on the Mount of Olives, the disciples came to him privately. "Tell us," they said, "when will this happen, and what will be the sign of your coming and of the end of the age?"

⁴Jesus answered: "Watch out that no one deceives you. ⁵For many will come in my name, claiming, 'I am the Christ,'ᵇ and will deceive many. ⁶You will hear of wars and rumors of wars, but see to it that you are not alarmed. Such things must happen, but the end is still to come. ⁷Nation will rise against nation, and kingdom against kingdom. There will be famines and earthquakes in various places. ⁸All these are the beginning of birth pains.

⁹"Then you will be handed over to be persecuted and put to death, and you will be hated by all nations because of me. ¹⁰At that time many will turn away from the faith and will betray and hate each other, ¹¹and many false prophets will appear and deceive many people. ¹²Because of the increase of wickedness, the love of most will grow cold, ¹³but he who stands firm to the end will be saved. ¹⁴And this gospel of the kingdom will be preached in the whole world as a testimony to all nations, and then the end will come.

¹⁵"So when you see standing in the holy place 'the abomination that causes desolation,'ᶜ spoken of through the prophet Daniel—let the reader understand— ¹⁶then let those who are in Judea flee to the mountains. ¹⁷Let no one on the roof of his house go down to take anything out of the house. ¹⁸Let no one in the field go back to get his cloak. ¹⁹How dreadful it will be in those days for pregnant women and nursing mothers! ²⁰Pray that your flight will not take place in winter or on the Sabbath. ²¹For then there will be great distress, unequaled from the

---

ᵃ39 Psalm 118:26   ᵇ5 Or *Messiah*; also in verse 23   ᶜ15 Daniel 9:27; 11:31; 12:11

beginning of the world until now—and never to be equaled again. ²²If those days had not been cut short, no one would survive, but for the sake of the elect those days will be shortened. ²³At that time if anyone says to you, 'Look, here is the Christ!' or, 'There he is!' do not believe it. ²⁴For false Christs and false prophets will appear and perform great signs and miracles to deceive even the elect—if that were possible. ²⁵See, I have told you ahead of time.

²⁶"So if anyone tells you, 'There he is, out in the desert,' do not go out; or, 'Here he is, in the inner rooms,' do not believe it. ²⁷For as lightning that comes from the east is visible even in the west, so will be the coming of the Son of Man. ²⁸Wherever there is a carcass, there the vultures will gather.

²⁹"Immediately after the distress of those days

" 'the sun will be darkened,
    and the moon will not give its light;
the stars will fall from the sky,
    and the heavenly bodies will be
        shaken.'*a*

³⁰"At that time the sign of the Son of Man will appear in the sky, and all the nations of the earth will mourn. They will see the Son of Man coming on the clouds of the sky, with power and great glory. ³¹And he will send his angels with a loud trumpet call, and they will gather his elect from the four winds, from one end of the heavens to the other.

³²"Now learn this lesson from the fig tree: As soon as its twigs get tender and its leaves come out, you know that summer is near. ³³Even so, when you see all these things, you know that it*b* is near, right at the door. ³⁴I tell you the truth, this generation*c* will certainly not pass away until all these things have happened. ³⁵Heaven and earth will pass away, but my words will never pass away.

The Day and Hour Unknown

³⁶"No one knows about that day or hour, not even the angels in heaven, nor the Son,*d* but only the Father. ³⁷As it was in the days of Noah, so it will be at the coming of the Son of Man. ³⁸For in the days before the flood, people were eating and drinking, marrying and giving in marriage, up to the day Noah entered the ark; ³⁹and they knew nothing about what would happen until the flood came and took them all away. That is how it will be at the coming of the Son of Man. ⁴⁰Two men will be in the field; one will be taken and the other left. ⁴¹Two women will be grinding with a hand mill; one will be taken and the other left.

⁴²"Therefore keep watch, because you do not know on what day your Lord will come. ⁴³But understand this: If the owner of the house had known at what time of night the thief was coming, he would have kept watch and would not have let his house be broken into. ⁴⁴So you also must be ready, because the Son of Man will come at an hour when you do not expect him.

⁴⁵"Who then is the faithful and wise servant, whom the master has put in charge of the servants in his household to give them their food at the proper time? ⁴⁶It will be good for that servant whose master finds him doing so when he returns. ⁴⁷I tell you the truth, he will put him in charge of all his possessions. ⁴⁸But suppose that servant is wicked and says to himself, 'My master is staying away a long time,' ⁴⁹and he then begins to beat his fellow servants and to eat and drink with drunkards. ⁵⁰The master of that servant will come on a day when he does not expect him and at an hour he is not aware of. ⁵¹He will cut him to pieces and assign him a place with the hypocrites, where there will be weeping and gnashing of teeth.

Matthew 24:35

God Is Eternal

"Heaven and earth will pass away, but my words will never pass away."

The Parable of the Ten Virgins

25 "At that time the kingdom of heaven will be like ten virgins who took their lamps and went out to meet the bridegroom. ²Five of them were foolish and five were wise. ³The foolish ones took their lamps but did not take any oil with them. ⁴The wise, however, took oil in jars along with their lamps. ⁵The

a29 Isaiah 13:10; 34:4   *b33* Or *he*   *c34* Or *race*   *d36* Some manuscripts do not have *nor the Son.*

bridegroom was a long time in coming, and they all became drowsy and fell asleep.

⁶"At midnight the cry rang out: 'Here's the bridegroom! Come out to meet him!'

⁷"Then all the virgins woke up and trimmed their lamps. ⁸The foolish ones said to the wise, 'Give us some of your oil; our lamps are going out.'

⁹"'No,' they replied, 'there may not be enough for both us and you. Instead, go to those who sell oil and buy some for yourselves.'

¹⁰"But while they were on their way to buy the oil, the bridegroom arrived. The virgins who were ready went in with him to the wedding banquet. And the door was shut.

¹¹"Later the others also came. 'Sir! Sir!' they said. 'Open the door for us!'

¹²"But he replied, 'I tell you the truth, I don't know you.'

¹³"Therefore keep watch, because you do not know the day or the hour.

The Parable of the Talents

¹⁴"Again, it will be like a man going on a journey, who called his servants and entrusted his property to them. ¹⁵To one he gave five talents*a* of money, to another two talents, and to another one talent, each according to his ability. Then he went on his journey. ¹⁶The man who had received the five talents went at once and put his money to work and gained five more. ¹⁷So also, the one with the two talents gained two more. ¹⁸But the man who had received the one talent went off, dug a hole in the ground and hid his master's money.

¹⁹"After a long time the master of those servants returned and settled accounts with them. ²⁰The man who had received the five talents brought the other five. 'Master,' he said, 'you entrusted me with five talents. See, I have gained five more.'

²¹"His master replied, 'Well done, good and faithful servant! You have been faithful with a few things; I will put you in charge of many things. Come and share your master's happiness!'

²²"The man with the two talents also came. 'Master,' he said, 'you entrusted me with two talents; see, I have gained two more.'

²³"His master replied, 'Well done, good and faithful servant! You have been faithful with a few things; I will put you in charge of many things. Come and share your master's happiness!'

²⁴"Then the man who had received the one talent came. 'Master,' he said, 'I knew that you are a hard man, harvesting where you have not sown and gathering where you have not scattered seed. ²⁵So I was afraid and went out and hid your talent in the ground. See, here is what belongs to you.'

²⁶"His master replied, 'You wicked, lazy servant! So you knew that I harvest where I have not sown and gather where I have not scattered seed? ²⁷Well then, you should have put my money on deposit with the bankers, so that when I returned I would have received it back with interest.

²⁸"'Take the talent from him and give it to the one who has the ten talents. ²⁹For everyone who has will be given more, and he will have an abundance. Whoever does not have, even what he has will be taken from him. ³⁰And throw that worthless servant outside, into the darkness, where there will be weeping and gnashing of teeth.'

The Sheep and the Goats

³¹"When the Son of Man comes in his glory, and all the angels with him, he will sit on his throne in heavenly glory. ³²All the nations will be gathered before him, and he will separate the people one from another as a shepherd separates the sheep from the goats. ³³He will put the sheep on his right and the goats on his left.

³⁴"Then the King will say to those on his right, 'Come, you who are blessed by my Father; take your inheritance, the kingdom prepared for you since the creation of the world. ³⁵For I was hungry and you gave me something to eat, I was thirsty and you gave me something to drink, I was a stranger and you invited me in, ³⁶I needed clothes and you clothed me, I was sick and you looked after me, I was in prison and you came to visit me.'

³⁷"Then the righteous will answer him, 'Lord, when did we see you hungry and feed you, or thirsty and give you something to

---

*a*15 A talent was worth more than a thousand dollars.

Always a Bridesmaid

Read: Matthew 25:1–13

DO YOU REMEMBER playing bride? Digging through the dress-up clothes to find the shiny white dress, high-heeled shoes and beautiful white veil? If you were playing with a group of friends, didn't you argue over who would "have to" be the bridesmaids and who would "get to" be the bride?

As we grew older, our imaginary play turned into the real event: picking the right dress, choosing the flowers and asking our sisters, friends and family members to serve as bridesmaids. But those women who remained unmarried were doomed to hear the tired old phrase "Always a bridesmaid, never a bride." But what's wrong with being a bridesmaid?

In the parable of the ten virgins, Jesus encouraged all believers to be like eager bridesmaids, ready and waiting for the coming of the bridegroom. In Jesus' wedding scenario, the wise bridesmaids, called "virgins," didn't carry bouquets of flowers; they carried oil-filled lamps. So why should we want to be like the bridesmaids? The secret is found in the symbolism behind the story.

The ancient Israelites considered marriage to be the greatest of life's events. When the time came for the wedding, the groom and his friends would dress in their finest clothes and parade to the home of the bride, usually by night, to bring the bride and her attendants to the groom's home. This was why it was so important for the bridesmaids to keep oil in their lamps . . . so they could light the way to the groom's home. Now you know where we probably got the idea for candlelight weddings!

But the oil in the lamps holds far more significance than its practical ability to illuminate the path or its romantic quality of providing ambience for the wedding. In Scripture, oil symbolizes the presence of the Holy Spirit (see 1 Samuel 16:13). Through this story, Jesus was symbolically reminding people that when he returns, he will be coming for those who are wise enough to be filled with the Holy Spirit. Are you ready? Are you like a wise bridesmaid with oil in your lamp?

Matthew 25:1–4

"At that time the kingdom of heaven will be like ten virgins who took their lamps and went out to meet the bridegroom. Five of them were foolish and five were wise. The foolish ones took their lamps but did not take any oil with them. The wise, however, took oil in jars along with their lamps."

reflection

1 How does this parable help you anticipate more fully Jesus Christ's return?

2 How do you know that the "lamp" of your heart is filled with the oil of the Holy Spirit?

3 Ask God to help you keep your lamp continually filled so you will be always ready and eagerly awaiting his coming.

RELATED READINGS

Acts 2:38–39;
Ephesians 5:15–18;
2 Timothy 1:13–14

Tuesday

Go to page 1197 for your next devotional reading.

drink? **38**When did we see you a stranger and invite you in, or needing clothes and clothe you? **39**When did we see you sick or in prison and go to visit you?'

40"The King will reply, 'I tell you the truth, whatever you did for one of the least of these brothers of mine, you did for me.'

41"Then he will say to those on his left, 'Depart from me, you who are cursed, into the eternal fire prepared for the devil and his angels. **42**For I was hungry and you gave me nothing to eat, I was thirsty and you gave me nothing to drink, **43**I was a stranger and you did not invite me in, I needed clothes and you did not clothe me, I was sick and in prison and you did not look after me.'

44"They also will answer, 'Lord, when did we see you hungry or thirsty or a stranger or needing clothes or sick or in prison, and did not help you?'

45"He will reply, 'I tell you the truth, whatever you did not do for one of the least of these, you did not do for me.'

46"Then they will go away to eternal punishment, but the righteous to eternal life."

The Plot Against Jesus

26 When Jesus had finished saying all these things, he said to his disciples, **2**"As you know, the Passover is two days away—and the Son of Man will be handed over to be crucified."

3Then the chief priests and the elders of the people assembled in the palace of the high priest, whose name was Caiaphas, **4**and they plotted to arrest Jesus in some sly way and kill him. **5**"But not during the Feast," they said, "or there may be a riot among the people."

Jesus Anointed at Bethany

6While Jesus was in Bethany in the home of a man known as Simon the Leper, **7**a woman came to him with an alabaster jar of very expensive perfume, which she poured on his head as he was reclining at the table.

8When the disciples saw this, they were indignant. "Why this waste?" they asked. **9**"This perfume could have been sold at a high price and the money given to the poor."

10Aware of this, Jesus said to them, "Why are you bothering this woman? She has done a beautiful thing to me. **11**The poor you will always have with you, but you will not always have me. **12**When she poured this perfume on my body, she did it to prepare me for burial. **13**I tell you the truth, wherever this gospel is preached throughout the world, what she has done will also be told, in memory of her."

Judas Agrees to Betray Jesus

14Then one of the Twelve—the one called Judas Iscariot—went to the chief priests **15**and asked, "What are you willing to give me if I hand him over to you?" So they counted out for him thirty silver coins. **16**From then on Judas watched for an opportunity to hand him over.

The Lord's Supper

17On the first day of the Feast of Unleavened Bread, the disciples came to Jesus and asked, "Where do you want us to make preparations for you to eat the Passover?"

18He replied, "Go into the city to a certain man and tell him, 'The Teacher says: My appointed time is near. I am going to celebrate the Passover with my disciples at your house.' " **19**So the disciples did as Jesus had directed them and prepared the Passover.

20When evening came, Jesus was reclining at the table with the Twelve. **21**And while they were eating, he said, "I tell you the truth, one of you will betray me."

22They were very sad and began to say to him one after the other, "Surely not I, Lord?"

23Jesus replied, "The one who has dipped his hand into the bowl with me will betray me. **24**The Son of Man will go just as it is written about him. But woe to that man who betrays the Son of Man! It would be better for him if he had not been born."

25Then Judas, the one who would betray him, said, "Surely not I, Rabbi?"

Jesus answered, "Yes, it is you."*a*

26While they were eating, Jesus took bread, gave thanks and broke it, and gave it to his disciples, saying, "Take and eat; this is my body."

27Then he took the cup, gave thanks and offered it to them, saying, "Drink from it, all of you. **28**This is my blood of the*b* covenant, which is poured out for many for the forgiveness of

---

*a***25** Or *"You yourself have said it"*   *b***28** Some manuscripts *the new*

Extravagant Love

Read: Matthew 26:6-13

"EXTRAVAGANT." "OVER THE TOP." "Totally in character for *her*," the disciples around the table might have thought. This woman did not follow convention. She didn't care that the men in the room were watching or what they thought. She just acted, and as a result, she is remembered to this day.

This scene continues to be an example of extravagant love. We know from John's Gospel that the woman mentioned here is Mary of Bethany, the sister of Lazarus and Martha. This event took place during the final week of Jesus' life, after he had raised Mary's brother from the dead and wept with her and her sister. Mary's life and faith must have undergone significant transformation in those following days and weeks. Although we can't know for sure what Mary was thinking, her act echoed the preparation of a body for burial. Mary's act wittingly or unwittingly foreshadowed Jesus' coming death on the cross.

Put yourself in Mary's shoes. Perhaps she had followed Christ and heard his predictions about the signs of the end times. Maybe she had heard him tell the parable of the ten virgins. She must have sensed something was different about Jesus that night. Although she may not have understood the full meaning of Jesus' words, Mary poured out her expensive perfume from an alabaster jar, anointing Jesus with her love. Most likely, she gave her Lord the most valuable thing she possessed. Though others criticized her, Jesus praised her for her extravagant expression of love for him, for preparing him for his burial in a symbolic way.

Abraham loved his son Isaac, yet he willingly offered him to God; and God gave him back as a blessing. Hannah offered Samuel to the Lord's service and has gone down in history as a woman most blessed. Mary had an alabaster jar of perfume. She broke it open and poured it out as a love offering. Jesus praised her actions and promised she would always be remembered.

What is your most precious possession? Are you willing to pour out your time? Your money? Your gifts? Your talents? When you give your best to Jesus, he will accept your offering of extravagant love with joy.

Matthew 26:10-12

Jesus said to them, "Why are you bothering this woman? She has done a beautiful thing to me. The poor you will always have with you, but you will not always have me. When she poured this perfume on my body, she did it to prepare me for burial."

reflection

1 What are you willing to offer Jesus today?

2 What are you holding back?

3 Do you ever worry about what others will think of your actions? Ask God for courage and willingness to act for Jesus no matter what others may think.

RELATED READINGS

Genesis 22:1-19;
1 Samuel 1:21—2:11;
Mark 14:3-9;
Luke 6:38

"We can do no great things—only small things with great love."

Mother Teresa

Wednesday

Go to page 1205 for your next devotional reading.

sins. [29]I tell you, I will not drink of this fruit of the vine from now on until that day when I drink it anew with you in my Father's kingdom."

[30]When they had sung a hymn, they went out to the Mount of Olives.

Jesus Predicts Peter's Denial

[31]Then Jesus told them, "This very night you will all fall away on account of me, for it is written:

" 'I will strike the shepherd,
    and the sheep of the flock will be
        scattered.'[a]

[32]But after I have risen, I will go ahead of you into Galilee."

[33]Peter replied, "Even if all fall away on account of you, I never will."

[34]"I tell you the truth," Jesus answered, "this very night, before the rooster crows, you will disown me three times."

[35]But Peter declared, "Even if I have to die with you, I will never disown you." And all the other disciples said the same.

Gethsemane

[36]Then Jesus went with his disciples to a place called Gethsemane, and he said to them, "Sit here while I go over there and pray." [37]He took Peter and the two sons of Zebedee along with him, and he began to be sorrowful and troubled. [38]Then he said to them, "My soul is overwhelmed with sorrow to the point of death. Stay here and keep watch with me."

[39]Going a little farther, he fell with his face to the ground and prayed, "My Father, if it is possible, may this cup be taken from me. Yet not as I will, but as you will."

[40]Then he returned to his disciples and found them sleeping. "Could you men not keep watch with me for one hour?" he asked Peter. [41]"Watch and pray so that you will not fall into temptation. The spirit is willing, but the body is weak."

[42]He went away a second time and prayed, "My Father, if it is not possible for this cup to be taken away unless I drink it, may your will be done."

[43]When he came back, he again found them sleeping, because their eyes were heavy. [44]So he left them and went away once more and prayed the third time, saying the same thing.

[45]Then he returned to the disciples and said to them, "Are you still sleeping and resting? Look, the hour is near, and the Son of Man is betrayed into the hands of sinners. [46]Rise, let us go! Here comes my betrayer!"

Jesus Arrested

[47]While he was still speaking, Judas, one of the Twelve, arrived. With him was a large crowd armed with swords and clubs, sent from the chief priests and the elders of the people. [48]Now the betrayer had arranged a signal with them: "The one I kiss is the man; arrest him." [49]Going at once to Jesus, Judas said, "Greetings, Rabbi!" and kissed him.

[50]Jesus replied, "Friend, do what you came for."[b]

Then the men stepped forward, seized Jesus and arrested him. [51]With that, one of Jesus' companions reached for his sword, drew it out and struck the servant of the high priest, cutting off his ear.

[52]"Put your sword back in its place," Jesus said to him, "for all who draw the sword will die by the sword. [53]Do you think I cannot call on my Father, and he will at once put at my disposal more than twelve legions of angels? [54]But how then would the Scriptures be fulfilled that say it must happen in this way?"

[55]At that time Jesus said to the crowd, "Am I leading a rebellion, that you have come out with swords and clubs to capture me? Every day I sat in the temple courts teaching, and you did not arrest me. [56]But this has all taken place that the writings of the prophets might be fulfilled." Then all the disciples deserted him and fled.

Before the Sanhedrin

[57]Those who had arrested Jesus took him to Caiaphas, the high priest, where the teachers of the law and the elders had assembled. [58]But Peter followed him at a distance, right up to the courtyard of the high priest. He entered and sat down with the guards to see the outcome.

[59]The chief priests and the whole Sanhedrin were looking for false evidence against Jesus so

[a]31 Zech. 13:7   [b]50 Or *"Friend, why have you come?"*

that they could put him to death. ⁶⁰But they did not find any, though many false witnesses came forward.

Finally two came forward ⁶¹and declared, "This fellow said, 'I am able to destroy the temple of God and rebuild it in three days.'"

⁶²Then the high priest stood up and said to Jesus, "Are you not going to answer? What is this testimony that these men are bringing against you?" ⁶³But Jesus remained silent.

The high priest said to him, "I charge you under oath by the living God: Tell us if you are the Christ,ᵃ the Son of God."

⁶⁴"Yes, it is as you say," Jesus replied. "But I say to all of you: In the future you will see the Son of Man sitting at the right hand of the Mighty One and coming on the clouds of heaven."

⁶⁵Then the high priest tore his clothes and said, "He has spoken blasphemy! Why do we need any more witnesses? Look, now you have heard the blasphemy. ⁶⁶What do you think?"

"He is worthy of death," they answered.

⁶⁷Then they spit in his face and struck him with their fists. Others slapped him ⁶⁸and said, "Prophesy to us, Christ. Who hit you?"

Peter Disowns Jesus

⁶⁹Now Peter was sitting out in the courtyard, and a servant girl came to him. "You also were with Jesus of Galilee," she said.

⁷⁰But he denied it before them all. "I don't know what you're talking about," he said.

⁷¹Then he went out to the gateway, where another girl saw him and said to the people there, "This fellow was with Jesus of Nazareth."

⁷²He denied it again, with an oath: "I don't know the man!"

⁷³After a little while, those standing there went up to Peter and said, "Surely you are one of them, for your accent gives you away."

⁷⁴Then he began to call down curses on himself and he swore to them, "I don't know the man!"

Immediately a rooster crowed. ⁷⁵Then Peter remembered the word Jesus had spoken: "Before the rooster crows, you will disown me three times." And he went outside and wept bitterly.

Judas Hangs Himself

27 Early in the morning, all the chief priests and the elders of the people came to the decision to put Jesus to death. ²They bound him, led him away and handed him over to Pilate, the governor.

³When Judas, who had betrayed him, saw that Jesus was condemned, he was seized with remorse and returned the thirty silver coins to the chief priests and the elders. ⁴"I have sinned," he said, "for I have betrayed innocent blood."

"What is that to us?" they replied. "That's your responsibility."

⁵So Judas threw the money into the temple and left. Then he went away and hanged himself.

⁶The chief priests picked up the coins and said, "It is against the law to put this into the treasury, since it is blood money." ⁷So they decided to use the money to buy the potter's field as a burial place for foreigners. ⁸That is why it has been called the Field of Blood to this day. ⁹Then what was spoken by Jeremiah the prophet was fulfilled: "They took the thirty silver coins, the price set on him by the people of Israel, ¹⁰and they used them to buy the potter's field, as the Lord commanded me."ᵇ

Jesus Before Pilate

¹¹Meanwhile Jesus stood before the governor, and the governor asked him, "Are you the king of the Jews?"

"Yes, it is as you say," Jesus replied.

¹²When he was accused by the chief priests

Matthew 26:64

God Is the Mighty One

"Yes, it is as you say," Jesus replied. "But I say to all of you: In the future you will see the Son of Man sitting at the right hand of the Mighty One and coming on the clouds of heaven."

ᵃ63 Or *Messiah*; also in verse 68   ᵇ10 See Zech. 11:12,13; Jer. 19:1–13; 32:6–9.

and the elders, he gave no answer. ¹³Then Pilate asked him, "Don't you hear the testimony they are bringing against you?" ¹⁴But Jesus made no reply, not even to a single charge—to the great amazement of the governor.

¹⁵Now it was the governor's custom at the Feast to release a prisoner chosen by the crowd. ¹⁶At that time they had a notorious prisoner, called Barabbas. ¹⁷So when the crowd had gathered, Pilate asked them, "Which one do you want me to release to you: Barabbas, or Jesus who is called Christ?" ¹⁸For he knew it was out of envy that they had handed Jesus over to him.

¹⁹While Pilate was sitting on the judge's seat, his wife sent him this message: "Don't have anything to do with that innocent man, for I have suffered a great deal today in a dream because of him."

²⁰But the chief priests and the elders persuaded the crowd to ask for Barabbas and to have Jesus executed.

²¹"Which of the two do you want me to release to you?" asked the governor.

"Barabbas," they answered.

²²"What shall I do, then, with Jesus who is called Christ?" Pilate asked.

They all answered, "Crucify him!"

²³"Why? What crime has he committed?" asked Pilate.

But they shouted all the louder, "Crucify him!"

²⁴When Pilate saw that he was getting nowhere, but that instead an uproar was starting, he took water and washed his hands in front of the crowd. "I am innocent of this man's blood," he said. "It is your responsibility!"

²⁵All the people answered, "Let his blood be on us and on our children!"

²⁶Then he released Barabbas to them. But he had Jesus flogged, and handed him over to be crucified.

The Soldiers Mock Jesus

²⁷Then the governor's soldiers took Jesus into the Praetorium and gathered the whole company of soldiers around him. ²⁸They stripped him and put a scarlet robe on him, ²⁹and then twisted together a crown of thorns and set it on his head. They put a staff in his right hand and knelt in front of him and mocked him. "Hail, king of the Jews!" they said. ³⁰They spit on him, and took the staff and struck him on the head again and again. ³¹After they had mocked him, they took off the robe and put his own clothes on him. Then they led him away to crucify him.

The Crucifixion

³²As they were going out, they met a man from Cyrene, named Simon, and they forced him to carry the cross. ³³They came to a place called Golgotha (which means The Place of the Skull). ³⁴There they offered Jesus wine to drink, mixed with gall; but after tasting it, he refused to drink it. ³⁵When they had crucified him, they divided up his clothes by casting lots.ᵃ ³⁶And sitting down, they kept watch over him there. ³⁷Above his head they placed the written charge against him: THIS IS JESUS, THE KING OF THE JEWS. ³⁸Two robbers were crucified with him, one on his right and one on his left. ³⁹Those who passed by hurled insults at him, shaking their heads ⁴⁰and saying, "You who are going to destroy the temple and build it in three days, save yourself! Come down from the cross, if you are the Son of God!"

⁴¹In the same way the chief priests, the teachers of the law and the elders mocked him. ⁴²"He saved others," they said, "but he can't save himself! He's the King of Israel! Let him come down now from the cross, and we will believe in him. ⁴³He trusts in God. Let God rescue him now if he wants him, for he said, 'I am the Son of God.'" ⁴⁴In the same way the robbers who were crucified with him also heaped insults on him.

The Death of Jesus

⁴⁵From the sixth hour until the ninth hour darkness came over all the land. ⁴⁶About the ninth hour Jesus cried out in a loud voice, *"Eloi, Eloi,ᵇ lama sabachthani?"*—which means, "My God, my God, why have you forsaken me?"ᶜ

⁴⁷When some of those standing there heard this, they said, "He's calling Elijah."

⁴⁸Immediately one of them ran and got a sponge. He filled it with wine vinegar, put it on

---

ᵃ35 A few late manuscripts *lots that the word spoken by the prophet might be fulfilled: "They divided my garments among themselves and cast lots for my clothing"* (Psalm 22:18)   ᵇ46 Some manuscripts *Eli, Eli*   ᶜ46 Psalm 22:1

a stick, and offered it to Jesus to drink. ⁴⁹The rest said, "Now leave him alone. Let's see if Elijah comes to save him."

⁵⁰And when Jesus had cried out again in a loud voice, he gave up his spirit.

⁵¹At that moment the curtain of the temple was torn in two from top to bottom. The earth shook and the rocks split. ⁵²The tombs broke open and the bodies of many holy people who had died were raised to life. ⁵³They came out of the tombs, and after Jesus' resurrection they went into the holy city and appeared to many people.

⁵⁴When the centurion and those with him who were guarding Jesus saw the earthquake and all that had happened, they were terrified, and exclaimed, "Surely he was the Son*a* of God!"

⁵⁵Many women were there, watching from a distance. They had followed Jesus from Galilee to care for his needs. ⁵⁶Among them were Mary Magdalene, Mary the mother of James and Joses, and the mother of Zebedee's sons.

The Burial of Jesus

⁵⁷As evening approached, there came a rich man from Arimathea, named Joseph, who had himself become a disciple of Jesus. ⁵⁸Going to Pilate, he asked for Jesus' body, and Pilate ordered that it be given to him. ⁵⁹Joseph took the body, wrapped it in a clean linen cloth, ⁶⁰and placed it in his own new tomb that he had cut out of the rock. He rolled a big stone in front of the entrance to the tomb and went away. ⁶¹Mary Magdalene and the other Mary were sitting there opposite the tomb.

The Guard at the Tomb

⁶²The next day, the one after Preparation Day, the chief priests and the Pharisees went to Pilate. ⁶³"Sir," they said, "we remember that while he was still alive that deceiver said, 'After three days I will rise again.' ⁶⁴So give the order for the tomb to be made secure until the third day. Otherwise, his disciples may come and steal the body and tell the people that he has been raised from the dead. This last deception will be worse than the first."

⁶⁵"Take a guard," Pilate answered. "Go, make the tomb as secure as you know how." ⁶⁶So they went and made the tomb secure by putting a seal on the stone and posting the guard.

The Resurrection

28

After the Sabbath, at dawn on the first day of the week, Mary Magdalene and the other Mary went to look at the tomb.

²There was a violent earthquake, for an angel of the Lord came down from heaven and, going to the tomb, rolled back the stone and sat on it. ³His appearance was like lightning, and his clothes were white as snow. ⁴The guards were so afraid of him that they shook and became like dead men.

⁵The angel said to the women, "Do not be afraid, for I know that you are looking for Jesus, who was crucified. ⁶He is not here; he has risen, just as he said. Come and see the place where he lay. ⁷Then go quickly and tell his disciples: 'He has risen from the dead and is going ahead of you into Galilee. There you will see him.' Now I have told you."

⁸So the women hurried away from the tomb, afraid yet filled with joy, and ran to tell his disciples. ⁹Suddenly Jesus met them. "Greetings," he said. They came to him, clasped his feet and worshiped him. ¹⁰Then Jesus said to them, "Do not be afraid. Go and tell my brothers to go to Galilee; there they will see me."

The Guards' Report

¹¹While the women were on their way, some of the guards went into the city and reported to the chief priests everything that had happened. ¹²When the chief priests had met with the elders and devised a plan, they gave the soldiers a large sum of money, ¹³telling them, "You are to say, 'His disciples came during the night and stole him away while we were asleep.' ¹⁴If this report gets to the governor, we will satisfy him and keep you out of trouble." ¹⁵So the soldiers took the money and did as they were instructed. And this story has been widely circulated among the Jews to this very day.

The Great Commission

¹⁶Then the eleven disciples went to Galilee, to the mountain where Jesus had told them to go. ¹⁷When they saw him, they worshiped him; but some doubted. ¹⁸Then Jesus came to them and said, "All authority in heaven and on earth

---

a54 Or *a son*

has been given to me. ¹⁹Therefore go and make disciples of all nations, baptizing them in*a* the name of the Father and of the Son and of the Holy Spirit, ²⁰and teaching them to obey everything I have commanded you. And surely I am with you always, to the very end of the age."

a19 Or *into*; see Acts 8:16; 19:5; Romans 6:3; 1 Cor. 1:13; 10:2 and Gal. 3:27.

1202

Mark

The story of Jesus' life, death and resurrection is told in the first four books of the New Testament. Of these four eyewitness accounts, the Gospel of Mark is *the most fast-paced narrative*. Historians are not exactly sure of Mark's identity, but most agree that he was a friend of Peter's, obtaining the information about the life of Jesus from him. Mark's excitement in telling his story is underscored by his repeated use of the words "immediately" and "at once."

The word *gospel* means "good news," and Mark emphasizes the "good news" of Jesus' ministry of salvation. *Mark is very clear about the deity of Christ* but also goes to great lengths to show his humanity. While he does not neglect recounting the teachings of Jesus, it is the actions of Jesus that stir his heart. The purpose of this Gospel is to tell Jesus' life story so that all will come to the conclusion that, *"Yes, Jesus is the Son of God."*

Author:
John Mark.

Audience:
Followers of Jesus. Mark wrote with a Roman audience in mind.

Date:
Probably between A.D. 55 and 65.

Setting:
Mark most likely wrote from Rome. Early church sources tell us the apostle Peter relayed information to Mark for his Gospel.

Verse to Remember:
Then a cloud appeared and enveloped them, and a voice came from the cloud: "This is my Son, whom I love. Listen to him!" (9:7)

John the Baptist Prepares the Way

1 The beginning of the gospel about Jesus Christ, the Son of God.*a*

²It is written in Isaiah the prophet:

"I will send my messenger ahead of you,
  who will prepare your way"*b*—

³"a voice of one calling in the desert,
 'Prepare the way for the Lord,
  make straight paths for him.'"*c*

⁴And so John came, baptizing in the desert region and preaching a baptism of repentance for the forgiveness of sins. ⁵The whole Judean countryside and all the people of Jerusalem went out

*a*1 Some manuscripts do not have *the Son of God.*   *b*2 Mal. 3:1   *c*3 Isaiah 40:3

to him. Confessing their sins, they were baptized by him in the Jordan River. ⁶John wore clothing made of camel's hair, with a leather belt around his waist, and he ate locusts and wild honey. ⁷And this was his message: "After me will come one more powerful than I, the thongs of whose sandals I am not worthy to stoop down and untie. ⁸I baptize you with*a* water, but he will baptize you with the Holy Spirit."

The Baptism and Temptation of Jesus

⁹At that time Jesus came from Nazareth in Galilee and was baptized by John in the Jordan. ¹⁰As Jesus was coming up out of the water, he saw heaven being torn open and the Spirit descending on him like a dove. ¹¹And a voice came from heaven: "You are my Son, whom I love; with you I am well pleased."

¹²At once the Spirit sent him out into the desert, ¹³and he was in the desert forty days, being tempted by Satan. He was with the wild animals, and angels attended him.

The Calling of the First Disciples

¹⁴After John was put in prison, Jesus went into Galilee, proclaiming the good news of God. ¹⁵"The time has come," he said. "The kingdom of God is near. Repent and believe the good news!"

¹⁶As Jesus walked beside the Sea of Galilee, he saw Simon and his brother Andrew casting a net into the lake, for they were fishermen. ¹⁷"Come, follow me," Jesus said, "and I will make you fishers of men." ¹⁸At once they left their nets and followed him.

¹⁹When he had gone a little farther, he saw James son of Zebedee and his brother John in a boat, preparing their nets. ²⁰Without delay he called them, and they left their father Zebedee in the boat with the hired men and followed him.

Jesus Drives Out an Evil Spirit

²¹They went to Capernaum, and when the Sabbath came, Jesus went into the synagogue and began to teach. ²²The people were amazed at his teaching, because he taught them as one who had authority, not as the teachers of the law. ²³Just then a man in their synagogue who was possessed by an evil*b* spirit cried out,

²⁴"What do you want with us, Jesus of Nazareth? Have you come to destroy us? I know who you are—the Holy One of God!"

²⁵"Be quiet!" said Jesus sternly. "Come out of him!" ²⁶The evil spirit shook the man violently and came out of him with a shriek.

²⁷The people were all so amazed that they asked each other, "What is this? A new teaching—and with authority! He even gives orders to evil spirits and they obey him." ²⁸News about him spread quickly over the whole region of Galilee.

Jesus Heals Many

²⁹As soon as they left the synagogue, they went with James and John to the home of Simon and Andrew. ³⁰Simon's mother-in-law was in bed with a fever, and they told Jesus about her. ³¹So he went to her, took her hand and helped her up. The fever left her and she began to wait on them.

³²That evening after sunset the people brought to Jesus all the sick and demon-possessed. ³³The whole town gathered at the door, ³⁴and Jesus healed many who had various diseases. He also drove out many demons, but he would not let the demons speak because they knew who he was.

Jesus Prays in a Solitary Place

³⁵Very early in the morning, while it was still dark, Jesus got up, left the house and went off to a solitary place, where he prayed. ³⁶Simon and his companions went to look for him, ³⁷and when they found him, they exclaimed: "Everyone is looking for you!"

³⁸Jesus replied, "Let us go somewhere else—to the nearby villages—so I can preach there also. That is why I have come." ³⁹So he traveled throughout Galilee, preaching in their synagogues and driving out demons.

A Man With Leprosy

⁴⁰A man with leprosy*c* came to him and begged him on his knees, "If you are willing, you can make me clean."

⁴¹Filled with compassion, Jesus reached out his hand and touched the man. "I am willing," he said. "Be clean!" ⁴²Immediately the leprosy left him and he was cured.

---

*a*8 Or *in* *b*23 Greek *unclean*; also in verses 26 and 27 *c*40 The Greek word was used for various diseases affecting the skin—not necessarily leprosy.

Expect the Extraordinary

Read: Mark 1:14–20

IT WAS A DAY LIKE ANY OTHER. It's likely the four men kissed their families good-bye and went down to the shore—just as they did every day. They probably told jokes, talked about their hopes and dreams, and bragged about how many fish they'd catch. This was the life they knew, the life they thought they were destined to live. Being fishermen was more than what they did; it was who they were.

Then something extraordinary happened. Jesus came on the scene.

When the divine intersects with the ordinary, everything changes. An ordinary man who catches fish becomes a disciple who fishes for people. A mother whose daily life consists of changing diapers and folding laundry becomes a shepherdess of young lives. A smart businesswoman becomes a spiritual leader. A teacher becomes a mentor. A friend becomes an intercessor. A student becomes a missionary. A tongue-tied wallflower blossoms into a gifted speaker. When Jesus enters the scene, we can expect the extraordinary.

The four Galileans could never have guessed the turn their lives would take that day. They were ordinary men living ordinary lives. But they recognized the extraordinary when they saw it, left everything they knew and chose to follow him.

There were other people at the lake that day who saw Jesus, other people who heard him speak. The father of James and John was there. So were some hired men. They heard and they saw, but they stayed with their nets and fished for fish.

When Jesus calls us to follow him, he is looking for people who are willing to let go of the ordinary and look for the extraordinary. Sometimes that means we're called to leave everything—our nets and our families—and go where he tells us. Other times, following him means we keep doing what we've been doing, only with a shift in our perspective: We still change diapers, but we focus on raising godly children. We still do laundry, but as we do, we remember that we serve the God of holiness. We still do business, but we remember that it's all kingdom business. We still go fishing, but now we fish for people as well as fish.

Go to page 1208 for your next devotional reading.

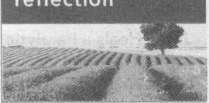

Mark 1:17

"Come, follow me," Jesus said, "and I will make you fishers of men."

reflection

1 When you heard Jesus' call for the first time, what changed for you?

2 Do you identify more with the men who left everything to follow Jesus or with those who stayed with their nets?

3 Jesus called fishermen to become "fishers of men." What is he calling you to do today?

RELATED READINGS

1 Corinthians 1:26–31; 1 Peter 2:9–10

43 Jesus sent him away at once with a strong warning: 44"See that you don't tell this to anyone. But go, show yourself to the priest and offer the sacrifices that Moses commanded for your cleansing, as a testimony to them." 45 Instead he went out and began to talk freely, spreading the news. As a result, Jesus could no longer enter a town openly but stayed outside in lonely places. Yet the people still came to him from everywhere.

Jesus Heals a Paralytic

2 A few days later, when Jesus again entered Capernaum, the people heard that he had come home. 2 So many gathered that there was no room left, not even outside the door, and he preached the word to them. 3 Some men came, bringing to him a paralytic, carried by four of them. 4 Since they could not get him to Jesus because of the crowd, they made an opening in the roof above Jesus and, after digging through it, lowered the mat the paralyzed man was lying on. 5 When Jesus saw their faith, he said to the paralytic, "Son, your sins are forgiven."

6 Now some teachers of the law were sitting there, thinking to themselves, 7"Why does this fellow talk like that? He's blaspheming! Who can forgive sins but God alone?"

8 Immediately Jesus knew in his spirit that this was what they were thinking in their hearts, and he said to them, "Why are you thinking these things? 9 Which is easier: to say to the paralytic, 'Your sins are forgiven,' or to say, 'Get up, take your mat and walk'? 10 But that you may know that the Son of Man has authority on earth to forgive sins..." He said to the paralytic, 11"I tell you, get up, take your mat and go home." 12 He got up, took his mat and walked out in full view of them all. This amazed everyone and they praised God, saying, "We have never seen anything like this!"

The Calling of Levi

13 Once again Jesus went out beside the lake. A large crowd came to him, and he began to teach them. 14 As he walked along, he saw Levi son of Alphaeus sitting at the tax collector's booth. "Follow me," Jesus told him, and Levi got up and followed him.

15 While Jesus was having dinner at Levi's house, many tax collectors and "sinners" were eating with him and his disciples, for there were many who followed him. 16 When the teachers of the law who were Pharisees saw him eating with the "sinners" and tax collectors, they asked his disciples: "Why does he eat with tax collectors and 'sinners'?"

17 On hearing this, Jesus said to them, "It is not the healthy who need a doctor, but the sick. I have not come to call the righteous, but sinners."

Jesus Questioned About Fasting

18 Now John's disciples and the Pharisees were fasting. Some people came and asked Jesus, "How is it that John's disciples and the disciples of the Pharisees are fasting, but yours are not?"

19 Jesus answered, "How can the guests of the bridegroom fast while he is with them? They cannot, so long as they have him with them. 20 But the time will come when the bridegroom will be taken from them, and on that day they will fast.

21"No one sews a patch of unshrunk cloth on an old garment. If he does, the new piece will pull away from the old, making the tear worse. 22 And no one pours new wine into old wineskins. If he does, the wine will burst the skins, and both the wine and the wineskins will be ruined. No, he pours new wine into new wineskins."

Lord of the Sabbath

23 One Sabbath Jesus was going through the grainfields, and as his disciples walked along, they began to pick some heads of grain. 24 The Pharisees said to him, "Look, why are they doing what is unlawful on the Sabbath?"

25 He answered, "Have you never read what David did when he and his companions were hungry and in need? 26 In the days of Abiathar the high priest, he entered the house of God and ate the consecrated bread, which is lawful only for priests to eat. And he also gave some to his companions."

27 Then he said to them, "The Sabbath was made for man, not man for the Sabbath. 28 So the Son of Man is Lord even of the Sabbath."

3 Another time he went into the synagogue, and a man with a shriveled hand was there. 2 Some of them were looking for a reason to ac-

cuse Jesus, so they watched him closely to see if he would heal him on the Sabbath. ³Jesus said to the man with the shriveled hand, "Stand up in front of everyone."

⁴Then Jesus asked them, "Which is lawful on the Sabbath: to do good or to do evil, to save life or to kill?" But they remained silent.

⁵He looked around at them in anger and, deeply distressed at their stubborn hearts, said to the man, "Stretch out your hand." He stretched it out, and his hand was completely restored. ⁶Then the Pharisees went out and began to plot with the Herodians how they might kill Jesus.

Crowds Follow Jesus

⁷Jesus withdrew with his disciples to the lake, and a large crowd from Galilee followed. ⁸When they heard all he was doing, many people came to him from Judea, Jerusalem, Idumea, and the regions across the Jordan and around Tyre and Sidon. ⁹Because of the crowd he told his disciples to have a small boat ready for him, to keep the people from crowding him. ¹⁰For he had healed many, so that those with diseases were pushing forward to touch him. ¹¹Whenever the evil*a* spirits saw him, they fell down before him and cried out, "You are the Son of God." ¹²But he gave them strict orders not to tell who he was.

The Appointing of the Twelve Apostles

¹³Jesus went up on a mountainside and called to him those he wanted, and they came to him. ¹⁴He appointed twelve—designating them apostles*b*—that they might be with him and that he might send them out to preach ¹⁵and to have authority to drive out demons. ¹⁶These are the twelve he appointed: Simon (to whom he gave the name Peter); ¹⁷James son of Zebedee and his brother John (to them he gave the name Boanerges, which means Sons of Thunder); ¹⁸Andrew, Philip, Bartholomew, Matthew, Thomas, James son of Alphaeus, Thaddaeus, Simon the Zealot ¹⁹and Judas Iscariot, who betrayed him.

Jesus and Beelzebub

²⁰Then Jesus entered a house, and again a crowd gathered, so that he and his disciples were not even able to eat. ²¹When his family heard about this, they went to take charge of him, for they said, "He is out of his mind."

²²And the teachers of the law who came down from Jerusalem said, "He is possessed by Beelzebub*c*! By the prince of demons he is driving out demons."

²³So Jesus called them and spoke to them in parables: "How can Satan drive out Satan? ²⁴If a kingdom is divided against itself, that kingdom cannot stand. ²⁵If a house is divided against itself, that house cannot stand. ²⁶And if Satan opposes himself and is divided, he cannot stand; his end has come. ²⁷In fact, no one can enter a strong man's house and carry off his possessions unless he first ties up the strong man. Then he can rob his house. ²⁸I tell you the truth, all the sins and blasphemies of men will be forgiven them. ²⁹But whoever blasphemes against the Holy Spirit will never be forgiven; he is guilty of an eternal sin."

³⁰He said this because they were saying, "He has an evil spirit."

Jesus' Mother and Brothers

³¹Then Jesus' mother and brothers arrived. Standing outside, they sent someone in to call him. ³²A crowd was sitting around him, and they told him, "Your mother and brothers are outside looking for you."

³³"Who are my mother and my brothers?" he asked.

³⁴Then he looked at those seated in a circle around him and said, "Here are my mother and my brothers! ³⁵Whoever does God's will is my brother and sister and mother."

> **Mark 3:35**
>
> *God Is Our Family*
>
> "Whoever does God's will is my brother and sister and mother."

The Parable of the Sower

4 Again Jesus began to teach by the lake. The crowd that gathered around him was so large that he got into a boat and sat in it out on the lake, while all the people were along the shore at the water's edge. ²He taught them

---

*a*11 Greek *unclean*; also in verse 30   *b*14 Some manuscripts do not have *designating them apostles*.   *c*22 Greek *Beezeboul* or *Beelzeboul*

Something Wonderful

Read: Mark 3:1–19

Mark 3:13

Jesus went up on a mountainside and called to him those he wanted, and they came to him.

reflection

1 What is God asking you to do that you are afraid to undertake?

2 What excuses have you been giving for not accepting the task?

3 What are the spiritual and physical resources you need to accept God's call? Ask God to give them to you.

RELATED READINGS

Exodus 3:1–12;
Romans 1:1–7;
1 Corinthians 1:26–31

"WHO, ME, LORD?"

"Yes, you. I'm calling you."

"But what you're asking of me is too difficult. I don't have the skills or the training. I can't possibly succeed at this!"

Does this conversation sound familiar? Many of us know the experience of being asked to take on a task that seems much too demanding for us. We're afraid of failure. We make excuses. But by doing so, we may miss the joy of being part of something wonderful.

In *The Purpose Driven Life*, author Rick Warren responds to those who make excuses concerning why they cannot serve the Lord: "Abraham was old, Jacob was insecure, Leah was unattractive, Joseph was abused, Moses stuttered, Gideon was poor, Samson was codependent, Rahab was immoral, David had an affair and all kinds of family problems, Elijah was suicidal, Jeremiah was depressed, Jonah was reluctant, Naomi was a widow, John the Baptist was eccentric to say the least, Peter was impulsive and hot-tempered, Martha worried a lot, the Samaritan woman had several failed marriages, Zacchaeus was unpopular, Thomas had doubts, Paul had poor health, and Timothy was timid."

The 12 men Jesus asked to be his apostles could have offered lots of reasons why they were not fit to serve. They were common men with no special standing in the eyes of the world. Yet when Jesus called, they came: fishermen, tax collectors and even revolutionaries. History shows that their faith and obedience to Jesus Christ changed the world profoundly.

When Jesus calls us to follow him, he's not looking for the smartest or the strongest or the most brave. He doesn't check our resume or call our list of references. Scripture is full of stories of women and men who were used powerfully by God despite their lack of experience or expertise. How about you? Is God asking you to accept an assignment that seems far beyond your comfort zone? Are you afraid that you might fail? Are you afraid that you might succeed?

Take heart from this account of those whom Jesus chose to be his closest companions—those who would carry on his work. They changed the world not because of what they had in themselves, but because of the One who empowered them. And they were part of something wonderful.

Friday

many things by parables, and in his teaching said: ³"Listen! A farmer went out to sow his seed. ⁴As he was scattering the seed, some fell along the path, and the birds came and ate it up. ⁵Some fell on rocky places, where it did not have much soil. It sprang up quickly, because the soil was shallow. ⁶But when the sun came up, the plants were scorched, and they withered because they had no root. ⁷Other seed fell among thorns, which grew up and choked the plants, so that they did not bear grain. ⁸Still other seed fell on good soil. It came up, grew and produced a crop, multiplying thirty, sixty, or even a hundred times."

⁹Then Jesus said, "He who has ears to hear, let him hear."

¹⁰When he was alone, the Twelve and the others around him asked him about the parables. ¹¹He told them, "The secret of the kingdom of God has been given to you. But to those on the outside everything is said in parables ¹²so that,

> "'they may be ever seeing but never
> perceiving,
> and ever hearing but never
> understanding;
> otherwise they might turn and be
> forgiven!'ᵃ

¹³Then Jesus said to them, "Don't you understand this parable? How then will you understand any parable? ¹⁴The farmer sows the word. ¹⁵Some people are like seed along the path, where the word is sown. As soon as they hear it, Satan comes and takes away the word that was sown in them. ¹⁶Others, like seed sown on rocky places, hear the word and at once receive it with joy. ¹⁷But since they have no root, they last only a short time. When trouble or persecution comes because of the word, they quickly fall away. ¹⁸Still others, like seed sown among thorns, hear the word; ¹⁹but the worries of this life, the deceitfulness of wealth and the desires for other things come in and choke the word, making it unfruitful. ²⁰Others, like seed sown on good soil, hear the word, accept it, and produce a crop—thirty, sixty or even a hundred times what was sown."

ᵃ12 Isaiah 6:9,10

A Lamp on a Stand

²¹He said to them, "Do you bring in a lamp to put it under a bowl or a bed? Instead, don't you put it on its stand? ²²For whatever is hidden is meant to be disclosed, and whatever is concealed is meant to be brought out into the open. ²³If anyone has ears to hear, let him hear."

²⁴"Consider carefully what you hear," he continued. "With the measure you use, it will be measured to you—and even more. ²⁵Whoever has will be given more; whoever does not have, even what he has will be taken from him."

The Parable of the Growing Seed

²⁶He also said, "This is what the kingdom of God is like. A man scatters seed on the ground. ²⁷Night and day, whether he sleeps or gets up, the seed sprouts and grows, though he does not know how. ²⁸All by itself the soil produces grain—first the stalk, then the head, then the full kernel in the head. ²⁹As soon as the grain is ripe, he puts the sickle to it, because the harvest has come."

The Parable of the Mustard Seed

³⁰Again he said, "What shall we say the kingdom of God is like, or what parable shall we use to describe it? ³¹It is like a mustard seed, which is the smallest seed you plant in the ground. ³²Yet when planted, it grows and becomes the largest of all garden plants, with such big branches that the birds of the air can perch in its shade."

³³With many similar parables Jesus spoke the word to them, as much as they could understand. ³⁴He did not say anything to them without using a parable. But when he was alone with his own disciples, he explained everything.

Jesus Calms the Storm

³⁵That day when evening came, he said to his disciples, "Let us go over to the other side." ³⁶Leaving the crowd behind, they took him along, just as he was, in the boat. There were also other boats with him. ³⁷A furious squall came up, and the waves broke over the boat, so that it was nearly swamped. ³⁸Jesus was in the stern, sleeping on a cushion. The disciples woke him and said to him, "Teacher, don't you care if we drown?"

³⁹He got up, rebuked the wind and said to the waves, "Quiet! Be still!" Then the wind died down and it was completely calm.

⁴⁰He said to his disciples, "Why are you so afraid? Do you still have no faith?"

⁴¹They were terrified and asked each other, "Who is this? Even the wind and the waves obey him!"

The Healing of a Demon-possessed Man

5 They went across the lake to the region of the Gerasenes.^a ²When Jesus got out of the boat, a man with an evil^b spirit came from the tombs to meet him. ³This man lived in the tombs, and no one could bind him any more, not even with a chain. ⁴For he had often been chained hand and foot, but he tore the chains apart and broke the irons on his feet. No one was strong enough to subdue him. ⁵Night and day among the tombs and in the hills he would cry out and cut himself with stones.

⁶When he saw Jesus from a distance, he ran and fell on his knees in front of him. ⁷He shouted at the top of his voice, "What do you want with me, Jesus, Son of the Most High God? Swear to God that you won't torture me!" ⁸For Jesus had said to him, "Come out of this man, you evil spirit!"

⁹Then Jesus asked him, "What is your name?"

"My name is Legion," he replied, "for we are many." ¹⁰And he begged Jesus again and again not to send them out of the area.

¹¹A large herd of pigs was feeding on the nearby hillside. ¹²The demons begged Jesus, "Send us among the pigs; allow us to go into them." ¹³He gave them permission, and the evil spirits came out and went into the pigs. The herd, about two thousand in number, rushed down the steep bank into the lake and were drowned.

¹⁴Those tending the pigs ran off and reported this in the town and countryside, and the people went out to see what had happened. ¹⁵When they came to Jesus, they saw the man who had been possessed by the legion of demons, sitting there, dressed and in his right mind; and they were afraid. ¹⁶Those who had seen it told the people what had happened to the demon-possessed man—and told about the pigs as well. ¹⁷Then the people began to plead with Jesus to leave their region.

¹⁸As Jesus was getting into the boat, the man who had been demon-possessed begged to go with him. ¹⁹Jesus did not let him, but said, "Go home to your family and tell them how much the Lord has done for you, and how he has had mercy on you." ²⁰So the man went away and began to tell in the Decapolis^c how much Jesus had done for him. And all the people were amazed.

A Dead Girl and a Sick Woman

²¹When Jesus had again crossed over by boat to the other side of the lake, a large crowd gathered around him while he was by the lake. ²²Then one of the synagogue rulers, named Jairus, came there. Seeing Jesus, he fell at his feet ²³and pleaded earnestly with him, "My little daughter is dying. Please come and put your hands on her so that she will be healed and live." ²⁴So Jesus went with him.

A large crowd followed and pressed around him. ²⁵And a woman was there who had been subject to bleeding for twelve years. ²⁶She had suffered a great deal under the care of many doctors and had spent all she had, yet instead of getting better she grew worse. ²⁷When she heard about Jesus, she came up behind him in the crowd and touched his cloak, ²⁸because she thought, "If I just touch his clothes, I will be healed." ²⁹Immediately her bleeding stopped and she felt in her body that she was freed from her suffering.

³⁰At once Jesus realized that power had gone out from him. He turned around in the crowd and asked, "Who touched my clothes?"

³¹"You see the people crowding against you," his disciples answered, "and yet you can ask, 'Who touched me?'"

³²But Jesus kept looking around to see who had done it. ³³Then the woman, knowing what had happened to her, came and fell at his feet and, trembling with fear, told him the whole truth. ³⁴He said to her, "Daughter, your faith has healed you. Go in peace and be freed from your suffering."

³⁵While Jesus was still speaking, some men

a 1 Some manuscripts *Gadarenes*; other manuscripts *Gergesenes*   *b* 2 Greek *unclean*; also in verses 8 and 13   *c* 20 That is, the Ten Cities

1210

A Mother's Request

CANAANITE WOMAN

"HOW DID HE HEAL ME, Mother? Were you there when it happened?"

"My daughter, you ask me to tell you a story you've heard many times."

"I know, Mother." The young girl paused as if she were in deep thought. "But I still don't understand how Jesus could heal me when he wasn't even there in my room."

"You speak of a great mystery as if I can tell you the answer. I don't know how he did it. I just know he did. Now, come. We have much to do today."

Her daughter was not quite ready just yet. She slowly lifted her eyes to meet her mother's. "You must have loved me very much to go to him."

"Yes, very much, my daughter." Her mother smiled and tousled the young girl's hair.

This Canaanite mother knew she would never be able to express just how much she loved her child. How much she'd risked to save her. How far she'd pushed. How great her faith.

She could hardly bear to think back to the time when her daughter had been so sick that she'd almost lost her. Her pale skin, now ruddy with health, had then made her look more like an old spirit than a young girl. Her worst fear had come true before her eyes: her daughter was dying.

Is it any wonder that this mother would not take no for an answer from Jesus? Her faith compelled her to push past any limits. Love propelled her to pursue him with all her heart. Despite the fact that Jews regarded Canaanites as longtime enemies and even subhuman, she dared to make her request. She was willing to risk being seen as a fool, a "dog" no less, if it meant her daughter would live.

The girl took up her basket. "I'm ready, Mother."

Her mother smiled. It was worth every risk. Every single one.

—Prayer—
God in heaven, when might I take a risk in the name of faith? I pray I will be ready when God opens the door.

> *Then Jesus answered, "Woman, you have great faith! Your request is granted." And her daughter was healed from that very hour.*
>
> Matthew 15:28

ASSIGNED READING:
Matthew 15:21–28;
Mark 7:24–30

Go to page 1215 for your next devotional reading.

Weekend

came from the house of Jairus, the synagogue ruler. "Your daughter is dead," they said. "Why bother the teacher any more?"

[36] Ignoring what they said, Jesus told the synagogue ruler, "Don't be afraid; just believe."

[37] He did not let anyone follow him except Peter, James and John the brother of James. [38] When they came to the home of the synagogue ruler, Jesus saw a commotion, with people crying and wailing loudly. [39] He went in and said to them, "Why all this commotion and wailing? The child is not dead but asleep." [40] But they laughed at him.

After he put them all out, he took the child's father and mother and the disciples who were with him, and went in where the child was. [41] He took her by the hand and said to her, *"Talitha koum!"* (which means, "Little girl, I say to you, get up!"). [42] Immediately the girl stood up and walked around (she was twelve years old). At this they were completely astonished. [43] He gave strict orders not to let anyone know about this, and told them to give her something to eat.

A Prophet Without Honor

6 Jesus left there and went to his hometown, accompanied by his disciples. [2] When the Sabbath came, he began to teach in the synagogue, and many who heard him were amazed.

"Where did this man get these things?" they asked. "What's this wisdom that has been given him, that he even does miracles! [3] Isn't this the carpenter? Isn't this Mary's son and the brother of James, Joseph,[a] Judas and Simon? Aren't his sisters here with us?" And they took offense at him.

[4] Jesus said to them, "Only in his hometown, among his relatives and in his own house is a prophet without honor." [5] He could not do any miracles there, except lay his hands on a few sick people and heal them. [6] And he was amazed at their lack of faith.

Jesus Sends Out the Twelve

Then Jesus went around teaching from village to village. [7] Calling the Twelve to him, he sent them out two by two and gave them authority over evil[b] spirits.

[8] These were his instructions: "Take nothing for the journey except a staff—no bread, no bag, no money in your belts. [9] Wear sandals but not an extra tunic. [10] Whenever you enter a house, stay there until you leave that town. [11] And if any place will not welcome you or listen to you, shake the dust off your feet when you leave, as a testimony against them."

[12] They went out and preached that people should repent. [13] They drove out many demons and anointed many sick people with oil and healed them.

John the Baptist Beheaded

[14] King Herod heard about this, for Jesus' name had become well known. Some were saying,[c] "John the Baptist has been raised from the dead, and that is why miraculous powers are at work in him."

[15] Others said, "He is Elijah."

And still others claimed, "He is a prophet, like one of the prophets of long ago."

[16] But when Herod heard this, he said, "John, the man I beheaded, has been raised from the dead!"

[17] For Herod himself had given orders to have John arrested, and he had him bound and put in prison. He did this because of Herodias, his brother Philip's wife, whom he had married. [18] For John had been saying to Herod, "It is not lawful for you to have your brother's wife." [19] So Herodias nursed a grudge against John and wanted to kill him. But she was not able to, [20] because Herod feared John and protected him, knowing him to be a righteous and holy man. When Herod heard John, he was greatly puzzled[d]; yet he liked to listen to him.

[21] Finally the opportune time came. On his birthday Herod gave a banquet for his high officials and military commanders and the leading men of Galilee. [22] When the daughter of Herodias came in and danced, she pleased Herod and his dinner guests.

The king said to the girl, "Ask me for anything you want, and I'll give it to you." [23] And he promised her with an oath, "Whatever you ask I will give you, up to half my kingdom."

[24] She went out and said to her mother, "What shall I ask for?"

a3 Greek *Joses*, a variant of *Joseph*   b7 Greek *unclean*   c14 Some early manuscripts *He was saying*   d20 Some early manuscripts *he did many things*

"The head of John the Baptist," she answered.

25 At once the girl hurried in to the king with the request: "I want you to give me right now the head of John the Baptist on a platter."

26 The king was greatly distressed, but because of his oaths and his dinner guests, he did not want to refuse her. 27 So he immediately sent an executioner with orders to bring John's head. The man went, beheaded John in the prison, 28 and brought back his head on a platter. He presented it to the girl, and she gave it to her mother. 29 On hearing of this, John's disciples came and took his body and laid it in a tomb.

Jesus Feeds the Five Thousand

30 The apostles gathered around Jesus and reported to him all they had done and taught. 31 Then, because so many people were coming and going that they did not even have a chance to eat, he said to them, "Come with me by yourselves to a quiet place and get some rest."

32 So they went away by themselves in a boat to a solitary place. 33 But many who saw them leaving recognized them and ran on foot from all the towns and got there ahead of them. 34 When Jesus landed and saw a large crowd, he had compassion on them, because they were like sheep without a shepherd. So he began teaching them many things.

35 By this time it was late in the day, so his disciples came to him. "This is a remote place," they said, "and it's already very late. 36 Send the people away so they can go to the surrounding countryside and villages and buy themselves something to eat."

37 But he answered, "You give them something to eat."

They said to him, "That would take eight months of a man's wages[a]! Are we to go and spend that much on bread and give it to them to eat?"

Mark 6:31

God Values Rest

Then, because so many people were coming and going that they did not even have a chance to eat, he said to them, "Come with me by yourselves to a quiet place and get some rest."

38 "How many loaves do you have?" he asked. "Go and see."

When they found out, they said, "Five—and two fish."

39 Then Jesus directed them to have all the people sit down in groups on the green grass. 40 So they sat down in groups of hundreds and fifties. 41 Taking the five loaves and the two fish and looking up to heaven, he gave thanks and broke the loaves. Then he gave them to his disciples to set before the people. He also divided the two fish among them all. 42 They all ate and were satisfied, 43 and the disciples picked up twelve basketfuls of broken pieces of bread and fish. 44 The number of the men who had eaten was five thousand.

Jesus Walks on the Water

45 Immediately Jesus made his disciples get into the boat and go on ahead of him to Bethsaida, while he dismissed the crowd. 46 After leaving them, he went up on a mountainside to pray.

47 When evening came, the boat was in the middle of the lake, and he was alone on land. 48 He saw the disciples straining at the oars, because the wind was against them. About the fourth watch of the night he went out to them, walking on the lake. He was about to pass by them, 49 but when they saw him walking on the lake, they thought he was a ghost. They cried out, 50 because they all saw him and were terrified.

Immediately he spoke to them and said, "Take courage! It is I. Don't be afraid." 51 Then he climbed into the boat with them, and the wind died down. They were completely amazed, 52 for they had not understood about the loaves; their hearts were hardened.

53 When they had crossed over, they landed at Gennesaret and anchored there. 54 As soon as they got out of the boat, people recognized Jesus. 55 They ran throughout that whole region and carried the sick on mats to wherever they

a 37 Greek take two hundred denarii

heard he was. 56And wherever he went—into villages, towns or countryside—they placed the sick in the marketplaces. They begged him to let them touch even the edge of his cloak, and all who touched him were healed.

Clean and Unclean

7 The Pharisees and some of the teachers of the law who had come from Jerusalem gathered around Jesus and 2saw some of his disciples eating food with hands that were "unclean," that is, unwashed. 3(The Pharisees and all the Jews do not eat unless they give their hands a ceremonial washing, holding to the tradition of the elders. 4When they come from the marketplace they do not eat unless they wash. And they observe many other traditions, such as the washing of cups, pitchers and kettles.*a*)

5So the Pharisees and teachers of the law asked Jesus, "Why don't your disciples live according to the tradition of the elders instead of eating their food with 'unclean' hands?"

6He replied, "Isaiah was right when he prophesied about you hypocrites; as it is written:

" 'These people honor me with their lips,
    but their hearts are far from me.
7 They worship me in vain;
    their teachings are but rules taught by
    men.'*b*

8You have let go of the commands of God and are holding on to the traditions of men."

9And he said to them: "You have a fine way of setting aside the commands of God in order to observe*c* your own traditions! 10For Moses said, 'Honor your father and your mother,'*d* and, 'Anyone who curses his father or mother must be put to death.'*e* 11But you say that if a man says to his father or mother: 'Whatever help you might otherwise have received from me is Corban' (that is, a gift devoted to God), 12then you no longer let him do anything for his father or mother. 13Thus you nullify the word of God by your tradition that you have handed down. And you do many things like that."

14Again Jesus called the crowd to him and said, "Listen to me, everyone, and understand this. 15Nothing outside a man can make

him 'unclean' by going into him. Rather, it is what comes out of a man that makes him 'unclean.'*f*"

17After he had left the crowd and entered the house, his disciples asked him about this parable. 18"Are you so dull?" he asked. "Don't you see that nothing that enters a man from the outside can make him 'unclean'? 19For it doesn't go into his heart but into his stomach, and then out of his body." (In saying this, Jesus declared all foods "clean.")

20He went on: "What comes out of a man is what makes him 'unclean.' 21For from within, out of men's hearts, come evil thoughts, sexual immorality, theft, murder, adultery, 22greed, malice, deceit, lewdness, envy, slander, arrogance and folly. 23All these evils come from inside and make a man 'unclean.' "

The Faith of a Syrophoenician Woman

24Jesus left that place and went to the vicinity of Tyre.*g* He entered a house and did not want anyone to know it; yet he could not keep his presence secret. 25In fact, as soon as she heard about him, a woman whose little daughter was possessed by an evil*h* spirit came and fell at his feet. 26The woman was a Greek, born in Syrian Phoenicia. She begged Jesus to drive the demon out of her daughter.

27"First let the children eat all they want," he told her, "for it is not right to take the children's bread and toss it to their dogs."

28"Yes, Lord," she replied, "but even the dogs under the table eat the children's crumbs."

29Then he told her, "For such a reply, you may go; the demon has left your daughter."

30She went home and found her child lying on the bed, and the demon gone.

The Healing of a Deaf and Mute Man

31Then Jesus left the vicinity of Tyre and went through Sidon, down to the Sea of Galilee and into the region of the Decapolis.*i* 32There some people brought to him a man who was deaf and could hardly talk, and they begged him to place his hand on the man.

33After he took him aside, away from the crowd, Jesus put his fingers into the man's ears.

---

*a*4 Some early manuscripts *pitchers, kettles and dining couches*   *b*6,7 Isaiah 29:13   *c*9 Some manuscripts *set up*   *d*10 Exodus 20:12; Deut. 5:16   *e*10 Exodus 21:17; Lev. 20:9   *f*15 Some early manuscripts *'unclean.'*   *16 If anyone has ears to hear, let him hear.*   *g*24 Many early manuscripts *Tyre and Sidon*   *h*25 Greek *unclean*   *i*31 That is, the Ten Cities

A Strong-Willed Woman

Read: Mark 7:24–36

SO WHAT DOES IT TAKE to have the distinction of being a genuinely strong-willed woman? After all, every woman has opportunities to use some degree of strong will at various times in her life . . . But for those of us who fit the description of the strong-willed woman, it can be said that we use our strong wills almost as often as we breathe. It is so deeply ingrained in us we often struggle to understand why everyone doesn't share the depth and strength of our convictions.

I met Emily after one of my learning styles seminars for public school teachers. She had not grown up in a Christian home, but she had attended a conservative church off and on during her youth. She thanked me, not only for the seminar but for weaving my faith into the presentation. Then she hesitantly asked me, "Do you believe it's even possible for a strong-willed woman to be a Christian?" I was startled by the question, and she went on to confess that she had very deliberately stayed away from church the past few years because she knew she had a stubborn and independent nature. Half of her was afraid God wouldn't even want her, and the other half was afraid he would demand she give up her strong will if she did decide to give her heart to Christ. Emily is certainly not alone. There are many strong-willed women whose hearts and souls long to know Christ but whose self-sufficient natures won't even consider the possibility of surrendering their hard-won independence. These are women who can and will change the world one way or another—and it's never been more important to find a way to recognize and validate their worth in the kingdom of God.

Many of us may have secretly wondered if there was something wrong with us, if perhaps we just weren't trying hard enough to be good, conforming Christian women. So let's come together and identify ourselves to each other and the world. Let's discover and celebrate the fact that God has placed in the heart of many of his human creations an undercurrent so strong and so solid it carries us from birth to death.

—Cynthia Ulrich Tobias

Mark 7:26–28

The woman was a Greek, born in Syrian Phoenicia. She begged Jesus to drive the demon out of her daughter. "First let the children eat all they want," he told her, "for it is not right to take the children's bread and toss it to their dogs." "Yes, Lord," she replied, "but even the dogs under the table eat the children's crumbs."

reflection

1. How did the woman in today's Scripture passage prove to be strong-willed? How did Jesus reward her for her determination?

2. Do you consider yourself a strong-willed woman? In what ways?

3. Ask God to make you strong enough to allow your will to become his will. Make your prayer the prayer of Jesus: "Not my will, but yours be done" (Luke 22:42).

RELATED READINGS

Matthew 15:21–28;
Ephesians 6:5–8

Monday

Go to page 1220 for your next devotional reading.

Then he spit and touched the man's tongue. **34**He looked up to heaven and with a deep sigh said to him, *"Ephphatha!"* (which means, "Be opened!"). **35**At this, the man's ears were opened, his tongue was loosened and he began to speak plainly.

36Jesus commanded them not to tell anyone. But the more he did so, the more they kept talking about it. **37**People were overwhelmed with amazement. "He has done everything well," they said. "He even makes the deaf hear and the mute speak."

Jesus Feeds the Four Thousand

8 During those days another large crowd gathered. Since they had nothing to eat, Jesus called his disciples to him and said, **2**"I have compassion for these people; they have already been with me three days and have nothing to eat. **3**If I send them home hungry, they will collapse on the way, because some of them have come a long distance."

4His disciples answered, "But where in this remote place can anyone get enough bread to feed them?"

5"How many loaves do you have?" Jesus asked.

"Seven," they replied.

6He told the crowd to sit down on the ground. When he had taken the seven loaves and given thanks, he broke them and gave them to his disciples to set before the people, and they did so. **7**They had a few small fish as well; he gave thanks for them also and told the disciples to distribute them. **8**The people ate and were satisfied. Afterward the disciples picked up seven basketfuls of broken pieces that were left over. **9**About four thousand men were present. And having sent them away, **10**he got into the boat with his disciples and went to the region of Dalmanutha.

11The Pharisees came and began to question Jesus. To test him, they asked him for a sign from heaven. **12**He sighed deeply and said, "Why does this generation ask for a miraculous sign? I tell you the truth, no sign will be given to it." **13**Then he left them, got back into the boat and crossed to the other side.

The Yeast of the Pharisees and Herod

14The disciples had forgotten to bring bread, except for one loaf they had with them in the boat. **15**"Be careful," Jesus warned them. "Watch out for the yeast of the Pharisees and that of Herod."

16They discussed this with one another and said, "It is because we have no bread."

17Aware of their discussion, Jesus asked them: "Why are you talking about having no bread? Do you still not see or understand? Are your hearts hardened? **18**Do you have eyes but fail to see, and ears but fail to hear? And don't you remember? **19**When I broke the five loaves for the five thousand, how many basketfuls of pieces did you pick up?"

"Twelve," they replied.

20"And when I broke the seven loaves for the four thousand, how many basketfuls of pieces did you pick up?"

They answered, "Seven."

21He said to them, "Do you still not understand?"

The Healing of a Blind Man at Bethsaida

22They came to Bethsaida, and some people brought a blind man and begged Jesus to touch him. **23**He took the blind man by the hand and led him outside the village. When he had spit on the man's eyes and put his hands on him, Jesus asked, "Do you see anything?"

24He looked up and said, "I see people; they look like trees walking around."

25Once more Jesus put his hands on the man's eyes. Then his eyes were opened, his sight was restored, and he saw everything clearly. **26**Jesus sent him home, saying, "Don't go into the village.*a*"

Peter's Confession of Christ

27Jesus and his disciples went on to the villages around Caesarea Philippi. On the way he asked them, "Who do people say I am?"

28They replied, "Some say John the Baptist; others say Elijah; and still others, one of the prophets."

29"But what about you?" he asked. "Who do you say I am?"

Peter answered, "You are the Christ.*b*"

---

*a***26** Some manuscripts *Don't go and tell anyone in the village*   *b***29** Or *Messiah*. "The Christ" (Greek) and "the Messiah" (Hebrew) both mean "the Anointed One."

³⁰Jesus warned them not to tell anyone about him.

Jesus Predicts His Death

³¹He then began to teach them that the Son of Man must suffer many things and be rejected by the elders, chief priests and teachers of the law, and that he must be killed and after three days rise again. ³²He spoke plainly about this, and Peter took him aside and began to rebuke him.

³³But when Jesus turned and looked at his disciples, he rebuked Peter. "Get behind me, Satan!" he said. "You do not have in mind the things of God, but the things of men."

³⁴Then he called the crowd to him along with his disciples and said: "If anyone would come after me, he must deny himself and take up his cross and follow me. ³⁵For whoever wants to save his life*a* will lose it, but whoever loses his life for me and for the gospel will save it. ³⁶What good is it for a man to gain the whole world, yet forfeit his soul? ³⁷Or what can a man give in exchange for his soul? ³⁸If anyone is ashamed of me and my words in this adulterous and sinful generation, the Son of Man will be ashamed of him when he comes in his Father's glory with the holy angels."

9 And he said to them, "I tell you the truth, some who are standing here will not taste death before they see the kingdom of God come with power."

The Transfiguration

²After six days Jesus took Peter, James and John with him and led them up a high mountain, where they were all alone. There he was transfigured before them. ³His clothes became dazzling white, whiter than anyone in the world could bleach them. ⁴And there appeared before them Elijah and Moses, who were talking with Jesus.

⁵Peter said to Jesus, "Rabbi, it is good for us to be here. Let us put up three shelters—one for you, one for Moses and one for Elijah." ⁶(He did not know what to say, they were so frightened.)

⁷Then a cloud appeared and enveloped them, and a voice came from the cloud: "This is my Son, whom I love. Listen to him!"

⁸Suddenly, when they looked around, they no longer saw anyone with them except Jesus.

⁹As they were coming down the mountain, Jesus gave them orders not to tell anyone what they had seen until the Son of Man had risen from the dead. ¹⁰They kept the matter to themselves, discussing what "rising from the dead" meant.

¹¹And they asked him, "Why do the teachers of the law say that Elijah must come first?"

¹²Jesus replied, "To be sure, Elijah does come first, and restores all things. Why then is it written that the Son of Man must suffer much and be rejected? ¹³But I tell you, Elijah has come, and they have done to him everything they wished, just as it is written about him."

The Healing of a Boy With an Evil Spirit

¹⁴When they came to the other disciples, they saw a large crowd around them and the teachers of the law arguing with them. ¹⁵As soon as all the people saw Jesus, they were overwhelmed with wonder and ran to greet him.

¹⁶"What are you arguing with them about?" he asked.

¹⁷A man in the crowd answered, "Teacher, I brought you my son, who is possessed by a spirit that has robbed him of speech. ¹⁸Whenever it seizes him, it throws him to the ground. He foams at the mouth, gnashes his teeth and becomes rigid. I asked your disciples to drive out the spirit, but they could not."

¹⁹"O unbelieving generation," Jesus replied, "how long shall I stay with you? How long shall I put up with you? Bring the boy to me."

²⁰So they brought him. When the spirit saw Jesus, it immediately threw the boy into a convulsion. He fell to the ground and rolled around, foaming at the mouth.

²¹Jesus asked the boy's father, "How long has he been like this?"

"From childhood," he answered. ²²"It has often thrown him into fire or water to kill him. But if you can do anything, take pity on us and help us."

²³"'If you can'?" said Jesus. "Everything is possible for him who believes."

²⁴Immediately the boy's father exclaimed, "I do believe; help me overcome my unbelief!"

a35 The Greek word means either life *or* soul*; also in verse 36.*

²⁵When Jesus saw that a crowd was running to the scene, he rebuked the evil*ᵃ* spirit. "You deaf and mute spirit," he said, "I command you, come out of him and never enter him again."

²⁶The spirit shrieked, convulsed him violently and came out. The boy looked so much like a corpse that many said, "He's dead." ²⁷But Jesus took him by the hand and lifted him to his feet, and he stood up.

²⁸After Jesus had gone indoors, his disciples asked him privately, "Why couldn't we drive it out?"

²⁹He replied, "This kind can come out only by prayer.*ᵇ*"

³⁰They left that place and passed through Galilee. Jesus did not want anyone to know where they were, ³¹because he was teaching his disciples. He said to them, "The Son of Man is going to be betrayed into the hands of men. They will kill him, and after three days he will rise." ³²But they did not understand what he meant and were afraid to ask him about it.

Who Is the Greatest?

³³They came to Capernaum. When he was in the house, he asked them, "What were you arguing about on the road?" ³⁴But they kept quiet because on the way they had argued about who was the greatest.

³⁵Sitting down, Jesus called the Twelve and said, "If anyone wants to be first, he must be the very last, and the servant of all."

³⁶He took a little child and had him stand among them. Taking him in his arms, he said to them, ³⁷"Whoever welcomes one of these little children in my name welcomes me; and whoever welcomes me does not welcome me but the one who sent me."

Whoever Is Not Against Us Is for Us

³⁸"Teacher," said John, "we saw a man driving out demons in your name and we told him to stop, because he was not one of us."

³⁹"Do not stop him," Jesus said. "No one who does a miracle in my name can in the next moment say anything bad about me, ⁴⁰for whoever is not against us is for us. ⁴¹I tell you the truth, anyone who gives you a cup of water

in my name because you belong to Christ will certainly not lose his reward.

Causing to Sin

⁴²"And if anyone causes one of these little ones who believe in me to sin, it would be better for him to be thrown into the sea with a large millstone tied around his neck. ⁴³If your hand causes you to sin, cut it off. It is better for you to enter life maimed than with two hands to go into hell, where the fire never goes out.*ᶜ* ⁴⁵And if your foot causes you to sin, cut it off. It is better for you to enter life crippled than to have two feet and be thrown into hell.*ᵈ* ⁴⁷And if your eye causes you to sin, pluck it out. It is better for you to enter the kingdom of God with one eye than to have two eyes and be thrown into hell, ⁴⁸where

"'their worm does not die,
and the fire is not quenched.'*ᵉ*

⁴⁹Everyone will be salted with fire.

⁵⁰"Salt is good, but if it loses its saltiness, how can you make it salty again? Have salt in yourselves, and be at peace with each other."

Divorce

10 Jesus then left that place and went into the region of Judea and across the Jordan. Again crowds of people came to him, and as was his custom, he taught them.

²Some Pharisees came and tested him by asking, "Is it lawful for a man to divorce his wife?"

³"What did Moses command you?" he replied.

⁴They said, "Moses permitted a man to write a certificate of divorce and send her away."

⁵"It was because your hearts were hard that Moses wrote you this law," Jesus replied. ⁶"But at the beginning of creation God 'made them male and female.'*ᶠ* ⁷'For this reason a man will leave his father and mother and be united to his wife,*ᵍ* ⁸and the two will become one flesh.'*ʰ* So they are no longer two, but one. ⁹Therefore what God has joined together, let man not separate."

¹⁰When they were in the house again, the disciples asked Jesus about this. ¹¹He answered,

---

ᵃ25 Greek *unclean*   *ᵇ29* Some manuscripts *prayer and fasting*   *ᶜ43* Some manuscripts *out,* ⁴⁴*where / "'their worm does not die, / and the fire is not quenched.'*   *ᵈ45* Some manuscripts *hell,* ⁴⁶*where / "'their worm does not die, / and the fire is not quenched.'*   *ᵉ48* Isaiah 66:24   *ᶠ6* Gen. 1:27   *ᵍ7* Some early manuscripts do not have *and be united to his wife.*   *ʰ8* Gen. 2:24

"Anyone who divorces his wife and marries another woman commits adultery against her. ¹²And if she divorces her husband and marries another man, she commits adultery."

The Little Children and Jesus

¹³People were bringing little children to Jesus to have him touch them, but the disciples rebuked them. ¹⁴When Jesus saw this, he was indignant. He said to them, "Let the little children come to me, and do not hinder them, for the kingdom of God belongs to such as these. ¹⁵I tell you the truth, anyone who will not receive the kingdom of God like a little child will never enter it." ¹⁶And he took the children in his arms, put his hands on them and blessed them.

The Rich Young Man

¹⁷As Jesus started on his way, a man ran up to him and fell on his knees before him. "Good teacher," he asked, "what must I do to inherit eternal life?"

¹⁸"Why do you call me good?" Jesus answered. "No one is good—except God alone. ¹⁹You know the commandments: 'Do not murder, do not commit adultery, do not steal, do not give false testimony, do not defraud, honor your father and mother.'ᵃ"

²⁰"Teacher," he declared, "all these I have kept since I was a boy."

²¹Jesus looked at him and loved him. "One thing you lack," he said. "Go, sell everything you have and give to the poor, and you will have treasure in heaven. Then come, follow me."

²²At this the man's face fell. He went away sad, because he had great wealth.

²³Jesus looked around and said to his disciples, "How hard it is for the rich to enter the kingdom of God!"

²⁴The disciples were amazed at his words. But Jesus said again, "Children, how hard it isᵇ to enter the kingdom of God! ²⁵It is easier for a camel to go through the eye of a needle than for a rich man to enter the kingdom of God."

²⁶The disciples were even more amazed, and said to each other, "Who then can be saved?"

²⁷Jesus looked at them and said, "With man this is impossible, but not with God; all things are possible with God."

²⁸Peter said to him, "We have left everything to follow you!"

²⁹"I tell you the truth," Jesus replied, "no one who has left home or brothers or sisters or mother or father or children or fields for me and the gospel ³⁰will fail to receive a hundred times as much in this present age (homes, brothers, sisters, mothers, children and fields— and with them, persecutions) and in the age to come, eternal life. ³¹But many who are first will be last, and the last first."

Jesus Again Predicts His Death

³²They were on their way up to Jerusalem, with Jesus leading the way, and the disciples were astonished, while those who followed were afraid. Again he took the Twelve aside and told them what was going to happen to him. ³³"We are going up to Jerusalem," he said, "and the Son of Man will be betrayed to the chief priests and teachers of the law. They will condemn him to death and will hand him over to the Gentiles, ³⁴who will mock him and spit on him, flog him and kill him. Three days later he will rise."

The Request of James and John

³⁵Then James and John, the sons of Zebedee, came to him. "Teacher," they said, "we want you to do for us whatever we ask."

³⁶"What do you want me to do for you?" he asked.

³⁷They replied, "Let one of us sit at your right and the other at your left in your glory."

³⁸"You don't know what you are asking," Jesus said. "Can you drink the cup I drink or be baptized with the baptism I am baptized with?"

³⁹"We can," they answered.

Jesus said to them, "You will drink the cup I drink and be baptized with the baptism I am baptized with, ⁴⁰but to sit at my right or left is not for me to grant. These places belong to those for whom they have been prepared."

⁴¹When the ten heard about this, they became indignant with James and John. ⁴²Jesus called them together and said, "You know that those who are regarded as rulers of the Gentiles lord it over them, and their high officials exercise authority over them. ⁴³Not so with you.

ᵃ19 Exodus 20:12–16; Deut. 5:16–20   ᵇ24 Some manuscripts *is for those who trust in riches*

Like a Lamb

Read: Mark 10:13–16

Mark 10:15–16

"I tell you the truth, anyone who will not receive the kingdom of God like a little child will never enter it." And he took the children in his arms, put his hands on them and blessed them.

reflection

1 What circumstance are you in right now in which you need to trust God as a child trusts her daddy?

2 Name some ways in which you know that your God—your *Abba*—protects you.

3 How can you become more like a child in the kingdom of God? Ask God to help you take the first step.

RELATED READINGS

Matthew 18:1–6;
21:14–16;
Romans 8:28–31;
1 John 3:1–3

AUTHOR AND SHEPHERD PHILLIP KELLER writes about coming home to his humble cottage one stormy night with a couple of shivering baby lambs. He wrapped them inside his big, wool jacket and snuggled them against his chest. Sleet, snow and chilling rain lashed against his body, but within his embrace, the lambs were safe and warm.

Children, like lambs, trust us to meet their needs and provide for their safety. With a natural tendency to believe, they don't weigh issues with cynicism like adults do. Jesus made it clear that the kingdom of God belongs to people with a childlike spirit—those who don't receive the kingdom like a child "will never enter it." This concept is hard for skeptical adults to accept. Many of us have grown oversophisticated, and our hearts have grown hard. Somewhere along the way we got tougher and more callous, turning to self-sufficiency and believing we could handle our lives by using our own resources. We've forgotten what it's like to believe as we might have when were little girls, looking up to God with childlike wonder and adoration.

Throughout Scripture, God continually encourages us to rely on him like a child relies on a parent. Some of us may have lost the ability to trust because our parents never provided adequately for our needs, while others of us may have lost our ability to trust through circumstances—a failed job, the death of a loved one, a lost desire. But God has revealed time and again that he can help us relearn that childlike faith if we let him. It's a matter of cultivating a relationship with him and letting him show himself faithful as he works good out of our circumstances.

Isaiah 40:11 paints a warm and inviting picture of perfect trust in Jesus: "He tends his flock like a shepherd: He gathers the lambs in his arms and carries them close to his heart."

Close your eyes and picture yourself resting your head on Jesus' chest. Can you hear his heart beating with love for you?

Tuesday

Instead, whoever wants to become great among you must be your servant, **44**and whoever wants to be first must be slave of all. **45**For even the Son of Man did not come to be served, but to serve, and to give his life as a ransom for many."

Blind Bartimaeus Receives His Sight

46Then they came to Jericho. As Jesus and his disciples, together with a large crowd, were leaving the city, a blind man, Bartimaeus (that is, the Son of Timaeus), was sitting by the roadside begging. **47**When he heard that it was Jesus of Nazareth, he began to shout, "Jesus, Son of David, have mercy on me!"

48Many rebuked him and told him to be quiet, but he shouted all the more, "Son of David, have mercy on me!"

49Jesus stopped and said, "Call him."

So they called to the blind man, "Cheer up! On your feet! He's calling you." **50**Throwing his cloak aside, he jumped to his feet and came to Jesus.

51"What do you want me to do for you?" Jesus asked him.

The blind man said, "Rabbi, I want to see."

52"Go," said Jesus, "your faith has healed you." Immediately he received his sight and followed Jesus along the road.

The Triumphal Entry

11 As they approached Jerusalem and came to Bethphage and Bethany at the Mount of Olives, Jesus sent two of his disciples, **2**saying to them, "Go to the village ahead of you, and just as you enter it, you will find a colt tied there, which no one has ever ridden. Untie it and bring it here. **3**If anyone asks you, 'Why are you doing this?' tell him, 'The Lord needs it and will send it back here shortly.' "

4They went and found a colt outside in the street, tied at a doorway. As they untied it, **5**some people standing there asked, "What are you doing, untying that colt?" **6**They answered

as Jesus had told them to, and the people let them go. **7**When they brought the colt to Jesus and threw their cloaks over it, he sat on it. **8**Many people spread their cloaks on the road, while others spread branches they had cut in the fields. **9**Those who went ahead and those who followed shouted,

"Hosanna![a]"

"Blessed is he who comes
in the name of the
Lord!"[b]

10"Blessed is the coming
kingdom of our
father David!"

"Hosanna in the highest!"

11Jesus entered Jerusalem and went to the temple. He looked around at everything, but since it was already late, he went out to Bethany with the Twelve.

Jesus Clears the Temple

12The next day as they were leaving Bethany, Jesus was hungry. **13**Seeing in the distance a fig tree in leaf, he went to find out if it had any fruit. When he reached it, he found nothing but leaves, because it was not the season for figs. **14**Then he said to the tree, "May no one ever eat fruit from you again." And his disciples heard him say it.

15On reaching Jerusalem, Jesus entered the temple area and began driving out those who were buying and selling there. He overturned the tables of the money changers and the benches of those selling doves, **16**and would not allow anyone to carry merchandise through the temple courts. **17**And as he taught them, he said, "Is it not written:

" 'My house will be called
a house of prayer for all nations'[c]?

But you have made it 'a den of robbers.'[d]"

18The chief priests and the teachers of the law heard this and began looking for a way to kill him, for they feared him, because the whole crowd was amazed at his teaching.

> ### Mark 10:45
>
> *God Loves Service*
>
> "For even the Son of Man did not come to be served, but to serve, and to give his life as a ransom for many."

---

a9 A Hebrew expression meaning "Save!" which became an exclamation of praise; also in verse 10   *b9* Psalm 118:25,26   *c17* Isaiah 56:7   *d17* Jer. 7:11

¹⁹When evening came, they*a* went out of the city.

The Withered Fig Tree

²⁰In the morning, as they went along, they saw the fig tree withered from the roots. ²¹Peter remembered and said to Jesus, "Rabbi, look! The fig tree you cursed has withered!"

²²"Have*b* faith in God," Jesus answered. ²³"I tell you the truth, if anyone says to this mountain, 'Go, throw yourself into the sea,' and does not doubt in his heart but believes that what he says will happen, it will be done for him. ²⁴Therefore I tell you, whatever you ask for in prayer, believe that you have received it, and it will be yours. ²⁵And when you stand praying, if you hold anything against anyone, forgive him, so that your Father in heaven may forgive you your sins.*c*"

The Authority of Jesus Questioned

²⁷They arrived again in Jerusalem, and while Jesus was walking in the temple courts, the chief priests, the teachers of the law and the elders came to him. ²⁸"By what authority are you doing these things?" they asked. "And who gave you authority to do this?"

²⁹Jesus replied, "I will ask you one question. Answer me, and I will tell you by what authority I am doing these things. ³⁰John's baptism—was it from heaven, or from men? Tell me!"

³¹They discussed it among themselves and said, "If we say, 'From heaven,' he will ask, 'Then why didn't you believe him?' ³²But if we say, 'From men'…" (They feared the people, for everyone held that John really was a prophet.)

³³So they answered Jesus, "We don't know."

Jesus said, "Neither will I tell you by what authority I am doing these things."

The Parable of the Tenants

12 He then began to speak to them in parables: "A man planted a vineyard. He put a wall around it, dug a pit for the winepress and built a watchtower. Then he rented the vineyard to some farmers and went away on a journey. ²At harvest time he sent a servant to the tenants to collect from them some of the fruit of the vineyard. ³But they seized him, beat him and sent him away empty-handed. ⁴Then he sent another servant to them; they struck this man on the head and treated him shamefully. ⁵He sent still another, and that one they killed. He sent many others; some of them they beat, others they killed.

⁶"He had one left to send, a son, whom he loved. He sent him last of all, saying, 'They will respect my son.'

⁷"But the tenants said to one another, 'This is the heir. Come, let's kill him, and the inheritance will be ours.' ⁸So they took him and killed him, and threw him out of the vineyard.

⁹"What then will the owner of the vineyard do? He will come and kill those tenants and give the vineyard to others. ¹⁰Haven't you read this scripture:

" 'The stone the builders rejected
has become the capstone*d*;
¹¹the Lord has done this,
and it is marvelous in our eyes'*e*?"

¹²Then they looked for a way to arrest him because they knew he had spoken the parable against them. But they were afraid of the crowd; so they left him and went away.

Paying Taxes to Caesar

¹³Later they sent some of the Pharisees and Herodians to Jesus to catch him in his words. ¹⁴They came to him and said, "Teacher, we know you are a man of integrity. You aren't swayed by men, because you pay no attention to who they are; but you teach the way of God in accordance with the truth. Is it right to pay taxes to Caesar or not? ¹⁵Should we pay or shouldn't we?"

But Jesus knew their hypocrisy. "Why are you trying to trap me?" he asked. "Bring me a denarius and let me look at it." ¹⁶They brought the coin, and he asked them, "Whose portrait is this? And whose inscription?"

"Caesar's," they replied.

¹⁷Then Jesus said to them, "Give to Caesar what is Caesar's and to God what is God's."

And they were amazed at him.

Marriage at the Resurrection

¹⁸Then the Sadducees, who say there is no resurrection, came to him with a question.

---

*a*19 Some early manuscripts *he*   *b*22 Some early manuscripts *If you have*   *c*25 Some manuscripts *sins.* ²⁶*But if you do not forgive, neither will your Father who is in heaven forgive your sins.*   *d*10 Or *cornerstone*   *e*11 Psalm 118:22,23

¹⁹"Teacher," they said, "Moses wrote for us that if a man's brother dies and leaves a wife but no children, the man must marry the widow and have children for his brother. ²⁰Now there were seven brothers. The first one married and died without leaving any children. ²¹The second one married the widow, but he also died, leaving no child. It was the same with the third. ²²In fact, none of the seven left any children. Last of all, the woman died too. ²³At the resurrection*a* whose wife will she be, since the seven were married to her?"

²⁴Jesus replied, "Are you not in error because you do not know the Scriptures or the power of God? ²⁵When the dead rise, they will neither marry nor be given in marriage; they will be like the angels in heaven. ²⁶Now about the dead rising—have you not read in the book of Moses, in the account of the bush, how God said to him, 'I am the God of Abraham, the God of Isaac, and the God of Jacob'*b*? ²⁷He is not the God of the dead, but of the living. You are badly mistaken!"

The Greatest Commandment

²⁸One of the teachers of the law came and heard them debating. Noticing that Jesus had given them a good answer, he asked him, "Of all the commandments, which is the most important?"

²⁹"The most important one," answered Jesus, "is this: 'Hear, O Israel, the Lord our God, the Lord is one.*c* ³⁰Love the Lord your God with all your heart and with all your soul and with all your mind and with all your strength.'*d* ³¹The second is this: 'Love your neighbor as yourself.'*e* There is no commandment greater than these."

³²"Well said, teacher," the man replied. "You are right in saying that God is one and there is no other but him. ³³To love him with all your heart, with all your understanding, and with all your strength, and to love your neighbor as yourself is more important than all burnt offerings and sacrifices."

³⁴When Jesus saw that he had answered wisely, he said to him, "You are not far from the kingdom of God." And from then on no one dared ask him any more questions.

Whose Son Is the Christ?

³⁵While Jesus was teaching in the temple courts, he asked, "How is it that the teachers of the law say that the Christ*f* is the son of David? ³⁶David himself, speaking by the Holy Spirit, declared:

"'The Lord said to my Lord:
  "Sit at my right hand
until I put your enemies
  under your feet."'*g*

³⁷David himself calls him 'Lord.' How then can he be his son?"

The large crowd listened to him with delight.

³⁸As he taught, Jesus said, "Watch out for the teachers of the law. They like to walk around in flowing robes and be greeted in the marketplaces, ³⁹and have the most important seats in the synagogues and the places of honor at banquets. ⁴⁰They devour widows' houses and for a show make lengthy prayers. Such men will be punished most severely."

The Widow's Offering

⁴¹Jesus sat down opposite the place where the offerings were put and watched the crowd putting their money into the temple treasury. Many rich people threw in large amounts. ⁴²But a poor widow came and put in two very small copper coins,*h* worth only a fraction of a penny.*i*

⁴³Calling his disciples to him, Jesus said, "I tell you the truth, this poor widow has put more into the treasury than all the others. ⁴⁴They all gave out of their wealth; but she, out of her poverty, put in everything—all she had to live on."

Signs of the End of the Age

13 As he was leaving the temple, one of his disciples said to him, "Look, Teacher! What massive stones! What magnificent buildings!"

²"Do you see all these great buildings?" replied Jesus. "Not one stone here will be left on another; every one will be thrown down."

³As Jesus was sitting on the Mount of Olives opposite the temple, Peter, James, John and

---

*a*23 Some manuscripts *resurrection, when men rise from the dead,*   *b*26 Exodus 3:6   *c*29 Or *the Lord our God is one Lord*   *d*30 Deut. 6:4,5   *e*31 Lev. 19:18   *f*35 Or *Messiah*   *g*36 Psalm 110:1   *h*42 Greek *two lepta*   *i*42 Greek *kodrantes*

Trusting in the Rock

Mark 12:41–42

Many rich people threw in large amounts. But a poor widow came and put in two very small copper coins, worth only a fraction of a penny.

1 What has suddenly disappeared from your life? How has it affected your ability to trust in God?

2 Who do you most identify with in this Scripture passage—the crowd who gave a portion of their income or the widow who gave sacrificially?

3 What is God asking you to put into his hands today?

RELATED READINGS

Deuteronomy 32:3–4;
Psalms 62:1–12;
95:1–11;
1 Timothy 6:17–19

IN MAY 2003 A HEAVY FOG covered the White Mountains of New Hampshire. When the dense haze lifted, residents were shocked to see that The Old Man of the Mountain had disappeared. The 40-foot-tall natural outcropping of granite ledges had looked like the profile of an old man. This natural wonder inspired Nathaniel Hawthorne's famous story, "The Great Stone Face," over 200 years ago. Its image graced New Hampshire license plates, quarters and tourist souvenirs. As the official state emblem, The Old Man of the Mountain had endured for centuries. But then the 700-ton face fell. New Hampshire's governor said: "This rugged yet beautiful monument fit the character of the pioneers who founded this state, the immigrants who built it, and the spirit of those who live here today. It was the ultimate symbol of those who would 'Live Free or Die.' "

Sometimes, like New Hampshire's state symbol, those things we trust disappear. They fade away in the night with one sudden phone call or car ride or decision. Perhaps we knew, deep down, that the person could not be counted on, the job could not last, the relationship would not weather the storm, but we decided to believe it was timeless anyway. When we carry many responsibilities—children, a marriage, a job, parents, a home—we often come to trust ourselves as well. *Who else will keep things going?* we wonder. So we hold on tightly to keep everything together, to stay in control.

God's desire is the opposite of our human inclination: He wants us to release our tight-fisted control. He wants us to give him the control of everything in our lives. The widow who gave two small copper coins showed her trust in God to provide for her, even if her every material possession was gone. The crowd who went before her gave a lot, but in proportion to what they owned, they gave but little. They were holding back. This faithful woman "put in everything—all she had to live on" (verse 44).

God wants you to place everything in his hands, not because he wants you to be empty, but because he wants to fill you to overflowing. Of all the things we look to for stability and permanence, he is the only true Rock who will never fall or fade away.

Wednesday

Andrew asked him privately, **4**"Tell us, when will these things happen? And what will be the sign that they are all about to be fulfilled?"

5Jesus said to them: "Watch out that no one deceives you. **6**Many will come in my name, claiming, 'I am he,' and will deceive many. **7**When you hear of wars and rumors of wars, do not be alarmed. Such things must happen, but the end is still to come. **8**Nation will rise against nation, and kingdom against kingdom. There will be earthquakes in various places, and famines. These are the beginning of birth pains.

9"You must be on your guard. You will be handed over to the local councils and flogged in the synagogues. On account of me you will stand before governors and kings as witnesses to them. **10**And the gospel must first be preached to all nations. **11**Whenever you are arrested and brought to trial, do not worry beforehand about what to say. Just say whatever is given you at the time, for it is not you speaking, but the Holy Spirit.

12"Brother will betray brother to death, and a father his child. Children will rebel against their parents and have them put to death. **13**All men will hate you because of me, but he who stands firm to the end will be saved.

14"When you see 'the abomination that causes desolation'*a* standing where it*b* does not belong—let the reader understand—then let those who are in Judea flee to the mountains. **15**Let no one on the roof of his house go down or enter the house to take anything out. **16**Let no one in the field go back to get his cloak. **17**How dreadful it will be in those days for pregnant women and nursing mothers! **18**Pray that this will not take place in winter, **19**because those will be days of distress unequaled from the beginning, when God created the world, until now—and never to be equaled again. **20**If the Lord had not cut short those days, no one

would survive. But for the sake of the elect, whom he has chosen, he has shortened them. **21**At that time if anyone says to you, 'Look, here is the Christ*c*!' or, 'Look, there he is!' do not believe it. **22**For false Christs and false prophets will appear and perform signs and miracles to deceive the elect—if that were possible. **23**So be on your guard; I have told you everything ahead of time.

24"But in those days, following that distress,

> "'the sun will be darkened,
>   and the moon will not give its light;
> **25**the stars will fall from the sky,
>   and the heavenly bodies will be
>   shaken.'*d*

26"At that time men will see the Son of Man coming in clouds with great power and glory. **27**And he will send his angels and gather his elect from the four winds, from the ends of the earth to the ends of the heavens.

28"Now learn this lesson from the fig tree: As soon as its twigs get tender and its leaves come out, you know that summer is near. **29**Even so, when you see these things happening, you know that it is near, right at the door. **30**I tell you the truth, this generation*e* will certainly not pass away until all these things have happened. **31**Heaven and earth will pass away, but my words will never pass away.

Mark 13:26

God Will Return With Power

"At that time men will see the Son of Man coming in clouds with great power and glory."

The Day and Hour Unknown

32"No one knows about that day or hour, not even the angels in heaven, nor the Son, but only the Father. **33**Be on guard! Be alert*f*! You do not know when that time will come. **34**It's like a man going away: He leaves his house and puts his servants in charge, each with his assigned task, and tells the one at the door to keep watch.

35"Therefore keep watch because you do not know when the owner of the house will come back—whether in the evening, or at midnight,

*a***14** Daniel 9:27; 11:31; 12:11   *b***14** Or *he*; also in verse 29   *c***21** Or *Messiah*   *d***25** Isaiah 13:10; 34:4   *e***30** Or *race*   *f***33** Some manuscripts *alert and pray* or when the rooster crows, or at dawn. [36]If he comes suddenly, do not let him find you sleeping. [37]What I say to you, I say to everyone: 'Watch!'"

Jesus Anointed at Bethany

14 Now the Passover and the Feast of Unleavened Bread were only two days away, and the chief priests and the teachers of the law were looking for some sly way to arrest Jesus and kill him. [2]"But not during the Feast," they said, "or the people may riot."

[3]While he was in Bethany, reclining at the table in the home of a man known as Simon the Leper, a woman came with an alabaster jar of very expensive perfume, made of pure nard. She broke the jar and poured the perfume on his head.

[4]Some of those present were saying indignantly to one another, "Why this waste of perfume? [5]It could have been sold for more than a year's wages[a] and the money given to the poor." And they rebuked her harshly.

[6]"Leave her alone," said Jesus. "Why are you bothering her? She has done a beautiful thing to me. [7]The poor you will always have with you, and you can help them any time you want. But you will not always have me. [8]She did what she could. She poured perfume on my body beforehand to prepare for my burial. [9]I tell you the truth, wherever the gospel is preached throughout the world, what she has done will also be told, in memory of her."

[10]Then Judas Iscariot, one of the Twelve, went to the chief priests to betray Jesus to them. [11]They were delighted to hear this and promised to give him money. So he watched for an opportunity to hand him over.

The Lord's Supper

[12]On the first day of the Feast of Unleavened Bread, when it was customary to sacrifice the Passover lamb, Jesus' disciples asked him, "Where do you want us to go and make preparations for you to eat the Passover?"

[13]So he sent two of his disciples, telling them, "Go into the city, and a man carrying a jar of water will meet you. Follow him. [14]Say to the owner of the house he enters, 'The Teacher asks: Where is my guest room, where I may eat the Passover with my disciples?' [15]He will show you a large upper room, furnished and ready. Make preparations for us there."

[16]The disciples left, went into the city and found things just as Jesus had told them. So they prepared the Passover.

[17]When evening came, Jesus arrived with the Twelve. [18]While they were reclining at the table eating, he said, "I tell you the truth, one of you will betray me—one who is eating with me."

[19]They were saddened, and one by one they said to him, "Surely not I?"

[20]"It is one of the Twelve," he replied, "one who dips bread into the bowl with me. [21]The Son of Man will go just as it is written about him. But woe to that man who betrays the Son of Man! It would be better for him if he had not been born."

[22]While they were eating, Jesus took bread, gave thanks and broke it, and gave it to his disciples, saying, "Take it; this is my body."

[23]Then he took the cup, gave thanks and offered it to them, and they all drank from it.

[24]"This is my blood of the[b] covenant, which is poured out for many," he said to them. [25]"I tell you the truth, I will not drink again of the fruit of the vine until that day when I drink it anew in the kingdom of God."

[26]When they had sung a hymn, they went out to the Mount of Olives.

Jesus Predicts Peter's Denial

[27]"You will all fall away," Jesus told them, "for it is written:

" 'I will strike the shepherd,
    and the sheep will be scattered.'[c]

[28]But after I have risen, I will go ahead of you into Galilee."

[29]Peter declared, "Even if all fall away, I will not."

[30]"I tell you the truth," Jesus answered, "today—yes, tonight—before the rooster crows twice[d] you yourself will disown me three times."

[31]But Peter insisted emphatically, "Even if I have to die with you, I will never disown you." And all the others said the same.

---

[a]5 Greek *than three hundred denarii*   [b]24 Some manuscripts *the new*   [c]27 Zech. 13:7   [d]30 Some early manuscripts do not have *twice*.

Worship and Witness

Read: Mark 14:1–72

OUR LORD JESUS CHRIST is the preeminent one and the head of the church. We worship him because he deserves all of our allegiance and our love. We sing, "He is Lord"; but is he truly *Lord*? Remember, Jesus is Lord *of* all, or not Lord *at* all. It is a contradiction in terms to say that Jesus is Lord of part of my life. He must be Lord of *all*!

We agree that first things must be first in our lives, but how many of us, if we carefully examined our hearts, would find that often the truly important things in life are last, and the least important things are right up there in first place?

More and more we need to realize that we have been saved for two great purposes in life—the first is to *worship,* and the second is to *witness.* If you and I are not a worshiping people, then the witness of our lives will be weak and fruitless. There are two aspects of worship that are vital. The first is the personal quiet place of communion with God. This is where we spend time in praise, adoration and thankfulness for all that God is and for all that our preeminent Lord Jesus has done for us. The second crucial aspect is our public worship, where we join with fellow believers in church and together worship God. Never treat public worship lightly.

Out of worship flows our witness. If Christ is preeminent in our hearts then "out of the overflow of the heart the mouth speaks" (Matthew 12:34). When Christ is Lord of all, the Holy Spirit fills our lives, and we can't help but overflow in witness (see John 7:38–39).

Dear heavenly Father, you have exalted your Son, Jesus, to be both Lord and Christ. Can I do anything less? I pray that he may have preeminence in every area of my life for his name's sake. Amen.

—*Barbara Hughes*

Mark 14:6–9

"She has done a beautiful thing to me. The poor you will always have with you, and you can help them any time you want. But you will not always have me. She did what she could. She poured perfume on my body beforehand to prepare for my burial. I tell you the truth, wherever the gospel is preached throughout the world, what she has done will also be told, in memory of her."

reflection

1 How did the woman in today's Scripture passage show that Jesus was Lord in her life?

2 How did this prove to be a lasting witness to him?

3 In what ways can you pour out your love to Jesus today in personal worship? To whom will you then witness about your love for the Lord?

RELATED READINGS
Psalm 45;
Matthew 28:16–20;
Acts 1:6–8

Thursday

Go to page 1231 for your next devotional reading.

Gethsemane

32They went to a place called Gethsemane, and Jesus said to his disciples, "Sit here while I pray." **33**He took Peter, James and John along with him, and he began to be deeply distressed and troubled. **34**"My soul is overwhelmed with sorrow to the point of death," he said to them. "Stay here and keep watch."

35Going a little farther, he fell to the ground and prayed that if possible the hour might pass from him. **36**"*Abba,*[a] Father," he said, "everything is possible for you. Take this cup from me. Yet not what I will, but what you will." **37**Then he returned to his disciples and found them sleeping. "Simon," he said to Peter, "are you asleep? Could you not keep watch for one hour? **38**Watch and pray so that you will not fall into temptation. The spirit is willing, but the body is weak."

39Once more he went away and prayed the same thing. **40**When he came back, he again found them sleeping, because their eyes were heavy. They did not know what to say to him.

41Returning the third time, he said to them, "Are you still sleeping and resting? Enough! The hour has come. Look, the Son of Man is betrayed into the hands of sinners. **42**Rise! Let us go! Here comes my betrayer!"

Jesus Arrested

43Just as he was speaking, Judas, one of the Twelve, appeared. With him was a crowd armed with swords and clubs, sent from the chief priests, the teachers of the law, and the elders.

44Now the betrayer had arranged a signal with them: "The one I kiss is the man; arrest him and lead him away under guard." **45**Going at once to Jesus, Judas said, "Rabbi!" and kissed him. **46**The men seized Jesus and arrested him. **47**Then one of those standing near drew his sword and struck the servant of the high priest, cutting off his ear.

48"Am I leading a rebellion," said Jesus, "that you have come out with swords and clubs to capture me? **49**Every day I was with you, teaching in the temple courts, and you did not arrest me. But the Scriptures must be fulfilled." **50**Then everyone deserted him and fled.

51A young man, wearing nothing but a linen garment, was following Jesus. When they seized him, **52**he fled naked, leaving his garment behind.

Before the Sanhedrin

53They took Jesus to the high priest, and all the chief priests, elders and teachers of the law came together. **54**Peter followed him at a distance, right into the courtyard of the high priest. There he sat with the guards and warmed himself at the fire.

55The chief priests and the whole Sanhedrin were looking for evidence against Jesus so that they could put him to death, but they did not find any. **56**Many testified falsely against him, but their statements did not agree.

57Then some stood up and gave this false testimony against him: **58**"We heard him say, 'I will destroy this man-made temple and in three days will build another, not made by man.'" **59**Yet even then their testimony did not agree.

60Then the high priest stood up before them and asked Jesus, "Are you not going to answer? What is this testimony that these men are bringing against you?" **61**But Jesus remained silent and gave no answer.

Again the high priest asked him, "Are you the Christ,[b] the Son of the Blessed One?"

62"I am," said Jesus. "And you will see the Son of Man sitting at the right hand of the Mighty One and coming on the clouds of heaven."

63The high priest tore his clothes. "Why do we need any more witnesses?" he asked. **64**"You have heard the blasphemy. What do you think?"

They all condemned him as worthy of death. **65**Then some began to spit at him; they blindfolded him, struck him with their fists, and said, "Prophesy!" And the guards took him and beat him.

Peter Disowns Jesus

66While Peter was below in the courtyard, one of the servant girls of the high priest came by. **67**When she saw Peter warming himself, she looked closely at him.

"You also were with that Nazarene, Jesus," she said.

68But he denied it. "I don't know or under-

---

*a*36 Aramaic for *Father*   *b*61 Or *Messiah*

stand what you're talking about," he said, and went out into the entryway.[a]

69When the servant girl saw him there, she said again to those standing around, "This fellow is one of them." **70**Again he denied it.

After a little while, those standing near said to Peter, "Surely you are one of them, for you are a Galilean."

71He began to call down curses on himself, and he swore to them, "I don't know this man you're talking about."

72Immediately the rooster crowed the second time.[b] Then Peter remembered the word Jesus had spoken to him: "Before the rooster crows twice[c] you will disown me three times." And he broke down and wept.

Jesus Before Pilate

15 Very early in the morning, the chief priests, with the elders, the teachers of the law and the whole Sanhedrin, reached a decision. They bound Jesus, led him away and handed him over to Pilate.

2"Are you the king of the Jews?" asked Pilate.

"Yes, it is as you say," Jesus replied.

3The chief priests accused him of many things. **4**So again Pilate asked him, "Aren't you going to answer? See how many things they are accusing you of."

5But Jesus still made no reply, and Pilate was amazed.

6Now it was the custom at the Feast to release a prisoner whom the people requested. **7**A man called Barabbas was in prison with the insurrectionists who had committed murder in the uprising. **8**The crowd came up and asked Pilate to do for them what he usually did.

9"Do you want me to release to you the king of the Jews?" asked Pilate, **10**knowing it was out of envy that the chief priests had handed Jesus over to him. **11**But the chief priests stirred up the crowd to have Pilate release Barabbas instead.

12"What shall I do, then, with the one you call the king of the Jews?" Pilate asked them.

13"Crucify him!" they shouted.

14"Why? What crime has he committed?" asked Pilate.

But they shouted all the louder, "Crucify him!"

15Wanting to satisfy the crowd, Pilate released Barabbas to them. He had Jesus flogged, and handed him over to be crucified.

The Soldiers Mock Jesus

16The soldiers led Jesus away into the palace (that is, the Praetorium) and called together the whole company of soldiers. **17**They put a purple robe on him, then twisted together a crown of thorns and set it on him. **18**And they began to call out to him, "Hail, king of the Jews!" **19**Again and again they struck him on the head with a staff and spit on him. Falling on their knees, they paid homage to him. **20**And when they had mocked him, they took off the purple robe and put his own clothes on him. Then they led him out to crucify him.

The Crucifixion

21A certain man from Cyrene, Simon, the father of Alexander and Rufus, was passing by on his way in from the country, and they forced him to carry the cross. **22**They brought Jesus to the place called Golgotha (which means The Place of the Skull). **23**Then they offered him wine mixed with myrrh, but he did not take it. **24**And they crucified him. Dividing up his clothes, they cast lots to see what each would get.

25It was the third hour when they crucified him. **26**The written notice of the charge against him read: THE KING OF THE JEWS. **27**They crucified two robbers with him, one on his right and one on his left.[d] **29**Those who passed by hurled insults at him, shaking their heads and saying, "So! You who are going to destroy the temple and build it in three days, **30**come down from the cross and save yourself!"

31In the same way the chief priests and the teachers of the law mocked him among themselves. "He saved others," they said, "but he can't save himself! **32**Let this Christ,[e] this King of Israel, come down now from the cross, that we may see and believe." Those crucified with him also heaped insults on him.

---

a68 Some early manuscripts *entryway and the rooster crowed*   *b72* Some early manuscripts do not have *the second time*.   *c72* Some early manuscripts do not have *twice*.   *d27* Some manuscripts *left, 28 and the scripture was fulfilled which says, "He was counted with the lawless ones"* (Isaiah 53:12)   *e32* Or *Messiah*

The Death of Jesus

³³At the sixth hour darkness came over the whole land until the ninth hour. ³⁴And at the ninth hour Jesus cried out in a loud voice, *"Eloi, Eloi, lama sabachthani?"*—which means, "My God, my God, why have you forsaken me?"*a*

³⁵When some of those standing near heard this, they said, "Listen, he's calling Elijah."

³⁶One man ran, filled a sponge with wine vinegar, put it on a stick, and offered it to Jesus to drink. "Now leave him alone. Let's see if Elijah comes to take him down," he said.

³⁷With a loud cry, Jesus breathed his last.

³⁸The curtain of the temple was torn in two from top to bottom. ³⁹And when the centurion, who stood there in front of Jesus, heard his cry and*b* saw how he died, he said, "Surely this man was the Son*c* of God!"

⁴⁰Some women were watching from a distance. Among them were Mary Magdalene, Mary the mother of James the younger and of Joses, and Salome. ⁴¹In Galilee these women had followed him and cared for his needs. Many other women who had come up with him to Jerusalem were also there.

The Burial of Jesus

⁴²It was Preparation Day (that is, the day before the Sabbath). So as evening approached, ⁴³Joseph of Arimathea, a prominent member of the Council, who was himself waiting for the kingdom of God, went boldly to Pilate and asked for Jesus' body. ⁴⁴Pilate was surprised to hear that he was already dead. Summoning the centurion, he asked him if Jesus had already died. ⁴⁵When he learned from the centurion that it was so, he gave the body to Joseph. ⁴⁶So Joseph bought some linen cloth, took down the body, wrapped it in the linen, and placed it in a tomb cut out of rock. Then he rolled a stone against the entrance of the tomb. ⁴⁷Mary Magdalene and Mary the mother of Joses saw where he was laid.

The Resurrection

16 When the Sabbath was over, Mary Magdalene, Mary the mother of James, and *Salome* bought spices so that they might go to anoint Jesus' body. ²Very early on the first day of the week, just after sunrise, they were on their way to the tomb ³and they asked each other, "Who will roll the stone away from the entrance of the tomb?"

⁴But when they looked up, they saw that the stone, which was very large, had been rolled away. ⁵As they entered the tomb, they saw a young man dressed in a white robe sitting on the right side, and they were alarmed.

⁶"Don't be alarmed," he said. "You are looking for Jesus the Nazarene, who was crucified. He has risen! He is not here. See the place where they laid him. ⁷But go, tell his disciples and Peter, 'He is going ahead of you into Galilee. There you will see him, just as he told you.'"

⁸Trembling and bewildered, the women went out and fled from the tomb. They said nothing to anyone, because they were afraid.

[The earliest manuscripts and some other ancient witnesses do not have Mark 16:9–20.]

⁹When Jesus rose early on the first day of the week, he appeared first to Mary Magdalene, out of whom he had driven seven demons. ¹⁰She went and told those who had been with him and who were mourning and weeping. ¹¹When they heard that Jesus was alive and that she had seen him, they did not believe it.

¹²Afterward Jesus appeared in a different form to two of them while they were walking in the country. ¹³These returned and reported it to the rest; but they did not believe them either.

¹⁴Later Jesus appeared to the Eleven as they were eating; he rebuked them for their lack of faith and their stubborn refusal to believe those who had seen him after he had risen.

¹⁵He said to them, "Go into all the world and preach the good news to all creation. ¹⁶Whoever believes and is baptized will be saved, but whoever does not believe will be condemned. ¹⁷And these signs will accompany those who believe: In my name they will drive out demons; they will speak in new tongues; ¹⁸they will pick up snakes with their hands; and when they drink deadly poison, it will not

---

a34 Psalm 22:1   *b39* Some manuscripts do not have *heard his cry and*   *c39* Or *a son*

Don't Be Afraid

Read: Mark 16:1–13

JESUS WAS DEAD. Crucified. And in his empty tomb sat an angel telling the grieving women who came to minister to their fallen master's body, "Don't be alarmed."

Of course, Jesus had told his followers what to expect. He would die . . . which he did. He would be buried . . . which he was. And in three days he would rise again. Now he wasn't in the tomb. And there was an angel who understated the situation by saying, "Don't be alarmed." Of course they were alarmed, afraid and distressed: The soldiers had crucified Jesus; he had lain in the tomb three days; the huge stone they had worried about had been rolled away; there was an angel standing there . . . talking to them!

It's easy to look at ancient Bible characters and second-guess their responses: "Why didn't they get it?" We like to think we would have gotten it. We would have understood Jesus words' about his death and resurrection. We'd have comprehended that he must first suffer as our Savior before he could return as King of kings. The knowledge that the sign of Jonah meant Jesus would lie three days in the tomb would have been a breeze for us to comprehend, or so we like to think.

But really, if we had been there, encountering an angel in a dark, empty tomb, we would have probably run away in terror or stood there quaking in our sandals. We might have been like the women who "said nothing to anyone, because they were afraid" (verse 8). What were they afraid of? Perhaps they were afraid of the Roman soldiers; they may have been afraid people would think they were crazy; they may have been afraid they wouldn't relay the angel's message correctly.

Do you hold back from telling people that Jesus is risen? Maybe you're afraid you'll be mocked or laughed at. Or maybe you're afraid people will think you've gone off the religious deep end. Or maybe you're afraid you won't know the right words to say. Listen to the angel's words again: "Don't be alarmed . . . He has risen!"

Mark 16:6

"Don't be alarmed," [the angel] said. "You are looking for Jesus the Nazarene, who was crucified. He has risen! He is not here. See the place where they laid him."

reflection

1 Put yourself in the women's shoes. What emotions other than fear might they have been feeling?

2 Are you afraid to tell others Jesus is risen?

3 Who needs to hear this Good News? Pray for the faith to overcome your fear.

RELATED READINGS

Romans 8:35–39;
1 Corinthians 15:54–58;
1 Peter 1:3–9;
1 John 4:16–18

Go to page 1235 for your next devotional reading.

hurt them at all; they will place their hands on sick people, and they will get well."

19After the Lord Jesus had spoken to them, he was taken up into heaven and he sat at the right hand of God. 20Then the disciples went out and preached everywhere, and the Lord worked with them and confirmed his word by the signs that accompanied it.

Luke

Luke, the physician, *meticulously researched the details* for his book, talking with people who had known Jesus well. The Gospels of Matthew and Luke record Jesus' birth, but Luke is the only one that reports Mary's song, *the Magnificat,* and the announcement to the shepherds. He shows Jesus' divinity, but emphasizes his humanity as well, calling him the *"Son of Man."* Luke spends much time telling us about common people's encounters with Christ through which we see Jesus' heart for people. Luke's Gospel concludes with the ascension, at which time Jesus was taken up to heaven. *The story then continues* in Luke's second volume, the book of Acts.

Author:
Luke, a doctor and a Gentile (Greek) Christian.

Audience:
Followers of Jesus. Luke appealed to the Gentiles.

Date:
Probably about A.D. 60.

Setting:
Luke wrote to the Gentiles from Rome or perhaps Caesarea, Achaia or Ephesus.

Verse to Remember:
"For the Son of Man came to seek and to save what was lost." (19:10)

Introduction

1 Many have undertaken to draw up an account of the things that have been fulfilled[a] among us, [2]just as they were handed down to us by those who from the first were eyewitnesses and servants of the word. [3]Therefore, since I myself have carefully investigated everything from the beginning, it seemed good also to me to write an orderly account for you, most excellent Theophilus, [4]so that you may know the certainty of the things you have been taught.

The Birth of John the Baptist Foretold

[5]In the time of Herod king of Judea there was a priest named Zechariah, who belonged to the priestly division of Abijah; his wife Elizabeth was also a descendant of Aaron.

[a]1 Or *been surely believed*

⁶Both of them were upright in the sight of God, observing all the Lord's commandments and regulations blamelessly. ⁷But they had no children, because Elizabeth was barren; and they were both well along in years.

⁸Once when Zechariah's division was on duty and he was serving as priest before God, ⁹he was chosen by lot, according to the custom of the priesthood, to go into the temple of the Lord and burn incense. ¹⁰And when the time for the burning of incense came, all the assembled worshipers were praying outside.

¹¹Then an angel of the Lord appeared to him, standing at the right side of the altar of incense. ¹²When Zechariah saw him, he was startled and was gripped with fear. ¹³But the angel said to him: "Do not be afraid, Zechariah; your prayer has been heard. Your wife Elizabeth will bear you a son, and you are to give him the name John. ¹⁴He will be a joy and delight to you, and many will rejoice because of his birth, ¹⁵for he will be great in the sight of the Lord. He is never to take wine or other fermented drink, and he will be filled with the Holy Spirit even from birth.ᵃ ¹⁶Many of the people of Israel will he bring back to the Lord their God. ¹⁷And he will go on before the Lord, in the spirit and power of Elijah, to turn the hearts of the fathers to their children and the disobedient to the wisdom of the righteous—to make ready a people prepared for the Lord."

¹⁸Zechariah asked the angel, "How can I be sure of this? I am an old man and my wife is well along in years."

¹⁹The angel answered, "I am Gabriel. I stand in the presence of God, and I have been sent to speak to you and to tell you this good news. ²⁰And now you will be silent and not able to speak until the day this happens, because you did not believe my words, which will come true at their proper time."

²¹Meanwhile, the people were waiting for Zechariah and wondering why he stayed so long in the temple. ²²When he came out, he could not speak to them. They realized he had seen a vision in the temple, for he kept making signs to them but remained unable to speak.

²³When his time of service was completed, he returned home. ²⁴After this his wife Elizabeth became pregnant and for five months remained in seclusion. ²⁵"The Lord has done this for me," she said. "In these days he has shown his favor and taken away my disgrace among the people."

The Birth of Jesus Foretold

²⁶In the sixth month, God sent the angel Gabriel to Nazareth, a town in Galilee, ²⁷to a virgin pledged to be married to a man named Joseph, a descendant of David. The virgin's name was Mary. ²⁸The angel went to her and said, "Greetings, you who are highly favored! The Lord is with you."

²⁹Mary was greatly troubled at his words and wondered what kind of greeting this might be. ³⁰But the angel said to her, "Do not be afraid, Mary, you have found favor with God. ³¹You will be with child and give birth to a son, and you are to give him the name Jesus. ³²He will be great and will be called the Son of the Most High. The Lord God will give him the throne of his father David, ³³and he will reign over the house of Jacob forever; his kingdom will never end."

³⁴"How will this be," Mary asked the angel, "since I am a virgin?"

³⁵The angel answered, "The Holy Spirit will come upon you, and the power of the Most High will overshadow you. So the holy one to be born will be calledᵇ the Son of God. ³⁶Even Elizabeth your relative is going to have a child in her old age, and she who was said to be barren is in her sixth month. ³⁷For nothing is impossible with God."

³⁸"I am the Lord's servant," Mary answered. "May it be to me as you have said." Then the angel left her.

Luke 1:37

God Can Do Anything

"For nothing is impossible with God."

Mary Visits Elizabeth

³⁹At that time Mary got ready and hurried to a town in the hill country of Judea, ⁴⁰where

---

ᵃ15 Or *from his mother's womb*   ᵇ35 Or *So the child to be born will be called holy,*

Waiting Game

MARTHA

THE DAYS SEEMED TO STRETCH on forever, and the nights were almost unbearable. The minutes turned into hours; one day turned into two—two of the longest days of her life. Certainly, the message that Lazarus was sick had reached Jesus by now. So, why wasn't he here already? Martha paced outside her home, deliberating the questions. She was confused by his delay. Didn't he care about her brother? Or *her* for that matter?

She decided to give him some more time. He was on his way, she felt sure. He had to be. Even when Lazarus's last breaths rattled in his chest, she kept casting her eyes toward the doorway. She expected Jesus to come through the door at any moment. And when he did, he would restore health and harmony in her family.

But he never came.

After Lazarus died, Mary (always the more emotional one) sobbed hysterically. The other mourners wrapped their arms around her in an effort to console her. Her body heaved with her loud sobs. Meanwhile, Martha responded as only Martha could. She made a mental list of what needed to be done to prepare her brother's body. She began at the top of her list and worked her way down. Mechanically, she sat and tore strips of material in which to wrap him. She fought against the tears welling in her eyes and bit her bottom lip until she thought it would bleed.

Later, she watched as the strong men shouldered her brother's body and carried it to its grave. She instinctively put her arm around her sister, and they both shuddered at the finality of the stone settling into place across the entrance. Martha silently crossed the last item off her list. It was over. Finished. There was nothing more to be done.

Just then, she saw a small crowd of people coming down the road toward her home. From a distance, she recognized a familiar figure striding toward her. In an instant, she knew who he was.

—Prayer—
Jesus, grant me patience in prayer and complete trust in your Word.

> "Lord," Martha said to Jesus, "if you had been here, my brother would not have died. But I know that even now God will give you whatever you ask."
>
> John 11:21–22

ASSIGNED READING:

Luke 10:38–42;
John 11:17–44

Weekend

she entered Zechariah's home and greeted Elizabeth. ⁴¹When Elizabeth heard Mary's greeting, the baby leaped in her womb, and Elizabeth was filled with the Holy Spirit. ⁴²In a loud voice she exclaimed: "Blessed are you among women, and blessed is the child you will bear! ⁴³But why am I so favored, that the mother of my Lord should come to me? ⁴⁴As soon as the sound of your greeting reached my ears, the baby in my womb leaped for joy. ⁴⁵Blessed is she who has believed that what the Lord has said to her will be accomplished!"

Mary's Song

⁴⁶And Mary said:

"My soul glorifies the Lord
⁴⁷   and my spirit rejoices in God my Savior,
⁴⁸for he has been mindful
        of the humble state of his servant.
    From now on all generations will call me
        blessed,
⁴⁹   for the Mighty One has done great
            things for me—
        holy is his name.
⁵⁰His mercy extends to those who fear him,
        from generation to generation.
⁵¹He has performed mighty deeds with his
        arm;
        he has scattered those who are proud in
            their inmost thoughts.
⁵²He has brought down rulers from their
        thrones
        but has lifted up the humble.
⁵³He has filled the hungry with good things
        but has sent the rich away empty.
⁵⁴He has helped his servant Israel,
        remembering to be merciful
⁵⁵to Abraham and his descendants forever,
        even as he said to our fathers."

⁵⁶Mary stayed with Elizabeth for about three months and then returned home.

The Birth of John the Baptist

⁵⁷When it was time for Elizabeth to have her baby, she gave birth to a son. ⁵⁸Her neighbors and relatives heard that the Lord had shown her great mercy, and they shared her joy.

⁵⁹On the eighth day they came to circumcise the child, and they were going to name him after his father Zechariah, ⁶⁰but his mother spoke up and said, "No! He is to be called John."

⁶¹They said to her, "There is no one among your relatives who has that name."

⁶²Then they made signs to his father, to find out what he would like to name the child. ⁶³He asked for a writing tablet, and to everyone's astonishment he wrote, "His name is John." ⁶⁴Immediately his mouth was opened and his tongue was loosed, and he began to speak, praising God. ⁶⁵The neighbors were all filled with awe, and throughout the hill country of Judea people were talking about all these things. ⁶⁶Everyone who heard this wondered about it, asking, "What then is this child going to be?" For the Lord's hand was with him.

Zechariah's Song

⁶⁷His father Zechariah was filled with the Holy Spirit and prophesied:

⁶⁸"Praise be to the Lord, the God of Israel,
        because he has come and has redeemed
            his people.
⁶⁹He has raised up a horn^a of salvation for us
        in the house of his servant David
⁷⁰(as he said through his holy prophets of
            long ago),
⁷¹salvation from our enemies
        and from the hand of all who hate us—
⁷²to show mercy to our fathers
        and to remember his holy covenant,
⁷³   the oath he swore to our father Abraham:
⁷⁴to rescue us from the hand of our enemies,
        and to enable us to serve him without
            fear
⁷⁵   in holiness and righteousness before
            him all our days.

⁷⁶And you, my child, will be called a prophet
        of the Most High;
        for you will go on before the Lord to
            prepare the way for him,
⁷⁷to give his people the knowledge of
            salvation
        through the forgiveness of their sins,
⁷⁸because of the tender mercy of our God,
        by which the rising sun will come to us
            from heaven
⁷⁹to shine on those living in darkness

---

^{a}69 *Horn* here symbolizes strength.

and in the shadow of death,
to guide our feet into the path of peace."

⁸⁰And the child grew and became strong in spirit; and he lived in the desert until he appeared publicly to Israel.

The Birth of Jesus

2 In those days Caesar Augustus issued a decree that a census should be taken of the entire Roman world. ²(This was the first census that took place while Quirinius was governor of Syria.) ³And everyone went to his own town to register.

⁴So Joseph also went up from the town of Nazareth in Galilee to Judea, to Bethlehem the town of David, because he belonged to the house and line of David. ⁵He went there to register with Mary, who was pledged to be married to him and was expecting a child. ⁶While they were there, the time came for the baby to be born, ⁷and she gave birth to her firstborn, a son. She wrapped him in cloths and placed him in a manger, because there was no room for them in the inn.

The Shepherds and the Angels

⁸And there were shepherds living out in the fields nearby, keeping watch over their flocks at night. ⁹An angel of the Lord appeared to them, and the glory of the Lord shone around them, and they were terrified. ¹⁰But the angel said to them, "Do not be afraid. I bring you good news of great joy that will be for all the people. ¹¹Today in the town of David a Savior has been born to you; he is Christᵃ the Lord. ¹²This will be a sign to you: You will find a baby wrapped in cloths and lying in a manger."

¹³Suddenly a great company of the heavenly host appeared with the angel, praising God and saying,

¹⁴"Glory to God in the highest,
and on earth peace to men on whom his favor rests."

¹⁵When the angels had left them and gone into heaven, the shepherds said to one another, "Let's go to Bethlehem and see this thing that has happened, which the Lord has told us about."

¹⁶So they hurried off and found Mary and Joseph, and the baby, who was lying in the manger. ¹⁷When they had seen him, they spread the word concerning what had been told them about this child, ¹⁸and all who heard it were amazed at what the shepherds said to them. ¹⁹But Mary treasured up all these things and pondered them in her heart. ²⁰The shepherds returned, glorifying and praising God for all the things they had heard and seen, which were just as they had been told.

Jesus Presented in the Temple

²¹On the eighth day, when it was time to circumcise him, he was named Jesus, the name the angel had given him before he had been conceived.

²²When the time of their purification according to the Law of Moses had been completed, Joseph and Mary took him to Jerusalem to present him to the Lord ²³(as it is written in the Law of the Lord, "Every firstborn male is to be consecrated to the Lord"ᵇ), ²⁴and to offer a sacrifice in keeping with what is said in the Law of the Lord: "a pair of doves or two young pigeons."ᶜ

²⁵Now there was a man in Jerusalem called Simeon, who was righteous and devout. He was waiting for the consolation of Israel, and the Holy Spirit was upon him. ²⁶It had been revealed to him by the Holy Spirit that he would not die before he had seen the Lord's Christ. ²⁷Moved by the Spirit, he went into the temple courts. When the parents brought in the child Jesus to do for him what the custom of the Law required, ²⁸Simeon took him in his arms and praised God, saying:

²⁹"Sovereign Lord, as you have promised,
you now dismissᵈ your servant in peace.
³⁰For my eyes have seen your salvation,
³¹   which you have prepared in the sight of
all people,
³²a light for revelation to the Gentiles
and for glory to your people Israel."

³³The child's father and mother marveled at what was said about him. ³⁴Then Simeon blessed them and said to Mary, his mother: "This child is destined to cause the falling and

---

ᵃ11 Or Messiah. "The Christ" (Greek) and "the Messiah" (Hebrew) both mean "the Anointed One"; also in verse 26.   ᵇ23 Exodus 13:2,12
ᶜ24 Lev. 12:8   ᵈ29 Or promised, / now dismiss

There was also a prophetess, Anna, the daughter of Phanuel, of the tribe of Asher. She was very old; she had lived with her husband seven years after her marriage, and then was a widow until she was eighty-four. She never left the temple but worshiped night and day, fasting and praying.

Coming up to them at that very moment, she gave thanks to God and spoke about the child to all who were looking forward to the redemption of Jerusalem.

No Age Barrier

Read: Luke 2:25–39

BY ANYONE'S DEFINITION, Anna was old. Married for only 7 years, a widow until age 84, Anna had witnessed the passing of decade after decade. Her world was not a large one, as she was consigned to living in the temple and devoted herself to fasting and prayer; she mostly worshiped and waited. The years of waiting were finally over when she spotted *him*: the precious infant lying in the young mother's arms. Angels had announced this child's birth. Now an aged woman became another in the line of those who sang the chorus of annunciation: The Messiah had come! What a beautiful message from a beautiful woman who had waited years to proclaim her prophetic message.

Nineteenth-century author and abolitionist Harriet Beecher Stowe once wrote, "So much had been said and sung of beautiful young girls, why don't somebody wake up to the beauty of old women?"

We live in a youth-oriented culture. American women spend millions of dollars each year on products designed to keep us young—or at least to help us appear that way. Older women can easily feel marginalized—as if their days of usefulness are past. Yet Scripture reminds us that God reserves some of his most significant assignments to women who have attained the maturity to handle them—like Anna the prophetess.

As the years pass, do you sometimes wonder whether the best ones are now behind you? Do your options seem limited and your value diminished? When you set your heart to serve God, you can continue to do so whatever your health, age or personal circumstances.

Angels and an elderly woman announced the birth of the Savior of the world. Approximately 33 years later, angels and a select group of women proclaimed the astounding news of his resurrection from the dead. Age and gender present no barrier when God entrusts us with a divine message or mission.

reflection

1 What encourages you about the story of Anna in the temple?

2 Physical limitations sometimes come with age, but what do you see as the positive aspects of advancing years?

3 How might your opportunities to serve God be broader now than they were when you were younger?

RELATED READINGS

Genesis 24:34–36;
Exodus 15:19–21;
1 Samuel 2:1–10;
Acts 2:14–21

Monday

Go to page 1241 for your next devotional reading.

rising of many in Israel, and to be a sign that will be spoken against, ³⁵so that the thoughts of many hearts will be revealed. And a sword will pierce your own soul too."

³⁶There was also a prophetess, Anna, the daughter of Phanuel, of the tribe of Asher. She was very old; she had lived with her husband seven years after her marriage, ³⁷and then was a widow until she was eighty-four.^a She never left the temple but worshiped night and day, fasting and praying. ³⁸Coming up to them at that very moment, she gave thanks to God and spoke about the child to all who were looking forward to the redemption of Jerusalem.

³⁹When Joseph and Mary had done everything required by the Law of the Lord, they returned to Galilee to their own town of Nazareth. ⁴⁰And the child grew and became strong; he was filled with wisdom, and the grace of God was upon him.

The Boy Jesus at the Temple

⁴¹Every year his parents went to Jerusalem for the Feast of the Passover. ⁴²When he was twelve years old, they went up to the Feast, according to the custom. ⁴³After the Feast was over, while his parents were returning home, the boy Jesus stayed behind in Jerusalem, but they were unaware of it. ⁴⁴Thinking he was in their company, they traveled on for a day. Then they began looking for him among their relatives and friends. ⁴⁵When they did not find him, they went back to Jerusalem to look for him. ⁴⁶After three days they found him in the temple courts, sitting among the teachers, listening to them and asking them questions. ⁴⁷Everyone who heard him was amazed at his understanding and his answers. ⁴⁸When his parents saw him, they were astonished. His mother said to him, "Son, why have you treated us like this? Your father and I have been anxiously searching for you."

⁴⁹"Why were you searching for me?" he asked. "Didn't you know I had to be in my Father's house?" ⁵⁰But they did not understand what he was saying to them.

⁵¹Then he went down to Nazareth with them and was obedient to them. But his mother treasured all these things in her heart. ⁵²And Jesus

grew in wisdom and stature, and in favor with God and men.

John the Baptist Prepares the Way

3 In the fifteenth year of the reign of Tiberius Caesar—when Pontius Pilate was governor of Judea, Herod tetrarch of Galilee, his brother Philip tetrarch of Iturea and Traconitis, and Lysanias tetrarch of Abilene— ²during the high priesthood of Annas and Caiaphas, the word of God came to John son of Zechariah in the desert. ³He went into all the country around the Jordan, preaching a baptism of repentance for the forgiveness of sins. ⁴As is written in the book of the words of Isaiah the prophet:

"A voice of one calling in the desert,
'Prepare the way for the Lord,
  make straight paths for him.
⁵ Every valley shall be filled in,
  every mountain and hill made low.
The crooked roads shall become straight,
  the rough ways smooth.
⁶ And all mankind will see God's
  salvation.'"^b

⁷John said to the crowds coming out to be baptized by him, "You brood of vipers! Who warned you to flee from the coming wrath? ⁸Produce fruit in keeping with repentance. And do not begin to say to yourselves, 'We have Abraham as our father.' For I tell you that out of these stones God can raise up children for Abraham. ⁹The ax is already at the root of the trees, and every tree that does not produce good fruit will be cut down and thrown into the fire."

¹⁰"What should we do then?" the crowd asked.

¹¹John answered, "The man with two tunics should share with him who has none, and the one who has food should do the same."

¹²Tax collectors also came to be baptized. "Teacher," they asked, "what should we do?"

¹³"Don't collect any more than you are required to," he told them.

¹⁴Then some soldiers asked him, "And what should we do?"

He replied, "Don't extort money and don't accuse people falsely—be content with your pay."

^a37 Or widow for eighty-four years   ^b6 Isaiah 40:3–5

¹⁵The people were waiting expectantly and were all wondering in their hearts if John might possibly be the Christ.ᵃ ¹⁶John answered them all, "I baptize you withᵇ water. But one more powerful than I will come, the thongs of whose sandals I am not worthy to untie. He will baptize you with the Holy Spirit and with fire. ¹⁷His winnowing fork is in his hand to clear his threshing floor and to gather the wheat into his barn, but he will burn up the chaff with unquenchable fire." ¹⁸And with many other words John exhorted the people and preached the good news to them.

¹⁹But when John rebuked Herod the tetrarch because of Herodias, his brother's wife, and all the other evil things he had done, ²⁰Herod added this to them all: He locked John up in prison.

The Baptism and Genealogy of Jesus

²¹When all the people were being baptized, Jesus was baptized too. And as he was praying, heaven was opened ²²and the Holy Spirit descended on him in bodily form like a dove. And a voice came from heaven: "You are my Son, whom I love; with you I am well pleased."

²³Now Jesus himself was about thirty years old when he began his ministry. He was the son, so it was thought, of Joseph,

the son of Heli, ²⁴the son of Matthat,
the son of Levi, the son of Melki,
the son of Jannai, the son of Joseph,
²⁵the son of Mattathias, the son of Amos,
the son of Nahum, the son of Esli,
the son of Naggai, ²⁶the son of Maath,
the son of Mattathias, the son of Semein,
the son of Josech, the son of Joda,
²⁷the son of Joanan, the son of Rhesa,
the son of Zerubbabel, the son of Shealtiel,
the son of Neri, ²⁸the son of Melki,
the son of Addi, the son of Cosam,
the son of Elmadam, the son of Er,
²⁹the son of Joshua, the son of Eliezer,
the son of Jorim, the son of Matthat,
the son of Levi, ³⁰the son of Simeon,
the son of Judah, the son of Joseph,
the son of Jonam, the son of Eliakim,

³¹the son of Melea, the son of Menna,
the son of Mattatha, the son of Nathan,
the son of David, ³²the son of Jesse,
the son of Obed, the son of Boaz,
the son of Salmon,ᶜ the son of Nahshon,
³³the son of Amminadab, the son of Ram,ᵈ
the son of Hezron, the son of Perez,
the son of Judah, ³⁴the son of Jacob,
the son of Isaac, the son of Abraham,
the son of Terah, the son of Nahor,
³⁵the son of Serug, the son of Reu,
the son of Peleg, the son of Eber,
the son of Shelah, ³⁶the son of Cainan,
the son of Arphaxad, the son of Shem,
the son of Noah, the son of Lamech,
³⁷the son of Methuselah, the son of Enoch,
the son of Jared, the son of Mahalalel,
the son of Kenan, ³⁸the son of Enosh,
the son of Seth, the son of Adam,
the son of God.

The Temptation of Jesus

4 Jesus, full of the Holy Spirit, returned from the Jordan and was led by the Spirit in the desert, ²where for forty days he was tempted by the devil. He ate nothing during those days, and at the end of them he was hungry.

³The devil said to him, "If you are the Son of God, tell this stone to become bread."

⁴Jesus answered, "It is written: 'Man does not live on bread alone.'ᵉ"

⁵The devil led him up to a high place and showed him in an instant all the kingdoms of the world. ⁶And he said to him, "I will give you all their authority and splendor, for it has been given to me, and I can give it to anyone I want to. ⁷So if you worship me, it will all be yours."

⁸Jesus answered, "It is written: 'Worship the Lord your God and serve him only.'ᶠ"

⁹The devil led him to Jerusalem and had him stand on the highest point of the temple. "If you are the Son of God," he said, "throw yourself down from here. ¹⁰For it is written:

"'He will command his angels concerning
you
to guard you carefully;
¹¹they will lift you up in their hands,

ᵃ15 Or *Messiah*   ᵇ16 Or *in*   ᶜ32 Some early manuscripts *Sala*   ᵈ33 Some manuscripts *Amminadab, the son of Admin, the son of Arni;* other manuscripts vary widely.   ᵉ4 Deut. 8:3   ᶠ8 Deut. 6:13

From Suffering to Serving

Read: Luke 4:1–44

LUKE, THE PHYSICIAN, tells us that Simon's mother-in-law was sick with a high fever. This was no ordinary cold. She was really, really sick and suffering. You know what it's like to have a fever. First you have the chills, so you pile the blankets high. Then you get too hot, so you throw the blankets off. Then you're hit with a blazing headache. Soon your whole body begins to ache. Finally, you're so worn out, you lay there lethargically, unable to move a muscle. It's miserable.

In this case, the disciples didn't run to the local apothecary; "they asked Jesus to help her" (verse 38). The Great Physician bent over the tired woman's body and told the fever to leave—and it left! Amazingly, she didn't need rest to recover from her ordeal. She wasn't just partially healed, she was so completely healed that "she got up at once and began to wait on them" (verse 39).

Now this was a no-nonsense kind of woman. She probably could have stayed on her sickbed for a few days, let other people wait on her, gotten a little more sympathy and emotional mileage out of that fever, and no one would have known (except Jesus). But some women have a gift for serving others, no matter what. They serve until they can't stand up anymore. And as soon as they're a bit better, they're up and at it again. They are always busy and always concerned for those around them. You know the type; they are often the silent strength behind those men and women who have the showier, more "glamorous" jobs.

You might *be* one of those women. You think, *I don't have time to rest, and I really don't have time to be sick.* But let's face it: sometimes our human bodies wear out. We get sick . . . or just sick and tired. That's when we can ask for help from the One who is the source of healing and strength. Jesus is still in the miracle business. Ask him to heal you body, mind and spirit. And keep in mind that there's nothing wrong with finding the healthy balance between meeting your own needs so you can continue to meet the needs of others.

reflection

1 Assess your life. Are you both serving others and caring for your own needs? How are you balancing the competing needs of those around you?

2 Are you chronically ill? How can you serve where you are?

3 Do you know someone who is sick and suffering? How can you pray for her? How can you help her in practical ways?

RELATED READINGS

Psalm 30:2;
Matthew 9:20–22;
James 5:14–16

"The definition of a servant: One who is doing the will of another with the resources of another for the benefit of another."

Cosette Conaway

so that you will not strike your foot against a stone.'[a]"

[12] Jesus answered, "It says: 'Do not put the Lord your God to the test.'[b]"

[13] When the devil had finished all this tempting, he left him until an opportune time.

Jesus Rejected at Nazareth

[14] Jesus returned to Galilee in the power of the Spirit, and news about him spread through the whole countryside. [15] He taught in their synagogues, and everyone praised him.

[16] He went to Nazareth, where he had been brought up, and on the Sabbath day he went into the synagogue, as was his custom. And he stood up to read. [17] The scroll of the prophet Isaiah was handed to him. Unrolling it, he found the place where it is written:

[18] "The Spirit of the Lord is on me,
    because he has anointed me
    to preach good news to the poor.
He has sent me to proclaim freedom for the prisoners
    and recovery of sight for the blind,
to release the oppressed,
[19]   to proclaim the year of the Lord's favor."[c]

[20] Then he rolled up the scroll, gave it back to the attendant and sat down. The eyes of everyone in the synagogue were fastened on him, [21] and he began by saying to them, "Today this scripture is fulfilled in your hearing."

[22] All spoke well of him and were amazed at the gracious words that came from his lips. "Isn't this Joseph's son?" they asked.

[23] Jesus said to them, "Surely you will quote this proverb to me: 'Physician, heal yourself! Do here in your hometown what we have heard that you did in Capernaum.'"

[24] "I tell you the truth," he continued, "no prophet is accepted in his hometown. [25] I assure you that there were many widows in Israel in Elijah's time, when the sky was shut for three and a half years and there was a severe famine throughout the land. [26] Yet Elijah was not sent to any of them, but to a widow in Zarephath in the region of Sidon. [27] And there were many in Israel with leprosy[d] in the time of Elisha the prophet, yet not one of them was cleansed—only Naaman the Syrian."

[28] All the people in the synagogue were furious when they heard this. [29] They got up, drove him out of the town, and took him to the brow of the hill on which the town was built, in order to throw him down the cliff. [30] But he walked right through the crowd and went on his way.

Jesus Drives Out an Evil Spirit

[31] Then he went down to Capernaum, a town in Galilee, and on the Sabbath began to teach the people. [32] They were amazed at his teaching, because his message had authority.

[33] In the synagogue there was a man possessed by a demon, an evil[e] spirit. He cried out at the top of his voice, [34] "Ha! What do you want with us, Jesus of Nazareth? Have you come to destroy us? I know who you are—the Holy One of God!"

[35] "Be quiet!" Jesus said sternly. "Come out of him!" Then the demon threw the man down before them all and came out without injuring him.

[36] All the people were amazed and said to each other, "What is this teaching? With authority and power he gives orders to evil spirits and they come out!" [37] And the news about him spread throughout the surrounding area.

Jesus Heals Many

[38] Jesus left the synagogue and went to the home of Simon. Now Simon's mother-in-law was suffering from a high fever, and they asked

---

Luke 4:18

God Cares for the Oppressed

"The Spirit of the Lord is on me . . . to preach good news to the poor. He has sent me to proclaim freedom for the prisoners and recovery of sight for the blind, to release the oppressed."

---

[a] 11 Psalm 91:11,12   [b] 12 Deut. 6:16   [c] 19 Isaiah 61:1,2   [d] 27 The Greek word was used for various diseases affecting the skin—not necessarily leprosy.   [e] 33 Greek *unclean*; also in verse 36

Jesus to help her. ³⁹So he bent over her and rebuked the fever, and it left her. She got up at once and began to wait on them.

⁴⁰When the sun was setting, the people brought to Jesus all who had various kinds of sickness, and laying his hands on each one, he healed them. ⁴¹Moreover, demons came out of many people, shouting, "You are the Son of God!" But he rebuked them and would not allow them to speak, because they knew he was the Christ.ᵃ

⁴²At daybreak Jesus went out to a solitary place. The people were looking for him and when they came to where he was, they tried to keep him from leaving them. ⁴³But he said, "I must preach the good news of the kingdom of God to the other towns also, because that is why I was sent." ⁴⁴And he kept on preaching in the synagogues of Judea.ᵇ

The Calling of the First Disciples

5 One day as Jesus was standing by the Lake of Gennesaret,ᶜ with the people crowding around him and listening to the word of God, ²he saw at the water's edge two boats, left there by the fishermen, who were washing their nets. ³He got into one of the boats, the one belonging to Simon, and asked him to put out a little from shore. Then he sat down and taught the people from the boat.

⁴When he had finished speaking, he said to Simon, "Put out into deep water, and let downᵈ the nets for a catch."

⁵Simon answered, "Master, we've worked hard all night and haven't caught anything. But because you say so, I will let down the nets."

⁶When they had done so, they caught such a large number of fish that their nets began to break. ⁷So they signaled their partners in the other boat to come and help them, and they came and filled both boats so full that they began to sink.

⁸When Simon Peter saw this, he fell at Jesus' knees and said, "Go away from me, Lord; I am a sinful man!" ⁹For he and all his companions were astonished at the catch of fish they had taken, ¹⁰and so were James and John, the sons of Zebedee, Simon's partners.

Then Jesus said to Simon, "Don't be afraid; from now on you will catch men." ¹¹So they pulled their boats up on shore, left everything and followed him.

The Man With Leprosy

¹²While Jesus was in one of the towns, a man came along who was covered with leprosy.ᵉ When he saw Jesus, he fell with his face to the ground and begged him, "Lord, if you are willing, you can make me clean."

¹³Jesus reached out his hand and touched the man. "I am willing," he said. "Be clean!" And immediately the leprosy left him.

¹⁴Then Jesus ordered him, "Don't tell anyone, but go, show yourself to the priest and offer the sacrifices that Moses commanded for your cleansing, as a testimony to them."

¹⁵Yet the news about him spread all the more, so that crowds of people came to hear him and to be healed of their sicknesses. ¹⁶But Jesus often withdrew to lonely places and prayed.

Jesus Heals a Paralytic

¹⁷One day as he was teaching, Pharisees and teachers of the law, who had come from every village of Galilee and from Judea and Jerusalem, were sitting there. And the power of the Lord was present for him to heal the sick. ¹⁸Some men came carrying a paralytic on a mat and tried to take him into the house to lay him before Jesus. ¹⁹When they could not find a way to do this because of the crowd, they went up on the roof and lowered him on his mat through the tiles into the middle of the crowd, right in front of Jesus.

²⁰When Jesus saw their faith, he said, "Friend, your sins are forgiven."

²¹The Pharisees and the teachers of the law began thinking to themselves, "Who is this fellow who speaks blasphemy? Who can forgive sins but God alone?"

²²Jesus knew what they were thinking and asked, "Why are you thinking these things in your hearts? ²³Which is easier: to say, 'Your sins are forgiven,' or to say, 'Get up and walk'? ²⁴But that you may know that the Son of Man has authority on earth to forgive sins…" He said to the paralyzed man, "I tell you, get up, take your mat and go home." ²⁵Immediately he stood up

---

ᵃ41 Or *Messiah*   ᵇ44 Or *the land of the Jews*; some manuscripts *Galilee*   ᶜ1 That is, Sea of Galilee   ᵈ4 The Greek verb is plural.
ᵉ12 The Greek word was used for various diseases affecting the skin—not necessarily leprosy.

in front of them, took what he had been lying on and went home praising God. 26Everyone was amazed and gave praise to God. They were filled with awe and said, "We have seen remarkable things today."

The Calling of Levi

27After this, Jesus went out and saw a tax collector by the name of Levi sitting at his tax booth. "Follow me," Jesus said to him, 28and Levi got up, left everything and followed him.

29Then Levi held a great banquet for Jesus at his house, and a large crowd of tax collectors and others were eating with them. 30But the Pharisees and the teachers of the law who belonged to their sect complained to his disciples, "Why do you eat and drink with tax collectors and 'sinners'?"

31Jesus answered them, "It is not the healthy who need a doctor, but the sick. 32I have not come to call the righteous, but sinners to repentance."

Jesus Questioned About Fasting

33They said to him, "John's disciples often fast and pray, and so do the disciples of the Pharisees, but yours go on eating and drinking."

34Jesus answered, "Can you make the guests of the bridegroom fast while he is with them? 35But the time will come when the bridegroom will be taken from them; in those days they will fast."

36He told them this parable: "No one tears a patch from a new garment and sews it on an old one. If he does, he will have torn the new garment, and the patch from the new will not match the old. 37And no one pours new wine into old wineskins. If he does, the new wine will burst the skins, the wine will run out and the wineskins will be ruined. 38No, new wine must be poured into new wineskins. 39And no one after drinking old wine wants the new, for he says, 'The old is better.'"

Lord of the Sabbath

6 One Sabbath Jesus was going through the grainfields, and his disciples began to pick some heads of grain, rub them in their hands and eat the kernels. 2Some of the Pharisees asked, "Why are you doing what is unlawful on the Sabbath?"

3Jesus answered them, "Have you never read what David did when he and his companions were hungry? 4He entered the house of God, and taking the consecrated bread, he ate what is lawful only for priests to eat. And he also gave some to his companions." 5Then Jesus said to them, "The Son of Man is Lord of the Sabbath."

6On another Sabbath he went into the synagogue and was teaching, and a man was there whose right hand was shriveled. 7The Pharisees and the teachers of the law were looking for a reason to accuse Jesus, so they watched him closely to see if he would heal on the Sabbath. 8But Jesus knew what they were thinking and said to the man with the shriveled hand, "Get up and stand in front of everyone." So he got up and stood there.

9Then Jesus said to them, "I ask you, which is lawful on the Sabbath: to do good or to do evil, to save life or to destroy it?"

10He looked around at them all, and then said to the man, "Stretch out your hand." He did so, and his hand was completely restored. 11But they were furious and began to discuss with one another what they might do to Jesus.

The Twelve Apostles

12One of those days Jesus went out to a mountainside to pray, and spent the night praying to God. 13When morning came, he called his disciples to him and chose twelve of them, whom he also designated apostles: 14Simon (whom he named Peter), his brother Andrew, James, John, Philip, Bartholomew, 15Matthew, Thomas, James son of Alphaeus, Simon who was called the Zealot, 16Judas son of James, and Judas Iscariot, who became a traitor.

Blessings and Woes

17He went down with them and stood on a level place. A large crowd of his disciples was there and a great number of people from all over Judea, from Jerusalem, and from the coast of Tyre and Sidon, 18who had come to hear him and to be healed of their diseases. Those troubled by evil*a* spirits were cured, 19and the people all tried to touch him, because power was coming from him and healing them all.

20Looking at his disciples, he said:

---

a18 Greek *unclean*

"Blessed are you who are poor,
for yours is the kingdom of God.
²¹ Blessed are you who hunger now,
for you will be satisfied.
Blessed are you who weep now,
for you will laugh.
²² Blessed are you when men hate you,
when they exclude you
and insult you
and reject your name as evil,
because of the Son of Man.

²³ "Rejoice in that day and leap for joy, because great is your reward in heaven. For that is how their fathers treated the prophets.

²⁴ "But woe to you who are rich,
for you have already received your comfort.
²⁵ Woe to you who are well fed now,
for you will go hungry.
Woe to you who laugh now,
for you will mourn and weep.
²⁶ Woe to you when all men speak well of you,
for that is how their fathers treated the false prophets.

Love for Enemies

²⁷ "But I tell you who hear me: Love your enemies, do good to those who hate you, ²⁸ bless those who curse you, pray for those who mistreat you. ²⁹ If someone strikes you on one cheek, turn to him the other also. If someone takes your cloak, do not stop him from taking your tunic. ³⁰ Give to everyone who asks you, and if anyone takes what belongs to you, do not demand it back. ³¹ Do to others as you would have them do to you.

³² "If you love those who love you, what credit is that to you? Even 'sinners' love those who love them. ³³ And if you do good to those who are good to you, what credit is that to you? Even 'sinners' do that. ³⁴ And if you lend to those from whom you expect repayment, what credit is that to you? Even 'sinners' lend to 'sinners,' expecting to be repaid in full. ³⁵ But love your enemies, do good to them, and lend to them without expecting to get anything back. Then your reward will be great, and you will be sons of the Most High, because he is kind to the ungrateful and wicked. ³⁶ Be merciful, just as your Father is merciful.

Judging Others

³⁷ "Do not judge, and you will not be judged. Do not condemn, and you will not be condemned. Forgive, and you will be forgiven. ³⁸ Give, and it will be given to you. A good measure, pressed down, shaken together and running over, will be poured into your lap. For with the measure you use, it will be measured to you."

³⁹ He also told them this parable: "Can a blind man lead a blind man? Will they not both fall into a pit? ⁴⁰ A student is not above his teacher, but everyone who is fully trained will be like his teacher.

⁴¹ "Why do you look at the speck of sawdust in your brother's eye and pay no attention to the plank in your own eye? ⁴² How can you say to your brother, 'Brother, let me take the speck out of your eye,' when you yourself fail to see the plank in your own eye? You hypocrite, first take the plank out of your eye, and then you will see clearly to remove the speck from your brother's eye.

A Tree and Its Fruit

⁴³ "No good tree bears bad fruit, nor does a bad tree bear good fruit. ⁴⁴ Each tree is recognized by its own fruit. People do not pick figs from thornbushes, or grapes from briers. ⁴⁵ The good man brings good things out of the good stored up in his heart, and the evil man brings evil things out of the evil stored up in his heart. For out of the overflow of his heart his mouth speaks.

The Wise and Foolish Builders

⁴⁶ "Why do you call me, 'Lord, Lord,' and do not do what I say? ⁴⁷ I will show you what he

---

Luke 6:35

God Shows Kindness

"But love your enemies, do good to them, and lend to them without expecting to get anything back. Then your reward will be great, and you will be sons of the Most High, because he is kind to the ungrateful and wicked."

Rock Solid

Luke 6:47–48

I will show you what he is like who comes to me and hears my words and puts them into practice. He is like a man building a house, who dug down deep and laid the foundation on rock. When a flood came, the torrent struck that house but could not shake it, because it was well built.

reflection

1 What storm is threatening to sway you?

2 How deep is your foundation in Jesus? How much deeper would you like it to go?

3 What will you do to develop a deeper and stronger foundation?

RELATED READINGS

1 Corinthians 3:10–16;
1 Peter 2:4–12;
Jude 20–21

Read: Luke 6:27–49

THE FUTURISTIC SPACE NEEDLE SPIKES from the Seattle skyline. Stretching approximately 605 feet into the sky, its spire pierces the clouds that often veil the earthquake-prone city. Although its height can seem frightening, especially when the Needle sways, it is actually safer than many tall buildings. The architects who designed the stunning structure kept one principle firmly in mind: the larger and higher the building, the stronger the base needs to be.

The Space Needle's foundation is 30 feet deep, weighs 5,850 tons and contains 250 tons of reinforcing steel. The foundation is as heavy as the Needle, enabling the airy structure to withstand a wind velocity of 200 miles per hour. In 2001 it withstood an earthquake of 6.8 on the Richter scale. It is estimated that it can endure even greater shocks because the architects doubled the 1962 building code requirements.

Jesus, the master builder of strong, resilient women, likens our spiritual foundation to a building with a strong, immovable base. In his analogy, he tells of a wise builder who "laid the foundation on rock" (verse 48). We know that sooner or later, floods *will* come in one form or another: illness, financial problems, a relationship breakdown, societal calamities, terrorism or natural disasters. If we don't take Jesus' words to heart and put them into practice, we are on shaky ground. But if we build our spiritual lives on what he says, we can withstand anything that shakes us.

And what strong words had Jesus given his followers? Love your enemies and be good to them (see verses 27–36). Exchange kindness for anger, silence for gossip, a sweet spirit for bitterness. Don't judge others but accept them as God has accepted you. Forgive, because you have been forgiven (see verse 37). Be generous, and generosity will come back to you when you most need it (see verse 38). Be more concerned with your own purity than about the purity of others (see verses 41–42). Care about the goodness of your heart because your words will reveal, no matter how good an actress you are, what's really inside (see verses 44–45). The rock solid foundation isn't an abstract notion. The "rocks," ironically, are a soft heart and a gentle spirit. And those can only come from the Rock of Ages, Jesus Christ.

Wednesday

Go to page 1250 for your next devotional reading.

is like who comes to me and hears my words and puts them into practice. ⁴⁸He is like a man building a house, who dug down deep and laid the foundation on rock. When a flood came, the torrent struck that house but could not shake it, because it was well built. ⁴⁹But the one who hears my words and does not put them into practice is like a man who built a house on the ground without a foundation. The moment the torrent struck that house, it collapsed and its destruction was complete."

The Faith of the Centurion

7 When Jesus had finished saying all this in the hearing of the people, he entered Capernaum. ²There a centurion's servant, whom his master valued highly, was sick and about to die. ³The centurion heard of Jesus and sent some elders of the Jews to him, asking him to come and heal his servant. ⁴When they came to Jesus, they pleaded earnestly with him, "This man deserves to have you do this, ⁵because he loves our nation and has built our synagogue." ⁶So Jesus went with them.

He was not far from the house when the centurion sent friends to say to him: "Lord, don't trouble yourself, for I do not deserve to have you come under my roof. ⁷That is why I did not even consider myself worthy to come to you. But say the word, and my servant will be healed. ⁸For I myself am a man under authority, with soldiers under me. I tell this one, 'Go,' and he goes; and that one, 'Come,' and he comes. I say to my servant, 'Do this,' and he does it."

⁹When Jesus heard this, he was amazed at him, and turning to the crowd following him, he said, "I tell you, I have not found such great faith even in Israel." ¹⁰Then the men who had been sent returned to the house and found the servant well.

Jesus Raises a Widow's Son

¹¹Soon afterward, Jesus went to a town called Nain, and his disciples and a large crowd went along with him. ¹²As he approached the town gate, a dead person was being carried out—the only son of his mother, and she was a widow. And a large crowd from the town was with her.

¹³When the Lord saw her, his heart went out to her and he said, "Don't cry."

¹⁴Then he went up and touched the coffin, and those carrying it stood still. He said, "Young man, I say to you, get up!" ¹⁵The dead man sat up and began to talk, and Jesus gave him back to his mother.

¹⁶They were all filled with awe and praised God. "A great prophet has appeared among us," they said. "God has come to help his people." ¹⁷This news about Jesus spread throughout Judea[a] and the surrounding country.

Jesus and John the Baptist

¹⁸John's disciples told him about all these things. Calling two of them, ¹⁹he sent them to the Lord to ask, "Are you the one who was to come, or should we expect someone else?"

²⁰When the men came to Jesus, they said, "John the Baptist sent us to you to ask, 'Are you the one who was to come, or should we expect someone else?'"

²¹At that very time Jesus cured many who had diseases, sicknesses and evil spirits, and gave sight to many who were blind. ²²So he replied to the messengers, "Go back and report to John what you have seen and heard: The blind receive sight, the lame walk, those who have leprosy[b] are cured, the deaf hear, the dead are raised, and the good news is preached to the poor. ²³Blessed is the man who does not fall away on account of me."

²⁴After John's messengers left, Jesus began to speak to the crowd about John: "What did you go out into the desert to see? A reed swayed by the wind? ²⁵If not, what did you go out to see? A man dressed in fine clothes? No, those who wear expensive clothes and indulge in luxury are in palaces. ²⁶But what did you go out to see? A prophet? Yes, I tell you, and more than a prophet. ²⁷This is the one about whom it is written:

"'I will send my messenger ahead of you,
    who will prepare your way before you.'[c]

²⁸I tell you, among those born of women there is no one greater than John; yet the one who is least in the kingdom of God is greater than he."

²⁹(All the people, even the tax collectors,

---

^a17 Or *the land of the Jews*   ^b22 The Greek word was used for various diseases affecting the skin—not necessarily leprosy.
^c27 Mal. 3:1

when they heard Jesus' words, acknowledged that God's way was right, because they had been baptized by John. 30But the Pharisees and experts in the law rejected God's purpose for themselves, because they had not been baptized by John.)

31"To what, then, can I compare the people of this generation? What are they like? 32They are like children sitting in the marketplace and calling out to each other:

"'We played the flute for you,
	and you did not dance;
we sang a dirge,
	and you did not cry.'

33For John the Baptist came neither eating bread nor drinking wine, and you say, 'He has a demon.' 34The Son of Man came eating and drinking, and you say, 'Here is a glutton and a drunkard, a friend of tax collectors and "sinners."' 35But wisdom is proved right by all her children."

Jesus Anointed by a Sinful Woman

36Now one of the Pharisees invited Jesus to have dinner with him, so he went to the Pharisee's house and reclined at the table. 37When a woman who had lived a sinful life in that town learned that Jesus was eating at the Pharisee's house, she brought an alabaster jar of perfume, 38and as she stood behind him at his feet weeping, she began to wet his feet with her tears. Then she wiped them with her hair, kissed them and poured perfume on them.

39When the Pharisee who had invited him saw this, he said to himself, "If this man were a prophet, he would know who is touching him and what kind of woman she is—that she is a sinner."

40Jesus answered him, "Simon, I have something to tell you."

"Tell me, teacher," he said.

41"Two men owed money to a certain moneylender. One owed him five hundred denarii,*a* and the other fifty. 42Neither of them had the money to pay him back, so he canceled the debts of both. Now which of them will love him more?"

43Simon replied, "I suppose the one who had the bigger debt canceled."

"You have judged correctly," Jesus said.

44Then he turned toward the woman and said to Simon, "Do you see this woman? I came into your house. You did not give me any water for my feet, but she wet my feet with her tears and wiped them with her hair. 45You did not give me a kiss, but this woman, from the time I entered, has not stopped kissing my feet. 46You did not put oil on my head, but she has poured perfume on my feet. 47Therefore, I tell you, her many sins have been forgiven—for she loved much. But he who has been forgiven little loves little."

48Then Jesus said to her, "Your sins are forgiven."

49The other guests began to say among themselves, "Who is this who even forgives sins?"

50Jesus said to the woman, "Your faith has saved you; go in peace."

The Parable of the Sower

8 After this, Jesus traveled about from one town and village to another, proclaiming the good news of the kingdom of God. The Twelve were with him, 2and also some women who had been cured of evil spirits and diseases: Mary (called Magdalene) from whom seven demons had come out; 3Joanna the wife of Cuza, the manager of Herod's household; Susanna; and many others. These women were helping to support them out of their own means.

4While a large crowd was gathering and people were coming to Jesus from town after town, he told this parable: 5"A farmer went out to sow his seed. As he was scattering the seed, some fell along the path; it was trampled on, and the birds of the air ate it up. 6Some fell on rock, and when it came up, the plants withered because they had no moisture. 7Other seed fell among thorns, which grew up with it and choked the plants. 8Still other seed fell on good soil. It came up and yielded a crop, a hundred times more than was sown."

When he said this, he called out, "He who has ears to hear, let him hear."

9His disciples asked him what this parable meant. 10He said, "The knowledge of the secrets of the kingdom of God has been given to you, but to others I speak in parables, so that,

a41 A denarius was a coin worth about a day's wages.

"'though seeing, they may not see;
        though hearing, they may not
        understand.'[a]

¹¹"This is the meaning of the parable: The seed is the word of God. ¹²Those along the path are the ones who hear, and then the devil comes and takes away the word from their hearts, so that they may not believe and be saved. ¹³Those on the rock are the ones who receive the word with joy when they hear it, but they have no root. They believe for a while, but in the time of testing they fall away. ¹⁴The seed that fell among thorns stands for those who hear, but as they go on their way they are choked by life's worries, riches and pleasures, and they do not mature. ¹⁵But the seed on good soil stands for those with a noble and good heart, who hear the word, retain it, and by persevering produce a crop.

A Lamp on a Stand

¹⁶"No one lights a lamp and hides it in a jar or puts it under a bed. Instead, he puts it on a stand, so that those who come in can see the light. ¹⁷For there is nothing hidden that will not be disclosed, and nothing concealed that will not be known or brought out into the open. ¹⁸Therefore consider carefully how you listen. Whoever has will be given more; whoever does not have, even what he thinks he has will be taken from him."

Jesus' Mother and Brothers

¹⁹Now Jesus' mother and brothers came to see him, but they were not able to get near him because of the crowd. ²⁰Someone told him, "Your mother and brothers are standing outside, wanting to see you."

²¹He replied, "My mother and brothers are those who hear God's word and put it into practice."

Jesus Calms the Storm

²²One day Jesus said to his disciples, "Let's go over to the other side of the lake." So they got into a boat and set out. ²³As they sailed, he fell asleep. A squall came down on the lake, so that the boat was being swamped, and they were in great danger.

²⁴The disciples went and woke him, saying, "Master, Master, we're going to drown!"

He got up and rebuked the wind and the raging waters; the storm subsided, and all was calm. ²⁵"Where is your faith?" he asked his disciples.

In fear and amazement they asked one another, "Who is this? He commands even the winds and the water, and they obey him."

The Healing of a Demon-possessed Man

²⁶They sailed to the region of the Gerasenes,[b] which is across the lake from Galilee. ²⁷When Jesus stepped ashore, he was met by a demon-possessed man from the town. For a long time this man had not worn clothes or lived in a house, but had lived in the tombs. ²⁸When he saw Jesus, he cried out and fell at his feet, shouting at the top of his voice, "What do you want with me, Jesus, Son of the Most High God? I beg you, don't torture me!" ²⁹For Jesus had commanded the evil[c] spirit to come out of the man. Many times it had seized him, and though he was chained hand and foot and kept under guard, he had broken his chains and had been driven by the demon into solitary places.

³⁰Jesus asked him, "What is your name?"

"Legion," he replied, because many demons had gone into him. ³¹And they begged him repeatedly not to order them to go into the Abyss.

³²A large herd of pigs was feeding there on the hillside. The demons begged Jesus to let them go into them, and he gave them permission. ³³When the demons came out of the man, they went into the pigs, and the herd rushed down the steep bank into the lake and was drowned.

³⁴When those tending the pigs saw what had happened, they ran off and reported this in the town and countryside, ³⁵and the people went out to see what had happened. When they came to Jesus, they found the man from whom the demons had gone out, sitting at Jesus' feet, dressed and in his right mind; and they were afraid. ³⁶Those who had seen it told the people how the demon-possessed man had been cured. ³⁷Then all the people of the region of the

---

[a]10 Isaiah 6:9   [b]26 Some manuscripts *Gadarenes*; other manuscripts *Gergesenes*; also in verse 37   [c]29 Greek *unclean*

Travels With the Messiah

Luke 8:25

"Where is your faith?"
[Jesus] asked his
disciples. In fear and
amazement they asked
one another, "Who is
this? He commands even
the winds and the water,
and they obey him."

reflection

1 As you've traveled with
Jesus, what has most
intrigued you about him?

2 Which of Jesus' mira-
cles would you most
like to have observed and
why?

3 What life experiences
have helped you to
trust Jesus more and fear
the world around you
less?

RELATED READINGS

Matthew 16:13–17;
John 2:1–11

Read: Luke 8:22–39

AS THE DISCIPLES TRAVELED with Jesus, there were a few
surprises along the way. First Jesus had turned water into wine at
a wedding. That was an "inside" secret because the guests never
knew what had happened. But the disciples knew that Jesus'
mother had urged him to do it. Then he started healing people.
Those healings were startling, clearly miraculous. This man who'd
called them to be his disciples didn't just heal people hidden away
for years in back bedrooms, unknown even to their neighbors. He
healed beggars known to the whole town, relatives of prominent
officials, men and women with obvious, disfiguring handicaps.

Still, the disciples needed to see a miracle that hit them closer
to home; they had to get to the point of really *personal* need
before they could understand the Master's true identity. It took a
storm at sea, and the disciples' own terror and helplessness, before
they really sat up and took notice that Jesus was not just a good
man but—could it be?—God *become* man. When their friend and
master stilled the angry sea with a single word, they were amazed
. . . and afraid. Suddenly, it wasn't the waves that were so intimidating, but the man in the boat with them who commanded the
waves.

As they continued their travels with Jesus, they would need
to know that he was more than a man . . . that he was the Christ.
They would need this awareness as they stepped ashore after their
traumatic boat trip. They would need to remember again and again
that the teacher who was so precious to them could command
the wind and waves. Because when they reached the shore, there
were no banners saying "Welcome, Jesus and Friends." No, their
welcoming committee was a screaming, naked man who lived
among the tombs. The demons within this poor man knew who
Jesus was and feared him. Perhaps now, after experiencing his
power to save them and calm the elements, the disciples feared
the demons less because they had grown to trust Jesus more
personally than ever before.

Go to page 1255 for your next devotional reading.

Gerasenes asked Jesus to leave them, because they were overcome with fear. So he got into the boat and left.

38The man from whom the demons had gone out begged to go with him, but Jesus sent him away, saying, 39"Return home and tell how much God has done for you." So the man went away and told all over town how much Jesus had done for him.

A Dead Girl and a Sick Woman

40Now when Jesus returned, a crowd welcomed him, for they were all expecting him. 41Then a man named Jairus, a ruler of the synagogue, came and fell at Jesus' feet, pleading with him to come to his house 42because his only daughter, a girl of about twelve, was dying.

As Jesus was on his way, the crowds almost crushed him. 43And a woman was there who had been subject to bleeding for twelve years,*a* but no one could heal her. 44She came up behind him and touched the edge of his cloak, and immediately her bleeding stopped.

45"Who touched me?" Jesus asked.

When they all denied it, Peter said, "Master, the people are crowding and pressing against you."

46But Jesus said, "Someone touched me; I know that power has gone out from me."

47Then the woman, seeing that she could not go unnoticed, came trembling and fell at his feet. In the presence of all the people, she told why she had touched him and how she had been instantly healed. 48Then he said to her, "Daughter, your faith has healed you. Go in peace."

49While Jesus was still speaking, someone came from the house of Jairus, the synagogue ruler. "Your daughter is dead," he said. "Don't bother the teacher any more."

50Hearing this, Jesus said to Jairus, "Don't be afraid; just believe, and she will be healed."

51When he arrived at the house of Jairus, he did not let anyone go in with him except Peter, John and James, and the child's father and mother. 52Meanwhile, all the people were wailing and mourning for her. "Stop wailing," Jesus said. "She is not dead but asleep."

53They laughed at him, knowing that she

was dead. 54But he took her by the hand and said, "My child, get up!" 55Her spirit returned, and at once she stood up. Then Jesus told them to give her something to eat. 56Her parents were astonished, but he ordered them not to tell anyone what had happened.

Jesus Sends Out the Twelve

9 When Jesus had called the Twelve together, he gave them power and authority to drive out all demons and to cure diseases, 2and he sent them out to preach the kingdom of God and to heal the sick. 3He told them: "Take nothing for the journey—no staff, no bag, no bread, no money, no extra tunic. 4Whatever house you enter, stay there until you leave that town. 5If people do not welcome you, shake the dust off your feet when you leave their town, as a testimony against them." 6So they set out and went from village to village, preaching the gospel and healing people everywhere.

7Now Herod the tetrarch heard about all that was going on. And he was perplexed, because some were saying that John had been raised from the dead, 8others that Elijah had appeared, and still others that one of the prophets of long ago had come back to life. 9But Herod said, "I beheaded John. Who, then, is this I hear such things about?" And he tried to see him.

Jesus Feeds the Five Thousand

10When the apostles returned, they reported to Jesus what they had done. Then he took them with him and they withdrew by themselves to a town called Bethsaida, 11but the crowds learned about it and followed him. He welcomed them and spoke to them about the kingdom of God, and healed those who needed healing.

12Late in the afternoon the Twelve came to him and said, "Send the crowd away so they can go to the surrounding villages and countryside and find food and lodging, because we are in a remote place here."

13He replied, "You give them something to eat."

They answered, "We have only five loaves of bread and two fish—unless we go and buy food for all this crowd." 14(About five thousand men were there.)

a43 Many manuscripts years, and she had spent all she had on doctors

But he said to his disciples, "Have them sit down in groups of about fifty each." 15 The disciples did so, and everybody sat down. 16 Taking the five loaves and the two fish and looking up to heaven, he gave thanks and broke them. Then he gave them to the disciples to set before the people. 17 They all ate and were satisfied, and the disciples picked up twelve basketfuls of broken pieces that were left over.

Peter's Confession of Christ

18 Once when Jesus was praying in private and his disciples were with him, he asked them, "Who do the crowds say I am?"

19 They replied, "Some say John the Baptist; others say Elijah; and still others, that one of the prophets of long ago has come back to life."

20 "But what about you?" he asked. "Who do you say I am?"

Peter answered, "The Christ[a] of God."

21 Jesus strictly warned them not to tell this to anyone. 22 And he said, "The Son of Man must suffer many things and be rejected by the elders, chief priests and teachers of the law, and he must be killed and on the third day be raised to life."

23 Then he said to them all: "If anyone would come after me, he must deny himself and take up his cross daily and follow me. 24 For whoever wants to save his life will lose it, but whoever loses his life for me will save it. 25 What good is it for a man to gain the whole world, and yet lose or forfeit his very self? 26 If anyone is ashamed of me and my words, the Son of Man will be ashamed of him when he comes in his glory and in the glory of the Father and of the holy angels. 27 I tell you the truth, some who are standing here will not taste death before they see the kingdom of God."

The Transfiguration

28 About eight days after Jesus said this, he took Peter, John and James with him and went up onto a mountain to pray. 29 As he was praying, the appearance of his face changed, and his clothes became as bright as a flash of lightning. 30 Two men, Moses and Elijah, 31 appeared in glorious splendor, talking with Jesus. They spoke about his departure, which he was about to bring to fulfillment at Jerusalem. 32 Pe-

ter and his companions were very sleepy, but when they became fully awake, they saw his glory and the two men standing with him. 33 As the men were leaving Jesus, Peter said to him, "Master, it is good for us to be here. Let us put up three shelters—one for you, one for Moses and one for Elijah." (He did not know what he was saying.)

34 While he was speaking, a cloud appeared and enveloped them, and they were afraid as they entered the cloud. 35 A voice came from the cloud, saying, "This is my Son, whom I have chosen; listen to him." 36 When the voice had spoken, they found that Jesus was alone. The disciples kept this to themselves, and told no one at that time what they had seen.

The Healing of a Boy With an Evil Spirit

37 The next day, when they came down from the mountain, a large crowd met him. 38 A man in the crowd called out, "Teacher, I beg you to look at my son, for he is my only child. 39 A spirit seizes him and he suddenly screams; it throws him into convulsions so that he foams at the mouth. It scarcely ever leaves him and is destroying him. 40 I begged your disciples to drive it out, but they could not."

41 "O unbelieving and perverse generation," Jesus replied, "how long shall I stay with you and put up with you? Bring your son here."

42 Even while the boy was coming, the demon threw him to the ground in a convulsion. But Jesus rebuked the evil[b] spirit, healed the boy and gave him back to his father. 43 And they were all amazed at the greatness of God.

While everyone was marveling at all that Jesus did, he said to his disciples, 44 "Listen carefully to what I am about to tell you: The Son of Man is going to be betrayed into the hands of men." 45 But they did not understand what this meant. It was hidden from them, so that they did not grasp it, and they were afraid to ask him about it.

Who Will Be the Greatest?

46 An argument started among the disciples as to which of them would be the greatest. 47 Jesus, knowing their thoughts, took a little child and had him stand beside him. 48 Then he said to them, "Whoever welcomes this little child

a 20 Or Messiah   b 42 Greek unclean

in my name welcomes me; and whoever welcomes me welcomes the one who sent me. For he who is least among you all—he is the greatest."

⁴⁹"Master," said John, "we saw a man driving out demons in your name and we tried to stop him, because he is not one of us."

⁵⁰"Do not stop him," Jesus said, "for whoever is not against you is for you."

Samaritan Opposition

⁵¹As the time approached for him to be taken up to heaven, Jesus resolutely set out for Jerusalem. ⁵²And he sent messengers on ahead, who went into a Samaritan village to get things ready for him; ⁵³but the people there did not welcome him, because he was heading for Jerusalem. ⁵⁴When the disciples James and John saw this, they asked, "Lord, do you want us to call fire down from heaven to destroy them[a]?" ⁵⁵But Jesus turned and rebuked them, ⁵⁶and[b] they went to another village.

The Cost of Following Jesus

⁵⁷As they were walking along the road, a man said to him, "I will follow you wherever you go."

⁵⁸Jesus replied, "Foxes have holes and birds of the air have nests, but the Son of Man has no place to lay his head."

⁵⁹He said to another man, "Follow me."

But the man replied, "Lord, first let me go and bury my father."

⁶⁰Jesus said to him, "Let the dead bury their own dead, but you go and proclaim the kingdom of God."

⁶¹Still another said, "I will follow you, Lord; but first let me go back and say good-by to my family."

⁶²Jesus replied, "No one who puts his hand to the plow and looks back is fit for service in the kingdom of God."

Jesus Sends Out the Seventy-two

10 After this the Lord appointed seventy-two[c] others and sent them two by two ahead of him to every town and place where he was about to go. ²He told them, "The harvest is plentiful, but the workers are few. Ask the Lord of the harvest, therefore, to send out workers into his harvest field. ³Go! I am sending you out like lambs among wolves. ⁴Do not take a purse or bag or sandals; and do not greet anyone on the road.

⁵"When you enter a house, first say, 'Peace to this house.' ⁶If a man of peace is there, your peace will rest on him; if not, it will return to you. ⁷Stay in that house, eating and drinking whatever they give you, for the worker deserves his wages. Do not move around from house to house.

⁸"When you enter a town and are welcomed, eat what is set before you. ⁹Heal the sick who are there and tell them, 'The kingdom of God is near you.' ¹⁰But when you enter a town and are not welcomed, go into its streets and say, ¹¹'Even the dust of your town that sticks to our feet we wipe off against you. Yet be sure of this: The kingdom of God is near.' ¹²I tell you, it will be more bearable on that day for Sodom than for that town.

¹³"Woe to you, Korazin! Woe to you, Bethsaida! For if the miracles that were performed in you had been performed in Tyre and Sidon, they would have repented long ago, sitting in sackcloth and ashes. ¹⁴But it will be more bearable for Tyre and Sidon at the judgment than for you. ¹⁵And you, Capernaum, will you be lifted up to the skies? No, you will go down to the depths.[d]

¹⁶"He who listens to you listens to me; he who rejects you rejects me; but he who rejects me rejects him who sent me."

¹⁷The seventy-two returned with joy and said, "Lord, even the demons submit to us in your name."

¹⁸He replied, "I saw Satan fall like lightning from heaven. ¹⁹I have given you authority to trample on snakes and scorpions and to overcome all the power of the enemy; nothing will harm you. ²⁰However, do not rejoice that the spirits submit to you, but rejoice that your names are written in heaven."

²¹At that time Jesus, full of joy through the Holy Spirit, said, "I praise you, Father, Lord of heaven and earth, because you have hidden these things from the wise and learned, and

---

[a]54 Some manuscripts *them, even as Elijah did* [b]55,56 Some manuscripts *them. And he said, "You do not know what kind of spirit you are of, for the Son of Man did not come to destroy men's lives, but to save them."* ⁵⁶And [c]1 Some manuscripts *seventy*; also in verse 17 [d]15 Greek *Hades*

revealed them to little children. Yes, Father, for this was your good pleasure.

²²"All things have been committed to me by my Father. No one knows who the Son is except the Father, and no one knows who the Father is except the Son and those to whom the Son chooses to reveal him."

²³Then he turned to his disciples and said privately, "Blessed are the eyes that see what you see. ²⁴For I tell you that many prophets and kings wanted to see what you see but did not see it, and to hear what you hear but did not hear it."

The Parable of the Good Samaritan

²⁵On one occasion an expert in the law stood up to test Jesus. "Teacher," he asked, "what must I do to inherit eternal life?"

²⁶"What is written in the Law?" he replied. "How do you read it?"

²⁷He answered: " 'Love the Lord your God with all your heart and with all your soul and with all your strength and with all your mind'ᵃ; and, 'Love your neighbor as yourself.'ᵇ"

²⁸"You have answered correctly," Jesus replied. "Do this and you will live."

²⁹But he wanted to justify himself, so he asked Jesus, "And who is my neighbor?"

³⁰In reply Jesus said: "A man was going down from Jerusalem to Jericho, when he fell into the hands of robbers. They stripped him of his clothes, beat him and went away, leaving him half dead. ³¹A priest happened to be going down the same road, and when he saw the man, he passed by on the other side. ³²So too, a Levite, when he came to the place and saw him, passed by on the other side. ³³But a Samaritan, as he traveled, came where the man was; and when he saw him, he took pity on him. ³⁴He went to him and bandaged his wounds, pouring on oil and wine. Then he put the man on his own donkey, took him to an inn and took care of him. ³⁵The next day he took out two silver coinsᶜ and gave them to the innkeeper. 'Look after him,' he said, 'and when I return, I will reimburse you for any extra expense you may have.'

³⁶"Which of these three do you think was a neighbor to the man who fell into the hands of robbers?"

³⁷The expert in the law replied, "The one who had mercy on him."

Jesus told him, "Go and do likewise."

At the Home of Martha and Mary

³⁸As Jesus and his disciples were on their way, he came to a village where a woman named Martha opened her home to him. ³⁹She had a sister called Mary, who sat at the Lord's feet listening to what he said. ⁴⁰But Martha was distracted by all the preparations that had to be made. She came to him and asked, "Lord, don't you care that my sister has left me to do the work by myself? Tell her to help me!"

⁴¹"Martha, Martha," the Lord answered, "you are worried and upset about many things, ⁴²but only one thing is needed.ᵈ Mary has chosen what is better, and it will not be taken away from her."

Jesus' Teaching on Prayer

11 One day Jesus was praying in a certain place. When he finished, one of his disciples said to him, "Lord, teach us to pray, just as John taught his disciples."

²He said to them, "When you pray, say:

" 'Father,ᵉ
hallowed be your name,
your kingdom come.ᶠ
³Give us each day our daily bread.
⁴Forgive us our sins,
for we also forgive everyone who sins
against us.ᵍ
And lead us not into temptation.ʰ' "

⁵Then he said to them, "Suppose one of you has a friend, and he goes to him at midnight and says, 'Friend, lend me three loaves of bread, ⁶because a friend of mine on a journey has come to me, and I have nothing to set before him.'

⁷"Then the one inside answers, 'Don't bother me. The door is already locked, and my children are with me in bed. I can't get up and give you anything.' ⁸I tell you, though he will not get up and give him the bread because he

---

ᵃ27 Deut. 6:5 ᵇ27 Lev. 19:18 ᶜ35 Greek *two denarii* ᵈ42 Some manuscripts *but few things are needed—or only one* ᵉ2 Some manuscripts *Our Father in heaven* ᶠ2 Some manuscripts *come. May your will be done on earth as it is in heaven.* ᵍ4 Greek *everyone who is indebted to us* ʰ4 Some manuscripts *temptation but deliver us from the evil one*

Too Busy

Read: Luke 10:38-42

WE FACE THE SAME CHOICE that confronted Martha. We can dismiss the implications of Jesus' words for us, especially when our time is limited and we are juggling so many other demands. Or we can face our need and begin working to know God better. Whatever we decide, we must not forget who puts this challenge before us and the depth of his concern. The real choice is not whether we will become thinkers or doers. We are called to be both. But we will be better at both if we heed Christ's call to dig deeply into the heart of God. This never means stepping out of life to devote ourselves to something abstract and useless; rather it means to plunge into the very essence of life. We were made for this, and it is only as we grow in our understanding of God that we will satisfy the deepest longings of our hearts and find the meaning we ache for.

But even more, we need to know him. Mary and Martha learned the hard way, and we do too. If my own struggles have taught me anything, it is that my greatest need is to know God better, and I am not alone. To be blunt, life is simply too demanding and overwhelming at times to think I can manage without knowing the one who rules the winds and waves that batter my little vessel. We ask too much of ourselves to try to trust a stranger. Neglecting our need to know him better is, as Dr. Packer so wisely warns, "to sentence ourselves to stumble and blunder through life, blindfolded, as it were, with no sense of direction and no understanding of what surrounds you." We hurt ourselves if we shrug our shoulders and walk away.

It is time we started. There is much to do and more to learn. Not even a lifetime will be enough to know God completely. But our smallest efforts will be richly rewarded, for "the time it takes to dig deep into the heart of God is often repaid by striking a vein of gold or an oil gusher. The effort is repaid with joy and power beyond all expectation."
—Carolyn Custis James

reflection

1 Do you consider yourself to be more like Mary or Martha?

2 How did this devotional help you to realize that you can be both a thinker and a doer?

3 What can you set aside right now in order to still your mind and hands long enough to listen for God's voice? Deliberately sit still for a few minutes and ask him to reveal himself to you in a new way.

RELATED READINGS

Psalm 46:10–11;
Matthew 6:25–34;
11:28–30;
Philippians 4:6–7

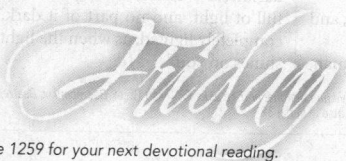

Go to page 1259 for your next devotional reading.

is his friend, yet because of the man's boldness[a] he will get up and give him as much as he needs.

9 "So I say to you: Ask and it will be given to you; seek and you will find; knock and the door will be opened to you. 10 For everyone who asks receives; he who seeks finds; and to him who knocks, the door will be opened.

11 "Which of you fathers, if your son asks for[b] a fish, will give him a snake instead? 12 Or if he asks for an egg, will give him a scorpion? 13 If you then, though you are evil, know how to give good gifts to your children, how much more will your Father in heaven give the Holy Spirit to those who ask him!"

Jesus and Beelzebub

14 Jesus was driving out a demon that was mute. When the demon left, the man who had been mute spoke, and the crowd was amazed. 15 But some of them said, "By Beelzebub,[c] the prince of demons, he is driving out demons." 16 Others tested him by asking for a sign from heaven.

17 Jesus knew their thoughts and said to them: "Any kingdom divided against itself will be ruined, and a house divided against itself will fall. 18 If Satan is divided against himself, how can his kingdom stand? I say this because you claim that I drive out demons by Beelzebub. 19 Now if I drive out demons by Beelzebub, by whom do your followers drive them out? So then, they will be your judges. 20 But if I drive out demons by the finger of God, then the kingdom of God has come to you.

21 "When a strong man, fully armed, guards his own house, his possessions are safe. 22 But when someone stronger attacks and overpowers him, he takes away the armor in which the man trusted and divides up the spoils.

23 "He who is not with me is against me, and he who does not gather with me, scatters.

24 "When an evil[d] spirit comes out of a man, it goes through arid places seeking rest and does not find it. Then it says, 'I will return to the house I left.' 25 When it arrives, it finds the house swept clean and put in order. 26 Then it goes and takes seven other spirits more wicked than itself, and they go in and live there. And the final condition of that man is worse than the first."

27 As Jesus was saying these things, a woman in the crowd called out, "Blessed is the mother who gave you birth and nursed you."

28 He replied, "Blessed rather are those who hear the word of God and obey it."

The Sign of Jonah

29 As the crowds increased, Jesus said, "This is a wicked generation. It asks for a miraculous sign, but none will be given it except the sign of Jonah. 30 For as Jonah was a sign to the Ninevites, so also will the Son of Man be to this generation. 31 The Queen of the South will rise at the judgment with the men of this generation and condemn them; for she came from the ends of the earth to listen to Solomon's wisdom, and now one[e] greater than Solomon is here. 32 The men of Nineveh will stand up at the judgment with this generation and condemn it; for they repented at the preaching of Jonah, and now one greater than Jonah is here.

The Lamp of the Body

33 "No one lights a lamp and puts it in a place where it will be hidden, or under a bowl. Instead he puts it on its stand, so that those who come in may see the light. 34 Your eye is the lamp of your body. When your eyes are good, your whole body also is full of light. But when they are bad, your body also is full of darkness. 35 See to it, then, that the light within you is not darkness. 36 Therefore, if your whole body is full of light, and no part of it dark, it will be completely lighted, as when the light of a lamp shines on you."

> **Luke 11:13**
>
> *God Gives His Spirit*
>
> "If you then, though you are evil, know how to give good gifts to your children, how much more will your Father in heaven give the Holy Spirit to those who ask him!"

---

a8 Or persistence   b11 Some manuscripts for bread, will give him a stone; or if he asks for   c15 Greek Beezeboul or Beelzeboul; also in verses 18 and 19   d24 Greek unclean   e31 Or something; also in verse 32

Six Woes

37When Jesus had finished speaking, a Pharisee invited him to eat with him; so he went in and reclined at the table. **38**But the Pharisee, noticing that Jesus did not first wash before the meal, was surprised.

39Then the Lord said to him, "Now then, you Pharisees clean the outside of the cup and dish, but inside you are full of greed and wickedness. **40**You foolish people! Did not the one who made the outside make the inside also? **41**But give what is inside the dish,*a* to the poor, and everything will be clean for you.

42"Woe to you Pharisees, because you give God a tenth of your mint, rue and all other kinds of garden herbs, but you neglect justice and the love of God. You should have practiced the latter without leaving the former undone.

43"Woe to you Pharisees, because you love the most important seats in the synagogues and greetings in the marketplaces.

44"Woe to you, because you are like unmarked graves, which men walk over without knowing it."

45One of the experts in the law answered him, "Teacher, when you say these things, you insult us also."

46Jesus replied, "And you experts in the law, woe to you, because you load people down with burdens they can hardly carry, and you yourselves will not lift one finger to help them.

47"Woe to you, because you build tombs for the prophets, and it was your forefathers who killed them. **48**So you testify that you approve of what your forefathers did; they killed the prophets, and you build their tombs. **49**Because of this, God in his wisdom said, 'I will send them prophets and apostles, some of whom they will kill and others they will persecute.' **50**Therefore this generation will be held responsible for the blood of all the prophets that has been shed since the beginning of the world, **51**from the blood of Abel to the blood of Zechariah, who was killed between the altar and the sanctuary. Yes, I tell you, this generation will be held responsible for it all.

52"Woe to you experts in the law, because you have taken away the key to knowledge. You yourselves have not entered, and you have hindered those who were entering."

53When Jesus left there, the Pharisees and the teachers of the law began to oppose him fiercely and to besiege him with questions, **54**waiting to catch him in something he might say.

Warnings and Encouragements

12 Meanwhile, when a crowd of many thousands had gathered, so that they were trampling on one another, Jesus began to speak first to his disciples, saying: "Be on your guard against the yeast of the Pharisees, which is hypocrisy. **2**There is nothing concealed that will not be disclosed, or hidden that will not be made known. **3**What you have said in the dark will be heard in the daylight, and what you have whispered in the ear in the inner rooms will be proclaimed from the roofs.

4"I tell you, my friends, do not be afraid of those who kill the body and after that can do no more. **5**But I will show you whom you should fear: Fear him who, after the killing of the body, has power to throw you into hell. Yes, I tell you, fear him. **6**Are not five sparrows sold for two pennies*b*? Yet not one of them is forgotten by God. **7**Indeed, the very hairs of your head are all numbered. Don't be afraid; you are worth more than many sparrows.

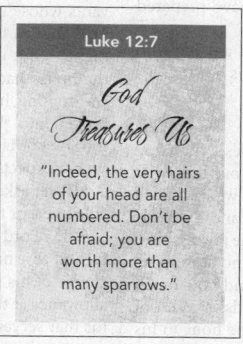

Luke 12:7

God Treasures Us

"Indeed, the very hairs of your head are all numbered. Don't be afraid; you are worth more than many sparrows."

8"I tell you, whoever acknowledges me before men, the Son of Man will also acknowledge him before the angels of God. **9**But he who disowns me before men will be disowned before the angels of God. **10**And everyone who speaks a word against the Son of Man will be forgiven, but anyone who blasphemes against the Holy Spirit will not be forgiven.

a41 Or what you have b6 Greek two assaria

11"When you are brought before synagogues, rulers and authorities, do not worry about how you will defend yourselves or what you will say, 12for the Holy Spirit will teach you at that time what you should say."

The Parable of the Rich Fool

13Someone in the crowd said to him, "Teacher, tell my brother to divide the inheritance with me."

14Jesus replied, "Man, who appointed me a judge or an arbiter between you?" 15Then he said to them, "Watch out! Be on your guard against all kinds of greed; a man's life does not consist in the abundance of his possessions."

16And he told them this parable: "The ground of a certain rich man produced a good crop. 17He thought to himself, 'What shall I do? I have no place to store my crops.'

18"Then he said, 'This is what I'll do. I will tear down my barns and build bigger ones, and there I will store all my grain and my goods. 19And I'll say to myself, "You have plenty of good things laid up for many years. Take life easy; eat, drink and be merry."'

20"But God said to him, 'You fool! This very night your life will be demanded from you. Then who will get what you have prepared for yourself?'

21"This is how it will be with anyone who stores up things for himself but is not rich toward God."

Do Not Worry

22Then Jesus said to his disciples: "Therefore I tell you, do not worry about your life, what you will eat; or about your body, what you will wear. 23Life is more than food, and the body more than clothes. 24Consider the ravens: They do not sow or reap, they have no storeroom or barn; yet God feeds them. And how much more valuable you are than birds! 25Who of you by worrying can add a single hour to his life*a*? 26Since you cannot do this very little thing, why do you worry about the rest?

27"Consider how the lilies grow. They do not labor or spin. Yet I tell you, not even Solomon in all his splendor was dressed like one of these. 28If that is how God clothes the grass of the field, which is here today, and tomorrow is thrown into the fire, how much more will he clothe you, O you of little faith! 29And do not set your heart on what you will eat or drink; do not worry about it. 30For the pagan world runs after all such things, and your Father knows that you need them. 31But seek his kingdom, and these things will be given to you as well.

32"Do not be afraid, little flock, for your Father has been pleased to give you the kingdom. 33Sell your possessions and give to the poor. Provide purses for yourselves that will not wear out, a treasure in heaven that will not be exhausted, where no thief comes near and no moth destroys. 34For where your treasure is, there your heart will be also.

Watchfulness

35"Be dressed ready for service and keep your lamps burning, 36like men waiting for their master to return from a wedding banquet, so that when he comes and knocks they can immediately open the door for him. 37It will be good for those servants whose master finds them watching when he comes. I tell you the truth, he will dress himself to serve, will have them recline at the table and will come and wait on them. 38It will be good for those servants whose master finds them ready, even if he comes in the second or third watch of the night. 39But understand this: If the owner of the house had known at what hour the thief was coming, he would not have let his house be broken into. 40You also must be ready, because the Son of Man will come at an hour when you do not expect him."

41Peter asked, "Lord, are you telling this parable to us, or to everyone?"

42The Lord answered, "Who then is the faithful and wise manager, whom the master puts in charge of his servants to give them their food allowance at the proper time? 43It will be good for that servant whom the master finds doing so when he returns. 44I tell you the truth, he will put him in charge of all his possessions. 45But suppose the servant says to himself, 'My master is taking a long time in coming,' and he then begins to beat the menservants and maidservants and to eat and drink and get drunk. 46The master of that servant will come on a day

*a*25 Or *single cubit to his height*

Scandalous Reckoning

MARY OF BETHANY

DAYS BEFORE CHRIST'S CRUCIFIXION, only one person seemed to understand the gravity of the situation: Jesus was going to die. Although he had said many times that he must come to Jerusalem to die, the disciples could not seem to grasp it. Mary of Bethany, at least in part, somehow understood.

That's why she chose to do something that shocked and confounded the men who followed Jesus. They didn't get it. But that didn't matter to Mary. She knew what she had to do.

The disciples were in denial. Their focus remained steadfastly in the present. They couldn't see that what she was doing was admirable. Instead, they worried about the cost of the perfume (it was worth a large sum of money); the customs of the day (it was traditional practice to give to the poor on the evening of the Passover); and their own opinions (without waiting for direction from Jesus, to whom the action was directed, they started to rebuke her).

Mary remained squarely transfixed on the horizon of events, though even she did not anticipate all that would transpire.

She could not have fully comprehended the significance; it was still the mystery of God. But the events taking place were not entirely lost on her, as they apparently were on the others. Intuitively, she sensed that what lay before her Lord was unimaginable pain, suffering and death. And she came to terms with it. Her ceremonial preparation for his burial confirmed her understanding.

As she carefully poured the nard on his head, the perfume traced the familiar features of his face: a brow she'd seen furrowed with concern; cheeks she'd seen wet with tears at the death of her brother; lips that had spoken truth to her. Her extravagance confounded the witnesses, but her comprehension of Christ's destiny touched the very heart of God.

"I tell you the truth, wherever this gospel is preached throughout the world, what she has done will also be told, in memory of her."

Matthew 26:13

ASSIGNED READING:

Matthew 26:6–13;
Luke 10:38–42;
John 11:17—12:11

—Prayer—

Dear God, I give everything I have to you, for you have made me rich with your love.

Weekend

Go to page 1261 for your next devotional reading.

when he does not expect him and at an hour he is not aware of. He will cut him to pieces and assign him a place with the unbelievers.

47 "That servant who knows his master's will and does not get ready or does not do what his master wants will be beaten with many blows. 48 But the one who does not know and does things deserving punishment will be beaten with few blows. From everyone who has been given much, much will be demanded; and from the one who has been entrusted with much, much more will be asked.

Not Peace but Division

49 "I have come to bring fire on the earth, and how I wish it were already kindled! 50 But I have a baptism to undergo, and how distressed I am until it is completed! 51 Do you think I came to bring peace on earth? No, I tell you, but division. 52 From now on there will be five in one family divided against each other, three against two and two against three. 53 They will be divided, father against son and son against father, mother against daughter and daughter against mother, mother-in-law against daughter-in-law and daughter-in-law against mother-in-law."

Interpreting the Times

54 He said to the crowd: "When you see a cloud rising in the west, immediately you say, 'It's going to rain,' and it does. 55 And when the south wind blows, you say, 'It's going to be hot,' and it is. 56 Hypocrites! You know how to interpret the appearance of the earth and the sky. How is it that you don't know how to interpret this present time?

57 "Why don't you judge for yourselves what is right? 58 As you are going with your adversary to the magistrate, try hard to be reconciled to him on the way, or he may drag you off to the judge, and the judge turn you over to the officer, and the officer throw you into prison. 59 I tell you, you will not get out until you have paid the last penny.a"

Repent or Perish

13 Now there were some present at that time who told Jesus about the Galileans whose blood Pilate had mixed with their sacrifices. 2 Jesus answered, "Do you think that these Galileans were worse sinners than all the other Galileans because they suffered this way? 3 I tell you, no! But unless you repent, you too will all perish. 4 Or those eighteen who died when the tower in Siloam fell on them—do you think they were more guilty than all the others living in Jerusalem? 5 I tell you, no! But unless you repent, you too will all perish."

6 Then he told this parable: "A man had a fig tree, planted in his vineyard, and he went to look for fruit on it, but did not find any. 7 So he said to the man who took care of the vineyard, 'For three years now I've been coming to look for fruit on this fig tree and haven't found any. Cut it down! Why should it use up the soil?'

8 " 'Sir,' the man replied, 'leave it alone for one more year, and I'll dig around it and fertilize it. 9 If it bears fruit next year, fine! If not, then cut it down.' "

A Crippled Woman Healed on the Sabbath

10 On a Sabbath Jesus was teaching in one of the synagogues, 11 and a woman was there who had been crippled by a spirit for eighteen years. She was bent over and could not straighten up at all. 12 When Jesus saw her, he called her forward and said to her, "Woman, you are set free from your infirmity." 13 Then he put his hands on her, and immediately she straightened up and praised God.

14 Indignant because Jesus had healed on the Sabbath, the synagogue ruler said to the people, "There are six days for work. So come and be healed on those days, not on the Sabbath."

15 The Lord answered him, "You hypocrites! Doesn't each of you on the Sabbath untie his ox or donkey from the stall and lead it out to give it water? 16 Then should not this woman, a daughter of Abraham, whom Satan has kept bound for eighteen long years, be set free on the Sabbath day from what bound her?"

17 When he said this, all his opponents were humiliated, but the people were delighted with all the wonderful things he was doing.

The Parables of the Mustard Seed and the Yeast

18 Then Jesus asked, "What is the kingdom of God like? What shall I compare it to? 19 It is like a mustard seed, which a man took and planted

a 59 Greek lepton

When Jesus Sees

Read: Luke 13:10–21

FROM AN EARLY AGE, we're taught to look away from those who are different. "Don't stare," we're told. "It's rude!" Often people with disabilities make us uncomfortable, so we learn to pretend we don't notice that someone has a deformity or scars or walks with a limp or moves around in a chair. Unfortunately, we sometimes take it one step further and pretend we don't see the person at all.

The woman in the synagogue had spent 18 years being overlooked. She was bent over like a question mark, staring at the ground and her own two feet. She couldn't see the faces behind the words, but she knew the tones, the jokes and the whispers. She could hear people hurrying past and skirting around her. And while plenty of people looked at her, many probably looked the other way. Only one truly saw her.

When Jesus saw her, he didn't turn away. He didn't pretend not to see her. Instead, he spoke to her and touched her. She was set free from her infirmity. Her 18 years of living with a crooked body dropped away, and she stood straight and tall, seeing Jesus face-to-face.

In that compassionate interaction, Jesus had an encounter with someone the world tends to overlook. He showed us that, first of all, we need to *see* others—to look at them and acknowledge their presence as God's creation, precious in his sight. When we look into their eyes, we'll see a human being and not a deformity, disability or limitation.

Second, we need to speak to that person as we would anyone. Conversing normally shows that we're not intimidated by the person's disability. Even if we're just talking about the weather, we are expressing our interest in the other person's words and opinions.

Third, we need to be willing to touch them if it's appropriate. Human touch is a mysterious, powerful tool that communicates worth and significance through something as simple as a handshake, a touch on the shoulder or a hug.

Everyone needs to know that they are valued. When we begin to see others as Jesus does—as human beings with value and significance—we might become the window through which they can see Jesus for themselves.

Go to page 1264 for your next devotional reading.

Luke 13:12

When Jesus saw her, he called her forward and said to her, "Woman, you are set free from your infirmity."

reflection

1 How do you tend to respond to people with disabilities?

2 What does Jesus' example with the woman teach you about relating to others with or without physical disabilities?

3 Whom do you need to see as Jesus sees them?

RELATED READINGS

1 Samuel 16:6–7;
2 Samuel 9:1–13;
2 Corinthians 4:16–18

"*I would rather be in this chair knowing him, than on my feet without him.*"

Joni Eareckson Tada

in his garden. It grew and became a tree, and the birds of the air perched in its branches."

20 Again he asked, "What shall I compare the kingdom of God to? 21 It is like yeast that a woman took and mixed into a large amount[a] of flour until it worked all through the dough."

The Narrow Door

22 Then Jesus went through the towns and villages, teaching as he made his way to Jerusalem. 23 Someone asked him, "Lord, are only a few people going to be saved?"

He said to them, 24 "Make every effort to enter through the narrow door, because many, I tell you, will try to enter and will not be able to. 25 Once the owner of the house gets up and closes the door, you will stand outside knocking and pleading, 'Sir, open the door for us.'

"But he will answer, 'I don't know you or where you come from.'

26 "Then you will say, 'We ate and drank with you, and you taught in our streets.'

27 "But he will reply, 'I don't know you or where you come from. Away from me, all you evildoers!'

28 "There will be weeping there, and gnashing of teeth, when you see Abraham, Isaac and Jacob and all the prophets in the kingdom of God, but you yourselves thrown out. 29 People will come from east and west and north and south, and will take their places at the feast in the kingdom of God. 30 Indeed there are those who are last who will be first, and first who will be last."

Jesus' Sorrow for Jerusalem

31 At that time some Pharisees came to Jesus and said to him, "Leave this place and go somewhere else. Herod wants to kill you."

32 He replied, "Go tell that fox, 'I will drive out demons and heal people today and tomorrow, and on the third day I will reach my goal.' 33 In any case, I must keep going today and tomorrow and the next day—for surely no prophet can die outside Jerusalem!

34 "O Jerusalem, Jerusalem, you who kill the prophets and stone those sent to you, how often I have longed to gather your children together, as a hen gathers her chicks under her wings, but you were not willing! 35 Look, your house is left to you desolate. I tell you, you will not see me again until you say, 'Blessed is he who comes in the name of the Lord.'[b]"

Luke 13:34

God Weeps for His People

"O Jerusalem, Jerusalem, you who kill the prophets and stone those sent to you, how often I have longed to gather your children together, as a hen gathers her chicks under her wings, but you were not willing!"

Jesus at a Pharisee's House

14 One Sabbath, when Jesus went to eat in the house of a prominent Pharisee, he was being carefully watched. 2 There in front of him was a man suffering from dropsy. 3 Jesus asked the Pharisees and experts in the law, "Is it lawful to heal on the Sabbath or not?" 4 But they remained silent. So taking hold of the man, he healed him and sent him away.

5 Then he asked them, "If one of you has a son[c] or an ox that falls into a well on the Sabbath day, will you not immediately pull him out?" 6 And they had nothing to say.

7 When he noticed how the guests picked the places of honor at the table, he told them this parable: 8 "When someone invites you to a wedding feast, do not take the place of honor, for a person more distinguished than you may have been invited. 9 If so, the host who invited both of you will come and say to you, 'Give this man your seat.' Then, humiliated, you will have to take the least important place. 10 But when you are invited, take the lowest place, so that when your host comes, he will say to you, 'Friend, move up to a better place.' Then you will be honored in the presence of all your fellow guests. 11 For everyone who exalts himself will be humbled, and he who humbles himself will be exalted."

12 Then Jesus said to his host, "When you give a luncheon or dinner, do not invite your friends, your brothers or relatives, or your rich

---

a 21 Greek three satas (probably about 1/2 bushel or 22 liters)   b 35 Psalm 118:26   c 5 Some manuscripts donkey neighbors; if you do, they may invite you back and so you will be repaid. ¹³But when you give a banquet, invite the poor, the crippled, the lame, the blind, ¹⁴and you will be blessed. Although they cannot repay you, you will be repaid at the resurrection of the righteous."

The Parable of the Great Banquet

¹⁵When one of those at the table with him heard this, he said to Jesus, "Blessed is the man who will eat at the feast in the kingdom of God."

¹⁶Jesus replied: "A certain man was preparing a great banquet and invited many guests. ¹⁷At the time of the banquet he sent his servant to tell those who had been invited, 'Come, for everything is now ready.'

¹⁸"But they all alike began to make excuses. The first said, 'I have just bought a field, and I must go and see it. Please excuse me.'

¹⁹"Another said, 'I have just bought five yoke of oxen, and I'm on my way to try them out. Please excuse me.'

²⁰"Still another said, 'I just got married, so I can't come.'

²¹"The servant came back and reported this to his master. Then the owner of the house became angry and ordered his servant, 'Go out quickly into the streets and alleys of the town and bring in the poor, the crippled, the blind and the lame.'

²²"'Sir,' the servant said, 'what you ordered has been done, but there is still room.'

²³"Then the master told his servant, 'Go out to the roads and country lanes and make them come in, so that my house will be full. ²⁴I tell you, not one of those men who were invited will get a taste of my banquet.'"

The Cost of Being a Disciple

²⁵Large crowds were traveling with Jesus, and turning to them he said: ²⁶"If anyone comes to me and does not hate his father and mother, his wife and children, his brothers and sisters—yes, even his own life—he cannot be my disciple. ²⁷And anyone who does not carry his cross and follow me cannot be my disciple.

²⁸"Suppose one of you wants to build a tower. Will he not first sit down and estimate the cost to see if he has enough money to complete it? ²⁹For if he lays the foundation and is not able to finish it, everyone who sees it will ridicule him, ³⁰saying, 'This fellow began to build and was not able to finish.'

³¹"Or suppose a king is about to go to war against another king. Will he not first sit down and consider whether he is able with ten thousand men to oppose the one coming against him with twenty thousand? ³²If he is not able, he will send a delegation while the other is still a long way off and will ask for terms of peace. ³³In the same way, any of you who does not give up everything he has cannot be my disciple.

³⁴"Salt is good, but if it loses its saltiness, how can it be made salty again? ³⁵It is fit neither for the soil nor for the manure pile; it is thrown out.

"He who has ears to hear, let him hear."

The Parable of the Lost Sheep

15 Now the tax collectors and "sinners" were all gathering around to hear him. ²But the Pharisees and the teachers of the law muttered, "This man welcomes sinners and eats with them."

³Then Jesus told them this parable: ⁴"Suppose one of you has a hundred sheep and loses one of them. Does he not leave the ninety-nine in the open country and go after the lost sheep until he finds it? ⁵And when he finds it, he joyfully puts it on his shoulders ⁶and goes home. Then he calls his friends and neighbors together and says, 'Rejoice with me; I have found my lost sheep.' ⁷I tell you that in the same way there will be more rejoicing in heaven over one sinner who repents than over ninety-nine righteous persons who do not need to repent.

The Parable of the Lost Coin

⁸"Or suppose a woman has ten silver coins[a] and loses one. Does she not light a lamp, sweep the house and search carefully until she finds it? ⁹And when she finds it, she calls her friends and neighbors together and says, 'Rejoice with me; I have found my lost coin.' ¹⁰In the same way, I tell you, there is rejoicing in the presence of the angels of God over one sinner who repents."

---

*a*8 Greek *ten drachmas*, each worth about a day's wages

Luke 15:10

"There is rejoicing in the presence of the angels of God over one sinner who repents."

reflection

1 What are some things that cause you to rejoice?

2 Jesus searched diligently for lost individuals. Who would you go out of your way to find?

3 When was the last time you felt spiritually lost? Do you feel lost right now? If you have lost your way, spend some time asking God to show you the way back home to him.

RELATED READINGS

Psalms 23:1–4; 139:1–24;
Luke 19:1–10;
John 10:14–16

Read: Luke 15:1–32

HERE'S AN INTERESTING BIT of trivia: According to the Department of Statistics, the average American spends one full year of their life looking for lost things. One year! Have you ever misplaced your car keys just when you urgently needed to get somewhere on time? or looked for those eyeglasses that were sitting on top of your head? or searched high and low for the book you wanted to take on vacation? You probably felt as if you searched an entire year just for one lost item.

Jesus spent *three* years searching . . . his entire ministry. But he did not search for material things, such as keys, glasses and books. No, Jesus looked for lost people. He searched among the sinners and found such unpopular people as Matthew, the tax collector, and Mary Magdalene, the woman tormented by seven demons. He searched in the region of Galilee and found the likes of Peter and John and many women followers. He searched among the rebellious and found Zacchaeus. He went into Samaria, an area shunned by orthodox Jews, and met the woman who lived in sin getting water at a well.

Jesus still searches for the lost. Where did he find you? At a nightclub? Living life as a rebel? Riding the subway in a big city? Buried under a pile of books at a university? Or perhaps he found you sitting in a church pew, convinced you had everything together, that you could set things right with God on your own terms . . . sort of like Nicodemus, the learned Pharisee and member of the Sanhedrin. Yet even to him, Jesus said, "You must be born again" (John 3:7).

Wherever you were, the Savior came looking for you because you are valuable to him. You are worth every moment of the search. For when you answered his call, he and the angels in heaven rejoiced. And now you are his beloved child, one of his "chosen people, a royal priesthood, a holy nation, a people belonging to God, that you may declare the praises of him who called you out of darkness into his wonderful light" (1 Peter 2:9).

There is so much, so very much for you to rejoice in.

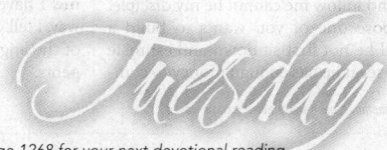

Go to page 1268 for your next devotional reading.

The Parable of the Lost Son

11 Jesus continued: "There was a man who had two sons. **12** The younger one said to his father, 'Father, give me my share of the estate.' So he divided his property between them.

13 "Not long after that, the younger son got together all he had, set off for a distant country and there squandered his wealth in wild living. **14** After he had spent everything, there was a severe famine in that whole country, and he began to be in need. **15** So he went and hired himself out to a citizen of that country, who sent him to his fields to feed pigs. **16** He longed to fill his stomach with the pods that the pigs were eating, but no one gave him anything.

17 "When he came to his senses, he said, 'How many of my father's hired men have food to spare, and here I am starving to death! **18** I will set out and go back to my father and say to him: Father, I have sinned against heaven and against you. **19** I am no longer worthy to be called your son; make me like one of your hired men.' **20** So he got up and went to his father.

"But while he was still a long way off, his father saw him and was filled with compassion for him; he ran to his son, threw his arms around him and kissed him.

21 "The son said to him, 'Father, I have sinned against heaven and against you. I am no longer worthy to be called your son.*a*'

22 "But the father said to his servants, 'Quick! Bring the best robe and put it on him. Put a ring on his finger and sandals on his feet. **23** Bring the fattened calf and kill it. Let's have a feast and celebrate. **24** For this son of mine was dead and is alive again; he was lost and is found.' So they began to celebrate.

25 "Meanwhile, the older son was in the field. When he came near the house, he heard music and dancing. **26** So he called one of the servants and asked him what was going on. **27** 'Your brother has come,' he replied, 'and your father has killed the fattened calf because he has him back safe and sound.'

28 "The older brother became angry and refused to go in. So his father went out and pleaded with him. **29** But he answered his father, 'Look! All these years I've been slaving for you and never disobeyed your orders. Yet you never gave me even a young goat so I could celebrate with my friends. **30** But when this son of yours who has squandered your property with prostitutes comes home, you kill the fattened calf for him!'

31 "'My son,' the father said, 'you are always with me, and everything I have is yours. **32** But we had to celebrate and be glad, because this brother of yours was dead and is alive again; he was lost and is found.'"

The Parable of the Shrewd Manager

16 Jesus told his disciples: "There was a rich man whose manager was accused of wasting his possessions. **2** So he called him in and asked him, 'What is this I hear about you? Give an account of your management, because you cannot be manager any longer.'

3 "The manager said to himself, 'What shall I do now? My master is taking away my job. I'm not strong enough to dig, and I'm ashamed to beg— **4** I know what I'll do so that, when I lose my job here, people will welcome me into their houses.'

5 "So he called in each one of his master's debtors. He asked the first, 'How much do you owe my master?'

6 "'Eight hundred gallons*b* of olive oil,' he replied.

"The manager told him, 'Take your bill, sit down quickly, and make it four hundred.'

7 "Then he asked the second, 'And how much do you owe?'

"'A thousand bushels*c* of wheat,' he replied.

"He told him, 'Take your bill and make it eight hundred.'

Luke 15:20

God Welcomes the Prodigal

"So he got up and went to his father. But while he was still a long way off, his father saw him and was filled with compassion for him; he ran to his son, threw his arms around him and kissed him."

---

*a***21** Some early manuscripts *son. Make me like one of your hired men.*   *b***6** Greek *one hundred batous* (probably about 3 kiloliters)
*c***7** Greek *one hundred korous* (probably about 35 kiloliters)

⁸"The master commended the dishonest manager because he had acted shrewdly. For the people of this world are more shrewd in dealing with their own kind than are the people of the light. ⁹I tell you, use worldly wealth to gain friends for yourselves, so that when it is gone, you will be welcomed into eternal dwellings.

¹⁰"Whoever can be trusted with very little can also be trusted with much, and whoever is dishonest with very little will also be dishonest with much. ¹¹So if you have not been trustworthy in handling worldly wealth, who will trust you with true riches? ¹²And if you have not been trustworthy with someone else's property, who will give you property of your own?

¹³"No servant can serve two masters. Either he will hate the one and love the other, or he will be devoted to the one and despise the other. You cannot serve both God and Money."

¹⁴The Pharisees, who loved money, heard all this and were sneering at Jesus. ¹⁵He said to them, "You are the ones who justify yourselves in the eyes of men, but God knows your hearts. What is highly valued among men is detestable in God's sight.

Additional Teachings

¹⁶"The Law and the Prophets were proclaimed until John. Since that time, the good news of the kingdom of God is being preached, and everyone is forcing his way into it. ¹⁷It is easier for heaven and earth to disappear than for the least stroke of a pen to drop out of the Law.

¹⁸"Anyone who divorces his wife and marries another woman commits adultery, and the man who marries a divorced woman commits adultery.

The Rich Man and Lazarus

¹⁹"There was a rich man who was dressed in purple and fine linen and lived in luxury every day. ²⁰At his gate was laid a beggar named Lazarus, covered with sores ²¹and longing to eat what fell from the rich man's table. Even the dogs came and licked his sores.

²²"The time came when the beggar died and the angels carried him to Abraham's side. The rich man also died and was buried. ²³In hell,ᵃ

ᵃ23 Greek *Hades*

where he was in torment, he looked up and saw Abraham far away, with Lazarus by his side. ²⁴So he called to him, 'Father Abraham, have pity on me and send Lazarus to dip the tip of his finger in water and cool my tongue, because I am in agony in this fire.'

²⁵"But Abraham replied, 'Son, remember that in your lifetime you received your good things, while Lazarus received bad things, but now he is comforted here and you are in agony. ²⁶And besides all this, between us and you a great chasm has been fixed, so that those who want to go from here to you cannot, nor can anyone cross over from there to us.'

²⁷"He answered, 'Then I beg you, father, send Lazarus to my father's house, ²⁸for I have five brothers. Let him warn them, so that they will not also come to this place of torment.'

²⁹"Abraham replied, 'They have Moses and the Prophets; let them listen to them.'

³⁰"'No, father Abraham,' he said, 'but if someone from the dead goes to them, they will repent.'

³¹"He said to him, 'If they do not listen to Moses and the Prophets, they will not be convinced even if someone rises from the dead.'"

Sin, Faith, Duty

17 Jesus said to his disciples: "Things that cause people to sin are bound to come, but woe to that person through whom they come. ²It would be better for him to be thrown into the sea with a millstone tied around his neck than for him to cause one of these little ones to sin. ³So watch yourselves.

"If your brother sins, rebuke him, and if he repents, forgive him. ⁴If he sins against you seven times in a day, and seven times comes back to you and says, 'I repent,' forgive him."

⁵The apostles said to the Lord, "Increase our faith!"

⁶He replied, "If you have faith as small as a mustard seed, you can say to this mulberry tree, 'Be uprooted and planted in the sea,' and it will obey you.

⁷"Suppose one of you had a servant plowing or looking after the sheep. Would he say to the servant when he comes in from the field, 'Come along now and sit down to eat'? ⁸Would he not rather say, 'Prepare my supper, get your-

self ready and wait on me while I eat and drink; after that you may eat and drink'? ⁹Would he thank the servant because he did what he was told to do? ¹⁰So you also, when you have done everything you were told to do, should say, 'We are unworthy servants; we have only done our duty.'"

Ten Healed of Leprosy

¹¹Now on his way to Jerusalem, Jesus traveled along the border between Samaria and Galilee. ¹²As he was going into a village, ten men who had leprosy*a* met him. They stood at a distance ¹³and called out in a loud voice, "Jesus, Master, have pity on us!"

¹⁴When he saw them, he said, "Go, show yourselves to the priests." And as they went, they were cleansed.

¹⁵One of them, when he saw he was healed, came back, praising God in a loud voice. ¹⁶He threw himself at Jesus' feet and thanked him— and he was a Samaritan.

¹⁷Jesus asked, "Were not all ten cleansed? Where are the other nine? ¹⁸Was no one found to return and give praise to God except this foreigner?" ¹⁹Then he said to him, "Rise and go; your faith has made you well."

The Coming of the Kingdom of God

²⁰Once, having been asked by the Pharisees when the kingdom of God would come, Jesus replied, "The kingdom of God does not come with your careful observation, ²¹nor will people say, 'Here it is,' or 'There it is,' because the kingdom of God is within*b* you."

²²Then he said to his disciples, "The time is coming when you will long to see one of the days of the Son of Man, but you will not see it. ²³Men will tell you, 'There he is!' or 'Here he is!' Do not go running off after them. ²⁴For the Son of Man in his day*c* will be like the lightning, which flashes and lights up the sky from one end to the other. ²⁵But first he must suffer many things and be rejected by this generation.

²⁶"Just as it was in the days of Noah, so also will it be in the days of the Son of Man. ²⁷People were eating, drinking, marrying and being given in marriage up to the day Noah entered

the ark. Then the flood came and destroyed them all.

²⁸"It was the same in the days of Lot. People were eating and drinking, buying and selling, planting and building. ²⁹But the day Lot left Sodom, fire and sulfur rained down from heaven and destroyed them all.

³⁰"It will be just like this on the day the Son of Man is revealed. ³¹On that day no one who is on the roof of his house, with his goods inside, should go down to get them. Likewise, no one in the field should go back for anything. ³²Remember Lot's wife! ³³Whoever tries to keep his life will lose it, and whoever loses his life will preserve it. ³⁴I tell you, on that night two people will be in one bed; one will be taken and the other left. ³⁵Two women will be grinding grain together; one will be taken and the other left.*d*"

³⁷"Where, Lord?" they asked.

He replied, "Where there is a dead body, there the vultures will gather."

The Parable of the Persistent Widow

18 Then Jesus told his disciples a parable to show them that they should always pray and not give up. ²He said: "In a certain town there was a judge who neither feared God nor cared about men. ³And there was a widow in that town who kept coming to him with the plea, 'Grant me justice against my adversary.'

⁴"For some time he refused. But finally he said to himself, 'Even though I don't fear God or care about men, ⁵yet because this widow keeps bothering me, I will see that she gets justice, so that she won't eventually wear me out with her coming!'"

⁶And the Lord said, "Listen to what the unjust judge says. ⁷And will not God bring about justice for his chosen ones, who cry out to him day and night? Will he keep putting them off? ⁸I tell you, he will see that they get justice, and quickly. However, when the Son of Man comes, will he find faith on the earth?"

The Parable of the Pharisee and the Tax Collector

⁹To some who were confident of their own righteousness and looked down on everybody

---

a 12 The Greek word was used for various diseases affecting the skin—not necessarily leprosy.   *b 21* Or *among*   *c 24* Some manuscripts do not have *in his day*.   *d 35* Some manuscripts *left.* *36 Two men will be in the field; one will be taken and the other left.*

Knocking on God's Door

Luke 18:7

"And will not God bring about justice for his chosen ones, who cry out to him day and night? Will he keep putting them off?"

reflection

1 Would you describe your prayer life as strong, weak or improving?

2 When God doesn't answer your prayer in the way you wanted, how do you handle it?

3 What specific steps will you take to grow in your prayer life?

RELATED READINGS

1 Samuel 1:1–20;
Isaiah 62:6–7;
Matthew 5:5; 7:7–11

Read: Luke 18:1–17

"I'VE BEEN LAID OFF AGAIN," said Jim.

"But that's the third time in five years," said Nan. "What will we do? Do you have severance pay?" Jim shook his head no.

Nan collapsed onto a kitchen chair, tears slipping down her cheeks. "I can't go through this again."

They were both middle-aged, and jobs were hard to find. They had children who needed clothing, parents who needed help. Together, they decided to place their future in God's hands and plead their case before him day and night. Every morning, they read God's Word together and prayed. At dinnertime they prayed too, asking God to provide a job.

Several weeks later, a woman they'd met at a job center told them about an opening. Armed with the knowledge that God is faithful and that he answers prayer according to his purpose, Jim applied for the job. Jim and Nan had knocked long and hard on heaven's door for job openings, and it took a long time for their prayers to be answered. This time, within a week, Jim was hired.

Unlike the widow in Jesus' parable who went before an unjust judge, Jim and Nan called upon a loving Father. The widow had no friend to speak for her, but Jim and Nan had Jesus—the One who lives to intercede. The widow only had access to the judge at certain times, while this couple had access to their heavenly Father morning, noon and night. In one area they were similar: like the widow, Jim and Nan were persistent; they did not give up.

And God answered.

You may be praying and waiting for something: a baby, a job, a husband, a ministry. Keep praying. Day and night. He will answer in the way that he sees fit. The answer may not look like what you were imagining, but it will be for your good.

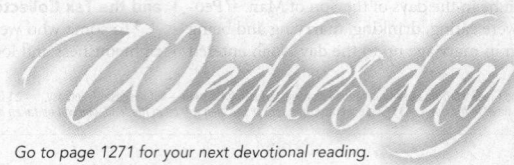

Go to page 1271 for your next devotional reading.

else, Jesus told this parable: [10]"Two men went up to the temple to pray, one a Pharisee and the other a tax collector. [11]The Pharisee stood up and prayed about[a] himself: 'God, I thank you that I am not like other men—robbers, evildoers, adulterers—or even like this tax collector. [12]I fast twice a week and give a tenth of all I get.'

[13]"But the tax collector stood at a distance. He would not even look up to heaven, but beat his breast and said, 'God, have mercy on me, a sinner.'

[14]"I tell you that this man, rather than the other, went home justified before God. For everyone who exalts himself will be humbled, and he who humbles himself will be exalted."

The Little Children and Jesus

[15]People were also bringing babies to Jesus to have him touch them. When the disciples saw this, they rebuked them. [16]But Jesus called the children to him and said, "Let the little children come to me, and do not hinder them, for the kingdom of God belongs to such as these. [17]I tell you the truth, anyone who will not receive the kingdom of God like a little child will never enter it."

The Rich Ruler

[18]A certain ruler asked him, "Good teacher, what must I do to inherit eternal life?"

[19]"Why do you call me good?" Jesus answered. "No one is good—except God alone. [20]You know the commandments: 'Do not commit adultery, do not murder, do not steal, do not give false testimony, honor your father and mother.'[b]"

[21]"All these I have kept since I was a boy," he said.

[22]When Jesus heard this, he said to him, "You still lack one thing. Sell everything you have and give to the poor, and you will have treasure in heaven. Then come, follow me."

[23]When he heard this, he became very sad, because he was a man of great wealth. [24]Jesus looked at him and said, "How hard it is for the rich to enter the kingdom of God! [25]Indeed, it is easier for a camel to go through the eye of a needle than for a rich man to enter the kingdom of God."

[26]Those who heard this asked, "Who then can be saved?"

[27]Jesus replied, "What is impossible with men is possible with God."

[28]Peter said to him, "We have left all we had to follow you!"

[29]"I tell you the truth," Jesus said to them, "no one who has left home or wife or brothers or parents or children for the sake of the kingdom of God [30]will fail to receive many times as much in this age and, in the age to come, eternal life."

Jesus Again Predicts His Death

[31]Jesus took the Twelve aside and told them, "We are going up to Jerusalem, and everything that is written by the prophets about the Son of Man will be fulfilled. [32]He will be handed over to the Gentiles. They will mock him, insult him, spit on him, flog him and kill him. [33]On the third day he will rise again."

[34]The disciples did not understand any of this. Its meaning was hidden from them, and they did not know what he was talking about.

A Blind Beggar Receives His Sight

[35]As Jesus approached Jericho, a blind man was sitting by the roadside begging. [36]When he heard the crowd going by, he asked what was happening. [37]They told him, "Jesus of Nazareth is passing by."

[38]He called out, "Jesus, Son of David, have mercy on me!"

[39]Those who led the way rebuked him and told him to be quiet, but he shouted all the more, "Son of David, have mercy on me!"

[40]Jesus stopped and ordered the man to be brought to him. When he came near, Jesus asked him, [41]"What do you want me to do for you?"

"Lord, I want to see," he replied.

[42]Jesus said to him, "Receive your sight; your faith has healed you." [43]Immediately he received his sight and followed Jesus, praising God. When all the people saw it, they also praised God.

Zacchaeus the Tax Collector

19 Jesus entered Jericho and was passing through. [2]A man was there by the name of Zacchaeus; he was a chief tax collector

---

[a]11 Or *to*   [b]20 Exodus 20:12–16; Deut. 5:16–20

and was wealthy. ³He wanted to see who Jesus was, but being a short man he could not, because of the crowd. ⁴So he ran ahead and climbed a sycamore-fig tree to see him, since Jesus was coming that way.

⁵When Jesus reached the spot, he looked up and said to him, "Zacchaeus, come down immediately. I must stay at your house today." ⁶So he came down at once and welcomed him gladly.

⁷All the people saw this and began to mutter, "He has gone to be the guest of a 'sinner.' "

⁸But Zacchaeus stood up and said to the Lord, "Look, Lord! Here and now I give half of my possessions to the poor, and if I have cheated anybody out of anything, I will pay back four times the amount."

⁹Jesus said to him, "Today salvation has come to this house, because this man, too, is a son of Abraham. ¹⁰For the Son of Man came to seek and to save what was lost."

> **Luke 19:10**
>
> *God Saves the Lost*
>
> "For the Son of Man came to seek and to save what was lost."

The Parable of the Ten Minas

¹¹While they were listening to this, he went on to tell them a parable, because he was near Jerusalem and the people thought that the kingdom of God was going to appear at once. ¹²He said: "A man of noble birth went to a distant country to have himself appointed king and then to return. ¹³So he called ten of his servants and gave them ten minas.ᵃ 'Put this money to work,' he said, 'until I come back.'

¹⁴"But his subjects hated him and sent a delegation after him to say, 'We don't want this man to be our king.'

¹⁵"He was made king, however, and returned home. Then he sent for the servants to whom he had given the money, in order to find out what they had gained with it.

¹⁶"The first one came and said, 'Sir, your mina has earned ten more.'

¹⁷"'Well done, my good servant!' his master replied. 'Because you have been trustworthy in a very small matter, take charge of ten cities.'

¹⁸"The second came and said, 'Sir, your mina has earned five more.'

¹⁹"His master answered, 'You take charge of five cities.'

²⁰"Then another servant came and said, 'Sir, here is your mina; I have kept it laid away in a piece of cloth. ²¹I was afraid of you, because you are a hard man. You take out what you did not put in and reap what you did not sow.'

²²"His master replied, 'I will judge you by your own words, you wicked servant! You knew, did you, that I am a hard man, taking out what I did not put in, and reaping what I did not sow? ²³Why then didn't you put my money on deposit, so that when I came back, I could have collected it with interest?'

²⁴"Then he said to those standing by, 'Take his mina away from him and give it to the one who has ten minas.'

²⁵"'Sir,' they said, 'he already has ten!'

²⁶"He replied, 'I tell you that to everyone who has, more will be given, but as for the one who has nothing, even what he has will be taken away. ²⁷But those enemies of mine who did not want me to be king over them—bring them here and kill them in front of me.' "

The Triumphal Entry

²⁸After Jesus had said this, he went on ahead, going up to Jerusalem. ²⁹As he approached Bethphage and Bethany at the hill called the Mount of Olives, he sent two of his disciples, saying to them, ³⁰"Go to the village ahead of you, and as you enter it, you will find a colt tied there, which no one has ever ridden. Untie it and bring it here. ³¹If anyone asks you, 'Why are you untying it?' tell him, 'The Lord needs it.' "

³²Those who were sent ahead went and found it just as he had told them. ³³As they were untying the colt, its owners asked them, "Why are you untying the colt?"

³⁴They replied, "The Lord needs it."

³⁵They brought it to Jesus, threw their cloaks on the colt and put Jesus on it. ³⁶As he went along, people spread their cloaks on the road.

ᵃ13 A mina was about three months' wages.

A Desirable Donkey?

Read: Luke 19:28–44

THINK OF THE ANIMAL that you most identify with. Perhaps you thought of a species that you physically resemble. Long neck? A giraffe. Sleek? A panther. Bookish? An owl. More than likely you picked an animal that shares a characteristic common to you: silly like a monkey, clever as a fox or resourceful like a squirrel. Answering this question reveals a lot about a person. Possums enjoy sleep. Birds crave freedom. And hyenas laugh from the belly. Which animal do you most closely resemble?

You probably didn't pick the donkey with its enormous ears, obstinate will and annoying bray. Notoriously stubborn and simpleminded, the donkey or donkey colt is mentioned frequently in the Bible. It served as the common beast of burden for the poor. Unlike the noble horse, which was coveted by the rich and royal, the donkey was an animal for blue-collar workers. Donkeys are low-maintenance animals with great endurance. They have the ability to live and work under hot, difficult conditions. Sometimes they were used for riding but mostly they pulled loads and carts, worked mills and threshers or carried heavy burdens.

Jesus chose to ride a donkey's colt when making his triumphal entry into Jerusalem. Although the King of kings deserved a fine steed, he humbly rode a big-eared burro. It was prophesied, "See, your king comes to you, gentle and riding on a donkey, on a colt, the foal of a donkey" (Matthew 21:5).

Doesn't that give you reassurance? If the Lord "needs" a stubborn, lowly donkey, perhaps he could use a whimsical woman. Maybe your plodding steadiness is just what he can use. Maybe your stubbornness looks more like persistence and perseverance to God. Perhaps your down-to-earth personality fits right into his plans. Paul said, "[God] chose the lowly things of this world and the despised things—and the things that are not—to nullify the things that are, so that no one may boast before him" (1 Corinthians 1:28–29).

Whether you resemble a parrot, a peacock or a porcupine, God needs you.

Go to page 1276 for your next devotional reading.

Luke 19:30–31

"Go to the village ahead of you, and as you enter it, you will find a [donkey's] colt tied there, which no one has ever ridden. Untie it and bring it here. If anyone asks you, 'Why are you untying it?' tell him, 'The Lord needs it.'"

reflection

1 What animal do you most identify with?

2 Why do you think Jesus chose a donkey to ride on into Jerusalem?

3 How might God use your personality traits for his glory?

RELATED READINGS

Proverbs 29:23;
Zechariah 9:9;
1 Corinthians 12:1–26

Thursday

37When he came near the place where the road goes down the Mount of Olives, the whole crowd of disciples began joyfully to praise God in loud voices for all the miracles they had seen:

38"Blessed is the king who comes in the
name of the Lord!"*a*

"Peace in heaven and glory in the highest!"

39Some of the Pharisees in the crowd said to Jesus, "Teacher, rebuke your disciples!"

40"I tell you," he replied, "if they keep quiet, the stones will cry out."

41As he approached Jerusalem and saw the city, he wept over it **42**and said, "If you, even you, had only known on this day what would bring you peace—but now it is hidden from your eyes. **43**The days will come upon you when your enemies will build an embankment against you and encircle you and hem you in on every side. **44**They will dash you to the ground, you and the children within your walls. They will not leave one stone on another, because you did not recognize the time of God's coming to you."

Jesus at the Temple

45Then he entered the temple area and began driving out those who were selling. **46**"It is written," he said to them, " 'My house will be a house of prayer'*b*; but you have made it 'a den of robbers.'*c*"

47Every day he was teaching at the temple. But the chief priests, the teachers of the law and the leaders among the people were trying to kill him. **48**Yet they could not find any way to do it, because all the people hung on his words.

The Authority of Jesus Questioned

20 One day as he was teaching the people in the temple courts and preaching the gospel, the chief priests and the teachers of the law, together with the elders, came up to him. **2**"Tell us by what authority you are doing these things," they said. "Who gave you this authority?"

3He replied, "I will also ask you a question. Tell me, **4**John's baptism—was it from heaven, or from men?"

5They discussed it among themselves and said, "If we say, 'From heaven,' he will ask, 'Why didn't you believe him?' **6**But if we say, 'From men,' all the people will stone us, because they are persuaded that John was a prophet."

7So they answered, "We don't know where it was from."

8Jesus said, "Neither will I tell you by what authority I am doing these things."

The Parable of the Tenants

9He went on to tell the people this parable: "A man planted a vineyard, rented it to some farmers and went away for a long time. **10**At harvest time he sent a servant to the tenants so they would give him some of the fruit of the vineyard. But the tenants beat him and sent him away empty-handed. **11**He sent another servant, but that one also they beat and treated shamefully and sent away empty-handed. **12**He sent still a third, and they wounded him and threw him out.

13"Then the owner of the vineyard said, 'What shall I do? I will send my son, whom I love; perhaps they will respect him.'

14"But when the tenants saw him, they talked the matter over. 'This is the heir,' they said. 'Let's kill him, and the inheritance will be ours.' **15**So they threw him out of the vineyard and killed him.

"What then will the owner of the vineyard do to them? **16**He will come and kill those tenants and give the vineyard to others."

When the people heard this, they said, "May this never be!"

17Jesus looked directly at them and asked, "Then what is the meaning of that which is written:

" 'The stone the builders rejected
has become the capstone*d,e*?

18Everyone who falls on that stone will be broken to pieces, but he on whom it falls will be crushed."

19The teachers of the law and the chief priests looked for a way to arrest him immediately, because they knew he had spoken this parable against them. But they were afraid of the people.

---

*a***38** Psalm 118:26   *b***46** Isaiah 56:7   *c***46** Jer. 7:11   *d***17** Or *cornerstone*   *e***17** Psalm 118:22

Paying Taxes to Caesar

20 Keeping a close watch on him, they sent spies, who pretended to be honest. They hoped to catch Jesus in something he said so that they might hand him over to the power and authority of the governor. 21 So the spies questioned him: "Teacher, we know that you speak and teach what is right, and that you do not show partiality but teach the way of God in accordance with the truth. 22 Is it right for us to pay taxes to Caesar or not?"

23 He saw through their duplicity and said to them, 24 "Show me a denarius. Whose portrait and inscription are on it?"

25 "Caesar's," they replied.

He said to them, "Then give to Caesar what is Caesar's, and to God what is God's."

26 They were unable to trap him in what he had said there in public. And astonished by his answer, they became silent.

The Resurrection and Marriage

27 Some of the Sadducees, who say there is no resurrection, came to Jesus with a question. 28 "Teacher," they said, "Moses wrote for us that if a man's brother dies and leaves a wife but no children, the man must marry the widow and have children for his brother. 29 Now there were seven brothers. The first one married a woman and died childless. 30 The second 31 and then the third married her, and in the same way the seven died, leaving no children. 32 Finally, the woman died too. 33 Now then, at the resurrection whose wife will she be, since the seven were married to her?"

34 Jesus replied, "The people of this age marry and are given in marriage. 35 But those who are considered worthy of taking part in that age and in the resurrection from the dead will neither marry nor be given in marriage, 36 and they can no longer die; for they are like the angels. They are God's children, since they are children of the resurrection. 37 But in the account of the bush, even Moses showed that the dead rise, for he calls the Lord 'the God of Abraham, and the God of Isaac, and the God of Jacob.'ᵃ 38 He is not the God of the dead, but of the living, for to him all are alive."

39 Some of the teachers of the law responded,

"Well said, teacher!" 40 And no one dared to ask him any more questions.

Whose Son Is the Christ?

41 Then Jesus said to them, "How is it that they say the Christᵇ is the Son of David? 42 David himself declares in the Book of Psalms:

" 'The Lord said to my Lord:
    "Sit at my right hand
43 until I make your enemies
    a footstool for your feet." 'ᶜ

44 David calls him 'Lord.' How then can he be his son?"

45 While all the people were listening, Jesus said to his disciples, 46 "Beware of the teachers of the law. They like to walk around in flowing robes and love to be greeted in the marketplaces and have the most important seats in the synagogues and the places of honor at banquets. 47 They devour widows' houses and for a show make lengthy prayers. Such men will be punished most severely."

The Widow's Offering

21 As he looked up, Jesus saw the rich putting their gifts into the temple treasury. 2 He also saw a poor widow put in two very small copper coins.ᵈ 3 "I tell you the truth," he said, "this poor widow has put in more than all the others. 4 All these people gave their gifts out of their wealth; but she out of her poverty put in all she had to live on."

Signs of the End of the Age

5 Some of his disciples were remarking about how the temple was adorned with beautiful stones and with gifts dedicated to God. But Jesus said, 6 "As for what you see here, the time will come when not one stone will be left on another; every one of them will be thrown down."

7 "Teacher," they asked, "when will these things happen? And what will be the sign that they are about to take place?"

8 He replied: "Watch out that you are not deceived. For many will come in my name, claiming, 'I am he,' and, 'The time is near.' Do not follow them. 9 When you hear of wars and revolutions, do not be frightened. These things

---

ᵃ37 Exodus 3:6   ᵇ41 Or *Messiah*   ᶜ43 Psalm 110:1   ᵈ2 Greek *two lepta* must happen first, but the end will not come right away."

10Then he said to them: "Nation will rise against nation, and kingdom against kingdom. 11There will be great earthquakes, famines and pestilences in various places, and fearful events and great signs from heaven.

12"But before all this, they will lay hands on you and persecute you. They will deliver you to synagogues and prisons, and you will be brought before kings and governors, and all on account of my name. 13This will result in your being witnesses to them. 14But make up your mind not to worry beforehand how you will defend yourselves. 15For I will give you words and wisdom that none of your adversaries will be able to resist or contradict. 16You will be betrayed even by parents, brothers, relatives and friends, and they will put some of you to death. 17All men will hate you because of me. 18But not a hair of your head will perish. 19By standing firm you will gain life.

20"When you see Jerusalem being surrounded by armies, you will know that its desolation is near. 21Then let those who are in Judea flee to the mountains, let those in the city get out, and let those in the country not enter the city. 22For this is the time of punishment in fulfillment of all that has been written. 23How dreadful it will be in those days for pregnant women and nursing mothers! There will be great distress in the land and wrath against this people. 24They will fall by the sword and will be taken as prisoners to all the nations. Jerusalem will be trampled on by the Gentiles until the times of the Gentiles are fulfilled.

25"There will be signs in the sun, moon and stars. On the earth, nations will be in anguish and perplexity at the roaring and tossing of the sea. 26Men will faint from terror, apprehensive of what is coming on the world, for the heavenly bodies will be shaken. 27At that time they will see the Son of Man coming in a cloud with power and great glory. 28When these things begin to take place, stand up and lift up your heads, because your redemption is drawing near."

29He told them this parable: "Look at the fig tree and all the trees. 30When they sprout leaves, you can see for yourselves and know that summer is near. 31Even so, when you see these things happening, you know that the kingdom of God is near.

32"I tell you the truth, this generation*a* will certainly not pass away until all these things have happened. 33Heaven and earth will pass away, but my words will never pass away.

34"Be careful, or your hearts will be weighed down with dissipation, drunkenness and the anxieties of life, and that day will close on you unexpectedly like a trap. 35For it will come upon all those who live on the face of the whole earth. 36Be always on the watch, and pray that you may be able to escape all that is about to happen, and that you may be able to stand before the Son of Man."

37Each day Jesus was teaching at the temple, and each evening he went out to spend the night on the hill called the Mount of Olives, 38and all the people came early in the morning to hear him at the temple.

Judas Agrees to Betray Jesus

22 Now the Feast of Unleavened Bread, called the Passover, was approaching, 2and the chief priests and the teachers of the law were looking for some way to get rid of Jesus, for they were afraid of the people. 3Then Satan entered Judas, called Iscariot, one of the Twelve. 4And Judas went to the chief priests and the officers of the temple guard and discussed with them how he might betray Jesus. 5They were delighted and agreed to give him money. 6He consented, and watched for an opportunity to hand Jesus over to them when no crowd was present.

The Last Supper

7Then came the day of Unleavened Bread on which the Passover lamb had to be sacrificed. 8Jesus sent Peter and John, saying, "Go and make preparations for us to eat the Passover."

9"Where do you want us to prepare for it?" they asked.

10He replied, "As you enter the city, a man carrying a jar of water will meet you. Follow him to the house that he enters, 11and say to the owner of the house, 'The Teacher asks: Where is the guest room, where I may eat the

a32 Or race

Passover with my disciples?' ¹²He will show you a large upper room, all furnished. Make preparations there."

¹³They left and found things just as Jesus had told them. So they prepared the Passover.

¹⁴When the hour came, Jesus and his apostles reclined at the table. ¹⁵And he said to them, "I have eagerly desired to eat this Passover with you before I suffer. ¹⁶For I tell you, I will not eat it again until it finds fulfillment in the kingdom of God."

¹⁷After taking the cup, he gave thanks and said, "Take this and divide it among you. ¹⁸For I tell you I will not drink again of the fruit of the vine until the kingdom of God comes."

¹⁹And he took bread, gave thanks and broke it, and gave it to them, saying, "This is my body given for you; do this in remembrance of me."

²⁰In the same way, after the supper he took the cup, saying, "This cup is the new covenant in my blood, which is poured out for you. ²¹But the hand of him who is going to betray me is with mine on the table. ²²The Son of Man will go as it has been decreed, but woe to that man who betrays him." ²³They began to question among themselves which of them it might be who would do this.

²⁴Also a dispute arose among them as to which of them was considered to be greatest. ²⁵Jesus said to them, "The kings of the Gentiles lord it over them; and those who exercise authority over them call themselves Benefactors. ²⁶But you are not to be like that. Instead, the greatest among you should be like the youngest, and the one who rules like the one who serves. ²⁷For who is greater, the one who is at the table or the one who serves? Is it not the one who is at the table? But I am among you as one who serves. ²⁸You are those who have stood by me in my trials. ²⁹And I confer on you a kingdom, just as my Father conferred one on me, ³⁰so that you may eat and drink at my table

in my kingdom and sit on thrones, judging the twelve tribes of Israel.

³¹"Simon, Simon, Satan has asked to sift you[a] as wheat. ³²But I have prayed for you, Simon, that your faith may not fail. And when you have turned back, strengthen your brothers."

³³But he replied, "Lord, I am ready to go with you to prison and to death."

³⁴Jesus answered, "I tell you, Peter, before the rooster crows today, you will deny three times that you know me."

³⁵Then Jesus asked them, "When I sent you without purse, bag or sandals, did you lack anything?"

"Nothing," they answered.

³⁶He said to them, "But now if you have a purse, take it, and also a bag; and if you don't have a sword, sell your cloak and buy one. ³⁷It is written: 'And he was numbered with the transgressors'[b]; and I tell you that this must be fulfilled in me. Yes, what is written about me is reaching its fulfillment."

³⁸The disciples said, "See, Lord, here are two swords."

"That is enough," he replied.

Jesus Prays on the Mount of Olives

³⁹Jesus went out as usual to the Mount of Olives, and his disciples followed him. ⁴⁰On reaching the place, he said to them, "Pray that you will not fall into temptation." ⁴¹He withdrew about a stone's throw beyond them, knelt down and prayed, ⁴²"Father, if you are willing, take this cup from me; yet not my will, but yours be done." ⁴³An angel from heaven appeared to him and strengthened him. ⁴⁴And being in anguish, he prayed more earnestly, and his sweat was like drops of blood falling to the ground.[c]

⁴⁵When he rose from prayer and went back to the disciples, he found them asleep, exhausted from sorrow. ⁴⁶"Why are you sleeping?" he asked them. "Get up and pray so that you will not fall into temptation."

Luke 22:20

God Covenants With Us

In the same way, after the supper he took the cup, saying, "This cup is the new covenant in my blood, which is poured out for you."

---

[a]31 The Greek is plural.   [b]37 Isaiah 53:12   [c]44 Some early manuscripts do not have verses 43 and 44.

Not My Will

Luke 22:41–42

[Jesus] withdrew about a stone's throw beyond them, knelt down and prayed, "Father, if you are willing, take this cup from me; yet not my will, but yours be done."

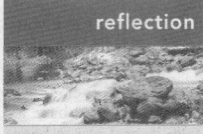

reflection

1 Describe the area of your life where you are struggling to accept the will of the Father.

2 How has this devotional helped you in understanding the difference between annihilating your will and submitting your will to God?

3 Can you now pray, "Nevertheless, not my will but thine be done"? Proclaim in faith that God's will is invariably the best thing for your life and the lives of those you love.

RELATED READINGS

Psalm 143;
Matthew 6:9–13;
John 10:15–18;
Romans 12:1–2

WHEN I WAS YOUNG I had the idea (I am sure I must have heard sermons on this) that I would somehow have to annihilate my own will before I could properly pray to God for his. "You must have absolutely no will of your own in the matter," someone had said. This sounded all right to me, and I spent a lot of time and energy trying to follow this advice. Finally I saw that no such thing was required. The struggle Jesus had in the Garden of Gethsemane showed me this. A conflict was taking place—not to annihilate his own will but to accept the will of the Father, which was *other* than his. It did not end with Jesus saying, "My will is now thine" but with, "Not my will but thine be done." The act of praying, far from divesting us of human desires, enables us to lay them before God as very real and pressing and say to him, "Not mine, Lord. Yours." (If we had gotten rid of them, there would be nothing to lay down.)

There is something terribly down-to earth about this. They are my own requests I am supposed to "make known" to God. They are things I feel strongly about. They may be sinful. If they are, making them known to God might make plain to me their true nature. But I start by making them known. I pray for what I want, as a child asks its father for whatever it wants. This is faith's legitimate activity.

Sometimes a father's answer to his child is no. If God, like a father, denies us what we want now, it is in order to give us some far better thing later on. The will of God, we can rest assured, is invariably a better thing, but our having asked for what we wanted now provides the occasion for us to say, "Nevertheless, not my will but thine be done."

—*Elisabeth Elliot*

Jesus Arrested

⁴⁷While he was still speaking a crowd came up, and the man who was called Judas, one of the Twelve, was leading them. He approached Jesus to kiss him, ⁴⁸but Jesus asked him, "Judas, are you betraying the Son of Man with a kiss?"

⁴⁹When Jesus' followers saw what was going to happen, they said, "Lord, should we strike with our swords?" ⁵⁰And one of them struck the servant of the high priest, cutting off his right ear.

⁵¹But Jesus answered, "No more of this!" And he touched the man's ear and healed him.

⁵²Then Jesus said to the chief priests, the officers of the temple guard, and the elders, who had come for him, "Am I leading a rebellion, that you have come with swords and clubs? ⁵³Every day I was with you in the temple courts, and you did not lay a hand on me. But this is your hour—when darkness reigns."

Peter Disowns Jesus

⁵⁴Then seizing him, they led him away and took him into the house of the high priest. Peter followed at a distance. ⁵⁵But when they had kindled a fire in the middle of the courtyard and had sat down together, Peter sat down with them. ⁵⁶A servant girl saw him seated there in the firelight. She looked closely at him and said, "This man was with him."

⁵⁷But he denied it. "Woman, I don't know him," he said.

⁵⁸A little later someone else saw him and said, "You also are one of them."

"Man, I am not!" Peter replied.

⁵⁹About an hour later another asserted, "Certainly this fellow was with him, for he is a Galilean."

⁶⁰Peter replied, "Man, I don't know what you're talking about!" Just as he was speaking, the rooster crowed. ⁶¹The Lord turned and looked straight at Peter. Then Peter remembered the word the Lord had spoken to him: "Before the rooster crows today, you will disown me three times." ⁶²And he went outside and wept bitterly.

The Guards Mock Jesus

⁶³The men who were guarding Jesus began mocking and beating him. ⁶⁴They blindfolded him and demanded, "Prophesy! Who hit you?" ⁶⁵And they said many other insulting things to him.

Jesus Before Pilate and Herod

⁶⁶At daybreak the council of the elders of the people, both the chief priests and teachers of the law, met together, and Jesus was led before them. ⁶⁷"If you are the Christ,ᵃ" they said, "tell us."

Jesus answered, "If I tell you, you will not believe me, ⁶⁸and if I asked you, you would not answer. ⁶⁹But from now on, the Son of Man will be seated at the right hand of the mighty God."

⁷⁰They all asked, "Are you then the Son of God?"

He replied, "You are right in saying I am."

⁷¹Then they said, "Why do we need any more testimony? We have heard it from his own lips."

23 Then the whole assembly rose and led him off to Pilate. ²And they began to accuse him, saying, "We have found this man subverting our nation. He opposes payment of taxes to Caesar and claims to be Christ,ᵇ a king."

³So Pilate asked Jesus, "Are you the king of the Jews?"

"Yes, it is as you say," Jesus replied.

⁴Then Pilate announced to the chief priests and the crowd, "I find no basis for a charge against this man."

⁵But they insisted, "He stirs up the people all over Judeaᶜ by his teaching. He started in Galilee and has come all the way here."

⁶On hearing this, Pilate asked if the man was a Galilean. ⁷When he learned that Jesus was under Herod's jurisdiction, he sent him to Herod, who was also in Jerusalem at that time.

⁸When Herod saw Jesus, he was greatly pleased, because for a long time he had been wanting to see him. From what he had heard about him, he hoped to see him perform some miracle. ⁹He plied him with many questions, but Jesus gave him no answer. ¹⁰The chief priests and the teachers of the law were standing there, vehemently accusing him. ¹¹Then Herod and his soldiers ridiculed and mocked

---

ᵃ67 Or *Messiah*   ᵇ2 Or *Messiah*; also in verses 35 and 39   ᶜ5 Or *over the land of the Jews* him. Dressing him in an elegant robe, they sent him back to Pilate. ¹²That day Herod and Pilate became friends—before this they had been enemies.

¹³Pilate called together the chief priests, the rulers and the people, ¹⁴and said to them, "You brought me this man as one who was inciting the people to rebellion. I have examined him in your presence and have found no basis for your charges against him. ¹⁵Neither has Herod, for he sent him back to us; as you can see, he has done nothing to deserve death. ¹⁶Therefore, I will punish him and then release him.ᵃ"

¹⁸With one voice they cried out, "Away with this man! Release Barabbas to us!" ¹⁹(Barabbas had been thrown into prison for an insurrection in the city, and for murder.)

²⁰Wanting to release Jesus, Pilate appealed to them again. ²¹But they kept shouting, "Crucify him! Crucify him!"

²²For the third time he spoke to them: "Why? What crime has this man committed? I have found in him no grounds for the death penalty. Therefore I will have him punished and then release him."

²³But with loud shouts they insistently demanded that he be crucified, and their shouts prevailed. ²⁴So Pilate decided to grant their demand. ²⁵He released the man who had been thrown into prison for insurrection and murder, the one they asked for, and surrendered Jesus to their will.

The Crucifixion

²⁶As they led him away, they seized Simon from Cyrene, who was on his way in from the country, and put the cross on him and made him carry it behind Jesus. ²⁷A large number of people followed him, including women who mourned and wailed for him. ²⁸Jesus turned and said to them, "Daughters of Jerusalem, do not weep for me; weep for yourselves and for your children. ²⁹For the time will come when you will say, 'Blessed are the barren women, the wombs that never bore and the breasts that never nursed!' ³⁰Then

"'they will say to the mountains, "Fall on us!"
and to the hills, "Cover us!"'ᵇ

³¹For if men do these things when the tree is green, what will happen when it is dry?"

³²Two other men, both criminals, were also led out with him to be executed. ³³When they came to the place called the Skull, there they crucified him, along with the criminals—one on his right, the other on his left. ³⁴Jesus said, "Father, forgive them, for they do not know what they are doing."ᶜ And they divided up his clothes by casting lots.

³⁵The people stood watching, and the rulers even sneered at him. They said, "He saved others; let him save himself if he is the Christ of God, the Chosen One."

³⁶The soldiers also came up and mocked him. They offered him wine vinegar ³⁷and said, "If you are the king of the Jews, save yourself."

³⁸There was a written notice above him, which read: THIS IS THE KING OF THE JEWS.

³⁹One of the criminals who hung there hurled insults at him: "Aren't you the Christ? Save yourself and us!"

⁴⁰But the other criminal rebuked him. "Don't you fear God," he said, "since you are under the same sentence? ⁴¹We are punished justly, for we are getting what our deeds deserve. But this man has done nothing wrong."

⁴²Then he said, "Jesus, remember me when you come into your kingdom.ᵈ"

⁴³Jesus answered him, "I tell you the truth, today you will be with me in paradise."

Jesus' Death

⁴⁴It was now about the sixth hour, and darkness came over the whole land until the ninth hour, ⁴⁵for the sun stopped shining. And the curtain of the temple was torn in two. ⁴⁶Jesus called out with a loud voice, "Father, into your

Luke 23:43

God Grants Salvation

Jesus answered him, "I tell you the truth, today you will be with me in paradise."

ᵃ16 Some manuscripts *him."* ¹⁷Now he was obliged to release one man to them at the Feast. ᵇ30 Hosea 10:8 ᶜ34 Some early manuscripts do not have this sentence. ᵈ42 Some manuscripts *come with your kingly power*

Nightmare

PILATE'S WIFE

SHE AWOKE WITH A START. Beads of sweat ran down the middle of her back. Her face was flushed, her breathing ragged and quick.

It took a few moments to reorient herself to her bedroom. Where was she? How long had she been sleeping?

She'd had the most terrifying nightmare. Even now, fully awake, the events seemed so real—she could recall every detail.

"Jesus . . ." she whispered to herself as she mindlessly smoothed the bed linens with her palms. Her dream had been about the man they called Jesus. He was a prisoner—brought before her husband, Pilate. But why? What crime had he committed?

Something about him in her dream led her to believe he was innocent. Completely innocent. She didn't know exactly how to explain it. She wasn't a Jew, and she couldn't begin to understand why these religious leaders had worked themselves into a frenzy over this man, but she knew without a doubt that they were dead wrong.

If only they could be more like the Romans . . . civilized, orderly, she thought to herself. Nevertheless, she was convinced. Her husband could be responsible for convicting an innocent man—to death!

Her stomach began to knot just thinking about it. Waves of nausea swept over her as she struggled out of bed. She knew what she had to do. She'd heard the commotion of the gathering crowd.

"It must be nearly time," she mumbled. She recalled her husband's annual duty to release one of the prisoners for Passover. "I have to hurry before it's too late . . ."

She called out for one of her aides. "Quick! Get a message to my husband immediately. He must not go ahead with the execution of that man. I don't care what you tell him, just tell him not to go through with it. He's innocent!"

The messenger left her chambers, and she collapsed back on the bed. Her mind raced with adrenaline, and her stomach ached as she wondered if the message would get to him in time.

—Prayer—
Lord God, help me to have a pure heart and to do what I know is right.

> While Pilate was sitting on the judge's seat, his wife sent him this message: "Don't have anything to do with that innocent man, for I have suffered a great deal today in a dream because of him."
>
> Matthew 27:19

ASSIGNED READING:
Matthew 27:11–26

Weekend

Go to page 1284 for your next devotional reading.

hands I commit my spirit." When he had said this, he breathed his last.

47 The centurion, seeing what had happened, praised God and said, "Surely this was a righteous man." 48 When all the people who had gathered to witness this sight saw what took place, they beat their breasts and went away. 49 But all those who knew him, including the women who had followed him from Galilee, stood at a distance, watching these things.

Jesus' Burial

50 Now there was a man named Joseph, a member of the Council, a good and upright man, 51 who had not consented to their decision and action. He came from the Judean town of Arimathea and he was waiting for the kingdom of God. 52 Going to Pilate, he asked for Jesus' body. 53 Then he took it down, wrapped it in linen cloth and placed it in a tomb cut in the rock, one in which no one had yet been laid. 54 It was Preparation Day, and the Sabbath was about to begin.

55 The women who had come with Jesus from Galilee followed Joseph and saw the tomb and how his body was laid in it. 56 Then they went home and prepared spices and perfumes. But they rested on the Sabbath in obedience to the commandment.

The Resurrection

24 On the first day of the week, very early in the morning, the women took the spices they had prepared and went to the tomb. 2 They found the stone rolled away from the tomb, 3 but when they entered, they did not find the body of the Lord Jesus. 4 While they were wondering about this, suddenly two men in clothes that gleamed like lightning stood beside them. 5 In their fright the women bowed down with their faces to the ground, but the men said to them, "Why do you look for the living among the dead? 6 He is not here; he has risen! Remember how he told you, while he was still with you in Galilee: 7 'The Son of Man must be delivered into the hands of sinful men, be crucified and on the third day be raised again.'" 8 Then they remembered his words.

9 When they came back from the tomb, they told all these things to the Eleven and to all the others. 10 It was Mary Magdalene, Joanna, Mary the mother of James, and the others with them who told this to the apostles. 11 But they did not believe the women, because their words seemed to them like nonsense. 12 Peter, however, got up and ran to the tomb. Bending over, he saw the strips of linen lying by themselves, and he went away, wondering to himself what had happened.

On the Road to Emmaus

13 Now that same day two of them were going to a village called Emmaus, about seven miles[a] from Jerusalem. 14 They were talking with each other about everything that had happened. 15 As they talked and discussed these things with each other, Jesus himself came up and walked along with them; 16 but they were kept from recognizing him.

17 He asked them, "What are you discussing together as you walk along?"

They stood still, their faces downcast. 18 One of them, named Cleopas, asked him, "Are you only a visitor to Jerusalem and do not know the things that have happened there in these days?"

19 "What things?" he asked.

"About Jesus of Nazareth," they replied. "He was a prophet, powerful in word and deed before God and all the people. 20 The chief priests and our rulers handed him over to be sentenced to death, and they crucified him; 21 but we had hoped that he was the one who was going to redeem Israel. And what is more, it is the third day since all this took place. 22 In addition, some of our women amazed us. They went to the tomb early this morning 23 but didn't find his body. They came and told us that they had seen a vision of angels, who said he was alive. 24 Then some of our companions went to the tomb and found it just as the women had said, but him they did not see."

25 He said to them, "How foolish you are, and how slow of heart to believe all that the prophets have spoken! 26 Did not the Christ[b] have to suffer these things and then enter his glory?" 27 And beginning with Moses and all the Prophets, he explained to them what was said in all the Scriptures concerning himself.

a 13 Greek *sixty stadia* (about 11 kilometers)   b 26 Or *Messiah*; also in verse 46

²⁸As they approached the village to which they were going, Jesus acted as if he were going farther. ²⁹But they urged him strongly, "Stay with us, for it is nearly evening; the day is almost over." So he went in to stay with them.

³⁰When he was at the table with them, he took bread, gave thanks, broke it and began to give it to them. ³¹Then their eyes were opened and they recognized him, and he disappeared from their sight. ³²They asked each other, "Were not our hearts burning within us while he talked with us on the road and opened the Scriptures to us?"

³³They got up and returned at once to Jerusalem. There they found the Eleven and those with them, assembled together ³⁴and saying, "It is true! The Lord has risen and has appeared to Simon." ³⁵Then the two told what had happened on the way, and how Jesus was recognized by them when he broke the bread.

Jesus Appears to the Disciples

³⁶While they were still talking about this, Jesus himself stood among them and said to them, "Peace be with you."

³⁷They were startled and frightened, thinking they saw a ghost. ³⁸He said to them, "Why are you troubled, and why do doubts rise in your minds? ³⁹Look at my hands and my feet. It is I myself! Touch me and see; a ghost does not have flesh and bones, as you see I have."

⁴⁰When he had said this, he showed them his hands and feet. ⁴¹And while they still did not believe it because of joy and amazement, he asked them, "Do you have anything here to eat?" ⁴²They gave him a piece of broiled fish, ⁴³and he took it and ate it in their presence.

⁴⁴He said to them, "This is what I told you while I was still with you: Everything must be fulfilled that is written about me in the Law of Moses, the Prophets and the Psalms."

⁴⁵Then he opened their minds so they could understand the Scriptures. ⁴⁶He told them, "This is what is written: The Christ will suffer and rise from the dead on the third day, ⁴⁷and repentance and forgiveness of sins will be preached in his name to all nations, beginning at Jerusalem. ⁴⁸You are witnesses of these things. ⁴⁹I am going to send you what my Father has promised; but stay in the city until you have been clothed with power from on high."

The Ascension

⁵⁰When he had led them out to the vicinity of Bethany, he lifted up his hands and blessed them. ⁵¹While he was blessing them, he left them and was taken up into heaven. ⁵²Then they worshiped him and returned to Jerusalem with great joy. ⁵³And they stayed continually at the temple, praising God.

John

Author:
The apostle John.

Audience:
Followers of Jesus.
John wrote to con-
vince unbelievers
and the doubting.

Date:
About A.D. 85–90,
before John's exile
to the island
of Patmos.

Setting:
John's eyewitness
account is presum-
ably the last Gospel
written.

Verse to Remember:
Jesus answered,
"I am the way and
the truth and the
life. No one comes
to the Father
except through
me." (14:6)

John's Gospel stands apart from the other three, shedding new light on what has by now become a familiar story. There are fewer parables, fewer instances of Jesus' public speaking and fewer miracles, but there are more conversations, more personal encounters and more interactions among the disciples. It is John who records *Jesus' seven "I am" statements* that give us tangible descriptions of who this Son of God is.

Nearly half of John's Gospel is devoted to the final week of Jesus' life. John is the only disciple who followed Jesus all the way to the cross, and as we look through his eyes, we feel his shock and deep grief, but we also experience something else—something that so overwhelmed John he incorporated it into how he described himself even years later when he wrote his Gospel. *We experience love.*

John always referred to himself as "the disciple whom Jesus loved," as though the concept still left him slack-jawed with awe. As we follow John's footsteps, listening to Jesus, witnessing his death and rejoicing at his resurrection, we experience that awe for ourselves. For we realize that we, too, are *the disciples whom Jesus loves.*

The Word Became Flesh

1 In the beginning was the Word, and the Word was with God, and the Word was God. **2** He was with God in the beginning. **3** Through him all things were made; without him nothing was made that has been made. **4** In him was life, and that life was the light of men. **5** The light shines in the darkness, but the darkness has not understood[a] it.

6 There came a man who was sent from God;

a5 Or darkness, and the darkness has not overcome

his name was John. **7**He came as a witness to testify concerning that light, so that through him all men might believe. **8**He himself was not the light; he came only as a witness to the light. **9**The true light that gives light to every man was coming into the world.*a*

10He was in the world, and though the world was made through him, the world did not recognize him. **11**He came to that which was his own, but his own did not receive him. **12**Yet to all who received him, to those who believed in his name, he gave the right to become children of God— **13**children born not of natural descent,*b* nor of human decision or a husband's will, but born of God.

14The Word became flesh and made his dwelling among us. We have seen his glory, the glory of the One and Only,*c* who came from the Father, full of grace and truth.

15John testifies concerning him. He cries out, saying, "This was he of whom I said, 'He who comes after me has surpassed me because he was before me.'" **16**From the fullness of his grace we have all received one blessing after another. **17**For the law was given through Moses; grace and truth came through Jesus Christ. **18**No one has ever seen God, but God the One and Only,*c,d* who is at the Father's side, has made him known.

John the Baptist Denies Being the Christ

19Now this was John's testimony when the Jews of Jerusalem sent priests and Levites to ask him who he was. **20**He did not fail to confess, but confessed freely, "I am not the Christ.*e*"

21They asked him, "Then who are you? Are you Elijah?"

He said, "I am not."

"Are you the Prophet?"

He answered, "No."

22Finally they said, "Who are you? Give us an answer to take back to those who sent us. What do you say about yourself?"

23John replied in the words of Isaiah the prophet, "I am the voice of one calling in the desert, 'Make straight the way for the Lord.'"*f*

24Now some Pharisees who had been sent **25**questioned him, "Why then do you baptize if you are not the Christ, nor Elijah, nor the Prophet?"

26"I baptize with*g* water," John replied, "but among you stands one you do not know. **27**He is the one who comes after me, the thongs of whose sandals I am not worthy to untie."

28This all happened at Bethany on the other side of the Jordan, where John was baptizing.

Jesus the Lamb of God

29The next day John saw Jesus coming toward him and said, "Look, the Lamb of God, who takes away the sin of the world! **30**This is the one I meant when I said, 'A man who comes after me has surpassed me because he was before me.' **31**I myself did not know him, but the reason I came baptizing with water was that he might be revealed to Israel."

32Then John gave this testimony: "I saw the Spirit come down from heaven as a dove and remain on him. **33**I would not have known him, except that the one who sent me to baptize with water told me, 'The man on whom you see the Spirit come down and remain is he who will baptize with the Holy Spirit.' **34**I have seen and I testify that this is the Son of God."

Jesus' First Disciples

35The next day John was there again with two of his disciples. **36**When he saw Jesus passing by, he said, "Look, the Lamb of God!"

37When the two disciples heard him say this, they followed Jesus. **38**Turning around, Jesus saw them following and asked, "What do you want?"

They said, "Rabbi" (which means Teacher), "where are you staying?"

John 1:14

God Reveals Himself

The Word became flesh and made his dwelling among us. We have seen his glory, the glory of the One and Only, who came from the Father, full of grace and truth.

---

*a*9 Or *This was the true light that gives light to every man who comes into the world*   *b*13 Greek *of bloods*   *c*14,18 Or *the Only Begotten*
*d*18 Some manuscripts *but the only* (or *only begotten*) *Son*   *e*20 Or *Messiah.* "The Christ" (Greek) and "the Messiah" (Hebrew) both mean "the Anointed One"; also in verse 25.   *f*23 Isaiah 40:3   *g*26 Or *in*; also in verses 31 and 33

John 1:7–9

[John] came as a witness to testify concerning that light, so that through him all men might believe. He himself was not the light; he came only as a witness to the light. The true light that gives light to every man was coming into the world.

reflection

1 What are your favorite types of light (lamps, candles, firelight, sunshine)? List them.

2 What positive feeling do you derive from each light source you listed?

3 How can you emit a Christlike light in your home or workplace?

RELATED READINGS

Matthew 5:14–16; John 3:16–21; 8:12

GURNET POINT LIGHT in Plymouth, Massachusetts, is distinct from any other lighthouse in the United States: It is associated with Hannah Thomas, the first female lighthouse keeper in America. When Hannah's husband went off to fight in the War for Independence, Hannah remained behind to keep the great lamp burning to guide ships out at sea.

In spiritual terms, women have been keepers of the light for centuries: Agnes of Rome was martyred for refusing to sacrifice to pagan gods. Glady Aylward was a missionary to China who shared the gospel in villages and prisons and among lepers. Rose Lathrop, daughter of Nathaniel Hawthorne, established homes in the late 1800s for young women suffering from cancer. Like John the Baptist, these women directed and guided others toward the true light that came into the world: Jesus.

Have you ever watched the sun reflecting off prisms hanging from a crystal chandelier? The prisms themselves are not the light; they merely reflect the light produced by the chandelier. Yet they are capable of throwing hundreds of sparkling rainbows throughout a room. In his book *Desiring God*, John Piper wrote, "We were made to be prisms refracting the light of God's glory into all of life. Why God should want to give us a share in shining with his glory—*shekinah*—is a great mystery. Call it grace or mercy or love—it is an unspeakable wonder!"

To reflect the light of God's presence in a dark and damaged world, we have to stay close to the source: the Son. The more we let his light shine into our eyes and reflect into the eyes of others, the more we become like him. "And we, who with unveiled faces all reflect the Lord's glory, are being transformed into his likeness with ever-increasing glory, which comes from the Lord, who is the Spirit" (2 Corinthians 3:18).

Let's be keepers of God's light—ensuring that the light of his love burns brightly. We can also reflect that light into the lives of others. It only takes a small beacon of light to dispel the darkness.

Monday

Go to page 1286 for your next devotional reading.

39"Come," he replied, "and you will see."

So they went and saw where he was staying, and spent that day with him. It was about the tenth hour.

40Andrew, Simon Peter's brother, was one of the two who heard what John had said and who had followed Jesus. 41The first thing Andrew did was to find his brother Simon and tell him, "We have found the Messiah" (that is, the Christ). 42And he brought him to Jesus.

Jesus looked at him and said, "You are Simon son of John. You will be called Cephas" (which, when translated, is Peter[a]).

Jesus Calls Philip and Nathanael

43The next day Jesus decided to leave for Galilee. Finding Philip, he said to him, "Follow me."

44Philip, like Andrew and Peter, was from the town of Bethsaida. 45Philip found Nathanael and told him, "We have found the one Moses wrote about in the Law, and about whom the prophets also wrote—Jesus of Nazareth, the son of Joseph."

46"Nazareth! Can anything good come from there?" Nathanael asked.

"Come and see," said Philip.

47When Jesus saw Nathanael approaching, he said of him, "Here is a true Israelite, in whom there is nothing false."

48"How do you know me?" Nathanael asked.

Jesus answered, "I saw you while you were still under the fig tree before Philip called you."

49Then Nathanael declared, "Rabbi, you are the Son of God; you are the King of Israel."

50Jesus said, "You believe[b] because I told you I saw you under the fig tree. You shall see greater things than that." 51He then added, "I tell you[c] the truth, you[c] shall see heaven open, and the angels of God ascending and descending on the Son of Man."

Jesus Changes Water to Wine

2 On the third day a wedding took place at Cana in Galilee. Jesus' mother was there, 2and Jesus and his disciples had also been invited to the wedding. 3When the wine was gone, Jesus' mother said to him, "They have no more wine."

4"Dear woman, why do you involve me?" Jesus replied. "My time has not yet come."

5His mother said to the servants, "Do whatever he tells you."

6Nearby stood six stone water jars, the kind used by the Jews for ceremonial washing, each holding from twenty to thirty gallons.[d]

7Jesus said to the servants, "Fill the jars with water"; so they filled them to the brim.

8Then he told them, "Now draw some out and take it to the master of the banquet."

They did so, 9and the master of the banquet tasted the water that had been turned into wine. He did not realize where it had come from, though the servants who had drawn the water knew. Then he called the bridegroom aside 10and said, "Everyone brings out the choice wine first and then the cheaper wine after the guests have had too much to drink; but you have saved the best till now."

11This, the first of his miraculous signs, Jesus performed at Cana in Galilee. He thus revealed his glory, and his disciples put their faith in him.

Jesus Clears the Temple

12After this he went down to Capernaum with his mother and brothers and his disciples. There they stayed for a few days.

13When it was almost time for the Jewish Passover, Jesus went up to Jerusalem. 14In the temple courts he found men selling cattle, sheep and doves, and others sitting at tables exchanging money. 15So he made a whip out of cords, and drove all from the temple area, both sheep and cattle; he scattered the coins of the money changers and overturned their tables. 16To those who sold doves he said, "Get these out of here! How dare you turn my Father's house into a market!"

17His disciples remembered that it is written: "Zeal for your house will consume me."[e]

18Then the Jews demanded of him, "What miraculous sign can you show us to prove your authority to do all this?"

19Jesus answered them, "Destroy this temple, and I will raise it again in three days."

20The Jews replied, "It has taken forty-six years to build this temple, and you are going to

---

[a]42 Both *Cephas* (Aramaic) and *Peter* (Greek) mean *rock*.   [b]50 Or *Do you believe...?*   [c]51 The Greek is plural.   [d]6 Greek *two to three metretes* (probably about 75 to 115 liters)   [e]17 Psalm 69:9

The Wedding Guest

John 2:9

The master of the banquet tasted the water that had been turned into wine. He did not realize where it had come from, though the servants who had drawn the water knew.

reflection

1 How has Jesus changed difficult circumstances for you in the past?

2 What would you exchange right now if you could—gladness for mourning, praise for despair, beauty for ashes? Invite Jesus to work a divine exchange for you as only he can.

3 Who will you share the knowledge of the joy of the Lord with today?

RELATED READINGS

Isaiah 61:1–3;
65:17–25;
Revelation 21:5

Read: John 2:1–11

YEARS AGO WHEN JOHNNY CARSON was the host of *The Tonight Show*, he interviewed an eight-year-old boy. The young man was asked to appear because he had rescued two friends from a coal mine outside his hometown in West Virginia. As Johnny questioned the boy, it became apparent to him and the audience that the young man was a Christian. So Johnny asked him if he attended Sunday school. When the boy said he did, Johnny asked, "What are you learning in Sunday school?" "Last week our lesson was about when Jesus went to a wedding and turned water into wine." The audience roared, but Johnny tried to keep a straight face. Then he said, "And what did you learn from that story?" The boy squirmed in his chair. It was apparent he hadn't thought about this. But then he lifted up his face and said, "If you're going to have a wedding, make sure you invite Jesus!"

Jesus' first miracle occurred at a wedding he'd been invited to. It clearly announced his nature, showing that he came to bring joy to his people. God delights in his children. Our joy pleases him. When we celebrate, he celebrates with us.

The hosts of the wedding celebration would have been embarrassed if the wine had run dry. Knowing this, Jesus' mother turned to the One who can turn sorrow into gladness. Jesus quietly worked behind the scenes to turn the water into wine. When the banquet master tasted the wine, he was surprised that it was better than what had been served at first.

When we invite Jesus into every aspect of our lives, he can exchange our past pain for present comfort and turn our deep sorrow into divine delight. He can take old wounds and turn them into fresh wisdom. He can turn stale, old thoughts into new ideas and creative ways to solve our problems. He can take a cold silence and turn it once again into a warm conversation. If we just ask, he can take those things that we are ashamed of and cast them into a sea of forgetfulness, allowing us to experience true and deep joy. He does not save the best for *last*, he saves the best for *now*.

Those who drew the water knew the secret: Jesus has the power to change things. Just imagine what he can change if you only issue the invitation. He's the guest who can never stay too long.

Tuesday

raise it in three days?" [21]But the temple he had spoken of was his body. [22]After he was raised from the dead, his disciples recalled what he had said. Then they believed the Scripture and the words that Jesus had spoken.

[23]Now while he was in Jerusalem at the Passover Feast, many people saw the miraculous signs he was doing and believed in his name.[a] [24]But Jesus would not entrust himself to them, for he knew all men. [25]He did not need man's testimony about man, for he knew what was in a man.

Jesus Teaches Nicodemus

3 Now there was a man of the Pharisees named Nicodemus, a member of the Jewish ruling council. [2]He came to Jesus at night and said, "Rabbi, we know you are a teacher who has come from God. For no one could perform the miraculous signs you are doing if God were not with him."

[3]In reply Jesus declared, "I tell you the truth, no one can see the kingdom of God unless he is born again.[b]"

[4]"How can a man be born when he is old?" Nicodemus asked. "Surely he cannot enter a second time into his mother's womb to be born!"

[5]Jesus answered, "I tell you the truth, no one can enter the kingdom of God unless he is born of water and the Spirit. [6]Flesh gives birth to flesh, but the Spirit[c] gives birth to spirit. [7]You should not be surprised at my saying, 'You[d] must be born again.' [8]The wind blows wherever it pleases. You hear its sound, but you cannot tell where it comes from or where it is going. So it is with everyone born of the Spirit."

[9]"How can this be?" Nicodemus asked.

[10]"You are Israel's teacher," said Jesus, "and do you not understand these things? [11]I tell you the truth, we speak of what we know, and we testify to what we have seen, but still you people do not accept our testimony. [12]I have

spoken to you of earthly things and you do not believe; how then will you believe if I speak of heavenly things? [13]No one has ever gone into heaven except the one who came from heaven—the Son of Man.[e] [14]Just as Moses lifted up the snake in the desert, so the Son of Man must be lifted up, [15]that everyone who believes in him may have eternal life.[f]

[16]"For God so loved the world that he gave his one and only Son,[g] that whoever believes in him shall not perish but have eternal life. [17]For God did not send his Son into the world to condemn the world, but to save the world through him. [18]Whoever believes in him is not condemned, but whoever does not believe stands condemned already because he has not believed in the name of God's one and only Son.[h] [19]This is the verdict: Light has come into the world, but men loved darkness instead of light because their deeds were evil. [20]Everyone who does evil hates the light, and will not come into the light for fear that his deeds will be exposed. [21]But whoever lives by the truth comes into the light, so that it may be seen plainly that what he has done has been done through God."[i]

John the Baptist's Testimony About Jesus

[22]After this, Jesus and his disciples went out into the Judean countryside, where he spent some time with them, and baptized. [23]Now John also was baptizing at Aenon near Salim, because there was plenty of water, and people were constantly coming to be baptized. [24](This was before John was put in prison.) [25]An argument developed between some of John's disciples and a certain Jew[j] over the matter of ceremonial washing. [26]They came to John and said to him, "Rabbi, that man who was with you on the other side of the Jordan—the one you testified about—well, he is baptizing, and everyone is going to him."

John 3:15–16

God Offers Eternal Life

"Everyone who believes in him may have eternal life. For God so loved the world that he gave his one and only Son, that whoever believes in him shall not perish but have eternal life."

---

[a]23 Or *and believed in him*   [b]3 Or *born from above; also in verse 7*   [c]6 Or *but spirit*   [d]7 The Greek is plural.   [e]13 Some manuscripts *Man, who is in heaven*   [f]15 Or *believes may have eternal life in him*   [g]16 Or *his only begotten Son*   [h]18 Or *God's only begotten Son*   [i]21 Some interpreters end the quotation after verse 15.   [j]25 Some manuscripts *and certain Jews*

No Condemnation

John 3:17

"For God did not send his Son into the world to condemn the world, but to save the world through him."

reflection

1 How have you experienced self-condemnation?

2 Reread the words and personalize them by filling in your name: "God did not send his Son into the world to condemn _____, but to save _____ through him."

3 How often do you feel judged by others throughout your day? Remember whose opinion really counts. Ask God to show you who you are in the light of his love.

RELATED READINGS

John 5:24;
Romans 8:1–4;
1 John 3:19–24

Read John 3:1–21

WE OFTEN GO THROUGH THE DAY feeling as if someone is looking over our shoulder ready to judge our actions. *My husband probably wonders why dinner isn't made yet . . . My boss is thinking I'm taking too long with that project . . . Amber's teacher doesn't understand why we were late this morning . . . This isn't how Mom would have done it . . .* And perhaps the voice we hear the most is our own: *Why aren't you good enough?*

Even if others praise us, the pressure we put on ourselves can drown out the latest acclaim. We put pressure on ourselves to do more—and do it better and quicker. *How could God be pleased with us,* we wonder, *when we feel so weak?*

Listen to the words in this chapter of John's Gospel. God wants a relationship with us—not to condemn us, but to free us. He offers redemption through Jesus—not because we have *done* something to deserve it, but because he loves us.

Though we may read those words again and again, they can be hard to believe. But try to wrap your brain around this truth: God does not condemn you. None of the pressure you feel throughout the day is from God. In truth, you may be trying to please others or achieve your own goals more than you are trying to please God. You may feel guilty because you keep changing the standard.

Richard Foster writes, "The less we are manipulated by the expectations of others, the more we are open to the expectations of God." Yes, we are weak. Yes, we often fail to meet our own expectations. But what does God expect of us today? To believe in his Son who set us free from sin. To believe that he is stronger than our doubts, fears, pride and ambition. To believe that he does not condemn us for who we were before we met his Son. To discover who we are in the light of his love, freedom and grace.

27To this John replied, "A man can receive only what is given him from heaven. 28You yourselves can testify that I said, 'I am not the Christ[a] but am sent ahead of him.' 29The bride belongs to the bridegroom. The friend who attends the bridegroom waits and listens for him, and is full of joy when he hears the bridegroom's voice. That joy is mine, and it is now complete. 30He must become greater; I must become less.

31"The one who comes from above is above all; the one who is from the earth belongs to the earth, and speaks as one from the earth. The one who comes from heaven is above all. 32He testifies to what he has seen and heard, but no one accepts his testimony. 33The man who has accepted it has certified that God is truthful. 34For the one whom God has sent speaks the words of God, for God[b] gives the Spirit without limit. 35The Father loves the Son and has placed everything in his hands. 36Whoever believes in the Son has eternal life, but whoever rejects the Son will not see life, for God's wrath remains on him."[c]

Jesus Talks With a Samaritan Woman

4 The Pharisees heard that Jesus was gaining and baptizing more disciples than John, 2although in fact it was not Jesus who baptized, but his disciples. 3When the Lord learned of this, he left Judea and went back once more to Galilee.

4Now he had to go through Samaria. 5So he came to a town in Samaria called Sychar, near the plot of ground Jacob had given to his son Joseph. 6Jacob's well was there, and Jesus, tired as he was from the journey, sat down by the well. It was about the sixth hour.

7When a Samaritan woman came to draw water, Jesus said to her, "Will you give me a drink?" 8(His disciples had gone into the town to buy food.)

9The Samaritan woman said to him, "You are a Jew and I am a Samaritan woman. How can you ask me for a drink?" (For Jews do not associate with Samaritans.[d])

10Jesus answered her, "If you knew the gift of God and who it is that asks you for a drink, you would have asked him and he would have given you living water."

11"Sir," the woman said, "you have nothing to draw with and the well is deep. Where can you get this living water? 12Are you greater than our father Jacob, who gave us the well and drank from it himself, as did also his sons and his flocks and herds?"

13Jesus answered, "Everyone who drinks this water will be thirsty again, 14but whoever drinks the water I give him will never thirst. Indeed, the water I give him will become in him a spring of water welling up to eternal life."

15The woman said to him, "Sir, give me this water so that I won't get thirsty and have to keep coming here to draw water."

16He told her, "Go, call your husband and come back."

17"I have no husband," she replied.

Jesus said to her, "You are right when you say you have no husband. 18The fact is, you have had five husbands, and the man you now have is not your husband. What you have just said is quite true."

19"Sir," the woman said, "I can see that you are a prophet. 20Our fathers worshiped on this mountain, but you Jews claim that the place where we must worship is in Jerusalem."

21Jesus declared, "Believe me, woman, a time is coming when you will worship the Father neither on this mountain nor in Jerusalem. 22You Samaritans worship what you do not know; we worship what we do know, for salvation is from the Jews. 23Yet a time is coming and has now come when the true worshipers will worship the Father in spirit and truth, for they are the kind of worshipers the Father seeks. 24God is spirit, and his worshipers must worship in spirit and in truth."

25The woman said, "I know that Messiah" (called Christ) "is coming. When he comes, he will explain everything to us."

26Then Jesus declared, "I who speak to you am he."

The Disciples Rejoin Jesus

27Just then his disciples returned and were surprised to find him talking with a woman. But no one asked, "What do you want?" or "Why are you talking with her?"

28Then, leaving her water jar, the woman went back to the town and said to the people,

---

*a*28 Or *Messiah*   *b*34 Greek *he*   *c*36 Some interpreters end the quotation after verse 30.   *d*9 Or *do not use dishes Samaritans have used*

29"Come, see a man who told me everything I ever did. Could this be the Christ^a?" 30They came out of the town and made their way toward him.

31Meanwhile his disciples urged him, "Rabbi, eat something."

32But he said to them, "I have food to eat that you know nothing about."

33Then his disciples said to each other, "Could someone have brought him food?"

34"My food," said Jesus, "is to do the will of him who sent me and to finish his work. 35Do you not say, 'Four months more and then the harvest'? I tell you, open your eyes and look at the fields! They are ripe for harvest. 36Even now the reaper draws his wages, even now he harvests the crop for eternal life, so that the sower and the reaper may be glad together. 37Thus the saying 'One sows and another reaps' is true. 38I sent you to reap what you have not worked for. Others have done the hard work, and you have reaped the benefits of their labor."

Many Samaritans Believe

39Many of the Samaritans from that town believed in him because of the woman's testimony, "He told me everything I ever did." 40So when the Samaritans came to him, they urged him to stay with them, and he stayed two days. 41And because of his words many more became believers.

42They said to the woman, "We no longer believe just because of what you said; now we have heard for ourselves, and we know that this man really is the Savior of the world."

Jesus Heals the Official's Son

43After the two days he left for Galilee. 44(Now Jesus himself had pointed out that a prophet has no honor in his own country.) 45When he arrived in Galilee, the Galileans welcomed him. They had seen all that he had done

in Jerusalem at the Passover Feast, for they also had been there.

46Once more he visited Cana in Galilee, where he had turned the water into wine. And there was a certain royal official whose son lay sick at Capernaum. 47When this man heard that Jesus had arrived in Galilee from Judea, he went to him and begged him to come and heal his son, who was close to death.

48"Unless you people see miraculous signs and wonders," Jesus told him, "you will never believe."

49The royal official said, "Sir, come down before my child dies."

50Jesus replied, "You may go. Your son will live."

The man took Jesus at his word and departed. 51While he was still on the way, his servants met him with the news that his boy was living. 52When he inquired as to the time when his son got better, they said to him, "The fever left him yesterday at the seventh hour."

53Then the father realized that this was the exact time at which Jesus had said to him, "Your son will live." So he and all his household believed.

54This was the second miraculous sign that Jesus performed, having come from Judea to Galilee.

The Healing at the Pool

5 Some time later, Jesus went up to Jerusalem for a feast of the Jews. 2Now there is in Jerusalem near the Sheep Gate a pool, which in Aramaic is called Bethesda^b and which is surrounded by five covered colonnades. 3Here a great number of disabled people used to lie—the blind, the lame, the paralyzed.^c 5One who was there had been an invalid for thirty-eight years. 6When Jesus saw him lying there and learned that he had been in this condition for a long time, he asked him, "Do you want to get well?"

> **John 4:42**
>
> *God Employs Women*
>
> They said to the woman, "We no longer believe just because of what you said; now we have heard for ourselves, and we know that this man really is the Savior of the world."

a29 Or Messiah b2 Some manuscripts Bethzatha; other manuscripts Bethsaida c3 Some less important manuscripts paralyzed—and they waited for the moving of the waters. 4From time to time an angel of the Lord would come down and stir up the waters. The first one into the pool after each such disturbance would be cured of whatever disease he had.

The Wellspring

Read: John 4:3–30

MOVING WATER HAS A FASCINATION of its own. Creeks gurgle, waterfalls plummet, springs bubble, ocean tides crash. The bubbles, foam and noise draw us. The water sustains us. We need water for our physical life, but it also somehow soothes our spirit.

Desert animals travel many miles to find a water hole. City birds cluster in birdbaths or rain puddles. Grocery shoppers pay several dollars for plastic bottles of water. For thousands of years springs and wells provided the only access to clean water. City planners designed their locations around reliable water sources. Hauling water from long distances was hard, thirst-inducing work.

When Jesus compared life with him to a never-ending, thirst-quenching spring, the image resonated with a hardworking Samaritan woman. Water got her attention, for she was thirsty. Though she had come to the well to draw water, Jesus knew she needed more than physical water; she needed him. She had tried to find satisfaction drinking from the wells of the world, but no man had truly quenched her thirst. Then she met Jesus, who knew everything she ever did. This man became a wellspring of life-giving truth that overflowed to her community.

What are you really thirsty for? Do you long to know the meaning of your life? Are you longing for the kind of love that fills you up rather than drains you? Are you forever trying to find acceptance and respect? Or are those longings so deep and buried that you can't even say what you want or need? Perhaps you can't even get beyond just feeling . . . empty.

Only Jesus can identify those deep longings and fill your thirsty soul. Seek out the One who offers you living water. Come to him. He won't be surprised at how empty you are. He knows everything you ever did. He's the wellspring who will fill you to overflowing with his goodness and love.

John 4:14

"Whoever drinks the water I give him will never thirst. Indeed, the water I give him will become in him a spring of water welling up to eternal life."

reflection

1 Would you describe your relationship with Jesus as a life-giving stream or a parched desert?

2 When and where do you feel closest to Jesus?

3 How has Jesus satisfied your spiritual thirst?

RELATED READINGS

Psalm 42:1–11;
John 7:37–39;
Revelation 7:16–17

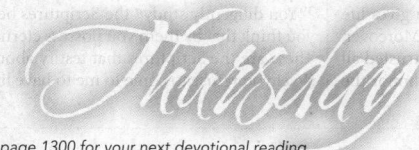

Go to page 1300 for your next devotional reading.

7"Sir," the invalid replied, "I have no one to help me into the pool when the water is stirred. While I am trying to get in, someone else goes down ahead of me."

8Then Jesus said to him, "Get up! Pick up your mat and walk." 9At once the man was cured; he picked up his mat and walked.

The day on which this took place was a Sabbath, 10and so the Jews said to the man who had been healed, "It is the Sabbath; the law forbids you to carry your mat."

11But he replied, "The man who made me well said to me, 'Pick up your mat and walk.'"

12So they asked him, "Who is this fellow who told you to pick it up and walk?"

13The man who was healed had no idea who it was, for Jesus had slipped away into the crowd that was there.

14Later Jesus found him at the temple and said to him, "See, you are well again. Stop sinning or something worse may happen to you." 15The man went away and told the Jews that it was Jesus who had made him well.

Life Through the Son

16So, because Jesus was doing these things on the Sabbath, the Jews persecuted him. 17Jesus said to them, "My Father is always at his work to this very day, and I, too, am working." 18For this reason the Jews tried all the harder to kill him; not only was he breaking the Sabbath, but he was even calling God his own Father, making himself equal with God.

19Jesus gave them this answer: "I tell you the truth, the Son can do nothing by himself; he can do only what he sees his Father doing, because whatever the Father does the Son also does. 20For the Father loves the Son and shows him all he does. Yes, to your amazement he will show him even greater things than these. 21For just as the Father raises the dead and gives them life, even so the Son gives life to whom he is pleased to give it. 22Moreover, the Father judges no one, but has entrusted all judgment to the Son, 23that all may honor the

Son just as they honor the Father. He who does not honor the Son does not honor the Father, who sent him.

24"I tell you the truth, whoever hears my word and believes him who sent me has eternal life and will not be condemned; he has crossed over from death to life. 25I tell you the truth, a time is coming and has now come when the dead will hear the voice of the Son of God and those who hear will live. 26For as the Father has life in himself, so he has granted the Son to have life in himself. 27And he has given him authority to judge because he is the Son of Man.

> ### John 5:26
>
> *God Is Life*
>
> "For as the Father has life in himself, so he has granted the Son to have life in himself."

28"Do not be amazed at this, for a time is coming when all who are in their graves will hear his voice 29and come out—those who have done good will rise to live, and those who have done evil will rise to be condemned. 30By myself I can do nothing; I judge only as I hear, and my judgment is just, for I seek not to please myself but him who sent me.

Testimonies About Jesus

31"If I testify about myself, my testimony is not valid. 32There is another who testifies in my favor, and I know that his testimony about me is valid.

33"You have sent to John and he has testified to the truth. 34Not that I accept human testimony; but I mention it that you may be saved. 35John was a lamp that burned and gave light, and you chose for a time to enjoy his light.

36"I have testimony weightier than that of John. For the very work that the Father has given me to finish, and which I am doing, testifies that the Father has sent me. 37And the Father who sent me has himself testified concerning me. You have never heard his voice nor seen his form, 38nor does his word dwell in you, for you do not believe the one he sent. 39You diligently study*a* the Scriptures because you think that by them you possess eternal life. These are the Scriptures that testify about me, 40yet you refuse to come to me to have life.

a39 Or Study diligently (the imperative)

41"I do not accept praise from men, 42but I know you. I know that you do not have the love of God in your hearts. 43I have come in my Father's name, and you do not accept me; but if someone else comes in his own name, you will accept him. 44How can you believe if you accept praise from one another, yet make no effort to obtain the praise that comes from the only God*a*?

45"But do not think I will accuse you before the Father. Your accuser is Moses, on whom your hopes are set. 46If you believed Moses, you would believe me, for he wrote about me. 47But since you do not believe what he wrote, how are you going to believe what I say?"

Jesus Feeds the Five Thousand

6 Some time after this, Jesus crossed to the far shore of the Sea of Galilee (that is, the Sea of Tiberias), 2and a great crowd of people followed him because they saw the miraculous signs he had performed on the sick. 3Then Jesus went up on a mountainside and sat down with his disciples. 4The Jewish Passover Feast was near.

5When Jesus looked up and saw a great crowd coming toward him, he said to Philip, "Where shall we buy bread for these people to eat?" 6He asked this only to test him, for he already had in mind what he was going to do.

7Philip answered him, "Eight months' wages*b* would not buy enough bread for each one to have a bite!"

8Another of his disciples, Andrew, Simon Peter's brother, spoke up, 9"Here is a boy with five small barley loaves and two small fish, but how far will they go among so many?"

10Jesus said, "Have the people sit down." There was plenty of grass in that place, and the men sat down, about five thousand of them. 11Jesus then took the loaves, gave thanks, and distributed to those who were seated as much as they wanted. He did the same with the fish.

12When they had all had enough to eat, he said to his disciples, "Gather the pieces that are left over. Let nothing be wasted." 13So they gathered them and filled twelve baskets with the pieces of the five barley loaves left over by those who had eaten.

14After the people saw the miraculous sign that Jesus did, they began to say, "Surely this is the Prophet who is to come into the world." 15Jesus, knowing that they intended to come and make him king by force, withdrew again to a mountain by himself.

Jesus Walks on the Water

16When evening came, his disciples went down to the lake, 17where they got into a boat and set off across the lake for Capernaum. By now it was dark, and Jesus had not yet joined them. 18A strong wind was blowing and the waters grew rough. 19When they had rowed three or three and a half miles,*c* they saw Jesus approaching the boat, walking on the water; and they were terrified. 20But he said to them, "It is I; don't be afraid." 21Then they were willing to take him into the boat, and immediately the boat reached the shore where they were heading.

22The next day the crowd that had stayed on the opposite shore of the lake realized that only one boat had been there, and that Jesus had not entered it with his disciples, but that they had gone away alone. 23Then some boats from Tiberias landed near the place where the people had eaten the bread after the Lord had given thanks. 24Once the crowd realized that neither Jesus nor his disciples were there, they got into the boats and went to Capernaum in search of Jesus.

Jesus the Bread of Life

25When they found him on the other side of the lake, they asked him, "Rabbi, when did you get here?"

26Jesus answered, "I tell you the truth, you are looking for me, not because you saw miraculous signs but because you ate the loaves and had your fill. 27Do not work for food that spoils, but for food that endures to eternal life, which the Son of Man will give you. On him God the Father has placed his seal of approval."

28Then they asked him, "What must we do to do the works God requires?"

29Jesus answered, "The work of God is this: to believe in the one he has sent."

30So they asked him, "What miraculous sign

---

a44 Some early manuscripts *the Only One*   *b7* Greek *two hundred denarii*   *c19* Greek *rowed twenty-five or thirty stadia* (about 5 or 6 kilometers) then will you give that we may see it and believe you? What will you do? [31] Our forefathers ate the manna in the desert; as it is written: 'He gave them bread from heaven to eat.'[a]

[32] Jesus said to them, "I tell you the truth, it is not Moses who has given you the bread from heaven, but it is my Father who gives you the true bread from heaven. [33] For the bread of God is he who comes down from heaven and gives life to the world."

[34] "Sir," they said, "from now on give us this bread."

[35] Then Jesus declared, "I am the bread of life. He who comes to me will never go hungry, and he who believes in me will never be thirsty. [36] But as I told you, you have seen me and still you do not believe. [37] All that the Father gives me will come to me, and whoever comes to me I will never drive away. [38] For I have come down from heaven not to do my will but to do the will of him who sent me. [39] And this is the will of him who sent me, that I shall lose none of all that he has given me, but raise them up at the last day. [40] For my Father's will is that everyone who looks to the Son and believes in him shall have eternal life, and I will raise him up at the last day."

[41] At this the Jews began to grumble about him because he said, "I am the bread that came down from heaven." [42] They said, "Is this not Jesus, the son of Joseph, whose father and mother we know? How can he now say, 'I came down from heaven'?"

[43] "Stop grumbling among yourselves," Jesus answered. [44] "No one can come to me unless the Father who sent me draws him, and I will raise him up at the last day. [45] It is written in the Prophets: 'They will all be taught by God.'[b] Everyone who listens to the Father and learns from him comes to me. [46] No one has seen the Father except the one who is from God; only he has seen the Father. [47] I tell you the truth, he who believes has everlasting life. [48] I am the bread of life. [49] Your forefathers ate the manna in the desert, yet they died. [50] But here is the bread that comes down from heaven, which a man may eat and not die. [51] I am the living bread that came down from heaven. If anyone eats of this bread, he will live forever. This bread is my flesh, which I will give for the life of the world."

[52] Then the Jews began to argue sharply among themselves, "How can this man give us his flesh to eat?"

[53] Jesus said to them, "I tell you the truth, unless you eat the flesh of the Son of Man and drink his blood, you have no life in you. [54] Whoever eats my flesh and drinks my blood has eternal life, and I will raise him up at the last day. [55] For my flesh is real food and my blood is real drink. [56] Whoever eats my flesh and drinks my blood remains in me, and I in him. [57] Just as the living Father sent me and I live because of the Father, so the one who feeds on me will live because of me. [58] This is the bread that came down from heaven. Your forefathers ate manna and died, but he who feeds on this bread will live forever." [59] He said this while teaching in the synagogue in Capernaum.

Many Disciples Desert Jesus

[60] On hearing it, many of his disciples said, "This is a hard teaching. Who can accept it?"

[61] Aware that his disciples were grumbling about this, Jesus said to them, "Does this offend you? [62] What if you see the Son of Man ascend to where he was before! [63] The Spirit gives life; the flesh counts for nothing. The words I have spoken to you are spirit[c] and they are life. [64] Yet there are some of you who do not believe." For Jesus had known from the beginning which of them did not believe and who would betray him. [65] He went on to say, "This is why I told you that no one can come to me unless the Father has enabled him."

[66] From this time many of his disciples turned back and no longer followed him.

John 6:37

God Doesn't Push Us Away

"All that the Father gives me will come to me, and whoever comes to me I will never drive away."

---

[a]31 Exodus 16:4; Neh. 9:15; Psalm 78:24,25   [b]45 Isaiah 54:13   [c]63 Or *Spirit*

⁶⁷"You do not want to leave too, do you?" Jesus asked the Twelve.

⁶⁸Simon Peter answered him, "Lord, to whom shall we go? You have the words of eternal life. ⁶⁹We believe and know that you are the Holy One of God."

⁷⁰Then Jesus replied, "Have I not chosen you, the Twelve? Yet one of you is a devil!" ⁷¹(He meant Judas, the son of Simon Iscariot, who, though one of the Twelve, was later to betray him.)

Jesus Goes to the Feast of Tabernacles

7 After this, Jesus went around in Galilee, purposely staying away from Judea because the Jews there were waiting to take his life. ²But when the Jewish Feast of Tabernacles was near, ³Jesus' brothers said to him, "You ought to leave here and go to Judea, so that your disciples may see the miracles you do. ⁴No one who wants to become a public figure acts in secret. Since you are doing these things, show yourself to the world." ⁵For even his own brothers did not believe in him.

⁶Therefore Jesus told them, "The right time for me has not yet come; for you any time is right. ⁷The world cannot hate you, but it hates me because I testify that what it does is evil. ⁸You go to the Feast. I am not yet*a* going up to this Feast, because for me the right time has not yet come." ⁹Having said this, he stayed in Galilee.

¹⁰However, after his brothers had left for the Feast, he went also, not publicly, but in secret. ¹¹Now at the Feast the Jews were watching for him and asking, "Where is that man?"

¹²Among the crowds there was widespread whispering about him. Some said, "He is a good man."

Others replied, "No, he deceives the people." ¹³But no one would say anything publicly about him for fear of the Jews.

Jesus Teaches at the Feast

¹⁴Not until halfway through the Feast did Jesus go up to the temple courts and begin to teach. ¹⁵The Jews were amazed and asked, "How did this man get such learning without having studied?"

¹⁶Jesus answered, "My teaching is not my own. It comes from him who sent me. ¹⁷If anyone chooses to do God's will, he will find out whether my teaching comes from God or whether I speak on my own. ¹⁸He who speaks on his own does so to gain honor for himself, but he who works for the honor of the one who sent him is a man of truth; there is nothing false about him. ¹⁹Has not Moses given you the law? Yet not one of you keeps the law. Why are you trying to kill me?"

²⁰"You are demon-possessed," the crowd answered. "Who is trying to kill you?"

²¹Jesus said to them, "I did one miracle, and you are all astonished. ²²Yet, because Moses gave you circumcision (though actually it did not come from Moses, but from the patriarchs), you circumcise a child on the Sabbath. ²³Now if a child can be circumcised on the Sabbath so that the law of Moses may not be broken, why are you angry with me for healing the whole man on the Sabbath? ²⁴Stop judging by mere appearances, and make a right judgment."

Is Jesus the Christ?

²⁵At that point some of the people of Jerusalem began to ask, "Isn't this the man they are trying to kill? ²⁶Here he is, speaking publicly, and they are not saying a word to him. Have the authorities really concluded that he is the Christ*b*? ²⁷But we know where this man is from; when the Christ comes, no one will know where he is from."

²⁸Then Jesus, still teaching in the temple courts, cried out, "Yes, you know me, and you know where I am from. I am not here on my own, but he who sent me is true. You do not know him, ²⁹but I know him because I am from him and he sent me."

³⁰At this they tried to seize him, but no one laid a hand on him, because his time had not yet come. ³¹Still, many in the crowd put their faith in him. They said, "When the Christ comes, will he do more miraculous signs than this man?"

³²The Pharisees heard the crowd whispering such things about him. Then the chief priests and the Pharisees sent temple guards to arrest him.

³³Jesus said, "I am with you for only a short

---

a8 Some early manuscripts do not have *yet.*   *b26* Or *Messiah*; also in verses 27, 31, 41 and 42 time, and then I go to the one who sent me. [34] You will look for me, but you will not find me; and where I am, you cannot come."

[35] The Jews said to one another, "Where does this man intend to go that we cannot find him? Will he go where our people live scattered among the Greeks, and teach the Greeks? [36] What did he mean when he said, 'You will look for me, but you will not find me,' and 'Where I am, you cannot come'?"

[37] On the last and greatest day of the Feast, Jesus stood and said in a loud voice, "If anyone is thirsty, let him come to me and drink. [38] Whoever believes in me, as[a] the Scripture has said, streams of living water will flow from within him." [39] By this he meant the Spirit, whom those who believed in him were later to receive. Up to that time the Spirit had not been given, since Jesus had not yet been glorified.

[40] On hearing his words, some of the people said, "Surely this man is the Prophet."

[41] Others said, "He is the Christ."

Still others asked, "How can the Christ come from Galilee? [42] Does not the Scripture say that the Christ will come from David's family[b] and from Bethlehem, the town where David lived?" [43] Thus the people were divided because of Jesus. [44] Some wanted to seize him, but no one laid a hand on him.

Unbelief of the Jewish Leaders

[45] Finally the temple guards went back to the chief priests and Pharisees, who asked them, "Why didn't you bring him in?"

[46] "No one ever spoke the way this man does," the guards declared.

[47] "You mean he has deceived you also?" the Pharisees retorted. [48] "Has any of the rulers or of the Pharisees believed in him? [49] No! But this mob that knows nothing of the law—there is a curse on them."

[50] Nicodemus, who had gone to Jesus earlier and who was one of their own number, asked,

[51] "Does our law condemn anyone without first hearing him to find out what he is doing?"

[52] They replied, "Are you from Galilee, too? Look into it, and you will find that a prophet[c] does not come out of Galilee."

[The earliest manuscripts and many other ancient witnesses do not have John 7:53—8:11.]

[53] Then each went to his own home.

8 But Jesus went to the Mount of Olives. [2] At dawn he appeared again in the temple courts, where all the people gathered around him, and he sat down to teach them. [3] The teachers of the law and the Pharisees brought in a woman caught in adultery. They made her stand before the group [4] and said to Jesus, "Teacher, this woman was caught in the act of adultery. [5] In the Law Moses commanded us to stone such women. Now what do you say?" [6] They were using this question as a trap, in order to have a basis for accusing him.

But Jesus bent down and started to write on the ground with his finger. [7] When they kept on questioning him, he straightened up and said to them, "If any one of you is without sin, let him be the first to throw a stone at her." [8] Again he stooped down and wrote on the ground.

[9] At this, those who heard began to go away one at a time, the older ones first, until only Jesus was left, with the woman still standing there. [10] Jesus straightened up and asked her, "Woman, where are they? Has no one condemned you?"

[11] "No one, sir," she said.

"Then neither do I condemn you," Jesus declared. "Go now and leave your life of sin."

The Validity of Jesus' Testimony

[12] When Jesus spoke again to the people, he said, "I am the light of the world. Whoever fol-

---

John 7:37

God Offers Fulfillment

On the last and greatest day of the Feast, Jesus stood and said in a loud voice, "If anyone is thirsty, let him come to me and drink."

---

[a] 37,38 Or / If anyone is thirsty, let him come to me. / And let him drink. [38] who believes in me. / As   [b] 42 Greek seed   [c] 52 Two early manuscripts the Prophet

lows me will never walk in darkness, but will have the light of life."

¹³The Pharisees challenged him, "Here you are, appearing as your own witness; your testimony is not valid."

¹⁴Jesus answered, "Even if I testify on my own behalf, my testimony is valid, for I know where I came from and where I am going. But you have no idea where I come from or where I am going. ¹⁵You judge by human standards; I pass judgment on no one. ¹⁶But if I do judge, my decisions are right, because I am not alone. I stand with the Father, who sent me. ¹⁷In your own Law it is written that the testimony of two men is valid. ¹⁸I am one who testifies for myself; my other witness is the Father, who sent me."

¹⁹Then they asked him, "Where is your father?"

"You do not know me or my Father," Jesus replied. "If you knew me, you would know my Father also." ²⁰He spoke these words while teaching in the temple area near the place where the offerings were put. Yet no one seized him, because his time had not yet come.

²¹Once more Jesus said to them, "I am going away, and you will look for me, and you will die in your sin. Where I go, you cannot come."

²²This made the Jews ask, "Will he kill himself? Is that why he says, 'Where I go, you cannot come'?"

²³But he continued, "You are from below; I am from above. You are of this world; I am not of this world. ²⁴I told you that you would die in your sins; if you do not believe that I am ⌊the one I claim to be⌋,ᵃ you will indeed die in your sins."

²⁵"Who are you?" they asked.

"Just what I have been claiming all along," Jesus replied. ²⁶"I have much to say in judgment of you. But he who sent me is reliable, and what I have heard from him I tell the world."

²⁷They did not understand that he was telling them about his Father. ²⁸So Jesus said, "When you have lifted up the Son of Man, then you will know that I am ⌊the one I claim to be⌋ and that I do nothing on my own but speak just what the Father has taught me. ²⁹The one who

sent me is with me; he has not left me alone, for I always do what pleases him." ³⁰Even as he spoke, many put their faith in him.

The Children of Abraham

³¹To the Jews who had believed him, Jesus said, "If you hold to my teaching, you are really my disciples. ³²Then you will know the truth, and the truth will set you free."

³³They answered him, "We are Abraham's descendantsᵇ and have never been slaves of anyone. How can you say that we shall be set free?"

³⁴Jesus replied, "I tell you the truth, everyone who sins is a slave to sin. ³⁵Now a slave has no permanent place in the family, but a son belongs to it forever. ³⁶So if the Son sets you free, you will be free indeed. ³⁷I know you are Abraham's descendants. Yet you are ready to kill me, because you have no room for my word. ³⁸I am telling you what I have seen in the Father's presence, and you do what you have heard from your father.ᶜ"

³⁹"Abraham is our father," they answered.

"If you were Abraham's children," said Jesus, "then you wouldᵈ do the things Abraham did. ⁴⁰As it is, you are determined to kill me, a man who has told you the truth that I heard from God. Abraham did not do such things. ⁴¹You are doing the things your own father does."

"We are not illegitimate children," they protested. "The only Father we have is God himself."

The Children of the Devil

⁴²Jesus said to them, "If God were your Father, you would love me, for I came from God and now am here. I have not come on my own; but he sent me. ⁴³Why is my language not clear to you? Because you are unable to hear what I say. ⁴⁴You belong to your father, the devil, and you want to carry out your father's desire. He was a murderer from the beginning, not holding to the truth, for there is no truth in him. When he lies, he speaks his native language, for he is a liar and the father of lies. ⁴⁵Yet because I tell the truth, you do not believe me! ⁴⁶Can any of you prove me guilty of sin? If I am telling the truth, why don't you believe me? ⁴⁷He

ᵃ24 Or *I am he*; also in verse 28   ᵇ33 Greek *seed*; also in verse 37   ᶜ38 Or *presence. Therefore do what you have heard from the Father.*
ᵈ39 Some early manuscripts *"If you are Abraham's children," said Jesus, "then*

who belongs to God hears what God says. The reason you do not hear is that you do not belong to God."

The Claims of Jesus About Himself

48The Jews answered him, "Aren't we right in saying that you are a Samaritan and demon-possessed?"

49"I am not possessed by a demon," said Jesus, "but I honor my Father and you dishonor me. **50**I am not seeking glory for myself; but there is one who seeks it, and he is the judge. **51**I tell you the truth, if anyone keeps my word, he will never see death."

52At this the Jews exclaimed, "Now we know that you are demon-possessed! Abraham died and so did the prophets, yet you say that if anyone keeps your word, he will never taste death. **53**Are you greater than our father Abraham? He died, and so did the prophets. Who do you think you are?"

54Jesus replied, "If I glorify myself, my glory means nothing. My Father, whom you claim as your God, is the one who glorifies me. **55**Though you do not know him, I know him. If I said I did not, I would be a liar like you, but I do know him and keep his word. **56**Your father Abraham rejoiced at the thought of seeing my day; he saw it and was glad."

57"You are not yet fifty years old," the Jews said to him, "and you have seen Abraham!"

58"I tell you the truth," Jesus answered, "before Abraham was born, I am!" **59**At this, they picked up stones to stone him, but Jesus hid himself, slipping away from the temple grounds.

Jesus Heals a Man Born Blind

9 As he went along, he saw a man blind from birth. **2**His disciples asked him, "Rabbi, who sinned, this man or his parents, that he was born blind?"

3"Neither this man nor his parents sinned," said Jesus, "but this happened so that the work of God might be displayed in his life. **4**As long as it is day, we must do the work of him who sent me. Night is coming, when no one can work. **5**While I am in the world, I am the light of the world."

6Having said this, he spit on the ground, made some mud with the saliva, and put it on the man's eyes. **7**"Go," he told him, "wash in the Pool of Siloam" (this word means Sent). So the man went and washed, and came home seeing.

8His neighbors and those who had formerly seen him begging asked, "Isn't this the same man who used to sit and beg?" **9**Some claimed that he was.

Others said, "No, he only looks like him."

But he himself insisted, "I am the man."

10"How then were your eyes opened?" they demanded.

11He replied, "The man they call Jesus made some mud and put it on my eyes. He told me to go to Siloam and wash. So I went and washed, and then I could see."

12"Where is this man?" they asked him.

"I don't know," he said.

The Pharisees Investigate the Healing

13They brought to the Pharisees the man who had been blind. **14**Now the day on which Jesus had made the mud and opened the man's eyes was a Sabbath. **15**Therefore the Pharisees also asked him how he had received his sight.

"He put mud on my eyes," the man replied, "and I washed, and now I see."

16Some of the Pharisees said, "This man is not from God, for he does not keep the Sabbath."

But others asked, "How can a sinner do such miraculous signs?" So they were divided.

17Finally they turned again to the blind man, "What have you to say about him? It was your eyes he opened."

The man replied, "He is a prophet."

18The Jews still did not believe that he had been blind and had received his sight until they sent for the man's parents. **19**"Is this your son?" they asked. "Is this the one you say was born blind? How is it that now he can see?"

20"We know he is our son," the parents answered, "and we know he was born blind. **21**But how he can see now, or who opened his eyes,

John 8:58

God Is Eternal

"I tell you the truth," Jesus answered, "before Abraham was born, I am!"

we don't know. Ask him. He is of age; he will speak for himself." ²²His parents said this because they were afraid of the Jews, for already the Jews had decided that anyone who acknowledged that Jesus was the Christ*a* would be put out of the synagogue. ²³That was why his parents said, "He is of age; ask him."

²⁴A second time they summoned the man who had been blind. "Give glory to God,*b*" they said. "We know this man is a sinner."

²⁵He replied, "Whether he is a sinner or not, I don't know. One thing I do know. I was blind but now I see!"

²⁶Then they asked him, "What did he do to you? How did he open your eyes?"

²⁷He answered, "I have told you already and you did not listen. Why do you want to hear it again? Do you want to become his disciples, too?"

²⁸Then they hurled insults at him and said, "You are this fellow's disciple! We are disciples of Moses! ²⁹We know that God spoke to Moses, but as for this fellow, we don't even know where he comes from."

³⁰The man answered, "Now that is remarkable! You don't know where he comes from, yet he opened my eyes. ³¹We know that God does not listen to sinners. He listens to the godly man who does his will. ³²Nobody has ever heard of opening the eyes of a man born blind. ³³If this man were not from God, he could do nothing."

³⁴To this they replied, "You were steeped in sin at birth; how dare you lecture us!" And they threw him out.

Spiritual Blindness

³⁵Jesus heard that they had thrown him out, and when he found him, he said, "Do you believe in the Son of Man?"

³⁶"Who is he, sir?" the man asked. "Tell me so that I may believe in him."

³⁷Jesus said, "You have now seen him; in fact, he is the one speaking with you."

³⁸Then the man said, "Lord, I believe," and he worshiped him.

³⁹Jesus said, "For judgment I have come into this world, so that the blind will see and those who see will become blind."

⁴⁰Some Pharisees who were with him heard him say this and asked, "What? Are we blind too?"

⁴¹Jesus said, "If you were blind, you would not be guilty of sin; but now that you claim you can see, your guilt remains.

The Shepherd and His Flock

10 "I tell you the truth, the man who does not enter the sheep pen by the gate, but climbs in by some other way, is a thief and a robber. ²The man who enters by the gate is the shepherd of his sheep. ³The watchman opens the gate for him, and the sheep listen to his voice. He calls his own sheep by name and leads them out. ⁴When he has brought out all his own, he goes on ahead of them, and his sheep follow him because they know his voice. ⁵But they will never follow a stranger; in fact, they will run away from him because they do not recognize a stranger's voice." ⁶Jesus used this figure of speech, but they did not understand what he was telling them.

⁷Therefore Jesus said again, "I tell you the truth, I am the gate for the sheep. ⁸All who ever came before me were thieves and robbers, but the sheep did not listen to them. ⁹I am the gate; whoever enters through me will be saved.*c* He will come in and go out, and find pasture. ¹⁰The thief comes only to steal and kill and destroy; I have come that they may have life, and have it to the full.

¹¹"I am the good shepherd. The good shepherd lays down his life for the sheep. ¹²The hired hand is not the shepherd who owns the sheep. So when he sees the wolf coming, he abandons the sheep and runs away. Then the wolf attacks the flock and scatters it. ¹³The man runs away because he is a hired hand and cares nothing for the sheep.

¹⁴"I am the good shepherd; I know my sheep and my sheep know me— ¹⁵just as the Father knows me and I know the Father—and

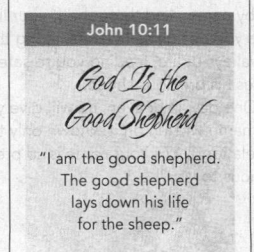

John 10:11

God Is the Good Shepherd

"I am the good shepherd. The good shepherd lays down his life for the sheep."

---

*a*22 Or *Messiah*   *b*24 A solemn charge to tell the truth (see Joshua 7:19)   *c*9 Or *kept safe*

He Knows Your Name

Read: John 10:1–18

John 10:3

"The watchman opens the gate for him, and the sheep listen to his voice. He calls his own sheep by name and leads them out."

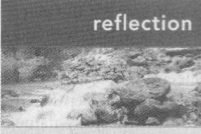

reflection

1 Spend some time thinking about Jesus' names. Which is your favorite and why?

2 How does it make you feel that Jesus knows and calls you by name?

3 What does it mean to you to know that he has a new, special name waiting for you?

RELATED READINGS

Psalm 23;
Isaiah 9:6;
Ezekiel 34:25–31;
Revelation 2:17

"The name we give to something shapes our attitude toward it."

Katherine Paterson

"THE SWEETEST SOUND in the world is the sound of a person's own name," wrote Dale Carnegie in his all-time bestseller *How to Win Friends and Influence People*. There's nothing more embarrassing than being at a social event and seeing someone you know and not remembering their name. There's nothing more humiliating than greeting someone you thought you knew well with a hug and a personal hello only to have them look back with the deer-in-the-headlights look. You just know they're thinking, *Now what is her name?*

Our name reflects who we are. It gives us a sense of belonging, a sense of identity. If someone knows our name, it means they know *us*. It's hard not to take it personally when someone forgets our name. Unfortunately, parents do it. They call us by our sibling's name or jumble our names into one long name: "JimmySueBob, get over here." Bosses do it. They point and say, "You, I need that report." Teachers do it. They mistakenly call us by our classmate's name. But if our closest friend, boyfriend or husband forgot our name—forget about it! It would be an almost unforgivable offense.

Thankfully, Jesus knows your name. In this passage of John we learn that Jesus calls us each "by name." The Creator of the universe, the One who determined the number of stars in the sky and called each of them by name, knows *your* name. Not only does he *know* your name, but he *calls* you by name.

When you were saved, Jesus spoke to you personally. He called you by name. And throughout your life, he calls your name as he leads you beside still waters, along the mountaintops and through the valleys of life, leading you to safe pastures as a shepherd guides his precious sheep.

One day, in heaven, he will give you "a white stone with a new name written on it, known only to him who receives it" (Revelation 2:17). Your name is so precious to Jesus. Is his name precious to you?

I lay down my life for the sheep. ¹⁶I have other sheep that are not of this sheep pen. I must bring them also. They too will listen to my voice, and there shall be one flock and one shepherd. ¹⁷The reason my Father loves me is that I lay down my life—only to take it up again. ¹⁸No one takes it from me, but I lay it down of my own accord. I have authority to lay it down and authority to take it up again. This command I received from my Father."

¹⁹At these words the Jews were again divided. ²⁰Many of them said, "He is demon-possessed and raving mad. Why listen to him?"

²¹But others said, "These are not the sayings of a man possessed by a demon. Can a demon open the eyes of the blind?"

The Unbelief of the Jews

²²Then came the Feast of Dedication*a* at Jerusalem. It was winter, ²³and Jesus was in the temple area walking in Solomon's Colonnade. ²⁴The Jews gathered around him, saying, "How long will you keep us in suspense? If you are the Christ,*b* tell us plainly."

²⁵Jesus answered, "I did tell you, but you do not believe. The miracles I do in my Father's name speak for me, ²⁶but you do not believe because you are not my sheep. ²⁷My sheep listen to my voice; I know them, and they follow me. ²⁸I give them eternal life, and they shall never perish; no one can snatch them out of my hand. ²⁹My Father, who has given them to me, is greater than all*c*; no one can snatch them out of my Father's hand. ³⁰I and the Father are one."

³¹Again the Jews picked up stones to stone him, ³²but Jesus said to them, "I have shown you many great miracles from the Father. For which of these do you stone me?"

³³"We are not stoning you for any of these," replied the Jews, "but for blasphemy, because you, a mere man, claim to be God."

³⁴Jesus answered them, "Is it not written in your Law, 'I have said you are gods'*d*? ³⁵If he called them 'gods,' to whom the word of God came—and the Scripture cannot be broken— ³⁶what about the one whom the Father set apart as his very own and sent into the world? Why then do you accuse me of blasphemy because I said, 'I am God's Son'? ³⁷Do not believe me unless I do what my Father does. ³⁸But if I do it, even though you do not believe me, believe the miracles, that you may know and understand that the Father is in me, and I in the Father." ³⁹Again they tried to seize him, but he escaped their grasp.

⁴⁰Then Jesus went back across the Jordan to the place where John had been baptizing in the early days. Here he stayed ⁴¹and many people came to him. They said, "Though John never performed a miraculous sign, all that John said about this man was true." ⁴²And in that place many believed in Jesus.

The Death of Lazarus

11 Now a man named Lazarus was sick. He was from Bethany, the village of Mary and her sister Martha. ²This Mary, whose brother Lazarus now lay sick, was the same one who poured perfume on the Lord and wiped his feet with her hair. ³So the sisters sent word to Jesus, "Lord, the one you love is sick."

⁴When he heard this, Jesus said, "This sickness will not end in death. No, it is for God's glory so that God's Son may be glorified through it." ⁵Jesus loved Martha and her sister and Lazarus. ⁶Yet when he heard that Lazarus was sick, he stayed where he was two more days.

⁷Then he said to his disciples, "Let us go back to Judea."

⁸"But Rabbi," they said, "a short while ago the Jews tried to stone you, and yet you are going back there?"

⁹Jesus answered, "Are there not twelve hours of daylight? A man who walks by day will not stumble, for he sees by this world's light. ¹⁰It is when he walks by night that he stumbles, for he has no light."

¹¹After he had said this, he went on to tell them, "Our friend Lazarus has fallen asleep; but I am going there to wake him up."

¹²His disciples replied, "Lord, if he sleeps, he will get better." ¹³Jesus had been speaking of his death, but his disciples thought he meant natural sleep.

¹⁴So then he told them plainly, "Lazarus is dead, ¹⁵and for your sake I am glad I was not

---

a22 That is, Hanukkah   *b24* Or *Messiah*   *c29* Many early manuscripts *What my Father has given me is greater than all*   *d34* Psalm 82:6

there, so that you may believe. But let us go to him."

16Then Thomas (called Didymus) said to the rest of the disciples, "Let us also go, that we may die with him."

Jesus Comforts the Sisters

17On his arrival, Jesus found that Lazarus had already been in the tomb for four days. 18Bethany was less than two miles*a* from Jerusalem, 19and many Jews had come to Martha and Mary to comfort them in the loss of their brother. 20When Martha heard that Jesus was coming, she went out to meet him, but Mary stayed at home.

21"Lord," Martha said to Jesus, "if you had been here, my brother would not have died. 22But I know that even now God will give you whatever you ask."

23Jesus said to her, "Your brother will rise again."

24Martha answered, "I know he will rise again in the resurrection at the last day."

25Jesus said to her, "I am the resurrection and the life. He who believes in me will live, even though he dies; 26and whoever lives and believes in me will never die. Do you believe this?"

27"Yes, Lord," she told him, "I believe that you are the Christ,*b* the Son of God, who was to come into the world."

28And after she had said this, she went back and called her sister Mary aside. "The Teacher is here," she said, "and is asking for you." 29When Mary heard this, she got up quickly and went to him. 30Now Jesus had not yet entered the village, but was still at the place where Martha had met him. 31When the Jews who had been with Mary in the house, comforting her, noticed how quickly she got up and went out, they followed her, supposing she was going to the tomb to mourn there.

32When Mary reached the place where Jesus was and saw him, she fell at his feet and said, "Lord, if you had been here, my brother would not have died."

33When Jesus saw her weeping, and the Jews who had come along with her also weeping, he was deeply moved in spirit and troubled. 34"Where have you laid him?" he asked.

"Come and see, Lord," they replied.

35Jesus wept.

36Then the Jews said, "See how he loved him!"

37But some of them said, "Could not he who opened the eyes of the blind man have kept this man from dying?"

Jesus Raises Lazarus From the Dead

38Jesus, once more deeply moved, came to the tomb. It was a cave with a stone laid across the entrance. 39"Take away the stone," he said.

"But, Lord," said Martha, the sister of the dead man, "by this time there is a bad odor, for he has been there four days."

40Then Jesus said, "Did I not tell you that if you believed, you would see the glory of God?"

41So they took away the stone. Then Jesus looked up and said, "Father, I thank you that you have heard me. 42I knew that you always hear me, but I said this for the benefit of the people standing here, that they may believe that you sent me."

43When he had said this, Jesus called in a loud voice, "Lazarus, come out!" 44The dead man came out, his hands and feet wrapped with strips of linen, and a cloth around his face.

Jesus said to them, "Take off the grave clothes and let him go."

The Plot to Kill Jesus

45Therefore many of the Jews who had come to visit Mary, and had seen what Jesus did, put their faith in him. 46But some of them went to the Pharisees and told them what Jesus had done. 47Then the chief priests and the Pharisees called a meeting of the Sanhedrin.

"What are we accomplishing?" they asked. "Here is this man performing many miraculous signs. 48If we let him go on like this, everyone will believe in him, and then the Romans will come and take away both our place*c* and our nation."

49Then one of them, named Caiaphas, who was high priest that year, spoke up, "You know nothing at all! 50You do not realize that it is better for you that one man die for the people than that the whole nation perish."

51He did not say this on his own, but as high

---

a18 Greek *fifteen stadia* (about 3 kilometers)   *b27* Or *Messiah*   *c48* Or *temple*

First and Last

MARY MAGDALENE

SEVEN. THAT'S THE NUMBER of demons who daily assaulted Mary of Magdala without remorse.

Unimaginable. That's what the tormented nights were like as Mary battled frightening forces she didn't understand—evil forces that brought fitful sleep and days filled with anguish. We'll likely never know the depth of relief she experienced at the healing hands of Jesus. Mary, changed by the power of love, was forever indebted to him. Following him was not an option; it was a necessity.

Three. That's the number of agonizingly long days Mary endured after Jesus' death; they must have seemed an eternity. She had stood at a distance from the cross, huddled together with her fellow sisters. None of them could believe the cruel scene unfolding before their eyes. The hands that had released indomitable power in her life, and in the lives of so many others, now hung limp on the wooden beams, pierced and bloody.

Last. That's what Mary was on Friday evening. She was one of the last to see Jesus alive. One of the last to leave his ravaged body and return home for Passover preparations. For all she knew, evil had just extinguished the light of the world forever. Lost without him, she stumbled home in the encroaching darkness that obscured her path and clung to her soul.

Among the first. That's what Mary was on resurrection morning. She was among the first at the tomb. Among the first to peer into the empty blackness of the cool enclosure. Among the first to see the glory of an angel, cleverly cloaked in the clothes of a gardener. She was first to ask the obvious and assume the worst. Ironically, the person God chose to see Jesus first was the last person most people would have expected to receive the honor (a demon-possessed woman?). Nevertheless, Mary Magdalene holds the envious position in history of being among the first—the first to see Jesus alive and the first to carry back to a waiting world the glorious gospel of Good News.

—Prayer—
Jesus, friend and Savior, thank you for the miracles you've worked in my life.

Mary Magdalene went to the disciples with the news: "I have seen the Lord!"

John 20:18

ASSIGNED READING:

Matthew 27–28;
Mark 15–16;
Luke 24:1–12;
John 19–20

Weekend

Go to page 1307 for your next devotional reading.

priest that year he prophesied that Jesus would die for the Jewish nation, **52**and not only for that nation but also for the scattered children of God, to bring them together and make them one. **53**So from that day on they plotted to take his life.

54Therefore Jesus no longer moved about publicly among the Jews. Instead he withdrew to a region near the desert, to a village called Ephraim, where he stayed with his disciples.

55When it was almost time for the Jewish Passover, many went up from the country to Jerusalem for their ceremonial cleansing before the Passover. **56**They kept looking for Jesus, and as they stood in the temple area they asked one another, "What do you think? Isn't he coming to the Feast at all?" **57**But the chief priests and Pharisees had given orders that if anyone found out where Jesus was, he should report it so that they might arrest him.

Jesus Anointed at Bethany

12 Six days before the Passover, Jesus arrived at Bethany, where Lazarus lived, whom Jesus had raised from the dead. **2**Here a dinner was given in Jesus' honor. Martha served, while Lazarus was among those reclining at the table with him. **3**Then Mary took about a pint*a* of pure nard, an expensive perfume; she poured it on Jesus' feet and wiped his feet with her hair. And the house was filled with the fragrance of the perfume.

4But one of his disciples, Judas Iscariot, who was later to betray him, objected, **5**"Why wasn't this perfume sold and the money given to the poor? It was worth a year's wages.*b*" **6**He did not say this because he cared about the poor but because he was a thief; as keeper of the money bag, he used to help himself to what was put into it.

7"Leave her alone," Jesus replied. "It was intended that she should save this perfume for the day of my burial. **8**You will always have the poor among you, but you will not always have me."

9Meanwhile a large crowd of Jews found out that Jesus was there and came, not only because of him but also to see Lazarus, whom he had raised from the dead. **10**So the chief priests

made plans to kill Lazarus as well, **11**for on account of him many of the Jews were going over to Jesus and putting their faith in him.

The Triumphal Entry

12The next day the great crowd that had come for the Feast heard that Jesus was on his way to Jerusalem. **13**They took palm branches and went out to meet him, shouting,

"Hosanna!*c*"

"Blessed is he who comes in the name of the Lord!"*d*

"Blessed is the King of Israel!"

14Jesus found a young donkey and sat upon it, as it is written,

15"Do not be afraid, O Daughter of Zion;
    see, your king is coming,
      seated on a donkey's colt."*e*

16At first his disciples did not understand all this. Only after Jesus was glorified did they realize that these things had been written about him and that they had done these things to him.

17Now the crowd that was with him when he called Lazarus from the tomb and raised him from the dead continued to spread the word. **18**Many people, because they had heard that he had given this miraculous sign, went out to meet him. **19**So the Pharisees said to one another, "See, this is getting us nowhere. Look how the whole world has gone after him!"

Jesus Predicts His Death

20Now there were some Greeks among those who went up to worship at the Feast. **21**They came to Philip, who was from Bethsaida in Galilee, with a request. "Sir," they said, "we would like to see Jesus." **22**Philip went to tell Andrew; Andrew and Philip in turn told Jesus.

23Jesus replied, "The hour has come for the Son of Man to be glorified. **24**I tell you the truth, unless a kernel of wheat falls to the ground and dies, it remains only a single seed. But if it dies, it produces many seeds. **25**The man who loves his life will lose it, while the man who hates his life in this world will keep it for eternal life.

---

*a*3 Greek a *litra* (probably about 0.5 liter)   *b*5 Greek *three hundred denarii*   *c*13 A Hebrew expression meaning "Save!" which became an exclamation of praise   *d*13 Psalm 118:25,26   *e*15 Zech. 9:9

²⁶Whoever serves me must follow me; and where I am, my servant also will be. My Father will honor the one who serves me.

²⁷"Now my heart is troubled, and what shall I say? 'Father, save me from this hour'? No, it was for this very reason I came to this hour. ²⁸Father, glorify your name!"

Then a voice came from heaven, "I have glorified it, and will glorify it again." ²⁹The crowd that was there and heard it said it had thundered; others said an angel had spoken to him.

³⁰Jesus said, "This voice was for your benefit, not mine. ³¹Now is the time for judgment on this world; now the prince of this world will be driven out. ³²But I, when I am lifted up from the earth, will draw all men to myself." ³³He said this to show the kind of death he was going to die.

³⁴The crowd spoke up, "We have heard from the Law that the Christ[a] will remain forever, so how can you say, 'The Son of Man must be lifted up'? Who is this 'Son of Man'?"

³⁵Then Jesus told them, "You are going to have the light just a little while longer. Walk while you have the light, before darkness overtakes you. The man who walks in the dark does not know where he is going. ³⁶Put your trust in the light while you have it, so that you may become sons of light." When he had finished speaking, Jesus left and hid himself from them.

The Jews Continue in Their Unbelief

³⁷Even after Jesus had done all these miraculous signs in their presence, they still would not believe in him. ³⁸This was to fulfill the word of Isaiah the prophet:

"Lord, who has believed our message
  and to whom has the arm of the Lord
    been revealed?"[b]

³⁹For this reason they could not believe, because, as Isaiah says elsewhere:

⁴⁰"He has blinded their eyes
  and deadened their hearts,

so they can neither see with their eyes,
  nor understand with their hearts,
  nor turn—and I would heal them."[c]

⁴¹Isaiah said this because he saw Jesus' glory and spoke about him.

⁴²Yet at the same time many even among the leaders believed in him. But because of the Pharisees they would not confess their faith for fear they would be put out of the synagogue; ⁴³for they loved praise from men more than praise from God.

⁴⁴Then Jesus cried out, "When a man believes in me, he does not believe in me only, but in the one who sent me. ⁴⁵When he looks at me, he sees the one who sent me. ⁴⁶I have come into the world as a light, so that no one who believes in me should stay in darkness.

⁴⁷"As for the person who hears my words but does not keep them, I do not judge him. For I did not come to judge the world, but to save it. ⁴⁸There is a judge for the one who rejects me and does not accept my words; that very word which I spoke will condemn him at the last day. ⁴⁹For I did not speak of my own accord, but the Father who sent me commanded me what to say and how to say it. ⁵⁰I know that his command leads to eternal life. So whatever I say is just what the Father has told me to say."

Jesus Washes His Disciples' Feet

13 It was just before the Passover Feast. Jesus knew that the time had come for him to leave this world and go to the Father. Having loved his own who were in the world, he now showed them the full extent of his love.[d]

²The evening meal was being served, and the devil had already prompted Judas Iscariot, son of Simon, to betray Jesus. ³Jesus knew that the Father had put all things under his power, and that he had come from God and was returning to God; ⁴so he got up from the meal, took off his outer clothing, and wrapped a towel around his waist. ⁵After that, he poured water into a

> **John 12:46**
>
> *God Is Light*
>
> "I have come into the world as a light, so that no one who believes in me should stay in darkness."

---

*a*34 Or *Messiah* *b*38 Isaiah 53:1 *c*40 Isaiah 6:10 *d*1 Or *he loved them to the last* basin and began to wash his disciples' feet, drying them with the towel that was wrapped around him.

⁶He came to Simon Peter, who said to him, "Lord, are you going to wash my feet?"

⁷Jesus replied, "You do not realize now what I am doing, but later you will understand."

⁸"No," said Peter, "you shall never wash my feet."

Jesus answered, "Unless I wash you, you have no part with me."

⁹"Then, Lord," Simon Peter replied, "not just my feet but my hands and my head as well!"

¹⁰Jesus answered, "A person who has had a bath needs only to wash his feet; his whole body is clean. And you are clean, though not every one of you." ¹¹For he knew who was going to betray him, and that was why he said not every one was clean.

¹²When he had finished washing their feet, he put on his clothes and returned to his place. "Do you understand what I have done for you?" he asked them. ¹³"You call me 'Teacher' and 'Lord,' and rightly so, for that is what I am. ¹⁴Now that I, your Lord and Teacher, have washed your feet, you also should wash one another's feet. ¹⁵I have set you an example that you should do as I have done for you. ¹⁶I tell you the truth, no servant is greater than his master, nor is a messenger greater than the one who sent him. ¹⁷Now that you know these things, you will be blessed if you do them.

Jesus Predicts His Betrayal

¹⁸"I am not referring to all of you; I know those I have chosen. But this is to fulfill the scripture: 'He who shares my bread has lifted up his heel against me.'ᵃ

¹⁹"I am telling you now before it happens, so that when it does happen you will believe that I am He. ²⁰I tell you the truth, whoever accepts anyone I send accepts me; and whoever accepts me accepts the one who sent me."

²¹After he had said this, Jesus was troubled in spirit and testified, "I tell you the truth, one of you is going to betray me."

²²His disciples stared at one another, at a loss to know which of them he meant. ²³One of them, the disciple whom Jesus loved, was re-

clining next to him. ²⁴Simon Peter motioned to this disciple and said, "Ask him which one he means."

²⁵Leaning back against Jesus, he asked him, "Lord, who is it?"

²⁶Jesus answered, "It is the one to whom I will give this piece of bread when I have dipped it in the dish." Then, dipping the piece of bread, he gave it to Judas Iscariot, son of Simon. ²⁷As soon as Judas took the bread, Satan entered into him.

"What you are about to do, do quickly," Jesus told him, ²⁸but no one at the meal understood why Jesus said this to him. ²⁹Since Judas had charge of the money, some thought Jesus was telling him to buy what was needed for the Feast, or to give something to the poor. ³⁰As soon as Judas had taken the bread, he went out. And it was night.

Jesus Predicts Peter's Denial

³¹When he was gone, Jesus said, "Now is the Son of Man glorified and God is glorified in him. ³²If God is glorified in him,ᵇ God will glorify the Son in himself, and will glorify him at once.

³³"My children, I will be with you only a little longer. You will look for me, and just as I told the Jews, so I tell you now: Where I am going, you cannot come.

³⁴"A new command I give you: Love one another. As I have loved you, so you must love one another. ³⁵By this all men will know that you are my disciples, if you love one another."

³⁶Simon Peter asked him, "Lord, where are you going?"

Jesus replied, "Where I am going, you cannot follow now, but you will follow later."

³⁷Peter asked, "Lord, why can't I follow you now? I will lay down my life for you."

³⁸Then Jesus answered, "Will you really lay down your life for me? I tell you the truth, before the rooster crows, you will disown me three times!

Jesus Comforts His Disciples

14 "Do not let your hearts be troubled. Trust in Godᶜ; trust also in me. ²In my Father's house are many rooms; if it were not so, I would have told you. I am going there to

---

ᵃ18 Psalm 41:9   ᵇ32 Many early manuscripts do not have *If God is glorified in him*.   ᶜ1 Or *You trust in God*

Servant Leaders

Read: John 13:1–17

NBC'S *DATELINE* NEWSMAGAZINE did a segment on a "revolutionary" idea for the business world: servant-leadership. Stone Phillips wondered, "Can humility and faith be good for business? Was Jesus the ultimate CEO? It's an image nearly 2,000 years old and a message that true leaders are servants first. It's an idea that's finding new disciples in corporate America."

Stone Phillips interviewed Larry Spears, who owns a worldwide nonprofit organization headquartered in Indianapolis. Larry suggested a leadership model based on sacrifice and service by those at the top toward those below them in the chain of command. He said, "Servant-leadership sort of challenges people to be brave and courageous, and to bring ideas like friendship and perhaps even love to the work place."

Jesus was the ultimate servant-leader. He knew he would be putting his mission in the hands of the disciples in the coming hours as he headed to the cross. It would soon be their turn to spread the Good News of the gospel message. So he demonstrated servant-leadership in a profoundly beautiful way. On the night before his trial and crucifixion, Jesus took the lead by humbly, lovingly kneeling at the feet of his followers and washing the dirt from their feet.

Perhaps he was thinking of how their feet would carry them to parts of the world they probably hadn't even yet heard about as they spread the Good News about the Messiah. Perhaps he reminisced about the places they had walked together. Perhaps he prayed that their feet would stand strong when they faced the persecution to come. This was surely a precious, intimate moment with his friends.

We women have grown accustomed to serving our friends and family. We serve dinner and wash dishes. We wash dirty faces. We wash loads and loads of laundry. As we carry out our roles as servants, may we humbly lead those we love to the servant-leader Jesus, the One who was willing to humble himself and wash us "whiter than snow" (Psalm 51:7).

Go to page 1309 for your next devotional reading.

John 13:15–16

"I have set you an example that you should do as I have done for you. I tell you the truth, no servant is greater than his master, nor is a messenger greater than the one who sent him."

reflection

1 Where are some of the places your feet have carried you for the Lord?

2 What leadership roles has God allowed you to undertake for him?

3 Knowing that Jesus was willing to washing his disciples' feet, how will you humbly serve those whom you lead?

RELATED READINGS

Matthew 23:8–12;
Mark 9:33–35;
Philippians 2:1–8

prepare a place for you. ³And if I go and prepare a place for you, I will come back and take you to be with me that you also may be where I am. ⁴You know the way to the place where I am going."

Jesus the Way to the Father

⁵Thomas said to him, "Lord, we don't know where you are going, so how can we know the way?"

⁶Jesus answered, "I am the way and the truth and the life. No one comes to the Father except through me. ⁷If you really knew me, you would know*a* my Father as well. From now on, you do know him and have seen him."

⁸Philip said, "Lord, show us the Father and that will be enough for us."

⁹Jesus answered: "Don't you know me, Philip, even after I have been among you such a long time? Anyone who has seen me has seen the Father. How can you say, 'Show us the Father'? ¹⁰Don't you believe that I am in the Father, and that the Father is in me? The words I say to you are not just my own. Rather, it is the Father, living in me, who is doing his work. ¹¹Believe me when I say that I am in the Father and the Father is in me; or at least believe on the evidence of the miracles themselves. ¹²I tell you the truth, anyone who has faith in me will do what I have been doing. He will do even greater things than these, because I am going to the Father. ¹³And I will do whatever you ask in my name, so that the Son may bring glory to the Father. ¹⁴You may ask me for anything in my name, and I will do it.

Jesus Promises the Holy Spirit

¹⁵"If you love me, you will obey what I command. ¹⁶And I will ask the Father, and he will give you another Counselor to be with you forever— ¹⁷the Spirit of truth. The world cannot accept him, because it neither sees him nor knows him. But you know him, for he lives with you and will be*b* in you. ¹⁸I will not leave you as orphans; I will come to you. ¹⁹Before long, the world will not see me anymore, but you will see me. Because I live, you also will live. ²⁰On that day you will realize that I am in my Father, and you are in me, and I am in

you. ²¹Whoever has my commands and obeys them, he is the one who loves me. He who loves me will be loved by my Father, and I too will love him and show myself to him."

²²Then Judas (not Judas Iscariot) said, "But, Lord, why do you intend to show yourself to us and not to the world?"

²³Jesus replied, "If anyone loves me, he will obey my teaching. My Father will love him, and we will come to him and make our home with him. ²⁴He who does not love me will not obey my teaching. These words you hear are not my own; they belong to the Father who sent me.

²⁵"All this I have spoken while still with you. ²⁶But the Counselor, the Holy Spirit, whom the Father will send in my name, will teach you all things and will remind you of everything I have said to you. ²⁷Peace I leave with you; my peace I give you. I do not give to you as the world gives. Do not let your hearts be troubled and do not be afraid.

²⁸"You heard me say, 'I am going away and I am coming back to you.' If you loved me, you would be glad that I am going to the Father, for the Father is greater than I. ²⁹I have told you now before it happens, so that when it does happen you will believe. ³⁰I will not speak with you much longer, for the prince of this world is coming. He has no hold on me, ³¹but the world must learn that I love the Father and that I do exactly what my Father has commanded me.

"Come now; let us leave."

The Vine and the Branches

15 "I am the true vine, and my Father is the gardener. ²He cuts off every branch in me that bears no fruit, while every branch that does bear fruit he prunes*c* so that it will be even more fruitful. ³You are already clean because of the word I have spoken to you. ⁴Remain in me, and I will remain in you. No branch can bear fruit by itself; it must remain in the vine. Neither can you bear fruit unless you remain in me.

⁵"I am the vine; you are the branches. If a man remains in me and I in him, he will bear much fruit; apart from me you can do nothing. ⁶If anyone does not remain in me, he is like a branch that is thrown away and withers; such

---

*a*7 Some early manuscripts *If you really have known me, you will know* means *cleans.* *b*17 Some early manuscripts *and is* *c*2 The Greek for *prunes* also

Faithfully Available

Read: John 14:1–31

WHAT ASSIGNMENT HAS GOD GIVEN YOU? Would you ask Him? I know He has one in mind for you because He told us clearly, through the words of the apostle Paul, that "we are God's workmanship, created in Christ Jesus to do good works, which God prepared in advance for us to do."

Don't dodge your assignment because it seems to lack any chance for success. Don't miss your assignment because it seems such an insignificant, small thing. The church in Europe was birthed when Paul spoke to a handful of women on a river bank. The size and scope of the assignment are up to Him, and the effectiveness and lasting impact of your service are also His responsibility. You and I are simply to be faithfully available . . . and obedient.

The assignments God has given me have taken me way beyond my comfort zone. While some of them have begun small and stayed small, others have begun small and grown larger, while still others were begun large and blossomed into major tasks.

There have been times when I have argued, resisted, procrastinated, and questioned, but in the end I always give in, because He is my Lord . . . I have "seen" Him . . . and I love Him. I don't serve Him because I have to. I serve Him because I want to do something for Him. And in the process of being obedient, I have come to know Him. He has "made known to me the path of life. He has filled me with joy in His presence, with eternal pleasures at His right hand."

With eagerness and enthusiasm, I put my feet in motion. I want to serve Him all the days of my life. I want to stay awake to His glorious vision forever. I am now on a passionate pursuit for more of Jesus. I embrace the Cross that shatters the stranglehold of self and enlarges my capacity to receive more. I long . . .

- ◆ to gaze on His visible face,
- ◆ to hear His audible voice,
- ◆ to feel His unmistakable touch,
- ◆ to become an eyewitness of His glory.

In the meantime, I refuse to sleep one more minute. I'm awake . . . with eyes opened, heart rended, and knees bent while I whisper, "Yes . . . Yes, Lord! . . . Yes, Sir!" then raise my hand as I move my feet. "I'm available for service. Send me. I'll go. I want to stay awake forever . . ."

—Anne Graham Lotz

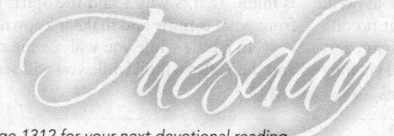

John 14:25–26

"All this I have spoken while still with you. But the Counselor, the Holy Spirit, whom the Father will send in my name, will teach you all things and will remind you of everything I have said to you."

reflection

1 What assignment has God given to you?

2 What is the first step of obedience you need to take in order to begin fulfilling that special assignment?

3 Whisper, "Yes . . . Yes, Lord!" and ask the Holy Spirit to teach you how to complete the assignment in a way that perfectly glorifies God and brings you to a greater knowledge of him.

RELATED READINGS

1 Chronicles 9:22–27;
Psalm 16;
Ephesians 2:4–10;
Hebrews 5:5–10

Go to page 1312 for your next devotional reading.

1309

branches are picked up, thrown into the fire and burned. [7]If you remain in me and my words remain in you, ask whatever you wish, and it will be given you. [8]This is to my Father's glory, that you bear much fruit, showing yourselves to be my disciples.

[9]"As the Father has loved me, so have I loved you. Now remain in my love. [10]If you obey my commands, you will remain in my love, just as I have obeyed my Father's commands and remain in his love. [11]I have told you this so that my joy may be in you and that your joy may be complete. [12]My command is this: Love each other as I have loved you. [13]Greater love has no one than this, that he lay down his life for his friends. [14]You are my friends if you do what I command. [15]I no longer call you servants, because a servant does not know his master's business. Instead, I have called you friends, for everything that I learned from my Father I have made known to you. [16]You did not choose me, but I chose you and appointed you to go and bear fruit—fruit that will last. Then the Father will give you whatever you ask in my name. [17]This is my command: Love each other.

The World Hates the Disciples

[18]"If the world hates you, keep in mind that it hated me first. [19]If you belonged to the world, it would love you as its own. As it is, you do not belong to the world, but I have chosen you out of the world. That is why the world hates you. [20]Remember the words I spoke to you: 'No servant is greater than his master.'[a] If they persecuted me, they will persecute you also. If they obeyed my teaching, they will obey yours also. [21]They will treat you this way because of my name, for they do not know the One who sent me. [22]If I had not come and spoken to them, they would not be guilty of sin. Now, however, they have no excuse for their sin. [23]He who hates me hates my Father as well. [24]If I had not done among them what no one else did, they would not be guilty of sin. But now they have seen these miracles, and yet they

have hated both me and my Father. [25]But this is to fulfill what is written in their Law: 'They hated me without reason.'[b]

[26]"When the Counselor comes, whom I will send to you from the Father, the Spirit of truth who goes out from the Father, he will testify about me. [27]And you also must testify, for you have been with me from the beginning.

16 "All this I have told you so that you will not go astray. [2]They will put you out of the synagogue; in fact, a time is coming when anyone who kills you will think he is offering a service to God. [3]They will do such things because they have not known the Father or me. [4]I have told you this, so that when the time comes you will remember that I warned you. I did not tell you this at first because I was with you.

The Work of the Holy Spirit

[5]"Now I am going to him who sent me, yet none of you asks me, 'Where are you going?' [6]Because I have said these things, you are filled with grief. [7]But I tell you the truth: It is for your good that I am going away. Unless I go away, the Counselor will not come to you; but if I go, I will send him to you. [8]When he comes, he will convict the world of guilt[c] in regard to sin and righteousness and judgment: [9]in regard to sin, because men do not believe in me; [10]in regard to righteousness, because I am going to the Father, where you can see me no longer; [11]and in regard to judgment, because the prince of this world now stands condemned.

[12]"I have much more to say to you, more than you can now bear. [13]But when he, the Spirit of truth, comes, he will guide you into all truth. He will not speak on his own; he will speak only what he hears, and he will tell you what is yet to come. [14]He will bring glory to me by taking from what is mine and making it known to you. [15]All that belongs to the Father is mine. That is why I said the Spirit will take from what is mine and make it known to you.

[16]"In a little while you will see me no more, and then after a little while you will see me."

---

[a]20 John 13:16   [b]25 Psalms 35:19; 69:4   [c]8 Or will expose the guilt of the world

---

John 15:7

God Gives Good Gifts

"If you remain in me and my words remain in you, ask whatever you wish, and it will be given you."

The Disciples' Grief Will Turn to Joy

17 Some of his disciples said to one another, "What does he mean by saying, 'In a little while you will see me no more, and then after a little while you will see me,' and 'Because I am going to the Father'?" 18 They kept asking, "What does he mean by 'a little while'? We don't understand what he is saying."

19 Jesus saw that they wanted to ask him about this, so he said to them, "Are you asking one another what I meant when I said, 'In a little while you will see me no more, and then after a little while you will see me'? 20 I tell you the truth, you will weep and mourn while the world rejoices. You will grieve, but your grief will turn to joy. 21 A woman giving birth to a child has pain because her time has come; but when her baby is born she forgets the anguish because of her joy that a child is born into the world. 22 So with you: Now is your time of grief, but I will see you again and you will rejoice, and no one will take away your joy. 23 In that day you will no longer ask me anything. I tell you the truth, my Father will give you whatever you ask in my name. 24 Until now you have not asked for anything in my name. Ask and you will receive, and your joy will be complete.

25 "Though I have been speaking figuratively, a time is coming when I will no longer use this kind of language but will tell you plainly about my Father. 26 In that day you will ask in my name. I am not saying that I will ask the Father on your behalf. 27 No, the Father himself loves you because you have loved me and have believed that I came from God. 28 I came from the Father and entered the world; now I am leaving the world and going back to the Father."

29 Then Jesus' disciples said, "Now you are speaking clearly and without figures of speech. 30 Now we can see that you know all things and that you do not even need to have anyone ask you questions. This makes us believe that you came from God."

31 "You believe at last!"[a] Jesus answered. 32 "But a time is coming, and has come, when you will be scattered, each to his own home. You will leave me all alone. Yet I am not alone, for my Father is with me.

33 "I have told you these things, so that in me you may have peace. In this world you will have trouble. But take heart! I have overcome the world."

John 16:33

God Has Overcome the World

"I have told you these things, so that in me you may have peace. In this world you will have trouble. But take heart! I have overcome the world."

Jesus Prays for Himself

17 After Jesus said this, he looked toward heaven and prayed:

"Father, the time has come. Glorify your Son, that your Son may glorify you. 2 For you granted him authority over all people that he might give eternal life to all those you have given him. 3 Now this is eternal life: that they may know you, the only true God, and Jesus Christ, whom you have sent. 4 I have brought you glory on earth by completing the work you gave me to do. 5 And now, Father, glorify me in your presence with the glory I had with you before the world began.

Jesus Prays for His Disciples

6 "I have revealed you[b] to those whom you gave me out of the world. They were yours; you gave them to me and they have obeyed your word. 7 Now they know that everything you have given me comes from you. 8 For I gave them the words you gave me and they accepted them. They knew with certainty that I came from you, and they believed that you sent me. 9 I pray for them. I am not praying for the world, but for those you have given me, for they are yours. 10 All I have is yours, and all you have is mine. And glory has come to me through them. 11 I will remain in the world no longer, but they are still in the world, and I am coming to you. Holy Father, protect them by the power of your

a31 Or "Do you now believe?"   b6 Greek your name; also in verse 26

Full of Joy

Read: John 17:1–26

John 17:13

"I am coming to you now, but I say these things while I am still in the world, so that they may have the full measure of my joy within them."

reflection

1 On a scale of one to ten, how would you rate your joy factor?

2 After reading Nadine's comments, do you relate to her when she talks about allowing imaginary troubles to interrupt joy?

3 What might you do today to experience more joy?

RELATED READINGS

Acts 14:15–17;
Romans 14:17–18;
Hebrews 1:8–9;
1 Peter 1:8–9

"I'D MAKE MORE MISTAKES next time," said 85-year-old Nadine Stair when asked what she would do if she had her life to live over again. "I'd relax. I would limber up. I would be sillier than I have been this trip. I would take fewer things seriously. I would take more chances. I would climb more mountains and swim more rivers. I would eat more ice cream and less beans. I would perhaps have more actual troubles, but I'd have fewer imaginary ones. You see, I'm one of those people who live sensibly and sanely hour after hour, day after day. Oh, I've had my moments, and if I had to do it over again, I'd have more of them. In fact, I'd try to have nothing else—just moments, one after another, instead of living so many years ahead of each day. I've been one of those persons who never goes anywhere without a thermometer, a hot water bottle and a raincoat. If I had to do it over again, I would travel lighter than I have. If I had my life to live over, I would start barefoot earlier in the spring and stay that way later in the fall. I would go to more dances. I would ride more merry-go-rounds. I would pick more daisies."

In his final prayer, Jesus prayed that his disciples would experience the full measure of his joy—now. He prayed for us to have his joy in the middle of rush-hour traffic, screaming kids and a darkening world. He doesn't want us to wait for heaven to be full of joy.

Jesus' joy has a divine purpose: to reveal him. He desires to fill us with overflowing joy, to proclaim his victory to the world over life's worst conditions—even in the face of hurricanes, plagues, terrorism and nuclear disaster.

But as Nadine tells us, joy flows from a foundation of *truth*. So many times we focus on imaginary troubles. But Jesus reminds us that joy comes from knowing the Father through the Son. As you reflect on your life, whether you're 18, 38, 48 or 88, choose to live in fullness of joy by taking the time to pick more daisies . . . and by living each moment fully aware of God's love for you.

Wednesday

Go to page 1316 for your next devotional reading.

name—the name you gave me—so that they may be one as we are one. 12While I was with them, I protected them and kept them safe by that name you gave me. None has been lost except the one doomed to destruction so that Scripture would be fulfilled.

13"I am coming to you now, but I say these things while I am still in the world, so that they may have the full measure of my joy within them. 14I have given them your word and the world has hated them, for they are not of the world any more than I am of the world. 15My prayer is not that you take them out of the world but that you protect them from the evil one. 16They are not of the world, even as I am not of it. 17Sanctify[a] them by the truth; your word is truth. 18As you sent me into the world, I have sent them into the world. 19For them I sanctify myself, that they too may be truly sanctified.

Jesus Prays for All Believers

20"My prayer is not for them alone. I pray also for those who will believe in me through their message, 21that all of them may be one, Father, just as you are in me and I am in you. May they also be in us so that the world may believe that you have sent me. 22I have given them the glory that you gave me, that they may be one as we are one: 23I in them and you in me. May they be brought to complete unity to let the world know that you sent me and have loved them even as you have loved me.

24"Father, I want those you have given me to be with me where I am, and to see my glory, the glory you have given me because you loved me before the creation of the world.

25"Righteous Father, though the world does not know you, I know you, and they know that you have sent me. 26I have made you known to them, and will continue to make you known in order that the love you have for me may be in them and that I myself may be in them."

Jesus Arrested

18 When he had finished praying, Jesus left with his disciples and crossed the Kidron Valley. On the other side there was an olive grove, and he and his disciples went into it.

2Now Judas, who betrayed him, knew the place, because Jesus had often met there with his disciples. 3So Judas came to the grove, guiding a detachment of soldiers and some officials from the chief priests and Pharisees. They were carrying torches, lanterns and weapons.

4Jesus, knowing all that was going to happen to him, went out and asked them, "Who is it you want?"

5"Jesus of Nazareth," they replied.

"I am he," Jesus said. (And Judas the traitor was standing there with them.) 6When Jesus said, "I am he," they drew back and fell to the ground.

7Again he asked them, "Who is it you want?"

And they said, "Jesus of Nazareth."

8"I told you that I am he," Jesus answered. "If you are looking for me, then let these men go." 9This happened so that the words he had spoken would be fulfilled: "I have not lost one of those you gave me."[b]

10Then Simon Peter, who had a sword, drew it and struck the high priest's servant, cutting off his right ear. (The servant's name was Malchus.)

11Jesus commanded Peter, "Put your sword away! Shall I not drink the cup the Father has given me?"

Jesus Taken to Annas

12Then the detachment of soldiers with its commander and the Jewish officials arrested Jesus. They bound him 13and brought him first to Annas, who was the father-in-law of Caiaphas, the high priest that year. 14Caiaphas was the one who had advised the Jews that it would be good if one man died for the people.

Peter's First Denial

15Simon Peter and another disciple were following Jesus. Because this disciple was known to the high priest, he went with Jesus into the high priest's courtyard, 16but Peter had to wait

---

a 17 Greek hagiazo (set apart for sacred use or make holy); also in verse 19 b 9 John 6:39

outside at the door. The other disciple, who was known to the high priest, came back, spoke to the girl on duty there and brought Peter in.

17"You are not one of his disciples, are you?" the girl at the door asked Peter.

He replied, "I am not."

18It was cold, and the servants and officials stood around a fire they had made to keep warm. Peter also was standing with them, warming himself.

The High Priest Questions Jesus

19Meanwhile, the high priest questioned Jesus about his disciples and his teaching.

20"I have spoken openly to the world," Jesus replied. "I always taught in synagogues or at the temple, where all the Jews come together. I said nothing in secret. **21**Why question me? Ask those who heard me. Surely they know what I said."

22When Jesus said this, one of the officials nearby struck him in the face. "Is this the way you answer the high priest?" he demanded.

23"If I said something wrong," Jesus replied, "testify as to what is wrong. But if I spoke the truth, why did you strike me?" **24**Then Annas sent him, still bound, to Caiaphas the high priest.*a*

Peter's Second and Third Denials

25As Simon Peter stood warming himself, he was asked, "You are not one of his disciples, are you?"

He denied it, saying, "I am not."

26One of the high priest's servants, a relative of the man whose ear Peter had cut off, challenged him, "Didn't I see you with him in the olive grove?" **27**Again Peter denied it, and at that moment a rooster began to crow.

Jesus Before Pilate

28Then the Jews led Jesus from Caiaphas to the palace of the Roman governor. By now it was early morning, and to avoid ceremonial uncleanness the Jews did not enter the palace; they wanted to be able to eat the Passover. **29**So Pilate came out to them and asked, "What charges are you bringing against this man?"

30"If he were not a criminal," they replied, "we would not have handed him over to you."

31Pilate said, "Take him yourselves and judge him by your own law."

"But we have no right to execute anyone," the Jews objected. **32**This happened so that the words Jesus had spoken indicating the kind of death he was going to die would be fulfilled.

33Pilate then went back inside the palace, summoned Jesus and asked him, "Are you the king of the Jews?"

34"Is that your own idea," Jesus asked, "or did others talk to you about me?"

35"Am I a Jew?" Pilate replied. "It was your people and your chief priests who handed you over to me. What is it you have done?"

36Jesus said, "My kingdom is not of this world. If it were, my servants would fight to prevent my arrest by the Jews. But now my kingdom is from another place."

37"You are a king, then!" said Pilate.

Jesus answered, "You are right in saying I am a king. In fact, for this reason I was born, and for this I came into the world, to testify to the truth. Everyone on the side of truth listens to me."

38"What is truth?" Pilate asked. With this he went out again to the Jews and said, "I find no basis for a charge against him. **39**But it is your custom for me to release to you one prisoner at the time of the Passover. Do you want me to release 'the king of the Jews'?"

40They shouted back, "No, not him! Give us Barabbas!" Now Barabbas had taken part in a rebellion.

Jesus Sentenced to Be Crucified

19 Then Pilate took Jesus and had him flogged. **2**The soldiers twisted together a crown of thorns and put it on his head. They clothed him in a purple robe **3**and went up to him again and again, saying, "Hail, king of the Jews!" And they struck him in the face.

4Once more Pilate came out and said to the Jews, "Look, I am bringing him out to you to let you know that I find no basis for a charge against him." **5**When Jesus came out wearing the crown of thorns and the purple robe, Pilate said to them, "Here is the man!"

6As soon as the chief priests and their officials saw him, they shouted, "Crucify! Crucify!"

---

a24 Or (Now Annas had sent him, still bound, to Caiaphas the high priest.)

But Pilate answered, "You take him and crucify him. As for me, I find no basis for a charge against him."

⁷The Jews insisted, "We have a law, and according to that law he must die, because he claimed to be the Son of God."

⁸When Pilate heard this, he was even more afraid, ⁹and he went back inside the palace. "Where do you come from?" he asked Jesus, but Jesus gave him no answer. ¹⁰"Do you refuse to speak to me?" Pilate said. "Don't you realize I have power either to free you or to crucify you?"

¹¹Jesus answered, "You would have no power over me if it were not given to you from above. Therefore the one who handed me over to you is guilty of a greater sin."

¹²From then on, Pilate tried to set Jesus free, but the Jews kept shouting, "If you let this man go, you are no friend of Caesar. Anyone who claims to be a king opposes Caesar."

¹³When Pilate heard this, he brought Jesus out and sat down on the judge's seat at a place known as the Stone Pavement (which in Aramaic is Gabbatha). ¹⁴It was the day of Preparation of Passover Week, about the sixth hour.

"Here is your king," Pilate said to the Jews.

¹⁵But they shouted, "Take him away! Take him away! Crucify him!"

"Shall I crucify your king?" Pilate asked.

"We have no king but Caesar," the chief priests answered.

¹⁶Finally Pilate handed him over to them to be crucified.

The Crucifixion

So the soldiers took charge of Jesus. ¹⁷Carrying his own cross, he went out to the place of the Skull (which in Aramaic is called Golgotha). ¹⁸Here they crucified him, and with him two others—one on each side and Jesus in the middle.

¹⁹Pilate had a notice prepared and fastened to the cross. It read: JESUS OF NAZARETH, THE

KING OF THE JEWS. ²⁰Many of the Jews read this sign, for the place where Jesus was crucified was near the city, and the sign was written in Aramaic, Latin and Greek. ²¹The chief priests of the Jews protested to Pilate, "Do not write 'The King of the Jews,' but that this man claimed to be king of the Jews."

²²Pilate answered, "What I have written, I have written."

²³When the soldiers crucified Jesus, they took his clothes, dividing them into four shares, one for each of them, with the undergarment remaining. This garment was seamless, woven in one piece from top to bottom.

²⁴"Let's not tear it," they said to one another. "Let's decide by lot who will get it."

This happened that the scripture might be fulfilled which said,

"They divided my
   garments among
   them
and cast lots for my
   clothing."*a*

So this is what the soldiers did.

²⁵Near the cross of Jesus stood his mother, his mother's sister, Mary the wife of Clopas, and Mary Magdalene. ²⁶When Jesus saw his mother there, and the disciple whom he loved standing nearby, he said to his mother, "Dear woman, here is your son," ²⁷and to the disciple, "Here is your mother." From that time on, this disciple took her into his home.

The Death of Jesus

²⁸Later, knowing that all was now completed, and so that the Scripture would be fulfilled, Jesus said, "I am thirsty." ²⁹A jar of wine vinegar was there, so they soaked a sponge in it, put the sponge on a stalk of the hyssop plant, and lifted it to Jesus' lips. ³⁰When he had received the drink, Jesus said, "It is finished." With that, he bowed his head and gave up his spirit.

³¹Now it was the day of Preparation, and the next day was to be a special Sabbath. Because

---

John 19:11

God Appoints Those in Authority

Jesus answered, "You would have no power over me if it were not given to you from above. Therefore the one who handed me over to you is guilty of a greater sin."

---

*a*24 Psalm 22:18

It Is Finished

John 19:30

Jesus said, "It is finished." With that, he bowed his head and gave up his spirit.

reflection

1 Have you accepted Jesus' death as full payment for your sins? How does it feel to be completely forgiven and free from eternal death?

2 Who are the people in your life who have not accepted Jesus' death as payment for their sins? Pray for those you know who haven't asked for his forgiveness.

3 What are different ways you can thank Jesus for the wonderful love gift that only he could give? Pray and thank him right now.

RELATED READINGS

Genesis 3:14–16;
Isaiah 53:1–12;
Hebrews 9:11–22

Read: John 19:25–42

ALL OF HUMAN HISTORY has been moving toward one climactic moment: the death of Jesus Christ. From the first hint in Genesis 3:15 that the serpent would strike the heel of the man to Simeon's prophecy to Mary that a sword would pierce her soul (see Luke 2:34–35), history has held its breath—waiting for the promise to be fulfilled. Those prophecies were finally, painfully fulfilled as the Lifegiver gave up his spirit on the cross.

All of the Old Testament sacrifices pointed to this moment. At this juncture, the great High Priest became the sacrificial Lamb. The symbolism and mysterious predictions became reality in the life and death of this man who was God. This God-man who turned himself over to death so that his murderers could be forgiven. This man-God whose death would remove the sins of his own mother, who watched with sorrow as the prophecies became reality on that hideous cross. This God-man whose willing sacrifice sufficiently, completely covered the sins of men and women past, present and future.

Angels, prophets and Jesus Christ himself predicted his death at the hands of sinners. But his death was also *for* those sinners. God's justice demands death for sin. God's mercy provided the willing, perfect sacrifice for sin. The cross is God's love gift. On that cross love made a man die so that his enemies could live. There, the only perfect human died so that we sinners can be forgiven. On that day, everything that separates people from God was torn in the brutal tearing of Christ's body.

He did it for you. This sacrifice was the only way your sins could be paid for without your own eternal death. Christ's death paid the price of your sin. When Jesus said, "It is finished," he meant there was nothing else to do, nothing left to pay. He paid it all—totally, completely, permanently.

It is finished.

Go to page 1318 for your next devotional reading.

the Jews did not want the bodies left on the crosses during the Sabbath, they asked Pilate to have the legs broken and the bodies taken down. ³²The soldiers therefore came and broke the legs of the first man who had been crucified with Jesus, and then those of the other. ³³But when they came to Jesus and found that he was already dead, they did not break his legs. ³⁴Instead, one of the soldiers pierced Jesus' side with a spear, bringing a sudden flow of blood and water. ³⁵The man who saw it has given testimony, and his testimony is true. He knows that he tells the truth, and he testifies so that you also may believe. ³⁶These things happened so that the scripture would be fulfilled: "Not one of his bones will be broken,"*a* ³⁷and, as another scripture says, "They will look on the one they have pierced."*b*

The Burial of Jesus

³⁸Later, Joseph of Arimathea asked Pilate for the body of Jesus. Now Joseph was a disciple of Jesus, but secretly because he feared the Jews. With Pilate's permission, he came and took the body away. ³⁹He was accompanied by Nicodemus, the man who earlier had visited Jesus at night. Nicodemus brought a mixture of myrrh and aloes, about seventy-five pounds.*c* ⁴⁰Taking Jesus' body, the two of them wrapped it, with the spices, in strips of linen. This was in accordance with Jewish burial customs. ⁴¹At the place where Jesus was crucified, there was a garden, and in the garden a new tomb, in which no one had ever been laid. ⁴²Because it was the Jewish day of Preparation and since the tomb was nearby, they laid Jesus there.

The Empty Tomb

20 Early on the first day of the week, while it was still dark, Mary Magdalene went to the tomb and saw that the stone had been removed from the entrance. ²So she came running to Simon Peter and the other disciple, the one Jesus loved, and said, "They have taken the Lord out of the tomb, and we don't know where they have put him!"

³So Peter and the other disciple started for the tomb. ⁴Both were running, but the other disciple outran Peter and reached the tomb first. ⁵He bent over and looked in at the strips of linen lying there but did not go in. ⁶Then Simon Peter, who was behind him, arrived and went into the tomb. He saw the strips of linen lying there, ⁷as well as the burial cloth that had been around Jesus' head. The cloth was folded up by itself, separate from the linen. ⁸Finally the other disciple, who had reached the tomb first, also went inside. He saw and believed. ⁹(They still did not understand from Scripture that Jesus had to rise from the dead.)

Jesus Appears to Mary Magdalene

¹⁰Then the disciples went back to their homes, ¹¹but Mary stood outside the tomb crying. As she wept, she bent over to look into the tomb ¹²and saw two angels in white, seated where Jesus' body had been, one at the head and the other at the foot.

¹³They asked her, "Woman, why are you crying?"

"They have taken my Lord away," she said, "and I don't know where they have put him." ¹⁴At this, she turned around and saw Jesus standing there, but she did not realize that it was Jesus.

¹⁵"Woman," he said, "why are you crying? Who is it you are looking for?"

Thinking he was the gardener, she said, "Sir, if you have carried him away, tell me where you have put him, and I will get him."

¹⁶Jesus said to her, "Mary."

She turned toward him and cried out in Aramaic, "Rabboni!" (which means Teacher).

¹⁷Jesus said, "Do not hold on to me, for I have not yet returned to the Father. Go instead to my brothers and tell them, 'I am returning to my Father and your Father, to my God and your God.'"

¹⁸Mary Magdalene went to the disciples with the news: "I have seen the Lord!" And she told them that he had said these things to her.

Jesus Appears to His Disciples

¹⁹On the evening of that first day of the week, when the disciples were together, with the doors locked for fear of the Jews, Jesus came and stood among them and said, "Peace be with you!" ²⁰After he said this, he showed them his hands and side. The disciples were overjoyed when they saw the Lord.

---

*a*36 Exodus 12:46; Num. 9:12; Psalm 34:20   *b*37 Zech. 12:10   *c*39 Greek *a hundred litrai* (about 34 kilograms)

Read: John 20:11–31

reflection

1 Do you think you *know* Jesus or just know *about* Jesus?

2 How much time each day do you spend with him?

3 How has time in his Word and in prayer helped you to know and love him more?

RELATED READINGS

John 3:16–21;
6:41–58;
1 John 5:1–5

IMAGINE JESUS SAVORING boiled fish for breakfast. See his face light up as he delights in a child's antics. Observe him as he keeps the party going, turning water at a wedding into choice wine.

This is the human Jesus—a man who cried, laughed, slept, conversed and shared affection freely. Few knew Jesus' personal habits like his 12 disciples. And John, who Jesus called "beloved," may have known him best of all.

As an insider, John offers an up-close view of seven of Jesus' miracles and shares the compelling details of Jesus' death and resurrection. After all of these real-life stories, John is quick to admit that Jesus did many more miracles: "But these are written that you may believe that Jesus is the Christ, the Son of God, and that by believing you may have life in his name" (verse 31).

"Trust me," John seems to say. "I knew him. I loved him. I watched him do miracles, die and come back to life again. Jesus is God's Son. He proved it!" Though we cannot walk beside the human Jesus today, millions have seen him through John's eyes.

Centuries later, a Jesus-follower named Sundar Singh said this about knowing Jesus Christ: "There are many Christians who do not feel his glorious presence as something real . . . only when someone surrenders his heart to Jesus can he find him." Singh knew in his mind who Jesus Christ was—but when he surrendered his heart, he found peace even while he was in prison.

How do you know Jesus? Knowing details about his life and ministry isn't enough. When you receive his forgiveness, you can go beyond knowing him to loving him. When you spend time with him in prayer, you can go beyond loving him to sensing his presence. Reflect today on how you can experience his presence in all of your daily moments. The real Jesus longs to hold a place in your heart.

"I must make a conscious, deliberate, daily choice to sit at His feet, to listen to His Word, to receive His love, to let Him change me and to pour out my heart's devotion to Him."

Nancy Leigh DeMoss

Go to page 1320 for your next devotional reading.

²¹Again Jesus said, "Peace be with you! As the Father has sent me, I am sending you." ²²And with that he breathed on them and said, "Receive the Holy Spirit. ²³If you forgive anyone his sins, they are forgiven; if you do not forgive them, they are not forgiven."

Jesus Appears to Thomas

²⁴Now Thomas (called Didymus), one of the Twelve, was not with the disciples when Jesus came. ²⁵So the other disciples told him, "We have seen the Lord!"

But he said to them, "Unless I see the nail marks in his hands and put my finger where the nails were, and put my hand into his side, I will not believe it."

²⁶A week later his disciples were in the house again, and Thomas was with them. Though the doors were locked, Jesus came and stood among them and said, "Peace be with you!" ²⁷Then he said to Thomas, "Put your finger here; see my hands. Reach out your hand and put it into my side. Stop doubting and believe."

²⁸Thomas said to him, "My Lord and my God!"

²⁹Then Jesus told him, "Because you have seen me, you have believed; blessed are those who have not seen and yet have believed."

³⁰Jesus did many other miraculous signs in the presence of his disciples, which are not recorded in this book. ³¹But these are written that you may*a* believe that Jesus is the Christ, the Son of God, and that by believing you may have life in his name.

Jesus and the Miraculous Catch of Fish

21 Afterward Jesus appeared again to his disciples, by the Sea of Tiberias.*b* It happened this way: ²Simon Peter, Thomas (called Didymus), Nathanael from Cana in Galilee, the sons of Zebedee, and two other disciples were together. ³"I'm going out to fish," Simon Peter told them, and they said, "We'll go with you." So they went out and got into the boat, but that night they caught nothing.

⁴Early in the morning, Jesus stood on the shore, but the disciples did not realize that it was Jesus.

⁵He called out to them, "Friends, haven't you any fish?"

"No," they answered.

⁶He said, "Throw your net on the right side of the boat and you will find some." When they did, they were unable to haul the net in because of the large number of fish.

⁷Then the disciple whom Jesus loved said to Peter, "It is the Lord!" As soon as Simon Peter heard him say, "It is the Lord," he wrapped his outer garment around him (for he had taken it off) and jumped into the water. ⁸The other disciples followed in the boat, towing the net full of fish, for they were not far from shore, about a hundred yards.*c* ⁹When they landed, they saw a fire of burning coals there with fish on it, and some bread.

¹⁰Jesus said to them, "Bring some of the fish you have just caught."

¹¹Simon Peter climbed aboard and dragged the net ashore. It was full of large fish, 153, but even with so many the net was not torn. ¹²Jesus said to them, "Come and have breakfast." None of the disciples dared ask him, "Who are you?" They knew it was the Lord. ¹³Jesus came, took the bread and gave it to them, and did the same with the fish. ¹⁴This was now the third time Jesus appeared to his disciples after he was raised from the dead.

Jesus Reinstates Peter

¹⁵When they had finished eating, Jesus said to Simon Peter, "Simon son of John, do you truly love me more than these?"

"Yes, Lord," he said, "you know that I love you."

Jesus said, "Feed my lambs."

¹⁶Again Jesus said, "Simon son of John, do you truly love me?"

He answered, "Yes, Lord, you know that I love you."

Jesus said, "Take care of my sheep."

¹⁷The third time he said to him, "Simon son of John, do you love me?"

Peter was hurt because Jesus asked him the third time, "Do you love me?" He said, "Lord, you know all things; you know that I love you."

Jesus said, "Feed my sheep. ¹⁸I tell you the truth, when you were younger you dressed yourself and went where you wanted; but when you are old you will stretch out your hands,

---

a 31 Some manuscripts *may continue to*   *b* 1 That is, Sea of Galilee   *c* 8 Greek *about two hundred cubits* (about 90 meters)

Some women were watching from a distance. Among them were Mary Magdalene, Mary the mother of James the younger and of Joses, and Salome.

Mark 15:40

ASSIGNED READING:

Mark 15:40; 16:1–8

SALOME HAD A STRANGE FEELING. Something told her that the climactic meeting in Jerusalem for Passover had a greater significance this year. Surely, as one of Jesus' closest followers and supporters, she was aware of the mounting controversy surrounding him at this time. People were more and more divided because of her Master. Most no longer perceived him as merely a popular miracle worker and generous benefactor. No. His recent messages about sacrifice and commitment were too intense and demanding for that description anymore.

She'd seen the reaction of the crowds. She'd observed how the religious leaders scowled and huddled in groups. Her intuition told her something was afoot.

Was she so surprised, then, when the assembly of Jews turned on him at the end of the week? After hearing of his predawn arrest in the garden of Gethsemane, she'd lingered nearby as they took him to the religious leaders and eventually to Pilate. She'd heard the commotion of jealous leaders shouting mercilessly for his execution.

Now, with the other women at the foot of the cross, this spiritual sisterhood formed the foundation for future Christian women's groups across the world. They could not have known history would record their names: Salome (probably the mother of James and John, Zebedee's sons), Mary Magdalene, Mary the wife of Clopas, Jesus' mother Mary and Mary the mother of James and Joses. Together, their synergy supported and encouraged Jesus on a regular basis. In pairs, triads and even as a group, they—and other women, such as Joanna, Mary of Bethany, Martha and Susanna—appear in Scripture alongside him on many occasions.

The last snapshot of Salome in Scripture is of her walking to the tomb on Sunday, spices in hand, to prepare Jesus' body. Perhaps on the way there, the strange feeling returned that she'd not been able to shake since arriving in Jerusalem. Only this time, by the time she reached the empty tomb, it brought an unexpected smile to her lips.

—Prayer—
Dear God, thank you for the women in my life who support me and love me.

Weekend

Go to page 1323 for your next devotional reading.

and someone else will dress you and lead you where you do not want to go." [19] Jesus said this to indicate the kind of death by which Peter would glorify God. Then he said to him, "Follow me!"

[20] Peter turned and saw that the disciple whom Jesus loved was following them. (This was the one who had leaned back against Jesus at the supper and had said, "Lord, who is going to betray you?") [21] When Peter saw him, he asked, "Lord, what about him?"

[22] Jesus answered, "If I want him to remain alive until I return, what is that to you? You must follow me." [23] Because of this, the rumor spread among the brothers that this disciple would not die. But Jesus did not say that he would not die; he only said, "If I want him to remain alive until I return, what is that to you?"

[24] This is the disciple who testifies to these things and who wrote them down. We know that his testimony is true.

[25] Jesus did many other things as well. If every one of them were written down, I suppose that even the whole world would not have room for the books that would be written.

Acts

Author:
Luke, a physician, and a Gentile (Greek) Christian.

Audience:
Specifically, Theophilus, whose name means "dear friend who loves God." He is the same high official for whom the book of Luke was written (see Luke 1:1).

Date:
Probably about A.D. 63.

Setting:
The gospel is spreading to all parts of the Roman Empire.

Verse to Remember:
"But you will receive power when the Holy Spirit comes on you; and you will be my witnesses in Jerusalem, and in all Judea and Samaria, and to the ends of the earth." (1:8)

The book of Acts, the second book written by Luke, *is full of firsts:* Peter's first sermon, the first mass evangelism meeting, the birth of the first church, the first martyr, the first Christian missionaries and the first Gentile additions to the new church. The new Christian church, composed of followers of Jesus, is a vibrant young church, *filled with the Holy Spirit* and quickly making a mark on the world. The arrival of the promised Holy Spirit makes the book of Acts exciting and unpredictable. Watch for *miracles and imprisonments and unexpected conversions.* See the Christians' hesitation as the persecuting Saul becomes the missionary Paul. *And watch persecution begin as the gospel* spreads to Gentiles and around the known world.

Jesus Taken Up Into Heaven

1 In my former book, Theophilus, I wrote about all that Jesus began to do and to teach ² until the day he was taken up to heaven, after giving instructions through the Holy Spirit to the apostles he had chosen. ³ After his suffering, he showed himself to these men and gave many convincing proofs that he was alive. He appeared to them over a period of forty days and spoke about the kingdom of God. ⁴ On one occasion, while he was eating with them, he gave them this command: "Do not leave Jerusalem, but wait for the gift my Father promised, which you have heard me speak about. ⁵ For

A Mother's Prayers

Read: Acts 1:1–14

MONICA NEVER STOPPED PRAYING for her son. She had raised Augustine in the Christian faith in their small town in Algeria, but when he was a teenager the family moved to Carthage in North Africa. Possessed of a brilliant intellect and an even stronger will, Augustine rejected his mother's faith and instead chose a life in pursuit of immorality. In his autobiographical book *Confessions*, Augustine spoke of his years of debauchery: "Years passed, in which I wallowed in the mire of that deep pit, and the darkness of falsehood . . . All which time that chaste, godly and sober widow . . . ceased not at all hours of her devotions to bewail my case unto You. And her prayers entered into Your presence . . ."

Three hundred years before the birth of Augustine, we can only imagine how another mother labored in prayer for her children. In addition to Jesus, her firstborn, Mary of Nazareth had several other children. And yet their family was spiritually divided. John's Gospel clearly tells us that "even his own brothers did not believe in him" (John 7:5). The skepticism of her younger sons toward their elder half brother must have pierced Mary's heart.

The black Friday when her oldest son hung on a Roman cross had to be the worst day of Mary's life. And the Sunday when he rose again was the very best. Among those to whom Christ appeared after his resurrection was his brother James. We don't need to know the words that passed between them. It's enough to know that when the disciples and the women gathered to pray in the upper room following Jesus' ascension into heaven, Mary was among them. And her other sons were with her! *Praying*. The One they had rejected in life was the One in whom they now placed their faith for eternity.

Monica's prodigal son Augustine became one of the most famously devout fourth-century Christians: the Bishop of Hippo. *The Confessions of St. Augustine* is a classic of the Christian faith. Mary's son James became leader of the church in Jerusalem and wrote the New Testament book that bears his name.

Do you have children, grandchildren or children whom you love—related to you or not—who have turned away from God? Years may pass without any apparent external change. But heaven hears your loving intercession on their behalf. Take heart! God hears your prayers for your children.

Acts 1:14

They all joined together constantly in prayer, along with the women and Mary the mother of Jesus, and with his brothers.

reflection

1 Speculate on why it wasn't until the resurrection that Jesus' brothers believed he was who he said he was.

2 If you have a prodigal or know a prodigal, how does this devotional offer you hope?

3 Spend some time praying for those who have walked away from the faith of their mothers. Ask God to hear your prayers and bring the straying children home.

RELATED READINGS

Matthew 18:12–14;
Luke 15:11–32;
2 Timothy 1:5–7

Monday

Go to page 1328 for your next devotional reading.

John baptized with[a] water, but in a few days you will be baptized with the Holy Spirit."

6So when they met together, they asked him, "Lord, are you at this time going to restore the kingdom to Israel?"

7He said to them: "It is not for you to know the times or dates the Father has set by his own authority. 8But you will receive power when the Holy Spirit comes on you; and you will be my witnesses in Jerusalem, and in all Judea and Samaria, and to the ends of the earth."

9After he said this, he was taken up before their very eyes, and a cloud hid him from their sight.

10They were looking intently up into the sky as he was going, when suddenly two men dressed in white stood beside them. 11"Men of Galilee," they said, "why do you stand here looking into the sky? This same Jesus, who has been taken from you into heaven, will come back in the same way you have seen him go into heaven."

Matthias Chosen to Replace Judas

12Then they returned to Jerusalem from the hill called the Mount of Olives, a Sabbath day's walk[b] from the city. 13When they arrived, they went upstairs to the room where they were staying. Those present were Peter, John, James and Andrew; Philip and Thomas, Bartholomew and Matthew; James son of Alphaeus and Simon the Zealot, and Judas son of James. 14They all joined together constantly in prayer, along with the women and Mary the mother of Jesus, and with his brothers.

15In those days Peter stood up among the believers[c] (a group numbering about a hundred and twenty) 16and said, "Brothers, the Scripture had to be fulfilled which the Holy Spirit spoke long ago through the mouth of David concerning Judas, who served as guide for those who arrested Jesus— 17he was one of our number and shared in this ministry."

18(With the reward he got for his wickedness, Judas bought a field; there he fell headlong, his body burst open and all his intestines spilled out. 19Everyone in Jerusalem heard about this, so they called that field in their language Akeldama, that is, Field of Blood.)

20"For," said Peter, "it is written in the book of Psalms,

"'May his place be deserted;
   let there be no one to dwell in it,'[d]

and,

"'May another take his place of
   leadership.'[e]

21Therefore it is necessary to choose one of the men who have been with us the whole time the Lord Jesus went in and out among us, 22beginning from John's baptism to the time when Jesus was taken up from us. For one of these must become a witness with us of his resurrection."

23So they proposed two men: Joseph called Barsabbas (also known as Justus) and Matthias. 24Then they prayed, "Lord, you know everyone's heart. Show us which of these two you have chosen 25to take over this apostolic ministry, which Judas left to go where he belongs." 26Then they cast lots, and the lot fell to Matthias; so he was added to the eleven apostles.

The Holy Spirit Comes at Pentecost

2 When the day of Pentecost came, they were all together in one place. 2Suddenly a sound like the blowing of a violent wind came from heaven and filled the whole house where they were sitting. 3They saw what seemed to be tongues of fire that separated and came to rest on each of them. 4All of them were filled with the Holy Spirit and began to speak in other tongues[f] as the Spirit enabled them.

5Now there were staying in Jerusalem God-fearing Jews from every nation under heaven. 6When they heard this sound, a crowd came together in bewilderment, because each one heard them speaking in his own language. 7Utterly amazed, they asked: "Are not all these men who are speaking Galileans? 8Then how is it that each of us hears them in his own native language? 9Parthians, Medes and Elamites; residents of Mesopotamia, Judea and Cappadocia, Pontus and Asia, 10Phrygia and Pamphylia, Egypt and the parts of Libya near Cyrene; visitors from Rome 11(both Jews and converts to Judaism); Cretans and Arabs—we

a5 Or in   b12 That is, about 3/4 mile (about 1,100 meters)   c15 Greek brothers   d20 Psalm 69:25   e20 Psalm 109:8   f4 Or languages; also in verse 11 hear them declaring the wonders of God in our own tongues!" ¹²Amazed and perplexed, they asked one another, "What does this mean?"

¹³Some, however, made fun of them and said, "They have had too much wine.ᵃ"

Peter Addresses the Crowd

¹⁴Then Peter stood up with the Eleven, raised his voice and addressed the crowd: "Fellow Jews and all of you who live in Jerusalem, let me explain this to you; listen carefully to what I say. ¹⁵These men are not drunk, as you suppose. It's only nine in the morning! ¹⁶No, this is what was spoken by the prophet Joel:

¹⁷" 'In the last days, God says,
    I will pour out my Spirit on all people.
  Your sons and daughters will prophesy,
    your young men will see visions,
    your old men will dream dreams.
¹⁸Even on my servants, both men and women,
    I will pour out my Spirit in those days,
    and they will prophesy.
¹⁹I will show wonders in the heaven above
    and signs on the earth below,
    blood and fire and billows of smoke.
²⁰The sun will be turned to darkness
    and the moon to blood
    before the coming of the great and glorious day of the Lord.
²¹And everyone who calls
    on the name of the Lord will be saved.'ᵇ

²²"Men of Israel, listen to this: Jesus of Nazareth was a man accredited by God to you by miracles, wonders and signs, which God did among you through him, as you yourselves know. ²³This man was handed over to you by God's set purpose and foreknowledge; and you, with the help of wicked men,ᶜ put him to death by nailing him to the cross. ²⁴But God raised him from the dead, freeing him from the agony

of death, because it was impossible for death to keep its hold on him. ²⁵David said about him:

" 'I saw the Lord always before me.
    Because he is at my right hand,
    I will not be shaken.
²⁶Therefore my heart is glad and my tongue rejoices;
    my body also will live in hope,
²⁷because you will not abandon me to the grave,
    nor will you let your Holy One see decay.
²⁸You have made known to me the paths of life;
    you will fill me with joy in your presence.'ᵈ

²⁹"Brothers, I can tell you confidently that the patriarch David died and was buried, and his tomb is here to this day. ³⁰But he was a prophet and knew that God had promised him on oath that he would place one of his descendants on his throne. ³¹Seeing what was ahead, he spoke of the resurrection of the Christ,ᵉ that he was not abandoned to the grave, nor did his body see decay. ³²God has raised this Jesus to life, and we are all witnesses of the fact. ³³Exalted to the right hand of God, he has received from the Father the promised Holy Spirit and has poured out what you now see and hear. ³⁴For David did not ascend to heaven, and yet he said,

" 'The Lord said to my Lord:
    "Sit at my right hand
³⁵until I make your enemies
    a footstool for your feet." 'ᶠ

³⁶"Therefore let all Israel be assured of this: God has made this Jesus, whom you crucified, both Lord and Christ."

³⁷When the people heard this, they were cut to the heart and said to Peter and the other apostles, "Brothers, what shall we do?"

Acts 2:33

God Pours Out His Spirit

"Exalted to the right hand of God, he has received from the Father the promised Holy Spirit and has poured out what you now see and hear."

ᵃ13 Or *sweet wine*   ᵇ21 Joel 2:28–32   ᶜ23 Or *of those not having the law* (that is, Gentiles)   ᵈ28 Psalm 16:8–11   ᵉ31 Or *Messiah.* "The Christ" (Greek) and "the Messiah" (Hebrew) both mean "the Anointed One"; also in verse 36.   ᶠ35 Psalm 110:1

38Peter replied, "Repent and be baptized, every one of you, in the name of Jesus Christ for the forgiveness of your sins. And you will receive the gift of the Holy Spirit. **39**The promise is for you and your children and for all who are far off—for all whom the Lord our God will call."

40With many other words he warned them; and he pleaded with them, "Save yourselves from this corrupt generation." **41**Those who accepted his message were baptized, and about three thousand were added to their number that day.

The Fellowship of the Believers

42They devoted themselves to the apostles' teaching and to the fellowship, to the breaking of bread and to prayer. **43**Everyone was filled with awe, and many wonders and miraculous signs were done by the apostles. **44**All the believers were together and had everything in common. **45**Selling their possessions and goods, they gave to anyone as he had need. **46**Every day they continued to meet together in the temple courts. They broke bread in their homes and ate together with glad and sincere hearts, **47**praising God and enjoying the favor of all the people. And the Lord added to their number daily those who were being saved.

Peter Heals the Crippled Beggar

3 One day Peter and John were going up to the temple at the time of prayer—at three in the afternoon. **2**Now a man crippled from birth was being carried to the temple gate called Beautiful, where he was put every day to beg from those going into the temple courts. **3**When he saw Peter and John about to enter, he asked them for money. **4**Peter looked straight at him, as did John. Then Peter said, "Look at us!" **5**So the man gave them his attention, expecting to get something from them.

6Then Peter said, "Silver or gold I do not have, but what I have I give you. In the name of Jesus Christ of Nazareth, walk." **7**Taking him by the right hand, he helped him up, and instantly the man's feet and ankles became strong. **8**He jumped to his feet and began to walk. Then he went with them into the temple courts, walking and jumping, and praising God. **9**When all the people saw him walking and praising God, **10**they recognized him as the same man who used to sit begging at the temple gate called Beautiful, and they were filled with wonder and amazement at what had happened to him.

Peter Speaks to the Onlookers

11While the beggar held on to Peter and John, all the people were astonished and came running to them in the place called Solomon's Colonnade. **12**When Peter saw this, he said to them: "Men of Israel, why does this surprise you? Why do you stare at us as if by our own power or godliness we had made this man walk? **13**The God of Abraham, Isaac and Jacob, the God of our fathers, has glorified his servant Jesus. You handed him over to be killed, and you disowned him before Pilate, though he had decided to let him go. **14**You disowned the Holy and Righteous One and asked that a murderer be released to you. **15**You killed the author of life, but God raised him from the dead. We are witnesses of this. **16**By faith in the name of Jesus, this man whom you see and know was made strong. It is Jesus' name and the faith that comes through him that has given this complete healing to him, as you can all see.

17"Now, brothers, I know that you acted in ignorance, as did your leaders. **18**But this is how God fulfilled what he had foretold through all the prophets, saying that his Christ[a] would suffer. **19**Repent, then, and turn to God, so that your sins may be wiped out, that times of refreshing may come from the Lord, **20**and that he may send the Christ, who has been appointed for you—even Jesus. **21**He must remain in heaven until the time comes for God to restore everything, as he promised long ago through his holy prophets. **22**For Moses said, 'The Lord your God will raise up for you a prophet like me from among your own people; you must listen to everything he tells you. **23**Anyone who does not listen to him will be completely cut off from among his people.'[b]

24"Indeed, all the prophets from Samuel on, as many as have spoken, have foretold these days. **25**And you are heirs of the prophets and of the covenant God made with your fathers. He said to Abraham, 'Through your offspring

a18 Or *Messiah*; also in verse 20   *b23* Deut. 18:15,18,19 all peoples on earth will be blessed.'ᵃ ²⁶When God raised up his servant, he sent him first to you to bless you by turning each of you from your wicked ways."

Peter and John Before the Sanhedrin

4 The priests and the captain of the temple guard and the Sadducees came up to Peter and John while they were speaking to the people. ²They were greatly disturbed because the apostles were teaching the people and proclaiming in Jesus the resurrection of the dead. ³They seized Peter and John, and because it was evening, they put them in jail until the next day. ⁴But many who heard the message believed, and the number of men grew to about five thousand.

⁵The next day the rulers, elders and teachers of the law met in Jerusalem. ⁶Annas the high priest was there, and so were Caiaphas, John, Alexander and the other men of the high priest's family. ⁷They had Peter and John brought before them and began to question them: "By what power or what name did you do this?"

⁸Then Peter, filled with the Holy Spirit, said to them: "Rulers and elders of the people! ⁹If we are being called to account today for an act of kindness shown to a cripple and are asked how he was healed, ¹⁰then know this, you and all the people of Israel: It is by the name of Jesus Christ of Nazareth, whom you crucified but whom God raised from the dead, that this man stands before you healed. ¹¹He is

"'the stone you builders rejected,
which has become the capstone.'ᵇ'ᶜ

¹²Salvation is found in no one else, for there is no other name under heaven given to men by which we must be saved."

¹³When they saw the courage of Peter and John and realized that they were unschooled, ordinary men, they were astonished and they took note that these men had been with Jesus. ¹⁴But since

they could see the man who had been healed standing there with them, there was nothing they could say. ¹⁵So they ordered them to withdraw from the Sanhedrin and then conferred together. ¹⁶"What are we going to do with these men?" they asked. "Everybody living in Jerusalem knows they have done an outstanding miracle, and we cannot deny it. ¹⁷But to stop this thing from spreading any further among the people, we must warn these men to speak no longer to anyone in this name."

¹⁸Then they called them in again and commanded them not to speak or teach at all in the name of Jesus. ¹⁹But Peter and John replied, "Judge for yourselves whether it is right in God's sight to obey you rather than God. ²⁰For we cannot help speaking about what we have seen and heard."

²¹After further threats they let them go. They could not decide how to punish them, because all the people were praising God for what had happened. ²²For the man who was miraculously healed was over forty years old.

The Believers' Prayer

²³On their release, Peter and John went back to their own people and reported all that the chief priests and elders had said to them. ²⁴When they heard this, they raised their voices together in prayer to God. "Sovereign Lord," they said, "you made the heaven and the earth and the sea, and everything in them. ²⁵You spoke by the Holy Spirit through the mouth of your servant, our father David:

"'Why do the nations rage
and the peoples plot in vain?
²⁶The kings of the earth take their stand
and the rulers gather together
against the Lord
and against his Anointed One.'ᵈ'ᵉ

²⁷Indeed Herod and Pontius Pilate met together with the Gentiles and the peopleᶠ of Israel in this city to

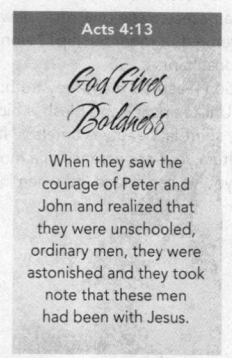

Acts 4:13

God Gives Boldness

When they saw the courage of Peter and John and realized that they were unschooled, ordinary men, they were astonished and they took note that these men had been with Jesus.

ᵃ25 Gen. 22:18; 26:4 ᵇ11 Or *cornerstone* ᶜ11 Psalm 118:22 ᵈ26 That is, Christ or Messiah ᵉ26 Psalm 2:1,2 ᶠ27 The Greek is plural.

Acts 4:13

When they saw the courage of Peter and John and realized that they were unschooled, ordinary men, they were astonished and they took note that these men had been with Jesus.

Read: Acts 4:1–37

reflection

1 Why were people so astounded by Peter and John's courage?

2 Based on your knowledge of the Bible, what had happened to transform them so radically?

3 How have you experienced a "faith-lift" since walking with Christ? How does it reflect outwardly?

RELATED READINGS

Psalm 149:1–9;
Isaiah 61:1–3;
1 Corinthians 1:26–31

WHEN WOMEN KINDLY ASK me to sign their copies of my books, I sometimes write, "To Susan the Beautiful!"

"Oh, no!" Susan (or Kathy or Linda) will protest, turning red. "I'm not beautiful."

"Sure you are," I insist, as I add my signature. "It says so right in the Bible." As further proof, I jot down "Psalm 149:4" and encourage them to look it up. You see, it's God's gift of salvation that makes us truly beautiful, inside and out. Nothing transforms a woman's appearance more than being covered from head to toe in the grace of God's Son.

I know this beautifying process is legitimate because I've seen it happen again and again. When women come to know the Lord in a real and personal way, their frown lines begin to soften. A sparkle appears in their eyes, and a radiance falls over their countenance.

We have proven scientifically that such physical changes occur when we fall in love: glowing skin, sparkling eyes, increased heart rate. And for some of us, similar improvements take place when we're expecting a child. Conventional wisdom says that "all brides are beautiful" and "pregnant women glow." It's chemical, hormonal, and very real.

Why not at the spiritual level too? When you allow the Lord to fill your heart with his boundless love, it shows on the outside. This beauty has nothing to do with cosmetics or plastic surgery. On the contrary, it's an inside job: A heart full of love produces a face full of joy.

When I stepped into a church for the first time as an adult, I was amazed to see pew after pew of attractive women. Is this a requirement of membership? I wondered. Maybe they're all Mary Kay consultants . . .

Soon I learned the happy truth: Such beauty is a gift from God. Unlike lipstick and blush, which seldom last longer than a few hours, spiritual beauty is timeless. It literally pours out of your pores and alters your appearance in a most appealing way. People will think you've had a face-lift, when in fact you've had a faith-lift.

—*Liz Curtis Higgs*

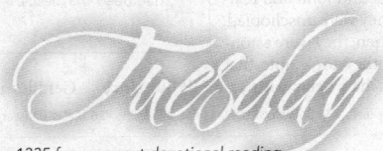

Tuesday

Go to page 1335 for your next devotional reading.

conspire against your holy servant Jesus, whom you anointed. [28]They did what your power and will had decided beforehand should happen. [29]Now, Lord, consider their threats and enable your servants to speak your word with great boldness. [30]Stretch out your hand to heal and perform miraculous signs and wonders through the name of your holy servant Jesus."

[31]After they prayed, the place where they were meeting was shaken. And they were all filled with the Holy Spirit and spoke the word of God boldly.

The Believers Share Their Possessions

[32]All the believers were one in heart and mind. No one claimed that any of his possessions was his own, but they shared everything they had. [33]With great power the apostles continued to testify to the resurrection of the Lord Jesus, and much grace was upon them all. [34]There were no needy persons among them. For from time to time those who owned lands or houses sold them, brought the money from the sales [35]and put it at the apostles' feet, and it was distributed to anyone as he had need.

[36]Joseph, a Levite from Cyprus, whom the apostles called Barnabas (which means Son of Encouragement), [37]sold a field he owned and brought the money and put it at the apostles' feet.

Ananias and Sapphira

5 Now a man named Ananias, together with his wife Sapphira, also sold a piece of property. [2]With his wife's full knowledge he kept back part of the money for himself, but brought the rest and put it at the apostles' feet.

[3]Then Peter said, "Ananias, how is it that Satan has so filled your heart that you have lied to the Holy Spirit and have kept for yourself some of the money you received for the land? [4]Didn't it belong to you before it was sold? And after it was sold, wasn't the money at your disposal? What made you think of doing such a thing? You have not lied to men but to God."

[5]When Ananias heard this, he fell down and died. And great fear seized all who heard what had happened. [6]Then the young men came forward, wrapped up his body, and carried him out and buried him.

[7]About three hours later his wife came in, not knowing what had happened. [8]Peter asked her, "Tell me, is this the price you and Ananias got for the land?"

"Yes," she said, "that is the price."

[9]Peter said to her, "How could you agree to test the Spirit of the Lord? Look! The feet of the men who buried your husband are at the door, and they will carry you out also."

[10]At that moment she fell down at his feet and died. Then the young men came in and, finding her dead, carried her out and buried her beside her husband. [11]Great fear seized the whole church and all who heard about these events.

The Apostles Heal Many

[12]The apostles performed many miraculous signs and wonders among the people. And all the believers used to meet together in Solomon's Colonnade. [13]No one else dared join them, even though they were highly regarded by the people. [14]Nevertheless, more and more men and women believed in the Lord and were added to their number. [15]As a result, people brought the sick into the streets and laid them on beds and mats so that at least Peter's shadow might fall on some of them as he passed by. [16]Crowds gathered also from the towns around Jerusalem, bringing their sick and those tormented by evil[a] spirits, and all of them were healed.

The Apostles Persecuted

[17]Then the high priest and all his associates, who were members of the party of the Sadducees, were filled with jealousy. [18]They arrested the apostles and put them in the public jail. [19]But during the night an angel of the Lord opened the doors of the jail and brought them out. [20]"Go, stand in the temple courts," he said, "and tell the people the full message of this new life."

[21]At daybreak they entered the temple courts, as they had been told, and began to teach the people.

When the high priest and his associates arrived, they called together the Sanhedrin—the full assembly of the elders of Israel—and sent to the jail for the apostles. [22]But on arriving at

a16 Greek *unclean*

the jail, the officers did not find them there. So they went back and reported, 23"We found the jail securely locked, with the guards standing at the doors; but when we opened them, we found no one inside." 24On hearing this report, the captain of the temple guard and the chief priests were puzzled, wondering what would come of this.

25Then someone came and said, "Look! The men you put in jail are standing in the temple courts teaching the people." 26At that, the captain went with his officers and brought the apostles. They did not use force, because they feared that the people would stone them.

27Having brought the apostles, they made them appear before the Sanhedrin to be questioned by the high priest. 28"We gave you strict orders not to teach in this name," he said. "Yet you have filled Jerusalem with your teaching and are determined to make us guilty of this man's blood."

29Peter and the other apostles replied: "We must obey God rather than men! 30The God of our fathers raised Jesus from the dead—whom you had killed by hanging him on a tree. 31God exalted him to his own right hand as Prince and Savior that he might give repentance and forgiveness of sins to Israel. 32We are witnesses of these things, and so is the Holy Spirit, whom God has given to those who obey him."

33When they heard this, they were furious and wanted to put them to death. 34But a Pharisee named Gamaliel, a teacher of the law, who was honored by all the people, stood up in the Sanhedrin and ordered that the men be put outside for a little while. 35Then he addressed them: "Men of Israel, consider carefully what you intend to do to these men. 36Some time ago Theudas appeared, claiming to be somebody, and about four hundred men rallied to him. He was killed, all his followers were dispersed, and it all came to nothing. 37After him, Judas the Galilean appeared in the days of the census and led a band of people in revolt. He too was killed, and all his followers were scattered. 38Therefore, in the present case I advise you: Leave these men alone! Let them go! For if their purpose or activity is of human origin, it will fail. 39But if it is from God, you will not

be able to stop these men; you will only find yourselves fighting against God."

40His speech persuaded them. They called the apostles in and had them flogged. Then they ordered them not to speak in the name of Jesus, and let them go.

41The apostles left the Sanhedrin, rejoicing because they had been counted worthy of suffering disgrace for the Name. 42Day after day, in the temple courts and from house to house, they never stopped teaching and proclaiming the good news that Jesus is the Christ.a

The Choosing of the Seven

6 In those days when the number of disciples was increasing, the Grecian Jews among them complained against the Hebraic Jews because their widows were being overlooked in the daily distribution of food. 2So the Twelve gathered all the disciples together and said, "It would not be right for us to neglect the ministry of the word of God in order to wait on tables. 3Brothers, choose seven men from among you who are known to be full of the Spirit and wisdom. We will turn this responsibility over to them 4and will give our attention to prayer and the ministry of the word."

5This proposal pleased the whole group. They chose Stephen, a man full of faith and of the Holy Spirit; also Philip, Procorus, Nicanor, Timon, Parmenas, and Nicolas from Antioch, a convert to Judaism. 6They presented these men to the apostles, who prayed and laid their hands on them.

7So the word of God spread. The number of disciples in Jerusalem increased rapidly, and a large number of priests became obedient to the faith.

Stephen Seized

8Now Stephen, a man full of God's grace and power, did great wonders and miraculous signs among the people. 9Opposition arose, however, from members of the Synagogue of the Freedmen (as it was called)—Jews of Cyrene and Alexandria as well as the provinces of Cilicia and Asia. These men began to argue with Stephen, 10but they could not stand up against his wisdom or the Spirit by whom he spoke. 11Then they secretly persuaded some men

a42 Or Messiah

to say, "We have heard Stephen speak words of blasphemy against Moses and against God." [12] So they stirred up the people and the elders and the teachers of the law. They seized Stephen and brought him before the Sanhedrin. [13] They produced false witnesses, who testified, "This fellow never stops speaking against this holy place and against the law. [14] For we have heard him say that this Jesus of Nazareth will destroy this place and change the customs Moses handed down to us."

[15] All who were sitting in the Sanhedrin looked intently at Stephen, and they saw that his face was like the face of an angel.

Stephen's Speech to the Sanhedrin

7 Then the high priest asked him, "Are these charges true?"

[2] To this he replied: "Brothers and fathers, listen to me! The God of glory appeared to our father Abraham while he was still in Mesopotamia, before he lived in Haran. [3] 'Leave your country and your people,' God said, 'and go to the land I will show you.'[a]

[4] "So he left the land of the Chaldeans and settled in Haran. After the death of his father, God sent him to this land where you are now living. [5] He gave him no inheritance here, not even a foot of ground. But God promised him that he and his descendants after him would possess the land, even though at that time Abraham had no child. [6] God spoke to him in this way: 'Your descendants will be strangers in a country not their own, and they will be enslaved and mistreated four hundred years. [7] But I will punish the nation they serve as slaves,' God said, 'and afterward they will come out of that country and worship me in this place.'[b] [8] Then he gave Abraham the covenant of circumcision. And Abraham became the father of Isaac and circumcised him eight days after his birth. Later Isaac became the father of Jacob, and Jacob became the father of the twelve patriarchs.

[9] "Because the patriarchs were jealous of Joseph, they sold him as a slave into Egypt. But God was with him [10] and rescued him from all his troubles. He gave Joseph wisdom and enabled him to gain the goodwill of Pharaoh king of Egypt; so he made him ruler over Egypt and all his palace.

[11] "Then a famine struck all Egypt and Canaan, bringing great suffering, and our fathers could not find food. [12] When Jacob heard that there was grain in Egypt, he sent our fathers on their first visit. [13] On their second visit, Joseph told his brothers who he was, and Pharaoh learned about Joseph's family. [14] After this, Joseph sent for his father Jacob and his whole family, seventy-five in all. [15] Then Jacob went down to Egypt, where he and our fathers died. [16] Their bodies were brought back to Shechem and placed in the tomb that Abraham had bought from the sons of Hamor at Shechem for a certain sum of money.

[17] "As the time drew near for God to fulfill his promise to Abraham, the number of our people in Egypt greatly increased. [18] Then another king, who knew nothing about Joseph, became ruler of Egypt. [19] He dealt treacherously with our people and oppressed our forefathers by forcing them to throw out their newborn babies so that they would die.

[20] "At that time Moses was born, and he was no ordinary child.[c] For three months he was cared for in his father's house. [21] When he was placed outside, Pharaoh's daughter took him and brought him up as her own son. [22] Moses was educated in all the wisdom of the Egyptians and was powerful in speech and action.

[23] "When Moses was forty years old, he decided to visit his fellow Israelites. [24] He saw one of them being mistreated by an Egyptian, so he went to his defense and avenged him by killing the Egyptian. [25] Moses thought that his own people would realize that God was using him to rescue them, but they did not. [26] The next day Moses came upon two Israelites who were fighting. He tried to reconcile them by saying, 'Men, you are brothers; why do you want to hurt each other?'

[27] "But the man who was mistreating the other pushed Moses aside and said, 'Who made you ruler and judge over us? [28] Do you want to kill me as you killed the Egyptian yesterday?'[d] [29] When Moses heard this, he fled to Midian, where he settled as a foreigner and had two sons.

---

[a]3 Gen. 12:1   [b]7 Gen. 15:13,14   [c]20 Or *was fair in the sight of God*   [d]28 Exodus 2:14

³⁰"After forty years had passed, an angel appeared to Moses in the flames of a burning bush in the desert near Mount Sinai. ³¹When he saw this, he was amazed at the sight. As he went over to look more closely, he heard the Lord's voice: ³²'I am the God of your fathers, the God of Abraham, Isaac and Jacob.'ᵃ Moses trembled with fear and did not dare to look.

³³"Then the Lord said to him, 'Take off your sandals; the place where you are standing is holy ground. ³⁴I have indeed seen the oppression of my people in Egypt. I have heard their groaning and have come down to set them free. Now come, I will send you back to Egypt.'ᵇ

³⁵"This is the same Moses whom they had rejected with the words, 'Who made you ruler and judge?' He was sent to be their ruler and deliverer by God himself, through the angel who appeared to him in the bush. ³⁶He led them out of Egypt and did wonders and miraculous signs in Egypt, at the Red Seaᶜ and for forty years in the desert.

³⁷"This is that Moses who told the Israelites, 'God will send you a prophet like me from your own people.'ᵈ ³⁸He was in the assembly in the desert, with the angel who spoke to him on Mount Sinai, and with our fathers; and he received living words to pass on to us.

³⁹"But our fathers refused to obey him. Instead, they rejected him and in their hearts turned back to Egypt. ⁴⁰They told Aaron, 'Make us gods who will go before us. As for this fellow Moses who led us out of Egypt—we don't know what has happened to him!'ᵉ ⁴¹That was the time they made an idol in the form of a calf. They brought sacrifices to it and held a celebration in honor of what their hands had made. ⁴²But God turned away and gave them over to the worship of the heavenly bodies. This agrees with what is written in the book of the prophets:

"'Did you bring me sacrifices and offerings forty years in the desert, O house of Israel?

⁴³You have lifted up the shrine of Molech
    and the star of your god Rephan,
    the idols you made to worship.
Therefore I will send you into exile'ᶠ
    beyond Babylon.

⁴⁴"Our forefathers had the tabernacle of the Testimony with them in the desert. It had been made as God directed Moses, according to the pattern he had seen. ⁴⁵Having received the tabernacle, our fathers under Joshua brought it with them when they took the land from the nations God drove out before them. It remained in the land until the time of David, ⁴⁶who enjoyed God's favor and asked that he might provide a dwelling place for the God of Jacob.ᵍ ⁴⁷But it was Solomon who built the house for him.

⁴⁸"However, the Most High does not live in houses made by men. As the prophet says:

Acts 7:49

God Is Infinite

"Heaven is my throne,
and the earth is
my footstool.
What kind of house will
you build for me?
says the Lord."

---

⁴⁹"'Heaven is my throne,
    and the earth is my
        footstool.
What kind of house will
        you build for me?
        says the Lord.
Or where will my resting
        place be?
⁵⁰Has not my hand made all these things?'ʰ

⁵¹"You stiff-necked people, with uncircumcised hearts and ears! You are just like your fathers: You always resist the Holy Spirit! ⁵²Was there ever a prophet your fathers did not persecute? They even killed those who predicted the coming of the Righteous One. And now you have betrayed and murdered him— ⁵³you who have received the law that was put into effect through angels but have not obeyed it."

The Stoning of Stephen

⁵⁴When they heard this, they were furious and gnashed their teeth at him. ⁵⁵But Stephen, full of the Holy Spirit, looked up to heaven and saw the glory of God, and Jesus standing at the

---

ᵃ32 Exodus 3:6   ᵇ34 Exodus 3:5,7,8,10   ᶜ36 That is, Sea of Reeds   ᵈ37 Deut. 18:15   ᵉ40 Exodus 32:1   ᶠ43 Amos 5:25–27   ᵍ46 Some early manuscripts *the house of Jacob*   ʰ50 Isaiah 66:1,2 right hand of God. [56]"Look," he said, "I see heaven open and the Son of Man standing at the right hand of God."

[57]At this they covered their ears and, yelling at the top of their voices, they all rushed at him, [58]dragged him out of the city and began to stone him. Meanwhile, the witnesses laid their clothes at the feet of a young man named Saul.

[59]While they were stoning him, Stephen prayed, "Lord Jesus, receive my spirit." [60]Then he fell on his knees and cried out, "Lord, do not hold this sin against them." When he had said this, he fell asleep.

8 And Saul was there, giving approval to his death.

The Church Persecuted and Scattered

On that day a great persecution broke out against the church at Jerusalem, and all except the apostles were scattered throughout Judea and Samaria. [2]Godly men buried Stephen and mourned deeply for him. [3]But Saul began to destroy the church. Going from house to house, he dragged off men and women and put them in prison.

Philip in Samaria

[4]Those who had been scattered preached the word wherever they went. [5]Philip went down to a city in Samaria and proclaimed the Christ[a] there. [6]When the crowds heard Philip and saw the miraculous signs he did, they all paid close attention to what he said. [7]With shrieks, evil[b] spirits came out of many, and many paralytics and cripples were healed. [8]So there was great joy in that city.

Simon the Sorcerer

[9]Now for some time a man named Simon had practiced sorcery in the city and amazed all the people of Samaria. He boasted that he was someone great, [10]and all the people, both high and low, gave him their attention and exclaimed, "This man is the divine power known as the Great Power." [11]They followed him because he had amazed them for a long time with his magic. [12]But when they believed Philip as he preached the good news of the kingdom of God and the name of Jesus Christ, they were baptized, both men and women. [13]Simon himself believed and was baptized. And he

followed Philip everywhere, astonished by the great signs and miracles he saw.

[14]When the apostles in Jerusalem heard that Samaria had accepted the word of God, they sent Peter and John to them. [15]When they arrived, they prayed for them that they might receive the Holy Spirit, [16]because the Holy Spirit had not yet come upon any of them; they had simply been baptized into[c] the name of the Lord Jesus. [17]Then Peter and John placed their hands on them, and they received the Holy Spirit.

[18]When Simon saw that the Spirit was given at the laying on of the apostles' hands, he offered them money [19]and said, "Give me also this ability so that everyone on whom I lay my hands may receive the Holy Spirit."

[20]Peter answered: "May your money perish with you, because you thought you could buy the gift of God with money! [21]You have no part or share in this ministry, because your heart is not right before God. [22]Repent of this wickedness and pray to the Lord. Perhaps he will forgive you for having such a thought in your heart. [23]For I see that you are full of bitterness and captive to sin."

[24]Then Simon answered, "Pray to the Lord for me so that nothing you have said may happen to me."

[25]When they had testified and proclaimed the word of the Lord, Peter and John returned to Jerusalem, preaching the gospel in many Samaritan villages.

Philip and the Ethiopian

[26]Now an angel of the Lord said to Philip, "Go south to the road—the desert road—that goes down from Jerusalem to Gaza." [27]So he started out, and on his way he met an Ethiopian[d] eunuch, an important official in charge of all the treasury of Candace, queen of the Ethiopians. This man had gone to Jerusalem to worship, [28]and on his way home was sitting in his chariot reading the book of Isaiah the prophet. [29]The Spirit told Philip, "Go to that chariot and stay near it."

[30]Then Philip ran up to the chariot and heard the man reading Isaiah the prophet. "Do you understand what you are reading?" Philip asked.

---

[a]5 Or Messiah [b]7 Greek unclean [c]16 Or in [d]27 That is, from the upper Nile region

³¹"How can I," he said, "unless someone explains it to me?" So he invited Philip to come up and sit with him.

³²The eunuch was reading this passage of Scripture:

"He was led like a sheep to the slaughter,
    and as a lamb before the shearer is silent,
    so he did not open his mouth.
³³In his humiliation he was deprived of
        justice.
    Who can speak of his descendants?
    For his life was taken from the earth."ᵃ

³⁴The eunuch asked Philip, "Tell me, please, who is the prophet talking about, himself or someone else?" ³⁵Then Philip began with that very passage of Scripture and told him the good news about Jesus.

³⁶As they traveled along the road, they came to some water and the eunuch said, "Look, here is water. Why shouldn't I be baptized?"ᵇ ³⁸And he gave orders to stop the chariot. Then both Philip and the eunuch went down into the water and Philip baptized him. ³⁹When they came up out of the water, the Spirit of the Lord suddenly took Philip away, and the eunuch did not see him again, but went on his way rejoicing. ⁴⁰Philip, however, appeared at Azotus and traveled about, preaching the gospel in all the towns until he reached Caesarea.

Saul's Conversion

9 Meanwhile, Saul was still breathing out murderous threats against the Lord's disciples. He went to the high priest ²and asked him for letters to the synagogues in Damascus, so that if he found any there who belonged to the Way, whether men or women, he might take them as prisoners to Jerusalem. ³As he neared Damascus on his journey, suddenly a light from heaven flashed around him. ⁴He fell to the ground and heard a voice say to him, "Saul, Saul, why do you persecute me?"

⁵"Who are you, Lord?" Saul asked.

"I am Jesus, whom you are persecuting," he replied. ⁶"Now get up and go into the city, and you will be told what you must do."

⁷The men traveling with Saul stood there speechless; they heard the sound but did not

see anyone. ⁸Saul got up from the ground, but when he opened his eyes he could see nothing. So they led him by the hand into Damascus. ⁹For three days he was blind, and did not eat or drink anything.

¹⁰In Damascus there was a disciple named Ananias. The Lord called to him in a vision, "Ananias!"

"Yes, Lord," he answered.

¹¹The Lord told him, "Go to the house of Judas on Straight Street and ask for a man from Tarsus named Saul, for he is praying. ¹²In a vision he has seen a man named Ananias come and place his hands on him to restore his sight."

¹³"Lord," Ananias answered, "I have heard many reports about this man and all the harm he has done to your saints in Jerusalem. ¹⁴And he has come here with authority from the chief priests to arrest all who call on your name."

¹⁵But the Lord said to Ananias, "Go! This man is my chosen instrument to carry my name before the Gentiles and their kings and before the people of Israel. ¹⁶I will show him how much he must suffer for my name."

¹⁷Then Ananias went to the house and entered it. Placing his hands on Saul, he said, "Brother Saul, the Lord—Jesus, who appeared to you on the road as you were coming here—has sent me so that you may see again and be filled with the Holy Spirit." ¹⁸Immediately, something like scales fell from Saul's eyes, and he could see again. He got up and was baptized, ¹⁹and after taking some food, he regained his strength.

Saul in Damascus and Jerusalem

Saul spent several days with the disciples in Damascus. ²⁰At once he began to preach in the synagogues that Jesus is the Son of God. ²¹All those who heard him were astonished and asked, "Isn't he the man who raised havoc in Jerusalem among those who call on this name? And hasn't he come here to take them as prisoners to the chief priests?" ²²Yet Saul grew more and more powerful and baffled the Jews living in Damascus by proving that Jesus is the Christ.ᶜ

²³After many days had gone by, the Jews

ᵃ33 Isaiah 53:7,8   ᵇ36 Some late manuscripts *baptized?"* ³⁷*Philip said, "If you believe with all your heart, you may." The eunuch answered, "I believe that Jesus Christ is the Son of God."*   ᶜ22 Or *Messiah*

"Get Up!"

Read: Acts 9:1–43

"GET UP!"

Did your parents use those words to rouse you out of sleep when you were a teenager? Are you now using those very words to wake those unwilling to rise from their warm, comfy beds in the morning? When you read through Acts 9, you'll notice that the phrase, "Get up," occurs in contrasting settings. A closer look moves these words from the commonplace to the compelling. Let's explore why this simple command warrants our attention.

On the road to Damascus, Saul was flattened to the ground by a blazing light and a surprising voice. After the Lord identified himself as Jesus, his first command to Saul was, "Now get up."

In the latter part of the chapter there are two accounts where Peter issued the command, "Get up." In the first, Peter instructed Aeneas, the paralytic in Lydda, to "get up and take care of your mat," after declaring, "Jesus Christ heals you" (verse 34).

Nearby in Joppa, a much-beloved saint named Tabitha, or Dorcas, had died. Peter went to the upstairs room where she lay. After he knelt and prayed, he turned toward the dead woman and said, "Tabitha, get up" (verse 40).

The Greek phrase "get up" has several meanings. It can be used in the sense of waking someone up from sleep. It can also mean to rise from a prone position as one who is ill. The deeper meaning is profound. It is the same root word used for resurrection—meaning to arise from the dead.

Saul, Aeneas and Dorcas were trapped in different realms of death—sin, paralysis and physical death—that required resurrection power. They heard the words, "Get up," and responded with immediate obedience.

Do you feel spiritually asleep—maybe even dead? As a wise person once counseled, "Just move your feet, and God will guide you where to go." But first, you have to "Get up!"

Acts 9:5–6

"Who are you, Lord?" Saul asked. "I am Jesus, whom you are persecuting," he replied. "Now get up and go into the city, and you will be told what you must do."

reflection

1 Spiritually, do you most relate to Saul, the opponent of Christ; Aeneas, the paralytic; or Dorcas, the woman who had died? Depending upon your answer, ask God to either knock you off your horse, heal you or resurrect you.

2 In what way is "getting up" a response of faith? What is keeping you from "getting up" to do what God has asked you to do?

3 Who in your life needs to know about Jesus' healing power? Whom can you be a "Peter" to? Pray for opportunities to talk with that person about Jesus.

RELATED READINGS

1 Kings 19:5;
Matthew 9:5;
Luke 8:49–56;
Acts 22:6–16;
Romans 1:1–4

Go to page 1338 for your next devotional reading.

conspired to kill him, **24**but Saul learned of their plan. Day and night they kept close watch on the city gates in order to kill him. **25**But his followers took him by night and lowered him in a basket through an opening in the wall.

26When he came to Jerusalem, he tried to join the disciples, but they were all afraid of him, not believing that he really was a disciple. **27**But Barnabas took him and brought him to the apostles. He told them how Saul on his journey had seen the Lord and that the Lord had spoken to him, and how in Damascus he had preached fearlessly in the name of Jesus. **28**So Saul stayed with them and moved about freely in Jerusalem, speaking boldly in the name of the Lord. **29**He talked and debated with the Grecian Jews, but they tried to kill him. **30**When the brothers learned of this, they took him down to Caesarea and sent him off to Tarsus.

31Then the church throughout Judea, Galilee and Samaria enjoyed a time of peace. It was strengthened; and encouraged by the Holy Spirit, it grew in numbers, living in the fear of the Lord.

Aeneas and Dorcas

32As Peter traveled about the country, he went to visit the saints in Lydda. **33**There he found a man named Aeneas, a paralytic who had been bedridden for eight years. **34**"Aeneas," Peter said to him, "Jesus Christ heals you. Get up and take care of your mat." Immediately Aeneas got up. **35**All those who lived in Lydda and Sharon saw him and turned to the Lord.

36In Joppa there was a disciple named Tabitha (which, when translated, is Dorcas*a*), who was always doing good and helping the poor. **37**About that time she became sick and died, and her body was washed and placed in an upstairs room. **38**Lydda was near Joppa; so when the disciples heard that Peter was in Lydda, they sent two men to him and urged him, "Please come at once!"

39Peter went with them, and when he arrived he was taken upstairs to the room. All the widows stood around him, crying and showing him the robes and other clothing that Dorcas had made while she was still with them.

40Peter sent them all out of the room; then

*a*36 Both *Tabitha* (Aramaic) and *Dorcas* (Greek) mean *gazelle*.

he got down on his knees and prayed. Turning toward the dead woman, he said, "Tabitha, get up." She opened her eyes, and seeing Peter she sat up. **41**He took her by the hand and helped her to her feet. Then he called the believers and the widows and presented her to them alive. **42**This became known all over Joppa, and many people believed in the Lord. **43**Peter stayed in Joppa for some time with a tanner named Simon.

Cornelius Calls for Peter

10 At Caesarea there was a man named Cornelius, a centurion in what was known as the Italian Regiment. **2**He and all his family were devout and God-fearing; he gave generously to those in need and prayed to God regularly. **3**One day at about three in the afternoon he had a vision. He distinctly saw an angel of God, who came to him and said, "Cornelius!"

4Cornelius stared at him in fear. "What is it, Lord?" he asked.

The angel answered, "Your prayers and gifts to the poor have come up as a memorial offering before God. **5**Now send men to Joppa to bring back a man named Simon who is called Peter. **6**He is staying with Simon the tanner, whose house is by the sea."

7When the angel who spoke to him had gone, Cornelius called two of his servants and a devout soldier who was one of his attendants. **8**He told them everything that had happened and sent them to Joppa.

Peter's Vision

9About noon the following day as they were on their journey and approaching the city, Peter went up on the roof to pray. **10**He became hungry and wanted something to eat, and while the meal was being prepared, he fell into a trance. **11**He saw heaven opened and something like a large sheet being let down to earth by its four corners. **12**It contained all kinds of four-footed animals, as well as reptiles of the earth and birds of the air. **13**Then a voice told him, "Get up, Peter. Kill and eat."

14"Surely not, Lord!" Peter replied. "I have never eaten anything impure or unclean."

15The voice spoke to him a second time,

"Do not call anything impure that God has made clean."

¹⁶This happened three times, and immediately the sheet was taken back to heaven.

¹⁷While Peter was wondering about the meaning of the vision, the men sent by Cornelius found out where Simon's house was and stopped at the gate. ¹⁸They called out, asking if Simon who was known as Peter was staying there.

¹⁹While Peter was still thinking about the vision, the Spirit said to him, "Simon, three*a* men are looking for you. ²⁰So get up and go downstairs. Do not hesitate to go with them, for I have sent them."

²¹Peter went down and said to the men, "I'm the one you're looking for. Why have you come?"

²²The men replied, "We have come from Cornelius the centurion. He is a righteous and God-fearing man, who is respected by all the Jewish people. A holy angel told him to have you come to his house so that he could hear what you have to say." ²³Then Peter invited the men into the house to be his guests.

Peter at Cornelius's House

The next day Peter started out with them, and some of the brothers from Joppa went along. ²⁴The following day he arrived in Caesarea. Cornelius was expecting them and had called together his relatives and close friends. ²⁵As Peter entered the house, Cornelius met him and fell at his feet in reverence. ²⁶But Peter made him get up. "Stand up," he said, "I am only a man myself."

²⁷Talking with him, Peter went inside and found a large gathering of people. ²⁸He said to them: "You are well aware that it is against our law for a Jew to associate with a Gentile or visit him. But God has shown me that I should not call any man impure or unclean. ²⁹So when I was sent for, I came without raising any objection. May I ask why you sent for me?"

³⁰Cornelius answered: "Four days ago I was in my house praying at this hour, at three in the afternoon. Suddenly a man in shining clothes stood before me ³¹and said, 'Cornelius, God has heard your prayer and remembered your gifts to the poor. ³²Send to Joppa for Simon who is called Peter. He is a guest in the home of Simon the tanner, who lives by the sea.' ³³So I sent for you immediately, and it was good of you to come. Now we are all here in the presence of God to listen to everything the Lord has commanded you to tell us."

³⁴Then Peter began to speak: "I now realize how true it is that God does not show favoritism ³⁵but accepts men from every nation who fear him and do what is right. ³⁶You know the message God sent to the people of Israel, telling the good news of peace through Jesus Christ, who is Lord of all. ³⁷You know what has happened throughout Judea, beginning in Galilee after the baptism that John preached— ³⁸how God anointed Jesus of Nazareth with the Holy Spirit and power, and how he went around doing good and healing all who were under the power of the devil, because God was with him.

³⁹"We are witnesses of everything he did in the country of the Jews and in Jerusalem. They killed him by hanging him on a tree, ⁴⁰but God raised him from the dead on the third day and caused him to be seen. ⁴¹He was not seen by all the people, but by witnesses whom God had already chosen—by us who ate and drank with him after he rose from the dead. ⁴²He commanded us to preach to the people and to testify that he is the one whom God appointed as judge of the living and the dead. ⁴³All the prophets testify about him that everyone who believes in him receives forgiveness of sins through his name."

⁴⁴While Peter was still speaking these words, the Holy Spirit came on all who heard the message. ⁴⁵The circumcised believers who had come with Peter were astonished that the gift

---

Acts 10:35

God Accepts People

"[God] accepts men from every nation who fear him and do what is right."

---

*a*19 One early manuscript *two*; other manuscripts do not have the number.

Is Good, Good Enough?

Read: Acts 10:1–48

Acts 10:22

The men replied,
"We have come from
Cornelius the centurion.
He is a righteous and
God-fearing man, who
is respected by all the
Jewish people. A holy
angel told him to have
you come to his house so
that he could hear what
you have to say."

reflection

1 How do you find yourself working to please God?

2 What steps did God take to bring the gospel to you? Who were his messengers?

3 What would your life look like if you truly believed Jesus was the only way to the Father?

RELATED READINGS

Matthew 7:21–23;
Romans 1:16–18

"There is no better measure of a person than what he does when he is absolutely free to choose."

Wilma Askinas

HOW MANY *GOOD* PEOPLE do you know? People who give to the poor, volunteer at the homeless shelter, travel on mission trips, tutor children in the projects, sort items at the relief agency or visit the elderly?

Cornelius the centurion was such a man. He was one of the *good* people. He had diligently worked his way through the ranks to take command of over 100 Roman soldiers. He was a God-fearing, devout man who gave to those in need. He was also a man of prayer. But though he was good, it was not enough.

That's the dilemma for all of us. No matter how good we try to be, being good is not the way to acceptance by a holy God, "for all have sinned and fall short of the glory of God" (Romans 3:23). But when God looked at Cornelius, he saw a willing and open heart. God knew that, though Cornelius longed to have an intimate relationship with him, he lacked information about Jesus. So God sent an angel to tell Cornelius that information could be attained from Peter in Joppa. Cornelius sent three men to find Peter. Then the Holy Spirit sent Peter a vision to prepare him for the mission ahead: to preach salvation to the Gentiles as well as the Jews. When Peter shared the Good News of Jesus' death and resurrection, Cornelius and his entire family received the gift of eternal life and the Holy Spirit.

Have you, like Cornelius, been working really hard to be good? That's good. But do you, like Cornelius, have a religion of good works without a real relationship with Jesus? Then God has the same message for you that he delivered to Cornelius and his family: "Everyone who believes in [Jesus] receives forgiveness of sins through his name" (verse 43). The only path to a relationship with the Father is to believe that Jesus is "the way and the truth and the life. No one comes to the Father except through [him]" (John 14:6).

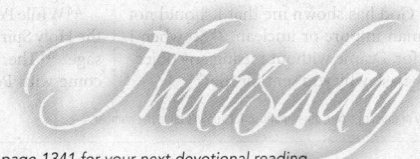

Thursday

Go to page 1341 for your next devotional reading.

of the Holy Spirit had been poured out even on the Gentiles. ⁴⁶For they heard them speaking in tongues[a] and praising God.

Then Peter said, ⁴⁷"Can anyone keep these people from being baptized with water? They have received the Holy Spirit just as we have." ⁴⁸So he ordered that they be baptized in the name of Jesus Christ. Then they asked Peter to stay with them for a few days.

Peter Explains His Actions

11 The apostles and the brothers throughout Judea heard that the Gentiles also had received the word of God. ²So when Peter went up to Jerusalem, the circumcised believers criticized him ³and said, "You went into the house of uncircumcised men and ate with them."

⁴Peter began and explained everything to them precisely as it had happened: ⁵"I was in the city of Joppa praying, and in a trance I saw a vision. I saw something like a large sheet being let down from heaven by its four corners, and it came down to where I was. ⁶I looked into it and saw four-footed animals of the earth, wild beasts, reptiles, and birds of the air. ⁷Then I heard a voice telling me, 'Get up, Peter. Kill and eat.'

⁸"I replied, 'Surely not, Lord! Nothing impure or unclean has ever entered my mouth.'

⁹"The voice spoke from heaven a second time, 'Do not call anything impure that God has made clean.' ¹⁰This happened three times, and then it was all pulled up to heaven again.

¹¹"Right then three men who had been sent to me from Caesarea stopped at the house where I was staying. ¹²The Spirit told me to have no hesitation about going with them. These six brothers also went with me, and we entered the man's house. ¹³He told us how he had seen an angel appear in his house and say, 'Send to Joppa for Simon who is called Peter. ¹⁴He will bring you a message through which you and all your household will be saved.'

¹⁵"As I began to speak, the Holy Spirit came on them as he had come on us at the begin-

Acts 11:21

God Guides People

The Lord's hand was with them, and a great number of people believed and turned to the Lord.

ning. ¹⁶Then I remembered what the Lord had said: 'John baptized with[b] water, but you will be baptized with the Holy Spirit.' ¹⁷So if God gave them the same gift as he gave us, who believed in the Lord Jesus Christ, who was I to think that I could oppose God?"

¹⁸When they heard this, they had no further objections and praised God, saying, "So then, God has granted even the Gentiles repentance unto life."

The Church in Antioch

¹⁹Now those who had been scattered by the persecution in connection with Stephen traveled as far as Phoenicia, Cyprus and Antioch, telling the message only to Jews. ²⁰Some of them, however, men from Cyprus and Cyrene, went to Antioch and began to speak to Greeks also, telling them the good news about the Lord Jesus. ²¹The Lord's hand was with them, and a great number of people believed and turned to the Lord.

²²News of this reached the ears of the church at Jerusalem, and they sent Barnabas to Antioch. ²³When he arrived and saw the evidence of the grace of God, he was glad and encouraged them all to remain true to the Lord with all their hearts. ²⁴He was a good man, full of the Holy Spirit and faith, and a great number of people were brought to the Lord.

²⁵Then Barnabas went to Tarsus to look for Saul, ²⁶and when he found him, he brought him to Antioch. So for a whole year Barnabas and Saul met with the church and taught great numbers of people. The disciples were called Christians first at Antioch.

²⁷During this time some prophets came down from Jerusalem to Antioch. ²⁸One of them, named Agabus, stood up and through the Spirit predicted that a severe famine would spread over the entire Roman world. (This happened during the reign of Claudius.) ²⁹The disciples, each according to his ability, decided to provide help for the brothers living in Judea.

---

[a]46 Or *other languages* [b]16 Or *in*

[30]This they did, sending their gift to the elders by Barnabas and Saul.

Peter's Miraculous Escape From Prison

12 It was about this time that King Herod arrested some who belonged to the church, intending to persecute them. [2]He had James, the brother of John, put to death with the sword. [3]When he saw that this pleased the Jews, he proceeded to seize Peter also. This happened during the Feast of Unleavened Bread. [4]After arresting him, he put him in prison, handing him over to be guarded by four squads of four soldiers each. Herod intended to bring him out for public trial after the Passover.

[5]So Peter was kept in prison, but the church was earnestly praying to God for him.

[6]The night before Herod was to bring him to trial, Peter was sleeping between two soldiers, bound with two chains, and sentries stood guard at the entrance. [7]Suddenly an angel of the Lord appeared and a light shone in the cell. He struck Peter on the side and woke him up. "Quick, get up!" he said, and the chains fell off Peter's wrists.

[8]Then the angel said to him, "Put on your clothes and sandals." And Peter did so. "Wrap your cloak around you and follow me," the angel told him. [9]Peter followed him out of the prison, but he had no idea that what the angel was doing was really happening; he thought he was seeing a vision. [10]They passed the first and second guards and came to the iron gate leading to the city. It opened for them by itself, and they went through it. When they had walked the length of one street, suddenly the angel left him.

[11]Then Peter came to himself and said, "Now I know without a doubt that the Lord sent his angel and rescued me from Herod's clutches and from everything the Jewish people were anticipating."

[12]When this had dawned on him, he went to the house of Mary the mother of John, also called Mark, where many people had gathered and were praying. [13]Peter knocked at the outer entrance, and a servant girl named Rhoda came to answer the door. [14]When she recognized Peter's voice, she was so overjoyed she ran back without opening it and exclaimed, "Peter is at the door!"

[15]"You're out of your mind," they told her. When she kept insisting that it was so, they said, "It must be his angel."

[16]But Peter kept on knocking, and when they opened the door and saw him, they were astonished. [17]Peter motioned with his hand for them to be quiet and described how the Lord had brought him out of prison. "Tell James and the brothers about this," he said, and then he left for another place.

[18]In the morning, there was no small commotion among the soldiers as to what had become of Peter. [19]After Herod had a thorough search made for him and did not find him, he cross-examined the guards and ordered that they be executed.

Herod's Death

Then Herod went from Judea to Caesarea and stayed there a while. [20]He had been quarreling with the people of Tyre and Sidon; they now joined together and sought an audience with him. Having secured the support of Blastus, a trusted personal servant of the king, they asked for peace, because they depended on the king's country for their food supply.

[21]On the appointed day Herod, wearing his royal robes, sat on his throne and delivered a public address to the people. [22]They shouted, "This is the voice of a god, not of a man." [23]Immediately, because Herod did not give praise to God, an angel of the Lord struck him down, and he was eaten by worms and died.

[24]But the word of God continued to increase and spread.

[25]When Barnabas and Saul had finished their mission, they returned from[a] Jerusalem, taking with them John, also called Mark.

Barnabas and Saul Sent Off

13 In the church at Antioch there were prophets and teachers: Barnabas, Simeon called Niger, Lucius of Cyrene, Manaen (who had been brought up with Herod the tetrarch) and Saul. [2]While they were worshiping the Lord and fasting, the Holy Spirit said, "Set apart for me Barnabas and Saul for the work to which I have called them." [3]So after they had

[a]25 Some manuscripts *to*

Praying Through

Read: Acts 12:1–17

DURING WORLD WAR II, Bible College of Wales founder Rees Howells regularly led his students in prayer. On September 9, 1943, the day the allies invaded Salerno, Italy, he called an extra prayer meeting at 9:45 P.M. and began with this message: "The Lord has burdened me between the meetings with the invasion of Salerno. I believe our men are in great difficulties, and the Lord has told me that unless we can pray through, they are in danger of losing their hold." The students fell to their knees and began praying. Then, at 11:00 P.M., they spontaneously began to sing, praising God for his intervention.

The next day the newspaper reported that the Nazis' artillery had been so heavy that establishing a beachhead required nothing short of a miracle. But a miracle had occurred. For no explainable reason, the enemy's artillery had ceased—at precisely 11:00 P.M.

Something mysterious takes place when we pray. God doesn't *need* our prayers, yet he uses them. In the inexplicable workings of heaven and earth, our prayers make a difference.

In this passage in the book of Acts, the believers who had gathered at Mary's house had just witnessed the death of James. They knew that Peter was next in line for Herod's sword, and they knew that they were powerless to do anything about it. But when they prayed to God for Peter, something miraculous happened. An angel stepped into the jail cell, Peter's chains fell off and the locked doors opened. On what might have been Peter's last night alive, God intervened in ways neither Peter nor the praying Christians could fathom.

We can never know how God will answer the prayers of his people. We only know that he tells us to pray about anything and everything. We may feel powerless in ourselves, but when we lift our prayers to God, when we "pray through" our difficulties, the door is opened for God to step in and do the miraculous.

Acts 12:5

So Peter was kept in prison, but the church was earnestly praying to God for him.

reflection

1 When has God answered your prayers in a way that exceeded your expectations?

2 Do you pray about everything or only about "big" things? Why or why not?

3 What difficulty might God be asking you to "pray through"?

RELATED READINGS

Matthew 7:7–11;
John 14:13–14;
1 Thessalonians 5:17;
James 5:13–16

"The more you pray, the more you will find to pray about."

Stormie Omartian

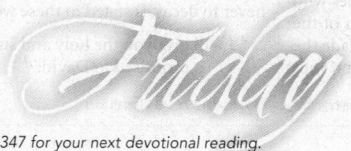

Go to page 1347 for your next devotional reading.

fasted and prayed, they placed their hands on them and sent them off.

On Cyprus

⁴The two of them, sent on their way by the Holy Spirit, went down to Seleucia and sailed from there to Cyprus. ⁵When they arrived at Salamis, they proclaimed the word of God in the Jewish synagogues. John was with them as their helper.

⁶They traveled through the whole island until they came to Paphos. There they met a Jewish sorcerer and false prophet named Bar-Jesus, ⁷who was an attendant of the proconsul, Sergius Paulus. The proconsul, an intelligent man, sent for Barnabas and Saul because he wanted to hear the word of God. ⁸But Elymas the sorcerer (for that is what his name means) opposed them and tried to turn the proconsul from the faith. ⁹Then Saul, who was also called Paul, filled with the Holy Spirit, looked straight at Elymas and said, ¹⁰"You are a child of the devil and an enemy of everything that is right! You are full of all kinds of deceit and trickery. Will you never stop perverting the right ways of the Lord? ¹¹Now the hand of the Lord is against you. You are going to be blind, and for a time you will be unable to see the light of the sun."

Immediately mist and darkness came over him, and he groped about, seeking someone to lead him by the hand. ¹²When the proconsul saw what had happened, he believed, for he was amazed at the teaching about the Lord.

In Pisidian Antioch

¹³From Paphos, Paul and his companions sailed to Perga in Pamphylia, where John left them to return to Jerusalem. ¹⁴From Perga they went on to Pisidian Antioch. On the Sabbath they entered the synagogue and sat down. ¹⁵After the reading from the Law and the Prophets, the synagogue rulers sent word to them, saying, "Brothers, if you have a message of encouragement for the people, please speak."

¹⁶Standing up, Paul motioned with his hand and said: "Men of Israel and you Gentiles who worship God, listen to me! ¹⁷The God of the people of Israel chose our fathers; he made the people prosper during their stay in Egypt, with

mighty power he led them out of that country, ¹⁸he endured their conduct[a] for about forty years in the desert, ¹⁹he overthrew seven nations in Canaan and gave their land to his people as their inheritance. ²⁰All this took about 450 years.

"After this, God gave them judges until the time of Samuel the prophet. ²¹Then the people asked for a king, and he gave them Saul son of Kish, of the tribe of Benjamin, who ruled forty years. ²²After removing Saul, he made David their king. He testified concerning him: 'I have found David son of Jesse a man after my own heart; he will do everything I want him to do.'

²³"From this man's descendants God has brought to Israel the Savior Jesus, as he promised. ²⁴Before the coming of Jesus, John preached repentance and baptism to all the people of Israel. ²⁵As John was completing his work, he said: 'Who do you think I am? I am not that one. No, but he is coming after me, whose sandals I am not worthy to untie.'

²⁶"Brothers, children of Abraham, and you God-fearing Gentiles, it is to us that this message of salvation has been sent. ²⁷The people of Jerusalem and their rulers did not recognize Jesus, yet in condemning him they fulfilled the words of the prophets that are read every Sabbath. ²⁸Though they found no proper ground for a death sentence, they asked Pilate to have him executed. ²⁹When they had carried out all that was written about him, they took him down from the tree and laid him in a tomb. ³⁰But God raised him from the dead, ³¹and for many days he was seen by those who had traveled with him from Galilee to Jerusalem. They are now his witnesses to our people.

³²"We tell you the good news: What God promised our fathers ³³he has fulfilled for us, their children, by raising up Jesus. As it is written in the second Psalm:

"'You are my Son;
today I have become your Father.'[b][c]

³⁴The fact that God raised him from the dead, never to decay, is stated in these words:

"'I will give you the holy and sure blessings promised to David.'[d]

---

[a]18 Some manuscripts *and cared for them*   [b]33 Or *have begotten you*   [c]33 Psalm 2:7   [d]34 Isaiah 55:3

35So it is stated elsewhere:

"'You will not let your Holy One see
decay.'ᵃ

36"For when David had served God's purpose in his own generation, he fell asleep; he
was buried with his fathers and his body decayed. 37But the one whom God raised from
the dead did not see decay.

38"Therefore, my brothers, I want you to
know that through Jesus the forgiveness of sins
is proclaimed to you. 39Through him everyone
who believes is justified from everything you
could not be justified from by the law of Moses.
40Take care that what the prophets have said
does not happen to you:

41"'Look, you scoffers,
wonder and perish,
for I am going to do something in your
days
that you would never believe,
even if someone told you.'ᵇ

42As Paul and Barnabas were leaving the
synagogue, the people invited them to speak
further about these things on the next Sabbath. 43When the congregation was dismissed,
many of the Jews and devout converts to Judaism followed Paul and Barnabas, who talked
with them and urged them to continue in the
grace of God.

44On the next Sabbath almost the whole city
gathered to hear the word of the Lord. 45When
the Jews saw the crowds, they were filled with
jealousy and talked abusively against what Paul
was saying.

46Then Paul and Barnabas answered them
boldly: "We had to speak the word of God to
you first. Since you reject it and do not consider
yourselves worthy of eternal life, we now turn
to the Gentiles. 47For this is what the Lord has
commanded us:

"'I have made youᶜ a light for the Gentiles,
that youᶜ may bring salvation to the
ends of the earth.'ᵈ"

48When the Gentiles heard this, they were
glad and honored the word of the Lord; and all
who were appointed for eternal life believed.

49The word of the Lord spread through
the whole region. 50But the Jews incited the
God-fearing women of high standing and the
leading men of the city. They stirred up persecution against Paul and Barnabas, and expelled
them from their region. 51So they shook the
dust from their feet in protest against them
and went to Iconium. 52And the disciples were
filled with joy and with the Holy Spirit.

In Iconium

14 At Iconium Paul and Barnabas went as
usual into the Jewish synagogue. There
they spoke so effectively that a great number
of Jews and Gentiles believed. 2But the Jews
who refused to believe stirred up the Gentiles
and poisoned their minds against the brothers.
3So Paul and Barnabas spent considerable time
there, speaking boldly for the Lord, who confirmed the message of his grace by enabling
them to do miraculous signs and wonders.
4The people of the city were divided; some
sided with the Jews, others with the apostles.
5There was a plot afoot among the Gentiles
and Jews, together with their leaders, to mistreat them and stone them. 6But they found
out about it and fled to the Lycaonian cities
of Lystra and Derbe and to the surrounding
country, 7where they continued to preach the
good news.

In Lystra and Derbe

8In Lystra there sat a man crippled in his
feet, who was lame from birth and had never
walked. 9He listened to Paul as he was speaking. Paul looked directly at him, saw that he
had faith to be healed 10and called out, "Stand
up on your feet!" At that, the man jumped up
and began to walk.

11When the crowd saw what Paul had done,
they shouted in the Lycaonian language, "The
gods have come down to us in human form!"
12Barnabas they called Zeus, and Paul they
called Hermes because he was the chief speaker.
13The priest of Zeus, whose temple was just outside the city, brought bulls and wreaths to the
city gates because he and the crowd wanted to
offer sacrifices to them.

14But when the apostles Barnabas and Paul
heard of this, they tore their clothes and rushed

ᵃ35 Psalm 16:10   ᵇ41 Hab. 1:5   ᶜ47 The Greek is singular.   ᵈ47 Isaiah 49:6

out into the crowd, shouting: **15**"Men, why are you doing this? We too are only men, human like you. We are bringing you good news, telling you to turn from these worthless things to the living God, who made heaven and earth and sea and everything in them. **16**In the past, he let all nations go their own way. **17**Yet he has not left himself without testimony: He has shown kindness by giving you rain from heaven and crops in their seasons; he provides you with plenty of food and fills your hearts with joy." **18**Even with these words, they had difficulty keeping the crowd from sacrificing to them.

19Then some Jews came from Antioch and Iconium and won the crowd over. They stoned Paul and dragged him outside the city, thinking he was dead. **20**But after the disciples had gathered around him, he got up and went back into the city. The next day he and Barnabas left for Derbe.

The Return to Antioch in Syria

21They preached the good news in that city and won a large number of disciples. Then they returned to Lystra, Iconium and Antioch, **22**strengthening the disciples and encouraging them to remain true to the faith. "We must go through many hardships to enter the kingdom of God," they said. **23**Paul and Barnabas appointed elders*a* for them in each church and, with prayer and fasting, committed them to the Lord, in whom they had put their trust. **24**After going through Pisidia, they came into Pamphylia, **25**and when they had preached the word in Perga, they went down to Attalia.

26From Attalia they sailed back to Antioch, where they had been committed to the grace of God for the work they had now completed. **27**On arriving there, they gathered the church together and reported all that God had done through them and how he had opened the door of faith to the Gentiles. **28**And they stayed there a long time with the disciples.

The Council at Jerusalem

15 Some men came down from Judea to Antioch and were teaching the brothers: "Unless you are circumcised, according to the custom taught by Moses, you cannot be saved." **2**This brought Paul and Barnabas into sharp dispute and debate with them. So Paul and Barnabas were appointed, along with some other believers, to go up to Jerusalem to see the apostles and elders about this question. **3**The church sent them on their way, and as they traveled through Phoenicia and Samaria, they told how the Gentiles had been converted. This news made all the brothers very glad. **4**When they came to Jerusalem, they were welcomed by the church and the apostles and elders, to whom they reported everything God had done through them.

5Then some of the believers who belonged to the party of the Pharisees stood up and said, "The Gentiles must be circumcised and required to obey the law of Moses."

6The apostles and elders met to consider this question. **7**After much discussion, Peter got up and addressed them: "Brothers, you know that some time ago God made a choice among you that the Gentiles might hear from my lips the message of the gospel and believe. **8**God, who knows the heart, showed that he accepted them by giving the Holy Spirit to them, just as he did to us. **9**He made no distinction between us and them, for he purified their hearts by faith. **10**Now then, why do you try to test God by putting on the necks of the disciples a yoke that neither we nor our fathers have been able to bear? **11**No! We believe it is through the grace of our Lord Jesus that we are saved, just as they are."

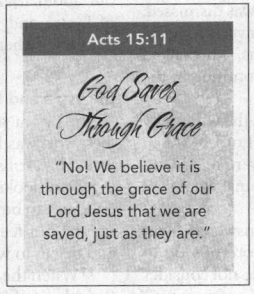

Acts 15:11

God Saves Through Grace

"No! We believe it is through the grace of our Lord Jesus that we are saved, just as they are."

12The whole assembly became silent as they listened to Barnabas and Paul telling about the miraculous signs and wonders God had done among the Gentiles through them. **13**When they finished, James spoke up: "Brothers, listen to me. **14**Simon*b* has described to us how God

---

*a*23 Or *Barnabas ordained elders*; or *Barnabas had elders elected*   *b*14 Greek *Simeon*, a variant of *Simon*; that is, Peter at first showed his concern by taking from the Gentiles a people for himself. ¹⁵The words of the prophets are in agreement with this, as it is written:

¹⁶ " 'After this I will return
    and rebuild David's fallen tent.
  Its ruins I will rebuild,
    and I will restore it,
¹⁷ that the remnant of men may seek the Lord,
    and all the Gentiles who bear my name,
  says the Lord, who does these things'ᵃ
¹⁸   that have been known for ages.ᵇ

¹⁹"It is my judgment, therefore, that we should not make it difficult for the Gentiles who are turning to God. ²⁰Instead we should write to them, telling them to abstain from food polluted by idols, from sexual immorality, from the meat of strangled animals and from blood. ²¹For Moses has been preached in every city from the earliest times and is read in the synagogues on every Sabbath."

The Council's Letter to Gentile Believers

²²Then the apostles and elders, with the whole church, decided to choose some of their own men and send them to Antioch with Paul and Barnabas. They chose Judas (called Barsabbas) and Silas, two men who were leaders among the brothers. ²³With them they sent the following letter:

The apostles and elders, your brothers,

To the Gentile believers in Antioch, Syria and Cilicia:

Greetings.

²⁴We have heard that some went out from us without our authorization and disturbed you, troubling your minds by what they said. ²⁵So we all agreed to choose some men and send them to you with our dear friends Barnabas and Paul— ²⁶men who have risked their lives for the name of our Lord Jesus Christ. ²⁷Therefore we are sending Judas and Silas to confirm by word of mouth what we are writing. ²⁸It seemed good to the Holy Spirit and to us

not to burden you with anything beyond the following requirements: ²⁹You are to abstain from food sacrificed to idols, from blood, from the meat of strangled animals and from sexual immorality. You will do well to avoid these things.

Farewell.

³⁰The men were sent off and went down to Antioch, where they gathered the church together and delivered the letter. ³¹The people read it and were glad for its encouraging message. ³²Judas and Silas, who themselves were prophets, said much to encourage and strengthen the brothers. ³³After spending some time there, they were sent off by the brothers with the blessing of peace to return to those who had sent them.ᶜ ³⁵But Paul and Barnabas remained in Antioch, where they and many others taught and preached the word of the Lord.

Disagreement Between Paul and Barnabas

³⁶Some time later Paul said to Barnabas, "Let us go back and visit the brothers in all the towns where we preached the word of the Lord and see how they are doing." ³⁷Barnabas wanted to take John, also called Mark, with them, ³⁸but Paul did not think it wise to take him, because he had deserted them in Pamphylia and had not continued with them in the work. ³⁹They had such a sharp disagreement that they parted company. Barnabas took Mark and sailed for Cyprus, ⁴⁰but Paul chose Silas and left, commended by the brothers to the grace of the Lord. ⁴¹He went through Syria and Cilicia, strengthening the churches.

Timothy Joins Paul and Silas

16 He came to Derbe and then to Lystra, where a disciple named Timothy lived, whose mother was a Jewess and a believer, but whose father was a Greek. ²The brothers at Lystra and Iconium spoke well of him. ³Paul wanted to take him along on the journey, so he circumcised him because of the Jews who lived in that area, for they all knew that his father was a Greek. ⁴As they traveled from town to town, they delivered the decisions reached

---

ᵃ17 Amos 9:11,12   ᵇ17,18 Some manuscripts things'— / ¹⁸known to the Lord for ages is his work   ᶜ33 Some manuscripts them, ³⁴but Silas decided to remain there by the apostles and elders in Jerusalem for the people to obey. ⁵So the churches were strengthened in the faith and grew daily in numbers.

Paul's Vision of the Man of Macedonia

⁶Paul and his companions traveled throughout the region of Phrygia and Galatia, having been kept by the Holy Spirit from preaching the word in the province of Asia. ⁷When they came to the border of Mysia, they tried to enter Bithynia, but the Spirit of Jesus would not allow them to. ⁸So they passed by Mysia and went down to Troas. ⁹During the night Paul had a vision of a man of Macedonia standing and begging him, "Come over to Macedonia and help us." ¹⁰After Paul had seen the vision, we got ready at once to leave for Macedonia, concluding that God had called us to preach the gospel to them.

Lydia's Conversion in Philippi

¹¹From Troas we put out to sea and sailed straight for Samothrace, and the next day on to Neapolis. ¹²From there we traveled to Philippi, a Roman colony and the leading city of that district of Macedonia. And we stayed there several days.

¹³On the Sabbath we went outside the city gate to the river, where we expected to find a place of prayer. We sat down and began to speak to the women who had gathered there. ¹⁴One of those listening was a woman named Lydia, a dealer in purple cloth from the city of Thyatira, who was a worshiper of God. The Lord opened her heart to respond to Paul's message. ¹⁵When she and the members of her household were baptized, she invited us to her home. "If you consider me a believer in the Lord," she said, "come and stay at my house." And she persuaded us.

Paul and Silas in Prison

¹⁶Once when we were going to the place of prayer, we were met by a slave girl who had a spirit by which she predicted the future. She earned a great deal of money for her owners by fortune-telling. ¹⁷This girl followed Paul and the rest of us, shouting, "These men are servants of the Most High God, who are telling you the way to be saved." ¹⁸She kept this up for many days. Finally Paul became so troubled that he turned around and said to the spirit, "In the name of Jesus Christ I command you to come out of her!" At that moment the spirit left her.

¹⁹When the owners of the slave girl realized that their hope of making money was gone, they seized Paul and Silas and dragged them into the marketplace to face the authorities. ²⁰They brought them before the magistrates and said, "These men are Jews, and are throwing our city into an uproar ²¹by advocating customs unlawful for us Romans to accept or practice."

²²The crowd joined in the attack against Paul and Silas, and the magistrates ordered them to be stripped and beaten. ²³After they had been severely flogged, they were thrown into prison, and the jailer was commanded to guard them carefully. ²⁴Upon receiving such orders, he put them in the inner cell and fastened their feet in the stocks.

²⁵About midnight Paul and Silas were praying and singing hymns to God, and the other prisoners were listening to them. ²⁶Suddenly there was such a violent earthquake that the foundations of the prison were shaken. At once all the prison doors flew open, and everybody's chains came loose. ²⁷The jailer woke up, and when he saw the prison doors open, he drew his sword and was about to kill himself because he thought the prisoners had escaped. ²⁸But Paul shouted, "Don't harm yourself! We are all here!"

²⁹The jailer called for lights, rushed in and fell trembling before Paul and Silas. ³⁰He then brought them out and asked, "Sirs, what must I do to be saved?"

³¹They replied, "Believe in the Lord Jesus, and you will be saved—you and your household." ³²Then they spoke the word of the Lord to him and to all the others in his house. ³³At that hour of the night the jailer took them and washed their wounds; then immediately he

Acts 16:31

God Saves Through Faith

They replied, "Believe in the Lord Jesus, and you will be saved—you and your household."

Little White Lie

SAPPHIRA

WHAT WAS THE PRICE we agreed to say we paid again?

Sapphira silently calculated the cost of the land once more for good measure.

Nine . . . plus . . .

Take away half . . . add . . . or was it add half and take away . . . ?

She muttered to herself as she made her way through the city streets. *I'm never going to get this right.* Her husband, Ananias, had been over this with her a hundred times, but still she tended to forget things whenever she was nervous. One little mistake, and their charade would be over.

"I'll go first and lay the money at the apostles' feet," he'd told her. "I'll tell them that the amount was the full price we got for the property. Then, if anyone asks you about it, you just back me up. Got it?"

She got it alright. How else were they going to make ends meet if they didn't keep a little kickback for themselves?

She'd been astonished lately at her friends and even perfect strangers. What had gotten into them? Everyone was out of their minds with generosity—selling houses and land as routinely as if they were eggs and butter.

Inside, she may have secretly wished she could be like the other churchgoers she admired.

But I'm just too practical, she reasoned. *Maybe when Ananias and I get ahead, then we'll be able to give like they do.*

In the meantime, she had to say that she was fairly impressed with the amount they *had* agreed to give to the church. She reassured herself on her way to meet Ananias. That gift would certainly outweigh any little white lie she or her husband would tell.

And maybe, with a little luck, Ananias would have already taken care of it and no one would ask her anything. Then she wouldn't have to tell a lie; she'd only have to live one.

—Prayer—

Heavenly Father, I am sorry for the lies that I participate in. Forgive me and help me to live a life of honesty.

Peter asked her, "Tell me, is this the price you and Ananias got for the land?" "Yes," she said, "that is the price."

Acts 5:8

ASSIGNED READING:

Acts 5:1–11

and all his family were baptized. [34]The jailer brought them into his house and set a meal before them; he was filled with joy because he had come to believe in God—he and his whole family.

[35]When it was daylight, the magistrates sent their officers to the jailer with the order: "Release those men." [36]The jailer told Paul, "The magistrates have ordered that you and Silas be released. Now you can leave. Go in peace."

[37]But Paul said to the officers: "They beat us publicly without a trial, even though we are Roman citizens, and threw us into prison. And now do they want to get rid of us quietly? No! Let them come themselves and escort us out."

[38]The officers reported this to the magistrates, and when they heard that Paul and Silas were Roman citizens, they were alarmed. [39]They came to appease them and escorted them from the prison, requesting them to leave the city. [40]After Paul and Silas came out of the prison, they went to Lydia's house, where they met with the brothers and encouraged them. Then they left.

In Thessalonica

17 When they had passed through Amphipolis and Apollonia, they came to Thessalonica, where there was a Jewish synagogue. [2]As his custom was, Paul went into the synagogue, and on three Sabbath days he reasoned with them from the Scriptures, [3]explaining and proving that the Christ[a] had to suffer and rise from the dead. "This Jesus I am proclaiming to you is the Christ,[a]" he said. [4]Some of the Jews were persuaded and joined Paul and Silas, as did a large number of God-fearing Greeks and not a few prominent women.

[5]But the Jews were jealous; so they rounded up some bad characters from the marketplace, formed a mob and started a riot in the city. They rushed to Jason's house in search of Paul and Silas in order to bring them out to the crowd.[b] [6]But when they did not find them, they dragged Jason and some other brothers before the city officials, shouting: "These men who have caused trouble all over the world have now come here, [7]and Jason has welcomed them into his house. They are all defying Caesar's decrees, saying that there is another king, one called Jesus." [8]When they heard this, the crowd and the city officials were thrown into turmoil. [9]Then they made Jason and the others post bond and let them go.

In Berea

[10]As soon as it was night, the brothers sent Paul and Silas away to Berea. On arriving there, they went to the Jewish synagogue. [11]Now the Bereans were of more noble character than the Thessalonians, for they received the message with great eagerness and examined the Scriptures every day to see if what Paul said was true. [12]Many of the Jews believed, as did also a number of prominent Greek women and many Greek men.

[13]When the Jews in Thessalonica learned that Paul was preaching the word of God at Berea, they went there too, agitating the crowds and stirring them up. [14]The brothers immediately sent Paul to the coast, but Silas and Timothy stayed at Berea. [15]The men who escorted Paul brought him to Athens and then left with instructions for Silas and Timothy to join him as soon as possible.

In Athens

[16]While Paul was waiting for them in Athens, he was greatly distressed to see that the city was full of idols. [17]So he reasoned in the synagogue with the Jews and the God-fearing Greeks, as well as in the marketplace day by day with those who happened to be there. [18]A group of Epicurean and Stoic philosophers began to dispute with him. Some of them asked, "What is this babbler trying to say?" Others remarked, "He seems to be advocating foreign gods." They said this because Paul was preaching the good news about Jesus and the resurrection. [19]Then they took him and brought him to a meeting of the Areopagus, where they said to him, "May we know what this new teaching is that you are presenting? [20]You are bringing some strange ideas to our ears, and we want to know what they mean." [21](All the Athenians and the foreigners who lived there spent their time doing nothing but talking about and listening to the latest ideas.)

[22]Paul then stood up in the meeting of the

---

*a*3 Or *Messiah*   *b*5 Or *the assembly of the people*

Reaching

Read: Acts 17:16–34

WHEN PEOPLE DREAM about what they can achieve, they are often told to "reach for the stars." Well, we all know one can reach, at least metaphorically, but never touch. The nearest star, our sun, is 93 million miles away, and if anyone even got much closer to it than we are now, they'd be incinerated. The temperature even on Venus, our next closest planetary neighbor, is 720 degrees Kelvin. The surface of the sun is a whopping 5800 degrees Kelvin. Does that tell you anything about the power of the Creator of the sun?

Happily, there's no danger of incineration when we reach for God. What Paul preached to the people of Athens is still true. Paul told them in chapter 17 that God revealed himself to us as the One who made everything and the One who dictates the rise and fall of nations. He revealed himself as the One in control of all things. Why does God go to such lengths to reveal himself? So that perhaps we might seek him. It's as if God is holding his breath, willing each and every person to reach out to him.

God promises that when we search for him, we'll find him and be satisfied. Living in God's realm is like being returned to our natural element. Our every breath is in his hands: "For in him we live and move and have our being" (verse 28). Otherwise we are spiritually like fish out of water; we can do nothing to help ourselves; we cannot move, and our spirits cannot stay alive.

Imagine the God of the universe wanting you to reach out to him—waiting in eager anticipation. Do you know what's really remarkable? As you begin reaching toward God, you'll find you don't need to reach at all. He is not far. There's no stretch. Our loving God is as close as your next breath—your next prayer. Jesus says, "Here I am! I stand at the door and knock. If anyone hears my voice and opens the door, I will come in and eat with him, and he with me" (Revelation 3:20).

Acts 17:27–28

"God did this so that men would seek him and perhaps reach out for him and find him, though he is not far from each one of us. 'For in him we live and move and have our being.' As some of your own poets have said, 'We are his offspring.'"

reflection

1 How is God revealing himself to you these days?

2 Can you remember what life was like before you first reached out to God? In what ways are you able to move and breathe and live in God?

3 Do you need to reach out to God now? If so, spend some time in his presence right now.

RELATED READINGS

1 Chronicles 16:10–11;
Isaiah 55:6–7;
Hebrews 11:6

Go to page 1352 for your next devotional reading.

Areopagus and said: "Men of Athens! I see that in every way you are very religious. 23For as I walked around and looked carefully at your objects of worship, I even found an altar with this inscription: TO AN UNKNOWN GOD. Now what you worship as something unknown I am going to proclaim to you.

24"The God who made the world and everything in it is the Lord of heaven and earth and does not live in temples built by hands. 25And he is not served by human hands, as if he needed anything, because he himself gives all men life and breath and everything else. 26From one man he made every nation of men, that they should inhabit the whole earth; and he determined the times set for them and the exact places where they should live. 27God did this so that men would seek him and perhaps reach out for him and find him, though he is not far from each one of us. 28'For in him we live and move and have our being.' As some of your own poets have said, 'We are his offspring.'

29"Therefore since we are God's offspring, we should not think that the divine being is like gold or silver or stone—an image made by man's design and skill. 30In the past God overlooked such ignorance, but now he commands all people everywhere to repent. 31For he has set a day when he will judge the world with justice by the man he has appointed. He has given proof of this to all men by raising him from the dead."

32When they heard about the resurrection of the dead, some of them sneered, but others said, "We want to hear you again on this subject." 33At that, Paul left the Council. 34A few men became followers of Paul and believed. Among them was Dionysius, a member of the Areopagus, also a woman named Damaris, and a number of others.

In Corinth

18 After this, Paul left Athens and went to Corinth. 2There he met a Jew named Aquila, a native of Pontus, who had recently come from Italy with his wife Priscilla, because Claudius had ordered all the Jews to leave Rome. Paul went to see them, 3and because he was a tentmaker as they were, he stayed and worked with them. 4Every Sabbath he reasoned in the synagogue, trying to persuade Jews and Greeks.

5When Silas and Timothy came from Macedonia, Paul devoted himself exclusively to preaching, testifying to the Jews that Jesus was the Christ.*a* 6But when the Jews opposed Paul and became abusive, he shook out his clothes in protest and said to them, "Your blood be on your own heads! I am clear of my responsibility. From now on I will go to the Gentiles."

7Then Paul left the synagogue and went next door to the house of Titius Justus, a worshiper of God. 8Crispus, the synagogue ruler, and his entire household believed in the Lord; and many of the Corinthians who heard him believed and were baptized.

9One night the Lord spoke to Paul in a vision: "Do not be afraid; keep on speaking, do not be silent. 10For I am with you, and no one is going to attack and harm you, because I have many people in this city." 11So Paul stayed for a year and a half, teaching them the word of God.

12While Gallio was proconsul of Achaia, the Jews made a united attack on Paul and brought him into court. 13"This man," they charged, "is persuading the people to worship God in ways contrary to the law."

14Just as Paul was about to speak, Gallio said to the Jews, "If you Jews were making a complaint about some misdemeanor or serious crime, it would be reasonable for me to listen to you. 15But since it involves questions about words and names and your own law—settle the matter yourselves. I will not be a judge of such things." 16So he had them ejected from the court. 17Then they all turned on Sosthenes the synagogue ruler and beat him in front of the court. But Gallio showed no concern whatever.

Acts 17:27

God Is Near

"God did this so that men would seek him and perhaps reach out for him and find him, though he is not far from each one of us."

---

*a*5 Or *Messiah*; also in verse 28

Priscilla, Aquila and Apollos

[18]Paul stayed on in Corinth for some time. Then he left the brothers and sailed for Syria, accompanied by Priscilla and Aquila. Before he sailed, he had his hair cut off at Cenchrea because of a vow he had taken. [19]They arrived at Ephesus, where Paul left Priscilla and Aquila. He himself went into the synagogue and reasoned with the Jews. [20]When they asked him to spend more time with them, he declined. [21]But as he left, he promised, "I will come back if it is God's will." Then he set sail from Ephesus. [22]When he landed at Caesarea, he went up and greeted the church and then went down to Antioch.

[23]After spending some time in Antioch, Paul set out from there and traveled from place to place throughout the region of Galatia and Phrygia, strengthening all the disciples.

[24]Meanwhile a Jew named Apollos, a native of Alexandria, came to Ephesus. He was a learned man, with a thorough knowledge of the Scriptures. [25]He had been instructed in the way of the Lord, and he spoke with great fervor[a] and taught about Jesus accurately, though he knew only the baptism of John. [26]He began to speak boldly in the synagogue. When Priscilla and Aquila heard him, they invited him to their home and explained to him the way of God more adequately.

[27]When Apollos wanted to go to Achaia, the brothers encouraged him and wrote to the disciples there to welcome him. On arriving, he was a great help to those who by grace had believed. [28]For he vigorously refuted the Jews in public debate, proving from the Scriptures that Jesus was the Christ.

Paul in Ephesus

19 While Apollos was at Corinth, Paul took the road through the interior and arrived at Ephesus. There he found some disciples [2]and asked them, "Did you receive the Holy Spirit when[b] you believed?"

They answered, "No, we have not even heard that there is a Holy Spirit."

[3]So Paul asked, "Then what baptism did you receive?"

"John's baptism," they replied.

[4]Paul said, "John's baptism was a baptism of repentance. He told the people to believe in the one coming after him, that is, in Jesus." [5]On hearing this, they were baptized into[c] the name of the Lord Jesus. [6]When Paul placed his hands on them, the Holy Spirit came on them, and they spoke in tongues[d] and prophesied. [7]There were about twelve men in all.

[8]Paul entered the synagogue and spoke boldly there for three months, arguing persuasively about the kingdom of God. [9]But some of them became obstinate; they refused to believe and publicly maligned the Way. So Paul left them. He took the disciples with him and had discussions daily in the lecture hall of Tyrannus. [10]This went on for two years, so that all the Jews and Greeks who lived in the province of Asia heard the word of the Lord.

[11]God did extraordinary miracles through Paul, [12]so that even handkerchiefs and aprons that had touched him were taken to the sick, and their illnesses were cured and the evil spirits left them.

[13]Some Jews who went around driving out evil spirits tried to invoke the name of the Lord Jesus over those who were demon-possessed. They would say, "In the name of Jesus, whom Paul preaches, I command you to come out." [14]Seven sons of Sceva, a Jewish chief priest, were doing this. [15]One day the evil spirit answered them, "Jesus I know, and I know about Paul, but who are you?" [16]Then the man who had the evil spirit jumped on them and overpowered them all. He gave them such a beating that they ran out of the house naked and bleeding.

[17]When this became known to the Jews and Greeks living in Ephesus, they were all seized with fear, and the name of the Lord Jesus was held in high honor. [18]Many of those who believed now came and openly confessed their evil deeds. [19]A number who had practiced sorcery brought their scrolls together and burned them publicly. When they calculated the value of the scrolls, the total came to fifty thousand drachmas.[e] [20]In this way the word of the Lord spread widely and grew in power.

[21]After all this had happened, Paul decided

---

[a]25 Or *with fervor in the Spirit*   [b]2 Or *after*   [c]5 Or *in*   [d]6 Or *other languages*   [e]19 A drachma was a silver coin worth about a day's wages.

Read: Acts 19:1–20

Acts 19:15–16

The evil spirit answered them, "Jesus I know, and I know about Paul, but who are you?" Then the man who had the evil spirit jumped on them and overpowered them all.

1 Have you ever been a name-dropper in some way? When?

2 Have you ever seen people call on God even though they didn't believe in him? What were the circumstances? What were the results?

3 In what ways can you bring honor to Jesus' name?

RELATED READINGS

Matthew 12:22–32;
Mark 16:15–18;
Luke 10:18–20

NAME-DROPPERS ARE KNOWN for annoying those who overhear their outrageous claims. Casually sprinkling their conversations with the names of famous people, they aim to impress their listeners. Some imply a familiarity with illustrious people, as if they are on a first-name basis.

In Acts 19, we meet the seven sons of Sceva, who employed name-dropping in their profession as exorcists. They incorporated the name of Jesus into their effort to drive out demons. But it backfired. The would-be exorcists were pummeled as the demon-possessed man overpowered them. The question is, if the disciples were able to cast out demons in Jesus' name, why couldn't the sons of Sceva? It was largely because they profaned God's name by taking it in vain. They knew the name of the Lord, but not the Lord of the name.

The demoniac's reply, "Who are you?" revealed that these men didn't have a personal relationship with Jesus nor did they believe Paul's teachings. Jesus had promised, "Signs will accompany those who believe: In my name they will drive out demons" (Mark 16:17). Tragically, these imposters thought they could use Jesus' name to work some magic.

The sons of Sceva presumptuously took Christ's name in vain. But there are other ways to take God's name in vain. Other forms of dropping God's name in a negative way:

♦ Repeating the Lord's name as a part of rote or routine (Matthew 6:7)

♦ Professing to be a Christian without obeying God's commands (Matthew 7:21–23)

♦ Praising God with the lips but not from the heart (Matthew 15:7–9)

There is power in God's name, but we can learn from this story to be careful not to drop God's name unless we have a personal relationship with him. The sons of Sceva were punished, beaten by the very demon they were trying to cast out. When we honor the Lord's name, we are honoring our Lord.

Tuesday

 Go to page 1361 for your next devotional reading.

to go to Jerusalem, passing through Macedonia and Achaia. "After I have been there," he said, "I must visit Rome also." **22**He sent two of his helpers, Timothy and Erastus, to Macedonia, while he stayed in the province of Asia a little longer.

The Riot in Ephesus

23About that time there arose a great disturbance about the Way. **24**A silversmith named Demetrius, who made silver shrines of Artemis, brought in no little business for the craftsmen. **25**He called them together, along with the workmen in related trades, and said: "Men, you know we receive a good income from this business. **26**And you see and hear how this fellow Paul has convinced and led astray large numbers of people here in Ephesus and in practically the whole province of Asia. He says that man-made gods are no gods at all. **27**There is danger not only that our trade will lose its good name, but also that the temple of the great goddess Artemis will be discredited, and the goddess herself, who is worshiped throughout the province of Asia and the world, will be robbed of her divine majesty."

28When they heard this, they were furious and began shouting: "Great is Artemis of the Ephesians!" **29**Soon the whole city was in an uproar. The people seized Gaius and Aristarchus, Paul's traveling companions from Macedonia, and rushed as one man into the theater. **30**Paul wanted to appear before the crowd, but the disciples would not let him. **31**Even some of the officials of the province, friends of Paul, sent him a message begging him not to venture into the theater.

32The assembly was in confusion: Some were shouting one thing, some another. Most of the people did not even know why they were there. **33**The Jews pushed Alexander to the front, and some of the crowd shouted instructions to him. He motioned for silence in order to make a defense before the people. **34**But when they realized he was a Jew, they all shouted in unison for about two hours: "Great is Artemis of the Ephesians!"

35The city clerk quieted the crowd and said: "Men of Ephesus, doesn't all the world know that the city of Ephesus is the guardian of the temple of the great Artemis and of her image, which fell from heaven? **36**Therefore, since these facts are undeniable, you ought to be quiet and not do anything rash. **37**You have brought these men here, though they have neither robbed temples nor blasphemed our goddess. **38**If, then, Demetrius and his fellow craftsmen have a grievance against anybody, the courts are open and there are proconsuls. They can press charges. **39**If there is anything further you want to bring up, it must be settled in a legal assembly. **40**As it is, we are in danger of being charged with rioting because of today's events. In that case we would not be able to account for this commotion, since there is no reason for it." **41**After he had said this, he dismissed the assembly.

Through Macedonia and Greece

20 When the uproar had ended, Paul sent for the disciples and, after encouraging them, said good-by and set out for Macedonia. **2**He traveled through that area, speaking many words of encouragement to the people, and finally arrived in Greece, **3**where he stayed three months. Because the Jews made a plot against him just as he was about to sail for Syria, he decided to go back through Macedonia. **4**He was accompanied by Sopater son of Pyrrhus from Berea, Aristarchus and Secundus from Thessalonica, Gaius from Derbe, Timothy also, and Tychicus and Trophimus from the province of Asia. **5**These men went on ahead and waited for us at Troas. **6**But we sailed from Philippi after the Feast of Unleavened Bread, and five days later joined the others at Troas, where we stayed seven days.

Eutychus Raised From the Dead at Troas

7On the first day of the week we came together to break bread. Paul spoke to the people and, because he intended to leave the next day, kept on talking until midnight. **8**There were many lamps in the upstairs room where we were meeting. **9**Seated in a window was a young man named Eutychus, who was sinking into a deep sleep as Paul talked on and on. When he was sound asleep, he fell to the ground from the third story and was picked up dead. **10**Paul went down, threw himself on the young man and put his arms around him. "Don't be alarmed," he said. "He's alive!" **11**Then he went upstairs again and broke bread and ate.

After talking until daylight, he left. ¹²The people took the young man home alive and were greatly comforted.

Paul's Farewell to the Ephesian Elders

¹³We went on ahead to the ship and sailed for Assos, where we were going to take Paul aboard. He had made this arrangement because he was going there on foot. ¹⁴When he met us at Assos, we took him aboard and went on to Mitylene. ¹⁵The next day we set sail from there and arrived off Kios. The day after that we crossed over to Samos, and on the following day arrived at Miletus. ¹⁶Paul had decided to sail past Ephesus to avoid spending time in the province of Asia, for he was in a hurry to reach Jerusalem, if possible, by the day of Pentecost.

¹⁷From Miletus, Paul sent to Ephesus for the elders of the church. ¹⁸When they arrived, he said to them: "You know how I lived the whole time I was with you, from the first day I came into the province of Asia. ¹⁹I served the Lord with great humility and with tears, although I was severely tested by the plots of the Jews. ²⁰You know that I have not hesitated to preach anything that would be helpful to you but have taught you publicly and from house to house. ²¹I have declared to both Jews and Greeks that they must turn to God in repentance and have faith in our Lord Jesus.

²²"And now, compelled by the Spirit, I am going to Jerusalem, not knowing what will happen to me there. ²³I only know that in every city the Holy Spirit warns me that prison and hardships are facing me. ²⁴However, I consider my life worth nothing to me, if only I may finish the race and complete the task the Lord Jesus has given me—the task of testifying to the gospel of God's grace.

²⁵"Now I know that none of you among whom I have gone about preaching the kingdom will ever see me again. ²⁶Therefore, I declare to you today that I am innocent of the blood of all men. ²⁷For I have not hesitated to proclaim to you the whole will of God. ²⁸Keep

watch over yourselves and all the flock of which the Holy Spirit has made you overseers.*ᵃ* Be shepherds of the church of God,*ᵇ* which he bought with his own blood. ²⁹I know that after I leave, savage wolves will come in among you and will not spare the flock. ³⁰Even from your own number men will arise and distort the truth in order to draw away disciples after them. ³¹So be on your guard! Remember that for three years I never stopped warning each of you night and day with tears.

³²"Now I commit you to God and to the word of his grace, which can build you up and give you an inheritance among all those who are sanctified. ³³I have not coveted anyone's silver or gold or clothing. ³⁴You yourselves know that these hands of mine have supplied my own needs and the needs of my companions. ³⁵In everything I did, I showed you that by this kind of hard work we must help the weak, remembering the words the Lord Jesus himself said: 'It is more blessed to give than to receive.'"

³⁶When he had said this, he knelt down with all of them and prayed. ³⁷They all wept as they embraced him and kissed him. ³⁸What grieved them most was his statement that they would never see his face again. Then they accompanied him to the ship.

Acts 20:21

God Saves

"I have declared to both Jews and Greeks that they must turn to God in repentance and have faith in our Lord Jesus."

On to Jerusalem

21 After we had torn ourselves away from them, we put out to sea and sailed straight to Cos. The next day we went to Rhodes and from there to Patara. ²We found a ship crossing over to Phoenicia, went on board and set sail. ³After sighting Cyprus and passing to the south of it, we sailed on to Syria. We landed at Tyre, where our ship was to unload its cargo. ⁴Finding the disciples there, we stayed with them seven days. Through the Spirit they urged Paul not to go on to Jerusalem. ⁵But when our time was up, we left and continued on our way. All the disciples and their wives and children accompanied us out of the city, and there on the beach we knelt to pray. ⁶After saying good-

---

ᵃ28 Traditionally *bishops*   *ᵇ28* Many manuscripts *of the Lord* by to each other, we went aboard the ship, and they returned home.

7 We continued our voyage from Tyre and landed at Ptolemais, where we greeted the brothers and stayed with them for a day. **8** Leaving the next day, we reached Caesarea and stayed at the house of Philip the evangelist, one of the Seven. **9** He had four unmarried daughters who prophesied.

10 After we had been there a number of days, a prophet named Agabus came down from Judea. **11** Coming over to us, he took Paul's belt, tied his own hands and feet with it and said, "The Holy Spirit says, 'In this way the Jews of Jerusalem will bind the owner of this belt and will hand him over to the Gentiles.' "

12 When we heard this, we and the people there pleaded with Paul not to go up to Jerusalem. **13** Then Paul answered, "Why are you weeping and breaking my heart? I am ready not only to be bound, but also to die in Jerusalem for the name of the Lord Jesus." **14** When he would not be dissuaded, we gave up and said, "The Lord's will be done."

15 After this, we got ready and went up to Jerusalem. **16** Some of the disciples from Caesarea accompanied us and brought us to the home of Mnason, where we were to stay. He was a man from Cyprus and one of the early disciples.

Paul's Arrival at Jerusalem

17 When we arrived at Jerusalem, the brothers received us warmly. **18** The next day Paul and the rest of us went to see James, and all the elders were present. **19** Paul greeted them and reported in detail what God had done among the Gentiles through his ministry.

20 When they heard this, they praised God. Then they said to Paul: "You see, brother, how many thousands of Jews have believed, and all of them are zealous for the law. **21** They have been informed that you teach all the Jews who live among the Gentiles to turn away from Moses, telling them not to circumcise their children or live according to our customs. **22** What shall we do? They will certainly hear that you have come, **23** so do what we tell you. There are four men with us who have made a vow. **24** Take these men, join in their purification rites and pay their expenses, so that they can have their heads shaved. Then everybody will know there is no truth in these reports about you, but that you yourself are living in obedience to the law. **25** As for the Gentile believers, we have written to them our decision that they should abstain from food sacrificed to idols, from blood, from the meat of strangled animals and from sexual immorality."

26 The next day Paul took the men and purified himself along with them. Then he went to the temple to give notice of the date when the days of purification would end and the offering would be made for each of them.

Paul Arrested

27 When the seven days were nearly over, some Jews from the province of Asia saw Paul at the temple. They stirred up the whole crowd and seized him, **28** shouting, "Men of Israel, help us! This is the man who teaches all men everywhere against our people and our law and this place. And besides, he has brought Greeks into the temple area and defiled this holy place." **29** (They had previously seen Trophimus the Ephesian in the city with Paul and assumed that Paul had brought him into the temple area.)

30 The whole city was aroused, and the people came running from all directions. Seizing Paul, they dragged him from the temple, and immediately the gates were shut. **31** While they were trying to kill him, news reached the commander of the Roman troops that the whole city of Jerusalem was in an uproar. **32** He at once took some officers and soldiers and ran down to the crowd. When the rioters saw the commander and his soldiers, they stopped beating Paul.

33 The commander came up and arrested him and ordered him to be bound with two chains. Then he asked who he was and what he had done. **34** Some in the crowd shouted one thing and some another, and since the commander could not get at the truth because of the uproar, he ordered that Paul be taken into the barracks. **35** When Paul reached the steps, the violence of the mob was so great he had to be carried by the soldiers. **36** The crowd that followed kept shouting, "Away with him!"

Paul Speaks to the Crowd

37 As the soldiers were about to take Paul into the barracks, he asked the commander, "May I say something to you?"

"Do you speak Greek?" he replied. [38]"Aren't you the Egyptian who started a revolt and led four thousand terrorists out into the desert some time ago?"

[39]Paul answered, "I am a Jew, from Tarsus in Cilicia, a citizen of no ordinary city. Please let me speak to the people."

[40]Having received the commander's permission, Paul stood on the steps and motioned to the crowd. When they were all silent, he said to

22
them in Aramaic[a]: [1]"Brothers and fathers, listen now to my defense."

[2]When they heard him speak to them in Aramaic, they became very quiet.

Then Paul said: [3]"I am a Jew, born in Tarsus of Cilicia, but brought up in this city. Under Gamaliel I was thoroughly trained in the law of our fathers and was just as zealous for God as any of you are today. [4]I persecuted the followers of this Way to their death, arresting both men and women and throwing them into prison, [5]as also the high priest and all the Council can testify. I even obtained letters from them to their brothers in Damascus, and went there to bring these people as prisoners to Jerusalem to be punished.

[6]"About noon as I came near Damascus, suddenly a bright light from heaven flashed around me. [7]I fell to the ground and heard a voice say to me, 'Saul! Saul! Why do you persecute me?'

[8]"Who are you, Lord?' I asked.

"'I am Jesus of Nazareth, whom you are persecuting,' he replied. [9]My companions saw the light, but they did not understand the voice of him who was speaking to me.

[10]"What shall I do, Lord?' I asked.

"'Get up,' the Lord said, 'and go into Damascus. There you will be told all that you have been assigned to do.' [11]My companions led me by the hand into Damascus, because the brilliance of the light had blinded me.

[12]"A man named Ananias came to see me. He was a devout observer of the law and highly respected by all the Jews living there. [13]He stood beside me and said, 'Brother Saul, receive your sight!' And at that very moment I was able to see him.

[14]"Then he said: 'The God of our fathers has chosen you to know his will and to see the Righteous One and to hear words from his mouth. [15]You will be his witness to all men of what you have seen and heard. [16]And now what are you waiting for? Get up, be baptized and wash your sins away, calling on his name.'

[17]"When I returned to Jerusalem and was praying at the temple, I fell into a trance [18]and saw the Lord speaking. 'Quick!' he said to me. 'Leave Jerusalem immediately, because they will not accept your testimony about me.'

[19]"Lord,' I replied, 'these men know that I went from one synagogue to another to imprison and beat those who believe in you. [20]And when the blood of your martyr[b] Stephen was shed, I stood there giving my approval and guarding the clothes of those who were killing him.'

[21]"Then the Lord said to me, 'Go; I will send you far away to the Gentiles.'"

Paul the Roman Citizen

[22]The crowd listened to Paul until he said this. Then they raised their voices and shouted, "Rid the earth of him! He's not fit to live!"

[23]As they were shouting and throwing off their cloaks and flinging dust into the air, [24]the commander ordered Paul to be taken into the barracks. He directed that he be flogged and questioned in order to find out why the people were shouting at him like this. [25]As they stretched him out to flog him, Paul said to the centurion standing there, "Is it legal for you to flog a Roman citizen who hasn't even been found guilty?"

[26]When the centurion heard this, he went to the commander and reported it. "What are you going to do?" he asked. "This man is a Roman citizen."

[27]The commander went to Paul and asked, "Tell me, are you a Roman citizen?"

"Yes, I am," he answered.

[28]Then the commander said, "I had to pay a big price for my citizenship."

"But I was born a citizen," Paul replied.

[29]Those who were about to question him withdrew immediately. The commander himself was alarmed when he realized that he had put Paul, a Roman citizen, in chains.

---

[a]40 Or possibly *Hebrew*; also in 22:2   [b]20 Or *witness*

Before the Sanhedrin

30The next day, since the commander wanted to find out exactly why Paul was being accused by the Jews, he released him and ordered the chief priests and all the Sanhedrin to assemble. Then he brought Paul and had him stand before them.

23 Paul looked straight at the Sanhedrin and said, "My brothers, I have fulfilled my duty to God in all good conscience to this day." 2At this the high priest Ananias ordered those standing near Paul to strike him on the mouth. 3Then Paul said to him, "God will strike you, you whitewashed wall! You sit there to judge me according to the law, yet you yourself violate the law by commanding that I be struck!"

4Those who were standing near Paul said, "You dare to insult God's high priest?"

5Paul replied, "Brothers, I did not realize that he was the high priest; for it is written: 'Do not speak evil about the ruler of your people.'*a*"

6Then Paul, knowing that some of them were Sadducees and the others Pharisees, called out in the Sanhedrin, "My brothers, I am a Pharisee, the son of a Pharisee. I stand on trial because of my hope in the resurrection of the dead." 7When he said this, a dispute broke out between the Pharisees and the Sadducees, and the assembly was divided. 8(The Sadducees say that there is no resurrection, and that there are neither angels nor spirits, but the Pharisees acknowledge them all.)

9There was a great uproar, and some of the teachers of the law who were Pharisees stood up and argued vigorously. "We find nothing wrong with this man," they said. "What if a spirit or an angel has spoken to him?" 10The dispute became so violent that the commander was afraid Paul would be torn to pieces by them. He ordered the troops to go down and take him away from them by force and bring him into the barracks.

11The following night the Lord stood near Paul and said, "Take courage! As you have testified about me in Jerusalem, so you must also testify in Rome."

The Plot to Kill Paul

12The next morning the Jews formed a conspiracy and bound themselves with an oath not to eat or drink until they had killed Paul. 13More than forty men were involved in this plot. 14They went to the chief priests and elders and said, "We have taken a solemn oath not to eat anything until we have killed Paul. 15Now then, you and the Sanhedrin petition the commander to bring him before you on the pretext of wanting more accurate information about his case. We are ready to kill him before he gets here."

16But when the son of Paul's sister heard of this plot, he went into the barracks and told Paul.

17Then Paul called one of the centurions and said, "Take this young man to the commander; he has something to tell him." 18So he took him to the commander.

The centurion said, "Paul, the prisoner, sent for me and asked me to bring this young man to you because he has something to tell you."

19The commander took the young man by the hand, drew him aside and asked, "What is it you want to tell me?"

20He said: "The Jews have agreed to ask you to bring Paul before the Sanhedrin tomorrow on the pretext of wanting more accurate information about him. 21Don't give in to them, because more than forty of them are waiting in ambush for him. They have taken an oath not to eat or drink until they have killed him. They are ready now, waiting for your consent to their request."

22The commander dismissed the young man and cautioned him, "Don't tell anyone that you have reported this to me."

Paul Transferred to Caesarea

23Then he called two of his centurions and ordered them, "Get ready a detachment of two hundred soldiers, seventy horsemen and two hundred spearmen*b* to go to Caesarea at nine tonight. 24Provide mounts for Paul so that he may be taken safely to Governor Felix."

25He wrote a letter as follows:

26Claudius Lysias,

To His Excellency, Governor Felix:

Greetings.

*a*5 Exodus 22:28   *b*23 The meaning of the Greek for this word is uncertain.

27This man was seized by the Jews and they were about to kill him, but I came with my troops and rescued him, for I had learned that he is a Roman citizen. 28I wanted to know why they were accusing him, so I brought him to their Sanhedrin. 29I found that the accusation had to do with questions about their law, but there was no charge against him that deserved death or imprisonment. 30When I was informed of a plot to be carried out against the man, I sent him to you at once. I also ordered his accusers to present to you their case against him.

31So the soldiers, carrying out their orders, took Paul with them during the night and brought him as far as Antipatris. 32The next day they let the cavalry go on with him, while they returned to the barracks. 33When the cavalry arrived in Caesarea, they delivered the letter to the governor and handed Paul over to him. 34The governor read the letter and asked what province he was from. Learning that he was from Cilicia, 35he said, "I will hear your case when your accusers get here." Then he ordered that Paul be kept under guard in Herod's palace.

The Trial Before Felix

24 Five days later the high priest Ananias went down to Caesarea with some of the elders and a lawyer named Tertullus, and they brought their charges against Paul before the governor. 2When Paul was called in, Tertullus presented his case before Felix: "We have enjoyed a long period of peace under you, and your foresight has brought about reforms in this nation. 3Everywhere and in every way, most excellent Felix, we acknowledge this with profound gratitude. 4But in order not to weary you further, I would request that you be kind enough to hear us briefly.

5"We have found this man to be a trouble-maker, stirring up riots among the Jews all over the world. He is a ringleader of the Nazarene sect 6and even tried to desecrate the temple; so we seized him. 8By*a* examining him yourself you will be able to learn the truth about all these charges we are bringing against him."

9The Jews joined in the accusation, asserting that these things were true.

10When the governor motioned for him to speak, Paul replied: "I know that for a number of years you have been a judge over this nation; so I gladly make my defense. 11You can easily verify that no more than twelve days ago I went up to Jerusalem to worship. 12My accusers did not find me arguing with anyone at the temple, or stirring up a crowd in the synagogues or anywhere else in the city. 13And they cannot prove to you the charges they are now making against me. 14However, I admit that I worship the God of our fathers as a follower of the Way, which they call a sect. I believe everything that agrees with the Law and that is written in the Prophets, 15and I have the same hope in God as these men, that there will be a resurrection of both the righteous and the wicked. 16So I strive always to keep my conscience clear before God and man.

Acts 24:15

God Will Resurrect

"I have the same hope in God as these men, that there will be a resurrection of both the righteous and the wicked."

17"After an absence of several years, I came to Jerusalem to bring my people gifts for the poor and to present offerings. 18I was ceremonially clean when they found me in the temple courts doing this. There was no crowd with me, nor was I involved in any disturbance. 19But there are some Jews from the province of Asia, who ought to be here before you and bring charges if they have anything against me. 20Or these who are here should state what crime they found in me when I stood before the Sanhedrin— 21unless it was this one thing I shouted as I stood in their presence: 'It is concerning the resurrection of the dead that I am on trial before you today.'"

22Then Felix, who was well acquainted with

*a*6–8 Some manuscripts *him and wanted to judge him according to our law.* 7*But the commander, Lysias, came and with the use of much force snatched him from our hands* 8*and ordered his accusers to come before you. By* the Way, adjourned the proceedings. "When Lysias the commander comes," he said, "I will decide your case." 23He ordered the centurion to keep Paul under guard but to give him some freedom and permit his friends to take care of his needs.

24Several days later Felix came with his wife Drusilla, who was a Jewess. He sent for Paul and listened to him as he spoke about faith in Christ Jesus. 25As Paul discoursed on righteousness, self-control and the judgment to come, Felix was afraid and said, "That's enough for now! You may leave. When I find it convenient, I will send for you." 26At the same time he was hoping that Paul would offer him a bribe, so he sent for him frequently and talked with him.

27When two years had passed, Felix was succeeded by Porcius Festus, but because Felix wanted to grant a favor to the Jews, he left Paul in prison.

The Trial Before Festus

25 Three days after arriving in the province, Festus went up from Caesarea to Jerusalem, 2where the chief priests and Jewish leaders appeared before him and presented the charges against Paul. 3They urgently requested Festus, as a favor to them, to have Paul transferred to Jerusalem, for they were preparing an ambush to kill him along the way. 4Festus answered, "Paul is being held at Caesarea, and I myself am going there soon. 5Let some of your leaders come with me and press charges against the man there, if he has done anything wrong."

6After spending eight or ten days with them, he went down to Caesarea, and the next day he convened the court and ordered that Paul be brought before him. 7When Paul appeared, the Jews who had come down from Jerusalem stood around him, bringing many serious charges against him, which they could not prove.

8Then Paul made his defense: "I have done nothing wrong against the law of the Jews or against the temple or against Caesar."

9Festus, wishing to do the Jews a favor, said to Paul, "Are you willing to go up to Jerusalem and stand trial before me there on these charges?"

10Paul answered: "I am now standing before Caesar's court, where I ought to be tried. I have not done any wrong to the Jews, as you yourself know very well. 11If, however, I am guilty of doing anything deserving death, I do not refuse to die. But if the charges brought against me by these Jews are not true, no one has the right to hand me over to them. I appeal to Caesar!"

12After Festus had conferred with his council, he declared: "You have appealed to Caesar. To Caesar you will go!"

Festus Consults King Agrippa

13A few days later King Agrippa and Bernice arrived at Caesarea to pay their respects to Festus. 14Since they were spending many days there, Festus discussed Paul's case with the king. He said: "There is a man here whom Felix left as a prisoner. 15When I went to Jerusalem, the chief priests and elders of the Jews brought charges against him and asked that he be condemned.

16"I told them that it is not the Roman custom to hand over any man before he has faced his accusers and has had an opportunity to defend himself against their charges. 17When they came here with me, I did not delay the case, but convened the court the next day and ordered the man to be brought in. 18When his accusers got up to speak, they did not charge him with any of the crimes I had expected. 19Instead, they had some points of dispute with him about their own religion and about a dead man named Jesus who Paul claimed was alive. 20I was at a loss how to investigate such matters; so I asked if he would be willing to go to Jerusalem and stand trial there on these charges. 21When Paul made his appeal to be held over for the Emperor's decision, I ordered him held until I could send him to Caesar."

22Then Agrippa said to Festus, "I would like to hear this man myself."

He replied, "Tomorrow you will hear him."

Paul Before Agrippa

23The next day Agrippa and Bernice came with great pomp and entered the audience room with the high ranking officers and the leading men of the city. At the command of Festus, Paul was brought in. 24Festus said: "King Agrippa, and all who are present with us, you see this man! The whole Jewish community has petitioned me about him in Jerusalem and here in Caesarea, shouting that he ought not to live any longer. ²⁵I found he had done nothing deserving of death, but because he made his appeal to the Emperor I decided to send him to Rome. ²⁶But I have nothing definite to write to His Majesty about him. Therefore I have brought him before all of you, and especially before you, King Agrippa, so that as a result of this investigation I may have something to write. ²⁷For I think it is unreasonable to send on a prisoner without specifying the charges against him."

26 Then Agrippa said to Paul, "You have permission to speak for yourself."

So Paul motioned with his hand and began his defense: ²"King Agrippa, I consider myself fortunate to stand before you today as I make my defense against all the accusations of the Jews, ³and especially so because you are well acquainted with all the Jewish customs and controversies. Therefore, I beg you to listen to me patiently.

⁴"The Jews all know the way I have lived ever since I was a child, from the beginning of my life in my own country, and also in Jerusalem. ⁵They have known me for a long time and can testify, if they are willing, that according to the strictest sect of our religion, I lived as a Pharisee. ⁶And now it is because of my hope in what God has promised our fathers that I am on trial today. ⁷This is the promise our twelve tribes are hoping to see fulfilled as they earnestly serve God day and night. O king, it is because of this hope that the Jews are accusing me. ⁸Why should any of you consider it incredible that God raises the dead?

⁹"I too was convinced that I ought to do all that was possible to oppose the name of Jesus of Nazareth. ¹⁰And that is just what I did in Jerusalem. On the authority of the chief priests I put many of the saints in prison, and when they were put to death, I cast my vote against them. ¹¹Many a time I went from one synagogue to another to have them punished, and I tried to force them to blaspheme. In my obsession against them, I even went to foreign cities to persecute them.

¹²"On one of these journeys I was going to Damascus with the authority and commission of the chief priests. ¹³About noon, O king, as I was on the road, I saw a light from heaven, brighter than the sun, blazing around me and my companions. ¹⁴We all fell to the ground, and I heard a voice saying to me in Aramaic,ᵃ 'Saul, Saul, why do you persecute me? It is hard for you to kick against the goads.'

¹⁵"Then I asked, 'Who are you, Lord?'

"'I am Jesus, whom you are persecuting,' the Lord replied. ¹⁶'Now get up and stand on your feet. I have appeared to you to appoint you as a servant and as a witness of what you have seen of me and what I will show you. ¹⁷I will rescue you from your own people and from the Gentiles. I am sending you to them ¹⁸to open their eyes and turn them from darkness to light, and from the power of Satan to God, so that they may receive forgiveness of sins and a place among those who are sanctified by faith in me.'

¹⁹"So then, King Agrippa, I was not disobedient to the vision from heaven. ²⁰First to those in Damascus, then to those in Jerusalem and in all Judea, and to the Gentiles also, I preached that they should repent and turn to God and prove their repentance by their deeds. ²¹That is why the Jews seized me in the temple courts and tried to kill me. ²²But I have had God's help to this very day, and so I stand here and testify to small and great alike. I am saying nothing beyond what the prophets and Moses said would happen— ²³that the Christᵇ would suffer and, as the first to rise from the dead, would proclaim light to his own people and to the Gentiles."

²⁴At this point Festus interrupted Paul's defense. "You are out of your mind, Paul!" he shouted. "Your great learning is driving you insane."

²⁵"I am not insane, most excellent Festus," Paul replied. "What I am saying is true and reasonable. ²⁶The king is familiar with these things, and I can speak freely to him. I am convinced that none of this has escaped his notice, because it was not done in a corner. ²⁷King Agrippa, do you believe the prophets? I know you do."

²⁸Then Agrippa said to Paul, "Do you think

ᵃ14 Or *Hebrew* ᵇ23 Or *Messiah*

The King and I

Read: Acts 26:1–32

THE KING AND I tells the story of an English widow named Anna who accepted the king of Siam's invitation to become his children's governess. Before she could meet the king, she had to learn court etiquette. One of the rules of the court was that her head always had to be lower than his. Upon meeting the king, he tested her by lowering his head closer and closer to the floor. Being used to a mere curtsy, which would have been adequate for meeting English royalty, Anna had difficulty managing her voluminous skirts and bobbing hoops as she went from curtsy to stooping to a prone position.

Paul's audience before King Agrippa defied protocol. He wore chains rather than formal attire, and he stretched out his hands rather than bowing his head. Paul didn't choose to talk about the weather or share a witty anecdote as if he were meeting royalty. If he had titled his audience before the king, it could have been called *The King of Kings and I*. Paul gave his testimony because he understood that telling a personal story could persuade both people and monarchs to follow Christ. His conversion story included three elements common to the stories of all who claim Christ as King:

(1) Encountering Christ in the present: Paul, breathing murderous threats, had bullied the disciples throughout Judea. But one day the light of Jesus' presence, "brighter than the sun" (verse 13), stopped him dead in his tracks. From then on, Paul called Jesus Lord instead of liar.

(2) Repenting of past sin: Paul confessed that he'd done many things in opposition to the name of Jesus (see verse 9), specifically, persecuting the church. Jesus took this personally, saying, "I am Jesus, whom you are persecuting" (verse 15). On that day, Paul's evil crusade ended when he turned from his sin and turned to Christ.

(3) Witnessing to others in the future: Paul was obedient to "the vision from heaven" (verse 19), declaring the gospel in Jerusalem, Judea and then to the Gentiles, "that they should repent" (verse 20). Because of Paul's obedience, the world heard Christ's message and was never to be the same.

Acts 26:14–15

"We all fell to the ground, and I heard a voice saying to me in Aramaic, 'Saul, Saul, why do you persecute me? It is hard for you to kick against the goads.' Then I asked, 'Who are you, Lord?' 'I am Jesus, whom you are persecuting,' the Lord replied."

reflection

1 Do you feel awkward or emboldened when telling others your *King of Kings and I* story?

2 How does your personal testimony include the same three elements as Paul's: encountering Christ, repenting of sin and witnessing to others?

3 What is your favorite way to address the King of kings, and what kinds of things do you discuss with him on a daily basis?

RELATED READINGS

Matthew 10:16–20;
Mark 13:9–11;
Acts 9:1–17

"The risen life is the best testimony to a risen Christ."

Unknown

that in such a short time you can persuade me to be a Christian?"

29 Paul replied, "Short time or long—I pray God that not only you but all who are listening to me today may become what I am, except for these chains."

30 The king rose, and with him the governor and Bernice and those sitting with them. 31 They left the room, and while talking with one another, they said, "This man is not doing anything that deserves death or imprisonment."

32 Agrippa said to Festus, "This man could have been set free if he had not appealed to Caesar."

Paul Sails for Rome

27 When it was decided that we would sail for Italy, Paul and some other prisoners were handed over to a centurion named Julius, who belonged to the Imperial Regiment. 2 We boarded a ship from Adramyttium about to sail for ports along the coast of the province of Asia, and we put out to sea. Aristarchus, a Macedonian from Thessalonica, was with us.

3 The next day we landed at Sidon; and Julius, in kindness to Paul, allowed him to go to his friends so they might provide for his needs. 4 From there we put out to sea again and passed to the lee of Cyprus because the winds were against us. 5 When we had sailed across the open sea off the coast of Cilicia and Pamphylia, we landed at Myra in Lycia. 6 There the centurion found an Alexandrian ship sailing for Italy and put us on board. 7 We made slow headway for many days and had difficulty arriving off Cnidus. When the wind did not allow us to hold our course, we sailed to the lee of Crete, opposite Salmone. 8 We moved along the coast with difficulty and came to a place called Fair Havens, near the town of Lasea.

9 Much time had been lost, and sailing had already become dangerous because by now it was after the Fast.[a] So Paul warned them, 10 "Men, I can see that our voyage is going to be disastrous and bring great loss to ship and cargo, and to our own lives also." 11 But the centurion, instead of listening to what Paul said, followed the advice of the pilot and of the owner of the ship. 12 Since the harbor was unsuitable to winter in, the majority decided that we should sail on, hoping to reach Phoenix and winter there. This was a harbor in Crete, facing both southwest and northwest.

The Storm

13 When a gentle south wind began to blow, they thought they had obtained what they wanted; so they weighed anchor and sailed along the shore of Crete. 14 Before very long, a wind of hurricane force, called the "northeaster," swept down from the island. 15 The ship was caught by the storm and could not head into the wind; so we gave way to it and were driven along. 16 As we passed to the lee of a small island called Cauda, we were hardly able to make the lifeboat secure. 17 When the men had hoisted it aboard, they passed ropes under the ship itself to hold it together. Fearing that they would run aground on the sandbars of Syrtis, they lowered the sea anchor and let the ship be driven along. 18 We took such a violent battering from the storm that the next day they began to throw the cargo overboard. 19 On the third day, they threw the ship's tackle overboard with their own hands. 20 When neither sun nor stars appeared for many days and the storm continued raging, we finally gave up all hope of being saved.

21 After the men had gone a long time without food, Paul stood up before them and said: "Men, you should have taken my advice not to sail from Crete; then you would have spared yourselves this damage and loss. 22 But now I urge you to keep up your courage, because not one of you will be lost; only the ship will be destroyed. 23 Last night an angel of the God whose I am and whom I serve stood beside me 24 and said, 'Do not be afraid, Paul. You must stand trial before Caesar; and God has graciously given you the lives of all who sail with you.' 25 So keep up your courage, men, for I have faith in God that it will happen just as he told me. 26 Nevertheless, we must run aground on some island."

The Shipwreck

27 On the fourteenth night we were still being driven across the Adriatic[b] Sea, when

---

[a]9 That is, the Day of Atonement (Yom Kippur)   [b]27 In ancient times the name referred to an area extending well south of Italy.

about midnight the sailors sensed they were approaching land. 28They took soundings and found that the water was a hundred and twenty feet*a* deep. A short time later they took soundings again and found it was ninety feet*b* deep. 29Fearing that we would be dashed against the rocks, they dropped four anchors from the stern and prayed for daylight. 30In an attempt to escape from the ship, the sailors let the lifeboat down into the sea, pretending they were going to lower some anchors from the bow. 31Then Paul said to the centurion and the soldiers, "Unless these men stay with the ship, you cannot be saved." 32So the soldiers cut the ropes that held the lifeboat and let it fall away.

33Just before dawn Paul urged them all to eat. "For the last fourteen days," he said, "you have been in constant suspense and have gone without food—you haven't eaten anything. 34Now I urge you to take some food. You need it to survive. Not one of you will lose a single hair from his head." 35After he said this, he took some bread and gave thanks to God in front of them all. Then he broke it and began to eat. 36They were all encouraged and ate some food themselves. 37Altogether there were 276 of us on board. 38When they had eaten as much as they wanted, they lightened the ship by throwing the grain into the sea.

39When daylight came, they did not recognize the land, but they saw a bay with a sandy beach, where they decided to run the ship aground if they could. 40Cutting loose the anchors, they left them in the sea and at the same time untied the ropes that held the rudders. Then they hoisted the foresail to the wind and made for the beach. 41But the ship struck a sandbar and ran aground. The bow stuck fast and would not move, and the stern was broken to pieces by the pounding of the surf.

42The soldiers planned to kill the prisoners to prevent any of them from swimming away and escaping. 43But the centurion wanted to spare Paul's life and kept them from carrying out their plan. He ordered those who could swim to jump overboard first and get to land. 44The rest were to get there on planks or on pieces of the ship. In this way everyone reached land in safety.

Ashore on Malta

28 Once safely on shore, we found out that the island was called Malta. 2The islanders showed us unusual kindness. They built a fire and welcomed us all because it was raining and cold. 3Paul gathered a pile of brushwood and, as he put it on the fire, a viper, driven out by the heat, fastened itself on his hand. 4When the islanders saw the snake hanging from his hand, they said to each other, "This man must be a murderer; for though he escaped from the sea, Justice has not allowed him to live." 5But Paul shook the snake off into the fire and suffered no ill effects. 6The people expected him to swell up or suddenly fall dead, but after waiting a long time and seeing nothing unusual happen to him, they changed their minds and said he was a god.

7There was an estate nearby that belonged to Publius, the chief official of the island. He welcomed us to his home and for three days entertained us hospitably. 8His father was sick in bed, suffering from fever and dysentery. Paul went in to see him and, after prayer, placed his hands on him and healed him. 9When this had happened, the rest of the sick on the island came and were cured. 10They honored us in many ways and when we were ready to sail, they furnished us with the supplies we needed.

Arrival at Rome

11After three months we put out to sea in a ship that had wintered in the island. It was an Alexandrian ship with the figurehead of the twin gods Castor and Pollux. 12We put in at Syracuse and stayed there three days. 13From there we set sail and arrived at Rhegium. The next day the south wind came up, and on the following day we reached Puteoli. 14There we found some brothers who invited us to spend a week with them. And so we came to Rome. 15The brothers there had heard that we were coming, and they traveled as far as the Forum of Appius and the Three Taverns to meet us. At the sight of these men Paul thanked God and was encouraged. 16When we got to Rome, Paul

---

a28 Greek *twenty orguias* (about 37 meters)   *b28* Greek *fifteen orguias* (about 27 meters)

The Power of Pain

Read: Acts 28:17–31

Acts 28:30–31

For two whole years Paul stayed there in his own rented house and welcomed all who came to see him. Boldly and without hindrance he preached the kingdom of God and taught about the Lord Jesus Christ.

reflection

1 How has suffering drawn you closer to God?

2 Has someone else's suffering impacted your life in a positive way?

3 How willing are you to allow God to use your pain for his glory? Pray now for willingness.

RELATED READINGS

Exodus 18:7–11;
2 Corinthians 4:7–18;
12:7–10

SUFFERING AND PAIN can lead to powerful ministry. Amy Carmichael established a home to rescue children from temple prostitution in India. When she fell ill and was confined to her bed, she wrote inspirational books and poems that continue to encourage generations of readers. Here's a beautiful example:

Our Father knows what's best for us, so why should we
complain?
We always want the sunshine, but he knows there must be
rain.
We love the sound of laughter and the merriment of cheer,
But our hearts would lose their tenderness if we never shed
a tear.
For growing trees are strengthened when they withstand
the storm,
And the sharp cut of the chisel gives the diamond grace
and form.
God never hurts us needlessly, and he never wastes our pain,
For every loss he sends to us is followed by rich gain.
And when we count the blessings that God so freely sent,
We'll find no cause for murmuring, and no time to lament.
For our Father loves his children, and to him all things are
plain,
So he never sends us pleasure when the soul's deep need
is pain.
So whenever we are troubled, and when everything goes
wrong,
We know God's working in our hearts, to make our spirit
strong.

When he was in chains, Paul preached to the Roman Jews and many of them believed in Jesus. He also wrote many letters, including the joy-filled letter to the Philippians, from a jail cell.

We all have experienced suffering. What is your unique story? No matter how universal the trauma, your situation and your response are personal to you. Others can learn from what you have gone through. Ask God for opportunities to share what you've learned about God's grace through your experience with suffering. Then stand back and be amazed at how God can use you to touch other people's lives.

Thursday

was allowed to live by himself, with a soldier to guard him.

Paul Preaches at Rome Under Guard

¹⁷Three days later he called together the leaders of the Jews. When they had assembled, Paul said to them: "My brothers, although I have done nothing against our people or against the customs of our ancestors, I was arrested in Jerusalem and handed over to the Romans. ¹⁸They examined me and wanted to release me, because I was not guilty of any crime deserving death. ¹⁹But when the Jews objected, I was compelled to appeal to Caesar—not that I had any charge to bring against my own people. ²⁰For this reason I have asked to see you and talk with you. It is because of the hope of Israel that I am bound with this chain."

²¹They replied, "We have not received any letters from Judea concerning you, and none of the brothers who have come from there has reported or said anything bad about you. ²²But we want to hear what your views are, for we know that people everywhere are talking against this sect."

²³They arranged to meet Paul on a certain day, and came in even larger numbers to the place where he was staying. From morning till evening he explained and declared to them the kingdom of God and tried to convince them about Jesus from the Law of Moses and from the Prophets. ²⁴Some were convinced by what he said, but others would not believe. ²⁵They disagreed among themselves and began to leave after Paul had made this final statement: "The Holy Spirit spoke the truth to your forefathers when he said through Isaiah the prophet:

²⁶ " 'Go to this people and say,
  "You will be ever hearing but never
      understanding;
    you will be ever seeing but never
      perceiving."
²⁷For this people's heart has become
      calloused;
    they hardly hear with their ears,
    and they have closed their eyes.
        Otherwise they might see
          with their eyes,
        hear with their ears,
        understand with their
          hearts
        and turn, and I would heal
          them.'*a*

²⁸"Therefore I want you to know that God's salvation has been sent to the Gentiles, and they will listen!"*b*

³⁰For two whole years Paul stayed there in his own rented house and welcomed all who came to see him. ³¹Boldly and without hindrance he preached the kingdom of God and taught about the Lord Jesus Christ.

Acts 28:28

God Extends Salvation

"Therefore I want you to know that God's salvation has been sent to the Gentiles, and they will listen!"

---

*a*27 Isaiah 6:9,10   *b*28 Some manuscripts *listen!"* ²⁹*After he said this, the Jews left, arguing vigorously among themselves.*

Romans

Author:
The apostle Paul.

Audience:
Followers of Jesus;
originally written to
Christians in Rome.

Date:
About A.D. 57.

Setting:
Paul wrote from
Corinth regarding
his pending visit
to Rome via
Jerusalem.

Verse to Remember:
"I am not ashamed
of the gospel,
because it is the
power of God for
the salvation of
everyone who be-
lieves: first for the
Jew, then for the
Gentile." (1:16)

The Christians in Rome had not yet met Paul, and he was excited about meeting them soon. But before he went to see them, he sent them this letter, perhaps his most straightforward theological essay in print. Starting with the sinfulness of humans and the wrath of God against sin, he moves on to tell of *God's grace in salvation,* which comes to us through God-given faith and not our works. He then tells of the future glory of the believer and gives some principles for God-centered living. *This is the book to read and study* to understand what God has given us freely through Christ. Whether you've not yet read through the whole Bible or you've studied it for years, the basics in this book are worth dwelling on. *God's gift of salvation is extraordinary.* And so is the new life we have begun.

1 Paul, a servant of Christ Jesus, called to be an apostle and set apart for the gospel of God— ²the gospel he promised beforehand through his prophets in the Holy Scriptures ³regarding his Son, who as to his human nature was a descendant of David, ⁴and who through the Spirit*a* of holiness was declared with power to be the Son of God*b* by his resurrection from the dead: Jesus Christ our Lord. ⁵Through him and for his name's sake, we received grace and apostleship to call people from among all the Gentiles to the obedience that comes from

*a*4 Or *who as to his spirit*   *b*4 Or *was appointed to be the Son of God with power* faith. **6**And you also are among those who are called to belong to Jesus Christ.

7To all in Rome who are loved by God and called to be saints:

Grace and peace to you from God our Father and from the Lord Jesus Christ.

Paul's Longing to Visit Rome

8First, I thank my God through Jesus Christ for all of you, because your faith is being reported all over the world. **9**God, whom I serve with my whole heart in preaching the gospel of his Son, is my witness how constantly I remember you **10**in my prayers at all times; and I pray that now at last by God's will the way may be opened for me to come to you.

11I long to see you so that I may impart to you some spiritual gift to make you strong— **12**that is, that you and I may be mutually encouraged by each other's faith. **13**I do not want you to be unaware, brothers, that I planned many times to come to you (but have been prevented from doing so until now) in order that I might have a harvest among you, just as I have had among the other Gentiles.

14I am obligated both to Greeks and non-Greeks, both to the wise and the foolish. **15**That is why I am so eager to preach the gospel also to you who are at Rome.

16I am not ashamed of the gospel, because it is the power of God for the salvation of everyone who believes: first for the Jew, then for the Gentile. **17**For in the gospel a righteousness from God is revealed, a righteousness that is by faith from first to last,*a* just as it is written: "The righteous will live by faith."*b*

God's Wrath Against Mankind

18The wrath of God is being revealed from heaven against all the godlessness and wickedness of men who suppress the truth by their wickedness, **19**since what may be known about God is plain to them, because God has made it plain to them. **20**For since the creation of the world God's invisible qualities—his eternal power and divine nature—have been clearly seen, being understood from what has been made, so that men are without excuse.

21For although they knew God, they nei-

ther glorified him as God nor gave thanks to him, but their thinking became futile and their foolish hearts were darkened. **22**Although they claimed to be wise, they became fools **23**and exchanged the glory of the immortal God for images made to look like mortal man and birds and animals and reptiles.

24Therefore God gave them over in the sinful desires of their hearts to sexual impurity for the degrading of their bodies with one another. **25**They exchanged the truth of God for a lie, and worshiped and served created things rather than the Creator—who is forever praised. Amen.

26Because of this, God gave them over to shameful lusts. Even their women exchanged natural relations for unnatural ones. **27**In the same way the men also abandoned natural relations with women and were inflamed with lust for one another. Men committed indecent acts with other men, and received in themselves the due penalty for their perversion.

28Furthermore, since they did not think it worthwhile to retain the knowledge of God, he gave them over to a depraved mind, to do what ought not to be done. **29**They have become filled with every kind of wickedness, evil, greed and depravity. They are full of envy, murder, strife, deceit and malice. They are gossips, **30**slanderers, God-haters, insolent, arrogant and boastful; they invent ways of doing evil; they disobey their parents; **31**they are senseless, faithless, heartless, ruthless. **32**Although they know God's righteous decree that those who do such things deserve death, they not only continue to do these very things but also approve of those who practice them.

God's Righteous Judgment

2 You, therefore, have no excuse, you who pass judgment on someone else, for at whatever point you judge the other, you are condemning yourself, because you who pass judgment do the same things. **2**Now we know that God's judgment against those who do such things is based on truth. **3**So when you, a mere man, pass judgment on them and yet do the same things, do you think you will escape God's judgment? **4**Or do you show contempt for the riches of his kindness, tolerance and patience,

a17 Or is from faith to faith   b17 Hab. 2:4

Not Ashamed

Romans 1:16

I am not ashamed of the gospel, because it is the power of God for the salvation of everyone who believes: first for the Jew, then for the Gentile.

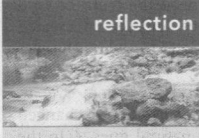

reflection

1 Would you describe yourself as easily embarrassed, extremely bold or somewhere in-between?

2 Are you ever in situations in which you don't want to seem "too Christian"? Who are you afraid of? What are you afraid of?

3 When were you ever embarrassed to share your faith? Describe how you felt. Ask God to help you be bold and unafraid to tell others about the gospel.

RELATED READINGS

Matthew 10:32–33;
Mark 8:34–38;
2 Timothy 1:8–12

"The Christian message is for those who have done their best and failed!"

Unknown

WHAT CAUSED YOUR CHEEKS to blush red in elementary school? Being picked last for recess games? Not knowing the answer when called on? Now think about your adolescent days. Were you embarrassed if a cute boy looked your way—or if he didn't? If someone pointed out that your clothes weren't like those of the other girls? Did you cower in humiliation if you were forced to give a speech or forgot your lines in the school play?

Today we might be ashamed if our children get in trouble or if we fail to keep our temper. We may feel ashamed if we neglect prayer or realize we haven't done much for anyone but ourselves for a long while. Not to worry, God has freed us to walk in this world unashamed. In Christ there is forgiveness and a new start. Later in the book of Romans Paul proclaimed, "There is now no condemnation for those who are in Christ Jesus" (Romans 8:1). In fact, there is only one real reason to be ashamed: if we're ashamed of the gospel message. Paul made sure his readers knew that he was not ashamed of the gospel of Christ. Indeed, he was eager to tell everyone about it—Greeks and non-Greeks, intellectuals and the uneducated, the wise and the foolish.

Maybe you're embarrassed to let people know you are a Christian. You think it might not be accepted in more "sophisticated" circles. You worry that you'll be labeled a "Jesus Freak," a "religious fanatic" or someone who needs a "crutch."

Maybe you don't share your faith because you think your credentials aren't good enough. You're afraid that you don't have the right education or that you haven't memorized enough Scripture or that you haven't been a believer long enough. But think of the many people who were saved in the Bible who immediately went and told others about their encounter with Christ. The key is that they told *their* story—and you know *your* story backward and forward.

If you're not ashamed of Jesus, the best way to overcome fear or speaking out is to "just do it." Keep it simple, keep it honest, but talk to your neighbors, tell your friends and family, and share the story about how Jesus redeemed you. The more you speak, the more your confidence will grow . . . and the more God will be glorified.

Go to page 1370 for your next devotional reading.

not realizing that God's kindness leads you toward repentance?

5But because of your stubbornness and your unrepentant heart, you are storing up wrath against yourself for the day of God's wrath, when his righteous judgment will be revealed. **6**God "will give to each person according to what he has done."[a] **7**To those who by persistence in doing good seek glory, honor and immortality, he will give eternal life. **8**But for those who are self-seeking and who reject the truth and follow evil, there will be wrath and anger. **9**There will be trouble and distress for every human being who does evil: first for the Jew, then for the Gentile; **10**but glory, honor and peace for everyone who does good: first for the Jew, then for the Gentile. **11**For God does not show favoritism.

12All who sin apart from the law will also perish apart from the law, and all who sin under the law will be judged by the law. **13**For it is not those who hear the law who are righteous in God's sight, but it is those who obey the law who will be declared righteous. **14**(Indeed, when Gentiles, who do not have the law, do by nature things required by the law, they are a law for themselves, even though they do not have the law, **15**since they show that the requirements of the law are written on their hearts, their consciences also bearing witness, and their thoughts now accusing, now even defending them.) **16**This will take place on the day when God will judge men's secrets through Jesus Christ, as my gospel declares.

The Jews and the Law

17Now you, if you call yourself a Jew; if you rely on the law and brag about your relationship to God; **18**if you know his will and approve of what is superior because you are instructed by the law; **19**if you are convinced that you are a guide for the blind, a light for those who are in the dark, **20**an instructor of the foolish, a teacher of infants, because you have in the law the embodiment of knowledge and truth— **21**you, then, who teach others, do you not teach yourself? You who preach against stealing, do you steal? **22**You who say that people should not commit adultery, do you com-

mit adultery? You who abhor idols, do you rob temples? **23**You who brag about the law, do you dishonor God by breaking the law? **24**As it is written: "God's name is blasphemed among the Gentiles because of you."[b]

25Circumcision has value if you observe the law, but if you break the law, you have become as though you had not been circumcised. **26**If those who are not circumcised keep the law's requirements, will they not be regarded as though they were circumcised? **27**The one who is not circumcised physically and yet obeys the law will condemn you who, even though you have the[c] written code and circumcision, are a lawbreaker.

28A man is not a Jew if he is only one outwardly, nor is circumcision merely outward and physical. **29**No, a man is a Jew if he is one inwardly; and circumcision is circumcision of the heart, by the Spirit, not by the written code. Such a man's praise is not from men, but from God.

God's Faithfulness

3 What advantage, then, is there in being a Jew, or what value is there in circumcision? **2**Much in every way! First of all, they have been entrusted with the very words of God.

3What if some did not have faith? Will their lack of faith nullify God's faithfulness? **4**Not at all! Let God be true, and every man a liar. As it is written:

"So that you may be proved right when you speak
and prevail when you judge."[d]

5But if our unrighteousness brings out God's righteousness more clearly, what shall we say? That God is unjust in bringing his wrath on us? (I am using a human argument.) **6**Certainly not! If that were so, how could God judge the world? **7**Someone might argue, "If my falsehood enhances God's truthfulness and so increases his glory, why am I still condemned as a sinner?" **8**Why not say—as we are being slanderously reported as saying and as some claim that we say—"Let us do evil that good may result"? Their condemnation is deserved.

---

a **6** Psalm 62:12; Prov. 24:12   *b* **24** Isaiah 52:5; Ezek. 36:22   *c* **27** Or *who, by means of a*   *d* **4** Psalm 51:4

Indisputable

DORCAS (TABITHA)

Peter sent them all out of the room; then he got down on his knees and prayed. Turning toward the dead woman, he said, "Tabitha, get up."

Acts 9:40

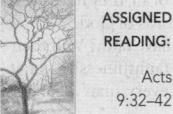

ASSIGNED READING:

Acts 9:32–42

"SHE WAS DEAD, I tell you." Several heads in the crowd of widows nodded.

"All of you were there and saw this with your own eyes?" asked the incredulous stranger. She was new in town and wasn't entirely convinced that these ladies weren't pulling her leg.

"Yes. I was there."

"Me too." The other voices in the crowd continued peppering their assurances.

One old woman stepped forward, clutching her robes so she would not step on the hem. "I've seen plenty of dead people in my day," she said with immitigable authority. "And I am certain she was *dead*."

Dorcas (the previously deceased and, thus, central figure in the story), was a staple of society and a well-known person in the community. Her generosity toward the poor was legendary, and her kindness seemed to know no bounds. She sewed robes and other clothing for widows in Joppa, staying up late into the evening until her fingers nearly blistered. Her death was a considerable loss to the community. No one could replace her. Not easily, anyway.

This is why it was such a miracle when Peter prayed for her and God brought her back to life. Not only was a dead woman now alive, but the dead woman was a treasure like Dorcas. Having her back in the world was a double delight.

But back to the doubting newcomer…

It was a fanciful story, of course. It's not every day that one hears about someone coming back from the dead. So, the doubters were not necessarily unexpected. Besides, the disciples definitely attracted their share of controversy. One never knew what was true nowadays. Rumors took flight in the town as often as the birds.

Only something irrefutable could prove their story beyond a doubt. And, as it turned out, while they were still talking, the irrefutable walked up and introduced herself to the newcomer.

"Hello and welcome," she said kindly. "My name is Dorcas. And you are?"

—Prayer—

I pray that I can be a witness to those who doubt in your power, Lord. I want to glorify your name.

Weekend

Go to page 1376 for your next devotional reading.

No One Is Righteous

⁹What shall we conclude then? Are we any better*ᵃ*? Not at all! We have already made the charge that Jews and Gentiles alike are all under sin. ¹⁰As it is written:

"There is no one righteous, not even one;
11   there is no one who understands,
        no one who seeks God.
¹²All have turned away,
        they have together become worthless;
    there is no one who does good,
        not even one."*ᵇ*
¹³"Their throats are open graves;
        their tongues practice deceit."*ᶜ*
    "The poison of vipers is on their lips."*ᵈ*
14   "Their mouths are full of cursing and
            bitterness."*ᵉ*
¹⁵"Their feet are swift to shed blood;
16   ruin and misery mark their ways,
¹⁷and the way of peace they do not know."*ᶠ*
18   "There is no fear of God before their
            eyes."*ᵍ*

¹⁹Now we know that whatever the law says, it says to those who are under the law, so that every mouth may be silenced and the whole world held accountable to God. ²⁰Therefore no one will be declared righteous in his sight by observing the law; rather, through the law we become conscious of sin.

Righteousness Through Faith

²¹But now a righteousness from God, apart from law, has been made known, to which the Law and the Prophets testify. ²²This righteousness from God comes through faith in Jesus Christ to all who believe. There is no difference, ²³for all have sinned and fall short of the glory of God, ²⁴and are justified freely by his grace through the redemption that came by Christ Jesus. ²⁵God presented him as a sacrifice of atonement,*ʰ* through faith in his blood. He did this to demonstrate his justice, because in his forbearance he had left the

sins committed beforehand unpunished— ²⁶he did it to demonstrate his justice at the present time, so as to be just and the one who justifies those who have faith in Jesus.

²⁷Where, then, is boasting? It is excluded. On what principle? On that of observing the law? No, but on that of faith. ²⁸For we maintain that a man is justified by faith apart from observing the law. ²⁹Is God the God of Jews only? Is he not the God of Gentiles too? Yes, of Gentiles too, ³⁰since there is only one God, who will justify the circumcised by faith and the uncircumcised through that same faith. ³¹Do we, then, nullify the law by this faith? Not at all! Rather, we uphold the law.

Abraham Justified by Faith

4 What then shall we say that Abraham, our forefather, discovered in this matter? ²If, in fact, Abraham was justified by works, he had something to boast about—but not before God. ³What does the Scripture say? "Abraham believed God, and it was credited to him as righteousness."*ⁱ*

⁴Now when a man works, his wages are not credited to him as a gift, but as an obligation. ⁵However, to the man who does not work but trusts God who justifies the wicked, his faith is credited as righteousness. ⁶David says the same thing when he speaks of the blessedness of the man to whom God credits righteousness apart from works:

7 "Blessed are they
        whose transgressions are
            forgiven,
        whose sins are covered.
8 Blessed is the man
        whose sin the Lord will
            never count against
                him."*ʲ*

⁹Is this blessedness only for the circumcised, or also for the uncircumcised? We have been saying that Abraham's faith was credited to him as righteousness. ¹⁰Under what circumstances was it credited? Was it after he was circumcised, or before? It was not after, but

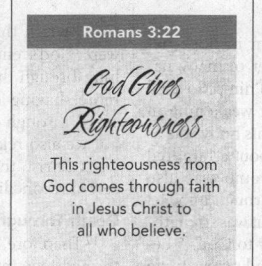

Romans 3:22

God Gives Righteousness

This righteousness from God comes through faith in Jesus Christ to all who believe.

*ᵃ*9 Or *worse*   *ᵇ*12 Psalms 14:1–3; 53:1–3; Eccles. 7:20   *ᶜ*13 Psalm 5:9   *ᵈ*13 Psalm 140:3   *ᵉ*14 Psalm 10:7   *ᶠ*17 Isaiah 59:7,8   *ᵍ*18 Psalm 36:1   *ʰ*25 Or *as the one who would turn aside his wrath, taking away sin*   *ⁱ*3 Gen. 15:6; also in verse 22   *ʲ*8 Psalm 32:1,2 before! ¹¹And he received the sign of circumcision, a seal of the righteousness that he had by faith while he was still uncircumcised. So then, he is the father of all who believe but have not been circumcised, in order that righteousness might be credited to them. ¹²And he is also the father of the circumcised who not only are circumcised but who also walk in the footsteps of the faith that our father Abraham had before he was circumcised.

¹³It was not through law that Abraham and his offspring received the promise that he would be heir of the world, but through the righteousness that comes by faith. ¹⁴For if those who live by law are heirs, faith has no value and the promise is worthless, ¹⁵because law brings wrath. And where there is no law there is no transgression.

¹⁶Therefore, the promise comes by faith, so that it may be by grace and may be guaranteed to all Abraham's offspring—not only to those who are of the law but also to those who are of the faith of Abraham. He is the father of us all. ¹⁷As it is written: "I have made you a father of many nations."ᵃ He is our father in the sight of God, in whom he believed—the God who gives life to the dead and calls things that are not as though they were.

¹⁸Against all hope, Abraham in hope believed and so became the father of many nations, just as it had been said to him, "So shall your offspring be."ᵇ ¹⁹Without weakening in his faith, he faced the fact that his body was as good as dead—since he was about a hundred years old—and that Sarah's womb was also dead. ²⁰Yet he did not waver through unbelief regarding the promise of God, but was strengthened in his faith and gave glory to God, ²¹being fully persuaded that God had power to do what he had promised. ²²This is why "it was credited to him as righteousness." ²³The words "it was credited to him" were written not for him alone, ²⁴but also for us, to whom God will

credit righteousness—for us who believe in him who raised Jesus our Lord from the dead. ²⁵He was delivered over to death for our sins and was raised to life for our justification.

Peace and Joy

5 Therefore, since we have been justified through faith, weᶜ have peace with God through our Lord Jesus Christ, ²through whom we have gained access by faith into this grace in which we now stand. And weᶜ rejoice in the hope of the glory of God. ³Not only so, but weᶜ also rejoice in our sufferings, because we know that suffering produces perseverance; ⁴perseverance, character; and character, hope. ⁵And hope does not disappoint us, because God has poured out his love into our hearts by the Holy Spirit, whom he has given us.

⁶You see, at just the right time, when we were still powerless, Christ died for the ungodly. ⁷Very rarely will anyone die for a righteous man, though for a good man someone might possibly dare to die. ⁸But God demonstrates his own love for us in this: While we were still sinners, Christ died for us.

⁹Since we have now been justified by his blood, how much more shall we be saved from God's wrath through him! ¹⁰For if, when we were God's enemies, we were reconciled to him through the death of his Son, how much more, having been reconciled, shall we be saved through his life! ¹¹Not only is this so, but we also rejoice in God through our Lord Jesus Christ, through whom we have now received reconciliation.

Death Through Adam, Life Through Christ

¹²Therefore, just as sin entered the world through one man, and death through sin, and in this way death came to all men, because all sinned— ¹³for before the law was given, sin was in the world. But sin is not taken into account when there is no law. ¹⁴Nevertheless,

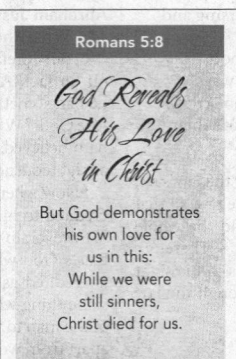

Romans 5:8

God Reveals His Love in Christ

But God demonstrates his own love for us in this: While we were still sinners, Christ died for us.

ᵃ17 Gen. 17:5   ᵇ18 Gen. 15:5   ᶜ1,2,3 Or *let us*

death reigned from the time of Adam to the time of Moses, even over those who did not sin by breaking a command, as did Adam, who was a pattern of the one to come.

¹⁵But the gift is not like the trespass. For if the many died by the trespass of the one man, how much more did God's grace and the gift that came by the grace of the one man, Jesus Christ, overflow to the many! ¹⁶Again, the gift of God is not like the result of the one man's sin: The judgment followed one sin and brought condemnation, but the gift followed many trespasses and brought justification. ¹⁷For if, by the trespass of the one man, death reigned through that one man, how much more will those who receive God's abundant provision of grace and of the gift of righteousness reign in life through the one man, Jesus Christ.

¹⁸Consequently, just as the result of one trespass was condemnation for all men, so also the result of one act of righteousness was justification that brings life for all men. ¹⁹For just as through the disobedience of the one man the many were made sinners, so also through the obedience of the one man the many will be made righteous.

²⁰The law was added so that the trespass might increase. But where sin increased, grace increased all the more, ²¹so that, just as sin reigned in death, so also grace might reign through righteousness to bring eternal life through Jesus Christ our Lord.

Dead to Sin, Alive in Christ

6 What shall we say, then? Shall we go on sinning so that grace may increase? ²By no means! We died to sin; how can we live in it any longer? ³Or don't you know that all of us who were baptized into Christ Jesus were baptized into his death? ⁴We were therefore buried with him through baptism into death in order that, just as Christ was raised from the dead through the glory of the Father, we too may live a new life.

⁵If we have been united with him like this in

ᵃ6 Or *be rendered powerless*

his death, we will certainly also be united with him in his resurrection. ⁶For we know that our old self was crucified with him so that the body of sin might be done away with,ᵃ that we should no longer be slaves to sin— ⁷because anyone who has died has been freed from sin.

⁸Now if we died with Christ, we believe that we will also live with him. ⁹For we know that since Christ was raised from the dead, he cannot die again; death no longer has mastery over him. ¹⁰The death he died, he died to sin once for all; but the life he lives, he lives to God.

¹¹In the same way, count yourselves dead to sin but alive to God in Christ Jesus. ¹²Therefore do not let sin reign in your mortal body so that you obey its evil desires. ¹³Do not offer the parts of your body to sin, as instruments of wickedness, but rather offer yourselves to God, as those who have been brought from death to life; and offer the parts of your body to him as instruments of righteousness. ¹⁴For sin shall not be your master, because you are not under law, but under grace.

Slaves to Righteousness

¹⁵What then? Shall we sin because we are not under law but under grace? By no means! ¹⁶Don't you know that when you offer yourselves to someone to obey him as slaves, you are slaves to the one whom you obey—whether you are slaves to sin, which leads to death, or to obedience, which leads to righteousness? ¹⁷But thanks be to God that, though you used to be slaves to sin, you wholeheartedly obeyed the form of teaching to which you were entrusted. ¹⁸You have been set free from sin and have become slaves to righteousness.

¹⁹I put this in human terms because you are weak in your natural selves. Just as you used to offer the parts of your body in slavery to impurity and to ever-increasing wickedness, so now offer them in slavery to righteousness leading to holiness. ²⁰When you were slaves to sin, you were free from the control of righteousness.

Romans 6:11

God Gives Our Spirits Life

In the same way, count yourselves dead to sin but alive to God in Christ Jesus.

²¹What benefit did you reap at that time from the things you are now ashamed of? Those things result in death! ²²But now that you have been set free from sin and have become slaves to God, the benefit you reap leads to holiness, and the result is eternal life. ²³For the wages of sin is death, but the gift of God is eternal life in*a* Christ Jesus our Lord.

An Illustration From Marriage

7 Do you not know, brothers—for I am speaking to men who know the law—that the law has authority over a man only as long as he lives? ²For example, by law a married woman is bound to her husband as long as he is alive, but if her husband dies, she is released from the law of marriage. ³So then, if she marries another man while her husband is still alive, she is called an adulteress. But if her husband dies, she is released from that law and is not an adulteress, even though she marries another man.

⁴So, my brothers, you also died to the law through the body of Christ, that you might belong to another, to him who was raised from the dead, in order that we might bear fruit to God. ⁵For when we were controlled by the sinful nature,*b* the sinful passions aroused by the law were at work in our bodies, so that we bore fruit for death. ⁶But now, by dying to what once bound us, we have been released from the law so that we serve in the new way of the Spirit, and not in the old way of the written code.

Struggling With Sin

⁷What shall we say, then? Is the law sin? Certainly not! Indeed I would not have known what sin was except through the law. For I would not have known what coveting really was if the law had not said, "Do not covet."*c* ⁸But sin, seizing the opportunity afforded by the commandment, produced in me every kind of covetous desire. For apart from law, sin is dead. ⁹Once I was alive apart from law; but when the commandment came, sin sprang to life and I died. ¹⁰I found that the very commandment that was intended to bring life actually brought death. ¹¹For sin, seizing the opportunity afforded by the commandment, deceived me,

and through the commandment put me to death. ¹²So then, the law is holy, and the commandment is holy, righteous and good.

¹³Did that which is good, then, become death to me? By no means! But in order that sin might be recognized as sin, it produced death in me through what was good, so that through the commandment sin might become utterly sinful.

¹⁴We know that the law is spiritual; but I am unspiritual, sold as a slave to sin. ¹⁵I do not understand what I do. For what I want to do I do not do, but what I hate I do. ¹⁶And if I do what I do not want to do, I agree that the law is good. ¹⁷As it is, it is no longer I myself who do it, but it is sin living in me. ¹⁸I know that nothing good lives in me, that is, in my sinful nature.*d* For I have the desire to do what is good, but I cannot carry it out. ¹⁹For what I do is not the good I want to do; no, the evil I do not want to do—this I keep on doing. ²⁰Now if I do what I do not want to do, it is no longer I who do it, but it is sin living in me that does it.

²¹So I find this law at work: When I want to do good, evil is right there with me. ²²For in my inner being I delight in God's law; ²³but I see another law at work in the members of my body, waging war against the law of my mind and making me a prisoner of the law of sin at work within my members. ²⁴What a wretched man I am! Who will rescue me from this body of death? ²⁵Thanks be to God—through Jesus Christ our Lord!

So then, I myself in my mind am a slave to God's law, but in the sinful nature a slave to the law of sin.

Life Through the Spirit

8 Therefore, there is now no condemnation for those who are in Christ Jesus,*e* ²because through Christ Jesus the law of the Spirit of life set me free from the law of sin and death. ³For what the law was powerless to do in that it was weakened by the sinful nature,*f* God did by sending his own Son in the likeness of sinful man to be a sin offering.*g* And so he condemned sin in sinful man,*h* ⁴in order that the righteous requirements of the law might be

---

*a*23 Or *through* *b*5 Or *the flesh; also in verse 25* *c*7 Exodus 20:17; Deut. 5:21 *d*18 Or *my flesh* *e*1 Some later manuscripts *Jesus, who do not live according to the sinful nature but according to the Spirit,* *f*3 Or *the flesh; also in verses 4, 5, 8, 9, 12 and 13* *g*3 Or *man, for sin* *h*3 Or *in the flesh* fully met in us, who do not live according to the sinful nature but according to the Spirit.

⁵Those who live according to the sinful nature have their minds set on what that nature desires; but those who live in accordance with the Spirit have their minds set on what the Spirit desires. ⁶The mind of sinful man*ᵃ* is death, but the mind controlled by the Spirit is life and peace; ⁷the sinful mind*ᵇ* is hostile to God. It does not submit to God's law, nor can it do so. ⁸Those controlled by the sinful nature cannot please God.

⁹You, however, are controlled not by the sinful nature but by the Spirit, if the Spirit of God lives in you. And if anyone does not have the Spirit of Christ, he does not belong to Christ. ¹⁰But if Christ is in you, your body is dead because of sin, yet your spirit is alive because of righteousness. ¹¹And if the Spirit of him who raised Jesus from the dead is living in you, he who raised Christ from the dead will also give life to your mortal bodies through his Spirit, who lives in you.

¹²Therefore, brothers, we have an obligation—but it is not to the sinful nature, to live according to it. ¹³For if you live according to the sinful nature, you will die; but if by the Spirit you put to death the misdeeds of the body, you will live, ¹⁴because those who are led by the Spirit of God are sons of God. ¹⁵For you did not receive a spirit that makes you a slave again to fear, but you received the Spirit of sonship.*ᶜ* And by him we cry, "Abba,*ᵈ* Father." ¹⁶The Spirit himself testifies with our spirit that we are God's children. ¹⁷Now if we are children, then we are heirs—heirs of God and co-heirs with Christ, if indeed we share in his sufferings in order that we may also share in his glory.

Future Glory

¹⁸I consider that our present sufferings are not worth comparing with the glory that will be revealed in us. ¹⁹The creation waits in eager expectation for the sons of God to be revealed. ²⁰For the creation was subjected to frustration, not by its own choice, but by the will of the one who subjected it, in hope ²¹that*ᵉ* the creation itself will be liberated from its bondage to decay and brought into the glorious freedom of the children of God.

²²We know that the whole creation has been groaning as in the pains of childbirth right up to the present time. ²³Not only so, but we ourselves, who have the firstfruits of the Spirit, groan inwardly as we wait eagerly for our adoption as sons, the redemption of our bodies. ²⁴For in this hope we were saved. But hope that is seen is no hope at all. Who hopes for what he already has? ²⁵But if we hope for what we do not yet have, we wait for it patiently.

²⁶In the same way, the Spirit helps us in our weakness. We do not know what we ought to pray for, but the Spirit himself intercedes for us with groans that words cannot express. ²⁷And he who searches our hearts knows the mind of the Spirit, because the Spirit intercedes for the saints in accordance with God's will.

More Than Conquerors

²⁸And we know that in all things God works for the good of those who love him,*ᶠ* who*ᵍ* have been called according to his purpose. ²⁹For those God foreknew he also predestined to be conformed to the likeness of his Son, that he might be the firstborn among many brothers. ³⁰And those he predestined, he also called; those he called, he also justified; those he justified, he also glorified.

³¹What, then, shall we say in response to this? If God is for us, who can be against us? ³²He who did not spare his own Son, but gave him up for us all—how will he not also, along with him, graciously give us all things? ³³Who will bring any charge against those whom God has chosen? It is God who justifies. ³⁴Who is he that condemns? Christ Jesus, who died—

Romans 8:28

God Works Good

And we know that in all things God works for the good of those who love him, who have been called according to his purpose.

---

*ᵃ*6 Or *mind set on the flesh*   *ᵇ*7 Or *The mind set on the flesh*   *ᶜ*15 Or *adoption*   *ᵈ*15 Aramaic for *Father*   *ᵉ*20,21 Or *subjected it in hope.* *ᶠ*21 For   *ᶠ*28 Some manuscripts *And we know that all things work together for good to those who love God*   *ᵍ*28 Or *works together with those who love him to bring about what is good—with those who*

Romans 8:26

In the same way, the Spirit helps us in our weakness. We do not know what we ought to pray for, but the Spirit himself intercedes for us with groans that words cannot express.

reflection

1 Describe your prayer life. Do you struggle with it or does it flow naturally? Is it structured or hit-and-miss?

2 Have you ever been at a loss for words during a time of prayer? How did the Holy Spirit intercede on your behalf? (For example: in song, in tears or in inexpressible ways.)

3 Examine your heart. What things in your life have you been unable to express to God? Now, let the Holy Spirit lift these struggles from you and carry them before the Father.

RELATED READINGS

Psalm 94:1–23;
Habakkuk 3:1–19;
Philippians 1:3–11

Read: Romans 8:26–27

BEADS OF PERSPIRATION form on your brow, your heart flutters, your mind swims. An endless loop replays in your head: the scathing, screaming argument with your mother; the prognosis from the doctor; a schedule so full you can't calm your thoughts enough to fall asleep at night.

You've probably been there at some point in your life: You rush before God like an eager child bursting into a room full of toys only to find that you have no idea how to begin to pray. You don't know if you should be asking for guidance, protection or forgiveness—or all of the above. And what about how to order your list? And should you say special words? How does this prayer thing work?

Maybe you've finally got a minute to yourself, so you grab your Bible, look up to the ceiling and think, *Now what?* That list you've been building in your mind goes blank. The phone rings. The kids cry. The TV blares from another room. The dog barks. Anything . . . everything interrupts the moment. *Help!* How do you pray when words fail?

Enter the Holy Spirit. He perceives our heart's agony and comforts us in our weakness. He knows our spiritual battle often burns hottest when we fight within ourselves. We wrestle with how to prioritize our prayers. We struggle with imposing our human agendas on a holy God. We cross our arms, grit our teeth and mentally stomp our feet when things don't turn out as we desperately prayed they would. Life's frustrations can mute us spiritually: "We do not know what we ought to pray for" (verse 26). But God does not stop hearing us when we're dumbstruck before him. Both in silence and when our words flow in a jumbled torrent, the Holy Spirit intercedes on our behalf to the Father. He *does* know what to pray for.

The next time your spirit groans with a weight heavier than you can bear, trust that even when you might not be able to find words to pray, God clearly hears your cries through the intervention of the Holy Spirit. He knows your heart, your thoughts and your greatest needs better than you do yourself. Though your words may fail, your intercessor will never fail you.

Go to page 1381 for your next devotional reading.

more than that, who was raised to life—is at the right hand of God and is also interceding for us. ³⁵Who shall separate us from the love of Christ? Shall trouble or hardship or persecution or famine or nakedness or danger or sword? ³⁶As it is written:

"For your sake we face death all day long;
we are considered as sheep to be
slaughtered."*a*

³⁷No, in all these things we are more than conquerors through him who loved us. ³⁸For I am convinced that neither death nor life, neither angels nor demons,*b* neither the present nor the future, nor any powers, ³⁹neither height nor depth, nor anything else in all creation, will be able to separate us from the love of God that is in Christ Jesus our Lord.

God's Sovereign Choice

9 I speak the truth in Christ—I am not lying, my conscience confirms it in the Holy Spirit— ²I have great sorrow and unceasing anguish in my heart. ³For I could wish that I myself were cursed and cut off from Christ for the sake of my brothers, those of my own race, ⁴the people of Israel. Theirs is the adoption as sons; theirs the divine glory, the covenants, the receiving of the law, the temple worship and the promises. ⁵Theirs are the patriarchs, and from them is traced the human ancestry of Christ, who is God over all, forever praised!*c* Amen.

⁶It is not as though God's word had failed. For not all who are descended from Israel are Israel. ⁷Nor because they are his descendants are they all Abraham's children. On the contrary, "It is through Isaac that your offspring will be reckoned."*d* ⁸In other words, it is not the natural children who are God's children, but it is the children of the promise who are regarded as Abraham's offspring. ⁹For this was how the promise was stated: "At the appointed time I will return, and Sarah will have a son."*e*

¹⁰Not only that, but Rebekah's children had one and the same father, our father Isaac. ¹¹Yet, before the twins were born or had done anything good or bad—in order that God's purpose in election might stand: ¹²not by works

but by him who calls—she was told, "The older will serve the younger."*f* ¹³Just as it is written: "Jacob I loved, but Esau I hated."*g*

¹⁴What then shall we say? Is God unjust? Not at all! ¹⁵For he says to Moses,

"I will have mercy on whom I have mercy,
and I will have compassion on whom I
have compassion."*h*

¹⁶It does not, therefore, depend on man's desire or effort, but on God's mercy. ¹⁷For the Scripture says to Pharaoh: "I raised you up for this very purpose, that I might display my power in you and that my name might be proclaimed in all the earth."*i* ¹⁸Therefore God has mercy on whom he wants to have mercy, and he hardens whom he wants to harden.

¹⁹One of you will say to me: "Then why does God still blame us? For who resists his will?" ²⁰But who are you, O man, to talk back to God? "Shall what is formed say to him who formed it, 'Why did you make me like this?'"*j* ²¹Does not the potter have the right to make out of the same lump of clay some pottery for noble purposes and some for common use?

²²What if God, choosing to show his wrath and make his power known, bore with great patience the objects of his wrath—prepared for destruction? ²³What if he did this to make the riches of his glory known to the objects of his mercy, whom he prepared in advance for glory— ²⁴even us, whom he also called, not only from the Jews but also from the Gentiles? ²⁵As he says in Hosea:

"I will call them 'my people' who are not
my people;
and I will call her 'my loved one' who is
not my loved one,"*k*

²⁶and,

"It will happen that in the very place where
it was said to them,
'You are not my people,'
they will be called 'sons of the living
God.'"*l*

²⁷Isaiah cries out concerning Israel:

---

*a*36 Psalm 44:22   *b*38 Or *nor heavenly rulers*   *c*5 Or *Christ, who is over all. God be forever praised!* Or *Christ. God who is over all be forever praised!*   *d*7 Gen. 21:12   *e*9 Gen. 18:10,14   *f*12 Gen. 25:23   *g*13 Mal. 1:2,3   *h*15 Exodus 33:19   *i*17 Exodus 9:16   *j*20 Isaiah 29:16; 45:9   *k*25 Hosea 2:23   *l*26 Hosea 1:10

"Though the number of the Israelites be
  like the sand by the sea,
  only the remnant will be saved.
[28] For the Lord will carry out
  his sentence on earth
  with speed and
  finality."[a]

[29] It is just as Isaiah said previously:

"Unless the Lord Almighty
  had left us descendants,
we would have become like
  Sodom,
we would have been like
  Gomorrah."[b]

Israel's Unbelief

[30] What then shall we say? That the Gentiles, who did not pursue righteousness, have obtained it, a righteousness that is by faith; [31] but Israel, who pursued a law of righteousness, has not attained it. [32] Why not? Because they pursued it not by faith but as if it were by works. They stumbled over the "stumbling stone." [33] As it is written:

"See, I lay in Zion a stone that causes men
  to stumble
and a rock that makes them fall,
and the one who trusts in him will never
  be put to shame."[c]

10 Brothers, my heart's desire and prayer to God for the Israelites is that they may be saved. [2] For I can testify about them that they are zealous for God, but their zeal is not based on knowledge. [3] Since they did not know the righteousness that comes from God and sought to establish their own, they did not submit to God's righteousness. [4] Christ is the end of the law so that there may be righteousness for everyone who believes.

[5] Moses describes in this way the righteousness that is by the law: "The man who does these things will live by them."[d] [6] But the righteousness that is by faith says: "Do not say in your heart, 'Who will ascend into heaven?'[e] (that is, to bring Christ down) [7] "or 'Who will descend into the deep?'[f] (that is, to bring Christ

up from the dead). [8] But what does it say? "The word is near you; it is in your mouth and in your heart,"[g] that is, the word of faith we are proclaiming: [9] That if you confess with your mouth, "Jesus is Lord," and believe in your heart that God raised him from the dead, you will be saved. [10] For it is with your heart that you believe and are justified, and it is with your mouth that you confess and are saved. [11] As the Scripture says, "Anyone who trusts in him will never be put to shame."[h] [12] For there is no difference between Jew and Gentile—the same Lord is Lord of all and richly blesses all who call on him, [13] for, "Everyone who calls on the name of the Lord will be saved."[i]

[14] How, then, can they call on the one they have not believed in? And how can they believe in the one of whom they have not heard? And how can they hear without someone preaching to them? [15] And how can they preach unless they are sent? As it is written, "How beautiful are the feet of those who bring good news!"[j]

[16] But not all the Israelites accepted the good news. For Isaiah says, "Lord, who has believed our message?"[k] [17] Consequently, faith comes from hearing the message, and the message is heard through the word of Christ. [18] But I ask: Did they not hear? Of course they did:

"Their voice has gone out into all the earth,
  their words to the ends of the world."[l]

[19] Again I ask: Did Israel not understand? First, Moses says,

"I will make you envious by those who are
  not a nation;
  I will make you angry by a nation that
  has no understanding."[m]

[20] And Isaiah boldly says,

"I was found by those who did not seek me;
  I revealed myself to those who did not
  ask for me."[n]

Romans 10:9

God Saves

That if you confess with your mouth, "Jesus is Lord," and believe in your heart that God raised him from the dead, you will be saved.

---

[a]28 Isaiah 10:22,23 [b]29 Isaiah 1:9 [c]33 Isaiah 8:14; 28:16 [d]5 Lev. 18:5 [e]6 Deut. 30:12 [f]7 Deut. 30:13 [g]8 Deut. 30:14 [h]11 Isaiah 28:16 [i]13 Joel 2:32 [j]15 Isaiah 52:7 [k]16 Isaiah 53:1 [l]18 Psalm 19:4 [m]19 Deut. 32:21 [n]20 Isaiah 65:1

²¹But concerning Israel he says,

"All day long I have held out my hands
   to a disobedient and obstinate people."*a*

The Remnant of Israel

11 I ask then: Did God reject his people? By no means! I am an Israelite myself, a descendant of Abraham, from the tribe of Benjamin. ²God did not reject his people, whom he foreknew. Don't you know what the Scripture says in the passage about Elijah—how he appealed to God against Israel: ³"Lord, they have killed your prophets and torn down your altars; I am the only one left, and they are trying to kill me"*b*? ⁴And what was God's answer to him? "I have reserved for myself seven thousand who have not bowed the knee to Baal."*c* ⁵So too, at the present time there is a remnant chosen by grace. ⁶And if by grace, then it is no longer by works; if it were, grace would no longer be grace.*d*

⁷What then? What Israel sought so earnestly it did not obtain, but the elect did. The others were hardened, ⁸as it is written:

"God gave them a spirit of stupor,
   eyes so that they could not see
   and ears so that they could not hear,
to this very day."*e*

⁹And David says:

"May their table become a snare and a trap,
   a stumbling block and a retribution for
      them.
¹⁰May their eyes be darkened so they cannot
      see,
   and their backs be bent forever."*f*

Ingrafted Branches

¹¹Again I ask: Did they stumble so as to fall beyond recovery? Not at all! Rather, because of their transgression, salvation has come to the Gentiles to make Israel envious. ¹²But if their transgression means riches for the world, and their loss means riches for the Gentiles, how much greater riches will their fullness bring!

¹³I am talking to you Gentiles. Inasmuch as I am the apostle to the Gentiles, I make much of my ministry ¹⁴in the hope that I may some-

how arouse my own people to envy and save some of them. ¹⁵For if their rejection is the reconciliation of the world, what will their acceptance be but life from the dead? ¹⁶If the part of the dough offered as firstfruits is holy, then the whole batch is holy; if the root is holy, so are the branches.

¹⁷If some of the branches have been broken off, and you, though a wild olive shoot, have been grafted in among the others and now share in the nourishing sap from the olive root, ¹⁸do not boast over those branches. If you do, consider this: You do not support the root, but the root supports you. ¹⁹You will say then, "Branches were broken off so that I could be grafted in." ²⁰Granted. But they were broken off because of unbelief, and you stand by faith. Do not be arrogant, but be afraid. ²¹For if God did not spare the natural branches, he will not spare you either.

²²Consider therefore the kindness and sternness of God: sternness to those who fell, but kindness to you, provided that you continue in his kindness. Otherwise, you also will be cut off. ²³And if they do not persist in unbelief, they will be grafted in, for God is able to graft them in again. ²⁴After all, if you were cut out of an olive tree that is wild by nature, and contrary to nature were grafted into a cultivated olive tree, how much more readily will these, the natural branches, be grafted into their own olive tree!

All Israel Will Be Saved

²⁵I do not want you to be ignorant of this mystery, brothers, so that you may not be conceited: Israel has experienced a hardening in part until the full number of the Gentiles have come in. ²⁶And so all Israel will be saved, as it is written:

"The deliverer will come from Zion;
   he will turn godlessness away from
      Jacob.
²⁷And this is*g* my covenant with them
   when I take away their sins."*h*

²⁸As far as the gospel is concerned, they are enemies on your account; but as far as election

---

*a*21 Isaiah 65:2   *b*3 1 Kings 19:10,14   *c*4 1 Kings 19:18   *d*6 Some manuscripts *be grace. But if by works, then it is no longer grace; if it were, work would no longer be work.*   *e*8 Deut. 29:4; Isaiah 29:10   *f*10 Psalm 69:22,23   *g*27 Or *will be*   *h*27 Isaiah 59:20,21; 27:9; Jer. 31:33,34 is concerned, they are loved on account of the patriarchs, ²⁹for God's gifts and his call are irrevocable. ³⁰Just as you who were at one time disobedient to God have now received mercy as a result of their disobedience, ³¹so they too have now become disobedient in order that they too may now[a] receive mercy as a result of God's mercy to you. ³²For God has bound all men over to disobedience so that he may have mercy on them all.

Doxology

³³Oh, the depth of the riches
of the wisdom and[b]
knowledge of God!
How unsearchable his
judgments,
and his paths beyond
tracing out!
³⁴"Who has known the mind
of the Lord?
Or who has been his
counselor?"[c]
³⁵"Who has ever given to
God,
that God should repay
him?"[d]
³⁶For from him and through
him and to him are
all things.
To him be the glory
forever! Amen.

Living Sacrifices

12 Therefore, I urge you, brothers, in view of God's mercy, to offer your bodies as living sacrifices, holy and pleasing to God—this is your spiritual[e] act of worship. ²Do not conform any longer to the pattern of this world, but be transformed by the renewing of your mind. Then you will be able to test and approve what God's will is—his good, pleasing and perfect will.

³For by the grace given me I say to every one of you: Do not think of yourself more highly than you ought, but rather think of yourself with sober judgment, in accordance with the measure of faith God has given you. ⁴Just as each of us has one body with many members,

and these members do not all have the same function, ⁵so in Christ we who are many form one body, and each member belongs to all the others. ⁶We have different gifts, according to the grace given us. If a man's gift is prophesying, let him use it in proportion to his[f] faith. ⁷If it is serving, let him serve; if it is teaching, let him teach; ⁸if it is encouraging, let him encourage; if it is contributing to the needs of others, let him give generously; if it is leadership, let him govern diligently; if it is showing mercy, let him do it cheerfully.

Love

⁹Love must be sincere. Hate what is evil; cling to what is good. ¹⁰Be devoted to one another in brotherly love. Honor one another above yourselves. ¹¹Never be lacking in zeal, but keep your spiritual fervor, serving the Lord. ¹²Be joyful in hope, patient in affliction, faithful in prayer. ¹³Share with God's people who are in need. Practice hospitality.

¹⁴Bless those who persecute you; bless and do not curse. ¹⁵Rejoice with those who rejoice; mourn with those who mourn. ¹⁶Live in harmony with one another. Do not be proud, but be willing to associate with people of low position.[g] Do not be conceited.

¹⁷Do not repay anyone evil for evil. Be careful to do what is right in the eyes of everybody. ¹⁸If it is possible, as far as it depends on you, live at peace with everyone. ¹⁹Do not take revenge, my friends, but leave room for God's wrath, for it is written: "It is mine to avenge; I will repay,"[h] says the Lord. ²⁰On the contrary:

"If your enemy is hungry, feed him;
if he is thirsty, give him something to
drink.
In doing this, you will heap burning coals
on his head."[i]

²¹Do not be overcome by evil, but overcome evil with good.

> ### Romans 11:33
>
> *God Cannot*
> *Be Fully*
> *Understood*
>
> Oh, the depth of the riches of the wisdom and knowledge of God! How unsearchable his judgments, and his paths beyond tracing out!

---

[a]**31** Some manuscripts do not have *now.* [b]**33** Or *riches and the wisdom and the* [c]**34** Isaiah 40:13 [d]**35** Job 41:11 [e]**1** Or *reasonable* [f]**6** Or *in agreement with the* [g]**16** Or *willing to do menial work* [h]**19** Deut. 32:35 [i]**20** Prov. 25:21,22

Scoot Down Low

Read Romans 12:1–21

"HUMBLE" COMES FROM THE WORD *HUMUS*, meaning "earth" or "brought down low." Yes, the Creator of the universe who flung the stars into space is also a very down-to-earth God. Why was Jesus "brought down low"—why did he come down to earth in our form?

I was pondering that thought one day as I was busy in the kitchen, my "hive of five" grandkids buzzing around the living room. I put dinner on the table and gave the "y'all come" signal. My grown children and their children began to make their way toward the feast and the smells of my home-cooked turnip greens, buttered carrots, okra gumbo, mashed potatoes, brisket, baked chicken and corn bread (with ice cream waiting in the freezer to top it all off a little later)!

But two of my darlin's were too busy playing to answer the call. "Alyssa! Alaya!" I called again. Still they paid no attention. So I did the only thing I could do. I went over to where they were engrossed in their baby dolls and scooted down on my achy knees to look them in the eyes.

Now I had their full attention. "Girls," I said with loving firmness, "did you not hear me calling you?"

They shook their heads no, their dark braids flying, their brown eyes wide with surprise.

"Well, sweet things, now that I have your attention, help your old Grammy up and let's go eat." Together the girls tugged on my arms and off we went toward the banquet.

As I walked with them, I thought about having to go to all that trouble, to physically scoot down low to get the attention of my granddaughters. It was then I realized that this is exactly what Jesus did for me.

God had a wonderful feast prepared for us in heaven and he called his people to come and eat and enjoy! But most often, caught up in their own little dramas, they ignored his call. So, in the form of his Son, Jesus "scooted down low" and became one of us. Why? To get our attention, to meet us eye to eye—to take us by the hand and lead us to the feast.

—*Carol Kent, Thelma Wells*

Tuesday

Go to page 1384 for your next devotional reading.

Romans 12:16

Live in harmony with one another. Do not be proud, but be willing to associate with people of low position. Do not be conceited.

reflection

1 How have you gotten caught up in "little dramas" that make it hard to live in harmony with others?

2 How does it help to remember that the Creator of the universe "scooted down low" to become one of us?

3 Do you need to "scoot down low" to make things right with someone? When and how will you do that so you can restore harmony to the relationship?

RELATED READINGS

Colossians 3:12–14; James 4:7–10

"What makes humility so desirable is the marvelous thing it does to us; it creates in us a capacity for the closest possible intimacy with God."

Monica Baldwin

Submission to the Authorities

13 Everyone must submit himself to the governing authorities, for there is no authority except that which God has established. The authorities that exist have been established by God. [2]Consequently, he who rebels against the authority is rebelling against what God has instituted, and those who do so will bring judgment on themselves. [3]For rulers hold no terror for those who do right, but for those who do wrong. Do you want to be free from fear of the one in authority? Then do what is right and he will commend you. [4]For he is God's servant to do you good. But if you do wrong, be afraid, for he does not bear the sword for nothing. He is God's servant, an agent of wrath to bring punishment on the wrongdoer. [5]Therefore, it is necessary to submit to the authorities, not only because of possible punishment but also because of conscience.

[6]This is also why you pay taxes, for the authorities are God's servants, who give their full time to governing. [7]Give everyone what you owe him: If you owe taxes, pay taxes; if revenue, then revenue; if respect, then respect; if honor, then honor.

Love, for the Day Is Near

[8]Let no debt remain outstanding, except the continuing debt to love one another, for he who loves his fellowman has fulfilled the law. [9]The commandments, "Do not commit adultery," "Do not murder," "Do not steal," "Do not covet,"[a] and whatever other commandment there may be, are summed up in this one rule: "Love your neighbor as yourself."[b] [10]Love does no harm to its neighbor. Therefore love is the fulfillment of the law.

[11]And do this, understanding the present time. The hour has come for you to wake up from your slumber, because our salvation is nearer now than when we first believed. [12]The night is nearly over; the day is almost here. So let us put aside the deeds of darkness and put on the armor of light. [13]Let us behave decently, as in the daytime, not in orgies and drunkenness, not in sexual immorality and debauchery, not in dissension and jealousy. [14]Rather, clothe yourselves with the Lord Jesus Christ, and do not think about how to gratify the desires of the sinful nature.[c]

The Weak and the Strong

14 Accept him whose faith is weak, without passing judgment on disputable matters. [2]One man's faith allows him to eat everything, but another man, whose faith is weak, eats only vegetables. [3]The man who eats everything must not look down on him who does not, and the man who does not eat everything must not condemn the man who does, for God has accepted him. [4]Who are you to judge someone else's servant? To his own master he stands or falls. And he will stand, for the Lord is able to make him stand.

[5]One man considers one day more sacred than another; another man considers every day alike. Each one should be fully convinced in his own mind. [6]He who regards one day as special, does so to the Lord. He who eats meat, eats to the Lord, for he gives thanks to God; and he who abstains, does so to the Lord and gives thanks to God. [7]For none of us lives to himself alone and none of us dies to himself alone. [8]If we live, we live to the Lord; and if we die, we die to the Lord. So, whether we live or die, we belong to the Lord.

[9]For this very reason, Christ died and returned to life so that he might be the Lord of both the dead and the living. [10]You, then, why do you judge your brother? Or why do you look down on your brother? For we will all stand before God's judgment seat. [11]It is written:

> "'As surely as I live,' says the Lord,
> 'every knee will bow before me;
> every tongue will confess to God.'"[d]

[12]So then, each of us will give an account of himself to God.

[13]Therefore let us stop passing judgment

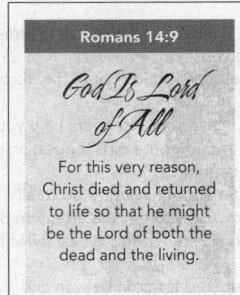

Romans 14:9

God Is Lord of All

For this very reason, Christ died and returned to life so that he might be the Lord of both the dead and the living.

---

[a]9 Exodus 20:13–15,17; Deut. 5:17–19,21   [b]9 Lev. 19:18   [c]14 Or *the flesh*   [d]11 Isaiah 45:23

on one another. Instead, make up your mind not to put any stumbling block or obstacle in your brother's way. **14**As one who is in the Lord Jesus, I am fully convinced that no food*a* is unclean in itself. But if anyone regards something as unclean, then for him it is unclean. **15**If your brother is distressed because of what you eat, you are no longer acting in love. Do not by your eating destroy your brother for whom Christ died. **16**Do not allow what you consider good to be spoken of as evil. **17**For the kingdom of God is not a matter of eating and drinking, but of righteousness, peace and joy in the Holy Spirit, **18**because anyone who serves Christ in this way is pleasing to God and approved by men.

19Let us therefore make every effort to do what leads to peace and to mutual edification. **20**Do not destroy the work of God for the sake of food. All food is clean, but it is wrong for a man to eat anything that causes someone else to stumble. **21**It is better not to eat meat or drink wine or to do anything else that will cause your brother to fall.

22So whatever you believe about these things keep between yourself and God. Blessed is the man who does not condemn himself by what he approves. **23**But the man who has doubts is condemned if he eats, because his eating is not from faith; and everything that does not come from faith is sin.

15 We who are strong ought to bear with the failings of the weak and not to please ourselves. **2**Each of us should please his neighbor for his good, to build him up. **3**For even Christ did not please himself but, as it is written: "The insults of those who insult you have fallen on me."*b* **4**For everything that was written in the past was written to teach us, so that through endurance and the encouragement of the Scriptures we might have hope.

5May the God who gives endurance and encouragement give you a spirit of unity among yourselves as you follow Christ Jesus, **6**so that with one heart and mouth you may glorify the God and Father of our Lord Jesus Christ.

7Accept one another, then, just as Christ accepted you, in order to bring praise to God.

8For I tell you that Christ has become a servant of the Jews*c* on behalf of God's truth, to confirm the promises made to the patriarchs **9**so that the Gentiles may glorify God for his mercy, as it is written:

> "Therefore I will praise you among the
> Gentiles;
> I will sing hymns to your name."*d*

10Again, it says,

> "Rejoice, O Gentiles, with his people."*e*

11And again,

> "Praise the Lord, all you Gentiles,
> and sing praises to him, all you
> peoples."*f*

12And again, Isaiah says,

> "The Root of Jesse will spring up,
> one who will arise to rule over the
> nations;
> the Gentiles will hope in him."*g*

13May the God of hope fill you with all joy and peace as you trust in him, so that you may overflow with hope by the power of the Holy Spirit.

Paul the Minister to the Gentiles

14I myself am convinced, my brothers, that you yourselves are full of goodness, complete in knowledge and competent to instruct one another. **15**I have written you quite boldly on some points, as if to remind you of them again, because of the grace God gave me **16**to be a minister of Christ Jesus to the Gentiles with the priestly duty of proclaiming the gospel of God, so that the Gentiles might become an offering acceptable to God, sanctified by the Holy Spirit.

17Therefore I glory in Christ Jesus in my service to God. **18**I will not venture to speak of anything except what Christ has accomplished through me in leading the Gentiles to obey God by what I have said and done— **19**by the power of signs and miracles, through the power of the Spirit. So from Jerusalem all the way around to Illyricum, I have fully proclaimed the gospel of Christ. **20**It has always been my ambition to

---

*a***14** Or *that nothing*   *b***3** Psalm 69:9   *c***8** Greek *circumcision*   *d***9** 2 Samuel 22:50; Psalm 18:49   *e***10** Deut. 32:43   *f***11** Psalm 117:1   *g***12** Isaiah 11:10

Overflowing Hope

May the God of hope
fill you with all joy and
peace as you trust in him,
so that you may overflow
with hope by the power
of the Holy Spirit.

reflection

1 Would you describe
your glass of hope as
empty, half full or over-
flowing?

2 What situation is God
asking you to endure
right now? How have you
found hope in the midst
of it?

3 If you could only have
one page of the Bible
to sustain you for the rest
of your life, what page
would it be?

RELATED READINGS

Lamentations 3:21–26;
Romans 5:3–5

Read: Romans 15:1–13

READING THE NEWSPAPER HEADLINES on any given day can
cause our hope to evaporate. Yet in Romans 15:13 Paul prays that
the "God of hope" will fill us with joy and peace so that we might
"overflow with hope." In the midst of a world filled with despair,
only God can fill us with hope. In verse 4, Paul revealed two keys to
hope: "Through endurance and the encouragement of the Scriptures we might have hope."

Key 1: Endurance. The Greek word for *endurance* means "to
bear up under pressure" or "to be courageous." It takes endurance
and courage to keep going when circumstances tempt us to give
up. But like athletes who know they will receive a prize, believers
can continue the race of faith fully confident that God will keep his
promises.

Key 2: Encouragement of the Scriptures. The Greek word for
encouragement means "comfort" or "solace." Reading God's
Word fills us with hope because it comforts our souls. We read of
God's ability to perform wonders and miracles in impossible situations and his power to turn intended evil to our good. We read
of God's ability to redeem, protect and heal us, his children. We
can rest, knowing that God loves us deeply and has our very best
interests in his big Abba Father's heart.

Years ago, a caravan crossed the north of India. A missionary
traveled with the group. As the caravan journeyed, a poor, old
man was overcome by the heat and labor of the trip. The heartless
caravan leader left him to perish alone on the road. The missionary
saw him and went to comfort the dying man. She knelt beside him
and whispered in his ear, "Brother, what is your hope?" With great
effort, the man replied, "The blood of Jesus, his son Christ . . . purifies . . . from all sin" (see 1 John 1:7).

As the missionary held the dying man in her arms, she saw a
piece of the Bible grasped tightly in his hands. It was a single page
of the Bible containing the passage from which these words were
found. The elderly man had walked a long journey, clearly enduring
until the very end with only a few words of Scripture to fill his heart
to overflowing with hope.

What is your hope?

Go to page 1389 for your next devotional reading.

preach the gospel where Christ was not known, so that I would not be building on someone else's foundation. ²¹Rather, as it is written:

"Those who were not told about him will see,
and those who have not heard will understand."ᵃ

²²This is why I have often been hindered from coming to you.

Paul's Plan to Visit Rome

²³But now that there is no more place for me to work in these regions, and since I have been longing for many years to see you, ²⁴I plan to do so when I go to Spain. I hope to visit you while passing through and to have you assist me on my journey there, after I have enjoyed your company for a while. ²⁵Now, however, I am on my way to Jerusalem in the service of the saints there. ²⁶For Macedonia and Achaia were pleased to make a contribution for the poor among the saints in Jerusalem. ²⁷They were pleased to do it, and indeed they owe it to them. For if the Gentiles have shared in the Jews' spiritual blessings, they owe it to the Jews to share with them their material blessings. ²⁸So after I have completed this task and have made sure that they have received this fruit, I will go to Spain and visit you on the way. ²⁹I know that when I come to you, I will come in the full measure of the blessing of Christ.

³⁰I urge you, brothers, by our Lord Jesus Christ and by the love of the Spirit, to join me in my struggle by praying to God for me. ³¹Pray that I may be rescued from the unbelievers in Judea and that my service in Jerusalem may be acceptable to the saints there, ³²so that by God's will I may come to you with joy and together with you be refreshed. ³³The God of peace be with you all. Amen.

Personal Greetings

16 I commend to you our sister Phoebe, a servantᵇ of the church in Cenchrea. ²I ask you to receive her in the Lord in a way worthy of the saints and to give her any help she may need from you, for she has been a great help to many people, including me.

³Greet Priscillaᶜ and Aquila, my fellow workers in Christ Jesus. ⁴They risked their lives for me. Not only I but all the churches of the Gentiles are grateful to them.

⁵Greet also the church that meets at their house.

Greet my dear friend Epenetus, who was the first convert to Christ in the province of Asia.

⁶Greet Mary, who worked very hard for you.

⁷Greet Andronicus and Junias, my relatives who have been in prison with me. They are outstanding among the apostles, and they were in Christ before I was.

⁸Greet Ampliatus, whom I love in the Lord.

⁹Greet Urbanus, our fellow worker in Christ, and my dear friend Stachys.

¹⁰Greet Apelles, tested and approved in Christ.

Greet those who belong to the household of Aristobulus.

¹¹Greet Herodion, my relative.

Greet those in the household of Narcissus who are in the Lord.

¹²Greet Tryphena and Tryphosa, those women who work hard in the Lord.

Greet my dear friend Persis, another woman who has worked very hard in the Lord.

¹³Greet Rufus, chosen in the Lord, and his mother, who has been a mother to me, too.

¹⁴Greet Asyncritus, Phlegon, Hermes, Patrobas, Hermas and the brothers with them.

¹⁵Greet Philologus, Julia, Nereus and his sister, and Olympas and all the saints with them.

¹⁶Greet one another with a holy kiss.

All the churches of Christ send greetings.

¹⁷I urge you, brothers, to watch out for those who cause divisions and put obstacles in your way that are contrary to the teaching you have learned. Keep away from them. ¹⁸For such people are not serving our Lord Christ, but their own appetites. By smooth talk and flattery they deceive the minds of naive people. ¹⁹Everyone has heard about your obedience, so I am full of joy over you; but I want you to be wise about what is good, and innocent about what is evil.

ᵃ21 Isaiah 52:15   ᵇ1 Or *deaconess*   ᶜ3 Greek *Prisca*, a variant of *Priscilla*

²⁰The God of peace will soon crush Satan under your feet.

The grace of our Lord Jesus be with you.

²¹Timothy, my fellow worker, sends his greetings to you, as do Lucius, Jason and Sosipater, my relatives.

²²I, Tertius, who wrote down this letter, greet you in the Lord.

²³Gaius, whose hospitality I and the whole church here enjoy, sends you his greetings.

Erastus, who is the city's director of public works, and our brother Quartus send you their greetings.ᵃ

²⁵Now to him who is able to establish you by my gospel and the proclamation of Jesus Christ, according to the revelation of the mystery hidden for long ages past, ²⁶but now revealed and made known through the prophetic writings by the command of the eternal God, so that all nations might believe and obey him— ²⁷to the only wise God be glory forever through Jesus Christ! Amen.

ᵃ23 Some manuscripts *their greetings.* ²⁴*May the grace of our Lord Jesus Christ be with all of you. Amen.*

1 Corinthians

Corinth was a wealthy and prosperous center
of commerce and trade when Paul wrote this letter.
Morally, however, it was bankrupt. The term *Corinthian*
came to be synonymous with immorality. And there, in
the center of this immoral society, was a young Christian
church struggling to survive.

Paul's words to the Corinthians are exceptionally modern in their *relevance to churches of today.* The
problems that surfaced in the congregation in Corinth are
the same problems that have plagued churches throughout the ages. There were divisions, questions about
marriage and divorce, concerns about how to relate to a
pagan world, lawsuits and immorality—difficult issues that
no one wanted to deal with.

Paul addresses these issues head-on, giving specific
advice about how to live as God's people in a fallen
world. Nothing ever really changes where human nature is
concerned, but Paul reminds us that we are not subjects
to the whims of that nature. He points us to the resurrection when we will all be changed, clothed with immortality
and bearing the likeness of Christ. He reminds us that
our lives are to be lived not for this world
but in preparation for that imperishable world that is
to come.

Author:
The apostle Paul.

Audience:
Followers of Jesus;
originally written to
the church in Corinth.

Date:
About A.D. 55.

Setting:
Paul wrote from Ephesus
to the church in Corinth, a
pagan cosmopolitan city
in Greece. He started this
church during his second
missionary journey.

Verse to Remember:
No temptation has seized
you except what is com-
mon to man. And God is
faithful; he will not let you
be tempted beyond what
you can bear. But when
you are tempted, he will
also provide a way out
so that you can stand up
under it. (10:13)

1 Paul, called to be an apostle of Christ Jesus by the will of God, and our brother Sosthenes,

2 To the church of God in Corinth, to those sanctified in Christ Jesus and called to be holy, together with all those everywhere who call on the name of our Lord Jesus Christ—their Lord and ours:

3 Grace and peace to you from God our Father and the Lord Jesus Christ.

Thanksgiving

4 I always thank God for you because of his grace given you in Christ Jesus. 5 For in him you have been enriched in every way—in all your speaking and in all your knowledge— 6 because our testimony about Christ was confirmed in you. 7 Therefore you do not lack any spiritual gift as you eagerly wait for our Lord Jesus Christ to be revealed. 8 He will keep you strong to the end, so that you will be blameless on the day of our Lord Jesus Christ. 9 God, who has called you into fellowship with his Son Jesus Christ our Lord, is faithful.

1 Corinthians 1:8

God Keeps Us Strong

He will keep you strong to the end, so that you will be blameless on the day of our Lord Jesus Christ.

Divisions in the Church

10 I appeal to you, brothers, in the name of our Lord Jesus Christ, that all of you agree with one another so that there may be no divisions among you and that you may be perfectly united in mind and thought. 11 My brothers, some from Chloe's household have informed me that there are quarrels among you. 12 What I mean is this: One of you says, "I follow Paul"; another, "I follow Apollos"; another, "I follow Cephas*a*"; still another, "I follow Christ."

13 Is Christ divided? Was Paul crucified for you? Were you baptized into*b* the name of Paul? 14 I am thankful that I did not baptize any of you except Crispus and Gaius, 15 so that no one can say that you were baptized into my name. 16 (Yes, I also baptized the household of Stephanas; beyond that, I don't remember if I baptized anyone else.) 17 For Christ did not send me to baptize, but to preach the gospel—not with words of human wisdom, lest the cross of Christ be emptied of its power.

Christ the Wisdom and Power of God

18 For the message of the cross is foolishness to those who are perishing, but to us who are being saved it is the power of God. 19 For it is written:

"I will destroy the wisdom of the wise;
    the intelligence of the intelligent I will frustrate."*c*

20 Where is the wise man? Where is the scholar? Where is the philosopher of this age? Has not God made foolish the wisdom of the world? 21 For since in the wisdom of God the world through its wisdom did not know him, God was pleased through the foolishness of what was preached to save those who believe. 22 Jews demand miraculous signs and Greeks look for wisdom, 23 but we preach Christ crucified: a stumbling block to Jews and foolishness to Gentiles, 24 but to those whom God has called, both Jews and Greeks, Christ the power of God and the wisdom of God. 25 For the foolishness of God is wiser than man's wisdom, and the weakness of God is stronger than man's strength.

26 Brothers, think of what you were when you were called. Not many of you were wise by human standards; not many were influential; not many were of noble birth. 27 But God chose the foolish things of the world to shame the wise; God chose the weak things of the world to shame the strong. 28 He chose the lowly things of this world and the despised things—and the things that are not—to nullify the things that are, 29 so that no one may boast before him. 30 It is because of him that you are in Christ Jesus, who has become for us wisdom from God—that is, our righteousness, holiness and redemption. 31 Therefore, as it is written: "Let him who boasts boast in the Lord."*d*

*a*12 That is, Peter   *b*13 Or *in*; also in verse 15   *c*19 Isaiah 29:14   *d*31 Jer. 9:24

The Foolish Things

Read: 1 Corinthians 1:18–31

THE LAWS OF NATURE as shown in cartoons are not to be trusted. Take the law of gravity, for instance. Aren't you amazed that a cartoon character can run off the edge of a cliff and keep running in place for several seconds before gravity finally kicks in? When gravity finally does regain its pull, why is it that the cartoon character's feet go first, stretching him to about ten times his original height, then the body goes, then the eyeballs follow a couple of seconds later?

And how is it those 200-foot falls are never fatal? Explosions don't kill either. No matter how many kilotons, the cartoon character never dies. He just turns black and smoky. After a second or two, even that goes away. Remarkable.

Nope, you can't trust the laws of nature in cartoon life.

Scripture teaches that we can't trust in our own cleverness any more than we can trust in our own righteousness. The fallen nature tells us that life is hard and then we die. If we have many resources, we might become hedonists and say "Eat, drink and be merry, for tomorrow we die." But just as the seemingly simple Roadrunner outwits the clever Wile E. Coyote every time, God's wisdom confounds the world's wisdom. The seemingly foolish things of God are really wise, while the seemingly wise things of the world really are foolish.

God used simple people to proclaim his simple message: Jesus Christ is our miraculous tunnel of escape from the curse of death issued when Adam and Eve fell. Any other route will leave us empty and forlorn. This may seem foolishly simpleminded to some, but it is the simple truth of the gospel; easy enough for a child to understand, yet profound enough for an intellectual to dwell on for eternity.

1 Corinthians 1:27

But God chose the foolish things of the world to shame the wise; God chose the weak things of the world to shame the strong.

reflection

1 When have you been considered foolish for believing the simple truth of the gospel?

2 How has God used your weakness to show himself strong?

3 This week, ask God to use you in spite of your weaknesses in the area he sees fit.

RELATED READINGS

Psalm 37:3–6;
1 Corinthians 3:18–23;
2 Corinthians 11:16–33

"Our Father stands with open arms and asks us to trust in His faithfulness...Truly, He is steady, and He firmly grasps us as we reach out to Him."

Cynthia Heald

Go to page 1394 for your next devotional reading.

2

When I came to you, brothers, I did not come with eloquence or superior wisdom as I proclaimed to you the testimony about God.[a] ²For I resolved to know nothing while I was with you except Jesus Christ and him crucified. ³I came to you in weakness and fear, and with much trembling. ⁴My message and my preaching were not with wise and persuasive words, but with a demonstration of the Spirit's power, ⁵so that your faith might not rest on men's wisdom, but on God's power.

Wisdom From the Spirit

⁶We do, however, speak a message of wisdom among the mature, but not the wisdom of this age or of the rulers of this age, who are coming to nothing. ⁷No, we speak of God's secret wisdom, a wisdom that has been hidden and that God destined for our glory before time began. ⁸None of the rulers of this age understood it, for if they had, they would not have crucified the Lord of glory. ⁹However, as it is written:

> "No eye has seen,
>   no ear has heard,
>   no mind has conceived
>   what God has prepared
>   for those who love
>   him"[b]—

¹⁰but God has revealed it to us by his Spirit.

The Spirit searches all things, even the deep things of God. ¹¹For who among men knows the thoughts of a man except the man's spirit within him? In the same way no one knows the thoughts of God except the Spirit of God. ¹²We have not received the spirit of the world but the Spirit who is from God, that we may understand what God has freely given us. ¹³This is what we speak, not in words taught us by human wisdom but in words taught by the Spirit, expressing spiritual truths in spiritual words.[c] ¹⁴The man without the Spirit does not accept the things that come from the Spirit of God, for they are foolishness to him, and he cannot understand them, because they are spiritually dis-

cerned. ¹⁵The spiritual man makes judgments about all things, but he himself is not subject to any man's judgment:

> ¹⁶"For who has known the mind of the Lord
>   that he may instruct him?"[d]

But we have the mind of Christ.

On Divisions in the Church

3

Brothers, I could not address you as spiritual but as worldly—mere infants in Christ. ²I gave you milk, not solid food, for you were not yet ready for it. Indeed, you are still not ready. ³You are still worldly. For since there is jealousy and quarreling among you, are you not worldly? Are you not acting like mere men? ⁴For when one says, "I follow Paul," and another, "I follow Apollos," are you not mere men?

⁵What, after all, is Apollos? And what is Paul? Only servants, through whom you came to believe—as the Lord has assigned to each his task. ⁶I planted the seed, Apollos watered it, but God made it grow. ⁷So neither he who plants nor he who waters is anything, but only God, who makes things grow. ⁸The man who plants and the man who waters have one purpose, and each will be rewarded according to his own labor. ⁹For we are God's fellow workers; you are God's field, God's building.

¹⁰By the grace God has given me, I laid a foundation as an expert builder, and someone else is building on it. But each one should be careful how he builds. ¹¹For no one can lay any foundation other than the one already laid, which is Jesus Christ. ¹²If any man builds on this foundation using gold, silver, costly stones, wood, hay or straw, ¹³his work will be shown for what it is, because the Day will bring it to light. It will be revealed with fire, and the fire will test the quality of each man's work. ¹⁴If what he has built survives, he will receive his reward. ¹⁵If it is burned up, he will suffer loss; he

---

1 Corinthians 2:9

God Plans a Wondrous Future

"No eye has seen,
no ear has heard,
no mind has conceived
what God has prepared
for those who love him."

---

*a*1 Some manuscripts *as I proclaimed to you God's mystery*   *b*9 Isaiah 64:4   *c*13 Or *Spirit, interpreting spiritual truths to spiritual men*   *d*16 Isaiah 40:13

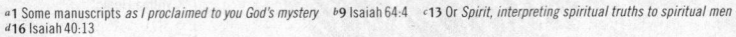

himself will be saved, but only as one escaping through the flames.

16Don't you know that you yourselves are God's temple and that God's Spirit lives in you? **17**If anyone destroys God's temple, God will destroy him; for God's temple is sacred, and you are that temple.

18Do not deceive yourselves. If any one of you thinks he is wise by the standards of this age, he should become a "fool" so that he may become wise. **19**For the wisdom of this world is foolishness in God's sight. As it is written: "He catches the wise in their craftiness"[a]; **20**and again, "The Lord knows that the thoughts of the wise are futile."[b] **21**So then, no more boasting about men! All things are yours, **22**whether Paul or Apollos or Cephas[c] or the world or life or death or the present or the future—all are yours, **23**and you are of Christ, and Christ is of God.

Apostles of Christ

4 So then, men ought to regard us as servants of Christ and as those entrusted with the secret things of God. **2**Now it is required that those who have been given a trust must prove faithful. **3**I care very little if I am judged by you or by any human court; indeed, I do not even judge myself. **4**My conscience is clear, but that does not make me innocent. It is the Lord who judges me. **5**Therefore judge nothing before the appointed time; wait till the Lord comes. He will bring to light what is hidden in darkness and will expose the motives of men's hearts. At that time each will receive his praise from God.

6Now, brothers, I have applied these things to myself and Apollos for your benefit, so that you may learn from us the meaning of the saying, "Do not go beyond what is written." Then you will not take pride in one man over against another. **7**For who makes you different from anyone else? What do you have that you did not receive? And if you did receive it, why do you boast as though you did not?

8Already you have all you want! Already you have become rich! You have become kings—and that without us! How I wish that you really had become kings so that we might be kings

with you! **9**For it seems to me that God has put us apostles on display at the end of the procession, like men condemned to die in the arena. We have been made a spectacle to the whole universe, to angels as well as to men. **10**We are fools for Christ, but you are so wise in Christ! We are weak, but you are strong! You are honored, we are dishonored! **11**To this very hour we go hungry and thirsty, we are in rags, we are brutally treated, we are homeless. **12**We work hard with our own hands. When we are cursed, we bless; when we are persecuted, we endure it; **13**when we are slandered, we answer kindly. Up to this moment we have become the scum of the earth, the refuse of the world.

14I am not writing this to shame you, but to warn you, as my dear children. **15**Even though you have ten thousand guardians in Christ, you do not have many fathers, for in Christ Jesus I became your father through the gospel. **16**Therefore I urge you to imitate me. **17**For this reason I am sending to you Timothy, my son whom I love, who is faithful in the Lord. He will remind you of my way of life in Christ Jesus, which agrees with what I teach everywhere in every church.

18Some of you have become arrogant, as if I were not coming to you. **19**But I will come to you very soon, if the Lord is willing, and then I will find out not only how these arrogant people are talking, but what power they have. **20**For the kingdom of God is not a matter of talk but of power. **21**What do you prefer? Shall I come to you with a whip, or in love and with a gentle spirit?

Expel the Immoral Brother!

5 It is actually reported that there is sexual immorality among you, and of a kind that does not occur even among pagans: A man has his father's wife. **2**And you are proud! Shouldn't you rather have been filled with grief and have put out of your fellowship the man who did this? **3**Even though I am not physically present, I am with you in spirit. And I have already passed judgment on the one who did this, just as if I were present. **4**When you are assembled in the name of our Lord Jesus and I am with you in spirit, and the power of our Lord Jesus

a19 Job 5:13 *b20* Psalm 94:11 *c22* That is, Peter

is present, [5]hand this man over to Satan, so that the sinful nature[a] may be destroyed and his spirit saved on the day of the Lord.

[6]Your boasting is not good. Don't you know that a little yeast works through the whole batch of dough? [7]Get rid of the old yeast that you may be a new batch without yeast—as you really are. For Christ, our Passover lamb, has been sacrificed. [8]Therefore let us keep the Festival, not with the old yeast, the yeast of malice and wickedness, but with bread without yeast, the bread of sincerity and truth.

[9]I have written you in my letter not to associate with sexually immoral people— [10]not at all meaning the people of this world who are immoral, or the greedy and swindlers, or idolaters. In that case you would have to leave this world. [11]But now I am writing you that you must not associate with anyone who calls himself a brother but is sexually immoral or greedy, an idolater or a slanderer, a drunkard or a swindler. With such a man do not even eat.

[12]What business is it of mine to judge those outside the church? Are you not to judge those inside? [13]God will judge those outside. "Expel the wicked man from among you."[b]

Lawsuits Among Believers

6 If any of you has a dispute with another, dare he take it before the ungodly for judgment instead of before the saints? [2]Do you not know that the saints will judge the world? And if you are to judge the world, are you not competent to judge trivial cases? [3]Do you not know that we will judge angels? How much more the things of this life! [4]Therefore, if you have disputes about such matters, appoint as judges even men of little account in the church![c] [5]I say this to shame you. Is it possible that there is nobody among you wise enough to judge a dispute between believers? [6]But instead, one brother goes to law against another—and this in front of unbelievers!

[7]The very fact that you have lawsuits among you means you have been completely defeated already. Why not rather be wronged? Why not rather be cheated? [8]Instead, you yourselves cheat and do wrong, and you do this to your brothers.

[9]Do you not know that the wicked will not inherit the kingdom of God? Do not be deceived: Neither the sexually immoral nor idolaters nor adulterers nor male prostitutes nor homosexual offenders [10]nor thieves nor the greedy nor drunkards nor slanderers nor swindlers will inherit the kingdom of God. [11]And that is what some of you were. But you were washed, you were sanctified, you were justified in the name of the Lord Jesus Christ and by the Spirit of our God.

Sexual Immorality

[12]"Everything is permissible for me"—but not everything is beneficial. "Everything is permissible for me"—but I will not be mastered by anything. [13]"Food for the stomach and the stomach for food"—but God will destroy them both. The body is not meant for sexual immorality, but for the Lord, and the Lord for the body. [14]By his power God raised the Lord from the dead, and he will raise us also. [15]Do you not know that your bodies are members of Christ himself? Shall I then take the members of Christ and unite them with a prostitute? Never! [16]Do you not know that he who unites himself with a prostitute is one with her in body? For it is said, "The two will become one flesh."[d] [17]But he who unites himself with the Lord is one with him in spirit.

[18]Flee from sexual immorality. All other sins a man commits are outside his body, but he who sins sexually sins against his own body. [19]Do you not know that your body is a temple of the Holy Spirit who is in you, whom you have received from God? You are not your own; [20]you were bought at a price. Therefore honor God with your body.

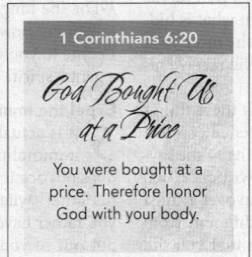

1 Corinthians 6:20

God Bought Us at a Price

You were bought at a price. Therefore honor God with your body.

---

[a]5 Or that his body; or that the flesh   [b]13 Deut. 17:7; 19:19; 21:21; 22:21,24; 24:7   [c]4 Or matters, do you appoint as judges men of little account in the church?   [d]16 Gen. 2:24

Marriage

7 Now for the matters you wrote about: It is good for a man not to marry.*a* ²But since there is so much immorality, each man should have his own wife, and each woman her own husband. ³The husband should fulfill his marital duty to his wife, and likewise the wife to her husband. ⁴The wife's body does not belong to her alone but also to her husband. In the same way, the husband's body does not belong to him alone but also to his wife. ⁵Do not deprive each other except by mutual consent and for a time, so that you may devote yourselves to prayer. Then come together again so that Satan will not tempt you because of your lack of self-control. ⁶I say this as a concession, not as a command. ⁷I wish that all men were as I am. But each man has his own gift from God; one has this gift, another has that.

⁸Now to the unmarried and the widows I say: It is good for them to stay unmarried, as I am. ⁹But if they cannot control themselves, they should marry, for it is better to marry than to burn with passion.

¹⁰To the married I give this command (not I, but the Lord): A wife must not separate from her husband. ¹¹But if she does, she must remain unmarried or else be reconciled to her husband. And a husband must not divorce his wife.

¹²To the rest I say this (I, not the Lord): If any brother has a wife who is not a believer and she is willing to live with him, he must not divorce her. ¹³And if a woman has a husband who is not a believer and he is willing to live with her, she must not divorce him. ¹⁴For the unbelieving husband has been sanctified through his wife, and the unbelieving wife has been sanctified through her believing husband. Otherwise your children would be unclean, but as it is, they are holy.

¹⁵But if the unbeliever leaves, let him do so. A believing man or woman is not bound in such circumstances; God has called us to live in peace. ¹⁶How do you know, wife, whether you will save your husband? Or, how do you know, husband, whether you will save your wife?

¹⁷Nevertheless, each one should retain the place in life that the Lord assigned to him and to which God has called him. This is the rule I lay down in all the churches. ¹⁸Was a man already circumcised when he was called? He should not become uncircumcised. Was a man uncircumcised when he was called? He should not be circumcised. ¹⁹Circumcision is nothing and uncircumcision is nothing. Keeping God's commands is what counts. ²⁰Each one should remain in the situation which he was in when God called him. ²¹Were you a slave when you were called? Don't let it trouble you—although if you can gain your freedom, do so. ²²For he who was a slave when he was called by the Lord is the Lord's freedman; similarly, he who was a free man when he was called is Christ's slave. ²³You were bought at a price; do not become slaves of men. ²⁴Brothers, each man, as responsible to God, should remain in the situation God called him to.

²⁵Now about virgins: I have no command from the Lord, but I give a judgment as one who by the Lord's mercy is trustworthy. ²⁶Because of the present crisis, I think that it is good for you to remain as you are. ²⁷Are you married? Do not seek a divorce. Are you unmarried? Do not look for a wife. ²⁸But if you do marry, you have not sinned; and if a virgin marries, she has not sinned. But those who marry will face many troubles in this life, and I want to spare you this.

²⁹What I mean, brothers, is that the time is short. From now on those who have wives should live as if they had none; ³⁰those who mourn, as if they did not; those who are happy, as if they were not; those who buy something, as if it were not theirs to keep; ³¹those who use the things of the world, as if not engrossed in them. For this world in its present form is passing away.

³²I would like you to be free from concern. An unmarried man is concerned about the Lord's affairs—how he can please the Lord. ³³But a married man is concerned about the affairs of this world—how he can please his wife— ³⁴and his interests are divided. An unmarried woman or virgin is concerned about the Lord's affairs: Her aim is to be devoted to the Lord in both body and spirit. But a married woman is concerned about the affairs of

*a*1 Or "*It is good for a man not to have sexual relations with a woman.*"

1 Corinthians 7:1–2

Now for the matters you wrote about: It is good for a man not to marry. But since there is so much immorality, each man should have his own wife, and each woman her own husband.

reflection

1 Are you surprised that God talks about sex in such a candid way? Why?

2 Do you find yourself focusing on God's restrictions rather than on what God encourages you to enjoy? How does this impact your view of God?

3 What has God called you to do right now? Ask God to give you joy in that thing and to keep Satan from tempting you away from the pleasures God's calling brings.

RELATED READINGS

Genesis 2:18–25;
1 Corinthians 6:12–20;
7:25–40;
1 Peter 3:1–7

Read: 1 Corinthians 7:1–17

WHAT ARE YOU DOING right now that is keeping you from enjoying what God has for you? Satan will turn this plot around in a number of ways. For example, he often tries to get us so bothered by the one thing we have been commanded by God not to do, that we spend far too much time thinking about it. Ultimately it distracts us from obeying God in other areas.

We become so preoccupied with certain restrictions that God has placed on our lives that we forget, just as Eve did, that those restrictions are for our own good. Without them we would be in big trouble. Sometimes single women and men are so consumed with "trying not to have sex," or at least trying not to go too far, that they are not enjoying the gift of being single. They see physical intimacy as something that they have to spend inordinate amounts of time and attention trying to avoid. Although they should indeed avoid having sex outside of marriage, singles often get so upset about the fact that they cannot have sex that they miss out on what God does want them to be doing in their relationship—learning about one another.

What joy there is in simply enjoying what God has for us right now. But in order to do that, we must not be consumed with what He has asked us *not* to do. The rate of adultery in our country has skyrocketed in recent years, and this can, at least in part, be attributed to a simple thing: Satan has dangled the carrot of single-ness before the eyes of those who are married, and they have been carried away by curiosity and craving.

If you are single, he tries to cause you to become powerless in your singleness. If you are married, he seeks to make you power-less in your marriage. If you are working in the ministry, he wants you to yearn for more money. If you have children, he wants you to long to be free to do whatever *you* want, at the risk of abandoning your family. Whatever it is that God has *not* called you to do right now in your life, Satan will do his best to entice you with that very thing. Beware!

—*Priscilla Evans Shirer*

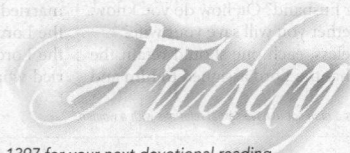

this world—how she can please her husband. ³⁵I am saying this for your own good, not to restrict you, but that you may live in a right way in undivided devotion to the Lord.

³⁶If anyone thinks he is acting improperly toward the virgin he is engaged to, and if she is getting along in years and he feels he ought to marry, he should do as he wants. He is not sinning. They should get married. ³⁷But the man who has settled the matter in his own mind, who is under no compulsion but has control over his own will, and who has made up his mind not to marry the virgin—this man also does the right thing. ³⁸So then, he who marries the virgin does right, but he who does not marry her does even better.^a

³⁹A woman is bound to her husband as long as he lives. But if her husband dies, she is free to marry anyone she wishes, but he must belong to the Lord. ⁴⁰In my judgment, she is happier if she stays as she is—and I think that I too have the Spirit of God.

Food Sacrificed to Idols

8 Now about food sacrificed to idols: We know that we all possess knowledge.^b Knowledge puffs up, but love builds up. ²The man who thinks he knows something does not yet know as he ought to know. ³But the man who loves God is known by God.

⁴So then, about eating food sacrificed to idols: We know that an idol is nothing at all in the world and that there is no God but one. ⁵For even if there are so-called gods, whether in heaven or on earth (as indeed there are many "gods" and many "lords"), ⁶yet for us there is but one God, the Father, from whom all things came and for whom we live; and there is but one Lord, Jesus Christ, through whom all things came and through whom we live.

⁷But not everyone knows this. Some people are still so accustomed to idols that when they eat such food they think of it as having been sacrificed to an idol, and since their conscience is weak, it is defiled. ⁸But food does not bring us near to God; we are no worse if we do not eat, and no better if we do.

⁹Be careful, however, that the exercise of your freedom does not become a stumbling block to the weak. ¹⁰For if anyone with a weak conscience sees you who have this knowledge eating in an idol's temple, won't he be emboldened to eat what has been sacrificed to idols? ¹¹So this weak brother, for whom Christ died, is destroyed by your knowledge. ¹²When you sin against your brothers in this way and wound their weak conscience, you sin against Christ. ¹³Therefore, if what I eat causes my brother to fall into sin, I will never eat meat again, so that I will not cause him to fall.

The Rights of an Apostle

9 Am I not free? Am I not an apostle? Have I not seen Jesus our Lord? Are you not the result of my work in the Lord? ²Even though I may not be an apostle to others, surely I am to you! For you are the seal of my apostleship in the Lord.

³This is my defense to those who sit in judgment on me. ⁴Don't we have the right to food and drink? ⁵Don't we have the right to take a believing wife along with us, as do the other apostles and the Lord's brothers and Cephas^c? ⁶Or is it only I and Barnabas who must work for a living?

⁷Who serves as a soldier at his own expense? Who plants a vineyard and does not eat of its grapes? Who tends a flock and does not drink of the milk? ⁸Do I say this merely from a human point of view? Doesn't the Law say the same thing? ⁹For it is written in the Law of Moses: "Do not muzzle an ox while it is treading out the grain."^d Is it about oxen that God is concerned? ¹⁰Surely he says this for us, doesn't he? Yes, this was written for us, because when the plowman plows and the thresher threshes, they ought to do so in the hope of sharing in the harvest. ¹¹If we have sown spiritual seed among you, is it too much if we reap a material harvest from you? ¹²If others have this right of support from you, shouldn't we have it all the more?

But we did not use this right. On the contrary, we put up with anything rather than hinder the gospel of Christ. ¹³Don't you know that

---

^a36–38 Or ³⁶*If anyone thinks he is not treating his daughter properly, and if she is getting along in years, and he feels she ought to marry, he should do as he wants. He is not sinning. He should let her get married.* ³⁷*But the man who has settled the matter in his own mind, who is under no compulsion but has control over his own will, and who has made up his mind to keep the virgin unmarried—this man also does the right thing.* ³⁸*So then, he who gives his virgin in marriage does right, but he who does not give her in marriage does even better.* ^b1 Or *"We all possess knowledge," as you say* ^c5 That is, Peter ^d9 Deut. 25:4

those who work in the temple get their food from the temple, and those who serve at the altar share in what is offered on the altar? [14]In the same way, the Lord has commanded that those who preach the gospel should receive their living from the gospel.

[15]But I have not used any of these rights. And I am not writing this in the hope that you will do such things for me. I would rather die than have anyone deprive me of this boast. [16]Yet when I preach the gospel, I cannot boast, for I am compelled to preach. Woe to me if I do not preach the gospel! [17]If I preach voluntarily, I have a reward; if not voluntarily, I am simply discharging the trust committed to me. [18]What then is my reward? Just this: that in preaching the gospel I may offer it free of charge, and so not make use of my rights in preaching it.

[19]Though I am free and belong to no man, I make myself a slave to everyone, to win as many as possible. [20]To the Jews I became like a Jew, to win the Jews. To those under the law I became like one under the law (though I myself am not under the law), so as to win those under the law. [21]To those not having the law I became like one not having the law (though I am not free from God's law but am under Christ's law), so as to win those not having the law. [22]To the weak I became weak, to win the weak. I have become all things to all men so that by all possible means I might save some. [23]I do all this for the sake of the gospel, that I may share in its blessings.

[24]Do you not know that in a race all the runners run, but only one gets the prize? Run in such a way as to get the prize. [25]Everyone who competes in the games goes into strict training. They do it to get a crown that will not last; but we do it to get a crown that will last forever. [26]Therefore I do not run like a man running aimlessly; I do not fight like a man beating the air. [27]No, I beat my body and make it my slave so that after I have preached to others, I myself will not be disqualified for the prize.

Warnings From Israel's History

10 For I do not want you to be ignorant of the fact, brothers, that our forefathers were all under the cloud and that they all passed through the sea. [2]They were all baptized into Moses in the cloud and in the sea. [3]They all ate the same spiritual food [4]and drank the same spiritual drink; for they drank from the spiritual rock that accompanied them, and that rock was Christ. [5]Nevertheless, God was not pleased with most of them; their bodies were scattered over the desert.

[6]Now these things occurred as examples[a] to keep us from setting our hearts on evil things as they did. [7]Do not be idolaters, as some of them were; as it is written: "The people sat down to eat and drink and got up to indulge in pagan revelry."[b] [8]We should not commit sexual immorality, as some of them did—and in one day twenty-three thousand of them died. [9]We should not test the Lord, as some of them did—and were killed by snakes. [10]And do not grumble, as some of them did—and were killed by the destroying angel.

[11]These things happened to them as examples and were written down as warnings for us, on whom the fulfillment of the ages has come. [12]So, if you think you are standing firm, be careful that you don't fall! [13]No temptation has seized you except what is common to man. And God is faithful; he will not let you be tempted beyond what you can bear. But when you are tempted, he will also provide a way out so that you can stand up under it.

1 Corinthians 10:13

God Is Faithful

And God is faithful; he will not let you be tempted beyond what you can bear. But when you are tempted, he will also provide a way out so that you can stand up under it.

Idol Feasts and the Lord's Supper

[14]Therefore, my dear friends, flee from idolatry. [15]I speak to sensible people; judge for yourselves what I say. [16]Is not the cup of thanksgiving for which we give thanks a participation in the blood of Christ? And is not the bread that we break a participation in the body of Christ? [17]Because there is one loaf, we,

[a]6 Or *types*; also in verse 11   [b]7 Exodus 32:6

Unbelievable

RHODA

"YOU'RE OUT OF YOUR MIND."

That's the first thing the other believers said when she ran into the room, stammering that Peter was standing at the front door.

"Excuse me . . . but it's . . . it's *him*."

"Who are you talking about, Rhoda?" they countered.

"Pet–P–P–Peter! He's there. I mean, he's here."

So much for being the bearer of good news. Instead of elation, they met her announcement with frustration. A servant girl did not always get a lot of respect. Sure, it was a lowly job. But why did they think she would lie about something like this?

Rhoda hardly knew what to do with their cavalier response. She even reached down and pinched herself to make sure she wasn't dreaming.

No, it was real. How could she get them to believe her?

Of course, she could hardly believe it herself. One minute several houseguests had gathered together at her mistress's house to pray for Peter's release from prison. The next minute, she'd heard Peter's authoritative voice just outside.

"Rhoda! Open the door!"

Could she dare to believe the power of God unfolding before her eyes? Would she? Should she? She knew James was already dead by Herod's decree. And Peter was scheduled to be next in line for public trial after the Passover. But she was certain it was Peter's voice she'd heard—alive and well. And that could only mean one thing: God himself had rescued Peter and sent him to their home, her home.

In an instant, she had flung open the door of her heart to believe in the miracle. But in her enthusiasm, she had left Peter standing outside.

"Rhoda! Open the door!"

—Prayer—

God, your blessings and miracles surround me every day. Open my eyes to the wonder of your presence.

When she recognized Peter's voice, she was so overjoyed she ran back without opening it and exclaimed, "Peter is at the door!"

Acts 12:14

ASSIGNED READING:

Acts 12:1–17

Weekend

Go to page 1401 for your next devotional reading.

who are many, are one body, for we all partake of the one loaf.

18 Consider the people of Israel: Do not those who eat the sacrifices participate in the altar? 19 Do I mean then that a sacrifice offered to an idol is anything, or that an idol is anything? 20 No, but the sacrifices of pagans are offered to demons, not to God, and I do not want you to be participants with demons. 21 You cannot drink the cup of the Lord and the cup of demons too; you cannot have a part in both the Lord's table and the table of demons. 22 Are we trying to arouse the Lord's jealousy? Are we stronger than he?

The Believer's Freedom

23 "Everything is permissible"—but not everything is beneficial. "Everything is permissible"—but not everything is constructive. 24 Nobody should seek his own good, but the good of others.

25 Eat anything sold in the meat market without raising questions of conscience, 26 for, "The earth is the Lord's, and everything in it."[a]

27 If some unbeliever invites you to a meal and you want to go, eat whatever is put before you without raising questions of conscience. 28 But if anyone says to you, "This has been offered in sacrifice," then do not eat it, both for the sake of the man who told you and for conscience' sake[b]— 29 the other man's conscience, I mean, not yours. For why should my freedom be judged by another's conscience? 30 If I take part in the meal with thankfulness, why am I denounced because of something I thank God for?

31 So whether you eat or drink or whatever you do, do it all for the glory of God. 32 Do not cause anyone to stumble, whether Jews, Greeks or the church of God— 33 even as I try to please everybody in every way. For I am not seeking my own good but the good of many, so that **11** they may be saved. 1 Follow my example, as I follow the example of Christ.

Propriety in Worship

2 I praise you for remembering me in everything and for holding to the teachings,[c] just as I passed them on to you.

3 Now I want you to realize that the head of every man is Christ, and the head of the woman is man, and the head of Christ is God. 4 Every man who prays or prophesies with his head covered dishonors his head. 5 And every woman who prays or prophesies with her head uncovered dishonors her head—it is just as though her head were shaved. 6 If a woman does not cover her head, she should have her hair cut off; and if it is a disgrace for a woman to have her hair cut or shaved off, she should cover her head. 7 A man ought not to cover his head,[d] since he is the image and glory of God; but the woman is the glory of man. 8 For man did not come from woman, but woman from man; 9 neither was man created for woman, but woman for man. 10 For this reason, and because of the angels, the woman ought to have a sign of authority on her head.

11 In the Lord, however, woman is not independent of man, nor is man independent of woman. 12 For as woman came from man, so also man is born of woman. But everything comes from God. 13 Judge for yourselves: Is it proper for a woman to pray to God with her head uncovered? 14 Does not the very nature of things teach you that if a man has long hair, it is a disgrace to him, 15 but that if a woman has long hair, it is her glory? For long hair is given to her as a covering. 16 If anyone wants to be contentious about this, we have no other practice—nor do the churches of God.

The Lord's Supper

17 In the following directives I have no praise for you, for your meetings do more harm than good. 18 In the first place, I hear that when you come together as a church, there are divisions among you, and to some extent I believe it. 19 No doubt there have to be differences among you to show which of you have God's approval. 20 When you come together, it is not the Lord's Supper you eat, 21 for as you eat, each of you goes ahead without waiting for anybody else. One remains hungry, another gets drunk. 22 Don't you have homes to eat and drink in? Or do you despise the church of God and humili-

---

a26 Psalm 24:1   *b28* Some manuscripts *conscience' sake, for "the earth is the Lord's and everything in it"*   *c2* Or *traditions*   *d4–7* Or *4 Every man who prays or prophesies with long hair dishonors his head. 5 And every woman who prays or prophesies with no covering of hair on her head dishonors her head—she is just like one of the "shorn women." 6 If a woman has no covering, let her be for now with short hair, but since it is a disgrace for a woman to have her hair shorn or shaved, she should grow it again. 7 A man ought not to have long hair* ate those who have nothing? What shall I say to you? Shall I praise you for this? Certainly not!

²³For I received from the Lord what I also passed on to you: The Lord Jesus, on the night he was betrayed, took bread, ²⁴and when he had given thanks, he broke it and said, "This is my body, which is for you; do this in remembrance of me." ²⁵In the same way, after supper he took the cup, saying, "This cup is the new covenant in my blood; do this, whenever you drink it, in remembrance of me." ²⁶For whenever you eat this bread and drink this cup, you proclaim the Lord's death until he comes.

²⁷Therefore, whoever eats the bread or drinks the cup of the Lord in an unworthy manner will be guilty of sinning against the body and blood of the Lord. ²⁸A man ought to examine himself before he eats of the bread and drinks of the cup. ²⁹For anyone who eats and drinks without recognizing the body of the Lord eats and drinks judgment on himself. ³⁰That is why many among you are weak and sick, and a number of you have fallen asleep. ³¹But if we judged ourselves, we would not come under judgment. ³²When we are judged by the Lord, we are being disciplined so that we will not be condemned with the world.

³³So then, my brothers, when you come together to eat, wait for each other. ³⁴If anyone is hungry, he should eat at home, so that when you meet together it may not result in judgment.

And when I come I will give further directions.

Spiritual Gifts

12 Now about spiritual gifts, brothers, I do not want you to be ignorant. ²You know that when you were pagans, somehow or other you were influenced and led astray to mute idols. ³Therefore I tell you that no one who is speaking by the Spirit of God says, "Jesus be cursed," and no one can say, "Jesus is Lord," except by the Holy Spirit.

⁴There are different kinds of gifts, but the same Spirit. ⁵There are different kinds of service, but the same Lord. ⁶There are different kinds of working, but the same God works all of them in all men.

⁷Now to each one the manifestation of the Spirit is given for the common good. ⁸To one there is given through the Spirit the message of wisdom, to another the message of knowledge by means of the same Spirit, ⁹to another faith by the same Spirit, to another gifts of healing by that one Spirit, ¹⁰to another miraculous powers, to another prophecy, to another distinguishing between spirits, to another speaking in different kinds of tongues,ᵃ and to still another the interpretation of tongues.ᵃ ¹¹All these are the work of one and the same Spirit, and he gives them to each one, just as he determines.

One Body, Many Parts

¹²The body is a unit, though it is made up of many parts; and though all its parts are many, they form one body. So it is with Christ. ¹³For we were all baptized byᵇ one Spirit into one body—whether Jews or Greeks, slave or free— and we were all given the one Spirit to drink.

¹⁴Now the body is not made up of one part but of many. ¹⁵If the foot should say, "Because I am not a hand, I do not belong to the body," it would not for that reason cease to be part of the body. ¹⁶And if the ear should say, "Because I am not an eye, I do not belong to the body," it would not for that reason cease to be part of the body. ¹⁷If the whole body were an eye, where would the sense of hearing be? If the whole body were an ear, where would the sense of smell be? ¹⁸But in fact God has arranged the parts in the body, every one of them, just as he wanted them to be. ¹⁹If they were all one part, where would the body be? ²⁰As it is, there are many parts, but one body.

²¹The eye cannot say to the hand, "I don't need you!" And the head cannot say to the feet, "I don't need you!" ²²On the contrary, those parts of the body that seem to be weaker are indispensable, ²³and the parts that we think are less honorable we treat with special honor. And the parts that are unpresentable are treated with special modesty, ²⁴while our presentable parts need no special treatment. But God has combined the members of the body and has given greater honor to the parts that lacked it, ²⁵so that there should be no division in the body, but that its parts should have equal concern for each other. ²⁶If one part suffers, every part

ᵃ10 Or *languages*; also in verse 28 ᵇ13 Or *with*; or *in* suffers with it; if one part is honored, every part rejoices with it.

27 Now you are the body of Christ, and each one of you is a part of it. **28** And in the church God has appointed first of all apostles, second prophets, third teachers, then workers of miracles, also those having gifts of healing, those able to help others, those with gifts of administration, and those speaking in different kinds of tongues. **29** Are all apostles? Are all prophets? Are all teachers? Do all work miracles? **30** Do all have gifts of healing? Do all speak in tongues*a*? Do all interpret? **31** But eagerly desire*b* the greater gifts.

Love

And now I will show you the most excellent way.

13 If I speak in the tongues*c* of men and of angels, but have not love, I am only a resounding gong or a clanging cymbal. **2** If I have the gift of prophecy and can fathom all mysteries and all knowledge, and if I have a faith that can move mountains, but have not love, I am nothing. **3** If I give all I possess to the poor and surrender my body to the flames,*d* but have not love, I gain nothing.

4 Love is patient, love is kind. It does not envy, it does not boast, it is not proud. **5** It is not rude, it is not self-seeking, it is not easily angered, it keeps no record of wrongs. **6** Love does not delight in evil but rejoices with the truth. **7** It always protects, always trusts, always hopes, always perseveres.

8 Love never fails. But where there are prophecies, they will cease; where there are tongues, they will be stilled; where there is knowledge, it will pass away. **9** For we know in part and we prophesy in part, **10** but when perfection comes, the imperfect disappears. **11** When I was a child, I talked like a child, I thought like a child, I reasoned like a child. When I became a man, I put childish ways behind me. **12** Now we see but a poor reflection as in a mirror; then we shall see face to face. Now I know in part; then I shall know fully, even as I am fully known.

13 And now these three remain: faith, hope and love. But the greatest of these is love.

Gifts of Prophecy and Tongues

14 Follow the way of love and eagerly desire spiritual gifts, especially the gift of prophecy. **2** For anyone who speaks in a tongue*e* does not speak to men but to God. Indeed, no one understands him; he utters mysteries with his spirit.*f* **3** But everyone who prophesies speaks to men for their strengthening, encouragement and comfort. **4** He who speaks in a tongue edifies himself, but he who prophesies edifies the church. **5** I would like every one of you to speak in tongues,*g* but I would rather have you prophesy. He who prophesies is greater than one who speaks in tongues,*g* unless he interprets, so that the church may be edified.

6 Now, brothers, if I come to you and speak in tongues, what good will I be to you, unless I bring you some revelation or knowledge or prophecy or word of instruction? **7** Even in the case of lifeless things that make sounds, such as the flute or harp, how will anyone know what tune is being played unless there is a distinction in the notes? **8** Again, if the trumpet does not sound a clear call, who will get ready for battle? **9** So it is with you. Unless you speak intelligible words with your tongue, how will anyone know what you are saying? You will just be speaking into the air. **10** Undoubtedly there are all sorts of languages in the world, yet none of them is without meaning. **11** If then I do not grasp the meaning of what someone is saying, I am a foreigner to the speaker, and he is a foreigner to me. **12** So it is with you. Since you are eager to have spiritual gifts, try to excel in gifts that build up the church.

13 For this reason anyone who speaks in a tongue should pray that he may interpret what he says. **14** For if I pray in a tongue, my spirit prays, but my mind is unfruitful. **15** So what shall I do? I will pray with my spirit, but I will also pray with my mind; I will sing with my spirit, but I will also sing with my mind. **16** If you are praising God with your spirit, how can one who finds himself among those who do not understand*h* say "Amen" to your thanksgiving, since he does not know what you are saying? **17** You may be giving thanks well enough, but the other man is not edified.

*a*30 Or *other languages*   *b*31 Or *But you are eagerly desiring*   *c*1 Or *languages*   *d*3 Some early manuscripts *body that I may boast*   *e*2 Or *another language;* also in verses 4, 13, 14, 19, 26 and 27   *f*2 Or *by the Spirit*   *g*5 Or *other languages;* also in verses 6, 18, 22, 23 and 39   *h*16 Or *among the inquirers*

One-Hit Wonderful

Read: 1 Corinthians 13:1–13

IN THE MUSIC INDUSTRY, a one-hit wonder is a musician famous for one smash hit. Their tunes are faddish and their popularity short-lived. Future generations adopt them because they define an era. Dancers know the moves to *Disco Duck*, *The Monster Mash* and *The Macarena*. The Surfaris' song *Wipe Out* captured California's beach scene in the 60s. People from the 70s can't forget Carl Douglas's *Kung Fu Fighting*. Those hits may have been great songs, but the musicians weren't able to keep the momentum going. And thus they aren't counted among the great acts of their eras.

In 1 Corinthians 13:1–3, Paul listed some attributes that fall into the great, but not greatest, category of one-hit wonders known to human beings: faith and hope. But nothing can compete with the greatest attribute of all: love. In God's book, love is one-hit wonderful. If you're going to be known for anything, let it be love. Your lifelong goal should be to embody the diverse characteristics of love found in 1 Corinthians 13.

Unfortunately, the English language is limited to only one word to describe the many types of love. As a result, our understanding of genuine love is inadequate; we tend to confuse one kind with another. The Greek language, however, has several words for *love*, such as *eros*, meaning romantic love, and *philia*, or friendship. And there are others. But Paul used the Greek word *agape* to describe love that is divine; this type of love originates with God. It is eternal; it never fails. Verses 4–7 describe the many facets of this preeminent type of love: patience, kindness, perseverance and hope.

Here's a challenge for you: Live today seeking the greatest of all attributes. Try to express the heart of Biblical love in all that you say and do. Let today be your love song, your one-hit wonderful to everyone you encounter.

Go to page 1404 for your next devotional reading.

1 Corinthians 13:13

And now these three remain: faith, hope and love. But the greatest of these is love.

reflection

1 How has God shown his love for you in a very tangible, personal way? How can you show him you love him in return?

2 Review verses 4–7. Which aspect of love is the most difficult for you to express?

3 How will you show love to those you encounter today?

RELATED READINGS

Matthew 5:43–48;
John 15:9–17;
1 John 4:7–21

"Love is . . . the gift of oneself."

Jean Anouilh

[18]I thank God that I speak in tongues more than all of you. [19]But in the church I would rather speak five intelligible words to instruct others than ten thousand words in a tongue.

[20]Brothers, stop thinking like children. In regard to evil be infants, but in your thinking be adults. [21]In the Law it is written:

> "Through men of strange
>   tongues
> and through the lips of
>   foreigners
> I will speak to this people,
>   but even then they will
>   not listen to me,"[a]

says the Lord.

[22]Tongues, then, are a sign, not for believers but for unbelievers; prophecy, however, is for believers, not for unbelievers. [23]So if the whole church comes together and everyone speaks in tongues, and some who do not understand[b] or some unbelievers come in, will they not say that you are out of your mind? [24]But if an unbeliever or someone who does not understand[c] comes in while everybody is prophesying, he will be convinced by all that he is a sinner and will be judged by all, [25]and the secrets of his heart will be laid bare. So he will fall down and worship God, exclaiming, "God is really among you!"

Orderly Worship

[26]What then shall we say, brothers? When you come together, everyone has a hymn, or a word of instruction, a revelation, a tongue or an interpretation. All of these must be done for the strengthening of the church. [27]If anyone speaks in a tongue, two—or at the most three—should speak, one at a time, and someone must interpret. [28]If there is no interpreter, the speaker should keep quiet in the church and speak to himself and God.

[29]Two or three prophets should speak, and the others should weigh carefully what is said. [30]And if a revelation comes to someone who is sitting down, the first speaker should stop. [31]For you can all prophesy in turn so that every-

one may be instructed and encouraged. [32]The spirits of prophets are subject to the control of prophets. [33]For God is not a God of disorder but of peace.

1 Corinthians 14:33

God Is Peaceful

For God is not a God of disorder but of peace.

As in all the congregations of the saints, [34]women should remain silent in the churches. They are not allowed to speak, but must be in submission, as the Law says. [35]If they want to inquire about something, they should ask their own husbands at home; for it is disgraceful for a woman to speak in the church.

[36]Did the word of God originate with you? Or are you the only people it has reached? [37]If anybody thinks he is a prophet or spiritually gifted, let him acknowledge that what I am writing to you is the Lord's command. [38]If he ignores this, he himself will be ignored.[d]

[39]Therefore, my brothers, be eager to prophesy, and do not forbid speaking in tongues. [40]But everything should be done in a fitting and orderly way.

The Resurrection of Christ

15 Now, brothers, I want to remind you of the gospel I preached to you, which you received and on which you have taken your stand. [2]By this gospel you are saved, if you hold firmly to the word I preached to you. Otherwise, you have believed in vain.

[3]For what I received I passed on to you as of first importance[e]: that Christ died for our sins according to the Scriptures, [4]that he was buried, that he was raised on the third day according to the Scriptures, [5]and that he appeared to Peter,[f] and then to the Twelve. [6]After that, he appeared to more than five hundred of the brothers at the same time, most of whom are still living, though some have fallen asleep. [7]Then he appeared to James, then to all the apostles, [8]and last of all he appeared to me also, as to one abnormally born.

[9]For I am the least of the apostles and do not even deserve to be called an apostle, because I persecuted the church of God. [10]But by the grace of God I am what I am, and his grace to

---

[a]21 Isaiah 28:11,12   [b]23 Or *some inquirers*   [c]24 Or *or some inquirer*   [d]38 Some manuscripts *If he is ignorant of this, let him be ignorant*   [e]3 Or *you at the first*   [f]5 Greek *Cephas*

me was not without effect. No, I worked harder than all of them—yet not I, but the grace of God that was with me. [11]Whether, then, it was I or they, this is what we preach, and this is what you believed.

The Resurrection of the Dead

[12]But if it is preached that Christ has been raised from the dead, how can some of you say that there is no resurrection of the dead? [13]If there is no resurrection of the dead, then not even Christ has been raised. [14]And if Christ has not been raised, our preaching is useless and so is your faith. [15]More than that, we are then found to be false witnesses about God, for we have testified about God that he raised Christ from the dead. But he did not raise him if in fact the dead are not raised. [16]For if the dead are not raised, then Christ has not been raised either. [17]And if Christ has not been raised, your faith is futile; you are still in your sins. [18]Then those also who have fallen asleep in Christ are lost. [19]If only for this life we have hope in Christ, we are to be pitied more than all men.

[20]But Christ has indeed been raised from the dead, the firstfruits of those who have fallen asleep. [21]For since death came through a man, the resurrection of the dead comes also through a man. [22]For as in Adam all die, so in Christ all will be made alive. [23]But each in his own turn: Christ, the firstfruits; then, when he comes, those who belong to him. [24]Then the end will come, when he hands over the kingdom to God the Father after he has destroyed all dominion, authority and power. [25]For he must reign until he has put all his enemies under his feet. [26]The last enemy to be destroyed is death. [27]For he "has put everything under his feet."[a] Now when it says that "everything" has been put under him, it is clear that this does not include God himself, who put everything under Christ. [28]When he has done this, then the Son himself will be made subject to him who put everything under him, so that God may be all in all.

[29]Now if there is no resurrection, what will those do who are baptized for the dead? If the dead are not raised at all, why are people baptized for them? [30]And as for us, why do we endanger ourselves every hour? [31]I die every day—I mean that, brothers—just as surely as I glory over you in Christ Jesus our Lord. [32]If I fought wild beasts in Ephesus for merely human reasons, what have I gained? If the dead are not raised,

> "Let us eat and drink,
>   for tomorrow we die."[b]

[33]Do not be misled: "Bad company corrupts good character." [34]Come back to your senses as you ought, and stop sinning; for there are some who are ignorant of God—I say this to your shame.

The Resurrection Body

[35]But someone may ask, "How are the dead raised? With what kind of body will they come?" [36]How foolish! What you sow does not come to life unless it dies. [37]When you sow, you do not plant the body that will be, but just a seed, perhaps of wheat or of something else. [38]But God gives it a body as he has determined, and to each kind of seed he gives its own body. [39]All flesh is not the same: Men have one kind of flesh, animals have another, birds another and fish another. [40]There are also heavenly bodies and there are earthly bodies; but the splendor of the heavenly bodies is one kind, and the splendor of the earthly bodies is another. [41]The sun has one kind of splendor, the moon another and the stars another; and star differs from star in splendor.

[42]So will it be with the resurrection of the dead. The body that is sown is perishable, it is raised imperishable; [43]it is sown in dishonor, it is raised in glory; it is sown in weakness, it is raised in power; [44]it is sown a natural body, it is raised a spiritual body.

If there is a natural body, there is also a spiritual body. [45]So it is written: "The first man Adam became a living being"[c]; the last Adam, a life-giving spirit. [46]The spiritual did not come first, but the natural, and after that the spiritual. [47]The first man was of the dust of the earth, the second man from heaven. [48]As

---

[a]27 Psalm 8:6   [b]32 Isaiah 22:13   [c]45 Gen. 2:7

Why the Resurrection Matters

1 Corinthians 15:54

When the perishable has been clothed with the imperishable, and the mortal with immortality, then the saying that is written will come true: "Death has been swallowed up in victory."

reflection

1 Have you ever experienced a loss like that of Sandra or C. S. Lewis? If so, what emotions and questions did you experience?

2 How does it help you to know that in heaven there is no sorrow?

3 If you don't currently live as if the resurrection is true, how could you begin to make it a daily source of encouragement and strength?

RELATED READINGS

Romans 6:4–11;
1 Thessalonians 4:13–18;
1 Peter 1:3–7;
Revelation 21:1–4

"Death is the golden key that opens the palace of eternity."

John Milton

Read: 1 Corinthians 15:1–58

SANDRA'S HUSBAND OF TEN YEARS died of a sudden heart attack last year, leaving her to raise three daughters alone. On certain days, she keeps busy enough to keep the tears at bay. But on others, she wonders if she'll ever recover from the loss. She misses her husband's arms around her, his head on the pillow beside her and his guidance in making big decisions. *God, why did he have to leave us so soon?* she asks. *Why didn't you heal him so he could live to watch his girls grow up?*

C. S. Lewis asked similar questions after he lost his wife, Joy, to cancer. In *A Grief Observed*, he wrote, "How often—will it be for always?—how often will the vast emptiness astonish me like a complete novelty and make me say, 'I never realized my loss till this moment'? The same leg is cut off time after time. The first plunge of the knife into the flesh is felt again and again."

It's normal—and healthy—to grieve when those we love are taken from us. But in 1 Corinthians 15, Paul explains why the resurrection of Jesus matters so much to those who believe: This earthly chapter is not the end of the eternal story; the pain of death will one day be only a memory.

When we leave our physical bodies behind at death, we'll be ushered into God's presence, where we'll feel his healing embrace. We'll be enveloped by his all-consuming love. And suddenly, in the light of God's face, and in the face of his passion for us, all our questions, our grief—and our sorrows—will fade away. And one day, at the resurrection, our perishable bodies will be "clothed with the imperishable." We'll be transformed so that we can live forever with Christ in holy joy.

If you are grieving, hold on to the promise of the resurrection. It will make all the difference in this world—and in the next.

was the earthly man, so are those who are of the earth; and as is the man from heaven, so also are those who are of heaven. [49]And just as we have borne the likeness of the earthly man, so shall we[a] bear the likeness of the man from heaven.

[50]I declare to you, brothers, that flesh and blood cannot inherit the kingdom of God, nor does the perishable inherit the imperishable. [51]Listen, I tell you a mystery: We will not all sleep, but we will all be changed— [52]in a flash, in the twinkling of an eye, at the last trumpet. For the trumpet will sound, the dead will be raised imperishable, and we will be changed. [53]For the perishable must clothe itself with the imperishable, and the mortal with immortality. [54]When the perishable has been clothed with the imperishable, and the mortal with immortality, then the saying that is written will come true: "Death has been swallowed up in victory."[b]

[55]"Where, O death, is your victory?
    Where, O death, is your sting?"[c]

[56]The sting of death is sin, and the power of sin is the law. [57]But thanks be to God! He gives us the victory through our Lord Jesus Christ.

[58]Therefore, my dear brothers, stand firm. Let nothing move you. Always give yourselves fully to the work of the Lord, because you know that your labor in the Lord is not in vain.

The Collection for God's People

16 Now about the collection for God's people: Do what I told the Galatian churches to do. [2]On the first day of every week, each one of you should set aside a sum of money in keeping with his income, saving it up, so that when I come no collections will have to be made. [3]Then, when I arrive, I will give letters of introduction to the men you approve and send them with your gift to Jerusalem. [4]If it seems advisable for me to go also, they will accompany me.

Personal Requests

[5]After I go through Macedonia, I will come to you—for I will be going through Macedonia. [6]Perhaps I will stay with you awhile, or even spend the winter, so that you can help me on my journey, wherever I go. [7]I do not want to see you now and make only a passing visit; I hope to spend some time with you, if the Lord permits. [8]But I will stay on at Ephesus until Pentecost, [9]because a great door for effective work has opened to me, and there are many who oppose me.

[10]If Timothy comes, see to it that he has nothing to fear while he is with you, for he is carrying on the work of the Lord, just as I am. [11]No one, then, should refuse to accept him. Send him on his way in peace so that he may return to me. I am expecting him along with the brothers.

[12]Now about our brother Apollos: I strongly urged him to go to you with the brothers. He was quite unwilling to go now, but he will go when he has the opportunity.

[13]Be on your guard; stand firm in the faith; be men of courage; be strong. [14]Do everything in love.

[15]You know that the household of Stephanas were the first converts in Achaia, and they have devoted themselves to the service of the saints. I urge you, brothers, [16]to submit to such as these and to everyone who joins in the work, and labors at it. [17]I was glad when Stephanas, Fortunatus and Achaicus arrived, because they have supplied what was lacking from you. [18]For they refreshed my spirit and yours also. Such men deserve recognition.

Final Greetings

[19]The churches in the province of Asia send you greetings. Aquila and Priscilla[d] greet you warmly in the Lord, and so does the church

---

> **1 Corinthians 15:57**
>
> *God Gives Victory*
>
> But thanks be to God! He gives us the victory through our Lord Jesus Christ.

---

[a]49 Some early manuscripts *so let us* [b]54 Isaiah 25:8 [c]55 Hosea 13:14 [d]19 Greek *Prisca*, a variant of *Priscilla*

that meets at their house. **20**All the brothers here send you greetings. Greet one another with a holy kiss.

21I, Paul, write this greeting in my own hand.

22If anyone does not love the Lord—a curse be on him. Come, O Lord[a]!

23The grace of the Lord Jesus be with you.

24My love to all of you in Christ Jesus. Amen.[b]

---

[a]22 In Aramaic the expression *Come, O Lord* is *Marana tha*.   [b]24 Some manuscripts do not have *Amen*.

1406

2 Corinthians

What would you write to your children or someone you loved if you knew they were facing difficult circumstances of their own making? This is the situation Paul was in. He had traveled to Corinth in the past and had already written a severe letter of correction to the church there. *Now he needed to confront them again.* He was distressed for their comfort and salvation (see 2 Corinthians 1:6). Like a father, Paul encouraged his spiritual children to *stand firm in the faith,* represent Christ well, give generously, beware of false prophets and take every thought captive to the obedience of Christ.

Paul told his brothers and sisters in Christ that they themselves were a "letter . . . known and read by everybody." We've often heard the saying, "Read my lips." Paul is saying that *others will "read our lives."* By our actions, words and deeds, we are living, walking, breathing letters from Christ for all to read.

Author:
The apostle Paul.

Audience:
Followers of Jesus; originally written to the church in Corinth.

Date:
About A.D. 55.

Setting:
False teachers in the church at Corinth were denying Paul's authority over them as an apostle.

Verse to Remember:
You yourselves are our letter, written on our hearts, known and read by everybody. You show that you are a letter from Christ, the result of our ministry, written not with ink but with the Spirit of the living God, not on tablets of stone but on tablets of human hearts. (3:2–3)

1

Paul, an apostle of Christ Jesus by the will of God, and Timothy our brother,

To the church of God in Corinth, together with all the saints throughout Achaia:

2 Grace and peace to you from God our Father and the Lord Jesus Christ.

The God of All Comfort

3 Praise be to the God and Father of our Lord Jesus Christ, the Father of compassion and the God of all comfort, **4** who comforts us in all our troubles, so that we can comfort those in any trouble with the comfort we ourselves have received from God. **5** For just as the sufferings of

Christ flow over into our lives, so also through Christ our comfort overflows. [6]If we are distressed, it is for your comfort and salvation; if we are comforted, it is for your comfort, which produces in you patient endurance of the same sufferings we suffer. [7]And our hope for you is firm, because we know that just as you share in our sufferings, so also you share in our comfort.

[8]We do not want you to be uninformed, brothers, about the hardships we suffered in the province of Asia. We were under great pressure, far beyond our ability to endure, so that we despaired even of life. [9]Indeed, in our hearts we felt the sentence of death. But this happened that we might not rely on ourselves but on God, who raises the dead. [10]He has delivered us from such a deadly peril, and he will deliver us. On him we have set our hope that he will continue to deliver us, [11]as you help us by your prayers. Then many will give thanks on our[a] behalf for the gracious favor granted us in answer to the prayers of many.

Paul's Change of Plans

[12]Now this is our boast: Our conscience testifies that we have conducted ourselves in the world, and especially in our relations with you, in the holiness and sincerity that are from God. We have done so not according to worldly wisdom but according to God's grace. [13]For we do not write you anything you cannot read or understand. And I hope that, [14]as you have understood us in part, you will come to understand fully that you can boast of us just as we will boast of you in the day of the Lord Jesus.

[15]Because I was confident of this, I planned to visit you first so that you might benefit twice. [16]I planned to visit you on my way to Macedonia and to come back to you from Macedonia, and then to have you send me on my way to Judea. [17]When I planned this, did I do it lightly? Or do I make my plans in a worldly manner so that in the same breath I say, "Yes, yes" and "No, no"?

[18]But as surely as God is faithful, our message to you is not "Yes" and "No." [19]For the Son of God, Jesus Christ, who was preached among you by me and Silas[b] and Timothy, was not "Yes" and "No," but in him it has always been "Yes." [20]For no matter how many promises God has made, they are "Yes" in Christ. And so through him the "Amen" is spoken by us to the glory of God. [21]Now it is God who makes both us and you stand firm in Christ. He anointed us, [22]set his seal of ownership on us, and put his Spirit in our hearts as a deposit, guaranteeing what is to come.

[23]I call God as my witness that it was in order to spare you that I did not return to Corinth. [24]Not that we lord it over your faith, but we work with you for your joy, because it is by faith you stand firm. [1]So I made up my mind that I would not make another painful visit to you. [2]For if I grieve you, who is left to make me glad but you whom I have grieved? [3]I wrote as I did so that when I came I should not be distressed by those who ought to make me rejoice. I had confidence in all of you, that you would all share my joy. [4]For I wrote you out of great distress and anguish of heart and with many tears, not to grieve you but to let you know the depth of my love for you.

Forgiveness for the Sinner

[5]If anyone has caused grief, he has not so much grieved me as he has grieved all of you, to some extent—not to put it too severely. [6]The punishment inflicted on him by the majority is sufficient for him. [7]Now instead, you ought to forgive and comfort him, so that he will not be overwhelmed by excessive sorrow. [8]I urge you, therefore, to reaffirm your love for him. [9]The reason I wrote you was to see if you would stand the test and be obedient in everything. [10]If you forgive anyone, I also forgive him. And what I have forgiven—if there was anything to forgive—I have forgiven in the sight of Christ for your sake, [11]in order that Satan might not outwit us. For we are not unaware of his schemes.

Ministers of the New Covenant

[12]Now when I went to Troas to preach the gospel of Christ and found that the Lord had opened a door for me, [13]I still had no peace of mind, because I did not find my brother Titus there. So I said good-by to them and went on to Macedonia.

[14]But thanks be to God, who always leads us

---

*a*11 Many manuscripts *your*   *b*19 Greek *Silvanus*, a variant of *Silas* in triumphal procession in Christ and through us spreads everywhere the fragrance of the knowledge of him. [15]For we are to God the aroma of Christ among those who are being saved and those who are perishing. [16]To the one we are the smell of death; to the other, the fragrance of life. And who is equal to such a task? [17]Unlike so many, we do not peddle the word of God for profit. On the contrary, in Christ we speak before God with sincerity, like men sent from God.

3 Are we beginning to commend ourselves again? Or do we need, like some people, letters of recommendation to you or from you? [2]You yourselves are our letter, written on our hearts, known and read by everybody. [3]You show that you are a letter from Christ, the result of our ministry, written not with ink but with the Spirit of the living God, not on tablets of stone but on tablets of human hearts.

[4]Such confidence as this is ours through Christ before God. [5]Not that we are competent in ourselves to claim anything for ourselves, but our competence comes from God. [6]He has made us competent as ministers of a new covenant—not of the letter but of the Spirit; for the letter kills, but the Spirit gives life.

The Glory of the New Covenant

[7]Now if the ministry that brought death, which was engraved in letters on stone, came with glory, so that the Israelites could not look steadily at the face of Moses because of its glory, fading though it was, [8]will not the ministry of the Spirit be even more glorious? [9]If the ministry that condemns men is glorious, how much more glorious is the ministry that brings righteousness! [10]For what was glorious has no glory now in comparison with the surpassing glory. [11]And if what was fading away came with glory, how much greater is the glory of that which lasts!

[12]Therefore, since we have such a hope, we are very bold. [13]We are not like Moses, who would put a veil over his face to keep the Israelites from gazing at it while the radiance was fading away. [14]But their minds were made dull, for to this day the same veil remains when the old covenant is read. It has not been removed,

because only in Christ is it taken away. [15]Even to this day when Moses is read, a veil covers their hearts. [16]But whenever anyone turns to the Lord, the veil is taken away. [17]Now the Lord is the Spirit, and where the Spirit of the Lord is, there is freedom. [18]And we, who with unveiled faces all reflect[a] the Lord's glory, are being transformed into his likeness with ever-increasing glory, which comes from the Lord, who is the Spirit.

Treasures in Jars of Clay

4 Therefore, since through God's mercy we have this ministry, we do not lose heart. [2]Rather, we have renounced secret and shameful ways; we do not use deception, nor do we distort the word of God. On the contrary, by setting forth the truth plainly we commend ourselves to every man's conscience in the sight of God. [3]And even if our gospel is veiled, it is veiled to those who are perishing. [4]The god of this age has blinded the minds of unbelievers, so that they cannot see the light of the gospel of the glory of Christ, who is the image of God. [5]For we do not preach ourselves, but Jesus Christ as Lord, and ourselves as your servants for Jesus' sake. [6]For God, who said, "Let light shine out of darkness,"[b] made his light shine in our hearts to give us the light of the knowledge of the glory of God in the face of Christ.

[7]But we have this treasure in jars of clay to show that this all-surpassing power is from God and not from us. [8]We are hard pressed on every side, but not crushed; perplexed, but not in despair; [9]persecuted, but not abandoned; struck down, but not destroyed. [10]We always carry around in our body the death of Jesus, so that the life of Jesus may also be revealed in our body. [11]For we who are alive are always being given over to death for Jesus' sake, so that his life may be revealed in our mortal body. [12]So then, death is at work in us, but life is at work in you.

[13]It is written: "I believed; therefore I have spoken."[c] With that same spirit of faith we also believe and therefore speak, [14]because we know that the one who raised the Lord Jesus from the dead will also raise us with Jesus and present us with you in his presence. [15]All this is

---

[a]18 Or *contemplate*   [b]6 Gen. 1:3   [c]13 Psalm 116:10

Humble Competence

Read: 2 Corinthians 3:4–18

2 Corinthians 3:4–5

Such confidence as this is ours through Christ before God. Not that we are competent in ourselves to claim anything for ourselves, but our competence comes from God.

reflection

1 How have you found your natural abilities insufficient?

2 How does knowing that you can rely on God's competence give you confidence?

3 What might you try to do for God's kingdom if you knew you could not fail?

RELATED READINGS

Exodus 4:10–12;
2 Corinthians 12:7–10;
James 1:16–18

YOU PROBABLY KNOW SOMEONE who overestimates her competence. She might be a member of your Bible study who has a subtle way of telling others how to run their lives. Maybe it's a coworker who takes control of everything around her.

On the other end of the scale are those (often women) who revel in false humility. They tell themselves and everyone else how incapable of anything they are.

In contrast, there are those who understand that their abilities are God-given. They realize that their talents are gifts, recognize their limitations and welcome others' input. They don't think of themselves as superior but consider others' needs before their own. Being around these people frees others to be the best they can be.

True competence begins with humility, recognizing our natural abilities but acknowledging that they can only carry us so far. With that knowledge, we begin to realize that our incompetence is merely a starting point. We don't have to be perfect; we have the freedom to be the uniquely gifted, talented and competent women God created.

Elisa Morgan, president of MOPS (Mothers of Preschoolers) International, wrote:

"I'm probably the least likely person to head a mothering organization. I grew up in a broken home. My parents were divorced when I was 5. My older sister, younger brother, and I were raised by my alcoholic mother.

"While my mother meant well—truly she did—most of my memories are of me mothering her rather than her mothering me. Alcohol altered her love, turning it into something that wasn't love . . .

"Ten years ago, when I was asked to consider leading MOPS International, a vital ministry that nurtures mothers, I went straight to my knees—and then to the therapist's office. How could God use me—who had never been mothered—to nurture other mothers?

"The answer came as I gazed into the eyes of other moms around me and saw their needs mirroring my own. God seemed to take my deficits and make them my offering."

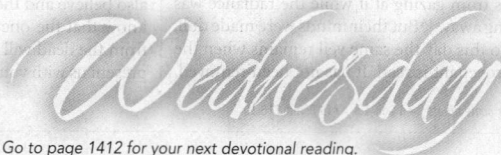

for your benefit, so that the grace that is reaching more and more people may cause thanksgiving to overflow to the glory of God.

16Therefore we do not lose heart. Though outwardly we are wasting away, yet inwardly we are being renewed day by day. 17For our light and momentary troubles are achieving for us an eternal glory that far outweighs them all. 18So we fix our eyes not on what is seen, but on what is unseen. For what is seen is temporary, but what is unseen is eternal.

Our Heavenly Dwelling

5 Now we know that if the earthly tent we live in is destroyed, we have a building from God, an eternal house in heaven, not built by human hands. 2Meanwhile we groan, longing to be clothed with our heavenly dwelling, 3because when we are clothed, we will not be found naked. 4For while we are in this tent, we groan and are burdened, because we do not wish to be unclothed but to be clothed with our heavenly dwelling, so that what is mortal may be swallowed up by life. 5Now it is God who has made us for this very purpose and has given us the Spirit as a deposit, guaranteeing what is to come.

6Therefore we are always confident and know that as long as we are at home in the body we are away from the Lord. 7We live by faith, not by sight. 8We are confident, I say, and would prefer to be away from the body and at home with the Lord. 9So we make it our goal to please him, whether we are at home in the body or away from it. 10For we must all appear before the judgment seat of Christ, that each one may receive what is due him for the things done while in the body, whether good or bad.

The Ministry of Reconciliation

11Since, then, we know what it is to fear the Lord, we try to persuade men. What we are is plain to God, and I hope it is also plain to your conscience. 12We are not trying to commend ourselves to you again, but are giving you an opportunity to take pride in us, so that you can

---

2 Corinthians 4:17

God Will Reward

For our light and
momentary troubles
are achieving for us an
eternal glory that far
outweighs them all.

---

answer those who take pride in what is seen rather than in what is in the heart. 13If we are out of our mind, it is for the sake of God; if we are in our right mind, it is for you. 14For Christ's love compels us, because we are convinced that one died for all, and therefore all died. 15And he died for all, that those who live should no longer live for themselves but for him who died for them and was raised again.

16So from now on we regard no one from a worldly point of view. Though we once regarded Christ in this way, we do so no longer. 17Therefore, if anyone is in Christ, he is a new creation; the old has gone, the new has come! 18All this is from God, who reconciled us to himself through Christ and gave us the ministry of reconciliation: 19that God was reconciling the world to himself in Christ, not counting men's sins against them. And he has committed to us the message of reconciliation. 20We are therefore Christ's ambassadors, as though God were making his appeal through us. We implore you on Christ's behalf: Be reconciled to God. 21God made him who had no sin to be sin*a* for us, so that in him we might become the righteousness of God.

6 As God's fellow workers we urge you not to receive God's grace in vain. 2For he says,

"In the time of my favor I heard you,
    and in the day of salvation I helped
        you."*b*

I tell you, now is the time of God's favor, now is the day of salvation.

Paul's Hardships

3We put no stumbling block in anyone's path, so that our ministry will not be discredited. 4Rather, as servants of God we commend ourselves in every way: in great endurance; in troubles, hardships and distresses; 5in beatings, imprisonments and riots; in hard work, sleepless nights and hunger; 6in purity, understanding, patience and kindness; in the Holy Spirit and in sincere love; 7in truthful

---

*a*21 Or *be a sin offering*   *b*2 Isaiah 49:8

Thursday

The "Me Disease"

Read: 2 Corinthians 5:1–21

2 Corinthians 5:15

And he died for all, that those who live should no longer live for themselves but for him who died for them and was raised again.

reflection

1 What causes you to become overly focused on your own life rather than looking out for the needs of others?

2 How will becoming less self-involved help you better live for Jesus Christ?

3 On whom can you shower God's love today?

RELATED READINGS

John 13:34–38;
Galatians 6:2–3;
Philippians 2:3–11;
1 John 3:16–18

LIKE A DEADLY VIRUS, the disease of self-centeredness permeates our culture. From the driver who blatantly cuts us off in traffic to the friend who talks only about her kids, her job, her *everything*, we're saturated with symptoms of the "Me Disease." The symptoms are rude behavior, selfish conversations and sheer indifference.

The deterioration in our society can be traced to decades of feeding the needs of the "me generation" that lives by the maxim, "I can do whatever I want as long as it doesn't hurt anyone." Unfortunately, the "me" attitudes aren't confined to secular society. Even many Christians quickly claim their "rights" when they're offended.

The antidote to this malady is found in today's Scripture passage: "Those who live should no longer live for themselves." But it doesn't stop there. We are instructed to live "for him who died . . . and was raised again." No higher price could have been paid to provide us with a life worth living.

So how do we follow this command in our busy and self-involved lives? How do we live for others—and, therefore, for Jesus Christ—rather than living for ourselves? We cannot physically anoint his feet with oil as the woman in Luke 7:46 did. And it isn't as if our Lord needs anything; he owns "the cattle on a thousand hills" (Psalm 50:10). The divine prescription for the "Me Disease" is this: Jesus said, "Whatever you did for one of the least of these brothers of mine, you did for me" (Matthew 25:40).

You live for Jesus when you take soup and muffins to a shut-in. You live for Jesus when you watch your neighbor's toddlers so she can run errands. You live for Jesus when you dare to look into the eyes of the down-and-out with respect and dignity. You live for Jesus when you speak up for the poor and stand up for justice. Today may our prayer be "to cease living for me and live only for Thee."

speech and in the power of God; with weapons of righteousness in the right hand and in the left; [8]through glory and dishonor, bad report and good report; genuine, yet regarded as impostors; [9]known, yet regarded as unknown; dying, and yet we live on; beaten, and yet not killed; [10]sorrowful, yet always rejoicing; poor, yet making many rich; having nothing, and yet possessing everything.

[11]We have spoken freely to you, Corinthians, and opened wide our hearts to you. [12]We are not withholding our affection from you, but you are withholding yours from us. [13]As a fair exchange—I speak as to my children—open wide your hearts also.

Do Not Be Yoked With Unbelievers

[14]Do not be yoked together with unbelievers. For what do righteousness and wickedness have in common? Or what fellowship can light have with darkness? [15]What harmony is there between Christ and Belial[a]? What does a believer have in common with an unbeliever? [16]What agreement is there between the temple of God and idols? For we are the temple of the living God. As God has said: "I will live with them and walk among them, and I will be their God, and they will be my people."[b]

[17]"Therefore come out from them
and be separate,
says the Lord.
Touch no unclean thing,
and I will receive you."[c]
[18]"I will be a Father to you,
and you will be my sons
and daughters,
says the Lord
Almighty."[d]

7 Since we have these promises, dear friends, let us purify ourselves from everything that contaminates body and spirit, perfecting holiness out of reverence for God.

Paul's Joy

[2]Make room for us in your hearts. We have wronged no one, we have corrupted no one, we have exploited no one. [3]I do not say this

to condemn you; I have said before that you have such a place in our hearts that we would live or die with you. [4]I have great confidence in you; I take great pride in you. I am greatly encouraged; in all our troubles my joy knows no bounds.

[5]For when we came into Macedonia, this body of ours had no rest, but we were harassed at every turn—conflicts on the outside, fears within. [6]But God, who comforts the downcast, comforted us by the coming of Titus, [7]and not only by his coming but also by the comfort you had given him. He told us about your longing for me, your deep sorrow, your ardent concern for me, so that my joy was greater than ever.

[8]Even if I caused you sorrow by my letter, I do not regret it. Though I did regret it—I see that my letter hurt you, but only for a little while— [9]yet now I am happy, not because you were made sorry, but because your sorrow led you to repentance. For you became sorrowful as God intended and so were not harmed in any way by us. [10]Godly sorrow brings repentance that leads to salvation and leaves no regret, but worldly sorrow brings death. [11]See what this godly sorrow has produced in you: what earnestness, what eagerness to clear yourselves, what indignation, what alarm, what longing, what concern, what readiness to see justice done. At every point you have proved yourselves to be innocent in this matter. [12]So even though I wrote to you, it was not on account of the one who did the wrong or of the injured party, but rather that before God you could see for yourselves how devoted to us you are. [13]By all this we are encouraged.

In addition to our own encouragement, we were especially delighted to see how happy Titus was, because his spirit has been refreshed by all of you. [14]I had boasted to him about you, and you have not embarrassed me. But just as everything we said to you was true, so our boasting about you to Titus has proved

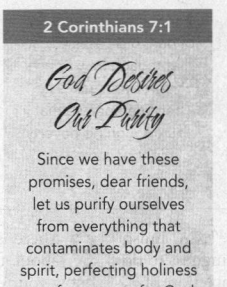

2 Corinthians 7:1

God Desires Our Purity

Since we have these promises, dear friends, let us purify ourselves from everything that contaminates body and spirit, perfecting holiness out of reverence for God.

---

[a]15 Greek *Beliar*, a variant of *Belial*   [b]16 Lev. 26:12; Jer. 32:38; Ezek. 37:27   [c]17 Isaiah 52:11; Ezek. 20:34,41   [d]18 2 Samuel 7:14; 7:8

to be true as well. ¹⁵And his affection for you is all the greater when he remembers that you were all obedient, receiving him with fear and trembling. ¹⁶I am glad I can have complete confidence in you.

Generosity Encouraged

8 And now, brothers, we want you to know about the grace that God has given the Macedonian churches. ²Out of the most severe trial, their overflowing joy and their extreme poverty welled up in rich generosity. ³For I testify that they gave as much as they were able, and even beyond their ability. Entirely on their own, ⁴they urgently pleaded with us for the privilege of sharing in this service to the saints. ⁵And they did not do as we expected, but they gave themselves first to the Lord and then to us in keeping with God's will. ⁶So we urged Titus, since he had earlier made a beginning, to bring also to completion this act of grace on your part. ⁷But just as you excel in everything—in faith, in speech, in knowledge, in complete earnestness and in your love for us*a*—see that you also excel in this grace of giving.

⁸I am not commanding you, but I want to test the sincerity of your love by comparing it with the earnestness of others. ⁹For you know the grace of our Lord Jesus Christ, that though he was rich, yet for your sakes he became poor, so that you through his poverty might become rich.

¹⁰And here is my advice about what is best for you in this matter: Last year you were the first not only to give but also to have the desire to do so. ¹¹Now finish the work, so that your eager willingness to do it may be matched by your completion of it, according to your means. ¹²For if the willingness is there, the gift is acceptable according to what one has, not according to what he does not have.

¹³Our desire is not that others might be relieved while you are hard pressed, but that

2 Corinthians 8:9

God Offers Spiritual Riches

For you know the grace of our Lord Jesus Christ, that though he was rich, yet for your sakes he became poor, so that you through his poverty might become rich.

there might be equality. ¹⁴At the present time your plenty will supply what they need, so that in turn their plenty will supply what you need. Then there will be equality, ¹⁵as it is written: "He who gathered much did not have too much, and he who gathered little did not have too little."*b*

Titus Sent to Corinth

¹⁶I thank God, who put into the heart of Titus the same concern I have for you. ¹⁷For Titus not only welcomed our appeal, but he is coming to you with much enthusiasm and on his own initiative. ¹⁸And we are sending along with him the brother who is praised by all the churches for his service to the gospel. ¹⁹What is more, he was chosen by the churches to accompany us as we carry the offering, which we administer in order to honor the Lord himself and to show our eagerness to help. ²⁰We want to avoid any criticism of the way we administer this liberal gift. ²¹For we are taking pains to do what is right, not only in the eyes of the Lord but also in the eyes of men.

²²In addition, we are sending with them our brother who has often proved to us in many ways that he is zealous, and now even more so because of his great confidence in you. ²³As for Titus, he is my partner and fellow worker among you; as for our brothers, they are representatives of the churches and an honor to Christ. ²⁴Therefore show these men the proof of your love and the reason for our pride in you, so that the churches can see it.

9 There is no need for me to write to you about this service to the saints. ²For I know your eagerness to help, and I have been boasting about it to the Macedonians, telling them that since last year you in Achaia were ready to give; and your enthusiasm has stirred most of them to action. ³But I am sending the brothers in order that our boasting about you in this matter should not prove hollow, but

*a*7 Some manuscripts *in our love for you*   *b*15 Exodus 16:18

that you may be ready, as I said you would be. [4]For if any Macedonians come with me and find you unprepared, we—not to say anything about you—would be ashamed of having been so confident. [5]So I thought it necessary to urge the brothers to visit you in advance and finish the arrangements for the generous gift you had promised. Then it will be ready as a generous gift, not as one grudgingly given.

Sowing Generously

[6]Remember this: Whoever sows sparingly will also reap sparingly, and whoever sows generously will also reap generously. [7]Each man should give what he has decided in his heart to give, not reluctantly or under compulsion, for God loves a cheerful giver. [8]And God is able to make all grace abound to you, so that in all things at all times, having all that you need, you will abound in every good work. [9]As it is written:

> "He has scattered abroad his gifts to the poor;
> his righteousness endures forever."[a]

[10]Now he who supplies seed to the sower and bread for food will also supply and increase your store of seed and will enlarge the harvest of your righteousness. [11]You will be made rich in every way so that you can be generous on every occasion, and through us your generosity will result in thanksgiving to God.

[12]This service that you perform is not only supplying the needs of God's people but is also overflowing in many expressions of thanks to God. [13]Because of the service by which you have proved yourselves, men will praise God for the obedience that accompanies your confession of the gospel of Christ, and for your generosity in sharing with them and with everyone else. [14]And in their prayers for you their hearts will go out to you, because of the surpassing grace God has given you. [15]Thanks be to God for his indescribable gift!

Paul's Defense of His Ministry

10

By the meekness and gentleness of Christ, I appeal to you—I, Paul, who am "timid" when face to face with you, but "bold" when away! [2]I beg you that when I come I may not have to be as bold as I expect to be toward some people who think that we live by the standards of this world. [3]For though we live in the world, we do not wage war as the world does. [4]The weapons we fight with are not the weapons of the world. On the contrary, they have divine power to demolish strongholds. [5]We demolish arguments and every pretension that sets itself up against the knowledge of God, and we take captive every thought to make it obedient to Christ. [6]And we will be ready to punish every act of disobedience, once your obedience is complete.

[7]You are looking only on the surface of things.[b] If anyone is confident that he belongs to Christ, he should consider again that we belong to Christ just as much as he. [8]For even if I boast somewhat freely about the authority the Lord gave us for building you up rather than pulling you down, I will not be ashamed of it. [9]I do not want to seem to be trying to frighten you with my letters. [10]For some say, "His letters are weighty and forceful, but in person he is unimpressive and his speaking amounts to nothing." [11]Such people should realize that what we are in our letters when we are absent, we will be in our actions when we are present.

[12]We do not dare to classify or compare ourselves with some who commend themselves. When they measure themselves by themselves and compare themselves with themselves, they are not wise. [13]We, however, will not boast beyond proper limits, but will confine our boasting to the field God has assigned to us, a field that reaches even to you. [14]We are not going too far in our boasting, as would be the case if we had not come to you, for we did get as far as you with the gospel of Christ. [15]Neither do we go beyond our limits by boasting of work done by others.[c] Our hope is that, as your faith continues to grow, our area of activity among you will greatly expand, [16]so that we can preach the gospel in the regions beyond you. For we do not want to boast about work already done in another man's territory. [17]But, "Let him who boasts boast in the Lord."[d] [18]For it is not the one who

---

[a]9 Psalm 112:9   [b]7 Or Look at the obvious facts   [c]13–15 Or [13]We, however, will not boast about things that cannot be measured, but we will boast according to the standard of measurement that the God of measure has assigned us—a measurement that relates even to you. [14]...[15]Neither do we boast about things that cannot be measured in regard to the work done by others.   [d]17 Jer. 9:24

commends himself who is approved, but the one whom the Lord commends.

Paul and the False Apostles

11 I hope you will put up with a little of my foolishness; but you are already doing that. ²I am jealous for you with a godly jealousy. I promised you to one husband, to Christ, so that I might present you as a pure virgin to him. ³But I am afraid that just as Eve was deceived by the serpent's cunning, your minds may somehow be led astray from your sincere and pure devotion to Christ. ⁴For if someone comes to you and preaches a Jesus other than the Jesus we preached, or if you receive a different spirit from the one you received, or a different gospel from the one you accepted, you put up with it easily enough. ⁵But I do not think I am in the least inferior to those "super-apostles." ⁶I may not be a trained speaker, but I do have knowledge. We have made this perfectly clear to you in every way.

⁷Was it a sin for me to lower myself in order to elevate you by preaching the gospel of God to you free of charge? ⁸I robbed other churches by receiving support from them so as to serve you. ⁹And when I was with you and needed something, I was not a burden to anyone, for the brothers who came from Macedonia supplied what I needed. I have kept myself from being a burden to you in any way, and will continue to do so. ¹⁰As surely as the truth of Christ is in me, nobody in the regions of Achaia will stop this boasting of mine. ¹¹Why? Because I do not love you? God knows I do! ¹²And I will keep on doing what I am doing in order to cut the ground from under those who want an opportunity to be considered equal with us in the things they boast about.

¹³For such men are false apostles, deceitful workmen, masquerading as apostles of Christ. ¹⁴And no wonder, for Satan himself masquerades as an angel of light. ¹⁵It is not surprising, then, if his servants masquerade as servants of righteousness. Their end will be what their actions deserve.

Paul Boasts About His Sufferings

¹⁶I repeat: Let no one take me for a fool. But if you do, then receive me just as you would a fool, so that I may do a little boasting. ¹⁷In this self-confident boasting I am not talking as the Lord would, but as a fool. ¹⁸Since many are boasting in the way the world does, I too will boast. ¹⁹You gladly put up with fools since you are so wise! ²⁰In fact, you even put up with anyone who enslaves you or exploits you or takes advantage of you or pushes himself forward or slaps you in the face. ²¹To my shame I admit that we were too weak for that!

What anyone else dares to boast about—I am speaking as a fool—I also dare to boast about. ²²Are they Hebrews? So am I. Are they Israelites? So am I. Are they Abraham's descendants? So am I. ²³Are they servants of Christ? (I am out of my mind to talk like this.) I am more. I have worked much harder, been in prison more frequently, been flogged more severely, and been exposed to death again and again. ²⁴Five times I received from the Jews the forty lashes minus one. ²⁵Three times I was beaten with rods, once I was stoned, three times I was shipwrecked, I spent a night and a day in the open sea, ²⁶I have been constantly on the move. I have been in danger from rivers, in danger from bandits, in danger from my own countrymen, in danger from Gentiles; in danger in the city, in danger in the country, in danger at sea; and in danger from false brothers. ²⁷I have labored and toiled and have often gone without sleep; I have known hunger and thirst and have often gone without food; I have been cold and naked. ²⁸Besides everything else, I face daily the pressure of my concern for all the churches. ²⁹Who is weak, and I do not feel weak? Who is led into sin, and I do not inwardly burn?

³⁰If I must boast, I will boast of the things that show my weakness. ³¹The God and Father of the Lord Jesus, who is to be praised forever, knows that I am not lying. ³²In Damascus the governor under King Aretas had the city of the Damascenes guarded in order to arrest me. ³³But I was lowered in a basket from a window in the wall and slipped through his hands.

Paul's Vision and His Thorn

12 I must go on boasting. Although there is nothing to be gained, I will go on to visions and revelations from the Lord. ²I know a man in Christ who fourteen years ago was caught up to the third heaven. Whether it was in the body or out of the body I do not know—God knows. ³And I know that this man—whether in the body or apart from the body I do not know, but God knows— ⁴was caught up to paradise. He heard inexpressible things, things that man is not permitted to tell. ⁵I will boast about a man like that, but I will not boast about myself, except about my weaknesses. ⁶Even if I should choose to boast, I would not be a fool, because I would be speaking the truth. But I refrain, so no one will think more of me than is warranted by what I do or say.

⁷To keep me from becoming conceited because of these surpassingly great revelations, there was given me a thorn in my flesh, a messenger of Satan, to torment me. ⁸Three times I pleaded with the Lord to take it away from me. ⁹But he said to me, "My grace is sufficient for you, for my power is made perfect in weakness." Therefore I will boast all the more gladly about my weaknesses, so that Christ's power may rest on me. ¹⁰That is why, for Christ's sake, I delight in weaknesses, in insults, in hardships, in persecutions, in difficulties. For when I am weak, then I am strong.

Paul's Concern for the Corinthians

¹¹I have made a fool of myself, but you drove me to it. I ought to have been commended by you, for I am not in the least inferior to the "super-apostles," even though I am nothing. ¹²The things that mark an apostle—signs, wonders and miracles—were done among you with great perseverance. ¹³How were you inferior to the other churches, except that I was never a burden to you? Forgive me this wrong!

¹⁴Now I am ready to visit you for the third time, and I will not be a burden to you, because what I want is not your possessions but you. After all, children should not have to save up for their parents, but parents for their children. ¹⁵So I will very gladly spend for you everything I have and expend myself as well. If I love you more, will you love me less? ¹⁶Be that as it may,

*a*1 Deut. 19:15

I have not been a burden to you. Yet, crafty fellow that I am, I caught you by trickery! ¹⁷Did I exploit you through any of the men I sent you? ¹⁸I urged Titus to go to you and I sent our brother with him. Titus did not exploit you, did he? Did we not act in the same spirit and follow the same course?

¹⁹Have you been thinking all along that we have been defending ourselves to you? We have been speaking in the sight of God as those in Christ; and everything we do, dear friends, is for your strengthening. ²⁰For I am afraid that when I come I may not find you as I want you to be, and you may not find me as you want me to be. I fear that there may be quarreling, jealousy, outbursts of anger, factions, slander, gossip, arrogance and disorder. ²¹I am afraid that when I come again my God will humble me before you, and I will be grieved over many who have sinned earlier and have not repented of the impurity, sexual sin and debauchery in which they have indulged.

Final Warnings

13 This will be my third visit to you. "Every matter must be established by the testimony of two or three witnesses."*a* ²I already gave you a warning when I was with you the second time. I now repeat it while absent: On my return I will not spare those who sinned earlier or any of the others, ³since you are demanding proof that Christ is speaking through me. He is not weak in dealing with you, but is powerful among you. ⁴For to be sure, he was crucified in weakness, yet he lives by God's power. Likewise, we are weak in him, yet by God's power we will live with him to serve you.

⁵Examine yourselves to see whether you are in the faith; test yourselves. Do you not realize that Christ Jesus is in you—unless, of course, you fail the test? ⁶And I trust that you will discover that we have not failed the test. ⁷Now we pray to God that you will not do anything wrong. Not that people will see that we

> **2 Corinthians 12:9**
>
> ### God's Grace Is Sufficient
>
> But he said to me, "My grace is sufficient for you, for my power is made perfect in weakness." Therefore I will boast all the more gladly about my weaknesses, so that Christ's power may rest on me.

Diamonds on Black Velvet

2 Corinthians 12:9

But he said to me, "My grace is sufficient for you, for my power is made perfect in weakness."

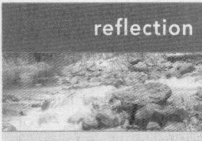

reflection

1 What would you say is your particular "thorn in the flesh"?

2 How might you have grown prideful had it not been for this "thorn"?

3 How has God proven himself strong on your behalf?

RELATED READINGS

Proverbs 18:12;
James 1:6–10;
1 Peter 1:6–7

Read: 2 Corinthians 12:7–10

"WHY WON'T GOD HEAL ME? Doesn't he love me?" Perhaps you've asked similar questions. Maybe you've been frustrated because God didn't answer a prayer the way you had hoped. Could it be that he is using those very difficulties to keep you dependent on him? Like placing sparkling diamonds on black velvet, our human weakness provides a contrasting backdrop against which God's power can be displayed.

Paul was faced with such a dilemma. He came from the best family line, studied at the best schools and encountered Jesus on the road to Damascus. He experienced revelations from God. It would have been easy for him to be proud. But Paul suffered a thorn in the flesh. Three times Paul asked God to remove his thorn. Three times God said no. Did that mean God didn't love Paul? Absolutely not! It simply meant that God decided to empower Paul despite his thorn, to keep Paul dependent on God's strength. God proved to Paul that God's power was made perfect in Paul's weakness.

Paul didn't tell his readers the nature of his thorn. If he had, we might be able to dismiss his words as not applying to us. Because he did not, we can identify with him—and wonder what our own thorns are. Is it a chronic illness, a debilitating disease we've suffered with or a painful injury we've sustained? Is it a chemical depression or bipolar illness? Is it cancer or chronic fatigue?

All of these "thorns" are hard to live with, especially if we've asked repeatedly for healing. They can make us feel weak and spiritually deficient. They can make us feel isolated, undeserving and ineffective. They can cause us to become self-absorbed and self-pitying. But there is another way to look at them: We can offer our illness or disability sacrificially to God and allow it to keep us on our knees, asking God for strength. We can allow God's love and power to push us through difficult and painful times, to use our "thorns" to make us more tenderhearted toward others. We can see them as the black velvet against which God's grace glitters.

Memorize God's words to Paul, and every time you are tempted to feel that your "thorn" disqualifies you from God's work, remember them: "My grace is sufficient for you, for my power is made perfect in weakness."

have stood the test but that you will do what is right even though we may seem to have failed. **8**For we cannot do anything against the truth, but only for the truth. **9**We are glad whenever we are weak but you are strong; and our prayer is for your perfection. **10**This is why I write these things when I am absent, that when I come I may not have to be harsh in my use of authority—the authority the Lord gave me for building you up, not for tearing you down.

Final Greetings

11Finally, brothers, good-by. Aim for perfection, listen to my appeal, be of one mind, live in peace. And the God of love and peace will be with you.

12Greet one another with a holy kiss. **13**All the saints send their greetings.

14May the grace of the Lord Jesus Christ, and the love of God, and the fellowship of the Holy Spirit be with you all.

Galatians

Author:
The apostle Paul.

Audience:
Followers of Jesus;
originally written to the
churches in Galatia.

Date:
About A.D. 50.

Setting:
Judaizers were falsely
telling Gentiles that they
had to obey the Jewish
laws in order to be
saved by Christ.

Verse to Remember:
I am astonished that you
are so quickly deserting
the one who called you
by the grace of Christ and
are turning to a different
gospel—which is really no
gospel at all. (1:6–7)

"Are you crazy?" It's hard to know how to answer such a question! Or what about, "How could you do something so stupid?" *Paul's question to his readers* is just as blunt: "Who has bewitched you?" (Galatians 3:1). One can picture him pulling on his hair in frustration or, if he were writing in English, using extra exclamation points. His readers knew the gospel. Yet they had willingly accepted a false gospel of human effort. So Paul looked in some detail at what the law can and cannot do. It can't save. It can't bring righteousness, before or after salvation. It can't provide any power at all, just a list of dos and don'ts. *Only the Holy Spirit provides the power* to keep the law.

No matter how hard we try, we cannot please God by our human effort, by following laws to earn "credit" with God. We could work 25 hours out of 24, and we'd still fall short. Our own efforts distract us from Christ and his glorious gospel. *Through him, we are saved by grace.* Without him, the law is only a list of legal obligations that remind us how far we fall short.

1

Paul, an apostle—sent not from men nor by man, but by Jesus Christ and God the Father, who raised him from the dead— ²and all the brothers with me,

To the churches in Galatia:

³Grace and peace to you from God our Father and the Lord Jesus Christ, ⁴who gave himself for our sins to rescue us from the present evil age, according to the will of our God and Father, ⁵to whom be glory for ever and ever. Amen.

No Other Gospel

⁶I am astonished that you are so quickly deserting the one who called you by the grace of

Christ and are turning to a different gospel—⁷which is really no gospel at all. Evidently some people are throwing you into confusion and are trying to pervert the gospel of Christ. ⁸But even if we or an angel from heaven should preach a gospel other than the one we preached to you, let him be eternally condemned! ⁹As we have already said, so now I say again: If anybody is preaching to you a gospel other than what you accepted, let him be eternally condemned!

¹⁰Am I now trying to win the approval of men, or of God? Or am I trying to please men? If I were still trying to please men, I would not be a servant of Christ.

Paul Called by God

¹¹I want you to know, brothers, that the gospel I preached is not something that man made up. ¹²I did not receive it from any man, nor was I taught it; rather, I received it by revelation from Jesus Christ.

¹³For you have heard of my previous way of life in Judaism, how intensely I persecuted the church of God and tried to destroy it. ¹⁴I was advancing in Judaism beyond many Jews of my own age and was extremely zealous for the traditions of my fathers. ¹⁵But when God, who set me apart from birth[a] and called me by his grace, was pleased ¹⁶to reveal his Son in me so that I might preach him among the Gentiles, I did not consult any man, ¹⁷nor did I go up to Jerusalem to see those who were apostles before I was, but I went immediately into Arabia and later returned to Damascus.

¹⁸Then after three years, I went up to Jerusalem to get acquainted with Peter[b] and stayed with him fifteen days. ¹⁹I saw none of the other apostles—only James, the Lord's brother. ²⁰I assure you before God that what I am writing you is no lie. ²¹Later I went to Syria and Cilicia. ²²I was personally unknown to the churches of Judea that are in Christ. ²³They only heard the report: "The man who formerly persecuted us is now preaching the faith he once tried to destroy." ²⁴And they praised God because of me.

Paul Accepted by the Apostles

2 Fourteen years later I went up again to Jerusalem, this time with Barnabas. I took Titus along also. ²I went in response to a rev-

elation and set before them the gospel that I preach among the Gentiles. But I did this privately to those who seemed to be leaders, for fear that I was running or had run my race in vain. ³Yet not even Titus, who was with me, was compelled to be circumcised, even though he was a Greek. ⁴This matter arose because some false brothers had infiltrated our ranks to spy on the freedom we have in Christ Jesus and to make us slaves. ⁵We did not give in to them for a moment, so that the truth of the gospel might remain with you.

⁶As for those who seemed to be important—whatever they were makes no difference to me; God does not judge by external appearance—those men added nothing to my message. ⁷On the contrary, they saw that I had been entrusted with the task of preaching the gospel to the Gentiles,[c] just as Peter had been to the Jews.[d] ⁸For God, who was at work in the ministry of Peter as an apostle to the Jews, was also at work in my ministry as an apostle to the Gentiles. ⁹James, Peter[e] and John, those reputed to be pillars, gave me and Barnabas the right hand of fellowship when they recognized the grace given to me. They agreed that we should go to the Gentiles, and they to the Jews. ¹⁰All they asked was that we should continue to remember the poor, the very thing I was eager to do.

Paul Opposes Peter

¹¹When Peter came to Antioch, I opposed him to his face, because he was clearly in the wrong. ¹²Before certain men came from James, he used to eat with the Gentiles. But when they arrived, he began to draw back and separate himself from the Gentiles because he was afraid of those who belonged to the circumcision group. ¹³The other Jews joined him in his hypocrisy, so that by their hypocrisy even Barnabas was led astray.

¹⁴When I saw that they were not acting in line with the truth of the gospel, I said to Peter in front of them all, "You are a Jew, yet you live like a Gentile and not like a Jew. How is it, then, that you force Gentiles to follow Jewish customs?

¹⁵"We who are Jews by birth and not 'Gentile sinners' ¹⁶know that a man is not justified by

---

*a15 Or *from my mother's womb*   *b18 Greek *Cephas*   *c7 Greek *uncircumcised*   *d7 Greek *circumcised*; also in verses 8 and 9   *e9 Greek *Cephas*; also in verses 11 and 14 observing the law, but by faith in Jesus Christ. So we, too, have put our faith in Christ Jesus that we may be justified by faith in Christ and not by observing the law, because by observing the law no one will be justified.

17"If, while we seek to be justified in Christ, it becomes evident that we ourselves are sinners, does that mean that Christ promotes sin? Absolutely not! 18If I rebuild what I destroyed, I prove that I am a lawbreaker. 19For through the law I died to the law so that I might live for God. 20I have been crucified with Christ and I no longer live, but Christ lives in me. The life I live in the body, I live by faith in the Son of God, who loved me and gave himself for me. 21I do not set aside the grace of God, for if righteousness could be gained through the law, Christ died for nothing!"*a*

Galatians 2:20

God Lives in the Christian

"I have been crucified with Christ and I no longer live, but Christ lives in me. The life I live in the body, I live by faith in the Son of God, who loved me and gave himself for me."

Faith or Observance of the Law

3 You foolish Galatians! Who has bewitched you? Before your very eyes Jesus Christ was clearly portrayed as crucified. 2I would like to learn just one thing from you: Did you receive the Spirit by observing the law, or by believing what you heard? 3Are you so foolish? After beginning with the Spirit, are you now trying to attain your goal by human effort? 4Have you suffered so much for nothing—if it really was for nothing? 5Does God give you his Spirit and work miracles among you because you observe the law, or because you believe what you heard?

6Consider Abraham: "He believed God, and it was credited to him as righteousness."*b* 7Understand, then, that those who believe are children of Abraham. 8The Scripture foresaw that God would justify the Gentiles by faith, and announced the gospel in advance to Abraham: "All nations will be blessed through you."*c* 9So those who have faith are blessed along with Abraham, the man of faith.

10All who rely on observing the law are un-

der a curse, for it is written: "Cursed is everyone who does not continue to do everything written in the Book of the Law."*d* 11Clearly no one is justified before God by the law, because, "The righteous will live by faith."*e* 12The law is not based on faith; on the contrary, "The man who does these things will live by them."*f* 13Christ redeemed us from the curse of the law by becoming a curse for us, for it is written: "Cursed is everyone who is hung on a tree."*g* 14He redeemed us in order that the blessing given to Abraham might come to the Gentiles through Christ Jesus, so that by faith we might receive the promise of the Spirit.

The Law and the Promise

15Brothers, let me take an example from everyday life. Just as no one can set aside or add to a human covenant that has been duly established, so it is in this case. 16The promises were spoken to Abraham and to his seed. The Scripture does not say "and to seeds," meaning many people, but "and to your seed,"*h* meaning one person, who is Christ. 17What I mean is this: The law, introduced 430 years later, does not set aside the covenant previously established by God and thus do away with the promise. 18For if the inheritance depends on the law, then it no longer depends on a promise; but God in his grace gave it to Abraham through a promise.

19What, then, was the purpose of the law? It was added because of transgressions until the Seed to whom the promise referred had come. The law was put into effect through angels by a mediator. 20A mediator, however, does not represent just one party; but God is one.

21Is the law, therefore, opposed to the promises of God? Absolutely not! For if a law had been given that could impart life, then righteousness would certainly have come by the law. 22But the Scripture declares that the whole world is a prisoner of sin, so that what was promised, being given through faith in

a21 Some interpreters end the quotation after verse 14.   b6 Gen. 15:6   c8 Gen. 12:3; 18:18; 22:18   d10 Deut. 27:26   e11 Hab. 2:4   f12 Lev. 18:5   g13 Deut. 21:23   h16 Gen. 12:7; 13:15; 24:7

Convert

LYDIA

"SO, YOU'RE PRETTY IMPORTANT in this church, huh?" The newcomer seemed intrigued.

Lydia, never one to seek prestigious titles, responded, "No, I was just following God's guidance when I accepted Paul's message by faith." Something she could not explain had happened when she'd heard Paul's words. "All I know is that I was changed. And I want to help others make the same discovery."

Lydia realized she may have seemed to her new friend as an unlikely candidate for conversion. She was a woman, and women rarely had the opportunity to sit at the feet of a highly trained and renowned teacher like Paul. But those closest to Lydia knew she seldom followed cultural norms or listened to what society said she should be or do.

"Seems like you've been cutting your own path for years," the newcomer remarked, as she heard more of Lydia's story.

"No, I wasn't a Jew," Lydia continued, as she shared her testimony with her guest. But she'd already found her way to the God of Israel, which is why some elements of Paul's message were already familiar to her. Before her guest could even ask it aloud, Lydia knew what she was thinking.

"Okay, then how did a Gentile, God-fearing woman from Asia Minor end up in Philippi?" There weren't even enough resident Jews to form a respectable synagogue there! It was hard to say. But it was out of the norm, and Lydia liked it that way.

"So, you see a day when many more of us will worship the true God?" her friend asked incredulously.

That was okay. Not everyone had to share Lydia's enthusiasm. She had reached the zenith of her profession in the clothing industry. Her company's P&L (profit and loss) statement read like a dream, and she enjoyed a position of influence among her peers and in the city. "So, why not dream big about the future of the church?" she countered. Now that she knew the full story of God's plan to redeem the world, she planned to be part of it.

—*Prayer*—

Dear God, thank you for bringing me into your faith family and adopting me as your child. You are a glorious Father indeed!

> *One of those listening was a woman named Lydia . . . The Lord opened her heart to respond to Paul's message.*
>
> Acts 16:14

ASSIGNED READING:

Acts 16:11–40

Jesus Christ, might be given to those who believe.

²³Before this faith came, we were held prisoners by the law, locked up until faith should be revealed. ²⁴So the law was put in charge to lead us to Christ[a] that we might be justified by faith. ²⁵Now that faith has come, we are no longer under the supervision of the law.

Sons of God

²⁶You are all sons of God through faith in Christ Jesus, ²⁷for all of you who were baptized into Christ have clothed yourselves with Christ. ²⁸There is neither Jew nor Greek, slave nor free, male nor female, for you are all one in Christ Jesus. ²⁹If you belong to Christ, then you are Abraham's seed, and heirs according to the promise.

4 What I am saying is that as long as the heir is a child, he is no different from a slave, although he owns the whole estate. ²He is subject to guardians and trustees until the time set by his father. ³So also, when we were children, we were in slavery under the basic principles of the world. ⁴But when the time had fully come, God sent his Son, born of a woman, born under law, ⁵to redeem those under law, that we might receive the full rights of sons. ⁶Because you are sons, God sent the Spirit of his Son into our hearts, the Spirit who calls out, *"Abba,[b]* Father."* ⁷So you are no longer a slave, but a son; and since you are a son, God has made you also an heir.

Paul's Concern for the Galatians

⁸Formerly, when you did not know God, you were slaves to those who by nature are not gods. ⁹But now that you know God—or rather are known by God—how is it that you are turning back to those weak and miserable principles? Do you wish to be enslaved by them all over again? ¹⁰You are observing special days and months and seasons and years! ¹¹I fear for you, that somehow I have wasted my efforts on you.

¹²I plead with you, brothers, become like me, for I became like you. You have done me no wrong. ¹³As you know, it was because of an illness that I first preached the gospel to you. ¹⁴Even though my illness was a trial to

you, you did not treat me with contempt or scorn. Instead, you welcomed me as if I were an angel of God, as if I were Christ Jesus himself. ¹⁵What has happened to all your joy? I can testify that, if you could have done so, you would have torn out your eyes and given them to me. ¹⁶Have I now become your enemy by telling you the truth?

¹⁷Those people are zealous to win you over, but for no good. What they want is to alienate you ₍from us₎, so that you may be zealous for them. ¹⁸It is fine to be zealous, provided the purpose is good, and to be so always and not just when I am with you. ¹⁹My dear children, for whom I am again in the pains of childbirth until Christ is formed in you, ²⁰how I wish I could be with you now and change my tone, because I am perplexed about you!

Hagar and Sarah

²¹Tell me, you who want to be under the law, are you not aware of what the law says? ²²For it is written that Abraham had two sons, one by the slave woman and the other by the free woman. ²³His son by the slave woman was born in the ordinary way; but his son by the free woman was born as the result of a promise.

²⁴These things may be taken figuratively, for the women represent two covenants. One covenant is from Mount Sinai and bears children who are to be slaves: This is Hagar. ²⁵Now Hagar stands for Mount Sinai in Arabia and corresponds to the present city of Jerusalem, because she is in slavery with her children. ²⁶But the Jerusalem that is above is free, and she is our mother. ²⁷For it is written:

> "Be glad, O barren woman,
>   who bears no children;
> break forth and cry aloud,
>   you who have no labor pains;
> because more are the children of the
>   desolate woman
>   than of her who has a husband."[c]

²⁸Now you, brothers, like Isaac, are children of promise. ²⁹At that time the son born in the ordinary way persecuted the son born by the power of the Spirit. It is the same now. ³⁰But

---

a24 Or *charge until Christ came*   *b6* Aramaic for *Father*   *c27* Isaiah 54:1

what does the Scripture say? "Get rid of the slave woman and her son, for the slave woman's son will never share in the inheritance with the free woman's son."[a] [31] Therefore, brothers, we are not children of the slave woman, but of the free woman.

Freedom in Christ

5 It is for freedom that Christ has set us free. Stand firm, then, and do not let yourselves be burdened again by a yoke of slavery.

[2] Mark my words! I, Paul, tell you that if you let yourselves be circumcised, Christ will be of no value to you at all. [3] Again I declare to every man who lets himself be circumcised that he is obligated to obey the whole law. [4] You who are trying to be justified by law have been alienated from Christ; you have fallen away from grace. [5] But by faith we eagerly await through the Spirit the righteousness for which we hope. [6] For in Christ Jesus neither circumcision nor uncircumcision has any value. The only thing that counts is faith expressing itself through love.

[7] You were running a good race. Who cut in on you and kept you from obeying the truth? [8] That kind of persuasion does not come from the one who calls you. [9] "A little yeast works through the whole batch of dough." [10] I am confident in the Lord that you will take no other view. The one who is throwing you into confusion will pay the penalty, whoever he may be. [11] Brothers, if I am still preaching circumcision, why am I still being persecuted? In that case the offense of the cross has been abolished. [12] As for those agitators, I wish they would go the whole way and emasculate themselves!

[13] You, my brothers, were called to be free. But do not use your freedom to indulge the sinful nature[b]; rather, serve one another in love. [14] The entire law is summed up in a single command: "Love your neighbor as yourself."[c] [15] If you keep on biting and devouring each other,

watch out or you will be destroyed by each other.

Life by the Spirit

[16] So I say, live by the Spirit, and you will not gratify the desires of the sinful nature. [17] For the sinful nature desires what is contrary to the Spirit, and the Spirit what is contrary to the sinful nature. They are in conflict with each other, so that you do not do what you want. [18] But if you are led by the Spirit, you are not under law.

[19] The acts of the sinful nature are obvious: sexual immorality, impurity and debauchery; [20] idolatry and witchcraft; hatred, discord, jealousy, fits of rage, selfish ambition, dissensions, factions [21] and envy; drunkenness, orgies, and the like. I warn you, as I did before, that those who live like this will not inherit the kingdom of God.

[22] But the fruit of the Spirit is love, joy, peace, patience, kindness, goodness, faithfulness, [23] gentleness and self-control. Against such things there is no law. [24] Those who belong to Christ Jesus have crucified the sinful nature with its passions and desires. [25] Since we live by the Spirit, let us keep in step with the Spirit. [26] Let us not become conceited, provoking and envying each other.

Galatians 5:22–23

God Changes Lives

But the fruit of the Spirit is love, joy, peace, patience, kindness, goodness, faithfulness, gentleness and self-control. Against such things there is no law.

Doing Good to All

6 Brothers, if someone is caught in a sin, you who are spiritual should restore him gently. But watch yourself, or you also may be tempted. [2] Carry each other's burdens, and in this way you will fulfill the law of Christ. [3] If anyone thinks he is something when he is nothing, he deceives himself. [4] Each one should test his own actions. Then he can take pride in himself, without comparing himself to somebody else, [5] for each one should carry his own load.

[6] Anyone who receives instruction in the word must share all good things with his instructor.

---

[a] 30 Gen. 21:10   [b] 13 Or *the flesh*; also in verses 16, 17, 19 and 24   [c] 14 Lev. 19:18

Galatians 5:18,25

But if you are led by the Spirit, you are not under law . . . Since we live by the Spirit, let us keep in step with the Spirit.

reflection

1 What steps is the Spirit prompting you to take today?

2 How have you resisted the Spirit's leading lately?

3 How strong is your desire to "keep in step with the Spirit"? Confess your resistance to his leading, and ask him to help you stay in step with him.

RELATED READINGS

Romans 6:6–14; 8:5–8;
1 Corinthians 3:16

Read: Galatians 5:13–25

"LET US KEEP IN STEP with the Spirit." It's as if Paul is describing those who are led by the Spirit as dancers who are in step with the perfect partner. In contrast, when moved by the flesh—impulses and thoughts that tell us to do as *we* desire—it's as if we are experiencing the clumsiness of a partner who keeps stepping on our toes and leading us in the wrong direction.

Like a dancer constantly tuned to the beat of the music, we must continually tune in to the voice of the Spirit and follow his lead. But, oh, how difficult it can be. The Spirit moves us to places where we might not feel quite comfortable, to step back when we want to step forward, to step forward when we want to step back. The rhythm might be too slow or too fast. Following the Spirit means resisting the urge to dance through life *our* way. It means relinquishing control.

How difficult it can be to be led by the Spirit and to hold our tongue. How difficult it is not to dance to the tune of popularity and to repeat that juicy piece of gossip we heard over coffee with friends. How humbling it is when the Spirit leads us to go low and say, "I'm sorry." How difficult it is to make the move to release resentment when we feel we've been wronged or unappreciated. When the enemy cuts in, he whispers in our ear, "What's a missed step here and there? No big deal. You can make up for it later," fueling the battle between flesh and Spirit.

Throughout the day we should ask ourselves, "Who am I being led by? My self, with its emotions, worries, pride, fears and selfishness? Am I being led by the enemy with his discordant tunes? Or am I being led by the Holy Spirit?"

Each time we move in step with the Spirit, we are saying yes to God. We're no longer bound to follow the whims of our flesh or the whisperings of the evil one. We can choose to move in sync with the Spirit.

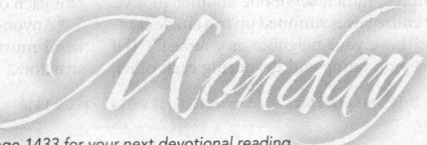

Monday

Go to page 1433 for your next devotional reading.

⁷Do not be deceived: God cannot be mocked. A man reaps what he sows. ⁸The one who sows to please his sinful nature, from that nature*a* will reap destruction; the one who sows to please the Spirit, from the Spirit will reap eternal life. ⁹Let us not become weary in doing good, for at the proper time we will reap a harvest if we do not give up. ¹⁰Therefore, as we have opportunity, let us do good to all people, especially to those who belong to the family of believers.

Not Circumcision but a New Creation

¹¹See what large letters I use as I write to you with my own hand!

¹²Those who want to make a good impression outwardly are trying to compel you to be circumcised. The only reason they do this is to avoid being persecuted for the cross of Christ. ¹³Not even those who are circumcised obey the law, yet they want you to be circumcised that they may boast about your flesh. ¹⁴May I never boast except in the cross of our Lord Jesus Christ, through which*b* the world has been crucified to me, and I to the world. ¹⁵Neither circumcision nor uncircumcision means anything; what counts is a new creation. ¹⁶Peace and mercy to all who follow this rule, even to the Israel of God.

¹⁷Finally, let no one cause me trouble, for I bear on my body the marks of Jesus.

¹⁸The grace of our Lord Jesus Christ be with your spirit, brothers. Amen.

a8 Or his flesh, from the flesh   b14 Or whom

Ephesians

Author:
The apostle Paul.

Audience:
Followers of Jesus;
originally written
to the church in
Ephesus.

Date:
About A.D. 60.

Setting:
Paul penned
this letter from
a Roman prison
to encourage all
the Christians in
Ephesus and
other areas.

Verse to Remember:
As a prisoner for
the Lord, then,
I urge you to live a
life worthy of the
calling you have
received. (4:1)

It is a high privilege to be saved by grace.

While we can never earn our salvation, it does come with responsibilities. We have a calling to live up to. What we do or don't do is a reflection on Jesus, either good or bad.

Paul wrote this letter to a young church set in the heart of a pagan society. Ephesus was a thriving commercial center, but in order for the church to thrive, its members needed to know how to live, how to *stand apart as different* and yet still be able *to influence* their society.

Paul covers a broad spectrum of conduct and relationships, for every part of our life is a part of our calling. He tells us to be imitators of God, a task that would be impossible except for one thing: *We are not alone.* We have the Spirit in our inner being, and we have the protection of the full armor of God. It's up to us, however, to use what we've been given. Paul's letter instructs us how to do that.

---

1 Paul, an apostle of Christ Jesus by the will of God,

To the saints in Ephesus,[a] the faithful[b] in Christ Jesus:

²Grace and peace to you from God our Father and the Lord Jesus Christ.

Spiritual Blessings in Christ

³Praise be to the God and Father of our Lord Jesus Christ, who has blessed us in the heavenly realms with every spiritual blessing in Christ. ⁴For he chose us in him before the creation of the world to be holy and blameless in his sight. In love ⁵he[c] predestined us to be

---

*a*1 Some early manuscripts do not have *in Ephesus.*   *b*1 Or *believers who are*   *c*4,5 Or *sight in love.* ⁵He adopted as his sons through Jesus Christ, in accordance with his pleasure and will— 6to the praise of his glorious grace, which he has freely given us in the One he loves. 7In him we have redemption through his blood, the forgiveness of sins, in accordance with the riches of God's grace 8that he lavished on us with all wisdom and understanding. 9And he*a* made known to us the mystery of his will according to his good pleasure, which he purposed in Christ, 10to be put into effect when the times will have reached their fulfillment—to bring all things in heaven and on earth together under one head, even Christ.

11In him we were also chosen,*b* having been predestined according to the plan of him who works out everything in conformity with the purpose of his will, 12in order that we, who were the first to hope in Christ, might be for the praise of his glory. 13And you also were included in Christ when you heard the word of truth, the gospel of your salvation. Having believed, you were marked in him with a seal, the promised Holy Spirit, 14who is a deposit guaranteeing our inheritance until the redemption of those who are God's possession—to the praise of his glory.

Thanksgiving and Prayer

15For this reason, ever since I heard about your faith in the Lord Jesus and your love for all the saints, 16I have not stopped giving thanks for you, remembering you in my prayers. 17I keep asking that the God of our Lord Jesus Christ, the glorious Father, may give you the Spirit*c* of wisdom and revelation, so that you may know him better. 18I pray also that the eyes of your heart may be enlightened in order that you may know the hope to which he has called you, the riches of his glorious inheritance in the saints, 19and his incomparably great power for us who believe. That power is like the working of his mighty strength, 20which he exerted in Christ when he raised him from the dead and seated him at his right hand in the heavenly realms, 21far above all rule and authority, power and dominion, and every title that can be given, not only in the present age but also in the one to come. 22And God

placed all things under his feet and appointed him to be head over everything for the church, 23which is his body, the fullness of him who fills everything in every way.

Made Alive in Christ

2 As for you, you were dead in your transgressions and sins, 2in which you used to live when you followed the ways of this world and of the ruler of the kingdom of the air, the spirit who is now at work in those who are disobedient. 3All of us also lived among them at one time, gratifying the cravings of our sinful nature*d* and following its desires and thoughts. Like the rest, we were by nature objects of wrath. 4But because of his great love for us, God, who is rich in mercy, 5made us alive with Christ even when we were dead in transgressions—it is by grace you have been saved. 6And God raised us up with Christ and seated us with him in the heavenly realms in Christ Jesus, 7in order that in the coming ages he might show the incomparable riches of his grace, expressed in his kindness to us in Christ Jesus. 8For it is by grace you have been saved, through faith—and this not from yourselves, it is the gift of God— 9not by works, so that no one can boast. 10For we are God's workmanship, created in Christ Jesus to do good works, which God prepared in advance for us to do.

One in Christ

11Therefore, remember that formerly you who are Gentiles by birth and called "uncircumcised" by those who call themselves "the circumcision" (that done in the body by the hands of men)— 12remember that at that time you were separate from Christ, excluded from citizenship in Israel and foreigners to the covenants of the promise, without hope and without God in the world. 13But now in Christ Jesus you who once were far away have been brought near through the blood of Christ.

14For he himself is our peace, who has made the two one and has destroyed the barrier, the dividing wall of hostility, 15by abolishing in his flesh the law with its commandments and regulations. His purpose was to create in himself one new man out of the two, thus making peace, 16and in this one body to reconcile both

---

*a*8,9 Or *us. With all wisdom and understanding,* 9*he*   *b*11 Or *were made heirs*   *c*17 Or *a spirit*   *d*3 Or *our flesh* of them to God through the cross, by which he put to death their hostility. **17**He came and preached peace to you who were far away and peace to those who were near. **18**For through him we both have access to the Father by one Spirit.

19Consequently, you are no longer foreigners and aliens, but fellow citizens with God's people and members of God's household, **20**built on the foundation of the apostles and prophets, with Christ Jesus himself as the chief cornerstone. **21**In him the whole building is joined together and rises to become a holy temple in the Lord. **22**And in him you too are being built together to become a dwelling in which God lives by his Spirit.

Paul the Preacher to the Gentiles

3 For this reason I, Paul, the prisoner of Christ Jesus for the sake of you Gentiles—

2Surely you have heard about the administration of God's grace that was given to me for you, **3**that is, the mystery made known to me by revelation, as I have already written briefly. **4**In reading this, then, you will be able to understand my insight into the mystery of Christ, **5**which was not made known to men in other generations as it has now been revealed by the Spirit to God's holy apostles and prophets. **6**This mystery is that through the gospel the Gentiles are heirs together with Israel, members together of one body, and sharers together in the promise in Christ Jesus.

7I became a servant of this gospel by the gift of God's grace given me through the working of his power. **8**Although I am less than the least of all God's people, this grace was given me: to preach to the Gentiles the unsearchable riches of Christ, **9**and to make plain to everyone the administration of this mystery, which for ages past was kept hidden in God, who created all things. **10**His intent was that now, through the church, the manifold wisdom of God should be made known to the rulers and authorities in the heavenly realms, **11**according to his eternal purpose which he accomplished in Christ Jesus our Lord. **12**In him and through faith in him we may approach God with freedom and

confidence. **13**I ask you, therefore, not to be discouraged because of my sufferings for you, which are your glory.

A Prayer for the Ephesians

14For this reason I kneel before the Father, **15**from whom his whole family[a] in heaven and on earth derives its name. **16**I pray that out of his glorious riches he may strengthen you with power through his Spirit in your inner being, **17**so that Christ may dwell in your hearts through faith. And I pray that you, being rooted and established in love, **18**may have power, together with all the saints, to grasp how wide and long and high and deep is the love of Christ, **19**and to know this love that surpasses knowledge—that you may be filled to the measure of all the fullness of God.

20Now to him who is able to do immeasurably more than all we ask or imagine, according to his power that is at work within us, **21**to him be glory in the church and in Christ Jesus throughout all generations, for ever and ever! Amen.

Unity in the Body of Christ

4 As a prisoner for the Lord, then, I urge you to live a life worthy of the calling you have received. **2**Be completely humble and gentle; be patient, bearing with one another in love. **3**Make every effort to keep the unity of the Spirit through the bond of peace. **4**There is one body and one Spirit—just as you were called to one hope when you were called— **5**one Lord, one faith, one baptism; **6**one God and Father of all, who is over all and through all and in all.

7But to each one of us grace has been given as Christ apportioned it. **8**This is why it[b] says:

> "When he ascended on high,
>   he led captives in his train
>   and gave gifts to men."[c]

9(What does "he ascended" mean except that he also descended to the lower, earthly regions[d]? **10**He who descended is the very one who ascended higher than all the heavens, in order to fill the whole universe.) **11**It was he who gave some to be apostles, some to be prophets, some to be evangelists, and some to be pastors and teachers, **12**to prepare God's people for

---

a15 Or *whom all fatherhood*   *b8* Or *God*   *c8* Psalm 68:18   *d9* Or *the depths of the earth* works of service, so that the body of Christ may be built up [13]until we all reach unity in the faith and in the knowledge of the Son of God and become mature, attaining to the whole measure of the fullness of Christ.

[14]Then we will no longer be infants, tossed back and forth by the waves, and blown here and there by every wind of teaching and by the cunning and craftiness of men in their deceitful scheming. [15]Instead, speaking the truth in love, we will in all things grow up into him who is the Head, that is, Christ. [16]From him the whole body, joined and held together by every supporting ligament, grows and builds itself up in love, as each part does its work.

Living as Children of Light

[17]So I tell you this, and insist on it in the Lord, that you must no longer live as the Gentiles do, in the futility of their thinking. [18]They are darkened in their understanding and separated from the life of God because of the ignorance that is in them due to the hardening of their hearts. [19]Having lost all sensitivity, they have given themselves over to sensuality so as to indulge in every kind of impurity, with a continual lust for more.

[20]You, however, did not come to know Christ that way. [21]Surely you heard of him and were taught in him in accordance with the truth that is in Jesus. [22]You were taught, with regard to your former way of life, to put off your old self, which is being corrupted by its deceitful desires; [23]to be made new in the attitude of your minds; [24]and to put on the new self, created to be like God in true righteousness and holiness.

[25]Therefore each of you must put off falsehood and speak truthfully to his neighbor, for we are all members of one body. [26]"In your anger do not sin"[a]: Do not let the sun go down while you are still angry, [27]and do not give the devil a foothold. [28]He who has been stealing must steal no longer, but must work, doing something useful with his own hands, that

> Ephesians 4:32
>
> *God Forgives*
>
> Be kind and compassionate to one another, forgiving each other, just as in Christ God forgave you.

he may have something to share with those in need.

[29]Do not let any unwholesome talk come out of your mouths, but only what is helpful for building others up according to their needs, that it may benefit those who listen. [30]And do not grieve the Holy Spirit of God, with whom you were sealed for the day of redemption. [31]Get rid of all bitterness, rage and anger, brawling and slander, along with every form of malice. [32]Be kind and compassionate to one another, forgiving each other, just as in Christ God forgave you.

5 Be imitators of God, therefore, as dearly loved children [2]and live a life of love, just as Christ loved us and gave himself up for us as a fragrant offering and sacrifice to God.

[3]But among you there must not be even a hint of sexual immorality, or of any kind of impurity, or of greed, because these are improper for God's holy people. [4]Nor should there be obscenity, foolish talk or coarse joking, which are out of place, but rather thanksgiving. [5]For of this you can be sure: No immoral, impure or greedy person—such a man is an idolater—has any inheritance in the kingdom of Christ and of God.[b] [6]Let no one deceive you with empty words, for because of such things God's wrath comes on those who are disobedient. [7]Therefore do not be partners with them.

[8]For you were once darkness, but now you are light in the Lord. Live as children of light [9](for the fruit of the light consists in all goodness, righteousness and truth) [10]and find out what pleases the Lord. [11]Have nothing to do with the fruitless deeds of darkness, but rather expose them. [12]For it is shameful even to mention what the disobedient do in secret. [13]But everything exposed by the light becomes visible, [14]for it is light that makes everything visible. This is why it is said:

> "Wake up, O sleeper,
>   rise from the dead,
> and Christ will shine on you."

---

[a]26 Psalm 4:4   [b]5 Or *kingdom of the Christ and God*

[15]Be very careful, then, how you live—not as unwise but as wise, [16]making the most of every opportunity, because the days are evil. [17]Therefore do not be foolish, but understand what the Lord's will is. [18]Do not get drunk on wine, which leads to debauchery. Instead, be filled with the Spirit. [19]Speak to one another with psalms, hymns and spiritual songs. Sing and make music in your heart to the Lord, [20]always giving thanks to God the Father for everything, in the name of our Lord Jesus Christ.

[21]Submit to one another out of reverence for Christ.

Wives and Husbands

[22]Wives, submit to your husbands as to the Lord. [23]For the husband is the head of the wife as Christ is the head of the church, his body, of which he is the Savior. [24]Now as the church submits to Christ, so also wives should submit to their husbands in everything.

[25]Husbands, love your wives, just as Christ loved the church and gave himself up for her [26]to make her holy, cleansing[a] her by the washing with water through the word, [27]and to present her to himself as a radiant church, without stain or wrinkle or any other blemish, but holy and blameless. [28]In this same way, husbands ought to love their wives as their own bodies. He who loves his wife loves himself. [29]After all, no one ever hated his own body, but he feeds and cares for it, just as Christ does the church— [30]for we are members of his body. [31]"For this reason a man will leave his father and mother and be united to his wife, and the two will become one flesh."[b] [32]This is a profound mystery—but I am talking about Christ and the church. [33]However, each one of you also must love his wife as he loves himself, and the wife must respect her husband.

Children and Parents

6 Children, obey your parents in the Lord, for this is right. [2]"Honor your father and mother"—which is the first commandment with a promise— [3]"that it may go well with you and that you may enjoy long life on the earth."[c]

[4]Fathers, do not exasperate your children; instead, bring them up in the training and instruction of the Lord.

Slaves and Masters

[5]Slaves, obey your earthly masters with respect and fear, and with sincerity of heart, just as you would obey Christ. [6]Obey them not only to win their favor when their eye is on you, but like slaves of Christ, doing the will of God from your heart. [7]Serve wholeheartedly, as if you were serving the Lord, not men, [8]because you know that the Lord will reward everyone for whatever good he does, whether he is slave or free.

[9]And masters, treat your slaves in the same way. Do not threaten them, since you know that he who is both their Master and yours is in heaven, and there is no favoritism with him.

The Armor of God

[10]Finally, be strong in the Lord and in his mighty power. [11]Put on the full armor of God so that you can take your stand against the devil's schemes. [12]For our struggle is not against flesh and blood, but against the rulers, against the authorities, against the powers of this dark world and against the spiritual forces of evil in the heavenly realms. [13]Therefore put on the full armor of God, so that when the day of evil comes, you may be able to stand your ground, and after you have done everything, to stand. [14]Stand firm then, with the belt of truth buckled around your waist, with the breastplate of righteousness in place, [15]and with your feet fitted with the readiness that comes from the gospel of peace. [16]In addition to all this, take up the shield of faith, with which you can extinguish all the flaming arrows of the evil one. [17]Take the helmet of salvation and the sword of the Spirit, which is the word of God. [18]And pray in the Spirit on all occasions with all kinds of prayers and requests. With this in mind, be alert and always keep on praying for all the saints.

[19]Pray also for me, that whenever I open my mouth, words may be given me so that I will fearlessly make known the mystery of the gospel, [20]for which I am an ambassador in

---

[a]26 Or *having cleansed*   [b]31 Gen. 2:24   [c]3 Deut. 5:16

Meeting the Enemy

Read: Ephesians 6:1–24

THE IDEA OF THE DEVIL more often solicits smirks than fear or caution in the world today. In his classic work *The Screwtape Letters*, C. S. Lewis writes from the point of view of a senior demon, Screwtape, giving advice to his protégé, Wormwood, on how to influence his target. Screwtape tells Wormwood, "The fact that 'devils' are predominately *comic* figures in the modern imagination will help you. If any faint suspicion of your existence begins to arise in his mind, suggest to him a picture of something in red tights, and persuade him that since he cannot believe in that (it is an old textbook method of confusing them) he therefore cannot believe in you."

The Bible is clear that the devil *is* real and his schemes can be traced back to Eden. Beyond our limited vision lies a spiritual realm where the war for souls is waged. Jesus Christ has already won the ultimate victory, but battles still rage as Satan tries to make Christians and Christianity ineffective and impotent. Those battles play out in various arenas. Paul described them as "rulers," "authorities," "powers of this dark world" and "spiritual forces of evil in the heavenly realms." Spiritual warfare in unseen realms is as real as the battles waged here on earth.

There are also battles that occur within our thoughts, our relationships, our attitudes and our everyday choices. If the devil can wear us down so that we snap at our children or belittle our husband or pass on a tidbit of gossip, he has weakened our witness.

For every battle we face, God provides us with a full set of spiritual armor. God's armor is based on truth and righteousness, faith and peace. He asks us to be armed with his attributes, not our own. Above all, we have prayer, which reaches into the spiritual realm and places the battle into the hands of the One who has already won the war.

The presence of evil need not make us suspicious or fearful. We don't need to look for a demon behind every door. But we should be alert and prayerful so that we are aware of the devil's schemes when they come and so we can fight the battle in the spiritual realm.

Go to page 1439 for your next devotional reading.

Ephesians 6:12

For our struggle is not against flesh and blood, but against the rulers, against the authorities, against the powers of this dark world and against the spiritual forces of evil in the heavenly realms.

reflection

1 How do you picture the devil and the battle in the spiritual realm?

2 What schemes of the devil have you seen in your own life?

3 What piece of God's armor do you most need right now?

RELATED READINGS

Hebrews 2:14–18;
1 Peter 5:8–9;
1 John 4:1–4

Tuesday

chains. Pray that I may declare it fearlessly, as I should.

Final Greetings

²¹Tychicus, the dear brother and faithful servant in the Lord, will tell you everything, so that you also may know how I am and what I am doing. ²²I am sending him to you for this very purpose, that you may know how we are, and that he may encourage you.

²³Peace to the brothers, and love with faith from God the Father and the Lord Jesus Christ. ²⁴Grace to all who love our Lord Jesus Christ with an undying love.

Philippians

Although he is in prison, this letter from Paul brims with the *theme of Christian joy*. Paul is joyful as he thinks of the Christians in Philippi. He rejoices that even his imprisonment advances the gospel. He is happy that his readers have willingly suffered for Christ as well, and *he finds great gain in Christ*. Paul is particularly pleased to hear of the Philippians' unity in Christ. They are like-minded, working together for the sake of the gospel and for one another, and Paul rejoices in that fact.

This book gives wonderful advice on putting perspective on life's bumps and bruises. The Christian life brings suffering, pain and even persecution. Yet the believer never suffers alone. *The presence of Christ Jesus brings joy* even in the midst of suffering. Read Philippians to see some of the many ways God shows himself faithful in hard times.

Author:
The apostle Paul.

Audience:
The church in Philippi and all followers of Jesus.

Date:
About A.D. 61.

Setting:
Under house arrest in Rome, Paul writes a letter to the believers in Philippi, the location of the first European church.

Verse to Remember:
Being confident of this, that he who began a good work in you will carry it on to completion until the day of Christ Jesus. (1:6)

---

1 Paul and Timothy, servants of Christ Jesus,

To all the saints in Christ Jesus at Philippi, together with the overseers*a* and deacons:

²Grace and peace to you from God our Father and the Lord Jesus Christ.

Thanksgiving and Prayer

³I thank my God every time I remember you. ⁴In all my prayers for all of you, I always pray with joy ⁵because of your partnership in the gospel from the first day until now, ⁶being confident of this, that he who began a good work in you will carry it on to completion until the day of Christ Jesus.

⁷It is right for me to feel this way about all of you, since I have you in my heart; for whether I am in chains or defending and confirming the gospel, all of you share in God's grace with me. ⁸God can testify how I long for all of you with the affection of Christ Jesus.

*a*1 Traditionally *bishops*

⁹And this is my prayer: that your love may abound more and more in knowledge and depth of insight, ¹⁰so that you may be able to discern what is best and may be pure and blameless until the day of Christ, ¹¹filled with the fruit of righteousness that comes through Jesus Christ—to the glory and praise of God.

Paul's Chains Advance the Gospel

¹²Now I want you to know, brothers, that what has happened to me has really served to advance the gospel. ¹³As a result, it has become clear throughout the whole palace guard[a] and to everyone else that I am in chains for Christ. ¹⁴Because of my chains, most of the brothers in the Lord have been encouraged to speak the word of God more courageously and fearlessly.

¹⁵It is true that some preach Christ out of envy and rivalry, but others out of goodwill. ¹⁶The latter do so in love, knowing that I am put here for the defense of the gospel. ¹⁷The former preach Christ out of selfish ambition, not sincerely, supposing that they can stir up trouble for me while I am in chains.[b] ¹⁸But what does it matter? The important thing is that in every way, whether from false motives or true, Christ is preached. And because of this I rejoice.

Yes, and I will continue to rejoice, ¹⁹for I know that through your prayers and the help given by the Spirit of Jesus Christ, what has happened to me will turn out for my deliverance.[c] ²⁰I eagerly expect and hope that I will in no way be ashamed, but will have sufficient courage so that now as always Christ will be exalted in my body, whether by life or by death. ²¹For to me, to live is Christ and to die is gain. ²²If I am to go on living in the body, this will mean fruitful labor for me. Yet what shall I choose? I do not know! ²³I am torn between the two: I desire to depart and be with Christ, which is better by far; ²⁴but it is more necessary for you that I remain in the body. ²⁵Convinced of this, I know that I will remain, and I will continue with all of you for your progress and joy in the faith, ²⁶so that through my being with you again your joy in Christ Jesus will overflow on account of me.

²⁷Whatever happens, conduct yourselves in a manner worthy of the gospel of Christ. Then, whether I come and see you or only hear about you in my absence, I will know that you stand firm in one spirit, contending as one man for the faith of the gospel ²⁸without being frightened in any way by those who oppose you. This is a sign to them that they will be destroyed, but that you will be saved—and that by God. ²⁹For it has been granted to you on behalf of Christ not only to believe on him, but also to suffer for him, ³⁰since you are going through the same struggle you saw I had, and now hear that I still have.

Imitating Christ's Humility

2 If you have any encouragement from being united with Christ, if any comfort from his love, if any fellowship with the Spirit, if any tenderness and compassion, ²then make my joy complete by being like-minded, having the same love, being one in spirit and purpose. ³Do nothing out of selfish ambition or vain conceit, but in humility consider others better than yourselves. ⁴Each of you should look not only to your own interests, but also to the interests of others.

⁵Your attitude should be the same as that of Christ Jesus:

⁶Who, being in very nature[d] God,
    did not consider equality with God
        something to be grasped,
⁷but made himself nothing,
    taking the very nature[e] of a servant,
    being made in human likeness.
⁸And being found in appearance as a man,
    he humbled himself
    and became obedient to death—
        even death on a cross!
⁹Therefore God exalted him to the highest place
    and gave him the name that is above
        every name,
¹⁰that at the name of Jesus every knee should bow,
    in heaven and on earth and under the earth,

---

[a]13 Or whole palace   [b]16,17 Some late manuscripts have verses 16 and 17 in reverse order.   [c]19 Or salvation   [d]6 Or in the form of
[e]7 Or the form

[11]and every tongue confess that Jesus Christ
is Lord,
to the glory of God the Father.

Shining as Stars

[12]Therefore, my dear friends,
as you have always obeyed—
not only in my presence, but
now much more in my ab-
sence—continue to work out
your salvation with fear and
trembling, [13]for it is God who
works in you to will and to act
according to his good purpose.

[14]Do everything without
complaining or arguing, [15]so
that you may become blameless and pure, children of God
without fault in a crooked and depraved generation, in which you shine like stars in the universe [16]as you hold out[a] the word of life—in
order that I may boast on the day of Christ that
I did not run or labor for nothing. [17]But even
if I am being poured out like a drink offering
on the sacrifice and service coming from your
faith, I am glad and rejoice with all of you. [18]So
you too should be glad and rejoice with me.

Timothy and Epaphroditus

[19]I hope in the Lord Jesus to send Timothy
to you soon, that I also may be cheered when
I receive news about you. [20]I have no one else
like him, who takes a genuine interest in your
welfare. [21]For everyone looks out for his own
interests, not those of Jesus Christ. [22]But you
know that Timothy has proved himself, because
as a son with his father he has served with me
in the work of the gospel. [23]I hope, therefore,
to send him as soon as I see how things go with
me. [24]And I am confident in the Lord that I myself will come soon.

[25]But I think it is necessary to send back to
you Epaphroditus, my brother, fellow worker
and fellow soldier, who is also your messenger,
whom you sent to take care of my needs. [26]For
he longs for all of you and is distressed because
you heard he was ill. [27]Indeed he was ill, and
almost died. But God had mercy on him, and
not on him only but also on me, to spare me

sorrow upon sorrow. [28]Therefore I am all the
more eager to send him, so that when you see
him again you may be glad and I may have
less anxiety. [29]Welcome him
in the Lord with great joy, and
honor men like him, [30]because
he almost died for the work of
Christ, risking his life to make
up for the help you could not
give me.

No Confidence in the Flesh

3 Finally, my brothers, rejoice in the Lord! It is no
trouble for me to write the
same things to you again, and
it is a safeguard for you.

[2]Watch out for those dogs,
those men who do evil, those
mutilators of the flesh. [3]For it is we who are the
circumcision, we who worship by the Spirit of
God, who glory in Christ Jesus, and who put
no confidence in the flesh— [4]though I myself
have reasons for such confidence.

If anyone else thinks he has reasons to put
confidence in the flesh, I have more: [5]circum-
cised on the eighth day, of the people of Israel,
of the tribe of Benjamin, a Hebrew of Hebrews;
in regard to the law, a Pharisee; [6]as for zeal, persecuting the church; as for legalistic righteousness, faultless.

[7]But whatever was to my profit I now
consider loss for the sake of Christ. [8]What is
more, I consider everything a loss compared
to the surpassing greatness of knowing Christ
Jesus my Lord, for whose sake I have lost all
things. I consider them rubbish, that I may gain
Christ [9]and be found in him, not having a righteousness of my own that comes from the law,
but that which is through faith in Christ—the
righteousness that comes from God and is by
faith. [10]I want to know Christ and the power
of his resurrection and the fellowship of sharing in his sufferings, becoming like him in his
death, [11]and so, somehow, to attain to the resurrection from the dead.

Pressing on Toward the Goal

[12]Not that I have already obtained all this, or
have already been made perfect, but I press on

Philippians 2:11

*God Is
Lord of All*

Every tongue confess
that Jesus Christ is Lord,
to the glory of
God the Father.

---

[a]16 Or *hold on to*

to take hold of that for which Christ Jesus took hold of me. [13]Brothers, I do not consider myself yet to have taken hold of it. But one thing I do: Forgetting what is behind and straining toward what is ahead, [14]I press on toward the goal to win the prize for which God has called me heavenward in Christ Jesus.

[15]All of us who are mature should take such a view of things. And if on some point you think differently, that too God will make clear to you. [16]Only let us live up to what we have already attained.

[17]Join with others in following my example, brothers, and take note of those who live according to the pattern we gave you. [18]For, as I have often told you before and now say again even with tears, many live as enemies of the cross of Christ. [19]Their destiny is destruction, their god is their stomach, and their glory is in their shame. Their mind is on earthly things. [20]But our citizenship is in heaven. And we eagerly await a Savior from there, the Lord Jesus Christ, [21]who, by the power that enables him to bring everything under his control, will transform our lowly bodies so that they will be like his glorious body.

4 Therefore, my brothers, you whom I love and long for, my joy and crown, that is how you should stand firm in the Lord, dear friends!

Exhortations

[2]I plead with Euodia and I plead with Syntyche to agree with each other in the Lord. [3]Yes, and I ask you, loyal yokefellow,[a] help these women who have contended at my side in the cause of the gospel, along with Clement and the rest of my fellow workers, whose names are in the book of life.

[4]Rejoice in the Lord always. I will say it again: Rejoice! [5]Let your gentleness be evident to all. The Lord is near. [6]Do not be anxious about anything, but in everything, by prayer and petition, with thanksgiving, present your requests to God. [7]And the peace of God, which transcends all understanding, will guard your hearts and your minds in Christ Jesus.

[8]Finally, brothers, whatever is true, whatever is noble, whatever is right, whatever is pure, whatever is lovely, whatever is admirable—if anything is excellent or praiseworthy—think about such things. [9]Whatever you have learned or received or heard from me, or seen in me— put it into practice. And the God of peace will be with you.

Thanks for Their Gifts

[10]I rejoice greatly in the Lord that at last you have renewed your concern for me. Indeed, you have been concerned, but you had no opportunity to show it. [11]I am not saying this because I am in need, for I have learned to be content whatever the circumstances. [12]I know what it is to be in need, and I know what it is to have plenty. I have learned the secret of being content in any and every situation, whether well fed or hungry, whether living in plenty or in want. [13]I can do everything through him who gives me strength.

[14]Yet it was good of you to share in my troubles. [15]Moreover, as you Philippians know, in the early days of your acquaintance with the gospel, when I set out from Macedonia, not one church shared with me in the matter of giving and receiving, except you only; [16]for even when I was in Thessalonica, you sent me aid again and again when I was in need. [17]Not that I am looking for a gift, but I am looking for what may be credited to your account. [18]I have received full payment and even more; I am amply supplied, now that I have received from Epaphroditus the gifts you sent. They are a fragrant offering, an acceptable sacrifice, pleasing to God. [19]And my God will meet all your needs according to his glorious riches in Christ Jesus.

[20]To our God and Father be glory for ever and ever. Amen.

Final Greetings

[21]Greet all the saints in Christ Jesus. The brothers who are with me send greetings. [22]All the saints send you greetings, especially those who belong to Caesar's household.

[23]The grace of the Lord Jesus Christ be with your spirit. Amen.[b]

---

[a]3 Or *loyal Syzygus*   [b]23 Some manuscripts do not have *Amen.*

A Gentle Spirit

Read: Philippians 4:1–13

IF YOU WALKED DOWN the street and asked five people what they thought the word *gentleness* meant, how many would say that a gentle person is docile, easily intimidated or passive? Or that gentleness would be a good quality for a pet or a horse? In our culture, assertiveness and forthrightness are more highly valued personality traits for human beings than gentleness.

But the Scriptures value gentleness. Here Paul explains what it means to be virtuous, especially in view of the disputes that had arisen among the Philippians. How were they to build unity? First, they were to rejoice. If they concentrated on rejoicing in the risen Christ, they would focus on their common joy rather than on the differences that could divide them. Next, they were to "let [their] gentleness be evident to all." Gentleness carries the idea of being reasonable. It does not mean that truth is compromised; rather, it means that the truth is defended with thoughtful consideration for the other's point of view. In other words, the people involved come to a meeting of the minds. There is a winsome quality in gentleness that diffuses anger and hostility.

A supervisor named Ann was gentle. She never raised her voice and never threatened. She had a steely calm about her. She smiled while explaining to vendors or employees exactly what was expected of them. She clearly stated the consequences if they didn't fulfill their obligations. But her subordinates never seemed defensive or discouraged; rather, they worked hard to live up to the expectations she laid out.

Paul reminded the Philippians that the key to peace was grateful prayer. He admonished them to give their every anxiety over to God as they gave thanks (verses 6–7). More than that, Paul encouraged his readers—including us—to focus on things that are beautiful, pure and positive (verses 8–9). Meditating on such things develops our ability to notice and appreciate small beauties and increases a sense of thanksgiving to God. A spirit of contentment and gratitude brings peace.

A woman who speaks words of encouragement and has an attitude of contentment is inviting; she draws people to her, even if she faces times of crisis and pain. When your gentleness is evident to all, others will know that the Lord is near and they, too, will rejoice.

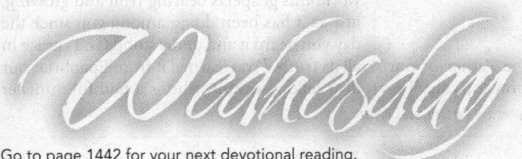

Go to page 1442 for your next devotional reading.

Philippians 4:4–5

Rejoice in the Lord always. I will say it again: Rejoice! Let your gentleness be evident to all. The Lord is near.

reflection

1 What three words do you think others would use to describe you?

2 What reputation would you most like to have?

3 What is currently challenging your ability to rejoice? How can you praise God anyway?

RELATED READINGS

Exodus 16:1–8; 17:1–7; Acts 16:16–40

"In the world's eyes, especially in the business world, gentleness is often thought of as wimpy, but God says, 'The unfading beauty of a gentle and quiet spirit…is of great worth in God's sight.'"

Judith Couchman

Colossians

Author:
The apostle Paul.

Audience:
The church in Colosse
(modern-day Turkey) and
all followers of Jesus.

Date:
About A.D. 60.

Setting:
Paul writes from house arrest in Rome to dispel false teachings in Colosse.

Verse to Remember:
And whatever you do,
whether in word or deed,
do it all in the name of
the Lord Jesus, giving
thanks to God the Father
through him. (3:17)

Jesus Christ is all you need; don't be distracted by lesser things. Christ is supreme, the Creator, the reconciler. Paul had heard of the Colossians' faith and love, but he wanted to be sure that they did not lose sight of Christ and focus on mere rules and religious traditions. If they focused on Christ, *Jesus could lead them on to maturity.*

The young church at Colosse had become a target of heretical attack. Some religious teachers insisted they had additional knowledge that was necessary for salvation. Paul's letter refutes the false teachers by *asserting the supremacy of Christ.*

1 Paul, an apostle of Christ Jesus by the will of God, and Timothy our brother,

2 To the holy and faithful[a] brothers in Christ at Colosse:

Grace and peace to you from God our Father.[b]

Thanksgiving and Prayer

3 We always thank God, the Father of our Lord Jesus Christ, when we pray for you, 4 because we have heard of your faith in Christ Jesus and of the love you have for all the saints— 5 the faith and love that spring from the hope that is stored up for you in heaven and that you have already heard about in the word of truth, the gospel 6 that has come to you. All over the world this gospel is bearing fruit and growing, just as it has been doing among you since the day you heard it and understood God's grace in all its truth. 7 You learned it from Epaphras, our dear fellow servant, who is a faithful minister

a2 Or *believing*   b2 Some manuscripts *Father and the Lord Jesus Christ* of Christ on our[a] behalf, **8**and who also told us of your love in the Spirit.

9For this reason, since the day we heard about you, we have not stopped praying for you and asking God to fill you with the knowledge of his will through all spiritual wisdom and understanding. **10**And we pray this in order that you may live a life worthy of the Lord and may please him in every way: bearing fruit in every good work, growing in the knowledge of God, **11**being strengthened with all power according to his glorious might so that you may have great endurance and patience, and joyfully **12**giving thanks to the Father, who has qualified you[b] to share in the inheritance of the saints in the kingdom of light. **13**For he has rescued us from the dominion of darkness and brought us into the kingdom of the Son he loves, **14**in whom we have redemption,[c] the forgiveness of sins.

The Supremacy of Christ

15He is the image of the invisible God, the firstborn over all creation. **16**For by him all things were created: things in heaven and on earth, visible and invisible, whether thrones or powers or rulers or authorities; all things were created by him and for him. **17**He is before all things, and in him all things hold together. **18**And he is the head of the body, the church; he is the beginning and the firstborn from among the dead, so that in everything he might have the supremacy. **19**For God was pleased to have all his fullness dwell in him, **20**and through him to reconcile to himself all things, whether things on earth or things in heaven, by making peace through his blood, shed on the cross.

21Once you were alienated from God and were enemies in your minds because of[d] your evil behavior. **22**But now he has reconciled you by Christ's physical body through death to present you holy in his sight, without blemish and free from accusation— **23**if you continue in your faith, established and firm, not moved from the hope held out in the gospel. This is

the gospel that you heard and that has been proclaimed to every creature under heaven, and of which I, Paul, have become a servant.

Paul's Labor for the Church

24Now I rejoice in what was suffered for you, and I fill up in my flesh what is still lacking in regard to Christ's afflictions, for the sake of his body, which is the church. **25**I have become its servant by the commission God gave me to present to you the word of God in its fullness— **26**the mystery that has been kept hidden for ages and generations, but is now disclosed to the saints. **27**To them God has chosen to make known among the Gentiles the glorious riches of this mystery, which is Christ in you, the hope of glory.

28We proclaim him, admonishing and teaching everyone with all wisdom, so that we may present everyone perfect in Christ. **29**To this end I labor, struggling with all his energy, which so powerfully works in me.

2 I want you to know how much I am struggling for you and for those at Laodicea, and for all who have not met me personally. **2**My purpose is that they may be encouraged in heart and united in love, so that they may have the full riches of complete understanding, in order that they may know the mystery of God, namely, Christ, **3**in whom are hidden all the treasures of wisdom and knowledge. **4**I tell you this so that no one may deceive you by fine-sounding arguments. **5**For though I am absent from you in body, I am present with you in spirit and delight to see how orderly you are and how firm your faith in Christ is.

Freedom From Human Regulations Through Life With Christ

6So then, just as you received Christ Jesus as Lord, continue to live in him, **7**rooted and built up in him, strengthened in the faith as you were taught, and overflowing with thankfulness.

8See to it that no one takes you captive through hollow and deceptive philosophy,

Colossians 1:17

God Superintends All

He is before all things, and in him all things hold together.

*a*7 Some manuscripts *your*   *b*12 Some manuscripts *us*   *c*14 A few late manuscripts *redemption through his blood*   *d*21 Or *minds, as shown by*

Colossians 1:22–23

But now he has recon-
ciled you by Christ's
physical body through
death to present you
holy in his sight, without
blemish and free from
accusation—if you
continue in your faith,
established and firm, not
moved from the hope
held out in the gospel.

reflection

1 What past sins have
caused you to feel
separated from God?

2 What are the outward
circumstances or in-
ward attitudes that may
threaten your present ac-
cess to God?

3 What are some steps
you can take to help
you continue steadfastly
in the faith?

RELATED READINGS

Romans 5:8–11; 8:35–39;
2 Corinthians 5:17–21

Read: Colossians 1:9–23

PRIMITIVE BRIDGES WERE MADE from logs or vines extending
across streams. According to historians, the first bridge was an arch
bridge built in Babylon about 2200 B.C. The ancient Chinese, Egyptians, Greeks and Romans also built arch bridges out of bricks and
stone. By modern times bridge builders began to use reinforced
concrete and steel so the bridges would be sturdy.

A bridge must be strong enough to support its own weight as
well as the people and vehicles that cross it. It must also be able
to resist natural forces, such as earthquakes, strong winds and
climate changes. Without bridges, people would be greatly incon-
venienced, needing boats to cross waterways or being forced to
travel long distances to traverse obstacles like canyons or ravines.
At the worst, without bridges, people would be more isolated from
one another.

The greatest bridge builder known to the world was and is
Jesus Christ. When Christ stretched out his arms over the cross,
he bridged the chasm that separates sinful people from a holy
God. Through his blood our sins were forgiven and God's justice
appeased.

But just like an expansion bridge, contrary forces can threaten
our access to God: unforgiveness, unconfessed sin and unclaimed
promises can corrode the foundation of our faith. Perhaps you've
received a phone call: "Your son's been in an accident"; or a diagnosis: "It's breast cancer"; or a letter: "It's over."

Life has a way of crashing in on us. That's why Paul exhorts
us to "continue in [our] faith, established and firm." Many times
we are tempted to turn back before we reach the other side. But
Christ's body and blood are strong enough to ensure our continued
access to God. No opposing force "will be able to separate us from
the love of God that is in Christ Jesus our Lord" (Romans 8:39).

Thursday

which depends on human tradition and the basic principles of this world rather than on Christ.

⁹For in Christ all the fullness of the Deity lives in bodily form, ¹⁰and you have been given fullness in Christ, who is the head over every power and authority. ¹¹In him you were also circumcised, in the putting off of the sinful nature,ᵃ not with a circumcision done by the hands of men but with the circumcision done by Christ, ¹²having been buried with him in baptism and raised with him through your faith in the power of God, who raised him from the dead.

¹³When you were dead in your sins and in the uncircumcision of your sinful nature,ᵇ God made youᶜ alive with Christ. He forgave us all our sins, ¹⁴having canceled the written code, with its regulations, that was against us and that stood opposed to us; he took it away, nailing it to the cross. ¹⁵And having disarmed the powers and authorities, he made a public spectacle of them, triumphing over them by the cross.ᵈ

¹⁶Therefore do not let anyone judge you by what you eat or drink, or with regard to a religious festival, a New Moon celebration or a Sabbath day. ¹⁷These are a shadow of the things that were to come; the reality, however, is found in Christ. ¹⁸Do not let anyone who delights in false humility and the worship of angels disqualify you for the prize. Such a person goes into great detail about what he has seen, and his unspiritual mind puffs him up with idle notions. ¹⁹He has lost connection with the Head, from whom the whole body, supported and held together by its ligaments and sinews, grows as God causes it to grow.

²⁰Since you died with Christ to the basic principles of this world, why, as though you still belonged to it, do you submit to its rules: ²¹"Do not handle! Do not taste! Do not touch!"? ²²These are all destined to perish with use, because they are based on human commands and

teachings. ²³Such regulations indeed have an appearance of wisdom, with their self-imposed worship, their false humility and their harsh treatment of the body, but they lack any value in restraining sensual indulgence.

Rules for Holy Living

3 Since, then, you have been raised with Christ, set your hearts on things above, where Christ is seated at the right hand of God. ²Set your minds on things above, not on earthly things. ³For you died, and your life is now hidden with Christ in God. ⁴When Christ, who is yourᵉ life, appears, then you also will appear with him in glory.

⁵Put to death, therefore, whatever belongs to your earthly nature: sexual immorality, impurity, lust, evil desires and greed, which is idolatry. ⁶Because of these, the wrath of God is coming.ᶠ ⁷You used to walk in these ways, in the life you once lived. ⁸But now you must rid yourselves of all such things as these: anger, rage, malice, slander, and filthy language from your lips. ⁹Do not lie to each other, since you have taken off your old self with its practices ¹⁰and have put on the new self, which is being renewed in knowledge in the image of its Creator. ¹¹Here there is no Greek or Jew, circumcised or uncircumcised, barbarian, Scythian, slave or free, but Christ is all, and is in all.

¹²Therefore, as God's chosen people, holy and dearly loved, clothe yourselves with compassion, kindness, humility, gentleness and patience. ¹³Bear with each other and forgive whatever grievances you may have against one another. Forgive as the Lord forgave you. ¹⁴And over all these virtues put on love, which binds them all together in perfect unity.

¹⁵Let the peace of Christ rule in your hearts, since as members of one body you were called to peace. And be thankful. ¹⁶Let the word of Christ dwell in you richly as you teach and admonish one another with all wisdom, and as

Colossians 3:4

God Is Life

When Christ, who is your life, appears, then you also will appear with him in glory.

ᵃ11 Or *the flesh* ᵇ13 Or *your flesh* ᶜ13 Some manuscripts *us* ᵈ15 Or *them in him* ᵉ4 Some manuscripts *our* ᶠ6 Some early manuscripts *coming on those who are disobedient* you sing psalms, hymns and spiritual songs with gratitude in your hearts to God. **17**And whatever you do, whether in word or deed, do it all in the name of the Lord Jesus, giving thanks to God the Father through him.

Rules for Christian Households

18Wives, submit to your husbands, as is fitting in the Lord.

19Husbands, love your wives and do not be harsh with them.

20Children, obey your parents in everything, for this pleases the Lord.

21Fathers, do not embitter your children, or they will become discouraged.

22Slaves, obey your earthly masters in everything; and do it, not only when their eye is on you and to win their favor, but with sincerity of heart and reverence for the Lord. **23**Whatever you do, work at it with all your heart, as working for the Lord, not for men, **24**since you know that you will receive an inheritance from the Lord as a reward. It is the Lord Christ you are serving. **25**Anyone who does wrong will be repaid for his wrong, and there is no favoritism.

4 Masters, provide your slaves with what is right and fair, because you know that you also have a Master in heaven.

Further Instructions

2Devote yourselves to prayer, being watchful and thankful. **3**And pray for us, too, that God may open a door for our message, so that we may proclaim the mystery of Christ, for which I am in chains. **4**Pray that I may proclaim it clearly, as I should. **5**Be wise in the way you act toward outsiders; make the most of every opportunity. **6**Let your conversation be always full of grace, seasoned with salt, so that you may know how to answer everyone.

Final Greetings

7Tychicus will tell you all the news about me. He is a dear brother, a faithful minister and fellow servant in the Lord. **8**I am sending him to you for the express purpose that you may know about our*a* circumstances and that he may encourage your hearts. **9**He is coming with Onesimus, our faithful and dear brother, who is one of you. They will tell you everything that is happening here.

10My fellow prisoner Aristarchus sends you his greetings, as does Mark, the cousin of Barnabas. (You have received instructions about him; if he comes to you, welcome him.) **11**Jesus, who is called Justus, also sends greetings. These are the only Jews among my fellow workers for the kingdom of God, and they have proved a comfort to me. **12**Epaphras, who is one of you and a servant of Christ Jesus, sends greetings. He is always wrestling in prayer for you, that you may stand firm in all the will of God, mature and fully assured. **13**I vouch for him that he is working hard for you and for those at Laodicea and Hierapolis. **14**Our dear friend Luke, the doctor, and Demas send greetings. **15**Give my greetings to the brothers at Laodicea, and to Nympha and the church in her house.

16After this letter has been read to you, see that it is also read in the church of the Laodiceans and that you in turn read the letter from Laodicea.

17Tell Archippus: "See to it that you complete the work you have received in the Lord."

18I, Paul, write this greeting in my own hand. Remember my chains. Grace be with you.

---

a8 Some manuscripts *that he may know about your*

1 Thessalonians

Is there any earthly relationship more tender than that of a mother and her baby or a father and the child on his knee? In this letter to the Thessalonians, Paul compares himself and *his love for the church* to both (see 1 Thessalonians 2:7,11). This was one of Paul's first letters to the churches, and it contains what Paul felt was of *paramount importance for new believers.* The letter came as a response to Timothy's visit and addresses some specific difficulties the church was facing: fierce opposition, efforts to undermine Paul's reputation and sincerity, uncertainty about Jesus' return, and confusion about how to live a life of holiness.

Every parent would love to be able to assure their children of a promising future, but predicting such is only conjecture. Paul, however, could assure his spiritual children of *Christ's return and ultimate eternal life* in God's presence as fact. How comforting to understand that no matter what difficulties we face in this life, *we know how the story is going to end.* "The one who calls you is faithful and he will do it " (1 Thessalonians 5:24).

Author:
The apostle Paul.

Audience:
The church in Thessalonica (modern-day northern Greece) and all followers of Jesus.

Date:
About A.D. 51.

Setting:
Paul wrote from Corinth to encourage the persecuted Christians in Thessalonica.

Verse to Remember:
For the Lord himself will come down from heaven, with a loud command, with the voice of the archangel and with the trumpet call of God, and the dead in Christ will rise first. (4:16)

1

Paul, Silas[a] and Timothy,

To the church of the Thessalonians in God the Father and the Lord Jesus Christ:

Grace and peace to you.[b]

Thanksgiving for the Thessalonians' Faith

[2] We always thank God for all of you, mentioning you in our prayers. [3] We continually remember before our God and Father your work produced by faith, your labor prompted by love, and your endurance inspired by hope in our Lord Jesus Christ.

[4] For we know, brothers loved by God, that he has chosen you, [5] because our gospel came to you not simply with words, but also with power, with the Holy Spirit and with deep conviction. You know how we lived among you for your sake. [6] You became imitators of us and of the Lord; in spite of severe suffering, you welcomed the message with the joy given by the Holy Spirit. [7] And so you became a model to all the believers in Macedonia and Achaia. [8] The Lord's message rang out from you not only in Macedonia and Achaia—your faith in God has become known everywhere. Therefore we do not need to say anything about it, [9] for they themselves report what kind of reception you gave us. They tell how you turned to God from idols to serve the living and true God, [10] and to wait for his Son from heaven, whom he raised from the dead—Jesus, who rescues us from the coming wrath.

Paul's Ministry in Thessalonica

2

You know, brothers, that our visit to you was not a failure. [2] We had previously suffered and been insulted in Philippi, as you know, but with the help of our God we dared to tell you his gospel in spite of strong opposition. [3] For the appeal we make does not spring from error or impure motives, nor are we trying to trick you. [4] On the contrary, we speak as men approved by God to be entrusted with the gospel. We are not trying to please men but God, who tests our hearts. [5] You know we never used flattery, nor did we put on a mask to cover up greed—God is our witness. [6] We were not looking for praise from men, not from you or anyone else.

As apostles of Christ we could have been a burden to you, [7] but we were gentle among you, like a mother caring for her little children. [8] We loved you so much that we were delighted to share with you not only the gospel of God but our lives as well, because you had become so dear to us. [9] Surely you remember, brothers, our toil and hardship; we worked night and day in order not to be a burden to anyone while we preached the gospel of God to you.

[10] You are witnesses, and so is God, of how holy, righteous and blameless we were among you who believed. [11] For you know that we dealt with each of you as a father deals with his own children, [12] encouraging, comforting and urging you to live lives worthy of God, who calls you into his kingdom and glory.

[13] And we also thank God continually because, when you received the word of God, which you heard from us, you accepted it not as the word of men, but as it actually is, the word of God, which is at work in you who believe. [14] For you, brothers, became imitators of God's churches in Judea, which are in Christ Jesus: You suffered from your own countrymen the same things those churches suffered from the Jews, [15] who killed the Lord Jesus and the prophets and also drove us out. They displease God and are hostile to all men [16] in their effort to keep us from speaking to the Gentiles so that they may be saved. In this way they always heap up their sins to the limit. The wrath of God has come upon them at last.[c]

Paul's Longing to See the Thessalonians

[17] But, brothers, when we were torn away from you for a short time (in person, not in thought), out of our intense longing we made every effort to see you. [18] For we wanted to come to you—certainly I, Paul, did, again and again—but Satan stopped us. [19] For what is our hope, our joy, or the crown in which we will glory in the presence of our Lord Jesus when he comes? Is it not you? [20] Indeed, you are our glory and joy.

3

So when we could stand it no longer, we thought it best to be left by ourselves in Athens. [2] We sent Timothy, who is our brother and God's fellow worker[d] in spreading the

---

[a]1 Greek *Silvanus*, a variant of *Silas*   [b]1 Some early manuscripts *you from God our Father and the Lord Jesus Christ*   [c]16 Or *them fully*
[d]2 Some manuscripts *brother and fellow worker*; other manuscripts *brother and God's servant*

Best of Parents

Read: 1 Thessalonians 1:1–10

ONE OF THE MOST ILLUMINATING names of God is the one especially revealed by our Lord Jesus Christ, the name of Father. I say especially revealed by Christ, because, while God had been called throughout the ages by many other names, expressing other aspects of His character, Christ alone has revealed Him to us under the all inclusive name of Father—a name that holds within itself all other names of wisdom and power, and above all [a name] of love and goodness, a name that embodies for us a perfect supply for all our needs. Christ, who was the only begotten Son in the bosom of the Father, was the only one who could reveal this name, for He alone knew the Father . . .

But before I go any farther I must make it plain that it is a Father, such as our highest instincts tell us a good father ought to be, of whom I am speaking. Sometimes earthly fathers are unkind, or tyrannical, or selfish, or even cruel, or they are merely indifferent and neglectful; but none of these can by any stretch of charity be called good fathers. But God, who is good, must be a good father or not a father at all . . . All of us have known good fathers in this world, or at least can imagine them. I knew one, and he filled my childhood with sunshine by his most lovely fatherhood. I can remember vividly with what confidence and triumph I walked through my days, absolutely secure in the knowledge that I had a father. And I am very sure that I have learned to know a little more about the perfect fatherhood of God, because of my experience with this lovely earthly father . . .

But God is not only a father, He is a mother as well, and we have all of us known mothers whose love and tenderness have been without bound or limit. And it is very certain that the God who created them both, and who is Himself father and mother in one, could never have created earthly fathers and mothers who were more tender and more loving than He is Himself. Therefore if we want to know what sort of a Father He is, we must heap together all the best of all the fathers and mothers we have ever known or can imagine, and we must tell ourselves that this is only a faint image of God, our Father in Heaven.

—Hannah Whitall Smith

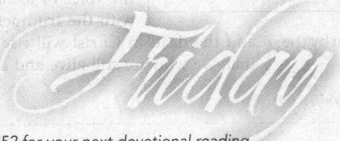

Go to page 1452 for your next devotional reading.

---

1 Thessalonians 1:3

We continually remember before our God and Father your work produced by faith, your labor prompted by love, and your endurance inspired by hope in our Lord Jesus Christ.

reflection

1 How do you typically address God? Do you call him Father, Lord or friend?

2 What things do you need from your heavenly Father?

3 Since Jesus revealed God as Father, pray to him as your *Abba* Father. Ask him to love you with the perfect father's love. If your earthly father has disappointed you, come to your heavenly Father with the expectation that he will never leave you nor forsake you.

RELATED READINGS

Exodus 15:1–5;
Matthew 6:9–13;
Galatians 4:1–6

"Trying to build the brotherhood of man without the fatherhood of God is like trying to make a wheel without a hub."

Irene Dunne

gospel of Christ, to strengthen and encourage you in your faith, ³so that no one would be unsettled by these trials. You know quite well that we were destined for them. ⁴In fact, when we were with you, we kept telling you that we would be persecuted. And it turned out that way, as you well know. ⁵For this reason, when I could stand it no longer, I sent to find out about your faith. I was afraid that in some way the tempter might have tempted you and our efforts might have been useless.

Timothy's Encouraging Report

⁶But Timothy has just now come to us from you and has brought good news about your faith and love. He has told us that you always have pleasant memories of us and that you long to see us, just as we also long to see you. ⁷Therefore, brothers, in all our distress and persecution we were encouraged about you because of your faith. ⁸For now we really live, since you are standing firm in the Lord. ⁹How can we thank God enough for you in return for all the joy we have in the presence of our God because of you? ¹⁰Night and day we pray most earnestly that we may see you again and supply what is lacking in your faith.

¹¹Now may our God and Father himself and our Lord Jesus clear the way for us to come to you. ¹²May the Lord make your love increase and overflow for each other and for everyone else, just as ours does for you. ¹³May he strengthen your hearts so that you will be blameless and holy in the presence of our God and Father when our Lord Jesus comes with all his holy ones.

Living to Please God

4 Finally, brothers, we instructed you how to live in order to please God, as in fact you are living. Now we ask you and urge you in the Lord Jesus to do this more and more. ²For you know what instructions we gave you by the authority of the Lord Jesus.

³It is God's will that you should be sanctified: that you should avoid sexual immorality; ⁴that each of you should learn to control his own body^a in a way that is holy and honorable, ⁵not in passionate lust like the heathen, who do not know God; ⁶and that in this matter no one should wrong his brother or take advantage of him. The Lord will punish men for all such sins, as we have already told you and warned you. ⁷For God did not call us to be impure, but to live a holy life. ⁸Therefore, he who rejects this instruction does not reject man but God, who gives you his Holy Spirit.

⁹Now about brotherly love we do not need to write to you, for you yourselves have been taught by God to love each other. ¹⁰And in fact, you do love all the brothers throughout Macedonia. Yet we urge you, brothers, to do so more and more.

¹¹Make it your ambition to lead a quiet life, to mind your own business and to work with your hands, just as we told you, ¹²so that your daily life may win the respect of outsiders and so that you will not be dependent on anybody.

The Coming of the Lord

¹³Brothers, we do not want you to be ignorant about those who fall asleep, or to grieve like the rest of men, who have no hope. ¹⁴We believe that Jesus died and rose again and so we believe that God will bring with Jesus those who have fallen asleep in him. ¹⁵According to the Lord's own word, we tell you that we who are still alive, who are left till the coming of the Lord, will certainly not precede those who have fallen asleep. ¹⁶For the Lord himself will come down from heaven, with a loud command, with the voice of the archangel and with the trumpet call of God, and the dead in Christ will rise first. ¹⁷After that, we who are still alive and are left will be

1 Thessalonians 4:16

God Will Call Us Home

For the Lord himself will come down from heaven, with a loud command, with the voice of the archangel and with the trumpet call of God, and the dead in Christ will rise first.

---

^a4 Or *learn to live with his own wife*; or *learn to acquire a wife*

caught up together with them in the clouds to meet the Lord in the air. And so we will be with the Lord forever. ¹⁸Therefore encourage each other with these words.

5 Now, brothers, about times and dates we do not need to write to you, ²for you know very well that the day of the Lord will come like a thief in the night. ³While people are saying, "Peace and safety," destruction will come on them suddenly, as labor pains on a pregnant woman, and they will not escape.

⁴But you, brothers, are not in darkness so that this day should surprise you like a thief. ⁵You are all sons of the light and sons of the day. We do not belong to the night or to the darkness. ⁶So then, let us not be like others, who are asleep, but let us be alert and self-controlled. ⁷For those who sleep, sleep at night, and those who get drunk, get drunk at night. ⁸But since we belong to the day, let us be self-controlled, putting on faith and love as a breastplate, and the hope of salvation as a helmet. ⁹For God did not appoint us to suffer wrath but to receive salvation through our Lord Jesus Christ. ¹⁰He died for us so that, whether we are awake or asleep, we may live together with him. ¹¹Therefore encourage one another and build each other up, just as in fact you are doing.

Final Instructions

¹²Now we ask you, brothers, to respect those who work hard among you, who are over you in the Lord and who admonish you. ¹³Hold them in the highest regard in love because of their work. Live in peace with each other. ¹⁴And we urge you, brothers, warn those who are idle, encourage the timid, help the weak, be patient with everyone. ¹⁵Make sure that nobody pays back wrong for wrong, but always try to be kind to each other and to everyone else.

¹⁶Be joyful always; ¹⁷pray continually; ¹⁸give thanks in all circumstances, for this is God's will for you in Christ Jesus.

¹⁹Do not put out the Spirit's fire; ²⁰do not treat prophecies with contempt. ²¹Test everything. Hold on to the good. ²²Avoid every kind of evil.

²³May God himself, the God of peace, sanctify you through and through. May your whole spirit, soul and body be kept blameless at the coming of our Lord Jesus Christ. ²⁴The one who calls you is faithful and he will do it.

²⁵Brothers, pray for us. ²⁶Greet all the brothers with a holy kiss. ²⁷I charge you before the Lord to have this letter read to all the brothers.

²⁸The grace of our Lord Jesus Christ be with you.

1 Thessalonians 5:24

God Is Faithful

The one who calls you is faithful and he will do it.

2 Thessalonians

Author:
The apostle Paul.

Audience:
The church in Thessalonica (modern-day northern Greece) and all followers of Jesus.

Date:
About A.D. 51 or 52, six months after the writing of 1 Thessalonians.

Setting:
The Christians in Thessalonica thought that Christ would return immediately. They became confused and disappointed when he didn't return on their timetable.

Verse to Remember:
"May the Lord direct your hearts into God's love and Christ's perseverance." (3:5)

The Thessalonians were enduring trials and growing in their faith. But a new trial had entered the scene and frightened some of them—the false teaching that the day of the Lord had already come. Paul writes to reassure them and to caution them to *beware of false teaching* and to tell them a little bit about the end times. He also counsels them to work hard, not to be idle and not to grow weary of doing good.

Correct teaching leads to correct living.

It was important that the Thessalonians base their actions on a true teaching. But it was also important that they *knew the truth* that God expected them to work to earn the food they ate. Notice how carefully and gently Paul corrects the believers who had been taught incorrectly but who wanted to know the truth.

1

Paul, Silas[a] and Timothy,

To the church of the Thessalonians in God our Father and the Lord Jesus Christ:

[2] Grace and peace to you from God the Father and the Lord Jesus Christ.

Thanksgiving and Prayer

[3] We ought always to thank God for you, brothers, and rightly so, because your faith is growing more and more, and the love every one of you has for each other is increasing. [4] Therefore, among God's churches we boast about your perseverance and faith in all the persecutions and trials you are enduring.

[5] All this is evidence that God's judgment is right, and as a result you will be counted worthy of the kingdom of God, for which you are suffering. [6] God is just: He will pay back trouble to those who trouble you [7] and give relief to you who are troubled, and to us as well. This will happen when the Lord Jesus is revealed from heaven in blazing fire with his powerful angels. [8] He will punish those who do not know God and do not obey the gospel of our Lord Jesus. [9] They will be punished with everlasting destruction and shut out from the presence of the Lord and from the majesty of his power [10] on the day he comes to be glorified in his holy people and to be marveled at among all those who have believed. This includes you, because you believed our testimony to you.

[11] With this in mind, we constantly pray for you, that our God may count you worthy of his calling, and that by his power he may fulfill every good purpose of yours and every act prompted by your faith. [12] We pray this so that the name of our Lord Jesus may be glorified in you, and you in him, according to the grace of our God and the Lord Jesus Christ.[b]

The Man of Lawlessness

2

Concerning the coming of our Lord Jesus Christ and our being gathered to him, we ask you, brothers, [2] not to become easily unsettled or alarmed by some prophecy, report or letter supposed to have come from us, saying that the day of the Lord has already come. [3] Don't let anyone deceive you in any way, for that day will not come until the rebellion occurs and the man of lawlessness[c] is revealed, the man doomed to destruction. [4] He will oppose and will exalt himself over everything that is called God or is worshiped, so that he sets himself up in God's temple, proclaiming himself to be God.

[5] Don't you remember that when I was with you I used to tell you these things? [6] And now you know what is holding him back, so that he may be revealed at the proper time. [7] For the secret power of lawlessness is already at work; but the one who now holds it back will continue to do so till he is taken out of the way. [8] And then the lawless one will be revealed, whom the Lord Jesus will overthrow with the breath of his mouth and destroy by the splendor of his coming. [9] The coming of the lawless one will be in accordance with the work of Satan displayed in all kinds of counterfeit miracles, signs and wonders, [10] and in every sort of evil that deceives those who are perishing. They perish because they refused to love the truth and so be saved. [11] For this reason God sends them a powerful delusion so that they will believe the lie [12] and so that all will be condemned who have not believed the truth but have delighted in wickedness.

Stand Firm

[13] But we ought always to thank God for you, brothers loved by the Lord, because from the beginning God chose you[d] to be saved through the sanctifying work of the Spirit and through belief in the truth. [14] He called you to this through our gospel, that you might share in the glory of our Lord Jesus Christ. [15] So then, brothers, stand firm and hold to the teachings[e] we passed on to you, whether by word of mouth or by letter.

[16] May our Lord Jesus Christ himself and

---

2 Thessalonians 1:6

God Is Just

God is just: He will pay back trouble to those who trouble you.

---

[a] 1 Greek *Silvanus*, a variant of *Silas*   [b] 12 Or *God and Lord, Jesus Christ*   [c] 3 Some manuscripts *sin*   [d] 13 Some manuscripts *because God chose you as his firstfruits*   [e] 15 Or *traditions*

Controversy

PRISCILLA

2 THESSALONIANS 2:16

There [Paul] met
a Jew named
Aquila . . . who
had recently come
from Italy with
his wife Priscilla,
because Claudius
had ordered
all the Jews to
leave Rome.

Acts 18:2

**ASSIGNED
READING:**

Acts
18:1–28;
Romans
16:3–5

"YOU'VE GOT TO BE KIDDING." Priscilla's neighbor was always getting the story wrong. She was sure that's what was happening now. No, her neighbor said emphatically, Emperor Claudius had served the entire neighborhood eviction notices. It was true.

Every Jew—each man, woman and child—received the royal edict to pack up and leave the Roman capital at once. Apparently, the emperor was weary of the Jews' arguments over the new Christian religion (inferred from the historical reference to "Chrestus"), so he summarily sent them packing.

Priscilla never forgot those first few panicked hours after the audacious ruling. Oh, the rush to get her and her husband Aquila's belongings together! As they joined their fellow deportees for a one-way ticket out of Rome, she cast one last glance at her home. "I wonder if I'll ever return home," she wondered, with tears threatening to spill.

Out of all the cities they could have chosen, the couple settled in the Greek city of Corinth, home to one of the largest gatherings of pagan worship on earth at that time.

"Lord, I know you can sometimes create controversy," she would later pray. "But I seem to be a magnet for it!"

Priscilla and her husband found themselves in a spiritual struggle between the overindulgent lifestyle of their neighbors and their Christian faith. On the way to the market or synagogue, she was assaulted by images and trinkets—ranging from the mundane to the obscene—all dedicated to the goddess of love, Aphrodite.

"Is it always going to be a tug-of-war? Why is it so hard to be a Christian?" Prayers filled her thoughts as she contemplated how her faith had affected the course of her everyday life.

When she and her husband moved to Ephesus to assist Paul in his missionary work, it didn't become any easier. Growing opposition, eventually erupting into full-scale rioting, tested her mettle. Priscilla could bear witness that being a Christian in the early church was not for the faint of heart. The social and political pressure likely claimed a number of spiritual casualties. However, with the encouragement of her husband, her friend Paul and a host of other new believers, her faith held fast and her legacy continues to this day.

—Prayer—
Lord, give me strength to do your will wherever my path leads.

Weekend

God our Father, who loved us and by his grace gave us eternal encouragement and good hope, [17]encourage your hearts and strengthen you in every good deed and word.

Request for Prayer

3 Finally, brothers, pray for us that the message of the Lord may spread rapidly and be honored, just as it was with you. [2]And pray that we may be delivered from wicked and evil men, for not everyone has faith. [3]But the Lord is faithful, and he will strengthen and protect you from the evil one. [4]We have confidence in the Lord that you are doing and will continue to do the things we command. [5]May the Lord direct your hearts into God's love and Christ's perseverance.

2 Thessalonians 3:5

God Directs Us

May the Lord direct your hearts into God's love and Christ's perseverance.

Warning Against Idleness

[6]In the name of the Lord Jesus Christ, we command you, brothers, to keep away from every brother who is idle and does not live according to the teaching[a] you received from us. [7]For you yourselves know how you ought to follow our example. We were not idle when we were with you, [8]nor did we eat anyone's food without paying for it. On the contrary, we worked night and day, laboring and toiling so that we would not be a burden to any of you. [9]We did this, not because we do not have the right to such help, but in order to make ourselves a model for you to follow. [10]For even when we were with you, we gave you this rule: "If a man will not work, he shall not eat."

[11]We hear that some among you are idle. They are not busy; they are busybodies. [12]Such people we command and urge in the Lord Jesus Christ to settle down and earn the bread they eat. [13]And as for you, brothers, never tire of doing what is right.

[14]If anyone does not obey our instruction in this letter, take special note of him. Do not associate with him, in order that he may feel ashamed. [15]Yet do not regard him as an enemy, but warn him as a brother.

Final Greetings

[16]Now may the Lord of peace himself give you peace at all times and in every way. The Lord be with all of you.

[17]I, Paul, write this greeting in my own hand, which is the distinguishing mark in all my letters. This is how I write.

[18]The grace of our Lord Jesus Christ be with you all.

---

a6 Or tradition

1 Timothy

Author:
The apostle Paul.

Audience:
Timothy, Paul's young protégé, young church leaders and all believers everywhere.

Date:
About A.D. 64, probably between Paul's first and second imprisonments in Rome.

Setting:
Timothy, the young pastor of the church of Ephesus, receives instructions from Paul on church management.

Verse to Remember:
Timothy, my son, I give you this instruction in keeping with the prophecies once made about you, so that by following them you may fight the good fight, holding on to faith and a good conscience. (1:18–19)

A friend in the faith is one of the greatest blessings God gives us. We need the companionship and encouragement of others, and we also need the loving honesty of someone *who wants us to grow* in our walk with Christ. That kind of friendship is what we see between Paul and Timothy in this first of the Pastoral Letters. In fact, Paul thought of Timothy as a son. Timothy had been Paul's loyal companion since joining him on his second missionary journey, staying with him even during Paul's imprisonment.

But *friends don't always get to remain together.* When Paul needed someone to pastor the church in Ephesus, he chose Timothy for the job. It meant they would no longer travel together as they once had, but it also gave Timothy an opportunity to grow in his faith and ministry. Paul's letter provides Timothy with the building blocks he needed to further the work in Ephesus. *He covers everything* from choosing leaders to caring for the needy. And he does it from one friend to another, seeking the best for Timothy and for the congregation he serves.

1 Paul, an apostle of Christ Jesus by the command of God our Savior and of Christ Jesus our hope,

²To Timothy my true son in the faith:

Grace, mercy and peace from God the Father and Christ Jesus our Lord.

Warning Against False Teachers of the Law

³As I urged you when I went into Ephesus so that you may command certain men not to teach false doctrines any longer ⁴nor to devote themselves to myths and endless genealogies. These promote controversies rather than God's work—which is by faith. ⁵The goal of this command is love, which comes from a pure heart and a good conscience and a sincere faith. ⁶Some have wandered away from these and turned to meaningless talk. ⁷They want to be teachers of the law, but they do not know what they are talking about or what they so confidently affirm.

⁸We know that the law is good if one uses it properly. ⁹We also know that law*a* is made not for the righteous but for lawbreakers and rebels, the ungodly and sinful, the unholy and irreligious; for those who kill their fathers or mothers, for murderers, ¹⁰for adulterers and perverts, for slave traders and liars and perjurers—and for whatever else is contrary to the sound doctrine ¹¹that conforms to the glorious gospel of the blessed God, which he entrusted to me.

The Lord's Grace to Paul

¹²I thank Christ Jesus our Lord, who has given me strength, that he considered me faithful, appointing me to his service. ¹³Even though I was once a blasphemer and a persecutor and a violent man, I was shown mercy because I acted in ignorance and unbelief. ¹⁴The grace of our Lord was poured out on me abundantly, along with the faith and love that are in Christ Jesus.

¹⁵Here is a trustworthy saying that deserves full acceptance: Christ Jesus came into the world to save sinners—of whom I am the worst. ¹⁶But for that very reason I was shown mercy so that in me, the worst of sinners, Christ Jesus might display his unlimited patience as an example for those who would believe on him and receive eternal life. ¹⁷Now to the King eternal, immortal, invisible, the only God, be honor and glory for ever and ever. Amen.

¹⁸Timothy, my son, I give you this instruction in keeping with the prophecies once made about you, so that by following them you may fight the good fight, ¹⁹holding on to faith and a good conscience. Some have rejected these and so have shipwrecked their faith. ²⁰Among them are Hymenaeus and Alexander, whom I have handed over to Satan to be taught not to blaspheme.

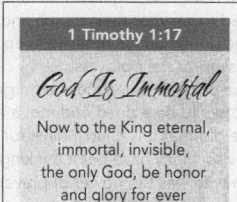

1 Timothy 1:17

God Is Immortal

Now to the King eternal, immortal, invisible, the only God, be honor and glory for ever and ever. Amen.

Instructions on Worship

2 I urge, then, first of all, that requests, prayers, intercession and thanksgiving be made for everyone— ²for kings and all those in authority, that we may live peaceful and quiet lives in all godliness and holiness. ³This is good, and pleases God our Savior, ⁴who wants all men to be saved and to come to a knowledge of the truth. ⁵For there is one God and one mediator between God and men, the man Christ Jesus, ⁶who gave himself as a ransom for all men—the testimony given in its proper time. ⁷And for this purpose I was appointed a herald and an apostle—I am telling the truth, I am not lying—and a teacher of the true faith to the Gentiles.

⁸I want men everywhere to lift up holy hands in prayer, without anger or disputing.

⁹I also want women to dress modestly, with decency and propriety, not with braided hair or gold or pearls or expensive clothes, ¹⁰but with good deeds, appropriate for women who profess to worship God.

¹¹A woman should learn in quietness and full submission. ¹²I do not permit a woman to teach or to have authority over a man; she must

*a*9 Or *that the law*

Prayer for All

1 Timothy 2:1–4

I urge, then, first of all,
that requests, prayers,
intercession and
thanksgiving be made
for everyone—for kings
and all those in authority,
that we may live peaceful
and quiet lives in all
godliness and holiness.
This is good, and pleases
God our Savior, who
wants all men to be
saved and to come to a
knowledge of the truth.

reflection

1 Describe a time when
you knew that your
prayers made a differ-
ence.

2 What priority does
prayer have in your
life?

3 How often do you
take the time to pray
for those around you? Do
you know someone who
needs prayer right now?
Then pray right now.

RELATED READINGS
Psalm 67:1–7;
Matthew 6:5–13; 7:7–12;
James 5:13–16

Read: 1 Timothy 2:1–15

WHEN THE YOUNG PASTOR went to visit his new church, five
women of all ages, shapes and sizes greeted him.

"We've been praying you would come," a spry 90-year-old
woman said with a smile. "I've been a member here since I was
a girl." They showed him into the small, country church that had
been at risk of closing its doors. She and her four friends had
decided to pray for their church and for those who would make
the decision about whether to keep its doors open. The pastor was
the answer to their prayers.

The pastor's colleagues had urged him not to accept the position. It would be a dead-end move for his career, they said. What
chance did that tiny church have for survival in such a remote area?
His advisers may have been thinking logically, but what they didn't
reckon with was the power of prayer. These five faithful women
believed that God could do the impossible—and he did. No one
could have predicted the large numbers of people who decided to
move from the city to the suburbs. Years later, the small, country
church has continued to grow into a thriving ministry under the
leadership of the man who felt compelled to accept the small
pastorate.

Paul's letter to Timothy encourages us to pray for everyone.
How easy it is to become complacent and believe that the prayers
of one person don't really matter. But wouldn't it be better to
spend our time praying, rather than giving up in frustration,
second-guessing or criticizing others?

Just imagine what would happen if each of us took on the serious business of praying for those around us. Not just *saying* we'll
pray, but *really* praying—asking for God's wisdom, guidance and
protection, and giving thanks for people's willingness to serve. Five
women prayed that God would make a difference in their church,
and he did. Think of what God might do when *you* commit to pray
for the people you know.

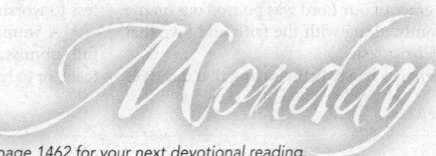

Monday

Go to page 1462 for your next devotional reading.

be silent. [13]For Adam was formed first, then Eve. [14]And Adam was not the one deceived; it was the woman who was deceived and became a sinner. [15]But women[a] will be saved[b] through childbearing—if they continue in faith, love and holiness with propriety.

Overseers and Deacons

3 Here is a trustworthy saying: If anyone sets his heart on being an overseer,[c] he desires a noble task. [2]Now the overseer must be above reproach, the husband of but one wife, temperate, self-controlled, respectable, hospitable, able to teach, [3]not given to drunkenness, not violent but gentle, not quarrelsome, not a lover of money. [4]He must manage his own family well and see that his children obey him with proper respect. [5](If anyone does not know how to manage his own family, how can he take care of God's church?) [6]He must not be a recent convert, or he may become conceited and fall under the same judgment as the devil. [7]He must also have a good reputation with outsiders, so that he will not fall into disgrace and into the devil's trap.

[8]Deacons, likewise, are to be men worthy of respect, sincere, not indulging in much wine, and not pursuing dishonest gain. [9]They must keep hold of the deep truths of the faith with a clear conscience. [10]They must first be tested; and then if there is nothing against them, let them serve as deacons.

[11]In the same way, their wives[d] are to be women worthy of respect, not malicious talkers but temperate and trustworthy in everything.

[12]A deacon must be the husband of but one *wife and must manage his children* and his household well. [13]Those who have served well gain an excellent standing and great assurance in their faith in Christ Jesus.

[14]Although I hope to come to you soon, I am writing you these instructions so that, [15]if I am delayed, you will know how people ought to conduct themselves in God's household, which is the church of the living God, the pillar and foundation of the truth. [16]Beyond all question, the mystery of godliness is great:

> He[e] appeared in a body,[f]
>   was vindicated by the
>   Spirit,
> was seen by angels,
>   was preached among the
>   nations,
> was believed on in the
>   world,
>   was taken up in glory.

Instructions to Timothy

4 The Spirit clearly says that in later times some will abandon the faith and follow deceiving spirits and things taught by demons. [2]Such teachings come through hypocritical liars, whose consciences have been seared as with a hot iron. [3]They forbid people to marry and order them to abstain from certain foods, which God created to be received with thanksgiving by those who believe and who know the truth. [4]For everything God created is good, and nothing is to be rejected if it is received with thanksgiving, [5]because it is consecrated by the word of God and prayer.

[6]If you point these things out to the brothers, you will be a good minister of Christ Jesus, brought up in the truths of the faith and of the good teaching that you have followed. [7]Have nothing to do with godless myths and old wives' tales; rather, train yourself to be godly. [8]For physical training is of some value, but godliness has value for all things, holding promise for both the present life and the life to come. [9]This is a trustworthy saying that deserves full acceptance [10](and for this we labor and strive), that we have put our hope in the living God, who is the Savior of all men, and especially of those who believe.

[11]Command and teach these things. [12]Don't let anyone look down on you because you are young, but set an example for the believers in speech, in life, in love, in faith and in purity. [13]Until I come, devote yourself to the public reading of Scripture, to preaching and to teaching. [14]Do not neglect your gift, which was

1 Timothy 3:16

God Became Human

Beyond all question, the mystery of godliness is great: He appeared in a body.

---

[a]15 Greek *she*   [b]15 Or *restored*   [c]1 Traditionally *bishop*; also in verse 2   [d]11 Or *way, deaconesses*   [e]16 Some manuscripts *God*   [f]16 Or *in the flesh*

given you through a prophetic message when the body of elders laid their hands on you. [15]Be diligent in these matters; give yourself wholly to them, so that everyone may see your progress. [16]Watch your life and doctrine closely. Persevere in them, because if you do, you will save both yourself and your hearers.

Advice About Widows, Elders and Slaves

5 Do not rebuke an older man harshly, but exhort him as if he were your father. Treat younger men as brothers, [2]older women as mothers, and younger women as sisters, with absolute purity.

[3]Give proper recognition to those widows who are really in need. [4]But if a widow has children or grandchildren, these should learn first of all to put their religion into practice by caring for their own family and so repaying their parents and grandparents, for this is pleasing to God. [5]The widow who is really in need and left all alone puts her hope in God and continues night and day to pray and to ask God for help. [6]But the widow who lives for pleasure is dead even while she lives. [7]Give the people these instructions, too, so that no one may be open to blame. [8]If anyone does not provide for his relatives, and especially for his immediate family, he has denied the faith and is worse than an unbeliever.

[9]No widow may be put on the list of widows unless she is over sixty, has been faithful to her husband,[a] [10]and is well known for her good deeds, such as bringing up children, showing hospitality, washing the feet of the saints, helping those in trouble and devoting herself to all kinds of good deeds.

[11]As for younger widows, do not put them on such a list. For when their sensual desires overcome their dedication to Christ, they want to marry. [12]Thus they bring judgment on themselves, because they have broken their first pledge. [13]Besides, they get into the habit of being idle and going about from house to house. And not only do they become idlers, but also gossips and busybodies, saying things they ought not to. [14]So I counsel younger widows to marry, to have children, to manage their homes and to give the enemy no opportunity for slan-

der. [15]Some have in fact already turned away to follow Satan.

[16]If any woman who is a believer has widows in her family, she should help them and not let the church be burdened with them, so that the church can help those widows who are really in need.

[17]The elders who direct the affairs of the church well are worthy of double honor, especially those whose work is preaching and teaching. [18]For the Scripture says, "Do not muzzle the ox while it is treading out the grain,"[b] and "The worker deserves his wages."[c] [19]Do not entertain an accusation against an elder unless it is brought by two or three witnesses. [20]Those who sin are to be rebuked publicly, so that the others may take warning.

[21]I charge you, in the sight of God and Christ Jesus and the elect angels, to keep these instructions without partiality, and to do nothing out of favoritism.

[22]Do not be hasty in the laying on of hands, and do not share in the sins of others. Keep yourself pure.

[23]Stop drinking only water, and use a little wine because of your stomach and your frequent illnesses.

[24]The sins of some men are obvious, reaching the place of judgment ahead of them; the sins of others trail behind them. [25]In the same way, good deeds are obvious, and even those that are not cannot be hidden.

6 All who are under the yoke of slavery should consider their masters worthy of full respect, so that God's name and our teaching may not be slandered. [2]Those who have believing masters are not to show less respect for them because they are brothers. Instead, they are to serve them even better, because those who benefit from their service are believers, and dear to them. These are the things you are to teach and urge on them.

Love of Money

[3]If anyone teaches false doctrines and does not agree to the sound instruction of our Lord Jesus Christ and to godly teaching, [4]he is conceited and understands nothing. He has an unhealthy interest in controversies and

[a]9 Or has had but one husband   [b]18 Deut. 25:4   [c]18 Luke 10:7

quarrels about words that result in envy, strife, malicious talk, evil suspicions [5]and constant friction between men of corrupt mind, who have been robbed of the truth and who think that godliness is a means to financial gain.

[6]But godliness with contentment is great gain. [7]For we brought nothing into the world, and we can take nothing out of it. [8]But if we have food and clothing, we will be content with that. [9]People who want to get rich fall into temptation and a trap and into many foolish and harmful desires that plunge men into ruin and destruction. [10]For the love of money is a root of all kinds of evil. Some people, eager for money, have wandered from the faith and pierced themselves with many griefs.

Paul's Charge to Timothy

[11]But you, man of God, flee from all this, and pursue righteousness, godliness, faith, love, endurance and gentleness. [12]Fight the good fight of the faith. Take hold of the eternal life to which you were called when you made your good confession in the presence of many witnesses. [13]In the sight of God, who gives life to everything, and of Christ Jesus, who while testifying before Pontius Pilate made the good confession, I charge you [14]to keep this command without spot or blame until the appearing of our Lord Jesus Christ, [15]which God will bring about in his own time—God, the blessed and only Ruler, the King of kings and Lord of lords, [16]who alone is immortal and who lives in unapproachable light, whom no one has seen or can see. To him be honor and might forever. Amen.

[17]Command those who are rich in this present world not to be arrogant nor to put their hope in wealth, which is so uncertain, but to put their hope in God, who richly provides us with everything for our enjoyment. [18]Command them to do good, to be rich in good deeds, and to be generous and willing to share. [19]In this way they will lay up treasure for themselves as a firm foundation for the coming age, so that they may take hold of the life that is truly life.

[20]Timothy, guard what has been entrusted to your care. Turn away from godless chatter and the opposing ideas of what is falsely called knowledge, [21]which some have professed and in so doing have wandered from the faith.

Grace be with you.

Timothy

Author:
The apostle Paul.

Audience:
Timothy and Christians everywhere.

Date:
About A.D. 66 or 67.

Setting:
Paul penned this, his last letter, from a Roman dungeon shortly before he was executed for his faith.

Verse to Remember:
Do your best to present yourself to God as one approved, a workman who does not need to be ashamed and who correctly handles the word of truth. (2:15)

Paul's letter to his young disciple, Timothy, is personal and tender. Paul is in prison in Rome and expects to die soon, and he has words of counsel for the young pastor. Addressing him as "my dear son," Paul exhorts Timothy to be faithful and *not to be ashamed of Christ.* He urges Timothy to stay true to his calling and to continue to teach others. More than anything else, *he is to preach the Word.* Paul gives his farewell and passes the baton, but he also urges Timothy to come to see him. His personal requests to this spiritual son come at the end of the letter.

After Paul's conversion, he lived a fruitful, busy—even hectic—life. Yet *he still found time* to invest personally in individuals.

1 Paul, an apostle of Christ Jesus by the will of God, according to the promise of life that is in Christ Jesus,

2 To Timothy, my dear son:

Grace, mercy and peace from God the Father and Christ Jesus our Lord.

Encouragement to Be Faithful

3 I thank God, whom I serve, as my forefathers did, with a clear conscience, as night and day I constantly remember you in my prayers. **4** Recalling your tears, I long to see you, so that I may be filled with joy. **5** I have been reminded of your sincere faith, which first lived in your grandmother Lois and in your mother Eunice and, I am persuaded, now lives in you also. **6** For this reason I remind you to fan into flame the gift of God, which is in you through the laying on of my hands. **7** For God did not give us a spirit of timidity, but a spirit of power, of love and of self-discipline.

8So do not be ashamed to testify about our Lord, or ashamed of me his prisoner. But join with me in suffering for the gospel, by the power of God, 9who has saved us and called us to a holy life—not because of anything we have done but because of his own purpose and grace. This grace was given us in Christ Jesus before the beginning of time, 10but it has now been revealed through the appearing of our Savior, Christ Jesus, who has destroyed death and has brought life and immortality to light through the gospel. 11And of this gospel I was appointed a herald and an apostle and a teacher. 12That is why I am suffering as I am. Yet I am not ashamed, because I know whom I have believed, and am convinced that he is able to guard what I have entrusted to him for that day.

13What you heard from me, keep as the pattern of sound teaching, with faith and love in Christ Jesus. 14Guard the good deposit that was entrusted to you—guard it with the help of the Holy Spirit who lives in us.

15You know that everyone in the province of Asia has deserted me, including Phygelus and Hermogenes.

16May the Lord show mercy to the household of Onesiphorus, because he often refreshed me and was not ashamed of my chains. 17On the contrary, when he was in Rome, he searched hard for me until he found me. 18May the Lord grant that he will find mercy from the Lord on that day! You know very well in how many ways he helped me in Ephesus.

2 You then, my son, be strong in the grace that is in Christ Jesus. 2And the things you have heard me say in the presence of many witnesses entrust to reliable men who will also be qualified to teach others. 3Endure hardship with us like a good soldier of Christ Jesus. 4No one serving as a soldier gets involved in civilian affairs—he wants to please his commanding officer. 5Similarly, if anyone competes as an athlete, he does not receive the victor's crown

unless he competes according to the rules. 6The hardworking farmer should be the first to receive a share of the crops. 7Reflect on what I am saying, for the Lord will give you insight into all this.

8Remember Jesus Christ, raised from the dead, descended from David. This is my gospel, 9for which I am suffering even to the point of being chained like a criminal. But God's word is not chained. 10Therefore I endure everything for the sake of the elect, that they too may obtain the salvation that is in Christ Jesus, with eternal glory.

11Here is a trustworthy saying:

If we died with him,
  we will also live with
    him;
12if we endure,
  we will also reign with
    him.
If we disown him,
  he will also disown us;
13if we are faithless,
  he will remain faithful,
  for he cannot disown
    himself.

A Workman Approved by God

14Keep reminding them of these things. Warn them before God against quarreling about words; it is of no value, and only ruins those who listen. 15Do your best to present yourself to God as one approved, a workman who does not need to be ashamed and who correctly handles the word of truth. 16Avoid godless chatter, because those who indulge in it will become more and more ungodly. 17Their teaching will spread like gangrene. Among them are Hymenaeus and Philetus, 18who have wandered away from the truth. They say that the resurrection has already taken place, and they destroy the faith of some. 19Nevertheless, God's solid foundation stands firm, sealed with this inscription: "The Lord knows those who are his,"a and, "Everyone who confesses the name of the Lord must turn away from wickedness."

> ### 2 Timothy 2:11–12
>
> *God Will Bring Us to Heaven*
>
> If we died with him,
> we will also live with him;
> if we endure,
> we will also reign
> with him.

---

a19 Num. 16:5 (see Septuagint)

From Cowardice to Compassion

2 Timothy 1:7

For God did not give us a spirit of timidity, but a spirit of power, of love and of self-discipline.

Read: 2 Timothy 1:7–14

reflection

1 In what situations have you suffered from the "Cowardly Lion" syndrome?

2 How does it make you feel to know that God has given you a spirit of love, power and self-discipline?

3 How would your perspective change if you knew you had only a month—or a day—left to tell those you love about Jesus?

RELATED READINGS

Psalm 40:5–10;
Acts 4:13–31;
Colossians 4:2–6

THREE TO ONE—that's God's ratio for success, according to 2 Timothy 1:7. A trio of God-given attributes—power, love and self-discipline—offsets one characteristic that doesn't come from him: timidity. The Greek word translated here as "timidity" also means "fear" or "cowardice." Can you relate? Who hasn't shrunk back, like the Cowardly Lion in *The Wizard of Oz*, when faced with opposition or an opportunity to speak about God to others?

But here's a refreshing perspective when confronting our own cowardice: Rather than looking at people with fear, we can see them as Jesus did. He was willing to go out and seek each one like a shepherd looks for a lost sheep. He saw each person's potential to become a child of God. We should see each person, not as a foe, but as a potential brother or sister. Do you see the difference such a change in perspective could make? It can move us from cowardice to compassion.

Who do you know that needs to hear about Jesus? A family member, a coworker, a next-door neighbor? Have they heard you speak on every subject except eternity? Regardless of what is holding you back, God has already replaced your timidity with power, love and self-discipline.

Power: We can be confident in sharing God's message because he offers us the very same power that raised Jesus from the dead. Paul reminded the Corinthians that he came "in truthful speech and in the power of God" (2 Corinthians 6:7). That same power is alive and real and available to you.

Love: God, who is love, can fill us so that we can invite others into his welcoming embrace. Love that "never fails" (see 1 Corinthians 13:8) gives us the desire to share the very best news with others.

Self-discipline: Self-discipline means that we have a sound mind, good judgment and discretion. These concepts dovetail to make us women who have the wisdom to tell others about Jesus. We will meet people where they are, discern what their needs are, sense where the "door" to their heart is, and walk through it with the gospel message.

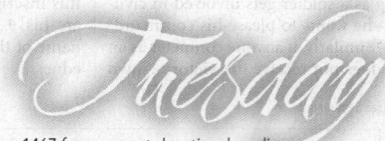

²⁰In a large house there are articles not only of gold and silver, but also of wood and clay; some are for noble purposes and some for ignoble. ²¹If a man cleanses himself from the latter, he will be an instrument for noble purposes, made holy, useful to the Master and prepared to do any good work.

²²Flee the evil desires of youth, and pursue righteousness, faith, love and peace, along with those who call on the Lord out of a pure heart. ²³Don't have anything to do with foolish and stupid arguments, because you know they produce quarrels. ²⁴And the Lord's servant must not quarrel; instead, he must be kind to everyone, able to teach, not resentful. ²⁵Those who oppose him he must gently instruct, in the hope that God will grant them repentance leading them to a knowledge of the truth, ²⁶and that they will come to their senses and escape from the trap of the devil, who has taken them captive to do his will.

Godlessness in the Last Days

3 But mark this: There will be terrible times in the last days. ²People will be lovers of themselves, lovers of money, boastful, proud, abusive, disobedient to their parents, ungrateful, unholy, ³without love, unforgiving, slanderous, without self-control, brutal, not lovers of the good, ⁴treacherous, rash, conceited, lovers of pleasure rather than lovers of God— ⁵having a form of godliness but denying its power. Have nothing to do with them.

⁶They are the kind who worm their way into homes and gain control over weak-willed women, who are loaded down with sins and are swayed by all kinds of evil desires, ⁷always learning but never able to acknowledge the truth. ⁸Just as Jannes and Jambres opposed Moses, so also these men oppose the truth— men of depraved minds, who, as far as the faith is concerned, are rejected. ⁹But they will not get very far because, as in the case of those men, their folly will be clear to everyone.

Paul's Charge to Timothy

¹⁰You, however, know all about my teaching, my way of life, my purpose, faith, patience, love, endurance, ¹¹persecutions, sufferings— what kinds of things happened to me in Antioch, Iconium and Lystra, the persecutions I endured. Yet the Lord rescued me from all of them. ¹²In fact, everyone who wants to live a godly life in Christ Jesus will be persecuted, ¹³while evil men and impostors will go from bad to worse, deceiving and being deceived. ¹⁴But as for you, continue in what you have learned and have become convinced of, because you know those from whom you learned it, ¹⁵and how from infancy you have known the holy Scriptures, which are able to make you wise for salvation through faith in Christ Jesus. ¹⁶All Scripture is God-breathed and is useful for teaching, rebuking, correcting and training in righteousness, ¹⁷so that the man of God may be thoroughly equipped for every good work.

4 In the presence of God and of Christ Jesus, who will judge the living and the dead, and in view of his appearing and his kingdom, I give you this charge: ²Preach the Word; be prepared in season and out of season; correct, rebuke and encourage—with great patience and careful instruction. ³For the time will come when men will not put up with sound doctrine. Instead, to suit their own desires, they will gather around them a great number of teachers to say what their itching ears want to hear. ⁴They will turn their ears away from the truth and turn aside to myths. ⁵But you, keep your head in all situations, endure hardship, do the work of an evangelist, discharge all the duties of your ministry.

⁶For I am already being poured out like a drink offering, and the time has come for my departure. ⁷I have fought the good fight, I have finished the race, I have kept the faith. ⁸Now there is in store for me the crown of righteousness, which the Lord, the righteous Judge, will award to me on that day—and not only to me,

2 Timothy 3:16

God Inspired Scripture

All Scripture is God-breathed and is useful for teaching, rebuking, correcting and training in righteousness.

but also to all who have longed for his appearing.

Personal Remarks

9Do your best to come to me quickly, **10**for Demas, because he loved this world, has deserted me and has gone to Thessalonica. Crescens has gone to Galatia, and Titus to Dalmatia. **11**Only Luke is with me. Get Mark and bring him with you, because he is helpful to me in my ministry. **12**I sent Tychicus to Ephesus. **13**When you come, bring the cloak that I left with Carpus at Troas, and my scrolls, especially the parchments.

14Alexander the metalworker did me a great deal of harm. The Lord will repay him for what he has done. **15**You too should be on your guard against him, because he strongly opposed our message.

16At my first defense, no one came to my support, but everyone deserted me. May it not be held against them. **17**But the Lord stood at my side and gave me strength, so that through me the message might be fully proclaimed and all the Gentiles might hear it. And I was delivered from the lion's mouth. **18**The Lord will rescue me from every evil attack and will bring me safely to his heavenly kingdom. To him be glory for ever and ever. Amen.

Final Greetings

19Greet Priscilla*a* and Aquila and the household of Onesiphorus. **20**Erastus stayed in Corinth, and I left Trophimus sick in Miletus. **21**Do your best to get here before winter. Eubulus greets you, and so do Pudens, Linus, Claudia and all the brothers.

22The Lord be with your spirit. Grace be with you.

a 19 Greek *Prisca*, a variant of *Priscilla*

Titus

Unfinished business can be extremely messy, and it tends to only grow worse with time if not attended to. The fledgling Christian community on the island of Crete had plenty of unfinished business after Paul's visit. A Cretan poet described his fellow citizens as "always liars, evil brutes, lazy gluttons" (Titus 1:12). But all people, brutes or otherwise, *need God's love,* and so when it was time for Paul to travel on, he left the unfinished business of sharing the gospel and building the church in the capable hands of his missionary companion Titus.

Paul's letter was written both to encourage Titus and to give him guidance in instructing these new believers. This book *contains sound advice* for anyone involved in the work of encouraging others, whether within our own families or within a larger circle of ministry. Paul reminds Titus and us, that we, too, were once like the Cretans, ignorantly wallowing in our sin. It is *only through Christ's mercy* that we have the hope of eternal life. It's a perspective that reminds us that Paul's words apply to us as much they do to those we are discipling.

Author:
The apostle Paul.

Audience:
Titus, a Greek Christian, and followers of Jesus everywhere.

Date:
Probably about A.D. 64.

Setting:
Paul left Titus in charge of the churches on the Mediterranean island of Crete.

Verse to Remember:
Remind the people to be subject to rulers and authorities, to be obedient, to be ready to do whatever is good. (3:1)

1 Paul, a servant of God and an apostle of Jesus Christ for the faith of God's elect and the knowledge of the truth that leads to godliness— ²a faith and knowledge resting on the hope of eternal life, which God, who does not lie, promised before the beginning of time, ³and at his appointed season he brought his word to light through the preaching entrusted to me by the command of God our Savior,

⁴To Titus, my true son in our common faith:

Grace and peace from God the Father and Christ Jesus our Savior.

Titus's Task on Crete

⁵The reason I left you in Crete was that you might straighten out what was left unfinished and appoint*ᵃ* elders in every town, as I directed you. ⁶An elder must be blameless, the husband of but one wife, a man whose children believe and are not open to the charge of being wild and disobedient. ⁷Since an overseer*ᵇ* is entrusted with God's work, he must be blameless—not overbearing, not quick-tempered, not given to drunkenness, not violent, not pursuing dishonest gain. ⁸Rather he must be hospitable, one who loves what is good, who is self-controlled, upright, holy and disciplined. ⁹He must hold firmly to the trustworthy message as it has been taught, so that he can encourage others by sound doctrine and refute those who oppose it.

¹⁰For there are many rebellious people, mere talkers and deceivers, especially those of the circumcision group. ¹¹They must be silenced, because they are ruining whole households by teaching things they ought not to teach—and that for the sake of dishonest gain. ¹²Even one of their own prophets has said, "Cretans are always liars, evil brutes, lazy gluttons." ¹³This testimony is true. Therefore, rebuke them sharply, so that they will be sound in the faith ¹⁴and will pay no attention to Jewish myths or to the commands of those who reject the truth. ¹⁵To the pure, all things are pure, but to those who are corrupted and do not believe, nothing is pure. In fact, both their minds and consciences are corrupted. ¹⁶They claim to know God, but by their actions they deny him. They are detestable, disobedient and unfit for doing anything good.

What Must Be Taught to Various Groups

2 You must teach what is in accord with sound doctrine. ²Teach the older men to be temperate, worthy of respect, self-controlled,

and sound in faith, in love and in endurance.

³Likewise, teach the older women to be reverent in the way they live, not to be slanderers or addicted to much wine, but to teach what is good. ⁴Then they can train the younger women to love their husbands and children, ⁵to be self-controlled and pure, to be busy at home, to be kind, and to be subject to their husbands, so that no one will malign the word of God.

⁶Similarly, encourage the young men to be self-controlled. ⁷In everything set them an example by doing what is good. In your teaching show integrity, seriousness ⁸and soundness of speech that cannot be condemned, so that those who oppose you may be ashamed because they have nothing bad to say about us.

⁹Teach slaves to be subject to their masters in everything, to try to please them, not to talk back to them, ¹⁰and not to steal from them, but to show that they can be fully trusted, so that in every way they will make the teaching about God our Savior attractive.

Titus 2:13

God Will Come Again

While we wait for the blessed hope—the glorious appearing of our great God and Savior, Jesus Christ.

¹¹For the grace of God that brings salvation has appeared to all men. ¹²It teaches us to say "No" to ungodliness and worldly passions, and to live self-controlled, upright and godly lives in this present age, ¹³while we wait for the blessed hope—the glorious appearing of our great God and Savior, Jesus Christ, ¹⁴who gave himself for us to redeem us from all wickedness and to purify for himself a people that are his very own, eager to do what is good.

¹⁵These, then, are the things you should teach. Encourage and rebuke with all authority. Do not let anyone despise you.

Doing What Is Good

3 Remind the people to be subject to rulers and authorities, to be ready to do whatever is good, ²to slander no one, to be peaceable and considerate, and to show true humility toward all men.

³At one time we too were foolish, disobedient, deceived and enslaved by all kinds of

ᵃ5 Or ordain   ᵇ7 Traditionally bishop

Lights in the Fog

Read: Titus 2:1–15

HAVE YOU EVER BEEN DRIVING down a road at night when the fog rolled in so thick you couldn't see five feet in front of you? It can be pretty scary. However, if you have a car's taillights ahead of you to guide you, suddenly it is not so frightening.

That is the message of Titus 2. Older women can serve as guiding lights for those coming after them. For many women, juggling all our roles—student, employee, boss, wife, mother—can be overwhelming, like walking through life in a fog. But God never intended for us to figure things out on our own—to simply muddle through. Just as he gave Ruth to Naomi and Mary to Elizabeth, God gives us each other to help, encourage and provide one another with companionship, to share ideas and wisdom and humor. When you live in community with others, you can see how other women raise and nurture their children. You can note how persistent someone is in cultivating and preserving her marriage and how it is serving her well. You can watch as women make their way in the marketplace with dignity and integrity.

It may be that the "older" woman isn't chronologically older at all. Perhaps God has gifted a younger woman with particular knowledge and wisdom that you might be in need of. We should be open to different generations reaching out to each other and bridging the years with love and laughter. We have more in common than we have differences.

In our day it's easy to become isolated and withdrawn. We don't often get together as women did in times gone by for quilting bees and church socials and over-the-fence visits. You may long for a woman to mentor you and advise you regarding how to handle your many roles and responsibilities. If so, ask God to send you someone who is wise and supportive. And keep your eyes open for such a woman so you can befriend her. She may need you as much as you need her. Perhaps God is nudging you to become a mentor to a younger woman. Pray that God will lead you to her and that you will have the courage to be a light in the fog.

Titus 2:3–5

Teach the older women to be reverent in the way they live, not to be slanderers or addicted to much wine, but to teach what is good. Then they can train the younger women to love their husbands and children, to be self-controlled and pure, to be busy at home, to be kind, and to be subject to their husbands, so that no one will malign the word of God.

reflection

1 What are the characteristics of your ideal mentor? Do you know someone who fits that description?

2 What are some ways that you can reach out to an older, wiser woman and invite her to be a part of your life?

3 What life experiences do you have to offer another woman? Ask God to show you someone open to being mentored.

RELATED READINGS

Proverbs 31:10–31;
Ephesians 5:21;
1 Peter 3:1–6

Wednesday

Go to page 1475 for your next devotional reading.

passions and pleasures. We lived in malice and envy, being hated and hating one another. ⁴But when the kindness and love of God our Savior appeared, ⁵he saved us, not because of righteous things we had done, but because of his mercy. He saved us through the washing of rebirth and renewal by the Holy Spirit, ⁶whom he poured out on us generously through Jesus Christ our Savior, ⁷so that, having been justified by his grace, we might become heirs having the hope of eternal life. ⁸This is a trustworthy saying. And I want you to stress these things, so that those who have trusted in God may be careful to devote themselves to doing what is good. These things are excellent and profitable for everyone.

⁹But avoid foolish controversies and genealogies and arguments and quarrels about the law, because these are un-

profitable and useless. ¹⁰Warn a divisive person once, and then warn him a second time. After that, have nothing to do with him. ¹¹You may be sure that such a man is warped and sinful; he is self-condemned.

Final Remarks

¹²As soon as I send Artemas or Tychicus to you, do your best to come to me at Nicopolis, because I have decided to winter there. ¹³Do everything you can to help Zenas the lawyer and Apollos on their way and see that they have everything they need. ¹⁴Our people must learn to devote themselves to doing what is good, in order that they may provide for daily necessities and not live unproductive lives.

¹⁵Everyone with me sends you greetings. Greet those who love us in the faith.

Grace be with you all.

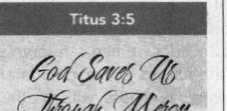

Titus 3:5

God Saves Us Through Mercy

He saved us, not because of righteous things we had done, but because of his mercy. He saved us through the washing of rebirth and renewal by the Holy Spirit.

Philemon

This little letter packs a big wallop. Paul's personal note to Philemon is *a fine example of how to deal gently* with a potentially tricky subject. One of Paul's new converts, Onesimus, was a slave who had run away from his master, Philemon, perhaps even stealing from him. Now Onesimus is a Christian, and Paul sends him back with this letter, urging that Philemon welcome his runaway slave as a Christian brother. To be sure that nothing would be held against the new convert, Paul promises that *he himself will pay any debt* that Onesimus may owe.

Between the lines of this letter is an appeal for trust and forgiveness, in Christ's name. When Paul instructs Philemon to charge a debt to him, Philemon knows he can trust Paul to pay it. And Paul is careful to tell Philemon that *Onesimus is a changed man,* deserving of forgiveness and acceptance.

Author:
The apostle Paul.

Audience:
Philemon, who was likely a member of the Colossian church, and all followers of Jesus.

Date:
About A.D. 60.

Setting:
Paul wrote to his friend Philemon, asking him to forgive a runaway slave, Onesimus.

Verse to Remember:
I appeal to you for my son Onesimus, who became my son while I was in chains. (10)

---

¹Paul, a prisoner of Christ Jesus, and Timothy our brother,

To Philemon our dear friend and fellow worker, ²to Apphia our sister, to Archippus our fellow soldier and to the church that meets in your home:

³Grace to you and peace from God our Father and the Lord Jesus Christ.

Thanksgiving and Prayer

⁴I always thank my God as I remember you in my prayers, ⁵because I hear about your faith in the Lord Jesus and your love for all the saints.

[6]I pray that you may be active in sharing your faith, so that you will have a full understanding of every good thing we have in Christ. [7]Your love has given me great joy and encouragement, because you, brother, have refreshed the hearts of the saints.

Paul's Plea for Onesimus

[8]Therefore, although in Christ I could be bold and order you to do what you ought to do, [9]yet I appeal to you on the basis of love. I then, as Paul—an old man and now also a prisoner of Christ Jesus— [10]I appeal to you for my son Onesimus,[a] who became my son while I was in chains. [11]Formerly he was useless to you, but now he has become useful both to you and to me.

[12]I am sending him—who is my very heart—back to you. [13]I would have liked to keep him with me so that he could take your place in helping me while I am in chains for the gospel. [14]But I did not want to do anything without your consent, so that any favor you do will be spontaneous and not forced. [15]Perhaps the reason he was separated from you for a little while was that you might have him back for good— [16]no longer as a slave, but better than a slave, as a dear brother. He is very dear to me but even dearer to you, both as a man and as a brother in the Lord.

[17]So if you consider me a partner, welcome him as you would welcome me. [18]If he has done you any wrong or owes you anything, charge it to me. [19]I, Paul, am writing this with my own hand. I will pay it back—not to mention that you owe me your very self. [20]I do wish, brother, that I may have some benefit from you in the Lord; refresh my heart in Christ. [21]Confident of your obedience, I write to you, knowing that you will do even more than I ask.

[22]And one thing more: Prepare a guest room for me, because I hope to be restored to you in answer to your prayers.

[23]Epaphras, my fellow prisoner in Christ Jesus, sends you greetings. [24]And so do Mark, Aristarchus, Demas and Luke, my fellow workers.

[25]The grace of the Lord Jesus Christ be with your spirit.

Philemon 15–16

God Can Unify All People

You might have him back for good—no longer as a slave, but better than a slave, as a dear brother. He is very dear to me but even dearer to you, both as a man and as a brother in the Lord.

---

[a]10 Onesimus means useful.

Hebrews

Most of the letters in the New Testament address the basics of the faith and Christian living. The book of *Hebrews addresses deeper theological issues.* It explains many Old Testament symbols of worship—the high priest, the sacrifices, the covenant—in the light of the new covenant brought by Jesus. Jesus is greater than the angels, greater than Moses, greater than any high priest, greater than the old covenant. *Jesus is the perfect and final blood sacrifice* for our sins.

Because of who Christ is and what he did on the cross, we can have full assurance and confidence to enter the presence of God. In the Old Testament Jewish tradition, only the high priest could enter behind the curtain into the holy presence of God once a year. The writer of Hebrews *flings wide the torn veil* that separated sinful humanity from God. He invites all of us to accept Christ as Savior and enter into a relationship with God with confidence and joy.

Author:
Unknown.

Audience:
Hebrew Christians and all followers of Jesus.

Date:
Sometime before the destruction of the temple in Jerusalem in A.D. 70.

Setting:
Jewish Christians were being persecuted, probably by both Jews and Romans, and were growing weary.

Verse to Remember:
Let us hold unswervingly to the hope we profess, for he who promised is faithful. (10:23)

The Son Superior to Angels

1 In the past God spoke to our forefathers through the prophets at many times and in various ways, ²but in these last days he has spoken to us by his Son, whom he appointed heir of all things, and through whom he made the universe. ³The Son is the radiance of God's glory and the exact representation of his being, sustaining all things by his powerful word. After he had provided purification for sins, he sat down at the right hand of the Majesty in heaven. ⁴So he became as much superior to the angels as the name he has inherited is superior to theirs.

⁵For to which of the angels did God ever say,

"You are my Son;
today I have become your Father*a*"*b*?

Or again,

"I will be his Father,
and he will be my Son"*c*?

⁶And again, when God brings his firstborn into the world, he says,

"Let all God's angels worship him."*d*

⁷In speaking of the angels he says,

"He makes his angels winds,
his servants flames of fire."*e*

⁸But about the Son he says,

"Your throne, O God, will last for ever and ever,
and righteousness will be the scepter of your kingdom.
⁹You have loved righteousness and hated wickedness;
therefore God, your God, has set you above your companions
by anointing you with the oil of joy."*f*

¹⁰He also says,

"In the beginning, O Lord, you laid the foundations of the earth,
and the heavens are the work of your hands.
¹¹They will perish, but you remain;
they will all wear out like a garment.
¹²You will roll them up like a robe;
like a garment they will be changed.
But you remain the same,
and your years will never end."*g*

¹³To which of the angels did God ever say,

"Sit at my right hand
until I make your enemies
a footstool for your feet"*h*?

¹⁴Are not all angels ministering spirits sent to serve those who will inherit salvation?

Warning to Pay Attention

2 We must pay more careful attention, therefore, to what we have heard, so that we do not drift away. ²For if the message spoken by angels was binding, and every violation and disobedience received its just punishment, ³how shall we escape if we ignore such a great salvation? This salvation, which was first announced by the Lord, was confirmed to us by those who heard him. ⁴God also testified to it by signs, wonders and various miracles, and gifts of the Holy Spirit distributed according to his will.

Jesus Made Like His Brothers

⁵It is not to angels that he has subjected the world to come, about which we are speaking. ⁶But there is a place where someone has testified:

"What is man that you are mindful of him,
the son of man that you care for him?
⁷You made him a little*i* lower than the angels;
you crowned him with glory and honor
⁸ and put everything under his feet."*j*

In putting everything under him, God left nothing that is not subject to him. Yet at present we do not see everything subject to him. ⁹But we see Jesus, who was made a little lower than the angels, now crowned with glory and honor because he suffered death, so that by the grace of God he might taste death for everyone.

¹⁰In bringing many sons to glory, it was fitting that God, for whom and through whom everything exists, should make the author of their salvation perfect through suffering. ¹¹Both the one who makes men holy and those who are made holy are of the same family. So Jesus is not ashamed to call them brothers. ¹²He says,

"I will declare your name to my brothers;
in the presence of the congregation I
will sing your praises."*k*

¹³And again,

"I will put my trust in him."*l*

And again he says,

---

*a*5 Or *have begotten you*   *b*5 Psalm 2:7   *c*5 2 Samuel 7:14; 1 Chron. 17:13   *d*6 Deut. 32:43 (see Dead Sea Scrolls and Septuagint)
*e*7 Psalm 104:4   *f*9 Psalm 45:6,7   *g*12 Psalm 102:25–27   *h*13 Psalm 110:1   *i*7 Or *him for a little while*; also in verse 9
*j*8 Psalm 8:4–6   *k*12 Psalm 22:22   *l*13 Isaiah 8:17

"Here am I, and the children God has given me."*a*

¹⁴Since the children have flesh and blood, he too shared in their humanity so that by his death he might destroy him who holds the power of death—that is, the devil— ¹⁵and free those who all their lives were held in slavery by their fear of death. ¹⁶For surely it is not angels he helps, but Abraham's descendants. ¹⁷For this reason he had to be made like his brothers in every way, in order that he might become a merciful and faithful high priest in service to God, and that he might make atonement for*b* the sins of the people. ¹⁸Because he himself suffered when he was tempted, he is able to help those who are being tempted.

Jesus Greater Than Moses

3 Therefore, holy brothers, who share in the heavenly calling, fix your thoughts on Jesus, the apostle and high priest whom we confess. ²He was faithful to the one who appointed him, just as Moses was faithful in all God's house. ³Jesus has been found worthy of greater honor than Moses, just as the builder of a house has greater honor than the house itself. ⁴For every house is built by someone, but God is the builder of everything. ⁵Moses was faithful as a servant in all God's house, testifying to what would be said in the future. ⁶But Christ is faithful as a son over God's house. And we are his house, if we hold on to our courage and the hope of which we boast.

Warning Against Unbelief

⁷So, as the Holy Spirit says:

"Today, if you hear his voice,
8 do not harden your hearts
as you did in the rebellion,
    during the time of testing in the
      desert,
⁹ where your fathers tested and tried me
    and for forty years saw what I did.
¹⁰That is why I was angry with that
      generation,
    and I said, 'Their hearts are always going
      astray,
    and they have not known my ways.'

¹¹So I declared on oath in my anger,
    'They shall never enter my rest.'"*c*

¹²See to it, brothers, that none of you has a sinful, unbelieving heart that turns away from the living God. ¹³But encourage one another daily, as long as it is called Today, so that none of you may be hardened by sin's deceitfulness. ¹⁴We have come to share in Christ if we hold firmly till the end the confidence we had at first. ¹⁵As has just been said:

"Today, if you hear his voice,
    do not harden your hearts
    as you did in the rebellion."*d*

¹⁶Who were they who heard and rebelled? Were they not all those Moses led out of Egypt? ¹⁷And with whom was he angry for forty years? Was it not with those who sinned, whose bodies fell in the desert? ¹⁸And to whom did God swear that they would never enter his rest if not to those who disobeyed*e*? ¹⁹So we see that they were not able to enter, because of their unbelief.

A Sabbath-Rest for the People of God

4 Therefore, since the promise of entering his rest still stands, let us be careful that none of you be found to have fallen short of it. ²For we also have had the gospel preached to us, just as they did; but the message they heard was of no value to them, because those who heard did not combine it with faith.*f* ³Now we who have believed enter that rest, just as God has said,

"So I declared on oath in my anger,
    'They shall never enter my rest.'"*g*

And yet his work has been finished since the creation of the world. ⁴For somewhere he has spoken about the seventh day in these words: "And on the seventh day God rested from all his work."*h* ⁵And again in the passage above he says, "They shall never enter my rest."

⁶It still remains that some will enter that rest, and those who formerly had the gospel preached to them did not go in, because of their disobedience. ⁷Therefore God again set a certain day, calling it Today, when a long time

---

a13 Isaiah 8:18   *b17* Or *and that he might turn aside God's wrath, taking away*   *c11* Psalm 95:7–11   *d15* Psalm 95:7,8
e18 Or *disbelieved*   *f2* Many manuscripts *because they did not share in the faith of those who obeyed*   *g3* Psalm 95:11; also in verse 5
h4 Gen. 2:2

later he spoke through David, as was said before:

"Today, if you hear his voice,
do not harden your hearts."[a]

⁸For if Joshua had given them rest, God would not have spoken later about another day. ⁹There remains, then, a Sabbath-rest for the people of God; ¹⁰for anyone who enters God's rest also rests from his own work, just as God did from his. ¹¹Let us, therefore, make every effort to enter that rest, so that no one will fall by following their example of disobedience.

¹²For the word of God is living and active. Sharper than any double-edged sword, it penetrates even to dividing soul and spirit, joints and marrow; it judges the thoughts and attitudes of the heart. ¹³Nothing in all creation is hidden from God's sight. Everything is uncovered and laid bare before the eyes of him to whom we must give account.

Jesus the Great High Priest

¹⁴Therefore, since we have a great high priest who has gone through the heavens,[b] Jesus the Son of God, let us hold firmly to the faith we profess. ¹⁵For we do not have a high priest who is unable to sympathize with our weaknesses, but we have one who has been tempted in every way, just as we are—yet was without sin. ¹⁶Let us then approach the throne of grace with confidence, so that we may receive mercy and find grace to help us in our time of need.

Hebrews 4:16

God Invites Us

Let us then approach the throne of grace with confidence, so that we may receive mercy and find grace to help us in our time of need.

5 Every high priest is selected from among men and is appointed to represent them in matters related to God, to offer gifts and sacrifices for sins. ²He is able to deal gently with those who are ignorant and are going astray, since he himself is subject to weakness. ³This is why he has to offer sacrifices for his own sins, as well as for the sins of the people.

⁴No one takes this honor upon himself; he must be called by God, just as Aaron was. ⁵So Christ also did not take upon himself the glory of becoming a high priest. But God said to him,

"You are my Son;
today I have become your Father."[c][d]

⁶And he says in another place,

"You are a priest forever,
in the order of Melchizedek."[e]

⁷During the days of Jesus' life on earth, he offered up prayers and petitions with loud cries and tears to the one who could save him from death, and he was heard because of his reverent submission. ⁸Although he was a son, he learned obedience from what he suffered ⁹and, once made perfect, he became the source of eternal salvation for all who obey him ¹⁰and was designated by God to be high priest in the order of Melchizedek.

Warning Against Falling Away

¹¹We have much to say about this, but it is hard to explain because you are slow to learn. ¹²In fact, though by this time you ought to be teachers, you need someone to teach you the elementary truths of God's word all over again. You need milk, not solid food! ¹³Anyone who lives on milk, being still an infant, is not acquainted with the teaching about righteousness. ¹⁴But solid food is for the mature, who by constant use have trained themselves to distinguish good from evil.

6 Therefore let us leave the elementary teachings about Christ and go on to maturity, not laying again the foundation of repentance from acts that lead to death,[f] and of faith in God, ²instruction about baptisms, the laying on of hands, the resurrection of the dead, and eternal judgment. ³And God permitting, we will do so.

⁴It is impossible for those who have once been enlightened, who have tasted the heavenly gift, who have shared in the Holy Spirit, ⁵who have tasted the goodness of the word of God

---

*a*7 Psalm 95:7,8   *b*14 Or *gone into heaven*   *c*5 Or *have begotten you*   *d*5 Psalm 2:7   *e*6 Psalm 110:4   *f*1 Or *from useless rituals*

The Throne of Grace

Read: Hebrews 4:1–16

DO YOU FIND IT DIFFICULT to approach God when you encounter a tempting situation? How quickly do you come to him when your attitude needs adjustment or when you are about to engage in a habit you know is unhealthy? What about those times you face difficult circumstances—a marital rift, a bad diagnosis, physical or emotional struggles? To whom do you turn? Do you turn to God or to human comforters?

Often our greatest comforters are those who have struggled with what we're facing. Why? Because they've been there. They've felt the pain, cried the buckets of tears, felt the anxiety and stayed up nights. They can sympathize in ways even our best friends cannot. But even their help is sometimes not enough. We need help from the throne of grace, the source of all comfort.

Throughout Jewish history, the high priest held the supreme position in the priestly hierarchy. The people looked to him to make the sin offering on the Day of Atonement. Only he could enter the most sacred place in the temple: the Most Holy Place, where the mercy seat rested. Jesus, as our high priest, offered the ultimate sacrifice of his own body so that no other sin offering will ever be required. When he hung on the cross, the curtain preventing access to the Most Holy Place ripped in two (see Matthew 27:51). Now everyone has access to the mercy seat. Our great high priest has opened the way for everyone to confidently enter the throne room of God.

No wonder Jesus extends amazing sympathy. He opened the way to forgiveness of sin and access to the Father. And beyond sympathy, Jesus offers empathy because he has suffered in ways no mere human has. Yes, Jesus encountered fear, exhaustion, weakness, abandonment and grief. He was misunderstood, mistreated, insulted, questioned, doubted, betrayed and so much more. He was "tempted in every way, just as we are—yet was without sin" (Hebrews 4:15). Moreover, he suffered all the horror and terrors of punishment for our sin.

Jesus knows. He feels what you feel; he sees deep into your soul. You can approach his throne with confidence, sit at his feet and weep with him. He's waiting for you.

Hebrews 4:15–16

For we do not have a high priest who is unable to sympathize with our weaknesses, but we have one who has been tempted in every way, just as we are—yet was without sin. Let us then approach the throne of grace with confidence, so that we may receive mercy and find grace to help us in our time of need.

reflection

1 When you encounter trials or temptations, to whom do you turn?

2 Do you feel confident that you will find an empathetic ear with Jesus?

3 Describe a time when you know, without a doubt, that Jesus answered your prayer for help in a time of need?

RELATED READINGS

Lamentations 3:22–23;
Matthew 27:50–54;
John 1:14–16;
Hebrews 2:10–18

Thursday

and the powers of the coming age, **6**if they fall away, to be brought back to repentance, because*a* to their loss they are crucifying the Son of God all over again and subjecting him to public disgrace.

7Land that drinks in the rain often falling on it and that produces a crop useful to those for whom it is farmed receives the blessing of God. **8**But land that produces thorns and thistles is worthless and is in danger of being cursed. In the end it will be burned.

9Even though we speak like this, dear friends, we are confident of better things in your case—things that accompany salvation. **10**God is not unjust; he will not forget your work and the love you have shown him as you have helped his people and continue to help them. **11**We want each of you to show this same diligence to the very end, in order to make your hope sure. **12**We do not want you to become lazy, but to imitate those who through faith and patience inherit what has been promised.

The Certainty of God's Promise

13When God made his promise to Abraham, since there was no one greater for him to swear by, he swore by himself, **14**saying, "I will surely bless you and give you many descendants."*b* **15**And so after waiting patiently, Abraham received what was promised.

16Men swear by someone greater than themselves, and the oath confirms what is said and puts an end to all argument. **17**Because God wanted to make the unchanging nature of his purpose very clear to the heirs of what was promised, he confirmed it with an oath. **18**God did this so that, by two unchangeable things in which it is impossible for God to lie, we who have fled to take hold of the hope offered to us may be greatly encouraged. **19**We have this hope as an anchor for the soul, firm and secure. It enters the inner sanctuary behind the curtain, **20**where Jesus, who went before us, has entered on our behalf. He has become a high priest forever, in the order of Melchizedek.

Melchizedek the Priest

7 This Melchizedek was king of Salem and priest of God Most High. He met Abraham returning from the defeat of the kings

and blessed him, **2**and Abraham gave him a tenth of everything. First, his name means "king of righteousness"; then also, "king of Salem" means "king of peace." **3**Without father or mother, without genealogy, without beginning of days or end of life, like the Son of God he remains a priest forever.

4Just think how great he was: Even the patriarch Abraham gave him a tenth of the plunder! **5**Now the law requires the descendants of Levi who become priests to collect a tenth from the people—that is, their brothers—even though their brothers are descended from Abraham. **6**This man, however, did not trace his descent from Levi, yet he collected a tenth from Abraham and blessed him who had the promises. **7**And without doubt the lesser person is blessed by the greater. **8**In the one case, the tenth is collected by men who die; but in the other case, by him who is declared to be living. **9**One might even say that Levi, who collects the tenth, paid the tenth through Abraham, **10**because when Melchizedek met Abraham, Levi was still in the body of his ancestor.

Jesus Like Melchizedek

11If perfection could have been attained through the Levitical priesthood (for on the basis of it the law was given to the people), why was there still need for another priest to come—one in the order of Melchizedek, not in the order of Aaron? **12**For when there is a change of the priesthood, there must also be a change of the law. **13**He of whom these things are said belonged to a different tribe, and no one from that tribe has ever served at the altar. **14**For it is clear that our Lord descended from Judah, and in regard to that tribe Moses said nothing about priests. **15**And what we have said is even more clear if another priest like Melchizedek appears, **16**one who has become a priest not on the basis of a regulation as to his ancestry but on the basis of the power of an indestructible life. **17**For it is declared:

"You are a priest forever,
    in the order of Melchizedek."*c*

18The former regulation is set aside because it was weak and useless **19**(for the law made

*a***6** Or *repentance while*   *b***14** Gen. 22:17   *c***17** Psalm 110:4

nothing perfect), and a better hope is introduced, by which we draw near to God.

²⁰And it was not without an oath! Others became priests without any oath, ²¹but he became a priest with an oath when God said to him:

"The Lord has sworn
    and will not change his mind:
'You are a priest forever.'"ᵃ

²²Because of this oath, Jesus has become the guarantee of a better covenant.

²³Now there have been many of those priests, since death prevented them from continuing in office; ²⁴but because Jesus lives forever, he has a permanent priesthood. ²⁵Therefore he is able to save completelyᵇ those who come to God through him, because he always lives to intercede for them.

²⁶Such a high priest meets our need—one who is holy, blameless, pure, set apart from sinners, exalted above the heavens. ²⁷Unlike the other high priests, he does not need to offer sacrifices day after day, first for his own sins, and then for the sins of the people. He sacrificed for their sins once for all when he offered himself. ²⁸For the law appoints as high priests men who are weak; but the oath, which came after the law, appointed the Son, who has been made perfect forever.

The High Priest of a New Covenant

8 The point of what we are saying is this: We do have such a high priest, who sat down at the right hand of the throne of the Majesty in heaven, ²and who serves in the sanctuary, the true tabernacle set up by the Lord, not by man.

³Every high priest is appointed to offer both gifts and sacrifices, and so it was necessary for this one also to have something to offer. ⁴If he were on earth, he would not be a priest, for there are already men who offer the gifts prescribed by the law. ⁵They serve at a sanctuary that is a copy and shadow of what is in heaven. This is why Moses was warned when he was about to build the tabernacle: "See to it that you make everything according to the pattern shown you on the mountain."ᶜ ⁶But the ministry Jesus has received is as superior to theirs as the covenant of which he is mediator is superior to the old one, and it is founded on better promises.

⁷For if there had been nothing wrong with that first covenant, no place would have been sought for another. ⁸But God found fault with the people and said ᵈ:

"The time is coming,
        declares the Lord,
    when I will make a new
        covenant
with the house of Israel
    and with the house of
        Judah.
⁹It will not be like the
        covenant
    I made with their
        forefathers
    when I took them by the
        hand
to lead them out of Egypt,
because they did not remain faithful to my
        covenant,
    and I turned away from them,
                declares the Lord.
¹⁰This is the covenant I will make with the
        house of Israel
    after that time, declares the Lord.
I will put my laws in their minds
    and write them on their hearts.
I will be their God,
    and they will be my people.
¹¹No longer will a man teach his
        neighbor,
    or a man his brother, saying, 'Know the
        Lord,'
because they will all know me,
    from the least of them to the
        greatest.
¹²For I will forgive their wickedness
    and will remember their sins no
        more."ᵉ

Hebrews 7:25

God Saves Completely

Therefore he is able to save completely those who come to God through him, because he always lives to intercede for them.

ᵃ21 Psalm 110:4 ᵇ25 Or *forever* ᶜ5 Exodus 25:40 ᵈ8 Some manuscripts may be translated *fault and said to the people.*
ᵉ12 Jer. 31:31–34

Prayer From A–Z

Hebrews 7:25

Therefore he is able to save completely those who come to God through him, because he always lives to intercede for them.

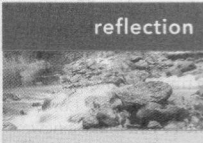

reflection

1 How would you rate your prayer life on a scale of one to ten?

2 Do you talk to God as much as you talk to your best friend? Why or why not?

3 How does it make you feel to know that Jesus lives to intercede for you? Spend time with him now, asking him to intercede on your behalf. Go through the alphabet of your needs.

RELATED READINGS

Daniel 9:17–23;
Luke 11:1–13;
Romans 8:26–27

"Prayer enlarges the heart until it is capable of containing God's gift of himself."

Mother Teresa

Read: Hebrews 7:11–28

AN ELDERLY GENTLEMAN passed his granddaughter's room one night and listened in as she repeated the alphabet in an oddly reverent way. He peeked in and asked her, "What on earth are you up to?" She explained, "I'm saying my prayers, but I can't think of exactly the right words tonight, so I'm just saying all the letters. Jesus will put them together for me because he knows what I'm thinking."

We've all been there. Our thoughts grow so muddled or our situations have grown so complicated that we don't know how to pray. We know we ought to pray. We feel the need to pray. But when we get on our knees or sit on our beds with our Bibles open, our minds go blank. *Lord, I don't even know where to start.*

What do you do when you don't know what to pray, how to pray or where to begin? Do you start cleaning the house? Do you make a mental to-do list? Do you cry? Do you just give up? The answer is found in Hebrews 7:25: Come to God through Jesus and ask him to intercede for you—he "lives to intercede for [you]."

Maybe you could take a cue from the little girl in the story and start your prayer alphabetically. A—appointments; B—busyness; C—children; D—deadlines; E—empty-nest . . . you get the idea. You can fill in the blanks. More importantly, Jesus can fill in the blanks. He knows what you need before you even utter the words.

Prayer is simply a conversation between you and God. You don't have to bend your knees, although you can. You don't have to bow your head—you can look up to heaven. You can pray with closed eyes, open eyes, hands clasped or lifted in praise. You can pray as you drive your car, as you wash your dishes or as you take your daily walk. You can make your life a continual conversation with God. As you commune with God, Jesus will intercede for you. He'll cover all the things you need, from A–Z. It's what he lives to do.

Go to page 1483 for your next devotional reading.

¹³By calling this covenant "new," he has made the first one obsolete; and what is obsolete and aging will soon disappear.

Worship in the Earthly Tabernacle

9 Now the first covenant had regulations for worship and also an earthly sanctuary. ²A tabernacle was set up. In its first room were the lampstand, the table and the consecrated bread; this was called the Holy Place. ³Behind the second curtain was a room called the Most Holy Place, ⁴which had the golden altar of incense and the gold-covered ark of the covenant. This ark contained the gold jar of manna, Aaron's staff that had budded, and the stone tablets of the covenant. ⁵Above the ark were the cherubim of the Glory, overshadowing the atonement cover.ᵃ But we cannot discuss these things in detail now.

⁶When everything had been arranged like this, the priests entered regularly into the outer room to carry on their ministry. ⁷But only the high priest entered the inner room, and that only once a year, and never without blood, which he offered for himself and for the sins the people had committed in ignorance. ⁸The Holy Spirit was showing by this that the way into the Most Holy Place had not yet been disclosed as long as the first tabernacle was still standing. ⁹This is an illustration for the present time, indicating that the gifts and sacrifices being offered were not able to clear the conscience of the worshiper. ¹⁰They are only a matter of food and drink and various ceremonial washings—external regulations applying until the time of the new order.

The Blood of Christ

¹¹When Christ came as high priest of the good things that are already here,ᵇ he went through the greater and more perfect tabernacle that is not man-made, that is to say, not a part of this creation. ¹²He did not enter by means of the blood of goats and calves; but he entered the Most Holy Place once for all by his own blood, having obtained eternal redemption. ¹³The blood of goats and bulls and the ashes of a heifer sprinkled on those who are ceremonially unclean sanctify them so that

they are outwardly clean. ¹⁴How much more, then, will the blood of Christ, who through the eternal Spirit offered himself unblemished to God, cleanse our consciences from acts that lead to death,ᶜ so that we may serve the living God!

¹⁵For this reason Christ is the mediator of a new covenant, that those who are called may receive the promised eternal inheritance—now that he has died as a ransom to set them free from the sins committed under the first covenant.

¹⁶In the case of a will,ᵈ it is necessary to prove the death of the one who made it, ¹⁷because a will is in force only when somebody has died; it never takes effect while the one who made it is living. ¹⁸This is why even the first covenant was not put into effect without blood. ¹⁹When Moses had proclaimed every commandment of the law to all the people, he took the blood of calves, together with water, scarlet wool and branches of hyssop, and sprinkled the scroll and all the people. ²⁰He said, "This is the blood of the covenant, which God has commanded you to keep."ᵉ ²¹In the same way, he sprinkled with the blood both the tabernacle and everything used in its ceremonies. ²²In fact, the law requires that nearly everything be cleansed with blood, and without the shedding of blood there is no forgiveness.

²³It was necessary, then, for the copies of the heavenly things to be purified with these sacrifices, but the heavenly things themselves with better sacrifices than these. ²⁴For Christ did not enter a man-made sanctuary that was only a copy of the true one; he entered heaven itself, now to appear for us in God's presence. ²⁵Nor did he enter heaven to offer himself again and again, the way the high priest enters the Most Holy Place every year with blood that is not his own. ²⁶Then Christ would have had to suffer many times since the creation of the world. But now he has appeared once for all at the end of the ages to do away with sin by the sacrifice of himself. ²⁷Just as man is destined to die once, and after that to face judgment, ²⁸so Christ was sacrificed once to take away the sins of many people; and he will appear a second

ᵃ5 Traditionally *the mercy seat* ᵇ11 Some early manuscripts *are to come* ᶜ14 Or *from useless rituals* ᵈ16 Same Greek word as *covenant*; also in verse 17 ᵉ20 Exodus 24:8

time, not to bear sin, but to bring salvation to those who are waiting for him.

Christ's Sacrifice Once for All

10 The law is only a shadow of the good things that are coming—not the realities themselves. For this reason it can never, by the same sacrifices repeated endlessly year after year, make perfect those who draw near to worship. ²If it could, would they not have stopped being offered? For the worshipers would have been cleansed once for all, and would no longer have felt guilty for their sins. ³But those sacrifices are an annual reminder of sins, ⁴because it is impossible for the blood of bulls and goats to take away sins.

⁵Therefore, when Christ came into the world, he said:

"Sacrifice and offering you did not desire,
 but a body you prepared for me;
⁶with burnt offerings and sin offerings
 you were not pleased.
⁷Then I said, 'Here I am—it
 is written about me
 in the scroll—
I have come to do your
 will, O God.'"ᵃ

⁸First he said, "Sacrifices and offerings, burnt offerings and sin offerings you did not desire, nor were you pleased with them" (although the law required them to be made). ⁹Then he said, "Here I am, I have come to do your will." He sets aside the first to establish the second. ¹⁰And by that will, we have been made holy through the sacrifice of the body of Jesus Christ once for all.

¹¹Day after day every priest stands and performs his religious duties; again and again he offers the same sacrifices, which can never take away sins. ¹²But when this priest had offered for all time one sacrifice for sins, he sat down at the right hand of God. ¹³Since that time he waits for his enemies to be made his footstool, ¹⁴because by one sacrifice he has made perfect forever those who are being made holy.

¹⁵The Holy Spirit also testifies to us about this. First he says:

¹⁶"This is the covenant I will make with
 them
 after that time, says the Lord.
I will put my laws in their hearts,
 and I will write them on their minds."ᵇ

¹⁷Then he adds:

"Their sins and lawless acts
 I will remember no more."ᶜ

¹⁸And where these have been forgiven, there is no longer any sacrifice for sin.

A Call to Persevere

¹⁹Therefore, brothers, since we have confidence to enter the Most Holy Place by the blood of Jesus, ²⁰by a new and living way opened for us through the curtain, that is, his body, ²¹and since we have a great priest over the house of God, ²²let us draw near to God with a sincere heart in full assurance of faith, having our hearts sprinkled to cleanse us from a guilty conscience and having our bodies washed with pure water. ²³Let us hold unswervingly to the hope we profess, for he who promised is faithful. ²⁴And let us consider how we may spur one another on toward love and good deeds. ²⁵Let us not give up meeting together, as some are in the habit of doing, but let us encourage one another—and all the more as you see the Day approaching.

Hebrews 10:23

God Is Faithful

Let us hold unswervingly to the hope we profess, for he who promised is faithful.

²⁶If we deliberately keep on sinning after we have received the knowledge of the truth, no sacrifice for sins is left, ²⁷but only a fearful expectation of judgment and of raging fire that will consume the enemies of God. ²⁸Anyone who rejected the law of Moses died without mercy on the testimony of two or three witnesses. ²⁹How much more severely do you think a man deserves to be punished who has trampled the Son of God under foot, who has treated as an unholy thing the blood of the cov-

ᵃ7 Psalm 40:6–8 (see Septuagint) ᵇ16 Jer. 31:33 ᶜ17 Jer. 31:34

enant that sanctified him, and who has insulted the Spirit of grace? **30**For we know him who said, "It is mine to avenge; I will repay,"*a* and again, "The Lord will judge his people."*b* **31**It is a dreadful thing to fall into the hands of the living God.

32Remember those earlier days after you had received the light, when you stood your ground in a great contest in the face of suffering. **33**Sometimes you were publicly exposed to insult and persecution; at other times you stood side by side with those who were so treated. **34**You sympathized with those in prison and joyfully accepted the confiscation of your property, because you knew that you yourselves had better and lasting possessions.

35So do not throw away your confidence; it will be richly rewarded. **36**You need to persevere so that when you have done the will of God, you will receive what he has promised. **37**For in just a very little while,

> "He who is coming will come and will not delay.
> **38** But my righteous one*c* will live by faith.
> And if he shrinks back,
> I will not be pleased with him."*d*

39But we are not of those who shrink back and are destroyed, but of those who believe and are saved.

By Faith

11 Now faith is being sure of what we hope for and certain of what we do not see. **2**This is what the ancients were commended for.

3By faith we understand that the universe was formed at God's command, so that what is seen was not made out of what was visible.

4By faith Abel offered God a better sacrifice than Cain did. By faith he was commended as a righteous man, when God spoke well of his offerings. And by faith he still speaks, even though he is dead.

5By faith Enoch was taken from this life, so that he did not experience death; he could not be found, because God had taken him away. For before he was taken, he was commended as one who pleased God. **6**And without faith it is impossible to please God, because anyone who comes to him must believe that he exists and that he rewards those who earnestly seek him.

7By faith Noah, when warned about things not yet seen, in holy fear built an ark to save his family. By his faith he condemned the world and became heir of the righteousness that comes by faith.

8By faith Abraham, when called to go to a place he would later receive as his inheritance, obeyed and went, even though he did not know where he was going. **9**By faith he made his home in the promised land like a stranger in a foreign country; he lived in tents, as did Isaac and Jacob, who were heirs with him of the same promise. **10**For he was looking forward to the city with foundations, whose architect and builder is God.

11By faith Abraham, even though he was past age—and Sarah herself was barren—was enabled to become a father because he*e* considered him faithful who had made the promise. **12**And so from this one man, and he as good as dead, came descendants as numerous as the stars in the sky and as countless as the sand on the seashore.

13All these people were still living by faith when they died. They did not receive the things promised; they only saw them and welcomed them from a distance. And they admitted that they were aliens and strangers on earth. **14**People who say such things show that they are looking for a country of their own. **15**If they had been thinking of the country they had left, they would have had opportunity to return. **16**Instead, they were longing for a better country—a heavenly one. Therefore God is not ashamed to be called their God, for he has prepared a city for them.

17By faith Abraham, when God tested him, offered Isaac as a sacrifice. He who had received the promises was about to sacrifice his one and only son, **18**even though God had said to him, "It is through Isaac that your offspring*f* will be reckoned."*g* **19**Abraham reasoned that God could raise the dead, and figuratively speaking, he did receive Isaac back from death.

---

*a***30** Deut. 32:35   *b***30** Deut. 32:36; Psalm 135:14   *c***38** One early manuscript *But the righteous*   *d***38** Hab. 2:3,4   *e***11** Or *By faith even Sarah, who was past age, was enabled to bear children because she*   *f***18** Greek *seed*   *g***18** Gen. 21:12

²⁰By faith Isaac blessed Jacob and Esau in regard to their future.

²¹By faith Jacob, when he was dying, blessed each of Joseph's sons, and worshiped as he leaned on the top of his staff.

²²By faith Joseph, when his end was near, spoke about the exodus of the Israelites from Egypt and gave instructions about his bones.

²³By faith Moses' parents hid him for three months after he was born, because they saw he was no ordinary child, and they were not afraid of the king's edict.

²⁴By faith Moses, when he had grown up, refused to be known as the son of Pharaoh's daughter. ²⁵He chose to be mistreated along with the people of God rather than to enjoy the pleasures of sin for a short time. ²⁶He regarded disgrace for the sake of Christ as of greater value than the treasures of Egypt, because he was looking ahead to his reward. ²⁷By faith he left Egypt, not fearing the king's anger; he persevered because he saw him who is invisible.

²⁸By faith he kept the Passover and the sprinkling of blood, so that the destroyer of the firstborn would not touch the firstborn of Israel.

²⁹By faith the people passed through the Red Sea[a] as on dry land; but when the Egyptians tried to do so, they were drowned.

³⁰By faith the walls of Jericho fell, after the people had marched around them for seven days.

³¹By faith the prostitute Rahab, because she welcomed the spies, was not killed with those who were disobedient.[b]

³²And what more shall I say? I do not have time to tell about Gideon, Barak, Samson, Jephthah, David, Samuel and the prophets, ³³who through faith conquered kingdoms, administered justice, and gained what was promised; who shut the mouths of lions, ³⁴quenched the fury of the flames, and escaped the edge of the sword; whose weakness was turned to strength; and

who became powerful in battle and routed foreign armies. ³⁵Women received back their dead, raised to life again. Others were tortured and refused to be released, so that they might gain a better resurrection. ³⁶Some faced jeers and flogging, while still others were chained and put in prison. ³⁷They were stoned[c]; they were sawed in two; they were put to death by the sword. They went about in sheepskins and goatskins, destitute, persecuted and mistreated— ³⁸the world was not worthy of them. They wandered in deserts and mountains, and in caves and holes in the ground.

³⁹These were all commended for their faith, yet none of them received what had been promised. ⁴⁰God had planned something better for us so that only together with us would they be made perfect.

God Disciplines His Sons

12 Therefore, since we are surrounded by such a great cloud of witnesses, let us throw off everything that hinders and the sin that so easily entangles, and let us run with perseverance the race marked out for us. ²Let us fix our eyes on Jesus, the author and perfecter of our faith, who for the joy set before him endured the cross, scorning its shame, and sat down at the right hand of the throne of God. ³Consider him who endured such opposition from sinful men, so that you will not grow weary and lose heart.

⁴In your struggle against sin, you have not yet resisted to the point of shedding your blood. ⁵And you have forgotten that word of encouragement that addresses you as sons:

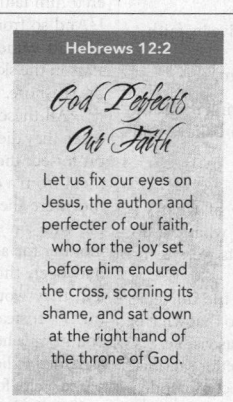

Hebrews 12:2

God Perfects Our Faith

Let us fix our eyes on Jesus, the author and perfecter of our faith, who for the joy set before him endured the cross, scorning its shame, and sat down at the right hand of the throne of God.

"My son, do not make light of the Lord's discipline,
  and do not lose heart when he rebukes you,
⁶because the Lord disciplines those he loves,
  and he punishes everyone he accepts as a son."[d]

---

[a]29 That is, Sea of Reeds   [b]31 Or *unbelieving*   [c]37 Some early manuscripts *stoned; they were put to the test;*   [d]6 Prov. 3:11,12

Conviction

BERNICE

CASUALLY RAISING HER BEJEWELED HAND to her cheek, she felt her face flush with color.

Why are you blushing? Bernice silently chastised herself. She assuaged her worries by assuring herself that it was, indeed, rather warm in here. She *couldn't* let this man get to her, what with his wild tale of desert visions, voices and people being raised from the dead. He was crazy. A lunatic.

So, why, at the same time, did his words ring with authenticity? Why did they seem to pierce her very soul and sear her conscience as if with a white-hot rod of steel?

Bernice was used to these occasional waves of guilt that coursed through her from time to time. After stifling whatever conviction she may have felt over the years, the guilt became less and less frequent, and now it was almost entirely absent. She was a married woman and carrying on as someone's mistress, but it didn't bother her, per se. It didn't even really concern her that the man beside her listening to Paul's testimony, Herod Agrippa II, was her lover. Or that he was also her brother. In her mind, being her brother's mistress was nobody's business but their own.

At least she didn't *think* it bothered her. Until now. Listening to Paul explain his faith in God, she felt faint. She was light-headed and almost nauseated.

Outwardly, she sneered at his absurdity, but inside she was a royal mess. At the most dramatic points of Paul's testimony, she felt inexplicably drawn and completely repelled at the same time. Of course, she would never breathe a word of this to anyone. She had an image to uphold. So, when it came time to pronounce an opinion on the matter, she sided with her brother's nonchalance. But she never forgot that hour in Caesarea.

—Prayer—

Almighty God, give me courage to share with others your message of love. Like Paul, help me be a gracious witness for you.

Paul replied, "Short time or long—I pray God that not only you but all who are listening to me today may become what I am, except for these chains."

Acts 26:29

ASSIGNED READING:

Acts 25:13— 26:32

Go to page 1485 for your next devotional reading.

Weekend

[7]Endure hardship as discipline; God is treating you as sons. For what son is not disciplined by his father? [8]If you are not disciplined (and everyone undergoes discipline), then you are illegitimate children and not true sons. [9]Moreover, we have all had human fathers who disciplined us and we respected them for it. How much more should we submit to the Father of our spirits and live! [10]Our fathers disciplined us for a little while as they thought best; but God disciplines us for our good, that we may share in his holiness. [11]No discipline seems pleasant at the time, but painful. Later on, however, it produces a harvest of righteousness and peace for those who have been trained by it.

[12]Therefore, strengthen your feeble arms and weak knees. [13]"Make level paths for your feet,"[a] so that the lame may not be disabled, but rather healed.

Warning Against Refusing God

[14]Make every effort to live in peace with all men and to be holy; without holiness no one will see the Lord. [15]See to it that no one misses the grace of God and that no bitter root grows up to cause trouble and defile many. [16]See that no one is sexually immoral, or is godless like Esau, who for a single meal sold his inheritance rights as the oldest son. [17]Afterward, as you know, when he wanted to inherit this blessing, he was rejected. He could bring about no change of mind, though he sought the blessing with tears.

[18]You have not come to a mountain that can be touched and that is burning with fire; to darkness, gloom and storm; [19]to a trumpet blast or to such a voice speaking words that those who heard it begged that no further word be spoken to them, [20]because they could not bear what was commanded: "If even an animal touches the mountain, it must be stoned."[b] [21]The sight was so terrifying that Moses said, "I am trembling with fear."[c]

[22]But you have come to Mount Zion, to the heavenly Jerusalem, the city of the living God. You have come to thousands upon thousands of angels in joyful assembly, [23]to the church of the firstborn, whose names are written in heaven. You have come to God, the judge of all men, to the spirits of righteous men made perfect, [24]to Jesus the mediator of a new covenant, and to the sprinkled blood that speaks a better word than the blood of Abel.

[25]See to it that you do not refuse him who speaks. If they did not escape when they refused him who warned them on earth, how much less will we, if we turn away from him who warns us from heaven? [26]At that time his voice shook the earth, but now he has promised, "Once more I will shake not only the earth but also the heavens."[d] [27]The words "once more" indicate the removing of what can be shaken—that is, created things—so that what cannot be shaken may remain.

[28]Therefore, since we are receiving a kingdom that cannot be shaken, let us be thankful, and so worship God acceptably with reverence and awe, [29]for our "God is a consuming fire."[e]

Concluding Exhortations

13 Keep on loving each other as brothers. [2]Do not forget to entertain strangers, for by so doing some people have entertained angels without knowing it. [3]Remember those in prison as if you were their fellow prisoners, and those who are mistreated as if you yourselves were suffering.

[4]Marriage should be honored by all, and the marriage bed kept pure, for God will judge the adulterer and all the sexually immoral. [5]Keep your lives free from the love of money and be content with what you have, because God has said,

"Never will I leave you;
    never will I forsake you."[f]

[6]So we say with confidence,

"The Lord is my helper; I will not be afraid.
    What can man do to me?"[g]

[7]Remember your leaders, who spoke the word of God to you. Consider the outcome of their way of life and imitate their faith. [8]Jesus Christ is the same yesterday and today and forever.

[9]Do not be carried away by all kinds of strange teachings. It is good for our hearts to be strengthened by grace, not by ceremonial foods,

---

[a]13 Prov. 4:26   [b]20 Exodus 19:12,13   [c]21 Deut. 9:19   [d]26 Haggai 2:6   [e]29 Deut. 4:24   [f]5 Deut. 31:6   [g]6 Psalm 118:6,7

The Meaning of Life

Read: Hebrews 13:1–21

AFTER DECADES OF RESEARCH, George Gallup Jr. listed the top spiritual needs of people today:

1. To believe that life is meaningful and has a purpose
2. To have a sense of community and deeper relationships
3. To be appreciated and respected
4. To be listened to
5. To feel they are growing in faith
6. To get practical help in developing a mature faith

Notice how many of the needs relate to relationships. That's because we are created to be relational people. God created us first to have a relationship with him and second to have relationships with one another. It is through our interactions with others that we find meaning in life. The Bible teaches that others will know whether our Christianity is genuine by looking at whether our love for each other is real (see John 13:35).

It's easy to love people who love us, but we are commanded to extend kindness and acts of service even to strangers. Doing so is a sign that our faith is dynamic and alive. God asks us to grow and mature by forgiving those who have wronged us. And Scripture instructs us to put others' needs ahead of our own, even if it's not convenient. That's how we show others we appreciate and respect them.

In Hebrews 13 the author instructs us concerning hospitality to strangers, marital relations and submission to authority—in essence, how to build relationships. But the whole catalog of interactions with others is rooted in, and gets its life source from, our relationship with Jesus. Our sacrifice of praise to God and our sacrifice of service to others are fundamentally linked to him. Our good works to others grow out of Christ's work *in* us, and that pleases him. None of our sacrifices for others are even comparable to the great sacrifice Jesus made in order to have a relationship with us. But the amazing thing is that when we offer the sacrifices of time, energy and good deeds to others, we not only grow closer to them, but we also grow closer to Jesus. In Christ, we find true meaning in our lives.

Hebrews 13:15–16

Through Jesus, therefore, let us continually offer to God a sacrifice of praise—the fruit of lips that confess his name. And do not forget to do good and to share with others, for with such sacrifices God is pleased.

reflection

1 Describe three incidents from Jesus' life on earth that depict how personal relationships were important to him.

2 In what ways have you put possessions, schedules or events ahead of people in your list of priorities?

3 Think of some practical ways you can show your family and friends this week that they are a priority to you.

RELATED READINGS

Job 29:11–17;
John 11:1–36;
3 John 1–4

Monday

Go to page 1490 for your next devotional reading.

which are of no value to those who eat them. [10]We have an altar from which those who minister at the tabernacle have no right to eat.

[11]The high priest carries the blood of animals into the Most Holy Place as a sin offering, but the bodies are burned outside the camp. [12]And so Jesus also suffered outside the city gate to make the people holy through his own blood. [13]Let us, then, go to him outside the camp, bearing the disgrace he bore. [14]For here we do not have an enduring city, but we are looking for the city that is to come.

[15]Through Jesus, therefore, let us continually offer to God a sacrifice of praise—the fruit of lips that confess his name. [16]And do not forget to do good and to share with others, for with such sacrifices God is pleased.

[17]Obey your leaders and submit to their authority. They keep watch over you as men who must give an account. Obey them so that their work will be a joy, not a burden, for that would be of no advantage to you.

[18]Pray for us. We are sure that we have a clear conscience and desire to live honorably in every way. [19]I particularly urge you to pray so that I may be restored to you soon.

[20]May the God of peace, who through the blood of the eternal covenant brought back from the dead our Lord Jesus, that great Shepherd of the sheep, [21]equip you with everything good for doing his will, and may he work in us what is pleasing to him, through Jesus Christ, to whom be glory for ever and ever. Amen.

[22]Brothers, I urge you to bear with my word of exhortation, for I have written you only a short letter.

[23]I want you to know that our brother Timothy has been released. If he arrives soon, I will come with him to see you.

[24]Greet all your leaders and all God's people. Those from Italy send you their greetings.

[25]Grace be with you all.

James

Hypocrisy is one of the biggest blights on the Christian faith. We say one thing, but we act in an entirely different manner. It was a problem in James's day, and it's a problem for us today. James tackles this issue in his letter, challenging his readers to examine both their beliefs and their actions. He goes beyond telling them what a Christian should do, however. Instead he shows them, illustrating with verbal pictures and vivid details, what *a life transformed by Jesus* looks like. It was a transformation he knew firsthand. As Jesus' half brother, he spent many years as a skeptic. It was only after Jesus' death and resurrection that *he became a true believer.*

The book of James is often categorized as wisdom literature—the "Proverbs" of the New Testament. His advice is extremely practical. It's the kind of teaching we can read and then clearly see how it should play out in our own lives. But it is also difficult. Knowing what to do and doing it are two different things, and James clearly understands that. He comes alongside us as a brother, challenging and encouraging us to live what we believe, putting our faith into action so that when the world looks at us *they'll know by what they see,* not just what we say, that we belong to Jesus.

Author:
James, the brother of Jesus.

Audience:
Early Jewish Christians scattered because of persecution and all followers of Jesus.

Date:
About A.D. 49.

Setting:
James encouraged the former members of the Jerusalem church, now scattered to various places because of persecution.

Verse to Remember:
As the body without the spirit is dead, so faith without deeds is dead. (2:26)

1

James, a servant of God and of the Lord Jesus Christ,

To the twelve tribes scattered among the nations:

Greetings.

Trials and Temptations

2Consider it pure joy, my brothers, whenever you face trials of many kinds, **3**because you know that the testing of your faith develops perseverance. **4**Perseverance must finish its work so that you may be mature and complete, not lacking anything. **5**If any of you lacks wisdom, he should ask God, who gives generously to all without finding fault, and it will be given to him. **6**But when he asks, he must believe and not doubt, because he who doubts is like a wave of the sea, blown and tossed by the wind. **7**That man should not think he will receive anything from the Lord; **8**he is a double-minded man, unstable in all he does.

9The brother in humble circumstances ought to take pride in his high position. **10**But the one who is rich should take pride in his low position, because he will pass away like a wild flower. **11**For the sun rises with scorching heat and withers the plant; its blossom falls and its beauty is destroyed. In the same way, the rich man will fade away even while he goes about his business.

12Blessed is the man who perseveres under trial, because when he has stood the test, he will receive the crown of life that God has promised to those who love him.

13When tempted, no one should say, "God is tempting me." For God cannot be tempted by evil, nor does he tempt anyone; **14**but each one is tempted when, by his own evil desire, he is dragged away and enticed. **15**Then, after desire has conceived, it gives birth to sin; and sin, when it is full-grown, gives birth to death.

16Don't be deceived, my dear brothers. **17**Every good and perfect gift is from above, coming down from the Father of the heavenly lights, who does not change like shifting shadows.

18He chose to give us birth through the word of truth, that we might be a kind of firstfruits of all he created.

Listening and Doing

19My dear brothers, take note of this: Everyone should be quick to listen, slow to speak and slow to become angry, **20**for man's anger does not bring about the righteous life that God desires. **21**Therefore, get rid of all moral filth and the evil that is so prevalent and humbly accept the word planted in you, which can save you.

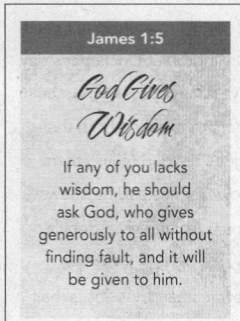

James 1:5

God Gives Wisdom

If any of you lacks wisdom, he should ask God, who gives generously to all without finding fault, and it will be given to him.

22Do not merely listen to the word, and so deceive yourselves. Do what it says. **23**Anyone who listens to the word but does not do what it says is like a man who looks at his face in a mirror **24**and, after looking at himself, goes away and immediately forgets what he looks like. **25**But the man who looks intently into the perfect law that gives freedom, and continues to do this, not forgetting what he has heard, but doing it—he will be blessed in what he does.

26If anyone considers himself religious and yet does not keep a tight rein on his tongue, he deceives himself and his religion is worthless. **27**Religion that God our Father accepts as pure and faultless is this: to look after orphans and widows in their distress and to keep oneself from being polluted by the world.

Favoritism Forbidden

2

My brothers, as believers in our glorious Lord Jesus Christ, don't show favoritism. **2**Suppose a man comes into your meeting wearing a gold ring and fine clothes, and a poor man in shabby clothes also comes in. **3**If you show special attention to the man wearing fine clothes and say, "Here's a good seat for you," but say to the poor man, "You stand there" or "Sit on the floor by my feet," **4**have you not discriminated among yourselves and become judges with evil thoughts?

5Listen, my dear brothers: Has not God chosen those who are poor in the eyes of the world to be rich in faith and to inherit the kingdom he promised those who love him? 6But you have insulted the poor. Is it not the rich who are exploiting you? Are they not the ones who are dragging you into court? 7Are they not the ones who are slandering the noble name of him to whom you belong?

8If you really keep the royal law found in Scripture, "Love your neighbor as yourself,"*a* you are doing right. 9But if you show favoritism, you sin and are convicted by the law as lawbreakers. 10For whoever keeps the whole law and yet stumbles at just one point is guilty of breaking all of it. 11For he who said, "Do not commit adultery,"*b* also said, "Do not murder."*c* If you do not commit adultery but do commit murder, you have become a lawbreaker.

12Speak and act as those who are going to be judged by the law that gives freedom, 13because judgment without mercy will be shown to anyone who has not been merciful. Mercy triumphs over judgment!

Faith and Deeds

14What good is it, my brothers, if a man claims to have faith but has no deeds? Can such faith save him? 15Suppose a brother or sister is without clothes and daily food. 16If one of you says to him, "Go, I wish you well; keep warm and well fed," but does nothing about his physical needs, what good is it? 17In the same way, faith by itself, if it is not accompanied by action, is dead.

18But someone will say, "You have faith; I have deeds."

Show me your faith without deeds, and I will show you my faith by what I do. 19You believe that there is one God. Good! Even the demons believe that—and shudder.

20You foolish man, do you want evidence that faith without deeds is useless*d*? 21Was not our ancestor Abraham considered righteous for what he did when he offered his son Isaac on the altar? 22You see that his faith and his actions were working together, and his faith was made complete by what he did. 23And the scripture was fulfilled that says, "Abraham believed God, and it was credited to him as righteous-

ness,"*e* and he was called God's friend. 24You see that a person is justified by what he does and not by faith alone.

25In the same way, was not even Rahab the prostitute considered righteous for what she did when she gave lodging to the spies and sent them off in a different direction? 26As the body without the spirit is dead, so faith without deeds is dead.

Taming the Tongue

3 Not many of you should presume to be teachers, my brothers, because you know that we who teach will be judged more strictly. 2We all stumble in many ways. If anyone is never at fault in what he says, he is a perfect man, able to keep his whole body in check.

3When we put bits into the mouths of horses to make them obey us, we can turn the whole animal. 4Or take ships as an example. Although they are so large and are driven by strong winds, they are steered by a very small rudder wherever the pilot wants to go. 5Likewise the tongue is a small part of the body, but it makes great boasts. Consider what a great forest is set on fire by a small spark. 6The tongue also is a fire, a world of evil among the parts of the body. It corrupts the whole person, sets the whole course of his life on fire, and is itself set on fire by hell.

7All kinds of animals, birds, reptiles and creatures of the sea are being tamed and have been tamed by man, 8but no man can tame the tongue. It is a restless evil, full of deadly poison.

9With the tongue we praise our Lord and Father, and with it we curse men, who have been made in God's likeness. 10Out of the same mouth come praise and cursing. My brothers, this should not be. 11Can both fresh water and salt*f* water flow from the same spring? 12My brothers, can a fig tree bear olives, or a grapevine bear figs? Neither can a salt spring produce fresh water.

Two Kinds of Wisdom

13Who is wise and understanding among you? Let him show it by his good life, by deeds done in the humility that comes from wisdom.

*a*8 Lev. 19:18   *b*11 Exodus 20:14; Deut. 5:18   *c*11 Exodus 20:13; Deut. 5:17   *d*20 Some early manuscripts *dead*   *e*23 Gen. 15:6   *f*11 Greek *bitter* (see also verse 14)

James 3:5

The tongue is a small part of the body, but it makes great boasts. Consider what a great forest is set on fire by a small spark.

reflection

1 Do you know someone whose life has been burned by gossip or harsh words?

2 On a scale of one to ten, how hot are your words?

3 How will you begin to use your tongue for healing rather than harm?

RELATED READINGS

Psalm 52:1–5;
Proverbs 11:11–13;
12:17–19;
James 1:22–26

"Gossips and talebearers set on fire all the houses they enter."

Unknown

IN 1944 THE NATIONAL FOREST SERVICE introduced the cartoon character Smokey Bear as the mascot for fire prevention. Soon afterward, a fire caused by human negligence ravaged 17,000 acres of forest in Capitan, New Mexico. During this fire, a tiny bear cub scampered up a tree. With badly burned paws and hind legs, the cub clung tenaciously to that pine tree until he was found by a firefighter. The cub was quickly dubbed Smokey Bear. School-age children were able to complete the phrase, "Only you . . ." with the concluding words ". . . can prevent forest fires." The phrase grew more popular than any other motto.

In the book of James we learn that our tongues can either be fire igniters or fire extinguishers. James pointed out that believers often engage in gossip, slander and backbiting. While working to build up the body of Christ with their actions, their tongues can insidiously cause fires throughout the church.

Lightning sometimes causes wildfires. But nine out of ten wildfires are caused by human negligence or arson. In the southwestern United States, a freight train threw sparks into ranch land, destroying 40,000 acres, along with an untold number of cattle. Word fires, like gossip, have split churches, ruined lives and can be just as scorching as forest fires. In California, landscape designers use ground cover as fire-retardant buffers around valuable property. Rather than using your words as combustible fodder, why not choose words that are fire resistant? Here are 12 words to quench a hot situation:

1: "Please" and **2, 3:** "Thank you:" Like water, these words refresh the listener.

4, 5: "I'm sorry." These two words quench the flames of heated arguments.

6, 7, 8: "I love you." These words carry tremendous power. They are the Niagara Falls of words.

9, 10, 11, 12: "I'm praying for you." These words let others know that you will ask God to give them the living water of Jesus and the Word. They will hydrate a dry and weary soul.

Go to page 1496 for your next devotional reading.

¹⁴But if you harbor bitter envy and selfish ambition in your hearts, do not boast about it or deny the truth. ¹⁵Such "wisdom" does not come down from heaven but is earthly, unspiritual, of the devil. ¹⁶For where you have envy and selfish ambition, there you find disorder and every evil practice.

¹⁷But the wisdom that comes from heaven is first of all pure; then peace-loving, considerate, submissive, full of mercy and good fruit, impartial and sincere. ¹⁸Peacemakers who sow in peace raise a harvest of righteousness.

Submit Yourselves to God

4 What causes fights and quarrels among you? Don't they come from your desires that battle within you? ²You want something but don't get it. You kill and covet, but you cannot have what you want. You quarrel and fight. You do not have, because you do not ask God. ³When you ask, you do not receive, because you ask with wrong motives, that you may spend what you get on your pleasures.

⁴You adulterous people, don't you know that friendship with the world is hatred toward God? Anyone who chooses to be a friend of the world becomes an enemy of God. ⁵Or do you think Scripture says without reason that the spirit he caused to live in us envies intensely?ᵃ ⁶But he gives us more grace. That is why Scripture says:

> "God opposes the proud
> but gives grace to the
> humble."ᵇ

⁷Submit yourselves, then, to God. Resist the devil, and he will flee from you. ⁸Come near to God and he will come near to you. Wash your hands, you sinners, and purify your hearts, you double-minded. ⁹Grieve, mourn and wail. Change your laughter to mourning and your joy to gloom. ¹⁰Humble yourselves before the Lord, and he will lift you up.

¹¹Brothers, do not slander one another. Anyone who speaks against his brother or judges

him speaks against the law and judges it. When you judge the law, you are not keeping it, but sitting in judgment on it. ¹²There is only one Lawgiver and Judge, the one who is able to save and destroy. But you—who are you to judge your neighbor?

Boasting About Tomorrow

¹³Now listen, you who say, "Today or tomorrow we will go to this or that city, spend a year there, carry on business and make money." ¹⁴Why, you do not even know what will happen tomorrow. What is your life? You are a mist that appears for a little while and then vanishes. ¹⁵Instead, you ought to say, "If it is the Lord's will, we will live and do this or that." ¹⁶As it is, you boast and brag. All such boasting is evil. ¹⁷Anyone, then, who knows the good he ought to do and doesn't do it, sins.

Warning to Rich Oppressors

5 Now listen, you rich people, weep and wail because of the misery that is coming upon you. ²Your wealth has rotted, and moths have eaten your clothes. ³Your gold and silver are corroded. Their corrosion will testify against you and eat your flesh like fire. You have hoarded wealth in the last days. ⁴Look! The wages you failed to pay the workmen who mowed your fields are crying out against you. The cries of the harvesters have reached the ears of the Lord Almighty. ⁵You have lived on earth in luxury and self-indulgence. You have fattened yourselves in the day of slaughter.ᶜ ⁶You have condemned and murdered innocent men, who were not opposing you.

Patience in Suffering

⁷Be patient, then, brothers, until the Lord's coming. See how the farmer waits for the land to yield its valuable crop and how patient he is for the autumn and spring rains. ⁸You too, be patient and stand firm, because the Lord's coming is near. ⁹Don't grumble against each other, brothers, or you will be judged. The Judge is standing at the door!

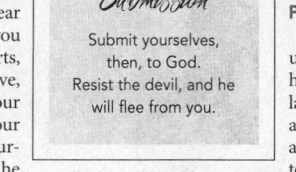

James 4:7

God Looks for Submission

Submit yourselves, then, to God. Resist the devil, and he will flee from you.

ᵃ5 Or *that God jealously longs for the spirit that he made to live in us*; or *that the Spirit he caused to live in us longs jealously*
ᵇ6 Prov. 3:34   ᶜ5 Or *yourselves as in a day of feasting*

¹⁰Brothers, as an example of patience in the face of suffering, take the prophets who spoke in the name of the Lord. ¹¹As you know, we consider blessed those who have persevered. You have heard of Job's perseverance and have seen what the Lord finally brought about. The Lord is full of compassion and mercy.

¹²Above all, my brothers, do not swear—not by heaven or by earth or by anything else. Let your "Yes" be yes, and your "No," no, or you will be condemned.

The Prayer of Faith

¹³Is any one of you in trouble? He should pray. Is anyone happy? Let him sing songs of praise. ¹⁴Is any one of you sick? He should call the elders of the church to pray over him and anoint him with oil in the name of the Lord. ¹⁵And the prayer offered in faith will make the sick person well; the Lord will raise him up. If he has sinned, he will be forgiven. ¹⁶Therefore confess your sins to each other and pray for each other so that you may be healed. The prayer of a righteous man is powerful and effective.

¹⁷Elijah was a man just like us. He prayed earnestly that it would not rain, and it did not rain on the land for three and a half years. ¹⁸Again he prayed, and the heavens gave rain, and the earth produced its crops.

¹⁹My brothers, if one of you should wander from the truth and someone should bring him back, ²⁰remember this: Whoever turns a sinner from the error of his way will save him from death and cover over a multitude of sins.

James 5:16

God Heals Prayer

Therefore confess your sins to each other and pray for each other so that you may be healed. The prayer of a righteous man is powerful and effective.

1 Peter

Your attitude toward others *represents Christ to them.* Peter wants his readers to understand this point. Be as gentle as you can, especially when dealing with unbelievers. Forgive their harshness. Answer those in authority respectfully, even if they don't treat you well. Whether you're dealing with a hard boss, an unbelieving husband or someone else who sometimes makes life difficult, *live for Christ* and don't assert your own rights. Let the unbelievers see your good deeds and notice that you are different.

Peter's readers were suffering, and he wanted them to be able to accept that suffering and to let the suffering itself help them reflect the gospel. If they accepted the suffering as part of their Christian experience rather than fighting it, the world would have a chance *to see that Christ offers hope.*

Author:
The apostle Peter.

Audience:
Early Jewish Christians scattered because of persecution and all followers of Jesus.

Date:
About A.D. 62–64, possibly written from Rome.

Setting:
The Roman emperor Nero was leading severe persecution of Christians.

Verse to Remember:
It is better, if it is God's will, to suffer for doing good than for doing evil. (3:17)

1

Peter, an apostle of Jesus Christ,

To God's elect, strangers in the world, scattered throughout Pontus, Galatia, Cappadocia, Asia and Bithynia, **2** who have been chosen according to the foreknowledge of God the Father, through the sanctifying work of the Spirit, for obedience to Jesus Christ and sprinkling by his blood:

Grace and peace be yours in abundance.

Praise to God for a Living Hope

3 Praise be to the God and Father of our Lord Jesus Christ! In his great mercy he has given us new birth into a living hope through the resurrection of Jesus Christ from the dead, ⁴and into an inheritance that can never perish, spoil or fade—kept in heaven for you, ⁵who through faith are shielded by God's power until the coming of the salvation that is ready to be revealed in the last time. ⁶In this you greatly rejoice, though now for a little while you may have had to suffer grief in all kinds of trials. ⁷These have come so that your faith—of greater worth than gold, which perishes even though refined by fire—may be proved genuine and may result in praise, glory and honor when Jesus Christ is revealed. ⁸Though you have not seen him, you love him; and even though you do not see him now, you believe in him and are filled with an inexpressible and glorious joy, ⁹for you are receiving the goal of your faith, the salvation of your souls.

¹⁰Concerning this salvation, the prophets, who spoke of the grace that was to come to you, searched intently and with the greatest care, ¹¹trying to find out the time and circumstances to which the Spirit of Christ in them was pointing when he predicted the sufferings of Christ and the glories that would follow. ¹²It was revealed to them that they were not serving themselves but you, when they spoke of the things that have now been told you by those who have preached the gospel to you by the Holy Spirit sent from heaven. Even angels long to look into these things.

Be Holy

¹³Therefore, prepare your minds for action; be self-controlled; set your hope fully on the grace to be given you when Jesus Christ is revealed. ¹⁴As obedient children, do not conform to the evil desires you had when you lived in ignorance. ¹⁵But just as he who called you is holy, so be holy in all you do; ¹⁶for it is written: "Be holy, because I am holy."ᵃ

¹⁷Since you call on a Father who judges each man's work impartially, live your lives as strangers here in reverent fear. ¹⁸For you know that it was not with perishable things such as silver or gold that you were redeemed from the empty way of life handed down to you from your forefathers, ¹⁹but with the precious blood of

Christ, a lamb without blemish or defect. ²⁰He was chosen before the creation of the world, but was revealed in these last times for your sake. ²¹Through him you believe in God, who raised him from the dead and glorified him, and so your faith and hope are in God.

²²Now that you have purified yourselves by obeying the truth so that you have sincere love for your brothers, love one another deeply, from the heart.ᵇ ²³For you have been born again, not of perishable seed, but of imperishable, through the living and enduring word of God. ²⁴For,

"All men are like grass,
   and all their glory is like the flowers of
      the field;
the grass withers and the flowers fall,
25   but the word of the Lord stands forever."ᶜ

And this is the word that was preached to you.

2 Therefore, rid yourselves of all malice and all deceit, hypocrisy, envy, and slander of every kind. ²Like newborn babies, crave pure spiritual milk, so that by it you may grow up in your salvation, ³now that you have tasted that the Lord is good.

The Living Stone and a Chosen People

⁴As you come to him, the living Stone—rejected by men but chosen by God and precious to him— ⁵you also, like living stones, are being built into a spiritual house to be a holy priesthood, offering spiritual sacrifices acceptable to God through Jesus Christ. ⁶For in Scripture it says:

"See, I lay a stone in Zion,
   a chosen and precious cornerstone,
and the one who trusts in him
   will never be put to shame."ᵈ

⁷Now to you who believe, this stone is precious. But to those who do not believe,

"The stone the builders rejected
   has become the capstone,ᵉ"ᶠ

⁸and,

"A stone that causes men to stumble
   and a rock that makes them fall."ᵍ

ᵃ16 Lev. 11:44,45; 19:2   ᵇ22 Some early manuscripts *from a pure heart*   ᶜ25 Isaiah 40:6–8   ᵈ6 Isaiah 28:16   ᵉ7 Or *cornerstone*
ᶠ7 Psalm 118:22   ᵍ8 Isaiah 8:14

They stumble because they disobey the message—which is also what they were destined for.

9But you are a chosen people, a royal priesthood, a holy nation, a people belonging to God, that you may declare the praises of him who called you out of darkness into his wonderful light. 10Once you were not a people, but now you are the people of God; once you had not received mercy, but now you have received mercy.

11Dear friends, I urge you, as aliens and strangers in the world, to abstain from sinful desires, which war against your soul. 12Live such good lives among the pagans that, though they accuse you of doing wrong, they may see your good deeds and glorify God on the day he visits us.

Submission to Rulers and Masters

13Submit yourselves for the Lord's sake to every authority instituted among men: whether to the king, as the supreme authority, 14or to governors, who are sent by him to punish those who do wrong and to commend those who do right. 15For it is God's will that by doing good you should silence the ignorant talk of foolish men. 16Live as free men, but do not use your freedom as a cover-up for evil; live as servants of God. 17Show proper respect to everyone: Love the brotherhood of believers, fear God, honor the king.

18Slaves, submit yourselves to your masters with all respect, not only to those who are good and considerate, but also to those who are harsh. 19For it is commendable if a man bears up under the pain of unjust suffering because he is conscious of God. 20But how is it to your credit if you receive a beating for doing wrong and endure it? But if you suffer for doing good and you endure it, this is commendable before God. 21To this you were called, because Christ suffered for you, leaving you an example, that you should follow in his steps.

22"He committed no sin,
   and no deceit was found in his mouth."[a]

23When they hurled their insults at him, he did not retaliate; when he suffered, he made no threats. Instead, he entrusted himself to him who judges justly. 24He himself bore our sins in his body on the tree, so that we might die to sins and live for righteousness; by his wounds you have been healed. 25For you were like sheep going astray, but now you have returned to the Shepherd and Overseer of your souls.

Wives and Husbands

3 Wives, in the same way be submissive to your husbands so that, if any of them do not believe the word, they may be won over without words by the behavior of their wives, 2when they see the purity and reverence of your lives. 3Your beauty should not come from outward adornment, such as braided hair and the wearing of gold jewelry and fine clothes. 4Instead, it should be that of your inner self, the unfading beauty of a gentle and quiet spirit, which is of great worth in God's sight. 5For this is the way the holy women of the past who put their hope in God used to make themselves beautiful. They were submissive to their own husbands, 6like Sarah, who obeyed Abraham and called him her master. You are her daughters if you do what is right and do not give way to fear.

7Husbands, in the same way be considerate as you live with your wives, and treat them with respect as the weaker partner and as heirs with you of the gracious gift of life, so that nothing will hinder your prayers.

Suffering for Doing Good

8Finally, all of you, live in harmony with one another; be sympathetic, love as brothers, be compassionate and humble. 9Do not repay evil with evil or insult with insult, but with blessing, because to this you were called so that you may inherit a blessing. 10For,

"Whoever would love life
   and see good days
must keep his tongue from evil
   and his lips from deceitful speech.
11He must turn from evil and do good;
   he must seek peace and pursue it.
12For the eyes of the Lord are on the
      righteous
   and his ears are attentive to their prayer,
but the face of the Lord is against those
      who do evil."[b]

a22 Isaiah 53:9   b12 Psalm 34:12–16

Suffering Well

Read: 1 Peter 2:4–25

1 Peter 2:20

But if you suffer for doing good and you endure it, this is commendable before God.

reflection

1 Does the concept of "suffering well" resonate with you? Why or why not?

2 Can you think of a time when God used a period of suffering to help you comfort another person?

3 How do you think suffering can make you more Christlike?

RELATED READINGS

Psalm 107:1–43; Isaiah 53:1–12; Romans 5:1–5; Philippians 3:7–11

"The Bible is a Christian's guidebook, and I believe the knowledge it sheds on pain and suffering is the great antidote to fear for suffering people. Knowledge can dissolve fear as light destroys darkness."

Philip Yancey

"WHAT GOOD IS SUFFERING?"

Have you ever asked that question? If so, you're not alone. The problem of pain and suffering in the world has turned many people away from faith in God and has inspired countless books and articles. Scholars and laypeople have tried for centuries to unravel the mystery of how God's plan can include evil in any form.

We live in a corrupt, fallen world in which illness occurs, violence happens and evil, for the time being, is allowed to run its course. Suffering is inevitable . . . our passage today even tells us we were "called" to suffer. It's not a matter of *if* we will suffer but *when* we will suffer. As believers in Jesus Christ, however, suffering offers the opportunity to display Christ's character and grace. For Christians, rather than asking, "Why does God allow suffering?" or even, "Why am *I* suffering?" we should ask, "How can I suffer *well*?"

Most of the early church leaders suffered violent deaths because of their outspoken and radical faith in Jesus. But every time one of them was martyred, the number of Christians grew. Why? Because people long to give themselves fully to a cause worth dying for. We all long for purpose and peace—and Jesus Christ offers both.

In his book *Velvet Elvis*, Bible teacher Rob Bell writes, "Ultimately our gift to the world around us is hope. Not blind hope that pretends everything is fine and refuses to acknowledge how things are. But the kind of hope that comes from staring pain and suffering right in the eyes and refusing to believe that this is all there is. It is what we all need—hope that comes not from going around suffering but from going through it."

Let's pray that God will allow us the privilege and strength of suffering well . . . for our sake, for his sake and for the sake of those who don't yet know him.

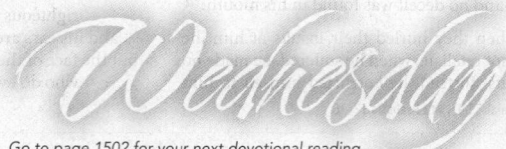

1496

Go to page 1502 for your next devotional reading.

¹³Who is going to harm you if you are eager to do good? ¹⁴But even if you should suffer for what is right, you are blessed. "Do not fear what they fear*a*; do not be frightened."*b* ¹⁵But in your hearts set apart Christ as Lord. Always be prepared to give an answer to everyone who asks you to give the reason for the hope that you have. But do this with gentleness and respect, ¹⁶keeping a clear conscience, so that those who speak maliciously against your good behavior in Christ may be ashamed of their slander. ¹⁷It is better, if it is God's will, to suffer for doing good than for doing evil. ¹⁸For Christ died for sins once for all, the righteous for the unrighteous, to bring you to God. He was put to death in the body but made alive by the Spirit, ¹⁹through whom*c* also he went and preached to the spirits in prison ²⁰who disobeyed long ago when God waited patiently in the days of Noah while the ark was being built. In it only a few people, eight in all, were saved through water, ²¹and this water symbolizes baptism that now saves you also—not the removal of dirt from the body but the pledge*d* of a good conscience toward God. It saves you by the resurrection of Jesus Christ, ²²who has gone into heaven and is at God's right hand—with angels, authorities and powers in submission to him.

Living for God

4 Therefore, since Christ suffered in his body, arm yourselves also with the same attitude, because he who has suffered in his body is done with sin. ²As a result, he does not live the rest of his earthly life for evil human desires, but rather for the will of God. ³For you have spent enough time in the past doing what pagans choose to do—living in debauchery, lust, drunkenness, orgies, carousing and detestable idolatry. ⁴They think it strange that you do not plunge with them into the same flood of dissipation, and they heap abuse on you. ⁵But they will have to give account to him who is ready to judge the living and the dead. ⁶For

this is the reason the gospel was preached even to those who are now dead, so that they might be judged according to men in regard to the body, but live according to God in regard to the spirit.

⁷The end of all things is near. Therefore be clear minded and self-controlled so that you can pray. ⁸Above all, love each other deeply, because love covers over a multitude of sins. ⁹Offer hospitality to one another without grumbling. ¹⁰Each one should use whatever gift he has received to serve others, faithfully administering God's grace in its various forms. ¹¹If anyone speaks, he should do it as one speaking the very words of God. If anyone serves, he should do it with the strength God provides, so that in all things God may be praised through Jesus Christ. To him be the glory and the power for ever and ever. Amen.

1 Peter 3:17

God Values Suffering

It is better, if it is God's will, to suffer for doing good than for doing evil.

Suffering for Being a Christian

¹²Dear friends, do not be surprised at the painful trial you are suffering, as though something strange were happening to you. ¹³But rejoice that you participate in the sufferings of Christ, so that you may be overjoyed when his glory is revealed. ¹⁴If you are insulted because of the name of Christ, you are blessed, for the Spirit of glory and of God rests on you. ¹⁵If you suffer, it should not be as a murderer or thief or any other kind of criminal, or even as a meddler. ¹⁶However, if you suffer as a Christian, do not be ashamed, but praise God that you bear that name. ¹⁷For it is time for judgment to begin with the family of God; and if it begins with us, what will the outcome be for those who do not obey the gospel of God? ¹⁸And,

"If it is hard for the righteous to be saved,
what will become of the ungodly and the sinner?"*e*

¹⁹So then, those who suffer according to God's will should commit themselves to their faithful Creator and continue to do good.

---

a14 Or *not fear their threats*   *b14* Isaiah 8:12   *c18,19* Or *alive in the spirit,* *19through which*   *d21* Or *response*   *e18* Prov. 11:31

To Elders and Young Men

5 To the elders among you, I appeal as a fellow elder, a witness of Christ's sufferings and one who also will share in the glory to be revealed: ²Be shepherds of God's flock that is under your care, serving as overseers—not because you must, but because you are willing, as God wants you to be; not greedy for money, but eager to serve; ³not lording it over those entrusted to you, but being examples to the flock. ⁴And when the Chief Shepherd appears, you will receive the crown of glory that will never fade away.

⁵Young men, in the same way be submissive to those who are older. All of you, clothe yourselves with humility toward one another, because,

"God opposes the proud
but gives grace to the
humble."*a*

⁶Humble yourselves, therefore, under God's mighty hand, that he may lift you up in due time. ⁷Cast all your anxiety on him because he cares for you.

⁸Be self-controlled and alert. Your enemy the devil prowls around like a roaring lion looking for someone to devour. ⁹Resist him, standing firm in the faith, because you know that your brothers throughout the world are undergoing the same kind of sufferings.

¹⁰And the God of all grace, who called you to his eternal glory in Christ, after you have suffered a little while, will himself restore you and make you strong, firm and steadfast. ¹¹To him be the power for ever and ever. Amen.

Final Greetings

¹²With the help of Silas,*b* whom I regard as a faithful brother, I have written to you briefly, encouraging you and testifying that this is the true grace of God. Stand fast in it.

¹³She who is in Babylon, chosen together with you, sends you her greetings, and so does my son Mark. ¹⁴Greet one another with a kiss of love.

Peace to all of you who are in Christ.

1 Peter 5:7

God Cares

Cast all your anxiety on him because he cares for you.

---

*a*5 Prov. 3:34   *b*12 Greek *Silvanus*, a variant of *Silas*

2 Peter

When spiritual leaders begin to draw people away from Christ, confusion results. Peter saw this happening among people he cared about, and he wrote this letter to remind them *to look at the Lord Jesus Christ* and not at their leaders if their leaders failed to follow Christ. The apostle Peter, one of the closest disciples to Jesus, continues to refer to Jesus throughout the letter with *titles that speak of respect:* Jesus is "our Lord and Savior" and "our Lord Jesus Christ." He is the One to be followed, no matter what anyone else says.

Peter tells us that people who follow Jesus for a short while and then choose a life of sin instead, leading others astray in the process, are worse off than those who never followed Christ in the first place. He warns his readers not to follow such false prophets into condemnation. He lists the spiritual virtues that Christ's followers should be striving for, and he tells us *to look to Jesus* —not other people— for the rewards of faith.

Author:
The apostle Peter.

Audience:
All followers of Jesus.

Date:
About A.D. 67.

Setting:
Shortly before his death, Peter wrote this letter to warn believers about false teachers.

Verse to Remember:
The Lord knows how to rescue godly men from trials and to hold the unrighteous for the day of judgment, while continuing their punishment. (2:9)

1 Simon Peter, a servant and apostle of Jesus Christ,

To those who through the righteousness of our God and Savior Jesus Christ have received a faith as precious as ours:

²Grace and peace be yours in abundance through the knowledge of God and of Jesus our Lord.

Making One's Calling and Election Sure

³His divine power has given us everything we need for life and godliness through our knowledge of him who called us by his own glory and goodness. ⁴Through these he has given us his very great and precious promises, so that through them you may participate in the divine nature and escape the corruption in the world caused by evil desires.

⁵For this very reason, make every effort to add to your faith goodness; and to goodness, knowledge; ⁶and to knowledge, self-control; and to self-control, perseverance; and to perseverance, godliness; ⁷and to godliness, brotherly kindness; and to brotherly kindness, love. ⁸For if you possess these qualities in increasing measure, they will keep you from being ineffective and unproductive in your knowledge of our Lord Jesus Christ. ⁹But if anyone does not have them, he is nearsighted and blind, and has forgotten that he has been cleansed from his past sins.

¹⁰Therefore, my brothers, be all the more eager to make your calling and election sure. For if you do these things, you will never fall, ¹¹and you will receive a rich welcome into the eternal kingdom of our Lord and Savior Jesus Christ.

Prophecy of Scripture

¹²So I will always remind you of these things, even though you know them and are firmly established in the truth you now have. ¹³I think it is right to refresh your memory as long as I live in the tent of this body, ¹⁴because I know that I will soon put it aside, as our Lord Jesus Christ has made clear to me. ¹⁵And I will make every effort to see that after my departure you will always be able to remember these things.

¹⁶We did not follow cleverly invented stories when we told you about the power and coming of our Lord Jesus Christ, but we were eyewitnesses of his majesty. ¹⁷For he received honor and glory from God the Father when the voice came to him from the Majestic Glory, saying, "This is my Son, whom I love; with him I am well pleased."ᵃ ¹⁸We ourselves heard this voice that came from heaven when we were with him on the sacred mountain.

¹⁹And we have the word of the prophets made more certain, and you will do well to pay attention to it, as to a light shining in a dark place, until the day dawns and the morning star rises in your hearts. ²⁰Above all, you must understand that no prophecy of Scripture came about by the prophet's own interpretation. ²¹For prophecy never had its origin in the will of man, but men spoke from God as they were carried along by the Holy Spirit.

False Teachers and Their Destruction

2 But there were also false prophets among the people, just as there will be false teachers among you. They will secretly introduce destructive heresies, even denying the sovereign Lord who bought them—bringing swift destruction on themselves. ²Many will follow their shameful ways and will bring the way of truth into disrepute. ³In their greed these teachers will exploit you with stories they have made up. Their condemnation has long been hanging over them, and their destruction has not been sleeping.

⁴For if God did not spare angels when they sinned, but sent them to hell,ᵇ putting them into gloomy dungeonsᶜ to be held for judgment; ⁵if he did not spare the ancient world when he brought the flood on its ungodly people, but protected Noah, a preacher of righteousness, and seven others; ⁶if he condemned the cities of Sodom and Gomorrah by burning them to ashes, and made them an example of what is going to happen to the ungodly; ⁷and if he rescued Lot, a righteous man, who was distressed by the filthy lives of lawless men ⁸(for that righteous man, living among them day after day, was tormented in his righteous soul by the lawless deeds he saw and heard)— ⁹if this is so, then the Lord knows how to rescue godly men from trials and to hold the unrighteous for the day of judgment, while continuing their punishment.ᵈ ¹⁰This is especially true of those who follow the corrupt desire of the sinful natureᵉ and despise authority.

Bold and arrogant, these men are not afraid

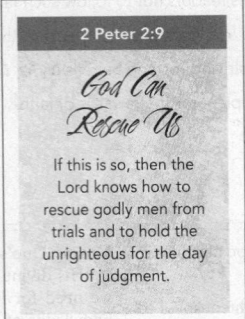

2 Peter 2:9

God Can Rescue Us

If this is so, then the Lord knows how to rescue godly men from trials and to hold the unrighteous for the day of judgment.

ᵃ17 Matt. 17:5; Mark 9:7; Luke 9:35 ᵇ4 Greek *Tartarus* ᶜ4 Some manuscripts *into chains of darkness* ᵈ9 Or *unrighteous for punishment until the day of judgment* ᵉ10 Or *the flesh* to slander celestial beings; [11]yet even angels, although they are stronger and more powerful, do not bring slanderous accusations against such beings in the presence of the Lord. [12]But these men blaspheme in matters they do not understand. They are like brute beasts, creatures of instinct, born only to be caught and destroyed, and like beasts they too will perish.

[13]They will be paid back with harm for the harm they have done. Their idea of pleasure is to carouse in broad daylight. They are blots and blemishes, reveling in their pleasures while they feast with you.[a] [14]With eyes full of adultery, they never stop sinning; they seduce the unstable; they are experts in greed—an accursed brood! [15]They have left the straight way and wandered off to follow the way of Balaam son of Beor, who loved the wages of wickedness. [16]But he was rebuked for his wrongdoing by a donkey—a beast without speech—who spoke with a man's voice and restrained the prophet's madness.

[17]These men are springs without water and mists driven by a storm. Blackest darkness is reserved for them. [18]For they mouth empty, boastful words and, by appealing to the lustful desires of sinful human nature, they entice people who are just escaping from those who live in error. [19]They promise them freedom, while they themselves are slaves of depravity—for a man is a slave to whatever has mastered him. [20]If they have escaped the corruption of the world by knowing our Lord and Savior Jesus Christ and are again entangled in it and overcome, they are worse off at the end than they were at the beginning. [21]It would have been better for them not to have known the way of righteousness, than to have known it and then to turn their backs on the sacred command that was passed on to them. [22]Of them the proverbs are true: "A dog returns to its vomit,"[b] and, "A sow that is washed goes back to her wallowing in the mud."

The Day of the Lord

3 Dear friends, this is now my second letter to you. I have written both of them as reminders to stimulate you to wholesome thinking. [2]I want you to recall the words spoken in the past by the holy prophets and the command given by our Lord and Savior through your apostles.

[3]First of all, you must understand that in the last days scoffers will come, scoffing and following their own evil desires. [4]They will say, "Where is this 'coming' he promised? Ever since our fathers died, everything goes on as it has since the beginning of creation." [5]But they deliberately forget that long ago by God's word the heavens existed and the earth was formed out of water and by water. [6]By these waters also the world of that time was deluged and destroyed. [7]By the same word the present heavens and earth are reserved for fire, being kept for the day of judgment and destruction of ungodly men.

[8]But do not forget this one thing, dear friends: With the Lord a day is like a thousand years, and a thousand years are like a day. [9]The Lord is not slow in keeping his promise, as some understand slowness. He is patient with you, not wanting anyone to perish, but everyone to come to repentance.

[10]But the day of the Lord will come like a thief. The heavens will disappear with a roar; the elements will be destroyed by fire, and the earth and everything in it will be laid bare.[c]

[11]Since everything will be destroyed in this way, what kind of people ought you to be? You ought to live holy and godly lives [12]as you look forward to the day of God and speed its coming.[d] That day will bring about the destruction of the heavens by fire, and the elements will melt in the heat. [13]But in keeping with his promise we are looking forward to a new heaven and a new earth, the home of righteousness.

[14]So then, dear friends, since you are looking forward to this, make every effort to be found spotless, blameless and at peace with him. [15]Bear in mind that our Lord's patience means salvation, just as our dear brother Paul also wrote you with the wisdom that God gave him. [16]He writes the same way in all his letters, speaking in them of these matters. His letters contain some things that are hard to

---

[a]**13** Some manuscripts *in their love feasts*   [b]**22** Prov. 26:11   [c]**10** Some manuscripts *be burned up*   [d]**12** Or *as you wait eagerly for the day of God to come*

Eternal Perspective

Read: 2 Peter 3:8–14

2 Peter 3:11–12

Since everything will be destroyed in this way, what kind of people ought you to be? You ought to live holy and godly lives as you look forward to the day of God and speed its coming.

reflection

1 If you knew the world would end tomorrow, how would you reprioritize your life?

2 How do you keep a positive outlook during discouraging times?

3 How will you go about making your life more godly and holy as you look toward eternity?

RELATED READINGS

Philippians 1:27–30;
3:18–21;
Titus 2:11–14

THESE VERSES FROM 2 PETER state clearly that earth's time clock is ticking. The world as we know it will come to an end one day. It may or may not occur in our lifetime, but it will occur one day because God has promised that it will. The important question is: How are you going to live until then? How will you spend your days?

Perhaps you or someone dear to you has been diagnosed with a life-threatening illness, and you know their life is winding down. Suddenly your perspective has shifted. What once seemed important no longer seems quite so important. We begin to ask the question Peter asked in verse 11: "What kind of people ought you to be?" We return to the realization that our relationships should come first—our relationship with God, our relationships with our family members and with fellow believers, friends and coworkers.

Thinking about the end of the world can seem frightening or depressing, especially when the signs can't be ignored: the deterioration of morality, growing violence and terrorism, unprecedented natural disasters, war, disease and famine throughout the earth. Watching the nightly news is enough to cause even the most optimistic woman to stay in bed and pull the covers over her head. The truth is that Peter is not asking us to dwell on end-time events but to consider how we will live our lives, right here, right now, while looking forward to a new heaven and a new earth.

How do we keep an eternal perspective while living on earth? Here are a few suggestions: Start each day by praying that God will use you for his purposes. Make it your ambition to please God in everything you do—whether you are packing your children's lunches, running a company or volunteering at church. Each night, thank God for the opportunities he's given you to serve him by serving others.

Living a holy and godly life not only ensures that you are at peace with God and with others, it also ensures that you are ready for whatever may come.

Thursday

understand, which ignorant and unstable people distort, as they do the other Scriptures, to their own destruction.

[17] Therefore, dear friends, since you already know this, be on your guard so that you may not be carried away by the error of lawless men and fall from your secure position. [18] But grow in the grace and knowledge of our Lord and Savior Jesus Christ. To him be glory both now and forever! Amen.

1 John

Author:
The apostle John.

Audience:
All the early churches and every follower of Jesus.

Date:
Between A.D. 85 and 95.

Setting:
Now an old man, this beloved disciple and close friend of Jesus writes to encourage the early churches.

Verse to Remember:
This is how we know what love is: Jesus Christ laid down his life for us. And we ought to lay down our lives for our brothers. (3:16)

We toss the word love around easily enough, but when it comes to defining it, to nailing down exactly what it means, we tend to stumble. We can come up with comparisons or things that it is like, but what is it really? When we strip away all the trappings, *what is love?*

That's the question the apostle John addresses in this letter. He wanted his readers to know beyond any doubt what love was. He wanted them to be secure in God's love, to know for certain where they stood with him. Through his words we again feel *the wonder of being loved by God.* John shows us that God's love is not a vague, intangible wisp we try to grasp, only to find it has slipped through our fingers yet again. *God's love is both solid and transforming.* We can look at our lives and see if we have God's love based on the tests he gives: how we handle sin, how we relate to others, what we do with false teaching and, above all else, what we believe about Jesus Christ. *It is through Jesus,* after all, that we are even able to know what love is.

The Word of Life

1 That which was from the beginning, which we have heard, which we have seen with our eyes, which we have looked at and our hands have touched—this we proclaim concerning the Word of life. [2] The life appeared; we have seen it and testify to it, and we proclaim to you the eternal life, which was with the Father and has appeared to us. [3] We proclaim to you what we have seen and heard, so that you also may have fellowship with us. And our fellowship is with the Father and with his Son, Jesus Christ. [4]We write this to make our[a] joy complete.

Walking in the Light

[5]This is the message we have heard from him and declare to you: God is light; in him there is no darkness at all. [6]If we claim to have fellowship with him yet walk in the darkness, we lie and do not live by the truth. [7]But if we walk in the light, as he is in the light, we have fellowship with one another, and the blood of Jesus, his Son, purifies us from all[b] sin.

[8]If we claim to be without sin, we deceive ourselves and the truth is not in us. [9]If we confess our sins, he is faithful and just and will forgive us our sins and purify us from all unrighteousness. [10]If we claim we have not sinned, we make him out to be a liar and his word has no place in our lives.

2 My dear children, I write this to you so that you will not sin. But if anybody does sin, we have one who speaks to the Father in our defense—Jesus Christ, the Righteous One. [2]He is the atoning sacrifice for our sins, and not only for ours but also for[c] the sins of the whole world.

[3]We know that we have come to know him if we obey his commands. [4]The man who says, "I know him," but does not do what he commands is a liar, and the truth is not in him. [5]But if anyone obeys his word, God's love[d] is truly made complete in him. This is how we know we are in him: [6]Whoever claims to live in him must walk as Jesus did.

[7]Dear friends, I am not writing you a new command but an old one, which you have had since the beginning. This old command is the message you have heard. [8]Yet I am writing you a new command; its truth is seen in him and you, because the darkness is passing and the true light is already shining.

[9]Anyone who claims to be in the light but hates his brother is still in the darkness. [10]Whoever loves his brother lives in the light, and there is nothing in him[e] to make him stumble. [11]But whoever hates his brother is in the darkness and walks around in the darkness; he does not know where he is going, because the darkness has blinded him.

[12]I write to you, dear children,
    because your sins have been forgiven on
        account of his name.
[13]I write to you, fathers,
        because you have known
            him who is from
                the beginning.
I write to you, young men,
        because you have
            overcome the evil
                one.
I write to you, dear
    children,
        because you have known
            the Father.
[14]I write to you, fathers,
        because you have known
            him who is from
                the beginning.
I write to you, young men,
        because you are strong,
        and the word of God lives in you,
        and you have overcome the evil one.

Do Not Love the World

[15]Do not love the world or anything in the world. If anyone loves the world, the love of the Father is not in him. [16]For everything in the world—the cravings of sinful man, the lust of his eyes and the boasting of what he has and does—comes not from the Father but from the world. [17]The world and its desires pass away, but the man who does the will of God lives forever.

Warning Against Antichrists

[18]Dear children, this is the last hour; and as you have heard that the antichrist is coming, even now many antichrists have come. This is how we know it is the last hour. [19]They went out from us, but they did not really belong to us. For if they had belonged to us, they would

1 John 1:9

God Purifies Us

If we confess our sins, he is faithful and just and will forgive us our sins and purify us from all unrighteousness.

---

[a]4 Some manuscripts *your*   [b]7 Or *every*   [c]2 Or *He is the one who turns aside God's wrath, taking away our sins, and not only ours but also*   [d]5 Or *word, love for God*   [e]10 Or *it*

have remained with us; but their going showed that none of them belonged to us.

20But you have an anointing from the Holy One, and all of you know the truth.*a* 21I do not write to you because you do not know the truth, but because you do know it and because no lie comes from the truth. 22Who is the liar? It is the man who denies that Jesus is the Christ. Such a man is the antichrist—he denies the Father and the Son. 23No one who denies the Son has the Father; whoever acknowledges the Son has the Father also.

24See that what you have heard from the beginning remains in you. If it does, you also will remain in the Son and in the Father. 25And this is what he promised us—even eternal life.

26I am writing these things to you about those who are trying to lead you astray. 27As for you, the anointing you received from him remains in you, and you do not need anyone to teach you. But as his anointing teaches you about all things and as that anointing is real, not counterfeit—just as it has taught you, remain in him.

Children of God

28And now, dear children, continue in him, so that when he appears we may be confident and unashamed before him at his coming.

29If you know that he is righteous, you know that everyone who does what is right has been born of him.

3 How great is the love the Father has lavished on us, that we should be called children of God! And that is what we are! The reason the world does not know us is that it did not know him. 2Dear friends, now we are children of God, and what we will be has not yet been made known. But we know that when he appears,*b* we shall be like him, for we shall see him as he is. 3Everyone who has this hope in him purifies himself, just as he is pure.

4Everyone who sins breaks the law; in fact,

sin is lawlessness. 5But you know that he appeared so that he might take away our sins. And in him is no sin. 6No one who lives in him keeps on sinning. No one who continues to sin has either seen him or known him.

7Dear children, do not let anyone lead you astray. He who does what is right is righteous, just as he is righteous. 8He who does what is sinful is of the devil, because the devil has been sinning from the beginning. The reason the Son of God appeared was to destroy the devil's work. 9No one who is born of God will continue to sin, because God's seed remains in him; he cannot go on sinning, because he has been born of God. 10This is how we know who the children of God are and who the children of the devil are: Anyone who does not do what is right is not a child of God; nor is anyone who does not love his brother.

Love One Another

11This is the message you heard from the beginning: We should love one another. 12Do not be like Cain, who belonged to the evil one and murdered his brother. And why did he murder him? Because his own actions were evil and his brother's were righteous. 13Do not be surprised, my brothers, if the world hates you. 14We know that we have passed from death to life, because we love our brothers. Anyone who does not love remains in death. 15Anyone who hates his brother is a murderer, and you know that no murderer has eternal life in him.

16This is how we know what love is: Jesus Christ laid down his life for us. And we ought to lay down our lives for our brothers. 17If anyone has material possessions and sees his brother in need but has no pity on him, how can the love of God be in him? 18Dear children, let us not love with words or tongue but with actions and in truth. 19This then is how we know that we belong to the truth, and how we set our hearts at rest in his presence 20whenever our hearts condemn

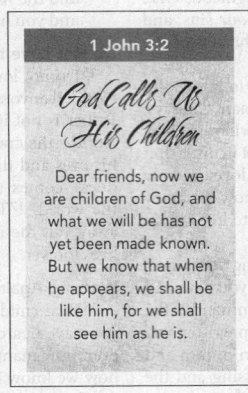

1 John 3:2

God Calls Us His Children

Dear friends, now we are children of God, and what we will be has not yet been made known. But we know that when he appears, we shall be like him, for we shall see him as he is.

---

*a*20 Some manuscripts *and you know all things*   *b*2 Or *when it is made known* us. For God is greater than our hearts, and he knows everything.

²¹Dear friends, if our hearts do not condemn us, we have confidence before God ²²and receive from him anything we ask, because we obey his commands and do what pleases him. ²³And this is his command: to believe in the name of his Son, Jesus Christ, and to love one another as he commanded us. ²⁴Those who obey his commands live in him, and he in them. And this is how we know that he lives in us: We know it by the Spirit he gave us.

Test the Spirits

4 Dear friends, do not believe every spirit, but test the spirits to see whether they are from God, because many false prophets have gone out into the world. ²This is how you can recognize the Spirit of God: Every spirit that acknowledges that Jesus Christ has come in the flesh is from God, ³but every spirit that does not acknowledge Jesus is not from God. This is the spirit of the antichrist, which you have heard is coming and even now is already in the world.

⁴You, dear children, are from God and have overcome them, because the one who is in you is greater than the one who is in the world. ⁵They are from the world and therefore speak from the viewpoint of the world, and the world listens to them. ⁶We are from God, and whoever knows God listens to us; but whoever is not from God does not listen to us. This is how we recognize the Spirit*a* of truth and the spirit of falsehood.

God's Love and Ours

⁷Dear friends, let us love one another, for love comes from God. Everyone who loves has been born of God and knows God. ⁸Whoever does not love does not know God, because God is love. ⁹This is how God showed his love among us: He sent his one and only Son*b* into the world that we might live through him. ¹⁰This is love: not that we loved God, but that he loved us and sent his Son as an atoning sac-

rifice for*c* our sins. ¹¹Dear friends, since God so loved us, we also ought to love one another. ¹²No one has ever seen God; but if we love one another, God lives in us and his love is made complete in us.

¹³We know that we live in him and he in us, because he has given us of his Spirit. ¹⁴And we have seen and testify that the Father has sent his Son to be the Savior of the world. ¹⁵If anyone acknowledges that Jesus is the Son of God, God lives in him and he in God. ¹⁶And so we know and rely on the love God has for us.

God is love. Whoever lives in love lives in God, and God in him. ¹⁷In this way, love is made complete among us so that we will have confidence on the day of judgment, because in this world we are like him. ¹⁸There is no fear in love. But perfect love drives out fear, because fear has to do with punishment. The one who fears is not made perfect in love.

¹⁹We love because he first loved us. ²⁰If anyone says, "I love God," yet hates his brother, he is a liar. For anyone who does not love his brother, whom he has seen, cannot love God, whom he has not seen. ²¹And he has given us this command: Whoever loves God must also love his brother.

Faith in the Son of God

5 Everyone who believes that Jesus is the Christ is born of God, and everyone who loves the father loves his child as well. ²This is how we know that we love the children of God: by loving God and carrying out his commands. ³This is love for God: to obey his commands. And his commands are not burdensome, ⁴for everyone born of God overcomes the world. This is the victory that has overcome the world, even our faith. ⁵Who is it that overcomes the world? Only he who believes that Jesus is the Son of God.

⁶This is the one who came by water and blood—Jesus Christ. He did not come by water only, but by water and blood. And it is the

> ### 1 John 4:16
>
> *God Is Love*
>
> And so we know and rely on the love God has for us. God is love. Whoever lives in love lives in God, and God in him.

---

*a*6 Or *spirit*   *b*9 Or *his only begotten Son*   *c*10 Or *as the one who would turn aside his wrath, taking away*

A Love Like No Other

1 John 4:16

And so we know and rely on the love God has for us. God is love. Whoever lives in love lives in God, and God in him.

Read: 1 John 4:7–21

LOVE'S DEEPEST DEFINITION is found in the simple but profound words, "God is love." But how can we transfer this amazing truth to our daily lives? Our finite minds can't understand a love so infinite, so fathomless, so unconditional, so beyond our imagining.

Perhaps a few illustrations of God's love can help us grasp the profound concept that God *is* love. First, consider the story of a farmer who had an unusual weathervane on his barn. Inscribed on the arrow were the words "God is love." A passerby asked the farmer, "What do you mean by that? Do you think God's love is changeable, turning in the wind like the arrow?" "Oh, no," replied the farmer, "I mean that whichever way the wind blows, God is still love." Think about it—God's love is unchanging.

But there is so much more to God's love than its immutability. A little girl and her mother were reading the New Testament one morning when they read, "For God so loved the world that he gave his one and only Son" (John 3:16). The mother stopped and asked the girl, "Don't you think it's wonderful how giving God is?" The child shook her head and said, "Why, no, Mommy, it would be wonderful if it were anybody else, but it is just like God." She knew that it is completely within God's loving character to be sacrificial.

We've all heard about Helen Keller, who was blind, deaf and mute as a child. Her teacher, Annie Sullivan, was determined to teach her to communicate through the sense of touch. Annie decided to tell her the story of Jesus Christ, using sign language. Helen responded, "Oh, I knew he must exist, but I didn't know his name!" Helen Keller is an example of God's amazing love and desire to reveal himself to anyone and everyone.

Though we may not grasp the true depth of the phrase "God is love," we know that he is unchanging and sacrificial, and he desires for every person to know him. No human love can compare with God's love—it's a love like no other.

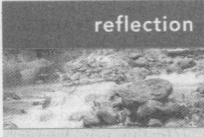

reflection

1 When was the last time you spent time dwelling on the truth that "God is love"? Prayerfully do so now.

2 What are some examples or stories from your life that are evidence of God's love for you?

3 Emphasize the words in the phrase "God is love" in different ways to help you grasp the significance: *God* is love. God *is* love. God is *love*.

RELATED READINGS

Psalm 107:1–43;
John 15:9–13;
Romans 5:6–8

Friday

Spirit who testifies, because the Spirit is the truth. 7For there are three that testify: 8thea Spirit, the water and the blood; and the three are in agreement. 9We accept man's testimony, but God's testimony is greater because it is the testimony of God, which he has given about his Son. 10Anyone who believes in the Son of God has this testimony in his heart. Anyone who does not believe God has made him out to be a liar, because he has not believed the testimony God has given about his Son. 11And this is the testimony: God has given us eternal life, and this life is in his Son. 12He who has the Son has life; he who does not have the Son of God does not have life.

Concluding Remarks

13I write these things to you who believe in the name of the Son of God so that you may know that you have eternal life. 14This is the confidence we have in approaching God: that if we ask anything according to his will, he hears us. 15And if we know that he hears us—whatever we ask—we know that we have what we asked of him.

16If anyone sees his brother commit a sin that does not lead to death, he should pray and God will give him life. I refer to those whose sin does not lead to death. There is a sin that leads to death. I am not saying that he should pray about that. 17All wrongdoing is sin, and there is sin that does not lead to death.

18We know that anyone born of God does not continue to sin; the one who was born of God keeps him safe, and the evil one cannot harm him. 19We know that we are children of God, and that the whole world is under the control of the evil one. 20We know also that the Son of God has come and has given us understanding, so that we may know him who is true. And we are in him who is true—even in his Son Jesus Christ. He is the true God and eternal life.

21Dear children, keep yourselves from idols.

2 John

Author:
The apostle John.

Audience:
All the early churches and every follower of Jesus.

Date:
Between A.D. 85 and 95.

Setting:
John addressed his letter to "the chosen lady and her children," who may have been a personal friend of John's or a metaphor for a church and its members.

Verse to Remember:
And this is love: that we walk in obedience to his commands. As you have heard from the beginning, his command is that you walk in love. (6)

Sometimes we are so intimately acquainted with someone that we don't have to identify ourselves before conversing. A child calls out across a busy store and the mother knows her child's voice. A friend calls on the phone and simply begins talking, with no need to identify herself. *That is the intimacy we see in this letter.* John addresses "the chosen lady and her children" without explaining who they are, implying a heart-to-heart relationship that the writer and recipient completely understand.

As in all of John's letters, there is heavy emphasis on "truth" and "love." Because we know the truth, Jesus Christ himself, we are recipients of God's love. And *because we know Jesus,* we are to be givers of God's love. As you read this short and intimate letter, see yourself as the "chosen lady" and allow John's words to wrap you in truth and love.

¹The elder,

To the chosen lady and her children, whom I love in the truth—and not I only, but also all who know the truth— ²because of the truth, which lives in us and will be with us forever:

³Grace, mercy and peace from God the Father and from Jesus Christ, the Father's Son, will be with us in truth and love.

⁴It has given me great joy to find some of your children walking in the truth, just as the Father commanded us. ⁵And now, dear lady, I am not writing you a new command but one we have had from the beginning. I ask that we love one another. ⁶And this is love: that we walk in obedience to his commands. As you have heard from the beginning, his command is that you walk in love.

7Many deceivers, who do not acknowledge Jesus Christ as coming in the flesh, have gone out into the world. Any such person is the deceiver and the antichrist. 8Watch out that you do not lose what you have worked for, but that you may be rewarded fully. 9Anyone who runs ahead and does not continue in the teaching of Christ does not have God; whoever continues in the teaching has both the Father and the Son. 10If anyone comes to you and does not bring this teaching, do not take him into your house or welcome him. 11Anyone who welcomes him shares in his wicked work.

12I have much to write to you, but I do not want to use paper and ink. Instead, I hope to visit you and talk with you face to face, so that our joy may be complete.

13The children of your chosen sister send their greetings.

3 John

Author:
The apostle John.

Audience:
Members of all
the early churches,
specifically a friend
named Gaius, and
all followers
of Jesus.

Date:
Between A.D. 85
and 95.

Setting:
Traveling pastors
relied on church
members'
hospitality.

Verse to Remember:
I have no greater
joy than to hear
that my children
are walking in the
truth. (4)

This short letter to Gaius from John was a quick note of support. John had noted Gaius's faithfulness, and he encourages him to *continue to do what is good.* The letter is short because it brought good news: John was on his way and would soon be able to speak with Gaius in person.

Sometimes it gets discouraging to do the right thing when others around us do not. It can be easy to join others in gossip, complaining or small acts of dishonesty. Be encouraged that even if others do not see your faithfulness, *God does.* And if you are struggling to be faithful, pray and ask him to help you do so. *Look for others who can be an example* to you, and seek out those whom you can thank for their actions that please God.

---

¹The elder,

To my dear friend Gaius, whom I love in the truth.

²Dear friend, I pray that you may enjoy good health and that all may go well with you, even as your soul is getting along well. ³It gave me great joy to have some brothers come and tell about your faithfulness to the truth and how you continue to walk in the truth. ⁴I have no greater joy than to hear that my children are walking in the truth.

⁵Dear friend, you are faithful in what you are doing for the brothers, even though they are strangers to you. ⁶They have told the

church about your love. You will do well to send them on their way in a manner worthy of God. [7]It was for the sake of the Name that they went out, receiving no help from the pagans. [8]We ought therefore to show hospitality to such men so that we may work together for the truth.

[9]I wrote to the church, but Diotrephes, who loves to be first, will have nothing to do with us. [10]So if I come, I will call attention to what he is doing, gossiping maliciously about us. Not satisfied with that, he refuses to welcome the brothers. He also stops those who want to do so and puts them out of the church.

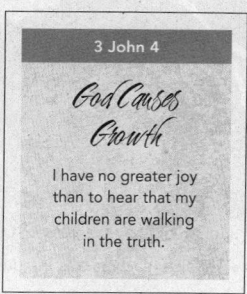

3 John 4

God Causes Growth

I have no greater joy than to hear that my children are walking in the truth.

[11]Dear friend, do not imitate what is evil but what is good. Anyone who does what is good is from God. Anyone who does what is evil has not seen God. [12]Demetrius is well spoken of by everyone—and even by the truth itself. We also speak well of him, and you know that our testimony is true.

[13]I have much to write you, but I do not want to do so with pen and ink. [14]I hope to see you soon, and we will talk face to face.

Peace to you. The friends here send their greetings. Greet the friends there by name.

Jude

Author:
Jude, brother of James and Jesus.

Audience:
Jewish Christians and all followers of Jesus.

Date:
About A.D. 65.

Setting:
Jude issued a warning about false teachers who lead people astray.

Verse to Remember:
Dear friends, although I was very eager to write to you about the salvation we share, I felt I had to write and urge you to contend for the faith that was once for all entrusted to the saints. (3)

Sin is never a pleasant topic. There are many things Jude might have discussed, but he felt that dealing with false teachers was the utmost importance. He no longer saw Jesus as the fanatical brother who refused to quietly blend in. *He now saw Jesus as the Messiah.* And he wanted to share that knowledge.

But as he smoothed his parchment, his thoughts were pierced by the realization that there were enemies in their midst, infiltrating the ranks. And they needed to be dealt with—now!

Jude reminds us that *the Christian life is a battleground.* When we take up our cross, we're inviting attack. From the world, yes, but unfortunately, the attack often comes from within the church as well. Believers don't have the option of drifting along quietly, undisturbed. We're in enemy territory, and we need to know how to fight. There are times for peaceful words of encouragement, and there are times for sharp words of rebuke. Jude reminds us that *we need to be alert* to both.

---

¹ Jude, a servant of Jesus Christ and a brother of James,

To those who have been called, who are loved by God the Father and kept by*ᵃ* Jesus Christ:

² Mercy, peace and love be yours in abundance.

The Sin and Doom of Godless Men

³ Dear friends, although I was very eager to write to you about the salvation we share, I felt I had to write and urge you to contend for the faith that was once for all entrusted to the saints. ⁴ For certain men whose condemnation was written about*ᵇ* long ago have secretly

ᵃ1 Or for; or in ᵇ4 Or men who were marked out for condemnation slipped in among you. They are godless men, who change the grace of our God into a license for immorality and deny Jesus Christ our only Sovereign and Lord.

⁵Though you already know all this, I want to remind you that the Lord[a] delivered his people out of Egypt, but later destroyed those who did not believe. ⁶And the angels who did not keep their positions of authority but abandoned their own home—these he has kept in darkness, bound with everlasting chains for judgment on the great Day. ⁷In a similar way, Sodom and Gomorrah and the surrounding towns gave themselves up to sexual immorality and perversion. They serve as an example of those who suffer the punishment of eternal fire.

⁸In the very same way, these dreamers pollute their own bodies, reject authority and slander celestial beings. ⁹But even the archangel Michael, when he was disputing with the devil about the body of Moses, did not dare to bring a slanderous accusation against him, but said, "The Lord rebuke you!" ¹⁰Yet these men speak abusively against whatever they do not understand; and what things they do understand by instinct, like unreasoning animals—these are the very things that destroy them.

¹¹Woe to them! They have taken the way of Cain; they have rushed for profit into Balaam's error; they have been destroyed in Korah's rebellion.

¹²These men are blemishes at your love feasts, eating with you without the slightest qualm—shepherds who feed only themselves. They are clouds without rain, blown along by the wind; autumn trees, without fruit and uprooted—twice dead. ¹³They are wild waves of the sea, foaming up their shame; wandering stars, for whom blackest darkness has been reserved forever.

¹⁴Enoch, the seventh from Adam, prophesied about these men: "See, the Lord is coming with thousands upon thousands of his holy ones ¹⁵to judge everyone, and to convict all the ungodly of all the ungodly acts they have done in the ungodly way, and of all the harsh words ungodly sinners have spoken against him." ¹⁶These men are grumblers and faultfinders; they follow their own evil desires; they boast about themselves and flatter others for their own advantage.

A Call to Persevere

¹⁷But, dear friends, remember what the apostles of our Lord Jesus Christ foretold. ¹⁸They said to you, "In the last times there will be scoffers who will follow their own ungodly desires." ¹⁹These are the men who divide you, who follow mere natural instincts and do not have the Spirit.

²⁰But you, dear friends, build yourselves up in your most holy faith and pray in the Holy Spirit. ²¹Keep yourselves in God's love as you wait for the mercy of our Lord Jesus Christ to bring you to eternal life.

²²Be merciful to those who doubt; ²³snatch others from the fire and save them; to others show mercy, mixed with fear—hating even the clothing stained by corrupted flesh.

Jude 21
God Brings Eternal Life

Keep yourselves in God's love as you wait for the mercy of our Lord Jesus Christ to bring you to eternal life.

Doxology

²⁴To him who is able to keep you from falling and to present you before his glorious presence without fault and with great joy— ²⁵to the only God our Savior be glory, majesty, power and authority, through Jesus Christ our Lord, before all ages, now and forevermore! Amen.

[a]5 Some early manuscripts *Jesus*

Working Hard

PHOEBE

I commend to you our sister Phoebe, a servant of the church in Cenchrea.

Romans 16:1

"YOU'RE GLOWING!" The older widow pointed out Phoebe's countenance.

"She is—look at her!" Now the other women in the church were pointing to her and smiling as she made her way past them. Wherever she went, Phoebe practically radiated Christ's love. It was in the way she greeted others on the street, in the way she took a hurting child in her arms, in the way she served food to the poor.

"She is never too busy to help . . ." one woman said.

". . . And never too preoccupied with her own life to see someone else's need," finished another. It was the way most people described Phoebe.

"You know, you can't love someone at arm's length," said another elderly woman, describing Phoebe's ability to embrace others. "That's what I learned from Phoebe."

"We've *all* learned from Phoebe," said another, and all agreed.

Phoebe had more than just a sunny disposition, as if all she did was delicately hover over life's circumstances—far removed from the grit and grime of tragedy and concern. Even with her positive outlook, she never shied away from the messiness of getting involved when she was needed.

In fact, Phoebe was entrusted with a difficult assignment: she was to deliver Paul's letter to the Roman church and serve as his representative. In the letter Paul commended her and noted her contributions to the other believers. Of course, they already could tell what kind of person Phoebe was. It was obvious.

ASSIGNED READING:

Romans 16:1–2

—*Prayer*—

Savior, I pray to you with sincerity and ask that you help me radiate your love wherever I go.

Weekend

Go to page 1519 for your next devotional reading.

Revelation

Visions of weird beasts. Candlesticks and sealed scrolls. Dragons and falling stars. Blood and violence. Glory. Majesty. Mystery. *The imagery of Revelation* can inspire and confuse. Interpreting it can stump the finest theologian or draw all-out theological warfare. *Revelation tells of the end times,* but exactly what it means has often been debated.

But one recurring image takes center stage. The risen Lord Jesus appears throughout the book. As a Lamb. As an awe-inspiring man. But always as the One who has conquered death and is now unquestionably the King. *Jesus Christ rules,* and he is in charge in these visions and letters of future battle and future triumph.

Look for Jesus in this book—for his words of exhortation and comfort, for his wrath against those who oppose him, but *especially for his promise* that he will soon return for his people and make all things new. That day is worth waiting for! Come, Lord Jesus.

Author:
The apostle John.

Audience:
Seven churches in Asia and all followers of Jesus.

Date:
About A.D. 95.

Setting:
John wrote about a vision he had while exiled on the island of Patmos near the end of his life.

Verse to Remember:
Then I heard every creature in heaven and on earth and under the earth and on the sea, and all that is in them, singing: "To him who sits on the throne and to the Lamb be praise and honor and glory and power, for ever and ever!" (5:13)

Prologue

1 The revelation of Jesus Christ, which God gave him to show his servants what must soon take place. He made it known by sending his angel to his servant John, ²who testifies to everything he saw—that is, the word of God and the testimony of Jesus Christ. ³Blessed is the one who reads the words of this prophecy, and blessed are those who hear it and take to heart what is written in it, because the time is near.

Greetings and Doxology

⁴John,

To the seven churches in the province of Asia:

Grace and peace to you from him who is, and who was, and who is to come, and from the seven spirits[a] before his throne, 5and from Jesus Christ, who is the faithful witness, the firstborn from the dead, and the ruler of the kings of the earth.

To him who loves us and has freed us from our sins by his blood, 6and has made us to be a kingdom and priests to serve his God and Father—to him be glory and power for ever and ever! Amen.

7Look, he is coming with the clouds,
    and every eye will see him,
    even those who pierced him;
    and all the peoples of the earth will
        mourn because of him.
                    So shall it be! Amen.

8"I am the Alpha and the Omega," says the Lord God, "who is, and who was, and who is to come, the Almighty."

One Like a Son of Man

9I, John, your brother and companion in the suffering and kingdom and patient endurance that are ours in Jesus, was on the island of Patmos because of the word of God and the testimony of Jesus. 10On the Lord's Day I was in the Spirit, and I heard behind me a loud voice like a trumpet, 11which said: "Write on a scroll what you see and send it to the seven churches: to Ephesus, Smyrna, Pergamum, Thyatira, Sardis, Philadelphia and Laodicea."

12I turned around to see the voice that was speaking to me. And when I turned I saw seven golden lampstands, 13and among the lampstands was someone "like a son of man,"[b] dressed in a robe reaching down to his feet and with a golden sash around his chest. 14His head and hair were white like wool, as white as snow, and his eyes were like blazing fire. 15His feet were like bronze glowing in a furnace, and his voice was like the sound of rushing waters. 16In his right hand he held seven stars, and out of his mouth came a sharp double-edged sword. His face was like the sun shining in all its brilliance.

17When I saw him, I fell at his feet as though

dead. Then he placed his right hand on me and said: "Do not be afraid. I am the First and the Last. 18I am the Living One; I was dead, and behold I am alive for ever and ever! And I hold the keys of death and Hades.

19"Write, therefore, what you have seen, what is now and what will take place later. 20The mystery of the seven stars that you saw in my right hand and of the seven golden lampstands is this: The seven stars are the angels[c] of the seven churches, and the seven lampstands are the seven churches.

To the Church in Ephesus

2 "To the angel[d] of the church in Ephesus write:

These are the words of him who holds the seven stars in his right hand and walks among the seven golden lampstands: 2I know your deeds, your hard work and your perseverance. I know that you cannot tolerate wicked men, that you have tested those who claim to be apostles but are not, and have found them false. 3You have persevered and have endured hardships for my name, and have not grown weary.

4Yet I hold this against you: You have forsaken your first love. 5Remember the height from which you have fallen! Repent and do the things you did at first. If you do not repent, I will come to you and remove your lampstand from its place. 6But you have this in your favor: You hate the practices of the Nicolaitans, which I also hate.

7He who has an ear, let him hear what the Spirit says to the churches. To him who overcomes, I will give the right to eat from the tree of life, which is in the paradise of God.

To the Church in Smyrna

8"To the angel of the church in Smyrna write:

These are the words of him who is the First and the Last, who died and came to life again. 9I know your afflictions and your poverty—yet you are rich! I know the slander of those who say they are Jews and are not, but are a synagogue of Satan.

---

a4 Or *the sevenfold Spirit*   b13 Daniel 7:13   c20 Or *messengers*   d1 Or *messenger*; also in verses 8, 12 and 18

Never the Same?

Read: Revelation 1:1–8

DO YOU EVER WISH that things could simply stay the same? Just when you figure out how to deal with a temperamental two-year-old, she moves into the terrific threes, and you begin to wonder who this small person is wearing your child's clothes . . . and, by the way, why don't those clothes fit anymore? Just when you get settled into your new home and neighborhood, you get transferred and have to begin packing and looking for another new home, new church and new friends. Just when you're collecting the travel brochures, an aging parent goes into the hospital and needs your constant care.

Wearily, you lay your head on the pillow and lament, "Doesn't anything ever stay the same?" An ancient Greek philosopher said, "There is nothing permanent except change."

But amidst the changes of life, if you listen very carefully, you can hear the voice of God speaking comfort to your soul: "[I am] the same yesterday and today and forever" (Hebrews 13:8). Though our children may change, though our job situations may be in flux, though our parents may have failing health, though circumstances may be unsettled, we can trust in the truth that our everlasting God never changes.

John's final book of the Bible, Revelation, tells of the changes that lie ahead. But John is quick to remind us that we have one constant in our lives: God. He is, and he was, and he is to come. He is the Alpha and the Omega, the beginning and the end. He bookends time. He is able to provide stability amidst the transitions of life.

If your legs feel unsteady because of the changes you face, look to God. He started everything, and he will finish what he started. His character never changes, his love never fails and his power never wanes. Yes, it's good to know that some things never change.

Go to page 1523 for your next devotional reading.

Revelation 1:8

"I am the Alpha and the Omega," says the Lord God, "who is, and who was, and who is to come, the Almighty."

reflection

1 When have the changes in your life seemed overwhelming?

2 Who has been a constant source of encouragement during the changing seasons of your life?

3 How has Jesus helped you weather the changes you've experienced?

RELATED READINGS

Psalm 136:1–26;
Hebrew 6:16–20;
James 1:17

"In a threatened world, in the kaleidoscope whirl of our life patterns, it can be enormously reassuring to remind ourselves that God is unchanging."

Gini Andrews

¹⁰Do not be afraid of what you are about to suffer. I tell you, the devil will put some of you in prison to test you, and you will suffer persecution for ten days. Be faithful, even to the point of death, and I will give you the crown of life.

¹¹He who has an ear, let him hear what the Spirit says to the churches. He who overcomes will not be hurt at all by the second death.

To the Church in Pergamum

¹²"To the angel of the church in Pergamum write:

These are the words of him who has the sharp, double-edged sword. ¹³I know where you live—where Satan has his throne. Yet you remain true to my name. You did not renounce your faith in me, even in the days of Antipas, my faithful witness, who was put to death in your city—where Satan lives.

¹⁴Nevertheless, I have a few things against you: You have people there who hold to the teaching of Balaam, who taught Balak to entice the Israelites to sin by eating food sacrificed to idols and by committing sexual immorality. ¹⁵Likewise you also have those who hold to the teaching of the Nicolaitans. ¹⁶Repent therefore! Otherwise, I will soon come to you and will fight against them with the sword of my mouth.

¹⁷He who has an ear, let him hear what the Spirit says to the churches. To him who overcomes, I will give some of the hidden manna. I will also give him a white stone with a new name written on it, known only to him who receives it.

To the Church in Thyatira

¹⁸"To the angel of the church in Thyatira write:

These are the words of the Son of God, whose eyes are like blazing fire and whose feet are like burnished bronze. ¹⁹I know your deeds, your love and faith, your service and perseverance, and that you are now doing more than you did at first.

²⁰Nevertheless, I have this against you: You tolerate that woman Jezebel, who calls herself a prophetess. By her teaching she misleads my servants into sexual immorality and the eating of food sacrificed to idols. ²¹I have given her time to repent of her immorality, but she is unwilling. ²²So I will cast her on a bed of suffering, and I will make those who commit adultery with her suffer intensely, unless they repent of her ways. ²³I will strike her children dead. Then all the churches will know that I am he who searches hearts and minds, and I will repay each of you according to your deeds. ²⁴Now I say to the rest of you in Thyatira, to you who do not hold to her teaching and have not learned Satan's so-called deep secrets (I will not impose any other burden on you): ²⁵Only hold on to what you have until I come.

²⁶To him who overcomes and does my will to the end, I will give authority over the nations—

²⁷'He will rule them with an iron
        scepter;
    he will dash them to pieces like
        pottery'ᵃ—

just as I have received authority from my Father. ²⁸I will also give him the morning star. ²⁹He who has an ear, let him hear what the Spirit says to the churches.

To the Church in Sardis

3 "To the angelᵇ of the church in Sardis write:

These are the words of him who holds the seven spiritsᶜ of God and the seven stars. I know your deeds; you have a reputation of being alive, but you are dead. ²Wake up! Strengthen what remains and is about to die, for I have not found your deeds complete in the sight of my God. ³Remember, therefore, what you have received and heard; obey it, and repent. But if you do not wake up, I will come like a thief, and you will not know at what time I will come to you.

⁴Yet you have a few people in Sardis

ᵃ27 Psalm 2:9   ᵇ1 Or *messenger*; also in verses 7 and 14   ᶜ1 Or *the sevenfold Spirit* who have not soiled their clothes. They will walk with me, dressed in white, for they are worthy. 5 He who overcomes will, like them, be dressed in white. I will never blot out his name from the book of life, but will acknowledge his name before my Father and his angels. 6 He who has an ear, let him hear what the Spirit says to the churches.

To the Church in Philadelphia

7 "To the angel of the church in Philadelphia write:

These are the words of him who is holy and true, who holds the key of David. What he opens no one can shut, and what he shuts no one can open. 8 I know your deeds. See, I have placed before you an open door that no one can shut. I know that you have little strength, yet you have kept my word and have not denied my name. 9 I will make those who are of the synagogue of Satan, who claim to be Jews though they are not, but are liars—I will make them come and fall down at your feet and acknowledge that I have loved you. 10 Since you have kept my command to endure patiently, I will also keep you from the hour of trial that is going to come upon the whole world to test those who live on the earth.

11 I am coming soon. Hold on to what you have, so that no one will take your crown. 12 Him who overcomes I will make a pillar in the temple of my God. Never again will he leave it. I will write on him the name of my God and the name of the city of my God, the new Jerusalem, which is coming down out of heaven from my God; and I will also write on him my new name. 13 He who has an ear, let him hear what the Spirit says to the churches.

To the Church in Laodicea

14 "To the angel of the church in Laodicea write:

These are the words of the Amen, the faithful and true witness, the ruler of God's creation. 15 I know your deeds, that you are neither cold nor hot. I wish you were either one or the other! 16 So, because you are lukewarm—neither hot nor cold—I am about to spit you out of my mouth. 17 You say, 'I am rich; I have acquired wealth and do not need a thing.' But you do not realize that you are wretched, pitiful, poor, blind and naked. 18 I counsel you to buy from me gold refined in the fire, so you can become rich; and white clothes to wear, so you can cover your shameful nakedness; and salve to put on your eyes, so you can see.

19 Those whom I love I rebuke and discipline. So be earnest, and repent. 20 Here I am! I stand at the door and knock. If anyone hears my voice and opens the door, I will come in and eat with him, and he with me.

21 To him who overcomes, I will give the right to sit with me on my throne, just as I overcame and sat down with my Father on his throne. 22 He who has an ear, let him hear what the Spirit says to the churches."

Revelation 3:21

God Grants Favor

To him who overcomes, I will give the right to sit with me on my throne, just as I overcame and sat down with my Father on his throne.

The Throne in Heaven

4 After this I looked, and there before me was a door standing open in heaven. And the voice I had first heard speaking to me like a trumpet said, "Come up here, and I will show you what must take place after this." 2 At once I was in the Spirit, and there before me was a throne in heaven with someone sitting on it. 3 And the one who sat there had the appearance of jasper and carnelian. A rainbow, resembling an emerald, encircled the throne. 4 Surrounding the throne were twenty-four other thrones, and seated on them were twenty-four elders. They were dressed in white and had crowns of gold on their heads. 5 From the throne came flashes of lightning, rumblings and peals of thunder. Before the throne, seven lamps were blazing. These are

the seven spirits*a* of God. ⁶Also before the throne there was what looked like a sea of glass, clear as crystal.

In the center, around the throne, were four living creatures, and they were covered with eyes, in front and in back. ⁷The first living creature was like a lion, the second was like an ox, the third had a face like a man, the fourth was like a flying eagle. ⁸Each of the four living creatures had six wings and was covered with eyes all around, even under his wings. Day and night they never stop saying:

"Holy, holy, holy
    is the Lord God Almighty,
who was, and is, and is to come."

⁹Whenever the living creatures give glory, honor and thanks to him who sits on the throne and who lives for ever and ever, ¹⁰the twenty-four elders fall down before him who sits on the throne, and worship him who lives for ever and ever. They lay their crowns before the throne and say:

¹¹"You are worthy, our Lord and God,
    to receive glory and honor and power,
for you created all things,
    and by your will they were created
    and have their being."

The Scroll and the Lamb

5 Then I saw in the right hand of him who sat on the throne a scroll with writing on both sides and sealed with seven seals. ²And I saw a mighty angel proclaiming in a loud voice, "Who is worthy to break the seals and open the scroll?" ³But no one in heaven or on earth or under the earth could open the scroll or even look inside it. ⁴I wept and wept because no one was found who was worthy to open the scroll or look inside. ⁵Then one of the elders said to me, "Do not weep! See, the Lion of the tribe of Judah, the Root of David, has triumphed. He is able to open the scroll and its seven seals."

⁶Then I saw a Lamb, looking as if it had been slain, standing in the center of the throne, encircled by the four living creatures and the elders. He had seven horns and seven eyes, which are

the seven spirits*a* of God sent out into all the earth. ⁷He came and took the scroll from the right hand of him who sat on the throne. ⁸And when he had taken it, the four living creatures and the twenty-four elders fell down before the Lamb. Each one had a harp and they were holding golden bowls full of incense, which are the prayers of the saints. ⁹And they sang a new song:

"You are worthy to take the scroll
    and to open its seals,
because you were slain,
    and with your blood you purchased men
        for God
    from every tribe and language and
        people and nation.
¹⁰You have made them to be a kingdom and
        priests to serve our God,
    and they will reign on the earth."

¹¹Then I looked and heard the voice of many angels, numbering thousands upon thousands, and ten thousand times ten thousand. They encircled the throne and the living creatures and the elders. ¹²In a loud voice they sang:

"Worthy is the Lamb, who was slain,
to receive power and wealth and wisdom
        and strength
    and honor and glory and praise!"

¹³Then I heard every creature in heaven and on earth and under the earth and on the sea, and all that is in them, singing:

"To him who sits on the throne and to the
        Lamb
    be praise and honor and glory and power,
        for ever and ever!"

¹⁴The four living creatures said, "Amen," and the elders fell down and worshiped.

The Seals

6 I watched as the Lamb opened the first of the seven seals. Then I heard one of the four living creatures say in a voice like thunder, "Come!" ²I looked, and there before me was a white horse! Its rider held a bow, and he was given a crown, and he rode out as a conqueror bent on conquest.

---

a5,6 Or the sevenfold Spirit

Once and for All

Read: Revelation 5:1–14

AT THE END OF THE DAY, how do you feel when you check off all the items on your to-do list? Great! What about the days you're only able to check off three out of ten? Ugh!

So much of our lives are spent trying to prove we are worthy—worthy of love, worthy of appreciation, worthy of value. The truth, especially for women, is that we battle feelings of unworthiness—as followers of Jesus, as leaders, as mothers, as students, as neighbors. No matter how hard we work at it, we never quite measure up to what we think we *should* be or do. We're all too aware of unmet goals, unmet expectations, shortcomings and failings. When we base our feelings of significance upon what we do, just a passing glance at our unfinished to-do list can depress us. Unworthy—that's how we often feel. Unworthy to receive God's love. Unworthy to be called righteous. Unworthy to be used by God.

The truth is that we can never prove we're worthy because in and of ourselves we're not. In Revelation 5 John cried out with great weeping at the realization that no one in heaven, on earth or under the earth was worthy to open the heavenly scroll.

Yet suddenly before John's eyes stood the only One worthy to open the scroll. "Worthy is the Lamb, who was slain, to receive power and wealth and wisdom and strength and honor and glory and praise!" (verse 12). By *his* blood—not by the blood, sweat and tears of our striving—we have been redeemed. We no longer have to prove our significance or earn our way. God has established our worth for all time.

In the light of eternity, it's good to know that your to-do list, the title on your business card, your clothing size, car or accomplishments have no bearing upon your worth. You have been made worthy not because of what you have or have not done, but because of what Jesus Christ has done on your behalf. Nothing you can do can make you any more or less loved, valued and precious to God. The sacrificial blood of Jesus, the only worthy One, has made you worthy.

Revelation 5:9

"You are worthy to take the scroll and to open its seals, because you were slain, and with your blood you purchased men for God from every tribe and language and people and nation."

reflection

1 In what situations do you most often feel unworthy?

2 How have you worked to "do a little more" to prove your worth?

3 Spend some time thanking Jesus for being the worthy One and for passing on his worth to you.

RELATED READINGS

Isaiah 43:2–4;
Romans 3:20–26; 5:1–2;
2 Corinthians 5:21

Go to page 1529 for your next devotional reading.

³When the Lamb opened the second seal, I heard the second living creature say, "Come!" ⁴Then another horse came out, a fiery red one. Its rider was given power to take peace from the earth and to make men slay each other. To him was given a large sword.

⁵When the Lamb opened the third seal, I heard the third living creature say, "Come!" I looked, and there before me was a black horse! Its rider was holding a pair of scales in his hand. ⁶Then I heard what sounded like a voice among the four living creatures, saying, "A quart*ᵃ* of wheat for a day's wages,*ᵇ* and three quarts of barley for a day's wages,*ᵇ* and do not damage the oil and the wine!"

⁷When the Lamb opened the fourth seal, I heard the voice of the fourth living creature say, "Come!" ⁸I looked, and there before me was a pale horse! Its rider was named Death, and Hades was following close behind him. They were given power over a fourth of the earth to kill by sword, famine and plague, and by the wild beasts of the earth.

⁹When he opened the fifth seal, I saw under the altar the souls of those who had been slain because of the word of God and the testimony they had maintained. ¹⁰They called out in a loud voice, "How long, Sovereign Lord, holy and true, until you judge the inhabitants of the earth and avenge our blood?" ¹¹Then each of them was given a white robe, and they were told to wait a little longer, until the number of their fellow servants and brothers who were to be killed as they had been was completed.

¹²I watched as he opened the sixth seal. There was a great earthquake. The sun turned black like sackcloth made of goat hair, the whole moon turned blood red, ¹³and the stars in the sky fell to earth, as late figs drop from a fig tree when shaken by a strong wind. ¹⁴The sky receded like a scroll, rolling up, and every mountain and island was removed from its place.

¹⁵Then the kings of the earth, the princes, the generals, the rich, the mighty, and every slave and every free man hid in caves and among the rocks of the mountains. ¹⁶They called to the mountains and the rocks, "Fall on us and hide us from the face of him who sits on the throne and from the wrath of the Lamb! ¹⁷For the great day of their wrath has come, and who can stand?"

144,000 Sealed

7 After this I saw four angels standing at the four corners of the earth, holding back the four winds of the earth to prevent any wind from blowing on the land or on the sea or on any tree. ²Then I saw another angel coming up from the east, having the seal of the living God. He called out in a loud voice to the four angels who had been given power to harm the land and the sea: ³"Do not harm the land or the sea or the trees until we put a seal on the foreheads of the servants of our God." ⁴Then I heard the number of those who were sealed: 144,000 from all the tribes of Israel.

⁵ From the tribe of Judah 12,000 were sealed,
   from the tribe of Reuben 12,000,
   from the tribe of Gad 12,000,
⁶ from the tribe of Asher 12,000,
   from the tribe of Naphtali 12,000,
   from the tribe of Manasseh 12,000,
⁷ from the tribe of Simeon 12,000,
   from the tribe of Levi 12,000,
   from the tribe of Issachar 12,000,
⁸ from the tribe of Zebulun 12,000,
   from the tribe of Joseph 12,000,
   from the tribe of Benjamin 12,000.

The Great Multitude in White Robes

⁹After this I looked and there before me was a great multitude that no one could count, from every nation, tribe, people and language, standing before the throne and in front of the Lamb. They were wearing white robes and were holding palm branches in their hands. ¹⁰And they cried out in a loud voice:

"Salvation belongs to our God,
   who sits on the throne,
   and to the Lamb."

¹¹All the angels were standing around the throne and around the elders and the four living creatures. They fell down on their faces before the throne and worshiped God, ¹²saying:

"Amen!

---

*ᵃ*6 Greek *a choinix* (probably about a liter)   *ᵇ*6 Greek *a denarius*

Praise and glory
and wisdom and thanks and honor
and power and strength
be to our God for ever and ever.
Amen!"

¹³ Then one of the elders asked me, "These in white robes —who are they, and where did they come from?"

¹⁴ I answered, "Sir, you know."

And he said, "These are they who have come out of the great tribulation; they have washed their robes and made them white in the blood of the Lamb. ¹⁵ Therefore,

"they are before the throne
    of God
  and serve him day and
      night in his temple;
and he who sits on the throne will spread
      his tent over them.
¹⁶ Never again will they hunger;
  never again will they thirst.
The sun will not beat upon them,
  nor any scorching heat.
¹⁷ For the Lamb at the center of the throne
      will be their shepherd;
  he will lead them to springs of living
      water.
And God will wipe away every tear from
      their eyes."

The Seventh Seal and the Golden Censer

8 When he opened the seventh seal, there was silence in heaven for about half an hour.

² And I saw the seven angels who stand before God, and to them were given seven trumpets.

³ Another angel, who had a golden censer, came and stood at the altar. He was given much incense to offer, with the prayers of all the saints, on the golden altar before the throne. ⁴ The smoke of the incense, together with the prayers of the saints, went up before God from the angel's hand. ⁵ Then the angel took the censer, filled it with fire from the altar, and hurled it on the earth; and there came peals of thunder, rumblings, flashes of lightning and an earthquake.

The Trumpets

⁶ Then the seven angels who had the seven trumpets prepared to sound them.

⁷ The first angel sounded his trumpet, and there came hail and fire mixed with blood, and it was hurled down upon the earth. A third of the earth was burned up, a third of the trees were burned up, and all the green grass was burned up.

⁸ The second angel sounded his trumpet, and something like a huge mountain, all ablaze, was thrown into the sea. A third of the sea turned into blood, ⁹ a third of the living creatures in the sea died, and a third of the ships were destroyed.

¹⁰ The third angel sounded his trumpet, and a great star, blazing like a torch, fell from the sky on a third of the rivers and on the springs of water— ¹¹ the name of the star is Wormwood.[a] A third of the waters turned bitter, and many people died from the waters that had become bitter.

¹² The fourth angel sounded his trumpet, and a third of the sun was struck, a third of the moon, and a third of the stars, so that a third of them turned dark. A third of the day was without light, and also a third of the night.

¹³ As I watched, I heard an eagle that was flying in midair call out in a loud voice: "Woe! Woe! Woe to the inhabitants of the earth, because of the trumpet blasts about to be sounded by the other three angels!"

9 The fifth angel sounded his trumpet, and I saw a star that had fallen from the sky to the earth. The star was given the key to the shaft of the Abyss. ² When he opened the Abyss, smoke rose from it like the smoke from a gigantic furnace. The sun and sky were darkened by the smoke from the Abyss. ³ And out of the smoke locusts came down upon the earth and were given power like that of scorpions of the earth. ⁴ They were told not to harm the grass of

---

Revelation 7:12

God Deserves Praise

"Praise and glory
and wisdom and thanks
and honor
and power and strength
be to our God for
ever and ever."

---

a 11 That is, Bitterness

the earth or any plant or tree, but only those people who did not have the seal of God on their foreheads. **5** They were not given power to kill them, but only to torture them for five months. And the agony they suffered was like that of the sting of a scorpion when it strikes a man. **6** During those days men will seek death, but will not find it; they will long to die, but death will elude them.

7 The locusts looked like horses prepared for battle. On their heads they wore something like crowns of gold, and their faces resembled human faces. **8** Their hair was like women's hair, and their teeth were like lions' teeth. **9** They had breastplates like breastplates of iron, and the sound of their wings was like the thundering of many horses and chariots rushing into battle. **10** They had tails and stings like scorpions, and in their tails they had power to torment people for five months. **11** They had as king over them the angel of the Abyss, whose name in Hebrew is Abaddon, and in Greek, Apollyon.*a*

12 The first woe is past; two other woes are yet to come.

13 The sixth angel sounded his trumpet, and I heard a voice coming from the horns*b* of the golden altar that is before God. **14** It said to the sixth angel who had the trumpet, "Release the four angels who are bound at the great river Euphrates." **15** And the four angels who had been kept ready for this very hour and day and month and year were released to kill a third of mankind. **16** The number of the mounted troops was two hundred million. I heard their number.

17 The horses and riders I saw in my vision looked like this: Their breastplates were fiery red, dark blue, and yellow as sulfur. The heads of the horses resembled the heads of lions, and out of their mouths came fire, smoke and sulfur. **18** A third of mankind was killed by the three plagues of fire, smoke and sulfur that came out of their mouths. **19** The power of the horses was in their mouths and in their tails; for their tails were like snakes, having heads with which they inflict injury.

20 The rest of mankind that were not killed by these plagues still did not repent of the work of their hands; they did not stop worshiping demons, and idols of gold, silver, bronze, stone and wood—idols that cannot see or hear or walk. **21** Nor did they repent of their murders, their magic arts, their sexual immorality or their thefts.

The Angel and the Little Scroll

10 Then I saw another mighty angel coming down from heaven. He was robed in a cloud, with a rainbow above his head; his face was like the sun, and his legs were like fiery pillars. **2** He was holding a little scroll, which lay open in his hand. He planted his right foot on the sea and his left foot on the land, **3** and he gave a loud shout like the roar of a lion. When he shouted, the voices of the seven thunders spoke. **4** And when the seven thunders spoke, I was about to write; but I heard a voice from heaven say, "Seal up what the seven thunders have said and do not write it down."

5 Then the angel I had seen standing on the sea and on the land raised his right hand to heaven. **6** And he swore by him who lives for ever and ever, who created the heavens and all that is in them, the earth and all that is in it, and the sea and all that is in it, and said, "There will be no more delay! **7** But in the days when the seventh angel is about to sound his trumpet, the mystery of God will be accomplished, just as he announced to his servants the prophets."

8 Then the voice that I had heard from heaven spoke to me once more: "Go, take the scroll that lies open in the hand of the angel who is standing on the sea and on the land."

9 So I went to the angel and asked him to give me the little scroll. He said to me, "Take it and eat it. It will turn your stomach sour, but in your mouth it will be as sweet as honey." **10** I took the little scroll from the angel's hand and ate it. It tasted as sweet as honey in my mouth, but when I had eaten it, my stomach turned sour. **11** Then I was told, "You must prophesy again about many peoples, nations, languages and kings."

The Two Witnesses

11 I was given a reed like a measuring rod and was told, "Go and measure the temple of God and the altar, and count the

---

a 11 *Abaddon* and *Apollyon* mean *Destroyer.*   *b* 13 That is, projections worshipers there. ²But exclude the outer court; do not measure it, because it has been given to the Gentiles. They will trample on the holy city for 42 months. ³And I will give power to my two witnesses, and they will prophesy for 1,260 days, clothed in sackcloth." ⁴These are the two olive trees and the two lampstands that stand before the Lord of the earth. ⁵If anyone tries to harm them, fire comes from their mouths and devours their enemies. This is how anyone who wants to harm them must die. ⁶These men have power to shut up the sky so that it will not rain during the time they are prophesying; and they have power to turn the waters into blood and to strike the earth with every kind of plague as often as they want.

⁷Now when they have finished their testimony, the beast that comes up from the Abyss will attack them, and overpower and kill them. ⁸Their bodies will lie in the street of the great city, which is figuratively called Sodom and Egypt, where also their Lord was crucified. ⁹For three and a half days men from every people, tribe, language and nation will gaze on their bodies and refuse them burial. ¹⁰The inhabitants of the earth will gloat over them and will celebrate by sending each other gifts, because these two prophets had tormented those who live on the earth.

¹¹But after the three and a half days a breath of life from God entered them, and they stood on their feet, and terror struck those who saw them. ¹²Then they heard a loud voice from heaven saying to them, "Come up here." And they went up to heaven in a cloud, while their enemies looked on.

¹³At that very hour there was a severe earthquake and a tenth of the city collapsed. Seven thousand people were killed in the earthquake, and the survivors were terrified and gave glory to the God of heaven.

¹⁴The second woe has passed; the third woe is coming soon.

The Seventh Trumpet

¹⁵The seventh angel sounded his trumpet, and there were loud voices in heaven, which said:

"The kingdom of the world has become
        the kingdom of our Lord and of his
        Christ,
                and he will reign for ever
                and ever."

¹⁶And the twenty-four elders, who were seated on their thrones before God, fell on their faces and worshiped God, ¹⁷saying:

"We give thanks to
        you, Lord God
        Almighty,
        the One who is and who
        was,
because you have taken
        your great power
        and have begun to reign.
¹⁸The nations were angry;
        and your wrath has come.
The time has come for judging the dead,
        and for rewarding your servants the
        prophets
and your saints and those who reverence
        your name,
        both small and great—
and for destroying those who destroy the
        earth."

¹⁹Then God's temple in heaven was opened, and within his temple was seen the ark of his covenant. And there came flashes of lightning, rumblings, peals of thunder, an earthquake and a great hailstorm.

The Woman and the Dragon

12 A great and wondrous sign appeared in heaven: a woman clothed with the sun, with the moon under her feet and a crown of twelve stars on her head. ²She was pregnant and cried out in pain as she was about to give birth. ³Then another sign appeared in heaven: an enormous red dragon with seven heads and ten horns and seven crowns on his heads. ⁴His tail swept a third of the stars out of the

> **Revelation 11:17**
>
> *God Reigns Over All*
>
> "We give thanks to you, Lord God Almighty, the One who is and who was, because you have taken your great power and have begun to reign."

sky and flung them to the earth. The dragon stood in front of the woman who was about to give birth, so that he might devour her child the moment it was born. ⁵She gave birth to a son, a male child, who will rule all the nations with an iron scepter. And her child was snatched up to God and to his throne. ⁶The woman fled into the desert to a place prepared for her by God, where she might be taken care of for 1,260 days.

⁷And there was war in heaven. Michael and his angels fought against the dragon, and the dragon and his angels fought back. ⁸But he was not strong enough, and they lost their place in heaven. ⁹The great dragon was hurled down—that ancient serpent called the devil, or Satan, who leads the whole world astray. He was hurled to the earth, and his angels with him.

¹⁰Then I heard a loud voice in heaven say:

"Now have come the salvation and the
        power and the
        kingdom of our
        God,
    and the authority of his
        Christ.
For the accuser of our
        brothers,
    who accuses them
        before our God day
        and night,
    has been hurled down.
¹¹They overcame him
        by the blood of the
        Lamb
    and by the word of their
        testimony;
    they did not love their lives
        so much
        as to shrink from death.
¹²Therefore rejoice, you heavens
        and you who dwell in them!
But woe to the earth and the sea,
        because the devil has gone down to you!
He is filled with fury,
        because he knows that his time is short."

¹³When the dragon saw that he had been hurled to the earth, he pursued the woman who had given birth to the male child. ¹⁴The woman was given the two wings of a great eagle, so that she might fly to the place prepared for her in the desert, where she would be taken care of for a time, times and half a time, out of the serpent's reach. ¹⁵Then from his mouth the serpent spewed water like a river, to overtake the woman and sweep her away with the torrent. ¹⁶But the earth helped the woman by opening its mouth and swallowing the river that the dragon had spewed out of his mouth. ¹⁷Then the dragon was enraged at the woman and went off to make war against the rest of her offspring—those who obey God's commandments and hold to the testimony

13 of Jesus. ¹And the dragon*ᵃ* stood on the shore of the sea.

The Beast out of the Sea

And I saw a beast coming out of the sea. He had ten horns and seven heads, with ten crowns on his horns, and on each head a blasphemous name. ²The beast I saw resembled a leopard, but had feet like those of a bear and a mouth like that of a lion. The dragon gave the beast his power and his throne and great authority. ³One of the heads of the beast seemed to have had a fatal wound, but the fatal wound had been healed. The whole world was astonished and followed the beast. ⁴Men worshiped the dragon because he had given authority to the beast, and they also worshiped the beast and asked, "Who is like the beast? Who can make war against him?"

⁵The beast was given a mouth to utter proud words and blasphemies and to exercise his authority for forty-two months. ⁶He opened his mouth to blaspheme God, and to slander his name and his dwelling place and those who live in heaven. ⁷He was given power to make war against the saints and to conquer them. And he was given authority over every tribe, people, language and nation. ⁸All inhabitants of the earth will worship the beast—all whose names have not been written in the book of life

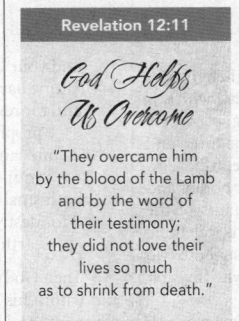

Revelation 12:11

God Helps Us Overcome

"They overcame him by the blood of the Lamb and by the word of their testimony; they did not love their lives so much as to shrink from death."

*ᵃ*1 Some late manuscripts *And I*

Imperfect Yet Forgiven

Read: Revelation 12:1–17

COMMON WISDOM HOLDS that we should never discuss two topics: religion and politics. Nevertheless, two travelers waiting for a delayed flight began a conversation about religion. One of them was a skeptic who was hostile to Christianity; the other was a timid girl who was undecided about her faith. The skeptic was trying to defend her lack of faith by exposing the evils historically afflicting Christendom: hypocrisy, covetousness, divisiveness and the corruption of well-known religious leaders.

Nearby, a Christian woman sat listening to the conversation. She knew the accusations were true—she had dealt with many of these issues in her own life. Soon, the skeptic loudly extended the circle of her audience and addressed the other travelers sitting nearby, including the Christian lady overhearing the exchange. "I can tell you are quick to condemn evil," the Christian lady replied. "You've just listed the things that make Christians human. I must tell you that I am a Christian and love Jesus. I won't speak a word in our defense since I have committed many of the sins you accuse us of. But I do challenge you to speak a word against Jesus Christ himself."

The skeptic was surprised. She seemed almost frightened as she sheepishly replied, "Well, no! I've read the Bible and I could not find fault with him. Even I know he was perfect." The timid girl looked at the Christian woman and smiled.

One of Satan's greatest tactics is to accuse believers. And most of his accusations are true. We *do* sin—we all fall short of the glory of God. The accuser of the Christian community doesn't have to look far to find accusations to hold against us.

Jesus overcame Satan at the cross and will one day hurl him into the lake of fire at the end of time. But today his accusations against believers carry no weight with God because our sins have been forgiven. As John tells us in the book of Revelation, the accuser was overcome by "the blood of the Lamb."

So the next time Satan or his minions accuse you of sin, don't grow defensive. Simply say, "You're right . . . but, hallelujah, I'm forgiven!"

Revelation 12:10–11

"For the accuser of our brothers, who accuses them before our God day and night, has been hurled down. They overcame him by the blood of the Lamb and by the word of their testimony; they did not love their lives so much as to shrink from death."

reflection

1 Do you grow defensive when someone accuses you of sin?

2 Based on your knowledge of Scripture, what tactics does Satan use to try to make you an ineffective Christian?

3 Spend some time thanking God for overcoming Satan. Ask him to give you strength to overcome and to be a good witness to those you encounter.

RELATED READINGS

Romans 16:20; James 4:7–10; 1 Peter 5:8–10

"Nothing in this world bears the impress of the Son of God so surely as forgiveness."

Alice Cary

Wednesday

Go to page 1535 for your next devotional reading.

belonging to the Lamb that was slain from the creation of the world.[a]

⁹He who has an ear, let him hear.

¹⁰If anyone is to go into captivity,
　　into captivity he will go.
If anyone is to be killed[b] with the sword,
　　with the sword he will be killed.

This calls for patient endurance and faithfulness on the part of the saints.

The Beast out of the Earth

¹¹Then I saw another beast, coming out of the earth. He had two horns like a lamb, but he spoke like a dragon. ¹²He exercised all the authority of the first beast on his behalf, and made the earth and its inhabitants worship the first beast, whose fatal wound had been healed. ¹³And he performed great and miraculous signs, even causing fire to come down from heaven to earth in full view of men. ¹⁴Because of the signs he was given power to do on behalf of the first beast, he deceived the inhabitants of the earth. He ordered them to set up an image in honor of the beast who was wounded by the sword and yet lived. ¹⁵He was given power to give breath to the image of the first beast, so that it could speak and cause all who refused to worship the image to be killed. ¹⁶He also forced everyone, small and great, rich and poor, free and slave, to receive a mark on his right hand or on his forehead, ¹⁷so that no one could buy or sell unless he had the mark, which is the name of the beast or the number of his name.

¹⁸This calls for wisdom. If anyone has insight, let him calculate the number of the beast, for it is man's number. His number is 666.

The Lamb and the 144,000

14 Then I looked, and there before me was the Lamb, standing on Mount Zion, and with him 144,000 who had his name and his Father's name written on their foreheads. ²And I heard a sound from heaven like the roar of rushing waters and like a loud peal of thunder. The sound I heard was like that of harpists playing their harps. ³And they sang a new song before the throne and before the four living creatures and the elders. No one

could learn the song except the 144,000 who had been redeemed from the earth. ⁴These are those who did not defile themselves with women, for they kept themselves pure. They follow the Lamb wherever he goes. They were purchased from among men and offered as firstfruits to God and the Lamb. ⁵No lie was found in their mouths; they are blameless.

The Three Angels

⁶Then I saw another angel flying in midair, and he had the eternal gospel to proclaim to those who live on the earth—to every nation, tribe, language and people. ⁷He said in a loud voice, "Fear God and give him glory, because the hour of his judgment has come. Worship him who made the heavens, the earth, the sea and the springs of water."

⁸A second angel followed and said, "Fallen! Fallen is Babylon the Great, which made all the nations drink the maddening wine of her adulteries."

⁹A third angel followed them and said in a loud voice: "If anyone worships the beast and his image and receives his mark on the forehead or on the hand, ¹⁰he, too, will drink of the wine of God's fury, which has been poured full strength into the cup of his wrath. He will be tormented with burning sulfur in the presence of the holy angels and of the Lamb. ¹¹And the smoke of their torment rises for ever and ever. There is no rest day or night for those who worship the beast and his image, or for anyone who receives the mark of his name." ¹²This calls for patient endurance on the part of the saints who obey God's commandments and remain faithful to Jesus.

¹³Then I heard a voice from heaven say, "Write: Blessed are the dead who die in the Lord from now on."

"Yes," says the Spirit, "they will rest from their labor, for their deeds will follow them."

The Harvest of the Earth

¹⁴I looked, and there before me was a white cloud, and seated on the cloud was one "like a son of man"[c] with a crown of gold on his head and a sharp sickle in his hand. ¹⁵Then another angel came out of the temple and called in a

---

[a]8 Or *written from the creation of the world in the book of life belonging to the Lamb that was slain*　　[b]10 Some manuscripts *anyone kills*
[c]14 Daniel 7:13

loud voice to him who was sitting on the cloud, "Take your sickle and reap, because the time to reap has come, for the harvest of the earth is ripe." [16]So he who was seated on the cloud swung his sickle over the earth, and the earth was harvested.

[17]Another angel came out of the temple in heaven, and he too had a sharp sickle. [18]Still another angel, who had charge of the fire, came from the altar and called in a loud voice to him who had the sharp sickle, "Take your sharp sickle and gather the clusters of grapes from the earth's vine, because its grapes are ripe." [19]The angel swung his sickle on the earth, gathered its grapes and threw them into the great winepress of God's wrath. [20]They were trampled in the winepress outside the city, and blood flowed out of the press, rising as high as the horses' bridles for a distance of 1,600 stadia.[a]

Seven Angels With Seven Plagues

15 I saw in heaven another great and marvelous sign: seven angels with the seven last plagues—last, because with them God's wrath is completed. [2]And I saw what looked like a sea of glass mixed with fire and, standing beside the sea, those who had been victorious over the beast and his image and over the number of his name. They held harps given them by God [3]and sang the song of Moses the servant of God and the song of the Lamb:

"Great and marvelous are
⠀⠀your deeds,
⠀⠀Lord God Almighty.
Just and true are your ways,
⠀⠀King of the ages.
[4]Who will not fear you,
⠀⠀O Lord,
⠀⠀and bring glory to your
⠀⠀⠀⠀name?
For you alone are holy.
All nations will come
⠀⠀and worship before you,
for your righteous acts have
⠀⠀been revealed."

[5]After this I looked and in heaven the temple, that is, the tabernacle of the Testimony, was opened. [6]Out of the temple came the seven angels with the seven plagues. They were dressed in clean, shining linen and wore golden sashes around their chests. [7]Then one of the four living creatures gave to the seven angels seven golden bowls filled with the wrath of God, who lives for ever and ever. [8]And the temple was filled with smoke from the glory of God and from his power, and no one could enter the temple until the seven plagues of the seven angels were completed.

The Seven Bowls of God's Wrath

16 Then I heard a loud voice from the temple saying to the seven angels, "Go, pour out the seven bowls of God's wrath on the earth."

[2]The first angel went and poured out his bowl on the land, and ugly and painful sores broke out on the people who had the mark of the beast and worshiped his image.

[3]The second angel poured out his bowl on the sea, and it turned into blood like that of a dead man, and every living thing in the sea died.

[4]The third angel poured out his bowl on the rivers and springs of water, and they became blood. [5]Then I heard the angel in charge of the waters say:

"You are just in these judgments,
⠀⠀you who are and who were, the Holy
⠀⠀⠀⠀One,
⠀⠀because you have so judged;
⠀⠀[6]for they have shed the
⠀⠀⠀⠀blood of your saints
⠀⠀⠀⠀⠀⠀and prophets,
⠀⠀and you have given them
⠀⠀⠀⠀blood to drink as
⠀⠀⠀⠀⠀⠀they deserve."

[7]And I heard the altar respond:

"Yes, Lord God Almighty,
⠀⠀true and just are your
⠀⠀⠀⠀judgments."

[8]The fourth angel poured out his bowl on the sun, and the sun was given power to scorch people with fire. [9]They were seared by the intense heat and they cursed the name of God, who had control over these plagues, but they refused to repent and glorify him.

Revelation 15:4

God Is Holy

"Who will not fear you,
O Lord,
and bring glory
to your name?
For you alone are holy."

[a]**20** That is, about 180 miles (about 300 kilometers)

¹⁰The fifth angel poured out his bowl on the throne of the beast, and his kingdom was plunged into darkness. Men gnawed their tongues in agony ¹¹and cursed the God of heaven because of their pains and their sores, but they refused to repent of what they had done.

¹²The sixth angel poured out his bowl on the great river Euphrates, and its water was dried up to prepare the way for the kings from the East. ¹³Then I saw three evil*ᵃ* spirits that looked like frogs; they came out of the mouth of the dragon, out of the mouth of the beast and out of the mouth of the false prophet. ¹⁴They are spirits of demons performing miraculous signs, and they go out to the kings of the whole world, to gather them for the battle on the great day of God Almighty.

¹⁵"Behold, I come like a thief! Blessed is he who stays awake and keeps his clothes with him, so that he may not go naked and be shamefully exposed."

¹⁶Then they gathered the kings together to the place that in Hebrew is called Armageddon.

¹⁷The seventh angel poured out his bowl into the air, and out of the temple came a loud voice from the throne, saying, "It is done!" ¹⁸Then there came flashes of lightning, rumblings, peals of thunder and a severe earthquake. No earthquake like it has ever occurred since man has been on earth, so tremendous was the quake. ¹⁹The great city split into three parts, and the cities of the nations collapsed. God remembered Babylon the Great and gave her the cup filled with the wine of the fury of his wrath. ²⁰Every island fled away and the mountains could not be found. ²¹From the sky huge hailstones of about a hundred pounds each fell upon men. And they cursed God on account of the plague of hail, because the plague was so terrible.

The Woman on the Beast

17 One of the seven angels who had the seven bowls came and said to me, "Come, I will show you the punishment of the great prostitute, who sits on many waters. ²With her the kings of the earth committed adultery and the inhabitants of the earth were intoxicated with the wine of her adulteries."

³Then the angel carried me away in the Spirit into a desert. There I saw a woman sitting on a scarlet beast that was covered with blasphemous names and had seven heads and ten horns. ⁴The woman was dressed in purple and scarlet, and was glittering with gold, precious stones and pearls. She held a golden cup in her hand, filled with abominable things and the filth of her adulteries: ⁵This title was written on her forehead:

MYSTERY
BABYLON THE GREAT
THE MOTHER OF PROSTITUTES
AND OF THE ABOMINATIONS OF THE EARTH.

⁶I saw that the woman was drunk with the blood of the saints, the blood of those who bore testimony to Jesus.

When I saw her, I was greatly astonished. ⁷Then the angel said to me: "Why are you astonished? I will explain to you the mystery of the woman and of the beast she rides, which has the seven heads and ten horns. ⁸The beast, which you saw, once was, now is not, and will come up out of the Abyss and go to his destruction. The inhabitants of the earth whose names have not been written in the book of life from the creation of the world will be astonished when they see the beast, because he once was, now is not, and yet will come.

⁹"This calls for a mind with wisdom. The seven heads are seven hills on which the woman sits. ¹⁰They are also seven kings. Five have fallen, one is, the other has not yet come; but when he does come, he must remain for a little while. ¹¹The beast who once was, and now is not, is an eighth king. He belongs to the seven and is going to his destruction.

¹²"The ten horns you saw are ten kings who have not yet received a kingdom, but who for one hour will receive authority as kings along with the beast. ¹³They have one purpose and will give their power and authority to the beast. ¹⁴They will make war against the Lamb, but the Lamb will overcome them because he is Lord of lords and King of kings—and with him will be his called, chosen and faithful followers."

¹⁵Then the angel said to me, "The waters you saw, where the prostitute sits, are peoples,

ᵃ13 Greek unclean

multitudes, nations and languages. ¹⁶The beast and the ten horns you saw will hate the prostitute. They will bring her to ruin and leave her naked; they will eat her flesh and burn her with fire. ¹⁷For God has put it into their hearts to accomplish his purpose by agreeing to give the beast their power to rule, until God's words are fulfilled. ¹⁸The woman you saw is the great city that rules over the kings of the earth."

The Fall of Babylon

18 After this I saw another angel coming down from heaven. He had great authority, and the earth was illuminated by his splendor. ²With a mighty voice he shouted:

"Fallen! Fallen is Babylon the Great!
    She has become a home for demons
and a haunt for every evil*ᵃ* spirit,
    a haunt for every unclean and detestable
        bird.
³ For all the nations have drunk
    the maddening wine of her adulteries.
The kings of the earth committed adultery
        with her,
    and the merchants of the earth grew
        rich from her excessive luxuries."

⁴Then I heard another voice from heaven say:

"Come out of her, my people,
    so that you will not share in her sins,
    so that you will not receive any of her
        plagues;
⁵ for her sins are piled up to heaven,
    and God has remembered her crimes.
⁶ Give back to her as she has given;
    pay her back double for what she has
        done.
    Mix her a double portion from her own
        cup.
⁷ Give her as much torture and grief
    as the glory and luxury she gave herself.
In her heart she boasts,
    'I sit as queen; I am not a widow,
    and I will never mourn.'
⁸ Therefore in one day her plagues will
        overtake her:
    death, mourning and famine.
She will be consumed by fire,

ᵃ2 Greek *unclean*

for mighty is the Lord God who judges
        her.

⁹"When the kings of the earth who committed adultery with her and shared her luxury see the smoke of her burning, they will weep and mourn over her. ¹⁰Terrified at her torment, they will stand far off and cry:

"'Woe! Woe, O great city,
    O Babylon, city of power!
In one hour your doom has come!'

¹¹"The merchants of the earth will weep and mourn over her because no one buys their cargoes any more— ¹²cargoes of gold, silver, precious stones and pearls; fine linen, purple, silk and scarlet cloth; every sort of citron wood, and articles of every kind made of ivory, costly wood, bronze, iron and marble; ¹³cargoes of cinnamon and spice, of incense, myrrh and frankincense, of wine and olive oil, of fine flour and wheat; cattle and sheep; horses and carriages; and bodies and souls of men.

¹⁴"They will say, 'The fruit you longed for is gone from you. All your riches and splendor have vanished, never to be recovered.' ¹⁵The merchants who sold these things and gained their wealth from her will stand far off, terrified at her torment. They will weep and mourn ¹⁶and cry out:

"'Woe! Woe, O great city,
    dressed in fine linen, purple and scarlet,
    and glittering with gold, precious stones
        and pearls!
¹⁷ In one hour such great wealth has been
        brought to ruin!'

"Every sea captain, and all who travel by ship, the sailors, and all who earn their living from the sea, will stand far off. ¹⁸When they see the smoke of her burning, they will exclaim, 'Was there ever a city like this great city?' ¹⁹They will throw dust on their heads, and with weeping and mourning cry out:

"'Woe! Woe, O great city,
    where all who had ships on the sea
        became rich through her wealth!
In one hour she has been brought to ruin!
²⁰ Rejoice over her, O heaven!

Rejoice, saints and apostles and
prophets!
God has judged her for the way she treated
you.'"

²¹Then a mighty angel picked up a boulder
the size of a large millstone and threw it into
the sea, and said:

"With such violence
the great city of Babylon will be thrown
down,
never to be found again.
²²The music of harpists and musicians, flute
players and trumpeters,
will never be heard in you again.
No workman of any trade
will ever be found in you again.
The sound of a millstone
will never be heard in you again.
²³The light of a lamp
will never shine in you again.
The voice of bridegroom and bride
will never be heard in you again.
Your merchants were the world's great
men.
By your magic spell all the nations were
led astray.
²⁴In her was found the blood of prophets and
of the saints,
and of all who have been killed on the
earth."

Hallelujah!

19 After this I heard what sounded like
the roar of a great multitude in heaven
shouting:

"Hallelujah!
Salvation and glory and power belong to
our God,
² for true and just are his judgments.
He has condemned the great prostitute
who corrupted the earth by her
adulteries.
He has avenged on her the blood of his
servants."

³And again they shouted:

"Hallelujah!
The smoke from her goes up for ever and
ever."

⁴The twenty-four elders and the four living
creatures fell down and worshiped God, who
was seated on the throne. And they cried:

"Amen, Hallelujah!"

⁵Then a voice came from the throne, saying:

"Praise our God,
all you his servants,
you who fear him,
both small and great!"

⁶Then I heard what sounded like a great multitude, like the roar of rushing waters and like
loud peals of thunder, shouting:

"Hallelujah!
For our Lord God Almighty reigns.
⁷ Let us rejoice and be glad
and give him glory!
For the wedding of the Lamb has come,
and his bride has made herself ready.
⁸ Fine linen, bright and clean,
was given her to wear."
(Fine linen stands for the righteous acts of the
saints.)

⁹Then the angel said to me, "Write: 'Blessed
are those who are invited to the wedding supper of the Lamb!'" And he added, "These are
the true words of God."

¹⁰At this I fell at his feet to worship him.
But he said to me, "Do not do it! I am a fellow servant with you and with your brothers
who hold to the testimony of Jesus. Worship
God! For the testimony of Jesus is the spirit
of prophecy."

The Rider on the White Horse

¹¹I saw heaven standing open and there before me was a white horse, whose rider is called
Faithful and True. With justice he judges and
makes war. ¹²His eyes are like blazing fire, and
on his head are many crowns. He has a name
written on him that no one knows but he himself. ¹³He is dressed in a robe dipped in blood,
and his name is the Word of God. ¹⁴The armies of heaven were following him, riding on
white horses and dressed in fine linen, white
and clean. ¹⁵Out of his mouth comes a sharp
sword with which to strike down the nations.

The Book of Life

Read: Revelation 20:1–15

THE DAY OF CHRIST will be a great and terrible day. Great for the righteous and terrible for the unrighteous. "In the end that Face which is the delight or the terror of the universe must be turned upon each of us either with one expression or the other."

I'm just grateful that Scripture speaks of that time as only "a day." It may mean the Great Judgment will be swift. After all, there are only two kinds of people in the end: those who say to God, "Thy will be done," and those to whom God says, in the end, "*Thy* will be done." All that are in Hell, choose it.

For all the people who insisted "My will be done!" God will not dissuade. He will no longer strive with them, either by pointing to His glory in creation or by preaching to them from the Gospel. For those who turn their backs on Christ, there is no heaven.

Yes, there is a hell.

It's unthinkable to talk about heaven without at least mentioning hell. Please note I didn't refer to it as "heaven's counterpart." Heaven has no counterpart. It has no opposite. Just as Satan is not God's opposite (for the devil is merely a created being—and a fallen one, at that!), neither does heaven have an opposite. In the vastness of God's infinite as well as cleansed and purified universe, hell may end up being only a speck. A trash heap. A garbage heap . . .

Rather than debate the census figures of heaven and hell, it is simply sufficient to say that hell exists; it's horrible, you don't want to go there, and you want to do everything in your power to keep others from choosing it. Jesus' teaching about hell with its wormwood and gall is meant to strike terror in our hearts, warning us that if heaven is better than we could dream, so hell will be worse than we can imagine.

Hell warns us to seek heaven.

It is its own best deterrent.

— Joni Eareckson Tada

reflection

1 How do you know that your name is written in the book of life? If you aren't sure, read Romans 10:9 and talk about it with your pastor.

2 Until the day of the Lord comes, there is time to tell others about Jesus. Who will you share the Good News of the gospel with?

3 Most people don't like to talk about hell. How did this devotional help you understand the warning that hell brings to an unbelieving world?

RELATED READINGS

Matthew 7:13–14;
Luke 16:22–31;
2 Peter 2:4–9; 3:10–17

"He will rule them with an iron scepter."*ª* He treads the winepress of the fury of the wrath of God Almighty. ¹⁶On his robe and on his thigh he has this name written:

KING OF KINGS AND LORD OF LORDS.

¹⁷And I saw an angel standing in the sun, who cried in a loud voice to all the birds flying in midair, "Come, gather together for the great supper of God, ¹⁸so that you may eat the flesh of kings, generals, and mighty men, of horses and their riders, and the flesh of all people, free and slave, small and great."

¹⁹Then I saw the beast and the kings of the earth and their armies gathered together to make war against the rider on the horse and his army. ²⁰But the beast was captured, and with him the false prophet who had performed the miraculous signs on his behalf. With these signs he had deluded those who had received the mark of the beast and worshiped his image. The two of them were thrown alive into the fiery lake of burning sulfur. ²¹The rest of them were killed with the sword that came out of the mouth of the rider on the horse, and all the birds gorged themselves on their flesh.

The Thousand Years

20 And I saw an angel coming down out of heaven, having the key to the Abyss and holding in his hand a great chain. ²He seized the dragon, that ancient serpent, who is the devil, or Satan, and bound him for a thousand years. ³He threw him into the Abyss, and locked and sealed it over him, to keep him from deceiving the nations anymore until the thousand years were ended. After that, he must be set free for a short time.

⁴I saw thrones on which were seated those who had been given authority to judge. And I saw the souls of those who had been beheaded because of their testimony for Jesus and because of the word of God. They had not worshiped the beast or his image and had not received his mark on their foreheads or their hands. They came to life and reigned with Christ a thousand years. ⁵(The rest of the dead did not come to life until the thousand years were ended.) This is the first resurrection. ⁶Blessed and holy are those who have part in the first resurrection. The second death has no power over them, but they will be priests of God and of Christ and will reign with him for a thousand years.

Satan's Doom

⁷When the thousand years are over, Satan will be released from his prison ⁸and will go out to deceive the nations in the four corners of the earth—Gog and Magog—to gather them for battle. In number they are like the sand on the seashore. ⁹They marched across the breadth of the earth and surrounded the camp of God's people, the city he loves. But fire came down from heaven and devoured them. ¹⁰And the devil, who deceived them, was thrown into the lake of burning sulfur, where the beast and the false prophet had been thrown. They will be tormented day and night for ever and ever.

The Dead Are Judged

¹¹Then I saw a great white throne and him who was seated on it. Earth and sky fled from his presence, and there was no place for them. ¹²And I saw the dead, great and small, standing before the throne, and books were opened. Another book was opened, which is the book of life. The dead were judged according to what they had done as recorded in the books. ¹³The sea gave up the dead that were in it, and death and Hades gave up the dead that were in them, and each person was judged according to what he had done. ¹⁴Then death and Hades were thrown into the lake of fire. The lake of fire is the second death. ¹⁵If anyone's name was not found written in the book of life, he was thrown into the lake of fire.

The New Jerusalem

21 Then I saw a new heaven and a new earth, for the first heaven and the first earth had passed away, and there was no longer any sea. ²I saw the Holy City, the new Jerusalem, coming down out of heaven from God, prepared as a bride beautifully dressed for her husband. ³And I heard a loud voice from the throne saying, "Now the dwelling of God is with men, and he will live with them. They will be his people, and God himself will be with them and be their God. ⁴He will wipe

ª15 Psalm 2:9

The Day Death Died

Read: Revelation 21:1–27

HAVE YOU READ the staggering statistics on death? One out of every one people dies! Yet despite the inevitability of death, people desperately try to avoid it. In fact, some are willing to pay a hefty price to prolong their life. Whether it's a year, a month or a day, those who attempt to cheat death go to great lengths. Some resort to cryonics, a technology in which ultra-cold temperatures are used to freeze their bodies so they can be restored at a later time. Celebrities seek the fountain of youth through vitamins, yoga and trendy diets. Yet every day, celebrities and ordinary citizens die. Health nuts and couch potatoes alike fall to the inevitability of death.

The good news is that there is a day coming when death will die. And death's companions—sorrow, tears and pain—will also meet their demise. The apostle John "heard a loud voice from the throne saying '. . . There will be no more death.' " What death did to Jesus was nothing compared to what Jesus did to death. His resurrection brought defeat to our enemies—the enemies of sadness, sin and death. In the future heavenly kingdom, they will have no hold over us.

Revelation 21 reveals that the true fountain of youth is Jesus. He said, "I am the Alpha and the Omega, the Beginning and the End. To him who is thirsty I will give to drink without cost from the spring of the water of life" (verse 6). If you want to cheat death, you must believe in Jesus, who promised, "I am the resurrection and the life. He who believes in me will live, even though he dies" (John 11:25). Knowing that death will die should affect the way you live. You don't need beauty products, exercise regimes or fad diets to add years to your life. Instead, Jesus adds life to your years.

For the believer, death holds no sting and the grave has no victory. Yes, we grieve when we're separated for a time from those we love. But in the face of death, we can be more hopeful than fearful, knowing that death isn't the end; it's the beginning of life ever more.

Go to page 1539 for your next devotional reading.

Revelation 21:4

"He will wipe every tear from their eyes. There will be no more death or mourning or crying or pain, for the old order of things has passed away."

reflection

1 How have you been more fearful than hopeful in the face of death?

2 How does the promise of death's demise give you hope for today?

3 How will you live differently based on the truths in this devotional?

RELATED READINGS

John 11:21–27;
Romans 6:8–10;
1 Corinthians 15:51–58

"In my end is my beginning."

Mary, Queen of Scots

every tear from their eyes. There will be no more death or mourning or crying or pain, for the old order of things has passed away."

[5] He who was seated on the throne said, "I am making everything new!" Then he said, "Write this down, for these words are trustworthy and true."

[6] He said to me: "It is done. I am the Alpha and the Omega, the Beginning and the End. To him who is thirsty I will give to drink without cost from the spring of the water of life. [7] He who overcomes will inherit all this, and I will be his God and he will be my son. [8] But the cowardly, the unbelieving, the vile, the murderers, the sexually immoral, those who practice magic arts, the idolaters and all liars—their place will be in the fiery lake of burning sulfur. This is the second death."

[9] One of the seven angels who had the seven bowls full of the seven last plagues came and said to me, "Come, I will show you the bride, the wife of the Lamb." [10] And he carried me away in the Spirit to a mountain great and high, and showed me the Holy City, Jerusalem, coming down out of heaven from God. [11] It shone with the glory of God, and its brilliance was like that of a very precious jewel, like a jasper, clear as crystal. [12] It had a great, high wall with twelve gates, and with twelve angels at the gates. On the gates were written the names of the twelve tribes of Israel. [13] There were three gates on the east, three on the north, three on the south and three on the west. [14] The wall of the city had twelve foundations, and on them were the names of the twelve apostles of the Lamb.

[15] The angel who talked with me had a measuring rod of gold to measure the city, its gates and its walls. [16] The city was laid out like a square, as long as it was wide. He measured the city with the rod and found it to be 12,000 stadia[a] in length, and as wide and high as it is long. [17] He measured its wall and it was 144 cubits[b] thick,[c] by man's measurement, which the angel was using. [18] The wall was made of jasper, and the city of pure gold, as pure as glass. [19] The foundations of the city walls were decorated with every kind of precious stone. The first foundation was jasper, the second sapphire,

the third chalcedony, the fourth emerald, [20] the fifth sardonyx, the sixth carnelian, the seventh chrysolite, the eighth beryl, the ninth topaz, the tenth chrysoprase, the eleventh jacinth, and the twelfth amethyst.[d] [21] The twelve gates were twelve pearls, each gate made of a single pearl. The great street of the city was of pure gold, like transparent glass.

[22] I did not see a temple in the city, because the Lord God Almighty and the Lamb are its temple. [23] The city does not need the sun or the moon to shine on it, for the glory of God gives it light, and the Lamb is its lamp. [24] The nations will walk by its light, and the kings of the earth will bring their splendor into it. [25] On no day will its gates ever be shut, for there will be no night there. [26] The glory and honor of the nations will be brought into it. [27] Nothing impure will ever enter it, nor will anyone who does what is shameful or deceitful, but only those whose names are written in the Lamb's book of life.

The River of Life

22 Then the angel showed me the river of the water of life, as clear as crystal, flowing from the throne of God and of the Lamb [2] down the middle of the great street of the city. On each side of the river stood the tree of life, bearing twelve crops of fruit, yielding its fruit every month. And the leaves of the tree are for the healing of the nations. [3] No longer will there be any curse. The throne of God and of the Lamb will be in the city, and his servants will serve him. [4] They will see his face, and his name will be on their foreheads. [5] There will be no more night. They will not need the light of a lamp or the light of the sun, for the Lord God will give them light. And they will reign for ever and ever.

[6] The angel said to me, "These words are trustworthy and true. The Lord, the God of the spirits of the prophets, sent his angel to show his servants the things that must soon take place."

Jesus Is Coming

[7] "Behold, I am coming soon! Blessed is he who keeps the words of the prophecy in this book."

---

[a]16 That is, about 1,400 miles (about 2,200 kilometers)   [b]17 That is, about 200 feet (about 65 meters)   [c]17 Or *high*   [d]20 The precise identification of some of these precious stones is uncertain.

Generations

EUNICE

"YOU MUST BE SO PROUD of Timothy." Her neighbor smiled. People were always saying things like that to her. Eunice took the compliments in stride and considered them some of the perks of motherhood.

Yes, she was extremely proud of her son. So much so, she had willingly paid the price of God entrusting her with such a unique gift. How many sunrises had she witnessed after praying through the night for him? Too many to count. She prayed for his personal purity, for his walk with God, for his future ministry and even for his future spouse—as confidently as if she could call her by name.

Thinking back through the years reminded her of her own special times with her godly mother, Lois. "You come from a long line of strong women," she remembered saying to Timothy, as the newborn slept in her arms.

Later, when he was older, she shared with him stories about his grandmother's stalwart faith. His eyes would gleam at the prospect of growing up to be like his hero. He wanted to be just like his grandmother—which was the same wish Eunice had had when she was a young girl.

In the absence of a spiritually strong male figure in Timothy's life, she felt that one of the most important prayers she ever prayed was one for a godly man to intersect Timothy's life. And God did not disappoint. Although Timothy came from two generations of faithful women, Paul was the spiritual father Timothy never had. And with that, Timothy committed to make his mother proud. He would raise the next generation in likewise fashion. How could she be more proud of him?

Although she realized God had his hand on Timothy's life, she likely never expected that his name and example would be included in the history of the early church. To his mother, he was just her little boy.

—Prayer—

Thank you, generous God, for all the blessings of this life and allowing me to enjoy them.

1 (Paul) have been reminded of your sincere faith, which first lived in your grandmother Lois and in your mother Eunice and, I am persuaded, now lives in you also.

2 Timothy 1:5

ASSIGNED READING:

Acts 16:1; 2 Timothy 1:5

Weekend

8I, John, am the one who heard and saw these things. And when I had heard and seen them, I fell down to worship at the feet of the angel who had been showing them to me. 9But he said to me, "Do not do it! I am a fellow servant with you and with your brothers the prophets and of all who keep the words of this book. Worship God!"

10Then he told me, "Do not seal up the words of the prophecy of this book, because the time is near. 11Let him who does wrong continue to do wrong; let him who is vile continue to be vile; let him who does right continue to do right; and let him who is holy continue to be holy."

12"Behold, I am coming soon! My reward is with me, and I will give to everyone according to what he has done. 13I am the Alpha and the Omega, the First and the Last, the Beginning and the End. 14Blessed are those who wash their robes, that they may have the right to the tree of life and may go through the gates into the city. 15Outside are the dogs, those who practice magic arts, the sexually immoral, the murder-ers, the idolaters and everyone who loves and practices falsehood.

16"I, Jesus, have sent my angel to give you[a] this testimony for the churches. I am the Root and the Offspring of David, and the bright Morning Star."

17The Spirit and the bride say, "Come!" And let him who hears say, "Come!" Whoever is thirsty, let him come; and whoever wishes, let him take the free gift of the water of life.

18I warn everyone who hears the words of the prophecy of this book: If anyone adds anything to them, God will add to him the plagues described in this book. 19And if anyone takes words away from this book of prophecy, God will take away from him his share in the tree of life and in the holy city, which are described in this book.

20He who testifies to these things says, "Yes, I am coming soon."

Amen. Come, Lord Jesus.

21The grace of the Lord Jesus be with God's people. Amen.

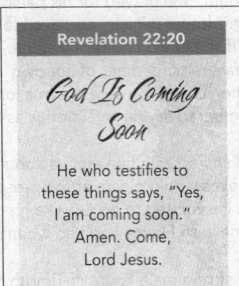

Revelation 22:20

God Is Coming Soon

He who testifies to these things says, "Yes, I am coming soon." Amen. Come, Lord Jesus.

Contents

Table of Weights and Measures

	BIBLICAL UNIT	APPROXIMATE AMERICAN EQUIVALENT	APPROXIMATE METRIC EQUIVALENT
WEIGHTS	talent (60 minas)	75 pounds	34 kilograms
	mina (50 shekels)	1¼ pounds	0.6 kilogram
	shekel (2 bekas)	²/₅ ounce	11.5 grams
	pim (²/₃ shekel)	¹/₃ ounce	7.6 grams
	beka (10 gerahs)	¹/₅ ounce	5.5 grams
	gerah	¹/₅₀ ounce	0.6 gram
LENGTH	cubit	18 inches	0.5 meter
	span	9 inches	23 centimeters
	handbreadth	3 inches	8 centimeters
CAPACITY Dry Measure	cor [homer] (10 ephahs)	6 bushels	220 liters
	lethek (5 ephahs)	3 bushels	110 liters
	ephah (10 omers)	³/₅ bushels	22 liters
	seah (¹/₃ ephah)	7 quarts	7.3 liters
	omer (¹/₁₀ ephah)	2 quarts	2 liters
	cab (¹/₁₈ ephah)	1 quart	1 liter
Liquid Measure	bath (1 ephah)	6 gallons	22 liters
	hin (¹/₆ bath)	4 quarts	4 liters
	log (1/72 bath)	¹/₃ quart	0.3 liter

The figures of the table are calculated on the basis of a shekel equaling 11.5 grams, a cubit equaling 18 inches and an ephah equaling 22 liters. The quart referred to is either a dry quart (slightly larger than a liter) or a liquid quart (slightly smaller than a liter), whichever is applicable. The ton referred to in the footnotes is the American ton of 2,000 pounds. Since most readers are more familiar with dry measures being given in weight rather than capacity (bushel, quart), dry measures have been converted in the footnotes to approximate weights.

This table is based upon the best available information, but it is not intended to be mathematically precise; like the measurement equivalents in the footnotes, it merely gives approximate amounts and distances. Weights and measures differed somewhat at various times and places in the ancient world. There is uncertainty particularly about the ephah and the bath; further discoveries may shed more light on these units of capacity.

One Year Through the Bible

DAY	PASSAGE	DAY	PASSAGE
January 1	Genesis 1—4	February 16	Numbers 22—24
January 2	Genesis 5—8	February 17	Numbers 25—26
January 3	Genesis 9—12	February 18	Numbers 27—29
January 4	Genesis 13—17	February 19	Numbers 30—32
January 5	Genesis 18—20	February 20	Numbers 33—36
January 6	Genesis 21—23	February 21	Deuteronomy 1—2
January 7	Genesis 24—25	February 22	Deuteronomy 3—4
January 8	Genesis 26—28	February 23	Deuteronomy 5—8
January 9	Genesis 29—31	February 24	Deuteronomy 9—11
January 10	Genesis 32—35	February 25	Deuteronomy 12—15
January 11	Genesis 36—38	February 26	Deuteronomy 16—19
January 12	Genesis 39—41	February 27	Deuteronomy 20—23
January 13	Genesis 42—43	February 28	Deuteronomy 24—27
January 14	Genesis 44—46	March 1	Deuteronomy 28—29
January 15	Genesis 47—50	March 2	Deuteronomy 30—32
January 16	Exodus 1—4	March 3	Deuteronomy 33—34
January 17	Exodus 5—7	March 4	Joshua 1—4
January 18	Exodus 8—10	March 5	Joshua 5—7
January 19	Exodus 11—13	March 6	Joshua 8—10
January 20	Exodus 14—16	March 7	Joshua 11—13
January 21	Exodus 17—20	March 8	Joshua 14—17
January 22	Exodus 21—23	March 9	Joshua 18—20
January 23	Exodus 24—27	March 10	Joshua 21—22
January 24	Exodus 28—30	March 11	Joshua 23—24
January 25	Exodus 31—34	March 12	Judges 1—3
January 26	Exodus 35—37	March 13	Judges 4—5
January 27	Exodus 38—40	March 14	Judges 6—8
January 28	Leviticus 1—4	March 15	Judges 9—10
January 29	Leviticus 5—7	March 16	Judges 11—13
January 30	Leviticus 8—10	March 17	Judges 14—16
January 31	Leviticus 11—13	March 18	Judges 17—19
February 1	Leviticus 14—15	March 19	Judges 20—21
February 2	Leviticus 16—18	March 20	Ruth 1—4
February 3	Leviticus 19—21	March 21	1 Samuel 1—3
February 4	Leviticus 22—23	March 22	1 Samuel 4—7
February 5	Leviticus 24—25	March 23	1 Samuel 8—12
February 6	Leviticus 26—27	March 24	1 Samuel 13—14
February 7	Numbers 1—2	March 25	1 Samuel 15—16
February 8	Numbers 3—4	March 26	1 Samuel 17—18
February 9	Numbers 5—6	March 27	1 Samuel 19—21
February 10	Numbers 7	March 28	1 Samuel 22—24
February 11	Numbers 8—10	March 29	1 Samuel 25—27
February 12	Numbers 11—13	March 30	1 Samuel 28—31
February 13	Numbers 14—15	March 31	2 Samuel 1—3
February 14	Numbers 16—18	April 1	2 Samuel 4—7
February 15	Numbers 19—21	April 2	2 Samuel 8—11

60 – Day Overview of the Bible

30 Days for Beginning Your Walk With Christ

DAY	DESCRIPTION	PASSAGE
☐	The Fall of Humanity	Genesis 3:1–19
☐	A People for God	Genesis 28:10–15; 32:22–28
☐	The Ten Commandments	Exodus 20:1–17
☐	Sacrifices Required Under Law . . .	Leviticus 5:14–19
☐	Punishments for Sin Under Law . .	Leviticus 20:7–27
☐	Obedience From Love	Deuteronomy 11:13–21
☐	Cycles of Disobedience	Judges 2:10–19
☐	The People Demand a King	1 Samuel 8:1–22
☐	Saul Fails and Is Rejected	1 Samuel 15:17–23
☐	Many Kings Fail	Jeremiah 1—17
☐	The Sin of the People	Ezekiel 20:5–26
☐	An Eternal King Promised	Jeremiah 23:1–6; Isaiah 9:6–7; Zechariah 9:9–10
☐	The Promised King Is Born	Luke 2:1–20
☐	The Word Became Flesh	John 1:1–18
☐	Signs and Miracles of Authority . . .	Matthew 9:1–8; Luke 13:10–17
☐	Jesus Fulfills the Law	Matthew 5:17–20; Romans 8:1–4
☐	Jesus Teaches About New Life	John 3:1–36
☐	Jesus Willingly Taken	John 18:1–11
☐	Jesus' Death and Resurrection	Luke 23:44—24:12
☐	Christ a Sacrifice for All	Hebrews
☐	God's Wrath Explained	Romans 1:18–32
☐	God's Judgment Explained	Romans 2:5–11
☐	Righteousness by Faith	Romans 3:9–26
☐	Life Through Christ	Romans 5:12–21
☐	Life by the Spirit	Romans 8:1–17; Galatians 5:16–26
☐	Living Sacrifices	Romans 12:1–21
☐	Walking in the Light	1 John 1—2
☐	Living for God	1 Peter 1—11
☐	Love for One Another	1 John 3:11–24
☐	Promise of Eternity	2 Corinthians 5:1–10; Revelation 21:1–4

30 Days With Jesus

30 Days in the Psalms

DAY	DESCRIPTION	PASSAGE
☐	Blessing	Psalms 67, 72, 84, 128
☐	Calling to God	Psalms 4, 5, 22
☐	Confidence	Psalms 27, 36, 71, 125
☐	Deeds of God	Psalms 9, 18, 118
☐	Doubt	Psalms 42, 73, 77
☐	Faithfulness of God	Psalms 105, 119:137–144, 146
☐	Fear	Psalms 37, 49, 91
☐	Glory of God	Psalms 19, 24, 29
☐	God Is a Helper	Psalms 54, 115, 119:169–176
☐	Identity	Psalms 8, 139
☐	Justice of God	Psalms 7, 26, 82
☐	Meditation	Psalms 119:9–16, 41–48
☐	Mercy	Psalms 13, 28, 86
☐	Music	Psalms 6, 149, 150
☐	Nature	Psalms 50, 104, 147, 148
☐	Peace	Psalms 23, 133, 119:161–168
☐	Power of God	Psalms 68, 93, 135
☐	Praise	Psalms 65, 98, 138
☐	Prayer	Psalms 17, 20, 102
☐	Protection	Psalms 59, 62, 124
☐	Safety in God	Psalms 11, 16, 142, 46
☐	Rejoicing	Psalms 30, 47, 97
☐	Righteousness	Psalms 1, 15, 112
☐	Salvation	Psalms 3, 14, 121
☐	Sin and Repentance	Psalms 25, 32, 38, 51
☐	Thanksgiving	Psalms 75, 106, 136
☐	Trust	Psalms 31, 40, 56
☐	Victory	Psalms 21, 76, 144
☐	Wisdom	Psalms 90, 107, 111
☐	Worship	Psalms 33, 34, 145

30 Days in Proverbs

DAY	PASSAGE
☐	Proverbs 1
☐	Proverbs 2
☐	Proverbs 3
☐	Proverbs 4
☐	Proverbs 5
☐	Proverbs 6
☐	Proverbs 7
☐	Proverbs 8
☐	Proverbs 9
☐	Proverbs 10
☐	Proverbs 11
☐	Proverbs 12
☐	Proverbs 13
☐	Proverbs 14
☐	Proverbs 15
☐	Proverbs 16
☐	Proverbs 17
☐	Proverbs 18
☐	Proverbs 19
☐	Proverbs 20
☐	Proverbs 21
☐	Proverbs 22
☐	Proverbs 23
☐	Proverbs 24
☐	Proverbs 25
☐	Proverbs 26
☐	Proverbs 27
☐	Proverbs 28
☐	Proverbs 29
☐	Proverbs 30–31

20 Not-So-Famous Bible Stories

30 Days With Paul

DAY	THEME	PASSAGE
☐	Elusive righteousness	Romans 3:9–26
☐	Peace and joy	Romans 5:1–11
☐	Sin and death	Romans 5:12–21
☐	Alive in Christ	Romans 6:1–14
☐	Battle with sin	Romans 7:7–25
☐	Being a conqueror	Romans 8:28–39
☐	A living sacrifice	Romans 12:1–8
☐	Running the race	1 Corinthians 9:19–27
☐	One body	1 Corinthians 12:12–31
☐	Love	1 Corinthians 13:1–13
☐	Resurrection	1 Corinthians 15:12–34
☐	Longing for heaven	2 Corinthians 5:1–10
☐	Christian hardships	2 Corinthians 6:3–13
☐	Weakness	2 Corinthians 12:1–10
☐	Christian freedom	Galatians 5:1–15
☐	Fruit of the Spirit	Galatians 5:16–26
☐	Incomparable grace	Ephesians 2:1–10
☐	Christian unity	Ephesians 4:1–16
☐	People of light	Ephesians 4:17—5:21
☐	Family dynamics	Ephesians 5:22—6:4
☐	Armor of God	Ephesians 6:10–20
☐	Imitating Jesus	Philippians 2:1–11
☐	Reaching the ultimate goal	Philippians 3:12—4:1
☐	Christ the head	Colossians 1:15–23
☐	Pleasing God	1 Thessalonians 4:1–12
☐	Jesus is coming	1 Thessalonians 4:13—5:11
☐	Avoiding idleness	2 Thessalonians 3:6–18
☐	Instructions for a young believer	1 Timothy 4:1–16
☐	Money	1 Timothy 6:3–10
☐	Staying strong	2 Timothy 3:10—4:8

30 Days of Promises

30 Days of Leadership

30 Days of Prayer

30 Days of Knowing God

30 Stories of Great Faith

Acknowledgments

RUTH HALEY BARTON
Devotion found on page 147

Taken from *Invitation to Solitude and Silence* © 2004 by Ruth Haley Barton.
Used with permission of InterVarsity Press, PO Box 1400,
Downers Grove, IL 60515. www.ivpress.com

KATIE BRAZELTON
Devotion found on page 326

Taken from *Pathway to Purpose for Women* © 2005 by Katherine F. Brazelton.
Used by permission of The Zondervan Corporation.

SALLY BREEDLOVE
Devotion found on page 67

Taken from *Choosing Rest* © 2002 by Sally Breedlove. Used by permission
of NavPress, Colorado Springs, CO. All rights reserved.

AMY CARMICHAEL
Devotion found on page 1092

Taken from *Thou Givest, They Gather* © 1958, pp 193–195.
Used by permission of CLC Publications.

Devotion found on page 259

Taken from *Candles in the Dark* © 1982, pp 41, 43.
Used by permission of CLC Publications.

JAN DRAVECKY
Devotion found on page 96

Taken from *Hope for Woman's Soul*, Grand Rapids, Inspiro, 2000, pp 11, 15.

ELISABETH ELLIOT
Devotion found on page 1276

Taken from *God's Guidance* © 1997 by Elisabeth Elliot. Used by permission
of Fleming H. Revell, a division of Baker Publishing Group.

LISA HARPER
Devotion found on page 1140

Taken from *Every Woman's Hope: Defined by Grace, Beloved by God* © 2001 by Lisa Harper.
Used by permission of Howard Books, a division of Simon & Schuster Adult Publishing Group.

LIZ CURTIS HIGGS
Devotion found on page 1328

Reprinted from *Rise and Shine* © 2002, 2004 by Liz Curtis Higgs. Used by
permission of Waterbrook Press, Colorado Springs, CO. All rights reserved.

BARBARA HUGHES

Devotion found on page 1227

Taken from *Devotions for Ministry Wives* © 2002 by Barbara Hughes.
Used by permission of The Zondervan Corporation.

CAROLYN CUSTIS JAMES

Devotion found on page 1255

Taken from *When Life and Beliefs Collide* © 2001 by Carolyn C. James.
Used by permission of The Zondervan Corporation.

NANCY KENNEDY

Devotion found on page 1077

Taken from *Praying with Women of the Bible* © 2004 by Nancy Kennedy.
Used by permission of The Zondervan Corporation.

CAROL KENT

Devotion found on page 1381

Taken from *Kisses of Sunshine for Sisters* © 2005 by Speak Up, Inc.
Used by permission of The Zondervan Corporation.

ANNE GRAHAM LOTZ

Devotions found on pages 847, 1309

Taken from *I Saw the Lord* © 2006 by Anne Graham Lotz.
Used by permission of The Zondervan Corporation.

PENNY PIERCE ROSE

Devotion found on page 292

Taken from *A Garden of Friends*, Ventura, Regal Books, pp 116–121.

EDITH SCHAEFFER

Devotion found on page 1000

Taken from *The Art of Life* © 1987 by Edith Schaeffer.
Used by permission of Crossway Books.

PRISCILLA EVANS SHIRER

Devotion found on page 1394

Taken from *A Jewel in His Crown* © 1999 by Priscilla Evans.
Used by permission of Moody Press.

HANNAH WHITALL SMITH

Devotion found on page 1447

Taken from *The God of All Comfort* © 1956 by Hannah
Whitall Smith. Used by permission of Moody Press.

ACKNOWLEDGMENTS

LUCI SWINDOLL

Devotion found on page 738

Taken from *The Best Devotions of Luci Swindoll* © 2001 by Women of Faith. Used by permission of The Zondervan Corporation.

JONI EARECKSON TADA

Devotion found on page 1535

Taken from *Heaven: Your Real Home* © 1995 by Joni Eareckson Tada. Used by permission of The Zondervan Corporation.

Devotion found on page 813

Taken from *The God I Love: A Memoir* © 2003 by Joni Eareckson Tada. Used by permission of The Zondervan Corporation.

MOTHER TERESA

Devotion found on page 231

Taken from *Mother Teresa, In the Heart of the World: Thoughts, Stories, & Prayers* © 1997. Used by permission of New World Library.

Additional benediction by Mother Teresa, original source unknown.

CYNTHIA ULRICH TOBIAS

Devotion found on page 1215

Taken from *Redefining the Strong-Willed Woman* © 2002 by Cynthia Ulrich Tobias. Used by permission of The Zondervan Corporation.

SHEILA WALSH

Devotion found on page 316

Taken from *Hope for a Woman's Soul: Meditations to Energize Your Spirit* © 2000 by New Life Clinics. Used by permission of The Zondervan Corporation.

Devotion found on page 379

Taken from *Honestly* © 1996 by Sheila Walsh. Used by permission of The Zondervan Corporation.

THELMA WELLS

Devotion found on page 1381

Taken from *Kisses of Sunshine for Sisters* © 2005 by Speak Up, Inc. Used by permission of The Zondervan Corporation.

CHRISTINE WYRTZEN

Devotion found on page 174

Taken from *Long Live the Child* © 2003 by Christine, Inc. Used by permission of The Zondervan Corporation.

Contributor Biographies

RUTH HALEY BARTON is a spiritual director, teacher and retreat leader. Ruth is co-founder of The Transforming Center providing leadership in the areas of vision, community building, teaching and content development. Ruth has served on the pastoral staff of several churches, including Willow Creek Community Church in South Barrington, Illinois, as associate director of spiritual formation.

SHARON BETTERS is executive director of MARK INC Ministries, a multimedia outreach designed to help turn broken people toward the heart of God. She has authored several books, including *Treasures of Encouragement, Treasures in Darkness, A Grieving Mother Shares Her Heart* and along with her husband, Chuck, *Treasures of Faith*.

JANET CHESTER BLY has authored 11 books and coauthored 18 with her husband, Stephen, both nonfiction and fiction. She writes and speaks on issues of a woman's heart. Her books include *Hope Lives Here* and *The Heart of a Runaway*.

KATIE BRAZELTON currently serves as Director of Women's Bible Studies at Saddleback Church. A licensed minister, Katie has earned a Ph.D. in Human Behavior/Leadership, an M.A. in Theology, an M.A. in Educational Administration, an M.A. in English, and is near completion of her Masters of Divinity. Katie has two adult children and one daughter-in-law.

SALLY BREEDLOVE is a frequent speaker at leadership conferences in North America and abroad. She has spoken to numerous groups, including Women Alive (Canada), Wycliffe Bible Translators (Asia), and Dixie Women (Alabama). Sally has been published in *Decision* magazine and written study notes for *The Women of Faith Study Bible* (Zondervan).

DIANNE E. BUTTS has written for over 50 Christian magazines and a dozen compilation books. Her writing has appeared in Great Britain, Bulgaria, Poland, Canada and Korea. She enjoys riding her motorcycle with her husband, Hal, and gardening with her cat, P. C. The trio lives in Colorado.

AMY CARMICHAEL (1867–1951) was born in Ireland, but spent her life serving the Lord as a missionary in India for 56 years, working with underprivileged children. She is the author of many books including, *God's Missionary* (CLC) and *You Are My Hiding Place* (Bethany House).

SUZIE CROSS markets books for a Christian publisher and has contributed writing for five devotional Bibles, including Zondervan's *True Images* teen Bible. Her writing reflects a mission and desire to help those experiencing pain find the hope and joy of Christ in and beyond their circumstances.

MARLENE DEPLER is a writer, inspirational speaker and "mentor" for young mothers. She has published numerous articles, devotionals, stories and poems in magazines such as *HomeLife*, *Woman's Touch*, *The Quiet Hour* and *Mature Living*. Marlene is the mother of three grown children and grandmother of six. She and her husband make their home in Colorado.

JENN DOUCETTE is a freelance writer and humorist who tries to find the funnies in the yuckies of life. She has authored *The Velveteen Mommy—Laughter and Tears from the Toy Box Years*, and coauthored *Live it Real—Devotions for Teens*. The Doucettes make their home in Snohomish, Washington.

JAN DRAVECKY co-founded Outreach of Hope Ministries with her husband, former baseball pitcher Dave Dravecky. She and Dave live in Colorado Springs. With Dave, she is the co-author of *Do Not Lose Heart* and *Stand by Me*.

PAIGE DRYGAS is a teacher, writer and editor who has helped develop Bible products including the *True Identity* and *True Images*. Paige lives outside Chicago with her husband.

CHERYL DUNLOP is the author of *Follow Me as I Follow Christ* and a freelance writer and editor. She loves to minister to children with troubled backgrounds and to explore God's creation.

DENA DYER is a wife, mom, writer and speaker from Texas. She loves to encourage women to find their hope, rest and joy in Jesus—our only true source of peace in the midst of a chaotic world. Her books include *Grace for the Race: Meditations for Busy Moms, The Groovy Chicks' Roadtrip to Peace* and *The Groovy Chicks' Roadtrip to Love*.

ELISABETH ELLIOT is best known for her classic book, *Through the Gates of Splendor* (Tyndale). She and her husband, Jim Elliot, served as missionaries in Ecuador, where Jim was killed by Auca Indians. She is a speaker and bestselling author of numerous other books, including *Passion and Purity* (Baker) and *A Chance to Die* (Baker). Elisabeth now lives with her husband, Lars Gren, in Magnolia, Massachusetts.

PAULA GAMBLE is an international worship leader, songwriter, author and intercultural training specialist with Campus Crusade for Christ, Intl. She is also the founder of *IseetheKing Productions*, which promotes enthusiasm for the King and world mission through Sojourney retreats and recordings.

STACY FRYE GRAVES is a freelance writer, corporate communications expert and former Bible Study Fellowship leader. She lives in Tyler, Texas, with her husband, Glen, and their two young sons, Landry and Luke.

GAYLE GRESHAM lives in Elbert, Colorado, with her husband and their two teenagers. Her articles have appeared in *Today's Christian Woman, The Lookout* and *Christian Standard*.

LISA HARPER was the creator and hostess of Renewing the Heart, Focus on the Family's conference series involving almost 200,000 women. She is the author of several books including *Relentless Love* and *Every Woman's Hope*.

RACHEL HAWKINS is employed at The Livingstone Corporation, located in Carol Stream, IL. She has contributed to the *New Women's Devotional Journal* (Zondervan).

LENYA HEITZIG is the author of *Holy Moments* and coauthor of the award-winning Bible study *Pathway to God's Treasure: Ephesians, Pathway to God's Plan: Ruth and Esther,* and *Pathway to Living Faith: James*. She founded Women at Calvary at Calvary Albuquerque Church and is currently the Women's Ministry Director at Ocean Hills Church in San Juan Capistrano where her husband, Skip Heitzig, is Senior Pastor. She has one son, Nathan.

LIZ CURTIS HIGGS is the author of 23 books, including her nonfiction bestseller *Bad Girls of the Bible* (Random House) and her fiction bestseller *Thorn in My Heart (Random House)*. Her children's Parable Series was awarded the ECPA Gold Medallion for Excellence in 1998. Liz has also presented more than 1500 inspirational programs for audiences in all 50 United States and 8 foreign countries.

BARBARA HUGHES has many years of experience as a pastor's wife. Married to Kent Hughes, pastor of College Church in Wheaten, Illinois, she is the author of *Disciplines of a Godly Woman* and co-author with her husband of *Liberating Ministry from the Success Syndrome* and *Common Sense Parenting*. She is the mother of four children.

CAROLYN CUSTIS JAMES travels extensively as a popular speaker for women's conferences, churches, colleges, seminaries and other Christian organizations. Her ministry organization, Whitby Forum, promotes thoughtful Biblical discussion to help men and women join forces in serving God together. She is author of *When Life and Beliefs Collide* (Zondervan) and *Lost Women of the Bible* (Zondervan). Carolyn lives in Orlando, Florida, with her husband and daughter.

SHARON JAYNES is a popular speaker at women's events internationally. She is the author of ten books including *Becoming a Woman who Listens to God*, *Ultimate Makeover*, *Your Scars are Beautiful to God* and *Becoming the Woman of His Dreams*. Her joy is bringing God's truth to today's woman.

JOAN JONES has served as a freelance consultant with The Livingstone Corporation in Carol Stream, IL. She is active in her church's children's ministry and is the mother of four. Joan lives in the Midwest with her husband and youngest daughter.

DEB KALMBACH is the coauthor of *Because I Said Forever: Embracing Hope in a Not-So-Perfect Marriage* and the author of a children's book, *Corey's Dad Drinks Too Much*. She is a vibrant and engaging speaker who gives hope and practical solutions to those who struggle with difficult relationships. Deb and her husband, Randy, make their home in Winthrop, Washington.

NANCY KENNEDY is an editor, feature writer and columnist for the *Citrus County Chronicle*. Her features have won several first place Excellence in Religious Writing awards from the Florida Press Club. Her books include *Praying With Women of the Bible* (Zondervan), *Between Two Loves* (Zondervan) and *When Perfect Isn't Enough* (Random House). Nancy and her husband live in Florida.

CAROL KENT is a popular writer, highly requested speaker and the president of Speak Up Speaker Services, a Christian speakers' bureau. She has numerous books to her credit including *When I Lay My Isaac Down* (NavPress) and *Becoming a Women of Influence* (NavPress). Carol lives with her husband, Gene, in Port Huron, Michigan.

ROSALIE KRUSEMARK is a freelance editor based in Minnesota.

MARY ANN LACKLAND is the founder and CEO of Fluency, specializing in communications consulting and fulfillment for ministries and nonprofits. She is a contributing author/editor of more than 60 published titles.

ANNE GRAHAM LOTZ, daughter of Billy and Ruth Graham, is the president and executive director of AnGeL Ministries, a nonprofit organization offering Christian outreach. Anne has spoken on all seven continents in more than 20 foreign countries. She has written many books, including *Just Give Me Jesus (Thomas Nelson)*, and *I Saw the Lord* (Zondervan). Anne and her husband, Daniel, reside in Raleigh, North Carolina.

KATHI MACIAS is a former pastor and counselor. She is a full-time writer/editor who has authored 17 books, as well as numerous short stories and magazine articles. Kathi is a mother and a grandmother and lives in Southern California with her husband, Al.

MARTHA MANIKAS-FOSTER served as the acquisitions editor of the first *Women's Devotional Bible,* and her writing has appeared in several national magazines. A radio announcer for the *Family Life Network,* Martha lives in western New York State with her husband, David, and their children, Connie and Peter.

SALLY MARCEY, a licensed clinical professional counselor and a licensed marriage and family therapist, is the author of two children's books: *The Underground Railroad* and *The Silverlake*

Stranger. She has contributed to works such as the *Soul Care Bible* and the *True Identity Bible*. She has worked in church ministry for the past 30 years, has been married for 34 years and has two grown children.

JANET HOLM MCHENRY is the author of 19 books and speaks about developing a stronger life of prayer. She has helped thousands across the country begin the practice of devotional prayerwalking. Her books include *PrayerWalk, Prayer Changes Teens: How to Parent From Your Knees* and *PrayerStreaming: Staying in Touch With God All Day Long*.

JUDY GORDON (MORROW) employs her love of words as a writer, speaker and editor. She has written books ranging from the topic of pregnancy loss to the theme of "Life's too short . . ." She also writes poetry, song lyrics and children's books. Judy has three grown sons and lives in the charming mountain town of Quincy, California.

LINDA NATHAN is the president of Logos Word Designs, Inc., a Christian writing, editing and marketing service. She writes and teaches with her husband Richard in an apologetics ministry and is the author of *The Dark Side of Karate*.

SARAH OVERTURF lives in Longmont, Colorado, with her husband and three children. She enjoys hiking and camping with her family, getting lost in a good story and taking moonlit walks with her dog.

STACEY PADRICK is the author of *Living With Mystery: Finding God in the Midst of Unanswered Questions*. As a writer, speaker and spiritual director, she loves to encourage women in their faith. She's written numerous articles for *Discipleship Journal, PRAY!, Today's Christian Women, The Upper Room* and more. She and her husband are about to adopt their first child.

TABITHA PLUEDDEMANN writes for freelance, as well as for the mission organization, SIM International. She lives in Charlotte, North Carolina, with her husband, Danny, and their son.

WHITNEY PROSPERI has a heart for teen girls. She is the author of *Life Style: Real Perspectives from Radical Women in the Bible* and *Girls Ministry 101*.

AMBER RAE has contributed to many Bible projects including *True Images* and *True Identity*. She is the author of the *True Images Devotional*. Amber leads her church's ladies ministry and is the mother of three small children.

RHONDA RHEA is the author of *Who Put the Cat in the Fridge* and other insanely funny books, including *I'm Dreaming of Some White Chocolate*. She is a radio personality and humor columnist and speaks at conferences and events nationwide. Rhonda lives in the St. Louis area with her pastor/husband and their five children.

PENNY PIERCE ROSE loves to study and teach God's Word. She has authored *A Garden of Friends* and coauthored the award-winning Bible study *Pathway to God's Treasure: Ephesians, Pathway to God's Plan: Ruth and Esther*, and *Pathway to Living Faith: James*. She is at home in Albuquerque, New Mexico, with her husband and three teens.

MAGGIE WALLEM ROWE is a speaker, dramatist, communications instructor and freelance writer who has contributed to a number of devotional Bibles for women and families. Maggie and her husband, Mike, a pastor, make their home in Wheaton, Illinois, where they serve First Baptist Church.

EDITH SCHAEFFER is the widow of philosopher Dr. Francis Schaeffer. Together they founded L'Abri Fellowship, an international study center and Christian community in

Switzerland. She has written many books including *L'Abri* (Crossway), *The Hidden Art of Homemaking* (Tyndale) and *A Celebration of Children* (Tyndale).

BETSY SCHMITT has worked with The Livingstone Corporation since 1999. She is an editor and writer who also heads up the New Product Development team for Livingstone. She is author of *Sticky Situations*, *Sticky Situations 2*, *The Big Book of Bible Fun* and the recently released *Trivia Twist Devotions*.

PRISCILLA EVANS SHIRER is the daughter of noted pastor, speaker and author Dr. Tony Evans and Lois Evans. Priscilla has been featured on Focus on the Family and is a corporate trainer with the Zig Ziglar Corporation. She hosts television and radio programs across the nation and speaks for major corporations and Christian audiences. She and her husband, Jerry, live in Dallas, Texas, with their young son.

CAROL SMITH is a writer and songwriter living in Nashville. She's the author of *Stranger Online*, a teen novel for girls, and contributes regularly to Bibles and Bible study products.

HANNAH WHITALL SMITH (1832–1911) was born into a strict Quaker home in Philadelphia and became a major influence in the Holiness movement of the late nineteenth century. Besides *The Christian's Secret of a Happy Life* (Baker), Smith also wrote *The God of All Comfort* (Moody).

ELISA STANFORD works as a writer and editor with Edit Resource in Colorado. She is the author of *Ordinary Losses: Naming the Graces That Shape Us*.

KAY MARSHALL STROM is the author of 31 books. She is also a sought-after speaker for conferences, retreats and special events. More and more her writing and speaking are taking her to countries around the world.

LUCI SWINDOLL is author of *Celebrating Life* and a co-author of various Women of Faith devotionals. She has served as a business executive of Mobil Oil Corporation and as vice president with Insight for Living. She lives in Palm Desert, California.

JONI EARECKSON TADA is the founder of Joni and Friends, an organization accelerating Christian outreach in the disability community that numbers 610 million people worldwide. Joni is also an artist and the author of numerous best-selling books, including *Diamonds in the Dust*, *More Precious Than Silver*, the Platinum award-winning *Joni*, *Heaven: Your Real Home*, *When God Weeps* and *The God I Love*.

ASHLEY TAYLOR is an editor with The Livingstone Corporation based outside Chicago, IL. Ashley has contributed to Bible projects such as *The Serendipity Study Bible*, *True Images*, and *True Identity*.

MOTHER TERESA OF CALCUTTA (1910–1997) is known around the globe for her indefatigable work on behalf of the poor, the sick and the dying. She devoted her life to giving hope to the hopeless in more than 120 countries. In 1979 she was awarded the Nobel Peace Prize for her work, and she continued to work faithfully until her death in 1997.

LINDA TAYLOR is the editorial director for The Livingstone Corporation based outside Chicago, IL. Linda is the author of *Does God Care if I Can't Pay My Bills?* and was a contributing editor to *The Life Application Study Bible*.

JESSICA THOMAS is a writer and exiled Southerner living in the great industrial towns of the Northeast and Midwest. Her reviews have appeared in the *Yale Review of Books*, the *New York Times Book Review* and the *Chattanooga Pulse*.

NANETTE THORSEN-SNIPES is a Georgia-based freelance writer and editor. She's published articles in more than 50 print magazines, including *Home Life*, *Mature Living*, and Focus on the Family's *Clubhouse*. She has published stories in more than 30 compilation books, including *Soul Matters*, *God's Way* and *Stories for the Heart* series. She is a freelance editor with The Christian PEN.

CYNTHIA ULRICH TOBIAS is founder and CEO of AppLe St. (Applied Learning Styles) and coordinates education and commerce programs throughout North America and internationally. She is a speaker and the best-selling author of several books including *I Hate School: How to Help Your Child Love Learning* (Zondervan), *Every Child Can Succeed* (Tyndale) and *Redefining the Strong-Willed Woman* (Zondervan). She lives near Seattle, Washington.

SHEILA WALSH is a speaker, author, singer and television talk show host. She is the author or coauthor of several books including *Honestly* (Zondervan), *Living Fearlessly* (Zondervan) and *Extraordinary Faith: God's Perfect Gift for Every Woman's Heart* (Thomas Nelson). She is also the creator of Children of Faith and the *Gnoo Zoo* (Thomas Nelson), a ministry to children that communicates God's love for them.

KARLA WARKENTIN is the author of the *Time-Stone Travelers* series for children (Cook Communications) and a student at Providence Theological Seminary. She draws her mission statement from Psalm 71: to "declare his power to the next generation, his might to all who are to come." Karla lives in Manitoba, Canada, with her husband and three children.

THELMA WELLS, a college professor at Master's Divinity School and Graduate School, was the first black woman to become assistant vice president of a commercial bank. She organized her own international speaking and consulting company, receiving the Small Business Administration's Entrepreneur of the Year Award, and implemented a national mentoring program for women in ministry. Thelma wrote *Listen Up Honey: Good News for Your Soul* (Thomas Nelson) and *Girl, Have I Got Good News for You* (Thomas Nelson).

CHRISTINE WYRTZEN is the founder and director of Daughters of Promise. Christine has been in ministry 28 years, has released 15 albums, as well as two books. Her daily radio program Daughters of Promise, can be heard each weekday on over 500 stations.

Subject Index

THE NIV *Women's* DEVOTIONAL BIBLE

General Editor
Penny Pierce Rose

Managing Editor
Ashley Taylor

Project Management and Editorial
Shari Vanden Berg

Editorial Assistance
Amy Ballor
Elisabeth Banks
Natalie Block
Mary Horner Collins
Ruth DeJager
Donna Huisjen
Mary Larsen

Production Management
Jake Barton
Phil Herich
Will Reaves

Art Direction
Jamie DeBruyn
Ron Huizinga
Kirk Lutrell

Cover Design
Brand Navigation and Jamie DeBruyn

Interior Design
Kirk Lutrell

Proofreading
Peachtree Editorial and Proofreading Service, Peachtree, GA

Interior Typesetting
The Livingstone Corporation, Carol Stream, IL
Kathy Ristow and Tom Ristow

Guarantee
We want to make sure you're satisfied with the quality of your purchase, and we stand behind the quality of all Zondervan Bibles. That's why we guarantee them for a lifetime against manufacturing defects. For more information on our quality guarantee and product care instructions, visit us at www.zondervan.com.

Care
We suggest loosening the binding of your new Bible by gently pressing on a small section of pages at a time from the center. To ensure against breakage of the spine, it is best not to bend the cover backward around the spine or to carry study notes, church bulletins, pens, etc. inside the cover. Because a felt-tipped marker will "bleed" through the pages, we recommend use of a ballpoint pen or pencil to underline favorite passages. Your Bible should not be exposed to excessive heat, cold or humidity. Protecting the gold or silver edges of the paper from moisture will avoid spotting, streaking or fading.